The Faber Companion to 20th-Century Popular Music

Phil Hardy has written extensively about music, the music industry and the cinema. He was editor of the innovative *Rockbooks* series (1971–2) and co-editor of one of the first significant reference books, the three-volume *Granada Encyclopaedia of Rock* (1976). He is the founder of MUSIC & COPYRIGHT (1992), generally accepted as the most authoritative and objective source of information about the international music business. He remains its editor. His film books include *Sam Fuller* (1972) and *Raoul Walsh* (1974). He is also the editor and main contributor to the Aurum Film Encyclopaedias. These include *The Western* (1994), *Horror* (1995), *Science Fiction* (1995), *Gangsters* (1998) and *War* (2001).

Phil Hardy lives among the rolling hills of North London. He has a footballing son, a singing daughter, a set-decorating girlfriend and two cats.

D1189211

The Faber Companion
to 20th-Century Popular Music

PHIL HARDY

faber and faber

THE WILSON LIBRARY
TRINITY SCHOOL
SHIRLEY PARK
CROYDON CR9 7AT
020 8656 9541

This book is dedicated to the memory of Carole James

First published in 1990
by Faber and Faber Limited
3 Queen Square London WC1N 3AU
Revised and updated in 1995
This revised and updated edition first published in 2001

Printed in Italy

A CIP record for this book is available from the British Library

ISBN 0–571–19608–X

10 9 8 7 6 5 4 3 2 1

Introduction

This book contains profiles of nearly 2,500 people who have contributed to the evolution of popular music in the twentieth century. They range from singers and songwriters through band-leaders, instrumentalists and vocal groups to the behind-the-scenes figures who invented the technology and created the companies that brought recorded music to the forefront of popular entertainment.

The potency of cheap music has often been commented on but it is less often acknowledged that it is the recording process that has given longevity to that potency. Recording is the element that links such disparate figures as Enrico Caruso, Bing Crosby, Sam Cooke, Danny O'Keefe, 2Pac Shakur and Robbie Williams. It was through their recordings that such singers had the chance of becoming international stars, and, increasingly as the century wore on, the strengths (and limitations) of the recording process came to mould the forms taken by popular music.

There are a number of reference works dealing with specific genres – the Broadway musical, jazz, country, rock'n'roll, the blues and so on – but the first edition of this book was among the first to bring together twentieth-century popular music in all its forms. Of course, there remain important distinctions between the different genres, but equally there are continuities and links between the most apparently disparate of singers and styles. The media and institutions of popular entertainment have of necessity been omnivorous, ignoring the niceties of distinction between genres. In the same way, throughout the century, performers absorbed influences across genre (and colour) lines. In the twenties, country pioneer Jimmie Rodgers drew extensively from the blues and popular music traditions just as, in the eighties, Prince reworked the imagery and sounds of white sixties rock. Moreover, while the surface styles and fashions of popular music change rapidly, the underlying structures move far more slowly. Though Elvis Presley's up-tempo rock'n'roll was undoubtedly a break with white pop traditions (but also a borrowing from certain black and country ones), he placed an equal weight on ballad singing, using a florid tenor that harked back to Mario Lanza and even Caruso himself. Without being overly polemical, one hope behind this book is that it will contribute to an understanding of the complex changes within popular music and a move away from the over-simplification of such concepts as that of a rock revolution.

The notion that the arrival of rock'n'roll in some way brought forth a new music lay behind the first reference book Dave Laing, my partner-in-crime for the first edition of the *Companion*, and I produced. Our three-volume *Encyclopaedia of Rock* (Panther, 1976) documented a music that began with rock'n'roll. One of the first reference books published about rock'n'roll and of the musics that followed in its wake, the *Encyclopaedia* did, of course, look back to the roots of the new music that emerged in the fifties. But it was essentially a forward-looking book, documenting and marking what was seen at the time to be a decisive shift from the past. A mark of how well established such a view was can be seen if one compares that book with Peter Gammond and Peter Clayton's *Guide to Popular Music* (Phoenix, 1960). Where our encyclopaedia looked forward, Gammond and Clayton's volume looked back. Casting its net far wider than jazz, vaudeville and Broadway and written some time after Elvis Presley and company had made their mark, it determinedly looked away from rock'n'roll to that strand of popular music which it defined as being 'in-between' genre musics, such as jazz and classical music. In its celebration of 'light' music, it even excluded the roots of rock'n'roll. Thus, the book had no entries on blues or country performers of the stature of Robert Johnson, Louis Jordan or Hank Williams.

Within a decade such a view became impossible to hold. When the *Companion* was first published in 1990, Janus-like it looked both backwards and forwards from the moment of rock'n'roll. It took for its brief the attempt to document, categorize and evaluate performers operating in the multitude of musical traditions that emerged in the twentieth century and which have been preserved through the recording process. The *Companion* was not alone in this. As historians uncovered the deep influence of the music of the pre-rock'n'roll era, so performers discovered continuities where breaks had previously been accepted. As a result, in the nineties there was a slew of albums by performers associated with contemporary music forms of 'classic songs from the Broadway era' and tribute albums to seminal figures in country, blues and so forth. In a similar fashion, music historians began to chip away at the idea that rock'n'roll was such a revolutionary moment.

At the same time there has been a proliferation of guides to rock music itself. This is a testament to the enduring interest the generations reared on rock have in the music and in the developments of that music. In marked contrast to earlier generations, who put aside the foolish things of youth when they grew up, the post-rock'n'roll generations have embraced the music that grew out of rock'n'roll and made it the soundtrack to their lives. In part merely another example of the potency of cheap music, at a deeper level it suggests the huge and growing impact that popular culture has on our lives. I still recollect the anger I felt in the late fifties and early sixties when I first noticed that the journalists who documented in great detail the arrival of the likes of Del Shannon and the glorious inanities of B. Bumble and the Stingers in the pop papers of the day always voted Ella Fitzgerald – who then meant nothing to me – best vocalist. That era, with its high-, middle- and low-brow debates, has gone. No longer is the rise of popular culture condemned out of hand and associated with an inevitable decline in moral standards. Nowadays in conversation people slip effortlessly from talk of Rogers and Hammerstein to Lyle Lovett and debate wittily over the dinner table about whether Dylan or Keats is the better poet, couching their arguments in terms that alternate between deep irony and profound concern. Even British High Court judges, the last bastions of ignorance about popular culture, know who Oasis are.

Another change that has occurred is the general acceptance of the importance of recordings. Once fragile pieces of shellac or easily scratched vinyl, the CD and the MP3 file have brought permanence to recordings. Indeed, so much so that many of the reference books about rock are now constructed around reviews of CD albums.

Many hundreds of thousands of artists have made records since Thomas Edison's invention of the phonograph in 1877. To choose only a fraction for inclusion in the *Companion* has not been easy. The criteria have been three-fold. First, whatever the quality of the music, it is impossible to ignore a certain level of commercial success or artists who are popular in the simple sense of having been 'liked by many people'. Secondly, there are those who were vital influences on the development of one stream or other of popular music. As well as the major stars of country music, for example, such as the Carter Family and Hank Williams, we have also included the likes of the Stanley Brothers and Lefty Frizzell, artists who, although not so well known outside country circles, nevertheless influenced its evolution. In particular, the book profiles several little-remembered pioneering recording artists and devotes space to songwriters, composers and performers associated with the cinema which, since the sound era, has become an important force in popular music. Finally, there are those whose artistic excellence cannot be ignored. In most cases such figures also qualify on grounds of success or influence. But, in the absence of either, artists like David Ackles demand a place in this book.

The boundaries of this book are in general those of Anglo-American popular music. Since the twenties, English-language songs and artists have dominated the world of popular music and this is reflected in the *Companion*. Nevertheless, the music of Europe, Latin America and, in the last few years, the contemporary music of Africa has also made its international mark. However, because this book is essentially historically oriented, only a few artists from those continents appear in these pages. Moreover, there are now several considered guides to world music.

Acknowledgements

The *Companion* has been an evolving work. The first two editions were overseen by Dave Laing and myself. We wrote the majority of the entries; however, many of the entries on country blues, early country music and artists of the dance-band era were written by Tony Russell, editor and publisher of the journal *Old Time Music*. Similarly, many of the soul music entries were written by Bob Fisher of Connoisseur Collection. For the second edition Tom Ferguson (rock) and Stan Britt (jazz) helped in the updating and writing of new entries. For this edition the main contributors have been Jim Washer, who is largely responsible for the dance entries, and Tom Jerome, who, while concentrating on the new rock entries, also helped revise and update the existing entries. Ian Bahrami copy-edited the book and oversaw its production with a patience and eye for detail that have benefited the *Companion* enormously.

I, of course, take full responsibility for the contents, but any credit is equally due to the contributors. Thank you all. And thank you, James.

Author's Note

Cross references to other entries in the *Companion* are given in **bold** type. Titles of singles appear in single inverted commas; titles of albums, films and shows appear in *italics*. An asterisk (*) after a title indicates it was a million-seller. From the eighties on, as million-sellers became commonplace, the practice of identifying them as such has been less closely observed.

Glossary of Styles and Genres

Most of the terms used in the *Companion* are self-explanatory. Below are capsule descriptions of some genres and styles of popular music that might be unfamiliar to the general reader. More detailed information on examples of each genre can be found in the entries referred to.

ALTERNATIVE COUNTRY a strand of COUNTRY music that emerged in the 1980s and which retained traditional country elements while adding a pop/rock edge. In the 1990s the name was given to groups whose sound was a blend of traditional country and contemporary alternative rock music; see **Lyle Lovett, Uncle Tupelo, Lambchop**.

AMBIENT an approach to music-making that eschews melody or rhythm for 'atmosphere'. In the eighties it was variously associated with New Age and avant-garde artists. In the nineties it became integrated with new dance musics (see TECHNO). See **Brian Eno**.

BEBOP (or BOP) the revolutionary jazz movement of the 1940s developed in New York and forming the basis of most subsequent modern jazz; see **Kenny Clarke, Dizzy Gillespie, Charlie Parker**.

BIG BAND JAZZ flourishing from the 1920s to the 1950s this was a highly arranged form of jazz, for orchestras of around twenty members; see **Count Basie, Duke Ellington, Fletcher Henderson, Woody Herman**.

BIG BEAT a form of dance music that emerged in the mid-1990s centred on playful, repetitive vocal/instrumental samples and fast drum loops; see **Fatboy Slim, Chemical Brothers**.

BLUEGRASS virtuoso COUNTRY music using mainly stringed instruments, originated by Bill Monroe in the 1940s; see **Bill Monroe, Flatt & Scruggs, Osborne Brothers**.

BLUES (COUNTRY BLUES) a fundamental element in secular black music, it emerged in the first decade of the century, taking a three-line, 12-bar format. The solo forms of country blues, played on guitar or piano were superseded in the 1940s by RHYTHM & BLUES; see **Fred McDowell, Robert Johnson, Blind Lemon Jefferson, Leroy Carr**.

BOOGIE-WOOGIE a percussive, rhythmic style of black piano-playing that flourished in the 1930s; see **Albert Ammons, Pete Johnson, Meade Lux Lewis**.

BRITISH BEAT the musical movement of the early 1960s spearheaded by **The Beatles**. With a repertoire grounded in ROCK'N'ROLL and RHYTHM & BLUES, beat groups characteristically comprised lead guitar, rhythm guitar, bass guitar and drums plus vocalist; see the **Move**, the **Searchers**, the **Hollies**.

BRITISH R&B the music created from the early and mid-1960s by young British imitators of the Chicago style of RHYTHM & BLUES; see **Alexis Korner, John Mayall, Eric Clapton**, the **Rolling Stones**.

BRITPOP a mid-1990s revival of guitar-led pop drawing on 1960s mod and beat groups from **The Beatles** to the **Small Faces**; see **Blur, Oasis**.

CAJUN a rhythmic accordion-led music from Southern Louisiana, mingling black styles with the traditions of the area's French-speaking population; see **Nathan Abshire, Doug Kershaw, Clifton Chenier**.

CLASSIC BLUES an important type of blues song, evolving in the 1920s, usually sung by women to a piano or jazz group backing; see **Ma Rainey, Bessie Smith**.

COUNTRY (COUNTRY & WESTERN, C & W) originally called hillbilly music, it is the commercial music of white rural (and much of urban) America; see the **Carter Family, Johnny Cash, Jimmie Rodgers, Hank Williams, Roy Acuff, Merle Haggard**.

COUNTRY BOOGIE a piano-based hybrid of COUNTRY and BOOGIE-WOOGIE, it was an important forerunner of ROCK'N'ROLL; see **Merrill Moore, Moon Mullican**.

COUNTRYPOLITAN the sweetened version of COUNTRY that emerged in the 1970s; see **Lynn Anderson**.

COUNTRY ROCK a style created in the late 1960s when rock groups turned for inspiration to COUNTRY; see the **Byrds**, the **Eagles, Gram Parsons**.

DISCO beginning in the 1970s, a strongly rhythmic and hypnotic dance music whose earliest popularity was in the discotheques of the era; see **KC & the Sunshine Band, Donna Summer, Giorgio Moroder**.

DOO-WOP the (mostly) black vocal music of the 1950s; see the **Ravens**, the **Orioles**, the **Platters, Dion and the Belmonts**.

DRUM'N'BASS a strand of dance music of the early 1990s characterized by fast, repetitive drums and deep bass tones; see **LTJ Bukem, Roni Size**.

DUB a type of REGGAE in which the record producer removes the vocal track, leaving only bass and drums; see **King Tubby**.

ELECTRONIC MUSIC the result of applying the increasingly sophisticated varieties of synthesizer to popular music; see **Pink Floyd, Kraftwerk, Can, Depeche Mode**.

FOLK a term which is applied to the pre-industrial 'music of the people' and its modern re-creation as well as the self-conscious attempt to create non-commercial or politically outspoken music; see **Cecil Sharp, Woody Guthrie, John Lomax, Pete Seeger, Kingston Trio**.

FOLK-ROCK a movement that occurred when rock bands of the mid-1960s turned for inspiration to FOLK; see the **Byrds, Bob Dylan, Fairport Convention, Steeleye Span**.

FUNK a polyrhythmic 1970s derivative of SOUL; see **Kool and the Gang, Earth Wind & Fire**. Sometimes also anarchic; see **George Clinton**.

FUSION attempts to merge jazz with other musical styles, notably Asian and classical; see **John McLaughlin, Narada Michael Walden**.

GARAGE initially a term for proto-punk US groups of the sixties – see **MC5** and **? and the Mysterians** – it later became the name of vocal house music that emerged in eighties, drawing its melodic and harmonic conventions from Black American sources, e.g. gospel, soul, R&B and jazz in the US. Speed/UK garage was a late 1990s hybrid incorporating the bass and percussion stylings of the UK jungle scene.

GOSPEL since the 1930s, the dominant church music of black America and a major influence on all black secular styles; see **Thomas A. Dorsey, Mahalia Jackson, Five Blind Boys of Mississippi, Sam Cooke, Ray Charles**.

GRUNGE A hard rock style originating in Seattle in the late eighties which mixed heavy metal with influences from punk rock. See **Nirvana, Pearl Jam**.

HEAVY METAL the result of one tendency in BRITISH R&B to emphasize volume and intensity, heavy metal was probably the most popular style of ROCK by the early 1990s; see **Black Sabbath, Iron Butterfly, Def Leppard, Ted Nugent**.

HIP-HOP with its derivative rap, hip-hop was the most important new black music of the 1980s. The style was developed by disc-jockeys who 'rapped' (spoke rhythmically) over records whose sound they modified through 'scratching'; see **Afrika Bambaataa, Grandmaster Flash**.

HONKY-TONK named after the taverns of the American Southwest, a form of COUNTRY featuring amplified steel and lead guitars in songs frequently dealing with adultery and drinking; see **Ernest Tubb, Lefty Frizzell, George Jones**.

HOUSE a form of disco-inspired, up-tempo, repeti-tive dance music that began to appear in the early 1980s; see **Masters at Work, Todd Terry**.

INDUSTRIAL a 1990s hard-rock style characterized by the merging of heavy, repetitive riffs and synthesized loops and beats; see **Nine Inch Nails, Marilyn Manson**.

JAZZ emerging from the cultural melting-pot of New Orleans, jazz became one of America's and black Americans' greatest art forms. Its eighty-year history has 'given rise to numerous sub-genres' including BIG BAND JAZZ, JAZZ-FUNK, BEBOP and JAZZ-ROCK; see **Buddy Bolden, Louis Armstrong, Paul Whiteman, Duke Ellington, Miles Davis, Ornette Coleman**.

JAZZ-ROCK one strand of the PROGRESSIVE ROCK movement of the 1960s, it brought together rock musicians seeking extra chords and tone-colours with jazz players looking for new energy; see **Blood, Sweat & Tears, Miles Davis, Weather Report**.

JUMP BLUES a hard-swinging transitional style of small group black music in the 1940s, it anticipated both RHYTHM & BLUES and ROCK'N'ROLL; see **Jimmy and Joe Liggins, Louis Jordan, Roy Milton**.

JUNGLE an early form of DRUM'N'BASS based around high-tempo drum rhythms overlaid by a soulful vocal track; see **Goldie**.

LATIN-AMERICAN MUSIC a generic name for dance rhythms originating in Mexico, the Caribbean, South and Central America which have had a sporadic influence on Anglo-American pop since the 1920s; see **Moises Simons, Xavier Cugat, Carmen Miranda, Edmundo Ros**.

MUSIC HALL comic songs and ballads performed by artists appearing in these British theatres in the half-century to 1930; see **Marie Lloyd, Gus Elen, Flanagan & Allen**.

NASHVILLE SOUND a 1950s trend where violins and vocal backing groups were added to the recordings of COUNTRY singers; see **Chet Atkins, Ray Price, Jim Reeves**.

NEW AGE more of a mood than a style, new age was soothing instrumental music of the 1980s, based on the softer kinds of classical, jazz and folk; see **John Fahey, Rick Wakeman, Ian Matthews**.

OPERETTA musical comedy theatre brought from Europe to the US at the end of the nineteenth century, and briefly revived with the advent of sound films; see **Victor Herbert, Sigmund Romberg, Rudolf Friml, Franz Lehár, Nelson Eddy**.

POP a broad term normally used for the softer, even more teenage-orientated sounds that emerged as ROCK'N'ROLL waned in the early 1960s. It is often contrasted with the tougher or more serious-minded ROCK; see **Bobby Vee, Dick Clark, Bay City Rollers, Stock, Aitken and Waterman.**

PROGRESSIVE ROCK a mid-1960s to mid-1970s trend characterized by ambitious attempts to expand the musical resources and thematic preoccupations of ROCK; see **Pink Floyd, Yes, King Crimson, Deep Purple.**

PSYCHEDELIC ROCK emerging in San Francisco in the mid-1960s, and often associated with the hippie ethos, it shared the experimental attitudes of PROGRESSIVE ROCK; see **Country Joe McDonald, Jefferson Airplane,** the **Grateful Dead,** the **Seeds.**

PUNK ROCK in America, the name given to the (amateurish) 'garage bands' that sprang up in imitation of The Beatles and Rolling Stones, punk was applied a decade later to a disruptive and highly publicized trend in British rock music; see **? And the Mysterians, MC5,** the **Clash,** the **Sex Pistols.**

RAGTIME a highly formal piano music with strong bass line and melodies derived from plantation songs and dances, ragtime flourished in the first decade of the century; see **Marvin Hamlisch, Scott Joplin.**

RAP Relentless rhythms supporting aggressive, chanted, rhyming lyrics characterize this highly influential genre. Beginning in New York (**Grandmaster Flash**), it evolved into 'gangsta rap' on the US West Coast (**NWA**). The style also spread to Europe and India (see **MC Solaar**).

REGGAE the general term for the main trends in Jamaican music since the late 1960s; see **Jimmy Cliff, Bob Marley, Prince Buster, Skatalites, UB40.**

RHYTHM & BLUES (R&B) a general name for the dominant black music forms of the 1950s; see **The Clovers, Bo Diddley, Ruth Brown, Muddy Waters.** In the 1990s the term R&B began to be used to describe the highly popular US style also known as 'New Jack Swing'. Essentially a dilution of hip-hop, it merged soulful, harmonic vocals with hook-laden rhythms; see **Blackstreet, En Vogue.**

ROCK a general name for the wide range of styles that have evolved from ROCK'N'ROLL; see **The Band, Creedence Clearwater Revival, Dire Straits, Dave Edmunds, The Who.**

ROCKABILLY an early fusion of black and country musics in the American South which just pre-dated ROCK'N'ROLL; see **Elvis Presley, Carl Perkins, Gene Vincent, Johnny Burnette, Charlie Feathers.**

ROCK'N'ROLL the mid-1950s synthesis of R&B and the HONKY TONK/ROCKABILLY side of COUNTRY which attracted a mass teenage audience for both black and white singers; see **Chuck Berry, Eddie Cochran, Fats Domino, Jerry Lee Lewis, Elvis Presley.**

SALSA a form of LATIN-AMERICAN MUSIC developed in New York by Puerto Rican and Cuban musicians in the 1950s and 60s; see **Ruben Blades, Celia Cruz, Tito Puente.**

SKA a forerunner of REGGAE which flourished in the mid-1960s adding elements of Jamaican mento music to RHYTHM & BLUES; see the **Skatalites, Laurel Aitken, Toots and the Maytals.** The term and music style was revived in the UK in the late seventies; see the **Specials, Madness.**

SKIFFLE first given to a form of 1920s black music in America, the name was adopted by a British 1950s style using improvised instruments (washboards, jugs, tea-chest bass) to perform American FOLK and BLUES songs; see **Chris Barber, Ken Colyer, Lonnie Donegan.**

SOUL the general name for the dominant form of black music in the 1970s, soul originated as a secularized version of GOSPEL; see **Bobby Bland, Solomon Burke, Aretha Franklin, Otis Redding, Percy Sledge.**

SPIRITUALS black equivalents to the Christian hymns sung by whites, spirituals lost ground to GOSPEL music from the 1930s onwards; see **Odetta, Paul Robeson.**

SWING a highly rhythmic style of BIG BAND JAZZ that was the main form of white American dance music during the late 1930s and early 1940s; see **Benny Goodman, Artie Shaw, Harry James.**

TECHNO One of several generic names for versions of the new dance music of the late eighties and nineties. See **Black Box.**

THRASH Otherwise known as 'hardcore', thrash is a more extreme mix of metal and punk than GRUNGE. It emphasizes guitar noise, speed and volume. See **Bob Mould, Sonic Youth.**

TRADITIONAL JAZZ the term for both the earliest, New Orleans styles of jazz and for the Anglo-American revival of the music (as 'trad') in the 1940s and 1950s; see **King Oliver, George Lewis, Acker Bilk, Ken Colyer.**

TRIP-HOP the term used to describe the slow, moody strand of British dance music based around slowed-down HIP-HOP beats and jazzy instrumentation that emanated from Bristol in the early to mid-1990s; see **Massive Attack, Portishead.**

VAUDEVILLE an American equivalent to the British music hall and the place where songs became hits in the era before radio, films and records were dominant; see **Nora Bayes, Al Jolson, Sophie Tucker, Ethel Waters.**

WESTERN SWING containing elements of JAZZ, BLUES and RAGTIME, as well as hillbilly and COUNTRY, this genre emerged in the American South-West in the 1930s and 1940s; see **Bob Wills, Milton Brown**.

WORLD MUSIC Originally a marketing term invented to help sell African, Asian and Latin American musics to European audiences, world music also refers to styles which mix those musics with contemporary studio or performance technology. See **Peter Gabriel, Youssou N'Dour**.

ABBA

Benny Andersson, b. 16 December 1946, Stockholm, Sweden; Agnetha Fältskog, b. 5 April 1950, Jönköping; Anni-Frid Lyngstad, b. 15 November 1945, Björkasen, Norway; Björn Ulvaeus, b. 25 April 1945, Gothenburg, Sweden

Experts in the dynamic pop single, Abba were the most commercially successful group of the seventies. However, like **Boney M**, another European group who based their music on American models, they were far less successful in America than elsewhere in the world. A mark of how appealing their well-crafted pop songs were was that in the nineties, long after the group had disbanded, collections of their hits sold in huge numbers and tribute recordings and tours by tribute bands were greeted warmly. The climax of this widespread affection for the group was the stage musical *Mama Mia* (1999). Constructed around 27 Abba songs by Catherine Johnson, it was both a critical and commercial success.

Ulvaeus was a founding member of the Hootenanny Singers, a **Kingston Trio**-inspired group that had a series of folky hits, including a Swedish-language version of 'The Green Green Grass of Home'. In 1967 he embarked on a solo career and in 1969 established a songwriting partnership with Andersson when the latter's group, the Hep Stars, folded. The Hep Stars had been Sweden's top rock'n'roll band of the sixties. By this time, Andersson was living with Lyngstad, who had recorded extensively but with little success in Sweden, and Ulvaeus with Fältskog, who had had several Swedish hits. In 1973 the foursome united as Abba (an acronym of the initials of their forenames) and set about recording in English, with Ulvaeus and Andersson as producers. They were signed by Polar, the label run by their manager and frequent songwriting partner of Andersson and Ulvaeus, Stikkan (Stig) Anderson (*b. 1931 Stockholm, d. 12 September 1997, Stockholm*).

Their first attempt at the Eurovision Song Contest, 'Ring Ring' (co-written by **Neil Sedaka**, who was as strong an influence on the music of Abba as was **Elton John** on their dress), failed in 1973. A year later, the confident, chirpy 'Waterloo' won, giving them their first million-seller and the first of eighteen consecutive Top Ten hits throughout Europe. Within a year came 'SOS' and then a trio of British No. 1s: 'Mamma Mia', 'Fernando' and the classic 'Dancing Queen' (all 1976), which would be the group's only

American No. 1. These records confirmed Abba's marvellous pop sensibilities. The dense, multi-layered productions alternated the sharp and perfectly matched lead vocals of Lyngstad and Fältskog with soaring, crashing choruses. The lyrics reworked the classic pop themes (dance, love and money, love and duty) in perfect Brill Building English. Abba's albums (particularly *Arrival*, 1976, and *Abba: The Album*, 1978) and tours were equally successful.

Unlike many acts Abba capitalized fully on their success. Polar Music licensed their material to different companies in different territories (Epic in the UK, Atlantic in America), even making bartering agreements with Eastern bloc countries. Despite a loss of £2 million on the oil spot market in 1977, the year of 'Knowing Me, Knowing You' and 'The Name of the Game', Polar was the most successful company in Sweden. In 1989 Stig Anderson sold Polar to PolyGram.

1978 saw the release of *Abba: The Movie*, an indulgent chronicle of their 1977 tour of Australia, and henceforth, though the hits continued unabated until 1980 (including 'Chiquitita' and 'I Have a Dream', 1979, and 'The Winner Takes It All' and 'Super Trouper', 1980), in the main they were brasher and had less imagination than the accompanying videos. Surprisingly (and in marked contrast to **Fleetwood Mac**), the strained personal relationships within the group – both couples parted – were never reflected in Ulvaeus's and Andersson's songs.

After several lesser hits in 1982, the group quietly disbanded, leaving the stage clear for the numerous imitators, such as **Buck's Fizz**, that they had inspired. Fältskog and Lyngstad made inconsequential solo albums, produced by Mike Chapman of **Chinn and Chapman** and **Phil Collins**, respectively, and, in 1983, Fältskog had an American Top Twenty hit with 'Can't Shake Loose'. Lyngstad subsequently returned to the Swedish charts with her first solo recording in a decade with *Djupa Andertag* (1996), which included a duet with **Roxette**'s Marie Fredriksson, 'All My Best Years'. In 1985 Ulvaeus and Andersson resurfaced as joint co-authors with **Andrew Lloyd Webber**'s early partner Tim Rice of the smash musical *Chess*. More substantial, although largely ignored outside Scandinavia, was their Swedish musical *Kristina Fran Duvelma* (1995).

The nineties saw a revival of interest in the group and their hits album *Abba Gold* (Polydor) sold over six million copies in Europe. Subsequently, as a back-catalogue act they finally conquered America, which they had been unable to when performing and recording. Around the world groups began to revive their songs, most notably **Erasure**, whose *Abba-esque* EP (Mute, 1992), a medley of Abba songs, was a hit throughout Europe. At the same time the Australian group Björn Again achieved a brief cult following for their loving and precise imitation of the Abba sound. Other examples of the warmth (and growing nostalgia) with which the band was viewed included the minor musical *Abba – The True Story* (1993), the forceful use of their music in the film *Muriel's Wedding* (1994), the various artists' tribute album by New Zealand indie groups, *Abbasalutely* (Flying Nun) – Abba's appeal has always been strong in Australasia – *Abbamania* (1999), in which a new generation of teen groups, such as Steps and **B*Witched**, offered their own interpretations of Abba classics, and, of course, *Mamma Mia*.

ABC

Martin Fry, b. 9 March 1958, Manchester, England; Mark Lickley; David Robinson; Stephen Singleton, b. 17 April 1959, Sheffield; Mark White, b. 1 April 1961, Sheffield

One of the most accomplished new romantic groups, ABC were an instant success in the early eighties through Fry's yearning lead voice and well-crafted songs. After a slump in popularity and inactivity because of Fry's illness, ABC returned to the British charts with the homage to **Berry Gordy**'s Motown sound, 'When Smokey Sings' (1987).

Sheffield-based Fry had previously edited the fanzine *Modern Drugs* through which he joined the synthesizer group Vice Versa. In 1980 he formed ABC with ex-Vice Versa members White (guitar) and Singleton (sax), plus Lickley (bass) and drummer Robinson. After 'Tears Are Not Enough' (1981) reached the Top Twenty on the independent Neutron label, the group was signed to Phonogram by Mark Dean (who later discovered **George Michael**).

Trevor Horn produced the chart-topping *The Lexicon of Love* (1982), which was heralded by critics as a return to the classic pop love song represented by Motown, **Phil Spector**, **Don Kirshner**'s Brill Building writers, and even **Frank Sinatra**. Fry's crooning and the group's lush harmonies gave ABC three hits in 1982: 'Poison Arrow' (also an American Top Twenty success on Mercury), 'The Look of Love' and 'All of My Heart'.

The concept video *Mantrap* and the album *Beauty Stab* (1983) suffered from a critical backlash, in part because of the political themes of 'Bite the Hand' and the British hit 'That Was Then but This Is Now'. After the less successful *How to Be a Zillionaire* (1985), whose 'Be Near Me' was an American Top Ten hit,

Fry's illness prevented further recording for two years.

Co-produced by **Nile Rodgers**' former partner in Chic, Bernard Edwards, *Alphabet City* (1987) proved to be a triumphant return. 'King without a Crown' and 'The Night You Murdered Love' were minor hits while 'When Smokey Sings' entered the Top Twenty. The tribute to **Smokey Robinson** confirmed Fry as the heir (along with **Paul Young**) to the British tradition of blue-eyed soul singing.

Up (1989) saw them experimenting with house music, but their biggest hit was the compilation *Absolutely ABC* (1990). After that the group moved to EMI to record *Abracadabra*, by which time it consisted of only Fry and White. The group's fortunes briefly revived when material was featured in the film *When Saturday Comes* (1997), which led to the album *Skyscraping* (deConstruction), but by the end of the decade Fry (sometimes with White) had become a staple item on the growing number of eighties revival tours. He also contributed a reading of 'Thunderball' to the album of James Bond cover themes, *Shaken, Not Stirred* (1998).

PAULA ABDUL

b. Paula Julie Abdul, 19 June 1962, Los Angeles, California, USA

Dancer and choreographer Paula Abdul was one of America's most successful singers of the early nineties. Her first three albums of lightweight pop-dance music offered a reassuring image, in contrast to the threatening one of **Madonna**, and sold a total of over ten million copies.

Abdul studied tap and jazz dancing from the age of ten and made her film début in *Junior High School* in 1978. She choreographed steps for the basketball dance squad the Laker Girls while still in college. In 1985 she choreographed several music videos and created the dance sequences for several **Janet Jackson** hits, including 'Nasty' (1986) for which she was given an MTV award in 1987. She subsequently choreographed videos for **Duran Duran**, **Debbie Gibson**, **Dolly Parton** and **ZZ Top** as well as working on Oliver Stone's film *The Doors*.

Abdul was signed to a recording contract by Virgin in 1988 but her first singles made little impact. The commercial breakthrough came with the album *Forever Your Girl*. Four singles from the album topped the US charts in 1989 and 1990. They were the title track, 'Straight Up', 'Cold Hearted' and 'Opposites Attract', which was composed by Oliver Leiber, son of Jerry Leiber (of **Leiber and Stoller**) and had a rap from Derrick Delite of Soul Purpose. *Shut Up and Dance (The Dance Mixes)* contained remixes of tracks from the début album and was issued in 1990. The producers included Family Stand (Peter Lord, Jeff

Smith and Sandra St Victor), **Don Was** and **L.A. and Babyface**.

By now Abdul was frequently seen at awards ceremonies, charity concerts (she contributed a track to the Disney album *For Our Children*, a fund-raiser for AIDS victims) and on high-profile advertising campaigns for Reebok shoes and Diet Coke. She designed a shoe line for the L.A. Gear clothes company. In 1991 backing singer Yvette Marine brought a case against Abdul and Virgin claiming she shared lead vocals on two of Abdul's recordings. The case was eventually dismissed in 1993.

Abdul's second album of new material was *Spellbound** (1991). It included compositions by **Prince** ('U') and **John Hiatt** ('Alright Tonight') and two US No. 1 singles, 'Rush Rush' and 'Spellbound'; 'Blowing Kisses in the Wind' was also a Top Ten hit, while 'Will You Marry Me?' featured **Stevie Wonder** on harmonica. *Head Over Heels** (1995), on which she was partnered by the likes of Color Me Bad and Haza, was less successful and Abdul turned increasingly to television and theatre, appearing in her first film, *In the Shadow of Evil*, in 1998 and taking the lead in a revival of **Dorothy Fields'** *Sweet Charity* (and choreographing the production) in 1999.

EWART ABNER
b. 1923, Chicago, Illinois, USA, d. 27 December 1997, Los Angeles

One of the few black record-industry executives, Abner helped mould the development of black music throughout the fifties and sixties, especially in Chicago where he was based.

In 1950, after graduating from Howard University with a degree in accountancy, he joined Chance, writing and producing for the **Flamingos** and **Harvey Fuqua**'s Moonglows and, in 1954, with record-store owners Vivian Carter, Jimmy Bracken and Calvin Carter, he formed Vee-Jay records, the first important black-owned record company of the post-war period. With Carter as a partner, Abner wrote and produced for many acts, including the **Dells**, Dee Clark, and the El Dorados (whose huge 1955 R&B hit 'At My Front Door', covered by **Pat Boone**, he co-wrote), but his forte was sales and marketing. In this capacity he nurtured and developed the careers of **Jimmy Reed**, **John Lee Hooker**, the Dells, **Gene Chandler**, **Jerry Butler** and the **Impressions**. A mark of his success was the renaming of the subsidiary Falcon label to Abner in 1957 and his promotion in 1960 to president of the company.

As president, he launched Vee-Jay into a period of unprecedented expansion for a black-owned company. In 1962 he signed the white vocal group the **Four Seasons**, who had a trio of million-selling singles while with the company – 'Sherry' and 'Big Girls Don't Cry' (both 1962) and 'Walk Like a Man' (1963) – and a decade later Abner signed the Seasons to Motown. In 1963 he signed **Hoyt Axton** and, at the suggestion of the Seasons' Bob Gaudio, he acquired the American rights to **The Beatles** from EMI when Capitol turned down its parent company's artists. As a result, in 1964 Vee-Jay had hits with 'Please Please Me' and 'Do You Want to Know a Secret?' when The Beatles finally broke through in America. Abner left the company in 1963 to concentrate on his own Constellation label, briefly returning to Vee-Jay in 1965, before family and financial problems brought Vee-Jay crashing down. Next Abner moved to Motown, the company that finally achieved what Vee-Jay had for so long seemed on the verge of doing when it transformed itself from a small R&B-based independent into a major company.

At Motown he became president in 1973, where he was responsible for renegotiating **Stevie Wonder**'s contract with the company in 1974. In 1975, following his departure from the company, Abner became Wonder's business consultant. In this capacity he was the guiding force behind Wonder's successful campaign to get Martin Luther King's birthday recognized as a national holiday in America. He was also one of the founders of The Black Music Association in 1978.

NATHAN ABSHIRE
b. 27 June 1913, near Gueydan, Louisiana, USA, d. 13 May 1981, Basile, Louisiana

Abshire was the best-known cajun accordionist of modern times.

A *mélange* of Old World French ballads and dance songs, Scots and Irish fiddle music and the blues, the cajun music of Southern Louisiana has been one of the most tenaciously regional and unassimilated idioms in the United States. On early recordings it was chiefly performed on fiddle or the diatonic one-row or two-row button accordion, or on both together. The status of the accordionists, however, was enhanced by the fact that one of them, Joseph F. Falcon, was the first cajun musician to make records, starting in 1927 with 'Allons à Lafayette' (Columbia). Falcon was one of the most popular artists in the first decade of recorded cajun music, under contract successively to Columbia, Bluebird and Decca.

Falcon apart, in the thirties accordion players were out of fashion. The most successful recording acts were fiddle-led stringbands like the Hackberry Ramblers – who as the Riverside Ramblers had a hit with 'Wondering' (1936), later picked up by **Webb Pierce** – and Leo Soileau with his Three (or Four) Aces; both groups recorded English as well as French songs in order to reach hillbilly record buyers.

4

Though he had a recording session for Bluebird in 1935, Nathan Abshire's career did not gain momentum until after the Second World War. In 1948, with a residency at the Avalon Club in Basile and a hit record in 'Pine Grove Blues' (O.T.), he not only improved his own prospects but brought the accordion back into public favour. The instrument's reputation was reinforced by the appearance of other excellent and popular players, including Lawrence Walker, Austin Pitre, and, in particular, Iry LeJune, but cajun musicians generally found it hard to keep even their local audience in the post-rock'n'roll fifties, and Abshire's fortunes ebbed once more. They recovered in the sixties with a series of superb singles for **Jay Miller**'s Kajun label and Floyd Soileau's Swallow. Both contracts produced remakes of the evergreen 'Pine Grove Blues', the Swallow period also providing Abshire with hits like 'The Lemonade Song' and even **Joe South**'s 'Games People Play' (1970).

On some of his Swallow recordings Abshire worked with the Balfa Brothers, Dewey (fiddle/vocal), Will (fiddle) and Rodney (guitar). Dewey Balfa, an articulate spokesman for cajun values, led the renaissance of cajun music in the seventies and eighties through his festival appearances, lecture tours and frequent recordings on Swallow, Sonet and other labels (notably *Under the Green Oak Tree*, Arhoolie, 1973) with accordionist (and accordion-maker) Marc Savoy and singer/guitarist D. L. Menard.

In the seventies Abshire was at first popular on the festival circuit, where his unforced emotional singing and blues-ridden playing were not tempered for the unfamiliar audience, but personal problems began to sap his abilities and his later recordings, though moving, are not representative. A PBS documentary, *The Good Times Are Killin' Me*, mapped this decline with almost too much candour.

Among Abshire's musical descendants are such players as Marc Savoy, Jo-El Sonnier, Bessyl Duhon, who regularly played with the pop-cajun artist Jimmy C. Newman on the *Grand Ole Opry*, Wayne Toups and Pat Savant. Sonnier had numerous country hits. Savant was a member of Lesa Cormier and the Sundown Playboys, whose 'Saturday Night Special' (Swallow, 1972), leased to **The Beatles**' Apple label, was the first cajun single ever issued outside the US.

AC/DC

Mark Evans, b. 2 March 1956, Melbourne, Australia (replaced by Cliff Williams, b. 14 December 1949); Philip Rudd, b. 19 May 1946, Melbourne, Australia (replaced by Simon Wright, b. 19 June 1963, Manchester, England, replaced by Chris Slade, b. 30 October 1946); Bon Scott, b. 9 July 1946, Kirriemuir, Scotland, d. 19 February 1980, London, England (replaced by
Brian Johnson, b. 5 October 1947); Angus Young, b. 31 March 1959, Glasgow, Scotland; Malcolm Young, b. 6 January 1953, Glasgow

Formed in Australia, AC/DC were one of the most successful heavy-metal groups of the seventies and eighties. Revelling in a 'bad boy' image, they sang frankly about sex while their distinctive stage act featured Angus Young in schoolboy cap and short trousers. In between his caustic guitar solos, he would occasionally 'moon' the audience.

The Youngs emigrated to Australia in the early sixties where their elder brother George was a member of the **Easybeats**. AC/DC was formed in 1973 at high school by guitarist Malcolm Young, and later joined by Angus Young (lead guitar) and vocalist Scott, a former drummer with the Valentines and Fraternity, who replaced Dave Evans as vocalist in 1974. By the time the group first recorded, drummer Rudd and Evans (bass) had become members.

High Voltage (1975) was produced by George Young and fellow Easybeat Harry Vanda. Both it and *T.N.T.* (1975) were Australian hits and the following year Atlantic released an amalgam of tracks internationally as *High Voltage*. During 1976–7 the group toured Europe and America, releasing *Dirty Deeds Done Dirt Cheap*, which included 'Big Balls' and 'Problem Child', before the aggressive *Let There Be Rock* established the band in the northern hemisphere. Williams, from former Columbia recording act Home, joined the group for *Powerage* (1978) and the live *If You Want Blood – You've Got It* (1978).

The band's first American Top Twenty hit was 'Highway to Hell' (1979), for which Robert John 'Mutt' Lange replaced Vanda–Young as producer. Soon afterwards Scott died following a drinking bout. The new lead singer was Johnson, formerly of Geordie, a British rock band whose hits had included 'All Because of You' (EMI, 1973) and 'Can You Do It'. His leather-lunged vocals graced the multi-million-selling *Back in Black* (1980), which included the British hit 'Rock'n'Roll Ain't Noise Pollution'.

For Those Who Are About to Rock (1981) found the band at the peak of its popularity, topping the American charts and providing more British hits in 'Let's Get It Up' and the title track. With heavy metal attracting a new generation of fans in the eighties, AC/DC achieved the status of elder statesmen of the genre. In 1983 Wright replaced Rudd, and was in turn replaced by Slade, who had previously played with **Manfred Mann's Earth Band** and **Gary Moore**, amongst others. The group's later albums included the Tony Platt-produced *Flick of the Switch* (1983) and *Fly on the Wall* (1985). *Who Made Who* contained songs from the soundtrack of *Maximum Overdrive*, a film based on a Stephen King novel.

Vanda and Harry Young returned as producers for *Blow Up Your Video* (1988). In the same year AC/DC had British hits with 'Heatseeker' and 'That's the Way I Wanna Rock'n'Roll'. *The Razor's Edge* (1990) included the Top Twenty UK hit 'Thunderstruck'. Another live album, *Live*, taken from the band's marathon 1990–1 world tour, followed in 1992, and in 1993 AC/DC had another UK hit with 'Big Gun', taken from the Arnold Schwarzenegger movie *Last Action Hero*. Even better was the Rick Rubin-produced *Ballbreaker* (1995), which saw drummer Rudd back in the group. The band embarked on a two-year tour in support of it. For *Stiff Upper Lip*, their first studio album in five years, George Young returned as producer. The highpoint of the engaging result was 'Can't Stand Still', which saw the band as entertaining as ever. *Bonfire* (1997) was a five-CD box set retrospective.

JOHNNY ACE
b. John Marshall Alexander Jnr, 9 June 1929, Memphis, Tennessee, USA, d. 23 December 1954, Houston, Texas

An R&B ballad singer in the style of **Nat 'King' Cole** and **Charles Brown**, Ace is now best remembered for the manner of his death: he shot himself playing Russian roulette in his dressing room at Christmas, 1954.

In the late forties he performed with Memphis band the Beale Streeters, whose most famous members were **B. B. King** and **Bobby Bland**. His first single for Duke, 'My Song', was No. 1 in the R&B charts in 1952. He followed up with six Top Ten R&B hits, all soothing baritone performances accompanied by subdued small combo arrangements, culminating in the posthumous chart-topper 'Pledging My Love' (1955). **Paul Simon**'s 1983 song 'The Late Great Johnny Ace' drew a parallel between Ace's tragic end and that of **John Lennon**. 'Pledging My Love' was later covered by **Elvis Presley** (1977) and Aaron Neville (1985), and Ace's original version was used in the film *Christine* (1986).

WILLIAM ACKERMAN
b. November 1949, Germany

Composer, guitarist and producer, Ackerman was the founder of Windham Hill Records, the first and most influential label in 'new age' music.

Ackerman moved to the US in 1958 when he was adopted by a Californian family. He learned guitar at the age of 12 and was influenced in developing an acoustic style by such players as Robbi Basho, **John Fahey** and Leo Kottke.

After dropping out of Stanford University, he worked as a boatbuilder, forming Windham Hill Builders. Ackerman also composed music for Stanford University theatrical productions and made a

privately financed album of these pieces in 1976, *In Search of the Turtle's Navel*. The delicate, restful feeling of Ackerman's playing set the tone for much of what was to be labelled 'new age' music in the eighties.

The album saw the launch of the Windham Hill label, for which Ackerman himself later made numerous albums, including *Childhood and Memory* (1979), *Past Light* (1983), the superior *Conferring with the Moon* (1986) and *Imaginary Roads* (1988). He also produced the first Windham Hill bestseller, *Autumn* (1981) by pianist George Winston. Ackerman produced later albums by Winston as well as recordings by other artists, including guitarist Michael Hedges and pianist/composer W. A. Mathieu.

Ackerman was chief executive officer of Windham Hill until 1986, when he stepped down to concentrate on directing the company's creative development. He continued to record into the nineties (*The Opening of Doors*, 1992). In 1992 he sold half of Windham Hill to BMG, which bought the other half in 1996, by which time Ackerman had largely retired from music. *Retrospective* (1993) is a collection of tracks from his eight albums.

DAVID ACKLES
b. 20 February 1937, Rock Island, Illinois, USA, d. 2 March 1999, Tujanga, California

Ackles was one of the many singer-songwriters to emerge in the late sixties whose critical success was never matched by their record sales.

Born into a showbusiness family, he was briefly a child star in a series of B-pictures featuring a dog called Rusty. After graduating in film studies from the University of Southern California he turned to songwriting. He joined Elektra as a staff songwriter in the mid-sixties and eventually persuaded the label to record him. His first two albums (*David Ackles*, 1968, and *Subway to the Country*, 1970) were marked by an eclecticism that was unusual for the time. His third album, *American Gothic* (1972), was a classic. Produced by **Elton John**'s lyricist Bernie Taupin (whose songs for John's 1971 album *Tumbleweed Connection* dealt with similar themes, as did many of the songs of **The Band** at the time), *American Gothic* was unique in the brooding intensity Ackles brought to his melancholic tales of rural despair and deprivation. Where others looked back with simple nostalgia, Ackles, his songs orchestrated in such a manner as to recall both Aaron Copland and **Kurt Weill**, looked back with the toughness that characterizes Willa Cather's treatment of the pioneers in her novels. The album sold badly and after one more on Columbia (*Five and Dime*, 1974) Ackles faded from view. His reputation as one of the more intriguing singer-songwriters of the seventies was confirmed with the reissue of his first three albums in 1994 to strong critical acclaim. By this time he was supporting himself by lecturing on songwriting and writing scores for student productions, including a critically applauded reworking of *The Threepenny Opera* in 1996 for which he also returned to the stage.

ROY ACUFF
b. 15 September 1903, Maynardville, Tennessee, USA, d. 23 November 1992, Nashville, Tennessee

If **Jimmie Rodgers** is the father of country music, Acuff, through his fifty-year association with the *Grand Ole Opry*, is the father of the country-music star system, of country-music publishing, and, to a great extent, of the entire Nashville industry. 'I'm a seller, not a singer,' he once said, and although he was referring to his way with a song, he could just as well have meant his skill with an image. A bizarre mark of his success occurred during the Japanese troops' attack on Okinawa in the Second World War. To demoralize and insult the defending Americans, the Japanese cried 'To hell with Roosevelt, to hell with Babe Ruth, to hell with Roy Acuff!'.

The son of a Baptist minister, and a star athlete at college (he was cheated of a career in baseball through illness), Acuff decided to go into music in his late twenties. After working in medicine-shows – often performing in blackface – where he developed a relaxed showmanship, he established himself on WNOX in Knoxville, Tennessee, on the *Midday Merry-Go-Round* – also an early step for Bill Carlisle and **Kitty Wells**. In 1936 he made his first recordings for ARC with his string band the Crazy Tennesseans. From this session came his two most enduring numbers, the primitive and powerful 'Wabash Cannonball' (actually sung on this original recording by Sam 'Dynamite' Hatcher) and the potent sacred song 'The Great Speckled Bird'. In marked contrast to the stark, wailing style Acuff would later employ, these recordings saw the group also performing softer versions of popular songs (such as **Gus Kahn** and **Walter Don-aldson**'s 'Yes Sir, That's My Baby').

Acuff joined the *Opry* in 1938 and within two years, sponsored by R. J. Reynolds' 'Prince Albert' Tobacco, was the show's star. During the forties he appeared in at least six movies, consolidating the fame he earned with wartime hit records on Okeh like 'Wreck on the Highway', 'Fireball Mail' (both 1942), 'Precious Jewel' and 'Pins and Needles' (both 1943). He was also gradually assembling one of the most talented and long-serving bands in country music, the Smokey Mountain Boys. They included fiddler Howdy Forrester and banjo- and dobro-player Bashful Brother Oswald.

In the forties Acuff made several attempts to enter politics, running for the governorship of Tennessee on the Republican ticket in 1944 and 1948. A more successful career move was the financing in 1942 of a music publishing company in partnership with **Fred Rose**. Acuff–Rose became the most securely established publishing house in Nashville, with vast holdings of Rose's and others' compositions, including those of **Marty Robbins, Felice and Boudleaux Bryant** and the entire catalogue of **Hank Williams**.

In many ways, Acuff's mournful mountain style was at variance with the growing sophistication of most country music, which was seeking to throw off its 'hillbilly' image. Significantly, though his tearful singing – he often cried during performances – won him a huge audience on the *Opry* broadcasts, his sales declined in the late forties and fifties. He moved without significant effect to MGM, Decca and Capitol, though he fared slightly better on Hickory, a label he co-owned with Rose. In 1962 he was the first living musician to be elected to the Country Music Hall of Fame, and in 1972 was honoured with a role in the **Nitty Gritty Dirt Band**'s project *Will the Circle Be Unbroken?*, a testament to the power and raw beauty of his forties records that his later clowning can never diminish.

Continually active in promoting Nashville as a centre of entertainment as well as music, he was involved in the Opryland project and presided over the 1974 opening of the new *Opry* house, at which he gave an on-stage lesson in playing the yo-yo to President Nixon. He continued to perform on the *Opry* every week, but spent most of his time at home in the heart of Opryland, close to his museum of country-music memorabilia.

BRYAN ADAMS
b. Bryan Guy Adams, 5 November 1959, Kingston, Ontario, Canada

An energetic hard-rock singer and guitarist, Adams was the most successful Canadian rock performer of the eighties and was responsible for the bestselling single in the world in 1991, '(Everything I Do) I Do It for You' (A&M). A diamond of rough-edged romanticism, the song topped the UK charts for 15 weeks, the longest period since **Frankie Laine**'s 18-week run in 1953 with 'I Believe'.

The son of English immigrants to Canada, Adams formed his first band in Vancouver in 1976, recording an album with rock band Sweeny Todd that year. Two years later he began songwriting with ex-Prism bass-player Jim Vallance, signing a contract with A&M Records' publishing arm, Rondor Music. Their compositions were recorded by **Kiss**, Bachman-Turner Overdrive, Prism and later **Joe Cocker** and **Bonnie Tyler**.

With a band that included Keith Scott (guitar) and

Dave Taylor (bass), Adams recorded an eponymous album for the Canadian branch of A&M in 1980. Produced by Bob Clearmountain, *You Want It, You Got It* (1981) was Adams' first international release, while his first hit came with the emphatic 'Straight from the Heart' from *Cuts Like a Knife* (1983). With Adams' hearty, slightly husky voice and a winning blend of pop tunes and unwavering rock rhythms, the album provided further successes with 'This Time' and the title track.

A world tour with **Tina Turner** helped to make *Reckless* (1985) an international bestseller. 'Run to You' reached the British Top Twenty and was the first of a series of six American hits taken from the album, including the No. 1 'Heaven', the nostalgic 'Summer of '69', 'One Night Love Affair' and 'It's Only Love', a duet with Turner.

In 1985 Vallance and Adams composed 'Tears Are Not Enough', the Canadian song for famine relief in Africa, and the following year Adams toured America on behalf of Amnesty International with **U2** and **Peter Gabriel**. *Into the Fire* (1986) included weightier songs on such topics as the demise of the American Indians ('Native Son') and the First World War ('Remembrance Day'). It provided hit singles with 'Heat of the Night', 'Into the Fire', 'Hearts on Fire' and 'Victim of Love'. But his greatest success came with the theme song to the Kevin Costner-starring vehicle *Robin Hood: Prince of Thieves*, '(Everything I Do) I Do It for You'* (1991). It was co-written by Robert John Lange, producer of the album *Waking Up the Neighbours*, which, helped by a two-year-long tour, sold over ten million copies worldwide. Subsequent hits included 'Can't Stop This Thing I've Started' and another duet with Turner, 'Thought I'd Died and Gone to Heaven'. A further hit was the plaintive ballad 'Please Forgive Me', once again co-written with his regular producer Lange, from *So Far So Good* (1993). After becoming the first rock star to perform in Vietnam since the war in 1994, Adams had two further US No. 1 singles with film themes: 'All for Love' from *The Three Musketeers*, on which he was partnered by **Rod Stewart** and **Sting**, and 'Have You Ever Loved a Woman?' (1995) from *Don Juan de Marco*.

In 1997 Adams achieved further international success with *18 'Til I Die*, his first solo album since *Waking Up the Neighbours*, on which he adopted a more rocking sound and image in an attempt to appeal to a younger demographic. Later the same year he issued a performance recorded for *MTV Unplugged*, which featured versions of many of his biggest singles, including the recent European hit 'Only Thing That Looks Good on Me Is You'. *On a Day Like Today* (1998) included a pair of UK hit singles in the title track and 'When You're Gone', a duet with **Spice Girl**

Melanie Chisholm. However, it was less successful in North America, failing to make the *Billboard* Hot One Hundred charts. The following year Adams released the greatest hits collection *The Best of Me*, and continued to try and maintain a harder-edged sound and image, opening for the **Rolling Stones** on their *No Sanctuary* tour.

BARRY ADAMSON
b. Manchester, England

A post-punk bassist turned composer of jazz-tinged themes to imaginary films, Adamson's musical career began in the late seventies as bass player in art-school punk band Magazine, fronted by ex-**Buzzcock** Howard Devoto. He followed this with a stint alongside another former member of the Buzzcocks, Pete Shelley, before joining the Bad Seeds, the backing group of Australian goth-rocker **Nick Cave**.

Leaving the Bad Seeds in 1987, Adamson turned his attention to writing jazzy, instrumental pieces in the style of **Ennio Morricone** and **John Barry**. His début solo album, *Moss Side Story* (1989), had little commercial impact, but its hip-hop-inspired sound provided inspiration for British trip-hop acts, including **Portishead**.

In the next few years Adamson fulfilled his dream of producing an actual film score with his work on *Delusion* (1991) and *Gas Food Lodging* (1992), before returning to his solo career with *Soul Murder* (1992) and *The Negro Inside Me* (1993), which included experimentation with ska and funk, respectively. *Oedipus Shmoedipus* (1996) revisited the sound of *Moss Side Story*, and featured an array of guest vocalists, including Jarvis Cocker (**Pulp**), Billy MacKenzie (formerly of the Associates) and old colleague Nick Cave.

After three of his compositions were included on the soundtrack to David Lynch's *Lost Highway* (1996) (which was produced by Trent Reznor of **Nine Inch Nails**), Adamson released his fifth album, *As Above, So Below* (1998), his most successful to date, which saw him sing for the first time. *The Murky World of Barry Adamson* (1999) compiled the best of his solo work.

CANNONBALL ADDERLEY
b. Julian Adderley, 15 September 1928, Tampa, Florida, USA, d. 8 August 1975, Gary, Indiana

A disciple of **Charlie Parker**, alto-saxophonist Adderley developed a rhythmic soul-jazz in the mid-sixties, notably on 'Mercy Mercy Mercy' (1966). Among the members of his group was **Weather Report** founder Joe Zawinul, while Adderley himself played on **Miles Davis**'s classic *Kind of Blue* (1959). With the more R&B-based **King Curtis**, Adderley was the key influence on the later school of rock saxophonists exemplified by **David Sanborn**.

After studying music at school in Tallahassee and college, Adderley became the musical-director of Dillard High School in Fort Lauderdale in 1948. While serving in the army in 1952–3 he led dance bands, moving to New York as a professional musician the following year. He first recorded with his trumpeter brother Nat and **Kenny Clarke** for Savoy in 1955. A quintet featuring Adderley's brother Nat (*b. 25 November 1931, Tampa, Florida, USA*) was commercially unsuccessful and in 1957 Cannonball joined Davis's group. Their first recording together was *Somethin' Else* (Blue Note, 1958), released under Adderley's name. When the Davis group became a sextet with the addition of **John Coltrane**, they recorded *Milestones* (Columbia, 1958), on which Adderley took one of his most praised solos on 'Straight No Chaser'. He also worked on the restrained *Kind of Blue* and the orchestral version of themes from **George Gershwin**'s *Porgy and Bess* (1960).

He left Davis in 1959 and during the early sixties recorded frequently for Riverside, having a jukebox hit with pianist Bobby Timmons' funky 'This Here' (1960) and reaching the R&B Top Thirty and pop Top Fifty with Galt MacDermot's 'African Waltz' (1961), a British hit for **John Dankworth**. 'The Jive Samba' (1963) also made the charts while Adderley went on to work with singer Nancy Wilson on records for Capitol.

His most famous quintet, comprising Nat Adderley, Zawinul (keyboards), Vic Gaskin (bass) and Roy McCurdy (drums) cut Zawinul's riff- and crescendo-laden 'Mercy Mercy Mercy' (Capitol, 1966), a Top Twenty pop hit. A vocal version of the tune was an R&B hit for Marlena Shaw on Cadet, while the Adderley Quintet had R&B success with the **Staple Singers'** 'Why Am I Treated So Bad' (1967). Adderley's 'Sack o'Woe' became a standard in the repertoire of later R&B and soul-jazz groups.

Adderley continued to record prolifically, with Zawinul's 'Country Preacher' (1970) an R&B success. Later group members included **Yusef Lateef** and **George Duke**, and Adderley's final records – *Phenix* (1975) and *Big Man* (1976) – were made for Fantasy.

KING SUNNY ADE
b. Sunday Adeniyi, 1946, Ondo State, Nigeria

Ade was a leading exponent of 'juju' music, a style which originated in the forties and fused traditional Yoruba music with highlife, the Ghanaian dance music. Adding electric instrumentation, guitarist and singer Ade and his African Beats frequently toured Europe in the seventies and eighties.

His father was an organist and his mother a church singer. Ade's own professional career began in 1965 as a musician with Moses Olaiya's travelling theatre troupe. Moving to the Nigerian capital Lagos, he played with highlife bands before forming the Green Spots. The group's first hit was a football song, 'Challenge Cup' (1967). In the same year he recorded the first of his twelve albums for Song Records, *Aluna Loluwa*.

After a dispute with Song in 1974, Ade went on to release numerous albums on his own Sunny Alade label, performing religious and socially-based songs with a guitar and vocal chorus group that numbered up to eighteen members. In 1975, the year Ade made his first trip to Britain and changed the name of his band to African Beats, Bob Aladeniyi, the band's deputy leader, left to form the Jungle Rock Stars. For much of the second half of the seventies Ade toured, bringing his guitar-led juju music with its tight harmonies and songs about Nigerian social issues to expatriate Nigerian audiences in the USA, Japan and Europe.

In 1981 Ade signed with Island Records for Europe and North America. His first records, *Juju Music* (1981) and *Synchro System* (1983), were critical successes as was *Aura* (1984), which included **Stevie Wonder** as a guest musician, but sales were small and Island dropped him in 1985. In the same year the African Beats broke up and Ade formed a new band, Golden Mercury, and returned to Nigeria. There he recorded solely for the domestic market and performed at his own club in Lagos, occasionally performing in the USA. *Live Ju Ju* (Provogue, 1988) was recorded in Seattle, Washington, USA. It was followed by the superior *The Return of the Juju King* (1989).

In 1994 Ade toured the USA and released *Live at the Hollywood Palace* through EMI, but for most of the nineties he remained in Nigeria, issuing a stream of reissues of his Green Spot days. The most notable of these were *Master Guitarist, Vols 1 & 2* (1994, 1995). In 1998 Ade made his first tour of Europe for some time and in 1999 performed once again in the US with sets that downplayed his social concerns in favour of the rhythmic delights of Juju. He followed that with *Seven Degrees North* (Mesa, 2000), on which he again centred on the exuberance of Juju on songs such as 'Congratulations' and 'Merciful God'.

LOU ADLER
b. 1935, Los Angeles, California, USA

Adler was one of the key figures in the development of California pop in the sixties, moving from bubble-gum pop to protest to rock, finally arriving in the seventies in Hollywood.

Having drifted into the music business through organizing dances at roller rinks in the Los Angeles area in 1958, Adler was soon writing and recording with **Herb Alpert**. In 1959 they wrote 'Baby Talk', which gave **Jan and Dean** their first Top Ten hit on the local Dore label and, in 1960, wrote 'Wonderful World' for **Sam Cooke**. The first was a nonsense song, the second a teen ballad; both were typical of their output. After briefly managing Jan and Dean and masterminding their move from Dore to Liberty, Adler was appointed West Coast manager first of publishers Screen Gems and then of Al Nevins' and **Don Kirshner**'s Aldon Music, thus putting him in regular touch with Brill Building songwriters such as **Carole King**, whose demos he pitched to record companies and artists. In 1963 he married Shelley Fabares, who in 1962 had a million-seller with the wistful 'Johnny Angel' (Colpix), and in 1964 he set up shop on his own with Dunhill Productions and Trousdale Music.

His key signings were Steve Barri and **P. F. Sloan**, who together and separately wrote and produced numerous records, ranging from the then current craze of surf music to protest songs. Dunhill quickly expanded as Adler signed the likes of **The Mamas and the Papas**, the Grass Roots (who had a steady stream of hits with producer Barri) and Richard Harris (who had an unlikely million-seller with **Jimmy Webb**'s 'MacArthur Park', 1968), while continuing to work as a producer with Jan and Dean and **Johnny Rivers**.

By now an established figure within the industry, Adler, with John Phillips (of The Mamas and the Papas), **Paul Simon**, Terry Melcher and Rivers, sponsored the 1967 Monterey Pop Festival that turned the spotlight on the emerging San Francisco groups. The same year, Adler sold Dunhill to ABC and formed Ode, on which Scott McKenzie had a million-seller with the hippie anthem 'San Francisco (Be Sure to Wear Flowers in Your Hair)' (1967) – a Phillips composition. Other Ode acts included **Spirit**, alternative comedians Cheech and Chong, and Carole King, whose epochal singer-songwriter album *Tapestry* was produced by Adler (1971). Thereafter, though he continued to produce King (including her *Speeding Time*, Atlantic, 1983), Adler's interests turned increasingly to films. He produced *Brewster McCloud* (1970), was involved in *Phantom of the Paradise* (1974), produced *The Rocky Horror Show* in Los Angeles and directed *Up in Smoke* (1979), the Cheech and Chong comedy.

In 1994 Adler briefly returned to the music business with a new label, Ode 2 Kids, and All God's Children, a 23-strong gospel choir of children aged between eight and eighteen.

AEROSMITH

Tom Hamilton, b. 31 December 1951, Colorado Springs, Colorado, USA; Joey Kramer, b. 21 June 1950, New York; Joe Perry, b. 10 September 1950, Boston, Massachusetts (replaced by Jim Crespo); Steve Tyler, b. Steven Tallarico, 26 March 1948, New York; Brad Whitford, b. 23 February 1952, Winchester, Massachusetts (replaced by Rick Dufay)

Once dubbed 'The Godfather of American Hard Rock', Aerosmith were part of the first wave of American heavy-metal groups. They were also among the most durable of bands, performing and recording for over two decades. In the course of their career, the simple high energy of their early work was transmuted into a sophisticated but still muscular hard-rock sound. Their songs have been covered by **R.E.M.** ('Toys in the Attic') and **Guns N' Roses** ('Mam Kin').

Clearly influenced by the **Rolling Stones** (Tyler closely resembled Mick Jagger) and the **Yardbirds**, Aerosmith was formed in New Hampshire in 1970 by singer Tyler and guitarist Whitford. With Perry (guitar), Hamilton (bass) and Kramer (drums), the group played the New England bar and club circuit and in 1972 signed to Columbia.

After the release of an eponymous début album co-written by Tyler and Perry, producer Jack Douglas supervised *Get Your Wings* (1974). Frequent live appearances throughout America took sales of *Toys in the Attic* (1975) to over a million and 'Sweet Emotion' was a minor hit while 'Dream on' (from the group's first album) reached the Top Ten in 1976. 'Walk This Way' and 'Last Child' from *Rocks* (1976) were also successful.

After releasing *Draw the Line* (1978), the group appeared in the film *Sgt Pepper's Lonely Hearts Club Band*, performing **The Beatles**' 'Come Together', which was a Top Thirty hit in 1978. The concert album *Live Bootleg* was released in 1979. Soon after the appearance of *Night in the Ruts*, Perry left to form the Joe Perry Project, recording *Let the Music Do the Talking* (Columbia, 1980) and *I've Got the Rock'n'Rolls Again* (1981).

With the additional loss of Whitford, who recorded one album with former **Ted Nugent** singer Derek St Holmes, and a serious motorcycle accident involving Perry, Aerosmith's next studio album, *Rock in a Hard Place*, did not appear until 1982. The album's relative lack of success brought about a reunion of the original line-up in 1985 when the group signed to Geffen for the commercially successful *Done with Mirrors*.

Aerosmith were associated with a surprise hit in the following year when the rap group **Run DMC** revived the band's 'Walk This Way', with Perry and Tyler appearing on the new version. The band's own next album was the Bruce Fairbairn-produced *Permanent Vacation* (1987), which included the hit single 'Dude (Looks Like a Lady)' and a version of the Lennon–McCartney song 'I'm Down'. Following a move to Geffen they charted in 1989 with 'Love in an Elevator' from *Pump*.

In many ways their most influential album, *Pump*, which included the ballad about an abused child 'Janie's Got a Gun', was celebrated both by old fans as marking a revitalization of the group and by the new wave of American hard rock acts, notably Guns N' Roses and **Nirvana** (whose *Incesticide* includes a joint tribute to them and **Led Zeppelin**, 'Aero Zeppelin'). The Bruce Fairbairn-produced *Get a Grip* (1993) was almost as successful, staying in the US charts for over a year. It was followed by the greatest hits collection, *Big Ones* (1994).

The release of their next album was delayed for three years due to a legal dispute between Geffen and the band's new label, Virgin. Eventually released in 1997, *Nine Lives*, which included several Eastern-flavoured tracks, débuted at No. 1 in the US *Billboard* charts, but failed to replicate the international success of its predecessors. They regained their European popularity the following year with the release of the Kevin Shirley-penned 'I Don't Wanna Miss a Thing', which remained in the UK Top Forty for 13 weeks. A live album, *A Little South of Sanity*, followed in 1999.

AFGHAN WHIGS

John Curley; Greg Dulli; Steve Earle (replaced by Paul Buchignani, replaced by Michael Horrigan); Rick McCollum

A soul-influenced grunge act, Afghan Whigs' career was hampered by the personal troubles of Dulli, the group's principal songwriter.

Guitarist/vocalist Dulli reportedly met lead guitarist McCollum in an Athens, Ohio, jail cell on Halloween in 1986. After recruiting drummer Earle (like Dulli and McCollum a student at the University of Cinncinati) and bassist Curley, a photographer with the *Cinncinati Enquirer*, the Afghan Whigs gained a loyal live following in the late eighties, and released their début album, *Big Top Halloween* (1988), on local independent label Ultra Suede. Combining seventies rock with *angst*-ridden lyrics, the album drew the attention of grunge label Sub Pop, who signed the band at the turn of the decade.

The Whigs' first Sub Pop release, *Up on It* (1990), produced by Jack Endino, was followed by a lengthy tour, on which Dulli developed pneumonia and marked paranoid tendencies. Retiring to his LA apartment, Dulli set to work on writing the band's next album, as well as a screenplay and several short stories. The result of this spurt of creativity was the underground hit *Congregation* (1992), which drew the attention of the major labels and saw the band sign to Elektra after releasing a final EP on Sub Pop, *Uptown Avondale* (1992), a selection of covers of R&B and soul standards, including Freda Payne's 'Band of Gold' and Dallas Frazier's 'True Love Travels on a Gravel Road'.

Gentleman (1993), the group's major label début, saw the band delve further into Dulli's personal traumas, and was again widely ignored by mainstream audiences, although the single 'Debonair' was heavily rotated on MTV. An extended break followed, before the release of *Black Love* (1996), another essay on self-loathing with heavy soul riffs. The first album to feature new drummer Paul Buchignani, *Black Love* included covers of **The Who**'s 'Quadrophenia' and 'Lets Get It on' by **Marvin Gaye**. Two further EPs followed on Elektra, *Honky's Ladder* and *Bonnie and Clyde*, before the band moved labels again, signing with Columbia and recruiting another drummer, Michael Horrigan.

Their sixth album, the soul-informed *1965* (1998), saw the band at last achieve a degree of commercial success, though it was marred by a brutal attack on Dulli at a Whigs' gig, which left him unable to perform for several months.

AFRIKA BAMBAATAA
See **Bambaataa, Afrika**

MILTON AGER AND JACK YELLEN
Milton Ager, b. 6 October 1893, Chicago, Illinois, USA, d. 6 April 1979, Los Angeles, California; Jack Yellen, b. 1892, Poland, d. 17 April 1991

Ager and Yellen composed 'Happy Days Are Here Again', which was later adopted by Franklin D. Roosevelt as his campaign song because of its anti-Depression sentiments.

Ager began as a song plugger and arranger for composers such as **Irving Berlin** and **Walter Donaldson**. While in the forces in the First World War he wrote 'Everything is Peaches Down in Georgia' with Grant Clark, which gave **Al Jolson** a big hit. After the war he teamed up in New York with Yellen.

Born in Poland, Yellen emigrated to America in 1897 and turned to songwriting as a means of working his way through college. The duo's best work included 'Ain't She Sweet?' (1927), 'Hard-Hearted Hannah' (1924) and 'Happy Feet', which with 'Music Hath Charms' was featured in the musical extravaganza *The King of Jazz* (1930), starring **Paul Whiteman** and his orchestra.

Despite the increase in the demand for songs for both stage and screen musicals in the thirties, the pair's output slackened. Where other songwriting teams built solid careers in Hollywood on strong Broadway foundations, Yellen and Ager, having drifted to Hollywood, simply drifted away. Thus, after the sale of their publishing company to Warner Brothers, Yellen virtually retired. His occasional work with Ager included the 1929 score for *Honky Tonk*, the film début of **Sophie Tucker**. Ager continued writing with various lyricists, but never as successfully as with Yellen. He too retired after the Second World War.

A-HA

Magne Foruholmen, b. 1 November 1962, Norway; Morten Harket, b. 14 September 1959, Norway; Pal Waaktar, b. 6 September 1963, Oslo

A Norwegian soft-rock band, A-Ha briefly were one of the most successful groups of the late eighties. The popularity of the band, like that of their Scandinavian predecessors **Abba**, reflected both the international character of pop music and the centrality of the English language, in which A-Ha both wrote and sang.

Influenced by **The Beatles** and the **Doors**, Foruholmen (keyboards) and Waaktar (guitar) played in Oslo groups Spider Empire and Bridges in the mid-seventies, releasing one self-financed album. They unsuccessfully travelled to London to seek a record contract in 1982 before recruiting vocalist Harket from soul band Soldier Blue.

Returning to England as a trio, A-Ha were signed to Warners, releasing 'Take on Me' (1985). The record was a hit in Europe and reached No. 1 in America some months later with the aid of a Steve Barron-directed video that included widely-admired animation effects. The band's status as teen-idols was established by the subsequent success of 'The Sun Always Shines on TV', 'Train of Thought' and 'Hunting High and Low', the title track from the band's 1986 début album.

Cliff Richard's producer Alan Tarney supervised *Scoundrel Days* (1986), which included the hit 'Manhattan Skyline' (1987). In the same year the group's lyricist Waaktar co-wrote the theme for the James Bond film *The Living Daylights* with **John Barry**. It provided A-Ha with a further Top Twenty hit in Britain.

In 1988 the group released *Stay on These Roads*, whose title track was another hit. Meanwhile A-Ha's former musical director, Dag Kolsrud, formed his own Scandinavian trio, One 2 Many, to release 'Downtown' (A&M, 1988).

In 1989 Harket starred in the film *Kamilla and the Thief*. *East of the Sun, West of the Moon* (1990) included the British Top Twenty single, 'Crying in the Rain', a revival of the **Everly Brothers**' 1961 hit. It was followed by the career retrospective *Headlines & Deadlines* (1991). They returned to the UK charts in 1993 with the single 'Dark Is the Night' and album *Memorial Beach*, after which the group members developed their solo careers. In the same year Harket changed direction to cut his first solo album, his own settings of twelve Norwegian poems about the life of Christ. Foruholmen turned to film scores with the

soundtrack to *Tikniver I Hjertet* (1995), Harket continued his solo career with *Wild Seed* (1995) and the Norwegian-only release *Vogts Villa* (1996), while Waaktar started recording under the name of Paul Savoy (*Mary Is Coming*, 1996; *Lacklustre Me*, 1997). The general failure of these projects led to the band officially re-forming in 1999 and releasing *Minor Earth, Major Sky* (2000), which won them good reviews and sales for its enchanting mix of Nordic gloom and jaunty pop tunes.

AIR

Jean-Benoit Dunckel, b. Versailles, France; Nicolas Godin, b. Versailles, France

Alongside **Daft Punk**, Air led the explosion of French pop/dance in the late nineties.

Dunckel and Godin met as students. With Etienne de Crecy they formed a short-lived indie band, Orange, but went their separate ways at the end of their education, with Dunckel going on to teach maths while Godin studied architecture. They were persuaded to reunite and record together by the Source record label, and contributed to the *Sourcelab* EP (1995).

Inspired by their *Sourcelab* contribution, Air cut a series of singles, including 'Modular Mix', and an EP, *Premières Symptomes* (1997). Their full-length début, *Moon Safari* (1998), was influenced by artists as diverse as the **Beach Boys** and Claude Debussy, and made use of ancient keyboards and modern-day electronica. Positively received, it also sold well. The success of the singles 'Sexy Boy' and 'Kelly Watch the Stars' prompted the band to embark on their first tour, with a band made up of musicians from their days at their Versailles college.

Air's follow-up to *Moon Safari* was the soundtrack to the Sofia Coppola-directed film *The Virgin Suicides* (2000).

AIR SUPPLY

Russell Hitchcock, b. 15 June 1949, Melbourne, Australia; Graham Russell, b. 1 June 1950, England; Ralph Cooper, b. 6 April 1951, Coffs Harbour, Australia; Frank Esler-Smith, b. 5 June 1948, London; Rex Goh, b. 5 May 1951, Singapore; David Green, b. 30 October 1949, Melbourne; David Morse, b. 5 November 1957, Adelaide

A soft-rock band whose name was chosen as a counterblast to heavy metal, Air Supply worked within the style pioneered in the seventies by **Bread**. With ten hit singles, the group was the most successful Australian band of the eighties on an international scale.

The group originally consisted only of singers Hitchcock and Russell, who were in the Australian cast of **Andrew Lloyd Webber**'s *Jesus Christ Superstar*. The former composed their earliest Australian hits, which included 'Love and Other Bruises' (Columbia, 1976). In 1979 they added the other members as instrumental backing, with Esler-Smith on keyboards and Morse and Goh on guitars, and switched labels to Arista.

A string of eight American Top Ten hits followed, including three million-sellers: the limpid 'All Out of Love' (1980 – their biggest hit in Britain), 'The One That You Love' (1981), an American No. 1, and the lush, operatic 'Making Love Out of Nothing at All' (1983). The last track was produced by Jim Steinman, who replaced earlier producers Robby Porter and Harry Maslin. 'Just as I Am' (1985) was an American hit, but *Hearts in Motion* (1986) sold poorly. In 1991 Air Supply moved to Giant for the lesser *Vanishing Race* (1993) and *Greatest Hits – Live* (1996). They continue to tour and are especially popular in South-East Asia, as evidenced by the number of karaoke-only releases of their material.

LAUREL AITKEN
b. 1928, Cuba

One of Jamaica's most versatile and popular singers in the fifties, Aitken was also one of the first to emigrate to England.

During the fifties he sang and recorded in various styles borrowed from American black music, notably the boogie tunes of **Louis Jordan**. Titles in this vein included 'Back to New Orleans' and 'More Whiskey'. When the Jamaican Broadcasting Corporation set up the island's first chart in 1959, Aitken's 'Boogie Rock' was one of the first records to reach No. 1. Other hits followed, including 'Little Sheila', for **Chris Blackwell**'s Starlight label (a foreunner of Island), which was the first Jamaican recording issued in Britain.

At the beginning of the sixties he moved to Britain (where several of his records had been issued on the Melodisc label since the mid-fifties). There he recorded some of the earliest ska songs for Island and then for Doctor Bird. Aitken tended to follow currently popular themes and styles, cutting Rastafarian anthems like 'Haile Selassie' and 'Deliverance Will Come', rude reggae ('Pussy Price'), skinhead themes ('Skinhead Train'), songs of social commentary ('Landlords and Tenants') and even reggae versions of white pop such as the songs of the **Everly Brothers**.

Aitken's only pop hit came at the height of the Two-Tone music phase in 1980. Backed by Unitone, he sang 'Rudy Got Married' (I Spy), an answer record to the **Specials**' 'Message to You Rudy'.

ALABAMA
Randy Yeull Owen, b. 13 December 1949, Fort Payne, Alabama, USA; Jeffrey Alan Cook, b. 27 August 1949, Fort Payne; Teddy Wayne Gentry, b. 22 January 1952, Fort Payne; Mark Joel Herndon, b. 11 May 1955, Springfield, Massachusetts

Alabama blended pop, rock and country to produce an exuberant style of music that, unusually, was as popular with traditional country-music fans as youthful audiences. As a result, they achieved an unparalleled run of seventeen consecutive country chart-toppers by 1986 and won the Country Music Association's 'Entertainer of the Year' award. In the eighties and nineties they had several pop hits without alienating their country audience.

The core of the group included three cousins, Owen, Cook and Gentry, who started playing together (with another cousin, Jackie Owen, on drums) in the Fort Payne area at dances as Wildcountry. They graduated to backing touring country stars in the early seventies before making their first record, 'I Want to Be with You' (GRT), as Alabama in 1977. From the beginning their records reflected both their traditional leanings and their background as a dance band – unusually for a country act, like rock groups, they played their own instruments on record, rather than relying on session players. With Herndon on drums, the group signed with MDJ Records and secured their first country Top Twenty record, with the autobiographical 'My Home's in Alabama' (1980), in which Owen's mellow lead singing was supported by traditional close harmonies and the driving beat of Southern rock. The success of this, written like most of the group's songs by Owen and Gentry, led to a contract with RCA in 1980, their first of numerous country chart-toppers, 'Why Lady Why', and their first Top Twenty hit, 'Feel So Right' (both 1981). These, in common with most of their hits, which include 'Love in the First Degree' (1982), 'The Closer You Get' (1983), 'There's No Way' (1985) and 'She and I' (1986), were romantic ballads, but equally important to Alabama's success, especially in live performance, were up-tempo numbers such as 'Mountain Music' and 'Tennessee River' featured on *Alabama Live* (1988).

Alabama's success prefigured that of **Ricky Skaggs**, **George Strait**, the **Judds** and other performers who emerged in the eighties and were even more committed to traditional styles of country music. In 1989 the band was named 'group of the decade' by the Academy of Country Music. Their hit albums of the early nineties included *Pass It on Down* (1991) and *American Pride* (1993), which included the hit single 'Hometown Honeymoon'. By the time of *In Pictures* (1995), their thirteenth album of original material, although their sound was predictable, it remained as popular as ever. 1998 saw the career retrospective, *For the Record: 41 Number One Hits*, which sold over 2 million units within the year and continued selling well in 1999.

THE ALBION BAND

Shirley Collins, b. 5 July 1935, Hastings, Sussex, England; Ashley Hutchings, b. 26 January 1945, Southgate, Middlesex; Dave Mattacks, b. 13 March 1948, London; Simon Nicol, b. 13 October 1945, London; John Tams; Graeme Taylor; Cathy LeSurf; Polly Bolton; Phil Beer

During the seventies, eighties and nineties former **Fairport Convention** and **Steeleye Span** bassist Hutchings led a series of groups with the Albion title. Dedicated to creating forms of English (rather than Celtic) electric folk music, the band included many leading folk instrumentalists and provided music for several National Theatre productions.

Hutchings' first Albion Country Band was put together to back his then wife Collins, a noted traditional singer who had also collected folk songs with **Alan Lomax**, on *No Roses* (Pegasus, 1971). The album included a version of the traditional 'Hal-an-Tow', which was later recorded by the Oyster Band (Cooking Vinyl, 1987), a leading group of the eighties folk-dance revival in England which Hutchings' pioneering work helped to inspire. Among the Country Band members were John Kirkpatrick (accordion) and guitarist **Richard Thompson**, who joined Hutchings to record *Morris on* (Island, 1972), which consisted of amplified versions of morris-dance tunes.

Kirkpatrick was also part of the later version of the Albion Country Band whose *The Battle of the Field* (Island, 1976) was recorded in 1973. The album included two Thompson compositions and contributions from **Martin Carthy** and Fairport Convention's Simon Nicol. That group was not a permanent one, and Hutchings formed a folk-dance band, the Etchingham Steam Band, with Collins but returned to the Albion theme in 1976 with the Albion Dance Band. This ensemble, whose shifting personnel included Nicol and drummer Mattacks, became a major attraction on the folk club and festival circuit, taking part in the National Theatre's production of *The Passion Play*, based on medieval mystery plays. In 1977 it signed to Harvest and released *The Prospect Before Us*, which introduced lead vocalist Tams.

A further name change, to the Albion Band, heralded a new emphasis on song rather than dance. The **Joe Boyd**-produced *Rise Up Like the Sun* (Harvest, 1978) was one of the most impressive electric folk albums of the period, mixing traditional songs like 'The Gresford Mining Disaster' with contemporary material. Guest vocalists included **Kate McGarrigle** and Andy Fairweather-Low. Among other regular members of the group were ex-**Soft Machine** violinist Ric Sanders and guitarist Taylor.

Later Albion Band recordings included *Lark Rise to Candleford* (Charisma, 1980), taken from the stage production of Flora Thompson's memoirs of Victo-

rian country life, *Shuffle Off* (Spindrift, 1983), released under the Albion Dance Band name, *Under the Rose* (1986) and *Stella Maris* (1987).

Tams later left the band to work on further plays and formed the Home Service, a folk-rock band that released *Alright Jack* (Making Waves, 1986) and *The Mysteries* (Coda, 1987), the music from the National Theatre production. Meanwhile, Hutchings performed and recorded a one-man show devoted to *Cecil Sharp* (1986) and led the Albion Band '89 on *Give Me a Saddle, I'll Trade You a Car* (Topic, 1989). *Live in Concert* (1993) melded performances from 1977 and 1982 to good effect.

Later members of the band's shifting line-up included singers Polly Bolton and Cathy LeSurf (the lead vocalist on the 1980 novelty hit 'Day Trip to Bangor' by Fiddler's Dram) and multi-instrumentalist Phil Beer.

ARTHUR ALEXANDER

b. 10 May 1940, Florence, Alabama, USA, d. 13 June 1993, Nashville, Tennessee

A short series of modestly produced but convincing and memorable records in the early sixties established Alexander as a source-figure for British rhythm and blues.

In his late teens, after some experience with a local gospel group, Alexander became associated with Muscle Shoals producer **Rick Hall** for whom he recorded 'You Better Move on' (Dot, 1961), which reached the Top Thirty in the USA. It was followed by the **Barry Mann**–Cynthia Weil composition 'Where Have You Been?' and his own 'Anna' (both 1962), his only R&B Top Ten entry. These and 'Go Home Girl' (1962) were taken up by innumerable British groups as readily assimilable down-home soul corollaries of contemporary **Drifters** or **Ben E. King** work. 'Anna' and 'You Better Move on' appeared on early records by **The Beatles** and the **Rolling Stones** respectively. (The latter was revived by **Ry Cooder**.) 'A Shot of Rhythm and Blues', the original flip-side of 'You Better Move on', also became a sub-cultural anthem and was memorably recorded by **Johnny Kidd**.

Subsequent unsuccessful records for Dot, Sound Stage 7 and Monument, and a period of illness, put Alexander out of the record business until 1972, when he recorded *Arthur Alexander* (Warners), which included 'Rainbow Road', **Dan Penn**'s fictionalized account of the singer's life. He had a minor hit with 'Every Day I Have to Cry Some' (Buddah, 1975), an earlier hit for Steve Alaimo (Checker, 1963), and recorded with **Carl Perkins** on Koala in 1979. He subsequently retired to become a busdriver in Cleveland. A posthumous album, *Lonely Just Like Me*, was issued in 1993 but his essential R&B legacy was assembled on *A Shot of Rhythm and Soul* (Ace, 1982).

ALICE IN CHAINS
Jerry Cantrell, b. 18 March 1966, Tacoma, Washington, USA; Sean Kinney, b. 26 May 1966, Seattle, Washington; Layne Staley, b. 22 August 1967, Bellevue, Washington; Mike Starr, b. 4 April 1966, Honolulu, Hawaii (replaced by Mike Inez)

A gloom-laden Seattle heavy-rock quartet that made extensive use of the heavy-metal vocabulary as practiced by **Black Sabbath**, Alice in Chains rose to international fame at the height of the grunge movement of the early nineties.

Vocalist/guitarist Staley, lead guitarist Cantrell, bassist Starr and drummer Kinney began performing in the Seattle area in 1987, signing to Columbia for the release of their début EP, *We Die Young*, in 1989, which became an underground hit. *Facelift* (1990) achieved gold status in the US, bolstered by the success of the single 'Man in the Box' and tours in support of **Megadeth** and **Iggy Pop**, before the band released the acoustic *Sap* EP (1992), which had a softer, acoustic feel.

Alice in Chains were recast as a grunge band after the success of **Nirvana**'s *Nevermind*, and achieved phenomenal success with their second full-length album, *Dirt* (Columbia, 1992), having also contributed to the *Singles* soundtrack. An intense essay on self-loathing and heroin addiction, the accusingly powerful *Dirt* soon reached multi-platinum status and spawned a pair of hit singles, 'Would?' and 'Rooster'. The album was quickly followed by the acoustic-led *Jar of Flies* (1993), which became the first EP to début at number one on the *Billboard* chart. The band soon announced a year-long hiatus as Staley performed with grunge supergroup Mad Season with members of the Screaming Trees and **Pearl Jam**. Alice in Chains reconvened in 1995 for their eponymous third album, before recording a highly successful MTV unplugged session, their first live show in three years. The performance was released as an album in 1996 but soon looked like being the group's final recording after Cantrell, whose claustrophobic lyrics were unusually well crafted for a heavy metal/grunge act, embarked on a solo career, backed by Inez and Kinney. His acclaimed *Boggy Depot* (1998) achieved widespread success in the US. It was followed by a box set Alice in Chains retrospective in 1999, *Music Bank*, which collected the best of the band's studio material with rarities and live recordings, and charted the growing elegance through which they presented their despairing vision.

ALICE COOPER
See **Cooper, Alice**

ALL SAINTS
Natalie Appleton, b. 14 April 1973, Canada; Nicole Appleton, b. 17 December 1974, Canada; Melanie Blatt, b. 25 March 1975; Shaznay Lewis, b. 14 October 1975, London, England

All Saints, one of the first wave of **Spice Girls** clones, soon gained recognition as a *bona fide* pop sensation in their own right. Their name comes from the London street on which they met.

The group originally consisted of just Blatt and songwriter Lewis, who recorded a single for ZTT Records with R&B vocalist Simone Rainford, 'Lets Get Started' (1995). When it failed, ZTT dropped the group and Rainford left.

Blatt and Lewis soon recruited two new members, Canadian sisters Nicole and Natalie Appleton, and under the guidance of manager John Benson signed to London Records, who matched the group with two big-name producers, Nellee Hooper (**Björk**, **Massive Attack**) and Cameron McVey (**Neneh Cherry**). Their first single as a four-piece, 'I Know Where It's At', reached number four in the British charts and sold well in Europe and Asia. The follow-up, 'Never Ever'* (1997), spent several months in the UK Top Ten before reaching No. 1. Their eponymous début album* consolidated their appeal, and included three further hit singles in 'War of Nerves', 'Bootie Call' and the double A-side 'Lady Marmalade'/'Under the Bridge', the latter a cover of a **Red Hot Chili Peppers** original that caused controversy when it was revealed to be about heroin.

All Saints' personal lives entered the public domain in 1998 as their popularity rose, with Nicole Appleton beginning an on–off relationship with **Robbie Williams** and Blatt having a baby with former **Jamiroquai** bassist Stuart Zender. The band won two Brit Awards and embarked on their first British tour, and took tentative steps towards an attempt at conquering the US. Blatt and the Appleton sisters took time off from the band the following year to take starring roles in the Dave Stewart-directed *Honest*, a would-be erotic/comic gangster movie set in 1960s London that garnered some of the worst reviews of any recent film. The group returned to the top of the UK charts in 2000 with 'Pure Shores', taken from the soundtrack to *The Beach*. They followed that with another UK hit single, 'Black Coffee', taken from the band's second album, the William Orbit-produced *Saints & Sinners*.

MOSE ALLISON
b. 11 November 1927, Tippo, Mississippi, USA

Middle-Class White Boy, the title of a 1982 Elektra album, aptly summed up the paradoxical quality of blues singer and idiosyncratic pianist Allison. A white Southerner, he grew up on a mixture of rhythm and blues and modern and big-band jazz. The result was an unusual style of blues music delivered in a laconic, breathy vocal mode.

In the fifties Allison, then deeply influenced by **Bud Powell**, accompanied a wide range of jazz performers including **Stan Getz** (1956–57 and 1959–60), with whom he recorded *Soft Swing* (Verve, 1957), **Gerry Mulligan** and Al Cohn. His piano style and occasional trumpet playing were very much in the bebop mainstream.

His first album for Prestige was the remarkable *Back Country Suite* (1957). Inspired by the approach of Bela Bartók's *Hungarian Sketches*, it mixed Allison originals with standards like 'Blueberry Hill'. It was followed by *Local Color*, which included 'Parchman Farm', Allison's song about the notorious Mississippi penal institution. The range of his work was quite extraordinary.

In addition to his own notable compositions ('Young Man's Blues', 'Moon & Cypress') his early recordings included **Willie Dixon**'s 'Seventh Son', **Duke Ellington**'s 'Do Nothing Till You Hear From Me', **Ray Noble**'s 'I Hadn't Anyone Till You' and **Charlie Parker**'s 'Yardbird Suite'. A selection of these is available on the CD *Mose Allison Sings & Plays* (1992). When Allison left Prestige in 1959 he recorded several albums for Columbia, including *I Love the Life I Live* (1960), before signing to Atlantic in 1962. The best of his ten albums for the label were *Mose Alive!* (1966) and *Mose in Your Ear* (1972).

After a six-year gap between recording contracts, he signed to Elektra, for whom he cut the 1983 album *Lessons in Living*, which included a remake of one of his earliest successes, 'Seventh Son'. That song and others like 'Parchman Farm' and 'I Love the Life I Live' made Allison an important influence on jazz-orientated British singers of the sixties such as **Georgie Fame**, who recorded Allison's version of 'Parchman Farm' on his first album. His 'Young Man's Blues' was a cult favourite among the mods of that time and was recorded by **The Who**. 'Everybody's Cryin' Mercy' was covered by **Bonnie Raitt**. In 1988 Allison guested on Pete Townshend's solo album *The Iron Man* and recorded new songs on *Ever Since the World Ended*. In 1990 he released the laconic *In My Back Yard* (Blue Note). He followed this with the even better *The Earth Wants You* (1994).

THE ALLMAN BROTHERS BAND

Duane Allman, b. 20 November 1946, Nashville, Tennessee, USA, d. 29 October 1971, Macon, Georgia; Gregg Allman, b. 8 December 1947, Nashville; Berry Oakley, b. 4 April 1948, Chicago, Illinois, d. 11 November 1972,

Macon; Richard Betts, b. 12 December 1943, West Palm Beach, Florida; Jai Johanny Johanson, b. John Lee Johnson, 8 July 1944, Ocean Springs, Mississippi; Butch Trucks, b. Jacksonville, Florida; Chuck Leavill (joined 1973); Lamar Williams (joined 1973, d. 25 January 1983); David 'Rook' Goldflies (joined 1980); Dan Toler (joined 1980)

Initially successful as the most effective underground heavy blues band of the early seventies, the Allman Brothers Band's longer-term significance lay in its willingness to draw on both blues and country roots, providing an impetus for such groups as **Little Feat**, as well as the host of Southern boogie bands that emerged in its wake. The group was also among the first in rock to feature twin lead guitarists, Betts and Duane Allman, one of the most gifted soloists of his generation, who was killed in a motorcycle accident in 1971 – as was bass-player Oakley a year later. In the nineties through almost constant touring they won themselves a second reputation as a blues roots band, their annual stay at New York's Beacon Theatre taking on almost the same stature as **Eric Clapton**'s regular Albert Hall appearances.

Before forming the band in 1969, Duane and Gregg had recorded as the Hour Glass for Liberty, and Duane had played on many sessions at **Rick Hall**'s Muscle Shoals studio for **Percy Sledge**, **Aretha Franklin**, **Wilson Pickett** (who recorded 'Hey Jude' at Duane's suggestion) and others. Some of this session work was later released on *Duane Allman: An Anthology* (Capricorn, 1972). The studio work brought Duane to the attention of **Jerry Wexler** and then Phil Walden, who signed him to the Macon-based Capricorn Records. The fluid blues riffs of *The Allman Brothers Band* (1969) and *Idlewild South* (1970) turned the band into a firm favourite at the giant rock festivals of the era. 'In Memory of Elizabeth Reed' and 'Midnight Rider' from the latter album best represent the band's melodic inventiveness.

Duane never again recorded in the studio with the band, though his live playing with the Allmans is preserved on *Live at the Fillmore East* (1971). But his best work was outside the band: as well as his earlier session work he was responsible for the justly famous 'full tile screech' slide guitar solos on **Eric Clapton**'s Derek and the Dominos album, *Layla* (Polydor, 1970).

The band continued without replacing Duane and achieved further success with the album *Brothers and Sisters*, in 1973. This contained the lyrical Betts instrumental 'Jessica' and the group's biggest single, the million-selling 'Ramblin' Man'. Leavill and Williams joined following Oakley's death, but the most potent period of the Allmans' career was over. Betts and Gregg Allman cut solo albums in 1974, but the latter's career disintegrated as he became better known as the man who married **Cher** twice. After a last hit on Capricorn, 'Crazy Love' (1979), Allman re-formed the band with Betts, Johanson, Trucks, Goldflies and Toler in 1980, and joined Arista for the minor *Reach for the Sky* and a surprising Top Forty single, 'Straight from the Heart'. Allman resumed his solo career with *I'm No Angel* (Epic, 1987) and *Just Before the Bullets Fly* (1989).

In 1988 Betts released *Pattern Disruptive* (Epic), which included 'Duane's Tune'. Several of the members of his backing group joined him and Gregg in re-forming the Allmans in 1990. The new group, featuring Johnny Neal (keyboards), Warren Haynes (guitar), Gregg Allman, Betts, Trucks, Jaimoe and Allen Woody (bass), recorded the workmanlike *Seven Turns*, produced by Tom Dowd. The impressive *Shades of Two Worlds* followed in 1991, and the live *An Evening with the Allman Brothers* in 1992, but the group's major release was the four-CD anthology set *Dreams* (1990), which confirmed the Allmans' status as the premier Southern rock group of their era. *2nd Set* (1995) marked a revival of their fortunes. Henceforth, new albums and reissues alternated. While the reissues tended to sell better, the group's live performances won them a new generation of fans, many of whom went on to buy Gregg Allman's increasingly fluid solo albums, the most notable of which was *Searching for Simplicity* (1977). Haynes and Woody left in 1995 to form Gov't Mule. Their eponymous début album (1995) was a simple heavy blues outing, but the later *Dose* (1998) was a far more assured example of blues-rock.

LAURINDO ALMEIDA
b. 2 September 1917, São Paulo, Brazil, d. 26 July 1995, Los Angeles, California, USA

Brazilian guitarist Almeida is credited with introducing the bossa nova rhythm to North America in 1953 and was involved in attempts to fuse Latin music with jazz.

Almeida's mother was a concert pianist and he took up guitar as a child, making his performing début on a Rio de Janeiro radio station. He visited Europe in 1936, seeing **Django Reinhardt** perform in Paris, and went to the United States in 1947 to join the **Stan Kenton** Orchestra, which was experimenting with 'progressive jazz', a controversial style incorporating atonality.

While with Kenton, he worked on the soundtrack of the **Danny Kaye** film *A Song Is Born* (1948), the first of dozens of Hollywood films in which Almeida's music was heard over the next three decades. His first solo album for Capitol was *Concert Creations for Guitar* and he went on to cut twenty more records of classical, film and popular material for the label.

In the mid-fifties Almeida formed a duo with bassist Ray Brown, exploring combinations of classical music and jazz on *Blues in Greens: Bach Ground*. Almeida also recorded with altoist Bud Shank in both a jazz vein (*Acertate Mas*, Pacific Jazz, 1952, produced by Richard Bock) and in classical manner (*Selected Classical Works for Guitar and Flute*, Concord, 1982). However his most influential albums were *Viva Bossa Nova* (1962), an American Top Twenty hit, and the Grammy-winning *Guitar from Ipanema* (1964).

With Charlie Byrd he recorded *Brazilian Soul* (Concord, 1981), which brought together Latin themes and rhythms with jazz techniques. Almeida's pioneering work in this area opened the way for later hits by **Stan Getz** and others.

In the eighties he made nine albums with the LA Four, which included Shanks, Brown and Sheeley Manne on drums, for Concord Jazz, and in 1989 reteamed with Byrd for the superior *Music of Brazilian Masters*.

MARC ALMOND
b. Peter Marc Almond, 9 July 1956, Southport, Lancashire, England

Almond once described himself as the 'Acid House Aznavour', emphasizing his twin passions for dance music and the French *chanson* tradition. An entertaining, camp torch singer who emerged from the new-romantic phase of British pop music, his career pursued an erratic course after he reached both the British and US Top Tens with his first record.

A cloakroom attendant at a Leeds club, he formed Soft Cell with synthesizer-player Dave Ball (b. 3 May 1959) in 1980. A self-produced EP (financed by Ball's mother) led to a contract with indie label Some Bizarre, who placed the group with Phonogram in Europe and Sire in America. Their first single, a revival of 'Tainted Love' (written by the **Four Preps'** Ed Cobb), was a dancefloor hit and then a British No. 1 that eventually spent fifteen weeks in the US charts in 1981.

What one critic called Soft Cell's 'electronic sleaze' brought British hits, such as 'Bedsitter' (1981), 'Torch' (1982) and 'Soul Inside' (1983), as well as Mike Thorne-produced albums including *Non-Stop Erotic Cabaret* (1982), *The Art of Falling Apart* (1983) and *This Last Night in Sodom* (1984). The latter titles referred to the dissolution of Soft Cell, when Almond moved on to other ensembles including the Immaculate Consumptives (with Lydia Lunch and Nick Cave) and the chaotic Marc and the Mambas with Matt Johnson of The The and Jim Foetus, which recorded *Torment and Torreros* (Some Bizarre, 1983). Ball released the undistinguished *In Strict Tempo* (1983).

Almond's solo career continued with *Vermin in Ermine* (1984) and *Stories of Johnny* (Virgin, 1985). In 1986 he recorded the poorly received *A Woman's Story: Compilation*, a sequence of covers of songs by Scott Walker (of the **Walker Brothers**), **Procul Harum**, **Mel Tormé** and others. The title track of *Mother Fist and Her Five Daughters* (Virgin, 1987) was a fey paean to masturbation. His only hit during this phase was the collaboration with Bronski Beat, 'I Feel Love' (London, 1985), one of Jimmy Somerville's last singles with the group before forming the **Communards**.

In 1988 he signed to EMI's Parlophone label, releasing *The Stars We Are* and 'Something's Gotten Hold of My Heart', a duet with the song's composer **Gene Pitney** which topped the British charts. In 1990 he recorded an album of songs by **Jacques Brel**, *Jacques*, and the lesser *Enchanted*. Far better was *Tenement Symphonies* (1991), produced by Trevor Horn, Dave Ball and Richard Norris. In the same year Almond published a book of poetry, *The Angel of Death in the Adonic Room*. In 1993 he recorded an uncharacteristic but beguiling live greatest hits album, *Twelve Years of Tears*, with a forty-piece orchestra at London's Royal Albert Hall. *Fantastic Star* (1996) was firmly in the mould of eighties electronica while 'Yesterday Has Gone' (1997) saw him duetting with sixties faded icon **P. J. Proby** to little effect.

HERB ALPERT
b. 31 March 1937, Los Angeles, California, USA

Co-founder of A&M Records, Alpert has sold more instrumental records than almost any other performer in history with his 'South of the Border' style of easy-listening music.

An ex-army trumpeter, after a brief solo recording career as Dore Alpert, Alpert joined forces with **Lou Adler** in 1958 to write songs for **Sam Cooke** and **Jan and Dean**. In 1960, again with Adler, he produced and recorded a Top Twenty cover-version of the **Dallas Frazier** song 'Alley Oop', under the name of Dante and the Evergreens for Larry Utall's Madison label. Then, in 1962, with Jerry Moss, Alpert set up A&M Records. For the first few years the company was virtually totally dependent on Alpert's recordings; by 1968 Alpert and his Tijuana Brass (Lou Paganini, Tonni Kalash, John Piasano, Nick Ceroli, Pat Senatore and Bob Edmundson) had sold over 20 million albums and the company's annual turnover was in excess of $50 million.

Alpert's first hit was 'Lonely Bull'* (1962), an evocation of a bullfight complete with crowd noises. It was written by Sol Lake, who over the years became a regular contributor of material to the Tijuana Brass. Alpert's quasi-Mexican music was quickly dubbed 'Ameriachi'. He didn't have another major hit single

until 1965 and 'A Taste of Honey', but by then he had also had four million-selling albums, *Lonely Bull* (1962), *South of the Border* (which features the **Jimmy Kennedy–Michael Carr** composition as its title track), *Whipped Cream and Other Delights* and *Goin' Places* (all 1965).

With both Sergio Mendes and the Sandpipers (who had similarly conceived Latin-tinged hits with the likes of 'Guantanamera', 1966) also on A&M, the label was briefly in danger of becoming typecast as merely easy-listening. Accordingly, Moss quickly and very successfully expanded the label's roster into the progressive rock area with the result that by the early seventies A&M was distributing Lou Adler's Ode label and was one of the biggest independent record companies in America. In 1968, the year before he stopped performing for some years, Alpert had his one hit as a vocalist with **Burt Bacharach**'s and Hal David's 'This Guy's in Love with You'*, the writers' first American No. 1.

The seventies saw Alpert far more willing to experiment. Thus he recorded with **Hugh Masekela** (1979) before securing the biggest hit of his career, the disco-tinged 'Rise'* (1979). The eighties saw him returning to the charts with 'Route 101' (1982) and recording with a variety of artists, including **UB40** (1986). *Keep Your Eye on Me* (1987) included the Top Ten hit 'Diamonds' with vocals by **Janet Jackson**. Alpert released *My Abstract Heart* in 1989. A&M meantime, courtesy of new acts like the **Police**, **Suzanne Vega**, **Bryan Adams** and Jackson, was more successful than ever. Its annual turnover had reached over $200 million when in 1989 Alpert and Moss sold the company to PolyGram.

His 1991 album *North on South Street* included hip-hop rhythms while his 32nd album *Midnight Sun* (1992), which included a new version of 'A Taste of Honey', was dedicated to the late **Stan Getz**, whose 1990 *Apasionado* album Alpert had produced. In 1994 he and Moss established a new record company, Almo Sounds, and in 1996 released the jazz-inflected *Second Wind*. *Passion Dance* followed in 1997.

AMAZING RHYTHM ACES
Howard R. Smith, b. 17 June 1949, Lafayette, Tennessee, USA; Billy Earheart, b. Tennessee; Barry Burton, b. Tennessee (replaced by Duncan Cameron, b. 1978, Tennessee); James Hooker, b. Tennessee; Jeff Davis, b. Tennessee; Butch McDade, b. 24 February 1946, Clarksdale, Missouri, d. 29 November 1998, Maryville, Tennessee

Like several groups of the seventies, the Amazing Rhythm Aces played a version of country music, melded with rock and R&B. However, their vision of country music was both more Southern and more relaxed than others. Thus, the group stood in marked contrast to the **Eagles**, who artfully recycled country motifs in the manner of a latter-day **Roy Rogers**. Similarly, the songs of Smith, the group's major songwriter, were far wittier and more comfortable than those of **Gram Parsons**. His corrosive blend of country and rock music stemmed not from the exuberance of an **Elvis Presley**, as did Smith's, but from the sombre verities represented by the likes of the **Louvin Brothers** and **Roy Acuff**. Where Smith celebrated illicit romance in 'Third Rate Romance', Parsons in 'Sin City' sang of God's vengeance on a failing flock who could not hide from him behind a 'gold-plated door'. Fittingly, Knox, the son of **Sam Phillips**, whose recordings with Presley best captured that earlier Southern exuberance, was associated with the group's classic recordings.

Smith and McDade and *ad hoc* members of the group that eventually became the Amazing Rhythm Aces backed **Jessie Winchester** during one of his tours while in exile in Canada. Winchester's recording of 'Third Rate Romance' led to the group officially forming. Signed to ABC, their first album, the superior *Stacked Deck* (1975), included 'Romance', which was a Top Twenty US hit, and 'Amazing Grace (Used to Be Her Favourite Song)', which was a country hit. The album itself mixed blues (a cover of **Bobby Bland**'s 'Who Will the Next Fool Be?') and ironic religiosity ('Life's Railway to Heaven') with the good-time sound of 'The Ella B'. A marginal success, it was followed by a clutch of impressive albums which won good reviews but poor sales. These included *Too Stuffed to Jump* (1976), which included the enigmatic 'The End Is Not in Sight', and *Toucan Do It Too* (1978), before Burton, who had acted as producer, quit in 1978. With Duncan Cameron as replacement the group recorded *Burning the Ballroom Down*, which featured guest appearances from the likes of **Joan Baez** and Tracy Nelson. After a final ABC album, *How the Hell Do You Spell Rhythm?* (1980), the group split, with Smith establishing himself as a Nashville songwriter, Cameron joining Sawyer Brown and Earheart becoming a member of **Hank Williams Jnr**'s backing band.

Then, in 1994, the group re-formed, without Burton, for *Ride Again* (1994) on their own Breaker Records, which featured fine versions of songs from their earlier (mostly the first two) albums. *Out of the Blue* (1997) featured new material, mostly from Smith, and in 1999 they issued a superior live album, *Concert Classics*, which included an impressive reworking of **Al Green**'s 'Love and Happiness'.

AMBROSE
b. Albert Ambrose, 1897, London, England, d. 12 June 1971, Leeds, Yorkshire

Ambrose was the leader of one of the most famous and longest-serving British dance bands. Known for its high level of musicianship, the Ambrose Orchestra was also one of the few British bands to win international recognition, notably in America where Ambrose had several hits in the thirties.

In his teens Ambrose travelled to America where he learned violin and played in cinema pit orchestras before in 1917 being appointed musical director of New York's Club de Vingt. In 1922 he formed his first British band at London's Embassy Club, recording for British Columbia in 1923. However, it was only after he moved to the Mayfair Hotel (at the then vast salary of £10,000 a year) and signed to Brunswick in 1927 that Ambrose won a wide following. Though his band was never a jazz band, Ambrose had a wider range of interest than most contemporary British bandleaders. Thus, in 1927 he gave the first public performance of **Fred Elizalde**'s *The Heart of the Nigger* suite, and his early bands invariably included a clutch of American sidemen, notably trumpeter Henry 'Hot Lips' Levine and clarinettist Danny Polo.

After a brief sojourn on HMV, Ambrose signed with Decca, for whom he made his best-known, jazzier recordings, and began to broadcast regularly. During the thirties Ambrose had his biggest American hits. These included 'Love Locked Out' (1934), 'I'm on a See-Saw' (1935), the show tune 'I'm in a Dancing Mood' (1936), and his version of **Michael Carr**'s and **Jimmy Kennedy**'s oft-recorded 'South of the Border' (1939). Throughout this period, his band included such luminaries as **Ted Heath**, George Chisholm and Billy Amstell (whose 1986 autobiography *Don't Fuss Mr Ambrose* includes an engaging account of his days with the band). Among the singers with the band were **Elsie Carlisle** and Sam Browne (whose comedy duets were a highlight of the band's broadcasts), **Vera Lynn**, **Anne Shelton** and the American vocalist Evelyn Dall.

In 1939 Ambrose lost most of his regular band to the RAF, where they became the nucleus of the Squadronaires. He later led mostly pick-up bands until he turned to artist management in 1956.

AMERICA
Dewey Bunnell, b. 19 January 1952, Yorkshire, England; Dan Peek, b. 1 November 1950, Florida, USA; Gerry Beckley, b. 12 September 1952, Texas

America were one of the most successful of the soft electric/acoustic harmony groups that sprang up in the wake of **Crosby, Stills and Nash**. Indeed their first hit, the transatlantic million-seller 'A Horse with No Name' (Warner Bros, 1972), was thought by many to be little but a pale imitation of Crosby, Stills, Nash and Young.

Formed in London in 1969 by the sons of US servicemen stationed in the UK, America returned to the US after their initial success. There, their quaintly mystical, if somewhat bland, self-penned love songs garnered them a series of Top Ten hits (including 'Ventura Highway', 1973; 'Tin Man', 1974; and 'Lonely People', 1975), climaxing in their second chart-topper, 'Sister Golden Hair' (1975). After 1974, their records were produced by **George Martin**, whose perfectionism echoed that of their own vocal harmonies. In 1977 Peek quit and America continued as a duo, enjoying continued but diminished success throughout the late seventies before signing with Capitol in 1980 and returning to the Top Ten with 'You Can Do Magic' (1982). This and *View from the Ground* (1983) were produced by Russ Ballard.

Perspective (1984) and *America in Concert* (1985) were the duo's last albums of the eighties, but they continued touring as America well into the nineties. They made guest appearances on records by the **Beach Boys**, **Dan Fogelberg** and television cartoon characters **The Simpsons**. A greatest hits album, *Encore*, was released on the Rhino label in 1991. It was followed by *Hourglass* (The American Gramophone Company, 1994) and *Human Nature* (Oxygen, 1998), but the group spent most of the decade on the nostalgia circuit, often appearing alongside the likes of the Beach Boys.

AMERICAN MUSIC CLUB
Mark Eitzel, b. 1962, Walnut Creek, California, USA; Dan Pearson, b. 1962, Danville, California; Vudi, b. 1958, La Honda, California; Matt Norelli (replaced by Tom Mallon, b. 1959, New York City); Brad Johnson; Mike Simms, b. 1966; Bruce Kaphan

The American folk-rock band American Music Club's albums were characterized by some of the most unremittingly pessimistic lyrics since the early work of **Leonard Cohen**.

The group was founded in San Francisco in 1982 by songwriter and lead singer Eitzel, who had formerly led Columbus, Ohio, punk bands the Cowboys and the Naked Skinnies. Originally an acoustic group with a shifting line-up, American Music Club played local clubs in the Bay area where Eitzel's aggressive attitude towards audiences brought them notoriety. By 1984 the line-up had solidified to include former country & western guitarist Vudi, drummer Norelli and bassist Dan Pearson (from the Ironics).

With the addition of Brad Johnson (keyboards), a début album, *The Restless Stranger*, was issued by Tom Mallon's label Grifter in 1985. After briefly moving to Germany, the group returned to California where Mallon produced and played drums on *Engine* (Frontier, 1987), which established Eitzel as a songwriter of desolation and anguish on compositions

like 'Nightwatchman' and 'Gary's Bar'.

With the addition of pedal-steel guitar by Kaphan, *California* (1988) showed a country music influence. This was followed by *United Kingdom* (Frontier, 1989) on which Simms played drums. There was then a dispute with the record company which halted American Music Club's career. During this period Eitzel played a solo concert in London which was recorded and issued as *Songs of Love* (Demon, 1991).

Bereavement was a major inspiration for Eitzel's consistently gloomy *Everclear* (1991) and *Mercury* (Virgin, 1992), the group's first album for a major record company. It also proved to be their final studio album, as the band announced their intention to disband following poor sales of the rarities collection *San Francisco* (1994). Eitzel continued his solo career with *West* (1997), which was produced by **R.E.M.**'s Peter Buck. He returned in 1998 with the affectionately titled *Caught in a Trap I Can't Walk Out 'Cause I Love You Too Much Baby*.

THE AMES BROTHERS
Joe, b. Joseph Urick, 3 May 1924, Malden, Massachusetts, USA; Gene, b. 13 February 1925, Malden; Vic, b. 20 May 1926, Malden, d. 23 January 1978; Ed, b. 9 July 1927, Malden

A smooth vocal group with five million-sellers to their credit, the Ames Brothers' career ran aground on the shores of rock'n'roll.

Signed to Coral in 1948, their first major success was 'Rag Mop'* (1950), a cover of Johnnie Lee Wills' (brother of **Bob Wills**) original country hit on Bullet. The differences between the two versions were significant: Wills' had a firm boogie beat, the Ames Brothers' was merely bouncy. Though the Brothers were clearly happier performing slow ballads, their biggest hits of the early fifties were rhythmic, including 'Undecided'* (1951) and 'You, You, You'* (1953), their first hit for their new label, RCA, which was co-written by Lotar Olias, the composer of most of **Freddy Quinn**'s hits.

By the mid-fifties, however, the Brothers' sound was far sweeter, as evidenced in their biggest-ever hit, 'The Naughty Lady of Shady Lane'* (1954), which had a similar lyrical twist to **Gilbert O'Sullivan**'s 'Clair' (the 'lady' was a baby), and 'Melodie d'Amour' (1957), an adaptation of a French song. In the same year they had a minor hit with 'Tammy', the theme song to the film *Tammy and the Bachelor* (1957).

After a series of minor hits, the group disbanded in 1960, and Ed Ames attempted a solo career as a singer and actor (he played Mingo in the *Daniel Boone* teleseries). He had a number of hits in the sixties, including 'My Cup Runneth Over' and 'Who Will Answer?' (both RCA, 1967), before turning to the club circuit.

ALBERT AMMONS
b. 23 September 1907, Chicago, Illinois, USA,
d. 2 December 1949, Chicago

Less of an extrovert or virtuoso than the other members of the 'Boogie Woogie Trio', **Pete Johnson** and **Meade Lux Lewis**, Ammons perhaps outdid his companions in rhythmic solidity and, at slow tempos, blues feeling.

After both solo and band experience in the twenties and early thirties, he formed his own Rhythm Kings, including Guy Kelly (trumpet) and Israel Crosby (bass), to play Chicago's Club DeLisa and record 'Boogie Woogie Stomp' and other titles for Decca (1936). With the boogie-woogie craze of 1938–9 came opportunities to record solos like 'Shout for Joy' (Vocalion, 1939) and duets with trumpeter **Harry James** (Brunswick, 1939). He also began his association with Johnson and Lewis, playing at New York's Café Society and Carnegie Hall. Sessions for Blue Note (1939, 1942) and Solo Art (1939) produced magnificent readings of 'Bass Goin' Crazy' and other tunes, while his 1941 Victor recordings with Johnson such as 'Cuttin' the Boogie' are among the finest of all boogie-woogie piano duets. For Commodore (1944) he led a new Rhythm Kings with Hot Lips Page (trumpet), Vic Dickenson (trombone) and Don Byas (tenor). Then with Mercury (1945–9), in a series of small-group recordings, he devised boogie translations of popular songs, such as 'Swanee River Boogie' (1946), 'Sheik of Araby' (1948) and 'You Are My Sunshine' (1948). On several of these he was partnered by his son, tenor saxophonist Gene (*b. 14 April 1925, Chicago, d. 23 July 1974*).

After his father's death Gene formed a two-tenor group with the **Charlie Parker**-influenced alto- and tenor-player Sonny Stitt. He later made a number of recordings on the borders of jazz and R&B, which were popular with black audiences. Based for most of his career in Chicago, he influenced a local school of saxophonists, including Johnny Griffin, who also spent his early playing days in rhythm and blues, with **Lionel Hampton** and trumpeter/bandleader Joe Morris.

TORI AMOS
b. Myra Ellen Amos, 22 August 1963, Newton, North Carolina, USA

The first of several successful female singer-songwriters to emerge in the 1990s, melding the lyrical venom of alternative rock to a distinctly seventies musical approach, Amos was unusual among her contemporaries for her reliance on the piano, rather than the guitar, as a rock instrument.

The daughter of a Methodist preacher, Amos was born in North Carolina but raised in Maryland. She began playing the piano and singing in the church choir at the age of four and aged five she won a scholarship to the Baltimore Peabody Conservatory. In her early teens she developed a love for rock'n'roll and, in particular, **Led Zeppelin**. Amos soon started to write her own songs, and began performing in local bars. Before she was 20 she had moved to LA and fallen in with the alternative rock scene.

In 1987 Amos was signed to Atlantic Records and released a forgettable pop–metal hybrid under the name 'Y Kant Tori Read?'. This sold poorly and was greeted with lukewarm critical appreciation. However, by the turn of the decade she had developed an entirely new style, which saw her returning to the piano to write a collection of atmospheric, sparsely arranged ballads, reminiscent of **Kate Bush** and **Joni Mitchell**.

In 1991 she played a series of concerts in Britain to mark the release of an EP, *Me and a Gun*, a harrowing, autobiographical tale of rape. It gained positive reviews in the media, prompting much interest in the live dates and strong sales of the EP. Later in the year Amos's first album as a singer-songwriter, *Little Earthquakes**, was released and sold strongly on both sides of the Atlantic. The album was followed by a covers EP, *Crucify Me* (1992), featuring her interpretations of songs including **Nirvana**'s 'Smells Like Teen Spirit' and 'Thank You' by **Led Zeppelin**.

A year-long tour was followed by the million-selling second album, *Under the Pink* (1994), which spawned two minor hit singles in 'Cornflake Girl' and 'God'. In 1996 Amos delivered her difficult third album, *Boys for Pele*, which in its lack of structure marked a departure from the fairly traditional sound of her preceding albums. Her most ambitious work to date, it included the single 'Professional Widow', which would later reach the top of the British charts after being remixed by Armand van Helden. She returned to the studio in 1998 for a further album of confessional balladry, *From the Choirgirl Hotel* (1998). The self-produced *To Venus and Back* (1999), a double-album of live recordings and new studio creations, included the hit single 'Bliss'. However, while the album was cutting edge in terms of marketing – it was introduced through a free digital download – in comparison with later confessional writers, such as **Alanis Morisette**, it seemed positively laid back.

LALE ANDERSEN
b. 23 March 1910, Bremerhaven, Denmark, d. 29 August 1972, Vienna, Austria

Andersen's husky-voiced recording of 'Lili Marlene'* (Electrola, 1939) was the original version of the most popular song of the Second World War.

A cabaret actress, Andersen first performed 'Lili

Marlene' in 1937. The lyric derived from a poem written by Hans Leip during the First World War, and was given a waltz setting by Rudy Link. However, when she came to record the song in 1939, composer Norbert Schultz provided a new tune and set the words against a marching tempo. The record was an immediate success – it was the first German million-selling disc, despite the fact that Andersen was persecuted by the Nazis during the war. The song was also taken up by the Allies and translated into over forty languages, including an English version by **Tommie Connor**, and was recorded by numerous artists, most notably by **Marlene Dietrich**.

After the war, Andersen's career went into decline and she briefly retired before returning to the European charts in 1960 with a German-language version of 'Jamais le Dimanche' (the Oscar-winning theme to *Never on Sunday*, which also provided American bandleader Don Costa with a million-seller with his English-language version). In 1961 Andersen won the Eurovision Song Contest.

The 1950 film *Lili Marlene* is loosely based on Andersen's wartime experiences, as is Rainer Werner Fassbinder's 1982 film, *Lili Marleen*. In their different fashions, both films and the use made by Dennis Potter of 'Lili Marlene' in his 1986 teleseries *The Singing Detective* testify to the resonances of the song and the surroundings that gave it birth.

BILL ANDERSON
b. 1 November 1937, Columbia, South Carolina, USA

Though he was enormously successful as a singer, businessman and television personality, Anderson's real importance lay in the songs he wrote in the late fifties and early sixties. With **Harlan Howard** (with whose ex-wife Jan Howard he would later regularly duet), **Willie Nelson** and Hank Cochran, Anderson brought a new realism to country songwriting, producing songs such as 'City Lights' and 'Once a Day' that detailed the personal pain, sense of isolation, moral confusion and anonymity that followed the growing urbanization of the South. The title of his first country hit best sums up his concerns: 'That's What It's Like to Be Lonesome' (Decca, 1959).

A graduate of the University of Georgia, Anderson turned briefly to journalism and work as a disc-jockey before **Ray Price** heard and recorded Anderson's 'City Lights', and sold a million copies in 1958. Anderson now turned full-time songwriter and performer, producing a string of similarly styled hits: '99 Years' (1959), 'Tips of My Fingers' (1960), and 'Po' Folks' (1961). His success with 'Mama Sang a Sad Song', his first country chart-topper in 1962, and the half-spoken 'Still', which made the national Top Ten in 1963 (and was his only major pop hit), both deeply sentimental

songs, won him the soubriquet 'Whispering Bill'. More importantly, success brought about a change of direction in his career. He wrote less – and the songs lacked the toughness of his earlier work – and turned his attention to becoming 'an all-round country entertainer', securing his own television programme, *The Bill Anderson Show* (and later presenting the *Funzapoppin* game show in 1980), and appearing in several low-budget country films, including *Las Vegas Hillbillies* (1966) and *The Road to Nashville* (1967).

He recorded extensively, but with lesser success, throughout the seventies (when Mary Lou Turner replaced Jan Howard as his duet partner). A serious accident in 1984 effectively ended his recording career but he continued to tour, his patriotic admonitions to audiences about long hair and the like signalling his profound conservatism. In 1989 he published an autobiography, *Whispering Bill*.

He continued to tour in the nineties, while at the same time he became the public spokesman for the Po Folks restaurant chain, named after his 1961 hit. He also began a new writing partnership with Steve Wariner, who, after securing a hit with his own version of 'Tips', went on to produce Anderson's 1998 outing, *Fine Wine*, which included a reworked 'Tips' on which Anderson was supported by Jan Howard, Jean Shepard and **Roy Clark**.

LAURIE ANDERSON
b. 5 June 1947, Chicago, Illinois, USA

A multi-media performance artist, Anderson is best remembered in pop music circles for her 1982 surprise European hit with the eight-minute single 'O Superman'.

A graduate student and then a teacher of sculpture and art history in New York, Anderson first performed her work in public in 1973. She was part of the loose circle of performance artists and musicians (**Brian Eno**, **Talking Heads**' David Byrne, and **Philip Glass** among them) who formed New York's avant-garde in the late seventies. Her shows typically involved mime, speech, music, film and special lighting effects.

'O Superman', first released on the New York independent label One Ten, used synthesizers, electronically treated voice, and tape loops, and appeared on Anderson's album, *Big Science* (Warners, 1982). The hit brought a large rock audience for her stage productions, such as the seven-hour stage show *United States*. A five-album live recording of the show, which typified Anderson's fascination with both the dangers and the textures of contemporary technology, was released in 1984.

Anderson's later albums for Warners were *Mister Heartbreak*, a collaboration with **Peter Gabriel**, and

Home of the Brave (1986). This included contributions from **Bill Laswell**, Chic's **Nile Rodgers** and author William Burroughs, whose concern with the manipulative power of language was an important influence on Anderson.

On *Strange Angels* (1989) she emphasized her singing voice and lost the impact of speech set against music which had characterized earlier recordings. In 1991 she issued the anti-censorship single 'Large Black Dick' and in 1993 Anderson published the book *Stories from the Nerve Bible* from which she read at solo concert performances. *Bright Sun* (1994) was produced by **Brian Eno**. It saw a return to speech in a series of provocative monologues, including one in partnership with **Lou Reed**. Reed also appeared on *Meltdown*, her major 1997 performance work. Far more impressive was her performance show *Songs and Stories from Moby Dick*, on which she took Melville's novel as a starting point for a character that, she suggests, outlasts his God in his pursuit of a revenge that becomes the defining element of his identity. Critically well received in the US, the show was viewed more cautiously in the UK, where the mixed media elements at *Moby Dick*'s centre had become commonplace factors in Britart.

LYNN ANDERSON
b. *26 September, 1947, Grand Forks, North Dakota, USA*

Though 'Rose Garden'* (Columbia, 1970), written by **Joe South**, was Anderson's only huge international hit, it remains one of the best examples of the countrypolitan trend of the seventies that saw numerous country acts sweetening their recordings in search of crossover success in the pop charts. What made her success all the more ironic was that she was the daughter of the traditionally orientated songwriter Liz Anderson (*b. 13 March 1930, Pine Creek, Minnesota*), who with such fine songs as 'My Friends Are Gonna Be Strangers' and 'I'm a Lonesome Fugitive' gave **Merle Haggard** the significant early hits that established his initial rebellious image.

Raised in California, Anderson won a regular place on **Lawrence Welk**'s weekly television show (1966–8). Signed by Chart Records, she had a country hit with her first release, her mother's composition 'Ride, Ride, Ride' (1966). In 1968 she moved to Nashville and married Columbia producer and songwriter R. Glenn Sutton, who became her producer when she joined the company in 1970. It was he who produced 'Rose Garden', its smooth sound perfectly suiting Anderson's clear, pop phrasing. A string of hits followed, including 'How Can I Unlove You?' (1971), 'Sing About Love' (1974) and 'Last Love of My Life' (1978). Her later recordings, including 'Even Cowgirls

Get the Blues' (1980) and the album *Outlaw is Just a State of Mind* (1980), saw Anderson, who had moved back to California, singing in an even poppier style but with little success. *What She Does Best* (Mercury, 1989) included a version of the **Drifters**' 'Under the Boardwalk'.

In the nineties she recorded rarely. The 1992 retrospective, *Greatest Hits*, drew together her best moments from the three previous decades. *Latest and Greatest* (Intersound, 1998) was a lacklustre outing.

JULIE ANDREWS
b. *Julie Elizabeth Wells, 1 October 1935, Walton-on-Thames, Surrey, England*

Like **Marlene Dietrich**, Andrews was engulfed by her earliest screen roles to the extent that her subsequent career was essentially a (bitter) commentary on the wholesome persona she created for *Mary Poppins* (1964) and *The Sound of Music* (1965).

A child performer, Andrews made her London stage début at the age of twelve. Her New York début, in an imported production of *The Boy Friend* in 1954, won critical praise for her cool, clear 'English' voice and aristocratic demeanour. In 1956 she created the role of Eliza Doolittle (which she played for some three years) in **Lerner and Loewe**'s *My Fair Lady*, the most influential Broadway musical of the fifties, and in 1960 she starred in their *Camelot*.

She lost the screen role of Eliza Doolittle to Audrey Hepburn, but secured the leads in both *Mary Poppins* (for which she won an Oscar) and *The Sound of Music*, roles which demanded wholesomeness rather than pertness, energy rather than delicacy. The songs for *Poppins*, written by Disney staff writers Robert and Richard Sherman, including 'Supercalifragilistic-expialidocious' (Andrews' only chart entry in 1965) and 'Chim Chim Cher-ee' were mostly novelty items. However, those written by **Rodgers and Hammerstein** for *Music* were more substantial and several have become standards, including 'My Favourite Things', 'Climb Ev'ry Mountain', 'Do-Re-Mi', and 'Edelweiss'. Moreover, *The Sound of Music* album was one of the most successful soundtrack albums ever, remaining on the charts until well into 1970.

But, though the roles made Andrews an international star, they also typecast her. After success with *Thoroughly Modern Millie* (1967), her performance as Gertrude Lawrence in *Star!* (1968) was roundly denounced. It was not until the late seventies, following her marriage to director Blake Edwards, that her screen career regained its impetus. The climax of this was the bitter comedy *S.O.B.* (1981) in which Andrews played a Mary Poppins lookalike transformed into a (briefly nude) vamp when her career flounders. Since then Andrews has eschewed purely musical roles in favour of dramatic comedy, although in 1992 she took the part of Anna in a recording of Rodgers and Hammerstein's *The King and I* by John Mauceri and the Hollywood Bowl Orchestra. In 1994 she further celebrated Richard Rodgers with *Richard Rodgers' Broadway* (Philips), a large-scale 'Broadway' album.

THE ANDREWS SISTERS
Patricia (Patti), b. 16 February 1920, Minneapolis, Minnesota, USA; Maxine, b. 3 January 1918, Minneapolis, d. 25 October 1995, New York; Laverne, b. 6 July 1915, Minneapolis, d. 8 May 1967

One of the most popular acts of the forties, the Andrews Sisters, who sold some 30 million discs in their career, recorded exotic, boogie novelties, such as 'Rhumboogie' and 'The Booglie Wooglie Piggie' and saccharine ballads in a brash, energetic, confident manner that remains appealing and surprisingly influential to this day.

The daughters of Norwegian and Greek parents, Patti, Maxine and Laverne were discovered by **Jack Kapp** and signed to his Brunswick label. Their second record was the phenomenally successful 'Bei Mir Bist Du Schön'* (1937), an adaptation of a Yiddish song by **Sammy Cahn** and Saul Chaplin. Queens of the radio, in 1940 they went to Hollywood and throughout the forties starred in more than fifteen (mostly B) movies as themselves; these include *Argentine Nights* (1940), *Give Out Sisters* (1942) and *Hollywood Canteen* (1944). Decca, the company to which they followed Kapp, regularly partnered the Sisters with other artists on the label. Thus as well as their own hits ('Boogie Woogie Bugle Boy'*, 1941 – which was revived to good effect by **Bette Midler** in 1973 – and 'Rum and Coca-Cola'*, 1944 – which was retitled 'Rum and Limonada' when released in the UK), they had hits with **Bing Crosby** ('Pistol Packin' Mama'*, a cover-version of **Al Dexter**'s country hit, and 'Jingle Bells'* in 1943; **Cole Porter**'s 'Don't Fence Me In'*, 1944; and 'South America, Take It Away'* in 1947), **Guy Lombardo** ('Christmas Island'*, 1947) and, on the country chart, with **Ernest Tubb** (including Tubb's own 'Don't Rob Another Man's Castle', 1949).

The Andrews Sisters neatly managed the transition from thirties sirens to forces' sweethearts in the forties, when the simple cheerfulness of songs such as 'Beer Barrel Polka' and 'I'll Be with You in Apple Blossom Time' were given greater resonance by the times. But in 1953 the trio broke up and Patti, who had always sung the lead parts – and had had a solo million-seller with a **Sammy Fain** song 'I Can Dream, Can't I?' (Decca) in 1949 – attempted a solo career. They regrouped for television and cabaret appearances in 1956, but henceforth their appeal was always nostalgic, as in their return with a 'borrowed' sister in the seventies Broadway musical, *Over Here*.

THE ANIMALS
Alan Price, b. 19 April 1942, County Durham, England; Hilton Valentine, b. 21 May 1943, North Shields; Bryan 'Chas' Chandler, b. 18 December 1938, Newcastle, d. 17 July 1996; John Steel, b. 4 February 1941, Gateshead; Eric Burdon, b. 11 May 1941, Newcastle; Dave Rowberry, b. 27 December 1943, Newcastle (joined 1965); Barry Jenkins, b. 22 December 1944, Leicester (joined 1966)

The Animals were one of the most impressive groups of the British beat boom of the mid-sixties. Their hit singles were drawn from the best American songwriters of the era and delivered with clarity and passion by Eric Burdon.

Originally a jazz combo led by keyboards-player **Alan Price**, the group became the Animals and turned to rhythm and blues with the arrival of singer Burdon in 1962. They soon became the leading band on Tyneside, were spotted by producer **Mickie Most** and moved to London's thriving club circuit in 1964.

Their first record was a version of 'Baby Let Me Take You Home' (EMI Columbia, 1964; MGM in America), taken from **Bob Dylan**'s first album. This was followed by the Animals' best-known recording, 'House of the Rising Sun'*, again culled from Dylan. Featuring Burdon's impassioned singing and Price's distinctive organ arpeggios, it was an international bestseller. The disc even impressed Dylan himself and contributed to his decision to work with electric instruments. It was a minor hit in Britain on its re-release in both 1972 and 1982.

Other hits followed, including 'I'm Crying' (1964), 'Please Don't Let Me Be Misunderstood' (written by **Nina Simone**), **Sam Cooke**'s 'Bring It on Home to Me', and 'We Gotta Get Out of this Place' by **Barry Mann** and Cynthia Weil (all 1965). At this point drummer John Steel left the band, following Alan Price who had formed his own band in May 1965. Dave Rowberry from jazz/R&B group the Mike Cotton Sound had replaced Price, while the new drummer was Barry Jenkins from beat group the Nashville Teens, who had made the charts with a version of **John D. Loudermilk**'s 'Tobacco Road'.

Under Burdon's leadership, the group moved to Decca and had a Top Ten hit in both Britain and the US with Gerry Goffin's and **Carole King**'s 'Don't Bring Me Down' (1966). Attracted by the new underground music of California, however, even Burdon wished to move away from the band's rhythm and blues roots. At the end of 1966 he re-formed the group as Eric Burdon and the Animals, retaining only Jenkins from the previous line-up. New members were John Weider (ex-**Family**) on guitar and violin, guitarist Vic Briggs from **Brian Auger**'s Steampacket and bass-player Danny McCullough. After their move to California, this band had a series of Top Twenty hits on MGM which reflected Burdon's enthusiasm for the hippie lifestyle. Supervised by Dylan producer Tom Wilson, these included 'When I Was Young', 'San Francisco Nights', 'Monterey' (all 1967), and 'Sky Pilot' (1968).

This Animals' line-up split up in 1969, leaving Burdon to follow a solo career which began promisingly in collaboration with soul band **War**: a hit single, 'Spill the Wine' (MGM, 1970) was followed by two albums, including the improbably titled *Black Man's Burdon*. He then cut an album with blues veteran **Jimmy Witherspoon** (*Guilty*, MGM, 1971), joined Capitol for three mediocre albums by the Eric Burdon Band (1974–5) and had a solo album produced by Chas Chandler (*Survivor*, Polydor, 1977).

Chandler, meanwhile, had become the most successful of the ex-Animals, as manager and producer of first **Jimi Hendrix** and then **Slade**. He also produced *Before We Were So Rudely Interrupted* (Jet, 1977), an unusually successful reunion album featuring the original five Animals. A second effort, *Ark* (IRS/A&M, 1983), was less impressive, and a subsequent live album, *Rip It to Shreds* (1983), was disappointing.

In 1986 Eric Burdon published an autobiography, *I Used to Be an Animal but I'm Alright Now*, and in 1988 released a solo album, *Wicked Man*. In the early nineties, he toured the US and Europe, occasionally with **Brian Auger**. He released a further solo album, *Misunderstood* (Aim) in 1995, while in 1997 original members Steel and Valentine put together yet another Animals line-up to tread the nostalgia circuit.

PAUL ANKA
b. 30 July 1941, Ottawa, Canada

A prolific songwriter and an astute businessman, Anka managed the transition from fifties teen-idol to mainstream showbusiness star with surprising ease.

The son of Lebanese immigrants, Anka entered showbusiness when he was ten and cut his first record, 'I Confess' (Modern), in 1956. A year later he signed to ABC and recorded his own composition, 'Diana'*. The rumba backing provided by Don Costa was far too inflexible to be truly plaintive, but the song's lyrics – featuring the classic complaint 'I'm so young and you're so old' – and Anka's baby-voiced intensity introduced one of the major themes of fifties balladry: teen *angst*. A mark of the song's popularity is that over 300 versions of it have been recorded and Anka's recording alone went on to sell 10 million copies. Though Anka's subsequent recordings, including 'You Are My Destiny'* (1958), 'Lonely

Boy'* and 'Put Your Head on My Shoulder'* (both 1959), and 'Puppy Love'* and 'My Home Town'* (both 1960), all of which he wrote, were increasingly melodramatic, he managed very successfully to be both clean cut (*à la* **Pat Boone**) and moody (*à la* **Elvis Presley**). The 1961 documentary *Lonely Boy* vividly captures Anka's period as a teen-idol.

In 1962 he left ABC for RCA (and bought back from ABC the rights to all his recordings). His hits continued on a lesser scale throughout the sixties, but he increasingly turned to concert appearances and songwriting. Among Anka's compositions were 'It Doesn't Matter Anymore' (recorded by **Buddy Holly**); the standard 'My Way' (recorded by **Frank Sinatra**, among many others), which he adapted from a French song co-written by recording star Claude François; 'She's a Lady' (recorded by **Tom Jones**); the theme to the film *The Longest Day* (1962), in which he also had a small part; and 'Johnny's Theme' for Johnny Carson's *Tonight* television show.

In 1970 he signed to United Artists and in 1974 had a No. 1 with the controversial 'You're Having My Baby', a duet with Odia Coates. At the same time, his compositions 'Puppy Love' and 'Lonely Boy', were successfully revived by Donny Osmond (of the **Osmonds**), the teen-idol of a new generation. The end of the decade saw Anka solidly established in Las Vegas and on the international cabaret circuit, and recording intermittently. In 1983 he had a surprise hit with 'Hold Me till the Mornin' Comes' (Columbia) and in 1992 he duetted with **Ofra Haza** on 'Freedom for the World'. He followed that in 1996 with the Latin-inflected album *Amigos*, on which he duetted with **Céline Dion**, **Kenny G** and Tom Jones, among others.

ADAM ANT
b. Stuart Leslie Goddard, b. 3 November 1954, London, England

A minor figure of British punk rock, Adam Ant enjoyed a brief period of success as a teenage idol in 1981–3 before launching a career as an actor.

Goddard had played with London bands Bazooka Joe and the B-Sides, whose Andy Warren (bass) and Lester Square (guitar) became members of Adam and the Ants. The band was inspired by the **Sex Pistols** and its early songs incorporated references to the standard motifs of punk style – including leather, bondage ('Whip in My Valise') and Nazism. 'Young Parisians' (1977) was issued by Decca and 'Xerox' (1978) by Do It, an independent label which also released *Dirk Wears White Sox* (1979).

Adam and the Ants, however, made little impact as an *echt*-punk band and in 1980 the group delivered itself into the hands of **Malcolm McLaren**. He took

Ants Matthew Ashman (guitar) and Dave Barbarossa (drums) to join Bow Bow Wow before remoulding Adam's image. Signing to Columbia, Adam and the Ants (now including Marco Pirroni on guitar) had the minor hit 'Kings of the Wild Frontier' (1980) before 'Dog Eat Dog' reached the Top Ten.

The new approach was intensely melodramatic with Adam Ant in fancy dress variously as highwayman, pirate or fop and starring in colourful videos directed by former TV producer Mike Mansfield. During 1981 he had six hit singles in Britain, including two No. 1s, 'Stand and Deliver' and 'Prince Charming'. Drawing on African (Burundi) drum rhythms and chanted choruses reminiscent of **Gary Glitter** or **Slade**, Adam Ant found a large following of pre-teenage fans who bought at least as many posters as records.

In 1982 Adam Ant launched himself as a solo artist with 'Goody Two Shoes', his first hit in America where his popularity had been achieved through the impact of video. Later British hits included 'Friend or Foe', the **Phil Collins**-produced 'Puss in Boots' (1983), inspired by the pantomime character, and 'Apollo Nine' (1984).

'Vive le Rock' (1985), the title track of his fourth Columbia album, was a commercial failure and Adam Ant shifted his attention to stage and screen. He returned to music with *Manners and Physique* (MCA, 1990) which produced a British hit single, 'Room at the Top'.

In 1993 he was reunited with Pirroni and the pair began working on a new album which appeared in 1994 as *Wonderful* (EMI). The continuing popularity of Ant's older hits was underlined when a 1993 'best of' album, *Antmusic*, reached the UK Top Ten.

ANTHRAX

Neil Turbin; Scott Ian, b. Scott Rosenfeld, 31 December 1963, New York, USA; Dan Spitz; Dan Lilker, b. 18 October 1964, New York; Charlie Benate, b. 27 November 1962, New York; Matt Fallon; Joey Belladonna, b. 30 October 1960, Oswego, New York; Frank Bello, b. 9 July 1965; John Bush

US group Anthrax were one of the pioneering speed metal/thrash bands to emerge in the early eighties. In a similar fashion to **Metallica** and **Megadeth** they helped reinvent heavy metal music for the nineties.

Formed in New York in 1981, the band drew on several non-musical sources, including skateboarding fashion and comic book imagery. The latter provided them with their breakthrough single in 1987, 'I Am the Law' (a line associated with comic-book character Judge Dredd). Founder members Lilker (bass) and Turbin (vocals) were joined by guitarists Ian and Spitz and drummer Benante for 'Soldiers of Metal'

(1983) on the independent label Megaforce, which preceded their début album, *Fistful of Metal* (1984). Around this time Ian and Lilker founded a spin-off group, Stormtroopers of Death (SOD, not to be confused with UK post-punk outfit, SOD/Spear of Destiny), which recorded and toured in its own right.

When Lilker left the band to join Nuclear Assault he was replaced by roadie Frank Bello. Turbin was next to leave, being replaced by Matt Fallon then by Joey Belladonna, with whom the band recorded the mini-album *Armed & Dangerous* (1985), which included a thrash reworking of the **Sex Pistols**' 'God Save the Queen'.

Anthrax charted in the UK with the Island album, *Among the Living* (1987), which included two Top Fifty singles, 'I Am the Law' and 'Indians', plus the groundbreaking speed metal/rap track 'I'm the Man', which sold over two million copies in the US alone. *State of Euphoria* and the Top Thirty single 'Make Me Laugh' further consolidated the band's position in 1988. *Persistence of Time* (1990) preceded their biggest hit, a cover of **Joe Jackson**'s 'Got the Time'.

The band parted company with Island after *Attack of the Killer B's* (1991), a collection of covers and B-sides. Anthrax's links with rap were cemented by the appearance of Chuck D and Flavor Flav on their version of **Public Enemy**'s 'Bring the Noise' and by a co-headlining tour with Public Enemy. New vocalist John Bush replaced Belladonna in time to appear on the band's first album for Elektra, *Sound of White Noise* (1993). The group appeared on the Kiss tribute album *Kiss My Ass* (1994), singing 'She', before releasing the raw-sounding *Stomp 442* (1995). However, by the time of *Volume 8 – The Threat Is Real* (Ignition, 1998) the once-threatening Anthrax sounded almost like a conventional rock group.

AQUA

Claus Norreen; Soeren Rasted; René Dif; Lene Nystrom

Scandinavian four-piece Aqua rose to fame in Scandinavia before achieving international success with their brand of high energy dance-pop.

Originally known as Joyspeed, the three-quarters Danish and one-quarter Norwegian band first began to work together in 1989. Signing to a small Swedish independent label, they achieved widespread recognition throughout Scandinavia, becoming a popular fixture in the Swedish pop charts with their up-tempo singles. However, the band became tired of their straightforward pop style, and in 1995 to mark their change in direction took the name Aqua, and added a hint of psychedelia to their sound.

The following year the newly named Aqua signed to the Swedish division of Universal, and released their first single, 'Roses Are Red', which topped the charts in both Sweden and Denmark. This was followed by 'My Oh My', which went gold within a week of release. However, the success of that was eclipsed by the 22 million-plus sales of their international début single 'Barbie Girl' (1997). The record (and video)'s mix of kitsch surrealism and giggly, dayglo eroticism propelled it to the top of the charts in 35 countries from Asia to Europe and made international stars of Aqua. Added help was given by Mattel, manufacturer of the Barbie doll, who sued Aqua and Universal for breach of copyright. This only gave the song's tag line – 'Come on Barbie. Let's go party' – a cod revolutionary element.

The follow-up release 'Witch Doctor', which was a little too camp for comfort, was almost as successful. More considered was Aqua's début album, *Aquarium* (1998). It went multi-platinum throughout the world and included more mature balladry alongside the youth-orientated pop of the single releases. Aqua achieved a third international hit with 'Turn Back Time' (1998), a song featured on the soundtrack to *Sliding Doors*, before crossing the Atlantic in an attempt to crack the American market. *Aquarius* (2000), which featured the hit single 'Cartoon Heroes', was firmly in the knowing camp style of its predecessor. While it understandably failed to achieve the success of their début album, with tracks like 'Good Guys' and the title song, the group demonstrated they were more than a clever video.

HAROLD ARLEN
b. Hyman Arluck, 15 February 1905, Buffalo, New York, USA, d. 23 April 1986, New York

One of America's best-known composers and songwriters, Arlen's greatest success came in Hollywood. He wrote for more than twenty films, most notably *The Wizard of Oz* (1939), which brought him and lyricist **Yip Harburg** an Oscar for 'Over the Rainbow', performed by **Judy Garland**. However, like such writers as **George Gershwin** and Doc Pomus (of the songwriting team **Pomus and Shuman**), Arlen at his best was deeply influenced by black music and throughout his career, whether composing for the famous Cotton Club revues or Hollywood films, his melodies had a melancholic, almost bluesy feel to them. As a result, he was a less witty but more impassioned composer than many of his contemporaries.

The son of a cantor, Arlen was given some formal musical training, but he quickly deserted classical music for ragtime and jazz, forming his first group (the Snappy Trio) while still in his teens. In 1929 Arlen, still set on a performing career, graduated to arranging, playing and singing in bands in New York, where he was hired by **Fletcher Henderson** to work as a rehearsal pianist on a show he was arranging for

Vincent Youmans. It was only when a piano doodle of his was transformed by lyricist Ted Koehler into 'Get Happy', which then became a massive hit for **Ruth Etting**, that Arlen accepted that he was a composer.

The Arlen/Koehler partnership was soon hired to replace **Dorothy Fields** and Jimmy McHugh as songwriters for a Cotton Club revue in 1931. Among the songs they produced for eight separate Cotton Club revues in the years 1931–43 were 'Between the Devil and the Deep Blue Sea' for Aida Ward, 'Minnie the Moocher's Wedding Day' for **Cab Calloway**, and the magnificent 'Stormy Weather' (later recorded by **Billie Holiday**) for **Ethel Waters**. Other compositions were 'I Got a Right to Sing the Blues', which was subsequently recorded by **Louis Armstrong** and **Jack Teagarden**, and the far poppier 'I've Got the World on a String' and 'It's Only a Paper Moon', the first Arlen song to be featured in a film, *Take a Chance* (1933).

Fearful of being typecast merely as a writer of jazz melodies, Arlen worked with Harburg and **Ira Gershwin** on the satiric revue *Life Begins at 8:40* (1934) and with Harburg wrote the score for the bitter musical *Hooray for What?* (1937) before heading for Hollywood. Among his first notable film songs were 'It's Only a Paper Moon' (1933), 'Last Night When We Were Young' (1936) and 'Over the Rainbow' (1939), a song as haunting in its way as 'Stormy Weather'. While Arlen's movie work was less substantial than his writing for the theatre, there were significant exceptions. The score for *Blues in the Night* (1941), written with **Johnny Mercer**, the third of his regular collaborators, gave **Jimmie Lunceford** a huge hit with the title song. Other highlights included 'Happiness Is a Thing Called Joe', written with Harburg for the all-black musical *Cabin in the Sky* (1943) and performed by Waters, 'The Man That Got Away', written with Ira Gershwin for *A Star Is Born* (1954), and, most surprising of all, 'That Old Black Magic', written with Mercer as a slow song for *Star Spangled Rhythm* (1942) and transformed by **Billy Daniels** into an up-tempo number. He also wrote with Mercer 'One for My Baby', introduced by **Fred Astaire** in *The Sky's the Limit* (1943) and appropriated in the fifties by **Frank Sinatra**, who made the song his own.

Back on Broadway, Arlen collaborated with Mercer on the all-black musical *St Louis Woman* (1946), which produced 'Come Rain or Come Shine'. In the fifties he brought Truman Capote's *House of Flowers* (1954) to the stage before resuming his partnership with Harburg for *Jamaica* (1957), starring **Lena Horne**. His last musical was *Saratoga* (1959) with Mercer, after which he restricted himself to the occasional movie, including *A Star Is Born* (1954), in which Garland sang his and **Ira Gershwin**'s 'The Man That Got Away', and another, lesser Garland vehicle, *I Could Go on Singing* (1963).

Like his frequent collaborator Johnny Mercer, Arlen also recorded many of his own compositions. Among his hits were 'Little Girl' (Brunswick, 1931), on which he was backed by **Joe Venuti**, 'Stormy Weather' (Victor, 1933), and 'Ill Wind' (1934), on which he was supported by **Eddy Duchin**'s orchestra. In 1966 he recorded again for the first time in over 25 years.

JOAN ARMATRADING
b. 9 December 1950, St Kitts, West Indies

A powerful and distinctive singer and songwriter, Joan Armatrading was consistently successful with British and European audiences from the mid-seventies, though her attempts to introduce a harder musical edge into her work drew mixed reactions. She was a major influence on the new generation of younger female singer-songwriters who emerged in the eighties and mixed personal and social concerns in their work, the most notable of these being **Tracy Chapman**.

She moved to Birmingham, England, at the age of eight and her first album, *Whatever's for Us* (Cube, 1972), with lyrics by Pam Nestor, showed a strong influence of acoustic folk-orientated songwriting. Neither that nor the following album made much impact and it wasn't until A&M teamed her with veteran producer Glyn Johns for *Joan Armatrading* in 1976 that she had her first chart success.

The album included two of her most durable songs, 'Down to Zero' and 'Love and Affection', which was a Top Ten hit. By now Armatrading had found her own individual style in songs whose lyrics combined reticence with intimacy and whose melodic shapes allowed full rein to a flexible, deep voice that had some affinity with **Nina Simone**'s. Johns also produced *Show Some Emotion* (1977), *To the Limit* (1978) and *Steppin' Out* (1979).

Their strong sales and Armatrading's growing confidence in live performance established a strong AOR following for her music. In addition, her studio and live bands featured many of the leading session musicians of the period, including Henry Spinetti (drums), Dave Markee (bass) and Tim Hinkley (keyboards). In 1978 Armatrading was the centre of controversy when she wrote and sang the theme song for *The Wild Geese*, a film about white mercenaries in South Africa.

The title track of her next album, *Me Myself I* (1980), gave her a second Top Ten single, in a style which employed heavier rock techniques. The producer of that album was Richard Gotterher, who had previously been successful with the **McCoys** and **Blondie**. *Walk Under Ladders* (1981) consolidated Armatrading's position as the most durable of British women songwriters and performers, with 'Drop the

Pilot' (1983) from *The Key* entering the Top Twenty.

Later records like *Back to the Night* (1984) and *Secret Secrets* (1985) showed a stronger rock influence. In 1988 she released *The Shouting Stage* and in 1990 the lesser *Hearts and Flowers*. The compilation *The Very Best of Joan Armatrading* reached the UK Top Ten in 1991, and 1992's *Square the Circle* was co-produced by songwriter Graham Lyle, who also co-wrote several of the songs. She moved to BMG for *What's Inside* (1995), which featured the Kronos Quartet on some tracks. However, that album was overshadowed by the retrospective *Love and Affection* (1997). More successful was the various artists compilation album she organized, *Lullabies with a Difference* (1998), in support of the charity Paces.

LOUIS ARMSTRONG
b. 4 July 1898, New Orleans, Louisiana, USA, d. 6 July 1971, New York

Armstrong's status in popular-music history rests on two distinct achievements. Through his genius for improvisation and his technical virtuosity on trumpet and cornet – most notably expressed on the 'Hot Five' recordings of 1926–8 – he made the greatest individual contribution to the evolution of jazz. He was also one of the best-known entertainers in showbusiness, with a distinctive gravelly singing voice, and a stage personality with roots in the vaudeville and minstrelsy eras. Through this persona, he signified 'jazz' to a global audience far larger than the *aficionados* of the genre.

Armstrong's early life was spent in Storyville, the red-light district of New Orleans and the birthplace of jazz. He first learned cornet in the Colored Waifs' Home, where he played in a brass band in 1913. As a teenager he worked delivering coal, while sitting in with various bands, including **Kid Ory**'s, where he briefly replaced **King Oliver** who had moved to Chicago. In 1919 he gained his first full-time job as a musician, playing in Fate Marable's band on the Mississippi riverboats with Johnny St Cyr (banjo) and drummer Baby Dodds.

With a growing reputation, Armstrong was brought to Chicago in 1922 to join Oliver's Creole Jazz Band, which performed for both black and white audiences at the Lincoln Gardens ballroom. Armstrong and Oliver developed a unique dual-cornet style that was the feature of many recordings made for Gennett, Okeh and Columbia in 1922–3. These included 'Working Man's Blues', 'Chimes Blues' (on which Armstrong played the first solo chorus) and 'Riverside Blues'.

In Oliver's band, he met pianist Lil Hardin (*1898–1971*), who became his second wife in 1924 and who guided his career throughout the twenties. At her prompting, Armstrong left Oliver and joined **Fletcher Henderson** in New York in 1924. His 'hot' style was a novelty within this highly arranged big-band format. With Henderson, he made his first vocal recording, 'Everybody Loves My Baby'. Armstrong was also in demand for small-group jazz recordings (with **Clarence Williams**) and as an accompanist for classic blues singers like **Ma Rainey**, Clara Smith and **Bessie Smith**, with whom his playing showed total empathy on such tracks as 'Reckless Blues' and **W. C. Handy**'s 'St Louis Blues'.

Armstrong returned to Chicago in 1925, and for the next four years played in various bands led by Lil Armstrong, Erskine Tate, Carroll Dickerson and (after 1927) himself. Parallel with this career as a popular dance-band soloist – as early as 1926 he was billed as 'the world's greatest trumpet player' – and singer with frequent radio appearances was his recording career as leader of the Hot Five and occasionally the Hot Seven. The first track released under Armstrong's name was 'My Heart' (Okeh, 1925) and in a three-year period he cut sixty tracks for Okeh with musicians including Lil Armstrong, St Cyr, Ory, Johnny Dodds (clarinet) and pianist **Earl Hines**. As well as a steady improvement in Armstrong's horn technique (during these years he changed from cornet to trumpet), they trace his mastery of, and decisive shift beyond, the New Orleans ensemble mode of playing. Among the classic recordings of this period are 'Melancholy Blues', 'Potato Head Blues' and 'Fireworks'. By 1928 and the renowned 'West End Blues', with its lengthy and intricate unaccompanied introduction, Armstrong had established full improvisation – the invention of new melody lines, not merely the paraphrase of existing ones – as the way forward for jazz.

His growing reputation in jazz circles was proved by the publication in 1927 of books of his *Jazz Breaks* and *Hot Solos*, transcribed from specially recorded cylinders, but he was also enjoying popular success in the 'race' market with the scat (wordless) vocals of 'Heebie Jeebies' (1926). The impact of the Depression on the Chicago nightclub scene led Armstrong to New York in 1930. There, he sang **Fats Waller**'s 'Ain't Misbehavin'' in the Broadway revue *Hot Chocolates*, and his recordings of current pop hits like 'Some of These Days' and 'I Can't Give You Anything but Love' were jukebox hits in Harlem. During a lengthy club engagement in California in the same year, Armstrong accompanied country-and-western star **Jimmie Rodgers** on a Los Angeles recording session and was briefly jailed for possessing marijuana. More significantly, he recorded a further series of ballads with a band that included the young **Lionel Hampton**. Among the titles were 'You're Driving Me Crazy', 'I'm Confessin'' and 'Sweethearts on Parade', a number featured by **Guy Lombardo**, whose sweet

dance-band sound Armstrong particularly admired.

From 1931 to 1947, Armstrong led a series of big bands under the successive musical direction of Zilner Randolph, Luis Russell, Joe Garland and Teddy McRae. He toured extensively in America and visited Europe in 1932 and 1934, doing much to popularize jazz there. After 1935, his career was under the firm control of manager Joe Glaser, who ensured a steady flow of recording dates and movie appearances.

Leon and Otis Rene's 'When It's Sleepy Time Down South' was recorded by Armstrong in 1932 and became his theme song for many years. Basically an updated 'coon' song, portraying happy black folk in a mythical South, it was evidence for the 'Uncle Tom' attitudes he was accused of adopting by younger blacks, particularly after 1945. Counter-evidence was provided in 1957 by Armstrong's highly publicized and impassioned attack on the US government's failure to act against school segregation in Arkansas.

The thirties also saw the transition from Armstrong jazz musician to Armstrong personality-entertainer. His singing came to dominate his live performances, whether of pop songs or novelty items like 'You Rascal You' or 'Old Man Moses'. After Glaser negotiated a recording contract with Decca's **Jack Kapp** in 1935, Armstrong's following among white audiences was strengthened by his pairing with a variety of other artists signed to the label. These included the **Mills Brothers**, **Tommy Dorsey**, **Louis Jordan**, Hawaiian guitarist Andy Iona and, most successfully, **Ella Fitzgerald**. Decca also had Armstrong re-record tunes from his Hot Five period during 1936–41.

His Hollywood film career began with *Pennies from Heaven* (1936), a musical by Arthur James Johnston and Johnny Burke in which his co-star was **Bing Crosby**. He appeared in several other films including *Cabin in the Sky* (1943), **Arthur Freed**'s all-black musical, before being cast in *New Orleans* (1947). The film was an unconvincing attempt to cash in on the Dixieland revival, but the band assembled for it, including former Armstrong associates Ory and clarinettist Barney Bigard, played a major New York concert to critical acclaim.

This success of a small-group jazz format plus the uncertain economic situation for big bands led to the formation of Louis Armstrong's All Stars in 1947. With Bigard, Hines and trombonist **Jack Teagarden**, he constructed an act that combined showmanship and jazz in equal amounts. Within two years, the All Stars was the highest-paid jazz group of its size. With various personnel changes, the group's fourteen-year career involved frequent tours to all parts of the world, including a 1960 forty-five-date African trip co-sponsored by the US government and Pepsi-Cola. The momentum of Armstrong's acting career was maintained in a further twenty films, including *High*

Society (1956), with the memorable 'Now You Has Jazz' duet with Crosby, *The Five Pennies* (1959) with **Danny Kaye** as cornettist **Red Nichols**, and *Hello Dolly* (1969) with **Barbra Streisand**.

'Hello Dolly'*, the title song from Jerry Herman's Broadway show, had reached No. 1 on Kapp in 1964, replacing **The Beatles** whose records had topped the chart for the preceding fourteen weeks. 'Hello Dolly' was one of the last in a series of post-war hits which began after Glaser re-signed him to Decca in 1948, where **Milt Gabler** took charge of his career. The **Gordon Jenkins** arrangement of 'Blueberry Hill' (1949) reached No. 1 and was followed by 'La Vie en Rose'/ 'C'est Si Bon' (1951) and 'Ramona' (1953). 'Blueberry Hill' was reissued in 1956 to capitalize on Armstrong's Columbia hit, **Kurt Weill**'s 'Mack the Knife'. Armstrong's final chart success was 'What a Wonderful World' (HMV, 1968). The song was again a hit after it was used in a British television commercial in 1988.

Apart from the hit singles, Armstrong's later recordings were many and varied. Gabler organized a series of recordings which celebrated Armstrong's lengthy career. In 1954 he cut an album of songs by W. C. Handy, while 1957 brought the four-album *Satchmo: A Musical Autobiography* ('Satchmo', like 'Pops', was a soubriquet acquired by Armstrong early in his career). With a linking narrative spoken by Armstrong himself, the re-recorded material included a number of obscure tunes from the earliest phases of his work.

After 1954 Armstrong recorded on a freelance basis for Verve, Columbia and Mercury as well as Decca. He collaborated with Ella Fitzgerald on selections from **George Gershwin**'s *Porgy and Bess* (Verve, 1960), with **Dave Brubeck** (1961) and with **Duke Ellington** (*Echoes of an Era*, Roulette). In 1970 a vocal album, *Louis and His Friends* (Audio Masterworks), included material as varied as Ellington's 'Mood Indigo' and **John Lennon**'s 'Give Peace a Chance' and guest players as diverse as **Miles Davis**, **Ornette Coleman** and **Eddie Condon**.

His final album was a selection of country songs recorded in Nashville. Despite serious health problems dating from a heart attack in 1959 and severe problems with his lip that limited his trumpet-playing, Armstrong continued to tour frequently until 1970. He died of heart and kidney failure. *Louis* by Max Jones and John Chilton (1971) is the definitive account of Armstrong's career.

DAVID ARNOLD
b. 1 January 1962, Luton, Bedfordshire, England

British film composer Arnold rose to prominence with his work on *The Young Americans* before taking on Hollywood.

A veteran of numerous unsung British rock bands in his youth, Arnold spent several years scoring British television drama series and documentaries. He also auditioned unsuccessfully for the **Clash** and the **Waterboys**. When his friend and colleague Danny Cannon moved from television to feature film direction with *The Young Americans* (1993), Arnold produced the score, including 'Play Dead', co-written and performed by **Björk**, which reached the British Top Ten.

With his career blossoming, Arnold travelled to LA, and the result was an invitation to provide the score to Roland Emmerich's big budget sci-fi adventure, *Stargate* (1994). The bombastic, unrelenting musical backdrop drew him many admirers, although some felt his style was overly traditional. Perhaps because of this criticism, his next score, *The Last of the Dogmen* (1995), was a more composed and sombre affair.

After his score for *Cut-throat Island* (1995) was rejected, Arnold returned to Emmerich for the high-profile science-fiction movie *Independence Day* (1996), which saw a stylistic return to the epic, large-scale production values of his work on *Stargate*. The following year Arnold wrote the score to the Bond movie *Tomorrow Never Dies* (1997), starring Pierce Brosnan. He also found time to work with the **Propellerheads** and Jarvis Cocker of **Pulp**, amongst others, on an album of James Bond themes, *Shaken, Not Stirred* (1997), as well as scoring *A Life Less Ordinary* and *The Visitor*, a US TV series. As grandiose as ever was his score for his third Roland Emmerich-directed film, the large-scale flop *Godzilla* (1998).

EDDY ARNOLD
b. 15 May 1918, near Henderson, Tennessee, USA

Despite his rural soubriquet 'The Tennessee Plowboy', Arnold, with sales of over 80 million records, was the first successful country-pop crossover artist, a status he achieved less with particular hit records than through the persistent application of a mellow crooning manner which country historian Bill C. Malone has described as being 'as appealing to bankers as to farmers'. He thus stands at the head of a line of singers that includes George Morgan, whose crossover hits included 'Candy Kisses' and 'Room Full of Roses' (Columbia, 1949), and, most notably, **Jim Reeves**.

Arnold first made a name on various Tennessee radio stations in the late thirties. In 1943 he joined the cast of the *Grand Ole Opry* as singer with **Pee Wee King**'s Golden West Cowboys, and in the following year he signed with RCA Victor. There followed a continuous stream of hits: 'I'll Hold You in My Heart' (1947), 'Bouquet of Roses' and 'Just a Little Lovin' Will Go a Long Long Way' (both 1948), 'Don't Rob

Another Man's Castle' (1949), 'Kentucky Waltz' and 'I Wanna Play House with You' (both 1951), 'Cattle Call' (1955), and many others. During the fifties he had his own TV shows and often guested on other, non-country programmes. His chart success continued well into the sixties, with 'Make the World Go Away' (1965) and 'I Want to Go with You' (1966) just two of his pop hits. In 1967 he was *Billboard*'s No. 1 Country Album Artist. He has been credited with record sales of over 70 million. In 1966 he was voted into the Country Music Hall of Fame. He continued to make the country charts regularly well into the eighties. In retirement he still occasionally recorded, including 'You Don't Miss a Thing' (1991).

MALCOLM ARNOLD
b. 21 October 1921, Northampton, England

A prolific composer of both light classical music and film scores, Arnold's melodic gift won him an Oscar for *The Bridge on the River Kwai* in 1957.

Unusually for a composer, he trained and started his professional career as an orchestral musician. Arnold studied trumpet at the Royal College of Music in London until 1941 when he joined the London Philharmonic Orchestra, eventually becoming principal trumpet. He left in 1954 to become a full-time composer.

Like **Kurt Weill** and Aaron Copland in an earlier era, Arnold devoted himself equally to large-scale classical works and popular material, principally for the cinema. With its whistled theme derived from the traditional march 'Colonel Bogey', *Kwai* was the prime example of Arnold's ingenuity in constructing film music. **Mitch Miller** had a hit with the tune in 1958 while British bandleader Cyril Stapleton reached the American Top Twenty with the 'Children's Marching Song' from Arnold's score for *The Inn of the Sixth Happiness* (London, 1959). Among the other films for which he wrote were *Hobson's Choice* (1954), *Tunes of Glory* (1960), *The Lion* (1962) and *David Copperfield* (1970). His closest brush with rock came in 1972 when he conducted a recording of **Deep Purple** organist Jon Lord's *Gemini Suite* (Purple) by the London Symphony Orchestra.

In the classical field, Arnold reworked traditional material in his *Suite of English Dances* and his arrangements of sea shanties. He wrote a *Guitar Concerto and Serenade* for the British virtuoso Julian Bream. In 1970 he wrote 'Fanfare for Louis' in celebration of **Louis Armstrong**'s seventieth birthday. Among his light classical pieces are 'Homage to the Queen', written for the 1953 coronation of Elizabeth II, and several compositions for brass bands, including the march 'Padstow Lifeboat', which was the 1974 National Championship test-piece.

ARRESTED DEVELOPMENT
Speech, b. Todd Thomas, 25 October 1968, Milwaukee, Wisconsin, USA; DJ Headliner, b. Timothy Barnwell, 26 July 1967, New Jersey; Montsho Eshe, b. Temelca Gaither, 23 December 1973, Georgia; Aerle Taree, b. Taree Jones, 10 January 1972, Milwaukee; Rasa Don, b. Donald Jones, 22 November 1968, New Jersey; Baba Oje, b. 15 May 1932, Mississippi; Nadriah, b. 1959

One of the most original of US rap and hip-hop groups, the Atlanta-based Arrested Development emphasized the African and rural Southern roots of their music. They have even called themselves 'agrarian rappers' as distinct from most rap performers and their urban concerns.

While studying at the Atlanta Art Institute, singer and rapper Todd Thomas and DJ Timothy Barnwell formed a gangsta rap group in 1987. They soon rejected the gangsta themes of violence and nihilism in favour of lyrics and a visual style highlighting African-American cultural heritage. Formerly known as DJ Peech, Thomas became known as Speech and he named the new band Arrested Development.

The group's distinctive clothing of bib overalls and dashikis was devised by Speech's cousin Aerle Taree, who also sang with the group. Other members included vocalist Nadriah, Rasa Don on drums and dancer Montsho Eshe. Baba Oje was listed as the band's 'spiritual advisor'.

Arrested Development's approach to rap evolved over three years, a period recalled in the title of their first album, *3 Years, 5 Months and 2 Days in the Life of . . .* (Chrysalis, 1993). The band's first single, 'Tennessee', which included samples of country fiddle music and bieol song was a Top Ten hit in 1992. It confirmed just how big a step forward Arrested Development represented for rap. This was followed by 'People Everyday' (a funky rewrite of **Sly Stone**'s 'Everyday People') and an appearance on MTV *Unplugged*. In 1993 Arrested Development became the first rap group to issue an album of their *Unplugged* performance. During that year the group had a further hit single with 'Mr Wendell'. They also took part in the Lollapalooza '93 tour of North America and played concerts in Europe. Speech produced the début album of Milwaukee rap group Gumbo in 1994, the year the group released *Zingalamundi*, which like *3 Years* put traditional rap concerns in a wider context, as on 'That's Mister Landlord' in which African gods are evoked to chase away a demanding landlord. Similarly, in nearly all the songs speech is always on the verge of becoming singing and the hard urban rhythms slip towards a more relaxed, jazzier feel.

In 1996 Speech contributed to the tribute album *Inner City Blues – The Music of Marvin Gaye* and released his first solo album, *Speech*. In 1998, by which time most of the group members had embarked upon a variety of solo products, Chrysalis issued *The Best of Arrested Development*.

ARROW
b. Alphonsus Cassell, Montserrat

One of the most popular calypso singers of the seventies, Arrow was the leading exponent of soca (soul calypso) music in the eighties.

The youngest child in a family of nine, he composed his first calypsos about teachers and schoolmates. While still at school he entered the King of Kings contest on the island of Antigua, performing the traditional calypso, 'Invitation to the Caribbean'. After being crowned Calypso King of Montserrat in 1971, he competed in the all-Caribbean competition in Antigua. Arrow later moved to Trinidad where he recorded *On Target* (1974) and developed an up-tempo calypso style on such compositions as 'Monique' (1975), which incorporated French influences from the nearby island of Guadeloupe.

Subsequent recordings included *Instant Knockout* (1981) and *Double Trouble* (1982). Arrow's international breakthrough came in 1983 when his carnival song 'Hot Hot Hot' became a UK hit. The single has sold over two million copies worldwide and the song is now acknowledged as a soca classic. In the US, Buster Poindexter (the former **New York Dolls** member David Johansen) had a hit with his version of 'Hot Hot Hot' adding a disco bass guitar pulse to calypso vocal stylings. The song was used as the official anthem of the 1986 soccer World Cup held in Mexico and it has been adapted for television commercials.

In 1988 Arrow signed a recording deal with Island's Mango subsidiary, releasing annual albums timed to coincide with the carnival seasons in the Caribbean and the UK, where he appeared at the Notting Hill Carnival in 1989 and 1990. *Knock Dem Dead* (1988) included the hip-hop flavoured 'Groovemaster'. This track was included in the soundtrack of the films *Casual Sex* and *The Mighty Quinn*. *Dance Soca Party* (1989) and *O La Soca* (1990) showed Arrow broadening his range to include tracks in zouk, African, rap and house styles, while *Zombie Soca* (1993), which included the insinuating 'Wine Yuh Body', was his best album for some time, a broad mix of dancehall music and social commentary.

He has toured widely in Europe, Japan, North America and Latin America. He was awarded the MBE for his services to Caribbean music.

ART ENSEMBLE OF CHICAGO
Roscoe Mitchell, b. 3 August 1940, Chicago, Illinois, USA; Joseph Jarman, b. 14 September 1937, Pine Bluff,
Arkansas; Lester Bowie, b. 11 October 1941, Frederick, Maryland; Malachi Favors, b. 27 August 1937, Lexington, Mississippi; Don Moye, b. 23 May 1946, Rochester, New York; Muhal Richard Abrams, b. 19 September 1930, Chicago

One of the most enduring avant-garde jazz organizations, the Art Ensemble grew out of the Association for the Advancement of Creative Musicians, founded in Chicago in 1965 by pianist and clarinettist Muhal Richard Abrams. Other members included **Anthony Braxton** and trumpeter Leo Smith. **Ornette Coleman** was an early influence on the AACM's collective improvisation, and several albums were cut for local blues label Delmark, including the ensemble piece *Little Suite (Sound)*, a free-form 'history' of jazz and black music.

The Art Ensemble was formed in 1968 by trumpeter Bowie, who had toured with soul singers like **Jerry Butler** and **Joe Tex**, saxophonists Mitchell and Jarman and bass-player Favors. From 1969 to 1972 the group was based in France, where it was joined by drummer Don Moye. Bowie's wife (soul singer **Fontella Bass** – her 'Rescue Me' reached No. 4 on Checker in 1965) was featured on several recordings, notably the film soundtrack *Les Stances à Sophie* (EMI Pathe, 1970). The band's live performances became progressively more theatrical in the style of African ceremonies while at the same time their music became increasingly Africanized in the course of the seventies. Wild vocal screams and African instruments (log-drums, whistles and gongs) were regularly featured in their performances. A triumphal return to the United States for the Ann Arbor Festival led to two albums for Atlantic, including *Fanfare for the Warriors*, for which Abrams joined the Ensemble. *Urban Bushmen* (ECM, 1982), a live recording of a 1980 concert, catches the band at its best during this period.

Mitchell, Bowie and Jarman all cut a number of solo albums, while *The Third Decade* (ECM, 1985) celebrated the group's twenty-year history with a range of material drawing on Irish melodies, tongue-in-cheek funk, American drumming and jazz balladry. Joe and Byron Bowie, Lester's trombone- and sax-playing brothers, were members of an equally avant-garde jazz-disco group, Defunkt, formed in 1980.

During the nineties the group and its members recorded on a part-time basis. The Ensemble released *Soweto* (DIW, 1991) and *Dreaming of the Master Suite* (1992), while Bowie recorded *Unforeseen Blessings* (Black Saint, 1990) with the Leaders, which included a witty version of 'Blueberry Hill'. Defunkt found an international audience in the dance clubs with *Heroes* (DIW, 1990).

MOE ASCH

b. Moses Asch, 1905, Warsaw, Poland, d. 19 October 1986, New York, USA

Through his Folkways label, Asch was the most important figure in recorded folk music in America for nearly forty years. The 2,000 or so albums he issued greatly contributed to the reservoir of material available to the young singers of the folk revival.

The son of novelist Scholem Asch, he grew up in Germany and in Brooklyn, where he worked on the installation of sound equipment in cinemas. He set up Asch Records in 1939 to release readings of his father's work.

During the early forties he became interested in blues, jazz and folk music, recording artists like **Burl Ives**, **Leadbelly**, **Coleman Hawkins** and **Woody Guthrie** for his shortlived Disc label. Folkways was set up in 1948 with Marion Distler and from the start it pursued an intensely independent policy, even pressing the records in-house.

In the fifties Asch recorded many albums by **Pete Seeger** and other contemporary singers, despite the existence of a blacklist in the entertainment industry. The catalogue also included ethnic music from Asia, Africa and Europe as well as the Americas. One of his more unusual titles was a recording of the testimony of playwright Bertolt Brecht before Senator McCarthy's Un-American Activities Committee. With the growth of the folk market Asch briefly produced a series of albums by the Blues Project (formed by **Al Kooper**) and others for the Verve company.

Asch prided himself on never deleting any album released on Folkways and its sister labels (RBF, Broadside and Asch). Shortly before his death he completed the sale of the catalogue to the Smithsonian Institution, an ethnographic foundation in Washington DC, whose director Ralph Rinzler, a former member of revival group the Greenbriar Boys and a song collector, was well qualified to maintain the Folkways tradition.

ASHFORD AND SIMPSON

Nickolas Ashford, b. 4 May 1943, Fairfield, South Carolina, USA; Valerie Simpson, b. 26 August 1948, Bronx, New York

Beginning with the **Ray Charles** hit 'Let's Go Get Stoned' (1966), Ashford and Simpson were one of black music's most successful songwriting teams. They provided hits for **Diana Ross**, **Marvin Gaye** and other artists from **Berry Gordy**'s Motown stable before launching their own careers as performers, where their romantic ballads found large audiences.

Former jazz dancer Ashford met gospel singer Simpson at a Harlem church in 1963. They recorded for Glover Records before joining Florence Greenberg's Scepter records in 1965 as songwriters. The success of 'Let's Go Get Stoned' led to a contract with Gordy's Jobete music publishing company and a move to Detroit. There, Ashford and Simpson wrote and produced material for Gaye and Tammi Terrell, including 'Your Precious Love' (1967), 'Ain't Nothing Like the Real Thing' (1968) and 'You're All I Need to Get By'.

The duo worked with **Gladys Knight and the Pips** but they had greater success with Ross, writing her first solo hits, 'Reach out and Touch (Somebody's Hand)' (1970), the No. 1 'Ain't No Mountain High Enough' (first recorded by Gaye and Terrell in 1967), and 'Surrender' (1971).

In 1971 Gordy reluctantly acceded to the pair's long-standing wish to become recording artists in their own right and Simpson's *Exposed!* was released to critical acclaim. Its sales, however, were poor and after recording *Keep It Comin'* as a duo, Ashford and Simpson moved to Warners while continuing to produce Ross, Knight and **Chaka Khan**.

I Wanna Be Selfish (1974) and *Come As You Are* (1975) were followed by the R&B hit 'Send It' (1977). The following year 'I'm Out of Your Life' was a minor success but their first major pop hit was 'I Found a Cure' from *Stay Free* (1979). Later Warner recordings were R&B hits but the duo did not cross over to the international pop market again until they moved to Capitol for *Street Opera* (1982) and the superior *Solid* (1985), the title track of which, an emphatic celebration of marital harmony, was a Top Twenty hit in both America and Britain. Later albums included *Love or Physical* (1989). The duo signed to Arista in 1991.

During the nineties they continued to supply songs to other artists, including Stephanie Mills, **Patti Labelle**, **Teddy Pendergrass** and Simpson's brother Ray, who had been a lead singer with the **Village People**.

ASIAN DUB FOUNDATION

Dr. Das, b. Aniruddha Das, London, England; Pandit G, b. John Pandit, London; Master D, b. Deedar Zaman; Bubble-E; DJ Sun-J

Eclectic five-piece Asian Dub Foundation draw on traditional and dance influences to create an 'Asian Punk Jungle' sound of their own.

The beginnings of the Asian Dub Foundation saw Das, assisted by Pandit, put together the Community Music Project in London, with the aim of breaking down racial barriers and introducing minority children to the basics of techno music. The duo formed the Asian Dub Foundation after the pair found Zaman through their music workshop in 1993. Adopting stage names soon after, the then three-piece band quickly gained a reputation for their frantic live performances and for the socio-political edge to Master D's rapping. In contrast to many other groups who adopted the cloak of social criticism, ADF remained true to their roots, organizing protests about selected issues (the Free Satpal Ram campaign) and setting up their own music-education workshops in imitation of the Community Music Project in London.

Signing to Nation Records within a year of their formation, ADF released an EP, *Conscious* (1994), and the 'Rebel Warrior' single, which saw the band recruit two new members, Bubble-E and DJ Sun-J. A further EP, *Facts and Fictions* (1996), followed as they began to gain a strong club following but failed to cross over into the mainstream market. This looked set to change with their move to Slash/Polygram for the release of the critically acclaimed *Rafi's Revenge* (1998), which spawned minor hit singles in 'Naxalite' and 'Free Satpal Ram', an Asian man whom the band felt had been unfairly jailed after killing an attacker in self-defence.

In 2000 they released the superior *Community Music*, a meld of influences as varied as **King Tubby** and **Public Enemy**, in which their blend of social criticism was as strong as ever, particularly in the opening tracks, which were coruscating attacks on the 'New' Labour government.

ASLEEP AT THE WHEEL

Ray Benson, b. 16 March 1951, Philadelphia, Pennsylvania, USA; Christine O'Connell, b. 21 March 1953, Williamsport, Maryland; Lucky Oceans, b. Rueben Gosfield, 22 April 1951, Philadelphia; LeRoy Preston; Floyd Domino, b. Jim Haber

Despite only ever grazing the charts and having some seventy members pass through the band over the course of twenty-five years, Asleep at the Wheel became a country institution. The group initially won attention for their revival of **Bob Wills**' Western Swing. However, over the years it won as much for its open-minded, traditional approach to country music as a whole, in which an **Eric Clapton** song ('Lay Down, Sally') was as easily countryfied as was a southern soul standard (Toussaint McCall's 'Nothing Takes the Place of You'). If the band's traditional aspirations denied them widespread success, its pair of tributes to Wills, *Tribute to the Music of Bob Wills* (Liberty, 1993), made with the collaboration of country stars **Lyle Lovett**, **Merle Haggard**, **Garth Brooks**, **George Strait** and others, and the even more adventurous *Ride with Bob* (Dreamworks, 1999), remain the most affectionate and revealing accounts of the joyful music Western Swing was at its best.

Benson (who would be the only member of the group in all its incarnations) formed the group in West Virginia in 1972 with steel guitarist Oceans and drummer Preston. With the addition of vocalist O'Connell and pianist Domino it won itself a reputation as a live act for its traditional approach to country music and a contract with United Artists in 1993. The resulting album, *Coming Right at Ya* (1973), mixed reworkings of songs associated with the likes of Wills, **Ernest Tubb** and **Moon Mullican** with equally affecting Benson originals. A critical success, albeit the first of many commercial failures, it led to the group relocating to Austin, Texas, where it established itself as a hugely popular draw. Their reputation survived the lacklustre eponymous Epic album (1975). They joined Capitol for *Texas Gold*, which featured their biggest almost hit, 'The Letter That Johnny Walker Read', and the delightful revival of **Count Basie**'s 'One o'Clock Jump'. However, their subsequent Capitol albums, which included the fine live outing *Served Live* (1979), failed to sell. After a massive change in personnel the band moved to MCA for *Framed* (1980) and *Asleep at the Wheel* (1985), which included more new compositions than previous outings and initiated the tradition of the group being augmented by guests such as **Bonnie Raitt** and **Willie Nelson** on individual tracks. A move to Arista (*Live & Kickin'*, 1991) and then Epic (*The Swinging Best of*, 1992) saw them extending their range to include more bluesy material but brought them no more success. In response Benson organized his ambitious 1993 Wills tribute for yet another label (Capitol). Despite the unevenness created by the stellar cast of guests, the album, like Haggard's earlier tribute, was both affectionate and enjoyable. However, neither it nor subsequent offerings were commercially successful and the band, its personnel ever changing, became increasingly a live act. Among the best of their later albums was *Back to the Future Live* (Sony, 1997), for which Benson reassembled the original group. More affecting was *Ride with Bob* (1999), on which Asleep was joined by a mix of old country (**Dwight Yoakam** and Haggard, among others) and new country (Lee Ann Womack and the Dixie Chicks).

Former Asleep members Oceans (*Lucky Steels the Wheel*, 1992), Preston (*Country Pedigree*, 1997) and Domino (*Boogie Woogie*, 1997) have all recorded in Western Swing style.

THE ASSOCIATION

Russ Giguere, b. 18 October 1943, Portsmouth, New Hampshire, USA; Jim Yester, b. 1941, Birmingham, Alabama; Ted Beuchel, b. 1943, San Pedro, California; Brian Cole, b. 1944, Tacoma, California, d. 2 August 1972; Terry Kirkman, b. 1941, Salinas, Kansas; Jules Alexander, b. 1942, Chattanooga, Tennessee (replaced by Larry Ramos Jr, b. Hilario Ramos Jr, 19 April 1942, Hawaii)

The Association were a successful sixties vocal-harmony group who, despite selling some 15 million copies of their singles, were unable to build a long-term career for themselves.

Formed around Kirkman (who had played with **Frank Zappa**) and Alexander in Los Angeles in 1965, the group from the start ploughed the path of soft, rather than hard, rock. Signed to Valiant in 1966, they had an immediate million-seller with the controversial 'Along Comes Mary' (despite its soft harmonies, the song was widely regarded, like the **Byrds**' 'Eight Miles High', as an ode to marijuana) and a second with the sentimental 'Cherish'. After the mildly psychedelic 'Pandora's Golden Heebie Jeebies' (1966), the group switched to Warner Brothers for 'Windy'* and 'Never My Love'* (both 1967). Alexander then left to meditate in India. His replacement was former New Christy Minstrel singer/guitarist Ramos. The Association's chart run tailed off after one more Top Ten hit, 'Everything that Touches You' (1968), and the theme to the film *Goodbye Columbus* (1969).

Despite a series of interesting progressive albums, including *The Association* (1970) and *Waterbed in Trinidad* (Columbia, 1972), by which time Richard Thompson had replaced Giguere, the group failed to find favour with the rock audience and turned to nightclubs for work. In 1981 they re-formed to tour and record the minor hit single 'Dreamer'. Giguere and Ramos continued to perform as the Association with new backing musicians throughout the eighties and nineties, but the group recorded only intermittently, including *A Little Bit More* (Track).

FRED ASTAIRE
b. Frederick Austerlitz, 10 May 1899, Omaha, Nebraska, USA, d. 22 June 1986, Los Angeles, California

When Astaire, already a star of the musical stage, was given a screen test the verdict was 'Can't act. Slightly bald. Can dance a little.' Yet within two years he had acquired legendary status in Hollywood, so much so that the mere mention of his name signalled excellence, as in **Cole Porter**'s 'You're the Top' which has the line, 'the nimble tread of the feet of Fred Astaire'. Astaire's talent was undeniably limited – he was, for example, far happier in white tie and tails than out of them – but he possessed the supreme ability of presenting sinuous movement to the camera. A few others could dance better, more could sing better, and many more handle light comedy better but Astaire (with weeks of rehearsal behind him) could simply sparkle on camera. Moreover, in his heyday as a screen star he introduced many of the wittiest songs of the thirties.

The son of Viennese immigrants, Astaire toured the vaudeville circuit as a child in a dancing act with his sister, Adele. The duo made their Broadway début in *Over the Top* (1917) and had their first big success with *The Passing Show of 1918*. For a decade the pair were firm favourites with New York and London audiences before Adele's marriage to Lord Charles Cavendish ended their partnership. In Hollywood, Astaire won a small part in *Dancing Lady* (1933) before being partnered with Ginger Rogers for *Flying Down to Rio* (1933). Rogers (*b. Virginia Katherine McMath, 16 July 1911, Independence, Missouri, USA*) sang and danced on the vaudeville circuit in her teens. Her first success came in 1928 when she teamed up with Jack Pepper as Ginger and Pepper. After appearances in the **Kalamar and Ruby** musical *Top Speed* (1929) and **George Gershwin**'s *Girl Crazy* (1930), in which she introduced 'Embraceable You', she went to Hollywood. First cast as a fast-talking blonde (*Hat Check Girl*, 1931), she returned to musicals when teamed by RKO with Astaire. In all, Rogers and Astaire made ten films together, including *The Gay Divorcee* (1934, derived from the musical *The Gay Divorce* in which Astaire had appeared on Broadway in 1932); *Top Hat* (1935); *Swing Time* (1936); and *The Story of Vernon and Irene Castle* (1939).

Though the plots varied, the films were essentially the same. Rogers was the bright object of the affections of Astaire's debonair, but essentially innocent, playboy and the courting was done on the dancefloor and the balcony where Astaire would serenade Rogers in one of numerous songs specially written for his reedy but pleasant voice. Among these were: 'Night and Day' and 'Begin the Beguine' (Cole Porter); 'The Continental' (the first song to win an Oscar, by Con Conrad and Herb Magidson); 'Cheek to Cheek' and 'Let's Face the Music and Dance' (**Irving Berlin**); 'A Fine Romance' and 'The Way You Look Tonight' (by **Jerome Kern** and **Dorothy Fields**); 'They Can't Take That Away from Me', 'They All Laughed' and 'Let's Call the Whole Thing Off' (all from *Shall We Dance*, 1937); 'A Foggy Day' and 'Nice Work If You Can Get It' (by George and **Ira Gershwin**). Equally important, Astaire's easy-going style of dancing transformed the film musical. Instead of vast production numbers, henceforth a couple dancing could provide the intensity so necessary to a musical without encumbering the plot with more than a dancefloor and a balcony.

Astaire's recordings of the songs he introduced in these films were huge hits, giving him eight No. 1s: 'Night and Day' (Victor, 1932), 'Cheek to Cheek' (Brunswick, 1935), 'I'm Putting All My Eggs in One Basket', 'The Way You Look Tonight', 'A Fine Romance' (1936), 'They Can't Take That Away from Me', 'Nice Work If You Can Get It' (1937) and 'Change Partners' (1938).

When Rogers left musicals for dramatic parts, Astaire danced his way through the forties and fifties with a variety of partners including: Rita Hayworth

(*You'll Never Get Rich*, 1941 and *You Were Never Love-lier*, 1942); Lucille Bremmer (*Yolanda and the Thief*, 1945); **Judy Garland** (*Easter Parade*, 1948); Jane Powell (*Royal Wedding*, 1951, which provided Astaire and Powell with a million-selling record, 'How Could You Believe Me When I Said I Loved You, When You Know I've Been a Liar All My Life'); and Leslie Caron (*Daddy Long Legs*, 1955, and *Funny Face*, 1956, which he choreographed himself). His greatest success came when Vincent Minnelli partnered him with Cyd Charisse in *The Band Wagon* (1953) and gave the pair the clever 'Micky Spillane' routine, which was more balletic than normal for Astaire.

After a few dramatic roles, including *On the Beach* (1959), Astaire emerged from semi-retirement for the fey *Finian's Rainbow* (1968). From then until his death, he alternated dramatic roles (such as *The Towering Inferno*, 1974, for which he won an Oscar) with TV specials.

In the forties and fifties Rogers established herself as a dramatic actress, winning an Oscar for *Kitty Foyle* (1940). In 1965 she returned triumphantly to Broadway when she replaced Carol Channing in Jay Herman's *Hello Dolly!* and in 1969 starred in the London production of the same author's *Mame*.

ASWAD
Brinsley Forde; Angus 'Drummie Zeb' Gaye; George Oban; Tony 'Gad' Robinson; Donald Benjamin; Courtney Hemmings; Ras George Levi; Vin Gordon; Karl Pitterson; Don Griffiths

The most successful UK reggae group to emerge in the late seventies, Aswad enjoyed several hits in the late eighties and early nineties when they played down their politically charged approach and espousal of Rastafarianism in favour of mainstream pop songs.

Formed in London in 1975 around the trio of Forde (guitar, vocals), Zeb (drums, vocals) and Oban, the group released their self-titled début album on Island Records in 1976. The commercial success of reggae at that time and the enthusiastic acceptance of the music by the burgeoning UK punk scene saw the band touring constantly for the next three years. By the time of their second album, *Hulet* (1979), released on the independent Grove Muzic label, Oban had left, replaced by 'Gad' Robinson, who took his place as the third creative member of the Aswad team. In 1980 Forde, who had been a child actor on the BBC TV children's series *The Double Deckers*, starred in the film *Babylon*, for which the band provided music. Later that year the band signed to CBS for two albums, *New Chapter* (1981) and *Not Satisfied* (1982), the latter reaching the UK Top Fifty.

The group re-signed to Island in 1983, releasing the in-concert album *Live and Direct*, which again

charted, and the following year enjoyed two minor hit singles with 'Chasing for the Breeze' and their revival of **Toots and the Maytals**' '54–46 (Was My Number)'. Another chart album, *Rebel Souls* (1984), followed on Island before they left to set up their own label, Simba. They released a collaboration with sound system legend Jah Shaka before *To the Top* (1986), but it was their return to the Island fold which would give them their greatest success. Signing to Island's Mango subsidiary, the band trimmed down to a three piece, and Zeb, whose voice was deemed more commercial than Forde's, was given lead vocal duties on 'Don't Turn Around' (1988). A pop song written by Albert Hammond and **Diane Warren**, it reached No. 1 in the UK, and the follow up 'Give a Little Love' reached the Top Twenty.

The album *Distant Thunder* (1988) reached the UK Top Ten, and the band enjoyed three further UK Top Forty singles over the following twelve months, but subsequent releases failed to capitalize on their break-through. *Too Wicked* (1990) was their last new album for Mango, although an album of remixes, *Firesticks*, did appear in 1993. A 1993 single 'How Long' (Big Life) with dance vocalist Yazz, attempting to revive her own career after her UK No. 1 'The Only Way Is Up' (Big Life, 1988), failed to reach the Top Thirty. 'Shine' from *Rise and Shine* (Bubblin', 1994) was more successful, while *Big Up* (1997) was nominated for a Grammy.

CHET ATKINS
b. Chester Burton Atkins, 20 June 1924, Lutrell, Tennessee, USA

As well as being an innovative and respected guitarist, as a producer Atkins was responsible for creating the 'Nashville sound', which represented a decisive shift in the sound of country music in the late fifties and early sixties.

Atkins was the son of a piano and voice teacher and his brother Jimmy was a member of the trio led by **Les Paul**. Chet took up the guitar when he was nine. His major influence was **Merle Travis**, whose finger-picking style, which made it possible for him to play melody and rhythm simultaneously, he adopted (with the difference that Atkins used three fingers rather than Travis's forefinger and thumb). In 1942 Atkins joined WNOX, backing comedian/vocalists Archie Campbell and Bill Carlisle, first on fiddle, then guitar. For some five years he played at various radio stations (spending much time in the music libraries making himself familiar with a wide range of music styles, which would later stand him in good stead). In 1946, while **Red Foley**'s guitarist, he made his first record, the modernistic 'Guitar Blues' (Bullet), in which his electric guitar was set against a bluesy clarinet, and in

1947 made his first recordings for RCA under the direction of Steve Sholes. Since he was seen as a competitor to Travis (a vocalist as well as guitarist), five of the eight tracks Atkins recorded on 11 August 1947 had vocals, but it was as a guitarist that he won favour. 'Canned Heat' (1947) and some of the recordings he made with the country comedy duo Homer and Jethro (who were also noted instrumentalists) in 1949, notably the exciting 'Galloping on the Guitar' and 'Main Street Breakdown', were used by disc-jockeys as incidental music. At the same time he was working as a featured sideman with the current version of the Carter Family, playing in a folkier mode.

Though he would make over thirty albums for RCA alone, the highpoint of Atkins' career as a guitarist was the early fifties. Having already proved himself the master of speed, he turned to melody with the delicate 'Chinatown, My Chinatown' (1952), in which he played in the manner of a steel guitarist, 'Country Gentleman' (1953), his best-known recording, and the charming 'Downhill Drag' (also 1953).

His record success was minimal, but his behind-the-scenes influence on the music coming out of Nashville was enormous. From 1949 Atkins had been a regular session guitarist on recordings made in Nashville, and from 1952 he was Sholes's assistant. When in 1955 RCA opened their own studio in Nashville, Atkins was appointed manager. Finally, in 1957, he was made head of RCA's Nashville operation. More significant than the titles were Atkins' activities in the studio. With the proliferation of studios in Nashville, there grew a need for versatile musicians adept at working with each other. Over the years, Atkins gathered such a group around him, including guitarists Grady Martin and Hank Garland, pianist Floyd Cramer, drummer Buddy Harmon, bassist Bob Moore and vocal quartet the Jordanaires.

As Atkins advanced from session arranger to session supervisor and finally producer, the sound he preferred, which was swiftly dubbed the 'Nashville sound', came more and more to dominate recordings made in Nashville. Piano and guitar took the lines normally played by fiddle and steel guitar and the resulting record, especially when sweetened with background vocals (or later strings), was lighter in feel, less harsh and closer to pop than most country music of the period. Among the artists with whom Atkins worked were the Everly Brothers, whose Cadence Records he played on and oversaw, Elvis Presley, all of whose early RCA recordings he supervised, the Browns, whose 'The Three Bells'* (1959) is a classic example of the Nashville sound at its most delicate and sugary, Skeeter Davis, for whom he produced 'The End of the World'* (1962), Don Gibson and Jim Reeves. The crossover success of these artists led to the Nashville sound quickly being standardized

and becoming a conservative rather than progressive influence.

By the sixties Atkins' own guitar work was for the most part similarly conservative and his recordings with the Boston Pops Symphony Orchestra and Ravi Shankar are professional rather than exciting. It was only with his protégé Jerry Reed (Me and Jerry, 1970), his reunions with his mentors Merle Travis (The Atkins–Travis Traveling Show, 1973) and Les Paul (Chester and Lester, 1976) and in duet with Doc Watson (Reflections, 1980) that his playing found its old sparkle.

Throughout the sixties and seventies Atkins took on progressively more administrative work for RCA – in 1968 he was appointed a divisional Vice-President of the company. As such he was responsible for signing Charley Pride, Connie Smith, Waylon Jennings and Dottie West. In 1973 Atkins was elected to the Country Music Hall of Fame.

In the late seventies Atkins resigned from all administrative work and in 1981 quit RCA for Columbia. Ironically, his Columbia recordings were no more adventurous than the bulk of his later work for RCA. On these, which included Street Dreams (1986) and Sails (1987), he played superior easy-listening music supported by a variety of star guests, such as George Benson.

Then, in 1990, he teamed up with Mark Knopfler of Dire Straits for the superior Neck and Neck. On this he mixed jazz with novelty tunes, like 'Yakety Axe', a tune best known as the theme music to Benny Hill's television comedy series, with marvellously understated readings of several country classics. In 1992 he recorded Sneakin' Around with fellow country veteran Jerry Reed and in 1994 he was the featured guitarist on Allen Toussaint's 'Southern Nights' on the various artists album Rhythm, Country and Blues, an American Top Twenty hit. A regular at awards ceremonies and one-off events throughout the nineties, he recorded only intermittently.

ATLANTA RHYTHM SECTION

Barry Bailey, b. 12 June 1948, Decatur, Georgia, USA; Paul Goddard, b. 23 June 1945, Rome, Georgia; J. R. Cobb, b. 5 February 1944, Birmingham, Alabama; Dean Daughtry, b. 8 September 1945, Kinston, Alabama; Robert Nix; Roy Yeager, b. 4 February 1946, Greenwood, Mississippi; Ronnie Hammond, b. Macon, Georgia

Unlike most of the Southern boogie bands of the early seventies who were proud of their live, 'rough' sound, the Atlanta Rhythm Section were as much at home in the studio as on the road.

The band was formed in 1970 around Daughtry, a one-time member of Roy Orbison's backing group the Candymen, Cobb and manager Buddy Buie, all of whom had been members of the Classics IV. Earlier the Classics IV had had a quartet of Top Twenty hits on Imperial ('Spooky' and 'Stormy', both 1968; 'Traces' and 'Everyday with You Girl', 1969), all smooth ballads sung with style by lead singer Dennis Yost. *Atlanta Rhythm Section* (MCA, 1972) marked a defiant break with the pop of the Classic IV, but by the time of *Dog Days* (Polydor, 1975) their sound had mellowed to include ballads and songs of social comment as well as straight-ahead Southern boogie.

Constant touring and a stream of well-crafted singles sung by Hammond, including the charming 'Doraville' (1974), a paean to the band's home town, 'So in to You' (1977), 'Imaginary Lover' (1978), and a remake of 'Spooky' (1979), resulted in several big-selling albums, the most successful of which was *Champagne Jam* (1978) on which Yeager replaced Nix as the group's drummer. They switched to Columbia in 1981 and had a final chart album, *Quinella*, and single, 'Alien', before disbanding.

WINIFRED ATWELL
b. 1914, Tunapuna, Trinidad, d. 27 February 1983, Sydney, Australia

Atwell, who sold some 20 million records in all, was the first and most successful of a series of pianists (the others being Joe 'Mr Piano' Henderson, Mrs Mills and Russ Conway) who held sway in the UK throughout the fifties.

Though trained as a classical pianist, Atwell turned to popular music soon after her arrival in London in 1946, playing medleys in an energetic ragtime style on what she called her 'honky-tonk' piano. Her first record (and biggest hit) in this style was a version of George Botsford's 'Black and White Rag'* (Decca, 1952), which was followed by a series of similar offerings, including 'Britannia Rag', 'Coronation Rag' and 'Flirtation Waltz' (all 1953), before she hit on the idea of recording a medley of songs in what was essentially a sing-along pub-piano fashion. The result was 'Let's Have a Party'* (Philips, 1953) and 'Let's Have Another Party'* (1954), and a rash of imitations, including Joe 'Mr Piano' Henderson's 'Sing It with Joe' (Polygon, 1955), Russ Conway's first chart record, 'Party Pops' (Columbia UK, 1957), and 'Mrs Mills' Medley' (Parlophone, 1961).

In 1955 she moved to Decca on which she had seven more Top Twenty hits, including a No. 1 with 'The Poor People of Paris' (1956), an American hit for **Les Baxter**. Though she attempted to confront it with 'Let's Rock 'n' Roll' (1957), the advent of rock'n'roll hastened the end of Atwell's chart career, and she drifted into television. Of the pianists who followed her, only Conway (briefly) outlasted rock'n'roll with 'Side Saddle'* and 'Roulette' (both 1959).

BRIAN AUGER
b. 18 July 1939, London, England

A stalwart of the British R&B scene in the sixties, Auger worked with **Rod Stewart**, among others, though his greatest commercial success came in partnership with singer Julie Driscoll. He later worked in jazz-rock and played on numerous recording sessions.

A poll-winning jazz pianist, he played with **John McLaughlin** before turning to R&B and Hammond organ with ex-Cyril Davies drummer Mickey Waller and Rick Brown (bass) in 1964. They were soon joined by former **Alexis Korner** and Cyril Davies singer Long John Baldry and Stewart. With the previously unknown Driscoll, the group became Steampacket, a touring blues revue featuring Auger's jazzy instrumentals by **Jimmy Smith** ('Back at the Chicken Shack') and **Jimmy McGriff** ('Kiko'), Driscoll's soul numbers ('I Know You Love Me Not'), Stewart's mixture of Motown and R&B, and Baldry's blues shouting. For contractual reasons Steampacket did not record but Auger's singles for EMI Columbia included **Mose Allison**'s 'Foolkiller' (1965) and **Booker T. and the MGs**' 'Green Onions'. Auger also played the harpsichord on the **Yardbirds** 'For Your Love' (1965) and accompanied **Sonny Boy Williamson**.

In 1966 Stewart left to join Shotgun Express, followed by Baldry, who launched a solo recording career. Steampacket gave way to the Brian Auger Trinity featuring Julie Driscoll, which recorded the eclectic *Open* (1967) for manager Giorgio Gomelsky's Marmalade label. It included versions of material by **Wes Montgomery**, the **Staple Singers** and **Donovan**, as well as Auger's own compositions. The following year Auger and Driscoll released a version of **Bob Dylan**'s 'This Wheel's on Fire'. Featuring Driscoll's strong, clear voice, the record was a British Top Ten hit. **David Ackles**' 'Road to Cairo' was less successful although the Auger–Driscoll duet 'Call Me' sold well in Europe.

The group released *Definitely What* (1968) and *Streetnoise* (1968) before Driscoll left, making occasional later records as Julie Tippett with her husband, jazz pianist Keith Tippett. These included *Blueprint* (RCA, 1972), *Frames* (Ogun, 1978), and *Couple in Spirit* (EG, 1988). Auger formed Oblivion Express with Jim Mullen (guitar) and future **Average White Band** drummer Robbie McIntosh. The band released six jazz-rock albums for RCA, with vocalist Alex Ligertwood (who later joined **Santana**) appearing on *Second Wind* (1972).

Auger's later work included studio sessions for Passport (1974) and jazz drummer Tony Williams (1979), while he wrote the Main Ingredient hit 'Happiness Is Just Around the Bend' (RCA, 1974). Later albums for Warners included *Happiness Heartaches* (1977) and *Encore* (1978), a reunion with Driscoll which included a version of **Steve Winwood**'s 'No Time to Live'. In 1985 Auger played as part of a reformed Spencer Davis Group, the band with which Winwood had begun his career.

He continued to play live into the nineties, notably with fellow sixties survivor Eric Burdon and a new version of Oblivion Express.

GENE AUSTIN
b. Eugene Lucus, 24 June 1900, Sibley, Louisiana, USA, d. 24 January 1972

Austin's silken baritone was a quintessential popular voice of the late twenties, both on radio, where he was nicknamed 'The Voice of the Southland', and on scores of Victor records, pre-eminently **Walter Donaldson**'s 'My Blue Heaven' (1927) – until **Bing Crosby**'s 'White Christmas', probably the bestselling popular record of all time.

Austin ran away from home in his teens to join a circus. In his early twenties, he learned to play piano and formed a dance band, but by 1923 he had gone into vaudeville with the singer Roy Bergere. He went solo the following year and in 1925 began his long association with Victor, during which he sold tens of millions of records, including among his hits 'Ramona' (1928) and 'Carolina Moon' (1929). He also wrote 'When My Sugar Walks down the Street', 'Lonesome Road' and 'How Come You Do Me Like You Do?'.

From 1933 he worked in a slightly jazzier vein with Otto 'Coco' Heimal (guitar) and Candy Candido (bass). In the early post-war years he retained enough of his fame to be signed by the Los Angeles independent label Four Star, but little was heard of him thereafter.

GENE AUTRY
b. Orvon Autry, 29 September 1907, Tioga Springs, Texas, USA, d. 2 October 1998, Studio City, California

Actor, singer, producer, songwriter and businessman, Autry was one of the most commercially successful popular artists of the twentieth century. Held in little regard in country-music circles or by film historians, his effect on the development of both country music and the Western has been decisive. There had been cowboy stars who sang before Autry (for example, Ken Maynard) and the likes of **Jimmie Rodgers** had done much to 'Westernize' country music, but it was Autry who created the notion of a singing cowboy, first on radio and record and then, even more influentially, on film.

His cinematic legacy was a host of singing cowboys, including Eddie Dean, Jimmy Wakely, Monte Hale, Rex Allen and his only real competitors, **Roy Rogers** and **Tex Ritter**. He had an equally powerful effect on country music: after Autry, Western-style clothes became *de rigueur* for performers and Western themes became prominent. Along the way, through his diverse investments, he made himself one of the richest men in America and revealed an obsession with Christmas which almost matched that of **Johnny Marks**: as well as selling more than 12 million copies of the Marks' composition 'Rudolph the Red-Nosed Reindeer' (CBS, 1949), Autry also had million-sellers with 'Here Comes Santa Claus' (1947), which he co-wrote with Oakley Haldeman, and 'Frosty the Snow Man' (1950).

Despite the legend, Autry had no cowboy connections. A farm boy, with a soft, nasal vocal style modelled on Jimmie Rodgers, Autry's first success came in partnership with Jimmy Long, a former workmate. Long was to be an important influence on Autry. He was a regular writing partner and occasionally recorded with him – they jointly wrote and performed Autry's first million-seller, 'That Silver Haired Daddy of Mine' (1931) – as well as introducing Autry to his future wife, Long's niece. In 1928, reportedly on the advice of Will Rogers, Autry travelled to New York where he spent two years as a radio singer before he was signed by **Art Satherley** to the American Record Corporation, which specialized in providing material for the many chain stores like Sears-Roebuck that had their own record labels.

Significantly, it was his sentimental recordings, rather than those in the style of, or from, the Rodgers repertoire, that brought him success and a succession of radio shows, culminating in the Sears-sponsored WLS ('World's Largest Store') Barn Dance in Chicago with which he remained until 1934. However, both his radio and record performances were still strongly influenced by Rodgers. To all intents and purposes Autry was a typically hillbilly performer of the period with the one exception that his promotional material increasingly spoke of a 'Western' and cowboy background rather than a country or rural one.

At the same time Autry was trying to get work in series Westerns, then in vogue in Hollywood. ARC owner Herbert Yates also ran Republic Studios and a role was found for Autry warbling in support of Ken Maynard in *In Old Sante Fe* (1934). He was then given the lead in the bizarre *Phantom Empire* (1935), which mixed elements of science fiction, the Western and Autry's own radio background with regular doses of serial action.

The serial was an enormous success. It fixed the image of the singing cowboy in the movies as a creature of fable, able to overcome the worst of dangers with a soothing song, his dandified outfit protecting him as if it were armour, and led to other film producers following Autry's example. At the same time, it offered country music a new route to success – the movies. For the most part country musicians grabbed the chance, unconcerned that Western motifs and terminology were replacing the traditional hillbilly images.

Supported for the most part by comedian Smiley Burnette and his horse Champion, Autry himself presented the unchanging fantasy of the singing cowboy in nearly a hundred movies (finishing with *Last of the Pony Riders*, 1953), on stage, at rodeos (in New York even!), on radio (his CBS radio show *Gene Autry's Melody Ranch* on which he was supported by Pat Buttram ran for some seventeen years from 1939), and on record. A prolific writer, he wrote over 200 songs, usually in collaboration with either Ray Whitley (with whom he wrote his theme song 'Back in the Saddle Again'), Frank Marvin or **Fred Rose**. Other Autry compositions include 'Have I Told You Lately that I Love You?' and 'I Hang My Head and Cry', while his million-selling discs included film title songs, such as 'Tumbling Tumbleweeds' (1935), 'South of the Border' and 'Mexicali Rose' (both 1939), and children's favourites, 'Peter Cottontail' (1949), 'Frosty' and 'Rudolph'.

In 1942, at the height of his popularity, Autry joined the Army Air Corps. When he returned to the screen and stage after the war, it was to find Roy Rogers had become the nation's No. 1 singing cowboy. From this point, Autry's relationship to country music was marginal – although he was elected to the Country Music Hall of Fame in 1969. From the fifties onwards he concentrated on his investments, which ranged from baseball (he owned the Los Angeles team), television, with his Flying A Productions, radio stations, music publishing and real estate, to oil. In 1988 he opened the Gene Autry Western Heritage Museum in Los Angeles.

FRANKIE AVALON

b. *Francis Avallone, 18 September 1939, Philadelphia, Pennsylvania, USA*

Avalon was one of a number of teen-idols of the late fifties whose stardom was shortlived. Unlike some of his contemporaries, however, he continued his career by becoming a personification of the fifties with cameo roles in such productions as the film *Grease*.

As a trumpet-playing child he won a talent contest and appeared on local television in the Philadelphia area. He later performed with Rocco and the Saints, a rock band signed to Chancellor, a label formed by Bob Marcucci and Peter de Angelis to supply potential teenage stars to **Dick Clark**'s *American Bandstand* TV show.

Avalon's first solo record, 'Dede Dinah', has been variously described as 'moronic' and an 'idiot chant', but it became a Top Ten hit in 1958. Seven more hits followed in the next two years, mostly written by Marcucci and de Angelis. The teen ballads 'Venus' and 'Why?' both reached No. 1 and the latter was his only British chart success.

In the sixties Avalon co-starred with Annette Funicello in a series of 'beach' movies, including *Beach Party* (1963), *Beach Blanket Bingo* (1965) and *How to Stuff a Wild Bikini* (1965). Soon after, he moved on from the teenage to the supper-club circuit and occasional TV appearances.

A 1976 disco remake of 'Venus' was a minor hit, but far better was his performance of 'Beauty School Dropout', one of the highlights of *Grease*, whose soundtrack album was one of the bestsellers of 1978.

In 1985 he, Bobby Rydell and Fabian toured as 'The Golden Boys of Bandstand' and in 1987 he and Funicello played parents of teenagers in *Back to the Beach*. Avalon returned to his first love when he played trumpet on *Dead Flowers* (1992) by Edan, a group that included his son and Edan, the son of Don Everly.

THE AVERAGE WHITE BAND (AWB)

Roger Ball, b. 4 June 1944, Dundee, Scotland; Malcolm Duncan, b. 24 August 1945, Montrose; Alan Gorrie, b. 19 July 1946, Perth; Onnie McIntyre, b. 25 September 1945, Lennox Town; Hamish Stuart, b. 8 October 1949, Glasgow; Robbie McIntosh, b. 1950, d. 23 September 1974, Los Angeles, USA; Steve Ferrone (joined 1974), b. 25 April 1950, Brighton, Sussex, England

Curiously anachronistic, although successful, the AWB was a white British group dedicated to emulating soul bands in styles ranging from Stax to the **Crusaders**.

Formed by musicians from the thriving soul scene in Glasgow, Scotland, the AWB came south to London and were signed by MCA in 1973. After a début album of considerable promise, *Show Your Hand*, they were signed by Atlantic. Produced by **Arif Mardin** (who was to work on the band's next six records), the first Atlantic album was full of well-crafted songs expertly sung by guitarist Stuart and bass-player Gorrie. It included the US No. 1 single. 'Pick up the Pieces'*. Soon afterwards drummer McIntosh died of a heroin overdose and was replaced by ex-Bloodstone member Ferrone.

The neat, immaculate arrangements of AWB tunes found a large American audience and the next album included 'Cut the Cake' (1975), another Top Ten hit. **Ben E. King** sang with the group on the disappointing *Benny and Us* (Atlantic, 1977) and AWB played on *Up* (Embryo, 1977) by British jazz-funk duo Dick Morrissey and Jim Mullen.

In 1980 AWB moved to RCA where they cut *Shine*

(1980) and *Cupid's in Fashion* (1982), produced by
Dan Hartman. 'Let's Go Round Again' from *Shine*
was a British hit. For most of the eighties the band
was defunct. Stuart joined **Paul McCartney**'s backing
group and wrote songs for **Chaka Khan**, Atlantic
Starr and others and Ferrone played with **Duran
Duran**, the **Christians** and **Eric Clapton**. The group
re-formed, minus Stuart, in 1989 for *Aftershock* (Polydor, 1989), which featured former **Santana** vocalist
Alex Ligertwood and guest vocals by Chaka Khan.
AWB returned to the concert circuit in the US in the
early nineties.

HOYT AXTON
b. 25 March 1932, Comanche, Oklahoma, USA,
d. 26 October 1999, Oklahoma

With **B. B. King**, **Elvis Presley**, **Joan Baez**, **Three Dog
Night**, the **Crusaders** and **Lynn Anderson** among the
dozens of artists who have recorded his material,
Axton's contemporary songs have been successful
with all kinds of audience, from blues to pop.

The son of respected country writer Mae Boren
Axton (composer of Presley's 'Heartbreak Hotel'), he
grew up in the Dust Bowl and his approach to songwriting – both traditional and radical – is close to that
of **Woody Guthrie**. He was part of the folk scene of
the late fifties, co-writing with Ken Ramsey the
Kingston Trio hit 'Greenback Dollar', and next
achieved success through the film *Easy Rider* (1969),
whose soundtrack featured **Steppenwolf**'s version of
his song 'The Pusher'. This and the later composition
'Snow Blind Friend' fell foul of the radio censors,
despite the fact they were exposing and not glorifying
drug habits.

The celebratory and the whimsical sides of Axton's
talent provided his next pop hits through Three Dog
Night's 'Joy to the World' (a No. 1 hit on Dunhill in
1971) and 'Never Been to Spain' (1972). In 1975 **Ringo
Starr** had a Top Ten record with Axton's 'No No
Song'.

With the success of the new Nashville songwriters,
he found it easier to return to his country background
in the mid-seventies, recording for A&M, MCA and
his own Jeremiah label. His best record of this period
is the double-album *Road Songs* (A&M), which
included many of his best-known compositions (on
several of which he duetted with **Linda Ronstadt**) and
featured guitarist **James Burton**. In 1979 he had Top
Twenty country hits with 'Della and the Dealer' and
'Rusty Old Halo', but in the eighties he turned
increasingly to films, appearing in *The Black Stallion*
(1982) and *Gremlins* (1984), among others. In 1991 he
released *Spin of the Wheel* on his own D.P.I. label.
Axton's last album was *Jeremiah Was a Bullfrog*, an
album of children's songs.

ROY AYERS
b. 10 September 1940, Los Angeles, California, USA

A former jazz vibraphone-player, Roy Ayers became a
leading figure in the jazz-funk crossover genre of the
late seventies.

He played piano and steel guitar before taking up
the vibes in high school where he formed the Latin
Lyrics, a group inspired by the Latin-jazz musician
Cal Tjader. After playing with Chico Hamilton, Gerald Wilson and others, Ayers rose to prominence as a
member of flautist Herbie Mann's band, with whom
he played between 1966 and 1970. Ayers contributed
to several of Mann's albums, including *Impressions of
the Middle East* (Atlantic, 1967) and *Memphis Two-
Step* (1971), while Mann produced Ayers' first solo
album, *Virgo Vibes* (Embryo, 1970).

Influenced by Mann's opportunistic ear for combining jazz with a whole range of other musics, Ayers
began to incorporate elements of soul, rhythm and
blues, and rock into his style. He also experimented
with the sound of the vibes, adding fuzztone and wah
wah pedal. In 1971 he formed his own group, Roy
Ayers' Ubiquity and signed to Polydor.

Among his numerous albums of the early seventies
were *He's Coming* (1972), *Change up the Groove* (1974)
and *Red Black and Green* (1975), which featured
Charles Tolliver (trumpet) and Sonny Fortune
(soprano sax). Among the artists who appeared on
Ubiquity albums were **George Benson** and singer Dee
Dee Bridgewater. The rise of disco and the growing
audience for jazz crossover music gave Ayers his first
R&B hit with 'Running Away' (1977), which became a
disco anthem throughout Europe. Later hits included
'Freaky Deaky' (1978) and 'Heat of the Beat' (1979).

Ayers toured Africa in 1979 and worked with **Fela
Kuti**, with whom he later recorded *Africa Centre of
the World* (1981). As disco fashions changed in the
eighties, his popularity waned and he switched labels
to Columbia. *In the Dark* (1984) was his most successful album of the decade. The following year he
released *You Might Be Surprised* and in 1987 *I'm the
One (For Your Love Tonight)*. Ayers' later releases
included 'Wake Up' (Ichiban, 1989) and a live album
recorded at Ronnie Scott's club in London.

ALBERT AYLER
*b. 13 July 1936, Cleveland, Ohio, USA, d. 25 November
1970, New York*

Probably the most uncompromising of new-wave
modern jazz musicians, saxophonist Ayler dismantled
both melody and harmony in favour of a music which
explored the physical properties of the instrument.
This avant-garde approach later gave way to Ayler's
commitment to re-create the marching bands of the

black music tradition and to message songs of peace and love.

His father, a semi-professional violinist and saxophonist, trained Ayler as a child. They played sax duets in church and by the mid-fifties Albert was playing with **Little Walter** and **Lloyd Price** on the R&B circuit. Between 1958 and 1961 he served in the army, playing tenor sax in a services band in Europe where he was introduced to free jazz playing as well as acquiring a taste for marches. After demobilization, Ayler returned to Europe, working with Cecil Taylor and recording a session for Danish radio in 1963 which showed him wrestling with the limitations of bebop in **Charlie Parker**'s 'Billie's Bounce'. The tracks were later released as *My Name is Albert Ayler* (Fantasy).

Returning to America, Ayler created his first masterpiece, *Witches and Devils* (Freedom, 1964) with drummer Sunny Murray. With each musician playing at his own speed, the album showed Ayler moving from the height to the depths of the saxophone.

He made more albums in 1964, characterized by the urgency and pace of his playing, inspired by what Ayler described as the 'hypnotizing' tone of **Sidney Bechet**'s soprano sax. After *Spiritual Unity* (ESP), Ayler, Murray and Henry Grimes were joined by **Don Cherry** on the film soundtrack *New York Eye and Ear Control* (ESP). Cherry also toured Europe with the Ayler group, playing on *The Hilversum Session* (Osmosis). In 1965 Ayler's brother Donald joined his group on trumpet and the music took on the flavour of New Orleans marching bands. *Spirits Rejoice* (ESP) included pieces based on 'La Marseillaise' and 'Our Prayer', a nineteenth-century hymn tune.

In 1966 Ayler signed with ABC/Impulse where Bob Thiele produced the more conventional jazz-rock album *New Grass* (1968), on which he was accompanied by drummer Pretty Purdie and **Canned Heat** guitarist Henry Vestine. By now Ayler was co-writing with harpist Mary Maria and singing lyrics with a religious basis. His final recordings, *Nuits de la Fondation Maeght* (Shandar, 1970), were made at a French festival and showed a return to the intensity of Ayler's earliest work.

Ayler died in mysterious circumstances: after being missing for several weeks, his body was found floating in New York's East River.

CHARLES AZNAVOUR
b. Shanaur Varenagh Aznavourian, 22 May 1924, Paris, France

The diminutive Aznavour is a raspy-voiced singer of (mostly self-composed) *chansons* and a sad-eyed actor who has come to be a personification of Frenchness for Anglo-Saxon audiences.

The son of a cook, Aznavour studied to become an actor. In 1942 he turned to songwriting (first with Pierre Roche, 'J'ai bu', a hit for George Ulmer) to support himself and with the encouragement of first **Maurice Chevalier** and then **Edith Piaf** (whose protégé he became) made a reputation for himself as a singer at the Paris Olympia Theatre. (He appeared in the 1957 documentary *Paris Music Hall.*) His most memorable films include Georges Franju's *La Tête Contre les Murs* (1958) and François Truffaut's *Tirez sur le Pianiste* (1960), in which he played the café entertainer. Both films highlighted the melancholy aspect of his personality. Since then he has appeared in a stream of films, both in France and Hollywood.

Aznavour's hits include 'Sur Ma Vie' (Barclay, 1955), 'Il Faut Savoir', 'Je Voyais Déjà' (both 1958), 'Je t'Attends' (1961) and 'La Mama'* (1963). This last song, co-written with Robert Gall, provided **Matt Monro** with a minor British hit in 1964 ('For Mama', with English words by Don Black). Since writing the operetta *Monsieur Carnival* (1965), Aznavour has concentrated on his film career, often writing the scores and/or songs for the films in which he appears. In 1974 he had a international hit with 'She' and a lesser hit with 'The Old-Fashioned Way'. In 1979 he published an autobiography, *Yesterday When I Was Young.*

AZTEC CAMERA
Roddy Frame, b. 29 January 1964, East Kilbride, Scotland

Essentially a flag of convenience for Scottish singer-songwriter Roddy Frame, Aztec Camera released a string of polished and varied pop/rock recordings throughout the eighties and into the nineties.

Formed in East Kilbride by Frame in 1980 with bassist Campbell Owens and drummer Dave Mulholland, Aztec Camera's first significant recordings were 'Just Like Gold' and 'Mattress of Wire' on the independent Postcard label in 1981. They moved to Rough Trade Records for two further singles and their début album, *High Land, Hard Rain* (1983). The album, with its striking blend of acoustic folk and jazzy rhythms, reached the UK Top Thirty and won acclaim for Frame's literate lyrics and fluent guitar playing. The departure of Owens and Mulholland precipitated regular changes in the band's line-up, with drummer Dave Ruffy (formerly of UK punk band the Ruts) becoming the longest-serving member. Malcolm Ross, formerly of Postcard labelmates Josef K and Orange Juice, joined as second guitarist after the album's release.

The critical and commercial success of the album and spin-off singles 'Oblivious' and 'Walk Out to Winter' prefaced a move to WEA, which reissued

'Oblivious', giving the band a UK Top Twenty single. Mark Knopfler of **Dire Straits** produced *Knife* (1984), which was nevertheless stylistically close to its predecessor, and again reached the UK Top Twenty. Frame's third album, *Love* (1987), recorded with session musicians in the US, initially had disappointing sales, but the hit singles 'How Men Are' and 'Somewhere In My Heart' revived it. Mixing dance, rock and Frame's trademark folkie stylings, it reached the UK Top Ten.

More touring followed, after which Frame again retreated to compose the fourth album, *Stray* (1990). Recorded with a set line-up of Paul Powell (bass), Frank Tontoh (drums) and Gary Sanctuary (keyboards), this was an even more eclectic record than its predecessor, and included a duet with Mick Jones (formerly of the **Clash** and Big Audio Dynamite), one of Frame's early influences, on the hit single 'Good Morning Britain'. The same schedule preceded the arrival of the 1993 album *Dreamland*, a collection, mainly of love songs, produced in collaboration with **Ryuichi Sakamoto**.

ERIC B AND RAKIM

Eric B, b. Eric Barrier, Queen's, New York, USA;
Rakim, b. William Griffin, 1969, Brooklyn, New York

One of the leading rap and hip-hop teams from the East Coast of the US, DJ Eric B and rapper Rakim were also the most focused, eschewing pop and crossover elements.

Eric B played trumpet and guitar as a child but became a DJ in the late seventies. By 1985 he was a mobile DJ for the New York radio station WBLS. He joined up with Rakim, a rapper and nephew of **Ruth Brown**, in 1986. Their first track was 'Eric B. Is President' (1987) and the début album, *Paid in Full*, was issued by Island's Fourth & Broadway label. The album was one of the first to sample tracks by James Brown (who took legal action against the duo) and included remixes by hip-hop pioneer Melle Mel, a former member of **Grandmaster Flash** & the Furious Five. In the UK, a remixed version by Coldcut of 'Paid in Full' was a 1987 hit. The duo joined the Def Jam Tour '87 alongside LL Cool J, **Public Enemy** and Whodini.

The second album, *Follow the Leader* (UNI, 1988), included 'Lyrics of Fury' and 'No Competition'. Jody Watley was the guest vocalist on 'Friends', a 1989 hit. It was followed by *Let the Rhythm Hit 'Em* (MCA, 1990) where Eric B used **James Brown** funk to back Rakim's gruff and pointed rapping on 'In the Ghetto' and 'No Omega'.

After a fourth album, *Don't Sweat the Technique* (1992), the duo split, Eric B re-emerging after a few years with his own label, 95th Street. Rakim's hiatus was longer, but he returned with a solo album, *The 18th Letter*, in 1997, preceded by a hit single, 'Guess Who's Back?'. Rakim's voice retained all the old authority of his finest years with Eric B, this time supported by the production skills of a variety of DJs, including Clark Kent, Pete Rock and **Gang Starr**'s DJ Premier.

THE B-52s

Kate Pierson, b. 27 April 1948, Weehawken, New Jersey, USA; Fred Schneider III, b. 1 July 1951, Newark, Georgia; Keith Strickland, b. 26 October 1953, Athens, Georgia; Cindy Wilson, b. 28 February 1957, Athens; Ricky Wilson, b. 19 March 1953, Athens, d. 13 October 1985

A quirky, ironic band whose early work relied heavily on fifties and sixties allusions – their name came from the Southern term for the bouffant hairstyles worn by Pierson and Cindy Wilson – the B-52s maintained an international cult following during the eighties.

Formed in Georgia in 1976, they attracted a following at Max's Kansas City in New York and in 1978 released the self-produced 'Rock Lobster', the tale of an underwater dance party. A British hit on its re-release in 1986, the record led to a contract with the British company Island, whose owner **Chris Blackwell** produced *The B-52s*, released on Warner Bros in the US. Praised by the critics for its arty trash aesthetic, it became a campus classic in America, selling over 500,000 copies, and remained on the Australian charts for nine months.

Wild Planet (1980) was a Top Twenty hit and the EP *Party Mix* (1981) of its songs was also successful. **Talking Heads'** David Byrne was brought in to produce the *Mesopotamia* (1982) EP, adding session musicians to provide a wider musical range. *Whammy* (1983) was followed by Schneider's solo album in 1984 and the Tony Mansfield-produced *Bouncing Off the Satellites* (1986). This album was completed shortly before Ricky Wilson's death from cancer. Their first album after his death, *Bouncing Off the Satellites* was arch and contrived but in 1989 they returned to the charts with 'Love Shack', part send-up and part homage to beach party music, from their most successful album ever, *Cosmic Thing*, produced by **Don Was**. *Good Stuff* (1992) was a lesser work, especially when compared with the remixed pairing of their two eighties EPs on one CD, *Party Mix/Mesopotamia* in 1991. Cindy Wilson left before the recording of *Good Stuff*. Her replacement was cult chanteuse Julee Cruise, best known for her work with filmmaker David Lynch. In 1994 the group had its biggest hit with the would-be camp theme song from the film *The Flintstones*, using the name BC-52s.

BABYFACE

b. Kenneth Edmonds, 10 April 1959, Cincinnatti, Ohio, USA

With **Jam and Lewis** and **Teddy Riley**, L.A. and Babyface were the leading members of the new generation of writer/producers in black music in the nineties. Together they formed La Face Records. Separately Babyface has worked with numerous acts, including **Bobby Brown, Sheena Easton, Whitney Houston, Aretha Franklin** and **Boyz II Men**. In this capacity he had some twenty US chart-toppers and fifty R&B

chart-toppers by 2000. He also developed a parallel career as a solo vocalist.

The pair met as members of Cincinnatti band the Deele in 1982. Guitarist and singer Edmonds' boyish looks had already gained him the nickname Babyface while drummer and bandleader Reid (b. *Antonio Reid, 7 June 1957, Cincinnatti, Ohio, USA*) was named L.A. because he always wore a Los Angeles Dodgers baseball cap. Signing to Solar Records, the group made their first album in 1983 but did not make an impact until the Reid–Edmonds ballad 'Two Occasions' was a hit in 1987. In the same year the Whispers were also successful with another L.A. and Babyface song, 'Rock Steady'. Deele's final hit was their biggest, 'Eyes of a Stranger' (1988).

However, by this time L.A. and Babyface had left the Deele to concentrate on songwriting and production. Their hits of this period included Easton's 'The Lover in Me' (No. 2 in 1988), Brown's 'My Prerogative' (No. 1 in 1989), Houston's 'I'm Your Baby Tonight' (No. 1 in 1990) and Johnny Gill's 'My My My' (No. 10 in 1990). The pair also worked with **Paula Abdul**, the **Jacksons** and Pebbles, whom Reid later married.

In 1991 they set up their own La Face label, producing and releasing recordings by Jermaine Jackson, Level 3 and **TLC**. The label's most important discovery was soul diva **Toni Braxton**, whose multi-million selling début album included such hits as 'Another Sad Love Song' and 'Love Shoulda Brought You Home'. The latter appeared in the film *Boomerang*, whose Reid and Edmonds-produced soundtrack also included Boyz II Men's chart-topper 'End of the Road' (1992).

Babyface began his solo singing career with *Lovers* (1986), which included a version of the **Stylistics**' 'You Make Me Feel Brand New'. On the hit album *Tender Lover* (Solar, 1989), Babyface mixed the dance rhythms of 'My Kinda Girl' and 'It's No Crime' with his trademark slow ballads. This was followed by *A Closer Look* (1991), a 'best of' selection which included duets with Pebbles and Karyn White, and *Babyface* (1993). He later recorded *For the Cool in You* (1993) and 'Take a Bow', a duet with **Madonna**, which he also wrote, for her album *Bedtime Stories* (1994). That year Reid and Edmonds severed their writing and production activities but remained business partners.

Babyface was the co-producer of *The Bodyguard* (1994) soundtrack, the biggest-selling soundtrack album of all time. Other productions from this period include *Just for You* (**Gladys Knight**), *II* (Boyz II Men), *I'm Ready* (Tevin Campbell), 'Willing to Forgive' (Aretha Franklin) and Toni Braxton's eponymous album (all 1994), *Reflections* (After 7) and the *Waiting to Exhale* soundtrack album (both 1995). In 1996 he widened his range, producing the **Eric Clapton** recording 'Change the World' for the film *Phe-*

nomenon. Clapton had previously guested on his bestselling album *The Day* and repeated that on *MTV Unplugged NYC* (1997). In 1998 he charted with the seasonal offering *Christmas with BabyFace*.

Although its hits declined in the second half of the decade, La Face was one of the most successful black labels of the nineties. In 1999 it had success with TLC ('No Scrubs', 'Unpretty') and Shanice ('When I Close My Eyes').

BURT BACHARACH
b. 12 May 1928, Kansas City, Missouri, USA

Artistically and commercially, Bacharach was one of the most successful composers of the modern era. In partnership with Hal David (and latterly Carole Bayer Sager), he wrote more contemporary standards than any songwriter since the era of **Cole Porter** and **George Gershwin**.

The son of a journalist, Bacharach grew up in New York and played in various amateur jazz groups. On his discharge from the army in 1952, he studied theory and composition at McGill University and then the Music Academy of the West. He became a pianist and later arranger to balladeers **Vic Damone**, **Steve Lawrence** and the **Ames Brothers** (during which time he first tried his hand at songwriting) and was **Marlene Dietrich**'s musical director (1956–8). In 1957 he entered into a brief partnership with lyricist Mack David which produced 'The Blob', the theme song of the cult science-fiction film and a Top Forty hit for the Five Blobs on Columbia. Next, he joined forces with David's younger brother Hal and they had immediate success with 'The Story of My Life', an American hit for **Marty Robbins** and a British one for Michael Holliday.

David (*b. 25 May 1921, New York*) began writing lyrics while in the army. On his discharge he wrote 'Four Winds and Seven Seas' (with Don Rodney), which gave bandleader **Sammy Kaye** a minor hit in 1949. Other early hits included 'American Beauty Rose' (with Redd Evans and Arthur Altman) for **Frank Sinatra**, 'Bell Bottom Blues' (with Leon Carr), a hit for **Teresa Brewer** in 1953, and 'My Heart Is an Open Book', which was recorded by several singers in 1957, and gave Carl Dobkins Jnr his only Top Ten hit in 1959. Although the duo of Bacharach and David followed 'The Story of My Life' with a million-seller, 'Magic Moments' (**Perry Como**, 1958), they did not work together regularly until 1962. In the interim, Bacharach completed his pop education, working extensively with the **Drifters**, arranging and scoring sessions for them and writing 'Mexican Divorce' and 'Please Stay' (both 1961) for them with Bob Hilliard, with whom he also wrote the superb 'Any Day Now' for Chuck Jackson (1962).

It was at a Drifters session that Bacharach met back-up singer **Dionne Warwick**, who became the vehicle into which Bacharach and David poured their creative energy from 1962 onward, starting with 'Don't Make Me Over'. Bacharach and David wrote and produced more than twenty Top Forty hits for Warwick, who by 1970 had sold 15 million records of their songs. Among her hits were 'Anyone Who Had a Heart' (covered in Britain by **Cilla Black**), 'Walk on By' (1964), the much-recorded 'Trains and Boats and Planes', 'I Just Don't Know What to Do with Myself' (1966), 'I Say a Little Prayer' (1967), 'Do You Know the Way to San José?' (1968), 'I'll Never Fall in Love Again' (1969) and 'Make It Easy on Yourself' (1970). As significant as the trio's commercial success was the excellence of the records. Warwick provided the light, lithe voice, David the literate, witty lyrics and Bacharach the imaginative melodies, unusual arrangements and complex rhythms that few singers other than Warwick could have managed: on 'Anyone Who Had a Heart', for example, she deftly weaves into and through 5/4 to 4/4 to 7/8.

Throughout this period Bacharach and David also supplied other artists with songs. These included **Gene McDaniels** ('Tower of Strength', Liberty, 1961), **Gene Pitney** ('The Man Who Shot Liberty Valance', 1962, and the superior 'Twenty-Four Hours from Tulsa', 1963), **Jackie DeShannon** ('What the World Needs Now Is Love', 1965), **Herb Alpert** ('This Guy's in Love with You', 1968), the Fifth Dimension ('One Less Bell to Answer', Bell, 1970) and the **Carpenters** ('Close to You', 1970).

'Liberty Valance', the title song to the John Ford film, presaged a move into films. Their first film score was *What's New Pussycat?* (1965), the title song of which provided **Tom Jones** with a Top Ten hit. 'Alfie' (1967) and 'The Look of Love' (from *Casino Royale*, 1967) won them Oscar nominations and they finally won an Oscar for 'Raindrops Keep Falling on My Head', which **B. J. Thomas** sang in *Butch Cassidy and the Sundance Kid* (1969). In the same year they wrote the long-running Broadway musical, *Promises, Promises*, which included 'I'll Never Fall in Love Again'. Then, in 1973, following the disastrous reception of the remake of *Lost Horizon*, which they scored, the pair quarrelled and parted amid a flurry of lawsuits. In 1980 David, who had always been active in the world of publishing, was elected president of ASCAP.

Throughout his career Bacharach had recorded his own songs himself (having minor hits with 'Saturday Sunshine', Kapp, 1963, and 'I'll Never Fall in Love Again', A&M, 1969). In the seventies he regularly appeared in TV spectaculars constructed around his songs and on the concert stage, and he made a series of albums on A&M, offering his own interpretations of his songs, including *Living Together* (1972), *Woman* (1979) and *Classics* (1987). These tend to be bland versions of his songs for other artists, often poorly sung by their composer. In 1981 he had his first hit for several years with the Oscar-winning song 'Arthur's Theme', written with Carole Bayer Sager, Peter Allen and **Christopher Cross**, who performed it. In 1982 he married Sager.

Sager (*b. 1946, New York*) joined Screen Gems as a lyric writer in the mid-sixties. Her first big success was 'Groovy Kind of Love' (1966), a million-seller for the Mindbenders in 1966, and a hit for **Phil Collins** in 1988, which she wrote with Toni Wine. In 1975 she wrote 'Midnight Blue' with Melissa Manchester (which gave Manchester her first hit), and in 1977 wrote the first of a series of songs with **Marvin Hamlisch**, 'Nobody Does It Better' (a hit for **Carly Simon**), which culminated in their writing the songs for Neil Simon's 1979 play, *They're Playing Our Song*, which was loosely based on their life together. Earlier, she recorded her first solo album, *Carole Bayer Sager* (Elektra, 1977), which gave her a British hit with the winsome 'You're Moving Out Today', co-written with **Bette Midler** and Bruce Roberts.

After Bacharach's marriage to Sager, the couple began collaborating and in 1986 wrote and produced a pair of American chart-toppers, 'That's What Friends Are for', the song written to help raise funds for research into AIDS (which re-united Bacharach with Warwick), and 'On My Own', by **Patti Labelle** and Michael McDonald of the **Doobie Brothers**. In 1998, after parodying himself as a lounge crooner in the spy spoof *Austin Powers*, he returned to performing, writing and producing *Painted from Memory* (Mercury) in partnership with **Elvis Costello**. While Costello had difficulties singing the complex rhythms Bacharach effortlessly conjured up, the result was an album that had clearly been seen by both as a challenge rather than a commercial exercise in the manner of **Frank Sinatra**'s *Duet* outings.

BACKSTREET BOYS
Nick Carter, b. 28 January 1980, Jamestown, New York, USA; Howie Dorough, b. 22 August 1973, Orlando, Florida; Brian Littrell, b. 20 February 1975, Lexington, Kentucky; AJ McLean, b. 9 January 1978, West Palm Beach, Florida; Kevin Richardson, b. 3 October 1972, Lexington, Kentucky

A hugely successful American boy-band, Backstreet Boys reversed the normal path of commercial success by finding fame in Europe before conquering their homeland.

The core membership of the Backstreet Boys – Carter, Dorough and McLean – first met at television auditions. After performing for several months as a trio, they recruited Richardson, then working at Disney World, and his cousin Brian Littrell. Their friendship with record producer Louis J. Pearlman secured them the services of management duo Donna and Johnny Wright, who arranged for them to tour. Snapped up by Jive Records in 1994, they began work on their début album with Veit Renn and Tim Allen.

*Backstreet Boys** (1995) was an instant success, reaching the Top Ten across Europe and spawning a big hit single, 'We've Got It Goin' on' (1996), the Boys being seen as a white **Boyz II Men**. However, in North America, where boy-bands were not as well established, only the Canadian market fell for the group's charms. With their second album, *Backstreet's Back** (1997), the band managed to crack the US market, and achieved three international hit singles with 'Quit Playin' Games (with My Heart)', 'As Long as You Love Me' and the title track, accompanied by a spectacular music video drawing influence from **Michael Jackson**'s 'Thriller'.

The Backstreet Boys took a year off in 1998 while Littrell had corrective heart surgery, but returned to the charts with their third album, *Millennium** (1999), which topped the US album charts and included the hit single 'I Want It That Way'.

BAD COMPANY
Paul Rodgers, b. 12 December 1949, Middlesbrough, England; Simon Kirke, b. 27 August, 1949, Wales; Mick Ralphs, b. 31 May 1944, Herefordshire; Boz Burrell, b. Raymond Burrell, 1946, Lincolnshire

A hugely successful British heavy blues group of the seventies, Bad Company were the prime example of a band tailored to supply a known audience demand.

Formed in 1973, Bad Company were a 'supergroup' of the time: singer Rodgers and drummer Kirke came from **Free**, guitarist Ralphs from **Mott the Hoople** and bassist Burrell from **King Crimson**. Signed to **Led Zeppelin**'s label SwanSong and handled by their manager, Peter Grant, the band's eponymous first album went Top Ten on both sides of the Atlantic, as did the first single, 'Can't Get Enough'.

The unswerving, ponderous rhythm perfectly set off Rodgers' hoarse vocals and set the pattern for another five albums. *Straight Shooter* (1975) and *Run with the Pack* (1976) rang the limited changes on the Bad Co. blueprint and were timed to coincide with lengthy stadium-rock tours. Among the group's hit singles were 'Feel Like Making Love' (1975) and a remake of the **Coasters**' 1957 hit 'Young Blood' (1976).

Increasingly resembling dinosaurs as the decade neared its close, the group nevertheless had their last hit single in 1979, 'Rock'n'Roll Fantasy' from *Desolation Angels*, the fifth album. The split came in 1982,

when Rodgers put together the Firm with Led Zeppelin's Jimmy Page and Ralphs toured with **Pink Floyd**'s Dave Gilmour.

Bad Company was relaunched in 1986 with ex-**Ted Nugent** vocalist Brian Howe replacing Rodgers for *Fame and Fortune*, *Dangerous Age* (both 1988) and *Holy Water* (1990). As the band continued to make annual US stadium tours, Burrell and Ralphs dropped out although the guitarist returned to the line-up in 1992. The following year Bad Company took part in The Last Rebel Tour with another re-formed seventies group **Lynyrd Skynyrd**. Later albums *Here Comes Trouble* (1992) and the live set *What You Hear Is What You Get* (1993) were also disappointing examples of formula rock.

In 1992 Rodgers formed the Law with ex-Faces/ **Who** drummer Kenny Jones before embarking on a solo career, releasing *Muddy Waters Blues* in 1993, a collection of **Muddy Waters** songs with guitar accompaniments by **Jeff Beck**, Gary Moore, Slash (of **Guns N' Roses**) and other luminaries. He also put together a touring band with ex-**Journey** guitarist Neil Schon and appeared at Woodstock '94 with a group including his former Free colleague Andy Fraser. It was followed by the surprising change of style, *Stories Told and Untold* (1996), which saw the group recording in a country-rock manner with guest appearances from **Kim Carnes**, Alison Krause and Poco's Timothy B. Schmidt. Rodgers' solo outing, *Now* (1998), was less challenging.

JOAN BAEZ
b. 9 January 1941, Staten Island, New York, USA

A central figure of the folk revival of the early sixties, Baez's unmistakable soprano and consistent commitment to pacifist-humanist politics in her music sustained a career spanning four decades.

Daughter of a Mexican-born physicist who was a consultant to UNESCO and a Quaker, Baez grew up in California and in Boston, where she came into contact with the New England folk scene of the late fifties. She was soon recognized as one of the most gifted interpreters of the traditional Child ballads. Accompanying herself on guitar, she was the hit of the 1959 Newport Folk Festival and the following year made the first of seventeen albums for Vanguard. It included songs from the **Carter Family** ('Wildwood Flower') and **Leadbelly** ('House of the Rising Sun'), as well as a riveting version of the tragic Scottish ballad 'Mary Hamilton'.

Like most of the younger folk singers, Baez was outspoken in support of causes such as nuclear disarmament and civil rights, whose anthem 'We Shall Overcome' was a feature of her concerts. But she did not perform any contemporary songs until she met

Bob Dylan, whom she introduced to her folk audiences on a 1963 tour. Baez became a prolific, if unoriginal, interpreter of his songs, recording a double-album of Dylan material – *Any Day Now* – in 1968. She enjoyed a hit single in Britain with Phil Ochs' 'There But for Fortune' in 1965.

As Dylan's work veered away from protest songs, Baez (in common with many of the folk revivalists) drifted away from him. Her political commitment was more practical than most: in 1965 she set up an Institute for Non-Violence in California and for several years withheld her taxes because of US defence spending. But the break was as much musical as political: unlike Dylan, Baez was never comfortable with the rock idiom, as was proven by her rendition of the Righteous Brothers' hit 'You've Lost That Lovin' Feeling' on Phil Spector's 1966 TV spectacular *The TNT Show*.

Instead, she broadened her horizons by recording six albums in Nashville from 1968 to 1973. With producer Norbert Putnam and other leading session players, Baez found an appropriate amplified mode for a repertoire that now included contemporary country and singer-songwriter material. *Any Day Now* was followed by *David's Album* (1969), dedicated to her husband David Harris, who was serving a prison sentence for refusing to be drafted.

The best of the Nashville albums was *One Day at a Time* (1970), which mixed old songs like 'Joe Hill' (about the turn-of-the-century labour leader Joe Hill) with the Rolling Stones' contemplative 'No Expectations' and contemporary social comment like Steve Young's 'Seven Bridges Road'. Alongside material by younger Nashville writers Mickey Newbury and Kris Kristofferson, *Blessed Are . . .* (1971) included a somewhat pedestrian styling of The Band's 'The Night They Drove Old Dixie Down', which brought Baez her only American Top Ten hit in 1971.

In the era of the Vietnam War, Baez was not neglecting her political ideals. The second side of *Where Are You Now My Son?* (A&M, 1973) was devoted to an extended piece which incorporated tapes she had made during an American air-raid on Hanoi that occurred while she was in Vietnam with a peace delegation.

During the seventies Baez developed her own writing, which produced the lucid and poetic 'Rider Please Pass By' (from *Where Are You Now My Son?*) as well as the moving confessional 'Love Song to a Stranger' (from *Come from the Shadows*, 1972) and 'Diamonds and Rust' (1975). The last was a minor hit and the title track of what was very much a contemporary Los Angeles rock album that also included a masterly reading of Jackson Browne's 'Fountain of Sorrow' and Dylan's 'Simple Twist of Fate', on which she imitated Dylan. 'Diamonds' was a powerful and

moving account of her sixties relationship with Dylan, with whom she was reunited on his Rolling Thunder Revue tour of 1976.

However, many of her compositions were merely prosaic and singer-songwriter albums such as *Blowin' Away* (1977), the first under a contract with Columbia's Portrait label, were disappointing. Baez's forte remained the live concert, accompanied only by her own guitar, and the most satisfying of her later albums were live recordings, notably *From Every Stage* (A&M, 1976), which showcased the generous range of her repertoire, from the gospel 'Amazing Grace' through country to Dylan and Leonard Cohen.

Into the eighties she continued to attract large international audiences for her performances, which continued to be frequently linked to political causes, such as that of the Sandinista revolution in Nicaragua, about which she made a 1982 film, *There but for Fortune*.

In 1988 she published a bestselling evocative autobiography, *And a Voice to Sing With*.

Later albums for Goldcastle included *Recently* (1987), with versions of Dire Straits' 'Brothers in Arms' and U2's 'MLK'; the live *Diamonds and Rust in the Bullring* and *Speaking of Dreams* (both 1989), on which she sang George Michael's 'Hand to Mouth' and her guest artists included Paul Simon and the Gipsy Kings. These are notably more comfortable, but less powerful, recordings than her sometimes fretful first essays into autobiography in the mid-seventies. She continued to be politically active into the nineties, visiting Bosnia and other trouble spots, and also toured regularly. In 1992 she released *Play Me Backwards*. Recorded in Nashville, it included 'Amsterdam', co-written with Janis Ian, and Mary-Chapin Carpenter's 'Stones in the Road'. The three-CD set *Rare, Live and Classic* (1993) included most of her classic recordings and several unreleased recordings made with Dylan, the Grateful Dead and Donovan, and serves as a testament both to her range and the importance of the body of her work. It was followed by the lesser *Gone from Danger* (1997).

DEFORD BAILEY
b. 1899, Carthage, Tennessee, USA, d. July 1982, Nashville, Tennessee

Deford Bailey was the only black cast member of the Nashville-based country radio show and touring troupe the Grand Ole Opry. His solo harmonica renderings of blues, old-time dance tunes and, in particular, train imitations like 'Pan American Blues' were first heard on Nashville radio in 1925, and when the WSM *Barn Dance* changed its name to the *Opry* in 1927, Bailey's 'Pan American' was the first performance to be broadcast. Billed as 'The Harmonica Wizard', he immediately became one of the show's leading acts, and his broadcasts, heard across the South, influenced younger players, both black (including Sonny Terry) and white.

Bailey also travelled widely on *Opry* tours in the thirties with **Uncle Dave Macon**, **Roy Acuff** and **Bill Monroe**. With the *Opry*'s growing status as the prime country radio showcase, however, Bailey's performances came to seem more and more archaic. By the late thirties his slot was an incidental indulgence, and by 1941 he was off the roster and running a shoeshine stand. Soured by his experience, he refused several TV, record and festival offers, and although he finally consented to participate in some of the *Opry*'s commemorative shows in the late seventies, he added no formal recordings to the small body of work he had cut in 1927–8. No other black country musician performed on the *Opry* until **Charley Pride** joined the show's cast some forty years later. In 1998 *The Legendary Deford Bailey: Country Music's First Black Star* (Revanant), a 26-track CD, was issued. It consisted of informal recordings made by Bailey in 1974 and revealed that Bailey had a wider range than his earlier recordings and performances had suggested. In the same year Warners issued a celebratory and informative compilation of black country performers, *From Where I Stand: The Black Experience in Country Music*, which fittingly began with Bailey's 'Pan American Blues'.

MILDRED BAILEY
b. Mildred Rinker, 27 February 1907, Tekoa, Washington, USA, d. 12 December 1951, Poughkeepsie, New York

Mildred Bailey's caressing treatments of ballads and her smoky, knowing style on blues were surprising accomplishments in a singer gifted with a small, high-pitched voice of limited range. After **Billie Holiday**, however, there were few vocalists better versed in the bitter-sweetness of popular song in the thirties.

A movie-house pianist in her teens, Bailey graduated to nightclubs, until her brother Al Rinker, a partner of **Bing Crosby** in **Paul Whiteman**'s Rhythm Boys, secured her a job as singer with the Whiteman band. Her 1932 recording of **Hoagy Carmichael**'s 'Rockin' Chair' (Victor) made her name – literally: she was known thereafter as 'The Rockin' Chair Lady'. Even more successful commercially were 'We Just Couldn't Say Goodbye' and 'All of Me' (1932).

She left Whiteman in 1933 to freelance and made records in the company of many leading jazz musicians, among them the xylophone- and vibraphone-player Red Norvo (*b. Kenneth Norville, 31 March 1908, Beardstown, Illinois*), whom she married. From 1936 to 1939 she sang with her husband's band – they were known as 'Mr and Mrs Swing' – often framed by the

arrangements of Eddie Sauter. Their joint hits included **Sammy Cahn**'s 'Please Be Kind' and **Frank Loesser**'s 'Says My Heart' (1938). On her own Bailey had hits with 'Don't Be That Way' (1933) and 'Trust in Me' (1937), among others. She later worked with **Benny Goodman**, and in 1944–5 had a popular radio show. Her career was often interrupted by illness, the legacy of a 1932 car accident. She died destitute.

PEARL BAILEY
b. 29 March 1918, Newport News, Virginia, USA; d. 17 August 1990, Philadelphia, Pennsylvania

An exuberant performer, Bailey was a comedienne and singer who moved between jazz, pop and musical theatre.

The daughter of a minister, she worked in vaudeville after winning a talent contest in Philadelphia as a dancer. Victory in another competition at the Apollo Theatre in Harlem launched her singing career in New York. She joined Noble Sissle's orchestra and made her first recording, 'Tessa's Torch Song' (Hit, 1944), with Cootie Williams' band.

Bailey moved into theatre when she deputised for **Rosetta Tharpe** in a **Cab Calloway** revue, subsequently singing with the Calloway band. She was a featured performer in **Johnny Mercer** and **Harold Arlen**'s Broadway musical *St Louis Woman* (1946). Later stage appearances included leading roles in *Bless You All* (1950), *Arms and the Girl* (1950), *House of Flowers* (1954) and a 1967 version of *Hello Dolly* with an all-black cast. During the forties, Bailey recorded duets with comedienne Moms Mabley ('Saturday Night Fish Fry', 1949) and trumpeter Oran 'Hot Lips' Page ('Huckleback' and 'Baby It's Cold Outside'), and made solo recordings with jazz arrangers Tadd Dameron and **Gil Evans**.

In the 1950s she recorded more pop-orientated material for Coral with Don Redman as musical director, including her biggest hit 'It Takes Two to Tango' (1952). Bailey's husband, the drummer Louis Bellson, became her musical director in 1961. Her later albums included *Come on, Let's Play with Pearlie Mae* (1962) and *All About Good Little Girls and Bad Little Boys* (1963).

Bailey appeared in a number of films, including *Variety Girl*, in which she sang 'Tired', *Carmen Jones* (1954), *That Certain Feeling* (1956), *St Louis Blues* (1958) and *Porgy and Bess* (1959). She published an autobiography, *The Raw Pearl*, in 1968 and continued to work, despite ill health, into the eighties.

ANITA BAKER
b. 20 December 1957, Detroit, Michigan, USA

One of the most stylish female soul singers of the

1980s, Anita Baker also composed most of the songs she recorded. She led the way for such younger song stylists as Regina Belle and **Toni Braxton**.

Baker's grandfather was a minister and she began as a gospel singer. She joined Chapter 8 in 1979, singing lead vocals on the R&B hit 'I Just Wanna Be Your Girl' (1979). When the group disbanded, Baker left music briefly before recording *The Songstress* (1983) for the Beverly Glen label. With string arrangements by **Gene Page** and produced by Patrick Moten and Otis Smith, it included the R&B hit 'Angel'.

Disputes with the label interrupted Baker's career and it was three years before the appearance of the landmark album *Rapture* (Elektra, 1986), on which former Chapter 8 keyboards-player Michael Powell co-wrote songs with Baker. The album included the hits 'Sweet Love' and 'Caught Up in the Rapture'. With its sultry synthesis of soul, R&B, jazz and gospel, *Rapture* was hailed as one of the classic albums of the decade.

The title track from the next album, the celebration of wedded bliss 'Giving You the Best That I Got', was equally successful in 1988 and the album itself, produced by Powell, topped the US charts. In 1990 Baker issued the lesser *Compositions*, on which she was accompanied by Greg Phillinganes and Nathan East from **Eric Clapton**'s band and Steve Ferrone from the **Average White Band**. Among her co-writers for the album were Gerald Levert and Marc Gordon from Levert. The same year she appeared at the Nelson Mandela Birthday concert in London, singing **Bob Dylan**'s 'Blowin' in the Wind' with **Bonnie Raitt**, Natalie Cole and others.

She was less active over the next three years, recording only one track, for a compilation album to celebrate the Barcelona Olympics in 1992. In 1994 she returned to the charts with *Rhythm of Love*. Co-produced by **Arif Mardin** it included songs by **Burt Bacharach** and **Carly Simon**, and was exceptionally relaxed in style.

ARTHUR BAKER
b. 22 April 1955

The increasing technological sophistication of music recording brought the 'remix' producer to the fore in the eighties. Originally specializing in New York dance and hip-hop music, Baker, who began as an engineer, was one of the leading remix operators of the period, working on tracks by **Bruce Springsteen**, **Cyndi Lauper**, **Diana Ross** and others.

Baker came to the fore through his work on **Afrika Bambaataa**'s early records. In the early eighties he became associated with the Tommy Boy label's hip-hop disco style, before mainstream rock artists started to come to Baker for new dance-based versions of their singles. In 1984 Springsteen's 'Dancing in the Dark' and Lauper's 'Girls Just Wanna Have Fun' were treated in this way. Baker also remixed material by **Bob Dylan**, **Pat Benatar**, **Gil Scott-Heron**, **Jimmy Cliff** and **Reuben Blades**. His pre-eminence was recognized when he was asked to co-produce, with Steve van Zandt, the anti-apartheid all-star record '(I Ain't Gonna Play) Sun City'.

Baker was less successful as a music businessman. He recorded New Edition for his own Streetwise company but the relationship ended in a flurry of lawsuits. In 1986 he set up another label, Criminal Records. Among its first releases was *Don't Push Your Luck* by Wally Jump Junior and the Criminal Element.

Among Baker's subsequent productions were tracks by **Jeff Beck**, Jeffrey Osborne and Will Downing's 'A Love Supreme' (Island, 1988), a vocal version of **John Coltrane**'s jazz composition. In the same year he signed to A&M to release his own records as Arthur Baker and the Backbeat Disciples. The first of these was *Merge* (1989), which featured guest vocals from **ABC**'s Martin Fry and Jimmy Sommerville, formerly of the **Communards**. **Al Green** guested on the single 'The Message Is Love' (1989). In 1990 Baker supervised the music for the documentary film *The Lives of Quincy Jones*, composing 'Listen Up' for the film. He wrote and produced the Wendell Williams hit 'Everybody (Rap)'. Al Green sang on the crusading *Leave the Guns at Home* (1991), Baker's contribution to the campaign to reform US gun laws. That track appeared on a later Backbeat Disciples album. Later productions include *Debravation* (Debbie Harry, 1992) and *Higher Power* (Big Audio, 1994).

JOSEPHINE BAKER
b. 3 June 1906, St Louis, Missouri, USA, d. 12 April 1975, Paris, France

Although Baker rose to stardom on the wave of French enthusiasm for jazz, it was as a music-hall star and patriot that she was deified in France.

Born in the slums of St Louis, where in 1917 she witnessed one of the worst race riots America has known, Baker joined a Philadelphia-based dance troupe in 1922. In 1923 she won a place in the chorus of the first black Broadway musical, **Eubie Blake**'s and Noble Sissle's *Shuffle Along*, in which she appeared among the chorus, scantily clad in the manner of the *Ziegfeld Follies*. Henceforth, exotic nudity was to be central to her career. She briefly appeared in *Chocolate Dandies* at the Cotton Club and in 1925 went to Paris in the chorus of *La Revue Nègre* with **Sidney Bechet**.

Both the show and Baker were enormous hits, opening Europe to a steady stream of black American artists and elevating Baker to stardom. Within a year she was a star of the *Folies Bergère* (where she intro-duced the Charleston to Europe, while clad only in a girdle of bananas) and recording for Odéon in a breathless, quavering voice. Her theme song was 'J'ai Deux Amours', the two lovers being France and America. She starred in several films, including *La Sirène des Tropiques* (1927), *Zou-Zou* (1930) and *Princesse Tam-Tam* (1935) and in Jacques Offenbach's opera *La Créole* (1934), each slowly shifting her on-stage character from American black to exotic for-eigner, a celebrity known as much for walking a leopard on a leash down the Champs-Elysées as any-thing else. In 1937 she became a naturalized French citizen, did volunteer work during the Second World War and in 1940 joined the Resistance. For this she was given the *Croix de Guerre* and the *Légion d'Hon-neur*, with the Rosette of the Resistance.

After the war she briefly and unsuccessfully visited America before settling once more in France with her 'rainbow family' of adopted children of various coun-tries, returning intermittently to the stage to support her family. Her death came four days after such a return.

LAVERN BAKER
b. 11 November 1929, Chicago, Illinois, USA, d. 10 March 1997, New York

One of the major R&B artists of the fifties, Baker began her career as a jazz singer and, though her later records presaged its arrival, she was one of the many R&B artists swept aside by the coming of soul.

Baker was originally billed as 'Little Miss Share-cropper', which suggests her style was more down home, but when she was signed to Columbia in the late forties, on the advice of **Fletcher Henderson**, she was recorded in the style of **Dinah Washington** and **Sarah Vaughan**. It was these recordings which reput-edly influenced **Johnny Ray**. Moving to King, she recorded up-tempo rhythm and blues with Todd Rhodes' band before joining Atlantic in 1953. Her third release for the company, the catchy 'Tweedlee Dee' (1954), was (then) the poppiest ever recording put out by Atlantic by a black act. It was a Top Twenty hit, despite being covered by Georgia Gibbs. Most of Baker's subsequent records took her back to an R&B base, most playfully on the Lincoln Chase composition 'Jim Dandy' (a Top Twenty hit in 1956 and coarsely revived in 1974 by **Black Oak Arkansas**, in which she invested the tale of her superhero with an eratic *frisson*), and most soulfully on 'Shake a Hand' (1959, and significantly an R&B, but not pop, hit).

Her biggest hit, 'I Cried a Tear' (1958), pointed the way forward to the soul ballad of the sixties. In the same year she recorded her best album, the heartfelt tribute *La Vern Baker Sings Bessie Smith*. Ironically, despite hits such as 'I Waited Too Long' (1959) and the pop-gospel version of **Leiber and Stoller**'s 'Saved' (1961), the coming of soul saw Baker's career swiftly decline. Her last major hit was 'See See Rider' (1963), after which her only success was in the R&B charts with the likes of the jazz-ballad standard 'Fly Me to the Moon' (1965). Her later records on Brunswick made little impact.

Baker subsequently performed infrequently but she recorded a concert for **Ruth Brown**'s television series *Bluestage* in 1990.

MICKEY BAKER
b. McHouston Baker, 15 October 1925, Louisville, Kentucky, USA

For most of the fifties, any noteworthy guitar part on a New York R&B record was probably the work of Mickey Baker. He played in what amounted to the Atlantic house band, worked as frequently for Savoy, King and other labels, and enhanced innumerable records by **Ruth Brown**, **Ray Charles**, the **Coasters**, the **Drifters** and others. Schooled in jazz – and even for a time calypso – he brought to R&B session work a fresh versatility of approach. Though often presented with musically limited material, which he might have played through with a jazzman's indifference, he chose to reshape it with a jazzman's ingenuity.

He had settled in New York in his mid-teens, taken up guitar about 1945, and by the beginning of the fifties had become an instructor in the instrument. In 1953, spurred by the success of **Les Paul** and Mary Ford, he formed a duo with a former student, Sylvia Vanderpool. As Mickey and Sylvia the pair had a million-seller with 'Love Is Strange' (Groove), which was based on an idea of **Bo Diddley**'s, and were seen widely on rock'n'roll package tours organized by **Alan Freed** and other promoters.

Baker emigrated to Europe in 1961, settling in Paris and working in jazz clubs and as a session guitarist. He teamed with his fellow émigrés **Memphis Slim** and **Champion Jack Dupree** and also worked with resident and visiting jazz musicians. During the sev-enties he toured other European countries and extended his repertoire to embrace Chicago-style band blues (*The Blues and Me*, Black and Blue, 1974), acoustic country blues (*Blues and Jazz Guitar*, Kicking Mule, 1977), and jazz-rock (*Jazz-Rock Guitar*, Kicking Mule, 1978). He has also published several guitar tutors and chord-books.

HANK BALLARD
b. 18 November 1936, Detroit, Michigan, USA

An arresting singer who was one of the most successful R&B artists of the fifties, Ballard's best-known composition is 'The Twist', a million-seller for **Chubby Checker** in 1960 and responsible for the biggest dance craze of modern times.

He first recorded with doo-wop group the Royals in 1951 for Federal, a subsidiary of **Syd Nathan**'s King Records. The group's original lead singer was Henry Booth, who performed ballads like **Johnny Otis**'s 'Every Beat of My Heart', a later (1961) hit for **Gladys Knight and the Pips**. In 1953 Ballard took over from Booth and the up-tempo 'Get It' was an immediate success.

The real breakthrough came with the **Ralph Bass** production 'Work with Me Annie', which spent six months in the charts during 1954. Ballard delivered the salacious lyrics with erotic gasps and cries which derived from the gospel tradition. The record inspired an answer disc from **Etta James** ('Roll with Me Henry'), and bowdlerized white cover-versions like Georgia Gibbs' 'Dance with Me Henry (Wallflower)', a No. 1 hit on Mercury in 1955.

By this time the group had changed name to the Midnighters and they produced a series of follow-up records which included 'Annie Had a Baby' and 'Annie's Aunt Fanny'. The group's next big hit was the searing blues ballad 'Teardrops on Your Letter' (1958), featuring a Ballard vocal that had all the characteristics of soul singing years before the term had been coined.

It was the B-side of that single, a throwaway dance number, which was to change Ballard's career. When covered by Checker, it was a massive hit and even the reissued version of Ballard's original made the pop Top Thirty in 1960. However, this led him to a series of novelty dance numbers of which only 'Finger Poppin' Time' was a major hit. A precursor of soul, Ballard chased after the teenage audience while others were perfecting the soul style.

He continued to perform, often as part of **James Brown**'s revue, and made his first British appearance in 1986. His recordings were sporadic and often, like 1974's 'Let's Go Streaking', forgettable.

AFRIKA BAMBAATAA
b. Kevin Donovan, 4 October 1960, South Bronx, New York, USA

Originally a disc-jockey, Afrika Bambaataa with **Grandmaster Flash** created the hip-hop genre. With such seminal recordings as 'Planet Rock' and 'Looking for that Perfect Beat', he later developed a style which combined the soul/funk of **James Brown** with the technological explorations of **Kraftwerk** and the politically aware lyrics of **Gil Scott-Heron**.

Originally the leader of a neighbourhood gang called the Black Spades, Bambaataa worked as a dee-

jay while at high school and in 1974 founded the Zulu Nation, a loose aggregation of dancers who performed with him at competitions and parties. The group had a broad political outlook influenced by the black nationalism of Malcolm X and the Black Panthers, and an anti-drug orientation. With Cosmic Force he recorded 'Zulu Nation Throwdown Part One' for Paul Winfield in 1980 and the following year signed to Tommy Boy. Produced by John Robie and **Arthur Baker**, Afrika Bambaataa and the Sonic Soul Force recorded the dance hit 'Planet Rock', which was a minor British hit on Polydor in 1982.

Bambaataa appeared in the movie *Beat Street* singing 'Looking for the Perfect Beat', which later formed the basis of the 1987 hit 'Beat Dis' by Bomb the Bass. 'Renegades of Funk' (1984) reached the British Top Thirty. With James Brown he recorded 'Unity' (1984) and later worked with ex-**Sex Pistols** singer John Lydon as Time Zone on 'World Destruction' (Celluloid). In 1986 Bambaataa released *Beware (The Funk Is Everywhere)*, which included a version of **MC5**'s 'Kick Out the Jams', after which he moved to EMI for *The Light* (1988). Its guest artists included ex-**Culture Club** singer Boy George, Nona Hendryx and **UB40**, who appeared on the British hit 'Reckless'.

In 1990 Afrika Bambaataa organized Hip-Hop Against Apartheid, whose members included **Queen Latifah** and the **Jungle Brothers**. This group recorded the fund-raising EP *Ndodemnyama – Free South Africa*. In 1991 he recorded the concept album *The Decade of Darkness (1991–2000)*. Conceived of as a blending of social consciousness and modern dance beats, it included a masterly reworking of James Brown's 'Say It Loud (I'm Black and I'm Proud)'. Less successful was the remix album *Don't Stop . . . Planet Rock* (1992), which attempted to give a hip-hop inflection to 'Planet Rock'. More recently, Bambaataa added his distinctive vocal and lyrical style to 'Afrika Shox', the first single from **Leftfield**'s 1999 *Rhythm and Stealth* album.

BANANARAMA
Sarah Dallin, b. 17 December 1961, Bristol, England; Siobhan Fahey, b. 10 September 1957, London (replaced by Jacqui Sullivan, b. 7 August 1960, London); Keren Woodward, b. 2 April 1961, Bristol

The most successful of British female vocal groups in the eighties, Bananarama specialized in lightweight revivals of earlier pop hits. But in contrast to many 'female vocal groups' of earlier eras, they took control of their own career at an early stage, projecting an image of autonomy and strength.

The original trio began singing *a cappella* at London clubs and parties in 1981, recording 'Ai A Mwana' (in Swahili) for **Elvis Costello**'s Demon

label. Produced by former **Sex Pistols** guitarist Steve
Cook, the single led to a long-term contract with
London Records.

Forming an alliance with ex-**Specials** group Funboy Three, Bananarama reached the British Top Ten
with a version of the Velvelettes' 1965 R&B hit 'He
Was Really Sayin' Somethin'' with backing vocals
from the male trio. In turn, Bananarama accompanied Funboy Three's equally successful revival of 'It
Ain't What You Do, It's the Way That You Do It'.

Later in 1982 Bananarama had a further Top Ten
hit with the Swain and Jolley-produced 'Shy Boy',
although the poor-selling slow ballad 'Cheers Then'
led them to revert to jaunty revivalism on 'Na Na Hey
Hey Kiss Him Goodbye' (1983), a bubblegum hit for
Steam (Fontana, 1970). Featured in the film *Karate
Kid*, 'Cruel Summer' became the group's first American hit, and was followed by the trio's most accomplished song, 'Robert de Niro's Waiting' (1984), a
tribute to the American film actor.

After two lesser singles, Bananarama's career was
revived in 1986 by the team of **Stock, Aitken and
Waterman**, who produced 'Venus', a disco-treated
updating of the 1970 British No. 1 by Dutch group
Shocking Blue. A Top Ten success in Britain, the
record was the group's first American No. 1. After the
disappointing 'More than Physical' and 'A Trick of
the Night' (1986), Bananarama were among the
singers on the SAW remake of **The Beatles**' 'Let It Be'
(1987), a benefit recording for the victims of the Zee-
brugge ferry disaster.

There were further hits in America ('I Heard a
Rumour') and Britain ('Love in the First Degree')
before Fahey, now married to Dave Stewart of the
Eurythmics, left the group. She later formed **Shake-
spears Sister** and co-wrote songs with Stewart ('If
You Should Go', recorded by the Fureys with Davey
Arthur, 1989).

With Jacqui Sullivan joining from the Shillelagh
Sisters, Bananarama began 1988 with two SAW originals, 'I Can't Help It' and 'I Want You Back', followed
by two of their more breathtaking cover-versions.
'Nathan Jones' was originally recorded by the
Supremes, to whom the British group had sometimes
been unrealistically compared, while 'Help' was a
charity fund-raising spoof version of The Beatles classic with British comediennes Dawn French and Jennifer Saunders.

Both records were dominated by Stock, Aitken and
Waterman's highly effective, if mechanical, dance
rhythms. In 1991 *Pop Life* was produced by Youth and
also in 1991 they released a version of the **Doobie
Brothers**' 'Long Train Runnin''. When Sullivan left
Bananarama in 1992, Dallin and Woodward continued as a duo, scoring minor hits in Britain with
'Movin' on' and 'Last Thing on My Mind' (1992) and
the album *Please Yourself* (1993). After that the band
separated.

THE BAND
*James Robbie Robertson, b. 5 July 1943, Toronto,
Canada; Richard Manuel, b. 3 April 1943, Stratford,
Canada, d. 4 March 1986, Florida, USA; Garth Hudson,
b. 2 August 1937, London, Canada; Rick Danko, b. 9
December 1942, Simcoe; Levon Helm, b. 26 May 1935,
Marvell, Arkansas, USA*

The Band made two decisive contributions to rock
music. Firstly, they helped **Bob Dylan** make the transition from acoustic to electric music in the mid-sixties,
when they backed him on several tours. Secondly,
their own work, particularly *Music from Big Pink*
(1968) and *The Band* (1969), was acclaimed by critics
as representing a 'maturing' of rock music. In contrast
to other sixties groups who spoke for the most part
only to their own generation and whose influences
were hardly skin deep, The Band placed themselves
firmly on the side of tradition rather than novelty.
Rather like the Irish film director John Ford whose
films collectively add up to an idealized portrait of a
long-lost America, The Band, all Canadians with the
exception of drummer Helm, looked at their new
home with a fresh eye and in their songs proudly celebrated America's down-trodden. 'Their music gave us
a sense that the country was richer than we guessed,'
wrote critic Greil Marcus.

The Band was pieced together in Canada by **Ronnie Hawkins**, whose 'Mary Lou' and 'Forty Days'
(Roulette, 1959) featured Helm on drums. One by
one, he recruited the future members of The Band as
his backing group, the Hawks. Their first recordings
together included **Bo Diddley**'s 'Who Do You Love?'
(1963), a Canadian hit which showcased Robertson's
stinging lead guitar. In 1964 Helm, who had occasionally sung lead (including **Bobby Bland**'s 'Further up
the Road', 1964), and the group left Hawkins to perform as Levon Helm and the Hawks.

By the mid-sixties their distinctive vocal and
instrumental interplay honed by continual touring,
the Hawks had won a cult following on the East
Coast. In 1965 they recorded with John Hammond Jnr
(*So Many Roads*, Vanguard, 1965) before being invited
by Dylan to back him (with Mickey Jones replacing
Helm as drummer) on his 1965–6 world tour. They
can be heard on the widely available bootleg album of
Dylan's 1966 concert at London's Albert Hall, giving
an ominous, thunderous backing to Dylan's screamed
vocals on 'Like a Rolling Stone' and other songs. Following Dylan's motorcycle crash, The Band joined
him in Woodstock in 1967 where they recorded *The
Basement Tapes* (widely bootlegged, 1967; officially
released, 1975) with Dylan, bringing a mellower edge

to his sound. Those recordings also saw Danko, Manuel and Robertson starting to write their own material, and collaborating with Dylan ('Tears of Rage' and 'This Wheel's on Fire', both of which surfaced in different versions on their début album).

Music from Big Pink (Capitol, 1968) was critically acclaimed for its natural sound (there was no overdubbing) and passionate singing, with Helm, Danko and Manuel often switching vocals within the same song. The songs themselves, which included a haunting version of 'I Shall Be Released', the jaunty 'We Can Talk', the oft-recorded 'The Weight' and 'Chest Fever', revealed a fondness for rural imagery and a Dylanesque way with metaphor. Even more impressive was *The Band* (1969), which included their biggest pop hit – the wryly humorous 'Up on Cripple Creek' – and the majestic 'The Night They Drove Old Dixie Down', later a hit for **Joan Baez** (1971). The album explored the simple verities of life through a range of traditional characters and stories ('Jawbone', 'Unfaithful Servant', 'King Harvest (Has Surely Come)'). *Stage Fright* (1970) added to these interests the tribulations of touring and included 'Time to Kill', the haunting 'Daniel and the Sacred Harp', 'The W. S. Walcott Medicine Show', 'All la Glory' and the fearful 'The Rumour'.

Cahoots (1971) was a lesser work, most notable for the guest appearance of **Van Morrison** and horn arrangements by **Allen Toussaint**, while the live album *Rock of Ages* (1972), which included a version of **Chuck Willis**'s 'Hang up My Rock'n'Roll Shoes', anticipated *Moondog Matinée* (1973). A superior collection of fifties standards, it included Bobby Bland's 'Share Your Love with Me', **Sam Cooke**'s 'A Change Is Gonna Come' and **Anton Karas**'s 'The Third Man'. Their best work of this period, however, was with Dylan with whom they recorded *Planet Waves* (1974) and the live album *Before the Flood* (1975). Tired of touring, after a pair of minor albums which confirmed their growing musical conservatism, the group decided to disband. With director Martin Scorsese they filmed and recorded their final concert, *The Last Waltz* (1978), which featured guest appearances from Dylan, **Bobby Charles**, **Neil Young**, **Dr John**, the **Staple Singers**, **Neil Diamond**, Ronnie Hawkins, and **Muddy Waters**, among others.

Helm was the first to record as a solo artist, forming Levon Helm and the RCO Allstars (which included Steve Cropper, Dr John and **Paul Butterfield**) to make a trio of lacklustre albums for ABC (1977–80), before in 1980 turning to acting with *Coalminer's Daughter*, the film biography of **Loretta Lynn**. Danko recorded an eponymous album for Arista (1978). Far better was Danko/Fjeld/Andersen (Stageway, Rykodisc, 1991) with Jonas Fjeld and Eric Anderson. Hudson and Manuel organized reunion

tours and turned to session work for most of the eighties. Robertson's subsequent career was more substantial. While a member of The Band he had worked as a producer (**Jesse Winchester**, Neil Diamond) and after *The Last Waltz* turned to films, writing the music for several of Scorsese's later films and writing, producing and starring in *Carney* (1980). He refused to join The Band reunion tours of 1984 and 1986. In 1987 he returned to recording with the hugely successful but musically conservative *Robbie Robertson* (Geffen), recorded with support from **U2** and **Peter Gabriel**. *Storyville* (1991), a loose concept album set in New Orleans' red light district, was less successful. Then, in 1994, Robertson released *Music for the Native Americans*, most of which he had conceived of as a soundtrack for a documentary about Indian history and culture. He followed that with *Contact from the Underworld of Redboy*, an album in the same vein with contributions from Priscilla Coolidge, among others.

To Kingdom Come (1989) was a superior retrospective compilation which detailed the group's career with intelligence and care. It was the prelude to *Jericho* (Pyramid, 1993), by a re-formed Band, minus Robertson of course. It was a surprisingly confident album, produced by John Simon who had supervised the first two Band albums. *Jericho* captured the spirit of their classic recordings without seeming either mannered or nostalgic. On it Danko, Helm and Levon were joined by Jim Weider (guitar), Richard Bell (a former Ronnie Hawkins pianist) and Randy Ciarlante (drums). The best songs were the title track and 'Country Boy', recorded in 1985 with Manuel singing lead. It was followed by a trio of lesser albums, *Live at Watkins Glen* (1995), *High on the Hog* (1996) and *Jubilation* (1998).

In 1993 two biographies of the group were published. Barney Hoskyns' *Across the Great Divide* for the most part saw Robertson as the creative centre, while Helm's *This Wheel's on Fire* was a more personal and splenetic account.

MOE BANDY
b. 12 February 1944, Meridian, Mississippi, USA

Like **George Strait**, John Anderson, Gene Watson and Mel Street, Bandy performed in a 'neo-honky-tonk' style. His material, with its tales of cheating, booze and lost love, was the traditional stuff of honky-tonk music of the forties and the sound harkened back to **George Jones** and beyond, but it was constructed around rhythms and with instruments that also showed a rock influence.

Brought up in a musical family, while in school in San Antonio, Texas, Bandy attempted a rodeo career but on graduating in 1962, he returned to music. He formed his first group, Moe and the Mavericks, and made several records for small labels, such as GP, Satin and Shannon while supporting himself as a sheet-metal worker. In 1973 he financed a session with producer Ray Baker that included the intense 'I Just Started Hatin' Cheatin' Songs Today', which made the country Top Ten when released on GRC Records. Further similarly styled hits followed: 'Honky Tonk Amnesia' (1973), 'It Was Always Easy to Find an Unhappy Woman' (1974), and the autobiographical 'Bandy the Rodeo Clown' (1975), which he wrote with **Lefty Frizzell**. In 1975 he joined Columbia and, after a further string of hits, in 1979 teamed up with Joe Stampley (b. 6 June 1943, Springhill, Louisiana), a singer even more influenced by rock'n'roll than himself. That partnership produced 'Just Good Ole Boys' (1979), 'Hey Joe, Hey Moe' (written for them by **Boudleaux Bryant**), 'Honky Tonk Queen' (both 1981), 'Where's the Dress?' (1984), a satire on pop music and transvestism, and 'Daddy's Honky Tonk'. Later solo country hits included 'It Took a Lot of Drinkin' to Get That Woman over Me' and 'Woman, Your Love' (1984). In 1987 he switched producers – from Ray Baker to Jerry Kennedy – for You Haven't Heard the Last of Me and henceforth his records would be slicker and slightly poppier than before. The change, however, had little impact and his best record of the nineties is the retrospective Honky Tonk Amnesia (Razor & Tie, 1996).

THE BANGLES

Susanna Hoffs, b. 17 January 1962, Newport Beach, California, USA; Debbi Peterson, b. 22 August 1961, Los Angeles, California; Vicki Peterson, b. 11 January 1958, Los Angeles, California; Annette Zilinskas (replaced by Michael Steele, b. 2 June 1954)

An all-female guitar group, the Bangles' melodic songs and catchy harmonies resulted in a series of international hits in the late eighties.

The group was formed in Los Angeles as the Colours in 1981 by guitarists Hoffs and Vicki Peterson, bass-player Zilinskas and drummer Debbi Peterson. Renamed the Bangles, the quartet made 'Getting Out of Hand' as the Bangs for their own Down Kiddie label. Objections from another group called the Bangs led to a further name change to the Bangles. After the group released a five-track mini-album on the independent IRS label, Zilinskas left to join Blood on the Saddle and later the Ringling Sisters. She was replaced by Steele.

In 1983 the Bangles signed a recording contract with CBS, issuing the David Kahne-produced All Over the Place. The group's first major success was 'Manic Monday', a sparkling pop song composed by **Prince**. This was the first of a series of hit singles which included the quirky 'Walk Like an Egyptian' (1986), written by Liam Sternberg, a version of **Paul Simon**'s 'Hazy Shade of Winter' (1988, produced by **Rick Rubin** for the film Less Than Zero) and 'In Your Room'.

With Hoffs on lead vocals, the softer ballad 'Eternal Flame' (1988) from Everything was a No. 1 hit on both sides of the Atlantic. Produced by Davitt Sigerson and co-written by Hoffs with Billy Steinberg and Tom Kelly, the song represented a change of style for the group. Soon afterwards the Bangles split up. Hoffs began a solo career with When You're a Boy, which included the minor hit 'My Side of the Bed' (1991), another collaboration with Steinberg and Kelly. She followed that with Susana Hoffs (1996), which also included a minor pop hit, 'All I Want'.

CHRIS BARBER

b. 17 April 1930, Welwyn Garden City, Hertfordshire, England

A jazz bandleader for over thirty years, British trombonist Barber played a key role in the growth of both the skiffle and R&B movements in the period 1955–63.

His first band included Monty Sunshine (clarinet), Pat Halcox (trumpet), **Lonnie Donegan** (guitar and banjo) and Ron Bowden (drums). Part of the growing trad jazz movement, the Barber band, following **Ken Colyer**'s lead, also included a small group within a group which played a set of folk and blues tunes in its performances. It was one of these, 'Rock Island Line', from the New Orleans Joys album (Decca, 1954), that became a Top Ten hit in 1956 for Lonnie Donegan, with Barber himself on bass.

When Donegan left to form his own group, Barber added Irish jazz and blues singer Ottilie Patterson to his line-up. As trad gained in popularity in Britain, the band had its only hit single, 'Petite Fleur' (Nixa, 1959), a **Sidney Bechet** tune played by Monty Sunshine, which was also a Top Ten hit on Laurie in America.

One of the first British jazz musicians to perform in the United States (at the Monterey Festival in 1959), Barber was also active in bringing American artists to Europe. Among those who were promoted by or toured with him were **Muddy Waters**, **Louis Jordan**, Alex Bradford, harmonica-player James Cotton, **Brownie McGhee and Sonny Terry** and **Dr John**, with whom Barber recorded on Black Lion in 1983.

As R&B grew in importance, the band became the Chris Barber Jazz and Blues Band, with the addition of electric guitarist John Slaughter. Gradually, too, the Barber band included mainstream as well as trad jazz in its repertoire and during the sixties and seventies it regularly toured throughout Europe, from Denmark to Hungary.

In more than three decades of its existence there have been surprisingly few line-up changes in the Chris Barber Band. Among the personnel have been Ian Wheeler (trumpet), John Crocker (clarinet), Vic Pitt (guitar) and Graham Burbidge (drums). Barber has recorded more than a dozen albums on various labels, including Decca, Pye-Nixa, Black Lion and Teldec.

In 2000 he was swept up in Donegan's attempt at a one-man skiffle revival, appearing alongside Donegan and **Van Morrison** on *The Skiffle Sessions – Live in Belfast*.

BARCLAY JAMES HARVEST
Stewart 'Woolley' Wolstenholme, b. 15 April 1947; Melvin Pritchard, b. 20 January 1948; Les Holroyd, b. 12 March 1948; John Lees, b. 13 January 1948

An archetypal progressive rock band of the early seventies, Barclay James Harvest survived without a change in style into the eighties principally through their large following in Germany.

The group was formed in Oldham, Lancashire, in 1966 by members of two local bands, the Sorcerers and the Keepers. Their early influences included **Love**, the **Byrds** and **Simon and Garfunkel**. In 1969 they signed to EMI's progressive label Harvest (which was said to have been named after the band) and the first eponymous album was produced by Norman 'Hurricane' Smith, the staff engineer who had a brief taste of pop glory with two Top Ten hits ('Don't Let It Die' and 'Oh Babe What Would You Say?') in 1971–2.

The band favoured symphonic rock music and featured Wolstenholme's mellotron alongside Lees' guitar. An orchestra led by Martyn Ford performed with the group on some gigs and on *Baby James Harvest* (1972), their fourth and final album for Harvest.

Now managed by Kennedy Street Management (who handled **10CC**) they signed to Polydor where Rodger Bain produced *Everyone Is Everybody Else* (1974) and a live album. A heavily criticized tour of South Africa was followed by the critically acclaimed *Time Honoured Ghosts*, produced by Elliot Mazer, whose other credits included **Neil Young** and Area Code 615.

Throughout the seventies and eighties Barclay James Harvest retained a cult following and albums were released on an annual basis. The 1982 live recording *A Concert for the People* was made in Germany, where the band retained its greatest support. After *Number 12* (1978) Wolstenholme left the group, recording a solo album, *Maestoso* (Polydor, 1980). In 1990, now known simply as BJH, they released *Welcome to the Show* and in 1992 celebrated their 25th anniversary with a sell-out UK tour and a 'best of' album (Polydor). It was followed by their last album

for Polydor, *Caught in the Net* (1993), after which they switched to Eagle, releasing *Nexus – Through the Eyes of John Lee* in 1999 after a protracted legal dispute. By the end of the decade the group's main audience was in Germany, where they regularly toured.

BOBBY BARE
b. 7 April 1935, Ironton, Ohio, USA

Bare had a million-seller with the self-penned gentle satire on rock'n'roll stardom, 'The All-American Boy' (Fraternity, 1958), under another name, had several crossover pop hits in the early sixties on RCA ('Shame on Me', 1962; 'Detroit City'* and '500 Miles Away from Home', 1963; and 'Miller's Cave', 1964), and was produced by the architect of the 'Nashville sound', **Chet Atkins**. However, the greatest influence on Bare was the narrative ballad, given a new impetus by the folk revival of the late fifties. But where the folk revivalists worked from an urban setting, Bare worked from a rural one, which gave extra weight to his performance of Ian Tyson's (of **Ian and Sylvia**) tale of Canadian migratory workers, 'Four Strong Winds'* (1964).

The son of poor farmers, Bare turned to music in his teens. Shortly before being drafted in 1959, he allowed boyhood friend, Bill Parsons, to take the credit for 'The All-American Boy', when Fraternity decided to issue the demo tape he'd sent them. Back from the army, he signed with RCA and recorded a stream of story songs that precisely pictured the emotional cost of rural immigration to the North. The best of these were Mel Tillis's and Donny Dill's 'Detroit City' with its classic line, 'By day I make the cars, by night I make the bars' and **Harlan Howard**'s very similar 'Streets of Baltimore' (1966), which was later revived to great effect by **Gram Parsons**.

A strong supporter of new writers and performers – he championed **Mickey Newbury**, **Kris Kristofferson** and **Waylon Jennings**, among others – he later worked closely with **Shel Silverstein**, charting with 'Marie Laveau' (1974), the ambitious concept album *Bobby Bare Sings Lullabies, Legends and Lies* (1975) and 'Red Neck Hippie Romance' (1976). That year he quit RCA for Columbia. The hits continued and in 1983 he provided the Nashville Network, a cable channel, with one of its best shows, *Bobby Bare and Friends*, in which he sang and interviewed other songwriters.

JIMMY BARNES
b. Scotland

The former leader of Cold Chisel, Barnes' classic rock voice made him one of Australia's leading singers.

Barnes formed Cold Chisel in Adelaide in 1974 with Ian Moss (guitar/vocals), Phil Small (bass), Don

Walker (piano/vocals) and drummer Steve Prestwich. Barnes' impassioned delivery and Walker's arresting lyrics informed such albums as *East* (1980) and *Circus Animals* (1982).

The group split in 1983 and both Walker and Barnes followed solo careers. Barnes formed a touring band that has included many of Australia's most proficient rock musicians. His solo recordings began with *Bodyswerve* (1984) and *Working Class Man* (1985), whose title track was one of his biggest hits.

Freight Train Heart (Geffen, 1985) had a more American sound and had songs by Mick Fleetwood, Desmond Child and Neil Schon of **Journey**. After the live *Barnestorming* (Mushroom, 1988) he released *Two Fires* (Atlantic, 1990). In 1991 he recorded 'Good Times' with **INXS**. *Love & Fear* (Mushroom, 2000), a concept/confessional album about marriage co-written with his wife, saw Barnes bellowing less to little effect. In the fashion of the times it was promoted by a free MP3 downloadable track, 'Love & Hate'.

CHARLIE BARNET
b. Charles Daly Barnet, 26 October 1913, New York, USA, d. 4 September 1991, San Diego

Known as the 'Mad Mab' and best remembered for his version of 'Cherokee', the much married Barnet was an important bandleader in the forties.

He was the first white bandleader to appear at the Harlem Apollo (in 1933) and among the first white leaders to employ black sidemen (such as trumpeter 'Peanuts' Holland) extensively.

The son of a corporate lawyer, Barnet, like **John Hammond** before him, decided on the jazz life early on, forming his own band at the age of sixteen to work on a transatlantic liner. A saxophonist, deeply influenced by **Coleman Hawkins** and **Johnny Hodges**, he formed his first big band in New York in 1933. In 1935 he briefly left music to attempt a career in Hollywood as an actor. But, after playing small parts in *Love and Hisses* and *Sally, Irene and Mary* (1936), he re-formed his band. Throughout the thirties he recorded mostly for small labels, such as Banner, Oriole and Melotone, until in 1939 he was signed by RCA Victor.

Barnet had an immediate hit with the **Billy May**-arranged version of **Ray Noble**'s 'Cherokee', a classic example of jazz- rather than pop-inflected swing, on RCA's Bluebird label. In general, Barnet's Bluebird recordings of 1939–41, which include many **Duke Ellington** compositions and some with **Lena Horne** as featured vocalist, are among the jazziest recordings by a white swing band. In 1942 Barnet joined Decca, on which he had a further hit with Dale Bennet's 'Skyliner' (1944), and in 1949, Capitol.

Following the post-war decline in interest in big bands, Barnet, who in 1958 entered personal management in Hollywood, organized bands for special occasions only.

RICHARD BARRETT
b. 1936, Philadelphia, Pennsylvania, USA

A writer, producer and manager as well as a performer, Barrett's career spanned three decades of black vocal-group music.

The son of middle-class parents, after his discharge from the army in 1954 Barrett was drafted in as lead singer of the Valentines. The group had a minor R&B hit with his composition 'Goodnight Kathleen' (Old Town, 1954), featuring his slurred vocals, and joined **George Goldner**'s Rama label for 'Lily Maybelle' (1955).

By 1958 the group was no more, but by then Barrett had become Goldner's right-hand man, bringing him **Frankie Lymon and the Teenagers** and the **Chantels** and producing a string of hits, including some of his own compositions – 'Creation of Love', by Lymon, and 'Maybe', the Chantels' biggest hit. During this time Barrett also recorded for MGM (1957–8), Gone (1959), 20th-Century Fox (1960) and Atlantic (1962), for whom he cut the frantic gospel-styled 'Some Other Guy' produced by **Leiber and Stoller**. Only a minor hit in America it was seen as a classic by British beat groups of the sixties and covered several times, most notably by the Big Three who had a Top Forty hit with it in 1963 (Decca).

Following the demise of Goldner's empire in 1963, Barrett returned to Philadelphia. There he unsuccessfully recorded Harold Melvin and the Blue Notes ('Get Out', 1964) for his own Landa label, before joining Swan as a producer. There he produced 'Gee Baby (I'm Sorry)' (1965) for the Three Degrees (who then consisted of Fayette Pinkney, Linda Turner and Shirley Porter) and, when Swan collapsed in 1966, he took over their management, slowly steering them to a lighter version of soul music. After a 1970 hit with a surprisingly powerful remake of 'Maybe' (Roulette), Barrett signed the group (which now comprised Pinkney, Sheila Ferguson and Valerie Thompson) to **Gamble and Huff**'s Philadelphia International label. The result was a series of hits, including 'Year of Decision' (1973), the haunting 'When Will I See You Again?'* (1974), which was an international chart-topper, and 'Take Good Care of Yourself' (1975), which saw them become international stars and the queens of the world's cabaret circuit – this last helped by Britain's Prince Charles' stated admiration of the group.

A change of label to Ariola in 1978 briefly saw them returning to soul ('Givin' Up Givin' in', 1978) but records like 'Woman in Love' and 'My Simple Heart' demonstrated they were far happier performing in their accustomed easy-listening style. In 1982 they and Barrett, who had devoted himself exclusively to the group since 1965, parted company. Since then Barrett has been largely inactive and the Three Degrees have continued to play the international cabaret circuit.

JOHN BARRY
b. John Barry Prendergast, 3 November 1933, York, England

A one-time rock'n'roll trumpeter and bandleader, Barry graduated to writing film music in the early sixties in the wake of the new-found interest of movie producers in pop music. He established the cool sound of British movies of the sixties with scores for *The Ipcress File* and *The Knack* (both 1965) and the Bond movies. Frequently his film scores – especially for the James Bond films, most of which he has written – have included successful theme songs.

Barry formed the John Barry Seven, an instrumental group, in 1957 to provide accompaniment for the growing number of rock'n'roll package tours crisscrossing Britain. An established arranger, he was also responsible for the pizzicato strings that made **Adam Faith**'s early records so distinctive. These can also be heard to good effect on 'Hit and Miss' (Columbia UK, 1960), the theme to the BBC's influential *Juke Box Jury* programme and a British Top Ten record for the John Barry Seven, one of the numerous minor hits the group had before Barry folded it in 1962.

His first film work was the score for *Beat Girl* (1959), which co-starred Faith. Five years later **Shirley Bassey** had a million-seller with her recording of the title song to *Goldfinger* (1964), which Barry wrote in collaboration with **Anthony Newley** and Leslie Bricusse. However, Barry's film work is far more varied than his close association with the Bond films might suggest. It includes *Born Free* (1966), the title song of which – written with lyricist Don Black – won an Oscar for Best Song and was an American Top Ten hit for pianist Roger Williams in 1966; the romantic, yet spare, score for *The Lion in Winter* (1968), which gave Barry a second Oscar; the elegiac Western *Monte Walsh* (1969); *The Day of the Locust* (1974); *King Kong* (1976); *The Black Hole* (1979); and *Out of Africa* (1985), which won Barry his third Oscar. In 1986 he scored the Francis Ford Coppola back-to-the-fifties film *Peggy Sue Got Married*, and in 1990 had a hit with the soundtrack to the award-winning *Dances with Wolves*, for which he won an Oscar. He wrote the music for the hit film *Indecent Proposal* (1993) and in the same year recorded *Moviola* (Epic), a collection of his non-Bond film themes. In the late nineties the revived interests in easy listening music and all things Bond culminated in renewed interest

in Barry's work and in the celebratory album *The Music of John Barry* (1999).

Barry has lived in America since 1970.

LIONEL BART
b. Lionel Begleiter, 1 August 1930, London, England, d. 3 April 1999, London

In the early sixties Bart, almost single-handedly, brought about a revolution in stage musicals similar to that wrought by **The Beatles** in the world of pop music or a decade earlier by the 'Angry Young Men' in the world of British theatre.

The youngest son of a family of Jewish immigrants, after completing his national service he joined the Communist Party and in the early fifties developed his theatrical skills writing cabaret-styled revues for the party's International Youth Group. Early shows included the tale of Robin Hood, told in the manner of Dostoevsky, and an agit-prop *Cinderella* for the Unity Theatre. His first fully fledged musical was a Ben Jonson take-off, *Willy Pone King of the Underworld*. Then, in 1956, Bart formed one of the first British skiffle bands with friends Mike Pratt and **Tommy Steele**. When Steele was signed to Decca and turned (briefly) into a rock'n'roller, the trio wrote Steele's early hits rather than relying on Tin Pan Alley songsmiths. These included 'Rock with the Cavemen' (1956), 'Water, Water' and 'A Handful of Songs' (both 1957) and, most dire of all, the jaunty 'Little White Bull' (1959), from the film *Tommy the Toreador*, which witnessed Steele's metamorphosis into an 'all-round entertainer'.

These songs were celebrated by *Absolute Beginners*' author Colin MacInnes as the first indications that rock'n'roll in Britain might produce a new kind of popular music rather than simply be inferior to, and endlessly imitative of, American models; though other Bart songs of the period, such as 'Livin' Doll'* (**Cliff Richard**'s first British chart-topper in 1959), hardly justified such claims. However, with his songs for Frank Norman's play about the Soho underworld, *Fings Ain't What They Used t'Be* (1959), Bart exceeded all expectations, producing a series of defiantly British songs, rich in cockney speech and humour. An enormous success, as was his collaboration with Laurie Johnson, *Lock up Your Daughters* (1959), *Fings* transferred to the West End, where it was soon followed by *Oliver* (1960), with book, music and lyrics by Bart.

Filmed in 1968 and one of the longest-running musicals ever staged in London, *Oliver* included a slew of memorable numbers: 'Food, Glorious Food', 'Consider Yourself', 'You've Got to Pick a Pocket or Two' and, most notably, the plaintive 'As Long as He Needs Me' (a British Top Ten hit for **Shirley Bassey** in 1960). This was followed by *Blitz* (1962), an evocation of the London of Bart's youth, that was more impressive in its staging than for its songs. By now, as one of the original creators of 'Swinging London', a media celebrity, his subsequent musicals, which included *Maggie May* (1964) and a return to the Robin Hood story with *Twang!!* (1965), all failed. Bart had invested his own money in them and went bankrupt as a result.

In 1969 Bart wrote *La Strada* which ran briefly in New York and in 1972 he contributed songs to *The Londoners* and *Costa Packet*. He returned in 1989 with 'Happy Endings' (EMI), his version of a song originally written for a TV commercial. In 1994 Cameron Mackintosh produced a lush revival of *Oliver* that seemed to be inspired more by the film than the musical. It was critically mauled but a commercial success. In the same year David Roper published his unauthorized biography, *Bart*.

DAVE BARTHOLOMEW
b. 24 December 1920, Edgard, Louisiana, USA

Trumpeter and bandleader Bartholomew was a powerful figure in New Orleans music in the forties and fifties. He co-wrote and arranged numerous hits for **Fats Domino**, and the shuffling rhythms of the Domino–Bartholomew sound were a potent influence on the development of Jamaican popular music.

The son of a noted Dixieland tuba player, Bartholomew played with Fats Pichon's riverboat jazz band until he was conscripted in 1942. On his return to New Orleans, he created one of the city's leading rhythm and blues bands, featuring drummer Earl Palmer and saxophonists Herb Hardesty and Alvin Tyler. He first recorded for David and Julius Braund's De Luxe label in 1947. An early R&B hit was 'Country Boy' (1949), recorded the year he was hired by Lew Chudd of Imperial to find and record New Orleans talent.

Bartholomew stayed with the label as A&R man, songwriter, arranger and producer until its sale to Liberty in 1963. The first of many hits were Jewel King's '3 × 7=21' (1950) and Domino's 'The Fat Man', whose mix of jump blues and Dixieland jazz set the pattern for much of Domino's recording success. Bartholomew also produced **Lloyd Price**'s 'Lawdy Miss Clawdy' (1952) and **Shirley and Lee**'s 'Let the Good Times Roll' (1956), and co-wrote 'I Hear You Knockin'' (1955) for **Smiley Lewis** (the song was revived in 1970 by **Dave Edmunds**).

The majority of Imperial's hits, however, came from Domino, most of whose songs were co-written with Bartholomew. Among the best known were 'Ain't That a Shame', 'I'm in Love Again', 'Blue Monday', 'I'm Walkin'', 'Walking to New Orleans' (on which Bartholomew introduced a shimmering string sec-

tion), and 'Let the Four Winds Blow'. Bartholomew also directed Domino's session and touring band, whose members included Hardesty, Palmer and drummer Walter Nelson.

Other Imperial artists produced by Bartholomew in the late fifties and early sixties included **Frankie Ford**, **Snooks Eaglin** and R&B guitarist Earl King. Among his own recordings were an early version of 'My Ding a Ling' (King, 1951), which **Chuck Berry** took to No.1 in 1972, and such instrumentals as 'The Monkey' (1957), which had a great impact in Jamaica, lending their relaxed rhythms to the evolution of ska music.

The partnership with Domino was broken when the singer moved to ABC but was briefly resumed in 1967 when the two formed the shortlived Broadmoor label. During later years, Bartholomew was in semi-retirement although he led Domino's touring band to Europe on occasion and in 1981 released an album of Dixieland jazz.

In 1992 EMI released a two-CD set, *Spirit of New Orleans*, devoted to his productions and recordings for Imperial that confirmed both his broad musical range and the majesty of his work with Domino.

COUNT BASIE
b. William Basie, 21 August 1904, Red Bank, New Jersey, USA, d. 26 April 1984, Hollywood, Florida

While other celebrated jazz orchestra leaders were renowned as composers or soloists, Basie spent over forty years perfecting the art of bandleading itself – the job of timing shifts of personnel and repertoire to ensure both continuity and change.

Although he formed his orchestra in 1936 in Kansas City, he had learned his piano style in Harlem from pianists like **James P. Johnson**, and Willie 'The Lion' Smith, and, above all, **Fats Waller**. Basie toured with vaudeville shows, ending up in Kansas City, where he accompanied silent movies before joining Walter Page's Blue Devils in 1927, a band whose leadership passed to Bennie Moten.

Following Moten's sudden death, the band broke up, but Basie brought together a number of its alumni in a new nine-piece group. The name 'Count' was given to him by a radio announcer who thought he deserved to rank with **Duke Ellington** and **Earl Hines**. At this point, Basie's was the top Kansas City band, bringing to perfection the powerful riffing 'territory' style, and combining it with his innovatory economical piano-playing.

Through **John Hammond**, Basie came to the notice of **Benny Goodman** and Decca recorded the band in 1936. These classic sides included 'One o'Clock Jump', later to become the band's theme tune. Featured players with this first version of the

Basie Orchestra included vocalist **Jimmy Rushing**, **Lester Young** (tenor saxophone) and Jo Jones (drums). Guitarist Freddie Green joined soon afterwards.

The unity of the rhythm section and the ensemble work of the horns in Basie's band inspired the swing music of white bands like those of Goodman and **Artie Shaw**. While those bands enjoyed wide commercial success, the Basie Orchestra toured the circuit of black dance halls and the clubs during the thirties and forties. Among its members were trumpeter Buck Clayton and **Billie Holiday**. The orchestra continued to record regularly for Columbia and topped the pop charts with 'Open the Door Richard', a 1947 novelty number featuring the singing of trumpeter Harry 'Sweets' Edison. It was also an R&B chart entry.

By 1950 financial problems had forced Basie to cut the size of his band to eight. With new composer/ arrangers Neal Hefti and Johnny Mandel, the big band was relaunched in 1952. During the fifties a succession of major soloists – including **Eddie 'Lockjaw' Davis** and Wardell Gray – kept the Basie band in the forefront of what was called mainstream jazz. The culmination of this phase was *The Atomic Mr Basie* (Roulette, 1959).

In later years, its innovatory period over, the band no longer nurtured new solo talent. Instead, after 1960, it took part in many studio collaborations with all the leading popular jazz vocalists, from **Ella Fitzgerald** to **Frank Sinatra**. At the same time Basie found a place in the show business mainstream, playing in Las Vegas and at the Royal Variety Performance.

The one new development in this last phase of his career came in the emphasis on Basie's own piano-playing. In a series of small-group recordings, he displayed solo skills which he had kept hidden for thirty years as a member of the Orchestra's rhythm section. Basie was still working up until his death.

After 1984 the orchestra continued to perform under the leadership of trumpeter Thad Jones. When Jones died in 1986, Frank Foster took over, recording *Long Live the Chief* (Denon, 1986), a Sonny Lester production which celebrated the fiftieth anniversary of the Basie band.

FONTELLA BASS
b. 3 July 1940, St Louis, Missouri, USA

An under-rated soul singer, Bass had an international hit with 'Rescue Me' before joining the avant-garde jazz group, the **Art Ensemble of Chicago**.

With a mother (Martha Bass) and grandmother who were both gospel singers, Bass's earliest musical experience was as a chapel organist. After success in a local talent contest, she was hired as a pianist for **Little Milton**'s band by its leader Oliver Sain. Touring

with Milton, Fontella Bass also began to sing.

Her first solo records were for local label Bobbin in 1961 and for **Ike Turner**'s Prann and Sonja labels. Continuing to tour with Sain when he split with Little Milton, Bass next recorded for Chess, when that company took over the bankrupt Bobbin. She had a major R&B hit in 1965 teamed with Bobby McClure on 'Don't Mess up a Good Thing', still a disco classic. Two more duet records followed before her greatest success a year later with the catchy 'Rescue Me', produced by Billy Davis, whose Motown-style arrangement was the perfect foil for Bass's singing, alternately breathy and piercing. Not only did this song top the R&B charts but it was a pop Top Ten hit in both the US and Britain. The follow-up 'Recovery' was only a minor hit.

She left Chess in 1968 and spent much of the seventies working in Europe with the Art Ensemble of Chicago. Some R&B singles were cut with Sain for Jewel/Paula and she also recorded unsuccessfully for Epic. In 1985 she returned to St Louis, appearing once more with Oliver Sain's band.

Bass is the sister of David Peaston, a soul singer who has recorded for Geffen and **Willie Mitchell**'s Waylor label. He performed with Bass and the Art Ensemble's Lester Bowie on the 1983 album *All the Magic*.

RALPH BASS
b. 1 May 1911, New York, USA, d. 1997, Nassau, Bahamas

A white New Yorker, Bass was a central figure in the evolution of R&B. He also produced many of the pioneering modern jazz records of **Charlie Parker** and others. In the fifties and sixties he moved into R&B and soul, working with such artists as **Muddy Waters**, **James Brown**, **Hank Ballard** and **Etta James**.

A former violinist in society bands, Bass went into production, supervising jazz recordings in the late thirties. He moved to Los Angeles and worked as a producer and talent scout for various labels, notably Paul Reiner's Black and White, for whom Bass made the hit 'Open the Door Richard' (1947) by Jack McVea. Bass also supervised jazz sessions for his own Bop and Portrait labels by **Erroll Garner**, Parker and **Dizzy Gillespie** and produced the first records by the Robins (later the **Coasters**) in 1949. In addition, Bass worked for Savoy on the early hits of **Johnny Otis**, **Esther Phillips** ('Double Crossing Blues', 1950) and others.

In 1950 Bass returned to New York to work for **Syd Nathan**'s King group of labels. Appointed to run Federal, he produced records by Phillips ('Ring-a-Ding-Doo', 1952), Little Willie Littlefield and the Dominoes ('60 Minute Man', 1951; 'Have Mercy Baby'). He supervised Hank Ballard's big hit 'Work with Me

Annie' and the **Five Royales**' 'I Think' before getting co-writer credits with the group's guitarist Lowman Pauling on the classic 'Dedicated to the One I Love', later revived by the **Shirelles** (1961), **The Mamas and the Papas** (1967) and others.

He discovered James Brown in 1955, producing such early successes as the influential 'Please Please Please' (1956) and 'Try Me' (1958). Bass moved to Chicago in 1960 to work for **Leonard Chess** of Chess Records. There he recorded hits by Etta James, **Ramsey Lewis**, Muddy Waters and others. He continued to produce blues records by Magic Slim, Sunnyland Slim and others into the seventies until Chess's Chicago office was closed.

SHIRLEY BASSEY
b. 8 January 1937, Cardiff, Wales

Bassey's powerful voice and vibrant personality made her an international cabaret star.

The daughter of a West Indian seaman, Bassey began singing in local working men's clubs and joined a touring revue at the age of sixteen, before bandleader turned impresario **Jack Hylton** gave her her first West End break in the revue Such Is Life (1955). A record contract with Philips produced a trio of early hits: 'Banana Boat Song' (a cover of the **Harry Belafonte** record, 1957), 'Kiss Me Honey, Honey, Kiss Me' and 'As I Love You' (both 1959). But it was only after a move to EMI's Columbia label and the **Lionel Bart** composition 'As Long as He Needs Me' that the mature Bassey style was established. Her big, booming voice and clear, melodramatic phrasing put her in great demand as an interpreter of show and film tunes. Hits in this vein include 'Climb Ev'ry Mountain' (1961), from **Rodgers' and Hammerstein**'s The Sound of Music, 'What Now My Love?' (1962), 'What Kind of Fool Am I?' (1963), from Leslie Bricusse's and **Anthony Newley**'s Stop the World I Want to Get Off, and the theme songs to the films Goldfinger* (1964), her only major hit in America, and Diamonds Are Forever (1972).

In 1967 she joined United Artists. Despite only the occasional hit single, she continued to sell albums in a steady fashion in the wake of regular concert tours and television appearances. In 1980 she went into semi-retirement in Switzerland but returned to record and perform sporadically. One of her more unlikely collaborations was with **Yello** on 'The Rhythm Divine' (1987). Keep the Music Playing (Dino, 1991) was her first album of new material in over a decade. In 1996 she had a club hit in tandem with **Chris Rea** with the film song 'Disco: La Passione' and in 1997 returned to the UK Top Twenty in collaboration with dance act Propellerheads with 'History Repeating'. In 1999 she released the live album The Birthday Concert and returned to Wales to appear at the opening of the Rugby World Cup. A year later she sought to translate her reputation as a source of dramatic samples into a fully fledged disco diva with Diamonds Are Forever: The Remix Album, on which dance rhythms were simply bolted on to previous recordings with mixed results.

MIKE BATT
b. 6 February 1950, Southampton, Hampshire, England

A British composer, arranger and producer, Mike Batt had considerably less success with his more 'artistic' projects than with commercial commissions such as the music for the children's television series The Wombles and the haunting ballad theme from the film Watership Down, 'Bright Eyes'*.

After making his professional début as a strip-club organist, Batt became staff songwriter and then A&R manager at Liberty Records in 1968. There he produced blues singer Jo-Ann Kelly and the first album by the Groundhogs. Leaving to be an independent producer, he worked on budget-priced orchestral versions of **Beatles**' songs and on advertising jingles. His first hit was with the children's television series theme 'The Wombling Song', (CBS) which reached No. 4 in 1974. A touring band was put together, with Batt dressed as Orinoco Womble. Several hit albums followed, each a pastiche on a musical style, such as rock'n'roll, minuets and surf music. Among the Wombles' singles were 'Remember You're a Womble', 'Minuetto Allegretto' and 'Wombling White Tie and Tails' (based on **Fred Astaire**'s film musical numbers). 'Summertime City', another TV theme, was also a Top Ten hit in 1975.

Batt later made a number of ambitious (some would say pretentious) concept albums, including Schizophrenia (Epic, 1977, with the London Symphony Orchestra), Tarot Suite (1979), Waves (1980) and The Hunting of the Snark (Adventure, 1986), based on the poem by Lewis Carroll. In contrast to their modest sales, he composed hit songs for Art Garfunkel ('Bright Eyes', which spent six weeks at No. 1 in Britain in 1979), **David Essex** ('A Winter's Tale', 1982) and Alvin Stardust ('I Feel Like Buddy Holly', 1984).

In 1989 Batt produced and arranged Classic Blue (Trax) by Justin Hayward of the **Moody Blues**. It included versions of the Batt compositions 'Bright Eyes' and 'Railway Hotel'. In 1992 he unsuccessfully mounted in London a musical version of Lewis Carroll's The Hunting of the Snark.

JOE BATTEN
b. 1885, London, England, d. 18 April 1955, London

With **Fred Gaisberg**, a pioneer record producer, Batten began his career in 1900 as an accompanist on cylinder recordings for Musiphone.

A self-taught pianist, the young Batten accompanied his father Albert, a comedian and balladeer, on his music-hall appearances for two years before setting up as a pianist and piano teacher in his own right. During the first decades of the twentieth century, when London was a key recording centre of popular music, Batten worked as an accompanist and recording director for some forty record companies. He recorded patriotic songs, marching bands, opera singers and leading balladeers of the day. Among those with whom he worked were **Peter Dawson**, **Stanley Kirkby**, **John McCormack** and **Harry Lauder**. In the twenties he helped build up a catalogue of classical music for Edison Bell, including the first complete recording of Elgar's *Dream of Gerontius* (1923), made at a time when the limited length of 78 r.p.m. records had made abridged versions of classical music the norm. In 1927 Batten joined Columbia Records as recording director where, in addition to overseeing most of the company's classical recordings, he worked with numerous British dance bands, including those of **Geraldo**, **Jack Payne** and Carroll Gibbons, and organized several original cast recordings of successful West End shows.

Following the merger of HMV and Columbia in 1931 to form EMI Batten set up EMI's Special Recording Department in 1935 to deal with film music, educational recordings, medical recordings, sound effects and church services, all of which helped extend the range of material found on gramophone records. During the war, with his son Bud, Batten organized the recordings of complete variety programmes which were then broadcast around the world to British troops by ENSA. Prior to his retirement from EMI in 1950, he established a network of 'sponsored' programmes on the Radio Luxemburg model which were sold throughout Australia and Canada.

His autobiography, *Joe Batten's Book*, was published posthumously in 1956. With Gaisberg's *Music on Record*, it is the most interesting account of the early days of recording.

LES BAXTER
b. 14 March 1922, Mexia, Texas, USA

Baxter is best remembered for his fifties work as an arranger, conductor and occasional hit-maker for Capitol Records.

He studied piano at Detroit Conservatory and in the late thirties moved to Hollywood where he found work as a member of Freddie Slack's band, as an arranger, and as one of **Mel Tormé**'s Mel-Tones vocal group. Signed to Capitol in 1950, he provided the orchestral accompaniment and arrangements for **Nat 'King' Cole**'s million-selling discs 'Mona Lisa' (1950) and 'Too Young' (1951). As a conductor his success began with 'Because of You' (1951, a bigger hit for **Tony Bennett**), 'Blue Tango' (1952), 'April in Portugal' (1953) and 'The Theme from the High and the Mighty' (1954). His biggest hits were 'Unchained Melody'* (1955), which also was a million-seller for **Al Hibbler**, and 'The Poor People of Paris'* (1956). In the early sixties he formed the commercial folk group Les Baxter's Balladeers. With David Crosby, later of the **Byrds** and **Crosby, Stills and Nash**, among its members, the group recorded unsuccessfully for **Frank Sinatra**'s Reprise label.

Most of Baxter's work was film related, but 'Paris' was an example of an Americanized European song. Written by Marguerite Monnot (who also wrote the music for Irma la Douce) and René Rouzaud, the song was originally a French hit for **Edith Piaf** as 'La Goulante du Pauvre Jean'. Since the end of the fifties Baxter has concentrated on writing film music, most often for director and producer Roger Corman, including *House of Usher* (1960), *The Raven* (1963), *Cry of the Banshee* (1970) and *I Escaped from Devil's Island* (1973).

THE BAY CITY ROLLERS
Derek Longmuir, b. 19 March, 1955, Edinburgh, Scotland; Alan Longmuir, b. 20 June 1953 (replaced by Ian Mitchell, b. 22 August 1958, Scotland, replaced by Pat McGlynn, b. 31 March 1958, Edinburgh); Eric Faulkner, b. 21 October 1955; Leslie McKeown, b. 12 November 1955; Stewart 'Woody' Wood, b. 25 February 1957

Briefly the pop sensation of the seventies, the Rollers, as they were nicknamed, were, like the **Osmonds**, one of the groups targeted specifically at the new generation of teenagers for whom the **Rolling Stones** were boring old men rather than excitingly dangerous.

Formed in Edinburgh in 1969 under the auspices of former bandleader turned mentor/manager Tam Paton, the Rollers honed their musical abilities reproducing Top Twenty hits in Edinburgh's clubs. The group's origins lay in the Saxons, a covers band whose members included bass-player Alan Longmuir. Paton changed the name and the personnel. Among those passing briefly through the ranks of the Bay City Rollers were Billy Lyall and David Paton who later found success as Pilot, notably with the UK hit 'January' in 1975. In 1971 the BCRs had a surprise hit with their **Jonathan King**-produced remake of the Gentrys' 1965 million-seller, 'Keep on Dancin'' (Bell). Subsequent records failed until 'Remember' (1974), the first to feature guitarist Wood and vocalist McKeown, and first of a string of hits written and produced for them by Bill Martin and **Phil Coulter**.

The subsequent successes included 'Shang-a-Lang', 'Summerlove Sensation' and 'All of Me Loves All of You' – all light, teen-orientated records. More significant than their music was the image created by Paton for the group by adapting the clothes of soccer's 'bovver boys' (including scarves and calf-length trousers) and emphasizing the group's Scottish origins with an excessive use of tartan.

A further change of producers (to Phil Wainman) and another remake (of the **Four Seasons**' 'Bye Bye Baby') won the group their first British No. 1 in 1975, and saw the beginning of fan hysteria comparable to that surrounding **The Beatles** in the early sixties. The hits and hysteria continued in the UK with 'Give a Little Love', 'Money Honey' (both 1975), 'Love Me Like I Love You' and a remake of the **Dusty Springfield** hit 'I Only Wanna Be with You' (1976). More surprisingly, they translated this British success to America in 1975, with the No. 1 'Saturday Night' (Arista), the first of six Top Thirty hits in three years (including 'Rock and Roll Love Letter', 1976, and 'You Made Me Believe in Magic', 1977).

Then, just as suddenly, the hysteria was replaced by ridicule virtually everywhere except Japan. In the eighties two versions of the Rollers existed, one fronted by McKeown and one by Faulkner, which included most of the original group. McKeown's played bars in America and elsewhere into the nineties, waiting for nostalgia to make them fashionable once more.

Faulkner's version of the band re-recorded versions of their hits for the British budget label Tring in 1993 and in 1995 they toured Japan to dwindling audiences.

NORA BAYES
b. Dora Goldberg, 1880, Joliet, Illinois, USA, d. 19 March 1928, New York

A vaudeville and Broadway star, Bayes was one of America's most successful pre-First World War recording artists.

A veteran of several touring vaudeville troupes, the deep-voiced Bayes was chosen by **Harry Von Tilzer** in 1902 to introduce his 'Down Where the Warzburger Flows' (with Tilzer himself playing the stooge to her from the balcony). The song was an immediate hit and made her a star (for many years she was called 'the Warzburger girl'). For the next five years she toured America and Europe, only returning to Broadway in 1907. Her biggest success, and the song always associated with her, came a year later when, with her second husband Jack Norworth (*b. 5 January 1879, Philadelphia, Pennsylvania, d. 9 September 1959, Laguna Beach, California*), she wrote 'Shine on Harvest Moon', which she introduced in *Follies of 1908*. Other songs Bayes introduced or made popular

in America included 'Has Anybody Here Seen Kelly?' (Victor, 1910), Richard Whiting's 'Japanese Sandman', Jack Shilkret's 'Make Believe' (Columbia, 1921) and various patriotic songs of the First World War, including **George M. Cohan**'s 'Over There' (Victor, 1917), 'The Man Who Put the Germ in Germany' and 'Someday They're Coming Home Again' (Columbia, 1918).

In the 1944 film loosely based on her life, *Shine on Harvest Moon*, she was played by Ann Sheridan and Norworth by Dennis Morgan.

THE BEACH BOYS
Brian Wilson, b. 20 June 1942, Hawthorne, California, USA; Dennis Wilson, b. 4 December 1944, Hawthorne, d. 26 December 1983, Santa Monica, California; Carl Wilson, b. 21 December 1946, Hawthorne, d. 7 February 1998, Los Angeles; Mike Love, b. 15 December 1941, Los Angeles, California; Al Jardine, b. 3 September 1943, Lima, Ohio; Bruce Johnston, b. 24 June 1945, Chicago, Illinois

The Beach Boys were the most commercially successful American group of the sixties. They continued recording and touring into the seventies and eighties, but compilations of early material such as *Endless Summer* (1974) – the first 'oldies' album to top the American charts – sold better than their new recordings. In the sixties, though their work grew in complexity and stature as Brian Wilson took control of their recording career, their best work, *Pet Sounds* (1966), retained the simplicity of their initial hits. Similarly, whereas their early work celebrated in great, almost sociological, detail the surf and sun leisure lifestyle of California's young, their later sixties work saw a new perspective in which (adolescent) anguish and loss of innocence (and wistful harmonies) took the place of the 'Fun, Fun, Fun' (1964) ethos (and brash harmonies) of their first hits as Brian Wilson pondered what would happen 'When I Grow Up (To Be a Man)' (1965). However, though these different perspectives can be isolated for the purposes of analysis, as Michael Wood has pointed out, 'the sad beauty of the Beach Boys' stems from the fact that 'there is a strange melancholy even in the early energetic songs, a note of mourning as they sing of the happy days a-surfin''. After *Pet Sounds*, the group had success with such intricate productions as 'Good Vibrations'* (1966) and 'Heroes and Villains' (1967) but, when Brian Wilson lapsed into writing alternately frivolous and over-ambitious (and largely unfinished) productions that puzzled rather than pleased audiences, the group were unable to find a way forward and drifted into semi-mystical songs – several of the group were believers in transcendental meditation – and hugely enjoyable, but derivative, reworkings of their earlier hits ('Do It Again', 1968).

Raised in a middle-class suburb of Los Angeles, the Wilson brothers, their cousin Love and friend Jardine performed variously as Kenny and the Cadets, Carl and the Passions (later an album title, 1972) and the Pendletones (in honour of the plaid shirt popular with California surfers) before recording 'Surfin' at the suggestion of Dennis Wilson in 1961. One of the first surfing songs (earlier recordings by such artists as Dick Dale and the Deltones – 'Let's Go Trippin'', Del-Tone, 1961 – had been instrumentals), the record made the lower reaches of the charts on Candix. Signed to Capitol in 1962 by Nick Venet, the group had immediate success with their hymns to sea, sand and cars: 'Surfin' Safari', 'Surfin' U.S.A.' (1963), a reworking of **Chuck Berry**'s 'Sweet Little Sixteen' in which the thought 'If everybody had an ocean' was offered as the solution to all teenage frustrations, and 'Little Deuce Coupe' from *Surfer Girl* (1963), the group's third album and the first to be produced by Brian. On these hits the group's driving harmonies were led by Love's nasal voice, but 'In My Room', also from *Surfer Girl*, and the wistful 'Don't Worry Baby' (1964) featured Brian's plangent falsetto and the beginnings of his melancholic romanticism. For the most part, this aspect was heard only on album cuts, while for the singles Brian produced a series of anthemic fantasies about the endless summer of California teenagers: 'Fun, Fun, Fun', 'I Get Around'*, the group's first No. 1 (though in 1963 Brian had co-authored and sung backing vocals on **Jan and Dean**'s No. 1 'Surf City'), 'Dance Dance, Dance' (1964), 'Help Me Rhonda' (another No. 1) and 'California Girls' (1965).

By the time of *The Beach Boys Today* and *Summer Days (and Summer Nights)* (1965), the group's approach was clearly schizophrenic, alternately rousing, on the singles, and delicate, on Brian's idealized accounts of romantic relationships ('Please Let Me Wonder', 'You're So Good to Me' and the *a cappella* fragment 'And Your Dream Comes True') on which the harmonies owed more to the **Four Freshmen** than the muscularity of the **Four Seasons**. Another feature of the albums was their sophisticated production, as Brian, under the influence of **Phil Spector**, found increasingly novel and unusual ways to showcase the densely layered vocal sound of the group. With **The Beatles** and the **Byrds**, Brian was in the forefront of the studio experimentation that dominated much of sixties rock. After almost losing his hearing in one ear in 1964 Brian had stopped touring with the group and spent even more time in the studio. He was replaced temporarily by **Glen Campbell** and then permanently by Johnston, who had recorded, with **Doris Day**'s son and future producer Terry Melcher as Bruce and Terry, 'Summer Means Fun' (Columbia, 1964).

The climax of this phase of the Beach Boys' career was *Pet Sounds*, created virtually single-handedly by Brian while the group were on tour. With lyricist Tony Asher, whose words tumbled around the melodies rather than propelled them, Brian fashioned a collection of songs encased in dreamily ethereal arrangements in which hope ('Wouldn't It Be Nice') gave way to puzzlement ('God Only Knows') and finally weary resignation ('I Just Wasn't Made for These Times'). Despite poor sales, the album's critical acclaim and the success of 'Good Vibrations', the group's first experiment with wholesale over-dubbing, led Brian to attempt a more ambitious realization of his concerns. In partnership with **Van Dyke Parks** he started work on the legendary *Smile* album. Never completed, due to Brian's growing drug dependency and the mental instability which would limit his contribution to the Beach Boys for much of the next ten years, tracks from it (notably the overwrought 'Surf's Up' and 'Cabinessence') appeared on subsequent albums.

Brian's diminished role within the group was marked by the production of *Smiley Smile* (1967) being credited to the Beach Boys. The group's hits continued on a lesser scale ('Wild Honey', 1967; 'Darlin'', 1968; a revival of the **Ronettes**' 'I Can Hear Music', 1969 – all songs harking back to the surfing era) but though they continued to release two albums a year and established their own Brother label, they turned increasingly to live performance, a move which further stranded them among their 'greatest hits'. They briefly recruited Ricky Fataar and Blondie Chaplin from the South African group Flame, whose eponymous début album (Brother, 1970) Carl Wilson, now emerging as the guiding light of the group, had produced. *Holland* (1972) included the affecting 'Sail on Sailor' (and an EP containing a fairy story written by Brian). By 1974, with Brian better known for his inactivity and erratic behaviour, and their biggest hits being the live recording *The Beach Boys in Concert* and the compilation album *Endless Summer*, the group seemed a spent force. Brian's own best work of this period was his production of the eponymous album of American Spring (UA, 1972), the group comprising Diane Rovell and her sister Marilyn (Brian's wife) who had previously recorded as the Rovells and the Honeys and had sung back-up vocals on many Beach Boys recordings. Tracks like 'This Whole World' and 'Forever' briefly recaptured the tone of *Pet Sounds*.

The group's commercial renaissance came with *15 Big Ones* (1976), on which they revived songs not associated with them. Among them were Chuck Berry's 'Rock and Roll Music', which gave the group its first Top Ten hit for a decade, the **Five Satins**' 'In the Still of the Night' and **Fats Domino**'s 'Blueberry

Hill'. But though Brian was once again contributing to the group, their new recordings took second place to their role as one of America's premier touring acts. Hits of this period included 'Good Timin'' (on their own Caribou label, 1979), a revival of the **Del-Vikings**' 'Come Go with Me' (1981) and 'Getcha Back' (1985). In 1988 the group had another American No. 1 with 'Kokomo' (Geffen), which was featured in the film *Cocktail*. It was produced by Terry Melcher and co-written by John Phillips of **The Mamas and the Papas**.

In 1992 the band released the unexceptional *Summer in Paradise*, their first studio album in seven years, on their own Brother records label.

From the late seventies onwards the members of the group began issuing solo records. Johnston's *Going Public* (1977) included a superior reworking of the evocative 'Disney Girls' and his own 'I Write the Songs', an American No. 1 for **Barry Manilow** (1975), and he produced albums by Terry Melcher and **Barry Mann**, among others. Dennis and Carl Wilson and Mike Love all made solo albums with only limited success. More surprising was Brian Wilson who in 1988, after some two years of work under the direction of his personal physician (and personal manager) Dr Eugene Landy, released the engaging, if eccentric, *Brian Wilson* (Sire), which musically picked up where *Pet Sounds* had left off.

However, legal battles soured the atmosphere around the Beach Boys in the nineties. In 1990 the group sued Wilson and Landy and in 1991 Mike Love sued Steven Gaines, author of *Heroes and Villains*, a biography of the group. Both cases were settled out of court, only for another suit to erupt in 1994 between Brian Wilson and Mike Love over the writing credits on seventy-nine of the group's songs. That was won by Love. In 1995 **Don Was** directed an affectionate documentary about Wilson, *I Just Wasn't Made for These Times*, and Capitol prepared to issue an assemblage of the legendary *Smile* album. Wilson also appeared on recordings by Van Dyke Parks, notably the critically well-received *Orange Crate Art* (1995), and Rob Wasserman, where he duetted with his daughter Carnie (b. 29 April 1968, Los Angeles). In 1989 she formed the vocal group Wilson Phillips with her sister Wendy (b. 16 October 1969, Los Angeles) and Chynna Phillips (b. 12 February 1968, Los Angeles), the daughter of **Mamas and Papas** members John and Michelle Phillips. For three years the trio enjoyed considerable success with such hits as 'Hold on', 'Release Me' and 'You Won't See Me Cry', all on SKB.

Wilson's reflective *Imagination* (Geffen, 1998) was an interesting addition to the singer's cannon of (teenage) angst. More intriguing was the brief live tour mounted in conjunction with Parks in which, supported by an orchestra, he offered readings of Beach Boys classics. Even more successful was *Live at the Roxy Theatre* (Brimel, 2000), in which with a band and back-up singer he re-created the feel of the Beach Boys' studio recordings. In the manner of the fashion of the times, it was first made available online from Brian Wilson's website. However, successful though these were, the best of his and the group's later albums was the four-CD set *The Pet Sounds Sessions* (1997), from which one could piece together the creation of what is now clearly the group's finest moment. The decade saw the brothers and group members return to the courts as the group's name was contested by various parties.

BEASTIE BOYS
King Ad-Rock, b. Adam Horovitz, 31 October 1966, New York City, USA; MCA, b. Adam Yauch, 15 August 1967, New York City; Mike D, b. Michael Diamond, 20 November 1965, New York City

Among the earliest hip-hop artists to gain notoriety, the Beastie Boys were also among the most successful white exponents of the genre. However, despite the punky white brat image which earned them international notoriety, the Beastie Boys' later recordings demonstrated a funky sensibility to rival any of their peers in 1990s hip-hop.

The trio first sang together while still at school, playing hardcore punk music in 1981 and recording the mini-album *PollyWog Stew* for a local independent label. These early tracks were reissued in 1994 as *Some Old Bullshit*.

By 1983 their style was incorporating rap influences and they added DJ Double RR as an on-stage disc-jockey to the line-up. The following year Double RR, aka **Rick Rubin**, formed his Def Jam label and issued a Beastie Boys single, 'Rock Hard'. The group next appeared in the rap movie *Krush Groove* and toured as support to **Madonna**. The first Beastie Boys album, *Licensed to Ill*, topped the US charts in 1987. It featured the raucous Top Ten hit '(You Gotta) Fight for Your Right (To Party)', as anthemic in its way as **Alice Cooper**'s 'School's Out'. Other hits from the album were 'No Sleep Till Brooklyn' and 'She's on It'.

The same year, the group's UK appearances led to disturbances at their concerts and to a short-lived craze for stealing emblems from Volkswagen cars after fans noticed that the trio wore VW medallions.

The Beastie Boys' career was in abeyance in 1988 in the wake of a dispute over royalties with Def Jam. During this period Horovitz played his first film roles in *Santa Ana Project* and *Lost Angels*.

In 1989 they moved to the Capitol label releasing *Paul's Boutique*, which showed their familiarity with a wide range of popular culture and was produced by the New York team the Dust Brothers (Matt Dike,

John King and Mike Simpson). *Check Your Head*, on which the group played their own instruments for the first time, was released in 1992.That was only a minor hit but it was followed after a lengthy delay by the superior *Ill Communication* (1994) on the group's own Grand Royal label, which was an enormous international hit and confirmed the group's ability to match their sound to the times with its spare, tough bass-heavy sound. Later signings to their Grand Royal label would include Sean Lennon, son of deceased former **Beatle** John Lennon.

Hello Nasty (1998), their first studio album in four years, was a huge success, débuting at No. 1 in the US in the *Billboard* charts and confirming the group's status as the most inventive of white rappers. It featured the hits 'Hold It Now Hit It' and 'Intergalactic'. A critical success as well, the album won praise not only for the band's lyrical science but also, surprisingly given their past, for its high production standards. Earlier they had released *The Inside from Way Out* (1996), a collection of funk instrumentals culled from the sessions for their previous two albums, through their fan club. In 1999 they took this a stage further, promoting their recordings and tours through Internet downloads. Initially their record company attempted to stop them 'giving away' recordings but later in the year, as the success of the promotions became clear, they joined forces with the group, offering purchasers the choice of the group's recordings in the form of an individualized *Best of*, which could be ordered online, custom pressed and mailed to them. The offer was made alongside the release of the two-CD retrospective *The Sounds of Science*, which was one of the bestselling records of 1999 in the US.

THE BEATLES

Pete Best, b. 1941, Liverpool, England (replaced by Ringo Starr, b. Richard Starkey, 7 July 1940, Liverpool); George Harrison, b. 25 February 1943, Liverpool); John Winston Lennon, b. 9 October 1940, Liverpool, d. 8 December 1980, New York, USA; James Paul McCartney, b. 18 June 1942, Liverpool; Stuart Sutcliffe, b. 1940, Edinburgh, Scotland, d. 10 April 1962, Hamburg, Germany

If greatness is measured in terms of commercial success and popularity, The Beatles are the greatest popular musicians of the century. Moreover, the changes in the music industry wrought by their success make it unlikely that their impact will be surpassed. Their artistic significance, however, is less certain. The musical genius of The Beatles lay less in innovation than in the ability to produce a synthesis of many pre-existing styles. In the end, it may be as songwriters rather than recording artists that they will best be remembered.

The group evolved from the Quarrymen, a band formed by Lennon with classmates at Quarry Bank high school in 1956. Unlike most of the skiffle groups of the era, whose repertoire was more folk-orientated, Lennon's band concentrated on rock'n'roll material like **Buddy Holly**'s 'That'll Be the Day' and **Gene Vincent**'s 'Be Bop a Lula', and reflected Lennon's adulation of **Elvis Presley**. In 1957 Lennon was introduced to the fourteen-year-old McCartney, who impressed him both with his musical knowledge and by the fact that he was already writing his own songs.

McCartney joined the group and soon began to compose with Lennon. Among their earliest collaborations were 'One After 909' (recorded in 1969 for the *Let It Be* album) and 'Hello Little Girl', a later hit for the Liverpool group, the Fourmost (Parlophone, 1963). At this early stage it was agreed that all compositions would be credited to Lennon–McCartney, even where only one of the them had been involved. By the time the first Beatles record was made, the pair had written more than eighty songs.

Before then, the Quarrymen had undergone several transformations. In 1958 Harrison joined on guitar and the following year a fellow student of Lennon's at Liverpool Art College, Sutcliffe, was enlisted on bass. The four-piece, drummerless band took part in a talent contest in Manchester in 1959 as Johnny and the Moondogs. Next they became the Silver Beetles, and finally The Beatles as they got their first regular gigs, playing lunchtime sessions at Liverpool's Jacaranda Club.

By this time, the Merseybeat style of guitar-based rock was evolving although The Beatles were not yet among the leading bands. The decisive stage of their development was a five-month period of work in Hamburg during 1960. A semi-professional band – Best had now been recruited on drums – they had to perform lengthy sets each day. Encouraged by the German club-owners to 'mak show' – put on a dynamic stage show – The Beatles turned themselves into a tightly knit, professional beat group, combining rock standards with their own songs.

Back in Liverpool, The Beatles soon gained the regular lunchtime spot at the Cavern and galvanized audiences. By the end of 1961, they had been voted top local band by the readers of the magazine *Mersey Beat* and had attended their first recording session: in Hamburg they backed singer Tony Sheridan on the traditional 'My Bonnie' on a Polydor session produced by **Bert Kaempfert**. They also recorded several titles themselves, including the old **Eddie Cantor** song 'Ain't She Sweet'. It was a request for 'My Bonnie' (credited to Tony Sheridan and the Beat Brothers) which attracted the attention of the manager of NEMS, Liverpool's leading record store. Brian Epstein soon became the group's manager and set about finding them a recording contract.

The demo tape – of rock standards rather than Lennon–McCartney songs – was turned down by four A&R men, because 'guitar groups are out of date'. Rejected, the group returned to Hamburg for the last time. This period of their development is documented on the live album *Rockin' at the Star Club*, recorded on their final Hamburg night, 31 December 1962. Released by Sony in 1991 after a lengthy legal dispute, the crude recording captures the raw power of The Beatles in performance and an early version of 'I Saw Her Standing There'.

Back in England the group was eventually signed by **George Martin** to EMI's Parlophone label, which was best known for comedy and novelty recordings. By this time Sutcliffe had left the band, deciding to stay in Hamburg to pursue his art studies (he died there of a brain haemorrhage). Sutcliffe's life and the Hamburg performances were the subject of the 1994 film *Backbeat*. With musical direction by **Don Was**, the sound of the early Beatles was re-created by a band including guitarist Thurston Moore (**Sonic Youth**), singer Greg Dulli (**Afghan Whigs**), R.E.M. bassist Mike Mills and **Nirvana** drummer Dave Grohl.

Martin provoked a further personnel change by insisting to Epstein that Best was not equipped to play on record. In 1962 he was replaced by Starr, the drummer from Rory Storme and the Hurricanes, who had in fact recorded with The Beatles on the privately made version of **George Gershwin**'s 'Summertime', sung by Storme's guitarist, Wally Eymond.

The first Beatles single, 'Love Me Do' was released in the autumn of 1962 and was a minor hit. It featured close harmonies influenced by the **Everly Brothers** and a harmonica solo by Lennon. With the next record, 'Please Please Me', the characteristic Beatles style was forged: the soaring falsetto harmonies, underlined by Harrison's lead guitar work, combined with simple yet precise love lyrics. Oddly, this major hit spent seven weeks in the British Top Five without topping the charts. However, the 'Fab Four' as the group had now been dubbed by the media, made up for it by reaching No. 1 three times in 1963. The songs were 'From Me to You', 'She Loves You' and 'I Wanna Hold Your Hand'*. The Beatles also had two No. 1 albums in that year. The first was *Please Please Me*. Beginning with the count in of '1 2 3 4' and ending with the 'rave-up' number 'Twist and Shout' (learned from the **Isley Brothers**), this captured the sound and spirit of the group's live Merseybeat performances and was recorded in only six hours. The earlier selections from *Live at the BBC* (1994), a collection of fifty-plus recordings made for the BBC radio programmes between 1962 and 1965, demonstrated the eclectic view The Beatles had of rock'n'roll.

Among the tracks were the **Coasters**' 'Young Blood', several **Carl Perkins** songs, **Johnny Burnette**'s 'Lonesome Tears in My Eyes', the obscure 'Clarabella', by former members of **Bill Haley**'s Comets, the Joolimars, as well as songs associated with **Chuck Berry** and **Little Richard**. The recordings (and the jokey asides) also confirmed the group's spirited approach to performance.

The second album, *With the Beatles*, also combined group originals with rock and R&B songs, including Barrett Strong's 'Money'. The same year saw 'She Loves You'*, their third UK No. 1 of 1963, which remained the biggest-selling single in Britain until McCartney's 'Mull of Kintyre'* in 1977.

By the end of 1963 The Beatles were the most popular artists all over Europe, setting fashions in hairstyles and clothing with their 'mop-tops' and collarless Beatle jackets, as well as selling records. But they had made no impact in the United States, mainly because EMI's American label, Capitol, refused to release their records, believing that nothing British would be successful in the US. The first four singles were thus issued by small labels, Vee-Jay and Swan. It was not until Epstein persuaded Ed Sullivan to feature the group on his network television show that Capitol agreed to release the fifth single, 'I Wanna Hold Your Hand'. Within a month it was No. 1 and with the re-release of the earlier singles, The Beatles had the top five places in the charts in March 1964, while even their Hamburg efforts made the charts, with 'My Bonnie' released by MGM and 'Ain't She Sweet' by Atco.

The next two years were the high point of 'Beatlemania'. The group undertook world tours and played to packed audiences which screamed so loud that none of The Beatles could hear himself play or sing. By the time they played what was to be their last public performance (in San Francisco on 28 August 1966), The Beatles had scored eight further No. 1 singles in the US including 'Can't Buy Me Love'* (1964), 'I Feel Fine'* and 'We Can Work It Out'* (1965) and 'Paperback Writer'* (1966). They had also made two critically acclaimed films by Dick Lester (*A Hard Day's Night*, 1964, and *Help!*, 1965) and released five further albums – *Beatles for Sale* (1964), *Rubber Soul* (1965) and *Revolver* (1966), in addition to the soundtracks. The Beatles had made fortunes for EMI, their music publishers (who included **Dick James**), and for the merchandizing company to whom the inexperienced Epstein had given ninety per cent of the income from Beatle wigs, dolls, and so on.

During those two years, too, their music underwent important changes. By now they had used the best of their pre-fame songs and were composing in a totally new environment. It was one in which their success virtually insulated them from the outside world but also one in which they were intensely aware of other developments in pop. Whether due to Dylan, dope, or both, from *Rubber Soul* onwards the songs of Lennon, in particular, show a greater self-consciousness about language. On that album, he contributed the elegiac 'In My Life' and the Dylanesque, comic 'Norwegian Wood'. It was in this period, too, that McCartney reached his peak as the consummate rock balladeer. His best songs were sad ones: 'Yesterday', 'Eleanor Rigby' and the under-rated 'For No One' (from *Revolver*).

Nor were The Beatles uninfluenced by cultural developments in the mid-sixties. Lennon's controversial remark of March 1966, that 'The Beatles are more popular than Jesus', was the harbinger of a hectic couple of years in which the group adopted with enthusiasm many of the tenets of 'flower-power' and the 'underground' while remaining essentially purveyors of the well-crafted three-minute song.

At this period, too, they were able to slow down the rate at which they were expected to produce new recordings. There was a year's gap between *Revolver* and the next album, *Sgt Pepper's Lonely Hearts Club Band* (1967). The new record and the remarkable single which combined Lennon's trance-like 'Strawberry Fields Forever' with McCartney's whimsical 'Penny Lane'* were products of the now widespread fascination of rock musicians with studio technology. Here, Martin played a vital role in translating the band's imaginative flights into unusual instrumentation and ingenious manipulation of tapes. Equally, as critics pointed out, these songs were the summation of a quirky, hothouse Englishness in the work of both Lennon and McCartney. Penny Lane and Strawberry Fields are both Liverpool place names, while the uniting concept of *Sgt Pepper* was an idealized North Country brass band, an image which also figured in the cartoon film *Yellow Submarine* (1969). While these nostalgic Anglicisms were impressively fused with a flower-power sensibility, much of The Beatles' work of this period, notably the widely criticized *Magical Mystery Tour* (1967), a quirky film made for television, now seems heavily dated, an historical curio which evokes an era without going beyond it.

In 1967 the band became followers of the Maharishi Mahesh Yogi and Epstein died. Though there were to be three more albums – *The Beatles* (aka *The White Album*) in 1968, *Abbey Road*, which took its name from the EMI recording studios, in 1969, and the **Phil Spector**-produced *Let It Be* (1970) – the group was no longer the cohesive unit which had soared to fame. This was clearly evident in the documentary film *Let It Be* (1970), which showed the making of that album. Of the songs from the final phase of the group's life, McCartney wrote twenty-three, Lennon twenty-two and Harrison eight (including his first hit, 'Some-

thing'*). All were solo efforts, as was much of the playing on the albums. These records did, however, produce a slew of classic songs, including 'I'm So Tired', 'Something', 'Here Comes the Sun', 'Get Back' and 'Let It Be'*.

From 1968 onwards The Beatles began to disintegrate in a slow, painful manner. To start with, they declared their economic independence by setting up Apple Corps, a kind of hippie capitalist enterprise designed to encourage creative projects of all kinds, but centred on a record label. Though Apple released **James Taylor**'s début album and successful records by **Mary Hopkin** and Badfinger, whose Top Ten hits included 'Come and Get It' (1970) and 'No Matter What' (1971), its disastrous financial management only compounded the business problems left by Epstein's death. Dick James also deserted, by choosing to sell his part of Northern Songs to Lew Grade's ATV rather than to Lennon and McCartney. In 1984 the catalogue was bought by **Michael Jackson**.

Meanwhile, already distanced by Lennon's relationship with **Yoko Ono**, McCartney and Lennon themselves were in dispute as to who should be brought in to salvage The Beatles' fortunes. McCartney favoured Lee Eastman, the father of his future wife Linda, while the other three Beatles preferred Allen Klein of ABCKO, a tough lawyer who had recently become the **Rolling Stones**' manager. Klein subsequently renegotiated the EMI contract, gaining a higher royalty rate. He also persuaded Lennon, Harrison and Starr to accept the principle of 'greatest hits' albums, something Epstein had strenuously opposed.

In later years, several re-releases of this type netted large sales, notably the so-called *Red* and *Blue* singles collections. In 1993 the *Red* and *Blue* albums became the last of The Beatles catalogue to be issued on CD. Their reissue had been delayed by a lengthy dispute between EMI and Apple.

Although the group members remained owners of Apple, their business partnership as individuals had formally ended when McCartney sought a court order to dissolve the group in 1970. But the artistic split had already happened. All four members went on in the next two decades to develop widely differing solo careers, which are detailed under each individual's name elsewhere in this book. In 1994 the remaining members of the group came together to record new instrumental tracks for a Beatles video documentary series, overseen by George Martin. In 1995 EMI/Apple released *Anthology*. A two-CD, 26-track album, it contained raw skiffle recordings ('That'll Be the Day') and unreleased tracks from 1956 to 1964, and confirmed both the power of the group at its youthful best and its development from an energetic performing unit to a skilled recording band. Less successful was 'Free as a Bird', on which the original group members added instrumentation to a Lennon demo track. *Anthology* was a huge commercial success and was followed by *Anthology 2*, which covered the period between 1965 and 1968, and also included another 'completed' Lennon song, 'Real Love', and *Anthology 3* (both 1996). Also commercial successes, their main point of critical interest was in showing how quickly the individual Beatles took control of their individual recordings. Moreover, in contrast to the **Beach Boys** set devoted to the making of *Pet Sounds* (*The Pet Sounds Sessions*, Capitol, 1997) where the individual tracks could be seen as the building blocks of the finished recordings, the out-takes and alternatives offered on *Anthology 2* and *3* were largely just that – alternatives. In 1999 EMI/Apple continued their plundering of The Beatles archives with a reissue of the *Yellow Submarine* soundtrack. Before that, producer Martin released *In My Life* (Echo, 1998), which included readings of (Martin-produced) Beatles songs by the likes of **Céline Dion** and Sean Connery, among others.

BEAUTIFUL SOUTH
Paul Heaton, b. 9 May 1962, Birkenhead, Lancashire, England; David Hemmingway, b. 20 September 1960; Briana Corrigan (replaced by Jacqueline Abbott); David Rotheray, b. 9 February 1961, Hull; David Stead; Sean Welch, b. 12 April 1960, Enfield, Middlesex

Generally unfashionable in the contemporary British pop world, despite the popularity of their pop/soul ballads, which often treated social and political themes, the Beautiful South is in many ways an extension of Heaton's former group, the Housemartins.

Guitarist, singer and songwriter Heaton formed the Housemartins in Hull in 1984 with guitarist Stan Cullimore (*b. 6 April 1962*) and drummer Hugh Whittaker. By the time of their first recording, 'Sheep', the band included ex-club DJ Norman Cook (aka **Fatboy Slim**, *b. Quentin Cook, 31 July 1963*) on bass.

Between 1986 and 1988 the Housemartins had six Top Twenty hits in Britain, including 'Happy Hour' and the No. 1 'Caravan of Love' (both Go! Discs, 1986), a revival of the gospel song first recorded by **Isley Brother** Jasper Isley. There were three Top Ten albums, *London 0 Hull 4* (1986), *The People Who Grinned Themselves to Death* (1987) and the compilation *Now! That's What I Call Quite Good* (1988).

When the group disbanded, Cook concentrated on creating, producing and remixing dance tracks, achieving vast worldwide successes in his Fatboy Slim persona. Heaton formed the Beautiful South with Hemmingway, songwriter and vocalist Rotheray, Sean Welch, former Housemartins roadie Dave Stead on bass and drums, and singer Briana Corrigan from the Anthill Runaways. The début album *Welcome to the Beautiful South* (1989) contained the big hits 'Song for

Whoever' and the British chart-topper 'A Little Time', a bleak picture of a marriage breakdown. Later albums included *Choke* (1990) with its attack on the multinational record companies 'I Think the Answer's Yes', and *0898* (1992).

Corrigan left the group before their fourth album *Miaow* (1994). Her replacement was Jacqueline Abbott but the band's sound or concerns had hardly changed. The group's greatest hits collection, the ironically titled *Carry on Up the Charts*, was one of the biggest sellers of 1994 in the UK. *Blue is the Colour* (1996) provided the band with further success, spawning the singles 'Rotterdam' and the bitter 'Don't Marry Her'. Lyrically, the album took a more sardonic approach than before, as did *Quench* (1998), which confirmed the band's reputation as one of Britain's most popular bands and included the UK Top Ten hit 'Perfect 10'.

GILBERT BECAUD
b. François Silly, 24 October 1927, Toulon, France

One of the leading *chansonniers* (singer-songwriters) of France in the fifties and sixties, Becaud's 'Et Maintenant' (1962) became an English-language standard as 'What Now My Love'.

As a youth he was a member of the Resistance and he began composing with lyricist Pierre Delanoe in 1946. Among their first successes was 'Je t'ai dans la Peau' (1950) for **Edith Piaf**. Becaud's own recording career began in 1952 when he had hits with 'Les Croix' and 'Mes Mains'. Among his other compositions were 'L'Orange', 'Nathalie' and 'Dimanche à Orly'. In 1958 his 'Le Jour où il Pluie Viendra' was an American and British hit for Jane Morgan as 'The Day the Rains Came Down' (Kapp). The following year Becaud and Delanoe wrote the opera *L'Opéra d'Aran*, which was produced in Paris. Becaud also wrote with Louis Amade and Maurice Vidalin.

Accompanied by Raymond Bernard's orchestra, Becaud's dramatic ballad 'Et Maintenant' was highly successful in France. With English lyrics by Carl Sigman, 'What Now My Love' became a hit for contrasting Anglo-Saxon artists. **Shirley Bassey**'s histrionic British Top Ten recording of 1962 was faithful to Becaud's original conception, but more divergent were Sonny and **Cher**'s duet and **Herb Alpert**'s 1966 instrumental version. In 1967 **Mitch Ryder** had a minor hit with the song, which was also covered by **Frank Sinatra**, **Barbra Streisand** and many other artists. Among other Becaud songs translated into English was 'The Importance of the Rose' with lyrics by **Rod McKuen**.

Becaud's only excursion into singing in English brought a British hit with 'A Little Love and Understanding' (Decca, 1975), which reached the Top Ten.

SIDNEY BECHET
b. 14 May 1897, New Orleans, Louisiana, USA,
d. 14 May 1959, Paris, France

Through his development of the soprano saxophone as a vehicle for improvisation, Bechet made a vital contribution to jazz. His full-blooded tone on clarinet also provided a model for later Dixieland-style players like Bob Wilber and Monty Sunshine of the **Chris Barber** band.

As a child Bechet became one of the most skilful clarinettists in New Orleans, playing in marching bands and groups led by his trombonist brother Leonard and Buddy Petit. He performed with **Bunk Johnson**'s Eagle Band before spending 1914–16 in touring bands throughout the South where, in one carnival show, he took his clarinet to pieces while continuing to play it.

On his return to New Orleans, he played with **King Oliver** whom he followed north to Chicago in 1917. He also worked in New York before touring Europe in 1919 with Will Marion Cook's Southern Syncopaters. Bechet first took up soprano saxophone in London, where he played for the Prince of Wales; that trip led to a series of visits to Europe which culminated in his decision to settle in Paris in 1951.

Bechet first recorded in 1923 with **Clarence Williams** and subsequently worked with Ford Dabney, Mamie Smith, **Duke Ellington** and **James P. Johnson** before returning to France with **Josephine Baker**'s *Revue Nègre* in 1925. He spent the next five years in Europe, touring Russia and Germany and playing with Noble Sissle in Paris.

The first significant group led by Bechet was the New Orleans Feetwarmers, which included Tommy Ladnier (cornet) and recorded such tracks as 'Blues in Thirds' and 'Nobody Knows the Way I Feel' in various sessions for Victor between 1932 and 1940. From 1934 to 1938 Bechet rejoined Sissle's orchestra, playing soprano sax on recordings of 'Polka Dot Rag' (1934) and 'Dear Old Southland' (1937), but the revival of interest in the New Orleans style in the late thirties and his appearance at **John Hammond**'s 'Spirituals to Swing' concerts in 1938 enabled him to pursue a solo career thereafter. His impassioned version of **George Gershwin**'s 'Summertime' initiated a much imitated melodic clarinet style.

After 1939 Bechet was in demand for live appearances and recording sessions. He recorded with **Jelly Roll Morton**, **Louis Armstrong**, Mezz Mezzrow (a fellow clarinettist and author of *Really the Blues*, 1946) for the latter's *King Jazz* (1945), and Albert Nicholas (Blue Note, 1946).

During the fifties Bechet became a celebrated figure in Paris, a symbol of jazz for the Left Bank intelligentsia. His records with Claude Luter's band for Vogue included the million-selling 'Les Oignons' (1949) and 'Petite Fleur' (1952), which in 1959 gave Barber's band a pop hit with Sunshine on clarinet. Bechet also recorded with visiting American musicians and appeared in the film *Blues* (1955). Bechet's autobiography *Treat It Gentle* was published in 1960, after his death from cancer.

BECK
b. Beck Hansen, 8 July 1970, Los Angeles, California, USA

An eclectic, multi-talented singer-songwriter, drawing on a variety of influences from hip-hop to folk-rock to create the quintessential example of nineties 'lo-fi' rock, typified by his 1994 hit single, 'Loser'.

The offspring of minor celebrity parents, the young Beck's environment bordered on the bohemian. The son of a bluegrass musician-turned-string arranger (for artists ranging from **Aerosmith** to **Hanson**), David Campbell, and an actress, Bibbe Hansen, Beck began to play the acoustic guitar in his teens and developed an interest in folk and blues.

After spending time in New York's East Village in the late eighties, Beck returned to LA and began to play in local bars, releasing several singles on the Bong Load record label, including 'Loser' (1993). 'Loser' was an alternative radio favourite in the US, which sparked a bidding war between the majors. Beck soon signed to DGC, who promptly put out his début album *Mellow Gold* (1994), which instantly received acclaim from a variety of sources for its assimilation of a plethora of influences from the folk-rock of **Bob Dylan** to the hip-hop sound of the **Beastie Boys**.

Before releasing an 'official' follow-up to *Mellow Gold*, Beck produced two albums for independent labels (his contract with DGC stipulated that he could release his more experimental output in this way). *Stereopathic Soul Manure* (Flipside, 1994) was a much more noisy, uncommercial-sounding album than his début, while *One Foot in the Grave* (K Records, 1994) embraced Beck's folk roots. While these two albums sold modestly, his début achieved gold status in the US.

While Beck spent much of the summer of 1995 on the Lollapalooza tour in the States, the release of his second major label album became an eagerly anticipated event. Produced by the Dust Brothers (of Beastie Boys fame), *Odelay* (1996) was more hip-hop orientated than its predecessors. It was greeted with universally exceptional reviews, topping most major album of the year polls and spawning two hit singles, 'Where It's At' and 'Devil's Haircut'. The following year Beck's contribution to the *A Life Less Ordinary* soundtrack, 'Deadweight', brought him another UK Top Ten single.

The release of *Mutations* (1998) was originally intended to be a low-key affair, distributed by Bong Load Records, but was snapped up by DGC as the official follow-up to *Odelay*. This resulted in legal action being taken by both labels and Beck briefly stopped recording. He returned to the charts with the well-received *Midnite Vultures* (DGC, 1999), which mixed old and new in his familiar manner, and returned to touring at the start of 2000.

JEFF BECK
b. 24 June 1944, Surrey, England

One of the most gifted British blues and rock guitarists, Beck's work with the **Yardbirds** influenced a generation of progressive-rock players. He later successfully led his own band with singer **Rod Stewart** but from the late seventies his career lost momentum as his recordings became infrequent.

He was inspired to take up guitar by the records of **Muddy Waters** and **Buddy Guy** and from 1963 played with Screaming Lord Sutch and in R&B groups like the Nightshift and the Tridents. In 1965 he replaced **Eric Clapton** in the Yardbirds, bringing to the group an experimental style with bent notes and fuzz-box distortion, best heard on the hits 'Heart Full of Soul' (1965) and 'Over Under Sideways Down' (1966).

Illness, as well as tension within the group when Jimmy Page became twin lead guitarist, led Beck to leave for a solo career in 1966. He formed his own group with **Rod Stewart** (vocals), Ron Wood (ex-the Birds) on bass and a variety of temporary drummers before Mickey Waller (ex-**Brian Auger**) joined. While the group made a name as a tough, exciting live act, Beck recorded a series of contrasting solo singles with producer **Mickie Most**. Written by Scott English (composer of the American Breed and Amen Corner hit 'Bend Me Shape Me' and 'Help Me Girl', an American success for the **Animals**), 'Hi Ho Silver Lining' (EMI Columbia, 1967) had a sing-along chorus combined with barbed lyrics about hippies. A Top Twenty hit in Britain, it was followed by future **10CC** member Graham Gouldman's 'Tallyman' and a faintly ludicrous version of Paul Mauriat's 'Love Is Blue' (1968). In each case the B-side was a hard-rocking blues by the Beck group, a style which permeated *Truth* (1968) and *Beck Ola* (1969). On the latter, Waller was replaced by Tony Newman (later to play with **David Bowie**) and pianist Nicky Hopkins, now a full-time group member, took a more prominent role than on the first album. Both albums reached the American Top Twenty.

The band broke up in 1969, with Hopkins and Waller returning to sessions and Stewart and Wood leaving to join the Faces. Beck was hospitalized following a road accident, and after a lengthy recupera-

tion period, recruited singer Bob Tench and keyboards-player Max Middleton to form a new Jeff Beck Group. With a line-up completed by drummer Cozy Powell and bassist Clive Chaman, they made *Rough and Ready* (Epic, 1971) and *Jeff Beck Group* (1972), the latter produced by Steve Cropper. Despite continuing success in America, Beck broke up the group in 1972 to join forces with the former **Vanilla Fudge** rhythm section as Beck, Bogart and Appice for an eponymous heavy-rock album which reached the American charts in 1973 and a subsequent *Live in Japan* album.

Beck's biggest sales came from the critically acclaimed instrumental album *Blow by Blow* (1975), produced by **George Martin**. Among the backing musicians were Philip Chen (bass) and Middleton, who went on to play with **Chris Rea** in the eighties. Like its predecessor, *Wired* (1976) displayed Beck's ability to combine solo dexterity with the heavy chording of British hard rock.

He moved further towards jazz-rock on *Jeff Beck Live with the Jan Hammer Group* (1977), the eighth Beck album to enter the American charts. For the next decade, however, Beck's activity was sporadic. He released only *There and Back* (1980) and *Flash* (1985) on which he was joined by Stewart, Hammer and producers **Arthur Baker** and **Nile Rodgers**. Despite their presence, the album left the impression of a master technician drifting from style to style. In 1989 Beck released *Guitar Shop* with Tony Hymas (keyboards) and ex-**Frank Zappa** drummer Terry Bozzio.

From the late sixties onwards, Beck was much in demand to play on other artists' albums, and he has appeared on recordings by **Donovan**, Mick Jagger, **Diana Ross**, Rod Stewart, **Tina Turner**, Roger Waters and **Stevie Wonder**, to name but a few. The boxed set *Beckology* (1992) was an acute distillation of his influential, albeit erratic, career. In 1993 he released the soundtrack to the TV mini-series *Frankie's House* (co-written with keyboards-player Jed Leiber, son of Mike Leiber of the **Leiber and Stoller** songwriting team) and an album of **Gene Vincent** songs with UK R&B revivalists the Big Town Playboys, *Crazy Legs*, a tribute to his hero, Blue Caps' guitarist Cliff Gallup. In the same year he contributed a reworking (with Seal) of 'Manic Depression' to the **Jimi Hendrix** tribute album, *Stone Free*. For much of the second half of the nineties Beck toured the US.

THE BEE GEES
Barry Gibb, b. 1 September 1946, Isle of Man, England; Robin and Maurice Gibb, b. 22 December 1949, Isle of Man

The Bee Gees enjoyed two distinct periods of stardom – as white pop stars in the late sixties and blue-eyed disco singers in the late seventies. In addition, Barry Gibb in particular enjoyed success as a writer of pop standards and as producer of recordings by such mainstream stars as **Barbra Streisand** and **Kenny Rogers**.

In 1958 the brothers emigrated from Britain to Australia with their showbusiness (bandleader and singer) parents. A Brisbane disc-jockey christened the close-harmony trio the Bee Gees and, following an appearance as support to **Chubby Checker**, they were signed by Festival Records in 1962. A string of poorly produced singles followed, mostly written by Barry. This early work was later repackaged as *Rare Precious and Beautiful* (Atco/RSO, 1968).

'Spicks and Specks' was a No. 1 in 1967, but by then the group had returned to Britain, where they were spotted by Robert Stigwood (*b. 1934, Adelaide, Australia*), the former manager of minor star John Leyton and now an executive of Brian Epstein's NEMS operation. Their first single for Polydor (Atco in the US) was 'New York Mining Disaster 1941'. It typified the Gibbs' penchant for narrative lyrics and tight, high-pitched harmonies. It reached the Top Twenty in both Britain and the US, the first of ten hits over the next two years. These included 'Massachusetts' and 'I've Gotta Get a Message to You', though the most popular with other singers was the plaintive 'To Love Somebody', memorably recorded by **Nina Simone** and **Janis Joplin**. In 1968 the brothers wrote 'Only One Woman', a UK hit for Australian group the Marbles.

Odessa (1969), the Bee Gees' attempt at a progressive album, was a commercial failure and Robin left to go solo, scoring a big hit with 'Saved by the Bell'. A reunion in 1971 produced two US million-sellers ('Lonely Days' and 'How Can You Mend a Broken Heart?' – their first American No. 1), but the group's **Beatles**-inspired approach had become outmoded. Its swansong came with the Bee Gees' contribution to the soundtrack of Lou Reisner's 1976 anti-war movie *All This and World War II*, on which they sang a selection of Lennon and McCartney numbers. A change of producer to Atlantic's **Arif Mardin** gave *Mr Natural* (1974) a recognizable soul tinge which was magnified on *Main Course* (1975), recorded at Criteria Sound, Miami. This included the disco favourite 'Jive Talkin''*, their first hit since moving to Stigwood's RSO label, as well as 'Come on Over', a hit for **Olivia Newton-John**.

New producers Criteria engineer Karl Richardson and Albhy Galuten gave *Children of the World* (1976) a fully fledged disco sound, heard at its best on the two million-selling singles, 'You Should be Dancing' and 'Love So Right'. But this was only a prelude to Stigwood's master stroke – the soundtrack of the movie of the craze. *Saturday Night Fever* (1977) became the biggest-selling soundtrack album ever, giving the Bee

Gees two mega-hits with 'Stayin' Alive'* and 'Night Fever'*.

The formula was repeated with diminishing success by Stigwood with *Grease*, the film version of a Broadway pastiche of fifties teen culture, and an overly cute dramatization of The Beatles' *Sgt Pepper's Lonely Hearts' Club Band*, which starred the brothers with **Peter Frampton**. *Grease* included two massive hits for Olivia Newton-John and John Travolta, while the title song, written by Barry Gibb, was a solo hit for the **Four Seasons**' Frankie Valli. The *Pepper* film was scorned by the critics.

A fourth brother, Andy (*b. 5 March 1958, Manchester, d. February 1988, Oxford*), also rode the disco boom, scoring five US million-selling singles in 1977–8. They included the three No. 1s, 'I Just Want to Be Your Everything', 'Love Is Thicker than Water' and 'Shadow Dancing'. He had two more hit singles in 1980 ('Desire' and 'Time Is Time') before drugs problems interrupted his career and he faded from view. He died in 1988.

The eighties opened with the Bee Gees suing Stigwood for $200 million and settling out of court. The 1981 album *Living Eyes* was lacklustre and Barry, Robin and Maurice turned to creating solo albums, none of which made much impact. Barry's *Now Voyager* was accompanied with a 'long-form' music video but it was still less successful than his collaborations with Barbra Streisand (*Guilty*, 1980), **Dionne Warwick** (for whom he wrote 'Heartbreaker' in 1982) and Kenny Rogers. Barry also recorded occasionally as the Bunburys, notably 'Fight (No Matter How Long)' which appeared on the 1988 Olympic Games album *One Moment in Time* and featured the playing of **Eric Clapton**.

In 1987 the group were reunited with Arif Mardin and cut their first Bee Gees album since 1980 (*E.S.P.*) for a new label, Warners, which yielded the UK No. 1 single 'You Win Again'. Subsequent recordings include *High Civilization* (1991) and the disappointing *Size Isn't Everything* (1993), with its UK Top Five single 'For Whom the Bell Tolls'. In 1996 the enduring appeal of their songs was evidenced when n-Trance had a North American hit with 'Stayin' Alive' and UK boy-band Take That had a European hit with 'How Deep Is Your Love'. The following year they had a hit with *Still Waters* and in 1999 Steps had a huge hit with their reworking of 'Night Fever'. In the same year *Saturday Night Fever* was reworked as a stage musical in London.

CAPTAIN BEEFHEART
b. Don Van Vliet, 15 January 1941, Glendale, California, USA

A true original, Beefheart melded an earthy comic-strip

surrealism with blues-based rhythms and vocals to produce a series of influential albums that marked out the avant-garde margins of rock in the sixties and seventies. His work anticipated and indeed influenced much post-punk new wave British and American music of the eighties, the decade in which he (largely) forsook music for art.

A child prodigy – for eight years, from the age of four, his clay sculptures were featured on a local television show – Beefheart moved with his family to Lancaster, California, in the Mojave desert in 1954. Deeply influenced by living in the desert (which would be a constant theme of his work), he went to school with **Frank Zappa** (another central influence) and drenched himself in blues and R&B, before forming various white R&B bands (including the Omens and the Blackouts) in the early sixties. Taking his name from a film he and Zappa (who was then scoring low-budget Westerns) planned but never made – *Captain Beefheart Meets the Grunt People* – Beefheart formed his first Magic Band in 1964.

Signed to A&M later that year as Captain Beefheart and the Magic Band (which comprised Alex St Clair, Jerry Handley, Doug Moon and Paul Blakeley), the band cut two singles, a version of **Bo Diddley**'s hit 'Diddy Wah Diddy', and 'Moonchild', written by producer David Gates, who was later to achieve success with **Bread**. These were only local hits and Beefheart moved to Buddah in 1966 to record *Safe As Milk* (1967) with the next incarnation of the Magic Band (which comprised **Ry Cooder**, John French, Jimmy Semens and Herb Bermann).

With the exception of Beefheart's gruff, mesmeric voice, the A&M singles sounded like standard British R&B fare, but *Safe As Milk* was (and remains) a remarkable album. The major stylistic influence was **Howlin' Wolf**, the power of whose 'Evil' Beefheart matched in his chilling recording of 'Electricity', making the song not a paean to technology but to a natural, frightening force. But Beefheart was far more than 'the best ever white blues singer' he was often commended as. Working within the sympathetic atmosphere provided by producer Richard Perry and with Cooder's emphatic slide guitar, Beefheart produced a series of mysterious songs, ranging from 'Where There's Woman' and 'Yellow Brick Road' to the R&B simplicity of 'Call on Me'.

A critical success, especially in the UK where Beefheart toured, the album was a commercial failure and *Mirror Man*, though recorded in 1968, was not released until 1970. Even worse *Strictly Personal* (1968), which includes the impressive 'Kandy Korn', was issued with phasing added to make it 'far out' by producer Bob Krasnow, on his own Blue Thumb label. Beefheart responded with his most experimental work to date, the double-album *Trout Mask*

Replica (1969), made for Zappa's Straight label. His only album created without any outside interference, *Trout Mask* featured a new Magic Band – Bill Harkelroad (Zoot Horn Rollo), Semens (renamed Antennae Jimmy Semens), Mark Boston (Rockette Morton) and Beefheart's cousin, the Mascara Snake. Recorded live, the album's twenty-eight songs were alternately abrasive ('Dachau Blues', 'My Human Gets Me Blues') and lyrical ('The Blimp'). Featuring Beefheart's free-form sax-playing, declamatory vocals and surreal songs, *Trout Mask* was a futuristic mix of avant-garde jazz and rock. However, though it won critical plaudits it was a commercial failure and after *Lick My Decals off Baby* (Reprise, 1970), which was made with Ed Marimba (Artie Tripp) replacing Semens, Beefheart's subsequent albums saw him edging back into the mainstream.

Clear Spot and *The Spotlight Kid* (both Reprise, 1972) were his most accessible and straightforwardly bluesy albums, but the Beefheart who toured extensively remained as 'experimental' as ever. As a result the melodic *Unconditionally Guaranteed* (Mercury/Virgin in the UK, 1974) was deemed too commercial by his fans. After this, the Magic Band quit to form the short lived Mallard, and Beefheart, who had sung on Zappa's *Hot Rats* (1969), toured with Zappa as a featured singer. *Bat Chain Puller* (Warner Brothers) was recorded with a new Magic Band in 1976, but wasn't released until 1978. Now signed direct to Virgin, Beefheart recorded *Doc at the Radar Station* (1980) and *Ice Cream for Crow* (1982), both of which recaptured the feel, if not the power, of the best of his sixties albums. But though, surprisingly, Beefheart survived into the eighties and became more influential than ever, it was at the cost of a marginalization of his own music-making. He made no further recordings and in 1985 he mounted the first in a series of successful art exhibitions which were as quirky as his music had been, with the added bonus of being commercially successful. In the nineties most of the early albums were re-released, often with much additional material, and in 1999 the retrospective five-CD set *Captain Beefheart and the Magic Band Grown Fins* documented their career in great detail.

BIX BEIDERBECKE
b. Leon Bix Beiderbecke, 10 March 1903, Davenport, Iowa, USA, d. 7 August 1931, New York

The first white musician to make a significant contribution to jazz, Beiderbecke's cornet and trumpet solos were emulated by a generation of players. His early death, from pneumonia, meant that he was at the height of his powers for only four years.

A self-taught pianist, Beiderbecke first heard jazz as a teenager through the records of the **Original Dix-**

ieland Jazz Band, though his enthusiasm for Ravel and Debussy also contributed to his highly individual style. In 1920–2 he learned at first hand from **Louis Armstrong** and other Chicago-based musicians, as well as playing on riverboats and in clubs while enrolled at military academy.

After his expulsion from the academy, Beiderbecke joined white collegian dance band the Wolverines, whose 'Copenhagen' (1924) and 'Fidgety Feet' already showed the cornet player to be far in advance of his pedestrian colleagues. He next played with Charlie Straight's orchestra in Chicago in 1925 before linking up with saxophonist Frankie Trumbauer, who became his closest musical colleague.

Occasional records during 1925–6, including his own 'Davenport Blues' with **Tommy Dorsey** on trombone, showed Beiderbecke's style maturing and in 1926 he and Trumbauer joined Jean Goldkette's orchestra. There he worked with **Eddie Lang** (guitar), **Joe Venuti** (violin) and **Jimmy Dorsey** (clarinet) who recorded with him as Bix Beiderbecke and his Gang on the ODJB's 'At the Jazz Band Ball' and **Clarence Williams**' 'Royal Garden Blues' (Okeh, 1927).

From late 1927 Beiderbecke was a member of **Paul Whiteman**'s orchestra, quickly establishing himself as the band's leading jazz soloist. He was featured on such records as 'Changes' (Victor, 1927), 'You Took Advantage of Me' (1928), 'Louisiana' and 'Mississippi Mud' with **Bing Crosby** on vocals. However, his more significant contributions came from recording dates independent of the Whiteman ethos.

With Trumbauer and Lang he made 'Singing the Blues' (1928), which contained his most influential solo, while 'In a Mist' (1928) was a piano solo which showed Beiderbecke's debt to Debussy. In 1930 he played on a **Hoagy Carmichael** session with Venuti, **Benny Goodman** and **Gene Krupa**, recording 'Rocking Chair' and 'Georgia on My Mind'. He also performed on 'Deep Harlem' (1929) by **Irving Mills**' Hotsy Totsy Gang.

Among those who modelled their trumpet styles on Beiderbecke were **Red Nichols**, Rex Stewart and Jimmy McPartland, who recorded *Shades of Bix* (Coral, 1953). Beiderbecke also received probably more literary attention than any other jazz musician. Dorothy Baker's novel *Young Man with a Horn*, filmed in 1950, was based on his life, while of several biographies *Bix: Man and Legend* (1974) by Sudhalter and Evans is acknowledged to be the most thorough.

HARRY BELAFONTE
b. Harold George Belafonte, 1 March 1927, Harlem, New York, USA

Best remembered for his highly successful recording career as 'The King of Calypso' in the late fifties, Bela-fonte's greater significance is arguably as a patron and supporter of black musicians, including **Miriam Makeba**, a role which culminated in his central part in the organization of the USA for Africa famine relief recording in 1985.

Having spent part of his childhood in Jamaica, he returned to the USA, joined the navy for three years and then became a member of the American Negro Theater Workshop. With the folk revival gathering momentum, Belafonte performed a selection of West Indian songs in the Village Vanguard nightclub in Greenwich Village. This led to a starring role in the film of Oscar Hammerstein's *Carmen Jones* and a recording contract with RCA Victor, who released the *Calypso* album in 1956. This contained a version of a traditional work song, 'Banana Boat Song'*, which was a Top Five hit on both sides of the Atlantic. A cover-version by white folk group the Tarriers on Glory (Philips in Britain) was even more successful, while **Stan Freberg** had a hit with a satirical version of the song in 1957. In 1988 the song was memorably featured in one of the set pieces of *Beetle Juice* when the film's characters are forced to mime to Belafonte's recording.

Belafonte went on to have seven more hits, including 'Island in the Sun' and 'Mary's Boy Child', the first single to sell a million copies in Britain, in 1957–8. He appeared in seven films, including *Carmen Jones* (1954) and *Island in the Sun* (1957), and during the sixties concentrated on occasional concert appearances, the most successful of which is captured on the live double-album *Belafonte at Carnegie Hall*. In 1981 he released *Loving You Is Where I Belong* (Columbia) which included **Bob Dylan**'s 'Forever Young' and **Ralph McTell**'s 'Streets of London'.

Accusations that he diluted traditional West Indian music were countered by Belafonte who argued that he was enabling the music to reach wider audiences. Unlike many who enjoyed success through the folk revival, he has retained a commitment to the advancement of black culture, not least through the control he maintains over his own artistic career. In 1985 he and his manager Ken Kragen played a leading role in organizing the USA for Africa charity recording 'We Are the World'* This led to the recording of *Paradise in Gazankulu* (EMI Manhattan, 1988) with black South African musicians. Less successful was *Belafonte '89* (1989), which highlighted his MOR inclinations.

THOM BELL
b. 1941, Philadelphia, Pennyslvania, USA

A writer, arranger and producer, Bell was a leading architect of the Philly soul sound of the seventies. He specialized in ethereal, string-filled backings for the falsetto lead voices of such groups as the **Delfonics** and the **Stylistics**.

Of middle-class West Indian parents, Bell studied classical piano as a child. A teenager friend of Kenny Gamble, Bell recorded with him as Kenny and Tommy ('Someday', Heritage, 1959) and together they formed the Romeos, which recorded unsuccessfully for Philadelphia label Arctic. A regular session player for Cameo Records, Bell was musical director for **Chubby Checker** on a British tour.

His first production work was for Brenda and the Tabulations and for the Delfonics on Moonshot and Cameo, but his first hit was the Showstoppers' 'Ain't Nothin' but a Houseparty' (Heritage, 1968), a British Top Twenty hit on Beacon. 'La La I Love You' (Philly Groove, 1968) was the first of ten Delfonics' hits arranged and produced by Bell. He also wrote many of the songs with Linda Creed, a former session singer of white French parentage. The first Creed–Bell composition was 'Free Girl', recorded by **Dusty Springfield** on the Bell-produced *Brand New Me* (Philips, 1970).

Reunited with producer Kenny Gamble, Bell arranged **Jerry Butler**'s 'Western Union Man' (1968) and 'Only the Strong Survive' (1969). Then, in 1970, **Hugo and Luigi** hired Bell and Creed to write for and produce the Stylistics for the Avco label. The result was a series of lush, literate soul ballads, including the million-selling 'Betcha by Golly Wow', 'You Make Me Feel Brand New', and 'Stone in Love with You'.

Together and separately, Bell and **Gamble and Huff** were responsible for most of the big soul hits of the period 1973–5. Bell arranged the **O'Jays'** 'Backstabbers' (1972), while for Atlantic he and Creed wrote successfully for the **Spinners** ('Could It Be I'm Falling in Love?', 1973) and the group's collaboration with **Dionne Warwick**, 'Then Came You'* (1974). Bell also arranged Ronnie Dyson's 'When You Get Right Down to It' (Columbia, 1974) and New York City's 'I'm Doin' Fine Now' (1973) for **Wes Farrell**'s Chelsea label. He was also in demand to work with older established artists, producing the **Johnny Mathis** album *I'm Coming Home* and a comeback record for **Little Anthony and the Imperials**. In 1973 he set up his own Tommy label, distributed by Columbia.

Among those Bell later worked with were **Elton John**, Deniece Williams on *My Melody* (1981) and *Niecy* (1982), Phyllis Hyman and James Ingram.

WILLIAM BELL
b. William Yarborough, 16 July 1939, Memphis, Tennessee, USA

One of the first artists signed to **Jim Stewart**'s and Estelle Axton's Satellite (later Stax) Records, Bell's recordings document the changes in Stax's version of Southern soul throughout the sixties.

Bell first recorded in 1957 as lead singer with the

Del Rios ('Alone on a Rainy Night', Meteor). When that group broke up he sang with the Phineas Newborn Orchestra before **Chips Moman** signed him to Stax and recorded Bell singing his own composition, the classic 'You Don't Miss Your Water' (1962). Bell's undemonstrative, plaintive vocal was clearly gospel influenced, as was the backing, but where later Stax records were driven by punchy horns, swirling organs and staccato guitar interjections, the accompaniment for 'Water' featured traditional piano triplets. Like many of the songs of **Joe Tex** and Moman and **Dan Penn**, 'Water' fused blues material with the moralizing narratives of country music. Interestingly, though 'Water' was a minor pop hit – because of its sales in the South – it was not an R&B hit, presumably because it was too down home for Northern blacks. And before the decade was out it would sound like a classic country song as performed by the **Byrds** on their influential country-rock album, *Sweetheart of the Rodeo* (CBS, 1969).

By the time of 'Share What You've Got' (1966), which ushered in a steady stream of rhythm and blues hits, Bell was accompanied by the full Stax sound. In contrast to **Otis Redding**, Stax's major act, Bell's controlled performances highlighted the lyrics of songs like 'Never Like This Before' (1966), 'Everybody Loves a Winner' (1967) and 'I Forgot to Be Your Lover' (1968), as well as their emotions. It was this quality that gave real dignity to his performance of his own composition 'A Tribute to a King' (1968), a moving testament to Redding after his untimely death. In the same year he scored his biggest ever hit, 'Private Number', a duet with Judy Clay which reached the American and British Top Ten.

Bell co-wrote nearly all his hits, usually with Booker T. Jones, and their songs for other artists included **Albert King**'s classic 'Born Under a Bad Sign'. After a stream of unsuccessful singles, Bell, like so many of Stax's acts, recorded a (self-produced) album of social comment, the deserving *Phases of Reality* (1972). When the company went into liquidation, he joined Mercury (where he recorded two albums and had a Top Ten hit with the superior 'Tryin' to Love Two', 1977). He subsequently set up his own production company, Peach Tree, in Atlanta in 1980 and later his own label, Wilbe. In 1986, now firmly in control of his own career, he returned to the R&B charts with *Passion*, a steamy essay in sexual politics which featured the duet with Janice Bullock, 'I Don't Want to Wake up Feeling Guilty'. In 1989 he released *On a Roll*.

THE BELLAMY BROTHERS
David Bellamy, b. 16 September 1945, Derby, Florida, USA; Howard Bellamy, b. 2 February 1941, Derby

Country-pop singers and songwriters, the Bellamy Brothers' most successful record was 'Let Your Love Flow' (1976). The song was later used in commercials and as the theme for the film *Little Darlings* (1980). In the eighties the duo had a series of country chart-toppers.

The son of a bluegrass musician, David Bellamy's early musical career included keyboards-playing with the Accidents soul band in the mid-sixties, when he backed **Percy Sledge** and others. In 1968 he and guitarist Howard formed the rock band Jerico, touring the South for three years.

The brothers next concentrated on jingle- and songwriting, with David composing Jim Stafford's novelty hit 'Spiders and Snakes'* (MGM, 1973). This led to a recording contract with Warners and the minor hit 'Nothin' Heavy' (1975). The following year, Stafford's producer Phil Gernhard supervised the brothers' version of Larry E. Williams' 'Let Your Love Flow'. With its close harmonies and acoustic guitars the record reached No. 1 in America and was a British Top Ten hit. However, the follow-up, 'Satin Sheets', written by Willis Alan Ramsey, was less successful.

They recorded *Plain and Fancy* (1977) and *Beautiful Friends* (1978) before achieving another pop hit with the coyly titled 'If I Said You Had a Beautiful Body Would You Hold It Against Me'.

Without modifying their airy harmonies, the Bellamy Brothers concentrated on country music during the eighties. Recording for **Mike Curb**'s organization, with releases through MCA, they had an early success in the country charts with 'Sugar Daddy' (1980). With David Bellamy contributing many of the songs, they had later hits with 'Dancing Cowboys' and 'When I'm Away from You' (1983).

The Bellamy Brothers' run of success continued in 1986 with 'Lie to You for Your Love' (MCA/Curb) and *Howard and David*. In 1987 'Kids of the Baby Boom' and the title track from *Crazy from the Heart* both reached No. 1 on the country charts. In 1988 they charted with 'Santa Fe' and *Rebels without a Clue*, produced by Jimmy Bowen. Emory Gordy Jnr produced their 1990 album *Reality Check*, which included the hit country single 'I Could Be Persuaded'. This was followed by a move to Atlantic for *Rollin' Thunder* (1991). *Take Me Home* (Branson Entertainment, 1994) contained new recordings of earlier Bellamy Brothers songs.

BELLE AND SEBASTIAN
Isobel Campbell; Richard Colburn; Mick Cooke; Stuart David; Chris Geddes; Stevie Jackson; Sarah Martin; Stuart Murdoch

Enigmatic Scottish octet Belle and Sebastian have achieved cult status with their brand of folk-rock

heavily influenced by **Nick Drake** and **Love**.

Formed in 1996 by principle members Murdoch and David, and augmented by cello and xylophone amongst more traditional instrumentation, Belle and Sebastian (named after an obscure children's TV series from 1997) recorded their début album as part of a Higher Education Certificate in Music Business and Administration at Stow College in Glasgow. The result, *Tigermilk* (1996), was completed in just five days and released on Jeepster Records as a limited edition of just 1,000 vinyl-only copies. The album, with its classic pop melodies and subtle orchestration, soon became a much sought after item, with original copies now worth as much as £800.

Tigermilk's successor, *If You're Feeling Sinister* (1997), the band's first album to be released internationally, was a critical if not commercial success, although word-of-mouth and the underground success of 'Lazy Line Painter Jane' and 'Stars of Track and Field' ensured a growing cult following for the band, who by now refused to communicate with the music press. The eagerly awaited follow-up, *The Boy with the Arab Strap* (1998), reached the UK Top Twenty, while 'This Is Just a Modern Rock Song' was Belle and Sebastian's first hit single.

1999 saw them named Best Newcomers at the Brit Awards, much to everybody's surprise, including the band's. Later in the year, *Tigermilk* was reissued on CD. After that founding member Stuart David left to concentrate on his Looper side-project, achieving underground success on both sides of the Atlantic with the albums *Up a Tree* (2000) and *The Geometrid* (2000). He had a minor hit single with 'Who's Afraid of Y2K?' and made his literary début with the often dreamlike *Nalda Said*. Cellist Campbell also recorded a solo album, *The Green Fields of Foreverland*, under the pseudonym the Gentle Waves.

The group returned the following year with 'Legal Man', which made the UK Top Thirty. Their fourth album, *Fold Your Hands Child, You Walk Like a Peasant*, built on the success of its predecessors, but its crossover appeal was hindered by the band's decision not to tour in support of it.

JESSE BELVIN
b. 15 December 1933, Texarkana, Arkansas, USA,
d. 6 February 1960, Los Angeles, California

The author of 'Earth Angel', America's best-loved doo-wop song, as a singer and arranger Belvin was a major influence on the development of West Coast black vocal music.

In 1949 Belvin joined Big Jay McNeely's band as vocalist and on his discharge from the army partnered Marvin Philips (as Jesse and Marvin) for 'Dream Girl' (Specialty, 1953), an R&B Top Ten hit. Subsequently he had solo hits, including the smooth 'Goodnight My Love' (Modern, 1953) and the **Nat 'King' Cole**-influenced soft-balladry of 'Funny' and 'Guess Who' (RCA, 1959). He made numerous solo discs, on Kent, Knight and Jamie and also sang with various doo-wop groups, including the Cliques ('Girl in My Dreams', Modern, 1956), Sharptones and the Sheiks (whose 'So Fine' on Federal was revived by the Fiestas in 1959). Most of these songs were written by Belvin.

His major work, however, remains 'Earth Angel' which sold over two million copies on Dootone in 1954 for the Penguins (Cleveland Duncan, Curtis Williams, Dexter Tisby and Bruce Tate). A perfect example of the idealized love ballad of the day, with its rumbling piano and strong hint of teen *angst* in the hesitant lead vocal of Duncan, 'Angel' caught the imagination of black and white teenagers alike.

Belvin's death in a car accident came after he had joined RCA, his first major label, and had R&B hits in 1959, the biggest of which was 'Guess Who'. *Blues Balladeer* (Specialty, 1990), a retrospective collection which includes several demo recordings, confirms his stature as both writer and vocalist.

BEN FOLDS FIVE
Ben Folds, b. Chapel Hill, North Carolina, USA; Darren Jessee; Robert Sledge

Oddly named, baby grand-led three piece Ben Folds Five have carved a unique niche in the indie-rock scene with their show-tune dramatics and **Randy Newman**-influenced pop.

Formed in 1993 by pianist/singer Folds, drummer Jessee and bassist Sledge, who claimed 'Five' sounded better than 'Three', the trio signed to Caroline to release their eponymous début album in 1995. *Ben Folds Five* had a kitsch sense of humour welcomed by US critics after the death of grunge rock. The band were widely ignored, however, until the singles 'The Battle of Who Could Care Less' and 'Brick' from their second album, *Whatever & Ever Amen* (1997), became college radio favourites, which sent the album to platinum status in the US. Both singles were also minor hits in the UK.

Ben Folds Five spent much of 1998 touring to support the release of *Naked Baby Photos*, a collection of B-sides, out-takes and live performances, before signing to Sony for the release of their acclaimed third studio album, *The Unauthorised Biography of Reinhold Messner* (1999).

PAT BENATAR
b. Patricia Andrzejewski, 10 January 1953, Long Island, New York, USA

With **Suzi Quatro** and, later, Lita Ford, Benatar was among the few women singers to find success with the heavy pop/rock style, which had been primarily a male preserve.

After early training in opera, Benatar became a singing waitress before taking jobs in cabaret where she performed ballads. After developing a more rock-orientated approach with guitarists Neil Giraldo and Scott St Clair Sheets, Roger Capps (bass) and Myron Grombacher (drums), she signed to Chrysalis in 1978. With Mike Chapman of **Chinn and Chapman** as producer and Giraldo as main songwriter, *In the Heat of the Night* included a version of **John Cougar Mellencamp**'s 'I Need a Lover' and the hit 'Heartbreaker'. With the aid of the dynamic Top Ten single 'Hit Me with Your Best Shot'*, *Crimes of Passion* (1980) repeated the success.

During the early eighties she modified her brand of brash heavy metal on the more melodic *Precious Time* (1981), which provided hits with 'Fire and Ice' (1981) and 'Shadows of the Night' (1982). Later Top Twenty entries included 'Little Too Late' (1983) and 'Love Is a Battlefield', Benatar's only British hit. Its narrative-based video, directed by Bob Giraldi, was the first of the genre to include spoken dialogue in addition to the song.

After 'We Belong' (1984), the film theme 'Invincible' (1985) and 'Sex as a Weapon', she took a break to start a family with Giraldo, whom she had married in 1982. Benatar returned in 1988 with her eighth album, the Geraldo/Peter Coleman-produced *Wide Awake in Dreamland*. She recorded a sincere, but lightweight, blues album, *True Love* (Chrysalis, 1991), which included a version of **B. B. King**'s 'Paying the Cost to Be the Boss'. Benatar returned to more familiar rock territory in 1993 with *Gravity's Rainbow*. Subsequent releases, which included *Innamarata* (1997), fared less well.

TONY BENNETT
b. Anthony Dominick Benedetto, 3 August 1926, New York, USA

Of all the singers who emerged before the arrival of rock'n'roll and who continued beyond it, Bennett was least influenced by the shifts in popular music around him.

The son of Italian immigrants, Bennett was drafted in 1944, and on his discharge turned professional singer after a two-year spell in Special Services, the army's entertainment branch. After singing in various New York clubs he was signed to Columbia and had immediate success with 'Because of You'* and a cover-version of **Hank Williams**' 'Cold, Cold Heart'* (both 1951). 'Because of You', on which Bennett's **Mario Lanza**-influenced singing was supported by swooping strings, pointed the way forward to

'Stranger in Paradise'* (1953), his most intense vocal performance, while his unhappiness with 'Cold, Cold Heart' was matched by his unease with the up-tempo 'Rags to Riches'* (1953). Henceforth, virtually all his recordings would set his chesty voice against a tinkling piano and sweeping strings. The best example of this, and one of the few new songs he recorded, was Douglas Cross and George Cory's 'I Left My Heart in San Francisco'* (1962), the song with which he is most associated. Other recordings in this vein included 'Firefly' (1958), 'I Wanna Be Around' (1962), 'Who Can I Turn to (When Nobody Needs Me)' (1964) and 'If I Ruled the World' (1965), the last two written by Leslie Bricusse.

While other popular performers, such as **Perry Como**, went into television or, like **Andy Willliams**, accommodated themselves to the rock-associated sounds and writers, Bennett never expanded his activities beyond touring and recording. Throughout the sixties, though his concerts continued to be well attended, his record sales declined and after arguments with Columbia (who wanted him to record more contemporary material) he left the label in 1972 for a brief sojourn with MGM. After that he briefly established his own record company, Improv, and spent the next decade without a recording contract until in a surprise move in 1986 Bennett rejoined Columbia and recorded *The Art of Excellence*, produced by his son (and manager) Danny and Ettore Stratta. The album, which included a surprising duet with **Ray Charles**, 'Everybody Has the Blues', utilized digital techniques to demonstrate Bennett's still thrilling dynamic range. More emotional was *Astoria: Portrait of the Artist* (1990), an autobiographical tribute to the New York neighbourhood in which he grew up. In 1991 Columbia released the boxed set *Forty Years – The Artistry of Tony Bennett* and the singer recorded a new collection of songs, *Steppin' Out*, in 1993.

Three marks of Bennett's new-found popularity with thirty-somethings were his 1994 American tour being sponsored by computer software company WordPerfect, his conscription to the ranks of those who have recorded *Unplugged* shows for MTV (1994) and his appearance at the 1998 Glastonbury Festival. His new-found audience had little effect on his recording choices. Hence his bestselling album of the nineties was *Here's to the Ladies* (1995).

GEORGE BENSON
b. 22 March 1943, Pittsburgh, Pennsylvania, USA

His global fame as a middle-of-the-road soul/pop crooner has all but obliterated Benson's status as one of the most technically brilliant guitarists of the last twenty-five years, and his contributions to the art of jazz guitar in particular. By 1980 producer **Quincy**

Jones could sum up Benson as no longer 'one of the world's great guitarists who can sing, but a great singer who is also the world's greatest guitarist'.

Benson began his career as a singer with various Pittsburgh R&B groups, but on the advice of jazz player Grant Green he moved to New York to become a session guitarist. He was first featured on Blue Note and Prestige recordings with organists **Jimmy Smith** and Brother Jack McDuff. He was signed to Columbia in 1965 by **John Hammond**, but albums there and for A&M had little success. However, a contract with Creed Taylor's CTI label in 1971 led to Benson establishing himself at the easy-listening end of the jazz market with albums like *White Rabbit* and *Good King Bad*.

Benson's vocal ambitions were not encouraged by CTI and in 1975 he signed to Warners. There producer Tommy Lipuma worked on combining his fluid guitar work with lush strings and occasional vocals. His first hit came with jazz guitarist Gabor Szabo's 'Breezin'', an instrumental track. A Top Ten record followed with a version of **Leon Russell**'s 'This Masquerade', featuring Benson's **Stevie Wonder**-like vocals.

Subsequent albums – *In Flight* and *Weekend in LA* – with their hit singles 'On Broadway', 'Nature Boy' and 'Love Ballad' propelled Benson into the superstar class. *Give Me the Night* (1980), one of four platinum albums, was produced by Quincy Jones. The international success of *In Your Eyes* (1983), *20/20* (1985) and *Tenderly* (1989) consolidated Benson's position as one of the greatest crossover artists of the era, in his ability to combine soul and jazz elements for both white and black audiences.

The cost of forever seeking that crossover success was seen on the bland *Big Boss Band* (1990), which he recorded with the **Count Basie** orchestra. In 1993 he returned to a soul jazz style for *Love Remembers*, which included his son Steven Benson Hue on keyboards. That was followed by *That's Right* (GRP, 1996) and *Standing Together* (1998). In the same year he charted with a duet with **Mary J. Blige** and recorded 'My Father, My Son', a song commissioned by Harrod's owner Mohamed Al Fayed in honour of his son Dodi, who was killed in a car crash alongside Diana, Princess of Wales. *Absolute Benson* (2000), which was as effortlessly smooth as ever, featured tasteful versions of **Donny Hathaway**'s 'The Ghetto' and **Stevie Wonder**'s 'Lately'.

BROOK BENTON
b. Benjamin Franklin Peay, 19 September 1931, Camden, South Carolina, USA, d. 9 April 1988, New York City

With sales in excess of 20 million records, Benton was one of the most successful black singers of the sixties. He was also one of the few to write his own material.

Benton followed the traditional path from gospel to rhythm and blues, singing first with the Camden Jubilee Singers, then in 1948, travelling north to join the New York-based Bill Landford Spiritual Singers before turning to R&B with the Sandmen in the mid-fifties. He recorded unsuccessfully for Vik and Epic, but more significantly he turned to songwriting with publisher Clyde Otis and arranger Belford Hendricks and sang on demos for Otis. In 1958 Benton supplied Top Ten hits for both Nat 'King' Cole ('Looking Back') and ex-Drifter, Clyde McPhatter ('A Lover's Question'). The demos for these reveal the contrasting sides of Benton – the Cole song is performed in a manner as smooth as velvet, while the song for McPhatter is far more in the gospel mould.

In 1959, through Otis (the first black director of A&R at a major label), Benton joined Mercury and had three huge hits, all written by Benton, Otis and Hendricks. 'It's Just a Matter of Time'*, 'Thank You Pretty Baby' and 'So Many Ways' all featured Benton's rich baritone set against the swirling strings provided by Hendricks. In 1960 he cut a classic pair of duets with Dinah Washington, 'Baby (You've Got What It Takes)'* and 'A Rockin' Good Way'*, which was issued complete with mistakes, so compelling is it. On both, Washington's carefree light voice bounced beautifully off Benton's macho baritone. Benton followed these songs with a pair of superior ballads, 'Kiddio' and Johnny Mercer's 'Fools Rush in'. In 1961 he had hits with the novelty 'The Boll Weevil Song' and the traditional 'Frankie and Johnnie'.

Though the hits continued, Benton was clearly out of sympathy with the heavier rhythms of soul and after some routine pop-soul outings, he quit Mercury for RCA (1965–7) and then Reprise, for whom he recorded the impressive Laura, What's He Got That I Ain't Got? (1967), which included a fine version of Bobbie Gentry's 'Ode to Billie Joe'. In 1970 he returned to the charts with an intense version of Tony Joe White's 'Rainy Night in Georgia'* (Cotillion).

After that, there were no more hits, despite releases on numerous labels, including MGM, Stax, All Platinum and Olde Worlde. Benton continued to tour successfully until his death.

IRVING BERLIN
b. Israel Baline, 11 May 1888, Temun, Russia,
d. 22 September 1989, New York, USA

Berlin was America's most successful and most representative songwriter of the first half of the twentieth century. The author of 'Alexander's Ragtime Band' (1911), 'White Christmas' (1942), with which Bing Crosby alone had sales of over 25 million discs, and 'God Bless America', America's unofficial national anthem best known in its recording by Kate Smith

(1939), Berlin demonstrated a complete mastery of popular song forms. He also had great success with scores for Broadway shows (including Annie Get Your Gun, 1946, in which Ethel Merman introduced 'There's No Business Like Show Business', and Call Me Madam, 1950) and films (including Top Hat, 1935, and Easter Parade, 1948) but it is primarily for his individual songs that Berlin will be remembered. They caught the spirit of the times, from the topical and ragtime songs in the century's first decades to the expressive ballads of the thirties and forties. Unlike many of his contemporaries, Berlin drew little from the European operetta tradition. His direct tunes and simple, but deftly constructed, lyrics were wholly American in feel, and situated in a direct line of descent from Stephen Foster. Berlin was unable to read or write music and could only play the piano in the key of F sharp major – he later had a piano made with a lever which allowed him to transpose keys without changing his fingering – but he turned these limitations to his advantage with his pragmatic, decidedly American, words and music.

Born in Russia, Berlin was raised in the lower East Side of New York where his family settled in 1892. In 1900 he ran away from home and made his stage début in The Show Girl (1902). After briefly working as a song plugger for Harry von Tilzer, he became a singing waiter at New York's Pelham café. There, with the café's pianist Nick Nicholson, he wrote his first published song 'Marie from Sunny Italy' (1907) and took Berlin as his professional name. 'Dorando', a topical Italian dialect song about the marathon runner, won him a contract with composer and publisher Ted Snyder. His first hits came in 1909 with the operatic parody 'Sadie Salome, Go Home' and 'My Wife's Gone to the Country (Hurrah! Hurrah!)' (recorded by Byron Harlan and Arthur Collins, who also recorded another early Berlin hit, 'That Mesmerizing Mendelssohn Tune', 1910). In the same year Berlin made his own first recording with the novelty song 'Oh! How That German Could Love' (Columbia). In 1910 he and Snyder appeared in the Broadway revue Up and Down Broadway and provided songs for Fanny Brice and Nora Bayes, among others.

By now an established songwriter, Berlin wrote 'Alexander's Ragtime Band' in 1911 for a revue held by George M. Cohan's Friars club. With its ragged military rhythms, simulated bugle calls and inviting introduction 'Come on and hear, Come on and hear', it bore little relationship to the classic ragtime of Eubie Blake and Scott Joplin. The song was taken up by vaudeville singer Emma Carus and was subsequently successfully recorded by Billy Murray (1911), Bessie Smith (1927), the Boswell Sisters (1935), Louis Armstrong (1937), Bing Crosby, Ray Noble (1938), and Al Jolson (1947), among others. It led to the similarly

styled 'Everybody's Doin' It' (1911), introduced by
Eddie Cantor, 'When That Midnight Choo-Choo
Leaves for Alabam'' (1912) and 'International Rag'
(1913), which Berlin himself introduced at the London
Hippodrome. In 1914 Berlin wrote his first complete
score for a Broadway revue, the 'ragtime' musical
Watch Your Step which, billed as 'A Syncopated Musical Show Made in America', starred **Vernon and
Irene Castle** and introduced 'Play a Simple Melody', a
hit for Billy Murray and Elsie Baker (1916). It was
revived in 1950 by Bing and Gary Crosby, **Jo Stafford**,
Phil Harris and Georgia Gibbs and **Bob Crosby**.
When drafted, he responded by writing and staging
on Broadway the show *Yip Yip Yaphank* (1918) in
which he sang his own 'Oh How I Hate to Get up in
the Morning' (a hit for **Irving Kaufman**).

After the war Berlin consolidated his success by setting up his own publishing company and buying back
his early copyrights. With Sam Harris he built his
own theatre, the Music Box, where he staged his own
revues, even appearing in the 1921 and 1923 editions.
At the same time Berlin was developing as a consummate ballad writer. He wrote his first ballad, the waltz
'When I Lost You', in 1912 after the death of his first
wife Dorothy Goetz and henceforth, Berlin devoted
himself to the ballad form – 'God Bless America'
which later provoked **Woody Guthrie** to write 'This
Land Is Your Land', though published in 1939, was
written in 1917 for *Yip Yip Yaphank*. The rise of the
ballad came at the time when record sales of songs
were growing at the expense of sheet-music sales. At
the same time, the requirements of theatre (and later
film) musicals and radio changed from novelty items
to production numbers (such as 'A Pretty Girl Is Like
a Melody' for *The Ziegfeld Follies of 1919*) and songs
that expressed a character's feelings ('Cheek to Cheek'
and 'Isn't This a Lovely Day' written for **Fred Astaire**
and Ginger Rogers in *Top Hat*, 1935).

During the Depression Berlin and Moss Hart wrote
the shows *For the Music* (1932) and *As Thousands
Cheer* (1935), which included 'Soft Lights and Sweet
Music' and 'Supper Time', introduced by **Ethel
Waters**, one of Broadway's first black stars. However,
following the success of 'Blue Skies', which Jolson
introduced in the first talking picture *The Jazz Singer*,
Berlin turned increasingly to films. Among the films
for which he wrote songs in the thirties were *Follow
the Fleet*, 1936 ('Let's Face the Music and Dance', a hit
for Astaire), *On the Avenue*, 1937 ('I've Got My Love
to Keep Me Warm', introduced by **Dick Powell** and a
hit for Ray Noble and **Billie Holiday** and revived by
Les Brown and the **Mills Brothers** in 1949) and *Carefree*, 1938 ('Change Partners', introduced by Astaire
and a hit for **Jimmy Dorsey** and **Lawrence Welk**).

In 1940 Berlin returned to Broadway with
Louisiana Purchase (filmed 1941) before once again

donning his First World War army uniform for the
patriotic revue *This Is the Army* (1942, filmed 1943) in
which he introduced 'This Is the Army, Mr Jones'. In
the same year he wrote the classic 'White Christmas',
introduced by Bing Crosby in *Holiday Inn* and subsequently recorded by such diverse artists as **Gordon
Jenkins** (1942), **Frank Sinatra** (1944), **Mantovani**
(1952), the **Drifters** (1954), **Pat Boone** (1957) and **Darlene Love** (1963).

Berlin's greatest theatrical success was *Annie Get
Your Gun* (1946), which was loosely based on the life
of the sharpshooter Annie Oakley. Producers **Rodgers
and Hammerstein** had originally asked **Jerome Kern**
to write the music with **Dorothy Fields**, but when he
died Berlin stepped in. The first of his pair of musicals
with **Ethel Merman** (who was replaced by **Betty Hutton** in the 1949 film version), *Annie*'s brash and
American subject matter inspired Berlin to produce
some of his most memorable songs. Among them
were 'Anything You Can Do', 'I Got the Sun in the
Mornin'', 'My Defences Are Down', 'The Girl That I
Marry' and the anthemic 'There's No Business Like
Show Business' which in 1954 was used as the title of
the film in which Marilyn Monroe sang Berlin's 'Heat
Wave'. That song was first performed in 1933, as were
several of the songs in *Easter Parade* (1948), notably
the title song and 'A Couple of Swells', both sung by
Astaire and **Judy Garland** in the film. Berlin's last two
hit shows, *Call Me Madam* (1950, filmed 1953) and
White Christmas (1954), also included a mix of old
and new songs. His last musical was *Mr President*
(1962) and his last notable song 'An Old-Fashioned
Wedding' (1966), after which he retired to supervise
the running of his publishing company.

Later a recluse, Berlin kept strict control over the
use of his songs, refusing to allow his works to be
used in commercials or given updated arrangements.

EMILE BERLINER
*b. 20 May 1851, Hanover, Germany, d. 3 August 1929,
Washington DC, USA*

Berliner was responsible for the introduction of the
flat disc in 1887. Previous 'records', such as those used
in **Thomas Edison**'s phonograph, had been cylinders.

Like Edison largely self-educated, Berliner emigrated
to America in 1870. He worked in a dry goods store in
Washington DC and began experimenting with electricity and acoustics. He invented an early electrical
microphone in 1877, which won him a position with
Bell Telephone, the company founded by Alexander
Graham Bell (who was later celebrated by **Sweet** in
their 1971 British hit 'Alexander Graham Bell').

Berliner patented his first gramophone, as he called
the machine upon which he played his flat records,
in 1887, and spent the next few years perfecting it,

developing the means of making multiple copies from an original recording and finding an appropriate substance out of which to make records. After briefly licensing his discoveries to a German toymaker (for whom Berliner, in the manner of Edison, recorded a deeply accented version of 'Twinkle, Twinkle, Little Star') in 1889, Berliner established his own record company, The United States Gramophone Company, in 1893. It is this company which, after a variety of changes of ownership and take-overs, was to be an influential element in the formation of the companies now known as EMI, BMG and PolyGram. Moreover, in **Fred Gaisberg**, Berliner employed the man who became in effect the first A&R man of the record industry.

BERT BERNS
b. Bert Russell, 1929, d. 31 December 1967, New York, USA

An important figure in New York music during the sixties, Berns composed such R&B and soul standards as 'Twist and Shout' (with Phil Medley) and 'Piece of My Heart'. During a brief foray into the British scene, he produced the first records of **Van Morrison**.

A former student of the Juilliard School of Music, Berns was nevertheless a classic product of Tin Pan Alley, working as a song-plugger and music copyist as well as composer, talent scout, A&R man and producer. His work also appeared under the names of Bert Russell and Russell Byrd. He operated at the interface of the new teenage pop and the emerging soul style. Thus, 'Twist and Shout', with the Latin-influenced rhythm typical of many Berns compositions was a hit both for black American group the **Isley Brothers** and for **The Beatles**. Similarly, his **Solomon Burke** soul songs ('Cry to Me' and 'Everybody Needs Somebody to Love') were taken up by groups like the **Rolling Stones**.

With **Jerry Ragavoy** he wrote the Garnett Mimms million-seller 'Cry Baby' (United Artists, 1963), and Berns productions appeared on a number of small New York labels, including his own Keetch, before he took over at Atlantic as resident songwriter/producer from **Leiber and Stoller** in 1963. There he was responsible for such classic **Drifters**' tracks as 'Under the Boardwalk' and 'Up in the Streets of Harlem', and for a number of hits by Burke.

It was the British enthusiasm for his work which brought Berns to London in 1964, where he recorded **Lulu**'s 'Shout' and a raw Irish rhythm and blues group, Them. Backed by Atlantic, he founded the Bang! label in 1965, scoring a pop hit with the McCoys' 'Hang on Sloopy' and producing the first solo album by Them's lead singer, Van Morrison.

Bang!'s sister soul label, Shout!, issued Erma Franklin's original version of 'Piece of My Heart', which was a 1968 rock hit for **Janis Joplin**'s Big Brother and the Holding Company. Franklin's own version was a belated UK Top Ten hit after it had been used in a television commercial in 1992.

Shortly before his death from a heart attack, he had recorded the first tracks by **Neil Diamond**.

ELMER BERNSTEIN
b. 4 April 1922, New York, USA

Known in the film circles as 'Bernstein West', to distinguish him from 'Bernstein East', **Leonard Bernstein**, Elmer is one of Hollywood's most prolific and versatile film composers with over ninety film scores to his credit. His score for *The Man with the Golden Arm* (1955) was one of the first to meld symphonic and jazz elements successfully.

On graduating from New York University, Bernstein attempted careers as a painter, actor and dancer before returning to music, which he had studied at the Juilliard School. While in the army during the Second World War, he wrote radio scores and arranged for **Glenn Miller**. On his discharge he worked briefly in radio before moving to Hollywood.

Though known for jazz scores, such as *Golden Arm*, the main title theme of which gave him a pop hit in 1956 (Decca), *Some Came Running* (1959) and *A Walk on the Wild Side* (1962), Bernstein was equally adept at producing brash and busy scores for epics and swashbucklers, in the manner of **Victor Young**, such as *The Ten Commandments* (1955) and *The Buccaneer* (1959), and melodic and atmospheric music for intimate films like *Birdman of Alcatraz* (1962) and *To Kill a Mockingbird* (1963). His one British hit was 'Theme to Staccato' (1959) from a teleseries about a jazz musician turned detective. He won an Oscar for his noisy but vibrant score for *Thoroughly Modern Millie* (1967). Much of his subsequent work, which includes the melancholy *The Shootist* (1976), *An American Werewolf in London* (1981), *Trading Places* (1983) and *Mad Dog and Glory* (1993) has not been so distinctive although his scores for *My Left Foot* (1989) and *The Grifters* (1990) were critically praised.

In 1993 he conducted the Royal Philharmonic Pops Orchestra on *Elmer Bernstein by Elmer Bernstein* (Denon), a selection of his most well-known movie themes. Film scores of the nineties included *Devil in a Blue Dress* (1995), *Buddy* and *The Rainmaker* (both 1997).

LEONARD BERNSTEIN
b. 25 August 1918, Lawrence, Massachusetts, USA, d. 14 October 1990, New York

One of the few composers since **George Gershwin** who could work with equal facility in classical and popular music, Bernstein's most renowned score was his collaboration with **Stephen Sondheim** on *West Side Story* (1959).

Following his graduation from Harvard and further studies, Bernstein was appointed Assistant Conductor of the New York Philharmonic Orchestra. His first concert, replacing Bruno Walter, was broadcast nationally and he became a national figure overnight. After other conducting assignments, he returned as Music Director of the Philharmonic from 1956 to 1969.

Bernstein pursued parallel careers as composer and educator – he became Professor of Music at Brandeis University in 1951. His first major works in the popular sphere were the music for the Broadway musicals *On the Town* (1944, filmed 1949) and *Wonderful Town* (1953), in collaboration with Betty Comden and Adolph Green. Bernstein next wrote the film score *On the Waterfront* (1955) before working with Sondheim on *Candide* (1956).

This led to *West Side Story*, the hit musical which transposed the *Romeo and Juliet* story to the world of New York street gangs. Later a successful film directed by Robert Wise in 1961, the show included several songs that became popular standards: the romantic ballad 'Maria' (a hit for **Johnny Mathis** in 1960 and **P. J. Proby** in 1965), the intense 'America' (of which the Nice recorded a rock version for Immediate in 1968), 'Tonight' and 'I Feel Pretty'. In 1985 Bernstein conducted a bestselling re-recording of the *West Side Story* score for Deutsche Grammophon, with opera stars **Kiri Te Kanawa** and Jose Carreras in the leading roles.

Among the most prolific of classical recording artists, Bernstein conducted for Columbia and Deutsche Grammophon all the symphonies of Mahler, Beethoven and Brahms, as well as the opera *Tristan und Isolde* (Philips, 1983). He was among the pioneers of the television presentation of music, creating the *Omnibus* series for the CBS network in 1954.

CHUCK BERRY
b. Charles Edward Berry, 18 October 1926, St Louis, Missouri, USA

Berry was the author of a way of songwriting and of a guitar style which still permeate rock. A major influence on **The Beatles**, **Bob Dylan**, the **Rolling Stones** and the **Beach Boys**, his own musical career was erratic, damaged by brushes with the law and by poor professional decisions.

He continues to be an enigmatic interviewee and many details of his early life remain obscure. He grew up in St Louis where his parents sang in a Baptist church choir and in his adolescence he spent time in a reform school following a conviction for robbery, and in night school, training as a beautician.

By the early fifties he was leading a blues trio in the St Louis area which featured pianist Johnny Johnson. During this period he integrated a range of influences into his own mature style. Among guitarists, he favoured the technical innovator **Les Paul** and jazz virtuoso **Charlie Christian**, but above all **T-Bone Walker**, whose single string guitar improvisations on such tracks as 'Strolling with Bones' (1950) Berry adapted to give a more insistent rhythm. His clearly enunciated vocals were free of the blues melisma and owed much to the examples of **Nat 'King' Cole** and **Louis Jordan**, whose witty humorous jump blues were a model for Berry's up-to-date lyric observations. Another songwriting source was the material supplied by Don Raye for **Ella Mae Morse**, like 'Down the Road Apiece' and 'House of Blue Lights', both of which Berry would later record.

His recording career began in 1955 in Chicago when **Muddy Waters** directed Berry and a demo tape of 'Ida Red' to **Leonard Chess**. It was based on a country-and-western record Berry had heard on the radio, and Chess made him re-record the song as 'Maybellene', a paean to a car with Berry's unusual clamorous guitar lines. Top disc-jockey **Alan Freed** (credited as co-writer) helped to popularize the record, which became one of the first rock'n'roll hits.

That neither Chess nor Berry was sure what had attracted the mass teenage audience to the record is clear from the fact that, of five singles released in 1956, only the magnificent hymn to the new music, 'Roll over Beethoven', was a hit. The other tracks lacked that teenage theme: 'No Money Down' was a Jordan-style complaint; 'Thirty Days', a conventional blues number; 'Brown Eyed Handsome Man', the first of the songs in which Berry starred as his own hero; and 'You Can't Catch Me', another car-race song.

In 1957–8 he had five Top Twenty successes and six more singles that appeared only in the lower reaches of the chart. In 1959–60 there were six small hits and five misses. All the big hits had themes tailored to a school-age, adolescent audience: 'Rock and Roll Music' reiterated the 'Beethoven' message, while 'Johnny B. Goode' was the story of a rock star; 'School Day' expressed the universal frustrations of those subjected to compulsory schooling, and 'Carol' and 'Sweet Little Sixteen' were teenage love songs.

But if most of these were not hits, they were hugely influential. As the next decade was to prove, the Berry *œuvre* was avidly studied by young musicians. In the fifties Berry's popularity as a live performer and on film was not diminished by his relative lack of chart success. He toured Australia, where his famous 'duck walk' – a crouching run across the stage during intricate solo passages – brought audiences to their feet. His live show was captured in the unlikely setting of the 1958 Newport Jazz Festival in the film *Jazz on a*

Summer's Day (1960), while under Freed's auspices he appeared in several rock films – *Rock Rock Rock* and *Mr Rock'n'Roll* (both 1957) and *Go Johnny Go* (1959).

In 1959 Berry was convicted on an immorality charge concerning a teenage girl employed at his nightclub. His first conviction was quashed on appeal but he was eventually sentenced and spent two years in an Indiana jail. By the time of his release, Berry's early work was more popular than ever thanks to a new generation of white rock bands. In Britain, both The Beatles and the Stones had acknowledged his importance by performing and recording his songs. 'Beethoven' and 'Rock'n'Roll Music' were on early Beatles' albums, while the Rolling Stones' club act ended with a rousing 'Bye Bye Johnny', and 'Come on', another witty complaint song, was their first single release. And when Decca released 'Memphis, Tennessee', one of Chuck Berry's finest blendings of blues feeling with a contemporary narrative by Dave Berry (born Grundy, he chose his stage name in honour of Chuck), Pye – the British licensee of Chess – retaliated by putting out the original, which became a Top Ten hit in 1963. In the same year in America, **Lonnie Mack**'s instrumental 'Memphis' was a big hit and the Beach Boys based 'Surfin' U.S.A.' on 'Sweet Little Sixteen', while Dylan's first Top Forty single 'Subterranean Homesick Blues' (1965) sounded like part two of one of Berry's greatest 'botheration' songs, 'Too Much Monkey Business'.

His first recordings after leaving jail included several classics – 'Nadine', 'No Particular Place to Go' (which captured the teen idyll in one line, 'Cruisin' and playin' the radio') and the perkily plaintive 'It Wasn't Me'. In 1966 Berry moved to Mercury for a $50,000 advance (his concern with money matters is legendary, and tales abound of his demanding payment in cash before he performs). By common consent, the five Mercury albums, which included *Golden Hits, St Louis to Frisco* and *Live at the Fillmore* (1967) are among his poorest work. Perhaps uncertain of the sixties audience, Berry re-recorded his hits 'in Memphis style', cut a heavy rock eighteen-minute instrumental 'Concerto in B Goode' and recorded a live album in San Francisco with the **Steve Miller** Band on which he courted the blues audience with versions of 'C. C. Rider' and 'Hoochie Coochie Man'.

A return to Chess in 1970 produced *Back Home*, which featured 'Tulane' and 'Have Mercy Judge', two story songs about drug busts, proving that his lyric skill remained. But it was a live recording which gave him a surprise transatlantic No. 1 in 1972. While in Britain to record *London Sessions* (1972) with an array of sixties guitar superstars in a similar format to earlier records by **Howlin' Wolf** and **Muddy Waters**, he cut 'My Ding-a-Ling'. On this mildly risqué version of 'My Tambourine', which he had recorded for Mer-

cury, he was backed by members of the **Average White Band**.

The song's success established Berry with a fresh teenage generation (the song even provoked an unsuccessful 'answer' record: 'My Pussycat' by Miss Chuckle Cherry). He continued to perform on rock revival shows and to record sporadically – *Rockit* (Atlantic, 1979), featuring Johnny Johnson's bluesy piano on 'I Need You Baby', was the best work of this period.

Berry's frayed relations with authority also continued. In 1979 he was sentenced to 100 days' imprisonment for tax evasion. He appeared in the 1977 movie *American Hot Wax*, based on Freed's career, and in 1987 starred in the autobiographical concert film *Hail Hail Rock'n'Roll* (whose musical director was Keith Richards), directed by Taylor Hackford, and published his autobiography which, unusually for rock stars, he also wrote.

His long time pianist Johnny Johnson recorded the solo albums *Johnny be Bad* (1991), with Keith Richards and **Eric Clapton** in support, and *That'll Work* (1993) with the Kentucky Headhunters. In the second half of the decade Berry's professional life was mostly taken up with celebratory performances and guest appearances at the Rock'n'Roll Hall of Fame, interspersed with brief tours.

RICHARD BERRY
b. 11 April 1935, New Orleans, Louisiana, USA,
d. 23 January 1997

A journeyman writer, producer and performer of the fifties and sixties, Berry wrote and recorded the original version of 'Louie Louie', one of rock'n'roll's greatest invocations of the power of music.

Berry moved to Los Angeles in the early forties and began writing songs with **Jesse Belvin**. He formed the Debonairs and with them was signed to Recorded in Hollywood by John Dolphin, who renamed them the Hollywood Bluejays. Renamed the Flairs when they moved to the Flair label, they recorded 'She Wants to Rock' (1953), produced by **Leiber and Stoller**, who later had Berry speak the narration of the Robins' version of the classic 'Riot in Cell Block No. 9' (Spark, 1955). Berry himself recorded a variant of the song 'The Big Break' (Flair, 1955), the year he duetted with **Etta James** on 'Roll with Me Henry', her answer record to **Hank Ballard** and the Midnighters' 'Work with Me Annie'. When the Flairs left Flair, the group became the Flares (without Berry) and had the Top Thirty hit 'Footstomping – Part 1' (Felsted, 1961).

Berry recorded solo for Modern and RPM before forming the Pharoahs and recording 'Louie Louie' (Flip, 1956). Although never a national hit, the song became part of the repertoire of the garage bands in

Washington state, where it had been a regional hit. Finally, when raucously re-recorded by the Kingsmen (Wand, 1963) at the height of Beatlemania, 'Louie Louie' sold a million copies and co-incidentally revived Berry's career. The song was later recorded by the **Kinks** (1965), the Sandpipers, whose soft-rock version was a hit in 1966 on A&M, and numerous others. Indeed so many acts recorded the song in different styles that in 1986 Rhino issued *Louie, Louie*, an album of versions of the songs. Later research has showed that there are over 1,200 recordings of the song. Berry only benefited from these in the nineties when he was returned the copyright of the song after a lengthy dispute. A further mark of the song's mysterious power was the FBI investigation into the song, which, according to papers released under the Freedom of Information Act, they considered to be either obscene or part of a rock'n'roll conspiracy.

Berry continued recording in the sixties, appearing on virtually every small Californian label, before in the seventies and eighties he restricted himself to appearances throughout the Los Angeles area.

B*WITCHED
Lindsay Armaou; Edele Lynch; Keavy Lynch; Sinead O'Caroll

Irish teen-pop quartet B*witched became the youngest girl group to have a UK No. 1 with their début release.

Inspired by the success of their older brother, **Boyzone**'s Shane, twin sisters Edele and Keavy Lynch and fellow members Armaou and O'Caroll signed to the Glow Worm label in 1997 and began to work with producer Ray Hedges (Boyzone, **Bros**). The extraordinary hype preceding their début release, 'C'est La Vie', understandable in view of the Lynch sisters' older relation, guaranteed its entry at number one in the British charts. However, the recording's traditional Irish instrumentation set it apart from the flood of girl- and boy-bands of the time.

The unrelenting barrage of publicity surrounding the group brought them a second number one hit with 'Rollercoaster', and their eponymous début album* soon followed suit. Their third single, 'To You I Belong', a mid-paced, festive ballad, also hit the top spot.

1999 saw B*Witched become the first group to go straight in at number one with their first four singles with the release of another light ballad, 'Blame it on the Weatherman'. They also embarked on a lengthy promotional tour of America, where their début release managed to climb into the Top Ten, echoing their immediate success in Britain. *B*Witched* was also a success in the US, remaining in the *Billboard* charts for most of 1999.

BIG COUNTRY
Stuart Adamson, b. 11 April 1958, Manchester, England; Bruce Watson, b. 11 March 1961, Ontario, Canada; Mark Brzezicki, b. 21 June 1957, Slough, England; Tony Butler, b. 2 February 1957, London, England

Formed by guitarist Stuart Adamson from the ashes of Scottish pop-punk band the Skids, Big Country enjoyed great success in the eighties with a string of anthemic singles and live shows which attracted a devoted following.

Adamson and vocalist Richard Jobson formed the Skids in Dunfermline, Scotland, in 1977. After one independent single, 'Charles', on their own label, No Bad Records, they signed to Virgin Records, recording three successful albums, including the 1980 Top Ten entry *The Absolute Game*, and several hit singles, including 'Into the Valley' and 'Masquerade' (1979). When Adamson left in 1981, Jobson kept the Skids' name alive for one more album, subsequently forming the Armoury Show with ex-Magazine/**Siouxsie and the Banshees** guitarist John McGeogh and releasing several albums of poetry before becoming a TV presenter.

Returning to Dunfermline, Adamson formed Big Country with childhood friend Watson, and with a temporary rhythm section recorded demos before recruiting bassist Butler and drummer Brzezicki (from Simon Townshend's On the Air) and signing to Phonogram in 1982. The band made the UK Top Ten with its second single, 'Fields of Fire' (1983). Two further hit singles, 'In a Big Country' and 'Chance', preceded the début album, *The Crossing*, which reached the Top Five in the UK and the Top Twenty in the US. The album was notable for the decidedly Scottish subject matter of Adamson's lyrics, a distinctive twin guitar sound and Steve Lillywhite's dynamic production.

'Wonderland' preceded *Steel Town* (1984), which was recorded with Lillywhite in chaotic circumstances in **Abba**'s Polar Studios in Stockholm. The album entered the UK charts at No. 1, testament to the band's popularity as a live attraction. Robin Millar took over as producer for the rootsier *The Seer* (1986), another UK Top Five album, which featured a guest spot from **Kate Bush** and delivered further UK hits, including 'One Great Thing', which won notoriety when used as the theme for a beer commercial the following year. Adamson and Watson also wrote the music for the Scottish film comedy *Restless Natives*.

The band's fourth album, *Peace in our Time* (1988), had a more Americanized sound, courtesy of producer Peter Wolf, in a bid to regain lost ground in the US, but the restrictions of the band's style were beginning to tell, and Brzezicki left Big Country in 1989, to be replaced by Pat Ahern. Experienced session drummer Simon Phillips played on *The Buffalo Skinners*

(1993), which marked a change of label (to Chrysalis imprint Compulsion) and a return to the sound of their early material. Shortly after its release, Brzezicki rejoined Big Country. They followed this with a live album of their hits, *Without the Aid of a Safety Net* (1994). *Why the Long Face* (1995) and a second live set, *Eclectic* (1996), featured a more stripped-down sound. It was followed by the punchier *Driving to Damascus* (1999), which featured a couple of songs by Ray Davies (formerly of the **Kinks**) and a duet with Eddi Reader (formerly of Fairground Attraction).

BIG DADDY KANE
b. Antonio Hardy, 10 September 1969, Brooklyn, New York, USA

Big Daddy Kane mixed the soul stylings of **Barry White** and **Marvin Gaye** to his own snappy rap technique to great commercial effect during the late 1980s and early 1990s. Kane has stated his aim was to be a cross between Marvin Gaye and Malcolm X, that is to say 'a sexy entertainer and a strong black leader', but he has generally promoted an image as the former at the expense of the latter.

Kane's career began in 1984, when as an aspiring rapper he was introduced to leading hip-hop producer Marley Marl via another New York rapper, Biz Markie. Markie was already signed to Marl's Cold Chillin Records, and Kane was added to the roster in 1987, releasing his début single 'Raw' the same year, and his first album, *Long Live the Kane*, in 1988.

His second album, *It's a Big Daddy Thing* (1989), saw the evolution of the sexy entertainer persona through hits like 'Smooth Operator', although a less charismatic attitude to women was also evident on 'Pimpin' Ain't Easy', recorded with Nice and Smooth. The album also contained the hit 'Ain't No Stoppin' Us Now'. As well as his own recording, Kane was also working as an in-house writer for other Cold Chillin acts, include Markie and Roxanne Shante.

Taste of Chocolate followed in 1990, featuring a collaboration with Barry White as well as a duet with Malcolm X's daughter, Camilla Shabazz. While recording with White clearly strengthened his romantic image, Kane also boosted his hardcore credentials with an appearance on 'Burn Hollywood Burn' on **Public Enemy**'s *Fear of a Black Planet*.

Prince of Darkness featured guest appearances from Busta Rhymes and **A Tribe Called Quest**'s Q-Tip, and maintained Kane's market position between rap and R&B audiences. It was followed by *Looks Like a Job for . . .* (1993) and *Daddy's Home* (1994).

Kane's recordings became less frequent as the 1990s progressed, as, in common with other rap stars, he began to develop a film career. He contributed 'Nuff Respect' to the soundtrack of *Juice*, co-starred in

Mario Van Peebles' black western *Posse* and also appeared in Robert Townsend's *Meteor Man*. Kane returned with 1998's *Veteranz Day*, but this failed to match the commercial success of his earlier recordings.

BIG MAYBELLE
b. Mabel Louise Smith, 1 May 1924, Jackson, Tennessee, USA, d. 23 January 1972

An accomplished performer in the new urban blues style of the fifties, Big Maybelle's uninhibited singing style contributed to the formation of the soul sound of the following decade.

After working with the Dave Clark Band in Memphis in the mid-thirties, she toured with the all-women Sweethearts of Rhythm. Her first solo records, for the King label in 1947, followed a spell with Christine Chatman's orchestra.

A move to Columbia's Okeh label led to her greatest commercial success, with three R&B hits in 1953. 'Grabbin' Blues', 'Way Back Home' and 'My Country Man' showcased Big Maybelle's ability to deliver both blues and ballads with raw emotional power or world-weary desperation. Her recordings seldom matched up to her live performances, however – she was a frequent and popular performer at Harlem's Apollo Theater – and she had only one more hit during the fifties, 'Candy' (Savoy, 1956). Part of her set at the Newport Jazz Festival in 1958 was included in the film *Jazz on a Summer's Day*.

Dubbed 'The Mother of Soul' in the sixties, she continued to record frequently with various labels including Epic, Scepter and Brunswick (who promoted her work as 'gospel soul'). Her only chart success came in 1966 with the minor R&B hits 'Don't Pass Me By' and '96 Tears'. The latter was written by Rudy Martinez, whose own recording as **? and the Mysterians** was a No. 1 pop hit and million-seller.

BIG YOUTH
b. Manley Augustus Buchanan, 1949, Kingston, Jamaica

A popular 'toaster' – a disc-jockey who ad-libbed over instrumental tracks – Big Youth developed a style heavily imbued with Rastafarian sentiments.

His first influence was toaster **U-Roy** and his first record was a deejay version of Errol Dunkley's 'Movie Star' for **Gregory Isaacs**' African Museum label. Big Youth found success with the novel 'S-90 Skank' (1972), a hymn of praise to a motorcycle on which producer **Keith Hudson** included the sound of the bike's engine. Big Youth's later songs were frequently topical in inspiration, like 'Foreman and Frazier' (1973), which dealt with a world-title boxing match.

Big Youth's most important recording was *Dread Locks Dread* (1975, released in Britain by Virgin in

1977). With titles like 'Marcus Garvey Dread' and 'Train to Rhodesia', it established a Rasta presence in the deejay style, in opposition to the sexual innuendo of performers like I-Roy. On later records Big Youth made deejay versions of such R&B and soul hits as **Ray Charles**' 'Hit the Road Jack' and **Marvin Gaye**'s 'What's Going on'.

Eventually, Big Youth turned to more conventional reggae singing on the **Prince Buster**-produced 'When Revolution Comes' and *Chanting Dread inna Fine Style* (Blue Moon, 1982). However, *Manifestations* (1988) was as uncompromising as ever and had little success outside Jamaica.

THE BIHARI BROTHERS

Joe, Jules, Lester and Saul Bihari ran Modern, one of the most important R&B record labels of the forties and fifties. Among those appearing on Modern and its associated labels were **B. B. King**, **John Lee Hooker**, **Howlin' Wolf**, **Elmore James**, **Jimmy Witherspoon** and **Ike and Tina Turner**.

Raised in Oklahoma, the Biharis moved to Los Angeles in 1941 where Jules operated jukeboxes in the city's black section. They set up Modern in 1945 to serve the massive influx of Southern blacks brought to the West Coast by the opportunities for war work. Jules supervised the recordings, Lester looked for talent, Joe did the marketing and Saul oversaw production and general business matters. In 1947 they bought a pressing plant and established a series of subsidiary labels including RPM and Crown.

The company's first R&B hit was Haddy Brooks' sultry version of 'That's My Desire' (1947), an even bigger hit for **Frankie Laine** later that year, but the Biharis recorded all types of black music from rural blues to the emerging vocal-group and instrumental R&B. Blues artists who provided hits for the company included Hooker with 'Boogie Chillun' (Modern, 1948) and King, whose 'Three o'Clock Blues' (1950) was the first success for the RPM label. Both were produced for the Biharis by local talent scouts – Hooker in Detroit by John Caplan and Leonard Besman and King in Memphis by Ike Turner. From Texas, Modern released tracks by Smokey Hogg, **Lightnin' Hopkins**, Pee Wee Crayton and Roy Hawkins, who wrote and first recorded 'The Thrill Is Gone' (1951), later a huge hit for B. B. King.

In Los Angeles itself, Modern was in competition with labels like Aladdin and Savoy for more contemporary R&B artists. Modern recorded Johnny Moore's Three Blazers with Floyd Dixon, whose own hits included 'Dallas Blues' (1949). Other successful records in the R&B charts were 'Blow Joe Blow' by sax-player Joe Houston, Young Jessie's 'Mary Lou', **Etta James**' 'Wallflower' (covered by Georgia Gibbs

on Mercury as 'Dance with Me Henry') and 'Good Rockin' Daddy' (1955), and 'Goodnight My Love' by **Jesse Belvin** (1956).

In the mid-fifties the company had the occasional pop hit with vocal groups like the Cadets ('Stranded in the Jungle') and the Teen Queens ('Eddie My Love'). By the end of the decade, however, the Biharis had placed their emphasis on repackaging the earlier records of Hooker, King and others on the budget-price Crown label, although soul and R&B by Ike and Tina Turner and others was released on the Kent label in the mid-sixties.

Though largely inactive in later years, Modern – unlike contemporaries like **Don Robey**'s Duke and **Syd Nathan**'s King – remained in its original ownership, despite Saul Bihari's death in 1975. On Jules's death in 1984, the rights in the label were sold to Virgin (US), Ace (UK) and Blues Interaction (Japan). Since then a vigorous reissue programme has been undertaken.

THEODORE BIKEL
b. 2 May 1924, Vienna, Austria

A screen and stage actor as well as folk singer, Bikel personified the cosmopolitan, cabaret aspect of the American folk revival of the early sixties.

He reached the United States via Palestine and London, where his stage appearances won him a part in the film *The African Queen* (1951). With his Jewish background, Bikel put together a repertoire of Eastern European, Russian and Yiddish songs. His first album for Elektra was the appropriately titled *Folk Songs from Just About Everywhere* (1958).

Bikel appeared at the 1960 Newport Folk Festival and in 1963, with **Pete Seeger** and others, he helped to reorganize the festival as a non-profit-making foundation. Though never a 'protest singer', he was outspoken in his condemnation of the blacklisting of Seeger and other artists which prevented them from appearing on US television in the fifties.

As an actor, Bikel appeared in more than a dozen films, including such diverse works as *My Fair Lady* (1964) and the **Frank Zappa** vehicle *200 Motels* (1971). On Broadway he starred with Mary Martin in *The Sound of Music* (1954). In 1977 Bikel was apppointed by President Carter to the National Council for the Arts.

ACKER BILK
b. Bernard Bilk, 28 January 1929, Pensford, Somerset, England

A bandleader and trad jazz clarinettist, Acker Bilk was the only British artist to top the American charts prior to **The Beatles** in the rock era. The disc was 'Stranger on the Shore' (EMI Columbia, Atco in

America, 1961), an instrumental ballad which had been the theme of a television series.

He spent four years with the band of purist New Orleans stylist **Ken Colyer** before forming Mr Acker Bilk's Paramount Jazz Band in 1958. With a sense of showmanship, elaborate publicity from the 'Bilk Marketing Board' and an exaggerated rural accent, Bilk benefited from the surge of popularity experienced by trad in the late fifties. Four Top Twenty hits, including 'Summer Set' (1960) and 'That's My Home' (1961), featuring Bilk's gravelly vocals – based on those of **Louis Armstrong** – preceded 'Stranger on the Shore'. 'Buona Sera' (1960) was a cover of **Louis Prima**'s American hit.

As trad gave way to the beat boom, Bilk's chart success waned, but the band continued to tour throughout Europe and to record on Pye/PRT and Polydor. In 1976 he had another Top Ten hit with 'Aria' (PRT), followed by a hit album, *Sheer Magic*. In the eighties he regularly appeared on television in Britain and toured intermittently.

BJÖRK
b. Björk Gudmundsdottir, 1965, Reykjavik, Iceland

An eccentric singer, Björk found fame fronting pop group the Sugarcubes before embarking on a successful solo career.

Music was a major focus of Björk's upbringing, and she began performing traditional Icelandic folk songs at a young age, releasing an album of standards soon after turning eleven. She spent her early teens in a series of punk bands, most notably Kukl, whose members later formed the core of the Sugarcubes. Founding members Björk, Siggi Baldurson and Einer Orn were joined by Magg Ornotfsdottir, Bragi Olagsson and Thor Eldon, with whom Björk had a son, Sindri, in 1987. Their début album, *Life's Too Good* (1986), made them superstars at home as well as winning them a cult following in the UK and US. After recording an album of Icelandic jazz, Björk became interested in dance music, which signalled the end of the Sugarcubes. Their final album, *It's It* (1992), collected together old material and dance remixes before the band split up.

Björk's first solo album, the aptly titled *Début* (One Little Indian, 1993), sold three million copies worldwide and spawned three hit singles: 'Big Time Sensuality', 'Human Behaviour' and 'Venus as a Boy'. Relocating to London, she outsold her début with *Post** (1995), which featured collaborations with Graham Massey of 808 State, Howie B and Tricky. This album featured her biggest hit single to date in 'It's Oh So Quiet', a cover of a 1930s jazz tune which reached the British Top Ten. Björk also charted with 'Army of Me', 'Isobel' and 'Possibly Maybe'.

After an album of remixes of tracks from *Post*, *Telegram* (1996), came the release of *Homogenic* (1997), widely viewed as her most consistent solo work, which merged together techno beats and orchestral arrangement, and featured an array of singles including 'Hunter', 'Bachelorette' and 'All Is Full of Love', the first single to be put out in DVD format.

In 1999 Björk turned to the cinema for the musical *Dancer in the Dark*, in which she appeared with Catherine Deneuve. The film, which won the Palme d'Or at Cannes, was controversial, with director Lars von Trier and Björk alternately celebrating and ridiculing each other, particularly for Björk's extreme identification with her part. *Selmasongs* (2000), which collected together her music for the film, included a duet with **Radiohead**'s Thom Yorke.

BLACK
Colin Vearncombe, b. 26 May 1951, Liverpool, England; Dave Dickie, Jimmy Sangster

Black is best remembered for the international hit 'Wonderful Life'.

Guitarist, keyboards-player and singer Vearncombe played in a local Liverpool punk group, Epileptic Tits, in 1977. He formed the first version of Black in 1981 and the following year met Dave Dickie, a former member of local band Last Chant and an engineer at Liverpool's Eternal studios. Dickie played keyboards and Jimmy Sangster joined on bass when Black toured with Orange Juice in 1983. Black's later activities were mostly studio-based. The unsuccessful singles 'Hey Presto' (1984) and 'More Than the Sun' were followed by the release of 'Wonderful Life' on a local label.

A turntable hit, it led to a recording contract in 1987 with A&M and the British hit 'Sweetest Smile'. A&M next issued a new version of 'Wonderful Life' with a stylish video and the song's yearning atmosphere and clever arrangement made it and its accompanying album among Europe's biggest-selling records of 1987.

The next album, *Comedy*, was co-produced by Dix and Robin Millar. However, neither it nor later singles like 'The Big One' and 'Feel Like Change' and the album *Black* (1991) were able to emulate the success of 'Wonderful Life'. The next Black release, *Are We Having Fun Yet?*, appeared on Vearncombe's own Chaos Reins label.

BLACK BOX

The *nom de disque* used by a trio of Italian house music producers, Black Box combined contemporary dance beats with soaring female vocals on the international hit 'Ride on Time'.

Known as Groove Groove Melody, the production

team consisted of club DJ Daniele Davoli, classical musician Valerio Simplici and computer and keyboards-player Mirko Limoni. Using a studio in the Reggio d'Emilia area, the trio used the voice of Katrine (born Catherine Quinol in Paris, France) and a sample of the US singer Loleatta Holloway (from 'Love Sensation') for the arresting lead singing on 'Ride on Time'. During 1989 the single headed national charts all over Europe and was an American hit as well. The Italian producers had to share their royalties with the owners of the Holloway track that had been sampled.

A similar formula was used in 1990 for 'I Don't Know Anybody Else' and 'Everybody Everybody', which appeared on the album *Dreamland*. The fourth Black Box hit, 'Fantasy', was a revival of an **Earth, Wind and Fire** song. Davoli, Limoni and Semplici were also responsible for dance records issued under several more names, such as Starlight ('Numero Uno', 1989).

The trio also produced US singer Lonnie Gordon ('Gonna Catch You') and a remix of **ABC**'s 1991 single, 'Say It'. In 1992 they issued a further album, *Mixed Up*.

THE BLACK CROWES
Chris Robinson, b. 20 December 1966, Atlanta, USA; Rich(ard) Robinson, b. 24 May 1969, Atlanta; Johnny Colt, b. 24 May 1966, Cherry Point, North Carolina; Steve Gorman, b. 17 August, 1965, Hopkinsville, Kentucky; Jeff Cease, b. 24 June 1967, Nashville, Tennessee; Marc Ford; Ed Hawrysch

US band the Black Crowes rose to prominence in the early nineties with a mix of hard rock and R&B that drew comparisons with the **Rolling Stones**, **Aerosmith** and (especially) **Rod Stewart** and the Faces.

Formed in Atlanta, Georgia, in 1984 (as the Greasy Little Toes, then Mr Crowe's Garden) around the songwriting partnership of the Robinson brothers, Chris (vocals) and Rich (guitar), the band also featured bassist Colt and drummer Gorman and the dual lead guitars of Robinson and Cease. It won a devoted local following, but the group was merely a local celebrity until picked up by the Def American label in 1989.

Producer George Droukalias captured the bourbon-soaked good-time atmosphere of the quintet's live performances on the début album, *Shake Your Money Maker*, which was released to lavish praise in 1990. It featured the band's break-through single, a no-holds-barred cover of **Otis Redding**'s 'Hard to Handle', and the cautionary tale of drug abuse, 'She Talks to Angels'. The album was a huge success in the US in great part because the band toured extensively to promote it, playing 350 dates and maintaining a

high profile. This helped keep *Money Maker* in the US charts for over 18 months, selling over five million copies in the process.

The constant touring was interrupted by the sessions for the second album, *The Southern Harmony and Musical Companion* (1992), recorded in only eight days, which saw the first appearance on record of new lead guitarist Ford (ex-Burning Tree), replacing Cease. Another hit album, it was also more adventurous (including, for example, a version of **Bob Marley**'s 'Time Will Tell'), but elsewhere kept to the rock/R&B blueprint. Again, intensive live work followed, including several major European festivals in the summer of 1993.

1994's hit album *Amorica* was only slightly more conservative, mixing seventies-style rock and Latin influences with aplomb. It was much criticized in America for its sleeve, which several retail chains refused to display. *Three Snakes & One Charm* (1996), which the band supported with a lengthy US tour, was far more enthusiastically received. The hard-rocking *By Your Side* (1999) was one of the first albums to be promoted through an Internet broadcast. In 2000 the group continued in this vein, teaming up with Jimmy Page of **Led Zeppelin** for *Jimmy Page and the Black Crowes Live at the Greek*, which was made available online through Musicmaker.com. The set introduced 'What Is and What Never Should Be', one of the first hit singles created online.

BLACK OAK ARKANSAS
Jim 'Dandy' Mangrum, b. 30 March 1948, Black Oak, Arkansas, USA; Ricky Reynolds, b. 29 October 1948, Manilan, Arkansas; Jimmy Henderson, b. 20 May 1954, Jackson, Mississippi; Stan Knight, b. 12 February 1949, Little Rock, Arkansas; Pat Daugherty, b. 11 November 1947, Jonesboro, Arkansas; Wayne Evans; Harvey Jett; Tommy Aldridge

Though they only had one major hit single, 'Jim Dandy' (Atco, 1974, a crude reworking of **Lavern Baker**'s 1956 hit), Black Oak Arkansas were one of the most successful touring acts of the seventies and formed a link between the (mostly Southern) boogie bands of that decade and the heavy-metal bands of the eighties.

The original band members all grew up in the vicinity of Black Oak and first came together as gang members before touring locally as Knowbody Else and recording one eponymous album for Stax in 1969. Later that year they settled in Los Angeles and signed to Atlantic as Black Oak Arkansas. Their early albums sold only moderately but through constant touring they slowly built an audience for their simple, riff-based boogie music, fronted by Mangrum's bare-chested machismo and mannered singing style. By the time of *High on the Hog* (1974) and *Raunch and Roll* (1975), the band had taken up residence in the album charts and in the stadiums of America.

Following a move to MCA in 1975, the band added female vocalist Ruby Star (with whom Mangrum also traded *doubles-entendres* on 'Jim Dandy'), who also recorded in her own right on MCA. By the late seventies and the growth of heavy metal their appeal started to wane, and with Mangrum the only remaining original member, they joined Capricorn for *Race with the Devil* (1977). During the eighties Mangrum, billed as Jim Dandy, toured and recorded as a solo act, moving further into heavy metal with releases like *Ready as Hell* (Heavy Metal Records, 1984).

BLACK SABBATH

Terry 'Geezer' Butler, b. 17 July 1949, Birmingham, England; Tony Iommi, b. 19 February 1948, Birmingham; Bill Ward, b. 5 May 1948, Birmingham; John 'Ozzy' Osbourne, b. 3 December 1948, Birmingham (replaced by Ronnie James Dio, b. 1940, USA, replaced by Dave Donato)

Arguably the band that invented heavy metal with their 1970 début record, twenty years later Black Sabbath had released over fifteen similarly constructed albums. By then, guitarist Iommi was the only remaining original member, vocalist Ozzy Osbourne having formed his own band in 1979, though in 1998 he rejoined for *Reunion*.

Originally a heavy blues band called Earth, the Birmingham group changed its name to Black Sabbath after drummer Butler had read a novel by occult thriller-writer Denis Wheatley. Their first eponymous album was produced by Rodger Bain and released by Vertigo. Quickly and crudely recorded, it nevertheless laid down the pattern of future work by Sabbath and many other bands – Osbourne's impassioned vocals and Iommi's crashing chords set off lyrics about destruction, war, drugs and the occult.

In the flower-power era, the ferocity of Sabbath's music caused protests from establishment figures. However, the second album, *Paranoid* (1970), and its title song were both Top Ten hits in Britain. The single was again a hit when reissued in 1980. The following three albums were also successful, with the musical pattern varied only by the addition of **Rick Wakeman** from **Yes** on keyboards for *Sabbath Bloody Sabbath* in 1973.

Later albums on NEMS in Europe and Warners in America included a choir and orchestra on some tracks and this dilution of the original heavy-metal approach has been cited as one reason why Osbourne finally left the band in 1979. He was replaced by Ronnie James Dio from Rainbow and the first album with the new vocalist, *Heaven and Hell* (Vertigo, 1980), was

Black Sabbath's most successful for some years.

The early eighties was an unsettled period for the band as first Dio and Ward and then Butler left. Ian Gillan (formerly of **Deep Purple**) sang on *Born Again* (1983), but by 1986, the *Seventh Star* album was entitled 'by Black Sabbath featuring Tony Iommi'. The vocalist was now Dave Donato.

In addition, the group's manager, Don Arden, was locked in dispute with Osbourne's manager (both Osbourne's wife and Arden's daughter). Ozzy's solo career had begun promisingly with a band featuring ex-**Uriah Heep** drummer Lee Kerslake and guitarist Randy Rhoads. It faltered in 1981 when a stage routine with a dead bat misfired, leaving Osbourne to undergo a course of anti-rabies inoculations, and hit a much more serious setback when Rhoads was killed in an air crash in 1982.

However, his lurid werewolf image for *Barking at the Moon* (Columbia, 1983) gave him two British hit singles and by 1986 he was at a new peak with the success of his fifth solo album, *The Ultimate Sin*. This was despite the unfavourable publicity from a court case when the parents of a teenage American suicide (unsuccessfully) claimed Ozzy's lyrics were responsible. That year also, he appeared in the horror film *Trick or Treat*, playing a fundamentalist preacher who campaigns against the evils of rock.

The original Sabbath quartet briefly reunited for a Live Aid performance, but the continuing rivalry between Iommi and Osbourne ensured that each would continue to produce his own separate version of classic heavy metal. The Iommi-led Black Sabbath released *The External Idol* (1987) and *Headless Cross* (1989), with former Trapeze and Deep Purple singer Glenn Hughes and produced by drummer Cozy Powell (*d. 5 April 1998*).

Osbourne followed *Tribute* (1987), a set of 1981 live recordings dedicated to Rhoads, with *No Rest for the Wicked* (1988), on which Zakk Wylde replaced guitarist Jake E. Lee. Wylde played on the live *Just Say Ozzy* (1990), recorded on the British leg of one of Osbourne's frequent tours of the late eighties and early nineties. In 1990 Osbourne helped out on Bill Ward's solo record *Ward One: Along the Way* (Chameleon). *No More Tears* was another US Top ten album, and he put in a cameo appearance in Penelope Spheeris's film *Decline of Western Civilization, Part 2* (1992).

Having overcome alcoholism, Osbourne attempted to overcome his addiction to touring, announcing his 1992 dates (from which 1993's *Live and Loud* was taken) would be his last, but in 1994 he began assembling a band for another farewell tour. Albums from this period include *Ozzmosis* (1995) and the retrospective *The Ozzman Cometh* (1997), while he and Iommi negotiated the reunion of Black Sabbath, which throughout the nineties had featured a much changed line-up.

In 1990, with a line-up of Iommi, Powell, much-travelled bassist Neil Murray and vocalist Tony Martin, Sabbath released *Tyr*, but another line-up change saw Dio back along with Iommi, Butler and veteran drummer Carmine Appice for *Dehumanizer* (1992). A one-off 1992 appearance by the three instrumentalists with Osbourne in the US led to speculation that Sabbath might re-form with Ozzy, but Iommi scotched the rumours by releasing *Cross Purposes* (IRS 1994) with yet another line-up of Black Sabbath. However, after *Forbidden* (1995) fared badly the economic rationale for a reunion grew stronger. After Osbourne appeared with the band several times in 1996 that happened in 1998 with the aptly titled *Reunion*.

BILL BLACK
b. 17 September 1926, Memphis, Tennessee, USA,
d. 21 October 1965, Memphis

Black's career provides a link between pre-rock'n'roll country music and sixties Southern soul. A string-bass session player for **Sam Phillips**, with Scotty Moore he played on all **Elvis Presley**'s Sun recordings and his early RCA tracks. In 1959 he formed the instrumental group, Bill Black's Combo, which influenced groups like **Booker T. and the MGs** with its bass-led rhythms.

Like Moore, Black was a member of the Starlite Wranglers with Doug Poindexter as vocalist. The group approached Sun Records and recorded the unsuccessful 'Now She Cares No More for Me'/'My Kind of Carrying on' (which, when issued in 1954, had 'Hillbilly' stamped across the label). Later Phillips hired Moore and Black to back Presley on the classic Sun records, in which R&B and country rhythms intertwined so successfully. When Black quit Presley in 1959, he mixed rock'n'roll and rhythm and blues with similar success. Starting with 'Smokie-Part 2'* (Hi, 1959) and ending with 'Twist-Her' (1962), he had eight pop hits, including two million-sellers, the best remembered of which is his version of the Presley hit 'Don't Be Cruel' (1960). In 1962 the Combo backed Gene Simmons on the Top Ten hit 'Haunted House' (Hi).

The original members of the band included Reggie Young (guitar), Martin Wills (sax), Carl McAvoy (piano), Jerry Arnold (drums) and Black on electric bass, but after Black's death from a brain tumour in 1965, guitarist Bob Tucker secured an agreement from his widow to keep the group going under Black's name. From *Solid and Country* (1975) on, the group became much more country orientated. By the eighties, having gone through some fifty personnel changes, they were a country-music institution.

CILLA BLACK
b. *Priscilla Maria Veronica White, 27 May 1943, Liverpool, England*

A singer whose career is a reminder of how unwise it is to make an absolute distinction between rock and showbusiness, Cilla Black's career began at the Cavern and by 1985 she was compère of the UK version of the TV game show *Blind Date*.

A Liverpool contemporary of **The Beatles**, she occasionally sang with Mersey groups and was signed to a management contract by Brian Epstein, who wanted to build on his early success with the Fab Four. She was given 'Love of the Loved', a Lennon–McCartney song for her first (unsuccessful) single on Parlophone, the same EMI label that had signed The Beatles.

Black's compellingly naive mezzo-soprano fared better when producer **George Martin** gave her **Dionne Warwick**'s US hit 'Anyone Who Had a Heart' to cover. This reached No. 1 in Britain in 1964. Thirteen more British hits followed in the next seven years, the most effective being the melodramatic 'You're My World' (a No. 1 in 1964) and Lennon–McCartney's oddly provincial 'Step Inside Love' (1968), delivered by Black in a manner reminiscent of a latterday **Gracie Fields**. She appeared in a number of undistinguished films, including *Work . . . Is a Four Letter Word* (1970).

Since the early seventies Black's musical contribution has been negligible. In 1985 she released the Dave Mackay-produced *Surprisingly Cilla* (Towerbell), which included remakes of some of her earlier hits and covers of **Phil Collins**' 'One More Night' and Tim Rice's, Björn Ulvaeus's and Benny Andersson's 'I Know Him So Well'. She entered the mainstream of British showbusiness, appearing regularly in television variety shows and pantomime. With *Blind Date* she achieved the distinction of becoming Britain's first female game show host.

A comeback album in 1993 garnered much media attention in the UK but few sales.

CLINT BLACK
b. *1962, Long Branch, New Jersey, USA*

One of the leading figures in contemporary country music, Black's songwriting and performing style mixes reflection with wry comment recalling that of **Merle Haggard** and **Jimmy Buffett**. With **Lyle Lovett**, Black is one of the most thoughtful and compelling of modern country writers

Black grew up in Houston, Texas, learning the guitar and harmonica. He worked as an iron worker and bait cutter on a fishing boat while playing local clubs where he formed a songwriting partnership with guitarist

Hayden Nicholas. Black was spotted by **ZZ Top** manager Bill Ham and signed a recording contract with RCA. His first single, 'A Better Man', an account of a failed relationship in which the narrator hopes he has learnt something for the future, went to No. 1 in the country charts as did four more songs from his début album *Killin' Time* (1989), including 'Nobody's Home' and 'Walkin' Away'. The album featured Nicholas on guitar.

The second album, *Put Yourself in My Shoes* (1990), included another country No. 1, 'Loving Blind', the sombre 'One More Payment' and 'Where Are You Now?'. In 1992 Black recorded *The Hard Way*, co-produced by James Stroud. In 1993 he issued *No Time to Kill*, which included the hits 'A Bad Goodbye' and 'No Time to Kill'. He also recorded a duet with Wynonna (formerly of the **Judds**), 'When My Ship Comes in'. The lesser *One Emotion* (1994) was his fifth album. It was followed by *Looking for Christmas* (1995), on which Black did the near impossible in producing an album of songs written or co-written by him. The album's stand-out track was the reflective 'The Kid', co-written with Haggard. The title song of *Nothing but the Tail Lights* (1997), his most successful album of the nineties, was a country chart-topper. More surprising was *D'Electrified* (2000) on which Black, with support from the likes of Edgar Winter, **Bruce Hornsby** and former member of Monty Python Eric Idle, embraced rock. The best track was a confident reworking of **Waylon Jennings**' classic 'Are You Sure Hank Done It This Way?'. A critical success, it sold poorly.

STANLEY BLACK
b. 14 June 1913, London, England

A leading figure in British popular music of the thirties and forties, Stanley Black was an orchestral conductor and a prolific arranger and composer of film, incidental and other light music.

At the age of twelve he had a composition broadcast by the BBC Symphony Orchestra. His own radio début was not until 1933, but in the interval he built a reputation as a pianist and arranger of dance-band music, contributing articles and arrangements to the *Melody Maker* and working with various bands. He recorded with visiting American jazz musicians such as **Coleman Hawkins**, Benny Carter and **Louis Armstrong**, and was commissioned to write material to be recorded by Hawkins and Carter. A visit with **Harry Roy** to South America in 1938 awoke his interest in Latin-American music, on which he became an expert.

In 1944 he took over as conductor of the BBC Dance Orchestra from Billy Ternent, a position he held until 1952. He also led the orchestra for **Anne Shelton**'s radio series *Introducing Anne*, and began a long association with Decca Records. In the fifties he worked on the radio series *Hi Gang* and *Much Binding in the Marsh*, among others, and wrote incidental music for BBC documentaries and signature tunes, including that for the **Goons**. In 1936 he started to compose for, and direct music for films, working eventually on more than fifty British films, including *Battle of the Sexes* (1959) and the **Cliff Richard** musical *Summer Holiday* (1963).

BUMPS BLACKWELL
b. Robert A. Blackwell, 23 May 1922, Seattle, Washington, USA, d. 9 March 1985, Whittier, California

A skilled arranger and composer, Blackwell is best known for masterminding the early hits of **Little Richard** and for his intermittent involvement in that artist's later career.

From a middle-class black family in Seattle, in the late forties he led a jazz group that included **Ray Charles** and **Quincy Jones**. He moved to Hollywood to study advanced composition under the composer Roy C. Harris, but soon took a job with **Art Rupe**'s Specialty label as arranger and producer. He cut records with **Larry Williams**, **Lloyd Price** and **Guitar Slim** before a demo tape from Little Richard arrived in 1955.

Blackwell wrote 'Good Golly Miss Molly', 'Ready Teddy' and 'Rip It Up' for Richard, providing material for the Frank Tashlin film, *The Girl Can't Help It* (1957), in which Richard sang the title song. He later produced **Sam Cooke**'s first secular recordings (composing 'You Send Me') and on leaving Specialty in 1957 took Cooke to the new Keen label. This was a nursery for such fledgling producers as **Lou Adler** and **Herb Alpert**.

Arguments with his partners led Blackwell to leave Keen to become West Coast A&R director for Mercury from 1959 to 1963. Here he signed **Billy Preston** and the Chambers Brothers, as well as recording some of Little Richard's best gospel performances. He became Richard's manager and continued to work on and off with the singer for the next decade.

CHRIS BLACKWELL
b. 22 June 1937, London, England

Founder of Island Records, the principal British independent record company, Blackwell played a major part in the emergence of British progressive rock in the sixties and, through his association with **Bob Marley**, the international popularity of reggae in the seventies. In the eighties Island signed U2, and American artists **Grace Jones** and the B-52s, as well as picking up the GoGo dance trend from Washington DC for international distribution.

Blackwell's family, associated with the Crosse & Blackwell food empire, was part of Jamaica's wealthy white community, and he was briefly aide-de-camp to the Governor-General before setting up Island to record a local jazz combo in 1959. Two years later he had his first hit with 'Little Sheila' by **Laurel Aitken**. Noticing the size of the expatriate market for Jamaican music in Britain, he moved to London in 1962, licensing material from other Kingston producers. He also licensed the American Sue label, whose material was in demand from both mod and R&B audiences. In 1968 Blackwell joined Lee Gopthal in setting up Trojan, which was to be Britain's most prolific reggae label for many years.

In 1964 he cut a pop hit, 'My Boy Lollipop', with Jamaican singer Millie Small, and on tour with her discovered Birmingham R&B band the Spencer Davis Group. Blackwell produced their early hits, leasing them to Philips. By the time **Stevie Winwood** set up Traffic in 1968, Island was fundamentally a progressive-rock label, with acts like **Fairport Convention**, **Emerson, Lake and Palmer**, **Cat Stevens**, Spooky Tooth, **Free** and **Jethro Tull**. Island was among the first to grasp that this was album rather than singles music, and promoted it accordingly. In the period 1968–72 the British album charts were dominated by progressive-rock bands.

Gradually, however, the production companies responsible for the rock acts – Chrysalis, Manticore, Bronze – set up their own labels and, in 1972, Island returned to its Jamaican roots when Blackwell signed and produced Bob Marley and the Wailers. Seeing in Marley the artist to give reggae an international audience, Blackwell worked with him to integrate rock elements into his music.

Later he concentrated on the corporate side of Island's activities, attempting to set up foreign branches and expanding into film production. Subsidiary labels like Antilles (jazz), Mango (Jamaican and African music) and 4th and Broadway (disco and dance music) were set up and he continued to produce a number of artists, notably Grace Jones and the B-52s.

In 1987, when Blackwell celebrated twenty-five years of Island's existence, the company employed 425 people and its turnover had topped $100 million. However, recurrent rumours that he wished to sell the company were confirmed in 1989 when PolyGram paid $272 million for Island Records. Blackwell remained with the company in an advisory capacity but devoted more time to property speculation (renovating art deco hotels in Miami) and, briefly, to film with Island Life. He also took the leading role in preserving Bob Marley's heritage by establishing the Bob Marley Foundation, which now owns the copyright to the singer's works in conjunction with the Marley family. He left PolyGram in 1998 to concentrate on Palm Pictures, his new music and film company.

OTIS BLACKWELL
b. 1931, Brooklyn, New York, USA

The writer of over 900 songs which sold over 30 million records, Blackwell was one of the greatest rock'n'roll composers.

He won local talent contests singing blues as a youth, but by his own admission was fascinated by cowboy singers such as **Tex Ritter**. It was perhaps this unusual combination of black and white influences that was the key factor in his success in the mid-fifties. Even his two most important pre-rock songs had cross-racial appeal. 'Daddy Rolling Stone' became a mod favourite in the version by the Jamaican singer Derek Martin and was recorded by **The Who** in 1965, while 'Fever' was a hit in 1955 for the white supperclub artist **Peggy Lee**, as well as **Little Willie John**.

This was only a prelude to Blackwell's greatest years when he supplied **Elvis Presley** not only with some of his best hit songs, but with a way of singing them, described by fellow songwriter **Doc Pomus** as containing a 'strange little tense passion'. Among these songs were 'Don't Be Cruel', 'All Shook Up' and 'Return to Sender'. Blackwell also supplied 'Great Balls of Fire' for **Jerry Lee Lewis** and 'Handy Man' for **Jimmy Jones**, the latter while working as a staff arranger for MGM.

Despite his close involvement in rock'n'roll, Blackwell operated as a songsmith of the Brill Building school and the arrival of **The Beatles** and sixties rock made him unfashionable. In 1977 he made some successful live appearances, followed by *These Are My Songs* (Inner, 1978) and a further solo album in 1981. By then, ironically, listeners saw a Presley influence on Blackwell, rather than the other way round. He had all but retired by the mid-eighties.

RUBEN BLADES
b. 16 July 1948, Panama City, Panama

One of the most controversial of the new salsa songwriters and singers of the eighties, Blades' socially committed songs began to reach English-speaking audiences following his signing to Elektra in 1984.

As a child in Panama, many of his earliest influences were American. They included **Glenn Miller**, **Duke Ellington** and, above all, rock'n'roll, which he sang with a band led by his brother. An incident in the Canal Zone in 1963 when American soldiers fired into a crowd of demonstrators, killing twenty-one people, had a formative impact on Blades' politics and his art. He ceased singing in English and returned to the Latin tradition for the songs on his first albums *A Los Seis a Nueva York Los Salvajes del Ritmo* (1969) and *De Panama a Nueva York* (1969), recorded in New York where he was pursuing his law studies.

On his return to Panama, Blades' musical success outstripped his work as a lawyer and in 1974 he moved to New York, the musical heart of the thriving salsa scene. He sang with Ray Barretto's band and in 1976 *The Good, the Bad and the Ugly* began a series of recordings with Willie Colon's band for Fania which included *Siembra* (1978), the highest-selling salsa album ever. Among the tracks on *Siembra* was one of Blades' best-known songs, 'Pedro Navaja', a 'Mack the Knife' tale of murder in the *barrio* (ghetto).

The success of Blades' socially conscious material brought the Elektra contract and *Buscando America* (*In Search of America*, 1984). The second album, *Escenas* (Scenes, 1985), included a duet with **Linda Ronstadt**, and in 1986 he starred in a critically acclaimed film, *Crossover Dreams*, as well as taking part in the anti-apartheid recording 'Sun City'. In 1987 Blades wrote and recorded with his band Los Seis Del Solar an album of songs inspired by the work of the Colombian novelist Gabriel García Márquez, *Agua de Luna*. *Nothing but the Truth* (1988) was his first English-language album and included songs co-written with **Lou Reed** and **Elvis Costello**.

However, by this time Blades' career was more film and politics than music orientated. He appeared in several films, ranging from *The Milagro Beanfield War* (1980) to *The Two Jakes* (1990), and, though he still recorded (*Caminando*, 1991), he set out to build upon his popularity in Panama by entering the political arena there. He was an unsuccessful candidate in the 1994 presidential election. In 1997 he appeared on stage (and on the accompanying album) in **Paul Simon**'s musical *The Capeman*. The show, one of the worst Broadway disasters ever, closing within a month after losing several million dollars, was an attempt at a grittier version of *West Side Story*, with the emphasis on the cost of gang membership. In 1999 he won a Grammy for *Tiempos* and in 2000 took the role of the painter Diego Rivera in Tim Robbins' superior film *Cradle Will Rock*. In the same year he also guested on **Gloria Estefan**'s Spanish language album *Almo Caribena*.

BLIND BLAKE

b. *Arthur Phelps, Jacksonville, Florida, USA, d. c. 1935*

One of the key figures in the growth of an urban blues music during the twenties and thirties, Blake accompanied many of the era's leading singers. Like many other handicapped blacks, he turned to street-corner busking to make a living.

He first came to prominence in Georgia in the twenties, performing rhythmic ragtime and dance tunes, then moved north to Chicago to record for **Mayo Williams** and Paramount. Beginning in 1926 with 'West Coast Blues' (whose opening line was 'Now we're gonna do that old country rock'), Blake recorded eighty sides for the label in four years, including blues, dance and novelty numbers like 'Lonesome Christmas Blues' (1929).

Among those with whom he collaborated on record at this period were **Gus Cannon** ('He's in the Jailhouse Now', 1927), the renowned jazz clarinettist Johnny Dodds ('Hot Potatoes'), **Ma Rainey** and Kid Sox Wilson, author of **Bessie Smith**'s famous number 'Gimme a Pigfoot'.

Blake's quick-fingered rags and delicately picked blues inspired both black and white guitarists in the rural South, while he was an important influence on younger singers, notably **Big Bill Broonzy** and **Josh White**, who was said to have been his 'lead boy'.

EUBIE BLAKE

b. *James Hubert Blake, 7 February 1883, Baltimore, Maryland, USA, d. 12 February 1983, New York City*

A legendary figure, Blake was an important ragtime pianist and the author, with lyricist Noble Sissle, of the first musical mounted on Broadway by blacks, *Shuffle Along* (1921).

The son of ex-slaves, Blake began playing piano in the local 'sporting house' when only fifteen. In 1899, the year **Scott Joplin** published 'Maple Leaf Rag', Blake composed his first rag, 'Charleston Rag'. The possessor of unusually large hands – he could span twelve notes where most pianists can hardly manage ten – Blake played at Atlantic City nightclubs in the summers and Baltimore hotels in the winters. Among his compositions from this period are 'The Chevy Chase' and 'Fizz Water'. Then, in 1914, while playing with Joe Porter's Serenaders, he began his ten-year collaboration with the band's new vocalist, Noble Sissle.

Sissle (b. *10 July 1889, Indianapolis, Indiana, d. 17 December 1975, Tampa, Florida*) was the son of a minister. On the death of his father, he joined the Jubilee Singers and then the Serenaders. In 1914 Sissle and Blake joined **James Europe**'s Society Orchestra, working as a piano-and-vocal team, and in 1917 Sissle took over the band, now called Europe's Army Band. After the war the pair went into vaudeville as the Dixie Duo (one of the first black acts to perform without burned cork) before collaborating on *Shuffle Along*, which they developed from various vaudeville sketches with fellow black vaudevillians Flournoy Miller and Aubrey Lyles. The show produced 'I'm Just Wild about Harry' (which was later used by Harry Truman when he campaigned for the Presidency) and 'Love

Will Find a Way' and briefly featured **Paul Robeson** as a member of a vocal quartet; the touring company included **Josephine Baker** in the chorus. In 1923 they wrote the score for another black musical, *Chocolate Dandies*, and in 1924 the pair produced 'You Were Meant for Me', before the partnership ended when Sissle went to Europe as a bandleader, continuing to lead orchestras until his retirement in 1960.

Blake and Andy Razaf wrote the score for *Blackbirds of 1930*, which produced his own favourite song, 'Memories of You'. Other songs from this period include 'You're Lucky to Me' and 'Lovin' You the Way I Do'. During the Second World War he worked as a USO entertainer and in the late forties retired to study composition. Then, in 1959, he released the album *The Wizard of Ragtime Piano* (20th-Century Fox) and resumed his partnership with Sissle for occasional concerts. In 1969 he recorded *The 86 Years of Eubie Blake* (Colombia), produced by **John Hammond**, and in 1978 renewed interest in ragtime led to the mounting of an adaptation of *Shuffle Along, Shuffling Along*, which later transferred to Broadway as *Eubie*. A legend, by virtue of his commitment to performing as much as for his longevity, Blake continued to appear at special events in his and ragtime's honour until a few months before his death.

ART BLAKEY
b. 11 October 1919, Pittsburgh, Pennsylvania, USA, d. 16 October 1990

With **Kenny Clarke** and **Max Roach**, Blakey was among the greatest bebop drummers. By the mid-fifties he was the leading exponent of hard bop drumming while his aggressive and subtle playing spurred on the young talent who passed through his group, the Jazz Messengers. In Britain in the eighties hard bop drummer Tommy Chase played a similar role in nurturing young musicians.

His first instrument was piano but by the late thirties he had taken up drums. Blakey moved to New York in 1942, playing with **Mary Lou Williams** and **Fletcher Henderson** before he joined **Billy Eckstine**'s orchestra in 1944. During his three years with the band, Blakey played with **Dizzy Gillespie**, **Charlie Parker**, **Miles Davis** and other leading bebop players and played on Eckstine's records for DeLuxe and National.

Betweeen 1947 and the formation of the Jazz Messengers in 1956, Blakey performed and recorded with numerous musicians. They included **Lucky Millinder**, trumpeter Fats Navarro, saxophonist James Moody and **Thelonious Monk**, with whom Blakey recorded 'Round about Midnight' (Blue Note, 1947) and further material in the fifties.

By that time Blakey's hard bop reputation had been established by such recordings as *A Night at Birdland* (Blue Note, 1954) with trumpeter **Clifford Brown** and Horace Silver (piano). In 1954–5 Silver and Blakey made *Horace Silver and the Jazz Messengers*, which included the pianist's gospel-tinged 'The Preacher' and 'Doodlin''.

When Silver left the group, Blakey became the undisputed leader, cutting the definitive *Hard Bop* (1956) with saxophonist Jackie McLean and trumpeter Bill Hardman. Blakey continued his collaborations with Monk and shared Roach's interest in large-scale percussion pieces (*Orgy in Rhythm*, 1957) while the Jazz Messengers maintained the gospel-flavoured approach with the arrival of pianist Bobby Timmons. His 'Moanin'' and 'Dat Dere' soon became jazz and R&B standards and he had even greater commercial success as a member of **Cannonball Adderley**'s group.

Blakey's assumption of the Muslim name Abdulla Ibn Buhaina gave the title to *Buhaina's Delight* (1961), which featured trumpeter Freddie Hubbard and Wayne Shorter, who later joined Miles Davis and founded **Weather Report**. This group stayed together until 1964 after which Blakey recruited such players as the young **Keith Jarrett** (*Buttercorn Lady*, 1966), **Stanley Clarke** and Woody Shaw.

In the early seventies Blakey toured with Gillespie and other bebop veterans but continued to run the Jazz Messengers as a nursery for emerging talent. Among those who passed through the group were alto-saxophonist Bobby Watson and trumpeter Terence Blanchard. Among the most remarkable of Blakey's later discoveries was **Wynton Marsalis**, who played on *Keystone 3* (Concord, 1982). In the late eighties the group included Philip Harper (trumpet) and Javon Jackson (tenor sax).

BOBBY BLAND
b. Robert Calvin Bland, 17 January 1930, Rosemark, Tennessee, USA •

One of the great stylists of popular music, Bland has variously been compared to **Frank Sinatra** and **Billy Eckstine**. Among black audiences for over thirty years he has been the only bluesman to rival **B. B. King** in popularity.

In contrast to other black performers, such as **Ray Charles**, **James Brown** and **Otis Redding**, who found international crossover success with emotive, passionate performances that drew heavily on gospel influences, the mark of Bland's style is restraint. His best work is characterized by a sombre, almost formal, quality, with Bland, in the words of one critic, laying out the words of a song 'with solemn, worldly resolve . . . like the markings on a highway'.

Raised in rural Tennessee, Bland moved to Memphis

in 1944, where, after briefly singing gospel, he became B. B. King's valet in 1949 and then a chauffeur for Roscoe Gordon (who in 1952 had a No. 1 R&B record, 'Booted', Chess). During this period he also performed with the Beale Streeters, who included **Johnny Ace**, and in 1951–2 recorded several sides, imitative of King and **T-Bone Walker**, produced by **Ike Turner** and **Sam Phillips** and leased to Chess and the **Bihari Brothers**' Modern and Kent labels. Signed to Duke Records in 1953, Bland was drafted after one release, 'Army Blues', and didn't record again until 1955, by which time Duke had been bought by **Don Robey** and relocated to Houston, Texas.

Robey paired Bland with bandleader Joe Scott, a former member of Bill Harvey's Orchestra and leader of Ace's band. Scott chose the singer's material (most of which was written specifically for Bland, bought outright by Robey and credited to his Deadric Malone pseudonym), fashioned the horn-led arrangements that showcased Bland's increasingly mellow baritone, and in effect created the Bland style of blues balladry. Bland's first hits were hard-edged blues, notably 'Further up the Road' (1957), but as he grew in confidence, his pliant voice alternately pleading and declaiming his songs of hurt, Scott and Bland created a style that hung midway between big-band blues and the emerging soul music of the sixties. Where other singers used melisma to create emotional effect, as a form of vocal punctuation Bland added short squawks and squeals, which were fully integrated by Scott into his increasingly formal arrangements. The first indications of the new mature Bland were 'I'm Not Ashamed' and 'I'll Take Care of You' (1959) and the culmination, the classic albums *Two Steps from the Blues* (1961) and *Call on Me* (1963). The first included 'Lead Me on' and 'I Pity the Fool', Bland's first R&B chart-topper, while *Call on Me* had 'The Feeling Is Gone', 'Share Your Love with Me' and 'Queen for a Day'. Equally remarkable was the live album *Here's the Man* (1962), with its mix of caressing love songs and statements of painful vulnerability, delivered with a dignified swagger which typified the enduring appeal of the Bland persona to black Americans.

His records sold in large quantities to black audiences – 'Call on Me' (1963) was a million-seller and between 1957 and 1975 Bland had some forty entries in the R&B charts, a record only bettered by James Brown, **Fats Domino** and Ray Charles – and throughout the sixties Bland toured constantly, generally making some 300 appearances a year at the clubs that comprise America's 'chitlin' circuit'. Then, in 1968, Scott (who died in 1979) and guitarist Wayne Bennett left Bland and his recordings lost direction. In 1971 Robey sold Duke to ABC and with a new bandleader, Mel Jackson, and producer, Steve Barri, Bland's career revived. His *California Album* (1973) and

Dreamer (1974), which included the superior '(Ain't No Love in the) Heart of the City', revived by hardrock band **Whitesnake** in 1980, saw Bland recording in a more sophisticated rock-inflected manner to good effect. However, when his hits declined ABC (and then MCA, which took over ABC) teamed Bland with B. B. King for the minor *Together for the First Time . . . Live* (1974) and *Together Again . . . Live* (1976) and attempted to move him further into the mainstream with a series of disappointing albums (*Come Fly with Me*, 1978, *Try Me I'm Real*, 1981). More significantly, MCA reissued his earlier albums which revived his flagging critical reputation.

Bland's fortunes further improved following a move to Tommy Couch's Malaco label, which had previously reinvigorated the careers of **Little Milton**, **Z. Z. Hill** and **Johnnie Taylor** by recording them in a basic R&B context. *Members Only* (1985), which included a memorable version of **Mac Davis**'s 'In the Ghetto', saw a return of the Bland style of blues balladry and while the lesser *Blues You Can Use* (1987) showed Bland's voice to be less pliable, his style remained as effective as ever.

Portrait of the Blues (1991) and *Years of Tears* (1993) each took over a year to record and saw Bland singing with undiminished authority. On *Years* in particular, his deliberate, formal readings of the lyrics (mostly by Malaco's house writers) gave them great resonance. While a trio of well put together career retrospectives – *I Pity the Fool* (1992), *Turn on Your Lovelight* (1994) and *That Did It* (1996) – brought Bland a new generation of mostly white fans, he continued recording (*Sad Street*, 1995, and the impressive *Live on Beale Stereet*, 1998) and touring to black audiences, a master stylist.

CARLA BLEY
b. Carla Borg, 11 May 1938, Oakland, California, USA

A composer of monumental works, such as the threealbum set *Escalator over the Hill*, Bley was also a catalyst in jazz–rock fusions of the most valid kind, where the musical forms interact yet maintain their identities.

The daughter of Swedish immigrants, she played piano and organ in church before moving to New York. Her earliest jazz works were performed in the early sixties by artists such as Art Farmer, her first husband Paul Bley and **George Russell**. She was soon involved with Cecil Taylor and **Sun Ra** in the Jazz Composers' Guild, a self-help organization for new music. In the same spirit she and trumpeter Mike Mantler, who became her second husband, formed the Jazz Composers' Orchestra in 1964 and the JCOA record label in 1966. Bley played piano with the Orchestra and contributed to important recordings by Clifford Thornton (*The Gardens of*

Harlem) and **Don Cherry** (*Relativity Suite*).

The jazz opera *Escalator over the Hill* was written with Paul Haines and took three years to record, appearing in 1972. Among those involved with the project were Cherry, **Charlie Haden**, **Jack Bruce** and Gato Barbieri. This led to a series of collaborations with rock musicians, including a 1975 tour with Bruce's band, the formation in 1977 of her own band with Hugh Hopper (ex-**Soft Machine**) and former **Frank Zappa** keyboards-player Don Preston, and an appearance on the 1981 album by **Pink Floyd**'s drummer, *Nick Mason's Fictitious Sports*.

Bley also continued to work with the Jazz Composers' Orchestra circle, releasing records through the Watt label, started by Mantler and herself. *Tropic Appetites* (1974) was another song cycle written with Haines, *Mortelle Randonnée* (1983) a film soundtrack released in France, and *I Hate to Sing* (1985) a typically witty and theatrical set of ensemble pieces. Bley has also sung on record, notably a suite of songs by avant-garde composer John Cage, produced by **Brian Eno** for his Obscure label.

Her later records included *Sextet* (ECM, 1987) and *Duets* (Watt, 1989) with Steve Swallow. Even more intriguing is the traditionally styled *Orchestra Siciliana Plays Carla Bley* (Watt/ECM, 1990). She continued touring with her big (9–10) band in the nineties but recorded only intermittently.

MARY J. BLIGE

b. 11 January 1971, New York, USA

Bronx native Mary J. Blige achieved mainstream success while retaining her credibility within the rap/hip-hop scene.

Discovered, in fairytale fashion, singing a version of **Anita Baker**'s 'Caught Up in the Rapture' in a karaoke studio, Mary J. Blige signed to Uptown Records for the release of *What's the 411* (1992)*. The album drew heavily on classic soul and included a version of **Chaka Khan**'s 'Sweet Thing', as well as featuring guest appearances from hip-hop artists Heavy D and **De La Soul**. Propelled by the success of 'Real Love' and 'Reminisce', Blige's début topped the US R&B chart and soon went platinum.

The hip-hop influence was more apparent on *My Life* (1994)*, which saw Blige move to MCA and was preceded by a remixed version of her first album. It spawned a hit single in 'Be Happy', and was followed by a more mellow-sounding record, *Share My World* (1997)*.

1998 saw the release of *The Tour*, recorded live during performances the previous year, while *Mary* (1999) featured collaborations with an array of big names, including **George Michael**, **Lauryn Hill** and **Elton John**.

BLIND MELON

Glen Graham; Shannon Hoon, b. 1967, d. 21 October 1995; Brad Smith; Roger Stevens; Christopher Thorne

A US rock band with hippie sensibilities, Blind Melon had a hit with 'No Rain' before the death of lead singer Shannon Hoon.

Blind Melon (also featuring twin guitarists Stevens and Thorne, drummer Graham and bass-player Smith) came together in the early nineties, signing to Capital at a time when every major label sought 'the next **Nirvana**'. The success of the single 'No Rain' (1993) sent their self-titled début to triple platinum status, but the band were unable to maintain those sales levels with their later releases.

Soup (1995), produced by Andy Wallace (Nirvana, **Jeff Buckley**), received much better reviews than its predecessor, but was a commercial failure, arriving at a time when rock audiences sought an antidote to grunge. In the middle of an extensive tour aimed to boost sales of *Soup*, Shannon Hoon was found dead on the band's tour bus, reportedly of a heroin overdose, the day after filming the promo video for the band's final single, 'Toes Across the Floor'.

After releasing a collection of rarities, *Nico* (1996), the remaining members of Blind Melon announced their intention to continue performing under a different name.

BLONDIE

Deborah (Debbie) Harry, b. 1 July 1945, Miami, Florida, USA; Chris Stein, b. 5 January 1950, New York; Clem Burke, b. 24 November, 1955, New York; Jimmy Destri, b. 13 April 1954, New York; Frank Infante; Gary Valentine (replaced by Nigel Harrison, b. 1953, Buckinghamshire, England)

Combining deft lyrics and production with Harry's glamour-girl image, Blondie, the most successful group to come out of the New York punk scene of the mid-seventies, had a surprising second taste of success in the nineties in Europe when they re-formed.

A one-time member of folk-rock band Wind in the Willows (they recorded an album for Capitol in 1968), Harry worked as a *Playboy* bunny and as a waitress in Max's Kansas City, before joining the Stilettos in 1972. The group featured three girl singers performing ironic versions of sixties pop. In 1973 Stein, a graduate of New York's School of Visual Arts, joined and under his and Harry's leadership the group evolved into Blondie. By 1975 they were performing regularly at CBGBs, the home of New York's burgeoning punk movement.

The band's eponymous 1976 album was independently produced by Richard Gottehrer and leased to Private Stock. If the group's art-rock leanings were reflected in titles like 'The Attack of the Giant Ants' and 'A Shark in Jet's Clothing' and Harry's deadpan singing style, they were promoted on the back of Harry's Marilyn Monroe-ish looks with more explicit singles: 'Rip Her to Shreds' and 'X Offender'. Following personnel changes and lack of success with Private Stock, the group moved to Chrysalis and had an immediate European hit with 'Denis' (1978), a witty remake of Randy and the Rainbows' 1963 Top Ten hit. Although the album it introduced, *Plastic Letters* (1978), was far darker in tone, it also sold well.

The group's breakthrough to megastardom came with *Parallel Lines* (1978), which saw them united with pop producer Mike Chapman (of **Chinn and Chapman**). He streamlined the group's sound, adding to the wit of their art-rock lyrics the wistfulness of pop, the whole made all the more powerful by Harry's pointedly unemphatic delivery. The album spawned four hit singles, 'Picture This', 'Hanging on the Telephone', 'Sunday Girl' and, most importantly of all, the disco-inflected 'Heart of Glass'*, which was Blondie's first American No. 1 in 1979. One of the first albums to be simultaneously conceived in video form, *Eat to the Beat* (1979), also produced by Chapman, was very much in the same style and garnered the group a trio of hit singles – 'Dreaming', 'Union City Blue' (which, confusingly, was not featured in *Union City*, Harry's 1979 impressive low-key acting début, for which Stein wrote the score) and 'Atomic'. By now, though all the group members were contributing songs, Harry, a celebrity rather than a mere star, had become the focus of Blondie, with her companion Stein elevated to the status of 'artist'. For the moment, the group survived, scoring their second American No. 1. with the **Giorgio Moroder**-produced 'Call Me'* from *American Gigolo* (1980), their third with their revival of the Paragons' reggae song 'The Tide Is High'* and their fourth with 'Rapture'*, a jokey venture into rap, these last both from the Chapman-produced *Autoamerican* (1980). Far better received in America than in Europe, *Autoamerican* marked the end of automatic success for Blondie.

In 1981 Harry released a disappointing solo album, *Koo, Koo*, made in collaboration with Chic's **Nile Rodgers** and Bernard Edwards, and in 1982 Blondie put out their last group album, *The Hunter*, which despite a hit in 'Island of Lost Souls' was generally dismissed. By then the group was little more than a name and in 1983 Blondie formally broke up. In 1994 a collection of out-takes and rarities, *Blondie and Beyond*, was released.

Throughout the eighties Blondie's members remained musically active. Destri released *Heart on the Wall* (1982) and Burke joined the **Eurythmics'** touring band and later played with Dramarama. Harrison became an A&R (artists & repertoire) executive

with Capitol Records. Harry successfully starred in *Videodrome* (1982) and appeared in the off-Broadway production of the comedy *Teaneck Tanzi* (which closed after one performance in 1983) before briefly retiring to help look after Stein, who was suffering from penphigus, a debilitating illness. She resurfaced in 1986 with the solo album *Rockbird* and the hit single 'French Kissin' in the USA'.

In 1987 she appeared in the eccentric film *Hairspray* and in 1989 released *Def Dumb and Blonde* with its hit single 'I Want That Man'. Producers of the album included Chapman and Tom Bailey of the **Thompson Twins**. Less successful was *Debravation* (1993), on which she was billed as Deborah Harry. A recovered Stein led Harry's touring band in the early nineties, though it seemed that in terms of records Blondie's nineties would be a series of best of and career retrospectives, in the manner of *Atomic* (1998). Then, after re-forming in 1999, the group had a massive hit with 'Maria' (RCA), making them one of the few groups to have European chart-toppers in the seventies, eighties and nineties. That introduced the equally successful *No Exit*, which was less ironic and far poppier than their early work. The live album *Livid* (2000) followed.

BLOOD, SWEAT AND TEARS

Randy Brecker, b. 27 November 1945, Philadelphia, Pennsylvania, USA; Bobby Colomby, b. 20 December 1944, New York; Jim Fielder, b. 4 October 1947, Denton, Texas; Dick Halligan, b. 29 August 1943, Troy, New York; Steve Katz, b. 9 May 1945, Brooklyn, New York; Al Kooper, b. 5 February 1944, New York; Jerry Weiss, b. 1 May 1946, New York; Chuck Winfield, b. 5 February 1943, Monessen, Pennsylvania (joined 1969); David Clayton-Thomas, b. 13 September 1941, Surrey, England (joined 1968); Lew Soloff, b. 20 February 1944, Brooklyn, New York (joined 1969)

Initially an experimental group fusing rock with jazz, blues and even classical music, Blood, Sweat and Tears ended its days as an easy-listening jazz-rock big band.

Intended as a vehicle for **Al Kooper**'s songs, the group was envisaged by him and fellow Blues Project alumnus Katz as a rock quartet (with drummer Colomby, who had played on the folk scene with **Odetta**) and bassist Fielder (ex-**Frank Zappa**). The horn section was recruited afterwards from the New York session scene. Their début album, *Child Is Father to the Man* (Columbia, 1968), was, accordingly, Kooper's vision of progressive music, circa 1967. It contained some of his best compositions ('My Days Are Numbered' and 'I Can't Quit Her'), as well as the pretentious 'Modern Adventures of Plato, Diogenes and Freud'.

Internal dissensions led to the exit of Kooper (to a solo career), Weiss and Randy Brecker of the **Brecker**

Brothers. Canadian white blues singer Clayton-Thomas was recruited, together with horn-players Winfield and Soloff for *Blood, Sweat and Tears* (1968). Produced by Jim Guercio (later to mastermind the rise of another jazz-rock band, **Chicago**), its mix of romantiç modern music (Erik Satie), jazzy songs (by **Laura Nyro** and **Billie Holiday**) and soulful rock made it a bestseller. Three 1969 million-selling singles were taken from the album: a revival of Brenda Holloway's 1967 hit 'You Made Me so Very Happy', Clayton-Thomas's 'Spinning Wheel' and Nyro's 'And When I Die', all showcasing Clayton-Thomas's big but featureless voice.

The hits continued in 1970–1 with **Carole King** and Gerry Goffin's 'Hi De Ho', Clayton-Thomas's bombastic 'Lucretia McEvil' and 'Go Down Gamblin''. The last was from the fourth album, the first to include all original material and the least successful of the post-Kooper records. With the arrival of Chicago and other bands featuring brass sections, Blood, Sweat and Tears was no longer unique and personnel changes started to multiply. By the time *No Sweat* (1973) was recorded, only Colomby and Fielder remained from the original line-up.

As vocalist, Clayton-Thomas was replaced first by Jerry Fisher and then by Jerry LaCroix. He rejoined in 1974 after an unsuccessful solo period in which he cut albums for Columbia and RCA. By now the band had found a niche on the Las Vegas nightclub circuit and, after three more albums, Columbia dropped them in 1976. This period of their career is best captured on the live album *Live and Improvised*, released in 1991. Even the presence of **Chaka Khan** and Patti Austin on *More than Ever* (1976) failed to rekindle the interest of record buyers.

Later albums were made for ABC (*Brand New Day*, 1976) and MCA (*Nuclear Blues*, 1980). By then, over forty musicians had passed through the band's ranks. During the eighties and early nineties Colomby and Clayton-Thomas led re-formed BST groups for live appearances. However, their only records of note were retrospectives such as the two-CD set *Greatest Hits* (1995).

MIKE BLOOMFIELD

b. 28 July 1944, Chicago, Illinois, USA, d. 15 February 1981, San Francisco, California

Bloomfield was a highly talented white blues guitarist who rose to prominence with **Paul Butterfield** and recorded with **Bob Dylan**. But despite his major influence on American rock bands, he failed to find lasting commercial success, recording mainly for small labels in his final years.

Living in Chicago, Bloomfield was able to hear **Muddy Waters**, **Buddy Guy** and other blues giants live. Briefly a rock-band guitarist, he worked as a folk-club manager and played his earliest acoustic gigs with fellow white blues fans Nick Gravenites (vocals) and Charley Musselwhite (harmonica). In 1965 he joined Paul Butterfield's Blues Band. The band's earliest recordings, released on the Elektra sampler *What's Shakin'?* (1965), were some of Bloomfield's finest, with his solos like lightning flashes illuminating the songs.

At the 1965 Newport Folk Festival, Bloomfield, plus Butterfield's rhythm section, was recruited at short notice to provide the controversial electric accompaniment for Dylan and later that year he played lead guitar on sessions for *Highway 61 Revisited*. It is Bloomfield that can be heard on 'Like a Rolling Stone'.

That performance and his contributions to Butterfield's first two albums established Bloomfield as the American guitar hero and a rival for such players as **Eric Clapton**. He left Butterfield to form the Electric Flag in 1966 with Gravenites, Buddy Miles (drums), Barry Goldberg (keyboards) and Harvey Brooks, a bassist who had played on many electric folk sessions for Dylan, **Phil Ochs** and **Judy Collins**, among others. *Long Time Comin'* (Columbia, 1968) was an uneasy mixture of jazz-rock and blues tracks, with Bloomfield at his best on strong versions of **Howlin' Wolf**'s 'Killing Floor' and Sticks McGhee's 'Wine'. Although the album sold well, Bloomfield left soon after its release. The band made one more album before splitting, with Miles joining **Jimi Hendrix** and Gravenites teaming up with **Janis Joplin** in Big Brother and the Holding Company. There was a 1974 reunion album, *The Band Kept Playin'*, produced by **Jerry Wexler** for Atlantic.

Based in San Francisco, Bloomfield now embarked on an erratic freelance career. The 1968 *Super Session* with **Al Kooper**, with whom he'd played on the Dylan tracks, and Stephen Stills set a trend for 'supergroup' recordings, and Bloomfield cut a similar album with John Paul Hammond and **Dr John** in 1973 (*Triumvirate*, Columbia). He also wrote and performed the scores for Haskell Wexler's *Medium Cool* (1970) and Alan Myerson's *Steelyard Blues* (1973). In 1975 MCA put together a further band, KGB, with ex-**Family** and Blind Faith bassist Ric Grech, Goldberg and Carmine Appice alongside Bloomfield. Once again, he left the group after the first (unsuccessful) album.

Never keen to tour and impaired by his drug use, Bloomfield retreated to the Bay Area where he played clubs, wrote further film scores (of which the most distinguished was the undistinguished *Andy Warhol's Bad*), and cut a series of low-key albums. *If You Love These Blues, Play 'Em as You Please* (Guitar Player, 1977) was a masterly instructional album, while *Count Talent and the Originals* (Clouds, 1978) reunited him with Gravenites and ex-Butterfield organist Mark

Nataflin. There were later records for Takoma, notably Between a Hard Place and the Ground.

Bloomfield was found dead in his car in February 1981. His last album was *Gospel Duets* for **Stefan Grossman**'s Kickin' Mule label although previously unreleased tracks from the mid-seventies were issued in 1990 as *Try It Before You Buy It* (One Way Records). His life is chronicled in Ed Ward's biography *Michael Bloomfield: The Rise and Fall of an American Guitar Hero*.

KURTIS BLOW
b. Kurt Walker, 9 August 1959, New York City, USA

The first rapper to record for a major label, Kurtis Blow's work became outmoded by the late 1980s when his middle-of-the-road style was outflanked by gangsta rap.

As a teenager Walker became programme director of the New York City College radio station and briefly worked as a DJ in Harlem with **Grandmaster Flash**. He was discovered by producers J. B. Moore and Robert Ford Jr, who provided lyrics for the first Kurtis Blow hit 'Christmas Rapping' (Mercury) at the end of 1979. An eponymous début album contained further raps such as the 1980 million-seller 'The Breaks' as well as a soul ballad and a version of Bachman Turner Overdrive's rock hit 'Takin' Care of Business'. Like 'The Breaks' the title track of *Deuce* (1981) was a slice of gritty social realism. On the five-track album *Party Time* (1983), Kurtis Blow fused rap vocals and hip-hop instrumental styles, working with Washington group EU. On live shows, Blow worked with DJ Davy DMX (Davy Reeves) until the mid-1980s. His later albums included *Ego Trip* (1984), with the novelty rap 'Basketball, America' (1985) and which contained the UK hit 'If I Ruled the World', *Kingdom Blow* (1986) and *Back by Popular Demand* (1988).

In 1985 he starred in the film *Krush Groove* and the following year organized a hip-hop tribute to Martin Luther King, 'King Holiday', by the King Dream Chorus & Holiday Crew. He later produced records for Oran 'Juice' Jones and recorded with Trouble Funk ('Break It Up', 1987).

BLUE OYSTER CULT
Eric Bloom, b. 1 December 1944; Albert Bouchard; Joe Bouchard, b. 9 November 1948; Allen Lanier, b. 25 June 1946; Buck Dharma (aka Donald Roeser), b. 12 November 1947

Initially a *jeu d'esprit* of two New York rock critics, Sandy Pearlman and Richard Meltzer, Blue Oyster Cult were the only successful art-rock heavy-metal group.

The band was formed at Stony Brook University by *Crawdaddy!* journalist Pearlman in 1967 with Roeser (guitar), Albert Bouchard (drums), Lanier (keyboards) and Meltzer (author of *The Aesthetics of Rock*) on occasional vocals. A vehicle for Pearlman's lyrics, the group went through various names including the Cows, Soft White Underbelly and Oaxoa before cutting an album for Elektra with Les Bronstein (author of the Peter, Paul and Mary song 'Big Blue Frog') on vocals.

The record was never released and with the addition of Joe Bouchard (bass) and Bloom (vocals) and a new name, Blue Oyster Cult signed to Columbia in 1971, with Pearlman now their manager and producer. The group's mystic logo (said to represent the god Chronos who ate his son the Grim Reaper) adorned their first eponymous album, whose songs included the demonic (Pearlman's 'Workshop of the Telescopes') and the weird (Meltzer's 'She's as Beautiful as a Foot'). But central to the album's sound was Roeser's high-tech guitar style, which inspired the BOC anthem 'Cities on Flame with Rock'n'Roll', and his haunting and elegant ballad, 'Then Came the Last Days of May'. The group toured with **Alice Cooper** and released *Tyranny and Mutation* (1973), which included 'The Red and the Black', an unlikely paean to the Royal Canadian Mounted Police.

Secret Treaties (1974) and the live *On Your Feet or on Your Knees* (1975) helped to build a following for the band while *Agents of Fortune* (1976) brought an unexpected hit single with Roeser's **Byrds**-inflected '(Don't Fear) The Reaper'. It also reached the British Top Twenty on its release there in 1978. As well as two songs and guest vocals by Lanier's girlfriend **Patti Smith**, *Agents of Fortune* contained a streak of mysticism which was extended on the esoteric *Specters* (1977). The live recording *Some Enchanted Evening* (1978), which included an unexpectedly respectful version of the **MC5**'s 'Kick Out the Jams', closed this experimental phase of BOC's career and ushered in a style which concentrated on heavier rhythms and a more standard heavy-metal image.

Annual albums followed and in 1981 the band had another hit, 'Burnin' for You'. After Albert Bouchard (the group's most prolific writer) had been replaced by Rick Downey, science-fantasy writer Michael Moorcock was briefly imported as a lyricist. The best of these later albums was *Imaginos* (1987), while Joe Bouchard left to join Deadringer in 1988. *Career of Evil* (1990) contained inferior live recordings of Blue Oyster Cult's better known songs.

The eighties also saw a series of Buck Dharma solo albums from Roeser, including *Fire of Unknown Origin* (1981), *Flat Out* (1982) and *Revolution by Night* (1983). A much changed group became a staple draw on the American club circuit while *Cult Classics* (1995) included the new group's take on several early Cult outings. It was followed by the well-documented retrospective *Workshop of the Telescopes* (1998).

THE BLUE SKY BOYS
Bill Bolick, b. 28 October 1917, Hickory, North Carolina, USA; Earl Bolick, b. 16 November 1919, Hickory, North Carolina

The Blue Sky Boys stand apart from the many other 'brother acts' of thirties and forties country music in their loyalty to traditional Appalachian song and manner, or at least to musical forms through which they could affirm traditional values without offending their sense of old-time style. Although they play the same instruments – Bill mandolin, Earl guitar – as the Monroe Brothers they echo neither their angular harmonies nor their hot playing; and unlike the Monroes, the **Carlisle Brothers** or the **Delmore Brothers** they evoke no sense of the blues. They thus represent the sober, conservative and other-worldly tradition in country music, the standpoint of the **Carter Family** rather than the playboy image of **Jimmie Rodgers**.

The brothers began playing together professionally in 1935, broadcasting over station WWNC in Asheville, North Carolina, and making personal appearances. Their career followed this pattern for fifteen years, varied by spells on other stations in Atlanta and Shreveport (the KWKH *Louisiana Hayride*) and by regular recording sessions for Bluebird, at which they made popular versions of 'Sunny Side of Life' (1936), 'Down on the Banks of the Ohio' (1936), 'Story of the Knoxville Girl' (1937), 'Are You from Dixie?' (1939), 'Turn Your Radio on' (their radio theme song) and 'Short Life of Trouble' (both 1940) and 'Kentucky' (1947). The poignant and beautifully integrated harmony singing on these and their scores of other records had a profound influence on later country acts such as the **Louvin Brothers**, Johnny (Wright) and Jack (Anglin), and especially the young **Everly Brothers**.

The Bolicks re-formed in the early sixties to record for Starday and Capitol, and again in 1976 for albums on County and Rounder.

BLUES TRAVELER
Brendan Hill, b. 27 March 1970, London, England; Chan Kinchla, b. 29 May 1969, Hamilton, Ontario, Canada; John Popper, b. 29 March 1967, Cleveland, Ohio, USA; Bobby Sheehan, b. 12 June 1968, Summit, New Jersey, USA

Blues Traveler spearheaded the revival of blues-based jamming with their harmonica-led rock.

Formed in 1983 by Hill (drums) and Popper (vocals/harmonica) at their New Jersey high school under the name Blues Band, the band moved to New York after adding Kinchla and Sheehan on guitar and bass. Hard work and Popper's startling harmonica solos found them a firm following on the blues club circuit, just as they decided to aim for success in the rock market rather than remain a cult blues act.

By now known as Blues Traveler, they put out their eponymous début in 1990, followed by *Travelers & Thieves* (1991), with which their fanbase began to grow. In the summer of 1992 Popper launched Horizons of Rock Developing Elsewhere (better known as H.O.R.D.E.), which consisted of a number of one-week tours featuring Blues Traveler and their contemporaries in the emerging blues-rock scene, including Phish and the Spin Doctors, but suffered a setback later in the year when he was involved in a serious car accident. *Save His Soul* (1993) was the band's first chart record in America, but by this stage it seemed as though the Spin Doctors would be the most likely of the H.O.R.D.E. bands to reach superstardom. *Four* (1994)* also looked like a commercial failure until the release of 'Run Around' (1995), which became one of the biggest-selling singles of the year and sent the accompanying album to multiple platinum status as the band toured solidly. In the same year the group recorded their emphatic version of 'Imagine' on the John Lennon tribute album *Working Class Hero*.

While they recorded the follow-up to *Four*, Blues Traveler released the two-disc set *Live from the Fall* (1996). Their fifth album, *Straight on 'Til Morning* (1997), was another big seller, and was followed by a successful arena tour in the US, on which they supported **Neil Young**.

BLUR
Damon Albarn, b. 23 March 1968, London, England; Graham Coxon, b. 12 March 1969, Rinteln, Germany; Alex James, b. 21 November 1968, Bournemouth, England; Dave Rowntree, b. 8 May 1963, Colchester

Leaders of the Britpop movement in the mid-nineties, Blur turned to introspective, lo-fi rock after becoming disillusioned with the public perception of them as novelty-pop hitmakers.

Originally known as Seymour, the band was formed in Colchester at the end of the eighties by art students Albarn (vocals), Coxon (guitar) and James (bass), with drummer Rowntree joining soon after. After a handful of gigs in and around London they signed to Food, an EMI subsidiary. Food boss Andy Ross urged the band to change their name, and they chose Blur from his list of suggestions.

The band's first two singles, 'She's So High' (1990) and 'There's No Other Way' (1991), and début album, *Leisure* (1991), were viewed by many as a cynical attempt to jump on the Madchester bandwagon. Blur moved away from the psychedelia of the baggy scene with 'Pop Scene' (1992), a horn-driven single punkier than their early material, which didn't fit in with the current musical climate and was a commercial failure.

An extended spell in the recording studio resulted in *Modern Life Is Rubbish* (1993), the first in a trilogy of album releases taking a cynical look at British lifestyles. Produced, as with their début, by Stephen Street, the album drew inspiration from classic British pop from the **Kinks** to **Madness**. The album sold well in the UK and spawned two hit singles, 'For Tomorrow' and 'Chemical World', but failed to make an impact on the American market. Its successor *Parklife** (1994) made Blur the biggest band in Britain, and featured a string of hits, including the title track, narrated by *Quadrophenia* star Phil Daniels, 'To the End' and the new wave-influenced 'Girls and Boys', which was also a minor hit in the US, where the album again failed to crack the charts.

Parklife's success paved the way for a glut of 'Brit-pop' bands in the mid-nineties, including **Oasis** and **Pulp**. Others found limited fame for a brief period before their target audience became bored of guitar-led pop-rock. In 1995 Blur began a high-profile feud with Oasis, blown up to ridiculous levels by the media, which came to a head when both bands released singles on the same day. Blur proved the victors on this occasion when their 'Country House' went straight in at Number One, but by the end of the year Oasis's *(What's the Story) Morning Glory?* had easily outsold *The Great Escape**, Blur's fourth album. It spawned three more hit singles in 'The Universal', 'Stereotypes' and 'Charmless Man', but by the end of the year the band seemed on the verge of splitting up.

Making a conscious decision to spend 1996 out of the public eye, Blur returned in 1997 with their eponymous fifth album*, which saw them move away from their British influences and embrace lo-fi American rock, of which Coxon was particularly fond. Although the album and lead-off single 'Beetlebum' reached the top of the charts in the UK, sales began to dwindle until the release of 'Song 2', which became their biggest international hit and led to the sale of over three million copies of *Blur* worldwide and at last brought the band a measure of success in the US, where they toured solidly.

1998 saw Blur work on individual projects. Coxon released a solo album, *The Sky Is Too High*, on his own Transcopic label, Albarn recorded the soundtrack to *Ravenous* with composer Michael Nyman and James worked alongside actor Keith Allen as Fat Les, hitting the UK Top Ten with the World Cup-themed single 'Vindaloo'.

The band's return to the studio resulted in *13* (1999), Blur's least commercial-sounding album to date, which featured nakedly personal lyrics from Albarn detailing the break up of his relationship with **Elastica**'s Justine Frischmann. Produced by William Orbit, *13* spawned another UK Number One single with the gospel-tinged 'Tender'.

The band spent much of 2000 working individually: Coxon issued a second lo-fi solo album, *The Golden D*, James had another hit with a football-themed cover of 'Jerusalem' as Fat Les, Albarn added vocals to three tracks on the Automator's *A Much Better Tomorrow* and Rowntree made a brief foray into animation. The band reconvened later in the year to mark their tenth anniversary with a 'best of' collection, featuring most of the single releases from their six studio albums and a new track, the upbeat 'Music Is My Radar'.

BOB AND MARCIA
Bob Andy, b. Keith Anderson, 1944, Kingston, Jamaica; Marcia Griffiths, b. Kingston

Among the first reggae artists to have pop hits in Britain, Bob and Marcia reached the Top Ten with their version of **Nina Simone**'s 'Young, Gifted and Black' (Harry J, 1970) and a remake of the Crispian St Peters song 'Pied Piper' (1971). Both, however, were already well established solo artists in Jamaica and have had lengthy careers.

Griffiths' first recordings for **Coxsone Dodd**'s Studio One label were cover-versions of American soul hits by singers like **Aretha Franklin** and **Dionne Warwick**. Andy started as a member of the Paragons before having a local solo hit, 'I've Got to Go Back Home', produced by Dodd. Another producer, Harry J, teamed them up for 'Young, Gifted and Black', reputedly the first reggae record with strings and a big influence on later attempts to sweeten reggae for the pop audience.

Poor management meant that Bob and Marcia were unable to capitalize on their UK success and after recording and performing in Germany, Griffiths returned to Jamaica, joining the I-Threes, the vocal backing group for **Bob Marley** and the Wailers, after cutting *Sweet Bitter Love* (Federal, 1972) another attempt at pop-reggae fusion.

Since Marley's death in 1980, Griffiths has developed a new solo career, writing her own material, such as the rasta-tinged 'Steppin' out of Babylon', produced by Sonia Pottinger. In 1986 she released *I Love Music* (Mountain Sound) and, in 1993, *Indomitable* (Penthouse). In that year she was given the Jamaican state award for services to music.

Andy has also pursued a solo career, releasing such albums as *Lots of Love and I* (1977) and *Song Book* (1988).

MARC BOLAN
b. Mark Feld, 30 July 1947, London, England, d. 16 September 1977, London

A singer and performer who inspired both glam-rock

artists and punk bands like the **Damned**, Bolan was
the most popular British teen-idol in 1970–2, when he
had ten hit singles. Although his own work was limited in scope, Bolan directly influenced artists as
diverse as **Gary Glitter**, the **Sex Pistols** and **Marc
Almond**.

The son of a truck-driver from London's East End,
guitarist Feld was a leading mod and fashion model
before recording 'The Wizard' (Decca, 1965) as Mark
Bowland and 'Third Degree' (1966) as Marc Bolan.
He next released 'Hippy Gumbo' (Parlophone) before
joining singer Andy Ellison in John's Children. The
group toured with **The Who** and recorded the guttural 'Desdemona' (1967) for Track, the label owned
by The Who's managers.

Bolan next became an exponent of flower-power
music, forming Tyrannosaurus Rex with Steve Pere-
grine Took (*b. 28 July 1949, London, England, d. 1980,
London*) on bongoes. They made the Tony Visconti-
produced 'Deborah' as a prelude to *My People Were
Fair and Had Sky in Their Hair but Now They're Content to Wear Stars in Their Brows* (Regal Zonophone,
1968). With additional vocals by disc-jockey John
Peel, it was a Top Twenty hit. 'One Inch Rock' (1968)
reached the Top Thirty while *Unicorn* (1969) and *A
Beard of Stars* (1970) were underground favourites.

After an unsuccessful American tour, Took was
replaced by Mickey Finn and, in a surprise move,
Bolan added an electric band for 'Ride a White Swan'
(Fly, 1970). No longer a flower child singing of magic
and mystery, Bolan was now the 'bopping elf' wielding an electric guitar. The single reached No. 2 in
Britain.

With simple, incantatory lyrics Bolan drew massive
teenage audiences for such songs as the British chart-
toppers 'Hot Love' (1971), 'Get It on' (his only American hit when retitled 'Bang a Gong'), *Electric Warrior*,
'Telegram Sam' (1972) and 'Metal Guru'. With the
arrival of fresh teen-idols in **David Cassidy** and the
Osmonds and of glam-rockers like Glitter, Bolan's
popularity waned after 1973. The film *Born to Boogie*
(1972), which also featured **Ringo Starr**, portrayed
Bolan at the height of his stardom.

In later years Bolan had intermittent hits with
'Teenage Dream' (1974), 'Zip Gun City' (1975) and 'I
Love to Boogie' (1976). With the arrival of punk, he
invited the **Damned** to tour with him and released
Dandy in the Underworld (1977).

Bolan had finished the last show in his television
series, *Marc*, shortly before his death in a car crash.
His final guest had been **David Bowie**. Since then, rare
tracks and reissues have been released in Britain with
occasional minor hits like 'You Scare Me to Death'
(Cherry Red, 1981) and 'Telegram Sam' (EMI, 1982)
confirming his cult status. *Best of the 20th Century Boy*
(1985) offers the best overview of his career. Its title

track ('20th Century Boy') was again a UK hit when
reissued in 1991 after its use in a television commercial.

BUDDY BOLDEN

*b. Charles Joseph Bolden, 6 September 1877, New
Orleans, Louisiana, USA, d. 4 November 1931, Jackson,
Louisiana*

Because he never recorded, Bolden remains a shad-
owy figure in the pre-history of jazz. The most successful New Orleans bandleader of the years
1895–1905, he is credited by many younger musicians
as the most important formative influence on New
Orleans jazz. 'Buddy Bolden Stomp' and 'Buddy
Bolden's Blues' were later composed and recorded in
his honour by **Sidney Bechet** and **Jelly Roll Morton**,
respectively.

He fused in his cornet playing the ragtime style,
dance rhythms such as the quadrille and early blues
like 'Make Me a Pallet on the Floor', one of the tunes
by which he was remembered by his sidemen like
Bunk Johnson. Known as 'King Bolden', he was also
reputed to have unusual strength, so that his playing
could sometimes be heard several miles away.

By 1907 he was in decline, and was committed to a
mental hospital, where he remained until his death.
Whatever his individual skills, it seems clear that
Bolden's expertise in organizing and promoting a
music regarded by many of his contemporaries as a
rowdy betrayal of Creole orchestras and marching
bands opened up the space in which **King Oliver**,
Louis Armstrong and others were able to flourish in
the years after 1910.

Donald M. Marquis's *In Search of Buddy Bolden*
(1978) dispels many of the myths that have accumulated around the bandleader.

MICHAEL BOLTON

*b. Michael Bolotin, 26 February 1953, New Haven,
Connecticut, USA*

After many years as a session singer, Bolton emerged
as a solo artist in the late eighties. A singer in the tradition of the **Righteous Brothers**, **Joe Cocker** and
Hall & Oates, he is proof of the permanent appeal of
blue-eyed soul.

During the mid-seventies he recorded *Michael
Bolotin* for RCA at Muscle Shoals, which showed the
influence of such singers as **Ray Charles** and **Marvin
Gaye**. Neither this or *Every Day of My Life* (1976) was
a commercial success and Bolotin joined hard-rock
band Blackjack as lead singer. The group's Polydor
albums were produced by Tom Dowd and Eddy
Offord.

When Blackjack disbanded, Bolotin signed a solo
recording deal with Columbia and changed his name

to Bolton. He maintained the hard-rock approach on his first two albums but returned to soul music on *The Hunger* (1987). This contained a version of **Otis Redding**'s 'Dock of the Bay' as well as the US Top Twenty hit 'That's What Love Is All About', co-written by Bolton and Eric Kaz, author of the rock standard 'Love Has No Pride', memorably recorded by **Bonnie Raitt**.

The 1989 album *Soul Provider* was an even more successful application of the blue-eyed soul formula, producing the No. 1 hit 'How Am I Supposed to Live Without You' and 'How Can We Be Lovers', composed by Bolton with Desmond Child and **Diane Warren**. Bolton and Warren co-wrote 'We're Not Making Love Anymore' for **Barbra Streisand** and Bolton himself composed four songs for **Cher**'s *Heart of Stone*.

The next album was *Time, Love and Tenderness* (1991), which reached the top of the US charts and included 'Steel Bars', co-written with **Bob Dylan**. Among the other tracks was 'Love Is a Wonderful Thing', composed by Bolton with Andy Goldmark. The song had the same title as an **Isley Brothers** composition from 1966, and the Isleys subsequently sued Bolton and Goldmark for plagiarism, winning the case in 1994.

There was no possibility of similar lawsuits aimed at *Timeless (The Classics)* on which Bolton joined the trend for singers to make albums of their favourite songs. It included versions of the **Bee Gees**' 'To Love Somebody' and **Dobie Gray**'s 'Drift Away'.

In 1993 Bolton issued *The One Thing*, which included another international hit, 'Said I Loved You . . . But I Lied'. Three of the album tracks were co-written and produced by a new collaborator, Robert John 'Mutt' Lange, best known for his work with **Bryan Adams** and **Def Leppard**. His most successful album of the nineties was *Greatest Hits, 1985–1995* (1995). It was followed by the cloying *This Is the Time – The Christmas Album* (1996) and an equally sentimental reading of operatic arias, *Secret Passion – The Arias* (1998), Bolton having recorded in an operatic vein before (for example, 'Vesti La Giubba' on *Pavarotti and Friends*, 1995). A commercial success, it was badly received by the critics.

BON JOVI

Jon Bon Jovi, b. John Bongiovi, 2 March 1962, Perth Amboy, New Jersey, USA; David Bryan, b. David Rashbaum, 7 February 1962, New Jersey; Richie Sambora, b. 11 July 1959; Alec John Such, b. 14 November 1956; Tico Torres, b. 7 October 1953

By the end of the eighties Bon Jovi had become America's leading hard-rock band, combining heavy-metal sounds with catchy pop songs, as **Queen** had

done a decade earlier. Despite competition from a new generation of metal and grunge bands, the group maintained its international following in the early nineties through lengthy world tours.

In the late seventies vocalist Jon Bon Jovi played in bar bands and worked briefly as an assistant at New York's Power Station studio. After recording a demo tape of 'Runaway', he put together the group with school friend Bryan (keyboards), Sambora (guitar) and Such and Torres on bass and drums. Among the group's early concerts was a support slot for **ZZ Top**. Signing to Mercury, the band released *Bon Jovi* (1984), which included small American hits in 'Runaway' and 'She Don't Know Me'. That album was co-produced by Lance Quinn, who also worked on *7800 Degrees Fahrenheit* (1985). A UK appearance with ZZ Top in that year paved the way for Bon Jovi's first British Top Twenty hit, 'You Give Love a Bad Name' (1986).

The track came from *Slippery When Wet**, which topped the American chart as did 'Livin' on a Prayer'. The album was supervised by former **Blue Oyster Cult** producer Bruce Fairbairn. On *New Jersey* (1988), the emphasis switched to big ballads like the epic 'Blood on Blood', a memoir of Jon Bon Jovi's adolescence. Like other Bon Jovi hits, the singles 'Bad Medicine' and 'Born to Be My Baby' were co-written by Desmond Child with Sambora and Jon Bon Jovi. Although it topped the US charts, *New Jersey* was less of an artistic success, pretentious rather than powerful.

In 1989 Bon Jovi headlined the first heavy-metal concert to be held at Moscow's Lenin Stadium and in 1990 Jon Bon Jovi released the solo album *Blaze of Glory*, which included soundtrack material from *Young Guns II*. On it he was supported by **Elton John** and **Little Richard**, among others. The next year Sambora issued his own solo album, *Stranger in this Town*, on which **Eric Clapton** appeared.

After a three-year gap the band regrouped for the UK number one album *Keep the Faith** (1993). Produced by Bob Rock, it included the hit singles 'Bed of Roses' and 'In These Arms'. On its *Keep the Faith* tour, Bon Jovi played to 2,500,000 people in 37 countries. In 1994 they returned to the international charts with *Crossroads*, a collection of their biggest hits, before releasing *These Days* (1995), which spawned the internationally successful singles 'Something for the Pain', 'Hey God', 'This Ain't a Love Song' and the title track.

The band took a four-year break in 1996, as Jon Bon Jovi began an acting career. After appearing in *Moonlight and Valentino* (1996) and *The Leading Man* (1997) the singer released his second solo album, *Destination Anywhere*, which included the UK hit single 'Midnight in Chelsea'. He also featured in several underground films, most notably alongside Lauren Holly and Ed Burns in *Long Time, Nothing New*

(1998). Richie Sambora also had a hit as a solo artist in 1998 with the title track from his second album, 'Hard Times Come Easy'. The group's 1998 album, *Undiscovered Soul*, was the least successful of their nineties' outings. It was followed by the minor but commercially successful *Crush* (2000). Far better was Jon Bon Jovi's performance in the film *U-571* in the same year.

GRAHAM BOND

b. 28 October 1937, Romford, Essex, England, d. 8 May 1974, London, England

A major figure in the British R&B scene of the mid-sixties, Bond's later career was artistically erratic and commercially disastrous. His heavy drug use contributed to his untimely death under the wheels of an underground train.

A former insurance agent, Bond's alto sax playing with the Don Rendell Quintet won him the title of New Jazz Star in the *Melody Maker* poll of 1961. The following year he replaced Cyril Davies in **Alexis Korner**'s Blues Incorporated, adding gritty vocals and impassioned keyboards work on his Hammond/Leslie organ to his saxophone solos. In 1963 he formed a trio with Korner's rhythm section, **Jack Bruce** and Ginger Baker to play an idiosyncratic blend of jazz, blues and soul. **John McLaughlin** joined the Graham Bond Organization before being replaced by tenor-sax-player Dick Heckstall-Smith. This quartet is represented on live recordings issued on Warners (1970) and Charly (1977) and on two EMI Columbia label albums, *The Sound of 65* and *There's a Bond Between Us* (1966).

At its best, the group was the most innovative R&B group of its era, with Bruce and Baker's solo work foreshadowing their later collaboration in **Cream**. Bruce left in 1965 and Baker in 1966, to be replaced by Mike Fellana (trumpet) and Jon Hiseman (drums). But lack of recording success and Bond's increasing involvement in drugs and black magic led to the band's demise in 1967.

Moving to Los Angeles, Bond cut two solo albums on Pulsar, backed by top session players Harvey Mandel (guitar) and Hal Blaine (drums). He returned to Britain in 1969, but the rest of his career was a series of failed attempts to create bands with his wife, the vocalist Diane Stewart. The shortlived Initiation was followed by Holy Magick, which featured Ghanaian percussionist Gaspar Lawal and which cut two albums for Vertigo. He played briefly with bands formed by Baker and Bruce before making his final recording with Bruce's lyricist Pete Brown, *Two Heads Are Better than One* (Chapter One, 1972). Shortly before his death, Bond had been working with Carole Pegg, from the folk-rock band Mr Fox.

JOHNNY BOND

b. Cyrus Whitfield Bond, 1 June 1915, Enville, Oklahoma, USA, d. 12 June 1978, Burbank, California

A singing cowboy, actor, performer and prolific song-writer, Bond was one of the few stars to bridge hill-billy and Hollywood notions of country music.

Born of poor farming stock, in 1934 Bond began broadcasting on local radio stations in the Oklahoma City area. In 1937 he joined the Bell Boys (led by Jimmy Wakely) and in 1940 travelled with Wakely to Hollywood where he joined **Gene Autry**'s *Melody Ranch* radio show, remaining with it until it ceased in 1956. By then Bond was established as a songwriter. Having already written 'Cimarron', a Western classic, and the haunting 'I Wonder Where You Are Tonight', he was signed to Columbia as a recording artist and was appearing regularly in films. In 1943, when Wakely left **Tex Ritter** to star in his own movies, Bond formed the Red River Valley Boys to back him.

However, Bond's greatest success was as a song-writer. Among his compositions (mostly published by the company he set up with Ritter) were 'I'll Step Aside', 'Tomorrow Never Comes' and 'Your Old Love Letters'. In the sixties he had a surprising pop hit with 'Hot Rod Lincoln' (Starday, 1960) and a country hit with the hilarious 'Ten Little Bottles' (1965). In the seventies he retired as a performer to supervise his publishing interests and work on behalf of the Country Music Association. In 1970 he wrote *The Tex Ritter Story*, and later published his own autobiography, *Reflections*.

GARY 'US' BONDS

b. Gary Anderson, 6 June 1939, Jacksonville, Florida, USA

Bonds' gruff, expressive voice graced a series of infectious and influential dance records of the early sixties, including the classic 'Quarter to Three'* (Legrand, 1961). Twenty years later, when most of his contemporaries were playing the rock'n'roll revival circuit, he returned to the Top Thirty with a pair of **Bruce Springsteen** productions.

The son of a college professor and music teacher, Bonds was brought up in Norfolk, Virginia. Through his singing with the Turks doo-wop group he came to the attention of record-store owner turned record producer and label owner Frank Guida in 1959. Guida's first success was one of the most bizarre novelty records ever made, 'High School USA'. Former member of **Gene Vincent**'s Bluecaps, Tommy 'Bubba' Facenda (*b. 10 November 1939, Norfolk, Virginia*) recorded twenty-eight versions of the song, each listing different high schools for different urban centres, which when leased to Atlantic made the Top Thirty in 1959. That record had a pronounced 'live' sound, which Guida would develop further in his work with Bonds.

Guida and his engineer and songwriting partner Joe Royster produced a decidedly rough, even muzzy, live sound through a primitive use of tape echo and phasing at a time when most pop records were sounding increasingly smooth. The results were particularly influential in Britain where beat groups up and down the country were similarly striving for live rather than processed sounds. Bonds' (as Guida renamed the singer without even telling him) string of hits began with 'New Orleans' (1960) and included 'Quarter to Three', for which Guida wrote a lyric to Gene Barge's earlier instrumental, 'A Night with Daddy G', and 'School Is Out' (1961), before Guida capitalized on the twist craze with 'Dear Lady Twist' and 'Twist Twist Señora' (1962). Both these records, like Jimmy Soul's 1963 million-seller 'If You Wanna Be Happy' (Legrand), despite their twist references, were derived from calypsos. 'Happy', for example, derives from 'Marry an Ugly Woman', which was recorded by its author, the calypso singer the Roaring Lion in 1934 (Banner).

Bonds continued to work during the sixties, recording for independent labels after Guida retired from the record business, and in the seventies worked briefly with Jerry Williams Jnr writing and (sometimes) producing for **Z. Z. Hill**, Johnny Paycheck and Doris Duke, among others. In the eighties Bonds was rescued from cabaret and the revival circuit by Springsteen, who regularly featured 'Quarter to Three' in his stage act. Signed to EMI-America, he had hits with Springsteen's productions of 'This Little Girl' (1981) and 'Out of Work' (1982) and his albums *Dedication* (1981) and *On the Line* (1982) saw him performing material by **Jackson Browne**, **Bob Dylan** and Springsteen, in a manner that combined the spirit of his Legrand recordings with Springsteen's contemporary sound. He produced *Standing in the Line of Fire* (1985), which sold poorly compared with the countless reissues of his classic material.

BONEY M

Marcia Barrett, b. 14 October 1948, St Catherines, Jamaica; Bobby Farrell, b. 6 October 1949, Aruba, West Indies; Liz Mitchell, b. 12 July 1952, Clarendon, Jamaica; Maisie Williams, b. 25 March 1951, Montserrat, West Indies

Created by German producer Frank Farian to take advantage of the European disco boom, Boney M went on to sell 50 million albums in three years, and were major stars everywhere except the United States. The group specialized in cover-versions of songs from such diverse sources as **Shirley Temple** and **Bob Marley**.

Following the success of another German disco group Silver Convention – whose 'Fly Robin Fly' was an American No. 1 on Midland in 1975 – Farian wrote and produced 'Baby Do You Wanna Bump?' under the name Boney M.

Its promising sales in the Netherlands led Farian to form a group to perform in clubs and discos as Boney M. Mitchell had replaced **Donna Summer** in the German cast of *Hair* while Farrell was a club disc-jockey. A long string of hits followed, featuring Farian's eclectic selection of raw material – including 'Ma Baker' and 'Rasputin' – (some of which he wrote himself, although most were old songs), his studio skill with synthesizers and mixing board and the kitsch, mildly sexy series of visual images created for album sleeves and television appearances.

Farian's sources included thirties musicals ('Hooray Hooray' was based on 'Polly Wolly Doodle', from the 1935 Shirley Temple vehicle *The Littlest Rebel*); British psychedelia (the Creation's 'Painter Man'); and Jamaican music. The Caribbean material was both authentic (the Melodians' 'Rivers of Babylon', Marley's 'No Woman No Cry', the traditional 'Brown Girl in the Ring') and pastiche: 'Mary's Boy Child', a No. 1 hit all over Europe at Christmas 1978 and previously recorded by **Harry Belafonte**, was composed by American arranger and conductor Lester Hairson in the forties. In the studio, however, Farian transformed these disparate songs into a single disco style, with robotic drum rhythms overlaid with further layers of synthesized sound.

For Britain and Europe, Boney M were signed to WEA International. In America, their records were released by Sire, without success. The failure to make an impact on the world's largest disco market contributed to the fading of the group, which had its last minor hit in Europe in 1981 with 'We Kill the World (Don't Kill the World)'. The group re-formed in 1989 and toured as a cabaret act in the early nineties with a 'Boney M Megamix' reaching the UK Top Ten in 1992.

THE BONZO DOG BAND

Vernon Dudley Bohay-Nowell; Dennis Cowan, b. 6 May 1947, London, England; Neil Innes, b. 9 December 1944, Essex; Rodney Desborough Slater, b. 8 November 1944, Lincolnshire; Roger Ruskin Spear, b. 29 June 1943, London; Sam Spoons, b. Martin Stafford; Vivian Stanshall, b. 21 March 1943, Shillingford, d. 5 March 1995, London; Larry 'Legs' Smith, b. 18 January 1944, Oxford

A whimsical and satirical band of the late sixties, the Bonzos' archetypally English sense of humour recalled both the **Goons** and **The Beatles**.

Founded in 1965 by art students Slater (saxophones) and Spear (kazoo, robots, mechanical toys), the group were originally the Bonzo Dog Dada Band, then Doodah Band before the final contraction of the name. An intensely visual comedy act, the band played the London college and club circuits and cut two singles for Parlophone before signing to Liberty for *Gorilla* (1966). Produced by future **Uriah Heep** manager Gerry Bron, the original material was composed by Innes (sardonic soft rock) and Stanshall (twenties surrealist nostalgia). The Bonzos' penchant for early jazz recalled other British groups like the Alberts and the Temperance Seven, who had reached the charts with a revival of **Walter Donaldson**'s 'You're Driving Me Crazy' (Parlophone, 1961), but the album also included delightfully savage renditions of **Tony Bennett**'s 'I Left My Heart in San Francisco' and **Julie Andrews**' saccharine 'The Sound of Music'.

Having appeared in The Beatles' film *Magical Mystery Tour*, the Bonzos had a surprise British hit in 1968 with the Innes composition 'I'm the Urban Spaceman'. The producer was **Paul McCartney**, under the pseudonym Apollo C. Vermouth. *The Doughnut in Granny's Greenhouse* (1968) contained 'Can Blue Men Sing the Whites?', the group's contribution to one of the key musicological debates of the era, comparable only to the Liverpool Scene's 'I've Got those Fleetwood Mac, Chicken Shack, John Mayall, Can't Fail Blues'. That album and *Tadpoles* (1969) were minor hits while the title of *Keynsham* (1969) referred to the hometown of Horace Batchelor, a legendary soccer tipster associated with Radio Luxembourg, for many years the only pop radio station to be heard in England.

The group split in 1970, with drummer Smith, guitarist Bohay-Nowell and percussionist Spoons joining jokey trad outfit Bob Kerr's Whoopee Band, while Spear went out as a novelty act with his machines and mechanical toys. Stanshall and Innes set out on contrasting solo careers before returning with bassist Cowan to cut one final Bonzos' album, *Let's Make Up and Be Friendly* (1972), with Liverpool Scene guitarist Andy Roberts and ex-**John Mayall** drummer Hughie Flint. With its early Beatle imitations and the Stanshall recitation 'Rawlinson End', it looked forward to the two leading members' later careers.

With Monty Python's Eric Idle, Innes created the Rutles, a spoof Fab Four, for a television show and a 1978 Warners album. Stanshall made several solo albums and featured as Master of Ceremonies on **Mike Oldfield**'s *Tubular Bells* (Virgin, 1973). He made the eccentric movie *Sir Henry at Rawlinson End*, which was also the title of his 1978 solo album. He also contributed lyrics to **Steve Winwood**'s *Arc of a Diver* (1981). During the seventies Innes had cut solo albums and occasionally performed with Grimms, a

comedy theatre ensemble including members of Scaffold, the Liverpool group whose novelty song 'Lily the Pink' (Parlophone, 1968) had been a No. 1 hit. He continued to record in the eighties and had his own UK TV series *The Innes Book of Records*, becoming a household face – if not name – through appearing in a series of TV advertisements for chocolates, later becoming a regular on TV celebrity game shows.

In the late eighties Stanshall and Innes recorded a one-off satirical single 'No Matter Who You Vote for, the Government Always Gets in', which remained unreleased until 1992, when it was issued by EMI on a three-CD history of the group, *Bestiality of the Bonzo Dog Band*.

The following year Stanshall was commissioned by BBC TV arts programme *The Late Show* to write an autobiographical musical. *Crank! – Vivian Stanshall, The Early Years* was premièred on BBC TV in 1993. He signed with Warner Bros in the UK and recorded extensively, but nothing was ever released.

BOO RADLEYS

Timothy Brown, b. 26 February 1969, Wallasey, England; Martin Carr, b. 29 November 1968, Thurso, Scotland; Steve Drewitt, b. Northwich, England (replaced by Rob Cieka, b. 4 August 1968, Birmingham); Sice, b. Simon Rowbottom, 18 June 1969, Wallasey

Psychedelic guitar-pop band the Boo Radleys, from Liverpool, had a massive hit single in the UK with 'Wake Up Boo' in 1995.

Taking their name from Harper Lee's classic novel *To Kill a Mockingbird*, Boo Radleys were formed in 1989 by schoolfriends Carr (guitar) and Rowbottom (vocals) and later augmented by bassist Brown and drummer Drewitt. Their independently released début *Ichabod and I* (1990) was followed by an EP on Rough Trade, *Every Heaven* (1991), after which the label collapsed and the band had to find a new home.

With Drewitt replaced by Cieka, they signed to Creation for *Everything's Alright Forever* (1992). Despite critical acclaim the album failed to meet sales expectations, but *Giant Steps* (1993) and the single 'Lazarus' found the band a niche in the market and a spot on the 1994 Lollapalooza tour.

Wake Up! (1995) saw the band cross over to mainstream success after the huge success of 'Wake Up Boo', which remained in the UK Top Ten for several months, stopping just short of the number one spot. *C'Mon Kids* (1996) spawned two minor hits in 'What's in the Box?' and the title track, but the rest of the album was purposefully uncommercial and saw the band return to mere cult status.

The commercial failure of *Kingsize* (1998) lead Martin Carr to the decision to bring the band's career to a halt with the intention of forming a new band.

BOOGIE DOWN PRODUCTIONS
KRS-One, b. Lawrence Krisna Parker, 20 August 1965, New York, USA; Scott La Rock, b. Scott Sterling, c. 1962, New York, d. 27 August 1987, South Bronx, New York

Boogie Down Productions were hip-hop contemporaries of **Public Enemy**, and rapper KRS-One rivalled Chuck D in terms of both his black radicalism and commitment to political rap.

Boogie Down Productions emerged from Scott La Rock and the Celebrity Three, who released one single, the anti-nuclear weapons rap 'Advance', in 1984. Contractual wrangles ultimately led the group to disband, but La Rock and KRS-One stayed together to form the Boogie Down Crew later in 1984.

In 1985 the pair recorded a one-off single on Sleeping Bag Records under the name 12:41. The track, 'Success Is the Word', was produced by **Mantronix** and became a local hit, after which the duo changed their name to Boogie Down Productions. La Rock and KRS-One, who at this stage was still homeless and living in a men's shelter in the Bronx, found little record company interest in their early demos, but one of those raps, 'South Bronx', gave the pair their breakthrough. 'South Bronx' appeared on B-Boy Records in 1986, and was a huge underground hit. A second single, 'The Bridge Is Over', enjoyed similar success, and was followed in 1987 by the album *Criminal Minded*.

The album had little in common with the party rap or bragging machismo of much contemporary hip-hop. Along with **Eric B & Rakim** and the **Ultramagnetic MCs**, BDP were using rap as a medium for telling tales of the street, of its poverty and violence. In their discussion of violence, BDP were a key influence on 'gangsta rap', although few of their imitators would match the intelligence of their approach. Then, in August 1987, La Rock was shot dead in the Bronx while trying to stop an argument. KRS-One changed labels to Jive, and as Boogie Down Productions released *By All Means Necessary* in 1988. The album included the hit single 'My Philosophy'.

La Rock's shooting prompted a greater focus in KRS-One's raps on the need for black self-education and the rejection of violence. This formed the central message of a national university lecture tour he embarked upon in 1989 ahead of the release of *Ghetto Music – The Blueprint of Hip Hop*. The album's emphasis of didactic rhymes rather than funky rhythms did not help it sell, but this was to some extent made up for with the follow-up, 1990's *Edutainment*, which featured the hit 'Love's Gonna Getcha'. 1991 saw Boogie Down Productions release rap's first live album, *BDP Live Hardcore*, as well as KRS-One guesting on **R.E.M.**'s *Out of Time*.

One more BDP album, *Sex and Violence*, followed in 1992, featuring the singles 'Duck Down', 'Thirteen and Good' and 'We in There'. After this, KRS-One simply used his own name for his recordings, releasing *Return of Da Boom Bap*, a return to a funkier, more street-level style, in 1993. 1995's *KRS-One* was preceded by the single 'MCs Act Like They Don't Know', a collaboration with **Gang Starr**'s DJ Premier.

In 1997 he released *I Got Next*, which included the hit 'Step Into a World' and 'Heartbeat', and in 1998 he guested on UK jungle star **Goldie**'s *Saturnz Return*.

BOOKER T. AND THE MGS
Booker T. Jones, b. 11 December 1944, Memphis, Tennessee, USA; Steve Cropper, b. 21 October 1941, Willow Spring, Missouri; Louis Steinberg, replaced by Donald 'Duck' Dunn, b. 24 November 1941, Memphis; Al Jackson Jnr, b. 27 November 1935, Memphis, d. 1 October 1975, Memphis

For over ten years the house band for Stax Records, Booker T. and the MGs (Memphis Group) were far more than a session band. The racially integrated group – Dunn and Cropper were white, Jones and Jackson, black – were the cornerstone of the lean soulful Stax sound, and of the company's success. Moreover, the group's tight and easy interplay, with Cropper's guitar slashing through the bluesy, percussive rhythms in which bass rather than drums was dominant, the whole held together by Jones' staccato organ, became synonymous with 'Southern soul'.

The nucleus of the group had the first of several hits with 'Last Night'* (Satellite, 1961) as the Mar-Keys (the name which they would use throughout their career whenever a horn section was added to the line-up). Their first hit as Booker T. and MGs followed in 1962 with the distinctive 'Green Onions'* (Stax), an insistent and surprisingly subtle dance tune and a hit again in Britain in 1979 when it was reissued. Other hits (with Dunn replacing Steinberg) include 'Chinese Checkers' (1963), 'Hip Hug Her' (1967), an instrumental version of the **Rascals** 'Groovin'', 'Soul Limbo' (1968), regularly used by BBC Television as the theme to its cricket coverage, and two Top Twenty film soundtrack hits in 1969, 'Time Is Tight' (from the thriller *Uptight* and the group's first major British hit) and 'Hang 'Em High'. In 1971 the band, which had always been an informal grouping, broke up, but by then the great days of Stax were over.

More significant than their own hits was Booker T. and the MGs contribution (and that of the individual members) to the Stax sound. As a rhythm section the group appeared on countless sessions by **William Bell**, **Otis Redding**, **Wilson Pickett**, Albert King, Carla and **Rufus Thomas**, **Sam and Dave** and Eddie Floyd, among others. As a songwriter, Jones wrote extensively with Bell. Their songs include 'Everybody

Loves a Winner', 'Private Number', and 'Tribute to a King' and 'Born Under a Bad Sign' for Albert King.

But it was Cropper who was the more influential and prolific as both instrumentalist and writer. Influenced by both **Bill Black** and the **Five Royales**' economical guitarist Lowman Pauling, Cropper's style was not one of embellishing a song, but contextualizing a tune as briefly as possible. Thus the short guitar burst on 'Green Onions' probably constitutes Cropper's longest-ever solo. Among the hits he co-wrote were 'In the Midnight Hour' and 'Ninety-Nine and One-Half (Won't Do)' for Wilson Pickett, 'Knock on Wood' for Eddie Floyd (with whom he wrote '634-5789' for Pickett), 'See Saw', which he wrote with **Don Covay** for **Aretha Franklin**, and a series of songs culminating in '(Sittin' on) the Dock of the Bay' for Otis Redding. Of all Stax's artists, Redding was the one with whom Cropper had the closest working relationship and whom he regularly produced, his guitar taking the place of the gospel choir and answering and echoing Redding's vocal pleas.

After the break up of the MGs, Jones married Priscilla (sister of **Rita**) **Coolidge** and moved to the West coast where he recorded with her for A&M. His biggest production success came with **Willie Nelson**'s *Stardust* (1978) and his biggest hit was the disco-tinged 'Don't Stop Your Love' (A&M, 1982). Dunn and Jackson remained in Memphis as session musicians, Jackson working at Hi studios (where he became a mainstay of the band that recorded with **Al Green**) as well as Stax, before his murder in 1975. Cropper, after cutting the pleasant solo album *With a Little Help from My Friends* (Volt, 1969), turned to production (most successfully with the **Temptations**, for whom he produced *House Party*, 1975, and the Cate Brothers, whose 1976 hit 'Union Man' and eponymous Asylum album he also played on). He also led several reunions of the MGs before, in 1977, (with Jones and Dunn) touring and recording with one-time member of **The Band** Levon Helm and his RCO Allstars. Then, in 1978, Cropper and Dunn joined the Blues Brothers – the band formed by comedians John Belushi and Dan Aykroyd in an attempt to 'hit out at preprogrammed electronic disco' – on whose hit remake of 'Soul Man' and *Briefcase of Blues* (Atlantic, 1978) they played. Both were also featured in the 1980 film *The Blues Brothers*.

Since then, Cropper has made a pair of solo albums for MCA (*Playing My Thing*, 1980, and *Night After Night*, 1982) and has played live with such artists as **Jimmy Buffett** and **Dave Edmunds**. For much of the eighties the members concentrated on individual projects. They re-formed briefly in 1990 to tour and in 1993 backed **Neil Young** on his world tour. In 1994, the year they released their first studio album in several years, *That's the Way It Should Be* (Columbia), it

was revealed that Dunn was suffering from throat cancer, and a series of dates with Young in the Far East were cancelled.

PAT BOONE
b. Charles Eugene Patrick Boone, 1 June 1934, Jacksonville, Florida, USA

After **Elvis Presley**, Boone was the most successful teenage singer of the fifties. But where Presley's greased hair, swivelling hips and pink cadillacs threatened, Boone's white buck shoes, polite voice, university background, pretty wife and four children, and series of cover-versions did much to dilute the explosive power of rock'n'roll for those 'twixt twelve and twenty' in the fifties.

Boone, who claims to be a descendant of frontiersman Daniel Boone, grew up in Nashville. While at university in the early fifties he recorded country songs for Republic, married country singer **Red Foley**'s daughter, Shirley, and began to appear regularly in local talent shows, displaying his warm baritone to good effect.

Signed to Dot by its owner Randy Wood in 1954, Boone was surprised by Wood's choice of song, 'Two Hearts, Two Kisses', then a huge R&B success for Otis Williams and the Charms on DeLuxe. This inaugurated Wood's policy of using Boone to produce bland, acceptable cover-versions of current black hits. Other labels, such as Mercury and Coral, would follow a similar policy but none so rigorously as Dot. As well as running Dot, Wood owned the largest mail-order record business in the South and so was able to discover what titles were selling and to whom. It was this that led to Wood specializing in covers for his artists. Thus, Dot's two other main acts of the period were the Fontane Sisters (who covered the Charms' 'Heart of Stone', 1954; Boyd Bennett's 'Seventeen', 1955; and the Teen Queens' 'Eddie My Love', 1956) and Gale Storm (who covered **Smiley Lewis**'s 'I Hear You Knocking', 1955; **Frankie Lymon** and the Teenagers' 'Why Do Fools Fall in Love?'; and the Charms' 'Ivory Tower', both 1956).

However, it was Boone's cover-versions that were the most successful and controversial. In 1957 several disc-jockeys, including **Alan Freed**, refused to play his cover of **Lucky Millinder**'s 'I'm Waiting Just for You', so incensed were they at his continued plundering of the work of black artists. Virtually all the records Boone made in 1955–6, the period in which he established himself, were covers: 'Ain't That a Shame'*, 1955 (**Fats Domino**); 'At My Front Door', 1955 (the El Dorados); 'I'll Be Home'*, 1956 (the **Flamingos**); 'Tutti Frutti' and 'Long Tall Sally', 1956 (**Little Richard**); 'I Almost Lost My Mind'* (**Ivory Joe Hunter**); and 'Chains of Love', 1956 (**Joe Turner**).

None of these songs is remembered as by Boone, whose versions (especially of the songs associated with Little Richard) were strained in comparison to the originals.

Late in 1956 he turned balladeer and was clearly more comfortable utilizing his smooth **Bing Crosby** crooning style on songs like 'Friendly Persuasion'* (1956), 'Anastasia' (1957), 'Love Letters in the Sand'* (1957) and 'April Love'* (1958), all of which were featured in films, the last two in films which also starred Boone, *Bernadine* and *April Love*. For the next five years, though Boone continued to offer teenagers homely advice in books like *Twixt Twelve and Twenty*, he sought a career in Hollywood and on television as a mainstream popular artist. However, like so many artists of the rock'n'roll era, Boone's career was virtually ended by the arrival of **The Beatles**. His last hits were the death song 'Moody River'* (1961) and the novelty song 'Speedy Gonzales' (1962).

Boone's few recordings of the sixties were of gospel and country music (including a brief stay on Motown's country label, Melodyland). In the seventies he toured and recorded with the gospel-based Pat Boone Family Show which included his wife and daughters. However, the most successful Boone of the decade was his daughter Debby (*b. 22 September 1956, Hackensack, New Jersey*). In 1977 her recording of the Oscar-winning title song 'You Light up My Life'* (Warners), which was written and produced by Joe Brooks, was the biggest-selling record in America for some twenty-five years, remaining at No. 1 for ten weeks. Since that time, apart from Pat's gospel albums on Light and Word and Debby's appearance in a touring version of the musical *Seven Brides for Seven Brothers* in 1982, neither Boone has been particularly active. Debby has followed in her father's footsteps and produced an autobiography, *Debby Boone . . . So Far*, liberally spiced with Christian advice. Boone himself continued to make occasional live appearances and in 1990 re-recorded his hits (*Greatest Hits*, Curb). In 1997 Boone returned to recording with the bizarre *In a Metal Mood: No More Mister Nice Guy*, on which he sang, with a big band-style backing, songs associated with the likes of **Deep Purple**, **AC/DC** and so forth. A commercial and critical failure, its release almost cost Boone his religious shows on evangelical broadcaster Trinity Broadcasting.

KEN BOOTHE
b. 1948, Kingston, Jamaica

Boothe was a skilful exponent of the pop-reggae style that brought the Trojan label over twenty British hits in the first half of the seventies.

Brought up in the Trench Town ghetto, Boothe's first record was 'World's Fair' (1964), followed by 'You're No Good', produced by Sonia Pottinger. He recorded with Stranger Cole before achieving success in the rock-steady era of reggae (1966–8). Produced by **Coxsone Dodd**, his hits included a cover-version of **Sandie Shaw**'s 'Puppet on a String' (1967).

Boothe toured Britain in 1967 with Alton Ellis and the Soul Vendors, rock-steady's supergroup. He had further Jamaican hits, including 'Freedom Street', before returning to Britain to record for Trojan, with Lloyd Charmers producing. His 1974 version of **Bread**'s 'Everything I Own' was a No. 1 hit, while the follow up 'Crying over You' also entered the Top Twenty. With albums like *Blood Brothers* (1978) and *Who Gets Your Love* (1979), Boothe continued to record for Trojan throughout the seventies. In 1986 he cut another cover-version of a pop hit with **Sam Cooke**'s 'Bring It on Home to Me'. While this was unsuccessful, **Culture Club**'s Boy George had his first solo hit in 1987 with 'Everything I Own', a remarkably faithful rendering of Boothe's 1974 arrangement.

EARL BOSTIC
b. 25 April 1913, Tulsa, Oklahoma, USA, d. 28 October 1965, Rochester, New York

Originally a jazz player, Bostic helped to form the hard-driving saxophone sound of R&B. He came into his own in the years immediately following the Second World War when scaled-down R&B bands played simple arrangements that depended on soloists (especially saxophonists) for their excitement. Soon, soloists like Bostic became as well known as the band-leaders.

At school and at Xavier University, New Orleans, he became proficient on guitar and trumpet, as well as his main instrument, alto sax. Bostic played with and arranged for various Midwest big bands before moving to New York in 1938. There he performed in various jazz orchestras, including **Don Redman**'s. He wrote 'Let Me Off Uptown' for **Gene Krupa** and did arrangements for **Artie Shaw** and **Louis Prima**. Bostic briefly led his own band, where he played trumpet and guitar as well as sax, before joining **Lionel Hampton**. He recorded with Hampton's big band in 1943–4, contributing to its drive and swing which paralleled the emerging rhythm and blues sound of the era.

Forming his own band in the late forties, he recorded for Majestic and Gotham ('Temptation', 1948) before scoring a No. 1 R&B hit on King with 'Flamingo', produced by **Ralph Bass** in 1951. Among Bostic's sidemen was the young **John Coltrane**. He recorded prolifically for King and among his most popular numbers were **Louis Jordan**'s 'Who Snuck the Wine in the Gravy?', 'Sleep' and '845 Stomp'. As well as honking R&B numbers, Bostic's records contained middle-of-the-road ballad material and show and film tunes (*The Great Hits of 1964*, for example, included 'Hello Dolly' and 'The Pink Panther').

Bostic moved to Los Angeles in the mid-fifties. A heart attack in 1956 kept him out of action for three years and he eventually died of another seizure following a club gig.

BOSTON
Brad Delp, b. 12 June 1951, Boston, Massachusetts, USA; Barry Goudreau, b. 29 November 1951, Boston; Sib Hashian, b. 17 August 1949, Boston; Tom Scholz, b. 10 March 1947, Toledo, Ohio; Fran Sheehan, b. 26 March 1949, Boston

One of America's biggest-selling rock bands, Boston was led by engineer Scholz, who also invented a miniaturized guitar amplifier.

The group's début album was based on tapes made by Boston-based Scholz, who over-dubbed twin guitar solos and harmony vocals. After being remixed by John Boylan, they were issued by Epic as *Boston* (1976) and went on to sell over eight million copies, with the single 'More Than a Feeling' reaching the Top Ten. To promote the album, Scholz toured the stadium circuit with local musicians Delp (vocals), Goudreau (guitar), Sheehan (bass) and Hashian (drums).

Don't Look Back (1978) and its title track sold only half the number of copies and a $20 million lawsuit caused a lengthy hiatus in Boston's career. During this time Goudreau made an eponymous solo album (Portrait, 1980) while Scholz formed a research company to develop his Rockman amplifier and also prepared material for *Third Stage*, released by MCA in 1986. Both it and the singles 'Amanda' and 'Can'tcha Say You Believe in Me' were huge American hits.

More legal problems followed, however, and the band's resurrection was short-lived. Goudreau and Delp formed the band RTZ, releasing *Return to Zero* (1991). Scholz won his multi-million dollar lawsuit against Sony/CBS and released a new album, *Walk on*, in the summer of 1994 to predictably high sales. It was only his fourth album in fifteen years and was followed by the equally successful *Greatest Hits* (1997).

THE BOSWELL SISTERS
Connie (later Connee), b. 3 December 1907, Kansas City, Missouri, USA, d. 11 October 1976, New York; Martha, b. 1908, New Orleans, Louisiana, d. 1958; Helvetia (Vet), b. 1902, New Orleans, d. 12 November 1988

American radio in the twenties and thirties boasted many 'blues singers', by which was usually meant Southern-born white *chanteuses* with an aptitude for what **Johnny Mercer**, in 'Blues in the Night', called 'the wail of a down-hearted frail'. Nobody sang this sort of blues with more authenticity and inventiveness than the Boswell Sisters.

They established a New Orleans reputation in the twenties as a radio and vaudeville trio, Connie playing cello, Martha piano and Vet violin, and made their first recordings for Victor in 1925. In 1930 they worked on station KFWB, Los Angeles, and in 1931 moved to New York to work at the Paramount Theater. **Jack Kapp** immediately signed them to Brunswick, where their cleverly arranged and 'bluesified' treatments of current popular songs like 'When I Take My Sugar to Tea' were enhanced by top jazz session musicians like **Joe Venuti**, **Eddie Lang**, Bunny Berigan and **Tommy** and **Jimmy Dorsey**. They also occasionally recorded with sweet orchestras like those of **Victor Young** and Jimmie Grier, the latter supporting them on a 1934 item titled 'Rock and Roll'. In 1932 they won a place on the radio show sponsored by Chesterfield cigarettes, beside **Ruth Etting** and **Arthur Tracy**, and in 1934–5 they became radio partners of **Bing Crosby**. They also appeared in the movies *The Big Broadcast of 1932, Moulin Rouge* and *Transatlantic Merry-Go-Round* (both 1934), and visited Britain in 1933 and 1935. This successful career was then disrupted by the marriages and subsequent retirement of Martha and Vet, but Connie continued as a solo artist in radio (until 1944), on records and in movies, such as *Syncopation* (1942), *Swing Parade* (1946) and *Senior Prom* (1959). For many years she worked from a wheelchair, having contracted polio as a child.

DENNIS BOVELL
b. 1953, St Peter, Barbados

Producer, group leader and master of dub production Bovell (aka Blackbeard) was among the most innovative reggae musicians of the seventies and eighties.

He formed his first group, Stonehenge, at school in England, where he spent the whole of his musical career. That band's **Jimi Hendrix**-inspired rock was superseded in 1972 by the funk and reggae of Matumbi. With Bovell on guitar, the line-up included Jah Bunny on drums and Webster 'Tasmanian' Johnson (keyboards). A troubled relationship with Trojan led to few releases until *Best of Matumbi* (1977), released after the group had joined EMI's 'progressive' label, Harvest. Two highly acclaimed albums – *Seven Seals* (1978) and *Point of View* (1979) – followed.

Bovell's production and solo career developed in parallel with his group work. Under various names (including Leggo and Blackbeard), he put together a series of dub albums, including *Strictly Dubwise* (Tempus, 1978) and *I Wah Dub* (More Cut, 1980). His masterpiece in this vein was the eclectic *Brain Damage* (Fontana, 1981) on which reggae mingled with calypso, rock and disco rhythms.

From the late seventies Bovell was among the most sought-after producers in British reggae and beyond. He was responsible for hits in the lover's-rock style by 15,16,17 ('Black Skin Boy') and Janet Kay ('Silly Games', Arawak, 1979). He also worked with the Birmingham reggae band Steel Pulse and with **Linton Kwesi Johnson**. During the punk era he produced albums by the Slits and the Pop Group. In 1984 Bovell worked on the Orange Juice album, *Texas Fever*, and he would regularly work with the band's founder, Edwin Collins, over the next five years.

DAVID BOWIE
b. David Robert Jones, 8 January 1947, London, England

A major influence on both glam-rock and punk through his stage shows and records of the early seventies, Bowie found international success with his disco- and dance-styled music of 1975 onwards. He brought disco rhythms, Philly soul and electronics into the vocabulary of mainstream rock. Even in the eighties the androgyny of **Michael Jackson** and the transvestism of **Culture Club**'s Boy George owed much to Bowie's pioneering of a decade earlier. In the nineties Bowie was the artist most identified with the Internet, with his 1999 album *hours . . .* being one of the first by a major artist and a major label (Capitol) to be offered as a digital download.

His early career gave little hint of what was to follow. Until 1969 he existed on the edge first of the British R&B scene and then of London's avant-garde underground. He took tenor sax lessons with noted jazz player Ronnie Ross and sang and played with various semi-professional groups before recording briefly as the King Bees (Vocalion, 1964), Mannish Boys (Parlophone, 1965) and Davy Jones and the Lower Third (Parlophone and Pye, 1965–6).

Changing his name to Bowie to avoid confusion with a **Monkees** member, he was persuaded by his manager Ken Pitt to write an album of mainstream pop songs. The result was *David Bowie* (Deram, 1967), a set of quirky songs with titles like 'Please Mr Gravedigger', 'Uncle Arthur' and 'The Laughing Gnome', performed in a light semi-cockney voice reminiscent of **Anthony Newley**. After Bowie's later success, the reissued 'Gnome' was a Top Ten hit in Britain in 1973.

Turning to Buddhism and the underground, Bowie studied with mime artist Lindsay Kemp. A spell with Kemp's troupe as musician and dancer was followed by the formation of an experimental trio, Feathers. These intensely theatrical experiences were to be crucial to the formation of Bowie's mature style.

Signing to Mercury in 1969, Bowie's first hit was his own composition, 'Space Oddity', a song chosen by BBC television to accompany its broadcast of the Apollo moon landing in July 1969. The album from which it came (released in the US as *Man of Words/ Man of Music*) was very much the work of a hippy singer-songwriter and by the time it appeared, the dream was over. Peace and love were out of fashion.

The Man Who Sold the World (Mercury, 1970; 1972 in the US) was a rock album, the first with his new collaborator, Hull guitarist Mick Ronson, a talented arranger and pianist. It was produced (as had been most of *Space Oddity*, apart from the title track) by American bassist Tony Visconti, later to co-produce several Bowie albums as well as records by **Marc Bolan** and many others. *The Man*'s songs were pessimistic portrayals of a world of mass murder and of dehumanized technology. It sold poorly, although **Lulu** later had a hit single in Britain with the title track (Polydor, 1974), produced by Bowie and Ronson.

1971 found Bowie with a new manager, Tony DeFries, and record label, RCA. In that year, too, Peter Noone (ex-Herman's Hermits) had a hit with one of his new songs, the deceptively light and sunny 'Oh You Pretty Things'. It typified *Hunky Dory*, which included songs of tribute to **Bob Dylan**, Andy Warhol and the **Velvet Underground**, whose leader Lou Reed's album *Transformer* Bowie produced the following year. He would also remix the third album by the Stooges (*Raw Power*, 1973) and later frequently collaborate with their frontman **Iggy Pop**. *Hunky Dory* was the prelude to his first great masterpiece, the song cycle *The Rise and Fall of Ziggy Stardust and the Spiders from Mars* (1972).

In July 1972 Bowie introduced his Festival Hall, London, gig with the words, 'I'm Ziggy', and for the next year he was to act out the persona of the alien who became a messianic rock star. The live shows with the Spiders (Ronson, bassist Trevor Bolder and drummer Mick 'Woody' Woodmansey) featured Bowie in his Ziggy outfit, green jump-suit, platform boots and spiky carrot-red hair. As rock theatre, the Ziggy shows were intended to feature Bowie acting the role of Ziggy. But the adulation he received brought the fusion of Bowie and Ziggy perilously close. This mental pressure and the fatigue of a heavy touring schedule led to his surprise announcement in July 1973 on the final night of the *Aladdin Sane* tour that he would give no more live shows.

The apocalyptic tone of the Ziggy songs had been carried over into *Aladdin Sane* (1973), whose title was a punning reference to madness. *Pin Ups* (1974) was Bowie's affectionate homage to his R&B and beat group contemporaries of a decade earlier. As well as **Yardbirds** and **Who** numbers, it included songs recorded by more obscure bands like the **Pretty Things** and the Merseys.

Nevertheless, his more sombre preoccupations remained. While cutting *Pin Ups* at the Château d'Hérouville near Paris, Bowie was already planning a musical version of George Orwell's futuristic novel, *1984*. Because the author's widow refused to release the rights, this project had to be abandoned but songs called '1984' and 'Big Brother' appeared on the next Bowie album, *Diamond Dogs*, his first since 1970 without Ronson, who embarked on a solo career before joining **Mott the Hoople**, whose 1972 hit single 'All the Young Dudes' Bowie had written and produced.

By the end of 1974, Bowie was one of the biggest rock stars in Europe. His last five studio albums and a live record (*David Live*, 1974) on RCA had all reached the Top Five in Britain, while the Ziggy character was a major inspiration for a number of artists who were swiftly categorized as glitter or glam rockers. They included Marc Bolan, **Suzi Quatro**, **Gary Glitter** and Alvin Stardust – who even used a similar name. More numerous were the hard core of Bowie fans who dressed like him and from whom came key figures in the foundation of British punk just a couple of years later. For punk, Bowie offered a prime example of visual excess and outrage, as well as an English-accented singing voice, distinct from the rock mainstream.

Though 'Space Oddity' had finally been a hit there in 1973, he remained only a cult figure in America. That position was to change in 1975, however, when first 'Young Americans' and then 'Fame'* (co-written with **John Lennon**, who sang backing vocals on it) were American hits. On these singles and the *Young Americans* album Bowie adopted a new persona. American-resident, he was now the white soul boy rather than sci-fi hard rocker. The album was cut in the Philadelphia studio used by **Gamble and Huff** with a new band including Main Ingredient guitarist Carlos Alomar, bassist Willie Weeks and **Luther Vandross** on backing vocals. This brand of neurotic funk was developed further on *Station to Station* (1976), which produced the hit single 'Golden Years'.

Bowie now toured again, in the persona of the 'thin white duke', with a fifties hipster hairstyle and casual clothes. The success of the tour was marred by Bowie's approving references to Hitler ('the first great rock star') in interviews. They combined his fascination with the idea of superior beings with the equal fascination which Germany – and, ironically, the twenties decadence and avant-garde culture which Nazism destroyed – held for him. They also coincided with a renewed public concern over a possible fascist revival in Western Europe.

That fascination was one reason why in 1977 Bowie moved to Berlin, where he lived for three years. There were also personal reasons, connected with his drug and alcohol use and the break-up of his marriage. Musically, his work now changed drastically. He produced three albums in collaboration with **Brian Eno**,

the respected avant-garde artist and producer, and also co-wrote and produced two 1977 albums for Iggy Pop. Bowie's own albums, *Low* (1977), '*Heroes*' (1977) and *Lodger* (1979) confused fans and critics and were among Bowie's least commercially successful records (1978's *Stage* largely consisted of live versions of tracks from *Low* and '*Heroes*'). In their exploration of instrumental and vocal sound and in the imaginative videos made for tracks from *Lodger*, however, they enabled Bowie to expand his musical range in preparation for his return to the mainstream.

This came with 'Ashes to Ashes', a sequel to the 'Space Oddity' narrative, and the 1980 album, *Scary Monsters*. These and the duet with **Bing Crosby**, 'Peace on Earth/Little Drummer Boy' (1982), were his last records under his RCA contract. Later that year Bowie signed to Capitol-EMI and offered another stylistic switch on *Let's Dance*, a collaboration with Chic's **Nile Rodgers**, which used a contemporary dance style.

On the subsequent 'Serious Moonlight' tour, Bowie dressed in a way reminiscent of the young **Frank Sinatra**. Dismissed by rock critics as 'family entertainment', *Let's Dance* produced three hit singles for Bowie. It was followed in 1984 by *Tonight*, while in 1985 Bowie and Mick Jagger had a massive hit with their version of **Martha and the Vandellas**' 'Dancing in the Street' from the Live Aid concert. At this period, Bowie also developed as a writer and performer for film soundtracks. With **Pat Metheny**, he composed the score for *The Falcon and the Snowman* (1985), and in 1986 he supplied songs for *Labyrinth* (including the hit single 'Underground'), *Absolute Beginners* and *When the Wind Blows*.

As a solo artist he released *Never Let Me Down* (1987) to coincide with the Glass Spider world tour, with **Peter Frampton** as lead guitarist. He then formed a band, Tin Machine, an attempt to recapture the spirit of the Stooges with the ex-Iggy Pop rhythm section of Hunt and Tony Sales. With guitarist Reeves Gabrels completing the line-up, they recorded an eponymous début in 1989, followed by *Tin Machine II* (1991) and the live *Oy Veh Baby* (1992).

Bowie resumed a solo career and his relationship with producer Rodgers by recording the electrodance oriented *Black Tie, White Noise* (Arista 1993), which included versions of **Cream**'s 'I Feel Free' and **Morrissey**'s 'I Know It's Going to Happen Someday'. The album re-united him with Ronson, who was to die of cancer a few months later. *Black Tie, White Noise* included the hit single 'Jump They Say' and was critically well received and topped the British chart. In 1994 Arista issued an interactive version of tracks from the album.

Bowie's second hit album of 1993 was the soundtrack for the BBC TV series *Buddha of Suburbia*, which featured the guitar playing of **Lennie Kravitz** on the title track. **Philip Glass** released a symphonic treatment of Bowie and Eno's *Low* in the same year. Bowie's next two studio projects highlighted his desire to embrace modern musical styles, with mixed results. 1995's *1. Outside*, produced by Eno, drew on the industrial rock sound of **Nine Inch Nails** and included the singles 'Hello Spaceboy' and 'The Heart's Filthy Lesson', while *Earthling* (1997) combined traditional rock-song structures with jungle beats. In between times Bowie released a single, 'Telling Lies', exclusively over the internet, contributed to the soundtrack of David Lynch's *Lost Highway* (1996) and was inducted into the Rock'n'Roll Hall of Fame.

In 1997 Bowie became the first artist to float his future royalties on the stock market, before setting up the BowieNet Internet Service Provider a year later. His fascination with new technology led him to make *hours...* (1999) digitally available before it was released as a physical CD. The album, which included a song co-written over the internet by a competition winner, marked a return to a more melodic, song-based approach, and was his most commercially successful release of the decade.

Bowie's recording career was punctuated by spells as an actor. He had starring roles in Nicolas Roeg's film of *The Man Who Fell to Earth* (1976), in David Hemmings' *Just a Gigolo* (1979) and in Oshima's *Merry Christmas Mr Lawrence* (1983). He made his stage début in the 1980 Broadway production *The Elephant Man*. In 1986 the wheel of his career seemed to have come full circle when he took a leading role in *Absolute Beginners*, Julien Temple's musical film of the Colin MacInnes novel set in the London of Bowie's youth. Bowie the family entertainer emerged as he took a role in Jim ('Muppets') Henson's fantasy, *Labyrinth*. In the nineties he appeared in *The Linguine Incident* (1991) and David Lynch's *Twin Peaks: Fire Walk with Me* (1992), as well as playing Andy Warhol in *Basquiat* (1996).

AL BOWLLY
b. Albert Alick Bowlly, 7 January 1899, Lourenço Marques, Mozambique, d. 17 April 1941, London, England

The most accomplished British dance-band singer of the thirties, Bowlly had a clear, distinctive voice, relaxed timing and a fulsome, romantic expressiveness beyond the reach, or taste, of his peers. He was one of the most individual exponents of the crooning style pioneered by **Bing Crosby**, a style Bowlly preferred to call 'the modern microphone manner'.

Growing up in Johannesburg, South Africa, he was a singing barber before joining the globetrotting Edgar Adeler and his Syncopators as banjoist and guitarist. After working in India and Germany, he

arrived in England in 1928 to join **Fred Elizalde**. In 1930 he became the vocalist of the **Roy Fox** band, appearing in BBC broadcasts and recording with studio bands organized by **Ray Noble**. Bowlly stayed with the Fox band (led by **Lew Stone**) from 1932 until 1934, when he joined Noble for a long and successful stay in New York.

Returning to London in 1936, Bowlly underwent a successful major operation for throat problems which enabled him to join Lew Stone's band and to make some excellent recordings with **Geraldo** in 1938. A further throat infection, however, limited his work during 1940–1 to a few record dates and a variety act with singer-guitarist Jimmy Mesene. He died when a German landmine exploded near his apartment.

Bowlly's recorded work amounted to more than a thousand items. He sang not only with his primary employers like Noble, Fox and Stone, but with many other bands, from concert orchestras to Hawaiian groups. Much of his work was uncredited or pseudonymous. Among his most popular songs were 'Time on My Hands' (1931), 'Goodnight Sweetheart' (1931), 'Love Is the Sweetest Thing' (1932), 'The Very Thought of You' (1934) – all recorded with Noble – and 'Never Break a Promise' (1938), with Geraldo. His signature tune was **Yip Harburg**'s 'Brother Can You Spare a Dime?', with its refrain, 'Say, don't you remember? They called me Al.' He broadcast frequently on both the BBC and European stations like Luxembourg, Hilversum and Lyons, and appeared in several feature and short films.

THE BOX TOPS
Alex Chilton, b. 28 December 1950, Memphis, Tennessee, USA; Bill Cunningham, b. 23 January 1950, Memphis; Danny Smythe (replaced by Tom Boggs), b. 16 July 1947, Wynn, Arkansas; John Evans (replaced by Rick Allen), b. 28 January 1946, Little Rock, Arkansas; Gary Talley, b. 17 August 1947

Best remembered for their 1967 recording of the Wayne Carson Thompson song 'The Letter'* (which later provided hits for both the Arbors and **Joe Cocker**, in 1969 and 1970 respectively) and the Spooner Oldham and **Dan Penn** composition 'Cry Like a Baby'* in 1968, the Box Tops were one of the few pop acts to emerge from soul-drenched Memphis in the sixties. Its successor band, Big Star, had a cult following among indie rock musicians of the eighties.

The group became the Box Tops when Chilton joined Ronnie and the De Villes as lead singer; they were spotted by Penn (who would produce their best work) and signed to Mala in 1966. Propelled by Chilton's grainy voice and Penn's gimmicky production – the record featured the sound of a jet airplane – their first single, 'The Letter', sold over four million copies. Henceforth, the group became a vehicle for Chilton and Penn's increasingly sophisticated productions: 'Cry Like a Baby', 'Choo Choo Train' and 'I Met Her in Church'. Their last major hit was another Thompson song, 'Soul Deep' (1969), produced by **Chips Moman** and Tommy Cogbill, soon after which Chilton left the group.

With fellow Mempheans Christopher Bell (*b. 12 January 1951, d. 27 December 1978*), Jody Stephens (*b. 4 October 1952*) and Andy Hummell (*b. 26 January 1951*) he formed Big Star and signed to Ardent in 1971. Though they had no chart success, the group's first two albums, *1 Record* (1972) and *Radio City* (1974, without Chris Bell) were notable for their progressive approach to pop and won much critical acclaim before the group disbanded in 1975 (their last album, *The Third Album*, was eventually released in 1978).

With countless bands citing Big Star as an influence, a live album from 1974 was issued in 1992. It was followed by the re-formation of the band in 1993 for a string of live dates at which *Columbia* was recorded. It featured Chilton and Stephens (Bell had been killed in a car crash in 1978). Chilton's erratic solo career included the ragged live album *One Day in New York* (1979) and the psychedelic *Like Flies on Sherbert* (Aura, 1980) and made him a cult hero, particularly in Britain. His wanderings through the eighties on independent label after independent label were pulled together by Rhino on *19 Years* (1991). Probably the most extreme of his eighties albums is *High Priest* (New Rose, 1987), on which he sings 'Volare', among other oddities.

That pointed the way to *Cliches* (1994, New Rose) a collection of cover-versions of classic songs from **Cole Porter**'s 'All of Me' to **Nina Simone**'s 'My Baby Just Cares for Me'.

In 1995 Chilton revived the Ardent label for *A Man Called Destruction*, which mixed originals ('Devil Girl') and versions of songs by others, notably the **Beach Boys**' 'New Girl in School'. The band reunited for *Tear Off* (Last Call, 1997), a collection of (mostly) R&B covers that was only released in France, and toured intermittently. Chilton continued his solo career with *Loose Shoes & Tight Pussy* (1999), another collection of covers, the best of which was his lugubrious reading of 'Goodnight My Love', a hit for the **Fleetwoods** in 1963.

JOE BOYD
b. 5 August 1942, Boston, Massachusetts, USA

Like Shel Talmy and Tony Visconti, Boyd was an American-born producer who played a large part in shaping the sound of British rock. With **Fairport Convention** and the **Incredible String Band**, he was one of the first to find a studio formula for acoustic

songs played on electric instruments. In the eighties he produced records by such artists as **R.E.M.** (their third album, *Fables of the Reconstruction*), **Billy Bragg** and 10,000 Maniacs, as well as maintaining his connection with ex-Fairport guitarist **Richard Thompson**.

As a student at Harvard University he promoted blues concerts and assisted at a **Jesse Fuller** recording session. In 1964 he went to Europe as tour manager for the American Folk Blues Festival package, returning the following year to set up a British arm of Jac Holzman's Elektra label. Boyd produced albums by **Martin Carthy** and Dave Swarbrick and the Incredible String Band before leaving to set up his own production company, Witchseason. He cut the first **Pink Floyd** single ('Arnold Layne') as well as six Fairport albums and records by other British performers of the late sixties, including John Martyn and **Nick Drake**.

Boyd spent much of the seventies back in America, working for Warners with a number of folk-related artists such as **Maria Muldaur**, **Kate and Anna McGarrigle** and Geoff Muldaur. The finest achievement of this period was *Kate and Anna McGarrigle* (1975), cut in Boyd's characteristic manner, 'live' in the studio with the minimum of over-dubs.

In 1981 Boyd set up his own label, Hannibal, for which he continued to produce the McGarrigles and resumed his partnership with Richard Thompson, with *Shoot Out the Lights* (1982) and *Hand of Kindness* (1983). In 1986 Hannibal released the highly regarded *Supply and Demand*, an album of songs by Bertolt Brecht, Hanns Eisler and **Kurt Weill** by ex-Henry Cow vocalist Dagmar Krause. The label additionally focused on folk, folk-rock and folk-jazz music from Hungary (Marta Sebastyen and Muzicsas) and Bulgaria (Ivo Papasov and Trio Bulgarka). After Hannibal merged with the US company Rykodisc, Boyd was able to put together even more ambitious projects such as the Thompson retrospective, *Watching the Dark* (1993), and the McGarrigles' classic, *Matapedia* (1996).

BOYZ II MEN
Wanya 'Squirt' Morris, b. 29 July 1973, Philadelphia, Pennsylvania, USA; Michael 'Bass' McCary, b. 16 December 1972, Philadelphia; Shawn 'Slim' Stockman, b. 26 September 1972; Nathan 'Alex-Vanderpool' Morris, b. 18 June 1971

One of the most popular young male R&B groups in the US, Boyz II Men represent Motown Records' latest attempt to re-create the success of the **Jacksons** in the label's heyday. Like their predecessors, Boyz II Men have mastered a variety of musical styles, ranging from hip-hop to nostalgic doo-wop ballads.

The four members of Boyz II Men met at the Philadelphia High School of Creative and Performing

Arts in 1988. They performed at local talent contests before being discovered by Michael Bivins of Bell Biv Devoe. Bivins signed the group to his Biv label, which was financed by Motown. The group's first US hits were 'Motownphilly' and 'It's So Hard to Say Goodbye to Yesterday'. Both were included on the début album *Cooleyhigh Harmony* (1991), which mixed soulful ballads with bright hip-hop tracks.

In 1992 the group recorded 'End of the Road' for the soundtrack of the Eddie Murphy film, *Boomerang*. The maudlin ballad stayed on top of the US charts for three months and also reached No. 1 in Britain. Boyz II Men also recorded the song in a Spanish language version, 'Al Fin del Camino'.

An album of seasonal songs, *Christmas Interpretations*, was issued at the end of 1993. It featured singer and composer Brian McKnight on the single 'Let it Snow'. The group later recorded a version of 'In the Still of the Night', the fifties doo-wop standard associated with the **Five Satins** for the television miniseries *The Jacksons* in 1993. The group had continued success in 1994 with *II*, which included 'I'll Make Love to You', which remained at the top of the US charts even longer than 1992's 'End of the Road'. The album eventually sold over seven million copies, while the **Mariah Carey** collaboration 'One Sweet Day' topped the US chart for a record-breaking sixteen weeks. After releasing *The Remix Collection* (1995), Boyz II Men performed before Pope John Paul II during his American visit of the same year and sang the national anthem at the closing ceremony of the 1996 Olympic Games in Atlanta, Georgia. Boyz II Men returned in 1997 with their third album, *Evolution*, which included the US No. 1 '4 Seasons of Loneliness'. Subsequent hits included 'Can't Let Her Go' (1998) and 'I Will Get There' (1999), which was featured in the film *Prince of Egypt*.

BOYZONE

Keith Duffy, b. 1 October 1974; Stephen Gately, b. 17 March 1976; Mike Graham, b. 15 August 1972; Ronan Keating, b. 3 March 1977; Shane Lynch, b. 3 July 1976

In the second half of the nineties Irish boyband Boyzone achieved vast success across Europe, Asia and Latin America with their brand of pop balladry.

Originally a six-piece who came together after replying to an advert in the *Irish Star*, Boyzone soon numbered five when Graham joined Duffy, Gately, Keating and Lynch after the departure of two founding members, Mark Walton and Richard Rock. Managed by Louis Walsh, the band hit the top of the Irish charts with a reworking of the **Osmonds**' 'Love Me for the Reason' (1994), later a British Number Two. Their début album, *Said and Done** (Polydor, 1995), also featured hit singles in 'Key to My Life', 'So

Good' and a cover of **Cat Stevens**' 'Father and Son'.

After successful tours of Europe and Asia, the group gained their first UK Number One with a cover of the **Bee Gees**' 'Words' from their second album, *A Different Beat** (1996). The album spawned further hits in 'Isn't It a Wonder' and the title track as the band tried to crack the Latin American market by releasing alternate versions of their songs in Spanish. Boyzone also released the theme songs to two movies, 'Picture of You' (from *Bean*) and 'Shooting Star' (from Disney's *Hercules*), as well as featuring on the BBC *Children in Need* version of **Lou Reed**'s 'Perfect Day'.

With *Where We Belong** (1998) the group became only the third act to have three No. 1s in the UK with consecutive albums (along with **Oasis** and **The Beatles**). In the same year two band members – Lynch and Keating – married their partners. They had two more UK No. 1 singles with 'All That I Need' and 'No Matter What'.

1999 saw Boyzone make a concerted effort to find success in America. They also had a further UK chart-topper with their version of 'When the Going Gets Tough', originally by **Billy Ocean**, which they recorded for the Comic Relief charity. In the same year Keating began a solo career with 'When You Say Nothing at All', which was featured in the hit movie *Notting Hill*. Band members Gately and Graham also began less successful solo careers in 1999. The group's greatest hits album, *By Request**, topped the charts across Europe in 1999–2000. In 2000 Keating released his first solo album, *Ronan*, which saw him attempting a more mature ballad style. In the fashion of the times the album, which included the European hit and UK chart-topper 'Life Is a Rollercoaster', was the work of several producers, including Steve Lipson, Steve Mac and Phil Thornley, and writers, including **Bryan Adams** and **Diane Warren**.

PERRY BRADFORD

b. 14 February 1893, Montgomery, Alabama, USA, d. 22 April 1970, New York

Perry Bradford was one of the first generation of twentieth-century black musical entrepreneurs, a contemporary of Harry Pace (whose Black Swan of 1921–4 was the first all-black record company) and **Mayo Williams**. His involvement with 'Crazy Blues', the first high-selling blues record, places him among the primary architects of the blues as commercial product.

Bradford grew up in Atlanta, Georgia, and became a vaudeville pianist, working with travelling minstrel shows. He moved to New York in 1910 and played in jazz bands, backing such singers as Mamie Smith (*b. 26 May 1883, Cincinnati, Ohio, d. 16 September 1946, New York*). He became Smith's musical director and featured her in his revue *Made in Harlem* (1918). In February 1920 he set up a recording date with Okeh at which Smith cut his composition 'That Thing Called Love', the first commercial recording of a black female artist. (The earliest examples of black recording were of gospel music, such as the 1902 Victor sides by the Dinwiddie Colored Quartet, or, more rarely, of 'coon' songs by male singers like **George W. Johnson**. In the nineteen-tens the only significant black recording artist was **Bert Williams**.)

The response to 'That Thing Called Love' from black Americans was immense, and did much to convince the white-owned record companies of the demand for records by black artists: what **Ralph Peer**, when later he initiated Okeh's 8000 series for blues and jazz material, called 'race records for the race'. In August 1920 Smith made 'Crazy Blues' (Okeh), the first vocal blues recording; Bradford wrote it and its reverse side, 'It's Right Here for You', and directed the session, for which, unlike its predecessor, he was able to hire a black band, including the cornet-player Johnny Dunn. The coupling is said to have sold more than 800,000 copies, prompting cover-versions on every rival label, among them treatments by Noble Sissle and **Eubie Blake** (Edison) and the **James Europe** band (Pathe).

Bradford was also associated with other popular blues artists of the day, including Alberta Hunter and Edith Wilson, and formed recording bands, including his Jazz Phools, for various labels. He also wrote for Bert Williams ('Unexpectedly', 1922). He was still active nearly twenty years later, when he claimed composer credit for 'Keep a Knockin'', which **Louis Jordan** had recorded. In 1965 he published the lively, anecdotal and highly selective autobiography *Born with the Blues*.

OWEN BRADLEY

b. 21 October 1915, Westmoreland, Tennessee, USA, d. 7 January 1998

Session musician, arranger, producer and studio owner, Bradley was one of the first to popularize Nashville as a recording centre and later, with **Chet Atkins**, was responsible for the development of the 'Nashville sound'.

By the late thirties Bradley was a pianist and guitarist, playing mostly pop music in pick-up bands in and around Nashville, graduating to the leadership of radio station WSM's orchestra in 1947. That same year, after playing on the first recording (a jingle) made at the first independent recording studio opened in Nashville, he was asked by Decca's Paul Cohen to build a studio specifically for recording purposes and guaranteed 100 sessions a year if he would. With the help of his brother Harold, who by the sev-

enties was one of Nashville's best-known session guitarists, Bradley built three studios in quick succession, each bigger than the other. He opened the first in 1952 and the most famous in 1955. This was the Quonset hut, better known as Bradley's Barn, which was eventually bought by Columbia when they moved their country operations to Nashville in 1962.

Though his work with **Ernest Tubb**, **Kitty Wells** and **Bill Monroe** and others remained traditional, Bradley's inclinations were towards the lusher sounds heard on the records he produced with **Patsy Cline** and **Brenda Lee**. Certainly, his 1956 recordings of **Buddy Holly** show him unsympathetic to Holly's raw rock'n'roll sound and the successful rockabilly records cut for Decca in Nashville by **Johnny Burnette** in 1956 were made independently of him. By now supervising sessions for Mercury and Dot as well as Decca, Bradley pioneered the use of strings and vocal choruses (usually either the Jordanaires or Anita Kerr Singers). In the sixties Bradley revitalized **Burl Ives**' recording career with his productions of 'A Little Bitty Tear' and 'Funny Way of Laughing', both international hits in 1962, and as the chief staff producer of MCA (as Decca became) he was responsible for producing **Loretta Lynn**, **Conway Twitty** and **Bill Anderson**.

Bradley had signed as a recording artist to Bullet Records in 1947, then joined Decca in 1949 where he continued recording as the Owen Bradley Quintet throughout the fifties. His first recordings, all instrumentals, mixed pop ('La Vie en Rose' and 'Blue Danube Waltz') with country songs ('Blue Eyes Crying in the Rain'), his only country hit being a version of 'Blues Stay Away from Me' (1949). But, ironically, his only significant hits came with his rock'n'roll-inflected instrumentals, 'White Silver Sands' (1957), later a Top Ten hit for **Bill Black**, and 'Big Guitar' (1958). He also recorded two albums of versions of numbers (mostly instrumentals) associated with rock'n'roll, *Bandstand Hop* (1958) and *Big Guitar* (1959). In the sixties he confined himself to production work.

In 1975 Bradley was elected to the Country Music Hall of Fame. He worked as an independent producer in the seventies. In 1988 he came out of retirement to produce *Shadowland* by **k. d. lang**, one of Patsy Cline's most ardent admirers among new country singers.

TINY BRADSHAW

b. Myron Bradshaw, 23 September 1905, Youngstown, Ohio, USA, d. 26 November 1958, Cincinnati, Ohio

Singer, pianist and drummer, Bradshaw led one of the bands of the forties and fifties that operated on the boundary of jazz and R&B.

At Wilberforce College, Ohio, he sang with a band led by **Fletcher Henderson**'s brother Horace. Moving to New York in the late twenties, Bradshaw played drums for the Savoy Bearcats, Luis Russell and the Blue Rhythm Band, a group organized by impresario **Irving Mills** to deputize for **Duke Ellington** and **Cab Calloway**.

He formed his own band in New York in 1934. Recordings for Decca the same year found Bradshaw singing 'The Sheik of Araby' and 'Darktown Strutter's Ball' in the Calloway style. Bradshaw had residencies at clubs in Chicago, Philadelphia and New York, but with the advent of the Second World War he was commissioned as a major and took a band to entertain US servicemen in many parts of the world. In 1944 Bradshaw's orchestra recorded for Regis.

Like many other bandleaders, Bradshaw was forced by the economic circumstances of the late forties to reduce the size of his band. With a stronger R&B emphasis, the Bradshaw small band had several hits on King in the early fifties. They included 'The Train Kept a Rollin'', 'Big Town' (with vocals by **Roy Brown**) and 'Soft', with its distinctive saxophone solo. Among other instrumentalists who played with Bradshaw were **Henry Glover**, Sil Austin, Red Prysock and **Art Blakey** sideman Sonny Stitt. **Lonnie Johnson** and **Arthur Prysock** were among the singers who recorded with the band.

PAUL BRADY
b. 10 May 1947, Strabane, County Tyrone, Northern Ireland

Brady is known both as an interpreter of traditional songs and as a contemporary songwriter. **Tina Turner** and **Bonnie Raitt** are among those who have recorded his compositions.

While studying in Dublin, he played guitar with local R&B band the Kult and later formed Rockhouse. In 1967 he joined the Johnstons, a leading Irish folk group who featured Adrienne Johnston's lead vocals. He stayed with the group until 1974, playing 12-string guitar and tin whistle and writing songs for the group.

He next joined Planxty and performed as a duo with Andy Irvine after the group split in 1975. Their only recording as a team, for Mulligan in 1976, included Brady's celebrated version of the traditional ballad 'Arthur McBride', which influenced **Bob Dylan**'s later recording of the song. During the late 1970s Brady collaborated with Irish instrumentalists such as fiddler Tommy Peoples and Kevin Burke and made a solo album of folk material, *Welcome Here, Kind Stranger* (1978), which featured 'The Banks of Pontchartrain'.

In the eighties Brady concentrated on songwriting and recording his own songs with rock-influenced

musicians. After *Hard Station* (1981), *True for You* (1983) and *Full Moon* (1984) he released the highly praised *Back to the Centre* (1986), on which he was accompanied by **Eric Clapton** and U2 drummer Larry Mullen. This contained some of his finest work in 'Deep in Your Heart' and 'The Island'. With Mark Knopfler of **Dire Straits** Brady co-wrote the soundtrack for the film *Cal* (1984).

Brady continued to release albums, notably *Primitive Dance* (1987) and *Trick or Treat* (1991) with its duet with Bonnie Raitt, but he achieved his greatest commercial impact through recordings of his songs by other artists. Among the Brady songs which have been successfully covered are 'Paradise Is Here' and 'Steel Claw' (Tina Turner), 'Luck of the Draw', 'Not the Only One', 'One Belief Away' (Bonnie Raitt), 'Night Hunting Time' (**Santana**) and 'The Island' (Dolores Keane). The career retrospective *Songs & Crazy Dreams* (1992) was followed by *Spirits Colliding* (1997).

BILLY BRAGG
b. Steven William Bragg, 20 December 1957, Barking, Essex, England

In 1975 Peter Jenner, former **Pink Floyd** and **Roy Harper** manager, forecast that the next thing in music would be someone 'with an acoustic guitar singing revolutionary songs in pubs'. His timing was out (punk came next) but ten years later, Billy Bragg fitted the description (and he was managed by Jenner). In fact, Bragg was unaware of leftist folk singers like Leon Rosselson and Dick Gaughan until he shared the stage with them at political benefit concerts. But in introducing their work to a new young audience, Bragg went some way to re-establishing the connection between political movements and contemporary folk song that had been broken in the seventies.

A songwriter who accompanied himself on ragged but effective electric guitar, Bragg caught the mood of a section of disaffected British youth in the early eighties. A spell with punk rock band Riff Raff and three months in the army were followed by the six-song album *Life's a Riot with Spy vs Spy* (Go Disc, 1984), which included 'A New England', a Top Ten hit for **Ewan MacColl**'s daughter Kirsty in 1985.

A second album, *Brewing Up with Billy Bragg*, was followed by the hit EP *Between the Wars*, whose title song was a fine example of Bragg's writing skill, juxtaposing the eighties with the thirties and the Second World War with a future war. In 1986 he helped to form Red Wedge, a loose grouping of rock performers who supported the Labour Party. His hit of that year, 'Levi Stubbs' Tears', combined a reverence for Motown music with a telling commentary on inner-city life. 1986's *Talking with the Taxman About Poetry* (a title taken from Soviet poet Mayakovsky) provided evidence of Bragg's ability to write love songs whose passionate realism matched that of his political lyrics. The album was released by Elektra in America.

He next released *Back to Basics* (1987) and *Workers' Playtime* (1988), produced by **Joe Boyd**. His charity version of The Beatles' 'She's Leaving Home' was a British No. 1 as a double A-side with 'With a Little Help from my Friends', sung by Scottish group **Wet Wet Wet**.

In 1989 he reactivated his Unity label to sign new talent and himself released *The Internationale* (1990). In 1991 he had his biggest hit album with *Don't Try This at Home*, which included the British hit single 'Sexuality' and featured guest appearances from members of **R.E.M.**, with whom he had regularly appeared.

After taking some time out of the business, Bragg returned with the highly acclaimed *William Bloke* (1996). His next project was the impressive *Mermaid Avenue* (1998, Elektra), on which, backed by new-country collective Wilco (an offshoot of **Uncle Tupelo**), Bragg performed a number of unreleased **Woody Guthrie** originals to which he and the group had written music. The album, which included such whimsicalities as 'Ingrid Bergman', confirmed that Guthrie's concerns were wider than just the political. This was even more the case with *Mermaid Avenue, Vol. 2* (2000), which saw Wilco take the musical lead in a deft celebration of romance ('Secrets of the Sea') and whimsy ('My Flying Saucer'). Before that was released Bragg issued the collection of rarities *Reaching to the Converted* (1999).

LAURA BRANIGAN
b. 3 July 1957, Brewster, New York, USA

An enthusiastic, big-voiced performer, Laura Branigan enjoyed substantial US success in the mid-eighties.

Born and raised in upstate New York, after a stint as an actress Branigan emerged in 1982 with her version of a European hit of the previous year, 'Gloria', written by Italian duo Umberto Tozzi and Giancar Bigazzi. It was a Top Five hit in the US and made the UK Top Ten. Her uninhibited performance of the song set the tone for her début album, *Branigan* (Atlantic, 1982), which sold over a million copies in the US. The follow-up, *Branigan 2*, repeated the success of the first album, and spawned another US hit, 'Solitaire', which reached the Top Ten the following year. From the same album, 'How Am I Supposed to Live Without You?' continued her run of US hits. The song was written by **Michael Bolton**, who went on to enjoy a massively successful career as a solo artist in the late eighties and nineties, and who topped the US chart with it in 1990.

Despite her continued success in her homeland,

Branigan found it difficult to build on her initial success overseas until 1984 when 'Self Control' made the UK Top Five. Its success propelled her third album, also titled *Self Control*, into the European charts. However, she was once again unable to follow up the breakthrough, and the next single 'The Lucky One' (taken from a US TV drama, *Uncommon Love*) was only a minor hit. The 1985 album *Hold Me* contained another US Top Forty hit, 'Spanish Eddie'. In 1987 she recorded a typically strident version of 'Power of Love', originally a UK No. 1 in 1985 for US vocalist Jennifer Rush. In 1993 she released *Over My Heart*, produced by Phil Ramone.

BRASS CONSTRUCTION
Sandy Billups; Michael Grudge, b. Jamaica; Randy Muller, b. Guyana; Wayne Parris, b. Jamaica; Larry Payton; Morris Price; Jesse Ward Jnr; Wade Williamson; Joseph Arthur Wong, b. Trinidad

Pioneers of jazz-funk, Brass Construction had some of the biggest-selling disco records of the late seventies.

From New York, the group was founded as the six-piece Dynamic Soul, led by songwriter and singer Muller with Ward on tenor sax and Price and Parris on trumpets, plus a rhythm section of Williamson (bass) and Payton (drums). Adding Grudge (sax), Wong (guitar) and Billups (percussion), they changed their name and signed to United Artists in 1976.

With a style derived from calypso and reggae as well as soul and jazz, Brass Construction scored a Top Twenty pop hit and an R&B No. 1 with their first single, 'Movin''. Later singles included 'Changin'' (1976), 'Ha Cha Cha' (1977) and 'L-O-V-E-U' (1978). The first three albums, produced by Jeff Lane and entitled simply *Brass Construction 1, 2* and *3*, were all big hits in America, though later albums on UA and, from 1983, Capitol did less well. Though they hardly recorded in the eighties several of their early hits were remixed, including 'Ha Cha Cha (Acieed Mix)' (1988).

Muller also worked as arranger for B T Express and produced records by Garnet Mimms and another New York band, Skyy, whose biggest hit was 'Call Me' (Salsoul, 1982). After Brass Construction ceased to record he set up his own production company and worked with such artists as Robyn Springer (*Makin' Moves*, Cardiac 1991).

ANTHONY BRAXTON
b. 4 June 1945, Chicago, Illinois, USA

A leading figure in improvised music, alto-sax-player Braxton worked with many of Europe's leading avant-gardists as well as such mainstream figures as **Chick Corea** and **Max Roach**.

Like the members of the **Art Ensemble of Chicago**, Braxton was a graduate of the Chicago-based Association for the Advancement of Creative Musicians (AACM). His first recording, *3 Compositions of New Jazz* (Delmark, 1966), demonstrated his original approach. A diagrammatical rather than melodic or rhythmic work, it reflected Braxton's interest in mathematics and chess. The album included contributions from other AACM alumni, trumpeter Leo Smith and violinist Leroy Jenkins, with whom Braxton toured Europe in 1969–70.

In Paris the group recorded two albums for BYG – *Anthony Braxton* (1969) and *This Time* (1970). Returning to New York, Braxton formed Circle with ex-**Miles Davis** keyboards-player Corea and bassist Dave Holland. Though less uncompromising than his former group, Circle produced some of the best collective improvisation of the era, notably on the double-album *Paris Concert* (ECM, 1972).

Braxton's solo activity remained resolutely exploratory. *For Alto* (Delmark, 1968) and *Saxophone Improvisations Series F* (America) were double-albums of solo saxophone-playing, most of the tracks being dedicated to musician friends or to influences like chess master Bobby Fischer, avant-garde composer John Cage and visionary architect Buckminster Fuller.

In 1974 he returned to the US and signed with Arista, mostly as a quartet with Dave Holland, Barry Altschul and Kenny Wheeler of George Lewis. His quartet music was his most jazz-related but the releases (for example *For Trio*, 1978, and *For Two Pianos*, 1982) were ill received in jazz circles. In 1976 he recorded a *Duets* album for Arista with AACM founder Richard Abrams. Braxton also spent some time in Europe, recording with guitarist Derek Bailey on *Duo* for Emanem and *Royal Vol. 1* (Incus, 1984).

While genuinely radical in his approach, Braxton did not want to destroy the past but rather to reinterpret or to shift it into new configurations. This was most evident in such varied works as the 1979 composition for string quartet recorded for Sound Aspects, *Birth and Rebirth*, with drummer Max Roach (Black Saint, 1979), and his mellow *Seven Standards* (1985), recorded for the Magenta subsidiary of New Age music label Windham Hill.

Later he began playing 'multiple logics music' in which the members of the quartet (now mostly Marilyn Crispin, Mark Dresser and Gerry Hemmingway) played several compositions simultaneously. Examples of this are *Quartet* (Birmingham) (1985) and *Quartet* (Willisau) (1991). Throughout this period Braxton wrote prolifically about his music while teaching at Wesleyan College Connecticut. Braxton's work is the subject of *Forces in Motion* by British critic Graham Lock.

TONI BRAXTON
b. 7 October 1968, Severn, Maryland, USA

US vocalist Braxton achieved phenomenal international success with her mixture of pop balladry and R&B, best instanced by her biggest hit of the nineties, 'Unbreak My Heart' (1996), and her exemplary reading of 'You're Making Me High' (1996).

Braxton's musical ability became apparent to her parents when she sang in church with her sisters, who entered her into numerous local talent contests, from which she invariably emerged victorious. While studying at Bowie Sate University with the intention of becoming a teacher, she caught the eye of LaFace Records owner **Babyface**, who signed her as the label's first female artist in 1991. A duet with Babyface, 'Give U My Heart' (1992), from the Eddie Murphy movie *Boomerang*, provided Braxton with an instant hit single, which she followed up with 'Love Shoulda Brought You Home'.

Neither single came close to the success of her eponymous début album, which sold 10 million copies worldwide. Spawning three more hit singles for Braxton in 'Another Sad Love Song', 'Breathe Again' and 'You Mean the World to Me', which all made the US Top Ten, the album won her three Grammy Awards, including Best New Artist.

With her second album release Braxton worked alongside an array of big names from the R&B world, including **R Kelly**, Tony Rich and, once again, Babyface. Alongside the **Diane Warren** composition 'Unbreak My Heart', *Secrets* (1996)* provided the singer with further international hits in the shape of 'Come on Over Here' and 'In the Late of the Night'. A lengthy dispute with her record company meant that she made no records between 1997 and 1999. She returned to recording in 2000 with the superior *The Heat*, which was a Top Ten hit in the US and Europe. It featured Warren's 'Spanish Guitar' and the hit single, the sultry 'He Wasn't Man Enough'.

BREAD
David Gates, b. 11 December 1940, Tulsa, Oklahoma, USA; James Griffin, b. Memphis, Tennessee; Robb Royer, b. Bell, California (replaced by Larry Knetchel); Mike Botts, b. Sacramento, California

The epitome of pop (as opposed to rock) at its best, Bread melded Gates' high, clear tenor with lush harmonies and cleverly constructed love songs to produce a string of million-sellers in the group's shortlived career.

Multi-instrumentalist Gates first recorded with **Leon Russell** for **Lee Hazelwood**'s East West label in the late fifties. Moving to Los Angeles, he established himself as a studio musician and producer and

worked with **Duane Eddy**, **Pat Boone**, **Captain Beefheart** and **Merle Haggard**, among others. With songwriters and musicians Royer and Griffin, who (under
the pseudonyms Robb Wilson and Arthur James) co-
wrote the 1970 Oscar-winning song 'For All We
Know', he was briefly a member of Pleasure Faire
before forming Bread in 1969.

The wistful 'Make It with You'* (Elektra, 1970)
gave them the first of ten American Top Twenty
records. These included 'If' (1971), the group's most
recorded song (which gave actor Telly Savalas a surprise international hit when he released a spoken version in 1975), 'Baby I'm a Want You' (1971), 'The
Guitar Man' and 'Everything I Own' (both 1972), all
of which were written and produced by Gates. In 1971
Botts joined on drums and session musician Knetchel
(who had played on million-sellers such as the **Byrds'**
'Mr Tambourine Man', 1965; Mason Williams' 'Classical Gas', 1968; and **Simon and Garfunkel**'s 'Bridge
over Troubled Water', 1970) replaced Royer, until the
group broke up in 1973.

Both Griffin and Gates pursued solo careers, with
Gates the more successful, producing a trio of Top
Forty hits, 'Never Let Her Go' (1975), 'Goodbye Girl'
and 'Took the Last Train' (both 1978). The last two of
these followed a short-lived reunion of Bread which
brought the group another huge hit, 'Lost Without
Your Love' (1976). In 1981 Gates, who had been largely
inactive since 1978, joined Arista to record *Take Me
Now*. He subsequently left music for ranching but
returned with *Love Is Always Seventeen* in 1994. He
also recorded in a New Age vein (*Urban Gypsy*,
Mountain Moods). Knetchel moved into New Age
instrumental music and played on **Elvis Costello**'s
Mighty Like a Rose (1991). Griffin had played with
Randy Meisner (ex-Poco) and **Billy Swan** as Black Tie
before becoming a founder member of country vocal
group the Remingtons, which recorded for BNA in
1992 (*Blue Frontier*). The success of the career retrospective *Anthology* (1996) led to the group re-forming
for a series of one-off tours in Japan and the US.

THE BRECKER BROTHERS
*Randy Brecker, b. Randal E. Brecker, 27 November 1945,
Philadelphia, Pennsylvania, USA; Michael Brecker,
b. 29 March 1949, Philadelphia*

One of the most notable features of the rise of 'adult
oriented rock' (AOR) in the seventies and eighties was
the rise of a new breed of highly skilled session musicians, whose services were much in demand by producers and singers. Like Tom Scott on the West
Coast, Mike and Randy Brecker were top session
players who went on to cut a series of albums with
their own band.

Trumpeter Randy began playing in Philadelphia

bar bands while studying the modern jazz of the forties, and a unique funk-bebop fusion still characterizes the Breckers' playing. In 1973 he went to New
York to form the pioneering and influential jazz-rock
band Dreams, with drummer Billy Cobham.

Joined by tenor saxophonist Mike Brecker, Randy
was soon in demand for recording sessions for both
jazz and rock artists. The Breckers' studio credits were
a roll call of top artists of the seventies, with **Paul
Simon**, **Aretha Franklin**, **Stevie Wonder**, **Lou Reed**,
John Lennon, **Charles Mingus** and Gato Barbieri
among those on whose albums they played.

In 1975 they signed as recording artists in their own
right to Arista. With a band that included fellow session star **David Sanborn** on sax, they cut 'Sneakin' up
Behind You', a minor hit. Their second album, *Back
to Back* (1976), included Patti Austin and **Luther Vandross** on vocals.

By 1981 the Brecker Brothers had cut six albums
together, and Randy had made a further two as a solo
artist. In 1986 Randy Brecker and his wife, singer
Elaine Elias, released *Amanda* (Sonet). In the eighties
Mike worked with avant-garde jazzman Kenny
Wheeler and with Mike Mainieri's Steps Ahead, a
contemporary bebop band, as well as recording with a
wide variety of performers from Charles Mingus to
Eric Clapton. In 1987 he began recording as a group
leader. Records include *Mike Brecker* (1987) and *Now
You See It . . . Now You Don't* (1991). In 1991 he was
also a featured soloist on **Paul Simon**'s *Rhythm of the
Saints*. Michael and Randy reunited in 1992 to record
Return of the Brecker Brothers (GRP) and *Out of Our
Loop* (1994).

JACQUES BREL
*b. 8 April 1929, Schaerbeck, Belgium, d. 9 October 1978,
Bobigny, France*

One of the few *chansonniers* (singer-songwriters) to
make an impact outside the French-speaking world,
Brel's stark poetic songs were recorded by such varied
artists as **Frank Sinatra** ('If You Go Away'), **David
Bowie** ('Amsterdam'), **Judy Collins** ('Marieke'), Alex
Harvey ('Next'), **Tom Jones**, **Marc Almond**, **Ray
Charles** and **Petula Clark**, although the most effective
interpreter of Brel's gritty, fatalistic lyrics was Scott
Walker of the **Walker Brothers**. Among his English-
language translators were **Rod McKuen** and Mort
Shuman (of **Pomus and Shuman**), who wrote a
musical about him.

The son of a wealthy Belgian industrialist, Brel
worked in the family firm until moving to Paris in
1953, intent on becoming a professional songwriter
and performer. His intense, involving stage presence
made him a French showbusiness star in the late
fifties and the live album *Music for the Millions (A*

l'Olympia) (Philips, 1964) found Brel at the height of his powers, conjuring up the characters depicted in his rough, direct lyrics. The songs included the bitter 'Les Bourgeois', the hymn to his native Flanders 'Marieke', and his best-known song, 'Ne Me Quitte Pas'. Brel wrote more than 400 songs, recording half of them for Barclay and Philips. He also appeared in films directed by Marcel Carné, Claude Lelouch and himself.

While Alasdair Clayre wrote English lyrics for the anti-war 'La Colombe', Brel's principal translators were McKuen and Shuman. The former wrote free adaptations of 'Ne Me Quitte Pas' ('If You Go Away') and 'Le Moribond', which as 'Seasons in the Sun' was a million-seller for Terry Jacks (Bell, 1974).

Shuman's versions were more faithful to Brel's original lyrics and in 1967 the American writer created and appeared in the stage show *Jacques Brel Is Alive and Well and Living in Paris*. Later recorded by Shuman and Elly Stone for Avant-Guard, it included 'If We Only Have Love', the picaresque tale of harbourfront life 'Amsterdam', 'Old Folks' and 'Jackie', a British hit in 1968 for Walker, who also recorded an album of Brel songs.

The fiercely moving 'Vieillir' ('If I Grow Old') anticipated Brel's death from cancer and the onset of the disease forced Brel to cease touring in 1967. His failing health limited his recording to a single album of bleak songs after 1974, *Brel* (1977). The last few years of his life were spent as a recluse in Polynesia.

After Brel's death, his daughter set up the Fondation Jacques Brel in Brussels. The definitive biography was written by French journalist Olivier Todd.

TERESA BREWER
b. 7 May 1931, Toledo, Ohio, USA

With **Johnny Ray**, **Frankie Laine** and **Kay Starr**, Brewer was one of a number of harder edged, more emotive singers who emerged in the pre-rock'n'roll fifties, supplanting the smoother stylists of the forties.

A child star – she first appeared on radio aged two – Brewer was a showbusiness veteran by 1950, the year of the first of six million-sellers, the shrill novelty number 'Music, Music, Music' (London). In 1952 she joined Coral and in 1953 co-starred with **Guy Mitchell** in *Those Redheads from Seattle*. Her hits, mostly brash up-tempo numbers, included 'Till I Waltz Again with You'* (1952), 'Ricochet'* (1953), 'I Gotta Go Get My Baby'* and 'Let Me Go Lover'* (both 1955) – the latter also a million-seller for Joan Weber who recorded the original version on Columbia – and 'A Tear Fell'* (1956). With the onset of rock'n'roll, Coral briefly used her to cover black hits, just as Dot used **Pat Boone**. Thus Brewer recorded unlikely and inferior (but commercially successful) versions of **Johnny**

Ace's 'Pledging My Love' in 1955 and **Sam Cooke**'s 'You Send Me' in 1957, before drifting slowly to the Las Vegas mainstream by the end of the decade when her hits came to an end. In the sixties she signed with Philips and turned briefly to country music before once more retiring to Las Vegas.

She made a surprising return to active recording in the seventies as a jazz singer. (Unlike **Rosemary Clooney**, who made a similar career move, she had never been a big-band singer.) She recorded with **Duke Ellington** the superior *It Don't Mean a Thing if It Ain't Got that Swing* (Columbia, 1973), and with **Count Basie** made the impressive *The Songs of Bessie Smith* (Doctor Jazz, 1983). Her recording with **Stephane Grappelli**, *On the Road Again* (Doctor Jazz, 1984), unusually featured violinist Grappelli on piano on one track. Even more interesting was *In London* (1987) on her husband and producer Bob Thiele's Signature label. With accompaniment by **Chas and Dave**, a pair of whose songs she sings, the album included a reworking of 'Music, Music, Music'. Brewer and Thiele later began an *American Music Box* series of recordings by leading composers. The first releases featured songs by **Irving Berlin** and **Harry Warren**.

FANNY BRICE
b. Fanny Borach, 29 October 1891, New York, USA, d. 29 May 1951, Hollywood, California

Fanny Brice was one of the best-loved figures of vaudeville thanks to the versatility with which she stepped back and forth from wisecracking Jewish comedy to tear-stained ballads of the Bowery.

The daughter of a New York barkeeper, she won first prize in a talent contest at the age of thirteen, singing 'When You Know You're Not Forgotten by the Girl You Can't Forget', and embarked on a theatrical career. In 1907 she was dismissed from the chorus line of **George M. Cohan**'s production of *Talk of New York* because she couldn't dance, and turned to singing in New York's burlesque houses, where she was discovered by Florenz Ziegfeld. She appeared on Broadway in his *Follies* of 1910 and many subsequent years, introducing such future standards as 'Second-Hand Rose', 'My Man' (both 1921) and 'Cooking Breakfast for the One I Love' (1930). After Ziegfeld's death in 1932 she continued to appear in the *Follies* produced by the Shubert brothers, in the 1934 show adding the new characterization Baby Snooks, a know-it-all child. Later in the thirties she transferred this role successfully to radio. She also appeared in films, among them *My Man* (1928) and *Be Yourself* (1930).

Her eventful life was dramatized in the 1939 film *Rose of Washington Square*, and in the 1964 Broadway musical *Funny Girl* (music by **Jule Styne**), in which she was played by **Barbra Streisand** – a role that did much to establish the latter's career. A film version, directed by William Wyler (1968), also starred Streisand. Brice was married to, and divorced from, the theatre producer Billy Rose.

JOHNNY BRISTOL
b. Morganton, North Carolina, USA

An important soul-music writer, arranger and producer first for Motown (where he worked with **Gladys Knight**, **Junior Walker** and **Stevie Wonder**, among others) and later for Columbia, Bristol's 'Hang on in There Baby' was an international disco hit in 1974.

His first records were made in 1961 with Jackey Beavers (as Johnny and Jackey) for **Harvey Fuqua** and Gwen Gordy's Tri-Phi label. They included the Beavers–Bristol–Fuqua compositions 'Do You See My Love (for You Growing)' – later a 1970 hit for Walker – and 'Someday We'll Be Together', a No. 1 hit for the **Supremes** in 1969. Bristol's is the male voice to be heard on the Supremes' record.

When financial problems brought Tri-Phi into the Motown empire of Gwen's brother **Berry Gordy**, Bristol became Fuqua's assistant as a staff writer and producer. He worked first with fellow Tri-Phi artists the Detroit Spinners, later the **Spinners** and, usually with Fuqua, wrote for or produced virtually all the top Motown artists. **Marvin Gaye** and Tammi Terrell's 'Ain't No Mountain High Enough' (1967), Wonder's 'Yester-Me, Yester-You' (1969), the **Four Tops**' 'What Is a Man' (1969), Edwin Starr's '25 Miles' (1969), David Ruffin's 'My Whole World Ended' (1969) and Knight's 'Daddy Could Swear, I Declare' (1973) were among his credits. But the group whose career Bristol did most to mould was Junior Walker and the All Stars.

He had discovered Walker in 1961 and brought him into the Fuqua stable. At Motown, Bristol produced many of Walker's records, including 'How Sweet It Is', 'Pucker up Buttercup', 'What Does It Take (to Win Your Love)' and 'Take Me Girl, I'm Ready' – another product of his writing partnership with Fuqua.

When Motown moved from Detroit to Los Angeles in 1973, Bristol followed Fuqua out of the company to become a producer for Columbia, where he worked with acts as diverse as O. C. Smith and **Boz Scaggs**. When Columbia rejected his proposal for a self-produced solo album, he took the project to MGM. His first release gave him a Top Ten hit with the heavily orchestrated 'Hang on in There Baby' (1974), a disco record in a similar style to Marvin Gaye's 'Let's Get It on'. The same year, his composition 'Love Me for a Reason' was a Top Ten hit for the **Osmonds**.

Later albums for Atlantic (*Bristol's Creme*, 1976) and Hansa (*Free to Be Me*, 1981) were unsuccessful.

As a producer, Bristol was responsible for Tavares' first album, but he also worked with middle-of-the road singers like **Tom Jones** and **Johnny Mathis**. After recording a 1981 album for Ariola, he remained relatively inactive. He produced a version of 'I'm Ready for Love' by the **Temptations** (1985), made 'Man in the Sky' (1989) for Ian Levine's British-based Motor City Records and released 'Come to Me' (Whichway, 1991).

ELTON BRITT
b. James Britt Baker, 7 July 1917, Marshall, Arkansas, USA, d. 23 June 1972, Connellsville, Pennsylvania

Although his name is most famously linked with his million-selling recording of the Second World War song 'There's a Star-Spangled Banner Waving Somewhere' (1942), Elton Britt had been a well-known country artist since 1932, when he signed with a country band on station KMPC, Los Angeles, which shortly afterwards became the original Beverly Hill Billies.

Moving to New York in 1933 he established himself as a radio and recording artist and songwriter specializing in Western and yodel numbers. Joining RCA Victor in 1939 he immediately scored with 'Chime Bells', thereafter a country yodelling standard, and worked closely with the songwriter and publisher **Bob Miller**. He had further hits in the forties and fifties, some with the singer Rosalie Allen. His twenty-two-year association with RCA Victor produced over 600 singles and fifty-six albums. He later recorded for ABC. Signing with Columbia Pictures in 1948, he appeared in *Laramie* (1949) and other films. He also made many network radio and TV appearances on the *Grand Ole Opry*, the WWVA (Wheeling, West Virginia) *Jamboree* and the **George Hamilton IV** TV show. Bestselling albums include *Yodel Songs* (RCA Victor, 1957), *Wandering Cowboy* (ABC, 1962) and *Beyond the Sunset* (ABC, 1963).

DAVID BROMBERG
b. 19 September 1945, Philadelphia, Pennsylvania, USA

A producer as well as performer on guitar, banjo, mandolin and fiddle, Bromberg played on albums by artists as diverse as **Bob Dylan** and **Chubby Checker**. He also led a series of bands characterized by their mix of American musics (blues, country, bluegrass, rock) and their leader's quirky sense of humour.

Raised in New York, Bromberg was a product of the folk revival. He was inspired to take up guitar by the **Weavers**, while later influences included **Big Bill Broonzy** and **Doc Watson**. After a year studying

musicology at Columbia University, he dropped out
to become guitar accompanist to a number of artists,
including gospel singer Brother John Sellers, Checker
and **Jay and the Americans**. He worked for two years
with **Jerry Jeff Walker**, playing guitar on the original
recording of 'Mr Bojangles'.

In 1970 he played on sessions for two Dylan albums,
Self Portrait and *New Morning*. Bromberg was also a
surprise hit at the 1970 Isle of Wight Festival. Appearing with folk singer Rosalie Sorrels, he stole the show
with his comic *tour de force*, 'Bullfrog Blues'.

A recording contract and four albums with Columbia followed, each of which included both original
and traditional or standard material from both blues
and white rural sources. the **Grateful Dead**'s Jerry
Garcia and Phil Lesh played on *Demon in Disguise*
(1972) and *Wanted Dead or Alive* (1974), but the best
was *Midnight on the Water* (1975), which featured
fiddle-player Jay Ungar and guest appearances from
the young **Ricky Skaggs**, **Dr John**, **Linda Ronstadt**
and the **Eagles**' Bernie Leadon.

In 1976 Bromberg moved to Fantasy, cutting the
double-album *How Late'll Ya Play 'Til?*, which
included live recordings of his eight-piece band. The
next year he cut a double-album of Western swing
with country fiddler Vassar Clements (*Hillbilly Jazz*,
Vols 1 and 2, Flying Fish).

The last Fantasy album, *You Should See the Rest of
the Band* (1980), included **The Band**'s Garth Hudson
on keyboards. After that Bromberg's live appearances
declined in number and he concentrated on making
violins. In 1990 he resumed his recording career with
Sideman Serenade (Rounder).

HERMAN BROOD
b. 5 November 1946, Zwolle, Netherlands

Herman Brood was a leading European singer and
writer of the punk era.

As an art student in Arnhem, Brood's earliest musical influences were **Fats Domino** and **Little Richard**.
He left college to work as pianist and singer in Moan,
a band touring American bases in Germany. In 1967
he joined Dutch group Cuby and the Blizzards,
recording two albums with them, *Groeten uit Grollo*
and *Live at Dusseldorf* (Philips, 1967).

. Sacked from the group because of a drug habit,
Brood travelled around Europe, returning to Holland
in 1974, where he recorded a solo album, *Showbiz
Blues*, before joining several groups. He finally
recorded *Streets* and formed his own band, Herman
Brood's Wild Romance, in 1976. The group included
Freddie Cavalli (bass), Peter Waaldrecht (drums) and
Danny Lademacher (guitar). The album *Schpritz* pro-
duced three Dutch hits: 'Saturday Night', 'Still
Believes' and 'Never Be Clever'.

Cha Cha (1978) inspired a film in which Brood
starred with British new-wave singer Lene Lovich
(whose 1979 hits included 'Lucky Number' and 'Say
When') and German punk figure Nina Hagen. She
and Brood were among many European artists
inspired by British punk rock. Others included Belgium's Plastic Bertrand ('Ça Plane Pour Moi', Sire,
1978) and Stinky Toys.

Herman Brood and his Wild Romance was released
in America in 1979. The album contained drugs songs
like 'R&R Junkie' and 'Dope Sucks' and was dedicated
to Lenny Bruce, **Frankie Lymon** and **Free**'s Paul Kossoff. *Wait a Minute* (Aves Int, 1980) included two
songs written with **Kim Fowley**. It was badly received
in the UK and led Brood to concentrate on continental Europe where his increasingly lightweight offerings (which include *The Brood*, 1984, and *Live*, 1985)
found a small but loyal audience. Produced by George
Kooymans of **Golden Earring**, *Yada Yada* (CBS, 1988)
reunited Brood with his former guitarist Danny
Lademacher.

After releasing *Freeze* in 1990, he concentrated on
his work as a painter and illustrator. He returned to
music in 1994 with *Fresh Poison* (Sony), on which he
was joined by members of his eighties band. In the
same year Brood starred in the film *Rock'n'Roll
Junkie*. Hagen had an erratic recording career, including the Zeus B. Held-produced *Nina Hagen* (Phonogram, 1989). She also published an autobiography, *I
Am a Berliner*.

ELKIE BROOKS
*b. Elaine Bookbinder, 25 February 1945, Manchester,
England*

One of the most consistently successful British
women singers of the seventies and eighties, Brooks
forged a style that combined rock and middle-of-the-
road elements.

After an apprenticeship that included work with
Humphrey Lyttleton's jazz band, Brooks joined
Dada, a jazz-rock band led by Pete Gage. With Gage,
she went on to form Vinegar Joe, which also featured
Robert Palmer, and cut three albums for Island in
1972–3. Her dynamic stage performance was compared to **Tina Turner**, but the band failed to reach a
large audience and split in 1974.

With Gage as musical director, Brooks signed a
solo contract with A&M. The first album, *Rich Man's
Woman*, stuck to the hard-rock format, but, with
Leiber and Stoller producing, *Two Days Away* (1977)
included two British hit singles: **Ellie Greenwich**'s
'Sunshine After the Rain' and 'Pearl's a Singer', with
its implied reference to the late **Janis Joplin**, which
enabled Brooks to marry her jazz and blues heritage
to a rock format.

Shifting ground towards a more mainstream pop formula, Brooks scored further hits with 'Don't Cry Out Loud' and a sensitive version of **Nina Simone**'s 'Lilac Wine' in 1978. In 1982 an emotive reading of **Chris Rea**'s 'Fool if You Think It's Over' from *Pearls*, which was heavily marketed through television, was also successful. Brooks' status as a major adult contemporary star in Britain was confirmed by her reworkings of the **Moody Blues**' 'Nights in White Satin' and **Rod Stewart**'s 'Gasoline Alley' (1983).

In 1984 she moved to EMI and released *Screen Gems*, a confidently rendered selection of standard ballads. In 1986 she had her first British Top Ten hit for a decade with the impassioned 'No More the Fool' (Legend), written by Russ Ballard. *Bookbinder's Kid* (Legacy, 1988), which included material by **Bryan Adams**, and *Inspiration* (Telstar, 1989) were less successful, and future recordings attempted to rework the *Pearls* formula to little effect. On 1993's *Round Midnight* she changed direction to sing a selection of jazz classics, but most of her nineties recordings were re-recordings of songs associated with her.

GARTH BROOKS

b. Troyal Garth Brooks, 7 February 1962, Yukon, Oklahoma, USA

The most successful of the 'Men in Hats' as the slew of new country music stars of the nineties were dubbed, Brooks' stage act and songwriting style incorporate elements of eighties stadium rock. A further mark of the breadth of his influences was his participation in the **Kiss** tribute album, *Kiss My Ass* (1994). After selling over 60 million albums in a decade and touring virtually non-stop at the end of the nineties, he signalled a dramatic career move with *In . . . the Life of Chris Gaines* (Capitol), in which he impersonated a rock singer, Gaines, whose career the album was presented as being a retrospective of.

The son of Colleen Carroll, a minor country singer of the fifties, Brooks performed while studying marketing at university in Oklahoma. His first visit to Nashville to seek a recording contract ended unsuccessfully but he formed his own band featuring his sister Betty Smittle on bass. After performing at Nashville's Bluebird Cafe in 1988 he was signed up by Capitol.

The début album, produced by Nashville veteran Allen Reynolds (**Don Williams, Crystal Gayle**), included a revival of a **Jim Reeves** hit ('I Know One') and some of his own songs, notably the plaintive 'If Tomorrow Never Comes' which topped the country music charts at the end of 1989. *No Fences* (1990) featured what was to become one of Brooks' best-known songs, 'Friends in Low Places', 'Unanswered Prayers' and a version of the **Fleetwoods**' 1961 hit 'Mr Blue'.

By this time, Brooks had established his dynamic stage act involving the use of a radio microphone and much running around the stage between songs. His touring band included Smittle as well as James Garver (lead guitar) and Steve McClure (steel guitar).

Ropin' the Wind (1991) sold over six million copies and produced further country No. 1 hits in 'The Thunder Rolls' and Brooks' version of **Billy Joel**'s 'Shameless'. The following year he recorded an album of Christmas songs, *Beyond the Season*.

The Chase had advance orders of five million copies in North America and included the hit 'We Shall Be Free', co-written with Stephanie Davis, as well as **Little Feat**'s 'Dixie Chicken'.

Brooks has tackled controversial subjects in his songs, most of which are co-written with established Nashville-based composers such as Pat Alger, who collaborated on 'The Thunder Rolls'. The song's video, in which Brooks portrayed a wife abuser, was banned by country music television networks in the US. Brooks' video for 'We Shall Be Free' was also withdrawn by television networks because of its alleged pro-gay sentiments.

In Pieces (1993) included the up-tempo hit 'Ain't Going Down (Til the Sun Comes Up)' and duets with Tricia Yearwood. Although Garth Brooks spent most of the year taking a break from public appearances, he continued having hits throughout 1993, including 'That Summer', 'Learning to Live Again' and 'Somewhere Other Than the Night'.

In 1994 Brooks toured Europe and Australia and issued the bestselling compilation album, *The Hits*. Brooks co-wrote all ten tracks of *Fresh Horses* (1995), his first studio album for two years. His least interesting album, it was nonetheless an enormous commercial success. Far more persuasive was *Sevens* (1997), which included 'Longneck Bottle', 'Belleau Woods' and 'Two Pina Coladas'. While *In . . . the Life of Chris Gaines*, which was received with a mixture of puzzlement and admiration, and a reduced work rate showed Brooks pondering his career direction, *Double – Live* (1998) and the easy-going *The Magic of Christmas* (1999) were big hits.

BIG BILL BROONZY

b. William Lee Conley Broonzy, 26 June 1893, Scott, Mississippi, USA, d. 15 August 1958, Chicago, Illinois

Like many blues artists who had careers as 'race' personalities, retired, and were then rediscovered by European *aficionados*, Big Bill Broonzy enjoyed a second musical life. Unlike the majority, however, he was valued by his new audience not for his previous accomplishments but largely in ignorance of, and to some extent despite, them.

Based in Chicago from 1920, Broonzy began to

record in the late twenties as a solo singer-guitarist or guitar accompanist, but almost from the start his country-styled work went hand-in-hand with membership of novelty groups like the Famous Hokum Boys. From the mid-thirties he was associated, as musician, songwriter and talent-scout, with most of the major urban-blues figures, among them **Memphis Minnie**, **Sonny Boy Williamson I**, Jazz Gillum and Washboard Sam. His own work, split between conventional small groups and slightly jazzier horn-and-rhythm bands, produced such hits as 'Trucking Little Woman' (1938), 'Just a Dream' (1939), 'Looking Up at Down' (1940), 'When I Been Drinking' and 'All by Myself' (1941). In 1939 he appeared instead of the murdered **Robert Johnson** as a 'primitive blues singer' in **John Hammond**'s 'Spirituals to Swing' concert in New York, a foretaste of the second career he would pursue in the fifties.

After the Second World War, he continued to be a fixture on the Chicago club scene, to which he helped introduce newcomers like **Muddy Waters**, and he made occasional New York concert appearances, but by 1950 he had retired from music to work as a janitor at Iowa State University. He re-emerged at the instigation of Chicago radio personality Studs Terkel, participating in the latter's concert series 'I Come for to Sing', and in 1951 made the first of several European tours.

The Big Bill introduced to European audiences was a 'folk-blues' artist, expected to perform solo, with acoustic guitar, in what was taken to be the style of the first-generation blues singers. Although his (now infrequent) American recordings – for Mercury (1951) and Chess (1955) primarily – followed the repertoire and small-band mode of his pre-war work, his sessions in Britain, France, Denmark and Italy were designed to elicit a mélange of traditional blues, gospel songs, narrations and, if possible, protest pieces like 'Black, Brown and White' and 'When Do I Get to Be Called a Man'. He recorded in a similar vein on his return to the US for Folkways (1956–7) and Verve (*Last Session*, 1957), and appeared at concerts with **Pete Seeger** and **Brownie McGhee and Sonny Terry**. His last European tour was in 1957 with gospel singer Brother John Sellers.

Though the European Big Bill seemed at times an anomaly, he performed with undiminished skill, and did much to accustom cultural strangers to the world of the blues. Club performances have been preserved in the documentary films *Low Light and Blue Smoke* (France, 1956) and *Big Bill Blues* (Belgium, 1956), and on albums for Storyville and Spotlite.

THE BROTHERS JOHNSON

George Johnson, b. 17 May 1953, Los Angeles, California, USA; Louis Johnson, b. 13 April 1955, Los Angeles

Produced by **Quincy Jones**, George and Louis Johnson scored two American million-sellers in 1976–7 with their pop-flavoured funk.

After leaving high school, they joined **Billy Preston**'s band, the God Squad, George on lead guitar and Louis on bass. They wrote Preston's 1974 hit 'Struttin'' before leaving to concentrate on their own career. Quincy Jones recorded four of their compositions on his 1975 album *Mellow Madness* and signed them to a contract with A&M.

All four albums produced by Jones sold over a million copies in America. Their hit singles included 'I'll Be Good to You' (1976), Shuggie Otis's 'Strawberry Letter 23' (1977) and 'Stomp' (1980). From 1981 the brothers took over production themselves and while they continued to have hits in the black music charts ('Welcome to the Club', 1982, 'Kick it to the Curb', 1988), their records no longer 'crossed over' to the Top Forty.

The brothers contributed 'Tomorrow' to Jones' 1989 album *Back on the Block*, which also included a new version of 'I'll Be Good to You'.

ARTHUR BROWN

b. Arthur Wilton, 24 June 1942, Whitby, Yorkshire, England

Brown was responsible for one of the most charming examples of psychedelia, the frenzied 'Fire'*, on which his demented vocals and Vincent Crane's swirling organ meshed perfectly.

A veteran of amateur blues groups, one-time university student Brown joined forces with Crane (*b. 1945, d. February 1989*) in 1967 and in the London clubs associated with the burgeoning underground movement the pair performed as the suitably titled Crazy World of Arthur Brown. Derived in equal parts from **Screamin' Jay Hawkins** (whose 'I Put a Spell on You' was a permanent feature of their act and was later recorded by them) and a parody of the silliest motifs of beads and bells psychedelia, the pair's antics won them a contract with Track Records. The label's owners, **The Who**'s managers Kit Lambert and Chris Stamp, encouraged them to further excesses until their show climaxed with Brown gyrating around the stage, his Sun robes flowing and his hair (actually a helmet) alight. For the group's hit single and only album, *The Crazy World of Arthur Brown* (1968), Carl Palmer, later of **Emerson, Lake and Palmer**, joined Brown and Crane.

However, the group's outrageousness soon became *passé*, and following the departure of Crane (to form Atomic Rooster and in the eighties to play with **Dexy's Midnight Runners**) and Palmer (to ELP), Brown disappeared from view. He resurfaced as the leader of Kingdom Come, another theatrical band, in

1971, and cut a solo record, *Dance with Arthur Brown* (Gull), in 1975. The same year he had a small part in the film *Tommy*. But by then such figures as **Alice Cooper** had far outreached Brown and brought rock theatre to the concert halls and stadiums of America.

After *Strangelands* (1988) Brown retired to become a carpenter and decorator in Austin, Texas. His partner was the former drummer with the Mothers of Invention, Jimmy Carl Black. He returned to live performance with a European tour in 1993 and in 1994 recorded an album with former **Cream** songwriter Pete Brown.

BOBBY BROWN
b. 5 February 1969, Roxbury, Massachusetts, USA

One of the most successful of a new breed of male soul stars, Bobby Brown's work artfully combined highly sophisticated production values with a street level image. In the nineties, after marrying **Whitney Houston**, his career was disrupted by legal and drug problems.

His earliest successes were as lead singer of teenage vocal group New Edition. Brown formed the group in 1983 with Ralph Tresvant and the future members of Bell Biv Devoe. Under the guidance of manager/writer/producer Maurice Starr, New Edition had a string of big hits, including the British No. 1 'Candy Girl' (1983), 'Cool It Now' (1984) and 'Mr Telephone Man'.

Brown left the group in 1986 to record the solo album *King of Stage* (1987). Its lack of commercial success led to LA and **Babyface** being brought in to write and produce *Don't Be Cruel* (1988), which featured Brown in a variety of styles including rap, soul ballads, funk and the 'New Jack' dance form associated with him. The album provided big hits in 'My Prerogative' and 'Every Little Step'. 'On Our Own' was taken from the soundtrack to *Ghostbusters II*, in which Brown took a small part.

In 1989 Brown's suggestive stage movements led to his arrest after a concert in Columbus, Georgia, on a charge of giving a sexually explicit performance. He was fined $562.

A four-year gap between studio albums was partly filled by the release of *Dance . . . Ya Know It!* (1990), a collection of remixes by Rita Liebrand and others, and 'She Ain't Worth It', a duet with Glenn Medeiros.

The first of the new Bobby Brown tracks to be issued was 'Humpin' Around', which became a US No. 1 in 1992, the year he married Houston. The long-awaited fourth album, *Bobby*, was issued in 1993 when 'Good Enough' and 'Get Away' became hits. In the same year he put out the remix album *Remixes in the Key of B*. There then followed a number of arrests for physical violence and drug usage. *Forever* (1997) was a minor hit.

CHARLES BROWN
b. 1920, Texas City, Texas, USA, d. 21 January 1999

'I'm driftin' and driftin', like a ship out on the sea . . .'. With 'Drifting Blues', one of the major R&B hits of the last days of the Second World War, Charles Brown introduced to the blues a new attitude, the melancholia not of deprivation but of frustration. It stood out against the bug-eyed jollity of the jump bands, and indicated a new stylistic path to many artists who until then had been committed to other modes, or to no mode in particular: notably the young **Ray Charles**, but also such singing and piano-playing acolytes as Floyd Dixon, Little Willie Littlefield and **Amos Milburn**.

The origins of Brown's crooning style (he calls himself not a blues singer but a 'blue ballad singer') were in voices of the thirties like the **Ink Spots** and Pha Terrell, singer with the Andy Kirk band, but more directly in the example of **Nat 'King' Cole**. Brown's public perceived him as bringing to the blues a sense of musical and social self-improvement that was more appealing than the working-class ruggedness of **Muddy Waters** or **Howlin' Wolf**.

College-educated in general musical practice, Brown had no stylistic direction in mind when, in 1944, he won a Los Angeles amateur show by playing **Earl Hines**' 'Boogie Woogie on St Louis Blues' and 'The Warsaw Concerto'. Shortly afterwards he joined Johnny Moore's Three Blazers as singer/pianist (with Moore on guitar and Eddie Williams bass) and played the Los Angeles club circuit. 'Drifting Blues' (Exclusive, 1945) made the band's name and in the following year they were voted Best R&B Trio by both *Cashbox* and *Billboard*.

Brown left the Blazers in 1949 to make his own name and was soon a major club and concert attraction, particularly after his R&B chart hit 'Black Night' (Aladdin, 1951). He had numerous lesser hits throughout the fifties, and on joining King in 1960 had a prompt seasonal success with 'Merry Christmas Baby', subsequently recorded by **Elvis Presley** and others. Commissioned to repeat this formula in 1961, he came up with 'Please Come Home for Christmas'*, which was revived in 1978 by the **Eagles**.

Brown lost some status during the sixties and seventies, in part because he was hardly valued at all by the new audience for blues and R&B; early magazines and reference books virtually ignored his work and its influence, though the latter had been affirmed by artists as diverse as the Chicago bluesmen Eddie Boyd and Baby Face Leroy Foster, and **B. B. King**. Occasional albums, including one for ABC-Bluesway

(1970), and US concert appearances sustained him until he found new popularity and respect in Europe in the late seventies.

During the eighties numerous albums of old and new material were issued by such European labels as R&B, Demon and Route 66. Then, in 1989, Brown issued a new album, the sprightly *One More for the Road* (Alligator), on which he was joined by Billy Butler, the guitarist on **Bill Doggett**'s 'Honky Tonk'. This was followed by *All My Life* (Bullseyes Blues, 1990), which featured **Dr. John**, *These Blues* (1994) and *Just a Lucky So and So* (1994). A mark of the affection and respect Brown was held in was that **Elvis Costello** wrote 'I Wonder How She Knows' for him and **Bonnie Raitt** (who often used him to open her shows), **John Lee Hooker** and **Ruth Brown** all appeared on record with him.

CLARENCE 'GATEMOUTH' BROWN
b. 18 April 1924, Orange, Texas, USA

Brown is a one-man definition of the omnivorousness of Texas music. Although much of his professional life and most of his recordings were in the blues field, he was raised by a father who played country fiddle and he maintained his affiliations with country, Western swing and cajun music, as well as Southwestern jazz. The fruits of these interests did not appear in token cameos but integrated into a rich, polymorphous music that narrowed the spaces between black and white vernacular idioms.

As a youth he learned fiddle, guitar, harmonica and drums, and it was as a drummer in South Texas bands that he began his professional career. Inspired by **T-Bone Walker**, he developed a blues guitar style similar to his model's but more clipped and aggressive. In the late forties, based in Houston, Texas, he worked in clubs and began a long association with Don Robey's Peacock label, often recording with saxophonist Jack McVea (*b. 5 November 1914, Los Angeles, California*) and his band; he had only one substantial hit in this period, 'Okie Dokie Stomp' (1955).

During the sixties he worked more in country music. In 1971 he toured in Europe, returning in 1973 to make an impressive appearance at the Montreux Jazz Festival, which led to several European record dates. His seventies albums are mixtures of blues, country, cajun and jazz, such as he had not had the opportunity to record before; they include *Blackjack* (Music Is Medicine, 1976) and *Makin' Music* (MCA, 1979), the latter a collaboration with the country guitarist **Roy Clark**. Subsequent albums for Rounder continued this policy with great success (notably *Texas Swing*, 1988) but also reaffirmed his command of a jump-blues band (*Alright Again!*, 1982, a Grammy award-winner, and *Standing My Ground*, Alligator,

1989) and the guitar skills which years before had so impressed other Southwestern players like Goree Carter, Lonnie Brooks and **Albert Collins**. *A Long Way Home*, despite the participation of **Eric Clapton** and **Maria Muldaur**, is a decidedly lesser affair.

CLIFFORD BROWN
b. 30 November 1930, Wilmington, Delaware, USA, d. 26 June 1956, Pennsylvania

The greatest of the younger hard bop-jazz trumpeters and famous for the light, airy quality of his playing, Brown's career was cut tragically short by his death in a car crash. He left behind a legend comparable to that of another trumpeter who died young, **Bix Beiderbecke**.

Given his first trumpet in 1945, Brown studied with Robert Lowery and played with **Miles Davis** and Fats Navarro in 1948. Hospitalized in 1950 following a road accident, his first records were made in 1952 with a rhythm and blues band, Chris Powell's Blue Flames. In 1953 he made some studio recordings with trombonist J. J. Johnson and pianist and arranger Tadd Dameron before touring Europe with **Lionel Hampton**'s orchestra. Despite Hamp's ban on individual recordings by his sidemen, Brownie (as he was nicknamed) left a Stockholm hotel by the fire escape to team up with trumpeter Art Farmer. Brown's solo on **Quincy Jones**' 'Stockholm Sweetnin'' is now regarded as a classic. Recordings made in Paris on the same tour were issued by Vogue.

Back in New York, Brown recorded with **Sarah Vaughan** and briefly joined the group led by pianist Horace Silver and **Art Blakey**, prior to the formation of the Jazz Messengers. The live recording *A Night at Birdland* (Blue Note, 1954) shows Brown fully at home in a hard bop setting, pitted against the power of Blakey's drumming.

Brown next travelled to Los Angeles to join another bebop drummer, **Max Roach**, in a quintet which reached its peak with the addition of **Sonny Rollins** in 1955. The purity and fluency of Brown's treatment of melody on his own 'Joyspring' and the standard 'Love Is a Many Splendored Thing' is shown to good effect on *Remember Clifford* (Mercury, 1954). The Rollins tune 'Pent-up House' on *Three Giants* (Prestige, 1956) demonstrates the perfect understanding between trumpeter and saxophonist. Four days after that recording Brown was dead.

His influence lived on in the work of a younger generation of trumpeters, notably Freddie Hubbard, Lee Morgan and Charles Tolliver.

DENNIS BROWN
b. February 1956, Kingston, Jamaica

One of the most consistently popular reggae singers

in Jamaica, Brown's attempts to emulate **Bob Marley** in reaching an international audience have been relatively unsuccessful.

Influenced by black American singers like **Nat 'King' Cole**, **Lou Rawls** and the **Temptations**, he cut his first hit, 'No Man Is an Island' for **Coxsone Dodd**'s Studio One label at the age of thirteen. His second Jamaican hit for Studio One was the plaintive 'If I Follow My Heart'. He performed with **Byron Lee**'s Dragonaires and had further hits with 'Baby Don't Do It' (1971) and 'Money in my Pocket' (1972), among others. His high tenor voice was well suited to these love ballads.

Brown is also a Rastafarian and his committed songs appeared on the 1977 Joe Gibbs productions *Wolf and Leopard* and *Visions of Dennis Brown*, which featured **Sly and Robbie** as well as veteran **Skatalites** saxophonist Tommy McCook. He also recorded for **Gregory Isaacs**' African Museum label. In 1975 he turned his hand to production and later set up the DEB label, which released work by British female lover's-rock singers 15, 16, 17.

From 1979 Brown's strategy was to divide his work between this roots music and an attempt to find a reggae crossover sound. In that year his re-recording of 'Money in My Pocket' (Lightning) was a British Top Twenty hit, while an appearance at the Montreux Jazz Festival was recorded and released on Laser. In 1980 he joined A&M and released *Foul Play* (1981) and *Love Has Found a Way* (1982). Despite touring America, he found no audience there, though the title track of his 1982 album was a minor hit in Britain.

In 1983 Brown moved to a funk-reggae mix, recording with members of **KC and the Sunshine Band** and having hits in Jamaica with 'Satisfaction Feeling' and 'Yvonne's Special Revolution'. He retained his popularity in Jamaica in the era of digital remixing in the mid-eighties with hits like 'Promised Land' and 'Love's Got a Hold on Me' (1986). Later album releases included *Wolves and Leopards* (Blue Moon, 1987) and *Judge Not* (Greensleeves, 1988), which included the hit single 'Big All Round' with Gregory Isaacs. It was followed by *Unchallenged* (1990).

JAMES BROWN
b. 3 May 1933, Barnwell, South Carolina, USA

Variously named 'The Godfather of Soul', 'Soul Brother No. 1' and 'the hardest-working man in showbusiness', Brown's gift for self-publicity cannot disguise his key role in the development of black American music since the sixties. His hoarse, gravelly singing, itself derived from such gospel models as the Sensational Nightingales' Rev. Julius Cheeks, paved the way for soul shouters like **Wilson Pickett** and **Otis Redding**. Equally, the taut, highly orchestrated

sound of Brown's records, in which repeated vocal phrases and slogans and complex churning rhythms predominated, formed the basis of the funk instrumental style of such musicians as **Sly Stone** and **George Clinton**. The strong social content which ran through his work from 'Say It Loud – I'm Black and I'm Proud' in 1968 through 'King Heroin' (1972) to 'Living in America' (1986) reflected a major strand of black American experience, 'from underprivileged isolation at the bottom of the heap to equivocal fraternisation with the White House', in the words of British critic Cliff White. In addition, Brown's determination to control his own career in both artistic and business terms provided a role model for later superstars like **Michael Jackson** and **Prince**. His continuing relevance to musical trends was underlined in the late eighties when James Brown had renewed chart success and his records were the most 'sampled' by a new generation of dance-record producers.

Raised by an aunt, Brown was convicted of a petty theft in 1949 and spent four years in prison. On his release he joined the Atlanta-based group the Gospel Starlighters, which also included Bobby Byrd, Johnny Terry, Sylvester Keels and guitarist Nafloyd Scott. By 1955 the group, now the Famous Flames, had moved into secular music and were signed by **Ralph Bass** to the Federal subsidiary of **Syd Nathan**'s King Records. The startling and impassioned 'Please Please Please'*, credited to James Brown and the Famous Flames, reached the R&B Top Ten, though follow-ups like 'Messing with the Blues' and the **Little Richard**-influenced 'Choonie on Chon' were unsuccessful.

Brown's next hit was the gospel-tinged ballad 'Try Me'* (1958). An R&B No. 1 and a minor pop hit, it started a string of R&B successes which stretched into the eighties. The first phase (1959–61) found Brown crystallizing his classic sound, combining frenzied lead vocals with split-second stop-start backing riffs on 'I'll Go Crazy' (1960), beginning to sloganize on 'Think', offering tear-jerking sobs on a revival of **Clyde McPhatter**'s Dominoes death song 'The Bells', and adding shouted lyrics to Jimmy Forrest's instrumental 'Night Train' (1962). One of Brown's most admired and copied records, 'Night Train' inspired a slew of ska instrumentals by such Jamaican artists as the **Skatalites** and the Melodians, while in Britain it was taken up by **Georgie Fame** and other soul-influenced members of the R&B movement.

Other singles from the early sixties included 'I Don't Mind' (1961), covered by **The Who** on their début album, the dance number 'Shout and Shimmy' (1962) and 'Prisoner of Love' (1963). Originally a 1946 hit for artists as varied as **Billy Eckstine**, **Perry Como** and the **Ink Spots**, the latter gave Brown his first pop Top Twenty hit. Initially, Nathan refused to record Brown with the singer's own musicians but after the backing group had made the R&B hit 'Mashed Potatoes' (1960) as Nat Hendrick and the Swans, Nathan relented and the Famous Flames played on later Brown sessions.

Brown's biggest-selling record of these years was *Live at the Apollo* (1962). It sold a million, an unprecedented feat for a live album by an R&B artist, and documented what had become the most dramatic and highly choreographed stage act in black music. With the supremely trained backing group led by Alfred (Pee Wee) Ellis, Brown would leap, dance, slither across the stage on his knees, and 'collapse', only to be revived wrapped in a regal cape.

Dissatisfaction with King's efforts on his behalf – Nathan had only agreed to issue the Apollo album after Brown paid for the recording himself – led Brown to release 'Out of Sight' (1964) on the Mercury subsidiary Smash. This led to a legal battle with Nathan which concluded with Brown returning to King with complete control of his career. There followed a series of innovative Top Ten pop hits which included 'Poppa's Got a Brand New Bag' (1965), 'I Got You (I Feel Good)', 'It's a Man's Man's Man's World' (1966) and 'Cold Sweat' (1967), which found Ellis and the Famous Flames honing their funk sound to perfection, introducing a Latin influence into the brief, chopping repetitive phrases.

The late sixties was the period of the black-power movement and Brown preceded **Marvin Gaye** and the **Temptations** in drawing on its slogans for 'Say It Loud – I'm Black and I'm Proud' (1968), as well as intervening to prevent ghetto riots after the death of Martin Luther King. His churning funk sound and folksy, nonsense or directly sexual lyrics brought further pop hits like 'Give It Up or Turnit a Loose' [*sic*] (1969), 'Mother Popcorn (You Got to Have a Mother for Me)' and 'Get Up I Feel Like Being a Sex Machine' (1970), the record most closely associated with the creation of 'funk'.

In 1971 Brown parted company with Ellis and the Famous Flames, several of whom, led by bassist William Bootsy Collins, joined George Clinton's Parliament/Funkadelic operation. Fred Wesley became the leader of his new backing group, the JBs, which featured Jimmy Nolan (guitar) and Maceo Parker on trumpet and saxophone. He also left King, which had been bought in 1970 by **Leiber and Stoller**, setting up his own production company first to release the 1971 hit 'Hot Pants (She Got to Use What She Got, to Get What She Wants)' on People and then sign a distribution agreement with Polydor.

His R&B hits continued throughout the seventies with such tracks as the No. 1s 'Talking Loud and Saying Nothing' (1972), 'Get on the Good Foot'*, 'The Playback'* (1974), 'My Thang' (1974) and 'Papa Don't Take No Mess – Part 1'. During the seventies Brown

also moved into films, acting in *Come to the Table* (1974) and providing music for *Black Caesar* and *Slaughter's Big Rip Off* in 1973.

By the start of the eighties Brown had been displaced by younger funk, hip-hop and rap artists – to whom he riposted with 'Rap Payback' (TK, 1981). He recorded *Soul Syndrome* (1980) for RCA, returned to Polydor for *Nonstop* (1981), and duetted with **Afrika Bambaataa** on 'Unity' (Tommy Boy, 1983), but the biggest success of the decade was the Dan Hartman-produced and oddly patriotic 'Living in America' (Scotti Brothers, 1986), the theme to *Rocky IV* and an international hit. The song appeared on *Gravity*, which also featured duets with white singers **Alison Moyet** and **Steve Winwood**. In 1988 the hip-hop vocal group Full Force produced Brown's *I'm Real* (Polydor), which included a guest appearance by Maceo Parker, and Full Force released its own *a cappella* 'Tribute' to the Godfather of Soul. In 1988, a year after he published his eponymous autobiography, he was imprisoned for drug offences. In the following year his career was interrupted by a jail sentence imposed for assault.

The album that followed his release, *Love Over-Due* (Scotti Bros, 1991), was a decisive return to form and while *Greatest Hits from the Fourth Decade* (1992) was a better concept than album it confirmed the enduring importance of Brown in the development of black music in the US.

In 1993 he released *Universal James*, which teamed him with contemporary black talent in the shape of producers Clivilles & Cole (also known as **C&C Music Factory**) and Jazzie B (of **Soul II Soul**). Less successful was *Live at the Apollo 1995*. His latest backing band, the New JBs, consisted of the West family, seven brothers and sisters from Washington D.C. The influence of Brown's instrumental sound was reflected in the increased recording opportunities for former JBs in the nineties. Parker, Wesley and Pee Wee Ellis (tenor sax) recorded as the J.B. Horns for Gramavision, while Parker cut the solo *Southern Exposure* (Novus 1994). While he continued to tour, Brown's best records of the nineties were mostly reissues of classic recordings and career retrospectives.

JOE BROWN
b. *Joseph Roger Brown, 13 May 1941, Swarby, Lincolnshire, England*

One of the first generation of British rock'n'rollers, Brown was a singer and accomplished guitarist whose subsequent career ran parallel to, though less successfully than, **Tommy Steele**'s.

Brown moved to Plaistow in London's East End at the age of two and formed the Spacemen skiffle group in 1956. The group auditioned for **Jack Good** and won a residency on the 1959 music teleseries *Boy Meets*

Girls as the backing group for visiting acts, with Brown also featured as an instrumentalist. With his blond spiky crewcut and open grin, Brown was (and remains) one of the most instantly recognizable figures of British pop. During this period Brown played the inventive Rockabilly-inspired lead guitar on **Billy Fury**'s *The Sound of Fury* (1960), one of the few classic albums of British rock'n'roll.

Signed to Decca, with the Spacemen now the Bruvvers and his backing band, Brown had his first hits in 1960 with a skiffle setting of Shelton Brooks' 1917 composition, 'The Darktown Strutters Ball' and a version of Ford Dabney's 1924 'coon' song, 'Shine', his first recording for Pye. The comic 'What a Crazy World We're Living in' was featured, along with Brown, in *What a Crazy World* (1963), one of the better British pop films, and gave him another minor hit, but his biggest hits came with a trio of country-inflected songs: 'A Picture of You', his best-remembered record, 'It Only Took a Minute' (both 1962), which was co-written by **Burt Bacharach**'s regular collaborator Hal David, and 'That's What Love Will Do' (1963). None of these were hits in America.

Though the arrival of **The Beatles** lost him his teenage following, Brown's easy-going stage manner and image of a cheerful cockney 'sparrer' won him a wider audience. He starred in the long-running West End production of *Charlie Girl* (1965) and henceforth concentrated on acting and television, only recording irregularly. Later recordings, which included the Lennon–McCartney composition 'With a Little Help from My Friends' (1967), and 'Hey Mama' (Ammo, 1973), were only minor hits and his countryish band, Brown's Home Brew, was short-lived.

In 1988 his daughter Sam Brown (*b. 7 October 1964, London, England*) recorded *Stop* (A&M), whose title track was a big hit in the UK and Europe. She began her career as a backing singer on records by **Adam Ant** and **Dexy's Midnight Runners** and toured with **Spandau Ballet**. Her other records included a version of 'Can I Get a Witness' (1989) and a duet with Jools Holland, formerly of **Squeeze**, 'Together Again' (1991).

LES BROWN

b. Lester Raymond Brown, 14 March 1912, Reinertown, Pennsylvania, USA

The leader of one of the more populist swing bands, Les Brown and his Band of Renown, Brown survived the end of the big-band era by moving into radio and television, working regularly with Bob Hope, on whose radio show his band had first found success in the forties.

From a musical family, clarinettist Brown organized his first band, the Duke Blue Devils, at Duke University in 1936. After working as a freelance

arranger, he was signed to Bluebird (an RCA subsidiary) in 1938 by Eli Oberstein, who with booking agent Joe Glaser secured Brown and his new band a New York residency. He also recorded for Decca and Okeh in this period. In 1940 **Doris Day** briefly joined the band as featured singer but it was not until her return that the band had its first taste of record success with 'Sentimental Journey'* (Columbia, 1945), co-written by Brown, Bud Green and Brown's regular arranger, Ben Homer. Homer was also responsible for the clever arrangement of the **Irving Berlin** standard 'I've Got My Love to Keep Me Warm' (1946), which gave Brown a second million-seller. However, by this time the big-band era was all but over – within a period of weeks at the beginning of 1947, the bands of **Benny Goodman**, **Woody Herman**, **Tommy Dorsey** and Brown and others broke up.

Brown shifted his interest to publishing. He settled in Hollywood, putting together bands for special occasions, the best of which was recorded in 1953 on *Live at the Hollywood Palladium* on Coral; he also supplied orchestral backings for several of Coral's singers, including the **Ames Brothers** and **Teresa Brewer**. In addition, Brown regularly supported Bob Hope, with whom he had been associated for over two decades, and **Dean Martin** on their TV specials. With the revived interest in big bands in the seventies, Brown began touring again, before retiring in 1981.

MILTON BROWN

b. 8 September 1903, Stephenville, Texas, USA, d. 18 April 1936, Fort Worth, Texas

Though it now seems unlikely that the epithet 'Father of Western Swing' will be wrested from **Bob Wills**, the fact remains that several contemporary bands were active, innovative and at least as popular as Wills's in the early thirties. One of them, Milton Brown's Musical Brownies, had not only recorded a substantial body of work before Wills's Texas Playboys first entered a studio, but in doing so had arguably laid down the ground rules of Western swing with a competence and decisiveness that Wills's musicians took some time to match.

Brown and Wills actually made their first issued recordings together, as the Fort Worth Doughboys in 1932, but some months later Brown left their sponsor to form his own band, which played the Crystal Springs Dance Pavilion and broadcast over Fort Worth's station KTAT. The line-up, of six to eight pieces, included fiddler Cecil Brower and jazz pianist Fred Calhoun. Two recording sessions for RCA Victor's Bluebird label in 1934 introduced the band's hot approach to blues and swing numbers. With the addition of Bob Dunn, a pioneer of amplified steel guitar, in late 1934 and fiddler Cliff Bruner in 1936 the Brownies were the strongest combination in this new style of hot string-band music, a placing ratified by their outstanding Decca sessions of 1935–6. These included superior versions of the blues ('St Louis Blues', 1935), conventional country tunes ('Sweet Jenny Lee', 1935), popular standards ('Ida Sweet as Apple Cider') and jazz standards ('Hesitation Blues'), virtually all performed with dancing in mind. Brown himself more or less determined the style of the Western swing vocalist, blending the mellowness of **Bing Crosby** with the jazz phrasing and jive mannerisms of **Cab Calloway**.

The band's promising future was destroyed by Brown's death following a car accident. It continued for two years under the leadership of his younger brother, guitarist Durwood, but core members like Dunn and Bruner had already left to create their own bands. The other Brownies eventually followed their example or joined other groups, in some of which (banjoist Ocie Stockard's Wanderers, for example), the Milton Brown manner was quite effectively preserved.

NACIO HERB BROWN
b. Ignacio Herbert Brown, 22 February 1896, Deming, New Mexico, USA, d. 28 September 1964, San Francisco, California

Just as a producer **Arthur Freed** did much to establish the form of the screen musical in the forties and fifties, so in the thirties he and composer Brown helped set the style for Hollywood film songs.

An early immigrant to Los Angeles – the family moved there in 1902 – Brown briefly worked as a piano accompanist before quitting music for first tailoring and then real estate, writing songs with Freed only as a relaxation. The pair were persuaded by producer Irving Thalberg to write the songs for *The Broadway Melody* (1929), the first real screen musical, promoted with the magical slogan 'All Talking! All Singing! All Dancing!'. Two songs in particular are worthy of note: 'You Were Meant for Me' and 'The Wedding of the Painted Doll'. The first is an early example of the lyrical and melodic clarity and simplicity that Hollywood would demand of its songsmiths (in contrast to the wit and dexterity Broadway demanded of its writers), while the second (as well as being a favourite of its writers – it derived from Brown's first instrumental success, 'Doll Dance' in 1921, and the pair would subsequently rewrite it in various guises) is an example of the exoticism that came to be a regular feature of Hollywood musicals.

Until Freed left writing for film production the pair wrote the scores for numerous musicals, including *The Hollywood Revue* and *The Pagan* (both 1929) which produced 'Singin' in the Rain' and 'Pagan Love Song' respectively; *Going Hollywood* (1933) which produced 'Temptation', a million-seller when dramatically revived by the **Everly Brothers** in 1961; and their reunion effort, the score for *Singin' in the Rain* (1952), whose subject – the coming of sound to the movies – both knew well, and which, as well as the title song, included the joyous 'Make 'Em Laugh'.

In addition to writing with Freed, Brown collaborated with **Gus Kahn** ('You Stepped out of a Dream', 1941), **Leo Robin**, Richard A. Whiting (with whom he composed the Broadway musical *Take a Chance*, 1932) and others. He retired to Mexico in 1943, but in 1948 returned to work in Hollywood, continuing with only occasional successes until his death.

NAPPY BROWN
b. Napoleon Brown, 1932, Charlotte, North Carolina, USA

A leading R&B singer of the fifties, Nappy Brown's rich baritone made him a precursor of such deep-soul singers as **Percy Sledge**.

Brown sang in gospel groups before moving to New Jersey in 1954. There he signed to Herman Lubinsky's Savoy label, cutting his own composition 'Don't Be Angry' (1955). The song was a hit for Brown but the cover-version by the white **Crew Cuts** sold even better.

He followed up with 'Pitter Patter', co-written by Charlie Singleton, who later collaborated with **Bert Kaempfert** on the **Frank Sinatra** hit 'Strangers in the Night' and who wrote the **Al Martino** hit 'Spanish Eyes'. Among later R&B hits were 'Little by Little' (1957), on which Brown used a hiccupping gimmick; 'It Don't Hurt No More' (1958), which had been a 1955 country hit for **Hank Snow**; and 'Cried Like a Baby' (1959). Brown's voice had a similar depth to jazz singer **Billy Eckstine**'s, although he was more emotionally forthright on ballads like 'The Right Time' (1958) and 'It's Really You', on which he screamed, wailed and even barked.

In 1961 his career was halted by a prison sentence and Brown did not record again until 1969 when he recorded *Thanks for Nothing* (Elephant) and *V*, on which he was supported by **Wilson Pickett**'s band. During the seventies Brown returned to gospel music, recording with the Bell Jubilee Singers for Stan Lewis's Jewel label. In 1984 he returned to secular music with the minor *Tore Up* (Alligator). Far superior were *Something's Gonna Jump Out of the Bushes* (Black Top, 1988) and *Apples & Lemons* (Ichiban, 1990) which displayed his gruff, humorous vocals to good effect.

ROY BROWN
b. 10 September 1925, New Orleans, Louisiana, USA, d. 25 May 1981, Los Angeles, California

The flamboyant emotionalism that so disgusted the guardians of musical values when they first encountered it in **Johnny Ray**, or a few years later in **Elvis Presley**, might have disturbed them even more had they known it was only a blurred copy of a typical display by Roy Brown – the voice of exploding passion that has gone on echoing from the throats of singers like **Jackie Wilson**, **Bobby Bland** and **B. B. King**.

Ironically, Brown's first idol was **Bing Crosby**. When Brown won an amateur show in Los Angeles in 1945 he was, despite a family background in church music, a pop balladeer, and it was only by accident that he stumbled upon success with the sexy shout number 'Good Rockin' Tonight' (1947). (It was later recorded to even more acclaim by **Wynonie Harris**, and subsequently by Presley.) His direction determined, he wrote and recorded (for DeLuxe) other raucous blues like 'Boogie at Midnight' (1949) which were R&B chart entrants, but his masterpiece was the harrowing 'Hard Luck Blues'* (1950) with its near-apocalyptic accompaniment by the Griffin Brothers Orchestra.

In 1952 Brown moved on to the King label, which had already taken over DeLuxe. He consolidated his record hits with extensive touring, often in set-up rivalry with Wynonie Harris. Lacking the flexibility to cope very adeptly with rock'n'roll, he left King in 1955 and after a spell with Imperial (1956–7) quit full-time musical work. Occasionally during the sixties he would make a locally distributed single, and in 1968 he cut *Hard Times* for ABC-Bluesway, but something more like a comeback occurred at the 1970 Monterey Jazz Festival, where he was featured with the **Johnny Otis** show. He toured England in 1978. At the time of his death he was engaged in a successful return to the US blues circuit.

RUTH BROWN
b. Ruth Weston, 30 January 1928, Portsmouth, Virginia, USA

Billed as 'Miss Rhythm', Brown was the most popular R&B artist of the fifties. Though she hardly figured in the pop charts, she sold over six million records, including three million-sellers: '5–10–15 Hours' (1952), '(Mama) He Treats Your Daughter Mean' (1953) and 'Lucky Lips' (1957), the **Leiber and Stoller** composition that also provided **Cliff Richard** with a million-seller when he revived it in 1963. In the eighties Brown returned to star in stage shows and to inspire the formation of the Rhythm & Blues Foundation.

The daughter of a choir director, Brown sang spirituals before briefly joining the **Lucky Millinder** band in 1944. In 1949 she was signed by Herb Abramson to the newly established Atlantic Records. Originally a balladeer – she'd won an amateur night contest at the Apollo with the **Bing Crosby** song 'It Could Happen to You' – her first few records were in the style of **Dinah Washington**. But success came with a pair of blues shouters by Rudolph Toombs, 'Tears from My Eyes' (1950), which **Louis Jordan** covered unsuccessfully, and '5–10–15 Hours', to which her lilting voice gave a sophisticated edge. Her most famous songs were"(Mama) He Treats Your Baby Mean', which heavily featured the exciting falsetto squeal that was her trademark, her version of Chuck Willis's 'Oh What a Dream' (1954), which topped the R&B charts and was covered by **Patti Page**, and 'Mambo Baby' (1954), one of many songs produced by the mambo craze of the early fifties.

As an established R&B star, rock'n'roll threatened Brown as much as it did Page. Though she continued to record successfully for Atlantic, her records of the second half of the decade were far more variable and decidedly more pop-orientated. Thus as well as the streetwise jive of the superior 'I Can't Hear a Word You Say' (1959), Leiber and Stoller also provided her with the froth of 'Lucky Lips', her biggest-selling record. Her best post-rock'n'roll record was the **Bobby Darin** composition 'This Little Girl's Gone Rockin'' (1958).

In 1962 she briefly recorded for Philips and then retired to raise a family. In the seventies she returned to performing, at jazz festivals and in musicals (including an all-black version of *Guys and Dolls* in 1975), and recording. Her later albums include *Sugar Babe* (President, 1976), *The Soul Survives* (Flair, 1982) and *Have a Good Time* (Fantasy, 1988). *Blues on Broadway* (1989) mixed versions of Brown's hits with earlier classics from the likes of **Billie Holiday**, such as 'Good Morning Heartache'. During this period she also starred in the Broadway revue *Black and Blue* and in **Allen Toussaint**'s off-Broadway show *Staggerlee*. She also had a cameo role in John Water's cult movie *Hairspray*.

After a successful battle to get back royalties for her fifties hits, Brown took a leading role in the formation of the Rhythm & Blues Foundation which provides financial and other help for older blues and soul artists and is supported by leading US record labels.

JACKSON BROWNE
b. 9 October 1948, Heidelberg, Germany

Singer-songwriter Browne was one of the few mainstream American rock artists to examine larger social issues consistently in his work. Like **Neil Young** and **Paul Simon**, he generally took his own life as his starting point, and the resulting work was an intelligent mix of introspection and social commitment.

Raised in Los Angeles, Browne was briefly a member of an embryonic version of the **Nitty Gritty Dirt**

Band. However, his first success came as a song-writer. His songs appeared on albums by one-time **Velvet Underground** member Nico (whom Browne supported on guitar in New York, 1967–8), **Tom Rush**, the Dirt Band, the **Byrds** and **Bonnie Raitt**, most of which were collected together on his first eponymous album (Asylum, 1972). That produced the hit 'Doctor My Eyes', but more significant was the song he co-wrote with Glenn Frey for the **Eagles**, 'Take It Easy' (1972), which established the group and its desperado image. Other Browne songs recorded by the Eagles include 'Nightingale', 'Doolin-Dalton' and 'James Dean'. However, by the time of *Late for the Sky* (1974), in his own, increasingly confident recordings he cut through the high romanticism of such songs and amplified the social concern implicit in his earlier material. Two songs from *Sky* illustrate these strands: 'Fountains of Sorrow' (later memorably recorded by **Joan Baez**), a personal song of acute observation, and the apocalyptic 'Before the Deluge'. Similarly, the sound of the album, with David Lindley's searing violin well to the fore, was far more urgent than previously.

The harrowing *The Pretender* (1976), recorded in the shadow of the suicide of Browne's wife, saw a return to introspection, while *Running on Empty* (1978) was a more openly reflective essay on the rigours of touring that climaxed with a pleasing reworking of **Maurice Williams**' 'Stay'. The transitional *Hold Out* (1980) was his most successful album hitherto, yielding a pair of hit singles, 'Boulevard' and 'That Girl Could Sing'.

Throughout the seventies Browne appeared in benefits for – mostly ecological – good causes and in 1979, with **Bonnie Raitt**, he helped organize a benefit concert for Musicians United for Safe Energy (MUSE), appearing with **Bruce Springsteen**, among others. Henceforth there would be a firm political dimension to his work. *Lawyers in Love* (1983) saw him satirizing the new cold-war warriors and his new-found 'yuppie' audience and still gave him a hit album and single. Even more forthright was *Lives in the Balance* (1986), which was recorded after a trip to Nicaragua and saw Browne attacking American foreign policy in Central America in songs like 'For America' and 'Soldier of Plenty'. *World in Motion* (1989) was similar in tone. The break-up of Browne's relationship with actress Daryl Hannah provided much of the inspiration for *I'm Alive* (1993), which saw a return to the personal issues that characterized his earlier work. That was followed by the socially reflective *Looking East* (1996).

THE BROWNS

James Edward Brown, b. 1 April 1934, Sparkman, Arkansas, USA; Bonnie Brown, b. 31 July 1937; Ella Maxine Brown, b. 27 April 1932, Sampti, Louisiana

Best remembered for 'The Three Bells'* (1959), the Browns' gentle three-part harmonies were derived both from the church and popular singing groups like the **McGuire Sisters** and the **Andrews Sisters**.

The children of a prosperous rancher, Jim Ed Brown and his elder sister Maxine became regular members of *The Barnyard Frolic* radio show broadcast from Little Rock and in 1953 recorded their own composition 'Looking Back to See' (Abbott) with **Jim Reeves** and **Floyd Cramer** among the backing group. In 1954 younger sister Bonnie joined them and they called themselves the Browns. While on Abbott, their material remained pure country, but after being signed to RCA by **Chet Atkins** in 1956 both the material and their sound grew poppier, culminating in 'The Three Bells' – an adaptation by Bert Reisfield of **Edith Piaf**'s huge French hit, 'Les Trois Cloches', written by Jean Villard – and 'The Old Lamplighter' (1960), a pop hit from 1946 written by Charles Tobias and Nat Simon. Both these songs, and the folksier 'Scarlet Ribbons' (1959), made the Top Twenty in both the country and pop charts.

Despite further hits, in 1967 Maxine and Bonnie quit to be with their families and Jim Ed continued as a solo act, his showmanship taking the place of his sisters' harmonies until 1976, when he started performing and touring with Helen Cornelius. Together they had several country hits, ranging from 'I Don't Want to Have to Marry You' (1976) to their version of **Neil Diamond**'s 'You Don't Bring Me Flowers' (1979), and 'The Bedroom' (1980). In 1981 the duo broke up and Brown briefly resumed his solo career.

DAVE BRUBECK
b. 6 December 1920, Concord, California, USA

With hit singles in the fifties, the Dave Brubeck Quartet popularized a form of chamber jazz that was scorned by many jazz critics and *aficionados*.

Brubeck had an academic musical training, studying under the classical composer Darius Milhaud. His famous Quartet grew out of an Octet recording made for Fantasy in 1946. The group included Paul Desmond (alto sax), Joe Morello (drums) and Norman Bates or Gene Wright (bass). Desmond (*b. 25 November 1924, San Francisco, d. 30 May 1977, New York*) was voted best new star on alto in the 1951 *Downbeat* critics' poll.

Their music was a kind of classicized jazz, with discernible influences in the harmonics of Bartók, the dignity of Bach and the romanticism of Rachmaninov. Like the music of the **Modern Jazz Quartet**, Brubeck's 'cool' bebop found a ready audience among college students who enjoyed the unusual time signatures and the music's sophistication. Such albums as *Jazz Goes to College* and *Jazz Goes to Junior College* helped to make the group regular poll-winners in the late fifties. In 1959 the Quartet joined forces with **Leonard Bernstein** and the New York Philharmonic to perform *Dialogue for Jazz Combo and Symphony*, composed by Brubeck's brother Howard.

Time Out (Columbia, 1960) contained 'Blue Rondo à la Turk' (in 9/8) and the international hit single 'Take Five', a catchy melody set in 5/4 time. 'Unsquare Dance' (1962) was also a hit in Britain. The Quartet split in 1967, reuniting shortly before Desmond's death in 1977. *25th Anniversary Reunion* was released by A&M in that year.

Brubeck's later records included albums with his sons Chris (electric bass), Darius and Danny, moving towards jazz-rock on *Brother, the Great Spirit Made Us All* (Atlantic). He also collaborated with avant-gardist **Anthony Braxton** and others (*All the Things We Are*, Atlantic, 1976). He continued to record throughout the eighties, offering tasteful versions of his earlier classic recordings. The best of these late records are *Moscow Night* (Concord, 1988), *Jazz Impressions of New York* (Columbia, 1990) and *Late Night Brubeck* (Telarc, 1994).

JACK BRUCE
b. 14 May 1943, Lanarkshire, Scotland

Widely regarded as the most accomplished bass player in rock music, Bruce was a member of **Cream** with **Eric Clapton** and Ginger Baker. After the group split up, he embarked on a solo career that was more varied and influential than successful.

As a child, Bruce learned Scottish folk songs from his mother and took up double bass at school. His first gigs were with Glasgow dance bands and in traditional jazz groups. In the early sixties he entered the London jazz scene where he met Baker and sax-player Dick Heckstall-Smith. Through them he played in early line-ups of **Alexis Korner**'s Blues Incorporated and joined the **Graham Bond** Organization in 1963. With Bond he recorded *The Sound of 65* (Decca, 1965) and *There's a Bond Between Us*, which featured Bruce's harmonica-playing and lead vocals as well as his bass-playing.

Bruce had brief spells with **John Mayall** and **Manfred Mann** before Cream was formed in late 1966. With poet-singer Pete Brown, Bruce composed the group's first record 'Anyone for Tennis', as well as many of its best-known songs, including 'White Room' and 'Sunshine of Your Love'. When Cream disbanded, Bruce embarked on a series of albums which placed further Bruce–Brown songs in complex, jazz-tinged arrangements. The superior *Songs for a*

Tailor (Polydor, 1969) was a Top Ten hit in Britain but *Harmony Row* (1971) and *Out of the Storm* (1974) sold less well.

For live performance he formed Jack Bruce and Friends with guitarist Larry Coryell and former **Jimi Hendrix** drummer Mitch Mitchell before briefly joining the jazz-fusion group **Tony Williams Lifetime**. Having sung on **Carla Bley**'s *Escalator over the Hill* (1972), Bruce next recorded three albums of heavy rock in 1972–4 with Leslie West and Corky Laing of **Mountain**.

He was less active in the latter part of the seventies, releasing only the solo album *How's Tricks* (1977) and touring as a bandleader in 1975 and 1980. *I've Always Wanted to Do This* (Epic, 1980) was a jazz-rock effort involving Billy Cobham (drums) and Clem Clempson (guitar), and the following year Bruce reverted to the rock/blues idiom in BLT, a collaboration with former **Procul Harum** guitarist Robin Trower and Bill Lordan (drums). The trio made two albums for Chrysalis in 1980–1.

During the rest of the eighties Bruce emerged occasionally to take part in such recordings as *Visions of Excess* (1986) by the Golden Palominos, a floating line-up group created by Anton Fier, formerly of Pere Ubu.

In 1989 he was reunited with Ginger Baker, whose post-Cream career had included recordings with his big band Airforce, the Baker-Gurvitz Army heavy rock band, the establishment of a studio in Nigeria and collaborations with **Bill Laswell** on the albums *Horses and Trees* (1986) and *Middle Passage* (1989). Bruce toured the United States with Baker and released *Will Power* (Polydor, 1989), which was followed by the lesser *A Question of Time* (Epic, 1990). 1993 saw the release of *Somethin Els* [*sic*], which featured contributions from Clapton, and Bruce toured extensively in support of it with a three-piece band featuring young guitarist Blues Sarenco, drawing immediate comparisons with Cream. A live album, *Cities of the Heart*, recorded on his 50th birthday, followed in 1994. Among the other musicians featured were Ginger Baker and guitarist **Gary Moore**, who joined with Bruce to form yet another blues-rock trio, BBM, and release an album later that year.

FELICE AND BOUDLEAUX BRYANT
Boudleaux, b. 13 February 1920, Shellman, Georgia, USA, d. 30 June 1987; Felice Scaduto, b. 7 August 1925, Milwaukee, Wisconsin

Essentially country songwriters – their 'Rocky Top' is one of the most recorded songs in the annals of country music – the Bryants produced a series of memorable hits for the **Everly Brothers** in the late fifties that neatly captured the narcissistic element so central to adolescent preoccupations.

From a musical family, Boudleaux Bryant briefly joined the Atlanta Symphony Orchestra as a violinist in 1938 before quitting to play first jazz and then country music as a member of **Hank Penny**'s band. In 1948 he married Scaduto and the pair began writing together – with the occasional song being credited solely to B. Bryant. Their first success was 'Country Boy', a Top Ten country hit for Little Jimmy Dickens in 1949. Signed by publisher **Fred Rose** of Acuff-Rose, they moved to Nashville in 1950 where they were among the few professional, non-recording songwriters. Several of their early compositions were first country and then pop hits when **Mitch Miller** produced cover-versions of them by artists such as **Tony Bennett** ('Have a Good Time') and **Frankie Laine** ('Hey Joe', originally recorded by Carl Smith in 1953). By the mid-fifties they were established country songwriters, regularly producing hits for **Eddy Arnold** ('I've Been Thinking' and 'The Richest Man', both 1955) and others.

Then, in 1957, Wesley Rose introduced them to the Everly Brothers, a traditional country duo, with instructions to produce teenage songs for them. The first was 'Bye Bye Love'* after which they provided the Everlys with six more million-sellers: 'Wake Up Little Susie' (1957), 'All I Have to Do Is Dream', 'Bird Dog' and 'Problems' (all 1958), and 'Take a Message to Mary' and 'Poor Jenny' (both 1959). These and other songs they wrote at this time – 'Raining in My Heart', recorded by **Buddy Holly** (1959), and the witty 'Let's Think About Living', which gave Bob Luman his only big hit in 1960 – have been compared to the songs of **Chuck Berry** and **Eddie Cochran** for their awareness of the mores of teenage life. But, in truth, compared to Cochran and Berry, such knowledge is limited. At their best what the Bryants' songs have is an (often unconscious) obsessional quality – as in 'All I Have to Do Is Dream', which less explicitly than Pete Townshend's 'Pictures of Lily' is a paean to masturbation – most evident in 'Love Hurts', a neurotic detailing of the cost of love. Among the numerous recordings of 'Love Hurts' the most significant are those by the Everlys, **Roy Orbison** and **Gram Parsons**, all of whom produced painfully 'knowing' versions, Jim Capaldi who had a British Top Ten hit with the song in 1975 and the hard-rock group **Nazareth** who reached the American Top Ten with it in 1976.

With the growing domination of pop music by New York publishers and artists who wrote their own material in the early sixties, the Bryants returned to writing mostly for country performers such as **Sonny James** ('Baltimore', 1964) and **Roy Clark** ('Come Live with Me', 1978). In 1979 they recorded an album of their own compositions, *Surfin' on a New Wave*, on the independent DB label.

PEABO BRYSON
b. Robert Peabo Bryson, 13 April 1951, Greenville, South Carolina

A soul ballad singer with a somewhat archaic crooning style, Bryson has enjoyed success with a series of duets with such artists as Natalie Cole, **Roberta Flack** and **Céline Dion**.

In 1971 he joined Moses Dillard and the Tex-Town Display and later worked as a session singer and writer for Bert Berns' Bang label in New York. Among his first recordings was 'Do It with Feeling' as lead singer of the Michael Zager Band.

Bryson's first solo album was *Reaching for the Sky* (Capitol, 1977), which included the soul standard 'Feel the Fire'. He next linked up with Natalie Cole, recording 'We're the Best of Friends' (1980). Bryson's first big hit was the romantic ballad 'Tonight I Celebrate My Love for You' (1984), a duet with Flack which reached No. 2 in Britain.

Between 1983 and 1988 Bryson recorded four albums for Elektra, including *Straight from the Heart* (1984, which included his biggest solo hit, 'If You're Ever in My Arms Again'), *Quiet Storm* (1986) – which shared its name with a new urban radio format – and *Positive* (1988), the title track of which was another hit duet, this time with Regina Belle. In 1993 Bryson was again teamed with Belle to sing Alan Menken and Tim Rice's 'A Whole New World', the main theme from Walt Disney's *Aladdin*.

In 1989 Bryson re-signed with Capitol and released *All My Love*. His later hits included 'Beauty and the Beast' (1992) with Dion and 'By the Time this Night Is Over' (1993) with saxophonist **Kenny G.**

JACK BUCHANAN
b. 2 April 1891, Helensburgh, Scotland, d. 20 October 1957, London, England

In the annals of musical comedy and revue, Jack Buchanan appears as an early British equivalent to **Fred Astaire**, offering his less remarkable skills as crooner and tap-dancer with self-deprecation. He embodied the elegant man-about-town of the pre-war British musical, wearing top hat, white tie and tails 'as though he were born in them' (according to one commentator) and dispensing in his fragile voice messages of wry humour and insouciance that sharply evoke their period.

He was established on the London stage by *Bubbly* (1917) and the Charlot revue *A to Z* (1921, with music by **Ivor Novello**), which also featured Beatrice Lillie and, in her first starring role, Gertrude Lawrence. The trio went on to Broadway success with *André Charlot's Revue* (1924) and *The Charlot Revue of 1925* (1926), in which Buchanan and Lawrence sang their one American hit 'A Cup of Coffee, a Sandwich and You' (Columbia). During the following decade Buchanan played in a series of musical comedies at the London Hippodrome with Elsie Randolph. These included *Sunny* (1926), *That's a Good Girl* (1928), *Stand Up and Sing* (1931) and *Mr Whittington* (1934), and introduced such hit songs as Novello's 'And Her Mother Came Too' (1921), 'Fancy Our Meeting', Al Hoffman's 'I'm in a Dancing Mood' (1936), and 'There's Always Tomorrow'.

His other American successes include the Broadway production of **Cole Porter**'s *Wake Up and Dream* (1929) with **Jessie Matthews**, and the films *Monte Carlo* (1930) with **Jeanette MacDonald**, Herbert Wilcox's *Goodnight Vienna* (1932) with Anna Neagle, and *Brewster's Millions* (1935). He directed one film, *That's a Good Girl* (1935), and produced several more, but his best film performance came in *The Band Wagon* (1953).

JEFF BUCKLEY

b. *Jeffrey Scott Moorhead, 17 November 1966, Anaheim, California, USA; d. 29 May 1997, Memphis, Tennessee*

Gifted singer-songwriter Jeff Buckley's vocal dexterity was strongly reminiscent of his father, **Tim Buckley**. His accidental drowning in 1997 provided another sharp parallel, with both lives ending prematurely.

Raised alone by his mother, Jeff was to meet his father just once, in 1976, weeks before his death from an accidental drug overdose. By this time, the young Buckley had taught himself to play his grandmother's guitar and had developed an obvious flair for singing. At seventeen he moved to LA, working with a variety of heavy rock and reggae bands with whom he soon became disinterested.

Moving to New York in 1990, Buckley met guitarist Gary Lucas, who had previously worked with **Captain Beefheart**, forming the short-lived band Gods and Monsters. After the band split, Buckley returned to solo performance on the city's Lower East Side, playing regularly at the Sin-E club, attracting attention from various record labels. After recording an EP, *Live at Sin-E* (1994), for Big Cat Records, Buckley signed to Sony.

His début album, *Grace* (1994), reflected a love for the music of **Led Zeppelin** and **Van Morrison**, with Buckley's powerful tenor adding an element of individuality to the mix. *Grace* featured the singles 'So Real' and 'Last Goodbye' and was followed by the *Live from the Bataclan* EP (1995), recorded during a lengthy world tour on which Buckley was backed by his regular band of Michael Tighe (guitar), Matt Johnson (drums) and Mick Grondhal (bass).

Buckley's accidental death in 1997 occurred when he drowned in the Mississippi River in the midst of preparing his second album. The double set *Sketches for My Sweetheart the Drunk* (1998) included tracks recorded by Tom Verlaine of **Television** in 1996, alongside home demos and a pair of live recordings. It provided Buckley with a posthumous UK Top Twenty hit, 'Everybody Here Wants You'. It was followed by *Mystery White Boy* (Columbia, 2000), a collection of live recordings made during his 1995–6 tour. More compelling than the originals, most of which can be heard better recorded elsewhere, are the versions of songs associated with other artists, especially the enchanting 'The Man that Got Away', sung by **Judy Garland** in *A Star Is Born* (1954).

TIM BUCKLEY

b. *Timothy Charles Buckley III, 14 February 1947, Washington DC, USA, d. 29 June 1975, Santa Monica, California*

Singer-songwriter Buckley possessed one of the most distinctive and lyrical voices of his generation. 'There is no name yet for the places he and his voice can go,' wrote critic Lillian Roxon. Buckley later abandoned folk-rock for a more exploratory and idiosyncratic approach, with mixed results.

Raised in Washington, he settled in California at the age of ten and by 1962 was playing guitar in country-and-western bands. Moving into folk music he formed a trio, the Bohemians, with poet and lyricist Larry Beckett and future **Blood, Sweat and Tears** bassist Jim Fielder. Through **Frank Zappa**'s manager Herb Cohen, Buckley was signed to Elektra in 1966, whose Jac Holzman produced his eponymous first album with Paul Rothchild.

With a West Coast backing group including **Van Dyke Parks**, this collection of Beckett–Buckley songs was one of the outstanding folk-rock albums of the period. Beckett's romantic lyrics on 'Valentine Melody' and 'Song Slowly Song' were a perfect foil for Buckley's singing, which managed to combine purity and passion.

While that album was a *succès d'estime*, the Jerry Yester-produced *Hello and Goodbye* (1967) was both a critical and commercial success. It contained the finest Beckett–Buckley song, 'Morning Glory' (later covered by Blood, Sweat and Tears and British group Decameron, among others), and the ambitious state-of-the-nation title song as well as Buckley's own poetic 'Once I Was'. His subsequent recordings moved away from folk-rock and became both more experimental and more introverted.

Happy Sad (1968) was co-produced by Yester and ex-**Lovin' Spoonful** guitarist Zal Yanofsky and featured a backing group pared down to a rhythm section. After the melancholic *Blue Afternoon* (Straight, 1969), Buckley turned towards jazz on *Lorca* (1970) and with *Starsailor* (1970) was using his voice as one more instrument in an ensemble whose sound Buckley himself compared to that of **John Coltrane**.

The Jerry Goldstein-produced *Greetings from LA* (1973) represented a further change of direction, towards funk and R&B. On 'Move with Me', 'Get on Top' and the relentless 'Nighthawkin'', the themes were aggressively sexual with one reviewer describing the album as 'made by a broken man still capable of desperate ecstasies'. *Sefronia* (Discreet, 1973) saw a return towards Buckley's earlier, more gentle approach and contained an impressive version of **Fred Neil**'s 'Dolphins'. It was followed by *Look at the Fool* (1974).

Buckley's death was due to an accidental drug overdose. His reputation was enhanced by the release of *Dream Letter* (Demon, 1990), a live recording from 1968 which set his impassioned and imaginative vocalizing against the sparest of backings. Other, more ragged, historical live recordings followed.

His son **Jeff Buckley**'s success also reinstigated interest in his father's material, leading to the re-release of his later albums and the issuing of an additional volume of live material, *Once I Was* (1999), which included a previously unheard version of 'I Don't Need It to Rain'.

BUCKS FIZZ
Jay Aston, b. 4 May 1961 (replaced by Shelley Preston, b. 14 May 1960); Cheryl Baker, b. Rita Crudgington, 8 March 1954; Bobby Gee, b. Robert Gubby, 23 August 1953; Michael Nolan, b. 7 December 1954

One of a number of vocal quartets formed in the wake of **Abba**'s success, Bucks Fizz adapted to changing trends and enjoyed a series of hits in the eighties, including three British No. 1s – 'Making Your Mind Up' and 'The Land of Make Believe' (both 1981), and 'My Camera Never Lies' (1982).

The group was formed by music publisher Nichola Martin and songwriter Andy Hill in 1981 to perform the UK Eurovision Song Contest entry 'Making Your Mind Up'. Baker was a former member of a previous Eurovision group, Coco. Bucks Fizz's energetic harmonies and mildly sexy stage show won the competition and gave them a chart-topper in Britain on RCA. 'Piece of the Action', 'One of Those Nights' and 'The Land of Make Believe' were further successes in that year.

The last single was from the album *Are You Ready?*, which included the 1982 hit 'My Camera Never Lies' and 'Now Those Days Are Gone'. *Hand Cut* (1983) included 'Run for Your Life' and 'Talking in Your Sleep' came from *I Hear Talk* (1984).

Nolan was severely injured in an accident to the group's bus in 1984, forcing Bucks Fizz to take a break from recording and performing. When they returned, Aston had been replaced by Preston and they had a new label, Polydor. *Writing on the Wall* (1986) included the hit singles 'New Beginning (Mamba Seyra)', 'Keep Each Other Warm' and 'I Hear Talk', but subsequent recordings failed to chart. The group released a live album, *At the Fairfield Hall, Croydon*, in 1991. By this time Gee and Nolan were partnered by Heidi Manton and Amanda Szwarc. In the nineties they became regulars on the UK's nostalgia circuit.

BUFFALO SPRINGFIELD
Ritchie Furay, b. 9 May 1944, Dayton, Ohio, USA; Dewey Martin, b. 30 September 1942, Chesterville, Canada; Bruce Palmer, b. 1947, Liverpool, Canada (replaced by Jim Messina, b. 5 December 1947, Maywood, California); Stephen Stills, b. 30 January 1945, Dallas, Texas; Neil Young, b. 12 November 1945, Toronto, Canada

In the wake of the **Byrds** and the **Lovin' Spoonful**, Buffalo Springfield attempted a fusion of the spirit of the Greenwich Village folk revival with rock forms and instrumentation. The eclecticism of their music, poor management and personality clashes contributed to the band's small commercial impact but its key figures, **Neil Young** and Stephen Stills, went on to **Crosby, Stills and Nash** (and Young) and to significant solo careers.

Guitarist/vocalists Stills and Furay had worked together in commercial folk group the Au Go Go Singers and met folk singer Young while on tour in Toronto. In 1965 Furay and Stills moved to Los Angeles where, inspired by **The Beatles** and other beat groups, they formed an amplified band with Young and bassist Palmer, whose earlier Toronto rock group, the Mynah Birds, had included **Rick James**.

With former Dillards drummer Martin and a name taken from a brand of steamroller, Buffalo Springfield performed original material by Young, Furay and Stills at LA's Whisky a Go Go club. They were signed by Sonny and **Cher**'s managers who placed the group with Atlantic. Their first release was Young's plaintive ballad 'Nowadays Clancy Can't Even Sing' (1966), followed by an eponymous album. This displayed the virtuosity of a group with three writers, three lead singers and two lead guitarists but it was only through the single 'For What It's Worth' that Buffalo Springfield came to national prominence.

Stills' song, with lead vocals by Furay and Young's restrained electric guitar work, described police action against Los Angeles teenagers and reached the Top Ten early in 1967. It should have provided a springboard for further success but 'Bluebird' and 'Rock'n'Roll Woman' were only minor hits while *Buffalo Springfield Again* (1967), on which Messina replaced Palmer, also made little impact. Its wide range of musical approaches foreshadowed the disintegration of the band as Furay's country-styled 'Child's Claim to Fame' vied with Stills' mainstream rock on the clamorous 'Mr Soul' and Young's melancholic 'Broken Arrow', an ambitious collage constructed by **Jack Nitzsche**.

Buffalo Springfield eventually split up two months before the release of *Last Time Around* (1968), a lesser work notable for Stills' move into Latin rhythms with 'Uno Mundo' and 'On the Way Home', the band's last single. The following year, Stills' combined with Graham Nash and David Crosby to create a new blend of acoustic/electric close-harmony rock while Young made two solo albums before joining the trio in 1970.

Meanwhile, Furay and Messina had formed the country-rock group Poco with pedal-steel-guitarist Rusty Young and Randy Meisner (bass), who later joined **Rick Nelson**'s band. After *Pickin' up the Pieces* (Epic, 1969), Messina left to go into production, before joining **Kenny Loggins** to form Loggins and Messina.

Adding guitarist Paul Cotton and Tim Schmidt (bass), Furay made four more pleasant but unsensational Poco albums before in 1973 he left the group to combine with ex-Byrds guitarist Chris Hillman and songwriter/singer John David Souther, co-author of the **Eagles**' 1976 No. 1 'New Kid in Town'*. The Souther–Hillman–Furay band's two Asylum albums made little impact and Furay went on to make such solo albums as the Michael Omartian-produced *I've Got a Reason* (Asylum, 1976), *Dance a Little Light* (1978) and *I Still Have Dreams* (1981).

JIMMY BUFFETT
b. 25 December 1946, Mobile, Alabama, USA

A singer-songwriter with a wry line in social observation, Buffett operated at the unlikely meeting point of Ernest Hemmingway, **Hank Williams** and **Xavier Cugat**. By the early nineties he had become one of America's top concert attractions.

A graduate in journalism, Buffett briefly worked for the music trade magazine *Billboard* before he signed with Barnaby in 1970. After one album (*Down to Earth*) he quit Nashville for Florida. His first album for Dunhill, *A White Sport Coat and a Pink Crustacean* (1973), whose title was a pun on **Marty Robbins**' 1957 million-seller 'A White Sport Coat and a Pink Carnation', featured **Steve Goodman** on guitar and established the easy-going, semi-autobiographical drunken-sailor persona that would form the basis of his best work. Buffett's songs neatly mixed cleverly rehearsed nostalgia ('They Don't Dance Like Carmen No More') and mock heroics ('The Great Filling Sta-

tion Holdup') with pensive lyrics ('Death of an Unpopular Poet').

He wrote and performed the music for *Rancho DeLuxe* (1974) and his next album, *Living and Dying in 3/4 Time* (1974), produced a Top Forty hit, 'Come Monday', but Buffett's commercial breakthrough didn't come until *Changes in Attitude* (1977) and its million-selling hymn to self-indulgence, 'Margaritaville'. Other hits included the album's title track, and the novelty song 'Cheeseburger in Paradise' (1978) and 'Fins' from *Volcano* (MCA, 1979). He recorded less frequently and more self-indulgently in the eighties, releasing albums like *Coconut Telegraph* (1981), *Last Mango in Paris* (1985) and *Hot Water* (1988). In 1987 Buffett became chairman of the Save the Manatee Committee. *Off to See the Lizard* (1989) and *Live Feeding Frenzy* (1991) saw Buffet sounding increasingly like **James Taylor**, who had guested on *Hot Water*. The retrospective set *Boats, Beaches, Bars & Ballads* (1992) highlighted the tourist and travelogue elements of Buffett's career at the expense of his far better (earlier) songs of literate social observation.

In 1989 he published his first novel, *Tales from Margaritaville*, followed in 1992 by *Where Is Joe Merchant?* Both made the *New York Times*' bestsellers' list. He tours once a year with his Coral Reefer Band and in 1992 formed his own label, Margaritaville Records, releasing a live album, *Margaritaville Cafe Light Night Menu* (1993), recorded at his own restaurant. In 1994 he released his first studio album in nearly six years, *Fruitcakes*.

In the second half of the nineties, he regularly toured the US, dabbled in book writing (including a couple of children's books written with his daughter and the autobiographical *A Pirate Looks at Fifty* [1998], which topped the *New York Times* bestseller list) and restaurant management, while at the same time recording several albums, most of whose songs celebrated indulgence and the pleasures of easy-goingness rather than hard work. Albums of the period included *Banana Wind* (1996) and *Don't Stop the Carnival* (1998). He also contributed to the Brian Wilson solo album *Imagination* (1998).

LTJ BUKEM
b. Daniel Williamson, 1968, England

LTJ Bukem was a leading figure in the UK jungle scene of the 1990s, first as a DJ and recording artist, and later as the head of a network of record labels promoting a more atmospheric, jazz-influenced form of drum'n'bass.

Brought up by adoptive parents, Williamson studied piano as a child, and developed an interest in jazz and fusion through a new music teacher when the family moved to Watford, north of London. These

new musical influences, including **Chick Corea** and
Roy Ayers, led Williamson to learn drums and trumpet, as well as inspiring an interest in DJing. He began
DJing as part of the local Sunshine sound system,
mixing jazz, soul and funk with heavier hip-hop and
reggae beats at parties around Watford, Slough and
High Wycombe. The acid house boom of 1988 drew
Williamson further into club and DJ culture, and in
1990 he got his big break, playing in front of 10,000
people at the Raindance rave party in Essex.

Now known as LTJ Bukem, he also began recording, releasing 'Logical Progression' on the independent Vinyl Mania label in 1990. He then released
'Demon's Theme' on his own Good Looking label in
1991. These and other early releases established
Bukem's trademark sound, a combination of the
speeded-up hip-hop beats he had heard at hardcore
raves with more soulful, jazz-influenced instrumentation, lifted from the jazz and funk he had listened to
as a teenager. His most notable releases during this
period were 'Music' (1993) and the magnificent 'Horizons' (1994). The release of 'Horizons' coincided with
Bukem's launching a drum'n'bass club night, Speed,
in central London. Speed would emerge as the genre's
most influential club, with Bukem and other DJs
including Fabio, Grooverider, **Goldie** and Alex Reece
helping drum'n'bass win wider mainstream coverage.

Bukem's entrepreneurial eye spotted an opportunity
to raise his label's profile at this point, and he licensed
a Good Looking compilation, *Logical Progression*, to
London Records in 1995. The set was a huge commercial success, a first introduction to drum'n'bass for
many listeners. Bukem at this stage controversially
quit Speed (which shut down soon after) to launch
Logical Progression club nights at UK house super-
clubs Cream and Ministry of Sound. He also developed a profile as a remixer, most notably with his
critically acclaimed reworking of Jodeci's 'Feenin'.

In the late 1990s Bukem's own music took a back
seat to his ever-expanding recording empire, which
now also included two other labels, Good Looking
and Earth Records, the latter focusing on more experimental drum'n'bass recordings. These labels have
been behind a number of compilation series, including *Earth*, *The Progression Sessions* and further *Logical
Progression* packages, which have showcased the
labels' ambient interpretation of drum'n'bass styles.
Following these, in 2000 he issued a six-volume series
of unissued tracks from Good Looking's vaults, *Points
in Time, Vols 1–6*, with further issues promised.

Until 2000 Bukem's only release under his own
name was the EP *Mystic Realms*. The two-CD set *Journey's Inward* (Good Looking Records) confirmed
Bukem's reputation as, in the words of one reviewer,
'the renaissance man of drum'n'bass'. An immediate
dance-club favourite, especially in the chill-out room,

Journey's Inward distilled much of what Bukem's own
rather sporadic recordings had offered during the preceding years. It had a sense of atmosphere and mood
that harked back to the seventies jazz-funk of Lonnie
Liston Smith and a taste for live sounds and instrumentation to accompany his drum'n'bass rhythms.
More intriguingly, it revealed growing interest in the
tempos of other genres, such as hip-hop (on the title
track) and house ('Feel What You Feel'). In support of
it he conducted a dee-jaying tour of North America.

SOLOMON BURKE
b. 1936, Philadelphia, Pennsylvania, USA

With **Sam Cooke** one of the greatest soul stylists of
the sixties, Burke was perhaps the most important
link between gospel and soul music. But where Cooke
brought a cool intensity to R&B balladry, Burke's soul
music, seen at its best in 'Everybody Needs Somebody
to Love' and the magisterial 'The Price' (1964), often
featured a harsher and more directly emotional version of the gospel sound. Significantly, Burke never
completely secularized his music, and alternated
preaching and soul singing throughout his career.

By the age of twelve, Burke was already a preacher
at his father's Philadelphia church, hosting a gospel
radio show and touring the circuit as 'The Boy Wonder Preacher'. In 1955 he joined Apollo Records and
recorded in both gospel and secular fashion, often
blending the two in the same performance. Though
stylistically confused, these records, which included
'No Man Walks Alone', 'Walking in a Dream' and
'You Can Run but You Can't Hide' (a song derived
from boxer Joe Louis' catchphrase), revealed both a
wide range of influence (from **Nat 'King' Cole** and
Elvis Presley to **Roy Hamilton**, whose 'You'll Never
Walk Alone' was clearly the model for many of his
recordings) and the sheer power of Burke's voice.
When these failed, Burke retired from showbusiness
and secured a degree in mortuary science.

In 1959 he returned to recording for Singular ('Be-
Bop Grandma') and in 1960, on the urging of *Billboard* columnist Paul Ackerman, he was signed to
Atlantic, just after the company had lost **Ray Charles**.
At Ackerman's suggestion he recorded the country
song 'Just out of Reach' in 1961, some three months
before Charles had his country-flavoured hit
'Unchain My Heart'. The record gave Burke his first
hit. Burke's other major country songs were 'Down in
the Valley', **Eddy Arnold**'s 'I Really Don't Want to
Know' (1962) and **Jim Reeves**' 'He'll Have to Go'
(1964). In 1962 **Jerry Wexler** teamed Burke with **Bert
Berns**, the man responsible for most of the best New
York deep soul recordings who would mastermind
Burke's subsequent work on Atlantic. The result was a
string of soul classics, including 'Cry to Me' (1962),

Wilson Pickett's 'If You Need Me' (1963), 'Got to Get You off My Mind' and 'Tonight's the Night' (1965), which Burke wrote with **Don Covay**, a regular collaborator. All showed off his big voice and his ability to sing with total control, whether passionately crooning or savagely preaching about lost love.

Dubbed 'The King of Rock and Soul', Burke was equally legendary for his entrepreneurial ability – at one point during an engagement at New York's Apollo he set up a popcorn stand outside the theatre – and his highly theatrical performances, at which, in the manner of **James Brown**, he would be crowned on stage. Though he had no chart success in the UK, he was a strong influence on the **Rolling Stones** who recorded his 'You Can Make It if You Try', 'Cry to Me' and 'Everybody Needs Somebody to Love', which was a staple of many British R&B groups' live performances. Before 1965, Burke had been Atlantic's most successful black act, but when his hits declined and the company began to re-orientate itself to rock music, he left in 1968.

He signed with Bell and had a huge hit with his soulful version of **Creedence Clearwater Revival**'s 'Proud Mary' (1969) before label-hopping his way through the seventies, recording for MGM ('Love's Street and a Full Road', 1972), Dunhill and Chess (for which he recorded inferior **Barry White** imitations like 'You and Your Baby Blues'). In 1979 Burke joined Infinity for whom he recorded the Jerry Williams Jnr-produced 'Sidewalks, Fences and Walls', which looked set to mark his return to the charts before the company collapsed.

In the eighties he formally returned to the church as Bishop Burke of the House of God for All People and recorded gospel songs for Savoy. He owned various businesses including a chain of mortuaries. In 1985 he had a surprise hit with the live album *Soul Alive* (Rounder), on which he reprised his past hits, giving them a strong gospel context, sermons and all. Sales of the studio album *A Change Is Gonna Come* (1986) confirmed a renewed interest in sixties soul and Burke's pre-eminent position as a soul stylist. *Love Trap* (Royalty, 1987) was less impressive but his versions of songs associated with **Roy Brown**, **Joe Turner** and **T-Bone Walker** on *Soul of the Blues* (Black Top, 1994) were both emphatic (in a soul manner) and distinctive in their own right. Burke, who subsequently became the owner of a chain of Californian mortuaries, continued to record, with the emphatic *Definition of Soul* (Pointblank, 1997) being among the best of his later albums.

JOHNNY BURNETTE

b. 25 March 1934, Memphis, Tennessee, USA,
d. 14 August 1964, Clear Lake, California

Best remembered for 'You're Sixteen'* (1960) with its succinct summary of teenage aspirations ('You're sixteen, you're beautiful and you're mine'), Burnette's short career was more substantial than his teen-idol status suggests. His aptly named Rock'n'Roll Trio recorded some of the most inventive rockabilly of the era and with his brother Dorsey he wrote several songs for **Ricky Nelson**.

Contemporaries of **Elvis Presley** – Johnny went to the same school as Presley and Dorsey (*b. 28 December 1932, Memphis, d. 19 August 1979, Canoga Park, California*) briefly worked with Presley at Crown Electric – the Burnette brothers, inspired by his success, formed the Rock'n'Roll Trio in 1956 with guitarist Paul Burlison (*b. 4 February 1929, Brownsville, Tennessee*). Rejected by **Sam Phillips** as too similar to Presley, the trio signed with Coral and had a minor hit with 'Tear It Up'. Other recordings of this period included a version of the **Delmore Brothers**' 'Blues Stay Away from Me' and **Tiny Bradshaw**'s 'Train Kept a-Rollin'' which featured a modernistic, distorted guitar solo from Burlison. In the same year they were featured (as the Johnny Burnette Trio) in the film *Rock, Rock, Rock* (1956).

In 1957 the trio disbanded and Dorsey and Johnny headed for Hollywood where they established themselves as songwriters. Together they wrote 'Waiting in School' (1957) and 'Believe What You Say' (1958) for Ricky Nelson, while Dorsey provided him with 'It's Late' (1959) and 'My One Desire' (1960). By this time the brothers had secured separate recording contracts, Dorsey with Era and Johnny with Liberty, where under the supervision of **Tommy 'Snuff' Garrett** he recorded a series of superior teen ballads. Among them were 'Dreamin'' (1960), 'You're Sixteen' (successfully revived by **Ringo Starr**, 1974), 'Little Boy Sad' and the patriotic '(For) God, Country and My Baby' (1961), before his career ground to a halt. At the time of his death in a boating accident, he was attempting a comeback on his own Magic Lamp label.

Dorsey was less successful as a teen balladeer – '(There Was a) Tall Oak Tree' (1960) being his only major hit – but in the seventies he found renewed success as a country singer and writer, providing songs for **Jerry Lee Lewis** and **Glen Campbell**, among others. His son Billy (*b. 8 May 1953, Memphis*) started his career playing in his father's band and recorded several country albums – including *Between Friends* (Polydor, 1979) and *Billy Burnette* (Columbia, 1980), with its new version of 'Tear It Up' – before graduating to rock in the eighties, joining **Fleetwood Mac** in 1987. Johnny's son Rocky (*b. 12 June 1953, Memphis*) also recorded, scoring a transatlantic hit with the neo-rockabilly song 'Tired of Toein' the Line' (EMI-America, 1980).

BURNING SPEAR
b. Winston Rodney, 1946, St Anns, Jamaica

One of the founders of modern reggae, Winston Rodney's vocal style and phrasing have been widely influential. Central to his music is a concern with black culture and history. His use of language, imagery and the Rastafarian philosophy of his songs have helped to create a vocabulary for two generations of musicians.

With a name taken from Kenyan independence leader Jomo Kenyatta, Burning Spear was originally a vocal trio comprising Rodney, Rupert Willington (bass), and Delroy Hines (tenor). Their first records (including 'Door Peeper', 1969) were produced by **Coxsone Dodd** and the first hits came in 1972 with 'Joe Frazier (He Prayed)'. In 1974 they signed with Jack Ruby's Ocho Rios productions. Their first records were 'Marcus Garvey' and 'Slavery Days', both huge local hits. With Rodney's spellbinding voice over steady bass and drums and the insistent, repeated question, 'Do you remember the days of slavery?', the *Marcus Garvey* album also sold well in Britain on Island. *Garvey's Ghost*, a dub version featuring Robbie Shakespeare (of **Sly and Robbie**), appeared in 1976, one of the first instrumental dub albums to be released outside Jamaica. In the same year Willington and Hines left, leaving Rodney to continue as a solo artist. He maintained a stream of albums on Island, including the mystical *Man in the Hills* (1977) and *Harder Than the Rest* (1979), a superior greatest hits collection. Later albums included the EMI-distributed *Hail H.I.M.* (1980) and *Farover* (1982), which was recorded at Rita Marley's Tuff Gong studio and included his Jamaican hit, 'Education'. A 1977 live album was made at London's Rainbow Theatre, where he was backed by **Aswad**.

By 1985 his records were distributed in Britain by Greensleeves, with *Revolution* (1985) and *People of the World* (1986) maintaining a high standard, with what one critic called Rodney's 'mantra-like vocal web' accompanied by the Rass Brass horns. In 1988 he recorded the slight *Mistress Music* (Slash), on which he was backed by rock musicians. His later Island albums *Mek We Dweet* (1990) and *Jah Kingdom* (1991) were more rewarding. *The World Should Know* was issued in 1993.

HENRY BURR
b. Harry H. McClaskey, 15 January 1882, St Stephen, New Brunswick, Canada, d. 6 April 1941, Chicago, Illinois, USA

Known as 'The Dean of the Ballad Singers', Burr, with **Al Jolson** and **Billy Murray**, was one of the most successful recording acts of the first quarter of the twentieth century.

He made his stage début as a boy soprano in 1898. Discovered by Giuseppe Companari, a former baritone with the Metropolitan Opera, Burr travelled to New York to study voice and sang as a church soloist. When he began recording popular songs in the days of cylinders, like many classically trained singers he believed it was beneath his dignity, so he took the pseudonym Burr (though he later reverted to his real name for selected Columbia and Pathe recordings). His recording career is complicated because he was both so prolific – reportedly, he made more than 12,000 recordings – and recorded for so many companies. His first major hit was 'Come Down, Ma Ev'ning Star' (1903) on Columbia. At the same time, he was recording as Irving Gillette for Edison – and under other pseudonyms for other labels, including Zon-O-Phone, Indestructible, Majestic and Imperial. He first recorded one of the songs most associated with him, 'In the Shade of the Old Apple Tree' (1905), as Gillette.

A soft-voiced tenor, Burr mixed sentimental offerings ('There's a Little Lane Without a Turning [On the Way to Home Sweet Home]', Victor, 1914, and 'M-O-T-H-E-R [A Word That Means the World to Me]', 1916), patriotic songs ('Good-Bye, Good Luck, God Bless You', 1916, and 'Just a Baby's Prayer at Twilight'*, 1918), and show songs. Among these were 'I Wonder Who's Kissing Her Now' (Columbia, 1909) and **Irving Berlin**'s 'What'll I Do' (1924).

As well as recording numerous duets (with Elizabeth Spencer, **Ada Jones** and Helen Clark, among others), Burr was a longstanding member of the Peerless Quartet which, with Billy Murray's American Quartet, was the most successful recording group of the early period. Formed in 1904 as the Columbia Male Quartet (and named after their record company), the group comprised Burr, Albert Campbell, Steve Porter and Tom Daniels, who was replaced by Frank Stanley in 1906 when they took the name Peerless. Later **Arthur Collins** replaced Porter and after Stanley's death in 1910, John Meyer joined the group and Burr took over lead vocals. All the group members recorded prolifically as solo artists. The group's first success was the barber-shop quartet classic 'Sweet Adeline' (1904), first introduced a year earlier by the Empire City Quartet and an even bigger hit for the Hayden Quartet (Victor, 1904) – the first vocal group to record extensively.

Other successes of the Peerless Quartet included 'Let Me Call You Sweetheart' (1911), 'My Bird of Paradise' (1915) and **George M. Cohan**'s 'Over There' (1917), one of the many patriotic songs they recorded in the course of the First World War. After the war their hits declined and in 1928 the group, which then consisted of Burr and three lesser known singers, formally broke up. While Stanley, undoubtedly the most popular bass of his day, was a member of the Peerless

Quartet, Burr recorded several successful duets with him, including an early version of **Nora Bayes**' 'Shine on Harvest Moon' (Indestructible, 1909). However, though Burr frequently partnered so many of the popular singers of the day, he only made one recording with Billy Murray and that late in their careers, 'I Wonder Where My Baby Is Tonight?' (Victor, 1926).

On their tours, the Peerless Quartet were often joined by Murray, pianist Frank Banta, saxophonist Rudy Wiedoeft and monologue specialist Monroe Silver (who after **Joe Hayman** was the most prolific recorder of the famous 'Cohen on the Telephone' comic sketches). The troupe was known as the Eight Popular Victor Artists (though the members recorded for other labels throughout their careers). In 1921 Burr's record sales started to falter and he began to perform on radio. But following the rise in popularity of dance music, Burr's nostalgic ballads increasingly seemed old-fashioned and after briefly recording first with **Art Landry** ('Sleepy Time Gal', Victor, 1925) and then Roger Wolfe Kahn ('Cross Your Heart', Victor, 1926), he retired in the early thirties. His death came after a long illness.

KENNY BURRELL
b. *Kenneth Earl Burrell, 31 July 1931, Detroit, Michigan, USA*

Influenced by **Charlie Christian**, Burrell was a prolific jazz guitarist. He recorded notably with **Gil Evans** and **Duke Ellington**.

From a musical family, Burrell learned guitar at the age of twelve and first recorded in 1951 with **Dizzy Gillespie** for Savoy. He learned classical guitar and played in small jazz groups before graduating from Wayne State University in 1955. He next briefly deputized for Herb Ellis in **Oscar Peterson**'s trio before moving to New York in 1956.

From the late fifties he was signed to the Blue Note label, where he played with organist **Jimmy Smith** on funky blues outings like *Back at the Chicken Shack* (1963) and *Midnight Blue*. When the label was re-launched in 1985, Burrell played at the reunion concert, audio and video recordings of which were later released.

A flexible accompanist, Burrell was in demand for a wide range of sessions in New York during the sixties. He recorded with **John Coltrane** for Prestige, vibes-player Terry Gibbs for Impulse (*Take It from Me*) and with Gil Evans on *Guitar Forms* (Verve), which included 'Greensleeves' and **George Gershwin**'s 'Prelude No. 2'.

Burrell continued to record frequently both as a sideman and as leader of his own small groups. Among later highlights of his career were *Ellington Is Forever* (Fantasy), a thoughtful tribute featuring

Jimmy Smith and Thad Jones; a 1972 jam with **B. B. King** at the Newport/New York Jazz Festival; and a duet album for the new Blue Note label with **Grover Washington Jnr** (*Togetherings*, 1985). Later albums include *Generations* (1987) and *Recapitulation* (1989). In 1994 he recorded *The Master* with Jimmy Smith.

GARY BURTON
b. *23 January 1943, Anderson, Indiana, USA*

A virtuoso performer on the vibraphone, Burton was a noted jazz bandleader, composer and teacher.

With a classically based training at the Berklee College of Music, Burton initially attracted attention because of his innovatory technique. He used four mallets instead of the customary two and he was able to 'bend' notes on the instrument.

He first recorded under his own name for Victor in 1961 and in 1963 as a member of George Shearing's quintet. His most important early collaboration was with **Stan Getz** for Verve in 1964, the year Shearing recorded an album of Burton's compositions, *Out of the Wood*. He formed his own band with guitarist **Larry Coryell** three years later, cutting a series of exploratory albums which drew on rock, country music and soul, as well as jazz. Among the RCA albums recorded at this time were *Lofty Fake Anagram* (1967), *Tennessee Firebird*, produced in Nashville by **Chet Atkins**, and an *In Concert* record which included a version of **Bob Dylan**'s 'I Want You'. The Burton Quartet played frequently at rock festivals in the underground era and Burton himself played on the first album by folk-rock artist **Tim Hardin**.

Moving to Atlantic, he made the country-tinged *Throb* with Sea Train violinist Richard Greene, *Paris Encounter* (1969) with veteran jazz violinist **Stephane Grappelli** and *Good Vibes* with a full line-up of R&B session players. Burton's best work of this period came on the **Carla Bley** composition *A Genuine Tong Funeral* (RCA, 1967), which also featured Gato Barbieri.

As the jazz-rock fashion receded, Burton seemed to search for his bearings. He found them in collaboration with German producer Manfred Eicher and his ECM label. His work for the label – beginning in 1973 with *Crystal Silence*, a duet with **Chick Corea** – re-emphasized his sense of form and penchant for a kind of 'chamber jazz'. The pair made further records together in 1979 and 1982.

Other associates in his ECM recordings included Steve Swallow, the bassist from the Burton Quartet, the young **Pat Metheny**, who partnered him on *Reunion* (1989), and composer/arranger Mike Gibbs, who conducted on *7 Songs for Quartet and Chamber Orchestra*. Burton continued to tour and make festival appearances, often including in his band students from Berklee, where he had returned to teach. His most recent albums for GRP include *Times Like These* (1988), *Right Time Right Place* (with Paul Bley, 1991), *Six Pack* (1992), on which Burton plays with six guitarists including **B. B. King** and Jim Hall, and a 1994 collaboration with singer Rebecca Parris.

JAMES BURTON
b. 21 August 1939, Shreveport, Louisiana, USA

Master of the Telecaster, Burton was one of the most admired guitarists of the fifties. Moreover, through his recordings with **Ricky Nelson** and later session work on the West Coast in the sixties and seventies he kept alive the hard-edged rockabilly style of guitar-playing. As such he was a key influence on many of the country-rock groups that appeared after the **Byrds**, the new 'Bakersfield sound' of **Buck Owens** and **Merle Haggard**, and the spare, surging sound of **Creedence Clearwater Revival**.

Burton's early influences were country guitarists but his first recording with Dale Hawkins (*b. 22 August 1938, Goldmine, Louisiana*), which produced the hit 'Suzie Q' (Checker) in 1957, was more notable for the growling, blues-styled solo he played. He also played with Bob Luman (*b. 5 April 1937, Nacogdoches, Texas, d. 27 December 1978, Nashville, Tennessee*), a country singer briefly turned rock'n'roller under the influence of **Elvis Presley**, before joining Rick Nelson's recording and touring band in 1958 with bassist James Kirkland. It was with Nelson on 'Believe What You Say', 'My Babe', 'Shirley Lee', and slower songs such as 'Hello Mary Lou' and 'Never Be Anyone Else but You', that Burton perfected his 'chickin' picking' style of playing in which he played single string runs with a staccato, almost percussive, effect. In 1964 Burton quit Nelson for session work, most notably with Haggard, providing support on 'The Bottle Let Me Down' and 'Swinging Doors' (both 1966), which were among the first country records to admit rockabilly as a positive influence. That same year he recorded *Corn Pickin' and Slick Slidin'* (Capitol) with steel guitarist Ralph Mooney.

In 1969, with pianist Glen D. Hardin, Burton joined Elvis Presley for some eight years, touring and recording with him, and in 1971 he cut a mediocre solo album, *The Guitar Sounds of James Burton* (A&M). More interestingly, Burton and Hardin formed the basis of the backing band for **Gram Parsons**' *Grievous Angel* (1972) and *GP* (1973), providing Parsons with a spare 'Bakersfield' country sound for his eerie songs of desperate hope and retribution. After Parsons' death in 1974, Burton and Hardin formed the Hot Band to back **Emmylou Harris** for a series of successful tours and albums, before both retreated to session work. In the eighties and nineties

Burton recorded with artists as diverse as **John Denver**, **Jerry Lee Lewis** and **Elvis Costello**.

BUSH
Robin Goodridge, b. 10 September 1966, Crawley, Sussex, England; Dave Parsons, b. 2 July 1965, Uxbridge; Nigel Pulsford, b. 11 April 1964, Newport, Wales; Gavin Rossdale, b. 30 October 1967, London

British grunge-rock band Bush amassed a huge following across America despite failing to find an audience in their homeland.

Formed in London in 1992, Bush signed to US indie label Trauma after failing to generate record company interest at home. Comprising singer-songwriter Rossdale, guitarist Pulsford, bassist Parsons and drummer Goodridge, their début album *Sixteen Stone* (1994) became a surprise hit with the success of lead-off single 'Everything Zen', heavily reminiscent of **Nirvana** with its raw guitars and extreme dynamics. The band had a US Number One with 'Glycerine' and sales of the album rose to seven million, helped by solid touring and the gimmicky enhanced CD *Little Things*, which included unreleased tracks and a Bush video game.

Bush worked with Steve Albini, producer of Nirvana's *In Utero*, on their second album, *Razorblade Suitcase* (1996)*, which saw them begin to develop their British fanbase beyond mere cult status. The album entered the US charts at Number One and spawned 'Swallowed', a hit single on both sides of the Atlantic and the most accessible track on an otherwise jagged, more complex-sounding record than its predecessor.

The album was followed by a collection of remixes by the likes of Tricky and **Goldie** entitled *Deconstructed* (1997), before finally in 1999 the much-delayed *The Science of Things*, with regular producers Clive Langer and Alan Winstanley in control, was released.

KATE BUSH
b. Catherine Bush, 30 July 1958, Welling, England

Bush was among the most distinctive British singer-songwriters to emerge in the wake of punk rock. Often idiosyncratic but rarely merely indulgent, her more recent albums have incorporated a wide range of ethnic sounds from Australasia, Europe and Africa.

From a middle-class background – her father was a doctor – she studied violin and piano as a child. Bush briefly led a pub band playing cover-versions, but it was her songwriting that attracted the attention of **Pink Floyd**'s David Gilmour. On his recommendation, she was signed by EMI Records.

Bush's first album, *The Kick Inside*, contained songs written over the previous three years and included 'Wuthering Heights' (EMI, 1978), the single inspired by Emily Brontë's classic novel. Produced by Andrew

Powell, accompanied by a balletic video and with Bush's voice swooping dramatically through four octaves, 'Wuthering Heights' reached No. 1 in Britain, Australia and several European countries.

Her next singles, the romantic ballad 'The Man with the Child in His Eyes' and 'Wow' (from the lesser *Lionheart*, 1978), were also big hits. In rock terms, Bush's stage act was no less original than her songs, involving mime and ballet whose style was influenced by Lindsay Kemp, a one-time associate of **David Bowie**. A live EP recorded on her début tour was a British hit in 1979.

In the eighties Bush prepared her albums meticulously, releasing them at the rate of one every two years. Each was greeted by a remarkable unanimity between critics and audiences, except in America, where only the 1985 single 'Running up That Hill (A Deal with God)' was a hit. *Never for Ever* (1980) contained the exuberant 'Babooshka' and unlikely guest artists in animal impressionist Percy Edwards and television personality Rolf Harris, whose own biggest hits were the Christmas record 'Two Little Boys' (1969) and a bizarre version of **Led Zeppelin**'s 'Stairway to Heaven' (1993). Bush also worked with **Peter Gabriel** on his 1980 solo album.

The Dreaming (1983) and the highly successful *Hounds of Love* (1985) were full of many-faceted compositions. The latter included orchestral arrangements by Michael Kamen and a 25-minute suite inspired by Celtic mythology and featured Bush's brother and collaborator Paddy on dijeridu, balalaika and fujare. In 1986 she recorded the original version of 'Don't Give Up' with the song's author Peter Gabriel and the following year a newly recorded Bush track, 'This Woman's Work', was included in the film *She's Having a Baby*.

The traditional music element of her music was further intensified on *The Sensual World* (1989), on which she was supported by the Bulgarian *a cappella* folk troupe Trio Bulgarka and the uillean pipes of Davy Spillane. The album included a literary adaptation of Molly Bloom's soliloquy from James Joyce's *Ulysses*.

In 1991 Bush contributed to **Roy Harper**'s album *Once* and sang 'Rocket Man' on *Two Rooms*, the tribute album to **Elton John** and Bernie Taupin. Her long-awaited seventh studio album, *The Red Shoes*, appeared in 1993. This time Bush turned to the cinema for inspiration, taking the album's title from Michael Powell's classic film about the emotional cost of artistic endeavour. The instruments used on *The Red Shoes* included the valiha, a Madagascan harp, while **Prince** remixed one track.

Although Bush has not toured since 1979, she has taken a creative role in the production of videos of her music. The dramatic scenario for 'Babooshka', 'Cloudbusting' (1985), which featured the actor Donald Sutherland, and the self-directed *Experiment IV* (1986) all appeared on the chart-topping video collection *The Whole Story* in 1987.

Inactive for most of the nineties, Bush was the subject of the tribute album *I Wanna Be Kate* (1998).

HENRY BUSSE
b. 19 May 1895, Magdeburg, Germany, d. 23 April 1955, Memphis, Tennessee, USA

As a trumpeter and writer Busse was one of the architects of the sweet jazz sound associated with **Paul Whiteman**, with whom Busse played from 1918 to 1928.

Busse emigrated to America in 1916, where he joined a cinema pit orchestra in New York. He formed a quintet before joining Whiteman in San Francisco in 1918. When the Whiteman orchestra was signed by Victor in 1920, its first recording (and first hit) was Busse's composition 'Wang Wang Blues' (written with fellow Whiteman sidemen, Gus Mueller and Buster Johnson). That recording was in the style, if not the spirit, of the **Original Dixieland Jazz Band**, but by the time of 'Hot Lips' (written with Henry Lange and Lou Davis in 1922 and later used by Busse as his own theme song), the Whiteman sound was far more formal. Busse's trumpet solo on 'When Day Is Done' (1927) was even sweeter.

In 1928 Busse left Whiteman to form his own band which recorded for Decca and toured throughout the thirties. Less symphonic in inclination than Whiteman, Busse's band featured his smooth, muted trumpet – he was among the first trumpeters to use a mute extensively – set against bright dance rhythms. He appeared as himself with Whiteman in *Rhapsody in Blue* (1945), a pedestrian film biography of **George Gershwin**, and in the minor musical *Lady, Let's Dance* (1944) before retiring in the late forties.

JERRY BUTLER
b. 8 December 1939, Sunflower, Mississippi, USA

One of soul music's most accomplished singers, Butler's greatest success came in the fifties and sixties with the **Impressions** and as a solo artist. He later collaborated with **Gamble and Huff** and formed a pioneering Writers' Workshop to nurture young talent. During the eighties the 'cool' sound of his rich, vibrant baritone was out of fashion and Butler concentrated on business and political careers.

He began singing with gospel choirs in Chicago before forming the Impressions with **Curtis Mayfield**. Their 'For Your Precious Love' (Falcon, 1958), which fused doo-wop and the emerging soul style, reached the Top Ten and launched Butler as a solo singer with Vee-Jay. He subsequently enjoyed a string of pop and R&B hits which included Mayfield's 'He Will Break

Your Heart' (1960); 'I'm a Telling You' (1961); 'Moon River' (1961), the **Henry Mancini–Johnny Mercer** song which was a British hit for Danny Williams; **Burt Bacharach**'s and Hal David's 'Make It Easy on Yourself' (1962), a 1965 British No. 1 for the **Walker Brothers**; 'Need to Belong'; and 'Let It Be Me' (1964), the first of many duets with **Betty Everett**.

When Vee-Jay collapsed in 1966, Butler moved to Mercury, Chicago's biggest label. After several attempts to find a direction for Butler's subtle, understated approach, the company paired him with Gamble and Huff. The string and vibraphone arrangements by **Thom Bell** and Bobby Martin on *The Ice Man Cometh* and *Ice on Ice* (1968) brought a series of pop hits. They included 'Never Gonna Give You Up', 'Hey Western Union Man' (1968), 'Only the Strong Survive'* and 'Moody Woman' (1969).

Perhaps inspired by the teamwork of Gamble-Huff's nucleus of writers and arrangers, Butler formed his Chicago-based Writers' Workshop, financed by Chappell Music. The enterprise launched such composers and performers as Charles Jackson, Marvin Yancey, Terry Callier and Brenda Eager, who duetted with Butler on the 1972 million-seller 'Ain't Understanding Mellow'.

In 1975 **Berry Gordy** brought Butler to Motown where he recorded the Top Ten soul hit 'I Wanna Do It to You' and the impressive concept album *Suite for the Single Girl* (1977), and a series of duets with Thelma Houston. A reunion with Gamble and Huff produced the uneven albums *Nothing Says I Love You Like I Love You* (Philadelphia International, 1979) and *The Best Love* (1980). By now, the cool style of 'The Ice Man' seemed anachronistic and his later recordings were restricted to a guest spot on *Touch the Feeling* (1982) by the **Crusaders**' Stix Hooper and *Ice'n'Hot*, an album on Butler's own Fountain label.

During the eighties he undertook a twenty-fifth anniversary tour with the Impressions, made radio and TV commercials, ran a beer distribution company and won political office in Chicago in 1986. He later signed to Ichiban and made occasional appearances in the nineties with the re-formed Impressions.

PAUL BUTTERFIELD

b. 17 December 1942, Chicago, Illinois, USA, d. 3 May 1987, Chicago

Leader of America's most important white blues band of the sixties, Butterfield's later excursions into Eastern music and blue-eyed soul made less impact.

As the first song on the epochal *Paul Butterfield Blues Band* (Elektra, 1965) put it, he was 'Born in Chicago', the son of a lawyer. He first heard the blues on the radio and learned to play harmonica and to sing from watching and later sitting in with the leading blues artists of the time. He later recorded with **Muddy Waters** on *Fathers and Sons* (Chess, 1969).

Formed in 1963 while Butterfield and guitarist Elvin Bishop were at the University of Chicago, his first band included **Howlin' Wolf**'s former rhythm section, Sam Lay (drums) and Jerome Arnold (bass), plus guitarist Smokey Smothers. Previously unreleased tracks by this line-up issued on Red Lightnin' in 1972 include a spirited version of the Waters classic 'Got My Mojo Workin''. Keyboards-player Mark Nataflin and young guitarist **Mike Bloomfield** were added after Smothers' departure. The band was recommended to producer Paul Rothchild, who signed them to Elektra and put two Butterfield tracks on an Elektra sampler, *What's Shakin'* (1965), which also featured **Tom Rush** and **Al Kooper**. He next spent long days in the studio with the group, experimenting with ways of recording this new amplified blues. Rothchild was also instrumental in Butterfield's signing a management deal with **Bob Dylan**'s manager Albert Grossman.

The group's début album was state-of-the-art contemporary Chicago blues, which explains why Butterfield was never very successful in Britain, where the blues revival was rooted in styles of a decade or more earlier. Underpinned by an authentic rhythm section that swung, Butterfield proved himself a true disciple of **Little Walter**, while Bishop and Bloomfield's work repaid their study of **B. B. King** and **Buddy Guy**.

Though sales were not spectacular, the album catapulted the band to fame in the blues and folk communities. In 1965 they were booked into the Newport Folk Festival, where the band, minus Butterfield, backed Dylan on his controversial electric début. The same year they played on a **Chuck Berry** recording session. In 1966 the band played in Britain, where Butterfield recorded with **John Mayall**, and released *East-West*, with its raga-like title track (complete with 'guitar hero' solos from Bishop and Bloomfield) and covers of **Cannonball Adderley**'s 'Work Song' and **Lee Dorsey**'s 'Get Out My Life Woman'.

That album and Bloomfield's departure shortly afterwards signalled the end of Butterfield's straight blues orientation and subsequent albums found him adding horns and exploring the varieties of R&B and soul, even using veteran deep soul composer-producer **Jerry Ragavoy** for *Keep on Moving* (1969). By this time all of the original members, apart from Butterfield himself, had left. The new lead guitarist was Buzzy Feiten.

Bishop (*b. 21 October 1942, Tulsa, Oklahoma*) formed his own band and recorded several albums for Columbia and Capricorn, having a Top Ten hit with 'Fooled Around and Fell in Love'* (Capricorn, 1976). The lead singer, Mickey Thomas, went on to join the **Jefferson Airplane** conglomeration.

Todd Rundgren, house producer at Grossman's Bearsville label, supervised a 1971 live album, and when the Blues Band disbanded in 1972, Butterfield moved to Woodstock, home of Bearsville. There he played on a number of albums (by Geoff and **Maria Muldaur**, **Jesse Winchester** and **Bonnie Raitt**) and formed a new band, Better Days, including New Orleans singer Ronnie Barron, guitarist Amos Garrett and **Bobby Charles**. Better Days made two albums in 1973–4 in the more laid-back style associated with Charles. Butterfield cut a further solo album, *Put It in Your Ear* (Bearsville, 1976), with veteran R&B producer **Henry Glover**. Among the many musicians on those sessions was **The Band**'s Levon Helm and Butterfield (who had performed at the *Last Waltz* concert) went on to tour with both Helm's RCO Band and with Rick Danko in the Danko–Butterfield Band.

He resumed his own recording career with *North-South* (Bearsville, 1981), produced in Memphis by **Willie Mitchell**, but serious illness now interrupted Butterfield's work and he made only one more album, *The Legendary Paul Butterfield Rides Again* (Amherst, 1986). After his death his classic albums were reissued by Rhino.

BUZZCOCKS
Pete Shelley, b. Peter McNeish, 17 April 1955; Howard Devoto, b. Howard Trafford (replaced by Garth Smith, replaced by Steve Garvey); Steve Diggle; John Maher

One of the leading British punk groups of the late seventies, the Buzzcocks influenced a later generation of US alternative rock groups and later successfully reformed in the early nineties.

From Manchester, the Buzzcocks were inspired to start playing by the example of the **Sex Pistols**. Devoto, a philosophy student, formed the band with Shelley, a former member of local group Jets of Air. The original line-up was completed by guitarist and bass-player Diggle and drummer Maher. After performing with the Pistols, the group issued the Martin Hannett-produced EP *Spiral Scratch* (1977) on their own New Hormones label.

Devoto left soon afterwards to form Magazine with guitarist John McGeogh (*b. 28 May 1955, Greenock, Scotland*). The group's major albums were *Real Life* (Virgin, 1978) and *Correct Use of Soap* (1980). In contrast to the jagged speed of punk, from *Secondhand Daylight* (1979) onwards Magazine offered eerie, haunting sounds set against Devoto's increasingly bizarre lyrics. The result was critical praise but few sales and in 1981 the band broke up. Before that McGeogh, who had regularly appeared with other groups, notably Visage, became a full-time member of **Siouxsie and the Banshees**. In 1983 Devoto began a brief solo recording career and in 1988 he recorded as

Luxuria. Devoto was replaced in the Buzzcocks by bass-player Smith. In turn, Smith was expelled from the band in 1978.

Now signed to United Artists, the Buzzcocks issued 'Orgasm Addict' as their first single. This was followed in 1978 by two Top Twenty albums in the UK, *Another Music in a Different Kitchen* and *Love Bites*. The Buzzcocks' most successful single was 'Ever Fallen in Love (With Someone You Shouldn't Have)' which epitomized the group's trademark twin buzz-saw guitar sound and memorable melodies. The song was revived in 1987 by **Fine Young Cannibals**.

This proved to be the peak of the Buzzcocks' popularity. After the release of *A Different Kind of Tension* (1979), which contained one of Shelley's best songs, 'You Say You Don't Love Me', the group issued only one more single and played a few live shows before splitting up in 1981. Shelley made three solo albums, *Homosapien* (1981), *XL1* (1983) and *Heaven and Sea* (1986). Diggle formed Flag of Convenience, later abbreviated to FOC. On a tour of Europe, Diggle found renewed interest in the Buzzcocks, and in the US grunge bands like **Nirvana** and alternative group Sugar were citing the group as a key influence. EMI issued *Product* (1989), a five-album box set of the group's work which included previously unissued live tracks.

In 1989 Maher and Garvey performed again with Diggle and Shelley. The reunited band played the Reading Festival in 1990 and recorded an EP, *Alive Tonight*. They toured the US before Maher and Garvey returned to their day-jobs. Shelley and Diggle reformed the band with bassist Tony Arber and drummer Phil Barker. An album recorded with **Bill Laswell** as producer remained unreleased but in 1993 Caroline Records issued *Trade Test Transmissions*. It showed extensive continuity with the group sound of over a decade earlier. It was followed by the retrospective box set *Product* (1995), the live album *French* (1996) and the superior studio outing *All Set* (1997).

MAX BYGRAVES
b. Walter Bygraves, 16 October 1922, London, England

A British all-round entertainer, Bygraves moved from the music hall to radio and then television through the skilful use of a jaunty persona that harked back to the good old days. The epitome of this was his twenty-strong series of singalong albums, commencing with *Singalongamax* (1971), in which he reprised, in medley form, past hits of popular music at a time when rock had become the mainstream music of the day.

While in the RAF Bygraves became known as Max after impersonating Max Miller in an amateur show. On his demob he made his début as a cockney comic on the music hall circuit, at one time touring with **Judy Garland**. In 1950 he joined the radio show *Educating*

Archie (whose unlikely star was a ventriloquist's dummy) and after singing on the show turned to recording with the comic 'Big 'Ead' (HMV). His first hit was 'Cowpuncher's Cantata' (1952), a medley of songs associated with **Frankie Laine**, including 'Mule Train' and 'Cry of the Wild Goose'. But the most important of his early recordings were the novelty songs 'Gilly Gilly Ossenfeffer Katzenellen Bogen By the Sea' (1954) and particularly 'You're a Pink Toothbrush', which was among the most requested records on the long-running *Children's Favourites* radio request programme that, even more than the charts, was the mark of a record's success in the immediate pre-rock'n'roll years. Other hits of this period included 'Meet Me on the Corner' (1955) and the film song 'The Ballad of Davy Crockett' (1956), an American hit for **Tennessee Ernie Ford** and the film's star, Fess Parker.

In 1956 Bygraves had a minor hit with 'Out of Town', specially written for his film *Charley Moon* by Leslie Bricusse (later the regular writing partner of **Anthony Newley**), which led to Bricusse tailoring 'A Good Idea Son' for Bygraves. His last major hit of the fifties was the self-penned 'You Need Hands' (1958). After 'Fings Ain't What They Used to Be' (1960) his hits declined and Bygraves concentrated on television. His recording career was revived by *Singalongamax* (Pye) whose nostalgic medleys of music hall and Broadway standards initiated a series of albums stretching to 1988 (*Singalongawaryears*) and even briefly was the name of his television series in the seventies. In the wake of that album he returned to the pop charts with an anodyne remake of 'Deck of Cards' (1973), previously a hit for **Phil Harris** (1984) and Wink Martindale (Dot, 1959). In 1976 he published his autobiography, taking for his title his catchphrase *I Wanna Tell You a Story*, and in 1983 became host of the game show *Family Fortunes*. Later recordings included *The Singalong Collection* (1987) and *Tulips from Amsterdam* (Arista, 1990).

THE BYRDS

Roger McGuinn, b. Jim McGuinn, 13 July 1942, Chicago, Illinois, USA; Chris Hillman, b. 4 December 1942, Los Angeles, California; Gene Clark, b. 17 November 1941, Tipton, Missouri, d. 24 May 1991, Sherman Oaks, California; David Crosby, b. David Van Cortland, 14 August 1941, Los Angeles; Michael Clarke, b. 3 June 1943, New York, d. 19 December 1993, Treasure Island, Florida

In the sixties the Byrds played a central role in the creation of both folk-rock and country-rock and were one of the first groups to experiment with studio technology. Their greatest period of commercial success, which produced two million-sellers (**Bob Dylan**'s 'Mr Tambourine Man', 1965, and 'Turn! Turn! Turn!', 1966) reflected their fusion of the wide-ranging repertoire of the folk revival with the beat-group approach of **The Beatles** into what became known as folk-rock. Subsequently never as commercially successful, the mastery of the studio they demonstrated on *Younger Than Yesterday* (1967) and *Notorious Byrd Brothers* (1968) and on the pioneering country-rock album *Sweetheart of the Rodeo* (1968) profoundly influenced later groups. The group's sound has influenced every subsequent generation of musicians and such artists as **Tom Petty** and **R.E.M.** have mined their repertoire and style. After the Byrds' demise, the group members made solo recordings and formed other groups (often with former Byrds) with varying degrees of critical and commercial success. With the possible exception of **Gram Parsons**' solo work, none of these was as influential as the group's key recordings of the mid-sixties.

In the early sixties McGuinn, Crosby and Clark worked within the commercial sector of the folk revival. McGuinn was a backing musician with the **Limeliters** and the Chad Mitchell Trio and in 1962 joined **Bobby Darin** when Darin introduced a folk spot in his live appearances. Crosby had been a **Les Baxter** Balladeer and Clark a member of the New Christy Minstrels before both turned to the coffeehouse circuit. In 1964, like other ex-folkies, they turned to beat music and formed the Jet Set. Augmented by Hillman, who had led a bluegrass group, the Hillmen, in the Los Angeles area, and drummer Clarke, the group became the Beefeaters and released the Beatles-influenced 'Please Let Me Love You' (Elektra, 1964), before signing with Columbia for the groundbreaking 'Mr Tambourine Man'.

Of the group's instruments, only McGuinn's twelve-string Rickenbacker was heard on the chart-topping 'Mr Tambourine Man'. Session musicians, including **Leon Russell**, provided the support to McGuinn's, Hillman's and Crosby's vocals. Yet, despite this start to their career (and the productive relationship with Dylan, whose material they regularly recorded in the course of their career), the Byrds were to function very much as a self-contained group. Like The Beatles, whose career they both paralleled and anticipated, the Byrds' strengths (and limitations) were those of a group, with the various members competing for control of the group sound and with each new album marking a cohesive new stage of development. Just as The Beatles' first albums reflected their influences (rock'n'roll and R&B) so *Mr Tambourine Man* (1965) and *Turn! Turn! Turn!* (1966), the title track of which – a biblical passage set to music by **Pete Seeger** – was a No. 1, demonstrated the roots of the Byrds' style. As well as the melancholic love songs of Clark ('It Won't Be Wrong', 'Set You Free This Time'), the albums included Dylan songs ('Lay Down

Your Weary Tune', 'All I Really Want to Do') and songs of the folk revival ('Satisfied Mind', 'The Bells of Rhymney'), plus crafted pop songs, new (**Jackie DeShannon**'s 'Don't Doubt Yourself') and old (**Vera Lynn**'s 'We'll Meet Again', **Stephen Foster**'s 'Oh! Susannah'). While the sound of the singles was of soaring harmonies and McGuinn's twelve-string, the albums were more complex. The stylization of much of the material suggested both an ironic weariness, which contrasted strongly with the music of their contemporaries, and a striving for formal perfection at the expense of a sense of excitement.

Following the departure of Clark – the group's major songwriter whose plaintive lead vocals had been a cornerstone of the Byrds' sound – for an erratic solo career, the group made *Fifth Dimension* (1966) and the classic *Younger Than Yesterday* (1967) as a foursome. Both were radically different in content – the albums included a series of songs ('Mr Spaceman', '5 D', 'C. T. A. 102') that briefly gave credence to the notion of 'space rock' – and influences – 'Eight Miles High', the group's last Top Twenty hit and one of the first rock songs to be banned for its drugs allusions, was a precursor of later psychedelic music and clearly influenced by **John Coltrane**. Both albums saw Crosby ('Everybody's Been Burned', 'Renaissance Fair') and Hillman ('Thoughts and Words', 'Time Between') establish themselves as writers and the group extend their innovatory, formal approach to control of the studio. However, while there were many differences from the sound of the earlier Byrds, there were also stylistic similarities, notably of tone, as evidenced in the ironic account of stardom, 'So You Want to Be a Rock'n'Roll Star'.

Notorious Byrd Brothers (1968), made after Crosby left to form **Crosby, Stills and Nash**, was one of the first and best high-technology studio albums. A homage to limiters and phasers, the album was a seamless web of pop songs (**Carole King**'s 'Goin' Back', 'Wasn't Born to Follow', featured in the film *Easy Rider*) and social attitudes ('Draft Morning', 'Change Is Now') which perfectly caught the 'right-on' stereo-headphone-listening habits of the times.

With only Hillman and McGuinn of the original members left, the Byrds, with the addition of Gram Parsons, then embarked on what was to be their most influential album, *Sweetheart of the Rodeo* (1968). It included songs by Dylan ('Nothing Was Delivered'), the **Louvin Brothers** ('The Christian Life'), **Woody Guthrie** ('Pretty Boy Floyd'), **William Bell** ('You Don't Miss Your Water'), **Merle Haggard** ('Life in Prison'), and Parsons' originals ('Hickory Wind'). Performed in a typically stylized manner, the album reintroduced to the rock mainstream a variety of regional musics that had been largely lost in the rock'n'roll revolution and virtually singlehandedly

created the country-rock genre that dominated much of American rock in subsequent years through the work of the **Eagles** and others.

In the wake of the departure of first Parsons and then Hillman (who together formed the Flying Burritto Brothers, which launched Parsons' later brief, but important, solo career), the Byrds became a vehicle for McGuinn. With an ever-changing line-up, whose most important members were former bluegrass instrumentalist Clarence White (who had played on *Sweetheart of the Rodeo*) and Skip Battin (who as part of Skip and Flip had chart success with the **Everly Brothers**-styled 'It Was I' and 'Cherry Pie', Brent, 1959, 1960 respectively), McGuinn released Byrds records for some five years with varying degrees of success. The most important albums of this period included *The Ballad of East Rider* (1969) and *Untitled* (1970), which included 'Chestnut Mare', a British Top Twenty hit, and 'Just a Season'.

After *Further Along* (1972), McGuinn disbanded the group to re-form the original Byrds for *Byrds* (Asylum, 1973), a lacklustre outing that only served to highlight the past contributions of Clark. More impressive was Clark's own *Roadrunner* (A&M, 1972), which featured the Byrds in support on most of the tracks. Since leaving the group Clark had attempted his own synthesis of rock and (traditional) country music in a pair of impressive albums with former bluegrass musician Doug Dillard (*The Fantastic Expedition of Dillard and Clark, Through the Morning Through the Night*, A&M, 1969) with little commercial success. After that Clark made the powerful singer-songwriter albums *White Light* (1971) and the lesser *No Other* (1974).

Following the failure of the Byrds' reunion album, McGuinn embarked on an erratic solo career, which included *Roger McGuinn* (1973), the hard-rock *Cardiff Rose* (1976) and *Thunderbyrd* (1977), and toured with Dylan's 'Rolling Thunder Revue' of 1975. Meanwhile, Hillman had a brief spell in Manassas, the band formed by Steve Stills (formerly of **Buffalo Springfield** and Crosby, Stills and Nash) and made a pair of albums in conjunction with songwriter J. D. Souther and another Buffalo Springfield alumnus, Ritchie Furay. Even at their best (*Trouble in Paradise*, Elektra, 1975) the group were clearly influenced by the Eagles, whose smooth version of the Byrds' country-rock sound brought great success. He next cut the pleasant solo albums *Slippin' Away* (Asylum, 1976) and *Clear Sailin'* (1977) before regrouping with McGuinn and Clark to make the smooth-sounding *McGuinn, Hillman and Clark* (Capitol, 1979) and *City* (1980). When Clark once again opted out, McGuinn and Hillman cut an eponymous album (1980), before going their separate ways.

After working as a session musician Hillman cut solo albums for Sugar Hill before returning to a more muscular country sound with the Desert Rose Band.

The group's 1987 début album featured Herb Pedersen on guitar and vocals and Jay Dee Maness on pedal-steel guitar and included a superior reworking of Hillman's 'Time Between'. The Desert Rose Band had several country hits before Hillman disbanded the group in 1994. He subsequently formed another country rock group, Rice, Rice, Hillman and Pedersen, which recorded two albums for Rounder, including an eponymous one (1999), which as well as a number of Hillman originals included a fine reworking of the **Grateful Dead** song 'Friend of the Devil'. While Hillman's voice was a touch too light to be completely convincing, his and Pedersen's celebration of the Californian country tradition, *Bakersfield Bound* (Sugar Hill, 1995), perfectly caught the spare dynamics of the Bakersfield sound (as created by **Buck Owens**' lead guitarist Don Rich and steel guitarist Tom Brumley) on reworkings of 'Playboy' and 'Close Up the Honk Tonks', among others. Even more impressive was the bluegrass album *Out of the Woodwork* (Rounder, 1997). Less successful was *Like a Hurricane* (2000), which despite its title was far too relaxed an affair.

McGuinn briefly toured as a folk singer before recording the impressive *Back from Rio* (Arista, 1990), on which he was supported by **Elvis Costello** and **Tom Petty**, amongst others. He subsequently released the lesser *Live from Mars* (1996), which relied too heavily on reworkings of earlier material. In 1987 Gene Clark returned to his folk-revival roots with the superior *So Rebellious a Lover* (Demon) in partnership with Carla Olson. Clark's *Silhouetted in Light* (Demon, 1992) was a live recording from 1990, while *American Dreamer* (Raven 1992) was a well-researched retrospective of all stages of his career, issued following his death in 1991. Michael Clarke, who had toured with his own version of the Byrds since the late eighties and had won a court case over the right to use the name, died of liver failure in 1993.

The Byrds' own career was summed up in the well-documented boxed set *The Byrds* (1990), which included four new recordings by Crosby, Hillman and McGuinn. Among them was a version of **Bob Dylan**'s 'He Was a Friend of Mine'. It remains the definitive retrospective. Their later career was covered in *12 Dimensions, 1965–1972* (Columbia, 2000), which included remastered versions (and out-takes) of *Byrdmaniax, Farther Along* and *Untitled*, and the previously unreleased *Live at the Fillmore, February 1969*. While the unreleased material from *Untitled* was interesting, *Live at the Fillmore* reminded one of how ragged the group could be in live performance. Moreover, recorded just after the group had lost Parsons and Hillman, the song selection confirmed the fundamental importance of them to the group: over half of the sixteen tracks were ill-performed versions of songs associated with the pair.

DAVID BYRNE
b. 14 May 1952, Dumbarton, Scotland

The founder and main creative force in **Talking Heads**, Byrne pursued solo projects from the mid-eighties. In addition to composing film music he championed Brazilian traditional music and produced several albums of it.

His family emigrated from Scotland to North America when Byrne was two years of age. He took up the guitar, violin and accordion while at high school in Baltimore. He formed bands while at the Maryland Institute College of Art, one of which evolved into Talking Heads. The group's career lasted from 1975 to 1991.

Byrne began his solo musical career in tandem with Talking Heads. In 1979 he collaborated with **Brian Eno** on *My Life in the Bush of Ghosts* and in 1981 he composed music for the Twylla Tharp ballet *The Catherine Wheel*.

He produced albums by the **B-52s** and the British group Fun Boy Three before staging a solo multimedia show, *The Tourist Way of Knowledge*, at the New York Public Library in 1985. In the same year Byrne recorded *Music for the Knee Plays*, a set of pieces with spoken and sung words which he had composed for an experimental drama by Robert Wilson. He followed this with his first film, the quirky *True Stories* (1986). In 1989 Byrne, **Ryuichi Sakamoto** and Cong Su were awarded the best soundtrack Oscar for their score for the film *The Last Emperor*. Byrne also scored the films *Married to the Mob* (1988) and *The Forest* (1991).

In 1989 he compiled *Beleza Tropical*, the first of four volumes of Brazil Classics issued on his own Luaka Bop label. These contained music by current Brazilian composers and performers such as Gilberto Gil, Jorge Ben and Caetano Veloso as well as lesser known traditional music. Byrne also made a television documentary about Brazilian music and recorded *Rei Mo Mo* (1989), an uneven solo album of original Latin-styled songs. **Celia Cruz**, Willie Colon and Kirsty MacColl were among the guest musicians. *Uh-Oh* (1992) was more effective in fusing pop and funk with Latin and Caribbean rhythms. He toured the US and Europe with Brazilian singer Margareth Menezes and a big band made up of New York-based Latin musicians.

Byrne's third solo album of his own compositions was the quirky *David Byrne*, issued in 1994. An introspective collection, it included 'Buck Naked', an elegy for an AIDS victim, and 'A Self-Made Man'. He moved to soundtrack music with *Blue in the Face* (1995), and in the same year published a book of photographs, *Strange Rituals*. The solo album *Feelings* (1997) was poorly received.

C&C MUSIC FACTORY

Robert Clivilles, b. 1960, New York, USA; David Cole, b. 1962, New York, d. 24 January 1995, New York

Among the most effective dance remixers of the late 1980s, C&C Music Factory's work was characterized by David Cole's gospel-inflected keyboard playing and by the eclectic range of the material on which they worked. This included deep soul (**Chaka Khan**), Latin music and rock.

In the mid-1980s Cole recorded 'You Take My Breath Away', a synth-pop dance tune. The duo first worked together in New York clubs, where Cole added his keyboard skills to Clivilles' DJing. They soon began to remix tracks by Natalie Cole, **Fleetwood Mac** and others. As writers and producers, Clivilles and Cole established themselves through records by female vocal group Seduction, whose album *Nothing Matters Without Love* (1989) included four R&B hits, Richard Valentine ('Come Back Lover') and Trilogy ('Love Me or Love Me Not'). The duo's other successes included 'Do It Properly' by Two Puerto Ricans, a Black Man and a Dominican. Among the artists they have produced are **James Brown** (*Universal James*, 1989), **Aretha Franklin** ('A Deeper Love', 1993), Chaka Khan (*Life Is a Dance*, 1989) and **Grace Jones** (three tracks on *Bulletproof Heart*, 1989).

In 1990 they renamed themselves C&C Music Factory. Mixing together funk, rock and hip-hip styles, they featured rapper Freedom Williams on 'Gonna Make You Sweat (Everybody Dance Now)', which was an international hit from the Top Ten album of the same name in 1990. The LP also featured former Weather Girls frontwoman Martha Wash. Also included on the album was the hit 'Here We Go', with vocals by Williams, who in addition graced their biggest UK hit, 1991's 'Things That Make You Go Hmmm'. Other guest vocalists on C&C Records included Zelma Davis ('Just a Touch of Love Everyday') and Deborah Cooper with Q Unique ('Keep It Comin'', 1992).

As Clivilles & Cole they recorded a Hi-NRG house version of **U2**'s 'Pride (In the Name of Love)' and the hit house anthem 'A Deeper Love', later covered by no less an R&B legend than **Aretha Franklin**. The pair also briefly worked with **Mariah Carey** before joining Columbia in 1994 for the album *Anything Goes*, which included the hit single 'Do You Wanna Get Funky?'.

The partnership was brought to an end by Cole's death from spinal meningitis early in 1995.

SAMMY CAHN

b. Samuel Cohen, 18 June 1913, New York, USA, d. 15 January 1993

On the printed page Cahn's lyrics may seem brash and over-emphatic, but on record, with melodies supplied by either Saul Chaplin, **Jule Styne** or **Jimmy Van Heusen** and vocals by the likes of **Frank Sinatra**, they work. With his ear for emotional slogans and headlines rather than witty sentiments, Cahn has been one of the most prolific and commercially successful lyricists of the century.

The son of Jewish immigrants, in his teens Cahn became an itinerant violinist, playing in various semi-professional bands around New York. He formed a songwriting partnership with Saul Chaplin (*b. Saul Kaplan, 19 February 1912, Brooklyn, New York*) after Chaplin set one of his lyrics to music. The only song to be published from this period was 'Shake Your Head from Side to Side' (1933) and the pair turned to writing speciality material for vaudeville acts, an activity Cahn maintained throughout his career by writing parodies of his own (and others') songs for celebrities to perform on special occasions. Their first success came in 1935 with 'Rhythm Is Our Business' written for **Jimmie Lunceford**, which the bandleader adopted as his signature tune after it had become a bestselling recording.

The pair celebrated by anglicizing their names. Significantly, their principal clients were record producers on the look-out for new material for their artists to perform, rather than the artists themselves. Thus it was Decca's **Jack Kapp** who demanded that Cahn and Chaplin produce an English-language version of a Yiddish song Cahn brought him. The result was 'Bei Mir Bist du Schön' (1937), the first million-seller for the **Andrews Sisters**. The pair travelled to Hollywood where they split up. Chaplin worked as film composer and orchestrator, receiving Oscars for his orchestrations of the music for *An American in Paris* (1951), *Seven Brides for Seven Brothers* (1954) and *West Side Story* (1961). In the sixties he produced such musicals as *The Sound of Music* (1965) and *Star!* (1968), the title song of which was written by Cahn and Van Heusen.

Cahn, meanwhile, teamed up with Jule Styne and worked on numerous films, including *Anchors Aweigh* (1944); *Romance on the High Seas* (1948), which provided 'It's Magic'* for **Doris Day**; *The Toast of New Orleans* (1949), which gave **Mario Lanza** his first million-seller, 'Be My Love' (written by Cahn and Nicholas Brodszky); and climaxed with *Three Coins in a Fountain* (1954), the title song of which won an Oscar and was their biggest success, the version by the **Four Aces** being a multi-million-seller. The pair also provided many songs for Sinatra, including 'Saturday Night Is the Loneliest Night of the Week', 'I Fall in Love too Easily' (from *Anchors Aweigh*), and 'Five Minutes More' (1946). They also wrote the long-running Broadway musical *High Button Shoes* (1947).

In 1956 Cahn and Van Heusen dissolved their respective writing partnerships to write together. Success came immediately with a series of up-tempo ballads, many of which were first aired by Sinatra. Among these were 'Love and Marriage' (1955), two Oscar-winning songs, 'All the Way' (1957) and 'High Hopes' (1959) – which Cahn would transform into John F. Kennedy's campaign song in 1960 – 'Come Fly with Me' (1958), 'The Second Time Around' (1960), 'Pocketful of Miracles' (1961), 'My Kind of Town' (1964) and 'The September of My Years' (1965).

They attempted two Broadway musicals, *Skyscraper* (1965) and *Walking Happy* (1966), and continued writing films throughout the sixties but after *Thoroughly Modern Millie* (1967) they worked less frequently. In 1970 Cahn and his old partner, Styne, wrote another Broadway musical, *Look to the Lilies*, and in 1974 Cahn took to the stage himself in a collection of his songs, *Words and Music*. The same year he published his autobiography, *I Should Care*.

J. J. CALE
b. Jean Jacques Cale, 5 December 1938, Oklahoma City, Oklahoma, USA

Master of the laid-back, yet insistent, bluesy guitar and mumbled, smoky vocals, Cale has been an important influence on such artists as **Eric Clapton** and **Dire Straits**.

Cale played in numerous high-school bands in the Tulsa area, including one with **Leon Russell**, before following Russell to Los Angeles in 1964, where a year later he recorded the first version of 'After Midnight' and played with the Russell-led Delaney and Bonnie tour on which he met Clapton. In 1967 he formed the short lived Leather Coated Mind and released (and co-produced) the opportunistic psychedelic album *A Trip Down Sunset Strip* (Viva) before returning to Tulsa.

Signed in 1969 by producer Denny Cordell to Shelter (which Cordell owned with Russell), Cale's career took off after Clapton had a Top Twenty hit with 'After Midnight' in 1970. A decade later Clapton had

another hit with Cale's 'Cocaine'. Cale's own first album, *Naturally* (1972), sold well and produced a hit single, 'Crazy Mama'. Produced by his manager, Audie Ashworth, the album defined the narrow path Cale would subsequently follow, as backed by the cream of Nashville's progressive session men (including David Briggs and Norbert Putnam) he created a series of relaxed, rolling chords and songs about 'taking it easy'.

His later albums include *Really* (1972), *Troubadour* (1976), *Shades* (1981), *Grasshopper* (1982) – his most successful album in the UK – and *Le Femme de Mon Pote* (Mercury, 1984). Always semi-detached from the music industry, Cale opted out of his recording contract and did not issue another album until signing with the UK-based Silvertone in 1989. *Travel Log* (1989) and *Number 10* (1992) followed. Less innovative than *Naturally*, Cale's later records nonetheless found a receptive audience, if only for the constancy of Cale's concerns and his determined spurning of the trappings of stardom. In 1994 he edged closer to the mainstream with *Closer to You* (Virgin). The self-produced *Guitar Man* (1997) fared badly compared to the retrospective *Anyway the Wind Blows* (1997).

JOHN CALE
b. 9 March 1942, Garnant, Wales

In the 25 years since he left the **Velvet Underground**, John Cale has maintained a reputation as one of popular music's least predictable and most unorthodox composers, performers and producers.

Having already combined formal classical training as a cellist with the study of avant-garde composition and the experience of playing rock, he recorded a trio of albums in the early seventies which displayed a similar eclecticism. The song collection *Vintage Violence* (Columbia, 1970) was followed by *Church of Anthrax* (1971), an improvising collaboration with avant-garde composer Terry Riley, whose minimalist sequence *A Rainbow in Curved Air* (1967) had been a considerable influence on progressive rock musicians. The third of Cale's solo albums was *The Academy in Peril* (Reprise, 1972), a more conventional classical exercise with the London Philharmonic Orchestra.

After working with members of **Little Feat** on another song collection, *Paris 1919* (1973), Cale moved to Island where he created a group of albums featuring a jagged, dissonant approach to rock. *Fear* (1974) was followed by *Slow Dazzle* (1975), which included what one critic called a 'perverse remake' of **Elvis Presley**'s 'Heartbreak Hotel', and *Helen of Troy* (1975).

Cale did not record again until the eighties when his records drew on punk (*Sabotage*, Spy, 1980) and bar-band music (*Caribbean Sunset*, Ze, 1984). Later records such as *Black Rose* (1985) and *Artificial Intelligence* (1986) appeared on the British label Beggars Banquet. He returned to the classical mode on *Words for the Dying* (Opal, 1989). Produced by **Brian Eno**, it included 'Falklands Suite', a setting of poems by Dylan Thomas.

During the seventies and eighties Cale was even more active as a producer of other people's work. He was involved in the early part of the solo career of fellow Velvets' alumnus Nico, playing keyboards on *Marble Index* (Elektra, 1968) and producing *Desert Shore* (Reprise, 1972) and *The End* (Island, 1974), with its controversial camp rendering of the Nazi anthem 'Deutschland uber alles'. Cale also took part in a live recording, *June 1 1974* (Island), with Nico, Eno and Kevin Ayers.

The character of his other production work was set by the eponymous first album by punk band Iggy and the Stooges (led by **Iggy Pop**) in 1969. Subsequently, Cale produced other punk or punk-influenced artists, including **Patti Smith** (the much respected *Horses*, 1975), **Jonathan Richman** (*The Beserkley Years*, 1987), Squeeze (their self-titled 1978 offering) and **Jennifer Warnes** (*Jennifer*, 1972).

The death of Velvet Underground mentor Andy Warhol inspired a reunion between Cale and **Lou Reed** for a tribute concert. This led to the composition of *Songs for Drella* (1990), an intricate song sequence about Warhol's life which was memorably performed by Reed and Cale with a spare, acoustic accompaniment. Cale later collaborated with Brian Eno on the less satisfactory *Wrong Way Up* (Opal, 1990) and issued a live album (*Fragments of a Rainy Season*, Hannibal, 1992) before taking part in the Velvet Underground reunion of 1993.

In 1994 Cale released an instrumental album, *23 Solo Piano Pieces for La Naissance de L'Amour*, and supervised the reissue of *Music for a New Society* on UK independent label Yellow Moon before issuing a collaboration with long-time **Bob Dylan** cohort Bobby Neuwirth (*Last Day on Earth*, MCA).

MARIA CALLAS
b. Maria Anna Kalageropoulos, 4 December 1923, New York, USA, d. 16 September 1978, Paris, France

The most lauded and most controversial operatic soprano of the post-Second World War period, Callas developed a highly individual style in which emotional intensity took precedence over technical perfection. Like **Enrico Caruso** and **Placido Domingo**, she was also well known to the general public, principally because of her well-publicized private life which confirmed her status as a 'prima donna'.

The daughter of Greek immigrants, Callas won talent contests as a child. In 1937 she moved to Greece,

studying at the National Conservatory in Athens. She made her professional début in 1940 but her career only began in earnest after the Second World War. Callas sang Ponchielli's *Gioconda* at Verona and *Tristan and Isolde* in Venice in 1947.

From 1948 she performed throughout Italy, thrilling audiences with her intensely dramatic style. Callas, however, divided the critics, some of whom described her voice as harsh and suggested she was a better actress than singer. Her first recordings were made for Cetra in 1950 – a selection of Wagner and Bellini arias – and in 1952 she recorded *Gioconda* and Verdi's *Traviata* for the label.

Callas moved to centre stage in world opera after Walter Legge signed her to EMI in 1953. For the remainder of her career, EMI's recording policy dominated her live appearances, which did much to establish Milan's La Scala as one of the world's great opera houses. *Cavalleria Rusticana* (1953) was the first of many collaborations with tenor Alfredo di Stefano, Tito Gobbi and conductor Victor de Sabata. *Tosca* (1954) was her first great critical and commercial success.

She rarely performed after 1960 and her career was increasingly punctuated by highly publicized rows with theatre managements. Callas continued to record prolifically – making over thirty albums for EMI – while a stormy relationship with Greek shipping tycoon Aristotle Onassis kept her in the headlines.

CAB CALLOWAY
b. Cabell Calloway, 25 December 1907, Rochester, New York, USA, d. 18 November 1994, Hosckessin, Delaware

With **Duke Ellington** the most commercially successful black bandleader of the thirties, Calloway was dubbed 'The King of Hi-De-Ho' for his scat-type vocals on songs like 'Minnie the Moocher'* (1931) which were notable for their hipster vocabulary. In the fifties he began a new career in musical theatre.

Raised in Baltimore and Chicago, he appeared in the all-black *Plantation Days* (1927). The following year he took over the leadership of the Alabams and in 1929 took the group to New York. There he also worked as a singer, entertainer and master of ceremonies before making his recording début on 'St Louis Blues' (1930) backed by the Missourians, as the Jungle Boys. The group had previously recorded **Jesse Stone**'s 'Ozark Mountain Blues' (1929) and included arranger and tenor-saxophonist Walter 'Foots' Thomas, trumpeter Lamar Wright, and alto-sax-player Andrew Brown, who would remain with Calloway throughout the thirties.

Managed by **Irving Mills**, the band changed billing to become Cab Calloway and his Orchestra and the leader's name was established by a long residency at

Harlem's Cotton Club in 1931–2. He was equally renowned for his songs, his showmanship and his extravagant clothes which included voluminous trousers, wide-brimmed hat, giant watch chain and long drape jacket. He recorded **Harold Arlen**'s and Ted Koehler's risqué 'Tickeration' (Brunswick, 1931) and their drug-related sequels to 'Minnie', 'Kicking the Gong Around' (1931) and 'Minnie the Moocher's Wedding Day'. Other recordings from this period are 'The Scat Song' (1932) and 'Jitter Bug' (1934).

In the mid-thirties the Calloway band was joined by trumpeter Doc Cheatham and arranger Eddie Barefield and briefly recorded for RCA Victor (1934) before moving to Vocalion where Calloway's biggest hit was the million-selling 'Jumping Jive' (1939). During this period Calloway and his band also appeared in several movies, including *The Big Broadcast of 1932*, *The Singing Kid* (1936) with **Al Jolson** and *Manhattan Merry-Go-Round* (1937), the title song of which was a hit for him. Although the Calloway Orchestra primarily featured Calloway's showmanship (he pioneered the zoot suit and frequently turned somersaults on stage) and his extravagant singing style, the 1939–42 orchestra was widely regarded as an outstanding jazz group.

It included such renowned instrumentalists as Latin trumpeter Mario Bauza (who later led **Machito**'s orchestra), saxophonist Chu Berry, drummer Cozy Cole (featured on 'Crescendo in Drums', 1939), and **Dizzy Gillespie**. With arrangements by Buck Ram, the recordings of the early forties included 'Bye Bye Blues' (Okeh, 1940) and Billy Strayhorn's composition for Duke Ellington 'Take the A Train'. Calloway also appeared in a number of films on his own, including *Stormy Weather* (1943), in which he sang 'Geechy Joe', and the **W. C. Handy** biopic *St Louis Blues* (1958), with **Eartha Kitt**, **Ella Fitzgerald** and **Nat 'King' Cole**.

The big band lasted until 1948, after which Calloway toured North and South America and Britain with occasional bands before joining the Broadway cast of **George Gershwin**'s *Porgy and Bess* as Sportin' Life in 1952. He appeared with Pearl Bailey and **Billy Daniels** in the all-black version of *Hello Dolly* (1974) and also toured with the Harlem Globetrotters basketball team. In 1973 he re-formed his big band for the Newport Jazz Festival and he appeared in the 1980 film *The Blues Brothers*, singing 'Minnie the Moocher'. He continued to make live appearances throughout the eighties and nineties. *Cab Calloway Stands in for the Moon* (America Clave, 1990) was a tribute album with contributions from **Allen Toussaint** and **Bobby Womack**, among others.

In 1993 Columbia reissued some of his classic recordings as *Cab Calloway – Best of the Big Bands* and *Cab Calloway – featuring Chuck Berry*.

CAMEO

Larry Blackmon, b. 24 May 1956; Tomi Jenkins; Gregory Johnson; Arnett Leftenant; Nathan Leftenant

Originally a twelve-strong funk band, Cameo made a major impact on pop and disco audiences in the mid-eighties. By the nineties, when the group's leader Blackmon founded his own label to produce other black artists, they had become a three-piece techno act.

Drummer-vocalist Blackmon had attended shows at Harlem's Apollo Theatre as a child. He led various soul groups, making his first recordings with the Players. He formed Cameo in 1977, signing to Chocolate City, a subsidiary of Casablanca. While 'Rigor Mortis' (1977) and 'It's Serious' (1978) were not hits, they influenced other black bands. Cameo's chart success began with the softer, ballad-orientated approach of 'I Just Want to Be' and 'Sparkle' from *Secret Omen* (1979). *Cameosis* (1980) reached No. 1 on the R&B charts while 'Freaky Dancin'' and *Knights of the Sound Table* (1981) were successful in the pop market.

Blackmon founded the Atlanta Artists label and reduced the group to five members in 1982. Cameo's first international success came the following year with *Alligator Woman* and 'She's Strange', which was accompanied by the first of a series of flamboyant videos directed by Amos Poe, which reflected Cameo's extravagant stage act in which Blackmon wore a red cod-piece. By 1985 the group was down to a trio and *Single Life* reached No. 1 in Britain. The album displayed Blackmon's mastery of studio techniques, mixing **Ennio Morricone** themes with black music's various genres, including hip-hop on 'Attack Me with Your Love'. The next album, *Word Up* (1986), went platinum and included the hits 'Candy' and 'Back and Forth'. *Machismo* was released in 1988. Even more basic in their commitment to dance grooves at the expense of melody were *Real Men Wear Black* (Arista, 1990), which included the hit 'I Want It Now', and *Emotional Violence* (Reprise, 1992). By this time Leftenant had left Cameo. A 'best of' album was released in 1993.

Among the performers produced by Blackmon for Atlanta Artists were Barbara Mitchell and Cashflow, whose 'Mine All Mine' was an international hit in 1986. Blackmon also produced tracks by **Otis Redding**'s sons the Reddings, Bonnie Pointer of the **Pointer Sisters**, **Bobby Brown** and **Chaka Khan**.

GLEN CAMPBELL

b. Glen Travis Campbell, 22 April 1936, Delight, Arkansas, USA

Campbell's sweet, soothing tenor voice perfectly represented the meeting point of country and pop music. Similarly, his success – his fifty or so albums on Capitol included twelve gold albums and seven platinum ones – demonstrated how profitable a meeting point that was for some performers.

From a musical family, Campbell was given his first guitar at the age of four. In his teens he toured the Southwest with his own country band, Glen Campbell and the Western Wranglers, before in 1960 he went to Los Angeles. There, his virtuoso guitar-playing quickly won session work with such diverse artists as **Frank Sinatra**, **Elvis Presley** and the **Beach Boys** (with whom Campbell toured briefly in 1965 when Brian Wilson was ill) and a contract with Capitol. The label saw him primarily as an instrumentalist – hence albums like *The Astounding 12-String Guitar of Glen Campbell* (1965) – despite his minor 1961 vocal hit, 'Turn Around Look at Me' (Crest).

Success came in 1967 with Campbell's version of the **John Hartford** composition 'Gentle on My Mind', and was confirmed by a trio of intriguingly wistful story songs, all written by **Jimmy Webb** and million-sellers, 'By the Time I Get to Phoenix' (1967), 'Wichita Lineman' (1968) and 'Galveston' (1969). Campbell next secured his own variety show, *The Glen Campbell Goodtime Hour*, co-starring roles in *True Grit* and *Norwood* (both 1969), and set about becoming an 'all-round entertainer' with strong country inclinations. His use of his position to introduce the songs of new writers like Kenny O'Dell and to popularize those of the likes of **Merle Haggard** outside the country audience contrasted with the occasional blandness of his work, such as his chart-topping versions of 'Rhinestone Cowboy' (1975) and 'Southern Nights' (1977), an **Allen Toussaint** composition.

His recording repertoire widened to include inspirational songs such as 'You'll Never Walk Alone' and 'Bridge over Troubled Water', as well as a leavening of pop standards, yet in duets with **Rita Coolidge**, **Tanya Tucker** and notably **Bobbie Gentry** ('Let It Be Me', 1969, 'All I Have to Do Is Dream', 1970), Campbell found an amalgam of country, folk and pop representative of real shifts within these idioms. With his record sales in decline, he left Capitol for Mirage in 1981 and afterwards later had country hits with Atlantic ('Faithless Love', 1984) and MCA (Webb's 'Still Within the Sound of My Voice', 1987). He returned to Capitol for the anodyne *Walkin' in the Sun* (1990) and then re-recorded his hits for Curb (1990).

Campbell toured with Hartford and Nicolette Larsen in 1991. His later albums included *Unconditional Love* (Capitol, 1991) and the Jerry Crutchfield-produced *Somebody Like That* (Liberty, 1993). In the wake of his autobiography *Rhinestone Cowboy* (1994), he was the subject of a number of 'best of's and career retrospectives, the best of which was *The Capitol Years* (1999).

CAN
Irwin Schmidt, b. 29 May 1937; Holgar Czukay, b. 24 March 1938; Michael Karoli, b. 29 April 1948; Jackie Liebesit, b. 26 May 1938; Damo Suzuki, b. 16 January 1950

With **Kraftwerk**, the most resilient and imaginative German avant-garde rock band, Can and its members were crucial in establishing Germany's role as a major production centre for electronically influenced music in the seventies.

Trained as jazz and classical musicians – keyboards-player Schmidt and bassist Czukay had studied with the composer Stockhausen – Can's ambition to produce a truly modern music based on rock was very much in the spirit of that time, 1968. Based in Cologne, the group recorded seven albums for United Artists between 1969 and 1974, including *Tapo Mago* (1971), *Ege Bamyasi* (1972) and *Future Days* (1973). All were characterized by electronic treatments of instruments and a use of hypnotic and repetitive rhythmic figures. Can was in demand for film music, scoring Skolimowski's *Deep End* (1970).

In 1974 Suzuki was replaced by Malcolm Mooney, who had been involved with Can in its early days. He sang on *Loaded* (1975), the group's most uncompromising album, released on the newly established Virgin label. The following year saw a more mainstream orientation with the addition of ex-Traffic members Reebop Kwaku Baah (percussion) and Rosko Gee (bass), plus two European hit singles, the novelty number 'I Want More' and a version of the Christmas carol 'Silent Night'. Reebop (who died in 1982) cut a solo album, *Trance*, in 1979.

At the end of the decade, Can ceased to exist as a unit while its members pursued solo projects. They formed their own Spoon label to release these and re-release the earlier group albums. Czukay made the acclaimed *Movies* in 1980, while Schmidt, guitarist Karoli and drummer Liebesit also cut solo albums. *Rome Remains Rome*, Czukay's 1986 album, included a cut-up of the Pope's voice on 'Blessed Easter'.

In 1986 the group re-formed to cut *Incandescence* (Virgin), which Schmidt produced. Karoli and Czukay shared production credits for *Rite Time* (Mercury/Phonogram, 1989). In 1991, with the group once more inactive, Czukay released another solo recording, a self-titled album on Virgin. He later made the atmospheric *Moving Pictures* (Mute, 1994). With the group no more, Mute released *Can Box*, a collection of unreleased performances from 1971–7, in 1999.

CANNED HEAT
Bob 'The Bear' Hite, b. 26 February 1943, Torrance, California, USA, d. 5 April 1981, Venice, California; Henry Vestine, b. 25 December 1944, d. 20 October 1997,

Paris, France; Al 'Blind Owl' Wilson, b. 4 August 1943, Boston, Massachusetts, d. 3 September 1970; Larry Taylor, b. 26 June 1942, Brooklyn, New York; Frank Cook; Adolpho 'Fito' de la Parra, b. 8 February 1948, Mexico City; Harvey Mandel, b. 1946, Detroit, Michigan

The only white American blues group to enjoy chart success, Canned Heat were fixtures of the rock festival scene of the late sixties.

Record collectors Wilson and Hite founded the band in 1966, naming it after a song by country blues singer Tommy Johnson. Adding Taylor on bass, Cook (drums) and Vestine (guitar), they recorded *Canned Heat* for Liberty in 1967. It contained solid versions of R&B standards like **Elmore James**' 'Dust My Broom' and **Howlin' Wolf**'s 'Goin' Down Slow'. The band's performance of 'Rollin' and Tumblin'' at the prototype rock festival was captured in D. A. Pennebaker's film *Monterey Pop*.

Cook was replaced by Fito de la Parra for *Boogie with Canned Heat* (1968), which included the atmospheric 'On the Road Again', first recorded by the Memphis Jug Band in the late twenties. Featuring Wilson's falsetto vocals, the song was a Top Twenty hit in America and reached the British Top Ten. *Livin' the Blues* (1968) produced another hit, 'Goin' Up the Country'.

This was the high point of Canned Heat's career and for two years they played the big outdoor festivals like Woodstock (1969) and the Isle of Wight (1970), cutting five more Liberty albums by 1970, including one with **John Lee Hooker**. That year produced a hit single, **Wilbert Harrison**'s 'Let's Work Together', but also the death of Wilson from a drug overdose. With first Taylor and then Mandel (the guitarist who had replaced Wilson) leaving to join **John Mayall**, Hite and Vestine struggled unsuccessfully to sustain the group's unusual blend of rural and urban blues. *Many Rivers to Cross* (Atlantic, 1974), produced at Muscle Shoals by Barry Beckett and Roger Hawkins, was Canned Heat's last significant recording although the band continued to perform in California until Hite's death. The nineties found Vestine playing in the Rent Party Band while Canned Heat was led by Taylor and de la Parra, with Mandel sometimes sitting in. *Reheated* (Dali, 1989) was a laid-back offering for those who followed them on such nostalgia circuit tours as *An Evening of California Dreamin'*. Later albums included *Internal Combustion* (1997) and *Blues Band* (1998).

FREDDY CANNON
b. Frederick Anthony Picariello, 4 December 1939, Revere, Massachusetts, USA

Cannon was one of the more talented of the Philadel-phia-based rock'n'rollers who achieved success through frequent appearances on **Dick Clark**'s *American Bandstand* television show.

The son of a dance-band leader, Cannon was a self-taught guitarist who by his teens (as Freddy Karmon) was backing groups touring the Boston area. In 1958 he sent a tape of his own recording of his mother's composition 'Rock'n'Roll Baby' to producers **Bob Crewe** and Frank Slay at Swan Records, who retitled it 'Tallahassie Lassie', added a party atmosphere (and their names to the song's credits) and secured Cannon, as they renamed Picariello, regular appearances on *Bandstand*. The result was a million-seller and the first of Cannon's series of eighteen straight hits. On subsequent outings, which included a raucous remake of the standard 'Way Down Yonder in New Orleans'* (1959), 'Jump Over' (1960), and 'Palisades Park'* (1962), Crewe and Slay retained the distinctive brassy live dance sound of 'Tallahassie' (a staid version of which was recorded by **Tommy Steele** in the UK), while Cannon's vocal style, which was oddly reminiscent of **Al Jolson**, remained as frantically naïve as ever. Unlike **Fabian**, another Philadelphia-based star, Cannon didn't attempt a movie career. However, he did outlast the 'British invasion' of the American charts spearheaded by **The Beatles**, with a pair of Top Twenty hits on Warner Brothers, 'Abigail Beecher' (1964) and 'Action'* (1965), the theme song to the teleseries *Where the Action Is*.

After recording for various small labels and playing the rock'n'roll revival circuit throughout the seventies, Cannon became a promotion man for Buddah Records, briefly returning to the lower reaches of the charts with 'Let's Put the Fun Back in Rock'n'Roll' in 1981.

GUS CANNON
b. 12 September 1883, Red Banks, Mississippi, USA, d. 15 October 1979, Memphis, Tennessee

A veteran of the black medicine-shows in the early years of the twentieth century, Cannon also led one of the finest of the Memphis jug bands.

From about the time of the First World War, he worked on travelling shows, singing, playing banjo and telling jokes; during this period he encountered the singer/guitarist Jim Jackson and the harmonica-player Noah Lewis (*b. 3 September 1895, Henning, Tennessee, d. 7 February 1961, Ripley, Tennessee*). With Lewis, guitarist Ashley Thompson and himself on banjo and jug, he formed Cannon's Jug Stompers and began recording for Victor in 1928. Later line-ups drew in Elijah Avery (guitar) and Hosea Woods (banjo, kazoo). The band's twenty-six sides, recorded in 1928–30, which embrace both blues ('Minglewood Blues', 'Viola Lee Blues') and earlier material like

'(My) Money Never Runs Out' and 'Bugle Call Rag', are an outstanding demonstration of jug-band principles. Lewis's harmonica-playing is especially fine. Cannon also recorded with guitarist **Blind Blake** for Paramount (1927) and with Hosea Woods (Brunswick, 1929).

He lived on in Memphis, though working chiefly outside music, and was occasionally contacted by visiting researchers: he recorded for Folkways in 1956 and Adelphi in 1969. In 1963 one of his old Jug Stompers sides, 'Walk Right in', became a No. 1 pop hit in a version by the Rooftop Singers (Vanguard). In its wake Cannon recorded an album of reminiscences and music for Stax, but few copies ever reached the market. He took part in several music documentaries.

Cannon's chief rival as a jug-band leader was Will Shade (*b. 5 February 1898, Memphis, Tennessee, d. 18 September 1966, Memphis*), who organized the Memphis Jug Band. Its personnel included Will Weldon (guitar), who in the thirties, as Casey Bill, was a leading steel guitarist; Charlie Burse (vocal/guitar/banjo); Shade himself (vocal/harmonica/guitar); and various lesser-known Memphians, as well as occasional guests like **Memphis Minnie**. The various MJB groups recorded nearly a hundred songs for Victor (1927–30), Gennett (1932) and Okeh (1934); the final group of recordings, with its swing rhythms and hot fiddling, offered both a model and a black parallel to the Western swing of **Bob Wills** – whose first band recording, 'Osage Stomp', was based on an MJB piece.

Other Memphis-area jug bands included harmonica-player Jed Davenport's Beale Street Jug Band and Jack Kelly's South Memphis Jug Band, while similar groups arose in Louisville, Kentucky (where the fashion may in fact have started), Birmingham, Alabama, Dallas, Texas and elsewhere. While some of those groups were essentially small blues bands, others were string bands that added a jug (or a jug-like cello or bowed string bass) in order to keep in step but did not change their repertoire. One such was Coley Jones' Dallas String Band, which played rags and old popular tunes like Ford Dabney's 'Shine'. Other jug bands were basically jazz units with a novelty angle, like the Dixieland Jug Blowers, with whom New Orleans clarinettist Johnny Dodds played.

Jug bands fell almost wholly out of favour in the post-Depression years, returning only with the skiffle vogue of the fifties and subsequent fashions in white folk-styled music; groups like the Even Dozen Jug Band and Jim Kweskin's Jug Band (with which **Maria Muldaur** sang) enjoyed some popularity. Occasionally novelty bands have had one-off pop hits with what are essentially jug-band performances; these include **Norman Greenbaum**'s Dr West's Medicine Show and Junk Band with 'The Eggplant that Ate

Chicago' (Go Go, 1966) and the British group Mungo Jerry ('In the Summertime', Dawn, 1970).

EDDIE CANTOR
b. Isidore Israel Itzkowitz, 31 January 1892, New York, USA, d. 4 October 1964, Hollywood, California

One of America's best-loved entertainers, whether in blackface, on Broadway or on screen, telling a joke or singing, Cantor's trademark was the boundless energy he poured into his performances, eyes forever rolling, feet never still and hands always gesticulating.

Orphaned at two, Cantor was reared by his grandfather. He left school at the age of fourteen, singing first on street corners and then as one half of a song-and-dance team in 1907, the year he took the name Cantor. He graduated to the job of a singing waiter in Coney Island (where he worked with pianist **Jimmy Durante**) before returning to vaudeville, working in blackface as a comedian and later as an assistant to Bendini and Arthur, a juggling act. It was during this time that Cantor first heard blackface minstrel Eddie Leonard's composition 'Ida (Sweet as Apple Cider)' which he would later dedicate to his wife and would become one of the many songs closely associated with him. From 1912 to 1914 he toured with one-time songwriter Gus Edwards' *Kid Kabaret* show (which also featured **George Jessel** and the young Walter Winchell), before heading the touring company in *Canary Cottage* and starring on Broadway in Florenz Ziegfeld's *The Midnight Frolics* in 1916. This led to his appearing in Ziegfeld's annual *Follies* in 1917–19 and starring in *Kid Boots* (1923), in which he sang 'Alabamy Bound', and, his greatest success, *Whoopee!* (1928), both of which were filmed (in 1926 and 1930, respectively).

Whoopee! was a landmark musical film. Co-produced by Ziegfeld and made in colour, it was the more faithful film version of any of Ziegfeld's stage shows and made the wisecracking Cantor a star, giving him two of his biggest hits with the **Walter Donaldson** and **Gus Kahn** compositions 'Making Whoopee' and 'My Baby Just Cares for Me'. It also introduced Busby Berkeley, who shot the dance numbers, and the overhead shot, which Berkeley would employ in countless films, to the musical. It led to a succession of musicals, all constructed around Cantor's energetic little-man persona, including *Roman Scandals* (1933), *Kid Millions* (1934), *Strike Me Pink* (1936) and *Ali Baba Goes to Town* (1937). His last major film was *If You Knew Susie* (1948), the title song of which, written by **Buddy Desylva**, was another of his best-known songs.

In the thirties he appeared in his own, highly popular, radio show and in 1941 returned to Broadway for his last major stage role as the star of *Banjo Eyes* (Cantor was known as 'Mr Banjo Eyes'). During the war –

like **Al Jolson**, whose career in many ways his paralleled – he travelled extensively, entertaining American
troops, and after the war was credited by President
Roosevelt with coining the phrase 'March of Dimes'
for his fund-raising activities on behalf of the treatment of infant paralysis. A heart attack in 1952
reduced his activities. In 1953 he was the subject of a
lacklustre biopic *The Eddie Cantor Story* in which he
was played by Keefe Brasselle, and in 1956 he was
awarded a special Oscar for 'distinguished service to
the film industry'. Among his books are two volumes
of autobiography, *My Life Is in Your Hands* (1928) and
Take My Life (1957).

CAPTAIN AND TENNILLE
Daryl Dragon, b. 27 August 1942, Los Angeles, Califor-
nia, USA; Toni Tennille, b. 8 May 1943, Montgomery,
Alabama

Like their label-mates the **Carpenters**, Captain and
Tennille personified the well-crafted pop harmonies
of the seventies, in the process having six million-
selling singles.

Keyboards-player Dragon (son of classical conductor Carmen Dragon) played in the Los Angeles house
band of *Mother Earth*, a rock musical co-written by
vocalist Tennille. They teamed up as backing musicians on a 1972 **Beach Boys** tour, later signing to
A&M, which released their self-produced single 'The
Way I Want to Touch You' in 1974.

The following year the duo recorded **Neil Sedaka**'s
'Love Will Keep Us Together'*, which reached No. 1.
Other Top Ten hits in 1975–6 were the re-released
'Touch'*, 'Lonely Night (Angel Face)'*, 'Muskrat
Love'* and a version of **Smokey Robinson**'s 'Shop
Around'. Their last major hit was the slinky No. 1 'Do
That to Me One More Time'* (Casablanca, 1979), but
by then their middle-of-the-road status had guaranteed them television success with first a primetime
ABC series and then an eighties daytime variety show
which Tennille hosted with Dragon as musical director. She later released solo albums, including *Moonglow* (1986), *All of Me* (Gaia, 1987) and *Do It Again*
(1990), a collection of classics by **Jerome Kern** and
George Gershwin. The following year Tennille
appeared on Broadway in *Stardust* and in 1992 she
released another nostalgic set, *Never Let Me Go*. In 1997
the pair reunited for *Twenty Years of Romance*, an
album consisting entirely of versions of songs recorded
by them earlier, before Captain joined the Beach Boys
Family & Friends touring ensemble in 1998 and Tennille took the lead in a revival of *Victor/Victoria*.

CAPTAIN BEEFHEART
See **Beefheart, Captain**

THE CARDIGANS
Lasse Johansson; Bengt Lagerberg; Nina Persson;
Magnus Sveningsson; Peter Svensson

A Swedish indie band, the Cardigans rose to international fame after contributing to the *Romeo and Juliet*
soundtrack. Although best known for the lightweight
pop of 'Lovefool' (1996), the band's diverse sound
takes in everything from jazzy trip-hop to **Black Sabbath** covers.

Formed in late 1992 by guitarist Svensson and
bassist Sveningsson, veterans of the Swedish music
scene having played together in various heavy-metal
bands, the Cardigans' line-up was completed by
Lagerberg (drums), Johansson (guitar/keyboards)
and singer Nina Persson. Their début album,
Emmerdale (1994), was a domestic success but the
band failed to gain international acclaim until the
release of *Life* (1995), which featured the minor hit
single 'Sick and Tired'. The album was repackaged the
following year with tracks from *Emmerdale* also
included, and sold over a million copies.

Having signed to Polygram, the Cardigans recorded *First Band on the Moon* (1996). The album was
generally darker in tone than its predecessors, with
the exception of the single 'Lovefool', which reached
the upper reaches of the charts across Europe and
Asia as well as in America and the UK after featuring
in Baz Luhrman's remake of *Romeo and Juliet*. This
brought total sales of the Cardigans' third album to
2.5 million copies.

Wishing to distance themselves from 'Lovefool',
the Cardigans experimented with trip-hop and electronica on the more keyboard-based *Gran Turismo*
(1998). Named after the band's favourite computer
game, it featured two hit singles in 'My Favourite
Game' and 'Erase/Rewind'.

MARIAH CAREY
b. 27 March 1970, Huntingdon, New York, USA

The bestselling female performer of the nineties,
Carey's record-breaking oeuvre takes in polished balladry and hip-hop influenced pop and has brought
her an astonishing thirteen Number One singles in
the US. Often likened to **Céline Dion** and **Whitney
Houston**, acts who like her have had success in virtually every corner of the world, unlike them Carey
wrote most of her own material.

Carey's mother was an opera singer and vocal
coach who named her daughter after the song 'They
Call the Wind Mariah' from *Paint Your Wagon*, by
Lerner and Loewe. Raised in upstate New York,
Carey moved to the city immediately after graduating
from high school and soon began writing songs with
keyboard-player Ben Margulies. After appearing as a

backing singer on a Brenda K. Starr record, she drew the attention of Tommy Mottola, the head of Columbia Records and subsequently head of Sony Music US.

Most of the songs on her début album *Mariah Carey* (1989) were co-written by Carey and Margulies (her regular writing partner until acrimony over royalties from the first album led to their breaking up). With production by Ric Wake and **Narada Michael Walden**, among others, the album provided four US No. 1 singles, 'Vision of Love', 'Love Takes Time', 'Someday' and 'I Don't Wanna Cry'. The album sold over six million copies in America alone and won Carey two Grammy Awards for Best New Artist and Best Female Performer. The follow-up release, *Emotions* (1991)*, saw Carey write more of the material herself, including the title track, her record-breaking fifth consecutive US Number One. The album also included the singles 'Can't Let Go' and 'Make It Happen', while the *MTV Unplugged EP* (1992) spawned another chart-topper, a cover of the **Jackson Five**'s 'I'll Be There'.

After marrying Mottola in a star-studded ceremony, Carey released her biggest-selling album to date, *Music Box* (1993)*, and had two further Number One singles, 'Hero' and 'Dreamlover'. Preceded by the festive hit 'All I Want for Christmas Is You' (1994), *Daydream* (1995) saw the singer begin to move away from pure pop and her worldwide audience grow. 'Fantasy' was only the second single to début at Number One in the US chart, while 'One Sweet Day', a duet with **Boyz II Men**, held on to the top spot for a record sixteen weeks, after which Carey began a lengthy world tour.

After her divorce from Mottola in 1997, her recordings took on a more soulful tinge. *Butterfly*⃰ (1997), which was co-produced by Sean Puffy Combs, included the US chart-topper 'Honey'. In 1998 she recorded 'When You Believe', a duet with Whitney Houston, for the *Prince of Egypt* soundtrack and released *#1's*⃰, which collected together her thirteen US chart-toppers. In 1999 she released the hugely successful *Rainbow*.

THE CARLISLE BROTHERS

Bill, b. William Carlisle, 19 December 1908, Wakefield, Kentucky, USA; Cliff, b. Clifford Raymond Carlisle, 6 May 1904, Taylorsville, Kentucky, d. 2 April 1983, Lexington, Kentucky

The Carlisles were not a country 'brother act' in the same way as the **Delmore Brothers** or **Louvin Brothers**: though they had similar musical goals, they often pursued them apart. Bill accompanied himself on standard guitar, while Cliff used a steel slide on the dobro mesonator guitar, then only recently developed.

Cliff's career began in earnest, on radio and records, in 1930, patterned upon **Jimmie Rodgers** (whom he once accompanied on record). Throughout the thirties he dealt in Rodgers' staple motifs, train songs (notably the fine 'Pan American Man'), heart songs and blue yodels, while recording successively for ARC, RCA Victor's Bluebird label and Decca, and broadcasting over WBT, Charlotte, North Carolina. With minor variations Bill's working life echoed his brother's, and the two frequently collaborated on records.

During the fifties, working together as the Carlisles with younger family members, they had country hits with 'No Help Wanted' (1953) and the much-recorded 'Too Old to Cut the Mustard' (1952, in which year it was also a hit for **Ernest Tubb**) and the comic 'No Help Wanted' (1953), written by Bill. He continued to head the group after Cliff's retirement, indulging his penchant for crackerbarrel comic numbers on the *Grand Ole Opry*, which the group joined in 1954. In 1966 he had a solo hit in the same vein with 'What Kinda Deal Is This?'.

Cliff, though out of professional music for the last twenty years of his life, was recognized as an influential dobro stylist and a transmitter of valued old songs. In these respects, he was an important progenitor of bluegrass.

BELINDA CARLISLE
b. 17 August 1958, Hollywood, California, USA

A former member of female rock band the Go-Gos, Belinda Carlisle has enjoyed a successful solo career based on jaunty and bright pop ballads.

Formed in Hollywood in 1978, the Go-Gos included Carlisle (lead singer), Charlotte Caffey (*b. 1953*, guitar, keyboards, vocals), Jane Wiedlin (*b. 1958*, guitar, vocals), Kathy Valentine (*b. 1959*, bass, vocals) and Gina Schock (*b. 1957*, drums). A new wave rock band, their first album was *Beauty and the Beat* (I.R.S., 1981).

After recording two further albums and touring the UK with **Madness**, the group split in 1985. The following year Carlisle's first single, 'Mad About You', and album, *Belinda*, were US hits. The next album was named after her best-known song, the anthemic 'Heaven Is a Place on Earth' composed by Ellen Shipley and the album's producer Rick Nowels, as well as the hits 'I Get Weak' and 'Circle in the Sand'.

The guest artists on *Runaway Horses* (1988) included former Go-Gos members Valentine, Schock and Caffey while **George Harrison** played slide guitar on the US hit single 'Leave a Light on' (1989). The Go-Gos reunited for several live appearances in 1990.

Carlisle's more recent recordings have included *Live Your Life Be Free* (1991), which included 'Little

Black Book', co-written with Marcella Detroit of **Shakespears Sister**, and *Real* (1993), with its UK hit single 'Big Scary Animal'. In 1996 she released *A Woman and a Man*.

ELSIE CARLISLE
b. c. 1902, Didsbury Lancashire, England, d. 5 September 1977

The pert, know-it-all flapper personified in American popular song of the twenties and thirties by **Ruth Etting**, Annette Hanshaw and Helen Kane had a coyer English cousin in the stage and recording artist and 'Radio Sweetheart No. 1' Elsie Carlisle.

Following a début at London's Metropolitan Music Hall in 1920 and several years of provincial touring, Carlisle began to make records in 1927, her first accompanist being the American pianist Carroll Gibbons (later leader of the Savoy Hotel Orpheans). She appeared in C. B. Cochran's London production of **Cole Porter**'s *Wake Up and Dream* (1929), singing 'What Is This Thing Called Love?'. She continued to record for several companies, her material ranging from sophisticated pieces like **Richard Rodgers** and **Lorenz Hart**'s 'Ten Cents a Dance' (1931) to romantic and comic songs and even, occasionally, suggestive blues numbers: she enjoyed some notoriety with a 1931 coupling of the Andy Razaf compositions 'My Handy Man' and 'My Man o' War', previously recorded by the black singers **Victoria Spivey** and Lizzie Miles. After a spell as band vocalist, alongside Sam Browne, with **Ambrose** (1932–5) she formed a double act with Browne, starring in the 1935 Radiolympia exhibition and the Royal Command Performance. She went on working, with Browne or solo, until her retirement during the Second World War.

HOAGY CARMICHAEL
b. Howard Hoagland Carmichael, 22 November 1899, Bloomington, Indiana, USA, d. 27 December 1981, Palm Springs, California

Composer, singer, lyricist and actor, Carmichael was the author of 'Star Dust', one of the most recorded standards of the twentieth century. Inspired by jazz, notably **Bix Beiderbecke**, and like **Harold Arlen** deeply immersed in the blues, forms which most of his songwriting contemporaries had little knowledge of, Carmichael's great achievement was the distillation of a distinctly Mark Twain-like vision of rural America in songs like 'Lazybones' (1933), 'Georgia on My Mind', 'Rocking Chair' (1930) and 'Memphis in June' (1945), songs which, though mostly better known through the recordings of other performers, relied for their sense of conviction on his folksy Midwestern nasal twang. It was this aspect of his work

that was usually featured in his occasional screen appearances, generally as a phlegmatic pianist with a cigarette invariably dangling out of his mouth.

Raised in Bloomington, Carmichael was a self-taught pianist. When the family moved to Indianapolis, he played ragtime in various clubs. At the University of Indiana, he supported himself by leading a five-piece band and booking other bands in which capacity he met his idol Bix Beiderbecke, who in 1924 recorded Carmichael's first composition 'Free Wheelin'' as 'Riverboat Shuffle' (a hit for **Isham Jones**, 1925, and **Red Nichols**, 1928) on the local Gennett label. After graduating in 1926, he briefly practised law in Miami, before Nichols' hit recording of 'Washboard Blues' (1927, with lyrics by Fred Callan) convinced him to return to music.

Back in Bloomington, he wrote the classic 'Star Dust' (1929), first recorded, with Carmichael on piano, by publisher **Irving Mills** and his Hotsy Totsy Band (1930) as a ragtime piece. Subsequently slowed down and with lyrics by Mitchell Parish, the song became one of the most recorded numbers of the century. Among those who had hits with 'Star Dust' were **Bing Crosby**, **Louis Armstrong** (1931), **Benny Goodman**, **Tommy Dorsey** (1936), **Glenn Miller** and **Artie Shaw** (1941). Other songs from this period recorded by Carmichael include 'Rockin' Chair' (Columbia, 1929), recorded as a duet with Armstrong, and 'Lazy River' (Victor, 1930), with a band that featured Beiderbecke, Tommy and **Jimmy Dorsey**, **Joe Venuti** and **Eddie Lang**. The wistful 'Georgia on My Mind' (1930) was a hit for **Mildred Bailey** (1932) and **Gene Krupa** (1941) and, after **Ray Charles'** million-selling version in 1960, was eventually adopted as the state song of Georgia.

In 1933 Carmichael, who unlike most songwriters never had regular collaborators, partnered **Johnny Mercer** on the hymn to indolence 'Lazy Bones' (a hit for **Ted Lewis** and Mildred Bailey, who had earlier taken 'Rockin' Chair' as her theme tune, and revived by **Jonathan King** in 1971). Though his melodies retained their strong jazz inflection – just as 'Star Dust' quotes from Armstrong's 'Potato Head Blues', so 'Skylark' (1942) is a pastiche of Beiderbecke – with the move to film music (with 'The Nearness of You' and 'Two Sleepy People', with **Frank Loesser**, 1938) his songs became more regular in construction. Later film songs included the atmospheric 'Memphis in June' (1945), 'Ole Buttermilk Sky' (1946) and the 1951 Oscar-winner 'In the Cool Cool Cool of the Evening' (written in 1939 with Mercer).

Following his role as Cricket in Howard Hawks' *To Have and Have Not* (1944), in which **Andy Williams** dubbed Lauren Bacall singing 'How Little We Know' and Carmichael sang the quirky 'Hong Kong Blues', Carmichael regularly appeared in films, most notably in *The Best Years of Our Lives* (1946), *Young Man with a Horn* (1950), the film loosely based on the life of Beiderbecke, and *Timberjack* (1955). Between 1959 and 1963 he also appeared in the Western teleseries *Laramie*, before retiring.

Carmichael wrote two autobiographies, *The Stardust Road* (1946) and *Sometimes I Wonder* (1966). One of his most devoted admirers was **Georgie Fame**, who recorded an album of Carmichael's songs (*In Hoagland*, 1981) and devised a live show based on them.

KIM CARNES
b. 20 July 1945, Los Angeles, California, USA

A product of the folk revival, writer and country-influenced singer Carnes won a Grammy award for her 1981 million-seller 'Bette Davis Eyes'.

A former member of pop-folk group the New Christy Minstrels (whose alumni included **Barry McGuire**, **Kenny Rogers** and Gene Clark of the **Byrds**), Carnes was signed as a writer by Jimmy Bowen before cutting *Kim Carnes* (1975) and the **Jerry Wexler**–Barry Beckett-produced *Sailin'* (1976) for A&M. A duet with Gene Cotton, 'You're a Part of Me' (Ariola, 1978), was a minor hit.

Among the artists who recorded compositions by Carnes and her husband Dave Ellingson were **Anne Murray**, **Barbra Streisand**, **Frank Sinatra** and Kenny Rogers, and her next hit, 'Don't Fall in Love with a Dreamer' (United Artists, 1980), was a duet with Rogers. It was the prelude to a series of solo hits on EMI America. 'More Love', a **Smokey Robinson** tune, reached No. 10 before the **Jackie DeShannon** song 'Bette Davis Eyes', produced by Val Garay, became the bestselling single of the year in America.

The biggest of Carnes' later hits was 'What About Me' (1984), recorded with Rogers and James Ingram, while she was also successful with 'Make No Mistake (He's Mine)', a duet with Barbra Streisand. As 'Make No Mistake (She's Mine)', the same song was a 1988 country hit for Rogers and Ronnie Milsap. In the same year Carnes released the Jimmy Bowen-produced *View from the House* (MCA). It included **Johnny Otis**'s 'Willie and the Hand Jive' and back-up singing from **Lyle Lovett** on the country hit 'Speed of the Sound of Loneliness', composed by **John Prine**. *Checkin' Out the Ghosts* (1995) was a Japanese-only release and *Gypsy Honeymoon* (1996) a retrospective set.

MARY-CHAPIN CARPENTER
b. 21 January 1958, Princeton, New Jersey, USA

One of the most talented of the new singer-songwriters to emerge in the eighties, Mary-Chapin Carpenter works within the US country music genre. Against a traditional backdrop of guitar, bass and drums she typically sings not of teenage *angst* but about mid-life crises.

She grew up in the Washington DC area where she won local talent awards. In 1986 she was signed to a recording contract by the Nashville office of Columbia Records. Her recording career has been shaped by producer/songwriter John Jennings.

Home Town Girl (1987) included a version of **Tom Waits**' 'Downtown Train', later a hit for **Rod Stewart**. *State of the Heart* (1989) was followed by *Shooting Straight in the Dark* (1990). Carpenter's own writing reached a peak on the hugely successful *Come on, Come on* (1991), which had a similar level of kinetic energy to **Bonnie Raitt**'s *Nick of Time* (1989). As well as the elegiac title track the album included the bitter social observation of 'He Thinks He'll Keep Her', the word-painting of 'I Am a Town', the exuberant 'I Feel Lucky' and a fine reading of **Lucinda Williams**' 'Passionate Kisses'. She followed that with the folkier and more introspective *Stones in the Road* (1994), which mixed exuberant romanticism ('Shut Up and Kiss Me') with bittersweet pragmatism ('House of Cards'). *A Place in the World* (1996) was closer to *Come on* in style, mixing spirited mid-life recollections of innocent dreams ('Hero in Your Own Hometown') with evocations of intimacy ('What If We Went to Italy') and plain simple observations ('Ideas Are Like Stars').

The compilation album *Party Doll and Other Favourites* (1999) also included several live recordings and her version of **John Lennon**'s 'Grow Old with Me', recorded for the 1995 tribute album *Working Class Hero*.

THE CARPENTERS
Richard, b. 15 October 1946, New Haven, Connecticut, USA; Karen, b. 2 March 1950, New Haven, d. 4 February 1983, Los Angeles, California

Their intimate harmonies and densely layered productions brought the brother and sister act ten million-selling singles and one of the biggest-selling albums ever, *The Singles: 1969–1973*.

Richard studied classical piano at Yale and in California after the family moved there in 1963. In 1965 he formed an instrumental trio with Wes Jacobs on bass and his sister Karen on drums that won a contract with RCA, for whom they recorded an unreleased album. In 1966 he and Karen formed the shortlived Spectrum (a member of which was John Bettis, later Richard's regular writing partner) before experimenting with over-dubbing to create subtle harmony effects.

Signed by **Herb Alpert** to A&M in 1969, the pair had a minor hit with the title track of their first album, a melodic version of **The Beatles** 'Ticket to Ride' (1969). Their next album, *Close to You* (1970), provided two million-sellers, the title track (a **Burt Bacharach** and Hal David composition, recorded earlier by **Dionne Warwick**), and the **Paul Williams** and Roger Nichols composition 'We've Only Just Begun'. Both songs characterized the Carpenters' sound, Karen's clear voice underpinned by Richard's delicate piano lines and surrounded by his sympathetic string arrangements.

Swept up in a wave of publicity that equated their wholesome harmonies with a clean-living image, the Carpenters produced a slew of hits, that for all their teenage themes made them middle-of-the-road performers, happiest appearing in Las Vegas or for President Nixon (in 1974). Their hits included 'For All We Know'*, 'Rainy Days and Mondays'* and 'Superstar'* (all 1971), 'Goodbye to Love'* (1972), 'Yesterday Once More'* (1973) and 'Top of the World'* (1973), all written by Richard and Bettis. 'Please Mr Postman'* (1974) demonstrated the cost of their search for studio perfection. In place of the ragged joy of the **Marvelettes** original, the Carpenters' version was so clever as to be almost heartless.

In 1974 Karen, suffering from anorexia nervosa, collapsed and the duo slowed down their frenetic work rate. At the same time, despite a ripening of their sound ('Calling Occupants of Interplanetary Craft', 1977, and *Made in America*, 1981), their hits declined. Following Karen's marriage to property developer Tom Burris, the duo virtually stopped recording in the eighties. After Karen's death, *Voice of the Heart* (1984) was released and Richard, who with Karen had produced most of the duo's work since 1973, turned to production. His solo album *Time* appeared in 1987.

In 1989 Cynthia Gibb starred in a television biopic, *The Karen Carpenter Story*, and *Lovelines*, an album of previously unreleased Carpenters recordings, was issued. During the nineties A&M released several Carpenters retrospectives. The 1994 tribute album *If I Were a Carpenter* included versions of the group's hits by such alternative rock artists as **Sonic Youth**. In 1996 Karen Carpenter's eponymous solo album was released. Produced by Phil Ramone it included a version of Paul Simon's 'Still Crazy After All These Years'. Brother Richard also released a solo album, *Pianist, Arranger, Composer, Conductor*, that year.

JAMES CARR
b. 13 June 1942, Memphis, Tennessee, USA

One of the finest exponents of Southern soul whose intense performances won him a strong cult following, Carr made the original versions of the often-recorded 'Pouring Water on a Drowning Man' (1966) and 'Dark End of the Street' (1967), the first song written by **Chips Moman** and Spooner Oldham. Like **O. V. Wright**, his influence was far greater than his success.

Raised in Shreveport, Louisiana, Carr sang with various gospel groups, notably the Soul Stirrers, before signing with country veteran Quinton Claunch's Memphis-based independent company Goldwax in 1966. The O. B. McLinton composition, 'You've Got My Mind Messed Up', in which his gospel quaver perfectly matched the song's message, was a surprise pop and R&B hit in 1966. By 1968 he had replaced the hoarse shouting of his earlier recordings, which was clearly influenced by **Otis Redding**, with the sophisticated pleading, more akin to **Percy Sledge**, of 'I'm a Fool for You' (1967) and 'A Man Needs a Woman' (1968), which marked the end of his pop hits. His last R&B entry was a version of the **Bee Gees**' 'To Love Somebody' (1969), after which he briefly recorded for Atlantic in 1971 and a couple of small Southern labels.

The victim of a rare mental disorder associated with deep depression, Carr was never able to capitalize on his success. A 1981 tour of Japan, where reissues of his Goldwax sides were very successful, failed when it became apparent that his illness prevented him performing. He has subsequently recorded only one album, *Take Me to the Limit* (Goldwax, 1991), produced by Claunch and Roosevelt Jamison.

LEROY CARR
b. 27 March 1905, Nashville, Tennessee, USA,
d. 29 April 1935, Indianapolis, Indiana

The early blues recording industry was galvanized by several high-selling records in the late twenties, one of the most notable of which was Leroy Carr's elegiac eight-bar 'How Long, How Long Blues' (Vocalion, 1928). Carr's cool and wistful singing and piano-playing, spiced by the single-string lines of his guitarist partner Scrapper Blackwell, extended the blues vocabulary by providing a new manner – urbane, self-questioning, deliberately poetic – and by furnishing it with a fresh kind of instrumental collaboration.

Carr and Blackwell worked together in clubs and theatres, first in Indianapolis and later in St Louis, while recording such popular numbers as 'Prison Bound Blues' (1928), 'Midnight Hour Blues' (1932), 'Mean Mistreater Mama' and 'Blues Before Sunrise' (both 1934), and 'When the Sun Goes Down' (1935), all of which were to become blues standards. Both the Carr–Blackwell method and Carr's care in composition stamped themselves upon such urban blues performers of the thirties as Bumble Bee Slim and Bill Gaither (who even called himself 'Leroy's Buddy'), as well as upon later artists like **Cecil Gant** and **Otis Spann**.

Carr died, from nephritis, not long after recording a moving solo blues, 'Six Cold Feet in the Ground'; Blackwell lived on as a respected elder of Indianapolis music until his death in 1967.

MICHAEL CARR

b. Maurice Cohen, 1904, Leeds, England, d. 16 September 1968, London

The songs written by Carr and lyricist **Jimmy Kennedy** in the thirties were the equal of the output of many American songwriting teams, and, individually, their careers survived the advent of rock'n'roll.

The son of boxer 'Cockney Cohen', Carr was brought up in Dublin. He spent the years 1924–30 in the United States, acquiring knowledge he would put to use in his later songs. On his return to London he turned to songwriting, collaborating on songs for **Gracie Fields** and others, but his biggest early success was 'Ole Faithful' (1934), a fake cowboy song which he wrote with Hamilton, brother of Jimmy, Kennedy. An early example of the Americanization of British culture, the song was a hit in both countries, and the duo followed it up with similar offerings, including 'The Wheel of the Wagon Is Broken' (1935) and 'The Sunset Trail' (1936).

Carr now linked up with Jimmy Kennedy, contributing songs for London shows as well as persevering with the Western theme in songs such as 'Cowboy' (1936) and the lilting 'South of the Border' (1939) – their biggest hit. Originally recorded by singing cowboy **Gene Autry** as the title song to his 1939 film, it has been subsequently recorded by more than one hundred artists. The duo's other great success, however, was decidedly British in spirit: the comic, patriotic, 'We're Going to Hang out Our Washing on the Siegfried Line' (1939). After this, their last hit together, Carr joined the army, where he was closely associated with the *Stars in Battledress* production.

In the fifties Carr had few hits until he concentrated on writing instrumental music, such as 'Man of Mystery' (1960), the theme from an Edgar Wallace teleseries which gave the **Shadows** their second British Top Ten hit and led to their recording another Carr composition, 'Kon-Tiki', a No. 1 in 1961.

THE CARS

Ric Ocasek, b. Richard Otcasek, 23 March 1949, Baltimore, Maryland, USA; Ben Orr, b. Benjamin Orzechowski, 9 August 1947, Cleveland, Ohio, d. 3 October 2000, Atlanta, Georgia; Elliot Easton, b. Elliot Shapiro, 18 December 1953, New York; David Robinson; Greg Hawkes

Like **Blondie**, the Cars were unusual among American bands of the late seventies in their ability to merge an art-rock approach with a mainstream pop-rock sound. The culmination of their appeal was the use of 'Drive' as the motif for the Live Aid concert in 1985.

Singer Ocasek and bassist Orr recorded as folk band Milkwood for Paramount in 1972. They played in various bands in the Boston area before forming the Cars in 1976. The other members were also veterans of the Boston scene, drummer Robinson having played with **Jonathan Richman**. Signed to Elektra, the band's first eponymous album was cut in London with **Queen** producer Roy Thomas Baker. Released in 1978, it contained three Top Forty hits including the rousing 'My Best Friend's Girl', which reached the Top Ten in Britain.

Commercially, the Cars were an album band, with each of their first five albums (all produced by Baker) selling over a million copies in America. The most dramatic success was that of *Heartbeat City* (on which Mutt Lange shared producer credits), whose three hit singles included the Live Aid-featured 'Drive' (1984) with lead vocals by Orr and 'Tonight She Comes' (1986). The band's career was given a boost at this point by an astute use of video (including one clip directed by Andy Warhol) at a time when the twenty-four-hour cable channel MTV was becoming increasingly popular. After the inconsequential *Door to Door* (1987) the group disbanded.

Since 1981 several band members had been developing their own projects. Ocasek, Robinson and Easton all produced other artists. Easton also formed his own group, Band of Angels, but Ocasek had the highest profile. He worked on (still unreleased) tracks with **Iggy Pop** and with influential electronic duo Suicide. Ocasek has also had an extensive career as a solo recording artist. He released two solo albums on Geffen, *Beatitude* (1983) and *This Side of Paradise* (1986), before moving to Warners for *Fireball Zone* (1991) and *Negative Theater* (1993). Ocasek later became a staff producer for Maverick, the label owned by **Madonna**, before moving to Columbia, for whom he recorded *Troubilizing* (1997) in the same capacity.

FIDDLIN' JOHN CARSON

b. 23 March 1868, Fannin County, Georgia, USA, d. 11 December 1949, Atlanta

Though not the first recording artist in the history of country music – Texas fiddler Eck Roberton preceded him by more than a year – Carson did offer in his June 1923 recording of 'The Little Old Log Cabin in the Lane' and 'The Old Hen Cackled and the Rooster's Going to Crow' (Okeh) the first example of Southern rural singing and the first country disc recorded in the South (at a makeshift studio in Atlanta).

Carson's singing and fiddling were immediately approved by his local audience, and the reception of the record and its successors did much to reveal a market for country records and to encourage the Northern-based companies to cater to it. Carson's other hits from this period included 'You Will Never Miss Your Mother Until She Is Gone', 'Fare You Well Old Joe Clark', a revival of 'Arkansas Traveler' (1924), a hit for **Len Spencer** in 1900, and 'Old Dan Tucker' (1925).

Carson continued to record until 1934, and his 150-plus sides, some solo, some with string band, others with his daughter Rosa Lee ('Moonshine Kate'), include valuable examples of antique fiddling style and comic routines. Carson then turned to politics, supporting Georgia populists Tom Watson and Eugene and Herman Talmadge, and was well known as a campaign entertainer – services for which he was rewarded with the post of elevator operator at the State Capitol in Atlanta.

THE CARTER FAMILY

Alvin Pleasant Carter, b. 15 April 1891, Maces Springs, Virginia, USA, d. 7 November 1960, Maces Springs; Sara Dougherty Carter, b. 21 July 1898, Flat Woods, Virginia, d. 8 January 1979, Lodi, California; Maybelle Addington Carter, b. 10 May 1909, Nickelsville, Virginia, d. 23 October 1978, Nashville, Tennessee

Genealogically the Carters are the 'first family' of American country music, extending vertically through three generations and horizontally into other influential clans, notably that of **Johnny Cash**. They were the first singing group to be widely popular, particularly on records, and they translated into a new commercial context an extensive body of traditional or quasi-traditional Southern song.

In the early twenties A.P. and his wife Sara sang informally at local functions in Southwestern Virginia, Sara playing autoharp. In 1926 they were joined by A.P.'s sister-in-law Maybelle, who sang and played guitar. In the following year they made their first records, for Victor, at the field session in Bristol, Tennessee, which also elicited the début sides of **Jimmie Rodgers**. Over the next seven years, guided by **Ralph Peer**, they recorded scores of Victor sides that sold extremely well throughout the South. The group's appeal lay in Sara's calm, deep-voiced singing and Maybelle's innovative guitar technique, whereby she picked the melody on the bass strings. Maybelle also sung second parts and A.P. an occasional, and unpredictable, third. Among the trio's most popular songs were 'Keep on the Sunny Side' (which became their theme), 'Bury Me Under the Weeping Willow', 'Wildwood Flower', 'I'm Thinking Tonight of My Blue Eyes' (which shares its melody with later country hits like **Roy Acuff**'s 'Great Speckled Bird', **Hank Thompson**'s 'Wild Side of Life' and

Kitty Wells' 'It Wasn't God Who Made Honky Tonk Angels') and 'Will the Circle Be Unbroken'.

The majority of the Carters' repertoire was lyric folk songs, Old and New World ballads and sacred songs – many of which A.P. collected from rural amateurs, rewrote or rearranged and claimed as his own compositions. Their output stands in sharp contrast to that of Jimmie Rodgers, their only commercial equal in the late twenties and early thirties. His stance was often that of a blues-singer, retailing humorous or bawdy episodes in the life of a 'good-time rounder'; the Carters stood firmly by the family virtues of sobriety, decency and old-time religion, their concerts announced by the reassuring advertisement 'The Program Is Morally Good'. Yet at Victor's instigation, in 1931, the two acts did record a couple of songs together, awkward humorous sketches that even include a barber-shop-quartet arrangement of 'There'll Be a Hot Time in the Old Town Tonight'.

The family later recorded for ARC (1935) and Decca (1936–8), adding to their repertoire as well as re-recording Victor successes. For much of 1938–41 they broadcast on Texas stations, including XERA in Del Rio; through these powerful but legally uncontrolled stations, whose transmitters were safely over the border in Mexico, they were heard by listeners far more widely spread than those they had reached with their records. By then the family group had been swelled by A.P. and Sara's daughter Janette (*b. 1923, Maces Springs*), who sang and played autoharp, and Maybelle's daughters Helen, June (*b. 23 June 1929, Maces Springs*) and Anita (*b. 31 March 1934, Maces Springs, d. 29 July 1939*), who were taking vocal spots on the family's programmes before they were in their teens. (A.P. and Sara had separated in 1932, but continued to work together.)

Sessions for Columbia (1940) and RCA Victor (1941) were the last by the original family, and their performing career ceased, after a couple of years on WBT Charlotte, North Carolina, in 1943. A.P. and Sara recorded in the fifties for the small Acme label with their children Janette and Joe (vocal/guitar), while Maybelle's children enjoyed some success as a more commercial country act, working with their mother first on radio in Virginia, Tennessee, Missouri and finally Nashville, where they joined the *Grand Ole Opry* in 1950. They also recorded as a trio for Columbia, and later separately: Anita for RCA Victor (1962, with **Hank Snow**), Mercury (1965) and Capitol (1972); June mostly with Johnny Cash, whom she married in 1968. After some years away from music, raising families, Helen and Anita rejoined June to perform on Cash's TV shows.

Sara and Maybelle were reunited as a duet for the 1967 Newport Folk Festival and made an album, *Historic Reunion* (Columbia), but thereafter Sara retired from public music-making. Maybelle resumed the autoharp (which she had played in her youth but never used on the family's recordings) and developed on that instrument a melody-picking style that was widely emulated. In 1971 she took an important role in the **Nitty Gritty Dirt Band**'s triple-album project *Will the Circle Be Unbroken* (United Artists). The original Carter Family was elected to the Country Music Hall of Fame in 1970.

Imitators of the Carters began to appear within a couple of years of their first recordings, but their most dedicated followers emerged after the original family had broken up: the A. L. Phipps Family of Barbourville, Kentucky, and the Canadian Romaniuk Family, both made numerous albums of implicit or explicit tributes. The Carters' influence beyond their own musical idiom has chiefly been in bluegrass, where many of the songs they popularized have been reshaped, for instance by **Flatt and Scruggs** (*Songs of the Famous Carter Family*, Columbia) and **Mac Wiseman**. Both Carter melodies and Maybelle's guitar style had marked influences on the music of **Woody Guthrie**, and songs from the Carter folio appeared in the early work of **Joan Baez**.

The Carter tradition was carried into a third generation by vocalist Carlene Carter, June's daughter by her first marriage to country singer Carl Smith. Recordings produced by her then husband **Nick Lowe**, *Musical Shapes* (1980) and *Blue Nun* (1981), were rock-orientated and rather diffuse but *I Fell in Love* (1990), produced by Howie Epstein of **Tom Petty**'s Heartbreakers, saw her cultivating her country and family roots: it even included a version of A.P.'s 'My Dixie Darling'. Her 1993 album *Little Love Letters* contained songs co-written with Bernie Taupin and Benmont Tench and was critically acclaimed as a nigh-perfect example of contemporary country.

CARTER THE UNSTOPPABLE SEX MACHINE
Jimbob, b. James Morrison, 22 November 1960; Fruitbat, b. Leslie Carter, 12 February 1958

One of the more adventurous products of British pop in the eighties, Carter combined a punkish irreverence with the sampling skills of the dance music scene.

Morrison and Carter had played in several South London bands, including the Ballpoints, the End, Peter Pan's Playground and Jamie Wednesday, which released the singles 'Vote for Love' and 'We Three Kings of Orient Aren't' on the independent Pink label.

Adding a drum machine for live shows, the duo took their new name from a newspaper headline and began to gain attention on the London club scene with a dynamic and unusual stage act. Their first single 'Sheltered Life' (Big Cat, 1988) was followed by

'Sheriff Fatman', a catchy attack on a notorious London landlord. The title of the group's first album, *101 Damnations* (1990), reflected their word-play and their fierce political stance.

30 Something (1991) was released by Rough Trade and became a Top Ten hit in the UK. The next year Carter moved to the major label Chrysalis but ran into legal difficulties over the use of a sample from the **Rolling Stones**' 'Ruby Tuesday' on 'After the Watershed'. The duo's third album, *1992 – The Love Album*, was less successful. *Post Historic Monsters* (1994) borrowed much of the imagery from the film *Jurassic Park*. *Worry Bomb* was released in 1995, accompanied as a limited edition with the superior *Doma Sportova . . . Live in Zagreb, 20/5/94*. Later the same year the band released the compilation volume *Straw Donkeys . . . The Singles*, which served as a companion piece to the B-sides set *Starry Eyed and Bollock Naked* (1994).

Carter announced their intention to split after the release of *A World Without Dave* (1997), recorded with new drummer Wez, with *I Blame the Government* (1998) serving as a fitting epitaph to their haphazard career. Morrison has continued to record as Jim's Super Stereoworld, while Carter has released a series of singles over the internet as Abdoujaparov. *LIVE* and *Sessions* were both issued posthumously in 1998.

CLARENCE CARTER
b. 14 January 1936, Montgomery, Alabama, USA

Carter is best remembered for his 1970 recording of the story-song 'Patches'* (which was originally recorded by **Chairmen of the Board** and written by that group's leader 'General' Norman Johnson). More typical of his blues-tinged Southern soul are the 1968 million-sellers 'Slip Away' and 'Too Weak to Fight', co-written and produced by **Rick Hall**, the producer of all his best records at Hall's Muscle Shoals studio.

Blind since childhood, Carter's background was the blues rather than gospel (though he sang in church briefly). He recorded for Duke and other labels with Calvin Scott as Clarence and Calvin and the C&C Boys before joining Hall's Fame label as a solo singer, writer, session guitarist and arranger – Carter holds a music degree – in 1965. His gravel voice regularly made the R&B charts and the lower reaches of the Hot Hundred throughout the late sixties and early seventies on Fame ('Thread the Needle', 1967) and from 1968 Atlantic ('Snatching It Back', 'Doing Our Thing', both 1969, and 'The Court Room', 1971). He also wrote songs for **Candi Staton**, to whom he was briefly married.

In 1975 Carter left Hall to join ABC and produce himself with little success, briefly returning to favour with *Let's Burn* on Venture in 1981. Throughout the eighties he played the chitlin' circuit, recording *Dr C.C.* (Ichiban, 1986) and other albums, including *Between a Rock and a Hard Place* (1990), whose title track was a soul hit for Ichiban. *Snatchin' It Back* (Rhino, 1992) is the definitive compilation set.

MARTIN CARTHY
b. 21 May 1940, Hatfield, Hertfordshire, England

The most influential guitar stylist of the English folk revival in the sixties, Carthy provided both **Paul Simon** and **Bob Dylan** with folk material. He contributed to the development of folk-rock through his work with **Steeleye Span** and the **Albion Band**.

A former boy soprano, Carthy's introduction to popular music came via **Lonnie Donegan**. After a brief period in the theatre, he worked as a musician in a London restaurant, dressed as an Elizabethan minstrel, before joining the Thameside Four in 1961. The repertoire was eclectic and Carthy's earliest influences included **Big Bill Broonzy** and **Rev. Gary Davis**, but his novel approach to the acoustic guitar accompaniment of traditional songs owed much to the Irish virtuoso uillean-piper Seamus Ennis, whose playing Carthy tried to translate into guitar techniques.

His first recording was made in 1963 for Decca's *Hootenanny in London*, an attempt to cash in on the burgeoning folk scene. At this period he was also resident singer at London's leading folk club, The Troubadour, where visiting Americans like Simon and Dylan also performed.

A further Decca album with the Three City Four, who included topical songwriter Leon Rosselson, led to a series of six albums for Fontana between 1965 and 1971. The first included 'Scarborough Fair', which Simon took as the basis for the **Simon and Garfunkel** recording of 'Parsley Sage Rosemary and Thyme' and Dylan for 'Girl from the North Country', as well as the traditional ballad 'Lord Franklin', whose melody was used in 'Bob Dylan's Dream'. The source of much of Carthy's ballad repertoire was the folk scholar and propagandist **A. L. Lloyd**.

The album also had fiddle accompaniment from Dave Swarbrick, later to become the mainstay of **Fairport Convention**. From 1966 to 1969 he and Carthy played the folk-club circuit as a duo and the third album, *Byker Hill* (1967), gave Swarbrick equal billing. *But Two Came By* (1968) included Sydney Carter's classic religious song 'Lord of the Dance' and the ballad 'Lord Lankin', later to be part of the repertoire of Steeleye Span, the electric folk group Carthy joined in 1969.

As singer and electric guitarist, Carthy made a vital contribution to the first two Steeleye albums before leaving in 1972, following a disagreement over musical policy. His later career saw him alternating between solo appearances and albums (for Pegasus, Deram

and Topic) and spells as a group member. With the exception of a 1977 Steeleye reunion, Carthy's bands have been markedly English in approach. These include Ashley Hutchings' Albion Band, the Watersons – the Hull-based vocal group that includes his wife Norma and daughter Eliza, with whom he made *For Pence and Spicey Ale* (1975) – and the John Kirkpatrick/Sue Harris group Brass Monkey, with whom he recorded *See How It Runs* (Topic, 1986). Carthy also took part in the recording of Peter Bellamy's folk-opera *The Transports* (Free Reed, 1977). *Right of Passage* (Topic, 1989) was Carthy's first solo album since 1983 and included a rare original composition, 'Company Policy', dealing with the Falklands conflict. In the same year he re-formed his duo with Swarbrick and they toured with Annie Briggs. An American live recording, *Life and Limb* (1990), was issued by Topic, which started a comprehensive reissue of Carthy's albums throughout the early nineties.

Waterson: Carthy (Topic, 1994) was a critically acclaimed recording with Norma and Eliza. In 1998 Carthy shocked the folk world with *Signs of Life* on which as well as traditional material ('Sir Patrick Spens') he included versions of the **Bee Gees**' 'New York Mining Disaster', **Elvis Presley**'s 'Heartbreak Hotel' and **Bob Dylan**'s 'Lonesome Death of Hattie Carrol'. Lugubrious and decidedly English, the readings were surprisingly affecting. His second album with his wife and daughter, *Broken Ground* (1999), was far more traditional.

Both Norma and Eliza Waterson had significant careers in their own right. Norma recorded in traditional style with her sister Lal (*A True Hearted Girl*, Topic, 1997), but her major recordings came when she broadened her range for *Norma Waterson* (Ryko, 1996) and offered marvellously measured readings of songs as various the **Grateful Dead**'s 'Muddy River', **Billy Bragg**'s 'St Swithin's Day' and **Richard Thompson**'s 'God Loves a Drunk'. She followed this with *The Very Thought of You* (1999), singing songs by **Queen**'s Freddy Mercury ('Love of My Life') and **Harold Arlen** ('Over the Rainbow') to remarkable effect. On *Heat, Light & Sound* (Topic, 1996) Eliza interrogated a set of traditional songs to interesting effect. She continued in this vein in her pair of 1998 albums, *Rice* and *Red*, on which her fiddle playing was even more prominent. Even more assured was *Angels & Cigarettes* (Warner, 2000).

ENRICO CARUSO
b. 27 February 1873, Naples, Italy, d. 2 August 1921, Naples

In his time the most popular operatic tenor in the world, Caruso was the first concert musician to understand the cultural and commercial possibilities of the gramophone. It was his recordings that shattered the view that records were little more than toys. His voice recorded well, its characteristics matching that of the acoustical recording diaphragm and its power drowning out much of the surface noise of the early discs. As **Fred Gaisberg**, who first recorded him in 1902, put it: 'He was the answer to a recording man's dream'. Fittingly, his 'Vesti la Giubba' (first recorded in 1902) was the first title to achieve a cumulative sale of a million copies.

From a large family, Caruso studied voice with Gugliemo Vergine and Vincenzo Lombardi and made his début in Morelli's *L'Amico Francesco* in 1894. By 1902, having already sung in Buenos Aires (1899), Rome (1899), Milan (1900) and at Covent Garden, and made a few cylinder recordings, he was an opera star on the verge of becoming a world celebrity. In March 1910 he recorded ten sides for Gaisberg for £100 outright and by the time of his death he had earned over £2 million in royalties. Since then, his estate has received the same amount. Issued with great success by the Gramophone and Typewriter Company (which later became EMI), these 1910 recordings also won Caruso a contract at New York's Metropolitan Opera Company when its director, Heinrich Conried, heard them.

In January 1904, after his début at the Met, Caruso signed with Victor (later RCA) – 'Caruso, the greatest tenor of modern times, makes records only for Victor' ran the ad copy – at the 'celebrity' rates of $4,000 for ten sides and $2,000 a year for five years for agreeing not to record for anyone else. These were among the records that inaugurated Victor's prestigious 'Red Seal' series. More expensive than popular recordings – the prices ranged from $1.50 to $7 per single-sided 12-inch record – the Red Seal recordings confirmed the cultural status of the phonogram and helped make Victor the leading record company in America. Though most of his recordings were of operatic arias, his last great popular success was a version of **George Cohan**'s patriotic 'Over There', an American No. 1 in 1918.

In all, Caruso recorded some 250 sides, including an orchestral version of 'Vesti la Giubba' in 1907, before his death in 1921. The release of the film *The Great Caruso* (1950), with **Mario Lanza** in the title role, stimulated sales of Caruso's records. In the seventies some of Caruso's earliest records were 'cleaned-up' by Dr T. G. Stockman of Utah University and issued by RCA.

JOHNNY CASH
b. John R. Cash, 26 February 1932, Kingsland, Arkansas, USA

Nicknamed 'The Man in Black', Cash, with his distinctive, slightly fluttery, baritone, was one of the few country performers widely known outside country music circles. Though he first achieved success in the rock'n'roll era and became a country superstar at a time when country performers were increasingly seeking to cross over into the pop market, Cash's music was largely unaffected by these trends. His style and concerns were always more folk-orientated (in the manner of **Woody Guthrie**). This approach led him to record with **Bob Dylan** and champion American Indian rights (notably *Bitter Tears*, 1964). In contrast to **Merle Haggard**, who in the course of his career established himself as a historian of country music, Cash in much of his work has functioned as a historian of the rural poor.

The son of a poor cotton farmer, Cash was raised on a Federal Government resettlement colony in Dyess, Tennessee (which was flooded in 1937, an event recalled in 'Five Feet High and Rising', Columbia, 1959). He took up the guitar and songwriting while stationed in the air force in Germany, and in 1954 in Memphis joined forces with bassist Marshall Grant and guitarist Luther Perkins (no relation to **Carl Perkins**), who had briefly played in his elder brother Roy's Delta Rhythm Ramblers. Billed as Johnny Cash and the Tennessee Two they were signed to **Sam Phillips**' Sun Records in 1955 and had an immediate country hit with 'Cry, Cry, Cry' and a pop hit with the pared-down simplicity of 'I Walk the Line'* (1956), his most representative Sun recording. In search of pop success Phillips paired Cash with writer/producer **Jack Clement**. The result was a trio of hits in 1958, 'Ballad of a Teenage Queen', 'Guess Things Happen That Way' and **Charlie Rich**'s sombre 'The Ways of a Woman in Love', the last two sweetened with vocal choruses.

Later that year, unhappy at Sun because Phillips wasn't interested in albums – a projected tribute to **Hank Williams** was never completed – Cash joined Columbia where he was assigned Don Law as producer. Law had produced artists as varied as **Robert Johnson** and **Flatt and Scruggs** and was more traditionally orientated than most producers. He encouraged Cash's folk inclinations and returned the singer to the spare sound of his first recordings. Cash's hits of this period included 'Don't Take Your Guns to Town' (1959) and 'Ring of Fire'* (1963). More striking, however, were his albums. These included *Ride This Train* (1960), a travelogue about America; *Blood, Sweat and Tears* (1963), an album in praise of the American working man which included **Harlan Howard**'s classic 'Busted' and 'The Legend of John Henry's Hammer', which revealed Cash's growing interest in folk material; *Bitter Tears* (1964), a collection of Indian protest songs by Peter La Farge and Cash, featuring 'The Ballad of Ira Hayes', the Indian who raised the flag at Iwo Jima and died an alcoholic; and *Orange Blossom Special* (1965), which included three Dylan songs. At the same time, for his personal appearances Cash (by now backed by the Tennessee Three with the addition of drummer W. S. Holland) established what one critic has called a 'folk troupe' to present a far wider range of American music than most country performers. Among its members were June Carter (the co-author of 'Ring of Fire', whom he married in 1968), assorted members of the **Carter Family** and Carl Perkins.

Cash's international breakthrough came with the live album *At Folsom Prison** (1968), his guest appearance on *Nashville Skyline* (1969), for which he wrote the liner notes and duetted with Dylan on 'Girl from the North Country', and his recording of **Shel Silverstein**'s humorous 'A Boy Named Sue' – a huge pop hit. Where previously Cash had been frowned upon by the Nashville establishment for his drug usage (which largely ended in 1967) and libertarian views, in the late sixties he was showered with honours and in 1969 secured a primetime television show. Country hits of this period included two duets with June Carter, 'Jackson' (1967), also a hit for **Lee Hazelwood** and Nancy Sinatra, and **Tim Hardin**'s 'If I Were a Carpenter' (1970), plus 'What Is Truth' (1970) and 'One Piece at a Time' (1976). In 1970 he appeared with Kirk Douglas in *A Gunfight*, a Western financed by the Jicarilla Apache tribe.

Though he recorded songs by **Kris Kristofferson** ('Sunday Morning Coming Down', 1970), Cash's strong commitment to religion (evidenced in a duet with evangelist Billy Graham on *The Man in Black*, 1971, and *Gospel Road*, 1973) kept him at some distance from the 'outlaw' movement in country music in the seventies. In the eighties, however, he recorded the highly successful concept album *Highwayman* (1986) with Kristofferson, **Waylon Jennings** and **Willie Nelson** and turned again to contemporary songwriters, including **Nick Lowe** ('Without Love', 1980) and **Bruce Springsteen** ('Highway Patrolman', 1983). At the same time he turned back to the music of the fifties (*Rockabilly Blues*, 1980; *The Survivors*, 1982, made with Carl Perkins and **Jerry Lee Lewis**). Sales of his own albums declined in this period and in 1986 he left Columbia for Mercury. **Paul McCartney** and **Emmylou Harris** were among the guests on *Water from the Wells of Home* (1987) and the breadth of his influence was confirmed in 1988 when a number of the new generation of folk artists, including Michelle Shocked, Brendan Croker and the Mekons, recorded the tribute album *'Til Things Are Brighter* (Red Rhino). In 1994 Cash teamed up with rock and hip-hop producer Rick Rubin for *American Recordings*, which includes songs by Lowe, **Tom Waits** and **Leonard Cohen**. Even better was *Unchained* (1996)

on which Cash was backed by **Tom Petty & the Heartbreakers** to great effect on a mix of traditional songs (from the likes of the **Louvin Brothers** and **Jimmie Rodgers**) and contemporary offerings. Prior to that, Cash recorded another Highwaymen album, *The Road Goes on Forever* (1995). In 1997 Cash published his autobiography. He was also diagnosed as suffering from Parkinson's Disease and since then has only worked intermittently. *Love, God, Murder* (2000) is the definitive box set of his Columbia years. Arranged thematically, rather than chronologically like 1993's *Essential Recordings*, the three-CD set confirmed the centrality of Cash to American music for some half a century.

Cash's younger brother Tommy pursued a singing career, recording prolifically, but with only limited success, throughout the sixties and seventies. Johnny's daughter **Roseanne Cash** and his stepdaughter Carlene Carter are among the most successful contemporary country singers and songwriters.

ROSEANNE CASH
b. 24 May 1955, Memphis, Tennessee, USA

One of the leading country music vocalists of the eighties, Roseanne Cash developed an impressive blend of rock and country over a series of albums written and produced by Rodney Crowell.

She was a back-up singer for her father **Johnny Cash** in the early seventies and studied acting in London before making her début album in Germany in 1978 for Ariola. Returning to Nashville, she signed to Columbia. The producer of *Right or Wrong* (1980) and her next five albums was Rodney Crowell (*b. 1950, Houston, Texas*), whom Cash had married the previous year.

She had a pop and country hit in 1981 with her own composition 'Seven Year Ache', the title track of the second Columbia album which also included the rockabilly tune 'My Baby Thinks He's a Train', composed by Leroy Preston, a former member of **Asleep at the Wheel**. *Somewhere in the Stars* (1982) included 'Ain't No Money' and 'I Wonder'.

Vince Gill added backing vocals to 'I Don't Know Why You Don't Want Me', a Cash–Crowell composition that was her fourth country No. 1.

Rhythm and Romance (1985) was critically acclaimed. It included the **Tom Petty**–Benmont Tench song 'Never Be You' (1986). Then came Cash's finest album to date, the country bestseller *King's Record Shop* (1987). It was the first record by a woman to produce four country chart-toppers: **John Hiatt**'s 'The Way We Make a Broken Heart', a revival of her father's 1962 hit 'Tennessee Flat Top Box', 'If You Change Your Mind', co-written by Roseanne and pedal-steel guitarist Hank de Vito, and **John Stewart**'s

'Runaway Train'. Cash's vocals were complemented by Steuart Smith's lead guitar parts.

Cash recorded a hit duet with Crowell ('It's Such a Small World', 1988) and a countryfied version of **The Beatles**' 'I Don't Want to Spoil the Party' in 1989 before the release of the bleak *Interiors* (1990). The album's songs of loss and anger were widely believed to have been inspired by the breakdown of the Crowell–Cash marriage. Cash later recorded *The Wheel* (1993). After *Retrospective* (1995) Cash left Columbia for Capitol, for whom she recorded *10 Song Demo* (1996), which she accompanied with a press release saying she was no longer a country singer. The album, sounding sparer than her Nashville-produced work, was notable for her continued examination of emotional matters.

DAVID CASSIDY
b. 12 April 1950, New York, USA

Like the **Osmonds** and the **Bay City Rollers**, Cassidy was briefly a seventies teen-idol.

The son of actor Jack Cassidy, he grew up in Hollywood and in 1970 secured the part of Keith Partridge in *The Partridge Family* teleseries, in which his stepmother Shirley Jones played the mother. Inspired by the **Cowsills**, the series (which ran until 1974) followed the weekly goings-on of a pop-singing family. To launch the series a single was released, 'I Think I Love You' (Bell, 1970). Featuring Cassidy on lead vocals, it sold a staggering six million copies and established him as a teen-idol, an image to adorn lunchboxes and be pinned to bedroom walls. Three more Top Twenty hits followed in 1971 – 'Doesn't Somebody Want to Be Wanted'*, 'I'll Meet You Halfway' and 'I Woke Up in Love This Morning' – and the group had a huge British hit with their version of **Neil Sedaka**'s 'Breakin' Up Is Hard to Do' in 1972, but once Cassidy began recording as a solo act, their success waned.

Cassidy's first hit, a bland remake of the **Association**'s 'Cherish'* (Bell, 1971), established the persona of a fellow teenager forever trembling on the edge of puppy love that he would titillate audiences with. For a short time, the hits flowed: 'Could It Be Forever?', 'How Can I Be Sure?', 'Rock Me Baby' (all 1972), the double-sided hit 'Daydreamer'/'The Puppy Song' (1973) – the definitive Cassidy outing – and 'If I Didn't Care' in 1974, the year he quit *The Partridge Family* and retired from teen-idoldom. He signed with RCA and recorded a series of unremarkable albums, including *Home Is Where the Heart Is* (1975). He was only briefly successful in the singles charts, first with ex-**Beach Boys** Bruce Johnston's composition 'I Write the Songs' (1975) and then with his version of the Beach Boys' 'Darlin''. He recorded intermittently thereafter, concentrating on acting

until his return to the British charts in 1985 with a remake of 'The Last Kiss' on which **George Michael** sang harmonies. In 1987 he replaced **Cliff Richard** in the London production of **Dave Clark**'s theatrical extravaganza, *Time*, and in 1990 released a solo album, *David Cassidy* (Enigma), which included the US Top Thirty hit 'Lyin' to Myself'. He made his Broadway début in 1993 starring with **Petula Clark** in *Blood Brothers* and in 1998 released his first album for eight years, *Old Trick, New Dog*.

While Cassidy's career was fading, that of his half-brother Shaun (*b. 27 September 1958, Hollywood, California*), the son of Jack Cassidy and Jones, was accelerating. Indeed, to some extent Shaun simply replaced David as the teen-idol of the late seventies. A veteran of several Hollywood teenage rock bands, Shaun was signed to Warner/Curb in 1975. His first hits came in Europe: 'Morning Gold' (1976) and his version of Eric Carmen's 'That's Rock'n'Roll'*, which was a huge American hit when issued there in 1977. His American career was launched when he starred in *The Hardy Boys* teleseries (1977–8) and his first hit was a cover of the **Crystals**' 1963 hit 'Da Doo Ron Ron'. But despite further hit singles ('Hey Deanie', 1977, and 'Do You Believe in Magic', 1978) and platinum albums (*Shaun Cassidy*), like his brother before him, Shaun found it impossible to graduate from being a teen-idol and by the eighties was concentrating on acting.

VERNON AND IRENE CASTLE
Vernon Blythe, b. 2 May 1887, Norwich, Norfolk, England, d. 15 February 1918, Fort Worth, Texas, USA; Irene Foote, b. 7 April 1893, New Rochelle, New York, d. 25 January 1969, Eureka Springs, Kansas

The Castles were the most influential ballroom dancers in the world. While they offered refined versions of the dances of their day, unlike **Victor Silvester** and the other masters of strict-tempo who followed them, they remained interpretive dancers and even danced to ragtime.

Trained as an engineer, Castle travelled to America with his actress sister, Coralie Blythe, and made an impression as a comic dancer in *The Girl Behind the Counter* (1907). He met and married Foote and the pair began dancing together at private functions. They had only limited success until they went to Paris as unknowns and returned in 1912 as the sensations of the day. They starred in **Irving Berlin**'s *Watch Your Step* (1914), inaugurated the *thé dansant*, formed their own band under the leadership of **James Europe** (who later was the first black bandleader to record) and set up their own school of ballroom dancing. They introduced numerous dance steps, notably the one-step, the turkey-trot, and several written especially for them by Ford Dabney and Europe (including 'The Castle Walk'), supervised a series of very successful dance records for RCA, and wrote the definitive book of dance steps, *Modern Dancing* (1914).

Other dancers followed in the Castles' footsteps as America's craze for dancing continued. These included Maurice and Walton, Joan Sawyer and Jack Jarrot, Mae Murray and Clifton Webb (later a movie actor) and G. Hepburn Wilson, who according to his publicity actually danced with a partner during the recording of the strict-tempo music issued by American Columbia under his supervision. However, few equalled the sinuous Castles or had the effect on fashion of Irene, who introduced bobbed hair to America.

In 1918 Vernon, who had distinguished himself as a pilot in France, died in a training accident. His widow, who retained her name through subsequent marriages, never fully resumed her professional career, instead devoting herself to animal welfare. In 1939 **Fred Astaire** and Ginger Rogers starred in *The Story of Vernon and Irene Castle*, and in 1948 Irene published her autobiography, *Castles in the Air*.

CATATONIA
Dafydd Ieuan (replaced by Aled Richards); Paul Jones; Cerys Matthews; Clancy Pegg (replaced by Owen Powell); Mark Roberts

Catatonia emerged in the midst of the Britpop boom of the mid-nineties, but were set apart from their peers by the dynamic range of Cerys Matthews' strikingly Welsh voice.

Formed in Cardiff by fellow buskers Matthews and Mark Roberts, Catatonia – also comprising bassist Jones, keyboardist Pegg and drummer Ieuan – gained a loyal following in their native Wales with the release of a pair of EPs, *For Tinkerbell* (1993) and *Hooked* (1994). Neither record was particularly remarkable, leaving Ieuan and Pegg to leave the band soon afterwards, to be replaced by Powell (guitar) and Richards (drums).

Having signed to Blanco Y Negro, the revamped membership recorded their début album, *Way Beyond Blue* (1996), from which they had a minor British hit, 'You've Got a Lot to Answer for'. After another low chart entry with 'I Am the Mob' (1997), Catatonia found themselves a mainstream fanbase with 'Mulder and Scully', which took its name from the principle characters in US TV series *The X Files* and reached the UK Top Five. The band won critical acclaim for their second album, *International Velvet* (1998), which went platinum and won the band a Brit Award. The album featured further British hit singles in 'Road Rage' and 'Strange Glue'.

In between successful tours of Britain and mainland Europe the band recorded *Equally Cursed and Blessed* (1999), which stuck to the same formula as its predecessor and achieved a similar level of success, spawning the singles 'Dead from the Waist Down' and 'Londinium'.

NICK CAVE
b. 22 September 1957, Victoria, Australia

From the unpromising start as leader of eighties Australian Stooges-copyists the Birthday Party, Nick Cave went on to produce an impressive canon of solo work and carve out a niche of his own, as influenced by the rural writings of Mark Twain as by the urban debauchery of **Lou Reed**.

As Boys Next Door, the Birthday Party was formed in Melbourne, Australia, in 1979. After one independent album under that name in 1980, the line-up of Cave (vocals), Roland S. Howard (guitar), Tracey Pew (bass), Mick Harvey (guitar, drums) and Phil Calvert (drums) relocated to London in 1981, recording an EP with New York performance artist Lydia Lunch and two albums, *Prayers on Fire* (1981) and *Junkyard* (1982), for the 4AD label before moving to Berlin. During this period, the band moved away from their Stooges soundalike phase. Calvert left in 1982 (to join the Psychedelic Furs), followed by Harvey, and the band broke up in 1983. Other Birthday Party recordings would later surface on the albums *The Bad Seed/Mutiny* and *Hee Haw*.

Cave embarked on a solo career, signing to Mute Records. His first solo album, *From Her to Eternity*, drew on the Birthday Party sound, but added a more controlled approach, notably on a cover of **Leonard Cohen**'s 'Avalanche' and the paean to Huckleberry Finn, 'Saint Huck'. The album, which reached the UK Top Forty, saw the introduction of Cave's new band, the Bad Seeds: Harvey, drummer Hugo Race, guitarist Blixa Bargeld (from Berlin band Einsturzende Neubauten) and bassist Barry Adamson (ex-Magazine). Cave's doomy lyrics, often set in a mythic American deep south, were well to the fore on the follow-up, *The Firstborn Is Dead*, laden with references to the Bible and **Elvis Presley** (both recurring obsessions) and featuring an inspired reworking of **John Lee Hooker**'s talking blues, 'Tupelo', which would become Cave's anthem. Race had left before *Firstborn* was recorded, but was not replaced until 1986's collection of cover versions (including songs by the **Seekers**, **Glen Campbell** and the **Velvet Underground**), *Kicking Against the Pricks*, which introduced Thomas Wylder. This line-up was at the core of *Your Funeral, My Trial* (1986), with ex-Cramps/Gun Club guitarist Kid Congo Powers joining for *Tender Prey* (1988), which remains Cave's most complete album.

Cave published his first novel, *And the Ass Saw the*

Angel, in 1989 (issued on CD in 1999), the year he made his acting début in the Australian prison film *Ghosts of the Civil Dead*, for which he provided the music (he had also appeared, with the Bad Seeds, in Wim Wenders' 1987 film *Wings of Desire*). Recorded in Brazil, *The Good Son* (1990) featured the band with a string backing, a successful experiment largely abandoned on the follow-up, 1992's excellent *Henry's Dream*. In 1993 *Live Seeds* captured Cave delivering a powerful set to an ecstatic audience. Even better was 1994's *Let Love in*, which treated love as both a positive and a destructive force. He followed that with the dark *Murder Ballads* (1996) and haunting *The Boatman's Call* (1997). In the same year he contributed a reading of 'Mack the Knife' to the tribute album *September Song: The Music of Kurt Weill* and published a new book, *King Ink*. In 1998 Mute issued a career retrospective, *The Best of Nick Cave*. In 2000 spoken-word label King Mob issued *The Secret Life of the Love Song*, a lecture about love songs in general and his own in particular that was given at London's Royal Festival Hall in 1999. The album also included Cave's renditions of some of his songs, notably 'Sad Waters Far from Me'.

FRANK CHACKSFIELD
b. 9 May 1914, Battle, Sussex, England, d. 9 June 1995

Arranger and orchestra leader Frank Chacksfield was a master of light mood music.

As a child Chacksfield studied piano and organ and while working as a solicitor's clerk began leading small bands in the South East. After the war he worked as an arranger on various radio shows and in 1948, the year he made his first recording, conducted **Henry Hall**'s orchestra and in 1949 **Geraldo**'s. In 1953 he formed his own orchestra and had his first hit with 'Little Red Monkey' (Parlophone). Later that year he switched to Decca and had international hits with Charlie Chaplin's 'Limelight' and another film theme, 'Ebb Tide'*, also hits for **Vic Damone** and **Roy Hamilton** and later revived by the **Platters** (1960) and the **Righteous Brothers** (1965).

His last Top Ten single success was yet another film theme 'On the Beach' (1954, 1960 in America), but more significant were the mood pieces 'In Old Lisbon' and 'Donkey Cart' (1956) which presaged the series of albums he made utilizing, like **Mantovani**, Decca's innovatory 'full frequency range recording' (ffrr) as part of its 'Phase 4' series. The first of these albums were these collections of film themes (*Film Festival*, 1968) before, in the seventies, Chacksfield made a number of easy-listening, tribute albums to songwriters. Among these, mostly titled *Frank Chacksfield Plays . . .*, were **Irving Berlin** (1976), Rodgers and Hart (1975), **Jerome Kern** (1976) and

Hoagy Carmichael (1977). He continued to record for Premier in the eighties. Later albums included *Love Is in the Air* (1984) and *A Little More Love* (1987), which included his arrangements of contemporary material like **Abba**'s 'Dancing Queen' and **Paul McCartney**'s 'Silly Love Songs'.

CHAIRMEN OF THE BOARD
'General' Norman Johnson, b. 23 May 1943, Norfolk, Virginia, USA; Eddie Curtis; Harrison Kennedy, b. Ontario, Canada; Danny Woods, b. 10 April 1944, Atlanta, Georgia

Protégés of ex-Motown writers **Holland, Dozier and Holland**, Chairmen of the Board scored several major hits in 1970–2, while lead singer Johnson enjoyed further success as a songwriter.

From Norfolk, Virginia, Johnson had been a member of the Showmen, who recorded his classic paean to rock'n'roll, 'It Will Stand' (Minit, 1961). A minor hit, the record was produced by **Allen Toussaint**, as was the equally fine follow-up, 'Country Fool'. After further releases for Minit and Swan, the group folded.

Johnson re-emerged in 1969 with Chairmen of the Board, essentially a showcase for his writing talent and distinctive gravelly vocals (although the other members occasionally sang lead). The group was one of the first to be signed to the Invictus label formed by the Holland brothers and Lamont Dozier who were looking for another **Four Tops**, with whom they had been so successful at Motown.

The Motown-flavoured first single, 'Give Me Just a Little More Time'*, was a Top Five hit in both Britain and America in 1970. The same year Johnson co-wrote, with Ronald Dunbar, the **Clarence Carter** hit 'Patches'. More success followed with 'Danglin' on a String', 'Pay to the Piper' and 'Everything's Tuesday'. Johnson also supplied songs to other H-D-H artists, including the anti-Vietnam war 'Bring the Boys Home' for Freda Payne and Honey Cone's three 1971 hits on Hot Wax: 'Want Ads'*, 'Stick-Up'* and 'One Monkey Don't Stop No Show'. Chairmen of the Board's last British hit was 'Working on a Building of Love' in 1972, after which they cut the **Sly Stone**-influenced 'black rock' album *Skin I'm In* (1974) before disbanding.

Johnson embarked on a solo career, releasing *General Johnson* (Arista, 1978), a set of his own compositions which included 'Patches' and the social commentary 'All in the Family'. He later recorded and produced disco material. Subsequently he briefly reunited with Woods for *Down at the Beach Club* (1980) and *On the Beach* (1981). The 'beach music' theme was maintained on 'Loverboy', which was a UK hit in 1986 after being remixed by Ian Levine. The definitive retrospective is *Greatest Hits* (1992).

HARRY CHAMPION
b. Harry Crump, 23 March 1866, London, d. 14 January 1942

The British music hall produced few more distinctive stylists than Champion, who sang cockney comic numbers very fast and staccato, like **Gilbert and Sullivan** patter songs in overdrive. Hoarse and bulbous-featured, he looked like the popular image of a coachman, in the tradition of Dickens' Sam Weller (and at one stage of his life he did own livery stables). His admirers regarded him, in the phrase of the early recording manager **Joe Batten** as 'the apotheosis of clean, honest vulgarity'.

Champion revealed little about his early life, but he first appeared on the London halls in 1888 as a black-face comedian under the name Will Conray. Changing to the cockney character, he launched into a series of anthems to working-class food: trotters and tripe, pies and pickles, hambone and sheep's heart. The best known is 'Boiled Beef and Carrots' (1909), a music-hall classic – as are 'Any Old Iron' (1911), revived by one-time **Goon** Peter Sellers in 1957; 'What a Mouth', revived to good effect by **Tommy Steele** in 1960; and 'I'm 'Enery the Eighth I Am' (1910), a million-seller for **Herman's Hermits** in 1965. Other Champion songs with a place in popular musical memory are 'Beaver', 'The End of My Old Cigar' and 'Ginger, You're Barmy', which was borrowed for the title of a novel by the English writer David Lodge.

In contrast to some of his contemporaries, Champion recorded prolifically and until late in life, especially for Regal. He also appeared at the Royal Variety Performances of 1932 and 1935. Traces of his legacy may be detected in the work of **Chas and Dave** and **Ian Dury**.

THE CHAMPS
Gene Alden, b. Cisco, Texas, USA (replaced by Jim Seals b. 17 October 1941, Sidney, Texas); Dave Burgess, b. Lancaster, California; Van Norman; Dale Norris, b. Springfield, Massachusetts; Chuck Rio, b. Daniel Flores, Rankin, Texas (replaced by Dash Crofts, b. 14 August 1940, Cisco, Texas)

A forceful instrumental rock'n'roll group of the late fifties, the Champs went on to greater success as solo or duo artists.

'Tequila', their first and greatest record, evolved from a studio jam at Challenge Records in Los Angeles involving five session musicians. Written by sax-player Rio and produced by label-owner Joe Johnson, the tune's mix of raucous saxophone and Latin rhythm took it to No. 1 in America and No. 5 in Britain in 1958. The track was revived in 1987 for the soundtrack of *Pee Wee's Big Adventure*. The follow-up 'El Rancho Rock' was less successful and Alden and Rio left, the latter to form a Champs-style group, the Originals.

The replacements were Texans Dean Beard, Jimmy Seals and Dash Crofts, whose earlier **Norman Petty**-produced singles had been released by Atlantic. With Seals on sax and such novelty titles as 'Mau Mau Stomp', 'Beatnik' and 'Rockin' Mary' (based on the nursery rhyme), the Champs tried in vain for another hit. More personnel changes followed as Bobby Norris replaced bass-player Norman, who was killed in a car crash, and Beard left to pursue a desultory recording career in Los Angeles and Nashville.

In 1962 the group tried to climb aboard the dance-craze bandwagon, releasing a *Great Dance Hits* album from which 'Limbo Rock' was a minor hit. By now Burgess had left the group to join **Gene Autry** and he was briefly replaced by session guitarist **Glen Campbell**. Challenge continued to release Champs singles (including a credible version of **Jimmy Reed**'s R&B classic 'Bright Lights Big City' in 1965) until the group dissolved 1964.

Seals and Crofts formed the Dawnbreakers and after their conversion to the Baha'i faith became a duo. They made numerous soft-rock albums during the seventies for Warner Brothers, scoring Top Ten hits with 'Summer Breeze' (1972), 'Diamond Girl' (1973) and 'Get Closer' (1976). They left the music business in 1978 but occasionally performed in later years.

GENE CHANDLER
b. Eugene Dixon, 6 July 1937, Chicago, Illinois, USA

Chandler was one of the most consistent soul performers, different facets of his music appealing to several generations of fans. The 1961 international million-seller 'Duke of Earl' was acclaimed as both a pop classic and the most mindless record ever. In the late sixties a string of hits produced by **Curtis Mayfield** won him critical acclaim, while seventies records like 'Get Down' were considered to be among the finest examples of disco music. By the mid-eighties the popularity of such artists as Freddie Jackson was proof that the mellow ballad style of which Chandler is a master still retained an audience.

An early career with various vocal groups led to a contract with Chicago's Vee-Jay label and 'Duke of Earl' with its catchy 'dook-dook-dook' bass refrain. Chandler was unable to follow up the hit and came under the wing of Mayfield, leader of the **Impressions**, who wrote and produced 'Rainbow', the first of a series of hits, in 1963. Shortly afterwards, Chandler moved to Vee-Jay's Constellation subsidiary, where Mayfield produced such Top Forty hits as 'Just Be True', 'Bless Our Love' (both 1964) and 'Nothing Can

Stop Me' (1965). By this time he was one of Chicago's premier R&B attractions.

In the late sixties Chandler formed his own labels, Bamboo and Mr Chand, enjoying hits with his own productions for Mel and Tim (Mel Harden and Tim McPherson), notably 'Backfield in Motion'*. At the same time he cut his own records for Mercury, scoring his biggest pop hit since 'Duke of Earl' with 'Groovy Situation'* (1970). During the seventies Chandler concentrated on his music-business interests, briefly recording for Mayfield's Curtom label and serving a short prison sentence for drugs offences in 1976.

His renaissance as an artist was the result of a contract with veteran Chicago producer Carl Davis. This produced Chandler's third million-seller, 'Get Down' (Chi-Sound, 1979). He remained with Davis's group of labels into the eighties, making a series of excellent recordings culminating in 'I'll Make the Living, If You Make the Loving Worthwhile' in 1984. In 1985 he signed with the independent Fastfire label, releasing *Your Love Looks Good on Me* and in 1991 recorded *Just Push Play*, with Eugene Church (of the **Chi-Lites**) producing. For most of the nineties he worked as an executive with Chi-Sound.

LEN CHANDLER
b. *Len Chandler Hunt Jnr, 27 May 1935, Akron, Ohio, USA*

One of the few black members of the folk revival of the early sixties, Chandler's efforts to encourage new talent gave a start to **Janis Ian**, among others.

His first musical training was on the oboe, but a high-school teacher introduced him to the heritage of the folk blues. He arranged folk songs for orchestral concerts in New Jersey before moving to New York in the late fifties. Chandler became resident singer at the Gaslight Café in Greenwich Village, where such artists as **Tom Paxton** made their début.

In 1962 he became involved in the civil-rights movement, writing many topical songs, including 'Going to Get My Baby out of Jail' and 'Which Side Are You on'. He later worked as a resident songwriter for a Los Angeles radio station before setting up the Alternative Songwriters' Chorus Showcase in 1971. This programme introduced many new artists, including Janis Ian, who first performed 'Society's Child' there.

Chandler recorded for Folkways, Blue Thumb and Columbia, among other labels.

THE CHANTELS
Arlene Smith, b. 5 October 1941, New York, USA; Sonia Goring, b. 1940, New York; Lois Harris, b. 1940, New York; Jackie Landry, b. 1940, New York; Rene Minus, b. 1943, New York

The Chantels were the first important female vocal group of the rock'n'roll era.

Discovered by **Richard Barrett** and signed to End in 1956 despite opposition from the label's owner **George Goldner**, their first records were made while they were still at school. 'He's Gone' (1957) typified the sound Barrett produced for them: lead singer Smith's voice wailing plaintively above gloomy piano chords and a simple beat with lashings of echo. That was written by Smith; their next, the superior 'Maybe'* (1958), was by Smith and Barrett. Subsequent releases 'Every Night' and 'I Love You So' (both 1958) were not as successful and in 1960 the group left End. Before this, they backed Barrett on the mawkish 'Summer's Love' (Gone, 1959).

In 1961 with Barrett again producing, but without Smith, the group moved to Carlton for 'Look in My Eyes' and 'Well, I Told You', an answer to **Ray Charles**' 'Hit the Road Jack', both Top Thirty hits, but far lighter in tone, before disappearing from sight. Smith signed with Big Top and recorded 'Love, Love, Love' with **Phil Spector** producing in 1961 before quitting the music business. In 1970 Barrett produced a new version of 'Maybe' featuring his new protégées the Three Degrees. He had previously remade another Chantels song, 'Look in My Eyes', with the Three Degrees.

HARRY CHAPIN
b. *7 December 1942, New York, USA, d. 16 July 1981, Jericho, New York*

A storyteller in the tradition of **Woody Guthrie** and **Phil Ochs**, Chapin was a singer of bitter-sweet tales – all his best songs are narratives – and an inveterate performer at benefit concerts. Sung in a plain, clear voice, his songs charted the pains of urban life.

The son of a dance-band drummer, Chapin sang in the Brooklyn Heights Boys Choir and in his teens played in a group with his brothers Tom and Stephen. After his brothers left the US to evade the draft in the sixties, Chapin pursued a career in film-making (a documentary he made with Jim Jacobs, *Legendary Champions*, was nominated for an Oscar), returning to music in the late sixties when he formed his own band with John Wallace, Ron Palmer and Tim Scott. Signed to Elektra in 1971, Chapin's début album, *Heads and Tails* (1972) was a hit, helped by the Top Twenty single, the six-minute-long 'Taxi'. The ambitious *Sniper and Other Love Songs* (1972) failed, but his next two albums, *Verities and Balderdash* (1973) and *Short Stories* (1974), which included the poignant 'Mr Tanner', sold well. Each was introduced by a hit single, respectively 'Cat's in the Cradle'* and 'W.O.L.D' (about the life and times of a deejay).

From *On the Road to Kingdom Come* (1976) onwards, Chapin's albums were either produced or arranged by his brother Stephen. His brother Tom recorded briefly for Fantasy. Though never explicitly political in his songs, Chapin's questioning doubt, best caught on *Dance Band on the Titanic* (1977), lost him the wider audience of his earlier work and in 1980 he quit Elektra for Boardwalk. His only hit for the label was the title track to *Sequel* (1981) which was literally a sequel to 'Taxi'. His death came in a car accident on the way to a benefit concert. In 1989 the album on which he had been working at the time of his death was released as *The Last Protest Singer*, and in 1990 an album of Chapin songs by such artists as **Bruce Springsteen**, **Richie Havens** and **Judy Collins** entitled *Tribute* was released. It had been recorded at a 1987 concert when Chapin was posthumously awarded the Congressional gold medal.

TRACY CHAPMAN
b. 30 March 1964, Cleveland, Ohio, USA

A politically committed songwriter in the mould of sixties performers, Chapman's first album brought her instant celebrity in the late eighties.

After playing guitar and writing songs at high school in Connecticut, Chapman joined an African drum group at Tufts University in Massachusetts. She also performed regularly in Boston folk clubs. Her recording contract with Elektra came when a fellow student played a tape of Chapman's songs to his father, a leading music publisher.

The first album, *Tracy Chapman*, was produced by David Kershenbaum and was issued in 1988 shortly before Chapman appeared at the televised Nelson Mandela tribute concert at Wembley Stadium in London. The impact of her impassioned performance took the album high in the UK and US charts. Her first single, 'Fast Car', was also a big transatlantic hit. The album's other highlights included 'Talkin' 'Bout a Revolution' and 'For My Lover'.

Chapman took part with **Peter Gabriel**, **Sting** and others in *Human Rights Now!*, a world tour for Amnesty International, before releasing *Crossroads* (1989). This repeated the formula of the début release, although Chapman was assisted by guest artists Scarlet Rivera on violin and **Neil Young**, who added a piano part to 'All that You Have Is Your Soul'. 'Freedom Now', dedicated to Nelson Mandela, was banned by South African radio.

The more muted and introverted *Matters of the Heart* was issued in 1992. Guest artists included **Bobby Womack** and Vernon Reid of Living Color. An austere outing, it included 'Bang Bang Bang' and

'Women's Work' and sold poorly. *New Beginning* (1995) saw Chapman returning to the simpler world of her earlier work, mixing intimate portraits (presumably drawn from her own life) with sweeping comments about the state of the world. 'Give Me One Reason' was a big hit. A regular performer at benefit concerts, Chapman in 1997 contributed a version of 'Holy Night' to the charity album *A Special Christmas*. She followed that with her first studio album in five years, the lacklustre *Telling Stories* (1999), on which she moved closer to the confessional mode.

THE CHARLATANS
John 'Day' Baker, b. 1969 (replaced by Mark Collins); Martin Blun, b. 1965; Jon Brookes, b. 1969; Rob Collins, b. 23 February 1963, Sedgley, Warwickshire, England, d. 23 July 1996 (replaced by Tony Rodgers); Barry 'Baz' Kettley (replaced by Tim Burgess, b. 30 May 1968, Salford, Lancashire)

A psychedelic, Hammond organ-driven rock band, the Charlatans were one of the few bands to outlive the 'Madchester' scene at the turn of the nineties, despite the death of keyboardist Rob Collins, who was initially seen as the linchpin of the group.

Starting life with a sound heavily indebted to punk rock, the Charlatans decided to head in a more pop-orientated direction after watching the **Stone Roses'** rise to fame. Ditching their original singer Baz Kettley in place of former Electric Crayons frontman Tim Burgess, the band – also including guitarist Baker, drummer Brookes and bassist Blunt alongside Hammond organ-player Collins – found themselves the subject of a bidding war between several labels after the release of their début single 'Indian Rope' (1990) on Dead Dead Good Records.

Eventually signing to Beggars Banquet, the Charlatans hit the UK Top Ten with their second single, 'The Only One I Know', a perfect encapsulation of the 'baggy' aesthetic with its bass-driven, rhythmic sound. Début album *Some Friendly* (1990) went straight in at the top of the British chart, but John Baker's subsequent departure and the personal problems of Blunt and Collins meant further material was delayed.

With a new guitarist Mark Collins (unrelated to keyboardist Rob), the group expected to continue where they left off, but found themselves generally ignored by a grunge-fixated audience with the release of their second album *Between 10th and 11th* (1992), in spite of the success of the lead-off single, 'Weirdo'. Later the same year Rob Collins was jailed for several months for his part in the robbery of an off-licence. On his release from prison the band completed *Up to Our Hips* (1994), which sold fairly well but failed to lift the group to stardom as expected.

The Charlatans returned late the following year with their eponymous fourth album, a UK Number One, which heralded a revamped sound reminiscent of the **Rolling Stones** and **Bob Dylan**. The album spawned three hit singles – 'Crashin' in', 'Just Lookin'' and 'Just When You're Thinkin' Things Over' – and included collaborations with the **Chemical Brothers**, but the band's progress was halted again when Rob Collins was tragically killed in a road accident as they began their fifth album.

Deciding to carry on without Collins (who was temporarily replaced by Martin Duffy from **Primal Scream** for live performances), the Charlatans' determination paid off as they reached new heights of popularity with the singles 'One to Another' and 'North Country Boy'. Their status as one of Britain's top bands was cemented by *Tellin' Stories* (1997), which featured new keyboardist Tony Rodgers and two further hit singles, the title track and 'How High?'.

In 1998 the Charlatans signed a new record deal with MCA after fulfilling their Beggars Banquet contract with the 'best of' compilation *Melting Pot*. They returned in 1999 with *Us and Us Only* and 'Forever', their first releases for new label Universal.

BOBBY CHARLES

b. Robert Charles Guidry, 1938, Abbeville, Louisiana, USA

From the fifties to the seventies Charles' recordings and songs were consistent in their languorous and unhurried quality. The major exception was his first record, 'Later Alligator' (1955), which borrowed freely from **Guitar Slim**'s Specialty recording, 'Later for You Baby'. Renamed 'See You Later Alligator' and recorded in a brash up-tempo manner by **Bill Haley**, it sold over a million copies in 1956.

Of Syrian descent, Charles was brought up in an atmosphere in which R&B, cajun and country musics overlapped. In 1955 he was the first white to be signed to Chess by Paul Gayten, the Chicago label's veteran New Orleans representative. Always a better balladeer than rocker, despite some engaging releases on Chess ('You Can Suit Yourself', 1957) and later Imperial ('On Bended Knee', 'Why Can't You', 1959), Charles was less successful as a recording artist than as a songwriter. He wrote the haunting million-seller 'I'm Walking to New Orleans' (1960) for **Fats Domino** (with Domino and **David Bartholomew**) and (with Gayton) the jaunty 'But I Do' for Clarence 'Frogman' Henry, which gave the singer his biggest ever hit in 1961 on Argo.

In the mid-sixties Charles turned to record promotion for Chess before recording country material for Jewel in 1967. In 1972 he recorded the critically acclaimed, relaxed *Bobby Charles* (Bearsville), a collection of well-crafted songs of social observation which included 'Small Town Talk' and the stately, wistful 'Tennessee Blues', on which he was backed by members of **The Band**, among others. Since then he has performed only intermittently. In 1987 he released *Clear Water*, an album in the style of *Bobby Charles*, but more hesitant.

RAY CHARLES

b. Ray Charles Robinson, 23 September 1930, Albany, Georgia, USA

Ray Charles is one of the greatest figures in post-war black music. The bold fusion of gospel and blues on his Atlantic recordings of the late fifties anticipated soul music, the extension of his repertoire to include country songs and pop ballads made him the 'crossover' artist supreme and the firm grip he kept on the business side of his career stands in stark contrast to those many artists who were victims of their own lack of judgement and the sharp practice of others. In addition, his singing inspired a generation of white singers, notably **Steve Winwood**, **Joe Cocker** and David Clayton-Thomas of **Blood, Sweat and Tears**.

He was blind at the age of seven and learned classical and jazz piano at a special school. He perfected imitations of the vocal styles of **Charles Brown** and **Nat 'King' Cole**, who were to remain his idols for the next decade. After playing in local dance, jazz and even country bands in Florida, Ray Robinson moved to Seattle on the West Coast in 1948. To avoid confusion with the boxing champion Sugar Ray Robinson, he now called himself Ray Charles. He made his first recordings with the McSon Trio for Jack Lauderdale's Los Angeles-based Swingtime label. The Cole-styled 'Baby Let Me Hold Your Hand' (1951) and 'Kiss Me Baby' (1952) were minor R&B hits. Two years touring as musical director for R&B artist **Lowell Fulson** ended when Charles signed to Atlantic in 1952. The following year he played on and produced Guitar Slim's hit 'The Things I Used to Do'* and formed his first small group, with David 'Fathead' Newman on tenor sax. The line-up of piano, bass, drums, two trumpets and two saxes became the model for all the great rhythm and blues bands to follow.

Five years of almost constant touring followed, along with growing record success in the R&B market. His first Atlantic hit was the novelty song 'It Should Have Been Me', but in the main Charles' uniquely rhythmic and joyous compositions were essentially gospel songs with secular lyrics. 'You Better Leave That Woman Alone' was originally 'You Better Leave That Liar Alone', while 'Lonely Avenue' and 'Talkin' About You' were adaptations of well-known gospel tunes.

He followed R&B hits like 'Mess Around' (1953) and 'I Got a Woman' (1954) with his first success with white listeners, 'Hallelujah I Love Her So' (1956). In that year, Atlantic's **Nesuhi Ertegun** organized the first of several jazz recordings for which Charles was joined by such luminaries as Milt Jackson (on *Soul Brothers*, 1959) and guitarist **Kenny Burrell**.

A year later, he simulated the call-and-response of the preacher and congregation by adding a female vocal trio, the Raelettes, led by former **Chuck Willis** backing singer Margie Hendrix. The band was also strengthened by the addition of Hank Crawford on baritone sax and this line-up cut the dynamic 'What'd I Say', a Top Ten pop hit in 1959. In that year, too, Charles recorded ballads with strings on *The Genius of Ray Charles* and scored a minor hit with a country-and-western song, **Hank Snow**'s 'I'm Movin' on'.

This mix of secularized gospel, ballads and country music, set the artistic pattern for the next decade. In 1959, however, Charles moved from Atlantic to ABC who offered him a producer's royalty and the ultimate ownership of his master tapes, terms which Atlantic could not match. He also set up his own music-publishing company, Tangerine.

In six years Charles had over twenty hits including three No. 1s which reflected the three sides of his work. **Percy Mayfield**'s 'Hit the Road Jack' (1961) was call-and-response with vocal banter between Hendrix and Charles, while **Hoagy Carmichael**'s slow ballad 'Georgia on My Mind' (1960) came from one of the first Charles concept albums, *Genius Hits the Road*, whose twelve songs had states' names in their titles. But the most epoch-making of the concept albums was *Modern Sounds in Country and Western Music* (1963), which contained 'I Can't Stop Loving You'*, the soulful version of **Don Gibson**'s song. This hit single was followed by other tracks from the album and a second volume, including 'You Don't Know Me' and 'Your Cheating Heart'. A more unexpected hit was 'One Mint Julep', from his finest jazz album, *Genius Plus Soul Equals Jazz* (1961), arranged by **Quincy Jones**.

In 1964 Charles was arrested on a drugs charge and he did not tour in the following year while he overcame his heroin addiction. From 1965 his records appeared on his own Tangerine label, which continued to be distributed by ABC until 1973. The ten albums from that period were more concepts (for example, *Sweet and Sour Tears*, 1964, a sad songs paired with a laughing songs collection) and more country with the exception of *A Message from the People* (1972), a somewhat fence-sitting collection of 'concerned' material which included the **Melanie** hit 'Look What They Done to My Song, Ma' as well as 'America the Beautiful'. His last Top Forty singles were 'Don't Change on Me' (ABC) and the instrumental 'Booty Butt' (Tangerine), in 1971.

From 1973 to 1977 Charles albums appeared on his Crossover label. The 1977 album *True to Life*, which covered **Johnny Nash**'s 'I Can See Clearly Now', marked a return to Atlantic, while from 1982 Charles' work was distributed by Columbia. The highlights of this period were a 1976 recording of *Porgy and Bess* with **Cleo Laine** and his first Nashville recording, *Wish You Were Here Tonight* (1982). This later work has tended to emphasize the Charles voice at the expense of musical innovation. In the mid-eighties he recorded a series of, mostly lacklustre, country albums for Columbia produced by **Billy Sherrill** that completely lack the fire of his ABC essays in country music. These include *Just Between Us* (1988) and *Seven Spanish Angels and Other Hits* (1989). In 1990 he moved to Warners for *Would You Believe* and *My World* (1993). In 1993 he guested with **INXS** on the hit single 'Please (You Got That . . .)'.

Charles has written for television commercials (Coca-Cola) and sang the theme songs for *The Cincinnati Kid* and *In the Heat of the Night* (1967). He appeared in *Ballad in Blue* (1964) and *The Blues Brothers* (1980). *Brother Ray*, his autobiography, written with David Ritz, was published in 1979.

Anthology (Rhino, 1989) collects together the most important of his recordings. A fuller career retrospective is the five-CD set *Genius & Soul* (Rhino). It was followed in 1998 by the collection of rarities *My Earlier Years*.

CHAS AND DAVE

Charles (Chas) Hodges, b. 28 December 1943, London, England; Dave Peacock, b. 24 May 1945, London; Mick Burt, b. 23 August 1943

The best of Chas and Dave's comic songs about working-class life in London, sung with fervent cockney accents over simple rock'n'roll riffs, brought the flavour of the music hall to the British charts in the eighties. Much of their more recent work has been in the lucrative but artistically barren fields of jingles and football songs.

Both were veterans of British rock'n'roll. Pianist Hodges was briefly a member of Mike Berry and the Outlaws – best remembered for British hits such as 'Tribute to Buddy Holly' (HMV, 1961) and 'Don't You Think It's Time' (1963) – and Cliff Bennett and the Rebel Rousers. Burt, who would later become Chas and Dave's drummer, was also a member of the group. Formed in 1961, the soulful Rebel Rousers, though they achieved little chart success ('Got to Get You into My Life' was their biggest hit on Parlophone in 1966), were one of the most respected groups of the British beat boom. In 1970–2 Hodges was a member of **Albert Lee**'s Heads, Hands and Feet, before joining forces with Peacock, then playing the rock'n'roll revival circuit, to write and perform songs with the feel, if not the sound, of traditional cockney pub sing-songs.

In 1975 they were signed to Retreat, a label owned by Big Jim Sullivan, a legendary British session guitarist, and recorded *One Fing 'n' Annuver* (1975). After Burt joined them, they produced *Rockney* (EMI 1977), which contained some of their best writing, in the manner of Ray Davies of the **Kinks** and **Squeeze**. Their first album included 'Woortcha!' which, when revived as 'Gertcha' in 1979, formed the basis for a string of television commercials for Courage beer. The song gave them a Top Twenty hit and the commercials fixed their image as purveyors of witty pub songs. They even briefly brought a touch of respectability to the sorry subgenre of the football song when, in 1981, they wrote (and performed with the Tottenham Hotspur football team) 'Ossie's Dream' and, in 1982, 'Tottenham Tottenham'. They composed later cup final efforts for the same club, including 'When the Year Ends in 1' (1991), and capitalized on the popularity of professional snooker with 'Snooker Loopy', a 1986 hit by the Matchroom Mob.

Their major hits included 'Rabbit' (1980), with the line 'you've got more rabbit [i.e. talk] than Sainsburys', 'Ain't No Pleasing You' (1982) and, in an attempt to moderate their image, 'My Melancholy Baby' (1983). However, by now they were regulars on television variety shows as well as the commercial breaks, and once a year released party records which were hugely successful, if crude compared to their earlier material.

CHUBBY CHECKER
b. Ernest Evans, 3 October 1941, Philadelphia, Pennsylvania, USA

The king of the twist, Checker was to the early sixties what **Vernon and Irene Castle** and **Victor Silvester** were to earlier generations of dancers. Indeed the twist craze temporarily restored the fortunes of the declining ballroom-dance schools originally set up by Silvester and others.

A former poultry plucker, Evans was signed to Cameo's subsidiary Parkway label by co-owner Kal Mann in 1958. Mann renamed the singer (as a variant on **Fats Domino**) and assigned him a Mann composition, 'The Class', to sing. A novelty item, in which Checker imitated Domino, **Elvis Presley** and others, it gave Checker a Top Forty hit in 1959. Checker's breakthrough came the following year when he recorded 'The Twist', already a hit for its composer, **Hank Ballard**. A million-seller, its success and that of Joey Dee and the Starliters' 'Peppermint Twist'* (Roulette, 1961), a song in honour of New York's Peppermint Lounge frequented by both adults and teenagers, made the dance the turkey-trot of its day.

Though Checker sold over ten million records in all, including a further five million-sellers ('Pony Time', 'Let's Twist Again' and 'The Fly' in 1961; 'Slow Twistin'' and 'Limbo Rock', in 1962), his career was tied to the dance craze(s) he had helped to promulgate. After 1965, apart from a 1975 hit with a reissue of 'Let's Twist Again', he no longer figured in the charts. He became a mainstay of first the nightclub and then the rock'n'roll revival circuits. In the eighties he recorded disco for MCA, including *The Change Has Come* (1982). He guested on the Fat Boys' revival of 'Let's Twist Again' (Tin Pan Apple, 1988) and in 1989 his hits were sampled on **Jive Bunny** and the Mastermixers' 'That's What I Like', a British No. 1.

THE CHEMICAL BROTHERS
Tom Rowlands, b. 1970, Henley-on-Thames, Oxfordshire, England; Ed Simons, b. 1971, London

The Chemical Brothers rose to popularity in the 1990s, marrying thundering hip-hop beats with distorted guitars and other random noises to win a following amongst dance and indie guitar fans alike.

Rowlands and Simons met while studying at Manchester University in England in the late 1980s. Sharing a love of both hip-hop and US garage guitar bands, the pair began DJing under the name of the Dust Brothers, in imitation of the US hip-hop production team of the same name. Their first recording, 'Song to the Siren', was picked up by influential UK dance DJ Andy Weatherall, and re-released on his Junior Boys Own label in 1993. Two EPs and remix work followed in 1994, before the band signed to Virgin in 1995. At this point, under threat of legal action from their US namesakes, they changed their name to the Chemical Brothers.

Their début album, *Exit Planet Dust* (1995), firmly established the Brothers' trademark hip-hop meets nasty guitar noises sound, and was a hit in both Europe and the US. As the Chemical Brothers, the band developed a reputation as a fine live act during 1995 and 1996, playing a number of large outdoor festivals, not normally fertile soil for dance-based acts. They also continued their remix work, and ran their own London club night, Heavenly Social.

In 1996 the band teamed up with **Oasis** guitarist and songwriter Noel Gallagher for the single 'Setting Sun', which was a No. 1 hit in the UK. A second UK No. 1 followed in 1997 with 'Block Rockin' Beats', ahead of a second hit album, *Dig Your Own Hole*. The pair released a DJ mix album, *Brothers Gonna Work It Out* (1998), before returning with their third studio album, *Surrender*, in 1999. The album, which included the hit single 'Hey Boy Hey Girl', again featured guest vocals from Noel Gallagher, as well as a contribution from **New Order**'s Bernard Sumner.

CLIFTON CHENIER

b. 25 June 1925, Opelousas, Louisiana, USA, d. 12 December 1987, Lafayette, Louisiana

For thirty years singer and accordionist Clifton Chenier dominated the zydeco music of Louisiana as **Bill Monroe** did bluegrass or **Muddy Waters** Chicago blues, but more commandingly. The first musician in the idiom to become familiar to the larger audiences of folk and blues, he was responsible almost single-handedly for its international recognition.

Zydeco, the dance music of the black French-speaking Southwest, developed from the cross-fertilization of the fiddle and accordion music shared by white (cajun) and black ('creole') inhabitants of southern Louisiana and the post-Second World War black idioms popular in the area, such as New Orleans R&B. The fiddle is nowadays found mostly in the more old-fashioned, rural bands, the characteristic sound of zydeco being the accordion, both the diatonic button accordion intrinsic to cajun music and, since Chenier, the chromatic piano accordion.

In the late forties and early fifties, based in Port Arthur, Texas, Chenier led weekend bands at clubs in the South Texas and Louisiana oilfield region, occasionally visiting transplanted black French communities in California, where he recorded for Specialty ('Ay-Tête-Fee', 1955). In the late fifties and early sixties he toured more widely and recorded some singles for Argo, Checker and Zynn, but the nucleus of his growing popularity was still in Southwest Texas and Louisiana. His most important and durable record connection, with Chris Strachwitz of Arhoolie, began in 1964 with a single, 'Ay Ai Ai'/'Where Did You Go Last Night'. Strachwitz released Chenier on Arhoolie albums for the white audience (he recorded at least a dozen albums over twenty years) and on Bayou 45s for the regional market. Early sidemen were pianist Elmore Nixon and Chenier's brother Cleveland on rub-board, a ridged metal singlet played with the fingers tipped by thimbles, in the manner of the skiffle washboard. Later bands moved towards a more conventional R&B line-up, with lead guitar and occasionally saxophone.

The Arhoolie association led Chenier on to the folk festival and club circuit, and in 1969 to appearances in Europe with the American Folk Blues Festival. In the seventies he alternated residencies in Southwestern clubs with tours and festivals, also featuring in the documentary films *Dry Wood and Hot Pepper* (1973, directed by Les Blank) and *Dedans la Sud de la Louisianne* (1974). Though still recording regularly for Arhoolie he appeared on **Huey P. Meaux**'s Crazy Cajun label and the local Maison de Soul and Jin labels, and on Tomato (*Cajun Swamp Music Live* from the Montreux, Switzerland, Rock/Blues Festival,

1977). He appeared in France in 1978 (recording for Free Bird), and on subsequent occasions. *I'm Here* (Alligator, 1984) won a Grammy award.

The 'King of Zydeco' had many would-be successors; the best known of them, who assumed the title of 'Crowned Prince of Zydeco', was singer and accordionist Rockin' Dopsie (*b. Alton Rubin, 10 February 1932, near Lafayette, d. 1993*), who toured internationally from the mid-seventies and recorded prolifically for Sonet. He also contributed to **Paul Simon**'s *Graceland* (1986), where he and his Twisters were called on to accompany Simon's panegyric to 'Clifton Chenier, the King of the Bayou' ('That Was Your Mother').

Rapidly making a name in eighties zydeco was singer/accordionist Buckwheat Zydeco (*b. Stanley Dural, 14 November 1947, Lafayette*), whose records on Rounder and Island with his Ils Sont Partis Band showed the more recent influence of soul and funk. Other significant figures in the genre included Michel Doucet (*Hot Chili Mama*, Arhoolie, 1993) a folklorist, fiddler and leader of the group Beau Soleil and Queen Ida & the Bon Temps Band. Clifton's son C. J. Chenier, who had joined his father's band in 1978, now leads his own Red Hot Louisiana Band.

CHER

b. Cherilyn Sarkasian LaPierre, 20 May 1946, El Centro, California, USA

Sonny and Cher were briefly American youth's ideal couple, first singing songs of teenage protest and then as wildly clothed conspicuous consumers on network television, before Cher's career outstripped that of her husband and erstwhile mentor. In the eighties she forged a successful career as a film actress before returning to music with immense success in the nineties.

After writing 'High School Dance', the B-side of **Larry Williams**' 'Short Fat Fannie'* (Specialty, 1957), Sonny (*b. Salvatore Bono, 16 February 1935, Detroit, Michigan, d. 5 January 1998, South Lake Tahoe, California*) joined Specialty as a staff producer and recorded as Don Christy for various labels. In 1963 he co-wrote 'Needles and Pins', later a million-seller for the **Searchers**, with **Jack Nitzsche** and worked as a writer and session arranger for **Phil Spector**. A back-up singer – she can be heard on the **Ronettes**' 'Be My Baby'* (Philles, 1963) – Cher recorded 'I Love You Ringo' (as Bonnie Jo Mason) for Spector in 1964, before the pair began recording in their own right, first as Caesar and Cleo and then as Sonny and Cher for Vault and Reprise.

Married in 1964, they signed to Atco in 1965, and had an immediate hit with their Los Angeles version of folk-rock, the teen anthem, 'I Got You Babe'* (successfully revived by **UB40** with the **Pretenders**'

Chrissie Hynde in 1986), written by Sonny. This was
followed by a series of hits, all of which capitalized on
the duo's comfortable, yet outrageous, image; Sonny
even recorded '(I'm Not the) Revolution Kind' (1965)
on his own. Their hits included 'Baby Don't Go'
(Reprise, 1965), 'But You're Mine' (1965) and 'The
Beat Goes on'* (1967). Produced by Sonny, the
records owed much to the arrangements of Harold
Battiste. At the same time, the pair had a series of solo
hits (also produced by Sonny and arranged by Battiste). Sonny's included 'Laugh at Me' (1965), while
on Imperial, Cher's hits included a cover of **Bob
Dylan**'s 'All I Really Want to Do' (1965), which was a
bigger hit than the **Byrds**' version, Sonny's composition 'Bang Bang (My Baby Shot Me Down)' (1966)
and 'You Better Sit Down Kids' (1967). As the hits
declined, the pair turned to films with the musical
fantasy *Good Times* (1967) and *Chastity* (1969), a vehicle for Cher's acting ambitions.

After a four-year absence they returned to the
charts with 'All I Ever Need Is You' (Kapp, 1971) and
'A Cowboy's Work Is Never Done' (1972). They followed this with a long-running television series, in
which Sonny played the foil to Cher's designer clothes
and witty put-downs, that established them as a Las
Vegas lounge act before the pair separated in 1974.
Sonny later went into politics and was elected to the
US Senate in 1994. Even before the split, it was apparent that Cher's career was blossoming at the expense
of Sonny's. With **Tommy 'Snuff' Garrett** producing,
she had a trio of American No. 1s – 'Gypsys, Tramps
and Thieves'* (Kapp, 1971), 'Half Breed'* (MCA, 1973)
and 'Dark Lady'* (1974) – all melodramatic narratives
in the manner of 'Bang Bang', which showcased her
powerful voice.

By now a Hollywood celebrity, as famous for her
liaisons with the likes of Gregg Allman (to whom she
was briefly married twice) and **Kiss**'s Gene Simmons
as her outrageous shows, Cher attempted a change of
direction with the **Jimmy Webb**-produced *Stars*
(1975), which featured her interpretation of songs by
Neil Young, **Eric Clapton** and **Jimmy Cliff**. She
turned to disco for the Top Ten hit 'Take Me Home'
(Casablanca, 1979), and was an uncredited featured
singer on **Meat Loaf**'s international hit, 'Dead Ringer
for Love' (Epic, 1981). But by then her acting career
had taken off with roles in *Come Back to the Five and
Dime, Jimmy Dean, Jimmy Dean* (1982), *Silkwood*
(1983), *The Mask* (1985), *The Witches of Eastwick*
(1987) and *Moonstruck* (1987), for which she won an
Oscar. Later films included *Tea with Mussolini* (1999).

In 1988 she returned to recording, with an epony-
mous album for Geffen which included the hits 'I
Found Someone' (co-written by **Michael Bolton**) and
'We All Sleep Alone', co-written and co-produced by
Jon **Bon Jovi**. The following year's 'If Could Turn

Back Time' (composed by **Diane Warren**), *Heart of
Stone** and 'After All', a duet with Peter Cetera from
the film *Chances Are*, were equally successful. *Love
Hurts* (Geffen, 1991) featured a lacklustre version of
the **Everly Brothers** hit and an energetic interpretation of 'The Shoop Shoop Song (It's in His Kiss)' – a
hit for **Betty Everett** in 1964. Taken from the film
Mermaids, in which she also appeared, it was an international bestseller. In 1992 the UK-only compilation
Greatest Hits 1965–1992 topped the UK chart. It initiated a period of recording in the UK for Warners with
limited success (for example, her version of the
Walker Brothers' 'The Sun Ain't Gonna Shine Anymore', 1996), before in 1998 she recorded *Believe*. A
carefully considered blend of big balladry with a
dance-beat inflection, it was a huge European hit.
Subsequently the title single topped the US charts in
1999, paving the way for the album's huge success
there.

DON CHERRY
b. 18 November 1936, Oklahoma City, Oklahoma, USA

A key associate of **Ornette Coleman** in the 'new-
wave' jazz of the sixties, trumpeter Cherry's own
bands later showed musical influences from Asia and
Africa.

Cherry and drummer Billy Higgins were members
of the Jazz Messiahs when they met Coleman in Los
Angeles in 1954. With bassist **Charlie Haden**, they
formed the nucleus for the epoch-making series of
recordings cut by Coleman between 1959 and 1963.
These included *Free Jazz* (Atlantic, 1960), a whole
album of continuous collective improvisation.

With Coleman, Cherry's thin tone on both orthodox and pocket trumpet was very much in the
leader's shadow. His début as a co-leader came with
the New York Contemporary Five, formed with
Archie Shepp in 1963, and the following year he
toured Europe and recorded with **Albert Ayler**.
Cherry's fully fledged intensely lyrical style was first
evident on *Complete Communion* (Blue Note, 1965),
which introduced the young Gato Barbieri. By now,
Cherry, like other apostles of the new jazz, was based
in Europe, where it was often easier to find appreciative audiences for avant-garde work.

Although he returned frequently to the United
States to record (for instance with Haden's Liberation
Music Orchestra and **Carla Bley**'s Jazz Composers
Orchestra) Cherry's relocation also encouraged his
interest in non-American musics. *Relativity Suite*
(JCOA, 1973) involved Tibetan bells and other sounds
garnered by Cherry during travels and studies in Asia
and Africa. He later formed the group Codona with
Colin Walcott (sitar) and Brazilian percussionist Nana
Vasconcelos to play his version of 'world music'.

In 1974 Cherry settled in Sweden, continuing to record with his early associates and making one ill-judged foray into 'fusion' music with *Here and Now* (Atlantic, 1976), produced by **Narada Michael Walden**. Don Cherry also occasionally recorded with rock musicians, including **Ian Dury**, Steve Hillage and **Lou Reed**. During the eighties he worked with Nana Vasconcelos in the Codono and Nu. His later records included *Art Deco* (A&M, 1989), *Multikulti* (1990), which had one track, 'Birdboy', dedicated to **Thomas Mapfumo**, and *A Tribute to Blackwell* (Black Saint, 1990).

In 1989 Cherry's daughter **Neneh** (*b. 10 March, 1964, Stockholm, Sweden*), a former member of the British post-punk avant-garde rock band Rip, Rig and Panic, with whom Cherry sometimes sat in, had a series of dance hits with singles from the exotic *Raw Like Sushi* (Circa). Her second album, *Homebrew* (1992), included contributions from US rap group **Gang Starr** and Michael Stipe of **R.E.M.** Neneh had an international hit single, 'Seven Seconds' with **Youssou N'Dour**, in 1994. Her half-sister Titiyo (*b. 1968*) had a Swedish hit with 'Talking to the Man in the Moon' (Telegram, 1989) and issued an epony-mous album in 1990, while their brother Eagleye enjoyed success as a youth TV presenter and, later, as singer-songwriter.

NENEH CHERRY
b. Neneh Mariann Karlsson, 10 March 1964, Stockholm, Sweden

Cherry, a groundbreaking performer of cosmopolitan origins, mixed hip-hop with the dance-pop of the eighties to create a sound which predated trip-hop and the alternative rap scene. She has managed to remain a big name in both mainstream and alterna-tive circles despite taking lengthy breaks between her three solo albums.

The daughter of West African percussionist Amadu Jah, Neneh Cherry was brought up by her mother and stepfather (jazz trumpeter **Don Cherry**) in Stockholm and New York before dropping out of school and moving to London at the age of fourteen. After work-ing with a series of punk groups, including the Cher-ries and the Slits, she joined Rip Rig and Panic, appearing on their last three albums, *God* (1981), *I Am Cold* (1982) and *Attitude* (1983). When the group split Cherry worked with one of its spin-offs, Float Up CP, on the album *Kill Me in the Morning* (1986) before deciding to embark on a solo career.

Spotted rapping in a London club, Cherry signed to Virgin subsidiary Hut and recorded her début sin-gle 'Stop the War' (1987), an attack on the conflict in the Falklands, and then featured on 'Slow Train to Dawn' by **The The**, attracting the attention of Booga

Bear (*b. Cameron McVey*), with whom she became romantically and professionally involved. The pair worked together on *Raw Like Sushi* (1989), Cherry's first solo album, which included three international hit singles – 'Buffalo Stance', 'Manchild' and 'Kisses on the Wind' – which fused the energy of **Public Enemy** with the pop nous of **Madonna**.

With the exception of her cover of 'I've Got You Under My Skin' (1990) from the charity album *Red Hot and Blue*, Cherry remained out of the limelight for the next three years as she battled Lyme disease. Her second solo album, *Homebrew* (1992), included appearances from **Gang Starr** and **R.E.M.**'s Michael Stipe, while Geoff Barrow gave 'Somedays' the same trip-hop feel he would later create as the chief musical force behind **Portishead**. She had another worldwide hit single in 1994 – 'Seven Seconds', a duet with **Yous-sou N'Dour**.

Cherry spent the next few years bringing up her two children before returning with *Man* (1996), which blended alternative rock with trip-hop and included a version of **Marvin Gaye**'s 'Trouble Man'. The album spawned two hit singles: 'Kootchi' and the string-drenched 'Woman'.

LEONARD CHESS
b. Lazer Schmuel Chez, 12 March 1917, Motol, Poland, d. 16 October 1969, Chicago, Illinois, USA

In the record company that bore their name, Leonard Chess and his brother Phil assembled most of the major artists in post-war Chicago blues, eliciting from them a body of work that was not only extremely suc-cessful in its own time but also significantly con-tributed to the later development of an international and multi-racial blues idiom.

The brothers arrived in the United States as immi-grants in 1928 and settled in Chicago. They went into the liquor business, and by the late thirties owned several clubs on the city's south side, the chief of which was the Macomba, which booked leading black entertainers of the day. Realizing that they were well placed to enter the reviving post-war record business, the brothers started a label, Aristocrat, and issued a controversial coupling by singer/saxophonist Andrew Tibbs, 'Bilbo Is Dead'/'Union Man Blues', the former side referring to an unadmired governor of Missis-sippi. Into a catalogue of mostly jump blues and vocal-group music, the country blues of the rural South was introduced in 1948 by **Muddy Waters**. Other important artists featured on Aristocrat include singer-pianist Sunnyland Slim and singer-guitarist Robert Nighthawk.

In 1950 the label's name was changed to Chess and a new numerical series began at 1425, the street-number of the family home on S. Karlov. (The initial release was by tenor-saxophonist Gene Ammons.) Waters' 'Rollin' Stone' was a hit that year, and Leonard Chess began to look for more southern-styled or down-home material from regional contacts like **Sam Phillips**, who supplied him (and at the same time the **Bihari Brothers**) with sides by Memphis-area artists such as Jackie Brenston ('Rocket "88"', 1951) and, most importantly, **Howlin' Wolf**. From Waters' Chicago circle came guitarist Jimmy Rogers, whose first recording was 'That's All Right' in 1950, and **Little Walter**, whose 'Juke' was a hit in 1952 on the sister-label Checker. Singer-pianist Willie Mabon was successful in the following year with 'I Don't Know' and 'I'm Mad', and 1952–3 generally was a profitable period for down-home blues on Chess, distinguished by superb, if not always commercially successful, recordings by **John Lee Hooker**, singer-guitarists Floyd Jones and John Brim and singer-pianist Eddie Boyd. Chess himself was soon recognized as an inventive and sympathetic producer who worked long to obtain the quality and effect he wanted, and the label acquired a recognizable house sound from its makeshift echo technique. Production and associated roles were frequently assigned to **Willie Dixon**.

Chess himself spent much of the first half of the fifties on the road in the South, establishing a widespread distribution network and radio contacts on stations like Nashville's WLAC. He also set up a music publishing company, Arc Music, in 1953. In 1955 **Sonny Boy Williamson II** joined the label, an acquisition somewhat eclipsed by the arrival in the same year of **Chuck Berry** and **Bo Diddley**, the former's 'Maybellene' giving Chess its first national hit. Williamson and Bo Diddley were assigned to Checker, on which the début recordings of **Otis Spann** (1955), and sides by **J. B. Lenoir** and **Lowell Fulson** – whose 'Reconsider Baby' (1954) initiated an eight-year stay – also appeared. Vocal groups like **Harvey Fuqua**'s Moonglows and the **Flamingos** were signed, as the down-home proportion of Chess/ Checker output decreased. A jazz label, Argo, also did well with pianists **Ramsey Lewis** and **Ahmad Jamal**.

The sixties saw Chess's interest in blues giving place to other concerns, such as his ownership, from 1963, of the Chicago station WVON. Session supervision passed to producer **Ralph Bass**, who had joined the company from King subsidiary Federal, and to Leonard's son Marshall. Founding figures like Waters, Wolf and Williamson remained on the roster, joined by younger artists like **Buddy Guy** and, briefly, **Otis Rush**, but their releases were less frequent and they moved, as the blues business in general was moving, towards album rather than single production. The label's reputation overseas – Chess material licensed to the British Pye International had had an enormous influence on British R&B bands – drew to its studios

such groups as **Fleetwood Mac** and led to international collaborations like Waters' and Wolf's London recordings. After Leonard Chess's death the company was sold to the tape corporation GRT, and soon afterwards Phil left to manage WVON, while Marshall worked for the **Rolling Stones**' eponymous label. Under the new proprietors the label was chiefly used for a series of reissue projects from the company's extensive holdings, a policy that survived further changes in ownership, to New York record man Joe Robinson and finally MCA.

ALBERT CHEVALIER
b. 21 March 1861, London, England, d. 11 July 1923

Known as 'The Costers' Laureate' ('though not, one imagines, by the costers themselves' according to Colin MacInnes), Albert Chevalier drew on cockney working-class life to write and sing some of the most highly coloured and best-loved songs of the Victorian music hall. Though he has been accurately described as 'that rarity in the halls before the First Great War, an outsider from the middle class' (another was George Robey), he was regarded by many of his contemporaries as a wholly credible interpreter of the cockney character, if less intrinsically authentic than, say, **Gus Elen** or Kate Carney.

That he slipped into the part so smoothly may be attributable to the fourteen years of straight acting that preceded his music-hall début in 1891. He was an immediate success with songs like 'The Future Mrs 'Awkins', 'Knocked 'Em in the Old Kent Road' (1891) and the enduring 'My Old Dutch' (1893), most of which he wrote himself, sometimes to music composed by his brother. 'My Old Dutch' included passages of spoken narrative, a form Chevalier developed in monologues like 'The Fallen Star', and in his last years he left the halls to deliver such recitations from the concert stage. He recorded a number of his monologues for HMV from 1911, including 'The Future Mrs 'Awkins' and 'Our Little Nipper'. He reflected on his career in the autobiographies *Albert Chevalier* (1896) and *Before I Forget* (1901).

MAURICE CHEVALIER
b. 12 September 1888, Menilmontante, France, d. 1 January 1972, Paris

A star of the French music hall, Chevalier became the best-known Frenchman outside France when he brought his romantic swagger and instantly identifiable crooning style to Hollywood.

Chevalier entered showbusiness as an acrobat at the age of twelve graduating to singing after an accident. Already a popular entertainer, in 1908 he partnered the legendary French music-hall star Mistinguett and started his film career with the silent short *Trop Créd-ule*. He returned to the music-hall stage after the First World War in the role of the straw-hatted, bow-tied *boulevardier* he would play for the rest of his career. After success in the operetta *Dedé*, he travelled to London for the revue *White Birds* and then to Hollywood. His first film there, *Innocents of Paris*, introduced the **Leo Robin** and Richard Whiting composition, the enduring 'Louise' whose opening line was made for Chevalier's accented crooning: 'Every little breeze seems to whisper Louise'. In *The Big Pond* (1930) he introduced the **Sammy Fain** composition, 'You Brought a New Kind of Love to Me'. There followed a series of Ruritanian operettas, the best of which were directed by Ernst Lubitsch, including *The Love Parade* (1929); *One Hour with You* (1932); *Love Me Tonight* (1932), which included an extended version of **Richard Rodgers**' and **Lorenz Hart**'s 'Isn't It Romantic'; and *The Merry Widow* (1934), the best version of **Franz Lehár**'s classic operetta. In these he was partnered by **Jeanette Mac-Donald**. Unhappy, however, with only being offered roles as a debonair lover, he returned to Paris.

Accused of collaborating with the Nazis during the Second World War, Chevalier's career suffered briefly in the forties, before he returned to film-making in France and commenced the highly successful series of one-man shows he mounted until 1968. Recalled to Hollywood to receive a special Oscar and appear in *Love in the Afternoon* (1957), he quickly assumed the persona of the *risqué* uncle for his second Hollywood career. *Gigi* (1958) gave him his best-remembered role and song, the **Frederick Loewe** composition 'Thank Heaven for Little Girls'. Throughout the sixties he alternated television, films and his one-man shows with regular appearances on the French stage.

THE CHI-LITES

Crendal Jones, b. 1939 St Louis, Missouri, USA (replaced by David Scott); Robert Lester; Eugene Record, b. 23 December 1940, Chicago, Illinois (replaced by Danny Johnson); Marshall Thompson, b. April 1941, Chicago, Illinois

Featuring the songs and warm, romantic voice of Eugene Record, the Chi-Lites were one of the most consistently successful soul vocal groups of the seventies.

Formed in 1960 and originally known as the Chanteurs and then Marshall and the Hi-Lites, the group of Thompson, Jones and Lester recorded for James Shelton Junior and other local Chicago labels before former cab driver Record joined them in the late sixties. Moving to Brunswick, the Chi-Lites used a falsetto-led style of group harmonizing for the R&B hits 'Give It Away' (1969) and 'Let Me Be the Man My Daddy Was'.

The group's smooth and immaculate harmonies first made an impact on the pop audience with the Top Thirty hit '(For God's Sake) Give More Power to the People' (1971), whose title echoed the political slogans of the Black Power movement. Their biggest hits, however, were the slow ballads 'Have You Seen Her' (1971) and 'Oh Girl', which reached No. 1 in America. For this song and the melancholic '(The) Coldest Days of My Life', Record surrounded his high, thin tenor with restrained but dramatic production effects in a manner reminiscent of **Gamble and Huff**. A number of the group's songs were co-written by Record with Barbara Acklin, whose own career included a Top Twenty hit with the Record–Acklin song 'Love Makes a Woman' (Brunswick, 1968).

The Chi-Lites had further R&B hits with 'A Letter to Myself' (1973), the joyous 'Stoned out of My Mind', 'Homely Girl' (1974) and 'Too Good to Be Forgotten' (1975). Later records – 'It's Time for Love' and 'You Don't Have to Go' (1976) – were British Top Ten hits but the group's run of success was halted by the demise of Brunswick amid payola accusations and the departure of Record for a solo career with Warners. This produced the acclaimed but uncommercial *The Eugene Record* (1977) and *Trying to Get You* (1978).

With Thompson reassuming the leadership, plus new members Johnson and Scott, the Chi-Lites moved to Mercury for *Happy Being Lonely* (1976) and *The Fantastic Chi-Lites* (1977). They made little headway against the disco boom, however, and in 1980 Record rejoined and the group made *Me and You* (20th Century Fox, 1981). In 1983 the Chi-Lites had a minor British hit with 'Changing for You' (R&B).

Their later recordings were *Steppin' Out* (Private I, 1984), *Hard Act to Follow* (Nuance, 1986) and 'Just Say You Love Me' (Ichiban, 1990). By this time Anthony Watson had replaced Record, who worked as a producer for **Gene Chandler** and others. The group continued to play cabaret venues into the nineties, recording *Help Wanted* in 1997.

CHICAGO

Peter Cetera, b. 13 September 1944, Chicago, Illinois, USA; Terry Kath, b. 31 January 1946, Chicago, d. 23 January 1978, Los Angeles, California; Robert Lamm, b. 13 October 1944, New York; Lee Loughnane, b. 21 October 1946, Chicago; Walter Parazaider, b. 14 March 1945, Chicago; James Pankow, b. 20 August 1947, Chicago; Walter Perry, b. 1945, Chicago; Danny Seraphine, b. 28 August 1948, Chicago

With **Blood, Sweat and Tears**, Chicago pioneered the blending of jazz and rock in the late sixties. The band's music settled into a more mainstream rock style in later years which was featured in a regular stream of albums titled only by numbers. All but two of them were million-sellers.

Guitarist Kath and horn-player Parazaider formed the Big Thing in 1967. Featuring the singing of bass-player Cetera and a brass section with Perry (saxes), Pankow (trombone) and Loughnane (trumpet), the group became Chicago Transit Authority and signed to Columbia. In 1969 an eponymous début album was produced in Los Angeles by Jim Guercio. As well as a version of **Steve Winwood**'s 'I'm a Man', it included a sequence based on the demonstrations at the 1968 Democratic Convention in Chicago.

The following year the band shortened its name and had three big hits. Pankow's 'Make Me Smile' and Lamm's '25 or 6 to 4' came from *Chicago II* (1970), while the ballad 'Does Anybody Really Know What Time It Is?', written by Lamm, had appeared on the début album. During the rest of the seventies Chicago perfected a smooth mainstream jazzy-rock approach and were rewarded with over a dozen Top Twenty hits. Of these, Lamm's 'Saturday in the Park' (1972), 'Just You 'n' Me' (1973) and the international No. 1 'If You Leave Me Now' (1976) were million-sellers.

The band's personnel remained remarkably stable during these years. Perry had left after the first album and Brazilian percussionist Laudir De Oliveira joined for *Chicago VII* (1974). After Kath's death in a shooting accident, guitarist Donnie Dacus and Chris Pinnick stayed briefly before Bill Champlin (guitar, keyboards) became a permanent member.

During the late seventies and early eighties Chicago's somewhat bland style was less effective and they were dropped by Columbia in 1981. Guercio had ceased producing the band after *Chicago XI* (1977), starting his own Caribou label as well as working with the **Beach Boys** and others. Chicago's career was revived, however, by Canadian songwriter and producer David Foster who supervised the American No. 1 'Hard to Say I'm Sorry' (Full Moon, 1982), from the film *Summer Lovers*, and its accompanying album *Chicago 16*, the band's biggest hit for years. Foster also masterminded the following two albums which provided more hits with 'Hard Habit to Break' (1984), 'You're the Inspiration' (1985) and 'Along Comes a Woman'.

1986 saw a major upheaval with Cetera leaving for a solo career which began with his own composition 'The Glory of Love' (theme from *The Karate Kid Part II*, Warners). He duetted with gospel singer **Amy Grant** on 'Next Time I Fall' (1986) and both *Solitude/Solitaire* (1986) and *One More Story* (1988) were best-sellers. 'After All', a 1989 duet with **Cher**, was a Top Ten hit. Later recordings, including 1992's *World Falling Down*, were less successful, however.

To replace Cetera, Chicago recruited bassist/vocal-ist Jason Scheff who appeared on *Chicago 18* (1986), but their most successful record of the year was a reissued '25 or 6 to 4'. However, Scheff featured on the 1987 hits 'Will You Still Love Me?' and 'She Would Have Been Faithful'. The Ron Nevison-produced *Chicago 19* (1988) continued the group's run of hits with the Albert Hammond–**Diane Warren** song 'I Don't Wanna Live without Your Love' (Reprise). 'Look Away' topped the American charts in the same year. A further hit was 'What Kind of Man Would I Be' (1989) while later albums included *Liberation* (1990) and *Twenty 1* (1991), once more produced by Ron Nevison. The only personnel change during this period was the replacement of original drummer Seraphine by Tris Imboden in 1992. *Night and Day* followed in 1995, but the bulk of the group's recordings in the nineties were retrospectives and 'best of's on a variety of labels, the group having kept the ownership of their masters. The best of these was *The Heart of Chicago, 1967–1997*.

THE CHIEFTAINS

Paddy Moloney, b. 1938, Dublin, Ireland; Sean Potts, b. 1930; Martin Fay, b. 1936, Dublin; Peadar Mercier, b. 1914; Derek Bell, b. 1935, Belfast; Sean Keane, b. 1946; Michael Tubridy, b. County Clare (replaced by Matt Molloy, b. Ballaghaderreen, County Roscommon); Kevin Conneff, b. Dublin

The group that played a major role in shifting the image of Irish folk music away from the raucous bawdiness associated with the Dubliners, the Chieftains' instrumental virtuosity mixed formal arrangements of traditional tunes with improvisations based upon them.

The group originated in the Coeltiori Cualann folk orchestra of Dublin composer and folklorist Sean O'Riada. An informal grouping including Moloney (uillean pipes and tin whistle), Potts (tin whistle), Fay (fiddle) and Tubridy (flute), they took the name Chieftains for their first record in 1963 for Garech Browne's Claddagh label. It included the slip jig 'Comb Your Hair and Curl It', a tune which became a favourite in the Dubliners' own repertoire as 'The Rocky Road to Dublin'.

There was a gap of six years before *Chieftains II* appeared, with the addition of Mercier – on bodhran (percussion) – and Keane, a classically trained violinist. An appearance at the 1970 Cambridge Folk Festival brought them wider recognition, but it was not until the group linked up with former **Steeleye Span** manager Jo Lustig in 1973 that the breakthrough to an international audience began.

Chieftains IV (1973) included the stately 'Morgan Magan', composed by the eighteenth-century blind harpist O'Carolan and played by classical harpist Bell,

who joined the band from the BBC Symphony
Orchestra in Belfast the following year. The O'Riada
composition 'Women of Ireland' formed part of the
score for Stanley Kubrick's *Barry Lyndon* (1975), and
won the group an Oscar in 1976. Lustig signed them
to Island for *Chieftains V* (1975), which recognized
common Celtic roots by including a set of Breton
tunes. The singer and bodhran-player Kevin Conneff
joined in 1976.

By now the Chieftains were in global demand,
touring North America, Japan, Australasia and
Europe. They played at open-air rock events alongside the **Grateful Dead** and **Eric Clapton** and Molony
played on sessions for **Paul McCartney** and Art Garfunkel, while the group provided traditional music
for a number of films. In 1979 the group performed
before was what claimed to be the biggest ever live
audience: the 1.3 million people who gathered in
Dublin's Phoenix Park for the Papal mass. In the
same year former Bothy Band violinist Matt Molloy
replaced Tubridy.

With another label switch (to Columbia) in 1978,
Chieftains' albums appeared at regular intervals, and
their music showed some willingness to encompass
other national traditions: most notably in 1985, when
the group was accompanied by a Chinese orchestra
during a visit to that country. The performance was
released as *Live in China* (Claddagh, 1985). In 1988 the
group regularly appeared in concert with **Van Morrison**, with whom they recorded the spritely *Irish
Heartbeat*, and signed to RCA Victor, releasing *A
Chieftains Celebration* (1989) to commemorate their
25th anniversary. *Over the Sea to Skye* (1991) was
recorded with **James Galway** while *Reel Music* (1991)
was a collection of the group's film music.

The Bells of Dublin (1991) and *An Irish Evening: Live
at the Grand Opera House, Belfast* (1992) continued
their tradition of playing with guest artists. The former, a collection of Christmas-related songs, included
Marianne Faithfull singing 'I Saw Three Ships a Sailing', the **McGarrigles** and performances of new songs
by **Elvis Costello** and **Jackson Browne**. *An Irish
Evening* featured **Nanci Griffith** and Roger Daltry of
The Who singing 'Behind Blue Eyes'. Even better was
1995's *The Long Black Veil*, on which they were joined
by Mick Jagger, **Van Morrison**, **Ry Cooder**, **Sting** and
Sinead O'Connor. It was followed by *Santiago* and the
authorized biography *The Chieftains* in 1997. The well-
received *The Long Journey Home* (1998) consisted of
music for the television documentary *The Irish in
America*, while *Tears of Stone* (1999) saw the group
operating as a back-up ensemble for a number of
women singer-songwriters (including **Mary-Chapin
Carpenter**, **Joni Mitchell**, the **Corrs** and **Bonnie Raitt**)
on a collection of love songs. They returned to centre
stage for *Water from the Well* (2000), an enjoyable

roots-based outing that includes 'The Lovely Sweet
Banks of the Moy' and other traditional offerings.

THE CHIFFONS
*Barbara Lee, b. 16 May 1947, Bronx, New York, USA,
d. May 15, 1992; Patricia Bennett, b. 7 April 1947, Bronx;
Sylvia Peterson, b. 30 September 1946, Bronx; Judy
Craig, b. 1946, Bronx*

One of the most distinctive girl groups of the sixties,
the Chiffons' sound was lighter than most.

The Chiffons met at high school and in 1960 had a
minor hit with a cover of the **Shirelles**' 'Tonight's the
Night' (Big Deal) before coming under the wing of
writer/manager Ronald Mack. In 1963 he took their
demo of his composition 'He's So Fine' to Phil and
Mitch Margo, Hank Medress and Jay Siegel, who as
the Tokens had had an American chart-topper with
'The Lion Sleeps Tonight'* (RCA, 1961), and were
operating as Bright Tunes Production Company.
Leased to Laurie, the Chiffons' recording was propelled to the top of the American charts on the
strength of its infectious 'doo lang, doo lang' intro
and Craig's sophisticated lead vocals. Later, **George
Harrison**'s biggest solo hit 'My Sweet Lord'* (Apple
1970) was judged to be derivative of Mack's song and
the Chiffons recorded their own version of Harrison's hit.
For their second Top Ten hit, 'One Fine Day' (1963),
their producers simply replaced Little Eva's vocals on
a recorded master with theirs. The group also
recorded for the Laurie subsidiary Rust as the Four
Pennies.

However, like so many of the girl groups of the sixties, the Chiffons were unable to build a solid career
on the basis of their chart hits. After the success of 'A
Love So Fine' (1963) , 'I Have a Boyfriend' (1964) and
the Motownish 'Sweet Talkin' Guy' (1966, and a reissued hit in Britain in 1972), they faded from view.
They appeared only locally in New York until 1989,
when they made a return on the US oldies circuit. In
1992 Barbara Lee died of a heart attack, and the group
stopped performing.

FRANCIS J. CHILD
*b. Francis James Child, 1 February 1825, Boston,
Massachusetts, USA, d. 11 September 1896, Boston*

The most important folk-song scholar of the nineteenth century, Child's codification of English and
Scottish material into the 'Child Ballads' became the
basic source for singers of traditional songs.

The son of a sail-maker, Child was a brilliant literary scholar who became a Harvard University professor at the age of twenty-six. His earliest interests were
in English and Scottish poetry, but these led him to
traditional verse. He published a volume on *English*

and Scottish Ballads in 1858 and in 1872 was commissioned to undertake a more exhaustive study. During the next twenty-four years, Child collected 305 traditional ballads, primarily from such printed sources as Bishop Percy's *Reliques of Ancient English Poetry* (1767). Publication of the ballads was completed two years after his death.

Child's collection was selective rather than exhaustive, with some songs excluded because of 'indecency' and others edited to emphasize their poetic aspects. However, it has remained the basic reference point for the singers of the folk revival who concentrate on traditional material. Thus, **Ewan MacColl**'s and Peggy Seeger's two ballad-recording projects, *The Long Harvest* and *Blood and Roses* (Blackthorne, 1982), refer to the songs by the numbers given to them in Child's work, for example 'The False Knight on the Road' (Child 3).

In the sixties Professor Bertrand Bronson compiled a four-volume work, *The Traditional Tunes of the Child Ballads*, which restored the melodies to Child's texts.

CHINN AND CHAPMAN
Michael Chapman, b. 16 May 1947, Brisbane, Australia; Nicholas Chinn, b. 13 April 1946, Bristol, England

Masters of the catchy, disposable pop song, Chinn and Chapman composed over fifty British Top Ten hits during the seventies. Chapman went on to produce rock acts, including **Blondie** and **Pat Benatar**.

Chapman moved to England and recorded for RCA with progressive rock band Tangerine Peel before meeting Chinn, who had written songs for the Peter Sellers' movie *There's a Girl in My Soup* (1970) with ex-**Manfred Mann** singer Mike D'Abo. Teaming up to write chart material inspired by American bubblegum hits like the Archies' 'Sugar Sugar', they embarked on fruitful partnerships with producers **Mickie Most** and Phil Wainman. The first Most hit was 'Tom Tom Turnaround' (RAK, 1971) by Australian band New World. The following year Most brought **Suzi Quatro** to Chinn and Chapman; they provided her with a series of ten hit songs, including 'Can the Can' (1973) and 'Devil Gate Drive' (1974).

The first Wainman-produced hits came from **Sweet**, whose ten chart entries appeared on RCA between 1971 and 1974. Like later Chinnichap bands Mud and Smokie, they were initially a competent bar band playing covers of Top Forty material on to whom the songwriters could graft a style and image. Sweet were glam and glitter, Mud (through singer Les Gray's creditable **Elvis Presley** impersonation) were rock'n'roll revival, and Smokie were Chapman's version of mid-seventies soft-rock.

Among Mud's dozen or so hits were two British

No. 1s written by Chinn and Chapman: the lugubrious ballad 'Lonely This Christmas' and the lively 'Tiger Feet'. After an abortive launch of Smokie as an album band – the BBC banned the title track 'Pass It Around' because of possible drug connotations – Chinn and Chapman reverted to targeting the singles chart. 'If You Think You Know How to Love Me' (RAK, 1975) was the first in a series of Top Twenty songs which continued until 1978. Smokie singer Chris Norman had a US hit duetting with Quatro on 'Stumblin' in' (RSO, 1979).

Sensitive to criticism that they were 'puppets' of Chinn and Chapman, both Sweet and Mud left to make their own records, though with little lasting success. By the mid-eighties Mud were recreating 'Tiger Feet' and the rest on the supperclub circuit.

Chapman, who had produced the Mud hits, moved to Los Angeles in the mid-seventies and in 1978–9 produced three American chart-toppers: Exile's 'Kiss You All Over'* (Warner Brothers), Nick Gilder's 'Hot Child in the City'* and the Knack's 'My Sharona'*. But his major (and most highly regarded) success was his work on three Blondie albums, *Parallel Lines* (1978), *Eat to the Beat* (1979) and *Autoamerican* (1980), where his pop sensibility was a perfect foil for the group's art-rock approach. His other work, with Pat Benatar, ex-**Abba** singer Agnetha Fältskog, **Tanya Tucker** and others, was less successful, as was Dreamland, a label set up with Chinn in 1979 which folded after two years.

Chapman's most successful productions of the eighties were for Lita Ford, former guitarist with **Kim Fowley** protegées, the Runaways.

THE CHORDETTES
Dorothy Schwartz, b. Sheboygan, Wisconsin, USA (replaced 1953 by Lynn Evans); Jinny Osburn, b. Sheboygan (replaced 1953 by Margie Needham); Janet Ertel, b. Sheboygan, d. 22 November 1988; Carol Bushman, b. Sheboygan

With their bright sound, the Chordettes both looked back to the **Andrews Sisters** and the big-band vocal groups and forward to the girl groups of the sixties.

The Chordettes began singing at college. They won an *Arthur Godfrey Talent Scouts* contest in 1949 and remained with the show for some four years. Signed by Archie Bleyer, the show's music director, to his Cadence label, they had a huge hit with the lullaby 'Mr Sandman'* in 1954 (Bleyer later married Janet Ertel). The song was covered in Britain by Max Bygraves and Dickie Valentine. In 1956 the Chordettes followed up with a bland cover of the Teen Queens' plaintive R&B hit, 'Eddie My Love', co-authored by **Maxwell Davis**. Other hits included 'Born to Be with You' (1956), 'Lay Down Your Arms' (1956), which, unusually for the time, was a cover of a British hit by **Anne Shelton**, and the strident 'Lollipop'* (1958), another cover of a black recording and their biggest hit. However, by the end of the fifties their sound was increasingly anachronistic and after releasing a version of the film theme song 'Never on Sunday' (1961), they moved to the cabaret circuit.

Osborn's decision to retire a few years later caused the group to split up. In 1988 Lynn Evans re-formed the Chordettes to appear in a doowop revival concert in New York. The other members were Nancy Overton (who had toured as a member of the Chordettes in the fifties), her sister Jean Swain and barbershop singer Doris Alberti.

CHARLIE CHRISTIAN
b. 29 July 1916, Dallas, Texas, USA, d. 2 March 1942, New York

Despite the brevity of his professional career, Christian did more than anyone else to create modern jazz guitar-playing, using the electric guitar for solos based on single-note runs and phrased like those of a horn. His impact on jazz was comparable to that of **Jimi Hendrix** on rock.

The son of a blind singer/guitarist, Christian grew up in Oklahoma City and built his first guitar from cigar boxes, to the amazement of his classmate, the future novelist Ralph Ellison. He played in his brother's band the Jolly Jugglers during the thirties, also working as a tap-dancer, baseball pitcher and prizefighter.

Christian was inspired to take up amplified guitar by seeing Eddie Durham, who had played the amplified instrument on **Jimmie Lunceford**'s 1935 recording, 'Hittin' the Bottle'. In 1937 he bought a Gibson ES-150, the best electric guitar on the market, which he played in bands led by Anna Mae Wilburn (later the conductor of the all-woman Sweethearts of Rhythm) and Alphonso Trent. Inspired by the long solo lines of tenor saxophonist **Lester Young**, Christian took the guitar out of the rhythm section and into the front line with trumpet and saxophone. He was to play with Young at **John Hammond**'s 'Spirituals to Swing' concert at the end of 1939. That year began with Christian refusing an offer from **Henry Busse**, after which he was heard by Hammond who recommended him to **Benny Goodman**. Initially sceptical, Goodman was so impressed by Christian's sophisticated improvisation that he reportedly let the first number they played together run on for over thirty minutes.

Christian's recordings with Goodman included 'Flying Home', a marvellously restrained version of **Hoagy Carmichael**'s 'Star Dust', 'Seven Come Eleven' and 'Solo Flight' (Columbia). The last (probably Christian's finest performance) was developed from 'Chonk Charlie Chonk', a theme worked out with drummer **Kenny Clarke** at Minton's, an afterhours club where Christian would go after his evening stint with Goodman at New York's Pennsylvania Hotel.

It was here that Christian contributed to the formation of bebop, a process documented on the aptly named 'Swing to Bop', a live recording with Clarke and **Dizzy Gillespie**, made by Jerry Newman, a fan, on his portable machine (*Harlem Jazz Scene 1941*, Esoteric). The Goodman recordings have been collected on two Columbia albums. He also recorded with **Lionel Hampton** and Ed Hall.

Christian was taken ill on a Midwest tour with Goodman in 1941. He died of tuberculosis the following year.

THE CHRISTIANS
Garry (Garrison) Christian, b. 1955, Merseyside, England; Roger Christian, b. 1950, Merseyside; Russell Christian, b. 8 July 1956, Merseyside; Henry Priestman, b. 21 June, Hull

In the eighties the Christians combined a tight, soulful harmony sound with sharp, socially aware lyrics, much as the **Impressions** or the **Staple Singers** had done in previous decades.

The three Christian brothers had performed as an *a cappella* soul trio under various names (performing on a TV talent show as Natural High in 1974) for several years before meeting up with songwriter and keyboard-player Henry Priestman (ex-the Yachts/It's Immaterial), a veteran of the Liverpool New Wave scene. The band signed to Island in 1986 and (now minus Roger) recorded their eponymous début album in 1987. It included three hit singles, 'Forgotten Town', 'Hooverville' and 'When the Fingers Point'. *The Christians* was Island's bestselling début album. A fourth hit single from the album, 'Ideal World', ended the year on a high. Roger Christian released a solo album, *Checkmate*, in 1989.

The following year saw the Christians touring to support the album, releasing two more hit singles, 'Born Again' and a version of the **Isley Brothers**' 'Harvest for the World', which reached the UK Top Ten. This was followed by an appearance on the charity single 'Ferry Cross the Mersey' (1989) along with other Liverpool artists, and by the band's eighth UK hit, 'Words'. The long-delayed second album, *Colour*, appeared in 1990, and gave the Christians another UK No. 1. The follow-up album, *Happy in Hell* (1992), followed the blueprint of its predecessors. In 1993 Island collected the band's hits to date on *The Best of the Christians*. The band defunct, Garry Christian released the poorly received solo album *Your Cool Mystery* in 1997.

LOU CHRISTIE

b. Lugee Geno Sacco, 19 February 1943, Glenn Willard, Pennsylvania, USA

Christie's mastery of the quavering falsetto gave him three million-sellers, all of which were stylistic throwbacks to the sound of **Del Shannon**.

Christie studied music and vocal technique before recording with the Classics and Lugee and the Lions on various local Philadelphia labels from 1959 onwards. It was for one of these, Co & Ce Records, that in 1962 he recorded 'The Gypsy Cried'*. It was written by Christie and Twyla Herbert, his regular writing partner whom press releases of the time described as 'a mystic twenty years Christie's senior'. Picked up by Roulette, the record was a huge hit in 1963, as was the equally melodramatic 'Two Faces Have I'*.

After two years in the army, he returned with his finest record, 'Lightnin' Strikes'* (MGM, 1966) and 'Rhapsody in the Rain' (1966), which was deemed to be sexually explicit and was banned by radio stations in the US and in the UK. After brief stays with Colpix ('Big Time', 1966) and Columbia ('Shake Hands and Walk Away Crying', 1967), during which time one of his old Co and Ce recordings, 'Outside the Gates of Heaven' (1966), was a hit, Christie joined Buddah for his last international hits, the frantic 'I'm Gonna Make You Mine' and 'She Sold Magic' in 1969. He later recorded for numerous labels, including Elektra, Three Brothers (*Zip-A-Dee-Doo-Dah*, 1974) and Lifesong, without success, and subsequently played the rock'n'roll revival circuit. In 1997 he released his first album of new material for twenty years, *Pledging My Love*.

THE CLANCY BROTHERS AND TOMMY MAKEM

Liam Clancy, b. 1936, Carrick-on-Suir, Ireland; Tom Clancy, b. 1923, Carrick-on-Suir, d. 7 November 1990, Cork; Paddy Clancy, b. 1922, Carrick-on-Suir, d. 10 November 1998, Carrick-on-Suir; Tommy Makem, b. 1932, Keady, County Armagh, d. 1990

The Clancy Brothers and Tommy Makem were the first group to popularize Irish traditional music in America, establishing the boisterous style in which it would generally be performed in the sixties and seventies.

While working as an actor in New York, Paddy Clancy was associated with **Moe Asch**'s Folkways label and Jac Holzman's Elektra Records in arranging and editing traditional material. He formed his own Tradition label, initially recording such artists as **Odetta** and **Josh White** in 1956. Tom, a former pop vocalist in Ireland, had also emigrated to America to pursue a career in the theatre.

Although there was a family background of tradi-

tional song, only Liam was involved in the folk-music scene. He moved to America in 1956 to collect songs in the Appalachian mountains, afterwards moving to New York. Multi-instrumentalist Makem had been discovered by Liam and also crossed the Atlantic, beginning a successful career as a solo folk artist.

After occasional live performances as a group, in 1959 the quartet recorded collections of rebel songs (*The Rising of the Moon*) and drinking songs (*Come Fill Your Glass with Us*). The rollicking, good-time harmony singing on such songs as 'The Jug of Punch' and 'The Leaving of Liverpool' established an image of Irish music on which the Dubliners would capitalize a decade later. It also led to criticism of the Clancys' approach from folk purists.

The success of these albums within the American folk scene led to engagements at Chicago's Gate of Horn and New York's Blue Angel club. A network television appearance on the *Ed Sullivan Show* increased their visibility still further. The group soon became an institution with annual St Patrick's Day concerts at New York's Carnegie or Philharmonic Hall and in 1961 began a series of albums for Columbia which included *The Boys Won't Leave the Girls Alone* (1962), *The Irish Uprising* (1966) and *Bold Fenian Men* (1969).

In 1969 Makem left to pursue a solo career in tandem with his acting roles on Broadway. He cut two solo albums for Polydor (*In the Dark Green Woods*, 1974, and *Ever the Winds*, 1975), which were arranged and produced by Donal Lunny, one of the new generation of Irish musicians, in a more reflective mode than the Clancy collaborations. In 1976 he cut *Tommy Makem and Liam Clancy* (Epic), which included Liam's version of Eric Bogle's contemporary folk classic 'The Band Played Waltzing Matilda', which reached No. 1 in Ireland. A contrasting version was recorded by 'rogue folk' band the **Pogues** on *Rum Sodomy and the Lash* (Stiff, 1985).

Tommy and Liam continued to record as a duo for Polydor Ireland and the US Shanachie label in the eighties. The Clancy Brothers continued to perform occasionally during the seventies, adding the English traditional singer Louis Killen. This line-up is featured on *Greatest Hits* (Vanguard, 1973). The original group re-formed for *Reunion* (1984) and performed at the Cambridge Folk Festival. After Tom's death in 1990, the remaining members appeared together occasionally in the nineties.

JIMMY CLANTON

b. 2 September 1940, Baton Rouge, Louisiana, USA

Jimmy Clanton was the only white rock'n'roll star created by the New Orleans R&B scene.

His first band, the Rockets, included his brother Ike, who later had two minor hits with 'Down the

Aisle' (Ace, 1960) and 'Sugar Plum' (Mercury, 1962). Spotted by New Orleans producer Cosimo Matassa, Jimmy was signed to Johnny Vincent's Ace label, for whom he recorded his own composition 'Just a Dream' in 1958. With a backing group which included Earl King on guitar and **Huey 'Piano' Smith**, the record sold a million, as did the follow-up, the **Johnny Ace**-influenced 'A Letter to an Angel'.

From this point, Clanton's records began to lose their R&B edge as he was increasingly promoted in line with the teen-balladeer role he played in the film *Go Johnny Go!* (1958). Clanton was Johnny Melody, a mysterious young singer whose demo disc is sending disc-jockey **Alan Freed**'s listeners frantic. 1959 brought the Top Ten single 'Go Jimmy Go' (written by **Pomus and Shuman**) and there were four smaller hits and another pop-singer film part (*Teenage Millionaire*, 1961) before he cut one of the classic teenage ditties, 'Venus in Blue Jeans' (1962). Written by **Neil Sedaka** and Howie Greenfield, the song was covered in Britain by Mark Wynter (Pye).

Clanton had one more minor success on Ace with 'Darkest Street in Town' (1963) before fading from view. He returned briefly to the charts in 1969 with 'Curly' on Laurie.

ERIC CLAPTON
b. 30 March 1945, Ripley, Surrey, England

The most talented white blues guitarist of his generation, Clapton was not only an expert copyist of such players as **B. B. King** and **Freddie King**; he also forged his own blues style during a career that had three distinct phases. The guitar hero of British R&B was followed by membership of the supergroup **Cream**. After 1973 and his recovery from heroin addiction, Clapton cultivated the role of unassuming journeyman singer, writer and instrumentalist. It was in this persona that he had his greatest success, with the album *Unplugged* (1992) and the poignant single 'Tears in Heaven', a song, like so many blues, crafted from personal pain, in this case the accidental death of Clapton's son.

He learned the blues while at art school from records by **Big Bill Broonzy**, **Muddy Waters** and others. In 1963 he joined Tom McGuinness, later of **Manfred Mann**, in shortlived groups the Roosters and Casey Jones' Engineers, before joining the **Yardbirds**. In less than two years with the band, Clapton earned a reputation as the most skilled instrumentalist on the rapidly growing London R&B scene, through his unrivalled ability to re-create the flowing modern guitar solos of the Kings. His sound at this time can be heard on *Five Live Yardbirds* (UK Columbia, 1964) and on the live recordings of the group with **Sonny Boy Williamson** (Fontana, 1964).

Clapton left the band in 1965 as the pop approach of their hit singles began to dominate their stage performances. Almost immediately he joined **John Mayall**, whose Bluesbreakers shared Clapton's purist attitude to Chicago blues. *Blues Breakers* (Decca, 1965) featured the whole range of Clapton's work from the searing slow blues of 'Have You Heard?' to the intricate up-tempo fingering on Freddie King's 'Steppin' Out'.

Although that album was a surprise Top Ten hit, Clapton remained little known outside the R&B sphere. This was to change after 1966 when he joined **Jack Bruce** and Ginger Baker to form Cream. The two years of the band's existence marked the high point of his career in terms of popularity and commercial success. Artistically, its value was questionable. The extended work-outs which were Cream's hallmark on stage encouraged Clapton to indulge in improvisational excesses whose technical brilliance often overshadowed any emotional statement. In the studio, however, he was able to create some of his finest performances; these include the poignant reading of **Robert Johnson**'s 'Crossroads' and the influential progressive-blues riffing on 'Sunshine of Your Love' and 'Strange Brew'. For the first time, he also began to develop a fragile yet effective singing voice.

Cream was followed by the shortlived Blind Faith, with Baker, Ric Grech and **Steve Winwood**. Clapton's musical activity for the next few years seemed to constitute a search for a new role away from the superstar limelight. He played briefly with **George Harrison** and with **John Lennon**'s Plastic Ono Band before working with white Southern soul duo Delaney and Bonnie Bramlett in 1970 and appearing on their Atlantic Album *On Tour!*

Among the Bramletts' band were Bobby Whitlock (drums), Carl Radle (*d. 30 May 1980*, bass) and Jim Gordon (drums), who formed the nucleus of Clapton's first band as a solo artist. With them he cut the low-key *Eric Clapton*, which included an American Top Twenty hit – **J. J. Cale**'s 'After Midnight' – and (as Derek and the Dominos) *Layla and Other Assorted Love Songs* (both Polydor/Atlantic 1970). 'Layla' (inspired by his then unrequited love for Patti Harrison, whom he later married) was Clapton's finest vocal performance to date and also featured impassioned guitar duetting with Duane Allman of the **Allman Brothers Band**, who had been introduced to Clapton by the album's producer **Tom Dowd**. The track was a Top Ten hit in Britain in 1972 and on its re-release a decade later.

An (eventually successful) fight against heroin addiction kept Clapton out of music for three years and when he re-emerged with a concert at London's Rainbow Theatre in 1973, his approach was closer to Cale's laid-back country soul than Allman's rock-flavoured blues. A live album of the concert was released, featuring Pete Townshend of **The Who** and guitarist Ron Wood of the Faces and later of the **Rolling Stones**.

His career was successfully relaunched and he went on to cut ten albums between 1974 and 1985. The new Clapton style was blues-based, rather than blues, although his many live performances were proof that he could still improvise with economy and imagination. The version of 'Rambling on My Mind' captured on the 1975 live album *E.C. Was Here* is a classic example.

Although primarily an album artist, Clapton went on to have several hit singles, including **Bob Marley**'s 'I Shot the Sheriff'* (from the 1974 album *461 Ocean Boulevard*), 'Lay Down Sally'* (from 1977's *Slowhand*, produced by Glyn Johns), and 'I Can't Stand It' (from *Another Ticket*, his last album for RSO, the label of his former manager Robert Stigwood). In 1983 he signed to Warner Brothers and released *Money and Cigarettes* followed by *Behind the Sun* (1985) and *August* (1986), a British Top Twenty hit.

The nucleus of Clapton's band throughout the seventies consisted of Radle, George Terry (guitar), Dick Sims (keyboards), and Jamie Oldaker (drums), with backing vocals by Yvonne Elliman and Marcy Levy, who (as Marcie Detroit) later formed **Shakespears Sister**. In 1984 Greg Phillinganes took over on keyboards and vocals with Nathan East on bass while **Phil Collins**, Andy Fairweather Low and Little Feat's Ritchie Hayward were among those who have toured and recorded with Clapton since the mid-eighties. *Crossroads*, a retrospective collection of seventy-three tracks from every phase of Clapton's career, was released by Polydor in 1988.

Journeyman (1989), a new studio album, featured his most intricate and thoughtful guitar playing for many years. In the same year he began an annual season at London's Albert Hall. In 1991 he performed there for twenty-four consecutive nights, an achievement marked by the release of the live album *24 Nights*. Among Clapton's guests were **Buddy Guy**, **Robert Cray**, **Albert Collins**, Johnny Johnson (**Chuck Berry**'s former pianist) and Michael Kamen, who composed a guitar concerto for the occasion. Clapton contributed to Kamen's soundtracks for *Lethal Weapon* 2 and 3 and the TV drama *Edge of Darkness* (1986). He also composed the music for the 1988 film *Homeboy*.

In 1992 came his biggest single in years, the lament 'Tears in Heaven', inspired by the death of his son, Conor, in 1991. *Unplugged*, the album it came from, was his most affecting, and commercially successful, album ever. Its follow-up *From the Cradle* (1994), a collection of blues standards given slightly too respectful renderings, saw Clapton withdrawing to his journeyman persona. It entered the US charts at No. 1. It was followed by a number of retrospectives and 'best of's (notably *The Clapton Chronicles*, 1999) and guest appearances by Clapton on tribute (notably *Dueces Wild* on which he partnered B. B. King on 'Rock Me Baby') and charity albums. The solo outing *Pilgrim* (1998), his poppiest record for some time, was issued in the same year that his drug rehabilitation centre, Crossroads, was opened in Antigua. Clapton partnered King again on *Riding with the King* (Reprise), a Top 5 album in 2000. Hardly a pioneering effort, the album had the advantage of seeming effortless in its meld of traditional and contemporary blues material.

THE DAVE CLARK FIVE
Dave Clark, b. 15 December 1942, London, England; Mike Smith, b. 6 December 1943, London; Rick Huxley, b. 5 August 1942, London; Lenny Davidson, b. 30 May 1944, London; Dennis Payton, b. 11 August 1943, London

The first British group (briefly) to match **The Beatles** in popularity in the British beat boom years, though the Dave Clark Five lacked the imagination of the Fab Four, in Clark they had a far more astute businessman than The Beatles' Brian Epstein. As a result, Clark was able to build a solid and lengthy career on slender talents, selling some 12 million records in the process.

Formed in 1958 in Tottenham by drummer Clark as a backing group for singer Stan Saxon, by 1961 the line-up of their hit years was established. Initially an instrumental group playing local dances, hence the emphasis on shouts and thumps that was to become their trademark, they recorded unsuccessfully for Ember ('Chaquita', 1961) and Piccadilly ('I Knew It All the Time', their first vocal outing, 1962) before signing with EMI's Columbia label in 1963. Their cover of the **Contours**' 'Do You Love Me?', a staple of the repertoire of many beat groups of the era, was only a minor hit (until it was released in America in 1964 in the wake of 'Glad All Over' when it sold a million copies). **Brian Poole and the Tremeloes** had the bigger hit with their version on Decca. But with 'Glad All Over' (1963), written by Clark and Smith, whose husky vocals were another of the group's trademarks, they secured the first of ten million-sellers.

Their toppling of The Beatles from the top of the British charts led to headlines in the British daily newspapers, but it was in America that the group were most successful. Promoted by more appearances on *The Ed Sullivan Show* than any other representative of the 'British invasion' they had a string of million-sellers on the Epic label, including "Bits and Pieces', 'Can't You See That She's Mine', 'Because', 'Any Way You Want It' (1964), all written or co-written by Clark, 'I Like It Like That' (a Top Ten hit for its composer, Chris Kenner, in 1961 on Instant), 'Over and Over' (a million-seller for its composer Robert Byrd, under the pseudonym of Bobby Day, on Class in 1958) and 'Catch Us If You Can' (1965) – the title song to the 1965 John Boorman film starring the group. Their American hits continued at a diminished level until 1967, fuelled by constant touring and, significantly, drawing on more cover-versions towards the end.

In Britain, the group struggled through to the seventies, recording first ballads (including Barry Mason's and **Les Reed**'s 'Everybody Knows', 1967, and Raymond Froggatt's 'Red Balloon', 1968) before joining the rock'n'roll revival movement with the medleys 'Good Old Rock'n'Roll' (1969) and 'More Good Old Rock'n'Roll' (1970). Then, in 1971, Clark folded the group, the members of which, except for Clark and Smith, retired from showbusiness. Smith formed a brief collaboration with one-time **Manfred Mann** singer Mike d'Abo and later worked as a producer (notably on Michael Ball's 1993 début album) while Clark, who owned the rights to the group's recordings, released a compilation, *25 Thumping Great Hits* (1975), to great success.

In the early eighties Clark started issuing to television edited highlights of *Ready Steady Go!*, the cult British rock music show of the sixties, and in 1986 mounted the musical extravaganza *Time*, which co-starred **Cliff Richard** and a hologram of Laurence Olivier, in London. Richard, **Leo Sayer**, Freddie Mercury of **Queen** and **Ashford and Simpson** were among those performing on **Dave Clark**'s *Time – The Album*.

In the early nineties, having gained control of his sixties catalogue, Clark began reissuing Dave Clark Five recordings through Hollywood Records in the US and EMI elsewhere.

DICK CLARK
b. 30 November 1929, Mount Vernon, New York, USA

America's oldest living teenager and a determined extrovert, Clark – who hosted the *American Bandstand* television show from 1956 – did his best to live up to the description of him in the Payola hearings of 1959 as 'the single most influential person' in the post-war popular music industry.

While at Syracuse University, Clark worked at radio station WRUN, graduating to his own show, *Dick Clark's Caravan of Music*, in Philadelphia in 1952. In that year *Bandstand* began with Bob Horn as host, as an afternoon replacement for English films on WFIL. By 1955 Clark's boyish looks and obvious knowledge of the music of the day, won him the host spot and when in 1957, renamed *American Bandstand*,

the show went national, Clark's association with rock was cemented for ever.

Like the British *Top of the Pops* (which came later), the show featured an audience dancing to records, but *Bandstand* made stars of the audience as well as the singers who lip-synched to their records. Regulars included **Connie Francis** and many Philadelphia-based acts (including **Chubby Checker**, **Fabian**, **Frankie Avalon** and **Bobby Rydell**, and others on Cameo-Parkway) in whose careers Clark had interests. (His substantial holdings in publishing and record companies made him a millionaire by 1959.) However, despite the obvious clash of interest, and in contrast to **Alan Freed**, Clark survived the Congressional Payola hearings of 1959, quietly divesting himself of interests in some thirty businesses along the way.

Throughout the sixties Clark continued to host *Bandstand*, which, unlike many of the acts it featured, survived the advent of **The Beatles**, while extending his career into screen acting (including *Because They're Young*, 1960, and *The Young Doctors*, 1961). In the seventies Clark branched out into independent television production, specializing in music-orientated projects, including *Elvis* (1979) and *The Early Beatles* (1981), and into game shows. By the nineties Dick Clark Enterprises was a fully fledged media company.

Taylor Hackford's 1980 film *The Idolmaker* told the fictionalized story of Clark's fifties career.

PETULA CLARK
b. 15 November 1932, Epsom, Surrey, England

One-time child star Clark, who sold over 30 million records in the course of her career, was one of the few British acts to conquer Europe and America, as well as the UK.

A popular child singer, on radio – she made her début aged nine – and in the concert hall, Clark graduated to a career as a child actor, making her film début, *A Medal for the General* (1944), at the age of twelve. In 1953, after a series of insipid roles, she abandoned films. She signed with Polygon (later Pye) and had her first British hit with 'The Little Shoemaker' in 1954. Other hits included 'Majorca' (1955), 'With All My Heart' (Pye, 1957, a cover of Jody Sands' American original) and 'Baby Lover' (1958), before at the end of the fifties she quit Britain for France, where she established herself as a concert artist and married record executive Claude Wolff. Henceforth her career would have a strong international element. Her first million-seller was 'Romeo' (1961), with music by Robert Stolz and an English lyric by **Jimmy Kennedy**, her second was 'Monsieur' (Vogue, 1962), which she sang in German, while she sang her third, 'Chariot' (Vogue, 1962), in French. (In America, Little Peggy March topped the charts with an English-language version of 'Chariot', 'I Will Follow Him'* on RCA.)

Her conquest of Europe complete, Clark and manager Wolff turned their attention to America. Written and produced by Pye's music director **Tony Hatch**, the jaunty 'Downtown'* (1965) was the first record by a British female singer since **Vera Lynn** to top the American charts. It was also the first of a series of international hits, including 'I Know a Place' (1965), 'My Love'* (1966), 'I Couldn't Live Without Your Love' (1966) and 'Don't Sleep in the Subway' (1967), all written by Hatch, which climaxed with her versions of Charles Chaplin's 'This Is My Song'*, the theme from *A Countess from Hong Kong* (1967), which she recorded in German, Italian, French and English.

In 1968 she starred in the musical *Finian's Rainbow* and, in 1969, in *Goodbye Mr Chips*.

In later years Clark continued to record and tour occasionally. Her records included *Warm and Tender* (1971), a 1983 live double-album and a 1988 dance-mix of 'Downtown' which was a British hit. In 1990 she wrote and appeared in the musical *Someone Like You* in London and in 1992 released *Treasures Vol. 1* on the US Scotti Bros label. In 1993 she appeared on Broadway with **David Cassidy** in the Willy Russell musical play *Blood Brothers*.

ROY CLARK
b. 15 April 1933, Meaherrin, Virginia, USA

The first country artist to perform in the Soviet Union (in 1976), Clark was best known as the co-presenter with **Buck Owens** of *Hee Haw*, the weekly television show constructed out of a marriage of hillbilly humour and country music, complete with the stereotype images of hay bales and overalls.

The son of a tobacco farmer, Clark was brought up from the age of eleven in Washington DC, then an important country music centre. After winning the Country Music Banjo Championship in 1949 and 1950, Clark played with **Jimmy Dean** and then joined *The Town and Country Jamboree* in 1955 as banjoist before joining **Wanda Jackson**'s band as arranger and guitarist in 1959. After unsuccessful records on Four Star and Debbie, he joined Capitol and secured his first country hit with **Bill Anderson**'s composition, 'Tips of My Fingers' (1963), a classic example of the 'Nashville sound' with its **Floyd Cramer**-like piano, vocal chorus and strings. Other hits followed, but more significantly, Clark was briefly host of the *Swinging Country* syndicated television show. This led to *Hee Haw*, where Clark's natural ebullience found a permanent home. The show helped Clark achieve his only significant pop hit, 'Yesterday, When I Was Young' (Dot, 1969). When the show was cancelled in 1972, only for its producers to syndicate it themselves,

Clark wrote an entertaining 'protest' song, 'The Lawrence Welk Hee-Haw-Counter-Revolution Polka'. Though he continued to make the country charts in the seventies, his career was constructed around his personality, rather than his singing. The culmination of this came in 1986 when he co-produced with Mel Tillis the comedy Western *Uphill All the Way* as a vehicle for Tillis and himself.

GUSSIE CLARKE
b. Augustus Clarke, 1953, Kingston, Jamaica

Gussie Clarke became one of the most influential reggae producers of the late eighties by introducing the latest studio techniques to the traditionally low-fi recordings of the local Jamaican music scene.

Clarke entered the music industry in the late sixties and early seventies cutting acetates, special pressings of reggae recordings, known as 'dub plates', for local sound systems (highly competitive Jamaican travelling discos). Each sound system would have its own DJs who would 'toast' or talk over the instrumental tracks Clarke and others provided. He moved into production in 1972, working with talkover pioneer **U-Roy**, whose 'The Higher the Mountain' (1972) was his first production, and his disciples **Big Youth** (*Screaming Target*) and I-Roy (*Presenting I-Roy*).

In the late seventies Clarke became an in-demand producer, and he also set up his own labels, Gussie and Puppy. He became increasingly involved with his various businesses, and by 1984 ran a small empire which included his studio, a music publishing company and his own distribution operation. Clarke's business-like approach, so different from the eccentricities of his predecessors, notably **Lee Perry**, led him to install the latest digital technology in his studio, which soon became the leading recording studio in Jamaica. His best production work from this period is captured on a trilogy of albums, *Music Works Showcase '88, 89* and *90*. Among the artists Clarke has produced are **Dennis Brown**, **Gregory Isaacs**, and the Mighty Diamonds. Other acts to take advantage of his studio facilities in the late eighties and early nineties included reggae crossover acts **Maxi Priest** and **Aswad**.

KENNY CLARKE
b. Kenneth Spearman Clarke, 9 January 1914, Pittsburgh, Pennsylvania, USA, d. 25 January 1985, Paris, France

Known as 'Klook', Clarke did most to develop bebop drumming, and was a founder member of the **Modern Jazz Quartet**. He moved to France in the fifties and was a key figure in the expatriate jazz world depicted in Bertrand Tavernier's film *Round Midnight* (1986).

With a father and brother who were musicians, Clarke joined his first band in 1930. In 1937–8 he toured Scandinavia with the Edgar Hayes Band, playing vibes and drums and making his first recordings in Sweden. He met **Dizzy Gillespie** in Teddy Hill's band in 1939, before becoming a house musician at Minton's, the New York club where bebop evolved.

With Gillespie, **Charlie Christian**, Tadd Dameron and others, Clarke experimented with new jazz techniques. It was his use of the bass drum pedal for special accents with the steady four beats maintained by the top cymbal which gave him the nickname 'Klook': another musician thought Clarke's playing sounded like 'klook-mop'. He composed 'Epistrophy' and other early bebop themes and can be heard on an amateur recording of the jam sessions at Minton's with Christian and **Thelonious Monk**, which has been variously re-released, most recently as *The Harlem Jazz Scene 1941* (Esoteric). He was also the house drummer for Savoy, the New York label which recorded many of the bebop pioneers.

Gillespie and Clarke worked with **Ella Fitzgerald** in 1942, working out the former's famous 'Salt Peanuts' routine, before Clarke was drafted in 1943. In Europe he met pianist John Lewis, who joined him in Gillespie's big band in the late forties. It was the rhythm section of this orchestra, including Ray Brown and Milt Jackson that formed the Modern Jazz Quartet in 1952.

After three years with the MJQ, Clarke joined French bandleader Jacques Helian and, based in Paris, worked all over Europe. In 1961 he formed a big band with Belgian pianist and arranger Francy Boland, which during the sixties was one of the most exciting and adventurous jazz orchestras in Europe. The band recorded more than a dozen albums for various labels during its ten years of existence, including a much acclaimed double-album for Polydor recorded live at **Ronnie Scott**'s Club in London in 1969.

During the sixties and seventies Clarke was at the centre of the community of expatriate American musicians in Paris, playing at clubs like the Blue Note, the Club St Germain and the Chat Qui Peche. Shortly before his death he was to be featured with Johnny Griffin in a Paris Reunion Band recording session organized by jazz writer Mike Hennessy, with the aim of recapturing the music of those clubs. With Billy Brooks replacing Clarke, *French Cooking* was released by Sonet in 1985.

STANLEY CLARKE
b. 30 June 1951, Philadelphia, Pennsylvania, USA

Originally a leading jazz string-bass-player, Clarke was a pioneer of jazz-rock, working with **Chick Corea** in Return to Forever (1972–6). A highly inventive

electric bassist, he was noted for his melodic playing and his unusual 'popping' effects, created by slapping rather than plucking the strings. As a performer and producer, Clarke later worked with artists as diverse as **George Duke**, Roy Buchanan and **Paul McCartney**.

Clarke studied violin, cello and double bass in Philadelphia before moving to New York in 1970. There he played with **Art Blakey**, **Stan Getz** and **Gil Evans** before recording *Return to Forever* (ECM, 1972) with keyboards-player Corea and Brazilian musicians Airto Moreira and Flora Purim. The success of this fusion music led to the permanent band named after that album.

Return to Forever recorded *Where Have I Known You Before* (Polydor, 1974) with guitarist Al Dimeola and *Romantic Warrior* (Columbia, 1976), on which lengthy solos were replaced by more formal structures. As a solo artist, Clarke signed to Atlantic, releasing *Stanley Clarke* (1974), with its Spanish flamenco influences, *Journey to Love* (1975), which included the R&B hit 'Silly Putty', and *School Days* (1976). *I Wanna Play for You* (Epic, 1979) included guest appearances by Getz, Moreira, **Jeff Beck** and singer Dee Dee Bridgewater.

Clarke's only pop hit was 'Sweet Baby' (Epic, 1981) from *The Clarke Duke Project*, the first of a series of collaborations with keyboardist Duke. His later solo albums included *Time Exposure* (1984), *Find Out* (1985) and *Hideaway* (1987).

As a producer, Clarke supervised Buchanan's *Loading Zone* (1977), Bridgewater's *Just Family* (1978), and Rodney Franklin's *Marathon* (1984). He became increasingly active as a film and television music composer. Among his credits are *The Five Heartbeats*, *Boyz N the Hood*, *Poetic Justice* and the Tina Turner bio-pic *What's Love Got to Do with It?*.

To perform his own compositions Clarke formed the trio Animal Logic in 1989 with ex-**Police** drummer Stewart Copeland and Los Angeles singer-songwriter Deborah Holland. He released the solo album *East River Drive* in 1992. Featuring the Cameroonian bassist Armand Sabal-Lecco, it encapsulated the range of styles for which Clarke had become known. This was followed by *Bolero* (Arista, 1993). The acoustic *Rite of Strings* (1995), which was made with Jean Luc Ponty and Al DiMola, was one of his few jazz recordings of the nineties.

THE CLASH
Terry Chimes (replaced by Nicky 'Topper' Headon, b. 1956, Dover, England); Mick Jones, b. 26 June 1956, London; Paul Simonon, b. 1956, London; Joe Strummer, b. John Mellors, 21 August 1952, Ankara, Turkey

One of the earliest British punk groups, the Clash

were also the most political in their choice of lyric themes. The group survived the demise of punk through their reputation as a tough, roots rock group.

In 1975 guitarist Jones and bassist Tony James formed rehearsal band London SS, whose various members included singer Simonon and drummer Headon. When James left, to join Chelsea and eventually form Generation X with **Billy Idol**, Jones and Simonon (bass) recruited Chimes (drums), guitarist Keith Levine and singer/guitarist Strummer. He had formerly led pub-rock group the 101-ers, which recorded 'Keys to Your Heart' (Chiswick, 1976).

Inspired by the **Sex Pistols**, the new band became the Clash and assembled a repertoire of tough, politically aware songs like 'White Riot', which became the band's first single after signing to the British branch of Columbia. By this time Levine had been sacked (he would later turn up in ex-**Sex Pistol** John Lydon's Public Image Ltd) amidst allegations of heroin use.

Revealing the band's hard-driving basic rock style and Strummer's cockney-accented vocals, the Mickey Foote-produced *The Clash* (1977) was a Top Twenty hit. It included a version of Junior Murvin's reggae hit 'Police and Thieves' as well as the caustic social commentaries 'London's Burning', 'I'm So Bored with the USA' and 'Janie Jones'. Chimes played on the album as 'Tory Crimes', but was ousted before its release in favour of Headon, who completed the band's classic line-up. Chimes later played in punk band London and in the Heartbreakers, the UK-based American band fronted by ex-**New York Dolls** guitarist Johnny Thunders. **Blue Oyster Cult** producer Sandy Pearlman supervised *Give 'Em Enough Rope* (1978), which provided the Clash's first Top Twenty hit in 'Tommy Gun' (1978).

The group toured America in 1979 and *London Calling* (1979), produced by Guy Stevens, included 'Train in Vain', a transatlantic hit. In the same year the Clash were featured in the film *Rude Boy*.

Sandinista! (1980) was a triple album which found the band extending its range, though sales were disappointing. A further change of producer to veteran Glyn Johns made *Combat Rock* (1982) an American hit and 'Rock the Casbah' reached the Top Ten. But with the band enjoying its greatest success, Headon was replaced by Peter Howard and Jones was expelled from the Clash. Headon released a soul/R&B album, *Wakin Up*, in 1985, but was jailed for 18 months for drug trafficking in 1987 and subsequently quit music. Jones went on to form Big Audio Dynamite with Don Letts and recorded *This Is Big Audio Dynamite* (Columbia, 1986). BAD released a further three moderately successful albums before Jones split the band, forming BAD II in 1990 and releasing *Kool Aid* (1990) and *The Globe* (1991). As Big Audio he recorded *Higher Power* in 1994. Strummer and Simonon hired two new guitarists and, after a lengthy period of inactivity, the Clash released *Cut the Crap* (1985), but its lack of impact led to the group's dissolution.

Strummer embarked on a series of solo projects, which included co-production on *No. 10 Upping Street* (Columbia, 1977), the second Big Audio Dynamite album. He also worked with film director Alex Cox, supervising the soundtrack albums of *Sid and Nancy* (MCA, 1986), the biopic about the Sex Pistols' Sid Vicious, and *Walker* (Virgin, 1988), as well as acting in *Straight to Hell* (1987). In 1988 he toured with his band Latino Rockabilly War and released the soundtrack album *Permanent Record*, one side of which featured Strummer and the band, his first sustained recording since the Clash. Some of the band also played on his début solo album, *Earthquake Weather* (1990). Strummer later produced the **Pogues**, and temporarily took over as lead vocalist for the band in 1991. Simonon based himself in America, playing on **Bob Dylan**'s album, *Down in the Groove* (1988). In 1991 he formed Havana 3am, who released an album on IRS.

In the same year the Clash's 'Should I Stay, Or Should I Go' was a reissued hit in the UK after being featured in a television commercial. The success of the single and the 'best of' album *The Story of the Clash Vol. 1* highlighted the lack of impact of the individual members' work. It sparked speculation that the Clash might re-form but neither Strummer nor Jones showed any interest in the idea. Indeed, most of their nineties records were compilations, including the three-CD set *On Broadway* (1995) and the superior *From Here to Eternity* (1999), a collection of live recordings made between 1978 and 1982. 1999 also saw the tribute album *Burning London*.

RICHARD CLAYDERMAN
b. Philippe Pages, 1954, Paris, France

A romantic light classical pianist who plays in a similar vein to **Liberace**, but with a pop-star image, Clayderman is said to have sold over 60 million records worldwide since the late seventies. In 1980, for example, he sold more records in France and Japan than any other artists.

He was the star pupil at the Paris Conservatoire before moving to the rock scene where he played with such singers as **Johnny Hallyday** and Michel Sardou. The turning point of his career came when he was signed by Olivier Toussaint and Paul de Sonneville to their Delphine label. His first recording, of de Sonneville's 'Ballade pour Adeline', was a hit in several European countries and became his theme tune, but it was not until 1978 that a massive touring schedule and promotional campaign led to widespread international recognition.

His repertoire, enshrined on a dozen albums for Delphine and Decca, was determinedly middle-brow, combining pop classics (Chopin, Beethoven, **George Gershwin**) with classic pops like **Paul Anka**'s 'My Way' and **Maurice Jarre**'s 'Lara's Theme' from the film *Dr Zhivago*. All were performed in the same manner, with Clayderman's relaxed piano-playing surrounded by soothing strings.

In 1982 Clayderman signed to Columbia, who attempted to emulate his European success in the United States and Britain. A series of carefully designed albums contained hits from musical shows: *Hollywood and Broadway* and *Love Songs of the World* (1986), which included several European tunes which had been American hits, notably Paul Mauriat's 'Love Is Blue' and **Domenico Modugno**'s 'Volare'. In 1989 he released an album of tunes by **Andrew Lloyd Webber** (Delphine). This was followed by *Together At Last*, on which Clayderman and **James Last** tackled the **Bryan Adams** hit '(Everything I Do) I Do It for You' (1992), and *Richard Clayderman Plays Abba* (1993).

He makes frequent international tours and was one of the first Western musicians to perform in China, which he visited with his *Oriental Melody* show in 1991.

JACK CLEMENT
b. Jack Henderson Clement, 5 April 1932, Memphis, Tennessee, USA

An influential producer and one of country music's most colourful characters, Clement helped shape the careers of **Johnny Cash**, **Charley Pride** and **Don Williams**, among others.

The son of a dentist and choirmaster, he began playing music professionally while in the marines, forming a bluegrass group with members of **Ernest Stoneman**'s band, first in Washington DC and then in Boston on his discharge in 1952. He returned to Memphis in 1954, working briefly as a dance instructor, before forming Fernwood Records with Slim Wallace. In 1956 they leased their first recording, 'Trouble Bound' by Billy Lee Riley, to **Sam Phillips**. Phillips promptly signed both Riley – who would later cut the rockabilly classic 'Flying Saucers Rock'n'Roll' (1957) – and Clement as an engineer, producer and session man.

At Sun, as well as cutting two unsuccessful singles, Clement was responsible for virtually all the label's country output, and produced records by **Roy Orbison** and **Jerry Lee Lewis** (including 'Whole Lotta Shakin' Goin' on'). He also masterminded Johnny Cash's new pop sound, writing and producing 'Ballad of a Teenage Queen' and 'Guess Things Happen That Way' (both Top Twenty hits in 1958). Later Clement would revive Cash's flagging career, producing 'Ring

of Fire' in 1963, another Top Twenty tune, and provide him with several of his comic songs, such as 'Everybody Loves a Nut' and 'The One on the Right Is on the Left'. Other Clement compositions include 'It'll Be Me' and '(I Wish I Had) Johnny's Cash and Charley's Pride'. In 1959 he left Sun, joined RCA as a producer and then, in 1961, quit to return to independent production with Bill Hall and Allen Reynolds. In 1966 he returned to Nashville to establish his own publishing and production company and promptly discovered Charley Pride. However, he did not restrict his work as a producer purely to country acts. He also produced albums by **Louis Armstrong** (*Louis, Country & Western*, 1971), Townes Van Zandt and Frank Yankovic. His production work is characterized by a commitment to natural sound.

In 1972 he formed the JMI label and (briefly) signed Don Williams and backed the movie *Dear Dead Delilah*, losing most of his money as a result. Following a period of retrenchment, Clement recorded the eccentric *All I Want to Do in Life* (Elektra, 1978). After 1980 he divided his time between his video business interests and record production. Among his productions was **Johnny Cash**'s *The Mystery of Life* (1991) while his studio is used regularly by **Garth Brooks**, who is produced by Allen Reynolds. Clement also worked on U2's *Rattle and Hum* (1991).

JAMES CLEVELAND
b. 1931, Chicago, Illinois, USA, d. 9 February 1991, Los Angeles, California

The author of more than 400 religious songs and producer of over 100 albums, the Rev James Cleveland was a leading figure in traditional black gospel music for over thirty years.

Cleveland's earliest musical experience was as a member of the congregation of **Thomas A. Dorsey**'s church. As a keyboards player in the Pilgrim Baptist Church he accompanied numerous visiting artists, including **Mahalia Jackson** and the Gospelaires.

He made his first vocal recordings, singing in a husky baritone, for Savoy in the early sixties. Among them was the million-selling 'Peace Be Still'. Cleveland led the trend towards recording soloists with choirs. Among those with whom he recorded with were the Salem Inspirational Choir, the Angelic Choir and the Southern California Community Choir, with whom he made *Having Church* (1990). He had his own label, King James, in the late eighties.

Cleveland produced **Aretha Franklin**'s *Amazing Grace* and he worked with **Quincy Jones** on the music for the television series *Roots*. Among those whose careers he launched were **Billy Preston** and Daryl Coley.

He was pastor and founder of the Cornerstone

Institutional Baptist Church of Los Angeles. In 1968 he founded the Gospel Music Workshop of America, the largest black religious music association in the world.

JIMMY CLIFF
b. *James Chambers, 1948, St Catherine, Jamaica*

With the exception of **Bob Marley**, Cliff has been the most internationally successful Jamaican singer-songwriter, combining reggae with soul stylings.

In 1962 Cliff wrote a song in praise of an ice-cream parlour and record store, 'Dearest Beverley', which persuaded one of the owners, **Leslie Kong**, to enter the record business. The result was a series of Jamaican hits, including 'Hurricane Hattie' and 'Miss Jamaica'. Produced by Kong, they were released in Britain on **Chris Blackwell**'s Island label. Cliff toured America with **Byron Lee**'s Dragonaires in 1964 before moving to England to record for Island. 'Give and Take' was a minor hit but his international success followed his performance at a Brazilian song festival which made 'Waterfall' a South American hit, before 'Wonderful World, Beautiful People' made the charts in both America and Britain in 1969.

The follow-up, the anti-war song 'Vietnam', made little impact but Cliff's version of **Cat Stevens**' 'Wild World' was a British hit in 1970. He was also successful with pop-reggae compositions for **Desmond Dekker** ('You Can Get It If You Really Want') and the Pioneers ('Let Your Yeah Be Yeah', Trojan, 1971).

In 1972 Cliff starred in Perry Henzell's film *The Harder They Come* as the Rude Boy who became a national hero. He was strongly featured on the soundtrack album, singing his own haunting gospel-ballad 'Many Rivers to Cross' (successfully revived in Britain by **UB40** in 1983) and 'Sitting in Limbo'.

Cliff's career in the seventies was marked by attempts to cross over into the international rock market, beginning with *Another Cycle* (Island, 1971), on which Cliff's songs (co-written with Panamanian composer Guilly Bright) were accompanied by the Muscle Shoals rhythm section. After 1972 he recorded in turn for EMI, Warner/Reprise and Columbia. *Follow My Mind* (Reprise, 1976) was typical of this later work, with half the album recorded in Jamaica and half in Los Angeles. Despite his concentration on trying to reach the world audience, Cliff continued to have hits in Jamaica throughout the seventies. On later records like *I Am the Living* (MCA, 1980), *Special* (Columbia, 1982) and *Cliff Hangar* (Columbia, 1985) he produced well-crafted socially and politically pertinent material. In 1980 he appeared in the film *Bongo Man* and in *Club Paradise* (1986).

Despite the controversy surrounding a 1982 tour of South Africa, Cliff and his band Oneness performed frequently throughout Africa in the eighties. Tracks for *Hanging Fire* (1988) were recorded in Congo with producer Ronald Bell of **Kool & the Gang**. *Images* (1989, with production by Ansel Collins) and *Save Our Planet Earth* (1990) were more reggae-orientated than his recent material, as was 1992's *Breakout*. The success of the movie *Cool Runnings* (1993) led to the soundtrack-featured 'I Can See Clearly Now' taking Cliff into the US Top Thirty for the first time in 15 years.

PATSY CLINE
b. *Virginia Patterson Hensley, 8 September 1932, Winchester, Virginia, USA, d. 5 March 1963, Camden, Tennessee*

Best known for heartbreak ballads, such as her classic recording of **Harlan Howard**'s and Hank Cochran's 'I Fall to Pieces' (1961), Cline was described by Don Hecht – composer of her first hit, 'Walking After Midnight' (1957) – as someone who could 'cry on both sides of the microphone'. But, in fact, the high emotional charge of her performances was the result of a remarkable vocal control and her skilful deployment of a wide range of vocal mannerisms, including sobs and sighs. In place of the regional whine and instinctive feel of earlier performers such as **Kitty Wells** and **Rose Maddox**, Cline's emotions were constructed in the recording studio – and were none the less authentic for it. As a result, though her style was unmistakably country, she had great success in the pop charts.

Cline sang on local radio from the age of fourteen and first recorded for Four Star in 1954, before signing with Decca in 1957. Her breakthrough was unusual for a country performer. It came with her performance of 'Walking After Midnight', a song originally written for **Kay Starr**, on the *Arthur Godfrey Talent Scouts* television programme. The song became a pop and country hit. Four years later came the archetypal 'I Fall to Pieces', which was followed by 'Crazy' (1961, an early **Willie Nelson** composition) and 'She's Got You' (1962), all country and pop hits. She died tragically in a plane crash that also killed **Hawkshaw Hawkins** and **Cowboy Copas** in 1963.

Interest in Cline remained strong after her death. In 1981, courtesy of a recording engineer, she duetted with **Jim Reeves** on 'Have You Ever Been Lonely' (RCA). She was portrayed in *Coalminer's Daughter* (1980), the film based on **Loretta Lynn**'s autobiography, in which Cline featured as both a help to and strong influence upon Lynn. In 1985 came *Sweet Dreams*, a biopic (titled after her first posthumous hit) about Cline in which Jessica Lange played the singer. Numerous reissues of Cline's recordings sold strongly and in 1994 *Always . . . Patsy Cline*, a music show featuring her hits, was chosen for the reopening of Nashville's Ryman Auditorium, the home of the Grand Ole Opry. Irish country singer Sandy Kelly starred with **George Hamilton IV** in a European show based on Cline's life. She was a strong influence on **k. d. lang**.

GEORGE CLINTON
b. 22 July 1940, Kannapolis, North Carolina, USA

Building on the 'black rock' of **Jimi Hendrix** and **Sly Stone**, Clinton developed a style and a philosophy called P-Funk during the seventies. Like a comic-strip version of **Sun Ra**, he built a cosmic mythology which was expressed through such bands as Parliament, Funkadelic, Brides of Funkenstein and Bootsy's Rubber Band. In his turn, Clinton influenced younger funk/rock musicians like **Rick James**, **Prince** and **Afrika Bambaataa**, with whom he collaborated on *The Light* (EMI, 1988). The sampling technology of recent years has enabled a new generation of rappers to incorporate Clinton's trademark sounds into their own works.

From the mid-fifties he led doo-wop group the Parliaments, recording unsuccessfully for several Detroit companies, including unreleased material for **Berry Gordy**'s Motown. The group's first pop hits were '(I Wanna) Testify' and 'All Your Goodies Are Gone' (Revilot, 1967) but after hearing the new music of Hendrix and Stone, Clinton made a drastic change of style.

He formed Funkadelic, whose eponymous début album for Westbound spawned the R&B hits 'Music for My Mother' and 'I'll Bet You' (1969). This was black rock of a kind even Stone had not envisaged, with over-amplified guitars, heavy-rock drumming and standard R&B vocalizing on bizarre lyrics.

In 1970 Funkadelic released *Free Your Mind and Your Ass Will Follow*, while Clinton also recorded *Osmium* (Invictus), the first record by Parliament – the plural had been dropped to discourage any association with conventional vocal groups. Later Funkadelic albums like *Maggot Brain* (1971) and *America Eats Its Young* (1972) focused on socio-political satire and the latter introduced a new rhythm section drawn from **James Brown**'s JBs, with William 'Bootsy' Collins (bass), Frankie Waddy, and Phelps Collins.

After *Standing on the Verge of Getting It* (1973), a dispute with Westbound led Clinton to transfer his energies to a re-formed Parliament, which signed to the new Casablanca label. *Up for the Down Stroke* (1974) showed Collins' influence in its use of the horn-led, sparse contemporary soul sound popularized by James Brown. Clinton now developed 'funk' into a mythology on albums like *Mothership Connection* (1975), with its loose concept involving the arrival

on earth of aliens on a mission to take back 'funk' to their home planet. The record included a Top Twenty hit in 'Tear the Roof off the Sucker (Give up the Funk)'.

The Clinton circle's recordings proliferated in the late seventies as Bootsy's Rubber Band signed to Warners, Clinton's backing vocalists signed to Atlantic as the Brides of Funkenstein and female group Parlet released tracks on Casablanca. Clinton made *Tales of Kidd Funkadelic* (1975) for Westbound before signing Funkadelic to Warners. Later records from that band and Parliament embodied a stream of characters, scenarios and neologisms with elaborate packaging, including posters and glossaries. Among them were Parliament's *Clones of Dr Funkenstein* (1976), *Funkentelechy vs the Placebo Syndrome* (1977), *Motor Booty Affair* (1978) and *Gloryhalastoopid* (1979), and *Hardcore Jollies* (1976), *One Nation under a Groove* (1978) and *Uncle Jam Wants You* (1979) from Funkadelic.

Only *One Nation under a Groove* was successful internationally (reaching the British Top Ten) and after the 1978 P-Funk Earth Tour, involving gigantic sets with flying-saucer landings and numerous costume changes, Clinton's popularity declined. While his singles were dancefloor successes, the albums required excessive effort to comprehend Clinton's proliferating private world. In 1981 he dissolved his empire and filed for bankruptcy, with Warners and PolyGram (who now owned Casablanca) as principal creditors.

Clinton lost the rights to his group names and Funkadelic was re-formed by some of his ex-associates to record for MCA. Clinton himself signed to Capitol as a solo artist, releasing *Computer Games* (1982), which used fragments of Motown hits, vocoders and synthesizers. It featured the R&B hits 'Loopzilla' and 'Atomic Dog'. With backing musicians drawn from his earlier groups, what Clinton called his 'Parliafunkedelicment Thang' was still intact and in 1986 he had minor hits with 'Do Fries Go with That Shake?' and 'Hey Good Looking'. Clinton also appeared on **Thomas Dolby**'s *Cube* (1985).

In 1989 he released *Cinderella Theory* on Prince's Paisley Park label. It included a new version of **Harry Belafonte**'s 'Banana Boat Song'. A second single, 'Tweakin'', followed. Clinton then signed his new Funkadelic to MCA, and the Incorporated Thang Band (which included his son Tracy, aka Trey Lewd) to Warners before issuing another solo album on Paisley Park, *Hey Man Smell My Finger* (1993). In 1994 UK band **Primal Scream** released the album *Give Out But Don't Give Up*, which featured several Clinton contributions.

In 1992 Clinton sued rapper Terminator X for unauthorized sampling of 'Body Language'. In general, however, he has been prepared to licence other acts to incorporate segments of his repertoire in new tracks. Among those using samples from Funkadelic or Parliament tracks on their own recordings have been **Hammer** ('One Nation Under a Groove'), **De La Soul** ('Not Just Knee Deep'), **Dr Dre**, **Ice Cube**, Snoop Doggy Dogg, **NWA** and Digital Underground. Clinton has welcomed this use of his older work and has issued collections of excerpts to encourage sampling under the title *Sample Some of Dis, Sample Some of Dat*. He has also released compilations of previously unreleased tracks from his archives under the title George Clinton & Family. The most imaginative of these was *Greatest Funkin' Hits*, a CD-ROM version of the album of 1996 that allowed eight tracks to be mixed individually by the buyer.

New recordings included *The Awesome Power of a Fully Operational Mothership* (1996) and *Live and Kickin'* (1998).

ROSEMARY CLOONEY
b. 23 May 1928, Maysville, Kentucky, USA

Clooney's wholesome big voice, clear diction and way with a novelty song made her one of the top female singers of the early fifties.

She began her singing career with her younger sister Betty as the Clooney Sisters. They sang first on radio in Cincinnati, where the family moved in 1941, and from 1946 with Tony Pastor's big band. In 1949 she was signed to Columbia by **Mitch Miller** and in 1951 was given 'Come-on-a My House' to record. The song was written by playwright William Saroyan and his cousin Ross Bagdasarian (who later as **David Seville** would lead the Chipmunks to fame), and Clooney's dynamic interpretation and the jangling harpsichord sound provided by Miller resulted in her first million-seller. Three more followed in 1952, 'Tenderly', 'Botch-a-Me', another example of Miller's fondness for folk-sounding songs, and 'Half As Much'. At the same time, Clooney briefly essayed a career in Hollywood, but with little success, her best film being *White Christmas* (1953) with **Bing Crosby**.

Her hits, however, continued unabated: 'Hey There'* (1954), 'This Ole House'* (1954) – her biggest hit – the novelty outing 'Mambo Italiano'* (1954), written by **Bob Merrill**, 'Memories of You', with the **Benny Goodman** trio from *The Benny Goodman Story*, and 'Mangoes' (1957) and 'Who Don Mon Man' (1958), both calypso-styled songs written for her in the wake of **Harry Belafonte**'s success with the genre. With the advent of rock'n'roll her career collapsed, her songs and singing style once described at the beginning of the fifties as sounding so new, now sounding old-fashioned. After records for RCA and Reprise in the early sixties, she retired to cabaret.

In 1977 she published her autobiography, *This for Remembrance*, which detailed in part her harrowing time in the psychiatric ward of a hospital. In 1978 this was dramatized on television as *Escape from Madness*.

At about the same time Clooney returned to the recording studio with *Everything's Coming Up Rosie* (Concord Jazz). Since the late seventies she has issued more than a dozen albums for the same company. Most were devoted to the works of such classic songwriters as **Cole Porter**, **Irving Berlin**, **Harold Arlen** and **Johnny Mercer**, but *Here's to My Lady* (1979) was a spirited tribute to **Billie Holiday**.

THE CLOVERS
Charles White, b. 1930, Washington DC, USA; John 'Buddy' Bailey, b. 1930, Washington DC; Harold Lucas; Thomas Woods; Mathew McQator; Bill Harris; Billy Mitchell

One of the most influential of vocal groups – they had seventeen consecutive hits on the R&B charts – the Clovers represented the transition from the sweet balladry of the **Ink Spots** and the **Orioles** to the fiercer R&B sounds of the fifties.

Discovered by Lou Krefetz singing in Washington's Rose Café in 1949, the Clovers recorded unsuccessfully for Rainbow before Krefetz placed the group with Atlantic in 1950. Their first two Atlantic records, both written by **Ahmet Ertegun**, topped the R&B charts in 1951. 'Don't You Know I Love You', featured cool singing against a pronounced bass line, but for 'Fool, Fool, Fool' lead singer Bailey adopted an intense blues style that matched the earthiness of the lyrics. It was this youthful fusion of blues and gospel (rather than the fusion of jazz and pop of earlier doo-wop groups) that helped lay the foundations for the soul music of the sixties.

Other hits of the early fifties included the original version of the much-covered Rudolph Toombs composition 'One Mint Julep' (1952), 'Ting-a-Ling' (1952), which was covered by **Kay Starr**, 'Good Lovin'' (1953) and 'Little Mama' (1954), both of which featured White's blues-drenched lead vocals, and the classic 'Your Cash Ain't Nothing but Trash' (1954).

Ironically the group are best remembered for two uncharacteristic ballads. 'Blue Velvet' (1955) garnered them a pop hit and **Bobby Vinton** a million-seller when he recorded it in 1963. Similarly, 'Devil or Angel' (1956) was a bigger hit for **Bobby Vee** in 1960. More significant for the group at the time, 'Love, Love, Love' (1956) saw Atlantic blending R&B with pop in an effort to tap the white rock'n'roll market. It made the pop charts, as did the cover by the **Diamonds**, but uncomfortable with the new sound, the group quit Atlantic for the wilderness of small labels, only returning to the R&B (and pop) charts with

Leiber and Stoller's humorous 'Love Potion No. 9' (United Artists, 1959), which would become a staple number of British beat groups of the sixties. The group split up in 1961, different groupings recording for various small labels and performing on the rock'n'roll revival circuit.

THE COASTERS

Carl Gardner, b. 29 April 1928, Tyler, Texas, USA; Billy Guy, b. 20 June 1936, Attasca, Texas; Bobby Nunn, b. 1925, Birmingham, Alabama, d. 5 November 1986; Leon Hughes; Young Jessie; Will 'Dub' Jones; Cornel Gunter, b. 14 November 1938, Los Angeles, California, d. 26 February 1990; Earl 'Speedo' Carroll, b. 1937, New York

The Coasters were virtually the creation of songwriters and producers **Leiber and Stoller**, whose comic playlets about ghetto, and then teenage, life were the mainstay of the group's repertoire during their period of greatest success. The million-sellers 'Searchin''/ 'Young Blood' (1957), 'Yakety Yak' (1958), 'Charlie Brown' and 'Poison Ivy' (1959) saw the members of the group creating (and reprising) vocal character parts, in the manner of the characters of the television situation comedies or animated cartoons of the period.

The Robins were formed in 1949 in Los Angeles when **Johnny Otis** added the deep-voiced Nunn to the A Sharp Trio. The group recorded prolifically for various labels, scoring a R&B Top Twenty hit ('If It's So Baby', Savoy, 1950) and No. 1 ('Double Crossin' Blues' which also featured Otis's protégée **Esther Phillips**). In 1951 the group recorded their first Leiber and Stoller composition ('That's What the Good Book Says', Modern) and in 1953 the writers' 'Ten Days in Prison' (RCA) in which, for the first time, the singers took character parts.

In 1954 Leiber and Stoller formed Spark Records and signed the Robins. 'Riot in Cell Block No. 9', which featured **Richard Berry** as narrator, and 'Framed' (1955) were firmly in the tradition of novelty blues numbers but 'Smokey Joe's Café' (1955), a vignette of low-life south of the border, saw Leiber and Stoller edging the group away from the feel, if not yet the sound, of R&B. On the basis of that record Leiber and Stoller were signed to the Atlantic subsidiary Atco as independent producers. When several members of the Robins declined to leave the West Coast for New York, bass Nunn and tenor Gardner, the two distinctive voices of the group, recruited Guy and Hughes (later replaced by Young Jessie), and took the name the Coasters.

'Down in Mexico' (1956) reprised the situation of 'Smokey Joe's Café' to even more exotic effect, but 'Searchin''/'Youngblood' (1957) were ground-breaking

classics. The former saw the Coasters comparing themselves to the detectives of popular culture and introduced the reflective attitude that would run through the best of Leiber and Stoller's work, while the latter was a hilarious portrait of lust with the group's gasping, leering voices the perfect equivalent of the huge eyeballs of comic strips.

With the group's move to New York, Gunter replaced Jessie and Jones (from the Cadets of 'Stranded in the Jungle', Modern, 1956, fame) replaced Nunn. At the same time saxophone solos by **King Curtis** became a regular feature of their recordings. The first was 'Yakety Yak' (1958), a song like **Eddie Cochran**'s 'Summertime Blues' (1958) and **Chuck Berry**'s 'School Day' (1957), which neatly captured the frustrations of teenage life and set the sound for future singles. Other hits of this period were 'Charlie Brown', 'Along Came Jones', 'Poison Ivy' (1959) and the classic 'Little Egypt' (1961), which marvellously caught the feel of burlesque. Equally noteworthy was 'Shoppin' for Clothes' (1960), the coolest- and blackest-sounding of their Atlantic recordings, and one of the few not written by Leiber and Stoller. In 1961 Carroll, former lead singer of the Cadillacs, best-remembered for their 1955 R&B hit 'Speedoo' (Josie), replaced Gunter who joined **Dinah Washington**'s revue before forming his own 'Coasters' who were subsequently sued for impersonation in 1971 by H. B. Barnum, by then manager of the legitimate group.

In 1963 Leiber and Stoller and the Coasters parted company and the group's sales slumped. In 1967, by now signed to Date, the group were reunited with Leiber and Stoller but 'Down Home Girl' and 'D. W. Washburn' failed and are better known through their recordings by Alvin Robinson (on Leiber and Stoller's Red Bird label, covered by the **Rolling Stones**, 1964) and the **Monkees**, respectively. The group's last hit came in 1971 with 'Love Potion No. 9' (Crown), a revival of the **Clovers**' 1959 hit. The Coasters later became a staple of the rock'n'roll revival circuit with Gardner, Guy, Jones and Gunter appearing at the 1988 New York celebration of Atlantic's 40th anniversary.

Although Leiber and Stoller were clearly the architects of the Coasters' success, the attempts by so many to duplicate their vocal mannerisms were testament to the deep influence of the group. Among the Coasters' recordings thus fêted have been 'Searchin'' (the **Hollies**, 1963), 'Poison Ivy' (the Rolling Stones, 1963); the Paramounts, from whom came **Procul Harum** (Parlophone, 1964); the Lambrettas (Rocket, 1980); and 'I'm a Hog for You Baby' (Screaming Lord Sutch, Decca, 1965 – a performer best remembered for his publicity-seeking attempts to enter parliament). 'There's a Riot Goin' on' was the title track of **Sly Stone**'s 1971 album and in the same year formed the basis of the **Beach Boys**' 'Student Demonstration Time'.

The group's story is told in great detail by Bill Millar in *The Coasters* (1974).

ERIC COATES
b. 27 August 1886, Hucknall, England, d. 21 December 1957, Chichester, England

Once called 'the uncrowned king of light music', Coates, with **Robert Farnon**, was one of the most successful composers of light classical music of the twentieth century. Although he was one of the first European composers to adopt syncopation, in all other respects Coates' music was decidedly British. His best-remembered works are the title march from *The Dam Busters* (1954) and the signature tunes to three long-running BBC programmes: 'By a Sleepy Lagoon' (1930) for *Desert Island Discs*; 'Knightsbridge' (1933) for *In Town Tonight*; and 'Calling All Workers' (1940) for *Music While You Work*.

The son of a doctor, Coates won a scholarship to the Royal Academy of Music in 1906. He played in various theatre orchestras in London before joining the Queen's Hall Orchestra in 1910. From 1912 onwards he was the principal viola, under Sir Henry Wood. In 1919, when neuritis in his left hand made playing the viola almost impossible, he turned to composition, from the beginning working in the tradition of polished light melodic music established by **Gilbert and Sullivan**. His first great success was 'The Merrymakers' overture in 1922. He was also a songwriter – Arthur Conan Doyle was among his lyricists – but it was his atmospheric mood pieces that secured his popularity. In contrast to the pastoral evocations of most other British composers, Coates was inspired by the city (particularly London) rather than the country, colouring his simple, warm melodies with a bustling modernity.

After 1939 he wrote less, concentrating on conducting his works throughout the world. In 1953 he published his autobiography, *Suite in Four Movements*.

EDDIE COCHRAN
b. 3 October 1938, Albert Lea, Minnesota, USA, d. 17 April 1960, Bristol, England

Perhaps the finest exponent of teenage rockabilly, Cochran wrote and recorded one of the classic adolescent anthems, 'Summertime Blues'. His early death cut short the career of a major guitar stylist as well as a potentially great rock songwriter. His best songs rivalled those of **Chuck Berry** and **Felice and Boudleaux Bryant** in the wit and precision with which they delineated the teenage experience.

A skilful guitarist, Cochran briefly recorded in 1955–6 with Hank Cochran (no relation) as the Cochran Brothers and as a solo artist for Sylvester Cross's small Los Angeles labels Crest and Ekko. His first release was 'Skinny Jim' (Crest, 1956). Like **Glen Campbell** a decade later, Cochran became known as a session guitarist before achieving prominence as a solo artist. His imaginative and innovatory solos can be heard on a score of obscure rockabilly singles from West Coast labels, such as 'Walking Stick Boogie' (Cash, 1956) by Jerry Capeheart (*b. 1929, d. 7 June 1998, Nashville, Tennessee, USA*), who became Cochran's writing partner and manager.

His big break came with a cameo role in *The Girl Can't Help It*, Frank Tashlin's witty satire on showbusiness. In the film Cochran sang the light, rhythmic 'Twenty Flight Rock'. Signing to Liberty, his first single, **John D. Loudermilk**'s 'Sittin' in the Balcony', was a Top Twenty hit in 1957. That and the minor hit 'Drive in Show' appeared on his first album, *Singin' to My Baby* (1957).

The following year 'Summertime Blues' was a hit in both America and Britain. With its witty but impassioned lyric of teen *angst*, the song has been successfully recorded by rock artists of later generations, including Blue Cheer (1968) and **The Who** (1970). 'C'mon Everybody' was less successful in the US but reached the British Top Ten in 1959. In that year he recorded 'Three Stars', the John D. Loudermilk tribute to **Buddy Holly**, the Big Bopper and **Ritchie Valens**. In 1963 Cochran received the same treatment from British songwriter Geoff Goddard, whose 'Just Like Eddie' (Decca) was a Top Ten hit for Heinz.

By now Cochran was a regular member of rock'n'roll package tours throughout America, Australia and Britain, where he was killed in a car accident travelling to London from a concert. He had posthumous British hits with 'Three Steps to Heaven' (whose B-side was the country-flavoured 'Cut Across Shorty') and 'Weekend', and for many years his English fan club organized pilgrimages to the roadside where he died. For a number of years after his death, obscure or previously unissued sides by Cochran were released.

More than a good-looking teen star, Cochran was adept in the studio, overdubbing instruments on his hit records. He also appeared in the films *Untamed Youth* (1957) and *Go Johnny Go* (1959). In the seventies contrasting versions of Cochran's songs were British hits for **Showaddywaddy** ('Three Steps to Heaven', Bell, 1975) and the **Sex Pistols** ('Somethin' Else' and 'C'mon Everybody', both Virgin, 1979).

The continuing British fascination with Cochran was illustrated by a scene in Chris Petit's film *Radio on* (1981), where **Sting** played a petrol-station attendant obsessed with the dead star, and by the use of 'C'mon Everybody' in a 1988 television commercial.

As a result the re-released song was a Top Twenty hit. In the same year Liberty issued the definitive retrospective: *Eddie Cochran: The Boxed Set*.

JOE COCKER

b. John Robert Cocker, 20 May 1944, Sheffield, England

Possessor of an impressive white soul voice, Cocker spent most of the seventies trying to recapture his successes of 1968–72. In 1982 he duetted with **Jennifer Warnes** on the Oscar-winning and chart-topping theme from *An Officer and a Gentleman*, but it was not until the early nineties that sales of his later records matched his continuing popularity as a live performer.

In the early sixties Cocker played with Sheffield band the Avengers, recording an unsuccessful version of the Lennon–McCartney song 'I'll Cry Instead' for Decca in 1963. By 1967 he was singing R&B and soul material with the Grease Band, which included Chris Stainton (keyboards) and guitarist Henry McCullough, who later joined **Paul McCartney**'s Wings.

Signed by producer Denny Cordell, he covered another Lennon–McCartney song, 'With a Little Help from My Friends' (Regal-Zonophone in Britain, A&M in America). Cocker's bellowed, **Ray Charles**-influenced version was a British No. 1 in 1968 and was followed by an eponymous album featuring **Steve Winwood** and **Led Zeppelin**'s Jimmy Page.

His eccentric performing style – flailing arms and contorted face – won attention in America where he appeared at the Woodstock Festival in 1969 and scored Top Ten hits in 1970 with the **Box Tops**' 'The Letter' and **Julie London**'s 'Cry Me a River'. By now Cocker was working with **Leon Russell**, whose 'Delta Lady' had given him a British hit in 1969. With Russell as musical director, Cocker undertook the chaotic Mad Dogs and Englishmen tour, which produced a film and a live double-album, but left the singer bankrupt and ravaged by alcohol and drugs.

A 1975 comeback produced the US Top Ten hit 'You Are So Beautiful', but was marred by further drink and drug problems. Later albums for A&M, Asylum and Island and a guest appearance on the **Crusaders**' *Standing Tall* preceded the duet with Warnes, 'Up Where We Belong', which reached No. 1 in America and was a British Top Ten record.

In 1984 he signed to Capitol, releasing *Civilised Man*, *Unchain My Heart* (1987) and the Dan Hartman-produced *One Night of Sin* (1989), whose title track was a revival of the 1956 Smiley Lewis song bowdlerized by **Elvis Presley** as 'One Night'. *Joe Cocker Live* followed in 1990 and he next contributed a version of 'Sorry Seems to be the Hardest Word' to *Two Rooms*, the tribute album to **Elton John** and Bernie Taupin.

Night Calls (1992) put Cocker back in the UK album chart, and the compilation *The Legend* later that year gave him a Top Five album for the first time in his career. Another duet, with Sass Jones on 'Trust in Me', appeared on the bestselling soundtrack to the film *The Bodyguard*. In 1994 he appeared at the Woodstock '94 event and released *Have a Little Faith*. *Organic*, produced by **Don Was** and featuring contributions from **Randy Newman** and Tony Joe White, as well as long-time associate Stainton, offered a mix of pared-down recordings of earlier hits and new material. The album was a huge hit in Germany, where Cocker's popularity was stronger than ever. He followed it with the lesser *Across from Midnight* (1998).

COCTEAU TWINS

Elizabeth Fraser, b. 29 August 1958, Grangemouth, Scotland; Robin Guthrie; Will Heggie; Simon Raymonde

The idiosyncratic, ethereal sounds of the Cocteau Twins attracted a sizeable cult audience in the late eighties with fans from the UK 'indie' rock scene and the ever-larger number of devotees of 'new age' music.

Guitarist Guthrie and bassist Heggie formed the Cocteau Twins in 1981 in the industrial town of Grangemouth, near Edinburgh. After Fraser joined they made several demo tapes setting her breathy vocals against a background concocted by Guthrie from tape-loops, electronic drums and effects-laden guitar. The tapes brought the band to the attention of London independent label 4AD, which released *Garlands* later that year. The Cocteaus' refusal to have their photographs displayed on their record sleeves together with Fraser's extraordinary singing style in which words often seemed to have been chosen for their sound rather than meaning (a technique previously employed by the **Velvet Underground** and **Pink Floyd**'s Syd Barrett), helped to quickly build a mystique around the band.

Heggie departed shortly after the first album's release, and the follow-up, *Head Over Heels* (1983), was recorded by Fraser and Guthrie as a duo. It was a more even album than its predecessor, with Guthrie concocting a multi-layered, lush backdrop for Fraser's vocal stylings. The duo joined a number of other 4AD artists on an album by This Mortal Coil, a loose conglomeration who recorded three albums for the label, containing various cover-versions. The highlight of the first album was a Fraser-sung version of **Tim Buckley**'s haunting 'Song to the Siren'.

The Cocteau's own 'Pearly-Dewdrops' Drops' gave them their first UK hit in 1984, followed by the Top Thirty album *Treasure*, the first to feature Heggie's replacement Simon Raymonde, the son of sixties record producer Ivor Raymonde. A confident, polished album, it set the standard for the group's next few releases, which would feature a fuller, richer sound. Guthrie and Fraser released the fourth Cocteaus' album in 1986. *Victorialand* featured a slimmed-down sound and gave the group their biggest album yet when it reached the UK Top Ten. The Cocteau Twins now released another EP, *Love's Easy Tears*, and collaborated with avant-garde composer and pianist Harold Budd on the album *The Moon and the Melodies* (1986). The Cocteaus toured the UK in 1986, but then took a sabbatical for the next two years, re-emerging with the impressive *Blue Bell Knoll* (1989), which finally saw them make some progress in the US. Even more accessible was *Heaven or Las Vegas* (1990), which reached the UK Top Ten.

Another pause in the band's career followed, during which Guthrie produced the début album of UK indie band Lush. *The Singles Collection* (1991) was followed by the first release for Fontana, *Four Calendar Café* (1993). It included the dreamy hit single 'Evangeline' and showed a new-found confidence in the use of more traditional song structures, combined with the trademark Cocteaus swirling backdrop.

The group took a two-year break before reconvening in 1994 to tour Europe, expanded by the addition of two drummers and two extra guitarists. In 1995 the Cocteau Twins released a pair of EPs which saw them exploring different directions. *Twinlights* was a subtle acoustic recording, while *Otherness* drew on ambient dance. *Milk and Kisses* (1996) was in the traditional Cocteaus vein, but proved to be their final recording when the band quietly decided to disband while attempting to record the follow-up. After the split, Fraser contributed vocals to several tracks on **Massive Attack**'s 1998 album *Mezzanine*. The two-CD set *BBC Sessions* was released in 1999, featuring tracks recorded for DJs John Peel and Mark Radcliffe.

DAVID ALLAN COE
b. 6 September 1939, Akron, Ohio, USA

One of many modern country singer-songwriters to be directly influenced by black music, Coe, like **Merle Haggard**, advanced his career in country music by using the experience of the many years he spent in prison.

As a teenager he was sent to reform school for theft and later sentenced to death for killing a fellow-prisoner in self-defence. Coe was saved by the abolition of the death penalty in Ohio and was paroled in 1967. He took the starkly realistic blues songs he had written in prison to producer Shelby Singleton, who released two albums on his SSS label: *Penitentiary Blues* and *Requiem for a Harlequin*.

Coe's commentary on current political scandals, 'How High's the Watergate Martha?' (Plantation,

1972), helped to establish his songwriting credentials and his first success came the following year when **Tanya Tucker**'s recording of his 'Would You Lay with Me (In a Field of Stone)' was a country No. 1. In 1974 he signed a recording contract with Columbia, releasing *The Mysterious Rhinestone Cowboy*, while his version of **Steve Goodman**'s 'You Never Even Called Me by My Name' was a country hit in 1975.

Coe was now recognized as an original talent, with wry, quizzical and offbeat songs. Among his albums were *Longhaired Redneck* (1976) and *Tattoo* (1977). He also wrote about the country music world itself in 'Willie, Waylon and Me' and 'If That Ain't Country'. In 1978 Johnny Paycheck had a massive hit with Coe's exhilarating 'Take This Job and Shove It'.

Later Columbia albums, including *Family Album* (1978) and *Castles in the Sand* (1983), sold well and in 1983 he topped the country singles chart with 'The Ride', a ghost story about a meeting with **Hank Williams**. The following year 'Mona Lisa's Lost Her Smile' was also a big hit. Later albums included *Son of the South* (1986) and *Songs for Sale* (1991). *For the Record* (1985) collected together the best of his Columbia recordings. In the nineties the German-based Bear Family records re-released several of his earlier records on CD, while Coe himself released *Standing Too Close to the Flames* (1995).

Coe's songs were recorded by many leading figures in country music, including **Johnny Cash**, **Tammy Wynette** and **George Jones**. In the mid-seventies he set up a music-publishing company with the aim of publishing material by prison inmates and in 1978 he wrote an autobiography, *Just for the Record*.

ALMA COGAN
b. 19 May 1932, Worthing, Sussex, England, d. 26 October 1966, London

Known as 'the girl with a chuckle in her voice' and for her extravagant, self-designed dresses, Cogan was one of Britain's most popular recording stars in the fifties.

The daughter of a haberdasher, she won a talent contest in her teens and sang with a local dance band. In 1947 she auditioned unsuccessfully for **Ted Heath** and in 1948 won a part in the chorus of the London production of **Jule Styne** and **Sammy Cahn**'s musical *High Button Shoes* alongside Audrey Hepburn. She had a minor acting role in *The Blue Lamp* (1949), but returned to singing when Wallace Ridley signed her to HMV in 1952, and she secured a regular guest spot on the radio show *Take It from Here*.

Her string of twenty hits, more than any other British female vocalist of the era, included 'Bell Bottom Blues' (a cover of **Teresa Brewer**'s 1953 American hit); 'I Can't Tell a Waltz from a Tango' (a cover of **Patti Page**'s hit) in 1954; 'Dreamboat', the only No. 1

by a British female singer in the fifties; 'Twenty Tiny Fingers' (1955); a cover of **Vaughn Monroe**'s 'In the Middle of the House' (1956); and a cover of the **McGuire Sisters**' 'Sugartime' (1958). Her last hit was 'Cowboy Jimmy Joe' (1961). Though her chart hits ceased, her chirpy personality guaranteed her regular British tours and TV appearances throughout the early sixties, when she also recorded an album of Lennon–McCartney songs.

Her death, from cancer, came after a long illness.

In 1992 the British writer Gordon Burn created a fictionalized account of her life in his novel *Alma Cogan*.

GEORGE M. COHAN

b. George Michael Cohan, 3 or 4 July 1878, Providence, Rhode Island, USA, d. 4 November 1942, New York

The debate about Cohan's birthdate is symptomatic. Sceptics have suggested that Cohan was born on 3 July, but adopted the later date (like the hero of his song, 'The Yankee Doodle'), so complete was his identification with America that was the dominant feature of his songs, plays and performances. However, Cohan's importance in the history of popular music is more than a matter of themes – 'America' was, after all, the theme of so many songwriters of the early part of the century. Cohan was responsible for a decisive shift in the development of the American musical stage and produced the first authentic example of that unique form, the Broadway musical: *Little Johnny Jones* (1904). Although he was a prolific writer – he wrote and directed some forty plays, was involved in a further 150 and published some 500 songs – much of his work is slight, but the central core, which includes such songs as 'The Yankee Doodle' and 'Give My Regards to Broadway' (both 1904) and 'Over There' (1917), is a remarkable exercise in brash, honest vulgarity, that captures everyday feelings to startling effect. Many of his songs have the flavour of the marches of **John Philip Sousa** with a little syncopation on the side, but though they are simple and use simple 'tricks' – for example, the triumphant repetition of 'over' in the last line of 'Over There', a song musically based on a bugle call – they are nonetheless memorable. His success was neatly pinpointed by Oscar Hammerstein II: 'Cohan's genius was to say what everybody was subconsciously feeling'. Moreover, he was luckier than most heroes of the twentieth century in having Jimmy Cagney (a one-time hoofer himself) play him with real verve, and win an Oscar in one of the best of Hollywood's biopics, *Yankee Doodle Dandy* (1942).

Born into a theatrical family, the self-taught George was a member by the time he was nine of the Four Cohans, a vaudeville act led by his father Jeremiah, a one-time minstrel. A songwriter by his teens, he had numerous attempts turned down before arriving in New York in the nineties where his sister Josie had secured a lengthy vaudeville engagement. By the end of the decade, he had established himself as a writer of coon songs and ragtime airs such as 'You're Growing Cold, Cold, Cold' (1897) which was advertised as 'the story of a coon with an iceberg heart' and, his first big success, 'I Guess I'll Have to Telegraph My Baby' (1898), which was introduced by Cohan's wife to be, Ethel Levy. Equally significantly, Cohan was now writing the material for the family shows. Before, they had been a simple mix of songs and patter, but after *The Governor's Son* (1901) – which included Cohan's first notable Broadway song, 'Too Many Miles from Broadway' – the shows were constructed around a plot which unified the various set-pieces. At that time, the only other musical shows to do this were the Ruritanian operettas imported from Europe. Cohan's breakthrough came with *Little Johnny Jones*, the story of an American jockey (played by Cohan himself) accused of throwing a race in England, who eventually clears his name. A failure when it opened on Broadway, Cohan toured America with it, rewriting as he went and bringing it back to the Great White Way in triumph in 1905. Heady with raucous jingoism ('The Yankee Doodle') and shameless presumption ('Give My Regards to Broadway', in which Cohan wrote as though he were one of its established inhabitants, was written when he was twenty-six and an outsider), *Little Johnny Jones* signalled the arrival of Cohan.

For the next fifteen years Cohan was the King of Broadway, initially putting on several hugely successful musicals a year before slowing down to one. Among these were *Forty Five Minutes from Broadway* and *George Washington Jnr* (both 1906), *The Man Who Owns Broadway* (1909), *Hello Broadway!* (1914, the year Cohan opened his own theatre) and *The Royal Vagabond* (1918). Cohan's influence waned after he took the side of the theatre managers and owners against the actors in their strike of 1919, one of the turning points in the history of Broadway. By then, anyway, Cohan was no longer an innovator. Indeed, though he still produced musicals, his best later work was as an author of melodramas, such as *Seven Keys to Baldpate* (1917) and *The Tavern* (1920), and as an actor, most surprisingly in Eugene O'Neill's *Ah, Wilderness!* (1933) and most notably playing Franklin Delano Roosevelt in George S. Kaufman's and Moss Hart's *I'd Rather Be Rich* (1937).

Several of Cohan's productions were filmed, including *Seven Keys to Baldpate* (five times between 1917 and 1947), *Little Johnny Jones* (1923, 1929) and *Song and Dance Man* and *The Home Towners* (both 1936), and he twice ventured briefly to Hollywood to make both silent – *Broadway Jones* (1917) – and sound films – *The Phantom President* (1932). But it was his songs and larger-than-life personality that Hollywood took notice of, first in numerous 'Broadway' musicals and then as the subject matter for *Yankee Doodle Dandy*.

In 1939 Cohan was awarded a Congressional Medal of Honor in recognition of the value of 'Over There' and 'You're a Grand Old Flag' (1907) during the First World War. One of his last published songs was 'We Must Be Ready' (1941), written some six months before Pearl Harbor. In 1959 a statue of him was erected on Broadway.

LEONARD COHEN
b. 21 September 1934, Montreal, Canada

Cohen was the archetypal sensitive singer-songwriter of the sixties. Surprisingly he found renewed critical and commercial success in the eighties with only slight changes to his spare style.

He was initially a poet who had recited his verse to jazz backings in the fifties, and a novelist who wrote the classic – albeit dated – sixties novel, *Beautiful Losers* (1966). In the same year **Judy Collins** recorded 'Suzanne', one of the finest of his song poems. An appearance at the 1967 Newport Folk Festival led to his first and most successful album, *Songs of Leonard Cohen* (Columbia, 1968). The lyrics embodied the same romanticism to be found in his literary work: eroticism mingled with religious imagery ('Sisters of Mercy'), wistful despair ('So Long Marianne') and esoteric intimations of mysticism ('Master Song'). Cohen softly intoned the words against a sparse acoustic backing and John Simon's production matched sound and meaning appropriately. Several of the songs later appeared on the soundtrack of Robert Altman's *McCabe and Mrs Miller* (1971).

Bob Johnston replaced Simon for *Songs from a Room* (1969), but the formula was the same, with 'Bird on a Wire' philosophically dispensing existential gloom and 'The Partisan' taking on issues of violence and politics. Cohen now began to tour, proving himself no musician but a skilful manipulator of audience emotions. Although not released until 1973, his live album (*Live Songs*) was recorded in 1970, the year of his third studio album, *Songs of Love and Hate*.

Following *New Skin for the Old Ceremony* (1974) Cohen retired to a Greek island, returning to live performance in 1976 and the following year releasing *Death of a Ladies Man*, produced by **Phil Spector**, who co-wrote the songs. A drastic and ambitious change in direction, towards rock, the record was a failure.

He released only two albums over the next decade. *Recent Songs* (1979) had vocal arrangements by **Jennifer Warnes**, who duetted with Cohen on several

tracks, while *Various Positions* (1985) showed a return to Cohen's original low-key, acoustic approach. He returned to recording with the self-produced *I'm Your Man* (1988), which saw him in a reflective mood about middle age and his middle European origins, and included additional vocals by Warnes. In 1991 **Nick Cave**, **John Cale** and **R.E.M.** were among those performing Cohen songs on the tribute album *I'm Your Fan*. This was the prelude to his greatest success, *The Future* (1992), a brooding look at the present – 'I have seen the future, brother it is murder'. Paradoxically, the album also included Cohen's most realistic and idealistic recordings of love songs. The former is his version of Frederick Knight's 'Be for Real', the latter his rendering of **Irving Berlin**'s 'Always'. *Cohen Live* (1994) offered equally brooding versions of the songs. In 1998 Columbia issued an eponymous album by Cohen's son Adam.

NAT 'KING' COLE
b. Nathaniel Adams Coles, 17 March 1919, Montgomery, Alabama, USA, d. 15 February 1965, Los Angeles, California

As a jazz pianist an important influence on **Art Tatum** and **Oscar Peterson**, Cole had even greater success as a singer. His smooth, warm, romantic baritone and relaxed singing style, with little trace of blues or gospel, won him six million-sellers and made several of his recordings, particularly 'Mona Lisa'* (1950) and 'When I Fall in Love' (1957), permanent features of late-night radio programming.

The son of a Baptist minister, Cole was raised in Chicago and studied piano as a child. He made his first recording with his older brother Eddie's band ('Honey Hush', Decca) in 1936. That showed the influence of **Earl Hines** but by the time of his 1939 recordings with his trio (Cole, guitarist Oscar Moore and bassist Wesley Prince) Cole was playing in the familiar single-note manner that marked the majority of his trio recordings for Decca (1940–1), several minor labels (1942) and Capitol, with whom they signed in 1943. Originally a wholly instrumental performer, Cole started singing in 1941 and by the time of his first hit on Capitol, his own composition 'Straighten Up and Fly Right' (1943), he was a singer/pianist rather than pianist/singer. For five years Cole continued to record with the trio, including '(I Love You) For Sentimental Reasons' (1946) and 'Harmony' (1947) with guest vocals from **Johnny Mercer**, but from the time of **Mel Tormé**'s 'The Christmas Song' (1946), his first recording with strings, and 'Nature Boy'* (1948, revived by **Bobby Darin**, 1961) Cole was increasingly recorded as a solo artist with orchestral backing. His last major recording with the trio was 'Little Girl'* (1948) the song initially popularized by **Guy Lombardo** and a hit for **Joe Venuti** with the songwriter **Harold Arlen** on vocals in 1931.

Les Baxter's orchestra supported Cole on the Oscar-winning film theme 'Mona Lisa'* (1950, revived in 1959 by Carl Mann on Philips, and **Conway Twitty** and later used as the title song to the 1986 British thriller) and 'Too Young'* (1951, revived by Donny Osmond of the **Osmonds**, 1972). These established Cole as a romantic balladeer and set the pattern of his subsequent career as a mainstream entertainer on stage, television, film and record, in collaboration with Baxter, **Nelson Riddle** and **Billy May**. In the late fifties he made the occasional opportunistic record ('When Rock'n'Roll Came to Trinidad', 1957) but for the most part he was unaffected by the musical revolution around him. Hits of the period include 'Answer My Love'* (1954, a British No. 1 for balladeer David Whitfield on Decca), 'A Blossom Fell'* (1955), 'When I Fall in Love' (1957, revived by British teen-idol Rick Astley in 1987 on PWL, and a hit again for Cole when reissued), 'Ramblin Rose' (1962) and the good-time-flavoured 'Those Lazy-Hazy-Crazy Days of Summer' (1963). A year before that the hit 'Let There Be Love', a collaboration with **George Shearing**, revived memories of Cole's trio days. Cole's last work in partnership, with Stubby Kaye singing 'The Ballad of Cat Ballou', provided a running commentary on the action of the comedy Western *Cat Ballou* (1965).

Cole's daughter Natalie (*b. 6 February 1950, Los Angeles*) had later success with a series of pop-inflected dance records. Among them were 'This Will Be' (Capitol, 1975), 'I've Got Love on My Mind'* (1977) and 'Our Love' (1978). In 1983 she recorded a tribute album to her father with **Johnny Mathis**, *Unforgettable*, and returned to the charts in 1988 with a glorious rendition of **Bruce Springsteen**'s 'Pink Cadillac'. Other hits included 'Miss You Like Crazy' (1989) and 'Wild Woman Do' (1990) before her biggest success *Unforgettable – With Love* (Elektra, 1991), another album of songs associated with Nat Cole. The title song, an electronically constructed duet with her father, was also a hit. On *Take a Look* (1993) she again sang a selection of standards before returning to songs associated with her father on *Stardust* (1996), which included another duet from beyond the grave, 'When I Fall in Love'.

ORNETTE COLEMAN
b. 19 March 1930, Fort Worth, Texas, USA

One of the most important individuals in popular music history, Coleman inaugurated the 'new-wave' jazz revolution of the sixties and remained one of the most inventive of contemporary saxophonists.

A Texas contemporary of **King Curtis**, Coleman

played in R&B bands before moving to New Orleans and then, in 1951, to Los Angeles. He spent the next seven years working on his new music with a small group of co-thinkers, including trumpeter **Don Cherry**, drummer Billy Higgins and bassist **Charlie Haden**. They met with hostility from other musicians because their playing ignored the jazz conventions of chord changes and keys established in the aftermath of the bebop revolution of the forties. But Coleman's music (played on a plastic alto sax) also involved a new emphasis on some of the most basic aspects of black music – the blues and the use of instruments to emulate human cries and shouts.

After a 1958 album for Contemporary, the Coleman group was signed by **Nesuhi Ertegun** to Atlantic, going on to cut the prophetically titled *The Shape of Jazz to Come* (1959) and seven others in three years. These included *Change of the Century* (1959), *This is Our Music* (1960) and *Ornette!*, on which Scott La Faro replaced Haden. In their combination of avant-garde forms and sounds derived from the roots of Afro-American music, these albums divided a generation of jazz players into those inspired to follow the Coleman path of free improvisation and those who fiercely resisted the 'new thing'. The most remarkable of the Atlantic recordings was *Free Jazz* (1960), on which eight musicians spontaneously and collectively improvised for thirty-six minutes.

After a two-year hiatus spent learning trumpet and violin, Coleman toured Europe in 1965 with bassist Davis Izenson and Charles Moffett on drums. His later work, based on what he termed a 'harmolodic' theory of music, focused on a series of attempts to broaden the standard American horizons of jazz. *Science Fiction* (Columbia, 1971) included Indian vocalist Asha Puthli, while *Skies of America* (Columbia, 1972) was a symphonic piece performed by the London Symphony Orchestra. Other collaborators in the seventies included Morocco's Master Musicians of Joujouka and electric guitarist James Blood Ulmer. *Dancing in Your Head* (A&M, 1977) featured Coleman in a free jazz-funk fusion mode with Prime Time, an electric band which included his son Denardo on drums. In 1986 he released *Song X* (Geffen), a collaboration with guitarist **Pat Metheny**.

The album *In All Language* featured one disc by Prime Time and a second by a re-formed version of the classic early sixties quartet. The 1988 Prime Time album *Virgin Beauty* was his most commercially successful. Subsequent albums include *Jazzbuhne Berlin* (1990) and *Naked Lunch* (1992).

ALBERT COLLINS
b. 3 October 1932 (or 1930), Leona, Texas, USA,
d. 24 November 1993, Las Vegas, Nevada

Collins was an exciting blues performer whose records conveyed the euphoria of a blues club on a good night. Initially influenced by **Clarence 'Gatemouth' Brown** and **T-Bone Walker**, he became a guitarist of comparable status and influence among both black and white musicians.

He grew up in Houston, Texas, forming his first band in his late teens but didn't record until 1958, with the locally popular instrumental 'The Freeze'. This was, for him, the birth of the cool: his subsequent singles for Bill Hall's labels in 1962–3 were all given titles like 'Frosty' and 'Sno-Cone' and later transferred to the album *The Cool Sound of Albert Collins*. His playing is characterized by the use of a D minor tuning and high capo positions, which yield a shrill and biting attack.

Elevated from the club circuit by the patronage of Bob Hite of **Canned Heat**, Collins moved to the West Coast in 1968 and played major folk and rock venues like the Ash Grove and Fillmore West. *Love Can Be Found Anywhere (Even in a Guitar)* (Imperial, 1968) represented his then largely instrumental act. Over the next decade he developed his singing while working extensively, much of the time without a supporting record label or even a regular band. In the Northwest, for example, he customarily hired the band led by singer/guitarist Robert Cray, whom Collins started on the path to an international reputation, notably with *Strong Persuader* (Mercury, 1986), the only blues album to make the higher reaches of the pop charts in the eighties.

In 1978 he signed with the Chicago independent label Alligator and began a series of albums that fully realized his abilities while incidentally preserving the 'cold' theme: *Ice Pickin'* (1978), *Frostbite* (1980) and so on. In 1985 he was the only blues artist to appear in the globally televised Live Aid concerts, as a guest of the white singer/guitarist George Thorogood; in the same year he joined Robert Cray and fellow Houstonian singer/guitarist Johnny Copeland for a 'reunion' album, *Showdown!* (Alligator). *Cold Snap* (Alligator, 1987) included a guest appearance by **Jimmy McGriff**, but far better were *Iceman* (Virgin, 1991) and *Collins Mix* (1992), on which **B. B. King** and Branford Marsalis were among the guests. During these years he frequently played as a guest on albums by such artists as **Jack Bruce**, **Gary Moore**, **David Bowie** and John Zorn. The retrospective *The Complete Imperial Recordings* (EMI, 1991) documented his early career with precision and care.

Collins died of lung cancer.

ARTHUR COLLINS
b. 7 February 1864, Philadelphia, Pennsylvania, USA, d. 3 August 1933

One of the pioneers of the American recording industry, Collins was a minstrel-style dialect-comedy singer. He is best remembered for his recording of 'The Preacher and the Bear' (Edison, 1905), the first monologue to sell a million copies.

He came to recording ('Zizzy Ze Zum Zee', Edison, 1898) after a career in vaudeville where, like **Len Spencer**, he specialized in novelty and dialect material. Among his early hits were **George M. Cohan**'s 'I Guess I'll Have to Telegraph My Baby' (1899), 'Bill Bailey, Won't You Please Come Home' (1902) and **Harry Von Tilzer**'s 'Down Where the Wurzburger Flows' (Victor, 1903). 'The Preacher and the Bear', which on its release in the UK was accompanied by a leaflet explaining the tale of a preacher chased up a tree after going hunting on Sunday, was written by publisher Arthur Longbrake under the pseudonym of Joe Arizona and successfully revived by **Phil Harris** (1947). The song was re-recorded by Collins for numerous labels, including Victor, Columbia, Everlasting, Indestructible and Zon-O-Phone. Though he never had such a big hit again, Collins recorded indefatigably between 1910 and 1920, notably ragtime and coon songs.

On many of these hits Collins was partnered by Byron G. Harlan (*b. 29 August 1861, d. 11 September 1936*), who was a close friend of **Thomas Edison**. Harlan's solo hits, mostly sentimental ballads, included **Leslie Stuart**'s 'Tell Me Pretty Maiden' (Columbia, 1901), Harry Von Tilzer's sequel to 'A Bird in a Gilded Cage', 'The Mansion of Aching Hearts' (Edison, 1902), and **Paul Dresser**'s 'My Gal Sal' (Victor, 1907). His recordings with Collins were more robust, mostly of ragtime and novelty songs. They included 'The Right Church but the Wrong Pew' (Columbia, 1909) and several by **Irving Berlin**. Among these were 'Alexander's Ragtime Band' (Victor, 1911), 'When That Midnight Choo Choo Leaves for Alabam'' (Columbia, 1913), 'Oh How She Could Yacki Hacki Wicki Wacki Woo (That's Love in Honolulu)' (Victor, 1916) and 'Dark Town Strutters' Ball' (Columbia, 1918), their last major hit.

Between 1909 and 1918 Collins also recorded, alongside **Henry Burr**, as a member of the Peerless Quartet. He was featured on their recording of 'Over There' (Columbia, 1917), one of the many versions of Cohan's patriotic song.

JUDY COLLINS
b. Judith Marjorie Collins, 1 May 1939, Seattle, Washington, USA

Collins was a major figure in popular song for two decades. Notable in the folk revival of the sixties for her encouragement of new songwriters like **Leonard Cohen** and **Joni Mitchell**, she devised a unique role as the interpreter of a repertoire that was in equal parts political, poetic and theatrical. That repertoire was encapsulated on the albums *In My Life* (Elektra, 1966), *Wildflowers* (1968) and *Who Knows Where the Time Goes?* (1969). In the seventies she broadened her scope to the extent of having a big hit with the definitive reading of **Stephen Sondheim**'s subtle show tune 'Send in the Clowns'. The record was in marked contrast to Collins' earlier chart success, the *a cappella* version of the spiritual 'Amazing Grace' (1971), which spent over a year in the British charts.

Her father Chuck Collins was a bandleader and disc-jockey in Denver, where she studied classical piano with Antonia Brica, about whom she made the film *Antonia: A Portrait of the Woman* in 1974. With the upsurge of interest in folk music in the mid-fifties, Collins was drawn into the Denver coffee-house scene and soon recognized for the clarity of her soprano voice.

In 1960 she was signed by Jac Holzman to Elektra and cut two albums which reflected the traditional song repertoire of the period. *A Maid of Constant Sorrow* (1961) included 'Wild Mountain Thyme' and 'I Know Where I'm Going', while *Golden Apples of the Sun* (1962) had 'Minstrel Boy' and 'The Silkie'.

By 1963–4 the established folk scene was feeling the impact of the new songwriters, led by **Bob Dylan** and **Tom Paxton**. Collins was no exception and *Judy Collins No. 3* (1963), with arrangements by Roger McGuinn (later of the **Byrds**), featured Dylan's 'Masters of War', and 'Come Away Melinda', an anti-war song by the under-rated Tim Rose, very much in the mould of his better-known 'Morning Dew'. The 1964 *In Concert* album included more Dylan as well as Paxton's 'The Last Thing on My Mind'.

This mixture of traditional and contemporary folk songs was continued with the *5th Album*, but *In My Life* marked a distinct shift of emphasis. With producer **Joshua Rifkin**, Collins programmed what was virtually a guide to the best current songwriters, without reference to genre. As well as Dylan and Cohen, there were **Randy Newman** ('I Think It's Going to Rain Today'), **The Beatles** ('In My Life'), **Jacques Brel** ('La Colombe') and two songs from radical music theatre: **Kurt Weill**'s and Bertolt Brecht's 'Pirate Jenny' and a song from Peter Weiss's *Marat/Sade*.

The versatility of Collins' singing enabled her to integrate such a wide range of material. A similarly unconventional selection was made for *Wildflowers*, which introduced Joni Mitchell – through 'Both Sides Now', a Top Ten hit for Collins. The album also included Collins' own songwriting for the first time, though this was shown to greater effect on the meditative 'My Father' from 1969's *Who Knows Where the Time Goes?*.

The main features of the six albums released during the seventies were the increasing confidence and quality of Collins' own songs and the steady encroachment of mainstream ballads and standards into her repertoire. Her writing reached a peak with *True Stories and Other Dreams* (1973). 'Che' was an elegiac and effective political song, while 'Secret Gardens' showed Collins' talent for writing autobiographical songs that were more than pages of a private diary.

The **Arif Mardin**-produced *Judith* (1975) included the hit 'Send in the Clowns', while *Bread and Roses* (1976) demonstrated Collins' continuing political commitment through the feminist title song and the inclusion of a composition by murdered Chilean songwriter Victor Jara. Later Elektra albums included *Times of Our Lives* (1982) and *Home Again* (1984), each of which underlined the continuing quality of her singing and her ability to surprise in her choice of repertoire.

In 1987 Collins signed to Danny Goldberg's Goldcastle label, releasing *Trust Your Heart*, which shared its title with her autobiography. Even better was *Fires of Eden* (Columbia, 1990), which included her own composition, the engaging 'Home Before Dawn'. In 1994 she released *Judy Sings Dylan . . . Just Like a Woman* (Geffen), a collection of Bob Dylan songs, and in 1995 she published her first novel, *Shameless*. It was followed by the two-CD retrospective *Forever* (1997).

PHIL COLLINS
b. 31 January 1951, London, England

Until he launched a solo career in 1981 Collins was a highly respected craftsman as drummer and singer with progressive rock band **Genesis**. His skill as a songwriter, blue-eyed soul singer and producer made him a rock superstar of the eighties. His status was symbolized by the fact that he was the only musician to perform in both London and Philadelphia during Live Aid, and by his leading role in the Prince's Trust, a charity patronized by the Prince and Princess of Wales. In the nineties he was better known for his wealth, which magazines estimated at being in the region of $400m.

Briefly a child actor, he recorded with rock band Flaming Youth for Uni before joining Genesis in 1970 and taking over as vocalist on *A Trick of the Tail* when **Peter Gabriel** left the group in 1976. In that year he also released *Unorthodox Behaviour* (Charisma) with jazz-rock group Brand X, which also included Percy Jones (bass), John Goodsall (guitar) and Rob Lumley (percussion). Collins played on six of the band's seven albums.

His success as a solo artist began with the release of *Face Value* (Virgin in Britain/Atlantic in America) in 1981. The passionate vocals (the recording coincided with the collapse of Collins' marriage), his crisp drumming and the addition of the brass section from **Earth, Wind and Fire** sent the album to No. 1 in Britain. The intense and gloomy 'In the Air Tonight' and 'I Missed Again' were hits on both sides of the Atlantic.

Hello I Must Be Going! (1982) provided his first British No. 1 single in the affectionate remake of the **Supremes**' 'You Can't Hurry Love'. Collins was now in demand as a producer and in 1982 he worked on albums by ex-**Abba** vocalist Anni-Frid Lyngstad and British guitarist-songwriter John Martyn. Later production credits included **Adam Ant**, **Howard Jones** and **Eric Clapton**. Collins was also approached to provide movie themes, one of which, 'Against All Odds', produced by **Arif Mardin**, was an American No. 1 in 1984. This began a run of six American hit singles in the next two years. Among them were two duets, one with Earth, Wind and Fire singer Philip Bailey ('Easy Lover', 1984), the other with Marilyn Martin (the film theme 'Separate Lives', 1985, from *White Nights*). The others were all taken from the 1985 album *No Jacket Required* and included the two American No. 1s 'Sussudio' and 'One More Night'. By now Collins had refined his style into the perfect crossover mélange of white rock and eighties soul music.

In the mid-eighties he began an acting career with a cameo role in the television series *Miami Vice*, whose theme tune gave Jan Hammer a No. 1 hit in 1985 (MCA). Collins' 'In the Air Tonight' also appeared on the *Miami Vice* (MCA) soundtrack album that topped the American charts. In 1988 he starred in *Buster* as train-robber Buster Edwards, and topped the UK charts with a revival of 'A Groovy Kind of Love', the 1966 hit for the Mindbenders (Fontana).

In 1989 he had a further international hit with the subdued song about the homeless 'Another Day in Paradise' from . . . *But Seriously**. This prefigured the most commercially successful period in his career. On his 1989 world tour he played to two million people in fifty-seven cities. His hit singles included 'Do You Remember' (1990), 'Hang in Long Enough' and 'That's Just the Way It Is', a response to the Northern Ireland situation with backing vocals by David Crosby. However, Collins' greatest success came with the albums . . . *But Seriously* (1989) and the superior *Serious Hits – Live* (1990). The concert recording, albeit re-edited in the studio, proved itself to have more emotional power than its studio counterpart. Then came *Both Sides* (1993), probably the definitive Collins album with its sombre reflection on the fragility of relationships and insistent calls for understanding. It included the hit 'Everyday'. In 1996 he formed the Phil Collins Big Band and released *Dance into the Light*. Far better received was the retrospec-

tive *Hits* (1997), and songs for the Disney animated film *Tarzan* (1999), which included the Oscar-winning 'You'll Be in My Heart'.

COLOSSEUM

Jon Hiseman, b. 21 June 1944, London, England; Dave Greenslade, b. 18 January 1943, Woking, Surrey; Tony Reeves, b. 18 April 1943, London; Dick Heckstall-Smith, b. 26 September 1934, Ludlow, Shropshire; James Litherland, b. 6 September 1949, Manchester; David 'Clem' Clempson, b. 5 September 1949; Chris Farlowe, b. 13 October 1940, London

British pioneers of jazz-rock fusion music, Colosseum never found for their ambitious music the mass acceptance of American counterparts such as **Chicago** and **Blood, Sweat and Tears**.

Colosseum was formed in 1968 by drummer Hiseman and sax-player Heckstall-Smith, who had previously worked together in the bands of **John Mayall** and **Graham Bond**. Reeves was also a Mayall alumnus, while guitarist Litherland was found through a *Melody Maker* advertisement.

Both *Those Who Are About to Die Salute You* (Fontana/Dunhill, 1969) and *Valentyne Suite* (Bronze, 1969) were Top Twenty hits in Britain and the band's lengthy pieces with extended solos made them favourites on the college circuit. By the time of the next album, *Daughter of Time* (1970), however, Litherland and Reeves had left, the former to join Mogul Thrash and later **Leo Sayer**'s backing band. The new members were Clempson (guitar) and Mark Clarke (bass) together with singer Farlowe, a former stalwart of the British R&B scene who had achieved a No. 1 with the Jagger–Richards' composition 'Out of Time' (Immediate, 1966).

Daughter of Time was the last studio recording, and Colosseum broke up in 1971, the year Bronze released a live album. Greenslade and Reeves formed a band called Greenslade, and went on to compose TV theme music. Clempson replaced **Peter Frampton** in Humble Pie, while Heckstall-Smith briefly had his own band before going on to a career which included gigs with **Jack Bruce**.

Hiseman and Clarke formed another jazz-rock band, Tempest, which cut two albums before the drummer put together Colosseum II in 1975. Ex-**Thin Lizzy** guitarist Gary Moore and Don Airey (keyboards), later to join **Deep Purple**'s Ritchie Blackmore, gave the group's three albums a heavier sound.

After the demise of Colosseum II in 1978, Hiseman concentrated on jazz-based projects, often with his wife, the saxophonist Barbara Thompson. Both also worked with **Johnny Dankworth** and **Andrew Lloyd Webber**.

JOHN COLTRANE
b. John William Coltrane, 23 September 1926, Hamlet, North Carolina, USA, d. 17 July 1967, New York

One of the most acclaimed figures in modern jazz, saxophonist Coltrane was a bridge between the bebop generation of **Charlie Parker** and the free-form avant-garde of **Ornette Coleman**. He played on some of **Miles Davis**'s best albums before forming his own quartet, which recorded prolifically in 1961–5. Like Parker, Coltrane inspired and influenced whole generations of younger musicians.

Coltrane was from a musical family: his mother was a church pianist and his father played violin. As a youth he learned clarinet and alto saxophone and he studied music in Philadelphia, where he moved in 1944. After two years in a navy band, Coltrane began his professional career in R&B groups. During 1947–8 he was a member of **Eddie Vinson**'s band and in 1949 he joined **Dizzy Gillespie**'s orchestra, with whom he made his first recordings (including 'The Champ', 1951). Drugs problems forced Coltrane to leave and he spent 1952–3 in the R&B band of saxophonist **Earl Bostic**.

After a switch of style to cool jazz with the **Johnny Hodges** group (1953–4), Coltrane joined Davis in 1955. In the space of a year the group made five albums for Prestige, including *Tallest Trees*. Tracks like 'Around Midnight' from *Tallest Trees* and 'If I Were a Bell' found Coltrane pushing at the limits of orthodox jazz, 'changing the notes of a chord around to see how many ways he can play it', as Davis said. Coltrane's continuing drugs problems led him out of the Miles Davis band and in 1957 he took time off to cure himself. He returned to perform with **Thelonious Monk**, recording with him for Milestone. At this period Coltrane developed what critic Ira Gitler called his 'sheets of sound' approach on a series of solo albums including *Blue Trane* (Blue Note, 1957), *Traneing In* (Prestige) and *Soultrane* (1958).

In 1958 Coltrane rejoined Davis and took part in such classic albums as the introverted *Kind of Blue* (1959) and the classic *Milestones* (1960). By now he had established his own individual approach, evident on the solo albums *Giant Steps* (Atlantic, 1959) and *My Favourite Things* (1960), where he introduced soprano sax on the **Rodgers and Hammerstein** title track. The peak of Coltrane's popularity was the early sixties when his quartet, with **McCoy Tyner** (piano), Jimmy Garrison (bass) and **Elvin Jones** (drums), released frequent albums on Bob Thiele's Impulse label to which he signed in 1961. Jones, in particular, showed complete empathy with the saxophonist's lengthy, complex solos on such tracks as the title piece from *Impressions*. Other highlights of this phase included *Live at the Village Vanguard* (1961) with **Eric Dolphy**, the big-band album *Africa/Brass* (1961) and *A Love Supreme* (1964). Widely regarded as the summit of the quartet's achievement, this suite reflected Coltrane's 'spiritual awakening' and was based around a four-note phrase chanted by the group at the close of the opening track.

By 1965 Coltrane was beginning to work with a newer generation of musicians and *Ascension*, with **Archie Shepp** and Pharoah Sanders, was a forty-minute improvisation sharing the approach of Coleman's highly influential *Free Jazz* (1961). During this final period of his career, Coltrane also worked closely with his wife, pianist Alice Coltrane, who had replaced Tyner. *Expression* (1967), the last album recorded by the saxophonist before his death from cancer, featured solos by Alice Coltrane and drummer Rashied Ali.

Those two carried on the Coltrane legacy by performing together after 1967, but equally important was a flood of unissued recordings whose release was supervised by Alice. In the seventies she was converted to Hinduism and her occasional later recordings incorporated Eastern religious elements.

RUSS COLUMBO
b. Ruggerio de Rudolpho Columbo, 14 January 1908, Philadelphia, Pennsylvania, USA, d. 2 September 1934, Hollywood, California

A crooner with a light baritone who specialized in romantic ballads, in the thirties Columbo briefly rivalled **Bing Crosby** in popularity.

The son of Italian immigrants, Columbo was a child prodigy, singing and playing the violin on stage from the age of four. In 1929 he joined Gus Arnheim's Coconut Grove Orchestra as a violinist and made his film début with a minor role in *Wolf Song*. He was heavily influenced by Crosby, who joined Arnheim's band in 1930 and was replaced as singer by Columbo when he left in 1931. Columbo's Valentino-like looks gave him a far sexier image than Crosby but his vocal style was remarkably similar. Later in 1931 Columbo himself left for a solo career, signing with Victor.

His first records, made with a studio band that included **Jimmy Dorsey** on clarinet, included the original versions of the standards 'I Don't Know Why' (by Fred Ahlert and Roy Turk, the composers of 'I'll Get By'), 'Prisoner of Love' (which he co-wrote with **Leo Robin** and Clarence Gaskill and was a million-seller for **Billy Eckstine** when he revived it in 1945) and 'Guilty'. In 1932 he followed in **Rudy Vallee**'s footsteps and formed his own orchestra (which included **Benny Goodman** and **Gene Krupa**), and in 1933 followed Crosby in attempting a film career. He starred in three films, *Broadway thru' a Keyhole* (1933), which also featured Blossom Seeley and Texas Guinan, *Moulin*

Rouge and *Wake Up and Dream* (1934). He died when an antique pistol he was examining went off and he was shot through the head.

KEN COLYER
b. 18 April 1928, Great Yarmouth, Norfolk, England, d. 11 March 1988, France

A pioneering figure in British traditional jazz, trumpeter Colyer exemplified the 'purist' approach to the genre. While former members of his band like **Chris Barber** and **Lonnie Donegan** went on to popular success, Colyer remained resolutely uncommercial. Through his early fifties performances with Donegan, **Alexis Korner** and others, Colyer also initiated the skiffle trend.

His first instrument was harmonica but in the late forties Colyer took up guitar-playing while in the merchant navy and, inspired by **Louis Armstrong** and **George Lewis**, formed the Crane River Jazz Band with Sonny Morris (trumpet). In 1952 Colyer went to New Orleans to meet and play with Lewis and other jazz veterans, recording *Ken Colyer in New Orleans* (Vogue, 1953) with clarinettist Emile Barnes.

Returning to Britain a hero of the growing trad movement, Colyer led a band which included Barber (trombone), Donegan (banjo) and Monty Sunshine (clarinet). They released *New Orleans to London* (Decca, 1954) before Colyer's strictly traditionalist attitude caused the remainder of the group to secede and form the Chris Barber Jazz Band.

Colyer's next band included **Acker Bilk** on clarinet and future **Stephane Grappelli** accompanist Diz Disley on guitar. They cut the rougher *Back to the Delta* (1954) while the Colyer Skiffle Group, with Korner on mandolin and guitar, released a version of **Leadbelly**'s 'Midnight Special' in the same year. *The Decca Skiffle Sessions 1956–7* were reissued in 1987 by British label Lake. Bilk formed his own group in 1958 while Colyer spurned the growing popularity of trad bands in funny clothes playing Dixieland versions of pop hits. During the late fifties he recorded for Decca, EMI Columbia and Tempo and accompanied George Lewis on a British tour.

From the early sixties traditional jazz lost its popularity and Colyer's later groups recorded only occasionally for labels like Vintage Jazz Music (VJM) (*Live at the Dancing Slipper*, 1969) and Happy Bird (*Winging and Singing*, 1975). In later years Colyer, in poor health, went into semi-retirement in the south of France.

COMMANDER CODY
b. George Frayne, 19 July 1944, Boise, Idaho, USA

Cody led the Lost Planet Airmen, one of several bands of the sixties to blend country and rock music. But where most, following the **Byrds**, took a folk approach or merely added country instruments and imagery to soft-rock harmonizing, Cody yoked together elements of Western swing, boogie-woogie and rockabilly into an anarchic country-rock firmly in the rock'n'roll tradition. The group's live performances were better received than their records and Cody's three hits were revivals of novelty songs, **Johnny Bond**'s 'Hot Rod Lincoln' (1960) and 'Beat Me Daddy Eight to the Bar' (earlier a pop hit for the **Andrews Sisters**, 1941) in 1972, and Tex Williams' and **Merle Travis**'s 1947 composition 'Smoke! Smoke! Smoke! (That Cigarette)' in 1973.

Frayne formed the group while studying art at Michigan University. Initially with a floating line-up, the group stabilized around pianist Cody (the name Frayne took), Andy Stein (fiddle, sax), Bill Kirchin (guitar, vocals), Bruce Barlow (bass), John Tichy (rhythm guitar) and Billy C. Farlow (vocals) and moved to San Francisco where Cody guested on the eponymous début album of New Riders of the Purple Sage (Columbia, 1971), the satellite country band of the **Grateful Dead**. In the same year the Lost Planet Airmen made *Lost in the Ozone* (Paramount). Though unevenly recorded, the album's mix of traditional material ('Family Bible'), mournful country ballads with unusual imagery ('Seeds and Stems'), rock'n'roll (**Eddie Cochran**'s '20 Flight Rock') and novelty songs ('Hot Rod Lincoln') drew critical praise. The better produced *Hot Licks, Cold Steel and Truckers Favorites* (1972) added to the group's concern with mock nostalgia ('The Kentucky Hills of Tennessee') and rock'n'roll (a rockabilly reworking of **Little Richard**'s 'Rip It Up'), what was to become an abiding interest in truck-driving songs, either read straight ('Diggy Liggy Lo') or as parodies ('Momma Hated Diesels').

Country Casanova (1973) was a lesser album but *Live from Deep in the Heart of Texas* (1974) captured their spirited stage show. Following a move to Warner Brothers, the group became less musically adventurous and after a trio of disappointing albums they disbanded. Cody recorded as a solo artist for Arista (*Midnight Man*, 1976), mostly in a boogie-woogie vein, before forming the Commander Cody band (which included Nicolette Larson, later a singing partner of **Neil Young**) for the minor *Rock'n'Roll Again* (1976) and *Flying Dreams* (1978). In 1980 he had European success with yet another novelty song, 'Two Triple Cheese (Side Order of Fries)' (MCA), and later continued to record as a solo act (*Let's Rock*, Special Delivery, 1987). In 1987 Cody formed a new band and recorded *Cody Returns from Outer Space*.

He returned to recording in 1995 with *Let's Rock* (Blind Pig).

THE COMMODORES

William King, b. 30 January 1949, Alabama, USA;
Ronald LaPread, b. 4 September 1946, Alabama;
Thomas McClary, b. 1950, Florida (replaced by J. D.
Nicholas, b. 12 April 1952, Watford, Herts, England);
Walter 'Clyde' Orange, b. 10 December 1947, Florida;
Lionel Richie Jnr, b. 20 June 1949, Tuskegee, Alabama;
Milan Williams, b. 28 March 1949, Mississippi

With record sales of over 40 million, the Commodores were one of the most successful black pop
bands of the seventies. They combined funky dance
music with languorous ballads expertly crooned by
lead singer **Lionel Richie**. The group survived Richie's
departure in 1982 and returned to the charts with
'Nightshift', a tribute to **Jackie Wilson** and **Marvin
Gaye**.

Formed from high-school groups in Tuskegee,
Alabama, the band originally performed as the Jays.
As the Commodores the group moved to New York
in 1969, cutting a cover-version of Alvin Cash's 'Keep
on Dancing' for Atlantic, produced by Jerry Williams
Jnr (aka Swamp Dogg). In 1971 they were booked as
the opening act for the **Jackson Five**'s world tour and
a Motown recording contract followed.

Produced by James Carmichael, who was to supervise all the Commodores' records, the synthesizer-
driven instrumental 'Machine Gun' (1974) was a hit
in Britain and America. The group subsequently
toured with **Stevie Wonder** and the **Rolling Stones**.

'Slippery When Wet' (1975) and 'Brickhouse' (1977)
were in the same disco-dance vein, but the bulk of the
group's singles featured the voice and writing of
Richie. 'Sweet Love' (1976) and 'Easy' (1977) were
American Top Ten hits, but the lazily romantic
'Three Times a Lady'* was No. 1 on both sides of the
Atlantic in 1978, the year the Commodores appeared
in the musical film *Thank God It's Friday*. Six more
Richie ballad hits followed, including 'Sail on' (1979),
the 1980 No. 1 'Still' and 'Oh No' (1981).

By now Richie was involved in solo ventures, which
included writing for and producing **Kenny Rogers**,
and duetting with **Diana Ross** on the movie theme
'Endless Love' (1981). He left the group in 1982 and
drummer Orange took lead vocals on *Commodores 13*
(1983). The following year McClary was replaced on
guitar and vocals by J. D. Nicholas from the UK-
based group **Heatwave**. *Nightshift* (1985) was the
Commodores' last album for Motown. Moving to
Polydor, the group released *United* (1986), which
included the soul hit 'Going to the Bank', and *Rock
Solid* (1988). In the same year they returned to the UK
charts when 'Easy' was reissued after being used in a
television commercial. Now consisting of the core of
King, Nicholas and Orange, the Commodores
released *No Tricks* in 1992, but sales were disappointing, although they continued to be a popular live
attraction.

THE COMMUNARDS

Richard Coles, b. 23 June 1962, Northampton, England;
Jimmy Somerville, b. 22 June 1961, Glasgow, Scotland

A successful British pop band of the mid-eighties, the
Communards were co-led by Somerville, who first
came to prominence with Bronski Beat – a trio which
caused a mild *frisson* by openly espousing a gay
lifestyle.

Reflecting their political approach, the Communards were named after the French revolutionaries of
1871. Somerville formed the group with pianist Coles,
with whom he had earlier worked on a documentary
film, and they performed with **Billy Bragg** and **Paul
Weller** on the Red Wedge tour in support of the
Labour Party. Both the eponymous album and the
first two singles by the band were hits, with 'Don't
Leave Me This Way' (London, 1986) becoming a
British No. 1 – with lead vocals shared by Somerville
and Sarah Jane Morris. The song had been a 1977 hit
for Thelma Houston in America and Harold Melvin
and the Bluenotes in Britain.

Bronski Beat had been formed by Somerville with
fellow Glaswegian Steve Bronski (*b. 7 February 1960*)
and Londoner Larry Steinbachek (*b. 6 May 1960*) in
1982. With Somerville's high-pitched, virtually falsetto
white soul voice backed by synthesizers, their first singles, 'Small Town Boy' (London, 1984), with lyrics
about the problems of gay youths, and 'Why?' were
Top Ten hits. The group followed up with two
revivals in 1985: **George Gershwin**'s 1935 show tune 'It
Ain't Necessarily So' and **Donna Summer**'s 1977 disco
classic 'I Feel Love'. The latter was a duet with **Marc
Almond**.

All four hits were included on the *Age of Consent*
album and following Somerville's departure early in
1985, *Hundreds and Thousands*, an album of remixes
containing only one new song, was released. Meanwhile John Foster from Newcastle band Bust was
drafted into Bronski Beat as lead vocalist. The new
line-up continued the run of hits with 'Hit that Perfect Beat' and 'C'mon C'mon' in 1986 before Foster
left the group.

Meanwhile the Communards maintained their success with 'So Cold the Night' (1986), 'Tomorrow' and
'Never Can Say Goodbye' (1987), a glorious remake of
Gloria Gaynor's 1974 disco hit. The album *Red*
reached the British Top Twenty before the duo
released further singles on gay themes in 'For a
Friend' (1988) and 'There's More to Love'.

By 1989 Somerville was appearing as a solo artist,
recording a version of Françoise Hardy's 'Comment
te dire Adieu' and *Read My Lips*. In 1990 Somerville

moved to San Francisco. He contributed a version of 'From this Moment on' to *Red Hot & Blue*, the compilation of **Cole Porter** songs released to raise money for AIDS charities. His version of the **Bee Gees**' 'To Love Somebody' was a UK Top Ten hit in 1990.

PERRY COMO
b. Pierino Como, 18 May 1912, Cannonsburg, Pennsylvania, USA

One of the most durable and successful of the second generation of crooners who came to prominence in the early forties, Como's warm baritone earned the singer twenty million-selling records and cumulative disc sales of over 50 million units. Stylistically influenced by **Bing Crosby**, 'Mr C', as Como was known in the fifties, smoothly managed the transition from big-band singer to solo performer and weathered the storm of rock'n'roll with the help of covers such as 'Ko Ko Mo (I Love You So)' (1955) and singalongs like 'Catch a Falling Star'* (1958). His career was helped along by a relaxed, natural manner which suited television.

The son of Italian immigrants, Como planned to be a barber before joining Freddie Carlone's band as featured singer in 1934. He toured the Midwest for three years with Carlone and then, in 1937, joined **Ted Weems**' band. After five years with the band, Como left to work as a solo singer and signed with RCA in 1943. Popular on radio for his rounded even tone, seen at its best in his ballad singing, he attempted a career in Hollywood, before recording success came in 1945. His first million-seller was 'Till the End of Time', a vocal version of Chopin's 'Polonaise in A' with which **Jose Iturbi** had already had an instrumental million-seller. Then came 'If I Loved You'* from **Rodgers and Hammerstein**'s *Carousel*; 'A Hubba-Hubba-Hubba'*, a novelty song from *Doll Face*, one of Como's better films; and his version of **Nacio Herb Brown** and **Arthur Freed**'s 'Temptation'*. Originally recorded by Como's mentor, Crosby, this inaugurated a policy of reviving past hits. Others in this vein included 'Prisoner of Love' (1946), the unabashedly sentimental 'When You Were Sweet Sixteen'* (1947), 'Because'* (1948) and 'If'* (1951), co-written by **Tolchard Evans** in 1934.

In contrast to **Dick Haymes** and **Frank Sinatra**, balladeers whose sales fell in the early fifties as a new breed of harder-voiced singers like **Frankie Laine** and **Johnny Ray** emerged, and whose records were highly produced, Como continued to sell vast quantities of records throughout the decade. Promoted on his television show, his hits included a judicious mix of novelty songs, such as 'Papa Loves Mambo'* (1954), 'Hot Diggity (Dog Ziggity Boom)'* (1956), 'Chee Chee-Oo-Chee (Sang the Little Bird)', a duet with Jaye P.

Morgan, and 'Delaware'* (1960) – 'What did Delaware, she wore a brand New Jersey . . .' – at which he was particularly adept. He also recorded an unlikely slick cover of Gene and Eunice's R&B hit 'Ko Ko Mo' (Aladdin, 1955), which was also covered by the **Crew Cuts** and **Tony Bennett**; formula ballads, such as 'The Girl with the Golden Braids' (1957); and relaxed numbers like 'Catch a Falling Star' and the Hal David and **Burt Bacharach** composition 'Magic Moments'* (1958).

In semi-retirement in the sixties and seventies, he recorded less frequently – but still had the occasional international success with romantic ballads like 'If' (1970) – and restricted his performing to Las Vegas clubs and to television.

EDDIE CONDON
b. Albert Edwin Condon, 16 November 1905, Goodland, Indiana, USA, d. 4 August 1973, New York

Once called 'the figurehead of Chicago jazz', Condon was a great organizer and publicist for the 'mainstream' jazz with which he grew up. Though never more than a competent guitarist, he set up recording sessions, ran clubs and wrote an acclaimed autobiography, *We Called It Music* (1948).

Originally a ukulele player, Condon changed to banjo to play with Horace Peavey's Jazz Bandits before moving to Chicago in 1922 to perform with **Bix Beiderbecke**. In 1924 he joined the Austin High School Gang, which included drummer **Gene Krupa** and clarinet-player Frank Teschemacher and developed Chicago-style Dixieland jazz.

Condon's first records were made with Red McKenzie in 1927 and the following year he recorded in New York with various racially integrated groups which included **Louis Armstrong** and **Fats Waller**, as well as making his first sessions as leader with the Feetwarmers ('Makin' Friends' with vocals by **Jack Teagarden**). During the thirties he was a busy figure in New York jazz circles, performing regularly with a variety of groups, recording for **Milt Gabler**'s Commodore in 1937 with his Chicagoans and in 1939 for Brunswick as the Summa Cum Laude in a style which attempted to recapture the youthful verve of a decade earlier. The band's outstanding soloist was tenor-sax-player Bud Freeman, who remained an associate of Condon's until the guitarist's death. Other members of the band, which appeared in the musical *Swingin' the Dream*, included Max Kaminsky (trumpet) and clarinettist Pee Wee Russell.

Primarily to keep alive the Chicago jazz epitomized by Beiderbecke, Condon came into his own as a jazz promoter in the forties. In 1942 he presented **Fats Waller** at Carnegie Hall, he was responsible for the first televised jam session, and he organized a series of concerts at New York's town hall with such artists as Russell and singer Lee Wiley. From 1945 to 1967 he ran his own jazz club, dedicated to the preservation of the Dixieland style. He published his bestselling auto-biography in 1948, the year of the television series *The Eddie Condon Floorshow*.

He continued to record prolifically, releasing such albums as *Ringside at Condon's* (Savoy, 1956), with Wild Bill Davison on cornet, and *Bixieland* (1958), a tribute to Beiderbecke. During the sixties Condon also toured Canada, Japan and England. He gave his name to *Eddie Condon's World of Jazz* (Columbia, 1972), a collection of jazz recordings from the twenties to the fifties by Condon and others produced by his biographer Hank O'Neal.

HARRY CONNICK JR
b. 11 September 1967, New Orleans, Louisiana, USA

Connick was one of the more unlikely stars of con-temporary American jazz. With more than a touch of the youthful **Frank Sinatra**, he combined elegant cocktail lounge piano playing with gently swinging vocals.

The son of a New Orleans district attorney, Con-nick learned the piano as a small child and made his first recording at the age of ten. One of his teachers was the legendary R&B pianist James Booker. Connick studied at the New Orleans Centre for Creative Arts with Ellis Marsalis (father of Wynton and Branford).

Connick evolved a 'retro' style of piano influenced by **Duke Ellington** and **Thelonious Monk** and adopted swing vocal stylings influenced by Frank Sinatra. A self-titled solo instrumental album appeared in 1987 followed by *20* (1989), on which he both played and sang. It included versions of **Hoagy Carmichael**'s 'Lazy River' and the Dixieland standard 'Basin Street Blues'. His work was brought to a mass audience by the film *When Harry Met Sally* (1989), which featured Connick's music on its soundtrack.

After further solo recordings of his own composi-tions with lyricist Ramsey McLean (*We Are in Love*, 1990, *Blue Light, Red Light*, 1991) he formed a big band for a concert tour. He recorded the Monk-influenced *Lofty's Roach Shuffle* in 1991 as the Harry Connick Jr Trio with Ben Wolfe (bass) and Shannon Powell (drums). He had a cameo role as a pianist in the film *Memphis Belle* (1990) and acted in *Little Man Tate* (1990). Connick also sang 'Promise Me You'll Remember', the theme song from *Godfather III*.

In 1992 he issued *25*, another collection of standard tunes from the 1930–55 era. Guest players included Ellis Marsalis, singer Johnny Adams and bassist Ray Brown. In the same year his début album of Dixieland tunes was re-released. He followed this in 1994 with *She*, which included the hit single '(I Could Only)

Whisper Your Name', and three lesser outings, *Whis-per Your Name* (1995), *Star Turtle* (1997) and *Come by Me* (1999). Far better was his return to acting in *Hope Floats* (1998).

RAY CONNIFF
b. 6 November 1916, Attleboro, Massachusetts, USA

A former big-band and recording session arranger, Conniff became king of easy-listening vocal-group records in the sixties. He made a long series of albums which combined recent hit songs with smooth close-harmony singing.

As a teenager Conniff learned trombone and stud-ied arranging through a correspondence course. In 1938 he joined Bunny Berigan's orchestra, playing solos on 'There'll Be Some Changes Made' (RCA Vic-tor, 1938) and other recordings. He went on to play with **Bob Crosby** and to provide arrangements for Teddy Powell – 'Feather Merchant's Ball' (Decca, 1939), a parody of **Woody Herman**'s 'Woodchopper's Ball' – and **Artie Shaw**. For Shaw, Conniff arranged a swing version of **George Gershwin**'s ''S Wonderful' (RCA Victor, 1945).

Conniff also worked with **Harry James** before **Mitch Miller** brought him to Columbia as a conduc-tor and arranger. He worked with such artists as **Johnny Mathis**, **Guy Mitchell** and **Marty Robbins** and produced crooner Don Cherry's 'Band of Gold'* (1956), a Top Ten hit in both Britain and America. In the same year Conniff began a recording career for the label, having a minor hit with a new version of ''S Wonderful' (1957).

By this time, he perfected his own sound in which a silky eight-piece vocal group was expertly blended with a light orchestral music. Later versions of the Ray Conniff Singers had thirteen male and twelve female voices. Annual albums like *Broadway in Rhythm* (1959) and *We Wish You a Merry Christmas* (1962) were bestsellers in America, with *Somewhere My Love** (1966) the most successful. With lyrics by P. F. Webster, the title song was a vocal version of **Maurice Jarre**'s 'Lara's Theme' from the film *Dr Zhivago*. It became Conniff's only Top Ten single. In Britain the track was successfully covered by the Mike Sammes Singers on HMV.

After a string of more than twenty-five Top Forty albums, Conniff's sales began to decline in the late sixties and he was persuaded by Columbia's Clive Davis to record current hit songs rather than stan-dards. The result was such records as *We've Only Just Begun* (1970), whose title track was a cover of the **Carpenters**' hit, *I'd Like to Teach the World to Sing* (1971), which featured the **New Seekers**' international hit, and *Clair* (1972), named after the **Gilbert O'Sulli-van** composition.

Ray Conniff in Moscow (1974) was the first American pop album to use Soviet musicians, while he extended his range with *The Nashville Collection* (1982), which included guest appearances by **George Jones**, **Charlie Rich** and Barbara Mandrell. Among later releases were the Spanish-language *Exclusivamente Latino* (1983) and *Always in My Heart* (1988), which included **Bob Dylan**'s 'Blowin' in the Wind' and **Abba**'s 'Fernando'.

TOMMIE CONNOR
b. Thomas P. Connor, 16 November 1904, London, England

Connor's simple, sentimental lyrics about such topics as mothers, Father Christmas and eskimos made him one of the most successful British songwriters of the thirties and forties.

Connor's first hit came with Little Mary Hagan's recording of 'My Home Town' (Decca, 1932). 'Jump on the Wagon' (1934), 'When the Guardsman Started Crooning on Parade' (1935) and other workmanlike songs followed, until a partnership with Eddie Lisbona, the pianist in **Ambrose**'s orchestra, brought Connor's first real success. Together they wrote 'It's My Mother's Birthday Today' (1935), a million-seller for **Arthur Tracy**; 'I May Be Poor But I'm Honest' (with Horatio Nicholls), one of the outstanding comedy numbers performed by Sam Browne and **Elsie Carlisle**; and numerous songs for shows, cabaret and films.

Connor also rivalled **Johnny Marks**, author of 'Rudolph the Red-Nosed Reindeer', in his ability to write Christmas songs. With **Michael Carr** and Jimmy Leach he wrote the tearjerker, 'The Little Boy that Santa Claus Forgot' (1937); with Spencer Williams (composer of 'Basin Street Blues' and 'Farewell to Storyville'), the patriotic 'I'm Sending a Letter to Santa' – a big hit for **Gracie Fields** in 1939; and alone he wrote 'I Saw Mommy Kissing Santa Claus' (1952), which sold over 11 million copies in Jimmy Boyd's version and is now a standard. In 1987 the song was given a cajun inflection by **John Cougar Mellencamp** on *A Very Special Christmas* (A&M), an album of Christmas songs by various artists, including **Bruce Springsteen** and **U2**, for charity.

Connor's other great international success was 'Lili Marlene', the classic song of the Second World War. His English words were written in 1944 to counter the effect of **Lale Anderson**'s recording. Before his retirement in 1956, Connor composed 'Never Do a Tango with an Eskimo', which gave **Alma Cogan** one of her biggest British hits in 1955.

THE CONTOURS
Joe Billingslea; Billy Gordon; Billy Hoggs; Hubert Johnson; Sylvester Potts; Huey Davis; Dennis Edwards; Joe Stubbs

One of **Berry Gordy**'s early Motown vocal groups, the Contours had a million-seller with 'Do You Love Me?', later a staple in the repertoire of British beat groups of the sixties.

Formed in Detroit in 1958, the group were taken up by Johnson's cousin **Jackie Wilson**, for whom Gordy had written songs. On Wilson's recommendation they were signed to the newly formed Gordy label. 'Whole Lotta Woman' (1961) was unsuccessful but the dance number 'Do You Love Me?' reached the Top Ten the following year. Written by Gordy himself, its novelty lyrics were sprinkled with the names of current dance crazes – twist, shake, mashed potato – and through its intense call-and-response vocal patterns, the record built to an exciting crescendo.

In Britain, where early Motown records were released on the small Oriole label and where the Contours toured in 1964, 'Do You Love Me?' attracted the attention of musicians rather than record-buyers. Like the **Isley Brothers**, the group had a hoarse, shouting vocal style that was more easily translated into a white idiom than the cooler singing of **Smokey Robinson** or **Marvin Gaye**. The song was recorded for Oriole in 1963 by Liverpool group Faron's Flamingos (who also covered the follow-up 'Shake Sherry') but the two hit versions came from **Brian Poole and the Tremeloes** (No. 1 on Decca in 1963) and the **Dave Clark Five**, whose version was an American hit in 1964.

Gordy tried the dance-song formula with subsequent records like 'Shake Sherry' (1963) and 'Can You Jerk Like Me' (1964) which were R&B hits but only minor successes in the pop charts. More interesting was the Contours' recording of the Smokey Robinson song 'First I Look at the Purse', with its coy line, 'What does every man look at first?'. The song was covered in 1971 by the **J. Geils Band**.

'It's So Hard Being a Loser' (1967) was the appropriate title of the Contours' last minor hit and in the following year they disbanded. Among the personnel changes over the group's ten-year history were the addition of Joe Stubbs, whose brother Levi was a member of the **Four Tops**, and Dennis Edwards, who later joined the **Temptations**.

The use of 'Do You Love Me' in the film *Dirty Dancing* led to the group re-forming to take part in a *Dirty Dancing* tour in 1987. Three years later the British producer Ian Levine issued a newly recorded Contours album, *Flashback*, on his UK Motorcity label.

RY COODER
b. Ryland Peter Cooder, 15 March 1947, Los Angeles, California, USA

A virtuoso guitarist, Cooder's music has been animated by his fascination with ethnic styles (ranging from Tex-Mex and calypso to folk music) and largely forgotten songs (such as standards from the depression and vaudeville 'coon' songs). As a result, Cooder has often been described as a living encyclopedia of American 'folk' musics. He had his greatest success in this guise in the nineties when he first put together the Buena Vista Social Club, a group of veteran Cuban musicians whose eponymous album (1997) was a huge hit. Subsequently he helped organize a documentary about the international tour that followed this success.

Cooder's parents were active in California blues and folk circles and when he took up the guitar, after losing his left eye in an accident, he was briefly taught by **Rev. Gary Davis**. After joining various shortlived folk and blues groups of the early sixties (including one with **Jackie DeShannon**), he formed the Rising Sons with fellow blues archivist **Taj Mahal**, only to leave the group after Taj Mahal's eponymous début album (Columbia, 1967). Briefly a member of **Captain Beefheart**'s Magic Band, he played slide guitar on the classic *Safe As Milk* (Buddah, 1967) before establishing himself as a key West Coast session musician, appearing on albums by the **Rolling Stones**, **Maria Muldaur**, **Randy Newman** and **Little Feat**, among others. Through his association with **Jack Nitzsche**, he was given the opportunity to work on the film scores of *Candy* (1968) and *Performance* (1970).

In 1969 he signed with Reprise. *Ry Cooder* (1970), co-produced by **Van Dyke Parks**, introduced Cooder the archivist. It featured a mix of little-known blues and hillbilly songs (**Sleepy John Estes**' 'Goin' to Brownsville' and 'How Can a Poor Man Stand Such Times and Live' by hillbilly singer Blind Alfred Reed) and equally little-known R&B numbers ('Alimony', a song by Tommy Tucker, better known for his composition 'Hi Heel Sneakers'). All were performed in a spare folk-blues manner with Cooder's strangled vocals well to the fore. Even more impressive was *Into the Purple Valley* (1971). Cooder's singing was more confident and the material – which ranged from R&B obscurities ('Teardrops Will Fall', originally recorded by Dicky Doo and the Don'ts) to songs of social comment ('Taxes on the Farmer Feeds Us All') – was more revealing of America's musical heritage. After *Boomer's Story* (1972), which featured an outstanding slide guitar version of Spooner Oldham's and **Dan Penn**'s 'Dark End of the Street', *Paradise and Lunch* (1974), on which Cooder duetted with **Earl Hines** on 'Ditty Wa Ditty', saw an increased sophistication in production and arrangement. The result was Cooder's most accessible album.

Chicken Skin Music (1976) and the live *Showtime* (Warners, 1977) found Cooder experimenting with Tex-Mex music in partnership with accordionist **Flaco Jimenez**, while *Jazz* (1978) reflected his interest in early jazz (it included compositions by **Bix Beiderbecke**), and the musics on its fringes, such as coon songs: Cooder gave added weight to 'Shine' by Ford Dabney and Cecil Mack by singing the usually omitted introduction. The album also included songs associated with Bahamian guitarist Joseph Spence. Less academic and generally livelier were Cooder's explorations of the world of R&B; *Bop till You Drop* (1979), *Borderline* (1981) and *The Slide Area* (1982), which featured songwriter **John Hiatt** on guest vocals. However, though well received, like Cooder's earlier work these albums did not sell in large quantities. In the eighties he turned increasingly to film work, producing atmospheric soundtracks to *The Long Riders* (1980), *Southern Comfort* (1981), Wim Wenders' highly successful *Paris, Texas* (1985), *Alamo Bay* (1985) and *Crossroads* (1987). The **Johnny Cash** title song from *Get Rhythm* (1987), on which he was joined by Parks and Larry Blackmon of **Cameo**, was a minor US hit in 1988. He produced and played on the rapturously received début album by his regular backing vocalists Bobby King and Terry Evans (*Live and Let Live!*, 1988) and followed this with the soundtrack *Johnny Handsome* (1989). In 1990 he toured with multi-instrumentalist David Lindley, and in 1992 he formed Little Village with **Nick Lowe**, John Hiatt and Jim Keltner. The group issued a disappointing eponymous album and toured briefly.

In the nineties Cooder's interest in world music was reflected in his collaborations with V. M. Bhatt (*A Meeting by the River*, 1993) and Malian singer/guitarist Ali Farka Toure (*Talking Timbuktu*, 1994), amongst others. He also continued to work on soundtracks, including *Geronimo* and *Trespass* in 1993 and *Primary Colours* in 1998. *Music by Ry Cooder* (1995) was a two-CD collection of his film music. Then, in 1997, he produced and played (in the company of his son) with the informal group of Cuban musicians dubbed the Buena Vista Social Club. The impact of the album released on World Circuit was as great as that of **Paul Simon**'s earlier *Graceland*, giving a huge impetus to roots/world music, and giving second careers to the club's members, who included Compay Segundo, Ibrahim Ferrer and Ruben Gonzalez, all of whom went on to record solo albums. The Wim Wenders-directed documentary neatly contrasted the fading glory of Havana, made even more so by overlighting, and charm of the musicians with the precision of their playing and their simple delight in the pleasures of travel that music made possible for them.

NORMAN COOK
See **Fatboy Slim**

SAM COOKE

b. Sam Cook, 22 January 1931, Clarksdale, Mississippi,
USA, d. 11 December 1964, Los Angeles, California

With **Ray Charles**, Cooke was the most important
precursor of soul music. Like **Brook Benton**, **Clyde
McPhatter** and **Jackie Wilson**, singers whose work
also pointed forward to soul, Cooke had a gospel
background, but where they (and Charles) interpolated elements from gospel music in their vocal styles,
Cooke hardly varied his style at all when he made the
transition to secular music. Whether his material was
a teen ballad ('Wonderful World'*, 1960), a novelty
dance song (the self-composed 'Twistin' the Night
Away'*, 1962) or a night-club standard (**George
Gershwin**'s 'Summertime') Cooke's high, pure tenor,
smooth delivery and mastery of restraint retained the
approach – though not the intensity of the magisterial
'Touch the Hem of His Garment' (1956) – of his work
with leading gospel group the Soul Stirrers. Moreover, in some of his later work, particularly the
epochal 'A Change Is Gonna Come' (1964), as uplifting a testament to the black experience of living in
America as any of his gospel recordings, Cooke found
a way to build on that intensity rather than compromise it in search of success in the pop market. Cooke
also wrote many of his thirty Top Forty entries and
was an important model within black music as someone who took control of his own career, forming his
own record, publishing and management companies.

One of eight children, Cooke was raised in Chicago
where his father was a Baptist preacher. In 1940 he
sang in the family gospel group the Singing Children
and in his teens joined the Highway QCs before in
1950 he was invited to replace R. H. Harris as lead
singer of the Soul Stirrers, one of the pioneering
groups of modern gospel music. In his recordings
with them for **Art Rupe**'s Specialty label (1951–6),
Cooke demonstrated both an ease and maturity, particularly in his vocal interjections and repetitions. His
live appearances revealed him to be the heart-throb of
the California gospel circuit and inevitably, with
prompting from his long-time mentor J. W. Alexander and producer **Bumps Blackwell**, Cooke turned to
secular music, initially under the pseudonym of Dale
Cook ('Lovable', 1957). When Rupe, who preferred
gospel to pop, refused to continue the experiment
Blackwell and Cooke moved to Keen, where the
singer's first release, 'You Send Me'* (1957), topped
both the pop and R&B charts. The lyric is pure confection, but from the introductory ululating 'Whoa-
oh-oh' Cooke's performance is thrilling. It was
followed by a string of lesser recordings, including 'I'll
Come Running Back to You'* (an earlier Specialty
recording), 'Lonely Island' (1958), 'Everybody Likes to
Cha Cha' and the oft-recorded 'Only Sixteen' (1959).

In 1960 Cooke signed to RCA. With producers
Hugo and Luigi Cooke had twelve Top Twenty hits in
the US before Hall (arranger of 'You Send Me') took
over production. Cooke demonstrated his ability to
be silky smooth on 'Wonderful World' (1960, and a
British hit again when re-released in 1986) and
'Cupid' (1961), relaxed on 'Another Saturday Night'
(1963 and 1986, again in Britain), and socially aware
('Chain Gang'*, 1960, 'Bring It on Home to Me', 1962,
on which he duetted with **Lou Rawls**, and 'A Change
Is Gonna Come'). Many of Cooke's other singles were
lightweight, but the albums *Night Beat* (1963), a collection of blues, and *Ain't That Good News* (1964)
were more considered and, unusually for the time,
conceived of as entities. At the same time, on *Live at
the Harlem Square Club* (recorded 1963, but not
released until 1986) Cooke showed the harsher side of
his voice, kept in check on most of his songs since the
Soul Stirrer days. Thus, his death – Cooke was killed
in a motel shooting incident – like that of **Buddy
Holly**, came just as he was on the verge of a new stage
of his career.

A mark of Cooke's deep influence is the number of
his songs that were hits in versions by other artists.
Among them were 'Cupid' (**Johnny Nash**, 1970; **Tony
Orlando** and Dawn, 1976); 'Only Sixteen' (a British
No. 1 for Craig Douglas in 1959; **Dr Hook**, 1976); 'Little Red Rooster' (the **Rolling Stones**, 1964); 'Bring It
on Home to Me' (the **Animals**, 1965; Eddie Floyd,
Stax, 1968); 'Wonderful World' (**Herman's Hermits**,
1965; Art Garfunkel with **Paul Simon** and **James Taylor**, 1978, and Cooke himself in the UK, 1986); and
'Another Saturday Night' (**Cat Stevens**, 1974). Among
the many recordings of 'A Change Is Gonna Come',
Prince Buster's perhaps best shows how deeply the
song affected other black musicians: recording the
song in Jamaica at a time when composers were not
often listed, Buster not only credited Cooke but at the
song's end added proudly 'This is Sam Cooke's song'.
The definitive biography is Daniel Woolf's *You Send
Me* (1995).

SPADE COOLEY

*b. Donnell Clyde Cooley, 17 December 1910, Pack Saddle
Creek, Oklahoma, USA, d. 23 November 1969, Oakland,
California*

Although recent revaluations assign the principal role
in the development of Western swing to **Bob Wills**,
there was great rivalry in the late forties between him
and Cooley, and it was in Cooley's rather than Wills's
publicity material that the epithet 'King of Western
swing' was first used. Cooley's orchestral approach –
what *Billboard* called 'Western tunes with sweet swing
arrangements' – was closer to that of conventional pop
bands, in that he employed a prominent fiddle section,

accordion and even harp, rather than the brass, reeds and hot fiddle soloists of the Wills aggregation.

Cooley began playing fiddle in the early thirties with country bands in southern California, notably Jimmy Wakely's. He went on to movie work in Hollywood, where he was a stand-in in Republic features for **Roy Rogers**, and made several Westerns in which he provided the musical accompaniment to the fisticuffs. These included *The Singing Sheriff* (1944) and *Square Dance Jubilee* (1949). By the early forties he was playing in bands at the large Venice Pier Ballroom in Venice, California, and on forming his own band had an immediate hit with 'Shame on You' (Columbia, 1945), which featured a vocal by Tex Williams. He subsequently held down popular residencies at the Riverside Rancho and Santa Monica Ballroom. He also established himself early on TV, with *The Hoffman Hayride* on KTLA-TV, Los Angeles, in 1948, on which **Hank Penny** was the featured comic.

Drinking and domestic problems hampered his career in the late fifties, culminating horrifically in July 1961 when he murdered his wife in front of their teenage daughter and was sentenced to life imprisonment. Freed, briefly, to attend another artist's benefit concert, he gave his performance, then died backstage of a heart attack.

RITA COOLIDGE
b. 1 May 1944, Nashville, Tennessee, USA

A clear-voiced interpretive singer best known for her recordings with **Kris Kristofferson**, Coolidge worked in the country, rock and easy-listening fields.

Children of a Baptist minister father and Cherokee Indian mother, Rita and her sister Priscilla first sang on radio jingles in Memphis, where she cut 'Turn Around and Love You' for Pepper. While Priscilla recorded with and married Booker T. Jones of **Booker T. and the MGs**, Rita moved to Los Angeles where she worked as a session singer for **Eric Clapton**, **Boz Scaggs**, Stephen Stills and many others.

In 1969 she joined Delaney and Bonnie and Friends, going on tour with **Leon Russell** and **Joe Cocker**'s Mad Dogs and Englishmen organization. 'Delta Lady', written by Russell and recorded by Cocker, was said to have been inspired by Coolidge. Her solo version of the **Carpenters**' 'Superstar' was a highlight of the show and in 1971 she signed a recording contract with A&M.

In the next fifteen years she recorded eleven solo albums, with producers David Anderle, Booker T. Jones and Andrew Gold as well as three duets with Kris Kristofferson, to whom she was married from 1973 to 1979. The early records contained material by newer country-rock writers like Steve Young, Eric Kaz

and Guy Clark, but she made little commercial impact until 1977 when the Anderle-produced *Anytime . . . Anywhere* provided three hit singles. Two were revivals of soul hits: **Jackie Wilson**'s 'Higher and Higher'* and the **Temptations** 'The Way You Do the Things You Do'*. The third was the Scaggs composition 'We're All Alone'.

After the success of the wistful 'I'd Rather Leave While I'm in Love' (1980), written by Carole Bayer Sager and Pete Allen, she moved closer to the middle-of-the-road with 'All Time High', the theme from the 1983 James Bond film, *Octopussy*. Her later recordings included 1988's lacklustre *Inside the Fire* and *Love Lessons* (1992).

With Kristofferson she appeared in a number of films, including Sam Peckinpah's *Pat Garrett and Billy the Kid* (1973).

ALICE COOPER
b. Vincent Furnier, 25 December 1945, Detroit, Michigan, USA

The popularizer of rock theatrics in the seventies, Alice Cooper's chief significance lay in his vital influence on the early members of the British punk-rock scene. It was to an Alice Cooper record that John Lydon (Johnny Rotten of the **Sex Pistols**) was miming when he was 'spotted' by **Malcolm McLaren**. Subsequently he became as well known for his appearances, in the manner of a **Bing Crosby**, on the golf course as in the recording studio.

Vocalist Furnier formed the Earwigs in Phoenix, Arizona, in 1965, and had a local hit in a **Who/Kinks** style with 'Don't Blow Your Mind'. The band became the Nazz and then, in 1967, Alice Cooper. This name was supposed to have been presented through a ouija board to the band, which now included Glen Buxton (guitar), Dennis Dunaway (bass), Michael Bruce (piano, guitar) and Neal Smith (drums). Performing in Los Angeles, they were seen by **Frank Zappa** and Shep Gordon, who signed them to Straight Records.

Trading on the sexual ambiguity of the band's name, the first album showed them in drag, but it wasn't until Alice Cooper signed with Warner Brothers in 1970 that they had a hit record, with 'Eighteen'. By this time, they had perfected a stage act which included simulated killings of a chicken and a doll.

A string of hits followed, of which the most effective were 'School's Out' (1972), a teenage anthem that is now a rock standard, 'Elected' (1972) and 'No More Mr Nice Guy' (1973). All featured Furnier's bellowed vocals which were to be so important for the future punk singers.

By 1975 Furnier so dominated the band that he alone was 'Alice Cooper'. He had become an American celebrity, with frequent chat-show appearances, a beer can never far from reach. With a new band including Josef Chrowski (keyboards), Dick Wagner (guitar), Penti Glan (drums) and Prakash John (bass), he had more American hits, notably 'Only Women Bleed' (1975, a British hit for Julie Covington) and 'I Never Cry'* (1976).

Despite a drink problem, Cooper continued to turn out albums – his fourteenth appeared in 1983. In 1986 he signed to MCA, releasing *Constrictor*, which included 'He's Back', the theme from the movie *Friday the 13th Part 6*. This was followed by *Raise Your Fist and Yell* (1987) and *Trash* and *Poison* (Epic, 1989), the title track of which was a Top Ten hit in Britain.

During the nineties he returned to the outrage of the earliest records, notably with 'Hey Stoopid' (1991), from which the cautionary title track was an international hit, but arguably his finest album remains *Love It to Death*, cut in 1971. 1994 saw the release of concept album *The Last Temptation*. His best album for many years, it was accompanied by a three-part comic book series published by Marvel Comics that perfectly caught the fairground melodramatics of the album. However, Cooper himself was far prouder of his hole-in-one in an Arizona golf tournament. *Temptation* was followed by a series of lesser outings, including the *X-Files*-inspired *Songs in the Key of X* (1996) and *A Fistful of Alice* (1997). *Brutal Planet* (2000), his first studio album in five years, offered a bleak, dystopian view of the future and won surprisingly warm reviews.

COWBOY COPAS
b. Lloyd Copas, 15 July 1913, Muskogee, Oklahoma, USA, d. 5 March 1963, Camden, Tennessee

A skilful guitarist and honky-tonk-styled country singer, Copas laid the foundations of his career in the Midwest during the thirties, playing one-night stands and small radio stations in the company of a musician known as Natchee the Indian Fiddler.

In 1938 he joined the *Boone County Jamboree* (later the *Midwestern Hayride*) on Cincinnati's station WLW. He signed with the new Cincinnati label King in 1945 and had an immediate hit with the war song 'Filipino Baby'. He followed this with 'Tragic Romance' (1946), 'Signed, Sealed and Delivered' (1947) and 'Tennessee Waltz' (1948), also a hit for its composer **Pee Wee King**, with whom Copas had been working since 1946 on the *Grand Ole Opry*.

Despite being named Top Country and Western Artist of 1948 by *Cashbox*, within a few years he was working in obscurity. His career was revived in 1959 by Don Pierce of Starday Records, and he had a substantial hit with 'Alabam' in 1960, followed by a new version of 'Signed, Sealed and Delivered' and a return to the *Opry*. Copas's revival ended when he died in

the plane crash that also killed **Patsy Cline** and **Hawkshaw Hawkins**.

JULIAN COPE
b. 21 October 1957, Deri, Glamorgan, Wales

One of the more idiosyncratic songwriters and performers to emerge from British punk, Cope won himself a cult following as he pursued his own idiosyncratic career in which, in the words of one critic, he mixed 'crackpot lyrics with eloquent tunes'.

Cope grew up in Liverpool, forming the Crucial Three with Ian McCulloch (later of **Echo and the Bunnymen**) and Pete Wylie. In 1978 Cope formed Teardrop Explodes, which had a series of UK hits, notably 'Treason (It's Just a Story)' and 'Reward' (Vertigo, 1981).

After their second album, the introverted *Wilder*, the group disbanded in 1983. Cope began a solo career with *World Shut Your Mouth* and *Fried* (1984), which won him comparisons with such artists as **Pink Floyd**'s Syd Barrett for their eccentricities.

A move to Island records brought Cope his first solo Top Twenty hit single, a new version of 'World Shut Your Mouth' (1986). The album *St Julian* was also a bestseller and inaugurated a brief period of near hit singles. These included 'Trampoline' and 'Eve's Volcano (Covered in Sin)' (1987) and 'Charlotte Anne' and 'Five O'Clock World' (1989). After the release of *My Nation Underground* (1988), his career was interrupted by ill health before he created his biggest hit, 'Beautiful Love', in 1991.

In the same year he released the double-album *Peggy Suicide* (1991), the first of a trilogy that he concluded with *Autogeddon* (1994). It was his most mainstream album and was well received. The second of the trilogy, *Jehovah Kill* (1992), an attack on conventional religion, was more intense but less compelling. *Autogeddon*, the first album to be released on Chrysalis's new Echo label, was even more eclectic than its predecessors, mixing straight rock (the title track) with simple dippiness. In 1994 he published a sprightly autobiography, *Head on*, and in 1995 released *Julian Cope Presents 20 Mothers* (Echo). The retrospective *Followers of Saint Julian* was issued by Island in 1997, the year Cope announced he was writing *The Modern Antiquarian: A Pre-Millennial Odyssey through Megalithic Britain*.

JOHNNY COPELAND
b. 27 March 1937, Haynesville, Louisiana, USA, d. 3 July 1997

A Texas blues guitarist and singer, Copeland benefited from the growth of interest in the blues among mainly white audiences in the eighties.

He was a professional boxer before turning to music

in the late fifties. Copeland's vocal style owed much to **Nappy Brown**. He played the clubs of Houston, Texas, and recorded local hits, including 'All Boy' (Mercury, 1958) and 'Down on Bending Knee' (Golden Eagle). During the sixties he recorded a version of **Bob Dylan**'s 'Blowin' in the Wind' (Wand, 1965).

In 1977 Copeland began a long relationship with the Rounder label, which issued *Copeland Special* followed by *Make My Home Wherever I Hang My Hat* (1982) and *Texas Twister* (1983). His most successful recording was *Showdown!*, a 1985 session with fellow-guitarists **Robert Cray** and **Albert Collins**. Despite its Dylanesque title, the 1986 album *Bringin' It All Back Home* was recorded in Africa. Copeland remained a favourite of the college and festival circuit into the nineties, making further albums such as *Boom Boom* (Rounder, 1990) and the hugely likeable *Jungle Swing* (Verve, 1996).

CHICK COREA
b. Armando Anthony Corea, 12 June 1941, Chelsea, Massachusetts, USA

Equally capable in avant-garde, classical and fusion styles, Corea was an extremely prolific jazz keyboards player. He led the innovatory jazz-rock band Return to Forever and was later involved in highly acclaimed collaborations with **Herbie Hancock** and **Gary Burton**.

His earliest gigs were with his father, a jazz trumpeter and arranger. Following a brief period at New York's Juilliard music school, he joined **Mongo Santamaria**'s Latin-jazz orchestra in 1962. He went on to join the bands of trumpeter Blue Mitchell and flautist Herbie Mann before making his first recording with **Stan Getz** (*Sweet Rain*, Verve, 1967), regarded by some as the saxophonist's best album.

This led to the most formative period of his career, as part of **Miles Davis**'s group between 1968 and 1971. Corea's move to electric Fender Rhodes piano on *In a Silent Way* and *Bitches Brew* (1969) played a key role in Davis's transition from acoustic to amplified music. Corea himself used this experience as the starting point for his own jazz-fusion band, but before doing so he spent a year in Europe recording classically influenced solo albums (*Piano Improvisations*) and group improvisations with avant-garde players **Anthony Braxton** and Dave Holland as Circle for the German label ECM.

Return to Forever was the title of a 1972 album by a group which included bassist **Stanley Clarke** and Brazilians Airto Moreira (percussion) and vocalist Flora Purim. When Moreira and Purim formed their own band in 1973, Corea formed the band Return to Forever with Lenny White (drums) and Bill Connors (guitar), who was replaced by Al DiMeola in 1974. Modelled on **John McLaughlin**'s Mahavishnu

Orchestra, the band cut five albums of light jazz-rock for Polydor and Columbia.

After Return to Forever broke up in 1976, Corea returned to acoustic piano work, touring with Hancock and recording with Burton (*In Concert, Zurich, Oct 28 1979*, ECM). Burton and a string quartet also recorded the first of Corea's extended compositions, the seven-movement *Lyric Suite for Sextet* (1983). In 1984 ECM released *Children's Songs*, a collection of twenty short piano solos, and in the eighties Corea recorded with Michael Brecker of the **Brecker Brothers**, saxophonist Steve Kajula, and others. In 1985 ECM released *Works*, a representative selection of his output for the label over the previous fifteen years. In later years, Corea divided his time between two groups. The Akoustic Band was a trio with John Patitucci (bass) and Dave Weckl (drums) with whom he recorded the sprightly *Akoustic Band* (GRP, 1989) and *Live* (1991). Corea's larger the Elecktric Band, made a series of lesser, more sedate, albums, including *Light Years* (1987) and *Beneath the Mask* (1991).

CORNELIUS
b. Keigo Oyamada, 27 January 1969, Tokyo, Japan

Japanese guitarist, composer and producer Cornelius has received international acclaim for his unique body of work, released on his own Trattoria record label, also home to Bill Wyman's back catalogue.

His musical career began in Lollipop Sonic and Flipper's Guitar, with whom he achieved moderate success domestically. In 1992, after the break up of his second band, he started Trattoria Records, on which he released a selection of mod and acid-jazz records by a variety of homegrown artists, as well as his own increasingly diverse solo material, an eclectic blend of discordant guitars reminiscent of **My Bloody Valentine**, hip-hop beats and **Beach Boys** harmonies. The albums *First Question Award* (1994) and *69/96* (1996) and a series of EPs, including a version of the **Rolling Stones**' 'You Can't Always Get What You Want', achieved him stardom across Japan, where he would regularly perform to audiences of over 10,000, flanked by a band of Cornelius clones.

Fantasma (1998), his first album to gain a full worldwide release, drew praise from the likes of **Beck** and the **Beastie Boys**, which helped Cornelius develop a cult following in Britain and the US. *FM: Fantasma Remixes* and *CM: Cornelius Remixes* (1999) collected reinterpretations of songs from the *Fantasma* album by artists such as Coldcut and UNKLE, and Cornelius's versions of their songs, respectively.

DON CORNELL
b. 1924, New York, USA

A big-voiced rather than emotive performer, Cornell had three million-sellers before his career was capsized by the first waves of rock'n'roll.

After singing with the bands of Bobby Hayes and the McFarland twins (George and Arthur), Cornell joined Sammy Kaye's band in 1942 as a singer and guitarist. On his discharge from the Army Air Corps in 1946, he rejoined the band before going solo in 1949, signing with Coral Records. He was backed by Kaye on his first major hit, a revival of the 1933 song 'It Isn't Fair'* (1950), the lyrics to which were written by **Sophie Tucker**'s bandleader Richard Himber. Other hits included 'I'm Yours'*, 'I' (1952), 'Heart of My Heart' (1953) on which he was joined by Alan Dale and Johnny Desmond, and 'Hold My Hand'* (1954) – his biggest hit in Britain – from the film *Susan Slept Here*. In 1955 he had a Top Thirty hit with 'Young Abe Lincoln', which was covered by **Hugo and Luigi**.

By 1956, like many other singers, Cornell was pushed by his record company into covering rock'n'roll material such as 'See-Saw' (originally by the Moonglows) and even **Lonnie Donegan**'s skiffle hit 'Rock Island Line', singing teen-orientated material like 'Teenage Meeting' and 'Mama Guitar' (1957) and making albums like *For Teenagers Only* (1958). These were only minor hits and in the sixties Cornell left Coral for the cabaret circuit.

THE CORRS
Andrea Corr, b. 17 May 1974, Dundalk, Ireland; Caroline Corr, b. 17 March 1973, Dundalk; Jim Corr, b. 31 July 1968, Dundalk; Sharon Corr, b. 24 March 1970, Dundalk

Sibling quartet the Corrs' blend of traditional Irish folk and US West Coast Rock in the vein of **Fleetwood Mac** has brought them multi-platinum sales across Europe and Asia as well as in Britain, Ireland and Canada.

After playing together since early childhood, the Corrs – consisting of guitarist Jim, singer Andrea, drummer Caroline and violinist Sharon – gained a recording contract with the Atlantic label after a series of lucky breaks drew their attention. Andrea won a small role in *The Commitments* (1992), with the band appearing at the related concert in Dublin. A chance encounter with Jean Kennedy Smith, the US Ambassador to Ireland, at a club gig lead to an invitation to perform at the opening ceremony of the 1994 World Cup.

Their début album, *Forgiven Not Forgotten* (1995), sold eight million copies on release across Europe, Asia, Scandinavia and Canada, although the band were ignored in Britain, and spawned the hit single 'Runaway'. The resulting world tour took in an appearance at the UK leg of the Fleadh festival and dates in Europe with **Céline Dion**. The follow-up, *Talk on Corners* (1997)*, was a more melancholy affair, featuring a guest appearance from the **Chieftains** on a version of **Jimi Hendrix**'s 'Little Wing'. It included several international hit singles, including 'What Can I Do'. Another hit was 'Dreams' (a Fleetwood Mac cover that was featured on the tribute album *Legacy: A Tribute to Fleetwood Mac's Rumours*). In the same year Andrea continued her acting career with a part in *Evita*.

In 1998 a reissued *Talk on Corners* (with extra tracks and remixes) gained the group a British Top Five hit with a remixed version of 'What Can I Do'. The act ended the year with two of the five top-selling albums in the UK. In 1999, to harden their image, they opened for the US leg of the **Rolling Stones**' *No Security* tour and in 2000 released *In Blue*, which in the fashion of the times saw five producers at the controls over various tracks, and which was agreeable rather than profound, hook-laden rather than compelling. The most intriguing track was the austere instrumental 'Rebel Heart', which was the theme of a television programme about the 1916 Irish Easter uprising.

LARRY CORYELL
b. 2 April 1943, Galveston, Texas, USA

Coryell was one of the most proficient guitarists of his era, exploring the possibilities of a fusion between jazz and rock. In the eighties he recorded several albums of popular classical pieces.

Coryell took up jazz guitar in 1957 and, after studying journalism at Washington University, moved to New York, making his first record with drummer Chico Hamilton (*The Dealer*, Impulse, 1966). He worked briefly with an early jazz-rock band Free Spirits before joining **Gary Burton** in 1967.

This was Burton's underground/psychedelic phase and Coryell contributed to albums like *A Genuine Tong Funeral* and *Lofty Fake Anagram*. He worked in other styles on flautist Herbie Mann's *Memphis Underground* (Atlantic, 1968), which included soul standards like 'Hold on I'm Comin'' and 'Chain of Fools', and Mike Mantler's *Jazz Composers Orchestra* (1968), where he used **Jimi Hendrix**-inspired feedback.

That influence was apparent on Coryell's first solo albums, *Lady Coryell* (dedicated to his lyricist wife Julie) and *Coryell* (Vanguard, 1969). Among the backing musicians was organist Mike Mandell, who joined Coryell in a touring band with **Jack Bruce** and ex-Hendrix drummer Mitch Mitchell. *Spaces* (1970) featured a line-up of future fusion stars, including **John McLaughlin**, **Chick Corea** and Billy Cobham.

Coryell now entered an unproductive heavy-rock phase which included an album recorded at Hendrix's Electric Ladyland studio (*Barefoot Boy*, Flying Dutchman, 1972) before *Offering* (1972) and *Real Great Escape* (1973) – which included the **Jimmy Webb** song 'P. F. Sloan' – righted the jazz-rock balance. The following year he launched his first fully fledged fusion group, Eleventh House, with ex-**Weather Report** and **McCoy Tyner** drummer Alphonse Mouzon. Signed to Arista, the band, whose other members included Randy Brecker of the **Brecker Brothers**, released three albums of restrained and flowing (if unchallenging) music.

He now embarked on a series of guitar duo projects. *Restful Mind* (Vanguard, 1975) was a mostly acoustic album recorded in Oregon with Ralph Towner, featuring Ravel's 'Pavane for a Dead Princess', an early hint of Coryell's interest in the classical repertoire. *Twin House* and *Splendid* (Elektra, 1977–8) found him working with Philip Catherine of the Dutch rock band Focus on material like **Django Reinhardt**'s 'Nuages' and Jimmy Guiffre's 'Train and the River'.

In the eighties Coryell cut three albums of solo guitar versions of classical works for Philips: *Bolero*, *Scheherazade* and *The Firebird and Petrouchka*. In 1985 he formed a new partnership with the young New York jazz guitarist Emily Remler, playing live and recording *Together* (Concord). 1990 saw him playing in a relaxed manner with Don Lanphere on *Coryell/ Lanphere*.

DON COSTA

b. 10 June 1915, Boston, Massachusetts, USA, d. 19 January 1983, New York

Costa was one of popular music's most versatile arrangers, conductors, composers and producers. The range of those he worked with stretched from **Little Anthony** to **Barbra Streisand**, the **Osmonds** to **Steve Lawrence**, and **Paul Anka** to **Frank Sinatra**.

The youngest of five children, he taught himself guitar at eight and by 1930 he was a staff musician at a local radio station. Determined to become a songwriter he moved to New York where his first success came with the orchestral arrangement for the **Vaughn Monroe** hit 'Red Roses for a Blue Lady' (1949). This was followed by a stint as Monroe's regular arranger and commissions to arrange sessions for such singers as **Sarah Vaughan**, **Vic Damone** and the **Ames Brothers**.

In the early fifties Costa joined the A&R department of ABC-Paramount records. Here he was associated with hits by **Lloyd Price** ('Stagger Lee' and 'Personality', 1959), Little Anthony & the Imperials and Lawrence and Eydie Gorme. His major triumph

at ABC was to sign the fifteen-year-old Anka. Under Costa's supervision Anka made a series of hits, including 'You Are My Destiny', 'Lonely Boy' and the multi-million selling 'Diana'. However, Costa was less successful either commercially or critically with Donny Osmond, most of whose seventies recordings he supervised.

The most successful of Costa's own orchestral recordings was a version of the film theme 'Never on Sunday' (1960) by the Greek composer Manos Hadjidakis. Costa played mandolin on the track.

All this was a prelude to Costa's highly accomplished work with leading ballad singers in the sixties. He scored **Sarah Vaughan**'s exquisite *Snowbound* (1961), **Tony Bennett**'s *Songs for the Jet Set* (1965) and Dinah Washington's *Drinking Again* (1962), but his finest arrangements were for Sinatra. During the same period Costa oversaw the recordings of **Trini Lopez**, whose 'If I Had a Hammer' he produced.

Costa was Sinatra's most important arranger/conductor of the decade. Some of his best writing appeared on *Sinatra and Strings* (1961) and Costa's versatility enabled him to keep up with the singer's numerous excursions into contemporary material such as *Cycles* (1968) and *My Way* (1969). Apart from a disastrous pseudo-Dixieland setting for **Paul Simon**'s 'Mrs Robinson', Costa was a pillar of reliability.

Costa continued to work with Sinatra in the seventies (*Ol' Blue Eyes Is Back* and the live *The Main Event*) and eighties (the middle portion of *Trilogy* and *She Shot Me Down*). Costa had a brief period of film work in the late sixties, scoring *Rough Night in Jericho* (1967), *Madigan* (1968) and *The Impossible Years* (1968).

Among the few recordings of his own were *Instrumental Versions of Simon and Garfunkel* (Mercury, 1968) and *Out Here on My Own* (1981), which featured his vocalist daughter Nikki Costa. He was preparing a second album with Nikki when he died of a heart attack.

ELVIS COSTELLO

b. Declan Patrick MacManus, 25 August 1954, London, England

British singer-songwriter and producer Costello emerged during the punk era. However, in contrast to most punk bands of the late seventies who expressed a generalized anger (through their appearance as much as their music), Costello's carefully crafted songs explored the classic themes of the difficulties of personal relationships and social issues with a controlled venom rarely found in rock. By the late nineties he had entered the mainstream, writing songs with the likes of **Paul McCartney** and recording songs for films (notably **Charles Aznavour**'s 'She', which was

featured in the romantic comedy *Notting Hill* [1999]).
However, he retained his sense of experimentation,
making albums in partnership with the Brodsky
Quartet (*The Juliet Letters*, 1992) and with **Burt
Bacharach** (*Painted from Memory*, Mercury, 1998).

The son of Ross MacManus, a singer with **Joe Loss**
and later a bandleader in his own right, Costello sang
with pub-rock band Flip City in the mid-seventies
before in 1977 he was signed by the independent Stiff
Records on condition he change his first name to
Elvis. His first two singles were 'Less Than Zero', a
bitter attack on the way in which British fascist
Oswald Mosley had become the object of fawning
media attention, and 'Alison', a chilling ballad in
which the singer harshly puts down a former girlfriend. They set the tenor of the **Nick Lowe**-produced
My Aim Is True (1977), on which Costello was backed
by American country-rock band Clover (but without
its lead singer **Huey Lewis**). The album included
other songs expressing the singer's anger, disgust and
sheer puzzlement at the ways of the world, notably
'Mystery Dance', 'Red Shoes' and 'Welcome to the
Working Week'. Even more impressive in its complex
delineation of emotional anguish through unusual
imagery and clever wordplay was Costello's first
British hit, 'Watching the Detectives'.

Following the formation of the Attractions (Pete
Thomas, drums, Bruce Thomas, bass, and Steve
Nieve, keyboards) as a permanent backing group,
Costello joined Radar (and Columbia in America).
The sound of *This Year's Model* (1978) was fuller,
complementing the harsh urgency of Costello's songwriting. Introduced by the hit 'I Don't Want to Go to
Chelsea', the album established Costello as a major
artist in both Britain and America where his songs
were widely covered (by **Linda Ronstadt**, among others). The lesser *Armed Forces* (1979) included
Costello's biggest British hit, 'Oliver's Army', and in
the same year he produced the **Specials**' début album.
In 1980 Costello and his manager Jake Riviera formed
their own F-Beat label, for which Costello recorded
the soul-inflected, ironically titled *Get Happy!!* with
its version of **Sam and Dave**'s 'I Can't Stand up for
Falling Down'. *Trust* (1981) included support from
members of **Squeeze**, whose *East Side Story* (1981)
Costello co-produced. His other production work
included the second album by the **Pogues** (*Red Roses
for Me*, 1985), whose bassist Cait O'Riordan he would
later marry, and **Nick Lowe** (*Nick Lowe and His Cowboy Outfit*, 1984).

Almost Blue (1981), produced in Nashville by **Billy
Sherrill**, was an album of mournful country songs
associated with **Merle Haggard**, **George Jones** (with
whom he'd duetted in 1980 on 'Stranger in the
House') and **Gram Parsons**, and included the British
hit 'Good Year for the Roses'. After *Imperial Ballroom*

(1982), Costello released the superior *Punch the Clock*
(1983) which included 'Shipbuilding', a magisterial,
oblique song inspired by the Falklands war that was
first recorded by **Robert Wyatt** (1982), 'Pills and
Soap', a strong attack on Britain's gutter press, and
his only major American hit, 'Everyday I Write the
Book', yet another account of personal relationships
in terms of power struggles. After the mellower *Goodbye Cruel World* (1984), Costello began working with
guitarist/producer T-Bone Burnett, whose influence
was to be found on *King of America* (1986), which featured Burnett and **James Burton**, with the Attractions
playing on only one track, and which saw Costello
directing his attention specifically to American matters. The lesser *Blood and Chocolate* (1987) found
Costello reunited with producer Nick Lowe while
Spike (Warners, 1989) included the trenchant 'Tramp
the Dirt Down', one of the most vengeful songs ever
written about a contemporary politician (Margaret
Thatcher), and the compassionate 'Baby Plays
Around'. The album featured two songs written with
Paul McCartney and the pair also collaborated on
songs for the latter's *Flowers in the Dirt*. Another song
from the collaboration was featured on *Mighty Like a
Rose* (1990), which included Costello's father on
trumpet. Far better was the music he composed as the
soundtrack to the series *GBH*. *The Juliet Letters*
(1992), an experimental collaboration with the Brodsky Quartet based on letters sent to Shakespeare's
heroine, was equally intriguing, making use of the
contrast between the singer's harsh voice and the
sombre sound of the string quartet.

The next year he contributed to *Weird Nightmare*,
Hal Willner's tribute to **Charles Mingus**, and wrote
all the songs for former Transvision Vamp singer
Wendy James' *Now Ain't the Time for Your Tears*.
1994's *Brutal Youth* saw Costello reunited with the
Attractions but to little effect: the anger seemed
forced and the sound, an uncanny re-creation of that
of the early albums, merely nostalgic. His bestselling
album for several years, its sales were dwarfed by reissues of his earlier albums, most of which included
numerous unreleased tracks. *Painted from Memory*
was a bold failure, Costello's voice not being equal to
the task of vaulting the gaps in Bacharach's complex
musical patterns. It was followed by the definitive retrospective *The Very Best of* (1999), which included his
biggest hit of the decade, the film song 'She'.

BILLY COTTON
*b. 6 May 1899, London, England, d. 25 March 1969,
London*

Though Cotton was one of the longest serving British
bandleaders, he is best remembered as a showman
and presenter of the radio series *The B... Cotton*

Band Show. Introduced by his bellowed 'Wakey-wakey!', this later became one of the most successful variety shows in the early days of British television.

Cotton joined the army in 1914, where he took up drums and bugle, and in 1918 the Royal Air Corps. In the twenties he drummed in various bands and played football for Brentford and Wimbledon before forming his own band in 1924 to play at the Wembley Exhibition. In 1928 an expanded band secured a residency at the Astoria and began recording for Regal Zonophone. By the thirties established as a touring and broadcasting band, the band in its recordings mixed attempts at hot jazz (**W. C. Handy**'s 'St Louis Blues', 1934) with more mainstream material (**Jimmy Kennedy**'s 'Isle of Capri', 1934, which featured singer Alan Breeze, a mainstay of Cotton's band since 1931). Though Cotton employed the likes of **Nat Gonella** in the thirties, he was more comfortable as a showman and during the Second World War perfected his brand of breezy comedy in ENSA shows for the troops.

After the war Cotton continued to record ('In a Golden Coach', **Tommie Connor**'s 'I Saw Mommy Kissing Santa Claus', Decca, 1953, 'Friends and Neighbours', 1954) but had greater success with the long-running *The Billy Cotton Band Show* (1949–68) which mixed novelty songs ('I've Got a Lovely Bunch of Coconuts') with comedy and became a national institution. In 1957 the show transferred to television with Cotton as its energetic centre and the band offering musical and comic support in equal measures. An avid sports fan, he died while watching a boxing match at Wembley.

Cotton's son, Bill Cotton Jnr, subsequently became controller of the BBC1 television channel, and later head of the television department of the Noel Gay organization.

PHIL COULTER
b. 1942, Londonderry, Northern Ireland

An important figure on the British pop scene in the seventies, Coulter was associated as writer, manager or producer with artists as varied as **Sandie Shaw**, the Dubliners, Billy Connolly and the **Bay City Rollers**. In the eighties he wrote one of the best songs inspired by the Northern Ireland situation and had orchestral hits in Ireland.

In the sixties he formed a songwriting partnership with Scotsman Bill Martin which brought No. 1 hits in Britain with two Eurovision Song Contest songs, Shaw's winner 'Puppet on a String' (1967) and **Cliff Richard**'s second-placed 'Congratulations' (1968). These successes led to a commission to write the England World Cup (soccer) Squad's official anthem 'Back Home' in 1970, another No. 1.

In parallel with his pop career, Coulter was also musical director for Irish folk band the Dubliners, whose ebullient style was inspired by the **Clancy Brothers**. Successful live performers in America, the group also had a British hit with the traditional songs 'Seven Drunken Nights' and 'Black Velvet Band' (Major Minor, 1967). They also performed songs of social comment by Coulter, including 'The Molly Maguires' and 'Free the People'. His 'The Old Man' was a later hit for the Fureys and Davey Arthur, Ireland's leading pop-folk group of the eighties.

In the mid-seventies Martin and Coulter rode the crest of the teeny-bop wave, revitalizing the Bay City Rollers' career with hits like 'Remember' and 'All of Me Loves All of You'. They also wrote and produced four hits for Kenny on RAK, including 'The Bump' (1974) and 'Julie Ann' (1975). 'Forever and Ever' (Bell, 1976) was a Martin–Coulter production which reached No. 1 for Slik, the Scottish group which included Midge Ure, later of **Ultravox**. In contrast, Coulter produced a series of records by Scottish comedian Billy Connolly, including his 1975 No. 1 'D.I.V.O.R.C.E.', a parody of **Tammy Wynette**'s country hit.

The partnership with Martin finished at the end of the decade and Coulter concentrated on orchestral recordings. He had cult Northern soul hits with re-issues of 'Good Thing Going' and 'Runaway Bunion' (Heat, 1983), but his most important project was two albums of Irish standard and traditional songs, *Classic Tranquillity* and *Sea of Tranquillity* (Panther, 1983–4) which were Irish hits and sold well in Britain and America. The former included Coulter's song 'The Town I Loved So Well', a moving ballad about the effects of 'the troubles' on his home town of Derry. In 1993 he recorded *Recollections*, orchestrated versions of material by such artists as Clannad, **Chris De Burgh**, **U2** ('Sunday Bloody Sunday') and Mark Knopfler of **Dire Straits** ('Cal').

COUNTING CROWS
Steve Bowman, b. 14 January 1967, Torrence, California, USA (replaced by Ben Mize); David Bryson, b. 5 November 1961, San Francisco, California; Adam Duritz, b. 1 August 1964, Baltimore, Maryland; Charles Gillingham, b. 12 January 1960, Torrence, California; Matt Malley, b. 4 July 1964, California

West coast rock band Counting Crows rose to fame with their brand of alternative rock, inspired by the experimental guitar bands of the seventies and **Van Morrison** and **The Band**.

Counting Crows came together in 1989 when Duritz (vocals) and Bryson (guitar) met in San Francisco and began to perform in bars and coffee houses together. Adding bassist Malley, keyboardist Gillingham and drummer Bowman to the line-up, the band moved from breezy acoustic rock to a darker sound, heavily influenced by progressive rock. Within a year they had built a live following in and around San Francisco, recording a demo which eventually saw them sign to DGC.

After a period of recording in a rented house in Hollywood, Counting Crows released *August and Everything After* (1993). Helped by the success of the single 'Mr Jones' and a year of solid touring, the album gradually climbed the US album chart, eventually selling over six million copies. In spite of the band's growing popularity, drummer Steve Bowman decided to leave the band to form Third Eye Blind, which later achieved major US success of its own. He was replaced by Ben Mize, formerly of rock band Cracker.

Another lengthy spell in the studio resulted in *Recovering the Satellites* (1996)*, which sold well in the States and saw the band begin to develop an international following. *Across a Wire: Live in New York City* (1998) was taped over dates the previous year.

DON COVAY
b. March 1938, Orangeburg, South Carolina, USA

One of the best soul songwriters of the sixties and early seventies, Covay, like **Joe Tex**, combined solemnity and humour, moralizing and wit, typified by the couplet, 'Without your reading writing and arithmetic/You're goin' out in the jungle fightin' lions with a toothpick . . .'.

The son of a Baptist minister, Covay grew up in Washington DC where he and his brothers formed a gospel quartet, the Cherry-Keys. In 1958 he joined the Rainbows, whose other members included John Berry, **Marvin Gaye** and Billy Stewart, whose later solo hits included revivals of **George Gershwin**'s 'Summertime' (Chess, 1966) and **Sammy Fain**'s 'Secret Love' (1966), before he died in a motor accident in 1970.

After recording with the Rainbows on Bobby Robinson's Red Robin label ('Mary Lee') and on Pilgrim, which was run by George Wein, later the promoter of the Newport Jazz Festival, Covay left the band to become warm-up man for **Little Richard**, who christened him Pretty Boy. Under this name, he cut the frantic 'Bip Bop Bip' (Atlantic, 1959) and as Don Covay and the Goodtimers he released a series of unsuccessful dance novelties on Sue, Columbia, Epic and Big Top between 1959 and 1961.

One of these, 'Pony Time' (written with John Berry), became a minor pop hit on the small Arnold label in 1961. It was quickly snapped up by Cameo in Philadelphia as a vehicle for **Chubby Checker**, and Covay joined the label, cutting 'Popeye Waddle' in 1962. In the same year, he enjoyed his first success as a soul-ballad writer with **Jerry Butler**'s recording of

'You Can Run' and with hit versions of 'Letter Full of Tears' by **Gladys Knight** in America and **Billy Fury** in Britain. Recording in a similar vein himself with New York label Rosemart, Covay reached the Top Forty with 'Mercy Mercy' (1964). The song quickly joined the repertoire of British R&B bands, with the **Rolling Stones** including it on their 1965 album *Out of Our Heads* and Mick Jagger's vocal sounding very similar to Covay's original.

Rosemart was distributed by Atlantic who quickly signed up Covay and released perhaps his most well-known song, 'See-Saw' (1965), recorded in Memphis and written with **Booker T.** guitarist Steve Cropper. It became a 1968 hit for **Aretha Franklin**, who had sold a million copies of Covay's 'Chain of Fools'. He also wrote hits in 1965 for Little Richard ('I Don't Know What You've Got [But It's Got Me]') and Tommy Tucker ('Long Tall Shorty').

Covay's own records were less successful. In 1969 he made the heavy blues album *House of Blue Lights* with the curiously named Jefferson Lemon Blues Band, and the following year returned to his funky moralizing on *Different Strokes*, which contained 'Why Did You Put Your Shoes Under My Bed' and 'Standing in the Grits Line'. Covay now joined Mercury as A&R man and recording artist, with the highly praised *Super Dude One* (1973) producing the American hit 'I Was Checkin' Out, She Was Checkin' In'. *Hot Blood* (1974) included a British hit, 'It's Better to Have'. In 1975 Covay wrote and recorded 'Rumble in the Jungle', a tribute to boxing champion Muhammad Ali.

Covay joined Philadelphia International in 1976 for *Travelin' in Heavy Traffic* and took part in a 1981 Soul Clan package tour with **Solomon Burke** and **Wilson Pickett**. He re-emerged in 1986 as a contributor to the Rolling Stones album *Dirty Work* and briefly signed with Island in 1990. In 1993 the Shanachie label issued a tribute album, *Back to the Streets*, on which a range of artists performed Covay's compositions.

NOËL COWARD
b. Noël Pierce Coward, 16 December 1899, Teddington, Middlesex, England, d. 26 March 1973, Port Maria, Jamaica

In addition to being one of the most influential figures of the British theatre as playwright and actor, Coward was an important songwriter. Indeed his own songs are both proof of the truth of his often quoted remark, 'Extraordinary how potent cheap music is', and examples of 'cheap music' at its most graceful and witty.

His first stage appearance was at the age of twelve and his first notable song, 'Parisian Pierrot', appeared in the 1923 show, *London Calling*, where it was introduced by Gertrude Lawrence. Coward became the young genius of the English stage and by the outbreak of the Second World War had written nine hit musicals. His first success as a lyricist came with 'Poor Little Rich Girl', sung by Alice Delysia in *On with the Dance* (1925), for which Philip Braham (composer of 'Limehouse Blues') wrote the music.

Coward frequently starred in his own plays and *This Year of Grace* (1928), with Beatrice Lillie, was his first Broadway hit. It contained two of his most popular songs, the brisk 'A Room with a View' and 'Dance Little Lady'. *Bitter Sweet* (1929) was Coward's attempt to construct a Viennese operetta, while his 'straight' play *Private Lives* featured only one song – 'Someday I'll Find You', a dramatic ballad sung on the London stage by Gertrude Lawrence.

The 1931 production *Cavalcade* (Coward's musical picture of the First World War) contained many songs of that period, including **Irving Berlin**'s 'Alexander's Ragtime Band' and **Ivor Novello**'s 'Keep the Home Fires Burning'. A Hollywood film (1933) of the play starred Clive Brook and Diana Wyngard. The best of his songs of the thirties include the comic numbers 'The Stately Homes of England', 'I Went to a Marvellous Party' and 'Mrs Worthington', with its immortal advice 'Don't put your daughter on the stage'; the romantic 'Mad About the Boy' and 'Mad Dogs and Englishmen', an urbane skit on the Empire mentality which was said to have been composed on a car trip from Hanoi to Saigon in 1930, and is probably the clearest example of the influence of **Gilbert and Sullivan** on him.

Coward spent much of the Second World War entertaining the troops and contributed songs for the war effort. 'London Pride', one of his best compositions, was saved from mawkishness by the precision of his imagery, while 'Don't Let's Be Beastly to the Germans' found him at his satirical best. The satire, however, was lost on both the BBC and EMI, who refused to broadcast or record it on the grounds that it was pro-German. *In Which We Serve* (1944), which won him an Oscar and was co-directed with David Lean, though propagandist in aim, remains Coward's most affecting portrait of the British.

After 1945 his career never recovered its momentum. In an age of austerity with the American cultural invasion in full swing, Coward's sophistication and languid Englishness were out of time. His own disillusion was expressed in the jaunty-sounding 'There Are Bad Times Just Around the Corner' (1952). Of the seven shows mounted by the mid-sixties, only *Sail Away* (1961) made a real impact, with Elaine Strich starring in the Broadway production.

Increasingly Coward turned to film acting, starring in ten movies, from satires like *Our Man in Havana* (1960) to comedy thrillers such as *The Italian Job*

(1969). His live shows placed him among the highest paid entertainers on the night-club circuit. His act is best captured on the 1955 live recording *Noël Coward in Las Vegas* (Columbia), which includes his risqué variation on **Cole Porter**'s 'Let's Do It', containing throwaway lines like 'Ernest Hemingway could . . . just do it'. In his pre-war heyday Coward recorded for EMI's His Master's Voice label and a selection of his most successful songs (*The Golden Age of Noël Coward*) remains in catalogue, along with several other collections, including *The Shows* and *The Revues* on EMI. In 1992 EMI released the definitive retrospective, the four-CD box set *The Master's Voice*. This was followed in 1998 by *Twentieth Century Blues*, in which the likes of **Sting**, **Robbie Williams**, the **Pet Shop Boys** and **Elton John** attempted to give a modern edge to Coward but to little effect.

COWBOY JUNKIES
Margo Timmins, b. 27 June 1961, Montreal, Canada; Michael Timmins, b. 21 April 1959, Montreal; Peter Timmins, b. 29 October 1965, Montreal; Alan Anton, b. Alan Alizojvodic, 22 June 1959, Montreal

In the seventies the likes of **Gram Parsons**, the **Eagles** and the **Pure Prairie League**, among others, sought to build upon country music, melding it and rock in (radically) different ways. In the eighties a second generation of acts, such as **k.d. lang, Lambchop** and the Cowboy Junkies, took another approach, seeking instead to strip down country music to its essence(s), which they could then re-present in various ways. The approach taken by the Junkies was a decidedly low-fi one – their seminal album, *The Trinity Sessions*, was recorded with one ambient microphone, and that philosophy imbues most of their subsequent recordings. That and the low-key vocals of Margo Timmins brought the country-tinged sad-café music of Cowboy Junkies a cult following.

Michael Timmins (guitar) and Anton (bass) had played in Hunger Project and Germinal before forming Cowboy Junkies, for which they recruited Timmins' sister Margo and brother Peter (drums) in Toronto in 1985. Their first album, *Whites Off Earth Now*, released on their own Latent label in 1988 (reissued on RCA, 1991), saw the group experimenting with reflective versions of mostly blues-based songs. The album also included an impressive reading of **Bruce Springsteen**'s 'State Trooper', marking their ability to renew other people's songs through interpretation. Their breakthrough album was their major label début, *The Trinity Sessions* (1988). On it they recovered the meanings of songs as disparate as **Patsy Cline**'s 'Walking After Midnight', **Hank Williams**' 'I'm So Lonely I Could Cry' and a memorable reworking of the **Velvet Underground**'s 'Sweet Jane', songs that had lost their meaning through the familiarity of unconsidered versions. Recorded in a Toronto church for some $500 and performed in a clearly considered manner that one critic suggested teetered between the hypnotic and the narcoleptic, the album was only a minor commercial success. However, Margo Timmins' trance-like vocals and the lo-fi approach the album represented were hugely influential. The group's haunting version of **Neil Young**'s 'Powderfinger', which was included in several alternative country compilations and thus reached a wider audience, was held in particularly high regard. That track was included on *The Caution Horses* (1990), which also included a pair of Michael Timmins' finest songs, 'Sun Comes Up, It's Tuesday Morning' and 'Cause Cheap Is How I Feel'.

Black Eyed Man (1992), another exercise in low-key style, included a duet from Margo Timmins and **John Prine**, 'If You Were the Woman and I Was the Man'.

After *Pale Sun, Crescent Moon* (1993) the group left RCA, who subsequently issued a pair of retrospective sets: the much regarded *Studio* (1996), on the cover of which was a photograph of the Calrec Ambisonic microphone that they had first used on *The Trinity Sessions*, and the two-CD live set *200 More Miles* (1995).

Signed to Geffen, the group released the superior *Lay It Down* (1996), which was hardly distinguishable from their RCA recordings. It was followed by *Miles from Home* (2000), which mixed up-tempo offerings with their signature down-tempo sound.

THE COWSILLS
Barbara, b. 1928, Newport, Rhode Island, USA, d. 21 January 1985; Bill, b. 9 January 1948, Newport; Bob, b. 26 August 1949, Newport; Dick, b. 26 August 1950, Newport; Paul, b. 11 November 1952, Newport; Barry, b. 14 September 1954, Newport; John, b. 2 March 1956, Newport; Sue, b. 20 May 1960, Newport

Billed as 'America's First Family of Song', the Cowsills and their squeaky-clean harmonies briefly dominated the American charts in the late sixties and were the inspiration for *The Partridge Family* teleseries which made **David Cassidy** a star.

The family group was transformed into a professional group by their father William 'Bud' Cowsill on his retirement from the navy in 1963. He acted as their manager, while his wife Barbara provided an extra voice. Bud got them a series of regular engagements at New York clubs in the mid-sixties. Signed to MGM by producer Artie Kornfeld in 1967, they had an immediate hit with Kornfeld's composition 'The Rain, the Park and Other Things'*. Radio programmers found their clean family image an attractive alternative to the psychedelia of the day and the Cowsills had a series of hits (including 'We Can Fly'

and 'Indian Lake' in 1968) that climaxed in their triumphant reworking of the hippie anthem 'Hair'* (1969), the title song of the Broadway show.

By now regular guests on American television variety shows – the group was never successful in Europe – and stars of the cabaret circuit, in 1970 they left MGM for London Records. However, where a couple of years before they had been unique, they were now in competition with family groups that had a greater impact, such as the **Osmonds** and **Jackson Five**. As suddenly as they had arrived, the group disappeared. After a desultory tour of American army bases in Europe, they disbanded in 1972. They regularly reformed for nostalgia tours, including one in 1991 and another in 1993.

FRANCIS CRAIG
b. 10 September 1900, Dickson, Tennessee, USA, d. 19 November 1966, Sewanee, Tennessee

Craig's recording of his and Kermit Goell's composition 'Near You'* on the independent Bullet label in 1947 was the first major pop hit made in Nashville.

Craig formed his own orchestra after the First World War, and for twenty-one consecutive years played at Nashville's Hermitage Hotel. In 1947 he approached Jim Bulleit, a one-time *Grand Ole Opry* announcer who had set up his own independent Bullet Records. Recorded at Castle recording studio, the first independent studio to be established in Nashville, and with Bob Lamm providing the vocals, 'Near You' was an immediate hit, eventually selling over two million copies to become the biggest-selling record of 1947 in America. The **Andrews Sisters** and Alvino Rey, among others, recorded versions. Craig followed it with his own composition, the 1948 hit 'Beg Your Pardon'. He subsequently recorded for Decca and Dot, for whom he made a new version of 'Near You' in 1958, after pianist **Roger Williams** scored a Top Ten hit with a revival of the song.

After the success of 'Near You', a straightforward pop song, Bulleit went on to produce a wealth of country material (and some blues, notably **B. B. King**). Among the artists involved were **Ray Price** (who made his first recordings for the label), Johnnie Lee Wills (the brother of **Bob Wills**, whose 1950 country hit 'Rag Mop' was a pop hit for the **Ames Brothers**) and Minnie Pearl. But, overcome by the harsh sound of rock'n'roll and the sweetness of the 'Nashville sound', the label disappeared from view in the late fifties.

FLOYD CRAMER
b. 27 October 1933, Shreveport, Louisiana, USA, d. 31 December 1997

Cramer's million-selling instrumental compositions

'Last Date' (1960) and 'On the Rebound' (1961) are definitive examples of the 'Nashville sound' masterminded by **Chet Atkins**.

Taught piano at the age of five, Cramer in his teens played in various groups. On graduating from high school in 1951, he joined the *Louisiana Hayride* radio show as an accompanist. After briefly recording for Abbott Records (1953–4), in 1955 Cramer moved to Nashville to work as a session man for Atkins, supporting **Elvis Presley**, **Jim Reeves** and others. The centrepiece of his spare yet ornamental style of playing was a distinctive right-hand 'slip note' technique which Cramer has compared to Maybelle Carter's guitar style and described as 'hitting a note and sliding almost simultaneously to another note . . . the result is a melancholy sound'. He borrowed this technique from pianist and songwriter Don Robertson's demo of 'Please Help Me I'm Falling' when he played on **Hank Locklin**'s 1960 recording of the song. The success of that and the haunting 'Last Date' led Cramer to make the technique his own.

After 1960 Cramer recorded over forty albums for RCA and garnered more hit singles, including 'San Antonio Rose', a Top Ten hit in 1961, and 'Stood Up' (1967). He has also performed with artists as diverse as **Johnny Cash** and **Perry Como**. Throughout this time he has continued to work as a session man, often in partnership with Atkins.

ROBERT CRAY
b. 1 August 1953, Columbus, Georgia, USA

With sales of over a million copies of his major label début, *Strong Persuader* (1986), Cray was both the most commercially successful blues artist of the eighties and the most innovative. His themes were the traditional ones of the blues, infidelity, passion and despair, but his melding of southern soul singing styles with spare, unadorned, yet powerfully expressive guitar lines revived and enlivened what seemed at one time to be a static form.

The son of a serviceman, Cray formed his first band, One Way Street, while in high school. In the sixties he listened to southern soul and **Jimi Hendrix**, rather than the blues, before hearing **Albert Collins** in 1969. Influenced by Collins' 'cool' guitar style, Cray started playing the blues in a variety of bands with bassist Richard Cousins, eventually forming the Robert Cray Band in 1974 in Eugene, Oregon. In 1976 the band toured with Collins as his backing group and in 1979 recorded *Who's Been Talkin'* for the independent Tomato Records (reissued, Charly, 1988) just before that company went bankrupt. Despite the inclusion of **O. V. Wright**'s soul standard 'I'm Gonna Forget About You', *Talkin'* was Cray's purest blues outing: the title track was by **Howlin' Wolf** and the

album also featured songs by, or associated with, **Willie Dixon** and **Freddie King**.

More innovatory were *Bad Influence* (Hightone, 1983), which added drummer Dave Olson as a regular member of the band, and *False Accusations* (1985), which saw keyboardist Peter Boe completing the line-up. Among the songs on these albums were 'Phone Booth', also covered by Collins, 'Bad Influence' which was recorded by **Eric Clapton** (who played with Cray when he toured England in 1986 and on whose 1989 album *Journeyman* Cray guested) and the cheating song 'Porch Light', his most representative recording of that period. In the wake of these albums he made *Showtime!* (Alligator, 1985) with Collins and guitarist Johnny Copeland.

The success of his solo albums led to Cray joining Mercury where, produced by Hightone's Bruce Bromberg and Dennis Walker, he recorded *Strong Persuader* (1986), which included the powerful 'Smoking Gun' and reached the American Top Twenty, the first blues record to do so since **Bobby Bland**'s *Call on Me* in 1963. Almost as successful was *Don't Be Afraid of the Dark* (1988), with **David Sanborn** on the saxophone. *Midnight Stroll* (1990) leaned towards Stax and soul and was recorded with the former Stax house band the Memphis Horns. After 1992's *I Was Warned*, Cray's eighth album, *Shame and Sin* (1993), was a return to the bluesier sound of his first recordings. Produced by Cray himself it featured him in duet with **Albert Collins** on **Albert King**'s 'You're Gonna Need Me'. The self-produced *Some Rainy Morning* (1995) was followed by the superior *Sweet Potato Pie* (1997), his most emphatic Southern soul outing. *Taking Your Shoes Off* (1999), his first record for Rykodisc, was similar in style.

The success of his records has made Cray much in demand as a guest artist. Among those with whom he has performed and recorded are **B. B. King**, Clapton and **John Lee Hooker**.

CREAM
Ginger Baker, b. Peter Baker, 19 August 1939, Lewisham, London, England; Jack Bruce, b. John Symon Asher Bruce, 14 May 1943, Lanarkshire, Scotland; Eric Clapton, b. 30 March 1945, Ripley, Surrey

Although in existence for only two years, Cream were the prototype for the kind of rock band that became enormously successful in the seventies. Loud, blues-based, instrumentally audacious and highly rhythmic, the group conquered America through the bombast of their lengthy live shows. It paved the way for myriad bands, including **Led Zeppelin**, **Mountain**, and the heavy-metal groups of the stadium-rock era. The group's sudden and immense success was, however, counter-productive for its members. Both **Jack Bruce** and Ginger Baker were inconsistent in their later work, while **Eric Clapton**'s recovery from the Cream trauma was slow although ultimately complete.

The group was formed in mid-1966 by three of the most experienced figures on the London rhythm and blues scene. Bruce and Baker had formed the rhythm section of **Alexis Korner**'s group in late 1962 and played together with **Graham Bond** in 1963-5 while Bruce had briefly partnered Clapton in **John Mayall**'s group. Immediately prior to Cream's formation, Bruce had been with **Manfred Mann** (playing on the British No. 1, 'Pretty Flamingo'), and Clapton was with Mayall.

On manager Robert Stigwood's Reaction label, the trio released the surreal Bruce–Pete Brown 'Wrapping Paper' backed by 'Cat's Squirrel', a harmonica feature for Bruce based on a traditional blues by Dr Ross. 'I Feel Free', whose scintillating guitar solo made it one of the group's stage favourites, was Cream's first British hit. It was followed by *Fresh Cream* (1967), which mixed blues standards like **Robert Johnson**'s 'Four Till Late' with quirky Pete Brown lyrics like 'Sleepy Time Time' and Baker's solo feature 'Toad'.

Frequent live performances in Britain gave Cream a more cohesive, harder sound which was evident on 'Strange Brew' (1967), a track on which Pete Brown's words were fused with Clapton's intense, exploding guitar lines with wah-wah effects to the fore. It was a taster for *Disraeli Gears*, which included the ecstatic 'Sunshine of Your Love'*, the sombre ballads 'We're Going Wrong' and 'World of Pain' (by producer Felix Pappilardi), as well as Clapton's psychedelic 'Tales of Brave Ulysses'.

After the band's first American tour in mid-1967, the balance in Cream's work swung away from these highly crafted studio tracks to marathon virtuoso live performances. At best an exhilarating collective improvisation previously unknown in rock, the Cream concerts often degenerated into over-extended solos from Clapton and Baker and sometimes from Bruce on harmonica or bass. The live tracks on *Wheels of Fire* (1968), which featured a finely structured fifteen-minute version of **Howlin' Wolf**'s 'Spoonful', also included the excesses of 'Train Time' and 'Toad''s seventeen minutes of drumming.

Wheels of Fire was a double-album whose studio half included the Bruce–Brown classic 'White Room', Clapton's 'Politician' and Baker's whimsical 'Pressed Rat and Warthog'. Soon after its release, Cream succumbed to the external pressures of success and internal dissensions. A lengthy American tour was followed by a farewell concert at London's Royal Albert Hall.

If the musicians were finished with Cream, the record company wasn't. *Farewell Cream* (1969), which mixed live material and new songs (of which only Clapton's 'Badge' was noteworthy), was followed in 1970 and 1972 by further volumes of *Live Cream*.

Meanwhile, each of the trio pursued a separate path. Bruce veered from Cream-like power trios (West, Bruce and Laing, BLT) to jazz-based work with **Carla Bley** and Tony Williams and his own highly regarded solo albums of Pete Brown songs. Clapton and Baker briefly reunited with **Steve Winwood** in Blind Faith in 1969 before the guitarist began a solo career which eventually made him a senior rock figure in the eighties.

After the demise of Blind Faith, Baker organized an unwieldy but exciting jazz-rock big band, Air Force, which released two Polydor albums in 1970. Its personnel included Bond, Winwood, ex-**Moody Blues** bassist Denny Laine and African drummer Speedy Acquaye. After the band split up, Baker set up a recording studio in Lagos, Nigeria, working with **Fela Kuti** on *Live!* (Signpost, 1972).

In the mid-seventies Baker returned to Europe to form the jazz-rock group Baker Gurvitz Army with singer-guitarist Adrian Gurvitz. Three albums were released in 1974-6 by Vertigo and Mountain. His musical activity in later years was spasmodic, although he recorded with Atomic Rooster (1980) and **Hawkwind** (*Levitation*, 1980). He released *From Humble Origins* in 1983 and *Horses and Trees* for the Celluloid label, produced by **Bill Laswell** in 1986. In the same year he recorded with ex-**Sex Pistols** vocalist John Lydon's Public Image Ltd on *Album*. Baker released the unremarkable *Middle Passage* in 1990 before joining Los Angeles heavy metal band Masters of Reality in 1992, recording one album with them. In 1993 Cream re-formed for a performance at a US awards show, paving the way for Baker and Bruce to form BBM with Gary Moore in 1994, promising a mixture of Cream classics, new material and lengthy on-stage jamming. However, Cream's best releases of the nineties were retrospective sets, the best of which was the four-CD compilation *Those Were the Days* (1997).

CREEDENCE CLEARWATER REVIVAL

John Fogerty, b. 28 May 1945, Berkeley, California, USA; Tom Fogerty, b. 9 November 1941, Berkeley, d. 6 September 1990, Scottsdale, Arizona; Stu Cook, b. 25 April 1945, Oakland, California; Doug Clifford, b. 24 April 1945, Palo Alto, California

The most popular rock band in America in the late sixties, Creedence found success with a churning, riff-based, modernist version of rockabilly. Their music melded nostalgia for a more innocent vision of America ('Proud Mary'*, 'Green River', 1969) with John Fogerty's increasingly acerbic songs about contemporary America ('Fortunate Son', 1969; 'Who'll Stop the

Train', 1970) and his reflective accounts of life on and off the road ('Lodi', 1969; 'Travelin' Band'*, 'Lookin' Out My Back Door'*, 1970).

The group was formed as the Blue Velvets (with Tom Fogerty singing lead) at El Cerrito junior high school in 1959. In 1961–2 they recorded for the San Francisco Orchestra label, before in 1964 they signed to Fantasy Records as the Golliwogs, recording several singles (most notably **Van Morrison**'s 'Brown-Eyed Girl') in a pastiche of the British group sound then swamping America. When that sound ebbed and psychedelia took root in San Francisco in 1967, Fantasy's new owner Saul Zaentz encouraged a turn to American roots music (rock'n'roll and country) and gave the band a new name – Creedence Clearwater Revival.

A 1968 reworking of Dale Hawkins' 'Suzie Q' (Checker, 1957) was a Top Twenty hit and their eponymous début album also included a revival of **Screamin' Jay Hawkins**' 'I Put a Spell on You'. These established the Creedence style with John Fogerty's fervent, rough vocals prominent over a solid, spare rhythm, but it was *Bayou Country* (1969) which included the oft-covered 'Proud Mary' (**Solomon Burke**, 1969; **Ike and Tina Turner**, 1971) that set the tenor for their subsequent releases. Just as **The Beatles** developed their sound through listening at a distance to American rock'n'roll and R&B, so John Fogerty, equally distanced from the American South that gave him inspiration, built from these influences a highly individual sound, climaxing in the classic *Willie and the Poor Boys* and *Cosmo's Factory* (1970). As well as reworkings of **Elvis Presley**'s 'My Baby Left Me', **Roy Orbison**'s 'Oooby Dooby' and **Marvin Gaye**'s 'I Heard It Through the Grapevine', the latter album included 'Lookin' out My Back Door', 'Long As I Can See the Light' and the chilling 'Run Through the Jungle'. Other hits of this period included 'Bad Moon Rising'*, 'Down on the Corner'* (1969), 'Up Around the Bend'* (1970) and 'Sweet Hitch-Hiker' (1971).

Following the lesser *Pendulum* (1971) John Fogerty relinquished control of the group and the flawed *Mardi Gras* (1972) saw the three members (Tom Fogerty left in 1971) sharing songwriting and vocals. Its artistic failure and dissension within the group and with Fantasy led to Creedence disbanding in 1972. Tom Fogerty recorded several solo albums for Fantasy (including *Excalibur*, 1973, and *Deal It Out*, 1981) and cut two albums with the group Ruby. Drummer Clifford and bassist Cook played with **Doug Sahm** on *Groovers Paradise* (1974) and from 1976 backed Don Harrison. Cook also moved into production with former lead singer of the Thirteenth Elevators Roky Erikson (*The Aliens*, Columbia, 1980), among others.

Far more successful was John Fogerty. His last recording for Fantasy was the solo album *Blue Ridge*

Rangers (1973) in which, in the guise of a group, he recorded a collection of country standards, ranging from **Merle Haggard**'s 'Today I Started Loving You Again' to **George Jones'** 'She Thinks I Still Care', two of which (**Hank Williams**' 'Jambalaya' and 'Hearts of Stone') were pop hits. After signing to Asylum he released *John Fogerty* (1975), which included more reworkings (**Jackie Wilson**'s 'Lonely Teardrops' and **Frankie Ford**'s 'Sea Cruise') and 'Almost Saturday Night' and 'Rockin' All Over the World', British hits for **Dave Edmunds** (1981) and **Status Quo** (1977), respectively.

Fogerty refrained from recording for a decade until he made the hugely successful *Centerfield* (Warners, 1985). Just how little his sound had changed was evident when Fantasy unsuccessfully sued him for infringing his own 'Run Through the Jungle' on the album's hit single 'The Old Man Down the Road'. 'Big Train (From Memphis)', a tribute to Sun Records (and later recorded by **Johnny Cash**, Roy Orbison, **Jerry Lee Lewis** and **Carl Perkins**, with Fogerty in support, on their 1986 reunion album, *Class of '55*) saw Fogerty looking backwards again but other tracks (notably 'I Saw It on TV') marked a growing bitterness about contemporary America in his writing. Less commercially successful was the even bleaker *Eye of the Zombie* (1986). He has been largely inactive since then, performing only at benefit events such as the San Francisco memorial concert for promoter Bill Graham in 1991. In 1998 he issued *Blue Moon Swamp*, which as its title indicated saw Fogerty pursuing Louisiana-styled musics. That was followed by the live *Premonition* (1999) and a return to touring in 2000 when he opened for Tina Turner.

THE CRESTS

Johnny Maestro, b. John Mastrangelo, 7 May 1939, Brooklyn, New York, USA; Jay Carter, b. 1939, Brooklyn (replaced by Eddie Wright in 1960); Harold Torres, b. 1940, Staten Island, New York (replaced by Chuck Foote in 1960); Tommy Gough, b. 1940, Staten Island (replaced by Leonard Alexander in 1960)

In contrast to most of the doo-wop groups of the fifties whose chart career was limited to a major hit and a couple of minor successes – more often than not in the R&B rather than the pop charts, for example, the Crows, the **Five Satins**, the Penguins and the Chords – the Crests managed to build a career on the basis of their big hit.

Formed in the late fifties, the racially mixed Crests were a typical New York vocal group. After briefly recording for Joyce Records ('Sweetest One', 1957), they signed to another independent, Coed. Their first hit was a paean to teenagedom, 'Sixteen Candles' (1958). A slow ballad featuring Maestro's light and wistful lead vocals, it was a Top Ten hit in both the pop and R&B charts. Other, equally melodic, Top Twenty hits included 'The Angels Listened In', 'Step by Step' (1959) and 'Trouble in Paradise' (1960), which featured a new line-up.

After a couple of minor hits in 1960, on which the group was billed as 'featuring Johnny Maestro', Maestro quit for a solo career that produced a couple of hits in 1961, 'Model Girl' and 'What a Surprise'. After several unsuccessful years, Maestro formed Brooklyn Bridge in 1968, and returned to the Top Ten for the first time in ten years with 'The Worst That Could Happen' (Buddah). Other, lesser, hits for the group included 'Welcome My Love' (1969) and 'Down by the River' (1970). In the seventies Maestro turned to the rock'n'roll revival circuit.

THE CREW CUTS

John Perkins, b. 28 August 1931, Toronto, Canada; Pat Barrett, b. 15 September 1933, Toronto; Rudi Maugeri, b. 27 January 1931, Toronto; Ray Perkins, b. 28 November 1932, Toronto

Described by one critic as singing 'rhythm and barber-shop harmony', the Crew Cuts specialized in cover-versions of R&B hits.

Formed at college in Toronto by the Perkins brothers and childhood friends Barrett and Maugeri, the group first called themselves the Canadaires. After an appearance on Gene Carroll's televised talent show, they were signed by Mercury in 1954 and given a new name to highlight their hairstyles. Their first hit, 'Crazy 'Bout You Baby' (1954), was written by Maugeri and Barrett, but real success came later that year with their million-selling cover of the Chords' classic 'Sh-Boom', which is often considered to be the first rock'n'roll hit. Introduced by the beguiling words 'Life could be a dream', the Chords' 'Sh-Boom' (on Atlantic's subsidiary Cat label) was a surreal collection of clichés sung over an infectious, bouncy rhythm; if the Crew Cuts' version was blander, because it had the advantages of national distribution it helped introduce the sounds of rock'n'roll to a wider, white audience. Thus, the Chords' record was a hit in the R&B charts and the Crew Cuts' in the pop charts.

In the few years before the arrival of white rock'n'roll styles in the wake of **Elvis Presley**, the Crew Cuts had a series of hits with covers of black recordings. These include 'Oop-Shoop' (originally recorded by Shirley Gunter on Flair), 1954; 'Earth Angel' (the Penguins); 'Ko Ko Mo', which was also covered by **Perry Como** (Gene and Eunice, Aladdin); 'Don't Be Angry' (**Nappy Brown**); 'A Story Untold' (the Nutmegs, Herald), all 1955; and 'Seven Days' (**Clyde McPhatter**, Atlantic) in 1956. Their hitmaking

days ended with a cover, not of a black but of a country recording. 'Young Love' (1956) was originally a hit for **Sonny James** and was a million-selling pop hit for Tab Hunter, who had better credentials than the Crew Cuts for a career as a teen-idol.

With the failure of such later attempts at bandwagon jumping as *Crew Necks and Khakis* and *The Crew Cuts Go Folk*, the group split up in 1963.

BOB CREWE
b. 12 November 1931, Newark, New Jersey, USA

Crewe began his music career as a demo singer before moving into production and becoming one of the most successful pop producers of the sixties.

He teamed with Frank Slay in 1953 as a writer, and as a singer recorded without success for Jubilee, Spotlight and many other labels. In 1956 the duo moved into production, working with doo-wop groups like the Rays, and in 1957 formed their own XYZ label. Their first hit, 'Silhouettes' by the Rays, was leased to Cameo Records in Philadelphia where the duo subsequently based themselves, eventually becoming partners in the Swan label and writing and producing hits for **Freddy Cannon**, Billie and Lillie and other Swan artists. In 1959 Crewe and Slay parted company and Crewe embarked on a solo career, scoring a minor hit with 'The Whiffenpoof Song' (Warwick, 1961), which had earlier been a hit for **Rudy Vallee** (1946) and **Bing Crosby** (1947). It was around this time too that Crewe met Frankie Valli and his group, using them for demos and for one-off releases under a variety of names, before eventually settling on the **Four Seasons**. Crewe recorded them under that name, first for Gone records ('Bermuda', 1962), then on an independent production leased to Chicago's Vee-Jay label ('Sherry', 1962).

That record's instant success (it went to No. 1) hurled Crewe into a non-stop round of writing and production, mainly in partnership with the group's Bob Gaudio. In the mid-sixties he formed New Voice and Dyno Voice records, producing hits for Norma Tanega ('Walking My Cat Named Dog') and a string of successes for **Mitch Ryder and the Detroit Wheels**, including 'Devil with a Blues Dress', 'Sock It to Me Baby' and 'Shake a Tail Feather'. He enjoyed his own biggest hit with the instrumental 'Music to Watch Girls By' (Dyno Voice) in 1966.

In 1969, when the Four Seasons' fame was in decline, he formed Crewe records, and had hits with Oliver ('Good Morning Starshine', from *Hair*, and 'Jean'*, 1969) before joining Motown as a producer, at the same time as the Four Seasons were signed to the label. Among the many items he co-wrote and produced there was the Valli comeback hit 'My Eyes Adored You'. In 1974 he returned to both independent production – scoring hits with Disco Tex and the Sex-o-lettes ('Get Dancin'', Chelsea) – and writing – with new partner Kenny Nolan, he penned hits like the chart-topping 'Lady Marmalade'* (Epic, 1975) for **Patti Labelle**'s Labelle.

The mid-seventies saw a flurry of writing and production work, built around the international comeback of the Four Seasons, and Crewe surrounded himself with many of the writers and producers he had nurtured during the sixties, including Denny Randell, Sandy Linzer and Charles Callello. In 1977, at the height of the disco craze, he signed a solo contract with Elektra and released *Motivation* (produced by **Jerry Wexler**) before being involved in a serious car accident.

THE CRICKETS

Jerry Ivan Allison, b. 31 August 1939, Hillsboro, Texas, USA; Sonny Curtis, b. 9 May 1937, Meadow, Texas; Glen D. Hardin, b. 18 April 1939, Wellington, Texas; Jerry Naylor, b. 6 March 1939, Chalk Mountain, Texas; Ric Grech, b. 1 November 1946, Bordeaux, France; Albert Lee, b. 21 December 1943, Leominster, England

Originally the group led by **Buddy Holly**, the Crickets split from him shortly before his death in 1959 to pursue careers as a pop band in the sixties and a country-rock group in the seventies.

Led by drummer Allison (who had recorded 'Real Wild Child' as Ivan in 1958, a song revived in 1987 by **Iggy Pop**) and guitarist Curtis, the group had seven chart entries in Britain between 1959 and 1964, due to their association with Holly, whose popularity was greater in Europe than America. These ranged over a variety of styles as the group followed the musical trends of the era. 'Love's Made a Fool of You' (Coral, 1958) was an unsubtle version of a Holly–Bob Montgomery song, with vocals by Earl Sinks, while 'More Than I Can Say' (1960), a Curtis–Allison composition, was sung in the manner of **Bobby Vee**, for whom it was a Top Ten hit. The Crickets recorded an album of Holly material with Vee in 1962.

Their best records of this era were the 'Peggy Sue'-styled 'My Little Girl' (from the 1963 British film *Just for Fun*), and the **Carole King**–Gerry Goffin song 'Don't Ever Change' (both Liberty, 1962). The lead vocalist on the latter was Los Angeles session man Naylor, while his songwriting partner **Glen Campbell** played guitar.

Now featuring pianist Hardin, later to play in **Elvis Presley**'s band, the Crickets cut a **Leon Russell** arrangement of the **Ritchie Valens** song 'La Bamba' (Liberty, 1964), which owed more than a touch to **The Beatles**' version of 'Twist and Shout'. It was featured in the 1965 movie *The Girls on the Beach*, whose music supervisor was Nik Venet.

In 1965 the group officially dissolved, with Naylor moving into television and Allison and Curtis concentrating on session work. When the group re-formed in 1971, it was rock revival time, as the title of their Barnaby album, *Rockin' 50s Rock'n'Roll*, showed. Their best recording of this period was Allison's song 'My Rockin' Days' from *Bubblegum, Bop Ballads and Boogie* (Philips, 1973). However, the seventies Crickets, which included songwriter Steve Krikorian and European musicians Lee (guitar) and Grech (bass), also purveyed low-key but effective country rock, notably on their final album, *A Long Way from Lubbock* (Mercury, 1974).

Paul McCartney's 1976 purchase of publishing rights in Holly songs led to occasional re-formations of the group in later years, but the Crickets did not record again until 1988's *Three Piece*. Released on Allison's own Rollercoaster label it became *T-Shirt* (1989) when reissued on CBS with the addition of a new title song, the winner of a song-writing contest organized by their British publisher Paul McCartney. The pared-down group now comprised Allison, Mauldin and singer-guitarist Gordon Payne.

JIM CROCE

b. 10 January 1943, Philadelphia, Pennsylvania, USA, d. 20 September 1973, Natchitoches, Louisiana

More intimate than **Neil Diamond** and less self-obsessed than **James Taylor**, Croce was an engaging singer-songwriter. His best-known songs were 'You Don't Mess Around with Jim' (1972) and 'Time in a Bottle'* (1973). His career was ended by a plane crash.

In 1961 Croce was a folk and blues disc-jockey at Villa-Nova university, where he met songwriter Tommy West and played in local rock bands. He later learned accordion and worked as a truck-driver before moving to New York in 1967.

Two years later Croce and his wife Ingrid signed to Capitol for *Approaching Day*. He was next produced by West and Jim Cashman on *You Don't Mess Around with Jim* (ABC, 1972). With rhythmic acoustic guitar accompaniment by Maury Muehleisen, both 'Operator' and the title track were American hits.

In the following year Croce released *Life and Times* and the story-song 'Bad Bad Leroy Brown'* reached No. 1 before he was killed. The posthumously released *I Got a Name* reached No. 2 while the ruminative 'Time in a Bottle' was used on the soundtrack of *The Last American Hero* and became his second No. 1.

Croce's releases continued to sell in 1974 when the gently melodic 'I'll Have to Say I Love You in a Song' reached the Top Ten and the light-hearted 'Workin' at the Car Wash Blues' was a minor hit. Cashman and West, whose own hits included 'Medicine Man' (Event, 1969) as the Buchanan Brothers and 'American City Suite' (Dunhill, 1972), later released the collections of Croce material *Photographs and Memories* (1975) and *The Faces I've Been* on their Lifesong label.

In 1993 his son A. J. Croce made his début as a recording artist with a jazz-influenced eponymous album produced by T-Bone Burnett on RCA Records.

CROSBY, STILLS AND NASH
David Crosby, b. David van Cortland, 14 August 1941, Los Angeles, California, USA; Stephen Stills, b. 3 January 1945, Dallas, Texas; Graham Nash, b. 2 February 1942, Blackpool, England

The epitome of 'laid-back' harmony singing in the progressive-rock era of the late sixties, Crosby Stills and Nash, with **Neil Young**, re-formed periodically to cater to a nostalgic demand among their audiences.

All three singer-songwriter-guitarists had been members of prestigious rock groups: Crosby had been with the **Byrds** until 1967, Stills with **Buffalo Springfield**, which split in 1968, and Nash had left the **Hollies** the same year. Through **Joni Mitchell**, whose first album Crosby had produced, they started jamming together and in 1969 recorded their eponymous first album for Atlantic.

Crosby Stills and Nash was a *tour de force* of close-harmony singing, with Nash taking the high tenor parts. It produced two hit singles, Nash's anthem of the hippie trail to north Africa, 'Marrakesh Express', and Stills' 'Suite: Judy Blue Eyes', dedicated to **Judy Collins**. Appropriately, one of their first live appearances was at the Woodstock Festival.

Instrumentally, the group's sound was semi-acoustic soft rock, but this became heavier when Young, with his harsher songs and electric guitar battles with Stills, joined the line-up in 1970. *Déjà Vu* (1970) had advance orders of over two million in America and was the classic statement of Woodstock era euphoria, with Mitchell's celebratory 'Woodstock' providing the group with a further Top Twenty hit. Other outstanding tracks were Crosby's paranoic 'Almost Cut My Hair' and the exultant 'Carry on' with its 'rejoice, rejoice, we have no choice' refrain. The rhythm section of Greg Reeves (bass) and Dallas Taylor (drums) was added for the album and live gigs.

Four Way Street (1971) was a double-album taken from those performances, which exposed the weakness of CSN and Y as a group as well as the brilliance of its individual members. Besides being a 'supergroup' it was a group of super egos, and personality clashes, particularly between Young and Stills, led to its dissolution at the end of 1970.

There was a reunion tour in 1974 and trio albums without Young: the listless *CSN* (Atlantic 1977), with its hit single 'Just a Song Before I Go', and *Daylight Again* (1982), from which 'Wasted on the Way' made

the Top Ten. But for most of the next decade each pursued a solo career. Nash recorded the critically acclaimed *Tales for Beginners* (Atlantic, 1971) and two further albums. He also cut two undistinguished duets with Crosby, whose solo output was confined to 1971's *If I Could Only Remember My Name*.

Stills was the most prolific, releasing six albums by 1978, the first two with Manassas, a group featuring ex-Byrd Chris Hillman. The Latin-flavoured 'Love the One You're With' was a hit on both sides of the Atlantic in 1971 for both Stills and the **Isley Brothers**.

The pattern was much the same during the eighties, with performances at anti-nuclear and anti-war benefits and one successful group album *Daylight Again* (1982) followed by the less successful live set *Allies* (1983). In that year Crosby was jailed on a firearms charge. A further sentence in 1986 for drugs offences was followed by a grand reunion with Stills, Nash and Young when they performed at a benefit with **Bruce Springsteen**, thus reaffirming their credentials as a part of rock's élite. Both Stills and Nash were quiet in the eighties, Stills releasing only one solo album (*Right by You*, WEA, 1984) and Nash two (*Earth and Sky*, 1980, and *Innocent Eyes*, Atlantic, 1986). Nash also briefly rejoined the Hollies in 1983. 1988 brought polite reviews for a new CSNY album, *American Dream*, which included Crosby's autobiographical 'The Compass'. The following year Crosby published his autobiography *Long Time Gone* (with Carl Gottlieb) and released *Oh Yes I Can* (A&M), which showed a welcome return to form. It was followed in 1993 by *Thousand Roads*, which included the minor hit 'Hero', a collaboration with **Phil Collins**. The minor CSN album *Live It Up* (1990) included a guest appearance by Branford Marsalis, while the group's history was documented in the four-CD boxed set *CSN* (1991).

After appearing at the Woodstock '94 festival, the group released *After the Storm*, a minor offering briefly enlivened by their sweet version of **The Beatles**' 'In My Life'. In 1999 the trio re-formed with Young clearly at the helm for *Looking Forward*, their bestselling album of new material in two decades. The group toured to sell-out audiences but, as on the album, in live performance the group seemed schizophrenic with CSN happy in nostalgia mood and Young, as ever, in the manner of **Bob Dylan**, re-examining his past and pondering the future. Aptly, the title song of the reunion album is his.

BING CROSBY
b. Harry Lillis Crosby, 2 May 1903, Tacoma, Washington, USA, d. 14 October 1977, Madrid, Spain

Affectionately known as 'The Old Groaner', Crosby was the most successful recording artist of the twentieth century and the most prolific. He recorded over 2,500 titles and sold more than 250 million records, including over twenty individual million-sellers. 'White Christmas' (1942) alone had sales of some 30 million. Moreover, Crosby's crooning represented a decisive shift in singing styles. In contrast to earlier singers who sang with a precise (often stilted) diction and phrasing, Crosby introduced a looser, more relaxed approach that formed the basis of the styles of singers as diverse as **Tony Bennett**, **Frank Sinatra** and **Perry Como**. Just as Crosby's innovatory singing style was made possible by the introduction of electrical recording (which required less volume and allowed more expression), so his career represented the coming together of the radio, recording and film industries. He first found stardom through radio and subsequently his film and recording career were mutually supportive, in great part because his resonant baritone voice and affable persona perfectly suited all three media.

Raised in Spokane, Crosby acquired the nickname Bing, after a cartoon character, while at high school. In 1920, while studying law at Gonzaga University, he joined the Musicaladers, a band organized by fellow student Al Rinker (the brother of **Mildred Bailey**). In 1925 he and Rinker toured as Two Boys and a Piano and in 1926 (after Crosby's first commercial recording, 'I've Got the Girl', Columbia) the pair were hired by **Paul Whiteman**, who teamed them with Harry Barris to form the Rhythm Boys vocal group. Between 1927 and 1929, when they appeared in *King of Jazz*, the trio were featured on several Whiteman recordings ('Side by Side', 'I'm Coming Home Virginia', 1927, and 'Changes', 1928, which also included **Bix Beiderbecke**'s most famous cornet solo with the Whiteman band).

In 1930 the Rhythm Boys left Whiteman and were featured in several films, including *Check and Double Check* (1930) in which they sang with the **Duke Ellington** Orchestra. Billed as Bing Crosby and the Rhythm Boys, they joined and recorded with Gus Arnheim's Hollywood-based orchestra before in 1931 Crosby went solo and signed to Brunswick. In September of that year Crosby started the nationally networked radio show which won him a huge following for his warm, relaxed, intimate singing style, best represented by the show's theme song 'Where the Blue of the Night Meets the Gold of the Day' (1931, based on **Gilbert and Sullivan**'s 'Tit-Willow' from *The Mikado*), which was also featured in the singer's starring film début, *The Big Broadcast of 1932*.

From the start of his solo career a high proportion of Crosby's recordings were of film and show songs. Initially these were cover-versions like the No. 1s 'Out of Nowhere' (1931), **Yip Harburg**'s 'Brother Can You Spare a Dime?' (1932), 'You're Getting to Be a Habit with Me' and 'Shadow Waltz', both by **Harry Warren**

and Al Dubin, 'The Last Round-Up' (1933) and **Nacio Herb Brown**'s 'Temptation' (1934). From 1934, when he signed with Paramount Studios, however, Crosby started recording material specifically written for his own films. Crosby's thirties films were light musicals in which he played the romantic lead. These included *Here Is My Heart* (1934), *Rhythm on the Range* (1936), *Waikiki Wedding* (1937), which featured his first million-seller, the Hawaiian-styled 'Leilani', and *Paris Honeymoon* (1939). Among his biggest hits of the period were 'Love in Bloom' (1934, one of his last Brunswick recordings before joining **Jack Kapp**'s newly established Decca later that year), 'June in January' (Decca, 1934), 'Soon', 'I Wished on the Moon', 'The Moon Got in My Eyes' (1935), 'I've Got a Pocketful of Dreams' and 'You Must have Been a Beautiful Baby' (1938), on which he was accompanied by the band of his brother, **Bob Crosby**.

In 1940 Crosby made *Road to Singapore*, the first of seven films in which, teamed with Bob Hope and Dorothy Lamour, he gently parodied his earlier romantic roles and established an easy-going screen persona to match his singing voice. The second *Road* film, *Zanzibar* (1941), included the hit 'It's Always You' by **Jimmy Van Heusen** who, with Johnny Burke (and later **Sammy Cahn**), would write songs for eighteen of Crosby's films. Among the hits they provided for Crosby were 'Moonlight Becomes You' (*Morocco*, 1942); 'Personality' (*Utopia*, 1945); the Oscar-winning 'Swinging on a Star'* from *Going My Way* (1944), for which Crosby also won an Oscar for his sentimental portrayal of a priest who brings hope to the slum children of New York; 'Aren't You Glad You're You' (from the sequel *The Bells of St Mary's*, 1945); and 'Sunshine Cake' (*Riding High*, 1950). His most successful film of the period was *Holiday Inn* (1942) with **Fred Astaire**, in which he introduced **Irving Berlin**'s 'White Christmas', the most popular secular Christmas song of all time. Crosby subsequently had success with other seasonal songs, 'Silent Night'* (1942), 'Jingle Bells'* (1943) and **Johnny Marks**' 'Rudolph the Red-Nosed Reindeer' (1950).

In the forties Crosby also regularly recorded material first popularized by country artists. 'Tumbling Tumbleweeds' (1940) was originally a hit for the **Sons of the Pioneers** (1934), 'New San Antonio Rose' (1941) came from **Bob Wills** (1940) and 'Pistol Packin' Mama'* (1944), the first of his six million-sellers with the **Andrews Sisters**, was originally a hit for **Al Dexter** (1943). With the Andrews Sisters Crosby also recorded **Cole Porter**'s parody of a cowboy song 'Don't Fence Me in'* (1944). In addition, Crosby recorded 'Irish' songs ('McNamara's Band'*, 1945; 'Galway Bay'*, 1947) and other exotica such as 'Now Is the Hour'* (1948), based on a traditional New Zealand Maori song.

Though the Andrews Sisters were Crosby's most frequent recording partners, throughout his career he recorded numerous duets with other artists. Among these were the **Mills Brothers** ('Dinah'; 'Shine', 1932), Connee Boswell of the **Boswell Sisters** ('Basin Street Blues', 1937; 'Alexander's Ragtime Band', 1938; 'An Apple for the Teacher', 1939), **Johnny Mercer** ('Mister Meadowlark', 1940), **Louis Jordan** ('My Baby Said Yes', 1945), **Les Paul** ('It's Been a Long, Long Time', 1945), **Judy Garland** ('Ya-Ta-Ta, Yah-Ta-Ta [Talk, Talk, Talk]', 1945), **Mel Tormé** ('Day by Day', 1946), **Al Jolson** ('Alexander's Ragtime Band'*, 1947), **Louis Armstrong** ('Gone Fishing', 1951; 'Now You Has Jazz', 1956), **Peggy Lee** ('Watermelon Weather', 1952), and even his son Gary ('Sam's Song'*, 1950; 'Down by the Riverside', 1954).

In the fifties Crosby played a dramatic film role in *The Country Girl* (1954), but his greatest success was in *High Society* (1954), a musical version of Philip Barry's Broadway play *The Philadelphia Story* (1939) with songs by Cole Porter, including Crosby's and Frank Sinatra's performance of 'Well Did You Evah'. The film also gave Crosby his last major hit, the duet with Grace Kelly, 'True Love'. After occasional film appearances in the sixties, notably in the last *Road* picture, *Hong Kong* (1960), Crosby retired. His last major role was as the on-screen narrator of *That's Entertainment* (1974).

BOB CROSBY
b. George Robert Crosby, 25 August 1913, Spokane, Washington, USA

Like his elder brother **Bing Crosby**, Bob was a singer, but his greater importance was as the leader of an orchestra that emphasized Dixieland jazz in an era dominated by swing.

He first sang professionally with Anton Weeks in San Francisco and in 1934 joined the orchestra led by **Tommy** and **Jimmy Dorsey**, recording 'Basin Street Blues' and other tracks with them for Decca. The following year Crosby was chosen to front a band made up from former members of Ben Pollack's orchestra. During the next seven years the Bob Crosby Orchestra became one of America's most popular jazz-inflected dance bands.

Through the arrangements of clarinettist Matty Matlock and bassist Bob Haggart, the band and its 'group within a group', the Bobcats, recorded numerous Dixieland jazz standards. These included 'Muskrat Ramble', **Louis Armstrong**'s 'Sugar Foot Strut' (Decca, 1936) and 'South Rampart Street Parade' (1937), the band's best-known number. A novelty version of 'Big Noise from Winnetka', on which drummer Ray Bauduc played on Haggart's strings, proved popular but the band's only million-

seller came when they backed Bing Crosby on a version of **Bob Wills**' Western ballad 'San Antonio Rose' (1940). Other hits of the period included 'Whispers in the Dark' (1937), **Johnny Mercer**'s 'Day in Day out' (1939) and **Harry Warren**'s and Mack Gordon's film theme 'Down Argentina Way' (1940).

Boogie-woogie and blues also featured in the Crosby band's repertoire. Pianist Bob Zurke was a fervent if sometimes mechanical boogie player and recorded **Meade Lux Lewis**'s 'Honky Tonk Train Blues' (1938), while in the same year the band covered **Big Bill Broonzy**'s 'Louise Louise' and Kokomo Arnold's 'Milk Cow Blues'.

The Crosby orchestra split up in 1942 and Crosby later led a services band. After 1945 he occasionally led new bands but he concentrated on a radio and TV career, and had his own Australian television series in the sixties. During the seventies Crosby re-formed his orchestra for festivals and concert tours while the small-group Dixieland style was maintained by the World's Greatest Jazz Band, led by ex-Bobcats Haggart and Yank Lawson (trumpet).

CHRISTOPHER CROSS
b. Christopher Geppert, 1951, San Antonio, Texas, USA

A vocalist, guitarist and songwriter, Cross was one of the most successful AOR ballad singers of the early eighties.

The son of an army officer, Cross formed Flash, a bar band specializing in covers of current hits, which by 1972 was San Antonio's top group. The following year he left the group to concentrate on songwriting. Demo recordings he made with a band led by Rob Meurer (keyboards) led to a contract with Warner Brothers in 1978. His eponymous first album produced by Michael Omartian was released in 1980. With vocal assistance from Michael McDonald of the **Doobie Brothers** and ex-**Eagles** Don Henley, plus guitar work by Larry Carlton of the **Crusaders**, the album produced four hit singles, including 'Ride Like the Wind' and the No. 1 'Sailing' (not the 1975 **Rod Stewart** hit). It also won Cross five Grammy awards.

In 1981 he scored his second American No. 1 and only British hit with the theme from the Dudley Moore movie, *Arthur*, 'Arthur's Theme (Best that You Can Do)', co-written with **Burt Bacharach** and Carole Bayer Sager. Further success came in 1983 with 'All Right', 'No Time for Talk' and 'Think of Laura', which was popularized through repeated plays on the teleseries *General Hospital*. The 1985 album *Every Turn of the World* and *Back of My Mind* (Reprise, 1988) made less impact. In 1992 he released the unexceptional *Rendezvous* (Ariola), which was less successful than a new version of 'Ride Like the Wind' by East Side Beat, which was a Top Ten hit in Britain in 1991.

ANDRAE CROUCH
b. 1 July 1942, Los Angeles, California, USA

One of the most successful contemporary gospel performers, Crouch duetted with **Stevie Wonder** and his
work was recorded by **Paul Simon**.

As a teenager, he played the piano and led the choir
in his father's church in east Los Angeles. His songwriting began when he organized a vocal group
among ex-addicts on a rehabilitation programme.
Crouch's first recordings were made with the COGIC
Singers on Vee-Jay, whose name came from the
Church of God in Christ tabernacle, from whose choir
the group was formed. Other members of the COGIC
Singers included **Billy Preston**, Crouch's twin sister
Sandra, and Edna Wright, later a member of the Hon-
eycone, a **Supremes**-style vocal group which had two
1971 million-sellers – 'Want Ads' and 'Stick-up' – on
Holland, Dozier and Holland's Hot Wax label.

Crouch next formed Andrae Crouch and the Disciples with Billy Thedford, recording *Take the Message
Everywhere* (Light, 1969) and *Keep on Singing* (1970).
Primetime television appearances brought a crossover
white audience which was consolidated by the Latin,
jazz and R&B elements added to *Soulfully*.

Throughout the seventies he continued a policy of
melding gospel messages and singing with current
rock and soul musical styles. Simon recorded his
'Jesus Is the Answer' on *Live Rhymin'* (1974) while
Leon Russell and the **Crusaders**' Joe Sample were
session players on *This Is Another Day* (1982). In 1981
Crouch recorded a single with Stevie Wonder ('I'll Be
Thinking of You') and a year later cut a solo album,
Don't Give Up (Warners).

In the eighties Crouch released live albums recorded
in New York and London while the singers on his
fourteenth release *No Time to Lose* (Myrrh, 1984)
included Krystle Edwards and ex-Motown artist Tata
Vega. In 1985 he produced a solo album by his sister
Sandra and was nominated for an Oscar for his contribution to the score of Steven Spielberg's *The Color
Purple*. By this time, Crouch had established a chain of
ministries and had become a middle-of-the-road evangelist, in the manner of Billy Graham and **Pat Boone**.

Mercy (1994), recorded for **Quincy Jones**' Qwest
label, was Crouch's first album for ten years.

SHERYL CROW
b. 11 February 1962, Kennett, Missouri, USA

Singer-songwriter Crow graduated from singing
backing vocals live with **Michael Jackson** to becoming one of America's top-selling female performers of
the nineties with a trio of albums steeped in R&B.

Growing up in the rural Mississippi region of the
US, Crow moved to St. Louis after she graduated

from high school and began to sing in R&B covers
bands. She spent much of the 1980s working as a
backing singer for such artists as **Rod Stewart** and **Joe
Cocker**, but became disillusioned with her career at
the turn of the decade. Her bluesy début, *Tuesday
Night Music Club** (A&M, 1993), was born out of a
series of weekly jams with local musicians, going
multi-platinum in the US after the success of the
upbeat 'All I Wanna Do'. Its commercial and critical
success was largely as a result of her ability to be both
mainstream and personal, to write intriguing verses
with strong hooks as their choruses.

Crow released her eponymous second album* in
1996, which included three big hits – 'If It Makes You
Happy', 'Everyday Is a Winding Road' and 'A Change
(Will Do You Good)' – and broke the singer in
Britain. The following year she wrote and performed
the title track to the James Bond movie *Tomorrow
Never Dies* (1997), and toured with the **Rolling Stones**.

The Globe Sessions (1998)* sold equally as well as its
predecessors and won Crow a Grammy Award for
Best Rock Album. The live album *Live from Central
Park* (2000), which saw her supported by the likes of
Rolling Stone Keith Richards, **Eric Clapton** (reportedly the subject of 'My Favourite Mistake') and the
Pretenders Chrissie Hynde, was essentially a holding
operation consisting of mostly relaxed versions of
classics ('White Room').

CROWDED HOUSE
*Neil Mullane Finn, b. 27 May 1958, Te Awamutu, New
Zealand; Paul Hester, b. Melbourne, Australia; Craig
Hooper; Nick Seymour, b. Melbourne; Tim Finn, b. 25
June 1952, Te Awamutu*

Probably the most successful New Zealand rock musicians, Neil and Tim Finn are noted for their melodic,
Beatles-influenced sound.

Crowded House was the successor group to Split
Enz, which had been formed in Auckland, New
Zealand, in 1972 by singer and pianist Tim Finn. The
band moved to Australia in 1975 and a year later to
England, where **Roxy Music** guitarist Phil Manzanera
produced the album *Second Thoughts* (Chrysalis).
Brother Neil Finn joined the group in 1977. Split Enz's
most successful album was *True Colours* (1979).

In 1985 Tim Finn left for a solo career while Neil
Finn, bass-player Seymour and drummer Paul Hester
formed a new band. Originally known as the Mul-
lanes, they settled on Crowded House in 1986. An
eponymous album was issued in that year on Capitol
for which the duo were joined by guitarist Hooper. It
was produced in Los Angeles by Mitchell Froom. A
big hit in the USA, it included the Top Ten single
'Don't Dream It's Over'.

Hooper had left the band by the time the less

accomplished *Temple of Low Men* was released in 1988. In 1989 an EP of recordings with Roger McGuinn of the **Byrds** was issued as *Byrdhouse*. The group temporarily disbanded in 1990 when Neil Finn and his brother worked together on new songs. These became the basis of *The Woodface*, a new Crowded House album for which Tim joined the group. The album produced big hits in Britain with 'Fall at Your feet' and 'Weather with You' (1992).

Once again a trio, Crowded House recorded *Together Alone* in New Zealand with producers Bob Clearmountain and Youth for release in 1993. The album included contributions from Polynesian drummers, a brass band and a Maori choir. Tim Finn issued a solo album *Before & After* in the same year, shortly after the Finn brothers had been awarded the Order of the British Empire for services to New Zealand music.

In 1994 Neil Finn took a break from playing with Crowded House to produce an album for Dave Dobbyn and work with Tim on their long awaited collaborative début, *The Finn Brothers* (1995). The following year he officially broke up Crowded House, releasing a highly successful compilation, *Recurring Dream: The Very Best of Crowded House*, and playing a final show with the band in front of 100,000 fans at the Sydney Opera House. Within a year Hester had formed a new band, Largest Living Things, to modest domestic success. Neil Finn had an international hit with his solo début, *Try Whistling This* (1998), which added programmed percussion to Crowded House acoustics.

ARTHUR 'BIG BOY' CRUDUP
b. 24 August 1905, Forest, Mississippi, USA, d. 28 March 1974, Nassawadox, Virginia

One of the bestselling blues artists of the forties, Crudup delivered scarcely modified field-hollers with an undertone of caressing sweetness. With their skeletal accompaniments – Crudup was a limited guitarist, and seldom used demonstrative sidemen – the performances were open and bare, ideal demo records of his insistently memorable compositions, which were widely taken up by blues and rockabilly artists. Most famous among these was **Elvis Presley**, whose first record for Sun in 1954 was Crudup's 'That's All Right' (originally recorded by its writer in 1946).

Crudup recorded regularly for RCA Victor from 1941 to 1954, producing such durable material as 'If I Get Lucky' (1941), 'Mean Old 'Frisco Blues' (1942), 'Who's Been Foolin' You' and 'Rock Me Mama' (1944), 'So Glad You're Mine' (1946) and 'My Baby Left Me' (1950). Presley also recorded these last two, while others of Crudup's compositions were reused or revised by **B. B. King**, **J. B. Lenoir**, Jimmy Rogers, and many others.

In the late forties and early fifties Crudup was a popular touring act in the South, often working with **Elmore James** and **Sonny Boy Williamson II** and sometimes broadcasting on KFFA, Helena, Arkansas. For most of the fifties and sixties he worked outside music, but he resumed his career in 1966 and in the following year began to appear at blues and folk festivals and made the album *Look on Yonder's Wall* (Delmark). In later years he toured Britain (1970) and Australia (1972), somewhat bemused by his billing – originally devised for an RCA reissue collection – as 'The Father of Rock'n'Roll'.

FRANK CRUMIT
b. 26 September 1889, Jackson, Ohio, USA, d. 7 September 1943, Longmeadow, Massachusetts

A jocular and inventive singer and writer of comic novelties, Crumit was a leading figure in stage, radio and recorded entertainment in the twenties and thirties.

After experience in vaudeville as a singer and ukulele player, he appeared in several Broadway shows, including *Greenwich Village Follies* and *Betty Be Good* (both 1920), *Tangerine* (1921) – his biggest hit, *Nifties of 1923* and *Moonlight* (1924). In some of these he worked alongside the actress/singer Julia Sanderson, whom he married in 1927. Transferred to radio in 1929, their partnership was particularly successful in 1933–4. From 1939 until his death Crumit hosted the radio game show *Battle of the Sexes*.

From 1919 onwards he recorded prolifically for Columbia and, from 1924, Victor, maintaining an output of conventional songs ('I'm Sitting on Top of the World', 1926, also a hit for **Al Jolson**, and later revived by **Les Paul**, 1953), novelty songs ('Crazy Words, Crazy Tune', 1927) and Broadway numbers ('Ida [Sweet as Apple Cider]', 1924, later revived by **Red Nichols** and **Glenn Miller**), while developing a speciality of reshaping traditional and minstrel-show songs. 'A Gay Caballero' and 'The Prune Song' (1928) were well-received examples in that vein, but by far his best-known number was the comic epic 'Abdul Abulbul Amir' (1928), which he re-composed from an original dating back to the Crimean War. Crumit also recorded the comic golfing numbers 'Donald the Dub' and 'And Then He Took up Golf', as well as 'Ukulele Lady' and the sentimental standard 'My Grandfather's Clock'.

In the eighties 'Abdul' was used as the basis for a television commercial for beer in Britain, where Crumit's records were reissued by ASV in 1981.

THE CRUSADERS
Wilton Felder, b. 31 August 1940, Houston, Texas, USA; Wayne Henderson, b. 24 September 1939, Houston; Stix

Hooper, b. Nesbert Hooper, 15 August 1938, Houston (replaced by Leon Ndugu Chancler); Joe Sample, b. 1 February 1939, Houston; Larry Carlton, b. 2 March 1948, Torrence, California; Robert Popwell

As the Jazz Crusaders, the group was a run-of-the-mill West Coast jazz band of the sixties. In the seventies they dropped 'jazz' from their name and became successful pioneers of jazz-funk.

Felder (bass, tenor sax), Hooper (drums) and Sample (keyboards) formed the Swingsters in Houston in the mid-fifties. With the addition of Henderson (trombone) and others, the group evolved into the Modern Jazz Sextet. In 1958 the four moved to Los Angeles, and under the name the Nighthawks worked as a dance band until they signed to World Pacific Jazz as the Jazz Crusaders in 1961. *Freedom Sound* (1961) was the first of fourteen albums recorded for the label during the sixties. None received critical acclaim or achieved significant sales and the Jazz Crusaders' members supplemented their income by session work, establishing themselves as among the most admired accompanists on their respective instruments.

The influences absorbed in these frequent pop and soul sessions contributed to the Crusaders' change of emphasis after 1970. The group signed first with Chisa, Motown's shortlived jazz label, before moving to Blue Thumb, a subsidiary of ABC. The catchy, rhythmic 'Put It Where You Want It' (1972) was a minor R&B hit and was covered in Britain by the **Average White Band**, whose sound was closely modelled on that of the Crusaders.

During the mid-seventies the group made two albums a year and had further singles successes with 'Don't Let It Get You Down' (1973) and 'Keep that Same Old Feeling' (1976). Henderson left the group in 1975 to concentrate fully on production and solo recordings for ABC and Polydor. The remaining trio brought in various West Coast session stalwarts including **Billy Preston**, bassist Chuck Rainey and Larry Carlton (guitar), who, with bassist Pops Popwell, became virtually a full-time member of the band. In 1975 the group toured with the **Rolling Stones** and the following year released the bestselling *Chain Reaction*.

From 1978 the individual Crusaders embarked on solo projects. Sample recorded *Rainbow Seeker* (1978) and *Carmel* (1979), Felder released *We All Have a Star* (1978), while Hooper's *The World Within* (1979) featured guest singer **Jerry Butler**. This 'guest-vocalist' approach was adopted by the Crusaders for their group albums beginning with *Street Life* (1979). The title track was sung by Randy Crawford (*b. Veronica Crawford, 1952, Macon, Georgia*) and became the Crusaders' only international pop hit, reaching the British Top Ten. Crawford toured with the group and

returned to a solo career, having further British chart success with 'One Day I'll Fly Away' (Warners, 1980), 'You Might Need Somebody' (1981) and her own composition 'Almaz' (1987).

In the late seventies the Crusaders helped to revitalize **B. B. King**'s career by accompanying him on the albums *Midnight Believer* (1978) and *Take It Home* (1979). King appeared with the band on the 1982 live in London album *Royal Jam*.

Other singers who recorded with the Crusaders were **Bill Withers** (on *Rhapsody and Blues*, 1980), **Joe Cocker** (*Standing Tall*, 1981) and **Bobby Womack**, whose appearance on Felder's 1985 album *Secrets* helped to relaunch his career.

In 1979 Carlton left the group to pursue a solo recording career which included the albums *Larry Carlton* (MCA, 1979) and *Last Nite* (1987), while Chancler replaced Hooper in 1983. During the eighties the group adapted to the demands of the disco market but albums like *Standing Tall* and *Ghetto Blaster* (1984) fell short of their best fusion work of the seventies.

Later releases included *The Good and Bad Times* (1986, with Nancy Wilson) and *Life in the Modern World* (1988). Marcus Miller produced *Healing the Wounds* (GRP, 1991), which included a new version of 'Mercy, Mercy, Mercy'.

In 1991 Henderson and Felder formed the Next Crusade, recording *Back to the Groove* and *Sketches of Life* (1992), which featured Lee Oskar of **War** on harmonica. Retrospectives followed in 1993 (*The Golden Years*) and 1996 (*Way Back Home*).

CELIA CRUZ
b. Santos Saurez, 21 October 1920, Havana, Cuba

Known as 'The Queen of Salsa', Celia Cruz was a major innovator and improviser in Latin music. During a career spanning four decades, she recorded with every leading salsa band and became only the second Latin musician to have a star on Hollywood Boulevard.

She grew up in a poor quarter of Havana, drawing on the music of Afro-Cuban cults in the formation of her style. She studied at the Havana Conservatory before winning an amateur singing contest sponsored by a local radio station in 1935. After this she became a full-time singer touring Mexico and Argentina in 1949 with Las Mulatas del Fuego. She made her first records in Mexico with band leader Memo Salamanca.

On her return to Cuba she became lead singer with the top Latin group La Sonora Matancera, making her début recording with the group in 1951, 'Cao, Cao, Mani Picao Seeco'. During her fifteen years with the band, Cruz recorded numerous hits, including 'Burundanga', 'El Cocoye' and 'Caramelos'.

In 1957 Cruz made her first appearance in New York and in 1960 she and Mantancera left Cuba following the revolution. She settled in New York and in 1962 married the band's trumpeter, Pedro Knight, who became her manager. She signed with Tico, for whom she made twelve albums, including seven with flautist **Tito Puente** and four recorded in Mexico with La Sonora Mantancera between 1966 and 1972. The last of these sold badly and her career was revived with a move to Vaya and her appearence on *Hommy* (1973), a Latin version of **The Who**'s *Tommy*. At Vaya flautist and percussionist Johnny Pachecho became her musical director. It was he who duetted with Cruz on the hit 'Cucula' from *Celia and Johnny* (Vaya, 1974), the first of their six albums together. Through producer Willie Colon, Cruz broadened her repertoire to include Brazilian-style songs like 'Berimbau', as well as Puerto Rican compositions.

'Bemba Colora', the song with which she invariably closed her shows, was recorded by Cruz with the Fania Allstars, which included Ray Barretto and **Mongo Santamaria** on percussion. In 1982 she was reunited on record with the Sonora Mantancera (*Feliz Encuentra*) and in 1989 sang live with the band. Among her later recordings with veteran bandleader Puente was *Homenaje a Benny More* (1986). She won a Grammy for *Ritmo en el Corazon* (1988), her second collaboration with Ray Barretto, and the later *Azucar Negra* (1993). In 1991 Cruz appeared in the film *The Mambo Kings Play Songs of Love* and in 1992 guested on Puente's hundredth album, *Mambo King*.

THE CRYSTALS
Dee Dee Kennibrew, b. Delores Henry, 1945, Brooklyn, New York, USA; Dolores 'Lala' Brooks, b. 1946, Brooklyn; Mary Thomas, b. 1946, Brooklyn (left 1962); Barbara Alston, b. 1945, Brooklyn; Pat Wright, b. 1945, Brooklyn (replaced by Frances Collins in 1964)

The first group signed to Philles in 1961, the Crystals were **Phil Spector**'s 'innocent image' girl group, their little-girl voices providing the still centre to the percussive storm of his 'wall of sound'.

Formed while still in high school at the encouragement of aspiring songwriter Leroy Bates, the Crystals met Spector while doing demo sessions for publishers Hill and Range. Their first hit was 'There's No Other (Like My Baby)' (Philles, 1961), which Spector reworked from Bates' original composition. Originally intended as the B-side of the more adventurous 'Oh Yeah Maybe Baby', 'No Other' was a plaintive ballad in the style of the **Chantels**. This was followed by the **Barry Mann** and Cynthia Weil song 'Uptown' (1962), for which Spector created a mini-symphony, replete with pizzicato strings, mandolins and castanets, about a man who after eking out a demeaning existence downtown during the day is made to feel like a king by his adoring woman when he comes

uptown. The group's next record was the controversial 'He Hit Me (and It Felt Like a Kiss)', which was withdrawn after protests.

Ironically, the Crystals' best-known record, the brooding, declamatory 'He's a Rebel'* (1962), does not feature them at all. This was a cover of the **Gene Pitney** song originally recorded by Vicki Carr on Liberty. In order to get his version out quickly, Spector recorded the song in Los Angeles with the more stately voice of **Darlene Love** singing lead, supported by the Blossoms, and simply credited it to the Crystals. Love and the Blossoms also performed on the Crystals' next release, 'He's Sure the Boy I Love' (1963). 'Da Doo Ron Ron'* and 'Then He Kissed Me', which made the Top Ten in America and established Spector's name as a producer internationally, featured lead vocals from Lala Brooks and the participation of the other members, but by then their voices were but one element in the sound Spector was creating. After two more minor hits, 'Little Boy' and 'All Grown Up' (1964), and a tour of the UK, where 'I Wonder' (London, 1964) charted, the Crystals bought their contract back from Spector, who was now more interested in Love and the harsher-sounding **Ronettes**.

They signed with United Artists and recorded a couple of Motown-flavoured singles in 1965. In the seventies they became regular members of the rock'n'roll revival circuit and even had a British hit with a reissue of 'Da Doo Ron Ron' in 1974. In 1977 Shaun Cassidy (the younger brother of **David Cassidy**) had an American No. 1 with a version of 'Da Doo Ron Ron'. In the nineties the Crystals comprised Kennibrew, Marcella Matthews and Deborah Sherman.

XAVIER CUGAT
b. Francisco de Asis Javier Cugat Mingall de Bru y Deulofeo, 1 January 1900, Gerona, Spain, d. 27 October 1990, Barcelona

The leader of the most popular Latin dance band of the forties, Cugat was also one of the most filmed bandleaders of all time. Frowned on by purists for blending the popular elements in Latin music with brash showmanship – the band wore flaming red jackets and always featured exotic dancers – Cugat's music lacked the passion and dynamism of **Machito**'s or **Tito Puente**'s. However, with **Perez Prado** and in Britain **Edmundo Ros**, he was largely responsible for the entry of Latin music into the mainstream of popular music.

Cugat's family emigrated to Cuba when he was four and in his youth he played the violin both in café and pit bands (at one time alongside **Moises Simons**, whose 'The Peanut Vendor' he later parodied as 'The Coconut Pudding Vendor', 1935) and the Havana Symphony Orchestra. In 1921 he moved to America and after a brief time working as a cartoonist formed a tango band, Xavier Cugat and His Gigolos, in the late twenties, making two of the first musical short films in 1927–8. While playing in the Hollywood area in the early thirties, Cugat made several film appearances and provided music for *Ten Cents a Dance* (1931) and other films, but it was only when he formed his Waldorf-Astoria Orchestra in 1935 that he had significant record success. At first he played what one critic called 'international light concert music', mixing Strauss waltzes with popular songs of the day ('Begin the Beguine', Victor, 1935) and some Latin music ('Para Vigo Me Voy', 1936), but increasingly Cugat Latinized his repertoire and presented it with visual aplomb, hiring Rita Hayworth (then still Margarita Cansino) and Rosario and Antonio as dancers and Carmen Castillo as a vocalist. Among his hits were 'The Breeze and I' (1940, with vocals by **Dinah Shore**), later a million-seller for **Caterina Valente** (1955), 'Brazil' (1943) and 'Balabu' (1944). In the late forties he appeared in several musicals (though only with **Carmen Miranda** once, *A Date with Judy*, 1948). Among these were *Holiday in Mexico* (1946), *This Time for Keeps* (1947) and *Luxury Liner* (1948).

In the fifties a personality (known as much for his wives, who included singers Abbe Lane and Charo, as his music), he appeared regularly on television. In 1971 a stroke ended his career.

CULTURE CLUB

Boy George, b. George Alan O'Dowd, 14 June 1961, London, England; Mikey Craig, b. 15 February 1960, London; Jon Moss, b. 11 September 1957, London; Roy Hay, b. 12 August 1961, Southend, Essex

With their combination of outrageous appearance (Boy George's flamboyant cross-dressing) and imitation of black musical styles, Culture Club sprang from a British tradition that stretched back to the early **Rolling Stones** and the **Kinks**. Like those bands, Culture Club became one of the biggest names in the USA. In 1983 they had three massive hits, including the haunting nonsense chant 'Karma Chameleon', which, greatly helped by an effective video set on a Mississippi riverboat, was No. 1 on both sides of the Atlantic. However, whereas the Stones and Kinks developed their own styles from their borrowings, Culture Club were more pop orientated and seemed content simply to return to rock's museum of styles for a new sound every few records. Another mark of their pop status was the fact that at the height of the band's career Boy George sold as many posters as records. After a much publicized struggle with drug addiction Boy George embarked on a solo career in 1987.

The band was the product of the post-punk disco and nightclub scene in the London of the early eight-

ies. George had worked in dress designing and was involved briefly with the **Malcolm McLaren**-managed group Bow Wow Wow. Bass-player Craig had been a disc-jockey, while guitarist Hay had played in Russian Bouquet and other semi-pro bands in Essex. Moss was a survivor from the punk era, having auditioned for the **Clash**, formed the band London and been briefly associated with both the **Damned** and **Adam Ant**.

Culture Club played their first gig in October 1981 and signed to Virgin Records six months later. Their third single, 'Do You Really Want to Hurt Me?', reached No. 1 in Britain late in 1982. Produced by Steve Levene and taken from the album *Kissing to Be Clever*, it featured George's tenor in a lovers' rock style. The 1983 album, *Colour by Numbers*, featured more hits, including 'Karma Chameleon' and 'Church of the Poison Mind', which was clearly a reworking of the early Motown sound and featured Helen Terry, whose soaring voice provided a stunning counterpoint to George's lead vocal. *Waking Up with the House on Fire* (1984) was a far weaker album and the singles from it – the silly 'War Song' and 'Medal Song' – were only minor hits, though 'War' briefly reached the British Top Ten.

By now Boy George had coarsened his image from the doll-like figure in print fabrics decorated with eclectically combined religious symbols to a semi-harridan. Culture Club's 1986 recording, *From Luxury to Heartache*, saw the group return to the charts, but the price of this success was that the group's own pop sensibility was downplayed in favour of **Arif Mardin**'s lush production. Similarly, the attempt to move to a more democratic notion of a group was foiled by Boy George's long sojourn on the front pages of the world's newspapers in the summer of 1986, following his public admission that he was a heroin addict.

The following year the group split (a greatest hits set, *This Time*, appeared in 1987) with George reaching No. 1 in Britain with his first solo record, a faithful rendition of **Ken Boothe**'s 1974 version of 'Everything I Own', composed by **Bread**'s David Gates. This was followed by the album *Sold* and in 1988 came 'No Clause 28', a protest at anti-gay discrimination by the UK government, plus the tepid 'High Hat'. Since then he has recorded as Jesus Loves You on his own More Protein label (*They Martyr Mantras*, 1991) but his most successful recording of the decade was a version of the Dave Berry 1964 hit 'The Crying Game', recorded for the soundtrack of the 1992 hit movie of the same name. During this period George also worked successfully as a DJ and remixer for the Ministry of Sound. Another 'best of' collection, *At Worst . . .*, followed in 1993, before like many groups before them Culture Club re-formed in the late nineties. The album *Don't Mind if I Do* (Virgin, 1999) saw the group rerunning their trademark reggae-influenced light rhythms set against Boy George's melancholic vocals to little effect.

MIKE CURB
b. 24 December 1944, Savannah, Georgia, USA

Producer, songwriter and company executive, Curb was one of the most successful record men of the sixties and seventies.

Brought up in Los Angeles, Curb turned to record production while at college in 1964, selling the finished product to established labels, notably the Capitol subsidiary, Tower. After writing a commercial slogan for motorcycles, 'You Meet the Nicest People on a Honda', he transformed the commercial into 'Little Honda' and the group into the Hondells and won his first Top Ten success on Mercury in 1964. The group had two further hits with 'My Buddy Seat' (1964) and a cover of the **Lovin' Spoonful**'s 'Younger Girl' (1966), and 'Little Honda' was recorded by the **Beach Boys**. By then, Curb had left college to form his own Sidewalk Productions. He put together soundtracks for virtually all of AIP's youth-orientated films, including *Wild Angels* (1966), *Riot on Sunset Strip* (1967) and *Psych-Out* (1968), which included early tracks by the Stone Poneys, the Electric Flag, the Chocolate Watch Band, the **Seeds** and the Strawberry Alarm Clock, which he released on his own Sidewalk label or leased to Tower.

In 1968 he sold Sidewalk to The Entertainment Company, remaining with the company as president. Curb's activities included scoring Hanna-Barbera cartoon series, running Together Records, which specialized in archive recordings of Los Angeles-based groups such as the **Byrds**, whose early recordings were released as *Pre-Flyte* (1969), and setting up co-production companies, notably with James William Guercio, producer of **Blood, Sweat and Tears** and **Chicago**. Then, in 1970, Curb joined MGM Records as president. In a blaze of publicity he announced MGM was dropping all artists associated with drug usage. In this way he got rid of most of the company's progressive groups (though he kept Eric Burdon, who was successful, and axed the **Cowsills**, who were not) and pointed it toward a middle-of-the-road policy with signings like the **Osmonds**. In the manner of **Mitch Miller**, he formed his own chorale, the Mike Curb Congregation, who had a Top Forty hit with the theme from *Kelly's Heroes*, 'Burning Bridges' (1971), and several country hits before Curb left MGM in 1973.

He next set up Curb Productions, and his own label distributed by Warners, Warner/Curb, on which he had two American No. 1s in 1977, the remake of the **Crystals**' 'Da Doo Ron Ron'* by Shaun Cassidy (the younger brother of **David Cassidy**) and 'You Light Up My Life'* by Debby Boone (the daughter of **Pat Boone**). In the eighties Curb was particularly successful in the country field, establishing a series of joint labels with other record companies and releasing material by artists signed to Curb Productions. These include **Hank Williams Jnr** (Warner/Curb), the Judds (RCA/Curb), **The Bellamy Brothers** (MCA/Curb) and Sawyer Brown (Capitol/Curb). After the mid-seventies Curb was active in the world of Republican politics. In 1978 he was elected Lieutenant-Governor of California.

On leaving office he established Curb Records, which became a leading country music label in the eighties and nineties through its deals with BMG, Warner and others.

THE CURE
Robert Smith, b. 21 April 1959, Crawley, Sussex, England; Laurence 'Lol' Tolhurst, b. 3 February 1959; Michael Dempsey; Simon Gallup, b. 1 June 1960; Mathieu Hartley; Steve Goulding; Phil Thornalley; Andy Anderson; Roger O'Donnell; Boris Williams; Perry Bamonte

With **New Order**, the Cure were one of the longest-lived of the UK 'post-punk' bands of the late seventies and early eighties. Their success a dozen years after their formation, despite endless line-up changes, was largely due to the idiosyncratic songwriting of Robert Smith. Like **Julian Cope** and **Morrissey**, Smith was a true obsessive, operating at a consistent level of poetic intensity.

Guitarist and vocalist Smith formed a band at school in Crawley, Sussex, in 1976 with drummer Tolhurst, bassist Dempsey and second guitarist Porl Thompson, briefly recruiting singer Peter O'Toole. After several name changes (and O'Toole's and Thompson's departure), the band signed to the Fiction label, run by Chris Parry, who also became the band's manager.

The Cure's début single, 'Killing an Arab', appeared in 1978. Smith's lyrics were based on an incident from Albert Camus's novel *L'Etranger*, but allegations of racism drew almost as much rock press attention as the record's sparse sound and chilling arrangement. Their début album, *Three Imaginary Boys* (1979), which included a startling version of **Jimi Hendrix**'s 'Foxy Lady', made the UK Top Fifty, and was subsequently reissued in the US (where the band signed to Elektra) with several track changes as *Boys Don't Cry*.

The band toured the UK in 1979 with **Siouxsie and the Banshees**, a band with a similarly 'gothic' style, and during the tour Smith temporarily joined the headliners when their guitarist and drummer quit. It was to be the first of several links between Smith and the Banshees. In the Cure, Dempsey was replaced by

Gallup after the tour and the band added keyboards-player Hartley. The band's second album, *Seventeen Seconds*, was a superior effort. It won the group a UK Top Twenty chart placing and a minor hit with 'A Forest'.

Faith (1981) was followed by the uncompromisingly doom-laden fourth album, *Pornography* (1982). Despite its grim content, the album made the UK Top Ten, but more line-up changes followed soon after, with bassist Goulding replacing Gallup and Tolhurst switching to keyboards – Hartley had left the group the previous year.

During 1982 Smith joined Siouxsie and the Banshees as a temporary replacement for guitarist John McGeogh, playing live and in the studio with them for the next eighteen months and also recording an album as the Glove with Banshees' bassist Steve Severin. During this period the Cure released only three singles, 'Let's Go to Bed', 'The Walk' and 'Love Cats', the last of which gave the band their first UK Top Ten single. The singles were compiled on the mini-album *Japanese Whispers* (1984). With producer Thornalley joining the band on bass and drummer Anderson completing yet another line-up, the Cure returned to the charts with the quirky, almost Syd Barrett-ish 'The Caterpillar' and its parent album *The Top* in 1984.

A stop-gap live album, *Concert*, appeared at the end of 1984, after which a line-up of Smith, Tolhurst, guitarist Thompson, bass-player Gallup and drummer Williams recorded what would become the band's breakthrough album, *The Head on the Door* (1985). The album entered the charts on both sides of the Atlantic and provided two hit singles, 'In Between Days' and 'Close to Me'. The band's singles, which

had been accompanied by a series of striking promotional videos directed by Tim Pope, were compiled in *Standing on a Beach* in 1986, after which the band toured extensively before recording the sprawling double set *Kiss Me, Kiss Me, Kiss Me* (1987), which further raised their profile in the US.

Tolhurst was fired by Smith and replaced by O'Donnell for the band's most successful album yet, *Disintegration* (1989), which provided the Cure with a huge US hit, 'Love Song'. After more touring, the band released a remix collection, *Mixed Up*, followed by a live mini-album, *Entreat*, in 1991. With former roadie Bamonte taking O'Donnell's place, the band recorded *Wish* (1992), which topped the UK chart and made the US Top Three. Helped by the hit single 'Friday I'm in Love', one of Smith's finest pop songs, it became the Cure's biggest-selling album.

The band were little seen in 1993 or 1994, the year in which Smith and manager Parry fought a court case unsuccessfully brought by Tolhurst, alleging that he was underpaid during his later years with the band. Also unsuccessful in 1994 was Parry's attempt (backed by Smith) to obtain a radio licence for an alternative rock station in London named XFM. The Cure ended the year in typical fashion, announcing the departure of yet another band member, drummer Williams. Their first studio album in four years was the surprisingly bright *Wild Mood Swings* (1996). It was followed by the compilation album *Standing on a Beach – The Singles* (1997) before *Bloodflowers* (2000) saw a return to the Gothic resignation of their earlier work with tracks like 'Out of the World' and the acoustic 'No If'. As ever, the album came with the promise/threat that it would be Smith's last with the band.

TED DAFFAN

b. Theron Eugene Daffan, 21 September 1912, Beauregarde Parish, Louisiana, USA, d. 6 October 1996, Houston, Texas

Though a steel-guitar player and country bandleader for more than a decade, Daffan is best known for composing and recording several major country hits of the forties, including 'Truck Driver Blues', the first truck-driving song, and a trio of honky-tonk classics – 'Worried Mind' (1940), 'Born to Lose' (1943), a bleak study of a country boy coming to terms with city life in the manner of **Harlan Howard**'s 'Streets of Baltimore', 'Detroit City' and **Gram Parson**'s 'Hickory Wind', and 'Headin' Down the Highway' (1945).

He grew up in Houston, Texas, where his interest in Hawaiian music and electronics led to his setting up a radio repair shop to which numerous country musicians came to experiment with amplification. Deeply influenced by **Milton Brown**, Daffan first played with the local country swing bands the Blue Ridge Playboys (for whom **Floyd Tillman** was the singer) and Bar-X Cowboys. In 1940, with his own band the Texans, he had the year's second biggest country seller with 'Worried Mind', but this was eclipsed by the double hit (recorded in 1942, released in 1943) 'No Letter Today'/'Born to Lose' (Okeh). He headed a large band at the Venice Ballroom, Los Angeles (1944–6), then returned to live in Texas.

In the fifties several of Daffan's compositions were hits for other country artists. They include 'I've Got Five Dollars and It's Saturday Night' by **Faron Young**, while his 1939 song 'I'm a Fool to Care' was a 1954 pop success for **Les Paul** and Mary Ford. He went into publishing, for a time with **Hank Snow** (who had a 1957 hit with Daffan's 'Tangled Mind'), and for some years also ran his own Houston-based Daffan label. 'Born to Lose' and others of his numbers were profitably recycled in the early sixties by **Ray Charles**, and most of them are now secure country standards.

DAFT PUNK

Thomas Bangaltar, b. 3 January 1975, France; Guy-Manuel De Homem Christo, b. 8 February 1974, France

Daft Punk were the most successful of the French dance acts, winning a Europe-wide audience with their disco-influenced house music towards the end of the 1990s. One element of Daft Punk's appeal lay in the artlessness of their approach. Furthermore, because they were not part of the house music revolution of the late 1980s, being rather the first stars of the genre's second generation, they have felt free to extend the range of influences on their 4:4 stew.

The pair met as schoolboys in Paris in 1987. Bangaltar's father was a songwriter who had written 1970s disco hits for the Gibson Brothers and Ottowan. Bangaltar Junior and Homem Christo soon began to collaborate musically. Their first recording was as an indie/new wave outfit, Darlin', releasing one single, 'Cindy So Loud', on Stereolab's Duophonic label. Although their influences included the **Beach Boys**, **Marc Bolan** and even **Barry Manilow**, by 1992 they had started going to clubs and were discovering, and starting to make, house music.

They attracted the attention of Scotland's Soma label in 1993, and a year later released their first single as Daft Punk, 'The New Wave'. This was followed by 'Da Funk', which was picked up by the **Chemical Brothers**, who promoted the track heavily in their DJ sets and asked Daft Punk to remix one of their tunes, 'Life Is Sweet'. As the popularity of 'Da Funk' grew, a bidding war began for the band, eventually won by Virgin. Further remix work, principally an unorthodox 3/4 reworking of Gabrielle's 'Forget About the World', followed in 1996, before the re-release of 'Da Funk', and their début album, *Homework*, in 1997. The album received a rapturous critical welcome, praised for its irreverent punk, pop and hip-hop-influenced house sound. Three more huge hit singles were pulled from the album: 'Around the World', 'Burnin'' and 'Revolution 909'.

Daft Punk's only recorded output in 1998 was a remix of Scott Grooves' 'Mothership Reconnection', but Bangaltar enjoyed huge success outside the group with Stardust, whose funky 'Music Sounds Better with You', co-written by Bangaltar, was the biggest house hit of the year.

VERNON DALHART

b. Marion Try Slaughter, 6 April 1883, near Jefferson, Texas, USA, d. 14 September 1948, Bridgeport, Connecticut

Although country music was established on record through the efforts of certain artists who were seen as belonging to, or speaking for, its own community – among them **Fiddlin' John Carson**, **Jimmie Rodgers**, and the **Carter Family** – a vital passage in its early history was steered by an artist with quite different musical credentials: a conservatory-trained singer with a background in opera and the all-purpose studio jobs of the young record industry. It was perhaps a matter of chance that Dalhart recorded country material at all, but, once he had proved himself at it with 'The Wreck of the Old '97', he not only determined the course of his own career but created the 'citybilly' strand of country music in which numerous other recording-studio professionals, including **Frank Luther** and **Carson Robison**, spent profitable and influential years.

Vernon Dalhart – he took his stage name from two Texas towns where, in his teens, he had worked as a cattle-puncher – attended the Dallas Conservatory of Music and then moved, in 1910, to New York, where he studied opera and secured roles in productions of Puccini's *Girl of the Golden West* (1912) and **Gilbert and Sullivan**'s *HMS Pinafore* (1913–14). In 1915 he began recording for Edison, though his first issued side was 'Can't You Heah Me Callin', Caroline?' in 1917. His voice suited the acoustic recording process and he was soon turning out popular songs, light operatic selections, Hawaiian and coon numbers for Edison, Columbia and Victor.

In 1924 he recorded for Edison an already old country 'event' song, 'The Wreck of the Old '97' (later the subject of involved legal actions over copyright). His Victor version of this was coupled with another old number, 'The Prisoner's Song' (later claimed in part by **Nat Shilkret**), which in the record-hungry climate quickly sold a million. Thereafter, Dalhart recorded almost exclusively hillbilly material, specializing in topical and tragedy songs like 'The Death of Floyd Collins' (1926), which he recorded for different labels. Many masters were pressed on a dozen or more labels, a process clouded by the use of scores of pseudonyms.

A somewhat factitious hillbilly instrumental flavour was provided by Dalhart's own harmonica and jew's-harp playing, violin, and the guitar and duet vocals of Carson Robison, with whom he collaborated from 1924 to 1928; when their association ended, Robison formed a similar act with singer Frank Luther. Towards the end of the twenties Dalhart expanded his repertoire to include social comment songs like 'Farm Relief Song' and **Bob Miller**'s '11 Cent Cotton, 40 Cent Meat', and in 1931, on a trip to London, he recorded a version of 'The Runaway Train' (Regal) – a favourite for many years on British children's radio. However, after 1933, he filled only one studio engagement, and by 1942 he was taking jobs as a small-town voice tutor, night watchman or hotel clerk. He died in obscurity, leaving a collection of recorded country songs several times greater than any other artist of his time.

THE DAMNED

Captain Sensible, b. Ray Burns, 23 April 1955, England; Brian James, b. Brian Robertson, 18 February 1955; Rat Scabies, b. Chris Miller, 30 July 1957, Kingston-upon-Thames, Surrey; Dave Vanian, b. David Letts, 12 October 1956; Robert 'Lu' Edmunds

The first British punk band to release a record, the Damned survived to celebrate their tenth birthday in 1986. While retaining a commitment to the ferocity of punk, they cultivated their penchant for English eccentricity, which was particularly evident on Captain Sensible's solo hit singles.

Drummer Scabies and guitarist James were originally members of London SS, a rehearsal band led by future **Clash** guitarist Mick Jones. The addition of bassist Sensible and singer Vanian with their fancy-dress stage outfits (tutu and Dracula clothes, respectively) made the group the most theatrical of early punk bands. Vanian's chosen image inspired the choice of name.

Their first single was 'New Rose', backed by a barely recognizable version of **The Beatles**' 'Help' – the first example of punk's penchant for cover-versions designed to destroy the original song. The single and album (*Damned Damned Damned*) were produced by pub-rock veteran **Nick Lowe** for the Stiff label in 1976. The songs were short staccato bursts of sound taken at breakneck speed, in the manner of the **Ramones**. Inexplicably, **Pink Floyd**'s Nick Mason (symbol of the music punk was intended to destroy) was brought in to produce *Music for Pleasure* (Stiff, 1977), on which the band became a five piece with the addition of second guitarist Lu. Its lack of success led to the first of several splits in the band. James left permanently to form first Tanz der Youth, then Lords of the New Church. The following year saw the group quit Stiff and briefly break up.

After shortlived separate projects, Sensible, Scabies and Vanian reunited in 1979, initially as the Doomed. Sensible moved to guitar and among the other musicians passing through the group was Jon Moss, later of **Culture Club**. Over the next seven years the Damned released seven albums on Chiswick, Bronze and MCA, scoring hits in 1980 with 'Love Song' and *The Black Album*, and in 1986 with a surprisingly respectful remake of Barry Ryan's 1968 hit 'Eloise'. A version of **Love**'s 'Alone Again Or' was a lesser hit in 1987.

By this point, Roman Jugg had replaced Sensible, whose zany solo version of **Rodgers and Hammerstein**'s 'Happy Talk' (A&M, 1982) was a British No. 1. He had further hits with 'Wot' in 1982 and 'Glad It's All Over' in 1984. The live *Final Damnation* (Restless, 1989) documented the 'final reunion' and featured all the original members of the group. In 1991 the band re-formed yet again around the core of Scabies, Vanian and James, and yet again in 1996 for *Not of this Earth* (in homage to Roger Corman, whose 1957 film of the same name was a cult classic).

VIC DAMONE
b. Vito Rocco Farinola, 12 June 1928, Brooklyn, New York, USA

A **Frank Sinatra** copyist in the forties, Damone later extended his range to become one of the few remaining practitioners of the art of romantic ballad singing.

After winning a place on *Arthur Godfrey Talent Scouts*, in 1947, he started singing regularly on the radio and at nightclubs, and signed with Mercury Records. 'I Have But One Heart' (1947) gave him a minor hit but his first big success was 'Again'* (1949) from the film *Road House* (1948). Another million-seller was 'You're Breaking My Heart' (1948), based on the turn-of-the-century ballad by Leoncavallo, composer of the opera *I Pagliacci*. Signed to a film contract (by MGM), like many singers of the time, Damone had an undistinguished screen career beginning with *Rich Young and Pretty* (1951) and ending with *Spree* (1967).

By the early fifties Damone was a moderately successful recording star. His hits included a revival of **Jerome Kern**'s 'Why Was I Born?' (1949); film songs such as 'Vagabond Shoes' and 'Just Say I Love Her' (1950); and even versions of 'Tzena, Tzena, Tzena' (originally a hit for **Mitch Miller**, the man who had signed Damone to Mercury) and 'Truly, Truly Fair' (1951, the bestselling version of which was by **Guy Mitchell**), produced by Miller on Columbia, for whom he now worked. These last two records saw Damone attempt to sing in a more muscular fashion, but the record that established his star status marked a return to traditional balladry. 'On the Street Where You Live' (Columbia, 1956) was from **Lerner's and Loewe**'s Broadway show *My Fair Lady*, which opened to great success in 1956. Subsequent records for Columbia, which included the theme songs to *War and Peace* (1956), *An Affair to Remember* (1957), one of the last songs written by **Harry Warren**, and *Gigi* (1958), were less successful, as were his sixties recordings for Capitol. A move to Warners garnered him only one hit, 'You Were Only Fooling' (1965).

Despite a lack of hit singles and a brief period of bankruptcy in the early seventies, Damone remained a regular at Las Vegas nightclubs and continued recording, most successfully on RCA (*Now*, 1981), throughout the eighties.

BILLY DANIELS
b. 12 September 1913, Jacksonville, Florida, USA, d. 7 October 1988, Los Angeles, California

Once described by columnist Walter Winchell as 'the sexiest singer of the day', Daniels' most famous recording was his up-tempo version of **Harold Arlen**'s and **Johnny Mercer**'s 'That Old Black Magic' (1948).

After singing in a church choir in his youth, Daniels travelled to New York to study law in 1930. To support himself he became a singing waiter in 1933. This led to his joining Erskine Hawkins' band as featured vocalist and a series of residencies at Harlem nightclubs where his energetic singing style and hip-swivelling performance won him immediate acclaim. He recorded for Victor's Bluebird subsidiary ('Symphony', 'Intermezzo') in the late thirties but with only limited success, his forte being live performance. After service in the marines during the Second World War, Daniels made his Broadway début in the musical *Memphis Bound* (1945) with dancer Bill Robinson and in 1948 recorded his version of 'That Old Black Magic' (Mercury), which he subsequently used as his signature tune. Though the recording never appeared in the charts, it is reputed to have sold in excess of five million copies over the years.

By now established on the nightclub and cabaret circuit, Daniels became one of the first entertainers to have his own television variety show (*The Billy Daniels Show*) in 1951. He attempted a film career with appearances in *Sunny Side of the Street* (1951), which co-starred **Frankie Laine**, and *Cruisin' down the River* (1953) with **Dick Haymes**, among others. In the sixties he toured extensively in Europe before returning to Broadway, co-starring with **Sammy Davis Jnr** in the long-running *Golden Boy* (1964). In 1975 he appeared in the all-black version of *Hello Dolly!* and in the eighties starred in the London production of *Bubbling Brown Sugar*.

THE CHARLIE DANIELS BAND
Charlie Daniels, b. 28 October 1943, Wilmington, North Carolina, USA; Joel Di Gregorio, b. Worcester, Massachusetts; Tom Crain; Charlie Hayward; Fred Edwards; Don Murray; Charlie Marshall

One of the first 'Southern rock' bands to emerge in the wake of the **Allman Brothers Band**, the Charlie Daniels Band proved adept at catching the mood of middle America. Thus, after 'The South's Gonna Do It', a definitive rebel-rouser and Top Thirty hit in 1975, they performed at President Jimmy Carter's inaugural ball in 1977 – a reward for the fund-raising benefits they had mounted for Carter. They returned to the Top Thirty with 'In America' (1980), put out in the middle of the Iran hostage crisis, and the Dan Daley composition 'Still in Saigon' (1982).

A member of various bluegrass groups, guitarist and fiddler Daniels turned professional musician at the age of twenty-one. His first group, the Jaguars, was named after the song they recorded for Bob John-ston in 1959, then an independent producer in Fort Worth. That group toured the South until 1967 when Daniels folded it to settle in Nashville as a session man and songwriter – **Elvis Presley** had already recorded his 'It Hurts Me' – at the invitation of John-ston, by now a leading producer with Columbia Records. Among the artists Daniels backed were **Bob Dylan** – on whose *Nashville Skyline* (1969), among other albums, he worked – and **Leonard Cohen**, with whom he also toured. He also tried production, supervising several albums for the **Youngbloods**, including *Elephant's Memory* (1969), and made a solo album for Capitol, *Charlie Daniels*.

In 1972 he formed the Charlie Daniels Band, aping the twin lead guitars (Daniels and Crain) of the All-man Brothers Band and adding to it two drummers (Edwards and Murray, who was replaced by Marshall in 1978). The band added to what would soon become the standard elements of Southern rock – blues, country, bluegrass, rock and a certain macho stance – a genuine feel for rural life (captured in 'Carolina [I Remember You]', Kama Sutra, 1981). Daniels' fiddle-playing was as much influenced by Western swing as bluegrass. They secured their first Top Ten hit, Daniels' own 'Uneasy Rider' – a talking bluegrass number – in 1973 and confirmed their regional popu-larity with 'The South's Gonna Do It', constant tour-ing and five albums, including *Way Down Yonder* (1974) and *Nightrider* (1975).

In 1975 they joined Epic and in 1979 had their biggest-selling single with Daniels' rousing adaptation of a traditional tune, 'The Devil Went Down to Geor-gia', from the platinum album, *Million Mile Reflec-tions*. In the eighties the band relaxed their touring schedule and the sale of their records, including *Me and the Boys* (1986), suffered accordingly.

They retained a strong country following, however, and had several hits, including 'Drinkin' My Baby Goodbye' (1985) and 'Boogie Woogie Fiddle Blues' (1988). The band had commented on political issues in 'Still in Saigon' (1982) and 'American Farmer' and their Southern populism was again expressed on the title track of the 1993 album *America, I Believe in You* (Liberty), which included a verse attacking the cre-ation of the North American Free Trade Area sung over a pounding southern boogie. Daniels joined **Johnny Cash** and **Travis Tritt** on top Nashville fiddler Mark O'Connor's 'The Devil Comes Back to Georgia' in 1994. The group's most important recordings of the decade were retrospectives: *A Decade of Hits* (1997) and *Fiddle Fire: 25 Years of the Charlie Daniels Band*.

JOHNNY DANKWORTH
b. 20 September 1927, London, England

One of the pioneers of modern jazz in Britain, saxo-phonist, composer and bandleader Dankworth became a leading exponent of chamber jazz. With his wife **Cleo Laine** he set up a music and arts centre for concerts and training courses.

Dankworth played in trad bands and studied clar-inet at the Royal Academy in London before taking part in early bebop experiments with **Ronnie Scott** and others. At the suggestion of bandleader **Ted Heath**, he formed the Johnny Dankworth Seven in 1950, with Don Rendell (tenor sax), Bill Le Sage (piano) and drummer Tony Kinsey, recording *A Lover and His Lass* (Esquire, 1952). Three years later Dankworth started a twenty-piece big band which featured vocalists Laine, Frank Holder and Tony Mansell. The Dankworth group also had two surprise hits with the witty 'Experiments with Mice' (Par-lophone, 1956), based on the nursery rhyme 'Three Blind Mice', and Galt McDermott's 'African Waltz' (EMI Columbia, 1961).

In 1958 Dankworth branched into cinema, writing some twenty scores for such British new-wave films as *Saturday Night and Sunday Morning* (1960), *The Criminal* (1960) and *The Servant* (1963). With **Dave Brubeck**, Scott and **Charlie Mingus** he appeared in the film *All Night Long* (1961), an updating of the *Oth-ello* story.

He also pioneered the jazz suite on a series of Fontana albums with concepts based on literary char-acters (*What the Dickens*, 1963, with solos by Tubby Hayes and Ronnie Scott), astrology (*Zodiac Variations*, 1964) and Shakespeare's songs (*Shake-speare and All That Jazz*), whose arrangements were composed for Laine.

With writer and former jazz saxophonist Benny Green, Dankworth composed the musicals *Boots without Strawberry Jam* (1968), a life of George Bernard Shaw, and *Colette* (1979), which starred Laine. For the London Philharmonic Society he com-posed *Improvisations for Jazz Band and Symphony Orchestra*. Dankworth also evolved a set of orchestral arrangements of popular music and conducted pro-grammes for major orchestras in North America and Britain. In 1985 he was appointed Principal Pops Con-ductor of the San Francisco Symphony Orchestra.

During the sixties Laine and Dankworth set up their Wavendon Allmusic Centre, dedicated to the couple's ideal of combining all forms of music. Many of Dankworth's recordings for Fontana and others were reissued on his own Sepia label. They included *Movies and Me*, *Octavius* and *Symphonic Fusions*, with the London Symphony Orchestra, and *Fair Oak Fusions* (1982), composed for cellist Julian Lloyd Webber.

Alec Dankworth, the son of John and Cleo, was one of Britain's leading young musicians of the nineties, playing bass with Stan Tracey as well as bands led by his father. Their daughter, Jacqui Dankworth, had a career as a singer and actress.

DANNY AND THE JUNIORS

Danny Rapp, b. 10 May 1941, Philadelphia, Pennsylvania, USA, d. 5 April 1983, Arizona; Dave White, b. David White Tricker, September 1940, Philadelphia (replaced by Bill Carlucci); Frank Maffei, b. November 1940, Philadelphia; Joe Terranova, b. 30 January 1941, Philadelphia; Lennie Baker

Danny and the Juniors recorded the paean to the high-school dance, the frantic 'At the Hop'* (ABC-Paramount, 1957), and the equally infectious, nostalgic chant 'Rock and Roll Is Here to Stay' (1958), written by group member White.

Formed in high school in 1955 as the Juvenairs, the group were introduced to the Philadelphia-based Singular Records by their manager Artie Singer. At the suggestion of **Dick Clark**, they changed the words of their first recording from 'Do the Bop', to 'At the Hop' and had an instant bestseller when it was leased to ABC-Paramount and promoted on Clark's *American Bandstand*. 'Rock and Roll Is Here to Stay' was almost as big a hit, but after 'Dottie' (1958) and 'Twistin' U.S.A.' (Swan, 1960) subsequent records were only minor hits. Most were dance orientated. Clark had pressed for them rather than **Chubby Checker** to record 'The Twist' and, though he failed, the logic of 'At the Hop' committed them to an endless series of dance records and even a 'Back to the Hop' (1961).

The group last charted in 1963 with 'Oo-La-La-Limbo' (Guyden) before splitting up. White went into production, working with Len Barry (for whom he wrote '1–2–3' with long-time associate Johnny Madara) and a number of Philadelphia acts, before releasing a solo album on Bell, *David White Tricker* (1971). Baker, the Juniors' saxophonist, co-founded the rock'n'roll revival group Sha Na Na, one of the hits of the film *Woodstock* (1970), in which they sang 'At the Hop'. Throughout the seventies both Sha Na Na and a version of the Juniors, who had another hit with 'At the Hop' in Britain when it was reissued in 1976, regularly played the revival circuit.

After Rapp's death, the group was led by Joe Terry, who sang on *Some Kind of Wonderful* (Topaz, 1987).

TERENCE TRENT D'ARBY

b. 15 March 1962, New York City, New York, USA

One of the most stylish pop-soul singers of recent years, the American-born Terence Trent D'Arby first found success in the UK.

The son of a minister, D'Arby grew up in Florida where he was an amateur boxing champion. He did not take up singing until he was stationed in Germany with the US army. In 1980 he joined local soul band Touch and in 1983 he moved to London after being discharged from the forces.

D'Arby was signed by CBS and his first releases, 'If You Let Me Stay', 'Wishing Well' and 'Sign Your Name', were all Top Ten hits in Britain. The début album *Introducing the Hardline According to Terence Trent D'Arby* (1987) was produced by **Heaven 17**'s Martyn Ware. It topped the UK chart and was a Top Five hit in America the following year.

Neither Fish nor Flesh (1989) divided both critics and consumers. Some admired its ambition while others saw it as merely pretentious – its subtitle was *A Soundtrack of Love, Faith, Hope and Devotion*. It sold poorly and it was three years before D'Arby released another album. Its title, *Terence Trent D'Arby's Symphony or Damn Exploring: The Tension Inside the Sweetness*, showed he had lost none of his self-confidence. The 1993 album, which was largely made in his own home studio, included the UK Top Twenty hits 'Delicate' (featuring Des'ree), 'She Kissed Me' and 'Let Her Down Easy', but it failed to find an audience in his native America. His recording of 'Wrong Way' appeared on the soundtrack of *Beverly Hills Cop 3*, while in 1995 his *Promised Land* television soundtrack album featured his recording of **Sam Cooke**'s 'A Change Is Gonna Come', on which he was backed by **Booker T. and the MGs**. That was followed by the self-produced *Vibrator*. A commercial failure it led to D'Arby leaving Sony for Java Records in 1997.

BOBBY DARIN

b. Walden Robert Cassotto, 14 May 1936, New York, USA, d. 20 December 1973, Los Angeles, California

With **Paul Anka**, Darin was most adaptable and successful of the teen-idols thrown up by rock'n'roll. Described by one critic as 'Melville's Confidence Man returning as a rock'n'roll trickster', so abrupt and complete was his change of identity from one series of records to the next, Darin reflected the speed of rock'n'roll's evolution and sketched out the possibilities for anyone who took firm control of his destiny.

Brought up by his mother (his father died before he was born), Darin could play drums, piano and guitar by his teens. He won a scholarship to Hunter College, but dropped out to play in New York's clubs and coffee-houses. A close friend of **Don Kirshner**, with whom he wrote his first song 'My First Love', in 1956, Darin, as he now called himself, signed with Decca and recorded an unsuccessful cover of **Lonnie Donegan**'s 'Rock Island Line'. In 1957, at the urging of Kirshner, Darin was signed to Atlantic's subsidiary Atco label, just as the company was re-orientating itself towards pop and away from the R&B that had brought it its initial success. 'Million Dollar Baby' and

'Don't Call My Name' (1957) failed, but in 1958 he wrote and recorded the novelty 'Splish Splash'*. Produced by **Ahmet Ertegun**, it was an instant hit and was followed by others: 'Queen of the Hop'* and (as the Rinky Dinks) 'Early in the Morning' (1958) and 'Plain Jane' (1959), records which despite their air of calculation retain their charm to this day. The climax of this phase of Darin's career was his own composition 'Dream Lover'* (1959). In spite of the song's clichéd theme and hackneyed chord changes, Darin's adolescent *angst* and the superior production transformed 'Dream Lover' into a classic rock ballad.

Darin's next record marked a complete change of direction. 'Mack the Knife' was written by **Kurt Weill** and Bertolt Brecht for their classic *Threepenny Opera*, which made its Broadway début in a Marc Blitzstein translation in 1954, and had provided **Louis Armstrong** with a Top Twenty hit in 1956. Darin's million-selling 1959 version saw him effortlessly assume the guise of a finger-clicking hipster and inaugurated the recording of a series of swinging standards: 'Beyond the Sea' (an adaptation by Jack Lawrence of Charles Trenet's 1945 classic 'La Mer'); Percy Montross's 'Clementine'; 'Won't You Come Home Bill Bailey?' (1960); **Hoagy Carmichael**'s 'Lazy River'; **Johnny Mercer**'s and **Harry Warren**'s 'You Must Have Been a Beautiful Baby'; and, most intriguing of all, eden ahbez's [*sic*] 'Nature Boy', which was first recorded by **Nat 'King' Cole**. So sure was Darin of his ability to create hits that he even released a piano solo, 'Beachcomber', which was a minor hit in 1960.

In 1960, like **Elvis Presley** and others, Darin moved to Hollywood where he began a second career as a screen actor, appearing in a wide variety of films, including the romantic *Come September* (1961), whose co-star, Sandra Dee, he married, the jazz film *Too Late Blues* (1962) and the racial drama *Pressure Point* (1962). Once again, his records changed style. He recorded an album of **Ray Charles** songs, including 'What'd I Say', which gave him another Top Thirty hit in 1962, and in the same year he wrote and recorded the witty exercise in pop, 'Multiplication', and recorded an album of duets of classic popular songs with **Johnny Mercer**, *Two of a Kind*. More successful was the self-composed laconic 'Things'* (1962) – his last hit for Atco – which reflected his growing interest in folk music.

In 1962 Darin joined Capitol and had an immediate hit with the forceful 'You're the Reason I'm Living' (1963), but most of his Capitol recordings, such as '18 Yellow Roses' (1963) and more Broadway tunes – including the theme tunes to Jay Herman's *Hello Dolly* (1964) and *Mame* (1965) – were less engaging. More interesting were his concert performances which saw him mixing standards, his rock'n'roll hits and folk songs, for which he was often backed by

Roger McGuinn (shortly before he formed the **Byrds**). When he returned to Atlantic in 1966, his hits were in the folk vein. These included **Tim Hardin**'s 'If I Were a Carpenter' (1966), his biggest hit of the late sixties, and 'The Lady Came from Baltimore' (1967).

Then, after working extensively for Robert Kennedy during his 1968 Presidential campaign, Darin left Atlantic and the mainstream of pop music. In 1969 he established the shortlived Direction Records for which he recorded the politically orientated *Born Walden Robert Cassotto* (1969), whose 'Long Line Rider' was a minor hit. In 1971 he rejoined the popular mainstream, signing with Motown, and once more took to regular appearances at Las Vegas. His only (minor) hit of this period was 'Happy' (1973), recorded the year of his death from a heart attack during surgery. His son Dodd wrote the biography *Dream Lovers* (1995) and in the same year Atlantic issued a four-CD retrospective, *As Long as I'm Singing*.

ERIK DARLING
b. 25 September 1933, Baltimore, Maryland, USA

A leading figure in the commercial stream of the American folk revival, Darling was an influential white exponent of the twelve-string guitar.

Inspired by the records of **Josh White** and **Leadbelly**, Darling formed the Tarriers with future film and television actor Alan Arkin. In 1956 they backed Vince Martin on his Top Ten hit 'Cindy Oh Cindy' (Glory), which was covered by **Eddie Fisher**. Adapting a Jamaican work song, the Tarriers reached No. 4 in the same year with 'Banana Boat Song'. The song was covered by the Fontane Sisters, **Sarah Vaughan** and **Steve Lawrence**, while **Harry Belafonte**'s different arrangement also reached the Top Ten (as, in 1957, did **Stan Freberg**'s satirical rendering). Later members of the group include banjoist Eric Weissberg, who with Steve Mandell had a 1973 hit with the 'Duelling Banjos' theme from the film *Deliverance*, and screenwriter Marshal Brickman.

In 1958 Darling replaced **Pete Seeger** in the **Weavers**, with whom he toured for four years before leaving to form the Rooftop Singers with Bill Svanoe and ex-**Benny Goodman** vocalist Lynne Taylor. Their version of the 1929 Gus Cannon Jug Stompers song 'Walk Right in' (Vanguard), featuring Darling's twelve-string, was a massive hit on both sides of the Atlantic in 1963. Its clean, enthusiastic harmonies were the essence of the commercial folk sound and contrasted with the rougher edges of Cannon's original. The follow-up, 'Tom Cat', also reached the American Top Twenty.

Darling also cut solo albums for Elektra, Vanguard (notably the influential *True Religion*, 1961) and

Atlantic, as well as appearing as accompanist on dozens of folk albums of the sixties. In the seventies Darling formed Border Town. His albums with them included *The Possible Dream* (Elektra, 1975) and *Border Town at Midnight* (Folk Era, 1976). Since then he has been largely inactive.

DARTS
George Currie; John Dummer; Griff Fender (b. Ian Collier); Bob Fish; Den Hegarty; Horatio Hornblower (b. Nigel Trubridge); Hammy Howell; Rita Ray; Ian 'Thump' Thompson

A British doo-wop revival band, Darts had a series of hit singles in the late seventies.

Bass-singer Hegarty, vocalists Fender and Ray and saxophonist Hornblower had been members of rock'n'roll band Rocky Sharpe and the Replays. In 1977 they regrouped with Thompson (bass), Currie (guitar) and drummer Dummer, who had led a blues band in the early seventies, recording four albums for Mercury, Philips and Vertigo. The line-up was completed by blues pianist Howell and ex-Mickey Jupp Band singer Fish.

Led by Hegarty, the group signed to Magnet in 1977 and recorded faithful versions of fifties hits, reaching the Top Twenty eight times in the next three years. A medley of the Rays' 'Daddy Cool' and **Little Richard**'s 'The Girl Can't Help It' (1977) was followed by 'Come Back My Love' (1978) and the Ad Libs' 'Boy from New York City'. After the ballad 'It's Raining' became their biggest hit, Hegarty was replaced by American-born Kenny Andrews and Howell left the group.

The hits continued with a revival of **Gene Chandler**'s 'Duke of Earl' (1979) but the **Four Seasons**' 'Let's Hang on' (1980) was Darts' final success. Soon afterwards the band left Magnet, releasing later records on their own Choicecuts label. Darts now began a new career in the theatre, appearing in *Yakety Yak*, a musical based on the songs of **Leiber and Stoller** that ran in the West End in 1983. By now Dummer had left the group to concentrate on projects like 'Blue Skies' (Speed, 1982) by Helen April, a novelty version of the **Irving Berlin** tune. Trubridge later became an official of the UK Musicians Union.

DAVE DEE, DOZY, BEAKY, MICK AND TICH
Dave Dee, b. David Harman, 17 December 1943, Salisbury, England; Dozy, b. Trevor Davies, 27 November 1944, Salisbury; Beaky, b. John Dymond, 10 July 1944, Salisbury; Mick, b. Michael Wilson, 4 February 1944, Salisbury; Tich, b. Ian Amey, 15 May 1944, Salisbury

Prolific British hitmakers in the second half of the sixties, DDDBM&T, as they were known, were the **Sweet** of their era.

Formed by former policeman Dee as Dave Dee and the Bostons in Salisbury in the early sixties, the group were signed in 1964 for management by songwriters Ken Howard and Alan Blaikley, who earlier that year had written a British No. 1 and international hit for the Honeycombs (the jaunty 'Have I the Right?' on Pye). Howard and Blaikley rejected the comic image of the group in favour of a series of increasingly melodramatic, bright pop hits. Produced by Steve Rowland, these included 'Hold Tight', 'Bend It', sung by Dee with tongue-in-cheek suggestiveness – though as one critic put it he owed more to seaside-postcard artist Donald Gill than **Elvis Presley** – and 'Save Me' (Fontana, 1966), climaxing with their best-remembered records 'Zabadak!' and their only British No. 1, 'Legend of Xanadu' (1967). Replete with extravagant sound effects and the image of whip-wielding Dee, the records were among the first to catch the attention of the new generation of pubescent pop fans for whom **The Beatles** and **Rolling Stones** meant nothing. Though they had hits in Europe, they failed to establish themselves in America.

After 'Xanadu', the hits were smaller and after 'Snake in the Grass' Dee quit the group for a short solo career ('My Woman's Man', 1970) before joining the British arm of Atlantic as head of A&R in 1973, and then Magnet Records. The group continued without him, touring sporadically during the next twenty years as Dozy, Beaky, Mick & Tich. They remained especially popular in Germany and Spain.

With the failure of DDDBM&T, Howard and Blaikley switched their attention to the Herd, who numbered **Peter Frampton** among their members. Their hits, also produced by Rowland, included 'From the Underworld', 'Paradise Lost' (Fontana, 1967) and 'I Don't Want Our Loving to Die' (1968). In the seventies Blaikley started working in the popular mainstream and by the eighties was established as a composer of television themes (including *Miss Marple*, 1986).

DAVE MATTHEWS BAND
Dave Matthews, b. 9 January 1967, Johannesburg, South Africa; LeRoi Moore, b. Charlottesville, Virginia, USA; Carter Beauford, b. Charlottesville, Virginia; Boyd Tinsley; Stefan Lessard, b. 1977, Virginia

Like **Phish**, the Dave Matthews Band both drew on the fluid pyrotechnics of the **Grateful Dead** and built its reputation by constant touring – often performing more than 150 gigs a year. However, where Phish leant more on the Dead's improvisatory attitude, the Dave Matthews Band took a more brooding stance, mixing poppier rhythms and world music riffs with increasingly sombre concerns to hypnotic effect, as on their best album, the guitar-driven *Before These Crowded Streets*.

Born and partly educated in South Africa, Matthews began performing in various pick-up bands in the Richmond area of Virginia after settling there in 1986. He formed the Dave Matthews Band with saxophonist Moore and drummer Beauford, both of whom played together in various jazz groups, violinist Tinsley and bassist Lessard in 1991 and the group quickly found itself a number of regular gigs in the area and became a student favourite. In 1993 the group released the self-financed live album *Remember Two Things* on the independent Bama Rags label. The album eventually sold in excess of 500,000 units, but its initial success with the burgeoning student audience more importantly won the group a contract with RCA. After two years of steady touring the band issued the surprisingly poppy Steve Lillywhite-produced *Under the Table and Dreaming* (1995), which included the hits 'Satellite', the funky 'What Would You Say' and 'Ants Marching'. In the wake of the album, which eventually would sell more than seven million copies, Matthews made the first of several tours with long-time collaborator Tim Reynolds, with whom he had regularly played before the formation of the Dave Matthews Band.

Crash (1996) and the live album *Live at Red Rocks 8:15:95* (1997) cemented the band's reputation, while forays to Europe, the UK and Brazil extended both their reputation and album sales, making them one of the most commercially successful bands of the nineties. *Before These Crowded Streets* (1998) included guest appearances by **Alanis Morissette**, on the atmospheric 'Spoon', and the Kronos Quartet. Despite its darker tone – slavery and the plight of Native Americans were among the issues broached – it was almost as commercially successful as *Crash*. It remained on the charts for over two years and sold some four million copies. After another acoustic tour with Reynolds, Matthews and Reynolds issued *Live at Luther College* (1999).

EDDIE 'LOCKJAW' DAVIS
b. 1921, New York, USA, d. 3 November 1986, Culver City, California

A prominent member of many of **Count Basie**'s bands from the fifties onwards, Davis was a big-toned tenor-saxophonist whose style showed the influence of both **Coleman Hawkins** and of bebop.

He served his apprenticeship with big bands, including those of Andy Kirk and the Chicago ex-disc-jockey **Lucky Millinder**. A 1946 recording with Fats Navarro ('Calling Dr Jazz', Savoy) revealed him to be a master of the raucous, powerhouse form of tenor-playing. Joining Basie in 1952, Davis was a semi-permanent member of the orchestra for twenty years, having an unusual contract which enabled him to take time off for solo performances and recordings. Among the latter were a series of bluesy tenor-organ duets with Shirley Scott, including *The Cookbook* (Prestige, 1956). His most renowned performances with Basie were on *The Atomic Mr Basie* (Vogue, 1959).

In the sixties Davis formed a successful partnership with Johnny Griffin, whose more orthodox bop style was a perfect foil for Lockjaw's booting sax. They cut the aptly named *Toughest Tenors* (Milestone). In later years Davis recorded for **Norman Granz**'s Pablo label and continued to tour extensively in both America and Europe.

REV. GARY DAVIS
b. 30 April 1896, Laurens, South Carolina, USA, d. 5 May 1972, Hammonton, New Jersey

Like **Leadbelly**, Gary Davis threw open a window on the world of rural black music other than the blues. A remarkably accomplished guitarist, he played a vast repertoire of rags, marches, turn-of-the-century square-dance tunes and old popular songs, in addition to the sacred music that was his chosen life-work. As a guitar teacher he inspired innumerable folk and blues players of the fifties and sixties, among them **David Bromberg**, **Ry Cooder**, Larry Johnson, Woody Mann, **Taj Mahal** and, his most loyal follower, **Stefan Grossman** (*b. 16 April 1945, Brooklyn, New York*), who produced many of his later records and himself became an influential tutor.

Partially blind since babyhood, totally so since the age of thirty, Davis worked as a street-singer in the thirties in the North Carolina tobacco cities of Asheville and Durham. He was ordained a Baptist minister in 1933. He recorded sacred songs and a couple of blues for the ARC in 1935, but the label chose to promote his sometime pupil **Blind Boy Fuller**, and Davis did not record again until after the Second World War. He was then living in New York, where he had moved in 1940, and was beginning to be known on the folk circuit through club appearances and records for Asch, Stinson, Riverside, Folkways and Prestige-Bluesville. It was for Prestige-Bluesville that he made the outstanding *Harlem Street Singer* (1960), which included such cornerstones of his repertoire as 'Pure Religion' and 'Twelve Gates to the City'. Other celebrated and often-recorded pieces were 'Get Right, Church', 'Oh Lord, Search My Heart' and the minstrel-era song 'Candyman', also a favourite of **Mississippi John Hurt**.

Rev. Davis visited Britain with the Blues and Gospel Caravan in 1964 and returned solo in 1965, 1969 and 1971. He also appeared at all the major US festivals on many occasions, and was the subject of at least three short films.

JIMMIE DAVIS
b. 11 September 1902, Beech Springs, Louisiana, USA, d. 5 November 2000, Louisiana

With a change of heart extreme even in country music, Davis turned from risqué numbers (such as 'Tom Cat and Pussy Blues' and 'Red Nightgown Blues') performed in the manner of **Jimmie Rodgers** – blue yodels in both senses – to mild country love songs (notably 'You Are My Sunshine') and thence, less surprisingly, to gospel music. In each idiom his work was distinguished by his clear, graceful singing.

After some singing experience at college, Davis became a radio performer in the late twenties on KWKH, Shreveport, Louisiana, which may have led to his being signed to RCA Victor in 1929. Over the next four years he recorded a Rodgers-like mixture of 'heart' songs, yodels, adapted traditional themes and, in particular, blues, such as 'She's a Hum Dum Dinger' (1930). He worked with a variety of guitar accompanists, including the black players Oscar Woods and Ed Schaffer.

In 1934 Davis signed with Decca and immediately recorded what was to become a country standard, 'Nobody's Darlin' but Mine'. The blues element faded from his work, which was now characterized by his hits 'It Makes No Difference Now' (1938), part-written by **Floyd Tillman**, and the undimmable 'You Are My Sunshine' (1940), to which – as to many other songs – Davis claimed a questionable writer's credit.

After some years in public office Davis ran, as a Democrat, for the governorship of Louisiana, a post he held in 1944–8 and again in 1960–4. In the first campaign he made great use of his musical reputation, travelling round the state with a country band that included **Moon Mullican**. In the fifties he began to devote himself to writing, publishing and performing country gospel songs and narrations (among them, 'Suppertime'). Most of his work since then has been in that idiom, except for occasional albums of secular country material. In 1969 he married Anna Carter of the famous country gospel family group the Chuck Wagon Gang, and in 1972 he became a member of the Country Music Hall of Fame. He recorded gospel songs and made live appearances at religious events until a heart attack in 1987 ended his career. *Country Music Hall of Fame* (MCA, 1991) is a useful retrospective, covering the period 1934–54.

MAC DAVIS
b. 21 January 1941, Lubbock, Texas, USA

In the early and mid-seventies Davis achieved massive success both as a songwriter – he wrote the classic 'In the Ghetto', recorded by **Elvis Presley** and **Bobby Bland**, among others – and as a performer, in both the country and pop charts, with records like 'Baby Don't Get Hooked on Me' (1972). But by the eighties his sound became blander and he seemed to lose touch with contemporary developments in country and pop and drifted into Las Vegas shows, easy-listening music and an attempted screen career.

In his teens, like **Buddy Holly** (also born in Lubbock) before him, Davis turned to rock, playing guitar in a number of amateur bands. He formed a rock group in 1960, and started writing songs, but quit performing to become an executive with Vee-Jay in 1961. In 1965 he joined Liberty and in 1966 was made head of Metric Music, the company's music publishing division in Hollywood. Within two years he had started selling to a variety of performers, including **Lou Rawls** ('You're Good to Me') and **Glen Campbell**, and in 1969 supplied Presley with the moving 'In the Ghetto' (Presley's first Top Ten hit for five years) and 'Don't Cry Daddy'. A year later **Kenny Rogers** had a Top Twenty hit with Davis's 'Something's Burning'.

Signed to Columbia in 1971, Davis topped the American charts in 1972 with 'Baby Don't Get Hooked on Me' and released the much-recorded 'I Believe in Music'. His Top Twenty hits were 'One Hell of a Woman', 'Stop and Smell the Roses' and 'Rock'n'Roll (I Gave You the Best Years of My Life)' (all in 1974). However, subsequent releases were less successful and in 1979, the year he made his screen début in *North Dallas Forty*, he left Columbia for Casablanca. That produced the minor hit 'It's Hard to Be Humble' (1980), which British television personality **Max Bygraves** regularly used as the closing number of his shows.

In 1981, still a frequent guest on television variety shows, he started to play Las Vegas regularly and made a second film, *Cheaper to Keep Her*, titled after **Johnnie Taylor**'s 1973 R&B hit.

MAXWELL DAVIS
b. Thomas Maxwell Davis, 14 January 1916, Independence, Kansas, USA, d. 18 September 1970, Los Angeles, California

As producer and arranger, Davis was a major influence on the West Coast rhythm and blues sound of the late forties.

Originally a violinist before changing to alto and tenor saxophone, Davis was steeped in the sound of Kansas City jump blues. He led his own band before joining first Eugene Coy and later **Jay McShann**, with whom he recorded in 1947–9. From 1947 he was closely associated with Eddie and Leo Mesner's Aladdin label, working with such artists as **Charles Brown**, Floyd Dixon and **Clarence 'Gatemouth' Brown**, who sang with the Maxwell Davis Combo before signing to the label. Davis composed **Amos**

Milburn's 1950 R&B No. 1 'Bad, Bad Whiskey', which began a cycle of songs that closed with 'Good Good Whiskey' in 1953.

In the fifties Davis played on sessions for the Federal and Modern labels, with such artists as **Etta James**, **Percy Mayfield** and Red Prysock. He arranged many of **B. B. King**'s recordings on Kent and also accompanied rock'n'roll singer **Ella Mae Morse** and dance-band leader Ray Anthony. He continued to create hits until 1967, when his arrangement of 'Tramp' for **Lowell Fulson** reached the Top Fifty on Kent. Shortly before his death Davis produced blues artist **Z. Z. Hill**.

MILES DAVIS
b. Miles Dewey Davis, 25 May 1926, Alton, Illinois, USA, d. 28 September 1991, Santa Monica, California

Miles Davis has been one of the most important figures in jazz since he participated with **Charlie Parker** in the formation of bebop in the late forties. As a bandleader and a highly influential improviser, he remained at the forefront of innovation through his pensive, subtle trumpet-playing. Davis's most far-reaching achievement was probably the jazz-rock fusion music of the seventies, which was nurtured in his group.

Born into a middle-class black family, Davis took up the trumpet at the age of thirteen and played briefly alongside Parker in **Billy Eckstine**'s orchestra in 1944. The following year he won a scholarship to the Juilliard School of Music in New York, but soon dropped out to play with Parker, then leading the bebop revolution in jazz. Although at this stage technically unimpressive, Davis learned quickly and practiced hard, and already possessed the ability to compress emotional statement into short solos. He recorded with Parker and with bebop groups led by **Charles Mingus**, Eckstine and others.

His first date as a leader came with *Birth of the Cool* (Capitol, 1949), a series of arrangements by **Gil Evans** and **Gerry Mulligan** for a nine-piece band which was the precursor of a school of West Coast 'cool' jazz in the fifties. During the early fifties Davis recorded with a range of small groups, perfecting his sparse, staccato trumpet style. The classic track from this phase was 'Bags' Groove', recorded for Prestige in 1954 at a session which involved well-publicized clashes between Davis and pianist **Thelonious Monk**.

The following year brought public recognition of Davis's commanding place in contemporary jazz. He was the hit of the Newport Jazz Festival and was signed by a major record company, Columbia, with whom he would be associated for the next three decades. Davis had a new group – featuring **John Coltrane**, pianist Red Garland, bassist Paul Chambers

and drummer Philly Joe Jones – and a new musical approach in which improvisation was built on modes not chords.

Sometimes using Gil Evans as arranger, Davis cut a series of acclaimed albums, culminating in 1959 with *Kind of Blue* and *Sketches of Spain*. The rhythm section was inspired, while the bustling solos of Coltrane and **Cannonball Adderley** were a perfect foil to the leader's introspective meditations.

The early sixties saw the rise of 'free jazz', associated with **Ornette Coleman**. Despite a common reaction against the jazz orthodoxy of the time, Davis and the young musicians around him rejected Coleman's innovations. Some of these younger players – **Herbie Hancock**, tenorist Wayne Shorter and drummer Tony Williams, among them – were key figures in the next great Davis quintet, which flourished in the mid-sixties. All three, who can be heard to good effect on the 1966 album *Miles Smiles*, later went into the jazz-rock field.

That field was opened up by Davis's most commercially successful record, *Bitches Brew* (1970). The previous album (*In a Silent Way*) had used a predominantly electric line-up, with **Chick Corea** and Joe Zawinul on keyboards, Dave Holland on bass and **John McLaughlin** on guitar. Now, Shorter's and Davis's solos were performed over a repetitive rhythm derived from contemporary West Coast underground rock. Followers of that music provided Davis with a new audience over the next two years, before his live performances were cut short by illness. Poor health dogged his career throughout the seventies and while his former sidemen made literally dozens of albums of fusion music, Davis released no studio recordings between *Get Up with It* (1974) and *The Man with the Horn* (1981). The latter coincided with a return to live performance with a small electric group.

In later years Davis renewed his partnership with Gil Evans (on *Star People*, 1983) and showed a penchant for pop ballads – **Cyndi Lauper**'s 'Time after Time' gave him his first hit single – and for singing. In 1986 he ended a thirty-year relationship with Columbia to sign to Warner Brothers for the acclaimed *Tutu* and *Amandla* (1988). He also provided solos on rock tracks by **Joni Mitchell** and **Scritti Politti**. *Aura* (1990) was his last CBS album. Composed by Danish trumpeter Palle Mikkelberg it featured **John McLaughlin** on guitar and Nils Peterson on bass. Davis duetted with **John Lee Hooker** on the soundtrack of the film *The Hot Spot* (1990) and the following year he starred in the film *Dingo-Dog of the Desert*, playing a trumpet player and performing music composed by **Michel Legrand**. The film was released after his death.

His final performance was at the Montreux Jazz Festival, where he returned to the Gil Evans arrangements of 'Sketches of Spain' with an orchestra directed by **Quincy Jones**. His final studio recording was *Doo Bop* (Warner, 1992), on which he attempted to synthesize jazz and rap.

SAMMY DAVIS JNR
b. 8 December 1925, New York, USA, d. 16 May 1990, Beverly Hills, California

Mimic, dancer, multi-instrumentalist and declamatory singer, Davis was firmly in the vaudevillian tradition, a flamboyant entertainer whose best work was done live rather than in the recording studio.

The son of vaudevillians, Davis first appeared on stage at the age of two. In 1931 he was featured in the **Ethel Waters** film *Rufus Jones for President*, and in 1932 joined his father, Davis Snr, and uncle, Will Mastin, in the family's song-and-dance stage act. It was during this period that Davis was tutored by Bill 'Bojangles' Robinson. By the end of the thirties Davis was the undisputed star of the show, billed as the Will Mastin Trio. After the Second World War, Davis rejoined the act and in 1946 the trio finally broke out of the chittlin' circuit to become headliners on regular variety shows. In the early fifties Davis went solo and, after losing an eye in an automobile accident in 1954, decided to concentrate on singing.

Already signed with Decca, he had his first hits with 'Hey There' from *The Pyjama Game* (1954), 'Something's Gotta Give' from the film *Daddy Long Legs*, 'Love Me or Leave Me', a revival of **Ruth Etting**'s 1928 hit, and 'That Old Black Magic', the **Harold Arlen** and **Johnny Mercer** composition made famous by **Billy Daniels** (all 1955). In 1956 he made his Broadway début in *Mr Wonderful* and in 1959 won critical acclaim as Sportin' Life in the film of **George Gershwin**'s *Porgy and Bess*, before appearing in a series of films with **Frank Sinatra** and his 'clan'. These include *Ocean's Eleven* (1960) and *Robin and the Seven Hoods* (1964). Of more artistic value was Davis's return to Broadway in 1964 to star alongside Billy Daniels (whose career in many ways prefigured Davis's) in *Golden Boy*, a musical adaptation of Clifford Odets' 1937 drama.

Having left Decca for Reprise Records (which was owned by Sinatra), Davis had his first million-seller with 'What Kind of Fool Am I' (1962) from Leslie Bricusse's and **Anthony Newley**'s musical *Stop the World I Want to Get Off*. Other hits from this period include **Lionel Bart**'s 'As Long as She Needs Me' (1963), 'The Shelter of Your Arms' (1965) and 'I've Gotta Be Me' (1969) from the musical *Golden Rainbow*, which Davis adopted as his theme song.

In 1970 he collapsed on stage during a Las Vegas concert and afterwards slowed down his work rate. His biggest record success came after he moved to MGM for whom he recorded 'Candy Man'*, his only American No. 1. The song was written by Bricusse and Newley for the film *Willy Wonka and the Chocolate Factory* (1971). He has published two volumes of autobiography, *Yes I Can* (1965) and *Hollywood in a Suitcase* (1980). In 1988 he partnered Gregory Hines and showed he could still dance in the evocative film *Tap*.

SKEETER DAVIS
b. Mary Frances Penick, 20 December 1931, Dry Ridge, Kentury, USA

Davis was one of the performers transformed by **Chet Atkins** from a traditional country singer into a pop star in the sixties.

The eldest of seven children, Davis began singing with a schoolmate, Betty Jack Davis (*b. 3 March 1932, Corbin, Kentucky, d. 2 August 1953*), as the Davis Sisters. After regular appearances on the *Kentucky Barn Dance*, in 1949 they were signed to RCA by Steve Sholes. In 1953 he supplied them with a traditionally styled country chart-topper, 'I Forgot More than You'll Ever Know', only for their career to be ended by a car crash which killed Betty Jack and severely injured Skeeter.

Her first two big solo hits, the self-penned '(I Can't Help You) I'm Fallin' Too' (1960) and 'My Last Date (With You)' (1961) were classic examples of both the 'Nashville sound' and of the current vogue for 'answer records': they were replies to hits by **Hank Locklin** and **Floyd Cramer**, respectively. But her most significant recording was the heartbreak ballad 'The End of the World'* (1962), whose lyric took the pathetic fallacy to its extreme. On the basis of that and 'I Can't Stay Mad at You' (1963), her last major pop hit, she briefly turned exclusively to pop, before returning to country, touring and recording with **Bobby Bare** and **George Hamilton IV**.

Though her records were less successful in the seventies and eighties, Davis continued to tour, particularly in the Far East. A devout Christian, she included a growing number of religious songs in her repertoire, which were reflected on the 1983 recording *Heart Strings* (Tudor). In surprising contrast was the live album of country pop with the New York group NBRQ, *They Play She Sings* (1985). In 1987 she married the group's bass-player Joe Staminato.

PETER DAWSON
b. 31 January 1882, Adelaide, Australia, d. 26 September 1961, Australia

Under his various aliases Dawson was, with **Stanley Kirkby**, one of the most prolific recording artists of all time, selling in excess of 25 million records before the LP era. The possessor of a flexible bass-baritone and perfect diction, he was able to sing anything from parlour ballads to grand opera, but he was at his best singing patriotic and sentimental ballads, songs by **Gilbert and Sullivan**, and the more muscular folk songs such as 'Waltzing Matilda'.

An amateur boxer in his youth, Dawson travelled to England in 1902 after winning a bass solo competition in Ballarat. There he studied voice under his fellow countryman, Sir Charles Santley. In 1904, as Leonard Dawson, he made his first recording, a cylinder, for Edison Bell, 'To My First Love', and later that year recorded 'Navajo', the first to be released under his own name for the Gramophone and Typewriter Company. In 1906 he first recorded as Hector Grant, in which capacity he regularly impersonated **Harry Lauder** on a variety of cheaper labels, singing Lauder's composition, 'For the Noo'. In the course of his long career Dawson made use of more than twenty aliases, including Peter Allinson, Geoffrey Baxter, Will Danby, Dick Denton, Charles Handy, Gilbert Munday, Charles Stander, Will Strong, Charles Webber and Robert Woodville. Ironically, it was this adaptability, which made him so popular with record companies, that prevented him from concentrating on a solo career as Peter Dawson. Thus, despite signing a series of exclusive contracts with the Gramophone and Typewriter Company, he continued to record under his various aliases for numerous other companies.

Dawson toured and performed on the radio throughout his career, making his last recording for EMI in 1955 and his final recording for Australian radio in 1958.

Songs associated with him include 'The Floral Dance', **Ivor Novello**'s first hit 'Till the Boys Come Home' (better known as 'Keep the Home Fires Burning'), 'Roses of Picardy', 'Bless this House' and 'The Lost Chord'.

DORIS DAY

b. Doris von Kappelhoff, 3 April 1924, Cincinnati, Ohio, USA

One of the most popular stars of the fifties and sixties – at one time she was paid the highest-ever recording advance by Columbia and was regularly in the chart of Top Ten Film Box-Office Stars – Day's intriguing voice was too often masked by **Mitch Miller**'s bright and bouncy productions, just as her screen career was deformed first by the tomboy image she was saddled with and later by being presented as America's perpetual virgin. Nonetheless, her recordings (which include seven million-sellers and numerous international hits) and films are far better (and more varied) than their reputation might suggest.

Trained as a dancer, Kappelhoff turned to singing

following an accident at the age of fifteen and joined Barney Rapp's band as featured singer in 1940. After a name change she joined the **Bob Crosby** band and then the **Les Brown** band, with whom she scored her first million-seller in 1945, 'Sentimental Journey' (Columbia). Her 1947 duet with Buddy Clark, 'Confess', produced a second. Then, in a typically Hollywood fairy story, following a performance at a party given by **Sammy Cahn** (who with **Jule Styne** had written the score), she was given the female lead in *Romance on the High Seas* (1948) as a replacement for the pregnant **Betty Hutton**. That film produced 'It's Magic'* and a screen career that included some forty films. Among these were *Young Man with a Horn* (1950), which was based on the life of **Bix Beiderbecke**; *Calamity Jane* (1953), a frontier comedy of sexual errors that produced the tremulous 'Secret Love'* (which won its writers, **Sammy Fain** and Paul Francis Webster, an Academy Award); the superior *Love Me or Leave Me* (1955), in which Day played **Ruth Etting** with real conviction; Hitchcock's *The Man Who Knew Too Much* (1956), which included 'Que Sera, Sera'*; and *Pillow Talk* (1959), the first and best of the series of sophisticated sex comedies that saw Day through the sixties.

Away from Hollywood, Day's recording career was masterminded by Columbia's autocratic head of A&R, Mitch Miller, until the sixties when her son, Terry Melcher, best known for his work with the **Byrds**, took over as producer. Thus, like **Guy Mitchell**, **Jo Stafford** and others, she was little but a foil for Miller's brash productions of his own selection of folk-orientated material. Examples of this include her 1952 duet with **Frankie Laine**, 'Sugarbush'*, and, most bizarre of all, 'A Man Is a Man'* (1951), which was based on the bawdy Second World War song 'A Gob Is a Slob' by folk singer Oscar Brand. Not surprisingly, though she remained hugely popular, after the advent of rock'n'roll she never sold records in the same quantities, though her last big hit, 'Move Over Darling' (which was co-written by her son), was successfully (and affectionately) revived by Tracy Ullman in 1984. She left Hollywood in 1968 on the death of her husband Marty Melcher when it was revealed that his mismanagement of her affairs had lost her $20 million, most of which she subsequently regained in damages from her former lawyer. In 1993 the TV-advertised *Singles Collection* returned her to the British album chart.

CHRIS DE BURGH

b. Christopher Davison, 15 October 1948, Argentina

A singer-songwriter whose penchant for religious and mythological themes recalled that of **Al Stewart**, De Burgh enjoyed modest success throughout Europe in the early eighties before his romantic ballad 'The Lady in Red' briefly won him an international audience.

From a British diplomatic family, he settled in Ireland and studied at Trinity College, Dublin, where his performing career began. He was discovered by songwriter Doug Flett and signed to A&M in 1974. The string-smothered *Far Beyond the Castle Walls* was released the following year. Despite a lack of sales in Europe, one track, 'Flying', was a No. 1 hit in Brazil.

His second album, *Spanish Train and Other Stories*, included a title track about playing cards with the Devil and a modern Christmas song, 'A Spaceman Came Travelling'. De Burgh's following grew steadily as he released five more albums by 1980, with four different producers, who included ex-**Yardbird** Paul Samwell-Smith and **Kate Bush**'s producer Andrew Powell. He enjoyed sizeable hits with his dramatic compositions in several European countries, as well as Canada and Brazil.

De Burgh's first British and American hit was 'Don't Pay the Ferryman' (1983), from the Rupert Hine-produced album *The Getaway*, but his commercial breakthrough came in 1986 with 'Lady in Red'. Taken from the album *Into the Light*, the song also made the American Top five. In its wake a re-release of 'A Spaceman Came Travelling' was a minor British hit. 'Missing You' continued his British hits while the 1988 album *Flying Colours* topped the UK charts.

Among De Burgh's later recordings were the compilation *From a Spark to a Flame* (1989), the live *High on Emotion*, *Power of Ten* (1992) and *Love Stories* (1998). They were better received than later albums, such as *Beautiful Dreams* (1995). In 1998 De Burgh was among the few performers asked to take part in the Princess Diana memorial concert.

DE LA SOUL
Posdnous, b. Kelvin Mercer, 17 August 1969, New York City, New York, USA; Trugoy, b. David Jude Jolicoeur, 21 September 1968, New York City; Pasemaster Mace, b. Vincent Lamont Mason Jr, 24 March 1970, New York City

An unconventional rap group, De La Soul found success by combining elements of flower-power culture with hip-hop beats.

Having taken a music business course at college, rapper Posdnous formed De La Soul in 1988, with the group's first single release, 'Plug Tunin'', following in 1989 on New York's influential Tommy Boy label. It was the release of their classic début, *Three Feet High and Rising*, later that year, that won the group international success. Even more than 1988's *Straight Out the Jungle* début from the **Jungle Brothers**, *Three Feet High . . .* added an anarchic sense of humour to rap's vocabulary, sounding more like a wacky hour-long radio show than a regular hip-hop record.

The group's preference for 1960s hippie imagery in the place of rap's usual gold chains and crotch-grabbing braggadocio set De La Soul apart from their peers, as did the origin of some of their samples. While **Run DMC** were basing tunes around riffs from **Aerosmith**, and **Public Enemy** were cutting up **James Brown** drumbeats for their own militant brand of hip-hop, De La Soul were using samples from soft white rock acts such as **Hall & Oates** and **Steely Dan** on 'Say No Go' and 'Eye Know'. Indeed they were even sued for their unauthorized use of an extract from the Turtles' mellow sixties hit 'Happy Together'.

With the Jungle Brothers, **A Tribe Called Quest**, **Queen Latifah** and Monie Love, De La Soul were part of the loose Native Tongues collective, rappers united in a positive, afro-centric outlook. De La Soul appeared on the Jungle Brothers' 'Doin' Our Own Dang' (1989) and had a hit with Queen Latifah with 'Mama Gave Birth to the Soul Children' (1990).

In reaction to the hippie image, the group's second album, *De La Soul Is Dead* (1991), had a tougher sound and harsher lyrics. The album legitimately sampled over 100 other records and included the Top 20 hit 'Ring Ring Ring (Ha Ha Hey)' and the funkily melodic 'Saturdays', which was as memorable for its sung female vocal chorus as for any of its rapping. The group's style continued to oscillate on its next two albums. 1993's *Buhloone Mindstate*, which featured contributions from Maceo Parker and Shortie No Mas (a female rapper whose own records were produced by De La Soul), saw a return to the frivolity of De La Soul's début album, to critical if not great commercial success. Like many of the group's early recordings, the album was produced by Prince Paul, formerly of Stetsasonic. The superior *Stakes Is High* saw a harder sound re-emerge. 'Pony Ride' harked back to 1989's 'Take It Off' in the informality of its chorus, 'Betta Listen' showed the group's humour was alive and well, while in the album's title track they produced one of the toughest combinations of rhymes and beats of their career. However, it was not a great commercial success and in 1999 De La Soul were to be found working with UK big-beat merchants the Propellerheads, recording '360 (Oh Yeah)' for an EP which also featured a Propellerheads collaboration with the Jungle Brothers.

Less experimental but more intriguing was the first album of the triple-CD set the group issued in 2000. Released in stages over a six-month period under the generic title of *Art Official Intelligence*, the first of the series was *Mosaic Thump*, which was constructed as a light-hearted party album and as such was in marked contrast to the reflective tone of *Stakes Is High*. Among the artists who guested on the album was **Chaka Kahn**.

DEAD KENNEDYS

Jello Biafra; East Bay Ray; Ted (replaced by Darren Peligro); Klaus Flouride

The missing link between the UK punk bands of 1976/77 and the later US hardcore scene of the eighties, the Dead Kennedys made some of the most politically charged recordings to emerge from the US in the late eighties.

Formed in San Francisco in 1977, the Dead Kennedys were led by the highly vocal Jello Biafra, and set their stall out with their high-octane 1979 début single 'California Uber Alles'. It was followed by a string of uncompromisingly incendiary singles, which although musically clichéd had a visceral power few US punk bands achieved. It gained the band a devoted following in the UK. The singles included 'Holiday in Cambodia', 'Kill the Poor' and the typically direct 'Nazi Punks Fuck Off'. The group released their début album, *Fresh Fruit for Rotting Vegetables* (1980), in the UK through independent label Cherry Red. Still their most successful album, it made the UK Top Forty. The following year their only hit single, 'Too Drunk to Fuck', reached the European charts. In the US it led to them being unsuccessfully prosecuted for indecency.

The band's second album, *Plastic Surgery Disasters* (1982), which featured new drummer D. H. Peligro, appeared, like all their subsequent releases, on their own Alternative Tentacles label, which also released material by bands like the Butthole Surfers. Later albums included *Frankenchrist* (1985) and *Bedtime for Democracy* (1986). The compilation *Give Me Convenience or Give Me Death* appeared in 1987, the same year that Biafra released the solo album *No More Cocoons*.

With the Kennedys defunct, Biafra continued his solo career with *High Priest of Harmful Matter* in 1989, followed by a collaboration with hardcore band Nomeansno, *The Sky Is Falling and I Want My Mommy* (1991). Biafra's next solo album was the typically forthright *I Blow Minds for a Living* (1991). In 1994 he teamed up with fellow maverick Mojo Nixon for the country-and-western parody *Prairie Home Invasion*.

Biafra's refusal to compromise his views led him into continued conflict with the status quo. In 1979 he unsuccessfully ran for mayor in San Francisco and in the eighties took a leading role in rock's fight against censorship, notably joining forces with **Frank Zappa**. In 1994 Biafra was injured in a fight in a club during a tour of Canada.

JIMMY DEAN

b. Seth Ward, 10 August 1928, Plainview, Texas, USA

Dean's speciality was the dramatic narrative, well exemplified in his two biggest hits, the self-penned 'Big Bad John' (1961)*, the story of a larger-than-life miner who sacrifices himself that his comrades might live, and 'P. T. 109' (1962), which related the heroic wartime exploits of John F. Kennedy.

Born into a poor rural family, Dean formed his first professional group while in the air force. On his discharge in 1948, he and his new group, the Texas Wildcats, signed to Four Star and had a Top Ten country hit with 'Bummin' Around' (1953). However, his biggest success in the fifties was as a television personality. He graduated from guest appearances to his own networked show, *The Jimmy Dean Show*, in 1957, a forerunner of **Roy Clark**'s *Hee Haw*.

His first pop hit (he was one of the first country artists to cross over) came with the novelty disc 'Little Sandy Sleighfoot' (Columbia, 1958). Then, in 1961, came the chart-topping 'Big Bad John' with its hammer sound effects and spare production. This was followed by five further Top Thirty hits in 1962, three of which were spoken narratives – 'Dear Ivan', 'The Cajun Queen' and 'To a Sleeping Beauty', 'P. T. 109' and 'Little Black Book' – before Dean returned to television in 1963–6. In 1966 Dean joined RCA but had little chart success, apart from a duet with Dottie West, 'Slowly' (1971), and in 1976 joined Casino, whereupon he bounced back with 'I.O.U.'*, another recitation which was also a hit when reissued on the Churchill label in 1983. But by then Dean's main occupation was the manufacture of pork sausages.

DEEE-LITE

Lady Miss Kier, b. Kieren Kirby, Youngstown, Ohio, USA; Super DJ Dimitry, b. Dimitry Brill, Kiev, Ukraine; DJ Towa Tei, b. Doug Wa-Chung, Tokyo, Japan

Deee-Lite shot to international success with 1990's 'Groove Is in the Heart', a catchy pop-dance crossover. However, despite a trio of fine albums, the band never matched the commercial appeal of this track.

Kier and Dimitry formed the group after meeting in New York in the early 1980s, Towa Tei joining in 1987 after moving to the city to study design. The absurdity of the group's image and composition – a post-Cold War marriage of Soviet, Japanese and US musical talent, sporting an extensive array of sixties fashion-disaster clothing – disguised the quality of the band's output.

Their début LP, *World Clique* (1990, Elektra), was a riot of bass-heavy, piano-led tunes, and featured contributions from funk horn legends Fred Wesley and Maceo Parker, a rap from **A Tribe Called Quest**'s Q-Tip, and ex-**James Brown** and **George Clinton** bass-player Bootsy Collins. As well as 'Groove Is in the Heart', the album also featured the hit 'The Power of Love'.

Like other acts arriving during the house music explosion of the late 1980s, Deee-Lite found success harder to maintain in the early 1990s. 1992's second LP, *Infinity Within*, offered the same high-quality mix of sweet vocal harmonies, big dance beats and sixties kitsch imagery, coupled with more socially concerned lyrics, embracing issues such as safe sex ('Rubber Lover') and the environment (the snappily titled 'I Had a Dream I Was Falling through a Hole in the Ozone Layer'). However, with audiences leaning more towards the tougher instrumental house acts such as **Leftfield** and **Underworld**, or towards the sixties guitar proclivities of Britpop, Deee-Lite found further commercial success elusive. Towa Tei left the group before their third album, *Dew Drops in the Garden* (1994), for which the now-married Kier and Dimitry recruited DJ Ani as his replacement. The album sold poorly, and after the release of a compilation, *Sampadelic Relics and Dancefloor Oddities* (1996), the group formally split.

The most successful of the band's members in the post-Deee-Lite years has been Towa Tei, who released his album *Future Listening!* in 1995, mixing Deee-Lite's humour with an even more catholic taste in rhythms and vocal styles. This was followed by a second solo album, *Sound Museum*, in 1998 and a third, the critically unpopular *Last Century Modern* (East West, 2000). Kier, meanwhile, settled for some time in London, where she became increasingly influenced by the emerging jungle scene. There was talk of a solo album, but by mid-1999 this had still to emerge.

DEEP PURPLE

Ritchie Blackmore, b. 14 April 1945, Weston-super-Mare, Avon, England (replaced by Tommy Bolin, b. 1951, Sioux City, Iowa, USA, d. 4 December 1976, Miami, Florida); Rod Evans, b. 1945 (replaced by Ian Gillan, b. 19 August 1945, Hounslow, Middlesex, England, replaced by Graham Bonnet, replaced by David Coverdale, b. 21 September 1951, Saltburn, Tyne and Wear); Jon Lord, b. 9 June 1941, Leicester; Ian Paice, b. 29 June 1948, Nottingham; Nick Simper, b. 1946, Norwood Green (replaced by Roger Glover, b. 30 November 1945, Brecon, Wales, replaced by Glenn Hughes)

One of the founders of heavy rock, Deep Purple were first noted for their hard-rock cover-versions of pop hits and for their rock/classics experiments. In the seventies and eighties guitarist Blackmore and singer Coverdale became leading figures of the heavy-metal genre.

During the early sixties Blackmore had played with Screamin' Lord Sutch and Neil Christian and the Crusaders before settling in Germany. He was recruited by former **Searchers** drummer Chris Curtis to join a new band with Simper (bass) and Lord (keyboards). Lord had previously been in R&B group the Artwoods while both had played in the backing group for the Flowerpot Men, a 'psychedelic' vocal group set up by John Carter and Ken Lewis whose biggest hit was 'Let's Go to San Francisco' (Deram, 1967). Curtis dropped out but the line-up was completed by Paice (drums) and singer Evans from the Maze.

After rejecting the name Concrete God, Deep Purple modelled themselves on **Vanilla Fudge**, playing tuneful songs in a heavy manner. While unsuccessful in Britain on Parlophone, the group's treatment of **Joe South**'s 'Hush' (1968) was a Top Ten hit in America, though **Neil Diamond**'s 'Kentucky Woman' fared less well. After recording *Shades of Deep Purple, Book of Talieysyn* and *Deep Purple* in only a year, Evans and Simper left the band.

Their replacements, Gillan and Glover, had played with Episode Six since 1963, recording harmony ballads for Pye, MGM and Chapter One, the label run by songwriter **Les Reed**. The new line-up indulged Lord's fusion tendencies by recording his *Concerto for Group and Orchestra* with the Royal Philharmonic Orchestra (1970) but it was Gillan's shrieking high notes on the driving 'Black Night' that brought the band's first British hit.

Deep Purple in Rock (1970) became the classic textbook of heavy rock with Blackmore's attacking guitar work complementing Gillan's stirring vocals on 'Speed King' and 'Child in Time'. The title track of *Fireball* (1971), the first record on the group's own Purple label, reached the British Top Twenty while 'Smoke on the Water' (1973) was a Top Ten hit in America.

At this high point, what was generally regarded as Deep Purple's most effective line-up was dissolved when Gillan and Glover left the group after differences with Blackmore. The bassist went on to a successful career as a producer (**Nazareth**, **Status Quo**) while Gillan formed a new group.

With Coverdale (vocals) and Hughes (bass) from Birmingham group Trapeze, Deep Purple cut the Top Ten albums *Burn* (1974) and *Stormbringer*, which showed Coverdale's blues and soul influences, before Blackmore quit in 1975. American guitarist Bolin joined for *Come Taste the Band* (1975) but his drug problems made his work erratic and eventually led to his death. *The California Rehearsals* (Pure, 2000) lovingly collects together the preparations for this album, including early versions of songs featured on *Come Taste*.

After Deep Purple disbanded in 1976, Lord and Paice linked up with keyboard-player Tony Ashton for *Malice in Wonderland* (Oyster, 1977), while

Coverdale formed the successful **Whitesnake**. Hughes rejoined Trapeze before embarking on a solo career, and Bolin formed his own band, recording for Warners. Meanwhile, Blackmore's Rainbow made eight albums between 1975 and 1983. The first four featured American-born vocalist Ronnie James Dio, whose previous band Elf had been signed to Purple Records, and veteran British drummer Cozy Powell also featured on four, joining for 1976's *Rainbow Rising*. All the albums were British hits, with *Down to Earth* (1979), with Graham Bonnet on vocals, and the Glover-produced *Difficult to Cure* (Polydor, 1981) among the most successful. The latter featured American vocalist Joe Lynn Turner, who also appeared on *Straight Between the Eyes* (1982) and *Bent Out of Shape*.

Gillan's post-Purple career had started with the Ian Gillan Band album *Child in Time* (1976), and he enjoyed considerable success with his own band, Gillan, releasing five hit albums between 1979 and 1982, the most successful being 1981's *Future Shock*. The band split in 1982, and Gillan then briefly joined **Black Sabbath** in 1983.

In 1984 Blackmore and Glover were reunited with Gillan, Lord and Paice to undertake a world tour and to record *Perfect Strangers* (Mercury). Glover produced the later Deep Purple album, *House of Blue Light* (1987), which was followed by another tour, during which the less successful live album, *Nobody's Perfect* (1988), was recorded. Gillan now left the band to record his first solo album, *Naked Thunder* (Atlantic), in 1989. This was followed by *Accidentally on Purpose* (1989), a collaboration with Glover. *Cherkazoo and Other Stories* (RPM, 1992) was a collection of Gillan's solo work from the seventies, previously only available in Japan.

Joined by former Rainbow vocalist Joe Lynn Turner, Deep Purple recorded *Slaves and Masters* (RCA, 1990) and toured in 1991. In 1993 Gillan, Blackmore et al. patched up their differences once again to record *The Battle Rages on* (RCA), and the 'classic' line-up set out on another world tour. However, before playing the last dates of the tour in Japan, Blackmore left and was briefly replaced by **Joe Satriani**. He in turn was replaced by Steve Morse (*b. 28 July 1954, Hamilton, Ohio, USA*), a former member of Kansas, for *The Final Battle* and *Come Hell and High Water* (1998). In 1999 the group re-recorded Lord's *Concerto for Group and Orchestra*, this time with the London Philharmonic Orchestra (Eagle Rock). It was as overblown as ever.

DEF LEPPARD
Frank Noon (replaced by Rick Allen, b. 1 November 1963); Steve Clark, b. 23 April 1960, d. 8 January 1991, *London (replaced by Vivian Campbell, b. 25 August 1963, Belfast, Ireland); Joe Elliott, b. 1 August 1959, Sheffield, Yorkshire, England; Rick Savage, b. 2 December 1960, Sheffield; Pete Willis (replaced by Phil Collen, b. 8 December 1957, London)*

The most successful British heavy-metal band of the eighties, Def Leppard paved the way for the new wave of heavy rock that began to dominate pop at the end of the decade.

As Atomic Mass, the group was formed at school in Sheffield by Elliott (vocals), Willis (guitar) and Savage (bass). Playing versions of **UFO** and **Thin Lizzy** hits, they became Def Leppard, adding drummer Noon and guitarist Clarke. With a loan from Elliott's father, in 1978 they recorded the EP *Getcha Rocks Off* for their own Bludgeon Riffola label. The record sold well and led to radio sessions and a recording contract with Phonogram. *On Through the Night* (1980) was produced by Tom Allom, reached the British Top Twenty and included the minor hits 'Wasted' and 'Hello America'.

Under the guidance of their American manager Peter Mensch, Def Leppard aimed the 'Mutt' Lange-produced *High 'n' Dry* (1981) at the US market, where it was a Top Forty hit. Henceforth, the band's material would be more dynamic and melodic than that of more conventional heavy-metal groups. During the recording of *Pyromania* (1983), Collen (formerly of Girl) replaced Willis and the group undertook a world tour to coincide with its release. With the American hits 'Photograph' and 'Rock of Ages', the album went to achieve sales of over seven million.

During preparations for the follow-up record, drummer Allen lost an arm in a car accident. With the aid of a Fairlight computer, he was able to complete the drum tracks for *Hysteria* and to play in later live performances. The use of the computer gave the album a firm techno element. This and Allen's more detailed arrangements made the 12-million-selling *Hysteria* a classic of melodic heavy metal. The release of the album was preceded by 'Animal', Def Leppard's biggest British hit to date. 'Pour Some Sugar on Me' was an American Top Five success before the album itself finally topped the US chart in 1988. The album quickly outsold *Pyromania*. After Clark's drug-induced death in 1991 the band decided not to replace him immediately, recording much of *Adrenalize* (1992) as a four-piece. The most mainstream of their albums, it was an enormous hit. The band recruited ex-**Whitesnake** and Dio guitarist Campbell in 1992 and toured heavily in support of the album. They had a US Top Ten hit with 'Two Steps Behind' from the film *The Last Action Hero* in 1993. In the same year the band released *Retroactive*, a compilation of rarities, unreleased songs and cover-versions. A Top Ten album on both sides of the Atlantic, it contained one song by **David Bowie**'s ex-guitarist Mick Ronson, at whose memorial concert in London in April 1994 Elliot and Collen played. The much-delayed *Slang*, on which Allen played an acoustic rather than electronic drum kit, was released to critical approval in 1996 and supported by a world tour.

DESMOND DEKKER
b. Desmond Dacris, 16 July 1942, Kingston, Jamaica

The first reggae artist to achieve sustained international recognition, Dekker's floating falsetto has remained one of the most popular sounds in Jamaican music.

A neighbour of **Bob Marley** in Kingston's Trench Town, Dekker first recorded for **Leslie Kong** with the Aces (Barry Howard and Sammy Jones). 'Honour Thy Father and Mother' (1963), released in Britain by **Chris Blackwell**'s Island label, was the first of a string of Jamaican hits.

From 1964, Dekker's songs commented on the 'rude boy' (street-gang) phenomenon, culminating in the James Bond-inspired '007', which was a 1967 British hit on Pyramid. He subsequently toured Britain and was later said to have influenced the skinhead youth culture style. The following year Dekker recorded his most well-known track, 'Israelites', a UK No. 1 and a Top Ten hit on Uni in America. Ironically, the lyrics, sung in Jamaican patois, expressed Rastafarian beliefs, implicitly opposed to the values of 'Babylon' (white society). 'It Mek' (1969) and **Jimmy Cliff**'s 'You Can Get It If You Really Want' (Trojan, 1970) were also successful.

Dekker had one more British pop hit – 'Sing a Little Song' (Cactus, 1975) – before cutting a misjudged Two Tone-styled album for Stiff (*Black and Dekker*, 1980), with backing from **Graham Parker**'s Rumour. His next record, the **Robert Palmer**-produced *Compass Point* (Stiff, 1981), was equally unsuccessful. In 1984 he was declared bankrupt, but he continued to tour in Europe into the nineties.

GEORGES DELARUE
b. 12 March 1925, Roubaix, France, d. 20 March 1992, Los Angeles, California, USA

One of the most prolific film music composers of the past 40 years, Delarue's career was spent in the film industries of France, Britain and the USA. He was known for his lyrical style.

After studying at the Paris Conservatoire, Delarue worked on films by several of the leading directors of the French 'new wave' cinema. Among these were François Truffaut's *Don't Shoot the Piano Player* (1960) and *Jules et Jim* (1962), Jean Luc Godard's *Con-*

tempt (1963) and Louis Malle's *Viva Maria* (1965).

During the sixties Delarue frequently worked on films shot in Britain. These included *A Man for All Seasons* (1966), *The Day of the Jackal* (1973) and *Women in Love* (1969). Among his most memorable European work was *The Conformist* (1970), by the Italian director Bernardo Bertolucci.

From the early seventies Delarue began to score Hollywood films. He won an Oscar for *A Little Romance* in 1979 and also worked with such directors as Oliver Stone (*Platoon*, 1986), John Frankenheimer (*The Horsemen*, 1971) and Mike Nichols (*Biloxi Blues*, 1988).

He also composed music for US television dramas and in 1985 he wrote and conducted a new score for Alexander Volkov's 1927 silent film epic *Casanova*. Several collections of his work have been issued, including two volumes of *Best Film Music of Georges Delarue* (Silva Screen, 1989) and *Music from the Films of François Truffaut* (Milan, 1989).

THE DELFONICS
Randy Cain, b. 2 May 1945, Philadelphia, Pennsylvania, USA (replaced by Major Harris, b. Richmond, Virginia, replaced by Bruce Peterson, b. Chicago); Wilbert Hart, b. 19 October 1947, Washington DC; William Hart, b. 17 January 1945, Washington DC; Ritchie Daniels

Produced by **Thom Bell**, the Delfonics were leaders of the sophisticated soul vocal-group movement of the late sixties. With Bell's swirling cushion of strings and woodwinds and William Hart's high, breathy tenor (reminiscent of **Little Anthony**), 'La La Means I Love You' (Philly Groove, 1968) spawned many imitators, just as the doo-wop hits of the fifties had done.

The group began as the Four Gents and were discovered by producer Stan Watson, a former member of the **Del-Vikings**, whose name inspired the change to the Delfonics. After Bell produced the local hits 'He Don't Really Love You' (Moonshot, 1967) and 'You've Been Untrue' (Cameo), Watson formed the Philly Groove label for the band.

Beginning with 'La La' William Hart co-wrote most of the songs with Bell. The major hits included 'Ready or Not Here I Come' (1968), the ethereal 'Didn't I (Blow Your Mind This Time)'* (1970) and 'Trying to Make a Fool of Me' (1970). After Bell shifted his attention to the **Stylistics**, Hart took creative control but *Walk Right Up to the Sun* (1971) and *Alive and Kicking* could not recapture earlier glories. By now Harris had joined the group but later records for **Curtis Mayfield**'s Curtom label were equally unsuccessful.

Harris had later pop hits with 'Love Won't Let Me Wait'* (Atlantic, 1975) and *All My Life* (1983). In one of the screen's best examples of how to use pop music, the Delfonics' music was used wonderfully in Quentin Tarantino's *Jackie Brown* (1997) to show the evolution of the Robert Forster character.

DELIRIOUS?

Stuart Garrard, b. 7 June 1966, Ipswich, England; Tim Jupp, b. 1 May 1966, Eastbourne; Martin Smith, b. 6 July 1970, Woodford Green, Essex; Stewart 'Stew' Smith, b. 27 January 1967, Shoreham-by-Sea; Jon Thatcher, b. 1 January 1976, Rustington, West Sussex

A Christian alternative rock band, Delirious? have steadily built up a fanbase in Britain and America despite a lack of airplay and media coverage because of their ideology.

The origins of Delirious? date back to 1993 when Garrard (guitar), Jupp (keyboards) and brothers Martin (vocals) and Stuart Smith (drums) began to play together in church services in Littlehampton, West Sussex. As word about the band spread they began touring the UK, adding bassist Thatcher to the line-up, and formed their own Furious? label. Over the next few years they released a series of albums of pop/worship, later collected on *The Cutting Edge* (1997).

Delirious?'s début album proper, *King of Fools* (1996), saw them alter their sound – becoming more akin to the stadium rock of U2 and **Manic Street Preachers** – while retaining a spiritual aspect in their lyrics. The album included the surprise hit 'Deeper', which reached the UK Top Twenty without any radio airplay, prompting EMI to sign the band. The following year saw Delirious? tour solidly in the US, where they sold 100,000 copies of their début album. The release of *Mezzamorphosis* (1999) drew comparisons with **Radiohead**'s *OK Computer* and saw the band gain new converts in both America and Britain, where they finally began to receive mainstream interest.

THE DELLS

Vern Allison; Chuck Barksdale; John Funches (replaced by Johnny Carter); Marvin Junior; Lucius McGill; Mickey McGill

With Marvin Junior's gospel-drenched lead vocals and Carter's stratospheric falsetto, the Dells were one of the most impressive soul vocal groups of the sixties. The group survived into the eighties, completing over thirty years of performing and recording.

They formed at a Chicago high school as the El Rays, cutting the *a cappella* 'Darling, Dear I Know' (Checker, 1953). Lucius McGill left before they signed to Vee-Jay as the Dells. The group recorded in the finger-popping style of Joe Carroll before enjoying their first R&B hit with the slow ballad 'Oh What a Night' (1956). The follow-ups – 'The Springer' and 'Jeepers Creepers' (both 1957) – were less successful and in

1958 Funches was replaced by the **Flamingos**' Carter after a car accident.

From 1962 to 1964 the Dells recorded for Chess – 'The Bossa Nova Bird' was a minor hit – but they rejoined Vee-Jay for the 1965 R&B classic 'Stay in My Corner'. When the label folded, the group signed to the Chess subsidiary Cadet in 1967. There they were provided with a dramatic and sophisticated soul sound by producer Bobby Miller and arranger Charles Stepney. Notable among the series of pop and R&B hits which followed were 'There Is' (1968), and re-recordings of 'Stay in My Corner', which reached the Top Ten in 1968, and of 'Oh What a Night' (1969). *There Is* (1968) remains one of the outstanding soul albums while *I Can Sing a Rainbow* contained elaborate arrangements of pop standards and provided the Dells' only British hit with a medley of the title track and a cover of Paul Mauriat's 'Love Is Blue'.

'Give Your Baby a Standing Ovation' (1973) was the group's final success before they moved to Mercury for *We Got to Get Our Thing Together* (1974) and *No Way Back* (1976). The group later recorded for ABC (1979), 20th Century-Fox (1980) and Private I (1981). Despite the changes in style in soul music during the eighties, the Dells retained a following on the nightclub circuit and recorded *One Step Closer* with producers Marvin Yancy and Chuck Jackson, and *The Second Time* (1988). The film *The Five Heartbeats* (1991) was loosely based on the group's early years and it helped to revitalize their career. They re-recorded 'Stay in My Corner' for the soundtrack album (Virgin) and had an R&B hit with 'A Heart Is a House for Love'.

THE DELMORE BROTHERS

Alton, b. 25 December 1908, Elkmont, Alabama, USA, d. 9 June 1964, Huntsville, Alabama; Rabon, b. 3 December 1916, Elkmont, d. 4 December 1952, Athens, Alabama

Among the brother acts of thirties country music the Delmores were exceptional on two counts: their success was largely founded on blues and, later, boogie-woogie material; and, rather than subsiding, it increased in the immediate post-war years, as they adapted, more adroitly than many of their contemporaries, to musical and technological change.

The Delmores rose to fame as cast members of the *Grand Ole Opry* (1932–8), their soft voices, close harmonies and well-contrived guitar-playing (Alton on standard and Rabon on the four-stringed tenor guitar) coming over especially well on the improved electrical radio microphones. They then moved to WPTF, Raleigh, North Carolina (1938–9) and WAPI, Birmingham, Alabama (1939–42), at the same time recording regularly for RCA Victor's Bluebird label (and later, briefly, Decca) and having steady-selling hits with 'Gonna Lay Down My Old Guitar' and, in particular, 'Brown's Ferry Blues' (both 1933). They also toured and recorded with *Opry* stars Fiddlin' Arthur Smith and **Uncle Dave Macon**.

In 1944, while on WLW, Cincinnati, Ohio, the Delmores joined the group of artists that launched **Syd Nathan**'s King label – others were Grandpa Jones and **Merle Travis** – and quickly became one of its leading country acts with a succession of boogie titles like 'Hillbilly Boogie' (1945) and 'Freight Train Boogie' (1946), capped by their 1949 hit 'Blues Stay Away from Me', based on a melodic figure usually associated with blues pianist **Jimmy Yancey**. During this period the Delmores also recorded in a gospel quartet, the Brown's Ferry Four, whose other members included, at different times, Grandpa Jones, **Red Foley**, Travis and **Cowboy Copas**. These recordings were influential for many years, and a quartet modelled on the Brown's Ferry Four, including some original members, appeared regularly on *Hee Haw*, the long-running US TV show devoted to country music.

Meanwhile, the brothers had been working on various Southern stations, notably WMC, Memphis (1945–7), and KPRC, Houston (1951–2). After Rabon's death Alton interspersed musical jobs with attempts at becoming a magazine short-story writer, and his last years were devoted to his autobiography *Truth Is Stranger than Publicity*.

THE DEL-VIKINGS

Norman Wright, b. 21 October 1937, Philadelphia, Pennsylvania, USA; Corinthian 'Kripp' Johnson, b. 1944, Cambridge, Maryland, d. 22 June 1990, Pontiac, Michigan; Donald 'Gus' Bakus, b. 1942, Long Island, New York; David Lerchey, b. 1946, New Albany, Indiana; Clarence E. Quick, b. 1944, Brooklyn, New York; Charles 'Chuck' Jackson, b. 22 July 1937, Winston Salem, South Carolina

The Del-Vikings were one of the first integrated doowop groups; others were the **Crests**, the Meadowlarks ('Heaven and Paradise', Dootone, 1955) and the **Marcels**.

The members met while stationed at an air force base in Pittsburgh in 1955 and recorded unsuccessfully for Luniverse in 1956. Then, after Johnson joined them, they cut Quick's composition 'Come Go with Me' independently and sold it to the small Fee-Bee Records. A local hit, the infectious chant was leased by Dot, who sold over a million copies in 1957, and was later a hit for **Dion** who gave it an even more raucous treatment in his 1962 revival. Their follow-up, 'Whispering Bells' (1957), also hit the Top Ten. Before that was released, however, all the group except Johnson had quit to become the Dell-Vikings (with an extra 'l') on Mercury, who had offered them more money than Dot. It was this group that had further hits with 'Cool Shake' and a version of the **Harptones**' 'Sunday Kind of Love' (1957). Johnson left Dot at the end of 1957, but various aggregations billing themselves as the Del- (and sometimes Dell-) Vikings appeared throughout the sixties. By the time of the rock'n'roll revival of the seventies Quick was the only original member of the group left.

One of the new members drafted in by Johnson when the others left to sign with Mercury was former gospel singer (with the Raspberry Singers) Jackson, who sang lead on the unsuccessful 'Willette' (1957). After that group disbanded, Jackson went solo, recording for Clock and Beltone before being signed to Wand in 1960 after Luther Dixon, a producer with the label, saw him appearing with **Jackie Wilson**. His first record for the label, the rich soul ballad 'I Don't Want to Cry' (which he co-wrote with Dixon), was a hit. But, henceforth, in search of pop hits, Wand teamed him with white pop songwriters. These included Wand's writer-in-residence **Burt Bacharach** ('I Wake Up Crying', 1961); Bacharach and Bob Hilliard (the soul classic 'Any Day Now', his biggest-ever hit in 1962); Gerry Goffin and **Carole King** ('I Need You', 1965); Tony Bruno (the heartfelt 'Tell Him I'm Not Home', 1963 – Jackson's best record); and **Leiber and Stoller** ('I Keep Forgettin'', 1962). The results were among the best examples of pop-soul of the period, as were his duets with Maxine Brown (best remembered for 'All in My Mind', Nomar, 1961, and the much-covered 'Oh No, Not My Baby', Wand, 1964), which included 'Something You Got' (1965) and a remake of **Shep and the Limelites**' 'Daddy's Home' (1967).

In 1967 Jackson left Wand for Motown, where he languished for some five years, making for the most part characterless records. He returned to the R&B charts in 1973, on ABC with 'I Only Get the Feeling', then moved on to All Platinum for 'I'm Needing You, Wanting You' (1975). In 1980 he had a minor R&B hit, 'I Wanna Give You Some Love', on EMI America, by which time he was an established star of cabaret soul. He performed at the inauguration of US president George Bush in 1989 and recorded 'All Over the World'.

JOHN DENVER

b. Henry John Deutschendorf, 31 December 1943, Roswell, New Mexico, USA, d. 12 October 1997, Monterey Bay, California

With more than twenty gold albums in the United States alone, Denver was a child of the sixties folk revival who became the archetypal middle-of-the-road singer-songwriter of the seventies.

From an air force family, he was a solo singer-guitarist in Los Angeles when he joined pop-folk group the Chad Mitchell Trio as a replacement for Mitchell himself in 1965. He toured with Joe Frazier and Mike Kobluk for four years, recording albums of both new and traditional songs for Mercury until 1969 when the group split up.

In the same year **Peter, Paul and Mary** had a massive translantic hit with the Denver ballad 'Leaving on a Jet Plane'. That success helped Denver to get a solo contract with RCA, where the Mitchell Trio arranger Milt Okun produced his first album, *Rhymes and Reasons* (1969). The record mixed sweet ballads like 'Jet Plane' with satirical attacks on President Nixon. Neither that nor two follow-up albums, which anthologized songs by folk-based artists like **Tom Paxton** and **Jacques Brel**, were successful. However, the 1971 record *Poems, Prayers and Promises* included the catchy 'Take Me Home Country Roads'*, co-written by Denver and Bill and Taffy Danoff. It reached No. 2 and was a British hit for **Olivia Newton-John** two years later.

Six more Top Ten hits (four of them No. 1s) followed by 1975, all of which displayed Denver's melodic talent on both sentimental ballads such as 'Annie's Song'* (later revived in an instrumental version by flautist **James Galway**, RCA, 1978) and jaunty songs like 'Thank God I'm a Country Boy'*. By now, he was in demand as a crossover star, appearing with **Frank Sinatra** and making his film début in *Oh God!* (1977). Denver cut four more RCA albums of his own material between 1977 and 1985, as well as a collaboration with opera star **Placido Domingo** (*Perhaps Love*, CBS, 1981). In 1976 he formed Windsong Records, signing the Danoffs, who had an immediate hit as the Starland Vocal Band with 'Afternoon Delight'. After being dropped by RCA he founded Windstar to release *Higher Ground* (1988), a country hit.

In the nineties Denver continued to perform and record. His albums include *Christmas Like a Lullaby* (American Gramaphone, 1990), the impassioned *The Flower that Shattered the Stone* (Windstar, 1991), on which he was accompanied by **James Burton**, and *Earth Songs* (MCA).

Despite the inevitable tendency of the MOR environment to emphasize the bland side of his writing and light tenor voice, Denver retained from his folk background a commitment to ecological causes, including conservation and opposition to nuclear energy. The B-side of the 1975 hit 'I'm Sorry'* was 'Calypso', named after the ship of marine biologist Jacques Cousteau, with whom Denver appeared in a television documentary.

In 1994 Denver was the first American musician to perform in Vietnam since the end of the war. He died in a plane crash in 1997.

DEPECHE MODE

Vince Clarke, b. 3 July 1961, Basildon, Essex, England (replaced by Alan Wilder, b. 1 June 1959); Andy Fletcher, b. 8 July 1961, Basildon; Dave Gahan, b. 9 May 1962, Epping, Essex; Martin Gore, b. 23 July 1961, Basildon

The most successful synthesizer pop group of the eighties, Depeche Mode had over twenty hit singles in Britain and Europe. By the nineties they had become part of the global stadium rock elite.

In 1980 Clarke (keyboards), Fletcher (guitar) and Gore (drums) formed Composition of Sound in their home town of Basildon. With the arrival of singer Gahan, Clarke added synthesizers, whose electro-pop sound dominated 'Dreaming of Me', made for Daniel Miller's independent Mute label. Soon afterwards *Speak and Spell* (1981) and its singles 'New Life' and 'Just Can't Get Enough' were British hits. Both singles were written by Clarke, who then left the band to form Yazoo with **Alison Moyet**. The hits, however, continued. Ex-Hitmen synthesizer specialist Wilder joined the band and Gore composed 'See You', 'The Meaning of Love' and 'Leave in Silence' for *Broken Frame* (1982).

Construction Time Again (1983) found Gore turning his attention to political themes on 'Two Minute Warning', 'Everything Counts' (an attack on multinational firms) and 'People Are People' – the band's first American hit, in 1985 on Sire. *Some Great Reward* (1984) included the British Top Ten success 'Master and Servant'. Further hits were 'Shake the Disease' (1985), 'It's Called a Heart' and 'A Question of Time' (1986).

Among the songs on *Music for the Masses* (1987) were 'Strangelove' and 'Never Let Me Down Again'. The group's 1988 American tour was filmed by D. A. Pennebaker and released as *101*, as a video and an album. The following year Gore released *Counterfeit EP*, a collection of versions of such songs as **Sparks**' 'Never Turn Your Back on Mother Earth' and the spiritual 'Motherless Child'. *Violator* (1990), produced by Flood, included the engaging 'Personal Jesus' and 'Enjoy the Silence', their biggest American hit so far. Other hits from the album included 'Policy of the Truth' and the haunting 'World in My Eyes'. Wilder released a solo album, *Bloodline*, using the name Recoil in 1992, as Fletcher began to take more of a managerial role for the band, giving up live work and appearing only fleetingly on the next album. In 1993 *Songs of Faith and Devotion* entered the US chart at No. 1, confirming the band's status as an unlikely member of rock's hierarchy. It was followed later that year by the in-concert album *Songs of Faith and Devotion – Live*.

However, while the tour was an unqualified success financially, it left the group in a state of disarray.

Wilder left the band in 1995 and Gahan attempted suicide the following year before entering rehabilitation to battle an addiction to heroin. Depeche Mode returned as a trio in 1997 with *Ultra*, which again topped the US charts and spawned the hit singles 'Barrel of a Gun' and 'It's No Good'. In 1998 they embarked on their first tour in four years to support the compilation release *The Singles '86–'98*. In 1999 they did the same in support of the equally successful *The Singles '81–'85*.

JACKIE DESHANNON
b. Sharon Myers, 21 August 1944, Hazel, Kentucky, USA

The author of numerous hits, DeShannon was one of the first songwriters of the rock era to develop a performing career in tandem with her writing. For the most part, DeShannon's work lacked the adolescent *angst* which characterized the work of such contemporaries as **Ellie Greenwich** and **Carole King**. Her songs were generally more reflective and folk-inflected.

The daughter of country music performers, DeShannon was singing regularly on the radio by the age of six and when the family moved to Chicago in the mid-fifties she secured her own show. In 1960, already an established performer and writer, DeShannon moved to California. Her early hit compositions include 'Dum Dum' (**Brenda Lee**, 1961), 'The Great Imposter' (the **Fleetwoods**, 1962), 'When You Walk in the Room' (the **Searchers**, 1964, and a minor hit for her) and 'Come and Stay With Me' (**Marianne Faithull**). She began recording as a member of the Nomads in 1960 and in 1962 signed with Liberty as a solo performer. Her first hit was a version of the country standard introduced by **Bob Wills**, 'Faded Love', and her recording of 'Needles and Pins' inspired the Searchers to make their million-selling version. However, her first major hit was her version of **Burt Bacharach**'s and Hal David's 'What the World Needs Now Is Love' (1965). By this time she was an important member of California's folk-rock circle, having formed an unrecorded group with **Ry Cooder** in 1963, toured with the **Byrds** (who recorded her 'Don't Doubt Yourself Babe' on their influential 1965 album, *Mr Tambourine Man*), and appeared at concerts with **Harry Belafonte** and **Bob Dylan**, as well as writing songs with **Jack Nitzsche** ('I Keep Wanting You'), **Randy Newman** ('She Don't Understand Him') and recording **Van Dyke Parks**' 'High Coin'.

Her own recordings fared less well until, in 1968, she had a minor hit with 'The Weight' from **The Band**'s début album and, in 1969, she scored a million-seller with her own composition, 'Put a Little Love in Your Heart'. She briefly moved to Capitol for

Songs (1971), which included 'West Virginia Mine', and then Atlantic (where she recorded a pair of superior albums, *Jackie*, 1972, and *Your Baby Is a Lady*, 1974). Her best album of the period was *New Arrangement* (Columbia, 1975), which featured her own, jaunty version of 'Bette Davis Eyes' (later a million-seller for **Kim Carnes** in 1981). Less intimate than Carole King's work, the album's concerns were broader and more delicately broached. However, it was a commercial failure, as was the inferior *You're the Only Dancer* (Amhurst, 1978). Since then she has concentrated on writing. Her hits for others include 'Breakaway' (Tracey Ullman, 1983), a revival of 'Put a Little Love in Your Heart' by **Eurythmics** member Annie Lennox in duet with **Al Green**, and a 1994 version of 'When You Walk in the Room' by country singer Pam Tillis.

DESYLVA, BROWN AND HENDERSON
Buddy DeSylva, b. George Gard DeSylva, 27 January 1895, New York, USA, d. 11 July 1950, Los Angeles, California; Lew Brown, b. Louis Brownstein, 10 December 1893, Odessa, Russia, d. 5 February 1958, New York; Ray Henderson, b. Raymond Brost, 1 December 1896, Buffalo, New York, d. 31 December 1970, Greenwich, Connecticut

Though they only operated as a songwriting partnership for a short period, composer Henderson and lyricists Brown and DeSylva perhaps best caught the spirit of the Jazz Age. They wrote with a sure grasp of vernacular American and showed complete faith in the icons of American popular culture in songs like 'Black Bottom', 'The Birth of the Blues' (both 1926), 'Varsity Drag', 'The Best Things in Life Are Free' (1927) – which was later used as the title of the 1956 biopic about them – 'You're the Cream in My Coffee' (1928), 'Button Up Your Overcoat' (1929) and 'If I Had a Talking Picture of You' (1930). Yet, at the same time, they could also produce the pure corn of 'Sonny Boy' (1929), which gave **Al Jolson** a multi-million-seller.

Each had written hits before forming their partnership in 1925. The son of Russian emigrants, Brown turned to songwriting in his teens. An introduction to Albert (brother of **Harry**) **von Tilzer** led to his first successes, 'Give Me the Moonlight, Give Me the Girl' (1917) which was later adopted by **Frankie Vaughan** as his signature tune, 'Oh, by Jingo' (1919) and 'Dapper Dan' (1920).

The son of a vaudevillian, DeSylva was brought up in Los Angeles. A talented child performer, he turned to lyric writing in his teens. Several of his early hits were introduced by Al Jolson. These included the **Gus Kahn** collaboration 'I'll Say She Does' (1918), 'April Showers' (1921, written with Louis Silver) and

'California Here I Come' (1924, with Joseph Meyer). Other successes were 'Nobody But You' (1920, written with **George Gershwin**), 'Look for the Silver Lining' (1920, with **Jerome Kern**) and 'A Kiss in the Dark' with **Victor Herbert**.

Henderson, the son of musicians, studied at the Chicago Conservatory of Music. In New York he worked as a staff pianist, arranger and song-plugger for several publishers while trying his hand at songwriting. His first hits were 'That Old Gang of Mine' (1923) with lyrics by Billy Rose and Mort Dixon, and 'Five Foot Two, Eyes of Blue' and 'I'm Sitting on Top of the World' (both 1925) with Sam Lewis and Joe Young. These were all huge hits, but more significant were 'Alabamy Bound' (1925), Henderson's first collaboration with De Sylva, and 'Don't Bring Lulu' (1925), written with Brown and Rose. That same year the newly formed partnership of DeSylva, Brown and Henderson was commissioned to write the songs for *George White's Scandals of 1925*.

That show flopped but the 1926 show is generally acknowledged to be the best of the eleven-strong series of revues. It produced 'Black Bottom', which sparked off the dance craze, and 'The Birth of the Blues', and led to the first of the trio's four Broadway musicals, *Good News!* (1927). This was followed by *Hold Everything!* (1928), *Following Thru* (1929) and *Flying High* (1930), all self-confident breezy comedies about modern fads. These in turn led to Hollywood. Unusually for the time, the trio set up their own publishing house. This enabled them to take complete control of their first musical, the innovative and influential *Sunnyside Up* (1929), producing and scripting it as well as supplying the songs. The failure of their science-fiction musical, *Just Imagine* (1930), led DeSylva, the ideas man of the partnership, to leave for a second career as a film producer, overseeing several of the classic **Shirley Temple** films. He also produced four Broadway shows from his own ideas and stories, including *Take a Chance* (1932) and *Louisiana Purchase* (1940), with songs by **Irving Berlin**, and subsequently was a co-founder of Capitol records. His last noteworthy song, for which he wrote both the music and lyrics, was 'Wishing', a 1939 hit for **Vera Lynn**.

Henderson and Brown continued to write together, producing material for such shows as *George White's Scandals of 1931* ('Life Is Just a Bowl of Cherries' and 'The Thrill Is Gone'), *Hot-Cha!* (1931) and *Strike Me Pink* (1933). *Scandals of 1931* was the first show to have its hit songs, sung by **Bing Crosby** and the Boswell Sisters, released by Brunswick on a single 12-inch record. Then Brown too retreated to Hollywood, leaving Henderson to write with Ted Koehler (*Say When*, 1934) and Jack Yellen (*George White's Scandals of 1935* and *Ziegfeld Follies*, 1943). His best-known song from this period is 'Animal Crackers', written for the Shirley Temple movie *Curly Top* (1935) with Koehler and Irving Caesar. Following the deaths of his erstwhile partners, Henderson retired in the fifties.

DEVO

Bob Casale; Jerry Casale; Alan Meyers (replaced by David Kendrick); Bob Mothersbaugh; Mark Mothersbaugh

Devo were a quirky art-rock band who enjoyed a critical and cult following in the early eighties.

Jerry Casale (bass) and Mark Mothersbaugh (vocals) met as fine art students at Kent State University in the seventies. Having invented a philosophy of 'de-evolution', they enlisted their guitarist brothers and drummer Meyers to form Devo in 1972. The group's first production was a prize-winning short video in 1975.

Released on the quintet's Booji Boy label, 'Jocko Homo' (1976) and 'Mongoloid' expressed Devo's introverted, allusive approach while their distant electronic sound made an impact with a version of the **Rolling Stones**' 'Satisfaction' (1977). **Brian Eno** produced *Q: Are We Not Men? A: We Are Devo* (1978), released by Warners in America and Virgin in Europe, probably their quintessential musical statement. It was followed by *Duty Now for the Future* (1979) and *Freedom of Choice* (1980), which provided a disco hit with the synthesizer-based 'Whip It'*.

In live performance the group developed uniforms which included flowerpot hats and featured Devo versions of such songs as **Johnny Rivers**' 'Secret Agent Man' and **Lee Dorsey**'s 'Working in the Coalmine', which they recorded for the National Lampoon movie *Heavy Metal* (1981). Their later records included *New Traditionalists* (1981), *Oh No! It's Devo* (1982), *Shout* (Warners, 1984) and *Total Devo* (Enigma, 1988), on which David Kendrick replaced Meyers.

After recording *Smooth Noodle Maps* (Enigma, 1990), which featured high-energy dance beats plus extracts from Bach and a version of **Tim Hardin**'s 'Morning Dew', the group split up with the band members turning to composing television themes and jingles. Ironically, the separation took place at a time when Devo's influence was being acknowledged by a new generation of bands including **Nirvana** and **Soundgarden**, both of whom recorded Devo tunes. This led to a comprehensive reissue programme from Rykodisc, *Hardcore Vol. 1, Vol. 2* (both 1994) and *Live: The Mongoloid Years* (1996), while the band themselves experimented with CD-ROM games, including *Devo Presents the Adventures of the Smart Patrol* (1995). In a surprise move the band recorded *The New Traditionalists* (1997, Infinity Records) and joined the alternative live Lollapalooza tour in the US that summer. *Pioneers Who Got Scalped* (Rhino, 2000) is the definitive retrospective.

Although Devo were sometimes compared to the mysterious San Francisco band the Residents, the goofiness of Devo's cover-versions were worlds apart from the avant-garde thoroughness of the Residents' *Third Reich 'n' Roll* (Ralph, 1975).

AL DEXTER
b. Albert Poindexter, 4 May, 1902, Jacksonville, Texas, USA, d. January 1984, Lake Dallas, Texas

If it were only for the extraordinary success of his 'Pistol Packin' Mama', one of the biggest of the early country-pop crossover hits, Al Dexter would have a secure listing in the historical gazetteer of country music. Though he never equalled that achievement, however, he repeatedly showed himself to be a master of the smooth Western swing/honky-tonk manner that came to dominate West Coast country music in the forties and early fifties. In this he was supported by Columbia A&R man **Art Satherley**.

Dexter had had regional hits since 'Honky Tonk Blues' (1936), but 'Pistol Packin' Mama' (1942) went national, quickly becoming a million-seller and triggering pop cover-versions by **Bing Crosby** and the **Andrews Sisters** – Decca's first release after the recording ban inaugurated by **James Petrillo** ended – and **Frank Sinatra**, among others. Its modern arrangement, with steel guitar, accordion and trumpet, influenced the recordings of other country artists like **Gene Autry** and **Johnny Bond**.

Dexter maintained a Texas following throughout the fifties and early sixties, running his own Bridgeport Club in Dallas and recording for Columbia, Decca, King, Capitol and other labels. He then retired to pursue real-estate and other business interests. His other influential compositions include 'Too Late to Worry', a seventies hit for **Ronnie Milsap**, and 'Take Me Back to Tulsa', for which he wrote the lyrics to a melody by **Bob Wills**, whose anthem it became.

DEXY'S MIDNIGHT RUNNERS
Kevin Rowland, b. 17 August 1953, Wolverhampton, England

Masterminded by Rowland, Dexy's Midnight Runners were one of Britain's most successful acts of the early eighties, in a style which switched from white soul to celtic folk.

Former leader of punk band the Killjoys, Rowland founded Dexy's in 1978 in Birmingham to re-create the soul sound of Britain's mod era of fifteen years earlier. With Al Archer (guitar), Peter Saunders (Hammond organ), Andy Growcott (drums), Pere

Williams (bass) and a brass section led by tenorist Jeff Blythe, Dexy's toured with the **Specials** before signing to EMI in 1979. Their first single, 'Dance Stance' was a minor hit but its follow-up, 'Geno', went to No. 1. 'Geno' was a catchy tribute to Blythe's ex-leader and British sixties soul artist Geno Washington, who had been a major live attraction despite having only minor hits with 'Hi Hi Hazel' and a cover of the **Doris Day** hit 'Que Sera, Sera' (Piccadilly, 1966).

Further hits followed in 1980 with 'There There My Dear' and the Pete Wingfield-produced *Searching for the Young Soul Rebels*. By now Rowland was a controversial figure in British rock, having bought advertisements to denounce journalists as 'dishonest and hippy' and withheld album tapes from EMI in an attempt to gain higher royalties.

The atmosphere of dispute spread to the band itself and six of the eight members walked out, leaving Rowland and trombonist Jimmy Paterson to recruit a new band in Birmingham, which included Micky Billingham (keyboards), Paul Speare (tenor sax), Billy Adams (guitar) and Seb Shelton (drums).

The ex-Dexys formed the Bureau and released 'Let Him Have It' while Rowland's new band (now on the Mercury label) had a Top Twenty hit with 'Show Me' before adding a fiddle section – the Emerald Express led by Helen O'Hara – on 'Come on Eileen'. This sing-along, pastiche folk-tune was Britain's bestselling record of 1982 and also an American No. 1.

A version of **Van Morrison**'s 'Jackie Wilson Said' reached the British Top Ten in the same year. Its companion album, *Too Rye Ay*, produced by Clive Langer and Alan Winstanley, was also successful. Rowland then went into retreat before returning with a new image (smart suits instead of gypsy costume) and *Don't Stand Me Down* (1985), an album which sold poorly despite being well reviewed. By now, only Adams, Shelton and O'Hara remained of the earlier line-up. In 1986 Dexy's Midnight Runners returned to the charts with a teleseries theme, 'Because of You', before in 1987 Rowland quit the group for a solo career which began inauspiciously with *The Wanderer* (1988). He was later declared bankrupt and in 1991 he recorded a new Dexy's album, *Manhood*, with Paterson.

In 1999, after undergoing drug rehabilitation and presenting himself as a cross-dresser, he signed to Creation. While the resulting album, *My Beauty*, was both confused and troubled, Rowland's mid-life crisis certainly gave new depths to songs like the **Four Seasons**' 'Rag Doll' and **Squeeze**'s 'Labelled with Love'.

NEIL DIAMOND
b. 24 January 1941, Brooklyn, New York, USA

A highly successful performer and composer, Diamond's best work has combined the qualities of fifties pop craftsmen and sixties singer-songwriters.

His earliest musical experience was with a folk group but in 1962 he took a job as staff songwriter with New York publisher Sunbeam Music. His first successes came in 1965–6 when Jay and the Americans reached the Top Twenty with 'Sunday and Me', the **Monkees** recorded his 'I'm a Believer' and Diamond's own version for Bang of 'Cherry Cherry' was a Top Twenty hit. He had four more hits in the following year, including 'Girl, You'll Be a Woman Soon' and 'Kentucky Woman', with which **Deep Purple** reached the Top Forty in 1968. British star **Lulu** also charted with Diamond's pop compositions at this time.

With artistic ambitions that went beyond Bang's hard-nosed pop approach, Diamond switched to the West Coast label Uni (later part of MCA) where his output of hits leavened simple love songs like 'Sweet Caroline'* and 'Cracklin' Rosie'* with the more substantial 'I Am . . . I Said' and 'Stones'. By 1972, when 'Song Sung Blue' became his second American No. 1, Diamond was an international star.

The live album *Hot August Night* (1972) was a Top Five album in the US, where it stayed on the chart for well over a year. Changing labels to Columbia, he composed the highly successful, if pretentious, soundtrack to the film version of Erich Segal's fable *Jonathan Livingston Seagull* (1973). The follow-up album, *Serenade* (1974), produced the Top Ten hit 'Longfellow Serenade' but Diamond's greatest critical success of the seventies was *Beautiful Noise* (1975). Produced by **The Band**'s Robbie Robertson, it was a fond evocation of the Brill Building songwriting of Diamond's early years.

Diamond appeared in *The Last Waltz*, Martin Scorsese's film of The Band's final concert, but the more usual setting for his live shows was Las Vegas. In 1977 he released another live album, *Love at the Greek**, recorded at the Greek Theatre in Los Angeles. Other highlights of this phase of his career were the hit duet with **Barbra Streisand** 'You Don't Bring Me Flowers'* (1978) and the remake of the film *The Jazz Singer* (1980), in which Diamond took the **Al Jolson** part. Though the movie was not a box-office smash, it produced three hit singles, of which 'Love on the Rocks' (1981) was the bestselling.

In the eighties Diamond was less prolific. *Heartlight* (1982) was noteworthy for its title song, co-written with Carole Bayer Sager and **Burt Bacharach** and inspired by the film *ET*.

Much of Diamond's subsequent work has been undistinguished. It has included *Primitive* (1984), *Headed for the Future* (1986) and the live *Hot August Night II* (1988). In 1989 he released *The Best Years of Our Lives*, produced by David Foster, who wrote several of the songs with Diamond. *Lovescapes* (1991) had numerous producers including Don Was and Pete

Asher. Far better was *Greatest Hits 1966–1992* (1992), even though it included live remakes of classics like 'Sweet Caroline'. A seasonal recording, *The Christmas Album*, made the US Top Ten in late 1992 (a *Christmas Album Vol. II* followed in 1994), and in 1993 Diamond returned to his roots with an affectionate album of cover-versions titled *Up on the Roof – Songs of the Brill Building*. Less successful was *The Movie Album: As Time Goes By* (1998), a double-album of movie themes.

THE DIAMONDS
Dave Somerville, b. Toronto, Canada; Bill Reed, b. Toronto (replaced by Evan Fisher, b. California, USA); Ted Kowalski, b. Toronto (replaced by John Felton, b. California); Phil Leavitt, b. Toronto (replaced by Mike Douglas, b. Toronto)

Of the sixteen hits by the Diamonds between 1956 and 1961, no less than ten were covers of black vocal group offerings. They have been much attacked for this practice by rock'n'roll purists. But though their records were cruder than the originals, the Diamonds attempted to reproduce – rather than soften – the sounds of doo-wop and they undeniably did much to accustom white ears to the wailing harmonies of black America.

Formed in high school in 1953 and signed to Mercury, the group had their first hit with a cover of **Frankie Lymon and the Teenagers**' 'Why Do Fools Fall in Love?' (1956). The Diamonds' version made the Top Twenty, but Lymon's original was the more successful. Henceforth the Diamonds' cover-versions would be more successful than the black originals. These included the Willows' 'Church Bells Will Ring', the **Clovers**' 'Love, Love Love', the G'Clefs' 'Ka-Ding-Dong' (1957), 'Little Darlin', by the Gladiolas (whose lead singer was **Maurice Williams**), the Rays' 'Silhouettes' and **Chuck Willis**'s 'The Stroll' (1957). Of these the most important was 'Little Darlin'', the Diamonds' biggest hit and the record which most closely approximated the sound of the original.

The group's last hit was a cover of the Danleers' elegiac 'One Summer Night' in 1961. Significantly, they did not long outlive the demise of the doo-wop style of black singing. In the early sixties, plagued by personnel changes, the group disbanded.

MANU DIBANGO
b. 10 February 1934, Douala, Cameroon

A pioneering figure in Afro-jazz fusions since the sixties, saxophonist, singer, pianist and arranger Dibango's efforts to combine African and American musics have been a strong influence on younger generations of performers.

He spent the years 1949–56 learning saxophone and classical piano in Paris, before moving to Brussels where he had a residency at the Black Angels Jazz club. Dibango moved to Zaire in 1960, playing with Joseph Kabalese and African Jazz for three years. Returning to Paris in 1965, he became a leading session and television performer, cutting a series of albums for Philips. These included *Manu Dibango* (1968), *O Boso* (1971) and *Soma Coba* (1972).

Dibango's best-known tune, 'Soul Makossa', was originally recorded as the B-side of the patriotic song 'Mouvement Ewondo', written to inspire the Cameroon soccer team in 1971. Two years later the track, which mixed traditional Cameroon dance rhythms with soul music, received airplay in New York and became an American hit on Atlantic. Later tracks like 'Big Blow' and 'Sun Explosion' were dance hits and during the seventies Dibango recorded prolifically for a number of labels. His albums included *Super Kiumba* (1974) and *Africadelic* (1975). He also began working as a film composer, initially for West African movies including *L'Herbe Sauvage* (Ivory Coast), *Ceddo* (Senegal) and *Le Prix De La Libert* (Cameroon).

In 1980 he signed to Island, making *Gone Clear* (1980) and *Ambassador* (1981) with producer Geoffrey Chung and rhythm section **Sly and Robbie**. He also continued his film work with the score for *Soft and Sweet* (1983). That year he also produced, performed on and arranged the three-CD set *Fleures Musicales du Camerooun*, which mixed traditional Cameroon music (and musicians) with newer musics, including pop-massaka, mangambe and bikusi (and musicians) to good effect. Dibango's later recordings were impressively varied. He made two albums of piano solos on African themes before working with producer Martin Meissonnier on the hip-hop influenced 'Abele Dance' (Celluloid, 1984). He next linked up with **Bill Laswell**, who used Dibango on his *Deadline* album and produced the Dibango solo album *Electric Africa* (Celluloid, 1985). In the same year Dibango organized 'Tam Tam Pour L'Afrique', a charity record by Paris-based African musicians to help famine victims in Ethiopia. Dibango played on **Herbie Hancock**'s *Electric Africa* before Laswell supervised *Afrijazzy* (1986), which included a new version of 'Soul Makossa'. In 1990 Dibango published his autobiography, *Trois Kilos de Café*, in Paris. He used the same title for an album of selected re-recordings of his seventies Pan-African hits, including 'Pata Pata' and 'Independence Cha Cha'.

Wakafrika (1994) included cameos from such celebrity guests as **Youssou N'Dour**, **Peter Gabriel** and **Sinead O'Connor**, while *Live '91* (Sterns, 1995) is a representative set of Dibango the sax player.

BO DIDDLEY
b. Elias Bates, 30 December 1928, McComb, Mississippi, USA

Diddley is the elaborator of the 'chink-a-chink-a-chink, a-chink-chink' beat, which critics have variously identified as a simple bump-and-grind shuffle and as being derived from African drum rhythms. Either way, though his 'jungle rhythms' proved too strong for the pop charts of their day, his songs and sound have been a lasting influence on the white blues-based groups that followed him.

Adopted by his mother's cousin and raised in Chicago, Bates assumed their family name, McDaniel, before taking the nickname Bo Diddley. He studied the violin briefly and spent his teens training to be a boxer and singing on street corners, often accompanying himself on guitar. By 1951 he had teamed up with harmonica-player Billy Boy Arnold and was a regular performer in the clubs of Chicago's south side and, in 1955, he signed with Chess and recorded the classic 'Bo Diddley'.

An R&B hit, the song introduced the characteristic Diddley style and content. Diddley's heavily amplified guitar, sometimes to the point of distortion, and his use of tremolo anticipated **Jimi Hendrix**'s experiments with feedback by more than a decade. His songs were less inventive than label-mate **Chuck Berry**'s (on many of whose classic recordings, including 'Memphis, Tennessee', Diddley played bass guitar). Diddley looked back to the streetwise humour of the likes of **Louis Jordan** to flesh out the blatantly macho celebration of himself rather than, like Berry, aiming at the new white teenage audience that was seeking out black music. But in live performance Diddley and his band (usually Jerome Green, **Otis Spann**, Arnold, Frank Kirkland and, from the sixties on, his half-sister 'The Duchess' on second guitar) were the epitome of the sweaty moment where the blues met rock'n'roll.

In the fifties few white groups performed his material (the exception being **Buddy Holly**, who recorded an exuberant version of 'Bo Diddley') but his songs became an essential part of the repertoire of many of the British R&B bands of the sixties. The **Rolling Stones**, **Yardbirds**, **Who**, **Pretty Things** (who took their name from one of his songs) and the **Animals** all played and recorded his material, with the Animals going so far as to lionize him in 'The Story of Bo Diddley' on their first, eponymous album. 'Say Man' (1959) and 'You Can't Judge a Book by the Cover' (1962) were his only major hits, but white artists popularized many of his songs. These include 'Mona', 'I'm a Man', 'Hey! Bo Diddley', 'Bring It to Jerome' and 'Who Do You Love?' (this last, recorded most famously by Ronnie Hawkins backed by the musicians who would later become **The Band** in 1963).

Diddley toured throughout the sixties and seventies, occasionally adopting the gimmicks of the day (hence the album *Bo Diddley Goes Surfing*, 1963) but never really changing his sound. His 1976 album, *20th Anniversary of Rock'n'Roll* (RCA), saw Diddley supported by numerous star names, but to little purpose. More significant were his 1979 tour with the **Clash** – which introduced his material to a new generation of rock fans – and his cameo role in *Trading Places* (1983), in which he effortlessly translated the 'Bo Diddley' persona from song to screen. In the late eighties he toured with Rolling Stones guitarist Ronnie Wood as the Gunslingers and released the live album *Live at the Ritz*. In 1989, with his profile at a new high following his appearance with baseball star Bo Jackson in a commercial for sports shoes, Diddley released his first studio album for fifteen years, *Breakin' Through the B.S.*. He continued to play live well into the nineties.

MARLENE DIETRICH
b. Maria Magdalene Dietrich, 27 December 1901, Berlin, Germany, d. 6 May 1992, Paris, France

Dietrich's screen image was the creation of director Josef Von Sternberg, with her playing a willing Trilby to his Svengali. Though her career as a *chanteuse* initially reflected the image of the seductive vamp, fixed by her role of Lola in *The Blue Angel* (1930), once she left Hollywood she produced a body of work in which her career and life were, in the manner of **Edith Piaf** and **Judy Garland**, the essential subject matter of her performances. Dietrich never simply sang, she performed.

The daughter of a Prussian officer, Dietrich studied with Max Reinhardt (and appeared in the chorus of several musical revues), then graduated to small parts in German films in the twenties. The role of Lola, songstress and temptress who brings Emil Jannings' schoolteacher to ruin, made her an international star and forever associated her with the song 'Falling in Love Again' (as 'Ich Bin von Kopf bis Fuss auf Liebe Eingestellt' was retitled for the English-language version of the film). The song was composed by Fredrich Hollander – who would work regularly with Dietrich in Hollywood – and Sammy Lerner from a German lyric by Robert Leibmann. Though Dietrich never used her husky, sensuous voice in musicals *per se*, a number of films cast her as an entertainer and demanded that she sing. Other songs associated with her include a pair by **Frank Loesser** and Hollander, 'The Boys in the Back Room' (from *Destry Rides Again*, 1939) and 'I've Been in Love Before' (from *Seven Sinners*, 1940), and **Cole Porter**'s 'The Laziest Gal in Town' (from *Stagefright*, 1950).

She became an American citizen in 1939 and during the Second World War worked extensively, entertaining the troops, in bond drives and, most importantly, at the request of the American Office of Strategic Services she recorded a version of 'Lili Marlene' to counter the popularity of **Lale Anderson**'s version. (She also recorded several American standards, including 'Miss Otis Regrets' and 'Surrey with the Fringe on Top' in German.) It was during this period that she developed the stage act she would turn to when she left Hollywood for cabaret in the fifties. With the assistance of lighting expert Joe Davis and musical director **Burt Bacharach** she concocted a show that evoked her past with both style and nostalgia. As well as singing the songs associated with her, she also made 'La Vie en Rose', 'Whatever Lola Wants', 'Le Chevalier de Paris' and **Pete Seeger**'s 'Where Have All the Flowers Gone?' her own. The latter, sung in German as 'Sag Mir Wo die Blumen Sind', gave her a substantial hit in West Germany in 1965 on Electrola.

For a quarter of a century Dietrich travelled the world with her cabaret show, making a large number of recordings in English, French and German of the shows and the songs. Among these are *Lili Marlene* (Columbia, 1983), which includes several of her wartime recordings, *The Legendary, Lovely Marlene* (MCA, 1972), a live recording of a concert, *Mythos* (Electrola, 1968), a collection of her German recordings, and *Marlene Dietrich at the Café Paris* (Columbia, 1964), on which she is introduced by **Noël Coward**. She retired in the late seventies and published her autobiography, *My Life Story*, in 1979.

DIMITRI FROM PARIS
b. Paris, France

One of the 'nouvelle vague' of successful French dance artists emerging in the second half of the 1990s, Dimitri's style combined jazzy, disco house with a strong element of 1960s-style easy listening/lounge music.

Dimitri worked as a club DJ in the mid-1980s in Paris, where he provided mixes for local radio stations. As his reputation grew, he began to do remix work, first just for French artists, but then for international stars including **Björk**, **Lisa Stansfield** and the Brand New Heavies. His work brought him to the attention of the Paris fashion houses, who commissioned him to provide soundtracks for their catwalk shows.

His real recording career began at the start of 1990s, with a single, 'Nitegroove', on Hi-Bias, and then an EP on another French label, Yellow Productions. He recorded as Dimitri From Paris to avoid confusion with both dutch techno house DJ Dimitri and **Deee-Lite**'s Dimitri Brill. An album, *Sacrebleu* (1996), followed on Yellow Productions, featuring the singles 'Sacre Francais' and 'Une Very Stylish Fille'. The record was well-received, critics warming to his ironic but affectionate mixture of 1990s house grooves and 1960s French pop kitsch.

On the back of the album's success, Dimitri DJed round the world, including the UK, US and Tokyo. He also renewed his acquaintance with the Paris fashion world, composing music for Yves Saint Laurent's new fragrance, 'Live Jazz', in 1998, as well as remixing rap crew **Stetsasonic**'s classic 'Talkin All that Jazz' for the Tommy Boy label's *Greatest Beats* compilation. In 1999 he remixed **Quincy Jones**' 'Soul Bossa Nova' for the second Austin Powers film, *The Spy Who Shagged Me*. Dimitri finally followed up *Sacrebleu* with *A Night at the Playboy Mansion* (2000), a compilation of deep-house grooves selected and mixed by the goateed Frenchman himself.

DINOSAUR JR.
Lou Barlow; Mike Johnston; J. Mascis; 'Murph'

With their distinctive sound and *angst*-ridden demeanour, Dinosaur Jr. heralded the emergence of the grunge revolution of the early nineties but never managed to achieve the commercial success of the scene's breakthrough acts.

Originally known simply as Dinosaur, the band's sound owed a debt to the heavy-rock experimentalism of **Sonic Youth** and Black Flag, two of the biggest names in the indie scene in the US at the time. Formed by singer-guitarist J. Mascis alongside bassist Barlow and drummer Murph, Dinosaur found instant recognition with their début album, *You're Living All Over Me* (1987), which sold steadily and proved inspirational to a generation of fans.

After the release of *Bug* (1988) (by which time the band had been forced to change their name by sixties act the Dinosaurs) Barlow left the band to concentrate on his own Sebadoh project. Undeterred, Mascis performed much of *Green* (1991) himself, before recruiting bass-player Johnston for *Without a Sound* (1994), which saw Murph leave. The album heralded a more accessible style, bringing the band a degree of mainstream success, while the follow-up, *Hand It Over* (1998), saw them return to their experimental roots.

With Sebadoh, Lou Barlow released seven albums of lo-fi rock, including *Rockin' the Forest* (1992) and *The Sebadoh* (1999), which included the UK hit single 'Flame'. Barlow also achieved success with his Folk Implosion side-project, gaining his highest US chart placing with 'Natural One' from controversial Larry Clark movie *Kids* (1996).

DION AND THE BELMONTS
Dion DiMucci, b. 18 July 1939, Bronx, New York, USA; Fred Milano, b. 22 August 1939, New York; Carlo Mastanglo, b. 5 October 1938, New York; Angelo D'Aleo, b. 3 February 1940, New York

Artistically and commercially, Dion and the Belmonts were the most successful white doo-wop group. For the most part they sang bright songs of adolescent *angst*, but Dion's instinctive, impassioned vocals gave an extra edge to their recordings and their choice of material was far more interesting than most. Similarly, unlike most fifties stars, Dion had a later solo career that was far more than a footnote to his days of rock'n'roll stardom.

The son of a singer and actress, Dion made his first professional appearance on **Paul Whiteman**'s *Teen Club* television show in 1954. He soon turned to doo-wop, the street-corner music of New York, and in 1957, joined forces with the Timberlanes to record 'The Chosen Few' for the independent Mohawk Records. In 1958 he formed the Belmonts (named after one of the main streets of the Bronx) and signed to Laurie. Success came instantly with 'I Wonder Why' and 'No One Knows' (1958), the first a jive-talking chant, the second a typical fifties essay in self-pity. But even the simplest sounding of their records were carefully constructed. 'Wonderful Girl' (1959), for example, which saw Dion celebrating the innocence of teenage love, backed by little more than a lazy sax, a solitary guitar and the cooing voices of the Belmonts, is a testament to his mastery of phrasing.

International success followed in 1959, with a wistful version of **Pomus and Shuman**'s clever teenage lament, 'A Teenager in Love'* (which was covered in the UK by Craig Douglas and **Marty Wilde**, who had the bigger hit). Then in 1960 came a trio of imaginative recastings of earlier hits – **Richard Rodgers**' and **Lorenz Hart**'s 'Where or When', and **Cole Porter**'s 'In the Still of the Night' and 'When You Wish upon a Star' – all of which made the Top Forty. In 1960 Dion left the Belmonts for a solo career and the group joined Sabrina Records where they had success with 'Tell Me Why' (1961) and 'Come on Little Angel'. But it was Dion whose career really prospered.

His first solo release, 'Lonely Teenager' (1960), was hardly different from his records with the Belmonts. Then came 'Runaround Sue'* and 'The Wanderer'* (1961). The macho masochism of the songs (written by Ernie Maresca who would achieve solo success with another of his compositions, 'Shout, Shout! [Knock Yourself Out]' on Seville in 1962) was a departure for Dion. But even more revolutionary was their sound. Dion adopted a gruff voice which was set against a chanting backdrop (by the uncredited Del-Satins), the whole made even more compulsive by the live feel to the recordings, a stylistic borrowing from **Gary US Bonds**' earlier hits 'New Orleans' and 'Quarter to Three'. At a time when most performers were softening their sound, Dion's was becoming harsher. Other hits in this style included 'Lovers Who Wander', 'Little Diane' and 'Love Came to Me' (1962).

In 1962 he joined Columbia, where if anything his records – which included versions of the **Drifters**' earlier R&B hits, 'Ruby Baby' and 'Drip Drop' and a rousing 'Donna, the Prima Donna' (all 1963) – became even fiercer. In 1964–5 he dropped from sight in an attempt to overcome his long-standing heroin addiction (which he only finally conquered in 1968). During this time he was introduced to a wide spectrum of black music, especially the blues, by Columbia's **John Hammond**, and released a series of R&B recordings, including 'Chicago Blues', 'Hoochie Koochie Man', 'Spoonful' and 'Johnny B. Goode', with which he had a minor hit in 1964, long before they became fashionable in American pop circles.

1967 saw a successful reunion with the Belmonts but the next stage of Dion's career began in 1968 with a return to Laurie. His gentle, folky recording of Dick Holler's 'Abraham, Martin and John'* (1968) was a rare example of a recording perfectly catching the mood of a country sunk in reflection after the assassination of Robert Kennedy. Even finer was the album *Dion* (1969), in which he interpreted songs by **Bob Dylan**, **Fred Neil**, **Joni Mitchell** and **Leonard Cohen** with conviction and attempted what can only be called a folk-psychedelic version of **Jimi Hendrix**'s 'Purple Haze'. There followed a series of mellow albums for Warners, including *Sit Down Old Friend* (1969) and *Sanctuary* (1971), which sold poorly. In 1973 Dion joined forces with the Belmonts again for the successful *Reunion*. A sojourn with **Phil Spector** resulted in the over-produced *Born to Be with You* (1975), which included an intense version of 'He's Got the Whole World in His Hands'.

That song presaged Dion's next move, to inspirational music. In the early eighties he signed with Word Records, for whom he has produced a series of superior Christian-themed albums, including *Inside Job* (1982) and the aptly titled *Kingdom of the Street* (1985). He returned to secular music in 1989 with the well-received *Yo Frankie* (Arista). Produced by **Dave Edmunds** it included a guest appearance by **Paul Simon** on a version of the Elegants' 1958 hit 'Little Star'. In the same year Dion was elected to the Rock and Roll Hall of Fame.

He later recorded a version of 'Mean Woman Blues' for an **Elvis Presley** tribute album, *The Last Temptation of Elvis* (1990). Inactive for most of the nineties, he returned to recording in 2000 with *Déjà Nu* (Collectables) on which, using fifties and early sixties recording techniques and equipment, he gave a

(mostly) doo-wop interpretation to more modern material, including a wonderful *a cappella* version of **Bruce Springsteen**'s 'If I Should Fall Behind'. *Bronx Blues* (1993) and *The Road I'm on* (1997) are the definitive retrospectives of his Columbia recordings, the first dealing with his early years with the label, the second with the period from 1962.

CÉLINE DION
b. 30 March 1968, Quebec, Canada

In her lengthy career Dion has made the transition from child star to French-language chanteuse and finally to internationally acclaimed ballad singer in English. Her albums *Falling Into You* and *Let's Talk About Love* were among the top ten most successful in North America in the nineties.

From a musical family (her parents played accordion and violin), Céline was the youngest of fourteen children. She made her first records at the age of thirteen for Quebec independent producer Rene Angeli. Her first hit in France as well as Quebec was 'D'Amour ou d'Amitié'.

By 1984 she was one of the best-known Francophone singers. She played a long season at the Olympia in Paris and sang for the Pope when he visited Canada. Three years later, at twenty, Dion changed record companies (to CBS) and exchanged her teenage image for an adult one. In 1988 she reached even bigger audiences by winning the Eurovision Song Contest, singing 'Ne Partez Pas Sans Moi' ('Don't Leave Without Me') as the representative of Switzerland.

The next big career move came in 1990 when **David Foster** and Chris Neil produced *Unison*, Dion's first album sung in English. In 1992 she recorded the film theme 'Beauty and the Beast' with **Peabo Bryson**. This was followed by *The Color of My Love* (1993), whose producers included Walter Afanasieff, **Mariah Carey**'s chief collaborator. Her first international hit, it included a revival of 'The Power of Love', the Jennifer Rush success of 1985, and 'Think Twice'.

Dion also recorded a version of the **Nat 'King' Cole** standard 'When I Fall in Love' with Clive Griffin for the soundtrack of the film *Sleepless in Seattle*. In 1994 she released *Dion Chante Plamondon*, a selection of songs by the veteran Québecois composer Luc Plamondon. After releasing a live album, *A l'Olympia*, and a further French-language collection, *D' Eux* (1995), Dion began working with production legend **Phil Spector**. The partnership was not a success and Spector left, explaining he could not work with someone so 'committed to mediocrity'. Ironically, Dion's next release, *Falling Into You* (1997), was her biggest hit to date, achieving vast international sales. It included 'Because You Loved Me', which was featured in the movie *Up Close and Personal*, and 'All By Myself', previously a hit for its writer Eric Carmen, the former lead singer of the **Raspberries**.

It was followed by Dion's biggest hit to date in 1998 with 'My Heart Will Go on', the love theme to James Cameron's record-breaking *Titanic*. Her success continued with *Lets Talk About Love*, *S'il Suffisait d'aimer* and the seasonal album *These Are Special Times* (all 1998). In 1999 she announced her intention to take a two-year break after the release of a greatest hits album, *All the Way . . . A Decade of Song*.

DIRE STRAITS

John Illsley, b. 24 June 1949, Leicester, England; David Knopfler, b. 1951 (replaced by Hal Lindes, b. 30 June 1953, Monterey, California, USA); Mark Knopfler, b. 12 August 1949, Glasgow, Scotland; Pick Withers (replaced by Terry Williams); Alan Clark, b. 5 March 1952, Durham, England; Guy Fletcher

One of the most successful bands of the eighties, Dire Straits embodied many of the virtues of sixties rock. Often evoking comparisons with **J. J. Cale** and **Eric Clapton** in his more mellow moods, leader Mark Knopfler combines a baroque blues guitar style with elaborate and sometimes offbeat lyrics delivered in a relaxed, drawling voice.

After studying at Leeds University, Mark Knopfler moved to London in 1973, briefly joining pub-rock group Brewer's Droop before taking jobs in journalism and teaching. By 1977 he was playing on the pub circuit when he cut a demo tape with David Knopfler (guitar), Withers (drums) and Illsley (bass). 'Sultans of Swing', an affectionate portrait of a pub jazz band, became a turntable hit when it was taken up by rock historian and Radio London deejay Charlie Gillett. The demo version of 'Sultans' was later issued on *The Honky Tonk Demos* by Gillett's own Oval label in 1979.

The band was subsequently signed to Vertigo, releasing an eponymous album produced by Muff Winwood in 1978. Mark Knopfler's drawling Dylanesque singing and plangent guitar-playing made a re-recorded 'Sultans of Swing' a Top Ten hit in both Britain and America. The caustic ode to a music journalist, 'Lady Writer', was less successful but *Communiqué* (1979), on which the track appeared, sold over three million copies worldwide. With the group signed to Warners in America, *Communiqué* was produced by **Jerry Wexler** and Barry Beckett. Mark Knopfler and Withers worked with the same producers on **Bob Dylan**'s *Slow Train Coming* (1979).

Before the recording of *Making Movies* (1980), David Knopfler left the group to follow a solo career, releasing albums on Peach River, Fast Alley, Making Waves and Greenhill. *Making Movies* included the eloquent love ballad 'Romeo and Juliet', which reached the British Top Ten. The group now included former Darling guitarist Lindes and keyboards-player Clark, who appeared on *Love Over Gold* (1982), which topped the British charts and included Dire Straits' biggest hit, 'Private Investigations'.

With ex-Man drummer Williams replacing Withers, a 1983 world tour yielded the double-album *Alchemy Live* but the next studio album, *Brothers in Arms*, did not appear until 1985. The first pop album to sell in considerable numbers on compact disc, it was also one of the biggest sellers of the decade. Knopfler's songs ranged from the moving utopianism of the title track to the sly dig at both MTV and popular attitudes to rock stardom of 'Money for Nothing', and the jaunty dance tune 'Walk of Life'. All three were British hits while 'Money for Nothing' topped the American charts.

After the 200-concert 'Brothers in Arms' world tour, for which Guy Fletcher joined on keyboards, Dire Straits went into hibernation as Knopfler concentrated on film and production work. He had earlier created the lyrical and evocative score for Bill Forsyth's *Local Hero* (1983), followed by *Cal* (1984) and *The Princess Bride* (1987). He produced albums by Dylan (*Infidels*, 1983), **Aztec Camera**, **Randy Newman** and Willy de Ville. As a solo artist Illsley made *Never Told a Soul* (Vertigo, 1984) and *Glass* (1988), as well as releasing a cover of ex-**Shadows** bassist Jet Harris's 'Diamonds' (1987) as K. Wallis B. and the Dark Shades of Night. In 1990 Knopfler returned to his pub-rock roots by recording with Leeds singer Brendan Croker as the Notting Hillbillies (*Missing . . . Presumed Having a Good Time*) and briefly touring with Croker, Steve Phillips and Dire Straits' manager, Ed Bicknell, on drums. In the same year he released *Neck and Neck*, a series of guitar and vocal duets with **Chet Atkins**. Dire Straits returned to live performance for the 1988 Nelson Mandela Birthday concert at Wembley Stadium. In 1991 the group began a two-year world tour in support of *On Every Street* (1991), which as before mixed witty attacks on consumerism ('Heavy Fuel'), dramatic songs ('Fade to Black') and easy-going utopianism ('How Long'). The touring band, which included Illsley, Fletcher, Clark, Phil Palmer (guitar) and Chris White (saxophone), recorded the live album *On the Night* (1993). *Golden Heart* (1996) was Knopfler's first non-soundtrack album. In the same year he recorded a version of 'Atlantis' for the Shadows tribute album *Twang!*. More substantial was his soundtrack for *Wag the Dog* (1998). For *Sailing to Philadelphia* (2000) Knopfler drew on **Van Morrison** (on 'The Last Laugh'), **James Taylor** (on the title track) and former members of **Squeeze** Chris Difford and Glen Tilbrook (on 'One More Matinee'). The result, in the words of one critic, was 'a model of tasteful understatement'

DIVINE COMEDY
Neil Hannon, b. 1970, Enniskillen, Northern Ireland

An extravagant pop project, the Divine Comedy became a cult hit in the nineties with a series of albums drawing on a range of influences from **Jacques Brel** to **Burt Bacharach**.

Having grown up in rural Northern Ireland the son of an Anglican bishop, Hannon formed the first incarnation of the band in 1989, influenced primarily by the indie scene of the mid-eighties. However, by the time *Liberation* (1993) and *Promenade* (1994) were released the Divine Comedy consisted merely of Hannon himself and sometime orchestral arranger Jody Talbot. Both albums were a heady mixture of **Kurt Weill** and Europop, introducing Hannon as a songwriter of wit and intellect, but failed to find an audience.

Hannon's break came with 'Something for the Weekend', which entered the UK Top Ten and featured on the album *Casanova* (1996). While Hannon's previous works had concerned literature and French cinema, *Casanova* saw him take the foppish title role in a series of tales of erotic abandon. The album went gold in Britain and spawned two further hit singles, 'Becoming More Like Alfie' and 'The Frog Princess'. The follow-up, *A Short Album about Love* (1997), had a more romantic tone, while *Fin de Siècle* (1998) saw Hannon tackle more serious issues for the first time, such as the troubles in his native Northern Ireland. He also found time in between to write the theme to the *Father Ted* television series and contributed a collaboration with composer Michael Nyman, 'I've Been to a Marvellous Party', to a **Noël Coward** tribute album.

A Secret History (1999) collected the best of Hannon's past material alongside two new singles, 'The Pop Singer's Fear of the Pollen Count' and 'Gin Soaked Boy'.

THE DIXIE HUMMINGBIRDS
James L. Davis; Willie Bobo; Ira Tucker, b. 1925, Spartanburg, South Carolina, USA; Paul Owens; Beechie Thompson; Howard Carroll; James Walker

The longest established gospel quartet, the Dixie Hummingbirds were a key religious influence on the formation of soul and later reached rock audiences through a collaboration with **Paul Simon**.

Baritone Davis, who grew up with **Josh White**, founded the group in Greenville, South Carolina, in 1928. Originally singing in the pre-gospel 'jubilee' style with barber-shop quartet harmonies, the group came to prominence in 1939 when 'Joshua Journeyed to Jericho' (Decca) was a regional hit. In the same year they won a song contest against the Heavenly Gospel Singers, whose bass Bobo subsequently joined

the group, as did teenage lead singer Tucker, from the Gospel Carriers.

In 1942 the Hummingbirds moved to Philadelphia, broadcasting regularly from radio station WCAC. With Tucker's histrionic, tortured singing and their choreographed performances – the group introduced the hip-slapping that became standard practice for male gospel quartets – they became leaders of the genre. With the addition of baritone Owens, the Hummingbirds recorded for Apollo in 1945 and four years later joined Gotham. There they cut such tracks as 'Standing out on the Highway', 'Move on Up a Little Higher' and 'Jesus Will Answer Prayer' with female group the Angelic Gospel Singers, with whom they also toured.

When **Don Robey**'s Peacock label signed the group in 1952, the Dixie Hummingbirds embarked on the most successful phase of their career. With guitarist Howard Carroll adding blues and jazzy touches and James Walker as alternate lead singer, the Hummingbirds' fifties hits included 'In the Morning' (with scat-singing from Tucker), the heavily syncopated 'Jesus Walked the Water' and 'My Prayer', with its orchestral arrangement. Tucker's dramatic, intense singing became a model for younger vocalists and his influence can be heard in the style of such soul and R&B singers as **Clyde McPhatter**, **Jackie Wilson** and **Bobby Bland**, whom Tucker briefly tutored. As a songwriter Tucker was responsible for the novelty pieces 'Christian Automobile' and 'Let's Go out to the Programs', which the Hummingbirds used in concerts to satirize the sound of younger rivals.

The group reached out to a wider secular audience with an appearance at the 1966 Newport Jazz Festival and in the late sixties began to record with a full rhythm section. The success of Paul Simon's 'Loves Me Like a Rock' (1973), on which the Hummingbirds provided vocal accompaniment, led to *We Love You Like a Rock*. The album mixed secular and religious material, including **Stevie Wonder**'s 'Jesus Children of America'. The instrumental backing ranged from tubas to synthesizer. Later crossover attempts were less impressive.

WILLIE DIXON
b. 1 July 1915, Vicksburg, Mississippi, USA, d. 21 January 1992, Los Angeles

As composer, producer, arranger, A&R man and general fixer, Dixon has been a dominant figure in Chicago blues since the mid-forties.

Before becoming chief house producer for **Leonard Chess**'s label in 1952, he performed as bassist and vocalist with such groups as the Five Breezes and the Big Three Trio. At Chess he supervised, accompanied, and often supplied material for, the recordings of such artists as **Howlin' Wolf** and **Muddy Waters**. **Otis Rush** and **Magic Sam** were among those with whom Dixon worked as a freelance producer in the late fifties.

During those years he wrote dozens of hits for these and other Chicago artists. They included '(I'm Your) Hoochie Coochie Man' (1953), 'Just Make Love to Me' (1953) and 'I'm Ready' (1954) for Waters; 'My Babe' (1955) for **Little Walter**; 'I Can't Quit You Baby' (1956) for Rush; and 'Spoonful' (1960), 'Wang Dang Doodle' (1960) and 'Little Red Rooster' (1961) for Wolf. Many of his songs were also taken up by white R&B bands. 'Rooster' was a British No. 1 for the **Rolling Stones** in 1964 while 'You Need Love' formed the basis of **Led Zeppelin**'s 'Whole Lotta Love'. Dixon's genius as a composer was to weave traditional elements, from black folklore and speechways as well as the heritage of the blues itself, into later blues and pop-blues forms. As well as succeeding with the black audiences of the fifties, Dixon's songs proved adaptable to other contexts, including those of the later periods of renewed interest in the blues.

In the sixties Dixon continued to work for Chess while capitalizing on the new enthusiasm for the blues, particularly in Europe. He performed in clubs and on foreign tours with **Memphis Slim**, as well as joining several American Folk Blues Festival tours of Europe. From 1968 he organized a series of all-star Chicago bands for club and concert work. This led to the formation of his own talent and recording agency, which Dixon ran while maintaining his frequent appearances throughout North America and Europe.

Dixon's solo records appeared on a number of labels, including Columbia (*I Am the Blues*, 1970) and Ovation, and he also recorded with Memphis Slim and with **Pete Seeger** for Folkways and Verve. His chief contribution to the blues, however, was behind the scenes, developing the careers of new artists or helping to maintain those of veterans. In the eighties he used the settlement from the lengthy plagiarism law suit over Led Zeppelin's use of 'You Need Love' to set up the Blues Heaven Foundation to further awareness of the blues and provide assistance for young musicians. In 1988 his album *Hidden Charms*, produced by T-Bone Burnette, won a Grammy and in 1989 he published his autobiography, *I Am The Blues*. The most important phase of his career was summarized by the Charly compilation, *A Tribute to Willie Dixon* (1991), which collected together twenty-four tracks he had either written and/or produced for Chess by the likes of Muddy Waters, **Bo Diddley** and Howlin' Wolf.

DR DRE
b. Andre Young, 1964, Los Angeles, California, USA

After the break-up of **NWA** in 1992, like fellow member **Ice Cube** Dr Dre began a prolific and highly controversial solo career. He was the house producer at Death Row Records, which he co-founded with Marion 'Suge' Knight. During its short four-year history the label was equally well known for its hits – it was responsible for some twenty million-selling singles – and the various encounters with the law of its key executives and acts, including Dre himself, whose outbursts of violence brought him several arrests.

Dre's first solo outing, the bestseller *The Chronic* (Death Row, 1993), was an exercise in high-octane funk. With its samplings from **George Clinton** and Leon Haywood, among others, it marked a decisive break from the simplicities of the gangsta rap of NWA. Hits from the album included 'Nuthin' but a "G" Thang' and the chart-topping 'Dre Day'. While a member of NWA Dre had been the house producer for fellow member Eazy E's Ruthless records, before breaking with Eazy E over unpaid royalties in 1991. That dispute led to a series of recorded personal attacks on each other. These included Eazy E's 'Muthaphuckkin G's', which was made in response to 'Dre Day'.

That song was also significant in introducing Snoop Doggy Dogg (*b. Calvin Broadus, 20 October 1972, Long Beach, California*), who also appeared rapping on several more tracks on *The Chronic*. In the wake of that Dre returned to production, supervising Dogg's début solo album, the multi-million-selling *Doggystyle* (Death Row, 1993). Featuring samples from **Curtis Mayfield** and a guest appearance by the Dramatics, the album spawned a series of classics, including 'Doggy Dogg World', 'Gin and Juice' and 'Murder Was the Case'. Dre did not produce Dogg's follow-up, *Doggfather* (1996), released the same year Dogg was acquitted of a charge of first-degree murder.

Dr Dre's productions for Death Row during this period included the Lady of Rage's 'Afro Puffs' (1994), Tha Dogg Pound's *Dogg Food* (1995) and **2Pac Shakur**'s 'California Love' (1996). However, by 1996, increasingly irritated by the people label president Knight wanted him to work with and uneasy about the atmosphere of institutionalized violence through which Knight ran the label and that he directed at 'rival' East Coast rappers, Dre quit to form his own Aftermath Entertainment. In the wake of Dre's acrimonious departure and the escalation of violence at Death Row that culminated in the murder of Shakur and the (unconnected) imprisonment of Knight, Death Row collapsed. The company's complex and lurid history is outlined in great detail in Rontin Ro's *Have Gun Will Travel*.

Aftermath's first release was the compilation album *Dr Dre Presents . . . The Aftermath* (1997). It included the rhetorical hit single 'Been There Done That', which was seen by most as his farewell to gangsta rap and Death Row. In 1999 Dre released *Dr Dre – 2001*. It was hugely successful, selling over five million copies, but even that success was overshadowed by the success of his discovery of white rapper Eminem, whose albums he produced and supervised. Over a surprisingly austere rhythm section, on *The Slim Shady LP* (Aftermath, 1998) and *The Marshall Mathers LP* (2000) Eminem offered the traditional misogyny and violence associated with rap. However, for all their lewdness and violence, many of the songs, in part because of the comic interjections, seemed defensive rather than provocative. *Marshall Mathers* included the hit single 'The Real Slim Shady', on which Eminem took a comic swipe at his mentor Dre.

Occasionally in the nineties Dre collaborated with his one-time partner in NWA, Ice Cube. In 1994 the pair made 'Natural Born Killaz' and in 2000 he guested on Ice Cube's *War and Peace Vol. II: The Peace Disc*, which included 'Hell Low' on which the pair rapped 'I started this gangsta shit/Is this the motherfuckin' thanks I get?'.

DR FEELGOOD
Lee Brilleaux, b. 1953, d. 7 April 1994; The Big Figure, b. John Martin, 1947; Wilko Johnson, b. John Wilkinson, 1947; John B. Sparks, b. 1953; John 'Gypie' Mayo (joined 1977); Johnny Guitar (joined 1981)

A British R&B revival band of the mid-seventies, Dr Feelgood bridged the gap between the London pub-rock bands like **Nick Lowe**'s Brinsley Schwarz (who were mostly interested in the past) and the punk groups with whom Dr Feelgood shared a high-energy approach.

As a teenager Johnson had played in an unsuccessful band on the same Essex circuit as the Paramounts (which included Robin Trower and Gary Brooker of **Procul Harum**). After studying at Newcastle University, he formed Dr Feelgood in 1971 with vocalist and harmonica-player Brilleaux and bassist Sparks. The Big Figure was a contemporary of Johnson's who was already a professional drummer with various groups, including Finian's Rainbow.

The group's name was taken from a song recorded by sixties group **Johnny Kidd and the Pirates**, whose guitarist Mick Green was the model for Johnson's rock'n'roll approach to the blues. The original version had been recorded in 1962 by Atlanta bluesman Willie Perryman (aka Piano Red) as 'Dr Feelgood and the Interns' and was a minor American hit on Okeh.

With a frantic stage act featuring Johnson's clockwork toy version of **Chuck Berry**'s duckwalk and a repertoire mixing fifties rock and R&B standards with their own compositions (such as 'Back in the Night') in the same vein, they built up a club and pub following which led to a contract with United Artists. Most

of *Down by the Jetty* (1975) was recorded in one take and faithfully reflects the group's live act. The more sophisticated *Malpractice* followed later that year, accompanied by much touring in Britain, Europe and America, which contributed to the success of the raw-sounding *Stupidity* (1976), recorded live, which reached No. 1 in Britain.

After *Sneakin' Suspicion* (1977), Johnson left to form the Solid Senders, who released an unsuccessful album, then joined **Ian Dury**'s band, playing on *Laughter* (1980). He went on to record several solo albums, including *Ice on the Motorway* (1980), *Watch Out!* (1985) and *Barbed Wire Blues* (1989). His replacement in Dr Feelgood was Mayo, another blues/rock player, who contributed the heavy riffs to the group's only hit single, 'Milk and Alcohol' (1979), from *Private Practice*. However, Brilleaux's determination not to modify the band's style left them increasingly isolated as punk gave way to softer pop sounds and subsequent albums for UA (five by 1981) sold poorly.

The group also went through a series of personnel changes with Mayo giving way to Johnny Guitar from fellow R&B band the Count Bishops, who in turn left in 1983. The Big Figure and Sparks departed in 1982 after *Fast Women and Slow Horses* (Chiswick, 1982), leaving Brilleaux as the sole survivor from the original band on later albums for I.D. (*Mad Man Blues*, 1985) and Stiff (*Brilleaux*, 1986).

In the late eighties the band formed their own label, Grand Records, to reissue their earlier recordings. The 1989 touring line-up included guitarist Steve Walwyn (from ex-**Small Faces** singer Steve Marriott's group), Phil Mitchell (bass) and drummer Kevin Morris. The band constantly played live, averaging well over 200 gigs a year, before the cancer which eventually killed him forced Brilleaux to give up live work in 1993. With Robert Kane and Steve Walwyn replacing Brilleaux and Wilko, the band continued to tour throughout the nineties. *Chess Masters* (EMI, 2000) saw them celebrating Chicago R&B with their usual speedfreak abandon. The results, as ever with Dr Feelgood, were mixed.

DR HOOK
Ray Sawyer, b. 1 February 1937, Chickasaw, Alabama, USA; Dennis Locorriere, b. 13 June 1949, Union City, New Jersey; William Francis, b. 16 January 1942, Mobile, Alabama; George Cummings, b. 28 July 1938, Meridian, Mississippi; John 'Jay' David, b. 8 August 1942, Union City; Richard Elswit, b. 6 July 1945, New York; Jance Garfat, b. 3 March 1944, California

Mixing humour, country harmonies and a bedraggled piratical image, Dr Hook built a solid career on the unlikely base of their parody of a pop song, 'Sylvia's Mother'*.

Formed in New Jersey in the mid-sixties as the
Chocolate Papers by ex-country singer Sawyer, who
had recorded 'I'm Gonna Leave' (Sandy, 1960), and
ex-folk singer Locorriere, the group were discovered
by Ron Haffkine, who became their manager and
producer. He put them in touch with songwriter and
cartoonist **Shel Silverstein**, who was writing the score
for *Who Is Harry Kellerman and Why Is He Saying All
Those Terrible Things about Me?* (1970). The group
appeared in the film and sang one song, 'Last Morning', on the strength of which they secured a contract
with Columbia. All the songs on their first album, *Dr
Hook and the Medicine Show* (1971), as the band was
then called, and their second, *Sloppy Seconds* (1972),
were written by Silverstein. The parodic 'Sylvia's
Mother' (1972) and witty 'The Cover of Rolling
Stone'* (1973), which was banned in Britain by the
BBC for 'advertising', won them an international following, but when they started writing their own songs
in the manner of Silverstein on *Belly Up* (1973) they
slipped badly. *Bankrupt* (1976), their first album for
Capitol, revealed strong Southern roots and a pop
sensibility on songs like 'Let Me Be Your Lover',
which perfectly fitted Locorriere's grainy vocals, but it
was their version of **Sam Cooke**'s 'Only Sixteen'* and
the title track of *A Little Bit More* (1976) that reinvigorated their career.

This was followed by a softening of their music. As
Dr Hook moved closer to the pop mainstream, their
success increased with the hits 'Sharing the Night
Together'* (1978), 'When You're in Love with a Beautiful Woman'* (1979), 'Sexy Eyes' (1980) and 'Baby
Makes Her Blue Jeans Talk' after their move to
Casablanca in 1982. With the departure of Sawyer,
whose eyepatch had given the band a focus, in 1983
and following a rash of personnel changes, the band's
hits ceased. Despite their shambolic image, Dr Hook
toured regularly and by the eighties were more successful in Europe than in America, even cutting *Live
in the UK* (1981) while on tour. The group disbanded
in 1985 following a final European tour, although
Sawyer formed a new 'Dr Hook' in 1988 for live performances. The lasting appeal of the band's best-
known material was demonstrated by the chart
success of the 1992 hits collection *Completely Hooked*.
'When You're in Love with a Beautiful Woman' was a
minor hit again in the UK when it was re-released in
1997. It led to the collection *Love Songs*, which was a
hit in the UK in 1999, and to Dr Hook's lead singer
Locorriere issuing a belated solo album, the minor
Out of the Dark (Track, 2000), in which he put satire
aside in favour of making a would-be perfect companion piece to a box of chocolates, even romanticiz-
ing such Hook favourites as 'Lucy Jordan' and
'Sylvia's Mother'. *Pleasure and Pain* (1996) is the
definitive box set.

DR JOHN
*b. Malcolm John 'Mac' Rebennack, 21 November 1941,
New Orleans, Louisiana, USA*

New Orleans songwriter and session man Rebennack
adopted the persona of 'Dr John the Night Tripper' in
the underground rock era, later becoming a respected
performer of classic New Orleans R&B piano styles.

As a baby he appeared on Ivory Soap boxes, and as
a teenager he learned guitar from Walter 'Papoose'
Nelson of **Dave Bartholomew**'s band. Rebennack
became the first white musician on the New Orleans
session scene, leading touring bands for white teen
pop stars Frankie Ford and Jerry Byrne (for whom he
wrote 'Lights Out') in the segregated South. He also
wrote 'What's Going on' for Art Neville, 'Losing Battle' for Johnny Adams and 'Lady Luck', a Top Twenty
hit for **Lloyd Price** in 1960.

Rebennack organized session bands for the Ace,
Ebb, Ric and Ron labels, and played on recordings
for Harold Battiste's AFO organization. But the collapse of many of the small labels and problems following a shooting incident with a promoter (which
left Rebennack with a hand injury) led him to follow
many of his New Orleans contemporaries to the
West Coast in 1963.

Through Battiste he played on numerous sessions
in Los Angeles, notably those of Sonny and **Cher** and
Phil Spector. Rebennack also set up the shortlived
Pulsar label as a Mercury subsidiary, recording tracks
by King Floyd and Alvin Robinson. With Jessie Hill
(whose 'Ooh Poo Pah Doo' had been a 1960 hit) and
Ronnie Barron, he organized groups to play in New
Orleans style on sessions and on the growing underground music scene. From these bands (including the
Zu Zu Band, which made *Zu Zu Man* for A&M in
1965, and Morgus and the Three Ghouls) came the Dr
John concept. *Gris Gris* (Atlantic, 1968), produced by
Battiste, featured saxophonist Plas Johnson with Hill
as Dr Poo Pah Doo. It was a potent mix of authentic
Creole and R&B music with hyped-up psychedelic
sorcery, and featured the much-covered song 'Walk
on Gilded Splinters'.

Three further albums in the same vein (*Babylon*,
1969, *Remedies*, 1970, and *The Sun Moon and Herbs*,
1971) were less impressive, mainly because of Rebennack's drug and managerial problems. The 1971
album, recorded in London, included **Eric Clapton**
and Mick Jagger among the backing musicians.
Rebennack next moved to Miami to work on sessions
for **Jerry Wexler** (he played organ on **Aretha
Franklin**'s 'Spanish Harlem'*) and to record *Gumbo*
(Atlantic, 1972) This was a straight re-creation of the
classic New Orleans rhythm and blues piano style of
Professor Longhair and **Huey 'Piano' Smith** and
gave Dr John a minor hit with 'Iko Iko', a remake of

the Dixie Cups' 1965 single. The title track from the **Allen Toussaint**-produced *In the Right Place* (1973) was his only Top Ten hit.

Though both albums established Dr John as a major roots artist, real commercial success eluded him. He played keyboards on **Bobby Charles**' 'Small Town Talk' and took part in a 'supersession' with **Mike Bloomfield** and John Hammond Jnr, which produced *Triumvirate* (Columbia, 1973).

Following the failure of *Desitively Bonnaroo* (1974), Rebennack put together his Rizzum and Blues Revue. Intended as an updated version of a medicine show its members included Barron, Robinson and New Orleans singer Tammi Lynn. Its only album, *Hollywood Be Thy Name* (United Artists, 1976), was given an inappropriate heavy-rock gloss by **Alice Cooper** producer Bob Ezrin. Dr John appeared on **The Band**'s farewell album, *The Last Waltz*, and made two albums for A&M's Horizon label before releasing the masterly solo piano album, *Dr John Plays Mac Rebennack* (Clean Cuts, 1981), which was a virtual inventory of New Orleans styles and includes the definitive reading of 'Memories of Professor Longhair'.

The well-titled *The Brightest Smile in Town* (1983) was an even better album. It saw Dr John extending his range to include a version of **Johnny Mercer**'s 'Come Rain or Come Shine' and a relaxed version of 'Average Guy' by Doc Pomus, formerly of **Pomus and Shuman**. As well as a pair of notable retrospectives, *The Ultimate Dr John* (1987) and *Mos' Scocious: Anthology* (1993), other records from this period included sessions with British jazz bandleader **Chris Barber** (Black Lion, 1982), while in 1986 Rebennack and Doc Pomus co-wrote and produced the **Jimmy Witherspoon** album *Midnight Lady Called the Blues* (Muse). In the wake of the critical success of these jaunty albums Dr John returned to a major label for the Grammy award-winning but disappointing *In a Sentimental Mood* (Warner, 1990). Intended as a tribute to **Ray Charles**, it saw Dr John swamped by the lush arrangements. He emphasized his jazz pedigree on *Bluesiana Triangle* (Windham Hill, 1990), with **Art Blakey** and David 'Fathead' Newman, and the album of historical jazz tracks *Goin' Back to New Orleans* (1992) was an improvement, but *Television* (GRP, 1994) was overdone. Far better was 'I'm on a Roll', his contribution to *Till the Night Is Gone: A Tribute to Doc Pomus* (1995), and *Afterglow* (1995), a set of bluesy big-band songs from the forties, which gave him space to stretch out vocally and on the piano with extended solos.

Back in the public eye, touring and often appearing as a special guest, he signed to EMI's Parlophone label, who immediately set about making him contemporary with *Anutha Zone* (1998), on which he was paired with **Portishead**, **Ocean Colour Scene** and **Paul Weller** to little effect. A commercial failure, John followed it with a far better but seemingly off-hand tribute to **Duke Ellington**, *Duke Elegant* (2000). Just prior to that he found time to guest on **Van Morrison**'s skiffle outing with **Lonnie Donegan** and **Chris Barber**, *The Skiffle Sessions – Live in Belfast*, where, clearly relaxed in a supporting role, his contributions shone out.

COXSONE DODD
b. Clement Dodd, 1932, Jamaica

One of the pioneers of the Jamaican record industry, Dodd was a producer and studio owner. Among the notable artists he worked with during the sixties and seventies were the **Skatalites**, **Bob Marley**, **Prince Buster**, **King Tubby**, **Desmond Dekker**, **Burning Spear** and Freddie McGregor.

In the early fifties Dodd was a migrant worker, cutting cane in the southern states of America. He returned to Jamaica with R&B records and set up a disc-jockey sound system, Sir Coxsone Downbeat, in 1954. Employing such figures as Prince Buster, **Lee Perry** and Count Machouki (the first deejay to 'toast' or talk over records), Dodd soon used local musicians to cut exclusive acetates in an R&B style for his four mobile sound systems.

At the beginning of the sixties he began to press copies of his acetates for general sale. Thus 'Freedom' by Clancy Eccles was recorded in 1959 for sound-system use and not released to the public on Dodd's Studio One label until 1961. Other early signings by Dodd were the Vikings (later **Toots and the Maytals**), rock-steady singer Norma Frazer, and Alton Ellis.

In 1963 Dodd built his own one-track studio and pressing plant, recording 'Phoenix City' and 'Guns of Navarone' by the Skatalites and using the group as his studio band. They backed Bob Marley and the Wailers on the 1964 hits 'Simmer Down' and 'It Hurts to Be Alone', while Marley acted as an A&R man, choosing songs for Dodd's artists to record.

The Wailers left Dodd after a dispute about money, something which also happened to the Maytals and to Perry, who each recorded songs about it ('Escape from Broadway' and 'People Funny, Boy'). Dodd was later sued by Marley when the producer leased albums of early Wailers' songs to Columbia for international release.

When the Skatalites disbanded in 1965, Jackie Mittoo became Dodd's house arranger, writing Alton Ellis's 'I'm Still in Love', which as 'Uptown Top Ranking' was a British No. 1 for Althia and Donna (Lightning, 1977). Mittoo organized house band the Soul Vendors, whom Dodd took on tour to England in 1967. Dodd productions, such as **Ken Boothe**'s version of **Sandie Shaw**'s Eurovision Song Contest winner 'Puppet on a String', were released in Britain by Trojan until 1969, when he set up the small Bamboo label with Junior Lincoln.

On his return to Jamaica he introduced the tape delay to reggae and upgraded his studio to eight tracks. During the seventies Dodd's Studio One label released records by Burning Spear, Marcia Griffiths (formerly of **Bob and Marcia**), the Wailing Souls, **Dennis Brown** and Freddie McGregor. In 1981 he left the Jamaican music industry and settled in New York where he continued to produce such artists as B. B. Seaton. In 1991 he returned to Jamaica to promote two shows to celebrate his thirty-five years as one of reggae's most influential figures.

BILL DOGGETT
b. William Ballard Doggett, 16 February 1916, Philadelphia, Pennsylvania, USA, d. 13 November 1996

Doggett's 'Honky Tonk'* was one of the bestselling records of the R&B era.

A pianist, he joined Jimmy Gorham's Band in 1935, briefly becoming leader in 1938, before relinquishing the band to **Lucky Millinder**. He worked as an arranger and pianist for the **Ink Spots** (1942–4) and performed with **Lionel Hampton**, whose alto saxophonist **Earl Bostic**'s career would later parallel his own. In 1949 he briefly replaced organist Wild Bill Davis in **Louis Jordan**'s Tympani 5 and took up the electric organ and toured and recorded with **Ella Fitzgerald** in 1951. In 1952 he formed his own band and signed with King, for whom he recorded prolifically for the next nine years. His biggest hit was 'Honky Tonk' (1956). An insistent dance riff written by the band – Berisford Sheperd, Billy Butler, Clifford Scott – and producer **Henry Glover**, and featuring relaxed guitar doodles by Butler and a rasping sax solo by Scott, the record was doubly unusual in that the riff was continued over both sides of the disc and it was recorded live. Its success inspired several similar instrumentals, including 'Raunchy' (Phillips International) by Bill Justis and 'Jivin' Around' (Cash) by Ernie Freeman, who also covered 'Raunchy', in 1957.

Doggett had further pop hits (notably 'Slow Walk', 1956, which was covered by Sil Austin on Mercury, and 'Soft', 1957) and a stream of R&B chart placings. These included a cover of Millinder's 'Ram-Bunk-Shush' (1957), which was also a hit for the **Ventures**, 'Hold It' (1958) and 'Rainbow Riot' (1959). During this period he also recorded in a jazz vein with Illinois Jacquet, Rex Stewart and Ike Quebec. In 1961 Doggett joined Warners. Subsequently he recorded for Columbia and ABC, among other labels, and regularly appeared as a sideman on French jazz and blues sessions.

THOMAS DOLBY
b. Thomas Morgan Robertson, 14 October 1958, Cairo, Egypt

A British synthesizer and keyboards player, Dolby's hits typified the rise of electronic pop in the mid-eighties. He also worked as a session musician, arranger and producer with such artists as **Grace Jones**, **Joni Mitchell** and **George Clinton**. Increasingly in the nineties he worked in new technologies and multimedia, experimenting with music-based programs for computer games such as Sega's *Double Switch*, which starred Deborah Harry of **Blondie**.

In the late seventies he was a sound-mixer for punk and new-wave bands like the UK Subs and the **Fall**. He briefly played with Bruce Woolley and the Camera Club before writing 'New Toy' (Stiff, 1981), a minor hit for German-born singer Lene Lovitch, whose biggest success was 'Lucky Number' (1979).

After playing keyboards on sessions for **Foreigner** and **Def Leppard**, Dolby formed the Venice in Peril label, releasing 'Windpower' and 'She Blinded Me with Science' from *The Golden Age of Wireless* (1981). Though only a minor hit in Britain, a reworked 'Science' reached the American Top Ten in 1983, attracting attention with a video which portrayed Dolby as a mad professor, using the voice of TV personality Dr Magnus Pyke. The visuals which accompanied 'Hyperactive' (1984), a British Top Twenty hit, drew on computer-generated graphics. The single came from *The Flat Earth*, which also included a version of **Dan Hicks**' 'I Scare Myself'. The shortlived studio band Dolby's Cube, which released 'Get Out of My Cube', included Clinton, Lovitch and members of **Earth, Wind and Fire**.

As a producer, Dolby worked with rap artists Whodini and, most frequently, British rock band **Prefab Sprout** (beginning with *Steve McQueen*, 1985). He co-produced Mitchell's *Dog Eat Dog* (1986). He played keyboards with **David Bowie** at Live Aid and composed soundtracks for films by George Lucas, Richard Brooks and Ken Russell (*Gothic*, 1987). In 1987 Dolby was unsuccessfully sued for trademark infringement by Dolby Laboratories, inventors of the tape noise reduction process.

For 'Airhead' and the album *Aliens Ate My Buick* (EMI, 1988), Dolby formed the Lost Toy People from Los Angeles-based musicians. On *Astronauts and Heretics* (Giant, 1992) Dolby's guests included Jerry Garcia and Bob Weir, **Ofra Haza** and Eddie Van Halen.

By the time of the release of the definitive compilation album, *Retrosectable* (1995), Dolby had virtually abandoned music for multi-media.

ERIC DOLPHY
b. Eric Allan Dolphy, 20 June 1928, Los Angeles, California, USA, d. 29 June 1964, West Berlin, Germany

A flautist and alto-saxophonist, Dolphy was a key associate of **John Coltrane** and **Ornette Coleman**. In developing his 'new thing' in the early sixties, Dolphy was particularly concerned to introduce the tonalities of Eastern music into jazz. His solos were increasingly built on principles of free association and his early death cut short a process of evolution that might have made Dolphy one of the greatest figures in modern jazz.

As a child he played clarinet and oboe and then alto-sax in a **Louis Jordan**-influenced band in the late forties. Influenced by **Charlie Parker**, he played in the big band led by Parker's ex-drummer Roy Porter, playing on 'Sippin' with Cisco' (1948). After army service, Dolphy returned to Los Angeles in 1953, where he first met Coltrane and Coleman. With his Men of Modern Jazz he had a club residency in 1956–7 before joining drummer Chico Hamilton's cocktail-jazz group in 1958.

At the end of 1959, Dolphy moved to New York where he played on 'Original Faubus Fables' by **Charles Mingus**. Dolphy made his own début album in 1960, *Outward Bound* (New Jazz), and also contributed on bass clarinet to Coleman's *Free Jazz*. The following year he recorded an unusual version of **Thelonious Monk**'s 'Round About Midnight' on **George Russell**'s *Ezz-Thetics* (Milestone).

Dolphy's first live dates as leader were recorded with Booker Little (trumpet) and pianist Mal Waldron on the triple-album *The Great Concert of Eric Dolphy* (Prestige, 1961). The same trio appeared with **Max Roach** on *Percussion Bitter Suite*.

After a European tour, Dolphy joined forces with Coltrane on whose *Ole* he had already played. He toured for six months with the saxophonist in 1961–2, recording the live albums *Impressions* (Impulse) and *Africa/Brass*, for which Dolphy did the orchestrations.

Leaving Coltrane, Dolphy recorded with Mingus, the **Modern Jazz Quartet**'s John Lewis, **Gil Evans** and critic/composer Gunther Schuller. Dolphy's next session as leader took place in 1963 when Alan Douglas produced *Iron Man* (Douglas International) and *Music Matador*. Drummer Tony Williams and trumpeter Freddie Hubbard were added for *Out to Lunch* (Blue Note, 1964), which proved to be Dolphy's final studio recording. It included perhaps his best bass-clarinet-playing on 'Something Sweet, Something Tender'.

He travelled to Europe for a tour with Mingus and later gave solo performances in France and the Netherlands, where *Last Date* (Limelight, 1964) was recorded. Dolphy died a month later from a heart attack associated with diabetes. A selection of his own private recordings, *Other Aspects* (Blue Note), was issued in 1987.

PLACIDO DOMINGO
b. 21 January 1941, Madrid, Spain

The flexibility of his voice and his outstanding acting ability made tenor Domingo one of biggest international opera stars of the seventies. In the manner of **Enrico Caruso** before him, Domingo 'crossed over' to the popular field in the eighties through solo recordings of popular material and duets with the likes of **John Denver**, which led to his recording 'El Mundial', the official theme song of soccer's 1982 World Cup. This was the prelude to his performance as one of the Three Tenors on the occasion of the World Cups of 1990 and 1994.

Domingo's parents were *zarzuela* (light opera) singers who settled in Mexico in the late forties. Domingo himself studied piano and sang baritone in musicals, including a Spanish translation of **Lerner and Loewe**'s *My Fair Lady*, which he recorded as *Mi Bella Donna* (1960). After joining the Mexican National Opera he switched to singing tenor and became the youngest-ever leading tenor when he took the part of Alfredo in Verdi's *La Traviata* in 1962.

Throughout the early sixties Domingo presented music shows on television. In 1965 he sang in Israel and made his American début in the following year. By now an international celebrity, Domingo performed in Hamburg, Vienna, Milan and London, making his first solo album for RCA in 1969. Domingo went on to take part in several opera recordings a year until the mid-seventies. He also made guest appearances on other labels, including EMI, Decca and Columbia, for whom he sang Lt Pinkerton in Puccini's *Madame Butterfly* in 1978.

Through producer Milt Okun, Domingo recorded *Perhaps Love* (Columbia, 1981), duetting on the title track with its composer, John Denver. The album also included versions of **John Lennon** and **Paul McCartney**'s 'Yesterday' and Denver's 'Annie's Song'. The success of that record led to a series of albums of mainstream popular material, beginning with *My Life for a Song* (1983), which included **Henry Mancini**'s 'Moon River' and **Johnny Mercer**'s 'Autumn Leaves'.

Christmas with Placido Domingo was recorded with the Vienna Symphony Orchestra and *Be My Love* (whose title tune had been a hit for **Mario Lanza**) with the London Symphony Orchestra. *Save Your Nights for Me* included a duet with Maureen McGovern, who had recorded the 1973 No. 1 'The Morning After' (20th Century), the theme to *The Poseidon Adventure*. Domingo also recorded several albums of popular songs from Spain, Mexico (*Adono*, 1982) and Argentina.

After the Mexican earthquake of 1983, Domingo spent a year performing only at charity events to raise money for the homeless. In 1985 he and Sarah Brightman had a British Top Ten album with **Andrew Lloyd Webber**'s *Requiem* (EMI), conducted by Lorin Maazel, and in 1989 he had a British Top Ten hit ('Till I Loved You') in an unlikely partnership with Jennifer Rush (best known for the melodramatic international hit, 'The Power of Love', CBS, 1985).

In the nineties Domingo continued to cultivate mainstream audiences with a series of albums that saw him performing popular ballads (*Be My Love*, 1990, and *The Broadway Album*, 1991). But his greatest success came with *The Three Tenors Concert* in 1990 with fellow opera stars José Carreras and Luciano Pavarotti (conducted by Zubin Mehta). Mounted in July 1990, on the eve of the World Cup football final, the concert of popular classical arias was an enormous success. The audio and video recordings of the event were multi-million-sellers, while Pavarotti had a British Top Ten hit in the same year with the aria 'Nessun dorma' from Puccini's *Turandot*, which had been used as a UK World Cup television theme.

In 1994 the three singers appeared in a similar concert in America for the next World Cup tournament, and the video of the performance, which included more popular standards than four years earlier, was equally successful. They repeated the process in 1998.

FATS DOMINO
b. Antoine Domino, 10 May 1929, New Orleans, Louisiana, USA

With sales of over 65 million records, pianist and singer Domino was the most popular exponent of the New Orleans style of R&B in the early fifties, finding a new worldwide audience with the arrival of rock'n'roll. Many of his recordings were covered by white artists and, with other New Orleans musicians, he was a prime influence on the development of Jamaican ska music.

The son of a violinist, he learned piano from his uncle, jazz banjo-player Harrison Verrett, and joined Billy Diamond's band in 1945. Although Domino inherited a local tradition of piano-playing exemplified by **Professor Longhair**, his most important influence was boogie-woogie player **Albert Ammons**. In 1949 **Dave Bartholomew** recorded Domino singing 'The Fat Man' for **Art Rupe**'s Specialty label. The eight-bar blues with rolling piano, Domino's rich, creole singing and a spirited sax solo from Herb Hardesty was one of the first records to sell a million in the R&B market.

Domino's next hit was the ballad 'Every Night About This Time' (1951), which introduced his char-acteristic repetitive triplet figure on piano, a technique introduced to rhythm and blues by Little Willie Littlefield. Later R&B successes, usually co-written by Domino and Bartholomew, included 'Goin' Home'* (1952), 'Goin' to the River'* (1953) and 'All By Myself'* (1955). Led and produced by Bartholomew, the immaculate session group on Domino's records throughout the fifties featured Hardesty, Earl Palmer (drums) and Frank Fields (bass).

He made his first impact on the nascent rock'n'roll audience with 'Ain't That a Shame' (Imperial, 1955); although only a minor hit for Domino, the song was swiftly and successfully covered by **Pat Boone**. It was later revived by the **Four Seasons** in 1963 and by Cheap Trick (Epic, 1979). The following year, five Domino singles reached the pop charts. As well as the original compositions 'I'm in Love Again' and 'Blue Monday', they included R&B versions of the standard ballads 'My Blue Heaven' and 'Blueberry Hill', which remained one of Domino's best-loved recordings.

With minimal changes to the formula, Domino remained a major figure in rock for five more years. His biggest hits included the infectious 'I'm Walkin'' (1957, covered by **Rick Nelson**), 'Valley of Tears', 'Whole Lotta Loving' (1958), 'I'm Gonna Be a Wheel Some Day'/'I Wanna Walk You Home' (1959), 'Be My Guest' and the loping 'Walking to New Orleans' (1960), which used a string section. More violins contributed to the success of the lazy ballad 'Natural Born Lover' (1960), which was followed by 'Let the Four Winds Blow' (1961), 'What a Party' and 'You Win Again' (1962). Domino's success with rock audiences was assisted by his cameo appearances in such films as *Shake Rattle and Roll* (1956), *Disk Jockey Jamboree* and *The Girl Can't Help It* (1957).

In 1963 he moved to the larger ABC-Paramount label, where he was produced by Felton Jarvis and **Bill Justis**. However, his record sales declined in an era dominated by **The Beatles** – though he enjoyed minor success with a cover of 'Red Sails in the Sunset' (1963). Later records were made for Mercury (*Live in Las Vegas*, 1965), Broadmoor (a shortlived label co-owned with Bartholomew) and Reprise, for whom Domino cut the Lennon–McCartney song 'Lady Madonna' (1968).

Universally accepted as a rock'n'roll legend in the seventies, he played at revival concerts in America and Europe and appeared in the film *Let the Good Times Roll* (1973). A later recording was *Sleeping on the Job* (Sonet), made in New Orleans in 1979.

In 1991 the definitive 100-track boxed set of his classic recordings, *They Call Me the Fat Man*, was issued by EMI. Among his few new recordings of the nineties was the seasonal album *Christmas Is a Special Day* (1995).

DON AND DEWEY

Don 'Sugarcane' Harris, b. 18 June 1938, Pasadena, California, USA, d. 30 November 1999; Dewey Terry, b. 1938, Pasadena

A West Coast vocal duo, Don and Dewey composed the rock standards 'I'm Leaving It (All) Up to You' and 'Farmer John', which became a staple of the British beat-group repertoire. Harris later played electric violin with **Frank Zappa** and **John Mayall**.

Harris studied classical violin from the age of six but first performed in public with Los Angeles group the Squires in the mid-fifties. He linked up with pianist Terry in 1955 and the duo made their first records for local labels Spot and Shade.

Next, **Art Rupe** signed Don and Dewey to his Specialty label. Beginning with 'Jungle Hop' (1957), they recorded a series of singles in both frantic rocking and bluesy ballad styles. Among the up-tempo songs were 'Big Boy Pete' (1959), a minor hit for the Olympics (Arvee, 1960), and 'Farmer John', later recorded by the **Searchers** (1963). 'When the Sun Begins to Shine' (1957) and 'I'm Leaving It (All) Up to You' were the best of the ballads. The latter was successfully revived by both Dale and Grace in 1963 (an American No. 1 on Montel) and by Donny and Marie of the **Osmonds** in 1974.

Don and Dewey toured with the **Johnny Otis** band in the late fifties, recording for Rush ('Soul Motion') and Highland, but split up in the early sixties. Harris joined **Little Richard**'s band and became a sought-after session musician, in 1970 appearing on Otis's *Cuttin' Up* (Epic), Zappa's *Hot Rats* and *Weasels Ripped My Flesh*, and Mayall's *USA Union* (1970).

After briefly re-forming Don and Dewey, Harris and Terry pursued solo recording careers in the seventies. Terry made *Chief* (Tumbleweed, 1973) and played keyboards on several of Harris's albums. These included *Fiddler on the Rock* (Polydor, 1970), *Cup Full of Dreams* (Epic, 1973) and *Sugarcane's Got the Blues* (BASF, 1973). On *New Violin Summit* (Metronome, 1971) Harris was joined by fellow violinists Jean-Luc Ponty and Michael Urbaniak. He later recorded with Los Angeles hardcore punk band Tupelo Chain Sex.

WALTER DONALDSON

b. 15 February 1893, Brooklyn, New York, USA, d. 15 July 1947, Santa Monica, California

Donaldson was one of the most prolific songwriters of his day.

A self-taught pianist, Donaldson turned to songwriting after a spell in a broker's office. His first big success was the elaborately titled 'Just Try to Picture Me Down Home in Tennessee' (better known as 'Back Home in Tennessee', 1915) with lyrics by William Jerome, one of his several songs with rural themes. On his discharge from the army he joined **Irving Berlin**'s music publishing company and had a huge hit with the brisk ragtime tune, 'How Ya Gonna Keep 'Em Down on the Farm'. Then came 'My Mammy', with lyrics by Joe Young and Sam Lewis, which, though it was not written for him, **Al Jolson** made his own (1919). That song sold over a million copies in sheet music, as did 'You're a Million Miles from Nowhere When You're One Little Mile from Home', 'My Buddy', 'Carolina in the Morning' (1922), 'Yes Sir That's My Baby' (all with lyrics by **Gus Kahn**) and 'My Blue Heaven' (1927), with lyrics by George Whiting. In 1928 Donaldson set up his own publishing company.

On occasion Donaldson wrote both words and music, notably on 'Little White Lies', 'You're Driving Me Crazy', a UK No. 1 for the Temperance Seven in 1961, and 'At Sundown', but he was happier collaborating with others. Though he made contributions to *Sweetheart Time* (1926) and with Kahn wrote the complete score to *Whoopee!* (1928), which starred **Eddie Cantor** and **Ruth Etting**, Donaldson saw himself as a song, rather than show, writer. In 1929, in company with many of his contemporaries, he went to Hollywood. Among his later songs were 'My Baby Just Cares for Me' from the 1930 film of *Whoopee!*, a big European hit in 1987 for **Nina Simone** with the reissue by Charly of her 1959 Bethlehem recording, 'Love Me or Leave Me', 'Sleepy Head' and 'Meadowlark', written with **Johnny Mercer**. He remained in Hollywood until ill-health forced him to retire in 1946.

LONNIE DONEGAN

b. Anthony James Donegan, 29 April 1931, Glasgow, Scotland

One of Britain's first teenage idols, Donegan's success with 'Rock Island Line' launched the skiffle boom of the fifties.

His father was a violinist with the National Scottish Orchestra and from his youth Donegan was immersed in music. He learned to play drums and guitar and played in amateur jazz bands before going into the army in 1949. There he played drums with the Wolverines jazz band and became committed to **Ken Colyer**'s authentic approach to New Orleans jazz, joining the band as banjoist on his discharge in 1951, and playing skiffle with **Chris Barber** and **Alexis Korner**. In 1952, after playing alongside his idol, **Lonnie Johnson**, he adopted the forename Lonnie and in 1953 joined Barber's jazz band.

In 1954, as part of the Barber band's *New Orleans Joy* album, Barber's skiffle group recorded 'Rock Island Line', learned from a **Leadbelly** record, and

'John Henry', which Decca finally released as a pair of novelty items under Donegan's name in 1956. The simple drama of 'Rock Island Line', which started slow and built to a breakneck climax, and its undisciplined vitality caused a sensation. By the end of the year Donegan had sold a million copies and found himself with an American Top Ten record and a parody version by **Stan Freberg**.

With the skiffle boom underway – by the end of 1956 there was estimated to be almost a thousand skiffle groups in London alone – Donegan left Barber for a solo career. He signed with Pye and his hits, which were noticeably folk- rather than blues-orientated, included 'Lost John' (1956), which was also an American hit, 'Cumberland Gap' and 'My Dixie Darling' (1958). Later that year he had a hit with a cover of the **Kingston Trio**'s 'Tom Dooley' and, in 1959, his last international success with the comedy song 'Does Your Chewing Gum Lose Its Flavour'*. Henceforth, he would oscillate between comedy ('My Old Man's a Dustman', 1960, his last British No. 1, an adaptation of the vulgar Liverpool folk song, 'My Old Man's a Fireman on the Elder-Dempster Line'), covers of hit American 'folk' songs (**Johny Horton**'s 'Battle of New Orleans', 1959, and the Highwaymen's American No. 1, 'Michael Row the Boat', 1961) and traditional songs ('Sal's Got a Sugar Lip', 1959, and 'Pick a Bale of Cotton', 1962). In the mid-fifties Donegan established his own music-publishing company and copyrighted the arrangements and new words to most of the traditional songs he recorded; for example, he changed 'Have a Whiff on Me' to 'Have a Drink on Me'. By the sixties his publishing interests were extensive, and included such material as the **Moody Blues**' 'Nights in White Satin'.

The Beatles (whose **John Lennon** and **Paul McCartney** were inspired by Donegan to form their first group together, the Quarrymen skiffle group) marked the end of Donegan's career as a star. He established himself on the cabaret and variety circuit. In 1978 he released the **Adam Faith**-produced *Puttin' on the Style* (Chrysalis) on which, supported by **Elton John**, **Ringo Starr**, **Leo Sayer**, **Albert Lee** and Ronnie Wood, he reprised his past hits. In 1980 he cut *Sundown*, a country album with **Doug Kershaw** which included a version of 'The Battle of New Orleans'. Following its commercial failure, he returned to the lucrative world of television and cabaret, returning to his skiffle roots to cut the live album *Jubilee Concert* (1981) and joining the Barber Band's fortieth anniversary tour in 1994. Encouraged by **Van Morrison**, who guested on a couple of tracks, he returned to his roots, releasing a skiffle album, *Muleskinner Blues* (Capo, 1999), and appearing alongside the likes of Barber and, in their skiffle identities, Adam Faith and **Rolling Stone** Bill Wyman in a sell-out Roots of British Rock concert at London's Albert Hall (1998). While the album wasn't a great commercial success, Donegan and company clearly enjoyed themselves and a year later with Barber and Morrison (with **Dr John** roped in for occasional support) they issued *The Skiffle Sessions – Live in Belfast* (Virgin).

DONOVAN
b. Donovan Leitch, 10 May 1946, Glasgow, Scotland

Initially accused of being a **Bob Dylan** imitator, Donovan developed his own whimsical style of flower-power singer-songwriting and enjoyed considerable popularity in the mid-sixties.

His family moved to Hatfield near London when he was ten and at the age of sixteen he dropped out of college into the world of British 'beats', a scene evoked in the best of his earliest songs. Donovan's break came with an appearance in 1965 on the television show *Ready Steady Go!*. With peaked cap and his acoustic guitar emblazoned with the slogan 'This machine kills' (an abridged version of **Woody Guthrie**'s original 'This machine kills fascists') he sang 'Catch the Wind'. He was soon signed to Pye and the song and the equally simple 'Colours' were hits, closely followed by his début album, *What's Bin Did and What's Bin Hid*. A TV documentary about him made soon afterwards showed the British 'beat' culture of the era, all roll-up cigarettes and singing round open fires on Cornish beaches. 'Try for the Sun' and 'Jersey Thursday' from *Fairy Tale* (1965) captured the mood of that culture even as their author was moving away from it into the life of 'swinging London', portrayed on the same album in 'Sunny Goodge Street'. 'Young Girl Blues' (in which Donovan caught the loneliness that was the darker side of swinging London) and 'Hampstead Incident' from *Sunshine Superman* (1966) were in the same vein, but it was the album's title song that pointed Donovan's way forward. Produced by **Mickie Most** with a gentle but insistent electric bass line, it reached No. 1 in America.

The song heralded a series of hit singles, expertly crafted by Most, which sometimes ran counter to the more meditative double-album *Gift from a Flower to a Garden* (1968). 'Mellow Yellow' (1968) was a stoned nonsense song in the style of Dylan's 'Everybody Must Get Stoned' while 'There Is a Mountain' (1967) used a light calypso rhythm and Harold McNair's flute to accompany a lyric that was like a Zen nursery rhyme. The first of Donovan's collaborations with another of Most's artists came on 'Hurdy Gurdy Man', where **Jeff Beck** played a heavily distorted fuzz-guitar solo. 'Atlantis' and the British hit 'Barabajagal' (1969) featured more conventional heavy-rock guitar from Beck.

In 1970 Donovan reverted to an acoustic format for *Open Road*. The following year he played the title role in David Puttnam's film of *The Pied Piper*. This was followed by *HMS Donovan*, a collection of children's songs and settings of poems by Yeats, Lewis Carroll and Edward Lear. *Cosmic Wheels* (Epic, 1972) found him with a new record label and reunited with Most. *Essence to Essence* (1973) was produced by former **Rolling Stones** manager Andrew Loog Oldham but was a confused mix of astrology and ecological homilies. More promising was the Norbert Putnam-produced *7-Tease* (1974). Backed by Nashville's leading session players, Donovan offered a concept album concerned with nothing less than the state of the world. His final Epic album was *Slow Down World* (1976). Most returned to produce Donovan for his own RAK label (1977) before the singer left the stage for a long rest during the punk era.

His next public appearances were in 1981 when he performed at the Cambridge Folk Festival. Many of Donovan's recordings of the eighties were not released in Britain. *Neutronica* (1981) and *Love Is the Only Feeling* (1981) were issued in Germany, while *Lady of the Stars* (Allegiance, 1983) was produced in America by **Jerry Wexler**. It included new versions of 'Sunshine Superman' and 'Season of the Witch'. In the early nineties there were signs of a revival of interest in his early songs in Britain. He returned to recording with *Rising* (1990) and in 1991 he toured with the **Happy Mondays**, who recorded a witty tribute, 'Donovan' (Factory). In the same year Donovan contributed to a parodic comic version of 'Jennifer Juniper' by UK television personalities Trevor and Simon. By 1992 and 1993 virtually all his material had been reissued on CD. His only album of new material in the nineties was *Sutras* (American Recordings).

His daughter Iona Skye became a film actress while his son Donovan Leitch (*b. 1967*) was lead singer of the Nancy Boys, a group which included Jason Nesmith, son of the former **Monkees** member. The Nancy Boys recorded *Johnny Chrome and Silver* (Equator, 1994).

JASON DONOVAN
b. 1 June 1968, Melbourne, Australia

Like **Rick Nelson** and Mickey Dolenz of the **Monkees**, Donovan was a child television star before becoming a teen pop idol.

The son of television actor Terence Donovan, Jason made his first small-screen appearance in the children's television series *Skyways*. Among his co-stars was **Kylie Minogue** and both joined the cast of daytime soap-opera *Neighbours* in 1986.

After the series had become one of the most popular programmes in the UK, first Kylie and then Jason were offered recording deals with leading songwriter-producers **Stock, Aitken and Waterman**. Donovan's début single 'Nothing Can Divide Us' (1988) inaugurated a three-year period during which he became Britain's leading teenage idol. His string of hits sung in a pleasant light tenor included a duet with Minogue ('Especially for You', 1989), SAW compositions such as 'Too Many Broken Hearts' (a 1989 chart-topper) and 'Hang on to Your Love', and new versions of older teen ballads like **Brian Hyland**'s 'Sealed with a Kiss' (1990) and the Cascades' 'Rhythm of the Rain' (1991). The album *Ten Good Reasons* was one of the biggest sellers of 1989 and *Between the Lines* (1990) was equally popular.

In 1991 Donovan moved to the stage to take the leading role in the London revival of **Andrew Lloyd Webber** and Tim Rice's *Joseph and the Amazing Technicolour Dreamcoat*. A recording of 'Any Dream Will Do' from the show topped the UK charts. Later records, no longer produced by Stock, Aitken and Waterman, such as *All Around the World* (1993) were less successful and by the end of the decade Donovan was more active in the theatre than in the recording studio. He appeared in revivals of *Camelot* (1996), *Night Must Fall* (1997) and *The Rocky Horror Show* (1999).

THE DOOBIE BROTHERS
Tom Johnston, b. Visalia, California, USA; John Hartman, b. 18 March 1950, Falls Church, Virginia (replaced by John McFee, b. Santa Cruz, California); Patrick Simmons, b. 23 January 1950, San Jose, California; Dave Shogren, b. San Francisco, California (replaced by Tiran Porter, b. Los Angeles, California); Michael Hossack, b. 18 September 1950, Patterson, New Jersey (replaced by Keith Knudsen, b. 18 October 1952, Ames, Iowa); Jeff 'Skunk' Baxter, b. 13 December 1948, Washington DC; Michael McDonald, b. 1952, St Louis, Missouri; Chet McCracken, b. 17 July 1952, Seattle, Washington

In the early seventies a successful West Coast boogie band noted for their harmony singing (they featured three lead singers), the Doobies effortlessly transformed themselves into an even more successful white funk band in the second half of the decade. The group's name comes from the Californian slang word for a marijuana cigarette.

Formed in 1970 by Johnston and Hartman and signed to Warners by Ted Templeman (a former member of **Harpers Bizarre** who would produce all their albums), the band found success with the release of their second album, *Toulouse Street** (1972). It established their sound – a strong, guitar-led beat and high, light harmonies – and included 'Listen to the Music', their first of fifteen Top Forty placings. Early hits include the much recorded 'Jesus Is Just Alright',

'Long Train Running' (both 1973), 'Black Water'* and
a spirited version of **Holland, Dozier and Holland**'s
'Take Me in Your Arms (Rock Me)' (1975), originally
a hit for Kim Weston in 1965. As well as their singles'
success, the group were a prominent concert attraction and both *The Captain and Me* (1973) and *What
Were Once Vices Are Now Habits* (1974) sold over a
million copies.

Vices saw the arrival of Baxter from **Steely Dan** and
a deepening of the band's sound. With the arrival of
McDonald (also from Steely Dan) in 1976, the group's
music shifted towards black rhythms and the meeting
place of funk and pop. The group's old songs were
recast, McDonald's impassioned vocals replaced the
high harmonies of Johnston and Hartman, and
McDonald wrote the majority of the band's new
material. With the multi-million success of *Minute by
Minute* (1978), which was introduced by 'What a Fool
Believes'* (with which **Aretha Franklin** also had a
minor pop hit), and a series of personnel changes,
McDonald's ascendancy within the band was confirmed. On *One Step Closer* (1980), which generated
another Top Ten hit, 'Real Love', the group were virtually McDonald's back-up band. By 1982 the group
had disbanded and McDonald, Johnston and Simmons were pursuing solo careers.

McDonald's first solo albums were *Michael
McDonald*, which included the huge hit single 'I Keep
Forgettin' (Every Time You're Near)', and *If That's
What It Takes* (1982), after which he recorded with
Elton John, **Christopher Cross**, **Kenny Loggins** (with
whom he wrote 'What a Fool Believes'), **Toto** and
Jackie DeShannon. In 1985 he released *No Lookin'
Back* (Warner Brothers) and, in 1986, had a pair of
international hits, 'Sweet Freedom' (the theme song
from *Running Scared*) and a duet with **Patti Labelle**,
'On My Own'* (MCA), which was written and pro-
duced by **Burt Bacharach** and Carole Bayer Sager.

In 1988 Johnston re-formed the Doobie Brothers
with Simmons, Hartman Porter and Hossack but
without McDonald. Some of the lead vocals were
taken by Cornelius Bumpus, an ex-Moby Grape
member who had been a Doobie Brother in the
period 1979–81. In 1989 this group recorded *Cycles*
(Capitol), which was surprisingly strong and gave
them a US Top Ten hit with 'The Doctor'. *Brotherhood* (1991) was less successful, but sales of a Doobie
Brothers 'best of' album were boosted in the UK by a
hit dance remix of 'Long Train Running' in 1993. The
band undertook a successful US tour in the same
year. *Rocking Down the Highway* (Sony, 1996) was a
live recording of their best-known numbers.

McDonald returned to recording in 2000 with *Blue
Obsession* (Sanctuary). His first album since 1993, it
included reworkings of **Neil Young**'s 'Down by the
River' and **Marvin Gaye**'s 'Ain't That Peculiar'.

THE DOORS

*John Densmore, b. 1 December 1945, Los Angeles,
California, USA; Robbie Krieger, b. 8 January 1946, Los
Angeles; Ray Manzarek, b. 12 February 1935, Chicago,
Illinois; Jim Morrison, b. 8 December 1943, Melbourne,
Florida, d. 3 July 1971, Paris, France*

The archetypal psychedelic art-rock band, the Doors
and leader Jim Morrison created a potent mix of lurid
poetry, effective organ/guitar backings and dramatic
live performance. Their recorded work inspired
members of each successive generation of musicians,
including **Iggy Pop**, **Alice Cooper**, the **Stranglers** and
Joy Division.

With romantic poetry as his earliest artistic influence, Morrison (vocals) was studying film at University College of Los Angeles when he met Manzarek,
keyboards player with Rick and the Ravens, who had
recorded for the local Aura label. With ex-Psychedelic
Rangers Krieger (guitar) and Densmore (drums),
they formed the Doors, a name suggested by Aldous
Huxley's quotation from William Blake, *The Doors of
Perception*.

In 1966 the group performed rock and R&B standards, plus **Kurt Weill**'s and Bertolt Brecht's
'Alabama Song' at Sunset Strip clubs, gradually introducing original material like 'When the Music's Over'
and the violent, apocalyptic and oedipal 'The End'.
Signing to Jac Holzman's Elektra label, they released
The Doors (1967), produced by Paul Rothchild. With
swirling keyboard arpeggios, 'Light My Fire'* reached
No. 1.

As well as the hit 'People Are Strange', *Strange Days*
(1967) included 'Horse Latitudes' – a high-school
poem of Morrison's set to a *musique concrète* backing
– and 'When the Music's Over' with its chanted
refrain 'we want the world and we want it – now!'.
1967 was the height of protest over the American war
in Vietnam and in an atmosphere where Victor Lund-
berg's lugubrious anti-draft-dodger monologue 'An
Open Letter to My Teenage Son' (Liberty) could
reach the Top Ten, Doors songs like 'Five to One' and
'The Unknown Soldier' (a minor hit in 1968) took on
strongly political connotations.

Morrison preferred to style himself an 'erotic
politician', however, and the million-sellers 'Hello I
Love You' (1968), the second No. 1 from *Waiting for
the Sun*, and the Doors' first major European hit, and
'Touch Me' (1969) had sexual themes. The latter
reached the Top Ten shortly after Morrison had been
charged with obscene behaviour at a concert in
Miami. After lengthy delays he was convicted but the
verdict was still under appeal at the time of his death.

As a result, the band made few live appearances
and Morrison's heavy alcohol and drug intake made
him increasingly erratic. Later albums included *The*

Soft Parade (1969), which used a string section, the well-received *Morrison Hotel* (1970) and *LA Woman* (1971), which included **John Lee Hooker**'s atmospheric blues 'Crawlin' King Snake' as well as the hits 'Love Her Madly' and the gentle, jazzy 'Riders on the Storm', which took on the aura of an epitaph after Morrison died in mysterious circumstances while on an extended vacation in Europe.

The Doors briefly continued as a trio, releasing the lacklustre *Other Voices* (1971) and *Full Circle* (1972). They reunited in 1978 to record backing tracks for *An American Prayer*, tapes of Morrison reading his poetry. Other albums of previously unreleased material were *Alive, She Cried* (1983) and *Live at the Hollywood Bowl* (1987). Both Krieger and Manzarek have enjoyed lengthy if unspectacular musical careers since the demise of the Doors. With Densmore, Krieger recorded with English singer Jess Roden as the Butts Band for Blue Thumb and ABC. Later Krieger made a series of solo albums for Blue Note and composed soundtrack music for such projects as a 1993 documentary on the Harley Davidson motorcycle. Manzarek made *The Golden Scarab* (Mercury, 1975) with **Crusaders** guitarist Larry Carlton while **Patti Smith** was guest vocalist on his *The Whole Thing Started with R'n'R* (1975). Between 1980 and 1983 Manzarek produced four albums on Slash and Elektra by Los Angeles band X as well as collaborating with **Philip Glass** on a version of Carl Orff's *Carmina Burana*. In 1993 he worked with Michael McClure on *Love Lion* (Shanachie), a poetry and music album.

The interest in Morrison was maintained in the eighties by a biography by Danny Sugerman and Jerry Hopkins (*No One Here Gets Out Alive*). Val Kilmer's portrayal of Morrison as a romantic hero in Oliver Stone's 1991 film *The Doors* was the catalyst for another Doors revival, which resulted in the group selling more records in the nineties (when their albums were re-issued hits) than in the sixties. *The Doors Box Set* (1997) included virtually everything the group had recorded. In 2000 Joel Lipman wrote the musical *Celebration of the Lizard*, in which a Jim Morrison-inspired character strides through a post-apocalyptic Los Angeles offering comments. Doors member Manzarek was the musical director of the show, which features some thirty songs from the Doors' catalogue.

JIMMY DORSEY

b. *James Francis Dorsey, 29 February 1904, Shenandoah, Pennsylvania, USA, d. 12 June 1957, New York*

Although he was an accomplished jazz saxophonist, Jimmy Dorsey's work as a bandleader was dominated by the popular ballad hits crooned by Bob Eberly and other singers.

He first played clarinet in his music-teacher father's band before forming Dorsey's Novelty Six as a teenager with his brother **Tommy Dorsey** and, later, the Scranton Sirens. Together, the brothers played with Jean Goldkette (1924) and **Paul Whiteman** (1926), where they recorded with **Bix Beiderbecke**, and other orchestras including that of **Ted Lewis**, which toured Europe in 1930. Jimmy Dorsey's clarinet and alto sax were also heard on records by **Jack Teagarden**, **Eddie Lang** and **Joe Venuti**.

In 1934 the Dorsey Brothers formed their own orchestra, playing a mixture of Dixieland tunes like 'St Louis Blues', popular ballads (sung by **Bob Crosby**) and **Benny Goodman**-style swing with arrangements by **Glenn Miller**. The band recorded for Decca but in 1935 the brothers fell out and Tommy left to set up his own band.

Jimmy Dorsey's orchestra grew in popularity during the late thirties and in 1937 had major hits with 'Change Partners' (1938) and 'The Breeze and I' (1941, later a million-seller for **Caterina Valente** in 1955) both sung by Bob Eberly. Eberly's younger brother Ray Eberle [*sic*] recorded prolifically as a vocalist with Glenn Miller (including the chart-topping 'Over the Rainbow', 1939). 1941 brought three million-sellers for the Jimmy Dorsey band and its vocalists Bob Eberly and Helen O'Connell: 'Amapola' and two Latin numbers, 'Green Eyes' and 'Maria Elena'. After further success with 'Blue Champagne' and **Johnny Mercer**'s 'Tangerine' (1941), the Dorsey organization had the first hit version of the much-recorded 'Besame Mucho' (1943), with vocals by Eberly and Kitty Kallen.

In addition to these pop dance numbers, the wartime Jimmy Dorsey band recorded jazz pieces like 'Mutiny in the Brass Section' and 'Waddlin'' at the Waldorf' (1944). They also appeared in such films as *The Fleet's In* (1942, in which they introduced the oft-recorded 'I Remember You'), *Four Jills and a Jeep*, and *Hollywood Canteen* (1944). In 1947 Jimmy was reunited with his brother for the biopic *The Fabulous Dorseys* and he continued to lead big bands until 1953. He then joined forces with Tommy to co-lead a touring group, the Fabulous Dorseys. After Tommy's death in 1956 Jimmy was sole leader but died of cancer in the year he had his last million-seller, 'So Rare' (Fraternity).

LEE DORSEY

b. *24 December 1924, Portland, Oregon, USA, d. 2 December 1986, New Orleans, Louisiana*

One of the most distinctive R&B singers of the sixties, Dorsey's best records were made in collaboration with **Allen Toussaint**.

As Kid Chocolate, Dorsey was a professional boxer in the forties before he moved to New Orleans in 1957. With Joe Banashak, he cut 'Lottie Mo' (ABC Paramount, 1960) before linking up with talent scout Marshall Sehorn and Toussaint, who placed Dorsey with Bobby Robinson's Fury label for the Harold Battiste-produced 'Ya Ya'. Based on a children's rhyme, the record was a Top Ten hit in 1961 and was covered as 'Ya Ya Twist' by **Petula Clark** in Britain. The equally catchy follow-up, 'Do-Re-Mi', was a minor hit shortly before Fury folded. Later records on Smash and Constellation sold poorly.

In 1965 his career revived when Toussaint and Sehorn signed him to Amy, a subsidiary of the New York pop label Bell. A string of hits, written by Dorsey and arranged and produced by Toussaint, followed. These included 'Ride Your Pony', 'Get Out of My Life Woman', 'Working in the Coal Mine' and 'Holy Cow', a British Top Ten hit on Stateside. The latter was also recorded by **The Band** (1973) and **Chas and Dave**.

With the exception of 'Everything I Do Gonna Be Funky', Dorsey's later singles were less successful. In a change of approach, Toussaint wrote and produced the superior concept album *Yes We Can* (Polydor, 1970), whose driving beat was the forerunner of Southern funk. The same team cut *Night People* (ABC, 1978). Several of Dorsey's songs from this period were successfully recorded by other artists, notably 'Sneaking Sally Through the Alley', the title track of **Robert Palmer**'s 1974 Toussaint-produced album. In 1976 Dorsey made a guest appearance on the début album of Southside Johnny and the Asbury Dukes.

In later years Dorsey devoted himself to running his New Orleans panel-beating company, but was tempted out of retirement to support the **Clash** on their 1980 American tour. He died from emphysema.

THOMAS A. DORSEY
b. 1 July 1899, Villa Rica, Georgia, USA, d. 23 January 1993, Chicago, Illinois

Like later singers such as **Little Richard** and **Al Green**, Dorsey was a classic example of a secular composer and performer who turned to sacred music at a high point in his career. Unlike those singers, however, his contribution to gospel music far outweighed his reputation as a popular musician.

He grew up in Atlanta with a Baptist minister father and an organist mother, learning popular piano styles from musicians at the 81 Theater. Moving to Chicago in 1916, he began to work with jazz bands, leading his own Wildcats to back **Ma Rainey** on her touring shows in 1924–8. He next became an arranger for a music publisher, a job which led to an association with the Brunswick/Vocalion record company, for whom Dorsey set up and played on many sessions.

His own recordings, as 'Georgia Tom', in partner-

ship with singer/guitarist Tampa Red (*b. Hudson Whittaker, 25 December 1900, Atlanta, d. 19 March 1987, Chicago, Illinois*) yielded the suggestive and catchy 'It's Tight Like That' (1928). Selling nearly a million copies, it was the major blues hit of its day, and was recorded by many other artists. For the next four years Dorsey wrote and recorded prolifically with novelty groups like the Hokum Boys ('Selling That Stuff', 1928) and as an accompanist to Rainey and other singers. His 'Terrible Operation Blues', sung by Jane Lucas (1930), was a 'point' number often revived on blues, hillbilly and 'party' records.

In 1932 Dorsey gave up Georgia Tom and left the blues business to work exclusively in gospel music, a term he is credited with inventing. He founded the National Convention of Gospel Choirs and Choruses in 1933 and went on to direct choirs and tour with them in many countries. Among his several hundred gospel compositions are the standards 'Precious Lord, Take My Hand', 'A Little Talk with Jesus', 'If You See My Savior' and 'Peace in the Valley'.

Dorsey's genius as a gospel composer is rooted in a wide experience of American vernacular music. His most enduring works combine elements of white popular and country music, as well as black idioms, and can be readily assimilated into those traditions. He received the National Music Award of the American Music Conference in 1976 and became one of the few black members of the National Gospel Singers Convention. Dorsey appeared in the documentary films *The Devil's Music* (1976) and *Say Amen Somebody* (1982).

TOMMY DORSEY
b. Thomas Francis Dorsey, 19 November 1905, Shenandoah, Pennsylvania, USA, d. 26 November 1956, Greenwich, Connecticut

Trombonist Tommy Dorsey led one of the leading swing and dance bands from 1935 to his death. The orchestra included numerous top jazz soloists as well as such vocalists as **Frank Sinatra** and **Jo Stafford**.

The son of a musician and younger brother of **Jimmy Dorsey**, he played in a family group before forming Dorsey's Novelty Six with Jimmy. By the early twenties the brothers had joined the New York dance-band and recording-session scene. They played on dozens of records by such artists as the California Ramblers, **Bix Beiderbecke**, **Joe Venuti**, **Hoagy Carmichael**, Jean Goldkette and **Paul Whiteman**, whose orchestra Tommy joined in 1926.

The brothers made their first recordings as leaders in 1929 and in 1934 formed a permanent band, the Dorsey Brothers Orchestra. With arrangements by **Glenn Miller** and vocals from **Bob Crosby**, the Orchestra played a mixture of Dixieland tunes, ballads

and up-tempo dance music. After a violent disagreement, Tommy left the group in 1935 to set up his own
orchestra, which was more strongly slanted towards
jazz and swing.

Initially his band was made up from former members of the Joe Haymes group and it had early success
with 'I'm Getting Sentimental over You' (RCA Victor,
1935), on which Dorsey took a trombone solo. With
singers Edythe Wright (featured on the chart-topping
'On Treasure Island', 1935, and 'The Music Goes
Round and Round', 1936) and Jack Leonard, the
band's popularity grew. Leonard's version of **Irving
Berlin**'s 'Marie' (1937) sold a million and introduced
a style of vocal refrain in which the band chanted
responses to the singer. Equally successful were a
series of swing versions of light classics such as Rubin-
stein's 'Melody in F' (1937), Rimsky-Korsakov's 'Song
of India' and Strauss's 'Blue Danube' (1937). In
marked contrast, 'Boogie Woogie', a version of black
pianist Clarence 'Pinetop' Smith's theme tune, was a
million-seller in 1938.

Dorsey's commitment to jazz was evident in the
formation of the Clambake Seven, a small group
within the orchestra which played in Dixieland style.
In 1938 he also organized the ambitious *Evolution of
Swing* concert at Carnegie Hall which included a pot-
ted history of jazz with performances in the style of
the **Original Dixieland Jazz Band**, Whiteman, Beiderbecke and **Fletcher Henderson**.

The early forties were the Dorsey Orchestra's heyday with the arrival of former **Jimmie Lunceford**
arranger Sy Oliver and the then unknown Sinatra,
who replaced Leonard in 1940. Oliver provided versions of **Dorothy Fields**' and Jimmy McHugh's 1930
song 'The Sunny Side of the Street' and 'Opus No. 1'*,
both big hits in 1944, the year **Gene Krupa** briefly
joined Dorsey. Sinatra's successful records with
Dorsey included 'I'll Never Smile Again' (1940),
'Dolores' (1941) and 'There Are Such Things'* (1942),
on which he was supported by the Pied Pipers. The
singer's jazz-flavoured style owed much to Dorsey's
trombone phrasing and in 1961 Sinatra recorded a
tribute album, *I Remember Tommy* (Reprise), with
arrangements by Oliver.

After Sinatra left for a solo career in 1942, Dorsey's
featured singers included Jo Stafford and **Dick
Haymes**. Among the orchestra's later recordings of
the forties were 'I Dream of You'* (1945), 'At Sundown' (1946) and 'Trombonology' (1947), which featured the leader. In the same year, both Tommy and
Jimmy appeared in the biopic *The Fabulous Dorseys*.

In 1950 the Tommy Dorsey Orchestra moved to
Decca and in 1953 he was reunited with Jimmy, who
had disbanded his own group. The two performed
together until Tommy's accidental death. When
Jimmy Dorsey died the following year, the orchestra

continued under the leadership of Warren Covington, who had a surprise hit with 'Tea for Two Cha
Cha'* (Decca, 1958). A 1964 version of the orchestra
included singer Frank Sinatra Jnr, while in the seventies the Tommy Dorsey Orchestra was led by Canadian trombonist Murray McEachern.

THE DOVELLS

*Len Barry, b. Leonard Borisoff, 6 December 1942,
Philadelphia, Pennsylvania, USA; Arnie Satin, b. 11
May 1943, Philadelphia; Jerry Summers, b. 29 December
1942, Philadelphia; Mike Dennis, b. 3 June 1942, Philadelphia; Danny Brooks, b. 1 April 1943, Philadelphia*

The Dovells are best remembered for 'Bristol Stomp',
one of a series of raucous dance records on Parkway
in the early sixties.

Formed in 1957 as a doo-wop group, a style they
returned to on album tracks, they recorded the wild
rocker 'Mope-Itty Mope' (Boss, 1958) as the Bosstones
before signing with Parkway, whose owners Kal Mann
and Dave Appell wrote 'Bristol Stomp' (1961) for
them. Harder-voiced and tougher-looking than most
of the Philadelphia teen-idols (though equally willing
to take advantage of regular appearances on **Dick
Clark**'s *American Bandstand*), they brought a degree
of commitment to the inane dance records they were
given. These included 'Do the New Continental',
'Bristol Twistin' Annie', 'Hully Gully Baby' (all 1962)
and a vocal version of **Phil Upchurch**'s 'You Can't Sit
Down' (1963), before their career came to an end with
the end of the dance craze of the early sixties and the
arrival of **The Beatles**.

With the demise of the group, lead singer Barry,
whose wavery, fierce voice was so distinctive, turned
to blue-eyed soul. He joined Decca, where he was
produced by John Madara and Dave White (a one-
time member of **Danny and the Juniors**). They supplied him with '1-2-3'* (1965) and 'Like a Baby' (1966),
both dance classics. When his hits dried up in 1967, he
temporarily abandoned rock for the cabaret circuit,
before following Madara and White into production.
He wrote and produced several minor disco hits in
the seventies and has had a long association with the
Philadelphia-based WMOT Productions, working
with such groups as Blue Magic, Fat Larry's Band and
Philly Cream.

TOM DOWD

b. 1925, New York, USA

As an engineer in the fifties, Dowd was a pioneer in
the development of recording techniques; in the sixties he recorded many of Atlantic's southern soul hits
and in the seventies and eighties was one of the most
respected producers in the industry.

The son of a concert-master and an opera singer, Dowd was a science graduate and classically trained musician. In 1946 he joined Apex studios and quickly became one of the most sought-after engineers in New York because he was able to engineer recordings with superior clarity, pitch and balance. He worked with Atlantic from the beginning. The first hits he engineered were Stick McGhee's 'Drinkin' Wine Spo-Dee-O-Dee' (1949) and **Ruth Brown**'s 'Teardrops from My Eyes' (1950), and in 1956 he joined the company exclusively. Before then he was regularly asked by Mercury to engineer covers of recordings that he'd engineered for Atlantic. Often, as in the case of Georgia Gibbs' covers of **Lavern Baker**'s R&B hits, he'd find that he was working with the same musicians and the same arrangers that had worked on the original recording.

Among the artists that Dowd worked with in the fifties and early sixties were **Joe Turner**, the **Clovers**, the **Drifters**, Laverne Baker, **Ray Charles** (including the famous *Ray Charles Live at Newport*, 1958), the **Modern Jazz Quartet** (whom Dowd recorded in stereo, long before it was common practice) and **Chuck Willis**. He usually worked in collaboration with **Jerry Wexler** and/or **Ahmet Ertegun**, and with **Nesuhi Ertegun** on the jazz projects. Towards the end of the decade Dowd engineered the first productions of **Leiber and Stoller**, most notably with the **Coasters**, on whose recordings Leiber and Stoller and Dowd experimented with multi-tracking.

In 1965 Dowd and Wexler oversaw the first Atlantic recordings made at the Stax Studio in Memphis and in 1966 they repeated the process at Muscle Shoals. Together the pair added a high gloss to the recordings of **Otis Redding** (notably *Otis Blue*, 1965 – which spawned the hits 'Respect' and 'Satisfaction' – and *Live in Europe*, 1967), **Wilson Pickett**, **Sam and Dave** and, most successfully of all, **Aretha Franklin**. By this time arranger **Arif Mardin**, Wexler and Dowd operated as a production triumvirate.

Dowd's first wholly autonomous production work was with the **Rascals** (then known as the Young Rascals), all of whose early hits he made. Later he worked with **Cream** (including *Disraeli Gears*, 1966, and *Wheels of Fire*, 1967, as engineer), **P. F. Sloan** (*Measure of Pleasure*, 1968), **King Curtis**, **Dusty Springfield**, **Jerry Jeff Walker** (*Mr Bojangles*, 1969) **Cher**, the **Allman Brothers Band** (*Eat a Peach*, 1972), Derek and the Dominos (*Layla*, 1970) and **Dr John**, before leaving Atlantic to freelance in 1972.

In the seventies and eighties, as well as producing many albums by **Eric Clapton** and **Rod Stewart**, Dowd worked with **Jackie DeShannon** (*Jackie*, 1972), **Lynyrd Skynyrd**, **Kenny Loggins** and Pablo Cruise, among others. His highest profile production in the early nineties was on the 'retro-rock' album by UK

band **Primal Scream**, *Give Out But Don't Give Up* (1994). Other nineties productions include *If We Fall in Love Tonight* (Rod Stewart, 1996) and *The Color of Love* (Earl Ronnie and the Broadcasters, 1997).

NICK DRAKE
b. 19 June 1948, Burma; d. 25 November 1974, Tamworth-in-Arden, England

Although singer-songwriter Drake was widely ignored in his own brief lifetime, his profile has risen considerably since his death in 1974. While his incantatory, breathy vocals and lush orchestral arrangements recall a young **Donovan**, Drake's songs are steeped in a sombre melancholy unrivalled by his contemporaries. His strong, rhythmic guitar style, rooted in the finger-picked blues of **Robert Johnson**, has also drawn praise.

Born to upper-middle-class parents in Burma, Nick Drake began to amass a collection of mournful acoustic-led songs while studying at public school in England. His performance at the 1967 May Ball at Fitzwilliam College, Cambridge, attracted the attention of producer **Joe Boyd**, who had recently set up his own Witchseason label, signing the likes of **Richard Thompson** and the **Incredible String Band**. The following year Drake recorded *Five Leaves Left* (1969), heavily reliant on the baroque string arrangements of Robert Kirby, also a student of Cambridge University. The album was a critical success and led to a series of live performances around Britain. However, Drake found the experience of touring so immensely painful that he would never perform in front of an audience again.

Drake's second album, *Bryter Layter* (1970), was given a jazzy air by members of **Fairport Convention** and was less self-pitying in mood than its predecessor. However, it was not a commercial success and sent the singer into a long period of depression. In 1972 he recorded his final studio album, *Pink Moon*, on which his frail voice was accompanied only by sparse acoustic guitar and piano. After the album's release Drake once again retired to his parents' home in Tamworth-in-Arden, making one final foray into the recording studio in early 1974.

In the months before his death Drake appeared to be beginning to overcome his personal difficulties, having agreed to write songs for French chanteuse Françoise Hardy during the last of his occasional trips to Paris. These plans would never reach fruition. Drake was found dead soon after, on 25 November 1974, by his mother in the family home, of an apparently accidental tranquillizer overdose.

Since his death Drake has achieved a growing cult following, particularly in the nineties, as artists including **Paul Weller** and **R.E.M.**'s Peter Buck have acknowledged his influence on their work. The four songs recorded in his final studio sessions appear alongside earlier unreleased material on the posthumous *Time of No Reply* (1979), while the *Fruit Tree* (1986) boxed set collects all of his recorded work.

In 1999 a tribute concert was arranged to mark the 25th anniversary of Drake's death. It included performances from **Beth Orton** and former **Suede** guitarist Bernard Butler.

PETE DRAKE
b. 8 October 1932, Augusta, Georgia, USA, d. 29 July 1988, Nashville, Tennessee

The foremost pedal-steel guitarist of the modern era, Drake's session work on **Bob Dylan**'s *John Wesley Harding* (1968) and *Nashville Skyline* (1969) made the steel guitar commonplace on rock as well as country albums.

A self-taught guitarist, Drake turned to steel guitar when he heard Jerry Byrd (a one-time member of **Red Foley**'s band and one of the first Nashville-based session musicians) in the late forties. He played with country groups on radio in Atlanta and on various television programmes before moving to Nashville in 1959. He was immediately in demand, giving country hits such as Roy Drusky's 'Anymore' and **George Hamilton IV**'s 'Before This Day Ends' a distinctive sound. From the early sixties on he issued instrumental albums on Smash, Starday (*For Pete's Sake* and *The Country Steel Guitar of Pete Drake*, both 1962), Cumberland (*Country Steel Guitar*, 1963) and Stop (which he co-owned). While continuing his session work, following the example of Alvino Rey, he experimented with a 'talking guitar', foreshadowing **Jeff Beck** and **Peter Frampton**. In 1964 he had a pop hit using the technique, 'Forever' (Smash).

In even greater demand after his sessions with Dylan, he worked with **George Harrison** (on *All Things Must Pass*, 1971), **Ringo Starr** (for whom he produced and played on *Beaucoups of Blues*, 1970), **Leon Russell**, Bill Medley of the **Righteous Brothers** and **B. J. Thomas** (whose *Great American Dream*, 1979, he produced), among others. He also worked regularly on country sessions in Nashville, producing albums for **Ernest Tubb** (*The Legacy and the Legend*, 1979) and Canadian country star, Ronnie Prophet (*Phantom of the Opry*, 1979).

PAUL DRESSER
b. Paul Dreiser, 21 April 1857, Terra Haute, Indiana, USA, d. 30 January 1906, New York

With **Charles K. Harris** and **Harry Von Tilzer**, Dresser was one of the founding fathers of Tin Pan Alley and modern commercial songwriting. Harris and Von Tilzer, however, pointed firmly to the future in their ability to write in a variety of styles (including ballads, dialect, coon, drinking and topical songs). Dresser's songs on the other hand were mostly narrative ballads harking back to the past, specifically to the sense of loss that runs through much of the work of **Stephen Foster**. Dresser's songs, like the novels of his younger brother Theodore Dreiser, have been described by critic Charles Hamm as 'human dramas sketched in verse . . . detailing the shift from a largely rural society to one dominated more and more by urban centres . . . and the new problems . . . in this new city life'.

After running away from home as a boy, Dresser worked in medicine- and minstrel-shows (in both white- and blackface) and as a journalist and sketch writer before settling in New York in the 1880s. There, he regularly appeared in vaudeville (as both a comic and singer), most notably at Tony Pastor's, which was rapidly becoming the meeting point of the new breed of songwriters. His first published song was 'Wide Wings' (1884) and his first hit the sentimental 'The Letter That Never Came' (1886).

Dresser's most enduring songs were 'Just Tell Them That You Saw Me' (1895), which was recorded by many singers including the Welsh baritone J. W. Myers (Columbia, 1895) and George J. Gaskin – 'the silver-voiced Irish tenor' – on several labels including Edison, Berliner and Columbia (1896); the rural idyll 'On the Banks of the Wabash' (1897), which was recorded by Gaskin (1897), Steve Porter (Berliner, 1898) and Harry MacDonough, second only to **Henry Burr** among the ballad singers of the early recording era (Victor, 1913), and later was adopted as the state song of Indiana; and 'My Gal Sal' (1905). That was recorded by Byron G. Harlan (Victor, 1907) and the Columbia Stellar Quartet (1921), among others. Interspersed with, and related to, these hits was a series of songs centred on young men and women who had left home, notably 'I Wonder Where She Is Tonight' (1899), 'She Went to the City' (1904) and 'The Town Where I Was Born' (1905). In marked contrast were Dresser's less impressive patriotic songs, such as 'The Blue and the Gray' (1900) and 'Mr Volunteer' (1901).

Dresser died virtually penniless at the home of his sister just before 'My Gal Sal' became one of his biggest ever hits.

THE DRIFTERS
Clyde McPhatter, b. 15 November 1933, Durham, North Carolina, USA, d. 13 June 1972, New York (replaced by Ben E. King, b. 28 September 1938, Henderson, North Carolina, replaced by Rudy Lewis, replaced by Johnny Moore, b. 1934, Selma, Alabama, d. 30 December 1998, London, England); Bill Pinkney, b. 15 August 1925,

Sumter, South Carolina (replaced by Ellsbury Hobbs);
Andrew Thrasher (replaced by Doc Green, d. 10 March
1989); Gerhard Thrasher (replaced by Charlie Thomas)

The first black vocal group of the rock'n'roll era to
have continued pop success, the Drifters included
among their lead singers two great – if contrasting –
stylists, the gospel-inspired **Clyde McPhatter** and the
sophisticated **Ben E. King**. Produced by **Leiber and
Stoller**, the Drifters were in the forefront of innovation in the late fifties and early sixties, introducing
Latin rhythms and string sections to the group genre.
With a frequently changing line-up, they were mainstays of the American and European supperclub circuits in later years.

The group was formed in 1953 by former Dominoes
singer McPhatter and the Thrashers, who had been
members of the family gospel quartet the Thrasher
Wanderers, whose 'Moses Smote the Water' was
issued by **Moe Asch** in 1947. Pinkney from the
Jerusalem Stars joined to sing bass. Managed by
Sarah Vaughan's husband George Treadwell, they
signed to Atlantic where **Ahmet Ertegun** produced
their first records. **Jesse Stone**'s 'Money Honey' (1953)
and McPhatter's 'Honey Love' (1954) topped the R&B
charts, **Johnny Ray** covered 'Such a Night', and the
Drifters' intense version of **Irving Berlin**'s 'White
Christmas' was widely regarded as one of the most
powerful vocal group recordings.

McPhatter left to begin a solo career in 1955 and
over the next three years the Drifters had four different lead singers, although only Johnny Moore
('Steamboat', 1956) brought R&B chart success. In
1958 Treadwell sacked the group and recruited the
Crowns, an R&B group that had recorded widely
since 1952, as his new Drifters. With Thomas, Green,
Hobbs and King, Leiber and Stoller put Latin percussion and strings on the poignant 'There Goes My
Baby' (1959). A big pop hit, it was followed by 'Dance
with Me' and 'This Magic Moment' (1960). King's
best-known performance with the Drifters, however,
was issued after he had left to seek solo success. Composed by **Pomus and Shuman**, 'Save the Last Dance
for Me' was a lilting romantic ballad, revived in 1989
by Bruce Willis (Motown).

Leiber and Stoller took King's departure in their
stride by recruiting ex-**Clara Ward** singer Lewis to
sing lead. Bland but effective, Lewis fronted a series of
immaculate pop hits with arrangements by **Phil Spector**, **Burt Bacharach** and **Bert Berns**. They included
'Please Stay' (1961), 'Some Kind of Wonderful',
Pomus and Shuman's 'Sweets for My Sweet' (later
covered in Britain by the **Searchers**), Gerry Goffin's
and **Carole King**'s 'When My Little Girl Is Smiling',
'Up on the Roof' (1962) and 'On Broadway' (1963).
Van McCoy's more pointed social comment 'Rat

Race' was a commercial failure, although the **Specials**
revived it in 1980.

Lewis died suddenly in 1964 and Moore rejoined
the Drifters to sing lead on Kenny Young's 'Under the
Boardwalk', produced by Berns. The song was a later
hit for Bruce Willis and the **Temptations** (Motown,
1987). Pop hits were sporadic in the mid-sixties but
Barry Mann's and Cynthia Weil's 'Saturday Night at
the Movies' (1964) reached the Top Twenty while
Goffin's and King's 'At the Club' (1965) and Mann's
and Weil's 'Come on over to My Place' were big
British hits when reissued in 1972.

Throughout the late sixties, the group drifted into
the supperclub circuit and recorded only occasionally.
The Berns production 'Up in the Streets of Harlem'
(1966) proved that the Drifters could create authentic
soul music but the revival of **Dean Martin**'s 1956 hit
'Memories Are Made of This' (a minor success in
1966) was more typical of their output.

In 1973 the group moved to Bell, where British
writers **Roger Greenaway** and Roger Cook produced
a string of hits with tuneful, jaunty pop ballads. These
included 'Kissing in the Back Row of the Movies'
(1974), 'There Goes My First Love' (1975), 'Can I Take
You Home Little Girl' and 'You're More Than a
Number in My Little Red Book' (1976).

While Moore's group, managed by Treadwell, continued to play oldies concerts and issued a new album
(*Too Hot*, 1989), the Original Drifters, led by Pinkney
and including Gerhard Thrasher, also toured Europe
in the eighties. Various versions of the band continued to play live well into the nineties. *Rockin' &
Driftin'* (1996) is the definitive retrospective.

JIMMY DRIFTWOOD

*b. James Corbett Morris, 20 June 1907, Mountain View,
Arkansas, USA, d. 12 July 1998*

As a schoolteacher in the rural Ozarks, Driftwood
used his lifelong interest in folk music to develop the
skills of both folklorist and songwriter. These skills
merged in his song 'Battle of New Orleans'. At the
same time, Driftwood was a vigorous public
spokesman for folk music and folk culture.

'Battle of New Orleans', a historical vignette of the
American War of Independence set to the fiddle tune
'Eighth of January', was included on Driftwood's first
album, *Newly Discovered Early American Folk Songs*
(RCA, 1958). The song was in turn covered by country
singer **Johnny Horton**, who had a pop and country
hit with it in 1959, **Lonnie Donegan** in Britain, and
Harpers Bizarre in 1968. 'Soldier's Joy' from the same
album, and similarly a story-song set to a traditional
fiddle tune, provided **Hawkshaw Hawkins** with a
country hit in 1959. 'Tennessee Stud', a Driftwood
composition from his next album, *The Wilderness*

Road and Jimmy Driftwood (RCA, 1959), was a hit for **Eddy Arnold** and has been much recorded since.

After 1961 Driftwood turned more towards promoting folk music. He was active in launching the Arkansas Folk Festival and later in winning federal funding for the Ozark Folk Center, an institution that has been particularly successful in the encouragement and study of regional folk life. Driftwood later directed a travelling troupe of local folk musicians, the Rackensack Folklore Society. In the seventies he recorded a pair of albums for his own Rackensack label, *Beautiful Buffalo River* and *I Hear Your People Singing* (both 1978).

EDDY DUCHIN

b. 1 April 1909, Cambridge, Massachusetts, USA,
d. 9 February 1951, New York

The most popular of several piano-playing bandleaders of the thirties and forties, Duchin, like **Liberace** after him, is better remembered for his pleasing personality and handsome good looks than his music. As a former sideman remarked, 'He was the only musician I've ever known who could play a thirty-two bar solo with thirty-two mistakes and get an ovation for it afterwards.'

In 1928 Duchin joined Leo Reisman's Orchestra as pianist. A sweet-sounding society band – it had a residency at New York's prestigious Central Park Casino – Reisman's band provided the backing for several of **Fred Astaire**'s biggest hits, notably 'Night and Day' (1932) and 'Cheek to Cheek' (1935). In 1931 Duchin, whose flourishes and embellishments had made him a huge crowd pleaser, formed his own orchestra and took over Reisman's residency. National popularity followed in 1932, the year he joined Columbia, and his Saturday tea dances were broadcast across America.

His first major hit was a cover of 'Night and Day' and most of his biggest hits were sweetened versions of film songs. These included **Harry Revel**'s 'Did You Ever See a Dream Walking?' (Victor, 1933), 'Let's Fall in Love' (which was composed by **Harold Arlen**, who had recorded his own 'Ill Wind', 1934, using Duchin's band as support), **Jerome Kern**'s 'I Won't Dance' (1935), **Nacio Herb Brown**'s 'You Are My Lucky Star' (1935), and **Cole Porter**'s 'It's De-Lovely' (1936). On most of these numbers Lew Sherwood, Duchin's trumpeter and musical director, handled the vocals.

By the end of the decade the more supple rhythms of swing took hold on America and Duchin's popularity began to slip. His last major hit was 'I Give You My Word' (Columbia, 1940). During the war he served in the navy and though afterwards he re-formed his band, illness interrupted his career. He died in 1951 of leukaemia. His memory was revived in the lugubrious biopic *The Eddy Duchin Story* (1956), which featured

Tyrone Power in the title role and Carmen Cavallaro's piano-playing. Earlier, Cavallaro had been Duchin's relief pianist and in 1945, in the wake of the interest in classical music sparked off by the success of *A Song to Remember*, he had a million-seller with his version of Chopin's 'Polonaise in A' (Decca), also a hit for **Jose Iturbi**. In the sixties Duchin's son Peter led a successful society dance band.

ANN DUDLEY

After enjoying chart success with the quirky Art of Noise, Ann Dudley became an arranger and film-music writer.

Her first job after leaving music school was as pianist on the BBC children's television show *Play Away*. She next recorded with future movie star Joanne Whalley-Kilmer as Cindy and the Saffrons. Their version of the **Shangri-Las**' 1966 track 'Past Present and Future' was a minor hit in 1981 on Stilleto.

Dudley subsequently became part of **Trevor Horn**'s studio team, working with such artists as **Yes**, **Frankie Goes to Hollywood** and **ABC**. In 1984 she collaborated with other Horn staff, J. J. Jeczalik (programmer and keyboards) and engineer Gary Langan, on an instrumental music project.

With a name taken from an avant-garde arts manifesto of the Italian Futurists, the Art of Noise embarked on a five-year career of witty and experimental dance and ambient music-making. Among the group's biggest successes were the club hit 'Close (to the Edit)' (1985), a remake of **Duane Eddy**'s 'Peter Gunn' featuring Eddy himself, and 'Kiss' (1988), a version of the **Prince** song featuring **Tom Jones**.

After the Art of Noise formally disbanded in 1990, Dudley started a new career as composer, arranger, producer and performer. She recorded *Songs from the Victorious City* in 1990 with Jaz Coleman, formerly of **Killing Joke**, and in the same year she conducted the orchestra at the **John Lennon** tribute concert held at Liverpool's Pier Head. In 1995 she released *Ancient and Modern*, a collection of religious music scored for full orchestra and chorus.

Most of her work has been in recording studios and film scores. Her film scores included *Buster* (1989, with **Phil Collins**), *Wilt* (1992), *The Crying Game* (1993) and *The Full Monty* (1997), for which she won an Oscar. Dudley has contributed to albums by **k. d. lang, Boy George**, the **Moody Blues**, Collins and Jones, amongst many others.

DAVE DUDLEY

b. David Darwin Pudraska, 3 May 1928, Spencer, Wisconsin, USA

With the success of his recording of 'Six Days on the

Road' (1963), Dudley helped establish the trucking song – in which truck-drivers and their world are the subject of unfettered macho admiration – as a genre in its own right. There had been earlier songs about truck-drivers, notably **Ted Daffan**'s 'Truck Driver Blues' (1939), but after Dudley trucking songs became an industry in themselves. Moreover, through the bar bands that performed the songs and the many movies that featured truckers, by the seventies the American trucker was given a mythical status, so much so that in 1972 **Commander Cody** could devote an entire album to truck songs. Later C. W. McCall had a huge pop hit with 'Convoy'* (MGM, 1975), which spawned a film of the same title in 1978.

A baseball pitcher in his youth, Dudley turned professional musician in 1953, graduating through radio shows and local performances to contracts with various small labels. After an automobile accident in 1960, he had his first country hits, 'Maybe I Do' (Vee, 1961) and 'Under the Cover of Night' (Jubilee), which culminated in 'Six Days', his only major pop hit, which he produced and released on his own Golden Wing label. 'Dudley's confident, quasi-rockabilly performance effectively captured both the boredom and excitement, as well as the swaggering masculinity, that often accompanied long-distance trucking,' wrote country-music historian Bill C. Malone, describing the song's appeal.

During his stay with Mercury (1963–75) Dudley recorded many trucking songs, including 'Two Six Packs Away' (1965), 'Trucker's Prayer' (1967) and 'One More Mile'. Several of his other country hits appealed to the same, conservative audience. These included his friend **Tom T. Hall**'s 'Mama, Tell Them What We're Fighting for' (1965), which takes the form of a soldier's letter from Vietnam, **Kris Kristofferson**'s 'Vietnam Blues' (1966) and his 1970 country No. 1, 'The Pool Shark'.

After leaving Mercury, Dudley recorded for small labels, having a minor hit in 1980 with 'Rolaids, Doan's Pills and Preparation H' on Sun. He worked for a while in radio and during the eighties held an annual country music festival at his lodge in Dudleyville, Wisconsin.

GEORGE DUKE
b. 12 January 1946, San Rafael, California, USA

A jazz-rock keyboards player, Duke became a successful producer for a wide range of artists in the eighties.

A virtuoso student of trombone and piano at San Francisco Conservatory, he turned to jazz and recorded his first album, *The Primal George Duke*, for MPS in 1966. Duke went on to play keyboards with **Dizzy Gillespie**, Don Ellis and French violinist Jean-Luc Ponty, contributing to the latter's Pacific Jazz

albums, notably *Electric Connection* (1968) and *King Kong* (1970).

In 1970 Duke made a decisive turn towards electronics and fusion music by joining **Frank Zappa**'s Mothers of Invention. He is featured on a number of Zappa albums, notably the film score *200 Motels* (1971) and *The Grand Wazoo* (1972). Now in demand as a sideman, Duke replaced Joe Zawinul in **Cannonball Adderley**'s band when Zawinul left to form **Weather Report**. He briefly joined drummer Billy Cobham's jazz-rock unit, recording *Live in Europe* (Atlantic, 1976).

The most impressive of Duke's own records was the Latin-jazz collaboration with Flora Purim and Airto, *A Brazilian Love Affair* (Epic, 1979). In the eighties a partnership with bassist **Stanley Clarke** yielded three albums and the Top Twenty hit 'Sweet Baby' (Epic, 1981). Though he changed labels to Elektra in 1985 for the well-received *Thief in the Night*, Duke made a greater impact as a producer. He worked on Deniece Williams' hit 'Let's Hear It for the Boy' (CBS, 1984) and on albums by **Miles Davis** (*Tutu*, 1986), Jeffrey Osborne and **Stanley Clarke** (1990). He produced the soundtrack to *The Five Heartbeats* (Virgin, 1991), the film based on the career of the **Dells**, and contributed to the soundtrack of the Steve Martin movie *Leap of Faith* (1992).

VERNON DUKE
b. Vladimir Dukelsky, 10 October 1903, Parafianovo, Russia, d. 16 January 1969, Santa Monica, California, USA

One of the several Broadway composers who also worked in films, Duke is best remembered for *Cabin in the Sky* (1940, filmed 1943) and the songs 'April in Paris' and 'I Can't Get Started without You'.

Dukelsky studied at the Kiev Conservatory of Music in his teens before in 1920 his family fled to America to escape the consequences of the Russian Revolution. In 1923 he returned to Europe, settling in London where he wrote both serious music (under his real name) and popular music (under his Duke pseudonym). Among his serious compositions was a setting of A. E. Housman's 'A Shropshire Lad' and music for Diaghilev's Ballet Russe. At the same time he contributed to several London musicals, notably *Yvonne* (1926) and *The Yellow Mask* (1928), his first complete score to a book by the prolific novelist Edgar Wallace. In 1929 he returned to America and had his first commercial success with 'I Am Only Human After All' (with lyrics by **Yip Harburg** and **Ira Gershwin**), which was introduced in *The Garrick Gaieties of 1930*. Other Duke and Harburg collaborations included the revue *Walk a Little Faster* (1932), which introduced the classic 'April in Paris', later memorably recorded by **Count Basie** (1956), among others, *The Ziegfeld Follies of 1934* and 'Autumn in New York', which **Frank Sinatra** revived in 1949. In partnership with Ira Gershwin, Duke contributed to *The Ziegfeld Follies of 1936*, which starred both **Fanny Brice** and **Josephine Baker** and introduced 'I Can't Get Started Without You', memorably recorded by Bunny Berigan (Vocalion, 1938) with **Artie Shaw** on clarinet.

As a Russian and writer of songs for revues, Duke was an unlikely choice to write the music for *Cabin in the Sky* (1940), a fantasy about black life, but he and lyricist John Treville Latouche (who had earlier supplied words to **Earl Robinson**'s 'Ballad for Americans') created a score that, though it drew hardly at all on black music, was surprisingly effective. The show (and later film) starred **Ethel Waters** and introduced 'Takin' a Chance on Love', a hit for both **Benny Goodman** and **Sammy Kaye** in 1943. Duke's other shows, which included the **Eddie Cantor** vehicle *Banjo Eyes* (1942) and *Sadie Thompson* (1944), written with Howard Dietz, were less successful. His last important songs, both with lyrics by the celebrated comic poet Ogden Nash, were 'Roundabout' and 'Out of a Clear Blue Sky' from the 1952 revue *Two's Company*.

Duke served in the Coast Guards during the Second World War and wrote 'the official fighting song of the US Coast Guard', 'The Silver Shield'.

CHAMPION JACK DUPREE

b. *William Thomas Dupree, 4 July 1910, New Orleans, Louisiana, USA, d. 21 January 1992*

Blues singer and pianist Dupree was at his most characteristic in club performance, where he deployed blues, boogies and reflective or humorous narrations in a manner suggesting a pre-rock'n'roll **Fats Domino**.

As a teenager he worked solo or with jazz bands in New Orleans. Moving north, he became a professional boxer (1932–40), returning to music in Indianapolis in 1939 and making his first records, for Okeh, in 1940. Based in New York from the early forties, he worked in clubs and recorded for many small labels, often with **Brownie McGhee**. Signing with King in 1953, he made several popular sides, some with guitarist **Mickey Baker**. He also recorded for the RCA Victor subsidiaries Groove and Vik (1956–7) with guitarist Larry Dale, but the peak of his fifties work was *Blues from the Gutter* (Atlantic, 1958), which included a version of his well-known drug song 'Junker's Blues'.

After a first tour of Europe in 1959 he settled in Zurich in 1960, moving to Copenhagen in 1965, Halifax (Yorkshire) in 1971, Sweden in 1974 and later Germany. During this period he became widely known in many European countries, making TV and film appearances and recording for Storyville (1959–63), Decca, Blue Horizon, Paris Album and other labels. He often worked with non-American musicians, including **Alexis Korner** (Atlantic, 1959), **Eric Clapton** and **John Mayall** (Decca, 1966), English clarinettist Monty Sunshine's band (Pinorrekk, 1982) and German guitarist Kenn Lending (Pinorrekk, 1983), but he was also reunited with Mickey Baker and **King Curtis** (Atlantic, 1973). Over the years he continued to observe and comment on social and political movements, some typical compositions including 'F. D. R. Blues' (Joe Davis, 1945), 'Free and Equal' (Storyville, 1961), 'Death of Luther King' (Vogue, 1968), 'I Want to Be a Hippy' (Blue Horizon, 1969), 'Vietnam Blues' (Sonet, 1971) and 'Freedom' (Free Bird, 1979). He toured Australia in 1990 and recorded *Live at Burnley* (JSP, 1990) at the British blues festival with support from The Big Town Playboys.

DURAN DURAN

Simon Le Bon, b. 27 October 1958, Hertfordshire, England; Nick Rhodes, b. Nicholas Bates, 8 June 1962; Andy Taylor, b. 16 February 1961, Wolverhampton (replaced by Warren Cuccurullo b. 1957 Brooklyn, New York City, USA); John Taylor, b. 20 June 1960, Birmingham; Roger Taylor, b. 26 April 1960, Birmingham

A product of the New Romantic backlash against punk, Duran Duran were the most popular and durable of eighties teeny-bop idols in Britain, causing what the press called 'Durandemonium' among their fans.

The band was formed in 1980 by club disc-jockey Rhodes (keyboards) and John Taylor (bass) with a name taken from a character in Roger Vadim's 1967 science-fiction spoof *Barbarella*, which starred Jane Fonda. With drummer Roger Taylor joining from the Scent Organs, guitarist Andy Taylor answering a *Melody Maker* ad and Le Bon, a drama student, they began playing the Birmingham club circuit.

After a tour with then top star Hazel O'Connor (whose hits included 'Eighth Day', A&M, 1980, and 'Will You', 1981), the group was signed to EMI, who saw them as a part of the current new-romantic trend alongside **Spandau Ballet**, **Gary Numan** and **Culture Club**. Their first single, 'Planet Earth', had the right trappings, with Le Bon's vague but evocative lyrics complemented by Russell Mulcahy's video. Mulcahy, with previous work for **Trevor Horn**'s Buggles ('Video Killed the Radio Star') and **Ultravox** ('Vienna'), went on to direct most of the band's videos, which were as crucial in establishing Duran Duran's film star/playboy image as the sleeve and merchandise designs of Malcolm Garrett.

The voyeuristic Godley and Creme video for 'Girls

on Film' was banned by both the BBC and MTV but the record gave Duran Duran their second British hit. They took off in America in 1982 with 'Hungry Like the Wolf' from their second album, *Rio*, its title redolent of the hedonistic lifestyle that was central to the Duran image. Other hits in that year were the album's title track and the ballad 'Save a Prayer', which was not released in America until 1985.

On *Seven and the Ragged Tiger* (1983), for which Alex Sadkin replaced Colin Thurston as producer, Le Bon's lyrics became more sombre. His preoccupation with a post-Holocaust breakdown of civilization was reflected in Mulcahy's video for 'Union of the Snake' and the later 'Wild Boys'. In 1983 Rhodes undertook the first spin-off project from the band, co-producing with Thurston the pop band Kajagoogoo, whose banal hits ('Too Shy', 'Ooh to Be Ah') seemed almost a parody of Duran Duran.

Internationally, 1984–5 was the band's peak, with 'The Reflex' reaching No. 1 in both Britain and America, and 'Wild Boys' and the James Bond film theme 'A View to a Kill' almost as successful. A live album (*Arena*, 1984) was an American million-seller, like its predecessors. At this point, however, Duran Duran took a sabbatical. Andy and John Taylor formed the Power Station with vocalist **Robert Palmer**, whose mainstream rock style was reflected in the titles of their American hits, 'Some Like It Hot' and 'Get It on'. The rest of the band recorded as the softer Arcadia (*So Red the Rose*, 1985), charting with 'Election Day'. In the same year Le Bon was involved in a near-fatal accident in his ocean racing yacht.

In 1986 Duran Duran regrouped for the successful album and single *Notorious*. Soon afterwards, Andy Taylor left to record as a solo artist for MCA, releasing a single, 'When the Rain Comes Down', and an album, *Thunder*, in 1987 with ex-**Sex Pistol** Steve Jones. He recorded an album of rock cover-versions, *Dangerous*, in 1990, including songs by **Mott the Hoople**, the **Kinks** and **AC/DC**.

Now a trio of Le Bon, Rhodes and John Taylor, Duran Duran released 'Meet el Presidente' in 1987 and in 1988 (briefly) changed their spelling to Duranduran for 'I Don't Want Your Love' from *Big Thing*. The *Decade* compilation (1990) was a minor success in the US, but in 1993 their career was revived with *Duran Duran (The Wedding Album)*, which included the hits 'Ordinary World' and 'Come Undone'. In 1994 the group released *Thank You*, an album of cover-versions of songs by such artists as **Lou Reed**, **David Bowie**, **Led Zeppelin** and **Neil Young**, with Roger Taylor playing on several tracks, before transmuting into Power Station for *Living in Fear* (1997). After that they resumed their Duran Duran identity for *Pop Trash* (Hollywood, 2000), on which they offered (mostly) grandiose balladry with a dash of camp.

JIMMY DURANTE
b. James Francis Durante, 10 February 1893, New York, USA, d. 29 January 1980, Santa Monica, California

Known as 'Schnozzola', because of his oversized, bulbous nose, Durante created one of the most engaging personas in showbusiness with his gravelly voice and raucous, often self-mocking, clowning as on his best-remembered recordings 'The Man Who Found the Lost Chord' and his theme song, his own composition, 'Inka Dinka Do'.

The son of a sideshow barker, Durante played ragtime piano in Coney Island and Bowery clubs in 1914, organizing his own group in 1916 and recording for Gennett and Okeh. In the twenties he teamed up with dancer Lou Clayton and vocalist Eddie Jackson and the trio became one of the hits of the New York cabaret circuit, graduating to Broadway in Florenz Ziegfeld's *Show Girl* (1929) and *The New Yorkers* (1930), in which they performed 'Wood'. After the trio broke up in 1931 Durante (with Clayton as his manager) went solo, signing with MGM. Among the numerous films in which he appeared were *Speak Easily* (1932), where he sang **Nacio Herb Brown** and **Arthur Freed**'s 'Singin' in the Rain'; *The Phantom President* (1932), the only film musical in which **George M. Cohan** appeared; *Palooka* (1934), in which he sang 'Inka Dinka Do' (Brunswick); *Little Miss Broadway* (1938); and *Music for the Millions* (1944), which produced the hit 'Umbriago' (Decca), fondly remembered for Durante's interpolated 'That note was given me by Bing Crosby, and boy was he glad to get rid of it.'

Durante also regularly appeared in Broadway musicals. His greatest success was in producer Billy Rose's mammoth production of *Jumbo* (1935, filmed as *Billy Rose's Jumbo* in 1962 with **Doris Day**) with music by Richard Rodgers (later of **Rodgers and Hammerstein**) and lyrics by **Lorenz Hart**. Among his compositions were 'I'm Jimmy the Well-Dressed Man', 'I Know Darn Well I Can Do without Broadway (But Can Broadway Do without Me?)' and 'I Ups to Him and He Ups to Me'.

In the fifties Durante moved into television (where he regularly closed his shows with 'Goodnight Mrs Calabash, wherever you are') and garnered another hit with 'Blackstrap Molasses' (1951), on which he was partnered by **Danny Kaye**, Groucho Marx and actress Jane Wyman. In the sixties he turned increasingly to cabaret and had a surprise minor hit with a version of **Kurt Weill**'s 'September Song' (Warner Brothers, 1963).

DEANNA DURBIN
b. Edna Mae Durbin, 4 December 1921, Winnipeg, Canada

Durbin saved Universal Studios from bankruptcy

with her classically trained voice and bubbling personality and went on to become Hollywood's highest-paid star.

Recommended to MGM, Durbin was teamed with fellow teenager **Judy Garland** in a musical short, *Every Sunday* (1936), in which she represented legitimate culture singing a light classical piece while Garland sang a pop song. MGM preferred Garland to her and she signed with Universal, where producer Joe Pasternak (who would later oversee the career of **Jose Iturbi**) constructed a series of light musical comedies around her wholesome image. These included *Three Smart Girls* (1936) and its various sequels: *100 Men and a Girl* (1938); *Mad About Music* (1939); *The Amazing Mrs Holliday* (1943); *Can't Help Singing* (1944), in which she sang the title song and 'More and More', both **Jerome Kern** and **Yip Harburg** compositions; *Up in Central Park*, in which she co-starred with **Dick Haymes**; and *For the Love of Mary* (1948). Even before the release of *Smart Girls*, Durbin was a star through her guest appearances on **Eddie Cantor**'s radio programmes.

No longer highly regarded, Durbin's films were very much of their time. Thus in *Smart Girls* she and her sisters reunite their divorcing parents, and in *100 Men* she persuades an unwilling Leopold Stokowski to conduct an orchestra of Depression-hit musicians. All were constructed as vehicles for her but when Pasternak left Universal for MGM and Durbin demanded more dramatic roles (such as that in *Christmas Holiday*, 1944, in which she introduced the **Frank Loesser** classic 'Spring Will Be a Little Late This Year'), she lost the affection of her audience. In 1948, aged 27, she suddenly retired to France and refused all entreaties to make a comeback.

IAN DURY
b. 12 May 1942, Billericay, Essex, England, d. 27 March 2000, London

Dury is the author of the seventies anthem 'Sex and Drugs and Rock and Roll' and numerous memorable character sketches, ranging from the intimate ('My Old Man') to the exuberant ('Billericay Dickie') that united the spirit of the English music hall with the sound of rock'n'roll.

Stricken by polio at the age of seven, Dury went to art school and while teaching formed his first band, Kilburn and the High Roads, in 1970. The band's defiant approach, in which Dury's deformities were flaunted at the audience, won them few fans until the mid-seventies when suddenly their attitude 'fitted' and the pub circuit provided them with suitable venues. Critic and disc-jockey Charlie Gillett briefly became their manager and signed them to the Anchor label, Raft, only for the label to fold before their

album was released. Now with a cult following, they joined Pye's progressive subsidiary Dawn and released *Handsome* (1974).

With the collapse of Dawn and the break-up of the band in 1975, Dury started working with Chaz Jankel, a former member of Byzantium, which had recorded unsuccessfully for A&M (including *Byzantium*, 1972). Jankel replaced Russell Hardy as the Kilburns' pianist and Dury's regular writing partner. They signed to the indpendent Stiff label, where *New Boots and Panties!!* (1977) was an immediate success, eventually selling over a million copies in the UK, and the song 'Sex and Drugs and Rock and Roll' (1977), though more ambiguous about the charms of rock'n'roll than its title might suggest, became a cult favourite. Dury's witty and inventive lyrics, his direct eroticism ('Wake up and Make Love with Me') and his affectionate accounts of London wideboys ('Clever Trevor') and his own heroes (in particular his reminiscence of the polio-stricken **Gene Vincent**, 'Sweet Gene Vincent') were perfectly highlighted by Jankel's arrangements. The album was followed by a trio of major hits, 'What a Waste', the British No. 1 'Hit Me with Your Rhythm Stick' (1978) and 'Reasons to Be Cheerful (Part 3)' (1979), a celebration of eccentricities (like 'England's Glory', which Dury wrote for music-hall comedian Max Wall). *Do It Yourself* (1979) with its smoother, jazzier sound, and tours with the Blockheads (as he named his group) confirmed Dury's status as a major British star, but the ragged *Laughter* (1980), which featured **Don Cherry** on pocket trumpet and was made after Jankel left to pursue a solo career, failed. After a move to Polydor for *Lord Upminster* (1981), the rejection by the United Nations of 'Spasticus Autisticus' as a contribution to the Year of the Disabled, and the unsuccessful *4,000 Weeks Holiday* (1984), Dury took a break from touring and recording.

After that, Dury divided his time between music and acting. His 'Profoundly in Love with Pandora' (EMI, 1985), the theme to the British teleseries *The Secret Diary of Adrian Mole Aged 13*, saw him reunited with Jankel. He appeared on television (*King of the Ghetto*, 1986), in films (*Pirates*, 1986, *Rocinante*, 1987, and *The Cook, the Thief, His Wife and Her Lover*, 1989) and plays (*Road*, 1987).

In 1989 he wrote (with former Blockhead Mickey Gallagher) and starred in the musical *Apples*. 1991's *Warts'n'Audience* was a live recording with Blockheads members made at a 1990 benefit concert for Blockheads drummer Charlie Charles, a victim of cancer. The gigs were so successful that Dury and the band played several more over the next two years, and members of the Blockheads played on 1993's *The Bus Driver's Prayer & Other Stories* (Demon), his best album since *Do It Yourself*. After that he turned to acting before, in 1998, after being diagnosed as suffering from cancer, he gave much attention to health matters, becoming a UN goodwill ambassador. In between his new careers as a UN spokesperson and voice-over star in television adverts, he recorded *Mr Love Pants* (1998), again with Jankel as his creative partner. Fittingly, after his death in 2000 his life was more often than not celebrated by people playing 'Reasons to Be Cheerful'.

BOB DYLAN
b. *Robert Allen Zimmerman, 24 May 1941, Duluth, Minnesota, USA*

'I like to stay a part of that stuff that don't change,' said Dylan in the notes to his retrospective five-record set *Biograph* (1985). And the key paradox of the work of Dylan, the most influential of the songwriters and singers of the sixties, is that his supreme originality was firmly rooted in his absorbing of traditions of music, poetry, and biblical myth and allegory. The impact of that originality on the direction taken by later popular music was two-fold. His work encouraged a serious attitude to rock music among pundits and practitioners alike. Dylan was the catalyst for the growing complexity in **The Beatles**' work after 1965, and he enabled critics and academics to claim the status of art for the music, as well as giving rise to a vast amount of scholarship, both professional and amateur, concerned to elucidate his own work and life. Secondly, Dylan was the first of the singer-songwriters. The appeal of his intensely personal and poetic utterances paved the way for the success of **Leonard Cohen**, **James Taylor**, **Joni Mitchell**, **Paul Simon**, **Neil Young** and myriad others. While the peak of his artistic success came in the sixties, three decades later he was still attracting large audiences for live shows in which he frequently subjected his own past repertoire to new versions and arrangements while making records, like *Time Out of Mind* (1997), that still challenged his audience. At the same time Sony's reissue programme made it clearer how his changes of styles in the sixties had become essential. Particularly revealing was *Bob Dylan Live 1996* (1998), which included both the acoustic and electric sets of his legendary Albert Hall Concert – which was actually recorded in Manchester. The acoustic set saw him straining for a manner of performance that needed a greater density of sound, while the electric set, for all its confusion and mayhem, gave a necessary urgency to his free-floating lyrics.

The son of a Jewish shopkeeper, he grew up in the Mid-west iron-mining town of Hibbing, an area of industrial decline described in his long ballad 'North Country Blues', recorded on 1964's *The Times They Are a-Changin'*. He played and sang in high-school rock band the Golden Chords and briefly played

piano with the Shadows, an early group led by **Bobby Vee**.

In 1959 Zimmerman enrolled at the University of Minnesota and took two important steps. He immersed himself in the college folk-revival scene and he chose a new name. He later said that the name was inspired by Western hero Matt Dillon, but by 1962 he was spelling it 'Dylan', in the same way as the British poet Dylan Thomas. Dylan soon dropped out of college, but he lived for another year in Dinkytown, Minneapolis's bohemia. There, he absorbed the classic radical mélange of the period – folk song, left-wing politics and beat poetry. Among his contemporaries were the blues musicians Spider John Koerner and Tony Glover (with Dave Ray they recorded albums for Elektra, including *Blues, Rags and Hollers*, 1964) and the journalist and critic Paul Nelson. Through these figures and others Dylan took in the recorded repertoire of such artists as **Robert Johnson**, **Ramblin' Jack Elliott** and, above all, **Woody Guthrie**.

His apprenticeship over, Dylan travelled to New York City in late 1960, partly to visit the severely ill Guthrie. He became one of many young singers performing at coffee-houses like Gerde's Folk City and the Gaslight in Greenwich Village. His first recording was as back-up harmonica player on **Carolyn Hester**'s eponymous début album for Columbia, the company to which he was signed by **John Hammond** in 1961. *Bob Dylan*, released early in 1962, gives a picture of his club act of the time. The only two original tracks were the wry, sardonic 'Talking New York' and the elegiac 'Song to Woody'. The remainder ran the gamut of American traditional music, from blues (**Jesse Fuller**'s 'You're No Good' and **Blind Lemon Jefferson**'s 'See That My Grave Is Kept Clean') and gospel ('The Gospel Plow') to the Appalachian mountain ballad 'Man of Constant Sorrow', whose title sums up the generally sombre tone of the album. Though it enjoyed only modest sales, the album was enormously influential, providing the **Animals** with substantial hits when they made blues group versions of 'Baby Let Me Follow You Down' (1964) and 'House of the Rising Sun'.

By 1962 Dylan was increasingly preoccupied with the growing civil-rights movement and with singers like **Len Chandler**, **Phil Ochs** and **Tom Paxton** was associated with the topical song magazine *Broadside*, which published 'Blowin' in the Wind'. It was the gentle **Peter Paul and Mary** version of this song, a Top Ten hit in June 1963, that first brought Dylan to public prominence, while within the growing folk audience his work was championed by **Joan Baez**.

All but two of the tracks on *The Freewheelin' Bob Dylan* (1963) were Dylan compositions and several were among the greatest of his political/apocalyptic songs. 'A Hard Rain's a-Gonna Fall' is a vision of a post-holocaust world which sets out from the **Child** ballad 'Lord Randal'. The finely controlled 'Masters of War' and 'Oxford Town' are among the greatest protest songs of any era, while 'Blowin' in the Wind' caught the urgency of the burgeoning youth politics of the period. *Freewheelin'* also introduced the characteristic Dylan love song, in the yearning yet sarcastic 'Don't Think Twice It's All Right'. His creative use of tradition was also evident on the gentle 'Girl from the North Country', based on a version of 'Scarborough Fair' learned from English singer **Martin Carthy**. Producer Tom Wilson introduced electric instruments on several tracks, three years before Dylan was to be virulently attacked for using an amplified backing group.

Dylan's position as the leading figure among the younger generation of folk singers was confirmed by a triumphant appearance at the 1963 Newport Folk Festival and underlined by the popularity of *The Times They Are a-Changin'* (1964). With more protest songs than any of his other albums, it included the apocalyptic 'Hollis Brown' (whose harrowingly realistic view of rural poverty looked forward to the Farm Aid concert two decades later), 'The Lonesome Death of Hattie Carroll' and the bitingly sarcastic 'With God on Our Side'. This was covered in a pop arrangement by **Manfred Mann** who, like the **Byrds**, regularly recorded Dylan songs, including 'Just Like a Woman' (1966) and 'Mighty Quinn' (1968).

By contrast, the aptly named *Another Side of Bob Dylan* (1964) was dominated by songs of personal relationships like the lyrical 'To Ramona' and the aggressive 'It Ain't Me Babe'. The record also included 'My Back Pages', whose refrain 'I was so much older then, I'm younger than that now' was interpreted as Dylan's farewell to folk protest. Others would create a lasting folk-rock synthesis based on Dylan and his songs but Dylan himself abandoned folk and folk-rock for rock itself.

Al Kooper's rolling organ chords on 'Like a Rolling Stone' (1965), a Top Ten hit and regarded by many as Dylan's finest single recording, typified the heady rock style which suffused *Bringing It All Back Home* (1965) and *Highway 61 Revisited*. The former included the mystic 'Gates of Eden', the poetic 'Love Minus Zero/No Limit' and 'Mr Tambourine Man', which reached No. 1 in a rock version by the Byrds. The highlight of *Highway 61* was the twelve-minute 'Desolation Row', a bleak allegory featuring a cast of characters drawn from history, mythology and medicine-shows. In this year, too, Dylan had two transatlantic Top Ten hits ('Rolling Stone' and 'Positively 4th Street'), plus two in Britain alone with 'The Times They Are a-Changin'' and the zany, **Chuck Berry**-inspired 'Subterranean Homesick Blues'.

In his wake came a brief folk-rock boom with hits from **Barry McGuire, Donovan**, Sonny and **Cher** (Dylan's own 'All I Want to Do'), the **Turtles** (Dylan's 'It Ain't Me Babe'), the **Animals** (**Barry Mann** and Cynthia Weil's 'We Gotta Get out of This Place') and the Byrds, who included Dylan material on each of their early albums. But Dylan also faced opposition to his new sound when his electric band (featuring Kooper with **Mike Bloomfield** and Sam Lay from **Paul Butterfield**'s group) was heckled at Newport in 1965 and booed on tour in England the following year. By then his touring band was made up of the Hawks, who later became **The Band**.

Although highly praised when it first appeared, the double-album *Blonde on Blonde* (1966) now seems very much limited by the horizons of the psychedelic era. While the lengthy, lullaby-like 'Visions of Johanna' and the sombre 'Just Like a Woman' were successes, on 'Sad-Eyed Lady of the Lowlands' the ambitious imagery and metaphor came dangerously close to incoherence. Recorded in Nashville as well as New York, the backing tracks were immaculate and the album gave Dylan hits with the raucous 'Rainy Day Women Nos 12 and 35' (with its nod towards **Ashford and Simpson**'s **Ray Charles** hit 'Let's Go Get Stoned') and the sprightly 'I Want You'.

A serious motorcycle accident in 1966 led Dylan to a period of withdrawal. He did not tour again for seven years, but continued to write and record. He began to work closely with The Band, composing the songs which were officially released in 1975 as *The Basement Tapes*, but which circulated as publishers' demo tapes in the late sixties. Among these songs were 'This Wheel's on Fire' (a 1968 British hit for Julie Driscoll and **Brian Auger** on Marmalade) and 'Mighty Quinn', a nonsense song which Manfred Mann took to No. 1 in Britain in the same year. The Band themselves put the elegiac 'I Shall Be Released' on their début album.

John Wesley Harding (1968), made with Nashville session musicians Charlie McCoy (bass), Kenny Buttrey (drums) and **Pete Drake** (steel guitar), showed a withdrawal from the lush poetics of *Blonde* and a shift towards parable and fable that took Dylan close to his early mentor Guthrie. The outstanding tracks included the moving 'I Pity the Poor Immigrant', the caustic 'Dear Landlord' (thought by some to refer to Dylan's manager Albert Grossman) and 'All Along the Watchtower' which was later transformed by **Jimi Hendrix**. As its title suggested, *Nashville Skyline* (1969) saw a decisive turn to country music. Dylan duetted in a deeper voice with **Johnny Cash** on a new version of 1963's 'Girl from the North Country', but it was the mellow yet trite 'Lay Lady Lay' that became Dylan's biggest-selling single.

Dylan had returned to live performance at Woody Guthrie memorial concerts in 1968 and at the Isle of

Wight Festival (1970) but the warm welcome which greeted him there was in stark contrast to the antagonism aroused by *Self Portrait* (1970). This collection of (mainly) other people's songs ranged from the curious crooning of **Lorenz Hart** and Richard Rodgers' 'Blue Moon' to the clipped delivery of Paul Simon's 'The Boxer' and the rockabilly lilt of Billy Grammer's 'Gotta Travel on'. However, Dylan redeemed himself in the ears of the critics with *New Morning* (1970), whose pastoral atmosphere introduced his first religious song ('Father of Night'), the jazzy 'If Dogs Run Free', and one of his best-known compositions, 'If Not for You', a 1971 million-seller for **Olivia Newton-John**.

His appearance with **George Harrison** at the 'Concert for Bangladesh' (1971) ushered in a phase which saw Dylan sitting in on recording sessions by such artists as **Doug Sahm**, **Steve Goodman** and former Electric Flag guitarist Barry Goldberg, whom Dylan produced. His own recording career took second place to the filming of *Pat Garrett and Billy the Kid* (1973), a Sam Peckinpah film in which Dylan had a minor role but for whose soundtrack album he wrote the intense 'Knockin' on Heaven's Door', a hit for him in 1973 and for **Eric Clapton** two years later.

Meanwhile, the closing years of his Columbia contract saw the release of a *More Greatest Hits* album (which despite its title included some new material) and *Dylan* (1973). Compiled by CBS after Dylan quit the label for Asylum/Island this was an undistinguished set of cover-versions that were out-takes from *Self Portrait*. *Planet Waves* (1974), a transitional set of love songs including the anthemic 'Forever Young' with The Band, was released by Asylum and in Europe by Island. Proof that Dylan's appeal remained undiminished, however, came when applications for five million tickets were received for a 1974 US tour with The Band. For the first time Dylan sang his old songs with new, often startling arrangements. Phil Ramone produced the album of the tour, *Before the Flood* (1974), Dylan's second release on Asylum/Island before he signed a new long-term deal with Columbia.

The mid-seventies proved to be among the most creative periods of Dylan's career with the imaginative 'Rolling Thunder Revue', a touring troupe which included poet Allen Ginsberg, Baez and Joni Mitchell as well as ex-**Mott the Hoople** guitarist Mick Ronson. *Hard Rain* (1976) was the album of the tour but before that Dylan released the highly regarded *Blood on the Tracks* (1975). It included the bitter, articulate 'Idiot Wind', the Western fable 'Lily Rosemary and the Jack of Hearts' and intricate tales of love gone wrong in 'Simple Twist of Fate' and 'Tangled Up in Blue'. On *Desire* (1976), made with new collaborators Jacques Levy (lyrics), Scarlet Rivera (violin) and **Emmylou Harris** (vocals), Dylan returned to topical protest on 'Hurricane', about the wrongful conviction of a former boxing champion, while 'Isis' went into the territory of myth and 'One More Cup of Coffee' was a return to his early laconic stance. *Street Legal* (1978) contained the stately 'Is Your Love in Vain' with its echoes of blues legend **Robert Johnson**, as well as the political 'Señor (Tales of Yankee Power)'.

In contrast, Dylan's work in the following decade was extremely uneven. *Live at Budokan*, a double-album recorded in Japan, documented the 1978 world tour which involved 115 concerts in ten countries. It coincided, however, with a new low point in critical esteem for Dylan. The elephantine four-hour extravaganza movie *Renaldo and Clara* (1978), which intercut live footage from 'Rolling Thunder' with curious semi-fictional scenes involving Baez, Sara Dylan and others, was widely attacked.

Even more shocking for some was *Slow Train Coming* (1979), the first of a trio of albums proclaiming Dylan's conversion to fundamentalist Christianity. Produced by **Jerry Wexler** and Barry Beckett, it included the impassioned 'Gotta Serve Somebody', which won a Grammy award. After *Saved* (1980), *Shot of Love* (1981) included the secular 'Every Grain of Sand' while *Infidels* (1984) was co-produced with Mark Knopfler of **Dire Straits**. *Empire Burlesque* (1985) was greeted by critics as a 'comeback album' but *Knocked Out Loaded* (1986), despite the mysterious 'Brownsville Girl', written with actor and playwright Sam Shepard, was generally unimpressive. The wide-ranging but enigmatically selective *Biograph* (1985) was a five-album set designed to provide a survey of his work over more than two decades. It included a number of previously unreleased tracks.

Dylan's high standing among his peers was shown by his role as the final artist at the Live Aid Concert, where his comments led to the organization of the Farm Aid shows in the same year. During the mid-eighties he continued to tour with **Santana** (1984), **Tom Petty** and Roger McGuinn (1986) and the **Grateful Dead** (1987), before, in another surprise move, he took the part of an ageing rock star in the inept *Hearts of Fire* (1987). The Dead's lyricist Robert Hunter co-wrote songs on *Down in the Groove* (1988), Dylan's twenty-fifth studio album. The live album *Dylan & the Dead* (1989) proved that the Grateful Dead were a better than adequate backing group, but not The Band.

At this point Dylan once again confounded the pundits by joining George Harrison, Tom Petty, **ELO**'s Jeff Lynne and **Roy Orbison** in the Traveling Wilburys (issuing two albums) and releasing the highly praised *Oh Mercy* (1989), supervised by **U2** producer Daniel Lanois. His most disciplined album for several years it included the outstanding 'Political World' and 'Where Teardrops Fall', and a powerful reading of 'What Was It You Wanted' in which Dylan faultlessly merged the sarcasm of an **Elvis Costello** with the cold detachment of a **Leonard Cohen** (on **Willie Nelson**'s album of duets, *Across the Borderline*, 1993, Dylan joined Nelson on a version of the song).

Dylan entered the nineties on the crest of a 'comeback' that looked set to last longer than previous ones. However, *Under the Red Sky* (1990), which included the infamous 'Wiggle Wiggle', was one of his lesser albums. This was despite, or possibly because of, its list of guests, which included George Harrison, **Bruce Hornsby**, **Elton John** and Al Kooper. Far more substantial was *The Bootleg Series, Vols 1–3* (1991), a superior collection of out-takes from all stages of his recording career that confirmed Dylan's willingness to experiment. During this period he continued touring to mixed reviews, alternating new versions of past anthems with hoarse – constant touring has severely roughened Dylan's voice – evocations of the original versions.

In 1992 he produced *Good As I Been to You*, his own version of an 'Unplugged' album when, supported by only his guitar and harmonica, he recorded a set of traditional folk songs ranging from 'Frankie and Johnnie' via the affecting 'Hard Times' to 'Froggie

Went A-Courtin''. He followed it with another acoustic album, the lesser *World Gone Wrong* (1993). The continued respect Dylan is held in by other musicians was reflected in the list of stars who lined up to appear at a 1992 tribute concert to mark the 30th anniversary of his signing to CBS. The concert and subsequent live album included appearances from such long-established artists as **Neil Young** and Eric Clapton as well as newer acts like **Pearl Jam**.

In 1994 Dylan underlined his capacity to surprise even his most ardent followers by permitting 'The Times They Are a-Changin'' to be sung by **Richie Havens** on a television commercial for an accountancy firm. He also performed at the Woodstock '94 festival. Critics tended to view much of Dylan's output of the nineties with disdain, especially in comparison to the historical recordings like *Bootleg* (1991) and *Live* (1998), but the spare sound of *Time Out of Mind* (1997), again produced by Lanois, which perfectly matched Dylan's stripped-down lyrics, was a major critical success. On songs like 'Not Dark Yet' and 'Tryin' to Get Heaven' Dylan suggested a ghostly, albeit stately, world in which the imminence of death and retribution was paramount. The result was Dylan's best album of new material for a decade.

THE EAGLES

Don Henley, b. 22 July 1946, Linden, Texas, USA; Glenn Frey, b. 6 November 1946, Detroit, Michigan; Bernie Leadon, b. 19 July 1947, Minneapolis, Minnesota (replaced by Joe Walsh, b. 20 November 1945, Cleveland, Ohio); Randy Meisner, b. 8 March 1946, Scottsbluff, Nebraska (replaced by Timothy B. Schmit, b. 30 October 1947, Sacramento, California); Don Felder, b. 1948, Gainsville, Florida

With sales of over 50 million albums, the Eagles were the most successful of the Californian rock bands of the seventies. To the studio intricacy of the earlier **Buffalo Springfield**, they added country-flavoured harmonies and yearning love songs, underpinned by a solid pop aesthetic.

The Eagles came together as part of **Linda Ronstadt**'s backing group in 1971. Frey had recorded with J. D. Souther (who would later collaborate on several songs for the group, including 'New Kid in Town', 1976) as Longbranch Pennywhistle; Henley was a one-time member of Shiloh; and Meisner had been a founding member of Poco before leaving to play with **Rick Nelson**. The most experienced was Leadon, who had played bluegrass with Chris Hillman (before Hillman joined the **Byrds**) and country-rock with former Byrds Gene Clark (in Dillard and Clark) and **Gram Parsons** (the Flying Burrito Brothers). Ronstadt's manager John Boylan put the quartet together and signed them to David Geffen's newly established Asylum label. The first album, *The Eagles* (1972), produced in the UK by Glyn Johns, yielded two American hits, 'Take It Easy' (by Frey and **Jackson Browne**) and 'Witchy Woman'. The first was an example of their polished brand of country-rock, far smoother than that of the Burrito Brothers, the second confirmed their rock leanings. It was followed by the concept album *Desperado* (1973), in which they paralleled the story of Western bandits Robert Dalton and Bill Doolin and that of the modern Western desperado, the rock'n'roll star, and introduced the standards 'Tequila Sunrise' and the title song. Its success decisively extended the Western clothing legacy of the singing cowboys of the thirties (notably **Gene Autry** and **Roy Rogers**) to rock.

For *On the Border* (1974), their breakthrough album, the group changed producers – to Bill Szymczyk, who had worked with the **J. Geils Band** and bluesman **B. B. King** – and managers – to Irving Azoff – and added session guitarist Felder. The new sound, harder but still pop orientated, gave them their first platinum album and first American No. 1, the ballad 'Best of My Love'. *One of These Nights* (1975) confirmed the group's huge success. The title track was their first European success and the album featured three Top Five American hits, including 'Take It to the Limit' and 'Lyin' Eyes'. By now their country leanings were minimal and Leadon (whose instrumental 'Journey of the Sorcerer' later was used as the theme music to the cult British radio series *The Hitchhiker's Guide to the Galaxy*) quit the band to become a respected session guitarist after a shortlived solo career. He was replaced by Walsh, for whom the Eagles (bar Leadon) had done backing vocals on his solo album *So What* (1974). He was also managed by Azoff.

Walsh made his name as a hard-rock guitarist with the James Gang (*Yer Album*, 1969, and the superior *The James Gang Rides Again*, 1970, both on ABC/Probe) and *Barnstorm* before going solo. His *The Smoker You Drink the Player You Get* (Dunhill/Probe, 1973) included a Top Thirty hit, the hard-rocking 'Rocky Mountain Way'. Walsh's arrival gave the Eagles a harsher, more electric sound that coincided on *Hotel California* (1976) with a series of gloomier songs that celebrated not the innocence of outlaws on the run but the decadence of life in Hollywood. Their most successful album, it spawned a trio of hit singles: 'New Kid in Town'*, 'Hotel California'* and 'Life in the Fast Lane'. Meisner left in 1977 to be replaced by Schmit (who had previously replaced him in Poco). After the lacklustre *The Long Run* (1979) and *Eagles Live* (1980), the group, disenchanted with the tribulations of success, ceased working and the members began to pursue solo projects. In 1982 the Eagles officially disbanded.

Even before leaving the Eagles, Walsh released the mordant *But Seriously Folks . . .* (1978), which included the laconic, self-mocking account of rock stardom 'Life's Been Good to Me' and the hit 'All Night Long' (Full Moon, 1980), from the film *Urban Cowboy*. His later work (which includes *There Goes the Neighborhood*, Asylum, 1981, and *You Bought It, You Name It*, Warners, 1983) was less successful. Meisner made an eponymous solo album (1978) and did session work for **Randy Newman** and **Bob Seger**, before signing with Epic in 1980 and making the Top Thirty with 'Deep Inside My Heart' (1980), 'Hearts on Fire' (1981) and 'Never Been in Love' (1982). All were firmly in the Eagles mould, to the extent that Henley and Frey sang back-up on Meisner's 1980 album, *One More Song*.

The most successful of the ex-Eagles were Henley and Frey. Henley teamed up with **Fleetwood Mac**'s Stevie Nicks for 'Leather and Lace' (Modern, 1981), and in 1982 had a massive hit with 'Dirty Laundry' from *I Can't Stand Still*. In 1985 he reappeared in the charts with 'The Boys of Summer' and 'All She Wants to Do Is Dance' from the thoughtful *Building the Perfect Beast* (Geffen). The *End of the Innocence* (1989) was equally successful. Much of Henley's energies during these years were devoted to environmental causes such as the preservation of Walden Pond, Massachusetts. He also made guest appearances on recordings by Roger Waters, Trisha Yearwood, Patty Smyth and **Elton John**. In 2000 he released the eco-friendly *Inside Job* (Warner).

After solo hits with 'I Found Somebody' and 'The One You Love' (1982), Frey, whose songs had always had the strongest storylines of the Eagles' hits, turned to writing film and TV themes. There were hits with 'The Heat Is on' from *Beverly Hills Cop* (1985) and 'Smuggler's Blues' and 'You Belong to the City' (1985), both from the teleseries *Miami Vice* (one of the first series to build in rock music as a central element) in which he also made his acting début, changing his cowboy denims of the seventies for the designer jeans of the eighties. Frey's solo albums included *The Allnighter* (1984) and *Soul Searchin'* (1988) with its Top Ten hit 'True Love'.

The Eagles' planned reunion for an American tour and album was delayed until 1994 but by then their reputation was even greater. In great part this was helped by *Common Thread: Songs of the Eagles* (Giant, 1993), on which a slew of 'new' country stars performed overly reverent versions of the Eagles' songs that had influenced them. It was a big hit in America. Even more commercially successful was the eight million-selling *Till Hell Freezes Over* (1994), the Eagles' own re-recordings of their best-known songs with four new tracks, which was issued half-way through their two-year reunion tour.

SNOOKS EAGLIN
b. Fird Eaglin, 21 January 1936, New Orleans, Louisiana, USA

Snooks Eaglin – blind, twenty-two years old and musically omnivorous – burst on to a folk-blues scene of the late fifties which was regarded by many onlookers as moribund. Touted as a 'modern street minstrel' (he also played in an R&B band, but less was made of that), he revitalized an idiom whose power had diminished with the death of **Big Bill Broonzy**. Indeed, rather like **Billy Bragg** with the English political folk song, Eaglin seemed almost to re-authenticate the form simply by being a young exponent of it.

New Orleans Street Singer (Folkways, 1958) introduced Eaglin's smoky, experience-stained voice, a strange orchestral style of guitar accompaniment and what one critic called 'an atmosphere of infinite sadness, of a private world of feeling', in numbers, often learned from radio or records, as motley as the jazz standard 'High Society' and **Charles Brown**'s 'Drifting Blues'. Further albums for Folk-Lyric, Prestige-Bluesville and Storyville drove him deeper into the role of street-singer. He tried to break out in 1960–1 by recording rhythm and blues singles with a band in the **Fats Domino** manner for Imperial, but these were not successful and his next album, a decade later, on Sonet found him back – in spirit, anyway – on the street corner, still synthesizing blues, gospel and pop. A few years on, however, the same label and producer (Sam Charters) let him throw off the folk mantle and strut in front of a New Orleans R&B combo again for *Down Yonder* (1978). He continued recording in this vein in the eighties for Black Top, issuing such albums as *Baby, You Can Get Your Gun!* (1987) and *Out of Nowhere* (1989).

STEVE EARLE
b. 17 January 1955, Fort Monroe, Virginia, USA

Unlike so many of those who offered up a rebellious image to the world, Earle, like **Merle Haggard** before him, lived such a life. However, whereas for Haggard music proved a salvation, Earle's (mostly drug) problems seriously retarded his commercial success. Indeed, in his recording career he has mined his familiarity with the other side of the tracks to great effect, creating in songs like 'Billy Austin' (1990) portraits that are as felt as they are observed. In his later work, particularly the impressive *El Corazón* (1997), he managed to build on this to create a unique blend of country and rock music in which social concern was always to the fore.

Raised on the outskirts of San Antonio, Texas, Earle quit school aged sixteen and travelled across the state playing bars to support himself. In Houston he met and was encouraged by songwriters **Jerry Jeff Walker** and Townes Van Zandt. Moving to Nashville in 1977, he briefly played bass for Guy Clark, but had no success as a songwriter. On Earle's return in 1979 **Carl Perkins** recorded his 'Mustang Wine' and Johnny Lee had a country hit with his 'When You Fall in Love'. Pairing up with Zip Gibson and Bullet Harris (who with later additions became the Dukes), Earle recorded the EP *Pink & Black* (LSI, 1982). Critically well received it resulted in a contract with Epic, who promptly rejected the neo-rockabilly album he recorded. It was later released, with material from

Pink & Black, as *Early Tracks* (1987). Signed to MCA by producer Tony Brown, he recorded the impressive *Guitar Town* (1986). The title track was a hit and its concerns suggested that Earle might take residence in the (then profitable) populist sector of heartland rock, as carved out by **Bruce Springsteen** and **John Mellencamp**. However, other tracks pointed toward the emerging new traditionalist movement (as evinced by the likes of **Randy Travis** and **Dwight Yoakam**). This confusion, and Earle's unrepentant radicalism and lifestyle, turned country audiences against him. This was further intensified by *Exit O* (1986) in which, in contrast to Nashville tradition, he recorded with his backing group, the Dukes, rather than session players.

The impressive and even rockier *Copperhead Road* (1988), which included the Vietnam War song 'Johnny Come Lately', recorded with the **Pogues**, was a hit with rock audiences but a miss with his one-time country audience. The even darker *The Hard Way* (1990), a tribute to the oppressed, which included the majestic 'Billy Austin', sold poorly and after the live album *Shut Up and Die Like an Aviator* (1991) and a number of highly public brushes with the law MCA dropped him. The culmination of this was his imprisonment in 1994 which led, after a period in a drug rehabilitation centre and the independently produced *Train a Comin'* (Winter Harvest, 1995), to a contract with Warner and the superior *I Feel Alright* (1996). Dealing with the same subject matter as *The Hard Way*, but lighter in tone and lacking the compressed sound of the earlier album, it was a critical success and for the first time saw Earle, in a modern fashion, writing in the manner of a **Hank Williams**, **Harlan Howard** or Haggard. The final song, 'You're Still Standing There', a duet with **Lucinda Williams**, introduced a note of affirmation for the first time.

It was followed by the even more impressive *El Corazón* (1997), which saw him moving even closer to the social concerns of **Woody Guthrie**. In the opening song 'Christmas in Washington', Guthrie is directly invoked while throughout the album Earle touches on the redemptive possibilities of love. This concern was even stronger on *The Mountain* (1999), the album he made with bluegrass outfit the Del McCoury Band. Generally regarded as the best bluegrass group of the nineties, the family band – it included two of McCoury's sons, Rob and Ronnie, amongst its members – had supported Earle on *El Corazón*'s 'I Still Carry You Around'. Among the stand-out tracks on the album were the murder ballad 'Carrie Brown' and the duet with Idris DeMent, 'I'm Still in Love with You'. Earle toured in support of the album, only to find his rock audience offended by the folksiness of the resulting sound. Far better received was *Transcendental Blues* (E-Square/Epic, 2000),

which largely returned to the sound of *El Corazón*. It was particularly noteworthy for its mature love songs, which included 'I Can Wait', 'Lonelier than This' and 'Halo 'Round the Moon'. The album also featured support from his brother Patrick and sister Stacey, with whom he duetted on 'When I Fall'. In the same year Stacey released her own album, *Dancin' with Them Brung Me Propper* (Gearle).

Ain't Ever Satisfied (HIPP, 1996) is the definitive early (1985–1991) career retrospective.

EARTH, WIND AND FIRE

Philip Bailey, b. 8 May 1951, Denver, Colorado, USA; Larry Dunn, b. 19 June 1953, Colorado; Johnny Graham, b. 3 August 1951, Kentucky; Ralph Johnson, b. 4 July 1951, California; Al McKay, b. 2 February 1948, Louisiana; Andrew Woolfolk, b. 11 October 1950, Texas; Freddie White, b. 13 January 1955, Chicago, Illinois; Maurice White, b. 19 December 1941, Memphis, Tennessee; Verdine White, b. 25 July 1951

One of the most successful black pop/soul bands of the seventies, Earth, Wind and Fire was the creation of drummer/producer Maurice White. Unlike the standard funk sound of the time, Earth, Wind and Fire's music was an imaginative mix of jazz, blues, soul and rock.

A Chicago session player, White recorded extensively in the sixties for such labels as Vee-Jay and Chess and with **Ramsey Lewis**, **Jimmy Reed** and **Little Milton**. He was a member of Lewis's trio from 1966 to 1970, taking part in world tours during which he became fascinated with Egyptology and astrology, which provided the name and inspiration for the group he formed in 1971.

Featuring former Vee-Jay solo singer Wade Flemons, Earth, Wind and Fire recorded two albums for Warners before disbanding and re-forming with a Columbia contract in 1973. The players on *Last Days and Time* included singer Bailey, Verdine White (bass), Dunn (keyboards), Graham (guitar), McKay (guitar), Woolfolk (saxophone) and Johnson (drums). Both that album and *Head to the Sky* (1973), which rooted their often pretentious lyrics in hard dance music, were bestsellers.

With Freddie White as second drummer, Earth, Wind and Fire released *Open Our Eyes* (1974) and supported **Santana** on a world tour, on which they often upstaged the headliners with such theatrical displays as suspending the bass player over the stage with wires and revolving the drumkits through 360 degrees.

The 1975 soundtrack album *That's the Way of the World* included a pop No. 1 in 'Shining Star'*, which was followed by further million-sellers 'Sing a Song' (1975) and 'Getaway' (1976). Earth, Wind and Fire's first British hit was 'Saturday Nite' (1977). The group appeared in the film of **The Beatles**' *Sgt Pepper's Lonely Hearts Club Band* (1978), singing 'Got to Get You into My Life'* which reached the Top Ten. This was the first of four million-sellers released by the group in the space of one year. The others included 'September', Bailey's mellifluous ballad 'After the Love Has Gone', and 'Boogie Wonderland', a collaboration with the **Emotions**.

'Let's Groove'* from *Raise* (1981) was the band's last major hit, but Bailey and Maurice White went on to distinguished solo careers. The singer recorded a chart-topping duet with **Phil Collins** on 'Easy Lover' (1985), while White built on his earlier production successes with Deniece Williams, the Emotions and Bailey, whose later solo albums included *Philip Bailey* (Zoo, 1994) and *Life and Love* (Eagle Rock, 1998). White's later productions included albums by Barbara Weathers and El DeBarge.

Earth, Wind and Fire re-formed in 1987, releasing *Touch the World*, their best album of the decade. They followed that with *Heritage* (1990), which was weighed down by guest appearances from such artists as **Sly Stone** and **Hammer**, and signed to Warners for the more consistent *Millennium* (1993). They toured for most of the nineties.

SHEENA EASTON
b. Sheena Orr, 27 April 1959, Glasgow, Scotland

First finding success through television exposure as a bright-voiced pop singer, Easton proved able to adapt to different trends in the manner of **Olivia Newton-John** before her.

Trained as a drama teacher, Easton's club singing brought her a recording contract with EMI and a 1980 BBC television documentary which portrayed her being groomed for stardom. Produced by Christopher Neil, the hymn to surburban domesticity '9 to 5' was subsequently a Top Ten hit in Britain and reached No. 1 in America the following year, where it was retitled 'Morning Train'* to avoid confusion with **Dolly Parton**'s 1980 hit single. An unsuccessful earlier single, 'Modern Girl', also became a hit in 1980.

The invitation to sing the title song from the James Bond film *For Your Eyes Only* (1981) heralded her arrival as the new MOR star, a status confirmed by her duet with **Kenny Rogers** ('We've Got Tonight', 1983). She reached the American charts regularly with singles like 'Telefone (Long Distance Love Affair)' (1983) and 'Strut' (1984) in the eighties, with only a controversy over the alleged obscenity of the **Prince** composition 'Sugar Walls' (1985) to disturb her progress.

In 1986 Easton released 'You're Still New to Me', a duet with Paul Davis on Capitol/Curb from the

Narada Michael Walden-produced album, and in 1987 had a hit with the duet with Prince, 'U Got the Look'. *The Lover in Me* (1988) saw Easton even more assiduously courting the R&B crossover audience with even greater commercial success. The individual tracks, produced by Jellybean, Prince and Babyface, were masterpieces of slick sexuality. The album's title track and that of *What Comes Naturally* (1991) were both American Top Ten hits. In 1989 Easton resumed her partnership with Prince for the American Top Forty hit 'The Arms of Orion'. In 1991 Easton appeared in a Chicago production of the musical *Man of la Mancha*. Produced by Patrice Rushen, 1993's *No Strings* saw her tackle a set of standards with mixed results. In 1997 she signed with MCA Records Japan.

THE EASYBEATS
George Young, b. 6 November 1947, Glasgow, Scotland; Gordon 'Snowy' Fleet, b. 16 August 1946, Bootle, Lancashire, England; Dick Diamonde, b. 28 December 1947, Hilversum, Holland; Harry Vanda, b. Harry Wandon, 22 March 1947, The Hague; Stevie Wright, b. 20 December 1948, Leeds, Yorkshire, England

Best remembered for 'Friday on My Mind' (1967), with **Eddie Cochran**'s 'Summertime Blues', the **Coasters**' 'Yakety Yak' (1958) and **Bob Geldof**'s 'I Don't Like Mondays' (1979), one of the most graphic expressions of teenage frustration, the Easybeats, like the **Bee Gees**, first established themselves as stars in Australia. However, unlike that group (or **AC/DC**, the group formed by George Young's younger brothers) the Easybeats were unable to translate that success into an international career and in the seventies Vanda and Young moved into production.

The group – all sons of European immigrants to Australia – was formed in 1963 and by 1965, with a repertoire initially similar to that of British beat groups, established themselves as Australia's leading group. Their Australian hits included 'She's So Fine', 'Sad and Lonely and Blue' and 'In My Book' (1965–6) before in 1966 they moved to the UK and with Shel Talmy (producer of the early recordings by the **Kinks** and **The Who**) cut the Vanda–Young composition 'Friday on My Mind', a British hit in 1966 (United Artists) and an American hit in 1967. Revived by **David Bowie** on *Pin Ups* (1973), it was the Easybeats' only international hit as the group moved between psychedelia ('We All Live Happily Together', 1967), soul (**Ray Charles**' 'Hit the Road Jack', 1967) and big balladry ('Hello How Are You', 1968), their last British hit.

In 1970, the year after their final American chart entry 'St Louis' (Rare Earth), the group disbanded. Vanda and Young, the writers of most of the group's material, went into production and formed a number of studio bands, including Paintbox, the Marcus Hook Roll Band (which recorded the frantic 'Natural Man', Regal Zonophone, 1972), and Flash in the Pan (*Pan-O-Rama*, Ensign, 1983). However, they had their greatest success with AC/DC, whose early albums they produced.

ECHO AND THE BUNNYMEN

Ian McCulloch, b. 5 May 1959, Liverpool, England; Will Sergeant, b. 12 April 1958, Liverpool; Les Pattinson, b. 18 April 1958, Ormskirk; Pete De Freitas, b. 2 August 1961, Port of Spain, Trinidad, d. 14 June 1989

In the tradition of the **Doors**, Echo and the Bunnymen successfully purveyed a superior adolescent *angst* to British audiences in the eighties.

The group was formed in Liverpool by guitarist and vocalist McCulloch with Sergeant (guitar), Pattinson (bass) and a drum machine named Echo. Their first single, 'The Pictures on My Wall' (1979), was released on the local Zoo label. With the addition of human drummer De Freitas, the Bunnymen's glossy songs of existential sadness – in which McCulloch's admiration for **Jacques Brel** and **Leonard Cohen** was apparent – attracted critical attention and in 1979 they were signed by Liverpool label Korova with Seymour Stein's Sire label holding American rights.

Crocodiles (1980) and *Heaven Up Here* (1981) were well received, but the first hit singles came with the Ian Broudie-produced *Porcupine* (1983), which included 'The Back of Love' and 'The Cutter', a British Top Ten hit. In 1984 the group were the first rock band to play major Liverpool venue St George's Hall since The Beatles in 1961. Further hits followed with 'The Killing Moon' and 'Seven Seas' from *Ocean Rain* (1984). *Songs to Learn and Sing* (1985) was a compilation of Echo and the Bunnymen singles. In the same year, De Freitas briefly left to form the Sex Gods and the Bunnymen released 'Bring on the Dancing Horses'. In 1987 Echo and the Bunnymen released the McCulloch song 'The Game' (WEA), taken from the band's eponymous fifth album.

'People Are Strange' (1988) was a revival of a Doors' song, produced by that group's Ray Manzarek. The following year McCulloch launched a solo career with the Ray Shulman-produced *Candleland*, dedicated to McCulloch's father and De Freitas, both of whom had died while McCulloch was working on the album. Elizabeth Fraser of the **Cocteau Twins** sang on the title track. The album was followed by the disappointing *Mysterioso* (1992). Sergeant and Pattinson continued to record as Echo & the Bunnymen until 1990, recruiting former member of Liverpool group St. Vitus Dance Noel Burke as their vocalist on the unremarkable *Reverberation* (1990).

After collaborating with Manchester dance act 808 State on 'Moses' (1994), McCulloch approached Sergeant with a view to working together again. The pair released one patchy album, *Burned*, as Electrafixion in 1995 before re-forming Echo and the Bunnymen with Pattinson. They returned in 1997 with the euphoric 'Nothing Lasts Forever', a UK Top Ten hit, and their acclaimed seventh album, *Evergreen*. It was followed in 1999 by *What Are You Going to Do with Your Life?* More surprising was McCulloch's involvement as co-writer of the official England theme-song for the 1998 Football World Cup, '(How Does It Feel to Be) On Top of the World'.

BILLY ECKSTINE

b. William Clarence Eckstein, 8 July 1913, Pittsburgh, USA, d. 8 March 1993, Pennsylvania

One of the most distinctive ballad singers, Eckstine was both a pivotal figure in the history of jazz (because of his commitment to bebop) and the first black singer to achieve lasting success in the pop mainstream.

After winning a talent contest in 1930 by imitating **Cab Calloway**, Eckstine sang briefly with Tommy Myles' band, before returning to college. On the recommendation of composer and tenor saxophonist **Buddy Johnson** (another important early supporter of bop) he joined **Earl Hines**' band in 1939 as singer (occasionally playing trumpet) and in turn encouraged Hines to sign up **Charlie Parker** and **Sarah Vaughan**. Eckstine's recordings with the band include 'Stormy Monday Blues' and his own 'Jelly Jelly' on RCA's Bluebird subsidiary. In 1943 he quit to go solo but in 1944 formed his own big band, a modern swing band committed almost exclusively to bebop, to the point where Eckstine's stylized vocals regularly took second place to the playing of **Dizzy Gillespie**, Dexter Gordon, **Art Blakey**, Charlie Parker, Fats Navarro, Gene Ammons and Kenny Dorham, among others. The band was badly recorded, by both National and Savoy, and badly managed and in 1947 Eckstine folded it to go solo. However, the support Eckstine gave bop musicians at that time was crucial, and, as since released radio transcriptions show (*Together*, Spotlite, 1983, which also featured Sarah Vaughan and **Lena Horne** as vocalists), the band was genuinely adventurous.

Even before folding his band, Eckstine had recorded solo to support it, scoring two million-sellers in 1945 with 'Cottage for Sale' and a revival of **Russ Columbo**'s 'Prisoner of Love' on the independent National label. Far more successful than his band recordings, though more mannered and pompously sung, these prefigured Eckstine's future career. Where before black bands had played ballads, jazz and dance music, in the immediate post-war years they had to choose. Lacking an interest in the blues and frustrated by the failure of his big band, Eckstine, at first reluctantly, turned to ballads. Henceforth his successes would be in the pop charts.

In 1947 he was one of the first signings to the newly established MGM Records and had immediate hits with revivals of 'Everything I Have Is Yours'* (1947), **Richard Rodgers** and **Lorenz Hart**'s 'Blue Moon'* (1948) and **Duke Ellington**'s Irving Mills and Juan Tizol's 'Caravan'* (1949). He had further success in 1950 with **Victor Young**'s theme song to *My Foolish Heart* and a revival of the 1931 **Bing Crosby** hit, 'I Apologize'*. However, unlike **Nat 'King' Cole** who followed him into the pop charts, Eckstine's singing, especially his exaggerated vibrato, sounded increasingly mannered and he was unable to sustain his recording success throughout the decade. His best record of the fifties was the thrilling duet with Sarah Vaughan, 'Passing Strangers', a minor hit on Mercury in 1957.

Eckstine later concentrated on live appearances, regularly crossing the world, and recorded only intermittently. In 1967 he briefly joined Motown and in 1981 recorded the impressive *Something More* (Stax).

DUANE EDDY
b. 28 April 1938, Corning, New York, USA

Rock'n'roll's first guitar hero, Eddy and his 'twangy' guitar sold over 25 million records in his heyday.

The son of a guitarist, Eddy was raised in Phoenix, Arizona, and by his teens was playing at local dances. In 1955 he met and regularly played with guitarists Al Casey and Jimmy Wyble (a one-time member of **Bob Wills**' Texas Playboys). Signed by disc-jockey turned producer **Lee Hazelwood** in 1957, Eddy, with Casey now in support, was placed with **Dick Clark**'s Jamie Records. Following the success of Bill Justis's 'Raunchy' (Phillips International, 1957) on which session guitarist Sid Manker played a melody on the bass strings, Hazelwood produced Eddy in a similar, but even more austere, style. The result, 'Movin' and Groovin'' (1958), was only a minor hit but the next release, the raucous 'Rebel Rouser'*, was an international hit. The song gave Eddy the name of his backing group, the Rebels, among whom were saxophonist Steve Douglas and pianist Larry Knechtel (later of **Bread**). Unlike earlier rock'n'roll guitarists like **Carl Perkins**, **Chuck Berry** and Scotty Moore, who made their instruments talk through their own mastery of technique, Eddy's simple, but resonant, guitar-playing was further amplified by Hazelwood's progressive production methods which utilized echo and tape delay to intensify the simple excitements of the tunes he and Eddy wrote.

Between 1958 and 1961, when they parted company, Eddy and Hazelwood had a string of hits, including '"Yep!"', 'Forty Miles of Bad Road' (1959), 'Because They're Young'* (1960) – the title music to his film début – a pared-down version of **Henry Mancini**'s 'Peter Gunn' (1960) and the title song to the film *Ring of Fire* (1961), his own composition. His own productions for Jamie (which included 'The Avenger', 1961) failed and in 1962 he joined RCA and had a Top Forty Hit with 'The Ballad of Paladin', the theme to the teleseries *Have Gun – Will Travel*, in which he was featured. This was followed by '(Dance with the) Guitar Man'* (1962), which saw him reunited with Hazelwood and for the first time featured a vocal chorus behind the 'twangy' guitar.

With the advent of **The Beatles** and the 'British invasion' of America, Eddy's career went into decline. He briefly signed to Colpix in 1967 (where he recorded *Duane Goes Dylan* and *Duane A Go Go*) before resurfacing as part of the rock'n'roll revival movement and turning to production (including Phil Everly's of the **Everly Brothers** *Star Spangled Springer*, 1973). Held in high regard in Britain where he was a great influence, Eddy found his recording career was given a boost by British producer **Tony Macaulay**, who wrote and produced the European hit 'Play Me Like You Play Your Guitar' (GTO) for him in 1975. He signed with Asylum in 1977, but despite recording with **Willie Nelson**, had no further commercial success until he was teamed with the Art of Noise for a remake of 'Peter Gunn' (China), which was a Top Ten hit in Britain in 1986. In 1987 he assembled an all-star supporting cast, including **Ry Cooder**, Jeff Lynne of **Electric Light Orchestra** and **Paul McCartney**, for *Duane Eddy* (Capitol).

NELSON EDDY
b. 29 June 1901, Providence, Rhode Island, USA,
d. 6 March 1967, Miami, Florida

Neatly described by one critic as the possessor of 'wavy blond hair, a slightly flabby face and assorted uniforms', Eddy was **Jeanette MacDonald**'s co-star in Hollywood's fling with operetta in the thirties. Once dubbed 'America's Singing Sweethearts', the duo's eight films are now considered high camp, but in their day they were among the most innocent of Hollywood's musicals.

A boy soprano, Eddy sang with the Philadelphia Civic Opera in 1924. From 1928 he concentrated on recitals and concerts until MGM signed him in 1932, only to leave him languishing in minor roles (including *Dancing Lady*, 1933, and *Student Tour*, 1934) before teaming him with MacDonald for *Naughty Marietta* (1935). Together the pair re-created the saccharine world of **Victor Herbert** (*Naughty Marietta*,

Sweethearts, 1938), **Rudolf Friml** (*Rose Marie*, 1936, from which their RCA recording of 'Indian Love Call' was the first show tune to sell a million copies) and **Sigmund Romberg** (*Maytime*, 1937), and even reduced **Noël Coward** to the same formula in *Bitter Sweet* (1938). Eddy appeared in other musicals, notably **Cole Porter**'s *Rosalie* (1937), in which he introduced 'In the Still of the Night', *Balalaika* (1939) and *The Chocolate Soldier* (1941), but could not throw off his wooden reading of lines and was always more successful supporting MacDonald. After their last film together, *I Married an Angel* (1941), his screen career declined and in 1947 he quit Hollywood for live performances.

In the fifties and sixties he toured, having most success reprising the love duets from his films with Gale Sherwood, and recorded occasionally, mostly re-creating his past hits.

THOMAS ALVA EDISON
b. 11 February 1847, Milan, Ohio, USA, d. 18 October 1931, West Orange, New Jersey

Known affectionately as 'The Wizard of Menlo Park', Edison could most authoritatively claim to be the man who invented the twentieth century (and patented it!).

An inveterate tinkerer, Edison became a telegraph operator in 1863, and in 1868 patented his first invention, a mechanical vote recorder. In 1870 he formed his own firm of consulting technologists and set about filling in the missing gaps in the communications explosion then underway, always basing his inventions on commercial concerns and social need (his vote recorder failed because Congress didn't want voting speeded up). In 1876 he moved to Menlo Park and, in 1877, demonstrated the phonograph, one of the few of his inventions that was not a refinement of another's earlier work. Interestingly, though Edison immediately saw the artistic possibilities of his later invention, the 'kinetograph', he conceived of the phonograph (and first sought to exploit it) primarily as a secretarial aide.

The machine into which Edison shouted the nursery rhyme 'Mary Had a Little Lamb' consisted of a cylinder around which was wrapped some tin foil upon which sound was 'imprinted' by means of a stylus connected to a mouth-piece. The cylinder was then played by a reproducing needle which converted these indentations back into sound. Thus, the primitive machine was both a recording and reproducing machine and the first records were cylinders rather than the flat discs that **Emile Berliner** would later popularize. Edison established a record company to issue recordings and retained his faith in the cylinder in the face of the disc's popularity until 1913, when he

issued his repertoire for the first time on disc. However, he continued issuing cylinders until 1929, when he finally left the record business.

Among Edison's other inventions and refinements were the electric light bulb and the storage battery. Fittingly for someone who laid the foundations of both the film and record industries – the sources of much of the best popular culture of the twentieth century – part of his legacy was cultural. He was responsible for changing the image of the 'inventor' from an isolated, cold, genius to that of a cheerful tinkerer.

DAVE EDMUNDS
b. 15 April 1944, Cardiff, Wales

A curator of the museum of rock'n'roll, Edmunds re-created with absolute precision the joys of slap-bass rockabilly and the overwhelming 'wall of sound' of **Phil Spector**. In contrast to, say, **Ry Cooder**, who was generally concerned to rediscover and re-present songs and musical styles, Edmunds aimed to re-create the recorded sounds of the past. Some of his most affecting music was made with **Nick Lowe**, their joint fascination with the past being combined with Lowe's rougher and readier approach to production and performance. In the eighties Edmunds turned increasingly to production.

After an eight-year apprenticeship in Welsh blues bands (and a début single for EMI Columbia of Tim Rose's 'Morning Dew' as the Human Beans), Edmunds formed Love Sculpture in 1967 with drummer Bob Jones and bassist John Williams. The group's repertoire consisted of rock'n'roll standards and adaptations of classical themes, a long-standing tradition in rock that had previously given rise to such hits as Nero and the Gladiators' adaptation of Grieg's 'In the Hall of the Mountain King' (Decca, 1961) and B. Bumble and the Stingers' irresistible abridgement of *The Nutcracker Suite*, 'Nut Rocker' (Rendezvous, 1962). Love Sculpture's breakneck version of Khatchaturian's 'Sabre Dance' (Parlophone), gave them a British Top Ten hit in 1968. After an American tour on which Terry Williams (who would reappear with Edmunds throughout his career before joining **Dire Straits**) replaced Jones, the group disbanded and Edmunds signed with Gordon Mills' MAM agency before returning to Wales to build his own recording studio, Rockfield.

He made the studio into a thriving concern, working with Brinsley Schwarz (for whom Nick Lowe played bass), the Flamin' Groovies, Ducks Deluxe, **Shakin' Stevens** and **Graham Parker**, among others. At the same time Edmunds spent months experimenting until he could reproduce his favourite records. The first results were a version of **Smiley Lewis**'s 1955 hit 'I Hear You Knockin''* (MAM, 1970), followed by his first solo album, *Rockpile* (EMI, 1972), which revealed a wide range of interests. A re-creation of Spector and the **Ronettes**' 'Baby I Love You' and a version of the **Chordettes**' 'Born to Be with You' in homage to Spector appeared on Edmunds' own Rockfield label in 1973. In 1975 he appeared in and wrote and played most of the pastiche score for the David Essex film *Stardust*, and released his second solo album, *Subtle as a Flying Mallet*, with Lowe on bass.

By now a veteran of the British pub-rock movement, Edmunds joined Swan Song, the label formed by **Led Zeppelin**, for *Get It* (1977), which produced another hit single, the **Chuck Berry**-inspired Lowe composition 'I Knew the Bride'. Edmunds also toured and recorded (*Seconds of Pleasure*, 1980) with Lowe, as Rockpile. *Repeat When Necessary* (1979) featured new songs from **Elvis Costello**, 'Girls Talk' (a British hit), and Graham Parker, 'Crawling from the Wreckage'. *Twangin'*, again with Rockpile's backing, was not released until after Edmunds and Lowe had parted company. It saw Edmunds return to mimicry with versions of 'Singin' the Blues' (a hit for **Marty Robbins** and **Guy Mitchell** in 1956), John Fogerty's 'Almost Saturday Night' and 'Baby Let's Play House', a song associated with **Elvis Presley**. Also on the album was a rockabilly version of 'The Race Is on', an early country hit for **George Jones**, on which he was backed by the Stray Cats. A rockabilly revival trio led by Brian Setzer, the Stray Cats had a series of multi-million-selling albums, produced by Edmunds, including *Stray Cats* (Arista, 1981) and *Rant'n'Rave with the Stray Cats* (1983) before their break-up in 1984.

In the early eighties he continued his solo career with *D.E. 7th* (Arista, 1982), which included a song specially written for him by **Bruce Springsteen**, 'From Small Things Big Things Come', *Information* (1983) and *Riff Raff* (1984), co-produced by Jeff Lynne of the **Electric Light Orchestra**, with whom he shared an affection for **Del Shannon**, both having produced 'comeback' albums for Shannon. Edmunds later concentrated on production, often supplying the artists he worked with with songs by John David (as Love Sculpture's Williams now called himself). Edmunds produced the studio reunion albums of the **Everly Brothers** (*The Everly Brothers* and *Born Yesterday*, both 1985), compiled the soundtrack for *Porky's Revenge* (1985), and co-ordinated a television tribute to **Carl Perkins**, which featured a rare performance by **George Harrison**. In America he produced the bestselling *Tuff Enuff* (Columbia, 1986) for Texas R&B revivalists the Fabulous Thunderbirds, and in Britain he produced the John David-written hits 'Red Sky' and 'Rollin' Home' from *In the Army Now* (1986) – **Status Quo**'s most successful album of the decade – and *Angel with a Lariat* (Sire, 1987) by Canadian 'new country' singer **k.d. lang**. In 1987 Edmunds embarked on his first extensive tour of the eighties in support of his live album *I Hear You Rockin'* (Arista). In 1989 he produced a comeback album by **Dion**, with whom he later toured, and in 1990 released the lacklustre *Closer to the Flame* (Capitol). Far better is his production work on Nick Lowe's 'comeback' album *Party of One* (1991). *Anthology* (Rhino, 1993) is the definitive retrospective.

CLIFF EDWARDS
b. 14 June 1895, Hannibal, Missouri, USA, d. 18 July 1972, Hollywood, California

As 'Ukulele Ike', Edwards was a leading vaudeville performer of the twenties, adept at both standard popular songs and black-styled hokum numbers. Later, he found renewed fame as one of the regularly heard voices in Walt Disney films and TV series, and on record.

He made his showbusiness début in his teens in St Louis saloons, but his break came about 1918 on the Chicago nightclub scene, from which he went on to New York and the vaudeville troupe of comedian Joe Frisco. By the mid-twenties he was a second-magnitude vaudeville star, working major theatre circuits, appearing in Florenz Ziegfeld's *Follies* and often heard on the radio with **Rudy Vallee**, the singer he would replace in 1936 as the star of *George White's Scandals*. He began recording for Pathé in 1923, accompanying himself on ukulele and kazoo, and over the next decade made some highly idiomatic hokum sides, somewhat in the vein of black singer-banjoist Papa Charlie Jackson. These included 'In on' (1924), 'Alabamy Bound' (1925) and the two-part 'Stack O'Lee' (1928). On most of his recordings made before 1928, the backing band included **Jimmy Dorsey**, **Red Nichols** and Miff Mole. He also recorded straightforward popular materials like **Gus Kahn** and **Isham Jones**' 1924 song 'It Had to Be You', and 'I'll See You in My Dreams'. In 1928 he signed a four-year contract with MGM and introduced **Nacio Herb Brown** and **Arthur Freed**'s 'Singing in the Rain' in *Hollywood Revue of 1929*.

He reputedly appeared in more than one hundred films, among them *George White's Scandals* (1935), *Gone With the Wind* (1939), *His Girl Friday* (1940) and *She Couldn't Say No* (1945), but it was his participation in Disney's *Pinocchio* (1940) that determined the course of his career for the next two decades. In the character of Jiminy Cricket he sang the Oscar-winning song 'When You Wish Upon a Star', and he went on to be the voice of Jim Crow in *Dumbo* (1941). From the mid-fifties he worked steadily for Disney

Productions, recording children's songs and appearing in the TV series *Mickey Mouse Club*. It was not a role that could have been predicted for the one-time singer of such party songs as 'I'm a Bear in a Ladies' Boudoir'.

JACKIE EDWARDS
b. Wilfred Edwards, 1938, Kingston, Jamaica,
d. 15 August 1992

An early associate of **Chris Blackwell**, Edwards was a veteran British-based reggae songwriter and singer.

During the fifties he was one of Jamaica's leading singers, with a style strongly influenced by **Nat 'King' Cole**. Among his early ballads were 'Tell Me Darling' and 'Heaven Just Knows'. When the island's JBC chart was introduced, Edwards was one of the first regular hitmakers with songs like 'Your Eyes are Dreaming' and 'We're Going to Love' (1960).

Edwards moved to Britain when Blackwell set up his Island label there and cut six albums in the mid-sixties, including *Stand Up for Jesus* (1964) and *Pledging My Love* (1966), with Millie Small. His greatest success, however, came as a songwriter when the Spencer Davis Group, produced by Blackwell, reached No. 1 with his 'Keep on Running' (Fontana, 1965) and 'Somebody Help Me' (1966). He also co-wrote 'When I Come Home' for the group with **Steve Winwood** and made his own records for Fontana.

Later albums were made for Trojan (*I Do Love You*, 1972) and Klik (*Do You Believe in Love?*, 1976). In 1975 he recorded 'Heavy Duty Festival', a song about that year's Jamaican Song Festival. Bunny Lee produced several Edwards albums for Third World in the late seventies and in 1982 he released three albums on Starlight, covering both roots reggae and pop standards.

TOMMY EDWARDS
b. 17 February 1922, Richmond, Virginia, USA,
d. 22 October 1969, Richmond

Songwriter Edwards is best remembered for his version of 'It's All in the Game'* (MGM, 1958). That recording was a revival and subsequently the song was successfully revived by **Cliff Richard** (who had a British hit in 1962 and his biggest American hit of the sixties with it in 1964) and the **Four Tops** (1970).

Edwards, who had a local radio show in Richmond, turned to songwriting in the early forties, writing the **Louis Jordan** R&B hit 'That Chick's Too Young to Fry' (1946). His demo records of his songs led to a contract with MGM and in 1951 he recorded his first version of 'It's All in the Game'. The melody was written by amateur musician General Charles Gates Dawes in 1912 as 'Melody in A Major'. (Dawes later became Vice-President of America during Calvin Coolidge's administration.) Carl Sigman added the words. Edwards' 1951 version was only a minor hit, as were contemporary recordings by **Dinah Shore** and Carmen Cavallaro. But in 1958 he re-recorded the song, singing it in the manner of **Nat 'King' Cole** with a heavier 'teen-ballad' backing. It was this version, the backing giving a specifically teenage interpretation to the trauma of romantic dreams – 'many a tear has to fall' – that sold over three million copies. Edwards' subsequent hits include his own composition 'Love Is All We Need' (1958), 'My Melancholy Baby' (1959) and 'I Really Don't Want to Know' (1960), before his career faded in the sixties.

EELS
Butch; Mark 'E' Everett; Tommy (replaced by Elton Jones)

A post-grunge trio, the Eels' lo-fi eclecticism and often bleak lyrical imagery drew comparisons with **Beck** and **Brian Wilson** and gained the band instant recognition internationally.

Eels were formed in the mid-nineties by singer-guitarist Everett, who had previously released two solo albums, *A Man Called E* and *Broken Toy Shop*. Also comprising bassist Tommy and drummer Butch, the band attracted the attention of the DreamWorks imprint after playing the club circuit in and around Los Angeles. *Beautiful Freak* (1996) brought the band instant acclaim in the States, where 'Novacaine for the Soul' became a college radio hit. Released the following year in Britain, the album's blend of lo-fi alternative rock and Wurlitzer wizardry spawned two further successful singles, 'Susan's House' and 'Lucky Day in Hell'.

The recording of *Electro-Shock Blues* (1998) was disrupted by the death of several members of Everett's family, reflected in the darker tone of songs such as 'Going to Your Funeral' and 'Elizabeth on the Bathroom Floor'. The album was also the first to feature new bassist Jones and included 'Last Stop: This Town', which made the UK Top Ten. *Daisies of the Galaxy* (1999), which saw the group reverting to the more immediate sound of *Beautiful Freak*, was critically well received.

ELASTICA
Justine Frischmann, b. 16 September 1969, Twickenham, England; Annie Holland, b. 26 August 1965, London (temporarily replaced by Sheila Chipperfield, b. 17 June 1976, London); Donna Matthews, b. 2 December 1971, Newport, Wales (replaced by Paul Jones); 'Mew'; Justin Welch, b. 4 December 1972, Nuneaton, England

A punk-pop band whose rise to fame coincided with the height of the Britpop explosion, Elastica's twisted sound, influenced by the **Fall** and **Wire**, later saw them credited with instigating the new wave of new wave.

After studying architecture at London University Frischmann spent a brief period as guitarist in an embryonic model of **Suede** before finding her creativity stifled and deciding to form her own group. Recruiting drummer Welch, guitarist Matthews and bass-player Holland through the classified pages of the *Melody Maker*, Elastica rehearsed for six months before a leaked demo tape gained them a recording contract with Deceptive Records.

The pre-release hype surrounding the limited edition of 'Stutter' (1993) ensured that all 1,500 copies sold within two days. Two EPs, *Line Up* and *Connection* (1994), saw the band develop a cult following, while their eponymous début album (1995) brought them mainstream recognition and became widely viewed as one of the best representations of the Britpop aesthetic. The album also brought them the threat of legal action due to the close similarity of 'Connection' and Wire's 'Three Girl Rhumba'. The band toured for the best part of two years, with Chipperfield replacing a pregnant Holland on bass, before disappearing into the studio amidst rumours of drug addiction.

Elastica finally re-emerged in 1999 with a harder sound and a radically altered line-up. Jones took over as lead guitarist, Holland returned to bass duties along with the addition of keyboardists Dave Bush and Mew. The *Elastica* EP (1999) collected six tracks recorded at various points over the band's three-year hiatus and featured Mark E. Smith of the Fall on two songs. Far more substantial was *Menace* (2000). **Blur**'s Damon Albarn (who reportedly had a hand in the writing of much of Elastica's first album) and Frischmann were once dubbed the Hugh Grant and Elizabeth Hurley of Britpop. He examined their break up on 13's 'Tender Is the Night'; on *Menace*, Frischmann does so on 'My Sex' and 'Mad Dog'. However, the album is far from a tit for tat exercise. Its driving force may have been personal but the album's impact lies in its evocation of failed love affairs in general, pictured with a Kinks-like observation of things British: 'What I want is a room with a three-bar fire.'

ELECTRIC LIGHT ORCHESTRA (ELO)

Bev Bevan, b. 25 November 1945, Birmingham, England; Melvyn Gale, b. 15 January 1952, London; Kelly Groucutt, b. 8 September 1952, London; Mik Kaminski, b. 2 September 1951, Harrogate, Yorkshire; Jeff Lynne, b. 12 December 1947, Birmingham; Richard Tandy, b. 26 March 1948, Birmingham

Originally an offshoot of the **Move**, ELO was designed to embody guitarist Lynne's vision of symphonic rock. With an energetic string section led by violinist Kaminski, the group found huge success in America and Europe during the seventies despite being attacked by critics for blandness and mercilessly pilloried by **Randy Newman**. ELO was less active in the eighties, with Lynne pursuing writing and production projects with such artists as **Del Shannon**, **Paul McCartney**, **Duane Eddy**, Newman and the Traveling Wilburys.

Before joining the Move in 1970, Lynne had led Birmingham group the Idle Race, which made two albums for United Artists in 1968–9. These critically acclaimed recordings showed both a leaning to dreamy romanticism ('Going Home' and the plangent 'Please No More Sad Songs') and eccentric humour ('Mr Crow and Sir Norman', 'Skeleton on the Roundabout').

Within the Move, Lynne, drummer Bevan and Roy Wood put together *Electric Light Orchestra* (United Artists, 1973), which provided a British hit with Lynne's '10538 Overture' (1972). Further success followed with 'Roll Over Beethoven', which combined the **Chuck Berry** song with the opening theme from the classical composer's Fifth Symphony. This track appeared on *ELO II* (1973), by which time Wood had left to form Wizzard and the group had been joined by Tandy (keyboards) and Kaminski.

Showdown (1973) found Lynne working towards a poppier sound and an American tour (captured on the live album *The Night the Light Went on in Long Beach*, 1974) helped the success of *Eldorado* (1974) and its hit single, the yearning 'Can't Get It out of My Head'. A similar combination of Lynne's keening vocals and churning strings took both 'Evil Woman' (1976) and 'Strange Magic' from *Face the Music* (1975) into the American Top Twenty.

The live *Ole ELO* (1976) was followed by *A New World Record* (1976), which became the band's most commercially successful recording. It included the haunting 'Telephone Line' and a new version of the Move's 'Do Ya', as well as ELO's biggest British hit 'Livin' Thing'. Kaminski and cellist Gale left the group before the release of the double-album *Out of the Blue* (1977), the last release on United Artists. Later ELO records appeared on Jet, the label owned by the group's manager Don Arden.

They included *Discovery* (1979), with its hits 'Don't Bring Me Down'* and 'Show a Little Love', *Time* (1981) and *Secret Messages* (1983). In 1980 Lynne wrote songs for the movie *Xanadu* and ELO performed on **Olivia Newton-John**'s version of the title song, which topped the British charts. The group then disbanded while Lynne concentrated on solo activities. In 1986 they re-formed to make *Balance of Power* (Epic), which provided a further hit with 'Calling America'.

Two years later Lynne formed a recording-only group with **Bob Dylan**, **Tom Petty**, **George Harrison** and **Roy Orbison**. *The Traveling Wilburys* (Warners) was an international success. Because of Lynne's commitment to personal projects (the sleek, slick *Armchair Theatre*, Reprise, 1989), ELO remained dormant until 1991. Then Bevan resuscitated the group as ELO II with original members plus Peter Haycock and former Climax Blues Band guitarist and orchestrator Louis Clark. This group toured Europe and released *Part Two*. Lynne 'constructed' **The Beatles**' recordings of **John Lennon**'s 'Free as a Bird' and 'Real Love' for *Anthology 1* (1995) and 2 (1996) from voice- and piano-only recordings by Lennon. Later he produced Paul McCartney's *Flaming Pie* (1997) album.

THE ELECTRIC PRUNES
James Lowe, b. San Luis Obispo, California, USA; Mark Tulin, b. Philadelphia, Pennsylvania; Ken Williams, b. Long Beach, California; Preston Ritter, b. Stockton, California; Weasel Spagnolo

With the **Seeds** one of the first Los Angeles garage bands of the psychedelic era, the Electric Prunes were responsible for the cult classic 'I Had Too Much to Dream Last Night'.

Formed in Los Angeles in 1965, the Prunes were signed to Reprise by producer Dave Hassinger in 1966, and in 1967 had an American Top Twenty hit with 'Dream'. The song's title perfectly captured the psychedelic mood of the times, as did Hassinger's production, which used fuzz and reverberation techniques to great effect. After an eponymous album and one more hit, 'Get Me to the World on Time' (1967), the group disbanded. A new group (which included John Herren, Mark Kincaid, Richard Whetstone and Brett Wade) took the name and released the previously recorded concept albums *Mass in F Minor* (1967), which came complete with a rosary on the cover, and *Release of an Oath: the Kol Nidre*, both written and arranged by David Axelrod. After one more album, the lacklustre *Just Good Old Rock'n'Roll* (1969), the group faded from view.

Rock critic, guitarist and producer, Lenny Kaye's compilation album *Nuggets* (Elektra, 1972) features 'Too Much to Dream' and several more garage-band classics, including singles by the Standells, the Chocolate Watch Band, the Magic Mushrooms and the Thirteenth Floor Elevators. Subsequently it was expanded to a multi-CD box set.

GUS ELEN
b. Ernest Augustus Elen, 22 July 1862, Pimlico, London, England, d. 17 February 1940, Balham, London

Few music-hall artists have caught the imagination of both their own and later generations as graphically as Gus Elen. His songs, and the costumes in which he performed them, had an almost documentary realism. They were as vivid a portrayal of working-class London life in Victorian times as the music hall had to offer.

Elen first appeared in the London halls in 1885 as an eccentric character singer, but in 1891 he discovered his aptitude for the coster role with 'Never Introduce Your Donah to a Pal'. Throughout the nineties he produced a succession of brilliant Cockney characterizations in ''E Dunno Where 'E Are', 'It's a Great Big Shame', ''Arf a Pint of Ale', 'The Golden Dustman', 'Down the Road', 'Wait Till the Work Comes Round' and the classic 'If It Wasn't for the 'Ouses in Between', written by Edgar Bateman and George Le Brun. Colin MacInnes wrote of 'his temperament, sturdy, laconic, tolerant and robust – so perfectly reflected in his harsh, friendly, sardonic, forthright voice', and if his audiences favoured the more studied impressions of **Albert Chevalier**, time has elevated Elen to a higher seat in the music-hall pantheon.

He retired from the halls during the First World War but returned in 1931–2 on the wave of music-hall revival, making short films and re-recording his most famous numbers. His last major appearance was in the 1935 Royal Variety Performance.

DANNY ELFMAN
b. 1954, Los Angeles, California, USA

Leader of the eccentric rock band Oingo Boingo, Elfman was one of the most sought-after film music composers of the nineties. His scores, usually synthesizer-based, are known for their playfulness and use of pastiche.

Singer and guitarist Elfman formed his band in Los Angeles in 1979 as the Mystic Knights. After a name change to Oingo Boingo, the group signed to A&M. Produced by Pete Solley (who had previously worked with British eccentric Reckless Eric), *Only a Lad* (1981) set the tone for later albums. The eight-piece band, which included Steve Bartek (guitar), Richard Gibbs (keyboards and trombone), Kerry Hatch (bass), John Hernandez (drums) and a horn section, skilfully presented Elfman's witty lyrics and arrangements.

Nothing to Fear followed in 1982 and Robert Margouleff of synthesizer pioneers Tonto's Exploding Headband produced *Good for Your Soul* (1983). The group's greatest commercial success came with *Dead Man's Party* (MCA, 1985), which caught the wave of dance music through such tracks as 'Weird Science'. After issuing a disappointing live album and the studio projects *Skeletons in the Closet* (1989) and *Dark at the End of the Tunnel*, Elfman disbanded the group to concentrate on his film career.

As a film composer, Elfman has worked closely with director Tim Burton, whose *Pee-Wee's Big Adventure* (1985) was his first score. He followed this with scores for *Beetlejuice* (1988), the highly acclaimed *Batman* (1989), *Edward Scissorhands* (1990), *Batman Returns* (1992) and the animated *The Nightmare Before Christmas* (1993), on which he sang the lead. He also wrote the score for the Warren Beatty–**Madonna** vehicle *Dick Tracy* (1990) as well as composing the theme for the animated television series *The Simpsons*. Later film scores included *Mars Attacks* and *Mission Impossible* (both 1996) and the playful *Men in Black* (1997).

In 1994 Elfman revived his band as Boingo with Hernandez and Bartek remaining from the original line-up. The first album, *Boingo* (Giant), included a version of **The Beatles**' 'I Am the Walrus' and a previously unreleased track from the Mystic Nights era.

FRED ELIZALDE
b. 12 December 1908, Manila, Philippines, d. 16 January 1969, Manila

In the twenties Elizalde was a pioneer of jazz in the UK, briefly performing in an uncompromising jazz style, until managements and recording directors restricted his opportunities.

The son of wealthy parents, Elizalde and his older brother Manuel were educated in America. In the twenties Fred led a dance band there and both sent reports on the jazz scene to London. When Manuel was sent to Cambridge in 1926, Fred accompanied him and formed a band, the Quinquaginta Ramblers, composed almost entirely of undergraduates with Manuel on saxophone and himself as pianist. In 1927 the band recorded for HMV. The label was taken by the novelty of the band being university based and including the likes of cricketer Maurice Allom (who in 1930 achieved a hat-trick in his Test début). Nonetheless, Elizalde's compositions, which included 'Stomp Your Feet' and the symphonic suite 'Heart of a Nigger' (retitled 'Heart of a Coon' when performed by **Ambrose** in 1927) were genuinely progressive compared to most British jazz of the period.

Later in 1927 Elizalde formed the Savoy Hotel Band, which included the Americans Adrian Rollini, Chelsea Quealey, and Bobby Davis from the California Ramblers, to perform at the Savoy. But though reviewed positively in the *Melody Maker*, and lionized by fellow musicians, the band only remained at the Savoy until 1929, after a series of compromises: initially Elizalde refused even to play waltzes. Although Elizalde himself was a social success, his music was not. His recordings on Brunswick and Parlophone included several with the young **Al Bowlly**, and the band appeared in the short film *Christmas Fantasy*

(1929); they were denied radio exposure, however (because listeners wanted dance music), and Elizalde's records were not a commercial success. Among his best recordings are 'Dixie', 'Tiger Rag', the introspective 'Grown Up Baby' (Parlophone, 1928), 'Singapore Sorrows' and 'Nobody's Sweetheart' (1929).

After recording for Decca, Elizalde left the UK in 1933 first for Spain, where he studied composition with de Falla, and then France, where he studied with Maurice Ravel. After this he returned to Manila where he became director of the Philippines broadcasting network, returning occasionally to Britain to give classical concerts.

DUKE ELLINGTON
b. Edward Kennedy Ellington, 29 April 1899, Washington DC, USA, d. 24 May 1974, New York

Widely regarded as America's greatest composer in any genre, Duke Ellington led his orchestra for over fifty years. He wrote literally thousands of works, ranging from standard ballads like 'Don't Get Around Much Anymore', through instrumentals ('Mood Indigo', 'Rocking in Rhythm') to full-scale suites such as *Black, Brown and Beige* and *Such Sweet Thunder*, his sequence of pieces based on Shakespearean characters. Ellington always composed with his orchestra members in mind and many of them stayed with him for twenty years or more. In the words of his veteran collaborator and arranger Billy Strayhorn, 'Ellington plays the piano, but his real instrument is his band'.

From a Washington middle-class background, Ellington took piano lessons as a child, played at dances and parties and wrote his first composition, 'Soda Fountain Rag', at the age of sixteen. After leaving school he worked as a sign-painter and a clerk while running his first band, which included Sonny Greer (drums) and Otto Hardwick (tenor sax). In 1922 the three moved to New York, where they played briefly with Wilbur Sweatman and Ellington learned jazz piano from **James P. Johnson** and Willie 'the Lion' Smith. The following year Ellington formed his first band for a nightclub engagement and with Jo Trent wrote the score for *Chocolate Kiddies*, a show which starred **Josephine Baker** and **Adelaide Hall** and enjoyed a long run in Berlin.

The band began to acquire an individual sound when James 'Bubber' Miley (trumpet) and Joe 'Tricky Sam' Nanton (trombone) were recruited. They developed growling and wah-wah tones through the use of mutes on their instruments. Ellington's first records were made for **Irving Mills** under a variety of names including the Jungle Band, Harlem Footwarmers and Whoopee Makers. Mills also managed the band for a decade from the late twenties as well as taking co-composer credits on many of Ellington's tunes.

The first great period of the Ellington Orchestra's work coincided with its 1927–31 residency at the Cotton Club in Harlem. The eleven-piece band now included two key figures who would be among its mainstays up to the sixties: Harry Carney on baritone sax and alto-player **Johnny Hodges**. Both the Cotton Club floorshow and Ellington's compositions of this period used 'jungle' motifs. Among the latter were 'Rockin' in Rhythm', 'Mood Indigo', 'The Mooch' and 'Creole Love Call', a musical portrait of **Bessie Smith** which featured Adelaide Hall singing wordless passages in harmony with Barney Bigard's clarinet.

During the thirties Ellington's growing reputation led to national and international tours. The band travelled America in two private Pullman coaches hired by Mills to avoid problems of racial segregation and to enable Ellington to write while on tour. He also played in London and Paris in 1933. Among the band's first film appearances were Amos 'n' Andy's *Check and Double Check* (1930) and *Murder at the Varieties* (1934), in which they performed an adaptation of Liszt's 'Ebony Rhapsody'. Ellington also composed music for the Marx Brothers' *A Day at the Races* (1936). Among his best-known compositions from this period were 'Sophisticated Lady', 'Caravan', and his first extended work, the twelve-minute 'Reminiscing in Tempo' written in 1934 in memory of his mother. He also received the first of many tributes from the 'straight' music world when **Percy Grainger** lectured in New York on his work.

In 1940 Billy Strayhorn joined the band and was soon co-authoring many of Ellington's compositions. Strayhorn's earliest solo works included 'Chelsea Bridge' and 'Take the A Train', which became a signature tune for the band. In the forties Ellington and Strayhorn wrote the first of their many suites or cycles of tunes. After *Blue Belles of Harlem* (1938) for **Paul Whiteman** and the 1941 civil rights show *Jump for Joy*, Ellington accepted a commission for a work to be premièred at New York's Carnegie Hall. *Black, Brown and Beige* (1943) was a musical history of American blacks and included work songs and the music of contemporary Harlem.

The success of that appearance led to annual concerts which featured such works as *Deep South Suite* (1946) and *Liberian Suite* (1947), recorded for Columbia, which Ellington joined after leaving RCA. The recording ban called by **James Petrillo**'s American Federation of Musicians and adverse economic conditions in the late forties affected the orchestra and by 1950, when recording restarted, Ellington was using a small group to cut sides for Mercer, a label run by his trumpeter son Mercer (*b*. 11 *March* 1919, *Washington*) and British-born critic **Leonard Feather**. Among the

important new members of the band in the forties and early fifties were Paul Gonsalves (tenor sax) and trumpeter William Alonzo 'Cat' Anderson, whose skill in very high registers became a feature of the Ellington sound.

In 1953–4 Ellington's recordings for Capitol include the uncharacteristically opportunistic 'Bunny Hop Mambo', but in 1955 he returned to Columbia, who recorded the orchestra's barnstorming performance at the Newport Jazz Festival. During the rest of the fifties Ellington and Strayhorn's creations included *A Drum Is a Woman* (1957), *Royal Ancestry* (a tribute to **Ella Fitzgerald**), the film score *Anatomy of a Murder*, and *Such Sweet Thunder*, in which characters from Shakespeare's plays were represented by soloists, with Hodges and Gonsalves 'playing' Romeo and Juliet. A 1959 tour of Britain inspired the *Queen's Suite*.

The sixties began with the score for *Paris Blues* (in which Sidney Poitier played a jazz musician) and another literary programme piece, *Suite Thursday*, based on John Steinbeck's works and commissioned by the Monterey Festival. It appeared on an album with Ellington's versions of Grieg's *Peer Gynt* which was publicized as 'swinging suites by Edward E. and Edward G.'. More classical variations were inspired by Tchaikovsky's *Nutcracker Suite* where the 'Russian Dance' became 'Volga Vouty' and 'Sugar Plum Fairy', 'Sugar Rum Cherry'. *My People* (1963), a major new work based on spirituals and blues, was written to celebrate the centenary of the emancipation of the slaves and featured the Swedish soprano Alice Babs. Ellington the pianist also began to record with other leading jazz figures, including **Count Basie**'s band, **Louis Armstrong**, **Coleman Hawkins** and **John Coltrane**.

The Ellington band's globe-trotting was reflected in such compositions as *Far East Suite* (1964), *Virgin Islands Suite* (1967) and *Latin American Suite* (1968). The orchestra visited Africa for the first time when they performed in 1966 at the World Festival of Negro Arts in Senegal. Ellington was later awarded the Emperor's Star by Haile Selassie of Ethiopia, one of the many awards and honorary degrees that came to him in the latter part of his career.

A new but increasingly central aspect of Ellington's work was his writing on religious themes. He composed and performed his first sacred concert in San Francisco in 1966 and regularly gave concerts in churches and cathedrals for the remainder of his career. Towards the end of the sixties the orchestra was hit by a series of deaths and departures. *And His Mother Called Him Bill* (1968) was Ellington's tribute to his closest colleague and it featured the poignant piano solo 'Lotus Blossom'. Hodges died in 1970 during the recording of the *New Orleans Suite*, with its musical portraits of Armstrong, **Mahalia Jackson** and **Sidney Bechet**.

During 1972–3 Ellington recorded a series of solo albums produced by **Norman Granz** and wrote an autobiography, *Music Is My Mistress*, published shortly before his death from cancer. Afterwards Mercer Ellington took over leadership of the orchestra, which made a successful appearance at Newport in 1976.

MISSY 'MISDEMEANOR' ELLIOT
b. Melissa Elliot, 1 July 1972, Portsmouth, Virginia, USA

A pioneering hip-hop star, Missy Elliot rose to fame writing and producing hits for a plethora of artists, including **Mariah Carey** and SWV, with long-term collaborator Timbaland before embarking on a solo career in which she reinvigorated the genre.

Missy Elliot's musical career began in her last year of high school, 1989, when she and Timbaland (*b. Tim Moseley, Portsmouth, Virginia*) created Sistas with three friends. The group signed with Jodeci svengali Devante Swing's label after meeting him on the swing-beat boy-band's 1990 tour, although they split soon after recording *4 All the Sistas Around Da World*, which was never released.

After several failed attempts at gaining a solo recording contract, Elliot decided to forge a career as a songwriter. Word soon began to spread of the production talents of Elliot and Timbaland when a demo tape found its way to Faith Evans. Their breakthrough hit was R&B diva Aaliyah's 'If Your Girl Only Knew', with the duo subsequently writing most of the singer's début, *One in a Million* (1996), one of the biggest hits of the year in the US. They went on to work with SWV ('Can We'), Mariah Carey, **Janet Jackson** and **Puff Daddy** as Elliot formed her own record label, The Gold Mind Inc.

This run of success prompted Elliot to make a second attempt at a solo career, resulting in *Supa Dupa Fly* (1997), a benchmark hip-hop album of the late nineties, featuring contributions from Timbaland, Busta Rhymes, Ginuwine and Aaliyah. The album sold over 1.5 million copies in the US alone and spawned the hit singles 'Sock It 2 Me' and 'The Rain'. Further production work followed – including **Spice Girl** Mel B's first solo release 'I Want You Back' and Timbaland's 'Up Jumps Da Boogie' – before Elliot recorded *Da Real World* (1999), on which she collaborated with Eminem and Destiny's Child.

RAMBLIN' JACK ELLIOTT
b. Elliot Charles Adnopoz, 1 August 1931, Brooklyn, New York, USA

A close associate of **Woody Guthrie**, Elliott bridged the generations between the post-Second World War folk artists and **Bob Dylan** and other new singers of the sixties folk revival.

The son of a Jewish doctor, Adnopoz was an early fan of cowboy music. Calling himself Buck Elliott, he ran away to join Colonel Jim Eskew's rodeo in 1947. On his return he went to college and took up guitar-playing. Elliott modelled himself on Guthrie, whom he met in Greenwich Village in 1951, and the pair remained close during Guthrie's long years of illness. His mimicry was so exact that Guthrie is reputed to have said 'he sounds more like me than I do!'. Guthrie's last recording was made with Elliott for **Moe Asch** in 1954.

In 1955, now Ramblin' Jack, he travelled to Europe, performing Guthrie's songs and a wide American folk and country repertoire which included **Hank Williams** songs. He played with such artists as Derroll Adams, **Ewan MacColl** and Peggy Seeger, and recorded for the British folk label, Topic.

On his return to America, he appeared at most of the major sixties folk festivals and recorded prolifically for Folkways, Fantasy, Everest and Prestige, producing several fine albums of Guthrie material including *Songs to Grow on* (Folkways), a collection of children's songs. A later reissue, *The Essential Jack Elliott* (Vanguard, 1976), captures his repertoire at this period well, with its mix of traditional songs ('House of the Rising Sun', 'Buffalo Skinner'), recent compositions by Dylan ('Don't Think Twice, It's Alright') and Adams ('Portland Town') and **Jesse Fuller**'s rousing 'San Francisco Bay'. In 1989 Fantasy reissued the sixties' albums *Sings Woody Guthrie* and *Ramblin'* as *Hard Travellin'*.

By this time a senior figure on the New York folk scene, Elliott befriended Dylan and other young performers. In 1968 he signed to Reprise for *Young Brigham*, an unsatisfactory attempt to update his music. In the same year he appeared at the Guthrie Memorial Concert at Carnegie Hall in New York.

In 1976 Elliott renewed his contact with Dylan, touring with him in the 'Rolling Thunder Revue' and appearing in his film *Renaldo and Clara*. In 1984 he issued the erratic *Jack Kerouac's Last Dream*.

SHIRLEY ELLIS
b. 1941, Bronx, New York, USA

Ellis is best remembered for her performance of the series of novelty dance hits she wrote with her husband Lincoln Chase in the mid-sixties.

While a member of the Metronomes, Ellis wrote 'One, Two, I Love You', recorded by the Heartbreakers on Vik. On leaving the group in 1958, she met fellow songwriter Chase, who wrote 'Such a Night' for the **Drifters** in 1954, and **Lavern Baker**'s biggest hit, 'Jim Dandy' (1956). Together they wrote the soul-flavoured nursery-rhyme-like ditty 'The Nitty Gritty', which when finally issued on Congress in 1963 made the American Top Ten and was successfully revived in 1969 by **Gladys Knight and the Pips**. Her subsequent hits, all similarly styled, included 'The Name Game' (1964), 'The Clapping Song' (1965) – which was also a minor British hit when reissued in 1978, and 'The Puzzle Song' (1965). However, she was unable to extricate herself from these formula songs and after the minor hit 'Soul Time' (Columbia, 1967), she retired.

British group the Belle Stars successfully revived 'The Clapping Song' (Stiff) in 1982.

JOE ELY
b. 9 February 1947, Amarillo, Texas, USA

A critics' favourite, Ely's brash high-energy blend of Texas honky-tonk styles and rock was an important influence on country performers at a time when the impetus behind much country music was the search for a crossover pop hit.

Raised in Lubbock, Texas, the birthplace of **Buddy Holly**, Ely left high school early to play the bars and cafés of West Texas, before forming an acoustic country group, the Flatlanders, with Butch Hancock (whose songs he would later regularly record) and Jimmie Dale Gilmour. The group recorded *One Road More* in 1972 – which remained unissued until released in Britain on Charly in 1980 – but it was only when Ely went electric for *Joe Ely* (MCA, 1976) that he found favour. The songs were mostly traditional honky-tonk material (including a trio of superior Hancock compositions, 'She Never Spoke Spanish to Me', 'Suckin' a Big Bottle of Gin', and the much-recorded 'Tennessee's Not the State I'm in') but performed in a manner that showed a pronounced blues and rock influence.

Subsequent albums included *Honky Tonk Masquerade* (1978), which featured the plaintive 'Because of the Wind' and the rocking 'Fingernails', *Musta Notta Gotta Lotta* (1981) and *Hi-Res* (1984). But though Ely was popular in Texas and the UK (where in the wake of the rockabilly revival, his music 'fitted', so much so that in 1981 he toured with the **Clash**), in America he proved too country for rock audiences and too rock for country audiences, and it was only in the mid-eighties that he began to make a real impact. In 1986, after MCA rejected the tapes of a projected album, he left the company and *Lord of the Highway* (1987), his best album for some time, was issued by the independent Hightone (Demon in the UK). He stayed with Hightone/Demon for the lesser *Dig All Night* (1988) before returning to MCA for the minor *Live at Liberty Lunch*. He toured with a band that included David Grisson (guitar), David McLaverty (drums) and Jimmy Pettit (bass) plus his former Flatlanders colleagues Gilmore and Hancock. In 1992 he released

Love & Danger with Ian Moore replacing Grisson. After *Twistin' in the Wind* (1998) he left MCA.

EMERSON, LAKE AND PALMER
Keith Emerson, b. 1 November 1944, Todmorden, Lancashire, England; Greg Lake, b. 10 November 1948, Bournemouth, Hampshire; Carl Palmer, b. 20 March 1951, Birmingham

ELP were the quintessential progressive rock band of the seventies, combining classical music influences with grandiose theatrical performances.

A veteran of British R&B, keyboards-player Emerson had been the focal point of the Nice, originally a backing group for ex-Ikette P. P. Arnold – they played on her 1967 hit recording of **Cat Stevens**' 'The First Cut Is the Deepest'. Leaving Arnold, the Nice developed a potent mixture of bravura playing and showmanship: during performances of **Leonard Bernstein**'s 'America' Emerson would set light to the American flag. In retaliation, the composer ensured that the Nice's recording of his song was not released in the USA. Their first British hit albums, on Charisma, included *Ars Longa Vita Brevis* (1968) and *Five Bridges Suite* (1970), a set of compositions by Emerson inspired by his home town of Newcastle-upon-Tyne.

With **King Crimson** bassist Lake and former **Arthur Brown** drummer Palmer, Emerson formed the new band in 1970. Their first appearance was at the 1970 Isle of Wight Festival, playing Emerson's version of Moussorgsky's *Pictures at an Exhibition* (with added lyrics which included the line 'Death is life'), which they recorded the following year. Signed to Island, and the Atlantic subsidiary Cotillion in America, they had two minor US hits with Lake's songs 'Lucky Man' and 'From the Beginning' (both 1972). These and lengthy, flamboyant tours made their albums bestsellers in America as well as Britain. The eponymous début record was followed by *Tarkus*, *Pictures* and *Trilogy* (1972).

In 1973 ELP formed their own label, Manticore, to release albums by Lake's writing partner and ex-King Crimson member Pete Sinfield, Italian band PFM (Preminta Formeria Marconi) and their own *Brain Salad Surgery*. The 1973–4 world tour, complete with laser light show and quadraphonic sound system, attracted two million customers. It was captured on the triple album *Welcome Back My Friends, to the Show that Never Ends* (1974).

But the show had ended. The group dispersed, with each member pursuing his own projects. Emerson had a British solo hit with the boogie-woogie standard 'Honky Tonk Train Blues' (1976), while Lake joined **Johnny Marks** as the writer of what seemed set to become one of the perennial Christmas songs ('I

Believe in Father Christmas'). As well as its 1975 success it was a minor hit in Britain on re-release in 1982 and 1983. When ELP re-emerged with the double-album *Works Vol 1* (1977), three sides were devoted to solo efforts – Emerson with his Concerto No. 1, Palmer with ex-**Eagles**' guitarist Joe Walsh and Lake with his own songs. From the album, ELP had their only British hit single with a treatment of Aaron Copland's 'Fanfare for the Common Man'. Another gigantic tour was embarked on, with full symphony orchestra.

Times, however, had changed and the response was disappointing. The group released *Love Beach* (1978), undertook a farewell tour plus live album in 1979, and bowed out. Emerson did film scores (*Inferno*, 1980, and *Nighthawks*, 1981), Lake a solo album (Chrysalis, 1981), while Palmer made an album with PM (Ariola, 1980) before joining **Yes** guitarist Steve Howe in a new supergroup, Asia, whose first album spent nine weeks at No. 1 in America in 1982.

In 1986 Emerson and Lake re-formed the group with former Richie Blackmore, **Jeff Beck** and Michael Schenker drummer Cozy Powell (*b. 29 December 1947, d. 5 April 1998*). The new ELP started where the old had left off: *Emerson Lake and Powell* (Polydor) included a rock version of 'Mars, the Bringer of War' from Gustav Holst's *Planets Suite*. With yet another drummer, Robert Berry, Emerson and Lake formed Three and released the poorly received *To the Power of Three* (Geffen, 1988).

In 1992 the original trio regrouped for a reunion tour and album, *Black Moon*, which included an ELP arrangement of Prokofiev's *Romeo and Juliet*. The tour produced yet another in concert album, *Live at the Royal Albert Hall* (Victory, 1993). That was followed by *In the Hot Seat* (1994) and the four-CD collection *The Return of Manticore* (1997).

THE EMOTIONS
Jeannette Hutchinson, b. 1951, Chicago, Illinois, USA (replaced by Teresa Davis, b. 22 August 1950, replaced by Pamela Hutchinson, b. 1958, Chicago); Wanda Hutchinson, b. 17 December 1951, Chicago; Sheila Hutchinson, b. 17 January 1953, Chicago

Employing soft harmonies in the manner of the **Supremes**, the Hutchinson sisters formed one of the few successful female vocal groups to record for the Memphis-based Stax label.

Based in Chicago, they were launched by their father Joe as a child gospel trio, the Heavenly Sunbeams, in the mid-fifties. Their repertoire was strictly sacred until the mid-sixties when they became first Three Ribbons and a Bow, then the Emotions. Through Pervis Staples of the **Staple Singers** (another secularized gospel group) they signed to the local Twinstacks label.

After the demise of Twinstacks, the group joined Stax where **Isaac Hayes** and David Porter provided them with several R&B hits, the biggest of which was 'So I Can Love You' (1969), with Wanda on lead vocals. In 1970 Jeannette was replaced by Davis. They appeared in the film *Wattstax* (1973), singing in an uncharacteristic fiery manner. After Stax folded in 1975, the Emotions signed to Columbia through Kalimba, the production company of **Earth, Wind and Fire**'s Maurice White, who supervised *Flowers* (1976) and *Rejoice* (1977), most of whose tracks were written by Wanda. On the latter album, which included the international disco hit 'Best of My Love' (1977), the youngest Hutchinson sister, Pamela, joined the group. They had a further Top Ten hit with 'Boogie Wonderland' (1979), in collaboration with Earth, Wind and Fire.

As White's star waned, so did that of his protégées. After releasing *Come into Our World* (1979) and *New Affair* (1981), they left Columbia to record for Red, an independent label based in their home town. They subsequently toured with Earth, Wind and Fire and the **Commodores** and in 1985 recorded 'If I Only Knew' (Motown). Since then, Wanda and Jeannette have sung on Earth, Wind and Fire's *Heritage* (1990) while Sheila sang on Gary Glenn's 'Feels Good to Feel Good' (1987).

BRIAN ENO
b. Brian Peter George St John de Baptiste de la Salle Eno, 15 May 1948, Woodbridge, Suffolk, England

A pioneer synthesizer player with **Roxy Music**, Eno later earned a reputation as a leading avant-garde figure in rock-music circles, and explored the potential of ambient music in such albums as *Music for Airports* (1979). In the eighties and nineties he worked as a producer with **David Bowie**, **Talking Heads**, U2 and others. He also wrote possibly the most-heard piece of music ever, the music welcoming a computer user to Microsoft's Windows.

Eno studied at art school in Ipswich and Winchester, where he discovered the work of avant-garde composer John Cage and wrote a book of music theory, *Music for Non Musicians*. As a member of Roxy Music in 1971–3, his role was to 'treat' the music electronically with a tape-recorder and VCS 3 synthesizer. His striking appearance in blue sequins and black boa provided a rival focal point to the suave **Bryan Ferry** and this contributed to his departure from the group after the release of *For Your Pleasure* (1973).

The first phase of a determinedly experimental solo career involved a swiftly changing array of musical styles. *No Pussyfooting* (Island, 1973) was a collaboration with **Robert Fripp** designed mainly to display tape-echo and delay techniques, while *Here Come the*

Warm Jets was a journey into **Lou Reed** territory, with appropriately perverse lyrics.

In 1974 Eno undertook what proved to be his last concert tour with the Winkies and also recorded the live *June 1 1974* with ex-**Velvet Underground** members Nico and John Cale, and Kevin Ayers, formerly of **Soft Machine**. The critically acclaimed *Taking Tiger Mountain (by Strategy)* (EG, 1974), with its modish Maoist title, was another collection of surprisingly strong songs, and *Another Green World* (1975) represented a return to the minimalism of John Cage. Eno announced that the music was composed according to the turn of cards from a pack called Oblique Strategies. With *Taking Tiger Mountain (by Strategy)*, it is probably his most influential recording.

The same year he recorded two albums with John Cale and set up Obscure Records to release his own increasingly stark and 'ambient' instrumental music (*Music for Films*, 1978; *Music for Airports*, 1979), creating a chic sound which led to frequent jobs as producer. After working with **Hawkwind**'s Robert Calvert, Eno supervised three albums in which David Bowie sought an alienating backing for his low-key lyrics: *Low* (1977), *Heroes* and *Lodger* (1978). He also released his own *Before and After Science* (1977).

These records and his production of Talking Head's *More Songs About Buildings and Food* (1978) brought Eno into contact with the avant-garde art world of New York, the city he made his base in the late seventies and early eighties. There, he produced further records by Talking Heads and **Devo**, as well as collaborating with David Byrne on the sound collage *My Life in the Bush of Ghosts* (1981). In New York Eno also began to work with 'video sculpture', producing *Manhattan Skyline* (1979).

The ambient aspect dominated his work from the mid-eighties when Eno was associated with such musicians as his guitarist brother Roger and Harold Budd (piano), with whom he made *The Plateaux of Mirror* (1980). Their work, sometimes classed as New Age although more challenging than most of the genre, was issued through Opal, a label set up by Eno and his wife Anthea Norton-Taylor. Among Eno's solo recordings for the company were *On Land* (1982) and *Thursday Afternoon* (1985). With the arrival of glasnost, Opal also began to issue material by Soviet avant-garde musicians. In 1990 Eno recorded *Wrong Way Up* with John Cale, whose previous album he had also worked on. He followed this with his own well-received album *Nerve Net* (1992) on WEA and the ambient sets *The Shutov Assembly* (1992) and *Neroli* (1993) on Opal – named after the natural oil derived from orange blossom. Other collaborative albums included *Wah Wah* (1994, with **James**) and *Spinner* (1995, with guitarist Jah Wobble), while *Songs in the Key of X* (1996) included a track made with **Elvis Costello**. In 1998 he recorded the only ever live performance of his celebrated ambient work *Music for Airports* (Point) and in 2000 created *Civic Recovery Centre Proposal (Quiet Club)* for the Hayward Gallery's exhibition of sound art, *Sonic Boom*.

In parallel with his own recordings and lecturing – he is a visiting professor at the London School of Art – Eno continued to accept production assignments, most notably the collaboration with **Daniel Lanois** on U2's bestselling *The Unforgettable Fire* (1984) and *The Joshua Tree* (1987).

ENYA
b. Eithne Brennan, 17 May 1961, Gweedore, County Donegal, Ireland

Enya and her collaborators have created some of the most successful New Age music, most of it featuring a strong Celtic folk music element.

Her father was a former showband leader and her elder siblings were founder members of traditional folk group Clannad, whose members included Maire Brennan (*b. 4 August 1952, Dublin, Eire*), Pol Brennan, Ciaran Brennan, Noel Duggan and Padraig Duggan. Enya joined the group in 1980. One of the most successful exponents of Irish traditional music of the eighties, Clannad specialized in providing atmospheric compositions for television and film.

The group was formed in 1973 by Maire (harp, vocals), Pol (flute, guitar, keyboards) and Ciaran (bass, synthesizer), the children of a former showband musician, Lee Brennan, now based in Gweedore, County Donegal, in the north-west of Ireland. Noel (guitar, vocals) and Padraig Duggan (mandola, guitar) were uncles of the three Brennans, making the name Clannad (Irish for family) highly apposite.

At first singing only in Irish, the group built up support in Ireland during the seventies and toured Germany and the US. In 1980 another sister, Eithne, joined on keyboards and vocals.

After recording selections of traditional tunes for local label Gael-Linn, Clannad was commissioned to provide the music for a television adaptation of *Harry's Game*, a thriller by Gerald Seymour with a Northern Ireland setting. Composed by Pol Duggan, the haunting 'Theme from *Harry's Game*' (featuring Maire's voice) was a UK Top Ten hit in 1982. The group also recorded the album *Magical Ring* for UK release by RCA. Soon after this Eithne Brennan (Enya) left the group. Ciaran Brennan composed the film music *Robin (the Hooded Man)* which appeared on the 1984 album *Legend*. This was followed by *Macalla* (1985) with guest vocals by Bono of **U2**, who had included the *Harry's Game* theme in their stage shows. American producers Greg Ladanyi and Russ Kunkel were brought in for *Sirius* (1987), which featured contributions from **Bruce Hornsby** and Steve Perry. *Atlantic Realm* (1989) contained more soundtrack music. Pol Duggan left the group before the release of *Anam* (1990). Clannad combined with **Paul Young** to record 'Both Sides Now' for the film *Switch* (1991). Maire Brennan issued a solo album, *Maire*, in 1992 and Clannad issued *Banba* in 1993.

Enya, after leaving Clannad, linked up with Irish producer Nicky Ryan and lyricist Roma Ryan. Collectively they contributed music to the film *The Frog Prince* (1985). This was followed by a commission to record the score for a BBC television series, *The Celts* (1987). BBC Records next issued her eponymous solo album. By this time Enya and the Ryans had developed a sound based on multi-layered synthesizer backings, Roma's mix of English and Gaelic and even Latin lyrics, and Enya's ethereal, floating soprano. Newly signed to the UK branch of Warner, Enya released the single 'Orinoco Flow'. Its insistent, hypnotic sound took it to the top of the charts and the accompanying album *Watermark* (1988) became an international hit. Music from *Watermark* was used in the films *L.A. Story* and *Green Card* (both 1991).

Using the same formula, *Shepherd Moons* was issued at the end of 1991. It included the UK hits 'Book of Days' and 'Caribbean Blue' and won a Grammy award in the US where it sold over three million copies alone.

ERASURE
Vince Clarke, b. 3 July 1960, Basildon, Essex, England; Andy Bell, b. 25 April 1964, Peterborough, Northants, England

Erasure were one of the leading pop/dance acts of the late eighties and early nineties. They shared a love of camp culture and classic pop with another synthesizer-driven duo, the **Pet Shop Boys**.

When main writer and keyboard-player Clarke left **Depeche Mode** in 1982, he immediately formed the duo Yazoo with vocalist **Alison Moyet**. Yazoo split in 1983 after two successful albums, and Clarke announced his next recording project would be the Assembly, which would feature an assortment of different singers, each picked according to their suitability for a particular song. Despite initially promising results with the UK Top Five hit 'Never Never' (featuring ex-Undertones vocalist **Feargal Sharkey**) in 1983, the project never came to fruition, and instead Clarke auditioned vocalists for a new act, Erasure.

Bell, a former choirboy and singer in bands in his native Peterborough, made his recording début on the Erasure single 'Who Needs Love Like That' (1985). It was a minor hit, but the duo's début album, *Wonderland*, only just scraped into the UK Top Seventy-Five. However, the European disco success of

'Sometimes' in the summer of 1986 was a prelude to its reaching the UK Top Five later that year. The follow-up 'It Doesn't Have to Be' (1987) was another hit, and the second album, *The Circus* (1987), reached the UK Top Ten.

These early recordings were heavily slanted towards the dancefloor, as a remix collection, *Two Ring Circus*, made clear in late 1987, but Clarke's feel for pop dominated the third album, *The Innocents*, which topped the UK chart in 1988. Helped by the US Top Twenty hits 'Chains of Love' and 'A Little Respect', the album climbed into the US Top Fifty.

The EP *Crackers International* (1988) and its lead track 'Stop' continued the success, and the duo's fourth album, *Wild!*, topped the UK chart on its week of release. By now Erasure were attracting headlines for their ever more extravagant and outrageous stage shows, which mixed elements of seventies trash culture with classic vaudeville and a camp approach. 'Blue Savannah' and 'Star' gave them further hits in 1990, 'Chorus' and 'Love to Hate You' carried on the winning sequence the following year, and the album *Chorus* was another chart-topper. A 1992 **Abba** tribute EP, *Abba-esque*, was their biggest hit yet and reached No. 1 in the UK singles chart, accompanied by promotional videos which featured the duo in drag affectionately parodying the seventies group. Erasure rounded off the year by releasing the hugely successful and optimistically titled *Pop! – The First 20 Hits*, which compiled all their singles to date.

1993 was a largely quiet year for the duo, although Bell did record a version of the **Donna Summer/ Barbra Streisand** hit 'No More Tears (Enough Is Enough)' with Canadian vocalist **k. d. lang**, like him a musician championing gay rights. The following year Erasure re-emerged with *I Say, I Say, I Say*, which again topped the chart despite receiving lukewarm reviews. After the failure of the reflective *Erasure* (1995) the pair signed to **Madonna**'s Maverick records for the camp *Cowboys* (1997). *Loveboat* (Mute, 2000) was a more successful mix of their synth-pop stylings and low-key moodiness.

AHMET AND NESUHI ERTEGUN
Ahmet, b. 1924, Turkey; Nesuhi, b. 1919, Turkey, d. 15 July 1989, New York City, USA

The Erteguns were among the founders of Atlantic, the most important independent American record company of the fifties and early sixties. While most other successful record-company bosses of the period either signed a few hit acts only to see their company fold when tastes changed, or survived by operating as paymasters (**Don Robey**, **Art Rupe**, **Syd Nathan**), for the most part leaving the creative decisions to producers and A&R men, the Erteguns, like **Sam Phillips** (of Sun) and **Leonard Chess** (of Chess), were the driving force behind their company, working as talent scouts, songwriters, producers and salesmen. Furthermore, where both Sun and Chess tended to operate within limited areas, Atlantic brought R&B into the popular mainstream. In the sixties and seventies Nesuhi produced dozens of jazz albums by **John Coltrane**, the **Modern Jazz Quartet**, **Ray Charles** and others while Ahmet oversaw the label's R&B output and signed **Cream** and **Led Zeppelin** to make Atlantic a leading progressive-rock company.

The sons of a Turkish diplomat and ambassador to the United States, the Ertegun brothers were keen jazz and blues fans. In the forties they collected records and wrote for small magazines as well as promoting jazz concerts in the Washington area. When their father died in 1944, the brothers decided to remain in America. In 1946 philosophy graduate Ahmet released a few titles, mostly jazz instrumentals, on the Quality and Jubilee labels with Herb Abramson, another keen jazz collector who, while A&R director at National Records, had been responsible for signing the **Ravens** and rejuvenating the career of **Joe Turner**. The following year they formed Atlantic Records, but though aware of the potential of harder-edged R&B and jump blues, the company's first releases were again jazz instrumentals from **Erroll Garner**, Johnny Griffen and one-time **Lionel Hampton** sideman Joe Morris with a band that included Ray Charles (later to be a mainstay of the company) on piano. More significantly, Atlantic hired **Tom Dowd** as engineer. He brought a clarity to the sound of the company's releases that made them technically far superior to most independent records of the day.

In 1949 the focus switched to R&B and Atlantic had its first hits with 'Drinkin Wine-Spo-Dee-OK-Dee' (a reworking by Stick McGhee, brother of **Brownie McGhee**, of an earlier release on **Mayo Williams**' Harlem label) and **Ruth Brown**'s 'So Long', both engineered by Dowd. In search of further rough-hewn R&B, Abramson and Ahmet went on field trips to the South. Though few of these signings, with the exception of **Professor Longhair**, were commercially successful, Atlantic set about toughening up the sound of their New York signings in the light of the New Orleans music. With **Jesse Stone** as arranger and Ahmet as occasional writer (under the pseudonym Nugtre) Atlantic had some thirty Top Ten R&B hits by 1953, including records by Ruth Brown, the **Clovers**, the Cardinals ('Shouldn't I Know', 1951) and Joe Turner. Following the arrival of **Jerry Wexler** in 1953, the company began recording its acts, notably **Lavern Baker**, Ray Charles and the **Drifters**, with more sophisticated backings (and sometimes irritating choruses) that were aimed at the pop as well as R&B charts. This policy was intensified in 1956 when

Leiber and Stoller joined as independent songwriter-producers and in 1959 the company had its first American No. 1 with **Bobby Darin**'s English-language version of Bertolt Brecht and **Kurt Weill**'s 'Mack the Knife'. This led Atlantic further into the pop field with such artists as Sonny and **Cher** and Nino Tempo and April Stevens.

In 1955 Wexler and Ahmet bought out Abramson, while Nesuhi, who while living on the West Coast had recorded **Kid Ory** for his Good Time Jazz label and Shelley Manne for Contemporary Jazz, joined the company to supervise its jazz roster. Over the next fifteen years Nesuhi recorded many of the most adventurous contemporary players, including Coltrane, **Ornette Coleman**, **Charles Mingus** and Eddie Harris. The company's biggest-selling jazz artists, however, were the MJQ, whose twenty Atlantic releases he also produced.

In the sixties Atlantic consolidated its position through production and distribution deals with **Jim Stewart**'s Stax company, whose acts included **Otis Redding**, **William Bell** and **Booker T. and the MGs**. Atlantic became the label most closely associated with 'Southern soul' through further distribution deals which gave it access to the recordings of **Joe Tex**, **Percy Sledge** and **Clarence Carter**, among others. At the same time Wexler produced numerous hits for Atlantic acts, including **Aretha Franklin**, **Wilson Pickett** and **Solomon Burke** at Stax's Memphis studios and other Southern studios (notably **Rick Hall**'s).

Meanwhile, in New York Ahmet signed a number of progressive rock acts, including the **Rascals**, **Iron Butterfly**, **Vanilla Fudge** and **Buffalo Springfield**.* However, his most spectacular success in this genre came from British groups. Ahmet had established British contacts as early as 1962, when he licensed **Acker Bilk**'s million-seller 'Stranger on the Shore', but in the wake of the British invasion led by **The Beatles**, Atlantic's association with British Polydor gave it access to such artists as Cream (and **Eric Clapton**'s subsequent work), the **Bee Gees** and Led Zeppelin. From **Chris Blackwell**'s Island label, Atlantic also secured the likes of **King Crimson** and **Emerson, Lake & Palmer**. The culmination of this process came in 1970 when Atlantic acquired distribution rights to the **Rolling Stones**' own label and issued the chart-topping live recording of the Woodstock Festival on its Cotillion subsidiary.

Atlantic's new broad base was also reflected in its change of ownership. In 1967 it was bought by Warner Brothers, which in turn was taken over by the Kinney Corporation in 1969 before in 1971 the company became Warner Communications. Throughout these changes Ahmet remained in charge at Atlantic, while in 1972 Nesuhi set up WEA International to manage the Atlantic, Warners and Elektra record companies outside America, at the same time becoming a key figure in the record industry's international trade association, IFPI. In 1987 he established his own East-West label for which he produced new albums by the MJQ.

While guiding Atlantic through the seventies and eighties, Ahmet continued to produce (including eponymous albums by **Danny O'Keefe**, 1970; **Manhattan Transfer**, 1973; Apache, 1981; and **Jimmy Yancey**, *Chicago Piano Vol. 1*, 1972).

DAVID ESSEX
b. David Albert Cook, 23 July 1947, London, England

Unlike **David Cassidy** and the **Bay City Rollers**, Essex survived his days as a teen-idol through a judicious mix of film and theatre projects that broadened the base of his career.

The son of a docker, Essex played drums in the Everons in his teens before beginning an unsuccessful solo recording career in 1964 that included singles for Fontana, MCA, Pye and Decca. He covered songs by **The Beatles**, **Ray Charles** and **Randy Newman**, even recording a novelty song about mini-skirts, 'Thigh High' (Fontana, 1966). He turned to acting in 1967, appearing in *A Smashing Time* and in 1970 understudied **Tommy Steele** in pantomime. In 1971 he secured the role of Jesus in the London cast of Stephen Schwartz's rock musical *Godspell* (which opened in New York a few months after Tim Rice's and **Andrew Lloyd Webber**'s similarly themed *Jesus Christ Superstar*). He left the cast for the lead in *That'll Be the Day* (1973), an affectionate but pointed account of the days of British rock'n'roll before The Beatles, in which he co-starred with Keith Moon and **Ringo Starr**. The score was produced by **Dave Edmunds**.

He signed to CBS, where his first release, the self-penned 'Rock on'* (1973), was an international success. It gave him his only major hit in America and led to a series of British hits that established Essex as a teen-idol. Mostly written by Essex and produced by Jeff Wayne, these included: 'Gonna Make You a Star', 'Stardust' (1974) – the theme to the, lesser, sequel to *That'll Be the Day*, 'Hold Me Close' and 'If I Could' (1975), all of which were performed in a decidedly theatrical manner.

In 1978 he shook off his teen-idol image by appearing in Rice and Lloyd Webber's *Evita* as Che and had a hit with 'Oh What a Circus' (Mercury) from the musical. But his subsequent lead in the film *Silver Dream Racer* and records (which included 'Hot Love', 1980, and 'Me and My Girl [Night-Clubbing]', 1982), though successful, failed to confirm this new image. Only by the mid-eighties was he able to throw off his teen-idol past completely with 'A Winter's Tale' (1983), co-written with Rice, and his ambitious con-

cept album *Mutiny* which spawned the hit 'Tahiti' (1983). In 1985 he mounted the well-received stage musical *Mutiny*, based on the album, which took for its subject the story of the mutiny on the *Bounty*. Later records, on his own Lamplight label, included *Centre Stage* (1986), a collection of show tunes, *Touching the Ghost* (1989) and 'The River' (1988), the theme from a TV sitcom in which Essex starred.

In 1990 Essex became president of Voluntary Service Overseas and recorded a fundraising album of 'world music'. He resumed his musical career by recording a selection of his favourite pop classics, *Cover Shot*, and in 1993 he acted in Oliver Goldsmith's comedy *She Stoops to Conquer* in London's West End. Most of his records of the decade were reissues.

GLORIA ESTEFAN
b. Gloria Maria Fajardo, 1 September 1957, Havana, Cuba

With her bandleader husband Emilio Estefan, Gloria Estefan created the most popular fusion of Latin music and English lyrics of the nineties.

The daughter of a policeman, she emigrated from Cuba to Miami at the age of three. While studying psychology at the University of Miami, she became the singer with Emilio Estefan's band, the Miami Latin Boys in 1975. Accordion-player Estefan (*b. 1953*) was himself was a Cuban immigrant. The following year the group changed names to Miami Sound Machine and made its first album, *Renancer*, a collection of Spanish-language songs.

Over the next six years the Miami Sound Machine became one of the best-known groups among Latin audiences. The group's crossover to global success began in 1984 when the English-language 'Dr Beat' was a Top Ten hit in Britain. The first US pop hits came in 1986 with 'Conga' and 'Bad Boy' and in the same year the group issued its first all English-language album, *Primitive Love*. The focus of attention was now firmly on Gloria's vocals and on *Let It Loose*, the credits changed to Gloria Estefan and the Miami Sound Machine (she had married Emilio in 1978). In addition to the emphatic 'Rhythm Is Going to Get You', this album included the ballad hits 'Can't Stay Away from You' and 'Anything for You', both written by Gloria.

The lesser *Cuts Both Ways* (1989) was issued as a Gloria Estefan solo album although the backings were provided by the Miami Sound Machine. Among its hits was the US No. 1 'Don't Wanna Lose You', another Gloria Estefan composition.

Her career was interrupted in 1990 by a serious injury sustained in a road accident but she returned to touring and recording the following year. Her recovery from her injuries coloured several songs on *Into the Light* (1991), whose other songwriters included **Jon**

Secada, at this time one of Gloria's backing singers. She later co-produced Secada's début album.

By now Gloria Estefan had become one of the music industry's leading figures and she participated in several charity albums, sang at the Superbowl and was given an award for her fundraising efforts to help hurricane victims. More recent recordings include 'Christmas Through Your Eyes' (1992), co-written with **Diane Warren**, and the highly acclaimed Spanish-language collection of mostly ballads *Mi Tierra* (1993), whose guest artists included **Tito Puente**. *Hold Me, Thrill Me, Kiss Me* (1994), as its title suggested, was far more pop-orientated. A collection of cover-versions of some of her favourite songs, it was also a huge international success, selling over two million copies worldwide. She followed it with the Spanish-language Christmas album *Abriendo Puertas* (1995) and the English-language albums *Destiny* (1996) and the dance-fuelled *Gloria!* (1998). *Almo Caribena* (2000), Estefan's third Spanish-language album, saw her supported by **Ruben Blades** on selected tracks ('No Me Dejes De Querer'). Low key, it lacked the broad-based appeal of *Mi Tierra*.

SLEEPY JOHN ESTES

b. John Adam Estes, 25 January 1899, Ripley, Tennessee, USA, d. 5 June 1977, Brownsville, Tennessee

Estes' special gift as a blues singer was to use the form as if he were a local newspaper reporter, dealing with the affairs of civic leaders and others of his town's personalities, black and white. 'Now Mr Clark is a good lawyer/He's as good as I ever seen/He's the first man that proved water run upstream' runs the verse of a laconic blues about a local lawyer ('Lawyer Clark Blues', 1964).

In the 'rediscovery' period of his career he extended this coverage to include his European admirers. Few other blues artists who have survived into modern times have preserved this function, once probably commoner in Southern black culture, of community journalism. Some of country singer **Tom T. Hall**'s songs function in this way.

In the twenties Estes was active in the Memphis area, where he began a series of broken-voiced, ungainly but moving records on Victor (1929–30). He later recorded for Decca (1935–40) and Bluebird (1941). The 1935 coupling of 'Married Woman Blues'/'Drop Down Mama' was even issued in Britain soon afterwards under the sponsorship of the Jazz Appreciation Society. Little was heard of him in the forties and fifties, and it was supposed that he had died. Certainly the fragile, wailing voice on his records implied so venerable a performer and so archaic a style that it was a shock when he was discovered, in 1962, to be alive, active and not even particu-

larly old. He then made the first of a series of albums for Delmark, *The Legend of Sleepy John Estes*, accompanied by his long-time associate, harmonica-player Hammie Nixon. *Brownsville Blues* (1964), devoted to friends and patrons in his home town, exemplifies his talent for reportage. Usually partnered by Nixon, he made many appearances, from 1963 onwards, at Newport and other folk and blues festivals. They toured Europe with the American Folk Blues Festival in 1964, 1966 and 1974, in the last year also visiting Japan. In 1972 Estes guested on **Ry Cooder**'s *Boomers Story*, which included Estes' own 'President Kennedy'.

RUTH ETTING

b. 2 November 1896, David City, Nebraska, USA, d. 24 September 1978, Colorado Springs, Colorado

By turns peppy, fragile and gallant, Ruth Etting evinced the contradictory spirits of America in the Depression: sometimes beaten down, sometimes bearing up, whenever possible blithe. Her radio audience knew her as 'America's Sweetheart of Song', while Tin Pan Alley recognized her interpretative power by giving her the first chance at some of the most potent songs of the day.

At the age of seventeen she went to work in Chicago as a singer and dancer, and by the mid-twenties she was singing with bands like Abe Lyman's on radio station WLS. Signing with Columbia Records in 1926, she initially made 'flapper' numbers like 'Varsity Drag' (1927). A part in Florenz Ziegfeld's *Follies of 1927*, starring **Eddie Cantor**, gave her the show-stopping **Irving Berlin** number 'Shakin' the Blues Away', and she worked with Cantor again the following year in *Whoopee!*, which provided what was to become one of her most celebrated numbers, 'Love Me or Leave Me', by **Walter Donaldson** and **Gus Kahn**.

By this time she was one of the nation's leading recording artists, her accompaniments often buttressed by the work of jazz musicians such as **Joe Venuti**, **Eddie Lang** and **Jimmy** and **Tommy Dorsey**. Her early boop-a-doop manner, similar to that of Helen Kane, was preserved in songs like 'Button Up Your Overcoat' (1929), but she more often adopted a moaning blues style, sliding down to blue notes like a 1929 share price; 'Body and Soul' (1930) and 'Ten Cents a Dance' – her poignant saga of a dance-hall hostess, hired out 'for exactly a dime a throw', by **Richard Rodgers** and **Lorenz Hart** from the 1930 musical *Simple Simon*.

Her last *Follies* appearance was in 1931, with **Helen Morgan**, when she revived the 1908 **Nora Bayes** number 'Shine on Harvest Moon'. In 1933 she was paired with Cantor again in the film *Roman Scandals*. As well as other movie appearances (*Gift of the Gab* and *Hips, Hips, Hooray*, both 1934) she made many short films and had long-running radio shows sponsored by Chesterfields, Kelloggs and Oldsmobile. Her part in the musical *TransAtlantic Rhythm* took her, in 1936, to London, where she recorded with the bandleader Jay Wilbur.

In 1937 she ended her fifteen-year marriage to the gangster Martin Snyder, 'Moe the Gimp'. The Gimp's parting shot was at his successor-to-be, the arranger Merle Alderman, but Alderman recovered to accompany Etting to the Colorado ranch for which she gave up showbusiness. In the 1955 biopic *Love Me or Leave Me*, she was played by **Doris Day**.

EUROPE
Joey Tempest; Kee Marcello; John Leven; Mic Michaeli; Ian Haughland

Swedish hard-rock band Europe enjoyed major success in 1987 with the worldwide hit single 'The Final Countdown', but were unable to build on their initial breakthrough, and sank into relative obscurity in the early nineties.

Vocalist Tempest and bassist Leven had teamed up in the Stockholm band Force along with guitarist John Norum in 1982. They won a national talent contest for rock bands, the prize being a local recording contract, and released their eponymous début in 1983. Highly derivative of US metal acts, it was nevertheless a Swedish Top Ten hit and when the band's second album, *Wings of Tomorrow*, also charted in their homeland, they were signed to Epic Records worldwide.

Norum left the band, now renamed Europe, and with guitarists Marcello, drummer Haughland and keyboard-player Michaeli, Tempest and Leven recorded *The Final Countdown*. Sung in English, and with a slant towards AOR rather than the heavy metal of the Force albums, it attracted enthusiastic reviews from the rock press, but it was the selection of the sci-fi themed title track for the soundtrack of the Sylvester Stallone film *Rocky IV* which sealed the album's success.

Already a hit in Europe, the keyboard-dominated single reached No. 1 in the UK in late 1986 and entered the US Top Ten three months later. A second single from *The Final Countdown*, 'Carrie', was an even bigger US hit later in 1987. The album was a major international success, and the band toured extensively to promote it, but the disappointing follow-up, *Out of this World* (1988), sold poorly in comparison, although it did provide 'Superstitious', a Top Forty hit in the UK and US. A third album, *Prisoners of Paradise*, appeared in 1991, but sales were even worse than its predecessor's, despite the presence of minor hits in 'I'll Cry for You' and 'Halfway to Heaven'. Dropped by Epic, the band subsequently fragmented following the departure of guitarist Marcello.

JAMES EUROPE
b. James Reese Europe, 22 February 1881, Mobile, Alabama, USA, d. 9 May 1919, Boston, Massachusetts

Europe was the first black bandleader to record.

Raised in Washington DC, where he studied piano and violin, Europe became an assistant director of the US Marine Band and in 1904 worked in New York as a pianist. In 1906 he was musical director of *Shoo-Fly Regiment*, which was billed as 'the first real American Negro play'. It was written by Robert Cole and James Rosamond Johnson, who later compiled, with his brother James Weldon Johnson, two influential collections of spirituals, *The Book of American Negro Spirituals* (1925) and *The Second Book of Negro Spirituals* (1926). Europe formed the Clef Club Orchestra in 1910 and then the Tempo Club Orchestra as clearing houses for black musicians. Both groups soon became society favourites for their spirited (rather than sedate) syncopated playing. However, Europe did not restrict himself to dance music: in 1914 he mounted a concert featuring 125 musicians and singers at Carnegie Hall.

The same year he met dancers **Vernon and Irene Castle** and subsequently his all-black orchestra regularly supported them. With Ford Dabney, the pianist in his band, he wrote numerous dance numbers for the Castles and others, including 'The Castle Walk' and 'Castle House Rag'. Dabney is best known as the author (with Cecil Mack) of the much-recorded 'Shine' (1910), one of the few songs to have outlived the fashion for 'coon' songs in the first decade of the twentieth century.

In 1914 Europe made several sides for Victor (most billed as 'under the personal supervision of Mr and Mrs Vernon Castle'), including 'Down Home Rag' and 'Too Much Mustard', which are among the earliest recorded examples of syncopated dance music. In 1919 he recorded more titles for American Pathé. On the entry of America into the First World War, Europe was commissioned as an officer in the American army and organized a fifty-strong black infantry band. Known as 'The Hell Fighters', this band toured France with great success in 1918, playing a mix of dance music and jazzier items ('Memphis Blues', 'St Louis Blues'). Europe and the band returned to America as heroes and in March 1919 set off on an American tour that was cut short when Europe was stabbed to death in Boston after an argument with band-member Herbert Wright.

EURYTHMICS
Annie Lennox, b. Griselda Anne Lennox, 25 December 1954, Aberdeen, Scotland; Dave Stewart, b. 9 September 1952, Sunderland, Tyne and Wear, England

One of the most dynamic rock bands of the eighties, Eurythmics won a large following through the combination of Stewart's well-crafted songs and Lennox's imposing androgynous stage persona and strong, clear voice. A master of most post-**Beatles** styles of songwriting, Stewart drew on such diverse influences as **Van Morrison**, the **Sex Pistols**, the **Ramones** and **Barclay James Harvest**. He later developed a second career as a producer of such luminaries as **Bob Dylan**, **Tom Petty** and Mick Jagger of the **Rolling Stones**.

After playing in folk clubs in the north-east of England, guitarist Stewart moved to London as a member of Longdancer, a soft-rock band which recorded *If It Was So Simple* for **Elton John**'s Rocket label in 1973. When the group split up he formed the Tourists with Peet Coombes and Lennox, then a student at the Royal College of Music.

The band toured with **Roxy Music** and then signed to Logo, releasing three albums and scoring a minor hit with 'The Loneliest Man in the World' (1979) before their version of **Dusty Springfield**'s 'I Only Want to Be with You' and 'So Good to Be Back Home Again' (1980) reached the Top Ten. The Tourists dissolved later the same year and Stewart and Lennox set about organizing a new group. As Eurythmics, they recorded *In the Garden* (RCA, 1982) with German producer Conny Plank, who had handled the later Tourists tracks. That album made little impact but *Sweet Dreams (Are Made of This)* (1983) and *Touch* (1984) provided five Top Ten hits in Britain and two in America. The mysterious and insistent 'Sweet Dreams'* (an American No. 1) and 'Love Is a Stranger' were followed by 'Who's That Girl', the exultant 'Right by Your Side' and 'Here Comes the Rain Again'. They also drew large audiences for their dramatic stage show which set off Lennox's hauteur against the bearded Stewart's ringing guitar solos and darting runs. Among the backing musicians on the 1984 world tour were **Blondie** drummer Clem Burke and backing singer Eddi Reader, who later formed Fairground Attraction whose 'Perfect' (RCA, 1988) was a No. 1 hit in Britain.

Work on the soundtrack for *1984* brought the group further success with the less impressive 'Sexcrime (Nineteen Eightyfour)' (Virgin, 1984). *Be Yourself Tonight* (RCA, 1985) included the hit singles 'Would I Lie to You', the exuberant 'There Must Be an Angel', which topped the British charts, and Lennox's powerful duet with **Aretha Franklin** 'Sisters Are Doing It for Themselves' (Arista). In the same year Stewart embarked on the first of his solo projects, producing **Feargal Sharkey**'s solo album.

Eurythmics' triumphant progress continued with 'Missionary Man' and *Revenge* (1986), after which Stewart concentrated on production for Dylan, the Ramones, **Bob Geldof**, Jagger and Daryl Hall of **Hall and Oates**, as well as setting up his own Anxious label which later had British chart success with London Beat, Curve and Candy Dulfer. The group reassembled to record *Savage* (1987), which included the hit singles 'Beethoven (I Love to Listen to)' and 'I Need a Man' (1988). Lennox later recorded another duet with a soul star, reviving **Jackie DeShannon**'s 'Put a Little Love in Your Heart' with **Al Green** on the soundtrack of *Scrooged* (1988). *We Too Are One* was released the following year. It included the international hit 'Don't Ask Me Why' and was their greatest commercial success. It was also the group's last, although a greatest hits collection topped the UK chart in 1991 and *Eurythmics Live 1983–1989* appeared in 1993.

Stewart released a solo album, *Dave Stewart & The Spiritual Cowboys* (1990), which featured **Pretenders** drummer Martin Chambers, before forming a working partnership with former **Specials** vocalist Terry Hall, releasing the self-titled album *Vegas* (1992). Lennox had an international bestseller with her first solo album, the melodramatic *Diva* (1992), which saw her giving more space to her voice to good effect. She followed that with *Medusa* (1995), a collection of largely disappointing cover-versions, including **Procul Harum**'s 'A Whiter Shade of Pale'. During this time Stewart grew more interested in film, establishing his own video company, Oil Factory, and producing and directing his first film, *Honest*.

Stewart's second solo album was the disappointing *Greeting from the Gutter* (1995). He followed it with *Slyfi* (1998). Finally, in 1999, after having re-formed for a number of special occasions, the pair recorded *Peace* as the Eurythmics, which while it hardly advanced the sound they had developed in the eighties, sounded, like the **Steely Dan** reunion album of the same year, as though they had hardly been away. Although it was a big success in Europe, it did not match the sales of *Greatest Hits* (1998). Stewart's directorial début, *Honest* (2000), was received far less generously. A would-be sixties-style gangster film starring members of girl group **All Saints** and whose release was accompanied by Stewart fulminating against the state of British film criticism and journalism, it was a critical and commercial failure.

BILL EVANS
b. 16 August 1929, New Jersey, USA, d. 15 September 1980

One of the most influential modern pianists, Evans had a distinguished solo career as a recording artist. His lyrical mode was a highlight of **Miles Davis**'s classic *Kind of Blue*. Evans qualified as a music teacher at Southeastern Louisiana College before joining Herbie Fields' big band in New York. He was drafted as an army bandsman and on return to civilian life was signed by Orrin Keepnews of Riverside Records, for whom he recorded until 1962. The first Evans album was *New Jazz Conceptions*, but he also played on sessions for **George Russell** (*Jazz Workshop*, RCA, 1957) and **Charles Mingus** (*East Coasting*, Bethlehem, 1957).

In 1958 Evans spent six months in Davis's group, returning the following year to record *Kind of Blue*. He played a pivotal role in establishing the brooding, elegiac tone of the album, co-writing the supremely introverted 'Blues in Green' with Davis. He then formed his own trio with Scott La Faro (bass) and drummer Paul Motian. The Evans Trio made several albums, beginning with *Portrait in Jazz* (Riverside, 1960), but their innovative approach to free melodic interplay was abruptly ended by La Faro's death in a car crash in 1961. Evans himself continued to record with other artists, notably Russell, Cannonball Adderley and Tony Scott. *Jazz in the Space Age* (Decca, 1960) included piano duets between Evans and Paul Bley.

After 1961 there were several personnel changes in the Evans group before he settled on Marty Morell (drums) and Eddie Gomez (bass), who eventually came to rival La Faro's technique and empathy. Highlights of Evans' recording career in the sixties included *Interplay* (Riverside, 1962), with Percy Heath (bass) and trumpeter Freddie Hubbard, and *Conversations with Myself* (Verve, 1963). On this album Evans overdubbed two further piano parts on his original solo track.

In 1970 he switched labels from Verve to Columbia, playing Fender-Rhodes electric piano on *The Bill Evans Album* and reuniting with Russell for the orchestral *Living Time*. Moving to Fantasy, Evans cut duet albums with Gomez (*Intuition, Montreux III*). His last recording was the live *The Paris Concert* (Elektra, 1979).

Evans' probing approach to rhythm and harmonics made a great impact on a generation of pianists who came to the fore in the seventies. They include **Keith Jarrett**, **Chick Corea**, **Herbie Hancock** and Joe Zawinul of **Weather Report**.

GIL EVANS

b. Ian Ernest Gilmore, 13 May 1913, Toronto, Canada, d. 20 March 1988, Mexico

A versatile jazz composer and arranger, Gil Evans was best known for his collaborations with **Miles Davis**, including *Sketches of Spain* (1960).

Of Australian parentage, Evans was inspired to take up jazz piano after hearing **Louis Armstrong**'s early records. From 1933 to 1941 he played in and led various big bands in California. Moving to New York, Evans became arranger for **Claude Thornhill**'s band, whose members were to include **Gerry Mulligan** and Lee Konitz.

A one-time room-mate of **Charlie Parker**, Evans was strongly influenced by bebop and when, in 1948, Thornhill laid off his band during the recording strike led by American Federation of Musicians leader **James Petrillo**, Evans joined a band formed by Mulligan, Konitz and Davis. The resulting recordings, released as 78 rpm singles in 1950, inaugurated the 'West Coast' school of jazz. They were later reissued as the album *The Birth of the Cool* (Capitol, 1957).

During the fifties Evans worked as a freelance arranger in New York, forming bands to record the Prestige albums *Big Stuff* (1957), *The Arranger's Touch* and *Pacific Standard Time*, on which **Cannonball Adderley** was the featured soloist in Evans' versions of jazz standards such as **Thelonious Monk**'s 'Round Midnight'. The partnership with Davis was resumed in 1957 for the big-band album *Miles Ahead*, which was followed by Evans' instrumental scoring of songs from **George Gershwin**'s *Porgy and Bess* (1959) and by *Sketches of Spain*. For the latter, Evans immersed himself in flamenco and Spanish art music, adapting works by Rodrigo and de Falla, as well as composing further pieces himself.

Evans' projects in the sixties emphasized his gift for creating memorable orchestral textures of great formal strength. They included *Out of the Cool* (Impulse, 1961), *The Individualism of Gil Evans* (Verve, 1964), which featured guitarist **Kenny Burrell**, and *Gil Evans* (Ampex, 1970). Plans for Evans to work with **Jimi Hendrix** were foiled by the guitarist's death, but *Gil Evans Plays Hendrix* (RCA, 1974), with Japanese guitarist Ryo Kawasaki, provided some idea of how the original project might have sounded. The big bands he put together in the seventies included younger soloists like David Sanborn (alto sax) and Hannibal Marvin Peterson (trumpet). Evans continued to record prolifically for Enja (*Blues in Orbit*), **Chris Blackwell**'s Antilles label (*Priestess*) and RCA (*There Comes a Time*). In 1986 he wrote the period score for Julien Temple's film of Colin MacInnes' fifties' novel *Absolute Beginners*. One of his last works was an arrangement of **Jimi Hendrix**'s 'Little Wing' for **Sting**.

TOLCHARD EVANS

b. Sydney Evans, 1901, London, England, d. 12 March 1978, London

Best remembered as the composer of 'Lady of Spain', Evans was one of the most successful British songwriters of the thirties.

From a musical family, Evans studied piano in his teens. In 1916 he joined music publisher **Lawrence Wright** as an office boy, while also working as a pianist in various bands, including one led by **Billy Cotton**. He published his first song, 'Candlelight', in 1919, and in 1926 had his first hit, 'Barcelona', published by Cecil Lennox Music, the company he set up with his regular lyricists, H. B. Tilsey, Stanley Damerell and Bob Hargreaves. Many British writers of the period responded to the flood of American songs about America by imitation. Thus Wright penned (under various aliases) 'Omaha', 'The Whispering Pines of Nevada' and 'Wyoming Lullaby'. Though Evans wrote a few such songs (including 'A Message from Missouri'), he also wrote a series of sturdy ballards that attempted, with some success, to romanticize Britain in a similar manner: 'The Road to Loch Lomond' (with Tilsey, 1926), 'Dreamy Devon' (with Hargreaves and Damerell, 1930) and 'Sunset down in Somerset'.

His biggest hit was the exotic 'Lady of Spain' (with lyrics by Erroll Reaves, 1931), which was introduced by **Jack Payne** and gave **Eddie Fisher** a million-seller in 1952. Almost as successful was 'If', another million-seller when revived in the fifties by **Perry Como**. His ballad 'The Bells of Normandy' was used by the commercial station Radio Normandy throughout the thirties. Evans also wrote special material for **Gracie Fields** and **George Formby**, and novelty songs, including 'The Organ Grinder Grinds All Day' and 'Let's All Sing Like the Birdies Sing' (1932), which **Henry Hall** made into a singalong hit and was revived in a jazzed-up manner by **Buddy Greco**.

Throughout his writing career Evans ran seaside bands, notably at Southend, and in the forties and fifties was often heard on BBC radio, where his *Tuneful Twenties* series was one of the first to look back at the history of popular music. Later he was a regular guest on *The Black and White Minstrel Show* and *The Billy Cotton Bandshow* teleseries. Como's and Fisher's success with his songs revived interest in Evans. His subsequent hit songs included 'Ev'rywhere' (1955), 'My September Love' (1956) and 'I'll Find You', all big hits for British balladeer **David Whitfield**. His death came after a lengthy illness.

BETTY EVERETT
b. 23 November 1939, Greenwood, Mississippi, USA

A full-throated pop-soul singer of the sixties, Everett had a series of effervescent hits.

Everett sang gospel music before moving to Chicago in 1956. There, she first recorded in a Chicago blues style for small companies including Cobra, Won-der Ful and CJ. In 1963 she signed to major Chicago independent label Vee-Jay and had an immediate R&B and pop hit with Clint Ballard's 'You're No Good'. A pallid cover-version by the **Swinging Blue Jeans** was a British hit the following year, while **Linda Ronstadt** had an American No. 1 with the song in 1975.

Everett's declamatory style was shown to even greater effect on 'The Shoop Shoop Song (It's in His Kiss)' (1964), whose infectious chorus took the record into the Top Ten. 'I Can't Hear You' and 'Getting Mighty Crowded' were minor hits in the same year, but when Vee-Jay teamed Everett with **Jerry Butler** on the **Felice and Boudleaux Bryant** standard 'Let It Be Me', she again reached the Top Ten.

A further duet with Butler, 'Smile' (1964), was a minor success but shortly afterwards Vee-Jay collapsed and Everett moved to ABC-Paramount and Uni, where she had a flurry of hits in 1969, with 'There'll Come a Time' the most successful. In the seventies Everett recorded for the West Coast label Fantasy. 'I Got to Tell Somebody' (1971) was a minor hit. On *Love Rhymes* (1974) and *Happy Endings* (1975), she worked with leading arranger **Gene Page**. In 1991 **Cher** had a huge hit with a revival of 'The Shoop Shoop Song'.

THE EVERLY BROTHERS
Don, b. 1 February 1937, Brownie, Kentucky, USA; Phil, b. 19 January 1939, Brownie

Though their looks and their songs about teenage *angst* identified them as rock'n'rollers, the Everlys' subdued, plaintive close harmonies and rich full-chorded acoustic guitar sound were pure country. The setting of Don's tenor against Phil's high, whining harmonies placed them in a tradition that stretched back to the thirties and the **Blue Sky Boys** and the **Louvin Brothers**. The only concession to the sound of rock'n'roll in their early recordings was the backbeat supplied by producer **Chet Atkins**.

The sons of country artists Ike and Margaret Everly, who had their own family radio show (a snatch of which can be heard on *Roots*, 1968), the brothers toured with their parents and appeared on radio when Don was eight years old. At one point Don had his own radio show on the same station, KMA, Shenandoah, Ohio, *The Little Donnie Show*.

In their childhood they absorbed a store of traditional country songs, many of which they returned to on the fine *Songs Our Daddy Taught Us* (1958), recorded in the middle of their string of pop hits on Cadence. On their parents' retirement and Phil's graduation from high school the family travelled to Nashville, where Don was signed by Atkins as a songwriter. He provided **Kitty Wells** with the country hit 'Thou Shalt Not Steal' in 1954, and in 1956 the duo signed with Columbia and recorded the Atkins-produced 'Keep on Loving Me'. Columbia dropped them within a year but in 1957 manager Wesley Rose introduced them to the songwriting team of **Felice and Boudleaux Bryant**, who provided 'Bye Bye Love', an immediate million-seller on their new record label, Cadence. Most of their subsequent

Cadence recordings were written by the Bryants and were country hits, but henceforth the Everlys were promoted as pop stars.

While on Cadence they had eight Top Ten hits: 'Bye Bye Love', 'Wake Up Little Susie'* (both 1957), 'All I Have to Do Is Dream'*, 'Bird Dog'*, 'Problems'* (1958), '('Til) I Kissed You'* (1959), 'When Will I Be Loved?' and 'Let It Be Me' (1960). The songs are classics, alternately witty and aching in their treatment of teenage *angst*, but it was the forceful, intense performances of the Everlys that burned them into the memory of a generation and influenced a host of performers from **Simon and Garfunkel** and **The Beatles** to **Gram Parsons**.

Following a dispute with Cadence over royalties in 1960, they left the label for a lucrative deal with the newly formed Warner Brothers Records and moved to Los Angeles. More significantly, the duo were deprived of the songs of the Bryants. Songwriters themselves – together and individually they'd written '('Til) I Kissed You' and 'When Will I Be Loved?' and went on to write 'Cathy's Clown' and 'So Sad' (1960), and 'The Price of Love' (1965) – that didn't seem important at first. Still produced by Atkins in Nashville their first record for their new company was their biggest-ever hit, 'Cathy's Clown'*, and other records sold well. These include 'Walk Right Back'* and its lachrymose B-side 'Ebony Eyes', 'Temptation' (1961) and 'Crying in the Rain' (1962). However, the sound behind their harmonies changed decisively, becoming poppier, more melodramatic (as on their version of **Nacio Herb Brown** and **Arthur Freed**'s 'Temptation' with its garish-sounding female backing singers), and sometimes simply more powerful as on 'Cathy's Clown', but always more assertive.

Like most established American acts, the Everlys were affected by the 'British invasion' of America following The Beatles. Suddenly their sound, like their image, was old-fashioned – it had been when they started but now it seemed conclusively so – and though they had the occasional hit, including 'The Price of Love' (1965) and 'Bowling Green' (1967), their recording career declined dramatically. Their best album from this period is *Roots* (1968), which saw them looking back to the past. Still in great demand for concert appearances, particularly in Britain, which they regularly visited throughout the sixties and seventies, the brothers' relationship became increasingly acrimonious. In place of the indistinguishable halves of a harmony act, they became distinct personalities: Phil lighter and poppier, Don (who later wrote and recorded a song entitled 'I'm Tired of Singing My Songs in Las Vegas'), darker and brooding. Finally, in 1973, just after joining RCA, the pair parted company dramatically on stage and vowed never to work together again.

Both recorded several solo albums, Don for Ode and Hickory and Phil, who was the more active, for RCA, Pye and Elektra, but neither achieved significant success as solo acts. Don's work was more country inflected, Phil's biggest success coming in a duet with **Cliff Richard**, 'She Means Nothing to Me' (Capitol, 1983), just before the duo reunited for a one-off concert at Wembley, London, in which they sang their hits, still in perfect harmony, to a doting audience. The live album derived from it, *Reunion* (Impressions, 1983), saw them back in the British and European album charts for the first time in over a decade. A contract with Mercury followed and two albums produced by **Dave Edmunds**, *The Everly Brothers* (1984) and *Born Yesterday* (1985), which mixed old and new songs, were issued. Though the **Paul McCartney** composition 'On the Wings of a Nightingale' reached the British Top Ten, neither was as successful as *Reunion*, signalling the inability of the Everlys, like so many of their generation of stars, to break free from the ties of nostalgia. Nonetheless they continued recording contemporary material with critical, if not commercial, success: for example, *Some Hearts* (1989).

In 1988 a statue of the brothers was unveiled in Central City, Kentucky.

EVERYTHING BUT THE GIRL
Tracey Thorn, b. 26 September 1962, Brookman's Part, Hertfordshire, England; Ben Watt, b. 6 December 1962, London

English duo Everything But the Girl built up an international following in the eighties with a series of albums of light, jazz-influenced acoustic pop before reaching new heights of popularity after heading in a more dance-orientated direction in the mid-nineties.

Thorn and Watt met at the University of Hull in 1981, having signed independently to Cherry Red Records the previous year. After collaborating on a cover of **Cole Porter**'s 'Night and Day', the pair released critically lauded solo albums in 1982, *A Distant Shore* (Thorn) and *North Marine Drive* (Watt), both of which topped the UK Indie Chart. They ended their respective solo careers in 1983 before recording *Eden* (1984), which gave them a hit single across Europe, 'Each and Every One'.

Love Not Money (1985) and *Baby* (1986) – recorded with a full orchestra and reminiscent of **Scott Walker** and **Phil Spector** – saw the band grow in stature across Europe and begin to develop a following in the US. *Idlewild* (1988) included a version of Danny Whitten's 'I Don't Want to Talk About It', another big hit in the UK, while *The Language of Life* (1990) featured contributions from **Stan Getz** and Omar Hakim. The album brought them a hit single in Japan and America, 'Driving', which lead to their first dates in Japan and a full US tour.

After recording *Worldwide* (1991) and the *Covers* EP (expanded and retitled *Acoustic* in the US and including a version of 'Tougher than the Rest' by **Bruce . Springsteen**), Watt was suddenly hospitalized with Churg Strauss Syndrome, leading to the cancellation of another lengthy tour. Two more albums – *Home Movies* (1993) and *Amplified Heart* (1994) – and a collaboration with cult filmmaker Hal Hartley in London followed before Thorn took time out from the band to work with Bristol-based trip-hop collective **Massive Attack** on their second album, *Protection*.

Prompted by the international success of the **Todd Terry** remix of 'Missing', Everything But the Girl's eighth album had a sound more akin to Thorn's work with Massive Attack than their previous material. *Walking Wounded* (1996) became their bestselling release to date. The band took a two-year hiatus while Thorn gave birth to twins before returning with *Temperamental* (1999), which continued in the same modern dance vein as its predecessor and included the hit single 'Five Fathoms'.

EXTREME

Nuno Bettancourt, b. 20 September 1966, Azores, Portugal; Gary Cherone, b. 24 July 1961, Malden, Massachusetts, USA; Paul Geary, b. 2 July 1961, Medford, Massachusetts; Pat Badger, b. 22 July 1967, Boston, Massachusetts

Nuno Bettancourt's intricate lead guitar work combined with anthemic close harmonies and melodic compositions made Extreme a highly successful metal/funk band for the nineties.

Bettancourt moved to the USA as a child. He played with Boston band Sinful and then linked up in 1985 with ex-Dream members Cherone (vocals) and Geary (drums). Adding bass-player Badger, the group's mix of funk and heavy metal attracted a following in clubs in the Boston area.

After winning a contest run by MTV, the group signed to A&M. A self-titled début album was only moderately successful but the more stylistically eclectic *Extreme II Pornograffitti* (1991) was a big hit on both sides of the Atlantic. A concept album with the subtitle 'A Funked Up Fairy Tale', it reached the Top Twenty in Britain while Cherone and Bettancourt's acoustic ballad 'More Than Words' briefly topped the US charts. 'Hole Hearted' and 'Song for Love' provided further hits and in 1992 the group participated in the tribute to **Queen**'s Freddie Mercury at Wembley Stadium in London.

The next album, *III Sides to Every Story*, appeared in 1992. It provided further hits in 'Rest in Peace' and 'Stop the World' before the pressures of the group's frequent international tours led Geary to leave in 1994. The lacklustre *Waiting for the Punchline* followed in 1995, after which the group broke up. Cherone joined **Van Halen** while Bettancourt issued the solo album *Schizophrenic* (1997).

FABIAN

b. Fabian Forte Bonaparte, 6 February 1943, Philadelphia, Pennsylvania, USA

In legend at least, Fabian was the archetypal manufactured teen-idol. He was signed by Chancellor Records because he looked like a cross between **Elvis Presley** and **Rick Nelson**, was heavily promoted by **Dick Clark**'s *American Bandstand*, and finally, as Clyde Ankle, he was the butt of **Stan Freberg**'s satire on rock'n'roll, 'The Old Payola Roll Blues'.

His first records for the Philadelphia-based Chancellor Records, 'I'm in Love' and 'Lillie Lou' (1958), failed miserably, but 'I'm a Man' (1959) – a **Pomus and Shuman** composition sung in emulation of Presley – fuelled by a series of appearances on *Bandstand*, hit the American Top Forty. Other 1959 hits in the same mould included 'Turn Me Loose', 'Tiger' and the title song to his first film, 'Hound Dog Man', which like 'Turn' was another Pomus and Shuman song. His move to films was decisive, and though he had hits in 1960 (notably 'About This Thing Called Love' and 'Kissin'' and 'Twistin'' [co-written by **Don Kirshner**, who would help create the manufactured idols of the next generation, the **Monkees**]), he stopped recording soon after.

Although he never became a major star, Fabian, like his one-time label-mate **Frankie Avalon**, continued to work regularly in films and television (including *North to Alaska*, 1960; *The Longest Day*, 1962; *A Bullet for Pretty Boy*, 1970; and *Disco Fever*, 1978). However, neither Fabian nor Avalon appeared in *Idolmaker* (1980), the film loosely based on the career of Chancellor's founder Bob Marcucci, in which their early careers figure largely.

JOHN FAHEY

b. 28 February 1939, Takoma Park, Maryland, USA

Fahey is an idiosyncratic but influential acoustic steel-stringed guitarist, with an unusual ability to assimilate a variety of American music styles. The creator of some twenty solo albums, he also owned the independent Takoma label.

A self-taught guitarist, Fahey's first love was traditional country music before, in 1956, he discovered the blues. In his twenties, often in the company of Henry Vestine (later of **Canned Heat**), Fahey travelled through the South in search of rare blues and country recordings. These trips resulted in the rediscovery of Bukka White and **Skip James** and formed the fieldwork for his MA in Folklore and Mythology on bluesman **Charley Patton**, which was eventually published as a book, *Charley Patton* (1970).

In 1959 he recorded the first version of *Blind Joe Death*, which was issued in a revised version on his own Takoma label in 1964, by which time Fahey had settled in California. Mixing the Episcopelian hymn 'In Christ There Is No East or West' with **W. C. Handy**'s 'St Louis Blues' and his own poetically titled formal, almost stately, blues-inspired offerings, 'Transcendental Waterfall' and 'On Doing an Evil Deed Blues', the album outlined the themes that Fahey would explore in his subsequent releases. Fahey also issued albums by guitarists Leo Kottke (whose later album for Capitol Fahey would produce) and Robbie Basho on Takoma. After six albums Fahey briefly signed with Vanguard in 1967 and then Reprise in 1969 (recording the superior instrumentally augmented essay in Dixieland, *Of Rivers and Religion*, 1972), before being dropped by the label in 1974. He returned to Takoma, releasing albums regularly. *Live in Tasmania* (1981) and *Railroads 1* (1984) are representative of his later work. Showing the impact of Brazilian guitarist Bolo Sete, *Rainforests, Oceans and Other Themes* (1985) was an influence on many of the instrumentalists who saw themselves as part of the New Age school that emerged in the wake of **Will Ackerman** in the eighties. In 1987 he released *I Remember Blind Joe Death* (Rounder) and, in 1990, *God, Time and Causality* and *Old Fashioned Love* (Shanachie). While *Return of the Repressed: Anthology* (Rhino, 1996) suffers from attempting to cover so broad a spectrum in its forty-two tracks, it remains the definitive retrospective. Most of *Hitomi* (Liv-House, 2000) was very much in the style of his sixties work, with the addition of a layer of echo. However, three of the tracks, billed as being by the John Fahey Trio, included overlaid electronic sounds and saw Fahey interacting with other musicians to intriguing effect.

SAMMY FAIN

b. Samuel Feinberg, 17 June 1902, New York, USA, d. 6 December 1989, Los Angeles

A prolific composer for the movies, Fain was the author of six million-selling songs.

A self-taught pianist, Fain began his career as a vaudeville entertainer while struggling to establish himself as a songwriter. His first hit, with lyrics by **Irving Mills** and Al Dubin, was 'Nobody Knows What a Redhead Mama Can Do' (1925). In 1927 he joined up with fellow vaudevillian Irving Kahal (*b. 5 March 1903, Houtzdale, Pennsylvania, d. 7 February 1942, New York*) and the two wrote together until Kahal's death. Their first hits were 'Let a Smile Be Your Umbrella' and 'I Left My Sugar Standing in the Rain' (1927), which was featured by **Paul Whiteman**'s Three Rhythm Boys, which then included the young **Bing Crosby**. (In 1949 Crosby had a million-seller with Fain and Bob Hilliard's 'Dear Hearts and Gentle People'.)

Fain and Kahal then moved to Hollywood, where their first notable film song was 'You Brought a New Kind of Love to Me' (performed by **Maurice Chevalier** in *The Big Pond*, 1930), after which they wrote numerous songs, but only rarely full scores, for films. These include 'By a Waterfall' (sung by **Dick Powell** in *Footlight Parade*, 1933); the torch song 'That Old Feeling' (co-written with Lew Brown, of **DeSylva, Brown and Henderson**, for *Vogues of 1938*); and the title song 'I'll Be Seeing You' (1944). In 1949 Patti Andrews (of the **Andrews Sisters**) had a solo million-seller with a revival of Fain's and Kahal's 1937 composition, 'I Can Dream Can't I?'.

Fain's biggest hits came after Kahal's death and most were associated with films: the Oscar-winning 'Secret Love' gave **Doris Day** a million-seller in 1954, and was subsequently successfully revived by Kathy Kirby (Decca, 1963) in the UK, Billy Stewart (Chess, 1966), and **Freddy Fender** in 1975; the Oscar-winning 'Love Is a Many Splendored Thing' was a million-seller for the **Four Aces** (1955); 'April Love' was a million-seller for **Pat Boone** (1957); and 'A Certain Smile'* was a big hit for **Johnny Mathis** in 1958. All of these were co-written by Paul Francis Webster.

Though Hollywood-based, Fain contributed to various Broadway shows, notably Olsen and Johnson's long-running *Hellzapoppin'* (1938). Throughout the sixties and seventies Fain continued to write songs for films (including *Made in Paris*, 1965, and *The Rescuers*, 1977) and Broadway (*Something More*, 1964).

FAIRPORT CONVENTION

Richard Thompson, b. 3 April 1949, London, England; Simon Nicol, b. 13 October 1950, London; Ashley Hutchings; Alexandra 'Sandy' Denny, b. 6 January 1948, Wimbledon, d. 21 April 1978, London; Martin Lamble, b. 1950, London, d. June 1969; Ian Matthews, b. Ian Matthews McDonald, 1946, Lincolnshire; Dave Mattacks, b. 1948, London (joined 1969); Dave Swarbrick, b. 5 April 1941, London (joined 1969); Dave Pegg, b. 2 November 1947 (joined 1969); Trevor Lucas, b. 25 December 1943, Australia (joined 1972), d. 4 February

1989, Australia; Jerry Donahue, b. 24 September 1946, New York, USA (joined 1972); Bruce Rowland (joined 1975); Martin Allcock, b. 5 January 1957, Manchester (joined 1985); Ric Sanders, b. 1952, Birmingham (joined 1985)

The most important of British folk-rock bands, Fairport Convention was the starting point for the careers of such artists as Sandy Denny, **Richard Thompson**, **Ian Matthews** and the **Albion Band**.

Bass-player Hutchings from Dr K's Blues Band and guitarist Nicol from the Ethnic Shuffle Orchestra formed the group with Thompson and singer Judy Dyble in 1967. Adding drummer Lamble and vocalist Matthews (formerly of harmony group Pyramid), they became regulars at clubs like Middle Earth and UFO on London's burgeoning underground scene. The first eponymous album for Polydor reflected their club set: it included tracks by **Joni Mitchell**, **Bob Dylan** and some original songs. It was produced by **Joe Boyd**, who was to supervise the first five Fairport albums.

The first of many personnel changes came shortly after the first album's release. Dyble left to join the pre-**King Crimson** group Giles, Giles and Fripp. Her replacement was folk-club singer Denny, who brought the traditional songs 'She Moved Through the Fair' and 'Nottamun Town' to *What We Did on Our Holidays* (Island, 1969). Featuring Denny's impassioned vocals and Thompson's sinuous electric guitar lines, the album was the first British recording of folk song set to rock music.

The new emphasis on traditional music caused the departure of Matthews early in the sessions for *Unhalfbricking* (1969), and the drafting in of violinist Swarbrick (previously half of a duo with **Martin Carthy**), initially as a backing musician on 'A Sailor's Life'. The album also included Denny's classic elegy, 'Who Knows Where the Time Goes?' (later recorded by **Judy Collins**), as well as a French version of the Dylan song, 'If You Gotta Go, Go Now'. As 'Si Tu Dois Partir', it became Fairport's only hit single.

Shortly before the release of *Unhalfbricking*, Lamble was killed in a motorway accident. Almost as a therapy, Fairport threw themselves into their next project, an album consisting of traditional material only. With former dance-band drummer Mattacks and with Swarbrick now a full member of the group, *Liege and Lief* (1970), like its predecessor, was a Top Twenty hit. A new feature of their work, live and on record, was the lengthy, climactic instrumental passages featuring Thompson and Swarbrick, notably on 'Meet on the Ledge'.

At this high point of Fairport's career and influence, two key members left to pursue separate projects. Hutchings, with his own idea of how electric folk should sound, formed **Steeleye Span**, later moving on to the various versions of his Albion Band. Denny formed the folk-rock band Fotheringay (also the title of one of her best songs) with Australian guitarist-singer Trevor Lucas, whom she later married.

Full House (1970), with Birmingham bassist Pegg (formerly a member of the Uglys with seventies rock-band leader Steve Gibbons), was notable mainly for another guitar/fiddle duel on Thompson's 'Sloth', and the same line-up was caught in full flight on *Live at the LA Troubadour*, not released by Island until 1977. In 1971 it was Thompson's turn to leave for a solo career, leaving a four-piece group with Nicol playing lead guitar.

For the rest of the group's career, Swarbrick was the only ever-present member. When his ideas alone animated Fairport's recordings the results varied between an imaginative attempt to make a folk-rock concept album (*Babbacombe Lee*, 1971) and *Rosie* (1973), which contained Swarbrick's efforts at pop love songs and received unflattering reviews. By this time Nicol and Mattacks had left to join Hutchings' Albion Country Band.

By then, however, Lucas and Fotheringay guitarist Jerry Donahue had brought new energy to the band and Denny returned for *Fairport Live* (1974) with its reprise of the earlier repertoire and *Rising for the Moon* (1975), where most of the songs were Denny compositions, in the mode she had developed on three solo albums, including *Like an Old Fashioned Waltz* (1973). Like Judy Collins, Denny was impressive on songs like 'Solo', a reflective look at her professional career and private life. Early in 1976 there was another upheaval with the Denny–Lucas–Donahue faction seceding. Denny returned to a solo career for *Rendezvous* (1977) before dying from a brain haemorrhage sustained after a bad fall. Donahue played sessions and later produced a well-received solo album, *Telecasting* (1986).

With ex-**Joe Cocker** player Bruce Rowland on drums and Breton guitarist Dan ar Bras (a colleague of Alan Stivell), Pegg and Swarbrick cut the undistinguished *Gottle O'Geer*. This was the end of the Island contract and seemed to be the end of the group until Nicol returned for the impressive *Bonny Bunch of Roses* (1977), which was leased to Vertigo and was followed by *Tippler's Tales* the following year. On both, the quartet followed the classic Fairport mix of traditional and new songs. By now, however, there was little chance of maintaining the group as a permanent unit. After *Farewell Farewell* (Simons, 1979), Pegg joined **Jethro Tull** and Swarbrick concentrated on solo records like *Smiddy Burn* (Logo, 1981).

Fairport Convention played annual reunion concerts during the eighties and nineties and recorded *Gladys' Leap* (Woodworm, 1985) and *Expletive Deleted*

(1986). On the latter Ric Sanders (violin) replaced Swarbrick, by now leading a new acoustic quartet, Whippersnapper. With Martin Allcock (keyboards) Fairport released *Red and Gold* (New Routes, 1989), whose title track was a story of the English Civil War composed by **Ralph McTell**, and in 1991 they issued *The Five Seasons*. *Jewel in the Crown* (Wormwood, 1995), their first studio album in four years, was followed by *Close to the Wind* (1998) and *The Wood & The Wire* (2000), by which time only Pegg and Nicol of the original members were in the group. However, by then the albums were merely adjuncts to the regular tours in which they mixed old and new material with ease for an ever-loyal audience.

FAITH NO MORE

Roddy Bottum, b. 1 July 1963, Los Angeles, California, USA; Mike 'Puffy' Bordin, b. 27 November 1962, San Francisco, California; Billy Gould, b. 24 April 1963, Los Angeles; Jim Martin, b. 21 July 1961, Oakland, California (replaced Dean Menta, replaced by Jon Hudson); Chuck Mosley (replaced by Mike Patton, b. 27 January 1968, Eureka, California)

A San-Francisco five-piece, Faith No More were one of the first bands to successfully mix heavy rock and rap elements while finding fame across Europe and America.

Gould (bass), Bordin (drums) and Bottum (keyboards) began playing together in 1981, working with a variety of singers, including Courtney Love (**Hole**), before settling on Chuck Mosley. After recruiting guitarist Jim Martin, Faith No More recorded *We Care a Lot* (1985) for Mordam Records. The album gained positive reviews but it was *Introduce Yourself* (Slash, 1987) that broke the band, earning them a loyal fanbase.

After the departure of Mosley in 1988 Faith No More brought in vocalist Mike Patton for their third album. Helped by the success of the single 'Epic', *The Real Thing* (1989) went platinum in the US. The eclectic *Angel Dust* (1992) was a big hit in Europe and Australia but saw the band return to cult status in their homeland. Martin left the band the following year and was temporarily replaced by Trey Spruance before the band's former roadie Dean Menta took over. *King for a Day, Fool for a Lifetime* (1995) became Faith No More's bestselling album in the US, but after they recorded *Album of the Year* (1997) the band split up. *Who Cares a Lot ? – The Greatest Hits* (1998) is the definitive career retrospective.

ADAM FAITH

b. Terry Nelhams, 23 June 1940, London, England

Second only to **Cliff Richard** as a British teen-idol in

the early sixties, Faith successfully extended his career into television and film in the seventies.

As a messenger boy for a film company, Faith worked in London's Soho area, where Britain's first skiffle clubs opened. Caught up in the energy of the new music, he formed the Worried Men skiffle group in 1956. Persuaded by **Jack Good** to go solo (as Adam Faith) with promises of appearances on *6.5 Special* (Britain's first teen-orientated teleseries), he recorded two unsuccessful singles for HMV in 1958, including a cover of **Jerry Lee Lewis**'s 'High School Confidential'. Early in 1959, on the recommendation of **John Barry**, he joined the cast of the television pop series *Drumbeat* as a regular singer and after more unsuccessful singles (on Top Rank) recorded the British No. 1, 'What Do You Want' (Parlophone).

'What Do You Want' was written by Johnny Worth (under the pseudonym of Les Vandyke), a one-time member of the Raindrops vocal group, who would be responsible for most of Faith's hits. But what was notable about the record was Faith's strangely appealing weak, mannered voice with its exaggerated hiccup, and Barry's pizzicato string arrangement. Unusually, Faith's recording, when issued in America was covered by **Bobby Vee**. Both records failed there, but in the UK the song dovetailed with Faith's gaunt, melancholy appearance and set the mood for a series of similarly constructed little-boy-lost hits. These included 'Poor Me', 'Someone Else's Baby', 'How About That' (1960), 'Easy Going Me' (1961) and 'Lonesome' (1962). During this time he also experimented with films (appearing in *Beat Girl*, 1959, and *Mix Me a Person*, 1962) and in a famous televised interview with John Freeman (*Face to Face*) demonstrated an intelligence that few expected from pop singers.

With the arrival of **The Beatles** and British beat, Faith joined forces with the Roulettes (among whose members were Russ Ballard, later of Argent, and Dave Courtney) for a series of lesser hits that carried him through to 1966. These included 'The First Time', 'We Are in Love' (1963) and 'Someone's Taken Maria Away' (1965). During this period Faith had his one American hit, 'It's Alright' (Amy, 1965), a track from the British album *On the Move* (1964). His biggest British hit of this period was a cover of the **Burt Bacharach** song 'Message to Martha' (1964), originally recorded by soul balladeer Lou Johnson.

His pop career over, Faith switched to acting. In 1971 his role as the perpetual loser in the teleseries *Budgie* was widely acclaimed (though a 1988 stage musical of *Budgie* written by Don Black and Mort Shuman, of **Pomus and Shuman**, flopped) and in 1974 he co-starred with **David Essex** in *Stardust*. He returned to music with the impressive *I Survived* (Warner Brothers, 1974), and his production (with

Courtney) of his discovery **Leo Sayer**'s début album, *Silverbird* (1973). In 1978 he revisited skiffle origins by producing **Lonnie Donegan**'s comeback album, *Puttin' on the Style*. However, by the eighties Faith seemed more interested in acting. In 1980 he co-starred with **The Who**'s Roger Daltry in *McVicar* and later regularly appeared on British teleseries like *Minder*. Faith returned to recording in 1991 with *Midnight Postcards*. In 1992 the British teleseries *Love Hurts* was specially written for him. By the end of the nineties Faith had redefined yet another persona, that of financial adviser, which he had attempted at the beginning of the decade as a columnist with the *Mail on Sunday*. In that capacity in 2000 he fronted the cable television Money channel.

PERCY FAITH
b. 7 April 1908, Toronto, Canada, d. 9 February 1976

The master of lush arrangements of popular songs, Faith's 'The Theme from *A Summer Place*'* was the bestselling record of 1960 in America.

After studying at the Toronto Conservatory and playing in several Canadian Orchestras, Faith was appointed staff conductor of the Canadian Broadcasting Company in 1933. During his last years with CBC, **Robert Farnon** joined the orchestra as a trumpeter and arranger. In 1940 Faith moved to the US as musical director of *The Contented Hour* radio series and in 1950 joined Columbia Records as an arranger and conductor of the label's staff orchestra. His first major successes were with **Tony Bennett**, who recorded 'Because of You'* (1950), 'Cold, Cold Heart'* (1952) and 'Rags to Riches'* (1953) at Faith's suggestion and under his supervision. Other Columbia artists for whom he provided arrangements included **Guy Mitchell**, **Rosemary Clooney**, **Frankie Laine** and **Doris Day**.

On his own, he had hits with 'I Crossed My Fingers' (1950), 'All My Love' (1951) and 'Delicado' (1952). His recording of 'The Song from *Moulin Rouge*'* (1953), better known as 'Where Is Your Heart', which featured vocals by Felicia Sanders and had an English lyric written by William Envick to Georges Auric's melody, was the bestselling record of 1953. **Mantovani** also had a hit with the tune. After a series of minor successes, Faith had another international hit with his million-selling version of the **Max Steiner** composition 'The Theme from *A Summer Place*' in 1960.

Although he had no other major hits, Faith's albums of mood music were enormously successful throughout the sixties. The best known of the fifty or so albums he made for Columbia were *Today's Themes for Young Lovers* (1961) and *Moods* (1962), and the best known of his film scores *Love Me or Leave Me* (1955).

MARIANNE FAITHFULL
b. 29 December 1946, London, England

A pop-folk ballad singer and associate of the **Rolling Stones** in the sixties, Faithfull returned with powerful post-punk protest material in the eighties.

The daughter of an Austrian baroness, Faithfull was a student at a Reading convent school but also, through her husband-to-be John Dunbar, part of 'swinging London', when she was discovered by Stones' manager Andrew Loog Oldham. A lush arrangement by future **Gary Glitter** producer Mike Leander coupled with Faithfull's quavering soprano took the Jagger–Richard ballad 'As Tears Go By' (Decca, 1964) into the British Top Ten and the American Top Thirty (on London).

An uninspired cover of **Bob Dylan**'s 'Blowin' in the Wind' flopped, but a switch to pop ballads with **Jackie DeShannon**'s sprightly 'Come and Stay with Me' was successful on both sides of the Atlantic. In 1965 Faithfull released two albums produced by Tony Calder – *Come My Way* and *Marianne Faithfull* – and had further hit singles with **John D. Loudermilk**'s 'This Little Bird' and 'Summer Nights'.

The following year, she shifted closer to middle-of-the-road music on *Faithfull Forever*. The album included **Michel Legrand**'s 'Theme from the Umbrellas of Cherbourg' as well as the first recording of 'Hampstead Incident' by **Donovan**, a singer whose period wistfulness was reminiscent of Faithfull's own. Apart from some singles produced by Oldham and Mick Jagger and a brief appearance on a **David Bowie** television show in 1973 (they duetted on Sonny and **Cher**'s 'I Got You Babe'), Faithfull's musical career was at a standstill for a decade. The reasons were an increasing drug problem, a heavily publicized liaison with Jagger and her determination to develop an acting career. She starred in *Girl on a Motorcycle* (1968) and *Hamlet* (1970).

In 1976, backed by **Joe Cocker**'s Grease Band, she made the country-flavoured but unremarkable *Dreamin' My Dreams* for NEMS, followed by *Faithless* (1978). Galvanized by punk, Faithfull went on to record a trio of impressive albums for Island. *Broken English* (1979) included bitter versions of **John Lennon**'s 'Working Class Hero' and **Shel Silverstein**'s 'Ballad of Lucy Jordan', as well as the angry anti-war sentiments of the title track. *Dangerous Acquaintances* (1981) was co-produced by **Steve Winwood**, while *A Child's Adventures* (1983) included songs by her second husband Ben Brierley and by Faithfull herself. With **Dr John** among her accompanists, Faithfull's *Strange Weather* (1987) included a haunting remake of 'As Tears Go By'.

Blazing Away (1990) was a live recording, with a band that included **The Band**'s Garth Hudson and **Dr John**, of songs associated with various phases of her career. In the same year Faithfull took part in the Berlin performance of former **Pink Floyd** member Roger Waters' *The Wall* and she later appeared and recorded with the **Chieftains**. In 1994 she published her autobiography, *Faithfull*, which was accompanied by a career retrospective, also called *Faithfull*. She followed that with the impressive *20th Century Blues* (1997), a collection of Berlin balladry by the likes of **Kurt Weill** and Fredrich Hollander. More focused than most reworkings of the past, the collection was also more pointed than comparable offerings by **Brian Ferry** and **George Michael.** It was followed a further career retrospective, *A Perfect Stranger* (1998).

THE FALL
Mark E. Smith, b. Mark Edward Smith, 1960, Manchester, England; Martin Bramah; Karl Burns; Marc Riley

The Fall began as part of the avant-garde wing of British punk. Smith's talent for producing spiky songs with perverse titles kept the band's momentum going despite the fact that the group only ever had a cult following.

The group was formed in Manchester in 1976 by vocalist Smith and guitarist Bramah, and their first single, 'Bingo Master's Breakout' (Step Forward, 1978), was a surreal tale intoned by Smith in a lugubrious manner akin to that of Manchester punk poet John Cooper Clarke. With Burns (drums) and guitarist Riley, the group released *Live at the Witch Trials* (1979). The producer was Bob Sergeant, later responsible for albums by the Beat and **Paul Young**'s Q Tips. A live album from this period was issued by Castle in 1992 as *Totales Turns*.

With the demise of Step Forward, the Fall moved to the premier British independent label Rough Trade in 1980, releasing a series of powerful post-punk singles including 'Totally Wired', 'How I Wrote Elastic Man' and 'Man Whose Head Expanded'. By 1982, when the punningly titled *Hex Enduction Hour* was a minor hit, Bramah had left and the band included Steve Hanley (bass) and guitarists Craig Scanlon and Paul Hanley.

Smith's then wife, American guitarist Brix, joined the Fall for the bitter and bleak *Perverted by Language* (1984). She later left to form her own band Adult Net, which covered sixties songs by Strawberry Alarm Clock and the **Shangri-Las** ('Remember') but while with the Fall Brix nudged them towards pop with chilling versions of 'There is a Ghost in the House' (1987, a hit for R. Dean Taylor in 1974) and the **Kinks**' 'Victoria' (1988). Now with Beggar's Banquet, the Fall released *This Nation's Saving Grace* (1985) and *Bend Sinister* (1986). Taking its title from a Vladimir Nabokov novel, the latter continued Smith's sideways commentary on contemporary matters with songs like 'Shoulder Pads' and 'Terry Waite Says'. By now his uncompromising stance had won him a place among a wider artistic community. Modern ballet dancer Michael Clarke choreographed and performed several Fall songs while Smith's first play, *Hey Luciani*, was produced in London in 1986.

Later albums included *The Frenz Experiment* (1988) and *Extricate* (Cog Sinister, 1990) by which time Brix Smith had severed all connection with the group. Her pop sensibility was missing on *Code Selfish* (1991) but by then Smith and the Fall's career as artists looked secure. In 1993 they signed to independent label Permanent Records and released *The Infotainment Scam*, which included a typically perverse cover of **Sister Sledge**'s 'Lost in Music'. *Middle Class Revolt* (1994), the Fall's eighteenth album, was as single-minded as ever. The definitive retrospectives are the two collections of singles, *458489 – A Sides* and *458489 – B Sides* (both 1991).

GEORGIE FAME
b. *Clive Powell, 26 June 1943, Leigh, England*

The earliest British exponent of the Hammond organ, vocalist and keyboards-player Georgie Fame mingled R&B, jazz and pop ballads in a career spanning more than three decades.

Pianist Powell was renamed by impresario Larry Parnes, who signed him as a member of **Billy Fury**'s Blue Flames. Leaving Fury in 1962, the Blue Flames, with Colin Green (guitar), Speedy Acquaye (congas), Red Reece (drums) and Tex Makins (bass), gained a residency at London's Flamingo Club. For a mainly black audience which included many GIs stationed in Britain, Fame developed a repertoire of wider-ranging R&B derived from **Mose Allison**, **Jimmy Smith** and **James Brown**, as well as ska – Fame recorded **Prince Buster**'s 'Madness' and Eric Morris's 'Humpty Dumpty'. *R&B at the Flamingo* (EMI Columbia, 1964), produced by songwriter and ex-**Shadows** member Ian Samwell, captured the Blue Flames live sound at this period, while *Fame at Last* (1964) found Fame creating his own sound from such disparate influences.

In 1965 Fame had a British No. 1 and American Top Thirty hit with the jazzy 'Yeh Yeh'*, a song composed by Jon Hendricks (of **Lambert, Hendricks and Ross**), who with Allison was a formative influence on his vocal style. Further success came with 'Get Away' (1966), adapted from a television petrol commercial, and covers of **Bobby Hebb**'s 'Sunny' and Billy Stewart's 'Sittin' in the Park'. Although the Blue Flames had by now been disbanded, Fame maintained his jazz credentials by recording *Sound Venture* (1966) with the Harry South Big Band and performing live in 1967 with **Count Basie**.

Moving labels to the recently established British branch of American Columbia, Fame cut the mainstream ballad 'Because I Love You' before the jaunty 'The Ballad of Bonnie and Clyde'* (1967). Written by **Mitch Murray** and Peter Callander, it was inspired by Arthur Penn's successful film. *The Faces of Fame* (1967) and *Third Face of Fame* (1968) were less effective attempts to present him as a glossy ballad singer, supported by the pick of British jazz instrumentalists, including **Ronnie Scott** and **John McLaughlin**.

Live performances and advertising jingles were more important than recording in Fame's work during the seventies, though a cabaret partnership with ex-**Animal** Alan Price yielded a hit with the catchy 'Rosetta' (1971). He recorded intermittently for Reprise, Island, Pye and Piccadilly and toured regularly with an enlarged Blue Flames, re-formed in 1974 and featuring trumpeter Eddie Thornton.

In Hoagland 81 (Bald Eagle, 1981) was the realization of a long-cherished project, a tribute to songwriter **Hoagy Carmichael**, which included vocals by Annie Ross. With bandleader Keith Smith, Fame turned the concept into a stage show, *Stardust Road* (1985). Its success led to a similar tribute to **George Gershwin**, *On 10th Avenue* (1986). His interest in Latin music was reflected in the release of an English-language version of Gilberto Gil's 'Sambo (Toda Menina Baiana)' (Ensign, 1986).

From 1989 on Fame regularly toured with **Van Morrison** as his musical director and played on several of his albums, including *Avalon Sunset* and *Too Long in Exile* (1993). Morrison returned the favour in 1991 on *Cool Cat Blues*, duetting with Fame on a version of 'Moondance'. The bulk of the album consisted of reworkings of songs associated with Fame, notably a reggae version of 'Yeh Yeh'. Subsequent Fame solo outings included *The Blues and Me* (1994), *Three Line Whip* (1995) and the collaboration with Mose Allison, *Tell Me Something* (1997).

FAMILY
Roger Chapman, b. 8 April 1944, Leicester, England; Ric Grech, b. 1 November 1946, Bordeaux, France, d. 17 March 1990, Leicester (replaced by John Weider, b. 21 April, 1947, replaced by John Wetton, b. 12 July 1949, Derby, England); Jim King, b. 1947, Northamptonshire (replaced by John 'Poli' Palmer, b. 25 May 1943); Rob Townshend, b. 7 July 1947, Leicester; Charlie Whitney, b. 24 June 1944, Skipton, North Yorkshire

Family were one of the more idiosyncratic British progressive rock bands of the sixties. After the group's demise, none of its individual members achieved comparable success.

The group rose from the ashes of Jim King and the Farinas, a Leicester soul band, in 1967. It drew audiences on the club and college circuit because of its unusual line-up – Grech played electric violin as well as bass, and guitarist Whitney drew on Indian musical forms in his compositions – and lead singer Chapman. Described by underground press luminary Richard Neville as resembling 'a demented Trotskyite with incredible stoned madman's eyes', he had a harsh, whinnying singing style to match.

From its sleeve design to Chapman's lucid and poetic lyrics, and dealing unblushingly with such issues as the meaning of life, *Music in a Doll's House* (Reprise, 1968) was a classic of the era, becoming a minor hit. The next three albums all reached the Top Ten: *Family Entertainment* (1969), with its hit single 'The Weaver's Answer', the live *A Song for Me* (1970) and *Anyway* (1970), which included Family's biggest hit, 'In My Own Time'. By now, multi-instrumentalist King and Grech had left, the latter to join **Steve Winwood** and **Eric Clapton** in Blind Faith. He later played with the **Crickets** and **Gram Parsons**. The replacements in Family, Palmer from Blossom Toes and bass/violin-player Weider from the **Animals**, brought a jazz influence and in 1971 the band appeared at the Montreux Jazz Festival.

Fearless (1971) included a song about the Irish situation ('Blind') and a four-part *a cappella* harmony on 'Larf and Sing'. The 1972 album *Bandstand* provided a British hit in 'Burlesque', but Family suffered further personnel changes with Palmer leaving in 1972 and John Wetton briefly replacing Weider before himself moving on to join **King Crimson**. The ever-present Chapman, Whitney and drummer Townshend recruited Jim Cregan and Liverpool veteran Tony Ashton (keyboards) for what was to be Family's last album, *It's Only a Movie* (Raft, 1973).

After the band split up in 1974, Ashton and Townshend joined Medicine Head, originally a two-man group recording for disc-jockey John Peel's Dandelion label. Ashton produced the hit single 'Slip and Slide' (Polydor, 1974). From 1974 to 1977 Chapman and Whitney cut five albums for Reprise and Vertigo (four under the name Streetwalkers), of which *Red Card* (Vertigo, 1976) was the most successful. Now one of the grand old men of British rock, Chapman recorded as a soloist for Arista (including *Chappo*, 1979) and RCA (*The Shadow Knows*, 1984) before moving to Germany, where he continued to record, usually with veteran guitarist Geoff Whitehorn, who became a member of **Bad Company** in the early nineties. Chapman was also a guest vocalist on **Mike Oldfield**'s *Island* (1987). Whitney and Townshend were members of Axispoint, an unimpressive rock band which made two albums for RCA in the late seventies. Townshend later joined the Blues Band fronted by ex-**Manfred Mann** singer Paul Jones.

Members of Family were the inspiration for characters in Jenny Fabian's thinly fictionalized memoir, *Groupie – A Sex-rock Odyssey* (1970).

FRANK FARIAN
b. 1942, Germany

One of Europe's most experienced pop producers, in **Boney M** and Milli Vanilli Farian twice created groups which successfully exploited current tastes in European dance music.

In the early sixties he led a beat group named after the British band the **Shadows** before moving to soul music and ballads. Recording for Hansa, he had several minor hits, including 'Dana My Love' (1972) and 'Rocky' (1976).

By the mid-seventies acts like Silver Convention had inaugurated a Euro-disco trend which Farian joined by producing 'Baby Do Ya Wanna Bump' with session musicians using the name Boney M. He subsequently recruited members to perform and record as Boney M, which had a five-year series of pan-European hits. Farian also produced disco singles by Eruption.

He was less active in the early eighties but he returned in 1987 with a new studio-created sound, that of Milli Vanilli. Beginning with 'Girl You Know It's True' and 'Baby Don't Forget My Number', Milli Vanilli's tracks were pop and dance hits in the USA as well as Europe. For public appearances, the group comprised Rob Pilatus and Fabrice Morvan. After the duo publicly claimed to have performed on Milli Vanilli recordings, Farian admitted that they hadn't. This led to the collapse of the group, although Farian next issued records by the Real Milli Vanilli which comprised the actual studio singers, Charles Shaw, Johnny Davis and Brad Howell.

In 1994 he issued a version of **Steely Dan**'s 'Rikki Don't Lose that Number' with Robin McCauley and he celebrated his twenty-fifth year in music with a *Greatest Hits* album.

RICHARD AND MIMI FARINA
Richard Farina, b. 1937, New York, USA, d. 30 April 1966, Carmel, California; Mimi Farina, b. Mimi Baez, 30 April 1945

The Farinas were pioneers of folk-rock whose work was distinguished by Richard's voluble, articulate lyrics and strong vocal harmonies. Also a novelist, Richard's cult book *Been Down So Long It Looks Like Up to Me* was published shortly before his death in a motorcycle accident.

Of Irish–Cuban parentage, Farina visited both countries before becoming an advertising copywriter and joining the Greenwich Village folk scene in the late fifties. Through **Carolyn Hester**, whom he married in 1960, Farina took up the dulcimer and began songwriting. His first recordings were made in London for Doug Dobell's Folklore label with Ric von Schmidt and **Bob Dylan** (billed as Blind Boy Grunt). *Dick Farina and Eric von Schmidt* (1963) included Farina's 'Christmas Island' and 'London Waltz'. He later appeared, with David Blue and Patrick Sky, on *Singer/Songwriter Project* (Elektra, 1964).

Now separated from Hester, he married and worked with Mimi, who shared the crystalline vocal quality of her elder sister **Joan Baez**. They appeared together at the 1964 Big Sur folk festival, after which they recorded *Celebration for a Gray Day* (Vanguard, 1965) which contained 'Pack up Your Sorrows' and 'Reno Nevada', the first of several Richard Farina compositions revived by **Ian Matthews**. Others were 'Hard Lovin' Loser' and 'Morgan the Pirate'.

Among the songs on *Reflections in a Crystal Wind* (1966) were the uncompromising 'Agitation Sell-Out Waltz' and 'Children of Darkness', later recorded by Joan Baez. Two years after Richard Farina's death, a further album, *Memories*, was released.

Mimi Farina later recorded with songwriter Tom Jans for A&M (*Take Heart*, 1971) before forming Bread and Roses, a music group named after James Oppenheim's feminist poem. Farina's setting of the poem was the title track of a **Judy Collins** album (1976) while Mimi also played on *Where Are You Now My Son?* (1972) by Joan Baez.

ROBERT FARNON
b. 24 July 1917, Toronto, Canada

Like **Eric Coates**, a highly successful composer of light music, Farnon was also an arranger and conductor who worked with **Frank Sinatra**, **Sarah Vaughan**, **Peggy Lee** and **Tony Bennett**, among others.

The son of a clothier, Farnon was educated at the Toronto Conservatory. By the time he was twenty-one, he was the lead trumpet and an arranger for **Percy Faith**, had written a symphony and was playing jazz with **Dizzy Gillespie** and **Charlie Parker**. Though most of his work since has been in the light classical field, it is this breadth of experience that distinguishes Farnon's work. During the Second World War, he went to Britain as conductor of the Canadian Band of the American Expeditionary Forces and settled there afterwards, writing numerous movie scores for Herbert Wilcox–Anna Neagle productions.

Like Coates, he wrote much mood music, including 'Jumping Bean', 'Westminster Waltz' and 'State Occasion', a piece that often accompanied newsreel of the Royal Family. In the fifties he released a series of albums of musical suites on Decca that were characterized by their superior arrangements. These included *Canadian Impressions, Songs of Britain* and *From the Highlands* (1957). His own setting of **George**

Gershwin's *Porgy and Bess* (1966) features probably his best jazz scoring. His music was arranged for brass bands and he conducted brass bands in programmes of his own works.

Throughout his career Farnon wrote film music. Among his scores were those for *Captain Horatio Hornblower* (1950), *Lilacs in the Spring* (1951), *The Truth About Spring* (1961), the satire on rock'n'roll *Expresso Bongo* (1959) and *Shalako* (1968). In the early sixties Farnon settled on the island of Guernsey and devoted himself to symphonic writing, before returning to arranging and conducting in the seventies and eighties, often in support of singers like Lee and Bennett (for whom he created a symphonic backdrop when he sang in London in 1986).

WES FARRELL
b. 1940, New York, USA

A songwriter, publisher, producer and label-owner, Farrell was an important behind-the-scenes figure in sixties pop and seventies disco music.

Hearing the blues while a Florida college student led Farrell to chose the music industry for a career. He became a Brill Building songwriter in New York, writing 'Boys' with Luther Dixon. The song was recorded by the **Shirelles** in 1962 and covered by the **Beatles** on their début album. The following year, Farrell set up his own publishing company, signing **Neil Diamond**, **Chip Taylor**, and Tommy Boyce and Bobby Hart. His own compositions from this time included 'Come a Little Closer' for **Jay and the Americans** and, with **Bert Berns**, 'Goodbye Baby (Baby Goodbye)' for **Solomon Burke** and 'My Girl Sloopy'. The latter, variously titled as 'Hang on Sloopy', was recorded by more than 150 artists and provided hits for the Vibrations, the **McCoys** and **Ramsey Lewis**.

Farrell's production company moved into bubblegum music in 1967, scoring one-off hits with 'Come on Down to My Boat' (MGM, 1967) by Every Mother's Son and 'Worst That Could Happen' (Buddah, 1969) by Brooklyn Bridge, featuring Johnny Maestro, lead singer of the **Crests**. More consistent hit-makers for Farrell were the **Cowsills** and the Partridge Family, the spin-off group from the teleseries sit-com that in turn spawned **David Cassidy**, whose 1972 hit 'Could It Be Forever' was co-written by Farrell.

In that year he formed his own label, Chelsea, and had a million-seller with its first release, Wayne Newton's lugubrious ballad, 'Daddy Don't You Walk So Fast'. More typical of Chelsea's output were the disco hits 'I'm Doin' Fine Now' (1973) by New York City and Disco Tex and the Sex-o-lettes' 'Get Dancin'' (1974). Further Chelsea successes included the Australian group Jigsaw, while its sister label Roxbury released records by Dee Clark and Jean Knight, as well as early sides by **Rick Springfield**. The labels folded in 1976.

Farrell later formed the Music Entertainment Group, whose subsidiaries included the contemporary Christian Benson Music Group.

FATBOY SLIM
aka Norman Cook, b. Quentin Cook, 31 July 1963, England

Under a variety of names and guises, DJ, remixer and producer Norman Cook's cheerfully versatile talent has provided a party soundtrack for the 1990s.

Cook grew up in Surrey, and began DJing as a student in Brighton. He first came to the public's attention as bass player in the Housemartins, who enjoyed chart success in the late 1980s. The first hint of his more dance-orientated future career came when Cook teamed up with D-Mob's Danny D as Double Trouble. The pair drew on samples from the **Jackson Five** and **Kool and the Gang** for their remix of **Eric B & Rakim**'s 'I Know You Got Soul', which was a Top Twenty hit in the UK in 1988.

With the Housemartins disbanded, Cook formed the loose Beats International collective, which enjoyed a UK No. 1 hit with 'Dub Be Good to Me' in 1990. The track was a good example of Cook's skills in utilizing parts of old songs to create something new, in this instance spicing up a cover of the SOS Band's 'Just Be Good to Me' with the bassline from the **Clash**'s 'Guns of Brixton'. Beats International went on to record two albums for Go! Discs, *Let Them Eat Bingo* (1990) and *Excursion on the Version* (1991), but failed to repeat the single success of 'Dub'.

After the demise of Beats International, Cook next joined forces with former Microgroove brass player and vocalist Ashley Slater to form Freakpower. Taking less of a pastiche approach than with Beats International, and attempting more genuine acid jazz-style songwriting, the pair released an album, *Drive Thru Booty*, on Island in 1994. The set contained the massive hit 'Turn on Tune in Cop out', whose commercial success was helped by its use in a Levi's ad campaign.

During a break from Freakpower's recording and touring, Cook embarked on yet another project, recording an album of party house tunes under the name Pizzaman. *Pizzamania* (1995) contained more pop and club hits, notably 'Sex on the Streets' and 'Happiness'.

Freakpower reassembled in 1996 for *More of Everything for Everybody*, which was popular in the clubs, but which Island did not heavily support or promote. Cook formed Skint Records in 1997 as the vehicle for his next incarnation, Fatboy Slim. Cook was a promi-nent figure within the UK's 'big beat' movement, DJing regularly at Brighton's Big Beat Boutique club nights, and his work as Fatboy Slim represented the apogee of this sound – crashing hip-hop beats, memorable, cut-up vocal samples and a rich mélange of musical accompaniment, from punk guitar to classical strings. *Better Living through Chemistry* (1997) sold reasonably and attracted good reviews, but it was 1998's *You've Come a Long Way, Baby* which gave Cook a seat at pop's top table. The first single from the album, 'Rockafella Skank', was a mammoth international hit, and was followed by three other huge single successes – 'Gangsta Tripping', 'Praise You' and 'Right Here Right Now'.

Cook's profile was also helped by his remix work – his remix of Cornershop's 'Brimful of Asha' was a UK No. 1 hit. Cook's sound seemed almost inescapable at times during 1998 and 1999, with his music also used enthusiastically in television and advertising. Soon after the release of *You've Come a Long Way, Baby*, his most commercially successful album, he married UK DJ Zoe Ball. The pair were often put forward as the presentable face of the new rock aristocracy of the era, in contrast to **Spice Girl** Posh and Manchester United footballer David Beckham.

ALICE FAYE
b. Alice Jeanne Leppert, 5 May 1912, New York, USA, d. 9 May 1998

With her hourglass figure, husky speaking voice, vibrant contralto and open smile, Faye was a major star of the thirties musical film.

The daughter of a policeman, Faye joined the Chester Hale Dance Group at the age of fourteen and the chorus of *George White's Scandals* in 1931. She was spotted by the show's star **Rudy Vallee**, who invited her to tour with his band and secured her the lead in the 1934 film version of *Scandals*. Seen initially as a Jean Harlow clone by Fox, she established herself in a series of wisecracking musicals before appearing in 1938 in a pair of melodramatic turn-of-the-century musicals. The first, *In Old Chicago*, was less notable than *Alexander's Ragtime Band*, a frothy confection constructed around some twenty songs by **Irving Berlin**, including 'Now It Can Be Told', 'Blue Skies', 'A Pretty Girl Is Like a Melody', 'Say It With Music' and 'Heat Wave'. These were followed by a string of similarly nostalgic period productions, climaxing in *Tin Pan Alley* (1940), in which Faye introduced **Harry Warren**'s 'You Say the Sweetest Things, Baby', before she was replaced, after a series of disputes with the studio, by Betty Grable, whose more aggressive image better suited the times.

Faye briefly retired before returning for two big successes, *Hello Frisco Hello* (1943), in which she introduced Warren's 'You'll Never Know', singing the song over the phone to John Payne, and *The Gang's All Here* (1943). After the disastrous *Fallen Angel*, she quit Hollywood in 1945. She occasionally performed with her husband, bandleader **Phil Harris**, throughout the fifties and, in 1962, returned to the screen as **Pat Boone**'s mother in the remake of *State Fair* and, in 1973, to Broadway for a successful revival of *Good News* with former screen lover Payne.

LEONARD FEATHER
b. 13 September 1914, London, England, d. 22 September 1994, New York, USA

Feather was the best-known and most influential jazz critic in America for almost fifty years. He also composed hundreds of jazz and blues numbers, produced many recording sessions, lectured, adjudicated in jazz competitions and wrote several books, including standard jazz reference works.

In his youth, while still living in England, he wrote for *Melody Maker* and other musical journals. He first visited the US in July 1935, where he became acquainted with **John Hammond** and **Milt Gabler**. Back in England, he produced recordings by Benny Carter (1936) and various British bands, often composing or arranging the repertoire and sometimes playing piano.

In 1939 he went to live in the US (he became a citizen in 1948) and contributed prolifically to the music papers *Metronome* and *Down Beat*, as well as to *Esquire*, with whose annual jazz poll he was associated from 1943. Throughout the forties he was heavily involved in recording work, producing **Charlie Parker**, **Dizzy Gillespie**, **Coleman Hawkins**, **Art Tatum**, **Duke Ellington**, **Louis Armstrong**, **George Shearing** and many others. He wrote **Dinah Washington**'s hits 'Evil Gal Blues' (Mercury, 1943) and 'Baby Get Lost' (1949), produced **Helen Humes**, and supervised a number of sessions by all-women bands which have become recognized as historically important. These include the International Sweethearts of Rhythm (*Girls in Jazz*, RCA, 1944) and the Beryl Booker Trio (*Cats vs Chicks*, MGM, 1954). He also championed bop and other developments in jazz, against the current of critical opinion.

An indefatigable journalist, Feather conducted his 'Blindfold Test', in which a musician comments on unidentified records, in *Down Beat* for more than thirty-five years. After 1965 he contributed a widely syndicated jazz column to the *Los Angeles Times*. He also compiled, with Ira Gitler, *The Encyclopedia of Jazz* (1960), *The Encyclopedia of Jazz in the Sixties* (1966) and *The Encyclopedia of Jazz in the Seventies* (1976). The autobiographical *The Jazz Years: Earwitness to an Era* was published in 1986.

CHARLIE FEATHERS
b. Charles Arthur Feathers, 12 June 1932, Myrtle, Mississippi, USA

Though never commercially successful, Feathers was an influential rockabilly stylist who benefited from the revival of interest in the genre in the seventies. So easily identifiable are the components in his union of black blues styles and country boogie that if he did not exist, musicologists would have been tempted to invent him in order to explain the origins of rockabilly.

The son of tenant farmers, Feathers learned guitar from Junior Kimbrough, a black sharecropper, and developed a style he called 'bluegrass rock'. It was one of several variants on the mix of black and white Southern musics that was to emerge as rockabilly from **Sam Phillips**' Sun Records studios in Memphis, where Feathers worked in the mid-fifties as session musician, songwriter and arranger. He made the demo disc and was co-author of 'I Forgot to Remember to Forget', recorded by **Elvis Presley** in 1955.

Feathers' own recording career began with two country singles in 1954–5 for Philips before he moved to Lester Bihari's Meteor label, cutting one record as Jess Hooper before releasing 'Tongue Tied Jill' (1956). Inspired by a stammering telephone operator, this novelty song introduced Feathers' unique repertoire of vocal gymnastics, with nonsense syllables and falsetto shrieks.

Though his singing influenced other Memphis artists and his songs (like 'Get with It' and 'Gone Gone Gone') were frequently recorded, Feathers himself drifted from label to label over the next fifteen years. From Meteor he went to King, Kay, Walmay, Memphis and in 1968 to Tom Phillips' Philwood ('Stuttering Cindy') and to Holiday Inn, a shortlived Sam Phillips label financed by the hotel company.

In the seventies he was 'rediscovered' by a new generation of record collectors. A British television documentary on Feathers led to records for small labels like Rollin' Rock, Barrelhouse, and his own Feathers. In Britain, Polydor reissued his Meteor singles with those of fellow cult hero Mac Curtis on *Rockabilly Kings* (1974) while *Rockabilly's Main Man* (Charly, 1978) was a selection of tracks documenting his career. Feathers continued to perform into the eighties in the Memphis area with his son Bubba on guitar and his daughter Wanda on backing vocals. In 1991 he once more played the historian when he recorded an eponymous album for Elektra's American Explorer series which encapsulated the genesis of rockabilly.

JOSE FELICIANO
b. 10 September 1945, Lares, Puerto Rico

A guitarist and jazz-tinged singer, Feliciano had twin

careers in Latin music and middle-of-the-road pop. His successful attempt to cross over to an English-language audience preceded those of **Julio Iglesias**, **Freddy Fender** and **Reuben Blades**.

Blind since birth, Feliciano moved with his family to Harlem in New York in 1950, making his first public appearance four years later. His varied early influences included soul singers **Sam Cooke** and **Ray Charles**, guitarists Luis Bonfa and **Django Reinhardt**, and pop vocalist **Frankie Laine**. Appearances in Greenwich Village folk clubs led to a recording contract with RCA in 1964. The novelty single 'Everybody Do the Click' was followed by *The Voice and Guitar of Jose Feliciano* (1965) and a series of recordings for the Latin market.

Feliciano made his first impact on English-speaking audiences in 1968 with a jazzy version of the **Doors**' 'Light My Fire' from *Feliciano!*, an album of cover-versions on which he was backed by West Coast jazz stalwarts Ray Brown (bass) and Jim Horn (flute). A rendition of Tommy Tucker's R&B song 'Hi Heel Sneakers' was also a hit in 1968. In that year he had major hits in Latin America with 'La Copa Rota' and 'Amor Gitana' and recorded in Argentina (*Una Voz, una Guitarra*), Venezuela (*Voz y la guitarra de Jose Feliciano*) and Mexico (*Mas Exitos des Jose Feliciano*). Less successful was his unconventional rendering of 'The Star-Spangled Banner' at the baseball World Series. With his wife and manager, Hilda Perez, he wrote 'Rain', a British hit for Bruce Ruffin in 1971.

By now established as a skilful, if mannered, interpreter of English-language material, Feliciano swiftly graduated to guest spots on mainstream television and Las Vegas nightclubs. His Latin audiences remained equally important, however, and for most of the seventies Feliciano had a television show syndicated throughout Latin America and the United States. After signing to Motown in 1980 he became the figurehead of the Latino label, cutting such albums as *Escenas de Amor* (1982) and *Los Exitos de* (1984). In 1987 he was nominated for a Grammy award in the Latin Pop category, for 'Lelolia'.

In 1972 Feliciano opened his own recording studio, and went on to attempt to recapture his earlier recording success by using such producers as Steve Cropper (*Compartments*, 1973) and **Jerry Wexler** and Barry Beckett (*Sweet Soul Music*, Private Stock, 1976). For *Romance in the Night* (1983) he was reunited with Rick Jarrard, producer of his early hits.

During the eighties Feliciano made a much greater impact with his Spanish-language recordings, which included *Escenas de Amor* (1983), *Tu Immenso Amor* (1987) and *Cielito Lindo* (1990). He won three Grammy awards for best Latin pop performance. Among his later English-language albums were *I'm Never Gonna Change* (1989), the jazz-styled *Steppin'*

Out (1990) and *Street Life '92* (1992). He followed that with the double-CD *The Big Three-O* (Fragile, 1996) before once again signing to a major label for *El Americano* (PolyGram, 1997).

FREDDY FENDER
b. *Baldemar G. Huerta, 4 June 1936, San Benito, Texas, USA*

Johnny Rodriguez was the first Chicano (Mexican-American) to achieve success in the country charts with 'Pass Me By' (Mercury, 1972). However, despite Rodriguez's occasionally dropping into Spanish, the dominant influence on him was **Merle Haggard**. In complete contrast, Fender, who hit both the country and pop charts with 'Before the Next Teardrop Falls'* in 1975, never deserted the rich amalgam that is Tex-Mex music. His speciality was the *conjunto*, a polka–waltz hybrid.

Born in a border town, Fender heard country, blues and Mexican music in his youth. In 1957 he turned professional (adopting the name Fender) and recorded for Duncan, a local San Antonio label. Records from this period include a Spanish version of **Elvis Presley**'s 'Don't Be Cruel' (1958), the rockabilly-styled 'Holy One', the original version of his own composition 'Wasted Days and Wasted Nights' (1959) – a local hit – and 'Crazy, Crazy, Baby' (1960). In 1960 a three-year jail sentence for possession of marijuana curtailed his career.

On his release from jail, he played the beer and tamale circuit, retiring for several years from 1969, before securing a contract with **Huey P. Meaux** in 1974. The combination of Meaux's productions, which mixed pedal-steel guitar, harpsichord and accordion, and Fender's choked, intense vocals made hits of 'Teardrop' and a remake of 'Wasted Days and Wasted Nights'* (ABC, 1975) – which Fender fittingly dedicated to his long-time friend, **Doug Sahm**. Other pop hits included an unlikely version of the **Doris Day** hit 'Secret Love' and a fine remake of the **Barbara Lynn** hit 'You'll Lose a Good Thing' (both 1975). Fender's later success has been restricted to the country charts (since 1979 on Meaux's Starflite Records and 1982 on Warner Brothers) with the likes of 'I'm Leaving It All Up to You' (1978) and 'Please Talk to My Heart' (1980). In 1987 he appeared with **Reuben Blades** in Robert Redford's film, *The Milagro Beanfield War*.

Since then he has increasingly concentrated on regional material in Spanish, while recording with Tex-Mex supergroup the Texas Tornados, whose other members are Doug Sahm, **Flaco Jimenez** and Augie Meyers (*Texas Tornados*, 1990, *Zone of Your Own*, 1991, and *Hangin' on a Thread*, 1993). In 1994 he signed with Arista as a solo artist.

LEO FENDER
b. 10 August 1909, Buenoa Park, California, USA,
d. 21 March 1991, Fullerton, California

Les Paul built the first solid-body electric guitar, but
it was Fender who built the first widely available
model, the Broadcaster, better known under its later
name, the Telecaster, a key element in both country
music and the sound of rock'n'roll.

A California-based guitar and amplifier manufacturer, Fender was continually asked by forties musicians to give them more volume and help them
eliminate screech and feedback. Independently,
Fender, Paul and Paul Bigsby (who built **Merle Travis**
his first solid-body guitar) came up with the solid
body as the solution. Fender's, christened the Broadcaster when it entered mass production in 1948, was
particularly known for its sharpness and attack and
found immediate favour with country musicians.
Guitarist Arthur Smith had an influential country hit,
'Guitar Boogie', with a prototype Broadcaster in 1947.
In 1950 the name was changed to Telecaster, and the
guitar has remained in production with few changes
since. In 1951 Fender introduced a solid body bass and
in 1956 the futuristic Stratocaster.

Fender sold his company to CBS in 1965 and in
1980 founded G&L Musical Products Ltd. In 1993 the
Stratocaster's fortieth birthday was celebrated in
Britain, with an all-star concert and a television docu-
mentary featuring Hank Marvin of the **Shadows**, **Eric
Clapton** and others.

Among those who have favoured the Telecaster are
James Burton, **Buck Owens**, Roy Nichols (the guitarist with **Merle Haggard**), Roy Buchanan, Stax session man Steve Cropper, and **Jeff Beck** (who coaxed
feedback from it). Stratocaster users have included
Buddy Holly, Marvin, Clapton and **Jimi Hendrix**.

KATHLEEN FERRIER
b. 22 April 1912, Higher Walton, Lancashire, England,
d. 8 October 1953, London, England

One of the most beloved singers of her times, Ferrier,
with her rich contralto, was equally at ease in opera,
lieder, oratorio and folk song.

The daughter of a schoolmaster, she studied piano
and in 1937 won the Carlisle Rose Bowl Festival.
Encouraged by Malcolm Sargent, she moved to London in 1942, and spent four years studying voice with
Roy Henderson. Benjamin Britten wrote the name
part in his opera *The Rape of Lucretia* for her and she
appeared in the role at Glyndebourne in 1946. After
this, she was in constant demand for concert tours,
operas and recording. Signed to Decca, she won popular success with her folk songs (notably her tender
recording of 'Blow the Wind Southerly' and her lilt-

ing version of 'My Bonny Lad', both of which were
staples of the seminal fifties radio programme *Two
Way Family Favourites*) and critical success for her
interpretations of Mahler and Gluck. She was stricken
with cancer in 1951 and died soon after her triumph in
Gluck's *Orpheo* in 1953, at Covent Garden.

BRYAN FERRY
b. 26 September, 1945, Washington, Tyne and Wear,
England

Lead singer and principal songwriter of **Roxy Music**,
Bryan Ferry pursued a parallel solo career from the
mid-seventies onwards.

His first album, *These Foolish Things* (Island, 1973),
was an eclectic selection of standard ballads and rock
songs, ranging from the title track, Eric Maschwitz's
elegant thirties love song, to **Bob Dylan**'s apocalyptic
'A Hard Rain's Gonna Fall' (a British hit). The distance between the singer and the songs set up by
Ferry's precise delivery made it an intriguing work.

Another Time, Another Place (1974) followed the
same pattern, producing two hit singles in **Dobie
Gray**'s 1965 song 'The In Crowd' and the sentimental
ballad 'Smoke Gets in Your Eyes', where Ferry's
singing affectionately quoted the **Platters**' 1958 version. The focus of his revivalism shifted to R&B in
1976 with a hit version of **Wilbert Harrison**'s 'Let's
Stick Together'. A hit EP of the same year, *Extended
Play*, included songs by **The Beatles** ('It's Only Love'),
Gallagher and Lyle ('Heart on My Sleeve') and
Shirley Goodman, formerly of **Shirley and Lee**
('Shame Shame Shame'). These tracks and a few re-
recorded Roxy songs were collected on the album
Let's Stick Together (1976), which heavily featured guitarist Chris Spedding. Ferry hired Spedding, Roxy
drummer Paul Thompson and bassist John Wetton
for live and studio work as the Bryan Ferry Band.

The next album, *In Your Mind* (Polydor, 1977), was
all Ferry's own work, with hit singles in 'This Is
Tomorrow' and 'Tokyo Joe'. The album and the tour
which followed reunited Ferry with former Roxy
Music member Phil Manzanera and paved the way
for the band's re-formation in 1978, the year Ferry
released *The Bride Stripped Bare*. The title, from a
sculpture by Marcel Duchamp, was an echo of Ferry's
art student origins. Though it contained its quota of
covers (**Lou Reed**'s 'What Goes on' and 'Hold on I'm
Comin'' by **Sam and Dave**), the Ferry compositions
were notably taut and intense.

His involvement with Roxy Music precluded any
further solo work until 1985 when *Boys and Girls* (Editions EG), with a sound close to Roxy's own, brought
major rock hits with 'Slave to Love' and 'Don't Stop
the Dance'. *Bête Noire* (Virgin, 1987) included the hit
single 'The Right Stuff', which was adapted from

'Money Changes Everything', an instrumental by the **Smiths**, whose guitarist Johnny Marr was featured on the album. Though he worked on an album of new material for quite a time, the lightweight *Taxi* (1993) was another collection of cover-versions, in the style of his earlier work on **David Bowie**'s *Pin Ups*. Among its tracks were the **Shirelles**' 'Will You Love Me Tomorrow?' and the **Hollies**' 'Just One Look'. Finally, in 1994, Ferry released the album of new material that he had been working on for some time, *Mamouna*. Co-produced by Robin Trower (formerly of **Procul Harum**) and featuring contributions from the likes of **Nile Rodgers** (of Chic) and former members of Roxy Music, including **Brian Eno**, *Mamouna* harked back to Roxy's *Avalon* in its gloomy examination of loneliness. The result was Ferry's best album for some time. Less successful was *As Time Goes By* (1999), a collection of ballads from the thirties and forties, such as **Gus Kahn**'s 'Love Me or Leave Me' and **Dorothy Fields**' 'I'm in the Mood for Love', presented in a rather over-orchestrated manner. This becomes even clearer if one compares **Dooley Wilson**'s wonderfully fragile, pared-down version of 'As Time Goes By' with Ferry's cluttered recording. Ferry's attempt is enjoyable, with the songs clearly seen as a challenge rather than a safe option, in the manner of so many reworkings of classic songs by rock stars, but simply lacks the sparkle of the earlier version.

DOROTHY FIELDS
b. 15 July 1904, Allenhurst, New Jersey, USA, d. 28 March 1974, New York

A librettist as well as a lyricist, Fields had a career which stretched from the twenties to the seventies. One of the many songwriters who travelled from Broadway to Hollywood, she specialized in literate love ballads, such as 'The Way You Look Tonight' which, sung by **Fred Astaire** in *Swing Time*, won her and **Jerome Kern** an Oscar in 1936.

The daughter of vaudevillian (and later Broadway producer) Lew Fields of Waters and Fields fame, she began her career writing 'instant' songs about current events for **Irving Mills** before forming a partnership with **Jimmy McHugh**. Their earliest successes included the classic 'I Can't Give You Anything But Love', the title and idea for which Fields reportedly got from eavesdropping on a couple window-shopping at Tiffany's. It was first featured in *Delmar's Revels* (1927) and though denounced by critics as 'puerile' was the hit of *Blackbirds of 1928*. They followed this with 'On the Sunny Side of the Street' and 'Exactly Like You' from *The International Revue* (1930) before moving to Hollywood. There Fields and McHugh wrote 'Cuban Love Song' (the title song of the 1931 film) and 'I'm in the Mood for Love', 'I Feel a Song

Coming on' (1941) and the wistful 'Don't Blame Me'.

Though she continued to write sporadically with McHugh, after the success of 'Lovely to Look At' and 'I Won't Dance' for the Astaire and Ginger Rogers musical *Roberta* (1935), Fields' favoured writing partner was Jerome Kern. To his stately melodies she added keenly observed lyrics about the transience of appearances that meshed perfectly with the musicals of the period: 'Lovely to Look At', 'Just Let Me Look at You' (1938) and, the best of their songs, 'The Way You Look Tonight', from the best of the Astaire and Rogers musicals, *Swing Time* (1936), which was successfully revived in 1961 by the **Lettermen**. Her other film collaborators included Oscar Levant, **Harry Warren** and **Harold Arlen**. In 1943 she appeared, as herself, in *Stage Door Canteen*.

Despite working in Hollywood, Fields continued to write Broadway shows. She wrote eight librettos with her brother Herbert, including *Let's Face It* (1941) and *Mexican Hayride* (1944) – which featured scores by **Cole Porter** – and, most successfully of all, *Annie Get Your Gun* (1946, filmed in 1950 with **Betty Hutton**) with a score by **Irving Berlin** for **Ethel Merman**. After Herbert's death, she teamed up with Cy Coleman for the decidedly modern *Sweet Charity* (1966, filmed in 1968), which included the raucous 'Big Spender' (a hit for **Shirley Bassey**, 1967). It was followed by the less successful *Seesaw* (1973).

GRACIE FIELDS
b. Grace Stansfield, 9 January 1898, Rochdale, Lancashire, England, d. 27 September 1979, Capri, Italy

'Coom on, lads and lassies, the factory's opened again . . . I've just got me clogs out of pawn.' With these words Fields introduced 'Sing as We Go', the climactic title number from the 1934 film (scripted by novelist J. B. Priestley) in which she leads laid-off mill-hands back to work. Innocent to the verge of silliness, the film and Fields' performance both typified the spirited, undaunted attitude which made her a major British star during the Depression years.

Fields began singing at the age of eight and joined various touring juvenile troupes before beginning a nine-year run in the revue *Mr Tower of London* in 1916. After marrying its producer Archie Pitt she made her first recordings in 1928. From the beginning, she mixed comic and sentimental songs, often poking fun at the content of a number like 'Sally' (her theme song which inspired the title of her film début, *Sally in Our Alley*, 1931) in live performances. But she is chiefly remembered for her absurdist comic narratives such as 'I Took My Harp to a Party', 'In My Little Bottom Drawer' and 'The Biggest Aspidistra in the World' as well as earthy numbers like 'In the Woodshed She Said She Would'. Despite her fine voice, her romantic songs – even the bestselling 'Isle of Capri' (the place she retired to in the fifties with her third husband, Boris Alperovici) – were less individual. Significantly, though she could always command enormous fees for live performances, her records never sold in large amounts.

With fellow Northerner **George Formby**, Fields was the most successful entertainer in the UK in the thirties, but enjoyed little success outside Britain. The four films she made specially for American audiences failed because they tried to fit her into a Hollywood glamour mould. More successful were *Holy Matrimony* (1943) and *Molly and Me* (1945), directed and written by her second husband, Italian Monty Banks. Many of the songs for these and her earlier films were written by Harry Parr-Davis, a prolific composer and, after writing 'Sing as We Go' for Fields, her regular accompanist.

During the Second World War, though based in America, she toured the world entertaining the troops with morale boosters like Parr-Davis's composition 'Wish Me Luck as You Wave Me Goodbye'. After 1945 she virtually retired, recording and giving live performances only occasionally. Her death came after she was made a Dame Commander of the British Empire.

FINE YOUNG CANNIBALS
Roland Gift, b. 28 May 1962, Birmingham, England; Andy Cox, b. 25 January 1960, Birmingham; David Steele, b. 8 September 1960, Birmingham

One of the most stylish of UK pop acts to emerge in the late eighties, the Fine Young Cannibals' success was built on the distinctive voice of Roland Gift and the talents of two musicians who had first tasted success during the short-lived ska revival of the late seventies and early eighties.

Guitarist Cox and bassist Steele first came to attention in the Beat, a Birmingham band which enjoyed considerable success from 1979 to 1983 as part of the so-called Two-Tone movement in the UK spearheaded by the **Specials**, on whose label the Beat's first single, 'Tears of a Clown' (a revival of the **Miracles'** hit), appeared in 1979. With a sound which grafted pop/rock stylings on to a ska backbeat, the band had a string of UK hit singles, including 'Hands Off She's Mine' (1980), 'Mirror in the Bathroom' (1980), 'Too Nice to Talk to' (1981) and 'Can't Get Used to Losing You' (1983). When the Beat split up in 1983, vocalists Dave Wakeling and Ranking Roger went on to form the largely unsuccessful General Public, keeping to the Beat blueprint, while Cox and Steele linked up with actor and singer Gift to perform their more R&B-slanted material.

Taking their name from a Robert Wagner movie,

the Fine Young Cannibals débuted via a self-made video on UK TV rock show *The Tube* in 1985, and were immediately signed to London Records, which released their first single, 'Johnny Come Home', that summer. A haunting hymn to a runaway youth, the single was a Top Ten hit and set the style for future releases, featuring Gift's plaintive vocal set to a pared-down guitar/bass/drums rhythm section.

Although the follow-up single, the politically oriented 'Blue', was a commercial failure, the début album was a hit, as was a version of the **Elvis Presley** hit 'Suspicious Minds' (1986). The band toured the US, where 'Johnny Come Home' was a minor hit, and the album reached the Top Fifty. During their visit film director Barry Levinson gave the band a cameo role in *Tin Men*.

Fine Young Cannibals next recorded a version of the **Buzzcocks'** 1978 hit 'Ever Fallen in Love' for the Jonathan Demme film *Something Wild*, but the group's activities now took second place to Gift's acting career. He appeared in the film *Sammy and Rosie Get Laid* (1987), while Cox and Steele branched out into production with US female rappers **Salt 'N' Pepa** and UK band Pop Will Eat Itself. They also scored a hit single in the UK as Two Men, a Drum Machine and a Trumpet with the dance track 'I'm Tired of Getting Pushed Around' (1988).

The band reunited to record the more dance-influenced *The Raw and the Cooked* (1989), which topped the UK album chart and provided them with an international hit, 'She Drives Me Crazy', a US No. 1. Further hits from the album included another US No. 1, 'Good Thing'. After touring extensively, the trio once again put Fine Young Cannibals on hold while Gift appeared in the British film *Scandal* (1989) and on stage with the Hull Truck theatre company. Cox and Steele took up more production work, working on tracks by female dance vocalist Monie Love as well as an album of their own remixes, *The Raw and the Remixed* (1990). Over the following three years, they sporadically worked on a new Fine Young Cannibals album, and produced several tracks on the acclaimed **Al Green** album *Don't Look Back*. Its sparse and soulful sound eerily re-created that originated by Green's legendary former producer **Willie Mitchell**, while shadowing the approach the duo had patented with the Fine Young Cannibals. *The Finest* (1996), which includes three new recordings, is the definitive retrospective.

EDDIE FISHER
b. Edwin Jack Fisher, 10 August 1928, Philadelphia, Pennsylvania, USA

Fisher's dynamic singing style formed a bridge between the intimate crooners of the forties and the

rock'n'roll singers of the fifties. One of the most successful recording artists of the first half of the fifties,
he was described by **Irving Berlin** as 'the closest thing
I have heard to **Al Jolson**'. Equally important was the
way in which the youthful Fisher, like **Frank Sinatra**
before him, appealed to a new generation of bobby-
sox fans. However, the advent of rock'n'roll and his
highly publicized series of unsuccessful showbusiness
marriages caused his career to go into decline after
1956.

The child of Russian Jewish immigrants, Fisher
made his first radio appearance on WFIL at the age of
twelve, becoming a regular on the *Magic Lady Supper
Club* children's show. In 1945 he sang briefly with
Charlie Ventura's band before performing at the
Copacabana and other nightclubs. He first recorded
for Columbia with the Martin Sisters in 1949 before
signing to RCA the following year.

With producer and arranger **Hugo Winterhalter**,
Fisher began a long series of hit singles with a cover of
Guy Mitchell's 'Thinking of You', which reached No.
1 in 1950. He followed this with 'Bring Back the Thrill'
and 'Turn Back the Hands of Time' before being
drafted. As an army entertainer, he performed in
Korea in 1952 while his records continued to be
released. He scored further hits with 'Anytime', the
first of his eight million-sellers, 'Tell Me Why', with
which the **Four Aces** had sold a million a year earlier,
a revival of **Tolchard Evans**' 'Lady of Spain' and Billy
Reid's 'I'm Walking Beside You' (1953). 'Oh Mein
Papa' (1953), probably Fisher's best-known recording,
was a million-selling instrumental hit on EMI's
Columbia label in Britain for Eddie Calvert, 'the man
with the golden trumpet'.

Fisher hosted the sponsored TV show *Coke Time* in
1953–6 but his recording career peaked in 1955 when
he had five American hit singles, including 'I Need
You Now'* (a British No. 1), '(I'm Always Hearing)
Wedding Bells' and 'Dungaree Doll'*. The following
year, Fisher's last major hits came from sources out-
side Tin Pan Alley. He covered the folky 'Cindy Oh
Cindy', first recorded by **Erik Darling**'s group the
Tarriers, and looked to Broadway for **Lerner** and
Loewe's 'On the Street Where You Live', from *My
Fair Lady*.

In 1956 Fisher married demure singing star **Debbie
Reynolds**, appearing with her in the film *Bundle of
Joy*. After that marriage failed, he married Elizabeth
Taylor, his co-star in *Butterfield 8* (1960). When he
separated from Taylor, he attempted to re-establish
himself on the cabaret circuit, cutting a live double-
album, *Eddie Fisher at the Winter Garden*, and scoring
a minor hit with a version of **Leonard Bernstein** and
Stephen Sondheim's 'Tonight' (Seven Arts, 1961). He
also recorded unsuccessfully for Dot and Ramrod
before returning to RCA for the minor hit 'Games

That Lovers Play' (1966). His final RCA album was a
tribute to **Al Jolson**, *You Ain't Heard Nothin' Yet*. Jolson remained perhaps the deepest influence on
Fisher, who, in the fifties, had used Jolson's former
associate Harry Askt as an accompanist.

Beset by drugs problems, Fisher filed for bankruptcy in 1970 and returned to cabaret. In 1976 he
joined a fifties revival tour. His daughter by Reynolds
is actress Carrie Fisher, who created the role of
Princess Leia in *Star Wars* (1977) and wrote several
novels including *Postcards from the Edge*, a fictionalized account of her drug problems, later a successful
movie.

ELLA FITZGERALD
*b. 25 April 1918, Newport News, Virginia, USA,
d. 15 June 1996*

For half a century Fitzgerald was the most technically
accomplished jazz singer and the one who commanded the largest popular following. While not as
intense as **Billie Holiday**, she sold millions of records
with her skilful scat singing and jazz-tinged versions
of pop standards.

After winning a *Harlem Amateur Hour* contest in
1934 by singing 'Judy', she joined **Tiny Bradshaw**'s
band before taking up a permanent post with drummer **Chick Webb**'s orchestra in 1935. Her first recording with Webb was 'Love and Kisses' (Decca, 1935)
and her biggest hit the million-selling 'A Tisket a Tasket' (1938).

With music by Al Feldman, the song's throwaway
lyrics were taken by Fitzgerald from a nursery rhyme,
and its success dominated Decca's recording plans for
her over the next decade. After Webb's death in 1939,
Fitzgerald led his band for two years and then went
solo. As well as ballads, she released novelty numbers
like 'My Wubba Dolly' (1939) and 'Melinda the
Mouse'. Decca's **Jack Kapp** also paired her with such
popular vocal groups as the **Mills Brothers** ('Big Boy
Blue', 1939), the Delta Rhythm Boys ('It's Only a
Paper Moon', 1945), **Louis Jordan** ('Baby It's Cold
Outside', 1949), **Louis Armstrong** ('You Won't Be
Satisfied Until You Break My Heart', 1946) and the
Ink Spots ('Into Each Life Some Rain Must Fall'*,
1944).

Fitzgerald's jazz singing was given more scope on
Norman Granz's 'Jazz at the Philharmonic' tours,
which she joined in 1946. Her scat singing on such
tunes as 'Flying Home' and 'How High the Moon'
were highlights of the concerts but apart from a
Gershwin Songbook album (1950), her Decca records
remained in the pop ballad category.

When her Decca contract ran out in 1955, Fitzgerald joined Granz's Verve label and in 1956 began a
long series of recordings based on the 'songbook'

concept. With orchestral backing by **Nelson Riddle** and others, she performed the works of such writers as **Jerome Kern**, **Cole Porter**, **Rodgers and Hart**, **Harold Arlen** and **Duke Ellington**. This was Fitzgerald at her best, her technical skill meshing with the polished lyrics of such songs as 'Manhattan', 'Love for Sale' and 'Ev'ry Time We Say Goodbye'.

A parallel set of albums found Fitzgerald paired with leading jazz musicians such as Ellington, **Oscar Peterson** and Louis Armstrong, with whom she made an album of songs from Gershwin's *Porgy and Bess* in 1960, while *Rhythm Is My Business* (1962) had arrangements by **Bill Doggett**, with whom she had previously recorded 'Crying in the Chapel' (1953). Now managed by Granz, Fitzgerald made her first film appearance in *Pete Kelly's Blues* (1955), with **Peggy Lee** making an album of songs from the film, followed by *St Louis Blues* (1958) and *Let No Man Write My Epitaph* (1960).

She also made the occasional hit single. Moe Koffman's 'Swinging Shepherd Blues' (HMV, 1958) reached the British Top Twenty while Fitzgerald had a transatlantic success with a live recording of **Kurt Weill**'s 'Mack the Knife' in 1960. Four years later her version of **The Beatles**' 'Can't Buy Me Love' was a minor hit in Britain.

Serious illness interrupted her career in the late sixties but Fitzgerald returned to recording with Granz's Pablo label in the seventies. Some of the finest of the later albums were made with guitarist Joe Pass (*Take Love Easy*, 1973) and pianist Tommy Flanagan – her regular accompanist on live dates. *Nice Work If You Can Get It* (1983) was a further selection of Gershwin material with **André Previn** on piano.

Fitzgerald underwent open-heart surgery in 1986 but returned to live performance the following year. In the nineties she recorded several pleasant albums that confirmed her unchallenged reputation as a stylist. These included *Jazz Around Midnight* (Polydor, 1990) and *The Intimate Ella* (1991). In 1993, however, she had further diabetes-related health problems, leading to the amputation of both legs.

FIVE BLIND BOYS OF MISSISSIPPI
Lawrence Abrams; Lloyd Woodard; Archie Brownlee, d. 8 February 1960, New Orleans, USA; Joseph Ford; Isiah Patterson; Roscoe Robinson; Big Henry Johnson

One of the first *a cappella* gospel 'quartets', the Five Blind Boys were renowned for leader Brownlee's dramatic screaming style which influenced the approach of many later singers, including **Sam Cooke**, **Ray Charles** and **James Brown**.

Piney Woods School for the Blind near Jackson, Mississippi, was a remarkable music centre, acting as the base for the all-female jazz group the Interna-

tional Sweethearts of Rhythm in the thirties and forties, as well as enjoying a reputation for religious music. From 1922 onwards, the school's principal, Laurence Jones, had organized a series of touring groups under the title the Cotton Blossom Singers to raise funds from wealthy whites. Brownlee led one such group which, after the members had left school, went on the road in 1944 as the Jackson Harmoneers.

Coached and managed by the Rev. Percell Perkins, the group recorded for Excelsior and Coleman before becoming the first gospel group to sign to **Don Robey**'s Houston-based Peacock label. They evolved a style in which the group sang a repeated phrase, building up the tension to highlight Brownlee's ecstatic falsetto, which could provoke scenes of religious hysteria in church and concert audiences.

Soon he was inspiring a series of bestsellers, beginning with 'Our Father', which headed the R&B charts in 1951 and was one of the most successful gospel records of all time. Other hit records included 'I'm a Soldier', 'Oh Way' and 'Where There's a Will There's a Way', which was later recorded by **Lonnie Mack**, whose laconic delivery was in total contrast to Brownlee's outpourings. In 1956 the Five Blind Boys switched labels to Vee-Jay.

After Brownlee's death from pneumonia, there were numerous personnel changes. The Blind Boys' tradition of fervent, unaccompanied gospel singing was maintained by such singers as Rev. Willie Mincy, Roscoe Robinson and Henry Johnson. The group made a first tour of Europe in 1965.

THE FIVE ROYALES
Lowman 'Pete' Pauling, b. Winston-Salem, North Carolina, USA, d. 1975; Curtis Pauling, b. Winston-Salem (replaced by Johnny Tanner 1950); Eugene Tanner, b. Winston-Salem; Clarence Pauling, b. Winston-Salem (replaced by Johnny Moore 1943); William Samuels, b. Winston-Salem (replaced by Obediah Carter 1950); Otto Jeffries, b. Winston-Salem

With the Dominoes and **Hank Ballard** and the Midnighters, the Five Royales were the most important fifties black vocal group to impart a distinct gospel flavour to their records.

Formed as a gospel group, the Royal Sons, in Winston-Salem in 1942, the group recorded for Apollo in 1948 as the Royal Sons Quintet (including 'Bedside of a Neighbor' and 'Journey's End'), before switching decisively to R&B as the Five Royales in 1952. Their second R&B outing, the intense 'Baby Don't Do It' (1952), written as most of their material would be by the group's guitarist and bass voice, Lowman Pauling, and featuring Johnny Tanner's rough, strong, intense lead vocals, topped the R&B charts in 1953. After several more R&B hits on Apollo, including 'Help Me

Somebody' (another R&B No. 1), 'Crazy, Crazy, Crazy' and 'Too Much Lovin'' (1953), all performed with a hard-edged urgency, the group switched to King Records in 1954.

At King, Pauling's blues-based guitar was even more strongly featured, most notably on 'Think', their biggest hit of 1957. Much covered by black artists – **Aretha Franklin** (1968) and **James Brown** (1960) are among those who have had big hits with the song – their recordings, in the words of a critic, represent 'R&B at its best, keeping the strength of blues lyrics and presenting them with the emotion of gospel singers'. Even more influential was their gritty recording of the song Pauling wrote with producer **Ralph Bass**, 'Dedicated to the One I Love' (1958). Only a minor hit for the Five Royales, it was subsequently a million-seller for both the **Shirelles** (1961) and **The Mamas and the Papas** (1967). Another of Pauling's songs was 'Tell the Truth', better known in the **Ray Charles** version. Generally, however, the Five Royales' recordings were too impassioned and their harmonies too rough to appeal to whites.

After leaving King, the group recorded for ABC, Vee-Jay and Smash, among others, with little success, before disbanding in the early seventies.

THE FIVE SATINS

Fred Parris, b. 26 March 1936, New Haven, Connecticut, USA; Rich Freeman, b. December 1940, New Haven; Al Denby, b. New Haven; Ed Martin, b. New Haven; Jessie Murphy, b. New Haven

The Five Satins' recording of 'In the Still of the Nite' (a song written by lead singer Parris, not the similarly titled **Cole Porter** song) is one of the best-loved doo-wop performances, a haunting ballad set against the surreal backdrop of a strange chant and a plodding piano that clearly ought not to belong together but do.

Parris formed the Scarlets (who recorded on Red Robin) in 1953 and the Five Satins in 1956. Signed to Standard, they recorded 'Still of the Nite' (1956) in a church basement and when leased to Ember the record was a huge hit. In 1960 and 1961, in the wake of successful versions of the song by **Dion and the Belmonts** and **Paul Anka**, respectively, the Five Satins had further minor hits with re-releases of the record. Soon after 'Still of the Nite''s release, Parris, who was in the army, was sent to Japan and Bill Baker was drafted in as lead singer for the more orthodox 'To the Aisle' (Ember, 1957). In 1958 Parris returned and the group had minor hits with 'Shadows' (1959) and 'I'll Be Seeing You' (1960), which they later revived *a cappella* fashion in the film *Let the Good Times Roll* (1973). During the sixties they recorded for Cub, Chancellor, Red Bird and United Artists with little success, until their career was boosted by the rock'n'roll revival.

In 1974, with Parris the only remaining original member, they signed with Kirshner Records and, billed as Black Satin, had a Top Forty R&B hit with 'Everybody Stand Up and Clap Your Hands' in 1976. In 1982 they signed with Elektra and had a minor pop hit with 'Memories of Days Gone By'.

ROBERTA FLACK

b. 10 February 1937, Asheville, North Carolina, USA

Roberta Flack had a series of solo and duet hits during the seventies and early eighties which featured a sophisticated vocal technique. With a jazzy feel and a certain reticence she was one of the first black singers of the era to develop a ballad style separate from the conventions of soul.

Flack's mother was a church organist and her father a jazz musician. She studied music at Howard University in Washington DC before becoming a teacher while singing and playing piano in Washington nightclubs. She turned professional in 1967 and was signed to Atlantic Records on the recommendation of jazz pianist Les McCann. *First Take* (1969) was produced by Joel Dorn and contained so impressive a reading of **Ewan MacColl**'s 'The First Time Ever I Saw Your Face' that even the **Fugees**' 1996 version could not overwhelm it. Also on the album was a fine version of **Leonard Cohen**'s 'Hey That's No Way to Say Goodbye'.

First Take Chapter Two followed in 1970 when Atlantic teamed Flack with **Donny Hathaway**. Co-produced by Dorn and **Arif Mardin**, their eponymous album included a cover of **James Taylor**'s recording of the **Carole King** song 'You've Got a Friend'. This was a minor hit and was followed in 1972 by 'Where Is the Love'*, a duet which reached the Top Ten.

In that year Flack had her first No. 1 record with a re-release of 'The First Time Ever I Saw Your Face'*, which had been featured on the soundtrack of the Clint Eastwood film *Play Misty for Me*. Another slow, melodic ballad was equally successful in 1973. 'Killing Me Softly with His Song'*, written by Norman Fox and Charles Gimbel, was reportedly inspired by **Don McLean**. 'Feel Like Makin' Love' (1974) was Flack's third No. 1.

During the mid-seventies she recorded little, concentrating instead on developing educational projects for disadvantaged young people. Shortly before Hathaway's death in 1979, she recorded the hit 'The Closer I Get to You'* with him, while a revival of the 1972 song 'Back Together Again' was a British hit for the duo in 1978. Flack's intermittent solo career produced further hits with 'If Ever I See You Again' (1978) and the film theme 'Making Love' (1982).

In 1980 she cut *Live and More* with Peabo Bryson,

whose R&B hits had included 'Underground Music' (Bullet, 1976) and 'Reaching for the Sky' (Capitol, 1978), and – with **Nat 'King' Cole**'s daughter Natalie – 'Gimme Some Time' (1979). This was followed by another Flack–Bryson collaboration, *Born to Love* (1983), which included the Gerry Goffin–Michael Masser hit single 'Tonight I Celebrate My Love'. Despite the involvement of **Quincy Jones, Ashford and Simpson** and writer Maya Angelou, *Oasis* (1988) sold poorly. In 1990 Flack produced and sang on *Tenor Saxophone* by Nino Tempo, best known for his 1963 hit version of 'Deep Purple' with April Stevens. She released the Arif Mardin-produced *Set the Night to Music* in 1991, with **Maxi Priest** providing guest vocals on the title track.

THE FLAMING LIPS
Wayne Coyne, b. 1960, Oklahoma, USA; Ronald Jones; Steven Drozd, b. Oklahoma, USA; Michael Ivins, b. Oklahoma, USA

A psychedelic rock band, the Flaming Lips spent a decade making a series of avant-garde albums layered in feedback before refining their sound to take in symphonic orchestration and music-hall schmaltz, which won them new admirers and universal acclaim.

The Flaming Lips date back to 1984, when singer/guitarist Coyne, inspired by **John Lennon**'s post-**Beatles** material, began to work with local musicians in Oklahoma. The ever-changing line-up of the eighties produced a series of garage-punk albums with song titles like 'One Million Billionth of a Milli-second on a Sunday Morning', the best of which later featured on *A Collection of Songs Representing an Enthusiasm for Recording 1984–1990* (Restless, 1998). By the time they released *In a Priest Driven Ambu-lance* (1990) – including contributions from Dave Fridmann and Jonathan Donahue, who went on to form **Mercury Rev** – the Flaming Lips had attracted the attention of WEA, to whom they signed in 1991.

The massive advance on their major label début afforded the band time to experiment in the studio. Now with a firm membership of Coyne, guitarist Jones, drummer Drozd and bassist Ivins they recorded *Hit to Death in the Future Head* (1992) and *Transmissions from the Satellite Heart* (1993), which were more focused than their previous material but failed to sell beyond the band's cult following. On the verge of being dropped by WEA, they had a surprise US hit with 'She Don't Use Jelly' (1994), finally giving the band a mainstream audience. 'Bad Days', from *Clouds Taste Metallic* (1995), saw the Flaming Lips gain further success after it was featured in *Batman Forever*, as their melodicism came to the fore ahead of discordance and feedback.

Zaireeka (1997) marked the beginning of a new kind of experimentation for Coyne's band, now down to a trio (Jones left in 1996 on a religious mission and never returned). A set of four CDs designed to be played simultaneously, the album coincided with a series of 'Boom Box Experiments', where Coyne would con-duct an 'orchestra' of forty pre-recorded tapes played by on-stage guests. The Flaming Lips found a wider audience in the UK with the release of their ninth album, *The Soft Bulletin* (1999), which featured their best collection of songs and a blend of traditional instrumentation – cello, harp and flugelhorn – and hi-tech recording equipment, taking in influences from **George Gershwin** to **My Bloody Valentine**.

THE FLAMINGOS
Sollie McElroy (replaced 1954 by Nathaniel Nelson, b. 10 April 1932, Chicago, Illinois, USA); John Carter (replaced by Tommy Hunt, b. 18 June 1933, Pittsburgh, Pennsylvania); Terry Johnson, b. 12 November 1935, Baltimore, Maryland; Ezekiel Carey, b. 24 January 1933, Bluefield, West Virginia; Paul Wilson, b. 6 January 1935, Chicago; Jacob Carey, b. 9 September 1926, Pulaski, Virginia

A fifties doo-wop group, the Flamingos survived the radical changes in music that overwhelmed many of their contemporaries, primarily because of the breadth of their influences, which ranged from hard gospel to the **Four Freshmen**.

Formed in Chicago's South side in 1952, from members of the same church, the group was signed to Chance in 1953. They had an R&B hit with 'Golden Teardrops' (1953) and recorded material written by **Ewart Abner** and Calvin Carter, before moving to Parrot (where they were among the many groups to cover Gene and Eunice's 'Ko Ko Mo', Aladdin, 1955) and then Checker, where they had their first national hit with the ballad 'I'll Be Home' (1956). Written by Fats Washington and Stan Lewis (who would later found Jewel Records), the song was very popular among the families of servicemen and an even bigger hit for **Pat Boone**. By this time McElroy had left and Carter had joined the **Dells**.

After a brief sojourn with Decca ('The Ladder of Love', 1957) the Flamingos returned to Checker, before signing with **George Goldner**'s End label in 1958. With 'Lovers Never Say Goodbye' (1958) they began a string of intensely romantic hits, which included their magisterial version of the **Harry War-ren** and Al Dubin composition 'I Only Have Eyes for You', **George Gershwin**'s 'Love Walked in' (1959) and 'Nobody Loves Me Like You' (1960). One of Amer-ica's favourite oldies from the fifties, 'I Only Have Eyes for You', which featured Hunt's lead voice (Nel-son having left to join the **Platters**) and the jazz-tinged 'be-bop-she-bop' backing phrase, was remade virtually note for note by Art Garfunkel on Columbia in 1975. The group adapted to the coming of soul and scored a hit with 'The Boogaloo Party' (Philips, 1966), their best-known song in Britain where it was popular among Northern soul fans, and later 'Buffalo Soldier' (Polydor, 1970), a paean to the black troopers of the US Cavalry.

FLANAGAN AND ALLEN
Bud Flanagan, b. Reuben Weintrop, 14 October 1896, Spitalfields, London, England, d. 20 October 1968; Chesney Allen, b. William Ernest Chesney Allen, 5 April 1894, Brighton, Sussex, d. 13 November 1982, London

Not even their devotees would award a high musical rating to the Crazy Gang, Britain's finest anarchic comedy team from the thirties to the fifties, and fore-fathers of the **Goons**, *Monty Python's Flying Circus*, *The Young Ones* and much else in the lineage of 'alter-native comedy'. In their midst, however, were Flana-gan and Allen, whose gentle, jog-along cockney duets not only had their place in the musical lore of the Sec-ond World War, but prefigured the cosier aspects of **Ian Dury**, **Chas and Dave** and even **Max Bygraves**.

Bud Flanagan started in showbusiness as a black-face comic (using the name 'Chick Harlem'). He worked in the USA in burlesque, and later as a come-dian in revues headed by **Florrie Forde**. He teamed up with Allen in 1924 to work in revue, and in 1931 they went into variety. It was in the following year that George Black, impresario at the London Palla-dium, conceived *Crazy Week*, featuring three estab-lished variety acts. Charles Naughton and Jimmy Gold had been a knockabout comedy act since 1908. Jimmy Nervo and Teddy Knox had been working together since 1919 as eccentric comics; they special-ized in burlesque ballets and slow-motion wrestling. To this team Flanagan and Allen were added in 1936 to form the Crazy Gang. A series of popular revues followed, beginning in 1937 with *Swing Is in the Air* and *London Rhapsody*. They broke up in the early for-ties but re-formed in 1947 and played in revue virtu-ally uninterrupted at London's Victoria Palace: *Knights of Madness* (1950), *Jokers Wild* (1954), *These Foolish Kings* (1956), *Young in Heart* (1960) and so on. 'Monsewer' Eddie Gray, originally a juggler, joined in 1956. The Gang finally disbanded in 1962.

Thirty years earlier Flanagan and Allen had made their musical name with Bud's affectionate London song 'Underneath the Arches', which became their signature tune. Their stage act consisted largely of punning routines punctuated by 'Oi!', but their vocal duets were sensitive and pretty, with light-as-a-feather harmonies. Among their successes, both in person and on record (chiefly for Columbia or Decca), were 'Dreaming', 'Umbrella Man' (1938) and

the wartime songs 'We're Gonna Hang out the Wash-ing on the Siegfried Line', written by **Jimmy Kennedy**, and **Michael Carr** and **Noel Gay**'s 'Run, Rabbit, Run'.

LESTER FLATT AND EARL SCRUGGS
Lester Flatt, b. 28 June 1914, Overton County, Ten-nessee, USA, d. 11 May 1979; Earl Scruggs, b. 6 January 1924, Cleveland County, North Carolina

The most famous duo in bluegrass, Flatt and Scruggs were the first alumni of the **Bill Monroe** band to break away and start an independent career, in which for a time they were considerably more successful than their ex-employer and to some extent usurped his position as the music's foremost public represen-tative. Each of them, even while with Monroe, laid down ground rules of bluegrass practice that were still followed more than forty years later.

Flatt became a professional singer and guitarist in 1939 and joined the band led by Monroe's brother Charlie, the Kentucky Pardners. He went over to Bill Monroe in 1944, followed shortly afterwards by Scruggs. They had an immediate effect on the Mon-roe band, which through its broadcasts and Columbia records promptly became the most influential tradi-tional band in country music. Scruggs' fast, bluesy and rhythmically exhilarating three-finger style on the banjo caught the ears of a generation of young pick-ers, while Flatt's relaxed – and often slightly flat – lead singing and trademark guitar runs also attracted many imitators.

The pair left Monroe in 1948 and signed with Mer-cury, recording tunes like 'Foggy Mountain Break-down' (1949), which gave their backing band its name, the Foggy Mountain Boys (and was later the hit theme tune of *Bonnie and Clyde*, 1967). By 1951 they were with Columbia, Monroe having switched to Decca. (Decades passed before Monroe publicly made peace with his ex-bandsmen.) Bluegrass standards-to-be, both banjo instrumentals and vocal numbers, poured out during the fifties and sixties: 'Flint Hill Special' (1952), 'Randy Lynn Rag', 'Crying My Heart Out over You', and their bestseller, 'The Ballad of Jed Clampett' (1962), the theme of the long-running TV series *Beverly Hillbillies*. They also maintained cast-member cards of the *Grand Ole Opry* from 1953 onwards, and also played such unaccustomed temples as New York's Carnegie Hall.

Musical differences threatened the duo from the early sixties, Flatt preferring the original acoustic bluegrass sound, while Scruggs wanted to experiment. Columbia, meanwhile, drew them into album proj-ects of songs by the **Carter Family** and **Bob Dylan**. They finally split up in 1969. Flatt led his Nashville Grass on the *Opry*, toured widely across the United

States and recorded regularly, for RCA – including duet albums with **Mac Wiseman** (*Lester 'n' Mac*, 1971, and *On the South Bound*, 1972) – and then for various bluegrass labels. He was working continuously until his final illness. The Nashville Grass, led by his old partner, singer and mandolinist Curly Seckler, continued to commemorate his style throughout the eighties.

Scruggs realized his wider ambitions by forming the Earl Scruggs Revue with his sons Randy and Gary (and later Steve), and playing the campus and folk-club circuit. The group recorded frequently for Columbia during the seventies, issuing two *Anniversary Albums* in 1975–6 to celebrate Earl's twenty-five years with the label; guest artists included **Johnny Cash**, **Billy Joel**, **Leonard Cohen** and **Buffy Sainte-Marie**. Later revue albums were produced by **Chips Moman**. In later years Scruggs was at pains to dissociate his music, and himself, from bluegrass, and was less active in public in the eighties, concentrating on producing tuition books and records.

FLEETWOOD MAC
Mick Fleetwood, b. 24 June 1942, London, England; Peter Green, b. Peter Greenbaum, 29 October 1946, London; John McVie, b. 26 November 1945, London; Jeremy Spencer, b. 4 July 1948, West Hartlepool (replaced 1971 by Bob Welch, b. 31 July 1946, California, USA, replaced 1974 by Lindsey Buckingham, b. 3 October 1947, Palo Alto, California); Danny Kirwan, b. 13 May 1950, London (replaced 1972 by Bob Weston); Christine Perfect McVie (joined 1970), b. 12 July 1943, Birmingham; Stevie Nicks (joined 1974), b. Stephanie Nicks, 26 May 1948, Phoenix, Arizona; Billy Burnete, b. 8 May 1953, Memphis, Tennessee; Rick Vito, b. 1950

One of the most tenacious organizations of the rock era, Fleetwood Mac evolved from a leading British blues band of the late sixties into an international best-selling soft-rock group of the seventies and eighties.

Guitarist Green, bassist McVie and drummer Fleetwood had met as members of **John Mayall**'s Blues-breakers. In 1967 they formed Peter Green's Fleetwood Mac, a name which reflected Green's status as a blues soloist, second only to **Eric Clapton**. Adding slide guitarist Spencer for the **Elmore James** numbers, the band was an immediate success on the British club and college circuit. Their 1968 epony-mous début album, produced by **Mike Vernon** for his Blue Horizon label, topped the album charts and included two minor hits, 'Black Magic Woman' (a big hit in 1970 for **Carlos Santana**) and the atmospheric blues number 'Need Your Love So Bad'.

Mr Wonderful (1968) included Green's Hawaiian-styled instrumental 'Albatross', which reached No. 1 and was a hit again when re-released in 1973 by

Columbia. Like the languid ballad 'Man of the World' (1969), 'Albatross' was atypical of Fleetwood Mac's live show, which, like the *Mr Wonderful* album, was still heavily blues-orientated. By now Kirwan (guitar, vocals) had joined the band. *Then Play on* (Reprise, 1969) included the hit single 'Oh Well', which like 'Green Manalishi' (1970) mixed obscure lyrics which diamond-hard blues solos from Green.

Soon afterwards Green left to cut a solo album for Reprise and then disappeared from view. He spent much of the seventies absorbed in what was variously described as fundamentalist religion or mental break-down, and did not record again until 1979 when *In the Skies* (PVK) inaugurated a series of albums for PVK and Creole. While lacking the fire of his earlier work, they contained passages of eloquent guitar-playing. In 1993 former **Cream** lyricist Pete Brown produced a homage to Green that included interpretations of his songs by former **Manfred Mann** vocalist Paul Jones and **Arthur Brown** among others. Green subsequently returned to touring and recording (including *Splinter Group*, 1997, and *The Robert Johnson Songbook*, 1998). However, his most affecting release of the period was the archive set *Pete Green's Fleetwood Mac: Live at the BBC* (1995), which was overseen by Mick Fleetwood. Also of interest was *Green & Guitar: The Best of Peter Green, 1977–81* (Music Club, 1996).

Without Green, Fleetwood Mac entered an unset-tled phase of frequent personnel changes. They cut the inconsequential *Kiln House* (1970) before adding ex-Chicken Shack singer-pianist Perfect (who later married McVie) and Welch, an American guitarist playing the Paris R&B clubs. Next, Spencer left abruptly during an American tour to join the reli-gious sect the Children of God, going on to record *Jeremy Spencer and the Children* (Columbia, 1972). Kirwan was asked to go, and attempted a solo career with three undistinguished albums for DJM between 1975 and 1979.

With a nucleus of McVie, Fleetwood and Perfect, Fleetwood Mac cut five albums in the years 1971–4, decisively moving away from the blues format. The pick of them were *Bare Trees* (1971) and *Mystery to Me* (1974), which featured guitarist Bob Weston. The band's loss of momentum was compounded by the behaviour of their former manager Clifford Davis, who formed another 'Fleetwood Mac' for an Ameri-can tour. The position was only resolved after lengthy litigation.

By 1974 the band seemed to be ready to fold when Fleetwood brought in Buckingham and Nicks, a duo who had previously performed with San Francisco group Fritz and with Don Everly of the **Everly Broth-ers**. Rejuvenated by the singing and writing of the new members, the group enjoyed its first American hit with 'Over My Head' (Reprise, 1975) from the album

Fleetwood Mac. That record produced further hits in 'Rhiannon (Will You Ever Win)' and 'Say You Love Me', but it was only the prelude to *Rumours*, which eventually sold over 25 million copies worldwide.

A skilfully crafted and melodic collection of songs of love and loss, the album had a similar impact to **Carole King**'s *Tapestry.* The confessional and confidential air was amplified by reports that the lyrics depicted the real-life romantic vicissitudes of the group. During 1977, *Rumours* provided Fleetwood Mac with four hit singles. Buckingham's 'Go Your Own Way' was followed by Nicks' 'Dreams'* and Christine McVie's 'Don't Stop' and 'You Make Loving Fun'.

Tusk (1979) was reputed to have cost over $1 million in studio time and was inevitably an anticlimax, although the title track, 'Sara' and 'Hold Me' were all hits. It was followed by a two-record live album and the studio production, *Mirage* (1982), which included the bestselling singles 'Gypsy' and 'Love in Store' in America and 'Oh Diane' in Britain.

During the eighties each member except John McVie released solo albums, the most unusual being Fleetwood's *The Visitor* (RCA, 1981), recorded with local musicians in Ghana. McVie belatedly issued a solo album, *Gotta Band,* in 1992. Though Christine McVie had one solo hit ('Get a Hold on Me', Warners, 1984), it was Nicks who became a solo superstar. *Belladonna* (Modern, 1981) reached the top of the American charts and *Wild Heart* (Atco, 1983) was only marginally less successful. Her hit singles included 'Edge of Seventeen' (1982), 'Stand Back' (1983) and a sequence of duets with **Tom Petty** ('Stop Draggin' My Heart Around', 1981), former member of the **Eagles** Don Henley ('Leather and Lace', 1981) and Sandy Stewart ('Nightbird', 1984). Nicks' records were consistent bestsellers through to 1986's 'Talk to Me', from the album *Rock a Little,* and *The Other Side of the Mirror* (EMI, 1989), produced by Rupert Hine. A 'best of' (*TimeSpace*, 1991) marked the end of her stay with EMI, and she moved to Atlantic for *Street Angel* (1994).

In 1987 Fleetwood Mac reunited for *Tango in the Night*.* Though the critical response was lukewarm, the album was their biggest-ever success, spawning a series of hit singles, including 'Little Lies', 'Big Love' and 'Everywhere', and topping the album charts in America and Britain. When, in 1988, Buckingham left to pursue a solo career, he was replaced by two younger musicians, Rick Vito (from **Bob Seger**'s band) and Billy (nephew of **Johnny**) **Burnette**. This line-up recorded the bland *Behind the Mask* (1990), which included the hit single 'Save Me'. Far better was Buckingham's third solo album *Out of the Cradle,* which melded catchy hooks and studio perfection with *élan.*

Although the *Rumours* line-up re-formed to play at the inaugural concert for president Bill Clinton in 1993, Nicks and Buckingham were absent from the 1994 touring line-up of Fleetwood Mac, which included former Traffic member Dave Mason and Bekka Bramlett, daughter of Delaney & Bonnie. *Legacy, A Tribute to Fleetwood Mac's Rumours* (1998) included contributions from **Elton John**, the **Corrs**, the Cranberries and others. However, by this time the band were in semi-retirement. Fleetwood, who had entered the music industry through investment distribution company The Point in 2000, established an Internet distribution company, resound.com.

THE FLEETWOODS
Gary Troxel, b. 28 November 1939, Centralia, Washington, USA; Barbara Laine Ellis, b. 20 February 1940, Olympia, Washington; Gretchen Diane Christopher, b. 29 February 1940, Olympia

A soft harmony trio in the mould of the **Chordettes**, the Fleetwoods were one of the few groups of the period to combine male and female voices.

High-school friends, the trio first called themselves Two Girls and a Guy when they joined forces in 1958. They signed with Dolton Records as the Fleetwoods and had an immediate million-seller with their own composition, 'Come Softly to Me'. Even better was their version of De Wayne Blackwell's 'Mr Blue'* later that year and their cooing revival of Thomas Wayne's 'Tragedy' (1961), their last Top Ten hit. After a series of minor hits, which included **Jackie DeShannon**'s 'The Great Impostor' (1962), they stopped recording in 1963 and retired from showbusiness.

DAN FOGELBERG
b. 13 August 1951, Peoria, Illinois, USA

A reflective singer-songwriter in the sixties mould, Fogelberg was a stalwart of the West Coast rock scene in the late seventies and eighties. In the nineties he was cited as an influence by **Garth Brooks** and other new stars of country music.

His earliest appearances were in folk clubs while he was studying art at the University of Illinois. Moving to Los Angeles, Fogelberg toured with **Van Morrison** before recording *Home Free* (Columbia, 1974) in Nashville with producer Norbert Putnam. His next album, *Souvenirs* (Epic, 1975), was produced by Joe Walsh and included the hit 'Part of the Plan'.

Fogelberg toured with the **Eagles**, with whom he shared a manager, Irving Azoff, later to be president of MCA Records. His own backing band, Fools Gold, cut albums for Arista and Columbia in 1976–7. Fogelberg's compositions were recorded by a number of other artists, including Walsh and ex-**Byrd** Roger McGuinn. His own releases included *Captured Angel*

(1975), *Netherlands* (1977) and a collaboration with
flautist Tim Weisberg, *Twin Sons of Different Mothers*
(Full Moon, 1978), which contained the hit 'The
Power of Gold'.

In the eighties Fogelberg's brand of soft rock with a
country tinge found a wider following and he had
nine American Top Thirty hits in five years, all on
Full Moon. They included his only British hit,
'Longer' (1980), the seasonal novelty 'Same Old Lang
Syne' (1980), 'Hard to Say' (1981) and 'The Language
of Love' (1984). A concept album dealing with childhood, *The Innocent Age* (1981), reached the Top Ten.
Like *Windows and Walls* (1984), it was produced by
Putnam and Marty Lewis. Fogelberg himself produced *Beauty Lies* (Full Moon, 1983) by Mike Brewer,
formerly of Brewer and Shipley, whose 1971 hit 'One
Toke over the Line' (Kama Sutra) had caused controversy because of drugs references in the lyrics.

Fogelberg's country leanings were emphasized by
his recordings with Earl Scruggs of **Flatt and Scruggs**,
and his version of the **Stanley Brothers**' 'Think of
What You've Done' on *High Country Snows* (1985).
Exiles was released in 1987. He also sang on the soundtrack of the 1980 film *Urban Cowboy*. He recorded
throughout the eighties with a degree of commercial
success on the country charts but the songs, though
often autobiographical, were increasingly bland. Later
albums included *The Wild Places* (1990), which
included a version of the Cascades' 1963 hit 'Rhythm
of the Rain', and the live recording *Greetings from the
West* (1991). In 1993 he released *River of Souls* and in
1995 *No Resemblance Whatsoever*, a further collaboration with Weisberg. Fogelberg, the subject of the
sixty-four-track retrospective *Portrait* (Sony, 1997),
continued to tour throughout the nineties.

FOGHAT

*'Lonesome' Dave Peverett, b. 1950, London, England;
Roger Earl, b. 1949; Rod Price (replaced by Eric
Cartwright); Tony Stevens, b. 12 September 1949,
London (replaced by Nick Jameson, replaced by Craig
MacGregor)*

A second-generation British blues band, Foghat were
one of the first to take up permanent residency in the
US and to regularly play the stadium circuit there.

Foghat was formed by Peverett and Earl, former
members of Savoy Brown, the first of the British blues
groups to transform themselves into headline stars in
the US through constant touring. As the blues boom
wound down, Savoy Brown – under the leadership of
Kim Simmonds – moved towards a harder (and
faster) rock sound on albums like *A Step Further*
(1969) and *Raw Sienna* (1970). Formed with the
American market in mind and signed to Albert
Grossman's Bearsville label, Foghat took that attitude

even further, producing at their best flowing, albeit
simplified, blues-based riffs, usually played at high
speed. Their first album, *Foghat* (1972), contained a
dramatic wah-wah reading of **Willie Dixon**'s 'I Just
Want to Make Love to You', which defined their style.
A minor hit in 1972, the song, in an abridged live version from *Live*, probably their best album, went Top
Forty in 1977, the year the group hosted a benefit concert for New York Public Library's Blues Collection.
By then, with five albums and countless tours of middle America under their collective belt, they were stadium superstars.

'Slow Ride', produced by one-time member Nick
Jameson, and their interpretation of the blues standard 'Drivin' Wheel' gave them hits in 1976, and they
had further hits with 'Stone Blue' (1978) and 'Third
Time Lucky (First Time I Was a Fool)' (1979). However, with the rise of heavy metal their once dynamic
boogies were outmoded and the group disbanded in
the eighties.

RED FOLEY

*b. Clyde Julian Foley, 17 June 1910, Blue Lick, Kentucky,
USA, d. 19 September 1968, Fort Wayne, Indiana*

Foley made his radio début in the early thirties on
Chicago's WLS *National Barn Dance*, where his clear,
trained-sounding voice and ingratiating manner made
him, like fellow Kentuckian **Bradley Kincaid**, an ideal
interpreter of Southern rural music to the station's
Midwestern audience. In the late thirties he worked
with programme director John Lair on the new *Renfro
Valley* [Kentucky] *Barn Dance*, later rejoining WLS
(1940–7) and then going on to the *Grand Ole Opry*
(1947–53) and the Springfield (Missouri)-based *Ozark
Jubilee* (1954–61).

Foley signed a lifetime contract with Decca in 1941
and in 1945 was one of the first country artists to
record in Nashville. Among his country hits were 'Old
Shep' (first recorded in 1935 and again in 1941, then
recycled by **Elvis Presley**); 'Foggy River' (1947); 'Tennessee Saturday Night' (1948); 'Chattanooga
Shoeshine Boy'* and, with guitarist Hank Garland,
'Sugarfoot Rag' (both 1950); 'Peace in the Valley'
(1951, written by **Thomas A. Dorsey** and the first ever
million-selling gospel recording); and 'One by One'
(1954). This last was one of several duets with **Kitty
Wells**. Foley also recorded a number of duets with
Ernest Tubb.

After a stint as a straight actor in the ABC-TV
series *Mr Smith Goes to Washington* (1961–2), Foley
based himself in Nashville, where in 1967 he was voted
into the Country Music Hall of Fame.

After the somewhat anodyne recordings he made
in the thirties, Foley's post-war work embodied quite
different strains. A declared fondness for black music

no doubt drew him to the boogie novelties for which he was known in the late forties; he even made an unreleased recording with the black pianist **Cecil Gant**. He also contributed to the rockabilly canon, often supported by Hank Garland (and hampered by the Anita Kerr Singers), with recordings like 'Crazy Little Guitar Man' (1958) and made a pair of interesting covers of R&B hits with 'Shake a Hand' (1953), originally a hit for Faye Adams on Herald in 1953, and 'Hearts of Stone' (1954), an earlier hit for the Charms on DeLuxe in the same year. Nonetheless, he is likely to be remembered for the gospel songs included in collections like *Beyond the Sunset* (Decca, 1956).

EMILE FORD
b. Emile Sweetman, 16 October 1937, Nassau, Bahamas

Ford was the first black British pop star.

One of the many West Indian immigrants to Britain in the fifties, Ford was educated in London. Discovered singing in Soho's skiffle clubs where he regularly performed with the Checkmates (which included his younger brothers and John Cuffley), he was signed by Pye and had an immediate million-seller with his infectious revival of the 1916 standard, 'What Do You Want to Make Those Eyes at Me for?' (1959). Subsequent British hits (none of his records even charted in America) included a revival of **Frank Loesser**'s 'On a Slow Boat to China', a version of Baker Knight's 'You'll Never Know What You're Missing' and Howie Greenfield's 'Counting Teardrops' (1960), his last Top Ten hit. However, beyond Ford's youthful exuberance, none of these recordings had much to do with rock'n'roll. After one more minor hit, 'What Am I Gonna Do' (1961), the Checkmates – now a seven-piece band with three girl singers called the Fordettes – left him to support Jimmy Justice (whose biggest hit would be a cover of the **Drifters**' 'When My Little Girl Is Smiling' on Pye in 1962). Ford continued to record unsuccessfully for a couple of years before turning to record production (he had been a sound engineer) and moving to Europe in the mid-sixties. In the eighties he regularly played the British cabaret circuit before emigrating to America.

FRANKIE FORD
b. 1941, Gretna, Louisiana, USA

A teenage rock'n'roll singer and would-be teen-idol, Ford recorded 'Sea Cruise', a fifties classic.

After singing with high-school bands in Gretna and Algiers, Ford was signed to Johnny Vincent's Ace label, based in Jackson, Mississippi. 'Cheatin' Woman' (1958) was a local hit but the follow-up, 'Sea Cruise', was a Top Twenty hit in 1959. Written by

New Orleans bandleader **Huey 'Piano' Smith**, whose vocal track was wiped and replaced by Ford's, the song opened with the sound of ship's bells and hooters before launching into a catchy and rhythmic verse and chorus. The song was especially popular in Jamaica, where New Orleans rhythm and blues played a vital role in the development of reggae, where it was associated with the emigrants' cruise to Britain. In 1971 Ace revived the song by using the same backing track behind the voice of Little Shelton.

Ford went on to have minor hits with the witty 'Alimony' (another Smith song) and 'Time after Time'. His success led Imperial to sign him in 1960, but the **Dave Bartholomew** arrangement of 'You Talk Too Much' was less successful than the version by the song's author, Joe Jones. He also recorded 'Seventeen' before army call-up in 1962 cut short his career as a budding teen-idol.

He later performed as a nightclub singer in New Orleans. In 1983 he joined a rock'n'roll revival show with **Bobby Vee** and Bobby Helms. He released the album *Growing Pains* in the same year. In later years he occasionally recorded his old material for Stan Lewis's Paula label. In the nineties he was a regular on the nostalgia circuit.

TENNESSEE ERNIE FORD
b. Ernest Jennings Ford, 13 February 1919, Bristol, Tennessee, USA, d. 17 October 1991, Fullerton, Virginia

With his big, booming voice and movie-star appearance, Tennessee Ernie Ford lent husky sex-appeal first to country songs in the immediate post-war period – when he scandalized purists by recording with **Kay Starr** ('I'll Never Be Free', and 'Nobody's Business', 1949) – then (decently muted) to gospel music, with which he was preoccupied for more than thirty years.

After working as a radio announcer (1937–41), Ford went to Southern California, where he met Cliffie Stone, who introduced him to Capitol Records. His hits for the label included 'Mule Train' (1949) – which, like 'Cry of the Wild Goose' was transformed into a million-selling pop record by **Frankie Laine** – 'Shotgun Boogie' (1950), 'Mister and Mississippi' (1951) and 'Blackberry Boogie' (1952). All, however, were mere curtain-raisers for the million-selling 'Sixteen Tons' (1955), written by fellow Capitol artist **Merle Travis**. He also pursued, and came to concentrate on, a career in gospel music, winning a Grammy for *Great Gospel Songs* (Capitol, 1964).

During the sixties and seventies he worked only sporadically, and in 1976 he broke with Capitol. Afterwards he worked exclusively in the gospel field, recording over twenty TV-marketed albums which reached a wide audience, undocumented by conventional record-industry research methods.

FLORRIE FORDE

b. Florence Flanagan, 14 August 1876, Fitzroy,
nr Melbourne, Australia, d. 18 April 1940, Aberdeen

A *grande dame* of the British music hall, Florrie Forde
specialized in rich, rounded renderings of chorus
songs. Consequently many of the numbers she popularized are among the best-remembered pieces of
early-twentieth-century popular music, though as a
personality she is recalled much less fondly or vividly
than, say, **Marie Lloyd**.

Her first appearances, in Sydney in 1893, were in
burlesque and pantomime, as well as on the legitimate stage. In 1897 she went to London, where she
initially took principal boy roles in pantomime. Her
success with the **Harry von Tilzer** composition
'Down at the Old Bull and Bush' (1903) determined
the kind of songs with which she would be most successful, and she followed it with 'She's a Lassie from
Lancashire' (1907), 'Oh! Oh! Antonio' (1908), 'Has
Anybody Here Seen Kelly' (1909) and 'Hold Your
Hand Out, Naughty Boy' (1914). She also originated,
at least for British audiences, two songs forever associated with the First World War, 'It's a Long Way to
Tipperary' (introduced in 1912) and 'Pack Up Your
Troubles' (1915). She made numerous recordings
through the first third of the century, and appeared in
the Royal Variety Performance of 1935.

FOREIGNER

Mick Jones, b. 27 December 1944, London; Ian McDon-
ald, b. 25 June 1946, London; Lou Gramm, b. 2 May
1950, Rochester, New York, USA; Dennis Elliott, b. 18
August 1950, London, England; Ed Gagliardi, b. 13 Feb-
ruary 1952, New York (replaced by Rick Wills), b. Al
Greenwood, New York

A highly successful mainstream stadium-rock group,
Foreigner, although American-based, was led by
British musicians.

Before performing with Spooky Tooth in 1971–4,
guitarist and singer Jones had spent five years as
musical director for French star **Johnny Hallyday**. He
briefly worked in New York with Leslie West before
linking up in 1976 with former **King Crimson** multi-
instrumentalist McDonald. Drummer Elliott had
played with the Hunter-Ronson Band and British
jazz-rock group If, while lead vocalist Gramm and
other members came from New York bands.

Offering an adult-orientated-rock formula, akin to
Boston and the **Cars**, Foreigner found a ready audi-
ence for their eponymous 1977 Atlantic début album.
It provided three hit singles written by Jones and
Gramm: 'Feels Like the First Time', 'Cold as Ice' and
'Long Long Way from Home'. *Double Vision* (1978)
consolidated the group's position with two million-

sellers, 'Hot Blooded' and the title track. For *Head
Games* (1979), Wills (formerly of King Crimson, the
Faces and **Peter Frampton**'s band) replaced Gagliardi
on bass.

The next album title, *4* (1980), referred both to the
group's sequence of releases and its personnel. By
now, McDonald and Greenwood had left and
Thomas Dolby and **Junior Walker** were guest players on the album. With Gramm's soaring blue-eyed
soul vocals, 'Waiting for a Girl Like You' was a hit on
both sides of the Atlantic. *Agent Provocateur* (1984)
contained the best known of Foreigner's songs, 'I
Want to Know What Love Is'*. Featuring the New
Jersey Mass Choir behind Gramm's plaintive lead
singing, the song – the supreme example of the
yearning romanticism and studio perfection which
were the band's trademark – reached No. 1 in both
America and Britain. *Inside Information* (1987) contained the Top Ten US hit 'I Don't Want to Live
Without You'.

In the mid-eighties the group's members pursued
separate projects. Jones co-produced **Van Halen**'s
5150, while Wills worked in radio and Gramm
released *Ready or Not* (Atlantic, 1987), a solo album
with Dan Hartman as producer and Nils Lofgren
among his accompanists. He followed it with *Long
Hard Look* (1989), before leaving in 1990 to form the
short-lived Shadowking with ex-**Whitesnake** and
future Def Leppard guitarist Vivian Campbell.

Jones released an eponymous solo album in 1989
and produced **Billy Joel**'s *Storm Front* (1989), before
reassembling Foreigner with new vocalist Johnny
Edwards for *Unusual Heat* (1991). It was a commercial
failure. Gramm rejoined in 1992, and the group
recorded some new tracks for the compilation *The
Very Best . . . Beyond*, released that year. A huge
American tour provided the album *The Classic Hits
Live* (1993). A new studio album, *Mr Moonlight*,
appeared the following year but by then the group's
back catalogue of car radio hits was regularly out-
selling their current releases.

GEORGE FORMBY

b. William Booth, 24 May 1904, Wigan, Lancashire,
England, d. 6 March 1961, Blackpool, Lancashire

Britain's highest-paid entertainer during the Second
World War and, with **Gracie Fields**, the most popular
screen star of the period, singer, ukelele-player and
comedian Formby – originally described as the
'gormless Lancashire lad' – was one of the few
regional entertainers to become nationally famous in
Britain.

The son of music-hall singer and comic George
Formby Snr, he was originally apprenticed as a
jockey, only turning to showbusiness on the death of

his father in 1921. After briefly working under his mother's maiden name of Hoy, he reluctantly took his father's stage name and much of his repertoire. Success came only after his marriage in 1924 to Beryl Ingham, a clog-dancer from Accrington, and the introduction of the ukulele into his act. Ingham (with whom Formby briefly appeared as a duo) subsequently masterminded his career, gradually transforming him from a toothy, Northern comedian to a classless figure in an evening suit, with brilliantined hair parted neatly in the middle to sanitize his risqué songs.

One of the first British radio stars, Formby graduated to films, starring in sixteen, beginning with *Boots! Boots!* (1934) and ending with *George in Civvy Street* (1946). *It's Turned Out Nice Again* (1941), titled after one of his stock phrases, was typical of these low-budget, simple-minded farces. The films' saving graces were Formby's performances and the songs (mostly co-written by him). Some, like 'Auntie Maggie's Remedy', were recognizable products of the urban folk tradition of his native Lancashire (as are the songs of comedian-singer Mike Harding, whose 'Rochdale Cowboy', was a surprise British hit in 1975 on Rubber). But even the sentimental hits, such as 'Leaning on a Lamp-post' (written by prolific British songwriter **Noel Gay**) or saucy songs like 'When I'm Cleaning Windows' (which was banned by the BBC) and 'With My Little Stick of Blackpool Rock', benefited from Formby's jaunty, throaty renditions. Similarly, his deft ukulele-playing brought a new popularity to the instrument.

Formby's popularity reached its zenith during the Second World War, when his travels to entertain the troops won him the Order of the British Empire. But after 1945 changes in popular taste led to a decline in his career. He turned successfully to the stage, starring in *Zip Goes a Million* in 1951, but thereafter he was dogged by ill-health. Formby died within three months of his wife, whose role had been crucial to his success. A mark of how far he entered the nation's consciousness was 1994's version of 'When I'm Cleaning Windows' by 2 in a Tent. The **Stock, Aitken** house-style production sampled the original Formby recording.

DAVID FOSTER
b. Victoria, British Columbia, Canada

Foster has been one of the most prolific songwriters and producers of pop and soul ballads in the last two decades.

After training as a classical pianist, he played in local rock bands before moving to Los Angeles as a member of Skylark, which had a US hit with 'Wildflower' (1971). When the band split up, Foster played piano in a production of *The Rocky Horror Show* and became a session musician.

He turned to songwriting and production in the late seventies, composing the **Earth, Wind and Fire** hit 'After the Love Has Gone'. Among his first studio jobs were albums by **Alice Cooper**, **Hall and Oates** and the **Average White Band**. He supervised **Chicago**'s sixteenth and seventeenth albums (composing the hit 'Hard to Say I'm Sorry') in the mid-eighties before finding a niche as writer-producer to leading adult contemporary solo artists.

In the mid-eighties he worked with **Barbra Streisand**, **Julio Iglesias** and **Anne Murray**. More recently Foster has co-produced recordings by Natalie Cole ('Unforgettable'), **Michael Bolton**, **Céline Dion** and Color Me Badd.

His credits as a film composer include songs for *St Elmo's Fire* (the John Parr American chart-topper 'Man in Motion', 1985), *White Nights* and *Quicksilver*. His 'The Glory of Love' was a big hit for Peter Cetera and appeared in *The Karate Kid Part II* (1986).

In 1993 he compiled and produced the multi-artist *The Christmas Album*. Among those contributing were Wynonna (formerly of the **Judds**), Bebe and Cece Winans and **Johnny Mathis**. Foster himself sang 'Carol of the Bells'.

Foster has recorded several solo albums. These include *Songwriters for the Stars* (1983), *David Foster* (1986) and *Symphony Sessions* (1988), on which he played his own 'Piano Concerto in G'.

STEPHEN FOSTER
b. 4 July 1826, Lawrenceville, Pennsylvania, USA,
d. 13 January 1864, New York

Foster was both America's first great popular songwriter and its first professional songwriter. He wrote some 200 songs and supported himself by his trade from 1850 until his early death in 1864. He was also one of the first white innovators to mine the deep seam of black music and culture, in however bowdlerized a fashion, that would be essential to the development of American (and hence the world's) popular music in the twentieth century. His deceptively simple, folk-like songs include the infectiously rhythmic 'Oh! Susannah' (1848), the cleverly crafted nostalgia of 'The Old Folks at Home' (1851), both classics of minstrelsy, and the wistful pleasures of the quintessential 'Irish' ballad 'Jeannie with the Light Brown Hair' (1854). His songs were among the first to be recorded on **Thomas Alva Edison**'s cylinders in 1890, along with the marches of **John Philip Sousa**, and have retained their popularity in the twentieth century through interpretations by artists as disparate as **Alma Gluck**, **Bing Crosby** and the **Byrds**.

The son of a well-to-do family, Foster was a largely

self-taught pianist. He composed his first song (the refined ballad 'Open Thy Lattice Love') in his teens and had it published in 1844. Then, during a stay in Cincinnati, he sold the rights to a batch of songs to publisher W. C. Peters. They included 'Susannah', which became the unofficial anthem of the California Gold Rush of 1849, and 'Old Uncle Ned', the first of his character sketches of black people. Both were minstrel songs, 'Susannah' being credited on the sheet music as from the repertoire of 'the Original Christy Minstrels', one of America's leading troupes of minstrel performers. This began a lengthy association between Foster and their leader, E. P. Christy, who would popularize many of the writer's songs. 'Ned' was similarly credited on sheet music as being from the repertoire of 'the Great Southern Sable Harmonists'.

Written in the heavy dialect of a white man's notion of black speech, Foster's songs echo many of the themes of early minstrelsy, depicting a mythical black as simple, amusing, illiterate and concerned only with pleasure. In this, they were surprisingly little different from the songs of America's first major black songwriter, James A. Bland, whose songs of plantation life, such as 'Carry Me Back to Old Virginny' (published in 1878 and later a million-seller for Alma Gluck) and 'Oh! Dem Golden Slippers' (1879), offered similarly sentimental and stereotyped portraits of blacks. As one critic has put it, 'Bland was a black Stephen Foster, as Foster was a white Bland.' However, though Foster's songs retained the patronizing attitudes of the era, he gradually brought new technical and emotional complexities to bear on his given subject. He introduced the idea of a chorus, rather than a mere refrain, and invested the black people he depicted in song with credible feelings and dignity. In 1853, when a stage adaptation of *Uncle Tom's Cabin* was mounted, several Foster songs, including 'The Old Folks at Home' – probably his best-known song – and 'My Old Kentucky Home' (1853), were interpolated. Among Foster's best songs of this type are 'Camptown Races' (1850), 'Massa's in de Cold, Cold Ground' (1852) and 'Old Dog Tray' (1853), by which time there is no mention of slaves or the South, and no trace of dialect. Moreover, the popularity of Foster's songs soon spread beyond minstrelsy: when singers like Adeline Patti toured America they invariably sang a Foster song as their encore.

The melancholy of many of Foster's minstrel songs – 'The morn of life is past' opens 'Tray' – found pure expression in the nostalgia of 'Jeannie', but with the notable exception of 'Beautiful Dreamer' (1864) hardly any of the similarly themed songs he wrote after moving to New York in 1860 are remembered today.

THE FOUR ACES
Al Alberts, b. Chester, Pennsylvania, USA; Dave Mahoney, b. Chester; Sod Voccaro, b. Chester; Lou Silvestri, b. Chester

With Alberts' rich baritone giving a melodramatic inflection to their barber-shop harmonies, the Four Aces sold some 20 million records in the fifties. But despite the fact that they were edging towards rock'n'roll in presentation and style, they were stranded on its shores.

After performing in the Philadelphia area in the late forties, they financed their own recording of the tantalizing ballad, 'Sin', on the local Victoria label and sold a million copies in 1951. Signed to Decca they had a further hit with 'Tell Me Why'* (1951), which was co-written by Alberts. After several minor hits, they sang **Sammy Cahn**'s and **Jule Styne**'s Oscar-winning film theme, the dramatic ballad 'Three Coins in the Fountain'* (1953), which set the pattern of their later recordings. These included 'Stranger in Paradise'* (1953), from the musical *Kismet*, and **Sammy Fain**'s 'Love Is a Many Splendored Thing'* (1955), another Oscar-winning song, before Alberts left for an unsuccessful solo career.

Without him to underpin their histrionic approach to harmony, the Four Aces faded from view by the end of the fifties after covers of 'Friendly Persuasion' (first recorded by **Pat Boone**, 1956), 'The World Outside' (a bigger hit for the Four Coins, another white vocal group of the period, in 1958), and the **Chordettes**' 'No Other Arms, No Other Lips' (1959). They made an unsuccessful attempt to climb aboard the rock'n'roll bandwagon with the awkward 'Rock and Roll Rhapsody' (1958).

THE FOUR FRESHMEN
Bob Flanigan, b. 22 August 1926, Greencastle, Indiana, USA; Ross Barbour, b. 31 December 1928, Columbus, Indiana; Hal Kratzch (replaced by Ken Errair, b. 23 January 1930, replaced 1956 by Ken Albers); Don Barbour, b. 19 April 1927, Greencastle, Indiana (replaced 1960 by Billy Comstock, replaced 1973 by Ray Brown)

A vocal and instrumental group known for their intricate four-part harmonies, the Four Freshmen were, with the Hi-Los, the most important of the jazz-orientated harmony groups of the fifties. In their time an influence on the **Four Preps**, the **Lettermen** and others, they were regular poll winners (even winning *Billboard*'s award for best vocal group of 1958, two years after their last chart hit). However, their influence on rock'n'roll group singing was minimal, until the **Beach Boys** recast their delicate harmonies in a more robust fashion in songs about the experiences of teenage America.

Formed in Indianapolis by the Barbour Brothers as the Toppers in 1948, the group toured the Midwest as the Four Freshmen. On the recommendation of **Stan Kenton** they were signed to Capitol in 1950 and had a series of minor hits, including 'Now You Know' and 'Pick up Your Tears', before recording 'It's a Blue World', their first major success, in 1952. Their other major hits were 'Day by Day', 'Charmaine' (1955) and the classic 'Graduation Day' (1956), which the Beach Boys used as a model for their own wistful songs about high school.

Unlike the more dramatically inclined Hi-Los who were unwilling to accommodate themselves to the changing times, the Four Freshmen in the course of their long career recorded over thirty albums, including *Freshman Favorites* (1956) and *Voices in Love* (1968), judiciously mixing standards and contemporary songs, and toured the world with their tight harmonies still intact.

THE FOUR LADS

Frank Busseri, b. Toronto, Canada; Bernard Toorish, b. Toronto; James Arnold, b. Toronto; Connie Codarini, b. Toronto

The Four Lads were one of the most commercially successful of the numerous white harmony groups of the early fifties.

Like the **Crew Cuts**, former choir boys from Toronto's Cathedral Choir School, the Four Lads were signed as back-up singers for recording sessions by Columbia in 1950. In this capacity they supported **Johnny Ray** on his 1951 million-seller 'Cry'. The group's own recording career began with the 1952 hit 'The Mocking Bird', a hit again when it was reissued in 1956 and a further hit when they re-recorded it in 1958. The song initiated a series of exotic songs that included 'Istambul' (1953) and 'Skokiaan' (1954) before Al Stillman and Robert Allen supplied the group with a pair of dramatic ballads, 'Moments to Remember'* (1955) and 'No, Not Much'* (1956). Subsequent hits included a swinging version of 'Standing on the Corner' (from *The Most Happy Fella*) and 'The Bus Stop Song' (from *Bus Stop*) in 1956, 'Who Needs You', 'Put a Light in the Window' (1957), 'There's Only One of You' and 'Enchanted Island' (1958). All were brash, up-tempo vocal workouts.

With a much changed line-up, the Four Lads continued to appear on television and in cabaret throughout the sixties.

THE FOUR PREPS

Bruce Belland; Glen Larson; Ed Cobb; Mary Ingram; Marvin Inabett; Don Clarke

An early influence on the **Beach Boys**, the Four Preps'

tight harmonies garnered them a couple of hits in the fifties. The group's shortlived career also prepared members Cobb and Larson and arranger Lincoln Mayorga for their diverse careers in showbusiness.

The group came together in the Hollywood High School Choir and made their début supporting **Rick Nelson** at Hamilton High School. Signed to Capitol, they had a minor hit in 1956 with 'Dreamy Eyes', before their sing-along rendition of Larson and Belland's '26 Miles (Santa Catalina)' sold over a million copies in 1958. Even more impressive was 'Big Man' (1958), also written by Belland and Larson, which featured arranger Mayorga's rich piano embellishments. The Four Preps now made a series of novelty records, including 'Got a Girl' (1960) and 'More Money for You and Me' (1961), a medley which was a genially cynical comment on rock'n'roll and included rewritten snippets of 'Mr Blue', 'A Teenager in Love' and 'Smoke Gets in Your Eyes', among others. Their last chart entry neatly identified the reason for their (and many of their contemporaries') lack of success, 'A Letter to The Beatles' (1964). With Canadian folk singer David Sommerville replacing Cobb in 1966, the Four Preps briefly became folkies, recording a version of Phil Ochs' 'Draft Dodger Rag' before disbanding in 1967.

Cobb and Mayorga had greater success as the producers and leaders of the Piltdown Men, a group of Capitol session men who had a series of novelty instrumental hits that mixed symphonic arrangements with booting saxes to good effect. In Britain, where arranger Harry Robinson (under the pseudonym of Lord Rockingham's XI) had earlier had a huge success with the raucous novelty record 'Hoots Mon' (Decca, 1958), the Piltdown Men were particularly appreciated. After 'Brontosaurus Stomp' (Capitol, 1960), which was only a minor American hit, they had a trio of Top Twenty records in Britain, 'McDonald's Cave' (1960), 'Piltdown Rides Again' and 'Goodnight Mrs Flintstone' (both 1961).

An established arranger and session pianist, Mayorga's first independent success came with Ketty Lester. A one-time torch singer who had toured with **Cab Calloway**, she recorded an emotional version of **Victor Young**'s film tune, 'Love Letters' (Era, 1962), for which Mayorga provided the memorable, austere piano accompaniment. Subsequent records, all with Mayorga at the piano, including 'But Not for Me' (1962), failed because they were too similar.

Mayorga was more successful in providing Brenda Holloway (*b. 21 June 1946, Atascardero, California*) with another majestic piano accompaniment for the anguished soul ballad 'Every Little Bit Hurts' (Tamla, 1964). Written by Cobb, the song has since become a standard. Holloway's other, lesser, hits include 'When I'm Gone' (1965) and her own composition 'You've

Made Me So Very Happy' (1967, later a million-seller for **Blood, Sweat and Tears**). Mayorga remained a respected session musician, working particularly closely with **Phil Ochs** (on *Tape from California*, 1967, and *Gunfight at Carnegie Hall*, 1971, among others) with whom he also toured. Mayorga also worked on albums by **Frank Zappa**, **Dusty Springfield**, **Ringo Starr**, Spring and Dory Previn. In the eighties he released a number of jazz-inflected albums, most notably with Amanda McBroom (*Growing up in Hollywood Town* and *West of Oz*, 1982). He also produced classical recordings.

Songwriter Cobb added production to his credits and by the mid-sixties was the linchpin of the Los Angeles garage-band scene. He wrote and produced a series of hits for the Standells (including the classic 'Dirty Water', 'Sometimes Good Guys Don't Wear White' and 'Why Pick on Me', 1966) and the Chocolate Watch Band ('Riot on Sunset Strip', 1967), among others, on Tower. His seventies production credits include the **Lettermen** (*Spin Away*, Capitol, 1972) and **Liberace** (*Mr Showmanship*, AVI, 1978). Cobb wrote and produced Gloria Jones' 'Tainted Love'. The song was a transatlantic hit in 1981 for Soft Cell (featuring **Marc Almond**).

The most commercially successful former Four Prep, however, was Larson. In the seventies he became an important Hollywood television producer-writer-director who specialized in borrowing concepts from hit movies and transforming them into teleseries. His successes included *McCloud*, *Alias Smith and Jones*, *Six Million Dollar Man* and *Battlestar Galactica*.

THE FOUR SEASONS

Frankie Valli, b. Francis Castellucio, 3 May 1937, Newark, New Jersey, USA; Bob Gaudio, b. 17 November 1942, Bronx, New York; Nick Massi, b. Nicholas Macioci, 19 September 1935; Tommy Devito, b. 19 June 1936

With the **Beach Boys**, the Four Seasons were the most successful American male vocal group of the rock era, selling some 80 million records in the course of their career. Frankie Valli had an instantly recognizable stratospheric falsetto voice and led the group through two decades of consistent hits, mainly built on the classic doo-wop sound of the fifties.

Valli began his career as a solo singer in 1952, but after little success joined the New Jersey-based Variatones, which included Massi, Devito and his brother. They renamed themselves the Four Lovers and signed with RCA in 1955. Although they charted the following year with 'Apple of My Eye', after one more single for Epic ('Pucker Up', 1958), they returned to the Jersey bar circuit.

Valli met producer **Bob Crewe** – then involved with the Philadelphia-based Swan label – in 1960. Crewe hired Valli and his group (which by now featured Gaudio, who while a member of the Royal Teens had composed their Top Ten ABC hit 'Short Shorts', 1958) as demo singers, promising them recording chances of their own. For two years, the group had releases on a variety of labels under several names, as well as providing background vocals for many Crewe productions. In early 1962 Crewe renamed the group the Four Seasons (after a local Jersey bowling alley) and produced 'Bermuda', the first record on which the group's distinctive sound was apparent. Leased to **George Goldner**'s End Label, 'Bermuda' failed but for their next release – the incantatory 'Sherry' in July 1962 – Crewe secured a production deal with Chicago-based Vee-Jay Records, then the largest black-owned company in America.

Within four weeks 'Sherry' was No. 1 on the chart and had sold in excess of a million copies. The Four Seasons then became the first group to achieve three consecutive No. 1 million-selling records, with 'Big Girls Don't Cry' (1962) and 'Walk Like a Man' (1963). Billed as the Four Seasons featuring the 'sound' of Frankie Valli, the group undertook a non-stop round of touring and television and, in order to have sufficient product for records, held a mammoth four-day recording session at New York's Bell sound studios. The material from these sessions – in the main covers of doo-wop and rock standards, with the odd Crewe–Gaudio composition – provided the bulk of their Vee-Jay releases over the next eighteen months. In late 1963 they sued Vee-Jay in a royalty dispute, won, and retrieved all their recordings, thereby becoming one of the earliest rock groups to have total control over their own material.

In 1964 they signed with Philips and returned to the charts with 'Dawn (Go Away)' which reached No. 2 (**The Beatles** held positions 1,3,4, and 5). With the Beach Boys, the Four Seasons were the only American group to survive the British invasion. For the next four years, they enjoyed an unbroken run of Top Twenty hits, which included the No. 1 'Rag Doll', **Bob Dylan**'s 'Don't Think Twice' (1965), under the pseudonym the Wonder Who, 'Let's Hang on' (1965), 'Working My Way Back to You' (1966), and a reworking of **Cole Porter**'s 'I've Got You Under My Skin'. Their 1968 attempt at social relevance with the album *Genuine Imitation Life Gazette*, a release better remembered for its complex sleeve design than its music, spelled the end of their hitmaking days and ushered in a lean period which lasted throughout the early seventies.

Members came and went with alarming regularity and Valli and Gaudio – the only stable elements – formed the Four Seasons' Partnership to control the masters that they retrieved after litigation with Philips. They signed with Motown's West Coast label Mowest in 1972, releasing the critically acclaimed, but commercially disastrous, *Chameleon*. However, after several more failed singles, they left Motown with a reputation as one of the top live concert draws in America still intact.

Valli purchased from Motown the master of a song in which he had faith, 'My Eyes Adored You', and obtained a deal for himself and the track with Private Stock records. Concurrently, he and Gaudio signed a version of the Four Seasons to Warner Curb records, and in 1974 Motown UK issued a track from *Chameleon*, 'The Night', which reached No. 7 in the UK in early 1975. It shared the chart with Valli's own 'My Eyes Adored You'*, which had by this time reached No. 1 in America; simultaneously, the group's first single for Warners, 'Who Loves You', was on its way to a Top Ten placing on both sides of the Atlantic. The group were again as famous as in their sixties heyday. The next Warners single, 'December 1963 (Oh What a Night)'*, was a No. 1 all round the world, and their biggest-ever hit; it was also unique for the fact that the majority of the vocals were taken by drummer Gerry Polci. The song was again a British hit in 1988. In 1978 Valli again reached No. 1 with the Barry Gibb theme from the movie *Grease*.

Gaudio gave up touring in the mid-seventies to concentrate on production. His work includes sessions for **Diana Ross**, **Roberta Flack**, Peabo Bryson, **Neil Diamond** (*The Jazz Singer*, 1980), **Barbra Streisand**, and the 1987 soundtrack to *Little Shop of Horrors*. Despite some dismal recordings, including an ill-advised flirtation with electro-funk on the MCA album *Streetfighter*, Valli and his various Seasons remained one of the most consistent live attractions in America and one of the most reissued. Among the group's members in the eighties were guitarist Larry Lingle, Robin Swenson (Keyboards), Rex Robinson (bass) and Chuck Wilson (drums). There were occasional recordings during this period, including a Ben Liebrand remix of 'December '63' for the film *Dirty Dancing II* and the 1992 album *Hope + Glory* (Curb), which featured Gaudio with Valli. *Anthology* (Rhino, 1987) is the best retrospective.

THE FOUR TOPS
Renaldo Benson, b. 1937, Detroit, Michigan, USA; Abdul Fakir, b. 26 December 1935, Detroit; Lawrence Payton, b. 1938, Detroit, d. 20 June 1997; Levi Stubbs, b. 6 June 1936, Detroit

The archetypal soul vocal group, the Four Tops retained their original line-up for over thirty years. Among their greatest hits was the classic 'Reach Out I'll Be There' (1966).

The group was formed in Detroit in 1952 as jazz vocal quartet the Four Aims. They recorded for Riverside, Singular, Chess and Columbia before joining **Berry Gordy**'s Motown in 1964. Their style was remoulded by the **Holland, Dozier and Holland** production team and their first single, 'Baby I Need Your Loving', reached the Top Twenty. The record introduced Stubbs' gruff, pleading lead vocal and the group's attractive harmony lines. The following year the Four Tops had their first No. 1 with 'I Can't Help Myself' and a Top Ten hit with 'It's the Same Old Song'.

The string of Motown hits continued until 1971. They included both Holland–Dozier–Holland compositions – 'Reach Out', 'Standing in the Shadows of Love' (1966), 'Bernadette' (1967) – and covers of pop hits like Left Banke's 'Walk Away Renee' (1968), **Tim Hardin**'s 'If I Were a Carpenter' (1968) and **Jimmy Webb**'s 'MacArthur Park' (1971). When the group joined Dunhill in 1972, Dennis Lambert, Brian Potter and Steve Barri provided further successes with 'Keeper of the Castle' (1972), 'Ain't No Woman (Like the One I've Got)'* and 'Are You Man Enough?' (1973) from the soundtrack of *Shaft in Africa*.

By now a pop institution, the Four Tops made frequent international tours during the seventies, signing to Casablanca in 1981. *Tonight* included a Top Twenty hit in 'When She Was My Girl', while 'Don't Walk Away' had similar success in Britain. In 1984 the group re-signed with Motown but neither *Magic* nor *Hot Nights* sold well. *Indestructible* (1988) was the début album for Arista with guest artists **Aretha Franklin** and **Phil Collins**, whose film *Buster* included 'Going Loco in Acapulco' by the Four Tops. The group also sang on Franklin's *Through the Storm* (1989).

In the nineties the Four Tops continued to tour the cabaret and nostalgia circuit. In 1992 they performed at the opening ceremony of the Eurodisney theme park near Paris.

KIM FOWLEY
b. 21 July 1942, Manila, Philippines

A grandson of **Rudolf Friml**, Fowley was a significant contributor to the Los Angeles music scene, from the days of black vocal groups in the fifties to the power pop of the seventies. Moreover, in common with Britain's **Jonathan King** (but across a far wider range of material), he demonstrated an unerring ear for gimmicky, novelty singles that earned him a cult status that lasted well into the nineties.

The son of actor Douglas Fowley (Doc in the *Wyatt Earp* teleseries and memorable as 'the director' in *Singing in the Rain*, 1952), he was brought up in Hollywood. In 1957 he sang with members of the **Jay-**

hawks (best known for their 1956 R&B hit 'Stranded in the Jungle' on Flash) and played with the Sleepwalkers, who then included **Sandy Nelson** and, legend has it, (briefly) featured **Phil Spector** on guitar. While working as a disc-jockey in Boise, Idaho, he produced the first recordings of **Paul Revere and the Raiders** ('Like Long Hair', Gardenia, 1961) before returning to Los Angeles where, often with schoolmates Gary Paxton and Skip Battin, he produced a series of records with shortlived groups. These included a pair of Top Twenty hits for Skip and Flip (as Paxton and Battin called themselves), 'It Was I' (Brant, 1959) and 'Cherry Pie' (1960), and the Paradons R&B hit 'Diamonds and Pearls' (Milestone, 1960). His biggest success came with his production of **Dallas Frazier**'s novelty song 'Alley-Oop'* (Lute, 1960) by the Hollywood Argyles, who were formed by Paxton and Bobby Rey, producer of the Safaris' 'Image of a Girl', a Los Angeles hit on Eldo in 1960. Fowley also produced 'Bumble Boogie' (Rendezvous, 1961) and 'Nut Rocker' (1962) by B. Bumble and the Stingers; 'Papa-Oom-Mow-Mow' by the Rivingtons (Liberty, 1962); and the Murmaids' version of **Bread**'s David Gates' 'Popsicles and Icicles' (Chattahoochee, 1963).

In 1965 Fowley turned his attention to the new rock music ushered in by **The Beatles**. He moved to Britain where he worked with **P. J. Proby** (as a choreographer) and produced sessions for **Family**, the Rockin' Berries, **Slade** (then called the 'N Betweens), **Cat Stevens** and **Soft Machine**, among others. On his return to Los Angeles, he joined **Frank Zappa**'s Mothers of Invention for their début album, *Freak Out* (1966), remixed **Johnny Winter**'s *Progressive Blues Experiment* (1969) and produced 'Don't Bogart that Joint' for Fraternity of Man, a song that appeared on the soundtrack of *Easy Rider* (1969). He looked back to the fifties by producing **Gene Vincent**'s *I'm Back and I'm Proud* (1969) as well as working with revivalist group Flash Cadillac and the Continental Kids. He produced Warren Zevon's début album, *Wanted Dead or Alive* (1969), and worked with the eccentric **Jonathan Richman**.

His self-produced solo albums, however, were as often infuriating and irritating as they were outrageous and charming. These included *Born to Be Wild* (Imperial, 1968), *I'm Bad* (Capitol, 1972) and *Snake Document Masquerade* (Island, 1979), a futuristic 'history' of the eighties. In the early seventies he concentrated on songwriting for the **Byrds** (especially when old associate Battin was a member), **Doug Sahm**, **REO Speedwagon** and **Helen Reddy**.

In 1975, in a calculated move, he recruited the all-female group the Runaways, who he garbed in black leather and presented as tough tomboys just out for fun. The image was ahead of its time and after a series of albums, mostly written by Fowley and the group, that sold only in Japan (including *The Runaways*, Mercury, 1976, and *Waitin' for the Night*, 1979), the group folded. Founder member **Joan Jett** formed her own group, Joan Jett and the Blackhearts, and had a series of American hits with similarly styled high-energy rock'n'roll. Since then Fowley has been largely inactive, although he has made occasional recordings, including the lacklustre *Sex, Cars & God* (Koch International, 1999).

ROY FOX
b. 25 October 1901, Denver, Colorado, USA, d. 20 March 1982, London, England

The American-born Fox was one of the most successful bandleaders in Britain in the thirties.

Raised in Hollywood, Fox took up the cornet at the age of eleven and played in various bands in the Los Angeles area before forming his own in 1920 to play at the Club Royale, Culver City. After a period travelling between residencies in New York, Miami and Hollywood, he was appointed musical director of the Fox Film Studio in 1928. Two years later Fox accepted an invitation to form a band for a season at London's Café de Paris. His sweet tone – he was known as 'the whispering cornettist', as much for his style of play as for his use of 'Whispering' as his signature tune – proved popular and he signed with Decca in 1931. His first major British band, which included **Nat Gonella**, Syd Buckman, Billy and Micky Amstell, Lew Stone and **Al Bowlly**, was regularly featured by the BBC. After Fox fell ill, Stone took over the band, and in 1933 Fox formed another band which included Buckman, Hughie Tripp, Harry Gold, Ivor Mairants, Andy Hodgkiss, Les Lambert and singer Denny Dennis.

Between 1933 and 1938, when he went to Australia, Fox toured Britain, recorded (for Decca and HMV) and regularly broadcast, his smooth sophisticated dance music finding special favour. He led small groups in New York during the war, returning to the UK in 1964 where he re-formed his band briefly, before leaving bandleading for management. In 1975 he published his autobiography, *Hollywood, Mayfair and All That Jazz*.

CHARLIE AND INEZ FOXX
Charlie, b. 29 October 1939, Greensboro, North Carolina, USA, d. 18 September 1998; Inez, b. 9 September 1944, Greensboro

A brother and sister R&B vocal duo, Inez and Charlie Foxx are best remembered for their 'call and response' novelty hit 'Mockingbird' (1963).

Their first public performance was with the Gospel Tide Choir in Greensboro, after which they played in local clubs before moving to New York in 1959. The Foxx's arrangement of 'Mockingbird', which was based on the same children's rhyme as the song 'Bo Diddley' and similar to **Shirley Ellis**' 'The Clapping Song', another song based on a child's rhyme, was released under Inez's name by Sue Records' Juggy Murray on his Symbol label. After it reached the Top Ten, Murray attempted unsuccessfully to repeat the formula with 'Hi Diddle Diddle' and 'Ask Me'.

However, 'Mockingbird' and the hypnotic 'Hurt by Love' (1964) established Inez and Charlie as a top R&B attraction and they had a further minor pop hit with another novelty song '(1–2–3–4–5–6–7) Count the Days' (Dynamo, 1968). Charlie Foxx concentrated on production in the late sixties and with Jerry Williams was responsible for **Gene Pitney**'s remarkable excursion into soul, 'She's a Heartbreaker' (Musicor, 1968).

After the duo split up at the end of the decade, Inez married producer Luther Dixon and recorded in Memphis for the Stax subsidiary Volt (*Inez in Memphis*, 1973). 'Mockingbird' was successfully revived in 1974 by **James Taylor** and **Carly Simon** and in 1982 by the Belle Stars.

PETER FRAMPTON
b. 22 April 1950, Beckenham, Kent, England

A 'guitar hero' of the seventies, Frampton had the bestselling live album of the decade.

He formed the Herd with Andy Bown on keyboards in 1966. Initially a rhythm and blues group, the Herd as recording artists were the vehicle for the poetic aspirations of **Dave Dee, Dozy, Beaky, Mick and Tich** writers Howard and Blaikley. In 1967 they had three hits on Fontana, including the impressive 'From the Underworld' (apparently inspired by the Orpheus myth) and 'Paradise Lost', which bore minimal resemblance to Milton's epic poem.

His fey good looks won Frampton a pop star following, but he was more comfortable with the heavy blues/rock band Humble Pie, which he set up with ex-**Small Faces** singer Steve Marriott in 1969. Extensive touring and the successful live album *Rockin' at the Fillmore* (A&M, 1971) established the band with American audiences, and provided a launch-pad for Frampton's solo career.

With Bown as session player, he recorded *Winds of Change* (A&M, 1972) and formed Frampton's Camel with former Spooky Tooth keyboards-player Mike Kellie and bassist Rick Wills, later to join **Foreigner**. Frampton's guitar pyrotechnics and coast-to-coast tours resulted in over six million sales for *Frampton Comes Alive!* (1976). Recorded in San Francisco, the album included backing musicians John Siomos (drums), Stanley Sheldon (bass) and Bob May (keyboards and guitar). Unusually for a live recording, it also produced hit singles including 'Show Me the Way', which featured the 'vocoder', a device which synthesized voice and guitar sounds, and 'Baby, I Love Your Way'.

The follow-up, *I'm in You* (1977), included **Ringo Starr** and **Stevie Wonder** among the backing musicians, and in 1978 Frampton took the role of Billy Shears in Robert Stigwood's inept film of *Sgt Pepper's Lonely Hearts Club Band*. Soon afterwards he was seriously injured in a car crash but returned to stadium tours in 1979 when 'I Can't Stand It No More' from *Where I Should Be* was a hit.

Frampton went on to record two further albums for A&M before going into semi-retirement. He returned to recording with *Premonition* (Atlantic, 1986), and briefly became lead guitarist for former schoolmate **David Bowie** in 1987. He released the unexceptional *When All the Pieces Fit* (1989), but a proposed Humble Pie reunion was scrapped on Marriott's death in 1991. Frampton and Marriott had recorded 'The Bigger They Come' for the film *Harley Davidson and the Marlboro Man* and two further tracks by the pair surfaced on the 1992 retrospective collection *Shine on*, while another provided a highpoint of 1994's *Peter Frampton* (Relativity). *Frampton Comes Alive II* (El Dorado, 1995) was less successful. He subsequently became a member of **Ringo Starr**'s All Starr band.

CONNIE FRANCIS
b. Concetta Franconero, 12 December 1938, Newark, New Jersey, USA

With a mixture of bouncy numbers and throbbing ballads whose only connection with rock'n'roll was her youthful exuberance, Francis was the most successful female artist of the fifties and early sixties, selling over 40 million records.

Francis learned the accordion at the age of four and first sang professionally at the age of eleven. After appearing on *Arthur Godfrey Talent Scouts*, she changed her name and embarked on a showbusiness career, singing standards in New York cocktail lounges. Signed to MGM in 1955, she had her first success duetting with **Marvin Rainwater** on 'Majesty of Love' in 1957. However, her solo records, which included 'Forgetting' (1956), failed until she cut an uptempo version of the standard 'Who's Sorry Now' (1958), written by **Kalamar and Ruby** and Ted Snyder in 1923. Boosted by her regular appearances on **Dick Clark**'s *American Bandstand*, the record went on to sell a million copies. Other standards which became hits for her include Betty Peterson's and Borney Bergantine's 'My Happiness'* (1958), which had already provided John and Sandra Steele with a million-seller in

1948 on Damon; Edgar Leslie's and Horatio Nicholls' 'Among My Souvenirs'* (1959); the Italian songs 'Mama'* (1960), later a million-seller for boy vocalist Heintje, and 'Jealous of You' (1960), which was originally titled 'Tango della Gelosia'; and DeSylva, Brown and Henderson's 1928 hit 'Together'.

More appealing than these florid reworkings were her gimmicky teen-orientated numbers, many of which were written by the new generation of New York songwriters. These included 'Stupid Cupid' (1958), written by Neil Sedaka and Howie Greenfield, 'Lipstick on Your Collar'* (1959), 'Robot Man' (1960) – a British hit only – and the American No. 1 'My Heart Has a Mind of Its Own', written by Greenfield with Jack Keller. 'Where the Boys Are'* (1961), another Sedaka–Greenfield composition, was the theme of the film in which she made her screen début.

Francis's success continued through the early sixties, with records such as 'Don't Break the Heart That Loves You' (1962) and 'Follow the Boys' (1963), but the arrival of The Beatles ended her residency in the charts and she embarked on a career as a nightclub singer. She found new audiences outside America, recording albums in French, German, Spanish, Italian and even Japanese, in the manner of Petula Clark, and collections of national and ethnic songs, including My Thanks to You (1959), a collection of songs by British songwriters recorded in London and Connie Francis Sings Great Jewish Favourites (Polydor, 1977).

Following a rape attack in 1974, she stopped performing for several years. In America, her most successful albums were collections of country songs, notably her duet with Hank Williams Jnr, Connie Francis and Hank Williams Jnr Sing Great Country Hits (Polydor, 1976). She returned to performing in the eighties and published an autobiography, Who's Sorry Now (1984). Later releases included Christmas in My Heart (Polydor, 1988) and Among My Souvenirs (Telstar, 1989), which included six new songs.

FRANCO
b. L'Okango La Ndju Pene Luambo Makiadi, 6 July 1938, Sona-Bata, Zaire, d. 12 October 1989, Brussels, Belgium

The best-known popular musician throughout Africa, Franco created 'soukous' music, which combined his fluid guitar style and songs of moral satire and social commentary. A bandleader and music businessman, he made more than 150 albums in a career spanning four decades.

Franco was born the son of a railway worker in the (then) Belgian colony of Congo. After his father's death in 1948, the family moved to the capital,

Léopoldville. Already a proficient guitarist, Makiadi's early style was influenced by Belgian jazz player and Django Reinhardt disciple Bill Alexander. His first recordings with the group Watam were made for Editions Loningsa in 1953. In 1956 he formed the first version of his group OK Jazz, named after the OK Bar whose owner financed the purchase of instruments for the nine-piece band. Vicky Longomba sang lead vocals on 'On Entre OK, On Sorte KO' (1957), which became one of Franco's most enduring catchphrases. The group's music at this stage was absorbing rumba and cha-cha rhythms.

With Independence in 1960, OK Jazz recorded 'Lumumba Héros National' (Pathe-Marconi) in praise of the nationalist leader. Franco then went on to record more than eighty singles for the Brussels-based Editions Populaires in the sixties and seventies. By the early sixties the group was fully amplified with electric bass and solid-bodied guitars.

Congolese music was splitting into two distinct styles, with artists like Dr Nico and (later) Tabu Ley producing a more internationally orientated sound, and Franco emphasizing the more folkloric 'roots' aspects of Zairean culture. This approach fitted the 1972 Africanization campaign of President Mobutu and Franco, who took the more 'authentic' name Luambo Makiadi, travelled with OK Jazz to support the campaign.

During these years, however, Franco was influenced by American soul artists and the horn arrangements of his music show his debt to James Brown. In the seventies Franco built a continent-wide following through appearances in fifteen countries at events like the Lagos FESTAC (1977), and he made the first of several European tours in 1978. In 1980 he formed his own African Sun Music and released recordings on the Edipop, Visa 80 and Choc labels. For a time in the early eighties OK Jazz was virtually based in Europe and in 1984 Franco made his first visit to America.

In 1985 Franco was one of the organizers of the famine relief Africa for Africa concert in Abidjan, Ivory Coast, and in 1986 he released a thirtieth-anniversary album, La Vie des Hommes (Choc).

In 1987 the band toured East Africa and Zambia and Franco recorded nearly twenty albums in the last three years of his life. The final records were Lukoli and For Ever, made with vocalist Sam Mangwana. After his death, Franco's body was flown to Zaire where four days of national mourning were declared. The turnover of members of OK Jazz was high during its thirty-year history, with Franco's former sidemen setting up rival bands like Orchèstre Vevey and Somo Somo. After his death OK Jazz continued under the leadership of Simaro Lutumba. A group of former associates formed the Brussels-based Champions of Zaire.

FRANKIE GOES TO HOLLYWOOD

Peter 'Pedro' Gill, b. 8 March 1960, Liverpool, England; Holly Johnson, b. William Johnson, 19 February 1960, Liverpool; Brian Nash, b. 20 May 1963, Liverpool; Marc O'Toole, b. 6 January 1964, Liverpool; Paul Rutherford, b. 8 December 1959, Liverpool

Propelled by **Trevor Horn**'s production skills and inspired video direction by Bernard Rose and Godley and Creme, Frankie Goes to Hollywood mixed Liverpool street credibility and a defiant affirmation of unorthodox sexuality to become Britain's pop sensation of 1984. In that year, their 'Relax'* became the biggest-selling single ever in Britain.

The group's roots lay in punk. Johnson, taking his first name from a character in **Lou Reed**'s 'Walk on the Wild Side', had been in Big in Japan and cut the solo singles 'Yankee Rose' and 'Hobo Joe' before forming the group with O'Toole (bass), Gill (drums) and guitarist Gerald O'Toole. They were joined by Rutherford from punk group Spitfire Boys, who had cut 'Mein Kampf' (RK Records, 1977).

Two stories have been given as the origin of the band's name. It either came from a caption to a photograph of the young **Frank Sinatra** or from a headline in a Liverpool paper about **Frankie Vaughan**. Either way the reference was highly ironic for their stage act resembled 'a leather-bound bordello of punk funk', according to one early reviewer. Two major labels, Arista and Phonogram, turned Frankie down before the band was signed by Horn and former rock journalist Paul Morley to their new ZTT label in 1983.

With a grandiose studio production in the manner of **Giorgio Moroder** or **Phil Spector**, 'Relax' reached the Top Ten before the BBC imposed a belated radio ban on the grounds of obscenity. On a wave of public outrage similar to that which had greeted the **Sex Pistols**' 'God Save the Queen', the single went to No. 1 in Britain and made the Top Ten in America. If the song's message – relax for better sex – was disturbing to some, Horn's surging disco rhythms were irresistible. With Morley masterminding media saturation, Britain was engulfed in a tide of 'Frankie Says' T-shirts, whose slogans veered between politics ('Arm the Workers') and sex in their attempt to cause outrage.

Allusions to nuclear war in the lyrics of the follow-up, 'Two Tribes', were amplified in Godley and Creme's video which showed a fist-fight between lookalikes of American and Soviet leaders. Like 'Two Tribes', 'The Power of Love' (1984) was a British No. 1. The title track of *Welcome to the Pleasuredome*, a name inspired by Coleridge's 'Kubla Khan', was another big hit. The album, although a bestseller, was padded out with thin cover-versions of **Bruce Springsteen**'s 'Born to Run' and the old **Gerry and the Pacemakers**' hit, 'Ferry Across the Mersey'.

Frankie's moment went when **George Michael**'s Wham! replaced them as pop sensation of 1985 and the band retreated to prepare *Liverpool* (1986). Although produced by Horn, this showed a shift to a heavy-metal style. The anthemic 'Rage Hard' was briefly a hit, and the album featured a monolithic rock epic ('Warriors of the Wasteland') and Johnson's opulent romanticism on 'Maximum Joy'.

The tepid critical response to *Liverpool* contributed to the decision in early 1987 to dissolve the group. Rutherford had a minor hit with 'Get Real' (1988) and he later formed Pressure Zone. Nash formed Low and recorded 'Tearing My Soul Apart' (1991). In 1988 Johnson signed to MCA after winning his freedom from ZTT through a bitterly contested court case with producer Horn. His solo career began promisingly with the hits 'Love Train' and 'Americanos' (1989) from the British No. 1 album *Blast!*. However, the follow-up, *Across the Universe* (1991), sold poorly and in 1994 he announced that he had been diagnosed as HIV positive. In the same year he published an autobiography, *Bone in My Flute*.

The continuing popularity of FGTH in Britain was underlined in 1993 when remixes of 'Relax' and *Bang!* – a greatest hits album – reached the Top Ten.

ARETHA FRANKLIN

b. 25 March 1942, Memphis, Tennessee, USA

The single most important female vocalist to emerge from the soul music boom of the mid-sixties, Franklin possesses one of the most moving and charismatic voices in popular music, and the role model for all subsequent gospel-based singers. If some of the emotive depth in her singing came from her far from contented childhood and troubled life, her dramatic style was firmly based in the church.

One of the five children of the Rev. C. L. Franklin, perhaps the most revered figure in black American preaching, Franklin was exposed from childhood to all the great figures in gospel music, including **Mahalia Jackson**, **Clara Ward** and **Sam Cooke**, all of whom were close friends of her father. With her sisters Carolyn and Erma, she sang in her father's church in Detroit. Her first recordings were made there when she was fourteen by the Detroit entrepreneur Joe Von Battle and leased to Checker Records in Chicago, the company which had issued more than fifty albums of her father's sermons.

In 1960 **John Hammond** signed her to a Columbia contract. Surprisingly, given Hammond's record in talent-spotting over the years (his successes include **Count Basie**, **Bob Dylan** and **Bruce Springsteen**), Franklin's Columbia years were filled with unexceptional covers of popular soul songs, poorly executed excursions into cocktail-lounge jazz and pointless, overblown arrangements of Broadway show tunes (such as her only pop hit 'Rock-a-Bye Your Baby With a Dixie Melody', 1961). Though she had several R&B hits ('Today I Sing the Blues', 1960; 'Operation Heartache', 1961), less than an album's worth of really interesting songs that hinted at her talent were recorded by Columbia. The best of these were 'Running Out of Fools' (1964) and 'Cry Like a Baby' (1966).

In 1966 she left Columbia for Atlantic and **Jerry Wexler**. Wexler, a long-time expert in black music, understood her capabilities, and flew her to Muscle Shoals where she cut Ronnie Shannon's 'I Never Loved a Man the Way That I Love You' and **Dan Penn** and **Chips Moman**'s 'Do Right Woman'. Both songs were unadulterated Southern soul, a genre far from natural for the city-bred Franklin. When released as a single in 1967 'I Never Loved a Man' was an immediate hit, reaching No. 9 on the pop, and No. 1 on the R&B, charts. The subsequent album was also a hit, as was her version of **Otis Redding**'s 'Respect' (1967), a No. 1 pop hit, and her first British chart entry. With a recording pattern now established, Wexler began to utilize a nucleus of writers, musicians and arrangers to complement Franklin's own songs and playing. Hits of this period include Shannon's 'Baby I Love You' (1967), **Don Covay**'s 'Chain of Fools', her own 'Think', **Burt Bacharach** and Hal David's 'I Say a Little Prayer' and Covay's 'See Saw' (1958). For her third album, *Lady Soul* (1968), Wexler used strings for the first time on the **Carole King**/Gerry Goffin song '(You Make Me Feel Like) A Natural Woman'.

During this period she was also divorced for the first time. The effect on her music was apparent: during 1969 she achieved little in the way of hit records. She returned to the charts in 1970 with 'Don't Play That Song' and her thrilling version of **Paul Simon**'s 'Bridge over Troubled Water' (1971). Other hits of the early seventies include a reading of the **Ben E. King** classic 'Spanish Harlem', her own 'Day Dreaming' (1972) and **Stevie Wonder**'s 'Until You Come Back to Me (That's What I'm Gonna Do)' (1974).

No longer working regularly with Wexler, Franklin's career became erratic and her personal life problematic. She worked with various producers for her seventies albums: *Let Me in Your Life* and *With Everything I Feel in Me* (both Wexler, 1974); *You* (Wexler/Franklin, 1975); *Sparkle* (**Curtis Mayfield**, 1976); *Sweet Passion* (Lamont Dozier, 1977); *Almighty Fire* (Curtis Mayfield, 1978) and *La Diva* (**Van McCoy**, 1979), before joining Arista (who by 1980 had revived the flagging career of **Dionne Warwick**). Her début for the label (*Aretha*, 1980) reunited her with **Arif Mardin** and Charles Jackson, who had both

worked with her at Atlantic. That album, and the Mardin-produced *Love All the Hurt Away* (1981), marked a major return to form, but it was the inspired coupling with **Luther Vandross** in 1982 that put her firmly back in the charts. A gold album (*Jump to It*) and a million-selling single in the title track brought Franklin's music to a new generation. The formula was repeated with less charm in 1983 on *Get It Right*.

After a year's hiatus she returned in 1985 with the **Narada Michael Walden**-produced album *Who's Zoomin' Who*, her biggest hit for fifteen years. The album, produced between 1985 and 1986, included four hit singles: the title track, 'Freeway of Love', 'Another Night' and 'Sisters Are Doing It for Themselves', a duet with the **Eurythmics**.

By the mid-eighties Franklin's recording popularity was clearly dependent on other catalysts, be it the producer, duettist or (in many cases) the remixer. Thus, in 1986 she had a hit with a remake of the **Rolling Stones**' 'Jumping Jack Flash', produced by Keith Richard, and in 1987 joined forces with **George Michael** for 'I Knew You Were Waiting'. Later that year she returned to her roots with the gospel double-album *One Lord, One Faith, One Baptism*, recorded in her father's Detroit church and featuring an impassioned sermon by the Rev. Jesse Jackson. It won her critical praise but sold poorly. The 1989 album *Through the Storm* included duets with the **Four Tops**, **Whitney Houston** and **James Brown**. *What You See Is What You Sweat* was an up-tempo album with its version of **Sly and the Family Stone**'s 'Everyday People' (1991).

In 1994 Arista issued a greatest hits album covering the years since 1980, with new tracks masterminded by Clivilles and Cole (of **C&C Music Factory**) and **Babyface**. In the same year Franklin had a hit with 'A Deeper Love' from the film *Sister Act II*. She re-signed with Arista, releasing *A Rose Is Still a Rose* (1998), which despite a stellar cast of contributors failed commercially. Far more successful was *Greatest Hits* (1998).

Aretha's two sisters were also professional singers. Erma recorded the original version of 'Piece of My Heart' (Shout, 1967), later a hit for **Janis Joplin** (1968). Erma's own version was a Top Ten hit in Britain in 1992 after it had been used in a television commercial. Carolyn (*b. 1945, d. 1988*) was a member of the Sweet Inspirations, who regularly backed Atlantic artists in the sixties and seventies and had their own hit with 'Sweet Inspiration' (1968).

DALLAS FRAZIER
b. 27 October 1939, Spiro, Oklahoma, USA

Frazier was one of the few country writers to deal with the past in a realistic, rather than romantic or nostalgic, manner in songs like 'California Cotton-fields' (recorded by him in 1969 but better known in the version by **Merle Haggard**). The song tells the story of his family's move from the Midwest to the Promised Land of California, and contains the bitter chorus, 'California cottonfields, where labour camps were filled with weary men with broken dreams.'

Frazier spent his teens in Bakersfield, California, and in 1952 won a **Ferlin Husky**-sponsored talent contest. This led to a contract with Capitol for whom he recorded children's novelty records before his nonsense composition 'Alley-Oop'* (Lute, 1960) topped the American charts by the Hollywood Argyles, an informal grouping of Los Angeles musicians including Sandy Nelson, Gary Paxton and Frazier himself, assembled by **Kim Fowley**. Another example of his ease at handling street argot was 'Mohair Sam', a hit for **Charlie Rich** in 1965.

By this time, Frazier had established himself in Nashville. He had a minor pop hit with the soul-inflected 'Hey Elvira' (Capitol, 1966) and a number of country hits on RCA (which he joined in 1969) but was far more successful as a writer. Many of his compositions were straightforward tearjerkers, such as 'There Goes My Everything' (a country hit for Jack Greene in 1966 and a pop hit for **Engelbert Humperdinck** in 1967) and the songs he supplied to **Jerry Lee Lewis** ('Another Hand Shakin' Goodbye'), **Charley Pride** ('Then Who Am I') and Connie Smith ('Ain't Love a Good Thing'), but a number of them showed a real ability to evoke rural life, akin to that of **Bobby Charles**. Among these were 'California Cottonfields' and 'The Son of Hickory Holler's Tramp', a pop hit for O. C. Smith in 1968; 'Big Table Murphy' (recorded first by Frazier but a country hit for Sue Thompson in 1975); and 'Beneath Still Waters', a country hit for **Emmylou Harris** in 1980.

In 1998 Frazier quit Nashville to become a minister.

STAN FREBERG

b. 7 August 1926, Los Angeles, California, USA

A brilliant satirist, Freberg recorded a series of memorable parodies of contemporary popular music in the fifties.

He entered showbusiness in his teens as a stooge for his magician uncle and then started doing vocal impersonations. On his discharge from the army in 1947, he created voices for many of the animated cartoons produced by Warner Brothers, Disney, Lantz and other studios. In 1949 he joined forces with comic Daws Butler, who became a regular collaborator over the years, for the *Time for Beany* children's teleseries and in 1950 signed with Capitol. His first hit was the satire 'John and Marsha' (1950), in which he repeated the two names for three minutes and captured the melodramatic intensity of the soap opera. He followed this with a savage parody of **Johnny Ray**'s 'Cry', 'Try' (1952), and his best-known records, a hilarious pair of children's fables told in the manner of the *Dragnet* teleseries, 'St George and the Drag-onet'* and 'Little Red Riding Hood' (1953).

In 1954 he turned his attention to rock'n'roll. In retrospect, the venom of his portraits of the Chords (whose 'Sh-Boom' he aped in 1954), **Elvis Presley** ('Heartbreak Hotel', 1956), **Lonnie Donegan** ('Rock Island Line', 1956) and the **Platters** ('The Great Pretender', 1955) indicated a distaste for the originals. The accuracy of his identification of the central elements of them (Presley's echo-laden voice, Donegan's lengthy spoken introduction to the song, the plodding piano in support of his hysterical Platters), however, reveals an understanding of the gimmickry that lay behind the best (as well as the worst) of much of rock'n'roll. Significantly, these were parodies not of songs but of recordings – they took as their central situation the making of a record. As such, they pinpointed the transition from the singer singing a song to the making of a record in which the song and singer were merely elements, which rock'n'roll highlighted through its new emphasis on production techniques. When Freberg saw excess in the mainstream of popular music, he was equally harsh. The classic examples of this are his version of **Mitch Miller**'s 'The Yellow Rose of Texas' (1955), which features an over-enthusiastic drummer, and 'Banana Boat (Day-O)' (1957) in which, with help from Peter Leeds' impersonation of a weary jazz session musician, he mercilessly punctured the fake folksiness of the fashion for calypso. On 'Wun'erful, Wun'erful!' he received assistance from **Peggy Lee** and Butler.

Undoubtedly his best record was his attack on the manufactured teen-idols that emerged in the wake of Presley, 'The Old Payola Roll Blues' (1960). The record introduced the unforgettable 'Clyde Ankle' (who was clearly modelled on **Fabian**) and explained his success in terms of lyrical inventiveness ('I was on my way to high school'), high notes (produced with the help of a man with a sharp stick) and, of course, payola, into which there was a current Congressional inquiry. In the UK, the **Goons** with 'Bloodnock's Rock'n'Roll' (Decca, 1956) and Peter Sellers with 'I'm So Ashamed' (1958) made similarly themed attacks on rock'n'roll but neither was as barbed nor as accurate as Freberg's.

He continued making comedy records, mostly albums, including *Stan Freberg Presents the United States of America* (1961) and *Freberg Underground Show No. 1* (1964), but these lacked the force of both his music parodies and the radio and television advertisements for which he became famous in the seventies. In the eighties he returned to his roots when he did the voices for *The Wozzles* children's cartoon series.

FREDDIE AND THE DREAMERS
Freddie Garrity, b. 14 November 1940; Pete Birrell, b. 9 May 1941; Roy Crewsdon, b. 29 May 1941; Bernard Dwyer, b. 11 September 1940; Derek Quinn, b. 24 May 1942

Though they came to prominence during the British beat boom, Freddie and the Dreamers' zany approach owned more to the variety-show tradition than to rock'n'roll.

After playing in the Red Sox skiffle group and working as a milk roundsman, Garrity formed the band in Manchester in 1962 with multi-instrumentalist Crewsdon, guitarist Quinn, Birrell (bass) and Dwyer (drums). Like their Liverpool counterparts, Freddie and the Dreamers' early repertoire was based on American rock and R&B songs, one of which, James Ray's 1961 Caprice hit 'If You Gotta Make a Fool of Somebody' (EMI Columbia, 1963), was their début single and a British hit. Like their subsequent records, it was produced by John Burgess.

Later songs were tailor-made for the group by **Mitch Murray** and 'I'm Telling You Now' and 'You Were Made for Me' perfectly suited Garrity's jaunty stage persona. The hits continued into 1964 with the Quinn composition 'Over You' and two revivals, **Paul Anka**'s 1957 song 'I Love You Baby' and 'I Understand', a syrupy ballad which had sold a million on Jubilee in 1954 for the Four Tunes.

As British audiences tired of Garrity's antics, 'I'm Telling You Now' was released by Tower in America, selling a million and reaching No. 1 in 1965 when **Herman's Hermits** also conquered America with their 'Englishness'. After **Chubby Checker** boarded the bandwagon with 'Let's Do the Freddie' (Cameo), Mercury – which held the rights to the group's later material – rush-released 'Do the Freddie', a swiftly recorded dance tune which referred to the stage movements of the lead singer as he leapt in the air, kicking his legs. 'You Were Made for Me' (Tower, 1965) was the band's final success in America.

In the same year Freddie and the Dreamers starred as a boy-scout troop in the low-budget film comedy *Cuckoo Patrol* with singer and comedian Ken Dodd, whose biggest hits were 'Tears' (EMI Columbia, 1965) and 'The River'. The group also appeared in *Seaside Swingers* (1965) in which Garrity sang the six-minute 'What's Cooking'. Later records included a cover of Dick and Deedee's 'Thou Shalt Not Steal' (1965), a minor British hit, *In Disneyland* (1966) and *King Freddie and His Dreaming Knights* (1967) with its version of **Paul Simon**'s '59th Street Bridge Song'.

By the end of the sixties the Dreamers had split up with Quinn becoming a clubowner and Dwyer going into management. Garrity and Birrell spent several years on the *Little Big Time* television show while in 1976 Garrity formed a new Dreamers group for summer seasons at seaside resorts and the occasional rock revival tour.

FREE
Paul Rodgers, b. 12 December 1949, Middlesbrough, Cleveland, England; Paul Kossoff, b. 14 September 1950, London, d. 19 March 1976, New York, USA; Andy Fraser, b. 7 August 1952, London; Simon Kirke, b. 27 August 1949, Wales; John 'Rabbit' Bundrick (joined 1972); Tetsu Yamauchi, b. 1946, Fukuoka, Japan (joined 1972)

Free's classic single 'All Right Now' was the epitome of the riff-based British heavy blues of the late sixties.

Alexis Korner gave the band its name when it formed in London in 1968 in the shadow of **Cream**. Vocalist and songwriter Rodgers had travelled from the north-east of England with the Roadrunners (who later formed Brown Sugar). Guitarist Kossoff was the son of actor David Kossoff and with drummer Kirke as the Black Cat Bones he had backed **Champion Jack Dupree** on *When You Feel the Feeling You Was Feeling* (Blue Horizon, 1968). Fraser had briefly played bass with **John Mayall**.

Following the release of the Guy Stevens-produced *Tons of Sobs* (Island, 1968), the group built a reputation on the club and college circuit, sometimes playing seven nights a week. They also toured America as support to Blind Faith. This experience was reflected in the new cohesion of the ensemble playing on *Free* (1969), co-produced by the band and **Chris Blackwell**. A minor hit in Britain, the album's success was eclipsed by the Rodgers–Fraser composition 'All Right Now', a Top Ten hit on both sides of the Atlantic. *Fire and Water* (1970), which contained a longer version of the single, was equally successful.

The lilting 'My Brother Jake' was a hit the following year, when internal tensions led to the group splitting temporarily, with Rodgers forming a group called Peace, Kossoff and Kirke recording with American keyboards-player Rabbit, and Japanese bassist Tetsu and Fraser rehearsing a trio called Toby.

These projects were abandoned when Free re-formed in 1972, initially for a farewell tour and live album, but in the event for a two-year period in which they had two more hit singles. 'Little Bit of Love' came from the 1972 album *Free at Last* while *Heartbreaker* (1973) included 'Wishing Well'. The latter had Tetsu and Rabbit performing instead of Fraser, who left in 1972 to form Sharks with session guitarist Chris Spedding. Kossoff, suffering from ill-health due to drugs problems, played on only half the tracks.

When Free finally split in 1973, Island re-released 'All Right Now', which became a hit again. Rodgers and Kirke put together **Bad Company**, while Tetsu joined **Rod Stewart**'s Faces. Fraser left Sharks shortly after the release of the acclaimed *First Water* (Island, 1973) and Kossoff recorded *Back Street Crawler* (Island, 1974), a solo album and the name of a band whose brief career ended when Kossoff died of drug abuse in 1976.

The continuing power of the band's work was underlined by further successful re-releases in Britain of their hits in 1978, 1983 and 1993. In 1991 a remix of 'All Right Now' was again a British Top Ten hit after the song had been used in a chewing-gum commercial. In the wake of that a slew of reissues followed during the decade.

ALAN FREED
b. 15 December 1922, Johnstown, Pennsylvania, USA,
d. 20 January 1965, Palm Springs, California

Though often dubbed the Pied Piper of rock'n'roll, Freed's major importance was as a supporter and champion of rhythm and blues. As a disc-jockey, Freed played a decisive part in broadening the audience for R&B to white teenagers in the early fifties. Later, in the rock'n'roll years, he supported many black acts, securing them appearances in films and concerts and regularly featured their records on his radio shows, at a time when white teen-idols were being aggressively promoted by the likes of **Dick Clark**. His career was effectively wrecked by the payola scandals of 1959.

Raised in Salem, Ohio, Freed played trombone at high school and was briefly a member of the Sultans of Swing jazz band. On his discharge from the army, he studied engineering and drifted into disc-jockeying, first playing classical records over WKST in New Castle, Pennsylvania. By 1951 his hoarse rasp and quick-fire delivery could be heard on the independent Cleveland station WJW hosting a programme sponsored by local record retailer Leo Mintz. Mintz convinced a reluctant Freed to play more R&B records by showing him white teenagers buying not the latest releases by **Perry Como** or **Kay Starr** but records by the **Clovers**, **Johnny Ace**, **Ruth Brown** and other R&B acts.

Freed changed his programme and its name (from *Record Rendezvous* to *The Moon Dog Rock'n'Roll Party*, preferring the name rock'n'roll because it did not have the black associations of R&B), and won instant success. In 1952 his understanding of the tastes of white teenagers was confirmed when he promoted a concert by black performers in Cleveland and sold almost 20,000 tickets for a hall that held only 10,000 people, half of them to whites. The success of his show took him to New York and station WINS in 1954 and in 1955 (a full year before **Elvis Presley** had his first national hit) he mounted a similar show (featuring **Joe Turner**, the **Harptones**, the **Drifters**, the Clovers and **Fats Domino**, among others) and again more than half the audience was white.

He didn't invent the term 'rock'n'roll', as he often claimed, but he did popularize it. Equally, he wasn't the first or the only white disc-jockey to play R&B – other early important disc-jockeys include Hunter Hancock, Gene Nobles, Hoss Allen, John 'R' Richbourg and Zenas 'Big Daddy' Sears – but it was Freed who was most closely associated with the rise of the new music. Freed broadcast twenty-seven hours of primetime a week, and his enthusiasm was apparent in his interjected screeches and his habit of thumping a telephone directory along with the beat of a record. He also became a powerful figure behind the scenes. Thus he received a number of dubious writer credits (including one on the Moonglows' 'Sincerely') and bribes, mostly from independent companies, though on occasion he did contribute to songs, notably **Chuck Berry**'s 'Maybellene'. He was also featured in a trio of films, *Rock Around the Clock* and *Rock, Rock, Rock* (both 1956) and *Don't Knock the Rock* (1957), and by 1958 was a national figure, the man who played what teenage America listened to. But already his star was on the wane. His espousal of black original versions – at one point he refused to play **Pat Boone**'s covers of black records – was both too progressive for the times and disliked by the industry, and his abrasive personality made him a difficult person to deal with. In 1958 his television show *Rock'n'Roll Dance Party* was cancelled when the camera showed **Frankie Lymon** dancing with a white girl, and later in the year he was charged with incitement to riot when riots broke out at a concert he promoted in Boston. The legal fees bankrupted him.

Then came the payola investigations. Sparked off by allegations that selected contestants had been given the answers to enhance the drama of TV quiz shows, the Congressional inquiries broadened to include music programming, where the practice of 'pay for play' was widely established. Freed was presented to the Congress as a scapegoat for the practices of many. Thus, in marked contrast to Dick Clark who had built an empire on his interests in the music he promoted on *American Bandstand* yet who survived the investigations unscathed, Freed's career was ruined. In 1959 he was sacked by WABC (sobbing his 'resignation' in the middle of **Little Anthony and the Imperials**' 'Shimmy Shimmy Ko-Ko-Bop'), and in 1962 he was found guilty of commercial bribery. In 1964, unemployed and virtually an alcoholic, he was charged with income tax evasion. He died before the case came to trial.

A sympathetic version of Freed's story forms the basis of the film *American Hot Wax* (1978), in which he was played by Tim McIntire.

ARTHUR FREED

b. Arthur Grossman, 9 September 1894, Charleston, South Carolina, USA, d. 12 April 1973, Hollywood, California

As a producer at MGM, Freed did more than anyone else to establish a new form of screen musical in the forties. Where thirties musicals were dominated by the 'putting on a show' formula, Freed encouraged directors Vincente Minnelli, Stanley Donen and Charles Walters, choreographer Michael Kidd, orchestrator **André Previn**, writers Betty Comden and Adolph Green, and the studio's art directors, among others, to concentrate on the imaginative possibilities of the dream and fantasy elements inherent in the screen musical. Among the actors and actresses he regularly worked with were **Judy Garland**, **Fred Astaire**, **Gene Kelly** and Cyd Charisse.

A song plugger in his teens, Freed turned to vaudeville where he worked with the Marx Brothers before the First World War. On his discharge, he started to write speciality material and songs, scoring his first hit with 'I Cried for You' (to music by Gus Arnheim and Abe Lyman) in 1923. He moved to Hollywood as a theatre director and started writing songs with **Nacio Herb Brown**. Their movie hits included 'You Were Meant for Me', 'You Are My Lucky Star', 'Singin' in the Rain', 'All I Do Is Dream of You', 'Temptation', 'Pagan Love Song' and 'Good Morning'. With other composers Freed produced 'Fit as a Fiddle' (Al Hoffman and Al Goodhart) and 'This Heart of Mine' (**Harry Warren**).

In 1939, after working as associate producer on *The Wizard of Oz*, Freed was made a producer by MGM and given control of his own unit. Among the classics he produced were *Cabin in the Sky* (1943); the hugely influential *Meet Me in St Louis* (1944), in which he also dubbed the singing voice of Leon Ames; the underrated *The Pirate*; and *Easter Parade* (1948), which featured seventeen songs by **Irving Berlin**. *On the Town* (1949) was the first musical to feature sequences shot on location at familiar landmarks, while the Oscar-winning *An American in Paris* (1951) featured a slew of songs by **George** and **Ira Gershwin** and a memorable seventeen-minute ballet sequence from Gene Kelly. Freed also produced the ever-popular *Singin' in the Rain* (1952), on which he and Brown reunited as songwriters, and *The Band Wagon* (1953), which featured the 'Girl Hunt' fantasy ballet sequence (a spoof on the work of Mickey Spillane), and introduced showbusiness's unofficial anthem, the **Arthur Schwartz** and Howard Dietz composition 'That's Entertainment'.

Later productions included *It's Always Fair Weather* (1955), which featured Previn's first songs, and *Gigi* (1958), Freed's second Oscar-winning picture.

Though he produced non-musicals after the sudden decline in popularity of the musical in the late fifties, these were undistinguished and in 1962 Freed retired to oversee the Academy of Motion Picture Arts and Sciences (the body which awards the Oscars).

RUDOLF FRIML

b. Charles Rudolf Friml, 7 December 1879, Prague, Austria-Hungary, d. 12 November 1972, Hollywood, California, USA

With **Sigmund Romberg**, Friml dominated Broadway in the decade after the end of the First World War. He composed a series of enormously successful, robust, but ultimately insubstantial, operettas which Friml himself described as possessing 'a full-bodied libretto with luscious melody, rousing choruses and romantic passions'.

After studying composition with Anton Dvořák in his teens, Friml toured Europe with violinist Jan Kubelik. In 1901 they gave their first recital in America and, after a successful performance of his 'Piano Concerto in B Major' in 1904, Friml settled in New York. In 1912, following a quarrel between **Victor Herbert** and Emma Trentini, the star of his *Naughty Marietta*, Friml won the commission to write the score for Trentini's next operetta, *The Firefly*. After the operetta's success, Friml devoted himself exclusively to Broadway. The best of the show's sophisticated melodies was 'Giannina Mia'; 'The Donkey Serenade', now the best-known number of *The Firefly*, was in fact written by Friml for the 1937 film.

In over twenty years he composed more than twenty Broadway shows, collaborating most frequently with **Otto Harbach**, the co-author of *The Firefly*. Among these were *High Jinks* (1913), *You're in Love* (1917) and *Sometime* (1918), in which Mae West introduced 'Any Kind of Man'. His best-known operettas were *Rose Marie* (1924) and *The Vagabond King* (1925). The former was notable for being set in exotic Canada rather than Europe and having songs were which integral to the action. It starred Dennis King and Mary Ellis (in the roles **Nelson Eddy** and **Jeanette MacDonald** would make their own in the 1936 film) and introduced the oft-recorded 'Rose Marie' and 'Indian Love Call', both of which would be successfully revived by **Slim Whitman** in the fifties. *The Vagabond King*, which was filmed in 1930 and 1956 (which also starred King as the poet François Villon) introduced the rousing 'Song of the Vagabonds', 'Only a Rose' and 'Some Day'. Friml's last significant success was the Florenz Ziegfeld-produced *The Three Musketeers* (1928) with its stirring, if decidedly old-fashioned, 'March of the Musketeers'.

In 1934 Friml travelled to Hollywood to work on film scores but, like Romberg, failed to establish himself there and after watching his operettas being reduced to a few numbers for MacDonald and Eddy, he retired.

ROBERT FRIPP
b. 9 May 1946, Wimbourne, Dorset, England

A founder member of **King Crimson**, Fripp's later career as a producer and guitarist included both avant-garde experiments and collaborations with rock artists like **Phil Collins** and Andy Summers of the **Police**.

His first work outside the Crimson group was *No Pussyfooting* (EG, 1972) with **Brian Eno**, an album based around a tape echo delay system developed by Eno. After King Crimson dissolved in 1974, Fripp and Eno recorded *Evening Star* (Island). In the same year Fripp became a follower of the Gurdjieffian philosopher J. G. Bennett and announced that his artistic aim was to work as a 'small, intelligent, highly mobile unit'.

Working mainly in New York in the late seventies, he was part of the minimalist avant-garde circle which included David Byrne of **Talking Heads** and **Philip Glass**. He played guitar on **David Bowie**'s *Heroes* and *Scary Monsters* albums, and contributed to records by Talking Heads (*Fear of Music*) and **Blondie** (*Parallel Lines*). As a producer, he was responsible for albums by female vocal group the Roches (Warners, 1979), the second **Peter Gabriel** album and Daryl Hall of **Hall and Oates** (*Sacred Songs*).

In 1979 Fripp released *Exposures*, an impressively cerebral solo album with accompaniment from Phil Collins, Hall and **Narada Michael Walden**. Announced as an exercise in 'Frippertronics', it was followed by *God Save the Queen/Under Heavy Manners* (1980). One side contained quirky instrumental variations on the British national anthem while the other represented Fripp's response to disco and featured vocals from Byrne. In 1981 Fripp included former post-punk band Gang of Four bassist Sara Lee in his group the League of Gentlemen, who released the double-album *The League of Gentlemen*.

Despite re-forming King Crimson the same year, Fripp maintained a separate recording career. With Andy Summers, a former colleague in the local Bournemouth beat-group scene of the sixties, he cut two lyrical and contemplative albums of guitar duets: *I Advance Masked* (A&M, 1982) and *Bewitched* (1984). After further re-releases and reworkings of earlier themes, the enterprising Fripp took a different direction with *Robert Fripp and the League of Crafty Guitarists* (Virgin, 1986). The album comprised per-

formances by members of his West Virginia guitar seminar. In 1986 Fripp married **Toyah** Willcox and worked on her albums *Desire* (EG, 1987) and *Prostitute* (1988). In 1991 he released another collaboration with the League of Crafty Guitarists, the charming *Show of Hands*. The same year, as Sunday All Over the World, he released *Kneeling at the Shrine* with Willcox, Trey Gunn (guitar) and Paul Beavis (drums). In 1993 Fripp released *The First Day*, a collaboration with vocalist **David Sylvian**. Then in 1994 he again reformed King Crimson for a short tour before returning to his intermittent series of experimental guitar albums. The best received of these include *A Blessing of Tears* (Discipline, 1995) and *The Gates of Paradise* (DGM, 1998).

LEFTY FRIZZELL
b. William Orville Frizzell, 31 March 1928, Corsicana, Texas, USA, d. 19 July 1975, Nashville, Tennessee

A digest of his recording career gives little impression of Lefty Frizzell's stylistic impact on country music since the fifties, which has been enormous and unfading. **Merle Haggard**'s vocal manner is deeply rooted in Frizzell's relaxed timing and startling melisma, while country singers of the eighties like **George Strait** (who recorded the fine commemorative song 'Lefty's Gone', 1982) and Randy Travis often echo Frizzell's drawl with a purist's fidelity.

Himself moulded by the styles of **Jimmie Rodgers** (many of whose songs he was later to refashion) and **Ernest Tubb**, Frizzell began performing in his teens. Some demos he sent to Dallas studio-owner Jim Beck reached Columbia A&R man Don Law, who signed him to the label. 'I Love You a Thousand Ways'/'If You Got the Money, Honey, I've Got the Time' (1950) began a series of recordings notable for their economical group sound, with an uncharacteristically prominent piano. 'Always Late', 'Mom and Dad's Waltz' and 'I Want to Be with You Always' (all 1951) consolidated his place among the leading style-makers of country music. Among his later successes were 'Long Black Veil' (1959) and 'Saginaw, Michigan' (1964). His career declined because of his drinking problems and was not commercially revived by a move to ABC in 1973, for whom he recorded the best of his late albums, *The Legendary Lefty Frizzell*.

Frizzell's younger brother David (*b. 26 September 1941*) had minor hits with 'You're the Reason God Made Oklahoma' (1981), a duet with Shelly West, and the solo 'I'm Gonna Hire a Wino to Decorate our Home' (1982).

THE FUGEES
Lauryn Hill, b. 26 May 1975, East Orange, New Jersey,

USA; Wyclef Jean, b. 17 October 1972, Haiti; Prakazrel 'Pras' Michel, b. 19 October 1972, Haiti

An alternative rap trio, the Fugees rose to superstardom with their version of 'Killing Me Softly', originally a hit for **Roberta Flack**, before achieving varied success as solo artists.

The Fugees were formed in 1992 in New York City when rapper Hill began to work with MCs Pras and Jean, first cousins who had grown up in New Jersey. In the group's formative years, when they were known as the Tranzlators, Hill also pursued a film career, starring in *Sister Act 2* (1992) before a deal with Ruffhouse/Columbia prompted her to let her music take preference. Finding another group were similarly named, the trio became the Fugees, a reference to Michel and Jean's refugee status.

Blunted on Reality (1994), heavily influenced by reggae, won the group a devoted underground following but failed to cross-over into the mainstream. With the jazz-tinged follow-up *The Score* (1996)* the Fugees achieved international acclaim, topping album charts in Europe and the US. The album featured four hit singles, 'Killing Me Softly', 'Ready or Not', 'Fugee La' and a version of 'No Woman No Cry'.

The success of *The Score* allowed the group to pursue their own solo projects. Wyclef Jean's *The Carnival* (1997) and Pras's *Ghetto Supastar* (1998) both sold well but were soon overshadowed by *The Miseducation of Lauryn Hill** (1998), which spawned hit singles in 'Doo Wop (That Thing)' and 'Everything Is Everything'. The album's sinuous mix of melodic flights of singing and social concern won Hill five Grammy Awards, including Album of the Year and Best New Artist, and garnered multi-million sales.

THE FUGS
Tuli Kupferberg, b. 28 September 1928, New York, USA; Ed Sanders, b. 17 August 1939, Kansas City, Missouri; Ken Weaver, b. Galveston, Texas

Described by one critic as 'a perfect mixture of sacrilege, scatology, politics and rock', the Fugs were among the earliest underground groups.

The band emerged from New York's East Village bohemia in 1964. Kupferberg and Sanders were beat generation poets, while Weaver was a Russian linguist and drummer. With various backing musicians they performed at small clubs and theatres, signing to avant-garde jazz label ESP in 1965. *First Album* contained a folk-rock setting of Blake's 'Ah Sunflower', as well as outrageous drug material ('I Couldn't Get High') and cheerful locker-room vulgarity ('Boobs a Lot'). The accompanists included guitarists Peter Stampfel and Steve Weber of the Holy Modal Rounders.

The Fugs (Kill for Peace) and *Virgin Fugs (for Adult Minds Only)* (1966) provided the same mixture of romantic poetry, energetic obscenity and anti-war satire. In 1967 the group signed to Reprise, and *Tenderness Junction* (1968), with a sleeve by noted photographer Richard Avedon, included 'Exorcizing the Evil Spirits from the Pentagon', a chant recorded live at a peace demonstration. With such instrumentalists as **Stefan Grossman** and **Carole King**, and collaborator Danny Kootch, the Fugs toured and cut three more Reprise albums. *It Crawled into My Hand, Honest* (1968) contained such songs as 'Marijuana' and 'Grope Need', while 'Flower Children' and 'Yodelling Yippie' were featured on *The Belle of Avenue A*. *Golden Filth* (1970) included re-recordings of the Fugs' best-known songs and appeared as the group disbanded. Sanders also released two self-produced solo albums on Reprise, *Sanders' Truckstop* (1972) and *Beer Cans on the Moon*.

During the seventies Sanders wrote *The Family*, the bestselling account of the murder trial of cult leader Charles Manson, while Kupferberg wrote and drew cartoons for the underground press and became a guerrilla theatre activist. In 1984 the duo re-formed the Fugs and released *Refuse to Be Burnt Out* (New Rose, 1985), recorded live at New York's Bottom Line club. Among their accompanists was Vin Leary, who had played guitar on the ESP albums. A new studio album, *No More Slavery*, was issued in 1986.

BLIND BOY FULLER
b. Fulton Allen, 1908, Wadesboro, North Carolina, USA, d. 13 February 1941, Durham, North Carolina

Fuller's role in the blues of the Southeastern United States, particularly the Carolinas and Georgia, is analogous to that of **Robert Johnson** in the Central South or **T-Bone Walker** in the Southwest and West. The clean execution of his guitar-playing, his crisp diction and the catchiness of many of his songs formed a stylistic model that was replicated by many younger or lesser figures, while it more subtly altered the approaches of even independent-minded contemporaries.

Fuller learned guitar in the mid-twenties and after losing his sight about 1928 became an itinerant musician, playing his loud steel-bodied National guitar on the streets of North Carolina cities like Winston-Salem, Durham, Burlington and Raleigh, where large black workforces served the warehouses and factories of the tobacco industry. In the mid-thirties he was part of a circle that included harmonica-player Sonny Terry (later of **Brownie McGhee and Sonny Terry**), singer/guitarist/washboard-player Bull City Red and **Rev. Gary Davis**, who probably deserves credit for at least some elements of his guitar style.

Fuller began recording for ARC in 1935, and one of his first sides, 'I'm a Rattlesnakin' Daddy', sold well and frequently appeared later in the repertoire of both black and white musicians, as did the even-better known 'Step It up and Go' (1940). Among other popular and imitated recordings were the raggy 'Truckin' My Blues Away' (1936), 'Mama Let Me Lay It on You' (1936) and 'Little Woman You're So Sweet' (1940). His evidently wide appeal – he recorded over 120 sides, all issued between 1935 and 1940 – was noted and in varying degrees emulated by other singer-guitarists of the region like Buddy Moss and Curly Weaver. After his death, Brownie McGhee – who was the leading Fuller-styled player of the immediate post-war years – issued a few recordings under the sobriquet 'Blind Boy Fuller No. 2'.

Other musicians who have been influenced by his approach include singer-guitarists Carolina Slim, Alec Seward and Ralph Willis, who, with McGhee, gave Southeastern acoustic blues some years of modest popularity in the New York area in the late forties.

JESSE FULLER
b. 12 March 1896, Jonesboro, Georgia, USA, d. 29 January 1976, Oakland, California

Like **Leadbelly**, Jesse Fuller drew on material that predated the arrival of the blues, and he passed on to the skiffle generation and beyond lively reminders of ragtime. His best-known song, a skiffle and jug-band standard, is the raggy 'San Francisco Bay Blues'.

After an adolescence spent wandering the United States in various jobs, Fuller settled in Los Angeles in the early twenties and became known to the Hollywood movie colony as a street vendor and occasional extra in, among other films, Douglas Fairbanks' *The Thief of Bagdad* (1924). He moved to Oakland, California, in 1929 and worked outside music until the forties, when he began to appear in San Francisco clubs as a singer and dancer, sometimes working with Leadbelly.

In the early fifties Fuller devised a one-man-band act in which he played guitar, harmonica, kazoo, washboard, cymbals and a foot-operated bass of his own invention, the 'fotdella'. This attracted the attention of local TV shows and record companies, and he recorded three albums of blues, minstrel songs and miscellaneous traditional and popular material for Good Time Jazz. By the early sixties he was familiar on the West Coast festival and coffee-house circuits, and in 1960–1 he first appeared in Europe. (There were further British tours in 1965 and 1967.) Subsequent years found him extending his touring to the East Coast and Canada, and he continued to work regularly until 1971.

LOWELL FULSON
b. 31 March 1921, Tulsa, Oklahoma, USA, d. 7 March 1999

In little over twenty years Fulson's music developed from the meandering country blues of the pre-war Southwest, by way of the cool California club music of the fifties, into an uncompromising synthesis of blues, soul and even, at times, Southern rock. Like **B. B. King** and to some extent **Muddy Waters**, though by different strategies, he exemplifies the dexterity of the blues-rooted musician who is determined to weather changing fashions without retreating into the safety of recycling his own past.

His early musical experiences included work with a black string band and as a country music performer, but he also travelled with the older blues singer Texas Alexander. In 1945 he moved to the West Coast, and in the following year began to record for the Oakland, California, songwriter and label-proprietor Bob Geddins, working either in a two-guitar format with his brother Martin or with a piano-led trio. He had R&B hits with 'Three o'Clock Blues' (1948), 'Every Day I Have the Blues' (1950) and 'Blue Shadows' (1950), collaborating with the skilled pianist and arranger Lloyd Glenn.

In 1954 Fulson signed with Phil and **Leonard Chess**'s Checker label and in that year enjoyed his biggest-ever hit, 'Reconsider Baby', now a blues standard and recorded by, among others, **Elvis Presley**. It was his only success in eight years with the label, but in the mid-sixties, when he had moved to the **Bihari Brothers**' Kent label, his fortunes blossomed again with 'Black Nights' and, especially, 'Tramp', written by Jimmy McCracklin (both 1966). The Kent (subsequently United) LPs of this period, *Soul, Tramp, Now!* and *Let's Go Get Stoned*, with their dime-store-psychedelic cover art and fashionably 'heavy' accompaniments, pointed the way to *In a Heavy Bag* (Jewel, 1968), generally regarded as the only worthwhile product of the brief 'psychedelic blues' phase. Recorded in Muscle Shoals with seasoned studio musicians, it even embraced **The Beatles**' 'Why Don't We Do It in the Road?'.

Fulson toured in Europe in 1969 and several times thereafter. During the eighties he recorded in Japan, France and Britain, customarily with small blues bands; the last of his more elaborately produced sessions was *The Ol' Blues Singer* (Granite, 1975), with Steve Cropper and others. In the nineties he recorded with small groups on fan-based labels like France's Blue Phoenix Records. His last albums were *Hold on* (1992) and *Them Update Blues* (1995). He continued working until illness forced his retirement in 1997.

Despite being limited in range, Fulson's songwriting produced several potent blues that have been taken up by admirers like B. B. King ('Three o'Clock Blues') and **Ray Charles**, who worked as his band-pianist in the early fifties.

FUN LOVIN' CRIMINALS
Fast; Huey; Steve

A mixture of hip-hop, blues and a *Pulp Fiction*-sampling single saw Bronx-based trio Fun Lovin' Criminals find critical and commercial acclaim in the mid-nineties.

The band formed in 1993 when keyboardist/bass-player Fast and drummer Steve, then part of a techno band, recruited ex-marine Huey (vocals/guitar) and began to play on the New York club circuit. A series of independently released EPs saw them labelled as **Beastie Boys** wannabes by the press, but their deter-mination landed them a deal with Chrysalis/EMI.

Come Find Yourself (1996) put paid to the Beastie Boys comparisons once and for all with its blend of smooth blues and rapping. The album sold steadily on the strength of the singles 'Fun Lovin' Criminal', 'King of New York' and 'Scoobie Snacks', which fea-tured extracts of dialogue from Quentin Tarantino's *Pulp Fiction*, giving the cult movie-maker a percent-age of the song's royalties. *100% Columbian* (1998) included a UK hit single in 'Love Unlimited', a soulful homage to **Barry White**, and consolidated the Fun Lovin' Criminals' success in Britain and the US.

HARVEY FUQUA
b. 27 July 1924, Louisville, Kentucky, USA

Founder and leader of the Moonglows and later a producer and head of A&R with Motown, Fuqua has played a key role in the development of black music since the fifties.

A relative of Charlie Fuqua of the **Ink Spots**, Har-vey Fuqua formed Crazy Sounds in 1952. The mem-bers, all of whom came from Louisville, comprised Alexander Graves (*b. 17 April 1930*), Prentis Barnes (*b. 1921*) and Bobby Lester (*b. 13 January 1930*). Featuring Barnes on lead vocals and Fuqua on bass, they were renamed the Moonglows by **Alan Freed** when he signed them to his Champagne label in 1952. After a couple of singles, they signed with **Ewart Abner**'s Chicago-based Chance label for whom they recorded prolifically until joining Chess in 1954.

Their first release on Chess was the doo-wop classic 'Sincerely'. Co-written by Freed and Fuqua and fea-turing Fuqua's dramatic lead singing set against a gentle babble of ethereal nonsense sounds, the record was an R&B hit for the Moonglows and a million-seller for the McGuire Sisters, whose bland cover-version was on Coral. Other hits included 'Most of All' (1955), 'See Saw' (1956), 'Please Send Me Someone

to Love' (1957) and 'The Ten Commandments of Love' (1958), while as the Moonlighters they recorded 'Shoo-doo-Bedoo' (Checker, 1955), an affectionate parody of the Chords 'Sh-Boom'.

In 1959 the Moonglows disbanded and Fuqua started working for Chess as a talent scout, producer and writer. Among his discoveries were **Etta James**, with whom he recorded, and the Marquees, whose featured singer was **Marvin Gaye**. After briefly recording the group as a new Moonglows in 1960, Fuqua quit Chess to set up first Anna and then, in 1961, the Harvey and Tri-Phi labels with **Berry Gordy**'s sister, Gwen (whom he later married), taking Gaye with him. Fuqua discovered and nurtured the talents of **Johnny Bristol**, **Junior Walker**, the **Spinners** and Shorty Long. When his labels fell into finan-cial difficulties, both were bought out by Berry Gordy and Fuqua joined Motown as head of promotion, quickly graduating to head of A&R. An integral part of Motown during its heyday, Fuqua produced, among others, the classic duets of Gaye and Tammi Terrell, 'Ain't No Mountain High Enough' (1967) and 'Your Precious Love' (1968), credits which placed him in the forefront of soul innovators of the sixties.

In 1971 Fuqua joined RCA, within which he formed his own production company and had great success with funk-soul bands the Nite-Liters ('K-Jee', 1971) and New Birth ('I Can Understand It', 1973, and 'Dream Merchant', after the group moved to Buddah in 1975). Fuqua later moved to San Francisco where he produced a trio of international disco hits for Sylvester on Fantasy ('Dance [Disco Heat]', 1978; 'You Make Me Feel [Mighty Real]' and 'I [Who Have Nothing]', both 1979). In the eighties Fuqua was reunited with Gaye and produced most of Gaye's Columbia recordings. He continued to perform with the Moonglows at revival shows.

BILLY FURY
b. Ronald Wycherly, 17 April 1941, Liverpool, England, d. 28 January 1983, London

Both pouting tough and appealingly wounded, Fury was in image halfway between Britain's major pop stars of the late fifties, **Cliff Richard** and **Adam Faith**. However, unlike either, and despite his considerable appeal, he was unable to adjust to the changes in pop and after a string of some twenty hits, his career stag-nated in the early sixties.

While working on the Mersey tugboats, Fury wrote songs and in the course of auditioning them for **Marty Wilde** in 1958, won himself a contract with Larry Parnes, then *the* impresario of British rock'n'roll. Affectionately known as 'Mr Parnes, Shilling and Pence', Parnes was a great believer in the power of a name. Thus Thomas Hicks became

Tommy Steele, Reginald Smith, Marty Wilde and Ronald Wycherly, Billy Fury. Before he left the pop business in the mid-sixties, Parnes' stable of stars included at one time or another **Georgie Fame**, Duffy Power, Dickie Pride, Vince Eager and the unlikely Johnny Gentle.

Parnes secured Fury regular bookings on **Jack Good**'s television shows *Oh Boy!* and *Boy Meets Girl* and signed him to Decca. His first single, the self-penned 'Maybe Tomorrow', was a hit in 1959, but even better was the rockabilly-inspired *The Sound of Fury* (1960), one of the few classics of British rock'n'roll, which featured **Joe Brown**'s inventive guitar and Fury's anguished singing. All the songs were written by Fury under his Wilberforce pseudonym, but the album was not a great commercial success at the time and after one more self-composed Top Ten single, 'Colette' (1960), Fury turned to the then common practice of covering American hits, mostly big brooding ballads. At the same time, his backing group (which was led by Georgie Fame) left to develop a career as one of Britain's pioneer R&B bands, and was replaced by the **Tornados**.

Fury's first significant covers of American hits were **Marty Robbins**' 'Don't Worry' and the more interesting 'A Thousand Stars' (1961). Originally recorded by doo-wop group the Rivileers (Baton, 1954) with Eugene Pearson (later a member of the **Drifters**) singing lead, this haunting ballad was a huge American hit for Kathy Young and the Innocents in 1960 on Indigo. Fury's best-remembered recording was his version of **Carole King** and Gerry Goffin's 'Halfway to Paradise' (1961), an American hit for **Tony** **Orlando**, which he followed with a revival of the thirties tango 'Jealousy' before covering another Orlando–King–Goffin hit, 'I'd Never Find Another You' (1961). Other covers included 'Letter Full of Tears' (1962), a **Don Covay** song that was originally a hit for **Gladys Knight** and the Pips, and a remake of **Conway Twitty**'s 'It's Only Make Believe' (1964). His British success declining in the wake of the success of fellow Liverpudlians **The Beatles**, Fury recorded covers with the Gamblers of two British beat classics, the **Dave Clark Five**'s 'Glad All Over' and the **Swinging Blue Jeans**' 'Hippy Hippy Shake' (itself a remake of Chan Romero's 1959 Del Fi recording), for the American market with no success.

Like Richard, Fury attempted a film career, but the films (*Play It Cool*, 1962, and *I Gotta Horse*, 1964, which was scored by David Heneker, who had co-authored *Half a Sixpence* for Tommy Steele) were lacklustre, surrounding Fury's brooding charm with cardboard antics. His last major hit, before he retired due to ill-health, was the moving, but decidedly old-fashioned, romantic ballad 'In Thoughts of You' (1965).

In the seventies Fury returned to the club circuit, singing his old hits, before his career was briefly revived by the **David Essex** film *That'll Be the Day* (1973) in which he reprised his past, playing rock'n'roll singer Stormy Tempest. After once more retiring, he started recording again in 1981 and scored a trio of minor hits, including a revival of 'Devil or Angel', earlier a hit for the **Clovers** and **Bobby Vee**. Produced by Stuart Colman, *The One and Only* was released posthumously.

KENNY G
b. Kenneth Gorelick, 1959, Seattle, Washington, USA

Playing a sanitized version of the jazz-funk saxophone style pioneered by **David Sanborn**, Kenny G has sold albums by the million in the USA and Asia but hardly any at all in Europe.

He formed his first groups at high school in Seattle and at seventeen sat in with **Barry White**'s Love Unlimited Orchestra. Kenny Gorelick's first professional job was with the Jeff Lorber Fusion and Lorber co-produced with Meco (Meco Monardo) the album *Kenny G* (Arista) in 1982.

His next collaboration was with composer-singer Kashif, who produced *G Force* (1983), which introduced the policy of alternating the unwavering mellow tone of his alto sax-playing with tracks by guest vocalists, and *Gravity* (1985). *Duotones* featured singer Ellis Hall from Tower of Power on 'What Does It Take' and 'Songbird' (1987), Kenny G's biggest hit single. *Silhouette* (1988) had guest vocals by **Smokey Robinson**.

In 1993 he released *Breathless*, which included the hit single 'By the Time This Night Is Over' with vocals by **Peabo Bryson**. It remained on the charts for over two years. Much sought after as a guest soloist Kenny G has contributed to recordings by **Whitney Houston**, the **Four Tops**, Johnny Gill and others. In 1994 he had a further hit with the seasonal offering *Miracles – The Holiday Album*, which was the first such item to top the US album charts since 1962. Even more successful was the same year's *Kenny G Live*. *Greatest Hits* (1997) is the definitive compilation.

MILT GABLER
b. 20 May 1911, New York, USA

Jazz *aficionado*, record-company owner and producer, Gabler was associated with such diverse figures as **Eddie Condon**, **Billie Holiday**, **Louis Jordan** and **Bill Haley**. He played a key role in bringing black rhythms to a wider audience.

The founder of the United Hot Clubs of America in 1936, which promoted jazz concerts and reissued classic jazz, and owner of the famous Commodore Music Shop in New York, a gathering place for jazz *aficionados*, Gabler established Commodore Records in 1938. He supervised sessions with Condon and various Dixieland aggregations, Billie Holiday, who recorded the original version of 'Strange Fruit' – her gruesome

account of a Southern lynching – on Commodore, **Jelly Roll Morton**, **James P. Johnson** and **Meade Lux Lewis**, among others. A further indication of the range of Commodore's releases was 'Private Jives', a parody of **Noël Coward**'s *Private Lives* with tenor saxophonist Bud Freeman in the Coward role, and the fifteen-minute improvisation (one of the first recorded) 'A Good Man Is Hard to Find'. Commodore was also one of the earliest companies to list personnel and date their recordings.

Then, in 1941, **Jack Kapp** hired Gabler to supervise 'race' (as black music was dismissively called then), jazz and 'hillbilly' (as country was equally dismissively called) music for Decca. In this capacity he oversaw a vast number of sessions by **Burl Ives**, the **Ink Spots**, the **Weavers**, **Red Foley**, **Louis Armstrong**, **Ella Fitzgerald** and **Guy Lombardo**, among many others. A major priority was Billie Holiday, whom he signed to the label, but Gabler had his greatest success with Louis Jordan, the biggest black recording star of the forties, whose jump beat was both central to the rise of R&B and laid the groundwork for the rhythms of rock'n'roll. When Jordan left Decca in 1954, Gabler signed Bill Haley and set about recording him firmly in the mould of Jordan (whose records he even played to Haley before sessions). For Haley Gabler produced 'Rock Around the Clock' (1954) and 'See You Later Alligator' (1955), pivotal records in the development of rock'n'roll, and even Jordan's own 'Choo Choo Ch'Boogie' (1956) and 'Caldonia' (1959).

In the sixties, while an executive producer with Decca, Gabler licensed his Commodore repertoire to Mainstream Records and in 1976, following his retirement from Decca, he revived the label and began reissuing material himself.

PETER GABRIEL
b. 13 February 1950, London, England

A former member of **Genesis**, Gabriel came nearest to achieving the ideal of seventies progressive rock in the eighties and nineties when he became one of the most popular rock artists while retaining an experimental approach to music.

After seven years as lead singer with the group, Gabriel left in 1975 to pursue a solo career, stating his belief that 'the use of sound and visual images can be developed to do much more than we have done.' Devoting himself to studio, rather than live, music he went on to produce a series of exploratory and contrasting studio albums, the first four entitled *Peter Gabriel*.

The first, released in 1977 by Charisma in Britain and Atlantic in America, contained the British hit, 'Solsbury Hill', an allegorical account of the split with Genesis. Gabriel's 1978 release, produced by **Robert Fripp**, was more experimental and influenced Atlantic's decision to reject its 1980 follow-up. Eventually released by Mercury in America, the album gave Gabriel two British and European hits in the angry tribute to the murdered black South African 'Biko' (which saw his first mixing of African rhythms with modern studio technology) and 'Games without Frontiers'. Using the title of a pan-European television game show, this song poked fun at nationalistic competition. Among the backing musicians were vocalists **Kate Bush** and former **Jam** member Paul Weller.

In the eighties Gabriel began to study non-Western musics, influences which showed on his 1982 album, renamed *Security* by his new American label, Geffen. The record included his video-led international hit, 'Shock the Monkey', which was accompanied by striking avant-garde visuals. The same year he underlined his new musical commitment by sponsoring the first in a series of WOMAD (World of Music and Dance) Festivals, which brought artists from several continents to perform and record in Britain. His only Genesis 'reunion' appearance took place to raise funds for WOMAD.

Peter Gabriel Plays Live (Charisma/Geffen, 1983) was followed by a soundtrack album to the Alan Parker film *Birdy* (1985). His most commercially successful album was *So*, which included the major international hit 'Sledgehammer', enhanced by a video created by noted British puppeteers and filmmakers the Quay Brothers. With Gabriel on Fairlight synthesizer, the album also featured Senegalese star **Youssou N'Dour**, who toured America with Gabriel, **Sting** and others on the 'Conspiracy of Hope' tour, a fund-raising effort for Amnesty International. In 1989 he released his music for the controversial film *The Last Temptation of Christ* on Real World, a WOMAD-sponsored label. He released a greatest hits album, *Shaking the Tree*, in 1990 and a collection of more introspective songs, *Us* (1992). Most of the songs, like the passionate 'Come Talk to Me', were reflections on his difficulties with personal relationships. Co-produced by **Daniel Lanois**, it included contributions from **Sinead O'Connor**, **Brian Eno** and African musician Manu Katche, on whose *It's About Time* Gabriel had performed.

Already one of popular music's most stylish video makers, in 1993 Gabriel produced *Xplora*, one of the first imaginative and stimulating music-based CD-ROMs. The following year he performed at the Woodstock '94 festival and released the *Secret World*

Live performance set. His first studio album in almost a decade was *Ovo* (Real World, 2000), a concept album chronicling the story of three generations of a family. Featuring contributions from such diverse sources as **Richie Havens**, the Black Dyke Mills Band and **Neneh Cherry**, *Ovo* was the music created for the Millennium Dome, a temporary structure built in Greenwich, London, to celebrate the millennium, which in the course of its short life was met with profound neglect by the British public and mounting hysteria by British politicians as, in the manner of Oliver Twist, it asked for more. Gabriel's music, a meld of ambient sounds and pained vocals with occasional thick chords from guitarist David Rhodes, was far better than the Dome itself, but hardly any more compelling.

SLIM GAILLARD
b. Bulee Gaillard, 4 January 1916, Detroit, Michigan, USA, d. 26 February 1991, London, England

Scat singer, guitarist, pianist and hipster comedian, Gaillard rose to prominence in the late thirties and the bebop era but his career continued into the nineties.

The son of a cruise-liner steward, Gaillard's first stage act involved him simultaneously tap dancing and playing guitar. In 1937 he began a six-year partnership with bassist Slam Stewart, who sang and bowed his instrument in unison. Appearing regularly on radio, Slim and Slam also had hit singles with 'Flat Foot Floogie', 'Cement Mixer', 'A-Reet-a-Voutie' and other songs using Gaillard's personal variant on jive talk, which he called 'vout'. The sheet music of 'Floogie' was among the items buried in a time capsule at the New York World's Fair in 1939.

Throughout the forties Gaillard led his own small group with a residency at Billy Berg's Hollywood nightclub, which was patronized by the movie élite and where he made several 'soundies' (short films of songs akin to the modern music video). He made cameo appearances in such films as *Hellzapoppin'* and *Star Spangled Rhythm* (1942). Among his best recordings from this era was 'Slim's Jam', which featured **Charlie Parker** and **Dizzy Gillespie**. This track was reissued in 1983 by Gaillard himself on *Roots of Vouty* (Putti-Putti). A cult hero to the emerging beat generation, Gaillard's club act was described in Jack Kerouac's novel *On the Road*. His children's song 'Down at the Station' was said to have inspired the *Thomas the Tank Engine* books of the Rev. W. Awdry.

In 1953 he appeared with **Billie Holiday** and **Coleman Hawkins** in **Norman Granz**'s 'Jazz at the Philharmonic' presentation and later toured with **Stan Kenton**. In the fifties and sixties Gaillard worked in cabaret as vocalist, comedian and master of ceremonies before moving into acting in various television drama series. These included *Charlie's Angels*, *Mission Impossible* and *Roots – the Next Generation*.

He retired to his California fruit farm, but was persuaded to return to the stage by Gillespie in 1982, the year he added hand-clapping to his son-in-law **Marvin Gaye**'s album *Midnight Love*. For a while Gaillard made London his base, performing his forties material to European audiences and appearing in the film *Absolute Beginners* (1986).

SERGE GAINSBOURG
b. Lucien Ginzburg, 2 April 1928, Paris, France, d. 2 March 1991, Paris

One of the most eccentric and controversial figures in the French *chanson* tradition, Gainsbourg was best-known internationally for the erotic 'Je T'aime . . . Moi Non Plus'.

The son of a pianist, he studied painting before joining the cast of the musical *Milord L'Arsoille*. During the fifties he composed a number of French hits, including 'La Javanaise' and 'La Chanson de Prevert'. He later supplied songs to **Johnny Hallyday**, Sacha Distel, **Petula Clark** and **Dionne Warwick**.

He also recorded in a guttural yet passionate voice, heard at its most effective on 'Je T'aime . . .'. Originally intended as a duet for Brigitte Bardot and himself, the piece was released as a duet with English-born actress Jane Birkin after Bardot withdrew from the project. It was an international *succès de scandale* in 1969 and Gainsbourg followed it with a 'fantasy ballad' album, *Melody Nelson* (1971).

Among his greatest commercial successes was the reggae-inflected *Aux Armes Etc.* (1979), whose unconventional version of 'La Marseillaise' led to Gainsbourg being almost lynched by angry paratroopers at a Strasbourg concert. His only English-language album was *Love on the Beat* (1984) recorded in New York. It included a duet with his daughter Charlotte on 'Lemon Incest'.

Gainsbourg also wrote film scores and occasionally acted in and directed movies, including *Je T'aime, Moi Non Plus* (1975), which starred Birkin and Gerard Depardieu.

FRED GAISBERG
b. 1 January 1873, Washington DC, USA, d. 2 September 1951, London, England

Gaisberg, who first recorded **Enrico Caruso** in 1902, was the most important talent scout and producer (though the term was not in use then) of the early recording era.

The son of German immigrants, Gaisberg was employed in 1891 by Columbia as 'Professor Gaisberg'

to provide piano accompaniment to numerous cylinder recordings, mostly of street musicians of the day. The most notable of these was **George Washington Johnson**, whose 'Laughing Song' (1891) is generally regarded as the biggest-selling cylinder of the 1890s. In 1894 Gaisberg joined **Emile Berliner**, for whom he worked as talent scout and accompanist, and in 1896 he supervised the first operatic vocal record (Ferruccio Giannini singing 'La Donna e Mobile' from *Rigoletto*). In 1897 Gaisberg established the first recording studio, in Philadelphia, and made further recordings with Giannini there. A year later he was sent to London to help establish the Gramophone Company and a studio (which he set up in Maiden Lane), and to find European talent. In this capacity, with his brother William (who died in 1918 after being severely gassed while recording the sounds of war in France) he travelled extensively in Europe.

As well as Caruso, whose first disc (rather than cylinder) recordings Gaisberg made in 1902, he was responsible for numerous important operatic recordings, including those by Dame Adelina Patti, Chaliapin and Beniamino Gigli, which helped give the gramophone and records a cultural status. Gaisberg was also responsible for numerous ethnic recordings, made during his travels in Russia, India and the Far East in the first decade of the century, all of which had to be shipped back to Hanover in Germany where the company's manufacturing plant was based.

It was these recordings and the companies set up around the world to market them that led to the dominant position the Gramophone Company (later EMI) soon established internationally. Gaisberg later became artistic director of HMV and after the formation of EMI in 1931 was responsible for much of its classical output, often working alongside **Joe Batten**.

GALLAGHER AND LYLE
Benny Gallagher, b. Largs, Scotland; Graham Lyle, b. Largs

Popular soft-rock songwriters and harmony singers, Gallagher and Lyle provided hits in the seventies for Art Garfunkel and **Elkie Brooks**, while Lyle's later songs were recorded by **Tina Turner**.

They first performed in a local soul band in their home town of Largs and set up a recording studio. Moving to London, the duo were signed by **Paul McCartney** as staff writers for Apple Records, where **Mary Hopkin** recorded their work, including the anthemic 'International', a song later recorded by **Jackie DeShannon**. Both were members of McGuinness Flint (1969–71), a band led by ex-**Manfred Mann** bassist Tom McGuinness and ex-**John Mayall** drummer Hughie Flint. Gallagher and Lyle wrote two jug-band-flavoured hits for the group, 'When I'm Dead and Gone' (Capitol, 1970) and 'Malt and Barley Blues' (1971). They also contributed songs to a solo album by the band's singer, *Dennis Coulson* (Elektra, 1973).

When the duo opted to cut their own records, they chose to work with McGuinness Flint producer Glyn Johns. An unsuccessful eponymous 1972 Capitol album was followed by a long-term contract with A&M. Johns produced three albums in 1973–4, including *Seeds*, which showed Gallagher and Lyle's talent for descriptive writing in 'Country Morning' and their sense of Scottish history in 'The Clearings'. They also wrote music for television documentaries. In 1974 they briefly joined Slim Chance, a band led by Ronnie Lane and dedicated to the same mix of good-time music as McGuinness Flint.

1976 brought their first chart success when American producer David Kershenbaum was brought in for *Breakaway*. The album included two British hits in 'I Wanna Stay with You' and the jaunty 'Heart on My Sleeve', but Garfunkel had even greater success in America with the title track. Perhaps the duo's best song, it married themes of loss and separation with a well-crafted melodic shape.

Love on the Airwaves (1976) included 'The Runaway', a topical song about Californian teenagers, which was successfully recorded by Elkie Brooks. Later albums, including *Showdown* (1978) and *Lonesome No More* (Mercury, 1979), made less impact and in 1979 they separated, reuniting only to record 'Putting the Heart back into the City' (A&M, 1988) to commemorate Glasgow's garden festival. Gallagher moved into production, while Lyle continued to write. With Terry Britton he composed Tina Turner's 1984 American No. 1 'What's Love Got to Do with It'*, her 1985 film theme, 'We Don't Need Another Hero (Thunderdome)' and **Michael Jackson**'s 'Just Good Friends'. Lyle also co-wrote Jim Diamond's 1984 British hit 'I Should Have Known Better'. *Heart on My Sleeve* (1991) was the definitive retrospective.

RORY GALLAGHER
b. 2 March 1949, Ballyshannon, Ireland, d. 17 June 1995

Gallagher was one of the most talented guitarists of the second wave of British blues musicians.

He performed with the Impact show band in Cork before forming his own rock'n'roll band in 1965. This evolved into Taste, a blues-based trio which included drummer John Wilson (b. 3 December 1947) and bassist Richard McCracken (b. 26 June 1948) when the group moved from Ireland to London in 1968. Featuring Gallagher's guitar pyrotechnics in the fashion of **Albert King** and **Buddy Guy**, Taste recorded several albums for Polydor in 1969–71, produced by Tony Colton. The most commercially successful was *On the Boards* (1970).

When McCracken and Wilson left to form Stud with guitarist Jim Cregan, Gallagher formed his own band with Irish musicians Gerry McAvoy (bass) and Wilgar Campbell (drums). The eponymous first album and *Deuce* (both 1971) were minor hits and Gallagher's extensive international tours ensured that *Live in Europe* (1972) reached the British Top Ten. In that year he was one of the British players who contributed to **Muddy Waters**' *In London* album.

In 1973 Rod de'Ath replaced Campbell and the addition of Lou Martin on keyboards added tonal colour to the leader's hard-driving compositions. After three more Polydor albums (including *Irish Tour 74*, which was filmed by director Tony Palmer) Gallagher moved to Chrysalis in 1975. *Calling Card* (1976) was produced in Munich by **Deep Purple**'s Roger Glover.

Disturbed only by several personnel changes – Ted McKenna joined on drums in 1978 and McAvoy finally left in 1980 – Gallagher retained his Europe-wide following with a series of consistent but predictable albums. *Jinx* (1982), his sixth for Chrysalis, was among the best. In 1977 he played on the comeback album of his early hero, **Lonnie Donegan**. From the mid-eighties Gallagher produced records on his own label, licensing *Defender* (1987) to Demon in Britain. *Fresh Evidence* (Castle, 1990) was intended as the first in a series of previously unreleased live recordings.

GALLIANO
Rob Gallagher; Crispin Robinson; Valerie Etienne; Constantine Weir

Galliano were the most intelligent and engaging of the bands to emerge from the UK's acid jazz scene of the late 1980s, characterized by Rob Gallagher's unapologetically English rap style. They enjoyed a huge and enthusiastic live following but failed to find the same level of success on record.

The band was built around Gallagher, who started creative life as a poet in the **Linton Kwesi Johnson** tradition, performing at poetry clubs around London. At one of these he encountered the jazz and funk sounds of the 'rare groove' scene and, critically, Gilles Peterson, who made Gallagher, as Galliano, his first signing when he set up the Talkin Loud label for Phonogram. Gallagher had recorded alone as Galliano, releasing *Welcome to the Story* on the Acid Jazz label in 1990, but added other musicians for his Talkin Loud début, 1991's *In Search of the Thirteenth Note*, which contained the hit 'Little Ghetto Boy'.

1992's *A Joyful Noise unto the Creator* was an acclaimed riot of melodramatic funk, ethnic percussion and positive and often hilarious lyrics. It spawned a number of hit singles, including 'Jus

Reach', 'Skunk Funk' and 'Prince of Peace'. Despite the obvious funk and soul influences on their music, the band also continued the tradition of bands like **Madness** in their lyrical and visual humour. A more serious tone was evident on *The Plot Thickens* (1994). Gallagher's lyrics took the pulse of contemporary Britain with a series of songs tackling issues such as the environment, consumerism, racism and religious bigotry. These themes were frequently put in the context of centuries of British and European history, notably on 'Was This the Time?' and the single 'Twyford Down'. Though critically well received, the album's stress on the band's more folky side at the expense of danceability was poorly timed, given that its release coincided with the mainstream emergence of jungle in the UK. The band's response later the same year was to release *A Thicker Plot*, a collection of remixes of material from their previous two albums.

The live interpretation of some of the songs from *The Plot Thickens* had suggested the band were becoming interested in the rhythmic possibilities of drum'n'bass, a suggestion confirmed by 1996's *4*, whose 'Freefall' mixed the band's song-orientated approach with drum'n'bass rhythms. However, neither *The Plot Thickens* nor *4* provided the band with a commercial breakthrough and later in 1996 the group broke up. Galliano's October 1996 farewell concert in London ended with a remarkable version of Mongo Santamaria and Oscar Brown's 'Afro Blue'.

JAMES GALWAY
b. 8 December 1939, Belfast, Northern Ireland

One of the leading classical flautists, James Galway crossed over into the popular field with a hit version of a **John Denver** tune. He followed this success with collaborations with figures like **Henry Mancini** and **Cleo Laine**.

From a Protestant working-class district of Belfast, Galway won flute championships as a child and became an apprentice piano tuner on leaving school. He won a scholarship to London's Royal College of Music in 1954 and later studied in Paris with Jean-Pierre Rampal. He also busked in the Métro.

During the sixties Galway built up his reputation as a member of the Sadlers Wells Opera and the BBC Symphony orchestras. In 1969 he joined the Berlin Philharmonic under Herbert von Karajan. He left to work as a soloist in 1975, signing a recording contract with RCA. Galway made six albums in two years and with successful world tours was promoted as 'The Man with the Golden Flute', the title of a compilation album released by RCA in 1978.

While recovering in hospital from a serious road accident in 1977, Galway heard Denver's 'Annie's Song'. Released in 1978, his instrumental interpreta-

tion was a Top Ten hit in Britain and launched him on a new career as an interpreter of pop melodies. In 1979 he recorded *Songs of the Seashore*, an album of Japanese tunes and Dan Hill's 'Sometimes When We Touch' was the title song of a 1980 album with Cleo Laine which reached the Top Twenty. This was followed by *The Pachelbel Canon*, an album of Australian material. With accompaniment by the Sydney Symphony Orchestra, it included 'Waltzing Matilda' and the **Bee Gees'** 'I Started a Joke'.

Later Galway albums included a collection of American songs, *The Wayward Wind* (1984), and *In the Pink* (1984), a selection of Mancini's film and television themes, *The Enchanted Forest* (1991), a collection of Japanese melodies, and *Wind Beneath My Wings* (1991), which included a piece specially written for him by **Elton John**. He made his first appearance in Russia in 1989.

He performed infrequently in the nineties.

GAMBLE AND HUFF
Kenny Gamble, b. 1941, Philadelphia, Pennsylvania, USA; Leon Huff, b. Camden, New Jersey

Songwriters and producers, Gamble and Huff made their Philadelphia International label the leading black record company of the seventies, emulating **Berry Gordy**'s achievement with Motown a decade earlier. Often with arrangements by **Thom Bell**, Gamble and Huff productions were notable for their sophisticated, highly orchestrated sound.

When they met in 1964, both had considerable experience as session players. Gamble had written Candy and the Kisses' minor dance hit 'The 81' (Cameo, 1964) and formed the Romeos with Bell (piano) and Roland Chambers (guitar). The group recorded unsuccessfully for Arctic, the label which took Barbara Mason to the national charts with 'Yes I'm Ready' (1965). In 1965 Bell was replaced by Huff, who had played piano on sessions for **Phil Spector**, written 'Mixed Up Shook Up Girl' for Patty and the Emblems (Herald, 1964) and recorded 'Little Eva' under the name the Locomotions on Swan.

When the Romeos split, Gamble and Huff formed their own label, successively called Excel and Gamble, to record the **Intruders**. Beginning with '(We'll Be) United', the group had a ten-year series of hits which included the million-seller 'Cowboys to Girls' (1968). That success brought the duo to the attention of other labels and their freelance productions included major hits for the white pop-soul band Soul Survivors ('Expressway to Your Heart', Crimson, 1968), Archie Bell and the Drells and **Jerry Butler**.

As leading Philadelphia labels Cameo-Parkway and Jamie wound up or concentrated solely on distribution, respectively, Gamble and Huff set up Neptune, a more ambitious company financed by **Leonard Chess** of the Chess Records group. Among its roster of artists were the Vibrations and the **O'Jays**, but when Chess was taken over by GRT after Leonard's death in 1969, Neptune folded.

Closing Gamble, the duo transferred the Intruders and the O'Jays to a new operation, Philadelphia International, which also recorded new signings Harold Melvin and the Blue Notes, **Billy Paul**, the Three Degrees and singer/writer/producer Bunny Sigler. In 1971 Gamble and Huff signed a deal with Columbia for international distribution and promotion of the 'Philly sound' and in 1972 they had Top Ten hits with Melvin's 'If You Don't Know Me By Now', Paul's 'Me and Mrs Jones'*, 'Backstabbers'* by the O'Jays and Johnny Williams' 'Slow Motion'. Following Gordy's Motown example, Gamble and Huff created an in-house team of publishers, management, writers, producers and studio musicians. Recording as MFSB (Mother, Father, Sister, Brother), the Philly musicians scored an instrumental No. 1 with 'The Sound of Philadelphia' (1974), the theme from television's *Soul Train*.

As Philadelphia International became the leading black music company of the mid-seventies, Gamble and Huff were in even greater demand for outside productions. They supervised hits by **Joe Simon** and **Wilson Pickett** and cut an album with **Barbra Streisand**. In 1982 they signed the **Five Blind Boys of Mississippi** to Peace International, a new gospel label. But despite further hits with the O'Jays, former Melvin lead singer **Teddy Pendergrass** and **Patti Labelle**, Gamble and Huff closed Philadelphia International when the Columbia contract expired.

In 1985 they re-formed the label, retaining their most popular act the O'Jays, and signing a worldwide distribution deal with EMI. Their first success was the million-selling 'Do You Get Enough Love', performed by Shirley Jones and written and produced by Sigler. This was followed by recordings by Phyllis Hyman (*Living All Alone*) and the **Dells**. The duo also recorded **Lou Rawls**' *Family Reunion* for their new Gamble and Huff label in 1987.

GANG STARR
Guru, b. Keith Elan, 18 July 1966, Boston, Massachusetts, USA; DJ Premier, b. Chris Martin, 3 May 1969, Brooklyn, New York

One of rap's more experimental outfits, Gang Starr were among the first rap groups to explore the use of jazz, both live and sampled, in hip-hop.

Guru begun his work in rap in Boston, before moving to New York in 1989. There he was put in touch with DJ Premier, at the time still at college in Texas. Through tapes and telephone communication, the

pair worked on tracks for a début album, *No More Mr Nice Guy* (1990). The album included the first overt statement on the pair's musical influences on 'Jazz Music', a track which attracted the attention of film director Spike Lee.

Lee put the band in contact with Branford Marsalis, who helped them put together a new track, the classic 'Jazz Thing', which featured on the soundtrack of Lee's next film, *Mo' Better Blues*. The group would later also contribute a track to the soundtrack of *White Men Can't Jump* (1992).

The critically acclaimed *Step in the Arena* (1991) continued the evolution of the duo's jazz-rap project, featuring samples from **The Band**, **Miles Davis** and **Kool and the Gang**. Rapper Guru took the jazz/rap synthesis one stage further with his *Jazzmatazz* project, which he described as 'an experimental fusion of hip-hop and jazz' and which resulted in an album in 1993. The long-player set Guru's raps against real instrumentation, rather than samples, and featured contributions from jazz luminaries such as **Donald Byrd**, **Roy Ayers** and **Courtney Pine**, as well as French rapper **MC Solaar** and former Young Disciples vocalist Carleen Anderson.

In the early 1990s the duo juggled solo work and Gang Starr recording. The Jazzmatazz project was preceded by a third Gang Starr LP, the harder *Daily Operation* (1992), followed up by *Hard to Earn* in 1994. A second Jazzmatazz LP, *Volume II – The New Reality*, followed in 1995, but three years passed before the next Gang Starr album, 1998's *Moment of Truth*, which maintained the high standards set by the group's earlier recordings. *Full Clip: A Decade of Gang Starr* (1999) compiled their best work to date.

CECIL GANT
b. 4 April 1913, Nashville, Tennessee, USA, d. 4 February 1951, Nashville

Gant's big R&B hit of 1944 'I Wonder' was to some extent responsible for the speedy recovery of the black record industry towards the end of the Second World War.

Like other wartime hits such as 'Saturday Night (Is the Loneliest Night of the Week)', 'I Wonder' captured the uneasy feelings of lovers separated – 'I wonder . . . my little darling . . . where can you be . . . again tonight' – and Gant's crooning of it undoubtedly owed something to **Nat 'King' Cole**. So popular was the song that disc manufacturers could not at first keep up with demand, while Gant, billed as the 'GI Sing-sation' and dressed in uniform, performed at savings bond drives, and, after the war, in Los Angeles clubs.

Though a crooner rather than a bluesman, Gant added to pop ballads, sung in a light and husky voice, jump-blues and boogie material. His piano-playing in the boogie idiom was particularly firm. The breadth of his musical interests was illustrated by a long series of records on Gilt Edge (1944–6). He was, however, unable to repeat the success of 'I Wonder'.

He also recorded for Four Star, Bullet, Imperial and other labels, and finally (1950–1) for Decca, where he anticipated rock'n'roll with titles like 'We're Gonna Rock' and 'Rock Little Baby', on which he was probably accompanied by country guitarist Hank Garland.

GARBAGE

Duke Erikson, b. Nebraska, USA; Steve Marker, b. New York; Shirley Manson, b. 3 August 1966, Edinburgh, Scotland; Butch Vig, b. 1964, Viroqua, Wisconsin, USA

An experimental, post-modern pop group formed by a Wisconsin-based production trio and augmented by Scottish vocalist Shirley Manson, Garbage achieved international acclaim with the release of their epony-mous début album in 1995.

The origins of Garbage date back to the early eight-ies when Vig and Erickson met at the University of Wisconsin and found common ground in their rural upbringing. They formed Spooner and recorded a demo with the help of Steve Marker, with whom Vig was to buy an eight-track recording system in 1984, marking the beginnings of Smart Studios.

While intermittently releasing garage rock albums as Spooner and then Firetown, the trio produced sin-gles for punk and rock bands on the Sub Pop and Twin Tone labels. Vig went on to produce a handful of groundbreaking alternative rock albums, including **Nirvana**'s *Nevermind*, **Sonic Youth**'s *Dirty* and the first two **Smashing Pumpkins** releases, *Gish* and *Siamese Dream*. By 1993, while they worked together remixing other artists, Vig, Marker and Erickson formed Garbage in the midst of endless studio experi-mentation, recruiting singer Shirley Manson after see-ing her on MTV with Angelfish.

The foursome spent the next year working at Smart Studios, resulting in *Garbage* (1995)*, which became an enormous success on the back of the singles 'Vow', 'Queer', 'Only Happy When It Rains' and 'Stupid Girl' and had a hi-tech sheen reminiscent of **My Bloody Valentine**'s *Loveless*. The album was followed by two years of relentless touring and 'Number One Crush' (1996), a track from the *Romeo and Juliet* soundtrack, which earned the band a trio of Grammy nominations. Another lengthy spell in the studio pre-ceded the release of *Version 2.0* (1998)*, echoing the success of *Garbage* and featuring four more hit sin-gles: 'Special', 'Push It', 'I Think I'm Paranoid' and 'Dumb'.

JUDY GARLAND

b. Frances Ethel Gumm, 10 June 1922, Grand Rapids, Minnesota, USA, d. 22 June 1969, London, England

Like **Marlene Dietrich**, whose move from the screen to the concert hall paralleled her own, Garland's art and life were tightly interwoven, but, unlike Dietrich, Garland was never in control of her career. Initially a cheerful innocent in a series of musicals with fellow child star Mickey Rooney and at the end of her screen career almost a parody of herself, Garland throughout her films, and later in concert, sang with moving intensity. Her vocal style was simple but affecting, the catch and her vibrato emphasized by her forever out-stretched hand all denoting her commitment to the material she sang. Her best performances included **Harold Arlen**'s 'Over the Rainbow'* (Decca, 1939), the song forever associated with her from *The Wizard of Oz*; Hugh Martin's and Ralph Blane's 'Have Your-self a Merry Little Christmas', which she sings to comfort Margaret O'Brien in *Meet Me in St Louis* (1944); and Arlen and **Ira Gershwin**'s 'The Man That Got Away' (Columbia, 1954), from *A Star Is Born*. On these, her passion helped forge an unusually intense relationship with her audience.

Though not quite 'Born in a Trunk' (as she sang in *A Star Is Born*), Garland was the daughter of vaude-ville parents and made her stage début at the age of three. Paired with her two elder sisters, she performed as the Gumm Sisters until, in 1936, now renamed Gar-land at the suggestion of **George Jessel**, she made her first recording ('Swing Mr Charlie' with **Bob Crosby** on Decca) and signed with MGM. Her screen début, *Every Sunday* (1936) in which she co-starred with **Deanna Durbin**, was not a success but her perform-ance of 'Dear Mr Gable' (a new introductory verse to the 1913 standard 'You Made Me Love You') was one of the highlights of *Broadway Melody of 1938* (1937). The verse was written by producer and lyricist Roger Edens, who became a close musical associate of Gar-land's: he played piano when she was screen-tested by MGM and later co-wrote 'Born in a Trunk' for her.

By now a juvenile star, Garland was teamed with Rooney for nine films, commencing with *Thorough-breds Don't Cry* (1937). Then in 1939, despite studio opposition, she was chosen by producer **Arthur Freed** for the part of Dorothy (originally intended for **Shirley Temple**) in *The Wizard of Oz*, one of the most engaging fantasies ever produced in Hollywood. Fol-lowing her marriage to orchestra leader **David Rose** in 1941, she made a series of backstage musicals, includ-ing *Strike Up the Band* (1940), *Babes on Broadway* (1941), in which she co-starred with **Gene Kelly**, *Ziegfeld Girl* (1941) and *Presenting Lily Mars* (1942), before she was teamed with director Vincente Minnelli (whom she married in 1945) for four superior films.

With Minnelli she made the wistful evocation of turn-of-the-century America, *Meet Me in St Louis* (1944), in which she was both brash ('The Trolley Song') and melancholic ('Have Yourself a Merry Little Christmas'), *The Clock* (1945), the amiable extravaganza *Ziegfeld Follies* (1946) and the witty *The Pirate* (1947) in which she sang **Cole Porter**'s triumphant 'Be a Clown' with Kelly. Though these and subsequent films, including *Easter Parade* (1948) in which she sang 'We're a Couple of Swells' with **Fred Astaire**, were successes, Garland – by now addicted to pills to keep her weight down, to sleep and to keep awake – earned the reputation of a temperamental star. After she broke down during the filming of *Annie Get Your Gun* and was replaced by **Betty Hutton**, she was fired by MGM in 1950, and in 1951 she divorced Minnelli.

In the summer of 1951 Garland made a triumphant appearance at the London Palladium which initiated a series of successful, highly emotional concert tours that reached its climax at Carnegie Hall in 1961. The recording of that performance, the double-album *Judy at Carnegie Hall* (Capitol, 1961), sold over two million copies and was the most successful of her numerous live albums. Before then she had returned to the screen for *A Star Is Born* (1954), the best of the films that echoed her life, and later appeared in three minor films, including *I Could Go on Singing* (1963), a parody of her career. She returned to the concert stage in the mid-sixties, but her appearances became more erratic. Her death was officially recorded as the result of an accidental overdose of sleeping pills, but as Ray Bolger (the Scarecrow in *The Wizard of Oz*) put it at her funeral, 'She just plain wore out'.

Two of her daughters, Liza Minnelli and Lorna Luft, followed Garland into showbusiness. Liza Minnelli (*b. 12 March 1946, Los Angeles, California, USA*) made her first screen appearance with her mother in 1949 (*The Good Old Summertime*) and, though her parents divorced when she was five, occasionally guested in her mother's concerts throughout the fifties. In 1963 she made her off-Broadway début and in the sixties established herself as a leading Broadway actress and cabaret performer. Her urgent, nervous singing style with its strong vibrato was strikingly reminiscent of her mother's but from the start (in the manner of **Barbra Streisand**) Minnelli's career was far broader based, mixing singing and dramatic roles in films and plays with cabaret and records. Nominated for an Oscar for *The Sterile Cuckoo* (1969), she won one for *Cabaret* (1972), Bob Fosse's reworking of Christopher Isherwood's novel *Goodbye to Berlin*, which made dramatic use of both her elfin charm and swaggering singing, particularly on the title song and 'Maybe This Time'. Minnelli's other major film was *New York, New York* (1977), Martin Scorsese's supe-

rior evocation of the big-band era of the forties in which she sang the title song.

Liza with a Z (Columbia, 1973), a soundtrack album from a television spectacular, captures Minnelli's cabaret style to good effect, especially on the tongue-twisting title track, 'Can't Help Loving That Man' and **George Gershwin**'s 'The Man I Love'. In a surprise move, Minnelli's *Results* (Epic, 1989) was a collaboration with the **Pet Shop Boys**.

Among the various accounts of Garland's life are *Judy* by Gerald Frank and *Rainbow* by Christopher Finch.

ERROLL GARNER
b. 15 June 1923, Pittsburgh, Pennsylvania, USA,
d. 2 January 1977

Garner's dazzling technique and commitment to melody made him the most commercially successful jazz pianist of the late forties and early fifties. His style was built on a combination of the percussive rhythmic directness of swing and the harmonic developments of bebop.

The son of a pianist, Garner was playing in local bands when, at the age of sixteen, he was discovered by **Mary Lou Williams**. He went to New York in the early forties, taking part in jam sessions with **Charlie Parker** and other pioneers of bebop. He first recorded for Savoy with **Slim Gaillard**'s associate Slam Stewart, a bassist whose speciality was to hum solos in unison with his playing. Garner accompanied vocalist Earl Coleman on 'This Is Always'.

Soon afterwards Garner formed his first trio, the format he would use for the remainder of his career. He recorded albums for Mercury and Disc before spending two years in California. There he cut sides for Ross Russell's Dial both with Parker and under his own name with bassist John Simmons and Alvin Stoller (drums). These included 'Loose Nut', 'Blues Garni' and 'Laura', his first great success.

Garner recorded prodigiously for Atlantic, Savoy, Rex and Signature before joining Columbia in the wake of his big success with 'Misty' (Mercury, 1954), his best-known tune and one of the most performed songs of the post-war years. With lyrics by **Jimmy Van Heusen**'s partner Johnny Burke, the song was a million-seller for **Johnny Mathis** in 1959 and was revived by **Lloyd Price** (1963) and **Ray Stevens** (1975). A series of bestselling albums followed of which the most notable was *Concert by the Sea* (1955). It exemplified Garner's approach, with its selection of Broadway show tunes and standard ballads with strong melody lines. They included 'Teach Me Tonight', **Johnny Mercer**'s 'Autumn Leaves' and **Vernon Duke**'s 'April in Paris'.

Garner continued to tour and record frequently, releasing albums on Columbia, Atlantic and London.

TOMMY 'SNUFF' GARRETT
b. 1938, Dallas, Texas, USA

For three decades Garrett was one of the most successful pop, country and middle-of-the-road producers.

As a teenager, he became a disc-jockey in Lubbock, where he championed **Buddy Holly**'s work, and Wichita Falls, before joining Liberty Records in Hollywood. At Liberty he was to work with the post-Holly **Crickets** but Garrett's first success was with **Johnny Burnette**, whose 'Dreamin'' he produced in 1960. He also discovered **Bobby Vee**, whom he first recorded at **Norman Petty**'s studio before concocting a series of string-laden hits in 1960–3 for the singer. Garrett also worked with **Gene McDaniels** but achieved his greatest commercial success with Gary Lewis and the Playboys.

Led by the son of comedy actor Jerry Lewis, the group had seven Top Ten hits in 1965–6, starting with 'This Diamond Ring'* and including 'Save Your Heart for Me' and 'She's Just My Style'. With arrangements by **Leon Russell**, Garrett produced five albums by the band. The Garrett–Russell team was also responsible for **Brian Hyland**'s 1966 hit, 'The Joker Went Wild'.

By this time, Garrett had left Liberty to form his own Viva label. His next chart success, however, came with his production for Kapp of Sonny and **Cher**'s 'All I Ever Need Is You' and 'A Cowboy's Work Is Never Done' in 1971–2, as well as Cher's million-selling solo hits, 'Gypsys, Tramps and Thieves' and 'Half-Breed'. Garrett was also responsible for the monologue 'If' by Telly Savalas, a 1975 No. 1 in Britain, where Savalas's teleseries *Kojak* had top ratings.

From the mid-sixties Garrett also recorded his own instrumental versions of film themes and pop hits in a series of Liberty albums by 'Tommy Garrett and his 50 Guitars'. As a producer, his later work was in the country field. He worked with **Tanya Tucker**, **Brenda Lee**, **Glen Campbell** and Phil Everly of the **Everly Brothers**, as well as cutting a solo album, *Snuff Garrett's Texas Opera Co.* (Rainwood, 1977). He briefly reactivated Viva as a Warners custom label in the eighties, with albums by **Ray Price**, Porter Wagoner, Shelly West and David (brother of **Lefty**) **Frizzell**, before retiring from the music business in 1983 to become a dealer in Western memorabilia and art.

NOEL GAY
b. Richard Moxon Armitage, 15 July 1898, Wakefield, Yorkshire, England, d. 3 March 1954, London

Gay was the composer of *Me and My Girl* (1937), Britain's longest-running musical of the thirties, in which Lupino Lane introduced one of the most famous 'cockney' songs of all times, 'The Lambeth Walk'. Though he wrote the music for some fifteen shows, Gay is best remembered for his novelty songs ('Run Rabbit Run', popularized by **Bud Flanagan**, 'I Took My Harp to a Party', a hit for **Gracie Fields**, 1933) and 'The Sun Has Got Its Hat on', introduced by Jack Hulbert in 1932.

From a prosperous family, Armitage was a musical prodigy. At the age of fourteen, he became honorary deputy organist at Wakefield Cathedral and a year later won a scholarship to the Royal College of Music. While a student at Cambridge, however, he turned to popular music, arranging dance music and writing songs for revues. This led to his being invited to write the score to *The Charlot Show of 1926*, in which **Jessie Matthews** scored her first major success, after which he took the pseudonym Noel Gay. His own first success came with 'All the King's Horses', which Cicely Courtneidge introduced in *Folly to Be Wise* (1931). Among his other hits were 'There's Something About a Soldier' (1935), 'Leaning on a Lamp-post' (1937), forever associated with **George Formby**, and 'Let the People Sing', one of the most popular songs of the Second World War.

In 1938, the year **Duke Ellington** had an American hit with his version of 'The Lambeth Walk', Gay established his own publishing house. After the war he suffered from deafness and wrote less, devoting most of his time to his publishing interests. In the eighties a revival of the old-fashioned *Me and My Girl*, the plot of which (much rewritten by British comedian and literary figure Stephen Fry) has a cockney barrow boy discovering he is the long-lost seventeenth Baron and eighth Viscount of Hareford, was one of the decade's biggest successes on Broadway.

MARVIN GAYE
b. Marvin Pentz Gay, 2 April 1939, Washington, DC, USA, d. 1 April 1984, Los Angeles, California

With **Smokey Robinson**, the **Temptations**, **Supremes** and **Four Tops**, Gaye was the epitome of what was known in the mid-sixties as the 'Motown sound'. He was also the most enigmatic of the artists signed to **Berry Gordy**'s label. Tied to Motown by marriage as well as contractually, Gaye's turbulent relationship with the Gordy family lasted almost twenty years. The possessor of what one critic has called 'an impressive vocal schizophrenia', his tenor could cover the range of expressions from simple pleasure through relaxed sensuality to gospel penitence. Despite the personal and financial problems which loomed large in his later life, and formed the basis of much of his later songwriting, he produced one of the most powerful bodies of work in the field of popular music.

The son of a Pentecostal minister, Gaye was schooled in the finer points of gospel from an early age. Like many, he turned to secular music in his youth, but his father's fierce authoritarian stance and failure as a minister gave an added dimension to Gaye's rebellion. Briefly a member of the Rainbows, Gaye enlisted in the US airforce in 1955 and on his discharge in 1957 he joined the Marquees, who recorded for Okeh ('Wyatt Earp', 1957). The group also backed Billy Stewart (whose later hits included the memorable 'Sitting in the Park', Chess, 1965) before they were discovered by **Harvey Fuqua** and hired by him as the new Moonglows. The group's only release featuring Gaye's lead voice was 'Mama Loocie' (Chess, 1959).

When Fuqua disbanded the Moonglows to set up as a producer in Detroit in 1960, Gaye went with him and, on the collapse of Fuqua's labels, was signed by Gordy in 1961 as a session singer and drummer (in which capacity he played on all the early hits of Robinson's Miracles). Soon afterwards, adding the 'e' to his name, he married Gordy's sister, Anna. His first recording for Tamla (Motown's sister label) *The Soulful Mood of Marvin Gaye* (1962) saw him singing standards (such as 'Mr Sandman', a hit for the **Chordettes**) but success came with the insistent dance record 'A Stubborn Kind of Fellow' (1962) and the even more heavily rhythmic 'Hitch Hike' (1963). If they were dance records in name, in spirit, like the even better 'Can I Get a Witness' (1963), they were heavily gospel influenced, even down to the tambourines and call-and-response choruses supplied by the Vandellas. By 1965, and 'I'll Be Doggone' and 'Ain't That Peculiar' (both co-written by Robinson), Gaye had developed a far more supple, controlled singing style to match the more complex beat that was the trademark of Motown. The climax of this stage of Gaye's career was the mysterious 'I Heard It Through the Grapevine' (1967), the singer's first international No. 1. The song was a reissued British hit in 1986 after being used in a jeans commercial.

Concurrent with these hits, Gordy utilized the 'lover man' image of Gaye by pairing him with the company's leading ladies. The result was another string of hits, first with **Mary Wells** ('What's the Matter with You Baby' and 'Once Upon a Time', both 1964), and then Kim Weston, the wife of Motown producer Mickey Stevenson ('It Takes Two', 1967), that climaxed with his partnership with Tammi Terrell. For the most part written and produced by the husband and wife team of **Ashford and Simpson**, Gaye and Terrell's records between 1967 and 1969 brought a new sensitivity to love balladry: 'Ain't No Mountain High Enough' (1967, and later a hit for **Diana Ross** in 1970), 'Your Precious Love', 'Ain't Nothing Like the Real Thing' (1968), and 'Good Lovin' Ain't Easy to Come by' (1969). In all, Gaye alone and in partnership with others had over sixty

American pop hits, a Motown record equalled only by Ross.

The seventies saw a radical shift in black music. The pioneering efforts of **Sly Stone**, **Curtis Mayfield**'s **Impressions** and **Isaac Hayes** both broached a new social awareness and saw black acts for the first time selling albums as well as singles in large quantities to the new rock audience. In contrast, Motown still operated a conveyor-belt production system and addressed its artists' albums to an imagined cabaret audience. Gaye, a recluse since the death of Terrell from a brain tumour in 1970, responded to these changes with 'What's Going on' (1971) and a self-produced album of the same title which, through the montage technique of over-dubbing, painted a picture of a blighted America, watched over by the sorrowful singer. Initially only half-heartedly promoted by Motown, the album hit a nerve with a Vietnam-torn America and spawned a further two massive hits, 'Mercy Mercy Me (the Ecology)' and 'Inner City Blues (Makes Me Wanna Holler)' (1971), both written, as were most of the songs, by Gaye himself. *What's Going on* gave Gaye his first major success in the album market. A mark of the impact it had on black performers is how many recorded songs from it. These include **Gil Scott-Heron**, Ross, **Aretha Franklin**, **Quincy Jones** and **Rahsaan Roland Kirk**. The effect on Motown was equally traumatic, producing a slew of socially concerned recordings, while Gaye's example eventually prompted **Stevie Wonder** to take complete control of his own career.

For Gaye himself, however, *What's Going on* only marked a transition. After 'He's the Man' (1972), a diatribe against President Nixon, and the jazz-orientated score for the minor blaxploitation thriller *Trouble Man* (1972), Gaye turned to the subject that was to obsess him for the rest of his career: the pleasures and pains of sex. With the production assistance of former singer Ed Townsend, Gaye created what many saw as the definitive late-night seduction album, *Let's Get It on* (1973). Though it was a huge success, like *Diana with Marvin* (which though recorded earlier was released after), Gaye's personal life was in a shambles. By 1974 his marriage to Anna Gordy was over and Gaye, deeply involved with drugs, had little interest in recording. Finally, in 1976, faced with mounting debts, he put his vocals over tracks laid down for a Leon Ware album, *I Want You*, and embarked on a world tour which only demonstrated how troubled he was. The disco outing 'Got to Give It Up' gave him his second American No. 1 in 1977, but he did not record again until 1979 when he produced the double-album *Here My Dear*. Made in compliance with a court order to give his divorced wife the proceeds of his 'next' album, it detailed, with glowing over-dubbed doo-wop harmonies, his painful relationship with Anna Gordy. Two years later, no longer a dependable hitmaker, Gaye left Motown and America to live in Belgium.

In 1981 he signed with Columbia and in 1982 delivered *Midnight Love*. Co-produced by his old mentor Fuqua and introduced by the majestic 'Sexual Healing'* (co-written by David Ritz, who would later write Gaye's biography, *Divided Soul*, 1985) the album once more took sex for its subject, this time set against reggae-inflected rhythms. *Midnight Love* gave Gaye his biggest-ever success. However, a diet of heavy touring and drugs did nothing to re-establish his composure and early in 1984 he returned to live with his parents in Los Angeles. There on 1 April, after an argument, he was shot dead by his father. After an autopsy revealed Gaye's cocaine addiction, Gaye Snr was found guilty of involuntary manslaughter. In 1985 Columbia released two posthumous albums, *Dreams of a Lifetime* and *Romantically Yours*, which included many of Gaye's hitherto unreleased recordings of standards. In 1986 Motown released *Motown Remembers Marvin*, a superior collection of hits and unreleased recordings, and in 1993 a collection of rarities and B-sides, *Seek and You Shall Find*. It was followed by the definitive retrospective, the four-CD *The Master* and the tribute album *Inner City Blues* (both 1995), to which the likes of **Madonna** and Stevie Wonder contributed.

Both his son (Marvin Jr) and his daughter Nona Gaye are recording artists.

CRYSTAL GAYLE
b. *Brenda Gail Webb, 9 January 1951, Paintsville, Kentucky, USA*

Gayle's international hit 'Don't It Make My Brown Eyes Blue'* (UA, 1977) was a landmark in the acceptance of the 'countrypolitan', middle-of-the-road style of country music. It was hailed as the first supperclub country song.

The youngest of eight children, Gayle (as she was renamed at the start of her recording career) was brought up in Wabash, 400 miles from the Kentucky mountains and mines that so shaped the career of her elder sister, Loretta Lynn. Though Gayle's interests lay in pop music, she joined her sister's touring show in 1970. After a brief stay with Decca, Gayle signed with United Artists in 1972, where she worked with producer Allen Reynolds, who provided her with a more sophisticated backing. The result was a stream of countrypolitan hits: 'Restless' (1972), 'Wrong Road Again' (1975), 'This Is My Year for Mexico' (1976), 'I'll Get over You' and 'I'd Do It All over Again' (1977), culminating in the crossover hit 'Brown Eyes', from *We Must Believe in Magic* (1977), the first album by a female country artist to sell over a million copies. The

song was composed by Richard Leigh, who had originally intended it to be recorded by **Shirley Bassey**. Her follow-up, 'Talking in Your Sleep'*, was equally successful. Her clear voice and dramatic phrasing set against Reynolds' spare production combined to give a sense of sophistication to traditional love songs.

In 1979 she moved to Columbia and had another pop hit, 'Half the Way', before moving on to Elektra in 1982 for the pop hit 'You and I', a duet with Eddie Rabbitt. That same year she worked with **Tom Waits** on the soundtrack for Francis Ford Coppola's film *One from the Heart*. Ironically, throughout this time, Gayle's material became increasingly countryfied. In 1981, for example, she had a big country hit with **Jimmie Rodgers**' 'Miss the Mississippi and You' and when by 1986 her pop success had dried up, she was still having country hits, including 'Cry' and the No. 1 'Straight to the Heart' (Warners, 1987).

In the nineties Gayle continued to tour and was the owner of a Nashville gift and jewellery business. *Ain't Gonna Worry* (1991) is the best of her modern country albums. Her 1993 *Best Always* (Curb) is mostly re-recordings, but *50 Original Tracks* is a fine collection of her material for UA and Liberty from 1974 to 1993.

GLORIA GAYNOR
b. *7 September 1949, Newark, New Jersey, USA*

Gaynor's 'Never Can Say Goodbye' (MGM, 1974) inaugurated the disco boom of the seventies, paving the way for such artists as **Donna Summer**. Unusually for a disco hit, her 'I Will Survive' (1979) became a feminist anthem because of its defiant assertion of independence.

One of seven children, Gaynor's recording career began in 1965 with an unsuccessful single for **Johnny Nash**'s Jocinda label. She next sang with the Soul Satisfiers and from 1967 was resident singer in a Newark nightclub. By 1973 her manager Jay Ellis had linked up with engineer Tony Bongiovi and arranger Meco Monardo to create a disco rhythm which was fronted by Gaynor's powerful voice. 'Honey Bee' (Columbia, 1973) was followed by *Never Can Say Goodbye* (MGM, 1974). The whole of one side of that album was continuous dance music and the driving title track, a revival of a 1971 **Isaac Hayes** and **Jackson Five** hit, reached the Top Ten in both America and Britain. The song was again revived by the **Communards** in 1987.

A disco version of the **Four Tops**' 'Reach Out I'll Be There' (1975) was a British hit but Gaynor's approach was soon eclipsed by the electronic pulse of **Giorgio Moroder**'s productions for Summer. She had a small hit with a revival of 'How High the Moon' (Polydor, 1976) and released such albums as *Experience* (1975) and *I've Got You* (1976), but she did not return to the spotlight until the release of 'I Will Survive' in 1979.

Originally the B-side of 'Substitute', the song was written and produced by Dino Fekaris and Freddie Perren, and became a multi-million-seller and a transatlantic No. 1. However, the follow-up, 'Let Me Know (I Have a Right)', was only a minor hit. During the eighties Gaynor recorded for Atlantic, Chrysalis ('I Am What I Am', 1983, from the musical *La Cage aux Folles*) and Fanfare. In 1994 she recorded new versions of disco classics, including, inevitably, 'I Will Survive'.

J. GEILS BAND

Jerome Geils, b. 20 February 1946, New York, USA; Peter Wolf, b. Peter Blankfield, 7 March 1946, New York; Stephen Jo Bladd, b. 13 July 1942, Boston, Massachusetts; Seth Justman, b. 27 January 1951, Washington DC; Danny Klein, b. 13 May 1946, New York; Magic Dick, b. Richard Salwitz, 13 May 1945, New London, Connecticut

A hard blues-rock group, the J. Geils Band had its greatest success in the seventies and eighties.

The group was formed in Boston in 1967 from an amalgamation of the J. Geils Blues Band (bassist Klein, Magic Dick on harmonica, and Geils himself on guitar) and two members of an art students' band, the Hallucinations (singer Wolf and drummer Bladd). Keyboards-player Justman joined the following year. Playing uncompromising rhythm and blues, in the manner of the early **Rolling Stones**, the band were soon popular on the New England club and college circuit.

The first eponymous album (Atlantic, 1970) contained a mixture of Wolf–Justman originals and covers of R&B numbers like **Otis Rush**'s 'Homework' and **John Lee Hooker**'s 'Serves You Right to Suffer'. Bill Szymczyk produced *The Morning After* (1971) and the group's next five studio albums. During this period the J. Geils Band had three Top Forty singles, 'Looking for a Love' (1972), 'Give It to Me' (1973) and 'Must of Got Lost' (1974). The group also played on the **Buddy Guy** and **Junior Wells** album, *Play the Blues* (Atlantic, 1972). Their live act is memorably captured on the in-concert sets *Full House* (1972) and *Blow Your Face Out!* (1976).

In 1978 the band switched labels to EMI-America, for the Joe Wissert-produced *Sanctuary*, which had a smoother rock sound. On *Love Stinks* (1980) Justman played synthesizer. That album included two minor hits but the more pop-orientated *Freeze-Frame* (1981) produced two million-sellers in the title track and 'Centerfold', Wolf's comment on the pin-up phenomenon, which reached No. 1.

After the hit 'I Do' in 1982, Wolf left the group – the first personnel change in their sixteen-year his-

tory. The title track of his first solo album, *Lights Out*, reached the Top Twenty in 1984. He later released *Come as You Are* (1987) and moved into production before signing to MCA as a solo artist for *Up to No Good* (1989).

In 1984 the J. Geils Band released *You're Getting Even While I'm Gettin' Odd*, with lyrics by Paul Justman, who directed the group's videos. Phoebe Snow sang lead vocals on several tracks, but the band split up shortly after its release. Geils set up a vintage car business but in 1991 he and Magic Dick formed a new blues band with Massachusetts musicians Jerry Miller (guitar), Rory McLeod (double bass) and Steve Ramsay (drums), recording *Bluestime* (Rounder, 1994). *Anthology* (1994) was exactly that.

BOB GELDOF
b. Robert Frederick Zenon Geldof, 5 October 1952, Dun Leoghaire, Ireland

Songwriter and singer with neo-punk band the Boomtown Rats, Geldof gained international fame as the organizer of Band Aid and the Live Aid concert in 1985. He subsequently re-established himself as a media person with his own very successful British television production company.

After working at several jobs, including journalism in Canada, Geldof joined the Nitelife Thugs in Dublin in 1976. With Gerry Roberts and Gerry Cott (guitars), Johnny Fingers (keyboards), Pete Briquette (bass) and drummer Simon Crowe, the group became the Boomtown Rats (a name Geldof found in **Woody Guthrie**'s *Bound for Glory*). With a style influenced by **Dr Feelgood**, the band built up a following in Ireland playing a mixture of R&B and punk.

The Boomtown Rats were signed by Nigel Grainge to his Ensign label, and Robert John 'Mutt' Lange produced an eponymous album in Germany. The first single, Geldof's bombastic 'Looking after No. 1' (1977), reached the Top Twenty and was followed by eight more hits in the next three years. Among them were 'Like Clockwork' (1978) and 'Rat Trap' from *A Tonic for the Troops* and Geldof's most dramatic lyric, 'I Don't Like Mondays'. Inspired by an American incident in which a teenage girl shot nine people, it topped the British charts in 1979 but sold poorly in America.

The accompanying album *Fine Art of Surfacing* provided another Top Ten single in 'Someone's Looking at You' but after the success of 'Banana Republic' (1980) the Boomtown Rats' career went into decline. Cott left the group in 1981 and the albums *V Deep* (1982) and *In the Long Grass* (1984) made little impact. Though the group remained in existence for several more years, Geldof became more involved with his solo career.

'He had already acted in Alan Parker's film of the **Pink Floyd** concept album *The Wall* (1982) but in 1984, galvanized by the Ethiopian famine, he organized the charity record 'Do They Know It's Christmas?'. With its anthemic refrain 'feed the world', the song was co-written with Midge Ure of **Ultravox** and recorded by Band Aid, an all-star group including **George Michael**, **Sting** of the **Police**, **David Bowie**, **U2**, **Status Quo**, **Culture Club** and **Duran Duran**. With over three million copies sold, it became the most successful single ever in Britain and the recording inspired similar efforts in America ('We Are the World'* composed by **Lionel Richie** and **Michael Jackson**, and produced by **Quincy Jones**), Canada (**Gordon Lightfoot** and **Bryan Adams**' 'Tears Are Not Enough'), the Netherlands and many other countries. A number of Paris-based African musicians recorded 'Tam Tam pour l'Ethiopie' while there were also heavy-metal, folk and reggae charity records. As well as the concern of the performers, this phenomenon reflected the music industry's growing sense of social responsibility with manufacturing and distribution profits also being donated to charity. In the late eighties the charity single became a widespread means of fund-raising.

In 1985 Geldof went on to organize Live Aid, a London- and Philadelphia-based concert which reached a worldwide television audience estimated at 1,000 million. Over fifty performers took part, among them **Paul McCartney**, **Bob Dylan**, the **Beach Boys**, **Neil Young**, **Phil Collins**, **Tina Turner** and **David Bowie**, whose duet with the **Rolling Stones**' Mick Jagger on **Martha and the Vandellas**' 'Dancing in the Streets' later became a hit single.

After guiding Band Aid for two years, during which he successfully oversaw the use of Band Aid funds and publicized the root causes of the famine, Geldof published an autobiography (*Is This It?*, 1987) and resumed his professional career. The solo album *Deep in the Heart of Nowhere* (Mercury, 1986) included the minor hit 'This Is the World Calling'. His second album, *The Vegetarians of Love* (1988), was more successful. In 1993 he resumed his musical career with the quirky *The Happy Club*. His 1994 single 'Crazy' was co-written by Dave Stewart of the **Eurythmics**. Subsequently Geldof moved into television, setting up Planet 24, which successfully bid for the *Big Breakfast* franchise. After that Geldof followed the next trend, the Internet, with an early dotcom company, deckchair.com.

GENESIS

Tony Banks, b. 27 March 1950, England; Peter Gabriel, b. 13 February 1950, London; Anthony Phillips (replaced by Steve Hackett, b. 12 February 1950); Mike Ruther-ford, b. 2 October 1950; Phil Collins (joined 1970), b. 31 January 1951, London

A seventies progressive rock band, Genesis evolved into one of the most successful mainstream rock groups of the mid-eighties.

The group originated in schoolboy bands at Charterhouse School involving Banks (piano), Rutherford (bass), Phillips (guitar) and Gabriel (vocals and flute). In 1967 a demo tape was sent to **Jonathan King**, an old boy of the school, who signed the band to Decca. Two singles and a concept album, *From Genesis to Revelation* (1969), were released. Written very much to King's blueprint, the album pretentiously traced 'the evolution of Man'.

In 1970, with John Mayhew on drums, Genesis were signed to Charisma and recorded *Trespass*. Soon afterwards Mayhew and Phillips left, the latter to pursue his music studies. He later released solo albums on Arista and RCA and *Tarka* (PRT, 1988), a suite based on Henry Williamson's otter book, co-composed with the author's son Harry. He was replaced by Hackett, while the new drummer was Collins, a former child actor and member of Flaming Youth with whom he had recorded *Ark 2* (Fontana, 1969).

Genesis now proceeded to develop a distinctive approach, centred on Gabriel's surreal lyrics – which followed the logic of rhyme-scheme rather than conventional narrative – and his theatrical performance involving mime and costume. *Nursery Cryme* (1971) was followed by *Foxtrot* (1972), which included the twenty-minute epic 'Supper's Ready' and was acted out on stage by Gabriel in a fox mask. The latter was a British hit, as were *Genesis Live* and *Selling England by the Pound* (1973).

In true art-rock style, Genesis had loftily ignored the pop charts, but 1974 brought their first hit single with 'I Know What I Like'. Later that year they undertook a hundred-date world tour to perform the double-album *The Lamb Lies Down on Broadway* with a stage show featuring special lighting and backdrop projection.

At this point, Gabriel left to pursue his individual vision and after auditioning 400 potential replacements, the group decided that Collins should handle lead vocals. Drumming on live performances was handled successively by Bill Bruford (a former member of **Yes** and **King Crimson**) and Chester Thompson, formerly of **Weather Report**. Both were featured on the live double-album *Seconds Out* (1977), which was preceded by *A Trick of the Tail* and *Wind and Wuthering* (both 1976).

Having cut a 1975 album (*Voyage of the Acolyte*), Hackett now departed for an undistinguished solo career, eventually joining former **Yes** guitarist Steve Howe in GTR in 1985. Once again there was no permanent replacement. Rutherford took over guitar on

recording sessions and American player Daryl Stuer-
mer joined for the 1978 world tour which promoted
Then There Were Three. Without Gabriel, Genesis had
moved steadily away from the 'concept album' idea
and this album included their first transatlantic hit,
'Follow You Follow Me'.

The transition to a more rhythmic mainstream
rock sound was complete on *Duke* (1980), which
included the first Collins compositions to be recorded
by Genesis and further hits with 'Misunderstanding'
and 'Turn It on Again'. The title track of *Abacab*
(1981) was successful in both America and Britain,
where the album entered the charts at No. 1. The 1983
album *Genesis* included an American hit in 'That's
All', while 'Mama' reached the British Top Ten. *Invisible Touch*, the trio's 1986 release, in turn produced its
crop of hit singles with 'In Too Deep', 'Tonight,
Tonight, Tonight', 'Throwing It All Away' and the
title track.

Even more successful, despite the five-year gap, was
1991's *We Can't Dance*, whose light and catchy title
track became another international hit. It was followed by two live albums, *Live: The Way We Walk*
('The Shorts' and 'The Longs', 1993). *Calling All Stations*, featuring former Stiltskins lead singer Ray Wilson (*b. 1969, Edinburgh, UK*), was the group's first
album of new material for five years. It was followed
by the four-CD box set *Archive: 1967–1975* (1998).

In addition to their work with Genesis, each member of the group developed a solo career. While
Collins recorded with Brand X as well as cutting his
own highly successful albums, Banks made *A Curious
Feeling* (1979), *The Fugitive* (1983), *Still* (1991) and
scored the 1983 film, *Wicked Lady*. Rutherford wrote
an album inspired by Peter C. Brown's novel, *Small-
creep's Day* (1980) and since 1985 has recorded as Mike
and the Mechanics. The eponymous first album
included two hits, 'Silent Running' and 'All I Need Is
a Miracle'. With vocals by former Ace singer Paul
Carrack, Mike and the Mechanics also released *The
Living Years* (Warners, 1988), whose moving title
track was co-written by Rutherford and B. A. Robertson, the disappointing *Word of Mouth* (1991) and the
far better *Beggar on a Beach of Gold* (1995). Carrack's
solo work included *Groove Approved* (1989).

BOBBIE GENTRY

*b. Bobby Lee Street, 27 July 1944, Chickasaw County,
Mississippi, USA*

Gentry is best remembered for her composition 'Ode
to Billie Joe'* (Capitol, 1967), a disquieting and enigmatic tale of suicide in a small Southern town.

Born in rural Mississippi, the setting of many of
her songs, Gentry moved to California when she was
thirteen. There, she studied music and began per-

forming in clubs in the early sixties. She signed with
Capitol in 1967 and her début record, 'Billie Joe', was
an immediate hit. It was dramatic and full of acute
observation – 'Papa said to Mama as he passed
around the blackeyed peas/"Well Billie Joe never had
a lick o'sense, pass the biscuits please"'. However, her
follow-ups, including 'Oklolona River Bottom Band'
and 'Chickasaw County Child', seemed forced and
lacked the drama of 'Billie Joe'. She only had one
more solo American pop hit, 'Fancy' (1970), and a
pair of duets with **Glen Campbell**, both versions of
Everly Brothers' hits, 'Let It Be Me' (1969) and 'All I
Have to Do Is Dream' (1970). In Britain she had a No.
1 with 'I'll Never Fall in Love Again' (1969), and a
long-running television series.

By the seventies she was a regular on the Las Vegas
circuit. Her career briefly revived in the wake of the
1976 film based on 'Billie Joe', which explained what
the song had left out, but by the eighties she had
largely faded from view.

GERALDO

*b. Gerald Bright, 10 August 1904, London, England,
d. 4 May 1974, Vevey, Switzerland*

Geraldo led one of the best-known British dance
bands of the forties. A cockney, fondly remembered
for his signing-off phrase during wartime radio
broadcasts, 'On behalf of me and the boys, cheerio
and thanks for list'nin'!,' he bizarrely found initial
success dressed in a theatrical costumier's idea of a
South American cowboy as the leader of Geraldo's
Gaucho Tango Band.

A child prodigy, Geraldo studied piano at the Royal
Academy of Music. After jobs as a relief pianist at a
cinema and a restaurant organist, he formed various
dance aggregations in the twenties. He toured Britain
and Europe before settling at the Hotel Majestic in St
Anne's-on-Sea, where he led the resident band for
five years and broadcast frequently. In 1930 he
unveiled Geraldo's Gaucho Tango Band at the Savoy
and quickly won the title of 'Tango King' and an
appearance at the Royal Command Performance in
1933, the year the band became Geraldo and His Sweet
Music.

As well as broadcasting, Geraldo recorded prolifically for Decca (as the Gaucho Tango Band) and later
for EMI in a swing style; in the early fifties he
recorded in an even jazzier vein. Appointed Director
of Dance Music at the BBC in 1940, Geraldo continued to experiment, launching a 'Sunday Night Swing
Club', for example. His various wartime broadcasts
included *Geraldo's Guest House*. Later appointed head
of the ENSA Band Division, he toured the Middle
East and Africa in 1944, the year **Ted Heath** left to
form his own band.

After the war Geraldo became involved in band management, supplying orchestras to various London theatres and Cunard liners, and was musical director of Scottish television. He retired in the mid-fifties.

GERRY AND THE PACEMAKERS

Gerry Marsden, b. 24 September 1942, Liverpool, England; Leslie McGuire, b. 27 December 1941, Wallasey; Les Chadwick, b. 11 May 1943, Liverpool; Freddie Marsden, b. 23 November 1940, Liverpool

Though their first album, *How Do You Like It* (1963), saw them mixing R&B (**Arthur Alexander**'s 'A Shot of Rhythm and Blues'), country (**Hank Williams**' 'Jambalaya') and rock'n'roll (**Chuck Berry**'s 'Maybellene') in the manner of the early **Beatles**, Gerry and the Pacemakers were far more pop-orientated than the Fab Four.

Formed by Marsden in 1959, the Pacemakers were one of the many Liverpool groups to learn their stagecraft in Hamburg. Signed by Beatles' manager Brian Epstein in 1962, and by **George Martin** to EMI's Columbia label in 1963, they topped the British charts with their first record, **Mitch Murray**'s chirpy 'How Do You Do It?'. They repeated this success with their second (Murray's similarly styled 'I Like It') and third singles (a revival of **Rodgers and Hammerstein**'s ballad 'You'll Never Walk Alone' from *Carousel*). The latter was quickly taken up by Liverpool's soccer fans and became Britain's most famous football anthem, so much so that in 1985 Marsden re-recorded it with an all-star backing as the Crowd to help raise money for the victims of the Bradford City football ground fire, on Spartan. Once more, the record reached No. 1, making Marsden the first artist to top the British charts with different versions of the same song.

The group's biggest international success was Marsden's own 'Don't Let the Sun Catch You Crying'* (a Top Ten hit in America on Laurie) in 1964. A year later the group starred with **Cilla Black** in the film *Ferry Across the Mersey*. One of Gerry's few compositions, the atmospheric title song was a Top Ten hit in both Britain and America and was affectionately revived by fellow Liverpudlians **Frankie Goes to Hollywood** on *Welcome to the Pleasuredome* (1985) and as a charity record in support of the survivors of the Hillsborough football disaster in 1989.

The group broke up in 1967 and Marsden, after a series of unsuccessful solo records on CBS, NEMS, Decca, Phoenix and DJM, began a career as a TV and cabaret entertainer. However, unlike **Tommy Steele**, he could never escape his pop past. He briefly replaced **Joe Brown** in the London musical *Charlie Girl*, before succumbing to the mood of nostalgia for the sixties and leading a re-formed Pacemakers on tours of America, Australia and Britain.

GEORGE GERSHWIN

b. Jacob Gershvin, 26 September 1898, Brooklyn, New York, USA, d. 11 July 1937, Beverly Hills, California

Gershwin was the only composer of the 'golden age of songwriting' to successfully transcend the limits of the popular song form. Though he wrote many standards (notably 'Swanee', 1919, 'They Can't Take That Away from Me' and 'They All Laughed', 1937), his high critical reputation rests on *Rhapsody in Blue* (1924) and the ground-breaking opera *Porgy and Bess* (1935). If **Irving Berlin** was the most representative American songwriter of the first half of the century, Gershwin was the most ambitious. Since his death his concern to extend the scope of musical theatre has been rivalled only by **Stephen Sondheim** and **Leonard Bernstein**.

With the exception that in his teens he studied piano with Charles Hambitzer, who gave him a firm knowledge of classical music and a technical mastery of the piano, Gershwin's background and early history were remarkably similar to the other popular songwriters of his generation. He worked as a song plugger in 1914, before becoming an accompanist to a number of vaudeville stars, including **Nora Bayes** (who in 1918 introduced the first song written by George and his brother **Ira Gershwin**, the rag-inflected 'The Real American Folk Song'). The following year he published his first song ('When You Want 'Em, You Can't Have 'Em, When You Have 'Em, You Don't Want 'Em' with a lyric by Murray Roth, a minor hit for **Sophie Tucker**) and by 1918 had supplied songs to several shows. Then in 1919 came George's first hit, 'Swanee' (with lyrics by Irving Caesar), which was popularized by **Al Jolson**. Between 1920 and 1924 Gershwin wrote songs for the annual editions of *George White's Scandals*. These included 'I'll Build a Stairway to Paradise' (a hit for both **Paul Whiteman** and **Ben Selvin**, 1923) and 'Somebody Loves You' (Whiteman, 1924), both with lyrics by Buddy DeSylva (of **DeSylva, Brown and Henderson**) and noticeably more sophisticated than Gershwin's earlier songs.

In 1924, with brother Ira now his regular lyricist, Gershwin wrote his first musical, *Lady, Be Good* (filmed 1941), which starred **Fred Astaire** and his sister Adele and introduced 'Fascinating Rhythm' (and originally included the haunting 'The Man I Love' before the song was dropped for being too melancholic). The Gershwins went on to write a series of witty musical comedies in which the songs took precedence over plot and character. Among them were *Oh, Kay!* (1926), which introduced 'Someone to Watch over Me' (a hit for Gershwin himself on Columbia); *Funny Face* (1927, filmed 1957), in which Astaire sang ''S Wonderful'; and the satirical *Of Thee I Sing* (1930).

The Gershwins also contributed songs to films, notably two for Astaire, who in many ways was the perfect vehicle for the sprightly rhythms and sophisticated *longueurs* of their best work. *A Damsel in Distress* (1937) included 'Nice Work if You Can Get It', while *Shall We Dance* (1937) introduced 'They Can't Take that Away from Me' (memorably recorded by Astaire and **Billie Holiday**), 'Let's Call the Whole Thing Off' (a hit for both Astaire and **Eddy Duchin**), and the title song.

From the twenties onwards Gershwin also experimented with extended pieces. The first of these, introduced in the 1922 edition of *George White's Scandals* was the twenty-minute 'jazz opera' *Blue Monday Blues* (with lyrics by DeSylva). More substantial was *Rhapsody in Blue*, which Gershwin first performed with an expanded Paul Whiteman Orchestra at Whiteman's 'Experiment in Modern Music' concert in 1924. A symphonic work, rather than the jazz piece it is often thought to be, *Rhapsody* (extracts from which Gershwin recorded with Whiteman in 1924 and 1927 for Victor, and which provided the title for the 1945 biopic about Gershwin) confirmed how much Gershwin had learned from his piano studies. Even more ambitious were *Concerto in F* (1925) and *An American in Paris* (1928), which formed the inspiration for the **Arthur Freed**-produced film of the same title (1951). Though performed by whites in blackface, *Blue Monday Blues* reflected both Gershwin's interest in black culture and musical idioms. The culmination of this interest was the folk opera *Porgy and Bess* (1935, filmed 1959), one of the major achievements in any American art form of the twentieth century. Based on DuBose Heyward's novel (and with the novelist, as well as Ira, contributing lyrics) the story of the inhabitants of Catfish Row was not an immediate popular success, but by the mid-fifties, after a successful Broadway revival (1953 with **Cab Calloway**), it had been produced in some thirty countries and its songs had been recorded by numerous artists. If, in retrospect, the story and lyrics derive too much from white stereotypes of blacks, the music, far more consistently than **Jerome Kern**'s for *Showboat* (1927) or **Vernon Duke**'s for *Cabin in the Sky* (1940), was triumphantly successful. Among the songs introduced in *Porgy and Bess* were 'Summertime' (a hit for **Billie Holiday**, 1936, and Billy Stewart, Chess, 1966), 'I Got Plenty o' Nuttin'', 'Bess, You Is My Woman Now', 'It Ain't Necessarily So' (**Bing Crosby**, 1938) and 'I Loves You Porgy'.

In 1937, with plans afoot for a new symphony, a musical cavalcade of American history, and an opera with a libretto by Lynn Riggs (whose 1931 play was the basis of **Rodgers and Hammerstein**'s *Oklahoma!*, 1943), Gershwin died of a brain tumour.

Since his death, Gershwin's works have been constantly performed, adapted and recorded. Among recent highlights are the 1989 recording of *Porgy and Bess* conducted by Simon Rattle with Willard White as Porgy, *Crazy for You*, a 1992 adaptation of of his 1930 musical *Girl Crazy* which opened to great critical acclaim on Broadway in 1992, and the Elektra recording of the 'restored' version of the original score of *Strike Up the Band*, George and Ira's 1927 musical satire on war profiteering with a libretto by George S. Kaufman. In 1994 the same label issued *G Plays G: the Piano Rolls*, a collection of Gershwin's own performances of his compositions. In striking contrast was *The Glory of Gershwin*, produced in London by George Martin and featuring harmonica virtuoso Larry Adler with a hotch-potch of partners ranging from **Elton John** to **Courtney Pine**.

IRA GERSHWIN
b. *Israel Gershwin, 6 December 1896, New York, USA, d. 17 August 1983, Hollywood, California*

The older brother of **George Gershwin**, Ira contributed lyrics to the majority of his brother's songs, bringing to them a dry, sophisticated elegance. After George's death he provided lyrics for **Jerome Kern**, **Kurt Weill** and **Harold Arlen**, among others.

The son of an itinerant New York businessman, Ira ignored the piano that was bought for him (which George took up with gusto) in favour of writing. He provided sketches for his college magazine and attempted a literary career. When he turned to lyric-writing he adopted the pseudonym Arthur Francis. Though he wrote 'The Real American Folk Song (Is a Rag)' with George in 1918, his first success came when, with **Vincent Youmans**, he wrote the Broadway show *Two Little Girls in Blue* (1921) which introduced 'Oh, Me! Oh, My!' a hit for **Frank Crumit** in 1922. In 1924 he collaborated with his brother on the unsuccessful *Be Yourself* and re-assumed his rightful name under which he supplied George with increasingly sophisticated lyrics.

After his brother's death in 1937, Ira collaborated with **Vernon Duke** (who took over work on *The Goldwyn Follies*, 1938, on George Gershwin's death), Kern (*Cover Girl*, 1944, which included 'Long Ago and Far Away', a hit for **Bing Crosby**, **Jo Stafford**, **Perry Como** and **Guy Lombardo**, among others) and Weill (the stage musical *Lady in the Dark*, 1941, filmed 1944, in which **Danny Kaye** introduced 'Tchaikovsky'). He later wrote with **Harry Warren** (*The Barkleys of Broadway*, 1949, with **Fred Astaire** and Ginger Rogers) and Harold Arlen (*A Star is Born*, 1954, in which **Judy Garland** introduced 'The Man That Got Away', also a hit as 'The Gal That Got Away' for **Frank Sinatra**).

In the sixties Ira retired to oversee the Gershwin catalogue.

STAN GETZ

b. Stanley Gayetzsky, 2 February 1927, Philadelphia, Pennsylvania, USA, d. 6 June 1991, Malibu, California

One of the most lyrical and technically proficient jazz tenor saxophone players, Getz enjoyed pop success with his arrangements of Brazilian bossa nova music in the sixties.

The son of Russian-Jewish immigrants, he took up saxophone in his teens and by 1943 he was playing professionally in New York. Influenced by **Lester Young**, he worked in the bands of **Jack Teagarden** (1943), **Stan Kenton** (1944–5), **Jimmy Dorsey** (1945), **Benny Goodman** (1945–6) and Randy Brooks, with whom Getz recorded 'How High the Moon' (Decca, 1946). The first records under his own name for Savoy ('Opus de Bop') and Sittin' In ('As I Live and Bop') were made at this period.

In the late forties Getz moved to the West Coast where he came to prominence as a leading member of **Woody Herman**'s Herd. Getz was featured on recordings of 'Cherokee Canyon' (Columbia, 1947) and Ralph Burns' magnificent 'Early Autumn', which established his reputation. Leaving Herman in 1949, Getz made small-group records with pianist Al Haig for Prestige before moving to **Norman Granz**'s Verve label.

During the fifties Getz was frequently paired on record with other top jazz names. These included **Lionel Hampton**, drummer Shelley Manne and a memorable session with **Dizzy Gillespie** where Getz switched from his normally temperate tone to a hard blowing style (*Diz and Getz*, Verve). Among his solo recordings was *Focus* (Verve, 1962), one of the few worthwhile jazz with strings projects. The arranger was Eddie Sauter, whose score for the film *Mickey One* (1965) was also played by Getz. He also recorded *The Steamer* (1956), in the year he appeared as himself in *The Benny Goodman Story*, and *The Soft Swing* (1957) with pianist **Mose Allison**, before in 1958 settling in Europe for several years.

When Getz's and guitarist Charlie Byrd's version of **Antonio Carlos Jobim**'s 'Desafinado'* (Verve, 1962) was a surprise hit, the tenor player made a series of albums based on bossa nova and other Latin material. The chart-topping *Jazz Samba* (1962) and *Jazz Samba Encore* were followed by *Getz–Byrd* (1963), made in partnership with Byrd, and *Getz–Gilberto* (1964). A collaboration with composer/guitarist Joao Gilberto, it provided another pop hit when 'The Girl from Ipanema' was released in 1964 with vocals by Gilberto's wife Astrud.

Although he retained his mainstream jazz approach, Getz frequently worked and recorded with the younger musicians of the sixties, including **Elvin Jones**, **Gary Burton** and **Chick Corea**. With the latter

he made *Sweet Rain* and *Captain Marvel* (Verve, 1972). By 1977, when he made the live *Stan Getz: Gold* in Copenhagen, his group included electric pianist Andy Leverne. In 1981 he released *The Dolphin* (Concord).

He signed to the reactivated Em Arcy label in the mid-eighties, recording *Anniversary* and *Serenity* in 1987 with a rhythm section led by Kenny Barron. Getz's final recordings were made with the same group in Copenhagen in 1991. *People Time* contained some of his most moving work and three months after the session he succumbed to cancer.

DEBBIE GIBSON

b. 31 August 1970, Long Island, New York, USA

A multi-talented teenager, Gibson became an international pop star in the late eighties.

A genuine child prodigy, Gibson learned piano from the age of five and reputedly composed her first song ('Make Sure You Know Your Classroom') at six. By the age of fifteen she had written over 100 songs as well as jingles for television commercials. Gibson signed a recording deal the following year and had her first hits in 1987 with 'Only in My Dreams' and 'Shake Your Love' from *Out of the Blue* (Atlantic). In 1988 'Foolish Beat' topped the US chart.

Like *Out of the Blue*, *Electric Youth* (1989) was entirely written and co-produced by Gibson. The title track and 'No More Rhyme' were Top Twenty hits and *Lost in Your Eyes* was another chart-topper, but the album and its follow-up *Anything Is Possible* (1990) sold less well than her début album. The title track of *Anything Is Possible* was co-written by Gibson and former Tamla Motown writer-producer Lamont Dozier (of **Holland Dozier Holland**).

On *Body and Soul* (1993) Gibson collaborated with further writers, including Carole Bayer Sager, **Narada Michael Walden** and Evan Rogers. By this time she was also developing a career in musical theatre. She played Eporine in the New York production of *Les Miserables* and in 1993 she opened as Sandy in the twentieth anniversary production of *Grease* in London. A duet with fellow-star Craig McLachlan on the showstopper 'You're the One That I Want' (previously an international hit for John Travolta and **Olivia Newton-John**) was a hit single in the UK.

DON GIBSON

b. 3 April 1928, Shelby, North Carolina, USA

The author of the epochal 'I Can't Stop Loving You', Gibson's tear-stained voice also produced some of the biggest country-pop hits of the fifties.

A professional musician by his teens, Gibson moved to Knoxville in 1946, where he became a featured performer on WNOX's *Tennessee Barn Dance* and recorded for local labels in a straight honky-tonk style. In 1954 he was signed as a songwriter to Acuff-Rose and in 1957, as a performer to RCA by **Chet Atkins**.

His first successes were as a writer. For **Faron Young** he wrote 'Sweet Dreams' (which later gave **Patsy Cline** her first posthumous hit and was the title of the 1985 film about her) and in 1958 provided **Kitty Wells** with the paean to unrequited love, 'I Can't Stop Loving You'. The same year saw Gibson achieve his first pop hits with the self-penned 'Oh Lonesome Me'* and 'Blue Blue Day', and in 1960 he reached the pop charts again with 'Just One Time'. With its sprightly beat and clean production, 'Oh Lonesome Me' was a classic example of Atkins' 'Nashville sound' but too many of Gibson's recordings set the sob of his voice against anodyne backings. Thus, his version of 'I Can't Stop Loving You' pales beside that of **Ray Charles**, while his rendition of his own '(I'd Be) A Legend in My Time' does not match **Ronnie Milsap**'s, and his version of 'One Day at a Time' is inferior to **Willie Nelson**'s. Significantly, neither Charles, Milsap nor Nelson succumb to the self-pitying aspects of the songs. One of Gibson's better recordings was 'Sea of Heartbreak', his last major pop hit in 1961, written by P. Hampton and Hal David (just before David became the regular writing partner of **Burt Bacharach**).

Gibson continued to make the country charts throughout the sixties, both alone and with Dottie West. In 1970 he left RCA for Hickory and duetted regularly with Sue Thompson, an artist who like Gibson had pop hits in the early sixties. These included 'Sad Movies (Make Me Cry)'* (1961), 'Norman'* and 'James (Hold the Ladder Steady)' (both 1962). Still a regular, if lesser, hitmaker, Gibson recorded for Warners and RCA in the eighties.

GILBERT AND SULLIVAN
Sir William Schwenck Gilbert, b. 18 November 1836, London, England, d. 29 May 1911, Harrow, Middlesex; Sir Arthur Seymour Sullivan, b. 13 May 1842, London, d. 21 November 1900, London

The authors of a series of highly popular comic operettas, Gilbert and Sullivan's works continued to be widely performed a century after they were first staged. Sullivan's success as a songwriter outlived his reputation as a leading classical composer in the Victorian era, while the satiric and facetious wit of Gilbert's lyrics added the adjective 'Gilbertian' to the English language.

Sullivan was the son of the bandmaster at Sandhurst military training school and by 1871, when the collaboration with Gilbert began, he had established a reputation as one of Britain's most promising young composers. The son of an author of children's books, Gilbert had already written comic and absurd tales for *Fun* and a number of dramas, the best of which (for example, *Engaged*, 1877), prefigured the fantastic comedy of the best of his work with Sullivan.

The first Gilbert and Sullivan play was the one-act *Thespis* (1871), but their first popular success was *Trial by Jury* (1875), a lampoon on the legal profession. It was produced by theatrical agent Richard D'Oyly Carte, whose company retained control over Gilbert and Sullivan productions until the works entered the public domain in 1961. In 1881 D'Oyly Carte opened the Savoy Theatre purely to stage the operettas. By that time *HMS Pinafore* (1878) – which dramatized a childhood kidnapping incident from Gilbert's own life – *The Pirates of Penzance* (1879) and *Patience* (1881) had consolidated the duo's reputation.

Sullivan was already well known in America through such songs as 'The Lost Chord' (1877). The duo's first success there came with *HMS Pinafore*, and the song 'Farewell My Own'. But due to a lack of copyright protection for foreign works, it was widely performed in unauthorized and Americanized versions. Accordingly, in 1879 the authors travelled to New York to organize an official production and to forestall similar problems with *Iolanthe* (1882), which opened simultaneously in London and New York.

The Mikado (1885) was the most popular of Gilbert and Sullivan's operettas, containing bestselling songs like 'Three Little Maids' and 'Tit Willow'. Its caricature of Japanese life brought a protest from that country's ambassador in London. The partnership produced six more operettas by 1896, notably *The Yeoman of the Guard* (1888) and *The Gondoliers* (1889), which included the ballad 'Take a Pair of Sparkling Eyes'.

Until the sixties, a conservative style of Gilbert and Sullivan productions was set by the D'Oyly Carte Company which remained firmly Victorian. Since the end of the monopoly control exercised by the Company, there have been a black *Mikado*, a 'camp' *Pirates of Penzance*, the 'Ratepayers'' *Iolanthe* and a 1986 *Mikado* directed by Jonathan Miller which used the full Sullivan score, which D'Oyly Carte had simplified. In 1982 **Linda Ronstadt** starred in a film version of *The Pirates of Penzance*, as she had done in the Broadway production.

Among the major series of recordings of the operettas were those conducted by Sir Malcolm Sargeant for HMV in the late fifties and early sixties and the D'Oyly Carte versions on Decca. The D'Oyly Carte Company closed in 1982, but reopened to perform Gilbert and Sullivan on a smaller scale five years later. In 1999 the film *Topsy Turvy*, directed by Mike Leigh (who was better known for his modern social satires), exposed the closed world of Gilbert & Sullivan to a charming mix of celebration and examination.

VINCE GILL
b. 4 April 1957, Norman, Oklahoma, USA

Gill's high, pure tenor made him one of the most admired new traditionalists in country music in the early nineties.

A skilled guitarist, Gill played in bluegrass bands such as the Bluegrass Alliance and Byron Berline's Sundance before joining **Pure Prairie League** in 1979. Gill sang and played guitar, banjo and fiddle on the band's *Firin' Up* (Casablanca, 1980) and *Something in the Night* (1981).

He next joined Rodney Crowell's band the Cherry Bombs (for which Tony Brown, then an A&R man for RCA, played keyboards) before signing a solo contract with RCA. Produced by Emory Gordy, he had minor country hits with 'Oklahoma Borderline', 'Everybody's Sweetheart' (1985), 'Cinderella' and 'If It Weren't for Him', a duet with **Roseanne Cash**.

The RCA recordings placed Gill in a conventional country setting. It wasn't until he moved to MCA in 1989 that Brown, who had arrived earlier as a staff producer, encouraged him to draw on Western Swing, bluegrass and pop-rock to develop a more individual approach. The result was a slew of successful albums and numerous Top Five country singles. *When I Call Your Name* (1989) included duets with Patty Loveless and **Reba McEntire** (on the title song). *Pocket Full of Gold* (1991) included the hits 'Take Your Memory with You' and 'Liza Jane'. The album also included a guest appearance by Mark Knopfler of **Dire Straits**; Gill had previously contributed to that band's *On Every Street*.

The multi-million selling *I Still Believe in You* (1992) produced two country No. 1s in 'Don't Let Our Love Start Slippin' Away' and the title track. 1994's *When Love Finds You** included the hits 'What Cowgirls Do' and the title track. In the same year he recorded the seasonal album *Let There Be Peace on Earth* and in 1995 duetted with **Dolly Parton** on a reworking of her 'I Will Always Love You'. Far better was his reflective *High Lonesome Sound* (1996), a thoroughly modern-sounding bluegrass-styled album. The seasonal *Breath of Heaven – A Christmas Collection* (1998) marked a growing conservatism in Gill. More interesting was *Let's Make Sure We Kiss Goodbye* (2000), a collection of (mostly) romantic ballads in honour of (and sometimes in partnership with, as on 'When I Look into Your Heart') his new wife **Amy Grant,** on which his keening voice gave substance to the lightweight lyrics.

DIZZY GILLESPIE
b. John Birks Gillespie, 21 October 1917, Cheraw, South Carolina, USA, d. 6 January 1993

One of the most substantial artists in modern jazz, Gillespie exerted an immense influence on a whole generation of jazz trumpeters. His approach was echoed in the early work of Fats Navarro, Howard McGhee and others. A leading bebop trumpeter and composer, as well as developing an inimitable mode of scat singing, he also originated the 'hipster's' uniform of beret and dark glasses.

The son of a bricklayer and spare-time bandleader, Gillespie won a music scholarship to Laurinburg Institute, North Carolina, before moving with his family to Philadelphia in 1935. After two years in Frank Fairfax's band, he joined Teddy Hill's orchestra in New York, where he replaced his early hero Roy Eldridge.

With Hill's band, Gillespie performed in Europe and gained his nickname 'Dizzy' because of his penchant for clowning. In 1939 he joined **Cab Calloway**'s popular orchestra and played on many recordings. Dismissed by Calloway in 1941, he spent brief periods with bands led by **Ella Fitzgerald**, **Fletcher Henderson**, **Earl Hines** and others before becoming musical director of **Billy Eckstine**'s orchestra in 1944.

During the early forties Gillespie also sat in with other experimentalists like **Kenny Clarke** and **Thelonious Monk** at Minton's Playhouse in Harlem, where the bebop style took shape. In 1944 he formed a small group with **Max Roach** and bassist Oscar Pettiford and cut 'Disorder at the Border' (Apollo) and other discs on which the new music was taking shape with **Buddy Johnson** and **Coleman Hawkins**. Eckstine's band united him with **Charlie Parker** and singer **Sarah Vaughan**, whose first record, 'East of the Sun', Gillespie arranged.

In 1945–6 Gillespie and Parker recorded together frequently for numerous small labels, including Guild, Manor, Dial, Stinson, Gotham, Musicraft and Prestige, with Gillespie sometimes using the pseudonym B. Bopstein for contractual reasons. Many of the tracks were classics of bebop, including his 'Groovin' High', a bop rearrangement of the standard ballad 'Whispering', the jagged phrasing of 'Salt Peanuts' and 'A Night in Tunisia'. His wit was apparent on 'He Beeped When He Should Have Bopped', with vocals by Alice Roberts. Gillespie occasionally performed with Parker in later years, notably at Carnegie Hall, New York, in 1947 and in Toronto in 1953, shortly before Parker's death.

From 1945 Gillespie also led his own big band, which toured throughout America, with arrangements by **George Russell**, Tadd Dameron and John Lewis (later of the **Modern Jazz Quartet**). With a basic swing-band approach, his band nevertheless incorporated bop solos as well as his fascination with Afro-Cuban music, a genre which Gillespie learned about from trumpeter Mario Bauza. For the remainder of his career, Gillespie led a variety of big bands and small groups, recording and touring frequently. From 1953 to 1961 he was signed to **Norman Granz**'s Verve label, cutting a memorable album with **Stan Getz** and recording with the young Lalo Schifrin on piano.

When Granz launched the Pablo label, Gillespie rejoined him and cut several notable albums in the seventies. *Big 4* (1975) featured guitarist Joe Pass and Ray Brown (bass), while his Latin interests were reflected on *Bahania* and *Afro-Cuban Jazz Moods*, a collaboration with **Machito**. *Dizzy* (1975) and *Montreux* (1980) were live recordings from the Montreux Jazz Festival.

During the eighties Gillespie assembled a United Nations Orchestra with musicians from many parts of the world.

MICKEY GILLEY

b. 9 March 1936, Natchez, Louisiana, USA

Like former evangelist Jimmy Lee Swaggart (an inveterate campaigner against the evils of rock music), Gilley is a first cousin of **Jerry Lee Lewis**. For much of his career, however, he lived in the shadow of Lewis until the movie *Urban Cowboy* (1980) made him a star.

Brought up in Ferriday with Lewis, Gilley gave up playing the piano until he heard a record by Lewis in Houston, where he'd settled, in 1956. His first records were simple Lewis imitations, but his Paula recordings, including his version of Warner Mack's 'Is It Wrong' (1959) and 'Lonely Wine' (1964), both local Houston hits, showed Gilley could be emotive without being mannered, as Lewis invariably was. In 1970, after performing in Houston clubs for ten years, he opened his own, Gilley's, and in 1974, had his first country No. 1 with 'Room Full of Roses' – originally a hit for George Morgan in 1949 – on Hugh Hefner's Playboy label. Then, in 1980, in the wake of *Urban Cowboy*, which was largely filmed at Gilley's and briefly made designer cowboy clothing and mores fashionable, he hit the pop charts with 'Stand by Me' (Full Moon), the first of three country chart-toppers that year. Johnny Lee, the bandleader at Gilley's, also had a hit with 'Lookin' for Love' (Full Moon), which was also featured in the film. Gilley moved to Epic and continued to make the country charts regularly throughout the eighties with such records as *It Takes Believers* (1985, with Charly McClain).

In 1994 he issued *Talk to Me* (Branson Entertainment), new recordings of his hits, but more indicative of his chosen career was his opening of new clubs in Branson and South Carolina.

GIPSY KINGS

Jahoul 'Chico' Bouchikhi; Nicolas Reyes, b. 1957; Andre Reyes; Tonino Baliardo; Canut Reyes

The 1989 hit 'Bamboleo' transformed the career of the Gipsy Kings, making the ensemble of flamenco players into one of the leading attractions in 'world music'.

From the gypsy community of the Camargue on the French–Spanish border, vocalist Nicolas Reyes was the son of Jose Reyes, a famous flamenco singer of the sixties and seventies who performed frequently with the internationally known guitarist Manitas de Plata. In 1976 he formed Los Reyes (the Kings) with four of his brothers. The group played at celebrity parties throughout Europe and added virtuoso guitarist Tonino Baliardo, a nephew of de Plata. In 1982 they recorded material in the Nueva Andalucia syle of flamenco, which was reissued in 1990 as *Allegria*.

In 1987 the group met French producer Claude Martinez, who persuaded them to update their sound with drums, bass guitar, percussion and synthesizer and to take the name Gipsy Kings. The pan-European discotheque success of 'Bamboleo' and 'Djobi Djoba' led to frequent tours and the well-publicized admiration of such artists as **Julio Iglesias**, **Eric Clapton** and **Peter Gabriel**. 'Bamboleo' was derived from a South American song and it inspired over a dozen cover-versions.

A self-titled album was issued in 1988, the first of a series of annual releases. In 1989 they released *Mosaique* and in 1990 'A Mi Manera', Reyes' flamenco version of 'My Way' sung in Gitan patois, was a big hit across Europe.

Este Mundo appeared in 1992, adding horns and strings to the Gipsy Kings' sound. On *Love & Liberty* (1993) Canut Reyes shared lead vocals with Nicolas. Produced by Gerard Prevost, the album included a Christmas anthem, 'Navidad', and the reggae-influenced 'Escucha Me'. The group moved to Atlantic for the lacklustre *Tierra Gitana* (1996) and the far better *Compas* (1997). However, neither album sold well and the group switched labels again. The more traditionally inclined *Cantos de Amor* (Nonesuch, 1998) was both a critical and commercial success.

PHILIP GLASS

b. 3 January 1937, Baltimore, USA

An avant-garde composer and performer, Glass's preoccupations have overlapped with those of a number of experimentalists in the popular field, including **Brian Eno**, **Mike Oldfield** and **David Byrne** of **Talking Heads**.

After gaining a master's degree at the Juilliard School, Glass moved to Paris to study in 1964. Dissatisfied with the academicism of Stockhausen, Boulez and the avant-garde of classicism, he discovered Indian music through **Ravi Shankar**. Glass was employed to transcribe Shankar's music for Conrad Rooks' film *Chappaqua* and became interested in its cyclic, repetitive rhythmic structures.

Returning to New York, he became part of the 'minimalist' circle of artists. This included master drummer Steve Reich, electronics composer Terry Riley (who recorded *A Rainbow in Curved Air*, Columbia, 1971) and La Monte Young. He formed the Philip Glass Ensemble to perform works such as 'One Plus One', rhythmic patterns tapped out on an amplified table top.

From the early seventies the focus shifted to repetition in melody and harmony and Glass's influence began to be heard in rock, notably on *Tubular Bells* by Oldfield, who also recorded the Glass composition 'North Star' on his 1979 album *Platinum*. The first recordings by the Ensemble were made for Glass's own Chatham Square label in 1972–3, but he found a wider audience with two Virgin albums, *Music in 12 Parts – Parts I & II* (1974) and *North Star* (1977). He also produced two albums for the new-wave group Polyrock on RCA.

Glass turned his attention to the stage and screen in the mid-seventies. He worked on the music for Samuel Beckett's *Toscando* with Arthur Russell, later to run the radical hip-hop label Sleeping Bag. A series of avant-garde operas began with the four-hour *Einstein on the Beach* (1976), followed by *Satyagraha* (1980, based on the life of Gandhi) and *Akhnaten* (1983). He scored the soundtrack for *Koyaanisqatsi* (1983), a documentary without words about contemporary America, and for Paul Schrader's *Mishima* (1984), which enabled him to explore Japanese music.

In 1982 Glass became the first composer since Stravinsky to sign an exclusive recording contract with CBS Masterworks. His albums for the label have included *Glassworks* (1982), *The Photographer* (1983) and *Songs from Liquid Days* (1986), a song collection with lyrics by Byrne, **Paul Simon**, **Laurie Anderson** and **Suzanne Vega**, and vocalists including **Linda Ronstadt** and Janice Pendarvis. *Dancepieces* (1987) was a collection of ballet scores written for the modern dance troupes of Twyla Tharp and others.

Glass found his largest audience in 1984 when he composed the music which accompanied the lighting of the flame at the opening ceremony of the Los Angeles Olympic Games. Subsequently he has had critical and commercial success with collaborations with artists as diverse as Allen Ginsberg and Doris Lessing. In 1992 he produced both an opera *The Voyage*, which was part of the celebrations of the 500th anniversary of Columbus' voyage of discovery to America, and *Low Symphony*, an orchestral fantasy

based on themes from **David Bowie**'s 1977 album of the same title. *Low* was issued on Glass's own Point label while a collaboration with Ravi Shankar, *Passages* (1990), appeared on Private Music. In 1993 Glass premièred *Orphée*, an opera based on Jean Cocteau's film version of the myth of Orpheus. The Kronos Quartet recorded an album of his music for Nonesuch in 1995.

GARY GLITTER
b. Paul Francis Gadd, 8 May 1940, Banbury, Oxfordshire, England

One of the more curious figures in British pop, Glitter's tongue-in-cheek stage act made him an unusual member of the 'glam' and 'glitter' rock movements, while his minimalist rock'n'roll, masterminded by producer Mike Leander, was one source for British punk.

As a schoolboy, Gadd led a skiffle group, Paul Russell and the Rebels, and cut his first record, 'Alone in the Night', as Paul Raven on Decca in 1960. In the same year he appeared in a documentary film, *Stranger in the City*. In 1961 **George Martin** produced Raven's unsuccessful cover of **Gene McDaniels**' 'Tower of Strength' for Parlophone.

After a spell warming up the audience for TV's *Ready Steady Go!*, Raven toured briefly with the Mike Leander Orchestra and formed Paul Raven and Boston International with trombonist John Russell to perform in Germany, where he played clubs from 1965 to 1970.

During this time he returned occasionally to Britain to record with Leander (*b. Michael Farr, 30 June 1941, d. 18 April 1996*). A former associate of Andrew Loog Oldham, Leander, who wrote the theme music to cult UK television pop programme *Ready Steady Go*, had been A&R man, arranger and producer for Decca, working with the **Rolling Stones**, **Marianne Faithfull**, **Billy Fury**, **Lulu**, **Marc Bolan**, Karl Denver, the Applejacks and Dave Berry. As a writer, he provided hits for Paul Jones ('I've Been a Bad Bad Boy' from the film *Privilege*), Peter and Gordon ('Lady Godiva'), and Vanity Fare ('Early in the Morning', Page One, 1969). In 1966 he was appointed to set up MCA's British branch. Leander had hits with New Zealand singer John Rowles ('If I Only Had Time', 1968) and was executive producer for the first recording of **Andrew Lloyd Webber**'s *Jesus Christ Superstar*, on which Paul Raven had a minor role. Raven also cut several unsuccessful singles for MCA, the oddest being 'We Are All Living in One Place' by Rubber Bucket (1970). Sung to the tune of 'Amazing Grace', this was inspired by a highly publicized hippie squat in Piccadilly and included a squatter choir singing along with Raven.

In 1970 Leander left MCA and worked with Raven

on creating a new sound, image and name. In Germany Raven had changed style from soul to rock'n'roll singing and 'Rock'n'Roll Parts 1 and 2' was built around this and Leander's fascination with the rhythm sounds of such artists as John Kongos (a white South African who had British hits on Fly with 'He's Gonna Step on You Again' and 'Tokoloshe Man', both 1971) and the 'creole voodoo' band Exhuma. Released in 1972 by Gary Glitter on Bell and at first only a dancefloor hit, 'Rock'n'Roll' reached No. 2 in Britain and was a massive international hit.

For live appearances, Glitter adopted an outfit of platform-heel boots and suits made from silver paper, while his backing band, the Glittermen, was directed by John Russell. Although the novelty soon wore off in America, Glitter had ten more hits in Europe and Britain, all co-written with Leander. They included 'Do You Wanna Touch Me (Oh Yeah!)' (which was successfully revived by Joan Jett in 1982), 'I'm the Leader of the Gang (I Am!)' (1973) and 'Remember Me This Way' (1974). Originally a 1959 hit on Colpix for James Darren, it was also the title of his third album and of a concert documentary film. Glitter's final hit during the seventies was 'Doing All Right with the Boys' (1975).

His backing group, successively retitled the Glitter Band and the G Band, also had a series of hits in 1974–6. These included a revival of 'Angel Face' (Bell, 1974), 'Goodbye My Love' (1975) and 'People Like You and People Like Me' (1976). They left Glitter to pursue a separate career before his brief retirement in 1976. He returned to recording with the minor hit 'It Takes All Night Long' (Arista, 1977), but his career was in decline and in 1980, by now a pop celebrity rather than a star, he was declared bankrupt.

Several 'comebacks' followed before his seasonal hit 'Another Rock'n'Roll Christmas' (Arista, 1984). In 1986 he worked with female heavy-metal band Girlschool, while a 1988 British No. 1, the Timelords' 'Doctorin' the Tardis', included extracts from Glitter's first hit. Frequent touring on the British college circuit in the eighties brought the Glitter experience to a new audience, who elevated him to the status of a camp icon. Over several years, his audience grew, and in the late eighties and early nineties his annual Christmas shows became an institution, held in ever larger venues. Unlikely to ever retire, he recorded intermittently throughout the nineties, including 'Red Hot (Reputation)' (Virgin, 1990), Leader (Attitude, 1991) – produced by his son Paul Gadd Jnr – and 'Through the Years' (EMI, 1992). His autobiography, Leader, was published in 1991 and in 1994 Leader!, a musical show based on his persona and career, opened in London. Ever preparing for a comeback, Glitter's career ended dramatically when he was found guilty of possessing child pornography in 1999.

HENRY GLOVER
b. 1922, Hot Springs, Arkansas, USA, d. 7 April 1991, New York

As assistant to **Syd Nathan** at King Records during the forties and fifties, Henry Glover was an influential A&R man, producer and arranger on innumerable rhythm and blues and country recordings by some of the most popular acts of the time. No other black executive of the period held a comparable position in so wide-ranging a company.

Glover studied at Wayne University in Detroit but left his course uncompleted to join the **Buddy Johnson** band as a trumpeter. He also worked in the mid-forties with the bands of Willie Bryant, **Tiny Bradshaw** and **Lucky Millinder**, leaving the last of these to join King. He was soon responsible for sessions by blues and R&B acts like Bullmoose Jackson (a Millinder bandsman), **Lonnie Johnson**, **Roy Brown**, **Wynonie Harris**, **Little Willie John**, **Champion Jack Dupree** and **John Lee Hooker**. He introduced first-rank jazz accompanists into many of these sessions, often engaging **Duke Ellington** or **Count Basie** sidemen when they were at hand. He also wrote material, sometimes in collaboration with Nathan (under the pseudonym Lois Mann); perhaps his most enduring number is 'Drown in My Own Tears', originally recorded in 1952 by Lulu Reed and then in 1956 by **Ray Charles**. At the same time he supervised country artists like **Moon Mullican**, **Cowboy Copas**, Grandpa Jones and others, feeding songs from the R&B catalogue into country sessions and vice versa. In 1956 he went to Roulette as a producer/arranger, working with Joey Dee, with whom he co-wrote the hit 'Peppermint Twist' (1961), and **Sam and Dave**. He rejoined King as vice-president in 1963 and remained with the company, through various changes of ownership, into the seventies.

ALMA GLUCK
b. Reba Fiersohn, 11 May 1884, Bucharest, Romania, d. 27 October 1938, New York, USA

Gluck's 1915 coupling of James A. Bland's 'Carry Me Back to Old Virginny' and **Stephen Foster**'s 'Old Black Joe' was the first of Victor's prestigious Red Seal discs to sell a million copies.

Brought up in New York, Gluck studied voice with Buzz-Peccia from 1906 and made a successful début at the Metropolitan Opera House in Massenet's Werther in 1909. She left the Met in 1912 for a career of concert work and signed with Victor's Red Seal label, recording duets with **Enrico Caruso** ('Brindisi' from La Traviata) and violinist Efrem Zimbalist, whom she later married (Massenet's 'Elégie' and Foster's 'The Old Folks at Home', 1915). But, like **Kathleen Ferrier**, she had her greatest impact and success with her recordings of 'folk songs', which included 'Comin' Thro' the Rye' and 'I'se 'Gwine Back to Dixie' (1917). She also recorded popular ballads of the day, including the 1909 adaptation of an American Indian song, 'From the Land of Sky-Blue Water' and 'Little Gray Home in the West' (1911).

Her revival of 'Carry Me Back to Old Virginny' led to renewed interest in Bland, who had died a pauper (and to the song eventually being adopted as the state song of Virginia). The first successful black American songwriter, Bland (*b. 22 October 1854, Flushing, New York, d. 5 May 1911, Philadelphia, Pennsylvania*) offered as sentimental a view of plantation life as Foster. A performer as well as songwriter, he joined the Original Black Diamonds in 1875 and graduated to the troupe led by Billy Kersands, the Original Georgia Minstrels. For them he wrote 'Carry Me Back to Old Virginny' (published 1878), 'Oh Dem Golden Slippers' (1879), 'In the Evening by the Moonlight' (1879) and 'Hand Me down My Walking Cane' (1880), among others. In 1881 he travelled to Britain with the Callander–Haverley minstrel show, where billed as 'The Idol of the Music Hall' he performed in front of Queen Victoria. In large part responsible for sustaining the popularity of the minstrel form in Britain (and Germany where he also toured successfully), Bland returned to America in 1890 only to find vaudeville replacing minstrelsy, just as in Britain the music hall had supplanted it.

ARTHUR GODFREY
b. 31 August 1903, New York, USA

If **Dick Clark**'s *American Bandstand* was the show most associated with promoting rock'n'roll in America in the fifties and early sixties, an appearance on Godfrey's televised talent show was the first stage in the careers of many of the recording artists who later graduated to *Bandstand*. Among those he 'discovered' were **Julius La Rosa**, **Steve Lawrence**, the **McGuire Sisters**, **Guy Mitchell** and **Johnny Nash**.

A one-time vaudeville banjoist, Godfrey became a radio announcer in 1930. With Al Jarvis and Martin Block, he was one of the first to establish the disc-jockey as a personality, someone who presented – rather than merely played – records. In the early forties Godfrey established the format of the talent show to which he devoted the rest of his career, first on radio, as *Arthur Godfrey Talent Scouts*, and then on television, as *Arthur Godfrey and Friends*. In 1947 Godfrey had a surprise million-seller himself with the humorous 'Too Fat Polka' (Columbia), but it was as a presenter of new talent that he was most important. Like the other major televised talent shows of the fifties (which were hosted by Jackie Gleason, Steve

Allen and Ed Sullivan), Godfrey's was essentially an all-purpose entertainment show. However, of the talent shows, his showed more rock'n'roll and R&B, and so gave further exposure to the new music.

The show's featured singer was **Julius La Rosa** and its musical director was Archie Bleyer, who in 1953 set up Cadence Records, one of the several successful independent record companies of the fifties. Among its roster were the **Everly Brothers**, **Andy Williams** (who eventually bought the company) and the **Chordettes**.

GOLDEN EARRING
George Kooymans, b. 11 March 1948, The Hague, Netherlands; Rinus Gerritsen, b. 9 August 1946, The Hague; Hans van Herwerden (replaced by Peter de Ronde); Fred van der Hilst (replaced by Jaap Eggermont, replaced by Cesar Zuiderwijk, b. 18 July 1948, The Hague); Frans Krassenburg (replaced by Barry Hay, b. 16 August 1948, Fyzabad, India)

Best known internationally for the hit 'Radar Love', with Focus and the Nits, Golden Earring are among Holland's most renowned rock bands.

The mainstay of the band has been guitarist and singer Kooymans and bass-player/vocalist Gerritsen. By the time of their first Dutch hit, 'Please Go' (1965), the group's other members were singer Krassenburg, de Ronde (bass) and Eggermont (drums). By the time of the band's third album *Magical Mirror* (1968) and its big hit 'Dong-Dong-Di-Ki-Di-Ki-Dong', multi-instrumentalist and singer Hay was a member of Golden Earring.

Playing in a progressive rock style, Golden Earring toured Europe and North America several times in the late sixties and early seventies. The peak of the group's international success was 1973–4 when 'Radar Love' was a worldwide hit. By then the group was a quartet of Kooymans, Gerritsen, Hay and Zuiderwijk, with the occasional addition of an extra guitarist. Albums from this period included *On the Double* (1969), *Eight Miles High* (1970) and *Moontan* (1973).

As the group opted for a classic hard rock sound it issued annual albums into the eighties when 'Twilight Zone' (1982) became a surprise US hit. Later albums have included *The Hole* (1986), Kooymans' *Solo* (1987), *Bloody Buccaneers* (1991) and *Face It* (1994), their twenty-fourth release.

THE GOLDEN GATE QUARTET
William Langford, d. 1970, Winston-Salem, North Carolina, USA (replaced 1940 by Clyde Riddick); Willie Johnson (replaced 1943 by Joe Johnson, 1943–4 by Alton Bradley, reinstated 1946, replaced 1948 by Orville Brooks, 1954 by Bill Bing, then Frank Todd, 1955 by

Julius Caleb Ginyard, later by Paul Brembly); Henry Owens, d. 1970 (replaced 1950 by Alton Bradley, 1951 by Eugene Mumford, 1954 by Clyde Wright, later by Calvin Williams); Orlandus Wilson (replaced 1943 by Clifford Givens, reinstated 1946)

The Golden Gate Quartet took the lead for more than half a century in popularizing 'jubilee', a style of black gospel singing much influenced by the caressing harmonies and the hot jazz phrasing of such black 'jive' or 'rhythm' vocal groups of the thirties as the **Ink Spots** and the **Mills Brothers**. Employing close harmony, scat-singing and a stylized narrative approach on a mixture of old gospel songs and modern popular tunes, the Gates (as they became known) profoundly influenced the black quartet tradition in both its religious and secular manifestations.

The original quartet of Langford (first tenor), Owens (second tenor), Willie Johnson (baritone), and Wilson (bass) was formed in 1934 in Norfolk, Virginia – home of their important predecessors the Norfolk Jubilee Quartet, who recorded prolifically from 1921 to 1940. The early Gates followed the Mills Brothers' device of vocally imitating instruments and soon became popular on radio, especially over WBT, Charlotte, North Carolina (1935–8); later they were nationally networked. Their first recording session, for Bluebird (1937), produced enduring favourites like 'Jonah' and 'Bedside of a Neighbor'. During 1938–9 they filled three record dates a year, having further successes like 'Travelin' Shoes' and 'Rock My Soul', and in 1939 they appeared at Carnegie Hall in **John Hammond**'s 'Spirituals to Swing' concert, after which they moved to New York to broadcast several times a week on the CBS network.

In 1940 the Gates partnered **Leadbelly** on record, then Langford left to form the Southern Sons. He later joined the Selah Jubilee Singers, and subsequently created the Langfordaires, of which **Brook Benton** was a member. Langford was replaced by Riddick, who was still with the group in the late eighties. The following year the group signed with Columbia. In 1943 Wilson and Johnson were drafted and Riddick took over the leadership. Around this time the Gates appeared in such films as *Star-Spangled Rhythm* (1942), *Hit Parade of 1943*, *Hollywood Canteen* (1944) and *Bring on the Girls* (1945). In 1946 Wilson and Johnson returned, and in 1947 the Gates regained their previous popularity with 'Shadrack', also appearing, with many jazz personalities, in Howard Hawks' *A Song Is Born* (1948).

Willie Johnson left in 1948 to head the Jubalaires and was replaced by ex-Jubalaire Brooks. The Gates also left Columbia for Mercury. In 1950 Owens left, his place being filled first by Bradley and then by Mumford, formerly of the Larks. There were further personnel changes in the fifties, a bad period for the Gates, who saw the storm signals of rock'n'roll. In 1955 they made a first trip to Europe, enjoying such success that in 1959 they moved permanently to France, where they undertook regular concert tours and made occasional records.

GOLDIE
b. 1964, Wolverhampton, Warwickshire, England

Goldie was the first artist from the UK's emerging jungle scene of the early 1990s to gain widespread mainstream coverage and recognition for his single 'Inner City Life' and album *Timeless*. His subsequent work has been more experimental and personal, but has won a more lukewarm critical reception.

Goldie grew up in the English Midlands town of Walsall, and as a teenager embraced hip-hop culture, particularly its graffiti art forms. He became a respected and well-known graffiti artist in the area, graduating to design pieces for the local council as the artform itself gained a modicum of respectability. His involvement in this branch of hip-hop culture took him to New York, where in 1986 he appeared alongside **Afrika Bambaataa** in the graffiti art movie *Bombing*. On his return to the UK in 1988 Goldie became involved in London's 'hardcore' scene, the breakbeat-rich strand of house that would eventually give birth to jungle. At first merely designing artwork for record labels, Goldie developed an interest in recording himself. This lead to his releasing 'Terminator' under the name Metalheadz on the Synthetic label in 1993.

'Terminator' was typical of the darker edge of breakbeat and hardcore tunes of the time, but eschewed the speeded-up vocals that normally accompanied the speeded-up beats. Later that year Goldie released 'Angel', which featured Dianne Charlemagne on vocals. *Timeless* was released on London Records in November 1994 and despite little press coverage débuted at No. 7 in the UK album charts. The album featured tracks making use of guitars and keyboards, and was a key step in expanding the lexicon of a still embryonic genre. The scope of his musical ambition was confirmed when the album's release was followed by a European and US tour, complete with large band including percussionist, bass player and guitarist. The broadening of musical horizons evident on *Timeless* was a critical stage in the development process of the drum'n'bass sound, a process that would lead to **Roni Size**'s *New Forms* and Alex Reece's *So Far*.

In addition to his own recordings, Goldie was by now also operating regular Metalheadz club nights in London, and running his successful Metalheadz label, which released a successful compilation series, *Platinum Breakz*.

Saturnz Return followed in 1998, preceded by the single 'Temper Temper', which featured **Oasis**'s Noel Gallagher. The album also featured a cameo by US rapper KRS-One on another hit single, 'Digital'. Elsewhere, the album featured vocal contributions from Dianne Charlemagne and, for the first time, Goldie himself. Uneven but ambitious, *Saturnz Return* continued the peculiar trend towards excessively long albums by drum'n'bass artists – Roni Size and 4 Hero were also guilty of this. One track, the quasi-classical and heavily autobiographical 'Mother', lasted over an hour.

By the end of the nineties Goldie's time was divided between musical interests and a nascent film acting career. He continued deejaying at Metalheadz both in London and on tour overseas, and mixed the jungle compilation *INCredible Sound of Drum'n'Bass*. On the screen, he appeared in *Everybody Loves the Sunshine* with **David Bowie** and had a cameo role in the James Bond film *The World Is Not Enough* (1999).

GEORGE GOLDNER
b. 1918, New York, USA, d. 15 April 1970, New York

The **Irving Mills** of the fifties, Goldner was an independent label-owner and publisher who specialized in R&B. In the words of historian Bill Millar, 'He was the original fifties bubblegum king, without a mind for stone blues. Nor was he entirely punctilious over royalty statements, but he cut a lot of wonderful records and did more for integration than the Supreme Court.'

A dance instructor and dance-hall proprietor in the forties, Goldner established Tico Records to specialize in Latin-American music in 1948. Among the artists he signed were **Tito Puente** and **Machito**. In 1953 he set up Rama to record black vocal groups in the hope of emulating the recent crossover success of the **Orioles**' 'Crying in the Chapel'. His first release, 'I Was Such A Fool' by the Five Budds, was a failure but within a year he had found the Crows (who comprised Sonny Norton, Bill Davis, Harold Major, Mark Jackson and Gerald Hamilton) and 'Gee'. Goldner recorded them in a far smoother style than most black vocal groups and the disc, often cited as the earliest rock'n'roll record, reached the Top Ten of both the pop and R&B charts in 1954.

Henceforth, Goldner combed the streets of New York for groups to record on his labels, Gone, Gee (named for the Crows hit), Rama and End. Among these were the Cleftones (who had an R&B hit with their first outing, 'You Baby You', 1956, and a pair of big pop hits in 1961 with their bright version of **Hoagy Carmichael** and **Johnny Mercer**'s 'Heart and Soul' and 'I Love You [for Sentimental Reasons]'); the Dubs ('This Could Be Magic', 1957); **Elvis Presley** imitator Ral Donner (who had a pair of Top Twenty hits in 1961, 'Girl of My Best Friend' and 'You Don't Know What You've Got'); the **Chantels**, **Little Anthony and the Imperials**, the **Isley Brothers** and the **Flamingos**. Less successful were the Valentines, signed in 1955, but by 1956 their lead singer **Richard Barrett** had become Goldner's right-hand man, arranger, producer, writer and talent finder and it was he who took creative control of most of Goldner's subsequent productions.

In 1962 Goldner, an inveterate gambler, sold his interests to Morris Levy with whom in 1956 he had set up Roulette Records. In 1964 he established the very successful Red Bird Records with **Leiber and Stoller** and, on its dissolution in 1969, he set up Firebird Records.

BOBBY GOLDSBORO
b. 18 January 1941, Marianna, Florida, USA

A nasal balladeer, somewhat reminiscent of **Gene Pitney**, Goldsboro is best remembered for 'Honey' (1968), a cloying tale of remembered love that went on to sell more than 10 million copies and became a staple of middle-of-the-road radio programming.

Goldsboro joined **Roy Orbison**'s touring band as a guitarist in 1960 and, in 1962, had his first hit with 'Molly' (Laurie). In 1963 he joined United Artists and in the following year had the first of four million-selling discs with the self-penned 'See the Funny Little Clown', produced by Bob Montgomery. Other hits included 'Little Things'* (which was covered in Britain successfully by Dave Berry on Decca) and 'Voodoo Woman' (both 1965), 'It's Too Late'* (1966), 'Honey', 'Watching Scotty Grow' and 'Summer (The First Time)' (1973), his last major pop hit.

All self-penned, except 'Honey' which was written by Bobby Russell, and 'Scotty' written by **Mac Davis**, the songs presented a clean-cut, idealized view of family love. Other artists have recorded successful versions of several of his compositions, notably 'With Pen in Hand', which was a hit for Vikki Carr in 1969.

During the seventies Goldsboro turned increasingly to country music (even recording a version of 'I Believe the South Is Gonna Rise Again', 1974), but despite label changes (to Epic in 1976 and then to Columbia in 1979) he did not repeat his earlier success.

JERRY GOLDSMITH
b. 10 February 1929, Los Angeles, California, USA

A prolific film composer, Goldsmith's eclectic approach to his work has resulted in film scores consisting entirely of sound effects (*The Planet of the Apes*, 1968), the lyrical romanticism of *The Blue Max* (1966) and the atonal dissonance of *Freud* (1962). An indication of just how prolific a film and television composer he has been is the estimate by one critic that every minute of every day a film or television programme featuring his music is being shown somewhere in the world.

After studying piano with Jacob Gimpel, Goldsmith studied composition with Mario Castelnuovo-Tedesco and film scoring with **Miklos Rozsa**. He began his professional career in radio (*Romance*) and graduated to television, writing scores for *The Man from UNCLE*, *Dr Kildare*, *The Twilight Zone* and *Gunsmoke*, among others. The first of over a hundred film scores was *Black Patch* (1957). Among his best scores are those for *Seconds* (1966), *The Detective* (1968), *Chinatown* (1974) – an atmospheric score in which he seamlessly melded in thirties tunes – and *The Omen* (1976), for which he won an Oscar. Far more macho in style were his scores for the Rambo series, beginning with *First Blood* (1982) and ending with *Rambo III* (1986).

Goldsmith also worked on such blockbusters as *Star Trek – The Motion Picture* (1979), *Papillon* (1973), *Gremlins* (1984), *Total Recall* (1990) and *Basic Instinct* (1992). Later scores included *Air Force One*, *LA Confidential* and *The Edge* (all 1997), the first muscular, the second evocative and the last amongst his most complex.

GOMEZ

Ian Ball, b. Stockport, England; Paul Blackburn, b. Stockport, England; Tom Gray, b. Stockport, England; Ben Ottewell, b. Derby, England; Olly Peacock, b. Stockport, England

A Sheffield-based five-piece, Gomez's rootsy, sixties-influenced sound brought them critical and commercial acclaim in Britain after they won the prestigious Mercury Music Prize for their début album.

Gomez began in 1996 at the University of Sheffield when singer-guitarist Ben Ottewell joined guitarists Gray and Ball, bassist Blackburn and drummer Peacock, who had been jamming together since their teenage years in Stockport. A shared fondness for US blues and Ottewell's unusually gruff, battered voice saw them develop a sound akin to **Tom Waits** and the **Grateful Dead**. The following year Gomez signed to Hut on the strength of their demo tapes, recorded on Ball's four-track machine, which prompted a minor bidding war.

Much of Gomez's début album *Bring It on* (1998) was taken from their original demo recordings, with additional instrumentation added in a Liverpool studio. The album drew comparisons with **Beck** and **The Band**'s *Music from Big Pink* and sold steadily on word of mouth until Gomez's surprise victory at the 1998 Mercury Music Awards, which brought them a degree of mainstream success and minor hit singles in 'Whip-

pin' Piccadilly' and 'Get Myself Arrested'. Gomez released their second album, *Liquid Skin*, in 1998, preceded by the hit singles 'Bring It on' and 'Rhythm and Blues Alibi'. A low-key EP, *Machismo*, followed in 2000, after which the band released *Abandoned Shopping Trolley Hotline*, a collection of radio sessions, rarities and a cover of **The Beatles**' 'Getting Better'.

NAT GONELLA
b. 7 March 1908, Islington, London, England

In the generation of British dance-band musicians whose playing was enlightened by the new American jazz, Nat Gonella was the most gifted and appreciative student of **Louis Armstrong** – whose small-group recordings of the twenties Gonella was to adapt and translate in the next decade into his 'cockney jazz' patois.

After an apprenticeship on the variety circuit Gonella joined the band of **Billy Cotton**, then resident at London's Ciro's Club, in 1930. The following year he joined **Roy Fox**'s orchestra at the Monseigneur, London; his vocal on the Fox recording of 'Oh Monah' (Decca, 1931) became popular and led to others, such as 'Georgia on My Mind' (1932), the number most closely associated with him. In 1934 he formed his own small group, the Georgians, and began a long series of recordings for Parlophone. The band toured Britain in 1935 and frequently thereafter. Also in 1935 Gonella published an instructional book, *Modern Style Trumpet Playing*.

In 1940 he formed a big band, the New Georgians, but by the fifties his style of jazz was out of fashion, and he had to wait until the sixties for a return to favour in the trad era. He recapitulated his past on *The Nat Gonella Story* (1961), and later in the decade toured Europe with **Acker Bilk**. In 1977 he enjoyed a surprise hit with a new version of 'Oh Monah' in Holland.

JACK GOOD
b. 1931, London, England

Like **Dick Clark**, Good discovered a successful formula for televising rock'n'roll. He produced Britain's *Oh Boy!* and America's *Shindig* in the sixties.

After studying at Oxford University, Good briefly formed a double act with actor and songwriter Trevor Peacock before joining BBC Television. In 1957 he became producer of *6.5 Special*, a Saturday evening show for young people. Under his guidance, the programme became the showcase for the first generation of British rock'n'roll artists like Terry Dene, **Marty Wilde** and Wee Willie Harris. The programme's resident band, Don Lang and his Frantic Five, had a British hit with 'Witch Doctor' (HMV, 1958).

Good next set up *Oh Boy!* (1958), the show which

introduced **Cliff Richard** to television audiences. He also produced the successor show *Boy Meets Girl*, hiring **Joe Brown** to lead the studio band. Good turned to record production with **Billy Fury**'s *The Sound of Fury* (Decca, 1959) and **Alexis Korner**'s *R&B from the Marquee* (1962). He also championed the fledgling British R&B movement in a weekly column for *Disc*.

He moved to America in 1962, devising *Shindig*, whose Hollywood-based house band included **Leon Russell** and **Glen Campbell**. The show gave their first television exposure to the **Righteous Brothers** and **Ike** and **Tina Turner**. Good also masterminded many television specials for **Andy Williams**, the **Monkees** and others. In 1963 he produced *Around the Beatles*, the group's first television spectacular. Among the guest artists was **P. J. Proby**, who later starred with Good himself in *Catch My Soul*, Good's rock version of Shakespeare's *Othello*. Patrick McGoohan's 1974 film of the show included songs from **Richie Havens**, Tony Joe White and Delaney Bramlett.

In the late seventies Good promoted a series of rock'n'roll revival concerts under the *Oh Boy!* tag. In 1977 he also devised a musical show based on the life of **Elvis Presley**, whose resident singers included **Shakin' Stevens**.

Good later retired to New Mexico but returned to Britain in 1991 to stage an autobiographical musical, *Good Rockin' Tonight*.

BENNY GOODMAN
b. Benjamin David Goodman, 30 May 1909, Chicago, Illinois, USA, d. 13 June 1986, New York

The leader of the greatest swing band of the thirties, Goodman was also a virtuoso clarinettist and a persuasive popularizer of jazz. Among his greatest achievements was to break the colour bar by working with black musicians **Teddy Wilson** and **Lionel Hampton**. In 1962 he became the first American musician since **Sidney Bechet** in the twenties to introduce jazz to audiences in the Soviet Union.

From a poor immigrant family, Goodman's first music lessons were at the local synagogue. His first musical hero was **Ted Lewis** and at the age of fourteen he joined Murph Podolsky's band. Goodman was soon part of the Chicago jazz scene, recording with various groups including **Red Nichols**' Charleston Chasers and the Five Pennies, which included future swing bandleaders **Glenn Miller**, **Tommy Dorsey** and **Gene Krupa**. For most of the period 1925–9 Goodman was a member of Ben Pollack's band, recording for Victor on tracks like 'Deed I Do' (1926) and 'Yellow Dog Blues' (1929). Although a dance orchestra, Pollack's band was a precursor of the swing era in the way its arrangements allowed scope for improvised solos.

After playing with Pollack in New York, Goodman left to follow a freelance career. In the next five years he played in theatre bands (*Girl Crazy*, 1930, starring **Ethel Merman**), performed on radio shows and took part in numerous recording sessions, including **Billie Holiday**'s début in 1933. Goodman formed a band in 1932 to accompany **Russ Columbo** but his first permanent orchestra was set up in 1934 with dance-hall and radio residencies. Its earliest Columbia recordings (including 'Cokey') showed the influence of **Pee Wee Hunt**'s Casa Loma Orchestra but playing opposite **Xavier Cugat** on the networked *Let's Dance* programme, Goodman developed the elements of swing. Among the ingredients of the new style were arrangements by **Fletcher Henderson** ('King Porter Stomp', RCA-Victor, 1935), his brother Horace and Edgar Sampson, plus the rhythmic excitement generated by Krupa and Bunny Berigan's hot trumpet solos on such tracks as 'Sometimes I'm Happy' (1935).

The swing craze was ignited by Goodman's 1935 national tour, which frequently caused riots among audiences, and the band subsequently had instrumental hits with 'Stomping at the Savoy' (1936), 'One o'Clock Jump', 'Sing, Sing, Sing', with Krupa's pyrotechnic drum break (the prototype of a thousand later jazz and rock drum solos), and 'Sugar Foot Stomp' (originally recorded by Henderson in 1925), which featured trumpeter **Harry James**.

The band also appeared in the film *The Big Band Broadcast of 1937* and the following year gave a famous concert at New York's Carnegie Hall. This included small-group jazz by Goodman's quartet (with Krupa, Wilson and Hampton) and a jam session with **Count Basie** and **Lester Young**. Goodman's concern to promote promising jazz players was underlined in 1940 when he hired electric guitarist **Charlie Christian**, who had been recommended by producer **John Hammond**. Goodman also sought to build bridges between popular and classical music, recording Alex Templeton's 'Bach Goes to Town' as well as clarinet pieces by Bartók (whom Goodman commissioned to write 'Contrasts for Clarinet, Violin and Piano'), Copland, Hindemith and Debussy (an adaptation of whose 'La Mer' he recorded in 1948 as 'Beyond the Sea').

In 1939, when Goodman's contract with Victor expired, several experienced musicians followed Krupa and James, who had left in 1938 to start their own big bands. Goodman responded by signing with Columbia and adding arranger Eddie Sauter and vocalist Helen Forrest. Together they made 'I Hear a Rhapsody', 'Perfidia' (1940) and 'Taking a Chance on Love' (1940, and a No. 1 hit in 1943). **Mildred Bailey** also recorded with Goodman ('Darn That Dream', a No. 1 in 1940). Among the instrumental successes of the period were 'The Man I Love' (1940), 'Clarinet à la King' (1941) and 'Mission to Moscow' (1941).

By 1942 **Peggy Lee** had replaced Forrest and her 'Why Don't You Do Right?' was a million-seller in 1943. Other vocal successes of the forties were **Dick Haymes**' 'Serenade in Blue' (1942), **Johnny Mercer**'s 'Moon-Faced, Starry-Eyed' (1947) and Al Hendrickson's version of 'Slow Boat to China'* (1948). During 1948–9, Goodman unsuccessfully tried to give his orchestra a bebop flavour and he disbanded it soon afterwards. After 1950, Goodman led a series of occasional bands, recording prolifically for Columbia, RCA, Capitol, London, and others. He had his own TV show in 1958–9 and worked on the soundtrack of the Walt Disney series *Make Mine Music*. His numerous foreign tours included trips to the Far East and Europe as well as Russia. His final recording was the soundtrack of a TV special, *Let's Dance* (Musicmasters, 1986).

His status as an elder statesman of jazz was confirmed in 1955 by the making of *The Benny Goodman Story*, which starred Steve Allen as the bandleader. Goodman also appeared in such films as *Hollywood Hotel* (1937), *The Powers Girl* (1942), *A Song Is Born* (1948) and *Stage Door Canteen* (1963).

STEVE GOODMAN
b. 25 July 1948, Chicago, Illinois, USA, d. 20 September 1984, Seattle, Washington

With a wry sense of humour and a satiric wit, Goodman was one of America's best singer-songwriters of the seventies. His best-known composition is 'City of New Orleans'.

Through the folk revival of the early sixties, Goodman absorbed folk song, blues and country music. A political science student at the University of Illinois, he left college to perform in Chicago's burgeoning club scene, where he met **John Prine**. Augmenting his income by writing advertising jingles, he was signed to Buddah which released his eponymous début album in 1971. Produced in Nashville by **Kris Kristofferson** and Norbert Putnam, it included 'City of New Orleans', which evocatively described a rail journey across America. In 1972 Arlo Guthrie had a hit single with the song, while its author was the hit of the Cambridge Folk Festival on his first visit to Britain.

Under the pseudonym Robert Milkwood Thomas, **Bob Dylan** played piano on the **Arif Mardin**-produced *Somebody Else's Troubles* (1973), which included the Vietnam protest song 'The Ballad of Penny Evans' and a cheerful satire on macrobiotic diets, 'The Chicken Cordon Bleus'. In 1975 Goodman moved to Asylum for *Jessie's Jig and Other Favorites*. *Words We Can Dance to* (1976) found him moving away from traditional song forms and included the sardonic political commentary 'Banana Republics', 'Death of a Salesman', his variant on the 'travelling

salesman' jokes, an energetic revival of Bobby Lewis's 'Tossin' and Turnin'' (Beltone, 1961).

Though Goodman's witty stage routine made him a popular figure at folk clubs and festivals, later Asylum albums like the Joel Dorn-produced *Say It in Private* (1978) and *Hot Spot* (1980) were disappointing. In 1983 he left Asylum and released *Artistic Hair* on his own Red Pyjamas label. Shortly after issuing *Santa Ana Winds* (1984), Goodman died of leukaemia.

RON GOODWIN
b. Ronald Goodwin, 17 February 1925, Plymouth, Devon, England

Goodwin was an arranger and orchestra leader in the fifties who later became known as a conductor and composer, mostly for his jaunty, martial film scores.

Educated in London, he learned the piano and trumpet and in his teens worked as a copyist and then staff arranger for various music publishers, while studying conducting at the Guildhall School of Music. Before forming his concert orchestra for radio broadcasts in 1951, he worked as an arranger for **Stanley Black**, **Geraldo** and **Ted Heath**, and in 1953 was signed by **George Martin** to EMI's Parlophone label. His British hits included an arrangement of Charlie Chaplin's 'Limelight' (1953) and his version of the theme to the teleseries *Medic*, 'Blue Star' (1955). His recording of 'Elizabethan Serenade' was one of the most successful pieces of light classical music of the decade. His album *Skiffling Strings* (1957) was retitled *Swingin' Sweethearts* (Capitol) for release in America where it was a surprise hit, with the title song entering the singles charts as well.

In 1958 Goodwin scored his first feature film, *Whirlpool*, and subsequently wrote the music for over sixty, mostly British, films. These included *Operation Crossbow*, *Those Magnificent Men in Their Flying Machines* (1965), *Where Eagles Dare* (1968), *Battle of Britain* (1969) and *Force Ten from Navarone* (1978). Most were lush, stirring symphonic scores, but his music for *Frenzy* (1972), Alfred Hitchcock's return to film-making in Britain after a thirty-year stay in America, was more dramatic.

In addition to his film work, Goodwin broadcast regularly throughout the seventies and conducted numerous albums of his film music (notably *The Very Best of Ron Goodwin*, EMI, 1977) and light classical music, including his own composition 'The New Zealand Suite' (on *Ron Goodwin Conducts the New Zealand Symphony Orchestra* in 1984) and *The Drake 400 Suite* (to commemorate the 400th anniversary of Sir Francis Drake's circumnavigation of the globe) on Chandos in 1980. In addition, he frequently conducted symphony orchestras in performances of luxuriant arrangements of pop songs.

In 1989 EMI issued *Fire and Romance*, a digitally remastered selection of Goodwin's and other composers' work. It included part of his *Beatles Concerto*, settings of Lennon–McCartney songs for orchestra and twin pianos.

THE GOONS

Spike Milligan, b. Terence Milligan, 16 April 1918, Admadnagar, India; Sir Harry Secombe, b. 8 September 1921, Swansea, Wales; Peter Sellers, b. Richard Henry Sellers, 8 September 1925, Southsea, Hampshire, England, d. July 1980

Britain's leading radio comedy team, the Goons had a series of hit records in the fifties. Two of its members, Secombe and Sellers, went on to contrasting solo recording careers.

Sellers' parents were music-hall artistes and he had performed as a drummer and a ukulele player before making his radio début as a mimic. Milligan was a promising jazz trumpeter whose nickname came from British jazz composer and critic Spike Hughes. He teamed up with Secombe while entertaining the troops during the Second World War.

In 1951, with Michael Bentine (who left the following year), they broadcast the first *Goon Show*. The anarchic, surreal programmes ran until 1960 with many later released in album form by BBC Records. Their first pop single was the absurdist 'Ying Tong Song' (Decca, 1956), which was followed by two Top Ten hits: 'I'm Walking Backwards for Christmas' and the mildly satirical 'Bloodnock's Rock'n'Roll'. 'Ying Tong' was also a hit when re-released in 1973. In the late fifties Sellers became a kind of British **Stan Freberg**, parodying both pop culture and pop music. He had a hit with a hilarious version of the music-hall song 'Any Old Iron' (Parlophone, 1957) and recorded the **George Martin**-produced *The Best of Sellers* and *Songs for Swinging Sellers*. The albums included skits on **Lonnie Donegan** ('Puttin' on the Smile'), cinema travelogues ('Balham, Gateway to the South') and pre-teen rock'n'rollers like Little Laurie London ('I'm So Ashamed').

After 1960, Milligan concentrated on theatre and television, in the early seventies recording occasionally with singer-songwriter Ed Welch, and narrating an orchestral setting of the Paul Gallico novel *The Snow Goose* in 1976. Sellers went into films. *The Millionairess* (1960) inspired a hit single in his comedy duet with Sophia Loren 'Goodness Gracious Me' (Parlophone) and led to an album, *Peter and Sophia*, and a further hit 'Bangers and Mash' (1961). Sellers later reached the British chart as a cast member of *Fool Britannia*. This satirical album, dealing with the Profumo sex and spies scandal also starred **Anthony Newley** and Joan Collins. Because of its controversial nature, Decca refused to release the record, which was issued by Jeff Kruger's independent Ember label. In 1964 Milligan, Sellers and Secombe regrouped to record another attempt at political satire, *How to Win an Election* (Philips). Sellers combined his gift for mimicry with his penchant for pop satire in 1965 when he recited **The Beatles**' 'A Hard Day's Night' in the style of Laurence Olivier's portrayal of Shakespeare's *Henry V*.

With a strong tenor voice, Secombe had reached the British Top Twenty in 1955 with 'On with the Motley' (Philips). From 1960 he concentrated on a career as a vocalist, taking lessons in opera singing. He starred in *Pickwick*, by Wolf Mankowitz, Leslie Bricusse and Cyril Ornadel, recording the hit song 'If I Ruled the World' (Philips, 1963). In 1967 both he and **Petula Clark** had hits with contrasting versions of 'This Is My Song'. For some years compère of television religious shows in the eighties, Secombe had a successful series of albums of sacred songs and songs from the shows, some duetting with Moira Anderson. He received a knighthood for his extensive charity work.

BERRY GORDY

b. Berry Gordy Junior, 28 November 1929, Detroit, Michigan, USA

Founder of Motown Records and the outstanding figure in the black music business, Gordy was an expert songwriter who created a pop music based on blues and gospel that became 'The Sound of Young America' in the sixties. Just as remarkable were his production methods. The hits of the **Supremes**, **Four Tops**, **Marvin Gaye**, **Stevie Wonder** and numerous others were created by the in-house writers, producers and musicians of what Gordy was proud to call the Hit Factory. Among those involved were **Smokey Robinson**, **Norman Whitfield**, **Holland, Dozier and Holland** and **Ashford and Simpson**. While some of his key staff and artists rebelled against Gordy's benevolent paternalism, he moved the company to Hollywood in a bid to conquer the film and MOR fields, mainly through **Diana Ross**, Wonder and his new star **Lionel Richie**. But the cost of economic independence was high and in 1988 Gordy followed **Don Robey**, whose Duke/Peacock group had been in some ways a forerunner of Motown, by selling his record company to a conglomerate (MCA).

A former professional boxer and a failed jazz record-store owner, Gordy turned to songwriting in the mid-fifties. His first success came when **Jackie Wilson** recorded his 'Reet Petite' (1957) and had further hits with such Gordy songs as 'This Is Why I Love You So' and 'I'll Be Satisfied' (1959). He next went into independent production, leasing **Marv**

Johnson's 'You Got What It Takes' (1959) and 'I Love the Way You Love' (1960) to United Artists and Barrett Strong's 'Money' (1960) to Anna, a label owned by his sister. 'Money' was covered by **The Beatles** and the Johnson songs were Top Ten pop hits, their mixture of gospel and pop looking forward to the 'Motown sound' which began when Gordy set up his own Tamla label in 1960.

Tamla's first million-seller was the Miracles' 'Shop Around', written by group member Smokey Robinson, among the first of the in-house writers, producers and session musicians brought together by Gordy to create the 'Motown sound'. Among the members of the Motown house band were James Jamerson and Carol Kaye (basses), Benny Benjamin (drums), Earl Van Dyke (keyboards) and guitarist Robert White. The result was music sung by black vocal groups and soloists which had a universal teenage appeal. By 1965, Tamla, Motown and the other Gordy labels had achieved forty-five Top Twenty hits and in 1966 seventy-five per cent of Motown singles reached the charts.

By the mid-sixties the company was also internationally triumphant. Initially licensed in Britain to the independent Oriole, Motown songs were taken up by The Beatles, **Brian Poole** and others. From 1965 EMI released Tamla-Motown material on its own label, giving the company an even higher profile.

As Motown grew, there were defectors from the Gordy empire. **Mary Wells**, in 1964, had been the first to leave the label and in 1967 Holland–Dozier–Holland set up their own labels. While Gordy continued to find new talent, like the **Jackson Five**, the more established artists looked for creative independence. In 1971 both Gaye and Wonder fought for control of their own work within Motown, and won. Others who left to find it were Whitfield, **Martha and the Vandellas**, **Gladys Knight**, the Four Tops and the Jacksons. Criticism of Gordy's treatment of his artists appeared in the first edition of a biography of **Michael Jackson** in 1991. After Gordy filed a lawsuit against author Randy Taraborelli these were deleted in later editions.

In 1971 Gordy moved the company to Los Angeles as part of a plan to broaden Motown into films and middle-of-the-road music. Linchpin of the scheme was Diana Ross, with her starring role in the Gordy-produced **Billie Holiday** biopic *Lady Sings the Blues* (1972). During the seventies, however, despite the individual success of Wonder, Gaye, **Rick James** and the **Commodores**, Motown was eclipsed by the Philadelphia soul of **Gamble and Huff**.

Two events signalled the decline in Motown's fortunes as the eighties began: Ross left Motown for RCA in 1980 and the label linked up with MCA for distribution. The proportion of Motown's income derived

from oldies increased with their ubiquitous use in TV commercials and on soundtracks like *The Big Chill* (1983). Finally, in 1988, Gordy sold the record company (but not the lucrative music publishing division, Jobete) to MCA and Boston Ventures, which in turn sold it to PolyGram in 1993. He published an autobiography, *To Be Loved*, in 1994.

LESLEY GORE
b. 2 May 1946, Tenafly, New Jersey, USA

Initially, like Britain's Helen Shapiro, merely another plaintive, if incisive, voice of female teen *angst* (exemplified on 'It's My Party'* and its sequel 'Judy's Turn to Cry', Mercury, 1963), Gore, in 1964, recorded the superb 'You Don't Own Me'*, one of the most forceful expressions of female independence in popular music, a record on a par with **Helen Reddy**'s 'I Am Woman' (1972).

The daughter of wealthy parents, Gore sang at high school with a band whose demos secured her (but not the band) a contract with Mercury in 1962. Her first record, produced – as would be all her Mercury recordings – by **Quincy Jones**, was 'It's My Party'. The song (successfully revived by Dave Stewart and Barbara Gaskin who topped the British charts with it in 1981 on Stiff) introduced the theme of the teenage love triangle (with Gore as the loser), the fat orchestral sound, and plaintive vocal style that dominated her early recording career. 'Judy's Turn to Cry' continued the story and her third Top Ten hit 'She's a Fool' (1963), which she co-wrote, was firmly in the same mould.

Though it sounded like Gore's previous hits, 'You Don't Own Me' (written by Johnny Madara and Dave White, a member of **Danny and the Juniors**) marked a decisive change. No longer was the singer either the passive recipient of a boy's affections or in conflict with another girl over them, instead she declaimed her independence. Her other major hits included two **Ellie Greenwich** and Jeff Barry compositions, 'Maybe I Know' (1964) and 'Look of Love' (1965). After a brief film career (which included *Ski Party* in which she sang **Marvin Hamlisch**'s 'Sunshine, Lollipops and Roses', 1965) and more mainstream records ('California Nights', her last major hit in 1967), she attempted a nightclub career.

In 1972 Gore recorded unsuccessfully with the Motown subsidiary Mowest, and in 1974 joined A&M. In 1978 she was reunited with Quincy Jones for *Love Me by Name*. She contributed lyrics (including 'Out Here on My Own', a Top Twenty hit for Irene Cara) to her brother Michael's music for the score of Alan Parker's *Fame* (1980). In the eighties and early nineties she performed occasionally on the American oldies circuit.

DAVY GRAHAM
b. 22 November 1940, Leicester, England

In the sixties Graham was the founder of a school of British acoustic guitar-playing whose later exponents included Bert Jansch and John Renbourn. His tune 'Angie' was the best-known guitar tune of the folk revival and a virtual test piece for budding virtuosi.

His father was a Scottish teacher of Gaelic and his mother came from Guyana. From the beginning, Graham's influences were varied, ranging from visiting blues artists like **Big Billy Broonzy** to classical guitarist Vincente Gomez. After starting his career in London folk clubs, Graham busked in Paris with Alex Campbell and played a jazz solo on a 1959 BBC arts programme produced by Ken Russell. He teamed up with **Alexis Korner** in 1961, recording a duet EP for Topic and very briefly playing guitar with Korner's Blues Incorporated.

Graham's unique ability to make connections between disparate musics found a wider audience when an arrangement of the Irish traditional song, 'She Moved through the Fair' as an Indian raga appeared on a live EP by the Thamesiders (Decca, 1963). After a budget instrumental record for Golden Guinea (*Guitar Player*, 1963), Graham made two key solo albums.

Folk Blues and Beyond (1965) lived up to its title with the accompaniment of 'Seven Gypsies' opening up the folk-baroque style of playing which Renbourn would perfect, and a version of **Charles Mingus**'s 'Better Git It in Your Soul' which showed Graham's skills as a jazz improviser. *Folk Roots, New Routes* (1965) was a collaboration with traditional singer Shirley Collins, where the guitarist's eclecticism was a foil for Collins' affecting contralto. Although rock was one guitar style without interest for Graham, this demonstration that old songs could be enhanced by new musical accompaniments was a lesson not lost on the folk-rock bands of a few years later.

Graham cut four more albums for Decca in the late sixties, including *Large as Life but Twice as Natural* (1969), which included 'Tristano', a tribute to the jazz pianist, and a version of **Joni Mitchell**'s 'Both Sides Now'. However, drugs problems kept him away from live performances. He did not record again until **Stefan Grossman** signed him to Kicking Mule in 1977. *The Complete Guitarist* (1978) recapitulated the eclecticism of his sixties work, with the addition of classical pieces by Vaughan Williams and de Visee. *Dance for Two People* (1979) found Graham playing Indian, Arabic and Turkish pieces on the appropriate instruments: oud, sarod and bouzouki.

In the eighties and nineties he made sporadic live appearances and issued occasional albums. The 1986 compilation *Folk Blues and All Points In Between* neatly encapsulates his most important recordings from the sixties.

PERCY GRAINGER
b. George Percy Grainger, 8 July 1882, Melbourne, Australia, d. 20 February 1961, White Plains, New York, USA

Originally a concert pianist, Grainger was the first person to use a phonograph to collect English folk songs. His later experiments with electronic 'Free Music' prefigured the progressive rock fusion music of the sixties.

He left Australia for Germany in 1895, and arrived in London in 1901. After attending a lecture by Lucy Broadwood of the Folk Song Society, Grainger collected songs in Lincolnshire and the west of England in 1906–9. His most famous discovery was Joseph Taylor, who provided 'Brigg Fair', which both Grainger and Frederick Delius arranged for piano – the latter included it in his *English Rhapsody*.

Grainger's use of recording equipment led to a controversy with **Cecil Sharp**. While Grainger felt that conventional music notation was inadequate to capture the precise details of folk singing, Sharp argued that the collector should be concerned only with the 'artistic effect' of a song, not the means by which the effect was produced. Ironically, Grainger's most popular folk tune arrangement, 'Country Gardens', was based on a song collected by Sharp himself. By the mid-twenties the sheet music was selling over 20,000 copies a year in North America alone and Grainger donated half his royalties to finance the publication of a full edition of songs collected by Sharp in the Appalachians. As 'English Country Garden', the tune was a British pop hit for **Jimmie Rodgers** (the son of **Hank Snow**) in 1962.

During the First World War Grainger settled in the United States and later became an American citizen. In 1921 he became the first concert pianist to perform in a movie theatre when he played four times a day between screenings at New York's Capitol Theater. **Duke Ellington**'s orchestra played in 1932 at an illustrated lecture where Grainger outlined his theory of Free Music. He saw Ellington's 'gliding tones' as exemplifying a desirable freedom from the constraints of conventional intervals and scales. Much of the last decade of Grainger's life was devoted to attempts to invent a machine to translate directly his musical ideas into sounds.

Grainger's recording career began with a series of piano pieces for the Gramophone Co. in 1908. From 1917 to 1931 he recorded for Columbia, while later albums of his compositions were conducted by Leopold Stokowski for RCA and Frederick Fennell for Mercury in the fifties. British pianist Martin Jones made new recordings of his folksong arrangements for Nimbus in the nineties, some of which were used on the soundtrack of the Merchant Ivory film of E. M. Forster's *Howard's End*.

GRAND FUNK RAILROAD

Mark Farner, b. 29 September 1948, Flint, Michigan, USA; Mel Schacher, b. 3 April 1951, Owosso, Michigan; Don Brewer, b. 3 September 1948, Flint; Craig Frost (joined 1972), b. 20 April 1948, Flint

Deploying simplified power chords, derived like those of their British contemporaries **Black Sabbath** from **Jimi Hendrix** and **Cream**, Grand Funk were the first and most successful American heavy-metal band of the seventies. Without radio play or critical support – the band's first albums were universally reviled by critics – Grand Funk achieved their sales of more than 20 million albums of high-volume stadium rock through constant touring and a cleverly orchestrated campaign by their manager Terry Knight (who promoted them as a people's band).

Farner and Brewer crossed paths as members of various bands in Michigan before joining disc-jockey turned singer Knight (*b. 9 April 1943, Flint*) in his group Terry Knight and the Pack. Knight had previously scored a Top Fifty hit with a revival of **Leiber and Stoller**'s 'I (Who Have Nothing)' (Lucky Eleven, 1966), a hit for **Ben E. King** and **Shirley Bassey** in 1963 (and later for **Tom Jones** in 1970). In 1968 they teamed up with Schacher (a one-time member of **? and the Mysterians** who had a No. 1 with the classic '96 Tears', Cameo, 1966) as Grand Funk Railroad and agreed to give Knight complete control if he would manage them. At a time when the headphone sound of progressive rock was dominant, Knight cut Grand Funk's sound to the bone, emphasizing simple riffs played at high volume, encouraged Farner (the group's main writer) to write populist chants (about music – 'Footstompin' Music'; against the war in Vietnam – 'Stop the War'; and pro-ecology – 'Save the Land', all from *E Pluribus Funk*, 1971) and, after a successful free performance at the 1969 Atlanta Festival, he sent the band on a lengthy tour of the stadiums of America.

Their début album, *On Time* (Capitol, 1969), sold over a million copies and in 1970, despite having only one Top Thirty single ('Closer to Home'), they reportedly sold more records than any other group in America. A further mark of Grand Funk's grass-roots popularity was that in 1971 they sold out New York's Shea Stadium in seventy-two hours, a feat which had taken **The Beatles** six weeks to accomplish. In 1972 there followed an acrimonious split with Knight and in 1973 (after Frost joined) they recorded *We're an American Band* with **Todd Rundgren** as producer.

The title track, a homage to life on the road, was their best record, sold a million, and gave them their first No. 1. Rundgren also produced their next album, *Shinin' on* (1974), which contained another chart-topper, a heavy-metal remake of **Carole King** and Gerry Goffin's 'The Loco-Motion'* (previously a No. 1 for Little Eva, Dimension, 1962). They continued to tour and record, now regularly scoring hit singles (including 'Some Kind of Wonderful', 1974, and 'Bad Time', 1975), but with the steady growth of heavy metal, their sound was no longer unique. After two more albums, including *Good Singin' Good Playin'* (MCA, 1976), produced by **Frank Zappa**, the group disbanded, only re-forming occasionally for charity functions, as in 1997 for the Bosnian-American Relief Fund.

Farner released a pair of lacklustre solo albums on Atlantic (*Mark Farner*, 1977, and *No Frills*, 1978) and in 1981 the group briefly re-formed (with Dennis Bellinger replacing Schacher) for *Grand Funk Lives* (Full Moon) and *What's Funk* (1983). They finally disbanded in 1983, when Brewer followed Frost and joined **Bob Seger**'s Silver Bullet Band. Farner recorded the gospel album *Just Another Injustice* in 1988. His later albums were all in a contemporary Christian vein and included *Wake Up* (1990) and *Some Kind of Wonderful* (1991).

GRANDMASTER FLASH

b. Joseph Saddler, 1 January 1958, Barbados, West Indies

Grandmaster Flash was one of originators of hip-hop, a key figure in the development of the role of the DJ in the genre, and an early master of the arts of mixing and scratching.

Barbados-born but raised in the Bronx, New York, Saddler became fascinated with DJ culture, attending parties in his neighbourhood in the 1970s. Applying himself to mastering and extending the DJ skills he observed at these parties, Saddler had towards the end of the decade established himself as the pre-eminent DJ around the Bronx, his speed on turntables and mixer earning him the nickname Flash. At this point he assembled a rapping and breakdancing team, the Furious Five, to front his mixing techniques. The team included Melle Mel (Mel Glover), Cowboy (Keith Wiggins), Creole (Danny Glover), Mr Ness (Eddie Morris) and Rahiem (Guy Williams). **Bobby Robinson**, who had stopped producing records a decade earlier, revived his Enjoy label in 1979 to release the group's 'Superrappin'', which became a local hit.

Flash and other mixers and rappers like **Afrika Bambaataa** and the Sugarhill Gang soon attracted the attention of larger record labels. Sylvia and Joe Robinson of Sugar Hill (formerly All-Platinum) were introduced to the phenomenon by their sons. They first signed the Sugarhill Gang, whose 'Rappers' Delight' (1979) was a Top Twenty hit, and then Grandmaster Flash.

His first Sugar Hill releases included 'Freedom' (1980), 'Flash to the Beat' and 'The Adventures of Grandmaster Flash on the Wheels of Steel', perhaps the finest recorded example of mixing and scratching techniques, which drew on records by Chic, **Blondie**, **Queen** and the Sugarhill Gang. The group followed these start-of-the-art mixes with the most successful of rap records, 'The Message' (1982). With socially conscious lyrics devised by Sylvia Robinson and Duke Bootee (aka Ed Fletcher), the record was a major R&B hit in America and reached the UK Top Ten.

The actual rappers Mel and Bootee received performer credits on 'Message 2 (Survival)' and the anti-drug rap 'White Lines (Don't Do It)', which was a UK hit in 1984. By then, Flash and Melle Mel had parted company in a flurry of lawsuits. Retitling himself Grandmaster Melle Mel, the latter cut further tracks for Sugar Hill, notably 'We Don't Work for Free' and 'Step Off', before the company's demise in 1986.

Flash signed a contract with the major Elektra label, releasing the unsuccessful albums *They Said It Couldn't Be Done* (1985), *The Source* (1986) and *On the Strength* (1988), which included a version of **Steppenwolf**'s 'Magic Carpet Ride'. Despite his stature as a leading figure in the genre, he was unable to sustain his career under the auspices of a big label. Like doo-wop in the 1950s, the best records of rap's first decade were produced by independent, not major, labels. Flash's best records of the nineties were all compilations, such as *Message from Beat Street* (1996). In 1998 he issued the lacklustre *Adventures of Wheels of Steel*.

GRANT LEE BUFFALO
Paul Kimble (replaced by Dan Rothchild); Joey Peters; Grant Lee Phillips

Folk-edged, alternative rock trio Grant Lee Buffalo built up a strong following in their native US, winning instant credibility when **R.E.M.**'s Michael Stipe offered his patronage.

Guitarist/songwriter Phillips and drummer Peters first played together alongside bassist James Brenner and singer Jeffrey Clark as Shiva Burlesque in the mid-eighties, releasing two albums of **Doors**-influenced rock – their eponymous début (1987) and *Mercury Blues* (1990) – on independent labels. The band broke up soon after releasing their second LP, with Phillips continuing to work with Peters. The pair recruited bassist/producer Kimble in 1991 and Grant Lee Buffalo was born.

Signing to Slash/Reprise the following year after generating interest in their live shows on the LA club scene, Grant Lee Buffalo recorded their début album, *Fuzzy* (1993), which won them instant success, particularly after Michael Stipe named it as one of his favourite records of the year. *Mighty Joe Moon* (1994) developed on the sound of *Fuzzy*, with Kimble's production adding a mystical, cinematic atmosphere to Phillips' storytelling and saw the band experiment with multi-tracked vocals and ancient keyboard sounds, recalling the studio wizardry of **Phil Spector** and the **Beach Boys**' Brian Wilson.

A high profile support slot on R.E.M.'s 1995 *Monster* world tour saw Grant Lee Buffalo's popularity grow, as did their contribution to the *Friends* soundtrack, a cover of the **Beach Boys**' 'In My Room'. *Copperopolis* (1996), their most folk-orientated album to date, was reminiscent of **John Lennon** and **Tom Petty** in places, and consolidated the band's success in the US while beginning to earn them an international fanbase. Kimble left soon after, leaving Phillips to mastermind *Jubilee* (1998), which included cameos from Michael Stipe and **Eels**' E and saw the band move to Warner Bros.

AMY GRANT
b. 25 November 1960, Augusta, Georgia, USA

America's 'first lady of contemporary Christian music', since 1985 Amy Grant has also enjoyed great success with her secular recordings, scoring pop hits on both sides of the Atlantic.

A doctor's daughter, Grant progressed from singing in her local church in Nashville to begin a career as a contemporary Christian recording artist at the age of fifteen under the tutelage of producer Brown Bannister. She was an immediate success in the Christian/gospel market, recording no fewer than eleven albums (including *Amy Grant, Age to Age, Father's Eyes, Never Alone* and *In Concert*) in the genre and picking up four Grammy awards. In 1982 she married Nashville songwriter and producer Gary Chapman. A tie-up between Myrrh Records, for whom she had recorded several albums, and A&M Records in 1984 saw the major label release the album *Straight Ahead* in the US later that year. A contemporary Christian set, it topped the *Billboard* inspirational charts (as all her albums have done) and was a small pop hit. Her next album for the label, *Unguarded* (1985), reached the US Top Forty and picked up a platinum disc, spinning off her first Top Forty single, 'Find a Way'. A&M released a further collection of Grant's inspirational recordings, *The Collection 1979–86*, the following year. In 1986 she had her first major single success with 'The Next Time I Fall', a duet with ex-**Chicago** vocalist Peter Cetera, which was a US No. 1. That was followed by the romantic *Lead Me on* (1988).

Grant devoted much of the following three years to bringing up her two children, before returning with a huge US tour and with her first genuinely secular set, *Heart in Motion* (1991), which established her as a major star. Mostly self-written and produced by Bannister, Michael Omartian (a fellow Myrrh artist) and Keith Thomas, the album provided her with the international hit single 'Baby Baby', which reached No. 1 in the US. Commitment to her family and her gospel activities curtailed Grant's secular career for the next two years, although she did record a highly successful album of Christmas songs, *Home for Christmas* (1992).

She duetted with country music star **Vince Gill** on the title track of *House of Love* (1994), which was featured in the film *Speechless* and included a version of **Joni Mitchell**'s 'Big Yellow Taxi'. *Beyond the Eyes* (1997) marked a step to introspection. She subsequently married Gill in 1999 and guested on his album *Let's Make Sure We Kiss Goodbye* (2000).

EDDIE GRANT
b. Edmond Montague Grant, 5 March 1948, Plaisance, Guyana

Grant was the most important Anglo-Caribbean rock artist of his generation. He developed a style which blended elements of reggae, pop, funk and African musics.

He emigrated to Britain in 1960. He played classical trumpet and made his first guitar in woodwork class before forming the Equals in 1965. It was one of the country's first mixed-race bands and included Dervin Gordon (vocals), Lincoln Gordon (guitar), Pat Lloyd (guitar) and John Hall (drums). First recorded as a 1966 B-side, Grant's 'Baby Come Back' (President, 1968) was a No. 1 for the group and in 1994 for Pato Banton with **UB40**. With Grant's flamboyant dyed white hair a feature of their dynamic stage act, the Equals had further hits with Grant's compositions 'Viva Bobby Joe' (1969) and 'Black Skinned Blue Eyed Boy' (1970).

Following a heart attack in 1971, Grant left the group to follow a career as a producer and solo artist. He worked on records by such reggae artists as 90 Degrees Inclusive and the Pioneers, as well as playing on sessions for albums by Mike Hugg and others. His first solo album was *Eddy Grant* (Torpedo, 1975).

By the mid-seventies Grant had his own Coach House studio in London and his own label, Ice. *Message Man* (1977) was the first album on which he played virtually every instrument. Although by now he had a growing audience in Africa and the Caribbean, 'Living on the Front Line' from *Walking on Sunshine* (1979) was Grant's first British solo hit. The title track was a 1982 hit for New York group Rocker's Revenge, while 'Police on My Back' was recorded by the **Clash** on their *Sandinista!* album.

Love in Exile (1980) was followed by *Can't Get Enough* (1981), whose title track was also a hit single. But his greatest success came with contrasting singles from *Killer on the Rampage* (1982). The ballad 'I Don't Wanna Dance' topped the British charts, while the heavily rhythmic 'Electric Avenue' evoked life in inner-city London and was his only American hit.

In 1981 Grant moved his headquarters to Barbados, where he built the Blue Wave studio. As well as preparing his own later albums, he recorded local artists such as soca singer Mighty Gabby ('This Beach Is Mine', 1982). Grant was commissioned to compose a title song for *Romancing the Stone*, and although it was not used in the film he included the track on *Going for Broke* (1984). In 1986 he released *Born Tuff* and in 1988 reached the British Top Ten with 'Gimme Hope Jo'Anna', an anti-apartheid song from *File under Rock* (Parlophone).

He acquired the rights to classic calypso material by such artists as **Mighty Sparrow**, Lord Kitchener and Roaring Lion and started to reissue it through Ice. He also recorded albums by contemporary calypsonians such as Calypso Rose (*Soca Diva*) and SuperBlue (*Flag Party*). In 1991 he recommenced his own recording career with *Paintings of the Soul* and *Soca Baptism* (1994), and in the mid-nineties attempted to buy up **Bob Marley**'s rights (as he had bought up many of the rights of the major calypso performers of the region) while at the same time having a repudiated manager seeking to regain control of his own career. These issues were resolved in 1998, after which Grant resumed his attempts to establish himself as a commercial guardian of Caribbean music.

GOGI GRANT
b. Audrey Brown, 20 September 1936, Philadelphia, Pennsylvania, USA

Grant is best remembered for her dramatic million-seller 'The Wayward Wind' (Era, 1956).

Raised in Los Angeles, Grant won a series of local talent contests in her teens and, on graduating from high school, turned professional singer in the early fifties. Signed to Era Records in 1955, she had an immediate hit with 'Suddenly There's a Valley'*, one of the few successes of the period on an independent label that had nothing to do with either rock'n'roll or R&B. Her follow-up 'The Wayward Wind' was even more successful, topping the American charts in 1956 and a hit again when reissued in 1961. Written by Herb Newman, the president of Era, the folk-like song and its dramatic production were similar in style to **Mitch Miller**'s series of hits with **Frankie Laine** and **Guy Mitchell**. **Tex Ritter** also had a hit with the song, while in Britain Jimmy Young (later a well-known radio talk-show host) covered it with moderate success in 1956 and **Frank Ifield** had a No. 1 with his 1963 revival. More interesting was **Neil Young**'s revival of the song on his *Old Ways* (1985).

Subsequent releases on Era (including 'You're in Love', 1956) fared less well and, after dubbing Ann Blyth's voice in the title role of *The Helen Morgan Story* (1957), Grant moved to RCA. She had a minor hit, 'Strange Are the Ways of Love' (1958), before moving to Liberty. In 1961, following the revival of 'The Wayward Wind', she briefly set up her own record label before retiring.

NORMAN GRANZ
b. 6 August 1918, Los Angeles, California, USA

A leading figure in modern jazz, Granz organized the 'Jazz at the Philharmonic' tours and started the successful Verve and Pablo record companies. He was the first person to release recordings of jazz concerts.

A former stock-exchange clerk and film editor, Granz opened Los Angeles' first de-segregated jazz club in 1941 after black fans of **Billie Holiday** were excluded from her shows. With the idea of presenting a concert as a 'jam session', Granz promoted a 'Jazz Concert at the Philharmonic' two years later, but had to drop the word 'Concert' to fit the title on posters. The first JATP tour took place in 1945 and until 1957 there were two ten-week tours a year, with all performances to mixed-race audiences. In 1944 he supervised the short film *Jammin' the Blues*, which was nominated for an Oscar.

Although JATP often featured up-tempo blowing by players like **Illinois Jacquet**, most of America's leading black and white musicians took part. They included **Lester Young, Ella Fitzgerald, Coleman Hawkins, Oscar Peterson** and the **Modern Jazz Quartet**. Granz also managed Fitzgerald and Peterson.

From the forties onwards Granz produced numerous records, first leasing them to **Moe Asch**'s Disc label (1944–5) and Mercury (1948–51) before setting up Clef (1951) and Norgran (1954). In 1957 he consolidated all his record releases on the Verve label. By the time it was sold to MGM for $2.8 million in 1961, Verve had built up an impressive jazz back catalogue with albums by **Count Basie, Fitzgerald, Dizzy Gillespie, Stan Getz**, Peterson, **Sarah Vaughan, Charlie Parker** (whom he signed to a long-term contract in 1948), and many others.

Angry at the neglect of many major jazz figures by record companies, Granz returned to record production in 1973 with the Pablo label, which released new work by Vaughan, Peterson, Freddie Hubbard and numerous others. In 1987 Pablo was sold to Fantasy in another multi-million-dollar deal.

STEPHANE GRAPPELLI
b. 26 January 1908, Paris, France, d. 1 December 1997

An associate of **Django Reinhardt**, Grappelli was one of the first virtuosi of the jazz violin. In a recording career of nearly 100 albums, he collaborated with musicians as diverse as **Duke Ellington**, Yehudi Menuhin and **Paul Simon**. He was made a member of the Legion of Honour by the French government in 1975.

Of French-Italian parentage, he was enrolled in Isadora Duncan's dancing school at the age of six and began playing violin at twelve. Two years later he was a member of a cinema band. Grappelli's earliest jazz influences were **Louis Armstrong** and **Joe Venuti** and in 1928 he joined Gregor and His Gregorians, a dance band modelled on **Jack Hylton**'s.

He met Reinhardt in 1934, and the pair formed an after-hours jazz group with bassist Louis Vola that was modelled in part on the earlier guitar-violin combination of **Eddie Lang** and Joe Venuti. As a quintet, the group played at the Hot Club of France organized by critic Hugues Panassie. The following year they recorded 'Tiger Rag' and 'Dinah' as the Quintet of the Hot Club of France. The group made dozens of records for Swing and Gramophone and Grappelli and Reinhardt worked with many leading American jazz musicians before war interrupted their career in 1939.

Grappelli spent the war years in Britain, performing with **George Shearing** for the troops. From 1946 until the guitarist's death in 1953 he was reunited with Reinhardt, and also played residencies in Paris. In the seventies Grappelli revived the Hot Club format in partnership with British guitarist Diz Disley. From the mid-fifties Grappelli gained a new Europe-wide audience through appearances at festivals, on television and on record.

Among his numerous albums from this period were collaborations with other violinists, including Stuff Smith (*Violins No End*, Pablo, 1957), a trio of fellow string players – Jean Luc-Ponty, Svend Amundssen and Smith (*Violin Summit*, Polydor, 1966) – Joe Venuti (*Venupelli Blues*, Affinity, 1979) and Yehudi Menuhin. Grappelli's recordings with the classical violin virtuoso Menuhin included *Tea for Two* (EMI, 1978) and *For All Seasons* (EMI, 1985). In 1988 he released *Stephane Grappelli Plays Jerome Kern* (GRP), produced by Ettore Stratta, and in 1990 *My Other Love*, produced by Bob Thiele and Tom Frost.

THE GRATEFUL DEAD
Jerry Garcia, b. Jerome John Garcia, 1 August 1942, San Francisco, California, USA, d. 9 August 1995, Forest Knolls, California; Bill Kreutzmann, b. 7 April 1946, Palo Alto, California; Phil Lesh, b. Philip Chapman, 15 March 1940, Berkeley, California; Rod Pigpen McKernan, b. 8 September 1945, San Bruno, California, d. 8

March 1973, San Francisco; Bob Weir, b. Robert Hall, 16 October 1947, San Francisco; Mickey Hart, b. 1950, New York; Donna Godchaux, b. 22 August 1947, San Francisco; Keith Godchaux, b. 14 July 1948, San Francisco, d. 23 July 1980, Marin County, California (replaced by Brent Mydland, b. 1952, Germany, d. 26 July 1990, Lafayette, California, replaced by Vince Welnick)

The premier psychedelic group of the sixties, the Grateful Dead were almost an anachronism in the high-technology eighties, the decade of their greatest commercial success. Primarily a live performance group, they bore the marks of their roots in the hippie lifestyle of sixties San Francisco throughout their career, most notably in the long improvisational shows featuring ragged harmonies and blues-based meandering guitar work by Weir and Garcia. Despite a five-year recording gap in the eighties, the Grateful Dead remained one of America's top concert attractions, mainly due to the successive generations of fans who, calling themselves Deadheads, flocked to see the band as if to somehow find again the sense of community the band had represented for three decades and that they as individuals had lost. After Garcia's death in 1995 the group disbanded and its members pursued solo projects.

The roots of the Grateful Dead lay in the 1960 meeting of Robert Hunter (later the Dead's non-performing lyricist) and Garcia, who played banjo and guitar on the West Coast folk circuit with **Country Joe McDonald** and others in the early sixties. In 1964 Garcia joined Mother McCree's Uptown Jug Champions within which guitarist Weir and keyboards-player McKernan performed folk and blues material. The following year they added Lesh (bass) and Kreutzmann (drums), became the Warlocks and went electric. Based in San Francisco's Haight-Ashbury district, the group became the Grateful Dead and evolved a free-form improvisatory style which fitted the mood of the fast-growing hippie culture. Hunter had previously participated in Stanford University's LSD tests, Garcia had become known as Captain Trips, and the Dead became the 'house band' at author Ken Kesey's Acid Test events. With LSD chemist Stanley Owsley in charge of their sound, the band's long rambling sets at numerous free concerts in the San Francisco area often included forty-minute versions of **Wilson Pickett**'s 'In the Midnight Hour', sung by Pigpen. With the addition of Hart on percussion, the band signed to Warners.

Their early recordings were issued much later as *History of the Grateful Dead* (MGM, 1971) but the band's first release was an eponymous album in 1967. This collection of short songs, though representative of the group's influences (**Sonny Boy Williamson**'s 'Good Morning Little Schoolgirl' and the traditional

'New, New Minglewood Blues'), was untypical of the group's live performances, which were more faithfully reflected in *Anthem of the Sun* (1968), the palindromically titled *Aoxomoxoa* (1969), which introduced 'St Stephen', and especially the double-album *Live Dead* (1969) with the majestic 'Dark Star' and a fifteen-minute rendition of **Bobby Bland**'s 'Turn on Your Lovelight'.

With lyricist Hunter coming to the fore, *Workingman's Dead* (1970) was a tighter, country-influenced album. Among its songs were 'Uncle John's Band' (a playful reference to the group's manager), 'New Speedway Boogie', the Dead's response to the Altamont incident where a fan was killed during a **Rolling Stones** concert, the sombre 'Black Peter' and a drug-culture reworking of 'Casey Jones', originally a hit for **Billy Murray** in 1910. The group maintained the same approach on *American Beauty* (1971) with the soft-rock 'Sugar Magnolia', the autobiographical 'Truckin'' and the philosophical 'Box of Rain' and 'Ripple'. Material from these two albums was regularly featured in the Grateful Dead's later concerts, while their greater commercial success enabled the group to develop in the seventies into an extended family of bands and musicians.

In 1972 the group formed their own Grateful Dead label and Round Records, for side projects by band members. The latter included New Riders of the Purple Sage and Garcia's bluegrass band Old and in the Way. For the Dead themselves, the early seventies was a period of musical consolidation as the live double-album *Grateful Dead* (1971), which included **Merle Haggard**'s 'Mama Tried', an extended version of **Buddy Holly**'s 'Not Fade Away' and **Kris Kristofferson**'s 'Me and Bobby McGee', outsold all their early work. Though it showed the group lacking in inspiration at times, the gargantuan triple-album *Europe '72* was also successful. There were personnel upheavals, however, as Hart left and Pigpen died of liver failure. Keith and Donna Godchaux (both vocalists) joined in 1972. Their career to this date is well documented in the compilation *What a Long Strange Trip It's Been* (Warner, 1977).

During the early seventies Garcia, Lesh and the Godchaux all made solo recordings, though perhaps the most interesting individual efforts were those of Hunter. Like his earlier lyrics for the Grateful Dead, the songs on *Tales of the Great Rum Runners* (Round, 1974), *Tiger Rose* (1975) and *Jack O'Roses* (Dark Star, 1980) confirmed an abiding interest in the underdogs of American life which Hunter shared with **The Band**'s Robbie Robertson.

The Grateful Dead's next studio albums, *Wake of the Flood* (1973) and *Blues for Allah*, appeared on the group's label but were as indecisive as the live recordings. By 1976 the momentum was gone and Clive

Davis signed the band to Arista, providing an arranger (Paul Buckmaster) and outside producers. Keith Olsen supervised the superior *Terrapin Station* (1977) while **Little Feat**'s Lowell George handled *Shakedown Street* (1978). By the time of *Go to Heaven* (1980) keyboards-player Mydland had replaced the Godchaux.

The following year brought *Reckoning* and *Dead Set*, both double-albums documenting live shows. The former was an all-acoustic set documenting the group's folk and country leanings, the latter the definitive eighties concert offering. For the remainder of the eighties, the band reverted to being one of rock's most popular live bands. Then in 1987 the group recorded the bestselling *In the Dark*, which spawned 'Touch of Gray', the Grateful Dead's first Top Ten hit in their twenty-three-year existence. In the same year the band toured with **Bob Dylan**, releasing the album *Dylan and Dead* (Columbia, 1989). Hart revived his solo career in 1989 with *Music to Be Born*, following it with *At the Edge* (1990) and *Planet Drum* (1991).

The Dead carried on with the aptly titled *Built to Last* (1989), which had Mydland singing lead on several tracks. Following his death in 1990 **Bruce Hornsby** briefly stepped in before Welnick was recruited full time. *Without a Net* (1991), a triple live set, neatly summed up the group's approach to performing. The same year, Garcia released the double live album *The Jerry Garcia Band* (Arista), on which he tackled songs by **The Beatles**, Dylan, **Los Lobos** and **Smokey Robinson**. From 1991 onwards, the Dead also began releasing a number of live albums from their huge archive of concert recordings, including *One from the Vault* (1991) and *Dick's Picks No. 1* (1993). In the early nineties it was revealed that through the charitable trust the Rex Foundation Lesh was financially supporting recordings of a number of British classical composers, including Havergal Brian and Robert Simpson.

A tribute album, *Deadicated* (1991), featured versions of the group's songs by such artists as Bruce Hornsby, **Midnight Oil** and **Elvis Costello**. *Dark Star* (1994) edited together numerous versions of perhaps the Grateful Dead's most famous compositions.

In 1995 Schanachie released the interesting *Roots of the Grateful Dead*. A collection of the original recordings of material associated with the group, it showed how broad was the range of influences upon them. It was followed by the compilation album *The Arista Years*, a three-CD live set, *Dozin' at the Knick*, and *Dick's Picks Vol 4* (all 1996). This last, a three-CD set, is considered by most critics to feature the group's best-ever recorded live show (New York, Feb 13–14, 1970). Made just as the band were to record *Workingman's Dead*, it melds material from that album with established favourites such 'Turn on Your Lovelight' and, of course, 'Dark Star'.

In the late summer of 2000 former Dead members Weir, Hart, Kreutzmann and long-time associate Hornsby, with Alphonse Johnson on bass, toured as the Other Ones to a rapturous critical and commercial reception.

DOBIE GRAY
b. Leonard Victor Ainsworth Jnr, 26 July 1942, Brookshire, Texas, USA

Best remembered for 'Drift Away'* (1973), a paean to the powers of rock'n'roll to soothe as well as excite, Gray was one of several black artists who recorded in both R&B and country styles.

The eighth son of a Texas sharecropper, Gray first achieved success with a series of cult dance records, including 'Look at Me', a minor hit on Cor Dak in 1963, 'The "In" Crowd', which he co-wrote, and its sequel 'See You at the "Go Go"' (both Charger, 1965). 'The "In" Crowd' was a cult classic among Britain's mods in the sixties and provided **Bryan Ferry** with a Top Twenty hit in 1974.

In the mid-sixties Gray turned to acting, working with Rip Torn in productions of *The Beard* and *The Balcony*, only returning to music in 1969 with the progressive rock group Pollution, with whom he recorded one album, *Pollution* (PSY, 1971). While cutting demos for songwriter **Paul Williams**, Gray met Paul's brother Mentor. With Mentor as producer, Gray made three relaxed albums of progressive country-soul for MCA, *Drift Away*, *Loving Arms* (both 1973), and *Hey Dixie* (1974), all featuring the songwriting talents of Troy Seals and Mentor Williams and Gray's smooth, sinuous voice. *Hey Dixie* sold badly and a move to Capricorn for *New Ray of Sunshine* (1975), which Gray produced with Seals, failed. However, the **Rick Hall**-produced 'You Can Do It' (Infinity, 1979) saw Gray return to the Top Forty, albeit in the guise of a disco artist. In 1986 Gray, once more writing with Seals, entered the country charts with 'The Dark Side of Town' (Capitol).

BUDDY GRECO
b. Armando Greco, 14 August 1926, Philadelphia, Pennsylvania, USA

Pianist, arranger and singer, Greco was a mainstay of the nightclub circuit for over twenty-five years. His best-remembered record is his finger-snapping version of **Lorenz Hart** and **Richard Rodgers**' 'The Lady Is a Tramp'* (Epic, 1962).

The son of a music critic and broadcaster, Greco regularly appeared on radio as both an actor and singer, before leading his own trio in 1944–9. During this period he recorded 'Ooh Look-a There, Ain't She Pretty' (1948) for the independent Musicraft label, which eventually went on to sell a million copies. In 1949 he joined **Benny Goodman** as a pianist and arranger and toured Europe and America. In 1952 Greco re-formed his trio to record for Coral (and later Kapp) in the manner of **George Shearing**, but found greater success on the nightclub circuit. Despite his lack of hit records, he soon graduated to the international cabaret circuit via television, where his finger-snapping cool won a large audience. Thus, although 'The Lady Is a Tramp' never figured on the American charts, it sold over a million copies in Europe. He had his only American chart hit with the **Bobby Vinton** composition 'Mr Lonely' (1962).

GREEN DAY

Billie Joe Armstrong, b. 17 February 1972, San Pueblo, California, USA; Mike Dirn, b. Mike Pritchard, 4 May 1972, California; John Kiffmeyer (replaced by Tre Cool, b. Frank Edward Wright III, 9 December 1972, Germany)

US punk-pop trio Green Day became one of the few American bands to maintain a significant level of success after the grunge rock scene came to an end in 1994. The rise of Green Day also signalled the emergence of a new breed of punk revivalists in the US.

Guitarist Armstrong and bassist Dirn began playing together whilst still in high school in Southern California, where they formed their first band, Sweet Children. After adding John Kiffmeyer to the line-up on drums they took the name Green Day – a reference to smoking marijuana. They released an EP, *1,000 Hours* (1989), and their power-pop début, *39/Smooth* (1990) (later collected together as *1039/Smoothed out Slappy Hours* [Lookout, 1991]) on local independent labels, amassing a strong fanbase within the Californian hardcore scene. With new drummer Tre Cool they recorded *Kerplunk* (1992), which broke the band across the US with the success of 'Welcome to Paradise'.

Signing to Reprise, Green Day released *Dookie* (1994), a much more powerful record than its predecessors, which sold over 12 million copies worldwide and won the band a Grammy for Best Alternative Performance. The album included four massive hit singles: 'Longview', 'Basket Case', 'When I Come Around' and a re-recorded version of 'Welcome to Paradise'. The follow-up, *Insomniac* (1995), was another commercial success, but was renounced by critics as being too similar to *Dookie*. A two-year break resulted in a more considered approach for *Nimrod* (1997), which sold well in the US and UK and gave Green Day another hit single, 'Hitchin' a Ride'. *Warning* (2000) added elements of folk to Green Day's trademark punk-pop sound, and included the international hit single 'Minority'.

AL GREEN
b. Albert Greene, 13 April 1946, Forrest City, Arkansas, USA

Green found international success in the seventies with a sound described by one critic as 'the living embodiment of a dying tradition, a unique distillation of cold fire, raw emotion and technical refinement'. In contrast to the slickness of much black music of the period, producer **Willie Mitchell** created for Green a backdrop of a slowish rolling tempo over a tight rhythm section which was further intensified by gospel-style organ fills, subdued horns and stabbing lead guitar lines in the manner of the best of Southern soul. Against this were set Green's sensual vocals, alternately teasing and testifying, that echoed the sweetness of **Sam Cooke** and the urgency of **Otis Redding**.

Green sang gospel with his brothers before in 1959 the family moved to Grand Rapids, Michigan, where Green formed the R&B group the Creations in 1964. As Al Greene and the Soul Mates he scored an R&B hit with 'Back Up Train' (1967) on the Hot Line Music Journal label formed by former Creations Curtis Rodgers and Palmer Jones. Subsequent recordings failed and Green played the chitlin' circuit until 1968 when he met Mitchell, who signed him to the Memphis-based Hi Records.

His first records (a cover of **The Beatles**' 'I Want to Hold Your Hand' and the **Isaac Hayes** composition 'One Woman', 1969) showed little individuality, but his bluesy reworking of the **Temptations**' 'I Can't Get Next to You' (1970) was an R&B hit. 'Driving Wheel', a revival of the Roosevelt Sykes blues standard (Regal, 1949) – and previously a hit for **Junior Parker** in 1961 – fared less well before the subdued 'Tired of Being Alone'* and the American No. 1 'Let's Stay Together'* (1971) brought Green international success. The sound of these records was heavily dependent on the Hi studio band, which included drummers Al Jackson (formerly of **Booker T. and the MGs**) and Howard Grimes, Teenie, Charles and Leroy Hodges on guitar, organ and bass, respectively, trumpeter Wayne Jackson and saxophonist James Mitchell. With the exception of Al Jackson (who died in 1975), these played on every Green recording until 1978, including six million-sellers, 'Look What You Done for Me', 'I'm Still in Love with You', 'You Ought to Be with Me' (1972), 'Call Me (Come Back Home)', 'Here I Am (Come and Take Me)' (1973) and 'Sh-La-La (Make Me Happy)' (1974).

From 1974 onwards, his personal life in turmoil, Green's songs increasingly had a gospel edge, as in 'Take Me to the River' (1974), revived by **Talking Heads** in 1978, 'Full of Fire' and *Truth and Time* (1978), Green's first album without Mitchell as producer. In 1976 he was ordained as a preacher and in

1980 finally quit secular music for gospel, signing to the Word label and recording only gospel material with great success for several years. In 1986 he was reunited with Mitchell for the minor *Going Away* (A&M) and in 1988 teamed up with Annie Lennox of **Eurythmics** for a version of **Jackie DeShannon**'s 'Put a Little Love in Your Heart'.

In 1989 he released *I Get Joy* (A&M), which mixed religious lyrics with dance beats to little effect and in 1991 recorded 'Leave the Guns at Home', a song written by **Arthur Baker** in support of firearms restrictions in the United States. He briefly returned to soul with the minor *Don't Look Back* (RCA, 1993), on which members of the **Fine Young Cannibals** sought to update the Willie Mitchell sound. His 1999 tour of the UK saw him performing both soul and gospel music with élan. The four-CD set *Anthology* (The Right Stuff, 1998) is the definitive retrospective.

ROGER GREENAWAY
b. 23 August 1938, Bristol, Avon, England

Often in partnership with Roger Cook, Greenaway composed some of the most popular songs of the sixties and seventies, notably 'I'd Like to Teach the World to Sing' (1971), a global hit for the **New Seekers** and better known as a Coca-Cola advertising theme. Greenaway was also a member of such vocal groups as David and Jonathan, Brotherhood of Man and the Pipkins.

After serving in the army he joined Bristol groups the Beltonaires and the Kestrels, where he met Cook (*b. 19 August 1941, Bristol*). The Kestrels recorded for Pye with Johnny Keating as musical director but by 1965 the Cook–Greenaway team were providing songs for other artists. Their first hit was 'You've Got Your Troubles' (Decca, 1965) by the Fortunes, for whom the duo also wrote 'This Golden Ring' (1966) and (with Albert Hammond and Mike Hazelwood) 'Freedom Come Freedom Go'. As David and Jonathan, the pair had their own hits in 1966 with a version of **The Beatles**' 'Michelle' and their own 'Lovers of the World Unite', which combined witty and allusive lyrics with falsetto harmonies.

Over the next decade Greenaway wrote more than thirty hit songs with Cook and with other composers and writers. Among them were such novelty songs as Whistling Jack Smith's 'I Was Kaiser Bill's Batman' (Deram, 1967); romantic ballads like **Gene Pitney**'s 'Something's Gotten Hold of My Heart' (1967), **Engelbert Humperdinck**'s 'The Way It Used to Be' (1968) and **Andy Williams**' 'Home Lovin' Man' (1970); the idealistic 'Melting Pot' by Blue Mink (Philips, 1969); and 'Softly Whispering I Love You' by the English Congregation (1971). Greenaway also wrote many long-running television jingles, including

one for Jacob's Club ('If you like a lot of chocolate on your biscuit join our Club'), British Gas ('Cookability, that's the beauty of Gas') and the ASDA ('Tap-Tap') jingle.

The biggest-selling Cook–Greenaway songs were 'I'd Like to Teach the World to Sing', with global sales of over 10 million and 'Long Cool Woman (In a Black Dress)'* (1972) recorded by the **Hollies**. During the seventies Greenaway also wrote and produced for David Dundas ('Jeans on', 1976 – another advertising jingle) and the **Drifters**, working with Cook on 'Kissin' in the Back Row of the Movies' (Bell, 1974) and producing the group's later hits, which included 'You're More Than a Number in My Little Red Book' (Arista, 1976), co-written with **Tony Macaulay**, and 'Like Brother Like Sister' with Geoff Stephens.

In the mid-seventies Cook emigrated to Nashville and wrote and published a series of hits for **Crystal Gayle**, including the country No. 1 'Talking in Your Sleep', **Don Williams** ('I Believe in You', 'Love Is on a Roll' and others). In 1980 Cook and Greenaway gave Gayle another country chart-topper with 'It's Like We Never Said Goodbye'.

After that Greenaway wrote little and served as Chairman of the Performing Right Society, before becoming Senior Vice President/International of the American Society of Composers, Authors and Publishers (ASCAP) in 1994.

NORMAN GREENBAUM
b. 20 November 1942, Malden, Massachusetts, USA

One of the most engaging one-hit wonders of the sixties, Greenbaum unexpectedly returned to the limelight when Dr and the Medics had a British No. 1 with a respectful revival of his 'Spirit in the Sky' (IRS, 1986).

After being on the edge of the folk scene while studying at Boston University, Greenbaum moved to Los Angeles in 1965, forming Dr West's Medicine Show and Junk Band with fellow folkies Bonnie Wallach, Jack Carington, and Evan Engber. Basically a jug band, fuelled by Greenbaum's interest in twenties music, they signed to local label Go Go in 1966 and scored a minor hit with the novelty tune 'The Eggplant That Ate Chicago'. By the time they toured on the back of the hit the band had been swamped by psychedelia and surprised audiences found not only the group's but their own faces being painted during performances.

Various members left to become full-time hippies, and Greenbaum drafted in rock players as well as ex-New Christy Minstrel Barry Kane (violin). At the end of 1967 Dr West split up and Greenbaum formed a succession of shortlived rock bands. He was spotted by producer Erik Jacobson and cut 'School for Sweet

Talk' as Dr Greenbaum before releasing 'Spirit in the Sky'* (Reprise, 1969). Featuring a fuzz-box built into the body of a guitar by Greenbaum's accompanist Robbie Robinson, the song was a Top Ten hit in America and reached No. 1 in Britain.

The quirky follow-ups, 'Canned Ham' and 'Don't Let the California Earthquake Scare You Away', failed to match 'Spirit''s impact and Greenbaum retired to run a goat milk business. In 1972 he returned with songs about farm life on *Petaluma*, which recalled the jug-band sound of the Dr West period and included **Ry Cooder** on some tracks.

The success of the revived 'Spirit in the Sky' was appropriate since Dr and the Medics were foremost among the so-called psychedelic revivalists in mid-eighties Britain. In 1991 country band the Kentucky Headhunters had a minor hit with yet another version of 'Spirit in the Sky'.

ELLIE GREENWICH
b. 23 October 1940, Brooklyn, New York, USA

Usually in partnership with Jeff Barry, Greenwich was one of the most prolific and skilled Brill Building songwriters of the early and mid-sixties.

At the age of fourteen, Greenwich demonstrated her songs to **Everly Brothers** and **Andy Williams** producer Archie Bleyer, but her professional career began only after graduation from college. Her first demo discs were made for **Leiber and Stoller** and featured songs later recorded by **Jay and the Americans** ('This Is It'), the Exciters ('He's Got the Power') and **Darlene Love** ('Today I Met the Boy I'm Going to Marry').

With Barry (*b. 1939*), the composer of the Ray Peterson death-song hit 'Tell Laura I Love Her' (RCA, 1960), she wrote and recorded as the Raindrops on Jubilee. The group's hits included 'What a Guy', 'The Kind of Boy You Can't Forget' and 'Hanky Panky', a million-seller for **Tommy James and the Shondells** in 1966.

In 1963 Barry and Greenwich started a successful partnership with **Phil Spector**. They composed hits for the **Crystals** ('Then He Kissed Me', 'Da Do Ron Ron'), the **Ronettes** ('Baby I Love You'), Darlene Love ('Wait Till My Bobby Gets Home') and **Ike and Tina Turner** ('River Deep, Mountain High'). They also continued to provide material for Leiber and Stoller, who had started their own label, Red Bird. The songs were again teen sagas for girl groups, notably the **Shadow Morton** production 'Leader of the Pack' by the **Shangri-Las** and 'Chapel of Love' for the Dixie Cups. 'Doo Wah Diddy Diddy', an American hit for R&B group the Exciters, reached No. 1 in Britain when covered by **Manfred Mann** in 1964.

The pair also produced many of **Neil Diamond**'s

early hits before dissolving their partnership in the mid-sixties. For a while Greenwich turned from songwriting to composing advertising jingles. She returned to music in 1973 with *Let It Be Written, Let It Be Sung* (MGM), a self-produced album of new versions of her sixties hits, plus two more recent compositions with Toni Wine. Her later recording, however, was limited to backing vocals on albums by artists including **Jim Croce**, **Blondie** (*Eat to the Beat*, 1979), **Gary US Bonds** and the Sorrows, a group including **Arthur Alexander** and Ellen Foley. Greenwich contributed two songs to Foley's 1983 solo album.

The paucity of Greenwich's later output suggested that her talents belonged to the sixties, a view confirmed in 1985 when a Broadway musical based on her life was staged. Titled *Leader of the Pack*, it starred Darlene Love and Greenwich herself.

NANCI GRIFFITH
b. 6 July 1953, Seguin, Texas, USA

A stylish songwriter and singer, Griffith's work crosses the boundaries between the country, folk and contemporary singer-songwriter genres.

She grew up in Dallas, Texas, and made her first performance as a singer at fourteen. After studying at the University of Texas, Griffith played clubs in Austin and Houston before moving to Nashville in 1984. During this time she recorded a live album, *There's a Light Beyond These Woods* (Philo, 1978), and a studio album, *Poet in My Window* (1982), of her compositions. Both were subsequently released by Rounder in 1986.

Bluegrass musician Jim Rooney produced *Once in a Very Blue Moon* (1984), which included guest vocals by **Lyle Lovett**. The album's critical success led to a contract with Rounder Records for *Last of the True Believers* (1985), which included 'Love at the Five and Dime', subsequently a hit for **Kathy Mattea**. This was the first of Griffith's recordings to be issued in Europe, where she would develop a large following.

In 1986 producer Tony Brown (who was largely responsible for widening **Vince Gill**'s repertoire) signed Griffith to MCA and produced the first of her five albums for the label. This was *Lone Star State of Mind*, whose tracks included one of the first recordings of Julie Gold's anthemic 'From a Distance'.

Griffith's next recordings were *Little Love Affairs* (1988), the live *One Fair Summer Evening* and *Storms* (1989), produced by Glyn Johns with contributions from **Albert Lee** and **Phil Everly**.

Although her reputation was steadily increasing in Europe, Griffith's work was seen as being too eclectic for US country audiences and after the poor sales of *Late Night Grande Hotel* (1991), MCA dropped her from its roster. Ironically, the next album, *Other*

Voices, Other Rooms (1993), was her most commercially successful. A collection of reworkings of favourite songs, often in partnership with their writers, it was produced by Rooney and featured Griffith with such artists as **Bob Dylan**, **John Prine**, **Emmylou Harris** and **Carolyn Hester**. She followed this with the lesser *Flyer* (Elektra, 1994), on which she largely returned to the confessional style of *Late Night*. *Other Voice Too (A Trip Back to Bountiful)* (1998), a sequel to the 1993 album, was equally successful. Its range was wide – from **Stephen Foster** to **Woody Guthrie** – as were its guest artists, which included **Lyle Lovett**, **Richard Thompson** and former member of the **Crickets** Sonny Curtis.

STEFAN GROSSMAN
b. 16 April 1945, Brooklyn, New York, USA

A virtuoso guitarist (and, later, head of Kicking Mule records), Grossman played an important role in the folk and blues revival of the sixties and seventies. He helped to bring **Rev. Gary Davis** to international audiences and also invented a special tablature designed to teach blues guitar-playing. Like **Ry Cooder**, he had an encyclopaedic knowledge of guitar styles, but his own records lacked the fire and intensity of Cooder's work.

In the early sixties he joined the Greenwich Village folk scene, learning blues and ragtime from Davis. Grossman formed the Even Dozen Jug Band with Peter Siegel, recording albums for Elektra and Legacy. In 1966 he wrote the first of many instructional books, *How to Play Blues Guitar*, before briefly joining the **Fugs** and Chicago Loop on electric guitar.

Grossman first visited Europe in 1967 and thereafter divided his time between both sides of the Atlantic. The first of numerous recordings, mostly intended to demonstrate various guitar styles, was *Yazoo Basin Boogie* (1970), released in Europe by Transatlantic. It was followed by *Ragtime Cowboy Jew* (1970) and *Those Pleasant Days* (1971).

In 1973 Grossman and former **Country Joe McDonald** manager Ed Denson launched Kicking Mule and embarked on an ambitious recording programme designed to showcase contemporary guitar virtuosi. Among those featured on the label were Duck Baker (*The King of Bongo Bong*, 1977), Charley Musselwhite (*Harmonica According to*, 1978), Sam Mitchell (*Bottleneck and Slide Guitar*, 1976), **Mickey Baker** (*Jazz Rock Guitar*, 1978), **Davy Graham** (*Dance for Two People*, 1979) and John Renbourn of **Pentangle**, with whom Grossman made a duet album in 1978.

Grossman's later solo albums included *Country Blues Guitar* (1977) and *Thunder on the Run* (1980), one of the last Kicking Mule releases.

DAVE GRUSIN
b. 26 June 1934, Littleton, Colorado, USA

An energetic composer, arranger, keyboards player and producer, Grusin co-founded GRP, the leading jazz-fusion record company.

He studied piano at the University of Colorado and Manhattan School of Music before touring as accompanist to **Andy Williams** in 1959. For some years he was musical director for Williams' television shows. Grusin also played on numerous studio recordings and began his own recording career with *Candy* (1961).

His greatest successes have come with film music, however. Grusin has composed scores for numerous movies since the sixties, including *The Graduate* (1967), *Heaven Can Wait* (1978), *On Golden Pond* (1981), *Tootsie* (1982), *The Fabulous Baker Boys* (1989) and *The Milagro Beanfield War*, for which he won an Oscar in 1989. Later scores included *Mulholland Falls* (1996) and *Selena* (1997).

In 1976 he and former drummer Larry Rosen founded Grusin/Rosen Productions, which evolved into GRP Records. GRP has since become the main focus of contemporary cross-over jazz, releasing albums by such artists as Lee Ritenour, **Chick Corea**, **Gary Burton**, Tom Scott and Diane Schuur. The label was sold to MCA in 1990 but Rosen and Grusin remained in executive control.

Among Dave Grusin's own GRP recordings are *Harlequin* (1985), *Cinemagic* (1987) and *Homage to Duke* (1993).

THE GUESS WHO
Randy Bachman, b. 27 September 1943, Winnipeg, Canada (replaced by Kurt Winter, b. 2 April 1946, and Greg Leskiw, b. 5 August 1947, replaced by Don McCullough, replaced by Dominic Troiano, b. 1945, Mondugno, Italy); Chad Allan, b. 1945, Winnipeg (replaced by Burton Cummings, b. 31 December 1947, Winnipeg); Garry Peterson, b. 26 May 1945, Winnipeg; Jim Kale, b. 11 August 1943 (replaced by Bill Wallace, b. 18 May 1949)

The first Canadian recording artists to have an American million-seller, the Guess Who used the novelty of their Canadian origins as a selling point for their music. Their mainstream rock music was a seventies' parallel to the sound of **Bryan Adams**, who achieved international stardom in the eighties.

From 1959 to 1965 guitarist Bachman and singer Allan played in various local Winnipeg bands before choosing Guess Who as a name. The decision was said to have followed Bachman's seeing **The Who** perform on a visit to Britain. With Peterson (drums) and bassist Kale, they had a hit in both Canada and the United States with a version of **Johnny Kidd**'s 'Shakin' All Over' (Scepter, 1965). The group toured North America on a **Dick Clark** package tour before Allan left to finish college and (later) become a chat-show host.

With new member Cummings (keyboards, vocals) as Bachman's writing partner, the Guess Who's records on MGM were hits inside Canada but US success eluded them until they signed with RCA and recorded 'These Eyes'* (1969) with producer Jack Richardson in New York. The album *Canned Wheat Packed by Guess Who* provided further hits in 'Laughing'* and 'Undun'.

The group's best-known song was the million-selling title track of *American Woman* (1970), replete with repetitive fuzz-guitar sounds from Bachman, whose conversion to Mormonism contributed to his decision to leave at this high point of the group's career. He was replaced by two guitarists and the Guess Who finished 1970 with another big hit, 'Share the Land'.

The next five years were marked by numerous personnel changes and a gradual decline in popularity. *So Long Bannatyne* (1971) included jazz influences and the hits 'Rain Dance' and 'Albert Flasher'. *No. 10* (1973) was notable only for 'Glamour Boy', an expression of Cummings' distaste for the glitterati **David Bowie** and **Lou Reed**. The Guess Who's last big hit was 'Clap for the Wolfman' (1974), a tribute to the famous deejay – Wolfman Jack – whose voice could be heard on the record.

Soon afterwards, one of Canada's most experienced guitarists joined the group. Troiano had played with **Ronnie Hawkins**, Mandala, Bush and the James Gang. He added instrumental vigour to *Flavours* (1974) and *Power in the Music* (1975), but when Wallace left in 1976, the group disbanded. It was re-formed a year later by original members Kale and Peterson and guitarists McDougall (1972–4) and Winter (1970–4), primarily as a vehicle for nostalgic re-creations of 'greatest hits' on occasional tours such as the 1979 *American Bandstand* tour organized by **Dick Clark**.

Both Bachman and Cummings went on to solo careers. After producing a Chad Allan solo album and recording his own *Axe* (RCA, 1970), Bachman formed Brave Belt with Allan, his brother Tim (drums) and Fred Turner (bass), cutting two Reprise albums. His first chart success came with his next band, Bachman-Turner Overdrive – Brave Belt minus Allan – whose 'You Ain't Seen Nothin' Yet'* (Mercury, 1974), a homage to The Who, was a massive international hit. The band's other successful pieces of workmanlike heavy rock included 'Taking Care of Business' (1974), 'Roll on down the Highway' (1975) and 'Take It Like a Man' (1976). Randy Bachman left the group in 1978 but returned with Peterson in 1983 to record for Compleat. In 1987 Bachman and Cummings mounted

a nostalgia tour to little interest and in 1993 Bachman made a solo album, *Any Road*, with guests **Neil Young** and Margo Timmins of the **Cowboy Junkies**.

Cummings' début solo album was produced by Richard Perry and included the ballad hit 'Stand Tall'* (Portrait, 1976). He made further albums on Portrait and Alfa and scored a minor hit with 'You Saved My Soul' (Alfa, 1981). The reunion album *All This for a Song* (1979) failed to save them from the nostalgia circuit.

GUITAR SLIM
b. Eddie Jones, 10 December 1926, Greenwood, Mississippi, USA, d. 7 February 1959, New York

A blend, perhaps unique in its day, of steamy gospel emotionalism and a calculatedly distorted electric guitar sound made 'The Things That I Used to Do' one of the most successful (it was No. 1 in the R&B chart for six weeks) and memorable records of 1954. It was the making of Guitar Slim's career, and he toured the South on the strength of it for the rest of his life. (It was also beneficial for its pianist and arranger, **Ray Charles**.)

Slim had been working in New Orleans clubs since the late forties, at first much under the influence of **Clarence 'Gatemouth' Brown**. Through public performance and a series of recordings for Specialty (1953–6) he developed an entirely personal style of playing and songwriting and a stage act of remarkable colour, energy and extravagance. Though he never matched the success of 'The Things That I Used to Do' – which has become a modern blues standard – he continued to make records of distinction for both Specialty, such as 'Something to Remember You By' (1956), and afterwards Atco. He died of pneumonia after collapsing during an Eastern tour.

GUNS N' ROSES
Axl Rose, b. William Bailey, 6 February 1962, Lafayette, Indiana, USA; Izzy Stradlin, b. Jeffrey Isbell, 8 April 1962, Lafayette (replaced by Robin Finck); Slash, b. Saul Hudson, 23 July 1965, Stoke-on-Trent, Staffordshire, England (replaced by Paul Hugo); Duff McKagan, b. Michael McKagen, 5 February 1964, Seattle, Washington, USA (replaced by Tommy Stinson); Stephen Adler, b. 22 January 1965, Cleveland, Ohio, USA (replaced by Matt Sorum, b. 19 November 1960, Mission Viejo, California, USA, replaced by Josh Freese)

For a brief period between the decline of the first two generations of heavy metal groups and the rise of grunge, Guns N' Roses were the most notorious rock band in the world. The subsequent loss of key members left the group's leader Axl Rose looking for a new role in the mid-nineties.

Rose played in Indiana bands as a teenager and moved to Los Angeles in 1985 to link up with guitarist Stradlin. The pair became involved in the local club scene, forming a series of groups with guitarist Tracii Guns. After leaving Guns they eventually formed a group with Slash (guitar), McKagen (bass) and Adler (drums). Playing heavy metal with punk attitude, Guns N' Roses quickly gained a following in the clubs of Southern California.

After issuing an EP, *Live?!*; *Like a Suicide*, on the local Uzi label, the group signed to Geffen Records in 1986. The following year they toured with **Iron Maiden** and **Motley Crüe** before issuing *Appetite for Destruction*. The album went on to sell over ten million copies worldwide. Its tracks included the US No. 1 single 'Sweet Child o' Mine', 'Paradise City' and 'Welcome to the Jungle', which was featured in the Clint Eastwood film *Dead Pool* (1988).

During the late eighties Guns N' Roses toured frequently and recorded only four new songs, which were issued with the EP tracks on *G N' R Lies* (1988). The group's reputation as the new 'bad boys' of rock was enhanced by a series of incidents, including a drunken appearance by Slash and McKagan on a televised awards show and the accidental death of two audience members during a Guns N' Roses performance at the Donington Monsters of Rock festival in the UK in 1988. After Rose leapt into the crowd at a Maryland concert in 1991, a riot ensued and three later performances on the tour were cancelled.

Four years after *Appetite for Destruction*, Guns N' Roses simultaneously issued two albums of new material, *Use Your Illusion I* and *Use Your Illusion II*, in 1991. Shortly afterwards Stradlin left the group to found his own band the Ju Ju Hounds. He released a solo album, *Izzy Stradlin and the Ju-Ju Hounds*, in 1992. Adler had been replaced by ex-Cult drummer Matt Sorum in 1990.

During 1992 and 1993 sales of the new albums, which included a number of hit singles, 'Don't Cry', 'November Rain' and a version of **Paul McCartney**'s James Bond film theme 'Live and Let Die', mushroomed. In 1993 Guns N' Roses paid tribute to the artists who had inspired their own early efforts on *The Spaghetti Incident*, a collection of punk songs originally recorded by such artists as **Iggy Pop**, **New York Dolls** and the **Damned**. Even this was not free of controversy; Rose included a song composed by convicted murderer Charles Manson.

Guns N' Roses' only output in 1994 was a cover of the **Rolling Stones**' 'Sympathy for the Devil', included on the soundtrack to *Interview with the Vampire*. Slash left the band soon after as the band clashed over musical directions. He issued a solo album, *Slash's Snake Pit*, the following year, rooted in 12-bar blues. Guns N' Roses remained inactive until 1999, when a

new line-up of the band (of which Rose was the only original member) contributed 'Oh My God' to the soundtrack of the lacklustre Arnold Schwarzenegger movie *End of Days*. In 2000 the band issued a double-CD set, *Live Era '87–'93*, much of which was performed by the original line-up of Rose, Slash, Stradlin, McKagan and Adler.

WOODY GUTHRIE
b. *Woodrow Wilson Guthrie, 14 July 1912, Okemah, Oklahoma, USA, d. 3 October 1967, New York*

The author of America's 'alternative' national anthem 'This Land Is Your Land' and many other classic songs of social comment and protest, Guthrie was the prime influence on the songwriters of the folk revival of the sixties. Among those who acknowledged their debt to him were **Bob Dylan**, **Phil Ochs** and **Tom Paxton**.

Guthrie's father was a district court clerk turned land speculator and local politician. After his mother's death from Huntington's chorea and the failure of his father's land deals, Guthrie moved to Pampa, Texas, where a fiddle-playing uncle kindled an interest in country music. Already an accomplished graphic artist and autodidact, he began to write new words to old tunes and made occasional radio broadcasts with the Corncob Trio.

A major dust storm in 1935 inspired his first great song, 'Dusty Old Dust', written to the tune of **Carson Robison**'s 'Ballad of Billy the Kid'. He spent the next two years travelling and developed a repertoire of material from many sources, including Appalachian ballads, hymns, blues, dance tunes and cowboy songs. Moving to Los Angeles in 1937, he co-wrote the country standard 'Oklahoma Hills' with his cowboy-singer cousin Jack Guthrie before performing regularly over KFVD. The show was a mixture of old-time music and Guthrie compositions, including many of his Dust Bowl ballads such as 'Dust Bowl Refugees' and 'I Ain't Got No Home'.

His benefit concerts for left-wing causes in California led to Guthrie's emergence on the New York folk scene in 1940. **Alan Lomax** recorded many hours of Guthrie's songs and stories for the Library of Congress, while an album of *Dust Bowl Ballads* was released by Victor. Guthrie also appeared on numerous radio programmes, often in association with **Leadbelly** and the young **Pete Seeger**. In 1941 he was commissioned to write a series of songs celebrating hydro-electric projects in the Pacific North-West. Among them were 'Grand Coulee Dam' and 'Pastures of Plenty', Guthrie's hymn to the migrant workers.

Because of his Communist associations, Guthrie was excluded from network radio but in 1943 the publication of his autobiography *Bound for Glory* brought him widespread recognition. In 1944 he embarked on a series of marathon recording sessions produced by **Moe Asch**. Some of the material was released on Folkways and on Herbert Harris's Stinson label. Among these recordings was an album of his songs for children, including 'Going to the Zoo' and 'Car Car'. In 1948 he composed 'Plane Wreck at Los Gatos (Deportees)' in response to the death of a plane load of immigrant workers; a memorable version of the song was included by **Dolly Parton** on her 1980 album *9 to 5*.

In 1950 the **Weavers** had a hit with 'So Long', a revised version of 'Dusty Old Dust', but by now Guthrie was entering a physical and mental decline which was diagnosed in 1952 as Huntington's chorea. He spent nearly the whole of his last fifteen years in hospital, while his reputation as one of the country's greatest songwriters increased. **Ramblin' Jack Elliott**, in 1951, was the first of many Guthrie imitators, who were to include Dylan, whose first album included a 'Song to Woody'. As the revival gathered momentum from 1958, every new artist or group included something by Guthrie in their repertoire and on their albums. When Elektra released a three-volume selection from the Library of Congress material in 1964, the royalties from Guthrie's compositions were over $50,000 a year.

Following Guthrie's death, Seeger and others organized memorial concerts with the participation of **Richie Havens**, **Country Joe McDonald** and **Judy Collins**, as well as Dylan, Paxton and **Joan Baez**. 'This Land Is Your Land', originally written as a radical counterblast to **Irving Berlin**'s 'God Bless America', became his best-known song. It was used in advertisements and as the theme for George McGovern's 1972 Presidential election campaign. Among those who have recorded it are **Peter Paul and Mary**, **Bing Crosby**, **Tex Ritter**, **Connie Francis** and **Bruce Springsteen**.

Guthrie's son Arlo (*b. 10 July 1947*) had a 1967 FM radio hit with the witty, subversive 'Alice's Restaurant' (Reprise), which is one of the few songs – **Bobbie Gentry**'s 'Ode to Billie Joe' is another – to form the basis of a film, *Alice's Restaurant* (1969). He went on to record a series of folk/country albums, one of which, *Hobo's Lullaby* (1973), included a Top Twenty hit in **Steve Goodman**'s 'City of New Orleans', and an impressive reading of his father's '1913 Massacre' that both echoed Woody Guthrie's rendering and showed how much Dylan's songs drew from Woody in both substance and style. Arlo also performed with Pete Seeger in the seventies, releasing together both a live album (*In Concert*) and *Precious Friend* (1981).

Hal Ashby directed the 1976 biopic *Bound for Glory* with David Carradine as Guthrie. An exhaustive biography, *Woody Guthrie, a Life*, by Joe Klein, was published in 1980. In 1988 **Willie Nelson**, Springsteen, Dylan and **U2** were among the artists who con-tributed their versions of Woody's songs to *Folkways: A Vision Shared*, a tribute album to Guthrie and kindred spirit Leadbelly. Even better was *'Til We Outnumber Them . . . The Songs of Woody Guthrie* (Righteous Babe Records, 2000) on which Springsteen ('Plane Wreck at Los Gatos') and others gave committed performances of Guthrie songs. The stand-out track is producer Ani DeFranco's melding of Guthrie's 'Do Re Mi' with the song of the same name written by **Rodgers and Hammerstein**.

Mermaid Avenue Vols 1 and *2* (Elektra, 1998, 2000) offered a timely reminder that Guthrie was more than a protest singer. On the pair of albums **Billy Bragg**, backed by new-country collective Wilco (an offshoot of **Uncle Tupelo**), performed a number of unreleased Guthrie originals to which he and the group had written music. The albums, which included such whimsicalities as 'Ingrid Bergman' and 'My Flying Saucer', and romantic outpourings such as 'Secrets of the Sea', confirmed that Guthrie's concerns were wider than just the political. A more traditional image of Guthrie was celebrated in **Steve Earle**'s powerful and moving 'Christmas Time in Washington' on his album *El Corazón* (1997).

BUDDY GUY
b. George Guy, 30 July 1936, Lettsworth, Louisiana, USA

The most successful and influential of the young singer-guitarists who stormed the Chicago blues establishment in the late fifties, Buddy Guy accommodated the early style of **B. B. King** to his own high-pitched, emotionally explosive singing and mercurial guitar-playing. After a long period without commercial success, Guy benefitted from the new interest in the blues of the early nineties.

With some local experience from Louisiana, Guy ventured on to the Chicago club scene in 1957, beginning, in the following year, what would prove to be a long association with Theresa's club. Also in 1958 he first recorded in his own name, for Artistic; two years later he signed with Chess and recorded a memorable début single, 'First Time I Met the Blues'.

In 1966 he began a partnership with the singer and harmonica-player **Junior Wells** that was to last for over two decades. The showmanship of their act secured them work on the college and festival circuits, and then further afield: in 1969 they toured Africa for the US State Department, and in 1970 they supported the **Rolling Stones** on a tour in Europe. They also recorded for Blue Thumb, Atco and Vanguard (Guy had previously been with Vanguard as a solo artist). The 1971 film *Chicago Blues* vividly captures their club performance.

Throughout the seventies and eighties Guy and Wells continued to work both at home and abroad, but Guy, at least, had no record-company support in the US at all: for more than a decade his new recordings were initiated by labels in Britain (JSP) and France (Black and Blue, Isabel), and it was only on JSP sets like *The Dollar Done Fell* (1980) that he recorded apart from Wells, revealing that his music, though still committed and exciting, was slow to progress, lacking the challenges of new playing partners or producers.

Guy's brother Phil, also a singer-guitarist, followed him to Chicago, and after working with him for a time eventually formed his own band. He toured in Europe and recorded several albums for British and French labels.

In the wake of the revival of interest in the blues after the success of **Robert Cray** and **John Lee Hooker**, Guy recorded the impressive *Damn Right I Got the Blues* (Silvertone, 1990) with support from **Eric Clapton**, **Jeff Beck** and Mark Knopfler of **Dire Straits**. A year later he recorded an equally well-received album with **Junior Wells**, *Alone and Acoustic* (Hightone). *Some Kind of Wonderful* (1993) included duets with **Bonnie Raitt** and Paul Rodgers, the former **Bad Company** singer. In 1994 Guy released the highly disciplined *Slippin' In*, a collection of songs associated with the likes of **Bobby Bland** and **Charles Brown** performed with real intensity.

CHARLIE HADEN

b. Charles Edward Haden, 6 August 1937, Shenandoah, Iowa, USA

The bassist with **Ornette Coleman**'s revolutionary free jazz quartet, Haden's later Liberation Music Orchestra provided an imaginative amalgam of music and politics.

Haden's parents were country singers who had a daily radio show. After studying music, he moved to Los Angeles where he played in the bands of Hampton Hawes, Art Pepper and Paul Bley. While with Bley, Haden first met **Don Cherry** and Coleman. In 1959 he moved to New York where he and drummer Billy Higgins joined Coleman, recording such epoch-making albums as *Change of the Century* (1959) and *Free Jazz* (1960). Following the earlier work of **Duke Ellington**'s Jimmy Blanton and Wilbur Ware (who played with **Thelonious Monk** and **Sonny Rollins**), Haden developed the melodic role of the bass.

After leaving Coleman's group, Haden embarked on a long series of collaborations with many of the key figures in the new jazz. As composer and leader, he recorded *Liberation Music Orchestra* (Impulse, 1969). This ambitious album consisted of **Carla Bley**'s arrangements of Spanish Civil War songs and Haden's own material such as 'Song to Che', a piece which caused Haden to be arrested in Portugal in 1971 after a performance in which he dedicated it to African freedom fighters. A second Liberation Music Orchestra album, *The Ballad of the Fallen* (ECM), was recorded in 1982 and included the Chilean resistance song 'A People United Will Never Be Defeated'.

In 1967 Haden rejoined Coleman, performing occasionally with him over the next decade and with Cherry formed Old and New Dreams, recording *Playing* (1983). He played with **Keith Jarrett** and **Archie Shepp** and cut *Closeness* (A&M, 1976), an album of duets with Alice Coltrane, Coleman and Jarrett. *Mágico* (ECM, 1979) and *Folk Songs* (1981) were the result of collective improvisations with Brazilian guitarist and pianist Egberto Gismondi and Norwegian saxophone-player Jan Garbarek. In 1983 he recorded *Rejoicing* (ECM) with electric guitarist **Pat Metheny** and in 1987 he released the forties-styled *Quartet West* (Verve) and toured with a new Liberation Music Orchestra featuring Dewey Redman on saxophone and playing music inspired by the political struggles of Central America. Haden recorded three more albums with Quartet West, successfully integrating sampled vocals and instruments on 1994's *Always Say Goodbye*, including the voice of actor Humphrey Bogart and the saxophone of **Coleman Hawkins**.

MERLE HAGGARD

b. 6 April 1937, Bakersfield, California, USA

A writer and performer of some complexity, Haggard is a giant of country music. He has been enormously successful with more than twenty-five country No. 1s. His musical breadth of vision is remarkable (as seen in his various tributes to the likes of **Jimmie Rodgers** and **Bob Wills**, which have established him as a custodian of country music's rich past). His assured songwriting resulted in a series of classics which include 'Sing Me Back Home', 'Today I Started Loving You Again', 'Hungry Eyes', 'Okie from Muskogee', 'The Bottle Let Me Down', 'I Threw Away the Rose' and 'If We Make It Through December'. Similarly, his husky, supple voice, which can be alternately smooth and strident, but always carrying a tremulous hint of despair and pain, enabled him to become a marvellous interpreter of songs. Lastly, Haggard was a profound influence on the country-rock of artists like **Gram Parsons** and many of the traditionally inclined country singers such as **George Strait** who emerged in the eighties and nineties.

Haggard's early life is the stuff of legend. He was born into a family of Dustbowl Oklahomans who migrated to California (like the characters of John Steinbeck's *Grapes of Wrath*) and lived in a converted boxcar. In 1946, when Haggard was nine, his father, an enthusiastic fiddler whose playing days were curtailed by a devout Christian wife, died. From the age of fourteen, Haggard roamed the Southwest, frequently being held in reformatories for various petty crimes, winding up in San Quentin in 1956 for armed robbery. Paroled in 1960, he returned to Bakersfield and, while working for his brother digging ditches, started playing country music. Deeply influenced by **Lefty Frizzell** (whose intonations can still be heard in his most recent recordings) and Wynn Stewart (whose backing band he joined in 1962), Haggard cut his first records for Lewis Talley's and Fuzzy Owen's Tally Records. His first country hit was Stewart's composition 'Sing Me a Sad Song' in 1963.

In 1965 he married Bonnie Owens (the ex-wife of Bakersfield's other major country star, **Buck Owens**) with whom he regularly recorded and toured. Later that year, following his success with Liz Anderson's

'(My Friends Are Gonna Be) Strangers' – he joined Capitol. His first country No. 1 was Anderson's 'I'm a Lonesome Fugitive' (1966). That song also fixed Haggard's image for the next few years as he wrote a' string of songs about being on the run and life in prison, including 'Branded Man', the powerful 'Sing Me Back Home' (1967) and 'Mama Tried' (1968), all country chart-toppers. At the same time Capitol's publicists for the first time 'revealed' Haggard's past. As a result, by the end of 1968, Haggard was a country superstar.

His early sound, like that of Buck Owens, was a straightforward mixture of honky-tonk and rockabilly, in which Ralph Mooney's strident pedal-steel-guitar work complemented the terse, staccato lead guitar of Roy Nicholls (or **James Burton**, who played lead on several early Haggard recordings). It was perfectly suited to songs of hard living and hard drinking. But Haggard's songwriting flowered and its range of topics widened to include reflections on the Okie migration to California ('Hungry Eyes', 1969, and the 1971 concept album, *Someday We'll Look Back*), wry observations and compassionate recollections ('Daddy Frank [the Guitar Man]' and 'Grandma Harp', both 1972) and simple, mature love songs ('Today I Started Loving You Again', 1968). With it, the Strangers' sound also developed so that, by the mid-seventies, horns were frequently to be heard on Haggard's recordings.

Another significant element was Haggard's series of tribute records, including *Same Train, a Different Time* (1969), a double-album salute to Jimmie Rodgers; *Land of Many Churches* (1972), a double-album of gospel hymns recorded with members of the **Carter Family**; and *I Love Dixie Blues* (1973). The most significant and affectionate of these tribute albums was *A Tribute to the Best Damn Fiddle Player in the World (or My Salute to Bob Wills)* (1970), for which Haggard learned to play the fiddle and which greatly helped rekindle interest in Wills and Western swing. He also supervised, sang and played fiddle on *For the Last Time* (UA, 1974), a double-album celebration of Wills. Taken as a group, these albums testify to Haggard's commitment to honouring and remembering the broad Southwest tradition of country music at a time when many Nashville country stars were foregoing their past in search of pop hits. At the same time, by looking back, Haggard forged a new synthesis that was both traditional and contemporary. Similarly, his songs with their directness and their realistic – rather than rose-tinted – looks at the past, echoed the best of traditional country songwriting.

In the early seventies, however, Haggard's keen ear for popular feeling briefly won him a completely different reputation outside the country market. His tongue-in-cheek recording of 'Okie from Muskogee'

(1969), a song defending the conservative virtues of small-town America against the vices of hippiedom, and the more directly patriotic 'The Fighting Side of Me' (1970) made him President Nixon's favourite country singer and an object of hate to many. Though he has refused to be drawn into making political statements, this populist edge has been a constant feature of Haggard's work. Many of his songs are about the lives of the blue-collar workers of America, such as the bleak 'If We Make It Through December', recorded in 1974 as recession briefly took a grip in America, and Haggard's only significant pop hit. The financial crisis in American farming in the eighties brought forth from Haggard the equally sombre 'Amber Waves of Grain' (1985) and a live album of the same title.

In 1977 Haggard left Capitol for MCA and in 1978 divorced Owens to marry Leona Williams, a back-up singer with the Strangers. Despite some success with MCA, including a tribute to **Elvis Presley**, *From Graceland to the Promised Land* (1977), and the superior *Serving 190 Proof* (1979), a collection of (mostly autobiographical) songs about troubled relationships, Haggard joined Epic in 1981 and published a bitter autobiography, *Sing Me Back Home*. Among his later records were duets with **George Jones**, *A Taste of Yesterday's Wine* (1982), and **Willie Nelson**, *Poncho and Lefty* (1983). Haggard's later solo albums were *A Friend in California* (1986), *Chill Factor* (1987), the bleak *5.01 Blues* (1990) and *Blue Jungle*. Despite being declared bankrupt in 1993, Haggard maintained a high profile as a live performer. He re-recorded his hits for Curb in 1993 but more important were Capitol's reissues of his classic albums. Ever loyal to Wills and Western Swing, he contributed to **Asleep at the Wheel**'s celebration of Wills, *Ride with Bob* (1999).

In 2000, in a surprise move, after quitting Curb in 1996 and being without a label for several years, Haggard signed with the Los Angeles-based Epitaph Records, which was better known for its punk acts, releasing *If I Could Only Fly* on the company's Anti label. Well received in alternative country circles, the mostly acoustic album was largely ignored by the country mainstream.

BILL HALEY
b. William John Clifton Haley, 6 July 1925, Highland Park, Michigan, USA, d. 9 February 1981, Harlingen, Texas

One of the founders of rock'n'roll, Haley contributed a strong cowboy and Western swing influence to the emerging music, while his group the Comets established many conventions of rock-group stagecraft. However, though his recording of 'Rock Around the Clock' was the biggest hit of the rock'n'roll era, selling more than 25 million copies, Haley possessed neither the writing ability of **Chuck Berry** nor the rebel-youth aura of **Elvis Presley** and he spent the last twenty years of his career repeating the hits of his *annus mirabilis*, 1955–6.

He grew up in Chester, Pennsylvania, and began his career as a yodelling cowboy, inspired by **Elton Britt**. In 1944 he replaced Kenny Roberts in Shorty Cook's Downhomers, touring the Midwest with the band for two years, before joining radio station WPWA in Chester as musical director. In 1948 he recorded country material, including versions of **Hank Williams**' 'Too Many Parties, Too Many Pals' and **Red Foley**'s 'Tennessee Border', for Jack Howard's Cowboy label in Philadelphia as Bill Haley and the Four Aces of Western Swing.

Next Haley formed the Saddlemen, who added a hard-edged rhythm to a mix of Western swing, yodel and polka. Billed as 'The Cowboy Jive Band', the group's singles for Keystone and Atlantic, with drums, showed Haley edging towards a new musical synthesis. This came closer with the 1951 cover of Jackie Brenston's 'Rocket 88', cut for Dave Miller's Holiday label. Brenston's original, which had topped the R&B charts on Chess earlier in the year, is often hailed as the first rock'n'roll record and was produced in Memphis by **Sam Phillips**, who later discovered Presley.

The following year Haley and the Saddlemen cut 'Rock the Joint', which showed the emergence of a distinctive style, featuring Haley's jive-talk, hipster lyrics and slap bass by Al Rex. Nevertheless the progress towards a potent mix of black and white music was slow. Thus, though in 1951 he recorded a fine version of **Memphis Slim**'s 'I'm Crying', 1952 saw him recording 'Jukebox Cannonball', a jive-talking version of **Roy Acuff**'s 'Wabash Cannonball', as well as his fiery version of Jimmy Preston's 'Rock the Joint' (a 1949 Gotham R&B hit). Finally, in 1953, Haley threw away his cowboy hat, changed the band's name to Comets and recorded 'Crazy Man Crazy', his first Top Twenty hit. The follow-up records, however, were dire versions of nursery rhymes ('Pat-a-Cake') or standards ('Chattanooga Choo-choo').

The catalysts for Haley's mature rock'n'roll sound were a new song and a new producer. In 1954 Haley's publisher James Myers signed him to Decca and presented him with 'Rock Around the Clock', a novelty tune written by Tin Pan Alley veteran Max Freedman (who also wrote 'Sioux City Sue') and Jimmy Dénight (Myers' pseudonym) that had been recorded unsuccessfully in 1952 by Sunny Dae. Decca's A&R chief, **Milt Gabler**, brought his experience with R&B jump-bandleader **Louis Jordan** to the recording session. His production was brighter and more emphatic than Haley's Essex recordings, building the tension on 'Rock Around the Clock' and arranging the rim shots from drummer Billy Guesack and the inspired guitar break from Danny Cedrone.

On its initial release, 'Rock' was only a minor hit, as was Haley's next single, a cover of **Joe Turner**'s rhythm and blues song 'Shake Rattle and Roll', for which Gabler bowdlerized the mildly risqué lyrics to ensure airplay on white radio stations. 'Dim, Dim the Lights' and the gimmicky 'Mambo Rock' provided further hits in 1954, but it was Hollywood that gave Haley's career the decisive push the following year. Appointed technical advisor to *The Blackboard Jungle* (1954) – a controversial drama about juvenile delinquency – Myers ensured that 'Rock Around the Clock' was used behind the opening credits.

Decca repromoted the single, which went to No. 1 in America, Britain, Australia and elsewhere. 'Rock Around the Clock' has since been recorded by more than a hundred artists and Haley's version re-entered the British charts three times, the last in 1974. Haley's career now took off, but without three of his original Comets who, dissatisfied with their financial position, left to form the Jodimars, recording unsuccessfully for Capitol. Bassist Al Rex remained from the original band and was joined by two former jazz players, guitarist Frank (Frannie) Beecher, who had played with **Benny Goodman**, and Rudy Pompilli, who had been voted best new saxophone player by *Downbeat* in 1953. Both were superb hot soloists, setting styles which were emulated by a generation of young musicians and they contributed to the Comets' athletic stage act, which involved Pompilli often playing lying on his back and Rex throwing his string bass around the stage.

There were ten hits in 1955–6. Some were in Haley's new jive-talking mould ('See You Later Alligator', 'Hot Dog Buddy Buddy', 'Razzle-Dazzle'), others were retreads of existing songs ('Saints Rock'n'Roll', 'Rockin' Through the Rye'). There was the film *Rock Around the Clock*, an innocuous showbiz tale which caused uproar in cinemas across the world when Haley and the Comets performed their hits. In addition, many of Haley's concerts were the scene of teenage hysteria and police brutality. The bemused Haley's response was to release the dire 'Teenager's Mother' and to star in *Don't Knock the Rock* with **Alan Freed** and **Little Richard**. In both he tried to explain that today's teenagers were only behaving as their elders had with the charleston or the jitterbug.

Haley was the first rock star to perform outside America. His 1957 world tour took in Australia, Jamaica and Britain and gave him a popularity there which long outlasted his success at home, where his star was on the wane. As the supply of new songs dried up, he cut ballads and novelties like the *Rockin' the Oldies* album with up-tempo versions of 'Dixie',

'Apple Blossom Time' and 'Rock Lomond'. His last hit was 'Skinny Minnie' in 1958, but he continued to tour for another decade, and made seven more visits to Europe.

With the golden age of rock over, Haley tried to revive his recording career by turning first to country with *Haley's Juke Box* (Warner Brothers, 1960) and then to the twist craze with the live *Twistin' Knights at the Round Table* (Roulette, 1962). His only success came in Mexico, where Haley lived for several years in the sixties and recorded for the Orfeon label. His final records were made for the Swedish Sonet label, who first cut two live albums after his 1968 European tour. Haley was assigned to producer Sam Charters, better known for his work with **Country Joe McDonald** and his blues field recordings. Cut in Nashville, *Rock Around the Country* (1971) included versions of **Kris Kristofferson**'s 'Me and Bobby McGee' and the **Creedence Clearwater Revival** song 'Who'll Stop the Rain', and was his best recording since his heyday.

But Haley was now in poor health and drinking heavily. Three further Sonet albums, concluding with *Everyone Can Rock and Roll* (1979), made in Muscle Shoals, were disappointing. His final tour was made to South Africa in 1980. He was posthumously inducted into the Rock and Roll Hall of Fame in 1987. Some of his former backing musicians occasionally played nostalgia concerts as Bill Haley's Comets. In 1990 Caprice International issued a previously unreleased fifties track, 'Football Rock'n'Roll'.

HALL AND OATES
Daryl Hall, b. Daryl Franklin Hohl, 11 October 1949, Pottstown, Pennsylvania, USA; John Oates, b. 7 April 1949, New York

Hall and Oates were the most successful blue-eyed soul singers of the eighties.

Hall had been lead singer of the Temptones, a white group of students from Philadelphia's Temple University inspired by the **Temptations**, who recorded 'Girl I Love You' (Arctic, 1966), produced by **Kenny Gamble**. He later cut solo records on Amy and Parallax for Len Barry's producer John Madara and formed soft-rock band Gulliver with Tim Moore, making one album for Elektra. In 1969 he began writing with Oates, who had previously sung with another Philadelphia-based soul band, the Masters.

With Hall on piano and Oates on acoustic guitar the duo began performing and a publishing deal with Chappell Music led to a recording contract with Atlantic. The **Arif Mardin**-produced *Whole Oates* (1972) was followed by *Abandoned Luncheonette*, which included the dramatic ballad 'She's Gone'. Initially only a minor hit for Hall and Oates, it was a No. 1 R&B single for Tavares in 1974 and a Top Ten record for Hall and Oates themselves when reissued in 1976. After the less successful *War Babies* (1974), produced by **Todd Rundgren**, they left Atlantic for RCA.

The eponymous début album for RCA included a glam-rock cover picture and a Top Ten US hit in 'Sara Smile'* (1976). In 1977 the dynamic 'Rich Girl'* gave Hall and Oates their first US No. 1, but *Beauty on a Back Street* (1977) and the David Foster-produced *Along the Red Ledge* (1978) were unexceptional, despite the presence of **George Harrison** on the latter. For *X-Static* (1979) a disco flavour was added, but Hall and Oates' career did not begin to pick up until *Voices* (1980), which they produced themselves and on which Sara and Janna Allen worked with them as songwriters.

The album's four hit singles included the duo's homage to their sixties predecessors in white-soul harmonies, the **Righteous Brothers**' 'You've Lost That Lovin' Feeling', and a further No. 1, 'Kiss on My List'*. The title track from *Private Eyes* (1981) also sold a million while 'I Can't Go for That (No Can Do)'* was No. 1 on both pop and R&B charts. Over the next four years (1982-5), Hall and Oates had ten more Top Twenty hits from the albums *HO* (1982), *Bim Bam Boom* (1984) and *Live at the Apollo* (1985), on which they were joined by two of their boyhood heroes, Eddie Kendricks and David Ruffin from the Temptations.

In 1986, amid reports of a split, Hall released his second solo album, *Three Hearts in the Happy Ending Machine* (the first, *Sacred Songs*, had been produced by **Robert Fripp** in 1976 but not released by RCA until 1980). Produced by the **Eurythmics**' Dave Stewart and with **Joni Mitchell** and **Bob Geldof** as guest vocalists, it included the hit single 'Dreamtime'. Hall and Oates returned to the studio for *Ooh Yeah!* (Arista, 1988), with its big hit 'Everything Your Heart Desires'. *Change of Season* (1990) saw the duo coasting. After contributing 'Philadelphia Freedom' to *Two Rooms*, the **Elton John**–Bernie Taupin tribute, they began work on a new album in 1992, but Hall subsequently decided to relaunch his solo career, signing to Epic and releasing the slick *Soul Alone* (1993). Now resident in London, Hall (with the Sounds of Blackness) recorded the theme song for the 1994 soccer World Cup, 'Gloryland', and *Can't Stop Dreaming* (1996). Next year the pair re-formed for *Marigold Sky*.

Other artists who successfully recorded Hall and Oates material have included **Diana Ross** ('Swept Away', 1984) and **Paul Young** ('Every Time You Go Away', 1985).

ADELAIDE HALL
b. 20 October 1909, Brooklyn, New York, USA, d. 7 November 1993, London, England

Not so much a jazz singer as a singer with jazz sympathies, often at her best with jazz accompanists, Adelaide Hall introduced some of the style of black American cabaret to thirties Europe, where she was prominent in the expatriate jazz community.

She made her theatrical début when still a schoolgirl in **Eubie Blake**'s *Shuffle Along* (1921). In 1927 she replaced Florence Mills, the recently deceased star of the show, in Lew Leslie's revue *Blackbirds*. She also made her recording début, providing the wordless vocal on **Duke Ellington**'s 'Creole Love Call' (Victor); its fame wrote her publicity for the rest of her career. As well as working with Ellington at the Cotton Club she appeared in the revue *Brown Buddies* (1930), and in 1931 made her cabaret début in Britain. (She had already visited Europe in the touring companies of *Chocolate Kiddies*, 1925, and *Blackbirds* of 1928.) Returning to the US, she worked with **Art Tatum** (1932–3) and Ellington again, then emigrated in 1936 to France, where she opened a Paris nightclub with her Trinidadian husband and manager Bert Hicks. She recorded there with the black American bandleader Willie Lewis, went on to tour Europe, and in 1938 resettled in London, where she quickly found work on the stage, in films and on records, with a series of attractive readings of contemporary popular songs (Decca, from 1939).

Hall's stage engagements continued into the fifties, both in London – *Kiss Me Kate* (1951), *Love from Judy* (1952) – and on Broadway, in *Jamaica* (1957, with **Lena Horne**). She continued to work in Britain, in clubs, at Ellington tribute concerts, and, since the film *Cotton Club* (1984), as a witness to the golden past of black American showbusiness.

HENRY HALL
b. 2 May 1898, Peckham, London, England, d. 29 October 1989, England

As director of the BBC Dance Orchestra, Hall was one of the most powerful figures in British popular music of the thirties.

The son of a blacksmith, Hall played in a Salvation Army band in his teens before studying piano at London's Trinity College and later at the Guildhall School of Music. After briefly working as a cinema pianist in the years immediately after the First World War, he led his first band at the Midland Hotel in Manchester, then became musical director of all the hotels owned by its proprietor, the London, Midland and Scottish railway company. He formed a band to play at the new hotel in the Scottish golfing resort of Gleneagles, where the BBC made an outside broadcast as early as 1924. He began his recording career in that year for British Columbia, switching to Decca in 1931, then back again to Columbia, for whom he made his best-known recordings, in 1932. In that same year, he succeeded **Jack Payne** as leader of the BBCDO. It was a controversial choice: the post seemed to call for a publicist, even a showman, yet it was filled by a man described as having 'the quiet dignity and unassuming demeanour of a family doctor or country solicitor' – in short, what the BBC would have believed impossible to find among London's Americanized dance-band musicians: an English gentleman.

In his new position, Hall gave the first dance-band broadcast from the newly built Broadcasting House in Portland Place. He also hosted *Henry Hall's Guest Night* which ran from 1934 until the fifties. The frequency and varied times of his broadcasts helped him to acquire a public drawn from several age- and interest-groups, though he seldom had much to offer to the fans of 'hot' jazz-influenced dance music. (He did, however, record some Benny Carter arrangements in 1936.) He had his greatest successes on record with novelties like 'Underneath the Arches' (1932), the refrain sung by **Flanagan and Allen**, the famous 'Teddy Bears' Picnic' (1932), which he sang himself, and 'The Music Goes 'Round and Around' (1936). In 1936, after starring in the film *Music Hath Charms* (1935), he directed the band on board the *Queen Mary*. The following year the BBCDO was disbanded and Hall took its members on tour under his own name, controversially removing from the band's repertoire all songs by Jewish composers for performances in Berlin in February 1938, before breaking up the band in summer 1939.

Among Hall's associates were Cyril Stapleton, who briefly played violin in the band before later becoming a prolific BBC bandleader himself, and the arrangers Sid Phillips, Van Phillips, Ronnie Munro, Arthur Lally and Paul Fenhoulet, who also led their own bands. During the Second World War, trombonist Fenhoulet led the Number One Balloon Centre Dance Orchestra, also known as the Skyrockets, one of the best of the forties hot dance bands.

After the war, Hall retired from bandleading to become a theatrical impresario and agent. From 1953 onwards, he was associated with the long-running television programme *Face the Music* and in 1955 published his autobiography *Here's to the Next Time*.

RICK HALL
b. 31 January 1932, Franklin County, Mississippi, USA

As an arranger, producer and studio owner, Hall was a key figure in the emergence of Southern soul in the sixties. In the seventies he was one of the most successful American producers.

The son of a sharecropper, Hall joined a local country band in Florence, Alabama, on his discharge from the army in 1957. He formed the Fairlanes in

1958 with **Billy Sherrill**, playing a mix of rock'n'roll and R&B and featuring the young **Dan Penn** as vocalist. With businessman Tom Stafford, Hall helped to establish Muscle Shoals as a production centre, setting up his own Fame studios in 1961, after disagreements with Sherrill (who went to Nashville). His first independent production was **Arthur Alexander**'s oft-covered 'You'd Better Move on' (1962) which he leased to Dot, before in 1964 setting up the Fame label with backing from Vee-Jay.

Fame's first release was the influential Top Twenty hit 'Steal Away' by Jimmy Hughes, which was successfully revived by **Johnnie Taylor** in 1970. The song was the first of a series of 'cheating songs' – a subgenre already well established in country music – by Southern soul performers that reached its climax with **James Carr**'s original recording of Penn and Spooner Oldham's 'Dark End of the Street' in 1967. 1964 also saw **Joe Tex** score his first million-seller with 'Hold What You've Got', produced by his manager, Buddy Killen, at Fame.

When Vee-Jay went bankrupt in 1965, the Fame label switched distribution to Atlantic, which for two years used the studio as an alternative to Stax's Memphis studio for its acts. Among the session musicians who regularly worked for Hall were Jimmy Johnson, Norbert Putnam, Albert Lowe, David Hood, Roger Hawkins, Jerry Corrigan, Spooner Oldham, David Briggs, **Chips Moman**, Eddie Hinton, Duane Allman of the **Allman Brothers Band**, Barry Beckett, Tommy Cogbill and Tommy Couch (who later set up the Malaco label along similar lines). And among those who recorded there after Hall helped place **Percy Sledge**'s 'When a Man Loves a Woman' (not recorded at Fame) with Atlantic, were **Wilson Pickett** ('Land of a Thousand Dances', '634-5789' and 'Hey Jude') and **Aretha Franklin** ('Do Right Woman'). When Moman and Cogbill left to set up their own AGP studios and Hall and Atlantic's **Jerry Wexler** fell out in 1968, Hall recorded **Etta James** for Chess in 1969, and joined forces with Capitol. He continued to produce **Clarence Carter**'s sixties hits (including 'Slip Away' and 'Patches') for Atlantic. Later that year Beckett, Hood and Johnson formed their own Muscle Shoals studio and Hall found a new rhythm section once more.

Hall wound up Fame Records in 1974, but continued to produce from his Fame studios. Throughout the seventies he had hit records with a variety of artists including **Bobbie Gentry**, **Paul Anka** ('[You're] Having My Baby'), the **Osmonds** ('One Bad Apple'), **Mac Davis** ('Don't Get Hooked on Me'), Liza Minnelli, **Tom Jones** and **Sammy Davis Jnr**.

TOM T. HALL
b. 25 May 1936, Olive Hill, Kentucky, USA

Regarded by many as one of country music's most observant songwriters, Hall's best work, which includes the bitter-sweet 'Trip to Hyden' and the moving 'The Year That Clayton Delaney Died' (1971), did much to revive the story-song in the seventies.

A former bluegrass musician and disc-jockey, Hall started writing songs when stationed in Germany during his military service in the late fifties. His first hit was 'D.J. for a Day', which reached the country Top Ten when recorded by cajun artist Jimmy C. Newman (Decca, 1963), after which Hall moved to Nashville. There he wrote some of the first songs about the Vietnam war, notably the patriotic 'Hello Vietnam' (Johnny Wright, Decca, 1965) and 'Mama, Tell Them What We're Fighting for' (**Dave Dudley**, 1965), before in 1967 he was signed to Mercury as a recording artist by Jerry Kennedy.

Hall's first great success came in 1968 when Jeannie C. Riley's recording of 'Harper Valley P.T.A.' (Plantation) topped the American charts and sold a million copies. Based on a true incident, the song about American small-town hypocrisy went one better than **Bobbie Gentry**'s 'Ode to Billie Joe' (1967) in prompting a film (1980) and a teleseries (1982), both starring Barbara Eden. Riley fared less well and, after a string of lesser country hits, became a born-again Christian in 1972.

Hall's own first country hit was the atmospheric 'Ballad of Forty Dollars' (1968), which was followed by several minor hits and two classic albums, *In Search of a Song* (1971), which included 'Clayton Delaney' and 'Hyden', and the equally bleak 'Feb 27, '71' and *The Storyteller* (1973), which included probably his best-known composition, 'Old Dogs, Children and Watermelon Wine'. Though on occasion the philosophizing that underpins these and other similar narratives seems naive, the observations they proceed from are often precise and unexpectedly revealing. In describing his philosophy of songwriting, Hall has said – in words that could almost paraphrase Agatha Christie's Miss Marple – 'Everything that has ever happened anywhere has happened at some time or another in Olive Hill [his home town]', and the rumour, gossip, and folklore of Middle America have continued to contribute to both the evocative and, occasionally, bathetic elements in his work.

In the seventies Hall also discovered and championed the Mexican-American country performer Johnny Rodriguez, whose first hit was 'Pass Me By' (Mercury, 1973), written by Hall's brother Hilton. Hall's 1976 bluegrass album, *The Magnificent Music Machine* included a revival of **Manfred Mann**'s 1968 hit 'Fox on the Run', a song that has become a perennial favourite with bluegrass groups. In 1977 Hall moved to RCA where he had less success. More successful were his books, *How I Write the Songs, How*

You Can and *The Storyteller's Nashville*, and the television show *Pop Goes the Country*, which he presented. On rejoining Mercury and his regular producer Jerry Kennedy, his career recovered with such characteristic pieces as 'Everything from Jesus to Jack Daniels' (1983) and 'P.S. I Love You' (1985). For the most part, however, Hall in the late eighties and nineties concentrated on writing stories and novels. Mercury collected together his best material in 1988 on *The Essential Tom T. Hall*, and the same year he released the collection *Country Songs for Kids*. *Homegrown* (1997), which featured the tribute song 'Bill Monroe for Breakfast', was a strong return to form.

WENDELL HALL
b. 23 August 1896, St George, Kansas, USA, d. 2 April 1969, Alabama

Hall earned vaudeville immortality in the early twenties with his nonsense song 'It Ain't Gonna Rain No Mo'', which was based on an old country dance tune. Merrily strumming his ukulele, he was a clear transatlantic forerunner of **George Formby**.

In the wake of his hit – which he recorded in the same month, October 1923, for Victor, Gennett and Edison – he worked on WLS, Chicago, and other radio stations, eventually directing the show *Majestic Theater of the Air* (1929). He later worked on the *Fitch Band Wagon* (1932–5) and *Gillette's Community Sing* (1936–7), the latter with comedian Milton Berle. Known as 'The Red-Headed Music Maker', the title of his 1924 Victor hit, Hall bowed out of recordings with a 1933 Bluebird date, which included 'New It Ain't Gonna Ran No Mo''– Part 3', and retired from show-business to become an advertising executive. Prior to that he recorded a series of duets with **Carson Robison**, including 'Whistling the Blues Away' (1924) and 'I'm Telling the Birds, I'm Telling the Bees (How I Love You)' (Brunswick, 1927).

JOHNNY HALLYDAY
b. Jean-Philippe Smets, 15 June 1943, Paris, France

France's only real rock'n'roll star, though he never had hits in either America or the UK, Hallyday has sold over 15 million records in Europe and built a lengthy career on what seemed at first to be shaky foundations as an interpreter of and guide to American popular culture.

Brought up by his aunt and American uncle who had a song-and-dance act, Hallyday travelled the world with them. In 1958 his blonde sideburns, **Elvis Presley**-like gyrations and reedy, wailing vocals with a decidedly melodramatic hiccup, led to France's first rock'n'roll riots and brought down the wrath of the establishment on his head, as much for his espousal

of an American-based culture as for his music. Other French rockers, notably Eddie Mitchell et les Chausettes Noires, had tapped into rock'n'roll before him, but it was Hallyday who made its rebellious image his own. Billed as the French Elvis and backed by the Golden Stars, Hallyday covered a wide variety of rock'n'roll hits in French, a practice generally known as 'ye-ye', with a decided penchant for black recordings. These included 'Roll over Beethoven' and 'Johnny B. Goode' (**Chuck Berry**), 'Tutti Frutti' and 'Long Tall Sally' (**Little Richard**), 'I'm Walkin'' (**Fats Domino**) – which Hallyday retitled 'Je Veux Me Promener' – and the **Everly Brothers**' 'Cathy's Clown', renamed 'Le P'tit Clown de ton Coeur'. Their success inspired a host of imitators.

In 1961 Hallyday had his only million-seller, a French-language version of **Chubby Checker**'s 'Let's Twist Again', 'Viens Danser le Twist' (Philips). Unlike so many rock'n'rollers who were swept away by **The Beatles**, Hallyday survived by becoming a living juke-box, performing songs from the whole spectrum of rock, singing in French the hits of **Bobby Vinton**, **Brian Hyland**, Presley, **Buddy Holly** and the **Ronettes** in the same performance. But his records, of which *Johnny Hallyday Sings America's Rockin' Hits* (1962) is a representative example, were far better than most cover-versions. One reason for this was that, from the mid-sixties on, Hallyday often recorded with English musicians of the calibre of Jimmy Page and **Peter Frampton**.

Though Hallyday never compromised his rebellious image, by the late sixties his popularity temporarily dipped with the rise of underground progressive music. He responded in the seventies by becoming a singer-songwriter, adapting material by writers like **Kris Kirstofferson**, writing his own songs and singing those American songwriter Mort Shuman (of **Pomus and Shuman**) wrote specifically for him. In the wake of **The Who**'s *Tommy* he recorded his own rock opera, *Hamlet*, as well continuing to record versions of rock classics, including the **Rolling Stones**' 'Honky Tonk Woman' and 'House of the Rising Sun', his biggest hit of the period which he took as his theme song.

In the eighties Hallyday had further hits with tributes to **Charlie Parker** ('Charlie Connais Pas') and playwright Tennessee Williams ('Quelquechose de Tennessee') and, in 1984, he travelled to Nashville to record an album on which he was supported by **Carl Perkins**, Tony Joe White and **Emmylou Harris**. That same year, he also began an acting career with an appearance in Jean-Luc Godard's *Détective* (1985). In 1986 he starred in the English-language science-fiction film, *The End of the Lion*, and the following year had a hit with a duet with English singer Carmel.

In 1993 Hallyday celebrated his fortieth anniversary

in showbusiness with ten shows at the Paris Olympia. PolyGram also issued a 25-CD set of his complete recordings for the label. *Lonely Town* (1994) was his first English-language album. Hallyday continued recording throughout the nineties, regularly finding European chart success with albums like *Sang Pour Sang* (Mercury, 1999). A mark of both his prodigious output and continued popularity was that in June 2000 Hallyday had nineteen titles in the seventy-five bestselling albums in France. Hallyday's son, David, is also a rock singer and leader of Blind Fish, who recorded *2000 BBF* (Scotti Bros, 1994).

GEORGE HAMILTON IV
b. 19 July 1937, Matthews, North Carolina, USA

Briefly a would-be rock'n'roller and teen-idol in the fifties, in the sixties Hamilton played a gentle, folky form of country and became the 'International Ambassador of Country Music'.

A veteran of numerous country radio shows by his teens, after appearing regularly on *Arthur Godfrey's Talent Scouts*, Hamilton turned to pop in 1956. He had an immediate million-seller with the **John D. Loudermilk** composition 'A Rose and a Babe Ruth' (ABC-Paramount) and a further one in 1958 with 'Why Don't They Understand'. Written by British writers Jack Fishman and Joe 'Mr Piano' Henderson, 'Understand' was typical of the songs of teenage *angst* of the time. His other hits of the period included 'Only One Love' (1957), 'Now and for Always' and 'I Know Where I'm Going' (both 1958). This last, which was his biggest hit in Britain, saw Hamilton returning to his folk-country roots. This move was consolidated by a label change to RCA in 1961.

His biggest hit on RCA was 'Abilene' (1963), but more significant was the growing folkiness of his brand of country music which led him to record songs by the Canadian **Gordon Lightfoot** (including 'Steel Rail Blues' and 'Early Morning Rain', both country hits for Hamilton in 1966). Hamilton toured Canada extensively, recording an album of Canadian songs, *Canadian Pacific* (1969), and making regular TV appearances there. This led to him becoming a front man on television shows featuring country music in both Canada and Britain throughout the seventies and eighties. In 1974 he was the first country artist to tour the Soviet Union and in 1978 he joined ABC, since when he has been most active in Christian music causes. His 1989 album *American Country Gothic* (Conifer) included a pair of Loudermilk songs produced by **Chet Atkins**. From the eighties onwards he regularly worked with his son, with whom he recorded *Country Classics* (1992). In 1994 he appeared in London with Sandy Kelly in *Patsy*, a musical tribute to **Patsy Cline**.

ROY HAMILTON
b. 16 April 1929, Leesburg, Georgia, USA, d. 20 July 1969

Hamilton was a leading rhythm and blues singer of the fifties, with a gospel-inflected style that made him one of the precursors of soul music.

As a teenager, his work as lead singer of Jersey City's' Searchlight Gospel Singers brought him a solo contract with Epic. Unusually, Hamilton's first R&B No. 1 was a Broadway show song, **Rodgers and Hammerstein**'s 'You'll Never Walk Alone' (1954), with which **Gerry and the Pacemakers** scored a pop hit a decade later. The tune suited his big, almost operatic, voice as did another song from *Carousel*, 'If I Loved You'.

The string of hits which made Hamilton a top attraction on the R&B circuit in 1954–5 also included 'Hurt', a revival of Robin's and Rainger's 1937 composition 'Ebb Tide', and the film theme 'Unchained Melody'. While Hamilton's version was the top R&B record of 1955 and a Top Ten pop hit, the song also provided hits for **Al Hibbler** and (in Britain) Jimmy Young. There were also successful instrumental versions by **Les Baxter** and **Liberace**.

Hamilton's more interesting work emphasized his gospel roots. 'Don't Let Go' was a Top Twenty hit in 1958, followed by a version of **Johnny Ace**'s 'Pledging My Love' and 'I Need Your Lovin''. His last hits for Epic came in 1961 with the original version of 'You Can Have Her', revived by Sam Neely in 1974, and 'You're Gonna Need Magic'.

He went on to record for MGM, RCA and AGP before his premature death from a heart attack.

MARVIN HAMLISCH
b. 2 June 1944, New York, USA

A composer, pianist and arranger, Hamlisch composed the score for *The Sting* (1973), which was largely responsible for a revival of interest in ragtime.

At seven, Hamlisch became the youngest ever student at the Juilliard School of Music. As a teenager, he turned to songwriting. 'Travelin' Man' was recorded by Liza Minnelli, and he had his first hit with **Lesley Gore**'s version of 'Sunshine, Lollipops and Roses' (1965).

In 1968 Hamlisch moved to Hollywood, undertaking the scores for films such as *The Swimmer* (1968), *Save the Tiger* (1972), and Woody Allen's *Take the Money and Run* (1969) and *Bananas* (1971). He received an Oscar nomination in 1971 for 'Life Is What You Make It', with lyrics by **Johnny Mercer**, and three years later won Oscars for his contributions to two films: his adaptation of **Scott Joplin** ragtime material for *The Sting* and the title song for *The Way We Were*, co-written with Marilyn and Alan Bergman. Both **Barbra Streisand** and **Gladys Knight and the Pips** had hits with the latter, while Hamlisch himself sold a million with 'The Entertainer' from *The Sting* (MCA, 1974).

With a new lyricist, **Carole Bayer Sager**, Hamlisch turned out further theme songs. **Carly Simon** recorded 'Nobody Does It Better' from the 1977 James Bond feature *The Spy Who Loved Me*, while 'If You Remember Me' from *The Champ* was a 1979 hit for ex-**Manfred Mann** vocalist Chris Thompson.

In the seventies he also wrote two stage musicals. The award-winning *A Chorus Line* (1975) was later filmed and included the ballad 'What I Did for Love', which was recorded by **Johnny Mathis**, **Shirley Bassey**, **Tony Bennett**, and many others. The show was filmed in 1985. With Neil Simon, he devised *They're Playing Our Song* (1979), a story about songwriters and based on his relationship with Bayer Sager. The score included their composition 'If He Really Knew Me'.

Among Hamlisch's Hollywood commissions in the eighties were the scores for *Sophie's Choice* (1982), *A Chorus Line* (1985), *Three Men and a Baby* (1987) and *January Man* (1989). He later acted as musical director for Barbra Streisand and co-wrote 'Ordinary Miracles' (1993) for her.

HAMMER
b. Stanley Burrell, 30 March 1962, Oakland, California, USA

One of the first rappers of the eighties to find crossover success, Hammer's soul revue style shows were soon outmoded by younger 'gangsta' rappers.

The youngest of seven children of a club manager, Hammer studied communications at college and was briefly a professional baseball player (where he acquired the nickname Hammer) before joining the US navy. After leaving the service in 1986 he formed a religious rap duo, the Holy Ghost Boys, and his own record label, Bustin'.

As MC Hammer, he issued 'Feel My Power' in 1987. A local hit, the track led to a contract with Capitol, who released the five-track *Let's Get It Started* (1988). The album was produced by Felton Pilate, a former member of the group Con-Funk-Shun, who would become Hammer's musical director and co-writer. *Let's Get It Started* topped the R&B charts and was followed by the multi-million-selling *Please Hammer Don't Hurt 'Em* (1988), which included Hammer's best-known track, 'U Can't Touch This'. The track used samples from the 1977 **Rick James** hit 'Super Freak' and elsewhere Hammer sampled music by **Queen** and **James Brown**. The album also included an undistinguished version of the **Chi-Lites**' soul ballad 'Have You Seen Her?' which was a Top Ten hit in both the US and UK.

Hammer's spectacular live performances in his trademark ultra-baggy trousers contributed to the success of the album, which sold nearly 20 million copies worldwide. His later work has not been able to match the impact of *Please Hammer Don't Hurt 'Em*. In 1991 he released *Too Legit to Quit*, on which he seemed to be moving away from samples-based rap towards mainstream R&B. In addition to his own compositions, it included a new version of Timmy Thomas' 1973 hit 'Why Can't We Live Together?' and the gospel song 'Do Not Pass Me By'.

A consummate businessman, he licensed his image to a television company which produced the cartoon series *Hammerman* and to Mattel for a Hammer doll. He was briefly the manager of heavyweight boxing champion Evander Holyfield before returning to the recording studio. In 1994 he moved to Giant Records for *The Funky Headhunter*, on which Hammer adopted a more sullen rapping style with samples from the Gap Band, **Prince** and **George Clinton** and guest appearances from **Dr Dre** of NWA and Snoop Doggy Dogg's Dogg Pound. Later recordings included the minor *Inside Out* (1995) and *Family Affair* (1997).

JOHN HAMMOND
b. 15 December 1910, New York, USA, d. July 1987, New York

One of America's leading record producers and talent scouts, Hammond played a key role in the careers of artists as varied as **Benny Goodman** and **Bob Dylan**.

From a wealthy family, Hammond dropped out of Yale to pursue his passion for jazz. In 1931 he became a columnist for British journals *The Gramophone* and *Melody Maker* and the following year financed a recording by pianist Garland Wilson. Throughout the thirties he was active as a reviewer, promoter and producer. Among those whose careers were advanced by Hammond were **Billie Holiday**, **Teddy Wilson**, **Count Basie**, **Charlie Christian** and Goodman. He was responsible for both Wilson and Christian joining Goodman's band, making it the first racially integrated jazz group, and he produced Holiday's first session where she sang with Goodman's band.

In a period of severe depression in the record business Hammond was hired by English Columbia to produce jazz recordings for the European collectors' market. He cut tracks by **Fletcher Henderson** and brought **Bessie Smith** back into the studio to cut 'Gimme a Pigfoot and a Bottle of Beer' (Columbia, 1933). During a brief spell working for **Irving Mills** he produced Red Norvo, **Artie Shaw** and **Mildred Bailey**. In 1938 and 1939 Hammond organized the 'Spirituals to Swing' concerts, at New York's Carnegie Hall. His purpose was to showcase every variety of black music and those appearing included the **Golden Gate Quartet**, Sonny Terry, **Sidney Bechet**, **Rosetta Tharpe**, **Big**

Bill Broonzy, Basie, Christian and Goodman.

Hammond acted as Assistant Director of Popular Recording at Columbia from 1939 until he entered the army in 1943. As well as many Goodman records, he supervised sessions by **Paul Robeson** and **Lena Horne**. In 1946 he was hired by Keynote Records where he worked with **Mitch Miller**. Hammond produced classical recordings of Igor Stravinsky conducting his own work, and Miller playing oboe concerti. When the company merged with Mercury, Hammond served briefly as Vice-President of the joint company. With club-owner George Wein and jazz historian Marshall Stearns, Hammond was one of the founders of the Newport Jazz Festival in 1954, serving on its board until 1970.

Vanguard, then a small classical label, brought in Hammond to develop a popular-music catalogue in 1953. Never sympathetic to bebop, he took the opportunity to record many mainstream jazz performers like **Jimmy Rushing**, Basie and Buck Clayton. Vanguard also issued albums of the 'Spirituals to Swing' concerts in 1958, shortly before Hammond rejoined Columbia.

Working initially on a reissue programme that featured **Robert Johnson** and Bessie Smith, Hammond also brought leading folk artists such as **Pete Seeger**, **Carolyn Hester**, and Dylan to the company. The poor sales of Dylan's early albums made him known as 'Hammond's Folly' at Columbia, but Hammond's later signings included **Leonard Cohen**, **George Benson** and **Bruce Springsteen**. He continued to produce veteran artists like **Eubie Blake** and blues singer Alberta Hunter. Consistently radical in his championing of black artists, Hammond covered the infamous Scottsboro Boys trial for *New Republic* in 1932 and served for many years on the board of the National Association for the Advancement of Colored People (NAACP).

His son John Paul Hammond (*b. 13 November 1943, New York*) was a leading white blues singer, recording nearly twenty albums for labels including Vanguard, Atlantic, Columbia, Capricorn and Rounder. The most successful was *Triumvirate* (Columbia, 1973), with **Dr John** and **Mike Bloomfield**. In 1970 he wrote and performed the soundtrack for Arthur Penn's *Little Big Man*. In 1992 he signed to Virgin Records' Pointblank label for the spirited *Got Live If You Want It*.

In 1977 Hammond published an autobiography, *John Hammond on Record*, co-written with Irving Townshend.

LIONEL HAMPTON
b. 12 April 1909, Louisville, Kentucky, USA

A leading exponent of the vibraphone, Hampton led successful big bands which combined swing rhythms with hard-driving R&B soloists.

He first played drums in the Chicago Defender Newsboys Band and learned vibes from percussionist Jimmy Bertrand. After playing with a number of Chicago groups, he moved to the West Coast in 1927, recording with Paul Howard's band for RCA in 1929, making his first disc as a singer on 'Moonlight Blues'. The following year he backed **Louis Armstrong** as a member of Les Hite's band. Hampton appeared as a masked drummer in the film *Pennies from Heaven* (1936). He briefly led his own band before a jam session led to an invitation to join **Benny Goodman**'s quartet in 1936. During his four years with Goodman, Hampton also cut records under his own name for RCA. For these he gathered together many of the leading jazz soloists of the period, including **Dizzy Gillespie**, **Charlie Christian** and **Coleman Hawkins**. These sides were some of the finest jazz recordings of the swing era.

The Hampton big band was founded in 1940 and for the next five decades he led similar groups. Hampton's extrovert showmanship and the raucous sax of **Illinois Jacquet** characterized the band's first and most famous recording, 'Flying Home' (Decca, 1942), co-written by Hampton and Goodman. His other hits included 'Hey! Ba-Ba-Re-Bop' (1945) and a 1949 version of Johnny Lee Wills' (brother of **Bob Wills**') 'Rag Mop', which was also a million-seller for the **Ames Brothers**. Among the booting horn players recruited by Hampton were **Earl Bostic**, Johnny Griffin and Arnett Cobb. Other members of the band included **Dinah Washington**, **Quincy Jones**, **Charles Mingus**, Johnny Griffin and **Wes Montgomery**.

In the fifties Hampton recorded for **Norman Granz**'s Clef and Norgran labels. He cut several records with **Oscar Peterson** and played some memorable sessions with Mezz Mezzrow in Paris in 1953. From the fifties he made frequent tours of Europe and Japan. In the early sixties he moved to Glad-Hamp, a label organized by his wife and manager Gladyse. In 1982 Teldec recorded a series of boogie-woogie duets between Hampton and the young German pianist Axel Zwingenberger. A recording of a '50th Anniversary Concert' held in Carnegie Hall was released on Carosella in 1983.

From the late seventies Hampton divided his time between performing and his growing business interests in music publishing and land development. In the mid-eighties his band included Doug Miller (tenor sax) and Richard Price (trumpet). During the nineties an annual Lionel Hampton Jazz Festival for young musicians was held at the University of Idaho.

HERBIE HANCOCK
b. 12 April 1940, Chicago, Illinois, USA

A versatile keyboards player, Hancock established his

reputation in **Miles Davis**'s group before moving on to jazz-rock and funk-rap fusion styles.

While studying engineering, Hancock played with trumpeter Donald Byrd and cut a solo album for Blue Note (*Takin' Off*, 1963). It included the soul-flavoured 'Watermelon Man', which became a hit single for **Mongo Santamaria**. For most of the sixties he played acoustic piano with Davis and a younger generation of sidemen, including Wayne Shorter, **Tony Williams** and **John McLaughlin**. Hancock contributed to such albums as *E. S. P.* (1965), *Miles Smiles* (1966) and *Filles de Kilimanjaro* (1968).

At the same time, he also pursued a solo recording career, releasing six Blue Note albums plus the soundtrack to Antonioni's *Blow Up* (MGM, 1968) before leaving Davis in 1968. Now recording with a sextet and with more expansive arrangements, showing his study of **Gil Evans**, Bartók and Stravinsky, Hancock released *Mwandishi* (Warners, 1971) and *Sextant* (Columbia, 1972) before *Headhunters* (Columbia, 1973) became his first bestseller. Dominated by a heavy R&B bass line, a revisited 'Watermelon Man' and the fifteen-minute 'Chameleon', the album established Hancock as a leading exponent of jazz-rock. *Thrust* (1974) and the soundtrack album *Death Wish* (1975) were in a similar vein. In 1976 Hancock formed VSOP with Davis alumni Ron Carter, Shorter and Williams plus trumpeter Freddie Hubbard. The group toured and recorded, playing sixties styles of small-group jazz. VSOP II, founded in 1984, included the brothers Branford and **Wynton Marsalis**.

Hancock also recorded a highly praised series of piano duets with **Chick Corea** for Polydor in 1979 but he made a greater impact with a series of disco records beginning with 'I Thought It Was You' from *Sunlight* (Columbia, 1978). A British Top Twenty hit, it featured a vocoder voice synthesizer, as did 'You Bet Your Love' (1979). In 1983 Hancock collaborated with New York electro-funk group Material on 'Rockit', another British hit. The album *Future Shock* (1983) also featured Sly Dunbar of **Sly and Robbie** and scratch artist Grand Mixer DST on turntables and vocals.

His next projects were contrasting. In 1985 he collaborated on *Village Life* with Foday Musa Soso, while he won an Oscar in 1987 for his soundtrack to *Round Midnight*, Bertrand Tavernier's film of the Paris jazz milieu of the fifties which starred Dexter Gordon.

Among his later recordings were *Perfect Funk* (1988) with Bootsy Collins and *A Tribute to Miles Davis* (Qwest, 1994) with Shorter and Tony Williams. *New Standard* (Verve, 1995) was his best record for some time. A collection of versions of songs by the likes of **The Beatles**, **Prince** and **Paul Simon**, the familiarity of the material gave Hancock (on acoustic piano) and his sidemen, who included Michael Brecker, licence to stretch out.

W. C. HANDY
b. William Christopher Handy, 16 November 1873, Florence, Alabama, USA, d. 28 March 1958, New York

Handy, the author of 'St Louis Blues' (1914) – the most recorded popular song of the twentieth century – was known as 'The Father of the Blues'. Though it is doubtful whether he wrote most of the pieces he copyrighted, Handy was the first person to publish jazz compositions, thereby giving structure and discipline to the emerging blues form. As critic Isaac Goldberg put it, Handy 'is not the inventor of the genre: he is its Moses, not its Jehovah. It was he who, first of musicians, codified the new spirit in African music and set it forth upon its conquest of the North.'

The son of a preacher, Handy became a cornet player in brass bands in Alabama, and was musical director of Mahara's Minstrels from 1896 to 1903. He studied composition and taught at Huntsville College. After leaving the minstrel show, Handy formed a nine-piece band and toured the Southern states.

Handy first heard blues music in rural Mississippi in the 1890s, and his later compositions were in the main based on this folk material. However, his first published work, 'Memphis Blues' (1912), was in fact a dance tune. Originally an electioneering song, 'Mr Crump', it was retitled to take advantage of the growing 'blues' craze. Handy later wrote 'Beale Street Blues', 'Yellow Dog Blues', 'St Louis Blues', and many others. 'St Louis' soon became a standard, and was recorded by dance and military bands as well as the leading blues singers of the era. In 1929 Handy and Kenneth W. Adams scripted a 17-minute dramatization of the song which starred **Bessie Smith** and was filmed by RCA Phototone.

Though he recorded intermittently between 1917 and 1945, Handy was most influential as a writer and publisher. With his partner Harry Pace, he moved to New York in 1918 and set up a successful music-publishing business, learning from the fact that he had earlier sold the rights to 'St Louis Blues' for $50. In 1921 Pace formed Black Swan, the first black-owned record company. With **Fletcher Henderson** as recording director, the label's earliest hits were city blues by **Ethel Waters** (the first woman to record 'St Louis Blues') but in 1924 the company was swallowed up by Paramount.

One of Handy's most significant contributions to an emergent black cultural consciousness was the publication of his *Blues: An Anthology* (1926), which had a great impact on the artists of the Harlem Renaissance. He also compiled a *Book of Negro Spirituals* (1939).

An eye disease left him totally blind in the twenties and he performed only occasionally thereafter. His sixty-fifth birthday was celebrated with a Carnegie Hall concert and in 1939 Handy made his last recordings with New Orleans clarinettist Edmond Hall. He published an autobiography, *Father of the Blues*, in 1941 and the **Nat 'King' Cole** film *St Louis Blues* (1958) was based on Handy's life. In 1969 the United States government commemorated Handy by issuing a postage stamp.

HANSON
Isaac Hanson, b. 17 November 1980, Tulsa, Oklahoma, USA; Taylor Hanson, b. 14 March 1983, Tulsa; Zachary Hanson, b. 22 October 1985, Tulsa

A sibling trio reared on rock and roll, Hanson began writing and performing in 1992 before rising to international superstardom with their 'MmmBop' single, gaining acclaim from teen-pop audiences and rock critics alike.

The Hanson brothers were raised in the oil-mining town of Tulsa before their father's job took them to Ecuador, Venezuela and Trinidad, where they began to discover the likes of the **Beach Boys**, **Chuck Berry** and **Bobby Darin** from a series of Time/Life compilations. Returning to the US they made two albums and began to perform live, with Isaac playing guitar, Taylor on keyboards and Zac on drums, but failed to find an audience until the release of 'MmmBop', from their major label début, *Middle of Nowhere* (Mercury, 1997)*, which was a huge success first in the US and then across Europe and Asia. The album spawned two further hit singles, 'Where's the Love' and 'I Will Come to You', and became one of the year's bestsellers.

Hanson spent much of the next year touring to promote *Middle of Nowhere*. In the wake of that album's success Mercury issued a pair of earlier recordings: *Three Car Garage: The Independent Recordings '95–'96* and *Live from Albertane* (1998), recorded in Seattle earlier in 1997.

The group's official follow-up album, *This Time Around*, was issued in 2000. An assured piece of guitar-driven pop, it included the hit single 'If Only' and a number of catchy tracks, such as 'Save Me' and 'Runaway Run'. As part of the promotion of the new album the group also demonstrated its commercial knowingness, offering fans a **David Bowie**-style subscriber-based Internet service, Hanson.net.

HAPPY MONDAYS
Shaun Ryder, b. 23 August 1962, Little Hulton, Lancashire, England; Paul Ryder, b. 24 April 1964, Manchester; Gary Whelan, b. 12 February 1966, Manchester; Mark Day, b. 29 December 1961, Manchester; Paul Davis, b. 7 March 1966; Mark 'Bez' Berry, b. 18 April 1964, Manchester

The epitome of the 'Madchester' scene of the late eighties, the Happy Mondays concocted dance music from an incongruous variety of sources. However, they owed their popularity as much to their 'acid house' image as to their musical imagination.

Taking their name from 'Blue Monday' by local heroes **New Order**, the group formed in 1984. Shaun Ryder was the singer with his brother Paul on bass, Whelan on drums, Day on guitar and Davis on keyboards. After performing at a talent contest at the Hacienda club, the group was signed to Factory Records (New Order's label) in 1985. The first single, 'Delightful', was produced by Mike Pickering, who would later find success as the founder of soul/dance group **M People**. Soon afterwards Berry joined as percussionist and dancer.

Over the next three years the Happy Mondays slowly built up a UK following, releasing the **John Cale**-produced *Squirrel and G-Man Twenty Four Hour Party People Plastic Face Carnt Smile (White Out)* in 1987 and *Bummed* in 1989, produced by Martin Hannett. It included the 1990 hit 'Step on', a version of the John Kongos song 'I'm Gonna Step on You Again' from 1971. The group's sound, which combined organ, disco-bass, congas and wah-wah guitar, and its dance rhythms appealed to audiences at the acid house rave parties which were a feature of teenage life of the time.

Helped by media publicity concerning Ryder's capacity for drug-taking, *Pills 'n' Thrills and Bellyaches* (1991) was a big commercial and critical success in the UK. It was reputedly inspired by the group's affection for **Donovan**, to whom they recorded the tribute song 'Donovan'. Reviewers compared the group with the **Rolling Stones**, **Mott the Hoople** and the **Faces**. Co-produced by acid house guru **Paul Oakenfold**, it included the hit singles 'Kinky Afro' and 'Loose Fit' as well as 'God's Cop', a raucous attack on the arch-conservative head of the Manchester police force. This was followed by the release of a live album and . . . *Yes Please* (1992), produced by former **Talking Heads** members Tina Weymouth and Chris Frantz.

Ryder's increasingly erratic behaviour and the collapse of Factory Records in 1992 contributed to the fragmentation of the Happy Mondays, who eventually split at the end of 1993. After a period of rehabilitation Ryder formed Black Grape with Bez and rapper Kermit, working with producer Danny Saber on a pair of acclaimed albums, *It's Great When You're Straight, Yeah!* (1995) and *Stupid, Stupid, Stupid* (1997). Both were a hi-octane blend of big beats, hip-hop breaks and rock guitar, and spawned a handful of hit singles including 'In the Name of the Father' and 'Reverend Black Grape', which drew criticism from religious leaders. Black Grape split under acrimonious circumstances in 1998, paving the way for a Happy Mondays reunion the following year, which included several appearances on the European festival circuit. The earlier 'best of' compilation *Loads* (1995) was reissued with the addition of the comeback single 'The Boys Are Back in Town', the band's reworking of the 1976 **Thin Lizzy** hit.

OTTO HARBACH
b. Otto Abels Hauerbach, 18 August 1873, Salt Lake City, Utah, USA, d. 24 January 1963, New York

A prolific librettist and lyricist, Harbach, unlike Oscar Hammerstein (of **Rodgers and Hammerstein**), with whom he collaborated in the twenties, was unable to establish his own identity and most of the shows with which he was associated are remembered as their composers', rather than his.

The son of Danish immigrants, Harbach became a professor of English before in 1901 he moved to New York to study at Columbia University for a Ph.D. He soon abandoned his studies for life as a reporter, copywriter and then songwriter. His first success was *Three Twins* (1908), with music by Karl Hoschna, which included 'Cuddle up a Little Closer, Lovey Mine', a hit for **Ada Jones** and **Billy Murray** and later for Kay Armen (Decca, 1949), the wife of **David Seville**. The duo's *Madame Sherry* (1910) included the hit 'Every Little Movement Has a Meaning of Its Own' (**Henry Burr**). After Hoschna's death in 1911, Harbach joined forces with **Rudolf Friml** as lyricist and librettist for *The Firefly* (1912). That was followed by ten further collaborations with the composer (including the landmark *Rose Marie*, 1924). In 1920 the young Hammerstein was apprenticed to him and together they worked with various composers, including Herbert Stothart (*Tickle Me*); Stothart and **Vincent Youmans** (*Wildflower*, 1923); Stothart and **George Gershwin** (*Song of the Flame*, 1925); **Jerome Kern** (*Sunny*, 1925); and **Sigmund Romberg** (*Desert Song*, 1926). During this period he also collaborated on his own with Youmans on *No, No, Nanette* (1925), one of the most successful musicals of the decade.

After *Sunny*, Harbach regularly worked with Kern, most successfully on *The Cat and the Fiddle* (1931), which included 'She Didn't Say "Yes"' and 'The Night Was Made for Love', and *Roberta* (1932), which included the oft-recorded 'Smoke Gets in Your Eyes' (a hit for **Paul Whiteman**, **Ruth Etting**, **Artie Shaw** in 1934 and a million-seller for the **Platters** in 1959), and 'The Touch of Your Hand'. After final collaborations with Romberg (*Forbidden Melody*, 1936) and Kern, *Hay Foot, Straw Foot* (1942), which failed to open in

New York, Harbach retired. Between 1950 and 1953, he was president of the American Society of Authors, Composers and Publishers (ASCAP).

E. Y. 'YIP' HARBURG
b. Isidore Hochberg, 8 April 1898, New York, USA, d. 5 March 1981, Los Angeles, California

Harburg was at the same time one of the most literate and whimsical ('Lydia the Tattooed Lady', written with **Harold Arlen**, 1939) and the most socially conscious (the Depression classic 'Brother Can You Spare a Dime?', with Jay Gorney, 1932) lyricists of the thirties and forties.

The son of Russian immigrants, Harburg went to school with **Ira Gershwin** and began writing parodies and light verse for the school paper. Deeply influenced by W. S. Gilbert of **Gilbert and Sullivan**, he continued as an occasional versifier while working as a successful electrical contractor throughout the twenties. When, in 1929, Harburg went bankrupt, Gershwin introduced him to Jay Gorney, who had just broken up with his writing partner, Howard Dietz (whose greatest successes were in collaboration with **Arthur Schwartz**). Harburg also wrote with **Vernon Duke** and with him (and Gershwin) produced his first success, 'I'm Only Human After All' for *The Garrick Gaieties* of 1930. For *Americana* (1932) he wrote 'Brother Can You Spare a Dime?', the lyrics of which – 'Once I built a railroad, made it run, made it race against time . . . now it's done, buddy can you spare a dime?' – were proof that the popular ballad tradition could be as socially conscious as protest songs. Other songs from this period include 'Only a Paper Moon' (1932), written with Arlen, and 'April in Paris' (1932) and 'I Like the Likes of You' (1934), with Duke. Another Depression song was 'Let's Take a Walk Around the Block' which he wrote with Arlen and Gershwin for *Life Begins at 8.40* (1934) and which was performed by Bert Lahr, who, along with Groucho Marx (who sang 'Lydia' in *At the Circus*, 1939), was Harburg's favourite vocalist.

By 1934, like Arlen, Harburg regularly travelled to and from Hollywood. With Arlen, he worked first for Universal then Warners (scoring the **Al Jolson** film, *The Singing Kid*, 1935, and *Gold Diggers of 1937*, 1936) before being assigned *The Wizard of Oz* (1939) by MGM. For this, seen by Harburg as a Depression fantasy, the pair wrote their best-known songs, 'Over the Rainbow', 'We're off to See the Wizard' and 'Follow the Yellow Brick Road'. Again with Arlen, he wrote 'Happiness Is a Thing Called Joe' for **Ethel Waters** in *Cabin in the Sky* (1943). During the war, his involvement in politics grew, and he wrote 'The Free and Equal Blues' with **Earl Robinson** and, with **Jerome Kern**, contributed 'And Russia Is Her Name' to what would later be seen as the highly controversial pro-Soviet *Song of Russia* (1944). On the occasion of Martin Luther King's death in 1968, he and Arlen wrote 'Silent Spring'.

For all his film success, Harburg was happiest working on Broadway where it was easier to write questioning shows rather than mere escapist fantasies. In this vein he wrote *Bloomer Girl* (1946) with Arlen, and the satirical *Finian's Rainbow* (1947) with Burton Lane, both of which were big hits. The latter, which was filmed in 1968 with **Fred Astaire**, included 'How Are Things in Glocca Morra', 'Old Devil Moon' and 'If This Isn't Love'. He continued to write, mostly Broadway shows (including *Jamaica*, 1957, with Arlen and *Darling of the Sun*, 1968, with **Jule Styne**) and a few film scores, notably the songs to the animated feature *Gay Purr-ee* (1962), which included his and Arlen's 'Paris Is a Lonely Town', but far less prolifically. Instead, he devoted his time to a variety of political and social concerns and returned to the often acerbic light verses of his youth.

TIM HARDIN
b. 23 December 1941, Eugene, Oregon, USA,
d. 29 December 1980, Los Angeles, California

Though he was an influential member of the folk revival of the sixties and the composer of several standards, Hardin had little success as a recording artist.

A distant relation of the outlaw John Wesley Hardin and the son of classically trained musicians, Hardin became a leading light in the Boston folk movement on his discharge from the marines in 1961. *This Is Tim Hardin* (Atco, 1966), featuring recordings made in 1962, shows the strong blues and jazz influence in his work of that period. In 1963, in Greenwich Village, he was part of the emerging folk-rock scene associated with the **Lovin' Spoonful**, whose mentor Eric Jacobsen later produced two of Hardin's albums.

In 1966 he won acclaim for his appearance at the Newport Folk Festival, and signed to Verve for whom he recorded *Tim Hardin* (1966) and the classic *Tim Hardin II* (1967), which included the wistful and evocative 'Reason to Believe' and 'If I Were a Carpenter'. 'Carpenter' was a Top Ten hit for **Bobby Darin** in 1966 – ironically Hardin's only hit was with Darin's composition 'Sing a Simple Song of Freedom' in 1969. The song was later successfully revived by the **Four Tops** in 1968, and **Johnny Cash** and June Carter in 1970. Among those who recorded 'Reason' were **Rod Stewart** and **Peter Paul and Mary**, while Hardin's 'Misty Roses' was a minor hit for **Johnny Mathis**. After a series of lesser albums Hardin joined Columbia in 1970 for the ambitious *Suite for Susan Moore and Damian* and *Bird on a Wire* (1971). Henceforth his career was blighted by drugs.

In 1970 he settled in Britain, recording the unimpressive *Painted Head* (1972) and *Nine* (Island, 1973). Back in America, he started recording an album in 1980 under the supervision of Don Rubin, co-producer of his 1967 Verve outing, only to die of a drugs overdose in the middle of the sessions. *Hang on to a Dream* (Verve, 1994) is the definitive retrospective.

BEN HARPER
b. 1969, Los Angeles, USA

American singer-songwriter Ben Harper has earned widespread acclaim for his use of traditional folk and blues on a series of heartfelt albums, made distinctive by his use of a Weissenborn acoustic slide guitar.

Harper grew up in the Inland Empire area of California, where he became proficient on the guitar at a young age. He signed to Virgin in 1993 after he was spotted performing live with blues legend **Taj Mahal**, who would later prove an important reference point in his solo material. His début album, *Welcome to the Cruel World* (1994), saw Harper gain instant recognition for his articulate portrayal of urban life, while 'Like a King', an ironic juxtaposition of Kings Martin Luther and Rodney, drew both praise and scorn in equal measure. The album also saw the singer use the Dobro to good effect on more funky tracks like 'Mama's Got a Girlfriend Now'.

Fight for Your Mind (1995) saw Harper's songs fleshed out more solidly by his backing band the Innocent Criminals, and led to a worldwide tour which saw him gain new admirers. Much of *The Will to Live* (1997) was recorded whilst Harper was still touring, reflected in the heavier rock sound utilized on the album.

ROY HARPER
b. 12 June 1941, Manchester, England

An iconoclastic singer and songwriter, Harper retained a cult following throughout Europe in the seventies and eighties.

He briefly enlisted in the air force at the age of fifteen, performing skiffle material in camp concerts before suffering a mental breakdown. During the early sixties he served a prison sentence in Liverpool before moving to London as a busker in 1964. Harper's intense lyrics and delivery won him a reputation on the folk-club circuit and in 1966 he released *The Sophisticated Beggar* on the small Strike label. This was followed by *Come Out Fighting Genghis Smith* (Columbia, 1967) and *Folkjokeopus* (Liberty, 1969).

Once Harper was an established regular at free concerts in London's Hyde Park, **Pink Floyd** manager Peter Jenner signed him to a long-term contract with

Harvest, EMI's underground label. Produced by Jenner, *Flat Baroque and Berserk* (1970) and *Stormcock* (1971) were the first in a series of albums on which Harper expounded his stoned hippie philosophy. He played a semi-autobiographical role in the 1972 film *Made*.

The accompaniment on the early albums was acoustic, but later records featured **Led Zeppelin**'s Jimmy Page on electric guitar. Page's respect for his work was evident in the naming of one track on *Led Zeppelin 3*, 'Hats off to Harper'. Pink Floyd similarly honoured him by bringing Harper in to sing lead vocals on 'Have a Cigar' from *Wish You Were Here* (1975).

While it was epics like 'I Hate the White Man' and 'Me and My Woman' that made Harper's name on the college circuit, some of his most effective compositions were quieter nostalgic pieces like 'When an Old Cricketer Leaves the Crease' from *HQ* (1975), on which he was accompanied by the Grimethorpe Colliery Brass Band, and 'One of Those Days in England' from *Bullinamingvase* (1977), his most commercially successful album. *The Unknown Soldier* (1978) included a powerful duet with **Kate Bush** ('You') and was his last Harvest recording.

In the late seventies Harper formed a series of bands to tour in Europe and America. Successively named Trigger, Chips and Black Sheep, their members included guitarists Chris Spedding and Andy Roberts and drummer Bill Bruford.

During the eighties Harper's status as a revered guru from an earlier era was underlined by the reissue of several albums on the small Awareness label. These included *Born in Captivity* (1985) and a collection of 1982 demo tapes which eventually became *Work of Heart* (1986). The collaboration with Page continued on *Whatever Happened to Jugula* (Beggar's Banquet, 1985). In 1986 Harper rejoined EMI, releasing *Descendants of Smith* and *Loony on the Bus* (1988). Far better were 1990's *Once* and 1992's *Death or Glory*.

HARPERS BIZARRE

Ted Templeman, b. 24 October 1944; Eddie James, b. Santa Cruz, California; John Peterson, b. 8 January 1945, San Francisco; Dick Scoppettone, b. 5 July 1945; Dick Yount, b. 9 January 1943, Santa Cruz

Harpers Bizarre were a vocal harmony group of the late sixties whose lead singer, Templeman, went on to become a leading rock producer.

Based in Santa Cruz, Harpers Bizarre were initially a four-member surf group, the Tikis, recording for Autumn. Following the demise of the label, the band recruited Peterson from the Beau Brummels and signed to Warners in 1967. Produced by Lenny Waronker with musical arrangements by **Leon Rus-**

sell, their version of **Simon and Garfunkel**'s '59th Street Bridge Song (Feelin' Groovy)' with its precision harmonies was a hit in both America and Britain.

Van Dyke Parks' 'Come to the Sunshine' was a further hit, but then the band changed policy to offer harmony versions of older standards. They had minor successes in 1967–8 with **Cole Porter**'s 'Anything Goes', **Harry Warren**'s 'Chattanooga Choo Choo' (a 1941 hit for **Glenn Miller**) and the 1959 **Johnny Horton** and **Lonnie Donegan** hit, 'Battle of New Orleans'. However, their recorded repertoire also included attractive versions of songs by new California songwriters like Parks and **Randy Newman** ('Simon Smith and His Amazing Dancing Bear').

The group continued to release albums – *Secret Life of Harpers Bizarre* (1968) and *Harpers Bizarre 4* (1969) – before disbanding in 1970. *As Time Goes By* (Forest Bay, 1976) was the fruit of an unsuccessful reunion in 1976, without Templeman or Peterson, who had taken part in a revival of the Beau Brummels.

As staff producer for Warners, Templeman was involved in myriad album projects during the seventies and eighties. His most notable successes came with **Van Morrison**, the **Doobie Brothers** and **Van Halen**.

THE HARPTONES

William Winfield, b. 24 August 1929, New York, USA; Bill Dempsey, b. New York; William Galloway (replaced 1954 by Jimmie Beckum); Bill Brown, b. 1936, New York, d. 1956; Nicky Clark, b. 1943, New York; Raoul Cita, b. 11 February 1928, New York

Though they had little commercial success, the Harptones remain one of the most highly regarded pioneer groups of the doo-wop era.

Formed by pianist and arranger Cita in 1953 in Harlem as the Harps, the group changed their name when they signed to Morty Craft's Bruce Records. Specialists in slow romantic songs featuring Winfield's ethereal tenor voice, they had an immediate hit with the classic, dreamy 'Sunday Kind of Love' (1953). Further records on Bruce included the Cita composition 'My Memories of You', before they switched to Paradise for 'Life Is But a Dream' (1953) and then to Rama in 1956 for cool versions of 'The Masquerade Is Over' and 'The Shrine of St Cecilia'. Plagued by contractual problems, they label-hopped their way through the fifties, scoring their only pop hit in 1961 on Companion with 'What Will I Tell My Heart', before disbanding in 1964. Winfield became a funeral director.

In 1982, after several temporary revivals of the name, Winfield and Cita briefly regrouped the Harptones and recorded the superior *Love Needs* (Ambient), which included harder-edged, but still vocally lush, reworkings of contemporary material such as **Jackson Browne**'s 'Love Needs a Heart'.

CHARLES K. HARRIS
b. 1 May 1867, Poughkeepsie, New York, USA,
d. 22 December 1930, New York

One of the founding fathers of Tin Pan Alley, Harris was the first major American songwriter actively to seek songwriting commissions, a fact he proudly proclaimed in the sign he hung outside his office 'Banjoist and song writer, songs written to order'. His major hit, the oft-recorded 'After the Ball' (1892) has been described with only a little exaggeration by historian Ian Whitcomb as 'the first [sheet music] million-seller to be conceived of as a million-seller and marketed as a million-seller'.

A self-taught musician (mostly from banjo instructional manuals), Harris was raised in Saginaw, Michigan, and Milwaukee, Wisconsin, where he displayed his famous sign in the 1880s. His first songs – which included 'If I Were the Chief of Police' – were promoted by amateur singers he met. When that tactic failed with 'After the Ball', according to his lengthy account of the song's history in *After the Ball: Forty Years of Melody* (1926), he paid ballad singer J. Aldrich Libby $500 to introduce the song. Essentially a Victorian ballad that is now remembered only for its still emotive chorus, the song was an immediate hit and was further popularized when **John Philip Sousa** regularly played it at the Chicago World's Fair. Among the earliest recordings of 'After the Ball' were those by George J. Gaskin (New Jersey, 1893) and the 'Artistic Whistler' John Yorke Atlee (Columbia, 1903) to a piano accompaniment by **Fred Gaisberg**. Subsequently, Harris himself recorded the song in 1929 in an early sound film and **Al Jolson** sang it in *The Jolson Story* (1946).

If the success of 'After the Ball' was an archetypal example of the creative and promotional practices that came to dominate Tin Pan Alley until the advent of radio, Harris also pointed the way forward for other songwriters when, after one publisher offered him $10,000 for the rights, he published himself with great financial success: in his instructional manual *How to Write a Popular Song*, Harris wryly advised 'know the copyright laws'. A prolific writer, Harris composed many songs that were popular in their time, though few of his songs are remembered today. Among those to be recorded were the Civil War song given the edge of topicality by the outbreak of the Spanish-American War, 'Break the News to Mother' (1897) – Gaskin (Columbia, 1898), the Edison Male Quartette (1898) and the Shannon Four (1917); 'Hello Central Give Me Heaven' (1901) – Byron G. Harlan (Edison, 1901); ''Mid the Green Fields of Virginia'

(1898) – Harry MacDonough (Edison, 1899) and Frank Stanley (Columbia, 1899); and his last major hit 'Always in the Way' (1903) – Harlan (Edison, 1903).

By the turn of the century, Harris's songs had fallen out of fashion. Though in his instructional booklet he commented 'styles in songs change as quickly as ladies' millinery', he himself was unable to adapt to the more strident rhythms of the new century and for the most part confined himself to publishing other people's hits.

EMMYLOU HARRIS
b. 2 April 1949, Birmingham, Alabama, USA

With her flawless soprano voice, Harris moved easily between rock and country music to become a highly successful recording artist in the seventies, eighties and nineties.

At the University of North Carolina, Harris played in a folk duo and later moved to Greenwich Village where she performed in clubs with artists like **Jerry Jeff Walker** and recorded *Gliding Bird* (Jubilee, 1969). As a club performer, she met the Flying Burrito Brothers' **Gram Parsons** and sang on his *GP* album (Warners, 1973). Harris joined his touring band and contributed to *Grievous Angel* (1973). On both records, her clear, sweet voice perfectly complemented Parsons' cracked singing style, giving his songs greater impact than they had on his solo recordings. After his sudden death, Harris formed her own Angel Band and evolved a country-rock repertoire closely based on Parsons' own.

Her first album for Warners, *Pieces of the Sky* (1975), included her best-known composition 'Boulder to Birmingham' (later a hit for **Dolly Parton**) and a remake of the **Louvin Brothers**' 'If I Could Only Win Your Love', which reached No. 1 in the country charts. The album was produced by Brian Ahern, known for his work with **Anne Murray**. In 1977 Harris married Ahern, who remained her producer until 1984.

While albums like *Elite Hotel* (1976), which included three Parsons compositions ('Sin City', 'Ooh Las Vegas' and 'Wheels'), and *Luxury Liner* (1977) sold well to rock audiences, Harris had a stream of country hits, including 'Sweet Dreams' and **Chuck Berry**'s '(You Never Can Tell) C'est la Vie'. Her touring band included such luminaries as Rodney Crowell, who co-wrote 'Amarillo' and 'Till I Gain Control Again' with Harris, **Albert Lee** and **Ricky Skaggs**. *Roses in the Snow* (1980) was Harris's most traditional album, mainly because of Skaggs' bluegrass arrangements.

Harris duetted with **Roy Orbison** on 'That Lovin' You Feelin' Again' (1980) and **Don Williams** on 'If I Needed You' (1981). Her only bestselling pop single was a revival of 'Mr Sandman' in 1981, but the country hits continued. In 1985 she recorded the concept album, *The Ballad of Sally Rose*, co-written with

British songwriter Paul Kennerley, whom she later married. On the album, a further examination of her formative relationship with Parsons, she is Sally Rose while Parson is represented by The Singer who inspires her and whose name she must carry on after his death. Among the guest artists on *Sally Rose* were **Linda Ronstadt** and Dolly Parton, with whom Harris recorded the hugely successful, if somewhat predictable, *Trio* (Warners, 1987). *13* (1987) included versions of **Merle Haggard**'s 'Today I Started Loving You Again' and the **Elvis Presley** hit 'Mystery Train', and in 1989 Harris released *Bluebird*. Far better was *Duets* (1990) on which she sang with such partners as **Neil Young**, **George Jones** and **John Denver**. Equally fine was the acoustic set *At the Ryman* (1992), in which she fronted a bluegrass-styled quintet, covering traditional, folksy, country tunes alongside songs by **Bruce Springsteen** and John Fogerty (of **Creedence Clearwater Revival**). In 1993 she released another impressive set, *Cowgirl's Prayer*. The Daniel Lanois-produced *Wrecking Ball* (1995), which saw her singing a broader range of material, from **Jimi Hendrix** to **Steve Earle**, won her a Grammy for Best Contemporary Folk album. *Trio II* (1999) was far more conservative. The three-CD set *Portraits* (1996) is the definitive retrospective.

In 1999 Harris oversaw production of the Gram Parsons tribute album *Return of the Grievous Angel* (Almo), on which she performed two duets, 'She' with the **Pretenders** and 'Sin City' with **Beck**. *Red Dirt Girl* (2000) on the independent Nonesuch label saw a return to the experimental style of *Wrecking Ball* with the difference that the (mostly) observational songs this time centred more on pain. Examples of this were 'Pearl', the title track and 'Tragedy', on which she duets with **Bruce Springsteen**.

PHIL HARRIS
b. 16 January 1904, Linton, Indiana, USA

A bandleader disposed towards jazz, Harris was best known for a series of forties' hits with novelty songs in a rasping Southern (sometimes Southern black) accent. The performances both recalled the early vaudevillian **Bert Williams** and also prefigured some of the ideas, a generation later, of **Randy Newman** and **Ry Cooder**.

He grew up in Nashville and played drums with local bandleader Francis Craig. Moving to the West Coast, Harris was leading his own band by 1931, by 1933 appearing in movies, and a year later commanding his own radio show. From 1936 to 1946 he was associated with Jack Benny's radio show, while from 1947 onwards he had his own slot with his wife, singer **Alice Faye**.

Harris recorded in the thirties for Vocalion,

Columbia, Decca and ARC, but it is his forties' Victor recordings that are most potent. They include such tales of Southern manners as 'The Darktown Poker Club' (1947), 'The Preacher and the Bear' (a 1947 revival of **Arthur Collins**' 1905 million-seller) and his trademark song 'That's What I Like About the South' (1947). He also recorded **Irving Berlin**'s 1911 composition 'Woodman, Woodman, Spare That Tree'. Frequently seen on television in the fifties – when he had his biggest hit with 'The Thing'* – Harris was also heard as the voice of Baloo the Bear in Walt Disney's cartoon adaptation of Kipling's *The Jungle Book*. From the late sixties he turned increasingly to country music.

WYNONIE HARRIS
b. 24 August 1915, Omaha, Nebraska, USA, d. 14 June 1969, Los Angeles, California

One of the most powerful and exuberant blues shouters of the forties and early fifties, Wynonie Harris was probably the most committed to the authentic spirit of the blues.

In his youth he was a dancer, drummer and singer with various Midwestern small groups. He moved to the West Coast in the early forties, where he worked with many jazz artists. Joining the band of **Lucky Millinder** he had his first hit record with 'Who Threw the Whiskey in the Well' (Decca, 1944). He also recorded for Aladdin, Hamp-Tone and Bullet, often supported by groups that included the likes of **Illinois Jacquet**, Jack McVea and **Johnny Otis**.

Signing with King Records in 1947, he promptly charted with 'Good Rockin' Tonight' (1948), a cover of the earlier hit by **Roy Brown**. This initiated a series of erotically inclined *double entendre* R&B hits, including 'I Like My Baby's Pudding' (1949), as well as 'Good Morning Judge' (1950), 'Blood-shot Eyes' (written by the country artist **Hank Penny**), 'Lovin' Machine' (1951) and 'Quiet Whiskey' (1953). He took part in many riotous package tours and maintained an amicable public rivalry with fellow King artist Roy Brown.

Though he stayed with King until 1957, his career declined in the middle and late fifties, and he left full-time music to become a café-owner in Brooklyn and, later, Los Angeles. He made occasional appearances on record and concert comebacks, but his voice had been impaired by years of hard use and his swaggering style was out of favour with both his audiences and a new generation of R&B band musicians.

GEORGE HARRISON
b. 25 February 1943, Liverpool, England

After **The Beatles** split in 1970, guitarist Harrison had

the most varied career of the Fab Four, working as recording artist, record-label owner, session player and film producer.

His first solo releases were the experimental *Wonderwall* (Apple, 1968) and *Electronic Sounds* (1970), but the **Phil Spector** production *All Things Must Pass* (1970) was a massive international success. The three-album set included 'What Is Life?' and the inspirational 'My Sweet Lord'*, which a court judgment later held was based on the **Chiffons**' 1963 hit, 'He's So Fine'.

Harrison's Hindu beliefs and interest in the Indian sub-continent led him to promote the 1971 'Concert for Bangladesh' in New York. With the involvement of **Bob Dylan**, **Eric Clapton**, **Ringo Starr** and **Leon Russell**, the album and film of the event (a precursor of Live Aid) eventually raised over $10 million for famine relief. Harrison's composition 'Bangla Desh' was a 1971 hit in both Britain and America.

Despite its devotional nature, *Living in the Material World* (1973) produced a No. 1 hit in 'Give Me Love (Give Me Peace on Earth)'. The following year Harrison undertook his final American tour to support *Dark Horse*, the first release on his own label of the same name. The title track was an American hit, and *Extra Texture (Read All About It)* (1975) included the successful 'You'. *33 1/3* (1976) was the last of his annual albums and Harrison turned his attention to other ventures.

His recording career was resumed with the lacklustre *George Harrison* (1979), which provided a hit in 'Blow Away'. In 1981 he released a tribute to **John Lennon**, 'All Those Years Ago', with contributions from Starr and **Paul McCartney**. Later albums, including *Somewhere in England* (1981) and *Gone Troppo* (1982), were released by Warners.

During the late sixties and seventies Harrison produced albums by a number of artists. Among them were Badfinger (*Straight Up*, Apple, 1972), Jackie Lomax (*Is This What You Want*, Apple, 1969), **Billy Preston**, **Ravi Shankar** and Splinter, who had a British hit with 'Costafine Town' on Dark Horse in 1974. He also added guitar to albums by Delaney and Bonnie, **Hall and Oates** and Dylan (*Desire*, 1976).

By the eighties Harrison was devoting most of his attention to his film production company, Handmade Films. Among the movies it financed were several Monty Python films and **Madonna**'s expensive flop, *Shanghai Surprise* (1986), for which Harrison was executive producer. In 1987 he returned to the charts with 'Got My Mind Set on You' and *Cloud Nine*, which included the reflective 'When We Was Fab'.

In the following year, Harrison joined Dylan, **Tom Petty**, Jeff Lynne of **ELO** and **Roy Orbison** to record *The Traveling Wilburys*, a collaborative album which included the hit 'Handle with Care'. A second

Wilburys album, *Volume 3*, appeared in 1990 but the project was abandoned after Orbison's death. In 1991 Harrison made his first tour for several years when he performed in Japan with a band featuring **Eric Clapton** (Harrison had played on Clapton's 1989 album *Journeyman*). *Live in Japan* (1992) was culled from it. In 1995 he teamed up with the remaining Beatles to record backing tracks for two of John Lennon's demo recordings for *Anthology* and repeated the process for *Anthology 2* (1996). In 1999 Harrison was wounded after an intruder broke into his UK mansion.

WILBERT HARRISON
b. 6 January 1929, Charlotte, North Carolina, USA, d. 26 October 1994, Spencer, North Carolina

A rhythm and blues singer and multi-instrumentalist, Harrison's most important records were the definitive version of 'Kansas City' and the original version of the widely recorded 'Let's Work Together'.

His earliest records were made for Rockin and De Luxe in Miami in the mid-fifties. Moving to New York, he recorded for Savoy and **Bobby Robinson**'s Fury, where Harrison's version of **Leiber and Stoller**'s 'Kansas City' (1959) was a surprise No. 1 hit.

Sometimes working (for economic reasons) as a one-man band, Harrison recorded sporadically in the sixties for many small labels, including Seahorn, Port, Neptune, Vest and Doc. At the close of the decade he teamed up with New York producer Juggy Murray for 'Let's Work Together' (Sue, 1969), previously recorded by Harrison as 'Let's Stick Together'. The strongly rhythmic anthem was a Top Forty hit and the album of the same name included a sinuous reading of **Richard Berry**'s 'Louie Louie' and a relaxed version of **Fats Domino**'s 'Blue Monday'. It was released in Britain on London.

White blues band **Canned Heat** covered 'Let's Work Together' the following year and in 1976 **Bryan Ferry** reached the British Top Ten with a revival of 'Let's Stick Together'.

Murray produced *Shoot You Full of Love* for his own Juggernaut label before Harrison began label-hopping again. 'My Heart Is Yours' came out on SSS International in 1971 and he cut later albums for Buddah (1972), **Wes Farrell**'s Chelsea (*Soul Food Man*), Wet Soul (*Anything You Want*), Brunswick and Hotline.

LORENZ HART
b. Lorenz Milton Hart, 2 May 1895, New York, USA, d. 22 November 1943, New York

Lorenz Hart, the lyricist partner of Richard Rodgers (later of **Rodgers and Hammerstein**), was, with **Cole Porter**, the most sophisticated of the Broadway songwriters. In their witty analyses of the problems and

pleasures of love, Hart's lyrics captured a heady
worldliness through a unique melding of learned references and internal rhymes. The high point of his
work with Rodgers, which included twenty-six Broadway musicals, was *Pal Joey* (1940). In relying on a
rogue as its central character, it was as revolutionary
in its way as **Jerome Kern** and Hammerstein's *Show
Boat* (1927).

The son of German immigrants, Hart began his
theatrical career (like **W. S. Gilbert**, an early influence) by translating German plays. In 1919 he met and
established a songwriting partnership with Richard
Rodgers. Their first published song was 'Any Old
Place with You' which producer Lew, the father of
Dorothy, Fields interpolated into his current Broadway show *A Lonely Romeo* (1919). Their future seemed
assured when Fields commissioned them to write
Poor Little Rich Girl (1920) and the show was well
received in Boston. When it transferred to Broadway,
however, Fields replaced most of their material with
songs by **Sigmund Romberg** and others and for the
next five years their efforts met with little success. The
turning point was *Garrick Gaieties* (1925). Originally a
revue to raise funds for the Theater Guild, it was one
of the hits of the year and introduced the pair's first
classic song, the intricately rhymed 'Manhattan', a hit
for **Paul Whiteman** and **Ben Selvin**. Their next show,
Dearest Enemy (1925), an operetta set during the War
of Independence and produced in the year of **Vincent
Youmans**' *No, No Nanette* and **Rudolf Friml**'s *The
Vagabond King*, was backward looking but the *Gaieties* edition of 1926 and *The Girl Friend* (1926)
marked a decisive break with the past. The former
included, as well as 'Mountain Greenery', a devastating parody of *Rose Marie* and the operetta tradition in
general, 'Rose of Arizona', while the story of the latter
was literally a dream.

As well as its title song, *The Girl Friend* introduced
'The Blue Room' (which, when revived by **Perry
Como** in 1949, gave him a hit). Equally successful was
A Connecticut Yankee (1927), which introduced 'Thou
Swell' and 'My Heart Stood Still' (both hits for Ben
Selvin and Paul Whiteman). Other hit shows of the
period include *Present Arms* (1928), which introduced
'You Took Advantage of Me'; *Spring Is Here* (1929),
which included 'With a Song in My Heart'; *Simple
Simon* (1930), whose 'Ten Cents a Dance' was a hit for
Ruth Etting; and *Ever Green* (1930), which was filmed
in 1934. In the UK, *Ever Green* was **Jessie Matthews'**
greatest British stage success and it provided bandleader **Jack Hylton** with an American hit with 'Dancing on the Ceiling' (1932).

From 1930–5 the pair worked in Hollywood, providing songs for musicals, including 'Isn't It Romantic' and 'Lover' for *Love Me Tonight* (1932), the
innovative *Hallelujah I'm a Bum* (1933), in which Hart

also acted, and *Hollywood Party* (1934), for which they
wrote an early version of the classic 'Blue Moon' only
to have it rejected by the producer. The only Hart–
Rodgers collaboration not introduced in either a film
or Broadway musical, 'Blue Moon' has since become
one of the most recorded popular songs of all time.
Among those to have had hits with it are **Al Bowlly**
and **Roy Noble** (1935), **Mel Tormé**, **Billy Eckstine**
(1949) and the **Marcels** (1961). In all, twelve of the
duo's Broadway musicals were transferred to the
screen. Among those who sang Hart's lyrics on screen
were **Jeanette MacDonald**, **Bing Crosby**, **George M.
Cohan**, **Maurice Chevalier**, **Judy Garland**, **Frank
Sinatra**, **Lena Horn**, **Doris Day** and **Jimmy Durante**.
While in Hollywood, Hart, for the only time, wrote
lyrics to music other than Rodgers' when he provided
new lyrics to **Franz Lehár**'s songs for *The Merry
Widow* (1934).

The pair returned to Broadway for the circus musical *Jumbo* (1935, filmed 1962), which featured Jimmy
Durante and the entire Paul Whiteman band and
'The Most Beautiful Girl in the World' (a hit for
Tommy Dorsey, 1953). But their thirties musicals
were less inventive and it was the songs rather than
the shows that lasted. Songs of note from this period
included 'There's a Small Hotel' (1936) and 'Falling in
Love with Love' (1938). Their most successful show
was *Babes in Arms* (1937, filmed 1939), a brash lets-
put-on-a-show-musical which included among its
numbers, the sombre, elegiac 'My Funny Valentine',
'Where or When', and the sardonic 'The Lady Is a
Tramp', a hit for **Sophie Tucker** and memorably
recorded by **Peggy Lee**.

Artistically more successful was *Pal Joey* (1940,
revived 1952, and filmed 1957). Based on a series of
short stories by John O'Hara and starring **Gene Kelly**
in his only major Broadway role, the show introduced
'Bewitched, Bothered and Bewildered' and 'Zip' in
which an 'intellectual' striptease artiste contemplates
the world: 'Zip! I was reading Schopenhauer last
night/Zip! and I think that Schopenhauer was right'.
It was followed by *By Jupiter* (1942), the pair's last collaboration. Radically different characters – Rodgers
was a workaholic while Hart led a Bohemian life –
their partnership ended when Hart turned down the
opportunity to transform Lynn Riggs' *Green Grow the
Lilacs* into a musical. That eventually became *Oklahoma!* (1943) and its success confirmed the new partnership of Rodgers and Hammerstein.

Hart died in 1943, soon after the triumphant reception of *Oklahoma!*. In the 1948 biopic *Words and
Music*, Mickey Rooney played Hart and Tom Drake,
Rodgers. Among the many later artists to pay tribute
to the pair were **Ella Fitzgerald**, with the two volumes
of her *Rodgers and Hart Songbook* (Verve), and the
Supremes (*The Supremes Sing Rodgers and Hart*, 1967).

JOHN HARTFORD
b. John Harford, 30 December 1937, New York, USA

A musical eccentric, Hartford is best known as the writer of 'Gentle on My Mind', a multi-million-seller for **Glen Campbell**.

Raised in St Louis, Hartford's first (and enduring) loves were bluegrass and riverboats. Proficient on fiddle, banjo and guitar by his teens, Hartford travelled to Nashville in 1965 after a brief interlude as a steamboat deckhand and radio announcer. There he found session work and a contract with RCA (who added the 't' to his name) in 1966. His recording of 'Gentle' on *Earthwords and Music* was a minor country hit in 1967 and, after Campbell's success with the song, many of his compositions were recorded by other artists.

Hartford's own recordings saw him retreating into charming eccentricity – thus his 1969 album *John Hartford* includes songs such as 'The Poor Old Prurient Interest Blues' – and in 1970 he left RCA for the more sympathetic Warner Brothers. *Areo-Plain* (1971) demonstrated his commitment to traditional bluegrass styles, while his distaste for the wholesale commercialization of country music and its institutions was evident in the lament 'They're Gonna Tear Down the Grand Ole Opry'.

In 1972 he retired to work on steamboats, before signing with the independent Flying Fish label in 1976. His subsequent albums, which include *Mark Twang* (1976) and *Headin' Down into the Mystery Below* (1979) as well as recordings with the Dillards, were traditionally orientated, as were his live performances, which featured clog dancing. He has also continued to write tongue-in-cheek songs such as 'Don't Leave Your Records in the Sun'. In 1986 he re-entered the mainstream with *Annual Waltz* (MCA). Subsequent releases, which include *Gum Tree Canoe* (1987), his most assured and controlled album for years, have been on Flying Fish. *A John Hartford Collection* (1987) collects together some of the best of his Flying Fish output. He continued recording into the nineties, mostly in historical mode – for example, *Cadillac Rag* (1992), an album of traditional fiddle tunes.

PJ HARVEY
b. Polly Jean Harvey, 9 September 1969, Yeovil, England

One of the most influential and original songwriters of the nineties, Harvey moved on from alt-rock frontwoman to bluesy solo artist, producing a series of critically acclaimed albums which dealt frankly with the themes of love and religion.

Polly Harvey grew up on a sheep farm in rural Yeovil, following in her mother's artistic footsteps by studying photography and learning to play the guitar

and saxophone. After stints in numerous local bands she formed PJ Harvey in 1991 with bassist Steve Vaughan and drummer Robert Ellis, taking centre-stage for the first time. The trio soon signed a deal with Too Pure, releasing the singles 'Dress' and 'Sheela-Na-Gig', which won much critical praise.

PJ Harvey earned considerable acclaim for their album début, *Dry* (1992), which saw the band build a fanbase in the UK, where they toured solidly, while also drawing interest from the US. The follow-up, *Rid of Me* (1993), was an even greater success. It was produced by grunge stalwart Steve Albini, whose noisy recording techniques perfectly complemented Harvey's unflinching lyrics. The sparse *4-Track Demos*, released later the same year, heralded the end of PJ Harvey as a band after the departure of Ellis and Vaughan at the end of the *Rid of Me* tour.

Harvey spent much of the next year in the studio, where she recorded her first album as a solo artist alongside multi-instrumentalists John Parish and Mick Harvey (one of **Nick Cave**'s Bad Seeds), guitarist Joe Gore (also a member of **Tom Waits**' band), drummer Eric Drew Feldman (**Pere Ubu**) and producer Flood. *To Bring You My Love* (1995) saw PJ Harvey move away from straight-ahead rock, taking instead a richer, bluesy sound. Hailed as a masterpiece by most critics, the album is Harvey's strongest body of work to date, as well as being her most commercially viable, bolstered by the success of 'C'Mon Billy' and 'Down by the Water'.

After touring for most of 1995 Harvey spent the next two years out of the limelight, apart from duetting with Nick Cave on his *Murder Ballads* album and singing on John Parish's side-project *Dance Hall at Louse Point*. She returned with *Is This Desire?* (1998), which saw a further change in direction, embracing the hi-tech methods of dance music in a more rhythm-based collection of songs. Harvey also made her acting début the same year as Mary Magdalene in Hal Hartley's *The Book of Life*. Her fifth studio album, *Stories from the City, Stories from the Sea* (2000), drew on the time Harvey had spent living in New York the previous year and included the singles 'Good Fortune' and 'This Mess We're in', one of three collaborations with **Radiohead** vocalist Thom Yorke.

TONY HATCH
b. June 1939, Pinner, Middlesex, England

Hatch was one of British pop music's most prolific arrangers, songwriters and producers of the sixties and seventies, often working with his wife Jackie Trent. He also composed one of the eighties' most ubiquitous tunes, the theme to the soap-opera *Neighbours*.

He studied at the London Choir School before joining a music publisher, and gaining his first studio

experience as an assistant producer with the Top
Rank label. During three years army service, Hatch
wrote band arrangements for the Coldstream Guards.

On his return to civilian life, Hatch had immediate
success as a songwriter. Both 'Look for a Star' (Garry
Mills) and 'Messing About on the River' (Josh
McCrae) were minor British hits in 1960. Hatch
became staff producer for Pye, working on records by
comedian Benny Hill (whose most popular single was
the 1971 British No. 1, 'Ernie [The Fastest Milkman in
the West]' on EMI's Columbia label), the Brook
Brothers ('Warpaint', 1961), **Emile Ford** and **Petula
Clark**.

For Clark, Hatch wrote the international bestseller
'Downtown' in 1964 and later hits including 'I Know
a Place' and 'Call Me'. He was equally proficient at
producing beat groups, and was responsible for Top
Ten hits by the **Searchers**, including 'Sweets for My
Sweet' (1963) and 'Needles and Pins' (1964). Hatch
himself had a minor hit with the instrumental 'Out of
This World' (1962).

In 1964 Hatch signed ballad singer Jackie Trent to
Pye and the couple wrote Trent's British No. 1,
'Where Are You Now?'. The Hatch–Trent team wrote
more hits for Clark, including 'Don't Sleep in the
Subway', 'I Couldn't Live Without Your Love' and
'The Other Man's Grass'. In 1968 Scott Walker of the
Walker Brothers reached the Top Ten with their
composition 'Joanna'. Hatch's later production suc-
cesses included David Parton's cover of **Stevie Won-
der**'s 'Isn't She Lovely' (Pye, 1977) and Sweet
Sensation's 1974 No. 1 'Sad Sweet Dreamer'.

In the seventies Hatch and Trent wrote two West
End musicals, *The Card* and *Rock Nativity*, but were
more successful as a cabaret and television act. They
later moved to Australia, where in 1986 Hatch contributed the theme song for *Neighbours*, the show
which was the springboard to success for **Stock,
Aitken and Waterman** protégés **Kylie Minogue** and
Jason Donovan. Earlier in Hatch's career he had written the music for the long-running British soap opera
Crossroads.

DONNY HATHAWAY

*b. 1 October 1945, Chicago, Illinois, USA, d. 13 January
1979, New York*

Best remembered for his duets with **Roberta Flack**,
Hathaway was also a talented composer and arranger.

As a child, he toured with his grandmother, gospel
singer Martha Pitts. Hathaway studied music at
Howard University in Washington DC before joining
Curtis Mayfield's Curtom label in Chicago as producer and arranger. He recorded with June Conquest
as June and Donnie before moving to Chess on a production contract. Hathaway also worked on a free-

lance basis with artists as diverse as **Jerry Butler**,
Woody Herman and the **Staple Singers**.

Through **King Curtis**, Hathaway signed a solo
recording deal with Atlantic in 1970. After *Everything
Is Everything* (1970), his eponymous second album
secured widespread media coverage as Atlantic promoted him as a black equivalent to singer-songwriters
like **Carole King** and **James Taylor**. 'The Ghetto'
(1970) was an R&B hit, but Hathaway's first major
pop success came when he was teamed with Flack on
'Where Is the Love' (1972), an airy ballad perfectly
suited to the restrained style of both singers.

In the same year *Donny Hathaway Live* reached the
Top Twenty. Often considered one of the best live
albums ever made, it was recorded at New York's Bitter End club by **Arif Mardin** and **Jerry Wexler**. The
album featured a crack New York session band on
such songs as **Marvin Gaye**'s 'What's Going on' and
John Lennon's 'Jealous Guy', plus reworkings of
Hathaway's own compositions. Hathaway scored the
1972 movie *Come Back Charleston Blue*, singing the
title song with Margie Joseph. He also had several solo
R&B hits in 1972–3, including 'Giving Up' and 'Love
Love Love', and released the semi-autobiographical
Extensions of a Man (1973).

Hathaway's volatile and depressive personality
meant that he worked only sporadically during the
mid-seventies. In 1978 Flack enticed him back into the
recording studio for their biggest success, 'The Closer
I Get to You'*. Their collaboration *Roberta Flack Featuring Donny Hathaway* (1979) was unreleased when
Hathaway fell to his death from a hotel window. One
of its tracks, 'Back Together Again', was a British hit
in 1980.

His daughter Lalah (*b. 1969*) began a singing career
with a self-titled solo album for Virgin in 1990.

RICHIE HAVENS

b. 21 January 1941, New York, USA

Havens was one of the few black singers associated
with the sixties folk revival, and a frequent performer
at the open-air rock festivals of the period.

His first professional performances were with the
McCrea Gospel Singers in 1955 but by the late fifties
he was writing poetry and attending beat poetry sessions in Greenwich Village clubs. There he heard traditional folk music and took up the acoustic guitar. In
the early sixties Havens was one of the best-known
café performers in New York, with his open guitar
tuning and distinctive versions of songs from many
folk and pop sources.

In 1965–6 he cut two albums for Douglas which
were released in Britain by Transatlantic. Following a
move to MGM's Verve-Folkways label, Havens'
Mixed Bag (1967) reflected his club act with songs by

Bob Dylan, The Beatles and Jesse Fuller. The impassioned naivety of his folk approach to the material was compelling and the album was a great success, so much so that when his career waned he released a similar-styled but less impressive sequel, *Mixed Bag II* (1976). Later albums, such as *Something Else Again* (1968) and *Richard P. Havens, 1983* (1969), showed a shift towards rock material, a development influenced by Havens' success at the Isle of Wight and Woodstock festivals in 1968–9. On the dark and oddly titled *Richard P. Havens, 1983*, Havens mixed reworkings of songs associated with **Donovan**, The Beatles, Bob Dylan and **Leonard Cohen** with his own compositions to good effect.

Between 1970 and 1974 Havens released six albums on his own Stormy Forest label. The highlights were his soulful interpretations of such songs as **George Harrison**'s 'Here Comes the Sun' from *Alarm Clock* (1971) – his only hit single – the **Bees Gees**' 'I Started a Joke' (*Stonehenge*, 1970) and Ervin Drake's 'It Was a Very Good Year' from the 1973 album *Portfolio*, which also included **Marvin Gaye**'s 'What's Going on'.

Later recordings included *Mirage* (1977), a mellow funk-tinged album for A&M, and *Connections* (Elektra, 1980). In the eighties Havens returned to Dylan and Beatles material for the bland Rykodisc album *Richie Havens Sings The Beatles and Dylan* (1987) and appeared with Dylan in the film *Hearts of Fire* (1987). His other film appearances were in **Jack Good**'s rock opera *Othello, Catch My Soul* (1974) and *Greased Lightning* (1972), with Richard Pryor.

Other albums for Rykodisc, mostly good-time versions of songs from the sixties in the manner of *Sings The Beatles and Dylan* included *The Collection* and *Now* (1991). In 1994 Havens was the first person to perform a Dylan song ('The Times They Are a-Changin'') on a television commercial (for Coopers & Lybrand) and he was one of the first acts to confirm his appearance at the 'Woodstock Revisited' festival. In the same year he released *Cuts to the Chase* (1994). He continued touring throughout the nineties and in 1998 contributed a track to the **Pete Seeger** celebratory album, *Where Have All the Flowers Gone*.

COLEMAN HAWKINS
b. 21 November 1901, St Joseph, Missouri, USA,
d. 19 May 1969, New York

The dominant voice on the tenor saxophone for more than half of the history of jazz, Hawkins created, virtually single-handedly, both a sound and a vocabulary for an instrument that had previously been little more than a novelty. His fluent and lyrical ballad playing, in particular, is among the most moving experiences jazz can offer, but equally remarkable was his ability to move with grace and flawless competence from one stylistic stage in jazz to the next.

He was playing in his teens and in 1921 joined singer Mamie Smith's Jazz Hounds. From 1924 to 1934 he was with the **Fletcher Henderson** orchestra, where he developed his speed, harmonic knowledge and improvisational skill. For the next five years he worked in Europe: in Britain with the bandleader **Jack Hylton**, in Holland with the Ramblers dance band, and in several other countries. In this period he recorded with many European musicians, among them **Django Reinhardt**, as well as fellow expatriates like Benny Carter.

Returning to the United States in 1939 and establishing himself on New York's 52nd Street, Hawkins had a surprise hit with a brilliant improvisation on Johnny Green's 1930 composition 'Body and Soul' (Bluebird), now an undisputed jazz classic. In the early forties he met the challenges of bebop with a confidence in his adaptability that proved justified. He worked with leading bop figures like **Thelonious Monk** and Fats Navarro and encouraged the young **Dizzy Gillespie**, but at the same time maintained his links with earlier styles by working with trumpeter Roy Eldridge. Throughout the fifties and sixties he played club and hotel engagements, appeared on **Norman Granz**'s 'Jazz at the Philharmonic' shows, and filled many record engagements. Of his albums from this period *The High and Mighty Hawk* (Felsted, 1957), produced by the English-born jazz enthusiast Stanley Dance, is outstanding and several sets for Prestige very good (notably *Duke Ellington meets Coleman Hawkins*, 1962, and *Today and Now*, 1963), but nothing to which Hawkins put his name is without interest, and few artists in the whole course of jazz have erected for themselves so massive and magnificent a monument.

EDWIN HAWKINS SINGERS
Edwin Hawkins, b. August 1943, Oakland, California, USA; Walter Hawkins; Tramaine Hawkins; Dorothy Coombs Morrison, b. 1945, Longview, Texas

Gospel arranger and choir-leader Hawkins recorded the 1969 international hit 'Oh Happy Day' and went on to become one of the leading figures in the gospel-music industry.

In 1967 Hawkins organized the North California State Youth Choir, drawing members from churches throughout the San Francisco area. To raise funds, they privately recorded and sold an album of devotional material. When a local disc-jockey began playing the old black Baptist hymn 'Oh Happy Day', it was picked up for release by Buddah, who renamed the choir the Edwin Hawkins Singers.

Featuring Morrison's impassioned solo vocals, the record was a Top Ten hit in America and Britain. When she left to pursue a solo career, appearing at the Big Sur Folk Festival in 1969, Hawkins began consciously to merge gospel with other musical forms. In 1970 he collaborated with **Melanie** on her first hit, 'Lay Down (Candles in the Rain)'. Early tours for the twenty-two-strong choir took in Playboy clubs and Las Vegas casinos while their albums included such secular material as **Bob Dylan**'s 'Blowin' in the Wind', as well as gospel songs. In 1982 Hawkins combined gospel with classical music on *Live with the Oakland Symphony Orchestra* (Myrrh).

By this time, his brother Walter Hawkins (whose 1976 Word album *Love Alive* had been a big gospel hit) and ex-wife Tramaine were receiving equal billing. She released *Tramaine* (Light, 1982), *Fall Down* (A&M), *The Joy That Floods My Soul* (Sparrow, 1989) and a 1990 live album with **Carlos Santana**, **Jimmy McGriff** and **Hammer**. Edwin Hawkins returned to a more conventional gospel approach for his later recordings. These included *Imagine Heaven* (1989), *Music and Arts Seminar Chicago Mass Choir* (1990) and *If You Love Me* (1993).

HAWKSHAW HAWKINS
b. Harold F. Hawkins, 22 December 1921, Huntington, West Virginia, USA, d. 5 March 1963, Camden, Tennessee

Hawkshaw Hawkins belonged to the new honky-tonk cadre of the forties, but unlike, say, **Ernest Tubb** or **Floyd Tillman**, he possessed the looks and personality of a hillbilly heart-throb. Though not an innovative stylist, he was among those who bridged the early, rudimentary honky-tonk and the mainstream country music of the second postwar decade.

His career began in his teens with a radio spot on station WSAZ in Huntington, West Virginia. In 1946 he joined the important WWVA (Wheeling, West Virginia) *Jamboree* and signed with King Records. His early releases were covers of Tubb's material, and his first hit came with the more individual 'Sunny Side of the Mountain' (1947), which later became a bluegrass standard. His bestseller was the **Pee Wee King** number 'Slow Poke' (1952).

In 1954 he joined the ABC-TV *Ozark Jubilee*, and in the following year the *Grand Ole Opry*, of which he was a cast member until his death. In 1962 he married fellow *Opry* performer Jean Shepherd. He also recorded for RCA-Victor and Columbia, but at the time of his death – in the plane crash which also killed **Patsy Cline** and **Cowboy Copas** – he had just returned to King and the country charts with 'Lonesome 7-7203'. *Hawk, 1953–1961* (Bear Family, 1991) is the definitive retrospective.

RONNIE HAWKINS
b. 10 January 1935, Huntsville, Arkansas, USA

One of the most consistent rockabilly artists, Hawkins is also remembered as the man who brought together the nucleus of **The Band**.

The first of his many Hawks groups was a country band but by 1957 Hawkins was singing rockabilly and auditioning unsuccessfully for **Sam Phillips**' Sun label. After army service, he made his recording début with a cover of 'Bo Diddley' on Quality (1958) in Toronto where he was based. The following year Joe Reisman signed him to the New York Roulette label and '40 Days', with Levon Helm on guitar, was a minor hit in the United States but a Top Ten record in Canada. The follow-up, 'Mary-Lou', was also successful. In 1960 Hawkins appeared on **Jack Good**'s British television show *Boy Meets Girl*.

Although he continued to record for Roulette (including *Folk Ballads*, 1960 – an unsuccessful attempt to ride the folk bandwagon), Hawkins' harsh, uncompromising style was unfashionable in the early sixties and he concentrated on live performance. By 1963 the Hawks included Canadians Robbie Robertson, Richard Manuel and Garth Hudson, as well as Helm. In that year the group cut a renowned version of **Bo Diddley**'s 'Who Do You Love', which featured outstanding guitar work from Robertson. This group also recorded *Mojo Man* (Roulette, 1964).

When Levon and the Hawks left him and later emerged as The Band, Hawkins found more young Canadians as backing musicians. Among them were Dominic Troiano, later a member of the James Gang and the **Guess Who**. Hawkins recorded for his own Hawk label, WLW (*Rrrracket Time*, 1965) and Yorkville before the success of The Band and his friendship with **John Lennon** helped to bring him a deal with Atlantic in 1970.

Ronnie Hawkins (Cotillion, 1970)' was recorded at Muscle Shoals with an all-star line-up including Duane Allman of the **Allman Brothers Band**, but neither it nor *The Hawk* (1971) sold well. In 1972 he moved to Monument and Nashville for *Rock'n'Roll Resurrection*, which included stirring sax-playing from Boots Randolph on a selection of oldies such as **Chuck Berry**'s 'Memphis Tennessee' and **Larry Williams**' 'Bony Moronie', and *Giant of Rock'n'Roll* (1974). Later records included another album called *The Hawk* (United Artists, 1979) with Garth Hudson on synthesizer and *A Legend in His Spare Time* (Quality, 1981), produced by Fred Mollin. A third album entitled *The Hawk* (Magnum Force, 1984) was a live set, recorded in England in 1982.

His appearance at The Band's 1976 farewell concert and on the *Last Waltz* album and film led to parts in **Bob Dylan**'s *Renaldo and Clara* (1977) and

Michael Cimino's *Heaven's Gate* (1980). He sang on the Canadian Band Aid Record, 'Tears Are Not Enough', and throughout the eighties recorded sporadically, mostly in a revivalist mode. Examples include *Making It Again* (1984) and *Hello Again . . . Mary Lou* (1991).

SCREAMIN' JAY HAWKINS
b. Jalacy Hawkins, 18 July 1929, Cleveland, Ohio, USA, d. 12 February 2000, Paris, France

One of the most bizarre R&B performers, Hawkins in his act combined surreal lyrics and vocal gymnastics with macabre garb and props.

A former boxing champion, he joined Tiny Grimes and his Rocking Highlanders as pianist and singer in 1952. Some of his records for Gotham with Grimes and with the bands of Leroy Kirkland and Teddy McRae were reissued on a British album, *Screamin' the Blues* by Red Lightning in 1982. In 1953 Hawkins recorded as a solo singer for Timely ('Baptize Me in Wine'), Apollo, Mercury ('[She Put the] Wamee [on Me]') and Grand.

His most famous sides, however, were for Okeh in the mid-fifties. They included 'I Put a Spell on You' (1956), with Herb Slotkin of Grand Records credited as co-writer, which was later memorably recorded by **Nina Simone** and **Alan Price**, for whom it was a British hit in 1966. While those versions make it an intense love song, the Hawkins original is replete with maniacal laughter, screaming and sobbing, and is almost a satire on horror-story conventions. The record was featured on the soundtrack of Jim Jarmusch's 1989 film *Strangers in Paradise*.

In keeping with the voodoo implications of the song, Hawkins' stage act involved skulls, a flaming coffin and gaudy robes. The best of the rest of his Okeh material included the magic potion recipe of 'Alligator Wine' and 'There's Something Wrong with You', which featured his gift for nonsense lyrics akin to those of **Slim Gaillard**. Wordless noises were the means by which Hawkins graphically portrayed his problem in 'Constipation Blues'.

At the height of the rock'n'roll era, Hawkins joined **Alan Freed**'s package tours and appeared in the film *Mister Rock'n'Roll* (1957). In the early sixties he toured Europe and made an indelible impact in England where his influence on eccentric figures like Screamin' Lord Sutch and **Arthur Brown** was evident. In 1969–70 he cut two albums for Philips with West Coast session stars like **Plas Johnson** (sax) and drummer Earl Palmer.

In later years Hawkins recorded for various labels including Mercury, Roulette, RCA and Decca, as well as appearing in the film *American Hot Wax* (1978). But his main activity remained his stage act, always in demand for club dates and international tours. In 1986 he released a live album with the Fuzztones on Midnight Music. The compilation album of his later material, *Cow Finger and Mosquito Pie* (Epic, 1990), is representative of his outlandish charms. In 1993 his version of **Tom Waits**' 'Heartattack and Vine' from 1991's *Black Music for White People* was used in a jeans commercial in Britain. Subsequent releases have all been compilations.

HAWKWIND
Dave Brock; Dik Mik; John Harrison (replaced by Thomas Crimble, replaced by Dave Anderson, replaced by Lemmy, b. Ian Kilminster, replaced by Paul Rudolph, replaced by Adrian Shaw, replaced by Harvey Bainbridge, replaced by Alan Davey); Terry Ollis (replaced by Simon King, replaced by Ginger Baker, replaced by Martin Griffin, replaced by Clive Deamer); Mick Slattery (replaced by Huw Lloyd Langton); Nik Turner; Del Dettmar (replaced by Simon House, replaced by Steve Swindells); Robert Calvert, d. 15 August 1988

In the seventies Hawkwind were the British epitome of the underground alternative rock band. In the eighties the band spawned **Motorhead**, one of the grossest heavy-metal groups.

Guitarists Brock and Slattery from Famous Cure and saxophone-player Turner from Mobile Freakout formed Group X in London's Ladbroke Grove (then the hippie quarter) in 1969. Adding Mik on synthesizers and drummer Ollis, they became Hawkwind and released an eponymous album on Liberty which was produced by former **Pretty Things** guitarist Dick Taylor.

A free performance outside the Isle of Wight Festival in 1970 confirmed Hawkwind as the mascots of Britain's underground media and burgeoning alternative society. After *In Search of Space* (1971), which highlighted the band's science-fiction obsessions, the group were joined by bass-player Lemmy.

Sci-fi author Bob Calvert wrote 'Silver Machine', the band's only Top Ten hit, in 1973. The accompanying album, *Space Ritual*, also sold well, but the following single, 'Urban Guerrilla', was withdrawn by Hawkwind's record label when London was a hit by a series of terrorist bombs. Grieg and a Ladbroke Grove café inspired the title of *Hall of the Mountain Grill* (1974), while fantasy writer Michael Moorcock contributed to 1975's *Warrior on the Edge of Time*.

In that year Lemmy was arrested on drugs charges during a North American tour and expelled from the band. He went on to form **Motorhead**. He was replaced by Rudolph from fellow underground band, Pink Fairies.

The group drifted through the rest of the seventies

with numerous personnel changes (including a brief tenure of the drum chair by Ginger Baker) and an uncertainty of musical direction. There were name changes (to Hawklords in 1978 and then back to Hawkwind) and switches of record label – to Charisma, RCA and Bronze. In the mid-eighties Brock was the only survivor from Group X and the band was recording for independent labels. Among its later eighties albums were *Bring Me the Head of Yuri Gagarin* (Demi-Monde, 1985), *Space Ritual 2* (APK, 1985), *Chronicle of the Black Sword* (Flicknife, 1986) and *Spirit of the Age* (1988). Their nineties recordings of new material included *Palace Springs* (1991), *It Is the Business of the Future to Be Dangerous* (1993) and *Future Reconstructions: Ritual of the Solstice* (1997), but their best-received release was the retrospective *Anthology* (Castle, 1992).

ISAAC HAYES
b. 6 August 1938, Covington, Tennessee, USA

As a songwriter, usually in partnership with David Porter, Hayes was responsible for several Southern soul classics recorded on **Jim Stewart**'s Stax label in the mid-sixties. As a recording artist in his own right, Hayes introduced on *Hot Buttered Soul** (1969) – which comprised only four tracks – extended mood-setting monologues (which one critic has described as 'a blend of soap-opera clichés and ghetto chic') and symphonic yet highly rhythmic backings. The album transformed the course of black music in the seventies and was a direct influence on **Barry White** and **Millie Jackson**, among others.

The son of a sharecropper, Hayes sang gospel as a child and in his youth formed a succession of groups (Valentine and the Swing Cats, the Teen Tones and Sir Isaac and the Doodads), all of which auditioned unsuccessfully for Stax. In 1964 he joined the company as a session musician and formed a writing partnership with Porter (*b. 21 November 1941, Memphis, Tennessee*) who, after a failed career as a singer, had become a staff writer at Stax in 1962. Their first successes came with **Sam and Dave** for whom they wrote and produced 'You Don't Know Like I Know', 'Hold on I'm Coming' (1966) and 'Soul Man'* (1967). Other hits included Carla Thomas's 'B-A-B-Y' (1966) and **Johnnie Taylor**'s 'I Had a Dream' (1967).

Presenting Isaac Hayes (1967), with its lengthy version of **Erroll Garner**'s 'Misty', saw the beginnings of the extended workout that climaxed on *Hot Buttered Soul* (1969), the most important black album since **James Brown**'s *Live at the Apollo* (1962). It included an eighteen-minute version of **Jimmy Webb**'s 'By the Time I Get to Phoenix' and an elaborate reworking of **Burt Bacharach**'s 'Walk on By' (originally recorded by **Dionne Warwick** in 1964). By 1971, after the minor

albums *The Isaac Hayes Movement* and *To Be Continued* (1970), Hayes' career seemed in decline. Despite the popularity of 'Never Can Say Goodbye' (also a hit for the **Jackson Five** and later revived by **Gloria Gaynor**, 1975), Barry White was having more success with his Hayes-derived seduction scenarios than Hayes himself. Then came the soundtrack for *Shaft* (1971), whose title track won Hayes an Oscar and topped the American charts, while the album (also a No. 1) set the pattern for the soundtracks of numerous blaxploitation thrillers, the best of which was ex-**Impression** Curtis Mayfield's for *Superfly* (1972). A disco version of 'Theme from Shaft' was a 1985 British hit for Eddy and the Southband (Phonogram).

Black Moses (1971) saw Hayes presenting himself as a black leader and confirmed the growing politicization of Stax which led to the 'Wattstax' concert and film (1973). Then, in 1974, the year Hayes scored and starred in *Truck Turner*, Stax went bankrupt. In 1975 Hayes signed with ABC with little success, only returning to the charts with **Roy Hamilton**'s 'Don't Let Go' (Polydor, 1979). *Royal Rappin's* (1979) saw him duetting with Millie Jackson, but for most of the eighties Hayes concentrated on production and acting. His only hit of the decade was the anti-drug song 'Ike's Rap' (Columbia, 1986). *Love Attack* was released in 1988, after which Hayes concentrated on an acting career, winning a degree of cult stardom with his role as Gandolf Finch in James Garner's much-loved tele-series *The Rockford Files*, while undertaking occasional live work. In 1998 Hayes won cult stardom with a new generation as the deep voice of Chef in the animated television series *South Park*.

JOE HAYMAN

Though Hayman wasn't the first to record comic Jewish monologues – that was probably Will N. Steele, who recorded 'Einstein on Fire' for Edison in 1900 – it was the huge success of his recording of 'Cohen on the Telephone' that launched the subgenre, one of the most extensive in the history of popular recording.

An American vaudevillian, Hayman travelled to Britain where he became a popular music-hall attraction in the first decade of the twentieth century. He recorded 'Cohen on the Telephone' in 1913 for British Columbia. Issued in America in 1914, the record reportedly sold over two million copies, a phenomenal number for the time. Its simple humour – 'Hullo! hullo! Are you dere? Hullo? Vot number do I vant? Well vot numbers have you got? Oh, excuse me, my mistook' – inaugurated a series of telephone misadventures of Mr Cohen. Hayman alone recorded over thirty monologues, including 'Cohen's Recruiting Speech', 'Cohen Calls His Tailor on the Phone' (1917),

'Cohen Buys a Wireless Set' (1922) and 'Cohen at the Prizefight' (1928), and numerous other companies issued their own 'Cohen' records. Thus, Barney Bernard was Victor's Cohen and George L. Thompson was Gennett's. The most prolific of Hayman's imitators was Monroe Silver – with **Henry Burr** one of the 'Eight Popular Victor Artists' – who recorded 'Cohen' monologues for over three decades on some twenty different labels and brought him to the radio. Cohen's misadventures were also brought to the screen in numerous silent shorts.

Following the rise of anti-Semitism in Europe in the mid-thirties, the self-deprecating humour of the Cohen series was no longer funny and it came to a natural end, though as late as 1942 Silver and **Billy Murray** recorded 'Cohen and Casey in the Army' (Beacon). The figure of Cohen is called to mind by the simple humour of Allen Sherman's 'Hello Mudduh, Hello Fadduh!' (Warners, 1963).

DICK HAYMES
b. Richard Benjamin Haymes, 13 September 1916, Buenos Aires, Argentina, d. 28 March 1980, Los Angeles, California

With his mellow, velvet baritone, Haymes was one of the most popular crooners of the forties.

Raised by his Irish mother, a singing teacher, in France, Britain, Switzerland and America, Haymes became a radio announcer in 1936. He quickly graduated to featured singer with the bands of Freddie Martin and Orin Tucker and in 1939, while trying to sell some of his songs to **Harry James**, was hired by him as a replacement for **Frank Sinatra**. A singer in the style of **Bing Crosby**, rather than Sinatra, Haymes' early records with James on Eli Oberstein's Varsity label revealed an archness in his phrasing that he would never lose. These include 'How High the Moon', 'Fools Rush in' (1940) and – their biggest hit together – 'I'll Get By' (1941).

In 1941 he left James and joined **Benny Goodman** before replacing Sinatra again in **Tommy Dorsey**'s band. Then, like so many band singers, Haymes went solo in 1943 on Decca, also signing a film contract with Fox. He had immediate success with his romantic version of **Harry Warren** and Mack Gordon's 1943 Oscar-winning song, 'You'll Never Know'* (from the film *Hello 'Frisco, Hello*), but was less successful as a screen star. His films included *Irish Eyes Are Smiling* (1944), in which he introduced Warren and Gordon's 'The More I See You' (revived successfully by **Chris Montez** in 1966); *State Fair* (1945), the only film for which **Rodgers and Hammerstein** wrote an original score together; *Do You Love Me* (1946), in which he starred with James and James' wife Betty Grable; and *The Shocking Miss Pilgrim* (1947), in which he and

Grable introduced **George** and **Ira Gershwin**'s 'For You, for Me, for Evermore'.

In 1948 Haymes returned to the cabaret circuit and had a million-seller with a revival of **Walter Donaldson**'s 1930 composition, 'Little White Lies' (Decca). In the fifties, however, he faced setbacks in both his personal life – he was married six times – and his career. He left America in 1953 with his then wife, Rita Hayworth, and was refused re-admission because he had registered as a resident alien to avoid the draft during the Second World War. He later twice went bankrupt. Comeback albums on Capitol (*Rain or Shine*, 1955, and *Moondreams*, 1956) failed and, despite sorting out his immigration problem, he settled in Ireland in the mid-sixties, touring America with muted success throughout the seventies. Haymes' final recording was *As Time Goes By* (1978) with the Louis McGlohon Trio.

OFRA HAZA
b. 19 November 1959, Israel, d. 23 February 2000, Israel

An outstanding singer trained in traditional Yemenite music, Ofra Haza, who was Israel's most successful international pop star, found new audiences in the era of 'world music' and dance beats.

She began performing the music of the Yemenite Jewish community at the age of thirteen. After two years army service she launched her solo career at nineteen and her acrobatic singing style and inventive songwriting, for example 'Tart's Song' (1979) with its slangy lyrics, won her considerable success. She represented the country four times in the Eurovision Song Contest, coming second in 1983 with 'Hi!' (which roughly means 'Stay Alive').

Haza recorded over a dozen albums for Israeli labels before she came to wider international attention with the passionate *Yemenite Songs* (1985), issued by the UK-based Globestyle. On that album she gave modern settings to deeply traditional material, including a devotional poem from the seventeenth century. The single 'Galbi' was a US dance hit and 'Im Nin Alu' was a European success in 1988. Haza's voice on the latter track was sampled by British producers Coldcut for their remix version of **Eric B** and **Rakim**'s 'Paid in Full' and for 'Pump Up the Volume' by M/A/R/R/S.

She signed to Warner's German branch and recorded *Shaday* (a mystical name for God), which sold over a million copies worldwide. The less interesting *Desert Wind* (1989) found Haza repositioned in the pop mainstream on songs produced by **Arif Mardin**, **Thomas Dolby** and others. This was followed by *Kirya* (1992). Produced by **Don Was**, this represented a return to traditional themes (the title track is an ancient Hebrew nickname for Jerusalem) with the addition of contemporary elements such as

Iggy Pop's vocal contribution on 'Daw Da Hiya'. In the same year she recorded an unlikely single with Sisters of Mercy, 'Temple of Love'. When in 1994 Yitzhak Rabin was awarded the Nobel Peace Prize (with Shimon Peres and Yasser Arafat) he asked her to sing at the award ceremony.

Her early death followed several years of illness.

LEE HAZELWOOD
b. 9 July 1929, Mannford, Oklahoma, USA

An important backroom figure in the fifties, Hazelwood found success as a producer (with **Duane Eddy**) and as a recording artist (with Nancy Sinatra).

A disc-jockey turned songwriter, Hazelwood independently produced Sanford Clark's big hit 'The Fool' (1956) and leased it to Dot. Further Dot productions were unsuccessful and in 1959 Hazelwood formed Jamie with music publisher Lester Sill and *American Bandstand* compère **Dick Clark**. One of the first masters supplied by Hazelwood from his Phoenix studio was 'Movin' and Groovin'' by Duane Eddy and the Rebels. The novelty of Eddy's echoing 'twangy' guitar sound made it a minor hit. There followed a series of instrumental hits, mostly co-written by Hazelwood and Eddy.

Again with Sill, he founded West Coast-based labels Trey and East West, which released some of **Phil Spector**'s earliest productions. Hazelwood himself went on to produce pop hits for Dino Desi and Billy ('I'm a Fool', Reprise, 1965) and Nancy Sinatra. The latter included two 1966 million-sellers written by Hazelwood, 'These Boots Are Made for Walkin'' and 'Sugar Town'. The following year, Hazelwood duetted with Sinatra on further examples of his quirky material. 'Jackson' and 'Lady Bird' reached the Top Twenty, while 'Some Velvet Morning' (1968) was only slightly less successful.

More experimental was a solo album, *Trouble Is a Lonesome Town* (1968), which was released on his own label, LHI, to which he devoted his energies in the late sixties. One of his signings was the International Submarine Band, **Gram Parsons**' innovative country-rock band whose *Safe at Home* (1967) Hazelwood supervised.

The eccentric *Poet, Fool or Bum* (Capitol, 1972) was Hazelwood's final recording before he retired from the music business in the mid-seventies. In the nineties he settled in Sweden and once more started recording in his experimental manner, touring the UK briefly in 1999.

HEART
Ann Wilson, b. 19 June 1951, San Diego, California, USA; Nancy Wilson, b. 16 March 1954, San Diego;

Roger Fisher, b. 1950; Steve Fossen (replaced 1980 by Mark Andes, replaced by Denny Carmassi)

Led by the songwriting Wilson sisters, Heart's mix of glamour and heavy rhythm made the group one of the most successful rock bands of the seventies and eighties. Unusually, their success continued, albeit in a lesser manner, into the nineties.

The Wilsons' earliest appearances were in folk clubs but they formed an electric band in Seattle with guitarist Fisher and Fossen on bass in 1972. The name was shortened from White Heart to Heart. Initially **Led Zeppelin** copyists, they moved to Vancouver, Canada, to enable their road manager to avoid the draft.

Signed to Shelley Siegel's Vancouver-based Mushroom label, they added Mike Derosier (drums) and Howard Leese (keyboards) for their million-selling début album *Dreamboat Annie* (1975). With Ann Wilson handling lead vocals on both ballads and hard-rock songs, 'Crazy on You' and 'Magic Man' were American hits in 1976. When Heart moved to Portrait, the CBS West Coast label, Siegel sued and released *Magazine*, a collection of unfinished tracks to compete with *Little Queen** (Portrait, 1977). The court ruling was that the band should be allowed to remix the Mushroom album.

Each album included one hit single: 'Barracuda' (Portrait, 1977) and 'Heartless' (Mushroom, 1978). The disappointing *Dog and Butterfly** (Portrait, 1979) included the hit 'Straight on' and was followed by Fisher's departure to form his own band. With Nancy Wilson moving to lead guitar, Heart recorded *Bébé le Strange** (Epic, 1980) and reached the Top Ten with a revival of Aaron Neville's (of the **Neville Brothers**) 'Tell It Like It Is'.

After a two-year hiatus, *Private Audition* (1982) was an American hit and for *Passion Works* (1983), ex-Jo Jo Gunne bassist Andes and drummer Carmassi joined the band. The only hit single of this period was a duet between Ann Wilson and Mike Reno of Canadian heavy-metal band Loverboy: 'Almost Paradise' (Columbia, 1984), the love theme from the film *Footloose*.

In 1985 the group moved to Capitol for the Ron Nevison-produced *Heart*, one of the year's biggest sellers. It saw the group firmly in the rock mainstream and gave the Wilsons a series of hits including 'What About Love', 'Never' and 'These Dreams'. The success continued with *Bad Animals* (1987), which contained Billy Steinberg and Tom Kelly's 'Alone', an American chart-topper and the band's first British Top Ten hit. After a three-year hiatus the band returned to the American charts with a trio of Top Twenty hits in 1990: 'All I Wannna Do Is Make Love to You', 'I Didn't Want to Need You' and 'Stranded' from

Brigade. Rock the House Live (1991) was a documentary of their 1990 tour rather than merely a greatest hits live offering. The Wilson sisters wrote most of the songs for *Desire Walks on* (1993), their bestselling album of the nineties, apart from the greatest hits collection, *These Dreams* (1997). In 1994 the group was one of the first to be the subject of a CD-ROM history. In 1999 Nancy released her first solo album, *Live at McCabe's Guitar Shop*.

TED HEATH

b. 30 March 1900, London, England, d. 18 November 1969, London

Heath's big band had several hits during the fifties, and in the forties and fifties was the only British big band to feature jazz material consistently. Many of Britain's leading jazz soloists were among its members.

A trombonist, Heath was one of the local musicians who played in 1921 with **Sidney Bechet**'s and Will Marion Cook's Southern Syncopated Orchestra on its British tour. He later became a member of the Metro-Gnomes, a band led by Ennis Parkes, who later married **Jack Hylton**. In 1928 Heath joined the dance orchestra led by **Ambrose**, soloing on 'Singapore Sorrows' (HMV, 1928). He remained with Ambrose for most of the thirties, but also played in the bands of Sydney Lipton, Maurice Winnick and **Geraldo**.

Inspired by the example of **Glenn Miller**, who was a lasting influence on his work, Heath left Geraldo in 1944 to form his own orchestra. Among its founder members were trumpeter Kenny Baker, pianist **Stanley Black** and drummer Jack Parnell, who sang on 'Route 66' and 'My Heart Goes Crazy', two of the Ted Heath Orchestra's earliest Decca recordings. Heath's composition 'I'm Gonna Love That Guy' gave the band its first American hit in 1948. **Ronnie Scott** joined Heath in 1946 but was dismissed less than a year later for failing to turn up at a gig.

The band's music was basically swing, with opportunities for brief solos from the jazz-orientated members. In 1953 the Ted Heath Orchestra played a concert at Carnegie Hall in New York. Among those who contributed arrangements for the orchestra were **Johnny Dankworth**, **Robert Farnon**, **George Shearing** and Tadd Dameron, whose 'Lyonia' and 'Euphoria' were recorded in 1949. Heath's hits included 'Vanessa' (1953), the TV theme 'Dragnet' (1953), 'Skin Deep' (1954), 'Faithful Hussar' (1956) – a minor American hit on London – and Moe Koffman's 'Swinging Shepherd Blues' (1958), also a hit for **Ella Fitzgerald**. Among the band's vocalists during the fifties were Dickie Valentine, Lita Roza and Dennis Lotis. Valentine left in 1954 for a successful solo career which included two No. 1 singles, 'Finger of Suspicion' and 'Christmas Alphabet' (Decca, 1955), while

Roza had a British No. 1 with a cover of **Patti Page**'s 'How Much Is That Doggie in the Window?' (Decca, 1953). Lotis appeared with Heath in the 1956 film *It's a Wonderful World*. Ted Heath's last minor hit was a version of the samba 'Sucu Sucu' in 1961.

During the fifties and sixties Heath made numerous albums for Decca, with a repertoire drawn from famous songwriters (including **Jerome Kern**, **George and Ira Gershwin**, **Richard Rodgers** and **The Beatles**) and other bandleaders, such as Glenn Miller and **Tommy Dorsey**. *Big Band Percussion* was a Top Twenty hit in 1962. Among Heath's arrangers during the fifties was Johnny Keating, who had a 1962 hit with the TV theme 'Z Cars'. The band's soloists included pianist Stan Tracey and trombonists Keith Christie and Don Lusher, who directed a re-formed Heath Orchestra after Ted Heath's death. The future of the orchestra was in doubt in 1994 when Heath's widow called for it to be disbanded.

HEATWAVE

Johnny Wilder, b. Dayton, Ohio, USA; Keith Wilder, b. Dayton; Rod Temperton, b. Hull, Humberside, England; Jessie Whitten, b. Chicago, Illinois, d. 1976, Chicago; Ernest 'Bilbo' Berger, b. Czechoslovakia; Mario Mantese, b. Spain; Roy Carter, b. England (joined 1976); Billy Jones (joined 1977); Calvin Duke; Keith Harrison; Derek Bramble

Heatwave were a European disco-soul band in the mould of **Earth, Wind and Fire**. Several members went on to greater success as songwriters, producers and vocalists.

Formed by expatriate Americans the Wilder brothers, the group gained popularity on the British club circuit, performing a mixture of current soul hits and original material. Heatwave signed to GTO in 1976. Their début album *Too Hot to Handle* (released on Epic in America) contained three hit singles. Written by keyboards-player Temperton and produced by Barry Blue, they were 'Boogie Nights'*, 'Too Hot to Handle' and the ballad 'Always and Forever'.

The second album *Central Heating* (1977) contained the ballad hit 'Mind Blowing Decisions'. Soon afterwards the first in a series of personnel changes occurred when guitarist Whitten was stabbed to death and bass-player Mantese was injured in a car crash. They were replaced by ex-Foundations guitarist Carter, and Bramble.

The next to leave was Temperton, who wished to concentrate on songwriting. Through his association with **Quincy Jones**, he provided hit material for **Michael Jackson** ('Thriller'), **George Benson** ('Give Me the Night') and the **Brothers Johnson**, becoming one of the eighties' most successful writers. Replaced in the band by Duke (from the Fatback Band), Temperton also continued to write for Heatwave: his 'The Groove Line' (1978) was an American million-seller.

The group released *Hot Property* (1978) before Johnny Wilder was severely paralyzed in a car crash. Although he continued to produce Heatwave's records and sing on them, he was replaced on stage by British-born J. D. Nicholson, who in turn joined the **Commodores** in 1983 when **Lionel Richie** went solo.

Heatwave continued to release albums – *Candles* (1981) and *Current* (1982) – but the group's only other hit was 'Gangsters of the Groove' in Britain in 1981. When the band split in 1982 Bramble moved on to produce hits for Lynx and for black British soul artist Jaki Graham, whose 1986 successes 'Set Me Free' and 'Breaking Away' he co-wrote. Bramble also worked with **David Bowie** on the latter's *Let's Dance* (1982). A re-formed Heatwave featuring Wilder, Jones and Tim Houpe enjoyed little success in 1991, when they released a new version of 'Mind Blowing Decisions'. *Dance Hits* (Sony, 1992) is the definitive 'best of'.

HEAVEN 17
Ian Craig Marsh, b. 11 November 1956, Sheffield, England; Martyn Ware, b. 19 May 1956, Sheffield; Glenn Gregory, b. 16 May 1958, Sheffield

One of the more imaginative British post-punk bands, Heaven 17 were one of the first groups to base their sound on synthesizers. They also played a vital role in the revival of **Tina Turner**'s career in the eighties.

Ex-computer operators Marsh and Ware were founder members of the **Human League** in 1977. The two synthesizer players left in 1981 to found the British Electric Foundation (BEF) with manager Bob Last. Heaven 17 – the name derives from the Anthony Burgess novel *A Clockwork Orange* – was its offshoot. With former stagehand Gregory on lead vocals, they released the controversial disco-protest track '(We Don't Need This) Fascist Groove Thang' (Virgin, 1981). Because the lyrics apparently referred to the President of the United States as fascist, the record was banned by British radio stations.

The group's first album *Penthouse and Pavements* included minor hits in 'Play to Win' and the title track and reached the Top Twenty. A mix of dance tracks and rock ballads, the album featured the **Crusaders**' Josie James as guest vocalist. *Music of Quality and Distinction* (1982) was a BEF 'various artists' project in which Marsh and Ware matched well-known singers with old songs. **Sandie Shaw** (with the **Dionne Warwick** standard 'Anyone Who Had a Heart'), Bernie Nolan of the Nolans vocal group (the **Supremes**' 'You Keep Me Hanging on'), **Gary Glitter** (**Elvis Presley**'s 'Suspicious Minds') and Tina Turner (the **Temptations**' 'Ball of Confusion') were among those involved. Marsh and Ware went on to produce

Turner's 1983 hit revival of **Al Green**'s 'Let's Stay Together'.

Heaven 17 had hit singles in 1983 with 'Temptation' (on which Carol Kenyon sang with Gregory), 'Come Live with Me' and 'Crushed by the Wheels of Industry', all taken from the album *The Luxury Gap*. In 1984 the group released *How Men Are*, and in 1986 a singles' collection, *Endless*. In the same year, *Pleasure One*, an album of new material, was poorly reviewed by the critics.

Ware took time out to co-produce the hit album *The Hardline According to Terence Trent d'Arby* (Columbia, 1987) before Heaven 17 released 'The Ballad of Go Go Brown' from *Teddy Bear Duke and Psycho* (1988). It was followed by a second volume of *Music of Quality and Distinction* (1991), again with a stellar cast which included **Chaka Khan**, Turner and Green of **Scritti Politti**. In 1992 a remix of 'Temptation' reached the British Top Five, prompting Virgin to release another hits collection, *Higher and Higher* (1993). In the same year Ware wrote a football song for the local Sheffield team, 'If It's Wednesday It Must Be Wembley'. In 1997 the original three members re-formed for *Bigger than America* (Warner). *Retox/Detox* followed in 1998. The live album *How Live Is* (Almafame, 1999) was doleful rather than soulful.

BOBBY HEBB
b. 26 July 1941, Nashville, Tennessee, USA

A songwriter and recording artist, Hebb had a global hit in 1966 with 'Sunny', which became a pop standard.

Equally influenced by black and country music, Hebb was a protégé of **Chet Atkins** and one of the first black artists to appear on the *Grand Ole Opry* radio show, when he performed with the Smoky Mountain Boys in 1953. When studying dental technology in Chicago he played with **Bo Diddley** and recorded for Battle in 1961 as Bobby and Sylvia with Sylvia Shemwell, who later joined the Sweet Inspirations, the group led by **Whitney Houston**'s mother Cissy.

Hebb went on to record for FM, Smash, Rich and Boom, before cutting 'Sunny' for Philips. The lilting melancholic ballad was inspired by the violent death in 1963 of his vocalist brother the day following President Kennedy's assassination. The song was a major success in both Britain and America and was later recorded by numerous artists, including **Georgie Fame**, **Cher** and Gloria Lynne. Richard Anthony also had a hit with a French translation of the song. The follow-up 'A Satisfied Mind' was less successful. In 1968 Hebb recorded in Philadelphia with **Gamble and Huff** and in 1973 he had a British disco hit with 'Love Love Love'.

Hebb's greatest impact, however, was as a writer. 'A

Natural Man' was a 1971 hit for **Lou Rawls** while other Hebb compositions were recorded by such artists as **Mary Wells**, **Marvin Gaye**, **Herb Alpert** and **Billy Preston**. In 1976 he had a minor soul hit with 'Sunny '76'.

FLETCHER HENDERSON

b. Fletcher Hamilton Henderson, 18 December 1897, Cuthbert, Georgia, USA, d. 28 December 1952, New York

In the twenties Henderson led one of the first black jazz orchestras. His later arrangements for **Benny Goodman** were vital to the emergence of swing.

Like his contemporary **Duke Ellington**, Henderson was a product of the black middle class: his father was a school principal and his mother a music teacher. He graduated in chemistry in Atlanta and moved to New York in 1920 to pursue further research. To supplement his income, he joined **W. C. Handy**'s music-publishing firm as a song demonstrator and never returned to his studies.

When Handy's former partner Harry Pace set up Black Swan records, Henderson became recording manager and formed a band to tour with the label's leading artist, **Ethel Waters**. This experience transformed his piano style from formal dance music to the stride approach of **Fats Waller** and **James P. Johnson**. Throughout the early twenties, Henderson was part of a loose group of session musicians which also included **Coleman Hawkins** and **Don Redman**. When a resident band was needed for a New York club in 1924, the group formed itself into the Fletcher Henderson Orchestra.

From 1924 to 1934 the band was resident at the Roseland Ballroom and made frequent tours. Its members included **Louis Armstrong** (1924–5), Hawkins, Rex Stewart and Benny Carter. After 1925 Henderson employed a second-string orchestra to tour colleges and smaller venues, performing the same repertoire of skilful arrangements by Redman, who left in 1927 to join McKinney's Cotton Pickers.

Henderson's band recorded frequently, beginning with Black Swan and Pathe before its first important sessions with Armstrong, which included 'Sugarfoot Stomp', and which Columbia kept in catalogue for ten years. 'Henderson Stomp' (1926) featured Fats Waller, while Stewart and Coleman were featured soloists on many sides cut for Harmony as the Dixie Stompers. Despite the virtual collapse of the record industry during the Depression, **John Hammond** produced tracks by Henderson for the European market in 1933. The orchestra's only hit record was 'Christopher Columbus' (1936).

Henderson's career as a freelance arranger began with Goodman in 1932. Adding call-and-response patterns to the contrasting brass and reed passages of Redman's charts, Henderson provided the blueprint for the swing sound of Goodman's orchestra on tunes like 'Honeysuckle Rose', 'Sometimes I'm Happy' and 'King Porter Stomp'. His arrangements were also played by other white bands including those of **Jack Hylton** and **Isham Jones**, and **Pee Wee Hunt**'s Casa Loma Orchestra. His younger brother Horace was also a gifted arranger who worked for **Tommy Dorsey**, **Earl Hines**, **Jimmie Lunceford** and Fletcher Henderson himself.

During the forties Henderson led a series of bands before joining Goodman as staff arranger in 1947 and reuniting with Ethel Waters the following year. A severe stroke in 1950 ended his professional career. In 1957 Rex Stewart organized the Fletcher Henderson All Stars to re-record the old arrangements on *The Big Reunion* (Jazztone). In the sixties Columbia compiled a four-album set of material from 1923–37. Its title, *A Study in Frustration*, reflected the view that Henderson's innovations and contributions to jazz had never been fully recognized.

JIMI HENDRIX

b. James Marshall Hendrix, 27 November 1942, Seattle, Washington, USA, d. 18 September 1970, London, England

Although his career was cut short by his sudden death, Hendrix was the most influential electric guitarist to date: every rock and jazz performer on the instrument since the sixties has been forced to take account of his technical innovations. An admirer of **Bob Dylan**, he was also the first black rock star, setting a visual style that would influence such later artists as **Michael Jackson** and **Prince**.

A self-taught musician, Hendrix acquired his first guitar at the age of twelve. Left-handed, he played a re-strung right-handed guitar throughout his career. After spending two years as a paratrooper, he got jobs in touring bands behind many of the top R&B and soul artists of the sixties. They included **B. B. King**, **Sam Cooke**, **Solomon Burke**, **Jackie Wilson**, **Little Richard** and the **Isley Brothers**, with whom he recorded. After his death, many albums containing Isley and Little Richard material with Hendrix as accompanist were issued. During these years (1961–4), he absorbed much of the flamboyant stagecraft which later inspired his live performances.

In 1964 Hendrix settled in New York, playing with Joey Dee, John Paul Hammond and Curtis Knight, with whom he co-wrote material that later appeared on *Get That Feeling* (Decca, 1967). He briefly formed his own band, Jimmy James and the Blue Flames, before former **Animals** bassist Chas Chandler invited him to England after seeing him perform in a New York club.

In London, he recruited ex-**Georgie Fame** drummer Mitch Mitchell (*b. 9 January 1947*) and bassist Noel Redding (*b. 25 December 1945*) and played clubs as the Jimi Hendrix Experience. Musicians like **The Who**'s Peter Townshend, **Eric Clapton** and Eric Burdon were impressed by his stage act (playing guitar with his teeth) and his technical pyrotechnics. In contrast to the white rock and blues orthodoxy, Hendrix made use of the wah-wah pedal and employed the tremolo arm to achieve an unprecedented control of feedback.

Chandler found Hendrix a recording contract with Track, the label run by The Who's management, and Hendrix's first single, 'Hey Joe', a cover of the Leaves' 1966 American recording, was a British Top Ten hit. It was followed by four others during 1967: the psychedelic classic 'Purple Haze', the bluesy ballad 'The Wind Cries Mary', 'The Burning of the Midnight Lamp' and a haunting version of Dylan's 'All Along the Watchtower'.

Hendrix made his first impact on America when he stole the show at the Monterey Pop Festival in July 1967. After completely recasting **Chip Taylor**'s 'Wild Thing', a number that came to form the centrepiece of his stage act, he climaxed the performance by setting fire to his guitar. This was followed by an abortive tour with the **Monkees**, whose teenybop audiences were nonplussed by Hendrix.

Hendrix's British success continued with the albums *Are You Experienced?* (1967) and *Axis: Bold as Love* (1968), masterly collections of blues, rock and psychedelic material. With the double-album *Electric Ladyland* (1968), on which he was joined by **Steve Winwood**, **Al Kooper**, **Buddy Miles** and others, he began the exploration of studio effects which came to dominate much of his later musical development. In contrast, Hendrix's live performances were reaching crisis point. Within the trio, relations between Hendrix and bassist Redding were deteriorating, and Hendrix was tiring of audience expectations that he emphasize showmanship above musicianship. Nonetheless he continued making live appearances throughout this period, including the Woodstock festival (1969) where he closed his act with an apocalyptic rendering of 'The Star-Spangled Banner'. More important to Hendrix himself though was the time spent in jam sessions at his New York studio with such musicians as **John McLaughlin** and Stephen Stills.

The Experience was replaced in 1970 by Band of Gypsies in which Hendrix was joined by Buddy Miles and bassist Billy Cox. The group recorded a live album, released on Capitol as part of a court settlement with a former manager, and Mitchell returned to replace Miles for what was to be Hendrix's final live show, the Isle of Wight Festival. This trio made the final authorized Hendrix studio album, *Cry of Love*. A few days after the Isle of Wight event, he died in his sleep from inhalation of vomit after drug-taking.

'Voodoo Chile' was a posthumous hit in Britain in 1970 and soon the market was flooded with many live and other recordings whose quality ranged from the execrable to the barely adequate. The task of editing the many hours of Electric Ladyland jam session tapes was entrusted to Alan Douglas, the veteran jazz producer who had supervised Hendrix's duets with McLaughlin. Remixing and adding other musicians, Douglas released *Crash Landing* (Polydor, 1974) and *Midnight Lightning* (Polydor, 1975). Studio out-takes from the London Track sessions were issued by Polydor in 1973 under the titles *War Heroes* and *Loose Ends*.

In the eighties and nineties Hendrix's reputation continued to grow, fuelled by several biographies, notably Charles Shaar Murray's admirable *CrossTown Traffic* (1990), which was one of the first books to focus on Hendrix the guitarist, and a continual stream of reissues and rediscovered, mostly live, recordings. Of these the best were *Radio One* (Castle, 1989) and *Live and Unreleased* (1989), two sessions recorded for BBC's Radio One, which confirmed his innovatory technique and willingness to experiment at almost any time. In 1994 Douglas oversaw the transfer of the catalogue in the US from Warner to MCA. The first 'new' release was the compilation *Blues* on which Douglas re-created Hendrix as a blues guitarist rather than the fusion guitarist of the seventies albums. Hendrix, of course, was both – and a rock guitarist; the quality of the album served to demonstrate again his versatility. In 1997, following a licensing agreement between the Hendrix estate and MCA, the Hendrix catalogue came under one record company. Since then a co-ordinated set of reissues has followed.

As well as being an influence on a wide range of guitarists, Hendrix also had a number of disciples. The most assiduous of these were former **Procul Harum** guitarist Robin Trower, and Frank Marino of Canadian heavy-metal band Mahogany Rush. Among the numerous artists who have performed Hendrix compositions were **Gil Evans**, who recorded a bigband album of his material, the classically trained Kronos Quartet, **Rod Stewart**, **Eric Clapton**, the **Pretenders** and the **Cure**.

VICTOR HERBERT

b. 1 February 1859, Dublin, Eire, d. 26 May 1924, New York, USA

Herbert was the first classically trained musician to involve himself in popular music in America. Though he wasn't influenced by any native American musics and, in turn, had little influence on those who followed him, he was the first important composer of the American musical stage.

The grandson of the Irish composer, painter and novelist Samuel Lover, Herbert was educated in Germany. He rose to become the first cellist in the Stuttgart Court Orchestra and studied composition with Max Siefritz. In 1886, with his wife, the soprano Therese Förster, he emigrated to America and joined the Metropolitan Opera House's orchestra. He also appeared as a solo cellist and his compositions, including *Concerto and Suite for Cello* (1887), won favour. Then, in 1893, Herbert was appointed director of the 22nd New York Regiment Band (founded by Patrick S. Gilmore, author of 'When Johnny Comes Marching Home').

Henceforth, though he continued to write serious music – and was chief conductor of the Pittsburgh Symphony Orchestra until 1904 – his energies were directed to composing in the popular idioms of the day. His musical education and experience of Viennese operetta soon led him to compose in this, the then dominant musical form of the American stage. For some twenty years he produced romantic scores (mostly with silly librettos) for more than fifty operettas that featured stirring marches, gliding waltzes and heroic ballads. The first, *Prince Ananias* (1894), was a relative failure, but the exotic *The Wizard of the Nile* (1895), written with Harry B. Smith – his most frequent librettist – and featuring 'Starlight, Star Bright', was a substantial success.

Herbert's greatest success was *Naughty Marietta* (1910), written with Rida Johnson Young, which included 'I'm Falling in Love with Someone', 'The Italian Street Song' and 'Ah Sweet Mystery of Life' (which later inspired the famous 'Mystery of Life' statue at Forest Lawn Memorial Park in Los Angeles), and was subsequently filmed in 1935 with **Nelson Eddy** and **Jeanette MacDonald**. Hits by Herbert include 'Gypsy Love Song' (1898), 'Kiss Me Again' (1905) and 'Because You're You' (1906). The Indian theme of *Naughty Marietta* was echoed in *Natoma* (1911), the better of his two grand operas, both of which failed. More significantly, Herbert wrote what was probably the first original musical score for a motion picture, *The Birth of a Nation* (1916).

If, in general, Herbert's musical legacy was negligible, with his work representing the end of an era rather than the beginning of one, in one respect he was genuinely progressive. Unlike most classically trained composers, Herbert actively marketed his works, which were published by M. Witmark and Sons. He was equally active in seeking to protect his copyrights. He was the leading light in the formation of the American Society of Composers, Authors and Publishers (ASCAP) and it was his suit against Shanley's Restaurant which led to the historic decision by Justice Oliver Wendell Holmes in the American Supreme Court in 1915 that a composer's works could not be publicly performed for profit without his permission.

WOODY HERMAN
b. Woodrow Wilson Herman, 16 May 1913, Milwaukee, Wisconsin, USA, d. 28 October 1987, Los Angeles

An important swing bandleader of the thirties, Herman organized some of the first modern jazz orchestras in the forties and continued to lead big bands into the eighties.

As a child Herman worked in vaudeville, joining Tom Gerun's dance bands on clarinet and alto saxophone in the late twenties. After two years with **Isham Jones**, Herman and other members of the band formed the Band That Plays the Blues, signing a Decca recording contract in 1936. Its repertoire included Herman's own blues vocals, popular ballads from a series of female singers and instrumentals, of which the Joe Bishop composition 'At the Woodchopper's Ball'* (1939) and 'Blues in the Night' (1941) were the most successful.

In the early forties Herman's work showed the influence of **Duke Ellington**, as both **Johnny Hodges** and **Ben Webster** recorded with his band, while 'Down Under' (1942) was one of **Dizzy Gillespie**'s first big-band compositions. The great leap forward in his work, however, was his 1945 recording for Columbia accompanied by what came to be known as the First Herd. With arrangements by Neal Hefti, and featuring pianist Ralph Burns and trumpeter Shorty Rogers, plus a bebop-inspired rhythm section, records like his version of **Louis Jordan**'s 'Caldonia' (with its five-trumpet unison passage), 'Apple Honey' and 'Wild Root' mixed modern jazz ideas with the standard big-band format. The Herman Herd's performances inspired modern classical composer Igor Stravinsky to write his *Ebony Concerto* for them. Stravinsky also conducted Herman's performance of the work at New York's Carnegie Hall in 1946.

During this period Herman reached an even larger public through his film appearances. These included *What's Cooking?* (1942) with the **Andrews Sisters** and *Earl Carroll Vanities* (1945), in which his band performed 'Apple Honey'. Later in 1945 he had a million-seller with his version of the theme from *Laura*.

In a gesture that was later to become routine, Herman broke up the First Herd in 1946, assembling a Second the following year. This featured the saxophone section of **Stan Getz**, Zoot Sims, Serge Chaloff and Al Cohn that became known as the 'Four Brothers' after a Jimmy Giuffre tune written for them. This group stayed together until 1949, but over the next four decades Herman toured and recorded with a series of orchestras. He visited Europe frequently, recording in 1959 with an Anglo-American Herd that included Don Rendell and Kenny Wheeler.

During the fifties he set up his own Mars label and in the sixties he attempted jazz-rock fusions on *Light My Fire* (Chess, 1968) with **Ramsey Lewis** arranger Richard Evans. He continued to record on Concord into the eighties with such albums as *My Buddy* (1983), which featured the singing of **Rosemary Clooney**, and *World Class* (1984), recorded live in Japan.

HERMAN'S HERMITS
Peter Noone, b. 5 November 1947, Manchester, England; Karl Green, b. 31 July 1946, Salford, Lancashire; Keith Hopwood, b. 26 October 1946, Manchester; Derek Leckenby, b. 14 May 1945, Leeds, Yorkshire, d. 4 June 1994; Barry Whitwam, b. 21 July 1946, Manchester

One of the more lightweight British beat groups of the sixties, Herman's Hermits were one of the most commercially successful. The exaggerated 'Englishness' of material like 'Mrs Brown, You've Got a Lovely Daughter' and music-hall star **Harry Champion**'s 1911 song 'I'm Henry the Eighth, I Am' made the group especially popular in America.

As the Heartbeats, they were an undistinguished Manchester group fronted by drama student Noone. Signed by **Mickie Most**, more for Noone's youthful good looks than their musical talents, they covered Gerry Goffin's and **Carole King**'s 'I'm into Something Good', reaching No. 1 in Britain on EMI's Columbia label in 1964. But Herman's Hermits' greater success came in America where the group had six Top Ten hits on MGM in 1965 alone, all coverversions or revivals delivered enthusiastically by the cheery, boyish Noone. They included Goldie and the Gingerbreads' 'Can't You Hear My Heartbeat?'*, 'Mrs Brown'* (a synthetic music-hall song written by Trevor Peacock for a 1963 television play), the Rays' 'Silhouettes'* (written by Frank Slay and **Bob Crewe**), **Sam Cooke**'s 'Wonderful World'*, 'I'm Henry the Eighth' and Kenny Young's 'Just a Little Bit Better'.

Noone and the group then appeared in the teen movies *When the Boys Meet the Girls* (1965) and *Hold on!* (1966). Their soundtracks yielded further hits, including **George Formby**'s 'Leaning on a Lamp-post' and 'Listen People', composed by Graham Gouldman, later of **10CC**. In 1966 the group cut a chirpy version of the **Kinks**' Ray Davies' bitter-sweet composition 'Dandy', and the following year had their last million-seller, the **Les Reed**–Geoff Stephens ballad, 'There's a Kind of Hush' (1967).

Set adrift by the rise of progressive rock, Noone launched a solo career under his real name, recording **David Bowie**'s 'Oh You Pretty Thing' (with the author on piano), a British but not American hit in 1971. Two years later, however, he was back with Herman's Hermits playing rock revival shows in America before retiring to live in France.

Noone made a further comeback in 1980, forming the Tremblers and recording *Twice Nightly* for **Beach Boy** Bruce Johnston's company (Epic in Britain). The album included material by **Elvis Costello**. He next played in **Gilbert and Sullivan**'s *The Pirates of Penzance* in America and Britain and cut a solo album, *One of the Glory Boys* (Columbia, 1982). Led by original members Leckenby (guitar) and drummer Whitwam, Herman's Hermits continued to play the nostalgia circuits of Europe and Australia. Noone also hit the oldies trail while developing a second career as a presenter on American cable TV. *The Best of the EMI Years Vol. 1* (1991) is the definitive collection.

BERNARD HERRMANN
b. 29 June 1911, New York, USA, d. 24 December 1975, Hollywood, California

Herrmann is generally regarded as the most important film composer operating in the symphonic tradition. His partnership with Alfred Hitchcock has been described as 'the greatest director/composer collaboration since Eisenstein and Prokofiev'. Herrmann's ominous (usually two-note) themes, characteristic major–minor chord changes and short impressionistic phrases, such as the stabbing, wild glissandos that conjure up the sound of birds shrieking in the murder scene in *Psycho*, are among the most intense film music ever written. However, though his most enduring scores are those he wrote for Hitchcock, Herrmann is also known for his scores for fantasy films and was one of the few film composers also to work regularly outside the cinema. As conductor of the Columbia Broadcast Symphony Orchestra (1940–58) he did much to broaden the appreciation of the classical repertoire and championed several (then) lesser known composers, notably Charles Ives whose works he frequently conducted in radio broadcasts. Among his own compositions were the cantata *Moby Dick* (1938), a symphony (1941) and the opera *Wuthering Heights* (1950).

Educated at New York University and the Juilliard School of Music, where he was taught by **Percy Grainger** among others, Herrmann founded the New Chamber Orchestra and in 1933 joined the Columbia Broadcasting network as a composer and staff conductor. There, he conducted the orchestra for Orson Welles' famous Mercury Theater radio presentation of *War of the Worlds* (1936) in which a 'real' radio programme was interrupted by news of the invasion from space. Herrmann's score for Welles' adaptation of *Dracula* was notable for its expressive use of strings and the major–minor chord changes which would become the composer's trademark. The association with Welles continued into film-making when Herrmann was commissioned to score *Citizen Kane* (1940) and *The Magnificent Ambersons* (1942). Other notable scores of this period were *The Devil and Daniel Webster* (1941), for which he won an Oscar, *Hangover Square* (1944), *The Ghost and Mrs Muir* (1947) and *The Day the Earth Stood Still* (1951).

In 1955 Herrmann began his association with Hitchcock with *The Trouble with Harry*. Their collaboration lasted for eight films and included *Vertigo* (1958), *Psycho* (1960) and *Marnie* (1963). *Vertigo*, his most sumptuous score, shows Herrmann's wit (during the title sequence as 'directed by Alfred Hitchcock' appears a low, fat D note is heard played on a tuba), his complex use of leitmotifs (with the motifs taking on new meaning as the plot unravels) and a dramatic understanding of Hitchcock's obsessional romanticism (notably in the lengthy kiss sequence which Herrmann has described as 'a long crescendo of emotional fulfilment'). The score for *Psycho*, written for an orchestra composed entirely of strings, is more visceral with melody abandoned in favour of menacing, unsettling fragments.

During the fifties Herrmann worked extensively in television, concentrating particularly on fantasy (notably *The Twilight Zone*). In 1960 his partnership with Hitchcock ended when his score for *Torn Curtain* was replaced and in the sixties Herrmann settled in London. The best of his later works include two scores for Brian De Palma, which built on his work with Hitchcock, *Sisters* (1973) and *Obsession* (1974), and *Taxi Driver* (1974), his last score.

One of the most recorded of film composers, Herrmann's albums include *Bernard Herrmann* (Decca, 1975), *The Mysterious Film World of* (1976), *Psycho* (Unicorn, 1975), *Sisters* (Entr'acte, 1975) and *Taxi Driver* (Arista, 1976).

CAROLYN HESTER
b. 1936, Waco, Texas, USA

Singer and guitarist Hester was a leading figure in the folk revival of the sixties.

A child actress, she first appeared on television, aged thirteen, and in 1956 moved to New York to study drama. With a repertoire of traditional songs and a powerful, dramatic vocal style, Hester was part of the Greenwich Village coffee-house and folk-club circuit, touring with the **New Lost City Ramblers**. She was briefly a member of a **Weavers**-style group, the Song Spinners, and a proto-**Peter Paul and Mary** trio with Bob Gibson and Ray Boguslav, before recording for Coral.

She recorded a well-received eponymous album for Tradition before signing to Columbia and using the then unknown **Bob Dylan** to play harmonica on *Carolyn Hester* (1961), a period-piece mixture of Appalachian mountain songs ('Swing and Turn Jubilee'), spirituals ('When Jesus Lived in Galilee') and a blues ('Come Back Baby') learned from Dylan. Hester married **Richard Farina** and in 1962 toured Britain with him.

In 1963 Hester and **Judy Collins** led a boycott of the television show *Hootenanny*, which had blacklisted **Pete Seeger**. As Dylan began the trend towards folk-rock, she formed the Carolyn Hester Coalition, an electric group, in the mid-sixties. After its commercial failure, Hester retired from music for several years, returning in the seventies to record for RCA and become a director of the annual folk festival in Kerrville, Texas. In 1993 she guested on **Nanci Griffith**'s acclaimed *Other Voices, Other Rooms* album.

NICK HEYWARD
b. 20 May 1961, Beckenham, Kent, England

The founder and lead singer of pop band Haircut 100, Heyward was briefly a British teen-idol in the early eighties.

Haircut 100 was formed in 1980 by Heyward and former schoolmates Graham Jones (guitar) and Les Nemes (bass). The group signed to Arista on the strength of a demo tape, and added session player Phil Smith (sax), Mark Fox (percussion) and ex-Eddie Floyd drummer Blair Cunningham to the line-up.

Written by Heyward and produced by Bob Sargeant, 'Favourite Shirts (Boy Meets Girl)' was an immediate success throughout Europe. 1982 brought three more British hits – 'Love Plus One', 'Fantastic Day' and 'Nobody's Fool' – featuring Heyward's airy vocals and whimsical lyrics. The album *Pelican West* was equally well received. Now a teen-idol and fan magazine pin-up, Heyward left the group in 1983 and released 'Whistle Down the Wind', a title borrowed from the 1961 Hayley Mills film for which **Malcolm Arnold** had written the music. Co-produced with Geoff Emerick, *North of a Miracle* contained two more hits, the infectious 'Take That Situation' and 'Blue Hat for a Blue Day'.

There followed a three-year gap before the next album, *Postcards from Home* (1986), during which time Heyward had only one minor hit, in 1984, the funky 'Warning Sign'. He signed to Warners in 1988, and 'You're My World' was a minor hit, but *I Love You Avenue* (1989) made little impact. Heyward was signed by Columbia in 1992, releasing the assured but formulaic *From Monday to Sunday*, which again sold poorly. He recorded two albums for Creation, *Tangled* (1996) and the intriguing *The Apple Bed* (1998), but neither sold well.

JOHN HIATT

b. 1952, Indianapolis, USA

John Hiatt, who had a moderately successful career as a solo performer and sideman from the mid-seventies onwards, won his greatest acclaim as a songwriter. His material was recorded by a plethora of artists from **Bob Dylan** to **Iggy Pop** and **Bonnie Raitt** to the **Neville Brothers**.

Hiatt played with various Indiana bands before moving to Nashville in 1970. A four-year spell as a staff songwriter for publishers Tree eventually brought him to the attention of Epic Records. *Hanging Around the Observatory* (1974), recorded in Nashville with session players, was a mixed bag of R&B, country and folk-rock, highlighting Hiatt's songwriting skills and shot through with his wry sense of humour. One song, 'Sure as I'm Sitting Here', was a US Top Twenty hit for **Three Dog Night** later that year. However, neither *Observatory* nor its follow-up, the more focused *Over-coats* (1975), sold well and Hiatt signed to MCA in 1978. *Slug Line* (1978), contained some of his best songs, including the title track, the **Elvis Costello**-like 'Take Off Your Uniform' and 'Washable Ink', memorably covered by the Neville Brothers. Despite favourable comparisons with Costello, **John Prine** and **Joe Jackson**, the album and its excellent follow-up, *Two Bit Monsters* (which contained the **Roseanne Cash**-covered 'Pink Bedroom'), once again failed to convert critical acclaim into sales. Hiatt next joined **Ry Cooder**'s band, touring and recording the *Borderline* album (1992) and soundtrack of *The Border*. The latter included the classic 'Across the Borderline', which **Willie Nelson** would record in 1993.

In 1982 Hiatt signed to Geffen records, who teamed him with (ex T-Rex/**David Bowie**) producer Tony Visconti for *All of a Sudden*, a polished set of songs including 'Something Happens' (later recorded by **Dave Edmunds**) and the brooding 'My Edge of the Razor'. The **Nick Lowe**-produced *Riding with the King* (1983) was followed by 1985's *Warming Up to the Ice Age*, which included a duet with Costello.

Beset by a growing dependence on alcohol, Hiatt spent the next two years away from music, before UK independent label Demon recorded him with a band of admirers and former collaborators (bassist/producer Lowe, guitarist Cooder and veteran drummer Jim Keltner). The resulting album, *Bring the Family*, was Hiatt's most successful yet, encouraging A&M subsequently to sign Hiatt to a long-term deal. The follow-up, *Slow Turning* (1988), featured Hiatt's touring band the Goners, who broke up shortly after slide guitarist Sonny Landreth left their ranks for a solo career. After the release of the less successful *Stolen Moments* (1990), Hiatt and the team that had made *Bring the Family* formed the low-key 'supergroup' Lit-tle Village, which released one eponymous album on Reprise in 1992. 1993 saw Hiatt continue his solo career with the well-received *Perfectly Good Guitar*. Subsequent recordings include *Walk on* (Capitol, 1995), on which Raitt guested, *Little Head* (1997) and the superior *Crossing Muddy Waters* (Sanctuary, 2000), made after his recovery from throat cancer.

AL HIBBLER

b. Albert Hibbler, 16 August 1915, Little Rock, Arkansas, USA

In the fifties Hibbler's bizarre use of vibrato and dramatic emphasis and his distorted accenting of words (which **Duke Ellington** described as 'tonal pantomime') briefly won him a wide audience.

Hibbler rose to fame as a vocalist with the bands of Dub Jenkins, **Jay McShann** (with whom he toured the Southwest in 1943) and Ellington, with whom he sang for eight years from 1943. While with Ellington he recorded R&B for various labels, including Miracle, Chess, RCA, Columbia and Atlantic ('Danny Boy', 1951). This last song saw him approaching the elaborate stylings he would employ on his recordings for Decca – the label he joined in 1955.

He had an immediate million-seller with 'Unchained Melody', from the film *Unchained* (1955), though significantly his mannered rendering was not as popular with the black audience as **Roy Hamilton**'s version of the song. For two years Hibbler's records, all dramatic ballads – including 'He' (1955), '11th Hour Melody', 'Never Turn Back' and 'After the Lights Go Low' (all 1956) – regularly made the Top Forty, before he drifted into obscurity.

In the mid-sixties Hibbler returned briefly to the club circuit in the wake of the **Righteous Brothers**' successful blue-eyed soul revivals of 'Unchained Melody' and 'He'.

DAN HICKS

b. 9 December 1941, Little Rock, Arkansas, USA

With his group the Hot Licks, Hicks produced an exhilarating blend of supperclub jazz, the **Andrews Sisters**, cowboy music and ragtime with a dash of wry humour and pseudo-nostalgia.

Raised in Santa Clara, California, Hicks joined the Charlatans, the first San Francisco rock group of the sixties, in 1965. He remained with the group, which is better remembered for its posters than its music – the Charlatans' lead singer was George Hunter, one of the best-known San Francisco poster artists – until 1968, when, with violinist David LaFlamme (who went on to form It's a Beautiful Day), he formed Dan Hicks and his Hot Licks.

Modelled on **Django Reinhardt**'s Hot Quintet, the

drummerless group (which now consisted of Hicks, Jon Weber, Sid Page, Sherry Snow, Christina Gancher and Jaime Leopold) was signed to Epic, for whom they recorded the classic *Original Recordings* (1969). Produced by Bob Johnston, the album defined Hicks's musical concerns and introduced his idiosyncratic songs, such as 'Canned Music', 'I Scare Myself', and 'How Can I Miss You When You Won't Go Away'.

When the album failed commercially, the group (with Hicks, Page and Leopold joined by John L. Girton, Maryann Price and Naomi Eisenberg) joined Blue Thumb in 1971, for whom they produced a series of engaging albums (*Striking It Rich*, 1971; *Where's the Money*, 1972; and *Last Train to Hicksville*, 1973). Their version of **Johnny Mercer**'s spoof 'I'm an Old Cow Hand (from the Rio Grande)' perfectly captures the mood of the song and the group. *Hicksville*, their only album with a drummer, was a surprise success but the ever-unstable group broke up, Page briefly joining **Sly Stone**, while Hicks made sporadic appearances in the San Francisco area. In 1978 Warner Brothers issued *It Happened One Bite*, a collection of Hicks songs recorded by the group as an intended soundtrack for a movie that was never released. During the eighties Hicks formed the Acoustic Warriors, which performed more frequently. In the nineties he returned to solo work in the San Francisco area but ventured as far as Los Angeles for the live recording *Straight Shootin'* (On the Spot, 1994), his first album for sixteen years. He followed that six years later with *Beatin' the Heat* (Surfdog Records), which featured original Hot Licks member Sid Page and Hicks duetting with **Elvis Costello**, **Rickie Lee Jones**, **Bette Midler** and **Tom Waits**, among others. Celebratory rather than innovative, the album included reworkings of old favourites ('I Scare Myself') and new Hicks compositions ('My Cello').

JOE HILL
b. Joel Emmanuel Haaglund (or Joseph Hillstrom), 1872, Sweden, d. 19 November 1915, Salt Lake City, Utah, USA

An important union organizer, Hill used folk song to build and strengthen the first American militant labour movement, the International Workers of the World (IWW or the 'Wobblies'). In this, he was one of the first people in the twentieth century to make social and critical use of folk song, and a forerunner of **Woody Guthrie** and **Bob Dylan**.

Little is known about Hill's early life. A seaman, he emigrated to America in 1902. By 1910 he was a member of the IWW – which had been formed five years earlier – and he took part in organizing strikes among dock workers in San Pedro, California, and in the

Mexican Revolution. During this period he was a regular contributor to IWW periodicals, *Solidarity* and *The Industrial Worker*, providing them with essays and, most importantly, songs, which were included in *The Little Red Songbook* after his death. Many were doggerel adaptations of contemporary hits and traditional material. His most famous song, 'The Preacher and the Slave', which introduced the phrase 'pie in the sky', was an adaptation of the Salvation Army hymn 'In the Sweet By-and-By' and 'Casey Jones – the Union Scab' was an adaptation of 'Casey Jones', the song about the 1900 Illinois train wreck which in 1910 was a huge hit for both **Billy Murray** and **Arthur Collins**. His other songs include 'There Is Power in the Union', 'Coffee An' and 'Rebel Girl', written for Hill's one-time love Elizabeth Gurley Flynn, who later became a leader of the American Communist Party.

In January 1914 he was arrested on a murder charge and found guilty on circumstantial evidence. Despite appeals by the Swedish government, President Woodrow Wilson and various labour leaders for a new trial, he was executed in November 1915. On the night before his death Hill sent his famous telegram to the IWW leadership: 'Don't waste any time in mourning. Organize.'

A direct influence on Woody Guthrie, Hill was later lionized in several songs, including 'Joe Hill' (1938, written by **Earl Robinson**, co-author of **Three Dog Night**'s 1972 American No. 1, 'Black and White'), recorded by **Joan Baez**, among others, and 'Joe Hill' by **Phil Ochs**. In 1971 he was played by Thommy Berggren in Bo Widerberg's romantic biopic, *Joe Hill*.

Z. Z. HILL
b. Arzell Hill, 29 September 1940, Naples, Texas, USA, d. 27 April 1984

The success of Z. Z. Hill's 'Down Home Blues' (1982) suggested that there was a black American audience who were still interested in, or at any rate who could be converted to, the blues – so long, perhaps, as it was judiciously placed in a wider context. For such a strategy Hill's experience had equipped him well.

In the late sixties and early seventies Hill was a well-regarded exponent of Southern deep soul who had several regional hits, notably 'I Need Someone' (1971), on Kent, working with the arranger **Maxwell Davis**. He also gained a cult following in Britain with albums like *The Brand New Z. Z. Hill* (1971). He worked for a number of major and minor labels, among them United Artists, with whom he recorded *Keep on Lovin' You* (1975), part-produced by **Allen Toussaint** and Lamont Dozier (of **Holland, Dozier and Holland**). After a period in the doldrums he signed with the Jackson, Mississippi, Malaco label in

1981 and embarked on a series of albums, including *Down Home* (1982) and *The Rhythm and the Blues* and *I'm a Blues Man* (both 1983). Though not formally blues records to the extent that their titles suggest, they skilfully mixed blues and deep-soul material in a manner that recalled **Bobby Bland** in his heyday; their success, in fact, mutely reproached the lost direction of Bland's own career, until that too was revived by a move to Malaco.

In 1994 Malaco marked the anniversary of Hill's death by issuing the tribute album *Z Zelebration*. Among the contributing artists were Denise Lasalle, Bobby Bland and **Little Milton**.

EARL HINES
b. Earl Kenneth Hines, 28 December 1903, Pittsburgh, Pennsylvania, USA, d. 22 April 1983, Oakland, California

The most influential jazz pianist of the thirties and forties, Hines played with **Louis Armstrong** on the 1929 Hot Five recordings and led a big band whose members included **Billy Eckstine** and **Charlie Parker**.

From a musical family, Hines toured with singer Lois Deppe in 1922 before moving to Chicago. There he played in the bands of Erskine Tate and Carroll Dickerson before joining Armstrong's Stompers, and partnering him in a brief venture as club owners in 1927. The renowned duets on such Hot Five titles as 'Weather Bird' showed the extent to which the mutual influence of Hines and Armstrong had made them the most advanced jazz players of the time. It was at this period that Hines perfected his 'trumpet' style in which the right hand played sequences which paralleled the phrasing of Armstrong's solos.

From 1929 Hines led his own band in residencies in Chicago with tours to New York and elsewhere. Nicknamed 'Fatha' in tribute to his pre-eminence as a pianist, he recorded for RCA (1929), Brunswick (1932–4) and RCA's Bluebird label (1939–42). The band reached its peak of popularity at the end of the thirties with hits like 'Boogie Woogie on St Louis Blues', 'Stormy Monday', 'Rosetta' (his best-known composition) and 'Jelly Jelly', which featured vocalist Eckstine. An earlier singer with the band had been Herb Jeffries, who went on to star in a short series of all-black Westerns that included *Harlem on the Range* (1939).

In 1942–3 Hines contributed to the foundation of bebop when Eckstine, **Sarah Vaughan**, Parker and **Dizzy Gillespie** were all band members and the orchestra featured the first arrangement of the bebop standard 'Night in Tunisia'. When Eckstine left to pursue a solo career, Hines briefly switched musical policy to include an all-female string section in a programme of semi-symphonic works.

Affected by the slump in the market for big bands,

Hines joined Armstrong's All Stars in 1948 to play small-group Dixieland jazz. He continued in the same vein after leaving Armstrong in 1951, touring Europe in a band with **Jack Teagarden** in 1957. From the sixties there was renewed recognition of his pioneering role when Hines cut a series of acclaimed solo albums, including *Earl Hines at Home* (Contact, 1964) and *Hines Plays Duke Ellington* (four albums, 1971–5).

He remained in demand for live appearances at clubs and festivals, continuing to lead a quartet until shortly before his death at the age of 79.

ROBYN HITCHCOCK
b. 1952, Cambridge, England

Singer-songwriter Hitchcock's career was dogged by comparisons with **Pink Floyd** leading light Syd Barrett, a recurring influence on his work, before establishing an identity for himself in the eighties. His reputation was boosted by the patronage of **R.E.M.**, who cited his former band the Soft Boys as a major influence.

Born and bred in Cambridge (as was Barrett), Hitchcock was the son of a writer, and subsequently went to art school, becoming involved in music in his late teens. He busked and played solo folk gigs, also joining a number of local bands, one of which, Dennis & the Experts, became the Soft Boys in 1976, with a line-up of Hitchcock, drummer Morris Windsor (aka Otis Fagg), bassist Andy Metcalfe and second guitarist Alan Davies. They recorded one EP, *Give It to The Soft Boys*, in 1977 for local label Raw before Davies was replaced by guitarist Kimberly Rew from another Cambridge band, the Waves.

Adding harmonica-player Jim Melton, they released their début album, *Can of Bees*, a mixture of live and studio cuts, in 1979. Melton left between the recording of the first album and the excellent *Underwater Moonlight* (Armageddon, 1980), on which Matthew Seligman replaced Metcalfe. It established the band with a loyal cult audience in the UK, with comparisons constantly made with a number of sixties bands, including **The Beatles**, **Byrds** and early Pink Floyd – the band recorded Syd Barrett's 'Vegetable Man' on the 1980 EP *Near The Soft Boys*. The band broke up in 1981. Several posthumous albums have since emerged, notably 1983's *Invisible Hits* and a 1993 compilation, *The Soft Boys 1976–81*, on the Rykodisc label. Seligman joined the **Thompson Twins** and later played with **David Bowie**, while guitarist Rew released two solo singles before re-forming his old band the Waves, fronted by US exile Katrina Leskanich. Changing their name to Katrina & the Waves, they had a Top Ten single on both sides of the Atlantic with 'Walking on Sunshine' (1985). Rew also

wrote 'Going Down to Liverpool', which was recorded by the **Bangles** in 1986.

Hitchcock embarked on a solo career in 1981 with
the album *Black Snake Diamond Role*, which included
some of the Soft Boys' last recordings and featured
Seligman in a supporting role, as did the follow-up,
Groovy Decay (1982). The 1985 set *Fegmania* saw the
first billing for his regular backing band the Egyp-
tians, which included ex-Soft Boys Metcalfe and
Windsor plus keyboard-player Roger Jackson.

By now Hitchcock had established himself on both
sides of the Atlantic as an 'eccentric English artist'.
Encouraged by Hitchcock's ever-rising profile, A&M
released *Globe of Frogs* (1988), which swiftly became a
favourite on the US college scene. A US-only collection, *Queen Elvis*, appeared in 1989, and *Perspex Island*
in 1991. It spawned a radio hit with the catchy pop
single 'So You Think You're in Love'.

In 1993 Hitchcock released *Respect*, his seventh solo
album, produced by John Leckie, who had also
worked with **XTC** – another band heavily influenced
by sixties British pop and psychedelia – and the man
who originally mixed Pink Floyd's 'Vegetable Man'.
Hitchcock's most direct album to date, shorn of many
of the cod-psychedelicisms which cluttered previous
efforts, it collected favourable reviews and included
another classic non-hit, 'Arms of Love', which was
swiftly covered by R.E.M. Although Hitchcock spent
an increasing amount of time in the US, living in
Washington DC, he recorded *Respect* in the UK and
returned again to take part in a one-off Soft Boys
reunion with Metcalfe, Rew, Seligman and Windsor
in London in early 1994. In 1995 Rhino in the US and
Sequel in the UK began a comprehensive reissue programme in which over ten albums, virtually all Hitchcock's solo and Egyptian work, were made available.
Each album also contained several previously unreleased tracks. The best of the albums were the live
Gotta Let This Hen Out and *Eye*. In 1996 he signed to
Warner for the more mainstream *Mixed Elixir*.

JOHNNY HODGES
*b. Cornelius Hodge, 25 July 1907, Cambridge, Massa-
chusetts, USA, d. 11 May 1970, New York*

With Benny Carter and Willie Smith, Hodges founded
the jazz alto-saxophone style. In the thirties and forties
his strong rhapsodic tone was an essential component
of the **Duke Ellington** sound. He influenced a whole
generation of forties saxophonists, from **Charlie Barnet** to Bruce Turner, alto-sax player with **Humphrey
Lyttelton**. Hodges also recorded with **Benny Goodman** and **Charlie Parker**, whose bebop alto style eventually became the model for later jazz generations.

Hodges' earliest instruments were drums and
piano but in 1921 **Sidney Bechet** tutored him on saxo-

phone. Based in Boston, his earliest professional
engagements were with stride pianist Willie 'The
Lion' Smith and with Bechet. In 1926 he joined drummer **Chick Webb**'s orchestra in New York, playing
frequently at the Apollo ballroom.

After a brief spell with Luckey Roberts, Hodges
began a twenty-year stay with Ellington in 1928. His
first recordings with the orchestra included
'Tishomingo Blues' (1928) and 'Hot Feet' (1929). Until
1951 Hodges was a featured soloist on dozens of
Ellington titles recorded with small groups as well as
big band for Victor, Musicraft and Columbia and
other labels. Among the most notable were 'Blue
Tune' (1932), 'In a Jam' (1936), with its instrumental
dialogue with Cootie Williams, 'Don't Get Around
Much Anymore' (1940), 'In a Mellotone', 'Come Sunday' (1941) and 'Magenta Haze' (1945).

Hodges also occasionally recorded away from
Ellington ('A Sailboat in the Midnight', Variety, 1937;
'Prelude to a Kiss', Vocalion, 1938). In 1938 he played
at Goodman's Carnegie Hall concerts. Among the
singers he accompanied were **Mildred Bailey** (1935),
Billie Holiday (1936), **Al Hibbler** ('White Christmas',
1943, on Mercer, a label run by Ellington's son) and
Ivory Joe Hunter. He also performed with **Woody
Herman** ('Perdido' 1944).

From 1951 to 1955 Hodges led his own group, whose
members included ex-Ellingtonians Sonny Greer
(drums) and Lawrence Brown (trombone) and,
briefly, the young **John Coltrane**. For Verve he made
The Jeep Is Jumping (1954) and collaborations with
Gerry Mulligan.

Rejoining Ellington's orchestra in 1955, Hodges
remained with them until his death.

HOLE
*Erik Erlandson; Jill Emery (replaced by Kristen Pfaff,
d. 1994, replaced by Melissa Auf der Maur); Courtney
Love, b. Love Michelle Harrison, 9 July 1965, San Francisco, USA; Caroline Rue (replaced by Patty Schemel)*

Probably still best known for being the band of Kurt
Cobain's widow, Hole produced some of the finest
music of the grunge era. Subsequently Courtney Love
went on to build a successful career as an actress.

Love formed Hole in 1989 after stints with a variety
of bands – including **Faith No More** and Babes in
Toyland – and a small role in *Sid and Nancy* (1985),
recruiting lead guitarist Erlandson, drummer Rue and
bassist Emery from an advert in *Flipside* magazine.
Hole soon gained a reputation for their frantic live
shows and released two EPs, *Retard Girl* and *Rat Bastard*, before recording their raw, abrasive début, *Pretty
on the Inside* (1991) with Kim Gordon of **Sonic Youth**.
While the album brought Hole an international cult
audience, Love's relationship with **Nirvana**'s Kurt

Cobain brought them attention from the mainstream media, and the band became one of the biggest rock acts in the US without making a new record. Cobain and Love were married on 24 February 1992, and had a child, Frances Bean, on 18 August, while the band replaced drummer Rue with Patty Schemel and bassist Emery with Kristen Pfaff, completing the definitive Hole line-up.

Live Through This (1994)*, a vibrant development on Nirvana's loud/soft dynamics, consolidated Hole's popularity but marked the beginning of a period of turbulence for the band. One week before the record's release Cobain committed suicide, and Love spent the next year falling apart in public. Meanwhile, the record company drew a series of hit singles from *Live Through This*, including 'Doll Parts', 'Violet' and 'Miss World', but had to replace bassist Kristen Pfaff with Melissa Auf der Maur after the former died of a heroin overdose.

Leaving the band on hold after overcoming her personal problems, Love embarked on a successful film career, starring in *The People vs. Larry Flint* (1996) alongside Woody Harrelson. Hole returned to the studio in mid-1997 with the **Smashing Pumpkins**' Billy Corgan at the helm. The result was *Celebrity Skin* (1998), which saw Hole find a mellower sound, almost reminiscent of **Fleetwood Mac**, and included two hit singles in 'Awful' and the title track.

After poor sales of *Celebrity Skin* and the departure of bassist Melissa Auf der Maur (who would go on to join the Smashing Pumpkins), Courtney took on two more leading film roles, *200 Cigarettes* (1998) and *Man on the Moon* (1999). In 2000 Hole contributed 'Be a Man' to the soundtrack to Oliver Stone's *Any Given Sunday*, before a dispute over digital downloads saw the band leave Geffen. The band then made a number of unreleased tracks available over the internet, including a version of 'Asking for It' (from *Live Through This*) featuring Cobain.

BILLIE HOLIDAY
b. Eleanora Holiday, 7 April 1915, Baltimore, Maryland, USA, d. 17 July 1959, New York

Widely regarded as the greatest of jazz vocalists, Holiday's genius was to imbue even the most banal lyric with a depth of feeling. Her most sustained period of achievement was the thirties and early forties when she received superb accompaniment from **Teddy Wilson**, **Lester Young** and others. Holiday's later years were dogged by drugs problems and her records were consequently uneven in quality.

The illegitimate daughter of guitarist and trumpeter Clarence Holiday, who left her mother soon after her birth, Holiday moved to New York as a teenager and took her first singing jobs in the early thirties. Record producer **John Hammond**, impressed with her vocal abilities, got Holiday her first recording session, 'Your Mother's Son in Law' (1933) with **Benny Goodman**.

In 1935 she cut 'What a Little Moonlight Can Do' with pianist Wilson, the first of eighty tracks she made for Brunswick and Vocalion in the following three years. Most were current pop tunes of little merit but, like the Sun recordings of **Elvis Presley**, they captured the joy of singing. On many of the sessions she was accompanied by leading jazz soloists like **Johnny Hodges** and Young, who gave her the name Lady Day. On such tracks as 'Mean to Me' (1937) and 'When You're Smiling', the rapport between Holiday and Young is total. Several of these songs, including 'I Cried for You' (1936) with Hodges, were jukebox hits.

In live performance Holiday sang with **Artie Shaw** and **Count Basie** before undertaking a residency at Café Society in New York where she introduced the brooding anti-lynching song 'Strange Fruit', composed by Lewis Allen, which she recorded for **Milt Gabler**'s Commodore label. A further Commodore track, her own composition 'Fine and Mellow' was a hit. Holiday's recordings from this period have a sombre ring. Among them were her own songs 'God Bless the Child', 'Gloomy Sunday' and 'I Cover the Waterfront'.

Holiday signed to Decca in 1944, and her records followed the label's pop-orientated policy. Although the string arrangements by **Gordon Jenkins** tended to emphasize the disparity between the material and the performance, such tracks as Ram Ramirez's 'Lover Man', her own 'Don't Explain' and 'Porgy' (1949) were outstanding.

Her first major solo concert took place at New York Town Hall in 1946 but the following year Holiday was convicted for drugs offences, spending nearly a year in jail. On her release she resumed a solo career that found her erratic in live performance. Her recording activity received a boost when **Norman Granz** signed her to Verve in 1952. The Verve recordings documented both the peaks and troughs of her final years and were reissued in ten volumes. Among the highlights were a 1954 concert with Basie, *Songs for Torching* (1955), *Velvet Mood* and *Songs for Distingué Lovers* (1958).

She published an embittered autobiography, *Lady Sings the Blues*, in 1956. **Diana Ross** played Holiday in the 1972 film of the same title which romanticized Holiday's life.

HOLLAND, DOZIER AND HOLLAND
Brian Holland, b. 15 February 1941, Detroit, Michigan, USA; Lamont Dozier, b. 16 June 1941, Detroit; Eddie Holland, b. 30 October 1939, Detroit

During the sixties Holland, Dozier and Holland wrote and produced many hit songs for the **Supremes**, **Marvin Gaye**, the **Four Tops** and other artists of **Berry Gordy**'s Motown stable. In 1968 they set up their own company, finding further success as producers and writers with **Chairmen of the Board**, Freda Payne and others. In later years they separated, with Dozier in particular producing and composing for a wide range of soul and pop singers.

Dozier had recorded unsuccessfully as Lamont Anthony for United Artists and Eddie Holland had been an early Tamla signing, making the Top Thirty with 'Jamie' (1962), before Gordy teamed them up with the latter's brother, who had already produced 'Please Mr Postman' (1961) by the **Marvelettes**. For **Martha and the Vandellas** the three wrote 'Come and Get These Memories' (1963), 'Heatwave' and 'Quicksand' but their greatest success came with the Supremes. After the insistent No. 1 'Where Did Our Love Go' (1964), Holland–Dozier–Holland supplied the group with six chart-toppers in the next three years. Among them were 'Baby Love' (1964), 'Stop! In the Name of Love' (1965), 'You Can't Hurry Love' (1966), 'You Keep Me Hanging on' (a 1968 hit for heavy-rock band **Vanilla Fudge**) and 'The Happening' (1967).

Motown artists who benefited from later material by the trio included the **Isley Brothers** ('This Old Heart of Mine', 1966), the Four Tops (the No. 1s 'I Can't Help Myself', 1965, and 'Reach out I'll Be There', 1966, as well as 'It's the Same Old Song' and 'Bernadette', 1969), Gaye ('Can I Get a Witness', 1963, 'You're a Wonderful One' and 'How Sweet It Is to Be Loved by You', 1964) and Martha and the Vandellas ('Nowhere to Run', 1965, and 'Jimmy Mack', 1967).

After a two-year legal battle, Holland–Dozier–Holland left Motown in 1968. Still based in Detroit, they launched the Invictus and Hot Wax labels. For contractual reasons, their first hits, Freda Payne's stirring 'Band of Gold'* (Invictus, 1970) and 'Give Me Just a Little More Time'* by Chairmen of the Board (Invictus, 1970), were credited to Dunbar and Wayne, but later million-sellers like Payne's anti-war 'Bring the Boys Home' (1971), Honey Cone's 'Want Ads' (Hot Wax, 1971) and 'Stick Up' and 'Somebody's Been Sleeping' by 100 Proof Aged in Soul (Hot Wax, 1970) bore the H–D–H name. Invictus also released 'Women's Love Rights' by Laura Lee, and Dozier and Brian Holland cut 'Why Can't We Be Lovers' (1972).

Further lawsuits followed Dozier's decision to break up the partnership in 1973. He had solo hits with 'Trying to Hold on to My Woman' (ABC, 1974) and 'Fish Ain't Bitin'' before recording such critically acclaimed albums as *Right There* (1976), *Peddlin'* (1977) and *Bittersweet* (1979) for Warners. **Odyssey** reached the British Top Ten in 1981 with a version of his 'Going Back to My Roots'.

During the eighties Dozier worked as a producer and writer with such artists as **Aretha Franklin**, **Ben E. King**, **Simply Red**, **Eric Clapton**, **Phil Collins** and Jon Anderson (of **Yes**). The Holland brothers also made occasional forays into the studio and briefly reunited with Dozier to write songs for the Four Tops.

THE HOLLIES

Allan Clarke, b. 15 April 1942, Salford, Lancashire, England (replaced by Michael Rickfors, b. Sweden); Bobby Elliott, b. 8 December 1943, Burnley; Eric Haydock (replaced by Bernie Calvert), b. 16 September 1944, Burnley; Tony Hicks, b. 16 December 1943, Nelson; Graham Nash, b. 2 February 1942, Blackpool (replaced by Terry Sylvester, b. 8 January 1945, Liverpool)

The Hollies were one of the most commercially and artistically successful of the British beat groups who emerged in the sixties.

Clarke and Nash first sang together in Manchester as the Two Teens in 1959. They formed the Deltas in 1962 with Haydock on bass and when guitarist Hicks joined the group it became the Hollies (named after the Christmas decoration, not **Buddy Holly**). Elliott joined on drums from Shane Fenton (the future Alvin Stardust) and the Fentones as the group were being signed to EMI's Parlophone label in 1963. They recorded 'Ain't That Just Like Me' and 'Searchin'', covers of **Leiber and Stoller** songs originally written for the **Coasters**.

The Hollies' first Top Ten hit was another R&B cover, 'Stay' by **Maurice Williams**. It featured the keening vocal harmonies of Clarke, Hicks and Nash which were to be the group's trademark. In the remainder of the decade the Hollies had seventeen British hit singles and, from 1966, a series of eight American successes. The earlier singles were mainly covers of American songs like **Doris Troy**'s 'Just One Look' (1964) and Mort Shuman's (of **Pomus and Shuman**) 'Here I Go Again', **Chip Taylor**'s 'I Can't Let Go' (1966) and 'I'm Alive', written by Clint Ballard Junior – the author of 'You're No Good', a hit for **Betty Everett** (1963) and **Linda Ronstadt** (1975). British material was provided by Graham Gouldman (later of **10CC**), who provided the ballad 'Look Through Any Window' and the terse 'Bus Stop'.

Arguably the Hollies' best songs of the era were those composed by Clarke, Hicks and Nash themselves. In 1966–7 they created a series of masterly pop songs with succinct lyrics and slightly off-beat themes. The frantic 'Stop Stop Stop' was followed by the serenity of 'On a Carousel' (1966), while the risky conceit of 'King Midas in Reverse' (1967) contrasted with the gentle love songs 'Carrie Anne' (1967) and 'Jennifer Eccles' (1968).

The singles came from two albums which emphasized the Hollies' intention to become part of the art- or progressive-rock trend of the period. *Evolution* (1966) also contained 'Lullaby to Tim', a piece which introduced the tremelo vocal effect later used by **Tommy James** on 'Crimson and Clover'. *Butterfly* (1967) went further in its use of electronic effects and Indian music. The group next proclaimed their admiration for **Bob Dylan** by recording *Hollies Sing Dylan*. However, the most progressive-minded of the band, Nash, had left for California, where he later formed **Crosby, Stills and Nash**, and the Hollies reverted to more standard pop material. 'Listen to Me' (1968) was a Tony Hazzard composition, while **Tony Macaulay** and Geoff Stephens were responsible for the chirpy 'Sorry Suzanne'.

The tone for the Hollies' greatest successes in the seventies was set by 'He Ain't Heavy, He's My Brother', a slow ballad delivered by Clarke's flawless tenor, which was followed by 'I Can't Tell the Bottom from the Top' (1970) and the up-tempo 'Long Cool Woman in a Black Dress'* (1971). Soon afterwards Clarke left to try a solo career, and was replaced by Swedish singer Rickfors, but after making three poor-selling albums including *My Real Name Is 'Arold* (RCA, 1972), Clarke rejoined the group to sing the ethereal lead on Albert Hammond's 'The Air That I Breathe' (Polydor, 1974). Clarke continued to cut solo albums for EMI, Atlantic and Curb during the seventies, while the group albums for Polydor in Britain and Epic in America included *Another Night* (1975, which featured a version of **Bruce Springsteen**'s '4th of July [Asbury Park]'), *Russian Roulette* (1976) and *A Crazy Steal* (1978). *The Hollies Sing Buddy Holly* (1980) was a selection of songs by the fifties rock star.

By now the group's live shows were catering mainly to a nostalgia market and in 1981, after the departure of Sylvester and Calvert, 'Holliedaze', which included disco versions of old Hollies' hits, was a minor success in Britain. In 1983 Nash and Clarke (who had left again in 1978) rejoined Elliott and Hicks to make *What Goes Around* (Atlantic), which produced an American hit with a remake of the **Supremes**' 'Stop in the Name of Love'. In 1987 the group released the minor 'This Is It'. Then in 1988 they again topped the British charts with a reissued 'He Ain't Heavy, He's My Brother' after the song had been featured on a television beer commercial before returning to the nostalgia circuit. The 1993 boxed set *Treasured Hits and Hidden Treasures* (EMI) had some newly recorded material, including songs by Richard Marx and **Nik Kershaw**. Two further archival sets followed, *At Abbey Road, 1963–1966* (1997) and *At Abbey Road, 1966–1970* (1998).

BUDDY HOLLY
b. Charles Hardin Holley, 7 September 1936, Lubbock, Texas, USA, d. 3 February 1959, Clear Lake, Iowa

Despite the brevity of his recording career (effectively just three years), Holly was one of the most influential rock performers. A master of rock'n'roll singing and guitar-playing, he drew on country and R&B styles to develop new song forms which provided the basis for the work of later generations of rock artists.

As a child he played piano and guitar, listening to blues and R&B, as well as country and western, on the radio. At high school Holly formed a duo with Bob Montgomery, performing as Buddy and Bob over local station KDAV. Though their repertoire included **Hank Ballard**'s 'Work with Me Annie', demonstration discs made by the two consisted of country and rockabilly songs mostly written by Montgomery. These tracks were later commercially released as *Holly in the Hills* (Decca, 1965).

In 1955 Buddy and Bob opened shows in Lubbock for **Ferlin Husky** and **Elvis Presley**. Holly was subsequently signed to Decca, travelling to Nashville to record with producer **Owen Bradley**. Although these tracks included an early version of 'That'll Be the Day', Decca released 'Blue Days – Black Nights' (1955) and 'Modern Don Juan' as singles; neither was successful. Montgomery went on to become a prolific country songwriter and producer working in the sixties and seventies with **Eddy Arnold**, the **Crickets**, **B. J. Thomas**, **Bobby Goldsboro**, **Slim Whitman** and others. He composed the oft-recorded 'Misty Blue', a hit for **Joe Simon** (1972) and revived by Dorothy Moore (Malaco, 1976).

After the failure of the Decca sessions, Holly formed a new band with Allison, Joe B. Mauldin (bass) and Niki Sullivan (guitar). Impressed by the hits **Norman Petty** had produced for Buddy Knox ('Party Doll'*, 'Hula Love', Roulette, 1957), the group travelled to Clovis, New Mexico, to record at his studio early in 1957. The resulting partnership was one of the most successful in pop music history.

Like **The Beatles**' producer **George Martin**, Petty was not overly fond of rock'n'roll. But instead of trying to soften Holly's sound, Petty encouraged the group to expand its musical vocabulary. Thus, 'Everyday' became a rock song with the feel of a minuet through the use of a celeste, Allison's hands slapping his knees as the only form of percussion, and Holly's nervous 'hiccuping' singing.

During the first half of 1957 Petty and the group recorded some twenty songs, most of which were later hits. On the strength of the new 'That'll Be the Day'*, Petty got a deal with Bob Thiele of Brunswick in New York and further arranged that the Clovis tracks would appear in two guises. Those with vocal backings were to be credited to the Crickets (a name chosen during a Clovis session) while others with double-tracked lead vocals and unusual instrumentation or rhythm would appear on Coral as by Buddy Holly.

By the end of 1957 the Crickets' 'That'll Be the Day' had reached No. 1 in America and the first Holly release, the frenetic 'Peggy Sue', was also a hit. By now the group had joined national package tours of rock'n'roll artists and further Crickets' hits followed in 1958 with the joyous 'Oh Boy', 'Maybe Baby' and 'Think It Over'.

The Buddy Holly singles were sometimes more successful in Britain where he toured in early 1958. The pensive, hypnotic 'Listen to Me', which was a commercial failure in America, reached the Top Twenty as did 'Rave on' and 'Early in the Morning', a **Bobby Darin** song recorded in New York. The albums *Chirping Crickets* and *Buddy Holly*, released in 1958, contained the remainder of the Clovis tracks, notably the innovative 'Words of Love', 'Look at Me' and 'Not Fade Away'.

By the end of the year Holly had moved to New York and was estranged from Petty and the Crickets. He had recorded with a string section on 'Moondreams' and on the **Paul Anka** song, 'It Doesn't Matter Anymore'. In early 1959 he began a major national tour with bassist **Waylon Jennings** (whose first single, 'Jole Blon', Holly had produced) and guitarist Tommy Alsup. He died a few weeks later when the small plane carrying Holly and fellow stars **Ritchie Valens** and the Big Bopper crashed.

Holly's current single 'It Doesn't Matter Anymore' soon reached No. 1 in Britain and the Top Twenty in America, where Coral quickly released *The Buddy Holly Story*. The next single release was the witty 'follow-up', 'Peggy Sue Got Married'/'Crying Waiting Hoping', both sides taken from demo tapes of new songs made by Holly shortly before his death. These tracks, which also included the pensive 'Learning the Game' and the mournful 'What to Do', showed a growing maturity in Holly's songwriting.

Notably in Britain, where his memory remained strongest, regular 'new' Holly material was issued over the next decade. For the most part these tracks were taken from the New York tapes or from even older unreleased tapes made by Holly at home in Lubbock. Backing tracks were added either by Coral in New York or by Petty, using the Fireballs, a Texas rock group. The songs were generally versions of rock classics, as in the British hits **Chuck Berry**'s 'Brown Eyed Handsome Man' (1963) and 'Bo Diddley'. The more substantial 'Reminiscing' (issued 1962) featured **King Curtis** on saxophone and had been the last Holly track produced by Petty in 1958.

The influence of Buddy Holly on later rock music was profound and long-lasting. The plane crash was commemorated by the sickly tribute record 'Three Stars' (Crest, 1959) by Tommy Dee (a pseudonym of **J. D. Loudermilk**) while the early sixties saw a spate of further tributes and imitations. **Bobby Vee** brought in the Crickets for his respectful *I Remember Buddy Holly* (1963) while **Tommy Roe** hiccupped his way through the 'Peggy Sue'-like 'Sheila'. In Britain, **Adam Faith** used a similar hiccupping mannerism and the pizzicato strings of 'It Doesn't Matter Anymore' on 'What Do You Want' (1959) while Mike Berry sang 'A Tribute to Buddy Holly' (HMV, 1961). Led by Allison and Mauldin, the Crickets continued to record and perform intermittently over the next three decades.

More importantly, Holly's approach to writing and recording was a formative influence on the British beat music of the early sixties. When The Beatles covered a Holly song, they chose not a standard rock'n'roll number but the gentle, unusual 'Listen to Me', while the **Rolling Stones** recorded the **Bo Diddley** shuffle 'Not Fade Away' and Blind Faith (with **Eric Clapton** and **Steve Winwood**) covered 'Well All Right'. The Holly legacy also stretched into the seventies when **Don McLean**'s 'American Pie' (1971) identified 'the day the music died' as the moment of the plane crash. Even later **Steeleye Span** covered 'Rave on' and **Linda Ronstadt** reached the Top Ten with 'It's So Easy' (1977), produced by Peter Asher who himself had recorded 'True Love Ways' as part of Peter and Gordon in 1965.

In 1978 Gary Busey starred in *The Buddy Holly Story*. The film was well received, though ex-Cricket Sonny Curtis was stung into writing and recording *The Real Buddy Holly Story* (Asylum). In 1990 the musical *Buddy*, first staged in London, transferred to Broadway. In 2000 it was still running in London.

The Complete Buddy Holly (1981) is just that, everything there was in the MCA vaults. Its critical and commercial success, especially on CD where the listener could programme out the tracks only of academic interest (but still have access to them if he wanted) laid the foundations for subsequent 'Complete . . .' compilations by other artists.

JOHN HOLT
b. 1947, Kingston, Jamaica

A leading reggae singer and writer, Holt specialized in love songs. He also composed 'The Tide Is High', an international hit for **Blondie** in 1980.

In 1962 Holt won the Vere John radio talent contest and made his recording début with 'Forever I'll Stay'. Three years later he joined Bob Andy (later of **Bob and Marcia**), Tyrone Evans and Harold Barrett in the Paragons vocal group, and had a series of Jamaican hits including 'Love at Last', 'Happy Go Lucky Girl' and 'On the Beach', all featuring his smooth tenor. After Andy left the group, they recorded 'The Tide Is High' (1966).

Holt's solo career began in 1968, when Duke Reid produced his hit 'Tonight'. Specializing in sentimental love songs, he recorded international pop material as well as his own compositions. During the early seventies, he recorded albums including *A Love I Can Feel* for **Coxsone Dodd** and the collection of love songs *Time Is the Master* (1973), which featured songs made famous by **Ivory Joe Hunter** and his stylistic mentor **Brook Benton**. It was the first album produced in Jamaica (by Harry A. Mudie) to feature a large string section. His greatest international success of the decade was a version of **Kris Kristofferson**'s 'Help Me Make It Through the Night', a British Top Ten hit on Trojan in 1975. Although he was no longer Jamaica's leading album artist, Holt continued to record prolifically throughout the eighties. Later albums include *Police in Helicopter* (1987) and *If I Were a Carpenter* (1989).

JOHN LEE HOOKER
b. 22 August 1917, Clarksdale, Mississippi, USA

The early work of John Lee Hooker marked him instantly as a singular bluesman. His blues were moaned or muttered chants, formally primitive – he seldom played in conventional time-divisions, and showed little interest in rhyme – and underpinned by hypnotically repetitious guitar figures in open tunings, which he interrupted with clanging solo passages out of rhythm. Like **Lightnin' Hopkins** and the young **Muddy Waters**, he turned aside from the jazz-influenced blues-band music of the late forties to revive, in an urban setting, the unpredictable individual voice of country blues. Such was the authority behind his recordings that after years of neglect he became in the late eighties and early nineties almost a talisman of the blues in the wake of his success with *The Healer* (1989).

After some playing around Memphis in his teens, Hooker moved to Cincinnati, where he worked chiefly with gospel quartets. In the late forties he worked with small groups in clubs in Detroit, where in 1948 he began to record for the **Bihari Brothers**' Modern label, frequently moonlighting for other companies like King, Savoy, Regal, Chance, Chess and Gotham under such pseudonyms as Birmingham Sam, John Lee Booker, Delta John and Texas Slim. His impact was immediate, 'Boogie Chillen' (Modern, 1948) becoming a blues standard. 'Hobo Blues', 'Crawling King Snake' (both 1949) and 'I'm in the Mood' (Modern, 1951) also reached the R&B charts.

After leaving Modern in 1954 he recorded for Specialty and then signed in 1955 with Vee-Jay, for whom he cut many singles and albums in his nine-year stay.

Now working with bands – earlier recordings had often been solos or accompanied only by a pianist or second guitarist – Hooker enlisted as his sidemen Chicago figures like **Jimmy Reed** and guitarist Eddie Taylor, and exchanged the haphazard excitement of his previous work for a more controlled – although still emphatically rhythmic – music. 'Dimples' (1956) and 'Boom Boom' (1962) were his hits of the period, the latter even charting in Britain in 1964. Between Vee-Jay sessions, Hooker cut albums for the folk-music market, playing acoustic guitar: *The Folk Blues of John Lee Hooker* (Riverside, 1959) was a solo set and *That's My Story* (Riverside, 1960) added jazz musicians Sam Jones (bass) and Louis Hayes (drums). Vee-Jay looked to a similar market with *The Folk Lore of John Lee Hooker* (1961), which included tracks recorded at the 1960 Newport Folk Festival, and *Concert at Newport* (1964).

His first visit to Europe was with the 1962 American Folk Blues Festival; he toured Britain on his own in 1964 and often thereafter. Having left Vee-Jay in 1964, he recorded album sessions for Impulse and Chess (both 1966), then signed with ABC-Bluesway and made *Live at Café au Go-Go* (1967) with the Muddy Waters band. The succeeding Bluesways albums *Urban Blues* (1968) and *Simply the Truth* (1969) – the latter including songs about miniskirts and Vietnam – won awards in international critics' polls. From 1970 he began to associate more with younger white blues and rock musicians, such as **Canned Heat** (*Hooker 'n' Heat*, Liberty, 1970), guitarist **Steve Miller** (*Endless Boogie*, ABC, 1971) and ex-**Paul Butterfield** bandsmen Elvin Bishop (guitar) and Mark Naftalin (piano) on *Never Get Out of These Blues Alive* (ABC, 1972) and *Born in Mississippi Raised Up in Tennessee*, both featuring guest appearances by **Van Morrison**. He also appeared in blues documentaries and *The Blues Brothers* (1980), contributed to the soundtrack of *Mister Brown* (1972) and *The Color Purple* (1986), and played many festivals in the US, Canada and Europe.

His working pattern remained similar through the eighties, but while his older material continued to be reissued, he made very few new recordings until a 1989 comeback with *The Healer* (Silvertone), on which he was joined by **Robert Cray**, **Santana**, Canned Heat, Los Lobos, George Thorogood and **Bonnie Raitt**. His most commercially successful album ever, it sparked off a Hooker-led blues revival that resulted in Hooker being, briefly, one of the most reissued artists ever. Even more extraordinary is the power of *The Healer* and its European hit sequel *Mr. Lucky*, which revealed both the depth of feeling of Hooker the bluesman and his unique ability, if not to reinvent himself *à la* **Bob Dylan**, to redefine his music. Both were band recordings but on neither was Hooker outshone by his famous guests. Such was the success of the albums that Hooker briefly became synonymous with the blues and was featured in advertisements. Signed to Virgin, he swiftly followed *Mr. Lucky* with *Boom Boom* (1992), a lesser, albeit still impressive set, from which the title track was a British Top Twenty hit. In 1993 Hooker recorded once again with Van Morrison on his album *Too Long in Exile*, with the extracted duet on a new version of Morrison's 'Gloria' returning him to the British Top Forty at the age of 75.

His next release was *Chill Out* (1994) with Carlos Santana as co-producer, while *Don't Look Back* (1997), which won him two Grammy awards, saw him working with Van Morrison, **Charles Brown** and **Los Lobos**. *The Complete '50s Chess Recordings* (1998) collects together many of his best recordings. However, because Hooker recorded so prolifically and for companies whose product is now available on lots of budget CDs, there is no comprehensive retrospective for Hooker.

SOL HOOPII
b. 1902, Honolulu, Hawaii, d. 16 November 1953, Seattle, Washington

During the twenties and thirties, as the Hawaiian guitar ceased to be a strictly indigenous instrument and edged towards the mainstream of American popular music, one of its leading authentic practitioners was Sol Hoopii. Through his work on films and recordings, and his early use of the electrified steel guitar, he did more than any of his contemporaries to determine and disseminate what were to become the standard forms of Hawaiian-American music.

Hoopii emigrated to the USA in 1919, settling first in San Francisco and later in Los Angeles. About 1925 he formed a trio with Lani McIntire and Glennwood Leslie to play in various Los Angeles nightclubs. Initially playing acoustic, he adopted the new electric Rickenbacker guitar in the early thirties and used it on recordings of popular tunes of the day ('Little Grass Shack', Brunswick, 1934) and in several movies. Among these were *Bird of Paradise* (1932), *Flirtation Walk* (1934), *Waikiki Wedding* (1937, with **Bing Crosby**) and *Song of the Islands* (1942, with Betty Grable). He also worked on soundtracks for the Charlie Chan series of movies.

In 1938 he became a travelling evangelist, but he did not entirely quit showbusiness, and in 1948 he returned to Hawaii for a tour. His influence upon both other island guitarists and such steel guitarists of the thirties and forties as Leon McAuliffe (with **Bob Wills**), Jimmy Helms (with **Hank Williams**) and Jerry Byrd has been considerable. *Master of the Hawaiian Guitar* (Rounder, 1990) is the definitive collection.

HOOTIE AND THE BLOWFISH
Mark Bryan, b. 6 May 1967, Gaithersburg, Maryland, USA; Dean Felber, b. 9 June 1967, Bethesda, Maryland; Darius Rucker, b. 13 May 1966, Charlston, South Carolina; Jim 'Soni' Sonefeld, b. 20 October 1964, Grand Rapids, Michigan

Briefly one of the most celebrated roots-orientated rock bands of the nineties, Hootie and the Blowfish earned international acclaim for their début, *Cracked Rear View*, which added to an **R.E.M.** sense of distance a sheer exuberance and crisp melodies that were decidedly out of fashion at the time.

Singer Rucker, guitarist Bryan, drummer Sonefeld and bassist Felber began playing together in the late eighties at the University of South Carolina, gradually gaining a following on the east coast with regular gigs on the club circuit. In 1993 the band won a deal with Atlantic Records on the strength of their live performances, and began recording their début with Don Gehman.

Cracked Rear View (1994) brought the band instant fame, with its acoustic guitar-led rock selling 15 million copies in the US alone. The album, which included three hit singles, 'Hold My Hand', 'Let Her Cry' and 'Only Wanna Be With You', won the band numerous Grammy Award nominations. Lacking the iconic status it had within the US, signalling there as it did the primacy of performance – seen in its essence in bar bands – over production, glamour or dance, the album was far less successful outside the US. In Europe the success of Hootie was mirrored by the growing success of local acts at the expense of international superstars.

Extensive touring preceded the release of *Fairweather Johnson** (1996), which sold well internationally but failed to match the success of *Cracked Rear View*. Hootie and the Blowfish returned in 1998 with *Musical Chairs**.

MARY HOPKIN
b. 3 May 1950, Pontardawe, Wales

An immediate sensation with her 1968 pop hit 'Those Were the Days', Hopkin tried unsuccessfully to establish herself as a middle-of-the-road star in the seventies.

A music and drama student with a flawless pop-folk voice, she came to prominence as a winner of the television talent contest *Opportunity Knocks*. **Paul McCartney** signed her to the newly formed Apple label in 1968 and produced 'Those Were the Days'. Based on a Russian folk song, it reached No. 1 in Britain and sold a million copies in America. The follow-up, 'Goodbye', written by McCartney and **John Lennon**, was equally successful. Her first album,

Postcard, which also contained songs by **Donovan**, was released in 1969.

Changing producers to **Mickie Most**, Hopkin had further hits in 1970 with 'Temma Harbour', the Eurovision Song Contest entry written by Geoff Stephens and John Carter, 'Knock Knock Who's There?' and 'Think About Your Children', composed by **Hot Chocolate**'s Errol Brown and Tony Wilson. She moved towards a contemporary folk sound for *Earth Song, Ocean Song* (Apple, 1971), with accompaniment from **Ralph McTell** and Dave Cousins of the Strawbs. The album was produced by Tony Visconti, whom Hopkin later married.

After four years in semi-retirement raising a family and singing backing vocals on albums by McTell, **David Bowie** and **Thin Lizzy**, Hopkin returned to recording with the Visconti production of an **Edith Piaf** song, 'If You Love Me' (Good Earth, 1976). In 1979 she released *The Welsh World of Mary Hopkin* (Decca), a collection of Welsh-language versions of folk material which included 'Guantanamera' and 'Turn Turn Turn'. Hopkin later recorded with **Peter Skellern** as Oasis (Warners, 1984), took part in **George Martin**'s 1988 recording of Dylan Thomas's verse play *Under Milk Wood* (EMI) and released an album of religious songs on Trax (1989). *Spirit* (1991) was overshadowed by the retrospective *Those Were the Days* (1995).

LIGHTNIN' HOPKINS
b. Sam Hopkins, 15 March 1912, Centerville, Texas, USA, d. 30 January 1982, Houston, Texas

Lightnin' Hopkins represents for many the truest function of the blues singer: a social reporter of and for his own community, instantaneous storyteller, and folk poet. Unlike, say, **Sleepy John Estes**, who wrote blues like a small-town newspaperman, Hopkins at first dealt more in autobiography, but gradually he looked to the world beyond his section of Houston for his subject matter, composing blues about natural disasters, the exploration of space, Korea and Vietnam. He told these stories in a half-sung, half-narrated form, drawing for accompaniment on characteristic guitar lines. At their best, voice and guitar united in an expressive medium of extraordinary intensity.

In his teens, already playing guitar, he travelled with the blues singer Texas Alexander, a frequent associate until the latter's death in about 1955. He made his first recordings in 1946 for Aladdin, in Los Angeles; then he signed with Gold Star in Houston, where he had his permanent base, and for the next three years alternated sessions for the two labels, generally recording solo with thunderously amplified guitar and interspersing slow blues with boogies.

Notable performances from this period include 'Short Haired Woman', 'Unsuccessful Blues' and the bitter 'Tim Moore's Farm'. About 1950 he signed with the **Bihari Brothers**' RPM, then Specialty, Sittin' in With (1951–2), Mercury (1952), Decca (1953) and other small labels. By 1956 he had evidently lost ground against rock'n'roll, and was not recording.

Blues researcher Sam Charters found him in Houston in 1959 and recorded his first album, *The Roots of Lightnin' Hopkins* (Folkways), which quickly led to similar sets, played with unamplified guitar for the folk-song market, on *Tradition, 77, Heritage* (all 1959), and a *Down South Summit Meetin'* with **Brownie McGhee and Sonny Terry** and **Big Joe Williams** (World Pacific, 1960). Also in 1960 he began a series of albums for Prestige-Bluesville, as well as filling one-off sessions for Fire and Candid (*Lightnin' in New York*, which includes a long folk-tale, 'Mister Charlie'). Managed for a time by local folklorist Mack McCormick, he played at folk festivals and clubs on the West Coast and in New York's Carnegie Hall; he also made his first appearance in documentary films and on TV, and in 1964 his first trip overseas, with the American Folk Blues Festival.

On later sixties recordings for Arhoolie, Verve-Folkways, Jewel and other labels, Hopkins was sometimes accompanied by rather unexpected people, including the folk singer Barbara Dane or trombonist John Ewing, but more often by fellow Houstonians like pianist Elmore Nixon or the harmonica-player Billy Bizor, who appeared with him in Les Blank's film *The Blues Accordin' to Lightnin' Hopkins* (1968). His response to late-sixties psychedelia was to record in mildly 'heavy' company like the Muscle Shoals crew on *The Great Electric Show and Dance* (Jewel, 1969).

Hopkins spent his remaining years in Houston, leaving it less often to play elsewhere – though he did visit Europe in 1977 – and recording less frequently than in his heyday. (By then nearly a hundred albums of his work had been issued.) Possibly his last session was for Charters again, *The Legacy of the Blues Vol. 12* (Sonet, 1974).

TREVOR HORN
b. 15 July 1949

A successful songwriter, Horn was Britain's most influential record producer of the early eighties. He was equally at home with progressive rock (**Yes**), Europop (Dollar) and disco-pomp (**Frankie Goes to Hollywood**).

Originally session musicians, Horn and Geoff Downes joined forces to record as Buggles, and had a No. 1 hit in Britain with the novelty song 'Video Killed the Radio Star' (Island, 1979). Horn also produced the duo's two albums, *The Age of Plastic* (Island, 1980) and *Adventures in Modern Recording* (Carrere, 1980). The Buggles' records introduced the surging bass-led rhythms which would make an even greater impact when applied to Frankie Goes to Hollywood's music. In 1980 Downes (keyboards) and Horn (guitar) joined Yes for a tour and album (*Drama*). Horn later produced *90125* for the group.

From 1981 he concentrated on 'backroom' activity. With Bruce Woolley (former leader of Camera Club, whose members had included **Thomas Dolby**), he composed 'Hand Held in Black and White' (WEA, 1981) and other hits for the vocal duo Dollar (former Guys and Dolls members Thereza Bazar and David Van Day). Horn paid homage to **Phil Spector** with his production of **ABC**'s *The Lexicon of Love* (Neutron, 1982) and gave an epic dimension to the group's romanticism on the hit singles 'Poison Arrow' and 'The Look of Love'. He also supervised **Malcom McLaren**'s piratical *Duck Rock* (Island, 1984), a collage of 'found sounds' from around the world.

In 1983 Horn, his wife Jill Sinclair and rock journalist Paul Morley founded their own ZTT label – the name came from a work by Italian futurist painter Marinetti. They had an immediate success with Frankie Goes to Hollywood, whose three No. 1s were Horn productions. The label also released work by the Art of Noise (*Into Battle*, 1984), which included **Ann Dudley**, and Ann Pigalle. It folded in 1994.

In the nineties Horn's greatest success came with **Mike Oldfield**'s *Tubular Bells II* and rock-soul singer-songwriter Seal, whose eponymous début album was a major hit in Britain and America. The follow-up, again called *Seal*, topped the British chart in the week of release in 1994.

Largely inactive in the nineties, his few productions for **Barry Manilow** (*I'd Really Love to See You Tonight*, 1997) and Goldi Render ('Nobody Lives without Love', 1995) were as mannered as ever. In 1997 he briefly re-formed the Art of Noise.

LENA HORNE
b. 30 June 1917, Brooklyn, New York, USA

An exciting singer and actress, Horne's career, especially as recounted in her 1981 one-woman Broadway show, *Lena Horne: The Lady and Her Music*, is a classic example of the invisible colour bar that has operated for the greater part of this century throughout the entertainment industry.

Raised by her actress mother, Horne dropped out of school to become a dancer at Harlem's Cotton Club in 1934, quickly graduating to singing. She toured with Noble Sissle's Orchestra (1935–6) and, after touring with **Charlie Barnet**'s band in 1940, appeared (and recorded to great acclaim) with **Teddy**

Wilson. Her satin-smooth voice was better suited to interpreting popular songs than jazz singing and she was always more at home in nightclubs than in front of a jazz band. Her exotic good looks and her performance in the film *The Duke Is Tops* (1938) and the black Broadway revue *Blackbirds of 1939* won her a long-term contract with MGM.

But if she was the first black performer to sign such a contract with a major studio, MGM were careful both to lighten her appearance with a special white make-up and to cast her in isolated guest spots in musicals which could be easily excised by Southern distributors. Her greatest Hollywood success was in the all-black musical *Cabin in the Sky* (1942), a superior film to *Stormy Weather* (also 1942) which was loosely based on the life of Bill Robinson. Her forties hits included 'Stormy Weather', 'One for My Baby (and One More for the Road)' and ''Deed I Do' (1948).

In the fifties she was blacklisted, in part because of her close association with **Paul Robeson** with whom, from the early forties, she had been prominent in the Civil Rights movement. For a decade she scarcely worked in either film or television. In 1955 she scored her biggest-ever hit record with her version of the title song to *Love Me or Leave Me* (RCA), based on the life of **Ruth Etting**. Her greatest success came on the concert stage and on Broadway where she appeared in *Jamaica* (1957), the musical by **Harold Arlen**, author of 'Stormy Weather' (which he wrote for **Ethel Waters** but which Horne made her own). In 1969 she returned to the screen in *Invitation to a Gunfighter* and in 1978 took the part of Glinda in the all-black remake of *The Wizard of Oz, The Wiz*.

The climax of her renewed success on the concert stage came with her extraordinary one-woman Broadway show, *The Lady and Her Music* (1981). It ran for over a year and was the most successful and self-conscious of the stream of all-black shows that appeared in the late seventies and early eighties. In 1984 she brought the show to London.

In 1994 Horne made her first album for the Blue Note label.

BRUCE HORNSBY
b. 23 November 1954, Williamsburg, USA

An accomplished session pianist, Hornsby carved out a distinguished career as a singer-songwriter in the late eighties, with recordings which in part tapped the same vein of rural Americana as the songs of **The Band**'s Robbie Robertson had in the seventies.

Starting on the Miami Beach barmitzvah circuit in the late seventies, Hornsby worked through bar bands, eventually becoming a house writer for 20th Century Fox before signing with RCA in 1985. His début album, *The Way It Is* (1986), included the anti-racist title track which gave him a massive worldwide hit. The album featured Hornsby's vocal and piano playing talents and a set of excellent songs (written with his lawyer brother, John) given an ultra-sympathetic backing by Hornsby's band, the Range (David Mansfield: violin/guitar/mandolin, George Martinelli: guitar, Joe Puerta: bass and John Molo: drums). The follow-up album, *Scenes from the South Side* (1988), was another finely crafted collection of piano-based songs mixing rock, country, jazz and blues and included the hit single 'The Valley Road', which he re-recorded with the **Nitty Gritty Dirt Band** in 1989.

By the time of the third album, *Night on the Town* (1989), Mansfield had left the Range to work on movie scores, to be replaced by Peter Harris. Mansfield appeared as a guest artist on the album, along with jazz bassist Charlie Haden, country singer Shaun Colvin and guitarist Jerry Garcia from the **Grateful Dead**. The album, which was less piano-dominated than its predecessors, was another commercial success. In 1990 Hornsby continued his relationship with Jerry Garcia by joining the Grateful Dead on a temporary basis as replacement for their late keyboard-player Brent Mydland. Over the next two years, Hornsby toured extensively, first with the Dead then with the Range, finding time to produce **Leon Russell** and fit in a number of guest session appearances along the way. He also wrote and performed, with jazzman Branford Marsalis, a song for the 1992 Barcelona Olympics, and played at the inauguration of US president Bill Clinton.

In 1993 he released his own fourth album, this time without the Range, featuring a trio of himself, Molo and bassist Jimmy Haslip (ex-Yellowjackets). The stylish *Harbour Lights* was a more adventurous work than its predecessors, recorded as a result of jamming in Hornsby's own studio with guest appearances from several jazz names including Marsalis and guitarist **Pat Metheny**. *Hot House* (1995), which included the US hit 'Walk in the Sun', was similar in style. Hornsby toured extensively within the US in 1998 and 1999. In 2000 he joined several former Grateful Dead members who toured as the Other Ones.

Hornsby has also written or co-written hits for a number of other artists, including **Huey Lewis** (who co-produced his début album) and Don Henley.

JOHNNY HORTON
b. 30 April 1927, Tyler, Texas, USA, d. 5 November 1960, Milano, Texas

Best remembered for his phenomenal success with the saga song 'The Battle of New Orleans'* (1959), Horton was also an important honky-tonk singer.

Brought up in east Texas, Horton turned profes-

sional musician in his teens, graduating to a spot on Shreveport's KWKH in 1948, billed as 'The Singing Fisherman' (a nickname he picked up because of his angling prowess). Recordings for Carman, Abbott, Mercury and Dot failed but, after joining Columbia, he had a country No. 1 with his own composition, the dance-hall classic, 'Honky Tonk Man' (1956), which was successfully revived by **Dwight Yoakam** in 1986. This and songs like 'Honky Tonk Hardwood Floor', though heavily rhythmic, remained country in style and content in a way that most rockabilly of the fifties was not.

Next, Horton, whose rich tenor allowed him to record romantic ballads as well as raucous numbers such as 'Ole Slewfoot' and 'Got the Bull by the Horns', was persuaded by his manager and bassist Tillman Franks to record a series of pseudo-historical saga songs. His first, a ballad about the death of a prospector in the Klondike, 'When It's Springtime in Alaska' (1959) was a country No. 1; a year later another, an abridged version of the **Jimmie Driftwood** composition 'The Battle of New Orleans', topped the pop charts (and provided **Lonnie Donegan** with a British hit). Other successes in this vein included 'Johnny Reb' (1959, one of the many songs written for the Centennial of the Civil War), 'Sink the Bismarck', which was inspired by the film of the same name, and the film title song, 'North to Alaska' (both 1960), before he died in a car crash.

Horton was survived by his wife, Billy Jean, who earlier had been widowed by the death of **Hank Williams**.

HOT CHOCOLATE
Errol Brown, b. 12 November 1948, Kingston, Jamaica; Tony Connor, b. 6 April 1947, Romford, Essex, England; Larry Ferguson, b. 14 April 1948, Nassau, Bahamas; Harry Hinsley, b. 19 January 1948, Northampton; Patrick Olive, b. 22 March 1947, Grenada; Tony Wilson, b. 8 October 1947, Trinidad

Mixing pop, soul and disco styles over nearly two decades, and featuring Brown's distinctive voice and shaven head, Hot Chocolate were one of Britain's most enterprising bands. In 1998 the dancefloor favourite 'You Sexy Thing' was given a further lease of life – and with it Brown's career – when it was featured in the hit film *The Full Monty*.

Brown emigrated to London as a child and in 1969 began writing songs with session musician Wilson, who had come to London as a student in 1961. **The Beatles**-owned Apple Records signed the duo as writers and they provided **Mary Hopkin** with a Top Twenty hit, 'Think About Your Children' (1970). They also recorded a reggae version of **John Lennon**'s 'Give Peace a Chance', under the name Hot Chocolate.

With no further encouragement from Apple,

Brown and Wilson moved to **Mickie Most**'s RAK stable, providing **Herman's Hermits** with 'Bet Yer Life I Do' and scoring a Hot Chocolate hit with the ballad 'Love Is Life'. A permanent band was organized with guitarist Hinsley from Cliff Bennett's Rebel Rousers plus semi-professionals Olive (percussion and bass), Ferguson (keyboards) and Connor (drums).

The combination of Most's expert production and Brown–Wilson's gift for simple but effective love songs brought eight hits on RAK in the next five years. Among them was 'Brother Louie' (1973), a tale of inter-racial love with **Alexis Korner** as the voice of the angry father (an American No. 1 for Stories). The disco-flavoured 'You Sexy Thing'* (1975) and 'Every One's a Winner' (1978) were Top Ten hits in America, where Hot Chocolate's records were released on Doug Morris's Big Tree label. The band's first album, *Cicero Park*, was released in 1974, its title track dealing with ecological issues.

Wilson left the group in 1976 to follow a solo recording career with Bearsville, releasing *I Like Your Style* (1976) and *Catch One* (1979). Hot Chocolate continued to have regular British hits, achieving their first No. 1 with the Russ Ballard song 'So You Win Again' (1977). Other Top Ten successes were 'Put Your Love in Me' (1977), 'No Doubt about It' (1980), 'Girl Crazy' and the memorable 'It Started with a Kiss' (1982), and 'What Kinda Boy You Lookin' for (Girl)' (1983).

Following the British success in 1987 of a remix of 'You Sexy Thing', Brown left the group to pursue a solo recording career with Warners, scoring a Top Thirty hit with 'Personal Touch' (1987). However, subsequent singles and the album *That's How Love Is* (1989) performed poorly. The lack of solo success enjoyed by Brown was only emphasized when a 1993 Hot Chocolate compilation *Their Greatest Hits* topped the British chart. After the failure of his second solo effort, *Secret Rendezvous* (1992), Brown was driven to the nostalgia circuit before *The Full Monty* resurrected his career.

SON HOUSE
b. Eddie James House Jnr, 21 March 1902, Riverton, Mississippi, USA, d. 19 October 1988, Detroit, Michigan

The intensity of performance intrinsic to Mississippi Delta blues can almost be measured by the yardstick of the music of Son House. His mature recordings are unsurpassed in their unity of voice and instrument and their tension of sacred and secular emotion.

House spent much of his youth and early manhood as a preacher, and although he left the church in his mid-twenties to become a blues singer and guitarist, he was drawn back to it on several occasions in his later life, and its echo may be heard in one of his famous 1930 recordings, 'Preachin' the Blues'. He was associated with **Charley Patton** and heard by the young **Robert Johnson**. This connection led to his being recorded by **Alan Lomax** for the Library of Congress in 1941–2. In 1943 he made his home in Rochester, New York, and for most of the next twenty years he was musically inactive. Traced in 1964 by blues researchers, he made an impressive and moving return to record with the album *The Legendary Son House/Father of Folk Blues* (1965) and to public performance with appearances at the Newport Folk Festival (1964–6, 1969) and many other events. He visited Europe in 1967 with the American Folk Blues Festival and on his own in 1970, but by that time his musical grasp had been weakened by ill-health, and after 1971 he seldom performed.

CISCO HOUSTON
b. Gilbert Vandine Houston, 18 August 1918, Wilmington, Delaware, USA, d. 29 April 1961, San Bernardino, California

Houston was a member of the leftist folk circle in post-Second World War New York, alongside **Woody Guthrie**, **Jack Elliott** and other Almanac Singers, but differed from these performers in having first-hand experience of working on Western ranches and learning cowboy songs, in which he was regarded as a specialist.

He grew up in Los Angeles, and in his teens left home to become an itinerant worker and singer. He first met Guthrie during one of the latter's spells in the West in the late thirties, and after a period of war service in the Merchant Marine rejoined him in New York, where they worked in clubs, on radio programmes and at union meetings. In 1944 they took part in a series of recording sessions for **Moe Asch**, often with Sonny Terry and Bess Lomax; subsequently Houston recorded, with and without Guthrie, for Stinson, Decca ('Rose, Rose I Love You', a hit in 1951 with orchestral backing by **Gordon Jenkins**) and Vanguard.

During the fifties he was frequently featured on folk-song concerts and radio and TV, and in 1959 he went on a State Department-sponsored tour of India, on his return from which he visited Britain. Soon afterwards he was forced by cancer to give up performing. He was held in great affection and admiration by other folk singers, and songs were written in his memory by **Tom Paxton**, Peter LaFarge and others. He was also an early influence on **Bob Dylan**.

WHITNEY HOUSTON
b. 9 August 1963, New Jersey, USA

Representing the second generation of a famous family

of soul and gospel singers, Whitney Houston was a leading black pop star of the eighties and nineties.

Her mother Cissy (*b. Emily Drinkard, 1932, Newark, New Jersey*) sang in the family gospel group the Drinkard Sisters before directing a group of backing singers that included her niece Dee Dee Myrna Smith, **Dionne Warwick** and Judy Clay (who later partnered **William Bell** on several duets). In the late fifties and early sixties they sang on records by such artists as **Solomon Burke**, **Wilson Pickett**, **Esther Phillips** and the **Drifters**. By 1967 Cissy had formed the Sweet Inspirations, who backed **Elvis Presley** and **Aretha Franklin** and had their own R&B hits on Atlantic. These included 'Let It Be Me' (1967) and 'Sweet Inspiration' (1968). As a solo artist, she recorded the original version of the **Gladys Knight** hit 'Midnight Train to Georgia' (Janus, 1971) and had a minor R&B hit with **Bobby Darin**'s 'I'll Be There' (1971), while her sister Thelma scored a No. 1 hit with the disco standard 'Don't Leave Me This Way' (Tamla Motown, 1977). Written by **Gamble and Huff**, it was successfully revived by British group the **Communards** in 1986. Thelma first recorded in 1969 (the **Jimmy Webb**-produced *Sunshower*, Dunhill) and after 'Don't Leave Me' had a further major hit with 'Saturday Night, Sunday Morning' (1979).

Whitney Houston pursued dual careers as fashion model and session singer (for **Lou Rawls**, **Chaka Khan**, the **Neville Brothers** and her mother) before reaching the charts in duets with **Teddy Pendergrass** and Jermaine Jackson. She signed a solo recording contract with Clive Davis of Arista in 1983. Her eponymous album was released in 1985 and by the end of 1986 it had sold more than 10 million copies worldwide, to become the most successful début album ever.

With tracks produced by Michael Messer, Jermaine Jackson, **Narada Michael Walden** and Kassif, plus further duets with Pendergrass and Jackson, the album offered smooth, sophisticated soul music, perfectly sung. It yielded four major hit singles: 'You Give Good Love', 'How Will I Know', 'The Greatest Love of All' and 'Saving All My Love for You', a 1986 No. 1 on both sides of the Atlantic.

In 1987 she reached the top again with 'I Wanna Dance With Somebody' from her second album *Whitney*. In the following year 'Where Do Broken Hearts Go' went to No. 1 and Houston's recording of 'One Moment in Time' was used as the theme for the Summer Olympics.

'I'm Your Baby Tonight' and 'All the Man That I Need' were both American chart-toppers in 1990. Such was her popularity that her version of 'The Star-Spangled Banner' was an American Top Twenty hit in 1991. But this was nothing compared with the impact of *The Bodyguard*. The film, in which she appeared as a threatened singer, was a huge success but the soundtrack album and its lead single, Houston's version of the **Dolly Parton** song 'I Will Always Love You', were amongst the biggest-selling records of all time – by 1995 the album had sold over 15 million units. In 1996 she contributed three tracks, including a chart-topping single ('Exhale [Shoop Shoop]') to the hit movie soundtrack *Waiting to Exhale* and in 1997 appeared in (and contributed to the bestselling soundtrack of) *The Preacher's Wife*. She duetted with **Mariah Carey** on 'When You Believe', which was featured in the animated movie *Prince of Egypt* (1998) and in the same year embarked on a two-year-long world tour in support of her first non-soundtrack album since 1990, *My Love Is Your Love*. Her hits collection, *The Greatest Hits* (2000), was less successful than expected.

HARLAN HOWARD
b. 8 September 1929, Lexington, Kentucky, USA

Howard is the author of numerous songs that became country standards.

Raised in Detroit, Howard started writing songs in his teens but it was not until he met **Johnny Bond** in Los Angeles and Bond recorded and published a song by him, that he became a professional songwriter. His first hit, written for **Ray Price** but given by Price to his protégé Charlie Walker, was the honky-tonk-styled ballad, 'Pick Me up on Your Way Down' (Columbia, 1958). Similarly styled songs of the period include 'Heartaches by the Number', a country hit for Price and a million-selling pop hit for **Guy Mitchell**, and 'Mommy for a Day', a hit for **Kitty Wells**.

He moved to Nashville in 1960 and composed a stream of hits, including 'Three Steps to a Phone' (**George Hamilton IV**, 1961); 'I Fall to Pieces', which he co-wrote with Hank Cochran (**Patsy Cline**, 1961); 'Don't Call Me from a Honky Tonk' (Johnny and Jonie Mosby, 1963); 'Busted', a country hit for **Johnny Cash** and a pop hit for **Ray Charles** in 1963; and the memorable 'Streets of Baltimore', which he co-wrote with Tompall Glaser of **Tompall and the Glaser Brothers** and was first recorded by **Bobby Bare** in 1966. Unlike many other songwriters who settled in Nashville, Howard's songwriting remained distinctively traditional. He was particularly favoured by **Buck Owens**, who began his chart career with a series of Howard compositions: 'Above and Beyond' and 'Excuse Me, I Think I've Got a Heartache' (both 1960) and 'Foolin' Around' (1961).

Howard attempted a singing career with albums on Monument, RCA and Nugget, but had only one minor hit, 'Sunday Morning Christian' (Nugget, 1971). Throughout the sixties he was married to the country singer Jan Howard, who often recorded her husband's compositions. By the eighties Howard was writing less ('Somewhere Tonight' for Highway 101) and working behind the scenes as a publisher in Nashville. However, he had renewed success in the nineties with the likes of 'Blame It on Your Heart' (a country chart-topper for Patty Loveless in 1993).

HOWLIN' WOLF
b. *Chester Arthur Burnett, 10 June 1910, West Point, Mississippi, USA, d. 10 January 1976, Hines, Illinois*

The most unswervingly archaic voice of Chicago blues, Howlin' Wolf brought into the rock era the throaty primitivism of pre-war Mississippi blues singers like **Son House**, **Charley Patton** and Booker White, expressed in a repertoire – often, and brilliantly, devised by **Willie Dixon** – full of the motifs of back-country folklore.

He spent his teens and early twenties as an itinerant singer-guitarist in and around the Mississippi Delta, first reaching a substantial audience when broadcasting, from 1948, on KWEM in West Memphis, Arkansas. In 1951 he began recording for **Sam Phillips**, who leased his work to both **Leonard Chess** and the **Bihari Brothers** of Modern Records. From 1952 he was based in Chicago and recording regularly for Chess. Sides like 'Evil Is Going on' (1954) and 'Smokestack Lightning' (1956) accorded with his imposing and even menacing stage presence and elevated him to membership, with **Muddy Waters** and **Sonny Boy Williamson**, of Chess's 'big three' down-home blues artists.

Wolf was particularly potent in the early sixties, recording such magnificent material as 'Wang Dang Doodle' (1960), 'The Red Rooster' (1961) and 'Goin' Down Slow' (1961), all contained in the remarkable collection *Howlin' Wolf* (Chess, 1962 – known, from the cover illustration, as 'the rocking chair album'). These songs and other work of the period were frequently covered by British R&B bands of the mid-sixties, 'Rooster' being a major hit for the **Rolling Stones** (1965). Of similar quality was 'Killing Floor' (1965), distinguished, as the earlier examples had been, by the sonorous lead-guitar work of Hubert Sumlin.

Wolf first visited Europe in 1964 with the American Folk Blues Festival. By the late sixties he was working the US festival and coffee-house circuits, and in 1969 he made a club tour of Britain. Separated from Willie Dixon's guidance he made the injudicious 'psychedelic' *The Howlin' Wolf Album* (Cadet Concept, 1969), *Message to the Young* (Chess, 1971) and *The London Howlin' Wolf Sessions* (Rolling Stones, 1971), the last with **Eric Clapton**, **Steve Winwood** and Rolling Stones Charlie Watts and Bill Wyman. *Back Door Wolf* (Chess, 1973) saw a return to more familiar values.

Wolf's legacy is discernible not only in the several occasional imitators who survive him in the blues field but in the calculated vocal distortions of various British and American alumni of the white blues school, such as **Captain Beefheart**.

KEITH HUDSON
b. *18 March 1946, Trenchtown, Jamaica, d. 14 November 1984, New York*

A leading figure in reggae music for three decades, Hudson produced many early dub records as well as developing his own career as a singer and writer.

In 1963 he wrote and produced the **Ken Boothe** hit 'Old Fashioned Way', and followed this with hits for **John Holt** ('Never Will I Hurt My Baby') and Delroy Wilson ('Run Run Run'). At the end of the sixties Hudson was the first to record the pioneering figure in 'toasting' or DJ music, **U-Roy** (Ewart Beckford), on 'Dynamic Fashioned Way', a variant of the earlier Boothe song. He went on to produce hits by Dennis Alcapone ('Spanish Omega'), Alton Ellis and **Big Youth**, whose 'Ace 90 Skank' included motorbike sounds recorded in the studio.

Pick a Dub, engineered by Osborne Ruddock (**King Tubby**) and produced by Hudson, was the first dub album, and consisted of rhythm tracks from former hits played by **Bob Marley**'s rhythm section, Carlton and Aston Barrett. Hudson's own recording career began in the early seventies with a series of albums concentrating on 'message' songs dealing with black consciousness. *Class and Subject* was followed by *Entering the Dragon* and *Flesh of My Skin* (Atra, 1975). With **Augustus Pablo** among the backing musicians, the title track dealt with the tribulations of black history.

In 1975 Hudson moved to New York and signed a recording contract with Virgin, releasing *Too Expensive* (1976), an account of his reaction to his new surroundings which was criticized as straying too far from Hudson's reggae roots. He left Virgin complaining that the company wished to turn him into the next Marley. *Rasta Communication* (Joint/Greensleeves, 1978) and *Steaming Jungle* (Vista Sounds, 1983) saw a return to his roots.

HUES CORPORATION
H. Ann Kelly, b. 24 April 1947, Fairchild, Alabama, USA; St Clair Lee, b. Bernard St Clair Lee Calhoun Henderson, 24 April 1944, San Francisco, California; Karl Russell, b. 10 April 1947, Columbus, Ohio; Fleming Williams, b. Flint, Michigan (replaced by Tommy Brown, b. Birmingham, Alabama)

The 1974 hit 'Rock the Boat' established the Hues Corporation as one of the earliest disco-soul vocal groups.

Kelly, Lee and Russell were a harmony trio singing on the Los Angeles nightclub circuit when they signed to RCA in 1973. Produced by John Florez, the title track of *Freedom for the Stallion* was a minor hit. But the second single from the album, Wally Holmes' 'Rock the Boat', became a million-seller in America and a major success in Europe. It was revived in 1983 by Forrest, who had a British Top Five hit with it on Columbia.

Lead singer Williams left the group before the release of 'Rockin' Soul' (1974), produced by Holmes, which was a lesser hit. The group moved away from the disco sound with the softer 'Love Corporation' (1975), when Brown and Russell left. Holmes then took the Hues Corporation to Warner/Curb for *I Caught Your Act* (1977) and *Your Place or Mine* (1978).

With no further hit records, the group returned to the cabaret circuit.

The band appeared in *Blacula* (1972), the first black horror movie, whose musical director was **Gene Page**.

HUGO AND LUIGI
Hugo Peretti, b. 6 December 1916, New York, USA, d. 1 May 1986, Englewood, New Jersey; Luigi Creatore, b. 21 December 1920, New York

Although they had a few hits as recording artists, Hugo and Luigi, as the cousins Hugo Peretti and Luigio Creatore came to be known as, were far more successful as producers, A&R men, songwriters and executives. Sales of their productions for artists as varied as **Perry Como**, the **Isley Brothers**, **Sam Cooke**, the **Stylistics**, Georgia Gibbs, Jimmie Rodgers, and the Tokens are estimated to be in excess of 50 million records.

The son of a classical violinist, Peretti was a trumpeter, arranger and one-time member of the orchestra of **Guy Lombardo** and **Charlie Barnet**. While working in New York in Broadway show bands and radio orchestras in the late forties, he joined forces with Creatore. They began writing children songs in the late forties, soon graduating to producing them as well. Then, in 1954, Mercury's Irving Green assigned them a number of productions. Their first hit was the Top Five outing 'The Little Shoemaker' (the Gaylords, 1954). As well as producing **Sara Vaughan** ('Whatever Lola Wants', 'Mr. Wonderful'), they proved adept at cleaning up R&B hits for the white market. Their biggest success in that vein was with former dance-band singer Georgia Gibbs, for whom they produced a bestselling version of **LaVern Baker**'s 'Tweedle Dee' (1955) and **Etta James**' 'Roll with Me Henry', this last under the politer title of 'Dance with Me Henry' (also 1955).

As recording artists their first success was the pop novelty 'Young Abe Lincoln' (Mercury), a minor hit in 1955. But by that time they were 'record men', having worked their way up to head of A&R for Mercury Records, replacing **Mitch Miller**. In 1957 they bought Roulette from **George Goldner** and concentrated on writing (usually under the pseudonym 'Mark Marwell') and producing. Their first great success was with Jimmie Rodgers (the son of **Hank Snow**), for whom they produced a trio of million-selling records: 'Honeycomb', 'Kisses Sweeter Than Wine' (both 1957) and 'Secretly' (1958), which they also co-wrote. Pop-folk productions, the records were as notable for their clean sound as for Rodgers' gimmicky 'Uh-oh!' vocal line. In 1959 they sold Roulette to **Henry Glover** and Morris Levy and joined RCA as independent producers and heads of A&R, in what for the times was an unprecedented deal, giving them both large salaries for the five-year term and a producers' royalty of a cent a record.

At RCA, their principal success was with Sam Cooke, many of whose records they supervised. At times the orchestral backings were unsympathetic to Cooke's sweet soul balladry but they were always clean, never fussy, and allowed Cooke's voice, alternately wistful and passionate, to stand out. Other successes included 'Shout'* by the Isley Brothers (1959) and 'The Lion Sleeps Tonight'* (1961) by the Tokens. This was adapted by Hugo and Luigi from the African folk song 'Wimoweh' – under which title it was a British Top Ten hit for Karl Denver in 1962 – which later resurfaced as a European disco hit for Tight Fit in 1982. Other productions from this period included 'Caterina' (Perry Como), 'I Will Follow Him' (Little Peggy March) and 'Tell Laura I Love Her' (Ray Peterson). In conjunction with George David Weiss, the duo also reworked Giovanni Martini's 'Plaisir d'Amour' for **Elvis Presley** as 'Can't Help Falling in Love'* (1961), while in 1959 they returned to the charts with 'La Plume de Ma Tante' and their biggest hit, 'Just Come Home', which reached No. 35 on the charts on RCA.

In the late sixties, with film producer Joseph E. Levine, they established Avco Records and when **Thom Bell** stopped producing the label's top act, the Stylistics, Hugo and Luigi took over and produced 'Let's Put It All Together' (1974). At the same time, with Weiss, they composed the score for the Broadway musical *Maggie Flynn* and the book and score for *The Jokers*. Afterwards, Creatore lived in semi-retirement in Florida. Peretti's death came after a lengthy illness.

THE HUMAN LEAGUE
Philip Oakey, b. 2 October 1955, Sheffield, England; Philip Adrian Wright, b. 30 June 1955, Sheffield; Martin Ware (replaced by Ian Burden, b. 24 December 1955, Sheffield); Ian Craig Marsh (replaced by Jo Callis, b. 2 May 1951, Glasgow, Scotland, replaced by Russell Den-

nett); Joanne Catherall, b. 18 September 1962, Sheffield; Susanne Sulley, b. 26 March 1963, Sheffield; Neil Sutton

The pop sensation of 1981, the Human League evolved from a 1977 avant-garde synthesizer band to become dance-music collaborators of **Jimmy Jam and Terry Lewis** in 1986.

Sheffield computer operators Marsh and Ware formed synthesizer group the Future with Addy Newton, who soon left to join experimentalist band Clock DVA. He was replaced as lyricist and singer by hospital porter Oakey and the name Human League was borrowed from a science-fiction game. Wright joined as 'visual technician', providing back projections of stills from *Star Trek* and *Batman* for the group's occasional live shows.

A first single, 'Being Boiled', was released on Bob Last's Edinburgh-based Fast Product label in 1978, making enough impact for Virgin to release *Reproduction* (1979). By the following year, the New Romantic vogue provided a large enough audience for *Travelogue* to reach the Top Twenty. Human League achieved further fame when the group's name was mentioned in **Feargal Sharkey**'s lyrics for the Undertones' 1980 hit 'My Perfect Cousin'.

There followed a major split, with Marsh and Ware setting up the British Electric Foundation and **Heaven 17**. They took with them the main experimental thrust of the group, leaving Oakey and Wright as fundamentally an electronic pop band, albeit a sophisticated one. They recruited Sheffield musician Burden, and brought in Catherall and Sulley as dancers and singers. The last arrival was Callis, former guitarist with Scottish punk band the Rezillos, who had had a 1978 hit, 'Top of the Pops' (Sire).

With Martin Rushent as producer, the new Human League turned out well-crafted love songs and scored four hit singles from the album *Dare* in 1981–2. The Oakey–Wright composition 'Boys and Girls' was followed by 'Sound of the Crowd' (Oakey–Burden), the summer hit 'Love Action', and 'Don't You Want Me'*. This narrative dialogue, sung by Oakey and Sulley, reportedly inspired by the film *A Star Is Born*, was a major international success, reaching No. 1 in America partly through the impact of its accompanying video, directed by Steve Barron.

An instrumental album of backing tracks from *Dare*, *Love and Dancing* was released by the League Unlimited Orchestra, but the only new recordings in the following two years were the singles 'Mirror Man' (1982) and 'Fascination' (1983). Oakey undertook a solo project with leading disco producer and composer **Giorgio Moroder** which included the hit 'Together in Electric Dreams' (Virgin, 1984) before the next Human League album, *Hysteria* (1984). Produced by Hugh Padgham, it had three more British

Top Twenty singles among its tracks: the uncharacteristic political statement 'The Lebanon', 'Life on Your Own' and 'Louise'.

After another lengthy gap during which Wright and Callis left the band, *Crash* was released in 1986. Four of its tracks were written by producers Jam and Lewis, who had supervised records by Patti Austin, Thelma Houston and **Janet Jackson**. These included the soul ballad hit single 'Human'. The remaining trio were joined by Sutton and Dennett for *Romantic?* (1990), which saw the group attempting to revive electronic disco to little avail. Its best track was the anachronistic Callis–Eugene Reynolds song 'Heart Like a Wheel'. In 1995 the group returned to the UK charts with *Octopus* and the hit single 'Tell Me When'. However, by the end of the decade they had moved to the nostalgia circuit, often in association with Heaven 17 and **Culture Club**.

HELEN HUMES
b. 23 June 1913, Louisville, Kentucky, USA, d. 9 September 1981, Santa Monica, California

An interpreter equally adept at blues, ballads and standards, Helen Humes possessed a light, flexible voice, an unerring sense of pitch and rhythm and a subtle touch in improvisation. Some critics place her, among women jazz singers, third only to **Billie Holiday** and **Ella Fitzgerald**.

With only brief and local experience behind her, Humes first recorded at the age of thirteen, singing blues of a distinctly adult character. In the middle and late thirties she worked as a band vocalist under several leaders, including **Harry James** and, from 1938 to 1942, **Count Basie** (replacing Holiday). From 1944, based on the West Coast, she travelled and recorded with a succession of blues/R&B bands, scoring hits with 'Be-Baba-Leba' (1945, with **Bill Doggett**) and 'Million Dollar Secret' (1950), recorded live at a Gene Norman concert in Los Angeles with **Roy Milton**'s band. She also worked with Buck Clayton, Dexter Gordon, the **Dizzy Gillespie** Orchestra (with whom she made several film shorts in 1947) and Basie again. In 1956 she spent a long and well-received stay in Australia with Red Norvo.

She worked less in the late fifties, but made several albums for Contemporary (1959–61) that displayed her command of a wide range of material. In 1962 she toured Europe with the first American Folk Blues Festival and in 1964 she again visited Australia, but from 1967 to 1973 she was in retirement. Her return was signalled by a series of European engagements and some French-made albums on Black and Blue, and she returned to hold regular residencies at the Cookery in New York City (1974–7), where she continued to charm audiences with her powers unimpaired.

ENGELBERT HUMPERDINCK
b. Arnold George Dorsey, 2 May 1936, Madras, India

Humperdinck was one of the roster of cabaret-orientated pop artists, which included **Tom Jones**, managed by Gordon Mills. Like Jones, Humperdinck turned frequently to country music for material.

Raised in Leicester, Gerry Dorsey was one of the last performers to start his career as a dance-band singer. After nearly ten years struggling he signed with Mills as manager in 1966. Mills was a former member of the Viscounts skiffle group who had graduated to songwriting (producing Top Twenty hits for **Johnny Kidd and the Pirates**) and thence to management with Jones. Mills came up with the name Humperdinck and turned him into a smoother, mat-inée-idol version of Jones. Signed to Decca, Humperdinck had his first million-seller with the country standard 'Release Me' (1967), a hit for **Ray Price** in 1954. This was followed by **Dallas Frazier**'s 'There Goes My Everything'* and the first of a series of songs written for him by **Les Reed** and Barry Mason, 'The Last Waltz'* (both in 1967). For the next few years he was rarely out of the charts: 'Am I That Easy to Forget', 'A Man without Love', 'Les Bicyclettes de Belsize' (all 1968), 'I'm a Better Man' (1969) and 'Winter World of Love' were among his successes.

Though the flow of hits stopped in the seventies, with the exception of 'After the Lovin'' (Epic), a surprise American Top Ten hit in 1976, Humperdinck, like Jones before him, turned to the cabaret circuit and television. *Remember I Love You* (RCA, 1987) was his first new album for over a decade and included a duet with **Gloria Gaynor**. However, whereas Jones discovered the ability to regularly reinvent himself, Humperdinck was unable to escape his matinée-idol image and thus remained trapped within the confines of his romantic repertoire and nostalgia audiences.

PEE WEE HUNT
b. Walter Hunt, 10 May 1907, Mount Healthy, Ohio, USA, d. 22 June 1979, Plymouth, Massachusetts

A Dixieland-style trombonist, singer and bandleader, Hunt found popularity during the post-Second World War revival of traditional jazz.

From a musical family, he learned banjo and trombone while studying at Ohio State University and Cincinnati Conservatory. He joined Jean Goldkette's band in 1927, and the following year, with Glen Gray (*b. 7 June 1906, Roanoke, Illinois, d. 23 August 1963, Plymouth, Virginia*) and others, formed the Casa Loma Orchestra.

With precise (though jazz-based), rather than swinging, arrangements by Gene Gifford, the Casa Loma group (named in honour of a hotel that never in fact opened) became one of the most prolific recording bands in America. Hunt was one of the featured soloists on sides recorded for Okeh (1929–31), Brunswick (1931–4) – including 'Casa Loma Stomp' (1931), 'Pardon My Southern Accent' and 'Dixie Lee' (1934) with Hunt on vocals – RCA Victor (1933), and Decca (1934–50). The Casa Loma Orchestra's greatest period of influence was the early thirties when its mix of ballads ('Blue Moon', 'When I Grow Too Old to Dream', both No. 1s in 1935) and swing numbers ('White Jazz') prepared the way for **Benny Goodman** and others. The orchestra also exerted a considerable influence on the development of dance music in Europe, where **Lew Stone** in London and James Kok in Germany played many Casa Loma arrangements.

Hunt left the orchestra in 1943 and after war service formed his own band, introducing a small group set which included 'Twelfth Street Rag', composed in 1914 by Euday L. Bowlay. The popularity of the piece (and Hunt's raucous trombone 'raspberries') with dancers at the Hollywood Palladium led **Johnny Mercer**'s newly formed Capitol label to release the tune under Hunt's name in 1948. It went on to sell a million.

He persisted with the good-time Dixieland formula into the fifties and sixties, having a further hit with Byron Gay's and Arnold Johnson's 1919 song 'Oh' (Capitol, 1953).

IVORY JOE HUNTER
b. 1911 (or 1914), Kirbyville, Texas, USA, d. 8 November 1974, Memphis, Tennessee

Although the early years of his professional career typed him as a blues artist, Ivory Joe Hunter had the ability and ambition to work in other fields. He eventually made the transition to ballads and country songs so successfully that he not only won a following among country audiences – and, through his songwriting, country artists – but was even awarded, shortly before his death, a benefit concert at the *Grand Ole Opry*.

In the late thirties, under the influence of **Duke Ellington** and **Fats Waller**, he worked as a singer and pianist with bands in southeast Texas. He moved to the West Coast in 1942, cutting his first record for his own Ivory label in 1945, accompanied by Johnny Moore's Three Blazers and for once yielding the piano stool to **Charles Brown**. He later started another label, Pacific, recording blues and boogies, but in 1947 he moved to King, where he worked with both black and white accompanists and made his first attempts at country material; these included 'Jealous Heart'. Signing in 1949 with MGM he developed his ballad style and had a No. 1 R&B hit with 'I Almost Lost My Mind'*; a lesser success was 'I Need You So', later recorded by **Elvis Presley**. In the early fifties he was in great demand as a touring attraction, with a sizeable band and a massive wardrobe.

Moving in 1954 to Atlantic he had his most enduring hit in 1956 with 'Since I Met You Baby' which sold a million copies despite being covered at the time by **Pat Boone** and since by countless pop artists. After further success with 'Empty Arms'* (Atlantic, 1957) and the **Bill Anderson** song 'City Lights' (Dot, 1959) his professional associations became more scattered and shortlived: he recorded for several labels during the sixties and early seventies, his final album being the defiantly titled *I've Always Been Country* (Paramount, 1974).

Among the admirers who performed at his *Opry* benefit were **George Jones**, **Tammy Wynette** and **Isaac Hayes**, a combination that accurately encapsulates the breadth of his appeal.

MISSISSIPPI JOHN HURT

b. 3 July 1893, Teoc, Mississippi, USA, d. 2 November 1966, Grenada, Mississippi

With his gentle, confiding voice and liltingly finger-picked guitar, John Hurt offered an intriguingly different blues from that of his Mississippi contemporaries **Charley Patton** and **Son House**. His work was proof that some black musicians first recorded in the twenties represented older styles and repertoires than those of country blues.

A self-taught player of only local celebrity, Hurt was recorded by Okeh in 1928 on the recommendation of better-known white musicians from his neighbourhood. He then disappeared from the musical scene until traced in 1963, whereupon he was brought to Washington DC to play in clubs and coffee-houses. Over the next three years he performed throughout the United States and Canada and recorded, in a style unchanged over nearly forty years, for Piedmont, Vanguard and other labels. Though the material was not issued until after his death, he also recorded for the Library of Congress. Among his best-loved numbers were 'Candy Man Blues', 'Spike Driver Blues' (a version of 'John Henry'), and 'Salty Dog', all of which were taken up by American folk guitarists. 'Richland Woman Blues' was memorably recorded by **Maria Muldaur** with Jim Kweskin's Jug Band.

FERLIN HUSKY

b. 3 December 1927, Flat River, Missouri, USA

Husky's tremulous tearjerker 'Gone'* (1957), replete with strings and a vocal chorus, was the quintessential country-pop record of the fifties.

Husky's first career was as a disc-jockey in St Louis. He only started performing seriously when he moved to Bakersfield, California, and became part of its thriving country scene in the forties. There he adopted the name Terry Preston (and the alias Simon Crum for his hayseed comic routines) and was signed to Capitol. Two Korean War-inspired duets with Jean Shepherd, 'Dear John Letter' and 'Forgive Me John' (1953), gave him his first hits. After 'Gone', Simon Crum had a country hit with 'Country Music Is Here to Stay' (1958) and Husky appeared, with **Faron Young** and Zsa Zsa Gabor, in the movie *Country Music Holiday* (1958). He then moved further away from mainstream country, hitting the pop charts in 1960 with the pop-gospel recording 'On the Wings of a Dove'.

Never again as successful in the pop charts, Husky continued to record for Capitol and, after 1973, ABC, and regularly made the country charts. After he suffered a stroke in 1977, Husky and his group, the Hush Puppies, toured less.

BETTY HUTTON

b. Elizabeth June Thornburg, 26 February 1921, Battle Creek, Michigan, USA

Known as 'The Blonde Bombshell', Hutton was the brash, energetic star of numerous Hollywood musicals.

She began singing with local dance bands in her teens to help support her family and joined the **Vincent Lopez** Orchestra in the late thirties. (Her sister Marion also became a big-band vocalist, most notably with **Glenn Miller**.) In 1940 Hutton appeared in the Broadway productions of *Two for the Show* and *Panama Hattie* (which featured songs by **Cole Porter**), which led to a contract with Paramount in 1942. After a series of madcap comedies with musical interludes, including *Star Spangled Rhythm*, *The Fleet's In* (both 1942) – in which she scored her first big hit with the **Johnny Mercer** composition, 'Arthur Murray Taught Me Dancing in a Hurry' – and *And the Angels Sing* (1944), for which she sang the Mercer title song, she graduated to dramatic roles. These included *Incendiary Blonde* (1945), based on the life of nightclub queen Texas Guinan, in which she sang 'Ragtime Cowboy Joe'.

In 1950 she landed the part of Annie Oakley in the hugely successful *Annie Get Your Gun* as a replacement for the ailing **Judy Garland**. Working with **Howard Keel** and singing songs by **Irving Berlin**, Hutton found a role to fit her zest and gusto perfectly. With Keel she sang 'Anything You Can Do I Can Do Better' and Berlin's hymn to his chosen career, 'There's No Business Like Show Business', and alone she warbled 'Doing What Comes Naturally' and 'You Can't Get a Man with a Gun'. After playing the lead in *The Greatest Show on Earth* and *Somebody Loves Me* (both 1952), which was based on the career of vaudeville star Blossom Seeley, Hutton quit Hollywood when she was not allowed to nominate her husband, choreographer Charles O'Curran, as the director of her films.

She made occasional stage and concert appearances throughout the fifties and sixties, and declared herself bankrupt in 1967. In 1974 she hit the headlines when it transpired that she had been living as a cook and cleaner in a rectory for several years, to which she returned after a shortlived attempt at a comeback.

BRIAN HYLAND
b. 12 November 1944, New York, USA

A teenage idol of the early sixties, Hyland lasted longer as a hitmaker than most of his contemporaries.

As a result of a demo disc by his group, the Delphis, Hyland was signed to Leader and reached No. 1 in America and the Top Ten in Britain with Paul Vance's and Lee Pockriss's novelty song, 'Itsy Bitsy Teenie Weenie Yellow Polka Dot Bikini' (Leader, 1960). A version of the song by UK children's TV presenter Timmy Mallett (as 'Bombalurina') was a UK No. 1 in 1990. Pockriss had previously written 'Seven Little Girls (Sittin in the Back Seat)', a 1959 hit for Paul Evans (who in turn wrote the **Kalin Twins**' 'When') and for Bombalurina in 1990, but the follow-up he provided for Hyland, 'Lop-sided, Overloaded and It Wiggled When I Rode It', flopped. Subsequent records for Kapp were also unsuccessful, but in 1961 he signed to ABC and had a Top Twenty hit with the yearning ballad 'Let Me Belong to You'.

In similar vein were his three big successes of 1962, written by Udell and Gold. Hyland crooned his way effectively through 'Ginny Come Lately' while 'Sealed with a Kiss' rivalled **Carole King**'s 'It Might as Well Rain until September' in its portrayal of the plight of teenage lovers parted by family holidays. The record was a British hit on its re-release in 1975 and in a version produced by **Stock, Aitken and Waterman** for soap opera star **Jason Donovan** on PWL in 1988.

The follow-up, 'Warmed over Kisses', also sold well, but like so many other American solo singers, Hyland in 1963 was floundering in the wake of the British group invasion of the charts. His next success was not until 1966 for Philips when **Tommy 'Snuff' Garrett** produced the **Leon Russell** arrangements of 'The Joker Went Wild' and 'Run Run Look and See'. Later Philips records made little impact and he moved to Dot (1969) before recording a surprise million-selling folky version of **Curtis Mayfield**'s 'Gypsy Woman', produced by **Del Shannon** (Uni, 1970).

Another revival, of **Jackie Wilson**'s 1959 hit 'Lonely Teardrops' (1971), only reached the lower end of the charts.

JACK HYLTON
b. 2 July 1892, Great Lever, Lancashire, England,
d. 29 January 1965, London

In the thirties Hylton led the most popular dance band in Europe.

A one-time boy soprano and pianist in a pierrot troupe, Hylton was a professional musician from his teens. In 1920 he joined a London dance band as a relief pianist, becoming its leader by dint of his musical knowledge in 1921, when the band recorded (with Hylton as arranger) for Zonophone as Jack Hylton's Jazz Band. The word jazz was inaccurate, since although a few of Hylton's later recordings (such as 'Black and Blue Rhythm', 1934) were jazz orientated and, in 1935, **Coleman Hawkins** toured with the band, Hylton's main influence was **Paul Whiteman**. Hylton saw Whiteman in London in 1923, and closely modelled the band he formed the following year specifically to tour Europe on that of·Whiteman, whose notions of 'symphonic jazz' Hylton actively championed as a European contribution to American music. Slightly jazzier were the looser recording aggregations Hylton sponsored, Jack Hylton's Rhythmagicians and Jack Hylton's Kit-Kat Band (the leader of which was Al Starita).

If Hylton's recordings (for HMV until 1931, then Decca, finally returning to HMV in 1935) were sedate and generally bland, they were also successful. In 1929 it is estimated he sold over three million records of tunes such as 'Shepherd of the Hills' and 'Me and Jane in a Plane'. The key to this success was his non-stop touring: between 1927 and 1938, Hylton undertook sixteen European tours, presenting a mix of light classics, popular hit songs, novelty numbers and speciality acts. Only occasionally did the band attempt the more ambitious works of arranger Billy Ternent.

After the outbreak of the Second World War Hylton turned briefly to broadcasting before breaking up the band in 1940 to concentrate on his parallel career as a theatrical impresario, producing shows on a regular basis for the Crazy Gang and importing and reviving American musicals such as *Annie Get Your Gun* (1947), *Kiss Me Kate* (1952), *Pal Joey* (1954) and *Camelot* (1964).

IAN AND SYLVIA

Ian Tyson, b. September 1933, British Columbia, Canada; Sylvia Fricker, b. September 1940, Chatham, Ontario

While the influence of country music on the folk revival was apparent through the **Carter Family** and **Woody Guthrie**, Ian and Sylvia were among the few folk artists to enter the country field in the seventies.

Tyson grew up in rural British Columbia, working on the land until he was introduced to folk song by visiting British singer Roy Guest while recuperating from a rodeo injury. He moved to Toronto in 1959 where he met Fricker singing in the city's folk clubs. The daughter of a music teacher, she teamed up with Tyson, both playing guitars and Fricker adding autoharp.

In 1960 Ian and Sylvia moved south to New York, where they were signed by Albert Grossman, manager of **Peter Paul and Mary** and **Bob Dylan**. He placed them with Vanguard, who released their first eponymous album in 1962. It was a typically eclectic selection of traditional material, but *Four Strong Winds* (1964) added contemporary songs – including Dylan's 'Tomorrow Is a Long Time' – to the Appalachian, French Canadian and gospel items. The album's title track became Tyson's best-known composition through versions by **Neil Young** and others. Its bittersweet narrative traces the annual path of Canada's migrant farmworkers, from the tobacco harvest of Ontario through the wheatfields of the Prairies to apple picking in British Columbia.

Fricker's most successful song, 'You Were on My Mind', appeared on *Northern Journey* (1964). It was a hit single in America for We Five (A&M, 1965), a group led by **John Stewart**'s brother Michael, and in Britain for Crispian St Peters (Decca, 1966). The title track of *Early Morning Rain* (1965) and 'For Lovin' Me' introduced the work of **Gordon Lightfoot**, a Toronto folk-scene colleague of Ian and Sylvia. *Play One More* (1966) and *Nashville* (1968) signalled the shift towards country music. The **Todd Rundgren**-produced *Great Speckled Bird* (Ampex, 1969, reissued Stony Plain, 1994) was an early example of the country-rock phenomenon. It featured leading Nashville session players David Briggs (piano) and Buddy Cage (steel guitar) alongside future **Maria Muldaur** guitarist Amos Garrett.

After a further album for Columbia (*You Were on My Mind*, 1972), the duo split up and returned to Canada where both began solo careers and worked in broadcasting. Fricker made *Woman's World* (Capitol, 1975) and Tyson recorded *Ol' Eon* (A&M, 1975) and *One Jump Ahead of the Devil* (Boot, 1979). He later became a key figure in the indigenous Canadian country-music scene, releasing a series of albums documenting the life of cowboys on the Canadian plains. Among these were *Cowboyography* (Stony Plain, 1986), which included the Canadian hit 'Navajo Rag', *I Outgrew the Wagon Train* (1990), *Stood There Amazed* (1991) and *Eighteen Inches of Rain* (1994). *All the Good Uns* (1996) was a distillation of the series, his warm voice bringing a sense of hope to even the bitterest of his tales.

Fricker also recorded solo, making eight albums in the eighties and nineties under her married name. The best of these included *Gypsy Cadillac* (1988), which featured a guest appearance by singer-songwriter Tom Russell, who regularly collaborated with both Tysons, and *You Were on My Mind* (1990). Since 1994 she has also recorded four albums as a member of Quartette. *River Road and Other Stories* (Salt Music, 2000) formed the basis of a theatrical production in which through songs she told the story of growing up in the fifties in provincial Canada.

JANIS IAN

b. Janis Eddy Fink, 7 May 1951, New York, USA

In the late sixties Janis Ian enjoyed brief celebrity as a teenage protest singer, before starting a second career as an intense singer-songwriter.

She grew up in New Jersey and New York, the daughter of a music teacher, and began composing songs on piano and guitar at the age of twelve. In 1965 the folk magazine *Broadside* published her 'Hair of Spun Gold', which led to club appearances and a recording contract with Verve. Produced by **Shadow Morton**, her first single was a controversial tale of inter-racial romance, 'Society's Child (Baby I've Been Thinking)'. Banned by some radio stations, it was featured by **Leonard Bernstein** on a television special about the 'rock revolution'.

'Society's Child' reached the Top Twenty in 1967 and was followed by an eponymous solo album containing other socially significant material like 'New Christ Cardiac Hero' and 'Janey's Blues'. Using a then fashionable folk-rock backing group (with **Richie Havens** on drums on some tracks), Ian cut two albums in 1968: *For All the Seasons of Your Mind* and *The Secret Life of J. Eddy Fink*. In 1969 she made the

Charles Callello-produced *Who Really Cares* and performed at the Newport Folk Festival.

The pressures of her career led the nineteen-year-old to go into retirement and she released only *Present Company* (Capitol, 1971) before returning to music full-time in 1974. In that year she released the reflective *Stars* (Columbia), whose title song was recorded by **Cher** and **Glen Campbell**, among others, while 'Jesse' gave **Roberta Flack** a 1973 hit. *Between the Lines* (1975) was produced by Brooks Arthur and included Ian's biggest hit, the impassioned song of experience 'At Seventeen'*. *Aftertones* (1975) was a Top Twenty hit but later albums such as *Miracle Row* (1977), produced by Ron Frangipane, and 1978's *Janis Ian* were less successful.

Night Rains (1979) showed a distinct jazz influence and featured pianist **Chick Corea**. It also included songs composed by Ian for the films *The Foxes* and *The Bell Jar*, and two tracks were produced by disco specialist **Giorgio Moroder**. In 1981 she released the Gary Klein-produced *Restless Eyes*.

After almost a decade of retirement Ian returned to performing in 1990 and made a short tour of Britain the following year. She subsequently signed to the Morgan Creek label, releasing *Breaking Silence* (1993), whose confessional stance and willingness to confront issues like domestic violence and the legacy of the Holocaust harked back to her earlier work. She followed that with *Hunger* (1997).

ABDULLAH IBRAHIM
b. Adolph Johannes Brand, 9 October 1934, South Africa

A leading jazz pianist and composer, Ibrahim was a prime mover in bringing the township jazz of South Africa and even older African folk modes into Afro-American music.

His grandmother was a church pianist and, in 1961, Dollar Brand (as he was then known) formed the Jazz Epistles in Cape Town with trumpeter **Hugh Masakela** and also saxophonist Kippi Moeketsi. The following year, with his wife the singer Sathima Bea Benjamin, he went into voluntary exile in Switzerland. There, Brand performed with **Duke Ellington**, who encouraged him to move to the United States.

With Ellington he recorded *Duke Ellington Presents the Dollar Brand Trio* (Reprise, 1963). More significant, however, were *Anatomy of a South African Village* (Fontana, 1965) and *The Dream* (Black Lion, 1965), both featuring Johnny Gertze (bass) and Makaya Ntshoko on drums. In the late sixties Brand established himself in Europe recording a mixture of tribute albums (*Ode to Duke Ellington*, 1969) and African-themed ones (*African Portraits*, 1968) before returning to South Africa in 1971. Then he recorded his most famous piece, 'Mannenberg', with sax-player

Basil Coetsee. The tune became an anthem for black South Africans during the Soweto uprising in 1976, the year Brand moved back to New York.

Many later albums by Ibrahim (the name he took after converting to Islam) and Benjamin were released on their own Enja label. They included *African Sketchbook* (1983), *Ekaya* (1983, and also the name of Ibrahim's group) and *African Piano*. He also recorded *Confluence* (Black Lion) with Argentinian saxophonist Gato Barbiere and in 1988 composed the score for Claire Denis's film *Chocolat*.

In the nineties his work included *No Fear No Die* (1993).

ICE CUBE
b. O'Shea Jackson, 15 June 1959, Los Angeles, California, USA

Since the break-up of **NWA**, Ice Cube has maintained his position as one of rap's most controversial figures, and also developed a career in films.

His first solo recording, *AmeriKKKa's Most Wanted* (1990), reinforced the image of a trigger-happy, streetwise gang leader, but added greater social commentary than his previous work. It included such tracks as 'The Nigga Ya Love to Hate' and 'It's a Man's World', in which his macho rhymes are countered by female rapper Yo-Yo. The album was produced by **Public Enemy**'s production team, the Bomb Squad.

After issuing the EP *Kill at Will*, Ice Cube had a US No. 1 hit with *Death Certificate* (1991), on which he sampled tracks by the **Average White Band**, the Meters and **Wilson Pickett**. The album alternated social comment on ghetto life with attacks on almost every category of American apart from young, straight, black males. Protests from Christian and Jewish groups that his lyrics promoted racial hatred and violence caused his UK label to delete two tracks from the album.

His later recordings have included *The Predator* (1992) and *Lethal Injection* (1993), whose tracks included a version of **George Clinton**'s 'One Nation under a Groove' and 'When I Get to Heaven', an attack on Christianity from an Islamic standpoint. Perhaps his most well-known song is the quietly menacing 'It Was a Good Day', a crossover hit in 1993. After producing rap artists Kam and Da Lench Mob for Warners, he set up his own label, Lench Mob. *Bootlegs and B Sides* was issued in 1995.

Ice Cube made his film début in John Singleton's *Boyz 'N the Hood* (1993), whose title was taken from a rap he had written for NWA. He later starred with **Ice T** in *Trespass*, and another Singleton film, *Higher Learning*. In 1996 he wrote and acted in the comedy *Friday*, and took a further step into cinema in 1998, directing *The Players Club*, which was a US hit. He also returned to recording that year, releasing an album, *War and Peace Vol. I: The War Disc*, his first in several years. In 1999 he starred alongside George Clooney in *Three Kings* and in 2000 released *War and Peace Vol. II: The Peace Disc*, which included 'Hell Low', on which, partnered by one-time former member of NWA **Dr Dre**, he rapped, 'I started this gangsta shit/Is this the motherfuckin' thanks I get?'. The album suggested that despite his burgeoning movie career Ice Cube remained as angry as ever.

ICE T
b. Tracey Morrow, 1959, Newark, New Jersey, USA

Although not the originator of the West Coast style of 'gangsta rap', Ice T was the first commercially successful exponent of it.

After serving a prison sentence for theft, he turned to rap music in 1986, taking his name from black author Iceberg Slim. *Rhyme Pays* (Sire, 1987) was an uncompromising collection of ghetto anecdotes. It was followed by *Power* (1988), which included the anti-drugs tirade 'I'm Your Pusher' and 'Girls L.G.B.N.A.F.', which drew the wrath of the Parents Music Resource Center censorship pressure group when they discovered the acronym stood for 'Let's Get Buck Naked and Fuck'.

That experience inspired the main themes of *The Iceberg/Freedom of Speech . . . Just Watch What You Say* (1989), on which Ice T chanted defiance against the forces in US society that wanted to ban rap. After recording *O. G. Original Gangster* (1991) he was forced to retreat in the face of pressures to censor his work. The song at issue was 'Cop Killer' from the album *Body Count* (1992), on which he added thrash metal to the musical mix. Although his record company resisted protests from police organizations, Ice T himself withdrew the track from the album. The furore had no impact on his popularity with both black and white fans of rap and he later toured with the Body Count metal band, which included twin guitarists Ernie C and D-Roc. In 1994 Body Count recorded *Born Dead*.

A dispute over the album cover design of *Home Invasion* (1993) caused Ice T to take the album to the independent Priority label for release. The title track dealt with the appeal of black rap to middle-class white teenagers and on 'Gotta Lotta Love' Ice-T included **Mike Oldfield**'s 'Tubular Bells' melody. It was another three years before his next album, *Return of the Real* (1996), which was a commercial disappointment.

Ice T's film appearances have included *New Jack City*, in which he played an undercover cop, *Ricochet* with Denzel Washington, *Trespass* and Ernest Dicker-

son's *Surviving the Game* (1994). He has also published a book of autobiography and personal philosophy, *The Ice Opinion* (1993).

BILLY IDOL
b. William Michael Albert Broad, 30 November 1955, Edgware, London, England

A minor figure in British punk rock, bottle-blonde Idol found success as a solo singer in America in the eighties with a highly produced mixture of mainstream rock and a glamourized punk image.

From a middle-class background, he was a student at Sussex University and one of the Bromley contingent of **Sex Pistols** fans when he joined (as a guitarist) punk band Chelsea with bassist Tony James (a former member of London SS, a proto-punk band that included the **Clash**'s Mick Jones). After a few months, the pair left along with drummer John Towe and set up Generation X, named after a sixties' book of pop sociology. Recruiting Bob Derwood Andrews (guitar), the group specialized in songs dense with references to rock, movies and TV. Their first three singles set the tone: 'Your Generation' (an answer song to **The Who**'s 1965 hit 'My Generation'), 'Ready Steady Go' (the title of a sixties TV rock show), and 'Wild Youth'. Former drummer with pioneering punk band Subway Sect Mark Laff joined after the first single. Their eponymous début album for Chrysalis was a minor hit in 1978, but *Valley of the Dolls* (1979), produced by former **Mott the Hoople** singer Ian Hunter, and *Kiss Me Deadly* (1981, credited to Gen X) made less impact. Generation X enjoyed four Top Fifty singles, the biggest hit being 'King Rocker' (1979).

Andrews and Laff quit in 1980, replaced by latter day Chelsea guitarist James Stephenson and ex-**Clash** drummer Terry Chimes. Generation X finally split in 1981, with James going on to play with ex-**New York Dolls** guitarist Johnny Thunders, later re-emerging with Sigue Sigue Sputnik in 1986. In a cynical attempt to commercialize the punk legacy, James signed the band to EMI amid much hype. After the heavily promoted **Giorgio Moroder**-produced *Flaunt It* gave the group only a minor hit with 'Love Missile F1-11', they faded from sight. In 1990 James joined 'Goth' band the Sisters of Mercy, but left in 1991 to pursue a solo career. Laff joined retro-rock outfit 20 Flight Rockers, who split up after an ill-advised move to Los Angeles, and Andrews formed Westworld, who had a British Top Twenty hit with 'Sonic Boom Boy' in 1987.

Idol moved to the United States to begin a solo career with his début album, *Don't Stop* (1981), produced by Moroder's associate Keith Forsey. The eponymous follow-up (1982) included the hit singles 'Hot in the City' (1982) and 'White Wedding' (1983), which was also a success in Britain two years later.

The songs were co-written by Idol and guitarist Steve Stevens.

Idol was one of a number of British acts to benefit in America from extensive exposure on the MTV twenty-four-hour video music channel. The ballad hit 'Eyes without a Face' (reportedly inspired by Gogol's novel *Dead Souls*) was typical of the morbid material on the bestselling *Rebel Yell* (1983). The album's title track gave Idol a British hit in 1985.

Whiplash Smile (1986), introduced by an audacious version of **William Bell**'s 'I Forgot to Be Your Lover', contained a similar mix of violence and glamour. By 1987 Idol was based in America where he topped the American charts with 'Mony Mony', a live revival of **Tommy James and the Shondells**' 1968 hit, and had further success with 'Don't Need a Gun' and 'Sweet Sixteen'. Idol's trademark sneer is flaunted to best effect on the compilation album *Vital Idol* (1987). *Charmed Life* (1990), which included the American Top Five 'Cradle of Love' and a version of the **Doors**' 'LA Woman', was made as Idol's interests turned more towards film and showed it. *Cyberpunk* (1993) showed a drift towards dance, exemplified by a bizarre version of the **Velvet Underground**'s 'Heroin'. By the end of the decade, although he was without a record contract, he regularly appeared on stage and film.

FRANK IFIELD

b. 30 November 1936, Coventry, Warwickshire, England

Briefly the most popular British balladeer of the sixties – he was the first British recording artist to have three British No. 1s with successive singles – Ifield, like **Engelbert Humperdinck**, borrowed much of his material from country acts.

Ifield emigrated to Australia when he was nine and went into showbusiness professionally in his teens. He had an early hit with 'Whiplash' (Festival, 1957) and in 1959 returned to Britain. His bright country-inflected voice, with its gimmicky falsetto and occasional yodel, was unusual. His first records were only minor hits but the **Victor Schertzinger–Johnny Mercer** composition, 'I Remember You' (EMI Columbia, 1962), with its hiccuping falsetto, gave him his first British chart-topper and million-seller. His records henceforth were mostly of country material: 'Lovesick Blues' (his second No. 1 in 1962) was a song associated with **Hank Williams** and 'The Wayward Wind' (his third No. 1 in 1963, originally recorded by **Gogi Grant**) with **Tex Ritter**. 'Nobody's Darling but Mine' and 'Mule Train' (both 1963) were also country songs.

However, Ifield lacked the personality of, say, **Andy Williams** or **Perry Como**, and made little of his enormous success. He was one of the many swept away by **The Beatles**. In the mid-sixties he had a few minor country hits in America on Hickory, including 'Call Her Your Sweetheart' (1966) and 'Good Morning Dear' (1970). Throughout the seventies and eighties Ifield appeared in cabaret and in oldies package tours.

IGGY (IGGY POP)

b. James Newell Osterberg, 21 April 1947, Ann Arbor, Michigan, USA

Former leader of the Stooges, an influential proto-punk group, Iggy Pop's erratic solo career initially developed in partnership with **David Bowie** and proved to be far longer than everyone expected, even if, like **Billy Idol**, at times he came dangerously close to self-parody.

He began as a drummer for local rock band the Iguanas (thereby acquiring his nickname) and blues group the Prime Movers, playing back-up for visiting artists such as **Junior Wells** and the **Shangri-Las**. In 1967 he formed the Stooges, with himself as lead vocalist plus guitarist Ron Asheton, drummer Scott Asheton and bassist Dave Alexander. Inspired by the **Doors**, the band evolved an outrageous stage act – with Iggy cutting himself with broken glass (much as **Sex Pistol** Sid Vicious would do a few years later) and diving into the audience – which brought headlines and a recording contract with Elektra. Produced by John Cale of the **Velvet Underground**, *The Stooges* (1969) included '1969', 'No Fun' and 'I Wanna Be Your Dog', all songs that became part of the British punk repertoire seven years later. *Funhouse*, produced by Don Gallucci, who had helmed the Kingsmen's classic 'Louie Louie', was released in 1970. A year later, after several line-up changes, the group split.

In 1972 Bowie's manager Tony DeFries signed Iggy Pop, who re-formed the Stooges (with James Williamson on guitar, Ron Asheton on bass and Scott Asheton on drums) to make the Bowie-mixed *Raw Power* (Columbia, 1972). Among the tracks were 'Search and Destroy', 'Penetration' and 'Death Trip'. After being dropped by CBS, the band undertook a gruelling touring schedule (as captured on the live album *Metallic KO*, 1977) before breaking up in early 1974. Drugs and mental health problems made the mid-seventies an unproductive period for Iggy, and he only recorded sporadically until 1977 when *The Idiot* was released by RCA. The first of a trio of collaborations with Bowie, it was supported by an American tour on which Bowie played keyboards in Iggy's band. *Lust for Life* (1977) was Iggy's most rock-orientated recording for some time while *TV Eye* (1978) was a live recording. In the same year recordings made with Williamson in 1974 were issued as *Kill City*. *New Values* (Arista, 1979) contained songs composed while Iggy was living in Berlin, including 'Tell Me a Story' and 'Billy Is a Runaway'.

The eighties was Iggy Pop's most prolific decade. He cut two further Arista albums – *Soldier* (1980) and *Party* (1981) – and in 1982 moved to Chris Stein's (of **Blondie**) Animal label for *Zombie Birdhouse*. There followed a further hiatus in which he again underwent a drugs cure while Bowie scored a worldwide hit with the Pop–Bowie composition 'China Girl' (1983). In 1985 he returned to work, co-writing and performing the title song for Alex Cox's film *Repo Man*, with ex-**Sex Pistol** Steve Jones on guitar. This led to the pair writing and recording songs which were released, together with five Pop–Bowie compositions, as *Blah Blah Blah* (A&M, 1986). Ironically the album's biggest hit was 'Real Wild Child', a revival of Australian rock'n'roll singer Johnny O'Keefe's 1958 Australian hit on Festival. The song had also been a minor American hit for the **Crickets**' Jerry Allison under the pseudonym Ivan. At the same time Pop turned to acting, appearing in the teleseries *Miami Vice* and films like *Sid and Nancy* and *The Color of Money* (1986). In 1988 Iggy released *Instinct*, another collaboration with Steve Jones. His contribution to the Aids benefit album *Red, Hot and Blue* (1989) was a duet with former member of **Blondie** Debbie Harry on **Cole Porter**'s 'Well Did You Evah?', He followed it with another duet, 'Candy' (Virgin, 1990), with Kate Pierson of the **B-52**'s, which gave him his biggest American hit to date. The album it came from, *Brick by Brick*, produced by **Don Was**, was his best outing since 1997's *Lust for Life*. For once Iggy wasn't overshadowed by his partners/guests and under Was's strict control he proved unexpectedly adept at melding different styles into an (almost) harmonious whole.

In 1993 he starred with **Tom Waits** in the Jim Jarmusch short film *Coffee and Cigarettes*. The same year he released the musically backward-looking *American Caesar*, which included a lyrically reworked 'Louie Louie' (an infamous version of which had appeared on *Metallic KO*) and 'Wild America', with guest vocals by **Henry Rollins**. A dynamic live performer, Pop's seemingly insatiable appetite for touring saw him playing to ever larger audiences in the late eighties and early nineties. Solo albums from this period include *Naughty Little Dogs* (Virgin, 1996). However, Iggy was more often found on tribute albums, including his own, *We Will Fall* (1997), and the James Bond celebration, *Shaken Not Stirred* (1998).

JULIO IGLESIAS
b. 23 September 1943, Madrid, Spain

Having been the most popular Spanish-language singer for two decades, Iglesias found appreciative English-speaking audiences in the eighties. While he continued to sell records in huge quantities in the nineties, his son Enrique sold even more.

He was a professional soccer player with Real Madrid before concentrating on a career in music. Signed to Columbia, he scored a long series of hits during the seventies in Spain and in Latin America with albums like *A Mis 33 Años*, *Emociones* and *Hey*. Iglesias entered the British charts in 1981 with a Spanish version of **Cole Porter**'s 'Begin the Beguine' and the album of the same name, which contained more English-language songs with translated lyrics, such as 'Island in the Sun'. Further British hits included 'Quiereme Mucho', 'Amor' and 'Julio' (1983). In that year Columbia awarded Iglesias a diamond disc for 100 million album sales.

The 1983 album *Julio* was multilingual with songs in French and English, as well as Spanish. But this was only a prelude to *1100 Bel Air Place* (1984), a calculated assault on the American market. All the material was performed in English and the album included two hit duets with top American artists: 'All of You' with **Diana Ross** and 'To All the Girls I've Loved Before'* with **Willie Nelson**, which topped the country charts. He maintained his hegemony over Latin markets with *Libra* (1985). In 1988 he duetted with **Stevie Wonder** on 'My Love' from *Non Stop*. In 1990 he released the Albert Hammond-produced *Starry Night* and in 1993 he was one of the many celebrities brought in to partner **Frank Sinatra** on his *Duets* album. The multilingual approach adopted by Iglesias has also involved his recording versions of his hits in French, Italian, German, Portuguese and Japanese. By 2000 Iglesias was reported to have sold over 200 million albums in seven languages.

However, Iglesias's best later albums were all Spanish-language offerings. These include *Carreterra* (1995), *Tango* (1996) and *Noche de Cuatro Lunas* (2000), all of which were less melodramatic than his English-language recordings suggested.

His son Enrique turned to recording at the beginning of the nineties and by the end of the decade was selling more albums than his father. As much influenced by rock as by Latin music, Enrique was signed to the Mexican-based Fonovisa label in 1995. His eponymous début (1995) signalled the start of a series of hit albums, including *Remixes* (1997), *Vivir* (1997), *Cosas del Amor* (1998) and *Bailamos* (1999), which generated sales of some 12 million in North America alone. In 1999 he moved to Universal for *Enrique* (1999).

THE IMPRESSIONS
Curtis Mayfield, b. 3 June 1942, Chicago, Illinois, USA, d. 26 December 1999, Roswell, Georgia; Jerry Butler, b. 8 December 1939, Sunflower, Mississippi; Sam Gooden, b. 2 September 1939, Chattanooga, Tennessee; Fred Cash, b. 8 October 1940, Chattanooga; Arthur Brooks, b. Chattanooga; Richard Brooks, b. Chattanooga

The Impressions were one of the most important and influential soul groups of the sixties. Their sound defined Chicago soul and their influence stretched to Jamaica where **Prince Buster**, in particular, made use of **Curtis Mayfield**'s allegorical song forms. Mayfield's parable of social awareness, 'It's All Right', and such songs as 'Gypsy Woman' and 'People Get Ready', highlighted by the group's gentle gospel harmonies, Johnny Pate's cool horn arrangements and Mayfield's hushed vocals and innovative guitar playing, marked a new level of sophistication in soul music.

A member of the Northern Jubileers gospel group, with **Jerry Butler**, Mayfield formed the Alphatones in 1953. In 1956 Mayfield and Butler joined forces with three members of the Roosters (Gooden and the Brooks brothers), a group that Butler had discovered. Signed to Vee-Jay's Abner subsidiary, as Jerry Butler and the Impressions, they had an immediate hit with 'For Your Precious Love' (1958), which was later revived by many artists, including Garnet Mimms (United Artists, 1964) and Linda Jones (All Platinum, 1972), whose impassioned version is one of the most dramatic examples of a complete reworking of a song. When Butler left the group for a solo career he was replaced by Cash (also from the Roosters) and following the group's return to the charts with 'Gypsy Woman' in 1961, and the departure of the Brooks brothers, the Impressions remained a trio.

The Impressions were dropped by Vee-Jay and almost broke up when Mayfield joined the successful Butler as guitarist, writer and arranger. After signing to ABC, however, the group had their first American Top Twenty hit with Mayfield's wistful 'Gypsy Woman'. The song introduced a stream of (almost) courtly love tales, including 'Minstrel and the Queen' (1962) and 'Isle of Sirens' (1967). More successful were Mayfield's reworkings of gospel imagery to create a series of songs which eloquently celebrated the growing sense of self-reliance of black America. These included 'It's All Right' (1963), which topped the R&B charts, 'I'm So Proud', 'Keep on Pushin' (1964), 'Amen' – the theme song to the film *Lilies of the Fields* and the only one of the series not written by Mayfield – and 'Meeting Over Yonder'. To these subtle songs of struggle, Mayfield added a unique sound, which took vocal arrangements from the **Swan Silvertones** and featured Pate's imaginative horn arrangements.

At the same time, Mayfield worked as a producer and writer with numerous other Chicago acts. Among these were **Gene Chandler**, Major Lance – for whom he wrote and produced a series of sinuous dance hits (including 'The Monkey Time' and 'The Little Girl' on Okeh, 1963, and 'Um, Um, Um, Um, Um, Um', 1964) – and Walter Jackson ('That's What Mama Say', Okeh, 1964). In 1966 he formed his own labels, Windy

C – on which he produced the teenage family group the Five Stairsteps, which had a series of hits starting with 'You Waited Too Long' (1966) – and Mayfield – on which he successfully produced the girl group the Fascinations ('Say It Isn't So', 1966).

Throughout the sixties Mayfield's stance grew more radical and the Impressions' songs became critical rather than merely inspirational. Nonetheless they continued to reach both the pop and R&B charts. Soon after 'We're a Winner' (1968), the Impressions left ABC and Mayfield set up Curtom, on which they had immediate success with the classic 'Choice of Colors' (1969), with the equally important 'Mighty, Mighty Spade and Whitey' on the B-side. Then, in 1970, Mayfield left the Impressions to be replaced first by Leroy Hutson (who in turn left to go solo in 1972) and then Reggie Torian and Ralph Johnson. This line-up remained intact until 1986 (when it recorded for MCA), with minor hits on the way on Curtom ('Finally Got Myself Together [I'm a Changed Man]', 1974, and 'First Impressions', the group's only British hit in 1976), Cotillion and Chisound.

The group continued to perform into the early nineties when the line-up was Gooden, Johnson, Cash and Smokey Hampton. *Anthology, 1961–1977* (1993) was the definitive retrospective.

THE INCREDIBLE STRING BAND
Mike Heron, b. 12 December 1942, Glasgow, Scotland; Robin Williamson, b. 24 November 1943, Glasgow; Clive Palmer; Christina 'Licorice' McKechnie; Rose Simpson; Malcolm Le Maistre; Gerard Dott

Cheerfully eclectic, mixing Celtic folk music with Indian and North African sounds, the Incredible String Band made some of the oddest and most enterprising music of the sixties.

Guitarist Heron met multi-instrumentalist Williamson at banjoist Palmer's Glasgow venue, Clive's Incredible Folk Club. As a trio, the Incredible String Band were signed to Elektra by **Joe Boyd**, who produced the first eponymous album in 1966.

Containing mostly original material, its eclectic promise was fulfilled by the remarkable *The 5000 Spirits or the Layers of the Onion* (1967), recorded without Palmer (who later recorded with the Famous Jug Band and COB, Clive's Own Band) and after Williamson had taken time out to travel to Morocco. With accompanists including sitarist Nazior Jarazbhoy and **Pentangle** bassist Danny Thompson, the album's wide-ranging material was by turns mysterious ('My Name is Death'), nostalgic ('First Girl I Ever Loved'), satirical ('Way Back in the 1960s'), and whimsical ('The Hedgehog's Song'). The music ranged from calypso to Middle Eastern to *a cappella* ballads.

The album was a minor hit but *The Hangman's Beautiful Daughter* (1968) caught the flower-power mood of the time and reached the Top Ten. With new members Simpson (bass) and McKechnie (vocals), the ISB offered a pastiche of **Gilbert and Sullivan** in 'Minotaur Song' and a pantheistic hymn in 'Water Song'. By this time, they were appearing in concert with such acts as **Pink Floyd** and joining the Anglo-American progressive-rock circuit.

The double-album *Wee Tam and the Big Huge* (1968) and *Changing Horses* (1969) were less successful and the group were reduced to a cult following by the time they recorded *U* (1970), the soundtrack to 'a surreal parable in dance and song' performed in collaboration with choreographer Le Maistre. The latter replaced Simpson in the group in 1971, when the Incredible String Band moved to Island for *Be Glad for the Song Has No Ending*, a soundtrack album to a film which combined concert footage with fantasy sequences. The next studio album, *Liquid Acrobat as Regards the Air*, showed a return to the genial eclecticism of their earliest work, and included reggae and traditional fiddle tunes. After *Earthspan* (1972), McKechnie was replaced by keyboards- and sax-player Dott (a former schoolmate of Heron) and the group moved towards a more conventional rock sound. *No Ruinous Feud* and *Hard Rope and Silken Twine* (1974) appeared before the band split up. One of their last performances was a London benefit with **Chick Corea** for the Church of Scientology which Heron and Williamson joined in 1968.

In the next decade Williamson settled in California, devoting himself to an exploration of Celtic music and forming his Merry Band with harp-maker Chris Caswell and Jerry McMillan from revivalist band Celtic Tradition, plus harpist Sylvia Woods. Williamson's Merry Band recordings for Flying Fish included *American Stonehenge* (1978) and *A Glint at the Kindling* (1979). He later wrote theatre and television music and recorded a series of spoken-word cassettes telling Celtic legends in 'modern bardic style'. In the early nineties he performed with ex-**Pentangle** guitarist John Renbourn.

Heron signed to the Neighbourhood label (owned by **Melanie** and Peter Schekeryk) and cut *Mike Heron's Reputation* in the same rock style he had employed for an earlier solo album, *Smiling Men with Bad Reputations* (Island, 1971). He later made *Diamond of Dream* (Bronze, 1977) and *Mike Heron* (Casablanca, 1980). *On Air* (1991) was an intriguing collection of recordings made for the BBC in the late sixties.

LUTHER INGRAM
b. 30 November 1944, Jackson, Tennessee, USA

Ingram, whose best-known recording is the original version of the standard 'If Loving You Is Wrong (I Don't Want to Be Right)'* (1972), had one of the most distinctive soul voices of the seventies.

He began singing in church choirs but in the early sixties moved to New York where **Leiber and Stoller** produced 'I Spy for the FBI' (Smash, 1965), later a hit for Jamo Thomas, and other unsuccessful singles. Ingram's luck changed after he was signed to Koko by Johnny Baylor in 1967. Distributed by Stax and using songs by the company's staff writers, Ingram had R&B hits with 'Pity for the Lonely' (1969), 'My Honey and Me' and 'Ain't That Lovin' You (for More Reasons Than One)' (1970).

The moralizing 'To the Other Man' (1970) was followed by the melancholic 'Missing You' (1971) before the release of the anguished 'If Loving You Is Wrong', composed by Carl Hampton, Raymond Jackson and former Minit recording artist Homer Banks. With a sparse backing, Ingram's committed vocals relayed a tale of marital infidelity which reached the pop Top Ten. The song was later covered by numerous artists including **Millie Jackson**, **Bobby Bland**, **Rod Stewart** and country singer Barbara Mandrell, for whom it was a pop hit in 1979 on ABC.

'I'll Be Your Shelter (in Time of Storm)' (1973) was a minor hit. After the collapse of Stax in 1974, Ingram continued to perform throughout the South and released occasional singles on Koko. After Baylor's death in 1985 he signed to the New York-based Profile label, recording the critically acclaimed *Luther Ingram* (1986), which included the R&B hit 'Baby Don't Go Too Far'.

THE INK SPOTS
Bill Kenny, b. 1915, d. 25 March 1978; Orville 'Hoppy' Jones, b. 17 February 1905, Chicago, USA, d. 18 October 1944, Chicago; Charlie Fuqua; Ivory 'Deek' Watson

With the **Mills Brothers**, the Ink Spots were the most popular and influential black vocal group in showbusiness in the thirties and forties. Their trademarks were Kenny's velvety high tenor and Jones' deep-voiced readings of the lyrics as mid-song recitations. They sang without effort in any tempo, in a manner that owed something to the jubilee style of gospel-quartet singing, and in its turn probably broadened it.

The original quartet, founded in 1934, were invited to Britain in that year by **Jack Hylton**. On their return to the US they became moderately well known, recording for Decca from 1936. For about three years they concentrated on jivey songs with strong jazz and blues elements like 'Stompin' at the Savoy' or Andy Razaf and Leon Berry's 'Christopher Columbus' (both 1936). The success of the slower and sweeter 'If I Didn't Care' (1939), however, drew them away from this path, and they turned instead to songs like 'My

Prayer' (1939), 'Whispering Grass' (1940) and 'Do I Worry?' (1940), though occasionally permitting themselves the light, quick touch of a 'Java Jive' (1940). In 1941 they appeared in the movie *Great American Broadcast* and in 1942 *Pardon My Sarong*; they were also popular on radio and at personal performances.

Soon after the success of 'Into Each Life a Little Rain Must Fall'* (made with **Ella Fitzgerald**), Jones died and was replaced by Kenny's brother, Herb, while Watson gave way to Billy Bowen. This line-up had two further million-sellers, 'To Each His Own' and 'The Gypsy' (1946), composed by British songwriter Billy Reid, who also wrote hits for Margaret Whiting ('A Tree in the Meadow', 1948) and **Eddie Fisher** ('I'm Walking Behind You', 1953).

By the early fifties there were two distinct Ink Spots, one including Fuqua, Watson and Bill Kenny from the original line-up with Jimmy Holmes and Harold Jackson. Later members were Leon Antoine and Isaac Royal. Groups bearing the Ink Spots' name continued to appear, both in America and overseas, and make records, into the eighties.

INNER CITY
Kevin Saunderson, b. 9 May 1964, Brooklyn, New York, USA; Paris Grey, b. Shanna Jackson, 5 November 1965, Glencove, Illinois

Inner City were the most commercially successful act to emerge from the Detroit techno scene of the late 1980s, bringing the city's tough new dance sound to a wider audience.

The band first came to prominence in 1988 with the hit 'Big Fun', at a time when the acid-house craze was opening European clubbers' ears to new dance sounds from across the Atlantic. The track also featured a year later on the group's début long-player, *Paradise*, one of the great dance albums of the eighties. The LP contained four hit singles, including 'Good Life', which became a dancefloor anthem, 'Ain't Nobody Better' and 'Do You Love What You Feel?'.

Inner City's second album, *Fire* (1990), was less critically and commercially successful, but the group returned to form with *Praise* (1992), which combined harder dance instrumentation with more gospel-influenced vocals and lyrics. It also brought further crossover pop success, with the hits 'Hallelujah' and 'Pennies from Heaven'.

After a diversion into instrumental techno experimentation on the single 'Ahnongay' in 1993, the group returned with two vocal house hits in 1994, 'Do Ya' and 'Share My Life'.

Despite their commercial achievements, Inner City never lost their genuine house music roots, partly through Saunderson's outside remix and production ventures, variously as Reese Project and E-Dancer.

The group's later work included the appearance of Saunderson's wife Ann – who had already co-written some of the group's earlier material – as joint vocalist with Grey, notably on the 1996 single 'Your Love'. In 1999 Saunderson made the questionable decision to re-release 'Good Life', re-sung in Spanish as 'Buena Vida', complete with flamenco guitar.

THE INTRUDERS
Samuel 'Little Sonny' Brown; Eugene Daughtry; Robert Edwards; Phil Terry

The eccentric but distinctive style of lead singer Little Sonny plus the arrangements of **Gamble and Huff** made the Intruders one of the most successful soul groups of the sixties and seventies.

In the early sixties they were a doo-wop group and elements of that anachronistic style persisted in the group's later sound. Their first records were made for local label Gowen (1961) and the New York-based Musicor, where 'All the Time' (1964) was produced by Huff. The quartet then recorded for Gamble and Huff's Excel company, which became Gamble Records in 1966.

In that year '(We'll Be) United' reached the R&B Top Twenty and was followed by further hits like 'Devil with an Angel's Smile', 'Together' (1967) and 'Baby I'm Lonely'. The breakthrough to the wider pop audience came in 1968 with the million-selling 'Cowboys to Girls'. Written by Gamble and Huff, it was their first major success. Employing the theme of growth from childhood to adolescence the song was sung by Brown in his nasal, almost bleating voice, supported by the group's mellow harmonies.

'(Love Is Like a) Baseball Game' was a lesser pop hit but later Intruders releases regularly entered the R&B Top Twenty. Among them were 'Slow Drag' (1969) and 'When We Get Married' (1970), after which Brown briefly left the group. His replacement Bobby Starr provided lead vocals on 'I'm Girl Scoutin'' (1971) before Brown returned for 'I Bet He Don't Love You' and '(Win Place or Show) She's a Winner' (1972), a pop hit in Britain in 1974. The group's final crossover hit was 'I'll Always Love My Mama' (1973) from *Save the Children*.

Energy of Love (1974) included cover-versions of the **Carpenters**' 'Rainy Days and Mondays' and **Mary Wells**' 'What's Easy for Two'. The group disbanded in 1975 but in 1984 Daughtry formed a new Intruders, recording *Who Do You Love* (1985), produced by Leon Bryant.

INXS
Garry Beers, b. 22 June 1957, Australia; Andy Farriss, b. 27 March 1959; Jon Farriss, b. 10 August 1961; Tim

Farriss, b. 16 August 1957; Michael Hutchence, b. 12 January 1959, Hong Kong, d. 22 November 1997, Sydney, Australia; Kirk Pengilly, b. 4 July 1958, Australia

During the eighties Australasian rock music came of age as bands such as New Zealand's Split Enz and Australia's **Air Supply**, **Midnight Oil** and **Men at Work** made a strong impact in both Europe and North America. The most spectacular of them was INXS, led by the charismatic Hutchence.

Originally known as the Farriss Brothers, the group included Tim (guitar), Andrew (keyboards) and Jon (drums) plus bassist Beers, guitarist Pengilly and lead singer Hutchence. They played local dates around Perth, Western Australia, before recording 'Simple Simon/We Are the Vegetables' (1980) as INXS for the independent Delux label. Later that year, 'Just Keep Walking' from the eponymous début album was a minor hit.

In 1981 RCA signed INXS, releasing *Underneath the Colours* with its Australian hits, 'Stay Young' and 'Loved One'. With the aim of breaking into the US market, the band switched to WEA, which released *Shabooh Shoobah* (1982) and set up an American tour in support of the **Kinks** and **Adam Ant**. As a result, 'The One Thing' reached the US Top Thirty in 1983.

Next INXS recorded 'Original Sin' in New York with producer **Nile Rodgers**. It was included on *The Swing* (1984), their first hit album in America. Chris Thomas came in to produce *Listen Like Thieves*, which included the band's first American Top Ten single, 'What You Need' (1986). However, the big breakthrough came in 1988 when 'Need You Tonight' topped the US chart and the ballad-driven *Kick* entered the Top Ten there. It provided the band with further big hits in 'Devil Inside' and 'Never Tear Us Apart'. *X* (1990) was virtually a remake of *Kick* and produced another two American Top Ten hits, 'Suicide Blonde' and 'Disappear'. *Live Baby Live* (1991) was recorded at the group's sell-out concert at Wembley Stadium, London. The soulful *Welcome to Wherever You Are* (1992), recorded after a lengthy break from touring, saw the band in a more relaxed and exploratory mood. Some tracks featured a large orchestra. In 1993 the group released the album *Full Moon, Dirty Hearts*, which was again followed by a lengthy world tour. The band reconvened in 1995 after a brief hiatus to record *Elegantly Wasted* (1996), which proved to be the original members' final album together after Hutchence's apparent suicide a year later in a Sydney hotel room, just hours after hearing that partner Paula Yates had lost custody of her children to ex-husband **Bob Geldof**. In 1999 the remaining members of INXS announced plans to continue with a new singer.

In 1989 Hutchence released the concept album *Max*

Q and he also attempted an acting career, starring in *Dogs in Space* (1986) and Roger Corman's *Frankenstein Unbound* (1990). *Michael Hutchence* (1999), which was released posthumously, included a duet with **U2**'s Bono.

IRON BUTTERFLY

Ron Bushy, b. 23 September 1941, Washington DC, USA; Darryl deLoach, b. San Diego, California; Doug Ingle, b. 9 September 1947, Omaha, Nebraska; Jerry Penrod, b. San Diego (replaced by Lee Dorman, b. 19 September 1945, St Louis, Missouri); Danny Weis, b. San Diego (replaced by Eric Braunn, b. 10 August 1950, Boston, Massachusetts, replaced by Mike Pinera, b. 29 September 1948, Tampa, Florida and Larry 'Rhino' Reinhardt, b. 7 July 1948, Florida)

Though musically undistinguished, Iron Butterfly had several bestselling heavy-rock albums in the late sixties, all of which featured lengthy tracks in the manner of **Vanilla Fudge**.

Led by church organist's son Ingle, the San Diego-based group were signed by Atlantic in 1967. Their appropriately named début album, the ponderous *Heavy*, was a minor hit but, with the addition of Dorman (bass) and Braunn (guitar), they achieved their greatest success with *In-a-Gadda-Da-Vida* (1968). The album went on to sell three million copies and an edited version of the seventeen-minute title track (a play on the phrase 'in the Garden of Eden') was a Top Thirty hit single. The follow-up album, *Ball* (1970), also reached the Top Ten.

After playing on the group's live album, Braunn departed and twin lead guitarists Pinera (from Blues Image, who had a Top Ten hit with 'Ride Captain Ride', Atco, 1970) and Reinhardt were hired. Both contributed to the optimistically titled but commercially disappointing *Metamorphosis* (1970), produced by Ritchie Podolor. The band split up soon afterwards with Pinera going on to play with Carmine Appice and Tim Bogert in Cactus.

Braunn and original drummer Bushy led a revived Iron Butterfly, which recorded the unimpressive *Sun and Steel* and the Denny Randell-produced *Scorching Beauty* (both MCA, 1975). In the eighties the band reformed again, but enjoyed little success. *Light & Heavy* (Rhino, 1993) is the definitive retrospective.

IRON MAIDEN

Paul Di'anno, b. 17 May 1959, Chingford, England (replaced by Bruce Dickinson, b. 7 August 1958, Worksop; replaced by Blaze Bayley); Steve Harris, b. 12 March 1957, London; Dave Murray, b. 23 December 1958, London; Doug Sampson (replaced by Clive Burr, b. 7 May 1957, replaced by Nicko McBrain, b. 5 June

1952); Dennis Stratton, b. 9 November 1954, London (replaced by Adrian Smith, b. 27 February 1957, London; replaced by Janick Gers, b. Newcastle, England)

An archetypal second-generation heavy-metal band, Iron Maiden, like **Black Sabbath** before them, built their success on an unswerving devotion to imagery of violence and horror, plus frequent live appearances.

Bassist and songwriter Harris, the son of a truck driver, formed the band in East London in 1976 with guitarist Murray, formerly of skinhead/punk band Secret. The band's name was taken from the medieval instrument of torture. Two years later a self-produced EP, *The Soundhouse Tapes*, led to a contract with EMI. The eponymous début album (1980) reached the Top Ten, spawning three minor hits, 'Running Free', 'Sanctuary' and 'Women in Uniform'.

By this point drummer Sampson had left and singer Di'anno was sacked to make way for the high-pitched vocals of Dickinson (christened the 'Air Raid Siren' by the band's followers). The Martin Birch-produced *Killers* (1981) was followed by a No. 1 album and hit single whose title was borrowed from satanist Aleister Crowley, *Number of the Beast* (1982). Crowley was also an influence on **Led Zeppelin**'s Jimmy Page.

By now the group's line-up had solidified with the arrival of veteran drummer McBrain from Trust and rhythm guitarist Smith. The 1983 album *Piece of Mind* provided their first major American success, as well as two British hit singles in 'Flight of Icarus' and 'The Trooper'. In 1984 the group began a mammoth 'World Slavery' tour of more than 200 concerts, to promote the *Powerslave* album, whose sleeve, designed by Derek Riggs, showed the band's mascot, a skeletal monster incongruously called Eddie, in an ancient Egyptian setting.

The tour resulted in the double-album *Live After Death* (1985) and a further British hit, 'Running Free', whose royalties were donated to anti-drug-abuse projects. Intimations of wide reading on Harris's part were confirmed by *Somewhere in Time* (1986), which acknowledged the influence of novelist Alan Sillitoe, science-fiction author Robert Heinlein and classical historian Pliny.

In 1988 the concept album *Seventh Son of a Seventh Son* topped the charts in the UK. Iron Maiden also had a trio of British Top Ten singles from it, 'Can I Play with Madness', 'Evil that Men Do' and 'The Clairvoyant'. The following year guitarist Smith released *Silver and Gold* with his band A.S.A.P., which included Zak Starkey (son of **Ringo Starr**) on drums. When Harris proposed a return to the group's early, harder, style Smith left and was replaced by Jannick Gers, a former guitarist with Gillan who had also played on Dickinson's solo album *Tattooed Millionaire* (1990). This line-up recorded the enormously

successful *No Prayer for the Dying* (1990), which included the British hits 'Holy Smoke' and 'Bring Your Daughter to the Slaughter', the latter issued in more (collectable) forms than any other new recording. It topped the British charts. In the same year Dickinson published a comic novel, *The Adventures of Lord Iffy Boatrace* (1990).

Fear of the Dark (1992) was very much in the style of the previous album with the twin guitars of Murray and Gers well to the fore. Its friendly reception by critics confirmed that the band was now seen as the acceptable face of heavy metal, almost the **Status Quo** of their time. Iron Maiden announced a world tour in 1992, followed in 1993 by European dates which Dickinson revealed would be his last with the band. His subsequent solo albums included *Accidents of Birth* (1997) and *The Chemical Wedding* (1998), before he rejoined the band in 1999.

The live albums *A Real Live One* and *A Real Dead One* were released in 1993, as was the record of their 1992 appearance at the British Monsters of Rock festival, *Live at Donington*. In 1994 Dickinson released his second solo album, *Balls to Picasso*. His replacement in Iron Maiden was Blaze Bayley, former lead singer of Wolfsbane. He was featured on the commercially successful *The X Factor* (1995) and the lesser *Virtual XI* (1998). In 1999 the band re-formed, raised over $20m in bonds on their back catalogue, and promptly returned to the fray with *Brave New World* (EMI, 2000). A commercial success, the much anticipated reunion of Smith and Dickinson, in the words of one critic, transmuted the anger of the seminal *Number of the Beast* into the *angst* of suburban armchair Vikings.

GREGORY ISAACS
b. 16 June 1950, Kingston, Jamaica

Known as the 'Cool Ruler', bitter-sweet crooner Isaacs possessed the most distinctive voice in Reggae after **Bob Marley**. Though most of his hits were in the lover's-rock vein, he never abandoned the social commentary and message songs that formed the backbone of reggae.

He first recorded with the Concords and cut his first solo single, 'Don't Let Me Suffer', in 1970 for Rupie Edwards' Success label. Isaacs made further records for **Prince Buster** ('Dancing Floor') and Phil Pratt before setting up his own African Museum label with Errol Dunkley in 1974. It issued his hits, including 'My Only Lover' and 'Lonely Soldier', as well as **Big Youth**'s first disc, a version of Dunkley's 'Movie Star'.

Isaacs had his first British reggae hit in 1974 with 'Love Is Overdue' (Attack), while the Alvin Ranglin-produced 'Innocent People Cry' was popular in Jamaica. Ranglin was also responsible for Isaacs' first album, *In Person* (1975). The following year, 'Extra

Classic' (African Museum) was a Jamaican No. 1. In 1977 he began a long association with fellow singer **Dennis Brown**, duetting with him on 'Let Off Sup'm' and cutting one of his best-known songs, 'Mr Know It All', for Brown's DEB label.

Over the next few years, Isaacs released frequent albums on a range of Jamaican and British labels. For Virgin's Front Line, he cut *Cool Ruler* (1979) and *Soon Forward*, backed by the Revolutionaries. Albums for Chrysalis's Pre label included *Lonely Lover* (1980, which contained one of his classic portrayals of ghetto life, 'Poor Natty') and *More Gregory* (1981). A contract with **Chris Blackwell**'s Island company produced his only British pop hit, *Night Nurse* (1982), one of the biggest-selling reggae albums of all time; *Out Deh* (1983), whose title track dealt with Isaacs' imprisonment on firearms charges; and *Reggae Greats* (1985). In 1985 Greensleeves also released the Gussie Clarke production *Private Beach Party*, which included a duet with Carlene Davis and had **Sly and Robbie** among the backing musicians.

During the eighties Isaacs frequently toured Britain, backed by the Roots Radics, led by guitarist Binghi Bunny (Eric Lamont). Gussie Clarke produced *IOU* (1989) and *Red Roses for Gregory* (1990). A 1994 album, *Dance Hall Don*, found Isaacs in the company of younger Jamaican rap artists.

CHRIS ISAAK
b. 26 June 1956, Stockton, California, USA

Blessed with the visual appeal of the young **Elvis Presley** and a voice which uncannily resembles **Roy Orbison**'s, Isaak achieved success in the late eighties and early nineties with a sound firmly rooted in the fifties.

While at university in the early eighties Isaak performed with his own band, the Silvertones. The line-up consisted of Isaak (vocals, guitar), James Calvin Wilsey (guitar), Rowland Salley (bass) and Kenney Dale Johnson (drums). Their vibrant mixture of country and rockabilly won them a Warner Bros contract in 1985. *Silvertone* (1985) caught the primitive feel of Isaak and the Silvertones' live set. Despite poor sales it picked up a number of enthusiastic reviews. The follow-up, *Chris Isaak* (1987), was more successful, and showed Isaak's songwriting developing into a brooding, cinematic style heavily influenced by Roy Orbison, particularly on the 'Blue Hotel' single, a small hit in Europe. *Heart Shaped World* (1989) failed to improve on the sales of its predecessors but garnered good reviews.

In 1990 maverick Hollywood director David Lynch used Isaak's 'Wicked Game' as the theme to his movie *Wild at Heart*, also using the song's haunting guitar figure (courtesy of Wilsey) as a recurring motif

throughout the film. The effect on Isaak's career was dramatic. The song became an international hit, giving him a Top Ten single in the UK and *Heart Shaped World*, repackaged as *Wicked Game* in 1991, was an international hit. The reissued single 'Blue Hotel' also was a hit in 1991. In the wake of this Isaak toured extensively before returning to the studio to record *San Francisco Days* (1993). The title song and 'Except the New Girl' were representative of the carefully worked out moodiness. It was followed by *Forever Blue* (1995), which, though it was equally drenched in mannered, echo-laden vibrato, somehow managed to be more affecting. It included 'Baby Did a Bad Bad Thing', which was later effectively featured in Stanley Kubrick's final film, *Eyes Wide Shut* (1999), the equally moody 'Graduation Day' and the sombre title track. More florid was *Baja Sessions* (1996) on which Isaak finally offered, with great success, his own version of Orbison's 'Only the Lonely', which had always been the template for his recordings. Less successful was 1998's *Speak of the Devil*.

Isaak, who had appeared in the films *Married to the Mob* (1988) and *Silence of the Lambs* (1991), had his first major role in Bernardo Bertolucci's *Little Buddha* (1994).

THE ISLEY BROTHERS
Rudolph Isley, b. 1 April 1939, Cincinnati, Ohio, USA; O'Kelly Isley, b. 25 December 1937, Cincinnati, d. 31 March 1986, Alpine, New Jersey; Ronald Isley, b. 21 May 1941, Cincinnati; Ernie Isley; Marvin Isley; Chris Jasper

With a career spanning thirty years, the Isley Brothers pioneered both the gospel-influenced soul music of the sixties and the black rock music of the seventies.

The original trio of Ronald, Rudolph and O'Kelly began as a gospel group in their home town of Cincinnati before moving in 1956 to New York and a career in secular music. The following year they recorded 'An Angel Cried' (Teenage) and in 1958 their reputation as live performers at such theatres as Harlem's Apollo and Chicago's Regal led to a series of singles for **George Goldner**'s Gone label.

The Isley Brothers' first hit was adapted from their improvised finale to the 1958 **Jackie Wilson** song 'Lonely Teardrops'*. 'Shout Parts 1 and 2'* was produced by **Hugo and Luigi** for RCA (1959). The song entered the repertoire of white beat groups and was a hit in America for Joey Dee and the Starliters (Roulette, 1962) and twice in Britain for **Lulu** (Decca, 1964 and 1986). While with RCA the Isleys also wrote and recorded 'Respectable', another beat standard which was recorded by the **Yardbirds**, among others.

In 1962 they briefly recorded for Atlantic before 'Twist and Shout' (Wand), an attempt to capitalize on the popularity of **Chubby Checker**'s dance hit, was a pop hit. **The Beatles**' version of the song on their début album brought the Isley Brothers international recognition. Among their other Wand recordings was the much-covered 'Nobody but Me'. After recording an album for United Artists (which included an early version of 'Who's That Lady') and a single for their own T-Neck label, the group, with new lead guitarist Jimmy James (**Jimi Hendrix**), joined Atlantic in 1964.

The late sixties found the trio signed to Motown Records, where writers and producers **Holland, Dozier and Holland** revived their career with the classic 'This Old Heart of Mine' (1968). They had three further hits in Britain, including Ivy Hunter's 'Behind a Painted Smile' and 'Put Yourself in My Place'. At this point, the Isley Brothers made a major switch in style. Influenced by the emergence of younger black rock artists like **Sly Stone** and Hendrix, they recruited younger brothers Ernie (guitar) and Marvin (bass) and cousin Jasper (keyboards). The result was their biggest hit, 'It's Your Thing'*, on the reactivated T-Neck label, distributed by Buddah. Next came *Giving It Back*, their first major album success which was a collection of rock songs, including **Bob Dylan**'s 'Lay Lady Lay' and Stephen Stills' 'Love the One You're With', a 1971 hit single for the Isleys.

From 1973 T-Neck was distributed by Columbia and during the next decade the Isley Brothers had a series of hit albums, from *That Lady* (1973) to *Between the Sheets* (1983). With a unique sound that mixed Ernie's Hendrix-influenced guitar and synthesizers initially programmed by Cecil and Margouleff (who had worked with **Stevie Wonder**) with the stylish, hard-edged singing of the elder brothers, they sold over 15 million albums in ten years. Among the Isleys' hit singles during this phase were two million-sellers, 'That Lady (Part 1)' (1973) and 'Fight the Power' (1975). The group were even more frequent visitors to the British charts, with 'Summer Breeze' (1974) and the passionate plea on the subject of global hunger, 'Harvest for the World' (1976) – revived in 1988 by British group the **Christians** – among their hits.

In 1984 the group split into two trios, with the younger members staying at Columbia as Isley, Jasper, Isley and the original Isley Brothers joining Warners. IJI's second album, *Caravan of Love* (1985), was a major pop and soul hit in America and in 1986 the Housemartins' *a cappella* cover of the title track on Go! Discs was the Christmas No. 1 in Britain. The Isleys' début for Warners, *Masterpiece*, was also a hit but its success was marred by eldest brother O'Kelly's sudden death from a heart attack. On *Smooth Sailin'*, produced by **Angela Winbush** (1987), Rudolph and Ronald included 'Send a Message', a powerful lament for him, while IJI's *Different Drummer* (1987) featured the pan-African anthem 'Brother to Brother'.

After the group had released *Spend the Night* (1988),

Ernie Isley made his début solo album, the Jimi Hendrix-influenced *High Wire* (Elektra, 1990). In the same year brother Ronald had an American Top Ten hit when he recorded a version of 'This Old Heart of Mine' with **Rod Stewart**. In 1992 came the group album *Tracks of Life*, which was followed by the in-concert set *Live* (Elektra, 1993). The following year the Isley Brothers won a court action against **Michael Bolton** for copyright infringement of their 1966 song 'Love is a Wonderful Thing'. *Mission to Please* (1996), produced by **R. Kelly**, was a monster hit. The group's career is documented in *Shout* (1990), which covers the Victor years, *The Isley Brothers* (1991), which covers their stay at United Artists, and *Forever Gold* (1990), which documents their stay at Columbia.

JOSE ITURBI
b. 28 November 1895, Valencia, Spain, d. 28 June 1980, Los Angeles, California, USA

Iturbi's appearances in films, always as himself, in the forties helped popularize classical music in general in America, while his million-selling recording of Chopin's 'Polonaise in B Flat' (Victor, 1945) – from the Chopin biopic *A Song to Remember* – led to a series of popular Chopin recordings and adaptations.

As a child, Iturbi played piano accompaniment to silent films. He made his début as a concert pianist in 1923 and emigrated to America in 1928, touring as a solo pianist. For several years he was conductor of the Rochester Philharmonic. In 1943 he appeared in *Thousands Cheer* and signed a contract with MGM, remaining in Hollywood until the end of the decade, when he returned to the concert stage. Among his films were *Adventures in Music* (1944) and *Anchors Aweigh* (1945), but it was his dubbing of Chopin's music in *A Song to Remember* (in which the composer was played by Cornel Wilde) that brought his greatest success and was most influential. Iturbi had a second million-selling record with Debussy's 'Clair de lune' (1945). That same year both Carmen Cavallaro and **Perry Como** had million-sellers with Chopin's 'Polonaise', Cavallaro with a rhythmic interpretation, Como with a vocal version, with lyrics by Buddy Kaye and Ted Mossman.

Iturbi's sister, Amparo, was also a pianist and actress.

BURL IVES
b. Burle Icle Ivanhoe, 14 June 1909, Hunt City, Illinois, USA, d. 14 April 1995, Anacorte, Washington

Among the New York folk singers of the forties like **Woody Guthrie** and **Pete Seeger**, Ives had perhaps the most winning and accessible way with a ditty, and in the early postwar years his soft, burry voice and capacious grab-bag of balladry wielded great influence on both perceptions and presentation of folk song.

Born into a tenant-farmer's family in rural Illinois, Ives spent his youth either wandering or attending teacher-training college, with occasional diversions into performing folk songs on small radio stations. He settled in New York in 1937 and found work in theatrical stock companies, landing a small part in **Richard Rodgers** and **Lorenz Hart**'s *The Boys from Syracuse* (1938). He also sang at clubs like the Village Vanguard and from 1940 to 1942 had his own CBS radio programme, *The Wayfaring Stranger*. After military service (1942–4) he returned to the theatre and song concerts like *Sing Out, Sweet Land*, in which he sang such staples of his repertoire as 'Foggy, Foggy Dew' and 'Blue-Tailed Fly'. He recorded albums of folk songs for Columbia and Decca, published an autobiography (*The Wayfaring Stranger*, 1948) and from 1953 onwards produced many printed collections of folk songs. His hits of this period include 'Blue-Tailed Fly' (Decca, 1948), recorded with the **Andrews Sisters**, 'Lavender Blue (Dilly Dilly)' and the original version of the oft-recorded 'Riders in the Sky' (1949).

During the fifties he was at least as well known as a character actor, his stage roles including Cap'n Andy in *Showboat* (1954) and Big Daddy in Tennessee Williams' *Cat on a Hot Tin Roof* (1955), a role he re-created in the 1958 film version. His other screen credits include *The Big Country* (1958), for which he received an Oscar for Best Supporting Actor, *East of Eden* (1955), *Desire under the Elms* (1958) and *Our Man in Havana* (1959).

In 1962 Ives rather surprisingly enjoyed a succession of country chart hits on Decca with 'A Little Bitty Tear', 'Call Me Mr In-Between' and 'Funny Way of Laughin'', the last of which received a Grammy as Best Country and Western Recording. These Nashville recordings were followed by themed albums of religious songs, Hawaiian material (*On the Beach at Waikiki*) and vaudeville standards (*My Gal Sal*). However, he may be best remembered for the perennial children's favourites, 'I Know an Old Lady (Who Swallowed a Fly)' and 'Big Rock Candy Mountain'. In the eighties he continued to give concerts in many countries, while maintaining his acting career with film and TV appearances. His most recent recording was *The Magic Balladeer* (Cornerstone, 1993).

THE JACKSON FIVE

Jackie Jackson, b. Sigmund Esco Jackson, 4 May 1951, Gary, Indiana, USA; Tito Jackson, b. Toriano Adaryll Jackson, 15 October 1953, Gary; Marlon David Jackson, b. 12 March 1957, Gary; Jermaine la Jaune Jackson, b. 11 December 1954, Gary; Michael Joe Jackson, b. 29 August 1958, Gary; Randy Jackson, b. Steven Randall Jackson, 29 October 1961, Gary

One of the most successful vocal groups in popular-music history, the Jackson Five had No. 1 hits with their first four singles. They proved longer-lasting than other teen idols of the period (notably the **Osmonds**, **Bay City Rollers** and **David Cassidy**). Of the group Michael, Jermaine and sister Janet all had significant solo careers.

Their father, Joe, had been guitarist with the Falcons (**Wilson Pickett**'s first group) and encouraged his five eldest sons to form a vocal group with Tito on guitar and Jermaine on bass. Though promoted as protégés of **Diana Ross**, they were discovered by Bobby Taylor of Motown group the Vancouvers, and signed to **Berry Gordy**'s label in 1969.

The following year the group scored chart successes with the scintillating dance tracks 'I Want You Back', 'ABC', 'The Love You Save' and 'I'll Be There'. The wailing lead vocals came from eleven-year-old Michael, with precision harmonies from the other brothers. The first Jacksons' hits were credited to 'The Corporation', a task force consisting of Freddie Perren, Fonso Mizell, Deke Richards and Gordy himself, whose job was to mould the group's image, sound and stage impact. Arrangements were by Motown veteran H. B. Barnum.

The year 1971 brought two No. 2 hits, 'Mama's Pearl' and 'Never Can Say Goodbye', and consistently high sales for later singles, which included a revival of Thurston Harris's 1957 hit 'Little Bitty Pretty One' (1972) and in Britain a Top Ten hit with a version of **Jackson Browne**'s ballad 'Doctor My Eyes'. Their final Motown hits were 'Dancing Machine' (1974) and 'I Am Love' (1975).

Despite a lawsuit from Gordy, the group – minus Jermaine (who was now Gordy's son-in-law) but with the addition of Randy – moved to Columbia's Epic label in 1975. *The Jacksons* (1976) – as they were now called – and *Going Places* (1977) were produced by **Gamble and Huff**, with 'Enjoy Yourself' (1976) becoming their first million-seller and 'Show You the Way to Go' their first British No. 1. Other singles were less successful, although the 1979 disco hit 'Shake Your Body'* (from *Destiny*) was written and produced by members of the group.

By this time, **Michael Jackson** was having increasing solo success but he rejoined the group for *Triumph** (1981) and its dance hit 'Lovely One'. Both he and Jermaine took part in the Pepsi-Cola sponsored 'Victory' tour of 1984, which played to two million Americans. The two brothers shared lead vocals on the hit 'Torture', while guest singer Mick Jagger duetted with Michael on 'State of Shock'* (1984). Soon afterwards the Jacksons signed to MCA, releasing the film theme, 'Time out for the Burglar'. The group later recorded *2300 Jackson Street* (Epic, 1989).

Jermaine's solo hits for Motown included a revival of **Shep and the Limelites**' 'Daddy's Home' (1973) and the **Stevie Wonder**–Lee Garrett song 'Let's Get Serious' (1980). His last Motown hit, 'Let Me Tickle Your Fancy' (1982), featured the backing vocals of cult group **Devo**. Moving to Arista, Jermaine had a pair of Top Twenty hits with singles from his eponymous album (1984), 'Dynamite' and 'Do What You Do'. He had a further hit with 'I Think It's Love'. His later records included *Don't Take It Personal* (Arista, 1989) and the lesser *You Said*.

In 1989 Jackie Jackson recorded his own solo album, *Be the One*, the title track of which was featured in the film *My Stepmother Is an Alien*.

After a starring role in the teleseries *Fame*, **Janet Jackson** signed with A&M in 1982 and began a highly successful solo career.

In 1992 the television drama *The Jacksons – An American Dream* was broadcast, following the family's life from the late forties up to 1984. A soundtrack album, *The American Dream*, sold poorly.

ALAN JACKSON

b. 17 October 1968, Newman, Georgia, USA

One of the newest stars of country music, Jackson's traditionalist approach is perhaps best represented by two of his biggest hits, 'Don't Rock the Jukebox', on which the singer asks for **George Jones** to be played on the jukebox rather than the **Rolling Stones**, and the paean to **Hank Williams**, 'Midnight in Montgomery'. That said, Jackson was also among the most romantic of the nineties generation of country stars, singing songs of loss which set his husky vibrato against a traditional sounding backdrop.

The son of a mechanic, Jackson moved to Nashville in 1986. He was discovered by **Glen Campbell**, who helped Jackson get a music publishing contract for his songs and a recording contract with Arista. Produced by Keith Stegall and Scott Hendricks, *Here in the Real World* was released in 1989. It gave Jackson a country No. 1 with 'I'd Love You All Over Again' while the title track, which was co-written by Jackson and Mark Irwin and whose lyrics contrasted what could be with what was, was a Top Five country hit. Other notable songs on the album were the title track and 'Chasin' that Neon Rainbow'. Among the backing musicians were session veterans Weldon Myrick (steel guitar) and Hargus 'Pig' Robbins (piano).

In 1991 Jackson released *Don't Rock the Jukebox*, whose title track was a heartfelt protest against the encroachment of rock sounds into contemporary country. The album gave Jackson a further chart-topper with 'Dallas'. *A Lot About Livin'* (1992), which included the country No. 1s 'Love's Got a Hold on You', 'She's Got the Rhythm' and 'Chattahoochee' (the most successful country single in the USA in 1993), sold over three million copies.

On *Who Am I?* (1994) he sang **Eddie Cochran**'s 'Summertime Blues', which was a country hit, as well as his own songs 'Job Description' and 'Let's Get Back to Me and You'. *Everything I Love* (1996) saw a return to the honky-tonk tradition he knew so well. He followed it with *High Mileage* (1998), which included 'I'll Go on Loving You' with its extended speech break, and *Under the Influence* (1999). At the same time Jackson proved himself able to mix the commercial necessities of the seasonal album with his own concerns, even gaining platinum sales for his untraditional *Honky Tonk Christmas* (1993).

Jackson's songs have been successfully recorded by other artists, including **Randy Travis** ('Better Class of Loser', 1991) and Clay Walker ('If I Could Make a Living', 1994).

FREDDIE JACKSON
b. 2 October 1956, Harlem, New York City, USA

A smooth, romantic soul singer, whose major subject is sex, Jackson's work shows the influence of **Jackie Wilson** and **Marvin Gaye**.

His mother was a singer and Jackson sang at Harlem's White Rock Baptist Church as a child. With Paul Laurence he formed the group LJE, and Jackson later sang and recorded with Los Angeles band the Mystic Merlins. Returning to New York, he and Laurence wrote songs for such artists as Howard Johnson and Melba Moore and he was subsequently recommended by Moore to Capitol Records.

Jackson's début album was *Rock Me Tonight* (1985). The title track became a hit on both sides of the Atlantic. This was followed by *Just Like the First Time* (1986) and *Don't Let Love Slip Away* in 1988.

Jackson also contributed as a duettist to albums by Melba Moore and Natalie Cole (*I Do*, 1990) before releasing his fourth album, *Do Me Again*. For this, Paul Laurence replaced Barry Eastmond as Jackson's songwriting partner.

Laurence was one of several producers of *Here It Is* (1993), Freddie Jackson's first album under a new recording deal with RCA. The album reached the Top Twenty of the US R&B chart.

JANET JACKSON
b. 16 June 1966, Gary, Indiana, USA

With *Control* (1986) and *Janet* (1993) Janet Jackson established herself as the funk queen of America.

A former member of the **Jackson Five**, like her brother **Michael Jackson**, Janet finally left the group to embark upon a solo career. She signed to A&M in 1982. Her first two albums, *Janet Jackson* (1982) and *Dream Street* (1984), produced a couple of minor pop hits ('Young Love', 1982, and 'Don't Stand Another Chance', 1984) but were not much better than dance club ready-mades. Her breakthrough came with *Control* (1986). Produced by **Jimmy Jam and Terry Lewis** it featured a backdrop of impeccably precise sinuous rhythms for Jackson's breathy vocalizing. The album also produced a slew of hit singles for Jackson: the title track, the carefully constructed 'When I Think of You', 'Let's Wait Awhile' and 'The Pleasure Principle'. She followed that with the lesser *Janet Jackson's Rhythm Nation 1814* (1989), which, though it produced even more hit singles ('Miss You Much', 'Rhythm Nation', 'Escapade', 'Alright', 'Come Back to Me', 'Black Cat' and 'Love Will Never Do [Without You]'), sacrificed spontaneity for straining after-effects. The album's statistical success (it was the first to generate seven Top Five singles) was followed by Jackson signing a record-breaking contract worth over $30m with Virgin. The first product of that deal was *Janet* (1993), which has sold over 10 million copies. Building on the sound of *Control*, *Janet* was even more fluent in its evocation of sexual and dance rhythms. Among the hits it spawned were 'That's the Way Love Goes', 'If', 'Again' and 'Any Time Any Place/And on and on'.

In 1996 Jackson signed a further multi-million dollar deal with Virgin, releasing her most sexually explicit album, *The Velvet Rope* (1997), for the company. A huge hit, it spawned a slew of hit singles, including 'Together Again', 'I Get Lonely' and 'Go Deep'.

JOE JACKSON
b. 11 August 1955, Burton-on-Trent, Derbyshire, England

Although he first found success as a new-wave songwriter, Jackson's later work was characterized by a stylistic range which included R&B, jazz and classical music.

He studied at the Royal College of Music in London and played saxophone in the National Youth Jazz Orchestra before becoming musical director of the Playboy Club in Portsmouth. There, he provided the backing for television talent contest winners Coffee and Cream and signed to A&M as a solo artist. The catchy 'Is She Really Going out with Him?' (1979) brought comparisons with **Elvis Costello** and was a hit on both sides of the Atlantic. Produced by David Kershenbaum, *Look Sharp* (1978) and *I'm the Man* (1979) also sold well in Britain where the ruminative 'It's Different for Girls' (1980) became his most successful single.

The year 1981 brought the first of his sudden shifts in style. *Jumpin' Jive* was an affectionate and spirited re-creation of the small-group rhythm and blues of **Louis Jordan**. Jackson toured with a group modelled on Jordan's Tympany Five, featuring alto-sax-player Pete Thomas, whose Deep Sea Jivers later became a regular feature of the London club scene.

The following year Jackson moved to New York and *Night and Day* was a pot-pourri of the music he found there. The album included examples of salsa, jazz, blues and disco music as well as rock and easy listening. Both 'Steppin Out' and 'Breaking Us in Two' were hits and the album reached the American Top Ten. The film soundtrack, *Mike's Murder* (1983), was less effective, but 1984's *Body and Soul*, recorded to get a 'live' sound, included the American hit 'You Can't Get What You Want (Till You Know What You Want)'.

In 1986 he released *Big World*, a live double-album with nothing on its fourth side. Its guitar-based songs like 'Wild West' and 'Man in the Street' harked back to his earliest recordings. Jackson again surprised his audience the following year with *Will Power*, a wide-ranging instrumental album with an orchestra conducted by George Manahan. It contained a pastiche of English Romantic composers like Elgar and Vaughan Williams and a 'Symphony in One Movement' that sounded like fifties' film music.

The double *Live* (1988) was followed by the soundtrack album *Tucker – the Man and his Dream* and the semi-autobiographical concept album *Blaze of Glory* (1989). A move to Virgin for *Laughter and Lust* (1990) saw him recording in a more mainstream manner, but with little commercial success. Thrash band **Anthrax** recorded his song 'Got the Time' in 1990, the same year A&M released the retrospective set *Steppin' Out*. *Night Music* (1994) saw Jackson moving towards instrumental music, a process that continued in the neo-classical *Heaven & Hell* (1997).

MAHALIA JACKSON
b. 26 October 1911, New Orleans, Louisiana, USA,
d. 27 January 1972, Chicago, Illinois

With her versatile contralto and a vocal approach which mixed sacred and secular techniques, Mahalia Jackson was the most popular solo gospel singer of her generation.

Growing up in New Orleans, Jackson was deeply influenced by the abandoned, heavily rhythmic African forms of worship of the Holiness Church. In 1927 she moved north to Chicago, and refusing an invitation from **Earl Hines** to sing blues, became lead vocalist with the Greater Salem Baptist Choir. Her down-home shouting style was influenced both by **Bessie Smith** and by the leading female gospel singer of the era, Willie Mae Ford Smith, an associate of **Thomas A. Dorsey**.

After cutting one single for Decca – 'God's Gonna Separate the Wheat from the Tares' in 1937 – she toured for a decade with Dorsey, the dominant figure in gospel music. Jackson's intense, allegedly 'flirtatious' stage presence had her banned from the more staid black churches. She resumed her recording career in 1946 with sides for Apollo with pianist Mildred Falls – her accompanist for the next twenty years. Among the first was 'Move on up a Little Higher', composed by Rev. W. H. Brewster and the first gospel record to sell a million copies. The follow-up, Kenneth Morris's 'Dig a Little Deeper', was also a big hit. Among her other well-known songs were 'In the Upper Room with Jesus' by Lucie Williams – the first female gospel composer – 'I'm on My Way to Canaan', 'How I Got Over' and 'Prayer Changes Things.'

When 'I Can Put My Trust in Jesus' won the French *disque d'or* in 1951, Jackson moved out towards white audiences, making her first European tour in 1952. In 1954 she left Apollo for Columbia after royalty disputes. Jackson cut fifteen albums for the label with **Mitch Miller** and **Percy Faith** adding strings to such albums as *The Great Mahalia Jackson*. She also sang with **Duke Ellington** on his suite *Black Brown and Beige* and recorded mainstream hymns such as 'Onward Christian Soldiers'. A pop-song collection, *What the World Needs Now*, included the **Marvin Gaye** and **Dion** hit 'Abraham, Martin and John' as well as the **Burt Bacharach**–Hal David title track and other material like **Jackie DeShannon**'s 'Put a Little Love in Your Heart'. In 1962 her singing of 'The Lord's Prayer' was a highlight of the film *Jazz on a Summer's Day*.

If by the sixties, however, Jackson had a mainly white audience and had become a businesswoman through her chain of Mahalia Jackson Chicken Diners, she retained her commitment to black causes. She endowed a Mahalia Jackson Scholarship Foundation and was a supporter of Dr Martin Luther King, singing 'Precious Lord, Take My Hand' at his funeral. The same hymn was sung at Jackson's own funeral by **Aretha Franklin**, one of the many major artists whom she had influenced.

MICHAEL JACKSON
b. 29 August 1958, Gary, Indiana, USA

The success of Michael Jackson's immaculate solo album *Thriller*, which was the biggest-selling album in music-industry history to date, confirmed the new centrality of black music in the eighties.

He first sang in public with his family group the **Jackson Five** at the age of six and began a solo career in 1971 in parallel with that of the group. *Got to Be There* produced hits with the title track and a revival of Bobby Day's 1958 song 'Rockin' Robin'. The following year he reached the British Top Ten with **Bill Withers**' song 'Ain't No Sunshine' and had an American No. 1 with the sentimental film theme 'Ben'.

Further albums from this period – *Music and Me* (1974) and *Forever* (1975) – were hampered by Motown's giving their young star sub-standard romantic material and oldies like 'Too Young'. His only hit single during the mid-seventies was 'Just a Little Bit of You'. Michael Jackson's career only began to gain momentum after his appearance with **Diana Ross** in *The Wiz*, a remake of *The Wizard of Oz* starring black actors. While the film was a critical failure, its musical director was **Quincy Jones**, whose production of Jackson on the dynamic 'You Can't Win' signalled the beginning of a major partnership.

The first fruits of the Jackson–Jones collaboration were the five hit singles from *Off the Wall* (Epic, 1979). The album included the dance classics 'Don't Stop (Till You Get Enough)' and 'Rock with You' by **Heatwave**'s Rod Temperton (both million-sellers), as well as the slow ballad 'She's Out of My Life'. Jones' high-definition production was embellished with string orchestrations and horn arrangements scored by Jerry Hey.

Motown capitalized on the revival of Jackson's career by re-releasing 'One Day in Your Life', which reached the British Top Ten in 1981, but Jackson underlined his pre-eminence as the most popular contemporary singer with *Thriller* (1982), whose title track was another Temperton composition. The verve and density of the sound disguised the rather sombre preoccupations of the lyrics of 'Billie Jean'* (the travails of a superstar) and the title track, whose horror-movie motifs were drawn out in the seventeen-minute *The Making of Michael Jackson's Thriller*. Claimed as the most successful music video ever, and directed by Hollywood super-brat Jon Landis, it fea-

tured inspired dance sequences with the singer made up as a zombie.

No less than six of *Thriller*'s nine tracks were American hits and another, the ballad 'The Girl Is Mine', was a British success. Not only was Jackson's 'Beat It' a million-seller but a coarse parody, 'Eat It' (Rock & R, 1984) by Weird Al Yankovic, also reached the charts. Both video and album strongly influenced fashion styles (Jackson's zoot suit and one gloved hand), choreography and contemporary black music, much of which sought to follow Jackson and cross over through such tactics as using well-known rock performers as guest artists, as Jackson did with Eddie **Van Halen**'s guitar solo on 'Beat It' and his duets with **Paul McCartney** on 'The Girl Is Mine' (Epic, 1982) and 'Say Say Say' (1983). He wrote the Diana Ross hit 'Muscles' (1982) and was the narrator of the soundtrack album of the film *E.T.* Jackson's megastar status was confirmed when, with **Lionel Richie**, he wrote 'We Are the World'* the USA for Africa all-star charity record, produced by Jones in 1985.

Now co-producer with Jones of his own records, Jackson was equally astute in business deals. In 1984 he signed a multi-million dollar contract for television advertising with Pepsi-Cola, who also sponsored the Jacksons' 'Victory' tour on which Michael was united with the group. In 1985 he purchased the publishing group ATV Music which held the rights to most of **The Beatles**' songs.

In classic Hollywood fashion, Jackson's reclusive behaviour gave rise to a series of rumours and myths about his private lifestyle. In 1986 he starred in *Captain Eo*, a short science-fiction film shown only in America's two Disneyland sites. In 1987 Columbia released 'I Just Can't Stop Loving You', a duet with Siedah Garrett, and the first single from his next album, *Bad*.

Again co-produced by Jones, *Bad* provided further hits with 'The Way You Make Me Feel', 'The Man in the Mirror' (written by Garrett and Glen Ballard with vocal backing by the **Andrae Crouch** choir), 'Dirty Diana', which contained a rock guitar solo by Steve Stevens, and 'Another Part of Me', from *Captain Eo*.

In 1988 Jackson published an autobiography, *Moonwalk*, named after his unique floating dance step. This was followed by the feature-length film *Moonwalker*, in which the star used superhuman powers to save the world. The storyline was created by Jackson himself.

He released *Dangerous* in 1992. Made for the most part with writer-producer **Teddy Riley**, it was less innovative than *Bad* and some of the songs, notably 'Heal the World', a reworking of 'We Are the World', were lacklustre. Far better were 'Remember the Time' and 'Black and White', with Jackson's voice floating around the intricate rhythm patterns created by Riley.

The creation of his own film company, Nation, in partnership with Sony in 1991 suggested a move into films but in 1993 Jackson's career all but collapsed in the wake of allegations concerning the sexual abuse of minors. These allegations received huge publicity. Subsequently Jackson cancelled live shows, and the Pepsi deal was not renewed.

However, despite the acres of bad publicity he had received, *HIStory: Past, Present and Future* (1995), which was supported by a lavish two-year international tour, was a massive success, spawning a number of hit singles including 'Scream', 'One More Time' and 'You Are Not Alone'. Later in the year Jackson ended his marriage with Lisa Marie Presley and Sony and Jackson merged their publishing interests. In 1996 **Pulp**'s Jarvis Cocker in protest disturbed a performance of the melodramatic and narcissistic 'Earth Song' at the UK Brit awards and Jackson announced he was about to become a father. *Blood on the Dancefloor*, a mix of new material and remixes, was released in 1997. In 1998 his girlfriend Debbie Rowe had a second child.

MILLIE JACKSON
b. 15 July 1943, Thompson, Georgia, USA

For a brief period in the mid-seventies Millie Jackson was the queen of soul music, with considerable vocal talents comparable to those of **Aretha Franklin**, **Esther Phillips** and **Nina Simone**. Her constant theme of sexual misbehaviour often resulted in stage shows which bordered on the obscene.

After an unsuccessful modelling career, Jackson was discovered in New Jersey by songwriter Billy Nichols, who signed her to MGM and, after one single, to the recently formed Spring label, which had enjoyed success with **Joe Simon**. Produced by Raeford Gerald, her début eponymous album (1972) included the R&B hits 'My Man a Sweet Man' and 'A Child of God' – a powerful depiction of ghetto life – plus the pop hit 'Ask Me What You Want'. The following year her biggest pop hit 'Hurts So Good' was included in the film *Cleopatra Jones*. A cover-version by lover's-rock reggae singer Susan Cadogan was a British hit on Magnet in 1975.

Jackson's fourth album, co-produced with Brad Shapiro at Muscle Shoals, launched her on the path to international fame. *Caught Up* (1974) was a loose concept album which took the contemporary trend for black music to deal with 'adult themes' such as adultery, and linked it with long spoken 'raps' like those popularized by **Barry White** and **Isaac Hayes**. The album sold nearly a million copies and Jackson's revival of the **Luther Ingram** hit 'If Loving You Is Wrong' was a major R&B hit.

Still Caught Up (1975) continued the saga with one side devoted to the wife's revenge and the other to the mistress's viewpoint. *Free and in Love* and *Lovingly Yours* (both 1976) were in a similar vein but by now Jackson had extracted the graphic sexual aspect of her recordings to provide the basis for a concert act that presented her as the sexually emancipated woman able to handle men on their own terms.

This change to a vaudeville-styled live performer proved shrewd as the rise of disco music drew sales away from the classic soul of *Feelin' Bitchy* (1977) and *Get It Outcha System* (1978). A 1979 pairing of Jackson with Hayes fared little better, though *Royal Rappin's* was successfully reissued in 1986.

By the beginning of the eighties Jackson had taken her raunchy show around the world and released it on a double-album, *Live and Uncensored* (1979), while her frequent British television appearances had incited the upright showbusiness personality **Max Bygraves** to protest. However, her albums of the early eighties, such as *For Men Only* (1980) and *Hard Times* (1982), were uninspired and Jackson's only hit came from a duet with **Elton John** on the raucous 'Act of War' (Rocket, 1985). In 1986 she signed to Jive, the American arm of British label Zomba, for *An Imitation of Love* and the characteristically outspoken *Back to the Sh.t* (1989). She later signed a recording contract with Ichiban.

She subsequently wrote a musical show based on her song 'Young Man, Older Woman' and in 1994 issued the less raunchy *Rock'N'Soul*.

WANDA JACKSON
b. Wanda Lavonne Jackson, 20 October 1937, Maud, Oklahoma, USA

Like **Brenda Lee** from a country music background, Jackson, who is best remembered for her Top Forty hit 'Let's Have a Party' (Capitol, 1960), was one of the few women to record rock'n'roll successfully. But whereas Lee's forte was the rock ballad, Jackson recorded in an altogether more exuberant, wild, rockabilly style.

From 1951 she sang country on Oklahoma City's KLPR radio station and in 1954 she toured with **Hank Thompson**. On the recommendation of Thompson's bandleader, Billy Gray, she was signed to Decca, recording mostly lachrymose ballads ('Tears at the Grand Ole Opry', 1955) and love songs ('The Right to Love', 1954), until a 1955 tour with **Elvis Presley** introduced her to rockabilly. Signed to Capitol, who saw her as a female **Gene Vincent**, she recorded a series of splendidly raucous sides, produced by Ken Nelson, on which her harsh, strident voice was supported by guitarists **Joe Maphis** and **Merle Travis** and pianist **Merrill Moore**. Among these were 'Honey Bop' (1956), the explosive 'Fujiyama Mama' (1958), 'Mean,

Mean Man' (1960) and 'Let's Have a Party', a spirited version of the song originally recorded by Presley. On that record she was backed by a band that included **Buck Owens** and black pianist Big Al Downing, who recorded the rockabilly classic 'Down on the Farm' (White Rock, 1958). Unusually for the period she also toured with Downing and continued recording rock'n'roll, including fine versions of 'Riot in Cell Block No. 9', 'Slippin' and Slidin'' and 'Whole Lotta Shakin' Goin' On' on her albums as late as 1962.

By then, however, Jackson's career was changing direction. In 1961 she had a big hit with her own composition 'Right or Wrong', which was produced by her bandleader **Roy Clark**, and henceforth recorded mostly country weepies as singles. The success of 'In the Middle of a Heartache' (1961) confirmed her status as a country star and throughout the sixties she regularly appeared on the country charts. She hosted her own syndicated television show, *Music Village*, and, like **Connie Francis**, extended her popularity abroad through recordings in German, Dutch and Japanese. In 1973 she left Capitol and later signed with Word Records to record a series of gospel records, including *Country Gospel* (1974), *Closer to Jesus* (1978) and *My Testament* (1982). In 1984 she recorded a live album of rock'n'roll standards in Sweden.

ILLINOIS JACQUET
b. Jean-Baptiste Jacquet, 31 October 1922, Broussard, Louisiana, USA

Jacquet was one of the archetypal 'Texas tenors' like Buddy Tate or Arnett Cobb with an essentially 'hot' sound and an affinity with the blues. His influence in the forties on countless honkers, screamers and other coarse-grained saxophonists was considerable, but his own work generally preserved more jazz decorum, and in ballads he showed the influence of **Coleman Hawkins** and **Ben Webster**. His own stylistic followers include **Eddie 'Lockjaw' Davis** and **King Curtis**.

He grew up in Houston, Texas. After experience in the late thirties with Milt Larkin's band, which then included Cobb and altoist **Eddie 'Cleanhead' Vinson**, he joined Floyd Ray, with whom his brother Russell was playing trumpet. Later that year (1941) he went to work for **Lionel Hampton**, and it was on a 1942 version of Hampton's biggest hit, 'Flying Home', that he played the long improvised solo which has passed into the jazz vocabulary. He subsequently worked with **Cab Calloway** (1943–5) and **Count Basie** (1945–6), and made a notable contribution to the 1944 short film *Jammin' the Blues*, alongside **Lester Young**. At 'Jazz at the Philharmonic' concerts he fought saxophone battles with tenor-player Flip Phillips, as in the 1947 Carnegie Hall 'Perdido' (Mercury).

In the middle and late forties he recorded for

Philo/Aladdin (including a 1947 big-band date with Fats Navarro and **Miles Davis**), Apollo, Savoy and Victor. His brother Russell Jacquet (*b. 1917*), who sometimes served in his bands, also led his own on dates for Globe, Modern, Savoy (with Dexter Gordon) and King (with Sonny Stitt). These recordings, like contemporary sides by Hampton, Jack McVea and other leaders, defined a kind of jazzy R&B that left an impression on early Northern rock'n'roll.

In the fifties Illinois Jacquet was more in the jazz mainstream, recording for **Norman Granz**'s Clef in the company of trumpeter Harry 'Sweets' Edison (*Groovin' with Jacquet*), among others, while in the sixties and seventies he formed small-group associations with organist/pianist Milt Buckner and organist Wild Bill Davis. He played in Hampton reunion bands in 1967, 1972 and 1980, worked frequently in Europe, and in 1984 formed his own Jazz Legends big band.

MAX JAFFA
b. 28 December 1912, London, England, d. 30 July 1991, London

In Britain almost an institution, the music of the Max Jaffa Trio became synonymous with the tea dance, sedate but still sparkling.

The son of a tailor, Jaffa was educated at the Guildhall School of Music and in 1928 started playing at London's Piccadilly Hotel. In 1929 he made his first broadcast with the Max Jaffa Saloon Orchestra and henceforth, with occasional interruptions, he led hotel bands. After the Second World War, with Reginald Kilbey and Jack Byfield, he formed the Max Jaffa Trio which was regularly heard in broadcasts from Scarborough, where he was musical director from 1959 to 1986.

Best remembered for his broadcasts, on the long-running *Music for Your Pleasure* and *Grand Hotel*, among others, he also recorded frequently, mostly collections of romantic songs on Valentine, Warwick and Bandleader Records and surprisingly with **Bert Weedon** in the fifties. His autobiography, *A Life on the Fiddle*, was published shortly before his death.

THE JAM
Rick Buckler, b. 6 December 1955, Woking, Surrey, England; Bruce Foxton, b. 1 September 1955, Woking; Paul John William Weller, b. 25 May 1958, Woking

A group whose inspiration was drawn equally from the mod era of the sixties and contemporary punk, the Jam had eighteen British hits in their five-year recording career before **Paul Weller** disbanded the group to form the Style Council.

Drummer Buckler and guitarist Weller formed

their first band at school in 1973. Joined by bassist Foxton and managed by Weller's building-worker father, the Jam launched themselves on the London club circuit in 1976. They signed to Polydor and their first album, *In the City* (1977), featured Weller's tough pictures of city life on 'Sounds from the Street' and 'Bricks and Mortar'. It was followed by the album *This Is the Modern World* (1977) and Top Twenty hits 'All Around the World' (1977) and 'Down in the Tube Station at Midnight' (1978). The latter came from *All Mod Cons*, whose title and the inclusion of the **Kinks**' 'David Watts' showed the group's debt to the music of the previous decade.

The group's 1979 hits, which included 'Strange Town' and 'Eton Rifles' (from *Setting Sons*), showed an increasing use of studio technology and a sharp awareness of social issues. In a period of rising youth unemployment, Weller's lyrics seemed timely and in 1980 the Jam had two No. 1s with 'Going Underground' and 'Start' from *Sound Affects*. Although the Jam's music was stylistically unrelated, their songs shared with those of most punk groups an intensely local frame of reference. Thus, despite continuing British hits with songs like 'Funeral Pyre' and 'Absolute Beginners' (a title inspired by Colin MacInnes' novel, but unconnected with the 1986 film of the book), the group had no more than a cult following in America.

1982 brought two No. 1 singles: 'Town Called Malice' and 'Beat Surrender', and a No. 1 album (*The Gift*), the Jam's final studio recordings. At the end of the year Weller broke up the group in order to go further into soul music with the Style Council. Two previously unissued live Jam albums appeared in 1983 (*Dig the New Breed*) and 1993 (*Live Jam*), along with an album of out-takes and rarities, *Extras* (1992). After the Jam's break-up, Foxton released the solo album *Touch Sensitive* (1983). He eventually joined Belfast punk veterans Stiff Little Fingers in 1990. Buckler joined the short-lived band Time UK.

JIMMY JAM & TERRY LEWIS

Jimmy Jam, b. James Harris, 1946, Minneapolis, Minnesota, USA; Terry Lewis, b. 1946, Minneapolis

Arguably the outstanding songwriter/producers in recent black music, Jam and Lewis combine a strong melodic sense with contemporary production values. Their most famous work has been with **Janet Jackson**.

The duo met as teenagers in Minneapolis when Jam was already a keyboards player and DJ while Lewis was a bass player and high school sports star. They played together in local group Flyte Time with drummer Jellybean Johnson. When **Prince** asked singer Morris Day to set up a recording and touring band, he formed the Time with Jam, Lewis and Johnson in 1981.

Although Prince had ruled that no member of the Time should take outside work, Jam and Lewis were hired to write and produce tracks for soul group the S.O.S. Band. When their involvement was made public, Prince fired them. Almost immediately, 'Just Be Good to Me' by the S.O.S. Band became a substantial hit and in 1982 Jam and Lewis launched their own production and publishing companies.

One of their first assignments was to mix 'The Coldest Rap', the début single by **Ice T**. During the mid-eighties they worked with such artists as Change, Cheryl Lynn, Cherelle, Patti Austin ('Heat of Heat') and fellow-Minneapolis musician **Alexander O'Neal**. Jam and Lewis wrote and produced his 1984 eponymous album, which was a Top Twenty hit.

The turning point in Jam and Lewis' career was *Control*, the 1986 album they wrote and produced for Janet Jackson. Her previous record had been poorly received and for *Control* Jam and Lewis changed their own way of working. Instead of providing Jackson with ready-made compositions, they built up each track around her vocals and relevant beats.

Control became a multi-million-seller and produced five hit singles. It moved the duo into the superstar league of producers, enabling them to choose projects to work on and to start their own label. They continued to produce Janet Jackson and O'Neal, worked with teenage black vocal group New Edition and, after its demise, former members Johnny Gill and Ralph Tresvant. Although it included the No. 1 hit 'Human', Jam & Lewis's production for UK group the **Human League** was less successful.

In 1991 they set up Perspective Records, which issued the bestselling soundtrack album *Mo' Money* and includes award-winning gospel group Sounds of Blackness on its roster. The group performed with Daryl Hall on the 1994 official World Cup song, 'Glorylands'. Perspective later became the black music division of A&M Records and Jam & Lewis added CeCe Peniston and others to the roster.

In the mid- to late nineties the pair's productions ranged even wider, including work with **Barry White** (*The Icon Is Love*, 1994), **Rod Stewart** (*If We Fall in Love Tonight*, 1996), **Boyz II Men** (*Evolution*, 1997) and **Mary J. Blige** (*Share My World*, 1997).

AHMAD JAMAL

b. 2 July 1930, Pittsburgh, Pennsylvania, USA

One of the most prolific modern jazz pianists, Jamal's work was an important influence on **Miles Davis** in the fifties. He later influenced the development of jazz-funk.

Jamal played with George Hudson's band in 1948

before forming his own trio, which was resident for many years at Chicago's Pershing Hotel. In 1951 he was signed to **Leonard Chess**'s Cadet label. Jamal's most successful album of the period was *At the Pershing* (1958), with Israel Crosby (bass) and Vernell Fournier (drums). It was particularly notable for its uses of pauses and silences as a melodic and dramatic trope.

Like fellow Pittsburgh pianist **Erroll Garner**, Jamal built his repertoire out of popular songs (**Cole Porter**'s 'Love for Sale', **George Gershwin**'s 'But Not for Me' and **Johnny Mercer**'s 'Autumn Leaves') and show tunes ('Surrey with the Fringe on Top' from **Rodgers and Hammerstein**'s *Oklahoma!*), as well as original compositions. He was also influenced by **Count Basie**'s economical style of playing which allowed an interplay between trio members within an overall jaunty rhythmic feel. An admirer of Jamal's approach, Miles Davis recorded his 'Ahmad's Blues' and 'New Rhumba'.

In the seventies Jamal led a quintet featuring guitarist Calvin Keys. He later recorded for ABC-Impulse (*The Awakening*, 1970), 20th Century (*One*, 1978), Motown (*Night Song*, 1980, which included 'Theme from MASH') and Gateway, which released *In Concert, MIDEM 81*, duets with **Gary Burton**. His nineties albums included the live *Chicago Revisited* (Telarc, 1992) and *I Remember Duke, Hoagy & Strayhorn* (1994).

JAMES

Tim Booth; Saul Davies; Andy Diagram (replaced by Michael Kulas); Paul Gilbertson (replaced by Larry Gott, replaced by Adrian Oxaal); Jim Glennie; Mark Hunter; Gavin Whelan (replaced by David Baynton-Powell)

A Manchester-based septet who had been on the cusp of superstardom since the baggy-inspired single 'Sit Down' (1991), James surprised everyone, including themselves, by selling over one million copies in the UK of their *Best of* album in 1998.

The original incarnation of James formed in 1982 when guitarist Gilbertson, bassist Glennie and drummer Whelan met singer Tim Booth at Manchester University. They released two EPs on Factory Records – *Jimone* (1983) and *James II* (1985), which saw them labelled as **Smiths** copyists – before signing with Sire Records. *Stutter* (1986) and the folk-tinged *Strip Mine* (1988) featured new guitarist Larry Gott (who replaced Gilbertson) and were accompanied by successful tours of the UK, but James so far failed to capitalize on their live following on record.

James released a live album, *One Man Clapping* (1989), on Rough Trade Records before joining Fontana with a radically altered line-up. Baynton-

Powell replaced Whelan on drums, while violinist/guitarist Davies, trumpeter Diagram and keyboard-player Hunter became members of an expanded James. *Gold Mother* (1990) became James' breakthrough album and included two hit singles, 'Come Home' and 'How Was it for You?'. By the time they released *Seven* (1992) 'Sit Down' had peaked at Number Two in the UK chart, and the band appeared to be on the verge of becoming one of Britain's biggest bands. The experimental *Laid* (1993), produced by **Brian Eno**, was a big success in America, but sold poorly in the UK, as did *Wah Wah* (1994), a collection of jams again recorded by Eno.

The group took an extended break after *Wah Wah* to rethink their sound, at which point Tim Booth worked on *Booth and the Bad Angel* (1996), a collaborative effort with Angelo Badalamenti, composer of the scores to *Twin Peaks* and *Blue Velvet*. Although the band were now virtually forgotten in America, *Whiplash* (1997) saw James begin to regain their British following. In spite of the departure of guitarist Larry Gott, the band had hits with 'She's a Star' and 'Tomorrow' before *The Best of James* (1998)* – including two new singles, 'Run Aground' and 'Destiny Calling' – went quadruple platinum and made James a household name in the UK. *Millionaires* (1999), again produced by Brian Eno, featured the recording début of two new members of James, guitarist Oxaal and multi-instrumentalist Kulas, and included the single 'I Know What I'm Here for'.

DICK JAMES

b. Richard Leon Vapnick, 12 December 1920, London, England, d. 1 February 1986, London

A band singer of the forties, James survived the rock era by moving into the publishing and record industries, achieving success through his association with **The Beatles** and **Elton John**.

The son of Polish immigrants, James served his apprenticeship as a crooner with local bands in North London before joining **Henry Hall** (where he was billed as Lee 'Amapola' Sheridan) and then **Geraldo** (who demanded he change his name to James) and finally Cyril Stapleton's orchestra. A jaunty rather than expressive balladeer, he was an early member of the Stargazers, a group whose British hits included 'Close the Door' and 'Twenty Tiny Fingers' (both Decca, 1955). An occasional songwriter, he numbered among his compositions 'White Wedding' and the novelty song 'You're a Pink Toothbrush, I'm a Blue Toothbrush', a hit for **Max Bygraves**, whose version was regularly requested on the BBC radio programme *Children's Favourites*.

In 1956 he was signed as a solo singer by producer **George Martin** to Parlophone and given 'Robin

Hood', the much-parodied theme tune to the British teleseries. Arranged by **Ron Goodwin**, it was James' only substantial hit. After the failure of his pallid cover of **Frankie Vaughan**'s British chart-topper, 'The Garden of Eden' (1956), James stopped touring and became a plugger for Sydney Bron (who later founded Bronze Records) and then formed his own publishing company, Dick James Music, in 1961.

An early copyright was Martin's instrumental composition 'Niagara Theme'. That was only a minor success but Martin's introduction of Brian Epstein and The Beatles to James in 1962 after the publishers of their first record, 'Love Me Do', had done nothing for the group was the making of James. He subsequently published most of the songs written by the artists managed by Epstein and, in 1965, set up Page One Records with Larry Page, scoring immediately with the **Troggs**' primitive million-selling recording of the **Chip Taylor** composition, 'Wild Thing'. In 1969, amid much rancour, James sold his interests in Northern Songs (the company he'd set up to publish the songs of **John Lennon** and **Paul McCartney**) for a profit of over £1 million and then dissolved his partnership with Page to set up DJM Records.

DJM's greatest success was with Elton John, who with Bernie Taupin, his songwriting partner, was also signed to James' publishing company. However, when John left in 1973, the company neither found a replacement nor was able to develop the kind of roster expected of a fully fledged record company. Indeed, John remained the company's main source of income throughout the seventies and eighties, and 1985 saw a lengthy court case between John and Taupin and DJM over disputed royalty payments. The DJM catalogue was subsequently sold to Poly-Gram.

ELMORE JAMES
b. 27 January 1918, Richland, Mississippi, USA,
d. 24 May 1963, Chicago, Illinois

The most influential bottleneck-style guitarist in the history of electric blues, Elmore James was also the composer or popularizer of several blues standards.

In his youth, James was acquainted with **Robert Johnson**, from whom he derived some of his most durable themes, and with **Sonny Boy Williamson**, whom he partnered in the late forties on KFFA, Helena, Arkansas and other Delta stations. From 1952 he appeared regularly in Chicago, where he was most often accompanied by pianist Johnny Jones, and his own cousin Homesick James on bass guitar.

James first recorded his trademark song 'Dust My Broom' (originated by Johnson) for Trumpet in 1952; sometimes titled 'I Believe My Time Ain't Long' and

by later copyists 'Dust My Blues', the song recurred throughout his subsequent sessions for Meteor (1953), Flair (1954–6), Chief (1957), Chess (1959) and **Bobby Robinson**'s Fire and companion labels (1959–62) in different versions. Also derived from Johnson was 'Standing at the Crossroads' – which Homesick James took on after Elmore's death – while 'Anna Lee' and 'It Hurts Me Too' were from fellow bottleneck guitarists Robert Nighthawk and Tampa Red, partner of **Thomas A. Dorsey**. Other much-covered James songs were 'The Sky Is Crying' (or 'The Sun Is Shining') and 'Look on Yonder Wall', which appeared on the first album by **Paul Butterfield**'s Blues Band.

James' singing, a slightly blurred scream, and torrential guitar figures heavily influenced Chicagoans like Hound Dog Taylor, J. B. Hutto and Johnny Littlejohn. He was also the model for **Johnny Winter** and for numerous British rhythm and blues guitarists, especially **Fleetwood Mac**'s Jeremy Spencer.

ETTA JAMES
b. Etta James Hawkins, 25 January 1938, Los Angeles, California, USA

Equally adept at singing blues, soul and supperclub pop, Etta James' career spanned five decades.

After singing with vocal group the Peaches, she was discovered by **Johnny Otis** in the early fifties and signed to the Modern label in 1955. Her first hit, co-written with Otis, was an answer record to **Hank Ballard**'s 'Work with Me Annie'. A cover-version of the salacious 'Roll with Me Henry' was a pop No. 1 and million-seller for white singer Georgia Gibbs as the retitled 'Dance with Me Henry'. James' later Modern recordings included the R&B hit 'Good Rocking Daddy' (1955).

In 1959 her contract expired and **Harvey Fuqua** arranged for James to join the Argo subsidiary of Chess Records. Her fifteen-year association with the label featured such classic R&B hits as 'All I Could Do Was Cry' (1960), 'At Last' (1961), the often-revived 'Something's Got a Hold on Me' (1962) and 'Pushover' (1963), her biggest pop hit of the era. 'Do I Make Myself Clear' (1965) and 'In the Basement' (1966) were duets with Sugar Pie DeSanto, who had enjoyed pop success on Chess in 1964 with the bluesy novelty songs 'Slip-in Mules' and 'Soulful Dress'. Many of these early Chess recordings were produced by **Ralph Bass**.

The most artistically satisfying phase of James' career began when **Leonard Chess** sent her to Muscle Shoals to record with **Rick Hall**. This partnership produced the original (and definitive) version of 'I'd Rather Go Blind' (1967) – a 1969 British hit for Chicken Shack featuring future **Fleetwood Mac** member Christine Perfect – as well as individual readings of such soul standards as **Clarence Carter**'s 'Tell Mama' (1967) and **Otis Redding**'s 'Security' (1968). Later Muscle Shoals hits were the country-music classic 'Almost Persuaded' (1969) – first recorded by David Houston and later a hit for **Tammy Wynette** – and 'Loser's Weepers' (1970).

At this point James seemed poised to join such contemporaries as **Aretha Franklin** and **Tina Turner** in breaking through to rock audiences. When Chess was sold to GRT in 1971, producer Gabriel Mekler gave her **Randy Newman**'s 'Leave Your Hat on' and 'Burn down the Cornfield', but the rise of disco and the demise of GRT deprived her of success. James' next recordings were not made until **Jerry Wexler** produced the uneven *Deep in the Night* for Warners in 1978. The album featured a spirited version of the **Eagles**' 'Take It to the Limit', which became a high point of her live shows. Her last major studio recording was *Changes* (MCA, 1980), produced by **Allen Toussaint**.

In the eighties James toured as a club act throughout America and Europe with a blues-inflected set and a band led by Chicago session player Cash McCall. She overcame a long addiction to heroin during this period and recorded only revivals of her old hits and some gospel material for K-Tel. In 1986, however, Fantasy recorded her live show, her best album for over a decade. With assistance from **Eddie 'Cleanhead' Vinson**, Brother Jack McDuff and Otis's guitarist son Shuggie, she released two albums, *Blues in the Night (the Early Show)* (1986) and *Blues in the Night (the Late Show)* (1987).

In 1989 James recorded *Seven Year Itch* (Island) produced by Barry Beckett, the keyboard player on her 1967 Muscle Shoals sessions. In 1990 she had a cameo role in the film *Bad Influence*, singing Tony Joe White's 'Out of the Rain'. Her 1991 album *Stickin' to My Guns*, again produced by Beckett, saw her recording country, blues and funk material with equal mastery. Produced by **Jerry Wexler**, *The Right Time* (1992) was a similarly classy collection. James followed this in 1994 with *Mystery Lady*, a collection of songs associated with **Billie Holiday**. *The Essential Etta James* (MCA, 1994) is the definitive retrospective, while *Love's Been Rough on Me* is a superior late recording which includes a fine reading of 'I've Been Loving You Too Long'.

HARRY JAMES

b. Harry Haag James, 15 March 1916, Albany, Georgia, USA, d. 5 July 1983, Las Vegas, Nevada

A trumpeter who was equally adept at pop schmaltz and jazz solos, Harry James led big bands for over forty years.

His first lessons on the instrument came from his father, who was conductor of the band of the Haag travelling circus, with which Harry played drums at the age of six. In 1931 the James family settled in Texas where Harry played with local groups before touring with Ben Pollack's orchestra in 1935. In 1937–9 he was a highly regarded soloist with **Benny Goodman**'s orchestra, playing on such recordings as 'Sing Sing Sing', 'Roll 'Em' and the **Fletcher Henderson** composition 'Sugar Foot Stomp'. During this period James also cut records with boogie-woogie pianists **Albert Ammons** and **Pete Johnson** and had his own recording band, which had a million-seller with **Count Basie**'s 'One o'Clock Jump' (Columbia, 1938).

In 1939 James formed Harry James and his Music Makers, which soon became one of the most popular bands of the swing era through live appearances, radio broadcasts and recordings for Columbia. Part of his success was due to a succession of featured vocalists, the first of whom was **Frank Sinatra**, who sang on the hits 'Ciribiribin'* (1939) and 'All or Nothing'* (1943). Other singers with the James band in the forties were Kitty Kallen, **Dick Haymes** and Helen Forrest, whose biggest successes were 'I Had the Craziest Dream' (1942) and **Sammy Cahn**'s 'I've Heard That Song Before' (1943).

It was as a dance band, however, that James' group attracted young audiences. His repertoire mixed up-tempo tunes with blues, boogie-woogie and virtuoso pieces for his brash but polished trumpet-playing. These included Rimsky-Korsakov's 'Flight of the Bumble Bee', 'By a Sleepy Lagoon', 'Carnival in Venice', 'You Made Me Love You' and 'Concerto for Trumpet'. As the forties progressed, James sweetened the band's sound by adding a string section.

During the forties James and his orchestra appeared in more than twenty Hollywood musicals. Among them were *Springtime in the Rockies* (1942) – which starred Betty Grable, whom James married the following year – *Two Girls and a Sailor* (1944), *Carnegie Hall* (1947) and *Young Man with a Horn* (1947), a fiction loosely based on the life of **Bix Beiderbecke**. While Kirk Douglas played the title role, James dubbed the trumpet-playing.

The orchestra continued to tour and record until 1954, playing a mixture of commercial dance music and swing-era jazz. Alto-sax-player Willie Smith was the outstanding soloist after James himself. James reorganized the band in 1957 and during the sixties had long residencies in Las Vegas with drummer **Buddy Rich** a featured player. The dominant influence on the orchestra was Count Basie, whose arrangers Neal Hefti and Ernie Wilkins also worked with James. During the seventies the band also toured Europe and James continued to perform until shortly before his death from a heart attack.

RICK JAMES

b. James Johnson, 1 February 1952, Buffalo, New York, USA

A leading black rock-funk artist of the early eighties, Rick James prefigured the sound of **Prince**.

His first important musical activity was in Canada, where he fled after deserting from the US army. In Toronto he formed the Mynah Birds with **Neil Young** and Goldy McJohn, later of **Steppenwolf**. Recordings for Motown were unreleased and James then spent some time in Europe, performing in England with a blues band, Main Line.

In the mid-seventies James returned to Buffalo and, influenced by the music of **George Clinton** and **Marvin Gaye**, successfully submitted demo tapes to Motown. These – including the paean to marijuana, 'Mary Jane' – were released in 1978 as *Come Get It!* by Rick James and the Stone City Band. Both the album and 'You and I' were hits for the company, then in something of a hit famine. James was given an unprecedented amount of attention at Motown and in 1979 released two albums (*Bustin' Out of L-Seven* and *Fire It Up*) as well as producing the début album of disco artist Teena Marie, *Wild and Peaceful*. In that year 'Bustin' Out' reached the pop Top Ten and three other singles were R&B hits.

After releasing the less popular *Garden of Love* and producing the Stone City Band's *In 'n' Out* (1980), James reached his peak in 1981 with *Street Songs**, whose finely crafted songs took in 'Ghetto Life' and 'Mr Policeman' as well as 'Fire and Desire' (a duet with Teena Marie). 'Super Freak (Part 1)' was his biggest pop hit, a song whose title aptly caught James' own image of beaded hair and heavily sequinned clothes.

Later records like *Throwin' Down* (1982) and (despite a guest appearance from **Smokey Robinson**) *Coldblooded* (1983) were disappointing but James had increasing success as a writer and producer for others. In 1982 he composed the **Temptations**' hit 'Standing on the Top' and the following year produced 'All Night Long', a British hit for the Mary Jane Girls, who went on to American success with 'In My House' (1985). He also produced the actor and comedian Eddie Murphy.

James' later career was marred by a contractual dispute with Motown and 1985's *Glow* was a commercial failure. In 1987 he left Motown to join Warners, where 'Loosey's Rap' (1988, with Roxanne Shante), from the minor album *Wonderful*, topped the R&B charts. **Hammer**'s 1990 hit 'U Can't Touch This' was based on James' 'Super Freak'. In 1993 he was given a prison sentence after being convicted of sexual assault. Released from prison in 1996, James began a comeback tour in 1997, the same year Motown issued the 'best of', *The Ultimate Collection*.

SKIP JAMES

b. Nehemiah James, 9 June 1902, Bentonia, Mississippi, USA, d. 3 October 1969, Philadelphia, Pennsylvania

One of the most powerful Mississippi blues performers, James was rediscovered by young white enthusiasts in the sixties.

The son of a Baptist preacher, James played piano and organ in his father's church. He attended high school in Yazoo City where he learned guitar. An itinerant worker, he travelled throughout Mississippi and Texas, performing in barrel-houses and at dances. He settled in Jackson and in 1930 auditioned for the Paramount Records scout H. C. Speir. The following year James travelled to the Paramount studios in Wisconsin and cut twenty-six tracks. They included such classic titles as 'Devil Got My Woman', 'Hard Time Killin' Floor Blues', '20-20 Blues' (which inspired **Robert Johnson**'s '32-20 Blues', 1936) and the spiritual 'I'm So Glad', which was recorded in the sixties by **Cream**. With an unusual rhythmic subtlety and a vocal range that included falsetto, James' style was highly distinctive.

Only a few singles by James were released before Paramount went out of business in 1932, defeated by the Depression. Disillusioned, he joined his father in Houston and devoted himself to religious activity as a preacher and organizer of gospel groups for the next two decades. In 1951 he returned to Mississippi to work as a sharecropper. It was there that **John Fahey** and Henry Vestine of **Canned Heat** tracked James down in 1964.

He was immediately booked for the Newport Folk Festival and spent the last five years of his life appearing at similar events and making new recordings of his classic repertoire for a number of labels. *Skip James: the Greatest of the Delta Blues Singers* (Melodeon, 1964) was followed by *Skip James Today!* (Vanguard, 1965) and *Devil Got My Woman* (Vanguard, 1968). All featured James' high, ghostly voice and pungent guitar accompaniment.

SONNY JAMES

b. Jimmie Loden, 1 May 1929, Hackleburg, Alabama, USA

In the mid-sixties and early seventies James had a string of sixteen consecutive country No. 1s. His most memorable record, however, was the teen ballad 'Young Love'* (1956). One of the first crossover hits, it topped both the country and pop charts.

From a musical background, James was playing fiddle in the family group by the age of four and in his teens won several fiddling contests. In the late forties he regularly broadcast on regional country shows and, after his army service, in 1952 signed with Capitol and had his first hit with 'For Rent' (1956). This was followed by 'Young Love'. Originally recorded by its co-writer Ric Carty (RCA), the song was covered (after James' success in the country charts) by actor Tab Hunter (Dot), whose million-selling version also topped the pop charts, and later revived by Donny Osmond of the **Osmonds** (1973). James' only other crossover hit was another teen ballad, 'First Date, First Kiss, First Love' (1957).

By the sixties James' clear voice and spare backing had won him the soubriquet 'The Southern Gentleman' and he had returned to more countryfied material. Hits of this period included 'The Minute You're Gone' (1963, a British No. 1 for **Cliff Richard** in 1965), 'You're the Only World That I Know' (1964) and 'Need You' (1966), the first of his string of consecutive No. 1s. Among the others were several revivals (including **Roy Orbison**'s 'Only the Lonely', **Johnny Preston**'s 'Running Bear' and **Ivory Joe Hunter**'s 'Since I Met You Baby', all in 1969, and **Brook Benton**'s 'It's Just a Matter of Time', 1970). In 1972 James switched to Columbia and had an immediate country No. 1 with 'When the Snow Is on the Roses', described by one critic as the quintessential celebration of home and hearth, and in 1973 he produced Marie Osmond's revival of 'Paper Roses'*, originally a hit for Anita Bryant (Carlton, 1960), who found renewed fame in the late seventies as a Christian crusader against gay rights and abortion.

During the eighties James recorded with less success for Monument and Dimension (*Innocent Lies*, 1982) before retiring from the music business.

TOMMY JAMES AND THE SHONDELLS

Tommy James, b. Thomas Gregory Jackson, 29 April 1947, Dayton, Ohio, USA; Joseph Kessler (replaced by Eddie Gray, b. 27 February 1948); Vincent Pietropaoli (replaced by Peter Lucia, b. 2 February 1947); George Magura; Ronald Rosman, b. 28 February 1945; Michael Vale, b. 17 July 1949

A successful American pop group of the sixties, Tommy James and the Shondells had fourteen hits in four years. Lead singer James went on to a less spectacular solo career.

James formed his first band in Niles, Michigan, in 1960 and went through numerous personnel changes before he and the Shondells cut the **Ellie Greenwich**–Jeff Barry song 'Hanky Panky' (first recorded by its writers as the Raindrops in 1964 for Jubilee) for the local Snap label. Picked up by Roulette, the record was a No. 1 hit and million-seller in 1966.

Produced by Ritchie Cordell, who also wrote or co-wrote many of the songs with James, the group's next successes included 'I Think We're Alone Now' (successfully revived by Tiffany in 1987 on MCA), 'Mirage'

(1967) and 'Mony Mony' (1968), a hit for **Billy Idol** in 1987. These were mainstream rock tracks, with 'Mony Mony', a British No. 1 and his only hit there, veering close to bubblegum music. Later songs, however, had more of a progressive rock or psychedelic tinge. There was a hypnotic use of phasing and echo on the 1968 No. 1 'Crimson and Clover' (successfully revived by **Joan Jett** in 1982) and mysterious (allegedly drug-inspired) imagery in 'Crystal Blue Persuasion' (1969). However, the group's intriguing progressive rock album, *Cellophane Symphony* (1969) fared less well commercially.

The Shondells' final hit before James left for a solo career was 'She' (1970), from *Travelin'*. Afterwards Gray (guitar), Lucia (drums), Vale (bass) and Rosman (keyboards) renamed themselves Hog Heaven and recorded one eponymous album (Roulette, 1971).

James wrote and produced Alive and Kicking's Top Ten hit 'Tighter, Tighter' (Roulette, 1970) before achieving solo success with 'Draggin' the Line' (1971). A cover-version by the **Dave Clark Five** was also a hit in Britain. He next essayed country music on the **Pete Drake**-produced *My Head, My Bed, My Red Guitar* (1972) and tried his hand as an interpreter of contemporary rock ballads on the Fantasy albums *In Touch* (1976) and *Midnight Rider* (1977), which was produced by Jeff Barry. His final hit record was 'Three Times in Love' (Millennium, 1980).

In 1987 James re-emerged with platinum-blonde pomaded hair, singing his hits on 'oldies' package shows with a new group of Shondells. They released the album *Hi-Fi* in 1989, the same year Rhino released the definitive retrospective, *Anthology*.

JAMIROQUAI

Wallis Buchanan, b. 29 November 1965; Jason 'Jay' Kay, b. 30 December 1969, Stretford, Lancashire, England; Derrick McKenzie; Toby Smith; Stuart Zender, b. 18 March 1974, Philadelphia, Pennsylvania, USA

The emergence of Jamiroquai in the early nineties with their hybrid of jazz, funk and seventies disco led to the reinvigoration of a British club scene which had become dominated by faceless DJs.

Kay formed the band in 1992, enlisting the help of McKenzie (drums), Smith (keyboards), Zender (bass) and Buchanan (vibes) for the release of 'When You Gonna Learn?' on the independent Acid Jazz label. Jamiroquai's tight, up-beat sound and the vocal similarities between Kay and **Stevie Wonder** prompted a bidding war between the majors, resulting in an eight-album deal with S2. *Emergency on Planet Earth* (1993) brought the band instant acclaim in the UK, entering the album charts at Number One, while *Return of the Space Cowboy** (1994) saw them find an audience in Japan and Europe.

Jamiroquai achieved international stardom with *Travelling Without Moving** (1996), which featured three hit singles, 'Virtual Insanity', 'Cosmic Girl' and 'Alright'. The album also broke the band in the US, where they won a Grammy and four MTV Awards. In 1998 Jamiroquai recorded a song for the *Godzilla* movie, 'Deeper Underground', which topped the British Chart, before bassist Zender left to have a child with **All Saints**' Melanie Blatt. Undeterred, Jamiroquai returned with *Synkronized* (1999), which consolidated their worldwide success and included 'Canned Heat', the band's thirteenth UK hit.

JAN AND DEAN
Jan Berry, b. 3 April 1941, Los Angeles, California, USA; Dean Torrence, b. 10 March 1940, Los Angeles

Close associates of the **Beach Boys**, harmony singers Jan and Dean successfully rode the crest of the surf-music wave in the mid-sixties.

High-school friends, they recorded 'Jennie Lee' (Arwin, 1958) with Arnie Ginsberg, future Beach Boy Bruce Johnston and two tape recorders in Berry's garage. With Torrence doing army service the record was released as by Jan and Arnie and was a national hit. 'Baby Talk' (1959) by Jan and Dean on **Lou Adler** and **Herb Alpert**'s Dore label also reached the Top Ten. Other minor hits included revivals of the Crows' 1954 doo-wop song 'Gee' (Dore, 1960), the Cleftones' 'Heart and Soul' (Challenge, 1961), and the **Harptones**' 'Sunday Kind of Love' (Liberty, 1962), before they found a theme to provide a focus for their sound and image.

Dick Dale and the Del-Tones' reverberating guitar on 'Let's Go Trippin'' (Deltone, 1961) had given surf music its own sound but it was the Beach Boys' Brian Wilson who pinpointed the cultural icons of surfing. With Berry, Wilson wrote 'Surf City', a paean to the idealized Southern Californian youth culture of sea, sex, surf and cars. Recorded by Jan and Dean for Liberty (with added vocal support from Wilson), the record was a 1963 No. 1. The accompanying album, *Surf City and Other Swinging Cities*, included such items as 'Way Down Yonder in New Orleans', 'You Came a Long Way from St Louis' and 'I Left My Heart in San Francisco'.

Reinforced by a spate of beach-party movies (Jan and Dean provided the soundtrack for the **Fabian** epic *Ride the Wild Surf*), the duo had seven more hits in less than two years. Some were set on the beach (the title song from the movie and 'Honolulu Lulu') while others focused on cars ('Drag City', 'Dead Man's Curve'); some had a humorous touch ('Little Old Lady from Pasadena', 'The Anaheim, Azusa and Cucamunga Sewing Circle, Book Review and Timing Association'); and there was one teenage love song

('New Girl in School'). All were delivered in Jan and Dean's precise, exhilarating, high-pitched harmonies.

As the surf boom subsided, Liberty tried unsuccessfully to push Jan and Dean towards other trends. *Folk 'n' Roll* (1965) found them singing **Bob Dylan**'s 'It Ain't Me Babe', **Barry McGuire**'s 'Eve of Destruction' and a song called 'Folk City'. *Filet of Soul* (1966) included covers of material by **The Beatles**, Len Barry and the **McCoys**. *Popsicle* (1966), however, returned to beach themes ('One Piece Topless Bathing Suit' and Wilson's 'Summer Means Fun'); the title track provided the duo's final hit.

In 1966 Berry suffered extensive brain damage as a result of a car crash. He made only a partial recovery and occasional attempts to perform and record were shortlived. Torrence made one solo album *Save for a Rainy Day* (1967) and in 1975 played a few concerts with surf-revival band Blue Pacific. He devoted himself to a career in graphics, specializing in album cover and poster art. A television movie biography of Jan and Dean, *Dead Man's Curve*, was screened in 1978. Berry recovered his health, and the duo toured America occasionally on the nostalgia circuit into the nineties. In 1980 the pair made the live album *One Summer Night* (Rhino) and in 1995 EMI released definitive retrospective, *Surf City*.

JAPAN
David Sylvian, b. David Batt, 23 February 1958, London, England; Steve Jansen, b. Steve Batt, 1 December 1959, London; Mick Karn, b. Antony Michaelides, 24 July 1958; Richard Barbieri, b. 30 November 1957; Rob Dean

An early example of glam-rock, Japan were one of the first groups of that genre to become popular in Japan itself, thereby paving the way for **Culture Club** and others. After the group split up, **David Sylvian** and Mick Karn devoted themselves to a variety of mostly avant-garde projects.

The group was formed at school in South London by Karn and the brothers Sylvian and Jansen in 1974. Betraying the influences of the **New York Dolls** in the lead singer's name and the band's androgynous appearance and of **Bryan Ferry** in Sylvian's singing, *Adolescent Sex* (Hansa, 1978) was an arty record in a punk era and made little impact. In 1979 and 1980 the group toured Japan itself where *Obscure Alternatives* (1980) sold well, with the album containing a flexidisc of Sylvian reading Japanese translations of his lyrics, written by fans.

With the band now handled by former **Yardbirds** manager Simon Napier-Bell, the title track of *Quiet Life* (1980) was the first of the group's nine British hits during 1981–2, the heyday of the new romantics in British rock. Shortly before the success of that single,

Japan had moved to Virgin and 'Art of Parties' and 'Life in Tokyo' from *Gentlemen Take Polaroids* (1980) were minor hits in 1981. The most successful of Japan's 1982 releases were the Top Ten singles 'Ghosts' (Virgin) and a revival of **Smokey Robinson**'s 'I Second That Emotion' (Hansa). *Tin Drum* (Virgin) reached the Top Twenty of the album charts in the same year.

Despite these successes, the group split up in 1982, with the live album *Oil on Canvas* (Virgin, 1983) their final release. Dean had already left to re-emerge later with **Gary Numan** but the three founder members retained the oriental connection. After his 'Forbidden House', recorded with **Ryuichi Sakamoto** of Japanese band Yellow Magic Orchestra, was included in the film *Merry Christmas Mr Lawrence* (among whose stars was **David Bowie**), Sylvian embarked on a solo career.

Jansen also worked with Japanese musicians before leaving music until he returned in 1987 with Barbieri as the Dolphin Brothers, releasing *Catch the Fall* (Virgin). Karn attempted to combine work as a sculptor with various musical projects. These included a collaboration with **Ultravox**'s Midge Ure and Dali's Car, a group formed with Pete Murphy from Bauhaus, which recorded *The Waking Hour*. Sylvian sang on Karn's solo effort *Dreams of Reason Produce Monsters*, whose title was taken from an etching by Goya.

In 1991 Japan reunited for one album, calling themselves Rain Tree Crow. After their eponymous album, however, Sylvian once again left to pursue his solo career, recording *The First Day* with **Robert Fripp**, and then his first real solo album for over a decade, *Dead Bees on a Cake* (1999).

JEAN-MICHEL JARRE
b. 24 August 1948, Lyons, France

Like **Mike Oldfield**, Jarre used complex electronic techniques to produce large-scale compositions which were usually musically undemanding, if highly popular. In the eighties he specialized in staging massive public spectacles for audiences of up to a million.

His father was film-music composer **Maurice Jarre** and his mother ran a Paris jazz club. He was influenced by Anglo-American rock music before studying at the Paris Conservatoire, and with electronic-music pioneer Pierre Schafer. Jarre's first electronic composition was performed at the Paris Opéra in 1971.

Over the next five years he wrote a wide range of music, including advertising jingles, film and ballet scores and pop material for such singers as Françoise Hardy and Patrick Juvet. His first album was *Oxygène* (Polydor, 1976), which was a No. 1 hit in France and sold several million copies worldwide. *Equinoxe* (1978) was equally successful and in 1979 a special perform-

ance was mounted in central Paris on Bastille Day.

After *Magnetic Fields* (1981), Jarre became the first Western pop artist to perform in China. *The Concerts in China* (1982) recorded the occasion. In contrast to the monumental nature of his other projects, *Music for Supermarkets* was issued in a limited edition of only one copy. With the master tape destroyed, the unique copy was auctioned in a Paris art gallery.

Zoolook (Dreyfus/Polydor, 1984) was more exploratory than Jarre's other work, and based on vocal lines created from a few phonemes and musical phrases taken from sounds 'sampled' on a Fairlight synthesizer. The 'Rendezvous Houston' project of 1986 was the pinnacle of Jarre's career to date. A \$2 million audiovisual spectacle with fireworks, lighting and lasers as well as music, it was marred by the absence of saxophone-playing astronaut Ron McNair, who had died in the US space shuttle *Challenger* several months before. The album *Rendezvous* pinpointed the limits of Jarre's approach. Abstracted from its context, the imagistic music was a symphonic pomp-rock soundtrack for an absent movie.

In 1988, following the release of *Revelations* (one of the tracks of which, 'London Kid', featured Hank Marvin of the **Shadows** on guitar), he mounted a concert in London's Docklands. He followed it with the album *Jarre Live* (1989) and *Waiting for Cousteau* (1990), a tribute to veteran marine biologist Jacques Cousteau. A 1990 performance in front of over two million people in Paris on Bastille Day was filmed. After mounting another massive outdoor concert in Sun City, South Africa, in 1992, Jarre released *Chronologie* (1993). In 1997, in the manner of Mike Oldfield, he revisited his most popular work, *Oxygène*, with *Oxygène 7–13*. Later albums included *Odyssey through O2* (1998) and *Metamorphoses* (1999).

MAURICE JARRE
b. 13 September 1924, Lyons, France

A composer of film music, Jarre is best known for his strong melodic, romantic scores for the epics *Lawrence of Arabia* (1962) and *Doctor Zhivago* (1965), both of which won him Oscars.

After studying at the Paris Conservatoire, Jarre wrote music for the concert hall. After working as the director of the Paris Théâtre National Populaire, he wrote his first score for Georges Franju's short, *Hôtel des Invalides* (1952), graduating to features with Franju's *La Tête contre les Murs* (1959). He quickly established himself, with **Michel Legrand**, as the leading French composer of film music.

In 1962 he wrote his first score for an American film, *The Longest Day*, which also featured a theme song written by **Paul Anka**. Later that year he had his first major international success with his score for

Lawrence of Arabia, the theme of which provided pianists Ferrante and Teicher with one of their many hits with film themes in 1963 on United Artists. Following his score for *Doctor Zhivago*, from which 'Lara's Theme' gave **Roger Williams** a hit in 1966, Jarre worked on numerous British and American films. Among his scores were those for *The Professionals* (1966), *Ryan's Daughter* (1970), *The Man Who Would Be King* (1975), *Winter Kills* (1979), *Witness* (1984) and *Mad Max: Beyond Thunderdome* (1985). In 1986 he recorded a selection of his film themes with the Royal Philharmonic Orchestra of London (Columbia). Later film work included the scores for *Fatal Attraction* (1987), *Dead Poets Society* (1989) and *Ghost* (1990).

He is the father of **Jean-Michel Jarre**.

AL JARREAU
b. 12 March 1940, Milwaukee, Wisconsin, USA

Jarreau was an outstanding jazz-influenced vocalist of the late seventies and eighties.

From a church-music background he formed the Indigoes vocal group while studying for a psychology degree, singing Hi-Los and **Lambert, Hendricks and Ross** arrangements and working with future jazz star **David Sanborn**. Moving to California in 1965, Jarreau performed with **George Duke** and the John Herd Trio. He formed a samba duo with guitarist Julio Martinez and made *We Got By*, his first album, for Warners in 1975. On the Tommy Lipuma-produced *Glow* (1976), Jarreau attempted individualistic versions of rock standards like **James Taylor**'s 'Fire and Rain' and **Elton John**'s 'Your Song'.

The live album *Look to the Rainbow* (1977) and *This Time* (1980) followed before Jarreau had a first hit single, 'We're in This Love Together' from *Breakin' Away* (1981). The album also included a vocal version of **Dave Brubeck**'s 'Blue Rondo à la Turk'; 'Mornin'', from 1983's *Trouble in Paradise*, was also a bestseller.

In 1984 he released the experimental *High Crime* and a further live album, *In London* (1985). By 1986 and his tenth album, *L Is for Lover*, Jarreau was moving towards the rock mainstream. The record was produced by **Nile Rodgers** and its title track composed by **Scritti Politti**'s Green Gartside. He had his biggest international hit in the same year when he recorded the theme song to the television series *Moonlightin'*. **George Duke** was the producer of *Heart's Horizon* (1988), which featured guitarist Earl Klugh.

He later contributed to albums by **Quincy Jones** and **Crusaders** member Joe Sample before recording *Tenderness* (1994). Produced by Marcus Miller, it included the standards 'Try a Little Tenderness' and 'Summertime'.

In 2000 Jarreau returned to the recording studio for the first time in six years for *Tomorrow Today* (GRP), which saw him luxuriating in the pop-jazz fusion he was so familiar with at a time when jazz (and pop) had moved on apace.

KEITH JARRETT
b. 8 May 1945, Allentown, Pennsylvania, USA

A virtuoso jazz pianist, Jarrett played with **Miles Davis** in the trumpeter's jazz-fusion period. He later concentrated on marathon acoustic piano recitals in which he drew freely on classical, rock and ethnic musics, as well as jazz.

Taking up piano as a small child, Jarrett toured at the age of sixteen with **Fred Waring**'s Pennsylvanians before briefly studying at the Berklee School of Music. Moving to New York, he played with **Art Blakey** and **Rahsaan Roland Kirk** before joining **Charles Lloyd**'s group in 1966. The flautist was at the height of his popularity with rock festival audiences and Jarrett played on the bestselling *Dream Weaver* (1966) and *Forest Flower* (1968).

The eclectic approach of the Lloyd recordings was carried over to the quartet formed by Jarrett in 1969. With **Charlie Haden** (bass), drummer Paul Motian and sax-player Dewey Redman he recorded *Backhand* (Impulse, 1969) and *Death and the Flower* (1970).

He next joined Davis to play on the controversial electric recordings *Live-Evil* and *Live at the Fillmore* (1970). Jarrett left Davis's group after only a year. He initially pursued a dual career, recording with his quartet *Expectations* (Columbia, 1972) and *Birth* (Atlantic, 1972), and in a change of direction signing to Manfred Eicher's German-based ECM in order to cut solo acoustic albums. The first of these was the highly influential *Facing You* (1971).

A compelling live performer, Jarrett released concert recordings, including the triple-album *Concerts Bremen and Lausanne* (1973) and *The Koln Concert*, which became a million-seller. He also collaborated with saxophonist Jan Garbarek (*Belonging*, 1975, and *My Song*, 1978) and composed neo-classical orchestral pieces which appeared on *In the Light* and *Arbour Zena* (1975).

In 1983 Jarrett formed a trio with drummer Jack de Johnette and Gary Peacock (bass). He toured with them into the nineties. The trio recorded *Changes* (1984) and *Standards*, which subjected such songs as **Vincent Youmans**' 'Stella by Starlight' and **Billie Holiday**'s 'God Bless the Child' to the Jarrett improvisational method. With Paul Motian replacing de Johnette, *Live at the Deer Head Inn* was a bestseller in 1994.

During the eighties Jarrett also made solo albums of jazz (*Dark Intervals*, 1987) and classical music (*Bach – Goldberg Variations*, 1989). In yet another approach,

Spirits (1986) was recorded in Jarrett's home studio with the artist playing a multiplicity of instruments including guitar, tabla, Pakistani flute and glockenspiel. In 1991 British musician and leader of **Nucleus**, Ian Carr, published a biography of Jarrett. The six-CD set, *Keith Jarrett at the Blue Note* (1994), collected together all trio recordings with bassist Gary Peacock and drummer Jack de Johnette to stunning effect.

JAY AND THE AMERICANS
Sandy Deane, b. Sandy Yaguda, 30 January 1943; Howie Kane, b. 6 June 1942; Marty Sanders, b. 28 February 1941; John Jay Traynor (replaced by David 'Jay' Black, b. 2 November 1941); Kenny Vance, b. 9 December 1943

In the opinion of one critic, 'a white and horribly gross version of the **Drifters**', vocal group Jay and the Americans had a series of hits throughout the sixties.

With Traynor as lead singer, the New York-based group were produced by **Leiber and Stoller** for United Artists in 1962. The title song from the album *She Cried* reached the Top Ten. Other tracks on the album included such Leiber–Stoller standards as **Ben E. King**'s 'Stand by Me' and the Drifters' 'Save the Last Dance for Me'.

Black, songwriting partner of guitarist Sanders, took over from Traynor for 'Only in America' (1963), a Leiber–Stoller composition originally written for the Drifters. The next hits, 'Come a Little Bit Closer' (1964) and the florid 'Cara Mia' (1965), were produced by **Wes Farrell**. To prove that anything could be processed through Black's bland, perfectly pitched singing, the group next recorded **Rodgers and Hammerstein**'s 'Some Enchanted Evening' and 'Sunday and Me', one of **Neil Diamond**'s first successful compositions.

Jeff Barry produced *Try Some of This* (1967), but Jay and the Americans' biggest hit was another Drifters' song, 'This Magic Moment'* (1969). After 'Walkin' in the Rain' reached the Top Twenty in 1970, the group's recording career was halted by a legal dispute with United Artists. However, they continued to perform during the early seventies, with Donald Fagen and Walter Becker of **Steely Dan** among their backing musicians. Both Vance and Black made solo albums for Atlantic in 1975, while Black appeared with **Frank Sinatra** in the 1977 telefilm *Contract on Cherry Street*.

During the seventies and eighties Black led the Americans at numerous 'oldies' concerts, climaxing in the twentieth anniversary of Richard Nader's pioneering revival shows in New York in 1989.

THE JAYHAWKS
Gary Louris; Mark Olson; Ken Callahan (replaced by Thad Spence in 1990, replaced by Tim O'Regan); Marc Perlman; Karen Grotberg; Kraig Johnson; Jesey Greene (replaced by Jen Gunderman)

Initially influenced by country as inflected by **Gram Parsons** and the **Louvin Brothers** rather than the **Eagles**, the Jayhawks by the nineties evolved into a more mainstream rock item with generic rather than specific country influences, in the manner of **Tom Petty**.

The group was formed in 1985 in Minneapolis, Minnesota, by folk/country writer Olson and bassist Perlman, with the addition of guitarist Louris from local rockabilly group Safety Last. In contrast to most other local groups who were under the influence of Hüsker Dü, from the start the Jayhawks toed a country line. Their eponymous self-produced album (Bunkhouse, 1986) won them comparisons with the Parsons-led Flying Burrito Brothers for its hard-edged country sense on tracks like 'The Liquor Store Came First' and 'Six Pack on the Dashboard'. Signed to Twin Tone records in 1989, a re-recorded version of that album, *Blue Earth*, won them further acclaim and a deal with Rick Rubin's American Recording label. Their first album for American was the hugely influential *Hollywood Town Hall* (1992), which included the **Neil Young**-influenced 'Waiting for the Sun' and cult favourite, the melancholic 'Two Angels', and won the group critical success for their fusion of rural and urban sounds. Following the arrival of Grotberg on keyboards, the group released the lusher *Tomorrow the Green Grass* (1994), which saw a mix of the enchanting ('Miss Williams' Guitar', a tribute to Olson's wife, singer-songwriter Victoria Williams) with the unexpected (a countrified version of fellow mid-Westerners **Grand Funk Railroad**'s 'Bad Time').

Tomorrow the Green Grass was a commercial success, but the change in direction led to Olson leaving the band to form the Original Harmony Ridge Creek Dippers with his wife and fiddler Mike Russell. That band issued a series of low-key country/folk albums in its own right (notably *Pacific Coast Rambler*, 1998) on its own Original Harmony Ridge Creek Dippers label, as well as a series of solo recordings by Williams, including the well-received *Musings of a Creekdipper* (1998).

In response to the departure of Olson the Jayhawks initially split, with individual members following solo projects, before in 1996 re-forming and releasing *The Sound of Lies* (1997). The first album written by Louris alone, it replaced the countrified sound of earlier efforts with a more mainstream rock sound and the more traditional subject of the break-up of a marriage (here Louris's). That album's 'Big Star', which echoed the **Byrds**' 'So You Want to Be a Rock and Roll Star', pointed to the group's wider acceptance of the rock mainstream. That move was completed with *Smile* (2000), which extended their influence to Petty (in the sombre 'What Led Me to This Town') and beyond in a number of guitar-driven tracks that, in the manner of later **Mary Chapin Carpenter**, saw the band trying to rock a tad too much.

JEFFERSON AIRPLANE

Signe Toly Anderson (replaced by Grace Slick, b. Grace Wing, 30 October 1939, Chicago, Illinois, USA); Marty Balin, b. Martyn Jerel Buchwald, 30 January 1942, Cincinnati, Ohio; Jack Casady, b. 13 April 1944, Washington DC (replaced by David Freiberg); Paul Kantner, b. 12 March 1942, San Francisco, California; Jorma Kaukonen, b. 23 December 1940, Washington DC (replaced by Craig Chaquico, b. 1955); Skip Spence (replaced by Spencer Dryden, b. 7 April 1943, New York, replaced by Joey Covington, replaced by John Barbata, replaced by Aynsley Dunbar, b. 1946, Liverpool, England, replaced by Don Baldwin); Papa John Creach, b. 28 May 1917, Beaver Falls, Pennsylvania, d. 22 February 1994; Mickey Thomas, b. 3 December 1949

Throughout their lengthy career, Jefferson Airplane remained one of the most adventurous and creative American rock bands. Founded in 1965 in San Francisco, the band mutated in 1974 into Jefferson Starship and bifurcated in 1985 into Starship and KBC.

The band was initially put together by dancer and folk singer Balin to perform folk-rock material at the Matrix, a club he ran with Bill Thompson, who was to become the group's manager. Singers Anderson and Kantner plus bassist Bob Harvey came from the folk scene, while Kaukonen was an electric guitarist who had performed with **Janis Joplin**. Drummer Spence had previously played guitar with local rock band **Quicksilver Messenger Service**. Casady, a Washington contact of Kaukonen, replaced Harvey as the band signed to RCA for the then high advance of $20,000. *Jefferson Airplane Takes Off* (1966) included Balin's 'Come up the Years' and 'It's No Secret'. Despite being subtitled 'The Jet Age Sound' it was a classic expression of folk psychedelia.

At this point, Spence left to form **Moby Grape**, Anderson left to have a baby and Slick from the Great Society joined Jefferson Airplane. Her powerful, raunchy voice and two songs she brought from her former band changed the band's music from the folky to the fully psychedelic. Both 'White Rabbit' (a retelling of the *Alice in Wonderland* theme) and 'Somebody to Love' were Top Ten hits and appeared on *Surrealistic Pillow** (1967), along with Balin's '3/5 of a Mile in Ten Seconds' with its hippie protest sentiment in which the singer wished to 'do away with people laughing at my hair'.

After Bathing at Baxters (1968) was an ambitious concept album which captured Jefferson Airplane's live sound on tracks like 'Won't You Try'/'Saturday Afternoon'. The title track of *Crown of Creation* (1968) was sung by Slick on the Smothers Brothers television show in black makeup and with clenched fist to show support for the black-power athletes at that year's Olympic Games. In terms of sound and songs, however, 1969 was the Airplane's peak. *Bless its Little Pointed Head* was the band's most musically accomplished album, with Dryden and Casady chopping the rhythm around behind Kaukonen's sitar-influenced guitar work. The album included **Donovan**'s 'Fat Angel' and, a nod to the group's folk roots, 'Other Side of this Life', a song by **Fred Neil**, who had been celebrated, with Winnie the Pooh, in 'Ballad of You and Me and Pooneil' on the *Baxters* album.

On *Volunteers*, Kantner's anthemic songs – notably 'We Can Be Together' – caught the era's mood of political utopianism, which he combined with science-fiction imagery on his solo album, *(It's a Fresh Wind That) Blows Against the Empire* (1970). With contributions from guest artists including David Crosby and Graham Nash from **Crosby, Stills and Nash**, the album was released as by Jefferson Starship and was nominated for a Hugo Award for sci-fi writing.

This was a period of chronic upheaval inside Jefferson Airplane. Mentally exhausted by the pressures of success, Balin left to pursue local projects in San Francisco, eventually recording *Bodacious DF* (RCA, 1974), while Dryden went to the New Riders of the Purple Sage. His replacement, Covington, was already playing with Kaukonen and Casady in their spare-time blues jamming band, Hot Tuna. Veteran black fiddle-player Creach also joined the group at this stage.

Perhaps perversely, much of Jefferson Airplane's energies in 1970–1 went not into musically integrating the new players, but into setting up their own label, Grunt. The first releases were more solo albums (by Creach and by Slick and Kantner, whose *Sunfighter* featured the **Edwin Hawkins Singers** on the title track), and *Bark*, one of the less-inspired group albums. *Long John Silver* (1972), however, included two of Slick's most scathing attacks on conventional wisdoms. 'Easter?' took Catholicism to task while 'Eat Starch, Mom?', did the same for health food fads.

But the band remained in the doldrums with more defections as Casady and Kaukonen left to work full-time as Hot Tuna, and ex-**Turtles** and Crosby Stills and Nash drummer Barbata and Quicksilver's singer, bass and keyboards-player Freiberg came in. With Creach also departing, the live *30 Seconds over Winterland* (1973) was the last Airplane album. Slick and Kantner meanwhile continued to turn out their own records. *Baron von Tollbooth and the Chrome Nun* (1973) was Crosby's nickname for the pair while *Manhole* (1974) was a Slick solo effort.

In 1974 the group was relaunched as Jefferson Starship. Without Kaukonen's originality, the sound was more conventional but more incisive and *Dragonfly* (1974) with ex-Steelwing guitarist Chaquico sold well. It also heralded the return of Balin who sang on one track but made a major contribution to *Red Octopus** (1975). His majestic ballad 'Miracles' was a No. 1 hit. *Spitfire** (1976) and *Earth** (1978) were also bestsellers, with the latter providing hit singles in 'Count on Me' and 'Runaway'.

The band reached another critical point with both Balin and Slick leaving, the latter to take a cure for alcoholism. Thomas (the singer on the 1976 Elvin Bishop hit 'Fooled Around and Fell in Love') was recruited to take lead vocals on *Freedom at Point Zero* (1981). After cutting two undistinguished solo albums, Slick sang backing vocals on *Modern Times* (1981) and took her customary leading role on *Winds of Change* (1982).

Nuclear Furniture (1984) turned out to be the swansong for the eighteen-year Kantner–Slick partnership. After legal action, Kantner received a $250,000 payoff while Slick retained the name Starship. With Thomas, Chaquico, Pete Sears (bass) and Denny Baldwin (drums), she recorded *Knee Deep in the Hoopla* (RCA, 1985). Produced by ex-**J. Geils Band** singer Peter Wolf, it included the No. 1 hit 'We Built This City on Rock'n'Roll'. With lyrics by Bernie Taupin, the song was a blast against the San Francisco administration, which had proposed to ban open-air concerts. In 1986 Kantner, Balin and Casady formed the KBC Band, releasing an eponymous album later that year.

In 1987 Starship scored their biggest hit with 'Nothin''s Gonna Stop Us Now' from the film *Mannequin*. The band followed it with the successful album *No Protection* (1987), but in a surprise volte-face in 1988 Slick and Kantner made up, re-forming Jefferson Airplane with Kaukonen and Casady. They released an eponymous album on Epic in 1989, but the reunion was brief, and the members returned to their own projects in 1990, after a critically savaged American tour. Starship returned to the charts in 1989 with 'It's Not Enough', from *Love Among the Cannibals* (1990), whose title track was an attack on Slick and Kantner by Thomas. By now Starship had none of its original Jefferson-era members. In 1992 Kantner, Casady and Creach joined forces once again, forming Jefferson Starship the Next Generation. Having recently released a solo album, *Better Generation*, Balin also joined in 1993. That line-up was responsible for *Deep Space/Virgin Sky* (1995). The compilation album *2400 Fulton Street* (RCA, 1987) documents Jefferson Airplane's early career.

BLIND LEMON JEFFERSON
b. July 1897, Couchman, Texas, USA, d. December 1929, Chicago, Illinois

Though not the first male blues singer to make records, Jefferson was the first to impose a significant amount of his own vocal and guitar style, and repertoire, upon the country-blues tradition. His extraordinary rhythmic powers, expressed in a high-pitched and freely moving vocal line, interspersed with unpredictably timed passages of solo guitar, not only distinguished his approach sharply from the firm duple rhythms of Mississippi contemporaries like **Charley Patton** but pointed the way, via **T-Bone Walker**, to the West Coast blues forms of later generations.

Jefferson began to travel in East Texas as a blind street-singer from his teens, and after the Second World War went farther afield; musicians in almost every part of the South report his passing through at some time in the twenties. In late 1925 or early 1926 he began recording for Paramount in Chicago, and reached an enormous audience with his second release, 'Got the Blues'/'Long Lonesome Blues'. Later recordings of special note include 'That Black Snake Moan' (Paramount, 1926; Okeh, 1927); 'Match Box Blues' (Paramount and Okeh, 1927), which has been recycled by black and white musicians, both before and since the well-known version by **Carl Perkins**; 'See That My Grave's Kept Clean' (Paramount, 1927 and 1928), recorded by **Bob Dylan** on his 1962 début album; and 'One Dime Blues' (Paramount, 1927). By his last sessions in 1929, however, he was largely repeating his own trademark phrases. He is believed to have had a heart attack and died on the streets of Chicago from exposure.

Many Southwestern singers and guitarists incorporated elements of Jefferson's work into their own, among them **Leadbelly**, **Lightnin' Hopkins**, **Mance Lipscomb** and Robert Pete Williams, a striking singer-guitarist first recorded when an inmate of the State Prison Farm at Angola, Louisiana. **B. B. King** has also spoken of his inheritance from Jefferson. Outside blues circles his influence has been by way of his repertoire rather than his style – even the white specialists in country-blues guitar have seldom taken him on – though his name has also been kept aloft (perhaps inadvertently) by **Jefferson Airplane**.

GORDON JENKINS
b. 12 May 1910, Webster Groves, Missouri, USA, d. 1 May 1984

As an arranger known for his lush orchestrations, and a musical director with Decca and then Capitol, Jenkins was an influential figure in popular music in the forties and fifties.

A multi-instrumentalist, Jenkins did arrangements for a St Louis radio station before being hired by **Isham Jones** as an arranger and pianist in the thirties. Jones' band, a sweet, rather than jazz, dance band, was known for its ensemble playing and gave Jenkins the opportunity to develop his technical skill and flair for melodic scoring on such tracks as the band's RCA Victor recording of his and Joe Bishop's 'Blue Prelude' (1932). On the band's break-up in 1936, Jenkins worked as a freelance arranger and songwriter (he was the author of the 1944 hit 'San Fernando Valley') and established his own orchestra and chorus before joining Decca in 1945.

In 1947 he had a million-seller with 'Maybe You'll Be There' and in 1949 had a huge hit with **Victor Young**'s film theme 'My Foolish Heart', which was also a success for **Billy Eckstine**. At the same time he regularly arranged for and conducted the orchestra for various Decca artists. These included **Dick Haymes** ('Little White Lies'*, 1947) and Patti Andrews of the **Andrews Sisters** ('I Can Dream, Can't I'*, 1949). Even more significantly, in 1949, by now musical director at Decca, Jenkins (who with his chorus had recorded several folky songs) was responsible for signing the **Weavers** (who were also sought by Columbia's **Mitch Miller**) against opposition from Dave Kapp. Their hits together included **Leadbelly**'s 'Goodnight Irene'* (1950), which was backed by Jenkins' own adaptation of the Israeli folk song, 'Tzena, Tzena, Tzena', 'The Roving Kind', 'On Top of Old Smokey' (1951), and the oft-recorded 'Wimoweh' (1952).

Moving to Capitol, Jenkins worked frequently with **Frank Sinatra** (notably on the 1959 album *No One Cares*) and **Nat 'King' Cole**, with whom he had his greatest successes. He was responsible for the lush arrangement of 'When I Fall in Love' (1957), one of Cole's best-known recordings, and the albums *Love Is the Thing* (1957) and *The Very Thought of You* (1958).

Jenkins later arranged Sinatra's *September of My Years* (1967) and his comeback album, *Ol' Blue Eyes Is Back* (1973). He also worked with **Nilsson** on *A Little Touch of Schmilsson in the Night*.

Jenkins was also a composer and songwriter. Among his compositions are 'Goodbye' (**Benny Goodman**'s signing-off tune), 'Blue Prelude', 'When a Woman Loves a Man' and 'Future', composed for Sinatra's 1979 concept album *Trilogy*.

WAYLON JENNINGS
b. 15 June 1937, Littlefield, Texas, USA

Part of the 'new Nashville', singer and writer Waylon Jennings championed songwriters like **Kris Kristofferson** and Billy Joe Shaver and, in collaboration with **Willie Nelson** and Tompall Glaser of **Tompall and the Glaser Brothers**, created the 'outlaw' strand of country music in the seventies.

From a musical family, Jennings was performing over radio station KDOV at the age of twelve. He became a disc-jockey in nearby Lubbock in 1955 and three years later **Buddy Holly** produced his first single, Harry Choates' cajun anthem 'Jole Blon' (Brunswick) with **King Curtis** on saxophone. Jennings played bass with Holly on the latter's final tour, giving up his plane seat to the Big Bopper on the night Holly died.

Shaken by the tragedy, Jennings returned to Lubbock to work as a dee-jay and singer, recording for local label Trend. In the early sixties he moved to Phoenix where he recorded an album for Ramco before signing to A&M where **Herb Alpert** tried to mould him into a pop-folk singer with material like **Tim Hardin**'s 'If I Were a Carpenter' and **Ian and Sylvia**'s 'Four Strong Winds'.

Bobby Bare encouraged **Chet Atkins** to record Jennings for RCA in a similar vein on *Folk Country* (1965), the first of thirty albums for the label. For the rest of the sixties he cut a variety of pop and standard country songs for RCA, scoring regular hits in the country charts. In 1966 he prefigured his later outlaw role by writing the music for and starring in the film *Nashville Rebel*. Among the outstanding albums from this period were *Waylon Jennings Sings Ol' Harlan* (1966), a selection of material by **Harlan Howard** which included 'Green River' and 'Heartaches by the Number', and *Love of the Common People* (1967), whose title track was a 1973 British hit for reggae singer Nicky Thomas. Jennings also recorded songs by **Lennon–McCartney** ('Norwegian Wood'), **John Hartford** ('Gentle on My Mind') and **Jimmy Webb**, whose 'MacArthur Park' was a minor pop hit for him in 1969.

His recorded repertoire expanded to include 'Sunday Morning Coming Down' and three other songs by the then unknown Kristofferson on *The Taker* (1970). *Ladies Love Outlaws* (1971) featured **Hoyt Axton**'s 'Never Been to Spain' and Alex Harvey's 'Delta Dawn', later a hit for **Tanya Tucker**. Then, in 1972, Jennings took full control of his recording career. With a New York manager, Neil Reshen, he negotiated a production deal virtually unprecedented in Nashville. The changes were immediate. Instead of Nashville session pickers, Jennings' touring band, the Waylors (featuring drummer Ritchie Allbright and steel-guitarist Ralph Mooney) played on *Honky Tonk Heroes* (1973). With a bass-driven sound derived from both honky-tonk music and rock, Jennings' passionate baritone delivered a set of Shaver's 'modern cowboy' songs. They included 'Willie the Wandering Gypsy and Me', a fulsome tribute to Nelson who, with producer Glaser and Jennings' wife Jessi Colter, featured on the 1976 *Outlaws** album, which reached the Top Ten of the pop charts and included a minor pop hit in the Colter–Jennings duet, 'Suspicious Minds'. *Ol' Waylon** (1977) was equally successful.

Despite a tendency to overemphasis in the projection of the outlaw image (wryly acknowledged by Jennings in 'Don't You Think This Outlaw Bit's Done Got out of Hand' on 1978's *I've Always Been Crazy*), Jennings had an unbroken series of major country hits over the next decade. They included duets with Nelson (*Waylon and Willie**, 1978) and with **Johnny Cash** ('There Ain't No Good Chain Gang', 1978); the teleseries theme 'The Dukes of Hazzard'* (also a pop hit); and a revival of **Little Richard**'s 'Lucille' from a 1983 fifties tribute album *It's Only Rock'n'Roll*. In that year, Jennings followed the current trend for duet records with *Waylon and Company*, on which his vocal partners included **Jerry Reed**, **Ernest Tubb**, Mel Tillis, **Emmylou Harris** and actor James Garner.

With Nelson, Cash and Kristofferson, Jennings made the concept album *Highwayman* (Columbia, 1985). *Turn the Page* (1985), with a **Bob Seger** title track and a version of **Fleetwood Mac**'s 'Rhiannon', was his final album for RCA. The following year he signed to MCA and released the superior *Will the Wolf Survive?* and followed it with *Hangin' Tough* (1987) and *Full Circle* (1988). After heart-surgery in 1988 he returned to recording with *The Eagle* (Epic, 1990) and a second Highwaymen album (*Highwayman 2*, 1990). He released *Clean Shirt* (1991) with Nelson and *Too Dumb for New York City – Too Ugly for LA* (1992) before returning to RCA to record a new album with producer **Don Was**. RCA also issued a two-CD retrospective set, *Only Daddy That'll Walk the Line*, in 1993. The superior outing *Right for the Time* (Justice, 1996) saw Jennings in fine voice meditating on the changes that had taken place in country music. In 1998 Jennings returned to the charts as a member of Old Dogs, a quartet comprising himself, **Mel Tillis**, Bobby Bare and **Jerry Reed**, with an eponymous album (Atlantic).

GEORGE JESSEL
b. George Albert Jessel, 3 April 1898, New York, USA, d. 23 May 1981, Los Angeles, California

Songwriter, actor, singer and producer, Jessel created the title role of *The Jazz Singer* in 1925 and appeared in over 1,000 performances on Broadway, only to lose the part to **Al Jolson** when Warners filmed the play in 1927.

The son of a failed playwright, Jessel began singing professionally in 1907. After touring for two years as a member of the Imperial Trio (with Walter Winchell, later to become famous as a newspaper columnist),

Jessel was teamed by songwriter and producer Gus Edwards with **Eddie Cantor** for *Kid Kabaret* and the pair played the vaudeville circuit until 1915. Jessel then travelled to England, and on his return to America in 1917 switched from singing to comedy with an act derived in part from the 'Cohen on the Telephone' monologues popularized by **Joe Hayman**. His opening line, 'Hello Momma', later gave him the title of his 1946 autobiography.

During this period Jessel also starred in several movies, most of which had a strong Jewish flavour. Among them were *Private Izzy Murphy* (1926), *Ginsberg the Great* (1927) and *George Washington Cohen* (1928). He also appeared in several revues, including *The Schubert Gaieties* (1919) and *The Passing Show* (1923), but his greatest success was with Samson Ralphaelson's non-musical play *The Jazz Singer*, about a cantor's son who can't give up the theatre. Though Jessel had made a couple of short sound films for Warners, when Warners filmed the play Jolson got the part because Jessel demanded too much money.

In the thirties Jessel divided his time between radio, nightclubs and Broadway, often writing and producing his shows (including *High Kickers*, 1941), before retiring from the stage in 1943. He moved to Hollywood where between 1945 and 1953 he worked as a producer for Fox. His films, mostly turn-of-the-century musicals, included *I Wonder Who's Kissing Her Now* (1947), which was loosely based on the life of composer Joe Howard; *Oh You Beautiful Doll* (1949), which gave Jessel his most substantial (and *Jazz Singer*-like) role, as a serious composer who finds fortune and fame in Tin Pan Alley; and *Tonight We Sing* (1953). At the same time he wrote numerous songs with composer Ben Oakland.

In the fifties he regularly appeared on television and in nightclubs, but devoted most of his time to charitable work. He was known as 'America's Toastmaster General' and in 1970 was awarded a special Oscar for his humanitarian efforts.

THE JESUS AND MARY CHAIN
James Reid, b. 1961, East Kilbride, Scotland; William Reid, b. 1958, East Kilbride; Douglas Hart; Murray Dalglish (replaced by Bobby Gillespie, b. 1964, Scotland); Richard Thomas; Ben Laurie; Matthew Parkin; Barry Blacker

One of Britain's more durable and influential postpunk bands, the Jesus and Mary Chain have maintained an admirable ability to simultaneously delight young audiences and outrage broadcasters and moralists on both sides of the Atlantic.

The Reid brothers' first music-making was done with the aid of a portastudio bought by their father from a redundancy payment. With Jim on vocals,

William on guitar and bassist Hart they recorded a demo tape in 1983 which evidenced their obsession with sixties psychedelia and garage band music. The tape was heard by Bobby Gillespie of **Primal Scream** and his enthusiasm helped to get the Jesus and Mary Chain a live booking in Glasgow.

This brought a recording contract with the independent Creation label and the first single 'Upside Down' (recorded with drummer Dalglish) was issued in 1984. With Gillespie sometimes sitting in on drums, the Jesus and Mary Chain played a series of controversial college gigs around Britain, sometimes performing only two songs and frequently provoking disorder.

The group's reputation as post-punk originals was consolidated by *Psychocandy* (1985), which reached the UK Top Forty. Despite (or because of) accusations of drug references, 'Some Candy Talking' was a Top Twenty hit in 1986. The next year the group, now reduced to the Reid brothers only, issued *Darklands*. With William singing lead on some tracks, the album was a Top Ten hit in Britain.

After the release of *Barbed Wire Kisses* (1988), a collection of out-takes and B-sides including 'Bo Diddley is Jesus', the group issued a new studio album, *Automatic*. It was once again a big UK hit but US success continued to elude them despite their undertaking a lengthy American tour in 1990 and joining the Lollapalooza II package tour of alternative bands in 1992.

By this point the Reids were supported by Laurie (guitar), Parkin (bass) and drummer Blacker on *Honey's Dead* (1992), the first album under a new contract with **Rick Rubin**'s Def Jam label. The band entered the headlines again when they were banned from performing their hit single 'Reverence' on *Top of the Tops* because it began with the line 'I wanna die just like Jesus Christ'. *The Sound of Speed* became the Jesus and Mary Chain's fourth UK Top Twenty album in 1993. The following year's *Stoned and Dethroned* was something of a departure for the band, taking a gentle acoustic tone and featuring their only US hit single, 'Sometimes Always', a duet with Mazzy Star's Hope Sandoval. *The Jesus and Mary Chain Hate Rock'n'Roll* was a collection of A-sides, including the newly recorded title track, which involved a temporary return to their raucous early material.

Returning to Creation Records in 1998 the group issued *Munki* (1998), which spawned a UK Top Ten single, 'Cracking Up'. The album proved to be the band's swansong, as the Reid brothers began working separately after fighting onstage in Los Angeles. Jim has since launched his new band, TV.69, while William's *Taster* (1999) offered a sampler of a variety of new projects, including Lazycame, who issued their début single, 'Finbegin', the following year.

JETHRO TULL

Ian Anderson, b. 10 August 1947, Edinburgh, Scotland; Mick Abrahams, b. 7 April 1943, Luton, Bedfordshire, England (replaced by Martin Barre, b. 17 November 1946); Clive Bunker, b. 12 December 1946 (replaced by Barrymore Barlow, b. 10 September 1949, replaced by Doane Perry); Glenn Cornick, b. 24 April 1947, Barrow-in-Furness, Cumbria (replaced by Jeffrey Hammond-Hammond, b. 30 July 1946, replaced by John Glascock, b. 1951, d. 17 November 1979, London, replaced by Dave Pegg, b. 2 November 1947, Birmingham); John Evan, b. 28 March 1948; David Palmer; Peter John Vettese; Martin Allcock

One of the most successful progressive rock bands of the seventies, Jethro Tull was for the most part a vehicle for the musical ideas and extravagant stagecraft of the intermittently brilliant Anderson.

Anderson formed his first bands – Blades and John Evan Smash, which featured Evan (keyboards), Hammond-Hammond (bass) and Barlow (drums) – in the resort town of Blackpool. In 1968 they made an unsuccessful attempt to break into the London blues scene, and split up. Anderson went on to form Jethro Tull (named after the eighteenth-century inventor of the seed drill) with Cornick (bass), Abrahams (guitar) and Bunker (drums). They recorded 'Sunshine Day' (MGM) before attracting attention through their performance at the Sunbury Festival. The band's managers, Chris Wright and Terry Ellis, signed them to Island for *This Was*, which featured Abrahams' blues-soaked solos on tracks like 'Cat Squirrel' and Anderson's folky flute on 'Serenade to a Cuckoo'.

The incongruity between the two styles led to the secession of Abrahams to set up Blodwyn Pig and later the Mick Abrahams Band. Barre joined for the haunting, nostalgic hit single 'Living in the Past' (1969) and an American tour which made *Stand Up* (1969) a minor hit in the United States (it reached No. 1 in Britain). The next single, 'Sweet Dream', was issued on Chrysalis, the label set up by Tull's management, and 'The Witch's Promise' (1970) was a Top Ten hit. Meanwhile, Anderson was gradually rejoined by his Blackpool colleagues. Evan returned for *Benefit* (1970) and Barlow and Hammond-Hammond also rejoined the band a year later. Bunker went on to form Jude with Robin Trower and Frankie Miller, while Cornick set up Wild Turkey and in 1976 joined Paris with ex-**Fleetwood Mac** guitarist Bob Welch.

With Anderson's manic stage presence (playing flute on one leg), Jethro Tull were a leading live band all over the world in the early seventies. *Aqualung* (1971) was the high point of this part of the group's career, with its anti-religious themes causing controversy. *Thick as a Brick* (1972), a concept album featuring the life of 'Gerald Bostock', an Anderson *alter ego*, reached No. 1 in America, and enabled a reissued 'Living in the Past' to become a hit there. An even more ambitious project, the multi-media show *A Passion Play*, was savaged by the critics for the pretentiousness of the concept (life after death) and the obscurity of the lyrics. Although the album still sold well, an outraged Anderson threatened not to tour again.

The 1974 album *War Child** was conceived as a film soundtrack and included a string section with arrangements by David Palmer. It included their last major American hit 'Bungle in the Jungle'. The undistinguished *Minstrel in the Gallery* (1975), which featured Anderson in a favourite role as a medieval troubadour, was the prelude to the most mismanaged of his ambitious projects. With Palmer now a permanent member of Jethro Tull, *Too Old to Rock'n'Roll, Too Young to Die* (1976) was intended as a stage musical on the hackneyed theme of an old rocker who eventually found himself a trendsetter. Emblazoned with a strip cartoon featuring an Anderson-like hero, the album found little favour with public or critics.

Jethro Tull's career revived with a turn to folk-rock on *Songs from the Wood* (1977). Perhaps inspired by his production work on **Steeleye Span**'s *Now We Are Six*, Anderson composed a set of songs like the minor hits 'Ring out Solstice Bells' and 'The Whistler', which balanced the rustic and the electric. Touring to support the album, however, his stage act was punctuated with verbal attacks on reviewers and an apparent nervousness in the face of the rise of punk.

By now Glascock had joined Jethro Tull on bass and vocals. *Heavy Horses* (1978) and *Stormwatch* (1979) completed a trilogy of folk-inspired albums. *A*, with **Fairport Convention**'s Pegg (who had stepped in when Glascock died after heart surgery) and Eddie Jobson (former keyboards player with **Roxy Music** and **Frank Zappa**), had been planned as a solo album. However, Chrysalis persuaded Anderson that it should be issued as a Jethro Tull record.

Broadsword and the Beast (1982) brought in producer Paul Samwell-Smith and keyboards-player Vettese, who also co-wrote material for *Walk into Light* (1983), the synthesizer-dominated album which was released under Anderson's name. With new drummer Perry, *Under Wraps* was issued in 1984. The following year Anderson developed a serious throat infection while touring America, curtailing his activity, although members of the band appeared on *A Classic Case – the Music of Jethro Tull* (RCA), with arrangements of the band's material conducted by Palmer.

Crest of a Knave (1987) was unexpectedly given a Grammy award as 'best heavy metal album'. *Rock Island* was released in 1989. Far better was the folk-inflected *Catfish Rising* (1991), which demonstrated the input of Fairport Convention members Dave Pegg (bass) and Martin Allcock (keyboards), who were

now also part of Jethro Tull. The acoustic live album *A Little Light Music* followed in 1992, and in 1993 the band released two career retrospectives, *25th Anniversary* and *The Other Box Set*, both containing a large number of previously unreleased tracks. New albums included *Roots to Branches* (1995), while band members Allcock and Anderson continued their solo careers. Allcock's *OX15* (New Day Records, 2000) included an ambitious reworking of the **Allman Brothers**' classic 'Jessica' as well as collaboration with Anderson ('Whenever We See the Dark') which sounded more Jethro Tull than the group themselves. Surprisingly successful was Anderson's acoustic *The Secret Language of Birds* (Papillon, 2000) which, despite its arch title and liner notes, was affecting in its observations.

JOAN JETT
b. 22 September 1960, Philadelphia, Pennsylvania, USA

Similar in style and image to **Suzi Quatro**, but threatening rather than playful, Jett found international success in the eighties, combining a pouting, rebellious tomboy image with heavy rock.

Educated in Hollywood, Jett was a founder member of the Runaways in 1975 with Sandy West, Cherie Currie, Lita Ford and Jackie Fox. Promoted by **Kim Fowley** as fallen angels in tight blue jeans playing hard rock, the Runaways, despite the enormous publicity their image garnered them, sold few records outside Japan. Their albums included *Queens of Noise* and *Waitin' for the Night* (Mercury, 1977). The band folded in 1979 when Jett, who had become its leader, quit after the heavy-metal onslaught of *And Now the Runaways!*. However, after her role in *We're All Crazy Now* (1979), an unreleased film loosely based on the group's career, with the other members played by actresses, Jett's career seemed in decline.

While working on the film, Jett met Kenny Laguna (producer of **Jonathan Richman**, among others) and Ritchie Cordell (writer of 'I Think We're Alone Now', 1967, and 'Mony, Mony', 1968, both hits for **Tommy James and the Shondells**). They co-produced Jett's solo album *Bad Reputation* (Boardwalk, 1981), which included three tracks recorded with ex-**Sex Pistols** Steve Jones and Paul Cook. That album did not sell but a year of touring with her backing group the Blackhearts turned *I Love Rock'n'Roll* (1982) into a huge hit. It spawned a million-selling title song and contained her remake of Tommy James and the Shondells' 1969 hit 'Crimson and Clover' and **Gary Glitter**'s 1973 hit 'Do You Want to Touch Me (Oh Yeah)'. This formed the prototype for British model turned rocker Samantha Fox's string of titillating hits which including 'Touch Me (I Want Your Body)' (Jive, 1986).

Jett's later hits included 'Fake Friends' and 'Every-day People' (1983). Ex-Runaway Ford re-emerged in the late eighties as a heavy metal guitarist/singer with a series of albums, including *Dancin' on the Edge* (1986), *Lita* (1988) and *Dangerous Curves* (1991). In 1986 Micki Steele, another former Runaway, reappeared (as Michael Steele) in the **Bangles**, who had international hits with 'Manic Monday', 'Walk Like an Egyptian' (Columbia, 1986) and 'Eternal Flame' (1989). Jett returned to acting in Paul Schrader's rock'n'roll film *Light of Day* (1987). Her 1990 album *Hit List* consisted entirely of cover-versions of the likes of **ZZ Top**'s 'Tush', the Sex Pistols' 'Pretty Vacant' and the Chambers Brothers' 'Time Has Come Today'. Though hardly reinterpretations of the songs, they were recorded with more verve than the *Notorious* (1991) set. Now signed to WEA, Jett released *Pure and Simple* in 1994. On it she collaborated with various members of female indie/rock bands L7, Babes in Toyland and Bikini Kill. The compilation *Fit to Be Tied* (1997) collects together most of her solo recordings.

JEWEL
b. Jewel Kilcher, 23 May 1974, Payson, Utah, USA

A folk-influenced singer-songwriter, Jewel sold over 10 million copies of her 1995 début to become one of the most successful female performers of the decade.

Jewel grew up in the rural town of Homer, Alaska, with her Swiss parents Atz and Nedra (who released two albums in the seventies). She often sang with them and began to perform alone at the age of six. After graduating from the Interlochen Fine Arts Academy in Michigan, Jewel spent a year living with her mother in San Diego before quitting her job and deciding to live in the back of her Volkswagen van. Continuing to play in small local venues, her song-writing ability and versatile vocal style started to attract a devoted following and in 1993 Jewel signed with Atlantic Records.

Jewel's début album was partly recorded at **Neil Young**'s home studio, with the rest of the album taped at the Innerchange, a Pacific Beach venue where she played regularly in the early nineties. *Pieces of You** sold poorly on its release in 1995 until the success of the singles 'Who Will Save Your Soul?' and 'You Were Meant for Me' sent it climbing up the US chart the following year. The album went on to sell 10 million copies worldwide as Jewel won Best New Artist at the American Music Awards.

After three years on the road, during which time she also contributed a version of 'You Make Loving Fun' to the **Fleetwood Mac** tribute album *Legacy* (1998) and published a collection of her poetry, *A Night without Armour* (1998), Jewel returned with the acclaimed *Spirit* (1999). In 1999 she also made her first

film, the well-received Civil War drama *Ride with the Devil*.

FLACO JIMENEZ
b. 11 March 1939, San Antonio, Texas, USA

The leading Tex-Mex accordionist, Jimenez came to international notice largely through his membership of **Ry Cooder**'s Chicken Skin Revue.

His father Santiago Jimenez – also nicknamed 'El Flaco' ('the skinny one') – was one of the foremost Tex-Mex accordionists and recording artists of the thirties and forties, developing, with fellow players such as Narciso Martinez, a driving music for bars and dance-halls. Called *conjunto* music (from the Spanish word for 'group'), it is typically fronted by an accordionist and filled out with *bajo sexto* (a form of twelve-string guitar), guitar(s), bass and drums. The repertoire consists of polkas (especially), *rancheras*, waltzes and occasional *huapangos* and mazurkas; songs (*canciones*) are usually sung in two-part harmony, and almost always in Spanish.

Inheriting this tradition, Flaco Jimenez enhanced it with both skill and flamboyance. For many years he was based in San Antonio, known only to Border audiences and recording exclusively for local labels. He became known among aficionados of American vernacular music through albums for Chris Strachwitz's Arhoolie label. The compilation *Flaco's First* (Arhoolie, 1995) details his mid-fifties recordings. He subsequently found fame through his association in the early and mid-seventies first with **Doug Sahm**, then Cooder, touring with the latter and playing on *Chicken Skin Music* and *Show Time*. He also appeared in Les Blank's documentary on Tex-Mex culture, *Chulas Fronteras*. Thereafter he frequently worked in Europe, recording for, among others, Sonet (*Tex-Mex Breakdown*, 1983, produced by Sahm and Augie Meyers) and the English independent Waterfront (*San Antonio Sound*, 1985), partnered on the latter, as often on tour, by American singer/guitarist/mandola-player and ex-**Bill Monroe** sideman Peter Rowan.

He subsequently made three albums with **Doug Sahm**, **Freddy Fender** and Augie Meyers as the Texas Tornados (*Texas Tornados*, 1990, *Zone of Our Own*, 1991, and *Hangin' on by a Thread*, 1992) continuing his solo career with *Ay Te Deju en San Antonio* (1991). The superior follow-up, *Partners* (1992), was an album of duets with an all-star cast which included Cooder, **Los Lobos**, **John Hiatt** and **Emmylou Harris**.

Flaco's younger brother Santiago Jimenez Jnr is also a respected singer/accordionist who has recorded for local labels and for Arhoolie. Outside the family, Flaco's chief rival is Esteban (Steve) Jordan, an imposing personality whose musical tastes stretch beyond Flaco's moderate traditionalism: he uses a phase shifter and synthesizers, and his repertoire incorporates other Latin-American forms, from South America and Cuba, as well as jazz and country music. (He had a local hit with a Spanish version of **Ray Charles**' 'Georgia on My Mind'.) Jordan was confined to a purely regional recording status, appearing on labels like Falcon, Freddie, Hacienda and his own El Parche, until he signed with RCA International in 1985 to make *My Toot Toot* (1985) and *Turn Me Loose* (1986). He appeared in **Talking Heads**' David Byrne's movie *True Stories* (1985).

JIVE BUNNY

The Jive Bunny character – a crudely drawn cartoon rabbit – was created to 'front' a string of UK hit singles during 1989–91 which followed the mastermix format patented by Dutch producer Jaap Eggermont in the early eighties. Session musicians were used to duplicate hits of the past which were then stitched together to a relentless disco backbeat.

Eggermont's formula had enjoyed worldwide success in the early eighties under the banner Stars on 45 (the 'artist' was Starsound), copying **Beatles** songs, **Stevie Wonder** songs and other hits of the sixties, and spawned a host of imitators. The novelty seemed to have worn off as the end of the decade approached, although there was still a demand from club DJs in the UK for 'mastermix' segued tracks.

In 1989 John Pickles, an electrical retailer in Doncaster, Yorkshire, who had been involved in the music business as an unsuccessful songwriter and advertising-jingles producer for several years, launched the first Jive Bunny single, 'Swing the Mood', as such a DJ-only 'mastermix'. The tracks had been created by local DJ Les Hemstock using excerpts from tracks by **Bill Haley**, **Little Richard**, **Glenn Miller**, **Elvis Presley** and the **Everly Brothers**. Copyright problems associated with commercial distribution of 'Swing the Mood' obliged Pickles to re-record much of the material using soundalikes. The Glenn Miller parts were recorded by the Belfast-based John Anderson Big Band.

When the single was released on Pickles's Music Factory label in June 1989, it was an immediate success, and climbed to the No. 1 slot in the UK. The next two singles, 'That's What I Like' and 'Let's Party', followed the same formula and also topped the UK chart that year, putting the Pickles imaginary quadruped on a par with **Gerry and the Pacemakers** and **Frankie Goes to Hollywood** as the only acts to have their first three singles reach No. 1 in the UK. *Jive Bunny – The Album* was issued and plans were announced for a series of books based on the Jive Bunny character with interest also being shown in an animated TV series.

After the success of 'That Sounds Good to Me' (1990) and 'Can Can You Party?' (1990), subsequent singles sold increasingly poorly. By the nineties Jive Bunny had joined the Smurfs and Wombles in the museum of cartoon and animal novelty acts.

ANTONIO CARLOS JOBIM
b. 1927, Rio de Janeiro, Brazil, d. 8 December 1994, New York City, USA

A prolific Brazilian composer of more than 300 tunes, Jobim was one of the founders of the bossa nova movement, writing such tunes as 'Desafinado' and 'Girl from Ipanema', both million-sellers in America.

Of French descent, Jobim's earliest influence was the big-band jazz of **Duke Ellington**, **Tommy Dorsey**, **Count Basie** and **Woody Herman**. His first major success came with the score for *Black Orpheus* (1958). Bossa nova ('new bump') was an attempt to combine the traditional samba dance rhythms with the cool jazz of **Gerry Mulligan** or Herbie Mann and was developed in the late fifties by Jobim, Joao Gilberto and others. The new music used staccato rhythms and breathy intimate vocals from singers like Astrud Gilberto and Elis Regina.

The bossa nova became an American craze after guitarist Charlie Byrd heard it during a tour of Brazil in 1961. His hit instrumental version with saxophonist **Stan Getz** of Jobim's 'Desafinado' (Verve, 1962) led to such 1963 novelty hits as Eydie Gorme's 'Blame It on the Bossa Nova' and **Elvis Presley**'s 'Bossa Nova Baby'. Byrd and Getz's *Jazz Samba* (1962) was also a bestseller and contained another Jobim tune, 'One Note Samba'.

Getz–Gilberto (1964) included 'Girl from Ipanema', composed by Jobim and Vinicuis de Moraes and sung by Astrud Gilberto. Her high-pitched vocals and Getz's gushing obbligatos made it an international hit. Other Jobim tunes which were widely performed in America included 'How Insensitive', 'Wave', 'Meditation' and 'Quiet Night of Quiet Stars'. Among those who recorded his music were **Ella Fitzgerald**, **Frank Sinatra**, **Dizzy Gillespie** and Gerry Mulligan. The bossa nova rhythm was used by Brazilian pianist Sergio Mendes on a long series of instrumental records of pop hits for A&M.

Jobim also made occasional recordings; these included *Elis and Tom* (Philips, 1974) with Elis Regina and *Um Homem de Aquarius* (Philips, 1980).

BILLY JOEL
b. 9 May 1949, Bronx, New York, USA

One of the most successful performers of the eighties and nineties, Joel combined the qualities of **Elton John** and **Bruce Springsteen**. Like Elton John, he was a showman who could draw on a range of past rock styles; while he shared with Springsteen that American rebel/youth/macho stance which can trace its lineage to **Presley** and James Dean and which, for many critics, is the essence of the 'rock tradition'.

Joel grew up in Hicksville, Long Island, and studied classical piano before joining his first rock band in 1964. His first records were with the Hassles for United Artists in 1968, work he later described as 'psychedelic bullshit'. As one-half of Attila, he cut an equally undistinguished album for Epic (1970). Next, Joel signed as a solo artist with Artie Ripp's Family Productions, who placed him with Gulf and Western's Famous label. The one resulting album, *Cold Spring Harbor* (1972, released by Philips in 1974 in the UK), revealed a genuine but still developing singer-songwriting talent.

The commercial failure of that album led Joel to move to the West Coast, where he played in bars under the name Bill Martin. That experience formed the basis for 'Piano Man', the title song of his first album for Columbia, for whom he signed in 1973. That gold album was followed by the less effective *Streetlife Serenade* (1974) which, like its predecessor, was produced in Hollywood by Michael Stewart.

Moving back to New York, Joel made *Turnstiles* (1976), which betrayed a wide variety of pop influences, including the **Phil Spector** sound on 'Say Goodbye to Hollywood', a song recorded the following year by Ronnie Spector as her comeback single. The rousing 'New York State of Mind' was also covered by a number of artists, including **Barbra Streisand** and **Bette Midler**.

Now established as a performer and songwriter in a variety of forms, Joel cut one album a year between 1977 (*The Stranger*) and 1983 (*The Nylon Curtain*), all of which reached high chart placings. Producer Phil Ramone contributed much to the overall impact of the records, but so too did Joel's ability to write effective if unsubtle songs on a range of themes. The most memorable included 'Allentown' (1982), dealing with unemployment, the classic love ballad 'Just the Way You Are' (1982), 'My Life', a rock generation equivalent to **Paul Anka**'s 'My Way', and the song which paid homage to the **Four Seasons**' Frankie Valli, 'Uptown Girl'. With a period video featuring Joel's fiancée Christie Brinkley, it was his biggest hit single.

His 1986 album *The Bridge* included duets with **Cyndi Lauper** and **Ray Charles**. After performing in the Soviet Union, Joel released the minor live album *Kohouept* (1987) and a version of **The Beatles**' 'Back in the USSR'. More in character was the witty up-tempo rocker and American chart-topper 'We Didn't Start the Fire' (1989) and its follow-up, 'I Go to Extremes', from *Storm Front*, which was produced by **Foreigner**'s Mick Jones. In the same year he began a

protracted lawsuit against his former manager Frank Weber. *Until the Night* (1991) was a minor offering but the confessional *River of Dreams* (1993), which entered the American charts at No. 1, was far better. It included 'No Man's Land' and 'Great Wall of China'. When it turned platinum in late 1994 it meant that Joel had the same number of platinum albums, eleven, as **The Beatles**. In 1997 his first classical piece, *Reverie*, was performed by Russian pianist Yuliya Gorennman, and in interviews Joel said that classical music would be his dominant concern in the future.

In 2000 Columbia issued *2000 Years: The Millennium Concert*, a double-CD of his New Year's Eve concert, which included virtually all his hits and playful cover-versions of a number of well-known songs by other acts, including the **Rolling Stones** ('Honky Tonk Woman') and **Sly Stone** ('Dance to the Music'). Less appealing was the large amount of stage patter.

ELTON JOHN
b. Reginald Kenneth Dwight, 25 March 1947, Pinner, Middlesex, England

With a large body of work that was by turns brash and sensitive, Elton John was one of the most popular performers and songwriters from the seventies to the nineties. With a persona that drew on **Liberace** and his love of soccer as much as on **John Lennon**, he personified the marriage of rock music and showbusiness. Perhaps the epitome of his complex image was his ability to survive numerous allegations about his (gay) sex life and then become the perfect celebrator of Princess Diana after her death with his affecting 'Candle in the Wind '97'.

His father had at one time played with dance band Bob Miller and the Millermen and as a child Reg Dwight attended master classes in piano at the Royal Academy of Music. On leaving school he worked for a music publisher while playing keyboards with Bluesology, a soul band which backed visiting American artists such as **Patti Labelle and the Blue Belles** and Billy Stewart. Dwight composed and sang 'Come Back Baby' (Fontana, 1965). In 1967 the group became the backing band for Long John Baldry with Dwight becoming Elton John, taken from the first names of Baldry and sax-player Elton Dean. He wrote the B-side of Baldry's No. 1 hit 'Let the Heartaches Begin'.

Leaving Bluesology, John teamed up with lyricist Bernie Taupin (*b. 22 May 1950, Sleaford, England*) and signed a publishing contract with **Dick James**. Some of their early material was recorded by Baldry, Roger Cook and **Three Dog Night**, while 'I Can't Go on Living without You' was an unsuccessful contestant for the British entry in the 1969 Eurovision Song Contest. During this period, John frequently sang anonymously on budget albums of current hits. This chapter in his career was later documented on *Reg Dwight's Piano Goes Pop* (RPM, 1994).

In contrast to the commercial numbers, the duo wrote singer-songwriter material for John himself to record, such as 'Lady Samantha' and his first album, *Empty Sky* (1969). He began to perform live with bassist Dee Murray and drummer Nigel Olsson, while *Elton John* was produced by Gus Dudgeon with intense string arrangements by Paul Buckmaster. The album contained two of Taupin's and John's most effective compositions, the romantic 'Your Song' and 'Border Song', but it made no impact until John's first American performances in 1970. His shows in Los Angeles, New York and Philadelphia won rave reviews and both the album and 'Your Song' were hits on Uni.

Over the next six years he released some fifteen albums and numerous singles. *Tumbleweed Connection* (1971) reflected Taupin's obsession with the Wild West, and was followed by the live *17-11-70* and *Friends*, the soundtrack from a Lewis Gilbert youth movie. On *Madman Across the Water* (1971), the band were joined by guitarist Davey Johnstone whose presence had brought extra impact to John's live shows. His on-stage histrionics, part Liberace, part **Little Richard**, made him one of the biggest draws of the era, while albums like *Honky Chateau* (1972) and *Don't Shoot Me, I'm Only the Piano Player* (1973) brought appreciation for Taupin's terse writing and John's melodic skill on material like 'Rocket Man'*, 'Daniel' and the nostalgic tribute to rock'n'roll (and American No. 1) 'Crocodile Rock'*.

Goodbye Yellow Brick Road contained the elegy for Marilyn Monroe 'Candle in the Wind', like 'Rocket Man' a prime example of Taupin–John's ability to give a fresh angle to a well-worn theme. *Caribou* (1974) provided hits with the ballad 'Don't Let the Sun Go Down on Me'* and the jaunty 'The Bitch Is Back'. 1975 found John at the peak of his popularity when both the autobiographical *Captain Fantastic and the Brown Dirt Cowboy* and *Rock of the Westies* (1974) entered the American charts at No. 1. Three million-selling singles also topped the hit parade: a cover of **The Beatles**' 'Lucy in the Sky with Diamonds' with John Lennon on guitar, 'Philadelphia Freedom' and 'Island Girl'. John's appearance in the film of **The Who**'s rock opera *Tommy* (1975), wearing giant boots and singing 'Pinball Wizard', captured the extravagant persona he adapted throughout this phase of his career.

By now relations with James had deteriorated and *Blue Moves* (1976) was the first John album to be released on Rocket, the label formed in 1972 by him and his manager John Reid. In 1982 Taupin and John began a three-year lawsuit against James for underpayment of royalties. One of the first signings to Rocket was vocalist Kiki Dee, whose hits included an English-language version of Véronique Sanson's 'Amoureuse' (1973) and 'I Got the Music in Me' (1974). By far her most successful record, however, was the 1976 duet with John, 'Don't Go Breaking My Heart'*, a massive international hit.

Exhausted by punishing touring and recording schedules, and reportedly demoralized by hostile reactions after he 'came out' as bisexual in a magazine interview, John took a break, concentrating on his chairmanship of Watford soccer club. When he returned to recording with *A Single Man* (1979), he had a new lyricist, Gary Osborne (Taupin had branched out, making an eponymous solo album and producing **David Ackles**' *American Gothic* in 1972). John resumed touring in 1979, with a spectacular series of concerts in the Soviet Union, accompanied only by percussionist Ray Cooper.

Throughout the eighties he continued to have hits, though the blockbuster songs were less frequent than in the seventies. 'Mama Can't Buy You Love'*, 'Little Jeannie'* (from *21 at 33*, 1980), 'I'm Still Standing', 'I Guess That's Why They Call It the Blues' (from *Too Low for Zero*, 1983), 'Sad Songs (Say So Much)' (from *Breaking Hearts*, 1984), 'Nikita' from 1985's *Ice on Fire* and 'I Don't Want to Go on Without You' were among them. In addition, he duetted with **Millie Jackson** on 'Act of War' (1985) and with **George Michael** on 'Wrap Her Up'.

The writing partnership with Taupin was resumed in 1980 but Taupin's separate career also blossomed. He recorded further solo albums, *He Who Rides the Tiger* (Asylum, 1980) and *The Tribe* (1987), and in 1986 he wrote No. 1 hits for **Heart** and Starship.

In 1986 Elton John released *Leather Jackets*, with its hit single 'Heartache All Over the World', followed by a live album recorded with the Australian Symphony Orchestra in 1987 which gave him another hit with another version of 1973's 'Candle in the Wind'. His success continued with 'Healing Hand' from *Sleeping With the Past* (1989) and the duet with **Aretha Franklin**, 'Through the Storm' (Arista, 1989). He had a further pair of British chart-toppers in 1990, 'Sacrifice' and the duet with George Michael 'Don't Let the Sun Go Down on Me'. In 1992 came *Two Rooms* (1992), a tribute album of John and Taupin songs by the likes of **Bon Jovi**, **Kate Bush**, **Rod Stewart**, **The Who**, Clapton and George Michael, which demonstrated that John's rating amongst his peers was as high as his commercial success. *The One*, John's own 1992 offering, was a mixed album. It included the thoughtful 'The Last Song', the 'Eleanor Rigby' pastiche 'Emily' and the disappointing collaboration with **Eric Clapton**, 'Runaway Train'. He followed that in 1993 with an album of duets, again with an all-star cast, which included Kiki Dee and **Paul Young**. In the same year he was awarded the title of Officer of Arts and Letters by the French government.

In 1995 he resuscitated his own Rocket label, releasing the critically well-received *Made in England*. He toured, in partnership with **Billy Joel**, but his most memorable performances were charity ones, mostly at AIDS benefits. In 1996 he turned to film music, writing 'Can You Feel the Love Tonight' for the Disney animated film *The Lion King*, and starred in the television documentary *Tantrums and Tiaras*, made by his partner David Furnish. Then, in 1997, he recorded a reworked 'Candle in the Wind' (with new lyrics by Taupin) in memory and celebration of Princess Diana after her sudden death. The record went on to be one of the bestselling singles ever. In the same year he released *The Big Picture*, the title indicating his growing interest in films. In 1999 he and Tim Rice (the former writing partner of **Andrew Lloyd Webber**, who had also started to write for Disney) rewrote *Aida* as *Elton John & Tim Rice's Aida*. In 2000 Disney staged the musical on Broadway to mixed reviews. In the same year John and Rice contributed songs to the minor animated feature *The Road to El Dorado*. John also recorded the soundtrack album, which included a carefully constructed duet with **Randy Newman**, 'It's Tough to Be a God'.

LITTLE WILLIE JOHN

b. *William Edward John, 15 November 1937, Lafayette, Arkansaas, USA, d. 26 May 1968, Walla Walla, Washington*

John was one of the most versatile and under-rated black artists of the fifties. In the manner of **Sam Cooke**, his recordings – which included the million-sellers 'Fever' (1956) and 'Talk to Me' (1958) – pointed forward to the emergence of soul in the sixties.

Raised in Detroit, John sang secular rather than gospel music from his early teens. In 1951, at the age of fourteen, he sang with **Count Basie** and won a talent contest sponsored by **Johnny Otis**. By 1954 he was recording for Prize ('Mommy What Happened to the Christmas Tree') and joined **Syd Nathan**'s King Records in 1955. His début disc, produced by **Henry Glover**, was an up-tempo bluesy cover of Titus Turner's 'All Around the World' (the song was later revived by **Little Milton** as 'Grits Ain't Groceries', 1969) and an R&B hit, as was the despairing 'Need Your Love So Bad', which demonstrated the melancholy side of John's singing. Featuring restrained guitar by **Mickey Baker**, the recording has since become a blues classic and the song, written by John's brother Mertis Jnr, has been revived by many artists, notably **Fleetwood Mac** who had a British hit with their recording of it in 1968. John's first major pop hit, the finger-snapping 'Fever', pseudonymously co-written

by **Otis Blackwell**, had a jazzier feel. Although the song was later revived by **Peggy Lee** (1958), the **McCoys** (1965) and others, most versions have replicated Glover's stark production.

'Talk to Me' (1958) and 'Sleep' (1960) saw John drifting towards pop balladry in search of further pop success, but more memorable were his up-tempo rockers ('Leave My Kitten Alone', 1959, later revived by **The Beatles**) and more soulful ballads (notably 'Let Them Talk', 1959; 'You Hurt Me', which saw John singing in the style of **Bobby Bland**; and the intense 'My Baby's in Love with Another Guy', 1962). Though he continued recording, his R&B hits ended in 1961 ('Take My Love') and by the middle of the decade John was a fading star. In 1966 he stabbed a railroad employee and was found guilty of manslaughter. He died in prison. **James Brown** recorded the tribute album *Thinking About Little Willie John and a Few Nice Things* (1968).

John's sister, Mable John, was a member of **Ray Charles**' backing group the Raelets and recorded for Motown and Stax ('Your Good Thing [Is About to End]', 1966).

JOHNNY AND THE HURRICANES

Johnny Paris, b. 1941; Tony Kaye (replaced by Bill Savitch, replaced by Lynn Bruce, replaced by Jay Drake); Lionel 'Butch' Mattice, b. 1941 (replaced by Bobby Cantrell); Paul Tesluk, b. 1941 (replaced by Eddie Fields); David Yorko, b. 1941 (replaced by Billy Marsh)

Johnny and the Hurricanes were a gimmick-laden instrumental group which flourished in the interregnum between the decline of rock'n'roll and the arrival of **The Beatles**.

Saxophone-player Paris formed his first band at high school in Toledo, Ohio, in 1958. As a university engineering student he recruited Yorko (guitar), Mattice (bass), Kaye (drums) and Tesluk (Hammond organ) to perform a summer residency at a local amusement park. After an audition backing singer Fred Kelley, Johnny and the Hurricanes were signed as an instrumental group by Detroit agent Irving Micahnik.

Their début record for Warwick, 'Crossfire', was a Top Thirty hit, but 'Red River Rock'* (1959) set the pattern for later hits. Based on the cowboy song 'Red River Valley', it featured the melody picked out on organ with raucous sax from Paris. Like later singles by the group, the arrangement was by Micahnik and his partner Harry Balk under the psuedonyms Tom King and Ira Mack. Later works given similar treatment were the army bugle call ('Reveille Rock', 1959) and the folk song 'Jimmie Cracked Corn' ('Beatnik Fly', 1960).

With the addition of Savitch from the Royaltones

(whose sole hit was 'Poor Boy', Jubilee, 1958), the group switched to Big Top and toured with label-mate **Del Shannon**. Later singles were only minor American hits but in Britain 'Rockin' Goose' – with a novelty honking sound from Paris – reached the Top Ten in 1960 on London. Later British hits were 'Ja-da' and 'Old Smokey', yet another adaptation of a folk song.

With another drummer (Bruce), Paris moved from old songs to new movies for source material, though 'Whatever Happened to Baby Jane', 'James Bond Theme' and 'Minesota Fats' were commercial failures. By 1963, when Johnny and the Hurricanes made a long-awaited European tour, only Paris of the original line-up remained.

In 1964 Paris signed with the Bell subsidiary Mala ('It's a Mad Mad Mad World') and during a Hamburg residency recorded an album for Heliodor which included Hurricanes arrangements of old German songs. He next set up his own Atila label and responded to the advent of The Beatles by wearing long hair and cuban heels, turning vocalist on 'The Saga of The Beatles' and releasing *Live at the Star Club Hamburg* (Atila, 1965). The last bandwagon Johnny and the Hurricanes were known to have jumped on came in 1967 when they recorded 'Psychedelic Worm' backed with 'Red River Rock 67'.

BLIND WILLIE JOHNSON

b. 1902, Marlin, Texas, USA, d. 1949, Beaumont, Texas, USA

Little is known about the musician generally regarded as the greatest performer of instrumentally self-accompanied black religious music in this century. A small body of recordings – no more than two albums' worth – reveals a singer of great power, particularly when using a shaman-like false bass, and a virtuoso bottleneck-style guitarist, whose highly vocalized playing harmonizes with, and at times takes over from, the sung lines.

Johnson recorded for Columbia between 1927 and 1930, submitting at his first session some of the songs for which he is best remembered: 'Jesus Make Up My Dying Bed' (taken up by **Bob Dylan** on his first album as 'In My Time of Dyin''), 'It's Nobody's Fault But Mine', 'Mother's [*sic*, for Motherless] Children Have a Hard Time' and 'If I Had My Way I'd Tear the Building Down'. On several of his records his wife Angeline sang an apt harmony. Also at his first session Johnson made the extraordinary recording of 'Dark Was the Night – Cold Was the Ground', a guitar solo with wordless vocalizing, which has been described as an exercise in 'pure sound rather than form'; it was used in the soundtrack of Pasolini's *The Gospel According to St Matthew* (1964).

'Keep Your Lamp Trimmed and Burning' (1928) was a performance often copied by later admirers, including **Fred McDowell**, while his vocal duetting with his wife inspired **Blind Willie McTell** to record sacred (and secular) songs with various female partners. In general, Johnson's singular musical vision has been easier to admire than to replicate, but **Ry Cooder** has recorded valued versions of his material, notably 'Dark Was the Night'.

BUDDY JOHNSON

b. Woodrow Wilson Johnson, 10 January 1915, Darlington, South Carolina, USA, d. 9 February 1977, New York

Buddy Johnson led one of the most popular black dance bands of the forties and fifties, also writing and arranging most of its material.

He went to New York in 1938, and initially worked as a pianist and arranger. In 1939 he formed his first band, a small bluesy jazz unit that began recording for Decca with his composition 'Stop Pretending' (later covered by the **Ink Spots**, among others). He had a hit the following year with 'Please Mr Johnson', sung by his sister Ella, an excellent stylist with elements of **Ella Fitzgerald** and **Billie Holiday**. She worked with him for many years and sang on such later hits as 'When My Man Comes Home', 'That's the Stuff You Gotta Watch' (1944), the classic 'Since I Fell for You' (1945), 'I'm Tired Crying over You' (1947) and 'Did You See Jackie Robinson Hit That Ball?' (1949) – one of a trio of chart hits about baseball players in that year, the others being Joe Di Maggio and Michael 'King' Kelly.

Later and larger groups – by 1944 he had sixteen pieces – became popular at New York's Savoy Ballroom and had a devoted and profitable following on the Southern and Midwestern ballroom circuits. Vocals were split between Ella, **Arthur Prysock** (who was with the band from 1943 to 1952), and Buddy himself, who sang 'Fine Brown Frame' (1944), a hit he shared with **Nellie Lutcher**. Moving in the fifties towards an R&B repertoire and sound, with an emphatic beat, Johnson, like **Lionel Hampton**, nurtured rock'n'roll. Though valued enough by Decca in 1949 to be given a three-year contract with guaranteed minimum royalties of $50,000, he joined Mercury when it expired. In 1956 he had a hit with the instrumental 'Doot Doot Dow'. Session musicians on his records at this period included Sam 'The Man' Taylor (tenor), jazz trombonist Slide Hampton and guitarist **Mickey Baker**. In the sixties, after a final minor hit with 'I Don't Want Nobody', which featured Ella on vocals, he gave up his band because of ill health.

BUNK JOHNSON

b. *William Geary Johnson, 27 December 1889, New Orleans, Louisiana, USA, d. 7 July 1949, New Iberia, Louisiana*

Trumpeter Johnson was a contemporary of the legendary **Buddy Bolden**. 'Rediscovered' in 1939, he became, with **George Lewis**, a symbolic figurehead of the revival of Dixieland and trad jazz, despite controversy over the quality of his work.

Like Bolden's, Johnson's early career is subject to debate. His own recollections were that he learned cornet from Wallace Cutchey and played with Adam Olivier's orchestra before joining Bolden's group around 1905. For the next three decades he gigged with a wide variety of touring groups in medicine-shows, circuses and theatrical troupes, returning periodically to New Orleans and other parts of Louisiana.

In 1933 Johnson settled in New Iberia, working as a caretaker and truck-driver. His name was mentioned by **Louis Armstrong** and **Clarence Williams** to jazz historians William Russell and Frederic Ramsey Jnr and they traced him in 1939. Johnson's ability to perform was hampered by the poor state of his teeth and the writers arranged for dentures to be fitted by **Sidney Bechet**'s dentist brother. After working as a music teacher, Johnson made his first recordings in 1942, at the age of fifty-three.

In 1943 he moved to California, the centre of the Dixieland revival. There he recorded with members of **Lu Watters**' Yerba Buena band. Returning to New Orleans, Johnson performed and recorded with other veteran players, including Alcide 'Slow Drag' Pavageau (bass), George Lewis (clarinet) and Baby Dodds (drums). He later played with Bechet before organizing his final recording session in late 1947, where he cut 'The Entertainer' and other ragtime pieces. Around this time he made the controversial claim, now rejected as indisputably false, that he had been Armstrong's teacher and major influence.

In 1948 Johnson suffered a stroke which paralyzed his left arm. He did not play again. His New Orleans revivalist group was later led by George Lewis.

GEORGE WASHINGTON JOHNSON

b. *1846, Virginia, USA, d. c. 1910*

Known in his day as 'The Whistling Coon', after one of his most successful recordings, Johnson was one of the first entertainers to record professionally. Though he gained a national reputation as a recording star, he remains a mysterious figure. His records were all deleted around 1910 after published reports (now believed to be false) that he had murdered his wife and been hanged. Nonetheless, his important place in the early days of recording is assured as the writer and

original recorder of 'The Laughing Song' (Columbia, 1891). The song was later a million-seller for English comedian Burt Shephard (Gramophone Company, 1910) and was the model for the perennially popular British novelty song 'The Laughing Policeman', first recorded in the early twenties by Charles Penrose.

Born into slavery on a Virginian plantation, Johnson moved to Washington DC, where he made his living whistling and singing, initially as a street performer. His recordings were so popular in the nineties that (because each copy had to be individually made) he had to record 'The Laughing Song' and 'The Whistling Coon' (Columbia, 1901) literally thousands of times. **Fred Gaisberg** supervised Johnson's recordings and described him thus: 'His whistle was low-pitched and fruity like a contralto. His laugh was deep-bellied, lazy like a carefree darky.'

JAMES P. JOHNSON

b. *James Price Johnson, 1 February 1894, New Brunswick, New Jersey, USA, d. 17 November 1955, New York City*

The first great jazz pianist, James P. Johnson was also a skilful composer for the musical theatre and concert hall.

Although he was classically trained, Johnson's first public performances were in Harlem at rent parties and dances for immigrants from the Southern states. From 1910 onwards he toured the vaudeville circuits and had residencies in Atlantic City and Toledo, Ohio. Piano rolls he made for the Aeolian Company and QRS in 1917–21 showed a style in which ragtime, blues and classical influences were all at work within a muscular percussive 'stride' sound.

During the twenties Johnson worked extensively in the theatre, as musical director and sometimes composer. In 1923 he took Charles Elgar's band to England to perform in the revue *Plantation Days*. He wrote the 1925 show *Running Wild*, which included 'Charleston' (which introduced the dance to the stage), 'Old Fashioned Love', and the title song, which became one of his most popular works. In 1926 he wrote 'If I Could Be with You One Hour Tonight' for **Ruth Etting**. With his one-time pupil **Fats Waller**, Johnson contributed material to the 1927 show *Shufflin' Along*. He also accompanied **Bessie Smith** on some of her finest recordings (including 'Backwater Blues' and 'Wasted Life Blues') and led the band for her short film, *St Louis Blues* (1929). Among Johnson's solo recordings during the twenties were 'Sugar', 'Harlem Chocolate Babies on Parade' and 'Carolina Shout', which swiftly became an essential part of the emerging jazz-piano repertoire.

Johnson's first symphonic work, *Yamekraw* (1928), was performed at Carnegie Hall. It was followed by the ballet music *Symphony Harlem* (1936), while he also worked with poet Langston Hughes on the short play *De Organiser*. In the thirties, Johnson briefly led big bands and played piano with Fess Williams, a comic performer on clarinet and sax.

With the revival of interest in earlier jazz styles, Johnson recorded frequently in the early forties for Asch, Signature, Decca and Blue Note. Among those with whom he recorded were **Eddie Condon**, Mezz Mezzrow and Edmond Hall. In 1943 he cut *Fats and Me*, a tribute to Waller.

Despite suffering a stroke in 1946 he continued to work, participating in a 1949 revival of his show *Sugar Hill*. A further stroke in 1951 left him unable to speak and effectively ended his musical career.

LINTON KWESI JOHNSON
b. 1952, Chapelton, Jamaica

A poet, playwright and black scholar, Johnson is a leading exponent of 'dub' poetry, intensely rhythmic verse declaimed to a reggae backing. Like his Jamaican contemporary the late Michael Smith (whose classic 'Me Cyan Believe It' was recorded for Island), he manages to combine literary skills with the rhythm, language and topics of 'yard' speech.

Johnson emigrated to England in 1963. A sociology graduate, he published two volumes of verse in the mid-seventies, including *Dread Beat 'n' Blood*, which was also the title of his first album. Billed as by Poet and the Roots, the recording had musical arrangements by **Dennis Bovell**. In 1979 Johnson signed to Island and recorded *Forces of Victory*, again with Bovell. The lyrics, in Jamaican patois or 'nation language', included the powerful 'What Fi Goh Rave'. This was followed by *Bass Culture* (1980), whose outstanding track was 'Inglan Is a Bitch', an account of the treatment of Afro-Caribbean immigrants to Britain. *Linton Kwesi Johnson in Dub* (1980) contained alternate versions of his earlier material.

He next wrote and narrated a highly praised BBC radio series tracing the history and social significance of reggae. His 1984 album, *Making History*, featured 'New Craas Massahkah', an angry account of a house fire that killed several black teenagers attending a party. A live album of Johnson reading his work was released by Rough Trade in 1985. Later recordings included *In Concert with The Dub Band* (1986) and *Tings and Times* (1990).

LONNIE JOHNSON
b. 8 February 1889 (or 1894), New Orleans, Louisiana, USA, d. 16 June 1970, Toronto, Canada

In the early years of blues recording Lonnie Johnson stood out as a city performer at a time when most male blues artists were rural or small-town acts. His unusual virtuosity on the guitar not only commanded the attention of other blues players but won him recording sessions with jazz figures as distinguished as **Louis Armstrong** and **Duke Ellington**. At the same time he enjoyed such frequent success with blues songs that by the arrival of the Depression he was the most prolific male blues artist in the recording business.

Johnson brought to the guitar (he played both six- and twelve-string models) a relatively sophisticated chordal vocabulary, metrical deftness and dramatic single-string vibrato. He played several other keyboard and string instruments, in particular the violin, on which he was also an influential performer. His first record in his own name, for Okeh in 1925, became a hit largely for its violin-accompanied 'Falling Rain Blues', which he frequently remade. As a singer he displayed a warm tone and excellent diction, but his delivery tended to be lugubrious and monotonous, although that was often in keeping with the rather humourless moralizing that typified his compositions, as in 'She's Making Whoopee in Hell Tonight' (Okeh, 1930) or 'Why Women Go Wrong' (Bluebird, 1939).

Based from 1925 in St Louis, Johnson spent the twenties playing the black vaudeville circuit and working as an Okeh staff musician, accompanying blues singers like Texas Alexander (1927-8), joining jazz units including Armstrong's ('Savoy Blues', 1927) and creating with **Eddie Lang** (under the pseudonym Blind Willie Dunn) a series of masterly guitar duet records (1928-9). He also toured with Bessie Smith in 1929.

After being out of music in the mid-thirties Johnson, now based in Chicago, returned to performing and recording (first for Decca, then Bluebird) in 1937. In 1947 he joined **Syd Nathan**'s King label and had a substantial hit with 'Tomorrow Night', an example of the pop ballads he was beginning to prefer to his rather unvarying blues. (He is said to have claimed that he copyrighted 148 songs with the same melody.) He made a lengthy tour of Britain in 1952 but by the end of the decade had left professional music again and was working as a hotel janitor in Philadelphia. He made a comeback in the early sixties on a series of Prestige-Bluesville albums, singing and playing standards as well as blues; on one of these he was reunited with **Victoria Spivey**. In 1963 he toured Europe with the American Folk Blues Festival and recorded for Storyville. In 1965 he settled in Toronto, where he appeared regularly in clubs until shortly before his death.

Johnson's unique 'singing' guitar lines were reflected in the work of innumerable later artists, among them **Robert Johnson**, **Lowell Fulson** and, especially, **B. B. King**. It is through King that Johnson's influence – seldom directly evident in rock-blues guitar-playing – extends into modern Chicago guitar styles.

MARV JOHNSON
b. 15 October 1938, Detroit, Michigan, USA, d. 15 May 1993, South Carolina

The first beneficiary of **Berry Gordy**'s writing and producing talent, Johnson played an important role in the evolution of the Motown sound.

A member of the Serenaders, Johnson was signed to an independent production deal by Gordy when **Jackie Wilson** stopped taking Gordy's songs. Their first record together was 'Come to Me', a Top Thirty hit in 1959, which Gordy leased to United Artists. Despite its churchy chorus and call-and-response structure, the record's clean production and Johnson's steady, rather than histrionic, vocal performance made it sound (in Motown historian Nelson George's words) 'as white as it did black'.

The song initiated an interesting series of pop and R&B hits for Johnson. These included 'You Got What It Takes' (1959), 'I Love the Way You Love' and '(You've Got to) Move Two Mountains' (1960), on which Gordy brought in writers **Smokey Robinson** and Brian Holland and Lamont Dozier (of the **Holland–Dozier–Holland** team). Though one of the foundations of the Motown empire, Johnson was only signed directly to the company when his career on United Artists was languishing. His biggest hits included 'I Miss You Baby' (1966) and 'I'll Pick a Rose for My Rose' (1968), a perennial favourite in Britain. His hitmaking days over, Johnson ran Motown's accounts department until the company moved to Los Angeles, when he remained in Detroit. He was later a regular on oldies' shows and in 1990 released 'Come to Me' on British producer Ian Levine's Motorcity label.

PETE JOHNSON
b. 24 March 1904, Kansas City, Missouri, USA, d. 23 March (or May) 1967, Buffalo, New York

In some respects the greatest boogie-woogie pianist of his day, Johnson had endless melodic inventiveness – he originated many of the classic themes and devices of boogie-woogie – and impeccable rhythmic drive. Unlike **Meade Lux Lewis** he was at ease with the role of a band pianist; unlike both Lewis and **Albert Ammons** he was a superb singer's accompanist.

In his teens he worked with pianists as a drummer, not taking up piano himself until he was twenty-two. In the early thirties he was hired to play at the Hawaiian Gardens club in Kansas City, where he met blues singer **Joe Turner**. They worked together in 1935–6 at the Sunset Crystal Palace, where one of their broadcasts attracted **John Hammond**, who invited them to New York. This and a second journey were unrewarding, but their 1938 visit for the 'Spirituals to Swing'

concert established them both: Turner went to work at Café Society, Johnson at the Famous Door. Over the next few years Johnson was closely associated with Ammons and Lewis, often playing duets or trios with them at Café Society and on records, broadcasts and in movie shorts like *Boogie Woogie Dream* (1941).

As well as accompanying Turner on his first recordings of his trademark pieces 'Goin' Away Blues' and 'Roll 'Em Pete' (Vocalion, 1938), Johnson recorded solos and band sides in his own name for Solo Art, Vocalion, Blue Note (all 1939) and Decca (1940–1), for whom he cut the celebrated 'Blues on the Downbeat', 'Kaycee on My Mind' and 'Death Ray Boogie'. In 1941 he recorded a set of masterly piano duets with Ammons (Victor). Distinguished jazz musicians like **Ben Webster** and 'Hot Lips' Page participated in his sessions for National (1946), and he also recorded boogies for Apollo and Down Beat while based on the West Coast in the late forties. He then worked in Detroit, Chicago, Pittsburgh, Toronto and Minneapolis, until in 1952 he lost part of a finger while changing a tyre. Thereafter he played only intermittently, but in 1955 he was back on record with Turner and **Jimmy Rushing**, and in 1958 he and Turner toured Europe with **Norman Granz**'s 'Jazz at the Philharmonic'. However, illness prevented him from building on this comeback.

PLAS JOHNSON
b. 21 July 1931, New Orleans, Louisiana, USA

One of the originators of the rock'n'roll saxophone sound, Johnson was heard on hundreds of records, from the hits of **Duane Eddy** to **Henry Mancini**'s theme for *The Pink Panther* (1963). Like **Maxwell Davis** he was a master of the brief instrumental break.

Johnson moved from New Orleans to Los Angeles in the early fifties and by the arrival of rock'n'roll had become part of the élite group of West Coast session musicians. From the late fifties he played tenor saxophone on numerous records, including the solo on 'Searchin'' by the **Coasters** (1959) and the lead part on the revival of **Glenn Miller**'s 'In the Mood' (Rendezvous, 1959) by the Ernie Fields Orchestra, as well as hits by the Piltdown Men, the group formed by former **Four Preps** member Ed Cobb and pianist Lincoln Mayorga.

He was equally at home with the R&B of **B. B. King** or Thurston Harris and the rock'n'roll of **Don and Dewey**, **Larry Williams** and fellow Capitol artists **Eddie Cochran** and **Gene Vincent**. However, the decline of heavy rhythm in the early sixties meant that Johnson's hard-blowing style was in less demand and he turned to film studio work.

With the return to popularity of rock music, Johnson's recording session bookings increased. After being recruited to play on **Frank Zappa**'s début album *Freak Out!* (1966), he accompanied such artists as former **Canned Heat** guitarist Harvey Mandel (1969), **Rita Coolidge** (1971), **Diana Ross** (*Lady Sings the Blues*, 1973), **Ry Cooder** (1974), **Carole King** (1974), **Steely Dan** and **Kate and Anna McGarrigle** (1975). Johnson had a featured role on **Maria Muldaur**'s *Sweet Harmony* (1976), which attempted to recreate the feel of forties jump-band music.

In later years Johnson continued to play on a wide range of sessions, including those of former **Guess Who** member Burton Cummings, R&B veteran **Etta James**, **Gladys Knight** and country-rock vocalist Nicolette Larson.

ROBERT JOHNSON
b. c. 1912, Hazlehurst, Mississippi, USA, d. 16 August 1938, Greenwood, Mississippi

According to one of his biographers, Robert Johnson 'is a chilling confrontation with aspects of the American consciousness . . . a visionary artist with a terrible kind of information about his time and place and personal experience'. The weight, scope and bluntness of this judgement is typical of Johnson criticism: few artists in blues history elicit so considerable and so nearly unanimous a respect, and of those none matches the charismatic effect of Johnson's music upon specialists, musicians and general listeners alike. In the history of blues style he is important as a transitional figure between the country blues of **Charley Patton** and **Son House** and the country-rooted Chicago idiom of **Muddy Waters**: his clear diction and suave boogie-based guitar lines suggest a younger **Big Bill Broonzy**, while his lack of vocal or emotional inhibition préfigures **Elmore James** and **B. B. King**.

In his late teens he learned a little from House and House's (and Patton's) associate Willie Brown. For much of the thirties he is believed to have travelled widely, not only in the South but to the East Coast and the Midwest; among his blues contemporaries he encountered **Howlin' Wolf**, **Sonny Boy Williamson II**, James and others. In two sessions for ARC, in November 1936 and June 1937, he recorded twenty-nine songs, almost all of which won admirers and imitators; among the most famous are 'Ramblin' on my Mind', 'Come on in My Kitchen', with its extraordinary, descriptive bottleneck guitar-playing, 'Cross Road Blues' (taken up by **Cream**, as was the lesser piece 'From Four Until Late'), the frenetic 'Preachin' Blues' and the reflective 'Love in Vain', reworked by the **Rolling Stones**. Attracted by these records, **John Hammond** tried to book Johnson for the December 1938 'Spirituals to Swing' concert at Carnegie Hall, only to discover that he had died a few months earlier, poisoned or stabbed at a country juke-joint.

Johnson was himself detectably influenced by **Lonnie Johnson** (as in 'Malted Milk' and 'Drunken Hearted Man') and **Leroy Carr** ('Love in Vain' follows the melody of Carr's 'When the Sun Goes Down'), and arguably also by the singer/pianist Peetie Wheatstraw and other contemporary recording artists. Among the innumerable artists for whom Johnson has been a model or inspiration are **Eric Clapton**, **Jimi Hendrix**, **Taj Mahal**, **Johnny Winter**, and his own stepson, Robert 'Junior' Lockwood (*b. 27 March 1915, Marvell, Arkansas*), who began recording in 1941 with 'Take a Little Walk with Me' (Bluebird), a variation on Johnson's 'Sweet Home Chicago', and through a long and distinguished blues career often redeployed elements of Johnson's music. In the seventies he formed a double-act with another Johnson devotee, singer/guitarist Johnny Shines whose 'Ramblin'' (JOB, 1952) and 'Dynaflow Blues' (Vanguard, 1965) are striking, Johnson-styled performances. A mark of his enduring importance was the enormous sales of Columbia's CD set *The Complete Recordings* (1990).

AL JOLSON
b. Asa Yoelson, 26 May 1886, Srednik, Russia, d. 23 October 1953, San Francisco, California

Jolson has often been acclaimed as the most complete entertainer of the twentieth century. As a recording artist he had million-sellers as early as 1912 and as late as 1950, and his career also encompassed minstrelsy, vaudeville, Broadway and the cinema. Yet, though his dramatic 'You Ain't Heard Nothing Yet' in *The Jazz Singer* (1927) launched the sound film, his career had a backward-looking quality to it. Jolson was always happier in front of a live audience, strutting down the ramps he had specially built so as to be even closer to them: when he started recording in 1911, he had to be restrained from moving around. Similarly, his sentimental, melodramatic singing style was complemented by pleading interjections and intensifying gestures (going down on bended knee, arms outstretched while singing 'My Mammy', for example). His booming voice, which with its rolled 'rrr's reflected both the operetta tradition and the exuberance of minstrelsy – traditions strong in turn-of-the-century America – was perfectly suited to acoustical recording. But his electrical recordings were less expressive when compared to the crooning of **Bing Crosby**. In short, in contrast to other entertainers whose careers spanned radio, the concert hall and the cinema, Jolson's image and style of performance was fixed in the past. Significantly, his career was in decline when it was revived by *The Jolson Story* (1946). Moreover, his continued use of blackface, long beyond the days of minstrelsy, was an embarrassing reminder of how crudely black culture has been represented by whites.

The son of a Jewish cantor, Jolson travelled to America at the age of seven and grew up in Washington DC. He began his showbusiness career in burlesque in 1898, singing from the gallery 'You Are My Jersey Lilly' to burlesque queen Aggie Beeler. His stage début was in Israel Zangwill's *The Children of the Ghetto* (1899), after which he toured in vaudeville with his brother Harry as Jolson, Palmer and Jolson. In 1905 he performed in blackface – which was to become his trademark – for the first time, billing himself as 'The Blackface with the Grand Opera Voice', and in 1908 joined Lew Dockstader's minstrel company. By 1910 the essentials of his act were in place, his habit of speaking directly to the audience, his blackface and his whistling. His self-confidence was absolute – 'You've never heard of me, but you will', ran one advert he placed in *Variety* at this period – all he needed was a hit song. That was supplied by his first Victor recordings, two songs from *Vera Violetta*, the 1911 operetta in which he appeared, 'Rum-Tiddle-Tiddle' and 'The Haunting Melody', written by **George M. Cohan**, who also started his career in blackface. Even more successful was 'Ragging the Baby to Sleep' (1912), his first million-seller, and a version of British music-hall star Billy Meerson's 'The Spaniard that Blighted My Life'* (1913). This last song provided Jolson with another million-seller in 1948 when he revived it in duet with Crosby (Decca).

His status on Broadway was assured by the success of *Sinbad* (1918) and *Bombo* (1921) in which, in blackface, he interpolated the ever-growing number of songs associated with him. These included 'Avalon', 'Rockabye Your Baby with a Dixie Melody', 'California Here I Come', 'Swanee' (**George Gershwin**'s first big success), 'My Mammy' (co-written by **Walter Donaldson**), 'April Showers', one of a number of songs written for Jolson by Buddy DeSylva (of **DeSylva, Brown and Henderson**) and **Gus Kahn**'s 'Toot, Toot, Tootsie! Goodbye'. (On several of these, Jolson was credited as co-author, a common practice, though it is unlikely that he made major contributions to the songs.)

By now billing himself as 'The World's Greatest Entertainer', he made the experimental sound short *April Showers* in 1926 for Warners and, in 1927, starred in the epochal *The Jazz Singer*. The phenomenal success of the story of a Jewish cantor's son who refuses to give up a showbusiness career, which was similar to Jolson's own (and to that of **George Jessel** who created the role in the long-running Broadway play), launched the talkies (and the demise of vaudeville) and Jolson's Hollywood career. *The Jazz Singer* film was remade in 1953, with Danny Thomas in the Jolson

role, and in 1980 with **Neil Diamond**. Jolson's second starring film, *The Singing Fool*, which featured him singing 'Sonny Boy'* (Brunswick, 1928), was even more successful, but few of Jolson's later films were of lasting interest. Two exceptions are *Hallelujah, I'm a Bum* (1933) – probably the only Hollywood musical to look at and deal directly with the Depression – and *Swanee River* (1940), a biopic of E. P. Christy, leader of one of America's most famous minstrel troupes and the man who introduced many of **Stephen Foster**'s classic songs.

A flamboyant and compulsive performer, Jolson was always ready to sing at benefits, and after his marriage to **Ruby Keeler** in 1928 helped her career by singing 'Liza' with her from the audience for part of the New York run of *Show Girl* (1929). During the thirties he regularly appeared in radio, launching the *Kraft Music Hall* in 1934, but his popularity ebbed with changing tastes. Like **Marlene Dietrich**, his career was boosted during the Second World War by his concerts for the American troops. This prompted *The Jolson Story* (1946) in which Larry Parks played Jolson, who supplied his own singing voice. A huge success, it led to a million-selling soundtrack album on Decca and five million-selling singles, including 'You Made Me Love You' and 'Anniversary Song', as well as a series of recordings with other Decca artists, such as Crosby, the **Mills Brothers** and the **Andrews Sisters**. The film's success spawned a sequel, *Jolson Sings Again* (1949), which in turn led to million-selling records of four of Jolson's songs, 'Swanee', 'California Here I Come', 'April Showers' and 'Rockabye Your Baby with a Dixie Melody'.

On news of his death, just after he returned from entertaining American troops in Korea, the lights on Broadway were turned out . . .

JON SPENCER BLUES EXPLOSION
Judah Bauer; Russell Simins; Jon Spencer

An energetic American three-piece, the Jon Spencer Blues Explosion have developed a loyal international fanbase for their punk-metal update of traditional blues.

After spending five years fronting Pussy Galore, with whom he made six albums, Jon Spencer formed the Blues Explosion with Simins (drums) and Bauer (guitar) in 1992. In the space of a year they made three albums of embryonic punk rock – *A Reverse Willie Horton*, *Crypt Style* and *The Jon Spencer Blues Explosion* – before signing to Matador and recording *Extra Width* (1993). The single 'Afro' brought the band nationwide exposure in their homeland, and was followed by *Orange* (1994), which saw them receive the patronage of the **Beastie Boys**. Their next release was the *Experimental Remixes EP* (1995), which saw **Beck**,

Moby, **Wu Tang Clan**'s Genius and the Beastie Boys' Mike D reinterpret their past material.

JSBX spent much of the next year working on other projects. Spencer worked on his wife Christina Martinez's Boss Hog project, while the trio reconvened to back original bluesman R. L. Burnside on his *An Ass Pocket o' Whiskey* album and subsequent tour. *Now I Got Worry* (1996) reflected the time spent with Burnside, making it the Explosion's most traditionally blues-styled album to date. Their next album, *Acme* (1998), saw the band begin to utilize hi-tech recording methods in place of the raw, improvisational quality of their early work, gaining JSBX new followers in the process.

ADA JONES
b. 1 June 1873, Lancashire, England, d. 22 May 1922

With her strong contralto and mastery of ethnic dialects, which she used to good effect in her duets with **Len Spencer**, Jones was, with **Nora Bayes**, one of the most popular female artists of the early years of recording.

After emigrating to America, Jones began recording in 1904 with Edison and had her first big hits in 1907, with 'I Just Can't Make My Eyes Behave' and the first of several duets with **Billy Murray**, 'Let's Take an Old Fashioned Walk' (Columbia). Among her many hits were 'The Yama, Yama Man' (Victor, 1909); 'Call Me Up Some Rainy Afternoon' (1910, on which she was supported by Murray's American Quartet); the novelty song 'Row! Row! Row!' (1913), which was co-written by **Harry Von Tilzer**; and 'On the Old Front Porch' (1914), a duet with **Henry Burr**.

Her most regular partners, however, were Murray and Spencer. With the former she sang a mix of comic songs and heart-wrenching ballads and with the latter (who had originally intended to record with Murray taking the female role) she created a long-running series of comic monologues and songs (mostly about Jewish and Irish characters) similar to those of **Joe Hayman** and **Arthur Collins**. Among their hits were 'Mr and Mrs Murphy' (Columbia, 1905), 'The Courtship of Barney and Eileen' (Edison, 1905), 'The Original Cohen' (Columbia, 1906), 'Herman and Minnie' (Victor, 1907), and a sequel to Spencer's biggest-ever hit 'The Arkansas Traveler', 'The Return of the Arkansas Traveler' (Columbia 1910). Jones also recorded frequently with Walter Van Brunt, **Thomas Edison**'s favourite tenor, whose biggest hit was 'Sympathy' (Victor, 1913) from **Rudolf Friml**'s first Broadway musical, *The Firefly*. Their duets include 'It's Got to Be Someone I Love' (Columbia, 1911) and 'Be My Little Bumble Bee' (1912).

Jones' last hit was 'When Frances Dances with Me' (Victor) in the year of her death.

ELVIN JONES
b. 9 September 1927, Pontiac, Michigan, USA

A leading modern jazz drummer, Jones came to prominence through his partnership with **John Coltrane**. He later recorded solo albums and led his own group.

From a musical family, Jones' elder brothers Thad (trumpet) and Hank (piano) were also jazz performers. After finishing army service in 1949 he played with various groups in Detroit before moving to New York in 1955 where he worked with **Charlie Mingus** and **Bud Powell**. He recorded with **Miles Davis** but first came to prominence in **Sonny Rollins**' group, demonstrating a polyrhythmic style of playing on *At the Village Vanguard* (1957).

Jones' post-bop style of drumming was eminently suited to the avant-garde approach of Coltrane, with whom he made a series of albums between 1960 and 1966, notably *A Love Supreme* (1964). Frequently, Jones and Coltrane duetted, as on *Africa/Brass* (1961), while the drummer often kept three distinct rhythms going behind other members of the group. 'The Drum Thing' from *Crescents* (1964) contained some of his best solo work.

After leaving Coltrane, Jones formed his own trio with Jimmy Garrison (bass) and Joe Farrell (sax) to make *The Ultimate* (Blue Note) and *Puttin' It Together* (1968). Jones made numerous recordings in the seventies and eighties with such players as the saxophonists Frank Foster, George Coleman and Dave Liebman, the most representative of which were *Soul Trane* (Denon, 1980) and *Earth Jones* (Palo Alto, 1982). His major recording of the nineties was *It Don't Mean a Thing* (Enja, 1992), a relaxed ensemble outing.

GEORGE JONES
b. 12 September 1931, Saratoga, Texas, USA

A country superstar for over twenty years and described by one critic as 'the last pure country singer', Jones deployed an array of vocal mannerisms (notably the alternating of low moans and high wails) and brought a unique intensity to his mournful songs of broken love. Though too many of his recordings featured choruses and lush backings, in the words of country-music historian Bill C. Malone 'these accoutrements . . . could not blunt or hide his distinctiveness'. His finest recordings include the archetypal 'She Thinks I Still Care' (1962) and 'The Grand Tour' (1974). For many listeners Jones' life and art became inextricably linked and many of his later hits were specifically written with this in mind (notably *The Battle*, 1975, which detailed the break-up of his marriage to **Tammy Wynette**).

From a musical family, Jones, inspired by **Roy**

Acuff as a youth, turned to singing, becoming a full-time performer after his discharge from the marines in 1952. In 1953 he signed with Starday, the label founded by his manager Harold 'Pappy' Daily. At first he sang in the style of **Hank Williams** (to whom he later recorded the tribute album *My Favorites of Hank Williams*, 1962) and, briefly, as 'Thumper Jones' and Hank Smith recorded in a rockabilly vein. But, following a move to Mercury in 1957, he reverted to the classic honky-tonk style, giving full rein to his blues-drenched East Texas twang. His first country No. 1 was the up-tempo novelty song 'White Lightning' (1959), written by J. P. Richardson (The Big Bopper) who also wrote **Johnny Preston**'s 1960 million-seller 'Running Bear', but more characteristic were 'Color of the Blues' (1957) and 'The Window up Above' (1960). In 1962 Jones moved to United Artists for whom he recorded 'She Thinks I Still Care', later a favourite with country-rock artists including John Fogerty of **Creedence Clearwater Revival**, 'A Girl I Used to Know' (1962) and 'The Race Is on' (1964), which was successfully covered by Jack Jones. During this period Jones began duetting with Melba Montgomery (reissued on *Vintage Collection*, Capitol, 1996) and recorded a duet album with **Gene Pitney** (Musicor, 1965, reissued Bear Family, 1995), which produced two small hits, 'I've Got Five Dollars and its Saturday Night' and 'Louisiana Man'.

Between 1965 and 1971 Jones recorded for Daily's Musicor label. Though many records from this period showed him at his best ('Walk Through This World with Me', 1967; 'Burn the Honky Tonk Down' and, most notably, 'A Good Year for the Roses', 1970, later revived by **Elvis Costello**), Daily's productions grew increasingly careless, often swamping the singer with strings. Jones' recording career was revived by producer **Billy Sherrill** when, after his 1969 marriage to Wynette, he joined her label, Epic. The duet 'We're Gonna Hold on' (1973) gave Jones his first country No. 1 since 1967 and introduced a series of hits which took for their subject the state of the Jones–Wynette marriage and climaxed with 'Golden Ring' and 'Near You' (1976) in the year Wynette remarried. Though Jones' drinking threatened his career, under Sherrill's skilful handling he prospered. Among his numerous hits were 'He Stopped Loving Her Today' (1980), 'If Drinking Don't Kill Me (Her Memory Will)' (1981), 'Who's Gonna Fill Her Shoes' (1985) and 'The One I Loved Back Then' (1986). At the same time Jones embarked on a series of adventurous duets. *My Very Special Guests* (1979) featured **Linda Ronstadt**, **Emmylou Harris**, **Willie Nelson** and Elvis Costello, among others, and in 1982 he recorded with **Merle Haggard** ('Yesterday's Wine') and **James Taylor** ('Bartender Blues'). Later albums included *Rockin' the Country* (1985), *Too Wild Too Long* (1987) and *One*

Woman Man (1989), probably the best of his later recordings. He made a guest appearance on Randy Travis's *Heroes and Friends* (1990) before resuming his own career with *Friends in High Places* (1990) on which he duetted with Emmylou Harris, **Buck Owens** and Travis. He moved to MCA for *And Along Came Jones* (1991), which he followed with *Walls Can Fall* (1992), *Rockin' Chair* (1992) and *High Tech Redneck* (1993). *The Essential George Jones* (1994), which draws from all stages of his career, is the definitive retrospective. *One* saw him reunited with Wynette. A commercial success it was followed by the intriguing remake of 'A Good Year for the Roses' (1996) in partnership with **Alan Jackson.** He published his autobiography *I Lived to Tell It All* the same year and in 1998 left MCA for Asylum Records.

GRACE JONES
b. 19 May 1952, Spanish Town, Jamaica

An image as much as a singer, Jones brought an unnerving sexual ambiguity to the disco boom of the early eighties.

The daughter of a minister and niece of a bishop in the Pentecostal church, she moved to Syracuse, New York, in 1964. Jones' height and striking androgynous looks brought her a career as a top Paris fashion model, and she appeared on the covers of *Vogue* and *Elle*.

Her recording career began with *Portfolio* (Island, 1976), produced by disco expert Tom Moulton. 'I Need a Man' and other songs from *Fame* (1978) and *Muse* (1979) were dancefloor favourites. Jones' gender-bending image, with undertones of sado-masochism, was moulded by her mentor and manager Jean-Paul Goude and she became the first singer to perform live at New York's leading discotheque, Studio 54.

Warm Leatherette (1980) was produced by **Chris Blackwell** and included the British hit 'Private Life', a cover of a composition by the **Pretenders'** Chrissie Hynde. The title track was by Daniel Miller of Mute Records, one of Britain's most successful independent labels in the eighties. The sleek and sophisticated *Nightclubbing* with a title track by **David Bowie** and **Iggy Pop**, gave Jones an R&B hit with 'Pull Up to the Bumper'.

Moving from a rock influence towards reggae, *Living My Life* (1982) was recorded in Jamaica and included 'Nipple to the Bottle', co-written by Jones and Sly Dunbar of **Sly and Robbie**. 'My Jamaican Guy' and 'The Apple Stretching' were further disco hits from the album. In 1985 Jones changed producers to **Trevor Horn** for the autobiographical *Slave to the Rhythm* (ZTT), whose title track entered the British Top Twenty. In the same year she appeared in the James Bond film *A View to a Kill*.

The following year she again switched label and

producer for *Inside Story* (Manhattan) with **Nile Rodgers**. *Bulletproof Heart* (Capitol) appeared in 1989. She was declared bankrupt in 1992 but returned to the charts and Island in 1993 with 'Sex Drive'.

HOWARD JONES
b. John Howard Jones, 23 February 1955, Southampton, Hampshire, England

A composer, singer and synthesizer player, Howard Jones' bright songs were firmly in the tradition of post-**Beatles** British pop.

He studied classical piano as a child and dropped out of music college in Manchester in 1976 to play in various groups, including 'classical-rock' band Warrior, new-wavers Bicycle Thieves and hard-rock group Skin Tite. After 1980 he built up a following around his home town of High Wycombe playing synthesizer as a solo act.

In 1983 Jones recorded sessions for BBC Radio One and signed to Warners. With a strong resemblance to **Peter Gabriel**'s 'Solsbury Hill', 'New Song' was a Top Ten hit in Britain and the following year reached the American Top Thirty. In 1984 he had four more British hits. The plaintive 'What Is Love' was the most successful, followed by 'Hide and Seek', 'Pearl in the Shell' and 'Like to Get to Know You Well'. His début album, the Rupert Hine-produced *Human's Lib*, topped the British charts.

To the despair of critics who railed against the shallow optimism of his world-view, Jones' run of hits continued in 1985 with 'Things Can Only Get Better', 'Look Mama' and 'Life in One Day', which was also a success in America. All came from *Dream into Action*, which contained 'Assault and Battery', a vegetarian protest song. Jones' brother Martin played bass on the album.

The 1986 album *One to One* was produced by **Arif Mardin**, who gave Jones a more sophisticated sound. The resulting singles, 'You Know I Love You . . . Don't You' and 'All I Want', were only minor hits. *Cross that Line* (1989) included a piano solo, but was equally unsuccessful. For *In the Running* (1992) Jones played piano more than synthesizer, but neither that nor the repackaging of his former hits on *The Best of Howard Jones* (1993) managed to revive his flagging career. He followed that with the live set, *Live Acoustic America* (1996), and *People* (1998), by which time he was a regular, along with the **Human League** and **Culture Club**, on the newly established eighties revival circuit.

ISHAM JONES
b. 31 January 1894, Coalton, Iowa, USA, d. 19 October 1956, Florida

A composer and instrumentalist, Isham Jones was leader of one of the earliest and most influential American dance bands.

His first instrument was bass but by 1914 he was leading a group in Saginaw, Michigan, on piano and saxophone. The following year he moved to Chicago, which was to remain his base for the next two decades. He first led a trio and then formed his first full-scale orchestra, with residencies at the Hotel Sherman and other venues. In 1924 the Isham Jones band played at the Kit Kat Club in London.

In parallel with San Francisco bandleader Art Hickman, Jones pioneered the instrumentation, arrangements and style of dance-band music. His group was renowned in the twenties for its flowing rhythmic and melodic approach. He first recorded for Brunswick in 1920 and 'Wabash Blues' (1922) was reputed to have sold over two million copies, while the cover-version by the Benson Orchestra on Victor sold over a million. By 1923 Jones was said to have earned some $500,000 in royalties. His next biggest hit was a ballad arrangement of **Hoagy Carmichael**'s 'Stardust' (1930) with violinist **Victor Young** as featured soloist. In the mid-thirties he signed to a new label, Decca.

From the mid-twenties Jones enjoyed the services of a series of top arrangers, including **Don Redman**, Jiggs Noble and **Gordon Jenkins**, who once described the Jones band as 'the greatest sweet ensemble of that or any other time'. Among the leading figures in the Isham Jones orchestra were Joe Bishop (tuba), Johnny Carlson (trumpet), vocalist Eddie Stone and Saxie Mansfield (sax). **Benny Goodman** was briefly a member and **Woody Herman** joined Jones in 1934. When the orchestra disbanded two years later, Herman, Bishop and other sidemen formed their own band. Although he occasionally performed and recorded after 1936, Jones concentrated on his songwriting.

A prolific composer, Jones was responsible for more than 200 songs. Among the best-known were 'I'll See You in My Dreams', 'It Had to Be You', 'Swinging Down the Lane', 'On the Alamo', 'Spain', 'There Is No Greater Love' and the band's theme tune, 'You're Just a Dream Come True'.

JIMMY JONES
b. 2 June 1937, Birmingham, Alabama, USA

A distinctive, shrill falsetto gave a real edge to Jones' two million-sellers, 'Handy Man' and 'Good Timin'' (1960). However, the excitement was dulled when the vocal gimmick was repeated too many times on lesser songs and his career stalled.

Educated in Birmingham, Jones moved to New York after his army discharge and recorded an early version of 'Handy Man' (Apollo, 1955) with the vocal group, the Sparks of Rhythm. He next recorded with the Pretenders (on Rama and **Bobby Robinson**'s Whirlin' Disc) and the Savoys (on Savoy) before attempting a solo career on Arrow and Epic. After **Otis Blackwell** heard a new demo of 'Handy Man', he signed Jones to MGM's R&B subsidiary Cub in 1959. His production of the song was an instant hit. Equally strong was the Clint Ballard and Fred Tobias-penned 'Good Timin'', one of the wittier, more literate songs of the era, but subsequent singles were distinctly minor ('That's When I Cried', 1960; 'I Told You So', 1961). Later that year Jones moved to Vee-Jay and Roulette where he made a series of soundalike recordings to little avail.

Though Jones' career quickly faded, 'Handy Man' has been frequently revived, most successfully by **Del Shannon** (1964) and **James Taylor** (1977).

QUINCY JONES

b. *Quincy Delight Jones Jnr, 14 March 1933, Chicago, Illinois, USA*

A trumpeter, composer, arranger and record producer, Quincy Jones' status as one of the music industry's most successful figures was confirmed by his production of the all-star charity recording 'We Are the World'* in 1985.

Growing up in Seattle, he joined a gospel quartet at the age of twelve, and two years later met the young **Ray Charles**. He studied at Schillinger House in Boston, the forerunner of the Berklee School of Music, paying his way through college with local jazz gigs. Moving to New York in the early fifties, Jones worked as a freelance arranger for **Dizzy Gillespie**, among others, before spending three years touring the world with **Lionel Hampton**'s band.

He spent the late fifties in Paris, as musical director for the Barclay label. He also studied composition with Nadia Boulanger, who had previously taught Stravinsky. He formed a big band for a show called *Free and Easy*, but his attempt to maintain it on a permanent basis was a financial disaster. Returning to New York, he became head of A&R at Mercury records from 1961 to 1968. Among the pop records he supervised were **Lesley Gore**'s string of hits, beginning with 'It's My Party'. Jones himself recorded the bestselling *Big Band Bossa Nova* (1962), taking advantage of the then current music craze. During this period he also worked as a freelance arranger and producer for numerous artists including **Billy Eckstine**, **Frank Sinatra**, **Johnny Mathis**, **Tony Bennett** and Charles, with whom he worked on the big-band classic *Genius + Soul = Jazz* (Impulse, 1961).

Jones' career as a prolific composer for films and television began with the 1965 Sidney Lumet movie *The Pawnbroker*. He went on to score more than forty films and 250 episodes of television drama series,

including *Ironside*, *I-Spy* and *Roots*. The most notable of his cinema soundtracks included *In Cold Blood* (1967), *In the Heat of the Night* (1967), *Bob and Carol and Ted and Alice* (1969) and *The Color Purple* (1986).

In 1969 he signed a solo contract with A&M and *Walking in Space* was the first in a series of albums in which Jones merged jazz brass sections with churning rock-funk rhythms. It was followed by *Gula Matari* (1970) and *Smackwater Jack* (1971), whose title track was a version of a **Carole King** song. Among the soloists on these records were Freddie Hubbard, **Rahsaan Roland Kirk** and Eric Gale. In 1971 Jones and Charles collaborated on the ambitious *Black Requiem*, performed with an eighty-voice choir and the Houston Symphony Orchestra.

His work on **Aretha Franklin**'s *Hey Now Hey* album (1973) showed a shift towards contemporary soul music, continued on Jones' own *Body Heat* (1974), *Mellow Madness* (1975), *I Heard That* (1976) and the 1978 million-seller *Sounds – and Stuff Like That*. The 1975 album featured vocals by the **Brothers Johnson**, who became the first of a number of new soul artists to be produced by Jones. Among the others were **Chaka Khan** and Rufus (*Masterjam*, MCA, 1979), **George Benson** (*Give Me the Night*, Warners, 1980) and **Michael Jackson**.

Jones met Jackson while working on the soundtrack of *The Wiz* (1978), Sidney Lumet's attempt to make a black version of *The Wizard of Oz*. He went on to produce *Off the Wall* (1980), then *Thriller* (1982) and *Bad* (1987), two of the biggest-selling albums in music-industry history. *Thriller* featured songs by another of Jones' protégés, former **Heatwave** keyboards-player Rod Temperton.

In 1981 Jones released *The Dude* (A&M), which contained three hit singles. Chas Jankel's 'Ai No Corrida' with vocals by Dune was followed by two songs featuring James Ingram, 'Just Once' and 'One Hundred Ways'. Ingram had a 1982 No. 1 with 'Baby Come to Me', a duet with another of Jones' session singers, Patti Austin. It was one of the first releases on Jones' own Qwest label. Ingram had further success with 'Yah Moh B There' (a 1984 duet with Michael McDonald) and 'There's No Easy Way' (1985).

Twenty-two years after his first No. 1 single with Lesley Gore, Jones repeated the feat with USA for Africa's 'We Are the World'. He arranged, organized and produced the session, which featured some thirty of America's leading pop artists, all of whom he instructed to 'check your egos at the door'.

In 1989 Jones recorded *Back on the Block*, an Afro-American musical history tour with guest support from a host of stars including **Miles Davis**, George Benson, **Ella Fitzgerald** and rapper **Ice T**. Since then he has largely concentrated on television production through a joint venture company he formed with

Time Warner. In 1991 he was the subject of the television documentary *The Lives of Quincy Jones*.

RICKIE LEE JONES
b. 8 November 1958, Chicago, Illinois, USA

Jones' style, fifties beat meets seventies folk in low rent scenarios, was established by her successful eponymous début album (1979) and its Top Five single 'Chuck E.'s in Love'. After it Jones spent most of the late eighties reinventing herself with only moderate success.

Like **Tom Waits**, with whom she was briefly romantically attached, Jones specialized in bohemian sub-culture observations. After former **Little Feat** creator Lowell George recorded her composition 'Easy Money' in 1979 she was signed to Warners. Her début album set out her stall with its glorious 'Chuck E.'s in Love', an American Top Five hit, and its series of songs describing after-hours life, including her own version of 'Easy Money'. After a two-year delay she released *Pirates*, which confirmed her beat sensibilities and finger-snapping attitude to life.

After the more up-tempo EP *Girl at Her Volcano* (1983) she released *The Magazine* (1984), which gave full flight to her gushing vocals and troubled lyrics, albeit in a restricted arena. *Flying Cowboys* (1989), produced by former member of **Steely Dan**, Walter Becker, was a more considered effort. Featuring assistance from British group the Blue Nile it saw a return to traditional song structures. Nonetheless, as her début outing for Geffen Records, it initially sold poorly. More accessible but a lesser work was *Pop Pop* (1991), a collection of cover-versions of songs that hardly seemed to matter to Jones. Among them were 'Up from the Skies' (**Jimi Hendrix**), 'Second Time Around' and 'Comin' Back to Me' (**Jefferson Airplane**). Far better was the self-produced *Traffic from Paris* (1993), which featured appearances by **Lyle Lovett** (on whose *Joshua Judges Ruth* she had appeared) amongst others, and the acoustic *Naked Songs* (1995), on which she runs through her back catalogue to stunning effect. Equally innovative was *Ghostyhead* (1997) which saw her experimenting with techno rhythms. In 2000 she essayed an album of covers, *It's Like This* (Epic). Duetting with **Dan Hicks**, **Joe Jackson**, Ben Folds and **Taj Mahal**, she created re-readings of songs as disparate as **George Gershwin**'s 'Someone to Watch Over Me' and **Marvin Gaye**'s 'Trouble Man', often to startling effect.

SPIKE JONES
b. Lindley Murray Jones, 14 December 1911, Long Beach, California, USA, d. 1 May 1965, Los Angeles, California

Spike Jones and His City Slickers were the best-known comedy band of the forties and fifties, reaching a worldwide audience through their recordings and movie appearances.

Jones took up drums at the age of eleven and in college organized a jazz band in the style of **Red Nichols**. From 1937 to 1942 he was a studio drummer in Hollywood, recording for most of the major labels behind artists like **Bing Crosby**, **Judy Garland** and **Fred Astaire**. He was also featured on **Ted Daffan**'s country hit 'Born to Lose' (1942). In early 1941 he formed a group to specialize in parody and musical lunacy, inspired by the Hoosier Hot Shots, who played quasi-hillbilly music with kazoos and washboards, and Freddie Fisher's Schnickelfritz Band, a comedy polka outfit that used cowbells and tuned motor-horns. (Jones himself, in earlier days, had reportedly relieved the boredom of dance-band engagements by playing a xylophone with his penis!) In August 1941 the band began to record, initially for Bluebird, but from 1944 for RCA Victor.

'Der Fuehrer's Face'* (1942), their first hit, was a sort of topical polka, but its successors found their fun in more purely musical jokes. The quintessential Jones technique was to take a sophisticated popular song, play it straight(ish) for a while, then destroy the mood with doubled tempos, gunshots, corny 'hot' jazz solos and passages played on motor-horns or a 'latrinophone' – a lavatory seat strung with piano wire. Of 'Cocktails for Two'* (1944), its writer Sam Coslow said that Jones 'desecrated one of his most beautiful songs'; **David Rose**, however, 'loved' the Jones version of his 'Holiday for Strings' (1945). 'You Always Hurt the One You Love' (1945) parodied the deep-voiced narrations of the **Ink Spots**; 'My Old Flame' (1947) threw in a take-off of the movie actor Peter Lorre; 1948's 'William Tell Overture' included a cod racing commentary; and 'I Went to Your Wedding' (1953) was in the adenoidal sobbing style of **Johnny Ray**. Other hits included a trio of Christmas novelties: 'All I Want for Christmas Is My Two Front Teeth'* (1948), which later formed the basis for actress Dora Bryan's comment on Beatlemania 'All I Want for Christmas Is A Beatle' (Fontana, 1963); a parody of **Gene Autry**'s million-selling version of **Johnny Marks**' 'Rudolph the Red-Nosed Reindeer' (1950); and a version of **Tommie Connor**'s 'I Saw Mommy Kissing Santa Claus' (1952). 'It looked like bedlam,' said one of the band's managers, 'but it was organized bedlam.'

Jones' collaborators, prodigally credited on the record-labels under such names as Sir Frederic Gas, Henrietta Pootwaddle and Horatio Q. Birdbath, included the vocalist and tenor saxophonist Red Ingle, who sang on 'Chloe'* (1945) and 'The Glow Worm'* (1946) and after leaving Jones was equally successful, in a similar vein, with 'Timtayshun' (Capitol, 1947), which also featured a pseudonymous **Jo Stafford**, and 'Cigarettes, Whusky and Wild, Wild Women' (Capitol, 1948). Carl Grayson specialized in the 'glug' effect heard on 'Cocktails'; banjoist Freddie Morgan wrote much of the band's material and did the comic-dialect vocals as on 'Chinese Mule Train' (1950); and Mickey Katz who, after two years' apprenticeship in the City Slickers, formed his comic *klezmer* band the Kosher Jammers to put over English-Yiddish parody numbers like 'Borscht Riders in the Sky'. (His son is actor Joel Grey, who starred with Liza Minnelli in *Cabaret*, 1972.)

Jones' 'Musical Depreciation Revue', featuring jugglers, roller-skaters, midgets, dead ducks and the leader conducting proceedings with an umbrella or toilet plunger, was featured in many films and radio and TV shows of the forties and fifties. The album era enabled Jones to develop his ideas more elaborately, as in *Dinner Music for People Who Aren't Very Hungry* (Verve, 1956), *Spike Jones in Stereo* ('Spooktacular in Screaming Sound') (Warners, 1959) and *60 Years of Music America Hates Best* (Liberty, 1960). By 1963, however, these comedy records were no longer selling, and Jones lent his name, though little else, to a 'New Band' which recorded the trad-jazz *Washington Square* (Liberty, 1963) and *Hank Williams Hits* (Liberty, 1964). He died from emphysema, leaving such unfinished projects as a series of parodies of **Leonard Bernstein**'s music lectures, a *Hootenanny Party* and a hot-rod version of *Dance of the Hours*, which he had already parodied in 1949.

TOM JONES

b. Thomas Jones Woodward, 7 June 1940, Treforest, Wales

Described by the British columnist Cassandra as 'sweat personified', by an American critic as 'the man who made the Chippendales possible' and often compared to **Elvis Presley**, Tom Jones was a bestselling recording star of the sixties who became one of the highest-paid vocalists on the television and cabaret circuits. In the late eighties and nineties he managed to reinvent himself and find chart and critical success again.

As Tom Woodward and Tommy Scott, he sang rock'n'roll and contemporary hit material in local clubs in the early sixties. He was discovered in 1964 by Gordon Mills, former member of the Viscounts vocal group, and composer of the **Johnny Kidd** hit 'I'll Never Get Over You'. Using the name Tom Jones and with breeches and pony-tail to echo the successful Tony Richardson film of the eighteenth-century novel, he took the brassy 'It's Not Unusual' (Decca/Parrot, 1964), written by Mills and Les Reed, to No. 1 in Britain and into the American Top Ten.

After minor successes with 'With These Hands' and the theme from the James Bond film *Thunderball*, Jones had a transatlantic hit with his high-volume reading of another film tune, **Burt Bacharach**'s and Hal David's 'What's New Pussycat' (1965). However, Jones' somewhat old-fashioned rock styling fitted uncomfortably with the current musical trends, until he found his niche with a remake of Porter Wagoner's tear-jerking 'Green Green Grass of Home' (1966). In 1967 he had further ballad hits with Mel Tillis's 'Detroit City', **Mickey Newbury**'s 'Funny Familiar Forgotten Feelings', Reed's and Barry Mason's 'I'm Coming Home' and **Lonnie Donegan**'s 'I'll Never Fall in Love Again'.

Jones' British and American hits continued into the early seventies. Their sources were varied: rousing Reed tunes ('Delilah', 1968, and 'Daughter of Darkness', 1970), revivals of old hits (**Clyde McPhatter**'s 'Without Love'*, 1969), and in 1970 the **Leiber–Stoller** song 'I (Who Have Nothing)' – a 1963 success for **Ben E. King** and **Shirley Bassey** – and **Paul Anka**'s 'She's a Lady'* (1971).

Beginning in 1969, his American television show for ABC had top ratings and he appeared live at Las Vegas and other prestige nightspots. There, he was able to indulge his tongue-in-cheek sexy stage movements, to the delight of his largely female audience. With the exception of the American hit 'Say You'll Stay Until Tomorrow' (Epic, 1977), Jones' later recordings veered from souvenirs of his performances such as *Live at Caesar's Palace* (1977) to unsuccessful moves into the country field. These included *Darlin'* (Polydor, 1981) and *Country* (Mercury, 1982).

After several years in semi-retirement, Jones returned in 1987 with *Matador* (Epic), an album of songs from a projected show by Mike Leander and Edward Seago about the famous bullfighter El Cordobes. The hit single 'A Boy from Nowhere' proved that his voice remained as powerful as ever. In 1988 he returned to the charts as the featured singer on the **Prince** song 'Kiss' by the Art of Noise (China), who in 1986 had revived 'Peter Gunn' featuring **Duane Eddy**, who had had the original hit in 1959.

Jones subsequently signed to Jive, releasing *At This Moment* from which 'Move Closer' was a minor hit. With a host of Welsh performers he appeared on **George Martin**'s recording of Dylan Thomas' *Under Milk Wood*. His 1991 album *Carrying a Torch* included four songs written and produced by **Van Morrison** as well as others by Albert Hammond. In 1993 Jones had another British Top Twenty hit with Dave Stewart (**Eurythmics**), a revival of **The Beatles**' 'All You Need Is Love', recorded for a children's charity.

The reinvention of the singer as a pop icon continued with *The Lead and How to Swing It*, recorded for **Trevor Horn**'s ZTT label in 1994. Among its producers and remixers were **Teddy Riley**, D. J. Battlecat and **Killing Joke**'s Youth. In 1996 he appeared in the cult film *Mars Attacks* and it was his reading of **Randy Newman**'s 'You Can Leave Your Hat on' that was used as striptease music in *The Full Monty* (1997). In 1999 he had the biggest hit of his career with *Reload* (Gut), a collection of duets with the likes of **Robin Williams** and Cerys Matthews of **Catatonia**, in which he attempted camp and pomp readings of songs like **Iggy Pop**'s 'Lust for Life' and **Talking Heads**' 'Burning Down the House'.

JANIS JOPLIN

b. 19 January 1943, Port Arthur, Texas, USA, d. 4 October 1970, Hollywood, California

The finest white blues and soul singer of her generation, Janis Joplin was a central figure of San Francisco rock in the late sixties.

Her first musical inspiration came from **Leadbelly** and **Bessie Smith** albums and in 1961 she left Port Arthur to study at the University of Texas in Austin. There she played in a bluegrass group at Threadgill's Club and, dropping out of college, spent the next few years on the folk scenes of Austin and San Francisco. In 1966 she settled in the latter and joined a blues band, Big Brother and the Holding Company. With bassist Peter Albin, guitarists Sam Andrews and James Gurley and drummer David Getz, Joplin recorded a poorly produced but nonetheless exciting eponymous album for Bob Shad's Chicago label Mainstream.

Their performance at the 1967 Monterey Pop Festival, with Joplin's raw, almost uncontrolled interpretation of **Big Mama Thornton**'s 'Ball and Chain' made them instant stars. With Albert Grossman as their manager, the group was signed by Columbia's Clive Davis, who was in the Monterey audience. The following year both *Cheap Thrills* and Joplin's reading of Erma Franklin's 1967 Shout recording 'Piece of My Heart' were big hits. Produced by John Simon, the album, which included **George Gershwin**'s 'Summertime', was criticized for the sometimes ragged character of the instrumental backing.

Shortly after the album's release, Joplin determined to launch a solo career, while Big Brother made two further Columbia albums, *Bee a Brother* (1970) and *How Hard It Is* (1971). With Sam Andrews and other San Francisco musicians, Joplin formed a soul-styled backing group which performed on the uneven but commercially successful *I Got Dem Old Kozmic Blues Again, Mama!*.

In 1970 she formed the Full Tilt Boogie Band with John Till (guitar) and Brad Campbell (bass), from the *Kosmic Blues* session group, plus Clark Pierson (drums) and former **Ronnie Hawkins** pianist Richard Bell. Her finest backing group, it provided sympa-

thetic accompaniment for the disciplined yet passionate vocals on *Pearl* (1971), produced by Paul Rothchild. Appearing shortly after Joplin's sudden death, both the album and her intense version of **Kris Kristofferson**'s 'Me and Bobby McGee' were No. 1 hits. *Pearl*'s other highlights were the chuckling, *a cappella* 'Mercedes Benz' and a majestic reading of **Dan Penn**'s and Spooner Oldham's 'A Woman Left Lonely'. By far Joplin's most accomplished recording, the album's impact made her death from a drugs overdose more poignant, despite the fact that it seemed to fit a romantic notion of the artist living life to excess.

In 1972 Columbia released *Janis Joplin in Concert*, which contained recordings from a number of live performances, while the 1974 documentary film *Janis* contained rare footage of her Austin folk-club days. In 1993 Sony released a comprehensive career retrospective, also titled *Janis*. The mythologizing of Joplin's career was complete in 1979 when **Bette Midler** starred in *The Rose*, a fictional film loosely based on Joplin's life and death. In 1973 Myra Friedman, a former Grossman staff member, published *Buried Alive*, the best of several biographies of Joplin. *Live at Winterland '68* (1998) was an archive set, while *The Ultimate Collection* (1998) was the definitive retrospective.

SCOTT JOPLIN

b. 4 November 1868, Texarkana, Texas, USA, d. 1 April 1917, New York

Known as 'The King of Ragtime', Joplin was the greatest ragtime composer. His work enjoyed a revival in the seventies when **Marvin Hamlisch** used his tune 'The Entertainer' in the score for the film *The Sting* (1973).

Joplin's father was a railroad worker, freed from slavery only five years before his son's birth, a violinist and former member of a plantation dance band. Joplin's mother was a singer and banjo-player. As a child, Joplin took piano lessons before leaving home in 1882 to wander Texas and Louisiana playing in bars, honky-tonks and travelling shows. In 1893 he performed at the Chicago World's Fair and two years later settled in Sedalia, Missouri. He conducted the Texas Medley Quartet, a vocal group who performed some of his earliest compositions.

His first and most successful instrumental was 'Maple Leaf Rag', written in 1897 and published two years later. It sold over a million sheet-music copies in Joplin's lifetime and was eventually recorded nearly a hundred times. Among the earliest discs were those by the US Marine Band and banjoist Fred van Eps.

Moving to St Louis, he published further works, including 'The Entertainer' (1902) and 'The Cascade'

(1904). He spent the final decade of his life in New York, where he appeared in vaudeville as 'The King of Ragtime Composers'. However, he was obsessed with writing and publishing *Treemonisha*, an opera whose score mixed ragtime, plantation songs and drawing-room ballads. Disappointment at its rejection by publishers contributed to the depressive illness which led to his death in a mental institution. The opera eventually received its première in Atlanta in 1971.

In contrast to the Tin Pan Alley versions of ragtime, Joplin's tunes were delicate and stately: in his 1908 book *The School of Ragtime* he wrote, 'Never play ragtime fast at any time.' Though he never recorded, pianola rolls of his playing were made and were re-issued by Riverside and Biograph. His influence was evident in the work of jazz performers like **Jelly Roll Morton** and Willie 'The Lion' Smith.

With renewed interest in ragtime during the seventies, a number of recordings of Joplin's work were made by modern pianists and arrangers. Among them were Ann Charters (Portents/Sonet), Knocky Parker (Audiophile), **Joshua Rifkin** (Nonesuch, 1971) and Gunther Schuller (Angel). Billy Dee Williams played the title role in the biopic *Scott Joplin* (1976), while a short documentary, *Scott Joplin, King of Ragtime Composers*, was directed by Amelia Anderson in 1977.

LOUIS JORDAN
b. 8 July 1908, Brinkley, Arkansas, USA, d. 4 February 1975, Los Angeles, California

An entertainer *par excellence*, Jordan's joyous, swing-inflected jump blues, described by one critic as 'jazz with a broad grin', was immensely popular with both black and white audiences in the immediate post-war years. Cited by numerous black performers of the early fifties as the man who made the blues jump, he was the single most important catalyst in the development of R&B. He was also a central influence on rock'n'roll, if only because Jordan's producer **Milt Gabler** based his records with **Bill Haley** on his work with Jordan. Several of Jordan's major hits were subsequently reworked by other artists, including the influential 'Let the Good Times Roll' (**Shirley and Lee**, 1956); 'Caldonia'* (**Woody Herman**, 1945); 'Choo Choo Ch'Boogie'* (Haley, 1956); and 'Is You Is (Or Is You Ain't My Baby)' (**Bing Crosby** with the **Andrews Sisters**, 1944). Others of Jordan's songs have remained in the repertoire of countless bar bands, notably 'Saturday Night Fish Fry'* (1949) which, in its laconic account of a police raid on a party, foreshadowed **Chuck Berry**'s witty approach to narrative.

As a child Jordan learned saxophone from his father and in his teens joined the Rabbit Foot Minstrels (with which **Ma Rainey** and **Bessie Smith** had once performed). In the early thirties he moved to

Philadelphia and, after singing with Charlie Gaines' and Joe Marshall's bands, in 1936 joined **Chick Webb**'s band, singing alongside **Ella Fitzgerald**. Jordan left the band in 1938 to form his Tympany Five Group (which name he continued to use despite its fluctuating size). Signed to Decca, Jordan's first recordings (which included the country singer **Carson Robison**'s 'Barnacle Bill the Sailor', 1938) were undistinguished, but by the time of 'At the Swing Cats Ball' (1939) Jordan had begun his rhythmic refinement of swing which reached its first mature expression in 1942's 'Five Guys Named Moe'. His 1944 recording of **Johnny Mercer**'s 'G.I. Jive' was his first million-seller and won Jordan the title of 'King of the Jukeboxes'.

Though subsequent Tympany Five recordings confirmed that the essential Jordan sound was a tight rhythm section in support of a close-knit sax and trumpet behind his irrepressibly good-humoured singing (as on 'Ain't Nobody Here But Us Chickens', 'Beans and Cornbread', 1947), so confident were Decca of his widespread appeal that they teamed Jordan with Crosby ('My Baby Said Yes', 1945), Ella Fitzgerald ('Baby It's Cold Outside', 1949) and **Louis Armstrong** ('Life Is So Peculiar', 1950). Jordan also appeared in several films, including *Junior Prom* (1946) and the bizarre all-black Western *Look Out Sister* (1949), in which he rode to the rescue singing 'Caldonia' in a clear parody of other singing cowboys.

By the end of the forties younger, rawer singers like **Wynonie Harris** and **Roy Brown** had broken Jordan's monopoly of the R&B charts, and in 1951, against the advice of Gabler, Jordan formed a fifteen-piece big band. That failed and in 1954, in poor health, Jordan left Decca, just as Gabler began producing Haley in a style closely modelled on Jordan's. Jordan label-hopped his way through the fifties and sixties, recording for RCA, Mercury (where he was produced by **Quincy Jones**), Ray Charles' Tangerine label and Black Lion (where he recorded with **Chris Barber**). In the seventies he re-formed the Tympany Five and in 1974 appeared at the Newport Jazz Festival. He made his last recordings for **Johnny Otis**'s Blues Spectrum label in the same year. *Five Guys Named Moe*, a musical featuring a selection of songs associated with Jordan, was a long-running hit in London's West End in the nineties.

JOURNEY
Prairie Prince, b. 7 May 1950, Charlotte, North Carolina, USA (replaced by Aynsley Dunbar, b. 1946, Liverpool, England, replaced by Steve Smith, b. Boston); Greg Rolie, b. 1948 (replaced by Jonathan Cain); Neal Schon, b. 27 February 1954, San Mateo, California; George Tickner; Ross Valory, b. 7 May 1950, San Francisco,

California; Robert Fleischman (replaced by Steve Perry, b. 22 January 1953, Hanford, California)

Journey blended pop harmonies and tunes with rock presentation to become one of the most successful American mainstream bands of the seventies and eighties.

Rolie had played keyboards with **Carlos Santana** and sung on his group's 1970 hits 'Evil Ways' and 'Black Magic Woman'. With guitarist Schon he left the band in 1972 and formed Journey with Tickner (guitar) and Valory (bass) from San Francisco band Frumious Bandersnatch. The group gained its name in a competition for radio listeners, and the first drummer was Prince from the Tubes. He was replaced by ex-**John Mayall**, **Jeff Beck** and **Frank Zappa** associate Dunbar for the eponymous début album released by Columbia in 1975.

Like *Journey*, the albums *Look into the Future* (1976) and *Next* (1977) (after which Fleischman joined on lead vocals) were unassuming, notable primarily for the quality of Rolie's and Schon's instrumental work. For *Infinity** (1978), produced by Roy Thomas Baker, Perry replaced Fleischman and two singles, 'Wheel in the Sky' and 'Lights', were minor hits. Dunbar was replaced by Smith (ex-Jean-Luc Ponty and Montrose) on *Evolution** (1979), which included Journey's first major hit, 'Lovin', Touchin', Squeezin''. Subsequently, Dunbar, who joined **Jefferson Starship**, sued for breach of contract.

After *Departure** (1980) and the live *Captured** (1980), *Escape** became the group's largest-selling album, due in part to the arrival of keyboards-player Cain, who co-wrote 'Who's Crying Now', one of the album's three Top Ten singles. The others were 'Don't Stop Believin'' and 'Open Arms'. In 1982 Perry charted with 'Don't Fight It', a duet with **Kenny Loggins**, while the next Journey album, *Frontiers* (1983), provided two further hits in 'Separate Ways (Worlds Apart)' and 'Faithfully'.

In 1984 Perry made the solo album *Street Talk* and reached the Top Ten with 'Oh Sherrie', while Journey recorded 'Only the Young' from the film *Vision Quest* (1985) and released *Raised on Radio* in 1986, with its hit 'Be Good to Yourself'. The band split up shortly afterwards. Schon and Cain formed the successful Bad English, while Rolie, Valory and Smith eventually joined forces again in 1991 as Storm. In 1992 Schon joined Hardline, who subsequently signed to MCA Records. In 1993 he toured with former **Bad Company** leader Paul Rodgers. The band re-formed for *Trial by Fire* (1996), which included the power-ballad 'When You Love a Woman'. In 1998, after the release of *Greatest Hits – Live*, Perry, whose health prevented him from touring, left the band for a solo career.

JUDAS PRIEST

K. K. Downing; Rob Halford, b. 25 August 1951, Birmingham, England; Ian Hill; John Hinch (replaced by Alan Moore, replaced by Simon Phillips, replaced by Les Binks, replaced by Dave Holland); Glen Tipton

With their twin lead guitars and a leather-clad singer who made his stage entrance on a motorcycle, Judas Priest were the essence of British heavy metal.

Originally a Birmingham-based pop band, Judas Priest's sound became heavier when Hill (bass) and Halford (vocals) joined the group in 1973. With guitarists Downing and Tipton, plus drummer Hinch, replacing the original members soon afterwards, the band became a fully fledged heavy-metal unit. Signing to the independent Gull label in 1974, they recorded *Rocka Rolla* (supervised by **Black Sabbath** producer Rodger Bain) and *Sad Wings of Destiny* (1976), on which Moore played drums.

With heavy metal only a fringe music in Britain's punk era, Judas Priest slowly built up a following and Rainbow and ex-**Deep Purple** bassist Roger Glover produced *Sin After Sin*, their first album for Columbia. Phillips took over on drums for that record only to be replaced by Binks on *Stained Class* (1978) and *Killing Machine* (1979), which was retitled *Hell Bent for Leather* in America, where it produced a minor hit in 'Take on the World'.

Recorded in Japan, *Unleashed in the East* celebrated the strobe, dry ice and mega-decibel excesses of Judas Priest's stage act. Pleading fatigue from the rigours of touring, Binks was replaced by Holland for *British Steel* (1980), released just as the group and the heavy metal genre came into their own. Without any perceptible concession to mainstream taste, Judas Priest had three British hits from that album: 'Living After Midnight', 'Breaking the Law' and 'United'.

Point of Entry (1981) also reached the British Top Twenty while *Screaming for Vengeance* (1982), produced by Tom Allom, sold more than two million worldwide. The group's later albums included *Defenders of the Faith* (1984), *Turbo* (1986) and *Live* (1987). *Ram It Down* (1988) was Judas Priest's next studio album. *Painkiller* (1990) with its speed guitar pyrotechnics saw the band resist the temptations of power-balladry which so many metal acts had succumbed to. In the same year a Nevada court ruled that the band was not responsible for the suicide of a teenage fan after listening to one of their songs. Halford left the band to form his own, Fight, in 1992. However, a legal dispute with Priest's label, Sony, kept him from recording. The other members of the band announced that they would continue as Judas Priest. *Metal Works 73–93* (1993) was a less than definitive retrospective. In 1997 the group released *Jugulator*, while a year later Halford's group, now called Two, issued *Voyeur*.

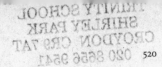

WYNONNA JUDD
b. 30 May 1964, California, USA

The eighties equivalent of the **Everly Brothers,** Wynonna and her mother Naomi were the most successful female duo of modern country music. However, when the duo broke up in the early nineties Wynonna's success continued unabated, unlike that of either of the Everlys. That said, like Phil and Don's, the Judds' sound, with its foregrounding of family harmonies over primarily acoustic instruments, was both a throwback and a confirmation of the rise of the new traditionalists.

As small children Wynonna and her sister Ashley sang together regularly with their mother Naomi (*b. 11 January 1946, Morrel, Kentucky, USA*). The family moved from California to Kentucky after Naomi's divorce and then to Nashville where Wynonna attempted a career as a solo singer. A meeting with hospitalized producer Brent Maher led to mother (who was a nurse) and daughter winning a contract with RCA. Their eponymous début outing (1984) included the memorable 'John Deere Tractor' but it was *Why Not Me* (1985) which showed off their impassioned harmonies to perfection. Its hits included the title track and the first of their many country chart-toppers 'Mama He's Crazy'.

Rockin' with the Rhythm (1985) saw the duo extend their repertoire (and their audience) with the respectful traditional song 'Grandpa (Tell Me About the Good Old Days)', being immediately followed by an emphatic version of the **Allen Toussaint** composition 'Working in the Coal Mine', best known as a hit for **Lee Dorsey**. The album established the duo as country superstars and allowed them to intersperse their (mostly) acoustic-based hits (which included 'Cry Myself to Sleep' and 'Guardian Angels') with an intriguing number of recordings with guest artists. These included **Dire Straits**' Mark Knopfler on 'Water of Love' (*River of Time*, 1989), **Bonnie Raitt** on 'Rompin' Stompin' Blues' (*Love Can Build a Bridge*, 1990) and **Emmylou Harris** on 'The Sweetest Gift' (*Heart Land*, 1987). The retrospective *The Judds Collection* (1983–1990) is one of the worst anthologies ever produced.

After *Build a Bridge* Naomi retired due to ill health and Wynonna continued on her own. *Wynonna* (1992), her first solo album, saw the hits continue unabated. It included three country chart-toppers, 'She Is His Only Need', 'I Saw the Light' and 'No One Else on Earth'. *Tell Me Why* (1993), a more confident set, saw Wynonna increasing her range. It included several hit singles, including 'Tell Me Why' and 'My Strongest Weakness'. In 1994 she had another major hit with **Mary-Chapin Carpenter**'s 'Girls with Guitars' and in 1997 released *Greatest Hits*. 2000's *New*

Day Dawning saw Wynonna joining Tony Brown and others as producer and attempting a number of versions of other people's songs, including **Joni Mitchell** ('Help Me') and Macy Gray. It also included a bonus EP of four tracks recorded with her mother. In general, the album saw Wynonna moving popwards. *Reunion Live* (2000) documented in too much detail – one critic noted that not a word was cut from the lengthy introductions to each song – the reunion of Wynonna and Naomi, and saw them singing together in wondrous harmony.

JUNGLE BROTHERS
Mike G, b. Mike Small, c. 1969, Harlem, New York, USA; Sammy B, b. Sammy Burwell, c. 1968, Harlem, New York; Afrika Baby Bam, b. Nathanial Hall, c. 1971, Brooklyn, New York

The Jungle Brothers came to prominence with the US East Coast rap scene of the late 1980s, mixing humour with the political consciousness and sense of Afro-American history of **Public Enemy** and **Boogie Down Productions**.

Rappers Mike G and Baby Bam and DJ Sammy B began performing together while still at school, and signed to the independent Warlock label in 1987, releasing their first single, 'Jimbrowski', later that year. This was followed in 1998 by the classic rap single 'Straight out the Jungle' and an album of the same name. The album was at once meaningful, intelligent, funky and fun, and as such stood out against the machismo and moral ambivalence of much of the rap output of the time. A third single, 'I'll House You', innovatively set hip-hop rhymes over a 4:4 house backbeat.

The début album featured a guest rap from Q-Tip of **A Tribe Called Quest**, which with the Jungle Brothers formed part of the loose Native Tongues collective of hip-hop artists promoting positivity through humour and eclectic beats. Others included **De La Soul**, **Queen Latifah** and Monie Love.

After the success of *Straight out the Jungle*, the band signed to Warner Bros and released *Done by the Forces of Nature* to a more subdued but still positive critical response in 1989. The album featured denser production and use of instrumentation and samples than its predecessor, as well as further guest appearances from the Native Tongues collective on the single 'Doin' Our Own Dang'. The album also established the Jungle Brothers within the context of recent black American progressive music: 'Good News Comin'' used African high-life guitars and rhythms as **Earth Wind & Fire** had done on 1975's 'It's the Way of the World', while 'Acknowledge Your Own History''s dissection of black America's past echoed **Stevie Wonder**'s *Black Man*.

After the experimental *JBeez Wit the Remedy* (1993), which displeased Warners and was underpromoted and sold poorly, the band members occupied themselves away from the Jungle Brothers over the next two years. In 1996 they released a comeback album, *Raw Deluxe*, on Gee Street, featuring mellower rhymes against beats and samples reminiscent of A Tribe Called Quest's *Low End Theory* period. Singles from the album included 'Brain' and 'Jungle Brother', both of which were remixed by trip-hop and jungle producers, expanding the group's potential audience.

In 1998 the band started work on a fifth album, produced by Alex Gifford of UK big-beat act the Propellerheads. One track, 'You Want It Back', billed as the Propellerheads featuring the Jungle Brothers, appeared on an EP at the end of 1998. It was followed by the album *V.I.P.* (1999).

BILL JUSTIS
b. 14 October 1927, Birmingham, Alabama, USA, d. 15 July 1982

As A&R man and producer, with Scotty Moore and **Bill Black**, Justis was one of the key figures in **Sam Phillips**' Sun Records operation.

He grew up in Memphis, learning music from his concert pianist mother. Justis took up jazz saxophone and formed his first dance band in 1942. He studied music at college and wrote arrangements before joining the Sun organization in 1957. Almost immediately, 'Raunchy' by Bill Justis and his Orchestra (the Sun session players) was a national hit on Phillips International. A watered-down blues with rasping sax from Justis and co-written with guitarist Sidney Manker, it was clearly inspired by **Bill Doggett**'s 1956 hit 'Honky Tonk' and was covered by Ernie Freeman (Imperial) and **Pat Boone**'s musical director **Billy Vaughn** (Dot), who also had big hits with the tune.

The follow-up, 'College Man' (1958), was a minor hit but *Cloud Nine* (1958) and other singles (which included 'Flea Circus', composed by future **Booker T. and the MGs** guitarist Steve Cropper) were unsuccessful. Justis also worked with many of Sun's artists but his most important discovery was **Charlie Rich**, whom he found singing jazz material in a bar. After giving Rich some **Jerry Lee Lewis** records and telling him to 'get that bad', Justis produced many of his records, including the memorable 1960 hit 'Lonely Weekends'.

Shortly before that record's success, Justis and **Jack Clement** had been fired by Phillips for 'insubordination'. Justis formed his own shortlived label (Play Me) and produced Ray Smith for Judd Phillips' Judd label before becoming staff producer for RCA Groove in 1961. There, he was reunited with Rich, producing a version of **Jimmy Reed**'s R&B hit 'Big Boss Man'.

Justis moved on to work for Fred Foster's Monument label and Sound Stage 7, where he produced the female vocal group the Dixiebelles on their hits '(Down at) Papa Joe's' (1963) and 'Southtown USA' (1964). In 1972 he released *Enchanted Sea* (Harmony).

BURT KAEMPFERT

b. 16 October 1923, Hamburg, Germany, d. 21 June 1980, Majorca, Spain

As well as being the first person to record **The Beatles**, Kaempfert was one of the most successful orchestra leaders of the sixties. Moreover, like Horst Jankowski – who had a million-seller with his own composition 'A Walk in the Black Forest'* (Philips, 1965) – and **James Last**, he was one of the few German artists to achieve international acclaim both as a conductor of easy-listening tunes in the manner of **Percy Faith** and as a composer.

A multi-instrumentalist, Kaempfert studied at the Hamburg School of Music and during the Second World War made his radio début with Hans Busch's orchestra. He subsequently formed his own orchestra and in the fifties had several hits in Germany on Loydor. He was also an arranger and producer for the company and as such he was responsible for such hits as **Freddy Quinn**'s 'Die Gittare und das Meer'* and Ivor Robic's 'Morgen'* (Laurie, 1959), the first American Top Twenty hit to be sung in German. Retitled 'One More Sunrise' and given English lyrics, the song also provided Dickie Valentine with a British hit (on Pye) and Leslie Uggams with an American hit (on Columbia). Kaempfert's own first million-seller was 'Wunderland bei Nacht' ('Wonderland by Night'), a hymn to Manhattan which topped the American charts in 1960 on Decca, despite covers by **Louis Prima** and Anita Bryant (Carlton). Kaempfert's other international hits, all melodic, easy-listening instrumentals include 'Tenderly' (1961), his revival of the 1948 song 'Red Roses for a Blue Lady'*, and 'Three o'Clock in the Morning' (1965). He regularly toured America and released numerous bestselling albums there, including *Lights Out, Sweet Dreams* (1963), *Magic Music* (1965), *Hold Me* (1967) and *Free and Easy* (1971).

Kaempfert was also responsible for The Beatles' oddest million-selling record. While they were in Hamburg he hired them to back Tony Sheridan singing 'My Bonnie Lies Over the Ocean' and 'When the Saints Go Marching In' in 1961. A hit in Germany where Sheridan was a star, the record sold poorly elsewhere until 1964 when in the wake of The Beatles' phenomenal success it charted in America (on MGM). The same year in the UK another Sheridan–Beatles collaboration, the old **Eddie Cantor** song 'Ain't She Sweet', on which **John Lennon** sang lead, was a minor hit on Polydor.

Kaempfert's greatest successes as a composer were 'Wooden Heart (Muss I' Denn)', which **Elvis Presley** sang in *GI Blues* (1961) and which gave Joe Dowell an American No. 1 on Smash in 1961; 'Spanish Eyes', which he recorded originally as the instrumental 'Moon over Naples' before, with a lyric by Eddie Snyder, it became a million-seller for **Al Martino** in 1965; and the oft-recorded 'Strangers in the Night' (also with words by Snyder), a million-seller for **Frank Sinatra** in 1966, which Kaempfert wrote for the first film he scored, *A Man Could Get Killed*.

GUS KAHN

b. 6 November 1886, Koblenz, Germany, d. 8 October 1941, Beverly Hills, California, USA

A prolific writer of Tin Pan Alley pop songs, Kahn, in conjunction with **Walter Donaldson** and others, also wrote for films and Broadway shows.

An immigrant to America at the age of four, Kahn was raised and educated in Chicago. In his youth he started writing special material for vaudeville acts and quickly graduated to songwriting on moving to New York. His first significant collaborator was fellow Chicagoan, Egbert Van Alstyne (co-author of 'In the Shade of the Old Apple Tree', 1905), with whom Kahn wrote 'Memories' (1915) and 'Pretty Baby' (1916), but more important was his association with **Al Jolson**, for whom he regularly wrote. With his wife, Grace LeBoy, Kahn wrote one of Jolson's first hits, 'Everybody Rag with Me' (1916) and he contributed 'I'll Say She Does' to Jolson's *Sinbad*, the Broadway hit of 1918.

Kahn's most successful partnership was with Donaldson, but in New York, and later in Hollywood, Kahn had a number of other collaborators. These included bandleader **Isham Jones** ('I'll See You in My Dreams' and 'It Had to Be You', 1925); **George** and **Ira Gershwin** (with whom he wrote *Show Girl*, which included 'Liza' and starred **Ruby Keeler**); **Vincent Youmans** (with whom he wrote several songs for the Latin extravaganza film musical, *Flying Down to Rio*, 1933); **Victor Schertzinger** ('One Night of Love', 1934); Arthur Johnson ('Thanks a Million', introduced by **Dick Powell** in the 1935 film of the same title); Bronislaw Kaper and Walter Jurmann ('Someone to Care for Me', sung by **Deanna Durbin** in *Three Smart Girls*, 1937, and 'All God's Chillun Got Rhythm' for the Marx Brothers' *A Day at the Races*, 1937); and **Nacio Herb Brown** ('You Stepped out of a

Dream', sung by **Tony Martin** in *Ziegfeld Girl*, 1941).

With Donaldson, Kahn wrote his most successful Broadway show and the only one transferred to the screen (in 1930); *Whoopee* (1928) featured the classics 'Makin' Whoopee' and 'Love Me or Leave Me' sung by **Eddie Cantor** and **Ruth Etting**. Other successful songs written by the pair were 'Yes Sir, That's My Baby' (1925) and 'My Baby Just Cares for Me' (1930). After his death, his life formed the basis of *I'll See You in My Dreams* (1951) in which he was played by Danny Thomas while **Doris Day** played his wife and some-time collaborator, Grace LeBoy.

THE KALIN TWINS
Harold Kalin; Herbie Kalin, b. 16 February 1939

A bright-voiced vocal duo, the Kalin Twins had major hits in 1958 and were among the first American rock'n'roll artists to tour Britain.

Signed to Decca on the advice of songwriter Clint Ballard Jnr, the Twins had their first hit with a version of Paul Evans and Jack Reardon's 'When', which reached the Top Ten in America and went to No. 1 in Britain on London. Evans, who also composed **Bobby Vinton**'s 'Roses Are Red', later scored his own big hit with the novelty 'Seven Little Girls Sittin' in the Back Seat' (Guaranteed, 1959).

The Kalins' second single, 'Forget Me Not', was also an American hit and in late 1958 they appeared in Britain headlining a package tour that included the then unknown **Cliff Richard**. In 1989 the twins in turn supported Cliff Richard in his London concerts. 'It's Only the Beginning' and 'Sweet Sugar Lips' were less successful in 1959 and Herbie and Hal (having turned twenty) made way for new teen-idols.

'When' remained popular and in 1975 the British group **Showaddywaddy** had a Top Ten hit with a new version of the song.

KALMAR AND RUBY
Bert Kalmar, b. 16 February 1884, New York, USA, d. 18 September 1947, Los Angeles, California; Harry Ruby, b. Harry Rubunstein, 27 January 1895, New York, d. 23 February 1974, Los Angeles

Screenwriters and songwriters, Kalmar and Ruby wrote the scores for nine Broadway musicals, three of which were filmed. Their best-known songs were 'Who's Sorry Now' (1923), a million-seller for **Connie Francis** when revived in 1958, and 'Three Little Words', introduced by **Bing Crosby** in *Check and Double Check* (1930) and later used as the title of the biopic in which **Fred Astaire** appeared as Kalmar and Red Skelton as Ruby.

Kalmar was a child magician in a tent show, and graduated to burlesque and vaudeville, often in a song

and dance team with his wife, Jessie Brown Kalmar. In 1911 **Arthur Collins** had a hit with 'In the Land of Harmony', written by Kalmar and Ted Snyder, and Kalmar established a publishing company with fellow vaudevillian Harry Puck. Another early hit was 'Oh What a Pal Was Mary', co-written with Edgar Leslie and recorded by **Henry Burr** (1919), among others. After an injury curtailed his performing career Kalmar formed a writing partnership with pianist Ruby, briefly a songplugger with Harry Cohn (later the head of Columbia pictures). After placing songs in several revues they wrote their first Broadway score, *Helen of Troy, NY*, in 1921 and had their first success with *The Ramblers* (1926, filmed as *The Cuckoos* in 1930 with Bert Wheeler singing 'I Love You So Much'). During this period the duo also worked with **Lorenz Hart**, Oscar Hammerstein (later of **Rodgers and Hammerstein**) and **Otto Harbach**. It was for one of these shows, *Good Boy* (1928), that the pair wrote 'I Wanna be Loved By You', a hit for **Ben Selvin** and later revived by Marilyn Monroe in Billy Wilder's *Some Like It Hot* (1959).

The success of *Top Speed* (1929, filmed 1930) and *Animal Crackers* (1928, filmed 1930) with the Marx Brothers, which introduced the classic 'Hooray for Captain Spaulding', led to Kalmar and Ruby scripting and writing songs for two further Marx Brothers films, *Horse Feathers* (1932) and the classic *Duck Soup* (1933), which included 'His Excellency Is Dead' and 'The Country Is Going to War'. In the forties the partnership broke up and Ruby wrote 'Give Me the Simple Life' with Rube Bloom. Introduced in *Wake Up and Dream* (1946), the song provided hits for **Benny Goodman** and Bing Crosby with **Jimmy Dorsey**.

JACK KAPP
b. 15 June 1901, Chicago, Illinois, USA, d. 25 March 1949, New York

A leading member of the American record industry establishment in the thirties and forties, Kapp's prime achievement was the founding of American Decca in 1934, which signalled the revival of the American record industry after the Depression.

Kapp first worked as a salesman for Columbia (1918–25), then moved in 1926 to Brunswick, where, as recording director (from 1930), he supervised sessions by many of its popular, 'race' and hillbilly artists. In 1933 he resigned to plan, with his brother Dave, an American equivalent of the British Decca label, finan-cially assisted by the latter's managing director Edward Lewis but remaining independent of the British com-pany. The new label appeared in the summer of 1934, with retail prices at 35 cents; previously most major-label records had been priced at 75 cents, but the post-

Depression way had been indicated in 1933 by Victor with their 35-cent Bluebird line. That, however, was a 'budget' label; what Decca offered were top stars at bargain prices. Kapp skilfully acquired cachet for the company by signing, at the outset, **Bing Crosby** and **Guy Lombardo**; they were shortly followed by the **Ink Spots**, the **Mills Brothers**, **Louis Armstrong**, **Louis Jordan**, **Lucky Millinder**, **Lionel Hampton**, **Jimmie Lunceford**, **Woody Herman** and the **Andrews Sisters**. Decca was also a pioneer of film soundtrack albums, its most successful being *The Wizard of Oz* (1939), featuring **Judy Garland**.

At first the 'race' and hillbilly catalogues relied heavily on artists Kapp had previously worked with at Brunswick or its sister-label Vocalion, but a forceful policy of talent-hunting, particularly on regular field-trips to the Texas cities of Houston, Dallas and San Antonio, soon gave the hillbilly catalogue great strength in Western swing (**Milton Brown**) and related material (**Jimmie Davis**, the Shelton Brothers, later **Ernest Tubb**). At the same time, the Chicago studio, overseen by **Mayo Williams** (who had also worked with Kapp in earlier times), recruited many of the leading blues artists of the late thirties, including Bumble Bee Slim, Leroy's Buddy (Bill Gaither) and Peetie Wheatstraw.

After his death in 1949, Decca significantly retreated from recording black artists for some years. In 1955 Dave Kapp left Decca to form Kapp Records, which had immediate success with pianist **Roger Williams** ('Autumn Leaves', 1955).

ANTON KARAS
b. 7 July 1906, Vienna, Austria, d. 9 January 1985, Vienna

Karas was the composer and performer (on the zither) of the million-selling 'Harry Lime Theme' (1949), the ominous title music to the film *The Third Man*. One of the first soundtrack successes after the Second World War, the music's phenomenal sales (which of the various recordings of the tune are estimated to be over 40 million) indicated the commercial possibilities of soundtrack recordings and initiated a series of similarly exotic-sounding film themes. A mark of the tune's instant recognizability and its long-term popularity was **The Band**'s inclusion of it on their album of revivals of fifties classics, *Moondog Matinee* (1973).

Karas learned to play the zither in his youth and from the age of eighteen earned his living playing the instrument in wine and beer gardens around Vienna. The director of *The Third Man*, Carol Reed, who wanted music appropriate to post-war Vienna, but not waltzes, heard Karas while on location and commissioned him to write the music. Karas composed

the 'Harry Lime Theme' by rearranging a practice piece from a zither tutor. In the wake of the film's success, Karas toured Europe and America (where **Guy Lombardo** had the bigger hit with his cover-version). Karas' tune was also used as the theme music to the teleseries *The Third Man*, starring Michael Rennie.

In the fifties Karas returned to Austria and opened his own wine house in Grinzing, 'The Third Man', at which he made regular guest appearances.

IRVING KAUFMAN
b. 1891, Syracuse, New York, USA, d. 3 January 1976, Indio, California

Like the Englishman **Stanley Kirkby**, Irving Kaufman possessed a strong, theatrical singing style that answered the demands of acoustic recording techniques. His voice was heard, though often uncredited or masked by pseudonym, on thousands of popular and novelty records made between 1910 and the end of the twenties. He came from the same melodramatic vocal tradition as **Al Jolson** and Harry Richman. He had perfect pitch, and was a favourite choice for vocal refrains on dance-band recordings by such prolific leaders as Sam Lanin, Ben Bernie and Lou Gold, or with the California Ramblers.

Kaufman began his showbusiness career as a boy soprano before becoming one of the first song pluggers to work for a record company rather than a music publisher. He worked for Edison, Victor and other labels simultaneously (and pseudonymously) before joining the stage and recording group the Avon Comedy Four – which also included Charles Dale, Harry Goodwin and Joe Smith – in 1916. In 1922 he became a vocalist with Gustave Haenschen's radio orchestra. Kaufman in addition worked with his brother Jack, also a prolific recording artist and sometimes was used, like **Vernon Dalhart** or **Frank Luther**, for novelty material on the fringes of hillbilly music, such as the 'bum' (hobo) songs popular about 1928.

In the thirties, under such aliases as Lazy Dan, Salty Sam the Sailor, Mr Jim and Happy Jim Parsons, Kaufman worked less in recording studios than on radio, where he appeared in *Broadway Vanities* (1934) and *Lazy Dan* (1935), and also had his own show. He was less active in the late thirties and the radio transcriptions he cut in 1946 are believed to have been his last recordings. In 1947 he returned to the stage in the musical version of Elmer Rice's *Street Scene*.

DANNY KAYE
b. David Daniel Kominski, 18 June 1913, Brooklyn, New York, USA, d. 3 March 1987, Los Angeles, California

A madcap entertainer, Kaye was known for his tongue-twisters and his rubber-faced mimicry. Though his greatest success was in Hollywood, his recordings of 'Thumbelina' and 'The Ugly Duckling' (1952) have become perennial favourites with children.

The son of Russian immigrants, Kaye worked as a waiter in Florida, graduating to singing and comedy on the Catskills 'Borscht Circuit' in the early thirties. An Oriental tour in 1934 encouraged him to develop his scat singing and pantomime. In 1939 he made his Broadway début in *The Straw Hat Revue* and in 1941 nightly stopped *Lady in the Dark* with his version of **Ira Gershwin** and **Kurt Weill**'s speciality song 'Tchaikovsky', in which he reeled off the names of fifty-four Russian composers, some real, some fictitious, in thirty-four seconds. He followed this with an appearance in **Cole Porter**'s *Let's Face It* (1941), for which his wife, Sylvia Fine, who wrote much of his comedy material and songs, supplied 'Melody in 4-F'.

Kaye's first film was *Up in Arms* (1944), in which he sang **Harold Arlen**'s 'Now I Know', and his first big success *The Secret Life of Walter Mitty* (1947), in which he played James Thurber's timid daydreamer. His other major films include an adaptation of Gogol's *The Inspector General* (1949) in which he sang speciality material written by Fine and **Johnny Mercer**; *Hans Christian Andersen* (1952), in which he introduced 'Thumbelina', 'The Ugly Duckling', 'The King's New Clothes', 'Inchworm' and 'Wonderful, Wonderful Copenhagen', all written by **Frank Loesser**; *White Christmas* (1954), in which he partnered **Bing Crosby**, **Rosemary Clooney** and Vera-Ellen on **Irving Berlin**'s title song; and *The Five Pennies* (1959), in which he played **Red Nichols**.

His record success began in 1947 with 'Bloop Bleep' (Decca), the first of a string of novelty hits which included 'The Woody Woodpecker Song' (1947), on which he was partnered by the **Andrews Sisters**, and 'I've Got a Lovely Bunch of Coconuts' (1952), better known in Britain in the version by **Billy Cotton**. He also recorded a straight version of 'C'est Si Bon' (1951). In the same year he made the first of many appearances as a mock conductor with the New York Philharmonic; in 1985 he entered the *Guinness Book of Records* for 'leading the world's biggest band', 3,500 musicians and a marching team of 2,000. In the late fifties and sixties he was away from music and film, devoting his time to working for UNICEF. In 1970 Kaye returned to Broadway in a revival of **Vincent Youmans**' *Tea for Two*.

SAMMY KAYE

b. 1910, Cleveland, Ohio, USA, d. 2 June 1987, Ridge-wood, New Jersey

Kaye's formula, encapsulated in his catchphrase

'music for romancing and dancing' made his sweet dance band one of the most successful of the big-band era.

The son of Czechoslovakian immigrants, he took up the saxophone and clarinet in his teens and after graduating from Ohio University in civil engineering formed his first band in Cleveland. Similar in style to **Kay Kyser**, with an emphasis on singers – at one point he featured as many as six; including **Don Cornell** – and sweet arrangements rather than instrumental solos, Kaye won a large audience in the Midwest from 1935 on through his radio broadcasts from Cleveland. He signed a contract with RCA in 1938.

Kaye's music, however, was less admired by swing band *aficionados* and **Charlie Barnet** recorded a devastating parody of his style, 'The Wrong Idea'. Kaye's first hit was his version of **Cole Porter**'s 'Rosalie' (Vocalion, 1937) from the film of the same name. Hits on RCA included the No. 1 'I'm a Big Girl Now' and 'The Old Lamplighter' (1946) – later a hit for the **Browns** in 1960; Tim Spencer's 'Room Full of Roses' (1949); Richard Himber's 'It Isn't Fair'* (1950), which featured Cornell on vocals; and his own patriotic 'Remember Pearl Harbor'. After moving to Columbia in 1950 he had another No. 1 with his version of **Jimmy Kennedy**'s 'Harbour Lights', which had originally been a hit for **Rudy Vallee** and was later successfully revived by the **Platters**. He went on to record for Decca and had a hit with **Henry Mancini**'s film theme 'Charade' (1964). By this time, however, his attention had turned to television. He hosted several television shows in the fifties, most notably his *So You Want to Lead a Band* (1954) game show, in which members of the audience conducted the band in competition for prizes.

In the seventies he acted as a band contractor and supervised his growing publishing and business interests.

KC AND THE SUNSHINE BAND

Harry Wayne Casey, b. 31 January 1951, Hialeah, Florida, USA; Rick Finch, b. 25 January 1954, Indianapolis, Indiana; Fermin Goytisolo, b. 31 December 1951, Havana, Cuba; Robert Johnson, b. 21 March 1953, Miami, Florida; Denzil Liptrot; Jerome Smith, b. 18 June 1953, Miami; Ronnie Smith, b. 1952, Hialeah; James Weaver; Charles Williams, b. 18 November 1954, Rockingham, North Carolina

A Florida-based soul group, KC and the Sunshine Band enjoyed a series of disco-dance hits in the seventies.

From the stable of TK label-owner and producer Henry Stone, the group was formed by white staff writers vocalist Casey (hence KC) and bassist Finch. They discovered the Sunshine Band in 1973, performing at

the wedding reception of TK artist Clarence Reid. The
R&B hit 'Blow Your Whistle' was released as KC and
the Sunshine Junkanoo Band, borrowing from the
'junkanoo' style of the Bahamas which mixed horns,
whistles and chants. After 'Sound Your Funky Horn'
also reached the R&B charts, the band released *Do It
Good* (1974).

'Queen of Clubs' from that album was a British hit
on Jayboy and in 1974 Casey and Finch devised
George McCrae's international disco hit 'Rock Your
Baby' (TK), which sold several million copies. The
Sunshine Band's pop hits began with 'Get Down
Tonight'*, 'That's the Way I Like It' (1975) and
'(Shake, Shake, Shake) Shake Your Booty' (1976), all
of which reached No. 1. The group's dominance of
the charts continued into 1977 with 'I'm Your Boogie
Man'* and 'Keep It Comin' Love'*.

Casey and Finch further contributed to TK's success in the seventies, signing disco artists Peter Brown,
T-Connection and Foxy, while Stone and his veteran
staff provided soul and blues material from such
artists as **Little Milton** and Lattimore. However, TK
suffered a financial collapse in 1979 shortly after KC
and the Sunshine Band's fifth American No. 1, the
ballad 'Please Don't Go'.

With the disappearance of TK and the decline of
the disco genre, Casey joined forces with Teri De
Sario for 'Yes I'm Ready'* (Casablanca, 1979) but had
no further success until he formed the Meca label to
release 'Give It Up', which was a British No. 1 on Epic
in 1983. The parent album, *All in a Night's Work*,
made the British Top Fifty, and the follow-up *KC
Ten*, credited to KC, made the American Top 100 in
1984, but there were no more hits, although Casey
continued to tour extensively in the United States.

A *Best of* album (1990) provoked little interest, but a
minor seventies revival and a hit version of 'Please
Don't Go' by KWS in 1992 saw KC and the Sunshine
Band's hits briefly back on the dancefloor in the early
nineties. An album, *Oh Yeah!* (1993), credited once
again to KC and the Sunshine Band, was swiftly released, containing a re-recorded 'Please Don't Go'. In the
same year dance act Cut'N'Move enjoyed a European
success with a revival of 'Give It Up', by which time
KC and the Sunshine Band had become just another
part of the eighties revival circuit. The definitive collection is *Get Down Tonight* (Rhino, 1998).

ERNIE K-DOE
b. Ernest Kador Jnr, 22 February 1936, New Orleans,
Louisiana, USA

With its rumbling piano, jaunty vocal and smile-mak-
ing lyrics, Ernie K-Doe's 'Mother-in-Law'* (1961) was
among the most catchy records ever to top the American charts.

The son of a Baptist minister, Kador sang gospel in
his teens. In Chicago he recorded in a blues vein for
United Records in 1953 and on his return to New
Orleans with the vocal group the Blue Diamonds for
Savoy ('Honey Baby', 1954) and solo for Specialty
('Do Baby Do', 1955) and Ember ('Tuff Enough',
1958), before signing with Minit and changing his
name to K-Doe in 1960. His first records failed but
the **Allen Toussaint**-written and produced 'Mother-
in-Law' was an immediate hit, despite being banned
by **Dick Clark**'s *American Bandstand* for its 'offensive
lyrics'. Featuring Benny Spellman's foghorn-like
moaning of the title phrase and with Toussaint's
piano well to the fore, the record has since become
one of the most-played golden oldies.

Though he had several minor hits ('I Cried My Last
Tear', 1961, and 'Popeye Joe', 1962), K-Doe was unable
to repeat the success of 'Mother-in-Law'. After
renewing his partnership with Spellman, with this
time Spellman's bass taking the lead on the similarly
styled 'Lipstick Traces' (Minit, 1962), K-Doe signed
with **Don Robey**'s Duke label, where he was unsuccessfully produced by **Willie Mitchell**. In 1970, with
Toussaint again producing, he recorded for Janus and
when that too failed he returned to singing in clubs in
New Orleans.

HOWARD KEEL
b. Harold Clifford Leek, 13 April 1917, Gillespie,
Ohio, USA

Keel's booming baritone and rugged good looks made
him a star of MGM's fifties film musicals and paved
the way for a second career as a reviver of adolescent
memories on television and the nightclub circuit in
the seventies and eighties.

The son of a coalminer, Keel was appointed the
Douglas aircraft company's (for whom he worked)
roving entertainer, which led to his musical stage
début in 1945 in a West Coast production of *Carousel*.
He starred in the London production of *Oklahoma!* in
1947 and, after bit parts in British films, made his
Hollywood début in *Annie Get Your Gun* (1950),
opposite **Betty Hutton**. That film's success launched
him on a career of, mostly outdoor, musicals. These
included *Show Boat* (1951); *Calamity Jane*; **Cole
Porter**'s *Kiss Me Kate* (1953), the last of the trio of
musicals he made with Kathleen Grayson; a remake of
Rudolf Friml's *Rose Marie* (1954), in which he and
Anne Blyth reprised the roles created on film by **Nelson Eddy** and **Jeanette MacDonald**; and *Seven Brides
for Seven Brothers* (1954), in which belted out 'Bless
Your Beautiful Hide'.

In the sixties Keel switched to straight acting parts,
mostly in action films, and in the seventies toured the
nightclub circuit (often with former co-star Kathleen

Grayson) before joining the cast of the *Dallas* tele-series and regularly releasing TV-promoted albums of love songs around the world. Among these was *Close to My Heart* (EMI, 1991). In 1994 he once more toured Britain.

RUBY KEELER
b. Ethel Hilda Keeler, 25 August 1909, Halifax, Nova Scotia, Canada

Tap and buck and wing dancer and singer Keeler is best remembered as the good-natured chorine in Warners' thirties backstage musicals who, with encouragement from **Dick Powell** (who partnered her seven times), at the last minute successfully replaced the show's ailing star.

Brought up in New York, Keeler took dancing lessons in her teens and in 1923 won a place in the chorus of **George M. Cohan**'s *The Rise of Rosie O'Reilly*. She had substantial parts in *Bye Bye Bonnie* and *Sidewalks of New York* (1927) and in 1928 married **Al Jolson**, who sang 'Liza' with her from the audience during her brief run in *Show Girl* (1929) before she moved with him to Hollywood.

Her first starring role was in *42nd Street* (1933), one of the most memorable of Busby Berkeley's essays in human geometry. Partnered by Powell, she introduced **Harry Warren** and Al Dubin's 'Shuffle Off to Buffalo' and just before the finale was given the immortal exhortation by Warner Baxter, 'You're going out a youngster, but you've got to come back a star.' A huge success, the film spawned two equally successful applications of the backstage formula later that year, with Warren and Dubin again providing the songs. *Gold Diggers of 1933* introduced 'We're in the Money', sung by Ginger Rogers, and 'Remember the Forgotten Man' for its finale, while *Footlight Parade* featured an energetic performance by James Cagney. Powell and Keeler continued their romance with *Dames*, in which Powell introduced the classic 'I Only Have Eyes for You' and was rewarded by Keeler's 'Gee, Jimmy, that's Swell', *Flirtation Walk* (1934), *Shipmates Forever* (1935) and *Colleen* (1936); Keeler also starred with Jolson in *Go into Your Dance* (1935), in which Jolson sang the Warren and Dubin title number. More memorable was the elaborate dance sequence she and Lee Dixon performed on a huge typewriter to **Johnny Mercer**'s and **Richard A. Whiting**'s 'Too Marvelous for Words' in *Ready Willing and Able* (1937).

She left Warners with Jolson and, after divorcing him in 1940, made one more B-musical, *Sweethearts of the Campus* (1941), in which she co-starred with **Rick Nelson**'s father, bandleader Ozzie Nelson, before marrying a real-estate broker and retiring in 1941. In the sixties, following the successful revival of

her thirties musicals, she returned to showbusiness. In 1971 she returned to Broadway after an absence of over forty years to star in a successful revival of **Vincent Youmans**' 1925 operetta *No, No, Nanette*, which was supervised by Busby Berkeley.

GENE KELLY
b. Eugene Curran Kelly, 23 August 1912, Pittsburgh, Pennsylvania, USA

Forever associated with the title song of *Singin' in the Rain* (1952), in which he did just that with marvellous aplomb, actor, dancer, singer, choreographer and director Kelly was, with **Fred Astaire** (whom he partnered in *Ziegfeld Follies*, 1946), the most inventive musical star to make his mark in Hollywood. Both had technically weak singing voices, but while Astaire epitomized dancefloor elegance, Kelly represented a more athletic, balletic form of dance that sprang from within the character in the Hollywood musical. As one critic wrote, 'Kelly made dancing seem the most natural activity – an extension of walking – with the street as his favourite stage.'

After graduating from Pennsylvania State University, Kelly supported himself with a variety of jobs before making it to the chorus line of the Broadway production of *Leave It to Me* (1938). Two years later he starred in **Lorenz Hart** and Richard Rodgers' (later of **Rodgers and Hammerstein**) innovatory *Pal Joey*, in which he introduced 'I Could Write a Book', a hit for **Eddy Duchin** in 1941, the year Kelly choreographed *Best Foot Forward*. That led to his Hollywood début in *For Me and My Gal* (1942), in which he scored his only major record hits, partnering **Judy Garland** in the title song and 'When You Wore a Tulip (And I Wore a Big Red Rose)'. He established himself as a dancer and Hollywood choreographer in *Cover Girl* (1944), in which he partnered Rita Hayworth, introduced **Jerome Kern** and **Ira Gershwin**'s 'Long Ago and Far Away' (subsequently a hit for **Bing Crosby**, **Jo Stafford**, **Perry Como** and **Guy Lombardo**, among others) and danced with himself (in the 'Alter Ego' sequence). His free-flowing attitude to dance was even more to the fore in the **Arthur Freed**-produced *Anchors Aweigh* (1945), in which he partnered **Frank Sinatra** and danced with Jerry the cartoon mouse, and Vincente Minnelli's *The Pirate* (1948), in which he introduced **Cole Porter**'s 'Be a Clown'.

By the time of *On the Town* (1949, the film version of the 1944 Broadway musical), which featured a score by **Leonard Bernstein** and Roger Edens, Kelly had graduated to co-director (with Stanley Donen) and sang 'New York, New York' with Sinatra and Jules Munshin. His finest moment came in *Singin' in the Rain* (1952), a story about the transition from silent movies to talkies built around a catalogue of songs by **Nacio Herb Brown** and producer Arthur Freed and co-directed by Donen and Kelly. In the film Kelly transformed the title song (previously sung in *Hollywood Revue of 1929*, by **Jimmy Durante** in *Speak Easily*, 1932, and Judy Garland in *Little Nellie Kelly*, 1940) and Donald O'Connor reworked 'Be a Clown' as 'Make 'Em Laugh'.

Increasingly a leading man and director rather than star of musicals, Kelly – after *An American in Paris* (1951), **Lerner and Loewe**'s *Brigadoon* (1954), in which he partnered Cyd Charisse, and *It's Only Fair Weather* (1955) – made his solo directing début, the poorly received musical without dialogue *Invitation to the Dance* (1956). Musical films, however, formed only a part of his subsequent career. Among those he directed were *Hello Dolly* (1969), starring **Barbra Streisand**, and the minor *Xanadu* (1980, starring **Olivia Newton-John**). More representative of his work was his narration of the compilation film *That's Entertainment* (1974) and its sequel *That's Entertainment Part Two* (1976). Both celebrated the finest moments of the Hollywood musical.

R. KELLY
b. Robert Kelly, 8 January 1969, Chicago, USA

As well as being one of the most successful solo artists of the nineties, R. Kelly has worked as producer and songwriter for artists including **Michael Jackson**, **Whitney Houston** and **Luther Vandross**.

After spending his teens busking with an electronic keyboard on the streets of Chicago, Kelly attracted the attention of Jive Records by winning a talent contest on the Big Break TV show. His first album, *Born into the '90s* (1992), recorded with his backing band Public Announcement, was an instant hit in the R&B world, but it was not until he released *12 Play* (1994) that Kelly achieved crossover success. The album spawned four hit singles: 'She's Got that Vibe', 'Your Body's Callin'', 'Sex Me' and 'Bump n' Grind', which reached the top of the US chart.

Having established his solo career, Kelly began to work with other artists. After producing *Age Ain't Nothin' but a Number* (1994) for Aaliyah, Kelly caused a stir by marrying the fifteen-year-old singer. In 1995 he helped revitalize Michael Jackson's career by writing 'You Are Not Alone' before releasing his acclaimed eponymous third album, which promptly went quadruple platinum in the US. Kelly had immense international success the following year with 'I Believe I Can Fly'*, from the movie *Space Jam*, his first UK chart-topper, which won three Grammy Awards. Kelly returned in 1998 with the double-album, *R*. A huge hit – it was the 30th most successful album of 1999 – it included a duet with **Céline Dion**.

JIMMY KENNEDY
b. 20 July 1902, Omagh, Northern Ireland, d. 10 April 1984, London, England

In collaboration with **Michael Carr**, Kennedy was one of the most successful of British songwriters ever. His lyrics had an emotional directness and dramatic power rare in British songwriters outside music-hall and rock music.

The son of a chief constable and a graduate of Trinity College, Dublin, Kennedy turned to songwriting after a spell in the colonial service. Before joining forces with Carr, he concentrated on providing English lyrics for continental songs – such as 'Play to Me Gypsy' (1934) – and on producing words for instrumental pieces, including 'The Teddy Bears' Picnic', a 1904 John W. Bratton tune written in celebration of Theodore Roosevelt's taking time off from campaigning for the presidency to go bear-hunting. Recorded by **Henry Hall** in 1933, the song became a children's classic. His most successful song of this type was 'My Prayer', an adaptation of George Boulanger's violin solo, 'Avant de Mourir', recorded first by **Gracie Fields** and in 1956 by the **Platters**. Fields also had a hit with 'The Isle of Capri', written in 1934 by Kennedy and Austrian refugee George Grosz.

The Kennedy–Carr hits, which began in 1935, varied in style from cowboy songs (like singing cowboys, then in vogue) such as 'South of the Border', show tunes (such as 'Home Town' for **Flanagan and Allen**, and 'There's a New World', both 1937) and a series of songs for Hall, including 'Why Did She Fall for the Leader of the Band' and 'Misty Islands of the Highlands' (both 1935). The climax to their partnership came with 'We're Going to Hang out Our Washing on the Siegfried Line' (1939), the 'Tipperary' of the Second World War.

Kennedy's success was not confined to Britain: in January 1940 he had the top two songs on *Variety*'s sheet-music chart, 'South of the Border' and 'My Prayer'. Kennedy worked equally successfully with other composers. With Grosz, now using the solidly English pseudonym of Hugh Williamson, he wrote 'Red Sails in the Sunset' (1935) and 'Harbour Lights' (1937), both of which were contemporary hits, the latter for **Rudy Vallee**, and, again, even greater hits when revived by the Platters 1960. He also continued his practice of adding lyrics to existing melodies, such as the fake cockney folk song 'The Hokey Cokey' (1942), set to a traditional tune, and translating foreign lyrics, including 'Love is Like a Violin' (a British hit for comedian Ken Dodd in 1960) and **Petula Clark**'s 1961 hit 'Romeo'.

In the fifties Kennedy settled in America. But, with the exception of the patriotic Korean War song 'The Red We Want Is the Red We've Got in the Old Red,

White and Blue', recorded by **Hugo Winterhalter**, few of his songs were significant hits. Returning to Europe, Kennedy retired to Switzerland in 1962.

STAN KENTON

b. Stanley Newcomb Kenton, 19 February 1912, Wichita, Kansas, USA, d. 25 August 1979, Los Angeles, California

Bandleader, composer and pianist, Kenton made excursions into what a later generation would call jazz-fusions (notably with classical and 'modern' music); these made him a controversial figure in forties and fifties jazz circles.

He grew up in California and during the late thirties played with a succession of big bands, including a spell as arranger for Gus Arnheim, who had played a leading role in **Bing Crosby**'s early career. In 1940 Kenton formed his own rehearsal band, which became a permanent unit the following year, recording initially for Decca and moving to Capitol in 1943.

While his reputation was built on experimental work, Kenton's concerts and broadcasts during the forties contained a judicious mixture of symphonic pieces and more orthodox big-band material. They featured such vocalists as **Anita O'Day** ('And the Tears Flowed Like Wine', 1944), and June Christy ('Tampico'* and 'Shoo-Fly Pie and Apple Pan Dowdy'*, 1945).

With arranger Pete Rugulo, who joined him in 1945, Kenton's engagement with the classics began in earnest with 'Artistry in Percussion' and 'Artistry in Bolero', jazz-based pastiches of Stravinsky and Ravel. More commercially successful was 'Artistry in Rhythm'* (1943), which became Kenton's theme song. In 1947 he turned to 'progressive jazz' with a new line-up that included guitarist **Laurindo Almeida**, drummer Shelly Manne, and arrangements by Neal Hefti and Shorty Rogers. Modernist composer Bob Graettinger wrote the atonal and dissonant 'City of Glass' for Kenton's orchestra; the tune's noise level and disregard for jazz orthodoxy alarmed critics but found audiences in colleges and concert halls. In 1950 he toured with a forty-piece orchestra, complete with string and woodwind sections. However, he still recorded with the likes of **Nat 'King' Cole** ('Orange Coloured Sky', 1950) and Chris Connor ('And the Bull Walked Around, Olay', 1953) and recorded film themes ('Laura', 1951) and songs ('Hush-a-Bye', from the 1953 version of *The Jazz Singer*).

One of Kenton's most popular recordings was a version of **Moises Simons**' 'Peanut Vendor' (1949), on which **Machito** played maracas, and his interest in Latin music was reflected in albums like *Cuban Fire* (1956). During the fifties the Kenton band toured extensively in America and abroad and among its members were Lee Konitz, Frank Rosolino and Jimmy Giuffre.

In the sixties Kenton fell out of favour with jazz *cognoscenti* but continued to find college audiences. His grandiosely named Mellophonium and Neo-phonic orchestras recorded prolifically, cutting *West Side Story* (1961), a 1964 album of themes from the operas of *Wagner* and a series of new works by Hugo Montenegro, film music composer **John Williams** and others (1965).

Kenton set up his own Creative World label in 1970 to record new work and to reissue his numerous albums recorded for Capitol over the previous three decades. In the nineties Capitol itself re-released many of his recordings on CD.

The fiftieth anniversary of Kenton's first band was celebrated in 1991 at a four-day convention in the USA, where an Alumni Band performed, led by Rugulo, Bill Russo, Rogers, Marty Paich and others. Among the soloists were O'Day, Connors and Lee Konitz. Among bandleaders who were influenced by his eclectic approach were his former trumpeter Maynard Ferguson, Don Ellis and British jazz player Vic Lewis.

JEROME KERN

b. 27 January 1885, New York, USA, d. 11 November 1945, New York

Following **Victor Herbert** but pre-dating **George Gershwin**, Kern, once described as 'a giant with one foot in Europe and the other in America', linked the European operetta tradition of the turn of the century with the modern American musical theatre. He established himself as a supplier of songs to be interpolated in American productions of European operettas in the first decades of the century, was a force in the creation of the sophisticated American musical comedy of the twenties (of which **Cole Porter** was the master), and it was his score for the hugely influential *Showboat* (1927) that decisively broke with the operetta and musical-comedy traditions to create the first wholly integrated musical with an American subject.

The son of a prosperous businessman, Kern started to write songs in his teens. After studying piano and composition at the New York School of Music and in Germany, he began writing songs in England. On his return to America in 1904 he worked as a song plugger and then rehearsal pianist and had his first success in 1905 with 'How'd You Like to Spoon with Me', which was interpolated in the English operetta *The Earl and the Girl*. Before his first full score, for *The Red Petticoat* (1912), Kern provided new songs to some twenty European operettas. It was such a song that brought Kern his first major success, 'They Didn't Believe Me' (1914, with lyrics by Herbert Reynolds). Even more significant was his joining forces with Guy Bolton and comic novelist **P. G. Wodehouse** in 1917 specifically to write modern (rather than costume) musical comedies about Americans. Among these were *Oh Boy!*, *Leave It to Jane*, one of the first musicals set on a college campus (1917), and *Oh Lady! Lady!!* (1918), in which Wodehouse and Kern introduced 'Bill', later to be one of the key songs of *Showboat*.

At the same time, Kern wrote scores for Florenz Ziegfeld's frothier revues, notably *Sally* (1920) and *Sunny* (1925), which marked his first collaboration with **Otto Harbach** and Oscar Hammerstein (later of **Rodgers and Hammerstein**). From this sprang Hammerstein and Kern's greatest work, *Showboat* (1927, filmed 1929, 1936 and 1951). Hammerstein adapted Edna Ferber's sprawling novel and wrote the lyrics while Kern provided a score that was inspired by, rather than sprang from, black music and culture, as in the show's opening number 'Ol' Man River', which was written specifically for **Paul Robeson** to sing after Kern had heard one of his gospel concerts. Other hits from the show included 'Bill' and 'Can't Help Loving That Man', both hits for **Helen Morgan** (Victor) who introduced them.

In the thirties satire became a prevailing trend in American musicals, but while other composers, like Gershwin and **Irving Berlin**, accommodated themselves to this trend, Kern retreated back into a sophisticated version of the operettas he had made his name with. Works in this vein include *The Cat and the Fiddle* (1931, filmed 1934), with Harbach, which introduced 'I've Told Ev'ry Little Star' and 'She Didn't Say "Yes"'; and *Roberta* (1933, filmed 1935 and 1952 as *Lovely to Look At*), also with Harbach, which introduced the classic 'Smoke Gets in Your Eyes', a hit for **Paul Whiteman**, **Ruth Etting** (1934), **Artie Shaw** (1941), the **Platters** (1959) and Blue Haze (A&M, 1972). Kern wrote two more shows (with Hammerstein), *The Three Sisters* (1934) and *Very Warm for May* (1939), which included 'All the Things You Are' (a hit for Shaw and **Tommy Dorsey**), but from 1934 onwards settled in Hollywood and wrote most of his new songs for the movies.

In Hollywood Kern's major collaborators were **Dorothy Fields** and **Johnny Mercer**. With Fields he wrote for *Swingtime* (1936) the wistful Oscar-winning 'The Way You Look Tonight' (a hit for the film's star **Fred Astaire**, **Billie Holiday**, **Guy Lombardo**, Goodman, 1942, and revived by the **Lettermen**, 1961), the sprightly 'Pick Yourself Up', and 'A Fine Romance'. Reunited with Hammerstein, for *High Wide and Handsome* (1937) he wrote the evocative 'The Folks Who Live on the Hill', a hit for Lombardo and memorably recorded by **Peggy Lee** (1957), and for *Lady Be Good* won a second Oscar for the evocative 'The Last Time I Saw Paris'. With Mercer he wrote songs for *You Were Never Lovelier* (1942) which, as well as the title song, included 'I'm Old Fashioned' and 'Dearly Beloved' (a hit for **Dinah Shore** and **Glenn Miller**). Kern's last major collaboration was with **Ira Gershwin**. For *Cover Girl* (1944) they wrote 'Long Ago and Far Away' (a hit for **Perry Como**, **Bing Crosby** and **Jo Stafford**, among others).

Following Kern's death in 1945, Robert Walker played him in the biopic *Till the Clouds Roll By* (1946).

DOUG KERSHAW
. b. *Douglas James Kershaw, 24 January 1936, Teil Ridge, Louisiana, USA*

A master cajun fiddler who did much to bring the genre to rock audiences in the seventies, Kershaw composed 'Louisiana Man', one of the most widely recorded country songs.

He grew up on an island in the Gulf of Mexico and made his first public appearance in 1944 with his guitarist mother. He formed the Continental Playboys with his brothers Pee Wee and Rusty in 1948. The group performed regularly on a Lake Charles television station. As a duo with Rusty, Kershaw appeared on the prestigious *Louisiana Hayride* radio show and recorded in 1953 for **Jay Miller**'s Crowley-based Feature label.

From 1955 Rusty and Doug recorded in Nashville for Hickory, accompanied by such luminaries as **Chet Atkins**, **Pete Drake** and **Floyd Cramer**. Their first country bestseller was **Boudleaux Bryant**'s rockabilly-flavoured 'Hey Sheriff' (1958), but their biggest success came with 'Louisiana Man', which was later recorded by more than 800 other artists, 'Diggy Liggy Lo' and their version of **Roy Acuff**'s 'Jole Blon' (1961). Later records made less impact and after releases on RCA and Princess the duo separated. Rusty's only solo album was *Cajun in the Blues Country* (Cotillion, 1970), made after a successful recovery from alcoholism.

Doug Kershaw's demonic instrumental style, however, made him much in demand for recording sessions. He played on **Bob Dylan**'s *Self Portrait* (1970) and with **John Stewart**, Longbranch Pennywhistle (a group which included future **Eagle** Glenn Frey and **Ry Cooder**), Earl Scruggs (of **Flatt and Scruggs**) and the heavy-rock band **Grand Funk Railroad** (on the 1973 album *Phoenix*).

Kershaw's solo recording career began with Mercury and MGM, before **Joe Tex**'s manager Buddy Killen secured him a Warners contract in 1969. The Killen-produced *The Cajun Way* (1969) was an uncomfortable attempt to straddle the country and rock audiences and many of Kershaw's later records suffered from similar problems. *Swamp Grass* (1972) had a heavy-rock emphasis while *Devil's Elbow* swung towards psychedelic music and *Douglas James Kershaw* (1973) was suffused with Nashville-style string arrangements. Although he was much in demand for rock festivals in the seventies, his live shows were often similarly uneven, descending from the high-energy virtuosity of his playing to some distinctly ordinary singing. The most effective of the Warners' albums was *The Ragin' Cajun* (1976), where Kershaw did just that, without regard for stylistic niceties.

He left Warners in 1979, later recording *Louisiana Cajun Country* (Starflyte, 1979) and *Instant Hero* (Scotti Bros, 1981), which included the country hit 'Hello Woman'. Kershaw's long dark hair and gaunt features also appealed to filmmakers. He had parts in *Zachariah* (1971), the Scorsese-produced 'underground' music movie *Medicine Ball Caravan* (1971), and *Days of Heaven* (1978). *The Best of Doug Kershaw* (Warner, 1989) is the definitive retrospective. *Hot Diggidy Doug* from the same year is only notable for the duet with **Fats Domino** on 'Toot Toot'.

NIK KERSHAW
b. 1 March 1958, Bristol, England

Dismissed by one commentator as 'a cuddly toy boy of modern pop', songwriter and singer Kershaw was briefly one of Britain's leading teen idols in the mid-eighties.

He grew up in Ipswich, where his mother led a local church choir, and was lead singer in heavy metal band Half Pint Hog before forming jazz-funk and cabaret band Fusion with keyboards-player Reg Webb, Ken Elson (bass) and Alan Clarke (drums). With Kershaw on guitar and vocals, Fusion recorded the undistinguished *Till I Hear from You* (Telephone, 1980) before splitting up.

Kershaw spent much of 1982 writing songs and recording the demo tapes which won him a contract with MCA the following year. Produced by Peter Collins, his first release, 'I Won't Let the Sun Go Down on Me', was unsuccessful but both 'Wouldn't It Be Good' and 'Dancing Girls' reached the British Top Twenty. In 1984 Kershaw's profile was further heightened by an invitation from **Elton John** to appear with him and Kershaw later played guitar on John's hit 'Nikita' (1985).

His début album, *Human Racing*, provided further hits with the title track and the re-released 'Sun'. Kershaw formed the Krew, a four-piece group to back him on stage, which included bassist Dennis Smith, formerly with mod group Secret Affair. In 1985 he had further chart success with 'Wide Boy', 'Don Quixote' and 'The Riddle', the title song of his second album and the best example of his lightweight but highly melodic approach to pop. However, despite international tours and an appearance at the Live Aid con-

cert, Kershaw's popularity remained limited to his native country.

In 1986 he recorded *Radio Musicola*, which enjoyed limited success. The same was true of *The Works* (1990). He had more success as a songwriter, being responsible for 'The One and Only' (1991), a massive British hit for Chesney Hawkes, the son of former **Tremeloes** singer Chip Hawkes.

KETELBEY
b. Albert W. Ketelbey, 4 August 1875, Birmingham, England, d. 26 November 1959, Isle of Wight

Like **Robert Farnon** and **Eric Coates** a prolific composer of mood music, Ketelbey specialized in musical panoramas and descriptive scenes. His best-remembered works are 'In a Monastery Garden' (1915) and 'In a Persian Market' (1920).

A musical prodigy, Ketelbey at the age of eleven composed a piano sonata that was praised by Sir Edward Elgar and after winning a scholarship to Trinity College, London, was appointed organist at St John's Church in London at the age of sixteen. His first works were classical but after being appointed director of the Vaudeville Theatre in 1897, he turned increasingly to light music. His first success was 'Phantom Melody' (1912) written just after he became musical director for Columbia Records. His speciality was exotic impressionistic pieces which conjured up (Western) images of foreign climes. As a publicity leaflet issued by his publishers in 1946 claimed, 'Ketelbey proved that there is a huge public ready to buy tuneful music which portrays interesting scenes and colourful incidents.' Among them were 'In a Chinese Temple Garden' (1925), 'By the Blue Hawaiian Waters' (1927), 'In the Mystic Land of Egypt' (1931), 'From a Japanese Screen' (1934) and 'Italian Twilight' (1951), as well as more familiar-sounding pictures ('Appy 'Ampstead', 1924). Few of these compositions were hits in individual recordings – an exception being Larry Clinton's 1938 Victor recording of 'In a Persian Market' – but they became familiar through their use as accompaniment to silent films and as background and mood music by tea-dance orchestras the length and breadth of Britain. He retired to the Isle of Wight in the early thirties.

KHALED
b. Cheb Khaled, 1960, Sidi-el-Houari, Algeria

In the eighties Khaled was the leading exponent of rai, the principal Algerian pop music style. In recent years he has experimented with rock–rai fusions.

He was born near the city of Oran, where the rai style originated in the thirties. The music absorbed various European and American influences and in

1976 produced its first teenage pop star in the actress Fadela Zalmat. Khaled's first instrument was harmonica but he came to prominence as a singer and accordionist. Like other teenage performers he prefixed his name with 'Cheb' ('young' or 'kid'). From the mid-seventies his songs of cars, sex, drugs and alcohol made him an idol of Algerian youth.

Although his music was ignored by Algerian radio, cheaply recorded cassettes of such songs as 'Hada Raykoum' and 'Sidi Boumedienne' regularly sold over 100,000 copies.

By the early eighties rai was becoming officially accepted and in 1985 the first officially endorsed festivals of the music were held in Oran and Algiers. There was also a growing audience for the music in France, where better facilities for recording were available.

In 1989 he released *Kutche*, a collaboration with the German-based North African musician Safy Boutella and produced by Martin Meissonier. Then, in 1992, French company Barclay signed Khaled. The eponymous album (1992), produced by **Don Was** and Michael Brook, included the hit single 'Didi', the first Arabic language song to become a Top Ten hit in France. It was also a big success in India and made Khaled's European reputation. 1993's *N'ssi* included several songs featured in Bertrand Blier's *1–2–3 Soleil* and won Khaled a Ceasar for the best soundtrack album in France. He followed that with *Sahara* (1996), which included the Francophone hit 'Aicha'.

CHAKA KHAN
b. *Yvette Marie Stevens, 23 March 1953, Chicago, Illinois, USA*

Originally lead singer of soul band Rufus, Chaka Khan became one of the most versatile female singers of the eighties, equally fluent in soul, rock and jazz styles.

She grew up in Chicago, forming her first group at the age of eleven and taking the African name Chaka Khan when she worked on a welfare programme sponsored by the Black Panthers. After singing with bar bands she formed Rufus in 1972 with Andre Fischer (drums) and keyboards-player Kevin Murphy, formerly with the American Breed, whose biggest hit was the 1968 No. 1 'Bend Me Shape Me' (Dot). The Scott English song was also a British hit for Amen Corner (Deram, 1968).

The novelty of a white soul band with a black singer won them a recording deal with ABC. After an eponymous début album (1973), Rufus reached the Top Ten with **Stevie Wonder**'s 'Tell Me Something Good'* from *Rags to Rufus* (1974), which provided a further hit in **Ashford and Simpson**'s 'You Got the Love'. *Rufusized* (1974) included the successful 'Once You

Get Started', while the title of *Rufus Featuring Chaka Khan* (1975) – which produced the million-selling 'Sweet Thing' – was recognition of the fact that Khan's singing was the key factor in the group's appeal.

Ask Rufus (1977) and *Street Player* (1978) maintained the soul-rock format, but in 1978 Khan opted for a solo career, recording *Chaka* (Warners). Produced by **Arif Mardin** and with a galaxy of backing musicians including Rufus guitarist Tony Maiden, Randy Brecker of the **Brecker Brothers**, **Phil Upchurch** and the **Average White Band**, it gave her a hit single in the Ashford and Simpson song 'I'm Every Woman'.

At this point, Khan broke from her established style to record with **Ry Cooder** (*Bop Til You Drop*, 1979), **George Benson** (the 1978 duet 'We Got the Love') and **Rick Wakeman** (*1984*, Charisma, 1981). After *Naughty* (1980), Khan recorded *What 'Cha Gonna Do for Me* (1981), with material ranging from **The Beatles**' 'We Can Work It Out' to bebop tune 'A Night in Tunisia', which featured a guest appearance by **Dizzy Gillespie**. She confirmed her skill in jazz singing on *Echoes of an Era* (Elektra, 1982), a project organized by drummer Lenny White to re-create jazz standards of the fifties with musicians including Freddie Hubbard and **Chick Corea**. *Chaka Khan* (1983) also included a 'Be-Bop Medley'.

She returned to the pop charts with 'Ain't Nobody' (1983), recorded with Rufus, with whom she was contractually obliged to cut a final album. Khan's next solo success was the artfully constructed title track of *I Feel for You* (1984). Written by **Prince**, it also included Stevie Wonder on harmonica and rapper Grandmaster Melle Mel. The album provided further hits in 'This Is My Night' and 'Eye to Eye'. *Destiny* (1986) included compositions by **Scritti Politti** and Mardin, as well as the ambitious 'Coltrane Dreams', whose bass and drum sounds were derived from Khan's singing sampled and processed through a Synclavier.

Khan's combination of technique and feeling made her the most renowned backing vocalist of the mid-eighties. In 1986 she sang with **David Bowie** on 'Underground', from the film *Labyrinth*, was a featured vocalist on **Robert Palmer**'s 'Addicted to Love' and duetted with **Steve Winwood** on 'Higher Love'. Khan also made a cameo appearance in the film *The Blues Brothers* (1980).

After 1988's *CK*, which was produced by Prince, she took a sabbatical from recording and moved to Europe. In 1989 a remix of 'I'm Every Woman' from the remix album *Life Is a Dance* reached the British Top Ten.

During the period in which she made no solo recordings, Khan enjoyed a trans-Atlantic hit with co-vocalist **Ray Charles** on **Quincy Jones**' 'I'll Be Good to You' and sang on **Paul Young**'s *Other Voices* in

1990. She also recorded in 1991 with the British Electric Foundation, a spin-off from **Heaven 17**, which itself was a splinter group from British electro-pop group the **Human League**.

Khan resumed solo recording with the minor British hit 'Love You All My Lifetime' and its parent album, the Grammy-winning *The Woman I Am* (both 1992), produced by Arif Mardin. In 1993 MCA issued *Sweet Things*, a greatest hits album from the Rufus years and the following year she recorded another solo album for Warner Bros. In 1995 she starred in London in the musical *Mama, I Want to Sing*. The single 'Love Me Still' (1995), co-written with **Bruce Hornsby**, was featured in the film *Clockers* and in 1996 the comprehensive retrospective *Epiphany* was released. She followed that with the **Prince**-produced *Come 2 My House* (1998) on her own Earth Song label.

KID CREOLE AND THE COCONUTS

Kid Creole (aka August Darnell), b. Thomas August Darnell Browder, 1951, Montreal, Canada; Coati Mundi, b. Andy Hernandez, 1950, New York, USA; Lori Eastside, b. Lori Smith; Adriana Kaegi, b. 1957, Switzerland; Carol Colman; Camilla Ansil; Cheryl Poirier; Taryn Haegy

An imaginative and witty blend of Caribbean music, rock, disco and forties big-band sounds brought Kid Creole and the Coconuts a brief period of celebrity in the early eighties.

With a Canadian mother and Trinidadian father, August Darnell grew up in the Bronx district of New York, forming rock bands the Strangers and the In-Laws with his half-brother Stony Browder. After qualifying as a drama teacher, he joined Browder in 1975 in the eccentric dance band Dr Buzzard's Original Savannah Band. With Hernandez on vibes and marimba, Corby Daye (vocals) and Micky Sevilla (drums), the group's eponymous RCA album produced the R&B and pop hit 'Cherchez la Femme'.

Dr Buzzard's later albums included *Dr Buzzard's Original Savannah Band Meets King Pennett* (RCA, 1978) and *James Monroe High School Presents DBOSB Goes to Washington* (Elektra, 1980). Their titles indicated the degree to which the group achieved only a minority appeal, but its attempt to create a melting-pot for a variety of New York street styles provided the basis for Darnell's next project.

After producing disco singles for Michael Zilkha's Ze Label, he and Hernandez put together the Kid Creole package in 1980. To the musical ideals of Dr Buzzard was added a spectacular stage show with a horn section, vocalist Eastside and the Coconuts, a trio of female singers and dancers – Swiss choreographer Kaegi, actress Poirier and former Guildhall School of Music student Haegy. The band toured with the **B-52s**

and **Talking Heads** before recording *Off the Coast of Me* (1980) and *Fresh Fruit in Foreign Places* (1981). Coati Mundi's (Hernandez) 'Me No Pop I' (1981) was a major hit in Latin America and a minor hit in Britain.

The following year the group had three British hits with tracks from *Tropical Gangsters*, released in Europe on Island. The sales of 'I'm a Wonderful Thing, Baby', 'Stool Pigeon' and 'Annie I'm Not Your Daddy' were boosted by the band's colourful live appearances with the men's gangster suits, the Coconuts' costume changes and the palm tree props. Darnell himself dominated the proceedings with a stage act inspired by forties heroes like **Cab Calloway**. There were lesser British hits in 1983 but the poor European sales of *Doppelganger* led to a hiatus in Kid Creole's career. Darnell concentrated on production, supervising 1983 albums by both Coati Mundi and the Coconuts and disco singles by Daisy Chain and Elbow Bones and the Racketeers.

Moving to Sire, Kid Creole and the Coconuts returned with *In Praise of Older Women . . . and Other Crimes* (1985) and *I, Too, Have Seen the Woods* (1987). Both albums embodied the Dr Buzzard 'mulatto music' philosophy. In the following year the group made a guest appearance on **Barry Manilow**'s *Swing Street*, before signing to Columbia in 1990.

The first single on the new label, 'The Sex of It' (1990), was written by **Prince** and was a minor hit. However, the parent album *Private Waters in the Great Divide* and *You Should Have Told Me You Were . . .* (1991) both sold poorly and Kid Creole moved to the nostalgia circuit. In 1994 British dance act Fire Island enjoyed a British Top Forty hit with the Kid Creole favourite 'There But for the Grace of God'.

JOHNNY KIDD

b. Frederick Heath, 23 December 1939, Willesden, London, England, d. 7 October 1966, Lancashire

With **Cliff Richard**, **Billy Fury** and Vince Taylor ('Brand New Cadillac', EMI Columbia, 1959), Kidd was one of the few British artists to sing rock'n'roll with any authority. In contrast to the others, however, Kidd's models were black rather than white, a factor which made him a lone precursor in the British pop of the early sixties of the Merseybeat and British R&B trends. Still active when those bandwagons rolled, Kidd did not benefit from them because his sound remained too much rooted in fifties rock to appeal to the new R&B purist and teenage audiences.

Kidd's first band, Captain Kidd and the Nutters, had been inspired by skiffle, but his career only prospered when, with a black eye-patch (the legacy of an accident with a broken guitar string), and a heavy-rock sound, Kidd formed the Pirates. With Alan Caddy on guitar, Kidd evolved a repertoire that mixed **Hank Williams**, **Bo Diddley** and **Arthur Alexander** with more conventional rock'n'roll material. He also wrote his own material, including his first hit, the dynamic 'Please Don't Touch' (HMV, 1959) and his best-known song, 'Shakin' All Over'.

Co-written with his manager Gus Robinson and featuring a rumbling tremolo guitar figure, 'Shakin' All Over' topped the charts in 1960. The song became a staple of the repertoire of the emerging generation of British beat groups and in 1965 was an American hit for the **Guess Who**. It was later recorded by **The Who** on *Live at Leeds* (1970). Kidd's follow-up, 'Restless', was also a hit.

In 1960 Caddy and drummer Clem Cattini left to play sessions for **Joe Meek** and form the **Tornados**, whose instrumental 'Telstar' was a 1962 No. 1. After various personnel changes, the best-known Pirates line-up of Mick Green (guitar), John Spencer (bass) and Frank Farley (drums) solidified in 1962. This group played on Kidd's next hits, 'I'll Never Get Over You' and 'Hungry for Love' (1963). Composed by Gordon Mills, these were beat ballads which foreshadowed 'It's Not Unusual' (1965), the first hit for Mills' protégé **Tom Jones**.

Although his work was shaped by many of the same Tamla Motown and R&B influences, Kidd did not prosper as **The Beatles** and the **Rolling Stones** took over. Despite frequent record releases, such as Diddley's 'I Can Tell' and 'Let's Talk About Us', he remained a fixture of the club circuit. He was killed in a car accident while returning from a club date in Lancashire.

Of the various members of the Pirates, Nick Simper (bass) went on to join the first version of **Deep Purple**, while Green reappeared in the early seventies with Shanghai, a group fronted by another early sixties rocker Cliff Bennett. In 1976 he re-formed the Pirates with Spencer and Farley. The trio cut two albums for Warners (*Out of Their Skulls*, 1977, and *Skull Wars*, 1978) and *Happy Birthday Rock'n'Roll* (Cube, 1979).

The most devoted disciple of Green's guitar style was Wilko Johnson of the mid-seventies band **Dr Feelgood**. That group's name was also inspired by Kidd's recording of the Willie Perryman (Piano Red) song. One of Kidd's achievements was to introduce to other British musicians R&B classics like that and Alexander's 'Shot of Rhythm and Blues'. In 1981 **Motorhead** and Girlschool combined on a heavy-metal revival of 'Please Don't Touch'. A decade later EMI issued a comprehensive compilation, *The Complete Johnny Kidd & The Pirates* (1992), which included two previously unreleased tracks.

KILLING JOKE

Jaz Coleman; Paul Ferguson; Youth, b. Martin Glover, 27 December 1960 (replaced by Paul Raven); 'Geordie' Walker, b. Newcastle-upon-Tyne, England

Killing Joke's brutal sound gained them a devoted cult following in the eighties. In the nineties, hailed as an influence on the contemporary 'grunge' scene, they re-formed to critical acclaim.

The band were formed in Cheltenham in 1979 when vocalist and keyboard-player Coleman and drummer Ferguson teamed up with former punk bassist Youth and Geordie, releasing the independent EP *Turn to Red*. Moving to London and signing to Island Records, they released 'Wardance' in 1980, the single appearing on the band's own label, Malicious Damage. They released their eponymous, self-produced début album on the EG label in 1980. A raw, uncompromising album, it captured the band's distinctive mixture of sixties idealism and seventies punk energy, a combination that was refined on the follow-up *What's THIS for . . .!* (1981).

Coleman temporarily left the band (and the country) in 1982, before the release of the doomy Conny Plank-produced *Revelations*, which made the UK Top Twenty. After its release, Coleman rejoined the band, which Youth had by now left. Youth went on to form the dance/pop act Brilliant, who had a minor UK hit with the **James Brown** cover 'It's a Man's Man's Man's World' (Food, 1985) and released *Kiss the Lips of Life* the following year. He enjoyed more success with his Blue Pearl project in 1990, reaching the UK Top Five with the dance track 'Naked in the Rain'. In the late eighties he became an in-demand mixer and producer, working with a range of artists who included **Bananarama**, **Paul McCartney** and **Crowded House**.

A stop-gap live album *Ha!* (1982) kept the Killing Joke name alive until the next studio set, *Fire Dances* (1983), which featured new bassist Raven. It was the band's most commercial-sounding album yet, and reached the Top Thirty. The follow-up, *Night Time* (1983), included their only Top Twenty single, the atmospheric 'Love Like Blood'. Dominated by Coleman's increasingly apocalyptic lyrics (he had become obsessed with the writings of satanist Aleister Crowley), *Brighter Than a Thousand Suns* (1986) was less successful, and during the recording of the patchy *Outside the Gate* (1988), Ferguson and Raven left the band. Drummer Martin Atkins, formerly of ex-**Sex Pistol** John Lydon's Public Image, joined for the musically unexceptional but lyrically acidic *Extremities, Dirt and Repressed Emotions* (1990), after which the band broke up.

Coleman recorded with classically trained musician **Ann Dudley** and announced plans to work on an opera and a book, before emigrating to New Zealand. A classically trained pianist, Coleman turned to symphonic work, writing and recording two symphonies, with the London and New Zealand Symphony Orchestras. However, the release of the compilation album *Laugh? I Nearly Bought One* (1992) and the recruitment of Youth to remix singles from it inspired a Killing Joke revival. In 1994 Coleman, Youth and Walker re-formed for the powerful and well-received *Pandemonium* (Big Life) and subsequent live work. *Democracy* (Zoo, 1996) was a lesser outing, especially compared to the anthology *Incomplete, 1980–1985* (EG, 1990).

BRADLEY KINCAID
*b. 13 July 1895, Garrard County, Kentucky, USA,
d. 23 September 1989, Springfield, Ohio*

Kincaid was the first American radio artist to popularize Anglo-American folk song among large, scattered and ethnically diverse audiences. His manner was friendly, and his singing clear and unobscured by a strong regional accent. He therefore appealed not only to transplanted Southerners aching at their separation from the music of their past but also to immigrants, responsive to lessons in the musical folklore of their new home.

College-educated at Berea, Kentucky, Kincaid moved to Chicago to continue his studies. Auditioning for the recently founded station WLS, he was given a slot to sing folk songs with his own simple guitar accompaniment. Rapid popularity led to a recording contract with Gennett (1927–9), for whom he made such typical numbers as 'Barbara Allen' (1928) and 'Sweet Kitty Wells' (1929). He subsequently recorded for Brunswick (1930), Bluebird (1933–4), Decca (1934), Bullet (1944), Majestic (1945) and Capitol (1950), logging a total of about 150 songs.

Much more effective in spreading Kincaid's name and repertoire, however, was his songbook *My Favorite Mountain Ballads and Old-Time songs* (1928), which quickly sold 100,000 copies and created the radio market for country song-folios from which many later artists were to profit. Kincaid issued a further eleven songbooks (the last published in 1945–6), the accumulated repertoire of which exceeded 300 songs. Many of these were secured by field-collecting similar to that of A. P. Carter of the **Carter Family**.

From WLS, Kincaid moved in 1930 to WLW, Cincinnati, in 1931 to KDKA, Pittsburgh, and over the next decade to one station after another, mostly in the East. In 1935–8 he teamed with Grandpa Jones, who later became popular as a singer, banjo player and comedian on the *Grand Ole Opry* and the TV series *Hee Haw*. In 1942 Kincaid returned to WLW and travelled with its *Boone County Jamboree*, and in 1944–9

he joined Nashville's WSM and the *Opry*, though he was somewhat overshadowed by the more expressive style and modern repertoire of **Roy Acuff** and others. Soon afterwards he virtually retired to manage a music store in Springfield, Ohio, though he re-emerged in 1963 to record, in a four-day session, 162 songs for the Bluebonnet label in Fort Worth. Six albums were issued, but more than half of the session's work remained untouched.

Kincaid's plain delivery of ballads and lyric folk songs had a widespread influence on innumerable country and folk performers, from **Mac Wiseman** to **Burl Ives**, but in his collecting and publishing he probably did more to disseminate native folk song than any other agent of his time.

KING CRIMSON
Robert Fripp, b. May 1946, Dorset, England; Mike Giles, b. 1942, Bournemouth, Dorset (replaced by Andy McCullough, replaced by Ian Wallace, replaced by Bill Bruford, b. 17 May 1949, England); Greg Lake, b. 10 November 1948, Bournemouth (replaced by Gordon Haskell, replaced by Boz Burrell, b. Raymond Burrell, 1946, Lincolnshire, replaced by John Wetton, b. 1950, Derby); Mel Collins; Jamie Muir; David Cross, b. 1948, Plymouth, Devon

Perhaps the archetypal progressive-rock band of the seventies, King Crimson steered an erratic course over three decades towards the realization of its leader **Robert Fripp**'s musical vision.

Giles, Giles and Fripp were a Bournemouth rock band which included guitarist Fripp and the Giles brothers, Mike on drums and Peter on bass. With singer Judy Dyble (later of **Fairport Convention**) and sax-player Ian McDonald they made *The Cheerful Insanity of Giles, Giles and Fripp* (Deram, 1968), produced by Wayne Bickerton. Dyble and Peter Giles left and bassist Lake joined before King Crimson was launched early in 1969.

One of the first groups to use a mellotron and playing (for the time) lengthy numbers with complex time-signatures, they achieved overnight fame through their performance at the **Rolling Stones**' free concert in London's Hyde Park. *In the Court of the Crimson King* (Island), pretentiously subtitled 'Some observations by King Crimson', appeared soon afterwards to acclaim from leading rock critics and was a British hit. Despite the overblown poetry of the lyrics (written by the band's then roadie Pete Sinfield), the title track and '21st Century Schizoid Man' had a symphonic grandeur little known in rock outside the work of such isolated figures as **Frank Zappa**.

A hastily arranged American tour caused the first of numerous personnel changes when McDonald and Giles left to make an eponymous album. When Lake left to set up **Emerson, Lake and Palmer** during the recording of *In the Wake of Poseidon* (1970), Fripp recruited Collins (sax) and drummer McCullough to complete the album. Jazz pianist Keith Tippett was brought in to play on the most curious track, 'Cat Food', Sinfield's vegetarian protest song. *Lizard* (1970) was a Sinfield–Fripp song cycle featuring Tippett and guest vocalist Jon Anderson of **Yes**.

A hard-blowing **King Curtis**-style player, Collins introduced fellow jazz-blues performers Burrell (vocals) and Wallace (drums) to the line-up. Fripp taught Burrell some bass guitar lines and a new King Crimson began to tour and record in 1971. This line-up made one studio album (*Islands*) and left behind a live recording (*Earthbound*, 1972) when Collins, Burrell and Wallace joined **Alexis Korner**'s Snape group.

If the early King Crimson had been a symphonic band and the second a 'blowing' band, Fripp's next group were noted for their improvisations. The 1972–4 outfit was built around the experienced rhythm section of Bruford from Yes and Wetton from **Family**. The group, which also included unorthodox percussionist Muir (who soon left to become a Buddhist monk) and Cross on violin and keyboards, cut the impressive *Larks' Tongues in Aspic* (1973). The album contained only three songs, a fact which may have contributed to Sinfield's departure to produce and record for ELP's label Manticore. The new lyricist for *Starless and Bible Black* (1974) was Richard Palmer-Jones, though the title was borrowed from Dylan Thomas.

Fripp now abandoned King Crimson to undertake a variety of musical projects, although he re-formed the group in 1981 when he toured with Bruford, bassist Tony Levin and Adrian Belew, a guitarist who had performed with **Talking Heads** and **David Bowie**. The new quartet maintained the King Crimson reputation for experimental work, combining New York avant-garde influences and African and Asian rhythms with more conventional rock and jazz improvisations. The group's recordings for Editions EG included *Discipline* (1981), *Beat* (1982) and *Three of a Perfect Pair* (1984).

While Fripp moved on to work with his wife, **Toyah Willcox**, and Andy Summers (of the **Police**), Bruford continued experimental work with former **Yes** keyboardist Patrick Moraz and his own group Earthworks, before returning to stadium rock with ex-Yes colleagues in Anderson, Howe, Bruford and Wakeman. Although the musical climate had changed many times since Crimson's heyday, enough interest still existed in the band's early work to justify a series of re-releases. These included *Boxed Set* (1986) and *The Essential King Crimson, Frame by Frame* (1991). In 1994 Fripp recorded a pair of solo albums, *The Bridge Between*, which was credited as by the Robert Fripp

String Quartet, and *Soundscapes, Live in Argentina* on Discipline Records. In 1993 the band re-formed and began touring. Their first recording was an EP, *Vroom* (1995). It was followed by *Thrak* and *THRaKaTTaK* (1996), in support of which they toured America, and the bootleg *B'Boom*.

ConstruKction of Light (2000) saw the group in archival mode, revisiting their past ('Frakctured', 'Larks Tongue in Aspic Part IV') but as angry as ever ('ProzaKc Blues', Heaven and Hell').

KING CURTIS
b. Curtis Ousley, 7 February 1934, Fort Worth, Texas, USA, d. 13 August 1971, New York

Appropriately nicknamed 'King', Curtis Ousley was the most formidable New York session saxophone player in the late fifties and sixties. Without losing his own instrumental voice he could adapt to the needs of rock'n'roll, jazz, soul or rock performances.

His father was a church guitarist with an interest in jazz, but Ousley's first idol was **Louis Jordan**. He took up first alto and then tenor saxophone and won a talent contest at the Harlem Apollo while on a visit to relatives in New York. After leading local bands in Texas, he returned to New York in 1954. Playing in a bar, he was spotted by **Jesse Stone**, who found him his first session work.

As an accompanist, Curtis was renowned for his work with the **Coasters**. From 'Yakety Yak' (1957) onwards, he provided brief, concise and apposite instrumental breaks for the cartoon-strip storylines of the songs written for the group by **Leiber and Stoller**. Curtis also worked with Leiber and Stoller on Sammy Turner's Top Ten hit 'Lavender Blue' (Big Top, 1959). As well as studio work, King Curtis led the orchestra on **Alan Freed**'s package tours, where he met **Buddy Holly**, who recorded 'Reminiscing' with Curtis in 1958. At the same session, the saxophonist played on **Waylon Jennings**' first single, 'Jole Blon'.

In the late fifties he began to make his own jazz and R&B recordings. *Soul Meeting* and *King Soul* (Prestige) featured Nat Adderley on trumpet and future **Miles Davis** pianist Wynton Kelly. Curtis cut R&B solos for such labels as Gem, Groove, Apollo and Crown. With organ accompaniment from Brother Jack McDuff, the instrumentals used a gruff style in the manner of Willis 'Gatortail' Jackson on standards like 'Honky Tonk', 'Fever' and 'The Hucklebuck'. Curtis also recorded a smoky reading of the ballad 'Harlem Nocturne', an R&B hit in 1960 for the Viscounts.

His first pop hit was the bandwagon-jumping 'Soul Twist' (1962), recorded for **Bobby Robinson**'s Enjoy label. Moving to Capitol, Curtis had lesser hits with 'Beach Party' (1962) and 'Soul Serenade' (1964). He was also featured on comedian Soupy Sales' hit, 'The Mouse' (ABC, 1965). From 1965, he recorded exclusively for Atlantic, cutting a long series of saxophone versions of current hit songs, from **Ben E. King**'s 'Spanish Harlem' (1965) through **Buffalo Springfield**'s 'For What It's Worth' (1967) to Jeannie C. Riley's 'Harper Valley PTA' (1968). The most outstanding of Curtis's numerous albums for Atlantic were *King Curtis Plays the Great Memphis Hits* (1967) and *Live at the Fillmore West* (1971), where he was backed by one of the finest East Coast rhythm sections: Bernard Purdie (drums), Cornell Dupree (guitar) and Gerald Jemmott (bass).

For most of the sixties Curtis was a key member of the label's A&R and studio team. He brought **Donny Hathaway** to Atlantic, acted as **Aretha Franklin**'s arranger and bandleader and played on albums with Delaney and Bonnie, the **Rascals**, **Champion Jack Dupree** and dozens of others. He also continued with freelance session work, notably on **John Lennon**'s *Imagine* (1971).

Curtis died after being stabbed while trying to stop a street fight.

KING TUBBY

b. Osborne Lawrence, 28 January 1941, Kingston, Jamaica, d. 6 February 1989, Kingston

A reggae sound-system operator, King Tubby was a central figure in the emergence of dub recordings, in which the vocal track was removed from an existing song and the bass and drum sound manipulated to achieve new instrumental sound shapes.

He entered the sound-system field in the Waterhouse district of Kingston in the late fifties through his work as a radio repairman. By the sixties he had his own sound system, Tubby's Home Town Hi-Fi, and was working as a disc cutter. While doing this he discovered he could make his own versions of records by dropping out the vocal and paring the sound down to bass and drums or alternatively adding in other instruments at will. The resulting versions could then be talked over by disc jockeys. In 1968 Ruddock's leading disc-jockey was **U-Roy**, whose 'toasting' (talking) over the Techniques' 'You Don't Care' became the signature tune of King Tubby's sound system. He began to experiment with echo and phasing and in 1971 worked with Carl Patterson on 'Psalm of Dub', the first commercially released dub record. He acquired a four-track studio and gained a reputation as a master engineer and mixer of dub records, working with **Keith Hudson** on *Pick a Dub*, the first album of dub versions of reggae hits.

With **Lee Perry**, Tubby took the lead in experimenting with reverb and delay echo to add extra layers of sound to the dub track, earning himself the nickname Scientist. From the mid-seventies he released numerous albums of his work, including *Dub from the Roots* (1974), *King Tubby Meets Roots Radics Dangerous Dub* (1981) and *Waterhouse Posse* (1983). *King Tubby's Specials* (1989) collects together some of his seminal seventies recordings.

He was murdered outside his home in 1989.

ALBERT KING

b. Albert Nelson, 25 April 1923, Indianola, Mississippi, USA, d. 20 December 1992

Although he made less commercial impact, Albert King was perhaps as influential as **Little Milton** and even **B. B. King** on the stylistic direction of black blues and blues-rooted music in the sixties and seventies. A singer and guitarist of great strength and solidity but quite narrow range, he was particularly fortunate in working with writers, producers and accompanists ideally suited to his approach.

For most of the period 1948–56 he worked among the In the Groove Boys in Osceola, Arkansas, leaving only to spend a couple of years (1952–4) around Chicago. Then from 1956 to 1964 he was based in St Louis. He recorded briefly for various labels until signing with Stax in 1966. Backed by **Booker T. and the MGs**, he made the superb *Born Under a Bad Sign* (1967), which included 'Laundromat Blues' and the Booker T. Jones–**William Bell** title song. It was followed by *Live Wire/Blues Power* (1968), recorded live at the Fillmore Auditorium in San Francisco, and *King, Does the King's Things* (1969), a collection of songs associated with **Elvis Presley**.

Now popular on the concert and festival circuits, particularly on the West Coast, King began to record in more funky settings, accompanied by the Bar-Kays and the Memphis Horns on *I'll Play the Blues for You* (Stax, 1972) and *I Wanna Get Funky* (1974). This process was maintained on productions for Utopia like *Truckload of Lovin'* (1976) and *Albert* (1976), and *New Orleans Heat* (Tomato, 1978), produced by **Allen Toussaint** and featuring members of the Meters. By the end of the seventies, however, though he was still commanding audiences both in America and in Europe, King had lost ground in the blues record market. He began to regain it with his Fantasy outing *San Francisco '83* (1983), followed by *I'm in a Phone Booth, Baby* (1986), with its **Robert Cray** title song. His last recording was the Alan Douglas-produced *Red House* (1991).

The chief mark of King's effect upon blues practice was the popularity, twenty years later, of the ensemble sound developed in his early Stax days. It was a sound approximated by many Southern bands and more distantly echoed in the work of Chicagoans like singer-guitarist Andrew Brown.

B. B. KING

b. Riley B. King, 16 September 1925, Itta Bena, Mississippi, USA

For fifty years an outstandingly influential figure in blues, King built bridges between the fifties bar-band music of Chicago, the cooler and more instrumentally sophisticated **T-Bone Walker** school in Los Angeles and the mixed milieu of Memphis where he himself began his career. Both his dramatic singing, which drew on such radically different styles as those of Walker and **Roy Brown**, and his more eclectic guitar-playing, rooted in Walker and **Lonnie Johnson**, virtually created blues traditions of their own. A huge influence on white blues guitarists, King rarely had the level of commercial success they had.

After starting out in a local gospel quartet, King began to work professionally in his early twenties singing in a Memphis café and on the city's new black station WDIA. Soon he was presenting a radio show, *Sepia Swing Club*, using the nicknames 'The Beale Street Blues Boy' or 'Blues Boy' King (whence B.B.). He first recorded in 1949 (the year he named his guitar 'Lucille', a fact which subsequently became a staple of his inter-song patter), for the Nashville Bullet label and in the following year he signed with the **Bihari Brothers**' RPM. 'Three o'Clock Blues' (1952), a revision of a **Lowell Fulson** record, topped the R&B chart for fifteen weeks, and he had further R&B Top Ten entries with 'You Didn't Want Me'/'You Know I Love You' (1952), 'Woke Up This Morning' (1953), 'Please Love Me' (1953), 'You Upset Me, Baby' (1954), 'Sweet Little Angel' (1956), 'Please Accept My Love' (1958) and 'Sweet Sixteen' (1960). Between 1950 and 1961 he recorded more than 200 sides for RPM and Kent, many of which were released on albums in the low-priced Crown catalogue; an outstanding example is *My Kind of Blues*, a 1960 session with pianist Lloyd Glenn.

King performed at major venues like New York's Apollo Theater, but the major part of his work was on the Southern black club circuit, which he travelled incessantly; in 1956 alone he played 342 one-night engagements.

In 1962 he signed with ABC and extended his recorded repertoire beyond the blues, but his best-regarded work of that time was the blues set recorded at a Chicago theatre in 1964, *Live at the Regal*. In 1967 he launched ABC's Bluesway series with *Blues Is King*. Now managed by the New York showbusiness accountant Sidney A. Seidenberg, he began to play venues like the Fillmores East and West, sharing the stage with such devotees of his music as **Mike Bloomfield** and **Johnny Winter**. 'The Thrill Is Gone', from *Completely Well* (Bluesway, 1969), reached No. 3 in the R&B charts and No. 15 in the pop charts, giving

him a foothold in a mass market, which he strengthened with work in TV commercials and on movie soundtracks.

Indianola Mississippi Seeds (ABC, 1970) included accompaniment from **Leon Russell** (piano), **Carole King** (piano) and Joe Walsh (guitar), among others, and produced minor pop hits in 'Hummingbird' and 'Chains and Things'. In 1971 he recorded a London session with **Alexis Korner**, **Ringo Starr** and others, and in 1972 an elaborately produced *L.A. Midnight* with jazz saxophonists Red Holloway and **Plas Johnson**, rock guitarists Walsh and Jesse Davis, and **Taj Mahal**. *Guess Who* (1972) drew its contents from pop sources like **Hoyt Axton** and the **Lovin' Spoonful**, a trend followed on *To Know You Is to Love You* (1973) and *Friends* (1974), while the blues constituency was awarded a couple of 'summit-meetings' with **Bobby Bland** (*Together for the First Time . . . Live*, 1974, and *Together Again*, 1976). King's progress flagged somewhat in the late seventies – though he continued to be well received on his many tours outside the US – but revived in 1979 with a move to MCA and *Take It Home*, a collaboration with the **Crusaders**. Though subsequent albums like the country set *Love Me Tender* (1982) were not successful, *Blues 'n' Jazz* (1983), which reunited him with Lloyd Glenn and also employed Arnett Cobb (tenor) and Woody Shaw (trumpet), affirmed King's continued interest in the forms on which he had founded his reputation.

King's appetite for live work was undiminished as he entered his sixties, regularly playing 250 gigs a year, and releasing frequent live albums. A 1991 *Live at the Apollo* set, recorded at the famous Harlem venue, found King playing to an urban black audience, a rarity in his later years during which his studio recordings have often been of variable quality as he attempted to blend traditional blues idioms into a modern AOR format for a largely white audience. He has also played on a catholic selection of records by other artists, including an unlikely trilogy of albums featuring cartoon characters **The Simpsons**, Garfield and Charlie Brown. In 1989 he appeared with **U2** on the hit single 'When Love Comes to Town', and in 1990 recorded with country artist **Randy Travis**. 1991's *There Is Always One More Time* was one of King's best later studio albums, and was followed by a lavish boxed set, *King of the Blues* (1992), which summed up his career to date. On the 1993 Grammy award-winner *Blues Summit*, King was joined by other blues luminaries such as **John Lee Hooker**, Irma Thomas and **Buddy Guy** while in 1994 he teamed up with jazz singer Dianne Schuur on the Phil Ramone-produced *Heart to Heart*.

King's influence on guitarists had first become apparent in the fifties work of the young Guy, and by the sixties he was being imitated to varying degrees by almost every second- and third-rank blues singer-guitarist, black or white, particularly in Chicago. By the eighties he had effortlessly deposed **Memphis Slim** as 'Ambassador of the Blues' and become, like **Louis Armstrong**, an international icon of black music, a position he maintained into the nineties. He continued his rigorous touring schedule in the nineties, reducing his appearances from 250 a year to a mere 200 a year. On the celebrity offering *Deuces Wild* (1998) King was paired with the likes of **Eric Clapton** ('Rock Me Baby'), **Tracy Chapman** ('The Thrill Is Gone'), **Willie Nelson** ('Nightlife') and **Bonnie Raitt** ('Baby I Love You'). Far better than it could have been, the album was overshadowed by the welter of reissues of his classic albums. More openly exuberant was *Let the Good Times Roll* (1999), King's tribute to **Louis Jordan**. Partnered by **Dr John,** King clearly enjoyed returning to the simple joys of 'Caldonia' and 'Saturday Night Fish Fry'. King partnered Clapton again on the Top Five album *Riding with the King* (Reprise, 2000), a comfortable but nonetheless rewarding mix of traditional and contemporary blues.

BEN E. KING

b. Benjamin Earl Nelson, 28 September 1938, Henderson, North Carolina, USA

More balladeer than soul singer, King was lead singer with the **Drifters** at their moment of greatest commercial success. His warm, romantic tenor can be heard on 'There Goes My Baby'* (Atlantic, 1959) and 'Save the Last Dance for Me'* (1960) and on a series of memorable solo recordings, including the classic and oft-covered 'Stand by Me' (1961), which he also co-wrote.

In New York, King formed the Four Bs and auditioned unsuccessfully for **Harvey Fuqua**'s Moonglows before in 1956 joining the Five Crowns, who recorded for Rainbow. In 1959, when the Drifters left manager George Treadwell, who owned the group's name, he promptly signed the Five Crowns and renamed them the Drifters. Thus it was that the Drifters made the difficult transition from the fifties to the sixties, by simply becoming a different group. As such they became heavily reliant on producers **Leiber and Stoller**. Where the Drifters' earlier records were notable for the vocals of **Clyde McPhatter**, what was noticeable about the 'new' Drifters was the overall sound of the records. The classic examples of this are their first record under the Drifters name, the innovatory 'There Goes My Baby', which mixed strings and percussive effects with Latin rhythms, and 'Save the Last Dance for Me', their biggest hit.

After leaving the Drifters in 1960, King's best solo records include the **Phil Spector**-supervised 'Spanish Harlem' (Atco, 1961) – later revived by many singers,

most successfully by **Aretha Franklin**, who also recorded another of King's hits, 'Don't Play That Song' – and 'Stand by Me' (1961), which King wrote with Leiber and Stoller. They set King's voice against vividly defined soundscapes which reflected warmth in 'Spanish Harlem' and starkness in 'Stand by Me'. 'Stand' became a standard, providing later hits for Spyder Turner (MGM, 1966), whose novelty version included impersonations of **Jackie Wilson** and others but not of King himself, **John Lennon** (1975) and **Mickey Gilley** (1980). Less impressive, though equally produced, were King's attempts at more mainstream balladry. These included 'I (Who Have Nothing)' (1963), which was covered in Britain by **Shirley Bassey** and successfully revised by **Tom Jones** in 1970, and Alan Jay Lerner's (of **Lerner and Loewe**) 'I Could Have Danced All Night'. In 1964, however, he briefly rivalled **Solomon Burke** for emotional excitement on 'It's All Over' and 'Seven Letters'.

When his hits dried up, King left Atlantic for Maxwell (in 1969) and then Mandala, but only returned to the Top Ten when he re-signed with Atlantic and recorded Gwen Guthrie's disco song, 'Supernatural Thing (Part 1)' (1975). King followed this with the superior *Benny and Us* (1977), which he recorded with the **Average White Band**, but despite a series of fine albums, including *Street Tough* (1981), he did not return to the charts again until 1986 when, after 'Stand by Me' was featured as the title track of a movie, it once more was reissued. In 1987, in Britain, where the song was also featured in a television campaign for Levi jeans, it topped the charts.

The renewed interest in King led to an undistinguished re-recording, *Save the Last Dance for Me* (EMI Manhattan, 1988), while Atlantic issued a remixed 'Supernatural Thing' in 1990. The following year he collaborated with **Bo Diddley** on a version of the Monotones' 'Book of Love', the title song of a film. King remains active as a live performer, and was a regular visitor to Europe into the nineties, playing both cabaret and concert venues. He signed with Ichiban in 1994. *Anthology* (Rhino, 1993) is the definitive retrospective.

CAROLE KING

b. Carole Klein, 9 February 1942, Brooklyn, New York, USA

King and Gerry Goffin were among the poets laureate of pop songwriting in the sixties. In the following decade her *Tapestry* (1971), which mixed intimacy and urgency to perfection, established the singer-songwriter sub-genre.

An accomplished pianist, King met Goffin (*b. 11 February 1939, Queens, New York*) at college and wrote tunes for his words when both joined the **Don**

Kirshner–Al Nevins office in the Brill Building. Before she composed a hit herself, she had one written to her by **Neil Sedaka**. King replied to his 'Oh! Carol' with the unsuccessful 'Oh! Neil' (Alpine, 1959).

With Goffin, however, she wrote primarily yearning but compact teenage love ballads, including the 1961 No. 1 hits for the **Shirelles** ('Will You Love Me Tomorrow?') and **Bobby Vee** ('Take Good Care of My Baby'). In the following year they composed Top Ten songs for Little Eva (the dance novelty 'The Loco-Motion', Dimension), the **Drifters** ('Up on the Roof'), **Steve Lawrence** ('Go Away Little Girl') and the Cookies ('Chains', a song covered by **The Beatles** on their début album). With Howie Greenfield, King also wrote the **Everly Brothers'** 1962 hit, 'Crying in the Rain', while 'It Might as Well Rain Until September' (Dimension, 1963) was the first hit recorded as well as written by King.

Goffin and King were extremely prolific in the early sixties, though some of their best songs failed to reach the top levels of the charts. These included the girl-group compositions, 'Don't Say Nothin' Bad About My Baby' (the Cookies) and 'He Hit Me', a **Phil Spector** production for the **Crystals** which was boycotted by radio stations because of its masochistic sentiments, as well as **Tony Orlando**'s 'Halfway to Paradise' (1961).

The duo weathered the arrival of The Beatles and other British artists better than many of their contemporaries. **Manfred Mann** ('Oh No, Not My Baby'), **Herman's Hermits** ('I'm into Something Good') and the **Animals** ('Don't Bring Me Down') successfully recorded their material, as did American rock group the **Byrds**, with 'Goin' Back' and 'Wasn't Born to Follow', which was featured in the film *Easy Rider* (1969). The last two songs indicated a growing away from teenage themes, though Goffin and King did provide one of the **Monkees'** biggest hits with 'Pleasant Valley Sunday' (1967).

In 1968 the professional and personal partnership was over and Goffin teamed up with former **Mike Bloomfield** keyboards-player Barry Goldberg to compose more country- and folk-orientated material that appeared on *It Ain't Exactly Entertainment* (Adelphi, 1973). Goffin–Goldberg also wrote **Gladys Knight**'s 1974 hit 'I've Got to Use My Imagination'.

King moved to Los Angeles where she formed a trio, the City, with Charles Larkey (bass) and Danny Kortchmar (guitar), recording a low-key album for **Lou Adler**'s Ode label. This was followed by *Carole King: Writer*, a solo album containing new versions of old hits and previously unrecorded Goffin–King compositions. *Tapestry*, however, contained a majority of new material, with either Toni Stern or King herself writing the lyrics. The reflective, mature mood of

'You've Got a Friend', a hit for **James Taylor**, 'So Far Away', the 1967 **Aretha Franklin** hit 'Natural Woman' and her own hit single 'It's Too Late'* found a massive new audience, whose tastes were later codified as FM rock or album-orientated rock. *Tapestry* was a worldwide hit, eventually selling in excess of 15 million copies. A further indication of its impact was the tribute album *Tapestry Revisited* (Sony, 1995), which included versions of the songs from it by **Rod Stewart**, **Céline Dion**, Aretha Franklin and others.

Like *Tapestry*, *Music* (1971) and its hit single 'Sweet Seasons' was produced by Adler with accompaniment by Larkey and drummer Russ Kunkel. Despite (or perhaps because of) their similar approach, *Rhymes and Reasons* (1972) and *Fantasy* (1973) did not repeat the success of *Tapestry*. However, *Wrap Around Joy* (1974) produced the hits 'Jazzman', which featured tenor sax-player Tom Scott, and 'Nightingale'. The album also included backing vocals by King's daughter Louise Goffin, who went on to her own recording career with the Kortchmar-produced *Kid Blue* (Asylum, 1979) and *Louise Goffin* (1981). In 1987 Louise signed to Warners and released *This Is the Place*.

After *Really Rosie* (1975) and *Thoroughbred* (1976), King changed labels to Capitol for *Simple Things* (1977), *Welcome Home* (1978) and *Touch the Sky* (1979). The following year she recorded *Pearls*, an album of Goffin–King oldies. Its revival of the 1963 **Chiffons'** hit 'One Fine Day' reached the Top Twenty. In the eighties she cut *One to One* (1983) and *Speeding Time* (1984), on which she was reunited with Adler, for Atlantic. From the mid-seventies King had also resumed occasional collaboration with Goffin and they wrote the 1986 **Anne Murray** hit 'Time Don't Run out on Me' as well as two songs on King's *City Streets* (1988). Her next album was *Color of Your Dreams* (Kings X, 1993), co-produced with Rudy Guess.

Carole King wrote the score for *Murphy's Romance* (1986) and contributed material to the children's cartoon film *The Care Bears Movie* (1985).

She made her Broadway début in 1994, starring opposite **David Cassidy** in *Blood Brothers*, the musical by British writer Willy Russell. In the same year Sony issued the boxed-set compilation *The Ode Years*. In 1995 British acting duo Robson and Jerome had a UK chart-topper with King's 'Up on the Roof', while in 1997 King contributed 'The Reason' to Céline Dion's *Let's Talk about Love* and in 1999 wrote 'Anyone at All' for the soundtrack of *You've Got Mail*.

FREDDIE KING
b. 3 September 1934, Gilmer, Texas, USA, d. 18 December 1976, Dallas

A stylistic heir of **T-Bone Walker** and **B. B. King**, Freddie King, with his fiery blues guitar-playing, was an important influence on **Eric Clapton** and a generation of British R&B instrumentalists.

He began learning guitar at the age of five and listened to records by **Big Bill Broonzy**, **Blind Lemon Jefferson** and **Louis Jordan**. In 1950 his family moved to Chicago, where King heard the work of **Muddy Waters** and B. B. King. In 1953 he joined the band of harmonica-player Little Sonny Cooper, recording with Cooper and Earl Payton's Blues Cats for Parrot. After the label folded, one of its owners, 'Lawyer' John Burton, founded El-Bee and recorded King as a soloist on 'Country Boy' (1956).

His growing reputation for technical brilliance led to a contract with Federal, a subsidiary of **Syd Nathan**'s King label. Rhythm and blues hits followed with a version of the B. B. King slow blues 'Have You Ever Loved a Woman' and the rocking instrumental 'Hideaway' (1960). With arrangements by pianist and A&R man Sonny Thompson, King went on to score a series of R&B bestsellers, notably the fluent, high-speed guitar solos 'The Stumble' (1961) and 'Driving Sideways' (1962), which were later recorded in Britain by **John Mayall**'s band, featuring Mick Taylor and Peter Green, respectively. Mayall also cut 'Hideaway' with Clapton on guitar.

While King's success ebbed in America in the mid-sixties, his status in Britain led to several tours, beginning in 1967 when he was accompanied by Chicken Shack, whose Stan Webb was perhaps his most ardent disciple. Meanwhile, he left Federal to record *Freddie King Is a Blues Master* (1969) and *My Feeling for the Blues* (1970) for Atlantic's Cotillion label, with producer **King Curtis**.

In the seventies King's recording career was orientated towards the white blues and soul audience. He signed to **Leon Russell**'s Shelter label for *Getting Ready* (1971), *Texas Cannonball* (1972) and *Woman Across the Water* (1973). He next joined RSO, where Clapton was a backing musician on the funk-flavoured *Burglar* (1974), produced in England by **Mike Vernon**. King's last album, the live *Larger Than Life*, found him performing in a more traditional R&B vein. He died of heart failure after being taken ill during a club performance in Dallas, where he had lived since 1963.

JONATHAN KING
b. Kenneth King, 6 December 1944, London, England

The British counterpart of **Kim Fowley**, King rose to fame as an eccentric pop personality in the sixties, was renowned in the seventies for such disposable pop productions as St Cecilia's 'Leap Up and Down and Wave Your Knickers in the Air' (Polydor, 1971) and in the eighties and nineties became a pop pundit and media personality.

While a Cambridge undergraduate, King had a sur-

prise transatlantic hit with his own composition, the wistful pseudo-protest song, 'Everyone's Gone to the Moon' (Decca, Parrot in the US, 1965). The same year he wrote and produced another transatlantic hit, 'It's Good News Week' for Hedgehoppers Anonymous (Decca/Parrot). Rather than pursue a performing career, he became personal assistant to Decca's founder, Edward Lewis, in which capacity he signed, named and produced the first album by **Genesis**, and made a series of engaging singles. These included the bizarre 'Let It All Hang Out' (1970), **Bob Dylan**'s 'Million Dollar Bash' and a surprisingly reverential version of **Hoagy Carmichael**'s 'Lazybones' (1971). In 1970 he set up his own production company and recorded a number of one-off pop songs, many of which were hits when leased to various companies. His 1971 successes included a heavy-metal version of the Archies' bubblegum classic 'Sugar Sugar' (Sakkarin, RCA), 'The Same Old Song' (the Weathermen, B&C) – both of which featured a pseudonymous King – 'Johnny Reggae' (the Piglets, Bell) and 'Keep on Dancing' (the **Bay City Rollers**' revival of the Gentrys' 1965 American hit).

In 1972 he set up UK Records, releasing a series of increasingly indulgent works, both under his own name – *Bubble Rock Is Here to Stay* (1972), *Pandora's Box* (1973), *J.K. All the Way* (1976) – and various pseudonyms – Shag ('Loop Di Love', 1972), 53rd and 3rd ('Chick a Boom', 1975) and 100 Ton and a Feather ('It Only Takes a Minute', 1976). King's biggest success was his cover of George Baker's 'Una Paloma Blanca' (1975), one of the first European summer-holiday pop hits, while in 1979 he recorded 'Gloria' (Ariola), later a huge hit for **Laura Branigan**. However, the mainstay of the label were 10CC with none of whose hits King was involved. All his other signings, including pub rockers the Kursaal Flyers and **Marty Wilde**'s son Ricky, failed to achieve chart success.

After winding up UK Records, King went on to become a pop pundit in the eighties. He presented a number of radio (*A King in New York*) and television (*Entertainment USA*) programmes, espousing increasingly populist and conservative views from his various platforms, including the *Sun* newspaper. In 1982 he published the novel *Bible Two* and subsequently unsuccessfully attempted to establish his own music paper, *Revvolution*. He was producer and presenter of the Brit Awards show, and in 1992 King released the album *Anticloning* on his own Sounds of Revvolution label. It attracted tabloid headlines because of the inclusion of the song 'Jason Donovan's Poof?' which berated media treatment of the Australian pop singer. King launched a music-industry only publication, *The Tip-Sheet*, in 1993. Since then he has regularly been active in organizing the UK's Eurovision Song Contest entry.

PEE WEE KING

b. Frank Anthony Kuczynski, 18 February 1914, Abrams, Wisconsin, USA, d. 7 March 2000, Louisville, Kentucky

Singer, accordionist and bandleader Pee Wee King is chiefly notable for securing and maintaining on the then traditionalist *Grand Ole Opry* a place for Western, or at least Midwestern, swing. He repaid the favour with 'Tennessee Waltz', a multi-million-seller for the country-music industry and a state song for Tennessee.

King first led a country-flavoured band in 1933 on WIS in Milwaukee, then moved in 1934 to WHAS, Louisville, Kentucky, where he named his band the Golden West Cowboys. It was probably at this time that he heard and marked the country-swing music of fiddler Clayton McMichen and his Georgia Wildcats. (McMichen had earlier been a member of **Gid Tanner**'s Skillet-Lickers.) After short stays on WLS, Chicago, and WNOX Knoxville, Tennessee, King moved in 1937 to WSM and the *Opry*. One of his band singers was **Eddy Arnold**, but the longest-serving was Redd Stewart.

After spells on Bullet (1945) and King (1945–6), King signed with RCA Victor in 1946. 'Tennessee Waltz', which he wrote with Stewart, went on to the country charts in versions by both himself and **Cowboy Copas**, but it was **Patti Page** who took it to the top of the pop charts in 1948, and in various recordings the number has sold over 10 million copies. King also reached the country charts with a modernized reading of the traditional fiddle tune 'Bonaparte's Retreat' (1948), and with 'Slow Poke' (1951) and 'Bimbo' (1954). At this period the Golden West Cowboys were frequently voted Best Country and Western Band by *Billboard* and *Cashbox*.

King left RCA Victor in 1961 and recorded for Briar (1962–4), Starday (1964–5) and Cuca (1966). He retired from performing in 1969 but managed country shows during the seventies. He was elected to the Country Music Hall of Fame in 1974 and was active as a director of the Country Music Foundation in Nashville.

THE KINGSTON TRIO

Dave Guard, b. 19 November 1934, Honolulu, Hawaii, USA, d. 22 March 1991 (replaced by John Stewart, b. 5 September 1939, San Diego, California); Nick Reynolds, b. 27 July 1933, San Diego; Bob Shane, b. 1 February 1934, Hilo, Hawaii

With smooth vocal lines, percussive acoustic-guitar accompaniments and well-groomed collegiate looks, the Kingston Trio set the tone for the folk revival of the early sixties. Their reign lasted until the arrival of **Bob Dylan** and a very different folk ambience.

Guard and Shane were high-school ukulele-playing friends in Hawaii. Reynolds met Guard at college in California and they began to perform in 1957 at San Francisco coffee-houses. The trio chose their name for its Caribbean flavour (this was the era of **Harry Belafonte**'s greatest popularity).

Signed to Capitol, the group released an eponymous first album which contained **Woody Guthrie**'s 'Hard Ain't It Hard' and showed the influence of the **Weavers**. But it was the choice of 'Tom Dooley'* as a single which ensured the Kingston Trio's success. First recorded on a 1952 Elektra album by collector Frank Warner (who had learned it from North Carolina singer Frank Proffitt), the doleful ballad described the fate of Tom Dula, condemned to death in 1868 for the alleged murder of his girlfriend. The record reached No. 1 in America and in Britain both **Lonnie Donegan** and the Kingston Trio had hit versions. A mark of its impact was that it was one of the first songs to inspire a movie (*The Legend of Tom Dooley*, 1959, in which the Trio's recording was heard), while in North Carolina, Dula's grave was restored.

Booked to appear at the 1959 Newport Folk Festival, the Trio aroused hostility among folk-music purists but inspired the formation of a host of other bland acoustic trios and quartets. Among the most successful were the Brothers Four (whose 'Greenfields' was a 1960 hit on Columbia) and the Highwaymen ('Michael' and 'Cottonfields', United Artists, 1961).

The Kingston Trio themselves had later hits in 1959 with 'The Tijuana Jail', 'MTA' (written by Bess Hawes, sister of **Alan Lomax**) and 'A Worried Man' before Guard left to form the Whiskeyhill Singers with Judy Henske. The group recorded for Capitol and performed the score for *How the West Was Won* (1962). Later Guard published several collections of children's stories. His replacement was songwriter **John Stewart** from the Cumberland Three, and the trio had further hits with **Pete Seeger**'s anti-war lament 'Where Have All the Flowers Gone?' (1962), **Hoyt Axton**'s 'Greenback Dollar' and Billy Edd Wheeler's 'Reverend Mr Black' (1963).

This move towards material by contemporary writers accelerated in the mid-sixties and the Kingston Trio recorded songs by **Jacques Brel**, **Rod McKuen**, and even **Lerner and Loewe** ('They Call the Wind Maria'). But despite the fact that they also cut Dylan's 'Blowin' in the Wind', by this period their approach had been superseded by the new breed of topical songwriters and harmony trios led by **Peter Paul and Mary**.

After recording some thirty albums, the trio disbanded in 1968, with Stewart going on to a career as a singer-songwriter and Reynolds retiring to his Oregon ranch. Shane organized a New Kingston Trio with Roger Gamble and George Grove. All six members of the old and new groups were reunited for a 1982 television special.

THE KINKS

Ray Davies, b. Raymond Douglas Davies, 21 June 1944, London, England; Dave Davies, b. David Russell Gordon Davies, 3 February 1947, London; Mick Avory, b. Michael Charles Avory, 15 February 1944, Hampton Court, Surrey (replaced by Bobby Henrit); Pete Quaife, b. 31 December 1943, Tavistock, Devon (replaced by John Dalton, b. 21 May 1943, replaced by Andy Pile, replaced by Jim Rodford, b. 7 July 1945); John Gosling (replaced by Ian Gibbons, replaced by Mark Haley)

One of Britain's leading beat groups in the sixties, the Kinks' guitar riff on 'You Really Got Me' (1964) became part of the musical language of rock. The group's later work was notable for Ray Davies' witty, passionate, incisive and often unfashionable songwriting. In the eighties the Kinks established themselves as a stadium-rock band in America, while in the nineties Davies was celebrated as the older brother of the new generation of art-school bands.

The Davies brothers learned guitar as children and formed their first amateur group with schoolmate Quaife, playing **Buddy Holly** and **Ventures** material until they heard their first **Chuck Berry** records in 1962. While an art student in London, Ray Davies was inspired by **Alexis Korner**'s Blues Incorporated band to join London R&B groups, but finally rejoined Dave Davies and Quaife to form a band variously called the Ravens and the Bo-Weevils. Through publisher/producer Larry Page (whose greatest success came with the **Troggs**), they cut a demo disc and were signed by independent producer Shel Talmy.

Using a vogue word of 'swinging London' ('kinky' was applied to everything from sexual perversity to fashion items), the group were renamed the Kinks and recorded **Little Richard**'s 'Long Tall Sally' and Ray's 'You Still Want Me' (Pye, 1964). With Avory, who had previously auditioned for the **Rolling Stones**, they toured with the **Dave Clark Five** and released 'You Really Got Me'. Its repeated phrase played on Dave Davies' fuzz guitar helped the record reach No. 1 in 1964. The sound influenced virtually every rock guitarist of the sixties and variations on it appeared in many later Kinks songs. *The Kinks*, a hastily assembled mix of Ray Davies originals and R&B standards, was rush-released and swiftly followed by a second Top Ten single, 'All Day and All of the Night'.

The commercial peak of the Kinks' career was 1965–7 when they had nine British and seven American hits. In 1965 'Tired of Waiting for You' was the first record to display Ray Davies' world-weary vocal style, while Dave achieved a then-revolutionary Indian-style drone sound on 'See My Friends'. The feature of the later material was Ray's emergence as a social commentator, by turns witty and compassionate. The genial satire on Carnaby Street ('Dedicated Follower of Fashion') and the *nouveau riche* popocracy ('Sunny Afternoon') was followed by resonant evocations of the urban environment (the melodic and wistful 'Waterloo Sunset') and traditional working-class lifestyles ('Dead End Street' and 'Autumn Almanac'). In 1967 Dave Davies had two solo hits with 'Death of a Clown' and 'Susannah's Still Alive'.

Away from the charts, however, the group was in crisis. An unresolved dispute with the American Federation of Musicians during a 1965 tour led to a ban on American appearances which lasted until 1969, while a British lawsuit over publishing rights began in 1967. These problems, coupled with the pressures of recording and touring caused internal tensions and in 1966 brought about Ray's collapse from nervous exhaustion.

After taking over production on *Something Else* (1967), which included both 'David Watts' (later revived by the **Jam**) and the melancholic 'Lazy Old Sun', Ray Davies responded to the new progressive and underground rock trends by writing his own 'concept album' in 1968. In *The Village Green Preservation Society* he developed one of the major themes of his work, a lament for a lost Edenic world submerged by modernity. Pete Quaife left the Kinks and emigrated to Canada in 1969, the year that the band released *Arthur*. Similarly themed to *Village Green* and subtitled 'The Decline and Fall of the British Empire' it portrayed an English family looking back over their experiences before emigrating to Australia. Among the best songs on these two albums were 'Walter', 'All of My Friends Were There', 'Victoria', 'Drivin'' and 'Shangri-La'.

With John Dalton installed on bass and undeterred by the lack of response from progressive-rock audiences, Davies pressed ahead with further album projects. The unattractively titled *Lola Versus Powerman and the Moneygoround, Part One* (1970) described the struggle of a rock band against the business but it included one of his biggest hits and most enduring songs. With a calypso lilt in his voice he sang in 'Lola' of a curiously compelling gender-blurring encounter in a 'club down in Old Soho'. The single was a Top Ten hit on both sides of the Atlantic and it assisted the group in its negotiations with RCA over a new recording deal.

The first albums for the new label were *Muswell Hillbillies* (1971), a partly autobiographical song sequence dealing with the uprooting of inner-city communities, and *Everybody's in Showbiz, Everybody's a Star* (1972). A double-album with one studio and one live record, its outstanding song was the gentle, melancholic 'Celluloid Heroes', dealing with the paradoxes of stardom through the central image of the stars' names set in paving stones on Hollywood Boulevard.

The live part of the record portrayed the new stage persona of the Kinks, a troupe of hard-drinking, wisecracking entertainers, which now included keyboards-player Gosling, backing singers and a horn section. The dramatic aspects of the live show were amplified in Ray Davies' ambitious writing and recording projects of the mid-seventies. The two-album *Preservation* (Part 1, 1973; Part 2, 1974), *Soap Opera* (1975) and *Schoolboys in Disgrace* (1976) were kinds of rock opera, though far removed from the high-tech splendour and fashionable mysticism of **The Who**'s *Tommy*. All were conceived with an eye on television or stage presentation but, despite some acerbic and moving moments, they found only a cult following.

In 1973 the Kinks asserted their autonomy by opening their own studio and forming a label, Konk, whose signings included Claire Hammill and Café Society. The latter group included **Tom Robinson**, who ironically later claimed that he had been mistreated financially by Konk, precisely the same complaint made by Ray Davies about his own relationship with the music business.

With *Schoolboys*, a semi-camp evocation of an English boyhood, the Kinks had returned to a simple rock-group format and sound. This approach formed the basis of the group's deliberate assault on the American market after being signed by Clive Davis to Arista in 1976. With Andy Pyle replacing Dalton on bass, they toured widely in support of *Sleepwalker* (1977) and *Misfits* (1978), which included 'Rock'n'Roll Fantasy', their first American hit for eight years. John Gosling and Pyle left after *Misfits*, replaced by Ian Gibbons (subsequently replaced in 1989 by Mark Haley) and Jim Rodford, respectively.

As *Low Budget* (1979) reached the American Top Twenty, the sixties Kinks were receiving tributes from a stream of revivals of their songs by **Van Halen** ('You Really Got Me', 1978), the **Jam** and the **Pretenders** ('Stop Your Sobbin'', 1979), whose lead vocalist Chrissie Hynde would become Davies' partner for four years. While he had earlier written music for the comedy film *Percy* (1971), the arrival of video finally provided Ray Davies with the appropriate visual form for his musical imagination, starting with the concert tape and album *One for the Road* (1980) and reaching a peak with Julien Temple's film for 'Predictable' (1981) and the transatlantic hit 'Come Dancing' (1982), which merged Davies' mastery of melody and his focused nostalgia.

Davies worked again with Temple in the film musical *Absolute Beginners* (1986), composing and singing 'Quiet Life', and created his own British television play with music, *Return to Waterloo*. He continued to rework his artistic motifs – personal identity, the loss of the past, the nature of the music industry – in later albums like *State of Confusion* (1983) and *The Road* (1988).

While remaining a core member of the group, Dave Davies resumed a solo recording career in 1980 with an eponymous album (RCA), *Glamour* (1981) and *Chosen People* (1983). Mick Avory was replaced by Bobby Henritt (ex-Argent) in the mid-eighties, after Henritt had played on *Word of Mouth* (1984), and in 1986 the Kinks signed to London Records, releasing *Think Visual*, *The Road* (1988) and *UK Jive* (1989).

As the Kinks approached their thirtieth anniversary, they signed a new recording contract with Columbia, releasing one minor Ray Davies classic, 'Did Ya' (1991), a nostalgic look back at sixties London. It was included on *Phobia* (1993), an otherwise undistinguished start to the latest stage in their career which saw the band return to the tour circuit. More interesting was Ray Davies' 1992 television documentary *Weird Nightmare*, about the making of **Hal Willner**'s tribute album to **Charlie Mingus**, and his intriguing part-fictionalized biography, *X-Ray* (1994). In the same vein was *To the Bone* (Konk, 1995), a stripped-down solo album by Davies. Featuring new material, the similarly styled *The Storyteller* (EMI) was released in 1998. In the same year Dave Davies published his own account of his days with the group, *The Outrageous Story of My Wild Years as the Founder and Leader of the Kinks*, and Castle Communications reissued all the Kinks' Pye albums to critical acclaim.

RAHSAAN ROLAND KIRK

b. 7 August 1936, Columbus, Ohio, USA, d. 5 December 1977, Bloomington, Indiana

A frequent winner of the 'miscellaneous' category in jazz polls of the sixties and seventies, Kirk was an important innovator. He introduced a new style of flute-playing as well as originating a method of playing two or three reed instruments simultaneously.

Accidently blinded as a small child, he took up tenor sax and flute, playing in R&B groups before in 1951 discovering the strich and manzello (woodwind instruments equivalent to alto and soprano saxophones). By developing a circular-breathing method, Kirk could play both these instruments simultaneously, often with a tenor sax in addition.

In the late fifties he played with the equally extroverted **Charles Mingus**, contributing to the memorable 'Hog Calling Blues' on *Mingus Oh Yeah* (1961). In the same year Kirk made the highly acclaimed *We Free Kings* (Atlantic). With Hank Jones on piano, the album demonstrated Kirk's combination of humming and breathy playing that made his flute style a key influence on such later performers as **Jethro Tull**'s Ian Anderson. The multi-instrumental technique was explored on *Rip Rig and Panic* (1965), whose title was used by a British eighties post-punk band which included **Don Cherry**'s daughter **Neneh**.

In 1968 Kirk released *Don't Cry Beautiful Edith*, with pianist Lonnie Smith, and *The Inflated Tear*, an album inspired by his childhood responses to blindness. Throughout his career Kirk also recorded tributes to jazz masters of the past, including **Billie Holiday** and **Lester Young**. Politically minded, he cut *Volunteered Slavery* with his Vibration Society in 1970, the year in which he helped to form the New York Collective of Black Artists and the Jazz and People's Movement, which undertook highly vocal protests at the lack of black musicians on American primetime television shows.

Leading his own small groups, Kirk toured frequently in the sixties and seventies and was reunited with Mingus for a 1974 Carnegie Hall concert. He suffered a severe stroke in 1975 but returned to tour Europe, playing one-handed, before a second stroke killed him.

STANLEY KIRKBY

With **Peter Dawson**, Stanley Kirkby was probably the most prolific artist of the British record industry, producing countless recordings of ballads, comic and novelty numbers, patriotic songs and other standard popular material. The early recording director **Joe Batten** wrote of him: 'He had the finest recording voice of all the artistes I have heard in recording studios. It was a pure baritone. His diction was perfect, and he had a versatility in interpretation that distinguished him from all others.'

He first made records in 1904. In 1907 both Kirkby and Dawson were among the cast that first recorded **Gilbert and Sullivan**'s *The Mikado* and by 1914 he was earning hundreds of pounds a week as a freelance. During the First World War, he specialized in patriotic subjects, and 'The Rose of No Man's Land', released by Edison Bell Winner in 1917, was the label's bestseller. He had further success on Winner with 'The Miner's Dream of Home', written by the music-hall singer Leo Dryden and ''Tis a Story That Shall Live Forever' (1913), a song about Captain Scott's tragic Antarctic expedition. He also recorded many titles for Regal and, under the pseudonym Murray Johnson, for HMV. In the twenties he specialized in comic oddities like 'Felix Kept on Walking' (1923) and 'Why Robinson Crusoe Got the Blues'.

As a journeyman in the demanding days of pre-electric recording, Kirkby had adaptability and stamina equalled on the American scene perhaps only by **Irving Kaufman** – about whom equally little is known.

DON KIRSHNER

b. 17 April 1934, Bronx, New York, USA

Songwriter, publisher, record-company owner and originator of the **Monkees**, Kirshner was an important force in the music business from the late fifties.

Raised in East Orange, New Jersey, Kirshner met **Bobby Darin** in 1956 and wrote songs and jingles with him (including 'I Want to Spend Christmas with Elvis') before Darin signed with Atlantic. Among those who sang on the demos was the young **Connie Francis**. In 1958 Kirshner and Al Nevins, a one-time member of the Three Sons, established Aldon Music specifically to publish songs for the teenage market. Together the pair signed up the cream of the new breed of songwriters, including **Neil Sedaka** and Howie Greenfield (who supplied the first Aldon-published hit when Connie Francis recorded their 'Stupid Cupid'), **Barry Mann** and Cynthia Weil, Jack Keller, **Carole King** and Gerry Goffin and later **Neil Diamond**, and set them to work in production-line conditions that aped those of the old Tin Pan Alley.

The result was a string of hit songs including 'Will You Love Me Tomorrow?', 'Take Good Care of My Baby' and 'Up on the Roof' (Goffin and King); 'You've Lost That Loving Feeling' and 'On Broadway' (Mann and Weil). Aldon quickly became a production company, recording and then leasing sides by Sedaka to RCA, Mann to ABC, and **Tony Orlando** to Epic before, in 1962, Kirshner established his own record company, Dimension. The label was instantly successful. Hits included Little Eva's recording of Goffin and King's 'The Loco-Motion'* (1962), a song that was revived successfully by **Grand Funk Railroad** in 1974 and by **Kylie Minogue** in 1988, and was a hit again in Britain for Little Eva when reissued in 1972 on London; 'Chains' (1962) by the Cookies, which was revived by **The Beatles** on their first album *Please Please Me*; and King's recording of her own 'It Might as Well Rain until September' (1962).

In 1963 Kirshner sold Aldon to Columbia Pictures–Screen Gems and was appointed president of the company's music division. His greatest success there was the Monkees, a pale imitation of The Beatles intended as a vehicle for Screen Gems songs and Columbia's burgeoning television division. The group surprisingly outlived their origins to become a popular and critical success. Following a dispute about royalty payments for *The Monkees* teleseries, Kirshner left Screen Gems and created a cartoon equivalent of the Monkees, the Archies, who accordingly could not argue back. The group's soundtrack featured Ron

Dante (later a successful producer, working with **Barry Manilow**, among others) as lead singer and had a series of hits on Kirshner's own labels. These included 'Bang-Shang a-Lang' (Calendar, 1968), 'Sugar Sugar'*, the bestselling record of 1969 in America, which was later covered by **Jonathan King** in Britain, 'Jingle Jangle'* (Kirshner, 1969) and 'Who's Your Baby' (1970).

In the seventies Kirshner established a pair of successful television programmes in America, *In Concert* and *Don Kirshner's Rock Concert*, while Kirshner Records developed into a briefly important independent label with Kansas (whose hits included 'Dust in the Wind'*, 1978) among its successful acts.

KISS

Peter Criss, b. Peter Crisscoula, 20 December 1947, Brooklyn, New York, USA (replaced by Eric Carr, b. Paul Caravella, 12 July 1953, Brooklyn, d. 22 March 1991); Ace Frehley, b. Paul Daniel Frehley, 27 April 1950, Bronx, New York (replaced by Vinnie Vincent, b. Vince Cusao, 1952, Brooklyn, New York, replaced by Mark St John, b. Mark Norton, 7 February 1956, Los Angeles, replaced by Bruce Kulick, b. 12 December 1953, New York); Gene Simmons, b. Gene Klein, 25 August 1949, Queens, New York; Paul Stanley, b. Paul Eisen, 20 January 1951, Queens

A curiosity of American rock music in the seventies and eighties, Kiss were inspired by superhero comic books and in turn inspired comics of their own.

Bass-player Simmons (formerly of New York group Rainbow) and guitarist Stanley (ex-Wicked Lester) found drummer Criss and guitarist/singer Frehley through magazine advertisements. Impressed by the **New York Dolls** and other glam-rock performers, they adopted high heels and face paint to create a visual package designed to simulate *Marvel* comic figures. With Simmons as 'Demon' and Stanley as 'Lover', they devised a spectacular stage show involving giant hell hounds with glowing eyes, exploding balls of fire and spitting 'blood'. Members of the band were never seen or photographed without their elaborate make-up.

Manager Bill Aucoin (who later handled **Billy Idol**) signed Kiss to Neil Bogart's Casablanca label. With predictable heavy-rock sentiments on songs like 'Strutter', 'Let Me Go Rock'n'Roll' and 'C'mon and Love Me', the material on *Kiss*, *Hotter Than Hell* (1974) and *Dressed to Kill* (1975) made little impact beyond the ranks of the Kiss army of teenage fans recruited through the group's constant touring. By 1976, however, that army was large enough to put a live version of their anthem 'Rock'n'Roll All Nite' into the Top Twenty and take its parent album *Alive!* into the US Top Ten.

Alice Cooper producer Bob Ezrin introduced orchestral backings on *Destroyer* (1976), and *Love Gun* (1977) provided the hit 'Beth'*. It was followed by a second live album, *Alive II* (1977), the band's fourth million-seller. In that same year Marvel Comics brought the comic-strip motif full circle by publishing a Kiss book while a full-length animated film, *Kiss Meets the Phantom of the Park*, was televised in 1978. Each group member issued his own million-selling solo album, but only Frehley's reached out beyond existing Kiss fans, producing a hit with a cover of British band Hello's 1975 song 'New York Groove'.

Dynasty (1979) included the million-seller 'I Was Made for Lovin' You' but after *Unmasked* (1980) Criss left (reportedly because the make-up was damaging his complexion). Coincidentally, the group went barefaced for *The Elder* (1981), a concept album which contained lyrics by **Lou Reed** and involved a shift to a milder new-romantic style. Its poor sales provoked a return to warpaint and heavy rock on *Creatures of the Night* (1982). On *Lick It Up* (1983), Vincent replaced Frehley, who formed his own group, Frehley's Comet. For 1984's *Animalize*, St John came in for Vincent, who later released *Invasion* (Chrysalis, 1986) with his own band of the same name, members of whom would later form the successful hard rock outfit Slaughter. Also in 1984 Simmons produced *W.O.W.* by ex-Plasmatics singer Wendy O. Williams.

With Simmons and Stanley still in command, Kiss released their sixteenth album, *Asylum*, in 1985. The title track of *Crazy Nights* (1987) was the group's biggest British hit to date. Simmons had meanwhile developed a second career as a character actor, utilizing his scary stage persona in such films as *Runaway* (1984) and *Never Too Young to Die* (1986). He also set up his own label, Simmons, but continued to record with Kiss. The group's later records included the lacklustre *Hot in the Shade* (1989) and the more impressive 'back to basics' set *Revenge* (1992). The latter was the band's first without Carr, who had died of cancer in 1991 and been replaced by Eric Singer, formerly with Badlands.

The new line-up recorded a version of Argent's 1973 UK hit 'God Gave Rock'n'Roll to You' for the hit movie *Bill and Ted's Bogus Journey*, which saw them back in the UK Top Five in 1992. With Simmons putting his extra-curricular activities on hold, the band celebrated their twentieth anniversary in 1993 with another rapturously received live album, titled, naturally enough, *Alive III*.

In 1994 a tribute album of versions of the group's songs, *Kiss My Ass*, was issued by Mercury. Those participating had been invited to do so by the band themselves. They included **Stevie Wonder**, **Anthrax** and country superstar **Garth Brooks**, reflecting the success of the band in attracting an audience far beyond hard-core heavy-metal fans. The band, dubbed by one critic as 'America's ultimate vaudeville act', re-formed for *Psycho Circus* (1998), which they supported with a sell-out US tour and promoted with an issue of US rock magazine *Spin* featuring four separate covers. All were collectors items within weeks; the album was far more disposable, its simple rebellion call – 'I pledge allegiance to the State of Rock'n'Roll' – needing the band's parodic live performance to bring it to life. In 2000 Kiss founders Simmons and Stanley were named official spokesmen for knac.com, the self-proclaimed home for hard rock on the Internet, which was also the sponsor of their farewell US tour that year.

EARTHA KITT
b. 26 January 1928, North, South Carolina, USA

Songstress and actress, Kitt developed a coquettish, self-mocking style – often performing reclining on a fur rug, for example – that recalled **Marlene Dietrich**. She found a new audience of dance music enthusiasts in the eighties.

Raised in New York, Kitt joined Katherine Dunham's dance troupe in 1946 and toured Europe. She settled in Paris where she developed her exotic nightclub act. Returning to America in 1951, she starred in New York clubs and in the Broadway production *New Faces of 1952*, making her screen début in the film version of the show, *New Faces* (1954). In the meantime, she signed with RCA and had hits in 1953 with her sultry versions of 'C'est Si Bon' and 'Santa Baby'. Her only other American hits came during the calypso boom, when she recorded 'Somebody Bad Stole the Wedding Bell' and 'Yellow Bird' (1959). In Britain, she had success with 'Under the Bridges of Paris' (HMV, 1955), which was also covered by **Dean Martin**, but was even more popular as a television and cabaret performer with her slinky interpretations of **Cole Porter**'s 'Let's Do It (Let's Fall in Love)', 'Just an Old Fashioned Girl', her theme song, and 'My Heart Belongs to Daddy'.

In Hollywood, she co-starred with **Nat 'King' Cole** in *St Louis Blues* (1958), a lacklustre biography of **W. C. Handy**, but failed to establish herself as a film actress and returned to the nightclub circuit and Europe, where she was hugely popular for most of the sixties, even starring in a film based on Harriet Beecher Stowe's classic novel, *Onkel Toms Hutte* (1965). Her camp appeal was utilized in America by the producers of the *Batman* teleseries in which she played Cat Woman. Kitt spent the early part of the seventies in Britain, touring the variety clubs of the north, before returning to America to star in *Friday Foster* (1975) and an all-black Broadway adaptation of *Kismet*, *Timbuktu* (1978). The eighties saw her back in Britain and, surprisingly, back in the charts with the **Giorgio Moroder** disco tune 'Where Is My Man' (Record Shack, 1983) and 'I Love Men' (1984). Only minor hits, both set her intoned suggestive lyrics against a backdrop of trance-like rhythm patterns.

Her first American recording for over a decade was *My Way: a Musical Tribute to Rev. Dr Martin Luther King* (1988) with a choir led by Rodena Preston, sister of **Billy Preston**. In 1989 she released *I'm Still Here* (Arista), another British-made album on which Kitt was accompanied by members of Bronski Beat. Kitt's 1994 album, *Back in Business*, placed her in a more conventional cabaret setting, performing songs by **Rodgers & Hart**, **Sondheim** and Porter.

THE KLF
Bill Drummond, b. William Butterworth, 29 April 1953, South America; Jimi Cauty, b. 1954

Under various names (JAMMS, the Timelords, KLF) Drummond and Jimmy Cauty recorded some of the most original dance-pop of the eighties before in the nineties they entered the even odder world of conceptual art with the K Foundation.

Drummond grew up in Scotland and in 1977 moved to Liverpool, where he became a member of Liverpudlian punk trio Big in Japan alongside Holly Johnson of **Frankie Goes to Hollywood** and Ian Broudie, who went on to lead the **Lightning Seeds**. In 1978 he founded Zoo Records with Dave Balfe and served as manager and producer for **Echo and the Bunnymen** and **Julian Cope**'s early band Teardrop Explodes before joining WEA as an A&R man in 1984. After making the solo albums *The Man* and *Bill Drummond* (1984), he began to work with Jimi Cauty, the former guitarist with Brilliant.

Naming themselves the Justified Ancients of Mu Mu (or JAMs for short), the duo gained notoriety for illegally sampling other artists – including **ABBA** and **The Beatles** – on the album *1987 (What the Fuck is Going on?)*. After being ordered to withdraw the album, the JAMs put out an alternate version, *1987 (The JAMs 45 Edits)*, featuring gaps where the samples originally lay and instructions to the listener on how to recreate the original LP.

Drummond and Cauty then renamed themselves the Timelords in 1988, releasing the *Doctor Who*-inspired single 'Doctorin' the Tardis', which became their first Top Ten single in the UK. They also wrote *The Manual*, a guide to writing and producing a Number One single, before becoming the KLF, or Kopyright Liberation Front, playing a major part in the revival of ambient music with *Chill Out* (1989). In the same year Cauty formed the **Orb** with Dr Alex Patterson.

The KLF had their biggest success with *The White*

Room (1991), featuring the 'Stadium House Trilogy' of singles, 'What Time Is Love?', '3AM Eternal' and 'Last Train to Transcentral', which were hits in Britain and the US, as was the majestic 'Justified and Ancient' (1992), a collaboration with **Tammy Wynette**. In the same year, after being named Best British Band, they gave an extreme performance at the Brit Awards ceremony, which included Drummond firing blanks from an automatic rifle at the audience and ended with the announcement that 'The KLF have left the music industry.'

Claiming that they would not make another record until peace reigned the world, the duo's subsequent activities have consisted of situationist-style pranks, mostly under the name of the K Foundation. Two of these involved donating £40,000 to the 'worst artist in Britain', Rachel Whiteread, who had just won the Turner Prize, and burning £1 million in cash on the island of Jura. As the K Foundation they honoured the 1994 accord between Yitzhak Rabin and Yasser Arafat with the limited edition single 'K Sera Sera', which was recorded with the Soviet Army Chorale and was made available in Israel only, and contributed a track to the *HELP* (1995) album under the guise of the One World Orchestra. After another two-year hiatus they returned with '***k the Millennium' (Mute, 1997). Drummond, with Mark Manning, published the bizarre novel *Bad Wisdom* (1996), a surreal account of the pair's attempt to erect a statue of **Elvis Presley** at the North Pole. As 2K Drummond and Cauty made one of their few live appearances of the nineties at London's Barbican Concert hall, where they masterminded a 'noise spectacle' featuring a massed male voice choir, a colliery brass band and Drummond and Cauty as a pair of elderly old men in electric wheelchairs. In 2000 Drummond published a book of essays, *45*, in which he published the details of planned 'art events', including the likes of *M25 for 25 Hours* – a planned drive around the M25 for 25 hours.

GLADYS KNIGHT AND THE PIPS

Gladys Knight, b. 28 May 1944, Atlanta, Georgia, USA; William Guest, b. 2 June 1941, Atlanta; Merald 'Bubba' Knight, b. 2 September 1942, Atlanta; Edward Patten, b. 2 August 1939, Atlanta

One of the longest-established soul vocal groups, Gladys Knight and the Pips' hits spanned four decades. Their style changed little over the years, with Knight's strong emotive vocals tinged with gospel feeling and expertly cushioned by the Pips' wistful and often complex backing harmonies.

A child prodigy, Gladys won the *Ted Mack Amateur Hour* television talent show in 1952, singing **Nat 'King' Cole**'s 'Too Young'. Already singing gospel, she formed the Pips with her brother Merald and cousins Guest and Patten. After unsuccessful recordings for Brunswick in 1957, they cut the **Johnny Otis** song 'Every Beat of My Heart' for the local Huntom label in 1961. The success of this and other Huntom singles in the R&B charts led to a contract with **Bobby Robinson**'s New York-based Fury label, for whom the group recorded a new version of 'Every Beat of My Heart'. Meanwhile Huntom leased the original to Vee-Jay, whose version reached the pop Top Ten and sold a million copies; the Fury disc was also a minor hit. However, 'Letter Full of Tears' (Fury, 1962) reached the Top Twenty.

In 1964 Gladys Knight and the Pips moved to Maxx where they were produced by **Van McCoy** on the impressive minor hits 'Giving Up' and 'Lovers Always Forgive'. While they were now established as a leading concert act, the group did not record again until **Berry Gordy** offered them a contract with Motown after their successful appearances with his Motortown revues.

'Everybody Needs Love' and Barrett Strong's 'Take Me in Your Arms and Love Me' (Soul, 1967) were R&B hits and the latter reached the British Top Twenty. They were followed by the **Norman Whitfield** production of the Whitfield–Strong song, 'I Heard It Through the Grapevine'* (1967), which broke through to the American Top Five, and 'The End of Our Road'* (1968). Over the next six years, Gladys Knight and the Pips were consistent entrants to the R&B Top Ten, reaching No. 1 with the **Johnny Bristol**, Clay Hinton and Joe McMurray production 'If I Were Your Woman' (1970) and 'Neither One of Us (Wants to Be the First to Say Goodbye)' (1973), both of which were also major pop hits.

The latter song and Knight's version of **Kris Kristofferson**'s 'Help Me Make It Through the Night' (1972) marked a move towards more sophisticated material with adult themes, and in 1973 the group left Motown, in part because of the company's habit of giving potential hits to other artists, as they had done with 'Grapevine' (to **Marvin Gaye**).

Signing to Buddah in 1973, they immediately had a massive pop hit with the moving 'Midnight Train to Georgia'* from *Imagination*. The song was written by Jim Weatherly, who also recorded two solo albums for Buddah in 1974–5. The album provided two more million-sellers in Gerry Goffin and Barry Goldberg's 'I've Got to Use My Imagination' (1973) and 'Best Thing That Ever Happened to Me' (1974). Further success followed with 'On and on' from **Curtis Mayfield**'s film score for *Claudine*, and a version of another film theme, 'The Way We Were' (1975).

While Knight's impassioned ballad-singing lost favour in America with the rise of disco, the group found success in Britain where 'Midnight Train to Georgia' reached the Top Ten in 1975, followed by

'Baby Don't Change Your Mind' (1977) and 'Come Back and Finish What You Started' (1978).

Knight's dissatisfaction with the group's drift towards cabaret, and legal disputes with both Buddah and Motown, caused a brief split with the Pips in the late seventies. After a lacklustre set by the Pips for Casablanca, the reunited group signed to Columbia in 1980. Despite impressive **Ashford and Simpson** productions on 'Taste of Bitter Love' (1980), 'Bourgie Bourgie', and the R&B hits 'Landlord' (1983) and 'Save the Overtime (for Me)' (1983), the group could not recapture their earlier pop success.

Leaving Columbia, Knight was briefly teamed with comedian Flip Wilson in an American television sitcom before the group signed a recording deal with MCA. In 1986 they were back in the R&B Top Ten with their first single for the label, 'Send It to Me', and in 1987 returned to the pop Top Twenty with Reggie Calloway's 'Lover Overboard' in the year they celebrated thirty years of recording together. It was to be the last group hit. Although Merald continued to work live with her, Gladys Knight signed to MCA as a solo artist in 1989. She enjoyed an immediate hit with the theme from the James Bond film *Licence to Kill* (1989). The MCA album *Good Woman* reached the American Top Fifty in 1991, and she made frequent television and live concert appearances in the early nineties. She sang 'Go on and on' for **Elton John**'s 1993 *Duets* album and for the various artists album *Rhythm, Country and Blues* she sang with country star Vince Gill on a remake of the **Marvin Gaye** & Tammi Terrell hit 'Ain't Nothin' Like the Real Thing'. Knight issued a new solo album, *Just for You*, in 1994. Motown issued *The Lost Live Album* (a 1974 concert whose tapes were reportedly lost) to critical acclaim in 1996 and in 1997 Knight published her autobiography, *Between Every Line of Pain and Glory*.

LESLIE KONG
b. 1933, Jamaica, d. 17 August 1971, Jamaica

One of the leading reggae producers during the sixties, Kong recorded such artists as **Jimmy Cliff**, **Bob Marley**, **Ken Boothe** and **Toots and the Maytals**.

Of Chinese extraction, Kong was a restaurant worker when he financed his first recording, **Derrick Morgan**'s 'Shake a Leg'. He set up his own label and record store, Beverly's Record and Ice Cream Parlour (subsequently shortened to Beverly's), in 1961. Cliff wrote and sang 'Dear Beverly' to persuade Kong to record him. His first hits included 'Miss Jamaica', 'Hurricane Hattie' and 'Daisy Got Me Crazy' (1962). Marley made his first record, 'Judge Not', for Beverly's in the same year. Another early hit produced and released by Kong was Derrick and Patsy's 'Housewives Choice'.

During the sixties Kong built up a strong roster of ska and rock-steady performers. Among those he produced were Bruce Ruffin ('Bitterness of Life', 1970), Delroy Wilson ('Gave You My Love', 1970), the Melodians ('It's My Delight', 1969), Ken Boothe ('Freedom Street', 1970) and the Maytals, whose 'Do the Reggay' (1967) was the first record to use the name 'reggae'. Kong also enjoyed international success with the Pioneers, whose 'Long Shot Kick the Bucket' (1969) was about the death of a famous racehorse. Unlike many Jamaican producers, Kong believed in developing artists as well as sounds. Thus, **Desmond Dekker**, whose British hits '007' (1967), 'The Israelites' (1969), the first international reggae hit, 'It Mek' (1969) and 'You Can Get It If You Really Want' (1970) were all Kong productions, first recorded for him in 1963 ('Honour Your Father').

Much of the impact of these records was due to the Beverly's All Stars, the studio band which featured former **Skatalites** guitarist Lynn Tait and bassplayer Lloyd Parkes. Other members included Bobby Ellis (trumpet), Paul Douglas (drums) and Ansell Collins (keyboards), who with his brother Dave had a British No. 1 with 'Double Barrel' (Technique, 1971).

Shortly before his sudden death from a heart attack, Kong was playing a key role in the internationalization of reggae. He organized the Jamaican sessions for **Paul Simon**'s 'Mother and Child Reunion' and recorded Cliff's songs and the Melodians' 'Rivers of Babylon' (a pop hit in 1978 for **Boney M**) for the soundtrack to the film *The Harder They Come*, in which he appeared in a cameo role.

KOOL AND THE GANG
Robert 'Kool' Bell, b. 8 October 1950, Youngstown, Ohio, USA; Ronald Bell, b. 1 November 1951, Youngstown; George Brown, b. 5 January 1949, Jersey City, New Jersey; Robert Mickens, b. Jersey City; Claydes Smith, b. 6 September 1948, Jersey City; James Taylor, b. 16 August 1953, South Carolina; Dennis Thomas, b. 9 February 1951, Jersey City; Rickey West, b. Jersey City (replaced by Curtis Williams, b. 11 December 1962, Buffalo, New York)

Among the founders of funk music, Kool and the Gang had numerous dancefloor and mainstream pop hits in the seventies. With the arrival of vocalist Taylor in 1978, the band added melodic soul ballads to their repertoire and enjoyed more success in the eighties.

With a jazz-loving father, bassist Kool and saxophonist Ronald Bell formed the Jazziacs at high school in 1964. With Smith (guitar), Thomas and Mickens (horns) plus West (keyboards) and drummer Brown, the group became the Soul Town Revue and the New Dimensions before signing to Gene Redd's De-Lite label in 1968.

Strongly influenced by the music of **Sly Stone** and **James Brown**'s JBs, 'Kool and the Gang' reached the R&B Top Twenty in 1969. Similar instrumental hits like 'Let the Music Take Your Mind' (1970) and 'Love the Life You Live' (1972) followed before *Wild and Peaceful* (1973) signalled a change in direction. Prefiguring their popularity with disco dancers, Kool and the Gang added vocal chants and (the previously unknown) whistles to make 'Funky Stuff' (1973), 'Jungle Boogie'* and 'Hollywood Swinging'* (1974) American pop hits.

Kool and the Gang were only partially successful during the disco boom, although their 'Open Sesame' appeared on the multi-million-selling soundtrack album *Saturday Night Fever* (1977). The late seventies was a period of uncertainty when Robert Bell flirted unsuccessfully with jazz again on *The Force* (1977) and then amid other personnel changes added lead singer Taylor.

A skilful ballad singer, Taylor led the group towards the crossover pop audience with *Ladies' Night* (1979). Co-produced by Brazilian keyboards-player Eumir Deodato (creator of the 1973 disco-style hit 'Also sprach Zarathustra [2001]', CTI), the album's title track was a million-seller, while 'Celebration'* (1980), the song that greeted the returning hostages from their 444 days in captivity in Iran, from *Celebrate* reached No. 1.

The group had found a winning formula, notably in Britain where Kool and the Gang had over twenty hits in the eighties and Kool and Taylor took part in the Band Aid recording. Among the group's successes were 'Ooh La La La (Let's Go Down)' (1982), 'Joanna', '(When You Say You Love Somebody) From the Heart' (1984) and 'Cherish' (1985). *Forever* (1986) sold several million copies worldwide and included the hit singles 'Victory' and 'Stone Love'.

By 1988 Ronald Bell had converted to Islam, calling himself Khalis Bayyan and Taylor had left, to be replaced on *Sweat* (1989) by singers Gary Brown and Skip Martin. The next year Taylor released a solo album, *Master of the Game* (MCA, 1989), with tracks produced by Deodata and **Narada Michael Walden**.

With the departure of Taylor the hits dried up, and the band's only subsequent successes were with remixed versions of their earlier hits, although their mid-seventies output enjoyed a revival in popularity with the sampling craze that dominated dance music in the early part of the nineties. They continued to tour and in 1993 released their first new album in three years, *Unite*, which featured new vocalist Odeen Mays. In the same year Taylor released his third solo album, *Baby I'm Back*. He briefly rejoined the group for *State of Affairs* (1997).

KOOL DJ HERC
b. Clive Campbell, 1955, Kingston, Jamaica

In many ways the Godfather of hip-hop, Kool DJ Herc pioneered the concept of the 'break', the brief rhythmic segment of a record which, manipulated and repeated, could be used to form a new, longer, more rhythmically intense groove. This technique became the basis of the hip-hop DJ's art.

Campbell grew up in Jamaica, under the twin musical influences of the island's reggae sound systems and the Motown and **James Brown** records his mother would bring back from her trips to New York. The family moved in 1967 to New York's run-down South Bronx district, where Campbell set about re-creating the Jamaican sound system model. He first used the name Kool Herc in 1970 when his sister asked him to play at a party she was organizing.

Herc quickly realized that reggae was less to the taste of his New York audiences than funk and Latin music, which he began playing instead. Herc noticed that the crowd reaction to these tunes was strongest during a track's drum break, when the vocal melody and instrumentation would drop out, leaving just the drum and percussion parts playing.

By spinning two copies of the same disc back to back, Herc could keep this 'break' from a track going indefinitely, cutting from one turntable to the other and extending the original 8- or 16-bar segment into a groove lasting several minutes.

'After observing the crowd and also observing the records I was playing, I noticed people were waiting for a certain point to come about,' Herc once explained. 'Some people would dance to start out with, but some people would just wait for that certain break. I thought, "Let me see what the effect's going to be if I put all of those records back-to-back and I'll call that segment the Merry-Go-Round".'

Herc's 'Merry-Go-Round' became known as the 'break', the manipulation of which would become central to the art of the hip-hop DJ. The concept of the 'break' also looked forward to the emergence of 'sampling', itself the foundation of much modern dance music.

From wildly popular performances at a series of block parties, Herc graduated to the New York clubs, beginning a residency at the Hevalo in 1974. From 1973 through to 1977, he was the premier DJ of the embryonic hip-hop scene, and a huge influence on other early hip-hop pioneers like **Afrika Bambaataa** and **Grandmaster Flash**.

Tragedy struck in 1977, however, when Herc was attacked after an argument at one of the clubs he was playing, the Executive Playhouse. He was stabbed four times, three times in the side and once through a hand. Although he recovered quickly, the incident had for Herc soured the atmosphere of the scene.

Herc has too infrequently been given his due by modern hip-hop artists, but his talent was finally captured on record in the late 1990s, on **Public Enemy** DJ Terminator X's 1994 *Godfathers of Threatt* album. He also travelled to the UK in 1997 to play as warm-up DJ to the **Chemical Brothers**.

KOOL MOE DEE
b. Mohandas Dewese, 1963, Harlem, New York, USA

Kool Moe Dee was part of the Treacherous Three, one of the original New York hip-hop crews, but later developed a successful solo rap career.

Kool Moe Dee's hip-hop career with the Treacherous Three began in the late 1970s, the group signing to the local Enjoy label and releasing their first single, 'The New Rap Language', in 1980. The track was a fine showcase for their high-speed rapping style. Further singles on Enjoy followed, before a move to Sugarhill Records in 1981.

The band broke up in the mid-1980s, Kool Moe Dee going to study communications at college in New York before deciding to return to hip-hop. His first single, 'Go See the Doctor', was produced by the then unknown **Teddy Riley**, and established the reputation of both men.

The track won Kool Moe Dee a solo deal with Jive in 1986, releasing his début album that same year. With the title track of his second album, *How Ya Like Me Now?* (1987), Kool Moe Dee began his on-record sparring with rival rapper LL Cool J. Despite the machismo of the LL Cool J duel, Kool Moe Dee retained an ethical dimension to his work, contesting the sexist and violent assumptions of gangsta rap and participating in the Stop the Violence movement.

Following the success of his third album, *Knowledge Is King* (1989), he became the first rapper to perform at the US Grammy music awards. He also featured that year on Quincy Jones' star-studded *Back on the Block* long-player.

Kool Moe Dee's fourth album, *Funke Funke Wisdom* (1991), proved a disappointment, and he parted company with Jive after the release of a *Greatest Hits* compilation in 1993. He recorded another album, *Interlude*, on DJ Easy Lee's label in 1994.

AL KOOPER
b. 5 February 1944, New York, USA

As musician, songwriter and producer Kooper was an important figure in the rock music of the sixties and seventies. With Blues Project, he was part of the early white blues movement and was a leading member of pioneering jazz-rock band **Blood, Sweat and Tears**. Kooper's later career as solo artist and producer included work with **Mike Bloomfield** and **Lynyrd Skynyrd**.

In the late fifties he had been a member of vocal groups the Casuals and Royal Teens (which also included the **Four Seasons**' Bob Gaudio), whose biggest hit was 'Short Shorts' (ABC-Paramount, 1958). Kooper next became a session guitarist for **Connie Francis**, **Dion** and others, also composing songs of which the most successful was the **Tommy 'Snuff' Garrett**-produced 'This Golden Ring' (Liberty, 1965), a No. 1 for Gary Lewis and the Playboys, co-written with Bob Brass and Irwin Levine.

By now Kooper was feeling the impact of **Bob Dylan**'s folk music and as Al Casey he began to play folk clubs. Through producer Tom Wilson he met Dylan and his swirling organ-playing was a key part of Dylan's sound in the mid-sixties, notably on 'Like a Rolling Stone'. Kooper performed with Dylan at the 1965 Newport Folk Festival and contributed to *Highway 61 Revisited* (1965), *Blonde on Blonde* (1966) and *New Morning* (1970).

During 1965 Kooper joined Blues Project, the experimental electric blues group formed by guitarist and ex-**Dave Van Ronk** associate Danny Kalb with jazz drummer Roy Blumenfeld and Steve Katz from the Even Dozen Jug Band. The group made three albums for Verve/Forecast, recording the Kooper composition 'I Can't Keep from Crying' on *Projections* (1966), before Kooper and Katz left to join Blood, Sweat and Tears.

Internal dissentions led to Kooper's departure from BS and T in 1967 and he joined Columbia as a producer. The following year he produced *Supersession*, a studio jam with Bloomfield and Stephen Stills, followed by a live album with Bloomfield, with **Carlos Santana** on guitar, recorded at the Fillmore in San Francisco in 1969. In the same year he produced the first solo album by Shuggie Otis, son of **Johnny Otis**.

Kooper also recorded a number of solo albums for Columbia, beginning with *I Stand Alone* (1969). *You Never Know Who Your Friends Are* included perhaps his most covered song, 'Brand New Day', sung by the **Staple Singers** on the soundtrack album for *The Landlord* (1970). The album was produced by Kooper and included further songs from Lorraine Ellison. As a session player he worked with **Taj Mahal** (*Nach'l Blues*, 1968), the **Rolling Stones** (*Let It Bleed*, 1969) and **Jimi Hendrix** (*Electric Ladyland*, 1968), and numerous other artists, ranging from the **Nitty Gritty Dirt Band** to **Leo Sayer** and **Alice Cooper**.

In 1972 he signed Lynyrd Skynyrd to MCA's new Sounds of the South label, producing the group's first three albums. His later production credits included the Tubes, **David Essex**, Nils Lofgren, the Johnny Van

Zandt Band, British pub-rock group Eddie and the Hot Rods (*Fish and Chips*, EMI, 1980), Green on Red and Billie Joe Shaver.

Kooper's own later albums included *Act Like Nothing's Wrong* (United Artists, 1977) and *Championship Wrestling* (Columbia, 1982). He toured with Dylan in 1981 and in 1983 organized a Blues Project concert, released as *Reunion in Central Park* (MCA).

During the early nineties he led Rock Bottom Remainders, an occasional band featuring the novelists Stephen King and Amy Tan. Kooper also published an autobiography, *Backstage Passes* (1976). In 1989 he helped put together the retrospective compilation *Al's Big Deal*. He returned to recording in 1994 with *ReKOOPERation* (Musicmasters Rock), an instrumental album of songs associated with **Booker T.**, **Ray Charles** and the Meters, among others.

KORN

Reginald 'Fieldy' Arvizu, b. Bakersfield, California, USA; Jonathan Davis, b. 18 January 1971, Bakersfield; James 'Munky' Shaffer, b. 6 June 1970, Rosedale, California; David Silveria, b. 21 September 1971, Bakersfield; Brian 'Head' Welch, b. 19 June 1970, Torrence, California

Californian quintet Korn have become one of the most successful American rock bands of the late nineties with a blend of the heavy rock of **Rage Against the Machine** and the aggression of rap trio **Cypress Hill**.

Guitarists Shaffer and Welch, bassist Arvizu and drummer Silveria began playing together in their home town of Bakersfield, California, as LAPD in 1992, before recruiting trainee mortician Jonathan Davis on vocals and relocating to Huntington Beach. Renaming themselves Korn, the band soon signed with Immortal/Epic and began work on their début album.

Korn (1994) sold slowly at first, but by the end of two years of touring in support of the likes of Ozzy Osbourne and **Marilyn Manson** the album had sold 700,000 copies in the US. The follow-up, *Life is Peachy* (1996), entered the album chart at No. 3, and included the hit single 'A.D.I.D.A.S.', which saw the band begin to cross over into the mainstream in spite of their heavy sound. Korn launched 'Family Values' two years later, a touring festival which the band headlined above a host of rock/metal acts. *Follow the Leader* (1998) managed to eclipse the sales of its predecessor by topping the US chart while also signalling the band's rise across Europe and the UK. It was followed in 1999 by a live album, *Family Values*, and the even more successful *Issues*, which topped the US charts with its repeated tales of deep dissatisfaction set against a thrash backing.

ALEXIS KORNER
b. 19 April 1928, Paris, France, d. 1 January 1984, London, England

A tireless propagandist for the blues, guitarist and bandleader Korner inspired a generation of young British musicians. From his pioneering Blues Incorporated group came the nuclei of the **Rolling Stones** and of **Cream**, while he also helped to form **Free** and **Led Zeppelin**. Korner himself recorded frequently and in later years established himself as a broadcaster.

Of Austrian–Greek–Turkish parentage, he grew up in France, Switzerland and North Africa before the onset of the Second World War brought the family to London. He learned boogie-woogie piano from **Jimmy Yancey** records and in the late forties joined **Chris Barber**'s traditional jazz band on guitar. In 1952 **Ken Colyer** formed a skiffle group within his band, with Korner, Barber and **Lonnie Donegan** as members. Korner recorded with the Colyer Skiffle Group ('Midnight Special', Decca, 1954), though it was Donegan who had a series of hits beginning with 'Rock Island Line' (1956).

During the fifties Korner also worked for the Melodisc and Decca record companies and, inspired by **Muddy Waters**, he and harmonica-player Cyril Davies began to perform amplified blues. With guitarist Jeff Bradford they recorded tracks in 1957 which were reissued on Doug Dobell's Folklore label in 1970. By 1961 they had gathered together a group of like-minded jazz musicians and opened their own club. Blues Incorporated had a floating membership and drew towards it such aspiring R&B musicians as future Stones Mick Jagger and Brian Jones, Paul Jones (of **Manfred Mann**), **John Mayall** and numerous others. In 1962, with singer Long John Baldry, pianist Keith Scott and saxophonist Dick Heckstall-Smith, Alexis Korner's Blues Inc. were recorded by **Jack Good** on *R&B from the Marquee* (Decca, 1962). The album mixed full-blooded versions of Waters songs with Korner originals like 'Finkel's Cafe', which drew on the soul-jazz of **Charlie Mingus** and **Cannonball Adderley**. Despite his central role in British rhythm and blues, Korner's own semi-acoustic guitar-playing harked back to **Lonnie Johnson** or **Big Bill Broonzy**, rather than the electric styles to which the younger British players were drawn.

Korner's jazz leanings caused a split with Davies, who formed his R&B All Stars in late 1962 to play hard Chicago blues like 'Country Line Special' (Pye, 1962), a scorching instrumental with Nicky Hopkins on piano. Baldry fronted the group in live performance and led it after Davies' death from leukaemia in March 1963.

The Korner group briefly included **Graham Bond**, **Jack Bruce** and Ginger Baker (tracks from this period

appeared on the collection *Bootleg Him*, Rak, 1972)
but by the time of *Alexis Korner's Blues Incorporated*
(Decca, 1964), the instrumental jazz side, featuring
Heckstall-Smith and fellow tenorist Art Themen, had
taken over. *Blues Incorporated* (Polydor, 1967)
included former Larry Parnes protégé Duffy Power
on harmonica and vocals and showed a shift back
towards country blues roots.

By this time, however, the blues boom in Britain
had moved in a different direction (towards the heavy
guitar-based sound typified by **Fleetwood Mac**) and
Korner became resident bandleader on the children's
TV show *Five o'Clock Club*. His live performances
were limited to small group work with Free at Last,
which included ex-John Mayall drummer Hughie
Flint, and the New Church, a collaboration with free
jazz exponents John Stevens and Evan Parker. Free at
Last suggested a name for Free, a band led by Korner
protégé Paul Kossoff, while another Korner alumnus
was Birmingham singer Robert Plant, who joined Led
Zeppelin in 1970. Korner's usual bassist in the late sixties was Colin Hodgkinson, who later led jazz-rock
outfit Back Door, who recorded four albums for
Warners in 1973–6.

Korner's popularity was greater in Europe than in
Britain and on a Danish tour he met Peter Thorup,
lead singer of blues band the Beefeaters. In 1970
Mickie Most persuaded Thorup and Korner to front
a studio band, CCS (Collective Consciousness Society), which had hits with big-band versions of the
Zeppelin song 'Whole Lotta Love' (1970), 'Walkin''
(1971) and 'Tap Turns on the Water'. The group also
made three albums for Most's Rak label. The effec-
tiveness of Korner's husky, gruff vocals on the CCS
hits brought him voice-over work on numerous jingles and commercials. He also had a speaking part on
the **Hot Chocolate** hit 'Brother Louis' (1973).

In 1972 Korner and Thorup toured America with
Humble Pie, where *Accidentally Born in New Orleans*
(Transatlantic, 1973) was recorded with **King Crimson** players Boz Burrell (bass) and Mel Collins (sax).
The line-up later toured as Snape but by the late seventies Korner was established as a BBC radio disc-
jockey and commentator on the blues. Many of his
final live appearances were in a duo with Hodgkinson, though in 1981 he recorded with Rocket 88, a
blues and boogie group featuring Bruce and Watts.

ERIC WOLFGANG KORNGOLD

*b. 29 May 1897, Brno, Czechoslovakia, d. 29 November
1957, Hollywood, California, USA*

Korngold was the most romantic of film composers.
His breathless, stirring scores for such films as *Captain Blood* (1935), *The Adventures of Robin Hood*
(1938), for which he won an Oscar, and *The Sea Hawk*

(1939), among others, led one critic to speculate that
'If Richard Strauss had scored motion pictures, his
film music might well have sounded like Korngold's.'
His influence on film composers can be heard in the
music of John Williams, which at times approaches
the grandiose heights of his own scores.

Korngold began composing at the age of six and
aged seven had his pantomine 'The Snowman' performed on the instructions of Emperor Franz Joseph.
In his teens he wrote a symphony and by the age of
nineteen three of his operas had been performed,
including the well-received *Die Tote Stadt*. In the thirties he collaborated with Max Reinhardt on several
film projects and was invited to America to adapt
Mendelssohn's music for Reinhardt's film version of
A Midsummer Night's Dream (1935). That led to
Korngold joining Warner Brothers, where he made
his name with a series of resonant, lush scores, most
notably for the studio's costume dramas and swash-
buckling movies. Among these were *Anthony Adverse*
(1936), for which he won his first Oscar, *The Prince
and the Pauper* (1937) and *The Private Lives of Elizabeth and Essex* (1939). In the late forties he retired
from film scoring to concentrate on symphonic writing, only returning in 1955 with the score to *Magic
Fire*. The film was based on the life of Richard Wagner, and in it, unlike most Hollywood films about
composers, Korngold used only Wagner's music and
in its original form.

Korngold wrote few songs. Among them were several with lyrics by Oscar Hammerstein II for the
musical *Give Us This Night* (1936) and his only popular success, 'Love Is Love', a hit for **Claude Thornhill**
(Columbia, 1947).

KRAFTWERK

*Ralf Hutter b. 1946, Krefeld, Germany; Florian Schnei-
der, b. Florian Schneider-Esleben b. 7 April 1947, Dusseldorf; Wolfgang Flur (replaced by Fritz Hijbert); Klaus
Roeder (replaced by Karl Bartos)*

Like **Can** and **Tangerine Dream**, Kraftwerk were an
innovative German electronic music group in the seventies. They were widely influential, inspiring British
electro-pop bands in the early eighties as well as
Afrika Bambaataa and other hip-hop artists, and
their recordings were widely sampled during the
nineties techno boom.

Hutter (organ) and Schneider (woodwind) met at a
jazz and improvised music course in Dusseldorf.
With Michael Rother (a later collaborator of **Brian
Eno** and film-score writer) and free jazz musician
Peter Brotzmann (who later played with **Bill Laswell**
in Last Exit) they performed at parties and art gal-
leries on the avant-garde circuit of the Ruhr. As Hutter and Schneider began to use tape loops, drum

machines, synthesizers and vocoders, their music drew on Stockhausen, **Pink Floyd**, Tangerine Dream and Terry Riley's repetitive, hypnotic *In C* (Columbia, 1969) and *Rainbow in Curved Air* (1970).

In the late sixties they set up their Kling Klang studio and recorded in 1970 as Organisation before signing to Philips as Kraftwerk. In 1971–2, two eponymous albums were released in Germany; both revealed a somewhat dour experimental approach concerned with the sounds and character of the modern industrial world. Produced by Conny Plank, who later worked with **Ultravox** and **Eurythmics**, they were issued in Britain as a double-album on Vertigo in 1973, but the group's international breakthrough came with the release of 'Autobahn' (1975). Edited from a twenty-two-minute album title track, the single was a hit in both Britain and America.

By this time percussionists Flur and Bartos had joined Kraftwerk, who moved to EMI for *Radioactivity* (1975), a concept album inspired by the complex of sounds to be found on the airwaves, which included a voice-over sequence reminiscent of the children's favourite 'Sparky's Magic Piano'. It was followed by *Trans Europe Express* (1977) and *Man Machine* (1978), a British Top Ten hit whose approach influenced the emergence in Britain at this period of the electronic dance music of the **Human League**, **Gary Numan**, **Orchestral Manoeuvres in the Dark** and Ultravox. Kraftwerk benefited from this trend in 1981 when 'The Model' from *Computer World* reached No. 1 in Britain. The follow-up, 'Showroom Dummies' (1982), was a minor hit, as was the sporting theme 'Tour de France' (1983).

In 1982 **Arthur Baker** and Afrika Bambaataa paid tribute to Kraftwerk by inserting motifs from 'Numbers' and 'Trans Europe Express' into their hit, 'Planet Rock'. The tribute became tangible when the German group successfully claimed copyright payments from the record.

After a three-year gap, Hutter and Schneider returned with *Electric Café* (1986), their most recent album of new material.

Following a handful of live dates to promote *Electric Café*, which drew headlines for the use of electronically animated lookalike mannequins in place of the band, Kraftwerk maintained a low profile. Their next recording was a remix of 'The Robots' (1990), a track from *Man Machine*, which reached the British Top Twenty. This was followed by an album of their best-known material, remixed for the dance market and titled *The Mix* (1991). In the meantime, Fritz Hijbert and Fernando Fromm-Abrentes replaced Flur and Bartos and the group made a brief British tour followed by one-off British appearances in 1992 (with **U2**), 1994 and 1998. In 1997 Flur recorded *Time Pie* as Mouse on Mars.

LENNIE KRAVITZ
b. 26 May 1964, New York City, USA

Although he was not born until the year of the 'British Invasion', Kravitz's classy recycling of the elements of sixties rock brought him commercial success as a recording artist in the nineties.

His mother was a television actress and Kravitz himself had child roles in *The Cosby Show* and various commercials. He grew up in Los Angeles where he was self-taught on piano, guitar, bass and drums. His recording début, *Let Love Rule* (1989), was heavily indebted to sixties rock and soul and became a minor hit. The following year Kravitz co-wrote and co-produced the **Madonna** hit 'Justify My Love'.

He next organized a benefit recording by an all-star Peace Choir of **John Lennon**'s 'Give Peace a Chance'. Lennon's younger son Sean Ono Lennon and **Guns N' Roses** guitarist Slash appeared on *Mama Said*, which established Kravitz in Britain where the album was a Top Twenty hit. It included the US hit single 'It Ain't Over Til It's Over'.

In 1992 Kravitz masterminded the English-language début of Vanessa Paradis, writing and producing her self-titled album and its European hit 'Be My Baby'. He also contributed to albums by Mick Jagger, **Aerosmith**, **Al Green** and **Curtis Mayfield** before releasing a third solo album, *Are You Gonna Go My Way*, in 1993. This was a big international success and Kravitz followed its release with his *Universal Love* tour, which included concerts in Europe, Japan and the US.

Despite beginning with the announcement that 'Rock 'n' Roll Is Dead', *Circus* (1995) was another international success. However, it was poorly received critically. Kravitz returned three years later with *5*, which took a more modern recording approach and spawned a Europe-wide hit single, 'Fly Away' (1999). Heavily featured in a Peugeot car commercial, it topped the UK charts.

KRIS KRISTOFFERSON
b. 22 June 1936, Brownsville, Texas, USA

By the eighties an international film star, Kristofferson was most influential in the seventies. He revolutionized Nashville with songs that mixed boozy romanticism with neatly observed and well-shaped accounts of life on the road and on the edge of despair, songs that were modern in their sympathetic treatment of the young but traditional in their form.

The son of a two-star general, Kristofferson grew up in army camps and, after studying at Pomona College, won a Rhodes Scholarship to Oxford University in 1958. There he attempted to become a novelist and, renamed Kris Carson by pop impresario Larry Parnes, briefly attempted a career as a 'genuine American rock'n'roller', before returning to America and in 1960 joining the army. On his discharge in 1965, intent on becoming a songwriter, he travelled to Nashville and after four years finally found success when **Roger Miller** recorded his 'Me and Bobby McGee' and **Johnny Cash** 'Sunday Morning Coming Down'.

Kristofferson's acceptance as a major new songwriter was confirmed when, in 1970, Sammi Smith topped the country charts with 'Help Me Make It Through the Night' (Mega). In 1973 **Gladys Knight** had a pop hit with the song. His first major pop hit came in 1971, when **Janis Joplin** topped the American charts with her million-selling version of 'Bobby McGee', which was a further success for **Jerry Lee Lewis** in 1972. Kristofferson's own recording career took off with 'Loving Her Was Easier (Than Anything I'll Ever Do Again)' (Monument, 1971) and 'Why Me'* (1973). His first two albums, *Me and Bobby McGee* (1970) and *The Silver Tongued Devil and I* (1971), contain the best of his songs. Few of his subsequent solo albums, which include *Jesus Was a Capricorn* (1973), *Easter Island* (1978) and *To the Bone* (1981), or his duets with **Rita Coolidge** (to whom he was married from 1973 to 1988), such as *Breakaway* (A&M, 1974) and *Natural Act* (1978), are their equal.

Far more substantial was Kristofferson's film work. After his début in *Cisco Pike* (1971), he co-starred with **Bob Dylan** in Sam Peckinpah's remarkable *Pat Garrett and Billy the Kid* (1973). His subsequent films include a remake of *A Star Is Born* (1976), with **Barbra Streisand**; *Convoy* (1978), which was inspired by C. W. McCall's 1975 international hit, 'Convoy'* (MGM); and *Heaven's Gate* (1980). In 1987 Kristofferson appeared in the controversial teleseries *Amerika* and released his first solo album for six years, *Repossessed* (Mercury). Coming after a duet with **Willie Nelson** (*Songwriter*, Columbia, 1985) and a successful collaboration with Nelson, **Waylon Jennings** and Cash (*Highwayman*, 1986), *Repossessed* and *Third World Warrior* (Mercury, 1990) – which featured Kristofferson's long-time associate **Billy Swan** on guitar – were superior collections of bitter songs about contemporary America.

In the early nineties Kristofferson balanced his acting career with live performances and his involvement in various 'green' environmental and political issues. He recorded and toured again with Cash, Jennings and Nelson (*Highwayman II*) and in 1994 he made a rare solo European visit, playing small clubs in a low-key tour. However, not signed to a major label, his recordings were mostly as a guest on various tribute albums, including **Otis Blackwell** (*Brace Yourself*, 1994, on which he sang 'All Shook Up') and **The Beatles** (*Come Together*, 1995, on which he sang

'Paperback Writer'). He returned to the studio in his own right in 1995 for *A Moment of Forever* (Karambolage), which was produced by **Don Was**. Far better was *The Austin Sessions* (1999), for which he revisited many of his hits in conjunction with the likes of **Steve Earle** and **Dire Straits**' Mark Knopfler, stripping away some of the gloss added to the original versions of 'Me and Bobby McGhee' and 'Help Me Make It Through the Night'. While not as dramatically revisionary as Dylan in his approach to the certainties of the past (as seen on the nostalgia circuit), Kristofferson managed to reinvigorate the songs to great effect.

GENE KRUPA
b. 15 January 1909, Chicago, Illinois, USA, d. 16 October 1973, Yonkers, New York

The best-known jazz drummer in swing and big-band jazz, Krupa played with **Benny Goodman** as well as leading his own bands in the thirties and forties. A consummate showman, he established the large-scale kit and the pyrotechnic drum solo as an essential part of big-band jazz.

Krupa came from a Polish Catholic family who intended him for the priesthood but he turned to music at the age of sixteen, playing with various dance bands as well as with **Eddie Condon** and the Austin High School Gang, which established the Chicago style of jazz. His first recording session was with the Condon-Red McKenzie Chicagoans (Okey, 1927) and he moved to New York in 1929, playing in 1929–30 on such tracks as 'Indiana', 'Dinah' and 'The Sheik of Araby' (Brunswick) with **Red Nichols**. During the next few years Krupa was in demand as a session drummer, recording with, among others, **Hoagy Carmichael**, **Bix Beiderbecke**, and singers Cleo Brown and Emmett Miller.

From 1932 he played with the commercial dance bands of **Russ Columbo**, Buddy Rogers and others before joining Goodman in 1934. During the next three years Krupa took part in the **John Hammond**-produced Goodman trio and quartet recordings for Victor with **Teddy Wilson** and **Lionel Hampton**. He also played a leading role in making the orchestra the top band of the swing era. 'Sing Sing Sing (With a Swing)', an arrangement by Jimmy Mundy, was the first tune to incorporate a sustained drum solo and was a highlight of Goodman's famous 1938 Carnegie Hall concert. Krupa's performance there made his name synonymous with extrovert drumming.

During the Goodman years Krupa made occasional records under his own name ('Swing Is Here', 1936) before in 1938 he formed his own big band. Apart from trumpeter Roy Eldridge the personnel were unknowns and the orchestra relied heavily on Krupa's drum soloing. Among its best-known pieces were 'Wire Brush Stomp' (1938), 'Drummin' Man' (1939), with vocals by Irene Day, 'Bolero at the Savoy' (1940) and 'Let Me off Uptown' (1941), sung by **Anita O'Day**. During the late thirties and early forties Krupa also made Chicago-style records with Condon and with the Metronome All-Stars.

In 1942 Krupa broke up his orchestra, playing briefly with Goodman and **Tommy Dorsey** before creating a new, jazz-orientated big band. Again featuring Eldridge and O'Day, the group showed bebop influences and drew on arrangements by **Gerry Mulligan** in numbers like 'Disc Jockey Jump' (1947). O'Day sang on 'How High the Moon' (1945) while 'What's This' (1945) featured scat vocals by Buddy Stewart and Dave Lambert, later of **Lambert, Hendricks and Ross**.

Economic problems forced the break-up of the big band in 1951 and during the next decade Krupa toured regularly with **Norman Granz**'s Jazz at the Philharmonic, often featuring in drum 'battles' with the equally uninhibited **Buddy Rich**. *The Big Band Sound of Gene Krupa* (Verve, 1959) re-created the orchestral line-up of the late forties with Mulligan's scores and in 1954 Krupa and fellow-drummer Cozy Cole founded a drum school in New York.

In 1959 he recorded the soundtrack for *The Gene Krupa Story* (renamed *Drum Crazy* in Europe) with Sal Mineo playing the title role. During the sixties he played mainly with small groups featuring saxophonists Eddie Shu and Charlie Ventura. Illness forced him into semi-retirement from the late sixties until his death from leukaemia.

KULA SHAKER

Alonza Bevan; Saul Dismont (replaced by Jay Darlington); Crispian Mills, b. 18 January 1963; Paul Winter-Hart, b. Somerset

A mixture of Eastern and Western influences brought English four-piece Kula Shaker immediate acclaim in their homeland, where they entered the album charts at Number One with their début, *K*.

The grandson of actor John and son of former television presenter Hayley, Crispian Mills spent five years playing guitar in various unsuccessful bands before travelling to India, where he underwent something of a spiritual awakening while working in a temple. Returning to Britain, he formed a band with bassist Bevan, drummer Winter-Hart and singer/keyboardist Dismont, taking inspiration from Sanskrit chanting and Eastern religious practices. They named themselves the Kays, believing the letter K to be magical.

Dismont left the band in 1994, replaced by Darlington, with Mills taking over lead vocal duties. After two more years of playing to disinterested audiences the quartet changed their name to Kula Shaker, soon signing with Columbia. Début single 'Grateful When You're Dead' was a minor hit, while the organ driven 'Tattva', sung mostly in Sanskrit, hit No. 4 in the charts. By the time the band released *K* (1996) they had become a household name in the UK, winning the Brit Award for Best Newcomer, but failed to gain recognition elsewhere. Kula Shaker's second album, *Peasants, Pigs and Astronauts* (1999), was preceded by a cover of **Deep Purple**'s 'Hush' (1997), after which they split up.

FELA KUTI
b. Fela Ransome-Kuti, 15 October 1938, Abeokuta, Nigeria, d. 2 August 1997

The creator of the Afrobeat style of music (in which African rhythms replaced American R&B and soul rhythms), Kuti was the most politically outspoken of the African musicians who found international success in the seventies and eighties.

While a distant relative, the Rev J. J. Ransome-Kuti, had recorded hymns for Zonophone in 1914, Fela Kuti's parents were a leading feminist politician and a headmaster. They sent Kuti to London to train as a doctor in 1958, but instead he studied music. There, he played piano with the Koola Lobitos, a jazz and highlife band on the London club circuit. After returning to Nigeria in 1962, he re-formed the group with drummer Tony Allen. From the mid-sixties they recorded for EMI.

During the sixties Kuti turned against the influence of **James Brown** and other soul musicians on Nigerian music and developed his Afrobeat style. This approach used 'broken English', or krio patois, in a call-and-response pattern of lyrics taken from traditional African music. Musically, Kuti used the Western instrumentation of horns and keyboards, but played with an African accent. By 1968 he was calling the music he made 'Afrobeat'.

In 1969 he moved to America, where he came into contact with the black-power ideas that infused many of the songs he composed after his return to Lagos. *69, The Los Angeles Sessions* (1969) documents this shift. Back in Lagos he renamed his group Nigeria 70 and then Afrika 70 and made a series of hit records · beginning with 'Jeun Ko'ku' (Eat and Die). He opened a club, The Afro Spot (later The Shrine), on the outskirts of Lagos, which he used as the base of his activities. He became increasingly outspoken on such albums as *Gentleman* (1973) and *Alagbon Close* (1974), which criticized the black élite and police brutality, respectively. In 1975 Kuti changed his middle name from the colonial Ransome to Anikulapo.

The political impact of Kuti's songs led to raids on

his commune in 1974 and 1977, when soldiers destroyed his equipment and recording studio. In response he declared the club and surrounding area the independent Republic of Kalaktu and refused to take part in the Pan African Cultural Festival that was held in Lagos in 1997. After a brief exile in Ghana, Kuti returned undaunted, composing such songs as 'Coffin for Head of State'– he also presented the outgoing regime with a replica of his mother's coffin; she had died from injuries that occurred during one of the raids on his club. Other political songs from this period included 'International Thief Thief' and 'Authority Stealing'. At the end of the decade he renamed his group Egypt 80. When EMI refused to release Kuti's 'Why Blackmen Dey Suffer' he left the company. His best albums from this period were *Black President* (1981) and *Underground System* (1982). In 1984–6 Kuti served a 20-month jail sentence for currency offences, during which time his son Femi led the band and **Bill Laswell** remixed his *Army Arrangements*.

Following his release, Kuti recorded *Teacher Don't Teach Me Nonsense* (Mercury, 1987) with producer Wally Badarou, *I Go Shout Plenty* (1988) and the powerful anti-apartheid track 'Beasts of No Nation', which attacked by name such Western leaders as Ronald Reagan and Margaret Thatcher. The best of his albums in the early nineties was the insistent *O D O O* (Shanachie, 1990). He followed this with a reworking of *Underground System* (1990), recorded in New York, and *Los Angeles Sessions* (Sterns, 1993), a set of Afro-jazz tunes. After his death Kuti's son Femi continued recording in his father's general style. However, *Shoiki Remixed* (Universal, 1999) showed him to be more willing than his father (who had rejected the offer of a record contract with Motown on the grounds that the time wasn't right) to meet the more obvious commercial demands of record companies.

KAY KYSER
b. 18 June 1906, Rocky Mount, North Carolina, USA, d. 23 July 1985, Chapel Hill, North Carolina

Among American dance bands of the thirties and forties, Kay Kyser's was regarded sometimes as a good novelty, sometimes as the worst kind of novelty. Among radio audiences it was known for its series *Kay Kyser's Kollege of Musical Knowledge*, broadcast from the Blackhawk Restaurant in Chicago, where patrons guessed song titles from extracts played by the band; suggestions were sent in by listeners, whose names were read out on the air.

Kyser formed his first band at the University of North Carolina. In 1929 he made some hot dance records for Victor, but his Blackhawk tenure, which began in 1934, made his name. Under the influence of **Guy Lombardo**, the Kyser band of the mid-thirties fell in with the corny instrumental effects of the so-called 'mickey-mouse' orchestra, and offered novelties featuring trumpeter Merwyn Bogue in the character of 'Ishkabibble'. Later work was novelty music of a better sort, and includes 'Three Little Fishes'* (1939) and the **Frank Loesser** composition 'Praise the Lord and Pass the Ammunition'* (1942). Other million-sellers for the band were **Johnny Mercer**'s 'Strip Polka', 'Who Wouldn't Love You', Frank Loesser's 'Jingle, Jangle, Jingle' (1942), the corny 'Woody Woodpecker's Song' and 'On a Slow Boat to China' (1948), which was revived in the rock'n'roll era by **Emile Ford**. The band appeared, with others, in the film *Stage Door Canteen* (1943), but during the Second World War Kyser's live engagements were strictly for services personnel.

Among the band's singers were Ginny Sims and Georgia Carroll; the latter became Kyser's wife shortly before he retired, in the early fifties, to devote himself to Christian Science.

PATTI LABELLE AND THE BLUE BELLES

Cindy Birdsong, b. 15 December 1939, Camden, New Jersey, USA; Sarah Dash, b. 24 May 1942, Trenton, New Jersey; Nona Hendryx, b. 18 August 1945, Trenton; Patti Labelle, b. Patricia Holt, 4 October 1944, Philadelphia, Pennsylvania

The career of this leading black vocal group had three phases. As 'girl group' Patti Labelle and the Blue Belles, they recorded a series of hit singles between 1962 and 1967. In 1971 the remodelled Labelle offered a progressive-rock-based sound on the million-selling 'Lady Marmalade'. When Labelle split up in 1977, both Hendryx and Patti Labelle went on to solo recording careers of note.

Labelle and Birdsong were in high school in Philadelphia when they formed the Ordettes in 1959. A year later promoter Bernard Montague combined the duo with Dash and Hendryx from the Del Capris. Producer Bobby Martin signed them to the local Newtown label and 'I Sold My Heart to the Junkman' by the Blue-Belles was a Top Twenty hit in 1962 while 'Down the Aisle' (1963) effectively mixed sentimentality and gospel fervour.

In 1964 Newtown was taken over by pop-orientated label Cameo and a year later, now renamed Patti Labelle and the Blue Belles, the quartet moved to Atlantic. There they recorded the original version of Carol Bayer Sager and Toni Wine's 'A Groovy Kind of Love' (covered in England by the Mindbenders and revived in 1988 by **Phil Collins**) and had minor hits with 'All or Nothing' (1965) and 'Take Me for a Little While' (1966).

Birdsong left to join the **Supremes** in 1968 and the remaining trio found a new glam-rock image under the guidance of British TV producer (*Ready Steady Go!*) Vicki Wickham. Renamed Labelle, the group made an eponymous album for Warners (1971) and backed **Laura Nyro** on her selection of sixties girl-group songs, *Gonna Take a Miracle* (1971). After further albums for Warners and RCA, the **Allen Toussaint**-produced *Nightbirds* (Epic, 1974) provided Labelle with the No. 1 hit 'Lady Marmalade'*, composed by Kenny Nolan and **Bob Crewe**.

With many songs composed by Hendryx, the group recorded *Phoenix* (1975) and *Chameleon* (1976) before splitting up. Patti Labelle cut a series of albums for Epic and worked with **Bobby Womack** and the B-52s until a move to Philadelphia International brought the R&B No. 1 'I'm in Love Again' (1983), produced by **Gamble**

and Huff. She starred with **Al Green** on Broadway and appeared in the film *A Soldier's Tale*. Patti Labelle later appeared at Live Aid before joining MCA for the hits 'New Attitude' (1985) and 'Oh People' (1986) and *Winner in You*, an international bestseller.

In 1986 Patti Labelle reached No. 1 with the Bayer Sager–**Burt Bacharach** song 'On My Own', a duet with former **Doobie Brothers** vocalist Michael McDonald. She enjoyed R&B hits with songs from the films *Outrageous Fortune* and *Dragnet* in 1987 and the following year sang the love theme from the James Bond movie *License to Kill*, 'If You Asked Me to'. In 1989 she released *Be Yourself* and she appeared in an all-star presentation of **The Who**'s rock opera *Tommy* in Los Angeles. This return to the stage preceded her appearance in the **Duke Ellington** musical *Queenie Pie*. In 1990 Patti Labelle was awarded a lifetime achievement award by the Congress of Racial Equality and in 1993 she was honoured with a star on the Hollywood Walk of Fame. A seasonal album, *This Christmas*, appeared in 1990, and in 1991 Labelle released her biggest-selling album in America for several years, the platinum-certified *Burnin'*. However, the follow-up in-concert set *Live!* was less successful. The next studio album was *Gems* (1994), with production by **Teddy Riley** and **Jimmy Jam and Terry Lewis**. In the same year she duetted with Travis Tritt on 'When Something Is Wrong with My Baby' on the *Rhythm, Country and Blues* compilation. She later (electronically) partnered **Frank Sinatra** on 'Bewitched' for *Duets II* (1994). Yet another guest appearance in the nineties was *The Songs of West Side Story* (1996). Just before that Patti released her own solo offering *Gems* (1994), *Flame* (1997) and the live set *Live! One Night Only* (1998).

Dash began a low-key solo career in 1978 with an American radio hit, 'Sinner Man', taken from her début album. *Ooh La La* followed in 1979, and she recorded sporadically through the eighties. In 1988 a move to the Manhattan label saw her reunited with Patti Labelle on the title track of *You're All I Need*. She sang on the **Rolling Stones**' *Steel Wheels* (1989) and ended the decade in Stones guitarist Keith Richards' part-time band, the X-pensive Winos, with whom she appeared on three albums: *Talk Is Cheap* (1988), *Live at the Hollywood Palladium* (1991) and *Main Offender* (1992).

Hendryx made a solo album, *Nona*, in 1977 followed by *Alter Nations* in 1979. She worked with **Bill Laswell** in New York group Material and recorded with **Talk-**

ing Heads on the albums *Remain in Light* (1980), *The Name of This Band Is Talking Heads* (1982) and *Speaking in Tongues* (1983); she also collaborated with the band's keyboard-player/guitarist Jerry Harrison on his solo début *The Red and the Black* (1981). Her own solo career continued with an attempted synthesis of rock, R&B and pop on the RCA albums *Art of Defense* (1984) and *The Heat* (1985). In 1995 Labelle re-formed for the one-off single 'Turn It Out'. After that Hendryx returned to her solo career. In 1987 she recorded *Female Trouble* (EMI) with producer Dan Hartman. The album included 'Winds of Change (Mandela to Mandela)', 'Why Should I Cry?' and 'Baby Go Go', written by **Prince**. This was followed by *Skin Diva* (Private Music, 1989). However, although attracting enthusiastic reviews it sold poorly and the early nineties saw little further activity from Hendryx. In 1992 she released an album with R&B/country veteran Billy Vera, *You Have to Cry Sometime*.

CLEO LAINE
b. Clementina Dinah Campbell, 27 October 1928, Middlesex, England

Laine and Annie Ross (of **Lambert, Hendricks and Ross**) are Britain's only world-class jazz vocalists. Laine also recorded extensively in the popular field and frequently appeared in stage musicals.

The daughter of a Jamaican immigrant father and white English mother, Laine began her professional career in 1952, with the **Johnny Dankworth** Seven, one of Britain's leading modern jazz groups. Originally a contralto, she stretched her vocal range to nearly four octaves under Dankworth's guidance. In 1958 Laine sang at Birdland in New York and married Dankworth before going on to tour the cabaret circuit and act in Sandy Wilson's West End musical *Valmonth*.

In 1960 she signed to Fontana, recording 'Let's Slip Away' before releasing her only Top Ten hit, a cover of **Patti Page**'s 'You'll Answer to Me' (1961). In that year Laine also played in the **Kurt Weill**/Bertolt Brecht opera *The Seven Deadly Sins*. *All about Me* (Fontana, 1963), with Johnny Keating's orchestra, was a collection of Broadway ballads. In 1964 she appeared in *Cindy-Ella*, a pantomime with an all-black cast, and on the cast album issued by Decca.

In the mid-sixties Laine began a new series of concept albums with Dankworth, recording *Shakespeare and All That Jazz* (1965), settings of songs from the plays by Dankworth, as well as *What the Dickens!*, based on characters created by the nineteenth-century novelist.

In the seventies she recorded the ballad collection *Feel the Warm* with the Harry Robinson Orchestra (EMI-Columbia, 1973) and with **Ray Charles** made a studio version of **George Gershwin**'s *Porgy and Bess*

(RCA, 1976), before making her Broadway début (*Cleo on Broadway*, 1977). She also appeared in the long-running London revival of **Jerome Kern** and Oscar Hammerstein's *Showboat* and in *Colette*, Dankworth's musical version of the French novelist's life. Laine recorded the songs from the latter in 1980.

Laine also collaborated on crossover projects with classical flautist **James Galway** (*Sometimes When We Touch*, RCA, 1980) and **Sky** guitarist John Williams (*Best Friends*, RCA, 1978). Her later records included *Gonna Get Through* (RCA, 1980) and *Smilin' Through* with actor/pianist Dudley Moore (Columbia, 1982).

In 1986 she won a Grammy award for *Cleo at Carnegie: The 10th Anniversary Concert* (DRG) and in 1988 Laine signed a long-term recording contract with RCA Red Seal, under which her first recording was an album of songs by women composers, *Woman to Woman* (1989). She followed that with an album of jazz standards, titled *Jazz*, in 1991. The next year Laine recorded with **Mel Tormé**. The orchestra on *Nothing Without You* (Concord Jazz) was directed by Dankworth.

Her autobiography, *Cleo*, was published in 1994.

FRANKIE LAINE
b. Frank Paul Lo Vecchio, 30 March 1913, Chicago, Illinois, USA

With cumulative sales of over 100 million discs, Laine was the most successful of the big-voiced balladeers – one contemporary reviewer described him as the possessor of 'steel tonsils' – who emerged in the forties. His success marked the end of the dominance of the crooning tradition of singing, while his records were among the first to reveal just how much sound could be manipulated by producers.

The son of Italian immigrants, Laine's first love was blues and jazz. Raised in Chicago, he worked as a teenager as a dance instructor – setting an endurance record in 1932 for dancing over 3,500 hours in less than three months – and sang with various pick-up jazz bands before in 1937 he briefly replaced **Perry Como** in Freddie Carlone's band. He left the band to become a solo artist and in 1944 teamed up with pianist and songwriter Carl Fischer, who, until his death in 1954, was Laine's closest musical associate. Spotted by **Hoagy Carmichael** in Hollywood, he was signed to Mercury in 1946 and in 1947 had a million-seller with **Mitch Miller**'s production of the 1931 song 'That's My Desire'. Sung in an intimate, caressing manner, the song (which was later successfully revived as an impassioned teenage plea by **Dion and the Belmonts**) was as popular with blacks as with whites. Laine's revival of Ford Dabney's 'coon' song 'Shine' (1948) showed off his voice in a big-band arrangement by Fischer and gave him a further million-seller.

The Laine sound, however, was not set until Miller's production of 'Mule Train'* (1949). Miller added a snapping bullwhip to the folksy lyric and intensified the tune's clippity-cloppity rhythm to highlight Laine's booming muscular voice. The result was one of the most dramatic pop records made up to that time and marked a decisive shift from a record as the recording of a performance of a song, to a record as a new sound created in the studio. Sometimes the recordings could be mannered ('That Lucky Old Sun'*, 1949), but more often Miller's gimmicks were innovative. These included alternating the sound of honking wild geese with French horns on 'The Cry of the Wild Geese'* (1950) – which, like 'Mule Train', was originally recorded by **Tennessee Ernie Ford**.

When Miller left Mercury for Columbia in 1951, Laine followed and together they notched up a lengthy series of million-sellers. These included dramatic versions of 'Jezebel' and 'Jalousie' (which was later revived by **Billy Fury** as 'Jealousy'); 'Rose, Rose I Love You', an adaptation of the traditional Chinese melody 'Mei Kuei', in 1951; and 'High Noon', a cover of **Tex Ritter**'s title song from the Fred Zinnemann western. Laine's success with this led to a series of similarly styled recordings, including 'Rawhide' (1959) – the theme song to the teleseries and a big hit in Britain – and 'Gunslinger' (1960). In 1952 he duetted with **Doris Day** on 'Sugarbush'*, which derived from a South African folk song, and in 1953 he had hits with his intense version of 'I Believe'* (a million-seller again on Decca in 1964 for the Irish vocal trio Bachelors, who specialized in folksy nostalgia) and 'Tell Me a Story'*, a duet with Jimmy Boyd, who in 1951 had had a huge hit with his version of **Tommie Connor**'s 'I Saw Mommy Kissing Santa Claus' (Columbia). Laine's last million-seller was 'Midnight Gambler' (1957).

During the fifties Laine appeared with little success in several movies, including *Sunny Side of the Street* (1951) and *Bring Your Smile Along* (1955). He had greater success on the cabaret and nightclub circuit where his ability to convey intimacy as well as power found favour throughout the sixties and seventies. After a short spell with Capitol he joined ABC, where he had occasional hits, including **Marty Robbins**' 'You Gave Me a Mountain' (1969). In 1975 he recorded the title song to Mel Brooks' comic Western *Blazing Saddles*, a song written and produced as a parody of Western film songs in general and his own recordings of 'High Noon' and 'Rawhide' in particular. In 1980 he signed to Polydor and released *Life Is Beautiful*.

LAMBCHOP
Paul Burch Jr; C Scott Chase; Dennis Cronin; John Delworth; Allen Lowery; Alex McManus; Jonathan Marx; *Mark Nevers; Paul Niehaus; Matt Swanson; Marc Trovillion; Deanna Varagona; Kurt Wagner*

Lambchop is a Nashville-based collective (collective rather than group because it boasts as many as fourteen members) that under the relaxed direction of leader Kurt Wagner has created a rich, timeless style that draws equally on country music, soul and orchestral pop. What makes the resulting sound unsettling, rather than MOR, are the odd sonic eruptions and the chilling tone of Wagner's almost spoken stories of quiet desperation in which the mundane (the weather) and the unusual (suicide) sit side by side in the manner of a David Lynch movie. Sometimes confusing, but always compelling (albeit in a catatonic way), Lambchop strains as much for grandeur, through the collective's preference for cellos, woodwinds and vibes as well as the mandatory steel guitar, as the feel of the everyday that Wagner repeatedly documents.

Lambchop came together in the early nineties around a core membership of singer/songwriter Wagner, drummer Lowery, bassist Trovillion and pedal-steel guitarist Niehaus. Their ambitious double-album début, *I Hope You're Sitting Down/Jack's Tulips* (Merge, 1994), was a curious blend of country- and rock-based song structures. Overlaid on this were Wagner's apparently stream-of-consciousness lyrics which mixed the surreal ('Cowboy on the Moon') and the morbid ('Soaky in the Pooper', which took as its subject suicide), delivered in a distanced style reminiscent of **Morrissey**. The follow-up, *How I Quit Smoking* (1995), introduced a seemingly more traditional, string-laden sound reminiscent at times of **Owen Bradley**'s productions, which, as ever, Wagner disturbed with his off-kilter observations. The sleeve also included pictures of Wagner's sculptures. The *Hank* EP (1996) was the band's most authentically country-styled set, despite featuring song titles like 'I Sucked My Boss's Dick'.

Wagner's playfulness continued apace on *Thriller* (1997), which lasted exactly 33 minutes and 33 seconds. Sonically, however, *Thriller* marked a departure from the band's earlier sound, adding Muscle Shoals brass and borrowings from seventies soul, while Wagner's vocals were a touch more impassioned, particularly on the opening tracks, the mournful 'Your Face, My Ass' and the up-tempo 'Your Sucking Funny Day'. Particularly fine is the lush 'The Old Fat Robin'. By this stage the band's membership had evolved into double figures, taking in a brass section and two drummers, alongside assorted guitarists, bassists and keyboard players. *What Another Man Spills* (1998) saw Lambchop sign with Chicago-based label City Slang, and added respectful readings of **Curtis Mayfield**'s 'Give Me Your Love' and Frederick Knight's 'I've

Been Lonely for So Long' to a collection of subtle, mournful originals.

Wagner spent time apart from Lambchop the following year, working in collaboration with songwriter Josh Rouse on the *Chester* EP (1999). The band reconvened in 2000 for their most ambitious work to date, the highly acclaimed *Nixon*. Its heartbroken tales swathed in orchestral splendour were given an even more soulful feel than previous outings. The result was their most atmospheric album to date, a symphony of confusion and ennui.

LAMBERT, HENDRICKS AND ROSS

Jon Hendricks, b. John Carl Hendricks, 16 September 1921, Newark, Ohio, USA; Dave Lambert, b. 1917, Boston, Massachusetts, d. 1966; Annie Ross, b. Annabelle Lynch, 25 July 1930, Mitcham, Surrey, England

Although each member had a solo career, as a trio Lambert, Hendricks and Ross were the most widely known exponents of 'vocalese', the setting of lyrics to well-known jazz instrumental solos.

With fellow vocalist Buddy Stewart, Lambert had recorded 'So What' (1945) with **Gene Krupa**'s orchestra, the first recording of a vocalese performance. During the early fifties he organized the Dave Lambert Singers and was the focus of vocal jam sessions out of which the trio grew in 1957.

A singer and drummer, Hendricks had played the jazz clubs of Toledo with artists like **Art Tatum** before moving to New York in 1955. His compositions were recorded by Art Pepper, **Louis Jordan** ('I Want You to Be My Baby', 1952), and others, but his first success came when Don Lang, bandleader for **Jack Good**'s British TV show *6.5 Special*, had a hit with his scat-flavoured 'Cloudburst' (HMV, 1955). The song was an early example of Hendricks' talent for putting lyrics to instrumental solos, following a method pioneered by Eddie Jefferson (whose best-known piece, 'Moody's Mood for Love', was based on a James Moody saxophone piece) and King Pleasure, who wrote words for 'Parker's Mood', a classic solo by **Charlie Parker**. 'Cloudburst' was taken from Sam 'The Man' Taylor's sax break on a 1954 R&B record by Claude Cloud and his Thunderclaps. The song had been unsuccessfully recorded by Hendricks himself and was later revived by **Barry Manilow**.

Ross had moved to Los Angeles as a child, studying in New York before singing briefly with **Lionel Hampton**. Her first vocalese recording was the Wardell Gray solo 'Twisted' (Prestige, 1952). With its sardonic lyric beginning 'My analyst told me . . .', the song was later revived by both **Bette Midler** and **Joni Mitchell**. In 1954 Ross moved to Britain to sing with Jack Parnell's band, linking up with Lambert and Hendricks on her return to New York.

Between 1959 and 1962 the trio took the jazz world by storm. With the men singing the reed and trombone parts and Ross re-creating trumpet or piano lines, two albums of vocalized **Count Basie** numbers were recorded for ABC-Paramount and Roulette, while *The Hottest New Group in Jazz* (Columbia, 1961) included Ross's *tour de force* 'Twisted'.

In 1962 Ross was replaced by Yolande Bavan but the trio split in 1964, two years before Lambert's death in a car crash. Hendricks, who had written most of the lyrics, performed in Europe for several years before organizing a new group, whose members included Bobby McFerrin (who had a surprise pop hit in 1988 with 'Don't Worry Be Happy' on EMI-Manhattan) and his wife and daughter Judith and Stephanie Hendricks.

His later compositions included 'Slightly out of Tune' based on the **Stan Getz** bossa nova hit 'Desafinado', lyrics for the **Weather Report** tune 'Birdland' and 'Love Me with a Feeling', a song featured in the Bette Midler vehicle *The Rose*. He recorded infrequently, cutting the Ben Sidran-produced *Tell Me the Truth* (Arista, 1979) and *Love* (Muse, 1985). An indication of Hendricks' standing among the jazz community was the presence on *Freddie Freeloader* (Denon, 1990) of **Wynton Marsalis** and **George Benson**. He appeared on **Manhattan Transfer**'s *Mecca for Moderns* (1981). In 1985 that group made *Vocalese*, an album of Hendricks compositions.

After leaving the group Ross settled in London, recording an eponymous album for Xtra (1963) of dramatic and satirical songs by poet Christopher Logue and jazz composer Tony Kinsey. The following year she released *A Handful of Songs* (Ember), a collection of standard ballads arranged by Johnny Spence. In later years Ross worked mainly in cabaret and as an actress, appearing in *Superman III* (1983) and *Short Cuts* (1993). She sang 'Hong Kong Blues' and 'My Resistance is Low' on **Georgie Fame**'s tribute to **Hoagy Carmichael**, *In Hoagland* (Bald Eagle, 1981).

In 1985 Hendricks and Ross reunited, with Bruce Scott taking the Lambert part. The influence of Lambert, Hendricks and Ross was strong on later generations of jazz vocalists, including Manhattan Transfer, Fame (who briefly worked with Hendricks in 1968) and **Al Jarreau**.

ART LANDRY
b. 1900

Landry was one of the earliest bandleaders to follow the example of **Paul Whiteman** and play special arrangements of songs, rather than merely repeating chorus after chorus, and one of the first to have a million-seller with a dance record, the Ted Koehler co-authored waltz 'Dreamy Melody' (Gennett, 1922).

A violinist, Landry formed his first band – Art Landry's Syncopatin' Six – in 1920. One of the most successful bands playing the Midwest dance-hall circuit, Landry and the Six joined the Richmond, Indiana-based Gennett Records, one of several companies specializing in jazz and dance music. However, Landry soon deserted jazz for sweeter sounds, changing the name of his band to Art Landry and the Call of the North to signify the new policy. It was under this name that he had his sole million-seller. He recorded prolifically for Gennett, under his own name and using pseudonyms, mostly in the sweet manner, and in 1924 moved to RCA Victor as Art Landry and His Orchestra. However, despite his numerous recordings – he is reported to have made over 2,000 in the course of his relatively short career – he was unable to repeat the success of 'Dreamy Melody' and after 1932 recorded only occasionally.

In the early fifties he emerged from retirement to perform regularly on a local radio station in Rutland, Vermont.

EDDIE LANG
b. Salvatore Massaro, 25 October 1902, Philadelphia, Pennsylvania, USA, d. 26 March 1933, New York

The pioneer of plectrum guitar-playing, Eddie Lang, more than anyone, was responsible for the instrument superseding the banjo as an indispensable element of dance bands and 'hot' jazz groups in the thirties.

The son of an instrument maker, Lang was a schoolfriend of violinist **Joe Venuti** and played violin as well as banjo and guitar in Charlie Kerr's band from 1920 to 1923 before, with Venuti, joining Bert Estlow's dance band. In 1924 he was briefly a member of the Scranton Sirens, whose members included **Tommy** and **Jimmy Dorsey**. Later that year Lang joined the Móund City Blues Blowers, a novelty kazoo and banjo group led by St Louis ex-jockey Red McKenzie which played in England and recorded an acclaimed version of the New Orleans standard 'Tiger Rag'.

In 1925 Lang moved to New York where, reunited with Venuti, he performed and recorded prolifically until his early death. His dynamic single-string guitar solos were evident on records with **Red Nichols**' Five Pennies and on the collaborations with trumpeter **Bix Beiderbecke** which included 'Singing the Blues' and 'For No Reason at All in C'. With Venuti, he cut more than seventy sides, creating many memorable examples of chamber jazz, including 'Doing Things' (RCA, 1928) – based on a theme by Debussy – and 'Stringing the Blues'. In 1928 Lang began to record under his own name in both jazz ('Eddie's Twister') and classical (Rachmaninoff's 'Prelude') idioms. As Blind

Willie Dunn he made his first blues recordings, including 'Church Street Sobbin' Blues'.

With blues player **Lonnie Johnson**, Lang recorded from 1929 the first and perhaps the greatest jazz guitar duets. Using the Blind Willie Dunn alias, he turned his technical poise into the perfect foil for the emotional intensity of Johnson's style on such tracks as 'Midnight Call Blues' and 'Blue Guitars' (Okeh). He also played incisive guitar on records by **Louis Armstrong**, **Jack Teagarden** and Tommy Dorsey, and worked with **Al Jolson** and other popular singers.

Outside the studio, Lang played in the big bands of Roger Wolfe Kahn, Adrian Rollini and **Paul Whiteman**, with whom he appeared in the film King of Jazz (1930). In 1932 he became accompanist to the young **Bing Crosby**, who was one of his greatest admirers. Lang died as a result of complications following a tonsillectomy.

K. D. LANG
b. Kathryn Dawn Lang, 1962, Consort, Alberta, Canada

Like **Lyle Lovett**, lang is an unusual country music star who has applied a distinctly distanced approach to her material. She first achieved cult success by presenting herself as a musical heir of **Patsy Cline** and confirmed her success by adopting an androgynous style of hair and dress before she confirmed that she was the first avowed lesbian country – and by then film – star. The most dramatic presentation of this was the Vanity Fair magazine cover, which showed her in a barber's chair being shaved by model Cindy Crawford.

A pharmacist's daughter, lang studied piano and guitar at college, and only turned to country music after her attempts to earn a living playing avant-garde music failed. She formed her first band, the Reclines, named in honour of Cline, in 1976. Signed to Canadian independent label Bumstead she recorded A Truly Western Experience (1984), which was notable for a tendency to parody country music styles in the manner of a **Malcolm McLaren**. That approach was curtailed on her first major label recording, Angel with a Lariat (Sire, 1987). Produced by **Dave Edmunds**, who was probably more responsible than lang for its straightforward, no-nonsense attitude, it won lang critical plaudits from rock critics and rejection from country fans, who found her ambiguous sexuality disconcerting. Her version of **Joe South**'s 'Rose Garden', best known in its version by **Lynn Anderson**, which dispensed with the affectations of the original, was representative of lang's approach. More mainstream was her duet with **Roy Orbison** on his 'Cryin''.

Her breakthrough album was Shadowlands (1988), a calculated tribute to Patsy Cline made with **Owen**

Bradley, Cline's original producer. As much a devotion as a celebration, lang was not overshadowed by the album's numerous guests, who included **Brenda Lee**, **Lorreta Lynn** and **Kitty Wells**. *Absolute Torch and Twang* (1989), though it included a fine version of **Chris Isaak**'s 'Western Stars', was mostly self-composed and won her the beginnings of a cult following outside country music as much as a stylist as a writer. The three-million-selling *Ingenue* (1992), her most successful album to date, blurred all distinctions between country and mainstream with its unique meld of influences. It included the striking 'Miss Chatelaine' and 'Save Me'. In the same year lang began her film career with a role in Percy Aldon's *Salmonberries*.

She next wrote and recorded the music for *Even Cowgirls Get the Blues*, Gus Van Sant's film of Tom Robbins' novel. She also contributed 'Teardrops' to **Elton John**'s *Duets* album and duetted with **Tony Bennett** on his highly successful MTV *Unplugged* show. Her own albums, which included *All You Can Eat* (1995) and *Drag* (1997), a concept album based on the theme of smoking, were more mannered and less successful. Far more enjoyable, but hardly experimental, was *Invincible Summer* (2000), an album of love songs delivered with precisely the lounge pop verities that Chris Isaak deployed on his more troubled love songs.

DANIEL LANOIS
b. 19 September 1951, Hull, Quebec, Canada

Daniel Lanois was one of the most sought-after producers of the eighties, noted for his atmospheric 'ambient' technique. He also had a brief career as a recording artist at the end of the decade.

Lanois first worked in local recording studios with his brother Bob before the pair set up their own studio. His first success was as producer on 'Echo Beach' (1980), the international hit by Canadian band Martha & the Muffins, and its parent album *Metro Music*. In the early eighties he began to work with **Brian Eno** on the latter's ambient recordings, including *On Land* (1982), the *Music for Films* series and Eno's album with composer Harold Budd, *The Pearl* (1984). This relationship would come to fruition in their work with U2. Lanois co-produced **Peter Gabriel**'s 1984 soundtrack album *Birdy*, and later that year teamed with Eno to produce U2's *The Unforgettable Fire*. The album marked a major change in the Irish band's style as Eno and Lanois encouraged U2 to experiment with sound and song structure in the studio.

In 1986 Lanois co-produced Gabriel's multi-platinum album *So*, followed in 1987 by U2's biggest-selling album to date, *The Joshua Tree*, and the acclaimed eponymous solo début from former member of **The Band**, Robbie Robertson. Lanois applied the experience of Eno's 'ambient' approach to recording when taking on his next major project, the **Neville Brothers**' *Yellow Moon* (1989), which resulted in the New Orleans veterans' most successful album, both critically and commercially. One of the stand-out tracks on *Yellow Moon* was a **Bob Dylan** song, 'With God on our Side', and Dylan himself was Lanois' next client. The resulting album, *Oh Mercy* (1989), was acclaimed as Dylan's finest effort in over a decade, with Lanois' production singled out for particular praise. Later that year, Lanois released his own début album, *Arcadie*, recorded in New Orleans with many of the musicians from the Dylan and Nevilles sessions, and he subsequently toured as a solo artist.

The start of the nineties again saw Lanois in the studio with Eno and U2, producing the *Achtung Baby* (1991) album, which was followed in 1992 by Peter Gabriel's *Us*, which he co-produced. In 1993 Lanois released his own second album, *For the Beauty of Wynona*, which like its predecessor seamlessly mixed folk, rock, world music and new age genres. In 1995 he helped revive the becalmed career of **Emmylou Harris** as the producer of *Wrecking Ball* and in 1996 he wrote the score for Billy Bob Thornton's film *Sling Blade*. In 1998 he reunited with Dylan for the superior *Time Out of Mind*.

MARIO LANZA
b. Alfredo Arnold Cocozza, 31 January 1921, Philadelphia, Pennsylvania, USA, d. 7 October 1959, Rome, Italy

A tragic figure, Lanza's thrilling, if undisciplined, tenor brought him two million-selling singles, 'Be My Love' (RCA, 1950) and 'The Loveliest Night of the Year' (1951), a million-selling album, *The Student Prince* (1954), and a brief screen career as the incarnation of the voice of opera.

The son of Italian immigrants, he taught himself singing from his father's collection of records by **Enrico Caruso** before briefly studying with Enrico Rossati and Giacomo Spandoni, former tutors of Caruso and Benjimino Gigli. This resulted in a contract with Columbia for a concert tour which was interrupted by Second World War service. On leaving the Air Force he joined MGM, then on the lookout for a romantic lead to star in musicals. In his first film, *The Midnight Kiss* (1949), he starred opposite Kathryn Grayson as a singing truck driver, in the kind of semi-autobiographical role from which he never really escaped. A success, the teaming was repeated by MGM for *The Toast of New Orleans* (1950), which produced Lanza's first million-seller, the **Sammy Cahn** and Nicholas Brodszky song 'Be My Love', before he starred as Caruso himself in *The Great Caruso* (1951). *Because You're Mine* (1952), featuring another song from Cahn and Brodszky, with Lanza in the role of an opera star drafted into the air force, was his last major starring role.

Henceforth, oddly anticipating the last years of **Elvis Presley**, problems with barbiturates, alcohol and obesity overshadowed his career. Thus for MGM's remake of **Sigmund Romberg**'s *Student Prince* (1954), Lanza's role was limited to dubbing the singing for Edmund Purdom. He made a few more movies, including the under-rated *Serenade* (1956), and continued to record in an increasingly popular vein – his last hit was a version of 'Ariverderci Roma' (1958) – before his death, at the age of thirty-eight, at a clinic in Rome.

JULIUS LA ROSA
b. 2 January 1930, Brooklyn, New York, USA

La Rosa was one of the several crooners who emerged in the early fifties but had their careers drastically shortened by the arrival of rock'n'roll.

While still in the navy (and in uniform), La Rosa made his first professional appearance on *Arthur Godfrey Talent Scouts* in 1951, quickly graduating to become the show's regular band singer. When in 1953 Archie Bleyer, the show's musical director, established his own record company (Cadence), La Rosa was one of the first artists signed and his recording of 'Anywhere I Wander' from the film *Hans Christian Andersen*, after heavy plugging by **Arthur Godfrey** on the show, was a big hit. Even more dramatic was Godfrey's on-air sacking of La Rosa for 'lacking in humility' on 19 October 1953, just before the release of La Rosa's biggest hit, his and Bleyer's transcription of the traditional Italian song 'Eh Cumpari'*. Other hits on Cadence included 'Domani' and 'Suddenly There's a Valley' (1955), before La Rosa switched to RCA where his attempts to record in both the popular and rock'n'roll veins ('Get Me to the Church on Time', 1956, and 'Mama Guitar', 1957) found little favour. His biggest hit of the period came in Britain where his cover of Renato Carosone's 'Torero', a hit in America on Capitol, reached the Top Twenty.

In the seventies La Rosa worked in radio, at one point hosting an afternoon show.

THE LA'S
Paul Hemmings; Lee Mavers; John Power; John Timson

An ill-fated pop quartet based in Liverpool, England, the La's drew on sixties beat pop rather than the psychedelia that inspired much of the Britpop movement, disintegrating soon after they recorded their exceptional eponymous début album.

Singer-songwriter Mavers formed the La's in 1986, recruiting guitarist Hemmings, bassist Power and drummer Timson from the local music scene. The band quickly attracted the attention of Go! Discs, with whom they signed the following year, releasing a pair of critically acclaimed singles – 'Way Out' and 'There She Goes' – before heading to the studio to begin working on their début. *The La's* (1990), which didn't emerge until three years later, at which point Mavers, ever the perfectionist, claimed the album had been rush-released and as a result could have been improved upon. The record-buying public didn't seem to agree, making a re-released version of 'There She Goes' a hit in Britain and the US, while the album was immediately described as a modern classic.

The La's spent much of 1991 on tour, but it had become clear that the band's future was uncertain soon after the release of their début. Mavers' behaviour became increasingly erratic as he began to cancel gigs and scrap recording sessions with alarming frequency. The band disappeared towards the end of 1991 on the premise that they were recording a new album, but by 1994 they had officially split.

While Mavers was not to be seen again in the music industry, bassist John Power went on to achieve considerable success in the UK with his own band, Cast. Like the La's, Cast were inspired principally by the beat pop of **The Beatles** and the **Hollies**, but also added a touch of garage rock to the mix. Cast released three popular albums – *All Change* (1996), *Mother Nature Calls* (1997) and *Magic Hour* (1999) – and had a series of hit singles, including 'Sandstorm' and 'Walkaway'.

JAMES LAST
b. Hans Last, 17 April 1929, Bremen, Germany

Known affectionately as Hansi to his legions of fans, Last sold in excess of 60 million albums of punchy, big-band arrangements of current hits. The albums were given greater immediacy by the songs being recorded without gaps between them, for 'non-stop dancing', and with hand-clapping and laughter added to increase the party atmosphere.

The son of an amateur musician, Last studied at the Bremen Music Academy and after the Second World War joined Hans-Günter Oesterreich's band as a bassist, playing American popular songs to the American soldiers stationed in Bremen. Soon afterwards, Last's brothers, Robert and Werner, joined the band, which became the Radio Bremen Dance Orchestra when Oesterreich secured a position with the radio station. Then, in 1948, Last quit to form his own band, the Becker–Last Ensemble, before in 1955 returning once more to radio as arranger of the North German Radio Dance Orchestra. He also worked as a freelance arranger for Polydor Records, arranging many of the European hits of **Freddie Quinn**, **Caterina Valente** and Helmut Zacharias.

In 1964 he formed his own orchestra, which included his brother Robert, signed with Polydor and in 1965 released the first of his twenty-strong series of *Non-Stop Dancing* albums, *Non-Stop Dancing 65*. Essentially a party record for parents, the album saw Last performing instrumental dance-band versions of the songs of **The Beatles**, **Rolling Stones**, **Chuck Berry** and the like. Interspersed with the *Non-Stop Dancing* series, Last produced a series of recordings of classical pieces, starting with *Classics up to Date* (1966) and, after his tours made him a star throughout Europe, a series of albums devoted to the traditional musics of different countries (*Last of Old England*, *In South America*, and so on). A master of avuncular showmanship, Last always kept his material up to date, but hardly changed his style after the mid-sixties. His only American hit single was 'The Seduction', from the film *American Gigolo*, in 1980.

Last maintained a high work-rate throughout the eighties, releasing three or four albums a year and regularly touring in Europe. In 1984 *James Last In Scotland* gave him his fiftieth British chart album. Towards the end of the decade the number of British releases lessened, although the frantic schedule was maintained elsewhere in Europe. His later records include *Classics by Moonlight* (1990), *Pop Symphonies* (1991), *Together at Last* with **Richard Clayderman** and *Viva Espana* (1992), timed to coincide with the Barcelona Olympics. In 1993 the chart success of *James Last Plays the Music of Andrew Lloyd Webber* confirmed Last's position as the artist with the second highest total of album chart entries in Britain, after **Elvis Presley**. His 1994 Christmas release featured **Engelbert Humperdinck**.

Last also wrote songs for other performers. They included 'Happy Heart' (recorded by **Andy Williams**), 'Games Lovers Play' (**Eddie Fisher**), 'Blame It on Me' (**Ray Charles**) and 'Fool' (Elvis Presley).

BILL LASWELL
b. 14 February 1950, Illinois, USA

One of the new breed of record producers of the eighties and nineties, Laswell regards songs as 'an old-fashioned primitive format'. He is renowned for ignoring stylistic and cultural boundaries in his work. As well as producing artists as diverse as Japan's **Ryuichi Sakamoto**, **Herbie Hancock** and **Fela Kuti**, Laswell has recorded his own compositions with avant-garde groups Material and Last Exit.

He grew up in Michigan, playing bass in local R&B bands at the age of fifteen, influenced by **James Brown** and **Wilson Pickett**. In 1979 he moved to New York where he joined the American branch of Jean Karakos's Celluloid label as house producer. He made

the first Material album, *Temporary Music* (1980), with a group that included future **Scritti Politti** drummer Fred Maher.

Laswell's greatest commercial success came with Herbie Hancock's 'Rockit' (1983), recorded with Celluloid artists including percussionist Daniel Ponce. As a result, Laswell worked on records by reggae artist Yellowman, Hancock (*Sound System*), Nona Hendryx and Mick Jagger (*She's the Boss*).

His credits for 1985 included albums by reggae artists **Sly and Robbie**, drummer Ginger Baker (*Horses and Trees*), **Yoko Ono** and the Golden Palominos. Laswell also worked with African musicians **Manu Dibango** and Fela Kuti, though his remix of the latter's *Army Arrangement* was criticized for editing out the artist's own guitar-playing.

Among Laswell's later work were Sakamoto's pan-Oriental *Neo Geo* (Columbia, 1987), Sly and Robbie's *Rhythm Killers* (4th and Broadway, 1987) and **Toure Kunda**'s *Natalia* (1985). His ability to bring together disparate artists was exemplified by 1985's 'Makossa Rock' by Deadline, whose personnel included Dibango, **Paul Butterfield** on harmonica and Steve Turre on the Australian aboriginal horn, the dijeridu, previously associated in Anglo-American music with Rolf Harris's novelty hit 'Sun Arise' (EMI Columbia, 1962).

Laswell made solo albums *Basslines* (1984) and *Hear No Evil* (1988) as well as *Lowlife*, a set of duets with free jazz saxophonist Peter Brotzmann, who was also a member of Last Exit with guitarist Sonny Sharrock and Ronald Shannon Jackson (drums). The group toured Europe in 1986 recording the unrelenting, free-form *Last Exit* (Enemy). Laswell's other group project was Material, a recording entity whose shifting personnel included guitarists Fred Frith and Sharrock, **Archie Shepp** and singers Hendryx and even the young **Whitney Houston**. Among the albums released by Material are *Memory Serves* (1982), *Seven Souls* (1989) and *Hallucination Engine* (1994), a collaboration with Palestinian oud- and violin-player Simon Shaheen. The latter was issued on Laswell's own Axiom label, which in the early nineties also issued recordings by guitarist Nicky Skopelitis (*Ekstasis*) and Chinese singer Liu Sola (*Blues in the East*).

YUSUF LATEEF
b. William Evans, 1920, Chattanooga, Tennessee, USA

A flautist and multi-instrumentalist, Lateef did much to introduce Oriental scales and metrical elements into modern jazz in the sixties and seventies.

He grew up in Detroit and toured with **Lucky Millinder** and **Dizzy Gillespie**, with whom he recorded in 1949. Lateef formed his first small groups during six years of study at Wayne State University in

Detroit and the Teal School of Music. In the early sixties he worked with **Charlie Mingus** and **Cannonball Adderley**. He was fluent on alto and tenor saxophone as well as flute, oboe and Asian and Middle Eastern woodwind instruments. His conversion to the Muslim faith impelled him to draw Eastern methods into jazz.

Among his first records was *Eastern Sounds* (Prestige, 1961) with his Detroit sidemen Barry Harris (piano), Ernie Farrow (bass and ribab) and Lex Humphries (drums). He also recorded in the sixties for Riverside, Savoy, Impulse (*The Golden Flute* and *Live at Pep's*, with trumpeter Richard Williams), Verve and Argo. In 1971 he signed to Atlantic. Among his albums for the label were *Gentle Giant*, *Hush 'n' Thunder* and *Part of the Search*.

In the eighties Lateef moved to Nigeria, where he taught music.

HARRY LAUDER
b. 4 August 1870, Portobello, Scotland, d. 26 February 1950, Strathaven

Dressed in fantastic tartans, with his twisted cromach and sporran always to the fore, Lauder came to be the personification of Scottish kitsch. His sentimental ballads and humorous songs (which included 'I Love a Lassie', 'Roamin' in the Gloamin'', 'A Wee Doech an' Doris', 'Stop Your Tickling Jock' and 'Glasgow Belongs to Me', and were mostly written by him) brought him international fame. On stage and on record he confirmed the traditional popular stereotypes of Scotland (melding a high romanticism with canny thriftiness). This image lasted into the sixties when Andy Stewart had British hits with 'Donald Where's Your Troosers' (Top Rank, 1960) and 'A Scottish Soldier' (1961), before a new generation of singers and comedians, such as Billy Connolly, countered it with more realistic versions of Scottish life.

The son of a potter, Lauder worked in the Lanarkshire flax mills and mines in his teens. After regularly performing as an amateur, he turned professional in 1894. He toured Scotland with concert-parties, eventually venturing further south, first singing Irish songs in England, fearful that his strong Scottish accent would be unintelligible, and in 1900 made his London début. With his 'Calligan' sketch (about an Irish tailor) and songs like 'Tobermory' and 'The Lass of Killiecrankie', he swiftly established himself as a leading figure of the music hall. In 1905 he made the first of numerous recordings for the Gramophone Company (most of which were of songs he first popularized on stage). So successful were his records that **Peter Dawson**, among others, impersonated Lauder on a number of budget labels singing his songs. In 1907 Lauder began his annual tours of America and the Dominions.

During the First World War, in which he lost his only son, he made famous the patriotic 'Keep Right on to the End of the Road', and performed for the troops, being knighted for his services in 1919. He made several films, the most notable of which was *Huntingtower* (1930), an adaptation of the John Buchan novel. In the twenties and thirties, though he remained immensely popular in concert and on radio, his record sales declined, his material becoming increasingly anachronistic.

CYNDI LAUPER
b. Cynthia Anne Stephanie Lauper, 22 June 1953, Brooklyn, New York, USA

Lauper was one of the most successful solo rock singers of the mid-eighties. Her image, slightly aggressive and cheerfully 'kooky' on her best-known hit 'Girls Just Want to Have Fun'*, was less threatening than **Madonna**'s, but still unusual for the period. By the nineties, of course, it had become the norm.

She was a singer with New York bar bands Doc West and Flyer – before laryngitis caused her retirement in 1977. With aid from voice coach Katie Agresta, Lauper regained her voice and in 1978 she formed the highly regarded rock band Blue Angel with John Turi (keyboards) and Arthur Neilson (guitar). Roy Halee produced an eponymous album for Polydor in 1980 but a legal dispute with a management company led to the group's demise in 1982 and Lauper's bankruptcy.

Lauper signed to Epic as a solo artist and her first single, 'Girls Just Want to Have Fun', was a major international hit. Propelled by a witty, fast-paced video and Lauper's rich, powerful, **Lesley Gore**-style pop voice, it established a genial scatterbrain image for her. It was followed by her delicate ballad 'Time After Time', co-written with Rob Hyman of Philadelphia group the Hooters, which became an American No. 1 and was later recorded on an instrumental version by **Miles Davis**. Both tracks appeared on the million-selling album *She's So Unusual*, as did two further 1984 hits, 'She Bop' and Jules Shear's 'All Through the Night'.

Her sequence of hits continued in 1985 with the film theme 'Goonies Are Good Enough'. In 1986 Lauper released a second album, *True Colors*, which included versions of 'Iko Iko' and **Marvin Gaye**'s 'What's Goin' on'. The title track and 'Change of Heart' were American hits. Her band at this time included noted guitarist Rick Derringer, ex-**Johnny Winter** and the **McCoys**, who was employed as Lauper's musical director.

After a two-year period in which she managed female wrestlers and became a born-again Christian, Lauper returned to music in 1989 when she released *A*

Night to Remember, with its hit single 'I Drove All Night' – the Billy Steinberg–Tom Kelly song which was also a posthumous hit for **Roy Orbison** in 1992. Although a disappointment after the first two albums, it reached the Top Ten in Britain. Lauper's interest in the visual element of her performances and promotional videos suggested a film career. However, her work in that area was restricted to appearances in a TV show for Walt Disney and two unsuccessful 1990 movies, *Paradise Paved* and *Off and Running*. She returned to recording with the 1992 soundtrack of the Tim Rice musical *Tycoon*, on which she sang two songs, including the hit single 'The World Is Made of Stone'. Her solo career resumed in 1993 with the album *Hat Full of Stars*. More successful was the greatest hits set, *Twelve Deadly Cins . . . and Then Some* (1994), which included a remixed version of 'Girls Just Want to Have Fun'. Less successful were *Sisters of Avalon* and the would-be ironic seasonal offering *Merry Christmas . . . Have a Nice Life* (1998), which was at considerable variance with her carefully constructed image.

STEVE LAWRENCE AND EYDIE GORME

Steve Lawrence, b. Steven Leibowitz, 8 July 1933, New York, USA; Eydie Gorme, b. 16 August 1931, New York

A soft-voice balladeer, Lawrence and his wife Eydie Gorme were among the first singers from the popular mainstream to record regularly the songs of the new breed of songwriters that emerged in the wake of rock'n'roll. Lawrence's only million-seller, 'Go Away Little Girl' (Columbia, 1962), was written by **Carole King** and Gerry Goffin, and Gorme's 'Blame It on the Bossa Nova'* (Columbia, 1963) was by **Barry Mann** and Cynthia Weil; their biggest joint hit, 'I Want to Stay Here' (1963), was also a Goffin and King composition.

The son of a cantor, Lawrence appeared on *Arthur Godfrey Talent Scouts* in 1952 and became a regular. In 1954 he graduated to the *Tonight* show and remained with the show for some four years. There he met and married fellow cast-member Gorme. He briefly recorded for King ('Poincianna', 1952) and was one of the many artists who covered **Harry Belafonte**'s 'Banana Boat Song', scoring a Top Twenty hit with his version (Coral, 1957). He went on to cover rock'n'roll songs regularly for Coral, including 'Party Doll' (originally recorded by Buddy Knox, Roulette, 1957) and 'Fraulein' (Bobby Helms, Decca, 1957), before in 1959 he had a pair of hits with original songs, 'Pretty Blue Eyes' (ABC), written by Teddy Randazzo, and Mann's 'Footsteps'. However, he was far more at ease with the lush romanticism of 'Portrait of My Love' (United Aritists, 1961), a cover of **Matt Monro**'s first British hit, and 'Go Away Little

Girl', his only American chart-topper. In 1963 Lawrence and Gorme had Top Forty hits with the duets 'Stay Here' and 'I Can't Stop Talking About It'.

Gorme's solo hits included 'Too Close for Comfort' (ABC, 1956) from the Broadway musical *Mr Wonderful*; a revival of **Gus Kahn**'s and **Victor Schertzinger**'s 1935 composition 'Love Me Forever' (1957), and 'You Need Hands' (1958), which was successfully covered in Britain by **Max Bygraves**, who made it his theme song. After her big hit with 'Blame It on the Bossa Nova', she returned to the subject with 'Can't Get Over (the Bossa Nova)' (Columbia, 1964) and had her last chart entry in 1969 with 'Tonight, I'll Say a Prayer' (RCA, 1969). By that time she and Lawrence were regular guests on television variety shows and stars of the cabaret circuit. In the seventies they briefly returned to the charts with 'We Can Make It Together' (MGM, 1972), on which they were supported by the **Osmonds**, but were far happier performing in Las Vegas.

LAYTON AND JOHNSTONE

Turner Layton, b. 1894, Washington DC, USA, d. 6 February 1978, London, England; Clarence Johnstone, d. 1953, New York

The black Americans Layton and Johnstone were the most popular close-harmony duet in Britain in the twenties and the thirties, singing a wide variety of popular songs with practised polish to Layton's tidy piano accompaniment.

The son of a music teacher Layton studied medicine but became a professional pianist in New York in the late nineteen-tens. With lyricist and vaudevillian Henry Creamer he wrote a series of popular hits, including 'After You've Gone' (1918), first recorded in a sentimental manner by **Henry Burr** and **Billy Murray** and subsequently established as a classic in the recordings of **Bessie Smith**, **Sophie Tucker** (1927), **Louis Armstrong** (1932) and **Benny Goodman** (1935); 'Dear Old Southland' (1921), a hit in contrasting styles for **Vernon Dalhart** and **Paul Whiteman** (1922); 'Trees', a hit for **Isham Jones** (1930); and the evocation of the cradle of jazz 'Way Down Yonder in New Orleans', another hit for Whiteman (1923) and later revived by **Frankie Laine** and **Jo Stafford** (1953) and **Freddy Cannon** (1960). The pair were responsible for the black musical comedy *Strut Miss Lizzie* (1922) and worked as a vaudeville act in both America and Europe. Layton also recorded in his own right on Black Swan in 1921.

In 1922 Layton teamed up with Johnstone and in 1924 they made their London début in *Elsie Janis at Home*. They remained in London for most of the following decade, broadcasting and recording prolifically for Columbia under the supervision of **Joe Batten**.

Reportedly they sold over ten million records, including 'It Ain't Gonna Rain No More', 'River Stay Away from My Door', 'We'll All Go Riding on a Rainbow' and 'Bye Bye Blackbird'. The partnership broke up in the wake of the scandal that occurred when Johnstone was cited in the divorce action of a white couple in 1935. Johnstone returned to America where he later died in obscurity. Layton remained in England, working and recording as a solo artist until the early fifties.

LEADBELLY
b. Huddie Ledbetter, 29 January 1889, Mooringsport, Louisiana, USA, d. 6 December 1949, New York

Physically massive, Leadbelly was also a colossus in the history of black American folk song. He possessed, and recorded, a repertoire of ballads, blues, dance songs ('reels'), minstrelsy and children's songs richer than that of any other performer, black or white, in this century. He sang and played them – accompanying himself on twelve-string guitar in a stirring style based on barrelhouse piano-playing – with a commanding presence that drew about him such diverse musicians as **Brownie McGhee** and Sonny Terry, **Woody Guthrie** and **Pete Seeger**.

Leadbelly (the origin of this corruption of his surname is undecided but it seems to have been an acknowledgement of his physical or temperamental toughness) grew up in Leigh, Texas, learning accordion as a child from his uncle Terrell Ledbetter and later guitar, harmonica and a little piano. In his late teens he became an itinerant worker and musician, and before the First World War he came across **Blind Lemon Jefferson**, whose guitar style he echoed in later blues recordings.

Leadbelly's middle years were partly spent in prison: he served a term for murder in Huntsville, Texas (1918–25), and another for attempted homicide in Angola, Louisiana (1930–4). It was at Angola that he was first recorded by **John Lomax** for the Library of Congress in 1933. Lomax's valuation of his ability, and songs that Leadbelly himself wrote as pleas for freedom, secured his release into Lomax's care in 1934, and he was launched upon the concert-halls and folk-song circles of the East Coast as an exemplar of the riches of black song. He recorded prolifically for the Library of Congress (over 200 pieces by 1942) and for the American Record Company, though few recordings were commercially released at the time. He also appeared with Lomax in reconstructed news footage for the radio series *The March of Time* (1935).

From 1937 Leadbelly lived in New York. He was again imprisoned, after an assault, in 1939–40; on his release he worked with combinations of musicians including Guthrie, McGhee and Terry and **Josh White**, and participated in a WNYC radio series, *Folk Songs of America*. As well as his work for the Library of Congress he recorded for Musicraft (1939), RCA Victor (1940, partnered on some sides by the **Golden Gate Quartet**), Asch (1941–2), Disc (1943), Stinson (1944) and Capitol (1944). In 1944 he moved to Hollywood, and in 1946 he toured the US with the political group People's Songs Inc. In 1947 he moved back to New York, where he spent the rest of his life, except for occasional concerts elsewhere and a visit to France in 1949 for the Paris Jazz Fair.

Of the many songs closely associated with him, some of the more famous are 'Goodnight Irene' (a nineteenth-century minstrel number); 'Midnight Special', 'Rock Island Line' and 'Cotton Fields', which became, with much else from his repertoire, root material for the British skiffle movement of the fifties; the blues ballad 'Boll Weevil' and the Old World ballad 'The Gallis Pole'; and, from his sometimes overlooked stock of blues themes, 'Good Mornin' Blues'. Like much of his repertoire these were all recorded repeatedly; representative collections are *Leadbelly* (Storyville, from Disc and Stinson masters), *Leadbelly* (Capitol, the 1944 session), *Last Session* and others (Folkways), *The Midnight Special* (RCA Victor, 1964, from 1940 masters) and *The Library of Congress Recordings* (Elektra, 1966).

The Leadbelly literature began with Lomax's *Negro Folk Songs as Sung by Lead Belly* (1936) and includes further song collections, a guitar tutor and a partly fictional biography. There was also a film biography, Gordon Parks' *Leadbelly* (1976); McGhee and Terry can be heard on the soundtrack, while the vocal role of Leadbelly was taken by the West Coast singer-guitarist Hi Tide Harris.

The songs and memory of Leadbelly have been nurtured in the United States by Seeger – whose version of 'Goodnight Irene' with the **Weavers** was a 1948 hit – and many others of the East Coast folk establishment, whence they reached **Bob Dylan**, whose early work was touched by them. In Britain his songs were championed by **Lonnie Donegan**, who had a Top Ten hit, his first, with 'Rock Island Line' in 1956 and followed it with more selections from the Leadbelly songbook. Through Donegan and other skiffle artists the Leadbelly legacy was passed to many musicians who later became prominent in folk music and R&B, among them two of the founding fathers of British blues, harmonica-player Cyril Davies and **Alexis Korner**. The most unusual 'cover' of a Leadbelly song was a hard-rock version of 'Black Betty' which was a big hit for Ram Jam in 1977 on Epic.

LED ZEPPELIN
John Bonham, b. 31 May 1948, Redditch, Worcestershire, England, d. 25 September 1980, Windsor, Berk-

shire; John Paul Jones, b. John Baldwin, 3 June 1946, Sidcup, Kent; Jimmy Page, b. 9 January 1944, Heston, London; Robert Plant, b. 20 August 1948, West Bromwich

The most successful – and the archetypal – rock quartet of the seventies, Led Zeppelin grew out of the British blues scene and inspired later generations of heavy metal groups (through Page's grandiloquent guitar-playing and Plant's leather-lung vocals) and progressive rock bands (through the obscure yet resonant mysticism of many of their songs).

Formed in 1968, the band was initially conceived by former **Yardbirds** guitarist Page and road manager Peter Grant as a successor to that group. Bass-player Jones was a youthful veteran of studio arrangements for such artists as **Alma Cogan** and the **Rolling Stones**, while Plant and drummer Bonham were unknown performers from a defunct Birmingham group, Band of Joy. Plant had cut unsuccessful singles for Columbia in 1967.

Initially billed as the New Yardbirds, the group took the name Led Zeppelin from a catchphrase of **The Who**'s Keith Moon. Signed to Atlantic, they recorded an eponymous début album which included such items from their live act as **Otis Rush**'s 'Can't Quit You' and **Willie Dixon**'s 'You Shook Me'. *Led Zeppelin II* (1969) included 'Whole Lotta Love', which featured Plant's full repertoire of gasps, grunts and groans. The track was a massive hit in America but in Britain the group decided it was inappropriate to release singles and the hit version on that side of the Atlantic was made by **Alexis Korner**'s CCS (RAK, 1970). The song was later covered by both **Tina Turner** and the London Symphony Orchestra, while in 1987 a plagiarism suit brought by Willie Dixon over similarities between his 'You Need Love' and 'Whole Lotta Love' was settled out of court.

The third album (*Led Zeppelin III*) was mostly prepared in a remote Welsh cottage and showed a broadening of sound (on the acoustically based 'That's the Way' and 'Tangerine') and theme – in 'Immigrant Song' Plant wrote of the Viking invasions of England. Like its predecessors, it topped the charts.

The title of the following record was made up of four mystic symbols, reflecting Page's interest in the mysticism of Aleister Crowley. Known variously as *Led Zeppelin IV, Untitled* or *Four Symbols*, the album included 'Stairway to Heaven', the group's perennial concert finale. Former **Fairport Convention** member Sandy Denny also appeared on the album, singing on the folk-tinged 'Battle of Evermore'. *Houses of the Holy* (1973) included the rollicking 'D'yer Maker' and the portentous 'No Quarter'. Next, Page was commissioned by American director Kenneth Anger to score his biker film *Scorpio Rising*, only to be later dismissed

when Anger claimed Page's attitude was 'contradictory' to the teachings of Crowley.

During 1974–5 Led Zeppelin set up their own label, Swan Song, signing **Bad Company** and the **Pretty Things**. The double-album *Physical Graffiti* (1975) became the group's biggest-selling recording and contained 'Kashmir', Page's Indian-influenced *tour de force*. Plant's injuries in a car crash postponed recording of *Presence* (1976), notable chiefly for its sleeve photographs of a mysterious obelisk in everyday settings. It also marked a return to the basic hard rock of the group's début album. In the same year, a concert film of the 1973 world tour, *The Song Remains the Same*, was released to a lukewarm critical response.

Led Zeppelin issued only one further studio album. Work on *In Through the Out Door* (1979) was held up when Plant withdrew from the sessions after the death of his son. When the record emerged, it included a diversity of material mostly masterminded by Jones and a further twist in the graphic-design saga as the album was issued with six different sleeves.

A European tour followed in 1980 but during rehearsals for a series of American concerts Bonham was found dead from alcohol poisoning. The remaining members decided to disband and the final Led Zeppelin release was *Coda* (1982), a collection of unreleased tracks spanning the whole of the band's career.

Jones retired from live performance, appearing occasionally as a producer (with the Mission) or string arranger, most notably on **R.E.M.**'s *Automatic for the People* (1992). In 1994 he performed and recorded with avant-garde diva Diamanda Galas (*The Sporting Life*). Plant and Page pursued busy recording careers during the eighties. Plant issued three solo albums, *Pictures at Eleven* (Swan Song, 1982), *The Principle of Moments* (Esparanza, 1983) and *Shaken and Stirred* (1985). 'Big Log' was a hit in Britain and America in 1983. He dallied with a side project, the Honeydrippers, which harked back to his days as an R&B singer and featured **Jeff Beck**, **Nile Rodgers** and, in a cameo role, Page. The Honeydrippers recorded a mini album *Volume 1*, and had American hits with revivals of Phil Philips' 1959 hit 'Sea of Love' (Esparanza, 1984) and 'Rockin' at Midnight' (1985), originally recorded by **Roy Brown** in 1948 and **Elvis Presley** in 1954.

Page wrote and recorded the score for *Death Wish II* (1982) and toured with a new heavy-rock quartet the Firm. Including ex-**Free** and Bad Company singer Paul Rodgers, Tony Franklin (bass) and Chris Slade (drums), the group had an American hit in 1986 with 'All the King's Horses' and released two albums.

In 1988 well-received solo albums were released by

both Page (*Outrider*, Geffen) and Plant (*Now and Zen*). Page subsequently toured with John Bonham's son, Jason, on drums while Plant toured with the young band featured on *Now and Zen*. The same line-up played on *Manic Nirvana* (1990), which showed Plant integrating their songwriting talents with his, but during the sessions for the next album Plant broke the band up, recruiting new musicians to complete *Fate of Nations* (1993). Despite its prolonged gestation, the album which emerged was hailed as his best solo work yet. The album's guest artists included **Richard Thompson**, Maire Brennan of Clannad and Nigel Kennedy.

Page, meanwhile, had concentrated on remastering the Led Zeppelin back catalogue for CD, resulting in an album *Remasters*, and a 4-CD box set, *Led Zeppelin*, in 1991, with a follow-up, *Remasters II*, in 1993. This led to speculation that a Zeppelin reunion might be imminent, but in 1993 Page teamed up with ex-**Whitesnake/Deep Purple** vocalist David Coverdale to form Coverdale Page, releasing an eponymous album which revived the classic Zeppelin sound.

Since the 1980 split, Led Zeppelin have re-formed for two concerts, Live Aid in 1985, with **Phil Collins** on drums, and the Atlantic Records' fortieth anniversary concert in New York when the drummer was Jason Bonham. He had formed his own group, Bonham, and recorded *The Disregard of Timekeeping* (WTG, 1989). By the early nineties the continuing success of Plant's solo work and the arrival of Coverdale Page meant that a Zeppelin reunion was unlikely. However, the enormous success of the 10-CD set *The Complete Studio Recordings* (1993) demonstrated the huge and ongoing appeal of the group and in 1994 Page and Plant reunited for *No Quarter* (Atlantic), which entered the US charts at No. 4. Almost as successful was the video of the MTV set that led to the album *Unleaded*. It was swiftly followed by *Encomium* (1995), which was voted both best and worst tribute album in a *Rolling Stone* readers poll, on which the likes of **Hootie and the Blowfish**, **Duran Duran** and **Henry Rollins** paid their dues to Led Zeppelin. In 1997 all the group's albums were reissued in a remastered form and the two-CD set *The BBC Sessions* was released. In 1998 Page and Plant recorded the surprisingly innovative *Walking into Clarksdale* to widespread critical approval. In 2000, the same year that Atlantic issued a further greatest hits, *Latter Days*, a sequel to the previous *Early Days*, Page teamed up with the **Black Crowes** for *Jimmy Page and the Black Crowes Live at the Greek*, which was made available online through Musicmaker.com. The set introduced 'What Is and What Never Should Be', one of the first hit singles created online.

ALBERT LEE
b. *21 December 1943, Leominster, Herefordshire, England*

A versatile British rock guitarist, Lee became one of the most respected country-rock instrumentalists in America from the late seventies on, playing with **Emmylou Harris** and the **Crickets**, among others.

He first came to prominence as lead guitarist with Chris Farlowe and the Thunderbirds, a leading R&B act on the London club circuit. Lee played a memorable solo on a version of **T-Bone Walker**'s 'Stormy Monday Blues' (Sue, 1965), originally released as by Little Joe Cook in an attempt to present Farlowe's voice as that of a black American. Leaving Farlowe in 1967, Lee played on sessions for **Joe Cocker** and others before joining Country Fever and playing the British country-and-western club circuit.

Lee next linked up with songwriter/producer Tony Colton and Ray Smith in 1969. With Chas Hodges (later of **Chas and Dave**), the group recorded as Poet and the One Man Band for Verve in 1969 before signing to Island. Now called Head, Hands and Feet, they contrived a skilful blend of country and rock, recording an eponymous album (1971) and *Tracks* (1972), which were released in America on Capitol. After *Old Soldiers Never Die* (Atlantic, 1973) had solidified Lee's reputation as one of the most accomplished contemporary guitarists, the group split.

He joined the revived Crickets, touring and playing on the Mercury albums *Remnants* (1973) and *Long Way from Lubbock* (1974). After briefly rejoining Farlowe, Lee moved to America where he became a key member of Emmylou Harris's Hot Band, touring with her in 1976–8 and playing on her later albums. Lee was also much in demand as a session player on guitar and mandolin, in both Britain and America. Among those whom he accompanied from the late seventies onwards were **Eric Clapton**, **Jackson Browne**, Herbie Mann, Juice Newton, Don Everly of the **Everly Brothers**, Marc Benno, **Dave Edmunds**, **Creedence Clearwater Revival**'s John Fogerty, **Jerry Lee Lewis** and Carlene Carter. He was instrumental in putting the reunited Everly Brothers band together in the mid-eighties, and continued to play with the duo alongside his other session/sideman work during the nineties.

Harris's producer Brian Ahern supervised Lee's first solo album, *Hidin'* (A&M, 1979). He later recorded an eponymous solo album for Polydor (1982) and *Speechless* (MCA, 1986). In 1994 he released an in-concert set recorded at the 1992 Montreux Jazz Festival with British quartet Hogan's Heroes, which included songs by **John Hiatt**, **Richard Thompson** and **Jimmy Webb**.

BRENDA LEE
b. *Brenda Mae Tarpley, 11 December 1944, Lithonia, Georgia, USA*

Like **Conway Twitty** and **Jerry Lee Lewis**, Lee returned successfully to her country roots to rebuild her career after, like that of so many rock'n'rollers, it collapsed in the wake of **The Beatles**. Nonetheless, despite her considerable later success in the country charts, it is for her records of the fifties and early sixties that she is best remembered. Sometimes raucous ('Let's Jump the Broomstick', Decca, 1958; 'Rockin' Around the Christmas Tree'*), sometimes knowing ('Sweet Nothin's'*, 1960), more often crying ballads full of melodramatic self-pity ('I'm Sorry'*, 1960; 'All Alone Am I'*, 1962; and 'Losing You'* 1963), all featured her remarkably pliant, husky voice, which, highlighted by **Owen Bradley**'s production, gave a sense of depth to the simple emotions she caressed.

A regular broadcaster on country shows in the Atlanta region since the age of seven, Lee was signed to Decca at the age of eleven by **Red Foley**'s manager Dub Albritton in 1956. One of her first recordings was the **Johnny Marks** composition 'Rockin' Around the Christmas Tree' which, with Bobby Helms' 'Jingle Bell Rock' (Decca, 1957), was one of the few successful Christmas novelty records of the rock'n'roll years. 'Christmas Tree' was a huge hit when finally released in 1960, by which time Bradley was recording Lee in a more dramatic and less exuberant style. After the relative failure of 'Dynamite' (1957) and 'Let's Jump the Broomstick', she modified her approach for 'Sweet Nothin's' which, as one critic put it, Lee 'sang with an intriguing mixture of childish innocence and mature innuendo'.

The even greater success of 'I'm Sorry' – which Lee sang in a manner similar to the crying style of **Patsy Cline** (who was also produced by Bradley), and like 'Sweet Nothin's' was written by former rockabilly singer Ronnie Self – confirmed this change of direction. A string of Top Ten hits followed. These included 'I Just Want to Be Wanted' (1960), 'Emotions', 'You Can Depend on Me', 'Dum Dum' (co-written by **Jackie DeShannon**) and 'Fool No. 1' (all 1961), and 'Break It to Me Gently' and 'Everybody Loves Me but You' (1962). Hugely popular in Europe, she had a pair of international million-sellers with English-language adaptations of foreign songs, the Greek 'All Alone Am I' (1962) and the French 'Losing You' (1963), but although her hits continued into the mid-sixties ('Coming on Strong' in 1966 was the last), her records were increasingly formula-ridden and, with the emergence of The Beatles, sounded distinctly old-fashioned.

After briefly attempting a career in cabaret, singing middle-of-the-road material, Lee returned to her country roots at the end of the sixties. Her first country success was 'If This Is Our Last Time' (1971) and she had further hits with **Kris Kristofferson**'s 'Nobody Wins' (1973), 'Big Four Poster Bed' (1974), 'He's My Rock' (1975), 'The Cowgirl and the Dandy' (1980) and an exuberant duet with **George Jones** on **Ray Charles**' 'Hallelujah I Love You So' (1984).

Lee's status as a *grande dame* of country was confirmed when she joined **Loretta Lynn** and **Kitty Wells** as guests on **k.d. lang**'s *Shadowlands* album in 1988. In the nineties Lee continued to tour. Later records include *Brenda Lee* (Warner, 1990), *Brenda Lee Christmas* (1991) and *Coming on Strong* (1995). She is a director of the Country Music Association.

BYRON LEE
b. *Ken Lazarus, Jamaica*

A leading bandleader, producer and label-owner in Jamaican music for over twenty years, Byron Lee offered a diluted, middle-of-the-road version of reggae which contrasted with the 'roots' approach of **Bob Marley** and others.

Originally a bass-player, Lee formed the Dragonaires, who recorded covers of American R&B hits which were released in Jamaica on future prime minister Edward Seaga's Federal label and in Britain in the late fifties on Siggy Jackson's Melodisc label. With the arrival of the ska style, the Dragonaires adapted to the trend, recording a softer folk-ska than the **Skatalites**, on calypso material like 'Yellow Bird' and 'Island in the Sun'.

In 1961 Lee moved into concert promotion, organizing tours of Jamaica on which the singers were backed by his band. He also promoted visits by such American artists as **Chuck Berry**, **Sam Cooke**, the **Drifters** and **Barbara Lynn**. When Seaga, now a government minister, organized a package to represent Jamaica at the 1964 World's Fair in New York, he sent Lee with **Jimmy Cliff** and Millie, to the chagrin of the more roots-based reggae artists. As a result of his American appearance, Lee and the Dragonaires recorded *Jump Up* (1965) for Atlantic.

Lee moved into record production in the mid-sixties by acquiring the West Indian (later Dynamic Sounds) studios. His most successful productions of this period were those of **Toots and the Maytals**. Dynamic Sounds later became the favourite Jamaican studio for visiting white artists like **Paul Simon** and **Joe Cocker**. In the seventies Lee expanded into licensing foreign recordings, notably those of PolyGram, Warners and Columbia.

He continued to record Dragonaires albums made up of instrumental versions of rock, calypso and reggae hits. These included *Disco Reggae* (Mercury, 1975), *Jamaica's Golden Hits* (State, 1979) and *The Best of Carnival* (Creole, 1984).

PEGGY LEE

b. Norma Egstrom, 26 May 1920, Jamestown, North
Dakota, USA

As a blues-influenced jazz singer, Lee's restrained yet
soulful, subdued singing style has been compared to
Billie Holiday. Her long singing career virtually
encompassed the history of American popular music
between 1940 and 1970. In addition, she acted in films
and revealed herself to be an accomplished songwriter.

Born on a farm, Lee sang with the Four of Us in
small clubs in the Mid-west and California, before
being discovered by **Benny Goodman** in Chicago in
1941 and joining his band as replacement for Helen
Forrest. Her first recordings with Goodman, including **Irving Berlin**'s 'How Deep Is the Ocean' (Columbia, 1941), were merely competent, but her 1942
recording of 'Why Don't You Do Right'* (1942)
revealed an individual style. Written by Lee herself, it
was based on a blues song by Lil Green. In 1943, after
her marriage to Goodman's guitarist David Barbour,
she left the band and retired to raise a family, only
occasionally recording. Among her first solo hits were
'Mañana'* (Capitol, 1948), written with Barbour, 'Bali
Ha'i' (1949) and 'Lover'* (1952), her spectacular
mambo version of **Lorenz Hart** and **Richard
Rodgers**' waltz, with an orchestral backing supplied
by **Gordon Jenkins**.

In the early fifties Lee formed a songwriting partnership with the Hollywood composer **Victor Young**,
which produced 'Where Can I Go Without You',
among other songs. In 1955 she demonstrated her versatility when she was nominated for an Oscar for her
performance as the fading singer in Peter Kelly's Blues
and lent her voice to Walt Disney for his first full-
length animated cartoon, The Lady and the Tramp, in
which she sang her own compositions 'He's a Tramp'
and 'The Siamese Cat Song'. On record, her material
ranged from show tunes like 'Mr Wonderful' and
'Joey, Joey, Joey' (Decca, 1956), to big band blues such
as 'Alright, Okay You Win' (Capitol, 1959), based on
Joe Williams and **Count Basie**'s interpretation. She
also sang rhythm and blues, including a fine version
of **Little Willie John**'s 'Fever'* (1958) and **Ray
Charles**' 'Hallelujah I Love Him So' (1959), and
recorded immaculate collections of popular ballads,
such as The Man I Love (1958), which included her
celebrated rendition of **Jerome Kern**'s 'The Folks
Who Live on the Hill' and her album with **George
Shearing**, Beauty and the Beat (1959).

Lee's openness to so many forms of music – she
even recorded an album of folk songs, Sea Shells (1956)
– led her to become one of the first mainstream performers to record material by **The Beatles** and other
contemporary songwriters. In 1969 she returned to the

Top Twenty with her highly formal version of **Leiber
and Stoller**'s 'Is That All There Is?', arranged by **Randy
Newman**. It was taken from an album of the duo's
songs, Mirrors (A&M). Throughout the seventies and
eighties her career was affected by serious illness but
she toured intermittently and appeared in Peg (1983),
an unsuccessful Broadway musical based on her life. In
1990 she released The Peggy Lee Songbook: There'll Be
Another Spring (Musicmasters), the first in a series of
reinterpretations of songs associated with her.

LEFTFIELD

Paul Daley; Neil Barnes

A leading group in the UK progressive house movement of the early to mid-nineties, and subsequently a
doyen of dub house cool, Leftfield also achieved
mainstream recognition with the Mercury Music
Prize-nominated Leftism album in 1995.

Daley and Barnes both came from a percussion/
drumming background. Daley had worked with a
variety of musicians in London's acid jazz scene in the
mid-eighties, including A Man Called Adam. Barnes
had already released one track under the name of
Leftfield, 'Not Forgotten', when he joined forces with
Daley to turn Leftfield into a duo at the end of the
eighties.

'More Than I Know' followed on the Outer
Rhythm label before in 1992 the pair formed their
own label, Hard Hands, and released the seminal singles 'Release the Pressure' and 'Song of Life', sparse
early classics of the genre that would become known
as progressive house. Their label also scored a coup
with the release of Dee Patten's proto-jungle classic
'Who's the Badman?' the same year.

'Song of Life' was a minor UK pop hit as well as a
huge club favourite, but real chart success followed in
1993, through a collaboration with former **Sex Pistols**
and Public Image Limited vocalist John Lydon. 'Open
Up' married Leftfield's bottom-heavy, dub-influenced
house rhythms with Lydon's familiar untutored
screech to powerful effect. The group's début album,
Leftism, emerged in early 1995. A critical and commercial success, it won the band a Mercury Music Prize
nomination in the UK. As well as featuring Lydon,
the album saw the band collaborating with another
singer, Curve vocalist Toni Haliday, on 'Original'. In
common with **Underworld**, their atmospheric instrumental sound leant itself well to film and television.
The downtempo track 'Melt' was used on television,
and the group also provided the soundtrack for the
film Shallow Grave.

The band's slowness in producing a follow-up led
to it becoming a subject of ridicule in the music press.
1999 finally saw fresh signs of life from the group,
with the contribution of the track 'Swords' to another

film, Doug Liman's *Go*. This was followed towards the end of 1999 by 'Afrika Shox', a collaboration with hip-hop legend **Afrika Bambaataa**. The track was a mesmeric marriage of Afrika's apocalyptic, vocodered vocals, crushingly heavy hip-hop rhythms and booming sub-bass. *Rhythm and Stealth* (1999) revealed Daley and Barnes' continued appetite for finding new ways of reworking their interest in dub reggae, hard house and hip-hop rhythms. In addition to 'Afrika Shox', the album's stand-out moments were 'Phat Planet', which gained a wider audience through its use in a TV commercial for Guinness, and 'El Cid', a hypnotic downtempo instrumental.

MICHEL LEGRAND
b. 24 February 1932, Paris, France

Legrand is a prolific film composer and songwriter, first in France and then Hollywood, and best known for his melodic scores. He is also an accomplished jazz pianist.

The son of Raymond Legrand, who wrote numerous scores for French films of the thirties and forties, Michel entered the Conservatoire National de Musique at the age of twelve. After graduation, he turned increasingly to popular music and from the early fifties onwards worked as an accompanist in live performance and on record, to such artists as **Maurice Chevalier**, **Jacques Brel** and Juliette Greco, and as a conductor and songwriter. One of his songs from this period, with an English lyric by **Johnny Mercer** and a new title, 'Once Upon a Summertime', was later recorded by numerous mainstream artists, including **Tony Bennett**, **Barbra Streisand** and **Andy Williams**.

In 1955 he wrote his first film score and in 1958 had a European success with the album *I Love Paris*, a collection of his own arrangements of popular French songs. International success came with his music for *Les Parapluies de Cherbourg* (1964) and *Les Demoiselles de Rochefort* (1967), both of which were entirely sung. Songs from both were given English lyrics by Norman Gimbel ('I Will Wait for You [If It Takes Forever]') and Alan and Marilyn Bergman, who subsequently became Legrand's regular songwriting partners ('You Must Believe in Spring'). That led to a move to Hollywood where he had immediate success with *The Thomas Crown Affair* (1968), one of the first films to build a sequence around a song specially commissioned for it. That song was 'The Windmills of Your Mind', sung by Noel, son of Rex, Harrison on the soundtrack and subsequently a hit for **Dusty Springfield** (1969).

Other films scored by Legrand include *The Summer of '42* (1971), for which he won an Oscar, *The Go-Between* (1971), *Lady Sings the Blues* (1971), in which **Diana Ross** played **Billie Holiday**, *Breezy* (1974) and

The Other Side of Midnight (1977). Songs of note from this period include 'Hands of Time' (1972), recorded by **Johnny Mathis** and **Sarah Vaughan**, among others; 'Happy' (1972), written with and recorded by **Smokey Robinson**; 'Summer Knows' (1971), recorded by Andy Williams; and 'What Are You Doing the Rest of Your Life' (1969), recorded by **Shirley Bassey**.

His jazz recordings included *After the Rain* (Pablo, 1983) and *Legrand Jazz* (Philips, 1986). In 1991 he scored *Dingo* in collaboration with **Miles Davis**, who also appeared in the film.

FRANZ LEHÁR
b. 30 April 1870, Komaron, Hungary, d. 24 October 1948, Bad Ischl, Switzerland

The composer of the hugely successful *The Merry Widow*, Lehár, with **Sigmund Romberg** and **Rudolf Friml**, had a decisive influence on the shaping of the stage musical in the first decades of the twentieth century.

The son of a military bandmaster, Lehár studied violin at the Prague Conservatory and became a bandmaster himself at the age of twenty, before turning to composition. After his first opera *Kukuschka* was produced in Leipzig in 1896, he moved to Vienna. There, working in the tradition established by the Strauss family, he brought a formal elegance to the operetta. His most popular success was *The Merry Widow*, the English libretto of which was written by (an uncredited) Basil Hood and the lyrics by Adrián Ross. Composed in 1905, and based on an earlier Viennese operetta, *Die Lustige Witwe*, it was an immediate hit throughout Europe, and was performed in some 450 theatres before being taken to London by impresario George Edwardes in 1907. Edwardes saw in the show a new kind of musical theatre to replace the ailing parades of 'Gaiety Girls' popularized by **Lionel Monckton** and others, and the declining interest in French light opera.

The Merry Widow was the hit of the 1907 season in London (where Lehár himself conducted the orchestra on its opening night) and then Broadway, where it revived the appeal of the European operetta. Numerous pastiches of the show's standout song, 'The Merry Widow Waltz' (as 'I Love You So' is better known), were published during the course of its lengthy runs in London and on Broadway and a parody of the show, *The Merry Widow Burlesque*, was mounted in 1908. Another mark of the show's success was the fashion for 'Merry Widow' hats and gowns it inspired. Often revived on stage, the operetta was filmed three times, in 1925, 1934 (with **Maurice Chevalier** and **Jeanette MacDonald** as the lovers) and 1952.

Few of Lehár's other operettas, which include *The*

Count of Luxembourg (1909), Eva (1911), Friedericke (1928) and Guidetta (1935), were popular in either Britain or America. The one exception was The Land of Smiles (1929), which included the song 'Yours Is My Heart Alone' ('Dein Ist Mein Ganzes Herz'), popularized by **Richard Tauber**, who later starred in Guidetta with great success in Europe. Tauber also recorded many of Lehár's operettas for Parlophone in the late twenties.

TOM LEHRER

b. Thomas Andrew Lehrer, 9 April, 1928, New York, USA

A Harvard professor of mathematics, Lehrer was unusual among popular recording artists of the fifties. His blackly funny and satirical songs were perfect expressions of 'sick' humour, artistic relations of the cartoons of Charles Addams or the stand-up comedy of Lenny Bruce, while his clipped, cheerful delivery and neat piano punctuation had enough of **Noël Coward** (or at least Bobby Troup) to reassure the musically conventional listener. Ironically, although little celebrated in the US, in the UK he was hugely influential, in tandem with calypso artists, as a topical songwriter. His heirs include both That Was the Week That Was and Monty Python.

After his discharge from military service, Lehrer, who had supported himself through college by singing his oddly satirical songs, found himself in demand as a cabaret act. After a couple of live performances were recorded, Lehrer, in the manner of folk groups of the time, had the idea of issuing a record – a 10-inch album – which he could then sell at his gigs. Thus was born Songs by Tom Lehrer (1957) on which he tested the audience with songs with such titles as 'The Masochism Tango', 'The Elements' and 'Poisoning Pigeons in the Park' – songs that became favourites among fifties intellectuals. In 1958 he performed in London and on the back of that success Decca bought the rights to Songs and issued it with great success; it even reached the UK Top Ten. That was followed by More of Tom Lehrer (1959), which included 'Be Prepared' ('the boy scouts' marching song'), 'The Old Dope Peddler' and more of that ilk. Subsequently the two albums were reissued as a single CD, Tom Lehrer in Concert (1994).

Although Lehrer went out of fashion quickly, by the mid-sixties he was rehabilitated, at least in Britain, and participated in satirical TV shows, writing new material in the same pungent style.

Britain had no parallel to Lehrer in his heyday. Audiences searching for an equivalent to his civilized wit, although with far less edge, turned to the stage and record recitals of comic songs by Michael Flanders and Donald Swann, the **George Martin**-produced At

the Drop of a Hat (HMV, 1959) and At the Drop of Another Hat (HMV, 1960); the sketches and character impressions of Peter Sellers (of the **Goons**), as on the enormously popular Songs for Swinging Sellers (Parlophone, 1959, also produced by Martin); or the nightclub naughtiness of singer/pianist Paddy Roberts. It was not until That Was the Week that the equivalent to Lehrer surfaced.

LEIBER AND STOLLER

Jerry Leiber, b. 25 April 1933, Baltimore, Maryland, USA; Mike Stoller, b. 13 March 1933, New York

Leiber and Stoller were among the most inventive and successful R&B and rock'n'roll songwriters and producers during the fifties and early sixties. Among those who recorded their work were **Elvis Presley**, the **Coasters** and the **Drifters**.

White boys fascinated by black music, they were introduced in Los Angeles in 1950 by Lester Sill of Modern Records. Their first recorded composition was 'Real Ugly Woman' by **Jimmy Witherspoon** (Modern, 1951) and their first R&B hit was 'Hard Times' by **Charles Brown** (Aladdin, 1952). Within two years more than twenty artists, including **Amos Milburn**, **Esther Phillips**, **Lucky Millinder** and Bullmoose Jackson, had cut Leiber and Stoller songs, but their first major success came in 1952 with **Big Mama Thornton** and 'Hound Dog' (Peacock) and Little Willie Littlefield's 'K.C. Lovin'' (Modern). Both were even bigger hits when revived by Presley (1956) and **Wilbert Harrison** (as 'Kansas City', 1959), respectively.

Leiber and Stoller set up the Spark label with Sill in 1954, signing the Robins, who became the Coasters when their mentors moved to New York as independent producers for Atlantic the following year. The duo's recordings with the Robins and Coasters saw a marked development in their writing and production techniques. For classic tracks like 'Riot in Cell Block No. 9' (1954), 'Smokey Joe's Cafe' (1955) and 'Searchin'' (1957), Leiber and Stoller wrote miniature dramas in which members of the group played different parts. As well as notching up eighteen hits for the group in seven years, the duo worked with such R&B artists as **Ruth Brown** ('Lucky Lips', 1957), **Joe Turner** ('The Chicken and the Hawk', 1955), **Lavern Baker** ('Saved', 1961) and the Drifters. In their work with the latter group, Leiber and Stoller successfully experimented with strings ('There Goes My Baby') and Latin rhythms ('Under the Boardwalk'). When the Drifters' lead singer, **Ben E. King**, went solo, Leiber and Stoller created the celebrated 'Spanish Harlem' and 'Stand by Me' (1961) for him.

Outside the Atlantic roster, the most important of the singers with whom they were associated was Presley, to whom they supplied 'Jailhouse Rock', 'King

Creole' and 'Baby I Don't Care'. Their other work was sometimes less impressive, primarily because Leiber and Stoller spread themselves across the whole pop spectrum from **Perry Como** ('Dancin'', RCA, 1957) to the teen pop group the Cheers ('Black Denim Trousers', Capitol, 1955) and the jazzy torch singer **Peggy Lee** ('I'm a Woman', Capitol, 1963).

During the early sixties Leiber and Stoller worked closely with the younger generation of writers and producers, basing themselves in New York's Brill Building and acting as mentors to tyro producer **Phil Spector**. In 1964 they set up the Red Bird and Blue Cat labels with **George Goldner** to exploit this talent. They released **Shadow Morton**'s classic **Shangri-La**'s material as well as records by the Dixie Cups and the Ad Libs ('The Boy from New York City', 1965). As well as this teenage pop material, Red Bird also recorded John Hammond Jnr, backed by Robbie Robertson and the nucleus of **The Band**, though the album was not released until 1968.

In the mid-sixties Leiber and Stoller dabbled in abortive stage and film musical projects, writing the impressive ballad 'Is That All There Is?' for Peggy Lee. They returned to the record industry in 1969 by purchasing **Syd Nathan**'s King/Starday group, whose catalogue included some of the earliest recordings of their own compositions. The attempt to repackage material and revitalize the company was not a success and in 1972 the duo returned to independent production, supervising recordings by British acts Stealer's Wheel ('Stuck in the Middle with You', 1973), **Procul Harum** (*Procol's Ninth*, Chrysalis, 1975) and **Elkie Brooks** ('Pearl's a Singer', 1976).

After producing Brooks' 1979 album *Live and Learn*, Leiber and Stoller concentrated on *Only in America*, a musical show containing thirty of their compositions. The play ran briefly in London in 1980 and a double-album of the duo's greatest recordings was released under the same title by Warners in 1980.

During the late eighties Leiber and Stoller were the subject of the film *Yakety Yak* and they scored the animated film *Hound Dog*. In the past decade they have been showered with awards from the Songwriters', Producers' and Rock'n'Roll Halls of Fame. They continued to work intermittently. Late productions included Tommy Hunt's *Biggest Man* (Kent, 1997) and **Gerry Rafferty**'s *Clowns to the Left, Jokers to the Right* (Raven, 1997).

Leiber's son Jed is a keyboard player and songwriter who has worked in the nineties with **Jeff Beck**, **Peter Frampton** and others.

LEMONHEADS
Evan Dando, b. 4 March 1967, Boston, Massachusetts, USA; Ben Deily (replaced by John Strohm); Jesse Peretz

(replaced by Julianna Hatfield, replaced by Nic Dalton, replaced by Bill Gibson); Doug Trachten (replaced by David Ryan, b. 20 October 1964, Fort Worth, Texas, replaced by John Strohm)

An influential group, the Lemonheads were briefly touched by stardom in the early nineties with their blend of alternative rock and **Gram Parsons**-esque country. Subsequently, band leader Evan Dando descended into severe drug addiction and the band lost their chance to break through into the mainstream.

Dando formed the Lemonheads at the end of his high-school career in the mid-eighties with guitarist Deily and bassist Peretz, recruiting drummer Doug Trachten in 1987 after the release of an EP, *Laughing All the Way to the Cleaners*, on the band's own Huh-bag label. The Lemonheads signed to Taang! on the strength of the EP, recording two albums, *Hate Your Friends* (1987) and *Creator* (1988), that veered towards the hardcore sound of Hüsker Dü. The band began to expand their fanbase with *Lick* (1989), scoring an underground hit with a cover of **Suzanne Vega**'s 'Luka', before rivalry between Dando and Deily saw them break up temporarily.

Now a three-piece, and with a new drummer, David Ryan, the Lemonheads signed to Atlantic Records, releasing the more melodic *Lovey* (1990). Their breakthrough came with *It's a Shame about Ray* (1992), which featured a cover of **Simon and Garfunkel**'s 'Mrs. Robinson' that became a big hit in the US. *Come on Feel the Lemonheads* (1993) was intended to be the album that brought the trio mainstream success, but Dando fell into heavy drug use and the band began to fall apart.

By the time of *Car Button Cloth* (1996), although Dando had cleaned up his act, the Lemonheads, now featuring bassist Gibson, guitarist Strohm and drummer 'Murph' (formerly of **Dinosaur Jr.**), were all but forgotten. After the release of a contract-fulfilling greatest hits album in 1998 they were dropped by Atlantic.

JOHN LENNON
b. John Winston Lennon, 9 October 1940, Liverpool, England, d. 8 December 1980, New York, USA

After the break-up of **The Beatles**, Lennon's solo work stood in marked contrast to that of **Paul McCartney**. Lennon's output was more controversial, distinctly erratic and less prolific, with six albums released in the decade prior to his death. Of these only *Imagine* (1971) was unquestionably a masterpiece, but while the majority of his songs showed little expansion of the passion and aggression that he had brought to The Beatles, the best of them showed a new maturity of approach.

Though The Beatles were not officially dissolved until 1970, Lennon's solo recordings had begun two years earlier when he and **Yoko Ono** made the avant-garde *Unfinished Music No. 1 – Two Virgins* with its censored sleeve photograph and *No. 2 – Life with the Lions*. In 1969 he further distanced himself from the other Beatles by forming a band to play at a Canadian rock'n'roll revival concert. Named the Plastic Ono Band, it included **Eric Clapton**, Klaus Voorman (bass) and drummer Alan White. Recorded and released as *Live Peace in Toronto* (Apple, 1969), the performance included new Lennon compositions (and 1969 hit singles), the anthemic 'Give Peace a Chance' and 'Cold Turkey', as well as rock standards like **Carl Perkins**' 'Blue Suede Shoes' and **Larry Williams**' 'Dizzy Miss Lizzie'.

Lennon's first full declaration of independence, however, was the stark *John Lennon/Plastic Ono Band* (1970). Often nakedly autobiographical, the album was made after he and Ono had followed a course of 'primal scream' therapy with Dr Arthur Janov. Produced by **Phil Spector** with a pared-down bass/guitar/drums instrumentation, the record included the bitter attack on the star and class system 'Working Class Hero', and 'Mother', a harrowing cry of pain.

That album was a necessary prelude to *Imagine* (1971), the most highly regarded set of the solo years. The title song and Lennon's reading of it conveyed a subtle utopian political vision which both contrasted with and matched the raucous agit-prop of 'Power to the People' (1971) and the seasonal 'Happy Xmas (War Is Over)' which was a hit in 1972, 1980 and 1981. 'Imagine' quickly became a standard, and was covered by numerous artists from **Joan Baez** to **James Last**, **Diana Ross** and **Nana Mouskouri**. Other tracks on the album included the intimate ballad 'Jealous Guy' (a hit for **Roxy Music** in 1981) and the sarcastic 'How Do You Sleep', widely taken to be as a thinly veiled attack on McCartney. Among the backing musicians on *Imagine* were **George Harrison** and pianist Nicky Hopkins.

Late in 1971 Ono and Lennon moved to New York. His next album was the less successful, heavily politicized *Some Time in New York City*, recorded with Elephant's Memory, led by saxophonist Stan Bronstein. The themes of Lennon's songs ranged from Ireland ('Sunday Bloody Sunday') to prison riots ('Attica State') and feminism ('Woman Is the Nigger of the World'). The combination of radical opinions and robust rock'n'roll backings made Lennon enemies among both critics and the US government, which attempted to deport him later in the seventies.

With its gentle title song, *Mind Games* (1973) marked a return to more conventional themes but its sales were outstripped by *Walls and Bridges* (1974), which included two American hits, 'Whatever Gets You through the Night' and 'Number Nine Dream'; the bluesy 'Nobody Knows You When You're Down and Out' was among the other tracks. A guest appearance at an **Elton John** concert in 1974 was Lennon's final live performance. *Rock'n'Roll*, an album of affectionate covers of fifties hits by **Fats Domino**, **Little Richard**, **Buddy Holly**, **Gene Vincent** and others, was released in 1975. *Menlove Avenue* (1986) contained previously unreleased tracks from this period.

A greatest hits collection, *Shaved Fish* (1975), was Lennon's last album to be released until shortly before his murder. After the birth of his son Sean in 1975 he retired from music, emerging only to co-write 'Fame' (1975) with **David Bowie**, the latter's first American No. 1. He returned to the studio with Ono in 1980 to make *Double Fantasy* (Geffen), which included 'Starting Over'. Following Lennon's shooting by Mark Chapman, 'Starting Over' went to No. 1 in both Britain and America and 'Woman' was also a hit. Further hits followed in the next few years, and Ono released six 1980 tracks by Lennon on *Milk and Honey* (1984). *Live in New York City* (a 1986 release of a 1972 concert recording) and *Menlove Avenue* (1986) were albums of previously unreleased material.

The fiftieth anniversary of his birth was commemorated in 1990 by a number of live events, including a concert at Liverpool's Pier Head. With **Dave Edmunds** as musical director, those taking part included **Ringo Starr**, **B. B. King**, **Wet Wet Wet** and **Hall and Oates**. In 1991 an all-star Peace Choir recorded 'Give Peace a Chance' with new lyrics by Lennon's younger son, Sean Ono Lennon.

Lennon's elder son Julian (*b. 8 April 1963, Liverpool*) began his own recording with *Valotte* (Virgin, 1984) and the hit 'Too Late for Goodbyes'. Subsequent albums included *Mr Jordan* (1989) and *Help Yourself* (Atlantic, 1991).

J. B. LENOIR
b. 5 March 1929, Monticello, Mississippi, USA,
d. 29 April 1967, Urbana, Illinois

Gifted with a high, clear voice of great beauty and poignancy, J. B. Lenoir carried into the Chicago blues of the fifties and sixties the expressive eloquence and fluent, relaxed guitar-playing of **Big Bill Broonzy**. Like Broonzy he wrote a number of explicit and bitter blues about racial oppression.

Lenoir went to Chicago in 1949 and in the following year began playing in clubs. Signing with Chess he recorded a 'Korea Blues' (1951), a theme he returned to in 1954 with 'I'm in Korea' (Parrot). He also made a topical hard-times blues, 'Eisenhower Blues' (Parrot, 1954), but in the same year and for the same label he was more successful with 'Mama Talk to Your Daughter', variants of which he often later recorded.

He also recorded for Job (1952–3) and Checker (1956–8), and later for USA, on many occasions accompanied by pianist Sunnyland Slim.

Lenoir came to international notice in 1965 when he toured Europe with the American Folk Blues Festival and recorded a powerful solo album, *Alabama Blues* (Columbia). He visited Europe again the following year, when an album of 'protest blues' and narratives, *J. B. Lenoir* (Polydor), was produced by **John Mayall**. Lenoir's music was also used as an acid commentary to the images in John Jeremy's documentary *Blues Like Showers of Rain* (1970).

LOTTE LENYA
b. Karoline Blamauer, 18 October 1898, Vienna, Austria, d. 27 November 1981, New York

For half a century Lenya was closely identified with the songs of Bertolt Brecht and her husband **Kurt Weill**. A singing actress rather than a singer, Lenya's cold, mannered performances capture the spirit of Weill's and Brecht's attempts to create in *Die Dreigroschenoper* (*The Threepenny Opera*, 1928) a socially relevant musical theatre rather than a musical or opera.

The daughter of a coachman and laundress, Lenya took to the stage at an early age, appearing in local circuses as a tightrope walker at the age of six. Briefly a member of the Zurich ballet company, she went to Berlin to continue her dramatic studies in 1920 and in 1924 met Weill. They married in 1926 and a year later she sang 'Alabama Song' (later revived by the **Doors**) in Brecht and Weill's *Mahagonny Songspiel*. Though she appeared in *The Threepenny Opera* as Jenny she did not sing 'Pirate Jenny', the song most identified with her, until the 1931 film version, directed by Pabst.

When the Nazis came to power Weill and Lenya fled to America where for most of the thirties and forties her career was eclipsed by that of her husband. In 1941 she made her Broadway début in *Candle in the Wind* and in 1945 appeared in Weill and **Ira Gershwin**'s uncharacteristic *The Firebrand of Florence*. Following Weill's death in 1950, Lenya established herself as the custodian of his works, always emphasizing the German period, in which she had a central role, at the expense of Weill's American work. In 1954 she had an enormous success in the Broadway revival of *The Threepenny Opera* in which she reprised her role of Jenny. She appeared in the original cast recording (MGM), supervised the 1958 German-language version (Columbia, considered by most to be the definitive recording), and throughout the fifties and sixties recorded several selections of songs by Weill, including *The Seven Deadly Sins* (Columbia, 1956), *Johnny Johnson* (MGM, 1957) and *Berlin Theatre Songs by Kurt Weill* (Columbia, 1955).

In the sixties she returned to acting, most memo-

rably as the villainess Rosa Kleb in the James Bond thriller *From Russia with Love* (1963), and in 1966 to Broadway in the hit musical *Cabaret*, for which John Kander's score echoed Weill's music. In the seventies she continued to give concerts of Weill's music.

LERNER AND LOEWE
Alan Jay Lerner, b. 31 August 1918, New York, USA, d. 14 June 1986, New York; Frederick Loewe, b. 10 June 1904, Berlin, Germany, d. 14 February 1988, Palm Springs, Florida

Following John F. Kennedy's assassination in 1963, his brief presidency was dubbed 'Camelot', after Lerner and Loewe's 1960 Broadway success which ended with the king, his life in ruins, telling a page to tell the story 'of the fleeting wisp of glory called Camelot'. The allusion, to a brief idyllic time now lost, was doubly fitting for it was also the recurring theme in Lerner and Loewe's work, which included *Brigadoon* (1947), *Paint Your Wagon* (1951), *My Fair Lady* (1956) – with *West Side Story* (1957) the most influential Broadway musical of the fifties – and the evocative film musical *Gigi* (1958).

The son of the Viennese tenor Edmund Loewe, Loewe was a piano soloist with the Berlin Symphony Orchestra at the age of thirteen. He studied composition with **Kurt Weill**'s teacher Ferrucio Busoni and wrote the European hit song 'Katrina' before in 1924 emigrating to America. There he was an unsuccessful concert pianist and drifted across America working at a variety of jobs (including cow puncher and prospector) before in 1935 forming a songwriting partnership with scriptwriter Earle Crooker. In the wake of their first hit ('A Waltz Was Born in Vienna', 1936), they wrote the unsuccessful Broadway musical *Great Lady* (1938), after which Loewe returned to working as a restaurant pianist until in 1942 he met another aspiring lyricist, Alan Jay Lerner.

From an affluent background, Lerner studied at the Juilliard School of Music and while at Harvard wrote songs for revues. On graduation in 1939 he became a radio scriptwriter before teaming up with Loewe for the unsuccessful *Life of the Party*. With *Brigadoon* (1947, filmed 1954), a fully integrated musical fantasy set in the Scottish highlands, the pair showed themselves to be the stylistic heirs of **Rodgers and Hammerstein**. The show included 'Almost Like Being in Love', a hit for **Frank Sinatra** and **Mildred Bailey**. After the failure of the unconventional *Love Life* (1948), written with Weill, Lerner returned to Loewe for the successful *Paint Your Wagon* (1951, filmed 1969 with additional songs by **André Previn** and Lerner). Replete with authentic incidents and the only Lerner and Loewe show set in America, it captured the robust days of the California Gold Rush and introduced the hit songs 'I Talk to the Trees' (which Clint Eastwood crooned in the film), 'Wand'rin' Star', a surprise million-seller (Paramount, 1970) for Lee Marvin and 'They Call the Wind Maria'.

The pair's greatest success came with *My Fair Lady* (1956, filmed 1964) based on George Bernard Shaw's *Pygmalion* (1913). Retaining much of Shaw's dialogue and writing many of the songs with an ear to Rex Harrison's limited vocal range, Lerner and Loewe produced a show in which the music and songs sprang from the characters. The original cast album, featuring Harrison, **Julie Andrews** and Stanley Holloway, sold over five million copies on Columbia. Nearly three decades later (Decca, 1987) the show was one of the first musicals to be recorded with opera stars (including **Kiri Te Kanawa** and Jose Carreras) singing the main roles. Among the numbers the show introduced were 'Wouldn't It Be Luverly', 'The Rain in Spain', 'I Could Have Danced All Night', 'Get Me to the Church on Time', the affecting 'I've Grown Accustomed to Her Face' and 'On the Street Where You Live', a hit for **Eddie Fisher**, **Vic Damone** (1956), **David Whitfield** (1958) and **Andy Williams** (1964).

Equally literate was Lerner and Loewe's next project, **Arthur Freed**'s penultimate screen musical production, *Gigi* (1958, adapted for Broadway in 1973). Based on a novella by Colette, the story of a tomboy (Leslie Caron, vocals by Betty Wand) transformed into a society beauty echoed the earlier musical and similarly gave its best songs to its elderly characters, notably **Maurice Chevalier** who alone sang 'Thank Heaven for Little Girls' and, with prompting from Hermione Gingold, 'I Remember It Well'. The pair's last Broadway success was the more sombre *Camelot* (1960), based on T. H. White's novel *The Once and Future King*, with Richard Burton and Julie Andrews, which introduced 'If Ever I Would Leave You'.

Following the dissolution of their partnership in 1962, Loewe retired and Lerner teamed up with Burton Lane for *On a Clear Day You Can See Forever* (1965, filmed 1970), with André Previn for *Coco* (1969), based on the life of Coco Chanel, and **Leonard Bernstein** for the unsuccessful *1600 Pennsylvania Avenue* (1976).

THE LETTERMEN

Bob Engemann, b. 19 February 1936, Highland Park, Michigan, USA; Jim Pike, b. 6 November 1938, St Louis, Missouri; Tony Butalo, b. 20 November 1940, Sharon, Pennsylvania

The Lettermen were the most commercially successful white close-harmony group of the sixties. As their college-derived name suggests, they were initially inspired by fellow label-mates the **Four Freshmen** and **Four Preps**.

Pike and Engemann sang together at Brigham Young University before joining up with the night-club singer Butalo in Los Angeles. Signed briefly to Warners, they moved to Capitol in 1961 and had immediate success with their cool version of **Jerome Kern** and **Dorothy Fields**' Oscar-winning song, 'The Way You Look Tonight' (first sung by **Fred Astaire** in *Swing Time*, 1936) and their tremulous recording of 'When I Fall in Love', an earlier hit for **Nat 'King' Cole** which was revived by Donny Osmond with success in the UK in 1973. 'Come Back Silly Girl' (1962) gave them a third Top Twenty hit.

Throughout the sixties the Lettermen continued to apply their smooth style to previous hits, including **Dion and the Belmonts**' 'Where or When' (1963), **Percy Faith**'s 'Theme from "A Summer Place"' (1965) and the **Flamingos**' classic 'I Only Have Eyes for You' (1966). Their last major hits were with remakes of **Little Anthony and the Imperials**' 'Goin' Out of My Head' (1967) and 'Hurt So Bad' (1968), the year Gary Pike (Jim's brother) replaced Engemann.

Though they had no more significant hits, they continued to record throughout the seventies, adapting their style to current trends, even recording some disco numbers in the late seventies. In 1982 they left Capitol for Applause.

LARRY LEVAN
b. Lawrence Philpot, 21 July 1954, d. 8 November 1992

Widely credited as the founder of modern house DJ culture, Levan was for more than a decade resident DJ at New York's legendary Paradise Garage.

Levan learned his trade at the start of the 1970s, playing at New York venues such as The Continental Baths and The Gallery, working with, amongst others, another soon-to-be dance music legend, Frankie Knuckles. In 1976 Levan became resident at the newly opened Paradise Garage. Levan and the club's sound engineer Richard Long put together an awesome, finely honed sound system at the club, perfect for the booming dance music Levan would be mixing.

Levan's influential mixing technique involved combining elements from two records at the same time to create something new. This could mean using two copies of the same record, for example laying an *a cappella* vocal part over an instrumental section or percussive interlude; or it could involve using two different records, and combining instrumental fragments from both. In this way, Levan created 'live' remixes of the tracks he was playing.

His evident creative talent as a club DJ made Levan an obvious choice to remix songs in a studio environment, and he was soon in demand as a remixer and producer. Over the next few years, he worked on a string of hits with several New York dance labels, most notably West End and Salsoul.

Levan's remix credits for Salsoul during this period included Instant Funk's 'I Got My Mind Made Up' (1978), Inner Life's cover of 'Ain't No Mountain High Enough' (1981) and First Choice's 'Double Cross'. He also reworked a series of releases by vocalist Tanaa Gardner for West End, including 'Work That Body', 'No Frills' and 'Heartbeat'. In the early 1980s Levan produced remixes for vocalist Gwen Guthrie, including 'Seventh Heaven, Peanut Butter and Padlock'. He teamed up with Guthrie again in 1986 for a memorable reworking of her hit, 'Ain't Nothing Going on but the Rent'.

Throughout this period, Levan remained a resident DJ at the Paradise Garage. The club would ultimately lend its name to a new dance genre – garage – generally taken to mean uplifting vocal house. But Levan's choice of material as a DJ at the club went far beyond this definition, embracing rock tunes like **The Who**'s *Eminence Front*, gospel, reggae and soul, as well as disco and house.

The club closed in 1987, with Levan there at the very end, but he was soon working on another club project, the Ministry of Sound, which was being set up by London DJ and Paradise Garage disciple Justin Berkmann.

After the Garage's closure, Levan lost his way, and became more frequent and less moderate in his use of drugs, particularly heroin and cocaine. He missed DJ gigs and studio work, and his health deteriorated. Levan went on a tour of Japan with longtime friend and fellow DJ François Kevorkian in 1992, and completed a remix of Loleatta Holloway's 'Strong Enough' for the tiny Active label a few months before his death from heart failure in November that year.

LEVEL 42

Boon Gould, b. 4 March 1955, Isle of Wight, England (replaced by Alan Murphy, d. 1988, replaced by Jakko Jakszyk); Phil Gould, b. 28 February 1957, Isle of Wight (replaced by Neil Conti, replaced by Gary Husband); Mark King, b. 20 October 1958, Isle of Wight; Mike Lindup, b. 17 March 1959, London

Level 42 were among the first British groups of the eighties to find international success playing a combination of pop, soul and jazz-funk, a style which had previously been virtually the exclusive preserve of American instrumentalists.

Bass-player King and the Gould brothers (Boon on guitar and drummer Phil) had played summer seasons in holiday camps on the Isle of Wight before forming Level 42 with Lindup (keyboards). The dancefloor success of 'Love Meeting Love' on the Independent Elite label led to the band signing to Polydor in 1980. Following groups like **Mike Vernon**'s Olympic Runners, Level 42 played in a 'Britfunk' style on their eponymous début album.

By 1982, when they released *The Early Tapes* and *The Pursuit of Accidents*, Level 42 were established as a leading band in British soul polls. After a series of minor hits, 'The Chinese Way' reached the Top Thirty in 1983 and 'The Sun Goes Down' was a Top Ten hit in Britain. The song was taken from *Standing in the Light*, produced in Los Angeles by **Earth, Wind and Fire** members Verdine White and Larry Dunn.

King's dextrous playing was a prime feature in Level 42's continued success as 'Hot Water' (1984) and the catchy and well-crafted 'Something About You' were further hits in Britain. The bestselling *World Machine* (1985) was co-produced by the band and Paris-based keyboards-player Wally Badarou, who also worked with **Grace Jones** and leading African musician **Fela Kuti** and composed film music, notably for *Kiss of the Spider Woman* (1986). Level 42's continuing shift towards mainstream pop music, evident on 'Something About You', was confirmed by 'Lessons in Love' (1986), from the Badarou-produced *Running in the Family*, whose title track brought Level 42 their first No. 1 the following year. In 1986 the group released the live double-album *A Physical Presence*.

During Level 42's 1987 World Tour, Phil Gould left the band and was temporarily replaced by Conti, who had previously played with **David Bowie** and **Prefab Sprout**. His permanent replacement was Husband. Guitarist Boon Gould also left the band in 1987, citing ill health, to be replaced by Murphy. Boon would later record as a solo artist.

Now based around the King–Lindup axis, the band recorded *Staring at the Sun* (1988). It included the hit singles 'Heaven in my Hands' and 'Take a Look'. A greatest hits collection, *Level Best*, appeared in 1989 and Lindup released a solo album, *Changes*, in 1990, before the band began recording a new album for Polydor. However, the label rejected the album, and Level 42 subsequently signed to RCA in 1991. The upheaval caused by the departure of Phil Gould and the death from Aids of Alan Murphy in 1989 seemed to have seriously affected King and Lindup, however, and when the Polydor-rejected album appeared later that year as *Guaranteed*, it received lukewarm reviews. Nevertheless, it made the British Top Five. Phil Gould returned to the fold in a writing/production role for the next album, the much-delayed *Forever Now* (1994), which was co-produced by Badarou. *The Very Best of Level 42* (1998) was released in the same year as Mark King's second solo album, *One Man*.

FURRY LEWIS

b. Walter Lewis, 6 March 1893, Greenwood, Mississippi, USA, d. 14 September 1981, Memphis, Tennessee

Furry Lewis, one of the first generation of Memphis-based songsters and blues singers, contributed distinctive blues, blues ballads and minstrel songs to the canon of recorded black music. He was also a notable guitarist in both finger-picking and bottleneck styles.

He grew up in Memphis where, he claimed, he was an associate of **W. C. Handy**. As a young man he worked on medicine-shows with the singer-guitarist Jim Jackson, who, though deploying at least as wide a repertoire as Lewis, was celebrated for his enormously popular two-part 'Jim Jackson's Kansas City Blues' (Vocalion, 1927).

Lewis lost a leg in a railroad accident in 1916. Later, he worked in Memphis with members of jug bands, including Will Shade and **Gus Cannon**. A striking selection of Lewis's music was preserved on records for Vocalion (1927, 1929) and Victor (1928), including two-part renditions of the blues ballads 'Kassie [i.e. Casey] Jones' (Victor) and 'John Henry' (Vocalion).

Traced by blues researchers in 1963, Lewis began to play at festivals, and in the late sixties he toured with the Alabama State Troupers rock show organized by Don Nix. As a key to the archives of Memphis's musical past he was often featured during the seventies in documentary films; he also had a cameo part in the 1975 feature *W.W. and the Dixie Dancekings*.

GEORGE LEWIS
b. George Louis Francis Zeno, 13 July 1900, New Orleans, Louisiana, USA, d. 31 December 1968, New Orleans

With **Bunk Johnson**, clarinettist Lewis was a 'rediscovered' figurehead of traditional New Orleans jazz when the music was revived by white enthusiasts in the forties.

In 1917 he joined a youth brass band, the Black Eagles, and played with leading New Orleans groups including those of **Kid Ory** and Buddy Petit before forming his own band in 1923. After five years, Lewis folded the group and joined the bands of Arnold DuPas and Evan Thomas, rather than following many of his contemporaries (including **Louis Armstrong** and **Sidney Bechet**) north to Chicago.

When Thomas was shot on the bandstand in 1932, Lewis retired from full-time music and worked as a stevedore in New Orleans. He continued to perform occasionally over the next decade but came to prominence when he made his first recordings as vocalist as well as clarinettist with Johnson for William Russell's American Music label and **Milt Gabler**'s Commodore in 1942. His own finest recordings as bandleader were the mix of blues ('See See Rider') and spirituals ('Just a Closer Walk with Thee') cut for Blue Note in 1943.

Lewis's intense blues style on clarinet made him a favourite of the revivalists, although there was some dispute over his tendency to go out of tune during solos: some argued that this was a feature of New Orleans style, others that this was a personal failing. In 1945 he worked with Johnson in New York and, after the latter's death in 1949, Lewis assumed the mantle of keeper of the flame of pure New Orleans jazz. During the fifties and early sixties he led a small group of veterans, including Alcide 'Slow Drag' Pavageau (bass) and Jim Robinson (trombone), on tours of Europe and Japan, where his last recordings were made in 1964. His 1957 and 1959 British appearances, where he was supported by **Ken Colyer**'s band, did much to stimulate the emerging trad jazz movement there.

HUEY LEWIS AND THE NEWS
Huey Lewis, b. Hugh Cragg, 5 July 1950, New York, USA; Sean Hopper, b. 31 March 1953, California; Chris Hayes, b. 24 November 1957, California; Johnny Colla, b. 2 July 1952, California; Mario Cipollina, b. 10 November 1954, California; Bill Gibson, b. 13 November 1951, California

A triumph of perseverance over inspiration, the eighties' success of Huey Lewis and the News followed its leader's long years in the amiable bar band, Clover. Lewis's popularity in America was part of a return to favour of an unassuming version of mainstream rock, epitomized in the title of his 1986 hit 'Hip to Be Square'.

A country-rock group, Clover was formed in California in 1968 by John McFee (pedal-steel guitar), Alex Call (guitar), John Ciambiotta (bass) and Mitch Howie (drums). Signing to the Bay Area label Fantasy, the group recorded an eponymous first album (1970) and *Forty-Niner* (1971), produced by Ed Bogas. With the addition of Sean Hopper (keyboards) and Louis (as his name was then spelt) on vocals and harmonica, Clover performed on the soundtrack of the Rip Torn country music drama *Payday* (1972). Without a recording contract, Clover played local gigs while McFee also played on recording sessions for **Van Morrison**, **Boz Scaggs** and **Steve Miller**.

Louis's love for R&B and Hopper's jazzy style gave Clover a more eclectic sound, and in 1976 the group was discovered by **Dr Feelgood** manager Jake Riviera, who persuaded the British Phonogram label to sign them. Clover recorded *Unavailable* (Vertigo, 1976), produced by Mutt Lange, and moved to London where they became popular performers on the pub-rock circuit. There they backed **Elvis Costello** on his first album, *My Aim Is True* (Stiff, 1977), and country singer Carlene Carter.

After Clover split up in 1979, Louis and Hopper returned to Marin County to form Huey Lewis and the News with ex-Soundhole members Hayes (guitar), Colla (guitar and saxophone), Mario Cipollina (bass) and Bill Gibson (drums). Signing to Chrysalis in 1980, the group found success for their genial mainstream rock sound when 'Do You Believe in Love' from the second album, *Picture This* (1982), was a Top Ten hit.

Sports (1984) became one of the biggest-selling albums of the era and included four hit singles in 'Heart and Soul' (1983), 'I Want a New Drug', 'The Heart of Rock'n'Roll' and 'This Is It' (1984). Lewis's first British hit was 'The Power of Love' (1985), the theme to Steven Spielberg's *Back to the Future* and Lewis's first American No. 1. With his relaxed stage manner and the golfing reference in the title of *Fore* (1986), Lewis seemed set to become the baby-boomers' **Bing Crosby**. The album spawned other American No. 1s with 'Stuck With You' and 'Jacob's Ladder', written by Bruce Hornsby. *Small World* (1988) and the hit 'Perfect World' maintained the momentum of the group.

In 1991 Huey Lewis and the News released *Hard at Play*, which was firmly in the mould of the band's previous albums, but sales were comparatively poor, and a greatest hits set, *The Heart of Rock'n'Roll*, was issued in 1992. This was the final Chrysalis album and Lewis and the News moved to Elektra to record *Four Chords and Several Years Ago* (1994). With versions of hits by such fifties and early sixties artists as **Don Covay**, **Lloyd Price** and the **Drifters**, the album found Lewis harking back to his earliest musical influences. In 1993 Lewis appeared in Robert Altman's acclaimed movie *Short Cuts*, which also featured appearances from fellow musicians **Tom Waits**, **Lyle Lovett** and Annie Ross, the veteran jazz vocalist who had been part of the trio **Lambert, Hendricks and Ross**. In 1995 Lewis sang 'Oh Darling' on the country tribute album, *Come Together, America Salutes The Beatles*.

JERRY LEE LEWIS
b. *29 September 1935, Ferriday, Louisiana, USA*

One of the greatest and most outrageous figures of fifties rock'n'roll, singer and pianist Lewis conveyed hysterical excitement with the controlled frenzy of his playing and whooping vocal style. He had a second career in country music during the seventies and eighties.

From a poor white family – his cousins were singer **Mickey Gilley** and television anti-rock evangelist Jimmy Lee Swaggart – Lewis played piano from the age of nine. His early influences were both white (**Moon Mullican**) and black (**Fats Domino**, Tampa Red), and the showmanship of **Al Jolson** also left its mark. His pounding playing won a Ted Mack talent show and a slot on WNAT Natchez, but at seventeen he briefly attended Waxahatchie Bible Institute, Texas, intending to become a preacher.

In 1956 **Sam Phillips** signed Lewis to Sun, releasing 'Crazy Arms' and sending him on tour throughout the South with **Johnny Cash** and **Carl Perkins**, on whose 'Matchbox Blues' Lewis played piano. His first hit was 'Whole Lotta Shakin' Goin' on' (1957). The song at first received little airplay and was initially banned as obscene. But a nationwide television appearance on the *Steve Allen Show* where Lewis stood up and kicked away his piano stool ensured its success.

Otis Blackwell wrote 'Great Balls of Fire' (1957) and 'Breathless', which were also Top Ten hits. Lewis appeared in the film *Jamboree* and sang the title song for *High School Confidential* (1958). His frantic, exciting style made him an international star until hostile publicity during a British tour in 1959 about his marriage to a thirteen-year-old second cousin destroyed his career.

Ignored by radio stations, Blackwell's 'Big Blon' Baby' (1959) and the traditional song 'Old Black Joe' (1960) sold poorly and Lewis also suffered from the decline of the Sun label, as Phillips took little interest in his artists. His only pop hit of this period was a spirited version of **Ray Charles**' 'What'd I Say' (1961), which like 'Whole Lotta Shakin'' also entered the country and R&B charts. However, Lewis remained a popular live performer and in 1961 took part in a 'battle of the bands' with **Jackie Wilson**.

His final Sun releases were unimaginative covers of **Chuck Berry**'s 'Sweet Little Sixteen' and **Little Richard**'s 'Good Golly Miss Molly' and his first releases for Mercury's Smash label which he joined in 1963 were equally ineffectual. Lewis's producer was Jerry Kennedy, a former session guitarist hired by Shelby Singleton to run Mercury's Nashville operation after the label was bought by the European Philips group in 1961. Among the artists whose work Kennedy supervised were **Dave Dudley**, **Faron Young**, **Tom T. Hall**, **Roger Miller**, **Mickey Newbury** and **Charlie Rich**.

With Lewis, he tried a variety of approaches, re-recording his rock'n'roll material (*Gold Hits*, 1964), moving towards country (*Country Songs for City Folks*, 1965), soul (*Soul My Way*, 1967) and R&B (*Return of Rock*, 1963). The best albums of these years were *The Greatest Live Show on Earth* (1965) and *More of the Greatest Live Show on Earth* (1966), mementoes of Lewis's perennially dynamic stage act.

Lewis even made a successful theatrical début in 1968 as Iago in *Catch My Soul*, a rock musical based on Shakespeare's *Othello* produced by **Jack Good**, with whom Lewis had worked in television in Britain and America. In the same year he moved decisively into the country field with the strong honky-tonk records 'Another Place, Another Time' and 'What Made Milwaukee Famous (Has Made a Loser Out of

Me)'. *She Even Woke Me up to Say Goodbye* (1969) was one of Lewis's best albums, with a notable version of Newbury's self-pitying title song.

Lewis remained in demand for rock revival events like the 1969 Toronto Festival and recorded a hit version of the Big Bopper's 'Chantilly Lace' (1972), as well as *London Session* (1973), with such luminaries as **Albert Lee**, **Peter Frampton** and **Rory Gallagher**. During the seventies, however, he primarily devoted himself to establishing his credentials as a leading country artist. Despite an increasingly erratic personal life involving shooting incidents, tax problems and two serious bouts of illness, Lewis recorded a long series of hits. Dealing in the classic country theme of marital travail, they included 'He Can't Fill My Shoes', 'Let's Put It Back Together Again' (1976), 'Middle Aged Crazy' (1977) and 'I'll Find It Where I Can' (1978).

A version of **Yip Harburg**'s 'Over the Rainbow' was Lewis's first hit for Elektra, for whom he cut the albums *Rockin' My Life Away* and *When Two Worlds Collide*. In 1983 he moved to MCA for *My Fingers Do the Talking* (1983) and *I Am What I Am* (1985). In Europe in particular, Lewis's reputation as a founding father of rock'n'roll was kept alive by frequent reissues of his Sun material, notably by the British label Charly, and he appeared live almost everywhere from Finland to Spain in the nineties. In 1989 he was impersonated by Dennis Quaid in the biopic *Great Balls of Fire* and in 1990 he contributed 'It Was the Whiskey Talking (Not Me)' to the soundtrack of the film *Dick Tracy*. *All Killer, No Filler* (Rhino, 1993) was a two-CD career retrospective. In 1995 he joined Elektra and released his first studio album in over ten years, *Young Blood*, a collection of songs first recorded by **Hank Williams** and **Jimmie Rodgers**.

MEADE LUX LEWIS
b. 4 September 1905, Chicago, Illinois, USA, d. 7 June 1964, Minneapolis, Minnesota

Perhaps the most versatile of the boogie-woogie piano's 'big three' (the others were **Albert Ammons** and **Pete Johnson**), Lewis's best performances brilliantly united speed, drive and invention. He also wrote some of the most enduring pieces in the boogie-woogie repertoire. An experimenter, he recorded boogies on other keyboard instruments, including harpsichord and celeste, and from time to time showed his skill at blues whistling.

Originally taught violin, Lewis was led to the piano by **Jimmy Yancey**. In the twenties he played round his home town, also working as a taxi-driver alongside Ammons. In 1927 he recorded 'Honky Tonk Train Blues' (Paramount), a classic and a test-piece of the boogie idiom. It became his most famous num-

ber, and when **John Hammond** brought him from obscurity in 1935 he cut a new version for the English Parlophone label, followed by Victor (1937) and Blue Note (1940) readings. Other admired compositions of this period were 'Yancey Special', dedicated to his first teacher, and 'Bear Cat Crawl'. With Ammons and Johnson he performed in New York at Carnegie Hall in 1938 and subsequently at Café Society; they also recorded piano duets and trios. In his own right he recorded for Vocalion (1938), Solo Art (1939) and Blue Note (1939–41), for whom he produced such solos as 'Six Wheel Chaser'.

He moved to the West Coast in 1941. He made several 'soundies' (short films for visual jukeboxes) in 1944, and appeared in *New Orleans* (1947), playing 'Honky Tonk Train Blues' and in *Nightmare* (1956). His later recordings, such as *Barrelhouse Piano* (Tops, 1956), were affected treatments of often trite material.

RAMSEY LEWIS
b. 27 May 1935, Chicago, Illinois, USA

A jazz pianist, Lewis had a series of pop hits in the sixties with a variant of the soul-funk style first developed by **Cannonball Adderley**.

After playing piano accompaniment in a Baptist church, he studied classical piano at Chicago Music College, leaving in 1955 to join the Clefs dance band. Soon afterwards he formed a trio with Eldee Young (bass) and drummer Isaac Holt, signing to Chess's Cadet label.

Showing the influence of label-mate **Ahmad Jamal**, the trio's albums included *Stretching Out* and *Never on Sunday* (both 1962) and *Sound of Spring* (1964), while Lewis also played with **Max Roach**, Clark Terry and Sonny Stitt. In 1965 he cut a percussive instrumental version of **Dobie Gray**'s pop hit 'The "In" Crowd'. Recorded live, the track included audience shouts and hand-clapping and reached both the R&B and pop Top Tens. The Ramsey Lewis Trio followed with further hits in the same vein, the **McCoys**' 'Hang on Sloopy' (1965) and **The Beatles**' film theme, 'A Hard Day's Night' (1966).

After a final hit with the gospel-tinged 'Wade in the Water', the drummer and bassist left to form Young-Holt Unlimited with Detroit pianist Ken Chaney. Recording for Brunswick in a similar style to Lewis's own, the group followed the minor success of 'Wack Wack' (1967) with the million-selling 'Soulful Strut', composed by Eugene Record of the Chi-Lites.

Lewis re-formed his trio with bass-player Cleveland Eaton and drummer Maurice White, who also played kalimba (African thumb piano). He left Lewis in 1969 to form **Earth, Wind and Fire**. Lewis continued to record prolifically, for Cadet until 1972 and thereafter for Columbia. *Funky Serenity* (1973) continued the policy of covering current hits, and **Booker T. and the MGs** guitarist Steve Cropper played on *Solar Wind* (1974). The most successful of the later albums was *Sun Goddess* (1975), produced by White.

After 1976 Lewis expanded the trio format to include flute and clarinet, explored classical forms on *Legacy* (1979), and recorded with singer Nancy Wilson on *The Two of Us* (1984). He also made the album *Keys to the City* (1987). Lewis's producer was former Earth, Wind and Fire member Larry Dunn. In the nineties he moved to the GRP label, recording *Sky Island* (1993) with his sons Frayne and Robert. He also hosted jazz radio and television shows.

SMILEY LEWIS

b. Overton Amos Lemons, 5 July 1913, DeQuincy, Louisiana, USA, d. 7 October 1966, New Orleans, Louisiana

Smiley Lewis is a classic example of a familiar type in R&B history: the undoubtedly talented and even innovative musician whose career in its prime coincides with that of a similar – even perhaps derivative – but more charismatic and commercially astute artist. The shadow across Lewis's path was that of **Fats Domino**, but he also lost potentially valuable songs to singers outside the world of rhythm and blues.

In the thirties Lewis worked as a speakeasy troubadour, accompanied only by his guitar; later he became a more established club attraction, heading a trio. He recorded for DeLuxe in 1947, then in 1950 signed with Imperial, becoming, over the next decade, one of the label's most prolific R&B acts. Usually accompanied by **Dave Bartholomew** bands, he recorded classic New Orleans blues sides like 'The Bells Are Ringing' (1952), which entered the R&B Top Ten, as did his most famous number, 'I Hear You Knocking' (1955). This was covered at the time by pop singer Gale Storm, who took it to No. 2, then later by Domino, and in 1970, in a precise re-creation, by **Dave Edmunds**, for whom it was a British No. 1. Lewis also recorded 'Blue Monday', in 1953, before Domino; 'One Night' (1955), which was covered by **Elvis Presley**; and 'Shame Shame Shame' (1956), which was featured on the soundtrack of Elia Kazan's *Baby Doll*.

Lewis left Imperial in 1960 and recorded for Okeh, Dot and Loma, for whom he re-cut 'The Bells Are Ringing', produced by **Allen Toussaint**.

TED LEWIS

b. Theodore Leopold Friedman, 6 June 1890, Circleville, Ohio, USA, d. 25 August 1971, New York

Known as 'The High Hatted Tragedian of Song' – from 1919 onward he wore a battered top hat while conducting – Lewis was a bandleader for fifty years,

playing a mix of comedy and syrupy dance music, spiced with jazz from the likes of such long-serving members of his various bands as Muggsy Spanier and George Brunis, and guests like **Fats Waller**.

A clarinettist, Lewis played in a local boys' band with his brother Edgar, a cornettist, before organizing his first band in 1910. In 1915 he travelled to New York and worked in vaudeville before joining Earl Fuller. In 1917 he formed his first professional band. In 1925 his was one of the first American bands to play jazz in Britain when he followed **Vincent Lopez** in a season at London's Kit Kat Club. Signed to Columbia, he recorded prolifically for the company between 1919 and 1933. It was his band that backed **Sophie Tucker** on her 1926 million-selling recording of 'Some of Those Days', and he often subsequently performed with Tucker. His biggest hits were his own composition 'When My Baby Smiles at Me'* (1920), a sentimental song which he talked rather than sang, and his version of Billy Rose's 'Me and My Shadow' (1927).

In 1929 Lewis made his first film, *Is Everybody Happy?*, titled after the question he regularly repeated during live appearances, and throughout the thirties appeared occasionally in films, both with his band and on his own. Other films included *Here Comes the Band* (1935), *Hold That Ghost* (1941) and *Follow the Boys* (1944). During this period he recorded for Decca. In the fifties he frequently appeared on television, reviving his band for social occasions and regularly reuniting with Tucker.

LIBERACE

b. Wladziu Valentino Liberace, 16 May 1919, West Allis, Wisconsin, USA, d. 4 February 1987, Palm Springs, California

With his glass pianos, candelabras, outrageous clothes and manner to match, Liberace was one of the most colourful entertainers in showbusiness. Though he never consistently sold records in vast quantities – his *métier* was TV and live performance – he was the most influential of the popular pianists of the fifties (who included **Roger Williams**, Ferrante and Teicher, **Winifred Atwell** and Russ Conway) and the link between them and the glitter of **Elton John**.

The son of a French-horn player who had played with **John Philip Sousa**, Liberace supported his classical piano studies by playing popular tunes under the name Walter Busterkeys before uniting both at a 1939 recital when he played 'Three Little Fishes' as an encore. Henceforth he would be a popular pianist. His repertoire consisted mostly of the popular classics, though much adapted – his version of Chopin's 'Minute Waltz' lasted only thirty-seven seconds because he preferred to 'leave out the dull parts' – played technically brilliantly and showcased by a genuinely friendly personality, a dimpled grin and a showmanship that became more knowing the camper he became. He adopted his trademark, a candelabra on his piano, from *A Song to Remember* (1945), the film which did much to popularize classical music in America in which **Jose Iturbi** played Chopin's music and Cornel Wilde Chopin.

By the late forties a success on the nightclub circuit, Liberace briefly essayed a film career before television made him a star. He reigned throughout the fifties, brushing aside homosexual insinuations, his melo-dramatic playing, with its plethora of trills and double octaves, his asides to his violin-playing brother George (Liberace's bandleader and the butt of many of his jokes), and his homilies to his mother, defusing the camp splendour of his act. In the sixties he retreated to Las Vegas, but in the seventies he appeared regularly on American television, and in the eighties his live shows were more successful than ever.

He recorded prolifically, most successfully for Columbia in the fifties, usually interspersing film and show tunes with his own arrangements of the classics. On the whole his albums were more successful than his singles, but in 1952 he had a Top Thirty hit with his ornate version of the **Kurt Weill** tune 'September Song'. In 1986, after a series of sell-out concerts con-firmed his star status, he re-signed with Columbia and the company issued *Liberace Piano Favourites*, a compilation of live performances from the fifties. His death was the result of Aids.

JIMMY AND JOE LIGGINS
Jimmy, b. 14 October 1922, Newby, Oklahoma, USA; Joe, b. 1915, Guthrie, Oklahoma, d. 1 August 1987, Lynwood, California

The Liggins brothers were successful jump-band lead-ers and recording artists of the late forties and early fifties, working in then current West Coast blues styles but rooted in the big-band music of the thirties.

The family emigrated to California during the Depression and the brothers were exposed to black bands through broadcasts from the Mexican border stations. Joe began playing in bands in 1933 around San Diego, as a trumpeter, drummer and finally pianist. In 1939 he went to Los Angeles, and in 1944 organized a six-piece group with saxophonist Little Willie Jackson. Despite its size, the band attained a big sound, and its skilful arrangements were much admired. Signing with Exclusive, Joe cut the infec-tious bestseller 'The Honeydripper' (1945). In its wake he was taken on by the powerful Harold Oxley agency and booked throughout the South.

After a brief boxing career (under the name 'Kid Zulu'), Jimmy had become Joe's driver, but had ambitions to become a guitarist and songwriter. He

left Joe in 1947 to lead his own band, which included the tenor saxophonist Harold Land, and record, with some success, for Speciality (1947–52); **Maxwell Davis** was employed as tenor saxophonist and arranger on some sessions.

Joe was also on Speciality, for whom he re-recorded 'The Honeydripper' and other earlier hits and had a first-time success with 'Pink Champagne' (1950). He left the label in 1954, thereafter briefly recording for Aladdin (which Jimmy had joined a couple of years earlier).

Both then stopped touring. Jimmy went into record distribution and later ran his own Duplex label, based from the mid-seventies in Durham, North Carolina. Joe played lounges as a singer-pianist round Los Angeles, often accompanied by Little Willie Jackson; they recorded together for **Johnny Otis**'s Blues Spectrum label in the seventies, and were featured in the Los Angeles blues episode of the British Channel 4 teleseries *Repercussions* (1984).

GORDON LIGHTFOOT
b. 17 November 1938, Orillia, Ontario, Canada

A prolific singer-songwriter for two decades, Light-foot was one of the most successful and distinctive Canadian artists of the seventies and eighties. His pre-eminence as a Canadian writer and performer was recognized in 1985 when he sang the opening line of 'Northern Lights', the all-Canadian charity recording for Ethiopian famine relief. Among those who recorded Lightfoot compositions in the seventies and eighties were **Bob Dylan**, **Elvis Presley**, **Anne Murray**, **Judy Collins**, **Barbra Streisand** and **Glen Campbell**.

Although his earliest successes were with folk, Lightfoot had studied music at Westlake College in Los Angeles and worked as a session singer and jingle producer. Influenced, however, by **Pete Seeger** and (especially) singer-guitarist Bob Gibson, Lightfoot plunged into the Toronto folk-club scene in the early sixties.

He had a minor Canadian hit on Chateau with the country-styled 'Remember Me' before **Ian and Sylvia** introduced his songs 'For Lovin' Me' and 'Early Morning Rain' to American audiences. The songs were successfully recorded by **Peter Paul and Mary** and soon their manager Albert Grossman took charge of Lightfoot's career. He signed to United Artists and released *Lightfoot* (1965), which contained 'Ribbon of Darkness', a country hit for **Marty Robbins**. This was followed by *The Way I Feel* (1967), which included the 'Canadian Railroad Trilogy', the first of a number of songs in which Lightfoot portrayed aspects of his native country's history and character. He also released *Did She Mention My Name?* (1968), *Back*

Here on Earth and *Sunday Concert* (both 1969), before switching labels to Reprise.

With a new producer (Lenny Waronker) and the participation of **Randy Newman** and **Ry Cooder**, *If You Could Read My Mind* (1970) added a West Coast gloss to Lightfoot's mix of romantic balladry and rural narrative. The album included the first recording of **Kris Kristofferson**'s 'Me and Bobby McGee', while Lightfoot's intense title track was a Top Ten hit. *Summer Side of Life* (1972) was recorded in Nashville but included some of Lightfoot's best 'Canadian' songs in 'Nous Vivons Ensemble' and 'Cotton Jenny', a jaunty portrayal of the textile communities of Ontario.

After *Old Dan's Records* (1973), he had a million-seller with the title track of *Sundown* (1974) and a further hit with 'Carefree Highway'. More chart success followed through the melancholic 'Rainy Day People' (1975), the narrative ballad 'Wreck of the Edmund Fitzgerald' (1976) and the tale of suspicion and jealousy 'The Circle Is Small (I Can See It in Your Eyes)' (1978).

Though he had no further major hits, the prolific Lightfoot continued to produce albums at frequent intervals throughout the eighties. They included *Shadows* (1982), *Salute* (1983) and his twenty-third album, *East of Midnight* (1986). There was a long gap before *Waiting for You* (1993), which included a version of Bob Dylan's 'Ring them Bells'. He followed that after another long delay with *A Painter Passing Through* (1998).

LIGHTNING SEEDS

Ian Broudie, b. 4 August 1958, Liverpool, England

The Lightning Seeds are a studio-based project masterminded by producer-auteur Ian Broudie, who achieved vast success in the nineties with his polished guitar-pop. They had their biggest hit with 'Three Lions', the official England team song for the Euro '96 football tournament.

After taking his first stab at the pop world as a teenager in the late seventies with Big in Japan, alongside future **KLF** founder Bill Drummond, Broudie turned to producing, creating a distinctive sound for several of the most popular indie bands of the time, including **Echo and the Bunnymen** and the **Fall**.

Broudie decided to have a second attempt at a pop career in 1989, recording *Cloudcuckoo Land*, the Lightning Seeds' début. Heavily reminiscent of his work with Echo and the Bunnymen and the **Pet Shop Boys**, the album spawned an international hit single, 'Pure'. The follow-up, *Sense* (1992), featured two further UK hits, 'Life of Riley' and the title track, while the success of *Jollification* (1994) prompted Broudie to put together a live band, which included keyboardist Ali Kane, drummer Chris Sharrock and bassist Martin Campbell.

The Lightning Seeds hit their peak, commercially and artistically, on *Dizzy Heights* (1996), featuring collaborations with **Terry Hall** and Nicky Wire of the **Manic Street Preachers**. The album gave Broudie five hit singles in the UK, including a cover of the **Turtles**' 'You Showed Me' and 'Sugar Coated Iceberg', as well as 'Three Lions'. The latter was a duet with comedians David Baddiel and Frank Skinner, which topped the British chart at the height of the football European Championships of 1996. They subsequently updated the football anthem for the World Cup football championship of 1998. The Lightning Seeds released a greatest hits album, *Like You Do*, in 1997.

THE LIMELITERS

Louis Gottlieb, b. 1923, Los Angeles, California, USA, d. 11 July 1996; Alex Hassilev, b. 11 July 1932, Paris, France; Glenn Yarbrough, b. 12 January 1930, Milwaukee, Wisconsin

A West Coast folk group of the early sixties, the cabaret-orientated Limeliters bridged the gap between the old-left purism of the **Weavers** and the pop approach of the **Kingston Trio**.

The trio was named after an Aspen, Colorado, club owned by multilinguist Hassilev and guitarist Yarbrough. Bass-player Gottlieb had previously worked with the Gateway Singers, formed in San Francisco in 1956 as part of the growing folk boom. The group recorded two albums for Decca in 1958 before Gottlieb left to form the Limeliters in the following year.

Combining Gottlieb's humorous introductions, Hassilev's cosmopolitan repertoire of Spanish, Russian and other material, and Yarbrough's clear tenor, the Limeliters were tailor-made for the soft centre of the folk scene. In their four-year career they made numerous broadcasts and live appearances, as well as recording a dozen albums for RCA. Their only hit was 'A Dollar Down' (1961).

With titles like *Folk Matinée, Fourteen 14K Folksongs, Sing Out* and *The Slightly Fabulous Limeliters*, the records mixed American folk songs ('John Henry') with foreign-language songs ('Aravah Aravah') and the occasional contemporary piece ('Spanish Is the Loving Tongue').

While Gottlieb retired to study musicology, Hassilev turned to production, supervising albums by **Theodore Bikel**, **Hoyt Axton** and Yarbrough, who had a Top Twenty hit with **Rod McKuen**'s 'Baby the Rain Must Fall' (1965). The latter went on to record for Elektra, Tradition, Warners and Stax, for whom the trio re-formed in 1974 to cut *Glenn Yarbrough and the Limeliters*. They re-formed again in 1988 for *Alive in Concert*.

LINDISFARNE

Rod Clements, b. 17 November 1947, North Shields, Tyne and Wear, England (replaced by Tommy Duffy); Simon Cowe, b. 1 April 1948, Tynemouth (replaced by Charlie Harcourt); Alan Hull, b. 20 February 1945, Newcastle, d. 17 November 1995; Ray Jackson, b. 12 December 1948, Wallsend; Ray Laidlaw, b. 28 May 1948, North Shields; Paul Nichols; Kenny Craddock; Marty Craggs

A rock band with strong regional folk roots, Lindisfarne enjoyed a brief period of success in the early seventies and remained popular favourites in the North-East of England after the group re-formed in the late seventies.

In 1967–8, Clements (bass), Cowe (guitar), Jackson (harmonica, mandolin) and Laidlaw (drums) were playing West Coast-influenced music at dances and in folk clubs in the Newcastle area as Downtown Faction and, later, Brethren. After backing songwriter Hull on recordings for the local Rubber label, they formed Lindisfarne with him. Named after a historic island off the Northumbrian coast, the group were signed by Tony Stratton-Smith to his Charisma label. The under-produced *Nicely out of Tune* (1970) was a showcase for Hull's catchy, colourful songs.

American producer Bob Johnston was brought in for the sharper-sounding *Fog on the Tyne* (1971), which included the jaunty pop hit 'Meet Me on the Corner', featuring Jackson's harmonica-playing. The ballad 'Lady Eleanor' also reached the Top Ten in 1972, while Hull's passionate protest song 'All Fall Down' was a minor hit in the same year.

With a good-time jug-band sound and sing-along choruses – especially on their finale number 'Fog on the Tyne' – Lindisfarne became one of the most popular live groups in Britain. However, the ambitious, 'progressive' album *Dingly Dell* was a commercial failure and in 1973, as Charisma released a live album, the group split in two. Laidlaw, Cowe and Clements formed Jack the Lad with Geordie writer-guitarist Billy Mitchell, later adding Walter Fairbairn and Phil Murray from electric-folk group Hedgehog Pie. The group recorded three albums for Charisma, including *The Old Straight Track* (1974) and *Jackpot* (United Artists, 1976).

With four experienced musicians who had also started out in Newcastle bands, Jackson and Hull retained the name Lindisfarne for *Roll on Ruby* (Charisma, 1973) and *Happy Daze* (Warners, 1974). When that group disbanded, the original quintet were persuaded to play a series of Christmas concerts in 1976. So great was the audience response to this nostalgic reunion that it became almost an annual affair and the group were signed to Mercury for a live recording (*Magic in the Air*, 1978) and an album of new songs, *Back and Fourth* (1978). This provided the hit 'Run for Home' that was also a minor success in America. Lindisfarne then released *The News* (1979), which included 'Dedicated Hound', Hull's attack on rock critics, and *Sleepless Nights* (LMP, 1982). In 1984 LMP released two albums of live recordings by the group, while *Dance Your Life Away* (Priority, 1986) contained new studio material.

The band hit its lowest point, artistically, in 1987 with the release of *C'Mon Everybody*, an album of rock'n'roll 'party' songs segued together. The far superior *Amigos* (Black Crow, 1989) also flopped. The band still had a devoted following in the North-East of England, however, and in 1990 teamed up with Newcastle-born footballer Paul Gascoigne for a 'rap' remake of their regional anthem 'Fog on the Tyne', which was a British Top Five hit. With a line-up of Laidlaw, Clements, Hull and Cowe augmented by sax-player Marty Craggs, Lindisfarne put their partytime image behind them for 1993's *Elvis Lives on the Moon* (Essential), which featured some of Hull's better late-period work, including the political songs 'Day of the Jackal' and 'Mother Russia'.

From the release of *Pipedream* (Charisma, 1973), Hull had also pursued an intermittent solo recording career. *Squire* (1975) included songs written for a television play while *Phantoms* (1979) was on **Elton John**'s Rocket label, which had earlier released *Isn't It Strange* (1977) by Radiator, a shortlived band including Hull, Laidlaw and Kenny Craddock. In the eighties he released only one solo album, *On the Other Side* (1983), and collaborated with Newcastle poet Tom Pickard on musical plays about local political and historical issues.

Jackson's solo career was dominated by a landmark lawsuit in which he successfully sued EMI (to whom he signed in 1977) for failing to attempt to develop his career. He later recorded *In the Night* (Mercury, 1980).

MANCE LIPSCOMB

b. 9 April 1895, Navasota, Texas, USA, d. 30 January 1976, Navasota

Like his contemporaries **Mississippi John Hurt** and **Furry Lewis**, Mance Lipscomb revealed through his recordings a rich vein of 'pre-blues' elements, such as ballads, dance songs and guitar rags. Like them, he was not recorded in his youth, so he neither attached special value to his blues pieces nor was he constrained to do so by collectors' tastes; it seems probable, therefore, that his recorded legacy accurately reflects the range of music enjoyed by his own community.

In his youth Lipscomb accompanied his father, a fiddler, at local events. Although he came across **Blind Lemon Jefferson** and Texas Alexander, he never played music for a living. In 1960 he was recorded by the folk-song enthusiasts Chris Strach-witz and Mack McCormick, and *Texas Sharecropper and Songster* was the first release on the former's Arhoolie label. After that, Lipscomb was in demand for folk festivals and Californian folk-song clubs. He made an album for Reprise (*Trouble in Mind*, 1961) but thereafter remained with Arhoolie, producing albums regularly until his death. The seven Arhoolie LPs – among which the first and *Texas Songster Volume 2* (1964) are outstanding – are little worlds of rural black music. They encompass ballads ('Ella Speed'), vaudeville numbers ('Ain't Gonna Rain No Mo'', 'Shine on Harvest Moon'), sacred songs in the style of **Blind Willie Johnson**, a variety of dance songs, and personalized versions of blues, both local and national. All are accompanied with guitar-playing of great springiness and verve.

Lipscomb's life and times, musical and agricultural, were movingly documented by the filmmaker Les Blank in *A Well Spent Life* (1971).

LITTLE ANTHONY AND THE IMPERIALS
Little Anthony, b. Anthony Gourdine, 8 January 1940, Brooklyn, New York, USA; Tracy Lord (replaced by Sam Strain, b. 9 December 1940); Ernest Wright, b. 24 August 1939; Clarence Collins, b. 17 March 1939; Glouster Rogers, b. 1940

Little Anthony and the Imperials were one of the few doo-wop groups to accommodate themselves success-fully to the changes in style of the sixties and seventies.

Gourdine joined the Duponts in 1955, and then formed the Chesters. Signed by **Richard Barrett** to End in 1958, and renamed the Imperials (with **Alan Freed** tagging Gourdine Little Anthony because of his size), the group had an immediate hit with 'Tears on My Pillow'*, which featured Gourdine's ethereal falsetto. This was followed by 'A Prayer and a Juke-box' (1959) and 'Shimmy, Shimmy, Ko-Ko-Bop' (1960), among others, before Gourdine, like label-mate **Frankie Lymon**, disbanded the group to pursue a shortlived solo career.

In 1963 Wright organized a re-formed Imperials (with Strain replacing Lord) and the group were signed to DCP by Teddy Randazzo – a former mem-ber of the Chuckles who had minor hits with 'The Way of a Clown' (ABC, 1960) and 'Big Wide World' (Colpix, 1963). Still singing doo-wop but with Gour-dine's dramatic falsetto set against a plush, sixties soul sound, they had five Top Forty records: 'I'm on the Outside (Looking In)', the intense 'Goin' out of My Head' (1964), 'Hurt So Bad', 'Take Me Back' and 'I Miss You So' (1965). 'Goin' and 'Hurt' were later revived by the **Lettermen**, while **Linda Ronstadt** also had a 1980 hit with 'Hurt So Bad'.

A move to Veep in 1966 and then to the main United Artists label in 1969 saw them still hitting the lower reaches of the pop charts (their recordings included a new version of the Moonglows' 'Ten Com-mandments of Love', 1969). They were also headliners in Las Vegas, before once again Gourdine left for a solo career and Strain joined the **O'Jays**. In 1977 Collins appeared in the UK with a new group of Imperials, who enjoyed their biggest ever hit, 'Who's Gonna Love Me' (Power Exchange). In the eighties Gourdine led yet another Imperials on the rock'n'roll revival circuit and recorded gospel material for MCA with little success.

LITTLE FEAT
Roy Estrada (replaced by Ken Gradney, b. New Orleans, Louisiana, USA); Lowell George, b. 13 April 1945, Hollywood, California, d. 29 June 1979, Arlington, Virginia; Richie Hayward, b. Ames, Indiana; Bill Payne, b. 12 March 1949, Waco, Texas; Paul Barrere, b. 3 July 1948, Burbank, California; Sam Clayton

Highly regarded for George's songs and guitar-play-ing, Little Feat were a California-based rock band of the seventies. Like **The Band**, they absorbed a range of American musical traditions (blues, jazz, country) and from them created their own romanticized vision of rural America.

With the exception of singer Payne, the original members were veterans of sixties rock. Drummer Hayward had recorded with George for Uni in folk-rock band Factory before joining Fraternity of Man, which recorded for ABC and Dot and performed the infamous 'Don't Bogart That Joint' on the soundtrack of *Easy Rider* (1969). George and bassist Estrada had played with **Frank Zappa**'s Mothers of Invention before forming Little Feat in 1969.

Little Feat (Warners, 1971) included blues and jazz influences as well as George's country-rock songs 'Truck Stop Girl' and 'Willing'. The former was later recorded by the **Byrds** and the latter by a number of artists, including **Linda Ronstadt** and **Commander Cody**. **Ry Cooder** and pedal-steel-guitarist Pete Kleinow also played on the album. The impressive *Sailin' Shoes* (1972) again featured George's evocative slide-guitar work and his distinctive husky singing. Soon after its release, Estrada joined **Captain Beef-heart** and Little Feat expanded to a six-piece band with conga-player Clayton (brother of regular **Bob Dylan** backing singer Merry) and guitarist Barrere. This line-up cut *Dixie Chicken*, which included Bon-nie Bramlett on vocals and showed a New Orleans R&B influence on such tracks as **Allen Toussaint**'s 'On Your Way Down'. The group then separated for a year during which George played on numerous ses-sions for such artists as **Jimmy Webb**, **Van Dyke Parks**, **Robert Palmer** and **Carly Simon**.

Little Feat regrouped for the commercially success-
ful *Feats Don't Fail Me Now* (1974) and *The Last
Record Album* (1975), which showed the jazz-rock
influence of Barrere and Payne. The band toured
Europe and America in the mid-seventies, releasing
Time Loves a Hero (1977) and the live double-album
Waiting for Columbus (1978).

While recording the material for *Down on the
Farm* (1979), the group split, with George releasing a
solo album, *Thanks I'll Eat It Here*. It included 'Easy
Money' by **Rickie Lee Jones**, a female singer-songwriter who reached the American Top Five with
'Chuck E's in Love' (Warners, 1979). George later
performed with his own nine-piece group but died of
drugs-related heart failure while on tour. *Hoy Hoy*
(1981) contained previously unreleased Little Feat
material.

During the eighties Barrere recorded a solo album
while Payne and Hayward concentrated on studio
work and joined the touring groups of such artists as
Joan Armatrading and **James Taylor**. Adding guitarist Fred Tuckett and ex-**Pure Prairie League/**
American Flyer singer Craig Fuller, the remaining
original members re-formed Little Feat in 1987 to tour
and release *Let It Roll* (Warners, 1988). The album
became their biggest seller in America, and was followed by *Representing the Mambo*. However, although
the musicianship on both that and 1991's *Shake Me
Up* was beyond reproach, the songs were not up to
the standard of the George era. Later albums included
Ain't Had Enough Fun (1995) and the double-album
set *Live from Neon Park* (1996). *As Time Goes By*
(1994) is the definitive retrospective.

LITTLE MILTON

b. *Milton Campbell, 7 September 1934, Inverness,
Mississippi, USA*

A chameleon-like blues singer and guitarist whose
recordings have often been too derivative of his influences (which include **Bobby Bland**, **B. B. King**, **T-
Bone Walker** and **Roy Brown**), Milton is best
remembered for his fusion of blues and soul in the
sixties on records like 'Who's Cheatin' Who?'
(Checker, 1965).

As a child, Milton sang in church before turning to
the blues in his teens. In the early fifties he led a blues
trio in the Memphis area and in 1954 joined **Sam
Phillips'** Sun label where, backed by **Ike Turner**, he
recorded in a variety of blues styles, even including
an imitation of **Fats Domino** ('Beggin' My Baby').
After further recordings on Meteor and Bobbin,
where he worked with bandleader Oliver Sain
('Lonely Man', 1958), Milton was signed by **Leonard
Chess** in 1961. His cover of Bland's 'Blind Man' gave
him his first national hit in 1965, but it was 'We're

Gonna Make It', arranged by **Donny Hathaway**, that
established Milton.

Other hits included 'Who's Cheatin' Who?' (1965)
and 'Grits Ain't Groceries' (1969), originally a hit for
Little Willie John, as 'All Around the World' – all
brassy blues numbers distinguished by Milton's rich,
growling vocal style. In 1971 he signed with Stax and
had a series of R&B hits with a more contemporary
sound (including his cover of **Charlie Rich**'s 'Behind
Closed Doors', 1974) before returning to a more
blues-based style with self-produced records on
Glades (including 'Friend of Mine', 1976, and 'Loving
You', 1977). In the eighties he joined Malaco, and
recorded a series of intense blues albums, including
Annie Mae's Café (1986), *Reality* (1991) and the masterly *Strugglin' Lady* (1992). Less successful was *I'm a
Gambler* (1997), which was overshadowed by an
anthology of his days at Chess, *Greatest Hits* (1997).

LITTLE RICHARD

b. *Richard Wayne Penniman, 25 December 1932 (or
1935), Macon, Georgia, USA*

In purely stylistic terms, Little Richard was the most
influential of the early stars of rock'n'roll, leaving his
mark on **Paul McCartney**'s singing and **Jimi
Hendrix**'s stagecraft as well as on soul singers **James
Brown** and **Otis Redding**. His hit records were also
frequently and profitably covered by white artists.
Like **Jerry Lee Lewis**, he was driven by a Southern
fundamentalist conscience that was both drawn to
and abhorred the ungodliness of rock, but, unlike
Lewis, Richard did not find another musical direction. Accordingly, he was doomed to repeat endlessly
his handful of matchless recordings of the fifties.

At the age of fourteen he was touring the South
with medicine-shows, and was first billed as Little
Richard when he sang with the B. Brown Orchestra.
He modelled himself on the flamboyant R&B singer
Billy Wright, whose influence was apparent on
Richard's first single, 'Every Hour' (RCA, 1951). His
wild, intense piano style was based on that of New
Orleans performer Esquerita (Eskew Reeder), and in
1952 he formed the Tempo Toppers with organist
Raymond Taylor. He recorded in Houston for **Don
Robey**'s Peacock label, releasing 'Fool at the Wheel'
(1953) and Taylor's 'Rice, Red Beans and Turnip
Greens' (1954).

With only poor record sales, Richard returned to
Macon, where he performed locally until **Lloyd Price**
advised him to send a tape to **Art Rupe** of Specialty
Records in Hollywood. This led to the 1955 recording
session which produced his first million-seller, 'Tutti
Frutti'. The song was based on a risqué number fea-
tured by Richard on stage, but with new lyrics by
Dorothy La Bostrie, a local songwriter called in by

producer Harold Battiste. Although **Pat Boone** had a bigger hit with his cover-version, he did not try to emulate Richard's manic screaming falsetto and Boone's recording is all but forgotten.

Boone also covered Richard's next single, schoolgirl Enortis Johnson's 'Long Tall Sally', although this time both records reached the Top Ten. The song was later recorded by numerous artists, from **Elvis Presley** and **The Beatles** onwards, and also started a fad for similarly titled songs like **Larry Williams**' 'Short Fat Fanny' and Long Tall Marvin's 'Have Mercy Miss Percy'. Richard released two more singles in 1956. 'Slippin' and Slidin'' was less successful but **Otis Blackwell**'s 'Rip It Up' reached the Top Twenty despite being covered by **Bill Haley**.

The following year, Richard appeared in two **Alan Freed** films, *Don't Knock the Rock* and *Mr Rock'n'Roll*, in which he sang 'Keep a Knockin''. His recording of the title song from *The Girl Can't Help It* reached the British Top Ten. His later American hits were 'Lucille' and 'Jenny Jenny' (1957) and the peculiarly intense 'Good Golly Miss Molly' (1958). With the Upsetters, featuring former Peacock session men Grady Gaines and Clifford Burks (saxes) and drummer Charles Connor, he toured extensively in America, Europe and Australia where, in 1958, Little Richard decided to give up rock'n'roll and turn to religion.

Returning to America he took counsel from bandleader turned evangelist Joe Lutcher and studied at a bible college in Alabama. Specialty continued to release rock'n'roll material until 1960, while Richard himself turned to gospel music, although he cut a few profane tracks with the Upsetters in 1960 which were released in 1962–3 on Little Star. His first sacred recordings were a series of poorly produced tracks for **George Goldner**'s End label (*Pray Along with Little Richard*, 1960) but he found a far more sympathetic setting at Mercury in 1961 where *The King of the Gospel Singers* (1962) was arranged and produced by **Quincy Jones**. More gospel material was cut for Atlantic in 1963 but by then Richard had returned to rock'n'roll in live performances in Britain in 1962–3, where he toured with the **Rolling Stones**.

Richard confirmed the end of his exile from rock by recording the dynamic 'Bama Lama Bama Lou' (Specialty, 1964), renewing his partnership with former Specialty A&R man **Bumps Blackwell** and relaunching his explosive stage act in America, where he became one of the most admired live performers of the decade, even appearing in Las Vegas in 1968. His sixties recordings, however, were disappointing. At Vee-Jay he cut new versions of his hits and made an album of other rock'n'roll standards (*Little Richard Is Back*, 1965). The backing musicians included **Don and Dewey** and Hendrix, who, as Maurice James, was briefly a member of Richard's band.

When Vee-Jay collapsed, Richard recorded for Modern with Stax session musicians in Memphis (*The Wild and Frantic Little Richard*, 1966) before moving to Okeh. With Williams producing, he made *The Explosive Little Richard* (1967) which included contemporary material like Chris Kenner's 'Land of 1000 Dances' and Shorty Long's 'Function at the Junction', as well as yet another *Greatest Hits* album.

The most important of his comeback albums, however, were the trio cut for Reprise between 1970 and 1972. Partly recorded in Sheffield, Alabama, *The Rill Thing* (1970) was a skilful modern soul album, while on *King of Rock'n'Roll* (1971) Little Richard left his mark on a series of contemporary hits, including the Rolling Stones' 'Brown Sugar' and **Martha and the Vandellas**' 'Dancing in the Street'. *The Second Coming* caught the New Orleans flavour of his early hits and featured Earl Palmer (drums) and Lee Allen (sax) among the backing musicians.

Outside the studio, however, it was the fifties Little Richard who was in demand. The early seventies was the heyday of Ralph Nader's 'rock revival' shows and Richard frequently starred in them, dressed in the robes of 'The King of Rock'n'Roll'. He also became a regular guest on television chat shows where his safe yet extravagant personality and ambiguous sexuality won him a new audience, but his recording career lost momentum.

A K-Tel re-recording of the old hits (*Little Richard Live*, 1976) was followed in 1977 by Little Richard once again turning his back on 'the devil's music' and his decadent lifestyle to rejoin the church. *God's Beautiful City* (World, 1979) was followed by preaching tours of the United States. In 1986 he signed to Warners and released *Lifetime Friend*, a mixture of gospel and rock material.

Richard later appeared in the film *Down and Out in Beverly Hills*, which included the minor hit 'Great Gosh A'Mighty', collaborated with the **Beach Boys** and Philip Bailey on film themes and sang 'Rock Island Line' on *Folkways: A Vision Shared*, the 1988 tribute to **Leadbelly** and **Woody Guthrie**. His only solo recording in recent years was *Lifetime Friends* (Warner, 1987), which included the near-hit 'Operator', although he sang on bestselling children's albums issued by Walt Disney Records in the nineties. In 1994 he made a guest appearance on MCA's concept album *Rhythm, Country and Blues*, singing 'Somethin' Else' with **Tanya Tucker**, contributed a charming reading of 'I Feel Pretty' to the tribute album *The Songs of West Side Story* (1996) and sang 'Good Golly Miss Dolly' at the opening of **Dolly Parton**'s theme park, Dollywood (1995). In 2000 he was the subject of the bio-pic *Little Richard*, directed by Robert Townsend, for which he was impersonated with some verve by Leon.

His story is told in *The Life and Times of Little Richard* (1984) by Charles White.

THE LITTLE RIVER BAND

Beeb Birtles, b. Gerard Bertlekamp, 28 November 1948, Amsterdam, Netherlands; Rick Formosa, b. Italy (replaced by David Briggs, b. 26 January 1951, Melbourne, replaced by Wayne Nelson); Graham Goble, b. 15 May 1947, Adelaide; Roger McLachlan, b. New Zealand (replaced by George McArdale, b. 30 November 1954, Melbourne, replaced by Barry Sullivan); Derek Pellicci, b. England; Glenn Shorrock, b. 30 June 1944, Rochester (replaced by John Farnham, b. Adelaide, Australia)

Like **Air Supply** in the eighties, the Little River Band were an Australian soft-rock group which had considerable commercial success in America.

Vocalist Shorrock emigrated as a child from England in 1956 and in the early sixties led the Adelaide-based Twilights, one of Australia's top **Beatles**-style rock groups. He returned to London in the early seventies, joining the Esperanto Rock Orchestra, which recorded three albums for A&M, including *Danse Macabre* (1974), produced by ex-**King Crimson** member Pete Sinfield.

In 1975 he teamed up with former members of the group Mississippi, Pellicci (drums) and guitarists Birtles and Goble. Adding McLachlan (bass) and Formosa (guitar), the Little River Band (named after a Melbourne suburb) signed to EMI's Harvest label. The self-produced, eponymous début album included the American hit 'It's a Long Way There' (1976), while *Diamantina Cocktail* (1977) brought further chart success with Shorrock's 'Help Is on Its Way' and 'Happy Anniversary', written by Birtles and guitarist Briggs and produced by John Boylan.

With the addition of McArdale and Briggs, the Little River Band's **Crosby, Stills and Nash**-influenced sound brought eight further Top Twenty hits by 1982. They included 'Reminiscing' (1978), 'Lonesome Loser' (1979), 'The Night Owls' (1981) and 'Take It Easy on Me' (1982), which was produced by **George Martin**.

Shorrock left to pursue a solo career in 1982, recording the Boylan-produced *Victim of the Peace* (Capitol, 1983). He was replaced by Farnham (whose *Uncovered*, 1981, had been produced by Goble), who sang on the 1983 hit 'We Two' which came from *The Net*. In 1986 Farnham left to follow a highly successful solo career, beginning with *Whispering Jack* (Wheatley), which contained the international hit 'You're the Voice', co-written by former **Procol Harum** member Keith Reid. After Shorrock rejoined in 1988, the Little River Band released *Monsoon*. In 1990 they signed with MCA for *Get Lucky* followed by *Worldwide Love* (1991). *Reminiscing* (Rhino, 1995) is the definitive retrospective.

LITTLE WALTER

b. Marion Walter Jacobs, 1 May 1930, Marksville, Louisiana, USA, d. 15 February 1968, Chicago, Illinois

Little Walter was probably the most accomplished and undoubtedly the most influential harmonica player in the history of the blues. His recordings in his own name and with **Muddy Waters** in the late forties and early fifties amount to a primer of amplified harmonica practice, on both diatonic (Vamper) and chromatic instruments, and it is doubtful if any player since his time has been untouched by his work. As a singer, though his voice was light and his manner unobtrusive, his admirers included Waters and **John Lee Hooker**.

Walter ran away from home in early youth to become an itinerant musician, and by his mid-teens was broadcasting from KFTA, Helena, Arkansas. In 1946 he went to Chicago where, the following year, he made his first records for the small and shortlived Ora Nelle label. He was then still heavily influenced by **Sonny Boy Williamson**, the greatest figure before him in blues harmonica-playing, but once he began recording with Waters for Chess, in 1949, he discovered a blaring, swooping style that did away with the instrument's accordion-like reediness and drew it closer to the sound of the saxophone.

After three years with Waters, Little Walter had a sudden R&B hit with the instrumental 'Juke' (Checker, 1952). He went out on his own, with great success for several years, and as well as participating in many tours had R&B chart entries, including 'Mean Old World' (1952), 'Blues with a Feeling' and 'Last Night' (both 1953) and – his best-known number – 'My Babe' (1955), written by **Willie Dixon**. In 1954 he was never out of the R&B Top Ten. All these recordings were included on his first album, *The Best of Little Walter* (Chess, 1958). He employed sidemen like Louis and David Myers, Robert Lockwood Jnr, Dixon and **Otis Spann**. He also recorded as a sideman himself, both with Waters (until the mid-fifties, and occasionally afterwards) and with other Chicago contemporaries, such as **Otis Rush**.

Walter visited Europe in 1962, Britain in 1964, and Europe again in 1967 with the American Folk Blues Festival. By that time he was in declining health – he had made what was to be his last recording in 1966 – and he died, the following year, after being injured in a street fight.

On many recording sessions with Waters, Walter worked interchangeably with his closest rival for harmonica stature, Walter 'Shakey' Horton (*b. 6 April 1917, Horn Lake, Mississippi, d. December 1981, Chicago*). Though a brilliant and stylistically independent player, Horton was somewhat overshadowed by Little Walter's more outgoing personality and superior singing, but for the last decade of his life he was acknowledged to be the leader in his field. He occasionally recorded with younger artists like John Nicholas (*Fine Cuts*, Blind Pig, 1978) or the Canadian band Hot Cottage (London, 1972), but his most lasting work was as a sideman, contributing immutable solos like that on Jimmy Rogers' 'Walking by Myself' (Chess, 1956).

DANDY LIVINGSTONE

b. Robert Livingstone Thompson, 1944, Kingston, Jamaica

A pop-reggae singer, Livingstone was one of the most successful British-based reggae artists during the seventies.

Moving to London at the age of fifteen, he formed with Tito Simon the ska vocal duo Sugar'n'Dandy, performing at the Flamingo Club in the early sixties. In the rock-steady era, Livingstone recorded as a solo artist and in 1967 cut 'We Are Rude', an answer record to **Prince Buster**'s attack on the 'Rude Boys' (the teenage street gangs of the era), and 'A Message to You Rudy', successfully revived by Two-Tone group the **Specials** in 1979.

He also recorded for Sonny Roberts' Planitone label and cut *Musical Doctor* before recording the British pop hit 'Suzanne Beware of the Devil' (Horse, 1972). 'Big City'/'Think About That' (1973) was a lesser hit and in 1973 he recorded *Conscious* (Mooncrest). Later recordings were released by Night Owl (*South African Experience*, 1978, and *Cartridge*, 1982).

A. L. LLOYD

b. 29 February 1908, London, England, d. 29 September 1982, London

A song collector, theorist and singer, Bert Lloyd was an important influence on the direction of the folk revival in Britain in the fifties and sixties. He was primarily responsible for the growth of interest in Eastern European music and in industrial folk songs, particularly those of the coal miners.

From a middle-class family in South London, he emigrated to Australia following his mother's death in 1924. While working on a sheep station Lloyd began to learn the songs of the itinerant shearing gangs and when he returned to England in 1935 he had a collection of 500 songs. He later recorded some of them on *The Great Australian Legend* (Topic, 1969) with accompanists who included **Fairport Convention** members Dave Swarbrick (violin) and Dave Pegg (bass).

Back in London, Lloyd researched folklore and worked as a translator before sailing to Antarctica in the whaling fleet in 1937. He recorded a selection of whaling ballads on *Leviathan* (Topic, 1968). During the forties he was a journalist on *Picture Post*, also publishing *The Singing Englishman* (1944), the first Marxist account of English folk song. In 1950 Lloyd became a full-time folklorist, studying and collecting material in the Balkans and compiling albums for Topic of Bulgarian and Albanian music.

Lloyd was a focal figure in the folk revival, specializing in adapting and re-creating fragmentary traditional ballads for use by the new generation of singers. Among these was 'Tam Lin', memorably recorded by Sandy Denny and Fairport Convention. With **Ewan MacColl** and **Alan Lomax** he worked on the radio series *Ballads and Blues* in the early fifties and in 1952 Lloyd published *Come All Ye Bold Miners*, a collection of songs from the British coalfields.

In the late fifties he contributed to MacColl and Charles Parker's series of *Radio Ballads* (singing the definitive version of MacColl's 'Shoals of Herring'). With the classical composer Ralph Vaughan Williams, Lloyd edited the *Penguin Book of English Folk Songs*. He sang selections from the book on a Philips album, but most of his recordings were made for the specialist Topic label in the late fifties and early sixties. These included collections of drinking songs (*All for Me Grog*), industrial songs (*The Iron Muse*, 1963), sea shanties and, with MacColl, English and Scottish traditional ballads. *First Person* (1966) was a solo album which showcased Lloyd's quavering yet compelling vocal style. *Folk Song in England*, Lloyd's major work of scholarship and theory, was published in 1967.

When controversy raged over the propriety of the folk-rock approach to traditional material, Lloyd generally favoured the electric-folk developments of the sixties, at one point even being mooted as a member of Fairport Convention.

CHARLES LLOYD

b. 15 March 1938, Memphis, Tennessee, USA

A disciple of **John Coltrane**, Lloyd's showmanship made him one of the most popular jazz musicians with progressive rock audiences of the late sixties.

While still at high school, he played saxophone with several rhythm and blues bands, including those of **B. B. King** and **Bobby Bland**. After studying at the University of Southern California, he replaced **Eric Dolphy** in drummer Chico Hamilton's group in 1960. With Hamilton and guitarist Gabor Szabo he recorded for Impulse, and played with **Cannonball Adderley**, recording *Dream Weaver* (1965) before forming his own quartet in 1966.

The quartet included Szabo and former **Miles Davis** rhythm section Ron Carter (bass) and Tony Williams (drums). The group performed a wide range of music from Adderley-style gospel-funk through rhythmic R&B material to free improvisation. The Lloyd quartet was signed to Atlantic by George Avakian, who promoted them like a rock act, emphasizing Lloyd's extrovert stage presence and colourful dress, which included the then fashionable kaftan.

A successful appearance at the 1966 Monterey Jazz Festival led to Lloyd's becoming the first jazz performer to play San Francisco's Fillmore West in 1968. By now, pianist **Keith Jarrett** and Jack de Johnette (drums) were in the group, which recorded *Forest Flower* (1966) and the modishly titled *Love-in* (1967), and toured Europe and the Soviet Union.

Lloyd spent the seventies in retirement from live performance, with his only musical activity a stillborn record-label project with Mike Love of the **Beach Boys**. He unexpectedly returned to jazz at the 1982 Montreux Festival, playing with young French pianist Michel Petrucciani. The following year he recorded for Blue Note with vocalist Bobby McFerrin. Later albums included *The Call* (ECM, 1993) and *All My Relations* (1995).

MARIE LLOYD

b. Matilda Alice Victoria Wood, 12 February 1870, Hoxton, London, England, d. 7 October 1922, Golders Green, London

Vivacious and direct, the personality of Marie Lloyd epitomized both the jollity and the joyousness of music hall. She was admired not only by her audiences of more than three decades but also by a remarkable succession of literary music-hall *aficionados*. George Bernard Shaw, Max Beerbohm, Compton Mackenzie, James Agate and Edmund Wilson praised her work (Arnold Bennett was a rare dissenting voice), while T. S. Eliot wrote in a celebrated essay: 'no other comedian succeeded so well in giving expression to the life of [her] audience, in raising it to a kind of art'.

She made her first appearance in public at the age of fifteen, and within a few months was playing at several of London's leading halls. Among her early successes were romantic songs like George Wake's 'The Boy in the Gallery' and the saucier 'Oh! Mr Porter' and 'A Little of What You Fancy (Does You Good)'. It was for the suggestive numbers that she became best known.

She appeared in pantomime at London's Drury Lane Theatre in *Humpty Dumpty* (1891), *Little Bo Peep* (1892) and *Robinson Crusoe* (1893), each time with Little Tich and Dan Leno. In 1893 she also played in France, and over the next twenty years she toured successfully in several European countries, South Africa (1896), Australia (1901), Canada (1913) and the United States (1907 and 1914).

She tried her hand once at revue, in *The Tivoli Revue* of 1902, and in 1908–9 experimented with musical comedy, but her genius was for the halls and she seldom left them for long. In 1907 she took a prominent part in the Variety Artists' Federation's strike against unfair management practices, and perhaps partly because of that she was excluded from the invited cast of the first Royal Command Performance in 1912, though her unfadingly 'blue' reputation was also a contributory factor.

It was a disappointment to add to an already afflicted life: she had been twice unhappily married – her second husband was the Cockney singer Alec Hurley – and was about to embark on a third and disastrous union. Though she continued to sing buoyant numbers like 'When I Take My Morning Promenade', 'Every Little Movement' and 'My Old Man Said "Follow the Van"', her private griefs were a subtext of her last outstanding song, 'One of the Ruins That Cromwell Knocked About a Bit', which she was delivering when she collapsed on the stage of the Edmonton Empire. She died shortly afterwards at her home.

Lloyd's recordings give little impression of her charisma. For a time, after her death, she was commemorated in performances by her sisters Alice, Grace and Daisy and her daughter, Marie.

ANDREW LLOYD WEBBER

b. 22 March 1948, London, England

With lyricist Tim Rice, Andrew Lloyd Webber composed the most successful rock musicals of the seventies. His highly melodic approach owed much to the traditions of operetta and the Broadway musical. After separating from Rice, Lloyd Webber had even greater success. Among his hits were *Phantom of the Opera* (1986) and *Sunset Boulevard* (1993). He also composed light classical works.

The son of classical composer William Lloyd Webber, director of the London College of Music, Andrew wrote his first classical work, 'The Toy Theatre Suite', in 1959. His first collaboration with Rice (*b. Timothy Miles Bindon Rice, 10 November 1944*), then an aide to EMI A&R man **Norrie Paramor**, was a musical biography of the Victorian philanthropist, Dr Barnardo.

Shortly afterwards, Lloyd Webber took a course in orchestration at the Guildhall College of Music and in 1968 the first performance of his and Rice's song cycle *Joseph and the Amazing Technicolour Dream Coat* was given in a London school; this was followed by a recording for Decca. During 1969 the pair worked on a more ambitious Biblical musical, which was to become *Jesus Christ Superstar*. A single of the title song by Murray Head was released by MCA Records, who put out an album in 1970. Produced by Mike Leander and featuring Yvonne Elliman as Mary

Magdelene singing 'I Don't Know How to Love Him', the album reached No. 1 in America in 1970, despite being denounced by evangelist Billy Graham. Robert Stigwood produced the stage version on Broadway and eventually the show was performed in more than forty countries. A film of the play, directed by Norman Jewison, was released in 1975.

With playwright Alan Ayckbourn, Lloyd Webber wrote *Jeeves* (1975), an unsuccessful musical based on the books of **P. G. Wodehouse**, before reuniting with Tim Rice to create *Evita* (1976). A glamorized version of the life of Eva Peron, wife of the Argentinian dictator, *Evita*'s music was again recorded by MCA, with hit singles by Julie Covington ('Don't Cry for Me Argentina') and Barbara Dickson ('Another Suitcase in Another Hall'). The studio album also included performances by Paul Jones, while the London stage production starred Elaine Paige and **David Essex**. When the musical was filmed in 1996 with **Madonna** in the title role, Lloyd Webber and Rice reunited to write 'You Must Love Me' for it. The orchestrations (by Lloyd Webber and David Cullen) brought a new sense of grandeur to the music, in particular the opening sequence, which virtually without words rehearses the story we are about to see.

After forming the Really Useful Company to retain control of his work, Lloyd Webber's next stage projects were *Cats* (1981), based on T. S. Eliot's poems *Old Possum's Book of Practical Cats*, and *Song and Dance* (1982), with choreography by Gillian Lynne. The latter included the song cycle *Tell Me on a Sunday*, recorded by Marti Webb. Lloyd Webber's later stage projects such as *Starlight Express* (1984), based on nostalgia for steam locomotives, and a new version of *The Phantom of the Opera* (1986), though commercial successes, lacked the dramatic zest of his work with Rice. Lloyd Webber also extended his reach into classical music with *Variations*, a set of pieces based on a theme by Paganini. His own version of the work, featuring Barbara Thompson and **Colosseum** leader Jon Hiseman was a British hit in 1978. It was also recorded by his cellist brother Julian. *Requiem* (HMV, 1985), a large-scale devotional work, found little favour with the critics. However, it included the song 'Pie Jesu', which gave Lloyd Webber's wife Sarah Brightman and boy soprano Paul Miles-Kingston a British Top Ten hit.

By now a knight, Sir Andrew transformed David Garnett's 1955 novel *Aspects of Love* into a musical in 1989, with lyricists Charles Hart and Don Black. Sung by cast member Michael Ball, the show's 'Love Changes Everything' was a hit on Lloyd Webber's own Really Useful label. A London revival of *Joseph* starring Australian pop idol **Jason Donovan** provided a British No. 1 with 'Any Dream Will Do' in 1991. After co-writing the pop hit 'Tetris' by Doctor Spin in 1992, Lloyd Webber's next theatrical project was a

musical based on the classic Billy Wilder movie *Sunset Boulevard*, with lyrics by Don Black. The show was taken off after several months and reopened in a new version with additional songs in 1994. In America the show's progress to vast commercial success was equally fraught. Actress Faye Dunaway's rejection by Lloyd Webber as not being able to sing well enough led to a lawsuit before Glenn Close's triumph on Broadway. Lloyd Webber set up his own film production company in early 1994 to turn five of his musicals into films, including an animated *Cats* and a big-screen *Phantom of the Opera*.

Whistle Down the Wind (1997), with lyrics from Jim Steinman – best known for his *Bat Out of Hell* collaborations with **Meat Loaf** – was loosely based on Keith Waterhouse and Willis Hall's script for the 1961 film of the same name about a group of children who think a murderer on the run is Jesus Christ. It was mauled by the critics but became a commercial success. For *The Beautiful Game* (2000) Lloyd Webber continued his attempts to surprise. He teamed up with stand-up left-wing comedian turned novelist and playwright 'Motor Mouth' Ben Elton and opera specialist director Robert Carsen for a musical set amongst the troubles of Belfast in 1969 as the conflict between Protestants and Catholics took root. Elton certainly provides a gritty and humour-strewn book – one critic noted that there are more laughs in *The Beautiful Game* than in the rest of Lloyd Webber's complete *oeuvre* – but his rhyming is somewhat rudimentary and his lyrics too often lost amid Lloyd Webber's bland balladry. The result is a musical pretending to be brave but too often settling for comfortable sermonizing in its take on a football club riven by sectarianism.

After *Evita*, Rice followed a varied career as broadcaster and author. He composed the musical *Blondel* (1983) before working with Benny Andersson and Björn Ulvaeus, formerly of **Abba**, on the hit musical *Chess*, whose most successful song was 'I Know Him So Well', a hit duet for Barbara Dickson and Elaine Paige in 1985. In 1989 he began work on an English-language version of the French musical *Starmania* by Michel Berger and Luc Plamondon, releasing an album from the project as *Tycoon* (1992), with guest vocalists including **Tom Jones**, **Kim Carnes** and **Cyndi Lauper**, who had a British Top Twenty hit with 'The World Is Stone'.

Rice wrote many songs for films from the seventies onwards and also worked with a number of collaborators, including **Rick Wakeman**, **Vangelis** and **Elton John**. His later film work for Walt Disney brought an Oscar for the song 'Whole New World', from the animated feature *Aladdin*. The song was a major international hit for **Peabo Bryson** and Regina Bell in 1993. In 1994 Disney's *The Lion King* was released, featuring five songs written by Rice with Elton John. In 1999 the pair reunited for *Elton John's Aida,* a musical based on the opera of that name, which was staged by Disney on Broadway in 2000. Much reworked, it was a commercial success.

LOS LOBOS
David Hidalgo, b. 1954, Los Angeles, California, USA; Conrad Lozano, b. 1952, Los Angeles; Luis Peres, b. 1953, Los Angeles; Cesar Rosas, b. 1954, Los Angeles; Steve Berlin, b. 1957, Philadelphia, Pennsylvania

In the eighties this 'band from East LA' was the first act of Mexican origins to enjoy major chart success in the US since **Ritchie Valens** in the fifties.

Formed in Los Angeles in 1974, Los Lobos came to national prominence in the US with their self-financed début album, self-mockingly titled *Just Another Band from East LA.* The individual members had all played in local covers bands. Strong local sales and enthusiastic reviews for the band's mixture of rock'n'roll and traditional Mexican music brought the band to the attention of leading LA independent label Slash, for whom they recorded an EP, *And a Time to Dance* (1983), which included a version of Ritchie Valens' 'Come on, Let's Go'. Slash teamed them with producers T-Bone Burnett and Steve Berlin (ex-the Blasters) for the EP and following album *How Will the Wolf Survive?* (1984), which brought Los Lobos to a wider audience. The album saw the introduction to the line-up of Berlin as saxophone player, and other members of the band began to crop up in supporting roles on albums by such artists as **Elvis Costello**, **Tom Waits** and **Ry Cooder**. At this time, they also played on **Paul Simon**'s *Graceland* album.

The follow-up album, *By the Light of the Moon* (1987), also charted on both sides of the Atlantic, but it was Los Lobos' contribution to the soundtrack of the Ritchie Valens bio-pic *La Bamba* which gave them their greatest success to date. Their version of Valens' 'La Bamba' made No. 1 in the UK and both it and the soundtrack album became massive international hits. The band responded by recording an album of Spanish-language and instrumental Mexican music, *La Pistola y el Corazon* (1988). Although failing to generate major sales, it again picked up excellent reviews.

The Neighborhood (1990) was a largely successful return to the style of *By the Light of the Moon.* However, it was the next album, *Kiko* (1992), which showed just how far they had developed since their début. It was a confident, assured set, which drew favourable comparisons with the very best of **The Band** and **Creedence Clearwater Revival**. It was followed by a superior and comprehensive two-CD compilation of their past successes along with some

new material, like the first album titled *Just Another Band from East LA* (1993). In 1995 the band contributed a stunning reading of 'Lonely Avenue' to the Doc Pomus tribute album, *Till the Night Is Gone.* After the children's album *Papa's Dream* (1996), the group released a sequel to *Kiko, Colossal Head* (1996). In 1997 Los Lobos joined forces with Peter Buck, Mike McCready and others to form the loose affiliation Tuatara, which released *Breaking the Ethers.*

JOSEPH LOCKE
b. Joseph McLaughlin, 23 March 1912, Londonderry, Ireland; d. 14 October 1999, Clane, County Kildare

A larger-than-life figure, Locke, while firmly in the tradition of **John McCormack**, brought a brash sentimentality (and in performance, sexuality – he was once called the **Tom Jones** of his day) to the repertoire of ballads he made his own. These included his theme song 'Hear My Song Violetta', 'I'll Take You Home Again Kathleen', 'Blaze Away' and the oft-recorded 'Come Back to Sorrento'. *Hear My Song* was also the title of the film loosely based on his career.

The son of a butcher, Locke sang in church and after serving in the Irish Guards joined the Royal Ulster Constabulary, earning himself the sobriquet 'The Singing Bobby' when he continued his amateur appearances. Dubbed Locke – because McLaughlin was considered too long to fit on posters – by band-leader turned impresario **Jack Hylton** when he became a professional in 1944, the singer found immediate success at Blackpool with his twinkling eyes, romantic voice and roguish manner. A staple on the Northern variety circuit – his style being deemed too simple for London – he started recording with regular success in 1947. He also appeared in several films, including *Holidays with Pay* (1954). However, although enormously successful, his gambling led to a growing debt with the Inland Revenue and in 1958, the day before he was to be arrested for the non-payment of £17,000 in owed taxes, he fled to Ireland.

While in enforced exile, a mystery singer, Mr X, toured the UK singing the songs associated with Locke with a remarkable facility and inviting the guess that he was in fact Locke. It is this period of his life that forms the backbone to Peter Chelsom's enchanting 1992 film *Hear My Song*, in which Ned Beatty impersonated Locke. Richard Thompson also explored this period in the singer's life with 'Joseph Locke'. Sung masterfully by Norma Thompson on *The Very Thought of You* (Hannibal, 1999), the song imagined an encounter in a pub with an inebriated singer pretending to be Locke.

Locke sang 'Danny Boy' at the film's London première and on the back of its release had a minor hit with a reissue of the title song and a more substantial one with a CD compilation of past recordings.

HANK LOCKLIN
b. Lawrence Hankins Locklin, 15 February 1918, McLellan, Florida, USA

Locklin's high tenor and rich vibrato made him, like **Slim Whitman**, a particular favourite in Ireland and, when allied to the 'Nashville sound' (as developed by **Chet Atkins**), won him a million-seller with 'Please Help Me I'm Falling' (RCA, 1960).

The son of a farmer, Locklin toured the Southern states and after the Second World War joined the cast of *Louisiana Hayride*. He signed with Decca, but only had hits after moving to Four Star. His first was 'The Same Sweet Girl' (1949), an unusual song in that though performed in the honky-tonk manner, it told a tale of fidelity rather than infidelity. More characteristic of his later recordings was 'Let Me Be the One' (1953). That song's success led to Locklin being signed to RCA, where Atkins gave a decidedly pop inflection to his records. Country hits included 'Geisha Girl' (1957) and the self-penned 'Send Me the Pillow You Dream on' (1958), which was subsequently successfully revived by **Johnny Tillotson** (1962) and **Dean Martin** (1965). That and Dale Robertson's 'Please Help Me', which provoked the answer record '(I Can't Help You) I'm Falling Too' by **Skeeter Davis**, are the songs most closely associated with Locklin. In 1970 he had a further country hit with an even poppier version of 'Please Help Me' with the Danny Davis Nashville Brass in support.

Though his only subsequent pop hits were a pair of British successes, 'We're Gonna Go Fishing' (1962) and 'I Feel a Cry Coming on' (1966), Locklin consistently had country hits throughout the sixties and seventies. In 1975 he joined MGM. The definitive retrospective is the four-CD set *Ivan M Tribe* (Bear Family, 1995).

LISA LOEB
b. Dallas, Texas, USA

After becoming the first unsigned artist to top the US *Billboard* charts with her single 'Stay', Loeb became a popular antidote to the nineties trend of female alternative rock performers.

Having learnt to play the guitar and piano as a child, Loeb studied music theory at Brown University, performing regularly alongside her roommate Liz Mitchell at local venues. After graduating, the duo formed Nine Stories with guitarist Tim Bright, bassist Joe Quigley and drummer Jonathan Feinberg, taking their name from a J. D. Salinger collection. After Mitchell left, Loeb met producer Juan Patiño, recording *The Purple Acoustic Tape* (1992), which she sold at gigs.

Loeb's breakthrough came when her actor friend Ethan Hawke asked her to contribute a track to his next movie, *Reality Bites* (1994). Originally featuring on the soundtrack album, 'Stay' climbed to the top of the US chart and sold over 750,000 copies worldwide, earning the singer a Grammy nomination and the Brit Award for Best International Newcomer. Loeb signed to Geffen for the release of her début album, *Tails* (1995)*. The follow-up, *Firecracker* (1997), proved equally successful and earned her another hit single, 'I Do'. She also appeared on the all-female Lilith Fair tour in 1997 and 1998.

FRANK LOESSER
b. 29 June 1910, New York, USA, d. 28 March 1969, New York

Composer, lyricist, librettist, producer and publisher, Loesser was one of the most versatile (and volcanic) Broadway songwriters. His best songs include the oft-recorded 'Praise the Lord and Pass the Ammunition' (1942), a million-seller for **Kay Kyser**; 'On a Slow Boat to China' (1948), revived by **Emile Ford** (1959); and the Oscar-winning 'Baby It's Cold Outside' (1949), memorably recorded by **Louis Jordan** and **Ella Fitzgerald**, and **Johnny Mercer** and Margaret Whiting, among others. His major film score was *Hans Christian Andersen* (1952), which provided **Danny Kaye** with several memorable songs, while his stage successes included the inventive *Guys and Dolls* (1953), *How to Succeed in Business Without Really Trying* (1963) and *The Most Happy Fella* (1966).

The son of a piano teacher, Loesser was briefly a newspaper reporter before in 1931 his first song ('In Love with the Memory of You') was published. After supporting himself as a pianist, in 1937 he moved to Hollywood where he wrote film songs with Burton Lane (best known for the 1947 Broadway musical *Finian's Rainbow*, which included 'How Are Things in Glocca Morra?', and *On a Clear Day You Can See Forever*, 1965, written with Alan Jay Lerner of **Lerner and Loewe**). His first successes came with **Hoagy Carmichael** ('Two Sleepy People', 1938, a hit for **Fats Waller**, **Sammy Kaye**, **Lawrence Welk** and the composer himself); Frederick Hollander ('See What the Boys in the Backroom Will Have', introduced by **Marlene Dietrich** in *Destry Rides Again*, 1939); Joseph Lilley ('Jingle, Jangle, Jingle', which provided **Gene Autry** with a hit in 1942); and **Jule Styne**, with whom he composed songs for Republic B-Westerns and 'I Don't Want to Walk without You Baby', a No. 1 for **Harry James** (1942).

In the same year Loesser had his greatest hit with 'Praise the Lord', the first song for which he wrote both words and music. That led to a series of patriotic war songs, including the humorous 'What Do You

Do in the Infantry', and the more straightforward 'Roger Young' and 'First Class Mary Brown' (1943). More representative of his literate romanticism was 'Spring Will Be a Little Late This Year' (1944) and 'Baby It's Cold Outside'.

In 1948 Loesser returned triumphantly to Broadway with his score for *Where's Charley*, a musical adaptation of Brandon Thomas's classic English farce, *Charley's Aunt*. That prepared the way for Loesser's adaptation of a series of stories by American humorist Damon Runyon, *Guys and Dolls* (1950, filmed 1955 with Marlon Brando and **Frank Sinatra**), for which Loesser wrote both the words and music. One of the most successful Broadway musicals of the fifties, it included the witty 'Luck Be a Lady' and the mock-revivalism of 'Sit Down You're Rocking the Boat', in which Loesser perfectly matched the intricate rhythms of Runyon's prose style. Equally impressive was the ambitious, operatic *The Most Happy Fella* (1956), for which Loesser wrote the book as well as the words and music. It included 'Standing on the Corner' (a hit for **Dean Martin** and the Four Lads, Columbia) and 'Happy to Make Your Acquaintance'. After the failure of *Greenwillow* (1960), Loesser had success again with the send-up of the Horatio Alger myth *How to Succeed in Business Without Really Trying* (1961, filmed 1967), which co-starred **Rudy Vallee** and included 'Brotherhood of Man'.

KENNY LOGGINS
b. 7 January 1948, Everett, Washington, USA

A songwriter, singer and guitarist, Loggins played mellow soft-rock with Jim Messina in the seventies and became a successful writer and producer of film soundtracks in the eighties.

In the mid-sixties Loggins played in Californian folk groups and the rock bands Second Helping and Gator Creek, recording for Viva and Mercury, respectively. He became a staff songwriter for the ABC Wingate publishing house and provided the **Nitty Gritty Dirt Band** with 'House at Pooh Corner'. When Loggins negotiated a recording contract with Columbia, Messina (*b. 5 December 1947, Maywood, California*) was assigned to him as producer. An experienced engineer, Messina had produced **Buffalo Springfield** and subsequently joined the band on bass, moving to Poco when the group split up. Such was his rapport with Loggins that they decided to record as a duo, releasing *Sittin' In* (1972), which included Loggins' 'Danny's Song', a hit for **Anne Murray**.

The eponymous second album provided a million-seller in 'Your Mama Don't Dance' (a hit for US heavy metal band Poison in 1989) and there were further hits in 1973 with 'Thinking of You' and 'My Music', from *Full Sail*. Later albums included *Mother*

Lode (1974), a miscalculated collection of fifties songs, *So Fine* (1975) and *Native Son* (1976).

Loggins and Messina separated in 1977, with Loggins setting out on a solo career with *Celebrate Me Home* (1977) and *Nightwatch* (1978), whose 'Whenever I Call You Friend', with harmony vocals by **Fleetwood Mac**'s Stevie Nicks, was a Top Ten hit. *Keep the Fire* (1979) also provided successful singles in 'This Is It' and the title track. In the same year Loggins co-wrote the **Doobie Brothers**' song 'What a Fool Believes'.

His career in movie themes began in 1980 with 'I'm Alright', from *Caddyshack*, followed by 'Footloose'* and 'I'm Free (Heaven Help the Man)' from *Footloose* (1984). Loggins' greatest Hollywood success, however, came with the 1986 fighter-pilot saga, *Top Gun*, for which he co-wrote several songs and sang the best-selling 'Danger Zone'. 'Nobody's Fool', from the film *Caddyshack 2*, was another big hit in 1988, although the album *Back to Avalon* failed to emulate the single's success. In 1989 Loggins decided to take a sabbatical from his recording career. He returned in 1991 with *Leap of Faith* and toured America in support. A later tour produced the 1993 live album *Outside: from the Redwoods*, on which he performed largely acoustic versions of his back catalogue, and in 1994 Loggins released *Return to Pooh Corner*, an album of songs for children.

Messina's solo albums included *Oasis* (Columbia, 1979) and *Messina* (Warner, 1981), after which he retired from performing and concentrated on running his recording studio operation. In 1989, however, he was reunited with his Poco colleagues for one successful album, *Legacy*. Loggins and Messina briefly reunited in 1992 for a handful of benefit concerts in their home town of Santa Barbara, California. *Greatest Hits* (Sony, 1998) is the definitive retrospective of the pair.

JOHN AND ALAN LOMAX
John Avery Lomax, b. 23 September 1875, Goodman, Mississippi, USA, d. 26 January 1948, Greenville, Mississippi; Alan Lomax, b. 15 January 1915, Austin, Texas

The Lomaxes, father and son, were the leading collectors of American folk song in the twentieth century. As curators, from its inception, of the Library of Congress's Archive of Folk Song, they gathered, or commissioned others to gather, what became the nation's most important collection of recorded folk music.

John A. Lomax was raised in the Southwest, where even as a teenager he collected songs from farmers and cowboys. At Harvard he encountered the folk-lorist George Lyman Kittredge, who, unlike other academics, encouraged his collecting, and he secured a travelling scholarship to make cylinder recordings in the Southwest (some of which survive). Drawing on this research, he published *Cowboy Songs and Other Frontier Ballads* (1910), a pioneering work, though not immediately recognized as such.

After spells in the worlds of academia and banking, Lomax embarked, in 1933, on a collecting trip with a new portable disc-recording machine; his eighteen-year-old son Alan accompanied him. It was on this venture that they met **Leadbelly**, as well as making important recordings of prison work songs. *American Ballads and Folk Songs* (1934) consolidated John Lomax's authority in the field and he became curator of the new Archive of Folk Song, assisted, from 1937 onwards, by Alan.

Among the material secured by the Lomaxes for the Archive were the sessions of music and reminiscences by **Jelly Roll Morton**; Anglo-American fiddle tunes, collected by Herbert Halpert and others; songs and narratives from the California labour camps, gathered by Charles Todd and Robert Sonkin; narratives of ex-slaves; early cajun field recordings; and music of several of the non-English-speaking immigrant communities.

In 1939 Alan produced a folk-music radio series for CBS, *Wellsprings of America*, the first of many. He collaborated with his father on the books *Our Singing Country* (1941) and *Folk Song, USA* (1947). He also developed folk-music catalogues for record companies like Decca (1945) and Columbia, for whom he edited the *World Library of Folk and Primitive Music* (seventeen volumes, 1951–7). In 1958 he made the first of his own records, *Texas Folk Songs* (Tradition). A lengthy recording project in 1959–60 produced almost a score of albums for Atlantic (*Southern Journey*) and Prestige (*Southern Folk Heritage*); it was on this trip that **Fred McDowell** was discovered.

During the sixties Alan was a director of the Newport Folk Festival and other events. He also began work on a worldwide survey of styles of performance of folk music, which led to the publication of *Cantometrics* (1976).

Alan's sister Bess had been active as a performer, associating herself in the late thirties with **Woody Guthrie**, **Burl Ives** and the circle that formed the Almanac Singers; she joined the group and married a fellow member, Butch Hawes. After the Second World War, she concentrated on teaching folk music, though she continued to perform publicly in California, where she moved in the fifties. Both she and Alan remained active in the folk-music establishment, and in 1993 Alan published an autobiography.

GUY LOMBARDO

b. Gaeterio Lombardo, 19 June 1902, London, Ontario, Canada, d. 5 November 1977, Houston, Texas, USA

Playing what he dubbed 'the sweetest music this side of heaven', Lombardo and his Royal Canadians were one of the most successful of the dance bands that emerged in the twenties. Though often attacked for its very sweetness – the band featured a large saxophone section, few brass instruments and a rhythm section that was felt rather than heard – the band's longevity (Lombardo never retired) and popularity were rooted in its instantly recognizable sound. A mark of the breadth of its appeal was that among the all-time attendance records it set, one was at Harlem's Savoy Ballroom. The band was hugely popular among blacks and Lombardo was often cited by **Louis Armstrong** as one of his favourite musicians.

Lombardo formed his first band in 1920 with his brothers Carmen, who until his death in 1971 was Lombardo's musical director, and Lebert (later a fourth brother, Victor, joined the band and a sister, Rose Marie, briefly sang with the orchestra). In 1927 Lombardo moved to Chicago. Only moderately successful at first, Lombardo's emphasis on smoothness and sweetness won a large audience when he began to broadcast from Chicago. During this period he is credited with having invented the instrumental medley, with brief arrangements of popular songs of the day, as a means of playing the many requests he received. Following his signing with the influential booking agency the Music Corporation of America, the pace of Lombardo's career increased significantly. In 1929 he made New York's Hotel Roosevelt his base, appearing there regularly until 1963.

Among the many songs Lombardo popularized were 'Coquette' and 'Sweethearts on Parade' (1928, written by Carmen); **Walter Donaldson**'s 'You're Driving Me Crazy' and 'Little White Lies' (1930); and Al Dubin and **Harry Warren**'s 'September in the Rain' (1937) and 'Auld Lang Syne', which Lombardo adopted as his theme song after the success of his first New Year's Eve broadcast. In the course of his career, which included spells with RCA Victor and Columbia, as well as Decca, where his recordings were mostly supervised by **Milt Gabler**, Lombardo sold more than 100 million records. His million-sellers included 'Humeresque' (Decca, 1946), an adaptation of Anton Dvořák's piece for solo piano; 'Winter Wonderland' (1946), which featured vocals by the **Andrews Sisters**; **Irving Berlin**'s 'Easter Parade' (1947); and his version of **Anton Karas**'s theme to *The Third Man* (1950).

Though he built up substantial interests in music publishing and property, Lombardo continued to tour throughout the sixties. After his death, Lebert briefly took over the leadership of the Guy Lombardo Orchestra.

JULIE LONDON

b. Julie Peck, 26 September 1926, Santa Clara, California, USA, d. 18 October 2000, Los Angeles, California

Although most of her working life was spent in film and, latterly, television, London is best remembered for her chillingly cold rendition of Arthur Hamilton's lachrymose ballad 'Cry Me a River' (Liberty), which sold a million copies in 1955, and was successfully revived by Mari Wilson in Britain in 1984. The dramatic effect of the record owed much to London's husband and producer, Bobby Troup (*b. 18 October 1918, Harrisburg, Pennsylvania*), who set her voice against the spare sound of the guitar of Barney Kessel and bass of Ray Leatherwood.

A statuesque blonde, London entered films in the late forties, graduating from B-feature quickies such as *Jungle Girl* (1944) to second leads in A-features, but never became a front-rank star. Her best films were *The Girl Can't Help It* (1956) – the classic film about rock'n'roll in which she performed 'Cry Me a River' – and Anthony Mann's violent *Man of the West* (1958). Though she regularly appeared in cabaret, in general she eschewed musicals, preferring dramatic roles.

In his own right, Troup was a singer, songwriter ('Route 66') and actor (he played **Tommy Dorsey** in *The Gene Krupa Story*, 1959). After London's recording career came to an end, she and Troup retired to television, starring in the series *Emergency* (1972–7), which was produced by her first husband, Jack Webb.

TRINI LOPEZ

b. Trinidad Lopez III, 15 May 1937, Dallas, Texas, USA

Best remembered for his exuberant version of 'If I Had a Hammer'* (1963), Lopez carved a career for himself with folky, Latin versions of contemporary hits.

A veteran of the club circuit of America's Southwest, Lopez was discovered in 1962 by record producer and one-time bandleader Don Costa while playing at Hollywood's PJ Club. Costa signed him to Reprise and recorded *Trini Lopez Live at PJ's* (1963). The album featured a party atmosphere, with gentle hand-clapping and enthusiastic yelps behind Lopez's vocals. 'Hammer', Lopez's version of the **Peter Paul and Mary** hit of 1962, was released as a single and was an immediate hit. Two other songs from the album, **Leiber and Stoller**'s 'Kansas City' and **Leonard Bernstein** and **Stephen Sondheim**'s 'America', were also hits. His other American hits, all similar in style, were 'Lemon Tree' (1965), 'I'm Coming Home Cindy', a version of **Ritchie Valens**' 'La Bamba' (1966) and, his last, 'Sally Was a Good Old Girl' (1968). He was more successful outside America with *Sing Along World* (1966), *Trini Lopez in London* (1967) and other albums, and throughout the sixties and seventies regularly toured both Europe and Latin America. In 1978 he released an ill-judged disco album in the UK, *Transformed by Time* (Pye International).

Unlike **Jose Feliciano**, however, Lopez was unable to build a more broadly based career, despite film work (including *The Dirty Dozen*, 1967), and occasional European hits, such as 'Trini Tracks' (RCA, 1981). In 1991 WEA Latina issued *25th Anniversary Album*, which included new versions of 'Hammer' and 'Lemon Tree' as well as Spanish language material. Lopez continued touring throughout the nineties.

VINCENT LOPEZ

b. 10 December 1895, Brooklyn, New York, USA, d. 30 April 1972, Miami Beach, Florida

Lopez was the first bandleader to be featured in a live outside radio broadcast when, in 1921, Radio WJZ transmitted part of his performance at New York's Pennsylvania Hotel. He led one of the most popular American radio dance bands of the twenties and thirties. Among those who played in his various bands were **Glenn Miller**, **Artie Shaw**, **Xavier Cugat** and **Betty Hutton**, whom he discovered.

Of Portugese extraction, Lopez was the son of a navy bandmaster. In his teens he started playing in New York bars and in 1916 led his first orchestra. His speciality was playing the piano novelties then in vogue, including Zez Confrey's 'Kitten on the Keys' and Felix Arndt's 'Nola', which Lopez adopted as his theme song. In 1925 his was one of the first American bands to perform in Britain and throughout the thirties and forties he broadcast from various New York hotels before making the Hotel Taft his base in 1941. He appeared in *The Big Broadcast* (1932) and numerous musical shorts.

On his retirement he published *Numerology* (1961), a reflection of his interest in numerology and astrology.

JOE LOSS

b. 22 June 1909, Liverpool, England, d. 6 June 1990

One of the most successful and longest-serving British orchestra leaders, Loss was the undisputed king of the ballrooms of the forties.

The son of a furniture-maker, Loss studied violin at both Trinity College of Music and the London School of Music, where he formed the Magnetic Dance Band. He turned professional musician in 1926 and played with various dance bands in Blackpool and London (including Oscar Rabin's) before forming his own seven-piece in 1930 to play at London's Astoria ballroom. In 1931 he became resident bandleader at the Kit Kat Club and in 1933 made his broadcasting début. Before he confined his activities to recording and tours of Britain's ballrooms during wartime, Loss alternated between residencies at various ballrooms and variety tours, appearing in circus tents and boxing rings, as well as theatres. Among his featured vocalists were **Adelaide Hall** and Chick Henderson, and in 1935 **Vera Lynn** made her broadcasting début with Loss's band. His most successful recordings of this period on Regal-Zonophone and later HMV included **Glenn Miller**'s 'In the Mood', which he adopted as his theme song, 'Woodchopper's Ball' and **Meade Lux Lewis**'s 'Honky Tonk Train Blues'. Technically perfect, Loss was at his best playing for a dancing audience at ballrooms rather than for a seated one at hotels. In 1940, in the course of one week, he played for 10,000 dancers at the Glasgow Playhouse ballroom.

Loss's popularity was little affected by the advent of rock'n'roll and in the sixties he had a series of dance-orientated British pop hits. These included 'Wheels Cha Cha' (HMV, 1961), 'Must Be Madison' (1962), and the highly unlikely 'March of the Mods' (1964). More typical of Loss's style were his series of strict-tempo dance albums, including *World Championship Ballroom Dances*, and his appearances on the popular television series *Come Dancing*. Popular in Europe and widely travelled – Loss led the first British band to play in China – Loss and his band regularly entertained the passengers on the *QE 2*'s annual world cruise from 1973 onwards. In 1978 he was awarded the OBE and his band continued to tour Britain in the eighties.

JOHN D. LOUDERMILK

b. 31 March 1934, Durham, North Carolina, USA

A prolific songwriter and occasional hitmaker in his own right, Loudermilk brought a definite folk inflection to his own performances and revealed an equally strong penchant for comedy and novelty in many of the songs he supplied to other performers.

The son of a carpenter, Loudermilk became a Salvation Army bandsman in his teens. A multi-instrumentalist, he made his radio début at the age of ten and his TV début two years later on a talent show hosted by **Tex Ritter**. While he was working for a local Durham TV station, **George Hamilton IV** recorded his composition 'A Rose and a Babe Ruth' (1956), which sold a million copies, and Loudermilk turned professional songwriter. Other songs from this period included 'Sittin' in the Balcony' (a hit for **Eddie Cochran** and recorded by Loudermilk as Johnny Dee); 'Waterloo' (a million-seller for Stonewall Jackson on Columbia in 1959); and 'Angela Jones' (a Top Thirty hit for Johnny Ferguson on MGM in 1960). As Tommy Dee, he recorded 'Three Stars' (Crest, 1959), a sentimental tribute to **Buddy Holly, Ritchie Valens** and the Big Bopper.

In the sixties he supplied the **Everly Brothers** with 'Ebony Eyes', Sue Thompson with the million-sellers 'Sad Movies (Make Me Cry)' (Hickory, 1961) and 'Norman' (1962), and had a series of pop and country hits himself. These included 'The Language of Love' (RCA, 1961), 'Thou Shalt Not Steal' and 'Road Hog' (1962), which were performed in a far sparer and folkier manner than other people's recordings of his songs. Representative albums of the time include *Suburban Attitudes* (1967) and *Country Love Songs* (1968). His most frequently recorded songs of the sixties were 'Abilene' (1963) and 'Break My Mind' (1967), which were originally recorded by George Hamilton, and the grim tale of rural poverty 'Tobacco Road', which gave British beat group the Nashville Teens a British and American Top Twenty hit in 1964 (on Decca and London, respectively). His last pop hit was 'Indian Reservation', which gave **Paul Revere and the Raiders** an American No. 1 in 1971 and was a British Top Ten hit for Don Fardon (Young Blood, 1970).

In the seventies and eighties Loudermilk spent much of his time studying ethnomusicology, recording only occasionally. *Sittin' in the Balcony* (Bear Family, 1995) is the definitive retrospective.

THE LOUVIN BROTHERS

Ira Louvin, b. 21 April 1924, Rainesville, Alabama, USA, d. 20 June, 1965, Jefferson City, Missouri; Charlie Louvin, b. 7 July 1927, Rainesville

The country songs and duet singing of the Louvin Brothers expressed the close ties of family life in the American rural South, a firm faith in God's word and a piercing sense of elemental joy and sorrow. More than any of their stylistic predecessors, such as the **Blue Sky Boys** or Charlie and **Bill Monroe**, the Louvins touched and changed the country and pop music that came after them, primarily through their direct influence upon the harmony singing of the **Everly Brothers**.

The brothers grew up in Henegar, Alabama, Ira taking up the mandolin and Charlie the guitar – an instrumental combination explicitly based on that of the Blue Sky Boys, Monroes and other country brother acts. In 1943 they won an amateur talent contest in Chattanooga, Tennessee, the prize for which was an early-morning radio show. Later in the forties they graduated to the prestigious *Midday Merry-Go-Round* on WNOX, Knoxville, Tennessee. In 1949 they signed to MGM, but their recording career was interrupted by Charlie's Korean War service. In 1951 they moved, at the instigation of **Fred Rose**, to Capitol.

By the mid-fifties the Louvin Brothers were major country stars: cast-members of the *Grand Ole Opry* and regular country chart-makers with hits like 'I Don't Believe You've Met My Baby' and 'You're

Running Wild' (both 1956). 'My Baby's Gone' (1959) also reached the Top Ten. In the late fifties and early sixties they recorded some twenty Capitol albums, about half of them of sacred songs; there was also a tribute set to the **Delmore Brothers**. Probably their most celebrated LP was *Tragic Songs of Life* (1956), which defined their transitional stance between old-time balladry and a modern 'realist' approach to emotional subjects.

The latter part of the Louvins' stay with Capitol was soured by their being forced to accede to more modern production ideas. Ira's mandolin was phased out, to be replaced by the polished guitar of **Chet Atkins**, and some of the brothers' bite was muzzled. Their own relationship, always changeable, also deteriorated, and in 1963 Charlie went solo, finding country chart success in the following year with 'I Don't Love You Anymore', and in 1965 with 'See the Big Man Cry, Mama'. In 1965 Ira, together with his wife Florence (who sang on his show, as Anne Young), was killed in a car crash. A solo album, *Ira Louvin* (Capitol), was released posthumously.

Charlie continued to work as a solo until 1970, when he formed a duet with Melba Montgomery, who also had singing partnerships with **Gene Pitney** and **George Jones**. The association only lasted until 1971, but Charlie remained a working country artist and was still an *Opry* regular during the eighties. In that decade, the Louvins' legacy of songs – many of which were written by them – began to be mined by other than pure country artists. **Emmylou Harris** recorded 'When I Stop Dreaming' and also occasionally performed in public with Charlie.

LOVE

Arthur Lee, b. 7 March 1944, Memphis, Tennessee, USA; John Echols, b. 1947, Memphis; Bryan MacLean, b. 25 September 1946, Los Angeles, California, d. 25 December 1998, Los Angeles; Ken Forssi, b. 1943, Cleveland, Ohio, d. 5 January 1998; Alban 'Snoopy' Pfisterer, b. 1947, Switzerland

With the **Doors**, the most hard-edged Los Angeles group of the psychedelic era, Love are best remembered for *Forever Changes* (1967). A classic album, it mixed lush, mysterious ballads ('Andmoreagain'), hippie philosophizing ('Old Man') and urgent, clearly drugs-related, songs ('Maybe the People Would Be the Times, or Between Clark and Hilldale'). The whole was tied together by swirling horns and exotic string arrangements with production techniques (notably phasing) that echoed the new emphasis on the studio following **The Beatles**' *Sgt Pepper's Lonely Hearts Club Band* (1967).

Raised in Los Angeles, Lee formed Arthur Lee and the LAGS (Los Angeles Group), inspired by **Booker T. and the MGs**. That group, which included later Love member Echols, recorded briefly for Capitol ('Ninth Wave') before in 1965 Lee assembled the first line-up of Love. Signed to Elektra, their eponymous début album (1966) saw them performing **Byrds**-inspired folk-rock material (bassist MacLean had been a roadie with the group) with a ferocity reminiscent of the early work of **The Who**, with its melding of acoustic and electric guitars over rapid drum patterns. Included on the album was the minor hit, a furious reworking of **Burt Bacharach**'s 'My Little Red Book', a version of Dino Valenti's 'Hey Joe' (a hit for the Leaves, Mira, 1966, and also recorded by the Byrds and **Jimi Hendrix**, 1967, with whom Lee would record an unreleased album in 1970) and the menacing ballad 'Signed D.C.'. *Da Capo* (1967) included the group's only major hit, '7 and 7 Is', and the indulgent 'Revelation', which lasted a whole side of the album and saw Lee perfecting a vocal stance that veered from the smoothness of a **Johnny Mathis** to the scream of a Mick Jagger. Then followed *Forever Changes*, whose critical success was not matched by sales; soon afterwards the group disbanded. MacLean occasionally teamed up with Lee in the future, and also played live as a solo artist before forming a duo with his half sister **Maria McKee**, which would eventually lead to the formation of Lone Justice. In 1990 she had an international hit with 'Show Me Heaven'.

Lee formed a second Love for *Four Sail* (1969) and *Out Here* (Blue Thumb, 1969, re-released with additional tracks as *Love*, MCA, 1982). With Jay Donnellan replacing Echols on lead guitar and George Suranovitch (drums) and Frank Fayad replacing Pfisterer and Forssi, these albums saw the exotic frothiness of Lee's earlier work pared down to little effect. *False Start* (1970) included a track from Lee's collaboration with Hendrix ('The Everlasting First') but, like Lee's solo outing *Vindicator* (A&M, 1972), it saw Lee equally directionless. On *Reel to Real* (RSO, 1974), recorded with yet another incarnation of Love, Lee was reduced to recording inferior versions of old Love songs. In 1977 Lee recorded an EP on the independent Da Capo label and in 1981 an eponymous solo album (Rhino), both of which were compared unfavourably to *Forever Changes* which, by the eighties, was firmly established as a classic rock album. During the eighties Lee and MacLean occasionally re-formed versions of Love to tour, while the **Damned**'s British hit with MacLean's best-known composition 'Alone Again Or' (1986) was evidence of Lee's continuing musical influence.

From 1989 onwards Lee played live as either Arthur Lee or Love. He signed as a recording artist to French label New Rose. The first album under the deal, *Arthur Lee & Love* (1992), was a pale imitation of former glories. After Lee was sentenced to 12 years imprisonment in 1995 for firearms offences, most

Love albums were reissued. The best of these was the two-CD set *Love Story* (1996). To much surprise, MacLean, who had become a born-again Christian in the seventies, released a solo album, *ifyoubelievein* (Sundazed). Consisting of demos he had put together over the years, it was well received critically.

DARLENE LOVE
b. *Darlene Wright, 1938, Los Angeles, California, USA*

As a session singer Love sang behind numerous stars and, under a variety of guises, took lead vocals on a number of classic **Phil Spector** productions, including 'Christmas (Baby Please Come Home)' (Philles, 1963). One of the few records issued under her own name, it is widely considered to be the most intense, if not the best, of Spector's 'little symphonies for the kids'.

The younger sister of Edna Wright, who as a member of Honey Cone had a pair of million-sellers, 'Want Ads' and 'Stick-Up' (Hot Wax, 1971), Love joined the Blossoms in 1958. The girl group recorded unsuccessfully for Capitol, **Gene Autry**'s Challenge label and Okeh, but had more success as a backing group. Love in particular was in great demand because of the strong emotional charge of her singing and sang on literally hundreds of records made in Los Angeles in the early sixties. In 1962 she was hired by Spector to sing the lead on 'He's a Rebel'*, which was issued under the **Crystals**' name – Spector was in conflict with the group – and in 1963 she sang lead on 'He's Sure the Boy That I Love', also issued under the Crystals' name.

In 1962 Spector put together Bob B. Soxx and the Blue Jeans, comprising Fanita James and Love from the Blossoms and **Clyde McPhatter** sound-alike Bobby Sheen. The group had big hits with his inventive reworking of the 1948 composition 'Zip-a-Dee-Doo-Dah' (1962) and 'Why Do Lovers Break Each Other's Heart?' (1963), before Spector decided to concentrate on Love as a solo artist. Her first two records, '(Today I Met) The Boy I'm Gonna Marry' and 'Wait 'Till My Bobby Gets Home' (1963), were Top Forty hits, but the pair's best collaboration was 'Christmas (Baby Please Come Home)'. Featuring an impassioned performance from Love and production from Spector which, unusually, surrounds but never dominates Love's voice, the recording – the only original song on Spector's legendary *Christmas* album – was not a hit, although it was issued in both 1963 and 1964. After a few more recordings, including the superior 'Stumble and Fall' (1964), Love and Spector parted company, she unhappy with his authoritarian attitudes and he displeased with her refusal to give up her session work or to leave the Blossoms, who were in great demand as back-up singers for live performances.

Love rejoined the Blossoms full-time, appearing regularly on the television show *Shindig* throughout the sixties. In the seventies the group toured with **Elvis Presley** and the individual members returned to their lucrative careers as session singers. In 1985 Love appeared on Broadway in *Leader of the Pack*, a show constructed around the songs of **Ellie Greenwich**, who had co-written many Spector-produced hits. She also acted in the *Lethal Weapon* series of films. In 1989 she released *Paint Another Picture* (Columbia), which included a version of her Crystals' hit, appropriately titled 'He's Sure the Man I Love'.

Love was a regular live performer in America in the nineties, with a show mixing gospel songs and her early hits. Those hits were compiled on a 1992 CD released by EMI. Later that year Love made a rare appearance on a new album when she appeared on the soundtrack album to the hit film *Home Alone II*, appropriately performing a Christmas song, 'All Alone This Christmas', backed by members of **Bruce Springsteen**'s E-Street Band. In 1997 she was awarded a little over $250,000 in back royalties from Spector.

LYLE LOVETT
b. *1 November 1957, Houston, Texas, USA*

The most intriguing of the modern generation of country singers, Lovett melds the traditional concerns of country music, introspective songs (in the manner of seventies singer-songwriters) with idiosyncratic narratives and incisive lyrics in a wholly compelling fashion. The dash of post-modernism (not to mention surrealism, for example, 'If I Had a Boat') this represents has meant that his songs have been better received than his recordings (which regularly feature a cello), delivered in his own cool, corner of the mouth vocalizing.

From a well-to-do background, while at university studying journalism in the seventies Lovett started writing songs and occasionally performing. He travelled to Europe in the late seventies and on his return became a regular feature of the Texas music circuit, often performing alongside **Nanci Griffith** who recorded his fatalistic 'If I Were the Woman You Wanted' (which Lovett subsequently recorded himself with a gender change) on *Once in a Very Blue Moon* (1984). On the recommendation of Texan recording artist Guy Clark, Lovett was signed to MCA/Curb, who released his eponymous début in 1986. Badly received in country circles, it included the meditative 'The Porch' and 'Closing Time', a hit for Lacy J. Dalton. Equally eclectic but far more controlled was *Pontiac* (1989), his best album to date. The title song was a chilling account of alienation, while 'If I Had a Boat' was a surreal homage to **Roy Rogers** and his fellow cowboy stars. If a disturbing edge was the keynote of these songs (and 'L.A. County'), 'Simple Song' and 'I

Loved You Yesterday' were moving love songs as much about love itself as the love in question, while 'Give Me Back My Heart' (in which redneckness is described as a disease: 'You catch it on your fingers and it crawls right up your sleeves') was simply joyful. Far more perplexing was *Lyle Lovett and his Large Band* (1989) which is both just that – Lyle Lovett with horns – and a strange essay in cover-versions, which include an affectionate version of doo-wop classic 'The Glory of Love' and a deadpan reading of **Tammy Wynette**'s 'Stand by Your Man'.

Joshua Judges Ruth (1992) was a decided return to form. His most commercially successful album, it included 'Church', another surreal story, this time about a never-ending sermon, the cowboy-inflected love song 'North Dakota' and the fatalistic love song 'She's Already Made Up Her Mind', all given an extra edge from Lovett's cool performance. It further enhanced Lovett's reputation as a songwriter and **Willie Nelson** (on *The Borderline*), amongst others, recorded songs by him. Lovett himself moved into films, appearing in *The Player* in 1992 and *Short Cuts* in 1993, where his odd physical appearance – he has a long face topped by a curly pompadour – was striking. In the same year he married actress Julia Roberts.

In 1994 he released *I Love Everybody*, which included songs written from the mid-eighties to the mid-nineties, to critical acclaim and (again) poor sales. *Road to Ensenada* (1996) was perhaps his most playful album – its first track included the line 'you can have my girl but don't touch my hat' and another **Bob Wills**-inflected song detailed the impenetrable charms of Texas. The two-CD set *Step Inside This House* (1998) was even more Texas-orientated. A collection of songs from the likes of Steve Fromholz, **Guy Clark** and Townes Van Zandt that Lovett described as having clung to him over the years, it captured the travails of small-time Texas life to perfection. Particularly affecting was Lovett's austere version of Fromholz's 'Texas Trilogy'. Far jollier was *Live in Texas* (1999) on which, with his large band, Lovett ran through his hits and misses with glee.

THE LOVIN' SPOONFUL

Steve Boone, b. John Stephen Boone, 23 September 1943, Camp Lejeune, North Carolina, USA; Joe Butler, b. Joseph Campbell Butler, 16 September 1943, Long Island, New York; John B. Sebastian, b. 17 March 1944, New York; Zal Yanofsky, b. 19 December 1944, Toronto, Canada (replaced by Jerry Yester)

Supplied by Sebastian with a stream of highly crafted and inspired songs, the Lovin' Spoonful in 1965–7 was arguably the leading American pop group. Their music drew equally on the 'British invasion' music of **The Beatles** and the eclectic energy of the Greenwich

Village folk scene, creating a blend of folk-rock which paralleled that of the **Byrds**. Sebastian's subsequent solo work seldom matched his early material.

The son of a respected classical harmonica player, Sebastian became a session player on the instrument for such folk artists as **Tom Rush**, **Judy Collins** and the Even Dozen Jug Band, of which (as John Benson) he was briefly a member. He met guitarist Yanofsky in the short-lived Mugwumps, a folk-rock band that also included future members of **The Mamas and the Papas** Cass Elliot and Denny Doherty. Encouraged by producer Eric Jacobsen, the pair formed a band with Boone (bass) and Butler (drums). Taking their name from a line in **Mississippi John Hurt**'s 'Coffee Blues', the Lovin' Spoonful played a mixture of folk-revival standards and Sebastian compositions such as the paean to rock music, 'Do You Believe in Magic?' (Kama Sutra, 1965). The group's début single, it was the first of ten American hits in two years.

On such love songs as 'You Didn't Have to Be So Nice' (1965), 'Darling Be Home Soon' (1966) and 'She Is Still a Mystery' (1967), Sebastian showed himself to be one of the few writers of the era who could stand comparison to **John Lennon** and **Paul McCartney**. His warm, clear singing delivered a poetic word-painting of a New York heatwave on the group's only No. 1, 'Summer in the City'* (1966), while 'Nashville Cats' eloquently saluted the 'Yellow Sun records' which had enthralled the young Sebastian, and 'Daydream' rivalled **Hoagy Carmichael**'s 'Lazybones' and the **Kinks**' 'Sunny Afternoon' in its relaxed evocation of supreme euphoria. The Lovin' Spoonful released three bestselling albums in this period: *Do You Believe in Magic?* (1965), *Daydreams* and *Hums* (both 1966). The group also provided soundtracks for two films, Woody Allen's *What's Up, Tiger Lily?* (1966) and Francis Ford Coppola's *You're a Big Boy Now* (1967).

The group's momentum was lost when Yanofsky left in 1967 under suspicion of being a police informer in a drugs case. He was replaced by former **Association** member and future **Tom Waits** producer Yester on *Everything Is Playing* (1968), which was commercially unsuccessful, despite the inclusion of two of Sebastian's best compositions, the ruminative 'Younger Generation' and the wry 'Boredom'. When Sebastian himself left the band soon afterwards, the Lovin' Spoonful story was effectively over, although Butler retained the name for *Revelation: Revolution '69* (1969) which featured **John Stewart**'s 'Never Goin' Back'.

Sebastian's solo career started strongly with appearances at the Woodstock and Isle of Wight Festivals in 1969, where – despite his 'granny' spectacles and tie-dye shirt – he poked fun at his audience with his challenging performance of 'Younger Generation'. He went on to have a hit with 'She's a Lady', which he wrote for the Broadway play *Jimmy Shine*. After a lawsuit with MGM, who claimed rights over his Kama Sutra contract, he released solo albums on Reprise in 1970 and 1971 but he performed and wrote only sporadically thereafter.

'Stories We Can Tell', memorably recorded by the **Everly Brothers**, was Sebastian's best composition of the seventies, though the most successful was the tele-series theme 'Welcome Back'* (Reprise, 1976), which gave him a No. 1 hit. In 1985 he composed sentimental songs for the soundtrack of the children's animated film *The Care Bears Movie* and in 1992 released *Tar Beach* (Shanachie), his first solo album for almost two decades. He followed that in 1996 with the lesser *I Want My Roots*.

The original members of the Lovin' Spoonful reunited to appear in **Paul Simon**'s film *One Trick Pony* (1980) while Boone, Butler, Jerry and Jim Yester toured as the Lovin' Spoonful in the nineties.

NICK LOWE
b. 25 March 1949, England

One of British rock's most active writers, producers and performers of the seventies and eighties, Nick Lowe's work was marked by a rare wit and sense of fun. In the nineties he transformed himself into a brooding singer-songwriter.

From 1969 to 1975 he was a member of Brinsley Schwarz, an under-rated pub-rock band. The nucleus of the group was Lowe (bass), his schoolfriend Schwarz (guitar) and Bob Andrews (keyboards), who first recorded for EMI in 1967 as Kippington Lodge. With Billy Rankin (drums) and guitarist Ian Gomm, Brinsley Schwarz recorded six albums for United Artists. Unusually for the progressive-rock era, the group distilled the rock'n'roll, country and soul music of an earlier period in original compositions like Lowe's 'Don't Lose Your Grip on Love', 'Nervous on the Road' and '(What's So Funny 'Bout) Peace Love and Understanding'. Despite (or because of) the glare of publicity which accompanied the launch of their first album – a planeload of British journalists were flown to see the group play at New York's Fillmore East – the group's albums sold poorly. The band found only cult success on London's developing pub-rock circuit.

Brinsley Schwarz split up in 1975, just as the new punk-rock bands were taking over London's pub-rock venues. Schwarz and Andrews joined **Graham Parker**'s band, while Gomm's solo career later yielded the American hit 'Hold on' (Stiff/Epic, 1979). Lowe's own solo début was intended as a joke. He wrote, produced and played 'We Love You Bay City Rollers' under the pseudonym of the Tartan Horde, which was an unexpected hit in Japan.

More significantly, with former Brinsleys' producer Dave Robinson, Lowe was unusual among his contemporaries in seeing potential in punk. When Robinson and Jake Riviera formed Stiff, Lowe's 'So It Goes'/'Heart of the City' was the company's first release and Lowe became the label's house producer, earning the sobriquet 'Basher' for his speedy, back-to-basics approach on such albums as the **Damned**'s *Damned Damned Damned* (1977), Graham Parker's *Howling Wind* (Mercury, 1976) and **Elvis Costello**'s *My Aim Is True* (1977), with whom he continued to work over the next few years. Other artists produced by Lowe in the late seventies were the **Pretenders**, **Dr Feelgood**, **Graham Parker** and Wreckless Eric.

With Costello he left Stiff for the newly formed Radar label, and resumed his recording career in 1978 with *Jesus of Cool* (renamed *Pure Pop for Now People* in America to avoid controversy). An expert recycling of classic sixties styles, the album included the British hit 'I Love the Sound of Breaking Glass' while 'Cruel to Be Kind' from *Labour of Lust* (1979) was a hit on both sides of the Atlantic.

During the eighties Lowe divided his time between performing and producing. He toured and recorded with **Dave Edmunds** and their group Rockpile, while continuing to release such albums as *Nick the Knife* (F-Beat, 1982), *The Abominable Showman* (1983), *Nick Lowe and His Cowboy Outfit* (1984), *Rose of England* (1985) and *Pinker and Prouder than Previous* (Demon, 1988). As a producer, Lowe had was reunited with Costello on *Blood and Chocolate* (1986), and his other eighties productions included *Suburban Voodoo* (1982) by Paul Carrack, a regular Lowe band-member and lead singer on Ace's 1975 hit 'How Long' and who charted again in 1986 with 'I Need You' (Epic) and *T-Bird Rhythm* (Chrysalis, 1982) by the Fabulous Thunderbirds. He also worked on albums by **John Hiatt** and country singer Carlene Carter (daughter of **Johnny Cash**), to whom he was married at the time.

In the nineties Lowe was less active as both performer and producer. He had played on John Hiatt's career-reviving *Bring the Family* (1987) in a band which included **Ry Cooder** and veteran drummer Jim Keltner, and he recruited the latter pair for his own next solo album, *Party of One*. The chemistry between the trio and Hiatt was such that they formed the short-lived Little Village, which released an epony-mous album in 1992 followed by a world tour. Solo once again, in 1994 Lowe teamed up with Costello, playing bass on his *Brutal Youth* before releasing his own album, *The Impossible Bird*, on the independent Upstart Records label. His most emotional album for some years, it included 'The Beast in Me', a song he wrote for Johnny Cash, **Dallas Frazier**'s 'True Love Travels on a Gravel Road' and **Ray Price**'s 'I'll Be There'. The minimalist *Dig My Mood* (1998) was, if anything, even bleaker, a superior, solemn contemplation of the possibilities of failure. Among the songs included were 'Faithless Lover', 'What Lack of Love Has Done' and 'Cold Grey Light of Dawn'.

LULU
b. Marie McDonald McLaughlin Lawrie, 3 November 1948, Glasgow, Scotland

Possessor of one of the best voices of the British beat boom, Lulu's recording career lost momentum as she opted for a role as a middle-of-the-road 'all-round' entertainer. The enthusiasm of a new generation of musicians saw her return to the British chart in the early nineties.

Among the many local beat groups snapped up by London record companies in the hope of emulating the success of **The Beatles** were Lulu and the Luvvers from Glasgow. Signed to Decca, they scored a Top Ten hit with a cover of the **Isley Brothers**' 'Shout' in 1964 but their version of **Bert Berns**' 'Here Comes the Night' flopped, despite Berns himself travelling from New York to produce the record. He was more successful a few months later when **Van Morrison**'s Them had a hit with the song.

Now detached from the Luvvers (whose bassplayer Jim Dewar went on to play with Stone the Crows and Robin Trower), Lulu found her soul material replaced by orchestral arrangements and mainstream British writers **Les Reed** and Geoff Stephens, who provided the 1965 hit 'Leave a Little Love'. After a series of unsuccessful singles, Lulu moved to EMI's Columbia label and independent producer **Mickie Most**.

With his ear for matching an artist's strengths to well-crafted material, Most coaxed a fiery reading of **Neil Diamond**'s 'The Boat That I Row' from Lulu. Both that and 'Let's Pretend' were British hits in 1967 before she made her greatest impact in America with the No. 1 'To Sir with Love', the theme from the film in which she starred with Sidney Poitier. The Most-supervised British hits continued through 1968 with Tony Hazzard's 'Me the Peaceful Heart', Howard's and Blaikley's 'Boy' and the peculiarly inane 'I'm a Tiger', written by **Marty Wilde** and Ronnie Scott. The climax of this phase of Lulu's career was her triumph in the 1969 Eurovision Song Contest with the a-lingual 'Boom-Bang-a-Bang'.

By now she was established in Britain as a television-show host, on a par with **Cilla Black**. But on record Lulu returned to her soul roots with *New Routes* (Atlantic, 1970). With Duane Allman of the **Allman Brothers Band** on guitar and co-produced by **Arif Mardin**, **Tom Dowd** and Bert Berns' former colleague **Jerry Wexler**, it included an American hit, 'Oh Me, Oh My, I'm a Fool for You Baby'. After *Melody*

Fair (Atlantic, 1970) she moved to **Wes Farrell**'s Chelsea label for *Make Believe World* (1973), with accompanists who included saxophonist Tom Scott and pianist Victor Feldman.

Lulu's only hit single during the seventies was a version of **David Bowie**'s 'The Man Who Sold the World' (Polydor, 1974), produced by the composer and his guitarist Mick Ronson. She later recorded for **Elton John**'s Rocket label (*Don't Take Love for Granted*, 1979) before an eponymous album for Japanese label Alfa brought an American hit in 1981 with 'I Could Never Miss You (More Than I Do)'. Like *Take Me to Your Heart Again* (Alfa, 1982), the album was produced by Mark London, co-author of 'To Sir with Love'. In 1986 her recording career came full circle when a re-recording of 'Shout' (Jive) was a British hit.

In the seventies and eighties Lulu continued to broadcast and also appeared on the London stage in *Guys and Dolls*. In the nineties she made a return to the UK Top Ten with the dance-slanted 'Independence' (1993) on Dome Records and co-wrote the **Tina Turner** hit 'I Don't Wanna Fight'. The album *Independence* (1993) failed to emulate the single's success, but later that year she topped the British chart as the featured vocalist on a version of producer/writer/ performer Dan Hartman's 'Relight My Fire' with teen pop idols Take That, none of whose members had been born when 'Shout' was first a hit. She was featured in Elton John's version of *Aida* (1999), but seemed more comfortable as a television host where her boundless enthusiasm never seemed out of place.

JIMMIE LUNCEFORD
b. James Melvin Lunceford, 6 June 1902, Fulton, Missouri, USA, d. 12 July 1957, Seaside, Oregon

Renowned for its showmanship and ensemble playing, the Lunceford Orchestra was one of the most exciting bands of the thirties. Its distinctive, loping 'two-beat' style of swing was created by arranger Sy Oliver.

After studying music with **Paul Whiteman**'s father Wilberforce in Denver, Lunceford graduated in music from Fisk University and played with the bands of Wilbert Sweatman and others in the early twenties, before becoming an instructor at a Memphis high school in 1927. There he recruited his own band from among his students. Though an accomplished pianist and proficient on all reed instruments, Lunceford rarely played with the band, preferring to conduct it. He briefly recorded for RCA in a hot style (notably 'Jazznocracy' and 'White Heat', 1930), but it was during a residency at New York's Cotton Club in 1934 that Lunceford's more relaxed style first emerged, following the arrival of Oliver in 1933.

Oliver (*b. 17 December 1910, Battle Creek, Michigan*),

a trumpeter and untrained arranger, brought a sense of wit to the band's music while Lunceford's strong sense of discipline, the assertive drumming of Jimmy Crawford and Willie Smith's leadership of the sax section ensured that Oliver's (and pianist Edwin Wilcox's) subtle arrangements were properly showcased. Signed to Decca in 1934, the Lunceford Orchestra's best-known recordings include **Harold Arlen**'s and **Johnny Mercer**'s 'Blues in the Night' (1941), which the band performed in the film of the same title, 'My Blue Heaven' (1936) and 'Margie' (1938); and Oliver's 'For Dancers Only' (1937) and 'Twenty-Four Robbers' (1941), which featured trombonist Trummy Young who was with the band between 1937 and 1943. The 1939 recording of 'Liza' was unusual in that it featured a rare instrumental appearance by Lunceford himself, on flute.

That year Oliver left to join **Tommy Dorsey** as arranger. Lunceford continued to record for Decca until 1945, then briefly for Majestic in 1946, but at the time of his death while on tour he was without a recording contract. During his last years with Decca, Lunceford recorded several sides (including 'I'm Gonna See My Baby' and 'That Someone Must Be You', 1944) with the Trenier Twins (later the Treniers when they expanded their line-up) whose scat style of singing was highly influential on the developing R&B vocal-group sound.

LUSCIOUS JACKSON
Jill Cunniff, b. 1968, New York, USA; Gabby Glaser, b. 1968, New York; Kate Schellenbach, b. 1967, New York; Vivian Trimble, b. New York

Although often referred to disparagingly as the female **Beastie Boys** (to whose label, Grand Royal, they are signed), Luscious Jackson perfected their guitar-driven hip-hop hybrid while their paymasters were still dabbling with alternative rap.

Although multi-instrumentalist Cunniff and guitarist Glaser had been friends since growing up together in New York City, they didn't form Luscious Jackson until 1991, recruiting keyboardist Trimble and Schellenbach, who had played with the punk incarnation of the Beastie Boys in 1982, on drums. The quartet released an EP, *In Search of Manny* (1992), and their début album, *Natural Ingredients* (1994), on Grand Royal, blending the looped grooves of ESG with delicately layered guitars and keyboards. The band's profile rose as they appeared at Lollapalooza and on **R.E.M.**'s *Monster* tour.

Luscious Jackson had their biggest success with their second album, *Fever in Fever out* (1996), which spawned a hit single, 'Naked Eye', and saw Cunniff and Glaser turn to lush, harmonic vocalizing in place of the pseudo-rap of its predecessors. Although Trim-

ble left in 1998, the band returned as a trio the following year with *Electric Honey*, which included a duet with **Blondie**'s Debbie Harry.

NELLIE LUTCHER
b. 15 October 1915, Lake Charles, Louisiana, USA

A small, even childlike voice, a sudden throaty vibrato, merry scat singing and a sassy way with some saucy material made Nellie Lutcher one of the most novel vocalists of the forties and stylistic forerunner of singers like **Lena Horne** and **Eartha Kitt**.

Her father, Isaac Lutcher, was a well-known bass player. She learned piano when she was young, listening to **Earl Hines** and **Teddy Wilson**, and played in local bands until 1935, when she moved to the West Coast to work as a club and lounge pianist. She was spotted at a 'March of Dimes' benefit concert in Los Angeles in 1947 and signed by Dave Dexter to Capitol. Her own composition, the breathless 'Hurry on Down' (based on the older song 'Bring It on Down to My House, Honey'), with its light-fingered jump piano, was a million-seller in 1947; it was followed in the same year by 'He's a Real Gone Guy' and in 1948 by 'Fine Brown Frame'.

On the strength of these successes, and prompted by Carlos Gastel – the manager she shared with **Nat 'King' Cole** – Lutcher was booked into New York's Café Society club, and in 1950 appeared in Britain. She continued to record for Capitol into the early fifties, mixing up-tempo pieces in the manner of her earlier hits with standards and novelties. She also recorded for Epic, Liberty and Imperial and filled club and theatre dates, but by the end of the fifties her name was fading, and much of her time in the sixties and seventies was spent in staff jobs at the Los Angeles Local 47 of the American Federation of Musicians. In 1973 she was recalled to New York by Barney Josephson, the one-time owner of Café Society, to work at his new Greenwich Village spot, the Cookery. She remained musically active into the eighties.

Her brother Joe Lutcher was a popular R&B singer, alto-saxophonist and bandleader around Los Angeles in the late forties and fifties. He recorded for Capitol and other labels before leaving music to found the LA Community Evangelistic Educational Center.

FRANK LUTHER
b. Francis Luther Crow, 4 August 1905, Larkin, Kansas, USA, d. 16 November 1980

Frank Luther was a conventional tenor singer who discovered on the freelance recording circuit of the twenties and early thirties an affinity with hillbilly song, and together with **Vernon Dalhart**, **Carson**

Robison and Frank Marvin formed the 'citybilly' recording clique. Later he nurtured a less opportunist interest in American folk music, and then in children's songs, in which field he became known as a composer, recording artist and radio executive.

After college, where he studied piano and voice, Luther became a singer at revival meetings, and in 1925 entered the ministry in Bakersfield, California. By the following year, however, he was playing piano and singing tenor in the DeReszke Singers quartet, and in 1927 he joined the popular radio and recording quartet the Revelers. In 1928 he embarked on a life in the recording studios of New York, where he cut popular and hillbilly numbers for virtually every company, often under such pseudonyms as Weary Willie or Lazy Larry. Many of his hillbilly recordings were duets with Robison (sometimes billed as Bud and Joe Billings), and these sides – including 'Wednesday Night Waltz' and 'When It's Springtime in the Rockies'/'Sleepy Rio Grande' (Victor, 1929) – were frequently among the bestsellers in the hillbilly lists. He also recorded with his brother Phil. He wrote some of his own material, including his best-remembered comic song 'Barnacle Bill the Sailor' (1928), of which there were numerous recordings, including an eccentric version by Hoagy Carmichael (Victor, 1929).

In the early thirties Luther most often recorded with his Trio, which initially consisted of himself, his wife Zora Layman and Leonard Stokes, but later included the singer and writer of cowboy songs Ray Whitley. By the mid-thirties the demand for hillbilly material had slackened, and Luther returned to quartet work, with the Men About Town. In a long spell with Decca (from 1934) he recorded folk songs, including a set of cowboy ballads including 'Home on the Range'; collections of songs associated with Stephen Foster and George M. Cohan; series of standards under titles like Gay Nineties, Songs of the South and Songs of the North; and, in particular, children's story-songs, which he wrote himself and recorded in several parts each so as to make three- or four-record sets. Among these were 'Snow White and the Seven Dwarfs' (1938), 'Mother Goose Rhymes' (1939–41) and songs about Babar the Elephant, based on the French children's stories by Jean de Brunhoff. By the mid-forties Luther had become director of children's programmes at a New York radio station. He went on to lecture on musical Americana and write Americans and Their Songs.

FRANKIE LYMON AND THE TEENAGERS
Frankie Lymon, b. 30 September 1942, New York, USA, d. 28 February 1968; Sherman Garnes, b. 8 June 1940, New York, d. 1978; James Merchant, b. 10 February 1940, New York; Joe Negroni, b. 9 September 1940, New York, d. 1977; Herman Santiago, b. 18 February 1941, New York

A youthful, black vocal group of the rock'n'roll era, Frankie Lymon and the Teenagers were a prototype for later 'teenybopper' bands like the Osmonds or the Jackson Five. Lymon's tragic career, scarred by drug addiction, was a model of a more sombre kind for later rock stars.

A street-corner harmonizing team, calling themselves the Premieres, the quintet were discovered by Richard Barrett, then lead singer of the Valentines. They won a talent contest run by George Goldner's Gee Records with 'Why Do Fools Fall in Love?', a song reportedly based on a school essay written by thirteen-year-old Lymon. The number opened with rhythmic nonsense syllables from bass singer Garnes and featured a saxophone solo by Jimmy Wright, while Lymon's piercing soprano took the song to the top of the R&B charts and into the pop Top Ten in 1956. It eventually sold a million copies.

The group's first album contained further R&B hits in 'I Promise to Remember', 'The ABCs of Love' and 'I Want You to Be My Girl', which also reached the pop Top Twenty. Managed by Morris Levy, Lymon pleaded his way through perhaps his most effective song, 'I'm Not a Juvenile Delinquent', in the Alan Freed film Rock Rock Rock (1956) and toured America, Australia and Britain, where 'Fools' had reached No. 1. In 1957 Lymon's brother Lewis recorded with the Teenchords.

In 1957 Lymon was persuaded to pursue a solo career but after the success of 'Goody Goody' his career took a downward turn. The Teenagers continued to record without Lymon but 'Flip Flop' (1957) aptly described their lack of impact. In 1960 Lymon made a brief comeback with a version of Thurston Harris's 'Little Bitty Pretty One' on Levy's Roulette label. For most of the sixties he was inactive, due to a heroin habit, which he conquered to return to performance in 1966 but two years later he died of an overdose. In the eighties Santiago and Merchant, now in their forties, formed a new Teenagers, with Pearl McKinnon taking Lymon's part, to sing on oldies shows.

'Why Do Fools Fall in Love?' eventually became a rock standard with later hit versions by the Happenings (BT Puppy, 1967) and Diana Ross (Motown, 1981). In 1986 the ownership of the estimated $1 million royalties earned by the song was the subject of a legal dispute between Lymon's widow and Morris Levy. Six years later the court found in favour of Lymon, Merchant and Santiago. After Levy sold Roulette to EMI in 1989, Lymon's classic was among the first tracks to be reissued. Best of (Rhino, 1993) is the definitive retrospective.

BARBARA LYNN

b. Barbara Lynn Ozen, 16 January 1942, Beaumont, Texas, USA

Lynn is best remembered for the 1962 R&B chart-topper and pop hit 'You'll Lose a Good Thing'. Written by Lynn (who also played guitar on the record), the lyric's sentiments were unusual for the time in that the singer is confident that her partner will be the loser by his leaving of her.

Discovered singing blues in Louisiana clubs by **Huey P. Meaux** (who produced virtually all her records), Lynn sang back-up vocals at Goldband studios before she recorded 'Good Thing' in New Orleans. Leased to Jamie, it inaugurated a series of rhythm and blues hits ('You're Gonna Need Me', 'It's Better to Have It', 'Oh Baby', later recorded by the **Rolling Stones**), mostly featuring assured, bluesy vocals supported by her simple, emphatic guitar-playing and a swirling horn section. In 1966 Meaux put her on his own Tribe label for **Dan Penn** and Rick Hall's 'You Left the Water Running' before signing her to Atlantic, on which she had a further pair of self-composed hits ('This Is the Thanks I Get', 1968, and '[Until Then] I'll Suffer', 1971), and released the superior *Here Is Barbara Lynn* (1968), the most carefully arranged and produced of her records. In 1976 **Freddy Fender** had a country hit with 'You'll Lose a Good Thing', produced by Meaux.

Lynn re-emerged in 1984 with the lacklustre *Live in Japan* (Avid, 1984) in which she was backed by the Japanese group the Backbeats. Far better was 1988's *You Don't Have to Go* on Ichiban. She has been largely inactive since then.

LORETTA LYNN

b. Loretta Webb, 14 April 1935, Butcher Hollow, Kentucky, USA

Lynn was a prolific and influential country hitmaker in the seventies. The commercial and critical success of the film of her 1976 autobiography *Coal Miner's Daughter* (1980), which won Sissy Spacek an Oscar for her portrayal of Lynn, did much to renew interest in traditionally rooted country music.

From a musical family – her younger sister is **Crystal Gayle** – Lynn was brought up in poverty in the coal-mining community of Butcher Hollow and married Oliver 'Mooney' Lynn at the age of thirteen. After moving to Custer, Washington, in the early fifties, she had four children and while raising them began writing songs and performing. She recorded her first song, 'I'm a Honky Tonk Girl' (Zero), in 1960 and she and Mooney promoted it themselves. After it charted, **Owen Bradley**, who had produced Lynn's major influence **Patsy Cline**, signed her to

Decca. Her early records, including 'Success' (1962) – her first country No. 1 – showed a debt to **Kitty Wells**, but later records (despite a noticeable softening of her vocal style) saw her develop into a major songwriter, and one of the few to address working-class women. As one critic put it, Lynn became 'the spokeswoman for every woman who had gotten married too early, pregnant too often, and felt trapped by the tedium and drudgery of life'. Songs in this vein included 'Don't Come Home a-Drinkin' (With Lovin on Your Mind)', 'You Ain't Woman Enough' (1966), 'First City' (1968), the autobiographical 'Coal Miner's Daughter' (1970), 'One's on the Way' (1971) and 'The Pill' (1975), which endorsed birth control. In 1972 she was the first woman to win the Country Music Association's Entertainer of the Year award.

In 1970 she began touring and regularly recording with **Conway Twitty**. Their joint hits included 'After the Fire Is Gone' (1971), 'Louisiana Woman, Mississippi Man' (1973) and 'As Soon as I Hang up the Phone' (1974).

Though her records were not pop successes, her compelling autobiography was a bestseller and hugely influential. Her depiction of Butcher Hollow and the travails of her early life reminded Americans of the rural origins of country music at a time when many country performers were deserting their musical roots in search of pop hits. The film's success led to a film biography of Cline, *Sweet Dreams* (1985). Ironically, despite her massive general exposure to the American public, Lynn's records still only reached the country charts. Her hits of the eighties included 'It's True Love' (1980) and 'I Lie' (1982). *Just a Woman* (MCA, 1988) was produced by Jimmy Bowen. Lynn was largely inactive on the recording front in the early nineties, concentrating on running her vast estate near Nashville which includes a town and a 'dude ranch' within its boundaries. In 1993, however, she teamed up with fellow veterans **Tammy Wynette** and **Dolly Parton** for *Honky Tonk Angels*, which returned her to the American album chart. Its success spurred MCA to issue the definitive three-CD box set, *Honky Tonk Girl: The Collection* (1994).

VERA LYNN

b. Vera Margaret Welch, 20 March 1917, London, England

Though she had hits both before and after the Second World War, Lynn is best remembered as 'The Forces' Sweetheart'. In the words of one critic, 'singing . . . simply and sincerely, all the silly, insincere songs about home and the little steeple pointing to a star and the brighter world over the hill', she captured and articulated the emotions of Britain at war. Like **Lale Anderson**, the **Andrews Sisters** and, especially, **Marlene Dietrich**, Lynn's career high-lighted the potency of cheap music in wartime, and the propaganda uses to which it could be put.

After singing regularly in working-men's clubs since the age of seven, Lynn joined Madame Harris's Kracker Kabaret Kids when she was eleven, remaining with them for four years. She began her career as a band singer with Howard Baker and made her first radio broadcast with **Joe Loss** four years later in 1935, the year she joined Charlie Kunz's band and made her first record, 'I'm in the Mood for Love' (Crown). In 1937 she joined **Ambrose**, with whom she had her first hit 'The Little Boy That Santa Claus Forgot' (1937), before going solo in 1940.

Her *annus mirabilis* was 1941, the year she starred in her first London revue, *Apple Sauce*, which produced 'Yours' (Decca) which eventually sold a million copies when reissued in 1952, and began her radio series, *Sincerely Yours*, in which she provided a link with home for service-men overseas. Singing to them in her striking, melodious voice and answering their letters, her impact was such that her sentimental manner was widely parodied in Britain and in 1944 Lynn attempted legal action to prevent the imperson-ations. Her key recordings of the period were 'We'll Meet Again', an optimistic song which gave the first of her trio of insubstantial films its title, the patriotic 'The White Cliffs of Dover' and 'Yours', a sentimental love song. By now Britain's biggest singing star, Lynn travelled to Burma in 1944 to entertain the troops. After the war she briefly retired to have a baby, returning to the studio to record 'Our Baby' (1947) and do a radio series with **Robert Farnon**.

In 1952 she starred in the revue *London Laughs* and was the first British artist to top both British and American charts, with 'Auf Wiedersehen Sweet-heart'*, a German tune with English lyrics by Jimmy Phillips and Geoffrey Parsons, after which she briefly attempted a career in America. But though her records sold well there – her hits included 'Such a Day' (1956) and 'Don't Cry My Love' (1958) – she never established herself as a star in America. In Britain she fared better, hosting several television shows and regularly touring the Commonwealth. She continued to have hits through the fifties. These included 'Forget Me Not' (1952), 'The Windsor Waltz' (1953), the chart-topping 'My Son, My Son' (1954) and 'A House with Love in It' (1956). During this period she also had her own long-running Radio Lux-embourg series, *Vera Lynn Sings*.

In 1960 she left Decca for EMI and recorded *Hits of the Sixties*, her first album of contemporary material which included songs by **Nilsson**, **Jimmy Webb** and **The Beatles**. She continued touring, hosting televi-sion specials and regularly appearing at soldiers' reunions throughout the seventies and eighties. In 1975 she was made a Dame of the British Empire and published her autobiography, *Vocal Refrain*.

In 1994 she gave a special concert during the com-memoration of the fiftieth anniversary of the D-Day landings. Her power as a national icon was further acknowledged when her objections to street parties in celebration of D-Day landings speeded their can-cellation.

LYNYRD SKYNYRD

Bob Burns (replaced by Artimus Pyle, b. Spartanburg, South Carolina, USA); Allen Collins, d. 23 January 1990, Jacksonville, Florida; Ed King (replaced by Steve Gaines, b. Seneca, Missouri, d. 20 October 1977, Gills-burg, Mississippi); Billy Powell; Gary Rossington; Ron-nie Van Zant, b. 15 January 1949, d. 20 October 1977, Gillsburg; Leon Wilkeson

A popular Southern 'boogie band' of the mid-seven-ties, Lynyrd Skynyrd's career was shattered when three of the group's members were killed in a plane crash, although a re-formed band found acceptance with fans in the early nineties.

The group began as a high-school band founded by Van Zant (vocals) with guitarists Collins and Rossing-ton. The name was inspired by that of a teacher, Leonard Skinner. Their blues and heavy-rock sound made Lynyrd Skynyrd successful in the Jacksonville, Florida, area and they made their first recordings in 1970–2. Including drummer Ricky Medlocke, who later found success as the singer on Blackfoot's 'High-way Song' and 'Train, Train' (Atlantic, 1979), these tracks were not released until 1978.

When the group was signed to a recording deal with **Al Kooper**'s newly formed Sounds of the South label, it included drummer Burns and bass-player Wilkeson. The Kooper production *Pronounced Lehn-erd Skinnerd* (1974) included material written by Van Zant over the previous four years and was an ener-getic blend of blues, honky-tonk music and the heavy boogie played by British bands like **Ten Years After** and Savoy Brown.

Second Helping (1975) contained the group's first hits, 'Sweet Home Alabama', a patriotic answer to **Neil Young**'s 'Southern Man', which had bewailed the redneck mentality, and 'Free Bird', with its high-speed guitar duets reminiscent of the **Allman Broth-ers Band**. Such songs as 'I'm a Country Boy' and 'Saturday Night Special' (a paean to guns) made *Nuthin' Fancy* (1975) a further stage in the mytholo-gizing of the Southern lifestyle. After *Gimme Back My Bullets* (1976), the group added a third guitarist in Gaines, while his sister Cassie became one of Lynyrd Skynyrd's backing singers.

One More for the Road was a live album and *Street Survivors* was released days before the Mississippi plane crash in which Van Zant, Gaines and his sister Cassie Gaines (one of the band's backing vocalists) died. The sleeve of *Street Survivors* – which showed the band surrounded by flames – was replaced and the album and single, 'What's Your Name', were bestsellers on both sides of the Atlantic.

Following the plane crash, the group split, their final release being the pre-Kooper material, *First and Last* (1978). Most of the band regrouped in 1980 as the Rossington–Collins Band, which made two albums for MCA. Collins was paralyzed from the waist down after a car accident in 1986, and died in 1990 following a prolonged bout of pneumonia. Pyle also formed his own band, releasing two albums, while Van Zant's younger brother Donnie found success leading 38 Special, a heavy-metal group whose biggest hits were 'Caught Up in You' (A&M, 1982) and 'If I'd Been the One' (1984).

In 1987 large audiences were attracted by a Lynyrd Skynyrd reunion tour on which the surviving members were joined by another Van Zant brother, Johnny, and guitarist Randall Hall. It was followed by the release of an album of out-takes and B-sides, *Legend*. A live double-album was released by MCA the next year. Legal problems over the use of the name prevented this group from recording again until 1991 when they emerged as Lynyrd Skynyrd 1991, releasing an album of the same name. In 1993, once more as Lynyrd Skynyrd, the band released the Barry Beckett-produced studio album *The Last Rebel* (Atlantic) to enthusiastic reviews. With a line-up of Rossington, Van Zant, Powell, Wilkeson, Hall and King, joined by drummer Custer, the group toured America and Europe with a set which included all the old Skynyrd favourites.

Alabama, **Wynonna Judd** and **Hank Williams Jr** were among the country artists who contributed to the 1994 tribute album, *Skynyrd Friends*. *Edge of Forever* (SPV) followed in 1999, showing the band to be as enthusiastic as ever. The *Boxed Set* (1992) is the definitive retrospective.

HUMPHREY LYTTELTON
b. 23 May 1921, Eton, Berkshire, England

A trumpeter, bandleader, broadcaster and author, Lyttelton was an important figure in the popularization of traditional and mainstream jazz in Britain during the fifties.

The son of a housemaster at Eton College, he col-

lected records as a youth and after war service in the Grenadier Guards joined George Webb's Dixielanders, a group in the **Lu Watters** mould, dedicated to preserving the New Orleans jazz of **Bunk Johnson** and **George Lewis**. When Webb disbanded the group, Lyttelton and clarinettist Wally Fawkes formed a new band under the trumpeter's name.

From 1949 the band recorded for EMI's Columbia and Parlophone labels, their repertoire consisting of standards as well as Lyttelton compositions like 'Blues for Waterloo' and 'Bad Penny Blues' (Parlophone, 1956), which reached the British Top Twenty. From this time onwards, the musical policy broadened with the formation of the ancillary Grant–Lyttelton Paseo Jazz Band, which played a mixture of jazz and calypso and featured the British-born calypsonian Freddie Grant on 'King Porter Stomp' and 'London Blues' (Columbia, 1952). This period of Lyttelton's career is deftly documented in the first two of his autobiographies, *I Play as I Please* (1954) and *Second Chorus* (1958). Lyttelton also appeared in the rock biopic *The Tommy Steele Story* (1957) and moved towards mainstream jazz with the addition to the band of soloists like Bruce Turner (alto sax), Tony Coe (tenor sax) and Kathy Stobart (tenor sax), who played on *Triple Exposure* (1959) and *Blues in the Night* (1960). In 1959 the Lyttelton band toured America.

In the sixties he made notable recordings with **Count Basie** trumpeter Buck Clayton for the 77 label, and in the seventies he assembled a nine-piece band which included Ray Warleigh (flute and alto sax) to record an album of *Duke Ellington Classics* (Black Lion). **Ellington** songs were featured on *Echoes of the Duke* (1985), sung by Helen Shapiro who as a teenager had scored pop hits with such **Norrie Paramor** productions as 'Don't Treat Me Like a Child', 'Walking Back to Happiness' and 'You Don't Know' (EMI Columbia, 1961). In 1987 Lyttelton released Shapiro's *The Quality of Mercer* – a collection of songs by **Johnny Mercer** – on his Calligraph label.

Outside music, Lyttelton pursued a career as a cartoonist (with Fawkes he wrote the long-running Trog strip), columnist and broadcaster, chairing panel games, most notably the parodic *I'm Sorry, I Haven't a Clue*, on which he was for ever on the verge of explaining the rules of the non-existent game Mornington Crescent, as well as introducing jazz programmes. In 1986 he took part in a television documentary which aimed to re-create the sound of **Buddy Bolden**'s early jazz bands.

M PEOPLE

Mike Pickering, b. 18 March 1958, Manchester, England; Heather Small, b. 20 January 1965, London; Paul Heard, b. 5 October 1960, London

M People grew out of the UK soul and house scene of the early 1990s, absorbing more and more mainstream elements as their commercial success grew during the decade.

Pickering, a lifelong dance and soul enthusiast, had been a DJ at Manchester's Hacienda nightclub and had enjoyed some recording success in the 1980s, notably as T-Coy with the underground house hit 'Carino'. In 1991 he linked up with Heard, who had previously recorded with Scottish pop-funk act Orange Juice and jazz revivalists Working Week, to write songs for a new soul/house project. Vocalist Small joined the pair shortly afterwards, leading to M People's first single release, 'Color My Life', on DeConstruction records in 1991. Both this and a second single, 'How Can I Love You More?', appeared on the group's début long-player, *Northern Soul* (1992). 'How Can I Love You More?' in particular was a huge club success, remixed into a booming house anthem by Sasha, one of the leading DJs from the north of England dance scene, from which M-People had themselves emerged.

The band achieved greater popular success across Europe with 1993's *Elegant Slumming*, which produced two huge hit singles, 'One Night in Heaven' and 'Movin' on Up'. It also gained the band unexpected critical approval, becoming the first dance album to win the UK's Mercury Music Prize. However, by the mid-nineties M People's mix of formulaic dance beats and hummable melodies began to seem unadventurous in comparison to the UK's emerging jungle, big-beat and speed-garage scenes. Subsequent recordings suggested a deliberate move away from the band's dance roots and towards a more mainstream sound. 'Search for the Hero', from 1994's *Bizarre Fruit*, was soft pop, anodyne enough to feature in a car advert, and a cover of the **Small Faces**' 'Itchycoo Park' made an unlikely single a year later. The diverse but unremarkable *Fresco* (1997) was followed in 1998 by a greatest hits collection, suggestive of a band whose best was behind them, although they scored another hit single in 1999 with 'Dreaming'.

TONY MACAULAY

b. Anthony Instone, 21 April 1944, London, England

Macaulay was one of the most successful British composers and producers of the sixties and seventies.

Trained as a civil engineer, Macaulay was a member of various skiffle groups in the fifties before joining Essex Music as a plugger in 1964. He changed his name because his cousin Anna Instone was head of the BBC's Gramophone Department, and in 1966 joined January Music as a writer, starting to produce for Pye in 1967. His first hit was 'Baby Now That I've Found You' (which he co-wrote with John McLeod, a one-time member of the Maple Leaf Four), a British No. 1 in 1967 and an American Top Twenty record in 1968 for the Foundations (on Pye and Uni, respectively). That song, along with 'Build Me Up Buttercup' (1968), a second million-seller for the group, written with Mike d'Abo, and 'In the Bad, Bad Old Days' (a Macaulay–McLeod song), were all emphatic beat ballads set firmly in the traditions of Tin Pan Alley, as were most of Macaulay's subsequent compositions and productions.

A more unlikely beneficiary of Macaulay and McLeod's talents was Long John Baldry. An early member of **Alexis Korner**'s Blues Incorporated, Baldry had been part of the British blues scene for some time and had performed with **Rod Stewart** as part of Steampacket before being tempted into pop by Macaulay, who provided him with the British No. 1 'Let the Heartaches Begin' (Pye, 1967) and his only other substantial hit, 'Mexico' (1968). In general, however, Macaulay worked with pop-orientated groups: **Herman's Hermits** ('I Can Take or Leave Your Loving', 1968), Pickettywitch ('That Same Old Feeling'; '[It's Like a] Sad Old Kinda Movie', 1970); the Paper Dolls ('Something Here in My Heart', 1968), and Edison Lighthouse ('Love Grows Where My Rosemary Goes'*, 1970). He also provided songs for established acts such as the **Hollies** ('Sorry Suzanne', 1969) and **Andy Williams** ('Home Lovin' Man', 1970).

In 1970 Macaulay tried to end his contract with January Music on the grounds that he had not been given independent legal advice when he had signed it and that the terms were unfair. After a lengthy battle which involved an appeal to the House of Lords in 1974, he won, thereby establishing an important precedent. During this period he was largely inactive, although he had some success with the New **Seekers**, whose 'You Won't Find Another Fool Like Me' (1973) and 'I Get a Little Sentimental Over You' (1974) he co-wrote with Geoff Stephens.

Macaulay's most successful collaborator, Stephens (b. 1 October 1934, London) had his first hit with 'Tell Me When', recorded by the Applejacks in 1964. In 1965 he wrote 'The Crying Game' for Dave Berry, like Baldry a one-time R&B singer turned balladeer, and in 1966 had his biggest success with the novelty song 'Winchester Cathedral'. Recorded by the New Vaudeville Band, a group of session musicians with Stephens taking lead vocals, the record sold over four million copies worldwide on Fontana. Another of Stephens' successful songs was 'There's a Kind of Hush', which Herman's Hermits recorded in 1967. Then, in 1969, Stephens joined forces with Macaulay to produce 'Sorry Suzanne'. Their most successful songs together were a series of hits for **David Soul**, including 'Don't Give Up on Us'* (1976), which topped both the British and American charts, 'Goin' in with My Eyes Open' and 'Let's Have a Quiet Night in' (both 1977).

Macaulay, in collaboration with **Roger Greenaway**, also revived the **Drifters**' British chart career with a series of amiable pop songs that, in the words of one critic, 'complemented rather than imitated the glories of their past'. These included 'Kissin' in the Back Row of the Movies' (1974) and 'You're More Than a Number in My Little Red Book' (1976). He was also responsible for reviving **Duane Eddy**'s chart career, writing 'Play Me Like You Play Your Guitar' (1975) for him.

In the late seventies and eighties Macaulay turned to the musical stage, developing projects with a variety of writers, without success.

PAUL McCARTNEY
b. James Paul McCartney, 18 June 1942, Liverpool, England

The most prolific of the ex-**Beatles**, McCartney's songwriting, after his split from **John Lennon**, emphasized the less abrasive aspects of Beatles' music. As a solo composer, McCartney's work has tended to oscillate between lush love songs and slighter, playful novelty pieces, the sublime and the ridiculous. He nevertheless established himself with new generations of listeners from the seventies onwards, becoming one of the most commercially successful singers and composers of the era. His work in the nineties has been more erratic, veering from classical (Standing Stone, 1997) to rock'n'roll revivalism (Run Devil Run, 1999).

Although the quartet had already ceased to work together, it was a lawsuit brought by McCartney which caused the dissolution of The Beatles partnership in 1970. He had already released McCartney (Apple, 1970), on which he marked his artistic independence by playing every instrument. The album

included 'Maybe I'm Amazed', one of his most effective and durable ballads.

Ram (1971), a collaboration between Paul and Linda McCartney (b. Linda Louise Eastman, 24 September 1942, Scarsdale, New York, USA, d. 17 April 1998, Tucson, Arizona), included hits in the wistful, melodic 'Another Day' and the novelty song 'Uncle Albert', which reached No. 1 in America. In the same year McCartney formed a touring band, Wings, with Linda on keyboards, former **Moody Blues** bassist Denny Laine and drummer Denny Seiwell. After playing some low-key college gigs, the group recorded Wild Life (Apple, 1972).

In 1972 McCartney deserted his thematic blandness to make two singles which were banned by the BBC. Recorded with new Wings guitarist Henry McCullough (formerly of **Joe Cocker**'s Grease Band), 'Give Ireland Back to the Irish' was thought to be politically inflammatory while 'Hi Hi Hi' was suspected of being a drug song. In retaliation McCartney released an arrangement of the nursery rhyme 'Mary Had a Little Lamb'. All three were British and American hits.

In the following year McCartney provided the theme song for the James Bond film Live and Let Die and recorded the Wings album Red Rose Speedway, which included the million-selling ballad 'My Love'. Despite the fact that Seiwell and McCullough left shortly before the sessions, Band on the Run became the finest achievement of McCartney's post-Beatles career. Recorded in Lagos with Linda and Laine, the album's title track and the vibrant 'Jet'* were both international hits.

For the rest of the decade a re-formed Wings, with a succession of drummers and guitarists, produced a series of high-gloss tuneful albums, each with its quota of hit singles. Venus and Mars (1975) included 'Listen to What the Man Said', At the Speed of Sound (1976) featured 'Silly Love Songs'* and 'Let 'Em In'*, and London Town (1978) provided 'With a Little Luck'. However, McCartney's greatest statistical (if not artistic) feat of this period was 'Mull of Kintyre', a lullaby-like sing-along piece. Released at Christmas 1977, it became the first single to sell more than two million copies in Britain.

After the hesitant start to his solo career, McCartney was by now firmly established as an elder statesman of pop. After Back to the Egg (1979) he dissolved Wings, McCartney II (1980) marking his return to solo status. Subsequent singles used the reliable formulae of seasonal sentiments ('Wonderful Christmastime', 1980) and celebrity duets in 'Ebony and Ivory' (with **Stevie Wonder**, 1982) and 'The Girl is Mine' (1982) and 'Say Say Say' (1983), both with **Michael Jackson**. The Wonder duet appeared on Tug of War, an album which made use of another well-worn ploy, the all-star backing group. In this instance, the musicians included ex-Beatles **George Harrison** and **Ringo Starr**.

The political message of the insipid 'Pipes of Peace' (a British No. 1 in 1983) was strengthened by its accompanying video which evoked the trenches of the First World War, while the British hit 'We All Stand Together', sung with the Frog Chorus, found McCartney working for the first time in the children's song area. The song itself appeared on the soundtrack of a cartoon film, *Rupert the Bear*.

The hit love song 'No More Lonely Nights' appeared in *Give My Regards to Broad Street* (1984), a musical film scripted by McCartney, but the movie itself was McCartney's first commercial failure for a decade. An ambitious, if formless, musical set in a dream structure, the film explored his relationship to the dead Lennon. Perhaps in response to that rejection, McCartney went into partnership with producer Hugh Padgham and songwriter Eric Stewart, formerly of **10CC**, for *Press to Play* (1986). The album was critically acclaimed as a return to McCartney's best form as was *Flowers in the Dirt* (1989), which included songs co-written with **Elvis Costello**. Prior to recording *Flowers*, he had recorded a selection of classic rock'n'roll songs which were released (initially exclusively in Russia) on *Choba B CCCP* (*Back in the USSR*) (1989).

The world tour which followed *Flowers in the Dirt* featured McCartney performing numerous Beatles numbers, including many never performed live by the band, and produced a triple live album, *Tripping the Live Fantastic* (1990). During the tour McCartney played to what was claimed to be the largest audience for a concert by one artist, 184,000 at the Maracana Stadium in Rio de Janeiro, Brazil. Among the musicians in the touring band were Hamish Stuart (ex-**Average White Band**) and Robbie McIntosh (ex-**Pretenders**). The same musicians played on the 1991 *Unplugged* album, the soundtrack to a live acoustic TV show. McCartney's next project was a venture into classical music with composer-conductor Carl Davis, *Liverpool Oratorio* (1991). The recording, which featured opera singer **Dame Kiri Te Kanawa**, topped the British classical charts. In 1993 McCartney released *Off the Ground*, which again featured collaborations with Costello. On it, he was backed by the 1990 touring band which now accompanied him on another lengthy tour, recorded as *Paul Is Live* (1993).

McCartney now ventured into ambient music, collaborating with producer Youth (**Killing Joke**) on *Strawberries Oceans Ships Forest*, which was released under the pseudonym the Fireman. Although it was initially favourably received, interest from the dance audience swiftly waned. In early 1994 the wheel seemed to have turned full circle when McCartney was reunited with Harrison and Starr to work on new

material for the soundtrack of a Beatles documentary, to be produced by **George Martin**, to accompany the *Anthology* CD reissue series. That was followed by *Flaming Pie* (1996), which featured **ELO**'s Jeff Lynne, Ringo Starr and **Steve Miller**. The album also featured a rare appearance by Linda McCartney, who had earlier been a regular collaborator with Paul. After her death in 1998, her *Wide Prairie* was issued.

Standing Stone (1997), described by McCartney as an oratorio and recorded with the London Symphony Orchestra, received mixed reviews. *Run Devil Run* (1999), a back to roots collection of rock'n'roll (and skiffle) songs, was more directly enjoyable. It and McCartney's return to the Cavern in Liverpool for a promotional live concert for the album which was broadcast over the Internet were greeted positively. Both album and concert featured McCartney supported by an assortment of veterans, including Dave Gilmour (of **Pink Floyd**), former **Pirate** Mick Green, Pete Wingfield and Dave Mattocks, attacking a varied assortment of fifties standards with real enthusiasm. It is the variety of the songs, cutting across the accepted histories of rock where musically **Rick Nelson**, **Gene Vincent**, the Vipers and **Chuck Berry** inhabit different worlds, that is appealing. On the album are neatly pared-down versions of 'Blue Jean Bop', 'Lonesome Town', 'Brown Eyed Handsome Man' and a clutch of McCartney originals, none of which seemed strained by being side by side. *Working Classical*, released later in the year, was his most successful classical album. Consisting of three orchestral pieces and a string quartet arrangement of love songs for Linda, the pieces were more melodic than McCartney's earlier classical attempts.

McCartney's own outside production work in the eighties and nineties was restricted to one 1987 album by **Duane Eddy**, his first such production since his work on Laine's *Holly Days* a decade earlier. However, he continued to be a regular guest on other people's records. Work in this vein included 'The Fireman' (1994, with Youth), 'Lady Madonna' (1995, with the Brodsky Quartet) and 'Help' (1995, a charity recording with members of **Oasis** and the **Jam**). Through his acquisition of the Edwin H. Morris catalogue in 1976, McCartney had become the publisher of **Buddy Holly**'s songs. During the eighties McCartney sponsored a number of Holly memorial events and his company produced a documentary video of the singer's career.

DELBERT McCLINTON
b. 4 November 1940, Lubbock, Texas, USA

Like Roy Head, **Doug Sahm** and Bruce Channel, McClinton was one of Texas's white blues and soul singers of the early sixties. His harmonica-playing directly influenced **John Lennon** in the sixties, while he scored a Top Ten hit in the eighties.

A member of the house band at a Fort Worth blues club, McClinton's first record (as Mac Linton) was a cover of **Sonny Boy Williamson**'s 'Wake Up Baby' on Major Bill Smith's Le Cam label in 1960. McClinton played the harmonica solo on former rockabilly singer Channel's hit single 'Hey Baby' (Smash, 1962), also produced by Smith. He accompanied Channel on a British tour in a bill that included **The Beatles**, and Lennon's playing on 'Love Me Do', the group's first single, recorded soon afterwards, is clearly indebted to McClinton. Later, McClinton repaid the borrowing by contribution to the country tribute to The Beatles, *Come Together* (1995), singing the title track. Channel's follow-up, 'Number One Man', was only a minor hit and he moved to Bell's Mala label in 1967, recording the *Keep on* album produced by Dale Hawkins. The title track, written by Wayne Carson Thompson, was a surprise British hit for him in 1968.

McClinton returned to the Texas bar-band circuit, joining the Ron-Dels, whose recording of his 'If You Really Want Me to, I'll Go' was a minor hit in 1964 and covered by **Waylon Jennings** and Sahm. In 1970 McClinton moved to California, where he made two albums for Atlantic's Clean label in partnership with Glen Clark, as Delbert and Glen (1972–3). Returning to Texas, he cut solo albums for ABC which mingled country, R&B and rock. Produced by Chip Young, they included *Victims of Life's Circumstances* (1975) and *Love Rustler* (1977). He then moved to Capricorn for *Second Wind* (1978) and *Keeper of the Flame* (1979) before reaching the Top Ten with 'Giving It up for Your Love' (Capitol, 1980). Up-tempo blue-eyed soul, with Bonnie Bramlett on backing vocals, the song came from *The Jealous Kind*, which included material by **Bobby Charles** and **Van Morrison** and was produced by Barry Beckett at Muscle Shoals. Though his only recording of the mid-eighties was as guest singer on Roy Buchanan's *Dancing on the Edge*, he remained a favourite on the Texas club circuit, with a live show captured on *Live from Austin* (Alligator, 1989).

In 1990 McClinton signed to Curb Records and released his first studio album for almost a decade, *I'm with You*, which was enthusiastically received and sold well in Europe. He won a Grammy award for his duet with fellow veteran **Bonnie Raitt** on 'Good Man, Good Woman', from her 1991 album *Luck of the Draw*, and released the track on his own next album, *Never Been Rocked Enough* (1991), which featured guest appearances by long-time admirers **Tom Petty** and Melissa Etheridge. Throughout his career, McClinton maintained a heavy schedule of live performances, regularly playing about 250 dates a year, and he carried on his live work at the same rate into the nineties. In 1995 he joined Rising Tide Records

and released *One of the Fortunate Few*, which included guest appearances from **Lyle Lovett, B. B. King** and **John Prine**, among others. It was his biggest commercial success of the decade.

Among McClinton's compositions are the **Emmylou Harris** 1978 country hit 'Two More Bottles of Wine' and 'B Movie Boxcar Blues', recorded by the Blues Brothers.

EWAN MacCOLL
b. William Miller, 25 January 1915, Auchterarder, Scotland, d. 22 October 1989, London, England

The singer whose example set the style for performing Scottish and English ballads in the folk revival, MacColl also composed the pop standard 'The First Time Ever I Saw Your Face'.

The son of an iron-moulder who moved from Scotland to Salford, Lancashire, in the late twenties, MacColl was a political artist from an early age, composing satirical verses for factory newspapers and performing with the Red Megaphones, a street theatre group. In the thirties he became a professional actor and writer, and worked with Joan Littlewood on 'Living Newspapers', designed as labour movement pageants, as well as the first British production of a Bertolt Brecht play. For radio, he wrote a documentary on the Chartist March, with music by Benjamin Britten.

In the forties he set up Theatre Workshop in London with Littlewood, who later devised the hit musical *Oh What a Lovely War!* and produced early plays by authors such as Frank Norman and **Lionel Bart**. It was through *Johnny Noble*, a Theatre Workshop production with traditional songs, that MacColl met American folklorist **Alan Lomax**. Together they devised a popular radio programme, *Ballads and Blues*, with **Big Bill Broonzy**, Jean Ritchie and **A. L. Lloyd** among the singers.

With the folk revival in England gathering momentum in the early fifties, MacColl organized live concerts with calypso singer Lord Kitchener, as well as folk quiz shows. Soon he and Peggy Seeger turned against the eclecticism of the revival and the skiffle movement. With Lloyd, Ralph Rinzler and others, they set up a folk club whose policy was that each singer should perform only material from their own 'native' culture. It was this 'Critics Group', formed with Bob Davenport, which set out to mould the revival in a traditionalist form. The dramatic, unaccompanied vocal style which evolved became known as the 'finger-in-the-ear' mode from MacColl's habit of cupping his hand over his ear when he sang. With Seeger, he recorded *The Long Harvest*, a ten-volume series of **Child** ballads for Argo during the sixties.

Parallel with this activity, the couple with producer

Charles Parker created a series of *Radio Ballads* for the BBC between 1958 and 1965. Dealing with such topics as a rail crash (*The Ballad of John Axon*), the fishing industry (*Singing the Fishing*) and young people (*On the Edge*), the programmes interwove tapes of actual speakers with songs composed out of the speech. Among the best-known MacColl compositions from the *Radio Ballads* are 'Shoals of Herring' and 'The Travelling People'.

As a songwriter, he achieved an American No. 1 in 1972 when **Roberta Flack** recorded his love song 'The First Time Ever I Saw Your Face', which was also cut by **Elvis Presley** and numerous other artists. 'Dirty Old Town', a song about Salford, became the theme tune of the British folk group the Spinners. It was a 1985 hit single for the **Pogues**, an Anglo-Irish group whose mix of punk and folk made them the eighties equivalent of the Dubliners, with whom they recorded a raucous version of 'The Irish Rover' in 1987.

MacColl had been one of **Bob Dylan**'s most outspoken critics and with the arrival in the seventies of electric folk music, his influence on the folk scene diminished. He and Seeger concentrated on collecting and editing the songs of a family of Scottish travellers (published as *The Stewarts of Blairgowrie*) and formed their own label, Blackthorne. They released a live album, *Saturday Night at the Bull and Mouth*, and *Cold Snap* and *Hot Blast*, two albums of their own compositions, mostly political songs with a forceful Marxist slant. Peggy Seeger's solo material was strongly feminist, and included 'I'm Gonna Be an Engineer', which appeared in *Different Therefore Equal* (1979). In 1979 MacColl and Seeger released *Blood Red Roses*, the first of an intended series of albums containing lesser known traditional ballads from Scotland and North America. His final recording, *Naming of Names* (Cooking Vinyl, 1990), and an autobiography, *Journeyman*, were published posthumously.

In the eighties MacColl's daughter Kirsty had pop hits with 'There's a Boy Down the Chip Shop Swears He's Elvis' (Polydor, 1981) and **Billy Bragg**'s 'A New England' (Stiff, 1985). She later sang with the Pogues on the 1987 Christmas hit 'Fairytale of New York' (Stiff) and reached the British Top Ten with a revival of the **Kinks**' 'Days'. Her next album was *Electric Landlady* (1991).

Ewan MacColl and Peggy Seeger's sons, Neill and Calum MacColl, were members of the Bible and Liberty Horses.

JOHN McCORMACK
b. 14 June 1884, Athlone, Eire, d. 16 September 1945, Dublin

McCormack was one of the most successful early recording artists, selling more than 200 million records in the course of his career. The possessor of a clear, soft, Irish tenor, he was acclaimed in America for his operatic work (notably in Verdi and Mozart) and in Europe for his recordings of sentimental ballads and drawing-room songs.

The fourth of eleven children, McCormack was studying for the Civil Service examination in Dublin when, in 1903, he won the singing prize at the Irish Music Festival. In 1904 he travelled to America to sing at the St Louis World's Fair and made his first recordings in London for Edison Bell and the Gramophone and Typewriter Company. Among these was his immensely popular recording of Thomas Moore's Irish ballad 'Believe Me If All Those Endearing Young Charms'. After studying in Milan, he recorded for Odeon in 1906, and in 1907 became the youngest tenor to sing a major role at Covent Garden (where he regularly appeared until 1914). Later in 1907 he made his first operatic recording for Odeon.

In 1909 he gave his first solo concert in America and in 1910 made his operatic début at New York's Manhattan Opera House. His Odeon contract was bought up by Victor, for whom he made a series of celebrity records that, like those of **Enrico Caruso**, confirmed that America, rather than Europe, had become the centre of operatic recording. His success can be gauged from the fact that, with a ten per cent royalty, in one year he earned over $300,000.

In Britain, he had his greatest success with ballads. These included 'I Hear You Calling Me' (which he recorded on numerous occasions), Moore's 'The Minstrel Boy', **Stephen Foster**'s 'Come Where My Love Lies Dreaming', 'The Irish Immigrant' and George Cooper's 'Genevieve'. In America, however, he had equal success with operatic arias ('Il Flor Che Aveci a Me', 1910; 'O Terra Addio', 1915), popular songs ('When Shadows Gather', 1910; 'The Sunshine of Your Smile', 1916), Broadway songs (**Victor Herbert**'s 'I'm Falling in Love with Someone', 1911; Jack Judge and Harry Williams' 'It's a Long, Long Way to Tipperary', 1915) and, like **George M. Cohan** and others, patriotic songs, including 'The Star Spangled Banner', **Ivor Novello**'s 'Keep the Home Fires Burning' (1917) and 'God Be with Our Boys Tonight' (1918).

During the First World War McCormack gave fund-raising concerts in America for the Red Cross and in 1919 he became an American citizen. In 1928 he was made a Papal Count by Pope Pius XI. Though a popular radio performer, he made only two films, both of which highlighted his Irish background. These were *Song o' My Heart* (1929) and Britain's first Technicolor film, *Wings of the Morning* (1937). He gave his last major concert in London in 1938 and made his last recordings in 1942.

VAN McCOY
b. 6 January 1940, Washington DC, USA, d. 6 July 1979

Session musician, songwriter and producer, McCoy's career paralleled the development of sixties soul into the disco music of the seventies, when he had his only major hit with the lush anthem to disco dancing, 'The Hustle'* (Avco, 1975).

McCoy studied piano from the age of four and performed locally with his elder brother, Norman, before recording with the Starlighters on End, and as a solo artist on his own Rockin' Records ('Hey Mr DJ', 1959). In 1961 he became a staff producer and writer with Scepter/Wand where he worked with the Shirelles, Chuck Jackson and others and in 1962 joined Leiber and Stoller as an arranger, working briefly with the Drifters, before signing with Columbia as a solo artist and writer.

His solo records, mostly sweet ballads, failed but he found success as a producer for Gladys Knight and the Pips ('Giving It Up', 1964), Chad and Jeremy ('Before and After', Columbia, 1964) and Peaches and Herb ('Close Your Eyes', Date, 1967). He had an even greater impact as a writer. 'Baby I'm Yours' gave Barbara Lewis a huge hit on Atlantic in 1965 and was subsequently covered by Peter and Gordon (EMI Columbia, 1965) and 'When You're Young and in Love' was a hit for Ruby and the Romantics (Kapp, 1964) and later for the Marvelettes (1967). Other artists who recorded his songs include Aretha Franklin, Bobby Vinton and Brenda and the Tabulations.

In 1967 he set up his own production company and had success with Jackie Wilson, whose recording of McCoy's 'I Get the Sweetest Feeling' (1968) was a huge hit (and as big a hit again when reissued in Britain in 1972 and 1986). The record prefigured McCoy's lush arrangements and productions for the Stylistics, whose records from 'Let's Put It All Together' (1974) he masterminded with Hugo and Luigi, after the departure of the group's original mentor Thom Bell. The instrumental album Disco Baby (Avco, 1975), billed as being by 'Van McCoy and the Soul City Symphony', included the transatlantic hit 'The Hustle' and established McCoy as a solo artist. Further hits included 'Change with the Times' (H&L, 1975), 'Party' (1976) and 'My Favorite Fantasy' (MCA, 1978). At the same time he continued to write and produce for others. For former member of the Temptations David Ruffin he wrote and produced Who Am I (Motown, 1975), which included the singer's only major international hit, 'Walk Away from Love', for Knight he wrote 'Baby Don't Change Your Mind' (1977) and he produced Franklin's La Diva (1979).

THE McCOYS
Randy Hobbs; Bobby Peterson; Randy Zehringer,

b. 1951, Union City, Iowa, USA; Rick Zehringer (also Derringer), b. 5 May 1947, Union City

With their hit 'Hang on Sloopy'* (1965), the McCoys were an archetypal garage band of the mid-sixties. Rick Derringer later played with Johnny Winter before following a solo recording career.

From 1962 the Zehringer brothers (Rick on guitar and Randy on drums) formed a series of high-school bands, including Rick and the Raiders, Rick Z Combo and the McCoys. In 1965 they played as support band to Bang label artists the Strangeloves, who enjoyed a Top Twenty hit with the bubblegum tune 'I Want Candy'. As a result, Bang's owner Bert Berns signed the McCoys, and the Strangeloves' Richard Gottehrer, Bob Feldman and Jerry Goldstein produced 'Hang on Sloopy' for them. Written by Berns and Wes Farrell, the song had earlier been unsuccessfully recorded by the Vibrations (Atlantic, 1964).

In Britain, the McCoys' energetic version of the song was the first success for Andrew Loog Oldham's Immediate label and in America it reached No. 1, while the group's revival of Otis Blackwell's 'Fever' (previously successful for Little Willie John and Peggy Lee) was a Top Ten hit. None of their later records emulated the first singles, though a revival of Ritchie Valens' 'Come on Let's Go' reached the Top Thirty in 1966. In 1968 the group moved to Mercury for the progressive-rock-orientated Infinite McCoys and Human Ball, but by this time they were reduced to performing as the house band at Steve Paul's New York club, the Scene.

Paul managed both the McCoys and Johnny Winter, and Rick (now Derringer) joined Winter's band and produced his first albums. In 1971 he toured with Edgar Winter's band White Trash and produced their No. 1 record 'Frankenstein' (Epic, 1973). Derringer's solo career began with All American Boy (Blue Sky, 1973), which included the minor hit 'Rock and Roll Hoochie Coo'. A new version of 'Sloopy' appeared on Spring Fever (1975), which was followed by Derringer (1976) and Sweet Evil (1977). The titles of If I Wasn't So Romantic, I'd Shoot You (1978) and Guitars and Women (1979) typified the mainstream machismo rock approach of his live band Derringer, which included Vinny Appice (drums) and Danny Johnson (guitar).

Face to Face (1980) was Derringer's final Blue Sky album. He followed that with the lesser Good Dirty Fun (1984) before he went on to produce the comic parody of Michael Jackson's 'Beat It' and 'Bad', 'Eat It' and 'Fat' by disc-jockey Weird Al Jankovic (Scotti, 1984, 1988). He also composed 'Real American', which became the theme tune of wrestling champion Hulk Hogan. In the nineties he worked as a guitarist in Cyndi Lauper's backing band while continuing with his solo career, releasing *Back to the Blues* (Blues Bureau Records, 1993), *Electra Blues* (1994) and *Tend the Fire* (Code Blue, 1996).

GENE McDANIELS
b. 12 February 1935, Kansas City, Missouri, USA

A dynamic vocalist with a pop-soul approach similar to that of **Dionne Warwick**, McDaniels was one of the few black singers to make an impact on white teenage audiences in the early sixties. He later recorded socially aware soul material.

The son of a minister, McDaniels played saxophone with gospel groups before pursuing a college career which included a period at Omaha Conservatory of Music. He signed to Liberty in 1960 where **Tommy 'Snuff' Garrett** guided his career. After releasing the unsuccessful singles 'In Times Like These' and 'The Green Door', he reached the Top Ten with the Luther Dixon–Elgin Rogers song 'A Hundred Pounds of Clay'* (1961). The religious love ballad was first banned in Britain (as sacrilegious) and then covered by Craig Douglas. McDaniels' next big hit was a powerful reading of **Burt Bacharach**'s melodramatic 'Tower of Strength', which became a British No. 1 for **Frankie Vaughan**.

He had further successes in 1962 with the catchy 'Chip Chip', **Carole King** and Gerry Goffin's 'Point of No Return', and 'Spanish Lace' all becoming American hits. During this phase McDaniels had a cameo role in the British film *It's Trad Dad!*, where he sang the dramatic 'Another Tear Falls'. His final minor hit for Liberty was 'It's a Lonely Town' (1963).

Now known as Eugene McDaniels, he shifted his attention to the soul market and in 1971 recorded *Outlaw* (Atlantic). Produced by Joel Dorn, the album included self-penned songs dealing with racism and other contemporary problems. His songs 'Mother Time' and 'Nature's Baby' were recorded by **Lena Horne** in 1971 and he supplied **Roberta Flack** with 'Feel Like Making Love'* (1974) and 'Love Is the Healing' (1975). Among those whose records were produced by McDaniels was **Gladys Knight**. In 1980 he opened his own recording studio in Seattle.

COUNTRY JOE McDONALD
b. 1 January 1942, El Monte, California, USA

Leader of Country Joe and the Fish, one of the first exponents of psychedelic rock, McDonald thereafter pursued an erratic but productive solo career as a political songwriter.

From a left-wing background, he was named after Josef Stalin and his earliest musical influences were folk writers like **Woody Guthrie**. After serving in the marines, McDonald attended college in Los Angeles

and published his first songs in a magazine, *Air Two*. In 1962 he moved to Berkeley and started the Rag Baby label with Ed Denson, releasing two EPs by the jug band Country Joe and the Fish in 1965. These EPs were reissued in 1992, when the disturbing power of 'Bass Strings' and 'Section 43' as aural equivalents of being high remained as strong as ever. The group had originally been a duo of McDonald and guitarist Barry Melton, then became the Instant Action Jug Band, performing at anti-war benefits in Berkeley. The group was featured in the chapter 'Frozen Jug Band' in Tom Wolfe's *Electric Kool-Aid Acid Test*.

By 1966, the year they signed to Vanguard, the group was an electric rock band. On *Electric Music for the Mind and Body* (1967), Melton and McDonald were joined by Bruce Barthol (bass), Gary 'Chicken' Hirsch (drums) and David Cohen (organ). Produced by blues scholar Sam Charters, the album included the sinister 'Not So Sweet Martha Lorraine' and a reworking of the mysterious 'Bass Strings' and was one of the formative recordings of the psychedelic era. McDonald's zany protest song 'Feel Like I'm Fixin' to Die Rag' provided the title for the group's next album, while 'Fish Cheer' ('gimme an F, gimme an . . . what's that spell?') gave them an irresistible theme song. In 1968 they released *Together* and McDonald wrote soundtrack music for a 'psychedelic Western', *Zachariah*, in which the band also appeared.

Here We Are Again (1969) featured 'Maria', an anti-war song in MOR ballad format, and introduced the new rhythm section of Peter Albin (bass) and David Getz (drums). The final recording before the group split up was *C. J. Fish* (1970), produced by Tom Wilson. At this point Melton retired before returning to work on **Grateful Dead** drummer Mickey Hart's *Rolling Thunder* (Warners, 1972).

During the next decade McDonald pursued a varied solo career. A selection of Guthrie material formed the basis for *Thinking of Woody Guthrie* (1969), and *Tonight I'm Singing Just for You* (1970), a selection of country standards, was recorded in Nashville with such session players as Norbert Putnam and Buddy Harmon. He also composed music for the film of Henry Miller's *Quiet Days in Clichy* and played in a rock group on *Hold on It's Coming* (1971) and as a solo artist on a live album recorded in New York (*Incredible! Live!*, 1972).

FTA (Free/Fuck the Army) was an agit-prop anti-war touring show in which McDonald worked with actors Donald Sutherland and Jane Fonda. The experience gave a subtler political dimension to *Paris Sessions* (1973). Described by McDonald as 'like a talking newspaper', the album was in the tradition of Guthrie and **Tom Paxton** in that it contained commentaries on contemporary issues, but was recorded in a rock, rather than folk, idiom. The accompanying musicians included Albin and three women players, Ann Rizzo (drums), Tucki Bailey (sax) and Dorothy Moscowitz, former keyboards player with cult avant-garde group United States of America.

In 1974 McDonald and Melton toured together in California and Country Joe signed a recording deal with Fantasy which resulted in a series of low-key albums. Among them were *Paradise with an Ocean View* (1975), *Love Is a Fire* (1976), *Goodbye Blues* (1977), *Rock'n'Roll from Planet Earth* (1978) and *Leisure Suite* (1979); *Reunion* (1977) featured the original Fish. With Ed Denson, McDonald revived the Rag Baby label in 1980, recording an acoustic album (*On My Own*) and records by Melton (*Level with Me*) and other Bay Area musicians. His later albums included *Child's Play* (1983) and *Peace on Earth* (1985).

In 1986 Country Joe and the Fish re-formed to perform 'Feel Like I'm Fixin' to Die Rag' for a 'Welcome Home Festival' for veterans of the Vietnam War, and in 1991 McDonald recorded *Superstitious Giants* (Rykodisc) with the **Grateful Dead**'s Jerry Garcia.

JEANETTE MacDONALD
b. 18 June 1903, Philadelphia, Pennsylvania, USA,
d. 14 January 1965, Houston, Texas

An accomplished comedienne, as pert as she was pretty, MacDonald was the definitive heroine of Hollywood's reinvention in the thirties of the lush, saccharine world of the operetta, as the object of desire of first **Maurice Chevalier** and then **Nelson Eddy**. In this role she was parodied mercilessly by comics of the time, but in later years her musicals were affectionately regarded as classic examples of high camp.

In 1920 MacDonald followed her sister Blossom into the chorus of *The Night Boat*. By 1923 she had progressed to leading roles and had her first real success in **George Gershwin**'s *Tip Toes* (1925). In 1929 she was signed by Ernst Lubitsch, against Paramount's wishes, to partner Chevalier in *The Love Parade*. The pairing was a success, and Lubitsch – after co-starring her with **Jack Buchanan** for *Monte Carlo* (1930), in which she introduced **Leo Robin**'s 'Somewhere Beyond the Blue Horizon' – repeated it three times, in *One Hour with You, Love Me Tonight* (1932) and, most successfully of all, *The Merry Widow* (1934). For the most part, these were sophisticated comedies and her singing was lighter and more knowing than it became later.

After *The Merry Widow*, she was trapped in a series of operettas with Eddy, in which, despite the matching of his rich baritone and her clear soprano, much of the liveliness of her earlier work was lost. However, if his wooden reading of his lines gave her nothing to spark off, the simple plot lines of the films – which

usually had her either fighting to prove his innocence or, on hearing news (albeit often false) of his death, singing through her tears to recollect their love – caught the tenor of the times, and together the pair were the most successful singing couple in the history of Hollywood. The eight films in which they co-starred included *Naughty Marietta* (1935) and *Sweethearts* (1938), which were based on the operettas by **Victor Herbert**; *Maytime* (1937) and *New Moon* (1940), based on works by **Sigmund Romberg**; and, best known of all, their version of **Rudolf Friml**'s *Rose Marie* (1936) from which their RCA recording of 'The Indian Love Call' became the first show tune to sell a million copies. In between working with Eddy, MacDonald teamed up with Clark Gable for *San Francisco* (1936), in which she finally played the opera singer she aspired to be, Allan Jones for Friml's *The Firefly* (1937) and her husband, Gene Raymond, for *Smilin' Thru* (1941). Her and Eddy's *The Girl of the Golden West* (1938), though based on the David Belasco play that Puccini adopted for his opera, had a new score written by Romberg and **Gus Kahn**.

Following a dispute with MGM over the dubbing of her voice in the foreign versions of her films, she left the studio in 1942 to attempt a career in opera. She returned briefly to Hollywood in various supporting roles later in the forties, before turning to cabaret and the musical stage in the fifties.

FRED McDOWELL
b. 12 January 1904, Rossville, Tennessee, USA, d. 3 July 1972, Memphis, Tennessee

Unlike most other blues musicians, Fred McDowell made his reputation without the help of revered vintage recordings. He was unknown to the world at large until 1960, but in his remaining twelve years he left the stamp of his music and his personality on many white blues players.

A self-taught guitarist, McDowell spent much of his life in farm work, but played intermittently in various parts of northern Mississippi and southwest Tennessee. Revealed to folklorists and blues *aficionados* through **Alan Lomax**'s field recordings, issued on the Atlantic *Southern Folk Heritage* and Prestige *Southern Journey* series, he was drawn on to the folk festival circuit in 1963 and recorded in the following year his first full album, *Delta Blues* (Arhoolie). Playing mostly with a steel slide, he added decorations on the upper strings to hypnotic bass figures, while accompanying himself on original songs or highly personalized versions of standard blues.

This set was followed by others for Arhoolie, as well as for similar documentary labels like Testament and Milestone. He visited Europe with the American Folk Blues Festival in 1965 and on his own in 1969, by which time he had taken up electric guitar. McDowell's amplified playing can be heard on the concert recordings *In London* (Transatlantic, two volumes), *Standing at the Burying Ground* (Red Lightnin') and on the studio set *I Do Not Play No Rock'n'Roll* (Capitol, 1969), which took its title from a humorous disclaimer that often prefaced his performances. He continued to be a favourite on the campus circuit on both coasts, but still played in his own community, accompanying singing groups in church.

His legacy survives in the playing of several British blues guitarists, notably Jo-Ann Kelly and her brother Dave; but it is most evident in the work of **Bonnie Raitt**, who recorded his 'Write Me a Few Lines' on *Taking My Time* (1973) and incorporated into her act a solo acoustic-guitar spot in his memory. The **Rolling Stones** included McDowell's 'You Gotta Move' on *Sticky Fingers* (1971).

REBA McENTIRE
b. 28 March 1954, Chockie, Oklahoma, USA

One of the most commercially successful new country acts of the eighties, with sales of over 30 million albums by 2000, McEntire built her lengthy career on her ability to mix traditional material, reworkings of pop ('Sunday Kind of Love') and soul ('Respect') songs, and her own songs with ease.

From a musical family, Reba, with her sister and brother, formed the Singing McEntires and recorded for the independent Boss label in 1972. Her father (as detailed in 'Daddy') was a rodeo rider and in 1974 McEntire sang 'The Star Spangled Banner' at the National Rodeo Finals. That led to a recording contract with Mercury and her first country hit, 'I Don't Want to Be a One Night Stand' (1976). That, like most of her Mercury outings, was firmly in the country-politan style. Her early recordings included a remake of 'Sweet Dreams', 'You Lift Me up to Heaven', the country chart-toppers 'I Can't Even Get the Blues' and 'You're the First Time I've Thought about Leaving' from her best Mercury album, *Unlimited* (1982).

With the switch to MCA in 1983 came a growing confidence and a far more traditional style to her recordings. *My Kind of Country* (1984) featured a number of acoustic tracks, including the superior 'How Blue' and 'Someone Should Leave'. *Have I Got a Deal for You?* (1985), which included the fine cheating song 'Only in My Mind', was followed by her best-known album, *Whoever's in New England* (1986), in which, like **K. T. Oslin**, she sang of sex and marriage from the woman's point of view. *Greatest Hits* (1987) includes all her early MCA Top Ten hits. After a pair of minor albums, *Reba* (1988) saw her widening her range with reworkings of the **Everly Brothers**' 'Cathy's Clown' and others sitting alongside new

songs. The 1989 outing *Live* included the hits 'Walk On' and 'You Lie'. It was followed by the bland *Rumour Has It* (1990), which was her biggest-selling album to date. Among its hits were the title song and 'Fallin' out of Love'. She followed that with *For My Broken Heart* (1991), her best album of the early nineties. *It's Your Call* (1992), which was almost as successful, included a pair of duets, 'Does He Love You' with Linda Davis and 'The Heart Won't Lie' with **Vince Gill**. Her hits in 1994 included 'Why Haven't I Heard from You?' and 'Till You Love Me' from *Read My Mind*. In the same year she published an autobiography, *Reba: My Story*.

Starting Over (1995), an album of cover-versions, presaged a fallow period before in 1997 she and Brooks & Dunn (then the most popular duo in country music) commenced a mammoth tour. On the back of it they released the chart-topping single 'If You See Him/If You See Her'. McEntire followed that with the Top Ten album *If You See Him* (1998), while Brooks & Dunn did the same with *If You See Her*. In 1999, as her country success dimmed, McEntire sought to further broaden her range. Thus *So Good Together* (1999) had three producers in an effort to widen her crossover appeal. The result was her most AOR album.

KATE AND ANNA McGARRIGLE
Kate McGarrigle, b. 1946, St Sauveur-des-Monts, Canada; Anna McGarrigle, b. 1945, St Sauveur-des-Monts

Songwriters and close-harmony singers, the McGarrigle sisters made some of the most poignant records of the seventies and eighties. The impact of their best work was due to the presence of folk rather than rock instrumentation, an aesthetic choice which extended to their songwriting and paradoxically gave their compositions a more realistic edge than those of many contemporary singer-songwriters.

With a French-Canadian mother and an Irish-Canadian father, the sisters grew up in a multi-cultural and highly musical family. With their elder sister Jane, they won a talent contest in 1958. In the early sixties the family moved to Montreal, where Kate and Anna formed a folk group, the Mountain City Four, with Peter Weldon and Jack Nissenson. While at college, the sisters wrote a song for a film celebrating Canada's centennial in 1967 but it was another five years before McKendree Spring made the first recording of Anna's haunting ballad 'Heart Like a Wheel'. The song was subsequently used in the film *Play It as It Lays* and became a hit when recorded in 1975 by **Linda Ronstadt**, who later, in partnership with **Dolly Parton** and **Emmylou Harris** (Trio, 1987), also recorded Anna's anguished 'I've Had Enough'.

In 1969 Kate McGarrigle began performing on the New York folk circuit. In 1971 she married **Loudon Wainwright III**, from whom she later separated. Among her compositions was the poetic meditation on plantation life and music 'Work Song', which was recorded in 1973 by **Maria Muldaur**, who also included Anna's 'Cool River' on *Waitress in a Donut Shop* (1974).

The growing awareness of their writing ability led to a recording contract for the sisters. Their eponymous début album was supervised for Warners by Muldaur's producer **Joe Boyd**. Released in 1976, it included 'Heart Like a Wheel' and other songs of loss in 'Mendocino' and 'My Town'. It brought a European following for Kate and Anna and, after a tour to Britain and Holland, they recorded *Dancer with Bruised Knees* (1977), which included the moving 'First Born'. Over the years these two came to be acknowledged as classic albums. *Dancer* was followed by the lesser *Pronto Monto* (1978). Kate McGarrigle also sang on *Rise up like the Sun* by the British folk-rock group the **Albion Band**.

When the Warners albums proved commercially disappointing, the sisters made *Entre la Jeunesse et la Sagesse*, an album of French-language songs for Kebec Disc (1980). This was later reissued as *French Record*. They signed to Polydor for *Love Over and Over* (1982), which included their own version of 'Work Song'. Although the sisters continued to play concerts and festivals, they did not release another album until 1990's *Heartbeats Accelerating* (Private Records), which included a haunting version of the cowboy's lament 'St James Hospital' (known in another form as 'Streets of Laredo'). The album successfully mixed their trademark acoustic stylings with more rock instrumentation, including synthesizers and drum machines. In 1992 their former producer and long-term admirer Joe Boyd re-released their early albums on his own label, Hannibal, to renewed critical adulation. In 1993 Kate and Anna were awarded the Order of Canada for their contribution to music.

Then, after a lengthy break, the McGarrigles returned with the wonderful *Matapedia* (1996). While the songs showed a return to the concerns of their earliest albums, albeit with an extra edge of desperation ('Why Must We Die?') and resignation ('I Don't Know'), the settings, largely by Michel Pepin, added a further level of intensity. The result was an enormous critical success. The sisters followed it with the charming *The McGarrigle Hour* (1998), in which with guests Linda Ronstadt, Emmylou Harris and Loudon Wainwright they recreated the feel of a Victorian evening of song, with repertoire that intertwined their own compositions with those of **Stephen Foster** and **Cole Porter** to perfect effect.

BROWNIE McGHEE AND SONNY TERRY

Brownie McGhee, b. Walter Brown McGhee, 30 November 1915, Knoxville, Tennessee, USA, d. 16 February 1996, Oakland, California; Sonny Terry, b. Saunders Terrell, 24 October 1911, Greensboro, North Carolina, d. 12 March 1986, New York

McGhee and Terry were the blues' leading partnership, as indivisible as Laurel and Hardy. McGhee was ingratiating, articulate, a suave singer and guitarist; the blind Terry coarser-voiced, but a singular genius of country blues harmonica, his playing highly personalized yet flexible enough to create a stylistic tradition of its own. For at least one generation of listeners, particularly in Europe, they were a first introduction to the blues.

The two met in Burlington, North Carolina, in 1939. For a time they were associated with the local blues singer **Blind Boy Fuller**, after whose death McGhee recorded for Okeh as Blind Boy Fuller No. 2. The pair moved to New York in the early forties (Terry had made an earlier trip to appear in **John Hammond**'s 1938 'Spirituals to Swing' concert) and joined the circle of folk and blues musicians around **Leadbelly** and **Woody Guthrie**. They made stage appearances – Terry played in the New York stage production of *Finian's Rainbow* (1947–8) – and broadcast for the Office of War Information, while recording prolifically for both 'race' and folk-music audiences, on labels like Savoy, Capitol and Disc. McGhee wrote or adapted much of their material, such as 'Walk on' (their theme song) and 'Sporting Life Blues'. They also accompanied **Champion Jack Dupree** and many lesser lights of early postwar blues in New York, such as singer-guitarists Ralph Willis and Stick(s) McGhee, Brownie's brother, who had a much-copied hit with 'Drinkin' Wine Spo-Dee-o-Dee' (Atlantic, 1951).

At various times during the forties and fifties they adapted their acoustic duet sound to the prevailing popular styles from Chicago and elsewhere, playing in small-band settings with pianists Dupree, Bob Gaddy or Harry Van Walls, and with McGhee using electric guitar. But they continued to record in older styles, both together and separately, for Elektra and Folkways. In 1955–7 they appeared in a New York production of Tennessee Williams' *Cat on a Hot Tin Roof*, and in 1957 McGhee contributed to the soundtrack of Elia Kazan's *A Face in the Crowd*.

The duo first visited Britain in 1958, working and recording with **Chris Barber**, and greatly influenced acoustic 'country'-style blues performers there. Throughout the sixties and early seventies they recorded regularly (for World Pacific, Prestige-Bluesville, Fantasy, Bluesway and Storyville) and toured frequently with the American Folk Blues

Festival tours of Europe in 1962, 1967 and 1970 and the American Blues Caravan of 1964. At home they worked the folk and blues festival and coffee-house circuits and did further movie soundtracks (*Buck and the Preacher*, 1972; *Book of Numbers*, 1972; *Leadbelly*, 1976).

By the mid-seventies the duo's relationship was strained, and although they worked together they seldom spoke to, or even acknowledged, each other. They finally parted at the end of the seventies to work independently. Terry cut the innovative *Whoopin'* (Mad Albino, 1984) where his collaboration with slide-guitarist (and producer) **Johnny Winter** recalled the early joint efforts of **Muddy Waters** and **Little Walter**. It was his last recording. McGhee spent much of the eighties in semi-retirement.

CHRIS McGREGOR

b. 24 December 1936, South Africa, d. 26 May 1990

With **Abdullah Ibrahim** (Dollar Brand) and **Hugh Masekela**, McGregor was one of the most distinguished South African jazz musicians living in exile. With the Blue Notes and the Brotherhood of Breath he fused the kwela (township jazz) of his native land with recent trends in avant-garde jazz.

The son of a Scottish-born white mission teacher, he studied modern classical music at Capetown College of Music while leading on piano a racially integrated hard-bop group, the Blue Notes, whose best-known Afro-jazz recording was 'Ponder Blues' (Gallotone, 1962). Including Dudu Pukwana (alto sax), Nick Moyake (tenor sax), Mongezi Feza (trumpet), Johnny Dyani (bass) and Louis Moholo (drums), the group won the jazz prize in 1963 at the prestigious Cold Castle Festival in Johannesburg. In 1991 Teal Records released a live set, *Jazz the African Sound*, of the band.

The harassment of the apartheid system led the Blue Notes to follow Ibrahim to Europe soon afterwards. Settling in London in 1965, they had a major impact on the British jazz scene. Their style evolved to encompass the newer free jazz trends and each member led his own group. Both Moholo and Pukwana remained respected figures in British jazz into the eighties; Feza died in 1975 and Dyani in 1986. Like them, McGregor did not live to see the defeat of the apartheid regime which had forced him into exile.

In 1970 McGregor assembled the first line-up of his big band, the Brotherhood of Breath, recording an eponymous album for RCA's Neon label in 1971 and releasing a live recording of a concert in Willisau, Switzerland (1972). With a nucleus of the original Blue Notes, the band also included such soloists from the British avant-garde scene as tenor-sax-player Evan Parker.

McGregor moved to France in the late seventies, organizing a new Brotherhood of Breath which recorded *Yes Please* (1981) on his own In and Out label. Later Brotherhood of Breath recordings included a tribute to Fezi and Dyani, *Blue Notes for Johnny* (1984), *Country Cooking* (1988), produced by **Joe Boyd** and *Live with Archie Shepp* (1991). The band toured Mozambique in 1984.

JIMMY McGRIFF

b. 3 April 1936, Philadelphia, Pennsylvania, USA

McGriff's swinging, bluesy Hammond organ-playing influenced a generation of rhythm and blues musicians in the sixties.

Originally a bass player with various local groups, he switched to organ under the influence of fellow-Philadelphian **Jimmy Smith**. McGriff mastered the now classic double-keyboard style where the melody and improvisation are played on the upper keyboard and a solid, contrapuntal bass line on the lower. With Morris Dow (guitar) and Jackie Mills (drums), he toured the East Coast with such singers as Don Gardner and **Arthur Prysock**.

In 1962 McGriff's trio recorded a throbbing instrumental version of **Ray Charles**' 'I Got a Woman' (Jell). Given national distribution by Juggy Murray's Sue label, the record was both a pop and an R&B hit. He had further R&B hits with 'All About My Girl' (1963) and 'The Last Minute' (1964). McGriff's compositions became part of the repertoire of **Georgie Fame** and other performers on the nascent British R&B scene.

He went on to record for Solid State (*Bag Full of Soul*, 1968), Blue Note (*Black Pearl*, 1970) and Groove Merchant, for whom he made some compelling jazz albums, both solo (*Fly Dude*, 1974) and with fellow organist Richard 'Groove' Holmes (*Giants of the Organ in Concert*). McGriff also collaborated with blues singer and harmonica-player **Junior Parker** on *Good Things Don't Happen Every Day* (Groove Merchant, 1972).

His later records included *Tail Gunner* (LRC, 1977), *Outside Lookin' In* (1978), *State of the Art* (1986) and *The Starting Five*. Best of all was his collaboration with veteran jazzman Hank Crawford on *Right Turn on Blues* (Telarc, 1994). They repeated the exercise a year later with *Blues Groove*.

THE McGUIRE SISTERS

Chris, b. 30 July 1929, Middletown, Ohio, USA; Dotty, b. Dorothy, 13 February 1930, Middletown; Phyllis, b. 14 February 1931, Middletown

The McGuire Sisters, like **Pat Boone** and the **Crew Cuts**, were among the numerous artists who began their recording career with covers of rock'n'roll songs originally recorded by black artists.

The sisters sang with local church choirs before forming a trio in their teens. After radio broadcasts in the Cincinnati area, they travelled to New York where they appeared on first **Kate Smith**'s radio show and then **Arthur Godfrey**'s televised talent show in 1953. Decca's **Milt Gabler** liked their hard-edged voices and signed them to the company's subsidiary label, Coral. In 1954 they had an immediate pop hit with a simplified version of the **Spaniels**' R&B hit 'Goodnight, Sweetheart, Goodnight' and followed it with a million-selling cover of the Moonglows' 'Sincerely'.

The group quickly diversified and had great success with a series of film songs, including 'Something's Gotta Give' (from *Daddy Long Legs*, 1955), their vocal version of 'The Theme from Picnic'* (1956) and 'Delilah Jones' (from *The Man with the Golden Arm*, 1956). They also partnered **Lawrence Welk** on 'Weary Blues' (1956) and recorded the bouncy 'Sugartime' (1958), which was covered in Britain by **Alma Cogan** and Jim Dale (Parlophone). When their own hits dried up, they returned to the practice of covering others'. Hence the string of minor hits which included 'Volare' (**Domenico Modugno**, 1958), 'Tears on My Pillow' (**Little Anthony and the Imperials**) and 'Just Because' (**Lloyd Price**) in 1961.

Their hitmaking days over, the trio retreated to cabaret. On the retirement of Chris and Dotty, Phyllis continued as a solo artist, regularly appearing in Las Vegas in the seventies.

BARRY McGUIRE
b. 15 October 1937, Oklahoma City, Oklahoma, USA

A former folk singer, Barry McGuire is remembered for his recording of 'Eve of Destruction', one of the most popular protest-style songs of the sixties.

In 1961 he joined the New Christy Minstrels, a group named after the nineteenth-century minstrel band which first popularized the songs of **Stephen Foster**. Other members included future **Byrds** member Gene Clark, **Kenny Rogers** and Randy Sparks, with whom McGuire wrote the Minstrels' first hit, 'Green Green' (Columbia, 1963). Their later hits included 'Saturday Night' (1963) and 'Today' (1964), from the film *Advance to the Rear*.

As the folk-rock era began, McGuire left the New Christy Minstrels and moved to California, where **Lou Adler** chose him to record songs by **P. F. Sloan**. Among the first of these was the **Bob Dylan**-inspired 'Eve of Destruction' (Dunhill, 1965), which, helped by McGuire's exaggerated, growling delivery, became a No. 1 hit. The song's somewhat pessimistic view of the future of the world inspired 'Dawn of Correction', an all-American response from the Spokesmen on

Decca. McGuire's album, *Eve of Destruction*, was followed by *This Precious Time* (1966), mostly written by Sloan and with the emergent **Mamas and the Papas** on backing vocals. In 1967 McGuire played a hippy rock singer in the film *The President's Analyst*.

He capitalized on that image by acting in the Broadway production of *Hair* while Adler released *The World's Last Private Citizen* (1967). That album's poor sales led McGuire into semi-retirement from which he emerged for *Barry McGuire and the Doctor* (Ode, 1971), which featured an impressive line-up of West Coast session musicians, including ex-Byrds Chris Hillman and Michael Clarke as well as future **Eagle** Bernie Leadon and Sneeky Pete Kleinow (steel guitar).

Soon afterwards McGuire became a born-again Christian and returned to recording in 1973 with the gospel album *Seeds* (Myrrh). He toured with the group David and released annual albums up to *Finer than Gold* (Sparrow, 1981).

JIMMY McHUGH
James Francis McHugh, b. 10 July 1894, Boston, Massachusetts, USA, d. 23 May 1969, Beverly Hills, California

McHugh was one of the many Broadway songwriters who went to Hollywood after the arrival of the talkies. Working most frequently with lyricists **Dorothy Fields** and Harold Adamson, he helped bring a new level of sophistication to Hollywood musicals.

A trained musician, McHugh was a rehearsal pianist at the Boston Opera House before becoming a song plugger for **Irving Berlin**'s publishing company. In 1921 he went to New York and wrote his first hit (with words by **Irving Mills** and **Gene Austin**), 'When My Sugar Walks Down the Street', though some sources suggest that the tune (and several others of McHugh's early successes) was in fact bought outright from **Fats Waller**. A general manager at Mills Music, he formed a partnership with Fields, one of the company's new signings, to write songs for *The Cotton Club Revue of 1929* and the pair had their first hits with the oft-recorded standard 'I Can't Give You Anything but Love', which was introduced by **Adelaide Hall** in *Blackbirds of 1928*. They followed this with 'On the Sunny Side of the Street' and 'Exactly Like You' from *The International Revue* (1930) before going to Hollywood. Among their early successes were 'Cuban Love Song' (which became the title song of the 1931 film), and 'I'm in the Mood for Love' and 'I Feel a Song Coming on', which were introduced by Frances Langford in *Every Night at Eight* (1935) and 'Don't Blame Me' (1934), later memorably revived by the **Everly Brothers**. By this time McHugh was working in partnership with Harold Adamson (*b. 10 December 1906, Greenville, New Jersey, d. 17 August 1980, Beverly Hills, California*).

The pair wrote songs for nineteen movies, including *Higher and Higher* (1943), which featured **Frank Sinatra** singing 'I Couldn't Sleep a Wink Last Night', and 'This is a Lovely Way to Spend an Evening', and *Calendar Girl* (1947), which included the song 'Have I Told You Lately That I Love You'. They were also responsible for the Second World War song 'Coming in on a Wing and a Prayer' (1943), which was later affectionately revived by **Ry Cooder**. In addition to his work with McHugh, Adamson collaborated with **Walter Donaldson** ('It's Been So Long', 1936), **Hoagy Carmichael** ('My Resistance Is Low', 1952) and **Victor Young** ('Around the World', 1956).

In the fifties McHugh wrote less and spent more time overseeing his publishing interests.

MARIA McKEE
b. 17 August 1964, Los Angeles, USA

McKee was one of the many roots-orientated country writers and performers to emerge in the eighties. If, unlike **Lucinda Williams**, she was unable to take control of her own career, she offered a fine contrast to the 'country hats' who emerged at the same time.

The daughter of an artist mother and a carpenter father, McKee had an early education in country and gospel music through her parents and was introduced to rock'n'roll as a child through her half-brother Bryan MacLean, guitarist with legendary sixties acid-rockers **Love**. At the age of sixteen, she sang in a band with MacLean, before forming a folk/country duo with guitarist Hedgecock in 1982. The pair played Los Angeles clubs before putting together, with MacLean's help, the first line-up of Lone Justice later that year with bassist Marvin Etzioni and drummer Don Heffington.

Praised by **Bob Dylan** and **Linda Ronstadt**, the band signed to Geffen Records the following year. Their eponymous début album, released in 1985, featured the keyboard playing and writing talents of Benmont Tench from **Tom Petty & the Heartbreakers**. Petty contributed material to the album, as did Bryan MacLean. His song 'Don't Toss Us Away' later became a country hit for Patty Loveless. The critical reception for the album was overwhelmingly favourable and the strength of McKee's writing was simultaneously reflected in the UK success of her 'A Good Heart', a No. 1 single for ex-Undertones vocalist **Feargal Sharkey** in 1985. However, despite a tour of the US with **U2** (Bono was another admirer of the band), sales of the album were disappointing.

For the second album, *Shelter* (1986), only Hedgecock was retained from the original line-up, the new members being bassist Sutton, guitarist Fontayne, drummer Richardson and ex-**Patti Smith** keyboard-player Bruce Brody. The album, effectively a McKee solo set, was more polished but sold fewer copies despite the presence of a minor hit single, 'I Found Love'. The band's new line-up was also a disappointment in live shows, and Lone Justice broke up in 1987. Brody would continue to work with McKee, while Hedgecock would eventually embark on a solo career. A live album taken from a BBC Radio 1 session, *Live in Concert*, featuring a spirited version of the **Velvet Underground**'s 'Sweet Jane', appeared in 1993.

McKee re-emerged as a solo artist with her eponymous début album in 1989. Featuring a more soulful sound than the Lone Justice albums, it included an affecting version of **Richard Thompson**'s 'Has He Got a Friend for Me?', which she followed with a brash reading of her own 'Drinking in My Sunday Dress'. McKee now based herself in Ireland and played a number of low-key Dublin gigs before beginning work on her second solo offering, the wonderfully titled *You Gotta Sin to Get Saved* (1993), her best album to date. It received ecstatic reviews, but had unimpressive sales. A mixture of R&B and country-rock styles, it included two **Van Morrison** songs. The best of these was McKee's version of Them's 'My Lonely Sad Eyes'. She followed this with *Life Is Sweet* (1996), which, in the manner of **Mary-Chapin Carpenter**'s later work, saw her seeking to return to the rock (rather than country/folk-rock) mainstream.

ROD McKUEN
b. Rodney Marvin McKuen, 29 April 1933, Oakland, California, USA

Poet, composer and writer McKuen had great success in the early seventies with a series of albums on which, in the manner of his fifties radio programme, 'Rendezvous with Rod', he dispensed advice to the lovelorn and homilies about life in general in an intimate, hoarse, half-sung, half-spoken manner, backed by lush strings.

During his teens McKuen wandered the Western states before returning to Oakland in 1949 to work as a disc-jockey. After serving in the army during the Korean War, about which he wrote his first book *Elephants in the Rice Paddies* (1954) and the song 'Soldiers Who Want to Be Heroes', he turned to songwriting and singing in a San Francisco nightclub. This led to his working as a composer of film music for Universal for two years, before in 1959 he moved to New York to write music for television and began recording.

McKuen composed the novelty hit 'The Mummy' (Bob McFadden and Dor, Brunswick, 1959) and had a minor hit with his own 'Oliver Twist' (Spiral, 1962). He then travelled to France where he perfected his *chansonnier* singing style. There he provided English lyrics for several **Jacques Brel** songs, most notably 'Ne

Me Quitte Pas' ('If You Go Away') and 'Le Mori-bund', which as 'Seasons in the Sun' was recorded by **Bobby Vinton** (1961) and the **Kingston Trio** (1964) and, a decade later, provided Terry Jacks (who in 1969 as a member of the Poppy Family had a million-seller with 'Which Way You Goin' Billy?' on London) with an American No. 1 (Bell) and another million-seller. He also translated songs by **Gilbert Becaud** and Georges Moustaki. Several of McKuen's own songs from this period were hits for other people, including Jimmie Rodgers ('World I Used to Know', Dot, 1963) and Glen Yarbrough ('Baby the Rain Must Fall', RCA, 1965, from *The Lonely Things*, an album of McKuen compositions). **Frank Sinatra** recorded *A Man Alone* (1969), an album of McKuen songs including 'Love's Been Good to Me'.

Even more successful were McKuen's poetry collections, which included *Listen to the Warm* (1967) and *Lonesome Cities* (1968). In the wake of these, which sold over two million copies, he recorded a series of bestselling albums for Reprise. Among them were *The Single Man* and *At Carnegie Hall* (1974), which included 'Jean', the Oscar-nominated theme from the film *The Prime of Miss Jean Brodie* (1969), whose score McKuen wrote. In the seventies McKuen formed his own mail-order company, Stanyon, through which he issued some fifty albums and twenty books of poetry.

SARAH McLACHLAN
b. 28 January 1968, Halifax, Nova, Canada

As well as being one of the most talented performers of her generation, McLachlan was also responsible for arranging the all-female Lilith Fair tour, which has established itself as a powerful force on the late nineties music scene in America.

McLachlan, who studied classical guitar and piano as a child, signed to Nettwerk Records at the age of seventeen, recording her début, *Touch* (Arista, 1989), three years later. The album won her immediate stardom in Canada, while the acclaimed *Solace* (1991), which mixed celtic influences with a decidedly pop-folk sound, brought her to international prominence. It was followed by *Live* (1992).

After a gruelling 16-month tour, McLachlan produced *Fumbling towards Ecstasy* (1994), which signalled an increased artistic maturity and included the hit single 'Hold on', inspired by a television documentary about an AIDS sufferer. 'Hold on' also featured on the *No Alternative* compilation album in support of the illness, while the singer also contributed a track to the soundtrack of the movie *The Brothers McMullen*. *The Freedom Sessions* (1995) collected demo versions of songs from *Fumbling towards Ecstasy* alongside a cover of **Tom Waits'** 'Ol' 55'.

As well as the release of her most successful album

to date, *Surfacing*, which spawned two further hits in 'Building a Mystery' and 'Sweet Surrender', 1997 saw McLachlan put together the inaugural Lilith Fair tour, which she headlined above an array of international female artists. The tour was reprised in 1998, when it included a date in the UK at the Royal Albert Hall, and 1999. Prior to that she had her biggest-ever US hit with the single 'Aida'. In 1999 she had further success with *Mirrorball*, which was one of the first albums to be promoted by free digital downloads.

MALCOLM McLAREN
b. Malcolm Robert Andrew McLaren, 1946

Manager and manipulator of the **Sex Pistols**, McLaren went on to pursue a recording career of his own, enjoying a surprising degree of success in the mid-eighties.

As an art student at various London colleges, he was involved in the protest movement of the mid-sixties. He was associated with the King Mob group, which espoused 'Situationist' ideas, aiming to shock people into an awareness of the 'boredom of everyday life'. With designer Vivienne Westwood, McLaren opened a boutique in Chelsea's Kings Road in 1971. As first Let It Rock and then Too Fast to Live Too Young to Die, it sold the then unfashionable Teddy Boy drapes to a new generation. In the mid-seventies, as Sex and then Seditionaries, the shop sold Westwood's bondage designs which were to become the uniform of the punk movement. McLaren's first taste of rock management was in 1974 with the **New York Dolls**, whom he dressed in Maoist Red Guard outfits to scandalize American audiences.

Returning to London, he turned several of the hangers-on at his shop into the Sex Pistols, signing the group to EMI in 1976. After an infamous televised confrontation between the group and television interviewer Bill Grundy, EMI cancelled the contract, paying £40,000 compensation. A&M next took on the band but soon dropped them, paying £75,000. In 1977 McLaren received £90,000 in advances from Virgin, who finally released the group's recordings.

The group split in 1978 and the following year lead singer Johnny Rotten successfully sued McLaren, claiming that unpaid royalties had been used to finance a film project that eventually became *The Great Rock'n'Roll Swindle* (1979), conceived by McLaren and directed by Julien Temple after sexploitation filmmaker Russ Meyer had withdrawn.

In 1980 McLaren planned **Adam Ant**'s successful new image and launched the group Bow Wow Wow, who had a minor hit with the paean to home taping, 'C30, C60, C90 Go' (EMI). They had great success in 1982 with 'Go Wild in the Country' and 'I Want Candy' (RCA), by which time McLaren was planning his own recording début. With producer **Trevor Horn**, he recorded *Duck Rock* (Charisma, 1983), a collection of songs based on 'field recordings' made in Africa and America, which led to McLaren being attacked for plagiarism. The album included the Top Ten hits 'Buffalo Gals' (the first British record to feature scratching) and the quirky 'Double Dutch'. After releasing *Would Ya Like More Scratchin'* (1984), he turned his attention less successfully to opera, releasing the hit single 'Madam Butterfly' and the album *Fans* (1985). *Swamp Thing* (1986) was a return to his earlier approach, mixing hip-hop and ethnic rhythms, while *Waltz Darling* (Epic, 1989) was recorded with the Bootzilla Orchestra. *Round the Outside! Round the Outside!* (Virgin, 1990) repeated the classics plus hip-hop formula and featured various American rappers.

In the nineties McLaren moved into television, directing commercials and, in 1991, his own Christmas show in Britain, the *Ghosts of Oxford Street*. It featured the **Pogues**, **Tom Jones** and Manchester band the **Happy Mondays** – appropriately described as the nineties answer to the Sex Pistols.

He returned to recording in 1993, when he signed to French jazz label Vogue. In the same year he secured himself a manager, **Elton John**'s John Reid. His first album for Vogue was *Paris* (1994), a clichéd evocation of the city as a bohemian paradise. It received a lukewarm welcome. The 1992 book *The Wicked Ways of Malcolm McLaren*, if only for its detailed account of his career, served to deflate McLaren's artistic pretensions and highlight his manipulative abilities. In 1999, in a surprise move, he announced his candidature to be London's mayor and found some support from a number of disaffected Labourites, including former Creation head and Oasis manager Alan McGhee.

JOHN McLAUGHLIN
b. 4 January 1942, Yorkshire, England

Originally a British R&B guitarist, McLaughlin became one of the most respected instrumentalists of the seventies, fusing jazz and Indian music in his Mahavishnu Orchestra.

A self-taught musician, he learned blues and flamenco styles in the fifties. McLaughlin's first professional work was with groups on the jazzy edge of British R&B. Among those with whom he played in the early sixties were **Alexis Korner**, **Graham Bond**, **Georgie Fame** and **Brian Auger**. A master technician, he evolved a style based on extremely long phrases played at high speed.

He made his recording début with Bond and also recorded with jazz saxophonist John Surman and bassist Dave Holland before making his solo début

with *Extrapolation* (Polydor, 1969). In that year he emigrated to America and joined **Miles Davis**'s group, with whom he recorded *In a Silent Way* (1969) and *Bitches Brew* (1970).

He also played with **Jack Bruce** in **Tony Williams'** Lifetime before recording *My Goal's Beyond* (1971), which featured over-dubbed guitar duets on famous jazz themes by Davis and **Charles Mingus**. The following year he formed the Indo-jazz-rock Mahavishnu Orchestra (the title means 'divine compassion, power and justice' in Hindi) with Billy Cobham (drums), Rick Laird (bass), Czech-born Jan Hammer (keyboards) and Jerry Goodman (violin). *The Inner Mounting Flame* (Columbia, 1972) was influential in its combination of strongly electric playing with the rhythms and themes of ragas. *Birds of Fire* (1973) was a Top Twenty hit.

After the live album *Between Nothingness and Eternity* (1973), the individual members of the group left to pursue solo careers. McLaughlin collaborated with fellow devotee of guru Sri Chimnoy **Carlos Santana** on *Love Devotion Surrender* (1973) and then re-formed Mahavishnu with violinist Jean-Luc Ponty and **Narada Michael Walden** (drums) to record *Apocalypse* (1974), which was produced by **George Martin** and featured the London Symphony Orchestra. With Ponty replaced by Stu Goldberg (keyboards), Mahavishnu went on to make *Visions of the Emerald Beyond* (1975) and *Inner Worlds* (1976).

McLaughlin next immersed himself in Indian music with Shakti ('creative intelligence, beauty and power'), a trio which included tabla and percussion players with the guitarist playing an adapted acoustic guitar designed to simulate the 'drone' sounds of the sitar. This group's Columbia albums included *Natural Elements* and *A Handful of Beauty* (1977). In 1980 McLaughlin formed an acoustic-guitar supergroup with flamenco star Paco de Lucia and Al Di Meola, recording a superior pair of albums, *Friday in San Francisco* (1981) and *Passion Grace and Fire* (1983).

Now recording for Warners, McLaughlin made the solo albums *Belo Horizonte* (1982) and *Music Spoken Here* before, with Billy Cobham, he put together a new Mahavishnu Orchestra in 1985 with Bill Evans (saxophone). In 1987 he recorded for ECM with percussionist Zakir Hussein and Norwegian saxophonist Jan Garbarek.

McLaughlin next formed a trio with Indian percussionist Trilok Gutu and bassist Kai Eckhardt, recording *Que Alegria* (Verve, 1992). He also developed jazz–classical fusions with his *Concerto for Guitar and Orchestra* (recorded in 1990 with conductor Michael Tilson Thomas) and in duets with classical pianist Katia Labeque. Later recordings included *Tokyo Live* (1993) and *After the Rain* (1995).

DON McLEAN
b. 2 October 1945, New Rochelle, New York, USA

Singer-songwriter McLean's 'American Pie'* and 'Vincent' are two of the most widely known songs of the seventies.

He made his professional début on New York's folk circuit in 1963 and later joined **Pete Seeger**'s Clearwater Project, an anti-pollution campaign based on a sloop in the Hudson River. Produced by Jerry Corbitt (formerly of the **Youngbloods**) and with arrangements by Ed Bogas, his first album *Tapestry* appeared in 1970 on United Artists' Media Arts label. The album, which sold poorly, included 'And I Love You So', a 1973 hit for **Perry Como**.

The eight-minute 'American Pie' (United Artists, 1972) was the title track from McLean's next album. A cryptic history of rock with its refrain 'the day the music died', the song was a No. 1 hit in America and reached No. 2 in Britain. The album also included 'Vincent', a highly romanticized tribute to the painter Van Gogh which became McLean's second hit. After 'Dreidel' (1973), McLean turned away from the singles market to record *Playin' Favorites*, an album of old folk, blues and country songs including 'Mountains of Mourne' and **Hank Williams**' 'Lovesick Blues'.

Touring frequently, McLean released further albums during the seventies. Among them were *Homeless Brother* (1974), which featured the narrative ballad 'Legend of Andrew McGraw', the live double-album *Solo* (1976), *Prime Time* (1977) and *Chain Lightning* (1979). He returned to the pop charts with a reverential revival of **Roy Orbison**'s 1962 hit 'Crying' (Millenium, 1981), 'Since I Don't Have You' (1981), originally a hit for the Skyliners (Calico, 1958), and a new version of 'Castles in the Air', his own composition, which had originally been the B-side of 'Vincent'.

During the eighties McLean repeated his successful formula, releasing a further live album (*Dominion*, EMI, 1982) and *Believers* (1982), which mixed a judicious selection of old pop hits (Ketty Lester's 'Love Letters', 1962; **Frankie Ford**'s 'Sea Cruise', 1959) with less impressive McLean compositions.

In 1988 he turned towards country music with *Love Tracks* (Capitol). Next he released *For the Memories Vols 1 & 2*, which featured standards from the thirties, forties and fifties. They made little impression, and his next release was an in-concert recording from his 1980 British tour, *Greatest Hits Live!* (1990). 'American Pie' had long been a staple of soft-rock programming, and in 1991 was reissued in Britain, reaching the Top Twenty and helping *The Best of Don McLean* (1991) into the album chart. With interest in his past recordings reawakened, McLean toured extensively, and a switch to Curb Records produced *Don McLean Christmas*, but new self-penned material was conspic-uous by its absence. In 2000 **Madonna** recorded a decidedly modernist version of 'American Pie'.

CLYDE McPHATTER
b. 15 November 1933, Durham, North Carolina, USA,
d. 13 June 1972, Tea Neck, New Jersey

Described by **Jerry Wexler** as 'the great, unique singer of all time', McPhatter's high tenor, heard first with the Dominoes, then the **Drifters** and on solo records after 1956, was one of the most distinctive and enduring sounds of fifties R&B.

The son of a Baptist minister, he formed the gospel group the Mount Lebanon Singers in 1947, and in 1950 joined the Dominoes. Formed by vocal coach Billy Ward from among his best students in 1950, the Dominoes were usually billed as Billy Ward's Dominoes, though Ward never sang with them. Signed to the King subsidiary Federal and produced by **Ralph Bass**, they were enormously influential in the early fifties. Other members were Bill Brown, Joe Lamount and James Van Loan. Bass-singer Brown sang lead on 'Sixty Minute Man', a risqué blues that was the biggest-selling R&B record of 1950, but it was McPhatter's soaring, crying vocals that won the Dominoes the adoration of fans on records like 'Have Mercy Baby' (1952) and the histrionic death song 'The Bells' (1953). Ward was a firm disciplinarian and following a row with him, McPhatter left the group in 1953 to be replaced by **Jackie Wilson**.

McPhatter signed with Atlantic and around him was formed the first line-up of the long-running Drifters. More successful and influential than any other black group of the period, with the exception of **Hank Ballard**'s Midnighters and the **Clovers**, the Drifters' first five records were all Top Ten R&B hits: the classic 'Money Honey' (1953), 'Such a Night', 'Honey Love' (1954 – one of McPhatter's few compositions), 'White Christmas' and 'What'Cha Gonna Do' (1955). The beauty of these records was the mixing of dramatic gospel phrasing with the more intimate harmonies of the doo-wop groups, seen at its most exciting on 'Money Honey' and its most spirited in 'White Christmas'. 'Christmas' opens with the bass singing lead (in the style of the **Ravens**) before McPhatter enters, using a range of vocal acrobatics in the manner of an improvising jazz musician that in their passion bring a new dimension to **Irving Berlin**'s song, better known through **Bing Crosby**'s sentimental version.

After army service in 1954–6, McPhatter went solo and had a further string of R&B and pop hits, including 'Treasure of Love' (1956) and the much-covered 'A Lover's Question'* (1958), before leaving Atlantic for MGM (in 1959), then Mercury. In contrast to the Drifters, who successfully accommodated themselves to the changes brought about by rock'n'roll, McPhatter, despite further hits (including his masterful version of **Billy Swan**'s 'Lover Please', 1962), struggled, each attempt to reach the new mass market bringing about a dilution in his unique vocal style. His later records (on Amy, Decca and B&C) were undistinguished.

GORDON MacRAE
b. 12 March 1921, East Orange, New Jersey, USA, d. 24 January 1986, Lincoln, Nebraska

A full-throated, handsome singer, MacRae is best remembered for his appearances in the film versions of *Oklahoma!* (1955) and *Carousel* (1956), in both of which he was partnered by Shirley Jones.

The son of early radio star 'Wee Willie' MacRae, MacRae worked as a child actor on radio. He later turned to singing, with Horace Heidt's Band, and then acting before joining the air force. After the war, he secured the lead in Ray Bolger's Broadway musical *Three to Make Ready* in 1946, and in 1947 was signed to Capitol Records and Warner Brothers. He began his screen career as a boxer in the crime melodrama *The Big Punch* (1948), but was soon starring in musicals, most successfully with **Doris Day** in films like *Young Man with a Horn* and *Tea for Two* (both 1949).

For a while his recording and film careers ran in parallel. His first million-seller was the **Sammy Cahn** and **Jule Styne** composition 'I Still Get Jealous' (1947), after which he teamed up with **Jo Stafford** for 'Say Something Sweet to Your Sweetheart'* (1948) and 'Whispering Hope'* (1949). Written in 1868 by music-publisher Septimus Winner (one of the most prolific nineteenth-century American songwriters) under the pseudonym of Alice Hawthorne, 'Whispering' was a sentimental exercise in close-harmony singing. But, following the success of *Desert Song* (1953), MacRae became wedded to the film musical. Thus he was given the lead in the film version of **Rodgers and Hammerstein**'s revolutionary stage musical *Oklahoma!* by Warners and then starred (in the role originally intended for **Frank Sinatra**) in *Carousel*, the duo's even more unlikely transformation of Ferenc Molnár's fantasy *Liliom* into a Broadway hit.

In his penultimate film, *The Best Things in Life Are Free* (1956), MacRae played songwriter Buddy DeSylva (of **DeSylva, Brown and Henderson**). He continued recording and in 1979 attempted an acting comeback with *The Pilot*.

CARMEN McRAE
b. 8 April 1920, New York City, USA, d. 10 November 1994

For much of her career overshadowed by her contemporaries **Ella Fitzgerald** and **Sarah Vaughan**, McRae's major and continuing influence was **Billie Holiday**.

While in her teens McRae studied piano and started songwriting, providing Holiday with 'Dream of Life' in 1939. Throughout the forties, she worked as an intermission singer and pianist at New York's Minton's jazz club. During this period she also briefly sang with **Count Basie**, Benny Carter's band (1944) and, under the name of Carmen Clarke (she was briefly married to drummer **Kenny Clarke**), made her first recordings with Mercer Ellington (1946–7). From 1948 onwards she became a regular on the jazz-club circuit, her unusually cold tone giving an edge to the lyrics of the ballads that were the staple of her repertoire. In 1953 she recorded (as McRae) for Stardust and Venus and in 1954, the year she won the *Down Beat* critics' poll as best newcomer, joined Decca.

From the sixties onwards she toured with her own trio and recorded regularly on her own (*Live at Bubba's*, 1982; *Live at Ronnie Scott's*, 1978) and in partnership with others (Cal Tjader, *Heatwave*; Chris O'Connor, *I Hear Music*, both 1983). A frequent visitor to Europe, where she played concert halls rather than jazz clubs, McRae, though she has occasionally sung and recorded contemporary material (**Billy Joel**'s 'New York State of Mind'; **Stephen Sondheim**'s 'Send in the Clowns'), was for the most part content to reinterpret the standards of her day. Later recordings included tribute albums to **Thelonious Monk** (1990) and **Sarah Vaughan** (1991).

JAY McSHANN
b. James Columbus McShann, 12 January 1909, Muskogee, Oklahoma, USA

In the forties McShann led a bluesy and rhythmically subtle Kansas City band whose excellence has been somewhat overshadowed by its having also propelled to fame the young **Charlie Parker**. McShann himself was a fine pianist in both band and solo settings, stylistically close to **Count Basie** but less laconic in his playing. He was also an inventive boogie-woogie player, singer and composer.

In the early thirties McShann worked in the Southwest with Eddie Hill's band, but from 1934 he was based in Kansas City, where he formed his own small group four years later. In 1939–43 he led a big band through whose ranks passed not only Parker but the **Lester Young**-like tenor saxophonist Paul Quinichette, later a Basie sideman, and the blues singer Walter Brown, whose recording of McShann's composition 'Confessin' the Blues' (Decca, 1941) was a hit and made the song a blues standard. McShann also recorded with vocalist **Al Hibbler** ('Get Me on Your Mind', 1943). Other enduring McShann compositions first recorded in 1941–2 include 'Hootie Blues', 'The Jumpin' Blues' and 'Dexter Blues'.

After a break for military service (1943–4) he formed a new band in 1945 and for a time was active on the West Coast, where he found a substitute for Brown in the young **Jimmy Witherspoon**. During the fifties and sixties he was based in Kansas City. He toured Europe in 1969 and frequently in the seventies and eighties, sometimes bandleading, sometimes as a piano soloist or with a trio. Records of note from this period include *The Big Apple Bash* (1971) and the tribute to Charlie Parker, *Paris All Star Blues* (1991).

BLIND WILLIE McTELL
b. 5 May 1901, Thomson, Georgia, USA, d. 19 August 1959, Milledgeville, Georgia

One of the most singular blues artists – he owes little to any known musician, and has had hardly more direct influence on any successor – McTell possessed a high, almost painstakingly distinct voice, which he employed on blues of great delicacy, sometimes wit and often seductiveness, underscored by rich yet subtle twelve-string guitar-playing.

Raised in Statesboro, Georgia (subject of one of his best-known blues, later recorded by the **Allman Brothers Band** and **Taj Mahal**), McTell ran away from home in his teens to work on travelling shows. After attending schools for the blind in Macon, Georgia, and New York (1922–6), he went on the road again, in 1927 meeting Victor's **Ralph Peer** in Atlanta, where he made his first records. He continued to record for Victor until 1932, meanwhile cutting slightly different material, chiefly guitar rags, for Columbia and Okeh under the pseudonyms Blind Sammie and Georgia Bill. He also worked as a travelling street-singer in partnership with **Blind Willie Johnson**. In 1933–6, now working for Vocalion and Decca, he recorded blues and gospel songs, on the latter sometimes duetting with his wife, Kate. He was part of a blues circle in Atlanta that also included singer/guitarists Buddy Moss and Curley Weaver.

In 1940 he was spotted street-singing in Atlanta by **John Lomax**, who recorded from him, on behalf of the Library of Congress, a session of blues, sacred songs, blues ballads and engrossing narratives about his life and the history of the blues. He continued to work in Atlanta through the forties and fifties, recording for Atlantic and Regal (1949–50). His last recordings, made for a local enthusiast in 1956, were later issued on Prestige-Bluesville (*Last Session*).

The English guitarist **Ralph McTell** chose his stage name in a homage to Willie McTell, while Bob Dylan wrote the celebratory song 'Blind Willie McTell', which included the lines 'I know one thing, no one can sing them blues like Blind Willie McTell.'

RALPH McTELL
b. Ralph May, 3 December 1944, Farnborough, Kent, England

Ragtime guitarist and composer of the standard 'Streets of London', McTell has been a leading figure on the British folk scene since the seventies.

A virtuoso instrumentalist, the young Ralph May took his stage name from the thirties blues player **Blind Willie McTell**. He spent a period busking in Paris in the late sixties before becoming a popular performer on the London club scene, signing to Transatlantic in 1968 and releasing *8 Frames a Second*. *Spiral Staircase* (1969) included 'Streets of London', whose potentially glib liberal message was delivered with convincing fervour by McTell.

After two further acoustic albums, McTell moved into the singer-songwriter sphere with the Gus Dudgeon-produced *You Well-Meaning Brought Me Here* (Famous, 1971). With arrangements by Tony Visconti, songs like 'Claudia' and 'Pick Up a Gun' showed McTell's ability to concretize such issues as racism and militarism. Visconti produced *Not Till Tomorrow* (Reprise, 1972), which included 'Sylvia', an elegy for the poet Sylvia Plath, and 'Zimmerman Blues', a meditation on the price of fame.

In 1974 a re-recorded 'Streets of London' reached the British Top Ten on Warners, while the follow-up, 'Dreams of You', with a tune based on Bach's 'Jesu Joy of Man's Desiring', was a minor hit a year later. McTell made several more albums for Warners, including *Right Side Up* (1976), which featured 'From Clare to Here', a portrayal of the feelings of Irish immigrants in London, and 'Naomi', which dealt with growing old, and the live *Ralph Albert and Sydney* (1977). *Slide Away the Screen* (1979) found McTell accompanied by such folk-rock luminaries as **Richard Thompson** and **Fairport Convention** members Simon Nicol and Dave Pegg, who co-produced the album.

During the eighties and nineties McTell concentrated on concert tours and appearances as compère and singer on children's television shows. He set up his own label, Mays, releasing such albums as *Water of Dreams* (1982), *Songs from Alphabet Zoo* (1983, a collection of TV material) and *Bridge of Sighs* (1987). In 1988 he returned to his roots with *Blue Skies Black Heroes* (Leola), a collection of classic blues and rags. He followed that album with *Stealin' Back* (1990) before embarking on the ambitious *The Boy with the Note* (1992). A concept album based on the life of Welsh poet Dylan Thomas, it was acclaimed as one of his best albums and served as a reminder of his still considerable song-writing talents. Equally fine was *From Clare to Here* (Red House, 1996).

MACHITO

b. Frank Grillo, 16 February 1912, Tampa, Florida, USA,
d. 15 April 1984, London, England

With **Tito Puente** and **Celia Cruz** one of the longest
established stars of Afro-Cuban music, Machito was
the first to incorporate jazz ideas in his music. He
dominated New York's Latin music scene from the
forties onwards and was also an early Latin influence
on jazz. Among those who recorded and played with
him were **Charlie Parker**, Herbie Mann, **Dizzy Gillespie** and Milt Jackson.

Raised in Cuba, Machito travelled to New York in
1937 and sang with various Latin groups, including
Xavier Cugat's, with whom he recorded, before
establishing his own band in 1940 with his brother-in-
law Mario Bauza (*b. 1912*), who had played with **Cab
Calloway** and **Chick Webb**, as his musical director.
His early recordings, such as 'Sopa de Pichon' (1940),
showed how adeptly Machito balanced American and
Cuban elements in his music. One of the first signings
of **George Goldner**'s Tico label, he quickly established
himself as the premier attraction among New York's
Latins. His influence on jazz and mainstream popular
music was at its greatest in the mid-forties and in the
wake of the mambo craze of the early fifties which
reawakened American interest in Latin music. In the
mid-forties, he was at the centre of the 'Cubop'
movement, recording and playing with Gillespie,
Parker (with whom he made the influential 'Tango' in
1947) and **Stan Kenton**, who in 1947 recorded
'Machito' in his honour. More memorably, Machito
guested on Kenton's influential recording of **Moises
Simons**' 'The Peanut Vendor' (1947), one of the most
successful examples ever of experimental jazz scoring
for an authentic Latin rhythm section.

Machito's continued musical openness led him
later to the emerging sounds of salsa. *Salsa Big Band
1982* (Timeless) won a Grammy Award in 1983. After
his death, his son, Machito Junior, took over the leadership of the Machito Orchestra and Quintet.

LONNIE MACK

b. Lonnie McIntosh, b. 18 July 1941, Harrison, Indiana,
USA

Mack's only million-seller was a terse, strongly
rhythmic, rockabilly-flavoured instrumental version
of **Chuck Berry**'s 'Memphis' in 1963. His other lesser
hits ('Wham' and 'Honky Tonk '65') were also
instrumentals, but Mack was far more than just
another guitar virtuoso. His music was an individual
blend of black (gospel, blues and soul) and country
music.

He formed his first band, playing country music, at
the age of thirteen, and graduated to playing

rock'n'roll in the mid-fifties before joining Troy Seals
as a sideman. It was at the end of a Seals session that
Mack cut 'Memphis'. A surprise hit – it was promoted
as 'surf music', then the rage – it led to the recording
of his finest album, the classic *The Wham of That
Memphis Man* (Fraternity, 1963). His guitar-playing
and singing on tracks like 'Why' and 'Where There's a
Will, There's a Way' reached moments of emotional
intensity akin to that of **Solomon Burke**. The album
did not sell and Mack retired from the music business
until 1968, when a laudatory account of the album in
the influential *Rolling Stone* magazine led to a recording contract with Elektra Records. *Wham* was reissued (in 1970) by Elektra and Mack recorded *Glad I'm
in the Band* (1969) and *Whatever's Right* (1970) for the
company, both fine albums in Mack's familiar intense
manner. A further album, *The Hills of Indiana* (1971),
featuring Don Nix, was gentler and more countrified,
suggesting a man at ease with himself.

Citing religious reasons, Mack once more withdrew
from the music business, cutting only a few singles
until his re-emergence in 1977 with *Home at Last*
(Capitol). For this he was once more backed by
Nashville session men, including Kenny Butry, David
Briggs, Norbert Putnam and Buddy Spiker, who had
collectively recorded as Area Code 615. In 1985 he
issued another of his occasional albums, the **Stevie
Ray Vaughan**-produced *Strike Like Lightning* (Alligator), which saw him returning to the roadhouse guitar style of *Wham* as did *Second Sight* (1986).
Roadhouses and Dance Halls (Epic, 1988) and *Live:
Attack of the Killer V* (1990) were lesser albums. *Lonnie on the Move* (Ace, 1992) is the definitive collection
of his Fraternity instrumentals.

UNCLE DAVE MACON

b. 7 October 1870, Cannon County, Tennessee, USA,
d. 22 March 1952, Readyville, Tennessee

In his later years Uncle Dave Macon, with his wing
collar, chin-whiskers and vaudeville routines, was the
member of the *Grand Ole Opry* best fitted for the role
of 'The Spirit of Country Music Past'. In the twenties,
however, he was a front-rank performer throughout
the South, an exuberant singer and banjo player
known not only from his broadcasts and tours but for
his scores of recordings, on which he reproduced
songs, tunes and jokes from the nineteenth-century
minstrel stage.

As a boy, he picked up such routines from show
people who stayed at his parents' Nashville hotel, but
he became a farmer and did not pursue a serious
musical career until he was almost fifty. In the late
1910s and early twenties he worked on the Southern
vaudeville circuits, eventually gaining the attention of
a Knoxville furniture-store owner who sponsored his

first recordings, for Vocalion in 1924. (In those days furniture stores, being outlets for phonographs, were also major record stockists.) On some of these recordings he was partnered by fiddler Sid Harkreader. Among these first sides was 'Hill Billie Blues', the first country record to use the term 'hillbilly'. Later Vocalion sessions introduced the superb blues and ragtime-influenced guitarist Sam McGee.

In 1926 Macon joined the cast of the then new *Grand Ole Opry* on WSM, Nashville, Tennessee, and quickly became the show's most charismatic performer, nicknamed 'The Dixie Dew-Drop'. He recorded regularly for Vocalion, and later Brunswick (1928–30), Okeh (1930), Gennett (1934) and Bluebird (1935–8), in a variety of formats: solo, with McGee or the **Delmore Brothers** (his frequent touring companions in the late thirties), or with a string band. Among his many highly personalized versions of traditional motifs were several that later became popular in folk-revival circles. They included 'Sail Away Ladies' (1927), whose refrain 'Don't you rock, di-de-o' underlay **Lonnie Donegan**'s 1957 hit 'Don't You Rock Me, Daddy-O'.

Macon remained an *Opry* stalwart until his death. He appeared in the 1940 Republic movie *Grand Ole Opry*, where his two-minute sequence, accompanied by his son Dorris on guitar, overshadowed the performances of **Roy Acuff** and others. Later in the forties he worked in *Opry* tent-shows with **Bill Monroe**. His work was reissued in the early sixties at the instigation of **Pete Seeger**, who conceived the collection' *Uncle Dave Macon* (RBF, 1963). Another influential early compilation was *Uncle Dave Macon: First Featured Star of the 'Grand Ole Opry'* (Decca, 1967), produced by Ralph Rinzler. In 1966 Uncle Dave Macon was voted into the Country Music Hall of Fame.

ROSE MADDOX

b. Roseea Arbana Brogdon, 15 August 1925, Boaz, Alabama, USA, d. 15 April 1998

Although **Kitty Wells** is often credited with raising the status of the female country singer to parity with the leading male artists, Rose Maddox was offering a dynamic woman's voice in country music several years earlier. She, however, was working in California rather than Nashville, and within the obscuring context of a family group.

The large Maddox family emigrated to Southern California in the early thirties. Rose's five brothers all played music: Cliff (mandolin), Cal[vin] (harmonica and guitar), Henry (guitar and mandolin), Fred (bass) and Don (fiddle). In 1937 they obtained a sponsor for a programme on the nearby KTRB, Modesto, station with Rose as singer and worked at local rodeos. In 1939 they won a contest organized by

KFBK, Sacramento, and with it a year's syndicated radio show reaching several Western states.

Regrouping in 1945 after an interruption for war service, the Maddox Brothers and Rose returned to KTRB. In the following year they signed with Four Star and began a four-year spell of recorded hilarity and pzazz. Rose's strong singing was supported by vigorous string-band playing – and interrupted by a stream of asides, cackles and brotherly rumpus – on material as disparate as 'Milk Cow Blues', rockabilly boogies, **Fred Rose**'s 'Blue Eyes Crying in the Rain', the moral tale 'Tramp on the Street' and sacred songs like 'Gathering Flowers for the Master's Bouquet'. They also recorded the original hit version of **Woody Guthrie**'s 'Philadelphia Lawyer' (1946). Non-family lead guitarists who played on the Four Star sessions included Jimmy Winkle, Roy Nichols (later **Merle Haggard**'s guitarist) and Gene Breeden.

Now billed as 'The Most Colorful Hillbilly Band in America' and costumed accordingly, the group signed with Columbia in 1951, at first preserving the knock-about atmosphere of the Four Star recordings. As this came to be seen as 'unrefined', Rose emerged from the family to record in her own (full) name. The band had two spells on the KWKH *Louisiana Hayride* in 1952–4 and worked in the Los Angeles area before breaking up in 1956. Among their last Columbia recordings were Don's novelty 'The Death of Rock and Roll' (1956) and Rose and Don's duet 'Love Is Strange' (1957), the Mickey and Sylvia R&B hit.

Rose signed as a solo artist with Capitol in 1959 and had a hit with 'Down, Down, Down'. 'Sing a Little Song of Heartache' and 'We're the Talk of the Town', a duet with **Buck Owens**, followed in 1963, as did the album *Rose Maddox Sings Bluegrass*, on which she had the support of Don Reno (banjo) and, anonymously, **Bill Monroe** (mandolin). *Cash Box* chose her as top female artist of 1963. The association with Owens yielded further hits in 1964 with 'Loose Talk' and 'Mental Cruelty'.

After some years of reduced activity Rose Maddox reappeared to record for Takoma (*Reckless Love and Bold Adventure*, 1972). Arhoolie reissued albums of the Four Star material (1976) and new recordings by Maddox in bluegrass and bluegrass-gospel style in the early eighties. She continued to make occasional appearances but in 1992 suffered a severe heart attack. *The One Rose: The Capitol Years* (Bear Family, 1993) is the definitive anthology.

MADNESS

Mike Barson, b. 21 April 1958, London, England; Mark Bedford, b. 24 August 1961, London; Chris Foreman, b. 8 August 1958, London; 'Chas' Smash, b. Carl Smyth, b. 14 January 1959; Graham 'Suggsy' McPherson,

b. 13 January 1961, Hastings, Sussex, England; Lee 'Kix'
Thompson, b. 13 January 1961, Hastings; Dan
Woodgate, b. 19 October 1960, London

Initially drawing on the ska style of reggae, Madness
were responsible for some of the finest British pop
records of the eighties. The group had twenty British
hit singles during an eight-year recording career
before splitting, then re-forming in the early nineties.

Formed in Camden Town, north London, by
pianist Barson, Thompson (sax) and guitarist Foreman as the Invaders, the group, with the addition of
singers Suggs and Smash, Bedford (bass) and
Woodgate (drums), became Madness in 1978. Named
after the 1963 **Prince Buster** bluebeat hit, they soon
gained a reputation for energetic live shows presenting their 'nutty sound', a mix of ska beat and anarchic
humour.

Their first record, a tribute to Buster, was 'The
Prince'. Released on the **Specials**' Two-Tone label it
reached the Top Twenty in 1979. Madness moved to
Stiff to cover Buster's own ska tune 'One Step
Beyond'. Produced by Clive Langer and Alan Win-
stanley, it was the title track of a 1980 album that
included further Top Ten songs in 'My Girl', 'Work
Rest and Play' and 'Baggy Trousers'.

Absolutely (1981) found them broadening their
songwriting horizons on successful singles like
'Embarrassment', 'Return of the Los Palmas Seven'
and 'Grey Day'. Madness also made a series of imaginative videos and *Take It or Leave It*, a full-length film
which brought the zany sixties antics of the **Monkees**
and **The Beatles** up to date.

Madness reached an artistic peak with *Rise and Fall*
(1982), a collection of portraits of inner-city London
life, notably the affectionate 'Our House', 'Primrose
Hill' (whose sense of place recalled that of The Beatles' 'Penny Lane'), the disillusion of 'Tomorrow's Just
Another Day' and the ferocity of Thompson's 'Blue
Skinned Beast', an attack on media jingoism.

Soon after Barson left to settle in Amsterdam,
Madness set up their own Zarjazz label (taking the
name from a sci-fi cartoon strip), signing Charm
School and ex-**Scritti Politti** member Tom Morley as
well as reaching the charts with Suggs and Foreman's
'Listen to Your Father', sung by **Feargal Sharkey**.
Their own *Keep Moving* (Stiff) provided hits with
Smash's 'Michael Caine' and Suggs and Foreman's
'One Better Day'.

Although both the caustic 'Uncle Sam' and a cover
of Scritti Politti's 'Sweetest Girl' made the Top Thirty,
Mad Not Mad (1985) was less successful than earlier
records. The failure of Zarjazz contributed to the tensions which led to the dissolution of Madness in 1986
with Barson returning to play on the final single,
'(Waiting for) The Ghost Train'. In 1988 Suggs,

Thompson, Foreman and Smyth resurfaced as The
Madness, releasing 'I Pronounce You' (Virgin) and
the album *The Madness* (1988), while Bedford formed
the jazzy Butterfield 8. Both he and Woodgate also
played with British-American indie-pop band Voice
of the Beehive, Woodgate becoming a permanent
member.

The Madness disbanded in 1990, with Suggs
becoming manager of Liverpool band the Farm, who
had two British Top Five hits in 1990. The other
members involved themselves with various projects,
of which Thompson and Foreman's the Nutty Boys
had the highest profile. Following the success of a
'best of' collection, *Divine Madness* (1992), the original members succumbed to pressure to re-form. They
headlined a day-long festival event in London and
their performance was recorded and released as *Madstock* (1992) by Go! Discs, the British independent
label where Smyth was employed as an A&R man.
Subsequently, Madness played Christmas gigs in
Britain in 1992 and 1993, but released only two new
recordings, 'The Harder They Come' (1992) and
'Night Boat to Cairo' (1993).

Suggs had limited success with his solo album *The
Lone Ranger* (Warner, 1995), which included the single 'Camden Town'. The success of a second compilation, *The Heavy Heavy Hits* (1998), increased the
pressure on the group to re-form. This they did for
Wonderful (Virgin, 1999). Including a duet with **Ian
Dury** ('Drip Fed Fred'), it saw the group marking
time.

MADONNA

b. Madonna Louise Vernon Ciccione, 16 August 1958,
Rochester, Michigan, USA

One of the most popular and iconoclastic teenage
idols of the eighties, Madonna's mix of self-assertion
and coquetry won her a following of millions of young
women (the 'wanna-bes') and caused heated debate
among their feminist elders. Having made her musical
mark through the use of current disco styles, she
sought to develop a career in films in the late eighties
and early nineties as a contemporary equivalent to
Marilyn Monroe. Madonna also set up her own record
company, Maverick, and signed **Alanis Morrisette**,
one of the nineties' most successful recording acts.

Originally intending to become a dancer, she won
a scholarship to the University of Michigan, moving
to New York in 1978 and appearing with the modern-
dance companies of Alvin Ailey and Pearl Lange.
After a brief period in Paris performing in the stage
musical *Born to Be Alive*, Madonna turned to music,
playing drums and singing with New York rock
bands Breakfast Club and Emmy with Steve Bray,
who co-wrote some of her later recordings.

Signing to Sire in 1982, she cut 'Everybody' and the Reggie Lucas-produced 'Burning Up' in the current disco mode before the John 'Jellybean' Benitez-produced 'Holiday' was first a dancefloor hit and then entered the Top Twenty in 1983. It was taken from the eponymous first album, which included further hits in 'Borderline' and 'Lucky Star' (1984).

The title track of the **Nile Rodgers**-produced *Like a Virgin* (1985) introduced Madonna's sex-kitten image and went straight to No. 1, as did the next two singles, 'Material Girl' and 'Crazy for You', from the soundtrack of *Vision Quest*. 'Into the Groove' (1985) was the year's definitive party record but Madonna was also adding other dimensions to both her image and her music ('Angel', 'Dress You Up', 1985), and becoming an international star. In 1985 she also had a critically acclaimed screen role in *Desperately Seeking Susan*.

True Blue (1986) was a bestseller in twenty-five countries; it too produced several hit singles, including 'Open Your Heart', 'Live to Tell', the defiant 'Papa Don't Preach' (whose tale of teenage pregnancy caused widespread controversy) and the determinedly romantic 'La Isla Bonita'. In 1986, the year her every move made news in the world's sensationalist press, she starred in the poorly received *Shanghai Surprise* with actor Sean Penn, to whom she was married from 1985 to 1988. The film was produced by **George Harrison**, who also wrote the score.

Madonna's progress continued into 1987 with a triumphant world tour, a zany comedy role in the film *Who's That Girl*, and hits with its title song 'Causing a Commotion' (written with Bray) and 'The Look of Love', co-written with producer Patrick Leonard. In 1989 she returned with *Like a Prayer*, whose controversial video for the title track (accused of sacrilege) caused Pepsi to withdraw its advertising contract with the artist. Nevertheless that song, 'Express Yourself' and 'Cherish' were massive international hits.

A world tour in 1990 coincided with the release of *I'm Breathless*, which was intended to cash in on her role in *Dick Tracy*, the private eye spoof in which she starred as Breathless Mahoney, alongside her then-current beau Warren Beatty. The album was another success, and provided her with the British No. 1 single 'Vogue'. A greatest hits album, *The Immaculate Collection* (1990), followed, with the newly recorded track 'Justify My Love' hitting No. 1 in America when released as a single, and stirring controversy with an overtly sexual video. The 1990 'Blond Ambition' world tour included equally erotic choreography and also produced a 'fly-on-the-wall' documentary, *In Bed with Madonna* (1991).

Madonna concentrated on non-recording activities for the next year, and in April 1992 signed a multimedia deal worth an estimated $60m with Time-Warner. As part of the agreement she set up her own label, Maverick, among whose first signings was the black American singer Me'shell Ndegé Ocello.

Madonna won good reviews for her appearance in the baseball movie *A League of Their Own* and bad ones for the erotic thriller *Body of Evidence* (1992). In the same year she published a 128-page coffee-table book, *Sex*, which featured large photographs of Madonna herself, generally nude in various soft-core porn poses, spiced by various illustrations incorporating elements of bisexuality and bondage, accompanied by her own text. The generally unfavourable press reaction – the book was seen as sensationalism for the sake of it – spilled over into reviews of the simultaneously released album *Erotica*. This was co-written and produced with Shep Pettibone and André Betts.

Nonetheless, another sell-out world tour followed in 1993. Billed as 'The Girlie Show', it contained a spectacularly presented but toned-down stage act which was perceived as a reaction to the upfront sexual nature of much of 1992's output. In 1994 Madonna returned to the charts on both sides of the Atlantic with the movie soundtrack single 'I Remember', whose almost-ambient sound reflected the awareness of trends which has characterized the whole of her career. More perplexing was the would-be confessional *Bedtime Stories* (1994), on which Madonna seemed unable to make her presence felt either as tease or as victim. Her collaborators included Nellee Hooper (producer of **Björk** and **Soul II Soul**), Dallas Austin (of **Boyz II Men**) and Dave Hall (of **Mariah Carey**).

In 1995 Madonna moved away from the overt sexuality of *Erotica* and *Bedtime Stories*, taking the role of Eva Peron in the movie adaptation of **Andrew Lloyd Webber**'s *Evita*. The singer also issued a second compilation volume, *Something to Remember*, and gave birth to a daughter, Lourdes, in late 1996, just as *Evita* went on general release. The movie was highly successful, winning Madonna the Golden Globe Award for Best Actress in a Musical or Comedy. She also scored hits with its attendant singles, Lloyd Webber's 'Don't Cry for Me, Argentina' and the freshly penned 'You Must Love Me'.

Madonna returned to her recording career in 1998 with the William Orbit-produced *Ray of Light*. Informed by electronica and trip-hop, the album proved to be her most successful release, both critically and commercially, since *Like a Prayer*. It spawned four hit singles, including the title track and the string-driven 'Frozen', as well as earning Madonna a plethora of Grammy and MTV Awards. By now almost a mainstream artist in the manner of **Sting** or **Elton John**, in 1999 she performed the main theme to *Austin Powers: The Spy Who Shagged Me*, 'Beautiful Stranger'. However, she lost none of her ability to shock, in 2000 releasing an arch dance version of of **Don McLean**'s classic account of rock'n'roll history, 'American Pie'. That was included on the emphatically titled *Music* (2000) in which, in the manner of her newfound sincerity she first essayed to talk of the delights of motherhood, she offered a simple paean to the pleasures of music, particularly the dancefloor. The result, despite its surprisingly thin sound, was a significant commercial success but only a modest critical success. Just as the second gangster film outing by her partner, UK film director Guy Ritchie, *Snatch* (2000), was compared unfavourably to his début feature, *Lock Stock and Two Smoking Barrels* (1998), so *Music* was seen by several critics as being more of the same, rather than the radical departure it was offered as.

MAGIC SAM
b. Samuel Maghett, 14 February 1937, Grenada, Mississippi, USA, d. 1 December 1969, Chicago, Illinois

With **Buddy Guy** and **Otis Rush** Magic Sam introduced the 'West Side sound' to Chicago blues in the late fifties, and although he died young, he had a great impact upon fellow blues singers and guitarists.

He moved to Chicago in his early teens and by 1955 was leading a club band. His first recordings, like Rush's were for Cobra, and 'All Your Love'/'Love Me with a Feeling' (1957) and 'Easy Baby' (1958) established his reputation as an exciting and above all modern stylist, without any over allegiance to the old-fashioned 'South Side' approach of **Muddy Waters**, **Howlin' Wolf** and others.

Magic Sam worked for a time with the singer and harmonica-player Shakey Jake in clubs and on record (Artistic, 1958), then spent a short and unhappy period in the army (1959–60). Some rather randomly conceived singles for Chief (1960–1) did not consolidate his reputation, and for several years he marked time in and around Chicago. The Delmark albums *West Side Soul* (1968) and *Black Magic* (1969) revitalized him and he began to work further afield, visiting Europe in the summer of 1969 with the American Folk Blues Festival, but he died, from a heart attack, later that year.

Of the many Chicago blues artists who followed his direction, perhaps the best known is the singer-guitarist Luther Allison, who earned a headline for being the first blues artist to be signed to the Motown Gordy label, for whom he recorded three albums between 1972 and 1976.

J. E. MAINER
b. Joseph E. Mainer, 20 July 1898, Weaversville, North Carolina, USA, d. 2 June 1971, Concord, North Carolina

As well as reinvigorating twenties-style string-band music on American Southern radio in the thirties and forties, J. E. Mainer stood at the centre of a talented troupe of country entertainers who worked in a variety of other styles. Mainer's Mountaineers, as they were called, thus exemplified in a single show – or, often, at a single recording session – the archaic, the novel and the constant themes and styles of country music.

As a young man Mainer was a cotton-mill worker, but towards the end of the twenties he began to play fiddle with his banjoist brother Wade. In 1934 they secured a radio slot on the powerful WBT, Charlotte, North Carolina. The following year they began a long association with RCA Victor's Bluebird label, scoring prompt success with 'Maple on the Hill' and 'Take Me in the Lifeboat'. Among the charter members of the recording band were Wade and the singer, yodeller and guitarist Daddy John Love.

Later in the thirties Wade led his own band, the Sons of the Mountaineers, and through it and the parent group passed such leading Southeastern musicians as the Morris Brothers (Wiley and Zeke) and the Hall Brothers (Roy and Jay Hugh). While some of the recordings from this circle recalled the fiddle-led string-band music of earlier figures like singer/banjoist Charlie Poole, the Wade Mainer–Zeke Morris duets were in the sober moralizing style of the **Blue Sky Boys**.

The various Mainer groups worked on many North Carolina stations in the thirties and forties, attracting large quantities of listeners' mail. In the late forties both J. E. and Wade recorded for King, though their air of a country variety act from the days of minstrelsy and medicine-shows gave them little grasp on the new market for bluegrass and rockabilly. Their material, however, proved attractive to many of the more traditional bluegrass bands, and several songs originally popularized by Mainer groups were taken up by, for instance, the **Stanley Brothers**.

In semi-retirement in the sixties and seventies, Mainer retained his links with music by making and repairing fiddles and sporadically recording what was eventually a lengthy series of albums for the California-based Rural Rhythm label. Wade came out of retirement in the seventies to play in public again and recorded a number of albums for Old Homestead, veering gently from re-creations of his thirties and forties music to a tentative bluegrass manner.

MIRIAM MAKEBA
b. Zensile Makeba, 4 March 1932, Johannesburg, South Africa

The best-known singer of black South African music, Makeba came to international stardom in the musical

King Kong and lived in voluntary exile in both America and Africa after 1960.

As a child she sang in both English and her native Xhosa, a language characterized by the 'clicking' sounds epitomized in one of her best-known pieces, 'Click Song'. Makeba performed with the Cuban brothers before in 1956 she joined the Black Manhattan Brothers, an eleven-strong vocal group which used close harmonies in the style of the **Mills Brothers**. She eventually became lead vocalist, recording albums of *mbaqanga* or Africanized jazz including *Tula Ndivile* (Gallotone), as well as forming her own female recording vocal quartet, the Skylarks.

After touring with the Brothers for three years, Makeba landed a leading role in *King Kong*, Todd Matshikiza's show about the tragic career of a black boxing champion which opened in Johannesburg in 1959. She travelled with the show to London and New York, where she decided to settle. Aided by **Harry Belafonte**, Makeba built a new career as a solo singer, giving concerts and recording for RCA (*Voice of Africa*, *An Evening with Harry Belafonte and Miriam Makeba*, 1965) and Reprise, for whom she cut the superior 1967 album *Pata Pata*, which included the hit single 'Pata Pata'.

Politically active in the anti-apartheid movements, Makeba married Black Power leader Stokely Carmichael and lived in Guinea for some years. In 1987 she toured with **Hugh Masekela** and **Paul Simon** following the release of the latter's *Graceland* album. Makeba also published an autobiography and recorded *Sangoma* (produced by Russ Titelman, Warners, 1988). *The Best of* (1992) is the definitive collection. In the nineties her most successful album was the evocative *Sing Me a Song* (Sonodisc, 1993). She followed that with the live album *Live from Paris and Conarky* (DRG, 1998) and the emotional *Homeland* (Punytamayo, 2000), in which she explored the pain of exile – she only returned to South Africa in 1990 after thirty-one years of exile – and the joy of returning home. The album also included a reworking of her earlier hit 'Pata Pata' as 'Pata Pata 2000'.

Makeba's daughter Bongi is also a professional singer, based in Paris.

THE MAMAS AND THE PAPAS
Denny Doherty, b. 29 November 1941, Halifax, Canada; Cass Elliott, b. Ellen Naomi Cohen, 19 September 1943, Baltimore, Maryland, USA, d. 29 July 1974, London, England; John Phillips, b. 30 August 1935, Parris Island, South Carolina; Michelle Gilliam Phillips, b. 6 April 1944, Long Beach, California

Although their close-harmony singing owed much to the vocal groups of the forties and fifties, the visual image and 'flower-power' lyrics of The Mamas and the Papas made them icons of the new hippie, underground music of the sixties.

The group's formation in Los Angeles in 1965 was described in 'Creeque Alley' (1967), one of John Phillips' most engaging compositions. Elliott and Doherty had been members of the shortlived Mugwumps, a New York folk-rock band that also included the **Lovin' Spoonful**'s John Sebastian and Zal Yanofsky. With Scott McKenzie (*b. 1 October 1944, Arlington, Virginia*), Phillips had been a member of the Journeymen, a **Kingston Trio**-style folk group that had recorded for Capitol in the early sixties.

The quartet first recorded as backing singers for **Barry McGuire** and were signed as a vocal group by Dunhill's **Lou Adler**. 'California Dreamin''* (1966), a touristic paean to the beauties of the state, was The Mamas and the Papas' first Top Ten hit. It was followed by 'Monday Monday'*, the yearning love song 'I Saw Her Again' and 'Look Through My Window'. Their début album, *If You Can Believe Your Eyes and Ears* (1966), contained a mixture of original songs and material by **The Beatles** ('I Call Your Name'), **Leiber and Stoller** ('Spanish Harlem') and Bobby Freeman ('Do You Wanna Dance?').

1967 brought five more hits for the group, of which the biggest were a revival of the **Five Royales**' 1958 success and the **Shirelles**' 1961 hit 'Dedicated to the One I Love', 'Creeque Alley' and John Phillips' 'Words of Love'. It was in this year that the group became indelibly linked with the hippie movement of San Francisco when the Phillips were among the organizers of the Monterey Pop Festival and John composed the Scott McKenzie hit 'San Francisco (Be Sure to Wear Some Flowers in Your Hair)'. The portentous lyrics ('a new generation/with a new explanation'), delivered in McKenzie's pure tenor, made the record a worldwide success, selling seven million copies and reaching No. 1 in Germany, Belgium, Denmark, Norway and Britain. Phillips also wrote McKenzie's follow-up, 'Like an Old Time Movie'.

By 1968 the group had split up. Elliott and John Phillips embarked on solo recording careers, the latter releasing *The Wolfking of LA* (Dunhill, 1970), backed by **James Burton** and the cream of Los Angeles session musicians. Elliott had a hit with the jaunty 'Dream a Little Dream of Me' (1968) and further success in 1969 with **Barry Mann**'s 'It's Getting Better'. She became a popular cabaret artist in America and Europe and her sudden death from heart failure followed a London performance. A live album, *Don't Call Me Mama Anymore*, was released posthumously. During the seventies Michelle Phillips began a career as a film actress and recorded *Victims of Romance* (A&M, 1977).

There were several Mamas and Papas reunions beginning with a lacklustre album, *People Like Us*

(1972). In the eighties a new quartet was formed by John Phillips and Doherty (later replaced by Scott McKenzie of 'San Francisco' fame) with Phillips' daughter McKenzie and Elaine 'Spanky' McFarlane, former lead singer of Spanky and Our Gang, whose 'Sunday Will Never Be the Same' (Mercury) had been a 1967 hit. They toured America extensively in the eighties, and a live album briefly appeared in Britain (although it gave no details of the personnel involved and was simply credited to The Mamas and Papas), but no studio recordings emerged. In 1988 Phillips co-wrote the **Beach Boys**' 'Kokomo', which topped the American chart.

Another Phillips daughter, Chynna, was a member of SBK recording group Wilson Phillips, which featured two daughters of Brian Wilson (Beach Boys) and briefly enjoyed considerable American success in the early nineties, selling over five million copies of their eponymous début album. The trio released a less successful follow-up, *Shadows and Light*, before the Wilson Sisters embarked on a career of their own.

Creeque Alley: The History of The Mamas and the Papas (1997) is the definitive retrospective.

HENRY MANCINI
b. 16 April 1924, Cleveland, Ohio, USA, d. 14 June 1994, Los Angeles, California

A prolific film composer, Mancini's success in the late fifties pinpoints the transition in Hollywood from music being conceived as a functional accompaniment to moving images to film (and TV) music being seen as potential record hits. He was also influential in modernizing the techniques of recording film music and introducing a new breed of studio musicians with a jazz, rather than classical, background.

The son of Italian immigrants, Mancini joined Tex Beneke's **Glenn Miller**-styled band as a pianist-arranger on graduating from the Juilliard School of Music in 1946. When his wife, Ginny O'Connor, a former back-up singer with **Mel Torme**, went to Hollywood he went with her to arrange library music for Universal's B-pictures. His first successes were the surreptitiously modernized arrangements for *The Glenn Miller Story* (1954) and *The Benny Goodman Story* (1956) and the jazz-inflected score for Orson Welles' *A Touch of Evil* (1958). His cool jazz compositions for the Blake Edwards-produced *Peter Gunn* teleseries in 1958 brought Mancini his first million-selling album, *Peter Gunn* (RCA), and began a long association with Edwards. 'Moon River' (with words by **Johnny Mercer**), the theme music for *Breakfast at Tiffany's* (1961), 'Days of Wine and Roses' (1963) – for which Mercer also wrote the words – and the instrumental theme 'The Pink Panther' (1964) all produced American Top Forty hits, the first two also winning Oscars.

In 1960 **Duane Eddy** had a British and American Top Thirty hit with a pared-down version of 'Peter Gunn' and in 1986, with the assistance of British avant-garde pop group the Art of Noise (whose members included **Ann Dudley**), Eddy had another hit with 'Peter Gunn'. Although most of Mancini's successes were light, bouncy and melodic, such as his 1969 chart-topping arrangement of **Nino Rota**'s *Love Theme from Romeo and Juliet* (from the film by Franco Zefferelli), the variety of his film work, which includes the sombre score for *The Molly Maguires* (1970) and the atmospheric score for *Nightwing* (1979), belied this reputation. In 1986 he teamed up with **Johnny Mathis** for a celebration of the golden age of *The Hollywood Musicals* (Columbia). His subsequent work has included the score for Blake Edwards' *Blind Date* (1987).

MANFRED MANN
Manfred Mann, b. Manfred Sepse Lubowitz, 21 October 1940, Johannesburg, South Africa; Mike Hug, b. 11 August 1940, Andover, Hampshire, England (replaced by Chris Slade, replaced by John Lingwood); Paul Jones, b. Paul Pond, 24 February 1942 (replaced by Mike d'Abo, b. 1 March 1944, replaced by Mick Rogers, replaced by Chris Thompson); Dave Richmond (replaced by Tom McGuinness, b. 2 December 1941, London); Mike Vickers, b. 18 April 1941, Southampton (replaced by Jack Bruce, b. 14 May 1943, Bishopsbrigg, Scotland, replaced by Klaus Voorman, b. 29 April 1940, Berlin, Germany, replaced by Colin Pattenden, replaced by Pat King, replaced by Matt Irving); Dave Flett (replaced by Steve Waller)

Manfred Mann was a leading British R&B group of the sixties. In the seventies the group that evolved out of that, Manfred Mann's Earthband, turned to progressive rock and in the eighties several original members of the group formed the Blues Band, which toured and recorded into the nineties.

Mann left South Africa in the late fifties and formed the Mann-Hug Blues Brothers in London with drummer Hug, bassist Richmond, Vickers (clarinet and alto sax) and singer and harmonica-player Jones, an Oxford University student who had played in short-lived groups with Brian Jones of the **Rolling Stones** in 1962. The group featured a succession of tenor-sax and trumpet players on material by the likes of **Charles Mingus** and **Cannonball Adderley**.

With the emergence of British R&B in 1963, the group became Manfred Mann and signed to HMV, making little commercial impact until '5 4 3 2 1' (1964), a novelty song featuring Jones' strident harmonica, was commissioned as the theme tune for the fashionable television pop show *Ready Steady Go!*.

The record was the first of a string of hit singles

recorded with new bassist McGuinness, who had pre-viously played with **Eric Clapton**. These continued with another novelty lyric (title courtesy of Shake-speare) 'Hubble Bubble Toil and Trouble' (1964), but for the most part they were versions of American uptown R&B songs like the 1964 No. 1, 'Do Wah Diddy Diddy', written by **Ellie Greenwich** and Jeff Barry for the Exciters (United Artists, 1962), 'Sha La La' (the **Shirelles**, 1962), and **Carole King** and Gerry Goffin's 'Oh No, Not My Baby' (Maxine Brown, Wand, 1964). 'If You Gotta Go, Go Now' (1965) was the first of Manfred Mann's hits with **Bob Dylan** songs.

Guitarist Bruce and horn-players Lyn Dobson and Henry Lowther arrived in 1965 when Vickers departed to write film music and jingles, and in 1966 Jones ('the one in the middle', as he described himself in a 1965 Manfred Mann song) left to pursue a solo career that included hits with 'High Time' and 'I've Been a Bad, Bad Boy', from the film *Privilege* in which he starred. Jones continued to work as an actor, returning to recording with the role of Peron in **Andrew Lloyd Webber** and Tim Rice's *Evita*.

In 1979 Jones reunited with McGuinness and slide-guitarist Dave Kelly in the R&B revivalist group the Blues Band, which recorded five albums in the early eighties before splitting in 1982, when Jones concen-trated on a stage career. They re-formed in 1985, releasing *Back for More* (RCA, 1989), and continued to record and tour on into the nineties and beyond. Later albums included *Homage* (Castle, 1993), which as the title suggests was a celebration of the band's heroes, given added interest in that it reflected a par-ticularly British view of the blues, and the equally impressive self-financed *Brassed Up* (Cobalt, 1999), on which the band added horns to good effect.

Jones' replacement in Manfred Mann was d'Abo from the Band of Angels. D'Abo appeared on a series of increasingly pop-orientated hits on Philips from 1966 to 1969. Beginning with Dylan's 'Just Like a Woman', they included Geoff Stephens' and John Carter's plangent 'Semi Detached Suburban Mr James' (1966, on which Mann played mini-Moog), a No. 1 with Dylan's 'Mighty Quinn', Tony Hazzard's 'Ha Ha Said the Clown' (1967) and 'Fox on the Run' (1968), which, incongruously, later became a favourite piece for modern bluegrass groups. After **Mitch Mur-ray**'s clichéd 'Ragamuffin Man' (1969), the group split, with d'Abo attempting a solo career whose high point was the 1972 album *Down at Rachel's Place* (A&M). He had greater success as a songwriter, com-posing 'Handbags and Gladrags', which was recorded by Chris Farlowe, **Jimmy Witherspoon** and **Rod Stewart**, and 'Build Me Up Buttercup', a British hit for the Foundations.

McGuinness and former **John Mayall** drummer

Hughie Flint formed McGuinness Flint, whose mem-bers included **Gallagher and Lyle**. Their hits included 'When I'm Dead and Gone' and 'Malt and Barley Blues'. Hug and Mann put together a new band, Manfred Man Chapter III. After two Vertigo albums featuring many leading British jazz soloists, Hug departed and the group became the progressive-rock styled Manfred Mann's Earth Band. With Slade (drums), Pattenden (bass) and Rogers (guitar), the group were popular on the European and American college circuits, recording more Dylan songs on *Glori-fied Magnified* (Vertigo, 1972) and achieving a British hit with 'Joybringer' (Vertigo, 1973). *Solar Fire* (Bronze, 1973) was a bestseller in Europe and *Roaring Silence* (1976) included an American No. 1 in **Bruce Springsteen**'s 'Blinded by the Light', sung by new member Thompson.

With occasional changes in line-up, Manfred Mann's Earth Band continued to record and tour until 1987. 'Davy's on the Road Again' (1978) was a British hit, while among the group's albums were *Angel Station* (1979), the concept album *Somewhere in Afrika* (1983) and the live recording *Budapest* (1984). *Criminal Tango* (10 Records, 1986) included Manfred Mann's versions of the **Jam**'s 'Going Underground' and other oldies.

Mann's last eighties album, *Masque* (1987), was recorded without vocalist Thompson, but made no impression on the charts. In 1979–80 Thompson had recorded two albums with the band Night, for the Planet label, and in 1986 he began his solo career with *High Cost of Living* (Atlantic).

Compilations from the two main parts of Mann's career appeared in the early nineties, when he was largely inactive, releasing only one album, the new age-influenced *Plains Music*. Recorded in Johannes-burg and London it included contributions from Smiles Makama on African hunting bows, saxophon-ist Barbara Thompson and ex-Moon singer Noel McCalla. *20 Years of Manfred Mann's Earth Band 1971–1991* (1990) encapsulated his later work, while *Ages of Mann* repackaged the sixties hits. The latter sold more copies, and the popular affection for the early Manfred Mann band material led five ex-members, including d'Abo and Jones, to play a short British tour in late 1992 as the Manfreds. This group, which was largely composed of members of the Blues Band, continued to tour into the nineties, changing their identity as required.

MANHATTAN TRANSFER

Eric Dickens (replaced by Alan Paul, b. 1949, Newark, New Jersey, USA); Tim Hauser, b. 1942, Troy, New York; Marty Nelson; Gene Pistilli (replaced by Janis Siegel, b. 1953, Brooklyn, New York); Pat Rosalia

(replaced by Laurel Masse, b. 1954, replaced by Cheryl Bentyne)

A sophisticated close-harmony vocal group which purveyed a mixture of jazz, swing, doo-wop and pop material, Manhattan Transfer were the most successful of a number of seventies groups who traded in nostalgia.

Hauser had played in high-school rock bands and college folk groups before he and Pistilli (co-author of Spanky and Our Gang's 1967 hit 'Sunday Will Never Be the Same') formed Manhattan Transfer in 1969. Named after a New York novel by John Dos Passos, the group recorded *Jukin'* (Capitol, 1971), a collection of forties material like 'You'se a Viper' and 'Java Jive'.

The commercial failure of the album hastened the disintegration of the band and Hauser formed a new Manhattan Transfer with Paul from the Broadway production of *Grease*, Masse and Siegel, who had recorded in the sixties with all-girl vocal group the Young Generation. Through **Bette Midler**'s manager Aaron Russo, they were signed to Atlantic by **Ahmet Ertegun**, who co-produced an eponymous album with Hauser. It provided hits in 'Operator' (1975) and, in Britain, the **Glenn Miller** tune 'Tuxedo Junction'.

Richard Perry took over as producer for *Coming out* (1976), which included a British and French No. 1 in Wayne Shanklin's schmaltzy ballad 'Chanson d'Amour'. **Jesse Stone**'s 'Don't Let Go' was a minor British hit. After the release of the appropriately titled *Pastiche* (1978), Masse was replaced by Bentyne and *Extensions* (1979) marked a change of emphasis for the group. Tracks like Siegel's arrangement of **Weather Report**'s Joe Zawinul's 'Birdland' and the Jon Hendricks (of **Lambert, Hendricks and Ross**) song 'Twilight Zone/Twilight Tone' were more contemporary and less nostalgic in approach.

Music for Moderns (1981) included Manhattan Transfer's biggest American hit, a revival of the Ad-Libs' 1965 success on Blue Cat, 'The Boy from New York City', but their next hit was from the leading soul writer Rod Temperton, who composed the transatlantic success 'Spice of Life' from *Bodies and Souls* (1984). *Bop Doo Wop* and *Vocalese* (1985) emphasized the group's jazz leanings, with the latter featuring guest vocalists Hendricks and Bobby McFerrin. In 1987 Siegel recorded *At Home* (Atlantic) with such jazz luminaries as Branford Marsalis and Cornell Dupree.

The group's later recordings included a collection of translated ballads by Brazilian songwriters (*Brasil*, 1987), *The Offbeat of Avenues* (1991), *Tonin'*, a 1994 album produced by **Arif Mardin**, and *Swing* (1997), on which the quartet were joined by **Stephane Grappelli**, **Asleep at the Wheel** and **Ricky Skaggs**.

MANIC STREET PREACHERS
James Dean Bradfield, b. 21 February 1969, Pontllanfraith, Wales; Richard 'Richey' James Edwards, b. 22 December 1967, Blackwood; Shaun Moore, b. 30 July 1970, Wales; Nicky Wire, b. Nicholas Allen Jones, 20 January 1969, Blackwood

The most politically charged British band of the nineties, the Manic Street Preachers started life as an energetic hybrid of the **Clash** and **Public Enemy**, gaining notoriety for their intelligent, outspoken sloganeering and winning a fanbase of unqualified devotion. After the disappearance of troubled lyricist Edwards the band took on a more conventional rock sound and gradually became one of the biggest bands in Britain.

The group was formed at the turn of the decade by cousins Bradfield (guitar/vocals) and Moore (drums) and their childhood friends Edwards (rhythm guitar) and Wire (bass), who had spent their teenage years immersed in music and literature. Early performances, under the name Betty Blue, included guitarist Miles 'Flicker' Woodward, while Edwards' role was akin to that of **Public Enemy**'s 'Minister of Information', Professor Grif. After releasing a pair of sub-Clash singles, 'New Art Riot' and 'Motown Junk', on independent labels the group signed with Columbia in 1991.

Generation Terrorists (1992), heavily influenced by **Guns N' Roses**' pomp-metal, saw the Manics find a cult audience around Britain on the back of a succession of minor hit singles, including 'Motorcycle Emptiness', 'You Love Us' and a version of 'Suicide Is Painless (The Theme from *Mash*)'. The patchy *Gold Against the Soul* (1993) was notable only for the singles 'From Despair to Where' and 'La Tristesse Durera', which both made the UK Top Thirty, as the band's sound edged, somewhat prematurely, towards the stadium rock of **Bon Jovi**.

The Manic Street Preachers reached their creative peak with *The Holy Bible* (1994), comparable both in its bleak tone and sparse discordance to Joy Division. Masterminded by Edwards, the album delved into such topics as the holocaust and American gun laws, while it soon became clear that the songs concerning anorexia and self-mutilation were autobiographical. Although Edwards had been publicly cutting himself since he carved '4 -Real' into his arm in the presence of an *NME* journalist, it was quite apparent that his troubles had worsened. He spent a brief period in the Priory psychiatric hospital in mid-1994 before disappearing without trace on the eve of a US tour, 1 February 1995.

After lengthy consideration, the band decided to continue as a trio. *Everything Must Go* (1996)* heralded a much more commercial feel than its predecessors, arranged in a style similar to **Phil Spector**'s Wall of Sound. 'A Design for Life', the lead-off single, reached No. 2 in the British chart, while the multi-platinum album spawned three further hits, 'Kevin Carter', 'Australia' and the title track. The following year the band were awarded Best Band and Best Album at the Brit Awards, a feat which they would repeat in 1999. *This Is My Truth: Tell Me Yours* (1998) echoed the success of its predecessor and gave the band their first chart-topping single in the UK, 'If You Tolerate This Your Children Will Be Next'. The trio returned in late 1999 with 'Masses Against the Classes', a return to the politically charged rock of their early material.

BARRY MANILOW

b. Barry Alan Pinkus, 17 June 1946, Brooklyn, New York, USA

Derided by critics as a 'peroxide puppet' and 'stuffed dummy', arranger-composer-crooner Manilow became the middle-of-the-road star of the rock generation in the mid-seventies. Before reaching that pinnacle of success, he had been a journeyman writer, accompanist and musical director. More recently, Manilow has extended his range to include jazz and Broadway musicals.

While studying music at the Juilliard School in New York, Manilow wrote for an off-Broadway show, *The Drunkard* (1964). He worked briefly in the mail-room at CBS-TV before moving upstairs to provide the music for various shows, including Ed Sullivan's. He also took up a lucrative career as a writer of advertising jingles for such products as Macdonald's hamburgers, Dodge automobiles and Carling beer. (Later, he included a medley of these compositions in his live shows.)

A job as accompanist at the gay venue the Continental Baths in 1972 led to a partnership with **Bette Midler**. Manilow played piano and did musical arrangements for her, as well as producing her first two albums. After opening the show for Midler on tour, Manilow signed to Bell as a solo artist in 1973. Neither his first single, 'Sweet Water Jones', nor an eponymous 1973 album sold well, but in 1975 he took a dynamic version of Richard Kerr's and Scott English's 'Mandy'* to No. 1 in America. As 'Brandy', the song had been a British hit for English on Horse in 1971.

Over the next decade, Manilow's unblushing romanticism and bright tenor voice brought more than twenty hit singles on Arista (the successor label to Bell). Among them were four million-sellers: 'I Write the Songs', composed by **Beach Boy** Bruce Johnston, Kerr's 'Looks Like We Made It' (1977), 'Can't Smile Without You' (1978) and 'Copacabana',

which was featured in the film *Foul Play* (1978). Later hits included a revival of the **Four Seasons**' 1965 song 'Let's Hang on' (1982), 'Memory' (1983) from **Andrew Lloyd Webber**'s musical *Cats*, and 'Read 'Em and Weep' (1983).

Manilow also toured frequently throughout America and Europe and appeared on numerous television specials, where his large nose and ingratiating manner were prominently featured. His dozen successful albums using piano, strings and horns to fill out the mid-tempo ballads in which he specialized were co-produced with Ron Dante, another New York veteran who had been the voice of Archie, leader of **Don Kirshner**'s sixties cartoon band the Archies.

In 1984, however, Manilow established his jazz credentials with *2.00 am Paradise Cafe*, on which **Gerry Mulligan**, **Sarah Vaughan** and **Mel Torme** also appeared. The following year he switched labels to RCA, who launched him at non-English-speaking markets. Manilow made recordings of hits translated into Spanish, Japanese, Italian, French and German. In 1987 he was reunited with Midler when she sang his composition 'Perfect Isn't Easy' on the soundtrack of the Walt Disney version of Dickens' *Oliver Twist*. He took a jazz theme for the classy but poor-selling album *Swing Street* (1988), whose guest artists included **Kid Creole** and **Stan Getz**, while *Barry Manilow* (1989) returned to the pop ballad formula.

In 1989 Manilow staged a highly successful one-man show on Broadway, releasing a live album from it in 1990. He continued the Broadway theme on *Showstoppers* (1991), a selection of hits from the musicals. His later records included *Hidden Treasures* (1993) and 'Let Me Be Your Wings' the theme from the animated film *Thumbelina* with Debra Byrd in 1994. In the same year he returned to the US charts with *Singin' with the Big Bands*, which found him accompanied by the current **Glenn Miller**, **Les Baxter** and **Tommy Dorsey** orchestras. He followed that with another concept album, *Summer of '78* (1996), on which he offered interpretations of seventies hits, and another tribute album, *Manilow Sings Sinatra* (1998). More interesting was the musical *Harmony* he wrote in partnership with Bruce Sussman about the thirties Jewish singing group in Germany, the Comedian Harmonists.

BARRY MANN

b. 9 February 1939, New York, USA

Usually in partnership with Cynthia Weil, Mann was one of the most prolific members of the Brill Building school of pop songwriters in the sixties. As well as penning such standards as 'On Broadway' and 'You've Lost That Lovin' Feeling', the duo were unusual for the period in that they also wrote a number of songs of social comment, including 'Uptown', 'We Gotta Get out of This Place' and 'Home of the Brave'.

Initially an architecture student, Mann turned to songwriting in 1959. His first successes came with 'She Say Oom Dooby Doom' (Mercury, 1959), **Steve Lawrence**'s 'Footsteps' (ABC, 1960) and 'I Love How You Love Me' by the Paris Sisters (Gregmark, 1961). With Howard Greenfield (**Neil Sedaka**'s regular writing partner), he composed 'War Paint', a British hit for the Brook Brothers on Pye in 1961.

In 1961 Mann met and married former actress Weil (b. 18 October 1937, New York). Working for **Don Kirshner**'s Aldon Music, the couple wrote 'Bless You' for **Tony Orlando** while Mann had his only hit as a recording artist with the novelty song 'Who Put the Bomp' (ABC-Paramount), which he had co-written with Gerry Goffin. The following year the **Crystals** had hits with 'Uptown' and 'He's Sure the Boy I Love'; other Mann–Weil successes included 'If a Woman Answers' (Leroy Van Dyke, Mercury, 1962), 'My Dad' (Paul Peterson, Colpix, 1962), 'Johnny Loves Me' (Shelley Fabares, Colpix, 1962) and 'I'm Gonna Be Strong' (**Gene Pitney**, Musicor, 1964).

While most of those songs were neat teenage pop material, Mann and Weil's versatility was shown by their equal facility in producing R&B epics like 'On Broadway' (the **Drifters**, 1963) and 'You've Lost That Lovin' Feeling' (1964), their most recorded song. Originally a hit for the **Righteous Brothers**, it was later covered by everyone from **Elvis Presley** to Telly Savalas. The best of their songs on social themes were 'We Gotta Get out of This Place' (1965), memorably recorded by the **Animals**, and the protest song 'Home of the Brave', a 1965 hit for Jody Miller on Capitol.

The pair had fewer hits in later years, though they supplied **Paul Revere and the Raiders** with 'Kicks' and 'Hungry' (1966), Cass Elliot of **The Mamas and the Papas** with 'It's Getting Better' and 'Make Your Own Kind of Music' (1969), and **B. J. Thomas** with the Top Ten singles 'I Just Can't Help Believing' (1970) and 'Rock'n'Roll Lullaby' (1972). Mann's last big hits of the seventies were **Dolly Parton**'s 'Here You Come Again' (1977) and 'Sometimes When We Touch' (20th Century, 1977), a romantic ballad co-written with the record's singer, Dan Hill.

Like fellow Brill Building alumni **Carole King**, Gerry Goffin and **Ellie Greenwich**, Mann recorded solo albums in the seventies, though Lay It All Out (Design, 1971), Survivor (RCA, 1974) and Joyride (United Artists, 1975) sold poorly. He also wrote songs for films, including An American Tail (1986) and Pinocchio and the Emperor of the Night (1987). Mann returned to recording in 2000 with Soul & Inspiration (Atlantic) on which, with assistance from Richard Marx and Daryl Hall (formerly of **Hall and Oates**), he offered his own versions of the hits others had had with his songs. However, unlike other songwriters (such as Carole King and **Jimmy Webb**) who produced alternate versions of well-known hits, Mann attempted to compete with the hit recordings themselves, to little effect.

MARILYN MANSON
b. Brian Warner, 5 January 1974, Canton, Ohio, USA

Borrowing as much from **Kiss** as **Alice Cooper**, Marilyn Manson became one of the most notorious and controversial performers of the nineties with his industrial Gothic rock and moral majority-baiting shock tactics cloaked in the language of a free-speech campaigner.

Warner worked as a music journalist in Tampa, Florida, before forming a band with Scott Mitchell in 1989. Warner (guitar/vocals) renamed himself after Marilyn Monroe and Charles Manson, while Mitchell (guitar) became Daisy Berkowitz. The pair were augmented by bassist Gidget Gein, keyboard-player Madonna Wayne-Gacy and drummer Sara-Lee Lucas and began to develop a fanbase in the Florida area. In 1993 they signed to **Nine Inch Nails**' Trent Reznor's Nothing Records, gradually gaining an international audience with Portrait of an American Family (1994) and Smells Like Children (1995), which included a minor hit, their cover of the **Eurythmics**' 'Sweet Dreams'. The band steadily gained notoriety, most notably after Manson tore up a copy of the Bible on stage and become a Reverend of the Church of Satan. In 1995 Gein and Berkowitz quit the band and were replaced by Twiggy Ramirez and Zim Zum.

In 1996 Manson proclaimed himself to be the 'Antichrist Superstar' on the album of the same name*. This provided him with his breakthrough into the mainstream, prompting widespread attack from the twin right-wing and religious fronts and regular picketing of his gigs. The following year Manson published his autobiography, The Long Hard Road Out of Hell, which drew as many detractors as supporters. For Mechanical Animals (1998)* Manson took an androgynous alien appearance reminiscent of **David Bowie**'s Aladdin Sane period on an album heavily influenced by mid-seventies glam rock. The singles 'I Don't Like the Drugs (But the Drugs Like Me)' and 'Rock Is Dead' (1999) were both minor hits in Britain.

Manson spent much of the next eighteen months out of the public eye after being held responsible for the Columbine High School massacre by the same right-wing groups who had attacked him in the past. He returned late in 2000 with Holy Wood (In the Shadow of the Valley of Death), a harder-edged, more rhythmic work than its predecessor, featuring the single 'Disposable Teens'. The album was intended as the third part of a trilogy, which had begun with *Antichrist Superstar*, tracing the rise and fall of mankind, and was released alongside a novel of the same name.

MANSUN

Dominic Brian Chad, b. 5 June 1973; Paul Draper, b. 26 September 1972, Chester, England; 'Stove' King, b. 8 January 1974; Andie Rathbone, b. 8 September 1971

Emerging at the end of the Britpop boom as a fairly disposable punk-pop quartet, Mansun developed into one of the most adventurous and technically proficient guitar bands in the UK.

Mansun were formed in 1995 by Draper (guitar/vocals), Chad (lead guitar) and King (bass), employing a succession of drummers until they secured the services of Rathbone the following year. Their first two singles, 'Skin Up Pin Up' and 'Take It Easy Chicken', were released on their own Sci-Fi Hi-Fi label and won the band large-scale media attention and a recording contract with Parlophone.

After spending much of 1996 building their profile in Britain and abroad with a series of self-produced EPs, most notable for 'Stripper Vicar' and 'Wide Open Space', Mansun entered the UK album chart at Number One with *Attack of the Grey Lantern* (1997). An astonishingly assured début, the album mixed the cinematic strings of **John Barry** with **Tears for Fears'** epic pop. Subsequently Mansun continued their series of four-track EPs with *Taxloss* and *Closed for Business*, which features a collaboration with ex-Magazine frontman Howard Devoto.

Mansun's second album, *Six* (1998), was in the same epic, progressive-rock vein as . . . *Lantern*, but saw them replace the orchestral sweeps with multi-layered, effects-laden guitars and experiment with complex song structures and changes in tempo. The album included the singles 'Being a Girl', 'Legacy', 'Negative' and 'Six', taking the band's tally of hits to eleven in just over three years. Mansun spent much of the following year out of the public eye before returning with *Little Kix* (2000), which featured the UK hit 'I Can Only Disappoint U'.

MANTOVANI

b. Annunzio Paolo, 15 November 1905, Venice, Italy, d. 29 March 1980, Tunbridge Wells, Kent, England

Mantovani was one of the most successful orchestra leaders of all time and one of the few British artists of the pre-**Beatles** era to achieve substantial success in America. His sweet, string-laden sound gave him seven million-selling albums and five million-selling singles.

The son of the first violinist at Milan's La Scala opera house, Mantovani emigrated with his family to Britain. At the age of sixteen he became a professional violinist under his mother's maiden name. He formed his first orchestra in 1925, and secured a residency at London's Hotel Metropole. In the thirties he began broadcasting and recording (for EMI's Regal Zonophone label) under the name of the Tipica Orchestra while playing at a variety of venues, including London hotels and Butlin holiday camps. At the same time he conducted for many stars, including **Noël Coward**, for whom he was briefly musical director. It was after joining Decca in 1940 that Mantovani began experimenting with the shimmering, ethereal sound for which he became known. Never recognized for his dance music, or his personality, Mantovani was one of the first popular artists associated with a recorded – rather than live – sound. His was a radically different sound from that of those who would follow him, but in that it was highly produced, it was similar in conception to that of, say, **Buddy Holly** or **Mitch Miller**. During the Second World War he made many broadcasts for the troops.

His first great success was with Ronald Binge's unusual arrangement of 'Charmaine'* (1951), full of cascading strings. The song had been one of the first to be popularized by the movies when it was used as the theme for the silent film *What Price Glory* in 1926. It was followed by a series of hit singles, in both Britain and America, where Mantovani regularly toured. These included 'Wyoming'* (1951), written by publisher **Lawrence Wright** under the pseudonym of Gene Williams; a silky adaptation of 'Greensleeves'* (1952); and the theme from 'Moulin Rouge'* (1953), which was also a hit for **Percy Faith**. In turn, Faith's adaptation of a piece by Swedish composer Hugo Alfven, 'Swedish Rhapsody'*, was a minor hit for Mantovani in 1953. Mantovani's last million-seller was 'Lonely Ballerina' (1954), co-written by **Michael Carr**; his later hits included the film themes 'Around the World in Eighty Days' (1957) and the oft-recorded 'Exodus' (1961). In 1954 he co-wrote (as Tulio Trapani) the Italianate ballad 'Cara Mia' for **David Whitfield** and backed him on his million-selling Decca recording.

Far more significant, however, was Mantovani's success with albums. He was one of the first popular artists to record albums rather than singles – 'Charmaine' was an album track – and throughout the fifties he had a series of hit albums. Among these were *Immortal Classics** (1954), *Songs from Theatreland** (1955), *Film Encores** (1957), *Gems for Ever** (1958 – more Broadway hits given the Mantovani touch) and *Exodus and Other Great Themes** (1960). So broad was Mantovani's appeal that he was used extensively by Decca when they sought to extend the market for stereo albums beyond the hi-fi enthusiasts. It was

Mantovani who established the market for 'mood music' when he was prominently featured in Decca's innovatory 'Phase 4' stereo releases and he became the first artist to sell a million stereo albums.

Mantovani continued to broadcast and record prolifically throughout the sixties and seventies. Among his later albums are *Film Encores* (1971), *From Mantovani with Love* (1971) – which included versions of 'Where Have All the Flowers Gone' and 'The Theme to Love Story' – and *Music for the Motorway* (1979), a cassette-only compilation.

A decade after Mantovani's death, veteran American conductor and producer Ettore Stratta was signed to Decca to create an updated version of the Mantovani sound.

THOMAS MAPFUMO
b. 2 July 1945, Marondera, Zimbabwe

The leading singer and songwriter in independent Zimbabwe, Mapfumo, known as 'The Lion of Zimbabwe', was one of the earliest modern African musicians to find an audience in Europe while maintaining a key role in Zimbabwean culture.

He began his career singing cover-versions of songs by such white rock artists as **Elvis Presley**, **Sam Cooke**, **The Beatles**, **Chicago** and **Blood, Sweat and Tears**, forming the Springfields in the early seventies. As the guerrilla liberation war intensified, Mapfumo began to write songs in Shona rather than English – a brave move for someone who had been taught that his own cultural traditions were backward – and developed a guitar-based music influenced by Zairean styles and by the political broadcasts of the underground radio station, Voice of Zimbabwe. One of his first songs in Shona was an adaptation of **Sam Cooke**'s anthemic 'A Change Is Gonna Come', which he recorded with the same impassioned dignity as Cooke and **Prince Buster**.

In 1973 he left the Springfields and formed the Hallelujah Chicken Run band, forsaking even Africanized versions of international songs in favour of Shona-based folk narratives and songs and African instruments, particularly the mbira (thumb piano). Singles like 1975's 'Morento', which was about the foreseen war, and 'Yarira' (1976), an exhortation to fight for civil rights, won the band a growing following. These were called *chimurenga* songs (*chimurenga* meaning struggle). In 1977 Mapfumo formed the Acid Band and released his first album, *Hokoyo* (1977). The title meant 'Watch Out'. The songs were characterized by ambiguous comments on the white regime and Mapfumo's music was banned by the government radio. He was detained without trial for ninety days.

In 1978 Mapfumo renamed the Acid Band Blacks Unlimited. Its members included Charlie Mayana

(bass, keyboards) and Jona Sitole (lead guitar) and representative singles were 'Africa', 'Black People' and 'Confusion'. After the creation of an independent Zimbabwe in 1980, Mapfumo maintained his critical political edge, refusing to merely become the voice of ZANU. His albums from this period included *Mabasa* (1984) and *Mr Music* (1985). *The Chimurenga Singles* (Earthworks, 1983) was a compilation of his seventies recordings.

His music took on reggae influences and two members of the British group Misty in Roots played on his 1986 album, *Chimurenga for Justice* (Rough Trade), recorded in England. His keen political eye was evident on the 1989 release *Corruption*, which contrasted the hotel bar, swimming-pool lifestyle of Harare's bureaucrats with that of Zimbabwe's rural and working classes. The later single 'Corruption', a calculated attack on the corruption and greed surrounding the Robert Mugabe government, was refused airplay. It was subsequently included in the bestselling *Chamunora* (1990) and the 1975–84 retrospective collection *Shumba*. At the height of the food riots in Harare in 1998 Mapfumo recorded 'We Are Slaves in Our Country'.

The definitive collection is *The Best of Thomas Mapfumo* (EMI, 1992).

JOE MAPHIS
b. 12 May 1921, Suffolk, Virginia, USA, d. 27 June 1986, Los Angeles, California

Known as 'The King of the Strings' for his lightning-fast finger-picking style, Maphis was one of the first and most influential country guitarists to play lead lines, rather than just rhythmic accompaniment. A strong influence on the developing sound of Californian country music that would climax in the careers of **Buck Owens** and **Merle Haggard**, he extended his impact beyond country music through his film work and his association with **Rick Nelson**, among others. Maphis even influenced the later surfing sound of Dick Dale and the Deltones.

From a musical family, Maphis was raised in Cumberland, Maryland, and joined his father's band, the Railsplitters, in 1932. While with the group (which played mostly up-tempo square-dance music), he built up the speed of his playing so as to be able to play the lead lines, commonly played on the fiddle, on his guitar. He became a professional musician in 1938, later joining Sunshine Sue Workman and her Rangers, and throughout the forties was a featured player on numerous country radio shows, including *Old Dominion Barn Dance* and *National Barn Dance*. He took up the electric guitar in 1947, the year he formed a duo with Rose Lee (b. 29 December 1922, Baltimore, Maryland) featuring her singing and his instrumental pyrotechnics. Together they wrote the honky-tonk classic 'Dim Lights, Thick Smoke (and Loud, Loud Music)' and, after their marriage in 1952, the pair moved to the television show *Town Hall Party*.

With his newly acquired double-necked guitar, in 1954 Maphis recorded the song most closely associated with him, 'Fire on the Strings' (Columbia), his adaptation of the traditional fiddle tune 'Fire on the Mountain' (later a pop hit in its own right for the Marshall Tucker Band on Capricorn in 1975). His speed and precision playing, on banjo and mandolin as well as guitar, secured him a steady stream of soundtrack work (including *God's Little Acre* and *Thunder Road*, 1958) and session work which included Rick Nelson's early recordings, such as 'Be Bop Baby', 'Stood Up' and 'Waiting in School' (all 1957), **Wanda Jackson**'s classic 'Let's Have a Party' (1960) and the **Four Preps**' '26 Miles' (1958). Maphis was also responsible for the distinctive sound of the themes to such teleseries as *Bonanza* and *The FBI*.

In the sixties he recorded for Capitol (*Fire on the Strings*, 1964) and with Rose Lee and alone for Starday (*Joe and Rose Lee Maphis, King of the Strings*) and toured extensively, and in the seventies recorded gospel songs for World Records. Maphis also helped promote the career of his niece Barbara Mandrell. Like Maphis a multi-instrumentalist, Mandrell became one of the most successful country artists in the seventies and eighties with her meld of country, soul and pop, even scoring a pop hit with her version of the soul standard '(If Loving You Is Wrong) I Don't Want to Be Right' (ABC, 1979).

THE MARCELS

Cornelius Harp, b. Pittsburgh, Pennsylvania, USA; Ronald 'Bingo' Mundy, b. Pittsburgh; Fred Johnson, b. Pittsburgh; Dick Knaus (replaced by Allen Johnson, b. Pittsburgh); Gene Bricker, b. Pittsburgh (replaced by Walt Maddox, b. Pittsburgh)

Best remembered for their 1961 million-selling version of Richard Rodgers (later of **Rodgers and Hammerstein**) and **Lorenz Hart**'s 'Blue Moon' with its infectious nonsense introduction by bass Fred Johnson ('Dang-a-dang-dang, ding-a-dong-ding'), the Marcels were one of the few racially integrated groups of the rock'n'roll era.

Named after the 'marcelled' wavy hairstyle of several of the group, the Marcels were signed to Colpix. Staff producer Stu Phillips masterminded their novelty version of 'Blue Moon', which had been successfully revived by **Elvis Presley** in 1956. An instant hit, it topped the charts in both America and Britain, and was followed by a series of less successful novelty versions of standards and an appearance in *Twist Around the Clock*. Their hits included **George Gershwin**'s

'Summertime', 'Heartaches' (1961) and 'My Melancholy Baby' (1962), by which time the Marcels had become an all-black group. Failing to overcome their tag as a novelty act to which Johnny Cymbal paid homage on his gimmicky 'Mr Bass Man' (Kapp, 1963), they disbanded in the mid-sixties. The group re-formed in the seventies to join the nostalgia circuit and were still occasionally performing in the nineties.

In 1980 film director John Landis featured their recording of 'Blue Moon', among several other 'moon' songs, in *An American Werewolf in London. The Best of the Marcels* (Rhino, 1993) is the definitive collection.

ARIF MARDIN
b. 15 March 1932, Istanbul, Turkey

An arranger and producer, Mardin contributed to the success of the Atlantic label in the sixties and seventies before becoming one of the most successful record producers of the eighties.

He became a jazz fan through hearing **Duke Ellington** records as a child and left Turkey to take up a **Quincy Jones** music scholarship at Berklee College in Boston. Moving to New York to work as a teacher and composer, Mardin was hired in 1962 by Atlantic's jazz chief **Nesuhi Ertegun** as his assistant and the company's archivist. After writing arrangements for **King Curtis**, he went on to produce both rock (Stephen Stills, **Danny O'Keefe**, the **Rascals**) and country music (**Willie Nelson**, **John Prine**).

However, Mardin's most successful work for Atlantic lay in the soul field. His first solo production was the US chart-topper by the (Young) Rascals, 'Good Lovin'' (1966), in which he overlaid a soft soul sound on a modern pop song. In 1972 he worked with **Tom Dowd** and **Jerry Wexler** on **Aretha Franklin**'s *Young, Gifted and Black*, for which he provided string and horn arrangements. He also produced work by **Brook Benton**, **Donny Hathaway**, **Roberta Flack**, **Wilson Pickett** and **Laura Nyro**. However, he had particular success with the **Average White Band,** with whom he repeated his trick with the Rascals of giving a white group a clearly black-inflected soul sound. He oversaw all their significant albums.

During the seventies Mardin was in demand as a freelance producer. He supervised *Main Course* (1975) by the **Bee Gees**. It was Mardin who was largely responsible for giving a soul feel to the group, best exemplified on 'Jive Talkin'' and 'Nights on Broadway'. Other productions then included **Judy Collins**' *Bread and Roses* (Elektra, 1976) and records by **Carly Simon** and **Ringo Starr**. His partnership with **Chaka Khan** began with *Chaka* (1978) and continued throughout the eighties. Mardin's ability to encompass new technologies was typified by Khan's 'I Feel for You' (1985), which used sampling techniques and arrangements by hip-hop musician Reggie Griffin. He also worked with such British rock performers as **Phil Collins** (*Separate Lives*, 1984), **Culture Club** (*From Luxury to Heartache*, 1986), **Scritti Politti** (*Cupid and Psyche*, 1985) and **David Bowie**. Mardin was a consistent hit-maker throughout the eighties, ending the decade with **Bette Midler**'s 'Wind Beneath My Wings' and her version of Julie Gold's anthemic 'From a Distance'.

Among the artists he has worked with in the nineties are Flack, the **Modern Jazz Quartet** (*A 40th Anniversary Celebration*, 1994), **Manhattan Transfer** and Linda Eder (Atlantic, *It's Time*, 1997).

Mardin's only recordings under his own name were the Atlantic albums *Glass Onion* (1969) and *Journey* (1974).

MARILLION

Fish, b. Derek William Dick, 25 April 1958, Scotland (replaced by Steve Hogarth); Brian Jelliman (replaced by Mark Kelly, b. 9 April 1961, Dublin, Eire); Steve Rothery, b. 25 November 1959, Brompton, Yorkshire, England; Diz Minnitt (replaced by Pete Trewavas, b. 15 January 1950, Middlesborough); Mick Pointer (replaced by Ian Mosley, b. 16 June 1953, London)

Fundamentally dedicated to reviving the seventies progressive rock of **Genesis** and **Yes**, Marillion achieved an unexpected popularity with their pomp-rock in Britain in the eighties, and their career survived the setback of the departure of charismatic vocalist Fish in 1988.

The group was formed in Aylesbury, Buckinghamshire, by Kelly (keyboards), Rothery (guitar) and bassist Minnitt in 1979 as Silmarillion, the title of a book by J. R. R. Tolkien. In 1981 former tree-feller and member of Cumbrian band Blewitt Fish took over as songwriter, face-paint artist and lead vocalist and they dropped the first syllable of their name and built a large club and college following. Having recorded sessions for BBC radio, they signed to EMI in 1982 with Trewavas replacing Minnitt.

'Market Square Heroes' was followed by the Nick Tauber-produced *Script for a Jester's Tears* (1983). This album included the hit singles, 'He Knows You Know' and 'Garden Party' (1983), which reached the Top Twenty. *Fugazi* (1984) included the hits 'Punch and Judy' and 'Assassing' while the live album *Real to Reel* (1984) was released following lengthy European and American tours. The group reached the peak of their British success in 1985 with the Top Ten singles 'Kayleigh' and 'Lavender' from *Misplaced Childhood*. Marillion's *Clutching at Straws* (1987) was produced by Chris Kimsey. Most of its songs were concerned with Fish's love-hate relationship with alcohol.

In 1988 Fish left the group for a solo career. As a

memento of the Fish years, Marillion released the live double-album *The Thieving Magpie (La Gazza Ladra)* before recruiting new vocalist Hogarth, a former member of the Europeans and How We Live. The first album with the new line-up, *Season's End* (1989), reached the British Top Ten. It featured a less 'mystical' approach, largely because of Hogarth's lyrics.

Fish contributed to **Mike Oldfield**'s *Earth Moving* before forming a new group with Oldfield pianist Mickey Simmonds and ex-Blewitt guitarist Frank Usher to record *Vigil in the Wilderness of Mirrors* (1990). It was a Top Five album in Britain, but shortly afterwards Fish left EMI to sign to Polydor Records. To steadily diminishing returns, he released *Internal Exile* (1991) and *Songs from the Mirror* (1992), an album of his favourite tracks from the sixties and seventies, which included songs from the **Kinks**, **Genesis** and Scottish rocker Alex Harvey. He left Polydor shortly after its release, issuing a double live album, *Sushi*, on his own label in 1994.

Marillion, meanwhile, were enjoying more success than in the Fish era. They released a second album, *Holidays in Eden* (1991), which again made the British Top Ten, and celebrated their tenth anniversary with a sell-out show at London's Wembley Arena in 1992. In 1994 they released their third successful Fish-free album, *Brave*. They followed that with *Made Again* (1994) and *Sunlight* (1995). The two-CD set *The Best of Both Worlds* (1997), in which one album featured Fish and the second was Fish-less, confirmed the continuing success of the Fish-less Marillion. Subsequent albums included *This Strange Engine* (Intact, 1997) and *Radiation* (Racket, 1998).

JOHNNY MARKS

b. 1903, Mount Vernon, New York, USA, d. 3 September 1985, New York

Writer and publisher Marks virtually cornered the Christmas novelty-song market single-handedly. His composition 'Rudolph the Red-Nosed Reindeer' reportedly sold 150 million records (of which 12 million alone are accounted for by **Gene Autry**'s 1949 recording) and eight million copies of sheet music. The song was based on Robert L. May's book of the same name. In addition Marks was responsible for three further seasonal million-sellers: 'I Heard the Bells on Christmas Day' (first recorded by **Bing Crosby**), 'Rockin' Around the Christmas Tree' (a hit for **Brenda Lee** in 1960) and 'A Holly Jolly Christmas' (first recorded by **Burl Ives**). A composer as well as lyricist, he scored several 'Rudolph'-related television programmes, including *Rudolph the Red-Nosed Reindeer* (a regular Christmas attraction in America, since 1964) and *Rudolph and Frosty*.

None of his other songs was as successful.

BOB MARLEY AND THE WAILERS

Bob Marley, b. Nesta Robert Marley, 6 February 1945,
St Anns, Jamaica, d. 11 May 1981, Miami, Florida, USA;
Bunny Wailer, b. Neville O'Riley 'Bunny' Livingston,
23 April 1947; Peter Tosh, b. Winston Hubert McIntosh,
9 October 1944, Westmoreland, Jamaica, d. 12 Septem-
ber 1987, Kingston

The only reggae artist to achieve international superstar status, Marley evolved a world music that, while
drawing on rock and African themes, was underpinned by the politics and theology of his Rastafarian
beliefs.

Of mixed-race parentage, Marley moved with his
black mother to the Trenchtown ghetto in Kingston
in 1957. He formed a vocal group in 1960 with Livingston, **Peter Tosh** and Junior Braithwaite. Basing
their style on American groups like the **Drifters** and
Impressions, they were coached by veteran singer Joe
Higgs. In 1962 Marley was introduced by **Jimmy Cliff**
to producer **Leslie Kong** and cut his first record,
'Judge Not' (Beverly).

Calling themselves the Wailing Wailers, the group
were signed by **Coxsone Dodd**, for whom they
recorded more than twenty hit singles between 1963
and 1967. 'Simmer Down', with backing by the
Skatalites and lyrics full of street aphorisms, reached
No. 1 early in 1964. Other hits included doo-wop ballads, ska versions of American songs like Aaron
Neville's (of the **Neville Brothers**) 'Ten Commandments of Love', and in 1965 a series of anthems to the
'Rude Boys' (street gangs) of Kingston, as well as a
version of **Bob Dylan**'s 'Like a Rolling Stone'.

In 1967 the group split from Dodd following a disagreement over unpaid royalties and set up their own
Wailing Soul label with producer Clancy Eccles.
Despite popular records like 'Hypocrite' and 'Stir It
Up', lack of airplay and poor distribution caused the
company to fold. At this point the Wailers were
signed as songwriters to Cayman Music, owned by
Johnny Nash and his manager. In the next four years,
they cut demo discs of eighty songs, several of which
appeared on Nash's 1972 hit album *I Can See Clearly
Now*. His version of Marley's 'Stir It Up' was a Top
Twenty hit in America in 1973.

In Jamaica, the Wailers recorded briefly for Kong
in 1969 before laying down a series of epochal tracks
with producer **Lee Perry**. Using his studio band the
Upsetters, he gave the group a new, tougher sound
which suited the militancy of Perry–Marley songs like
'Duppy Conqueror' and 'Small Axe' and Tosh's anti-
colonial '400 Years'. 'Trench Town Rock', released on
the band's Tuff Gong label, was No. 1 in Jamaica for
five months during 1971.

Through Nash, CBS in Britain released Marley's
'Reggae on Broadway' and the Wailers travelled to

London, where **Chris Blackwell** of Island Records
signed them to a long-term contract. *Catch a Fire*
(1972) was the first reggae record conceived as an
album and the first Anglo-Jamaican record, with
Blackwell over-dubbing guitar and speeding up the
rhythm track of the songs cut by the Wailers with **Sly
and Robbie**, Carlton 'Family Man' Barrett (*b. 17
December 1950, Kingston, Jamaica, d. 17 April 1987,
Kingston, Jamaica*) and his brother Aston from the
Upsetters along with vocalists Rita Marley, Marcia
Griffiths (formerly of **Bob and Marcia**) and Judy
Mowatt. The album, with its judicious blend of rock,
soul, blues and funk with reggae, was a critical success.

Major tours of rock venues in Britain and North
America took place in 1973, with Livingston, who disliked foreign travel, leaving to be temporarily replaced
by Joe Higgs. *Burnin'* (1973) included songs by him as
well as 'Get Up, Stand Up' and 'I Shot the Sheriff'.
The latter (a hit for **Eric Clapton** in 1974) was among
several Marley compositions recorded by other artists
at this time. They included 'Guava Jelly' (**Barbra
Streisand**) and 'Slave Driver' (**Taj Mahal**).

The soul-reggae ballad 'No Woman No Cry' was
the outstanding track on the 1974 album *Natty
Dread*. Again produced by Blackwell, it featured
American guitarist Al Anderson and African drummer Remi Kabaka. Blackwell now had Marley set into
the rock pattern of an album a year supported by
regular international tours with a Wailers which no
longer included Tosh. The 1975 *Live* album, cut in
London, was followed in 1976 by *Rastaman
Vibration*.

Marley's roots, however – his religion and his Tuff
Gong operation – remained in Jamaica. He responded
to the death of Haile Selassie in 1975 by cutting 'Jah
Live' under the pseudonym Hugh Peart and by basing
'War' on *Rastaman Vibration* on one of the Ethiopian
ruler's speeches. 1976 was a violent, tense election year
in Jamaica and though Marley remained politically
neutral he was shot and wounded by unknown gunmen in December, only a few weeks before the 'Smile
Jamaica' concert he had organized to reconcile the
opposing political leaders. He recovered sufficiently to
appear. Both Peter Tosh and Carlton Barrett would
later be murdered by gunmen.

His international career resumed with *Exodus*
(1977), which included two British hit singles, the title
track and the disco-tinged 'Jamming'. The B-side of
the latter was 'Punky Reggae Party', on which Marley
appeared to give his blessing to the emergent punk
rock movement. Further tracks from the *Exodus* sessions formed the basis of *Kaya* (1978), whose bright
mix brought accusations that his music was becoming
too cosmopolitan. 'Is This Love' from the album was
a British Top Ten hit. The same year a second live
album, *Babylon by Bus*, appeared.

Marley now found new inspiration from Africa. His 1978 world tour took him to Gabon, an experience reflected in *Survival* (1979), which included 'Zimbabwe', a liberation anthem taken up by many African musicians. Such was Marley's status that he was invited to perform at the country's independence celebrations in 1980. That year's album, *Uprising*, showed that African musical elements, such as Junior Murvin's highlife guitar on the UK hit 'Could You Be Loved' were beginning to replace the rock elements in his work. The album was Marley's last recording. In September 1980 he collapsed during an American tour. He was diagnosed as having cancer and despite extensive treatment he died eight months later. The Jamaican government, which had awarded him the title Honourable, organized a state funeral.

Rita Marley took over the running of Tuff Gong, which released albums by Bob's mother Cedella Booker (*Redemption Songs*, 1985) and by his children, Ziggy Marley and the Melody Makers. Born David Marley, Ziggy followed his father in developing a crossover mix of classic reggae and rock. His recordings included *Play the Game Right* (1985), *Hey World* (EMI, 1987), *Conscious Party* (Virgin, 1988), produced by Tina Weymouth and Chris Frantz of **Talking Heads**, and *Joy and Blues* (1993).

Rita faced a legal challenge over the ownership of the label from Bunny Wailer, who had continued to produce a series of classic solo reggae albums through his Solomonic Productions, including *Blackheart Man* (1976) and *Marketplace* (1986). In 1981 he recorded a tribute album to Marley, *Bunny Sings the Wailers* while an album of the Studio One ska sides by the original Wailers was reissued in 1982. Bunny was also behind an attempt to create a Wailers 'reunion' album using guitar and vocals demo tapes cut by Bob Marley in the Wailin' Soul period, with Tosh, Braithwaite and Bunny over-dubbed.

After Marley's death, the posthumously finished *Confrontation* was released in 1983, and the British chart-topping compilation *Legend* in 1984. An album of rarities, *Rebel Music*, followed in 1986 and another, *Talkin' Blues* in 1991. A box set, *Songs of Freedom* (1992), offered a fine summary of the man's talents. The legal wrangling over Marley's assets was ended by a Jamaican court decision which in 1991 accepted a joint bid of just under $12m from Blackwell and Rita Marley. That settlement led eventually to the release of *Chant Down Babylon* (Tuff Gong/Island, 2000), a collection of eleven Marley tracks remixed and added to by the likes of Busta Rhymes, Lauryn Hill, Erykah Badu and (an uncredited) Betty Wright, under the supervision of the family. The result, a sort of hip-hop version of reggae, is interesting rather than respectful, but finally irrelevant to Marley's body of work.

MARMALADE

Junior Campbell, b. 31 May 1947 (replaced by Hughie Nicholson); Pat Fairlie, b. 14 April 1946 (replaced by Garth Watt Roy); Dean Ford, b. William McAleese, b. 5 September 1946 (replaced by Sandy Newman); Graham Knight, b. 8 December 1946; Raymond Duffy (replaced by Alan Whitehead)

Formed by ex-members of Glasgow beat groups, Marmalade found success in the late sixties with records made in the well-crafted pop song mode pioneered by the **Hollies** and others a few years earlier.

As Dean Ford and the Gaylords, the group released cover-versions of **Shirley Ellis**'s 1965 hit 'The Name Game' (EMI Columbia) and the **Coasters**' 1961 record 'Little Egypt'. In 1968 as Marmalade they signed to the newly established British branch of Columbia. That year, 'Lovin' Things' reached the Top Ten while a cover of **The Beatles**' spoof reggae number 'Ob-La-Di Ob-La-Da' was a No. 1 hit.

After recording **Tony Macaulay**'s 'Baby Make It Soon', the group moved to Decca where they had a series of hits written by guitarist Campbell and lead singer Ford. The gentle 'Reflections of My Life' (1969) was followed by 'Rainbow' (1970) and 'My Little One' (1971) before Campbell left to record as a solo artist, achieving British success with the soul-styled 'Hallalujah Freedom' (Deram, 1972) and 'Sweet Illusion' (1973).

Marmalade's new songwriter was Nicholson, formerly with the Poets who recorded in the mid-sixties for Immediate and Decca, scoring a minor hit with the intricate 'Now We're Thru' (Decca, 1964). He composed the jaunty 'Cousin Norman' (1971) and 'Radancer' (1972) before the band's alleged sexual excesses were exposed by a newspaper. The group had bookings cancelled and Nicholson left to form Blue with ex-Poets bassist Ian Macmillan and American drummer Timi Donald. With updated beat-group harmonies, the new band recorded two well-received albums for RSO and two for Rocket. Their only hit was 'Gonna Capture Your Heart' (1977), produced by **Elton John**.

After 'Our House Is Rockin'' (EMI, 1974), Ford in turn left Marmalade for a solo recording career with EMI. He later sang on the **Alan Parsons** Project album *Pyramid* (1978). With new members Newman and Roy, bassist Knight and drummer Whitehead had a hit with the appropriately titled 'Falling Apart at the Seams' (Target, 1976) from *Only Light on My Horizon Now* (1977). The group split soon afterwards, though Knight later put together a new Marmalade to play the old hits on the nostalgia package tours of the eighties and nineties.

WYNTON MARSALIS

b. 18 October 1961, Kenner, Louisiana, USA

The most acclaimed young trumpeter of the eighties, Marsalis recorded classical works as well as adopting a classicist approach to jazz, basing his style on that of the early **Miles Davis**.

His father Ellis Marsalis was a jazz pianist who had played in the band of trumpeter Al Hirt. Hirt's band had two million-selling hit instrumentals with **Allen Toussaint**'s 'Java' (RCA, 1963) and 'Sugar Lips' (1964), written by **Billy Sherrill** and Buddy Killen, **Joe Tex**'s manager. Marsalis named his son after pianist Wynton Kelly.

Wynton Marsalis studied classical trumpet and played in various marching bands and jazz groups before making his professional début with the New Orleans Philharmonic Orchestra. In 1979 he won a scholarship to the Juilliard School of Music in New York. There he played in the pit band for **Stephen Sondheim**'s Broadway musical *Sweeney Todd* before his growing reputation led to an offer to tour with **Art Blakey**'s Jazz Messengers in 1980. This was followed by concerts and recordings with groups led by **Herbie Hancock**, whose members included bassist Ron Carter and drummer Tony Williams.

Hancock produced Marsalis's eponymous début album for Columbia which was released in 1982, the year he won the 'Musician of the Year' title in *Downbeat* magazine's readers' poll. *Think of One* (1983) was produced by Marsalis himself. He achieved greater recognition in 1984 when he won Grammy awards in both the jazz and classical music categories. *Hot House Flowers* contained string accompaniments to his immaculate interpretations of such standards as **Hoagy Carmichael**'s 'Stardust' and 'When You Wish Upon a Star', while *Trumpet Concertos* included works by Haydn and Hummel. In 1986 Wynton again released both jazz and classical recordings: *J. Mood* and *French Concertos*. These were followed by *Live at Blues Alley* (1987) and *Marsalis Standard Time*.

His older brother Branford played saxophones on Marsalis's next recording, *Black Codes (From the Underground)* (1984). Branford went on to tour with **Sting** of the **Police**, playing on *The Dream of the Blue Turtles* (1985), and made his own album of light classical pieces by Ravel, Satie and Stravinsky, *Romances for Saxophone* (CBS Masterworks, 1986). With Terence Blanchard he later recorded the soundtrack for Spike Lee's film, *Mo' Better Blues*. The brothers also collaborated with Ellis Marsalis on *Fathers and Sons* and appeared on *Pontius Pilate's Decision* (Arista, 1992), composed and performed by their younger brother, the trombonist Delfaeyo.

Wynton Marsalis has sometimes been criticized for masking emotional depth with technical virtuosity and leaning too heavily on outdated styles. However, *The Majesty of the Blues* (1989) is a highly emotive work and it treats the blues as an evolving form rather than a museum piece. It initiated a series of recordings which saw Marsalis meditating on the past rather than being in thrall to it. Among these were the three-volume series *Soul Gestures in Southern Blue* (1991), the *Standard Time* series, particularly Volume 3 (1990), the heavily **Duke Ellington**-inflected *Tune in Tomorrow* (1990), *In This House on This Morning* (1992) and the superb *On Movement* (1993), which includes the score Marsalis wrote for the modern ballet *Griot New York*. In 1999 he recorded *Big Train*, an impressionistic account of a train ride across America.

MARTHA AND THE VANDELLAS
Martha Reeves, b. 18 July 1941, Detroit, Michigan, USA; Rosalind Ashford, b. 2 September 1943, Detroit; Annette Sterling

The most earthy and exciting of Motown's girl groups (in contrast to the cool charms of the **Supremes**), Martha and the Vandellas had success with a series of intense dance records in the sixties. The best-remembered were 'Heatwave' (1963) and 'Dancing in the Street', subsequently recorded by **The Who**, **Linda Ronstadt** ('Heatwave'), **Van Halen** and Mick Jagger and **David Bowie** ('Dancing').

A former Motown secretary, Reeves pestered boss **Berry Gordy** to allow her to record and was eventually rewarded with back-up work, most notably with **Marvin Gaye** ('Stubborn Kinda Fellow', 1962; 'Hitch Hike', 1964). With two other secretaries, Ashford and Sterling, she formed Martha and the Vandellas and recorded **Holland, Dozier and Holland**'s 'Come and Get These Memories' (1963). A hit, the record was followed by more HDH productions: 'Heatwave', 'Quicksand', 'Live Wire' and, perhaps the most famous of all early Motown records, 'Dancing in the Street' (all 1964). The hits continued with 'Nowhere to Run', 'Jimmy Mack' and 'Honey Chile'. Always popular in England, the group (despite charting with 'Dancing' in 1964) did not have a major hit there until the record was re-released in 1969, and reached No. 4. This began a short run of hits which included the 1971 Top Twenty entry 'Forget Me Not', an earlier failure in America.

By this time the line-up of the group had completely changed. Martha Reeves was the only original member with her sister Louis and Sandra Tilley in support. However, despite these changes the group ceased to make an impact in the USA. Embittered by what she saw as a deliberate attempt by Motown to ignore her career in favour of such singers as **Diana Ross**, Reeves left the label in 1974 and signed to MCA. There, she was produced by Richard Perry on what was to be renowned as the most expensive album recorded to that date. The album, *Martha Reeves*, was a commercial failure and prompted Reeves to move to Arista where again her recordings failed to attract attention. After one more album for Fantasy (*We Meet Again*, 1978), she turned to the oldies circuit with various 'Vandellas' line-ups.

In 1989 Reeves and the original Vandellas (Sterling and Ashford) toured Britain where they took part in an ex-Motown recording project organized by producer-songwriter Ian Levine. The trio returned to Britain in 1992 and 1993, performing with other Motown survivors including the **Temptations** and the original **Four Tops** in shows billed as the Giants of Motown. In 1994 Reeves published her autobiography *Dancing in the Streets* and in 2000, in tandem with fellow Motownees Mary Wilson of the Supremes and Edwin Starr, she returned to the UK for a six-week tour.

DEAN MARTIN
b. *Dino Paul Crocetti, 7 June 1917, Steubenville, Ohio, USA, d. 25 December 1995*

Actor, singer and, with **Frank Sinatra** (of whose 'Rat Pack' Martin was a well-known member), one of the original investors in Reprise Records, Martin had one of the most varied careers of all the balladeers who emerged in the forties. Originally a romantic crooner and later the straight man to crazy comedian Jerry Lewis, Martin deftly used his Italian background and much publicized liking for a drink – he even portrayed a caricature of himself (Dino) in Billy Wilder's *Kiss Me Stupid* (1964) and jokily recorded 'Little Ole Wine Drinker Me' (Reprise, 1967) – to build a multi-faceted career in showbusiness.

A former prize-fighter, steel-mill labourer and croupier, he joined Sam Watkins' Band in Cleveland. After a name change to Dino Martini, he became a solo singer, similar in style to, but less distinguished than, **Bing Crosby**. His relaxed, easy-going charm won him only moderate success until in 1946, as Dean Martin, he teamed up with Lewis. After great success on television, the pair signed to Paramount and made seventeen films together between 1949 and 1956. Signed to Capitol, Martin had a number of minor hits, including 'I'll Always Love You' (1950) and 'If' (1951), before 'That's Amore'* (1953), the **Harry Warren** song from *The Caddy*. His first No. 1 was the folky 'Memories Are Made of This'* (1956), in the year he broke up with Lewis. The song was co-written by Terry Gilkyson, who had earlier provided **Frankie Laine** with 'The Cry of the Wild Geese' and in 1957 had his own Top Ten hit, 'Marianne' (Columbia). Martin's film career briefly floundered after the break with Lewis, but in 1958 he had renewed record success with his romantic interpretation of 'Return to Me'*, which was co-written by **Guy Lombardo**'s brother Carmen, and his cover of **Domenico Modugno**'s

'Volare' with English lyrics by Mitchell Parish. In 1959 he had film success with *Some Came Running* and *Rio Bravo*, in both playing dramatic roles carefully modelled on his public persona.

Martin successfully mixed cabaret and film work for several years but had no further record success until 1964, when he reached No. 1 with 'Everybody Loves Somebody'* (Reprise), which became the theme of his long-running television series, *The Dean Martin Show*. The song was written by Irving Taylor and Ken Lane (who conducted the orchestra on Martin's recording) and had been previously recorded by Sinatra, **Peggy Lee** and **Dinah Washington**. Martin's version was produced by Jimmy Bowen, the co-author of Buddy Knox's 1957 million-seller, 'Party Doll' (Roulette), and a respected producer of country acts in the seventies and eighties (he worked with **Merle Haggard** and **Hank Williams Jnr**, among others). Most of Martin's subsequent recordings were in a similar countryish vein. These included a version of **Hank Locklin**'s 'Send Me the Pillow You Dream on', which had earlier provided the **Browns** (1960) and **Johnny Tillotson** (1962) with pop hits, **Lee Hazelwood**'s 'Houston' (1965), **John Hartford**'s 'Gentle on My Mind' (1969) and Mel Tillis's 'Detroit City' (1970), before he was reunited with Bowen, who produced *The Nashville Sessions* (Warners, 1983).

At the same time, Martin continued his television, cabaret and film careers, playing Matt Helm in a series of spy films, the first of which was *The Silencers* (1966), inspired by the success of the James Bond movies, among other roles. From the eighties onward he performed less frequently. His son, Dino, was a member of Dino, Desi and Billy, whose pop hits, including 'I'm a Fool' and 'Not the Lovin' Kind' (Reprise, 1965), were produced by Lee Hazelwood.

Music writer Nick Tosches published *Dino*, an unauthorized biography of Martin, in 1992. In the wake of his death Martin's baroque latinery won him a newfound audience as king of easy-listening music.

FREDDY MARTIN
b. *9 December 1906, Springfield, Ohio, USA, d. 1 October 1983*

The leader of a band in the sweet style popularized by **Guy Lombardo**, Martin's speciality was dance-band adaptations of the classics. His greatest success in this vein was a version of the opening theme to Tchaikovsky's Piano Concerto No. 1 in B Flat Minor, which with words by Bobby Worth and retitled 'Tonight We Love' gave him a million-seller in 1941.

Orphaned at the age of four, Martin studied drums and saxophone and played with local bands before forming his first band while a student at Ohio State University. Through his friendship with the Lombardo brothers, he found local gigs and then worked as a sideman until 1932, when he turned professional, established himself as a hotel bandleader and signed with Brunswick. Initially featuring three saxophones, set against the trombone of Russ Morgan and the vocals of Elmer Feldkamp (and later Eddie Stone and pianist Merv Griffen), he developed a more individual style after joining RCA in 1940. His first major success was 'Tonight We Love', arranged by Ray Austin, which sparked numerous cover-versions, including one entitled 'Concerto for Two' by **Claude Thornhill**, a former pianist with Martin's band. Martin's million-seller was the forerunner of other classical adaptations of the forties, including Martin's own 'I Look to Heaven' (based on a Grieg concerto) and, most notably, **Jose Iturbi**'s great success with versions of Chopin (Polonaise in A Flat) and Debussy ('Claire de Lune') in 1945. In the meantime, Martin had further million-sellers with **Irving Berlin**'s Oscar-winning song 'White Christmas' (from *Holiday Inn*, 1942) and the novelty song 'I've Got a Lovely Bunch of Coconuts' (1949), first popularized by **Billy Cotton** in Britain in 1948.

From the fifties onwards Martin regularly appeared on television and in the seventies, following the revived interest in big-band music, he frequently toured America with **George Shearing** and **Bob Crosby**, among his featured soloists.

GEORGE MARTIN
b. 3 January 1926, London, England

Arranger, producer and A&R executive, Martin is best known for his work as producer of most of **The Beatles**' recordings.

After studying oboe and composition at the Guildhall School of Music, he joined EMI Records where from the mid-fifties he was head of the Parlophone label. There, the versatile Martin recorded jazz (**John Dankworth, Humphrey Lyttelton**), cabaret (Michael Flanders and Donald Swann), Scottish dance music (Jimmy Shand), skiffle (the Vipers) and ballad singers like **Matt Monro** and **Shirley Bassey**.

His particular forte was comedy. Among the comics whose records he supervised were former **Goon** Peter Sellers (*Best of Sellers*, 1959; *Songs for Swinging Sellers*, 1960), Bernard Cribbins ('Hole in the Ground' and 'Right, Said Fred', both 1962), and the cast recordings of *Beyond the Fringe* (1961) and *That Was the Week That Was* (1964). It was with these recordings that Martin began the experiments with sound effects, in the manner of **Stan Freberg**, which would prove so valuable in his later work with The Beatles, whom he signed to Parlophone in 1962.

Martin acted as producer on all the group's recordings up to *Abbey Road* (1970). After their first single 'Love Me Do' was a minor hit, he unsuccessfully tried to persuade them to record **Mitch Murray**'s 'How Do You Do It?' instead of 'She Loves You'. His objections to Pete Best's drumming were heeded, however, and Ringo Starr was brought in as a replacement. As the group became more artistically ambitious, Martin's knowledge of musical and studio techniques became invaluable. It was he who added the string quartet to 'Yesterday' and advised on the construction of such later tracks as 'Strawberry Fields Forever'. Martin also scored the first Beatle film, *A Hard Day's Night* (1964), and recorded his instrumental versions of the group's material on *Off the Beatle Track* (Parlophone, 1964) and *The Beatle Girls* (United Artists, 1966).

During the sixties he produced other Liverpool artists managed by Brian Epstein, including **Gerry and the Pacemakers** (who *did* record the hit version of 'How Do You Do It?'), **Cilla Black** and Billy J. Kramer. By 1965 Martin's reputation was such that he was able to leave EMI to become an independent producer, opening his own studios in London and on the Caribbean island of Montserrat. Following the devastation of the island in 1989, Martin organized the fund-raising album *After the Hurricane* (Chrysalis), which contained tracks by numerous artists who had recorded at Air Montserrat, including **Paul McCartney**, the **Police**, **Dire Straits** and the **Rolling Stones**.

Martin's greatest success in the seventies was with **America**. He also worked with Ringo Starr (*Sentimental Journey*, 1970), English folk-rock eccentrics Stackridge (*The Man in the Bowler Hat*, MCA, 1974), **Jeff Beck** (*Blow by Blow*, 1973; *Wired*, 1974), **Jimmy Webb** (*El Mirage*, 1977) and **Neil Sedaka** (*A Song*, 1977).

He maintained his Beatles connections by supervising the post-production of the live album *At the Hollywood Bowl* (1977) and producing the soundtrack album to The Beatles-inspired film *Sgt Pepper's Lonely Hearts Club Band* (1978). In the eighties Martin worked with Paul McCartney on *Tug of War* (1982) and *Pipes of Peace* (1983).

In 1988 Martin produced a recording of Dylan Thomas's verse play *Under Milk Wood* (EMI), which featured among the cast **Mary Hopkin** and **Bonnie Tyler**. With his studio now part of the Chrysalis group, Martin continued occasionally to produce new artists such as Andy Leek (*Say Something*, Atlantic, 1988).

In the eighties Martin was largely occupied with running the Air Studios group, personally supervising the building of a second London studio which opened in 1993. His first major production of the decade was the Broadway cast version of **The Who**'s *Tommy* (RCA, 1993). In the nineties Martin oversaw The Beatles' three-volume *Anthology* project, produced McCartney's *Flaming Pie* (1997), amongst other albums, and released the concept album *In My Life* (Chrysalis, 1999), in which various guests interpreted songs associated with Martin/The Beatles.

JIMMY MARTIN
b. 10 August 1927, Sneedville, Tennessee, USA

At his best a superb bluegrass lead singer, a strong guitarist and an extrovert front man, Martin never quite attained the status appropriate to his talents, partly because of personal abrasiveness and partly because he spent too much time trying to turn ephemeral novelties into surprise hits.

He began singing on the radio in 1948, and in 1949 was hired by **Bill Monroe** to replace **Mac Wiseman**. He worked with Monroe for two spells between 1949 and 1954, participating in several Decca recording sessions and singing the lead on sides like 'The Little Girl and the Dreadful Snake' and 'A Voice from on High'. It is doubtful if, Lester Flatt (of **Flatt and Scruggs**) aside, Monroe ever employed a better lead singer. He also worked in 1951–2 with Bobby Osborne of the **Osborne Brothers**, their King recordings of 'Blue-Eyed Darlin'' and 'You'll Never Be the Same' being superb examples of bluegrass duet-singing. Then, in 1954, after leaving Monroe, he worked with both Osbornes as the Sunny Mountain Boys, an exceptionally fine band captured on that year's RCA recordings '20/20 Vision' and 'Save It! Save It!'.

The Osbornes left him in 1955 and in 1956 Martin signed with Decca, while working on many of the leading radio shows, including the *Grand Ole Opry* and the *Louisiana Hayride*. His sound, which he characterized as 'good 'n' country' (also the title of an early Decca album), was developed in collaboration with such instrumentalists as mandolin-player Paul Williams and banjoist J. D. Crowe, who became a prominent bluegrass bandleader himself in the seventies and eighties. Others to have passed through the Martin band – the leader was reputedly hard to work for and the playing repetitious, and few stayed long – included Bill Emerson (banjo), Alan Munde (banjo), later a member of Country Gazette, Doyle Lawson (mandolin), whose Quicksilver was a leading bluegrass, and, in particular, bluegrass-gospel, group of the eighties. Among Martin's more successful Decca sides were 'Widow Maker' (1964), 'Sunny Side of the Mountain' (1965) and 'Freeborn Man' (1968). In 1976 he was dropped by MCA (Decca's new owners) and afterwards recorded for Gusto/Starday and Rounder (*You Don't Know My Mind*, 1990).

TONY MARTIN
b. Alvin Morris Jnr, 25 December 1912, Oakland, California, USA

A romantic balladeer, Martin began his career as a band singer in the thirties, graduated to romantic leads in Hollywood and had his greatest record success in the forties and early fifties.

Martin started out under his real name as a saxophonist in Anson Weeks' band in San Francisco in the early thirties and later played alongside **Woody Herman** in Tommy Gerun's band. He made his radio début as a singer on *The Lucky Strike Hour* and went to Hollywood in 1936. There, he starred in a string of light musicals, including *Sing Baby Sing* (1936), *Ziegfeld Girl* (1941), in which he introduced **Nacio Herb Brown** and **Gus Kahn**'s 'You Stepped out of a Dream', and *The Big Store*, in which he played the romantic lead to the Marx Brothers' inspired lunacy and sang 'The Tenement Symphony'. He recorded with **Ray Noble** on Columbia before his first chart success, **Freddy Martin** and Bobby Worth's 'Tonight We Love' (Decca, 1941), which had been featured in the 1938 film, *Romance in the Dark*. After the war he had even greater success with 'To Each His Own'* (Mercury, 1946), before joining RCA in 1948. Though his screen career faltered in the early fifties, he had continued record success with his version of **Edith Piaf**'s 'La Vie en Rose' (1950), 'I Get Ideas' (1951) and the dramatic 'Kiss of Fire' (1952). His last major hit was 'Walk Hand in Hand' (1956).

In the sixties Martin formed a double act with his wife Cyd Charisse and the pair toured the cabaret circuit. In 1976 they published an autobiography, *The Two of Us*.

AL MARTINO
b. Alfred Cini, 7 October 1927, Philadelphia, Pennsylvania, USA

The coolest of the dramatic Italian balladeers to emerge in the fifties, Martino most closely identified with his background. Thus, it was fitting that he was chosen for the role of Johnny Fontane, the popular Italian singer (reputedly based on **Frank Sinatra**), in Francis Ford Coppola's *The Godfather* (1971).

The son of Italian immigrants, Martino was a boyhood friend of **Mario Lanza** who encouraged him to become a singer. After appearing in local nightclubs, he recorded 'Here in My Heart'* for the small BBS label in 1952. The record topped both the American and British charts and won Martino a contract with Capitol. His old-fashioned style denied him further significant record success in America throughout the fifties, though he continued to chart in Britain ('Now', 1953; 'Wanted', 1954; 'The Man from Laramie', 1955 – a bigger hit for Jimmy Young). His career was revived by a version of Leon Payne's 1949 country hit, 'I Love You Because' (1961) and 'I Love You More and More Every Day' (1964). In 1965 he had his biggest hit, 'Spanish Eyes'*, when Eddie Snyder wrote an English lyric to a tune written and recorded by **Bert Kaempfert** as 'Moon Over Naples'.

A star attraction of the cabaret circuit after his role

in *The Godfather*, he further consolidated his once more fashionable Italian image with 'To the Door of the Sun (Alla Porte del Sol)' and a remake of **Domenico Modugno**'s 'Volare' (1975).

THE MARVELETTES
Katherine Anderson, b. 1944; Juanita Cowart, b. 1944; Georgeanna Tillman, b. 1944, d. 6 January 1980, Detroit, Michigan, USA; Gladys Horton, b. 1944 (replaced by Anne Bogan); Wanda Young, b. 1944

After the **Supremes**, the Marvelettes were the most successful female group on **Berry Gordy**'s Motown roster during the sixties. Unlike their sweet-voiced colleagues, however, their records often retained the rough edges of R&B and gospel singing.

Formed at Inkster High School in Detroit as the Casinyets, the Marvelettes gave Gordy his first American No. 1 with 'Please Mr Postman' (Tamla, 1961), which featured Horton's gospel-tinged lead singing. **The Beatles** covered the song on *With the Beatles* (1964), and it reached No. 1 again when revived by the **Carpenters** in 1975.

Following the departure of Tillman and Cowart, the Marvelettes' career was masterminded by **Holland, Dozier and Holland**, who wrote and produced the group's Top Twenty singles, 'Playboy' and 'Beechwood 4-5789', in 1962. The Marvelettes continued to have R&B hits with 'Someday Someway', 'Strange I Know' and 'I'll Keep Holding on' (1965), but their next major pop success came in 1966 with the softer 'Don't Mess Around with Bill', written by **Smokey Robinson**. This was recorded after they had rejected 'Baby Love', which became a massive hit for the Supremes.

Robinson supplied further pop hits with 'The Hunter Gets Captured by the Game' (1967) and 'My Baby Must Be a Magician' (1968). The group's only British success came with **Van McCoy**'s languorous ballad 'When You're Young and in Love' (1967). In 1969 Horton was replaced by a new lead singer, Bogan, and with further changes in personnel the Marvelettes continued to tour during the seventies. Unlike **Gladys Knight and the Pips**, however, they seemed unable to adapt to the new trends in black music.

In 1989 original members Rogan and Horton plus Echo Johnson and Jean McLain recorded in disco mode for Ian Levine's British-based Motor City Records ('Holding on with Both Hands' and *Now*).

HUGH MASEKELA
b. 4 April 1939, Witbank, Johannesburg, South Africa

An exile for thirty years, trumpeter Hugh Masekela did most to introduce South African township jazz to foreign audiences. His most popular work mixed African jazz with Western pop or rock elements.

Masekela's early influences were **Louis Armstrong**, **Count Basie** and **Duke Ellington**. As a boy, he was a gifted soccer player as well as a musician and his first trumpet was provided by Father Trevor Huddleston, a radical priest who was later expelled from South Africa and became a British bishop. He formed the Merry Makers of Spring in 1955, but as apartheid was strictly enforced the band found it increasingly difficult to travel and find venues, and in 1958 Masekela folded the band. He joined various African jazz and variety package tours before finding a job in the pit orchestra of the hit musical *King Kong* (1959) which starred **Miriam Makeba**, whom he later married. In 1959 he founded the Jazz Epistles. They quickly became the country's leading jazz group. Members included pianist Dollar Brand (**Abdullah Ibrahim**).

In 1960, after the Sharpeville Massacre, Masekela left South Africa to study music in London, where he played with **John Dankworth** and **Cleo Laine**. Under a scholarship scheme initiated by **Harry Belafonte**, he travelled to New York to study at the Manhattan School of Music from 1964 to 1967. He also started recording. Albums from this period include *Trumpet Africa* (1962), *The Americanization of Oooga Booga* (1964) and *The Emancipation of Hugh Masekela* (1966). He appeared at the 1967 Monterey Pop Festival and formed his own label, Chisa, to release such records as 'Grazing in the Grass'*, a 1968 instrumental hit. With lyrics by Harry Elston the song was also a million-seller for the Friends of Distinction on RCA the following year.

During the seventies Masekela worked frequently in Africa, playing in Nigeria and Ghana with **Fela Kuti**'s Africa 70 and recording *I Am Not Afraid* with Ghanaian Afro-rock band Hedzoleh Sounds. He was briefly signed to Motown (*Reconstruction*, 1970). He recorded with London-based South African exile Dudu Pukwana (*Home Is Where the Music Is*, Chisa, 1972) and **Herb Alpert** (*Alpert and Masekela*, A&M, 1978).

In the eighties he performed in Zimbabwe and in Botswana, where he set up a recording studio to make *Technobush* (Jive Africa, 1984) with his Kalahari Band. While some of Masekela's records have been criticized for blandness, the strengths of his fusion of Jo'burg township jazz and Afro-beat dance rhythms was evident on *Tomorrow* (Warners, 1987), which featured 'Bring Him Back Home', dedicated to the imprisoned nationalist leader Nelson Mandela. In 1987 he toured with Makeba and **Paul Simon**, who had recorded most of *Graceland* with South African musicians. This led to further Masekela records for Jive (*Waiting for the Rain*, 1988) and Novus. In 1989 he wrote the music to the township musical *Sarafina*, which was filmed in 1992 with Whoopi Goldberg, and released *Up Township*.

Masekela first returned to South Africa in 1990 and in 1993 made *Hope*, a live recording of some of his most famous tunes with an all-star band of South African musicians. He followed that with *Black to the Future* (Triloka, 1996), recorded with a new generation of South African musicians.

MASSIVE ATTACK
Daddy G., b. Grant Marshall, 1959; 3D, b. Robert del Naja, 1966; Mushroom, b. Adrian Vowles, 1968, Bristol, England

Massive Attack were one of the most important UK recording groups of the nineties. The band drew on a wide variety of sources, including US hip-hop, Jamaican reggae, soul, funk and even punk, as the basis for their hugely influential sound.

The band had its origins in the Wild Bunch, a New York-style sound system that developed out of the legendary Bristol club, the Dug Out, in the early eighties. Marshall was already established as a DJ at the club, and formed the original Wild Bunch line-up with Miles Johnson and Nellee Hooper. Hooper would later go on to form another sound system collective, **Soul II Soul**, in London with Jazzie B. To that original Wild Bunch trio was added del Naja, a noted local graffiti artist and aspiring rapper, and later still the younger Vowles, a hip-hop fanatic.

The Wild Bunch played the Dug Out, organized warehouse parties around Bristol, and also played at parties in London. After a Wild Bunch trip to Japan in 1987, del Naja was thrown out of the group and Johnson and Hooper signed a deal with Island as the Wild Bunch, recording two singles, 'The Look of Love' and 'Friends and Countrymen', which were released in the US. A row between Johnson and Hooper saw the latter join up with Jazzie B to form Soul II Soul, while Johnson returned to Japan and then moved to New York.

Back in Bristol, meanwhile, del Naja, Vowles and Marshall decided to form Massive Attack, originally conceived as a Soul II Soul offshoot to be produced by Hooper. The trio signed a management deal and financed a single, 'Any Love', on their own label in 1988. A recording deal with Virgin followed, and in 1991 the band released their début album, *Blue Lines*. The album put on record much of the original Wild Bunch style and sound – reggae and hip-hop beats, breaks and samples from Marshall's extensive record collection, and rapping from 3D, Marshall and another collaborator, Tricky (*b. 1964*). In addition, the album featured singers Shara Nelson and veteran reggae vocalist Horace Andy. Nelson lent her powerful and emotive voice to two singles from the album, 'Safe from Harm' and the classic 'Unfinished Sympathy', which was later remixed to devastating effect for the

clubs by **Paul Oakenfold**. The album was a commercial success, and was viewed critically as a landmark in British black music. Its marriage of US hip-hop techniques with reggae and soul stylings gave it a very contemporary, but also very non-American, feel.

After *Blue Lines*, Massive Attack parted company with Nelson, who signed with Cooltempo, releasing *Down That Road* (1993) and *Friendly Fire* (1995). Two of the best British soul albums of the nineties, they were notable for Nelson's fine melodies, intelligent lyrics and innovative choice of songwriting collaborators. Nelson subsequently worked with UK deep-house guru Charlie Webster as Presence, releasing the single 'Sense of Danger' in 1999.

Massive Attack returned with *Protection* (1994), an altogether lusher set than their début, which met with commercial success but more restrained critical approval. The album, produced by Nellee Hooper, featured Nicolette and **Everything But the Girl**'s Tracey Thorn on vocals, as well as Andy on an eccentric cover of the **Doors**' 'Light My Fire'. Another key collaborator was the film composer Craig Armstrong, who added exquisite string arrangements and piano melodies to two tracks. The band released another version of the album, *No Protection*, remixed by dub reggae DJ the Mad Professor, in 1995. Another lengthy silence ensued before a new single, 'Risingson', saw the light of day in 1997. The track hinted at a yet darker sound, and this was confirmed with *Mezzanine* (1998). Far more sombre than its predecessors, the album almost entirely buried the band's dance music background beneath – on several tracks – layers of heavy, sinister rock guitar. The set again featured Andy on vocals plus two more new singers, Sara Jay and the **Cocteau Twins**' Liz Fraser. Fraser featured on the single 'Teardrop', a UK hit. Other singles from the album were 'Angel' and 'Inertia Creeps'.

MASTERS AT WORK
Lil' Louis Vega; Kenny 'Dope' Gonzalez

New York's Masters at Work were the leading house and garage remix and production team of the nineties, mixing irresistible swinging house rhythms with a feeling for live instrumentation which drew widely on black musical history. Moreover, Masters at Work were an important influence on the 'nu-house' trend in UK dance music towards the end of the nineties, most notably on the work of producers like Ashley Beedle and Basement Jaxx.

Vega grew up in the Bronx and Gonzalez grew up in Brooklyn. Both were of Puerto Rican parentage. In the early eighties Vega and Gonzalez were noted DJs around New York, though Vega was immersed in house, garage and Latin music while Gonzalez was strictly a hip-hop fan. Gonzalez was working as a mobile DJ under the name Masters at Work and had founded his own Dope Wax label. He worked on production for a number of major New York dance labels, including Strictly Rhythm and Nervous, and in 1987 loaned out the Masters at Work name to **Todd Terry** for the 1987 single 'Alright Alright'. In return Terry introduced Gonzalez to Vega. The pair decided that their contrasting musical interests might be more than the sum of their parts and released their first joint production, 'Blood Vibes', on Cutting Records in 1991 and subsequently an eponymous album later that year on the same label. The album featured vocalists including Jocelyn Brown and Vega's wife India, as well as guest roles for producers Terry and Maurice Joshua.

The pair enhanced their reputation over the next few years by several high profile remixes, working the MAW magic on mainstream pop artists such as **Michael Jackson**, **Madonna**, **Deee-Lite**, **Lisa Stansfield** and, perhaps most notably, **St Etienne** for 'Only Love Can Break Your Heart'. At the same time the pair's profile outside the club circuit began to develop with their first recording as Nu Yorican Soul, 'The Nervous Track' (1993), a stunning achievement that mixed sophisticated Latin percussion into a throbbing 4:4 groove. They followed that with 'Love and Happiness' (recorded as River Ocean) and 'I Can't Get No Sleep', the latter two featuring vocals from Vega's wife India. Gonzalez found equal commercial success with his Bucketheads side project, which enjoyed huge club and pop hits in 1995 with the Chicago-sampling 'The Bomb (These Sounds Fall into My Mind)' and 'Got Myself Together'.

'Nervous' attracted the interest of UK Talkin Loud owner Gilles Peterson, who encouraged the pair to complete a Nu Yorican Soul album. The resulting set, *Nu Yorican Soul* (1997), won unanimous critical acclaim and was the most eloquent artistic statement yet by the pair. The album featured guest appearances from a number of black music legends, including **Roy Ayers** (on a re-recording of 'Sweet Tears'), **George Benson**, **Tito Puente**, Dave Valentin and Jocelyn Brown. Hits from the album included 'You Can Do It Baby', a collaboration with Benson, 'Runaway', featuring India on vocals again, and 'I Am the Black Gold of the Sun', which, like 'Runaway', was a reworking of a seventies classic and was remixed beautifully by UK drum'n'bass crew 4 Hero.

The pair's collaborations with India continued with 'To Be in Love', also in 1997, and 'I Love the Night Life', a cover of Alycia Bridges' disco classic which featured in the film *Last Days of Disco*. The richness of their talent was further demonstrated on their version of 'Pienso en Ti', which showed a skilful handling of Latin-style percussion arrangements. Exquisitely realized collaborations with the stars continued into the new millennium, notably with Benson on a cover of

Donny Hathaway's 1970s soul anthem 'The Ghetto', and with Roy Ayers and former **Shalamar** vocalist Jody Watley on 'I Love to Love'.

JOHNNY MATHIS
b. 30 September 1935, San Francisco, California, USA

The master of love balladry, or as one writer more forcefully put it, 'The King of Necking Music', Mathis had a tender, slightly husky voice and sang in a manner akin to the later **Nat 'King' Cole**. At his best – on tracks like 'The Twelfth of Never' (1957), 'A Certain Smile' (1958) and 'Misty' (1959), aided by **Mitch Miller**'s ethereal soundscapes – Mathis created a magical, private other world for his listeners in which young love would always endure.

The son of a vaudevillian, Mathis, though he sang from an early age, was an outstanding athlete and planned a career in physical education before he was signed to Columbia by George Avakian in 1955. He recorded unsuccessfully in a jazz vein until Miller, Columbia's head of A&R, took control of his career. In contrast to his dramatic productions for **Frankie Laine** and others, Miller gave Mathis caressing love songs and surrounded them with sympathetic sounds that highlighted Mathis's poignant reading of the lyrics. The result was a series of huge hits, commencing with 'Wonderful! Wonderful!'* (1956), 'It's Not for Me to Say' and the classic double-sided disc, 'Chances Are'/'Twelfth of Never'* (1957), that stretched to 1963. Other major records included 'Come to Me', the tremulous 'A Certain Smile' (1958), co-written by **Sammy Fain**, **Erroll Garner**'s 'Misty' (1959), 'Gina' (1962) and 'What Will Mary Say' (1963).

More revealing of Mathis's huge appeal to young lovers was the phenomenal success of *Johnny Mathis' Greatest Hits** (1958). One of the first 'greatest hits' albums, it was released when Mathis's busy schedule prevented him recording a new album and remained on the *Billboard* charts for almost ten years. It was followed by *Heavenly** (1959) which was almost as successful. However, though hugely popular in live performance, Mathis's lack of singles' success led him to leave Columbia briefly for Mercury in 1963.

On his return to Columbia, he started regularly recording and performing contemporary material – most of his previous recordings had been of songs by veteran Tin Pan Alley songsmiths – by such writers as **Carole King** ('It's Too Late') and **Carlos Santana** ('Evil Ways'). The culmination of this development was his American No. 1, 'Too Much, Too Little, Too Late'* (1978), a duet with Deniece Williams. A one-time member of **Stevie Wonder**'s Wonderlove backing group, Williams had earlier had a hit with 'Free' (Columbia, 1977) and later had her own million-seller with 'Let's Hear It for the Boy' (1984), the theme song from the film *Footloose*. The Mathis and Williams' pairing was one of the first of many; in the eighties the strategy became an established industry marketing ploy to aid flagging careers and extend the audience for newer signings. Mathis himself was paired with Paulette McWilliams and Angela Bofill before returning to the charts with **Dionne Warwick** ('Friends in Love', 1982). His later albums included *The Hollywood Musicals* (1986, with **Henry Mancini**) and *Once in a While* (1988). He continued to tour and record in the nineties (*In a Sentimental Mood*, 1990, and *Better Together*, 1991, a collection of duets).

KATHY MATTEA
b. 21 June 1959, Cross Lanes, West Virginia, USA

One of the most consistent younger country singer-songwriters, Kathy Mattea has developed a country-pop style in the tradition of **Crystal Gayle** and **Lynn Anderson**.

Mattea sang in a bluegrass band at college before moving to Nashville in 1982. There she worked as a guide at the Country Music Hall of Fame and as a session singer before signing a recording contract with Mercury. Allen Reynolds produced *Kathy Mattea* (1985) and *From My Heart* (1985) but her commercial breakthrough came with the far folkier acoustic album *Walk the Way the Wind Blows* (1986), whose hits included **Nanci Griffith**'s 'Love at the Five and Dime' and 'Train of Memories'.

Her first country No. 1 was 'Goin' Gone' in 1988 from the album *Untasted Honey*. That also included the equally successful 'Eighteen Wheels and a Dozen Roses', a trucking song by Paul and Gene Nelson. In the same year she married songwriter Jon Venzer, who became her regular writing partner. *Willow in the Wind* (1989) included 'Come from the Heart', 'Burnin' Old Memories' and 'She Came from Fort Worth'.

Her subsequent albums include *Time Passes By* (1991), which included her version of 'From a Distance', *Lonesome Standard Time* (1993), made after she had vocal-chord surgery and which drew on her bluegrass background, and *Walking Away a Winner* (1994), of which the title track was one of her biggest hits of the decade. A regular campaigner for AIDS awareness (which was not common among country acts) in 1994 she also helped organize and appeared on the AIDS charity album, *Red Hot & Country*. She recorded less frequently thereafter. Later albums included *Love Travels* (1997).

IAN MATTHEWS
b. Ian Matthews MacDonald, 16 June 1946, Lincolnshire, England

Though none of his solo albums matched the commercial success of his work with **Fairport Convention** or Matthews Southern Comfort, with his tenor voice and penchant for sensitive, wistful songs Matthews was one of the most intelligent singer-songwriters to emerge in the seventies.

After recording with the **Beach Boys**-styled the Pyramid for Deram ('Summer of Last Year', 1967) Matthews joined Fairport Convention, leaving the group in 1969 when it started to emphasize traditional folk material, rather than the folk-rock that had brought its initial success. He formed Matthews Southern Comfort and made a trio of accomplished country-rock albums (*Matthews' Southern Comfort*, which included 'I've Lost You', a hit for **Elvis Presley** in 1970; *Later That Year* and *Second Spring*, Uni, 1970). Many of the songs on these albums were pseudonymously written and produced by Ken Howard and Alan Blaikley, who were better known for their work with **Dave Dee, Dozy, Beaky, Mick and Tich**. However, Matthews Southern Comfort had their greatest success with **Joni Mitchell**'s anthemic 'Woodstock', which topped the British charts in 1971. This came just before Matthews left the group for a solo career. That resulted in two albums for Vertigo, *If You Saw Thro' My Eyes* and *Tigers Will Survive* (which gave the singer a minor hit with his *a cappella* version of the **Crystals**' 'Da Doo Ron Ron') in 1971, and established Matthews' low-key approach. In 1972 he formed the shortlived Plainsong with guitarist Andy Roberts and recorded the concept album *In Search of Amelia Earhart* (Elektra, 1972), an album inspired by the story of the American aviator.

In 1973 Matthews settled in America where he recorded the superior *Valley Hi* (produced by former **Monkee** Mike Nesmith for his own Countryside label) and the self-produced *Somedays You Eat the Bear* (1974). Both mixed Matthews' own compositions (notably 'Keep on Sailing' and 'The Fault') with some of the best songs by contemporary writers, including **Jackson Browne**'s 'These Days', **Richard Thompson**'s 'Shady Lies', Steve Young's 'Seven Bridges Road', **Tom Waits**' 'Ol' 55' and **Jesse Winchester**'s 'Biloxi'. Though these were critical successes, they failed comñercially and Matthews adopted a more up-tempo sound for *Go for Broke* (Columbia, 1976), which even included a brash version of **Van Morrison**'s 'Brown-Eyed Girl'. His only major chart success came in 1978, with 'Shake It' from his début album for producer Sandy Roberton's independent Rockburgh Records, *Stealin' Home*, made on his return to Britain. Further releases included the folky *Siamese Friends* (1979) and *Discreet Repeat* (1980), a compilation of his recording history that emphasized its richness. It remains the definitive Matthews retrospective.

In the eighties Matthews turned to A&R work until

in 1988 he was the first vocalist to record for Windham Hill, the New Age label founded by **Will Ackerman**. *Walking a Changing Line* was a selection of songs by Jules Shear.

Matthews moved to Austin, Texas, in 1989, releasing a cassette-only, live album with guitarist Mark Hallman, *Ian Matthews Live* (1989). Matthews next signed to the Goldcastle label in 1990. He released the albums *Pure and Crooked* (1990), *Nights in Manhattan – Live* (1991) and *Orphans and Outcasts Vol. 1*, before the label closed down. A second volume of *Orphans and Outcasts* was issued by American magazine Dirty Linen in 1993. In 1992, with former Plainsong colleague Roberts, who had played with Matthews at the Cambridge Folk Festival in 1990, he released the album *Dark Side of the Room* as Plainsong. Later that year, he released *Skeleton Keys* on American independent label Mesa. Tinged with melancholy ('Living in Reverse', 'Compass and Chart') it was hailed as his best work in years. In 1994 he released the superior *The Dark Ride* (Watermelon), which included a reworking of **Tim Buckley**'s 'Morning Glory' and a sequel to his own 'Tigers Will Survive', 'Darcy's Song'. He followed that with the acoustic *The Tiniest Wham* (Perfect Pitch, 2000). In addition to his studied melancholy ('Secret Storm') the album showed Matthews adept at nimble wordplay (in the manner of performers like **Dan Hicks** and **Danny O'Keefe**) on songs like 'Sister' and 'The Power and the Glory'.

Excerpts from Swine Lake (1998) is a retrospective of his later work.

JESSIE MATTHEWS
b. 11 March 1907, London, England, d. 20 August 1981, London

The star of West End and film musicals in the thirties when she was known for her graceful dancing and tremulous singing, Matthews won new acclaim in the sixties in the title role of the long-running BBC radio soap opera, *Mrs Dale's Diary*.

Born in London's Soho district, Matthews made her first professional stage appearance at the age of ten and throughout her teens appeared in the choruses of London revues. She appeared on Broadway when British-based impresario André Charlot took his revue to New York in 1924 and starred in the Charlot-produced 'international edition' of *Earl Carroll's Vanities* (1927) and *Wake Up and Dream!* (1930). Her greatest success, however, came in Britain, notably in *This Year of Grace!* (1928), in which she introduced **Noël Coward**'s 'Room With a View', and Richard Rodgers' (later of **Rodgers and Hammerstein**) and **Lorenz Hart**'s *Ever Green* (1930), in which she sang 'Over My Shoulder' – later to become her theme song and the title of her 1974 autobiography –

and 'When You've Got a Little Springtime in Your Heart'. In 1931 she made her first major film, *Out of the Blue*, and went on to make some twenty more, including her greatest success, *Evergreen* (1934, a reworking of *Ever Green*), *Head over Heels* (1936), in which she sang 'May I Have the Next Romance with You', *Sailing Along* (1938) and *Tom Thumb* (1958).

When her career as a musical star came to an end, Matthews found renewed success on radio when in 1963 she took over the title role in the long-running *Mrs Dale's Diary* – the show was first broadcast in 1948 – for its last six years.

BILLY MAY
b. William E. May, 10 November 1916, Pittsburgh, Pennysylvania, USA

Trumpeter, composer, bandleader and arranger, May is best remembered for his arrangements for **Frank Sinatra**, notably the influential *Come Fly with Me* (1958) which included the singer's classic recordings of 'Moonlight in Vermont' and 'It's Nice to Go Traveling'.

May made his professional début with Gene Olson's Polish-American Orchestra in 1933. He worked as a trumpeter and arranger with **Charlie Barnet** (1938–9), for whom he arranged 'Cherokee' and wrote 'Wings over Manhattan', **Glenn Miller** (1940–2), playing the trumpet solo on the classic 'American Patrol', and Alvino Rey, before in the early forties settling in Hollywood where he worked with **Rick Nelson**'s father Ozzie and **Phil Harris**. He recorded for Capitol and had a Top Fifty hit with the theme from *The Man with the Golden Arm* (1956). *Naughty Operetta* (1955) featured his witty, modern arrangements of songs from the world of operetta. Among the musicians in his studio orchestras were Maynard Ferguson, Si Zentner, Barney Kessel and Alvin Stoller. May briefly formed his own band and acted in (and did the arrangements for) the film *Nightmare* (1956) but by the end of the fifties he had settled down to a career as a freelance arranger, working with **Anita O'Day**, **Nat 'King' Cole**, **Peggy Lee**, **Mel Tormé** and **Sinatra**, among others. In 1985 he recorded a 'reunion' album with members of his orchestras, *You May Swing* (Intersound).

JOHN MAYALL
b. 29 November 1933, Macclesfield, Cheshire, England

With **Alexis Korner**'s Blues Incorporated, John Mayall's Bluesbreakers played a central role in British R&B in the sixties, at different times including such figures as **Eric Clapton** and the founders of **Fleetwood Mac**. With their leaders' unwavering commitment to the blues, both bands schooled a generation of musicians.

Unlike Korner, however, Mayall persevered with the blues-band formula well into the nineties.

After national service in the RAF, Mayall attended art school, and in the mid-fifties formed the Powerhouse Four, a group which in 1961 became the Blues Syndicate. Encouraged by Korner, Mayall moved to London and formed his first Bluesbreakers with John McVie (bass), Bernie Watson (guitar) and Martin Hart (drums), who was soon replaced by the Blues Syndicate's Hughie Flint. Signed to Decca, Mayall released the **Mike Vernon**-produced 'Crawling Up a Hill' (1964), featuring his organ and harmonica-playing. Mayall was virtually alone among the burgeoning white rhythm and blues artists of the period in writing his own material, something highlighted on the live album *John Mayall Plays John Mayall* (1965), on which Roger Dean played guitar.

The Bluesbreakers' greatest popular success came soon afterwards when Clapton replaced Dean. Having left the **Yardbirds** because they were becoming too pop-orientated, the guitarist eagerly agreed to join one of the most uncompromising R&B groups on the circuit. *Blues Breakers – John Mayall with Eric Clapton* (1966) was both an artistic and commercial triumph, reaching the Top Ten. An intense and skilful attempt to re-create contemporary black American R&B, the album was notable for the slow blues 'Have You Heard', which featured Mayall's strangled falsetto (*à la* **Otis Rush**) and Clapton's articulate, immaculate guitar solo.

Later in 1966 Mayall and Clapton cut 'Lonely Years' for Vernon's Purdah label and Mayall played all the instruments on *The Blues Alone* (1967) before Clapton left to form **Cream**. His replacement was Peter Green from Shotgun Express, and Aynsley Dunbar, formerly with such Liverpool groups as the Merseysippi Jazz Band and the Mojos, took over on drums when Flint joined Korner and then set up McGuinness Flint. A more controlled, economical player than Clapton, Green's début on *A Hard Road* (1967) was nonetheless impressive on such tracks as **Freddie King**'s 'The Stumble' and that album too reached the Top Ten. The best Mayall–Green collaboration, though, came on the guitarist's last single with the group, which coupled **Elmore James**' 'It Hurts Me Too' with Rush's 'Double Trouble' (1967).

Mayall's decision to record these songs was part of his determination that black Americans should get due recognition from white blues audiences, a policy he spelt out on *Crusade* (1967), which included material by **Buddy Guy** and **Albert King**, among others. This album featured the eighteen-year-old Mick Taylor from the Gods on guitar, drummer Keef Hartley, and sax-players Chris Mercer and Rip Kant. Over the next year the turnover of musicians increased while Mayall released two albums. The double *Diary of a*

Band was a curious mixture of live recordings and such documentary material as tuning-up sessions and on-stage witticisms, while *Bare Wires* mixed semi-confessional Mayall compositions with a jazz-inflected group including future **Colosseum** players Dick Heckstall-Smith, Jon Hiseman and Tony Reeves.

The autobiographical approach formed the basis of *Blues from Laurel Canyon* (1968), a virtual diary of a trip to California. The record marked the end of the first phase of Mayall's career. With the expiry of his contract with Decca, he decided to drop the Bluesbreakers name and the last of his superhero guitarists graduated as Taylor left to join the **Rolling Stones**.

Now signed to Polydor, Mayall dropped electric guitar and drums altogether on the aptly named *The Turning Point* (1969), which was recorded by a quartet including Johnny Almond (saxes, flute) and acoustic guitarist John Mark. The album also contained the first of a long line of sermonizing lyrics with 'The Laws Must Change', which was followed by 'Plan Your Revolution' on *Empty Rooms* (1970), and 'Nature's Disappearing' from *USA Union* (1970). The latter title referred both to Mayall's decision to base himself in California and to his use of an all-American band, comprising ex-**Don and Dewey** violinist Don Harris and former **Canned Heat** musicians Harvey Mandel (guitar) and Larry Taylor (bass). *Back to the Roots* (1971) was an uneasy rendezvous of some of Mayall's former sidemen (Clapton, Taylor, Almond, Hartley) with his new style of songs ('Mr Censor Man', 'Television Eye').

For the next few years, Mayall was intent on a *Jazz-Blues Fusion*, the title of a 1972 live album made with former **Stan Getz** trumpeter Blue Mitchell and blues guitarist Freddie Robinson. This group also made *Moving on* and *Ten Years Are Gone* (1973). With Mayall's flair for choosing precise if banal titles, *New Year, New Band, New Company* (1975) announced his move to ABC with a band which for the first time included another vocalist, Dee McKinnie, who also featured on the **Allen Toussaint** production *Notice to Appear* (1975) and *Banquet in Blues* (1976). After cutting a final album for ABC, *Last of the British Blues* (1978), Mayall signed to **Dick James**' DJM label, for whom he recorded three albums in 1979–81.

In 1982 Mayall made a brief Bluesbreakers reunion tour of America and Australia with McVie and Taylor before forming a new Bluesbreakers with guitarists Coco Montoya and Walter Trout, bassist Bobby Haynes and drummer Joe Yuele. They recorded two live albums before Mayall signed to Island and released *Chicago Line* (1988), again featuring Montoya. Trout went to go on to enjoy a successful solo career with albums on the Provogue label. In 1990 Mayall released his second Island album, *A Sense of Place*, a minor hit in America. He continued to tour and recorded *Wake Up Call* (Silvertone, 1993). With contributions from guitarists **Buddy Guy**, Mick Taylor, Coco Montoya and singer Mavis Staples (of the **Staple Singers**), it was acclaimed as his best album for many years. He followed it with two lesser outings on Silvertone, *Spinning Coin* (1995) and *Blues for the Lost Days* (1998).

Mayall's son Gaz became a London disc-jockey and label owner (Gaz's Rockin' Records) in the late eighties, releasing mainly ska revival material.

CURTIS MAYFIELD

b. 3 June 1942, Chicago, Illinois USA, d. 26 December 1999, Roswell, Georgia

One of the giants of black music, Mayfield has had a prolific career as singer, composer and label owner since leaving the **Impressions** in 1970.

Mayfield's first solo album, *Curtis* (1970), spawned the European (but not American) hit 'Move on Up', but his biggest success came with *Superfly* (1972), the soundtrack to the blaxploitation movie of the same name. An impressionistic meld of Mayfield's falsetto and percussive effects bound tightly together, the album produced two million-sellers for Mayfield, 'Freddie's Dead' and 'Superfly' (1972), and opened the door for a series of inferior soundtrack albums (including *Let's Do It Again*, 1975, and *Short Eyes*, 1977, in which he also appeared). For the most part, Mayfield's albums of the seventies and eighties were similarly flawed, his often incisive lyrics ('There's No Place Like America Today', 1975, and 'Dirty Laundry', 1982) spoiled by clichéd arrangements and backings.

In 1983 he joined forces with Butler, Cash and Gooden for a successful Impressions twenty-fifth anniversary tour. While the Impressions were later regulars on the cabaret circuit, Mayfield played small clubs in both Europe and America as a solo act, reworking his past hits more in the manner of a **Bob Dylan** than a soul star. In 1989 he released *Something to Believe in* (Curtom), which included both a reworking of 'It's All Right' and the poignant, Impressions-like ballad 'Never Let Me Go'.

In 1990 Mayfield was paralyzed from the neck down after an on-stage accident, but he continued to record and work on new projects. Two tribute albums to Mayfield were subsequently compiled. *People Get Ready* (Shanachie) was released in 1993, featuring contributions from a cast of artists which included **Huey Lewis and the News**, Bunny Wailer and **Jerry Butler**. **Bruce Springsteen**, **Whitney Houston**, **Elton John** and **Aretha Franklin** contributed to a similar 1994 compilation, *A Tribute to Curtis Mayfield* (Warner). The definitive career retrospective is *People Get Ready!* (Rhino, 1996), and in the same year Mayfield recorded the well-received *New World Order*.

PERCY MAYFIELD

b. 12 August 1920, Minden, Louisiana, USA, d. 11 August 1984, Los Angeles, California

Mayfield was among the most poetic of blues composers, writing such R&B standards as 'Please Send Me Someone to Love', 'Hit the Road Jack' and 'River's Invitation'.

He grew up in Houston and moved to Los Angeles where he approached the Supreme label with songs intended for **Jimmy Witherspoon**. Instead, Mayfield himself recorded 'Half Awake' and 'Two Years of Torture'. The records' success led to a contract with **Art Rupe**'s Specialty label where **Maxwell Davis** produced 'Please Send Me Someone to Love' (1950). The song was a No. 1 R&B hit and for two years Mayfield was one of the West Coast's leading black singing stars. His other hits from 1951–2 included 'Lost Love', 'What a Fool I Was', 'Cry Baby' and 'The Big Question', while he also composed such classic blues as 'Strange Things Happening' and 'Life is Suicide'.

At the height of his popularity, Mayfield suffered severe facial injuries in a car accident. His live performances were curtailed and he concentrated on songwriting, while continuing to record between 1955 and 1960 for Chess, Cash, Imperial and Seven Arts. Mayfield's most productive period as a writer, however, was the early sixties when he composed exclusively for **Ray Charles**, producing a body of work now considered pivotal to the development of soul music. Among the Charles material were 'Hit the Road Jack', 'Hide Nor Hair' and 'Danger Zone'.

When Charles set up his Tangerine label in 1962, Mayfield released *My Jug and I* which spawned 'River's Invitation', his first R&B hit for a decade. He next recorded for Brunswick and then cut three albums for RCA, including *Weakness Is a Thing Called Man* (1970) and *Blues and Then Some* (1971), and had a minor hit with 'To Live in the Past' (1970). His final release for a major label was a mid-seventies single produced by **Johnny 'Guitar' Watson** for Atlantic.

With the eighties revival of interest in West Coast blues, Mayfield toured Europe in 1982 and was gaining renewed attention in America at the time of his death.

MAZE FEATURING FRANKIE BEVERLY

Frankie Beverly, b. Philadelphia, Pennsylvania, USA; Vernon Black; William Bryant; Robin Duhe; Wayne Linsey; Roame Lowery; Ron Smith; Billy Johnson; McKinley Williams

Featuring the classic soul vocals of bandleader and composer Beverly, Maze represents a late flowering of the R&B revue stage extravaganza. The group has retained a loyal following in the US and Europe for two decades.

During the late sixties Beverly was a popular figure on the Philadelphia soul scene, performing as Frank Beverly and the Butlers and recording with singers/percussionists Lowry and Williams as Raw Soul for producers **Kenny Gamble** and **Leon Huff**.

The trio moved to San Francisco where they formed the nine-piece Maze. Among the group's members over the next decade were keyboards-players Philip Woo, Linsey and Bryant, former **Patti Labelle** guitarist Smith and Duhe (bass). The band toured with **Marvin Gaye** (one of the biggest influences on Beverly's vocal style) before signing to Capitol in 1976. A self-titled début album was followed in 1978 by *Golden Time of Day*, which reached the R&B Top Thirty. *Inspiration* (1979) and *Joy and Pain* (1980) were equally successful.

Frequently compared to **Earth, Wind and Fire**, Maze never achieved that band's success in attracting mainstream white audiences in the US but their impressive live shows were captured on *Live in New Orleans*. This double-album included several studio recordings, including the R&B hit 'Running Away'.

The group toured Japan and Europe regularly and they became cult favourites with UK clubgoers. Recordings of 'Before I Let You Go' and 'Golden Time of Day' from the band's London début in 1981 were issued as a single and *We Are One* (1983) was a Top Forty hit in Britain.

After releasing *Can't Stop the Love* (1985) and another live recording, Maze were inactive for a few years. In 1989 they returned to touring and signed to a new record label, Warner Bros. The title track of *Silky Soul* (1989) was Beverly's homage to Gaye and the album contained one of the most effective of Beverly's message songs, 'Mandela'. In the same year Capitol issued a Greatest Hits album which featured remixes of 'Joy and Pain' (with rapper **Kurtis Blow**) and 'Before I Let Go' by Hank Shocklee. The former was a minor hit in the UK when issued as a single.

In 1993 Maze issued *Back to Basics*, which included the single 'Laid Back Girl', and became one of the band's biggest R&B hits.

After leaving Maze, Wayne Linsey released *Perfect Love* (Virgin, 1992) with his wife, vocalist Lynne Fiddemont-Linsey.

MC5

Rob Tyner, b. 12 December 1944, Detroit, Michigan, USA, d. 17 September 1991, Detroit; Wayne Kramer, b. 30 April 1948; Fred 'Sonic' Smith, b. 1949, West Virginia, d. 6 November 1994, Detroit; Michael Davis; Dennis Thompson

The MC5, originally called the Motor City Five, represented a political strand of the underground music of the sixties and prefigured the concerns of the punk

movement of the seventies, when their albums found a new audience.

Formed in Detroit, the group became the house band for John Sinclair's revolutionary White Panther Party. Sinclair's sense of the outrageous – he had the band appearing on stage wearing American flags and shouting revolutionary slogans and profanities – won the group a contract with Elektra in 1968, after a performance in support of anti-war demonstrators at the Democratic Convention.

The result was *Kick Out the Jams* (1969), which caused controversy for its title track on which the group clearly sang 'Kick out the jams, motherfuckers' – eventually an alternative version of the song, substituting 'brothers and sisters' for the offending phrase, was released – and Sinclair's highly political sleeve note. The album was quickly deleted by Elektra and was only restored to the catalogue in the eighties. After Sinclair was jailed for marijuana possession the band, disillusioned with revolutionary fervour but still committed to the revolutionary power of rock'n'roll, signed to Atlantic and recorded *Back in the USA* (1970). Produced by rock critic Jon Landau (who later produced and managed **Bruce Springsteen**), the album's hard-edged, energetic sound won the group great acclaim, but like *High Time* (1971), it sold poorly and the group broke up in 1972.

The various members embarked on separate projects throughout the seventies. Kramer played guitar battles with **Ted Nugent** before being jailed on drugs charges in 1974, while Smith performed with (and in 1980 married) **Patti Smith**. He was working with Patti on a new album when he died of a heart attack in 1994. Bassist Davis played briefly with ex-Stooges Ron Asheton and James Williamson in Destroy All Monsters. But their greatest success came with the reissue of the band's first two albums in the aftermath of the punk movement which claimed them as heroes. However, unlike the similarly outrageous **Iggy Pop**, none of the former members of the MC5 was able to translate their cult status into pop success.

Both Kramer (*Wayne Kramer's Deathtongue*, 1992; *The Hard Stuff*, 1996 and *Citizen Wayne*, 1997) and Tyner (*Blood Brother*, 1991) made solo albums in the nineties. Tyner died shortly after writing the notes for the 1997 CD reissue of *Kick Out the Jams*. In 2000 Kramer joined online music company MusicBlitz.com as an artist, producer and A&R man. In this last capacity he signed former **Ramone** Dee Dee and Pere Ubu to the label.

MC SOLAAR
b. Claude M'Barali, 1969, Senegal

France's best-known rap artist, Solaar's work combined intelligent, fluid rhymes with a hip-hop backing which mixed funk beats and elements of the French *chanson* tradition.

Solaar grew up in a single-parent family in Paris, absorbing musical influences as diverse as **Serge Gainsbourg** and **Bob Marley**. Inspired by US models, he developed a rap style to deal with such topics as homelessness, fashion victims and unrequited love. Accompanied by the 501 Special Force Posse, Solaar made his first album for Polydor in 1990. Entitled *Qui Seme le Vent Recolte le Tempo*, the album produced four hit singles in France, but also gave Solaar a profile elsewhere in Europe, enhanced by a series of acclaimed live performances. Collaborations with other artists followed, including **Gang Starr**'s Guru on his Jazzmatazz project and UK hip-hop group Urban Species.

Solaar's début LP was picked up in the UK by Gilles Peterson's Talkin' Loud label, which also released its follow-up, *Prose Combat*, in 1994. Like his first, it was produced by DJ Jimmy Jay and Boom Bass (aka Hubert Blanc-Francard). Using acid-jazz rhythm tracks, Solaar's themes included the limits of stardom in 'Temps Mort' and street violence in 'La Concubine de l'Hemoglobine'. The album provided further French hits in 'Nouveau Western' and 'Obsolete'.

In 1995 Solaar fittingly provided one track, 'Comme Dans un Film', for the soundtrack of *La Haine*, a compelling slice of modern urban realism which dealt with the themes of inner-city despair and violence tackled by Solaar in his lyrics.

Solaar's third album, *Paradisiaque*, appeared on Mercury in 1997 and featured the hits 'Gangster Moderne' and 'Les Temps'. This was quickly followed up in 1998 by an eponymous (and very short, lasting 37 minutes) fourth studio album, and by a live album, *La Tour de La Question*.

MEAT LOAF
b. Marvin Lee Aday, 27 September 1947, Dallas, Texas, USA

A powerful heavy-rock singer, Meat Loaf came to prominence as a star of the *Rocky Horror Picture Show* (1975), a movie which gently guyed both the horror film genre and the teen-beat ballads of the late fifties. In collaboration with writer/producer Jim Steinman (who later went on the work with **Andrew Lloyd Webber**) he recorded the oft-re-released bestselling *Bat Out of Hell* (1978) and its 1993 sequel, before, following in the path of **Alice Cooper**, transforming himself (and his image by losing a lot of weight) into the guy next door.

During the late sixties the bulky vocalist worked with Popcorn Blizzard and toured with various artists including **Ted Nugent**, on whose 1976 album *Free for All* he sang lead vocals. He first recorded for **Berry Gordy**'s Rare Earth label as Stoney and Meat Loaf (1971). Moving to New York, Meat Loaf appeared in an off-Broadway musical *Rainbow in New York* and in Steinman's *More than You Deserve*. After filming Jim Sharman's screen version of Richard O'Brien's *Rocky Horror Show*, Meat Loaf and Steinman toured with the *National Lampoon Show*.

The **Todd Rundgren**-produced *Bat Out of Hell* (Cleveland International/Epic, 1977) grew out of *Never Land*, a Steinman musical based on the *Peter Pan* story. Frenetic but tuneful hard rock, the album provided the million-selling 'Two Out of Three Ain't Bad' and lesser hits with 'You Took the Words Right Out of My Mouth' and 'Paradise by the Dashboard Light', which featured noted baseball announcer Phil Rizzuto and singer Ellen Foley. The album's dramatic title track reached the British Top Twenty in 1979.

Meat Loaf's acting career continued with appearances in *Americathon* (1980) and *Roadie* (1981), in which he took the title role. In 1981 he released the Stephan Galfas-produced *Dead Ringer* from which the pulsating 'Dead Ringer for Love' (a duet with an uncredited **Cher**) was a British hit. Steinman's solo album *Bad for Good* appeared in the same year but soon afterwards his partnership with Meat Loaf ended in a flurry of lawsuits.

Steinman went on to write and produce **Bonnie Tyler**'s 1983 hit 'Total Eclipse of the Heart' and her later duet with Rundgren, 'Loving You's a Dirty Job (But Someone's Gotta Do It)'. He also worked with **Barry Manilow**, **Barbra Streisand**, the Sisters of Mercy and **Def Leppard**. Steinman wrote and performed songs for the Walter Hill rock'n'roll fable movie *Streets of Fire* before assembling a cast of female vocalists including *Bat* . . . singer Foley, who had enjoyed only moderate success in a solo career, for his next project, Pandora's Box. *Original Sin* (Virgin, 1989) was another concept album and featured Steinman's trademark Wagnerian sound, but was a poor seller.

Meat Loaf's British success continued with the title track of *Midnight at the Lost and Found* (1983, produced by **Tom Dowd**) and 'Modern Girl' from his début album for Arista, *Bad Attitude* (1984). The former **Boney M** producer **Frank Farian** supervised *Blind before I Stop* (1986), which saw the singer's sales begin to slump in Britain. A lacklustre live album, *Live at Wembley* (1987), followed, but as the decade drew to a close, Meat Loaf was becoming better known as a television personality than as a musician. The successful re-release of 'Bat Out of Hell' in 1991 helped to reverse the trend, and paved the way for a reconciliation between Meat Loaf and Steinman, who masterminded *Bat Out of Hell II: Back into Hell* (Virgin), which appeared in 1993. A return to the sound of the first album, it was an immediate success, selling over

10 million copies worldwide within six months and topping the charts on both sides of the Atlantic. The single 'I Would Do Anything for Love (But I Won't Do That)', accompanied by a suitably outrageous video, topped the European charts for over a month in 1993. He followed that with the lesser *Welcome to the Neighbourhood* (1995). Subsequently, by now a media figure as much as a rock star, he appeared in the Spice Girls film *Spice World* (1998). The next year he issued 'Is Nothing Sacred', a British hit.

HUEY P. MEAUX
b. 10 March 1929, Kaplan, Louisiana, USA

Producer, record-company owner and deal-maker, Meaux, with Floyd Soileau and George Khoury, gave Cajun music a pop dimension in the early sixties. In his later work with **Doug Sahm** and **Freddy Fender**, Meaux found further success with pop- and rock-inflected productions of Tex-Mex music.

A French-speaking cajun, Meaux, named after Louisiana's infamous Governor Huey P. Long, played drums with his father, who was an accordionist, and with **Moon Mullican** while working as a barber, before branching into record production. His first label was Crazy Cajun, on which he recorded himself, and his first productions of regional material, until 1959 when he produced two pop hits, Rod Bernard's 'This Should Go on for Ever' and Jivin' Gene's 'Breaking up Is Hard to Do'. Leased to Argo and Mercury, respectively, both were intense, almost dirge-like performances, only a step away from the wailing sound of the cajun ballad, as was his 1961 production of Joe Barry's **Fats Domino**-inspired version of the **Ted Daffan** song, 'I'm a Fool to Care' (Mercury). Meaux's best productions of this time, however, were with **Barbara Lynn**. Among these were the superior 'You'll Lose a Good Thing' (1962) and 'Oh Baby (We've Got a Good Thing Going)' 1964, subsequently covered by the **Rolling Stones**). Throughout this period, Meaux also operated as a talent scout and deal-maker for major record labels, placing independent productions with them. The most successful of these included Roy Head's rocking 'Treat Her Right' (Backbeat, 1965) and **B. J. Thomas**'s first hit, 'I'm So Lonesome I Could Cry' (Scepter, 1966).

Meaux's greatest discovery of the sixties, however, was Sahm, who as the leader of the Sir Douglas Quintet had an international hit with 'She's About a Mover' on Meaux's own Tribe label in 1965. One of the many songs inspired by **Ray Charles**' 'What'd I Say', 'She's About a Mover' – and most of Sahm's later work – reflected the almost bewildering array of musical influences (blues, country, Mexican music) present in the south of Texas. Where other producers and managers might have sought to discipline the erratic Sahm,

Meaux, during their lengthy association (which included *Together After Five*, 1970, and *Texas Rock for Country Rollers*, 1976) allowed him his head. The consequence was that Sahm, though a considerable and enduring influence on many, never achieved significant commercial success after 'Mendocino'* (1968).

In marked contrast to his handling of Sahm was Meaux's approach to Fender, whom he guided to success in the seventies and eighties. After 'Before the Next Teardrop Falls' (1975), Meaux for the most part restricted Fender to an impassioned, old-fashioned approach to country ballads. His other hits with the singer included 'Wasted Days and Wasted Nights' (1975) and a remake of Lynn's 'You'll Lose a Good Thing' (1976), the year he produced Kinky Friedman's scabrous country album *Lasso from El Paso* (Epic). His cameo appearance as the disc-jockey in *True Stories* (1986), the film by **David Byrne**, testified to the high regard in which Meaux was held by those concerned with the fringes, as well as the mainstream, of popular music. In 1996 that image was destroyed when Meaux was arrested for child pornography.

JOE MEEK
b. Robert George Meek, 1929, Newent, Gloucestershire, England, d. 3 February 1967, London

With Denis Preston one of the first independent British producers, Meek was responsible for numerous hits in the sixties, most notably with John Leyton ('Johnny Remember Me') and the **Tornados** ('Telstar'*), all of which featured a highly constructed sound in the manner, though not the style, of **Phil Spector**.

After working as an RAF radio technician, in 1953 Meek became an engineer at IBC Studios, one of the few independent studios then operating in Britain. There he worked on records by **Frankie Vaughan**, Denis Lotis, **Anne Shelton**, **Petula Clark** and others. In 1956 he joined Preston at Lansdowne Studios, and engineered hits by **Lonnie Donegan** and recordings by **Chris Barber** and **Humphrey Lyttelton** (including his hit, 'Bad Penny Blues', Parlophone, 1956), as well as Preston's calypso productions, which were among the first to be made in Britain. In 1960 he left to establish his own RGM Sound, a tiny studio built above a shop in North London, and Triumph Records, on which he had an immediate hit with his own production of Michael Cox's cover of Johnny Ferguson's American hit, 'Angela Jones' (MGM, 1960). Other releases on Triumph by the instrumental group the Flee-Reckers fared less well and Meek subsequently leased his productions to major companies.

His first big success was the echo-laden production of 'Johnny Remember Me' (Top Rank, 1961), written by Geoff Goddard (who became Meek's house writer)

and sung by actor turned singer Leyton. The trio followed this with 'Wild Wind', 'Son This Is She' (1961) and 'Lonely City' (1962), all eerie mystical songs given their edge by Meek's production. Meek also produced Mike Berry's unusually effective recording of Goddard's 'Tribute to Buddy Holly' (HMV, 1961), his biggest hit 'Don't You Think It's Time' (1963), and several lesser hits by Berry's backing group, the Outlaws, including 'Swingin' Low' and 'Ambush' (1961).

The Outlaws, who included **Deep Purple** founder Ritchie Blackmore among their members, operated as session musicians for several Meek productions, as did the Tornados, who achieved international success with their recording of Meek's swirling instrumental 'Telstar' (1962). Despite further hits with the Tornados and one-time member Heinz, notably a tribute to **Eddie Cochran**, 'Just Like Eddie' (Decca, 1963), and a British No. 1 for the Honeycombs ('Have I the Right', Pye, 1964), Meek was out of sympathy with the music that emerged in the wake of **The Beatles** and the **Rolling Stones**. In a fit of depression after shooting and killing his landlady, he committed suicide on the anniversary of **Buddy Holly**'s death.

Since his death, Meek's contribution to developing production techniques and to establishing the concept of the independent producer have been widely recognized, and a cult following has built up around his work. In the early nineties independent British label RPM began releasing a series of albums of Meek's complete works, while John Repsch published an exhaustive biography.

MEGADETH
David Ellefson, b. 12 November 1964, Jackson, Michigan, USA; David Mustaine, b. 13 September 1961, La Mesa, California; Chris Poland (replaced by Jeff Young, replaced by Marty Friedman); Gars Samuelson (replaced by Chuck Behler, replaced by Nick Menza)

A thrash metal quartet led by former **Metallica** frontman Dave Mustaine, Megadeth became one of the biggest-selling American heavy-rock acts of the eighties and early nineties.

After being fired by Metallica in 1983, allegedly for persistent drug abuse, Mustaine recruited bassist Ellefson, guitarist Poland and drummer Samuelson, recording the acclaimed *Killing Is My Business . . . and Business is Good* (Combat, 1985), which earned the band a deal with Capitol. *Peace Sells . . . But Who's Buying?* (1986), which mixed comments on war-mongering and the environment to vitriolic effect, is considered one of the best thrash albums of the eighties. Propelled by the band's constant touring, it went platinum.

Before recording *So Far, So Good . . . So What?* (1988) Mustaine sacked Poland and Samuelson,

replacing them with Jeff Young (guitar) and Chuck Behler (drums). The band's third album included a hit cover of the **Sex Pistols**' 'Anarchy in the UK'. Another lengthy tour followed before Mustaine was arrested in a drugs-related incident and ordered to enter rehabilitation.

Megadeth re-emerged with Marty Friedman and Nick Menza in place of Young and Behler for *Rust in Piece* (1992), which achieved platinum status, as did *Countdown to Extinction* (1992). While the songs, particularly 'Ashes in Your Mouth', showed the band to be as angry as ever, in their construction they revealed a growing sophistication.

Youthanasia* (1994) was the band's biggest-selling album internationally, while *Hidden Treasures* (1995) collected rarities from their twelve-year career. Megadeth returned after a two-year hiatus with *Cryptic Writings* (1997) before embarking on their first tour since the release of *Youthanasia*. In 1999 the band released *Risk*, which saw them experiment with acoustic guitars and string arrangements for the first time.

MELANIE
b. Melanie Safka, 3 February 1947, New York, USA

A gifted and idiosyncratic singer, Melanie became a symbol of the 'peace and love' style of the Woodstock era.

With a Ukranian father and an Italian mother who had been a professional jazz singer, Safka became a New York drama student, occasionally singing in Greenwich Village clubs. With independent producer Peter Schekeryk (whom she later married) she recorded *Born to Be* (1969) for Neil Bogart's Buddah label. As well as Melanie originals, it included **Bob Dylan**'s 'Mr Tambourine Man' and the children's song 'Christopher Robin'. *Affectionate Melanie* (1969) appeared before she performed at the Woodstock Festival.

That experience inspired her first hit song 'Lay Down (Candles in the Rain)', on which she was accompanied by the **Edwin Hawkins Singers**. This was followed by the hippie philosophizing of 'Peace Will Come (According to Plan)' and her biggest hit, the mildly *risqué* novelty piece 'Brand New Key'*, which was No. 1 in America at Christmas 1971. Released on Neighborhood, a label formed by Safka and Schekeryk, the song was successfully revived in a hayseed parody ('Combined Harvester') by the British group the Wurzels on EMI in 1976. Melanie's *Candles in the Rain* (1970) included one of her best **Edith Piaf**-styled compositions, 'What Have They Done to My Song, Ma' (a British hit in 1970 for the New **Seekers**) and a revival of the **Rolling Stones**' 'Ruby Tuesday', which became a major British hit.

Although later Neighborhood albums like *Madru-gada* (1973) and *Sunset and Other Beginnings* (1975) showed Melanie to be a thoughtful interpreter of lyrics, the 'flower child' era had passed and they sold poorly. Her later albums included the **Ahmet Ertegun** co-production *Photograph* (Atlantic, 1976), *Phono-genic* (Midsong, 1978), *Arabesque* (RCA, 1982), *Seventh Wave* (Neighborhood, 1983), *Cowabonga* (1989), *Precious Cargo* (1991), *Freedom Knows My Name* (1993) and *Old Bitch Warrior* (1996).

DAME NELLIE MELBA

b. Helen Porter Mitchell, 19 May 1861, Melbourne, Australia, d. 23 February 1931, Sydney

The possessor of a clear soprano voice, Melba, with **Enrico Caruso**, was one of the greatest and most popular opera stars of the first decades of the twentieth century. Her recording career lasted only from 1904 to 1926 – when her farewell performance at London's Covent Garden was recorded – but her popularity was such that albums of her historic recordings sold in huge quantities long after her death. The most successful of these were *Dame Nellie Melba** (HMV, 1961) and the five-album set *The London Recordings** (1976).

The daughter of Scottish immigrants, Melba travelled to Britain in 1886. After studying in Paris, she took the name Melba (in honour of her birthplace) and had her first great success in Verdi's *Rigoletto* in Brussels in 1887. She made her Covent Garden début in 1888 in Donizetti's *Lucia di Lammermoor* and toured the world to great success, notably in Italian opera and *Hélène* (the title role of which Saint-Saëns wrote specially for her). While in America in the eighteen-nineties, she made several private recordings for Gianni Bettini on his specially adapted phonograph, which contemporary critics considered notable for their clarity. None of these recordings has survived.

In 1904 Melba made her first official recordings for the Gramophone and Typewriter Company (later EMI) in London. So popular was she that the records, each in their own mauve sleeve with a picture of the diva on the rear, were priced at a guinea (£1.05p), then the most expensive records to be released. In America, issued by Victor, the company for which she subsequently recorded, similarly packaged, they sold for $5. During this period the price of a record reflected its prestige value. Thus the recordings of opera stars were the most expensive, even more so when in duet, and those of comics and popular singers the cheapest. Another mark of the esteem in which Melba was held was that she laid the foundation stone of the Gramophone and Typewriter factory at Hayes, Middlesex, in 1907.

Among her best-known recordings were 'O Soave Fanciulla', a duet with Caruso, and numerous arias from *La Bohème*, *Traviata* and *Otello*. She also recorded some popular songs, including **Stephen Foster**'s 'The Old Folks at Home' and traditional folk songs, such as 'Auld Lang Syne' (accompanied by the Coldstream Guards) and 'Coming Thro' the Rye'.

During the First World War she raised money for the Red Cross and after her retirement in 1926 returned to Australia. She published her reminiscences *Melodies and Memories* in 1925 and was made a Grand Dame of the British Empire in 1927.

JOHN MELLENCAMP

b. John Mellencamp, 7 October 1951, Seymour, Indiana, USA

A mainstream rock songwriter and performer, Mellencamp reverted to his real name midway through his career, emphasizing the post-**Springsteen** social realism of many of his mid-eighties songs.

As Johnny Cougar, his teen-idol good looks brought him to the attention of **David Bowie**'s then manager Tony DeFries, who signed him to MCA. The resulting album, *Chestnut Street Incident* (1976), flopped, as did the follow-up, *The Kid Inside* (1977). Cougar moved to Riva, the label owned by **Rod Stewart**'s manager, Billy Gaff, releasing *A Biography* (1978), which included the track 'I Need a Lover'. The album did not sell, however, but tracks from it were included on the US album *John Cougar* (1979) from which 'I Need a Lover' was issued as a single, reaching the US Top Thirty. Former **Booker T**. guitarist Steve Cropper produced two further successful singles, 'This Time' (1980) and 'Ain't Even Done with the Night' (1981) from the album, *Nothin' Matters and What if It Did*.

1982 was Cougar's most successful year, proving that the clichéd, strutting rock-hero style was not outmoded. *American Fool* was No. 1 album for two months and, aided by video exposure on the new MTV channel, it spawned two million-selling singles, 'Hurts So Good' and the story-song 'Jack and Diane', which gave him his breakthrough in Britain.

He reverted to 'Mellencamp' for his stage name, as part of a strategy of 'authenticity', which also involved recording albums quickly, cheaply and 'live' in the studio. Songs such as 'The Face of the Nation' stressed the plight of the Midwest working class and Mellencamp performed at the Farm Aid benefit concerts held to raise funds to help destitute American farmers.

The Springsteen aura and his own past success kept the hits coming. *Uh-huh* (1984) included three hits in 'Pink Houses', 'Crumbling Down' and 'Authority Song' and *Scarecrow* (1985) provided further Top Twenty success through 'Lonely Ol' Night', 'Small Town' and the tribute to sixties music, 'R.O.C.K. in the USA'. *Conspiracy of Hope* (Phonogram, 1986) continued his run of successes.

In 1987 Mellencamp released *The Lonesome Jubilee*, which spawned hits with 'Paper in Fire' and 'Cherry Bomb'. In the following year he sang **Woody Guthrie**'s 'Do Re Mi' on *A Vision Shared*, a tribute to Guthrie and **Leadbelly**. *Big Daddy* followed in 1989, with another American hit in 'Pop Singer', before Mellencamp took time off from his musical career to make his début movie, *Souvenirs*, in 1990.

He directed his own movie, *Falling from Grace*, which had its première in 1992, before returning to the recording studio for *Whenever We Wanted* (1991). It was a continuation of the rootsier, more acoustic-orientated style Mellencamp had pursued since *Scarecrow*, and sold over a million copies in America. He toured throughout 1992 and released the brooding *Human Wheels* in 1993 followed by *Dance Naked* (1994), a return to a mainstream rock approach which heavily featured guitarist Andy York, a former member of Nashville country-rock band Jason & the Scorchers. In the same year he duetted with Me'Shell Ndegé Ocello (a protégée of **Madonna**) on a version of **Van Morrison**'s 'Wild Night'. The dance-based *Mr Happy Go Lucky* saw Mellencamp achieve success with a dramatic a change in style, while his version of 'Gamblin' Bar Blues' on the **Jimmie Rogers** tribute album masterminded by **Bob Dylan** sought to stress once again his roots identity. The art book *Selected Paintings* (1998) revealed yet another side to the artist, while *The Best I Could Do, 1997–1988* (1997) is the definitive career retrospective. In 1998 he signed with Columbia records and released the self-written and self-produced *John Mellencamp*.

MEMPHIS MINNIE
b. *Lizzie Douglas, 3 June 1897, Algiers, Louisiana, USA, d. 6 August 1973, Memphis, Tennessee*

Memphis Minnie was the only female blues artist who successfully rivalled her male contemporaries as both singer and instrumentalist. The Chicago blues scene of her time could boast singers like Lil Johnson, Merline Johnson ('The Yas Yas Girl') and Lil Green, and there were singers of comparable stature in St Louis and other blues centres, but none seems to have been a skilled instrumentalist. Memphis Minnie challenged the men on what was considered their instrument, the guitar. According to **Big Bill Broonzy**, whom she once beat in a contest, she could 'pick a guitar as good as any man . . . make a guitar cry, moan, talk and whistle the blues.'

She was singing and playing guitar and banjo on the streets of Memphis perhaps before the First World War; certainly by the early twenties, after some experience with travelling tent-shows, she was working the bars of Beale Street. With her husband Kansas Joe McCoy (b. *11 May 1905, Raymond, Mississippi, d.*

28 January 1950, Chicago, Illinois) she recorded a series of exciting vocal/guitar duets for Columbia and Vocalion (1929–32), including the hit 'Bumble Bee' (1930). By 1933 she and McCoy were based in Chicago, but two years later they divorced. Minnie had a series of club residencies, the best known being at Ruby Lee Gatewood's Tavern, where she held 'Blue Monday' parties. She recorded for Decca (1934–5), Bluebird (1935) and Vocalion/Okeh/Columbia (1935–49), exchanging the two-guitar country-blues format of her previous recordings for a contemporary Chicago band sound with piano and sometimes trumpet.

From 1939 she was joined on records by her new husband, singer/guitarist Ernest 'Little Son Joe' Lawlars (b. *18 May 1900, Hughes, Arkansas, d. 14 November 1961, Memphis, Tennessee*). She had a sequence of especially potent sides in the early forties, 'Nothing in Rambling' (1940), 'Me and My Chauffeur Blues' (1941) and 'Looking the World Over' (1941). (The reverse side of the last, 'Black Rat Swing' by Little Son Joe, was also a race hit and has been recorded by many other artists.) In the forties Minnie lived in Indianapolis and Detroit, but she returned in the early fifties to Chicago, where she re-recorded 'Me and My Chauffeur', by now her trademark number, for Checker (1952). It failed to secure her place in the new Chicago blues generation of **Muddy Waters** and **Howlin' Wolf**, and after a final recording for JOB (1954) she retired and spent her remaining years in Memphis.

MEMPHIS SLIM
b. *Peter Chatman, 3 September 1915, Memphis, Tennessee, USA, d. 24 February 1988, Paris, France*

For almost thirty years a member of the community of black American musicians in France, Memphis Slim did more than any other artist to educate Europeans in the history of the blues. A highly skilled rather than outstanding pianist, he was sufficiently versatile to anthologize several periods of blues and boogie-woogie piano-playing in a single set. His singing, though formed in the declamatory mould of his predecessor Roosevelt Sykes, acquired its own distinction, and he was also an adept and amusing storyteller, but he owed his charisma less to particular abilities than to his imposing self-confidence and air of urbane cultivation.

Self-taught, he spent his late teens and twenties as an itinerant piano player before settling, in 1937, in Chicago, where he worked in clubs with **Big Bill Broonzy** and recorded for Okeh and Bluebird ('Beer Drinking Woman', 1940). In the first postwar decade he recorded prolifically with small jump bands for Miracle (1947–9), King (1949), Premium (1950–1), Mercury (1951), Chess (1952) and United (1952–4). Among his more popular numbers were 'Grinder

Man Blues' and 'Mother Earth'. Two albums made in the summer of 1959 epitomized the duality of his career: *The Real Boogie Woogie* (Folkways) was a historical survey of that idiom in the form of a solo recital, while *At the Gate of Horn* (Vee-Jay) was a vigorous club set by a seven-piece band. In the same year he played Carnegie Hall, the Ash Grove in Los Angeles and the Newport Folk Festival. He recorded further Folkways albums, either solo or with **Willie Dixon**, and visited Europe with Dixon in 1960–1, recording in England (for Collector with **Alexis Korner**, and Fontana), France (Agorilla) and Denmark (Storyville). Meanwhile, in the US, he made albums for Folkways and Prestige-Bluesville, including a session for the latter with West Coast guitarist Lafayette Thomas; two for Candid with fellow veterans Jazz Gillum (harmonica) and Arbee Stidham (guitar); and a band date for Strand with his guitarist partner of former years, Matt Murphy. In Autumn 1961 he moved permanently to Paris.

During the sixties and seventies he appeared in virtually every European country, often giving concerts titled 'The Story of the Blues' in which he played the best-known songs of predecessors like Broonzy and **Leroy Carr**. He joined the 1962 and 1963 American Folk Blues Festivals, touring after the latter with fellow participant **Sonny Boy Williamson II**. He worked in the United States in 1965–6 and made occasional return visits in later years, but his performing and recording activity was chiefly in France, where he made thematic albums for Barclay, including *Old Times, New Times*, which united him with his original model, Roosevelt Sykes, but also placed him among Chicagoans like **Buddy Guy**. Subsequent recordings appeared on Blue Star, Isabel and Milan. He suffered from kidney failure in 1986 but recovered to fulfil touring commitments in Africa, Israel and the United States before a recurrence of the illness proved fatal.

MEN AT WORK
Greg Ham, b. 27 September 1953, Australia; Colin James Hay, b. 29 June 1953, Scotland; John Rees, b. Australia; Jerry Speiser, b. Australia; Ron Strykert, b. 18 August 1957, Australia

Men at Work was one of the few Australian bands to achieve international success during the eighties. Unlike the more orthodox **Air Supply** and the **Little River Band**, however, Men at Work was the product of the new wave and pub-rock trends in Australian music.

Songwriter and singer Hay had emigrated to Australia in the early sixties and played in various bands while studying at La Trobe University, Melbourne. From these emerged Men at Work in 1979, with Strykert on guitar, Ham on keyboards and saxophone and a rhythm section of Speiser (drums) and Rees (bass).

The group became the biggest draw on the Melbourne pub circuit and were signed to Columbia in 1981.

Featuring Hay's quirky lyrics and eclectic rhythms, *Business as Usual* (1982) was produced by Peter McIan. 'Who Can It Be Now'* and the alternative view of Australia 'Down Under'* reached No. 1 there and in America, where the latter benefited from a witty video incorporating aspects of the stereotypical Aussie lifestyle. The album also topped the American charts for fifteen weeks.

Hay wrote eight of the songs on *Cargo* (1983), including the album's three hit singles, 'Overkill', 'It's a Mistake' and 'Dr Heckle and Mr Jive'. Rees and Speiser left the band before the recording of *Two Hearts* (1985), which repeated the formula of the earlier albums. In 1987 Hay launched a solo career with *Looking for Jack*, produced by Robin Millar. He later released *Wayfaring Sons* (MCA, 1990), before establishing his own label, Lazy Eye, for *Topanga* (1995).

JOHNNY MERCER
b. John Herndon Mercer, 18 November 1909, Savannah, Georgia, USA, d. 25 June 1976, Los Angeles, California

Singer and record-company founder, Mercer was one of the most successful lyricists of the twentieth century, winning four Oscars in the course of his long career. His facility was such that he could write pure corn, such as the pastiche cowboy song 'I'm an Old Cowhand from the Rio Grande' and sophisticated lyrics ('Too Marvelous for Words', 'Ac-cent-tchu-ate the Positive') with equal ease. However, his best work, like that of **Harold Arlen**, with whom he wrote the magisterial 'Blues in the Night', had a bluesy, yearning feel. A white Southerner, Mercer's heritage (of black as well as white music) is reflected in his flair for description (for example, his words to 'Lazybones', the mysterious phrase 'my huckleberry friend' in 'Moon River' and the central situation of 'One for My Baby') which gave his work a decidedly different American emphasis from that of his fellow songwriters, most of whom were city-based, Jewish immigrants.

The son of a lawyer who suffered bankruptcy, Mercer travelled to New York in 1928 to seek work as an actor. He failed but placed 'Out of Breath and Scared to Death of You' (with music by Everett Miller) in *The Garrick Gaieties* (1930) and by 1932 was regularly singing with and writing (mostly novelty) material for **Paul Whiteman** on his *Kraft Radio Show*. Songs from this period include 'Fair Thee Well to Harlem' and 'Christmas in Harlem' (with **Jack Teagarden**), 'Lazybones' (with **Hoagy Carmichael** in 1932) and 'Pardon My Southern Accent' (with Matty Malneck, 1934). He resurrected his acting ambitions with appearances in *Old Man Rhythm* (in which he sang his own 'I Never Saw a Better Night') and *To Beat the Band* (1935), before returning to songwriting. His first major film success came with 'I'm an Old Cowhand' which, with 'Something's Gotta Give' (1955), was one of several songs to which he wrote both words and music. It was introduced by **Bing Crosby** in *Rhythm on the Range* (1938). Other early film successes included 'Too Marvelous for Words' (1937) and 'Hooray for Hollywood' (1938), both with **Richard Whiting**. While in Hollywood, he hosted his own radio show and in 1942 he and record-shop owner Glenn Wallichs, with financial support from Buddy DeSylva (of **DeSylva, Brown and Henderson**) formed Capitol Records. Among Mercer's signings to the label was **Nat 'King' Cole**. In 1954 the company was sold to EMI.

A prolific recording artist in his own right, Mercer had several successes with his own interpretations of his compositions. Among these were 'Mister Meadowlark' (Decca, 1940), a duet with Crosby; 'Ac-cent-tchu-ate the Positive' (Capitol, 1945); 'Candy' (1945), on which he was partnered by **Jo Stafford** and the Pied Pipers; and 'Personality' (1946) – all No. 1s – and 'Moon Faced, Starry-Eyed' (1947), with **Benny Goodman**, and 'Baby It's Cold Outside' (1949) with Margaret Whiting.

At the same time, Mercer continued to write. His major collaborators included **Harry Warren**, who co-wrote 'Jeepers Creepers', 'You Must Have Been a Beautiful Baby' (1938) and the Oscar-winning 'On the Atcheson, Topeka and the Sante Fe' sung by **Judy Garland** in *The Harvey Girls* (1946) and a hit for Mercer himself in 1945. With **Jerome Kern** he wrote 'Dearly Beloved', 'You Were Never Lovelier', and 'I'm Old Fashioned', sung by **Fred Astaire** in *You Were Never Lovelier* (1942). With Rube Bloom he produced 'Fools Rush in' (1939), recorded originally by **Glenn Miller** and revived by **Rick Nelson** in 1963; and with **Victor Schertzinger**, 'Tangerine', 'I Remember You', a hit for **Jimmy Dorsey** and a million-seller when revived by **Frank Ifield** in 1962, and the witty 'Arthur Murray Taught Me Dancing in a Hurry', introduced by **Betty Hutton** in *The Fleet's in* (1942). With Carmichael he produced 'Skylark' (1942), 'How Little We Know' (1944) and another Oscar-winning song, 'In the Cool Cool Cool of the Evening' (1951).

However, Mercer's most distinctive work of this period was with Arlen. Together they wrote the outstanding 'Blues in the Night' (1941), in which Mercer made evocative use of vernacular ('My Momma don' tol' me') and poetic use of American place names ('From Natchez to Mobile, from Memphis to St Joe'), 'That Old Black Magic', 'Hit the Road to Dreamland' (1942), 'One for My Baby' (1943) and 'Let's Take the Long Way Home' (1944). The pair also wrote the Broadway musicals *St Louis Woman* (1946), which introduced 'Come Rain or Come Shine' (impressively revived by **Ray Charles** in 1968) and 'Any Place I

Hang My Hat Is Home', and *Saratoga* (1959). More jaunty and more successful were the screen musical *Seven Brides for Seven Brothers* (1954) and the Broadway show *Li'l Abner* (1956, filmed 1959), both written with Gene de Paul. He first introduced the oft-recorded 'Bless Your Beautiful Hide' and 'Sobbin' Women' and the second 'Jubiliation T. Cornpone', described by one critic as 'a fine Gilbertian celebration of a local equivalent of the Duke of Plaza-Toro'.

In the sixties Mercer recorded with and wrote material for such artists as **Bobby Darin** (*Two of a Kind*, Capitol, 1962), and Bing Crosby and **Louis Armstrong** (*Bing and Louis*). After leaving Capitol he recorded albums on Submarine and Artistic which emphasized the haunting quality of his best songs. He also, less successfully, continued to write shows, including an adaptation of J. B. Priestley's *The Good Companions* (1974) with music by **André Previn**. He had far greater success in partnership with **Henry Mancini**. They won Oscars with 'Moon River' (from *Breakfast at Tiffany's*, 1961), probably the best-known of Mercer's songs, and the title song to *The Days of Wine and Roses* (1962), which provided hits for **Jerry Butler** and **Andy Williams**, respectively, as well as Mancini himself. Like so many of his earlier songs, both have become standards.

MERCURY REV
David Baker; Jimmy Chambers; Jonathan Donahue; David Fridmann; Sean 'Grasshopper' Mackowiak; Suzanne Thorpe

Like their close colleagues the **Flaming Lips**, Buffalo, New York-based Mercury Rev have progressed from avant garde, feedback-layered experimentation to producing an acclaimed album of symphonic pop drawing on a century of American musical history.

After contributing to the Flaming Lips' *In a Priest Driven Ambulance* (1990), Donahue (guitar) and Fridmann (bass) formed Mercury Rev alongside vocalist Baker, lead guitarist Grasshopper, flautist Thorpe and drummer Chambers. They spent a year soundtracking their own home-made movies before releasing the psychedelic space-rock of *Yerself is Steam* (1991). Described by one critic as 'seventies art rock performed with a nineties post-modernist stance', it won them an underground following. Support slots with **My Bloody Valentine** and **Spiritualized** preceded the departure of Baker, leading Donahue to assume chief songwriting and vocal duties. *Boces* (1993) and *See You on the Other Side* (1995), both produced by bassist Fridmann, were highly acclaimed but failed to expand Mercury Rev's cult fanbase.

The band took an extended break after touring in support of their third album, during which time Thorpe and Chambers left to pursue other projects, while Fridmann continued to work with the band as a producer only. *Deserter's Songs* (1998), the result of two years' work, was immediately declared a modern classic by the majority of critics, achieving gold status in the UK and selling well internationally. The resulting world tour saw the formation of a new Mercury Rev line-up, featuring keyboardists Justin Russo and Adam Snyder, bassist Jason Russo and Jeff Mercel on drums, alongside Donahue and Grasshopper, while Dave Fridmann produced highly praised albums for **Mogwai** and the Flaming Lips in 1999.

ETHEL MERMAN
b. Ethel Zimmerman, 16 January 1909, Astoria, New York, USA, d. 5 February 1984, New York

Best known for her declamatory rendition of **Irving Berlin**'s anthem, 'There's No Business Like Show Business' (which she introduced on Broadway in 1946 and sang in the 1954 film of the same title) and for her extravagant stage manner, Merman won her title as the first lady of American musical comedy by, in the words of Stanley Green, 'portraying a gutsy dame whose heart of gold is revealed through a voice of brass'.

Merman worked as a secretary and sang in nightclubs before winning overnight fame with her arresting rendition of **George** and **Ira Gershwin**'s 'I Got Rhythm' in the Broadway show *Girl Crazy* (1930). Equally notable was the calibre of the show's orchestra. Led by **Red Nichols**, it included **Jimmy Dorsey**, **Benny Goodman**, **Glenn Miller**, **Jack Teagarden** and **Gene Krupa**. Merman followed *Girl Crazy* with a triumph in the 1931 edition of *George White's Scandals*, in which she introduced Brown and Henderson's (of the **DeSylva, Brown and Henderson** team) 'Life Is Just a Bowl of Cherries' and 'My Song', and *Take a Chance* (1932), in which she performed **Nacio Herb Brown** and **Richard Whiting**'s 'Eadie Was a Lady'. The song was so popular that its lyrics were printed in the *New York Times* the day after the show's opening.

Though she recorded for Victor and Decca with some success (in the seventies she even recorded a disco version of 'Show Business'), Merman's greatest success was on stage. She appeared in no less than five musicals with scores by **Cole Porter** (*Anything Goes*, 1934, filmed with Merman and **Bing Crosby** in 1936; *Red, Hot and Blue*, 1936; *DuBarry Was a Lady*, 1939; *Panama Hattie*, 1940; and *Something for the Boys*, 1943) and two with scores by Berlin (*Annie Get Your Gun*, 1946; and *Call Me Madam*, 1950, filmed 1953). *Annie Get Your Gun* (which she revived briefly in 1966) marked the peak of her success. As well as 'Show Business', she sang 'They Say It's Wonderful', 'Doin' What Comes Naturally' and 'You Can't Get a Man with a Gun'. **Jule Styne** and **Stephen Sondheim**'s *Gypsy* (1959), in which she played the ambi-

tious mother of famed American stripper Gypsy Rose Lee, provided her brassiest role.

She appeared in some twelve films, but few had the impact of her stage performances. In the sixties she appeared regularly in cabaret and on television and in the seventies was the voice of the Wicked Witch in *Journey back to Oz* (1972) and provided the commentary for *Rudolph and Frosty's Christmas in July* (1979).

BOB MERRILL
b. Henry Robert Merrill Lavan, 17 May 1921, Atlantic City, New Jersey, USA, d. 17 February 1998

A prolific writer of pop songs in the fifties for **Guy Mitchell**, **Patti Page** and **Rosemary Clooney**, among others, Merrill turned to Broadway with great success in the sixties, writing *Carnival* (1961) and co-writing *Funny Face* (1964) with **Jule Styne**.

Raised in Philadelphia, Merrill travelled to New York in 1942 to seek work as an actor. During the war, while in the army, he produced shows and wrote sketches for the troops and afterwards became a television writer and director for first NBC and then Columbia. But following the success of Eileen Barton's million-selling recording of his and Al Hoffman's 'If I Knew You Were Coming I'd've Baked a Cake' (National, 1950), which was also a hit for **Bing Crosby**, Merrill turned decisively to songwriting.

Columbia's head of A&R, **Mitch Miller**, teamed Merrill with singer Guy Mitchell and instructed Merrill to write songs in the manner of Terry Gilkyson, author of **Frankie Laine**'s 'The Cry of the Wild Geese' (1950), songs which, as one critic put it, 'sounded as if they had folk origins'. The result was a series of hits for Mitchell, including the million-sellers 'My Truly, Truly Fair' (1951) and 'There's a Pawnshop on a Corner in Pittsburgh, Pennsylvania' (1952). Other singers to benefit from Merrill songs were Page ('How Much Is That Doggie in the Window'*, 1953, which was a British chart-topper for Lita Roza on Decca), Clooney ('Mambo Italiano'*, 1954, also recorded by **Dean Martin**), **Jimmy Rodgers** ('Honeycomb' 1957) and **Perry Como** ('Love Makes the World Go Round', 1958). However, by the end of the fifties, Merrill was concentrating not on individual pop songs but on shows.

In 1961 'Love Makes the World Go Round' reappeared as part of *Carnival*, Merrill's most successful musical as lyricist and composer. In 1964 he had an even greater success with the songs to *Funny Girl* which he wrote with Jule Styne. The show, loosely based on the early life of **Fanny Brice** and produced by Ray Stark, Brice's son-in-law, made a star of **Barbra Streisand**, who introduced 'People' and 'Don't Rain on My Parade', which became standards. Subsequent shows, both on his own (*Henry, Sweet Henry*,

1967) and with Styne (*Sugar*, 1972) fared less well. He died after a self-inflicted gunshot wound in 1998.

METALLICA

James Alan Hetfield, b. 3 August 1963, Los Angeles, California, USA; Lars Ulrich, b. 26 December 1963, Copenhagen, Denmark; Lloyd Grand; Ron McGovney; Jef Warner; David Mustaine; Kirk Hammett, b. 18 November 1962, USA; Clifford Lee Burton, b. 10 February 1962, USA, d. 27 September 1986; Jason Newstead, b. 4 March 1963, Battle Creek, Minnesota, USA

One of the most original and inventive bands to emerge from the American thrash-metal scene in the eighties, Metallica recorded a series of albums which continually redefined the genre, selling some 65 million copies worldwide along the way.

Drummer Ulrich and guitarist/vocalist Hetfield formed Metallica in Los Angeles in 1981 with bassist McGovney and lead guitarist Grand, who was briefly replaced by Mustaine then by Warner then by Hammett, and bass-player Burton replaced McGovney before the band relocated to San Francisco in 1983. A further move to New York preceded the arrival of the first album, *Kill 'Em All*, on the independent Megaforce label, which won instant acclaim from rock critics.

The band's intense live performances and the strong sales of the first album led to their being signed by Elektra, and the second album, *Ride the Lightning* (1984), spent almost a year on the US album chart. The third album, *Master of Puppets* (1986), saw the band expanding on the thrash blueprint. It introduced the band to a much wider audience worldwide. While on tour in Scandinavia in 1986 the band's coach skidded off the road, killing Burton instantly. The others returned to the US and recruited Newstead from Phoenix band Flotsam & Jetsam, embarking on a series of dates through the rest of 1986 and into 1987.

The first recording with Newstead was an EP of favourite cover-versions, including songs by Budgie and **Killing Joke**, *The $5.98 EP – Garage Days Revisited*, which entered the UK singles chart – the band had previously refused to release singles – and sold over 3 million copies worldwide. A series of European festivals in 1987 preceded the arrival of . . . *And Justice for All* (1988), their most sophisticated and successful album yet. The band now began to release singles, and enjoyed several hits in the UK. More extensive touring followed before the release of the multi-platinum *Metallica* in 1991, produced by Bob Rock (**Bon Jovi, Motley Crüe**). It remained in the US charts for over three years and saw the band confirmed as a major act worldwide, spinning off several hit singles, including 'Enter Sandman' and 'Wherever

I May Roam'. A heavy touring schedule including stadium dates with **Guns N' Roses** followed, and the album went on to sell over 12 million copies.

Firmly lodged in the upper echelons of rock, Metallica acknowledged their status as a major live act by releasing a massive, expensively packaged three album/two video boxed set of live material in 1993 as *Live Shit! Binge & Purge*. The band appeared at Woodstock '94, the rain-soaked twenty-fifth anniversary festival. Their next studio release was the two-disc *Load* (1996), on which the band moved towards a more polished alternative rock sound. Metallica also underwent something of an image makeover, which saw them cut their hair and have their publicity photographs taken by Anton Corbijn. After headlining the 1997 Lollapalooza festival the band released *Reload*, a collection of out-takes from the *Load* sessions coupled with new studio material. *Garage Inc* (1998) was a second set of covers, featuring Metallica's interpretations of songs by artists ranging from **Thin Lizzy** to **Nick Cave**. The live double-album *S&M* (1999) was equally innovative. The acronym stood not for sadomasochism, but Symphony and Metallica, and the album paired them with the San Francisco Symphony orchestra. For the project, which included symphonic versions of favourites such as 'Enter Sandman' and 'Masters of Puppets', the orchestrations were provided by Michael Kamen, with whom the band had worked before on their 1991 hit 'Nothing Else Matters'. In 2000 the group sued the Napster file-sharing service in the US, alleging it encouraged copyright theft. As a result it was commended by music-industry bodies and spokespersons, but faced protests from its own fans.

PAT METHENY

b. 12 August 1954, Lee's Summit, Missouri, USA

Working in the interstices between jazz, rock and electronic music, Metheny is one of the most proficient and versatile contemporary guitarists.

He grew up in Kansas City, and took up trumpet before learning guitar at the age of ten. He played in modern jazz groups while still at high school and went on to study and teach music at the University of Miami and Berklee School. In 1973 he joined **Gary Burton**'s group and in 1976 made his first album, *Bright Size Life* (ECM) with bassist Jaco Pastorius. He next formed the Pat Metheny Group with composer and keyboards-player Lyle Mays. Together they recorded *Watercolors* (1977) and *The Pat Metheny Group* (1978) before Metheny joined Pastorius to accompany **Joni Mitchell** on her 1979 tour.

Resuming his recording career, Metheny made contrasting albums in the pastoral, almost new-age styled *New Chatauqua* (1979) and the jazz-rock collection

American Garage (1980). This was followed by a more conventional series of jazz improvisations with such artists as bassist **Charlie Haden**, Michael Brecker of the **Brecker Brothers** and Dewey Redman on *80/81* (1980). *As Falls Wichita, So Falls Wichita Falls* (1981) was an album of collaborations with Mays and Brazilian percussionist Nana Vasconcelos, who was also featured on the live double-album *Travels* (1983).

That was preceded by Metheny's most commercially successful album, *Offramp* (1982), on which he undertook dazzling experiments with the Synclavier guitar-synthesizer. *Rejoicing* (1983), a jazz trio record made with Haden and drummer Billy Higgins, was the prelude to Metheny's most controversial work of the eighties, *Song X* (1986). Described as 'unlistenable' by some critics, this free-form blowing session with Haden and **Ornette Coleman** led to live performances by a Metheny–Coleman group.

Metheny, however, also maintained his interest in Latin and jazz-rock music. The airy *First Circle* (1984) was based on Brazilian rhythms while on the soundtrack album *The Falcon and the Snowman* (1985) he worked with **David Bowie**, collaborating on the hit single 'This Is Not America'.

In 1987 Metheny and Mays left the avant-garde label ECM and recorded the Latin-influenced *Still Life (Talking)* for Geffen. Without Mays Metheny recorded the more conventional *Letter from Home* (1989) and *Questions and Answers* (1991), his most accessible album. *Secret Story* (1992) was an ambitious autobiographical concept album with string orchestra. Metheny subsequently worked with fellow guitarist John Scofield on the bestselling *I Can See Your House from Here* and in 1994 released *Zero Tolerance for Silence*. 1995's *We Live Here*, the first group recording for several years, saw Metheny in a poppier mood than normal. After that he moved into film scores, most successfully with his evocative score for *A Map of the World* (1999), before in 2000 returning to the trio format with *Trio 99–00* (Warner). A hugely satisfying album, it saw Metheny revisiting his earlier compositions ('Travels', 'Beyond the Missouri Sky'), milestones such as **John Coltrane**'s 'Giant Steps', mixed with new compositions, such as the sinewy '(Go) Get It'.

GEORGE MICHAEL
b. Georgious Panayiotou, 25 June 1963, London, England

Formerly of teenybop disco duo Wham!, George Michael became the most successful white soul singer and songwriter of the eighties. His records regularly topped both the pop and black music charts. A further mark of his huge fanbase was that despite his career being halted in the early nineties when he

embarked on a landmark lawsuit against his record label, he recommenced his career later with his popularity intact. Indeed, in the manner of **Elton John**, his reputation was hardly affected when he was arrested for making homoerotic advances to a Los Angeles policeman.

As schoolboys Michael and Andrew Ridgeley (*b. 26 January 1963*) formed ska band Executive in Bushey, Hertfordshire, in 1979. As Wham!, with Michael singing and Ridgeley on guitar, they signed to the Innervisions label, releasing 'Wham! Rap (Enjoy What You Do?)' (1982), supervised by British soul producer Bob Carter. 'Young Guns (Go for It)' reached the Top Ten and was the first of a series of light disco hits that ceased only when the duo separated in 1986.

Wham!'s hits in 1983 included 'Wham Rap', 'Bad Boys', 'Club Tropicana' and 'Club Fantasia Megamix'. Like **Duran Duran**, the duo's image reflected the post-punk hedonism of the disco scene, with Michael in particular becoming a teen-idol.

A contractual dispute with their record label led to Wham! acquiring manager Simon Napier-Bell, who had formerly worked with the **Yardbirds** and **Japan**. They moved to Epic where the more forthright 'Wake Me Up Before You Go Go' (1984) became their first No. 1 in both Britain and America. Michael next released the solo single 'Careless Whisper'* before Wham!'s 'Freedom' and 'Last Christmas'. The album *Make It Big* also reached the Top Ten. In 1985 the duo became the first rock band to perform in China, a tour which was filmed by director Lindsay Anderson. They topped the British charts at Christmas with the up-beat 'I'm Your Man'. The same year, Michael also sang on the Band Aid charity record 'Do They Know It's Christmas?' and on Elton John's 'Wrap Her Up'.

The last Wham! release included 'Wham! Rap '86' (1986) after which Michael embarked on a solo career. He released 'A Different Corner' (1986) before recording the restrained soul duet 'I Knew You Were Waiting (For Me)' with **Aretha Franklin**. After a gap of a year, he returned with *Faith* (1987), which provided six hit singles in America. They began with the controversial 'I Want Your Sex' (1987), which was banned by radio stations and appeared on the soundtrack of *Beverly Hills Cop 2*. The pop No. 1 'Faith' was backed by the R&B hit 'Hard Day', and was followed by the ballads 'Father Figure' (1988) and the sixties-soul-flavoured 'One More Try'. 'Monkey' had an anti-drugs message. *Listen without Prejudice Vol. I* was released in 1990 and gave Michael another multi-platinum success on both sides of the Atlantic. A second volume was reportedly already recorded, and Michael announced that from now on he intended to avoid the album–tour treadmill. Accordingly, his next live appearances were in the form of various brief tours on which he mostly performed favourite soul songs.

In 1992 he began working on an album of these songs featuring guest vocalists, titled *Trojan Souls*, and contributed material to an Aids benefit album, *Red Hot & Dance*. Shortly after its release, Michael began a court action to free himself from his contract with Sony Entertainment, which had acquired CBS, the label to which he had originally signed. The legal action, which he eventually lost in 1994, dominated Michael's life for the next two years, and his only record release was an Aids fund-raising live EP which included two **Queen** songs recorded at a 1992 memorial concert for vocalist Freddie Mercury, who had died from Aids. Released by Hollywood Records, it topped the British singles chart in 1993.

Having successfully negotiated a deal with Virgin, through which he set up his own Aegean imprint the previous year, Michael released *Older* (1996). The album was a mature blend of soulful balladry and up-beat dance tracks, and included the UK No. 1 singles 'Jesus to a Child' and 'Fastlove'. In 1998 the singer was arrested for lewd conduct in a public toilet near his Beverly Hills home, an incident which he brushed aside with comic effect on 'Outside' after revealing himself to be homosexual on CNN. Later the same year he issued a highly successful hits collection, *Ladies and Gentlemen: The Best of George Michael*, which again made reference to his arrest in its title. The album was divided between his ballads and dance tracks on two discs, 'For the Heart' and 'For the Feet'. *Songs from the Last Century* (1999), a reworking of past hits, was equally successful but poorly received critically. While the eclecticism of the choices, which ranged from **Rodgers** and **Hart**'s 'Where or When' to 'Secret Love', a 1953 hit for **Doris Day**, via the Depression standard 'Brother Can You Spare a Dime' and the **Police**'s 'Roxanne', is intriguing, the performances bring nothing extra to the songs. The result is an album in which Michael eschews his usual exploratory stance for mere celebration.

BETTE MIDLER
b. 1 December 1945, Paterson, New Jersey, USA

Talking dirty and mixing camp and swagger with a broad musical repertoire, the self-styled 'Divine Miss M' propelled herself from the chorus line and the sixties to leading parts in Hollywood movies in the eighties with a flurry of hit records in the seventies.

Raised in Hawaii, Midler sang in her teens in a female folk group, the Pieridine Three, and acted. In the late sixties she travelled to New York and appeared in the chorus line of several shows, eventually graduating to a featured part in *Fiddler on the Roof*. In the early seventies, with **Barry Manilow** as

her musical director, she won a cult following at the gay men's club, the Continental Baths, with her mix of show tunes, blues, contemporary songs and pastiche versions of old-time pop songs. Signed to Atlantic in 1972, she had a trio of hits in 1973: a remake of 'Do You Want to Dance' (originally a hit for Bobby Freeman in 1958 on Josie), a version of the **Andrews Sisters**' 'Boogie Woogie Bugle Boy' and Buzzy Linhart's 'Friends'. All were from her début album, *The Divine Miss M* (1972). Though a media sensation, Midler's subsequent albums, which included songs by **Bob Dylan**, **Tom Waits**, **John Prine** and a version of **Edith Piaf**'s 'La Vie en Rose', were less successful. Then, in 1979, she had a huge success with her first film, *The Rose*, which was loosely based on the life of **Janis Joplin**. It led to an Oscar nomination and a million-seller with the title song and a further chart entry with her revival of **Percy Sledge**'s 1966 hit 'When a Man Loves a Woman' (1980).

In the eighties, apart from the concert film and album *Divine Madness* (1980), Midler largely concentrated on her screen career, most successfully with *Down and Out in Beverly Hills* (1986) in which she reprised her 'Divine Miss M' persona to great comic effect. In 1989 Midler made legal history by winning damages for the use of a 'soundalike' in a TV commercial. She returned to the charts in 1989 with 'Wind Beneath My Wings' from the film *Beaches*, produced by **Arif Mardin**. Her 1991 album *Some People's Lives* made the Top Ten in America and Britain and included a hit version of Julie Gold's much-recorded 'From a Distance'. The soundtrack album from *For the Boys* (1991), in which she starred as a war-time entertainer, was less successful. Another movie, *Hocus Pocus*, followed in 1993, as did the compilation *Experience the Divine: Greatest Hits*. It reached the Top Five in Britain, giving Midler her biggest British hit album. Less critically successful was *Bed of Roses* (1996), her first non-soundtrack album for several years. She returned to film for 'Go Help the Outcasts' from the animated film *The Hunchback of Notre Dame* (1996). She followed that with *Bathhouse Betty* (1998).

MIDNIGHT OIL
Peter Garrett, b. 1954, Sydney, Australia; Jim Moginie, b. Sydney; Martin Rotsey, b. Sydney; Dwayne Hillman, b. New Zealand; Rob Hirst, b. Sydney

A politically inspired rock band, Midnight Oil were one of several Australian artists to achieve international recognition in the late eighties.

The origins of the band lay in a Sydney group, Farm, which included the teenage guitarists Moginie and Rotsey plus drummer Hirst. After recruiting law student and singer Garrett from Rock Island Line and bassist Hillman from the swingers, the group became Midnight Oil in 1975.

Over the next five years they were probably the most hard-working band in Australia, playing hundreds of live shows and issuing the bestselling *Head Injuries* (1979) and *Bird Noises* (1980). Many of Garrett's lyrics focused on environmental issues. After recording *Place without a Postcard* (1981) with producer Glyn Johns in England, the group signed an international recording deal with CBS.

During the rest of the eighties, Midnight Oil built up a global following through their dynamic live appearances and by releasing three critically acclaimed albums: *Red Sails in the Sunset* (1982), *10,9,8,7,6,5,4,3,2,1* (1983) and *Diesel and Dust* (1986), which was the band's first worldwide hit, reaching the US Top Twenty. It included the hard rocking 'The Dead Heart' and 'Warakurna', and the hit single 'Beds Are Burning' which deals with the situation of Australia's aboriginal population.

Even better was *Blue Sky Mining* (1990) whose title track angrily described the plight of fatally ill asbestos miners in Western Australia. Its other highlights include the anthemic 'Forgotten Years' and the low-key 'Bedlam Bridge'. In 1991 the group contributed a version of 'Wharf Rat' to *Dedicated*, a collection of songs in celebration of the **Grateful Dead**.

Later albums included *Scream in Blue: Live* (1992), a selection of concert performances from 1982–1990, and *Earth & Sun & Moon* (1993). Its hymn to republicanism, 'Truganini', with its vision of the 'the Union Jack in flames', was, perhaps surprisingly, a Top Thirty hit in Britain. The definitive retrospective is *20,000 Watts R.S.I.* (1997). The group followed that with *Redneck Wonderland* (1998).

Outside music, Garrett ran for the Australian senate on an anti-nuclear platform, became president of the Australian Conservation Foundation and has published *Political Blues* (1988), a selection from his outspoken newspaper column.

THE MIGHTY CLOUDS OF JOY

Joe Ligon, b. Troy, Alabama, USA; Johnny Martin, b. Los Angeles, California; Paul Beasley; Elmo Franklin; Richard Wallace

After the **Staple Singers**, the Mighty Clouds of Joy were the most commercially successful black gospel group.

Formed in Los Angeles in the late fifties, the group's two lead voices melded the urgent, hard sounds of Ligon – who was decisively influenced by Rev. Julius Cheeks of the Sensational Nightingales – with the smoother urban sophistication of Martin. Signed to **Don Robey**'s Peacock label in 1959, the group were aggressively promoted, and given a flashy image to match, by Robey. Soon the company's most

successful gospel group, the Mighty Clouds edged closer to soul throughout the sixties, finally crossing the boundary from 'gospel' to 'inspirational' music in 1974 when their new label ABC released *It's Time*, produced by Dave Crawford in Philadelphia and featuring that city's premier session men.

Despite the traditional non-mixing of gospel acts with pop music, their singles – 'Time' (1974), 'Mighty Cloud of Joy' (1975) and 'Mighty High' (1976) – reached the R&B Top Forty. All message-orientated recordings, they featured heavy disco-style arrangements, but even they could not swamp the power of the vocals.

In the late seventies the group returned to gospel, signing with Myrrh, a subsidiary of the worldwide conglomerate of Christian music, Word Records.

MIGHTY SPARROW
b. Slinger Francisco, b. 9 July 1935, Grenada, West Indies

The most important figure in the development of calypso music since the fifties, Mighty Sparrow brought a new melodic emphasis to the form.

He was the heir to a tradition of topical songs reaching back to the nineteenth century in the Caribbean islands of Trinidad and Tobago. The first competitions to find the king of calypso were held at carnival time in Port of Spain, the Trinidad capital, at about the time of the First World War.

From the forties calypso was Americanized (through pop versions by the **Andrews Sisters** and folk versions by **Harry Belafonte**) and it flourished in Britain in the fifties through immigrants like Lord Kitchener and Lord Beginner. However, the most creative figures in the genre came from its homeland.

Having moved to Trinidad from Grenada at the age of two, Francisco improvised verses at school, sang in church and played in a steel band. His early influences as a singer included **Nat 'King' Cole** and the **Mills Brothers**. His first calypso composition was 'The Parrot and the Monkey'.

Taking the name Mighty Sparrow he won the title of calypso king at the Trinidad carnival for the first time in 1956, dressed as a schoolboy and singing 'Dan Is the Man in the Van'. He went on to repeat that victory on numerous occasions during the next twenty years with a variety of material commenting on sexual behaviour, political trends ('High Cost of Living') and other topics ('Race Track'). He returned after an eighteen-year absence to win the calypso king award in 1992. The following year he was defeated by Mighty Chalkdust, Hollis Liverpool, who holds a PhD in musicology.

Mighty Sparrow has made over forty albums. In the fifties he recorded for Vita Disc, and in the sixties for RCA, releasing such albums as *The Calypso King of Trinidad* and *Sparrow Come Back*. Among his later recordings are the popular 1972 ballad 'Only a Fool Breaks His Own Heart', 'Hot and Sweet' (1974), produced by **Van Dyke Parks**, *King of the World* (Dynamic, 1986) and *25th Anniversary* (Charlie's, 1989). Many of Sparrow's classic calypsos have been reissued by **Eddie Grant**'s Ice label. The first and most important of these, *Vol. 1* (1994), collected together the best of his fifties' recordings. It was followed by another three similarly titled albums. Ice also released a new recording, *Dancing Shoes*, in 1993. Grant also included versions of Sparrow's 'Ten to One It's Murder' and 'Good Citizen' on his own *Soca Baptism* (1994).

AMOS MILBURN

b. 1 April 1926, Houston, Texas, USA, d. 13 January 1980, Houston

One of the most influential blues artists of the Texas–West Coast axis, Milburn specialized in romping boogies about drinking and partying. His ideas, based upon the work of figures like **Pete Johnson** and **Charles Brown**, were developed in their turn by contemporary singer/pianists like **Fats Domino**, Floyd Dixon and Little Willie Littlefield, and his best-known song, 'Chicken Shack Boogie'*, became an R&B standard. In the eighties his style deeply affected British and American R&B bar bands.

After Second World War service he played with his own small groups in clubs around Houston, securing a contract with Aladdin in 1946 and recording piano boogies and blues. 'Chicken Shack Boogie' (1948), a celebration of black night-life larded with hep-talk, was an enormous hit and gave him country-wide status as a club act and recording artist. He was voted Top R&B Artist by *Billboard* in 1949 and 1950. Others of his numerous R&B chart entries included 'Hold Me Baby' (1948), 'Roomin' House Boogie' (1949), 'Bad Bad Whiskey' (which reached No. 1 in 1950) and 'Let Me Go Home Whiskey' (1953). On much of his Aladdin output he collaborated with the arranger and tenor saxophonist **Maxwell Davis**.

In 1954 he broke up his band and worked solo on rock'n'roll package tours for the Shaw agency. His later Aladdin sessions reflected the success of Fats Domino and were often held in New Orleans with local musicians. He left the label in 1956 and worked as a duo with Charles Brown, recording for Ace (1959). In 1963 he cut an album for Motown. For much of the sixties he worked in and around Cincinnati and Cleveland, Ohio, his club act embracing not only his old material but pop standards. He suffered a series of strokes and in 1972 retired to obscurity in Houston. On a 1973 session for Blues Spectrum, not released until 1977, he played the right-hand piano part and his old friend **Johnny Otis** the left; these were his last recordings.

BUDDY MILES

b. George Miles, 5 September 1946, Omaha, Nebraska, USA

A high-profile rock and soul drummer and occasional vocalist, Miles played with such luminaries as **Jimi Hendrix**, **Mike Bloomfield** and **Carlos Santana**.

As a teenager he became a session drummer and played live with the **Ink Spots** and **Wilson Pickett**. In 1967 Miles joined Electric Flag with Bloomfield and bassist Harvey Brooks. After recording two albums, the group split and Miles took trumpeter Marcus Doubleday with him to form the Buddy Miles Express whose *Expressway to Your Skull* (Mercury, 1968) and *Electric Church* (1969) were modelled on the Electric Flag's soul/blues/rock sound.

In 1970 Miles joined Hendrix's Band of Gypsys and after Hendrix's death he and fellow-Gypsy Billy Cow (bass) recorded the hit album *Them Changes*. With ever-changing personnel, Miles cut three more Mercury albums before signing to Columbia in 1972. There he collaborated with Carlos Santana on a live album recorded in Hawaii (1972), while **Johnny Bristol** produced a superior soul album, *All the Faces of Buddy Miles* (1974).

He later recorded *More Miles per Gallon* (1975) and *Bicentennial Gathering* (1976) for Casablanca and in 1978 formed a band while in jail for theft. In 1981 Miles resumed his professional career, recording *Sneak Attack* (Atlantic). In 1988 he was the voice of the California Raisins on an album of rock'n'roll standards that was a spin-off from a successful television commercial.

BOB MILLER

b. 20 September 1895, Memphis, Tennessee, USA, d. 26 August 1955, New York

For a quarter of a century Bob Miller was, in the words of the *Saturday Evening Post*, the 'undisputed non-stop song-writing champion [of hillbilly music]. **Irving Berlin** and others have written a thousand songs. Miller makes them look hesitant.' In 1928 he wrote 450 hillbilly numbers; by 1950 he had passed 7,000. This would be less momentous if they were all of the stature and memorability of his 'Dry Votin' – Wet Drinkin' – Better Than Thous, Hypocritical Blues' (1929), but Miller's body of work includes such accurately targeted numbers as the prisoner's lament 'Twenty-One Years', the senior citizens' standard 'Rockin' Alone (In an Old Rockin' Chair)' and many other country hits first heard in the thirties and far from moribund in the nineties.

He grew up in Memphis, becoming a pianist on the riverboats in his teens, then leading an orchestra and writing and publishing jazz and blues compositions like the 'Beale Street African Opera Series' (1923) which included 'Strut Your Material'. By 1928 he was based in New York, where he offered record companies his three-way service of writing, publishing and, if necessary, recording their hillbilly catalogue. His own first record, 'Eleven Cent Cotton Forty Cent Meat' (Columbia, 1928), found immediate favour in the South for its sardonic comments on the farmers' worsening lot. Oddly for a hillbilly hit, this was a vocal/piano solo; subsequent recordings used small groups with fiddle, guitar, banjo and kazoo. In 1928 too Miller wrote 'Sipping Cider', a minor hillbilly success for **Vernon Dalhart** which reappeared in the sixties as a hit for the Danish pop duo Nina and Frederick.

For the next five years Miller was phenomenally productive in all his capacities. He wrote songs about farm relief, prohibition, chain-stores, bank failures and, in the best broadsheet tradition, crime. On this subject, he ranged from the Lindbergh kidnapping case, which inspired 'There's a New Star up in Heaven (Baby Lindy Is up There)' (Columbia, 1932), to the deaths of 'Legs' Diamond and John Dillinger and, later, the assassination of Louisiana governor Huey P. Long – a subject he first speculated on in song two years before the actual event. At the same time he was producing more standard hillbilly repertoire like 'Little Red Caboose Behind the Train' (1929) and 'Little Sweetheart of the Prairie' (1931). 'Twenty-One Years' (1930) and 'Rockin' Alone (In an Old Rockin' Chair)' (1932) were recorded with most success by **Carson Robison**, and the serio-comic 'Seven Years with the Wrong Woman' (1932) – apparently based on a rueful reminiscence of fellow recording mogul **Art Satherley** – by Cliff Carlisle and others.

Miller worked in 1930–1 as a recording manager for Columbia and Okeh, and, after their absorption into it, for ARC. He developed new artists, providing songs by himself or writers in his stable and producing sessions on which he sometimes played piano. One of these 'Miller men', **Elton Britt**, had the biggest country hit of the Second World War with 'There's a Star Spangled Banner Waving Somewhere', published by Miller from his premises in the Brill Building. He maintained offices in the Broadway song-factory for another fifteen years, supported more by his old copyrights than by a foothold in the world of Nashville-dominated country music.

GLENN MILLER

b. Alton Glenn Miller, 1 March 1904, Clarinda, Iowa, USA, d. 15 December 1944, over English Channel

Miller led the most popular commercial swing band of the late thirties whose sound was best represented by 'In the Mood' (1939) and his signature tune, 'Moonlight Serenade'. After his wartime death, his music lived on through later versions of his orchestra and the 1954 biopic starring James Stewart.

He grew up in rural Nebraska, getting his first trombone at the age of thirteen and playing in local dance bands. When Miller studied at the University of Colorado, he appeared in Denver with Boyd Senter's band. In 1926 he moved to Los Angeles, playing in Ben Pollack's dance band, for whom he arranged ''Deed I Do' (1926) and made his first recordings. After performing in New York in 1928, he left Pollack to work on the East Coast, playing and arranging for **Red Nichols**, Bert Lown, **Victor Young**, **Pee Wee Hunt** and Glen Gray's Casa Loma Orchestra, Ozzie Nelson (father of **Rick Nelson**) and the orchestra led by **Tommy Dorsey** and his brother **Jimmy**. For the Dorseys, Miller composed 'Dese Dem Dose' and made a proto-swing arrangement of 'Stop, Look and Listen', whose call-and-response pattern and use of a fade-in and fade-out looked forward to his own later style.

Miller's penchant for gimmicky writing was evident in 'Bugle Call Rag', recorded by English bandleader **Ray Noble**, which included snippets of Ravel's 'Bolero' and other tunes. Miller's work with Noble, for whom he assembled an American orchestra in 1934, also showed him developing the combination of clarinet and four saxophones that would become a trademark of his own swing recordings.

Although Miller made his first records for Columbia in 1935, as leader of a recording band playing swing with a string section, it was not until he formed his third orchestra that he found a large audience. The Glenn Miller Orchestra's first live performances took place in New York in 1938. From the beginning, the audience reaction was overwhelming as the band was mobbed by jitterbugging teenagers.

In the three years 1939–42 Miller had more than a dozen hits. The most famous was the riff-based 'In the Mood'* (Bluebird, 1939), written by tenor saxophonist Joe Garland and **Fats Waller**'s lyricist Andy Razaf (the tune was taken up as a theme tune by British bandleader **Joe Loss**). Other million-sellers for Miller included the Bill Finegan arrangement of R. A. Eastburn's 1869 song 'Little Brown Jug' (1939); 'Moonlight Serenade', which began with a trombone solo based on Miller's warming-up exercise; 'Pennsylvania 6-5000' (1940), co-written by the band's arranger Jerry Gray; 'Tuxedo Junction'; and the **Harry Warren** novelty film songs 'Chattanooga Choo-Choo' (1941) and 'Kalamazoo' (1942), sung by Tex Beneke and Marion, sister of **Betty Hutton**, in Sun Valley Serenade and Orchestra Wives, respectively.

The variety of the band's repertoire was evident

from its No. 1 hits, which included the classical adaptation 'Moon Love' (1939), **Harold Arlen**'s 'Over the Rainbow', the Walt Disney song 'When You Wish upon a Star' (1940), the riff-laden 'Tuxedo Junction', 'Fools Rush in' (revived in 1963 by **Rick Nelson**), 'Blueberry Hill' (a later hit for **Fats Domino** in 1956), the Russian folk tune 'Song of the Volga Boatmen' and 'Don't Sit Under the Apple Tree' (1942). Among the vocalists featured with Miller's band were **Kay Starr** and Ray Eberle, who sang Andre Kostalanetz's 'Moon Love' and 'The Story of a Starry Night', both based on themes from Tchaikovsky.

His last big hit was an adaptation of the 1891 march 'American Patrol'* (1942). Shortly afterwards Miller was drafted into the air force where he led a famous service band, performing in America and England. Miller's plane disappeared en route to France.

After his death, various 'Glenn Miller Orchestras' emerged to perpetuate his music and the trombonist's estate nominated the band led by clarinettist Buddy de Franco as the official Miller band. Glenn's brother Herb formed a band to perpetuate the Glenn Miller sound in 1981. This orchestra is now led by John Miller, Herb's son. In Britain, the Syd Lawrence Orchestra specialized in the fifties and sixties in imitating Miller's original recordings. More important was Miller's influence on such later bandleaders as **Nelson Riddle**, **Ted Heath** and Paul Weston.

The success of *The Glenn Miller Story* (1954) kept his memory bright as did the hit versions of 'In the Mood' by Miller copyist Ernie Fields (Rendezvous) in 1959 and by Miller himself in a re-release which returned the song to the British charts in 1976. Two years later the vocal group Tuxedo Junction reached the American Top Forty with a revival of 'Chattanooga Choo-Choo' (Butterfly). In 1995 recordings made in London by Miller for broadcasting to Germany in 1944 were issued for the first time on CD.

JAY MILLER
b. Jay D. Miller, 5 May 1922, El Campo, Texas, USA

Throughout the fifties and sixties Jay Miller was the most commercially successful record producer in Southern Louisiana, concurrently engaged in the pop, blues, R&B, country, cajun and comedy fields.

His involvement with local music began in the mid-thirties when he sang cowboy songs on KPLC, Lake Charles. When his family moved to Crowley in 1937 he met popular string-bands like the Hackberry Ramblers, Leo Soileau's Four Aces and Happy Fats and the Rayne-Bo Ramblers, and played guitar or mandolin with similar line-ups.

In 1946 he started the first Louisiana-based record label, Fais Do Do, with releases by Happy Fats and fiddler Doc Guidry. It was followed in 1947 by Feature, a primarily country label which introduced the smooth Al Terry and the more honky-tonk-styled Lou Millet and went on to launch **Doug Kershaw** and the pop-cajun singer Jimmy C. Newman, author of 'Alligator Man' (1961), who later recorded prolifically for MGM and Decca. Miller supported his ventures with the royalties on **Kitty Wells**' 1952 recording of his 'It Wasn't God Who Made Honky Tonk Angels', an answer song to **Hank Thompson**'s 'Wild Side of Life' (1952).

In 1954 Miller recorded his first commercially successful blues artist, singer/guitarist Lightnin' Slim. After a few releases on Feature ('Rock Me Mama', 'New Orleans Bound', 1954) Miller leased Slim's output to Ernie Young's Excello, a Nashville-based blues label associated with the powerful station WLAC. The resulting sales encouraged Miller to develop a blues catalogue. Lazy Lester, the harmonica player on the best Lightnin' Slim sides, began recording in his own name in 1958 and had a hit the following year with 'I'm a Lover Not a Fighter'/'Sugar Coated Love'. Another singer/harmonica player, Slim Harpo, had his biggest hit with his first Miller/Excello recording, 'I'm a King Bee' (1957), later recorded by the **Rolling Stones** (1964). 'Rainin' in My Heart' (1961) and 'Baby Scratch My Back' (1966) ensured a measure of international fame before his death in 1970. Miller also introduced to the blues audience the singer/guitarists Lonesome Sundown and Silas Hogan, and the gruff singer and harmonica-player Moses 'Whispering' Smith.

Miller recorded cajun music on his own Cajun Classics and Kajun labels, plus rock'n'roll and R&B on Rocko and Zynn. He also leased material to larger companies, such as Warren Storm's 1958 hit 'Prisoner's Song' (Nasco). Owning the best-equipped studio in southern Louisiana, he engineered or produced many successful sides for other local operators, such as Floyd Soileau, whose 1959 swamp-pop hit 'This Should Go on Forever' by Rod Bernard was recorded in Miller's studio and leased to **Leonard Chess**'s Argo. Soileau's Ville Platte operation housed the labels Swallow, which had regional hits by **Nathan Abshire**, Vin Bruce and Belton Richard, and Jin, best known for Johnnie Allan's reworking of **Chuck Berry**'s 'The Promised Land', a minor hit in Britain in 1974 (Oval). Other important Louisiana producers of the period included George Khoury, whose Khoury's and Lyric labels were active from 1950, and Eddie Shuler, a one-time cajun bandleader whose Goldband label had successful cajun releases by Cleveland Crochet ('Sugar Bee', 1961) and the Hackberry Ramblers ('Cajun Pogo', 1963).

By 1966 Miller's association with Excello had ended and blues sales were declining and he launched his Rebel label: 'subtle rib-tickling satire for those who take a conservative position on integration issues'. The first release, 'Flight NAACP 105' by the Son of Mississippi (Joe Norris), sold nearly a quarter of a million copies. Other releases included 'Kajun Klu [sic] Klux Klan' and 'Move Them Niggers North' by Johnny Rebel (Clifford 'Pee Wee' Trahan) and the pro-war 'Birthday Thank You Tommy from Vietnam' by veteran cajun singer Happy Fats. Rebel's output was collected on the album For Segregationists Only.

At the end of the sixties Miller turned his attention to civic affairs, and the management of his labels, record store and Master-Trak studio was taken over by his son Mark. The Kajun label was reactivated for local French bands, while zydeco and other regional black music appears on Blues Unlimited. The studio continued to be used for cajun and zydeco sessions by companies outside Louisiana, such as Rounder and Sonet, while Jay Miller's vast back catalogue was systematically reissued on more than fifty albums by the British Flyright label.

MITCH MILLER
b. 4 July 1911, Rochester, New York, USA

One of the most successful recording artists of the fifties with his series of sing-along singles and albums, Miller was even more influential as a producer. In his work with **Frankie Laine**, **Rosemary Clooney**, **Johnny Ray**, **Guy Mitchell** and **Johnny Mathis**, among others, he developed the notion of a record being more than a mere recording of a performance. His dramatic productions featured a unique mix of sound effects (a snapping bullwhip, honking geese) and unusual instrumentation (cellos, French horns, a jangling harpsichord) that was intended to intensify the listening experience. Few of his productions could be faithfully reproduced by their singers in live performance. Miller, who had a penchant for folk-sounding songs, was, with **Gordon Jenkins** (his rival at Decca), also influential in widening the audience for folk music beyond that of the folk revival. He was also one of the first producers to make cover-versions of established country hits.

After graduating from the Eastman School of Music in 1932, Miller became an oboist with the Rochester Philharmonic Orchestra and in 1936 joined the CBS Symphony Orchestra and played with the orchestras of **Percy Faith** and Andre Kostelanetz, among others, over a period of eleven years.

In 1948 he was appointed by **John Hammond** as head of the pop division of the newly formed Mercury Records and had immediate success with his productions for Laine. The most important of these were 'Mule Train'* (1949) and 'The Cry of the Wild Geese'* (1950), in which Miller set Laine's big voice against a dramatic soundscape. Their success led to

Miller's being appointed head of A&R at Columbia in 1950. Both of these songs had originally been recorded by country singer **Tennessee Ernie Ford** and at Columbia Miller continued the policy of covering previous country hits. Thus, in 1951, he gave **Tony Bennett Hank Williams**' 'Cold, Cold Heart', had a pop hit and in 1952 repeated the process for Rosemary Clooney ('Half As Much') and **Jo Stafford** ('Jambalaya'). But his greatest success with this ploy was 'Singing the Blues'. After **Marty Robbins** had a country No. 1 with the song, Miller turned it into both a pop and R&B hit for Mitchell and then repeated the process, only marginally less successfully, with Robbins' next recording, 'Knee Deep in the Blues'.

At Columbia, Miller also began his own recording career. His first hit was a cover of Gordon Jenkins' million-selling adaptation of the Israeli folk song 'Tzena, Tzena, Tzena' (1950) which featured a cheerful chorus and spare instrumentation. His recording of the song presaged the jaunty sing-along formula that would bring him such success throughout the fifties. His major hits included an adaptation of the Civil War marching song 'The Yellow Rose of Texas'* (1955), which was memorably parodied by **Stan Freberg** (1955), and 'March from Bridge on the River Kwai'* (1957), written by **Malcolm Arnold**. Miller extended the formula to albums, in the process becoming the most successful album artist of his time. These included Sing Along with Mitch*, Christmas Sing Along with Mitch*, More Sing Along with Mitch* (all in 1958, the year he began his successful television sing-along series) and a further four million-selling albums by 1960, by which time the formula was overworked and tired.

Miller's strong and publicly stated opposition to rock'n'roll, which he misunderstood and crudely characterized as being about 'pony-tail ribbons, popsicles and peanut brittle' rather than 'Music', left Columbia in the mid-sixties with a middle-of-the-road attitude to pop that cost the company dearly. Of all the major labels in the fifties and early sixties, Columbia made the least rock'n'roll signings: Miller turned down both **Elvis Presley** and **Buddy Holly** when they were offered to him. His authoritarian attitude was also in part responsible for the company losing **Frank Sinatra** (whom Miller recorded in 1950 singing **Leadbelly**'s 'Goodnight Irene', backed by Miller's sing-along chorus!)

However, as a producer Miller's work was decidedly progressive. Though many of the songs he assigned to artists were covers (thus Clooney's 'Come on-a My House'*, 1951, was taken from Kay Armen's Decca recording of the **David Seville** song, and Ray's 'Just Walking in the Rain'*, 1956, a cover of the Prisonaires' Sun recording), and others were derived from folk songs (Mitchell's 'The Roving Kind'*, 1950,

Doris Day's 'A Guy Is a Guy'*, 1952) or were artificial folk songs (such as **Bob Merrill**'s series of hits for Mitchell), as conceived by Miller they were entirely new, records rather than mere performances. Moreover, though he was mostly associated with brash, big-voiced balladeers and dramatic productions, his work with Mathis (such as 'The Twelfth of Never', 1957) showed Miller to have an equally delicate touch.

In the sixties Miller, a millionaire from his singalong albums, retired.

ROGER MILLER

b. *Roger Dean Miller 2 January 1936, Forth Worth, Texas, USA, d. 25 October 1992, Los Angeles, California*

One of the most successful country singer-songwriters of the sixties, Miller's best songs brought country humour and language ('Dang Me'*, 'Chug-a-Lug'*, 1964) and a bemused, wry rural eye ('England Swings', 1965) to the mainstream of American popular music.

Raised in Erick, Oklahoma, Miller was deeply influenced by **Hank Williams** and started singing and writing in his teens. In the mid-fifties he went to Nashville and had his first songwriting success when **Ray Price**, whose touring show he joined as a comedian, recorded his 'Invitation to the Blues' (1958). Signed to RCA in 1960, he had a country hit with 'When Two Worlds Collide' (1961) and joined **Faron Young**'s band as a drummer in 1962. Signed by producer Jerry Kennedy to Smash in 1964, Miller had immediate success with the comic 'Dang Me' and 'Chug-a-Lug'. More influential outside country circles, however, were the more relaxed 'King of the Road' (1965) – which was subsequently recorded by numerous artists including the Proclaimers in 1990 and inspired an answer song, 'Queen of the House' (Capitol, 1965), from Jody Miller (no relation) – and the gentle 'England Swings' (1965), an ironic comment on the media's creation of the 'swinging London' phenomenon. Both 'King' and 'England' were substantial pop hits all over the world. Miller had continued success throughout the sixties, alternating comic novelty items ('Husbands and Wives', 'You Can't Roller Skate in a Buffalo Herd', 1966) with folksy musings that were decidedly blander than his earlier songs. These included 'Walkin' in the Sunshine' (1967) and the oft-recorded 'Little Green Apples', which was also a hit for O. C. Smith (Columbia, 1968), a former singer with **Count Basie**.

Miller label-hopped through the seventies, securing few hits, either pop or country, along the way. A notable exception was 'Old Friends' (Columbia, 1982) on which he was partnered by Price and **Willie Nelson**. But by this time his interests lay elsewhere. He

sang in the Disney cartoon *Robin Hood* (1973) and in 1984 wrote all the songs to *Big River*, a successful Broadway adaptation of Mark Twain's *The Adventures of Huckleberry Finn*.

STEVE MILLER

b. *5 October 1943, Milwaukee, Wisconsin, USA*

One of the most durable of American musicians, Miller's career has spanned four decades. His style is best summarized as a genial mix of blues and mainstream rock.

The son of a jazz- and blues-loving doctor, Miller formed his first band, the Marksmen Combo, which included **Boz Scaggs**, in 1955. By the early sixties the group had become the Ardells and were playing Motown and R&B material. With organist Barry Goldberg, Miller formed the shortlived Miller–Goldberg Blues Band in Chicago in 1963 and the nucleus of this group accompanied **Chuck Berry** on *Live at the Fillmore* (1967).

By this time Miller had moved to San Francisco and was performing locally as the Steve Miller Blues Band with Scaggs (guitar, vocals), Jim Peterman (keyboards), Lonnie Turner (bass) and Tim Davis (drums). This line-up played on the soundtrack of *Revolution* (1969), performed at the Monterey Pop Festival, and were signed by Capitol in 1967 for a then unheard of advance of $50,000, plus full artistic control of their record releases.

At Miller's insistence, *Children of the Future* (1968) and *Sailor* (1969) were produced in England by Glyn Johns, who made imaginative use of special effects and other studio techniques. *Sailor* included Miller's first minor hit, 'Livin' in the USA'. Scaggs left and keyboards-player Ben Sidran joined the band for *Brave New World* (1969), which reached the Top Forty. The main feature of *Your Saving Grace* (1970), the Nashville-recorded *Number 5* (1971) and *Rock Love* (1972) was the rapid turnover of personnel in what was now called the Steve Miller Band.

The following year, Miller reached No. 1 with the title track from the self-produced *The Joker*. A change of style from his blues-based songs, it was a relaxed, witty slice of mainstream rock. A long period of silence was ended in 1976 when Miller returned with two albums recorded at the same time, *Fly Like an Eagle* (1976) and *Book of Dreams* (1977). Both were major hits and each spawned a clutch of successful singles including the No. 1 'Rock'n'Me', 'Fly Like an Eagle'* and 'Jet Airliner'.

At this point Miller retired to set up his own studio in Oregon where he recorded another pair of albums, the disappointing *Circle of Love* (1981) and *Abracadabra* (1982), whose sprightly title track sold a million in reaching No. 1. The band now included

drummer-songwriter Gary Mallaber and guitarists
Kenny Lewis and John Massaro. This line-up was featured on a 1983 live album. In 1984 the Steve Miller
Band released the lacklustre *Italian X-Rays* while
1987's *Living in the 20th Century* was dedicated to
blues singer **Jimmy Reed** and included three of his
songs. A version of **Lee Dorsey**'s 'Ya Ya' was among
the tracks on *Born 2 B Blue* (1988).

In 1990, following its use in a jeans commercial, a
reissued 'The Joker' topped the British singles chart,
prompting the release of *The Best of Steve Miller
1968–1973*. The next two years saw Miller tour regularly, and in 1992 he released his first new studio
album for four years, the unexceptional *Wide River*.

The three-CD set *Steve Miller Band Box Set* (1994)
is the definitive retrospective. It was followed by
Greatest Hits (1998).

LUCKY MILLINDER

*b. Lucius Millinder, 8 August 1900, Anniston, Alabama,
USA, d. 28 September 1966, New York*

Bandleader, expansive showman and occasional
vocalist, Millinder's various orchestras included leading jazz, bebop and R&B figures over three decades.

He grew up in Chicago where he became a well-
known master of ceremonies in ballrooms and clubs
in the late twenties. In 1931 he fronted a touring band
and in 1932 moved to New York. After leading the former Congo Knights of Ralph Cooper during a residency on the French Riviera in 1933, Millinder took
over the leadership of **Irving Mills**' Blue Rhythm
Band.

Founded as a second-string group to deputize for
Mills' star orchestras led by **Cab Calloway** and **Duke
Ellington**, the Blue Rhythm Band also recorded for
Decca in its own right, and accompanied such singers
as Mamie Smith and **Sister Rosetta Tharpe** on
'soundies', short films for visual juke boxes. Millinder
led the band until 1938 when he took over **Bill
Doggett**'s orchestra with Doggett remaining as
pianist. When that venture was a financial failure,
Millinder formed a new band which provided the
soundtrack music for *Paradise in Harlem* (1940). He
recorded for Decca throughout the forties, with
singers Tharpe (secular material like 'Trouble in
Mind') and **Wynonie Harris**, and with soloists
including **Eddie 'Lockjaw' Davis**, Lucky Thompson
and **Dizzie Gillespie** ('Little John Special', 1942). Less
impressive was the patriotic instrumental 'We're
Gonna Have to Stop the Dirty Little Jap'.

Millinder had R&B hits on RCA with 'D' Natural
Blues' (1949) and 'I'll Never Be Free' (1950) before
joining **Syd Nathan**'s King label where Millinder's former trumpeter and songwriting partner **Henry Glover**
had become A&R director in 1947. 'I'm Waiting Just

for You' (King, 1951) was Millinder's biggest hit and
his orchestra soon became a house band for the label,
providing accompaniment on many rhythm and blues
hits by Harris, Bullmoose Jackson and others.

After 1952 Millinder's big-band activities were
infrequent and he worked as a disc-jockey, salesman
and fortune-teller.

THE MILLS BROTHERS

*John, b. 11 February 1911, Piqua, Ohio, USA, d. January
1936 (replaced by John Mills Snr, b. 1882, Piqua, d. 8
December 1967); Herbert, b. 12 April 1912, Piqua, d. 12
April 1989, Las Vegas, Nevada; Harry, b. 9 August 1913,
Piqua; Donald, b. 29 April 1915, Piqua, d. 13 November
1999*

The Mills Brothers, like the **Ink Spots**, adapted the
early black jubilee quartet style into a medium for
sweet, and occasionally hot, harmonized treatments
of popular songs. To this approach they added vocal
impressions of instruments: though their records
have 'trumpet', 'bass' and other such sounds, the only
actual instrument used was a guitar.

As boys, they worked in vaudeville and had a radio
show on WLW, Cincinnati. From 1930 they were
heard on nationwide radio from New York and their
first record, 'Nobody's Sweetheart'/'Tiger Rag'
(Brunswick, 1931), was a million-seller. Film appearances followed, in *The Big Broadcast of 1932*, *Operator
13* (1933) and *Twenty Million Sweethearts* (1934, with
Dick Powell), and they played in Britain in 1934 and
several times thereafter. Other successful recordings
included their theme song 'Goodbye Blues' and, with
Duke Ellington and his orchestra, 'Diga Diga Doo'
(both Brunswick, 1932). In 1934 they moved to the
newly founded Decca label.

When John Mills, the guitarist and singer of the
'bass' lines, died in 1936, he was replaced by his father;
the guitar role, for a time, fell to the jazz musician
Bernard Addison. The group continued to tour,
appear on radio – often in **Bing Crosby**'s shows – and
record. In 1943 they had a hit with 'Paper Doll'*
(Decca) and appeared in the movie musicals *Chatter-
box*, *He's My Guy* and *Reveille with Beverly*. Other
million-sellers included 'You Always Hurt the One
You Love' (1944), a revival of **Hoagy Carmichael**'s
'Lazy River' (1948), and 'Glow Worm' (1952), which
earlier had been a big hit for **Spike Jones**. John Mills
Snr retired in 1956 and the brothers then worked as a
trio with a guitar accompanist, maintaining their
popularity as a nightclub act and recording several
albums for Dot.

Like the Ink Spots, the Mills Brothers had an incal-
culable effect on doo-wop, but they were also listened
to attentively farther away: their style was often reproduced by South African township groups, at least one

of which in the fifties was actually called the African Mills Brothers.

IRVING MILLS
b. 16 January 1894, Russia, d. 21 April 1985, Palm Springs, Florida, USA

Mills was a publisher, manager (of **Duke Ellington**, the **Mills Brothers** and **Cab Calloway**, among others), booking agent and general fixer. Though his accounting procedures and business methods might have been questionable, he did more to promote black talent in the thirties than virtually any other white man.

Mills began his career in music in 1912 as a song plugger and in 1916, with his elder brother Jack, established Mills Music. In 1919 he organized his own band, Irving Mills and His Hotsy Totsy Gang, briefly employing **Benny Goodman**, **Tommy Dorsey** and **Artie Shaw** as sidemen, before in 1926 he met Ellington. Mills first employed Ellington as a bandleader and arranger but within a year he folded his own band to manage him. By this time Mills Music was one of the most important publishers specializing in jazz. Moreover, with Mills managing Ellington, Calloway and **Lucky Millinder**, Mills Music quickly became a focus of black musical activity in New York.

Following the collapse of the American record industry in the thirties, Mills actively subsidized recordings of his artists' copyrights in order to increase Mills Music's earnings (and his own earnings: many Mills Music copyrights such as Ellington's 'Mood Indigo', 'Sophisticated Lady' and 'It Don't Mean a Thing if It Ain't Got That Swing', and Calloway's 'Minnie the Moocher' had their lyrics credited to Mills, though it is unclear if he actually wrote them). Similarly he briefly published *Melody News* (on which **John Hammond** worked in 1934–5) to publicize his artists and jazz in general, and in 1937 established the Master and Variety labels on which a number of small jazz groupings from within the bands of Ellington, Calloway and **Charlie Barnet** recorded. In 1939 Ellington left Mills, who henceforth concentrated on his growing management and publishing empires, though he found time to help produce the stage (1942) and film (1943) versions of *Stormy Weather*.

In 1966 Mills sold Mills Music to an investment consortium. Before he finally retired to Florida, he briefly returned to the music business in the seventies by buying **Norman Granz**'s publishing catalogue.

RONNIE MILSAP
b. 16 January 1944, Robbinsville, North Carolina, USA

Milsap's best records have been those that reflected the breadth of his musical vision (*Ronnie Milsap,*

Warner Brothers, 1971, and his early sides for RCA in a honky-tonk style), but he has had his greatest success with a series of pop-inflected country ballads.

Born blind, Milsap could play several instruments by the time he was ten. While at school he formed a rock'n'roll group, the Apparitions, and after briefly attending college decided on a career in music. He played with **J. J. Cale** before forming his own band in 1965 and signing with Scepter Records. His first records for the label (which included 'Never Had It So Good', 1965) were in an R&B vein and Milsap toured the South with such artists as **Bobby Bland**, rather than country or rock performers.

After settling in Nashville in 1969, he turned increasingly to country music, scoring his first hit with 'Loving You Is a Natural Thing' (Chips, 1970). The **Dan Penn**-produced *Ronnie Milsap* (Warners) was a mix of rock'n'roll (**Chuck Berry**'s 'Sweet Little Rock and Roller'), contemporary country (**Kris Kristofferson**'s 'Please Don't Tell Me How the Story Ends'), impassioned balladry (**Roy Orbison**'s 'Crying') and included Penn and Spooner Oldham's reflective 'Blue Skies of Montana'. However, the album sold poorly and Milsap moved to RCA in 1973. His first recording, the superior honky-tonk-styled 'I Hate You', was a hit but by the time of his definitive recording of Bob Gibson's '(I'd Be) A Legend in My Time' (1974), his records were being swamped by strings. This crossover sound brought Milsap phenomenal success in the country charts throughout the seventies and eighties and into the nineties. His country No. 1s include 'Day Dreams about Night Things' (1975), '(I'm a) Stand by My Woman Man' (1976), 'It Was Almost Like a Song' (1977), 'Nobody Likes Sad Songs' (1979), 'Am I Losing You' (1980), 'Any Day Now' (1982), 'Show Her' (1983), 'Still Losing You' (1984), the duet with **Kenny Rogers** 'Make No Mistake She's Mine' (1987) and 'A Woman in Love' (1989). Several of these were also pop hits. Among his later albums were the intriguing collection of fifties standards *Lost in the Fifties Tonight* (1986) and *Back to the Grindstone* (1991).

The *Essential Ronnie Milsap* (RCA, 1995) is the definitive compilation of his RCA days, while *Sings His Best for Capitol* (1996) is a re-recording of his best-known songs.

ROY MILTON
b. 31 July 1907, Wynnewood, Oklahoma, USA, d. 18 September 1983, Los Angeles, California

A bandleader highly respected by his contemporaries, Milton achieved the sound and swing of a big band sound with a six- or seven-piece group, thereby contributing to **Louis Jordan**'s blueprint for an R&B format that would be both flexible and economical and would in other hands prove readily adaptable to the requirements of rock'n'roll.

He grew up in Tulsa, Oklahoma, gaining some band experience as a vocalist and drummer with Ernie Fields (1931–3) before moving, in 1935, to the West Coast, where he formed his Solid Senders in 1938 to work clubs in Los Angeles. At evening engagements he played standards and current popular numbers for white clientele, then in black after-hours sessions he would reveal his blues and boogie influences. Among the Solid Senders were the boogie pianist Camille Howard, tenor-saxophonist Buddy Floyd and altoist Jackie Kelso. Milton did most of the singing, in an easy-going crooning manner.

In 1945 he recorded for Gladys and **Lionel Hampton**'s Hamp-Tone label and for **Art Rupe**'s Juke Box, the forerunner of Speciality. 'R.M. Blues'*, a riff-based number hastily composed for the first Rupe session, was the biggest R&B hit of 1946, staying at No. 1 for twenty-six weeks. Milton also issued sides on his own Roy Milton label, which was later renamed Miltone, showcasing artists associated with the owner and featuring descriptive record-label art by the cartoonist William Alexander.

For the next eight years Milton worked across the United States, and was firmly established among the leading R&B acts: as a 1952 *Down Beat* headline put it, 'One Squeal Shy of Jordan, a Beat from Hamp'. Leaving Speciality in 1954 he recorded for Dootone (1955), King (1956–7) and Warwick (1960) before retiring in the early sixties. He made a comeback in 1970, appearing with the **Johnny Otis** show at the Monterey Jazz Festival and on Otis's Epic albums derived from the event. He also appeared with Otis on occasions in the seventies, and recorded with him for Kent and Blues Spectrum. On a European tour in 1977 he recorded *Instant Groove* (Black and Blue), with guitarists Billy Butler (veteran of the **Bill Doggett** band) and Roy Gaines.

CHARLES MINGUS

b. 22 April 1922, Nogales, Arizona, USA, d. 5 January 1979, Cuernavaca, Mexico

Like later avant-gardists such as the **Art Ensemble of Chicago**, Mingus's innovations as bass player, composer and bandleader were aimed at reintegrating the earliest forms of black music into contemporary jazz as well as at seeking new approaches. Like **Duke Ellington**, his works were frequently of a programme music type, inspired by and aiming to embody political, personal or artistic events or attitudes. But unlike Ellington, Mingus's idiosyncratic method of teaching his musicians their parts – aurally rather than in writing – often turned his best recordings into a form of collective improvisation.

He grew up in the Watts district of Los Angeles and absorbed church music before learning trombone and cello. At high school he switched to jazz double bass and studied with Red Callender. Mingus played in vibes-player Red Norvo's trio after moving to New York in 1951, where he performed in bands with a variety of styles, ranging from New Orleans (**Louis Armstrong**) through big bands and swing (**Lionel Hampton**) to bebop (**Bud Powell** and **Charlie Parker**). He took part in the Toronto live recording which reunited Parker and **Dizzy Gillespie** in 1953. The resulting album was issued on Mingus's own Debut label, which he formed with drummer **Max Roach**.

Jazz Experiment (Bethlehem, 1954) with tenor-sax-player (and future producer of **Miles Davis**) Teo Macero provided the first evidence of Mingus's conceptual originality. It was followed by a free jazz duet with drummer Roach on *Percussion Discussion* (Prestige, 1955) and the remarkable *Pithecanthropus Erectus* (Atlantic, 1956), whose title track, with Jackie Maclean on alto, aimed at tracing the evolution of the human species.

The next five years represented the peak of Mingus's explosive creativity as he released a series of albums which were both original in their overall structure and crammed with arresting solos. Among them were *East Coasting* (1957), which featured trumpeter Clarence Shaw, and *Tijuana Moods*, a suite which brilliantly evoked the experience of a lost weekend in the Mexican border town and introduced demonic drummer Danny Richmond, a former R&B sax player who worked with Mingus for the remainder of his career. *Duke's Choice* and *Reincarnations of a Lovebird* were Bethlehem albums dedicated to Ellington and Parker, while on *Blues and Roots* (Atlantic, 1958) such tracks as 'Wednesday Night Prayer Meeting' (with **Eric Dolphy**'s impassioned soprano sax solo) and 'Moanin'' found Mingus distilling the essence of black American music. Other albums from this era included *Mingus Oh Yeah* (Atlantic), *Mingus Ah Um* (Columbia), with its affectionate **Lester Young** tribute, 'Goodbye Pork Pie Hat', *Tonight at Noon* (Atlantic) and *Black Saint and Sinner Lady* (Columbia, 1963). He also wrote the score for John Cassavetes' *Shadows* (1958).

In the early sixties Mingus's live performances were marked by his collaboration with Dolphy. The best of the numerous recordings later released of European and American concerts were *The Great Concert of Charles Mingus* (Prestige, 1964) and *Town Hall Concert* (Fantasy, 1964). Disagreements with record companies and an attempt to set up a permanent jazz workshop meant Mingus was less visible in the late sixties but in the seventies he returned to recording with a group featuring Richmond, George Adams (sax) and Don Pullen (piano) on *Changes One* and *Changes Two* (Atlantic).

During the final year of his life, he embarked on an unlikely collaboration with **Joni Mitchell**. Although they did not record together, Mitchell's lyrics to his compositions appeared on her album, *Mingus* (Asylum, 1979). Mingus died of Huntington's chorea.

Mingus published an autobiography, *Beneath the Underdog*, in 1971. **Leonard Cohen**, **Rolling Stones** Charlie Watts and Keith Richards and **Dr John** were among the contributors to *Weird Nightmare: Meditation on Mingus*, a tribute album produced by Hal Willner in 1992. Ray Davies of the **Kinks** directed a film about the making of Willner's album.

KYLIE MINOGUE
b. 28 May 1968, Melbourne, Australia

Minogue was briefly one of the most successful female singers in UK chart history in the eighties courtesy of a succession of pop singles crafted by the production/songwriting team of **Stock, Aitken and Waterman**. Her bright sound formed the template for the more sophisticated offerings of the boy and girl groups that followed in her wake.

She began her TV acting career at the age of eleven. By the age of eighteen, she was a veteran of several Australian television soap operas, including *The Sullivans* and *The Hendersons*, before she joined the cast of *Neighbours* in 1986. This became a massive success in the UK, regularly drawing audiences of about 14 million viewers. She was signed by Australian label Mushroom Records in 1987, enjoying immediate success with a version of the 1962 Little Eva hit, 'The Locomotion'.

She was subsequently signed to Stock, Aitken and Waterman's PWL label in the UK, and hit the No. 1 slot in the UK with her début single, 'I Should Be so Lucky' (1988). 'Lucky' was a slick, formulaic dance/pop single, typical of SAW's output, and set the tone for a series of similar titles. Her début album, *Kylie* (1988), was an immediate success, containing four UK hit singles. Success in the US followed, with 'Lucky' reaching the Top Thirty and 'Je Ne Sais Pas Pourquoi' the Top Five before a remixed version of 'Locomotion' made the No. 1 slot. Minogue's début album also made the US Top Five, although subsequent success in America was muted.

A duet with fellow *Neighbours* star **Jason Donovan**, 'Especially for You', saw Minogue's year out in style, reaching No. 1 in the UK. The second album, *Enjoy Yourself*, also appeared in 1989, and was another UK success. The following year brought a string of efficiently marketed singles, giving her five further Top Five hits, including the chart-toppers 'Hand on Your Heart' and 'Tears on My Pillow', a new version of the

1958 song by **Little Anthony and the Imperials**. A third album, *Rhythm of Love*, appeared in 1990. As time went on, however, Minogue became increasingly disenchanted with her squeaky-clean, perennial teenager image, and 1991 saw her attempt to change, with a move to a sexier, vamp-like image.

The attempted change of image was only partly successful and 1991 was a disappointing year for Minogue, culminating in the failure of the single 'Keep on Pumpin' It' (featuring a more heavily dance-orientated sound) to reach the UK Top Forty. A return to a poppier sound on 'If You Were with Me Now' (a duet with Keith Washington) and a revival of the **Chairman of the Board**'s 'Give Me Just a Little More Time' saw Minogue back in the upper regions of the singles chart. She next broke away from SAW to sign with UK dance label deConstruction, releasing an emphatic dance (rather than pop) album in 1994. Among the eponymous album's hit singles were 'Put Yourself in My Place' and 'Confide in Me'.

Minogue's next appearance on record was a duet with fellow Australian star **Nick Cave** on 'Where the Wild Roses Grow', from his *Murder Ballads* (1996) album, which saw the singer aim for a more adult market. Her next solo project, a second eponymous album (1997), included several tracks co-written by Minogue with **Manic Street Preachers**' James Dean Bradfield and Sean Moore, notably the single 'Some Kind of Bliss'. However, the album was a commercial failure, leading Minogue to reconsider her future image. *Kylie*, published in 1999, a watered-down version of **Madonna**'s *Sex*, pointed one way. That undoubtedly was the animus behind her would-be ironic re-creation of the famous Athena poster of the seventies of a female tennis player scratching her bare behind. More successful was her reinvention of herself as a dance diva with the hit single (and UK chart-topper) 'Spinning Around' for her new record label Parlophone. The subsequent album, *Light Years* (2000), included the Robbie Williams composition 'Loveboat', but its ambience was better captured by the **Village People** tribute 'Your Disco Needs You'.

CARMEN MIRANDA
b. Maria do Carmo Miranda da Cuhna, 9 February 1909, Marco de Canavezes, Portugal, d. 5 August 1955, Hollywood, California, USA

Known as 'The Brazilian Bombshell', and remembered in equal parts for her high-speed samba and rumba dancing, tongue-twisting singing and her towering head-dresses of fruit, Miranda was one of the more unlikely musical stars of the forties. Almost a creature of pure fantasy, she was remembered with affection in **Jimmy Buffett**'s delightful 'They Don't Dance Like Carmen No More' (1973) and in **Bette**

Midler's stage act, the centrepiece of which included a parodic impersonation of her.

Raised in Brazil, Miranda was a nightclub singer and recording star, and starred in several domestic films (including *Alo Alo Brasil*, 1934, and *Banana de Terra*, 1938) before she travelled to New York for a featured part in the Broadway show *Streets of Paris* (1939), in which she sang Al Dubin and **Jimmy McHugh**'s 'South American Way'. That led to a contract with Fox and her Hollywood début, *Down Argentine Way* (1940), in which she repeated 'South American Way'. She followed this with a series of musicals in which she was invariably cast as an exotic, fiery 'other woman' with whom the likes of Don Ameche and **Perry Como** (who partnered her in *Doll Face*, 1945, and *If I'm Lucky*, 1946) briefly dallied. All geared to the South American market (the war having closed Europe to American films), her other movies included *That Night in Rio* (1941), in which she sang Dubin and **Harry Warren**'s 'Yi Yi Yi Yi'; *The Gang's All Here* (1943), in which she duetted with **Benny Goodman**; and *Copacabana* (1947), in which Groucho Marx played her agent. Miranda recorded virtually all her film songs for Decca, as well as several duets with the **Andrews Sisters**, including 'Cuanto Le Gusto' and 'The Wedding Samba'.

As realism replaced the escapist fantasy element of musicals in the late forties, so Miranda's career declined and after a few more films, including *Scared Stiff* (1953, her last in which she co-starred with Jerry Lewis and **Dean Martin**), she retreated to cabaret. In Brazil her death was cause for national mourning. In 1994 producer Nelson Motta organized a tribute album, *The Living Legend of Carmen Miranda*, with contributions from Marisa Monte, Gal Costa and Caetano Veloso.

GUY MITCHELL
b. Al Cernik, 21 February 1927, Detroit, Michigan, USA, d. 12 July 1999

One of the many beneficiaries of **Mitch Miller**'s production expertise in the fifties, Mitchell is best remembered for his chirpy version of 'Singing the Blues'* (Columbia, 1956).

The son of Yugoslavian immigrants, Mitchell was briefly signed to Warners as a child actor and singer. After navy service, he joined Carmen Cavallaro's band as a featured vocalist in 1946 and in 1949 won an *Arthur Godfrey Talent Scouts* before being signed by Miller to Columbia. His first hit, 'My Heart Cries for You'* (1950), the tune of which was adapted by **Percy Faith** from a traditional French melody, projected him as merely another big-voiced balladeer, but with his hearty, jocular version of 'The Roving Kind' (1951) Mitchell found an individual voice. The song, origi-

nally recorded by the **Weavers**, was an adaptation of an English sea shanty, 'The Pirate Ship', by Jessie Cavanaugh and Arnold Stanton and Mitchell's performance was the model for Miller's own later sing-along records. Its success led to Miller providing Mitchell with a series of songs that sounded as if they had folk origins. These included 'Sparrow in the Tree Top', 'My Truly, Truly Fair'* (1951), 'Pittsburgh, Pennsylvania'* and 'Feet Up (Pat Him on the Po-Po)' (1952), all written by **Bob Merrill**.

When Mitchell's 'folk' hits dried up, Miller turned to country material and in the process gave Mitchell his greatest success, 'Singing the Blues' (1956). Originally recorded by **Marty Robbins**, the song was a pop and R&B hit in America for Mitchell and in Britain gave both Mitchell and **Tommy Steele** (who, like Mitchell, also covered Robbins' follow-up, 'Knee Deep in the Blues') No. 1 records. Henceforth, Mitchell recorded mostly in a country vein and had his last big hit with **Harlan Howard**'s 'Heartaches by the Numbers'* (1959), originally a hit for **Ray Price**.

In the sixties he recorded only sporadically and in the seventies retired.

JONI MITCHELL
b. Roberta Joan Anderson, 7 November 1943, Fort McLeod, Alberta, Canada

The archetypal singer-songwriter of the seventies, Mitchell treated the studio as a confessional in her early recordings. However, her work was sharper than the majority of the genre, her eloquent lyrics offering what she called an 'anatomy of the love crime'. In her later recordings she developed a more complex approach, blending idiosyncratic jazzy singing with skilful melodies.

Originally an art student in Calgary, Mitchell took up folk singing and moved to Toronto. She married fellow singer Chuck Mitchell in 1965 and began performing on the Detroit and New York club circuits. She first came to prominence through **Judy Collins**' recording of the meditative 'Both Sides Now', the best of her early compositions. Most of the songs on Mitchell's début album *Songs to a Seagull* (Reprise, 1968), produced by David Crosby, suffered from a decorative 'folksy' romanticism. In contrast, *Clouds* (1969) contained 'Both Sides Now' and a number of more profound expressions of sadness and longing, such as 'I Don't Know Where I Stand' and 'That Song About the Midway'.

The title of *Ladies of the Canyon* (1970) reflected Mitchell's status as one of the new rock aristocracy of Southern California. It was at her house that **Crosby, Stills and Nash** first sang together and she provided backing vocals for **James Taylor**'s 'You've Got a Friend'. Her songs by now showed a wider thematic and emotional range. As well as the conventionally poetic 'Circle Game' (memorably recorded by **Tom Rush**), there were compositions focusing on a London street busker and the contrasting 'plight' of the rock star ('For Free'), dealing jauntily with urban redevelopment ('Big Yellow Taxi') and articulating the ideals of love and peace in 'Woodstock', a British No. 1 for **Ian Matthews**' group Southern Comfort.

Blue (1971) was both the most impassioned and the most adventurous in formal terms of Mitchell's earlier albums, containing the exultant 'A Case of You' and the elegiac 'The Last Time I Saw Richard'. Mitchell moved further away from conventional song forms with *For the Roses* (1972), which included her first Top Thirty hit, the skittish 'You Turn Me on, I'm a Radio', as well as 'People's Parties', an acute portrait of the disillusionment of the Woodstock generation. Greater commercial success greeted *Court and Spark* (1974) where Tom Scott's swirling sax lines echoed Mitchell's swooping vocals on two more hits, 'Help Me' and 'Free Man in Paris'. The increasing jazz influence on Mitchell's vocal style was acknowledged by the inclusion on *Court and Spark* of a version of Annie Ross's (of **Lambert, Hendricks and Ross**) vocalese piece 'Twisted'. The contribution of Scott's band LA Express was highlighted on *Miles of Aisles* (1974), a double-album recorded on Mitchell's 1973 world tour.

With *The Hissing of Summer Lawns* (1975), Mitchell turned her attention to middle America, whose lifestyle she observed in a dazzling series of songs. This was her last Top Ten album and in the late seventies Mitchell's compositions became more abstract, concerning themselves less with melody than with rhythm and timbre. Her collaborators on *Hejira* (1976) were drawn primarily from the jazz world and included the innovatory bass-player Jaco Pastorius, **Crusaders**' guitarist Larry Carlton and arranger Mike Gibbs. This phase reached its peak with *Mingus* (1979). Planned as a collaboration between Mitchell and **Charles Mingus**, the project was curtailed by the latter's death, leaving Mitchell to write and record lyrics to 'Goodbye Pork Pie Hat' and other Mingus tunes. Her accompanists included **John McLaughlin**, **Gerry Mulligan** and Jan Hammer. Pastorius and **Pat Metheny** played on the 1980 live album *Shadows and Light*.

In the eighties Mitchell seemed more involved in art than music and her infrequent recordings showed a move to a more conventional rock sound. *Wild Things Run Fast* (Geffen, 1982) included a duet with **Lionel Richie** and an ill-advised version of **Leiber and Stoller**'s rock'n'roll classic 'Baby I Don't Care'. Of greater import was the **Thomas Dolby**-produced *Dog Eat Dog* (1985) which, for the first time, found Mitchell dealing with such political topics as TV

evangelists and the Ethiopian famine. *Chalk Mark in a Rain Storm* (1988), on which she duetted with **Peter Gabriel** and was supported by **Tom Petty** and **Willie Nelson**, was an altogether more lyrical offering, giving full rein to her drifting, multi-tracked vocals. Now more involved with painting than music, Mitchell's recordings were rarer. *Night Ride Home* (1991) was largely acoustic and included 'Slouching Towards Bethlehem', a musical setting of the poem by W. B. Yeats. *Turbulent Indigo* (Reprise, 1994), which included many reproductions of her paintings, sounded remarkably close to *Blue*. It included a version of the Dan Hartman-composed song 'How Do You Stop', a hit for **James Brown** in 1987. Her reputation was further enhanced by the release of two retrospective collections in 1996: *Hits*, which included just that, and the equally intriguing *Misses*, which were just that – personal Mitchell favourites that had failed commercially. She returned to recording with the lesser *Taming the Tiger* (1998) on which she was supported by Wayne Shorter. More interesting was the concept album *Both Sides Now* (2000) in which against an orchestral backing she sang a selection of classic love songs, ranging from 'Stormy Weather', 'You're My Thrill' and a pair of her own compositions ('Both Sides Now' and 'A Case of You'), to tell the story of a love affair that goes wrong.

WILLIE MITCHELL
b. 1928, Ashland, Tennessee, USA

Bandleader and composer Mitchell was the musical director of Hi Records in the seventies where he produced such soul artists as **Al Green**, **O. V. Wright** and **Ann Peebles**.

He played trumpet at high school and formed his first band in 1954. Mitchell played on sessions organized by **Ike Turner** for Modern and by the end of the fifties his group was house band for Reuben Cherry's House of the Blues label. In 1963 Mitchell moved to the newly formed Hi label and recorded a series of R&B instrumental hits, including 'Buster Brown' (1965), 'Bad Eye' (1966) and 'Soul Serenade' (1968). He later arranged and produced records by Wright, Otis Clay (notably 'Trying to Live My Life without You'), Syl Johnson and Denise Lasalle, whose records were released on the Chicago-based Westbound label. Her successes included the R&B No. 1 'Trapped By a Thing Called Love' (1971) and the humorous 'Man Sized Job' (1972).

Mitchell's session band was based on veteran **Booker T. and the MGs**' drummer Al Jackson and the Hodge brothers, Leroy (bass), Charles (keyboards) and Tennie (guitar), and this group provided the taut, immaculate backing for Green's first hit, 'Tired of Being Alone' (1971). Mitchell produced a dozen more hits for Green over the next five years, co-writing some, including 'Let's Stay Together' (1972). He also created the tense backing for Peebles' atmospheric 'I Can't Stand the Rain' and produced the Syl Johnson hit, 'Take Me to the River' (1975). Johnson was originally a Chicago blues harmonica player who moved into R&B in the early sixties and was signed to Hi by Mitchell in 1970.

In the mid-seventies Green abandoned soul for the church and gospel music. Mitchell continued to produce Peebles and Wright, but the Hi label folded in 1980. After producing albums by **Jesse Winchester** and **Paul Butterfield** for Bearsville, he set up his own Waylo label in 1983. Among the artists he produced there were Peebles, Clay and Lanier and Co. Mitchell renewed his partnership with Green in 1986, producing *Going Away* (A&M). He later worked with a British pop group for the first time, producing the début album by **Wet Wet Wet** (*Popped in, Souled out*, 1987).

MOBY GRAPE
Skip Spence, b. 18 April 1946, Windsor, Ontario, Canada, d. 16 April 1999; Peter Lewis, b. 15 July 1945, Los Angeles, California, USA; Jerry Miller, b. 10 July 1943, Tacoma, Washington; Bob Mosley, b. 4 December 1942, Paradise Valley, California; Don Stevenson, b. 15 October 1942, Seattle, Washington

Like Brinsley Schwarz (the group that counted **Nick Lowe** among its members), Moby Grape are sure of a place in the history of popular music, if only for the overkill marketing of their first albums which largely overshadowed their subsequent careers. Columbia issued five singles at the same time from Moby Grape's eponymous début album (1967), all of which failed. Moby Grape's musical significance is that they were one of the few San Francisco groups to perform and record structured pop songs rather than jams, a group in the mould of the **Byrds** rather than the **Grateful Dead**.

The group was formed in 1966 by one-time **Jefferson Airplane** member Spence and ex-Airplane manager Matthew Katz, with guitarist Lewis (from the Cornells) and bassist Mosley (from Los Angeles group the Misfits). The name was taken from a well-known nonsense joke ('what is purple and lives at the bottom of the sea?'). Such was the interest in San Francisco among record companies at the time that, after their first Fillmore Ballroom appearance, fourteen expressed interest in signing them. Signed to Columbia for a huge sum, they made the tightly controlled *Moby Grape* (1967). However, with its twin lead guitars, three-part harmonies and eclectic songs ('Omaha', '8.05', 'Fall on You'), the album failed amidst the hype that surrounded its release.

Wow (1968), which saw Columbia continue its

bizarre marketing strategy – it included a track that could only be played at 78 r.p.m. and a bonus album that featured a live jam session with **Mike Bloomfield** and others – lacked the control of the first album. Nonetheless it reached the Top Twenty. Soon after, Spence left to record the mysterious *Oar* (Columbia, 1968) and the group settled down as a quartet to record *Grape 69* (1969), notable for its sleeve note in which the group blamed themselves for the hype of the past. Following its failure, the group began the process of breaking up and re-forming, only intermittently recording in the seventies. Their albums included the countryish *Truly Fine Citizen* (1970), *20 Granite Creek* (Reprise, 1972) and *Grape Live* (Escape, 1979). More significant was the reissue of *Moby Grape* (Edsel, 1984), which won them a favourable critical reassessment.

Disputes over the ownership of the group name led to the original members (minus Spence) recording as the Melvilles (after the author of *Moby Dick*) for the West Coast label Herman in 1991. They re-formed intermittently in the nineties, sometimes with Spence, who was diagnosed a paranoid schizophrenic, sitting in with them when well enough. A re-release of *Oar* brought the album renewed cult status for its mix of whimsy and psychedelia and led to *More Oar* (1999), which included performances from **Tom Waits**, **R.E.M.** and **Beck** in tribute to the Spence original.

THE MODERN JAZZ QUARTET
Kenny Clarke, b. Kenneth Spearman Clarke, 9 January 1914, Pittsburgh, Pennsylvania, USA, d. 25 January 1985, Paris, France (replaced by Connie Kay b. Conrad Henry Kirnon, 27 April 1917, Tuckahoe, New York, d. 30 November 1994, New York); Percy Heath, b. 30 April 1923, North Carolina; Milt Jackson, b. Milton Jackson, 1 January 1923, Detroit, Michigan; John Aaron Lewis, b. 3 May 1920, LaGrange, Illinois

The virtual creators of chamber jazz during the fifties and sixties, the MJQ's best work rested on the tension between Lewis's shapely, severe, baroque structures and Jackson's more fluid playing.

A fastidious pianist and arranger, Lewis studied anthropology at the University of New Mexico before working in New York with such pioneers of bebop as **Charlie Parker** and **Dizzy Gillespie**, for whose big band Lewis wrote and played in 1946–8. He later helped to formulate **Miles Davis**'s 'chamber jazz' project of 1949–50.

Jackson was the first bebop vibraphone player, working with Gillespie and **Thelonious Monk** before recording with Lewis and Cuban drummer Chano Pozo for the Detroit Sensation label in 1948. He went on to play with **Woody Herman** and Gillespie's big band before rejoining Lewis in 1951. Their first records were released on Gillespie's Dee Gee label as by the Milt Jackson Quartet. When the group signed to Bob Weinstock's Prestige label in 1952, they became the Modern Jazz Quartet. With fellow bebop players **Kenny Clarke** on drums and Heath (bass), the MJQ's first release was Lewis's classically inspired fugue 'Vendome' (1953). It typified the band's intention to graft classical music on to jazz and to produce a chamber-jazz version of collective improvisation.

The group's sound was based on Jackson's unusual approach to vibes-playing which treated the instrument more like a horn than a piano and on Lewis's introspective, gentle style as a pianist. This commitment to classical form caused controversy in critical circles and in 1955 Kay replaced Clarke, who was dissatisfied with the group's baroque approach. In the same year **Nesuhi Ertegun** signed the group to Atlantic. The next five years were the high point of the MJQ's career. Among their albums were *Fontessa* (1956), which included Jackson's 'Bluesology', Lewis's score for the Roger Vadim film *No Sun in Venice* (1957) and the double-album *European Concert* (1960). Less successful, though much performed, was *Django* (1956), Lewis's tribute to **Django Reinhardt**.

During the sixties Lewis's compositions were less inspired and the group were frequently guilty of repeating past successes. The best records of the decade were a selection of pieces from **Gershwin**'s *Porgy and Bess* (1964); *Collaboration*, with guitarist **Laurindo Almeida**, which included an adagio by Spanish classical composer Rodrigo, also recorded by Miles Davis on his *Sketches of Spain*; and *Blues at Carnegie Hall* (1965). With *Blues on Bach*, Lewis went all the way over to the European art music tradition, and emulated the French musician Jacques Loussier, whose own jazz-tinged versions of Bach had been influenced by the MJQ.

Last Concert (1974) commemorated the dissolution of the MJQ, with Lewis going into jazz education, Jackson recording extensively for **Norman Granz**'s Pablo and Kay playing with Dixieland bands. The bassist formed a jazz-funk group with his brothers Jimmy (alto sax) and Albert (drums). The Heath Brothers recorded for Columbia.

The MJQ reunited in 1981 for a triumphant performance at the Newport Jazz Festival and toured regularly thereafter. The group returned to recording for Nesuhi Ertegun's East-West label, releasing *For Ellington* (1988), a tribute to **Duke Ellington**. A fortieth anniversary album was produced in 1992 by **Arif Mardin**.

DOMENICO MODUGNO

b. 9 January 1928, Polignano a Mare, Italy, d. 6 August 1994, Lampedusa

Modugno is best remembered as the author and singer of the 1958 multi-million-selling 'Volare' (as 'Nel Blu Dipinto di Blu' is better known), which remains the most successful popular Italian recording internationally. Modugno's total worldwide sales are in excess of 20 million records.

In his teens, Modugno travelled to Rome in search of film stardom and supported himself as a balladeer (in which role he was cast in *Il Mantello Rosso*). While he never rose above bit parts in films, his singing won him regular work on radio and a contract with Fonit Records and his compositions, at first in the Sicilian dialect, were widely recorded. Among these were 'La Piscipada', 'La Donna Riccia' (1956) and 'Lazzarella' (1957), which won second prize at the Neapolitan Song Festival. His greatest success came in 1958 when he won the prestigious San Remo Song Festival with 'Nel Blu Dipinto di Blu'. An enormous hit in Italy for Modugno (despite being covered by Marino Marini on Durium), the song was released in America on Decca later that year and topped the charts. With its powerful melodic chorus, the song was the culmination of the trend of Italianate ballads that echoed through the fifties in America. Among the many cover-versions, mostly using the English-language lyric by Mitchell Parish, were recordings by **Dean Martin**, whose version was the most successful after Modugno's own, **Jesse Belvin** and **Nelson Riddle**. In Britain, as well as Modugno, Marini and Martin, comedian Charlie Drake (Parlophone) had a hit with the song. **Bobby Rydell** (1962) and **Al Martino** (1975) later successfully revived the song and it has since been recorded by innumerable artists. In 1985 it was the natural choice of Italian stars when they got together in the manner of Band Aid to raise money for charity.

However, though Modugno had considerable further success in Italy (notably winning the San Remo Festival three more times with 'Piove', 1959, 'Addio, Addio', 1962, and 'Dio Come Ti Amo', 1966), he had little elsewhere. Only 'Piove', better known as 'Ciao Ciao Bambino' with an English lyric by Parish, brought him international success in 1959: this time, the cover-versions, by Marini in Britain and Jack Noguez in France and America (Jamie), were more successful. Modugno appeared in seventeen films and in 1987 was elected to the Italian parliament.

MOGWAI

Dominic Aitchisin, aka Demonic, b. Glasgow, Scotland; Stuart Braithwaite, aka pLasmatroN, b. Glasgow; Martin Bulloch, aka Bionic, b. Glasgow; Barry Burns, b. Lanarkshire, Scotland; John Cummings, aka Capt. Meat, b. Glasgow; Brendan O'Hare, aka The Relic

Scots instrumental quartet Mogwai's experimental

soundscapes, based on the loud–soft dynamics of alternative rock, have earned them acclaim and a burgeoning international fanbase.

Mogwai were formed in 1995 by guitarists Braithwaite and Cummings, bassist Aitchisin and drummer Bulloch, releasing a series of singles on independent labels (gathered together on *Ten Rapid*, 1996) before signing with Chemikal Underground Recordings. Having recruited former **Teenage Fanclub** drummer Brendan O'Hare, Mogwai took on the pseudonyms Demonic, pLasmatroN, Bionic, Capt. Meat and the Relic for the recording of their full-length début, *Young Team* (1997). The album's expansive structures and ethereal tone were praised by critics worldwide as the band began to develop a cult fanbase in Britain and the US, bolstered by the *Summer* and *Mogwai Fear Satan* (1998) EPs. O'Hare left the band shortly after recording the album.

After a lengthy world tour to support *Young Team* Mogwai released an album of remixes by a selection of underground artists, including μ-ziq and David Holmes, *Kicking a Dead Pig* (Eye-Q, 1998), and their most successful EP to date, *No Education = No Future (Fuck the Curfew)*. They recorded their second album, *Come on Die Young* (1999), with **Mercury Rev**'s Dave Fridmann, in Buffalo, New York, dispatching the heavy guitar sounds of their début in favour of xylophones and keyboards. The album also marked the recording début of multi-instrumentalist Barry Burns, a former music teacher and flautist. It was followed by an eponymous EP, which included a collaboration with a brass band and featured a track dedicated to the late film director Stanley Kubrick.

MOLLY HATCHET

Danny Joe Brown, b. 1951, Jacksonville, Florida, USA (replaced by Jimmy Farrar, b. La Grange, Georgia); Bruce Crump (replaced by Barry Borden, b. 12 May 1954, Atlanta, Georgia); Steve Holland, b. 1954, Dothan, Alabama; Dave Hlubek, b. 1952, Jacksonville; Duane Roland, b. 3 December 1952, Jeffersonville, Indiana; Banner Thomas (replaced by Riff West, b. 3 April 1950, Orlando, Florida)

In the tradition of Southern heavy rock deriving from the **Allman Brothers Band** and **Lynyrd Skynyrd**, Molly Hatchet were notable for the longevity of their commercial success and the origin of the group's name: Hatchet Molly was a legendary character who specialized in decapitating her lovers.

The group was formed in 1971 by Holland (former rhythm guitarist of Ice) lead guitarist Hlubek and Thomas (bass). By the time the band signed to Epic in 1977, the line-up included drummer Roland and ex-Rum Creek singer Brown. The eponymous début album was supervised by **Ted Nugent**'s producer

Tom Werman and sold a million copies, while *Flirtin' with Disaster** (1979) was even more successful, reaching the Top Twenty.

Relying for their popularity on constant touring, rather than hit singles or media exposure, Molly Hatchet's success continued with *Beatin' the Odds* (1980) and *Take No Prisoners* (1981), which sported a sleeve drawing showing the band members as muscle-bound heroes of a sword-and-sorcery B-movie. For those albums Brown was replaced by Farrar but he rejoined the band for *No Guts . . . No Glory* (1983), by which point Borden and West had become the band's rhythm section.

Molly Hatchet's brand of macho rock continued to attract American followers with *The Deed Is Done* (1985). They signed with Capitol in 1989 and founding member Hlubek left and was replaced by Bobby Ingram. The resulting album, *Lightning Strikes Twice* (1990), compared badly with Epic's *Greatest Hits*, issued in the same year.

CHIPS MOMAN
b. 1936, LaGrange, Georgia, USA

Session musician, writer and producer Moman was, in the sixties with **Rick Hall** and Steve Cropper, one of the architects of the sound that came to be known as 'Southern soul'. In the seventies he became one of the most successful producers working in the country field.

After working briefly as a session guitarist in Los Angeles and touring with **Gene Vincent** and **Johnny Burnette**, Moman settled in Memphis and with **Jim Stewart** and Estelle Axton helped set up Stax Records in 1958. The company's house producer in the early days, he was responsible for Carla Thomas's sweet-sounding 'Gee Whizz' (Atlantic, 1961) and the Mar-Keys 'Last Night' (Satellite, 1961), one of the first records to display the Stax sound. Moman signed **William Bell** and others to Stax, before in 1964 he fell out with Stewart and Axton over money and set up his own American studios in Memphis.

There he produced the Gentrys' hit 'Keep on Dancing' (MGM, 1965, later revived by the **Bay City Rollers**) and with **Dan Penn** wrote the classic cheating song 'Dark End of the Street' (first recorded by **James Carr** in 1967 and subsequently by numerous artists including **Percy Sledge**, **Roy Hamilton**, **Linda Ronstadt**, **Ry Cooder** and **Richard Thompson**). He later formed the production company AGP with Penn and songwriter and session musician Spooner Oldham. With them he also worked as a session musician on first **Wilson Pickett**'s and then **Aretha Franklin**'s sessions at Hall's Fame Studios, writing (with Penn) the classic 'Do Right Woman – Do Right Man' for Franklin. Other Moman compositions include

'Another Somebody Done Somebody Wrong Song', 'Everybody Loves a Rain Song' and 'Luckenbach Texas'.

During his three-year association with Penn and Oldham, Moman produced over a hundred records which entered the Top Hundred, including 'The Letter'* (1967), 'Cry Like a Baby'* (1968) and 'Soul Deep' (1969) for the **Box Tops**, a pair of huge country hits for **Sandy Posey** ('Born a Woman' and 'Single Girl', both 1966), **Elvis Presley**'s *From Elvis in Memphis* (1969), one of the best of Presley's later albums, and Merrilee Rush's hit version of **Chip Taylor**'s 'Angel of the Morning' (Bell, 1968).

In the seventies Moman left Memphis for Nashville where he produced albums for **Waylon Jennings**, Jennings' wife, Jessie Colter, **Willie Nelson**, **Ronnie Milsap** and **B. J. Thomas**, among others. He next supervised the highly successful *Highwayman*, which featured **Johnny Cash**, **Kris Kristofferson**, Nelson and Jennings before returning to Memphis in 1985. Moman's later productions included *Highwayman II* (1987), *Are You Sure Hank Done It This Way?* (Waylon Jennings, 1992), *Midnight Mover* (**Bobby Womack**, 1993) *The Nashville Sessions* (**Petula Clark**, 1995) and *In My Lifetime* (**Neil Diamond**, 1996). In 1996 he retired from production to play golf in Georgia.

LIONEL MONCKTON

b. 18 December 1861, London, England, d. 15 February 1924, London

One of the most prolific composers of British musicals in the first decade of the twentieth century, Monckton, with Howard Talbot and Arthur Wimperis, was the author of *The Arcadians* (1909), probably the first English musical in which songs were fully integrated into the plot.

The son of a civil servant and an actress, Monckton abandoned a career in law for the world of musical theatre in the mid-1890s. He worked first as a theatre critic (for the *Daily Telegraph*, among other newspapers) and then as the composer of occasional tunes which theatrical impresario George Edwardes interpolated into his productions at the Gaiety Theatre. The high points of these plotless productions were parades by the Gaiety Girls, as the chorus was called. Their popularity can be gauged from the fact that several of the Gaiety Girls married into the aristocracy, including (after his death) Monckton's wife, Gertie Miller. In all, Monckton wrote the music for more than twenty shows, including *A Runaway Girl* (1898); *A Toreador* (1901), the first of eleven to star Miller; *A Country Girl* (1902); *The Orchid* (1903), which became very successful when mounted later on Broadway; *The Girls of Gotenberg* (1907); and *The Arcadians* (1909). Seen by many as the best of his work, *The*

Arcadians was a fitting end to the 'Gaiety musicals' which were replaced by the craze for operetta triggered off by the phenomenal success of **Franz Lehár**'s *The Merry Widow* (1907). With the coming of ragtime, the audience for Monckton's essentially sedate music disappeared and in the last years of his life he wrote no music at all.

Many of Monckton's songs were recorded by Miller, including 'Moonstruck' (HMV, 1909), 'A Quaker Girl' (1910) and 'Chalk Farm to Camberwell' (1916).

THELONIOUS MONK

b. Thelonious Sphere Monk, 11 October 1917, Rocky Mount, North Carolina, USA, d. 17 February 1982, Englewood, New Jersey

Despite having been one of the founder figures of bebop, Monk's advanced harmonic and rhythmic ideas led to his neglect by jazz audiences until the late fifties. However, he received full recognition in the following decade and was a major influence on some of the most original pianists of later generations.

He grew up in New York and played church organ before studying the jazz piano-playing of **Fats Waller**, **Earl Hines** and **Art Tatum**. His first paid work was at rent parties but in the late thirties he spent two years with a travelling evangelist's show. In 1940 he joined drummer **Kenny Clarke** in the house band at Minton's in New York. With Clarke, he wrote 'Epistrophy', one of the first bebop anthems. Monk and his protégé **Bud Powell** developed a keyboard style appropriate to accompanying such key players as **Charlie Parker** and **Dizzy Gillespie**. His recording début was as accompanist to guitarist **Charlie Christian** in 1941.

Later in the forties he played briefly with **Lucky Millinder** and **Coleman Hawkins**, with whom he recorded for Joe Davis. Monk's first records as a leader were made with **Art Blakey** for Blue Note in 1947. 'In Walked Bud' and 'Round About Midnight' were among the many titles recorded in order to beat the 1948 American Federation of Musicians ban. The revolutionary character of his work and the difficulty of finding work following a 1951 drugs conviction made the early fifties a lean period for Monk and he recorded only a few tracks in 1952–4 for Prestige with **Sonny Rollins** and **Max Roach** before Orrin Keepnews of Riverside signed him to a long-term contract in 1955.

Among the Riverside records was *Brilliant Corners* (1957) with Rollins and Roach, on which Monk displayed his sardonic and witty approach to the sentimentality of such love songs as 'I Surrender Dear', in a more sophisticated version of Waller's sarcastic way with such compositions. He also recorded with **John**

Coltrane on *Monk's Music* (1957), which included 'Crepuscule with Nellie', dedicated to his wife, and Johnny Griffin (*Misterioso*, 1960).

From 1962 to 1968 Monk recorded for Columbia, often with a quartet which included tenor saxophonist Charlie Rouse, but after his path-breaking work of earlier years these albums often seemed formulabound. He was reunited with Blakey in 1971 for *Something in Blue* and *The Man I Love* (Black Lion), and made a world tour with Gillespie's Giants of Jazz (1971–2) but his musical activity was curtailed by illness in the mid-seventies. Monk gave his last performance in 1976 and died of a stroke six years later.

In 1984 A&M issued *That's the Way I Feel Now*, which featured musical tributes to Monk by performers ranging from **Gil Evans** and **Carla Bley** to **Joe Jackson** and **Dr John**. A more vibrant witness to the quality of his work lay in the later pianists whom he influenced, among them Cecil Taylor, Randy Weston and Stan Tracey.

Monk's son T. S. Monk was a jazz and R&B drummer who recorded *Take One* (Blue Note, 1992). T. S. Monk was also chairman of the Thelonius Monk Institute, which holds talent contests for young pianists. Among the winners has been Marcus Roberts, now a recording artist with RCA.

THE MONKEES

Mickey Dolenz, b. 8 March 1946, Los Angeles, California, USA; Davy Jones, b. 30 December 1945, Manchester, England; Peter Tork, b. Peter Thorkelson, 13 February 1944, Washington DC; Michael Nesmith, b. 30 December 1942, Houston, Texas

For many critics the Monkees were judged by the manner of the group's formation – the group was deliberately designed by television executives to capitalize on the success of **The Beatles**. However, the Monkees made some of the most attractive pop singles of the late sixties, and later one of the group – Nesmith – attempted with some success to make idiosyncratic country-rock albums in a solo career of some distinction. Moreover, the successful reunion undertaken by the other three members in 1986 indicated that the Monkees had struck a genuine nerve.

Inspired by the zany style of *A Hard Day's Night!*, TV producers Bert Schneider and Bob Rafelson (later a major film director – for example, *Five Easy Pieces*, 1970) sold the concept of a television series to **Don Kirshner** and Columbia Pictures. Auditions were held in Hollywood in 1965 to find a suitably photogenic quartet. Jones and Dolenz were former child actors (in **Lionel Bart**'s *Oliver!* and the TV series *Circus Boy*, respectively), while Tork and Nesmith had been guitarists in rock bands. The television series, with a theme song by Tommy Boyce and Bobby Hart,

was an immediate success when launched in 1966. As a result the group had eight hit singles on Colgems in the next eighteen months. Among the six million-sellers were the Monkees' first releases, Boyce and Hart's 'Last Train to Clarksville' and **Neil Diamond**'s 'I'm a Believer'. The eponymous début album topped the charts on both sides of the Atlantic early in 1967.

The rush release of *More of the Monkees* a few months later angered Nesmith and after 'A Little Bit Me, A Little Bit You' became the group's third hit single, Kirshner – the series' musical director – resigned and the Monkees plus Chip Douglas produced *Headquarters* (1967). One track, Dolenz's 'Randy Scouse Git', was a British hit as 'Alternate Title' (the change was due to protests from the BBC) but the group's next American success came with **Carole King** and Gerry Goffin's 'Pleasant Valley Sunday'*.

The artistic high point of the Monkees' career was the Douglas-produced *Pisces, Aquarius, Capricorn and Jones Ltd* (1967), which included Jones' best vocal performance on a thoughtful version of **John Stewart**'s ballad 'Daydream Believer', another million-selling hit single. In 1968 the second series of Monkees films had finished and the group were on the way down. 'Valleri', an early Boyce and Hart production, was their last Top Ten single and the artistic freedom of the fully self-produced *The Birds, the Bees and the Monkees* (1968) impressed neither critics nor record-buyers. The album exposed the wide gulf between the countrified Nesmith and Jones' taste for sentimental ballads. In the same year the Monkees booked **Jimi Hendrix** as the opening act of their American tour only to see him booed off stage.

1968 ended with the commercial failure of *Head*, an anti-war comedy feature produced by Rafelson and Jack Nicholson. The soundtrack album contained some of the group's best music – Tork's 'Can You Dig It' and Nesmith's 'Circle Sky' – but it and the accompanying single of Goffin and King's psychedelic-style 'Porpoise Song' were equally unsuccessful. Early in 1969 Tork left the group and the remaining trio recorded two further albums, *Instant Replay* (which included **Neil Young** as a guest artist) and *The Monkees Present*. At the end of 1969 Nesmith also quit and Dolenz and Jones released *Changes* (1970), which was dominated by Jeff Barry compositions, before formally winding up the Monkees in 1971.

Dolenz initially followed a stage and TV career, appearing in the London production of **Nilsson**'s *The Point*. He went on to produce and direct such television programmes as the children's show *Metal Mickey* (1983) and in 1993 released a kids album, *Mickey Dolenz Puts You to Sleep*. Jones appeared in *Godspell* while Tork led the New Monks, a New York City rock group.

With a more substantial musical background,

Nesmith – who before leaving the group had written **Linda Ronstadt**'s first hit, 'Different Drum' (1967) and recorded the instrumental album *Wichita Train Whistle Sings* (Dot, 1968) – embarked on a solo career as a country-rock artist. Forming his First National Band with pedal-steel-guitarist Red Rhodes, he recorded three albums for RCA: *Magnetic South* (1970), which included his first hit with the wistful 'Joanne', *Loose Salute* (1971) and *Nevada Fighter* (1972). These innovative records, which offered a gentle meld of country and rock, won Nesmith a significant cult reputation. A Second National Band with **Gene Vincent** guitarist Johnny Meeks cut *Tantamount to Treason Vol. 1* (1972) and *And the Hits Just Keep on Comin'* (1972). *Pretty Much Your Standard Ranch Stash* was the final RCA album, and Nesmith set up Countryside, a shortlived label which released albums by **Ian Matthews** and Rhodes. After the eccentric concept album *The Prison* (1975), Nesmith recorded sporadically for his own Pacific Arts label. He increasingly turned his attention to video, winning the first Grammy given for music video with *Elephant Parts* (1981). Pacific Arts became a leading video production house and Nesmith was also involved with such independent films as *Timerider* (1983). In 1990 Rhino issued the well-received retrospective albums *The Older Stuff*, which consisted of material from his country albums, and *The Newer Stuff*, a compilation from his later recordings. Later records included *The Garden* (1994).

Jones and Dolenz had attempted to revive the group with Boyce and Hart in 1975 (recording a Capitol album in 1976) but it was not until ten years later, after the independent Rhino label had successfully reissued the Monkees' albums and MTV had broadcast their TV shows non-stop, that they agreed to reunite with Tork. A 1986 tour was a huge success as was *Then and Now* (Arista), which mixed old and new material and gave the group a hit with 'That Was Then, This Is Now'. *Pool It!* (Rhino, 1987) was a lacklustre album of new material produced by Roger Bechirian. The group toured the United States and Britain in 1989 but disbanded soon afterwards. In the nineties Tork briefly essayed a solo career with the lacklustre *Stranger Things Have Happened*.

Listen to the Band (Rhino, 1991) is the definitive career retrospective, while *Justus* (Rhino, 1996) was a full group reunion. Fittingly, revivals of the television series won far better reviews.

MATT MONRO
b. *Terry Parsons, 1 December 1930, London, England, d. 7 February 1985, Cambridge*

Monro was one of the few balladeers to emerge after the advent of rock'n'roll. Among his hits of the early

sixties was the lush romantic ballad 'Softly as I Leave You' (Parlophone, 1962), later recorded by his major musical influence, **Frank Sinatra**.

He made his first broadcast while in the army and through the intervention of **Winifred Atwell** (after whose father he took his stage name) secured a contract with EMI's Parlophone label and joined Cyril Stapleton as a featured singer. So similar in style was Monro to Sinatra that, billed as Fred Flange, he guested on one-time **Goon** Peter Sellers' *Songs for Swinging Sellers* (1959) impersonating Sinatra. His first big British success was Norman Newell's 'Portrait of My Love' (1960), which was covered in America by **Steve Lawrence**, and was followed by his major international hit, the Leslie Bricusse composition 'My Kind of Girl' (1961). Other hits included 'From Russia with Love' (1963), the theme song to the James Bond film; 'Walk Away' (1964), his only other American hit; and his version of **The Beatles**' 'Yesterday' (1965). Ironically, his recording of the title song to the film *Born Free* (1965), though it won its authors Don Black and **John Barry** an Oscar and subsequently has become one of the songs most closely associated with Monro, was not a hit for the singer. It was dropped from most prints of the film and provided hits for pianist **Roger Williams** (1966) and the Hesitations soul group (Kapp, 1968). Though his later albums, notably *I Have Dreamed* (1965), sold well, his only singles chart success was 'And You Smiled' (EMI, 1973).

Throughout the seventies and early eighties Monro regularly appeared on television and toured the international cabaret circuit, headlining at the Sands, Las Vegas, in 1983. In Britain, he seemed on the verge of a comeback before his death in 1985 from cancer.

BILL MONROE
b. *William Smith Monroe, 13 September 1911, near Rosine, Kentucky, USA, d. 9 September 1996*

'The Father of Bluegrass Music' is the sort of legend that usually screams from a show-poster, but it is a truer billing than most of its kind: certainly nobody has ever challenged Bill Monroe's right to it. Though the roots of bluegrass lay in the string-band music and harmony-singing traditions of the Southeast, and some of its specific aspects were developed by individuals, such as the intricate three-finger banjo playing of Earl Scruggs (of **Flatt and Scruggs**) or the Hawaiian/blues contribution of Josh Graves on the Dobro resonator guitar, it is a matter of record – in both senses – that Monroe conceived the idea of the bluegrass sound, brought it into being and nurtured it, sometimes almost alone in the field, for more than forty years.

Monroe left his rural Kentucky home to work

around Chicago and Detroit in the late twenties. While there he began to play music with his brother Charlie (b. 4 June 1903, Rosine, d. 27 September 1975, Reidsville, North Carolina). They secured jobs on the WLS Chicago National Barn Dance, though as dancers rather than musicians; later they worked on Indiana stations in Hammond and Gary. Bill was playing mandolin and Charlie guitar, a combination possibly suggested to them by the established WLS acts Mac and Bob and Karl and Harty.

In 1934–5 the brothers worked on stations in the Midwest and North Carolina, and in 1936 gained the sponsorship of the Crazy Water Crystals Co. on WBT, Charlotte, North Carolina (alongside **J. E. Mainer** and many other country acts of the day). Their popularity brought a contract with RCA Victor's Bluebird label, for which they recorded several dozen fast and intense versions of sacred numbers and traditional songs like 'On the Banks of the Ohio'. In 1938 they split, Charlie going on to lead his Kentucky Pardners with considerable success over the next three decades; it was in that group that Lester Flatt began his career. Bill formed the first of his line-ups called the Blue Grass Boys and in 1939 secured a place on the Grand Ole Opry roster which he held for the next half century. Recordings for Bluebird in 1940–1 show a group struggling to force together ideas from blues, old-time fiddling and even Western swing; either Monroe's conception of what he intended to do was not yet clear to him, or he had failed to impose it on his bandsmen.

Something closer to what would later be called bluegrass was attained in 1945 when Monroe signed with Columbia and recorded, among others, the first version of 'Kentucky Waltz', though the presence of a piano-accordion (played by Sally Ann Forrester, wife of the fiddler Howdy Forrester, who would himself later work with Monroe) braked Monroe's progress to a wholly new sound. Everything changed with the 1946 band, the first, and epoch-making, true bluegrass line-up, with Scruggs (banjo), Flatt (guitar), Chubby Wise (fiddle) and Howard Watts (bass). Over the next year this group recorded such 'core' bluegrass songs as 'Blue Moon of Kentucky', 'Mother's Only Sleeping' and 'Molly and Tenbrooks', with Monroe singing either solo or in a sky-scraping tenor harmony over Flatt's more soft-edged lead, while Scruggs and Wise impelled and accentuated the rhythm with an emphasis entirely new to country music.

Flatt and Scruggs left Monroe in early 1948 to lead their own group, and after a 1949 Columbia recording Monroe left the label for Decca. He had earlier quit Victor because he did not want to be on the same label as his brother, and his new move was to dissociate himself from a company that had taken on a band he believed to be imitating him, the **Stanley Brothers**

– though Carter Stanley did briefly work with Monroe in 1951. Other distinguished bluegrass musicians who passed through Monroe's band in the fifties and sixties included **Jimmy Martin**, fiddlers Vassar Clements and Buddy Spicher (later to become prolific Nashville session musicians) and banjoist Sonny Osborne of the **Osborne Brothers**. During this period Monroe made several albums now regarded as primers of bluegrass practice, among them Knee Deep in Bluegrass (1958), I Saw the Light (1958) and Bluegrass Instrumentals (1965).

More sophisticated recording techniques also clarified Monroe's own contribution to the bluegrass sound. His mandolin-playing combined a flexible, blues-derived sense of timing and accent with relentless drive, exemplified on instrumental showpieces like 'Rawhide' (1951) and 'Roanoke' (1954). As a singer he left a similar stamp upon the idiom: his ringing head-tones, bluesy flattenings and shrill yodelling were not so much an individual's trademarks as the basic devices of bluegrass vocals. His recordings of 'New Mule Skinner Blues' (1950), 'Blue Moon of Kentucky' (1954) and other pieces were so nearly definitive that it is hard to perform – and not easy to imagine – those songs in a different manner.

At times in the sixties Monroe's band featured younger musicians of an untypical background, city-bred and college-educated, such as Richard Greene (fiddle), Bill Keith (banjo) and Peter Rowan (guitar/vocal). Greene and Rowan subsequently worked together in the folk-rock band Sea Train (1969–72) and the more bluegrass-orientated Muleskinner, and were associated with mandolinist and bandleader David Grisman, an architect of the jazz-influenced 'new acoustic' music that sprang up on the West Coast in the seventies. Keith, like Greene, worked in the sixties with Jim Kweskin's Jug Band, and became the major influence after Scruggs upon bluegrass banjo-playing, devoting much of his time in the eighties to tuition, though he toured outside the US intermittently with singer/guitarist/record-producer Jim Rooney.

Interest in Monroe's music began to develop not only among younger musicians but also in campus folk-song clubs. In 1963 this audience was made aware of Monroe, and he of it, by his manager Ralph Rinzler, himself an ex-member of a folk-scene bluegrass band, the Greenbrier Boys. Rinzler's sleevenotes on Monroe's albums helped to expound bluegrass's inheritance from traditional music and free it from associations with the 'commercialized' country music emanating from Nashville. (Yet all Monroe's records at this time were being made in a major Nashville studio under the direction of producers like **Owen Bradley**, and some employed session professionals like bass-player Ernie Newton and guitarist Grady Martin.) Monroe's first exposure to a college audience was at the University of Chicago Folk Festival in 1963.

Soon after this came the start of the purely bluegrass festival, a movement with Monroe at its centre. In 1967 he instituted his own event at Bean Blossom, Indiana, which became the biggest draw of the bluegrass year. He had appeared in England in 1965 and frequently played there and in other overseas countries throughout the sixties and seventies. In 1970 he was elected to the Country Music Hall of Fame. Still associated with Decca (later MCA), he continued to produce albums of high quality like *Bill Monroe's Uncle Pen* (1972), dedicated to the fiddle-playing relative who first inspired him to become a musician, and *Master of Bluegrass* (1981). On *Bill Monroe and Stars of the Bluegrass Hall of Fame* (MCA, 1986) he gathered round him in a genial reunion both contemporaries – Ralph Stanley of the Stanley Brothers, Jim and Jesse McReynolds, Mac Wiseman, Carl Story – and followers like the Washington DC-based band the Country Gentlemen. It amounted to a declaration of his equanimity in accepting the hard-won role of 'Father of Bluegrass'.

Despite heart problems, Monroe made occasional live appearances into the nineties, celebrating his fiftieth anniversary as a member of the Grand Ole Opry by recording the album *Live at the Opry* (MCA, 1989). In the nineties Monroe's classic recordings were systematically re-released. *The Music of Bill Monroe* (MCA, 1994) is the definitive career retrospective.

VAUGHN MONROE

b. 7 October 1911, Akron, Ohio, USA, d. 21 May 1973, Stuart, Florida

A bandleader, remembered for his good looks and his operatic singing style, Monroe had his greatest success in the forties. In the fifties he extended his career through appearances in series Westerns and covers of R&B songs.

In the thirties Monroe studied voice and worked as a trumpeter with the bands of Gibby Lockhard, Austin Wylie and Larry Funk before forming his own band on Boston in 1940. Signed to Victor, he had an immediate hit with 'Racing with the Moon'* (1941) and henceforth Monroe's singing and that of his vocal group the Moon Maids took precedence over the band's playing. Other successes included 'There I've Said It Again'* (1945) and 'Ballerina'* (1947). More significant was his backing of the **Sons of the Pioneers** on 'Cool Water' (1948) which prefigured his involvement with cowboy music. In 1949 he had his last million-seller with '(Ghost) Riders in the Sky', which was based by Stan Jones on the Civil War Tune 'When Johnny Comes Marching Home'. The song was successfully revived in the style of **Duane Eddy** by

the Ramrods (Amy, 1961) and later by the **Shadows** (1980). Monroe strengthened his association with Western imagery by a cover of 'Mule Train' (1949), though **Frankie Laine** (who cited Monroe as one of his influences) had the bigger hit, and then, at a time when the singing cowboy genre was in its death throes, made a pair of Westerns in which he starred as a two-fisted singing sheriff, *Singing Guns* (1950) and *The Toughest Man in Arizona* (1952).

Monroe continued his association with Western themes with covers of 'On Top of Old Smokey' (1951, better known through its recording by the **Weavers**), 'In the Middle of the House' (1956, originally recorded by Rusty Draper on Mercury) and **Johnny Horton**'s 'Battle of New Orleans' (1959). But he had his most unlikely hit of the fifties with a cover of 'Black Denim Trousers' (1955), an R&B hit for the Cheers whose 1955 Capitol recording was the first major pop hit written and produced by **Leiber and Stoller**.

Monroe retired to Florida in the early sixties.

PATSY MONTANA

b. Rubye Blevins, 30 October 1914, Hot Springs, Arkansas, USA, d. 3 May 1996

Singer and yodeller Montana was the first female country artist to make a national name on radio and records, thereby laying the trail that was followed in the fifties by the women pioneers of modern country music, **Kitty Wells** and **Patsy Cline**.

After a brief connection with **Jimmie Davis**, whom she partnered, singing, yodelling and playing fiddle, on a 1932 Victor recording session, she joined the Prairie Ramblers, a four-man string band then establishing itself on WLS, Chicago. In 1935 she recorded with them 'I Wanna Be a Cowboy's Sweetheart' (ARC) and became the first woman in country music to have a million-seller. She followed it with many other songs on Western themes with yodel refrains, including at least half-a-dozen with 'Montana' in their title. Through the thirties the Prairie Ramblers were more and more influenced by Western swing, and Montana's songs became somewhat jazzy, as in 'Swing Time Cowgirl'. She also worked with the group outside the studio, touring constantly under the WLS aegis, particularly in the Midwest, though it has been claimed that they played county fairs in every state of the US.

Contemporary with Montana, and also on WLS, were her chief, though friendly, rivals in the cowgirl stakes, the Girls of the Golden West (Millie and Dolly Good). They sang a similar repertoire to Montana's in sweet harmony, with twin yodelling, but preferred slow and medium tempos and used only a single guitar for accompaniment. There were numerous other cowgirl duos and trios in this period, perhaps most notably the DeZurik Sisters, who used harmonized yodelling to imitate Hawaiian guitars and also broadcast for Purina chicken-feed as the Cackle Sisters.

The Prairie Ramblers, who recorded prolifically from 1935 to 1941 on the ARC-Vocalion-Okeh series of labels, also had a subsidiary career on record as the Sweet Violet Boys, recording *risqué* material like 'I Haven't Got a Pot to Cook in' (1936), 'Sweet Violets' (1937) and 'I Love My Fruit' (1939), possibly the first gay hillbilly song. It is not reported whether this influenced Montana's decision to part company with them, which she did in 1941, signing with Decca and remaking some of her earlier numbers. In 1946–7 she had her own ABC radio show, *Wake Up and Smile*. She also organized a family act with her pre-teen daughters Judy and Beverly. For much of the fifties and sixties she was not occupied with music, but she returned to music in the seventies, visiting Europe on several occasions, and continued to be intermittently active.

CHRIS MONTEZ

b. 17 January 1943, Los Angeles, California, USA

Best known for 'Let's Dance'* (Monogram, 1962), an insistent dance record in the vein of **Ritchie Valens'** 'La Bamba', Montez returned to the charts with softer Latin-flavoured material in the manner of **Jose Feliciano** and **Trini Lopez**.

After graduating from high school, Montez had a local hit with 'All You Had to Do Was Tell Me' (Monogram, 1962), a duet with Kathy Young, whose earlier national hit had been the ethereal 'A Thousand Stars' (Indigo, 1960). His follow-up was 'Let's Dance', an international hit which featured Montez's chanted chicano vocals and a repetitive organ riff. In Britain it was successful again when reissued in 1972 and 1979. Like the equally successful 'Some Kinda Fun'* (1962), 'Let's Dance' was written and produced by Monogram's owner Jim Lee. Future releases on Monogram failed and Montez only returned to the charts after joining A&M in 1966. His first hit for the new label was the romantic 'Call Me' which he followed with revivals of **Harry Warren** and Mack Gordon's film songs 'The More I See You' and 'There Will Never Be Another You' (1966) and **Jule Styne** and **Sammy Cahn**'s 'Time After Time' (1966).

From the late sixties onwards he appeared regularly in cabaret.

WES MONTGOMERY

b. John Leslie Montgomery, 6 March 1925, Indianapolis, Indiana, USA, d. 15 June 1968

Particularly noted for his single note runs and his thumb- (as opposed to plectrum-) or finger-picking,

Montgomery was one of the most influential jazz guitarists. **George Benson** and **B. B. King** are among those who have acknowledged his technical prowess, while his successful jazz-pop records for Verve and A&M anticipated Benson's later crossover efforts.

A self-taught musician, Montgomery's first influence was **Charlie Christian**. In the mid-forties he played in groups with his brothers Buddy and Monk before, in 1948, he joined **Lionel Hampton**'s band and toured with him for two years. He spent most of the fifties in obscurity in Indianapolis but travelled to Los Angeles to make such tracks as 'Finger Pickin'' and 'Old Folks' with tenor-sax-player Harold Land for Pacific Jazz.

Through **Cannonball Adderley**, Montgomery was signed to Riverside where producer Orrin Keepnews worked with him on a series of pathbreaking albums. After leading his own group on *Go!* and *Incredible Jazz Guitar* (both 1960), he was partnered with **George Shearing** (*Wes and Friends*) and Nat Adderley (*Work Songs*).

Montgomery next moved to Verve where producer Creed Taylor gave him more commercial settings, with strings and choruses. Among the Verve recordings were *Bumpin'* (1964), *Goin' Out of My Head* (Montgomery's biggest-selling album) (1965) and *Jimmy and Wes* (1966), a collaboration with organist **Jimmy Smith**. He later recorded for A&M in a similar vein, scoring a minor hit with 'Windy' (1967) and taking a **Beatles** song for the title track of *A Day in the Life* (1967), his most commercially successful record.

He died of a heart attack.

THE MOODY BLUES

Graeme Edge, b. 30 March 1942, Rochester, Kent, England; Denny Laine, b. Brian Hines, 29 October 1944, Jersey (replaced by Justin Hayward, b. 14 October 1946, Swindon, Wiltshire); Mike Pinder, b. 19 December 1942, Birmingham (replaced by Patrick Moraz, b. 24 January 1948, Morges, Switzerland); Ray Thomas, b. 29 December 1942, Stourport, Worcestershire, England; Clint Warwick, b. 25 June 1949, Birmingham (replaced by John Lodge, b. 20 July 1945, Birmingham)

Originally a British beat group, the Moody Blues became one of the most successful exponents of progressive rock, judiciously combining self-consciously poetic lyrics with string and mellotron backings and skilful melodies.

The group was formed in 1964 by ex-members of other Birmingham bands. Guitarist and singer Laine had led the Diplomats, while keyboards-player Pinder had been with the Crew Cats and harmonica- and flute-player Thomas with El Riot and the Rebels. Signed to Decca in 1964, they reached No. 1 in Britain and the American Top Ten the following year with a faithful cover-version of Bessie Banks' soul ballad 'Go Now'. A rendition of the **Drifters** 'I Don't Want to Go on without You' and 'From the Bottom of My Heart' were less successful and in 1966 Laine and bassist Warwick were replaced by Birmingham bassist Lodge and Hayward, who had previously recorded for Pye as a solo singer. Laine later joined **Paul McCartney**'s Wings where his performance of 'Go Now' was a highlight of their live shows.

After a period of hibernation, the Moody Blues returned with *Days of Future Passed* (1967), one of the concept albums (it traced the progress of one day) which defined the possibilities of the new progressive genre. Like **The Beatles** with **George Martin**, the Moody Blues benefited from collaboration with a skilled musician from a non-rock background. Peter Knight had been an arranger with the dance bands of **Ambrose** and **Geraldo** and had been hired to work with the Moody Blues on a rock version of Dvořák's *New World Symphony*. Instead, the group persuaded him to provide them with instrumental passages and string charts which fitted the airy lead voices of Hayward and Thomas and the dream-like character of their lyrics. The outstanding song was Hayward's intensely romantic 'Nights in White Satin', which reached the Top Twenty and was even more successful when reissued in 1972 (following its belated success in America) and 1979. It was also a hit for the Dickies (A&M, 1979) and **Elkie Brooks** (A&M, 1982)

In Search of the Lost Chord (1968) was an unadulterated dose of hippie philosophy and included 'The Best Way to Travel' (which was thinking) and two minor British hits, 'Voices in the Sky' and 'Ride My See-Saw'. The symphonic-rock approach was pursued on *On the Threshold of a Dream* and *To Our Children's Children's Children* (both 1969), the first album to be released on the band's own Threshold label. *A Question of Balance* (1970) contained a bestselling single in the catchy, urgent 'Question', written by Hayward.

After *Every Good Boy Deserves Favour* (1971) and *Seventh Sojourn* (1972), with its hits 'Isn't Life Strange' and the coy 'I'm just a Singer in a Rock and Roll Band', the individual members of the Moody Blues concentrated on solo projects, the most successful of which was *Blue Jays* (1975), a collaboration between Hayward and Lodge with its British hit 'Blue Guitar'. Ignoring the rise of punk, which was dedicated to the overthrow of progressive rock, the group reassembled to record *Octave* in 1978. The healthy sales of the album led to an international tour the following year for which Pinder was replaced by former **Yes** keyboards-player Patrick Moraz.

In the eighties the Moody Blues continued to release albums on a regular basis, though the frequency was now every three years instead of annually. While reviewers sneered at the group as 'middle-aged

rockers', their hits continued with *Long Distance Voyager* (1981), 'Your Wildest Dreams' from their first album for Polydor, *The Other Side of Life* (1986), and 'I Know You're out There Somewhere' from *Sur La Mer* (1988). In the nineties the band continued to tour and record, albeit at a leisurely pace. They released *Keys of the Kingdom* (1991) and the live album *Live at Red Rocks* (1993). After a legal action with Decca in an attempt to gain control of their back catalogue, the group released *Live at Red Rock* (1993) and then the definitive retrospective, *Time Traveller* (1994), an eighty-track compilation, including *Red Rock* as a bonus album.

Hayward's later solo efforts included *Night Flight* (1980), produced by Jeff Wayne, on whose concept album *The War of the Worlds* (1978) Hayward had sung 'Forever Autumn', *Classic Blue* (1989) with **Mike Batt** and *The View from the Hill* (1996). In 1995 Pinder released a solo album, *Among the Stars*. During the nineties the band continued touring, particularly in America. In 2000 they issued a live greatest hits collection, *Hall of Fame* (Ark), recorded at London's Albert Hall with the support of a full orchestra.

CHRISTY MOORE
b. 1946, Newbridge, County Kildare, Ireland

A leading figure in Irish contemporary folk music in the nineties, Moore was also a member of two of the country's most innovative bands, Planxty in the seventies and Moving Hearts in the eighties.

From a musical family he worked as a bank clerk before taking up folk music, inspired by the **Clancy Brothers** and Dominic Behan, the singer-songwriter brother of Irish playwright Brendan Behan. Moore's earliest appearances were on the English folk circuit and Behan co-produced his début album, *Paddy on the Road*, in London in 1968.

Returning to Dublin Moore made several solo albums for Irish label Tara in the early seventies. Among these was *Prosperous* on which he was accompanied by Andy Irvine from the influential folk band Sweeney's Men (mandolin), Liam O'Flynn (uillean pipes) and Donal Lunny (guitar and bouzouki). The sound of *Prosperous*, its mix of Eastern European instruments with Irish traditional and contemporary folk compositions, led directly to the formation of the most highly regarded of Irish modern folk bands, Planxty.

The group lasted only three years (1973–5) but it made three albums which showed a new direction for the presentation of Irish folk music. They included *The Well Below the Valley* (1973) and *Cold Blow and the Rainy Night* (1974). The group briefly re-formed in 1979.

During the late seventies Moore worked as a solo

performer with a repertoire focused on social and political issues, although a 1977 self-titled album on Tara contained several traditional songs. Other albums from this period included *Live in Dublin* and *The Iron Behind the Velvet* (both 1978). In 1981 he returned to the group format by forming the electric folk band Moving Hearts. Other members included Lunny, Declan Sinnott (guitar), Keith Donald (saxophones) and the uillean piper Davy Spillane, who has since developed a solo recording career. The group released *Moving Hearts* (1981) and *Dark End of the Street* (1982). Moving Hearts continued to perform until 1984 and recorded an acclaimed instrumental album, *The Storm* (1985).

Moore himself recorded *The Time Has Come* (1983) before finding his mature style on *Ride on* (1984). With Lunny producing, this was a superlatively sung selection of songs ranging from a W. B. Yeats lyric to ballads by the Northern Ireland MP and hunger striker Bobby Sands. *Ride on* also included 'Lisdoonvarna' the first of Moore's comic monologues that comment on the Irish music, political and social scene.

The poignant title track of *Ordinary Man* (1987) was a hit single in Ireland. The original version of the album also included 'They Never Came Home', which dealt with a fatal fire at a Dublin discotheque. The track was withdrawn after threats of libel actions from the disco's owners.

By now a leading figure at European folk festivals, Moore recorded *Unfinished Revolution* (1987) and *Voyage* (1989), among whose tracks were compositions by **Elvis Costello** and **Ewan MacColl**. The bestselling *Smoke and Strong Whiskey* (1991) included a version of the **Pogues**' Shane McGowan's 'Fairytale of New York' as well as the autobiographical 'Encore'. In 1993 he released *King Puck*. In 1994 he released *Live at the Point*, which included a stunning version of 'Fairytale of New York'. In the same year Tara issued a compilation of Moore's long out-of-print earlier recordings, *The Christy Moore Folk Collection*.

GARY MOORE
b. 4 April 1952, Belfast, Northern Ireland

One of Britain's most talented rock and blues guitarists, Moore was best-known for his work with **Thin Lizzy** before he unexpectedly found a large following throughout Europe in the nineties for his straight-ahead blues music.

His first band was Skid Row, formed in 1969 with Phil Lynott (guitar, vocals), Brendan Shiels (bass) and Noel Bridgeman (drums). Lynott soon left to form Thin Lizzy and the remaining trio recorded two albums of heavy blues-rock for Decca. After Skid Row split up, Moore made one album as the Gary Moore Band (*Gringing Stone*, 1973) before spending three

separate periods as a member of Thin Lizzy between 1974 and 1979, working with **Colosseum** and playing numerous recording sessions.

Since 1979 he has followed a solo career which began with the melodic hit 'Parisienne Walkways' with Lynott on vocals. Moore next formed the short-lived G-Force in Los Angeles before signing to Virgin as a soloist. His subsequent albums included *Corridors of Power* (1982), *Victims of the Future* (1984) and *Wild Frontier*, a UK Top Ten hit in 1987.

Like those albums, *After the War* (1989), with guest vocalists Ozzie Osbourne and Sisters of Mercy, remained within a heavy-rock format. But Moore now made a decisive return to the electric blues of his formative years, enlisting **Albert Collins** and **Albert King** to contribute to the multi-million selling *Still Got the Blues* (1990), whose sales were boosted by Moore's frequent live performances throughout Europe.

With co-producer Ian Taylor and guests **B. B. King** and Collins, Moore next issued the equally well-received *After Hours* in 1992. In 1993 he re-recorded his old hit as 'Parisienne Walkways 93' and released a live album, *Blues Alive*. After playing with **Jack Bruce**'s band at a German festival (recorded on *Cities of the Heart*, CMP, 1993), in 1994 he joined Bruce and Ginger Baker in BBM, a power trio which reprised the hits of **Cream**, with Moore ably filling in the **Eric Clapton** parts, and also gave Moore a chance to play some more orthodox blues numbers. In the same year Virgin released the career retrospective *Ballads & Blues*. After contributing to the tribute album for **Fleetwood Mac** founder Peter Green, *Blues for Greeney* (1995), Moore took a more restrained, mainstream direction with *Days in Paradise* (1997).

GRACE MOORE
b. Mary Willie Grace Moore, 5 December 1901, Slabtown, Tennessee, USA, d. 26 January 1947, Copenhagen, Denmark

An imposing blonde soprano, Moore was partly responsible for the brief popularity of opera singing in thirties screen musicals.

In the twenties Moore appeared on Broadway (including the *Music Box Revues* of 1923 and 1924) and at the Metropolitan Opera House (1928–31) before travelling to Hollywood. Her first film was *A Lady's Morals* (1930) which was based on the life of the Swedish soprano Jenny Lind and included several operatic selections. She followed it with an excursion into operetta, **Sigmund Romberg** and Oscar Hammerstein II's *New Moon* (1931), in which she partnered Lawrence Tibbet, another classically trained singer. Her greatest success was **Victor Schertzinger**'s *One Night of Love* (1934) in which she introduced **Gus**

Kahn and Schertzinger's Oscar-winning title song, as well as singing excerpts from *Lucia Di Lammermoor*, *Carmen* and *Madame Butterfly*. It was that film's success that inspired MGM to team **Nelson Eddy** and **Jeanette MacDonald**. After *Love Me Forever* (1935), which also featured Moore singing opera, she retreated to operetta for *The King Steps Out* (1937). Her later films were less well received.

She died in a plane crash over Copenhagen during a European concert tour. In 1953 Kathryn Grayson played her in the film biography, *So This Is Love*.

MERRILL MOORE
b. 26 September 1923, Algona, Iowa, USA

A country-boogie pianist like **Moon Mullican**, Moore was an important link between boogie-woogie and Western swing and the early rock'n'roll sounds of **Bill Haley** and **Jerry Lee Lewis**.

While at high school Moore discovered boogie-woogie through listening to **Meade Lux Lewis**, and Western swing through **Bob Wills**. Based in San Diego after the Second World War, he began to combine the two musics first in solo appearances and then in 1950 with the appropriately named group, Merrill Moore and his Saddle, Rock and Rhythm Boys. Signed to Capitol by Ken Nelson in 1952, Moore showed a similar mix of country and R&B music, with his left hand playing boogie-woogie bass lines while his right hand improvised wildly in the manner of an R&B saxophonist. His recorded material was similarly varied, including Western swing standards (Wills' 'She's Gone' and **Hank Thompson**'s 'Doggie House Boogie'), **Jelly Roll Morton**'s 'King Porter Stomp', country songs ('Barrel House Bessie'), boogie-woogie classics ('Down the Road Apiece') and even piano novelties such as Felix Arndt's 1916 composition 'Nola' (best-known in its recording by **Vincent Lopez**).

Moore's hillbilly rhythm and blues, at its best on recordings like 'Rock-Rockola' (1955), a tribute to the Rockola jukebox, 'House of Blue Lights' (1953), his most successful record, 'Down the Road' (1955) and 'Red Light' (1953), was both exciting and moving. A selection of his Capitol recordings was re-released in Britain on two Ember albums, *Bellyful of Blue Thunder* (1967) and *Rough-House 88* (1969).

While with Capitol, Moore also worked as a session pianist, recording with **Wanda Jackson** and Tommy Sands, among others. In 1958 he left the label to work the club circuit. *Boogie My Blues Away* (Bear Family, 1990) includes all his fifties Capitol recordings.

MORAN AND MACK
George Moran, b. 1881, Elwood, Kansas, USA,
d. 1 August 1949, Oakland, California; Charles E. Mack,
b. Charles E. Sellers, 1888, White Cloud, Kansas,
d. 11 January 1934, Mesa, Arizona

The long history of the blackface cross-talk act, a staple of minstrelsy and vaudeville for more than a century, produced only a few recording teams of lasting memory. Among the most important of these were Moran and Mack.

Dubbed 'The Two Black Crows', Moran and Mack were initially famous through their appearances on stage and radio (*The Majestic Theater Hour*) and then familiar in countless American and British homes from their fourteen-part series of Columbia recordings (1927–9) in which they exchanged views on what were supposed to be characteristic occurrences of black life. The first in the series, 'The Early Bird Catches the Worm'* (1927), was one of the fastest-selling records of the twenties and was followed by 'Curiosities on the Farm', 'In Jail', 'In Hades' and 'Foolishments'. Mack also recorded, on his own, 'Our Child' (Columbia, 1927), accompanied by the distinguished New York ragtime and stride pianist Charles Luckeyth ('Luckey') Roberts, tutor to **James P. Johnson**, writer of musical comedies and rival to **Eubie Blake**.

Equally well known were Charles J. Correll and Freeman F. Gosden, who recorded, for Victor, first in their true names or as Sam'n'Henry, then from 1928 as Amos'n'Andy. Under this billing they had their biggest hit, 'Is Everybody in Your Family as Dumb as You Is?', and became one of America's best-loved radio acts. Later their adventures were turned into magazine stories and their antics were still featured on TV as late as the fifties.

A large number of lesser-known blackface duos were active on stage, radio and records in the USA up to the Second World War, including Snowball and Sunshine, who were based in Texas, and Lasses (White) and Honey (Wilds), heard on the *Grand Ole Opry*. In the post-war era such routines tended to be found only on the Southern rural circuit, though the blacked-up and overalled bass player, a descendant of the Amoses and Andys (and kin to the comic stooge Rochester – Eddie Anderson – who worked with Bob Hope), continued to be seen in bluegrass bands for a little longer.

In Britain the blackface tradition was upheld in the twenties by acts like John Henry and Blossom and Alexander and Mose, the latter team being the actor James Carew and the comic monologist Billy Bennett ('Almost a Gentleman'), who in his own persona, starched shirtfront and army boots delivered recitations like 'The Green Tie on the Little Yellow Dog' – a parody of the Kiplingesque 'The Green Eye of the Little Yellow God', popularized by the actor Bransby Williams – and 'Christmas Day in the Cookhouse'.

Elements of the style survived into the sixties, along with other blackface trappings, in the popular British TV and stage variety production *The Black and White Minstrel Show*.

DERRICK MORGAN
b. 1937, Kingston, Jamaica

A leading reggae singer, Morgan adapted his style to each phase of Jamaican music from the fifties to the seventies.

Like other vocalists of the fifties, Morgan modelled his singing on American R&B artists and styles. His earliest hit, 'Fat Man' (1960), was inspired by **Fats Domino**'s song of the same name while 'Look Before You Leap' was sung in the style of **Ben E. King** and 'I Pray for You' (1961) echoed the gospel fervour of the early Clyde McPhatter. In 1960 he teamed up with his sister as Derrick and Patsy, recording 'Housewives' Choice' which became one of first bestsellers for **Chris Blackwell**'s Island label in Britain. Island went on to release Morgan's *Forward March* (1963), the title track of which was an anthemic celebration of Jamaican independence, and several other albums.

Morgan was indirectly responsible for **Leslie Kong**'s entry into the music industry when Kong financed his 1962 recording 'Shake a Leg'. This alliance with a businessman from the Chinese community so enraged Morgan's previous producer, **Prince Buster**, that he recorded '30 Pieces of Silver' and 'Black Head Chinee Man'. Morgan counter-attacked with 'Blazing Fire' and the 'answer record' sequence continued with 'Creation' (Buster), 'Love Natty' (Morgan) and 'Praise without Raise' (Buster).

The two singers were also involved in the sequence of records devoted to the 'rude boy' phenomenon of the rock-steady era. While Buster assumed the mantle of 'Judge Dread', Morgan, like **Bob Marley**, was one of those performing pro-rudie songs, notably 'Rudies Don't Fear'. During this period Morgan also recorded the rock steady classic 'Greedy Gal'. With the rise of Rastafarianism in the early seventies, Morgan remade the song as 'Rasta Don't Fear'.

Morgan's only British success came with 'Moon Hop' (Crab, 1970), which was caught up in the enthusiasm for reggae shown by white skinheads. Among his later records were a version of Max Romeo's 'Wet Dream' (1975), *People Decession* (Third World, 1977) and *The Conqueror* (Vista Sounds, 1985).

HELEN MORGAN
b. Helen Riggins, 2 August 1900, Danville, Ohio, USA, d. 8 October 1941, Chicago, Illinois

A star of Broadway and New York's nightclubs in the twenties and thirties, Morgan was a torch singer whose troubled life echoed the tragic heroines she made her speciality.

The daughter of a farmer, Morgan worked as a shop girl and manicurist before becoming a singer, first in carnival sideshows, then in small clubs in Chicago and finally New York's finest speakeasies. Completely untrained, she won instant fame through her emotional 'tear-stained' style of singing. After appearing in the chorus of the touring version of **Jerome Kern**'s *Sally* (1924), she had featured roles in *George White's Scandals* (1925) and *Americana* (1926) before being offered the part of Julie in Kern and Oscar Hammerstein II's *Showboat* (1927), one of the most influential musicals of the twentieth century, which marked a radical break with the twin traditions of operetta and simple musical comedy in favour of character and plot. Morgan introduced Kern and **P. G. Wodehouse**'s 'Bill' and repeated her role in the 1929 film of the show and James Whale's 1936 film.

Though she appeared in several films, few bar *Showboat* and Rouben Mamoulian's *Applause* (1929), the bitter-sweet story of an ageing burlesque star in which Morgan sang **Yip Harburg**'s 'What Wouldn't I Do for That Man', were significant. Among her other films were *Roadhouse Nights* (1930), *Go into Your Dance* and *Frankie and Johnnie* (1935). Her career was ruined by alcoholism which caused her early death in 1941. However, when the biopic *The Helen Morgan Story* (1957) was made with Ann Blyth in the title role and **Gogi Grant** dubbing her singing voice, love rather than drink was presented as the cause of Morgan's troubles.

ALANIS MORISSETTE
b. Alanis Nadine Morissette, 1 June 1974, Ottawa, Canada

The most successful of the mid-nineties breed of female singer-songwriters, Morissette sold over 15 million copies of her breakthrough album, *Jagged Little Pill**, which featured her highly individual version of confessional recordings in which pop slickness and aggressive posturing were mixed in equal proportion.

Morissette won her first break into the music industry at the age of ten, landing a presenting role on the Nickelodeon TV series *You Can't Do That on Television*, and subsequently releasing her début single, 'Fate Stay with Me'. She spent the next four years performing around the country, eventually earning a deal with MCA. Morissette's 1991 eponymous début was a collection of mild dance-pop songs, achieving platinum status in Canada; the follow-up, *Now Is the Time* (1992) flopped, leading the singer to seek a new direction.

After finishing high school, Morissette left Canada for Los Angeles, where she met Glen Ballard, acclaimed songwriter for artists such as **Michael Jackson** and **Paula Abdul**. The pair soon began to work together, moving away from the teen-pop of Alanis's earlier recordings towards a darker rock sound. Morissette's demo tape earned her a deal with **Madonna**'s Maverick label and she began work on *Jagged Little Pill* (1995). On the strength of the singles 'You Oughta Know', 'Hand in My Pocket', 'Ironic' and 'All I Really Want' the album was a phenomenal worldwide success, winning the singer four Grammys. Morissette's much-anticipated follow-up, *Supposed Former Infatuation Junkie** (1998), which included the singles 'Thank U' and 'Joining You', was another international hit but inevitably failed to reach the sales levels of its predecessor. In the same year her previously unavailable recording of 'Uninvited' helped the soundtrack album *City of Angels* to the top of the US charts.

She remained as controversial as ever, less for her songs in 1999 than for having her tour sponsored by MP3.com, then under attack from the US recording industry for allegedly significantly contributing to the spread of Internet piracy. *Unplugged* (1999), despite including more than just the hits, has the sound of a stop-gap album with its mix of acoustic folkery and air-headed philosophy.

GIORGIO MORODER
b. 26 April 1940, Oristel, Italy

Popularizer of the synthesizer and sequencer and producer of **Donna Summer**'s classic disco track 'Love to Love You'* (Oasis, 1975), Moroder also worked with such artists as **Blondie** and **David Bowie** on his various film projects, and was briefly one of the most successful and inventive producers of the eighties.

Raised in Italy, Moroder played bass in several groups before settling in Munich where he teamed up with producer and lyricist Peter Bellotte. Specializing in dance-orientated music, the pair had several hits in Germany including 'Nachts Schient die Sonne' (Oasis, 1971), which gave Chicory Tip a million-seller when translated as 'Son of My Father' (Columbia, 1972). Moroder's breakthrough record was the epic – it lasts just under seventeen minutes – and erotic 'Love to Love You' (1975), with its synthesizer-dominated rhythms and Summer's simulation of the sounds of orgasm. It was the first example of what later became known as Eurodisco music and was a massive American hit when released on Neil Bogart's Casablanca label. Equally influential was the delayed follow-up 'I Feel Love' (1997).

Moroder went on to produce further Summer albums (including *Four Seasons of Love*, 1976, and *Bad Girls*, Casablanca, 1979) as well as records by **Janis Ian**, the Three Degrees, **Sparks** and Sigue Sigue Sputnik, whose début album (*Flaunt It*, 1986) he oversaw. More experimental were his own solo records, which included the first digitally recorded and mastered album, $E = MC^2$ (Casablanca, 1979). His hit singles included 'Theme from Here to Eternity' (1977) and, with the **Human League**'s Phil Oakey, 'Together in Electric Dreams' (Virgin, 1984), from Moroder's score to the film *Electric Dreams*.

Moroder's film music included *Midnight Express* (1979), for which he won an Oscar, *American Gigolo*, which included his production of Blondie's 'Call Me'*, *Cat People* (1982) and *Flashdance* (1983), which won him another Oscar and included Irene Cara's 'Flashdance . . . What a Feeling'* and **Joan Jett**'s 'I Love Rock'n'Roll'*. More interesting (and controversial) was Moroder's restoration and re-editing of Fritz Lang's classic silent film *Metropolis* (1984), which included hits by **Bonnie Tyler** ('Here She Comes') and **Queen**'s Freddie Mercury ('Love Kills'). During the eighties Moroder was much in demand to provide rock soundtracks to Hollywood films and in response he set up Music Team, a group of producers to create soundtrack packages for film producers. His most notable success, and one of the most successful soundtrack albums ever, was *Top Gun* (Columbia, 1986). A No. 1 album in both Britain and America, it included the hit singles 'Take My Breath Away' by Berlin and 'Danger Zone' by **Kenny Loggins**.

The *Top Gun* score was a collaboration with Tom Whitlock. Other members of Music Team included Richie Zito, Harold Faltermeyer (who had his own European hit with 'Axel F' on MCA in 1985 and wrote the music for the 1985 film *Fletch*) and Keith Forsey, Moroder's former session drummer and producer of albums by **Billy Idol**, former **Eagle** Glenn Frey and **Simple Minds**. In 1988 Moroder produced and co-wrote Koreana's 'Hand in Hand' (PolyGram), the official song of the Seoul Olympics.

ENNIO MORRICONE
b. 11 October 1928, Rome, Italy

A prolific composer for over 300 movies, Morricone brought a new dimension to film scoring in his work on numerous Italian Westerns of the sixties, most notably those of Sergio Leone. He radically affected the practice of writing musical themes for characters, replacing the themes with motifs, which often involved startling use of percussion and chorus.

A graduate of the Conservatorio di Santo Cecilia, Morricone studied trumpet and composition and wrote classical and experimental music in the late fifties. He began to write film scores in the early sixties, but his first significant work was the score for *Per un Pugno di Dollari* (1964). Just as Leone's film (entitled *For a Few Dollars More* when dubbed into English) redefined the Western, so, in place of what one critic has called the 'heroic style' which dominated American Western scoring, Morricone brought a 'surrealistic panorama of strange cries, savage guitar chords, jangling bells and the cracking of whips'. The results have been described as sounding 'like **Mitch Miller** on dope'. As well as scoring all Leone's films, Morricone composed the music to numerous Italian films of the sixties and seventies, releasing many soundtrack albums on RCA.

From the late seventies onwards he wrote scores for Hollywood and international productions, including *Quemada!* (1969), *Exorcist II* (1977), *Days of Heaven* (1978) and *The Mission* (1985), for which he won an Oscar. Ironically, Morricone's only major hits came from accompanying **Paul Anka** on the Italian-language recording 'Ogni Volta'* (RCA, 1964) and as the writer and performer of the theme to the British teleseries *The Life and Times of David Lloyd George*, 'Chi Mai' (BBC, 1981). In 1987 he co-wrote 'It Couldn't Happen Here' with the **Pet Shop Boys** and Virgin released *Film Music 1966–87*, a double-album of new recordings of his most notable themes. The same company issued an album of his *Chamber Music* in 1988.

Morricone has subsequently maintained his prolific output, scoring such films as *The Endless Games* (1989), Zefferelli's *Hamlet* (1990), *Money* (1991), *State of Grace* and *In the Line of Fire* (1993). Later nineties film scores included *Nostromo* (1997) and *U Turn* (1998).

VAN MORRISON

b. George Ivan Morrison, 31 August 1945, Belfast, Northern Ireland

One of the greatest vocal stylists in rock music, Morrison's early work showed a mastery of blues and soul singing. From the eighties onwards, while his songs have showed a growing preoccupation with spiritual themes, his singing style become more improvisatory and jazz-inflected, forever suggesting a sense of mystery, perhaps best summed up in the title of one of his many late albums, *Inarticulate Speech of the Heart* (1983). In the manner of few artists – **Bob Dylan** and **Neil Young** spring to mind – Van Morrison has managed to make compelling and affecting music at every stage of his ever-changing career.

The son of American music enthusiasts, Morrison grew up in a working-class area of Belfast listening to records by such artists as **Woody Guthrie**, **Jimmy Rodgers**, **Leadbelly** and **Hank Williams**. He learned to play guitar and saxophone and was a member of various local skiffle and rock'n'roll bands. On leaving school in 1960 he became sax player with the Monarchs, touring Britain and Germany where the group cut an instrumental single, 'Twingy Baby' (1963).

Back in Belfast, Morrison formed an R&B group, Them, with ex-Monarchs guitarist Billy Harrison. A successful residency at the Maritime Hotel led to a contract with Decca. Slim Harpo's 'Don't Start Crying Now' was followed by a frenetic version of the blues standard 'Baby Please Don't Go' which was chosen as theme tune for the television show *Ready Steady Go!* and reached the British Top Ten in 1964.

The group moved to London where Decca brought **Bert Berns** from New York to produce their version of his 'Here Comes the Night'. The song was a big hit in 1965 in both America and Britain. The group's later singles included the Morrison compositions 'Mystic Eyes' (a minor American hit) and the raucous 'Gloria', which inspired garage bands on both sides of the Atlantic and was successfully covered in America by one of them, the Shadows of Knight (Dunwich, 1966). In 1966 Them toured America where Morrison jammed with his namesake Jim, lead singer of the **Doors**.

Soon afterwards, the group broke up and Morrison returned to Belfast to write new songs before Berns invited him to record in New York in 1967. The lilting 'Brown Eyed Girl' (Bang, 1967) was a Top Ten hit, and was followed by the less successful 'Ro Ro Rosey'. However, Bang's hasty release of two albums (*Blowing Your Mind* and *The Best of Van Morrison*) alienated Morrison from Berns even before the latter's sudden death ended their partnership.

Based in Cambridge, Massachusetts, Morrison started to perform with a jazz guitar/flute/bass trio. He was signed to Warners in 1968 and recorded one of the definitive sixties concept albums, *Astral Weeks*. Produced by Louis Merenstein with backing musicians including **Modern Jazz Quartet** drummer Connie Kay and John Payne (flute), the album included the swirling melodies of 'Cypress Avenue' and 'Madame George', songs inspired by memories of Belfast.

Morrison himself produced the superior *Moondance* (1970), which included ex-Colwell-Tilton Blues Band player Jack Schroer (saxes), Jeff Labes (keyboards) and John Platania, from former Bang group Silver Bicycle, on guitar. All became mainstays of Morrison's band over the next five years. The album showed a greater diversity of styles, from sophisticated ballad (the title track) to the triumphal R&B of 'And It Stoned Me', another nostalgic memory of childhood. The mysterious, sweet-sounding 'Into the Mystic' prefigured the elliptical writing of Morrison's later songs.

His Band and Street Choir (1970) included 'Domino', Morrison's first Top Ten single since leaving Bang. For the first time his backing group was billed as the Caledonia Soul Orchestra, the name pulling together Morrison's Irish roots and his black American influences. Among the Street Choir were

Martha Velez and Judy Clay, erstwhile partner of **William Bell**.

In 1971 Morrison moved to California and with Clover steel guitarist John McFee and Ronnie Montrose (guitar) recorded the mellow *Tupelo Honey*, produced by Ted Templeman. It contained the Top Thirty hit 'Wild Night' and the romantic 'I Wanna Roo You', improbably covered by comic actress Goldie Hawn. Other singers who recorded material from *Tupelo Honey* included **Richie Havens** (the title track), Martha Reeves of **Martha and the Vandellas** ('Wild Night'), **Dusty Springfield** and **Jackie deShannon** (both 'I Wanna Roo You'). In the same year Morrison also worked with **The Band**, co-writing '4% Pantomime' and singing it with Robbie Robertson on *Cahoots*.

The masterpiece of this phase of Morrison's career was *St Dominic's Preview* (1972), whose widescreen cinematic title song, cutting between Belfast and West Coast rock culture, captured the singer poised between two worlds. With Bernie Krause on Moog, the album's other highlights were the vocal *tour de force* 'Listen to the Lion', which found Morrison roaring and purring, using his voice as one instrument in the band, and 'Jackie Wilson Said (I'm in Heaven When You Smile)'. This sprightly tribute to the great soul singer was a 1982 British hit for **Dexy's Midnight Runners**.

Hard Nose the Highway (1973) was a lesser work which nevertheless confirmed Morrison's move towards longer songs: 'Autumn Song' lasted for ten minutes. Its choice of material, however, seemed odd. 'Purple Heather', a reworking of the Irish folk song 'Wild Mountain Thyme', stood next to 'Being Green', Kermit the Frog's song from *Sesame Street*. Morrison's highly acclaimed live shows were captured on the double-album *It's Too Late to Stop Now* (1974), which was followed by *Veedon Fleece*, an enigmatic song sequence inspired by a return visit to Ireland.

There followed a long gap in Morrison's recording career before the prosaically, but accurately, titled *A Period of Transition* appeared in 1977. Co-produced with **Dr John**, the album seemed to indicate that Morrison was still seeking a fusion between his blues-jazz music and the deepening spirituality which inspired much of his songwriting. Religious imagery and literary allusions multiplied on later albums like *Wavelength* (1978) and *Into the Music* (1978), his first album for Mercury, while *Common One* (1980) included the shimmering, mystical 'Summertime in England'. The outstanding songs on *Beautiful Vision* (1982), a further collection of Belfast memories, were the title track, 'Van Lose Stairway' and 'Cleaning Windows', in which Morrison paid homage to his blues and country music heroes as well as novelist Jack Kerouac. The aptly titled *Inarticulate Speech of*

the Heart (1983), containing 'Rave on John Donne' (a reference to the seventeenth-century metaphysical poet), was followed by a 1984 live album, recorded in Belfast, while 1985's *A Sense of Wonder* included a powerful setting of William Blake's poem 'Let the Slave (Price of Experience)'. Among the backing musicians were the Irish group Moving Hearts.

Morrison's considerable following provided the basis for frequent live appearances during the eighties and his recording activity was equally prolific. Later albums included *No Guru No Method No Teacher* (1986), a title which referred to Morrison's leaving the Scientologists, and *Poetic Champions Compose* (1987). In 1988 he collaborated with the Chieftains on *Irish Heartbeat* (Polydor) while *Avalon Sunset* (1989) had **Georgie Fame** on Hammond organ and **Cliff Richard** as guest vocalist.

In the nineties Morrison's work-rate showed no sign of slowing. With Fame now his musical director, he toured regularly and released *Enlightenment* (1990), which included the autobiographical 'In the Days before Rock'n'Roll' as well as lyrics by Irish poet Paul Durcan, and *Hymns to the Silence* (1991), both of which reached the British Top Five. In 1991 he collaborated with **Tom Jones** and **John Lee Hooker**. Two 'best of' albums, concentrating on his later career, appeared in 1990 and 1993, the year that he released what most critics saw as his finest album in a decade, *Too Long in Exile*, which included a reworking of 'Gloria' and featured a guest appearance from Hooker. In 1994 he released the live *A Night in San Francisco*, which included his daughter Shana and the young Irish singer-songwriter Brian Kennedy on backing vocals. The album's finest moments (particularly a superb version of **James Brown**'s 'It's a Man's Man's World') confirmed Morrison's continuing artistic regeneration. The same year saw the release of *No Prima Donna*, a tribute album of Morrison's songs performed by such artists as **Sinead O'Connor**, **Lisa Stansfield**, **Marianne Faithfull** and **Elvis Costello**. The album was compiled by Van Morrison himself.

The uplifting *Days Like This* (1995) was followed by *Tell Me Something*, a tribute to **Mose Allison**, and his contribution to *The Songs of Jimmie Rodgers* (1997), on which he sang 'Mule Skinner Blues', prefiguring his later rebirth as a skiffler. In the same year he released *The Healing Game*. Even more intriguing was *The Philosopher's Stone* (1998), a double-album compilation of unreleased recordings made between 1971 and 1988 that showed his complete mastery of the anecdotal song. After *Back on Top* (Virgin, 1999), Morrison completely surprised his audience with the charming *The Skiffle Sessions – Live in Belfast* (1999), on which, partnered by **Chris Barber** and **Lonnie Donnegan** and with a little help from the nineties everyman Dr John, he tried with some success to recapture the moment of skiffle. More importantly, the album confirmed Morrison's endless willingness to try something new. Morrison continued his flurry of collaborations with *You Win Again* (2000), a collection of rock'n'roll and country covers, including two of Hank Williams' songs made in partnership with Linda Gail Lewis, the sister of **Jerry Lee Lewis**.

MORRISSEY
b. Steven Patrick Morrissey, 22 May 1959, Manchester, England

After a successful period with the **Smiths**, Morrissey had mixed fortunes as a solo performer in the nineties.

In 1988 Morrissey released the solo album *Viva Hate* (HMV), which made the US Top Fifty, and reached the UK Top Ten with 'Suedehead', co-written with producer Stephen Street. The following year he switched producers to Clive Langer and Alan Winstanley on 'Ouija Board, Ouija Board'. A string of hit singles and their B-sides were collected on *Bona Drag* (1990), which, like its successor *Kill Uncle*, made the UK Top Ten. Morrissey's cult status in the US had progressed to the stage where he could sell out New York's Madison Square Garden, and 1992's *Your Arsenal* saw him break into the US Top Thirty. His most successful album, it was produced by ex-**David Bowie** and **Mott the Hoople** guitarist Mick Ronson and incorporated elements of seventies glam rock with Morrissey's abiding fascination with rockabilly. The album was followed by the live set *Beethoven Was Deaf* (1993).

Morrissey had built a devoted following in the UK, but in the mid-nineties there were signs that his constant (albeit ambiguous) flirtation with nationalism and neo-fascist imagery on songs like 'Suedehead', 'The National Front Disco' and 'Asian Rut' were beginning to alienate his strongest supporters in the media. The issue came to a head in 1992 when, draped in a union flag at an outdoor concert in London's Finsbury Park, he drew a torrent of abuse from fans. He marked the release of *Vauxhall and I* (1994) by remarking in interviews that he believed that the extreme right-wing British National Party should be allowed to air its views in the interests of free speech. The retrospective set *The World of Morrissey* (Parlophone, 1995) was a big hit in the UK.

Southpaw Grammar, released later the same year, included the minor UK hit 'Dagenham Dave' but was met with open hostility by the music press. *Maladjusted* (1997) – the UK pressing of which lacked the damning 'Sorrow Will Come in the End', apparently aimed at Morrissey's former Smiths bandmembers – was a commercial failure, despite the release of the comic 'Satan Rejected My Soul' as a single. It was followed by two further compilation volumes, *Suedehead:*

The Best of Morrissey (1997) and *My Early Burglary Years* (1998). The singer returned to the public eye the following year with a full-scale tour of the UK.

ELLA MAE MORSE
b. 12 September 1924, Mansfield, Texas, d. 16 October 1999

An exuberant singer, Morse's 1942 recording of 'Cow Cow Boogie' was the first million-seller for the newly established Capitol label.

Morse began singing with the small band run by her parents. In 1939 **Jimmy Dorsey** heard her and signed her briefly to his band. While with him, she met pianist Freddie Slack (*b. 7 August 1910, La Crosse, Wisconsin, d. 10 August 1965, Hollywood, California*) and joined his band in 1941. A notable boogie-woogie pianist, Slack heard **Ella Fitzgerald** singing 'Cow Cow Boogie' – Don Raye's adaptation of Charles 'Cow Cow' Davenport's 'Cow Cow Blues' – in the film *Ride 'Em Cowboy* (1941) and recorded it with Morse, who in turn sang it in *Reveille with Beverly* (1943). Her subsequent records, including several more boogie-woogie songs, sold only moderately. Among them were 'Mr Five by Five' (1942), with guitar accompaniment by **T-Bone Walker**, and Raye's 'House of Blue Lights' (1946), which was later revived by **Merrill Moore**, among others. Morse retired at the end of the forties. Her comeback record was 'Blacksmith Blues'* (1952) on which **Nelson Riddle**'s accompaniment featured a hammer clinking on an anvil to good effect.

Morse retired again in the mid-fifties. Her hits were issued on CD by Capitol in 1992. However, the definitive retrospective was *Barrelhouse, Boogie & the Blues* (1997).

JELLY ROLL MORTON
b. Ferdinand Lemott, 20 October 1890, New Orleans, Louisiana, USA, d. 10 July 1941, Los Angeles, California

With **Louis Armstrong**, Morton was the most important exponent of New Orleans jazz. But while the trumpeter's technical brilliance and career strategy made him a leading figure in popular music, Morton had little commercial success. That fact, and his penchant for exaggeration (he once claimed to have invented jazz), have sometimes obscured the extent of his achievement. As a composer and arranger he provided the most important link between ragtime and the pot-pourri of Spanish, creole and other New Orleans traditions and the mainstream jazz of the thirties. Morton's orchestrations introduced the instrumental break and the background riff that were central to big-band jazz while such pieces as 'Milenburg Joys' and 'King Porter Stomp' were staples of the swing-band repertoire.

He began playing piano professionally in New Orleans in 1906 and for nearly two decades lived and worked all over the United States. Morton toured with a vaudeville troupe, led his own bands in Chicago (1914) and Vancouver (1917) and played solo piano as well as having brief spells as a hotel keeper and boxing promoter.

In 1923 Morton settled in Chicago, performing and touring occasionally (notably with **W. C. Handy** in 1926), as well as working for the Melrose publishing company. Most importantly, over the next six years he recorded prolifically as soloist and group leader, creating the music upon which his reputation rests. In 1924 he made a series of piano rolls of such titles as 'King Porter Stomp', 'Mr Jelly Lord' and 'Tom Cat Blues' as well as cutting tracks in duet with **King Oliver**. Between 1923 and 1926 Morton recorded for Gennett ('Wolverine Blues', 1923), Paramount, Vocalion and Autograph ('High Society', 1924).

He signed a four-year exclusive deal with Victor in 1926 and embarked on a series of band recordings with his Red Hot Peppers, a group featuring George Mitchell (trumpet) and Omer Simeon (clarinet), while **Duke Ellington** trumpeter Bubber Miley appeared on some of the twenty-five tracks made by the group. Among the highlights were 'Blue Blood Blues', 'Mournful Serenade', 'Shoe Shine Drag', 'Jelly Roll Blues' and 'Doctor Jazz', on which Morton also sang.

His preference for small group jazz out of fashion, Morton scarcely recorded again until 1938 but his compositions were taken up by many leading swing bands. 'Milenburg Joys' was recorded by **Tommy Dorsey**, **Don Redman** and the British bandleader **Lew Stone**, Bunny Berigan did 'Jelly Roll Blues' while 'King Porter Stomp' was a hit for **Fletcher Henderson** (1933) and **Benny Goodman** (1935). Financial problems dogged Morton's own career and in 1936–8 he performed at Washington clubs until **Alan Lomax** recorded many hours of Morton playing, singing and reminiscing for the archives of the Library of Congress. The results were later issued as a twelve-album series and Morton's conversations formed the basis of Lomax's biography *Mr Jelly Roll* (1950).

With the renewed interest in traditional jazz, Morton recorded with his New Orleans Jazzmen (Victor, 1939), a group with **Sidney Bechet** on soprano sax. Poor health meant he did not record again, but his tunes took on a further lease of life as the trad movement gathered momentum in the forties and fifties.

SHADOW MORTON
b. George Morton, 1942, Richmond, Virginia, USA

Morton was an innovative record producer of the early sixties. Like **Phil Spector**, he understood that the studio could be used as a laboratory for experiments with sound, but while Spector's grand structures were 'little symphonies for the kids', Morton's finest records with the **Shangri-Las** and others were dramatic vignettes of teenage street-life set to music.

He grew up in Brooklyn and in the early sixties was a member of the Gems, a vocal group which occasionally backed singer Ellie Gay. After Gay became successful (as songwriter **Ellie Greenwich**), Morton approached her about producing records. His first attempt was 'Remember (Walking in the Sand)' by the Shangri-Las with its atmospheric seagull cries and eruptions of emotive singing by the group's leader Mary Weiss. Released on **Leiber and Stoller**'s and **George Goldner**'s Red Bird label, it was a Top Ten hit in 1964. It was followed by his masterpiece, 'Leader of the Pack'*, on which bird sounds were replaced by motorcycle engines as Weiss told her shocked girlfriends of her love for a greasy biker. It reached No. 1 and inspired the parody, 'Leader of the Laundromat' by the Detergents (Roulette, 1964), whose lead singer was Ron Dante, later of the Archies.

Over the next year, Morton was responsible for ten more hits, including more songs by the Shangri-Las (notably the doleful 'I Can Never Go Home Anymore') and records by the Ad Libs ('The Boy from New York City'), Dixie Cups ('Chapel of Love'), Tradewinds ('New York's a Lonely Town') and Jelly Beans ('I Wanna Love Him So Bad').

Morton's next assignment was the début album by teenage protest singer **Janis Ian**, from which 'Society's Child' (MGM, 1967) became a big hit. He also supervised the recording career of a very different New York act, **Vanilla Fudge**. The epitome of riff-laden heavy rock, the group reached the Top Ten with Morton's production of their treatment of the **Supremes**' 'You Keep Me Hangin' on' (Atlantic, 1968).

At the end of the sixties Morton left music to indulge his passion for car racing, but that career ended after he suffered a serious accident. He returned to the studio in 1971 to produce **Mott the Hoople**'s 'Midnight Lady' and in 1974 the **New York Dolls**' *Too Much Too Soon* (Mercury), the second album by the glam-rock/punk group. He later worked on albums by the all-female group Isis (Buddah) and by Tom Pachecho (RCA) before leaving the music business.

MICKIE MOST
b. Michael Peter Hayes, June 1938, Aldershot, Hampshire, England

Most was one of the most successful pop-orientated producers of the post-**Beatles** era. Among the artists with whom he worked were the **Animals**, **Lulu**, **Donovan**, **Jeff Beck**, **Hot Chocolate** and **Suzi**

Quatro, most of whom were signed to his RAK record company.

Raised in North London, Most formed the Most brothers in 1958 with Alex Wharton (who later, as Alex Murray, produced the **Moody Blues**' first hit, 'Go Now', in 1964), recorded unsuccessfully for Decca and in 1959 went to South Africa. There he formed Mickie Most and the Playboys and churned out successful covers of rock'n'roll (including **Chuck Berry**'s 'Johnny B. Goode' and **Buddy Holly**'s 'Rave on'), in the process learning how to produce. On his return to Britain in 1963, he had a minor hit as Mickie Most and the Gear with 'Mr Porter', before setting up as an independent producer. His first signing was the Animals, for whom he selected material as well as producing their first seven hits, including 'Baby Let Me Take You Home' (EMI Columbia, 1964), an adaptation of the old blues song 'Baby Let Me Follow You Down', previously revived by **Bob Dylan**, and 'The House of the Rising Sun'* (a hit again when reissued in 1972 and 1982 on RAK). Other artists Most produced at this time were the Nashville Teens ('Tobacco Road' and 'Google Eye', Decca, 1964, both **John D. Loudermilk** compositions), **Brenda Lee** ('Is It True', 1964), Lulu ('The Boat That I Row', 1967) and **Herman's Hermits**, whose string of American hits he was responsible for. These included 'Mrs Brown You've Got a Lovely Daughter'* and 'I'm Henry the Eighth, I Am'* (1965).

However, if Herman's Hermits provided Most with his greatest commercial success until Hot Chocolate in the seventies, his work with Terry Reid, Donovan and Beck was more creative. He gave blue-eyed soul singer Reid a fittingly sparse sound, while on *Sunshine Superman* (1966) and *Mellow Yellow* (1967) he provided a sympathetic backdrop for Donovan's gentle songs, and on *Truth* (1968) a dynamic soundscape for Beck's guitar pyrotechnics. Most was also responsible for Beck's uncharacteristic pop hits, 'Hi-Ho Silver Lining' (1967) and his cover of Paul Mauriat's 'Love Is Blue' (1968).

In 1969 Most formed RAK and, with **Chinn and Chapman** as his in-house producers and writers, the label had a string of pop successes with Smokie (whose hits included 'Living Next Door to Alice', 1976, and a revival of the **Searchers** 'Needles and Pins', 1977); Mud (who had a trio of British No. 1s, 'Tiger Feet'*, the **Elvis Presley** parody 'Lonely This Christmas', 1974, and 'Oh Boy', 1975); Quatro ('Can the Can', 1973, and 'Devil Gate Drive', 1974); New World ('Tom Tom Turnaround', 1971); Racey ('Lay Your Love on Me', 1978); **Alexis Korner**'s CCS ('Walkin'' and 'Tap Turns on the Water', both 1971); and Hot Chocolate, who had more than twenty hits. Most also oversaw the first hits of **Marty Wilde**'s daughter Kim (including 'Kids in America', 1981, and

'View from a Bridge', 1982), before she left RAK for MCA in 1983.

As well as running RAK, Most became a pop pundit on the television talent show *New Faces* (1973–8) and produced the shortlived *Revolver*, one of the few television pop programmes to feature punk extensively. After a period of retirement he briefly reactivated the RAK label in 1988, producing 'I Don't Wanna Fight' by Perfect Stranger (aka ex-**Uriah Heep** singer Peter Goalby).

MOTLEY CRÜE

Vince Neil, b. Vincent Neil Wharton, 8 February 1961, Hollywood, California, USA; Tommy Lee, b. Thomas Lee Bass, 3 October 1962, Athens, Greece; Mick Mars, b. Robert Deal, 3 April 1955, Terre Haute, Indiana, USA; Nikki Sixx, b. Frank Carlton Serafino Ferrano, 11 December 1958, San José, California, USA; John Corabi

Motley Crüe, along with their compatriots Ratt, were at the forefront of a wave of new (mainly Los Angeles-based) heavy metal bands to emerge in the eighties. They had sales of over 25 million albums and found a huge audience worldwide with their combination of no-frills hard rock and flamboyant, glam-rock image. The well-documented over-indulgence by group members in drugs and alcohol did little to dent their popularity; however, the on–off relationship of Lee and Pamela Anderson deflected much of the group's rebelliousness.

Bassist Sixx and drummer Lee first joined forces as Christmas in 1980, having previously played in unsuccessful hard rock bands London and Suite 19, respectively. The pair added guitarist Mars and eventually discovered vocalist Neil in local LA Top Forty band Rock Candy. Renamed Motley Crüe, the band recorded 'Stick to Your Guns' for their own Leathur label in 1981, followed by the album *Too Fast for Love*. A high-octane and outrageous stage act involving chainsaws and burning clothes helped to gain a recording deal with Elektra in 1982. Setting their agenda as the preoccupations of American youth ('sex, drugs, pizza and more sex'), the band toured heavily around the release of their second album, *Shout at the Devil* (1983), a US Top Twenty hit.

Motley Crüe toured throughout 1984, but the year ended in tragedy when Neil was involved in a car crash which killed one of his passengers, drummer Nick Dingley, better known as Razzle from Scandinavian **New York Dolls** clones Hanoi Rocks. The band regrouped in 1985 to record *Theatre of Pain*, which was less metallic than its predecessors and drew comparisons with **Aerosmith**. It included a hit cover-version of 'Smokin'' in the Boys Room', a 1973 US Top Five single for Brownsville Station.

Girls Girls Girls (1987) was another million-seller

which provided hit singles with the title track and 'You're All I Need'. However, their extensive tour schedule was halted when Sixx had a near-fatal drink and drug overdose. In 1988 the band were largely inactive with various members undergoing treatment for their drink and drugs problems before reconvening to record *Dr Feelgood* (1989). By this point Neil was experimenting in areas outside the band, with a cameo role in the movie *The Adventures of Ford Fairlane* and a growing interest in driving racing cars. In 1991 the band recorded three new tracks including an unlikely cover of the **Sex Pistols**' 'Anarchy in the UK' for the career retrospective *Decade of Decadence*, another huge seller.

In 1992 Neil was sacked from the band and replaced by vocalist/guitarist Corabi, formerly of Scream. Reportedly unhappy with a proposed change in musical direction, Neil unsurprisingly harked back to the style of classic Crüe on his début solo album, *Exposed* (1993). The new line-up made its début on *Motley Crüe* in 1994, which saw the band attempt to move on from their established style. While the album was commercially successful, from this point on the Lee–Anderson relationship would take centre stage. In 1996 the pair sued *Penthouse* for selling a tape of them having sex and in 1998 Anderson sued for divorce for a second time. During this period, Neil issued *Carved in Stone* (1995) and the band released *Generation Swine* (1997). In 1999 Lee quit the band and made a full reconciliation with Anderson and in 2000 the band, still minus Lee, released the revivalist *New Tattoo* to bad reviews.

MOTORHEAD

Larry Wallis (replaced by 'Fast' Eddie Clarke, replaced by Brian Robertson, b. 7 February 1956, Clarkston, Scotland, replaced by Wurzel, b. Michael Burston, 27 October 1949, Cheltenham, Gloucestershire, England); Lemmy, b. Ian Kilminster, 24 December 1945, Stoke-on-Trent, Staffordshire; Lucas Fox (replaced by Phil Taylor, b. 21 September 1954, Chesterfield, Derbyshire, replaced by Peter Gill, b. 9 June 1951, Sheffield, Yorkshire); Phil Campbell, b. 7 May 1961, Pontypridd, Wales

Proudly boasting a 126-decibel live sound, Motorhead's late seventies hard rock helped prepare the way for the heavy-metal trend of the eighties.

The group was formed in 1975 and took its name from a song written by bassist Lemmy for his former group **Hawkwind**; in the sixties he had played in the Motown Set and the Rockin' Vickers, who recorded the **Kinks**' 'Dandy' (Columbia, 1966), produced by Shel Talmy, and Sam Gopal's Dream (*Escalator*, Stable, 1969). Through journalist and former leader of the Deviants Mick Farren, he met ex-Pink Fairy Wallis (guitar) and Fox (drums). The trio created an

uncompromising heavy-rock music, akin to that of **Ted Nugent** in America. Abortive recording deals with United Artists and Stiff were followed by an eponymous début album on pub-rock label Chiswick, by which time ex-Curtis Knight guitarist Clarke and Taylor had joined the band.

A minor hit, the album led to a contract with Bronze where Motorhead's cover of the Kingsmen's 'Louie Louie' (1978) emphasized the group's affection for the earlier and simpler forms of rock'n'roll. *Overkill* (1979) lived up to its title and, like 'Bomber' (1979), was a Top Forty hit.

The group's greatest period of success came in 1980–1 when the Top Twenty records *The Golden Years* (an EP) and 'Ace of Spades' (the title track from an album) were followed by the live album *No Sleep Til Hammersmith* (1981), which went to No. 1 in Britain. In that year Motorhead also recorded the bestselling *St Valentine's Day Massacre* EP with female heavy-metal group Girlschool (the lead track was a revival of **Johnny Kidd**'s 'Please Don't Touch'), and the jokey 'Don't Do That' with mainstream vocal group the Nolans.

After the Top Ten album *Iron Fist* (1982), former **Thin Lizzy** guitarist Robertson brought a melodic sophistication to *Another Perfect Day* (1983). His displacement in 1984 by twin lead guitarists Wurzel and Campbell re-established the traditional Motorhead sound on *Orgasmostron* (1986), the first album for GWR following the bankruptcy of Bronze. *Rock'n'Roll* (GWR, 1987) included the film title song 'Eat the Rich' (1987) and was further proof of Lemmy's irreverent anarchism. It was followed by a second ear-blasting live album, *No Sleep at All* (1988). By 1990, when the band signed with Epic, Taylor, who had left and rejoined the band several times, was back in the fold.

The first release for the major label, the intriguing *1916*, found the band experimenting with their trademark HM sound – the anti-war title track featured Lemmy actually singing (as opposed to roaring) against a string quartet backing. Although acclaimed by critics and hardcore fans, its sales were unexceptional, and when the 1992 follow-up *March or Die* (recorded without Taylor) failed to reach the British Top Fifty, the band were dropped by the label. Undaunted, they released their own comment on the Epic experience with *Bastards* (1993), yet another slab of uncompromising, no-frills hard rock. *Overnight Sensation* (1996) and *Snake Bite Love* (1998) were in a similar vein. However, they were overshadowed by the four-CD retrospective *Protect the Innocent* (1997). Throughout this period the band continued to tour, particularly in the US and Germany, where they recorded the live *Everything Louder than Everything Else* (1999). *We Are Motorhead* (SPV, 2000) included a version of the **Sex Pistols**' 'God Save the Queen', but to all intents and purposes its ambience was determined by the six-minute track 'One More Fucking Time', which mixed tiredness and dissolution to Motorhead perfection.

MOTT THE HOOPLE
Verden Allen, b. 26 May 1944 (replaced by Morgan Fisher); Dale 'Buffin' Griffin, b. 24 October 1948; Mick Ralphs, b. 31 March 1948, Hereford, England (replaced by Ariel Bender, b. Luther James Grosvenor, 23 December 1949, Evesham, Worcestershire, replaced by Mick Ronson, b. Hull, Humberside, d. 29 April 1993, replaced by Ray Major); Stan Tippens (replaced by Ian Hunter, b. 3 June 1946, Shrewsbury, Shropshire, replaced by Nigel Benjamin); Overend Pete Watts, b. 13 May 1947, Birmingham

A leading British rock band of the seventies, Mott the Hoople were noted for their close relationship with **David Bowie**, who wrote their biggest hit ('All the Young Dudes') and with whom Ronson played guitar before joining Mott.

The nucleus of the group were the Hereford musicians, guitarist Ralphs, vocalist Tippens, drummer Griffin and Watts (bass), who had comprised the Doc Thomas Group which toured Italy in the mid-sixties and recorded there. After the group folded, several members backed **Jimmy Cliff** before re-forming as Silence and signing to Island in 1969. Producer Guy Stevens had recently read the novel *Mott the Hoople* by Willard Manus and gave the name to the group. He also auditioned lead singers, choosing Hunter, who had played in Nottingham rock bands and been a staff songwriter for a London music publisher.

Their eponymous début album was released in 1969 and revealed an organ-based sound reminiscent of **Bob Dylan**'s *Blonde on Blonde* (1968). It was followed by the manic *Mad Shadows* (1970) and the gentler *Wildlife* (1971). The hard-rock-styled *Brain Capers* contained what would become an Ian Hunter stage staple in 'Sweet Angeline' alongside the epic 'The Journey' and the heavy riffing 'Death May Be Your Santa Claus'.

Although a considerable live attraction, record sales were poor, and the band had decided to split up when long-time fan David Bowie intervened. Mott the Hoople were signed by Bowie's manager to CBS and Bowie himself produced *All the Young Dudes* (1972). With Hunter transformed from a Dylanesque singer to a Bowie/**Lou Reed** stylist, Mott the Hoople had their first hit with the album's Bowie-written title track. The most artistically successful album was *Mott* (1973), recorded after Allen left the group. It contained hits in 'Honaloochie Boogie' and the paean to rock'n'roll 'All the Way from Memphis', which

appeared on the soundtrack of Martin Scorsese's *Alice Doesn't Live Here Anymore* (1975).

The band toured America, an experience described in Hunter's book *Diary of a Rock'n'Roll Star* (1974), and gradually began to make headway there. In Britain they had further hits with the anthemic 'Roll Away the Stone', after which Ralphs departed to form **Bad Company**, and 'Golden Age of Rock'n'Roll' from the otherwise disappointing *The Hoople* (1973). The group recruited former Spooky Tooth guitarist Grosvenor (renamed Ariel Bender by Hunter) in 1973. Onetime Love Affair keyboards-player Fisher was also added for *The Hoople*, which reached the American Top Thirty. After further touring, Bender was sacked, although he did appear on *Mott the Hoople – Live* (1974), another American hit. He was briefly replaced by ex-David Bowie guitarist Ronson, who toured Europe with the band and recorded what would be their farewell single, 'Saturday Gigs' (1974).

At the end of 1974 Hunter and Ronson left the band to form their own group. Hunter released a solo album in 1975 which reached the Top Thirty before he split with Ronson, who went on to work with **Bob Dylan** and the **Byrds**' Roger McGuinn. Griffin, Watts and Fisher recruited Benjamin (vocals) and Major (guitar), changed their name to Mott, and recorded *Drive on* (1975) and *Shouting and Pointing* (1976). They then replaced Benjamin with ex-Medicine Head vocalist John Fiddler for two albums as the British Lions before splitting up. Griffin would later become a BBC staff producer while Fisher continued an erratic recording career. His most interesting album was *Minatures* (Pipe, 1980), a collection of over fifty tracks, each under a minute long, by the likes of **Robert Wyatt**, George Melly, the **Damned**'s Dave Vanian and the Residents.

Hunter went on to record the solo albums *All American Alien Boy* (1976) and *Overnight Angels* (1977), before teaming up with Ronson again for *You're Never Alone with a Schizo* (Chrysalis, 1979), *Welcome to the Club* (1980) and *Short Back and Sides* (1981), co-produced by Mick Jones of the **Clash**; they returned to CBS for the disappointing *All of the Good Ones Are Taken* (1983), on which Ronson's contribution was minimal. The duo split, with Ronson concentrating on production work, but in 1989 they were reunited and signed to Mercury, releasing *YUI Orta*. They toured over the following eighteen months, but in 1991 Ronson was diagnosed as having liver cancer. He produced the successful album *Your Arsenal* for **Morrissey** and appeared on David Bowie's *Black Tie White Noise* (1993), but finally succumbed to his illness in April 1993. Hunter was one of many stars who appeared at a 1994 memorial concert for him in London. Hunter also worked as producer for Ellen Foley (with Ronson), American singer Genya Ravan and

Billy Idol's former group Generation X. *The Collection* (1993) is the best summary of Hunter's solo work on Columbia. He later went on to release *Dirty Laundry* (Citadel, 1995) and *The Artful Dodger* (1997).

BOB MOULD
b. 1960, New York State, USA

Songwriter and guitarist Mould pioneered the hardcore genre which was the US response to British punk rock with his band Hüsker Dü. Later a major influence on the 'grunge' bands of the early nineties, Mould nonetheless could not emulate the success of the acts he had inspired, such as **Pearl Jam**, **Soul Asylum** and **Nirvana**.

A hard-rock fan in his early teens, Mould's musical perspective was irreversibly altered by the arrival of punk in 1976. Inspired by US trail-blazers such as the **Ramones**, **Patti Smith** and **Television** as well as slightly later UK acts such as the **Sex Pistols**, the **Clash** and the **Buzzcocks**, he formed Hüsker Dü in 1978 while at university in Minnesota. With a line-up completed by bassist Greg Norton and drummer Grant Hart, the band released their first single, 'Statues', in 1981 on a small independent label. Like most of their early material, it was written by Hart and was a brief, frenetic thrash. The album *Land Speed Record* (1982) contained seventeen songs in the same vein, but the EP *In a Free Land* (1982) saw the band beginning to expand their musical horizons.

The second Hüsker Dü album, *Everything Falls Apart* (SST, 1982), drew acclaim from British critics, and the EP *Metal Circus* and album *Zen Arcade* confirmed their critical standing. The latter, released in 1984, was a double set, featuring the band's trademark punky thrashes alongside more involved material, including the fourteen-minute 'Recurring Dream'.

By this point, Hart and Mould were both contributing as songwriters, and the obvious quality of the material on 1985's *New Day Rising* and *Flip Your Wig* led to a recording contract with Warner Bros. The peerless *Candy Apple Grey* (1986) included Mould's acoustic epic 'Hardly Getting Over It'. However, disagreements between Hart and Mould dogged the recording of the double-album *Warehouse and Other Stories* (1987), and the strain of a heavy touring schedule plus Hart's drug problems brought the band's career to an end in 1988. A live album, *The Living End*, released in 1994, is a fitting epitaph to a most influential group.

After the disbanding of Hüsker Dü, both Hart and Mould continued as solo artists. Hart made several albums which gained critical acclaim but little commercial success, most notably 1994's eponymous début with a new band, Nova Mob. Mould resurfaced in 1989 on the Virgin label with *Workbook*, which was dominated by a more contemplative, acoustic sound than had previously been evident. Adored by critics, it sold poorly, as did the follow-up, the maudlin *Black Sheets of Rain* (1990), and he was subsequently dropped by the label. A compilation of tracks from the two albums plus live material, *Poison Years*, was issued in 1994.

After touring as a solo acoustic act, Mould formed another powerful trio, Sugar, with drummer Malcolm Travis and bassist David Barbe, signing to the US independent Rykodisc, and in the UK to Creation Records. In the wake of the 'grunge' explosion that Hüsker Dü had partly inspired, Sugar's début album, *Copper Blue* (1992), was an immediate hit on both sides of the Atlantic. *Beaster* was a half-hour suite of darker, more improvisational material, recorded at the *Copper Blue* sessions. More ecstatic reviews greeted the second full Sugar album in 1994. Displaying Mould's wry appreciation of his newfound commercial success, it was titled *File Under Easy Listening*.

Having issued the rarities collection *Besides* (1995), Mould announced that Sugar was on hold. The following year he released an eponymous third solo album, on which he played all the instruments himself. In 1998 Mould issued *The Last Dog and Pony Show*, which he supported with a solo acoustic tour, by which point it had become apparent that Sugar would not be re-forming.

MOUNTAIN
Steve Knight; Corky Laing, b. 28 January 1948, Montreal, Canada; Felix Pappalardi, b. 1939, New York, USA, d. 17 April 1983; Leslie West, b. Leslie Weinstein, 22 October 1945, New York

Featuring guitarist West, Mountain was formed to fill the void left by the demise of **Cream**, the virtuoso trio comprising **Eric Clapton**, Ginger Baker and **Jack Bruce**; Bruce recorded with West and Laing after the demise of Mountain.

Pappalardi had been a folk revival backing guitarist for such artists as **Fred Neil** and **Tom Rush**. He graduated to production with **Joan Baez**, **Tim Hardin** and the **Youngbloods**, and in 1967 supervised Cream's *Disraeli Gears*. He met West when he was asked to produce the Vagrants, a New York group which had recorded 'Respect' (Atlantic, 1966) and for whom the 250lb West played lead guitar.

The group disbanded soon afterwards and Pappalardi went on to produce and play bass on the solo album *Leslie West – Mountain* (Windfall, 1969). As a result a group was formed with N. D. Smart (drums) and Knight (organ). After Mountain's triumphant performance at the Woodstock Festival with their bombastic power-trio rock, Laing replaced Smart on *Mountain Climbing* (1970) and the hit 'Mississippi Queen'.

Nantucket Sleighride (1971) and *Flowers of Evil*

(1972) successfully repeated the formula but soon afterwards Pappalardi returned to studio work. A live album and *The Road Goes on Forever* (1973) were subsequently released but by now West and Laing had teamed up with Bruce for *Why Dontcha* (1972) and *Whatever Turns You on* (1973). Pappalardi briefly returned for the Mountain reunion *Avalanche* (1974) but afterwards each member pursued an undistinguished solo career.

West made *The Great Fatsby* (1975), produced by Bob D'Orleans, and *The Leslie West Band*, while Laing released *Makin' It on the Street* (Elektra, 1977). Pappalardi's production credits included Back Door (led by **Alexis Korner** alumnus Colin Hodgkinson) and Jesse Colin Young of the Youngbloods. He also combined with a Japanese rock group to cut *Felix Pappalardi and Creation* (A&M, 1976) and released *Don't Worry Mum* in 1979. West and Laing re-formed the group with bassist Matt Clarke (formerly of Rainbow, with whom the new Mountain toured in 1985) for the minor *Go for Your Life*. The group split up soon afterwards.

West took part in Miles Copeland's instrumentalists' No Speak tour and played on *Guitar Speaks* (Illegal, 1988).

NANA MOUSKOURI
b. 10 October 1936, Athens, Greece

A multilingual ballad singer, instantly recognizable from her horn-rimmed spectacles, Mouskouri based herself in Paris during the sixties. A frequent star of concerts and television specials, she sold huge quantities of records throughout Europe.

Her early training was in classical music but in 1958 she first sang on Greek radio and met composer Manos Hadjidakis, who wrote the international hit 'Never on Sunday'. In 1961 she recorded another of his film songs, 'The White Rose of Athens', in German ('Weisse Rosen Aus Athen') for Philips. An adaptation of a Greek traditional tune, it sold a million copies throughout Europe. The lyrics of Mouskouri's later English-language version were by Norman Newell.

Mouskouri went on to record frequently in five languages, having hits in France with a version of 'Les Parapluies de Cherbourg' in conjunction with **Michel Legrand**, as well as 'Guantanamera' (1967) and 'C'est Bon la Vie'.

In Britain she had considerable success with such albums as *Over and Over* (Fontana, 1969) with its version of **Ewan MacColl**'s 'The First Time Ever I Saw Your Face', *The Exquisite Nana M* (1970), *British Concert* (1972), which included **Simon and Garfunkel**'s 'Bridge over Troubled Water', and the greatest hits collection *Passport* (1976), which reached the Top Ten. On all these records, Mouskouri skilfully mixed folk and folk-like songs, performing them with an accentuated sincerity that won her a large mainstream following. Her most successful single was the television theme 'Only Love' (Carrere, 1986). Later recordings include *Classical Nana* (1990) and *Oh Happy Day* (1991). In 1994 she was elected as a member of the European Parliament.

THE MOVE
Roy Oliver Ulysses Wood, b. 8 November 1946, Birmingham, England; Bev Bevan, b. 25 November, 1945, Birmingham; Trevor Burton, b. 9 March, 1944, Birmingham (replaced by Rick Price, b. 10 June 1944, Birmingham); Christopher John 'Ace' Kefford, b. 10 December 1944, Birmingham; Carl Wayne, b. 18 August 1944, Birmingham (replaced by Jeff Lynne, b. 30 December 1947, Birmingham)

Even more in thrall to **The Beatles** than their beat-group contemporaries the **Hollies**, the Move were one of the glories of British pop music of the sixties. If their records always bordered on the pastiche, their sideways (and backwards) looks were nonetheless genuinely innovative. Whereas the **Kinks** and **The Who** quickly discovered their own styles and themes, the Move, in record after record, recapitulated the stages of The Beatles' development. Finally, after the Fab Four created an *alter ego* in Sgt Pepper's Lonely Hearts Club Band, the Move evolved into the **Electric Light Orchestra**, a group formed with the idea of re-creating in live performance the post-*Sgt Pepper* recorded sounds of The Beatles.

Liverpool was not the only city to support a flourishing beat-group scene in the early sixties; nor was **John Lennon** the only would-be rock'n'roller to go to art school. Just as Manchester and Newcastle had highly organized beat scenes, so Birmingham gave birth to 'Brum Beat'. A key figure was Wood, a former student of Moseley School of Art who, while a member of Mike Sheridan and the Nightriders, learned the need to 'mak show' – in a white wig he did **Dusty Springfield** impersonations. Among the group's records for Pye were covers of **Charlie Rich**'s 1960 hit 'Lonely Weekends' and the **Marvellettes**' 1961 hit 'Please Mr Postman'.

In late 1965 the Move was formed from among members of the Nightriders, the Mayfair Set and Carl Wayne and the Vikings. They dressed as Chicago gangsters and won immediate attention for their stage act, which included the destruction of TV sets. Their first record was a pastiche of the main theme to Tchaikovsky's '1812 Overture', 'Night of Fear' (Deram, 1967). A hit, it was followed by a pair of jaunty, yet threatening, juvenile versions of psychedelia that demonstrated Wood's flair for melody and his tongue-in-cheek pop aesthetic. These were 'I Can Hear the

Grass Grow' (1967) and 'Flowers in the Rain' (Regal Zonophone, 1967) the first pop record played on the BBC's new pop network, Radio One. It was promoted by manager Tony Secunda with a photomontage of Prime Minister Harold Wilson naked in a bath tub, which resulted in a highly publicized libel suit against the group. Though hits in Britain, the records failed in America where the Move won only a cult following.

In 1968 both Kefford and Burton left, the former to pursue an abortive solo career and the latter to join the Uglies led by Steve Gibbons, an under-rated Birmingham rock singer and writer who later recorded for Wood's Wizard label (*Short Stories*, 1971) and RCA. Though the Move's eccentric albums (*The Move*, 1968, and *Shazam*, 1970, by which time the group consisted of Wood, Lynne, Bevan and Price) were only minor hits, they continued to have hit singles. These included 'Fire Brigade' (1968), a witty account of the explosive power of love; the delightful cameo 'Curly' (1969); and, best of all, the sombre, wistful 'Blackberry Way' (1968), Wood's response to The Beatles' 'Penny Lane' and 'Strawberry Fields' and the group's only No. 1. With its prominent cello and symphonic sound, it presaged the evolution of the Move into ELO, which followed the arrival of Lynne from Birmingham progressive group the Idle Race. Before this the Move had further hits, including 'Brontosaurus' (1970), Wood's pastiche of the then current British fifties revivalist trend; the exotic 'Chinatown' (Harvest, 1971); and – their only American hit – Lynne's frantic 'Do Ya'. The Move's last album, *Message from the Country* (1971), made following the departure of Price, saw Wood as eclectic as ever. It included affectionate parodies of **Elvis Presley** ('Don't Mess Me Up'), **Rudy Vallee** ('My Marge') and **Johnny Cash** ('Ben Crawley Steel Co').

Wood soon tired of ELO and after its eponymous début album (1971), he left to form Wizzard with a new set of Birmingham musicians, including Price, Bob Brady and Nick Pentelow. In the manner of **10CC** and **Dave Edmunds**, Wizzard had a series of hits with pastiches of earlier styles, notably **Phil Spector**'s 'wall of sound'. Among these were the flamboyant 'Ball Park Incident' (1972), 'See My Baby Jive' and 'Angel Fingers' (both 1973 chart-toppers), and 'I Wish It Could Be Christmas Everyday' (1973, and a hit when reissued in 1981 and 1984). Wood's subsequent records with Wizzo, the Helicopters, or solo (notably 'Dear Elaine', from his solo album, *Boulders*, on which he played every instrument, and 'Forever', 1973), though moderately successful, saw him operating increasingly in a time warp. He also produced albums by **Darts** and Annie Haslam in the late seventies.

During the eighties Wood's intermittent recordings included *Starting Up* (Legacy, 1987), on which he again played all the instruments. *Great Move* (1993) is the definitive retrospective of the group's EMI days while *Movements: The 30th Anniversary Anthology* (Sequel, 1998) collects together their later work.

ALISON MOYET
b. Genevieve Alison Moyet, 8 June 1961, Basildon, Essex, England

A powerful, jazzy singer Moyet enjoyed success in the eighties, both with Yazoo and as a solo artist.

She sang with local R&B bands on the Essex pub-rock circuit and was also influenced by punk singer Poly Styrene, leader of X-Ray Spex who reached the Top Twenty with 'Germ-Free Adolescence' (EMI, 1978). However, it was her blues style that was featured in Yazoo, a duo formed with ex-**Depeche Mode** keyboards-player Vince Clarke in 1981. 'Only You' (Mute, 1982) placed Moyet's rootsy singing against the backdrop of Clarke's electronics and was a Top Ten hit. A year later, the Flying Pickets' softer *a cappella* version topped the British charts on 10 Records. Yazoo's next records – 'Don't Go', 'The Other Side of Love' and *Upstairs at Eric's* – were equally successful.

Moyet herself wrote the group's final hit, 'Nobody's Diary', and shortly before the release of *You and Me Both* (1983), Yazoo split up. Clarke went on to further success with singers **Feargal Sharkey** ('Never Never', 1983, as the Assembly) and Andy Bell (*b. 1956, Middlesbrough, England*) with whom he formed **Erasure**. The duo's hits included 'Sometimes' (Mute, 1986), 'Victim of Love' (1987) and 'A Little Respect' (1988).

Contractual problems delayed the launch of Moyet's solo career with Columbia but in 1984 she released 'Love Resurrection'. Written by Lamont Dozier (of **Holland, Dozier and Holland**, and produced by Steve Jolly and Tony Swain (who had supervised 'Just an Illusion', R&B 1982, and other hits by British disco-soul group Imagination), it was the first of a series of Top Ten entries.

'All Cried Out' appeared on the million-selling *Alf* (1984) and was followed by a version of 'That Ole Devil Called Love', arranged by John Altman, who led the jazz big band with which Moyet performed in 1985. *Raindancing* (1986) returned to the AOR rock-ballad approach. Produced by Jimmy Iovine, it provided hits with 'Is This Love' and 'Weak in the Presence of Beauty'.

In 1987 Moyet had further success with a revival of 'Love Letters', using the arrangement that had given Ketty Lester a million-seller in 1962. The 1991 album *Hoodoo*, containing songs composed by Moyet with Pete Glenister, was patchy and Moyet later expressed dissatisfaction with it. In 1994 she returned with the hit single 'Whispering Your Name', written by American singer-songwriter Jules Shear, whom she had supported on a 1992 United States tour, and the album

Essex. In the nineties she made various guest appearances on other people's albums, including the **Lightning Seeds**' *Jollification* (1994) and Tricky's *Nearly God* (1996), but her major success was the compilation album *Singles* (1995), which topped the UK charts on its release.

MARIA MULDAUR
b. Maria Grazia Rosa Domenica D'Amato, 12 September 1942, New York, USA

A gifted interpreter of folk, blues and jazz songs, Muldaur came to prominence in the mid-seventies with a series of solo albums for Reprise and Warners.

At high school she formed the Cashmeres vocal group but attending a concert by **Doc Watson** converted her to folk music. As a fiddler and singer she was part of the Greenwich Village folk scene in the early sixties. She first recorded with John Sebastian (later of the **Lovin' Spoonful**), **Joshua Rifkin**, **Stefan Grossman** and Steve Katz (a founder member of **Blood, Sweat and Tears**) as the Even Dozen Jug Band (Elektra, 1964).

When that group split up, she joined the Jim Kweskin Jug Band which had a repertoire of blues, ragtime and folk material, occasionally adding **Leiber and Stoller** songs. There she met folk guitarist Geoff Muldaur (whose *Sleepy Man Blues*, Prestige, 1963, featured **Dave Van Ronk** in support), whom she later married. Between 1964 and 1969 the group recorded several albums, including *See Reverse Side for Title* (Vanguard, 1966) and *Garden of Joy* (Reprise, 1967). When harmonica-player Mel Lyman formed a religious sect and took Kweskin with him, the band dissolved. Violin-player Richard Greene went on to a distinguished career with Seatrain (1969–73), the Blue Velvet Band, and his own Greene String Quartet (*Molly on the Shore*, Hannibal, 1988).

The Muldaurs made *Pottery Pie* (Reprise, 1969) and *Sweet Potatoes* (Warners, 1972) as a duo before separating. Geoff went on to play with **Paul Butterfield** and made solo albums for Warners and Flying Fish, including *Geoff and Amos* (1978) and *Blues Boy* (1979). Maria made an eponymous album produced by **Joe Boyd** and Lenny Waronker (Reprise, 1974), which for the first time displayed the versatility of her singing. Her high-pitched timbre, reminiscent of jazz singer **Mildred Bailey**, was used to good effect on **Kate McGarrigle**'s 'Work Song', a tragi-comic look at plantation life; the sassy 'Don't You Feel My Leg', by New Orleans jazz guitarist Danny Barker; and **Dolly Parton**'s 'My Tennessee Mountain Home'.

The album also included a Top Ten hit in David Nichtern's sophisticated, slinky 'Midnight at the Oasis', with its relaxed guitar solo by Amos Garrett. Muldaur had further success in 1975 with a revival of

Leiber and Stoller's 'I'm a Woman' (originally a hit for **Peggy Lee** in 1963) from *Waitress in a Donut Shop*. Later albums for Reprise and Warners included *Sweet Harmony* (1976) and *Open Your Eyes* (1979), which, unusually for Muldaur, included a contemporary soul song, **Betty Wright**'s 'Clean Up Woman'.

In the eighties Muldaur turned to gospel music, releasing *Gospel Nights* (Takoma, 1980), *There Is a Love* (Myrrh, 1982) and *Sweet and Low* (Spindrift, 1984). She later recorded the secular *Transblucency* (Uptown, 1986) and *Live in London* (Making Waves, 1987). She moved to another independent label, Music for Little People, for the jazzy *On the Sunny Side* (1991), followed by the equally enjoyable *Louisiana Love Call* (1993), which included a duet with Aaron Neville, and *Jazzabelle* (1994).

Her daughter Jenni Muldaur (*b. 1967*) sang backing vocals with **Todd Rundgren** before making her eponymous début album in 1993 with producer Russ Titelman.

MOON MULLICAN
b. Aubrey Mullican, 27 (or 29) March 1909, Corrigan, Texas, USA, d. 1 January 1967, Beaumont, Texas

Under the sobriquet 'King of the Hillbilly Piano Players' Moon Mullican deployed a simple but swinging keyboard technique – his 'two-finger style' – on a large number of records by Western swing bands in the late thirties and forties. He also sang, in an amiable bluesy manner somewhat like **Jack Teagarden**'s, on many of these and, later, his own recordings, which are valued as early examples of country rockabilly.

At the end of the thirties Mullican was playing and recording with such South Texas groups as the Blue Ridge Playboys (who also included **Floyd Tillman**), the Modern Mountaineers and Cliff Bruner's Texas Wanderers. It was with Bruner that he first recorded what would become a staple of his repertoire, 'Pipe Liner's Blues' (Decca, 1940), which had special appeal for the oilmen in the Gulf cities of Beaumont and Galveston. He also worked with the popular Shelton Brothers (Joe and Bob), and with **Jimmie Davis**, whom he accompanied on the political-musical campaign trail in 1944.

Later in the forties Mullican worked on KPAC, Port Arthur, Texas, and had a 1947 No. 1 and million-seller with the country novelty 'New Jole Blon' – an English translation (and augmentation) of the regional hit in cajun French by the singer and fiddle-player Harry Choates ('Jole Blon', Gold Star, 1946). This was followed by 'Sweeter than the Flowers' (1948), 'Goodnight Irene' (1950), 'I'll Sail My Ship Alone'* (1950 – another No. 1, and Mullican's best-known composition, which was later revived by **Jerry Lee Lewis**), 'Mona Lisa' (1950) and 'Cherokee Boogie'

(1951). For the next ten years or so he remained active on tours and on Texas radio and TV.

GERRY MULLIGAN

b. *Gerald Mulligan, 6 April 1927, Long Island, New York, USA, d. 20 January 1996*

One of the most prominent jazz musicians of the fifties, Mulligan was also the foremost exponent of the baritone saxophone.

He grew up in Philadelphia and found his first professional work as an arranger and tenor saxophonist with Elliot Lawrence's band. Moving to New York in 1946, Mulligan wrote 'Disc Jockey Jump' and arranged the bebop anthem 'How High the Moon' for recordings by **Gene Krupa**'s swing band. In 1947 he went on to play with **Claude Thornhill**'s band and met **Gil Evans**, through whom he wrote for and played on the **Miles Davis** *Birth of the Cool* (Capitol, 1950) album. The following year Mulligan made his first recordings as a leader for Prestige.

His decision to move to Los Angeles in 1952 gave rise to the appellation 'West Coast jazz' for the precise music made by Mulligan's new quartet, which included trumpeter Chet Baker but no pianist. Their records for Prestige were characterized by the interweaving empathy between the two horn players. Mulligan next recorded with Lee Konitz and wrote arrangements for **Stan Kenton** before forming his most illustrious quartet with trombonist Bob Brookmeyer, Red Mitchell (bass) and drummer Frank Isola. One of the most popular mainstream jazz leaders of the era, Mulligan appeared in the films *I Want to Live* (1958) and *The Subterraneans* (1960) while his group was featured in the Newport Festival movie *Jazz on a Summer's Day* (1960).

Never involved in the new waves of jazz during the sixties and seventies, Mulligan continued to lead bands which performed his relaxed mix of bop and swing. A gregarious musician, he recorded frequently, his collaborators ranging from bop innovator **Thelonious Monk** through lyrical horn-player **Stan Getz** to eighties fusion musicians like Mike Brecker of the **Brecker Brothers** and keyboards-player Dave Grusin (*Little Big Horn*, 1988). One of his last albums was *Re-Birth of the Cool* (GRP, 1992), in which a mix of those on the original record and others offered new versions of the original tracks. Davis, who had planned to appear, died just before the making of the album. His place was taken by Wallace Roney.

ANNE MURRAY

b. *20 June 1944, Springhill, Nova Scotia, Canada*

Possessor of one of the purest and most versatile voices in the popular music of the seventies and eighties, Murray's career strategy won her large audiences on the borderline between adult-orientated-rock and countrypolitan music.

She made her first appearance alongside **Guess Who** on Canadian TV's *Let's Go* while training to be a physical education teacher in the mid-sixties. Murray became a regular on another television programme, *Singalong Jamboree*, and the show's musical director, Brian Ahern, produced her first album, *This Way My Way*, for local label ARC.

Moving to Capitol, she recorded 'Snowbird', a country-styled song that reached the American Top Ten in 1970. A wholesome image was fostered by subsequent (and less successful) albums, *Honey Wheat and Laughter* and *Straight, Clean and Simple* and a sequence of duets with **Glen Campbell** (1971). However, the 1973 albums *Danny's Song* and *Love Song* offered a more varied repertoire and presented Murray as a dynamic performer, notably on a live version of Barbara George's 1961 hit 'I Know', included on the former. She enjoyed big hits with two **Kenny Loggins** songs, the lullaby for a new-born nephew 'Danny's Song' and 'Love Song', and in 1974 reached the Top Ten with a revival of **The Beatles**' 'You Won't See Me'.

Murray had a break from recording while she started a family, but returned in 1978 with a new producer, Jim Ed Norman, and an American No. 1, the intense slow ballad, 'You Needed Me'*. This was followed by three more pop Top Twenty singles, 'I Just Fall in Love Again', the country No. 1 'Broken Hearted Me' (1979) and a revival of **John Stewart**'s 1967 hit for the **Monkees**, 'Daydream Believer'.

Throughout the eighties Murray released albums on an annual basis but her records sold best to country-music audiences. 'A Little Good News' (1983) won a Grammy award, while later country hits included the duet with Dave Loggins 'Nobody Loves Me Like You Do' (1984), from the bestselling album *Heart over Mind*, a title which aptly summed up the sentimental character of the bulk of her later material. *Something to Talk About* (1986) involved a change of producer from Norman to the triumvirate of **David Foster**, Jack White and Keith Diamond, and a shift of focus towards the pop radio audience. She later released *Songs of the Heart* (1987) and *Harmony* (1989) and *Yes I Do* (1991), but much of her time was taken up by her involvement in Canada's Save the Children Fund charity. She left Capitol for SBK Records and recorded *Croonin'* in 1993, a tribute album to female singers of the fifties, whose softer sounds she clearly was in sympathy with. Her bestselling album of the period was *An Intimate Evening with Anne Murray . . . Live* (1998).

BILLY MURRAY

b. 25 May 1877, Philadelphia, Pennsylvania, USA,
d. 17 August 1954

The most popular recording artist of the first two
decades of the twentieth century in America, Murray
introduced a more casual, natural style of singing,
though he never completely broke with the European
ballad style personified by **Henry Burr**. This is particularly evident in his recordings of the songs of **George
M. Cohan**, virtually all of which he recorded in his
lengthy career, and in his 'conversational' duets with
Ada Jones.

Raised in Denver (hence the early nickname, 'The
Denver Nightingale'), Murray sang in vaudeville
before making his first recording in 1903, 'Tessie (You
Are the Only, Only)' (Columbia). His clear tenor won
him immediate popularity with songs like 'Meet Me
in St Louis, Louis' (Edison, 1904) and the topical
songs 'Come Take a Trip in My Air-Ship', which was
inspired by the Wright Brothers' historic flight at
Kitty Hawk, and 'In My Merry Oldsmobile' (Victor,
1905), which commemorated an Oldsmobile winning
the first transcontinental auto race. But it was his
interpretation of, and close identification with, the
songs of Cohan that established Murray. This began
with his recordings of 'Yankie Doodle Dandy', 'Give
My Regards to Broadway' (1905) and 'You're a Grand
Old Flag' (1906), which, though Murray also recorded
it for Columbia, International, Zone-O-Phone and
Edison, among others, was Victor's biggest-selling
record of the decade. In 1908 Murray made the most
popular version of the oft-recorded 'Take Me Out to
the Ball Game', written by **Nora Bayes**' husband Jack
Norworth and Albert, brother of **Harry Von Tilzer**.

In 1907 Murray joined the Hayden (originally
Haydn) Quartet, which with the American and Peerless Quartets was the most important American
vocal-harmony group of the period. The group originally comprised John Bieling, Harry Macdonough,
S. H. Dudley and William F. Hooley and first
recorded in 1898. That recording was of 'She Was
Bred in Old Kentucky' on **Emile Berliner**'s Berliner
label and the group subsequently recorded the most
popular versions of the barber-shop quartet classics
'In the Good Old Summer Time' (Victor, 1903) and
'Sweet Adeline' (1904). Among the songs they
recorded with Murray were 'Put on Your Old Gray
Bonnet' (1909) and 'By the Light of the Silvery Moon'
(1910). Before the group officially disbanded in 1914,
Murray formed the American Quartet (which was
known as the Edison Premier Quartet when it
recorded on Edison) with Bieling, Hooley and Steve
Porter. That group's first great success was 'Casey
Jones' (Victor, 1910). Based on a 1900 train crash, it
predated **Vernon Dalhart**'s similarly inspired 'Wreck

of the Old '97'* (Victor) by some fourteen years.
Other hits included 'Play that Barber-Shop Chord'
(1910), 'Oh You Beautiful Girl' (1911) and 'Moonlight
Bay' (1912, which was one of the many songs they also
recorded for Edison). 'It's a Long, Long Way to Tipperary' (1914) and 'Goodbye Broadway, Hello France'
(1917) were two of the patriotic songs they recorded.
With the addition of counter-tenor Will Oakland the
group recorded as the Heidelberg Quintet ('Waitin'
for the Robert E. Lee', 1912, 'By the Beautiful Sea',
1914).

Murray's solo recordings and those with Jones,
however, were his most influential. His own were
more dramatic and emotional than most of his contemporaries'. Similarly, his duets with Jones, which
range from the comic to the melodramatic, were far
more light-hearted and relaxed. Their hits, mostly
show tunes, included 'Let's Take an Old Fashioned
Walk' (Columbia, Zon-O-Phone, 1907), 'Cuddle up a
Little Closer, Lovely Mine' (Victor, 1908), the
sprightly 'Be My Little Baby Bumble Bee' (1912) and
one of the earliest versions of 'What Do You Want to
Make Those Eyes at Me for?' (1917). Murray also
recorded several songs with Elsie Baker, on which
Baker was usually credited as Edna Brown.

Murray's own hits included such comic songs as
'I'm Looking for the Man that Wrote the Merry
Widow Waltz' (1908), one of the many songs inspired
by **Franz Lehár**'s operetta; 'Cousin Caruso' (1909);
and an early version of 'He'll Have to Get Under –
Get Out and Get Under (to Fix up His Automobile)'
(1914), as well as numerous show songs by Cohan and
others. Among these were 'Harrigan' (1907), 'Baghdad' (1913), 'Baby' and 'I Love a Piano' (1916). In the
late 1910s and early twenties Murray turned increasingly to novelty records. Among these were 'The
Vamp' (1919), which he recorded in duet with Harry
Macdonough; 'Yes We Have No Bananas' (1923),
which he whistled and sang as part of the Great White
Way Orchestra; and 'Charley My Boy' (1924), on
which he was backed by Jack, brother of **Nat Shilkret**.
One of his last hits was his only duet with Burr, his
nearest rival in popularity ('I Wonder Where My
Baby Is Tonight?', 1926).

MITCH MURRAY

b. 30 January 1940, Hove, Sussex, England

A master of the simple pop song, Murray was one of
the most successful British songwriters of the sixties.

Murray's first success was 'How Do You Do It?'
(1963), which was recorded but not released by **The
Beatles**. Subsequently **George Martin** persuaded
Gerry and the Pacemakers to record it. The song was
a British chart-topper and American Top Ten for the
group and the follow-up, 'I Like It', also topped the

British charts. Murray then collaborated with Freddie Garrity, the lead singer of the Manchester group **Freddie and the Dreamers**, to produce the happy-go-lucky 'I'm Telling You Now' – an American No. 1 on Tower in 1965 and British No. 2 on EMI's Columbia label in 1963. Murray himself wrote 'You Were Made for Me', a British Top Ten record in 1963 and American Top Thirty record in 1965.

In 1967 Murray wrote his first major hit with Peter Callander, 'Even the Bad Times Are Good', a British hit for the Tremeloes (formerly **Brian Poole and the Tremeloes**). Callander (*b. 10 October 1939, Hampshire*) had previously written 'Walking Tall' for **Adam Faith** in 1963, and co-written with **Les Reed** a pair of British hits for Paul and Barry Ryan ('Don't Bring Me Your Heartaches', Decca, 1965, and 'I Love Her', 1966). His speciality was writing English lyrics to continental hits. These included 'A Fool Am I' and 'Don't Answer Me', for **Cilla Black** in 1966; 'Give Me the Time' for **Dusty Springfield** in 1967; 'Suddenly You Love Me' for the Tremeloes in 1968; and 'Monsieur Dupont' for **Sandie Shaw** in 1969. Among the songs written by Callander and Murray were 'The Ballad of Bonnie and Clyde', a million-seller for **Georgie Fame**, 'Goodbye Sam, Hello Samantha' (co-written with Geoff Stephens) for **Cliff Richard** in 1970, 'I Did What I Did for Maria' (MCA, 1971) for Tony Christie, and a series of hits for Paper Lace, which they also produced and released on their own Bus Stop label. These included the British No. 1 'Billy Don't Be a Hero' (1974) and the Top Twenty sequels 'The Night Chicago Died' (also a US No. 1) and 'The Black Eyed Boys' (1974). 'Billy' was subsequently an American No. 1 for Bo Donaldson and the Heywoods. Callander also wrote, with Geoff Stephens, 'Daddy Don't You Walk So Fast', which was a British hit for Daniel Boone on Penny Farthing and an American Top Ten for Wayne Newton on Chelsea in 1971.

By the eighties Murray's Tin Pan Alley notion of pop was decidedly old-fashioned. He briefly turned his attention to television jingles, then produced and presented British Telecom's 'Dial-a-Disc' service, before establishing himself as a leading humorous speech writer. He has written many books of ad-libs and speeches, including *The Mitch Murray Book of One-Liners for Weddings*.

MY BLOODY VALENTINE
Dave Conway (replaced by Bilinda Butcher); Debbie Googe; Colm O'Ciosoig; Kevin Shields, b. Queens, New York, USA

Dublin-based sonic pioneers My Bloody Valentine won widespread acclaim for their innovative studio techniques, which have proven inspirational to a number of artists and producers in the late eighties and nineties, most notably **Garbage** and **Ride**.

My Bloody Valentine were formed in Dublin in 1984 by Shields (guitar/vocals), Conway (vocals), O'Ciosoig (drums), adding bassist Googe after the release of *This Is Your Bloody Valentine* (1985), which drew comparisons with the **Jesus and Mary Chain** and **Sonic Youth**. Further EPs, including *The New Record by MBV* (1986) and *Ecstasy* (1987), saw the band begin to develop a ferocious wall of sound, while Conway was replaced by guitarist/singer Butcher, who added a harmonic edge as well as boosting the quartet's live sound.

The band's full-length début, *Isn't Anything* (1988), was immediately proclaimed as one of the most influential underground albums of the decade. Their first release since signing a recording contract with Creation, the album was built around layers of guitar and keyboard dissonance offset by dream-like vocals. The band were soon referred to as the leaders of the 'shoegazing' scene – also numbering Ride, the **Boo Radleys**, Slowdive and Lush – so named because they barely moved or looked at their audience whilst on stage.

After releasing two more experimental EPs, *Glider* (1989) and *Tremolo* (1990), My Bloody Valentine recorded their second album, *Loveless* (1991), which, like its predecessor, was instantly lavished with the highest praise. The album was a clear development from *Isn't Anything*, held together by powerful effects loops and shimmering guitar tones, and was hugely influential on nineties record production, particularly Garbage's eponymous début. In spite of its critical admiration, the album failed to meet commercial expectations, and having cost a reported £300,000 to record it almost sent the band's label into liquidation.

My Bloody Valentine returned to the studio in 1992 to begin work on a new albumbut, despite persistent rumours about imminent new material, the band, now simply Shields and Butcher, produced no follow-up to *Loveless*. Although the band never officially split, Shields subsequently became a semi-permanent member of **Primal Scream** in 2000, playing on and producing several tracks on their acclaimed *XTRMNTR*.

JOHNNY NASH
b. 19 August 1940, Houston, Texas, USA

A soul and pop singer with a high, clear voice akin to that of **Johnny Mathis**, Nash had two distinct periods of popularity. In the fifties he was a successful teen-ballad star, while in the seventies he had hits with reggae-tinged material and was the first American artist to record **Bob Marley**'s songs.

As a child, he sang in Houston churches and appeared on local television and from 1956 on the networked **Arthur Godfrey** radio show. Nash's first recording was 'A Teenager Sings the Blues' (ABC Paramount, 1957) and the following year he reached the Top Thirty with 'A Very Special Love' and joined **Paul Anka** and **George Hamilton IV** on the sickly Christmas hit 'The Teen Commandments', an 'inspirational' talk from the trio.

Nash went on to record poor-selling ballad albums for Warners, Groove and Argo, but he also branched out as an actor and label-owner, starring in *Take a Giant Step* (1958) and *Key Witness* (1960). With promoter Danny Sims he set up the JODA and JAD labels and he also composed 'What Kind of Love Is This' for Joey Dee and the Starliters (Roulette, 1962), the group which, with **Chubby Checker**, spearheaded the twist dance craze with such records as 'Peppermint Twist'.

In 1967 Sims and Nash moved to Jamaica, recording *Hold Me Tight* (JAD). The record's soft, reggae-influenced sound brought a hit single in 1968 with the title song (a Nash composition), while 'You Got Soul' and a version of **Sam Cooke**'s 'Cupid' (1969) were British hits on Major Minor. The lilting title song of *I Can See Clearly Now* (Epic, 1971) was an American No. 1 and a million-seller, while the album also included 'Stir It Up' and 'Guava Jelly' by Marley, whom Sims and Nash had signed to a publishing contract.

My Merry Go Round and *Celebrate Life* (1974) found Nash uneasily mingling reggae with soul but 'Tears on My Pillow' (1975) was a British No. 1. The following year Nash had a further British hit with a faithful revival of Cooke's '(What a) Wonderful World', but he was unable to sustain the success and faded from view in the eighties. Then in 1989 a remixed version of 'I Can See Clearly Now' made the British charts and in 1991 'Stir It Up' was a reissued hit after it was used in a television coffee commercial.

SYD NATHAN
b. 27 April 1904, Cincinnati, Ohio, USA, d. 1968, Florida

As the founder and active manager of King Records – one of the leading American independent labels of the forties and fifties – Syd Nathan played a part in crucial developments in R&B and hillbilly music and, as such, helped build many of the foundations of rock'n'roll. In contrast, however, to Sun Records' **Sam Phillips**, who consciously yoked together black and white traditions in his guidance of the recordings of **Elvis Presley**, Nathan was a tough and economical businessman rather than a creative producer. As such, he had uneasy relationships with many of his artists, often initially rejecting their choices of material. Thus he considered **James Brown**'s 'Please, Please, Please' (1956) as unreleasable and only allowed Brown to record the epochal *Live at the Apollo* (1962) when Brown agreed to pay the recording costs.

After trying various ventures, including running a jewellery store, a shooting gallery and a pawnshop, Nathan opened Syd's Record Shop in Cincinnati in 1938. There, he came into contact with some of the hillbilly artists working on the local radio stations, including **Merle Travis** and Grandpa Jones who collaborated on the first records issued with a King label in 1943. The company was formally created in 1944, with Nathan's brother Sam as treasurer, and incorporated, as well as the record label, a pressing plant, a sleeve-printing factory and a publishing company, Lois Music, named after Nathan's wife Lois Mann – an identity he often borrowed as a songwriting pseudonym. (Another was Sally Nix.) At first King was a strictly hillbilly label – its early signings included the **Carlisle Brothers**, the **Delmore Brothers**, **Cowboy Copas** and **Hank Penny** – while 'race' material was issued on Queen, but this division was abandoned in 1947 and everything was released on King. The material was distinguished by label colour: blue for 'race', maroon for hillbilly.

Though Nathan himself supervised hundreds of recordings, from 1947 **Henry Glover** produced much of the black music on King, working with **Earl Bostic**, **Tiny Bradshaw**, **Roy Brown**, **Bill Doggett**, **Champion Jack Dupree**, **Wynonie Harris**, Bullmoose Jackson, **Lucky Millinder**, Todd Rhodes and **Eddie 'Cleanhead' Vinson**. It was Glover who guided King in the direction of big-band R&B – the label was noticeably less successful with solo singers – in the forties and then smaller group R&B in the fifties, the defining feature of both being the honking sax that epitomized one of King's biggest sellers, Doggett's 'Honky-Tonk' (1956). In 1951 **Ralph Bass** joined the company to run the Federal label (James Brown, **Johnny 'Guitar' Watson**); other labels in the family included Deluxe, originally owned by Jules and David Braun in Linden, New Jersey; Glory (gospel); Bethlehem (jazz); and Audiolab, a budget-album line of repackaged King material in a variety of idioms.

King continued to grow through the fifties and early sixties, adding **Hawkshaw Hawkins**, **Moon Mullican**, Wayne Raney, Reno and Smiley and the **Stanley Brothers** to its hillbilly roster and **Albert King** and **Freddie King** to its bluesmen. There were also ventures into pop (**Steve Lawrence**) and rockabilly (**Charlie Feathers**, Mac Curtis). Nathan vigorously pursued the album market, and the company art department created a colourful – if 'tacky' in its use of visual clichés and racial stereotypes – house style, particularly for the many 'concept' albums of trucking and hot-rod songs. In 1967, aware of his imminent death, Nathan – a record man to the end – recorded a farewell to his employees in which he also offered them business advice.

In 1970 King was sold to Starday Records of Nashville. After a time, Starday-King was bought by **Leiber and Stoller**, then in 1975 by Gusto Records, also of Nashville. Gusto launched, or occasionally licensed to other companies, various reissue programmes of blues R&B and the more commercially viable hillbilly and bluegrass names.

NAZARETH
Peter Agnew; Manny Charlton; Zal Cleminson; Dan McCafferty; Darrel Sweet

Firmly in the **Led Zeppelin** mould, Nazareth specialized in creating heavy-rock interpretations of such unlikely songs as **Boudleaux Bryant**'s 'Love Hurts', **Joni Mitchell**'s 'This Flight Tonight' and the **Rolling Stones**' 'Ruby Tuesday'.

Singer McCafferty, drummer Sweet and bassist Agnew founded the Shadettes in Dumfermline, Scotland, in 1961. With the addition of lead guitarist Charlton in 1969, the group became Nazareth (inspired by the first line of **The Band**'s 'The Weight'). They signed to B&C Records and *Nazareth* was released in 1971 on the Pegasus label. After *Exercises* (1972), McCafferty's hoarse, urgent singing gave Nazareth three British hits on Mooncrest in 1973. 'Broken Down Angel' was followed by 'Bad Bad Boy' and 'This Flight Tonight' from the bestselling *Loud and Proud*, which, like its predecessor, was produced by former **Deep Purple** bassist Roger Glover. In 1974 McCafferty had a solo hit with Mick Jagger and Keith Richards' 'Out of Time', previously a No. 1 in 1966 for British R&B singer Chris Farlowe.

Although the group toured America as well as Europe, their only US hit came with 'Love Hurts'

(A&M, 1975), the same year that a revival of Tomorrow's 'My White Bicycle' reached the British Top Twenty. With the collapse of Mooncrest, later Nazareth records were issued on Mountain, a label formed by the band's management. Later success was, however, sporadic, with only 'May the Sun Shine' and *No Mean City* (1979) reaching the British Top Twenty. For the latter, Cleminson, former guitarist with the Sensational Alex Harvey Band, joined Nazareth. Harvey (*1935–81*) was a seminal figure on the Scottish rock and R&B scene from the late fifties on. With Cleminson and the highly theatrical SAHB, Harvey enjoyed substantial British success in the mid-seventies with albums such as *Next . . .* (1973), on which he provided the definitive version of the **Jacques Brel** title song, and *Tomorrow Belongs to Me* (1975).

Nazareth continued into the eighties, moving to NEMS for *Fool Circle* (1981), produced by the **Doobie Brothers**' Jeff Baxter, and the live *Snaz* (1981), on which the original quartet were augmented by ex-**Spirit** member John Locke (keyboards) and Glaswegian guitarist Billy Rankin. Locke left after *2XS*, with Rankin taking over his keyboard role, and the band released *Sound Elixir* (1983), *The Catch* (Vertigo, 1984) and *Play the Game*, but by the mid-eighties they seemed to have become part of rock history, with Sahara reissuing six of their early albums. They concentrated on touring in the Americas and Europe in the late eighties but, following their championing by **Guns N' Roses** vocalist Axl Rose, returned to the studio in 1992 to record *No Jive*. Guns N' Roses covered the title track from 1975's *Hair of the Dog* on their 1993 album *The Spaghetti Incident?*

YOUSSOU N'DOUR
b. 1 October 1959, Dakar, Senegal

Of the many African musicians to receive exposure in Europe and North America as a result of the 'world music' trend, Youssou N'Dour achieved the greatest artistic and commercial success. Through collaborations with **Peter Gabriel** and others he has married his mastery of traditional forms with contemporary recording and performing technologies.

The eldest of nine children, his mother was a *griot*, part of a caste of professional singers. Youssou began singing at twelve with a local drama group. He joined the Super Diamono band at fifteen and in 1976 became leader of the Star Band in Dakar. Here he evolved a style mixing traditional folk and religious music with Latin rhythms.

In 1981 Youssou N'Dour formed his own group, Super Etoile de Dakar, with arranger and bassist/keyboards-player Habib Faye to play his version of 'mbalax', a modern electronic version of Senegalese traditional music.

He made Paris his recording base and made his first tour of Europe with a thirteen-piece Super Etoile de Dakar in 1984, releasing the highly acclaimed *Immigrés* and *Nelson Mandela*. This led to an invitation from Peter Gabriel to join his world tour and to appear on Gabriel's album *So*. Subsequently N'Dour joined the Amnesty International Human Rights Now tour with Gabriel, **Sting**, **Bruce Springsteen** and others, and sang on **Paul Simon**'s *Graceland*.

In 1988 he signed a recording contract with Virgin, recording *The Lion* (1989) on which he rearranged material first recorded on some of the eighteen cassettes he had recorded for the Senegal market. *The Lion* also included 'Shakin' the Tree', co-written and performed with Gabriel partly in English and partly in the Senegalese Wolof language. For *Set* (1989) he returned to live studio recording with his Super Etoile band. The album included 'Toxiques', a protest song about the export of chemical waste to third world countries.

In 1992 he made a new recording agreement with 40 Acres and a Mule, the label owned by US film-maker Spike Lee. Recorded in N'Dour's own studio in Dakar, *Yes Open* found him singing in French and English as well as Wolof and mingling synthesizers, funk riffs and rock guitar with the 'tama', the talking drum. He followed with *Wommat* (1994), which included 'Seven Seconds Away', a duet with **Neneh Cherry**, which became a big European hit. N'Dour also appeared at Woodstock '94.

The Guide (1994) saw N'Dour moving into the mainstream, while the superior *Joko* (Columbia, 2000), its much delayed sequel, was even more mainstream. Featuring duets with Sting ('Don't Walk Away') and Gabriel and members of the **Fugees**, it even included a reworking of the **Temptations**' recording 'Don't Look Back'. Even 'Birima', a reworking of his famous song in praise of an ancient African king, mixed traditional instruments with programmed sounds.

FRED NEIL
b. 1937, St Petersburg, Florida, USA

Neil was an important folk songwriter with an influential introspective, confidential vocal style, comparable to **J. J. Cale** in approach. However, his songs were best known in recordings by others, and include **Nilsson**'s 'Everybody's Talkin'', which was featured on the soundtrack of *Midnight Cowboy* (1969); **Roy Orbison**'s dramatic version of 'Candy Man' (1961); the classic 'Other Side of This Life', recorded by the **Lovin' Spoonful**; and 'The Dolphins', the most memorable version of which was by **Tim Buckley**. Others who recorded his songs include **Frank Sinatra**, **Jose Feliciano** and **Jefferson Airplane**, whose 'The Ballad

of You and Me and Pooneil' was dedicated to Neil.

In his teens, Neil took up guitar and songwriting and moved to New York, where he found immediate success when **Buddy Holly** recorded 'Come Back Baby' in 1958. In New York, Neil immersed himself in the Greenwich Village folk scene, winning acclaim for his twelve-string guitar-playing and mature, bluesy interpretations of his own and traditional material. However, after appearing on a pair of Folkways collections and recording the classic *Bleecker and Mac-Dougal* (Elektra, 1965, reissued as *Little Bit of Rain*, 1970), on which he was supported by John Sebastian and which included the original versions of 'Other Side of This Life' and 'Blues on the Ceiling', Neil returned to Florida. There he lived the life of a recluse in Coconut Grove, only returning for the superior *Fred Neil* (Capitol, 1966) which included 'Everybody's Talkin'', his own fine version of 'The Dolphins', 'That's the Bag I'm in' and 'Sweet Cocaine'. Subsequent recordings included *Everybody's Talking* (1969), *The Other Side of This Life* (1970), which featured **Gram Parsons** on piano, and *Sessions* (1971). He has not recorded since.

BILL NELSON
b. 18 December 1948, Wakefield, Yorkshire, England

One of Britain's most accomplished rock guitarists, Nelson won acclaim during the seventies and eighties for his work with Be Bop De Luxe and as a soloist.

He founded Be Bop in Wakefield, Yorkshire, in 1972 as a vehicle for his flamboyant, **Jimi Hendrix**-inspired guitar-playing and his melodic songs. Following a recommendation from deejay John Peel, the group were signed to EMI's progressive rock label, Harvest, in 1974. After *Axe Victim*, Andrew Clark (keyboards), Simon Fox (the former drummer with Hackensack) and New Zealander Charlie Tumahai (bass) replaced Nelson's former sidemen and played on *Futurama* and *Sunburst Finish* (1976). The former included Be Bop De Luxe's best-known number 'Maid in Heaven', while the latter reached the Top Twenty and included the hit single 'Ships in the Night'.

The group found a niche in the contemporary glitter/futurist rock trend and *Modern Music* (1976) and the double-album *Live! In the Air Age* (1977) were their most successful records. In 1979, however, Be Bop De Luxe was disbanded and Nelson and Clark formed the electronically inclined Red Noise with Ian Nelson (sax), Rick Ford (bass) and Steve Peer (drums). After *Sound on Sound* (1979), Harvest refused to release *Quit Dreaming and Get on the Beam*. The album eventually appeared on Phonogram in 1981 and was a Top Ten hit.

Nelson subsequently set up his own label, Cocteau,

to issue a series of experimental and idiosyncratic records. Among them were *Das Kabinett* (1981), inspired by the classic silent film, *The Cabinet of Mr Caligari*; *Sounds the Ritual Echo* (1985); *Cocteau Signature Tunes* (1986); and *Map of Dreams* (1987), a television soundtrack album in an atmospheric New Age style. He also maintained a parallel recording career with major companies, releasing material on Phonogram in 1982–3 and signing to Columbia's Portrait label in 1986. Among Nelson's recordings for the latter were *Getting the Holy Ghost Across* and *Living for the Spangled Moment* (1986). His own Cocteau label reissued many of Nelson's recordings in 1989.

Later original recordings were sporadic and unsuccessful, and Nelson concentrated on film and TV soundtrack work in the late eighties and early nineties. In 1994 he formed Channel Light Vessel with keyboards-player Roger Eno (brother of **Brian Eno**) and vocalist Kate St John. Subsequent solo albums included *After the Satellite Sings* (1996) and *Atom Shop* (1998).

RICK NELSON

b. Eric Hilliard Nelson, 8 May 1940, Teaneck, New Jersey, USA, d. 31 December 1985, De Kalb, Texas

Although his success as a teen-idol was built as much on his looks as on his musical ability, Nelson's early singles, such as 'It's Late' and 'Hello Mary Lou', were well-crafted recordings featuring leading session guitarist **James Burton**. He went on to make a series of well-received country-rock albums in the seventies.

His father was the singing bandleader Ozzie Nelson and his mother the band's featured singer. They recorded prolifically in a sweet style during the thirties for Brunswick ('I Still Get a Thrill', 1930; 'It Was So Beautiful', 1932; 'And Then Some', 1935) and Bluebird ('Roses in September', 1937; 'Little Skipper', 1939; 'Alice Blue Gown', 1940). They had greater impact with a family radio series *The Adventures of Ozzie and Harriet*, which started in 1944. The parts of their children were played by actors until 1949 when Ricky and his brother David joined the cast. The series moved to television in 1952 and in 1957 Ricky Nelson became the first television soap star to graduate to a recording career.

With the aid of this built-in publicity, his début single, which coupled a bouncy version of **Fats Domino**'s 'I'm Walkin'' with 'A Teenager's Prayer' and included Barney Kessel on guitar, became a double-sided hit on Verve. Over the next seven years Nelson had more than thirty American hit singles. After another Verve hit, 'You're My One and Only Love', he moved to Imperial where **Joe Maphis** played the spirited rockabilly guitar solo on 'Be Bop Baby' (1957). In late 1957 Burton replaced Maphis and added important touches

to 'Stood Up' (1957), 'Believe What You Say' and Sharon Sheeley's 'Poor Little Fool' (1958). During the same year Nelson starred in the John Wayne Western *Rio Bravo*. Although his performance was critically acclaimed, Nelson's later screen appearances were sporadic.

The pattern of combining a rock'n'roll song with a ballad on each Nelson release continued into 1959 when Baker Knight's 'Never Be Anyone Else But You' was coupled with Dorsey and **Johnny Burnette**'s uptempo 'It's Late'. Both were Top Ten hits. As rock'n'roll proper lost momentum, so Nelson's songs lost their harder edges. His chart success faltered during 1960 but the following year he had a No. 1 with the relaxed 'Travellin' Man' whose B-side, **Gene Pitney**'s 'Hello Mary Lou', with its double-tracked vocals and sing-along chorus, became one of Nelson's best-remembered records. Although by now he had changed his name from Ricky to the more mature Rick, 'Everlovin'' (1961), Jerry Fuller's 'Young World' and 'It's Up to You' (1963) were in a similar vein.

In 1963 Nelson left Imperial for Decca where he recorded standards like **Johnny Mercer**'s 'Fools Rush in' and Burke and Dubin's 'For You' before the deep influence of rockabilly on his work led him towards country music in a move which predated the country-rock movement. *Bright Lights and Country Music* (1966) and *Country Fever* (1967) were collections of songs by such luminaries as **Willie Nelson**, **Glen Campbell** and **Doug Kershaw** and both featured Burton on dobro.

Nelson next turned to singer-songwriters for his material. Produced by John Boylan, *Another Side of Rick* (1968) and *Perspective* (1969) featured compositions from **Tim Hardin**, **Nilsson** and **Randy Newman**. Inspired by **Bob Dylan**'s *Nashville Skyline*, Nelson formed the Stone Canyon Band with ex-Poco guitarist Randy Meisner in 1970. With ex-**Buck Owens** steel-guitarist Tom Brumley he created his own country-rock synthesis on a version of Dylan's 'She Belongs to Me', which was a minor hit in 1970. This was followed by *In Concert* (MCA, 1970) and *Rick Sings Nelson* (1970), the first album on which all the songs were written by Nelson himself.

After releasing *Rudy the Fifth* (1971), Nelson had his final hit with the million-selling 'Garden Party'. Including the lines 'If memories were all I sang/I'd rather drive a truck', the song described his mixed feelings at being expected only to play his old hits at revival shows. From the mid-seventies Nelson's recording career went into decline. *Windfall* (1974) was his last album for MCA and he released only two further records, *Intakes* (Epic, 1977) and *Playing to Win* (Capitol, 1981). He continued to tour in the eighties and died in a plane crash *en route* to a booking.

His twin sons Gunnar and Matthew (*b. September*

1967) recorded *After the Rain* (DGC, 1990) as Nelson, while his daughter Tracy is a television actress.

SANDY NELSON
b. Sander L. Nelson, 1 December 1938, Santa Monica, California, USA

The only rock drummer to have solo hits, Nelson's 'Let There Be Drums' (1961) influenced later generations of percussionists.

He attended the same Los Angeles high school as **Jan and Dean** and **Phil Spector** and made his first records for Ebb and Challenge with Kip Tyler and the Flips. Nelson played drums for Spector on the Teddy Bears' 'To Know Him Is to Love Him' (1958) and also recorded with **Gene Vincent**.

In 1959 he recorded the punchy, riff-laden 'Teen Beat' for local label Original Sound and the single reached the Top Ten in America and Britain. Nelson signed to Lew Chudd's Imperial company but such follow-ups as 'Drum Party' (1960) and 'Cool Operator' (1961) were unsuccessful until 'Let There Be Drums' was released. The single's repeated thundering phrase was frequently borrowed by later drummers and appeared on Cozy Powell's 'Dance with the Devil' (1974) and **Boney M**'s 'Rasputin' (1978). In 1980 B. A. Robertson, whose earlier hit 'Cool in a Kaftan' had poked fun at psychedelia, included a two-minute history of drumming on his début album *Initial Success* (Asylum). Entitled 'Eat Your Heart Out Sandy Nelson', it naturally began with the words 'let there be drums!' The composition itself was covered in 1988 by British group Boss Beat.

Despite the fact that he had lost a foot in a car accident, Nelson was able to record 'Drums Are My Beat' and 'Drummin' up a Storm', which were lesser hits in 1962. His later recording career, like that of his labelmates the **Ventures**, consisted predominantly of big-beat versions of pop hits. Thus *Be True to Your School* (1964) included the **Coasters**' 'Charlie Brown' while *Beat That *?!! Drum* [*sic*] (1966) had a version of **Donovan**'s 'Sunshine Superman'.

In the eighties Nelson formed his own label, Vee-bltronics, to release recordings of his drum improvisations.

WILLIE NELSON
b. 30 April 1933, Abbott, Texas, USA

One of the most significant figures in modern country music, Nelson's music is decidedly Texan, with strong honky-tonk and Western swing influences. He was a prolific and hugely successful writer in the fifties, mostly of sombre ballads. In the seventies, after a period in which he was recorded unsympathetically, he became the original Nashville 'outlaw'. He took control of his own recording career and found country (and pop) success with a spare, intense sound that ran counter to the countrypolitan trend of the time. Thus, for example, his breakthrough hit, 'Blue Eyes Crying in the Rain' (Columbia, 1975) featured only Nelson's voice and an acoustic guitar. He moved to Austin, Texas, and through his annual 4 July celebrations, in which he showcased country rock bands and new performers hostile to the countrypolitan movement, as well as traditionally inclined artists, made it an alternative capital of country music to Nashville. Nelson's own success continued into the eighties, expanding to include films and a long series of duets, the most unlikely being with **Julio Iglesias** ('To All the Girls I've Loved Before'*, 1984). More significant was the emergence of a slew of traditionally inspired country acts in the eighties, including the Judds, Dwight Yoakam, **George Strait** and **Ricky Skaggs**, all of whose careers in some part were made possible by the new openness forced upon Nashville in the wake of the commercial success of Nelson and his fellow outlaws.

Raised on a farm, Nelson formed his first band while at high school. This included his sister Bobbie, who has regularly performed with Nelson throughout his career. After his discharge from the air force in 1952, Nelson drifted through a succession of jobs before becoming a disc-jockey. During this time he started songwriting seriously and on the proceeds of his first published song, 'Family Bible', in 1959 travelled to Nashville. There, he was signed by Texan honky-tonk star **Ray Price** to his publishing company Pamper Music, eventually joining Price's backing band as bassist. Among the country standards he wrote were 'Crazy', a country No. 1 for **Patsy Cline** (1961), which was later successfully revived by **Linda Ronstadt**; 'Hello Walls', a country No. 1 for **Faron Young**; and 'Night Life' (1963), which Ray Price made his theme song; **Roy Orbison** had a pop hit with the sad Christmas song, 'Pretty Paper' (1963). These and other songs like 'The Party's Over' (a UK Top Ten hit for **Lonnie Donegan** in 1962), 'Funny How Time Slips Away', 'Darkness on the Face of the Earth' and 'The Healing Hands of Time', all memorably recorded by Nelson himself in the sixties for RCA, were inflected with the weatherbeaten directness of a **Hank Williams** and were perfect examples of that strand of country music which has been described as 'white man's blues'.

He recorded prolifically throughout the sixties for Liberty and RCA (where he was generally produced by **Chet Atkins**), but Nelson was unhappy with the way in which his unusual jazz-inspired phrasing (reminiscent of **Hoagy Carmichael** at times) was frequently made to compete with lavish strings. In 1970 he quit Nashville for Austin and started to mix with younger, more rock-inspired artists, notably **Waylon Jennings** and **Kris Kristofferson**. In 1972 he left RCA and joined Atlantic's newly established country division for whom he recorded the seminal *Shotgun Willie* (1973), produced by **Arif Mardin**, and *Phases and Stages* (1974), produced by **Jerry Wexler**. Made in New York and at Muscle Shoals, respectively, and featuring support from such rock musicians as **Doug Sahm**, the albums had a stark sound in which for the first time Nelson's rough, whiskey-soaked interpretations of his songs were appropriately showcased. Furthermore, *Phases and Stages*, which related the break-up of a marriage, one side from the husband's perspective, the other from the wife's, saw Nelson successfully extending the range of his writing. However, though the albums were crucial to Nelson's development and critical successes, they failed commercially and when Atlantic closed down its country division, Nelson moved to Columbia.

Guaranteed complete creative control, Nelson's first album for Columbia was the epochal *Red Haired Stranger** (1975). A concept album about a bittersweet romance set in 'the old West', it included Nelson's first-ever pop hit, **Fred Rose**'s 'Blues Eyes Crying in the Rain', first recorded by **Roy Acuff** in the forties. Equally significant was *Wanted: The Outlaws** (RCA, 1976). The album, made in collaboration with Jessi Colter, Waylon Jennings (whose duet with Nelson, 'Good Hearted Woman', was a pop hit) and Tompall Glaser of **Tompall and the Glaser Brothers**, all Nashville rebels who adopted the 'outlaw' image and found a crossover rock audience (rather than the middle-of-the-road audience 'countrypolitan' Nashville stars were seeking). Its success helped break down many of the conservative barriers in Nashville while at the same time the 'outlaw' image testified to the potency of the cowboy mythology which had become a central element of the music since the innocent days of **Gene Autry**. The album had a further significance for Nelson: henceforth a great number of his recordings would be collaborations with others. These include *Waylon and Willie** (1978), *One for the Road* (1979, with **Leon Russell**), *San Antonio Rose* (1980, with Ray Price), *Poncho and Lefty* (1982, with **Merle Haggard**) and *Highwayman* (1986, with **Johnny Cash**, Kristofferson and Jennings), as well as his duet with Iglesias.

By now a country superstar, Nelson established himself as an actor in a series of films in which he played roles carefully patterned on his own persona. These included *The Electric Horseman* (1979), *Honeysuckle Rose* (1980), whose million-selling soundtrack album included the hit 'On the Road Again', *Barbarossa* (1982) and a telefilm version of *Red Headed Stranger* (1987). However, few of his recordings in the eighties were of his own compositions. Among the

best of these was *To Lefty from Willie* (1977), a tribute to **Lefty Frizzell**; *Stardust** (1978), a collection of popular songs which included sympathetic versions of Hoagy Carmichael's title song and 'Georgia on My Mind' and **Irving Berlin**'s 'Blue Skies'; and *Somewhere over the Rainbow* (1981). *What a Wonderful World* (1987) was another covers set and gave Nelson another American hit with Iglesias on 'Spanish Eyes'. Though this material saw him edging away from strictly country material and he often performed in cabaret at Las Vegas and elsewhere, Nelson's style made few concessions to such changes in venue.

In 1989 he released the appropriately named *Born for Trouble*, before rejoining Cash, Kristofferson and Jennings for *Highwayman II* (1990). That same year, however, Nelson ran into serious tax troubles and the American tax office, the IRS, seized his estate to settle nearly $17m of tax debts. In an effort to raise money to pay his debt, he issued an album of unreleased material, *Who'll Buy My Memories?* (1991) and toured again with the Highwaymen before settling with the IRS in 1993. Later that year he released one of his finest albums yet, *Across the Borderline* (Columbia), again largely containing other peoples' songs, on which he was joined by **Bob Dylan**, **Paul Simon**, **Bonnie Raitt** and **Mose Allison**, among others. With state of the art production by **Don Was**, it introduced Nelson to a new audience. For his next album, *Moonlight Becomes You* (1994), a collaboration with guitar virtuoso Paul Buskirk, Nelson returned to the formula of *Stardust*, releasing another jazz-tinged selection of standards like 'Sentimental Journey' and 'Please Don't Talk About Me When I'm Gone'. *Healing Hands of Time* (Liberty, 1995) included a new version of 'Funny How Time Slips Away'. Most of Nelson's releases of the nineties, however, were either retrospectives of various stages of his career or stripped-down reworkings of past hits or thematic material. The first included his stay with Liberty (*The Early Years*, 1994), with Columbia (*Revolutions of Time*, 1995) and RCA (*The Essential Willie Nelson*, 1996), while the latter included *Spirit* (1996) and the gospel album *How Great Thou Art* (1997). More experimental was the instrumental album *Night and Day* (SPV, 2000) on which with veteran country fiddler Johnny Gimble playing **Stephane Grappelli** to Nelson's **Django Reinhardt** the pair gave a decidedly Texan inflection to the jazz excursions of the Hot Club of France. Among the numbers were 'Nuages', 'September in the Rain' and a carefree version of 'Sweet Georgia Brown'. In the same year the ever productive Nelson issued a blues album, *Milk Cow Boogie* (Island), on which he duetted with **B. B. King**, **Dr John** and Keb Mo among others on a mix of songs associated with them ('The Thrill Is Gone') and reworkings of Nelson originals ('Night Life').

THE NEVILLE BROTHERS

Aaron, b. 24 January 1941, New Orleans, Louisiana, USA; Art, b. 17 December 1938, New Orleans; Charles, b. 28 December 1939, New Orleans; Cyril, b. 10 January 1950, New Orleans

The Neville Brothers formed the nucleus of **Allen Toussaint**'s studio band in the sixties and early seventies, producing an intense rhythmic sound that presaged the later arrival of funk. The group belatedly found an international rock audience in the late eighties.

Art and Aaron Neville's recording career began while they were still at school. With a vocal group, the Hawketts, Art recorded 'Mardi Gras Mambo' (Chess, 1954), a novelty R&B hit. With its hypnotic rhythms the record became one of the signature tunes associated with New Orleans' annual *mardi gras* festival. The Hawketts played local clubs but did not record again. Aaron joined the band in 1958, but Art then joined Lee Diamond's band, recorded 'Cha Dooky Doo' and 'Ooh Wee Baby' and was the pianist on Jerry Byrne's rock'n'roll hit 'Lights Out' (Specialty, 1958). While Aaron reached the R&B charts with the Toussaint-produced 'Over You' (Minit, 1960), Art later made the haunting ballad 'All These Things' (Instant, 1962).

Aaron's biggest hit came with the bluesy 'Tell It Like It Is' (Parlo, 1966), written by Diamond and arranger George Davis. 'She Took You for a Ride' was a minor hit and when Parlo collapsed soon afterwards Art and Aaron played in New Orleans as the Neville Sounds before forming the nucleus of Toussaint's studio band, playing on numerous Toussaint-produced hits. From that band Art Neville formed the Meters in 1969 with Leo Nocentelli (guitar), George Porter (bass), and Joseph 'Ziggy' Modeliste (drums). With a sound based on **Sly Stone**'s and masterminded by Toussaint, the instrumentals 'Sophisticated Cissy' and 'Cissy Strut' (Josie, 1969) were minor pop hits while 'Look-Ka Py Py' (1969) and 'Chicken Strut' (1970) were R&B hits.

The group next signed to Reprise, releasing *Cabbage Alley* (1972), while continuing to work on Toussaint productions, including albums by **Dr John**, **Robert Palmer** and **Patti Labelle**'s group Labelle. The Meters later recorded *Rejuvenation* (1974), *Fire on the Bayou* (1975), for which Cyril Neville joined the group, and *Trick Bag* (1976). On *The Wild Tchoupitoulas* (Island, 1976) they accompanied George and Amos Landry to re-create the ceremonial music of *mardi gras*. The album marked the first time all four Nevilles had teamed up on disc.

Dissatisfaction with Toussaint in 1977 led to David Rubinson producing *New Directions* but a legal dispute with Toussaint caused the Meters to split soon

afterwards. As a result, the Neville Brothers formed, with the addition of Aaron and saxophonist Charles. After the **Jack Nitzsche**-produced eponymous album (Capitol, 1978), they moved to A&M for *Fiyo on the Bayou* (1981) and the live *Neville-ization* (1984). In 1986 they participated in the 'Conspiracy of Hope' tour for Amnesty International, with **Joan Baez**, **Peter Gabriel** and **Sting** of the **Police**, among others. A brief stay with EMI produced the guest-star-heavy and disappointing *Uptown* (1987). However, a return to A&M produced their finest album, *Yellow Moon* (1989), produced by **Daniel Lanois** (producer of **U2**). It included songs by **Link Wray** and **Bob Dylan**. The same year Aaron duetted with **Linda Ronstadt** on the hit 'Don't Know Much' (Elektra) and album *Cry like a Rainstorm, Howl like the Wind*. He also appeared on Lanois' solo album, *Acadie* (1989), singing 'Amazing Grace', the hymn which had long been a staple of the Nevilles' stage act.

With their profile at its highest point the band toured extensively, although European audiences were somewhat confused by a set which ignored many of the highlights of *Yellow Moon* in favour of the oldies medleys which peppered the Nevilles' regular shows at their own New Orleans club, Tipitina's. A lesser companion to *Neville-ization*, *Live at Tipitina's Vol. II* appeared on American independent label Spindletop in 1990, preceding the follow-up to *Yellow Moon*, *Brothers' Keeper* (A&M, 1990). Lacking Lanois' atmospheric production, it was still an excellent album, particularly when compared to 1992's poor *Family Groove*. Aaron meanwhile reactivated his solo career, releasing two patchy albums, *Warm Your Heart* (1991, produced by Ronstadt) and *The Grand Tour* (1993), followed by an unexceptional seasonal collection, *Aaron Neville's Soulful Christmas*. He also appeared as a guest on albums by **Kenny G**, **Maria Muldaur** and others. In 1994 the Neville Brothers appeared at Woodstock '94 and released the in-concert set *Live on Planet Earth*, mixing oldies and a few highlights from their own career. A far better resumé of their early solo and band material was offered by the 1987 compilation *Treacherous* (Rhino).

NEW KIDS ON THE BLOCK

Donnie Wahlberg, b. 17 August 1969, Dorchester, Massachusetts, USA; Danny Wood, b. 14 May 1971, Boston, Massachusetts; Jordan Knight, b. 17 May 1971, Worcester, Massachusetts; Jonathan Knight, b. 29 November 1968, Worcester; Joey McIntyre, b. 13 December 1972, Needham, Massachusetts

New Kids on the Block were the world's most successful teenage vocal group of the late eighties.

The group was put together by Maurice Starr, the creator of New Edition, whose members included

Bobby Brown and the trio Bell Biv Devoe. Starr's aim was to produce a white equivalent to the teen-idol vocalizing of New Edition. His first recruit was Wahlberg, who brought in his brother Mark, Wood and the Knight brothers. Mark Wahlberg soon left the line-up and later formed his own recording band, Marky Mark and the Funky Bunch.

Starr first called his new group Nynuk but changed the name to New Kids on the Block after signing a recording deal with CBS in 1985. The first single 'Be My Girl' and a self-titled début album were commercially unsuccessful and it took three years of touring for the group to attract attention from teenage audiences.

The breakthrough came in 1989 with a marathon US tour and the hit single 'You Got It (The Right Stuff)'. The group's slickly choreographed stage moves and boyish good looks brought eight million sales in the US for the somewhat inappropriately-titled *Hangin' Tough*, produced by Starr. Other hit singles from the album included a lacklustre cover-version of the **Delfonics**' 'Didn't I (Blow Your Mind)', the gushing 'This One's for the Children' and the title track. The group also issued a seasonal *Merry, Merry Christmas* the same year.

New Kids mania began in Britain towards the end of 1989 and accelerated when the quintet toured there the following year. The tour preceded the European release of *Merry, Merry Christmas* and of the new album, *Step by Step*.

In 1991 the group joined the current fashion for releasing remix albums with *No More Games/Remix Album*. **Arthur Baker** and Clivilles & Cole (aka **C&C Music Factory**) were among the contributors. The group continued its global touring although Wahlberg found time to produce the US chart-topping 'Good Vibrations' for his brother's group with Loleatta Holloway as the featured singer.

By the close of 1992 the band's 'never-ending tour' was winding down and the New Kids on the Block disappeared from view. Maurice Starr had ceased to manage them and they spent much of 1993 preparing a comeback album under their new name of NKOTB. *Face the Music* was issued the following year. It featured a grown-up hip-hop-orientated sound courtesy of producer/writers **Teddy Riley** and **Narada Michael Walden**. Wahlberg produced four of the album's tracks, including the first single, 'Dirty Dawg'. In contrast to their earlier albums, *Face the Music* only just scraped into the US Top Forty.

THE NEW LOST CITY RAMBLERS
Mike Seeger, b. 1933, New York, USA; John Cohen, b. 1932, New York; Tom Paley, b. 19 March 1928, New York (replaced by Tracy Schwarz, b. 1938, New York)

Formed in the explosion of interest in folk music in the United States in the fifties and sixties, the New Lost City Ramblers stood out by their uncompromising advocacy of traditional, pre-Nashville country music, in particular the old-time string-band sounds of the twenties and thirties. Their representation of this music was so attractive and convincing that it led many of their contemporaries, and even more of the next generation of players, to adopt the same models and construct a similar musical value-system. Few American musicians of the early sixties who had the slightest leaning towards folk music were unaffected by the NLCR, and many were, at least short-term, devotees.

Seeger, son of the ethno-musicologist Charles (an early academic supporter of hillbilly and blues music) and half-brother of **Pete Seeger** absorbed traditional music through family associations and learned to play all the string-band instruments. In the fifties he began to collect folk music himself, making contact with veteran recording artists like banjoist Dock Boggs and fiddler Eck Robertson (*b. 20 November 1887, Amarillo, Texas*). It was Robertson who made the first recordings of Southern fiddle music, for Victor in New York in 1922 (the first Southern-made recordings of hillbilly music were cut the following year by **Fiddlin' John Carson**).

Cohen had become interested in folk music while at Yale, and afterwards sang in New York coffee-houses as well as pursuing a career as a photographer. He too went South to collect traditional music, and on a field trip to Kentucky met the singer, banjoist and guitarist Roscoe Holcomb, whose subsequent recordings for Folkways influenced the young **Bob Dylan**. Holcomb was also the chief subject of Cohen's *The High Lonesome Sound* (1962), the first of a series of documentary films about traditional music in both North and South America.

Paley came from a classical music background – his mother was a piano teacher – but took up folk music in early fifties while pursuing an academic career as a mathematician. Unlike the musically restless Seeger and Cohen, he concentrated on just two instruments, banjo and guitar, attaining a skill and sense of traditional style that he later passed on, as a teacher, to such younger players as **Ry Cooder**.

Formed in 1958, the NLCR recorded a début album for Folkways, drawing on material originally recorded by artists like **Gid Tanner**'s Skillet-Lickers, **Uncle Dave Macon** and Charlie Poole. Subsequent albums for Folkways, *Songs of the Depression* (1960) and four more eponymous volumes (1960–3), supplied abundant material for the string-band revival. The band also appeared at the first Newport Folk Festival (1959) and many of its successors, and was well-known throughout the US on the campus and coffee-house circuit. In 1962 Paley left the NCLR and moved to England, where he led the New Deal String Band with Janet Kerr (fiddle) and Joe Locker (banjo), and recorded for Argo and Kicking Mule. His replacement, Schwarz, who played fiddle, banjo and guitar, had also discovered folk music while at college, but had studied in Washington DC where he had been exposed to country and bluegrass music in its habitat, and was able to slacken a little the purism of the Ramblers' approach.

The NLCR Mark II continued its Folkways catalogue with *American Moonshine and Prohibition Songs* (1963) and *Gone to the Country* (1964), among others. Cohen and Seeger edited a collection from their repertoire, *The New Lost City Ramblers Song Book* (1964), a valuable source of musical, theoretical and pictorial information about old-time music. By the late sixties, however, the NLCR were working together less, all its members pursuing their own projects. Seeger resumed his collecting but recorded occasionally for Folkways, Vanguard and Mercury. In the seventies he worked for a time with his then wife, singer and instrumentalist Alice Gerrard, who also worked with the singer Hazel Dickens and later in the Harmony Sisters. He also organized annual old-time music festivals at Rockbridge, Virginia.

Cohen played sporadically with groups, including the Putnam String County Band, while teaching and making films, among them *Mountain Music of Peru* (1984). Schwarz continued to play music full-time, often in a family group with his wife Eloise and various children. A lover of cajun music, he played and recorded with Louisiana musicians, including fiddler Dewey Balfa. Paley, still based in England, played fiddle and continued to work much of the year in Europe and the US, where he joined the others at a folk festival in a 1988 NLCR reunion.

NEW ORDER

Bernard Albrecht (aka Sumner), b. Bernard Dicken, 4 January 1956, Salford, England; Ian Curtis, d. 18 May 1980, Macclesfield, Cheshire; Peter Hook, b. 13 February 1956; Steven Morris, b. 28 October 1957, Macclesfield; Gillian Gilbert, b. 27 January 1961, Manchester

Originally Joy Division, a leading British new-wave group specializing in twentieth-century gothic imagery, New Order was formed after the death of lead singer Ian Curtis and found huge success with a mixture of dance and indie rock in the eighties.

Inspired by the **Sex Pistols**, Albrecht (guitar) and Hook (bass) formed punk group Warsaw with Curtis (vocals) and drummer Morris in Manchester in 1977. Renaming themselves Joy Division (after Nazi concentration-camp prostitutes), they released the EP *An Ideal for Living* (Enigma, 1978).

In 1979 they signed to Factory, the local label set up by television journalist Tony Wilson. With Curtis's dirge-like vocals and obscure but unsettling lyrics, *Unknown Pleasures* (produced by Martin Hannett) was an intense evocation of depression and paranoia. Critical champions of the post-punk wave of British music were entranced, not least by Joy Division's live performances and Curtis's staccato stage movements.

After recording *Closer* (1980), Curtis committed suicide. Shortly afterwards 'Love Will Tear Us Apart' (later included by **Paul Young** on his 1983 album *No Parlez*) reached the Top Twenty. A final Joy Division collection, *Still* (1981), consisted partly of live recordings and was a Top Ten hit.

The remaining members chose New Order as their new name and recruited keyboards-player Gillian Gilbert. 'Ceremony' (1981) saw a shift towards an electronic style, a move confirmed by *Movement* (1981). The following year, 'Temptation' was a minor hit, while the more rhythmic 'Blue Monday' (1983) reached the Top Ten. It was an international hit in countries as diverse as Poland and New Zealand and inspired one of the best 'scratch' videos, by the Duvet Brothers.

Further British hits followed with 'Confusion' (1983, produced and co-written by **Arthur Baker**) and 'Thieves Like Us' from *Power Corruption and Lies* (1983). *Low Life* (1985) continued the evolution of the New Order sound with lyrical wit and a more melodic approach. *Brotherhood* (1986) used a range of stylistic clichés and quotations from **Lou Reed**, **Ennio Morricone** and country music to underpin enigmatic lyrics.

A 'best of' collection, *Substance*, accompanied 'True Faith' (1987), which was New Order's most successful British single to date (also reaching the American Top Forty) and a **Quincy Jones** remix of 'Blue Monday' sold equally well the next year. *Technique* was issued in 1989, débuting at No. 1 in Britain and making the American Top Forty. After recording the unlikely British No. 1 single 'World in Motion' with the England football team in 1990, the band concentrated on solo projects.

Sumner enjoyed the most success with his duo Electronic, formed with ex-**Smiths** guitarist Johnny Marr. Their eponymous début album reached the British Top Five and provided three hit singles. Hook formed the rockier Revenge, releasing the mini-album *One True Passion* (1990) and Gilbert and Morris recorded as the Other Two, releasing the album *The Other Two and You* in 1994. New Order's own next album, *Republic*, had a prolonged gestation period, which was cited as one of the reasons for the collapse of Factory Records in 1992. The band subsequently signed to London Records, releasing the album in 1993.

New Order would not work together again until

1998, once more spending the intervening years working on solo material. After disbanding Revenge, Hook
formed Monaco with guitarist David Potts, who later
rejected an offer to join **Oasis** as bassist. Monaco had
a minor UK hit in 1997 with *Music for Pleasure*, which
included the single 'What Do You Want from Me?'
Electronic issued two further albums, *Raise the Pressure* (1996) and *Twisted Tenderness* (1999), both of
which were modestly successful. New Order reconvened in 1998 to perform live for the first time in five
years, headlining at the Reading Festival. Their first
recorded output since 1993 was 'Brutal', which
appeared on the soundtrack to the movie adaptation
of Alex Garland's *The Beach* in 2000.

THE NEW YORK DOLLS

*David Johansen, b. 9 January 1950, New York, USA;
Arthur Kane, b. 3 February 1951; Billy Murcia, b. 1951,
New York, d. 6 November 1972, London, England
(replaced by Jerry Nolan, b. 7 May 1951, New York City,
d. 14 January 1992, New York City); Rick Rivets
(replaced by Sylvain Sylvain, b. Syl Mizrahi); Johnny
Thunders, b. John Genzale, 15 July 1954, d. 23 April 1991,
New Orleans*

An innovative rock group, the New York Dolls were
highly influential in the development of punk rock in
the late seventies and inspired the 'glam-metal' scene
in the eighties. However, in retrospect, it may be that
their lasting influence lies in their shambolic performances and in the excesses of the individual lives,
which in the manner of the **Sex Pistols** gave new
meaning – and impetus – to the rock'n'roll lifestyle
of the eighties.

Raised on New York's Lower East Side, guitarist
Thunders (initially known as Johnny Volume) joined
his first band, Actress, with Rivets (guitar), Murcia
(drums) and Kane (bass). Singer Johansen joined
soon afterwards from Fast Eddie and the Electric Japs
and after Kane met Sylvain at a screening of Russ
Meyer's notorious *Beyond the Valley of the Dolls*, the
group had acquired a new name and a new rhythm
guitarist.

Visually, the Dolls were strongly influenced by
glam-rock as epitomized by **Marc Bolan** and **David
Bowie** and performed a mixture of original songs and
R&B oldies dressed in high heels, lurex tights, feather
boas and make-up. In the process they transformed
the glitter of glam-rock into something more threatening. Other groups, including Wayne County, the
Brats (formed by Rivets), Teenage Lust and **Kiss** followed in their wake, creating a New York glitter-punk
movement.

Having recorded demos (posthumously released as
Lipstick Killers (ROIR), in 1972 the Dolls visited England to record and support **Rod Stewart** and the

Faces, but during the trip Murcia died of a drink and
drugs overdose. With new drummer Nolan, the
group recorded an eponymous début album for Mercury in 1973. Produced by **Todd Rundgren**, it contained such adolescent anthems as 'Trash',
'Personality Crisis' and a version of **Bo Diddley**'s
'Pills'.

Shadow Morton was brought in to produce *Too
Much Too Soon* (1974) but the result was uneven,
matching up to the Dolls' live sound on only a few
tracks, such as 'Puss 'n' Boots', 'Human Being' and
'Babylon'. Sales were poor and from early 1975 the
group was managed by future Sex Pistols manager
Malcolm McLaren, who changed their image by
dressing them as Maoist Red Guards for several New
York gigs. Disillusioned with the continued lack of
success, Thunders and Nolan left the group to form
the Heartbreakers with ex-**Television** bassist Richard
Hell and guitarist Walter Lure, although Johansen
and Sylvain continued to tour until 1977, using
replacement musicians. Several live recordings of the
Dolls subsequently emerged, the best being *Seven Day
Weekend* (Receiver, 1992), rehearsal tapes from
1973–4.

The original group had split just before the emergence of their most dynamic disciples, the musicians
and fanzine writers of the British punk scene of
1976–8. Accordingly, with Hell replaced by Billy Rath,
the Heartbreakers moved to London and recorded
L.A.M.F. (1977) for British label Track. Adopted by
the London punk fraternity, they toured heavily, but
shortly after Nolan had been replaced by ex-**Clash**
drummer Terry Chimes, they split up at the end of
1977. A typical live show of the period was released as
D.T.K. by Jungle Records in 1982.

Thunders recorded *So Alone* (1978) in London with
an all-star cast including Steve Marriott, **Thin Lizzy**
leader Phil Lynott and Sex Pistols Steve Jones and
Paul Cook. Probably his finest solo moment, it failed
to sell, and although he toured constantly and
released a further six albums (on New Rose and Jungle), Thunders never recaptured the momentum of
1976–7 in a career blighted by the heroin addiction
which contributed to his death in mysterious circumstances in 1991. Several posthumous live albums subsequently appeared. Nolan, having played on and off
with Thunders throughout the eighties (notably on a
1984 Heartbreakers reunion), died from stroke-
related pneumonia less than a year later.

Sylvain released solo albums on RCA in 1979 and
1981 and occasionally appeared live with Thunders in
the late seventies and early eighties. Thunders apart,
the most significant solo contribution from an ex-
New York Doll was Johansen's. An eponymous solo
album (*Blue Sky*, 1978) was followed by the soul-
inspired *In Style* (1979) and *Here Comes the Night*

(1981). Sylvain was a regular member of Johansen's band during 1978–9, and was heavily featured on *In Style*. The excellent live album *Live It up* (1982) was followed by the lesser *Sweet Revenge* (1984). Increasingly Johansen began to concentrate on an acting career, but in 1985 re-emerged in the guise of tuxedo-clad cabaret singer Buster Poindexter, winning several categories at the first New York Music Awards ceremony the following year. In 1987 he released a version of Trinidad singer **Arrow**'s soca hit 'Hot Hot Hot' (RCA), followed by two tongue-in-cheek albums of cover-versions which mixed R&B with the big-band jazz of **Cab Calloway** (*Buster Goes Berserk*, 1989; *Buster's Happy Hour*, 1994). His film appearances included *Scrooged* (1988), *Married to the Mob* and *Freejack* (1992), with Mick Jagger.

The New York Dolls' influence continued into the nineties, with **Morrissey** covering the first album's 'Trash' and, in 1993, **Guns N' Roses** releasing versions of 'Human Being' and Thunders' theme song 'You Can't Put Your Arms around a Memory' on the US chart-topping album *The Spaghetti Incident?*. *Rock'n'Roll* (1994) collects together the best of their early material and out-takes with a scholarly eye rather than a fan's commitment.

MICKEY NEWBURY
b. 19 May 1940, Houston, Texas, USA

Newbury, with **Kris Kristofferson**, **Willie Nelson** and **Tom T. Hall**, among others, was one of the most successful of the new breed of rock-inflected country songwriters to emerge in the late sixties. He is the writer of 'An American Trilogy' (an arrangement of 'Dixie', 'Battle Hymn of the Republic' and 'All My Trails'), memorably recorded by **Elvis Presley** and Newbury himself, and the classic country weepie 'She Even Woke Me Up to Say Goodbye'. However, where Kristofferson and Nelson would have an impact on the world outside country music, Newbury's influence was contained within it and was further blunted by the advent of the new traditionalism of the eighties.

Raised in Houston, where he listened to black as well as country music in the fifties, Newbury travelled to Nashville on his discharge from the air force. His first success came with 'Funny, Familiar, Forgotten Feelings', a country hit for **Don Gibson** (1966) and a pop hit for **Tom Jones** (1967), and 'Just Dropped in (To See What Condition My Condition Was in)', which gave **Kenny Rogers** his first major hit in 1968. Both anticipated the typical word and emotional play of 'She Even Woke Me up to Say Goodbye'. First taken up by **Jerry Lee Lewis**, the song was later recorded by numerous artists. Signed briefly to RCA and then Elektra, Newbury's own recordings failed until he released the atypical, haunting 'An American Trilogy' (1971).

In the seventies his songs were recorded by a wide variety of artists, including **Joan Baez**, whose *Diamonds and Rust* (1975) included 'Frisco Mabel Joy' and two other songs, **Andy Williams** ('Sweet Memories', 1968), **Willie Nelson** and **Ray Charles**. Newbury's own recordings (on RCA, *Harlequin Melodies*, 1968, and Mercury, *Looks Like Rain*, 1969) fared less well and in 1970 he moved to Elektra. Recording in a more muscular style, as, for example, on *Heaven Help the Child* (1973), he still failed to find success and retreated to a sweeter style on records for ABC/Hickory (*The Sailor*, 1979) and MCA (*Sweet Memories*, 1985). More interesting was the independently produced *In a New Age* (Airborne, 1988), which saw Newbury singing against the sparest of backings. Since then he has performed and recorded only intermittently.

ANTHONY NEWLEY
b. 24 September 1931, London, England, d. 14 April 1999

The co-author and star of the influential musical *Stop the World, I Want to Get Off!* (1961), Newley had an unusually varied career. A former child actor, he briefly turned to rock'n'roll to launch his recording career in the late fifties before forming a successful writing partnership with Leslie Bricusse in the sixties and seventies, when he also became a film director. However, if the avenues he pursued were various, the themes of his work were constant: loneliness and unhappiness.

After a theatrical apprenticeship, Newley graduated to films. His most memorable juvenile part was as the Artful Dodger in David Lean's *Oliver Twist* (1949), before he established himself as a character actor in a series of British adventure pictures in the early fifties. His appearance in the revue *Cranks* (1955), which took him briefly to Broadway, gave him a taste for the theatre. Then in 1959 he sang and played the part of a conscripted rock'n'roller in *Idol on Parade*. His recording of the title song and the plaintive 'I've Waited So Long', both of which he co-wrote, were British hits and launched him on a brief and eccentric recording career. His hits included two No. 1s ('Why' and 'Do You Mind', 1960 – chirpy ballads performed in a quavering voice) and oddities like the traditional songs 'Strawberry Fair' (1960) and 'Pop Goes the Weasel' (1961), which are noteworthy for their influence on such early **David Bowie** efforts as 'The Laughing Gnome' (a hit when re-released in 1973).

Newley's most significant hit was 'What Kind of Fool Am I?' (1961) from *Stop the World*, the first of the musicals he wrote with Bricusse (*b. 29 January 1931, London*). While at Cambridge University Bricusse wrote for and appeared in revues mounted by the Footlights club and made his West End début in *An Evening with Beatrice Lillie* (1955). **Max Bygraves** had hits with a pair of Bricusse songs ('Out of Town' and 'A Good Idea, Son') in 1956, and in 1958 Bricusse wrote his first musical, *Lady at the Wheel*, with Robin Beaumont. His greatest early successes were 'My Kind of Girl', a hit for **Matt Monro** in 1960 and later recorded by numerous singers, including **Frank Sinatra**, and 'If I Ruled the World' (co-written with Cyril Ornadel), a hit for one-time **Goon** Harry Secombe in 1963 after being featured in the musical *Pickwick*.

Filmed in 1966 and again in 1978 (as *Sammy Stops the World*), *Stop the World* was described by one critic as an 'allegorical musical'. It starred Newley as the little man attempting to defeat the system and introduced 'Gonna Build a Mountain' and 'Once in a Lifetime' as well as the oft-recorded 'What Kind of Fool' (with which **Shirley Bassey** and **Sammy Davis Jnr**, who starred in the 1978 film, also had hits in 1962). The show was revived on the London stage in 1989. In 1965 the pair produced the similarly styled hit musical, *The Roar of the Greasepaint, the Smell of the Crowd*, which introduced 'Who Can I Turn to?', an American hit for **Tony Bennett**. The year before, in collaboration with **John Barry**, they had written the hit title song to the James Bond film, *Goldfinger*; henceforth, together and separately, the pair concentrated on films. With **Henry Mancini**, Bricusse wrote the title song for *Two for the Road* (1966) and on his own wrote the lyrics and complete score for *Doctor Doolittle* (1967), in which Newley had a featured part. However, despite winning an Oscar for 'Talk to the Animals', the film, then one of the most expensive musicals ever mounted, was a commercial and critical failure, as were *Goodbye Mr Chips* (1969), which starred **Petula Clark**, and *Scrooge* (1970).

On his own Newley also stumbled disastrously. *Can Heironymus Merkin Ever Forget Mercy Humpe and Find True Happiness?* (1969), which he wrote, directed, produced and starred in (opposite his then wife Joan Collins), was an extravaganza in which Newley presented himself as the tortured artist. Newley and Bricusse were more successful with their songs for *Willy Wonka and the Chocolate Factory* (1971), one of which, 'Candy Man', was a million-seller for Sammy Davis Jnr. Other performers they wrote for include Sergio Mendes ('The Joker'), **Nina Simone** ('Feeling Good') and **Barbra Streisand** ('Look at That Face'). They later wrote *The Good Old Bad Old Days* (1971) and songs for the 1976 television adaptation of *Peter Pan*, while Bricusse wrote the musical *Beyond the Rainbow* (1978).

In 1991 Newley staged *Once upon a Song*, a revue featuring his songs, in Miami. In 1994 he toured Britain in a revival of *Scrooge*. After his death RCA issued an intriguing career retrospective, the ironically titled *On a Wonderful Day Like Today* (2000), which brought to the fore his success at lounge-styled passion, in which hurt was counterpoised with lush, sweeping orchestrations.

RANDY NEWMAN
b. Gary Newman, 28 November 1944, New Orleans, Louisiana, USA

In marked contrast to most other singer-songwriters of the seventies, Newman didn't sing sweetly about (his own) personal relationships. Instead, with his cracked voice, he created a wide range of unpleasant and demented characters through whose mouths Newman addressed contemporary issues in America. This distance resulted in some of the most ironic and witty songs of the era, songs that reach back to the concerns and style of songwriters as varied as **George** and **Ira Gershwin** and **Yip Harburg**. Newman's melodies were similarly complex. As a result, though his songs were recorded successfully by several performers, his own recordings only brought Newman a cult audience. In addition, though as both writer and recording artist he was careful to situate himself on the edges of the mainstream of popular music, his best work confirmed the vitality of that mainstream and drew extensively from it. In the nineties, as the window of opportunity for his idiosyncratic views narrowed, he turned, with great success, to film music, winning three Oscar nominations in 1999 for his contributions to three different films.

Raised in Hollywood in a musical family – his uncles Lionel, Emil and Alfred Newman were noted film composers – Newman joined Metric Music as a staff writer in 1962. There he worked with **Jackie DeShannon**, **Leon Russell**, David Gates and others before becoming a staff arranger at Reprise in 1967, eventually being signed to the label in 1968. The deeply sad 'I Think It's Gonna Rain Today', recorded by **Judy Collins** in 1966, and the satiric whimsy of 'Simon Smith and His Amazing Dancing Bear' – a British hit for **Alan Price** in 1967 – illustrate the different sides of Newman's early songwriting.

Newman's eponymous début album (1968), which featured his songs set in complex orchestral arrangements and his second, *12 Songs* (1969), a collection of demos which included 'Mama Told Me (Not to Come)', a million-seller for **Three Dog Night** in 1970, were commercial failures. However, Newman won himself a high critical reputation and in 1970 **Nilsson** recorded a whole album of his songs, *Nilsson sings Newman*. His own album from this period was *Live* (1970). With only his piano for support, Newman recorded the definitive versions of the cream of his early compositions: 'Lonely at the Top', a parody of a showbusiness song, 'Old Kentucky Home', a parody of **Stephen Foster**, 'Davy the Fat Boy', 'Rain Today', 'Yellow Man' and 'I'll Be Home'. *Sail Away* (1972) had greater commercial success and saw Newman extending his range, adding a twist of social awareness and bitterness to songs like 'Burn on', about a river so polluted it was literally afire; 'Political Science', a vivid attack on the 'better dead than red' mentality; 'God's Song', a fierce denunciation of religion; and the satiric title song, in which in the character of a slave-ship captain he extols the great life awaiting black Africans in America as slaves. This was followed by the concept album, *Good Old Boys* (1974), a much misunderstood collection of songs about the South which evoked the times of the complex figure of Huey P. Long, governor of Louisiana.

In 1977, with vocal backing from members of the **Eagles**, Newman made his most commercially successful album, *Little Criminals*. It included the ironic anthem 'I Love L.A.' – 'Sixth Street – we love it' – the satiric 'Short People', which despite being attacked for bigotry sold a million copies, and 'Baltimore', which was also recorded by **Nina Simone**. *Born Again* (1979), which included the witty attack on **ELO**, 'The Story of a Rock and Roll Band', was a lesser album, but *Trouble in Paradise* (1983), which featured guest appearances from **Linda Ronstadt** and members of **Fleetwood Mac**, saw a return to the stance of world-weariness just this side of cynicism and gave Newman a minor hit with his duet with **Paul Simon**, 'The Blues'.

Newman's film work, which began when he contributed songs to *Performance* (1970), was lighter. His best film scores were for *Ragtime* (1979) and *The Natural* (1984), while his growing interest in cinema was signalled with his involvement in the comedy Western *Three Amigos!* (1986). Newman co-wrote the script, wrote several songs for the film and appeared in it as 'The Singing Bush'. The superior *Land of Dreams* (1988) mixed autobiographical memories ('Dixie Flyer', 'Four Eyes') with further portrayals of the red-neck mentality (the powerful 'Roll with the Punches', the title being the advice a bigot offers a black child) and a typically Newman double-edged celebration of things American ('Follow the Flag'). The album's co-producer was Mark Knopfler of **Dire Straits**.

Newman concentrated on film and TV soundtrack work in the nineties, contributing songs to the soundtracks of *Her Alibi* and *Major League* and music for the Robert De Niro movie, *Awakenings*. In 1991 he won an Emmy award for his music from the teleseries *Cop Rock*. In 1994 he wrote the score for the James Garner movie *Maverick* and, following the critical mauling of his reworking of the Faust legend, *Faust* (1995), he retreated to film music for much of the decade. While much of this was merely adequate (*James and the Giant Peach*, 1995), some was deeply affecting (*Toy Story*, 1997), a reminder that one of

Newman's great abilities was to write in character. The great example of this was his score for *Pleasantville* (1998), one of the three films for which he was Oscar-nominated in 1998; the others were *Babe: Pig in the City* and *A Bug's Life*. His *Pleasantville* score, like the film, echoed, in a distorted way, other Hollywood celebrations of small-town America. In 1999 he wrote the affecting score for *Toy Story 2*, giving melody to its fear of loss, which over the years has come to be one of the major, albeit hidden, themes of Newman.

Faust, which was in part conceived as a stage musical, was over-burdened with high concept and guests, including **Bonnie Raitt**, **Elton John**, **James Taylor** and Linda Ronstadt. Far better was *Bad Love* (1999), Newman's first solo album since 1998. The opening song, 'My Country', caught exactly the complex relationship of a man and his country and a parent and his family, while 'I'm Dead', supposedly sung by a rock star well past his sell-by date – 'Each record that I'm making/Is like a record that I've made/Just not as good' – reminds one of the venom in Newman's lyrics. Similarly, the complex emotions of 'My Country' testify to Newman's ability, like Robbie Robertson of **The Band**, to find the pulse of America. Critically well received, it sold poorly. In contrast, his song for *Toy Story 2* (1999) was again Oscar-nominated. In 2000 writers Michael Roth and Jerry Patch mounted *The Education of Randy Newman*, a musical (loosely based on *The Education of Henry Adams*) in which Newman's own life and songs formed the basis of a meditation on America. Michael Roth, who was the musical director of Newman's *Faust* musical, repeated that role for the show.

OLIVIA NEWTON-JOHN
b. 26 September 1948, Cambridge, England

A chameleon among vocalists, Newton-John found success with three different singing styles. She began as a bright-voiced folk-tinged pop singer, next becoming a successful country/middle-of-the-road artist and in 1978 emerged as a film star through her appearance with John Travolta in the film *Grease*, which led to a series of harder-edged hit records.

The daughter of an academic, she moved to Melbourne, Australia, in 1953. At the age of sixteen Newton-John's perfect pitch and purity of tone won her first prize in a talent contest judged by Johnny O'Keefe. Dubbed 'The Wild One' for his frantic stage act, O'Keefe was the most successful Australian rock'n'roll singer, recording cover-versions of American songs as **Johnny Hallyday** did in France, and topping the charts with 'She's My Baby' (Festival, 1959). His 1957 hit 'Real Wild Child' was successfully revived by **Iggy Pop** in 1987.

Newton-John returned to Britain in 1964, teaming

up in a vocal duo with Pat O'Carroll. She recorded **Jackie DeShannon**'s 'Till You Say You'll Be Mine' (Decca, 1966) before joining the shortlived Toomorrow, a **Don Kirshner** group modelled on the **Monkees**, making her screen début in the lightweight science-fiction film *Toomorrow* (1970), before becoming a regular on **Cliff Richard**'s television show. This exposure led to a contract with Pye, where she was produced by **Shadows**' bass-player John Farrar on a cover of **Bob Dylan**'s 'If Not for You' (1971). A minor hit on MCA in America, the record reached the British Top Ten as did the follow-up, a version of the traditional song 'The Banks of the Ohio'. Later British hits included **George Harrison**'s 'What Is Life' (1972) and **John Denver**'s 'Take Me Home Country Roads' (1973). However, the first phase of Newton-John's career ended in anticlimax when her performance of 'Long Live Love' only came fourth to **Abba** in the 1974 Eurovision Song Contest.

In the same year, the ballad 'Let Me Be There' (EMI) sold a million copies to both pop and country listeners in America and brought Newton-John awards as top country vocalist. Although strongly criticized by many conservative country performers, her success confirmed the countrypolitan trend of the period. Her later hits in this vein included 'I Honestly Love You'* (1974), 'Have You Never Been Mellow'* and 'Please Mr Please'* (1975).

'Sam' (EMI 1977) was Newton-John's first British success for three years and was the prelude to two multi-million-selling duets on RSO with Travolta taken from the fifties pastiche *Grease*, in which she played the female lead. 'You're the One That I Want' topped the charts on both sides of the Atlantic and 'Summer Nights' was a British No. 1. *Grease* also provided a solo hit for Newton-John in 'Hopelessly Devoted to You'*.

She now exchanged the innocence of her *Grease* role for a less cloying and more forceful image which brought considerable success in the eighties, often with film-related songs. Her biggest hits in this vein included 'A Little More Love'* (1978), 'Magic'* and (with the **Electric Light Orchestra**) 'Xanadu', from the 1980 movie *Xanadu*, 1981's 'Physical'* whose accompanying video neatly capitalized on the aerobics craze, and 'Twist of Fate' (1984) from the film *Two of a Kind*, in which she was reunited with Travolta. Her 1980 duets with Cliff Richard ('Suddenly') and Andy Gibb ('I Can't Help It') were gentler ballads. With her long-serving producer Farrar, Newton-John also reached the American Top Twenty with 'Soul Kiss' (1985), the title song from her twelfth album. With a title track by **Elton John** and Bernie Taupin, *The Rumour* was released in 1988.

Concentrating on non-music activities, including her work as a goodwill ambassador for the UN envi-

ronment programme, Newton-John did not release another album until 1990's *Warm and Tender*, a cloying album of lullabies and nursery rhymes inspired by her three-year-old daughter. The 1992 compilation *Back to Basics* contained four new recordings. She followed that with another personal record, *Gaia: One Woman's Journey* (1995), but in the main restricted her later recording to guest appearances, as on the *Highlights from the Main Event* (1998), a live album of the Australian tour she made with John Farnham and Anthony Warlow. In 2000 she was reunited with Farnham when the pair were chosen to sing 'Dare to Dream' at the opening ceremony of the Olympic games.

RED NICHOLS
b. Ernest Loring Nichols, 8 May 1905, Ogden, Utah, USA, d. 28 June 1965, Las Vegas, Nevada

One of the first white musicians to play jazz seriously, Nichols was the most active recording bandleader of the twenties and the leader of the hugely influential Five Pennies.

The son of a professor of music, Nichols played in his father's brass band before deserting 'serious' music for jazz under the influence of the **Original Dixieland Jazz Band** and **Bix Beiderbecke**. In 1923 he travelled to New York and joined Johnny Johnson's orchestra on cornet. Between 1925 – when songwriter **Harry Warren** made his vocal début with a Nichols band – and 1932, Nichols ran his own jazz band while working for Sam Lanin, **Paul Whiteman** and others and at the same time led his own pit orchestra for Broadway shows. The band he put together for **George** and **Ira Gershwin**'s *Strike Up the Band* (1930) included such luminaries as **Benny Goodman**, **Gene Krupa**, **Jack Teagarden**, **Jimmy Dorsey** and **Glenn Miller**. More influential were the series of records he made starting in 1926 as Red Nichols and the Five Pennies. Prior to that he had recorded under a variety of pseudonyms (including the Charleston Chasers, the Arkansas Travellers, the California Redheads and the Louisiana Rhythm Kings). Among the members of the Five Pennies (which despite the band's name generally consisted of between six and ten members) were Jimmy Dorsey, **Eddie Lang**, Miff Mole, Adrian Rollini, **Joe Venuti** and Goodman, with arrangements contributed by Miller. Their records, which included a million-selling version of the **Eddie Cantor** hit 'Ida Sweet as Apple Cider' (Okeh, 1927) and featured Nichols' romantic cornet- and fine ensemble-playing, introduced many musicians and listeners to jazz.

The thirties saw Nichols leading a big dance band and (under the name of Loring Nichols) pit and radio orchestras for such artists as Bob Hope and **Ruth Etting**. In 1944, after briefly retiring from music, he became the featured soloist with **Pee Wee Hunt** and Glen Grey's Casa Loma Orchestra. In 1945 he moved to Los Angeles, formed a small group and signed with Capitol. Then in 1959 *The Five Pennies* was released. A sentimentalized, gaudy biopic with **Danny Kaye** as Nichols and a guest appearance by **Louis Armstrong**, among others, the film's huge success made Nichols a star for the second time. In the words of **Leonard Feather** he 'acquired a loyal following of bankers, brokers, baseball players and assorted Broadway celebrities . . . appealing to their weakness for nostalgia by offering a bland variation . . . of the music that had been associated with him three decades earlier'.

He toured Europe and America in the sixties, delighting audiences with his sweet version of Dixieland until his death.

NILSSON

b. Harry Edward Nelson III, 15 June 1941, New York City, USA, d. 15 January 1994, Agoura Hills, California

A leading pop songwriter of the late sixties and early seventies, Nilsson's two biggest hit recordings came with other composers' material. Nilsson never fully developed his talent for strong, melodic composition, preferring instead to pursue an erratic lifestyle in the late seventies with **John Lennon**, **Ringo Starr** and other nightclubbers.

Nilsson began to write songs while working in a California bank, providing 'Paradise' and 'Here I Sit' for the **Phil Spector**-produced **Ronettes**. When the **Monkees** cut his 'Cuddly Toy' as an album track in 1967, Nilsson secured a recording contract with RCA. *Pandemonium Shadow Show* (1967) contained 'She Sang Hymns out of Tune' and covers of two **Beatles** songs, while *Aerial Ballet* (1968) included a version of **Fred Neil**'s 'Everybody's Talkin'', which was chosen for the soundtrack of the hit movie *Midnight Cowboy* and gave Nilsson an American Top Ten hit in 1969. The film also featured Nilsson's ironic 'I Guess the Lord Must Be in New York City' and in the same year **Three Dog Night** had a million-seller with his composition 'One'.

By now Nilsson's wry, tuneful pieces had won the public approbation of Lennon and his songs were in demand. He composed the score for Otto Preminger's *Skidoo* (1968), while 'Puppy Song' from *Harry* (1969) provided a British hit for **David Cassidy**. In the first of several unexpected moves, Nilsson devoted his next album to the work of **Randy Newman** (*Nilsson Sings Newman*, 1970) and followed it with a set of songs from a whimsical television full-length cartoon, *The Point* (1971), which included the hit 'Me and My Arrow'.

His most commercially successful album was *Nilsson Schmilsson* (1971), which included his biggest hit,

the emotive ballad 'Without You'*, written by Pete Ham and Tom Evans of the British group Badfinger, and further successful singles in 'Jump into the Fire', 'Coconut' and 'Spaceman'. During the next few years, Nilsson's output was eccentrically varied. A collection of his own songs (*Son of Schmilsson*, 1972) was followed by *A Little Touch of Schmilsson in the Night* (1973), a set of standard ballads including **Gus Kahn** and **Walter Donaldson**'s 'Makin' Whoopee' and 'As Time Goes By', the song most closely associated with **Dooley Wilson**, who sang it in *Casablanca* (1942). The album was recorded with the **Gordon Jenkins** orchestra.

Nilsson then collaborated with Starr on the film score *Son of Dracula* (1974) and made *Pussy Cats* (1974). Produced by Lennon, this album included versions of **Bob Dylan**'s 'Subterranean Homesick Blues' and **Bill Haley**'s 'Rock Around the Clock'. This burst of productivity came to an end with *Knnillssonn* (1977). In 1980 wrote the score for Robert Altman's *Popeye* and released *Flash Harry*, which included songs co-written with Lennon, Starr and others.

His later recordings were even more sporadic. In 1988 a collection of out-takes from *Nilsson Schmilsson* was issued as *A Touch More Schmilsson* and in 1992 he contributed to the soundtrack of the Jeff Bridges/Robin Williams movie *The Fisher King*. He had finished recording his first complete album of new material since 1976 shortly before his death some months after he had suffered a major heart attack. A long overdue reissue of his RCA material was released as *Personal Best* in 1995. The forty-eight recordings were personally selected by Nilsson before his death from his RCA recordings. It was followed after his death by the tribute album *For the Love of Harry* (1995) on which the likes of **Randy Newman, Jimmy Webb** and **Joe Ely** sang his songs.

NINE INCH NAILS

Trent Reznor, b. Erie, Pennsylvania, USA

Nine Inch Nails' Trent Reznor played a key role in the development of industrial music in the nineties, as well as inspiring a generation of teens to wear dark trenchcoats and black eyeliner.

Having spent his childhood on a farm in Pennsylvania, Reznor moved to Cleveland and performed in a variety of local rock bands before beginning his Nine Inch Nails project alongside an ever-changing group of session players. His self-produced début, *Pretty Hate Machine* (TVT, 1989), drawing as much on mid-period **David Bowie** as it did on the contemporary industrial rock scene, spent the best part of two years on the US *Billboard* chart and became the benchmark by which other albums of its genre were judged. Later that year Reznor and TVT embarked upon an extended lawsuit that had the effect of stopping him recording. However, the lack of new material failed to stunt the growth of his ever-expanding fanbase.

Reznor eventually negotiated a deal in 1992 to form his own Nothing label and quickly released a pair of EPs, the superior *Broken*, with its high anger quotient, and *Fixed*, a collection of remixes. His second full-length album, *The Downward Spiral* (1994), was a more diverse affair than its predecessors, with a selection of more tranquil pieces providing a break from the relentless pounding beat of the heavier tracks. The US chart-topping album was soon accompanied by *Further Down the Spiral* (1995), an extended EP of other artists' interpretations of NIN songs. By this time Reznor's Nothing Records was also beginning to grow in stature with the addition of **Marilyn Manson** to the roster. After touring to support *The Downward Spiral* for much of 1995 Reznor returned to his studio, resurfacing only to contribute to David Lynch's *Lost Highway* film soundtrack before the eagerly anticipated release of *The Fragile* (1999).

NIRVANA
Kurt Cobain, b. 20 February 1967, d. 9 April 1994; Chris Novoselic, b. 16 May, 1965; Dave Grohl, b. 14 January 1969; Chad Channing; Jason Everman; Pat Smear

Pioneers of the American 'grunge' style of the late eighties which married punk and heavy metal, Nirvana achieved global success while garnering drug lifestyle headlines the likes of which had not been seen since the heyday of the **Rolling Stones**.

The original line-up of guitarist/vocalist Cobain, bassist Novoselic and drummer Channing had formed in Aberdeen, Washington, in 1988, releasing a single, 'Love Buzz'/'Big Cheese', on the influential Seattle label Sub Pop in 1989. For the band's début album, *Bleach* (1989), a second guitarist, Everman, was recruited, but he left the band in 1990, as did Channing. Dan Peters from labelmates Mudhoney played drums on the 1990 single 'Silver', but he had been replaced by Grohl by the time the band signed to Geffen Records in 1991.

The first album under the new deal, *Nevermind* (1991), was a huge success in the US, topping the album chart, and picking up critical plaudits worldwide for its mixture of punk, metal and pop. In the wake of the Top Twenty single 'Smells Like Teen Spirit' (1991), *Nevermind* also became a major success in the UK, with two further hit singles, 'Come as You Are' and 'Lithium', taken from the album. In 1992 Cobain's drug problems and those of his wife Courtney Love (vocalist with grunge band **Hole**) threatened to tear Nirvana apart. At the same time, law suits had been filed against the band from members of English

sixties band Nirvana over the use of the name, and from UK post-punk outfit **Killing Joke**, alleging that the guitar part of 'Smells Like Teen Spirit' was lifted from one of their songs, 'Love Like Blood'. In the absence of any new tracks, a compilation of out-takes and demos was released, *Incesticide* (1992). During this period, Cobain also worked on a spoken-word EP with avant-garde writer William Burroughs, released in 1993 as *The Priest, They Called Him*.

In 1993 Nirvana released *In Utero*, preceded by the hit single, 'Heart Shaped Box'. The album marked a distinct change of direction for the band, with a much more sombre mood than its predecessor. It caused some consternation when previewed to US audiences during shows in which the band experimented with the addition of a second guitarist, Smear, formerly of the Germs, and a cello player. Nevertheless *In Utero* topped the charts on both sides of the Atlantic. Subsequent pressure from censorship groups in America led Geffen to change the cover artwork (which included images of human foetuses) and the title of one track, 'Rape Me', to 'Waif Me'. In April 1994, a few weeks after Cobain's drug overdose in Rome curtailed the group's European tour, Cobain committed suicide. In the wake of his death Nirvana's back catalogue recharted en masse and his wife's band, Hole, had success with *Live Through This* (Geffen, 1994).

In November 1994 MTV's *Unplugged in New York* entered the US charts at No. 1. Further posthumous releases included the *Singles* boxed set (1995) and a live recording, *From the Muddy Banks of the Wishkah* (1996), taped at various points between 1989 and 1994. In 1998 Nick Broomfield's documentary *Kurt and Courtney* caused controversy over its claims that Love was partly responsible for her husband's death, which have since been almost unanimously refuted. The following year Cobain was dubbed 'icon of the nineties' by *Rolling Stone* magazine, who had previously published an anthology in tribute to the singer, *Cobain: By the Editors of Rolling Stone Magazine* (1995).

After Cobain's death, Grohl formed the Foo Fighters, performing all of their eponymous début (Roswell, 1995) himself. Grohl recruited latter-day Nirvana colleague Smear alongside former Sunny Day Real Estate rhythm section Nate Mendel (bass) and William Goldsmith (drums) for live performances, scoring a handful of hit singles with 'This Is a Call', 'I'll Stick Around' and 'For All the Cows'. Foo Fighters had further success with *The Colour and the Shape* (1997) and *There Is Nothing Left to Lose* (1999), despite frequent line-up changes which eventually saw all of the band's original membership replaced within three years.

Novoselic took a more low-key approach to his post-Nirvana output, releasing one eponymous album with his new band Sweet 75 in 1998. He has also spent several years collating material for a forthcoming definitive Nirvana boxed set.

THE NITTY GRITTY DIRT BAND
Jeff Hanna, b. 11 July 1947, Detroit, Michigan, USA; Jimmie Fadden, b. 9 March 1948, Long Beach, California; John McEuen, b. 19 December 1945, Long Beach; Bruce Kunkel; Ralph Taylor Barr; Leslie Steven Thompson; Chris Darrow; John Cable; Jackie Clark

The Dirt Band's widely acclaimed triple-album, *Will the Circle Be Unbroken?* (1972), recorded in Nashville with **Roy Acuff**, **Merle Travis**, **Doc Watson**, Maybelle Carter (of the **Carter Family**) and Earl Scruggs (of **Flatt and Scruggs**) among the guests, is a seminal work. Like the **Byrds**' *Sweetheart of the Rodeo* (1968), it confirmed the interest in country music by rock musicians (and the rock audience). However, unlike the Byrds, who virtually created country-rock overnight with *Sweetheart*, the Dirt Band approached country music from a more traditional, folk perspective, seeing it above all as 'American music'.

The band, originally called the Illegitimate Jug Band, was formed in 1965 in Long Beach with McEuen's brother, William, a disc-jockey and producer, as manager. Signed to Liberty Records in 1966, their first recordings featured an electric mixture of blues, jug-band music, bluegrass – John McEuen was one of the first people to play the five-stringed banjo in a rock context – and original songs by themselves and new songwriters such as **Jackson Browne** (briefly a band member), **Kenny Loggins** and **Randy Newman**. Following the modest hit 'Buy Me for the Rain' (1967), they made an appearance in the film version of *Paint Your Wagon* (1968) before recording *Uncle Charlie and His Dog Teddy* (1970), which gave them their first Top Ten single with the **Jerry Jeff Walker** composition 'Mr Bojangles'. Lighter in feel and more traditionally inclined than **The Band**, but equally concerned with America as their subject matter, the group's *Uncle Charlie* and *All the Good Times* (1971) are among their most engaging works.

In 1972 John McEuen, who regularly worked as a solo performer, initiated and wrote the sleeve note for United Artists' (the restructured Liberty) reissue of its **Bob Wills**' recordings, *Hall of Fame, Bob Wills and Tommy Duncan*. Following *Will the Circle Be Unbroken?*, the band's sound became even more country-fied, though their influences remained wide-ranging: thus comedian Steve Martin first performed 'King Tut', later a Top Twenty single for him in 1978, with the band. In 1977 they were the first American rock band to tour the Soviet Union and in 1980, they secured their second Top Twenty single with the title song from their eleventh album, 'An American Dream', which featured **Linda Ronstadt** singing harmony. The album produced another hit, 'Make a Little Magic', but henceforth they featured in the country, rather than the pop charts. In 1985 they had four country hits, including 'Modern Day Romance' and 'High Horse' and recorded the emphatically traditional album, *Plain Dirt Fashion*, on their new label, Warner Brothers. The retrospective *Twenty Years of Dirt* made the charts in 1986. Subsequently the group moved to Warners, where they recorded the superior *Workin' Band* (1988). More successful was the double-album *Will the Circle Be Unbroken, Volume 2* (MCA, 1989), which, like the 1972 volume, was recorded with numerous guests. Among them were **John Denver**, **John Prine**, **Emmylou Harris** and former **Byrds** Chris Hillman and Roger McGuinn.

Later Nitty Gritty Dirt Band recordings included the Randy Scruggs-produced *Rest of the Dream* (1990), with a title track composed by **John Hiatt**, *Not Fade Away* (1992) and the folksy *Acoustic* (1994). They returned to the charts again with 'Bang Bang'.

JACK NITZSCHE
b. Bernard Nitzsche, 22 April 1937, Michigan, USA, d. 25 August 2000, Los Angeles, California

An eclectic arranger, composer and producer, Nitzsche's career spanned three decades and included collaborations with figures as varied as **Phil Spector** and **Neil Young**.

Raised on a Michigan farm, Nitzsche travelled to Los Angeles in 1955 as a would-be jazz saxophonist but soon drifted into working in the city's burgeoning pop-music industry. In 1959 he wrote 'Bong, Bongo, Bongo' (Original Sound), which was a minor hit for percussionist Preston Epps, and worked as a musical copyist with Sonny Bono (later to become better known for his partnership with **Cher**) at **Art Rupe**'s Speciality label. Nitzsche's big break came when he arranged the **Crystals**' 'He's a Rebel' for Spector in 1962. The following year he had a solo hit with the instrumental 'The Lonely Surfer' on Reprise, for whom he also recorded a series of ephemeral albums such as *Hits of The Beatles* (1964) and *Chopin '66* (1966). More significantly, Nitzsche worked on many of Spector's recordings of the mid-sixties, including 'Da Doo Ron Ron' and 'Then He Kissed Me' (the Crystals), 'Be My Baby' and 'Walking in the Rain' (the **Ronettes**) and 'River Deep Mountain High' (Ike and **Tina Turner**). As a songwriter, with Sonny Bono he was responsible for 'Needles and Pins', a world-wide hit for the **Searchers** in 1964. He also played piano on the **Rolling Stones**' *Out of Our Heads* (1965), *Aftermath* (1966) and *Sticky Fingers* (1971), and composed the score for *Performance* (1970), in which Rolling Stone Mick Jagger had a starring role.

Nitzsche's partnership with Young began when he

produced **Buffalo Springfield**'s 'Expecting to Fly' (1967). He later arranged Young's first solo album and played in his backing group Crazy Horse, whose eponymous 1971 album he produced. His penchant for large-scale arrangements, apparent on the string parts written for Young's 'A Man Needs a Maid' (on *Harvest*, 1972), was given full rein on *St Giles Cripplegate* (Reprise, 1972). Recorded with the London Symphony Orchestra, the album consisted of a series of neo-classical instrumental pieces.

In the mid-seventies Nitzsche concentrated on writing for films. His scores included *The Exorcist* (1974), *One Flew Over the Cuckoo's Nest* (Fantasy, 1975) and *Blue Collar* (MCA, 1978). However, he later returned to the recording studio to produce between 1978 and 1981 three albums for rock band Mink de Ville, as well as works by **Graham Parker** (the superior *Squeezing Out Sparks*, 1979), the **Neville Brothers**, Michelle Phillips (formerly of **The Mamas and the Papas**, whose retrospective *Creeque Alley* he also produced in 1991) and **Rick Nelson** (*Playing to Win*, 1981).

He later returned to film work, providing music or acting as music supervisor for such movies as *An Officer and a Gentleman* (1982), for which he co-authored with his wife, **Buffy Sainte-Marie**, the Oscar-winning song 'Up Where We Belong'. The song was subsequently a worldwide hit for **Joe Cocker** and **Jennifer Warnes**. Other soundtracks included *Breathless* (1983), *Starman* (1984), *9½ Weeks* (1986), *Stand by Me* (1986) and *The Hot Spot* (1990), whose soundtrack included contributions from **Miles Davis** and **John Lee Hooker**. In the nineties he oversaw many retrospective sets, particularly of artists he had earlier worked with, such as the Neville Brothers and Graham Parker. More personal was his production of John Hiatt's *Living a Little, Laughing a Little* (Raven, 1996).

NO DOUBT
Tom Dumont; Tony Kanal, b. India; John Spence, d. December 1987; Eric Stefani; Gwen Stefani; Adrian Young

Ska/New Wave-influenced four-piece No Doubt's uplifting guitar pop was something of an antidote to the relentless anger of much of the nineties' alternative rock bands.

No Doubt were formed in Anaheim in 1987 by twin vocalists Spence and Gwen Stefani with her brother Eric on keyboards, picking up Dumont (guitar), Kanal (bass) and Young (drums) while playing the local party circuit. John Spence committed suicide later the same year, but No Doubt decided to continue, with Stefani becoming the lone singer. The band's profile steadily rose with support slots for the

Red Hot Chili Peppers and Ziggy Marley, attracting the attention of Interscope Records, who signed them in 1991.

No Doubt released their eponymous début album in 1992, a diverse mix of seventies rock guitar and **Madness**-inspired two-tone/pop, but it failed to sell in a grunge-dominated market. In the midst of a feud with their record label over poor sales the band distributed the raw, punk-influenced *Beacon Street Collection* (1994) themselves.

Now reduced to a quartet after the departure of Eric Stefani to pursue a burgeoning career in animation, No Doubt had their breakthrough with *Tragic Kingdom* (1996), which spawned the hit singles 'Just a Girl' and 'Spiderwebs' and served as an aural document of the end of a seven-year relationship between Gwen Stefani and Tony Kanal. 'Don't Speak' (1997) topped the British chart as the band became a big hit on the international stage. No Doubt returned with the epic-styled 'New' in 1999. That was included in the muted *Return of Saturn* (2000). Produced by Glenn Ballard, best known for his collaboration with **Alanis Morissette**, it continued the odd marriage of screeching vocals and pop songs ('Ex-Girlfriend') to good effect.

RAY NOBLE
b. Stanley Raymond Noble, 17 December 1903, Brighton, Sussex, England, d. 4 April 1978, London

Bandleader and songwriter Noble led one of the most popular and sweetest-sounding British recording bands of the early thirties. He was also the first British bandleader to establish himself in America.

Noble started writing songs while still at school. His first hit was 'Nobody's Fool but Your Own' (1928), but after winning an arranging contest sponsored by *Melody Maker* he had greater success as a recording artist and arranger. He worked briefly as an arranger with **Jack Payne** in 1929 before being appointed musical director of HMV. For five years with the New Mayfair Orchestra, HMV's 'house band' (in fact the pick of London's musicians, many from **Lew Stone**'s band), Noble produced the smoothest sounding dance music in Britain and was one of the few British artists to sell records in large quantities in America. Once established as a recording artist, he recorded many of his own compositions, invariably with **Al Bowlly** on vocals until they parted company in 1936. These included 'Good Night Sweetheart' (1931), 'By the Fireside', the much-recorded 'Love Is the Sweetest Thing' (1932), which was successfully revived by **Peter Skellern** in 1978, 'The Very Thought of You' (1934), which gave **Rick Nelson** and **Tony Bennett** hits in 1964 and 1965, respectively, 'The Touch of Your Lips' (1936) and 'Cherokee' (1938).

Noble also contributed songs to several British films of the period, including *Princess Charming* (1934).

His strong American record sales led to an invitation to perform there, and in 1934, taking only Bowlly and drummer Bill Harty, Noble went to New York where **Glenn Miller** put together a band of top American musicians for him. Noble was a success in America, but his recordings, despite a million-selling revival of the 1909 composition 'By the Light of the Silvery Moon' (Columbia, 1941), with vocals by Snooky Lanson, later the featured singer on *Your Hit Parade*, were generally inferior. In England, he worked with adaptable session musicians, in America with individual stylists, such as Charlie Spivak on trumpet and George Van Eps on guitar, who were unwillingly to bend their playing to Noble's style. Nonetheless, he prospered, appearing in films (including *The Big Broadcast of 1936*, in which **Bing Crosby** and **Ethel Merman** duetted in his 'Why the Stars Come out Tonight', and *A Damsel in Distress*, 1937, with **Fred Astaire**) and on radio (with ventriloquist Edgar Bergen) where his silly-ass persona won him a wide audience.

In the early fifties, Noble ended his lengthy association with Bergen and retired to Santa Barbara.

IVOR NOVELLO
b. David Ivor Davies, 15 January 1893, Cardiff, Wales, d. 6 March 1951, London

In many ways Novello's career paralleled that of **Noël Coward**. Both were songwriters, playwrights, actors, producers (and owners of houses in Jamaica), and both were transitional artists, whose (musical) work most often looked back to old forms while laying the groundwork for new ones. Thus, though in Sheridan Morley's phrase, 'Ivor smiled on until 1951', his heyday was the thirties when, with his soulful good looks, he was the epitome of the matinée idol.

The son of a music teacher, Novello went to Magdalen College, Cambridge, as a choral scholar, but quickly turned from a career in serious music to the theatre. His first song, 'Spring of the Year', was published in 1910, and his first hit came later that year with 'The Little Damozel', before he became a celebrity overnight as the composer (with words by Lena Guilbert Ford) of the stirring, patriotic 'Till the Boys Come Home' (better known as 'Keep the Home Fires Burning') in 1914. For the most part, however, his songs were firmly in the operetta tradition until 1921 when he composed the score for *A–Z*, in which **Jack Buchanan** introduced the witty novelty 'And Her Mother Came Too'.

During the twenties and thirties Novello combined writing musicals (generally with lyricist Christopher Hassall) with a career as an actor-manager, mostly producing melodramas and comedies, and a film career, in which he appeared in such diverse works as *Bonnie Prince Charlie* (1923) and Alfred Hitchcock's *The Lodger* (1926). The first important Novello musical was *Glamorous Night* (1935). Not an integrated musical in the contemporary American style, it used songs evocatively to punctuate a melodramatic plot. His major musicals were *Crest of a Wave* (1937), which included 'Rose of England'; *The Dancing Years* (1939), a bitter-sweet romance with topical references to Nazism which was filmed in 1950; and *Perchance to Dream* (1945), for which Novello wrote both music and lyrics. *Perchance* included his best-remembered song, 'We'll Gather Lilacs', whose theme of lovers parting and hoping to meet again captured the mood of the last days of the Second World War.

In 1947 Novello was a founding member of the Songwriters' Guild (since renamed the British Academy of Songwriters, Composers and Authors), formed by a group of British composers to campaign for greater broadcast time to be given to British material – at the time the proportion of British songs played on the BBC was as low as fifteen per cent. After Novello's death, the academy instituted the Ivor Novello awards, granted annually for outstanding contributions to British popular music.

NUCLEUS
Ian Carr, b. 21 April 1933, Dumfries, Scotland; Jeff Clyne (replaced by Roy Babbington); Karl Jenkins (replaced by Dave MacRae); John Marshall; Brian Smith; Chris Spedding, b. 17 June 1944, Sheffield, Yorkshire, England (replaced by Allan Holdsworth)

A pioneering jazz-rock band led by trumpeter Carr, Nucleus included many leading British instrumentalists of the seventies in its ranks.

With his brother Mike, Carr led modern jazz group the EmCee Five in Newcastle in the early sixties. The band also included future synthesizer pioneer and member of Tonto's Expanding Head Band, Malcolm Cecil, on bass. Carr became one of the most highly regarded British jazz musicians through a lengthy collaboration with tenor-sax-player Don Rendell and in 1969 he founded Nucleus. Intended to explore the borderline of jazz and rock through the use of electronics and amplification, the band was an immediate success, winning first prize at the Montreux Jazz Festival and appearing at the Newport Jazz Festival in 1970. In the same year, Nucleus signed to Vertigo, Philips' newly established 'progressive' label.

Elastic Rock and *We'll Talk About It Later* (1970) featured Jenkins on keyboards and baritone sax, the rhythm section of Marshall (drums) and Clyne (bass) and the rock guitar of Spedding, whose previous credits had included **Jack Bruce**'s *Songs for a Tailor* album. After *Solar Plexus* (1971), whose title track was commissioned from Spedding by the Arts Council, all left Nucleus. Marshall and Jenkins joined jazz-fusion group **Soft Machine** while Spedding formed rock band Sharks before moving on to a prolific session and touring career.

With the ever-present Smith (clarinet), Carr recorded six more albums for Vertigo before moving to Capitol in 1977 for *In Flagrante Delicto* and *Out of the Long Dark* (1979). In 1978 Nucleus toured India and in 1984 the group performed in Latin America. From the mid-eighties Carr concentrated on teaching at London's Guildhall School of Music, composing such pieces as 'Spirit of the Place' (1986) and writing about jazz.

In 1973 Carr published *Music Outside*, an account of the group's genesis in the context of the British jazz scene. He also wrote biographies of **Miles Davis** (1982) and **Keith Jarrett** (1991), and with Digby Fairweather and Brian Priestley compiled the authoritative reference work *Jazz, the Essential Companion* (1987).

TED NUGENT
b. 13 December 1948, Detroit, Michigan, USA

One of heavy-metal's founding fathers, Nugent showed unwavering devotion over twenty years to the genre's basic elements. Although a dextrous guitarist, his commitment to the precept 'if it's too loud, you're too old' left him partially deaf by the eighties while his songs seldom deviated from the twin macho themes of aggression and misogyny.

The son of an army sergeant, he played in high-school bands the Royal High Boys and the Lourds, which once opened for the **Supremes**. In 1964 Nugent formed the Amboy Dukes, named after a fictional street gang. Their first recordings, for the Detroit-based Mainstream label, included a minor hit with a garage-band version of the R&B standard 'Baby Please Don't Go' (1967). The group had a Top Twenty hit with the title track from *Journey to the Center of the Mind* (1968), which featured singer Rusty Day and Rick Lober on keyboards. In 1968–9, the Amboy Dukes toured with **Jimi Hendrix** and **Cream**. After *Migration* (1969), the group moved to Polydor for *Marriage on the Rocks* (1970) and *Survival of the Fittest* (1971).

By this time, Nugent's high-energy guitar solos were the focus of the band and in the early seventies, ever publicity conscious, he staged guitar duels with such rivals as Wayne Kramer of the **MC5** and **Iron Butterfly**'s Mike Pinera as part of the band's stage act. Another label change took Nugent and the Amboy Dukes to Discreet but the resulting albums sold poorly. In 1975 Nugent signed a solo contract with Epic and recorded an eponymous album with Derek

St Holmes (vocals and guitar), Rob Grange (bass) and drummer Cliff Davies.

Record sales improved with *Free for All* (1976), which introduced **Meat Loaf** as guest vocalist, while *Cat Scratch Fever* (1977) was Nugent's most successful album, reaching the American Top Twenty. He went on to make six more albums for Epic, all of which sold in considerable numbers to heavy-metal listeners in Europe and America. Despite a label change to Atlantic for *Nugent* (1982), *Penetrator* (1984) and *Little Miss Dangerous* (1986), Nugent's fundamentalist approach remained unchanged, although sales gradually diminished. After one more album for Atlantic, *If You Can't Lick 'Em . . .* (1988), he formed the lighter Damn Yankees with ex-**Styx** guitarist Tommy Shaw, bassist Jack Blades and drummer Michael Cartellone. Their eponymous début (1990) made the American Top Twenty, as did its follow-up, *Don't Tread* (1992). *Out of Control* (1993), a double-album retrospective of his days at Sony, was his most noteworthy release of the nineties. It was followed by the anti-gun control *Spirit of the World* (1995).

GARY NUMAN
b. Gary Anthony James Webb, 8 March 1958, London, England

Numan was a precursor of the wave of synthesizer-based music which washed over the British charts in the early eighties. But despite his long string of hits, he left little mark on later musicians. His prime achievement was as an entrepreneur, employing family members as his staff and investing his earnings from music in boats and aircraft. Unsurprisingly, he was one of the few rock performers to give fulsome public support to Margaret Thatcher's re-election campaign of 1983.

He began as a punk guitarist with the Lasers, who became Tubeway Army and cut two singles for Beggars Banquet in 1979. By now Numan was entranced with the electronic sounds of **Kraftwerk**, **Ultravox** and **David Bowie** and the group split, with the recalcitrant punk element forming Station Bombers. With bassist Paul Gardiner and his uncle Jess on drums, Numan released *Tubeway Army* (1979).

Replicas (1979) contained the song about robots 'Are "Friends" Electric?', whose repetitive 'futurist' sound took both single and album to No. 1 in Britain. A few months later, Numan repeated the process with *The Pleasure Principle* and 'Cars', his only American hit. Also in 1979, he provided songs for **Robert Palmer**'s album, *The Clue*. The electronics plus sci-fi lyrics formula provided more hits over the next three years. They included 'I Die You Die' (1980), 'She's Got Claws' (1981), 'We Take Mystery (To Bed)' (1982) and 'Warriors' (1983), which included guest appearances by **Japan**'s Mick Karn and Roger Taylor of **Queen**. In 1984 Numan set up his own Numa label, releasing the live double-album *White Noise* and *The Fung* (1985).

The Numa records sold poorly but in 1986 he returned to the Top Twenty with a remixed version of 'Cars'. In 1988 he signed to Illegal, releasing *Metal Rhythm*. Further albums followed: *Skin Mechanic* (1989), *Outland* (1991) and *Machine and Soul* (1993). Largely sticking to the gloomy synth-pop formula of his earlier material, none of his later albums of original material, which included *Sacrifice* (1994) and *Exile* (1997), made any significant impression on the charts, although his annual tours were well attended by his loyal cult following. The retrospective *Premier Hits* (1996) was far more successful, reaching the UK Top Twenty. He followed that with *Pure* (Eagle, 2000), another essay in doomed gothicism.

NWA

Dr Dre, b. Andre Young, 1964, Los Angeles, California, USA; Ice Cube, b. O'Shea Jackson, 1959, Los Angeles; Eazy-E, b. Eric Wright; MC Ren, b. Lorenzo Patterson, Compton, Los Angeles; DJ Yella, b. Antoine Carraby, Compton

The most notorious and well-publicized of the new school of US rap, NWA sold equally well to black and white teenagers. Since the group split up, most of its members have had successful solo careers.

Prior to the formation of NWA, **Dr Dre**, MC Ren and DJ Yella had been members of the hip-hop group World Class Wreckin' Cru, while **Ice Cube** had fronted CIA with producer Sir Jink and K-Dee. With the arrival of rapper (and former drug dealer) Eric Wright (Eazy-E), the group became NWA (Niggaz With Attitude). Their début single, Ice Cube's 'Boyz N the Hood', was released in 1986 on Eazy-E's Ruthless label. It was followed by 'Dope Man' (1987) and *Straight Outta Compton* (1989). With these tracks, NWA launched the West Coast style of 'gangsta rap'. The uncompromising lyrics of such tracks as 'Boyz N the Hood', 'Gangsta Gangsta' and 'Fuck the Police' luridly described life on the streets of the Compton ghetto of Los Angeles without the distancing political or religious perspective of East Coast rap. The group's videos were banned by MTV and in some cities they were prevented from performing by local police officials.

Ice Cube left the group to start a solo career shortly before NWA followed up with *Efil4Zaggin* (1991). It entered the US pop charts at No. 2 and was the subject of an unsuccessful prosecution for obscenity in the UK. In 1992 they released *Appetite for Destruction*, an appropriate title for Dre who has several convictions for assault.

Several members of NWA had issued solo records in parallel with the group's work and after the group split each member followed a solo career. Dr Dre's and Ice Cube's prolific output is dealt with in separate entries. Eazy-E issued *Eazy Duz It* (1989) and in 1993 *It's on (Dr Dre 187um) Killa*, a direct attack on his former colleague. MC Ren made the EP *Kizz My Black Azz* before recording *Shock of the Hour* (1993), a mix of gangsta and Islamic songs whose producers included the Danish duo Solid Productions.

LAURA NYRO

b. 18 October 1947, New York City, USA, d. 8 April 1997

An inventive singer-songwriter of the seventies, Nyro forged a style that fused gospel and New York pop-soul. With a singing range of three octaves, her vocal gymnastics rivalled those of **Joni Mitchell** and foreshadowed **Kate Bush**.

The daughter of a jazz trumpeter, Nyro's precocious songwriting ability – she began composing at the age of eight – led to a recording contract with Verve in 1966. Produced by Milt Okun, *More Than a New Discovery* sold poorly but contained material which later provided hits for other artists. 'Wedding Bell Blues' was a 1969 No. 1 for the Fifth Dimension, 'And When I Die' was a million-seller for **Blood, Sweat and Tears** while **Barbra Streisand** recorded 'Stoney End' in 1970.

She appeared at the 1967 Monterey Pop Festival inappropriately dressed in an outfit that looked forward to glam-rock and was a failure, but under the managerial guidance of David Geffen she signed to Columbia and between 1968 and 1971 recorded a highly regarded series of albums. *Eli and the 13th Confession* (1968), produced by former **Four Seasons** member Charles Callello, introduced Nyro's characteristic mix of Catholic and street-corner imagery and also included further hits for the Fifth Dimension ('Stoned Soul Picnic' and 'Sweet Blindness') and **Three Dog Night** ('Eli's Coming').

New York Tendaberry (1969), co-produced by Roy Halee with arrangements by Jimmy Haskell, contained more intense and idiosyncratic material like the dark and violent 'Tom Cat Goodbye' and the forbidding 'Captain Saint Lucifer'. The producer of *Christmas and the Bead of Sweat* (1970) was **Arif Mardin** and the backing musicians included Alice Coltrane and Duane Allman of the **Allman Brothers Band**. It was followed by *Gonna Take a Miracle* (1971). Containing cover-versions of such songs as **Martha and the Vandellas**' 'Dancing in the Street', the album was Nyro's tribute to the New York music of the sixties which had inspired her own work. Among the highlights were *a cappella* versions of the **Crystals**' 'Da Doo Ron Ron' (under the title, 'I Met Him on a

Sunday') and the Miracles' 'You Really Got a Hold on Me', on which Nyro was joined by **Patti Labelle** and her trio Labelle.

She did not record again until *Smile* (1975), which contained sharply observed songs of marital disintegration and a disillusioned commentary on the music business. *Season of Light* (1977) was an uneven live album but *Nested* (1978) included 'My Innocence' and the elegiac 'American Dreamer', songs which matched the best of Nyro's earlier work. In 1984 she released *Mother's Spiritual* which added a pantheistic note to her work. *Live at the Bottom Line* (1989) found Nyro in good voice and it produced eight new songs, including the ecologically-minded 'The Wild World', and the zany 'Japanese Restaurant Song'.

Her only original of the nineties was *Walk the Dog & Lite the Lite* (Columbia, 1994), which recalled *Smile* and set her always intriguing lyrics against a sparse backdrop.

PAUL OAKENFOLD
b. 1961, Mile End, London, England

Paul Oakenfold was arguably the most successful international DJ to emerge from the 1988 house-music explosion. He was a key figure in the early years of the genre, through his various London club nights and his production and remix work. He later became the leading exponent of the 'trance' house sound.

Oakenfold grew up in north London, studying cookery at college and then working as a chef. In the early 1980s he moved to New York, where he worked for a number of record companies and developed a taste for the early house sounds being played at the Paradise Garage club by **Larry Levan**.

Moving back to London, Oakenfold worked in A&R for record labels including Def Jam and Champion, for whom he first remixed on Fresh Prince's 'Girls Ain't Nothing but Trouble'. Under the influence of DJ friend Trevor Fung, he also began learning how to DJ. At this time Oakenfold and Fung also began visiting the Mediterranean island of Ibiza. A trip to the island in 1987 with Fung and others including Danny Rampling exposed Oakenfold to the sounds of acid and Chicago house. Returning home, Oakenfold and Rampling sought to bring this 'Balearic' sound back to the UK – Rampling through his legendary Shoom club, Oakenfold through his Future and Spectrum club nights. These were both critical clubs in the development of house music in Britain. Spectrum was a pure acid-house party, but Future saw dance beats mixed up with indie guitar bands like the **Stone Roses** and the **Happy Mondays**.

The nights established Oakenfold as a leading DJ in the UK, and also made him an in-demand remixer and producer. In 1989 and 1990 he worked with the Happy Mondays, remixing their 'Wrote for Luck' single and then producing their third album, *Pills 'n' Thrills and Bellyaches*. He also produced classic remixes of the Shamen's 'Pro-Gen' – later retitled 'Move Any Mountain' – and **Massive Attack**'s 'Unfinished Sympathy'.

In 1989 Oakenfold had set up his own label, Perfecto, which through the 1990s established itself as a home for the 'Goa trance' sound, a mainly instrumental style of house music heavily dependent on sweeping, ethereal synthesizer sounds and a classically European – as opposed to Afro-American – sense of melody. The label's most successful signings included BT and Grace.

Oakenfold would bring this trance style to bear on future remix work, notably his reworking of **U2**'s 'Even Better than the Real Thing' in 1991. His relationship with U2 extended to him accompanying the band on their Zoo TV world tour in the early 1990s, acting as their warm-up DJ and thereby becoming perhaps the world's first 'stadium DJ'. In 1997 he began a DJ residency at the Cream club in Liverpool which lasted two years and confirmed him as the premier British DJ of his generation.

OASIS
Paul 'Bonehead' Arthurs, b. 23 June 1965, Manchester, England (replaced by Gem Archer); William John Paul Gallagher, b. 21 September 1972, Manchester; Noel Thomas Gallagher, b. 29 May 1967, Manchester; Tony McCaroll (replaced by Alan White); Paul 'Guigsy' McGuigan, b. 9 May 1971 (replaced by Andy Bell)

Drawing on thirty years of British rock, from their much-cherished **Beatles** to **T Rex** and the **Jam**, and borrowing the tough image of the **Rolling Stones**, Oasis were one of the most popular bands of the mid-nineties. The mixture of exuberance and anger, crafted in anthemic-like recordings, won them an audience that spanned 10 Downing Street and the queues for unemployment benefits and made them a fixture in media articles by journalists determined to understand what was happening to British youth. The group's Britishness was their only limiting feature, meaning that although they had significant success outside the UK, they meant less overseas. Oasis were also responsible for returning guitar-pop to the British charts.

Liam Gallagher (vocals), Arthurs (guitar), McGuigan (bass) and McCaroll (drums) formed Rain in 1993, before Liam's older brother Noel (lead guitar/vocals) joined, renaming the band Oasis and taking over all songwriting duties. The band rehearsed intensively for a year before signing with Creation Records. The band's profile rose significantly on the strength of their early singles, 'Supersonic', 'Shakermaker' and 'Live Forever', with first album *Definitely Maybe* (1994), a raw document of life on the dole with ambitions of superstardom, entering the UK chart at Number One and becoming the fastest-selling début in British history. The album also reached the US *Billboard* charts as the band toured solidly, and hit number two back home with the string-led 'Whatever'.

Oasis began 1995 with further promotional work in

America, before replacing drummer McCaroll with Alan White, the only member of the band not to hail from Manchester. The band topped the British chart with 'Some Might Say' before beginning a (PR-created) feud with **Blur**, which culminated in both bands releasing new singles on the same day. While Blur's 'Country House' beat 'Roll with It' to the number one spot, Oasis outperformed their rivals with (What's the Story) Morning Glory? (1995), a more acoustic guitar-led collection which became one of the bestselling British albums ever. The album spawned two further hit singles, 'Wonderwall' and 'Don't Look Back in Anger' (1996), and reached the US Top Ten, leading to a successful world tour which culminated in two huge shows at Knebworth in the summer of 1996, drawing the largest-ever audience for a British concert. Noel Gallagher topped the charts again later in the year with the **Chemical Brothers** on their 'Setting Son' collaboration.

Oasis spent the best part of a year recording their third LP, Be Here Now (1997), which was hugely popular initially but lead to a vast media backlash after failing to live up to the impossible hype that had preceded its release. The album included two more UK Number One singles, 'D' You Know What I Mean' and the epic 'All Around the World', heavily reminiscent of The Beatles' 'Hey Jude' and with an accompanying video based on Yellow Submarine. Another worldwide tour followed before the band disappeared into the studio, as the media became fixated with the relationship between Liam Gallagher and pop star-turned-actress Patsy Kensit.

The B-sides collection, The Masterplan (1998), was intended as a stop-gap before the release of Oasis's fourth studio album. Arthurs and McGuigan left the band amicably in 1999 after the completion of the album, leaving the Gallagher brothers as the only original members of the group. The new group, with Andy Bell and Gem Archer, formerly of Heavy Stereo, replacing McGuigan and Arthurs, released Standing on the Shoulder of Giants in 2000.

Released into a new environment, in which the likes of **Shania Twain**, the **Backstreet Boys** and Norman '**Fatboy Slim**' Cook better reflected the interests of British youth, on a new label, Big Brother, which replaced Creation after its founder and their manager Alan McGhee quit the record industry in disgust, and at a time where Liam Gallagher's public private life was garnering more column inches than the group's music, the album was much attacked on its release. A mark of how limited were its ambitions was the general concern with sounding contemporary that ran through the album, most noticeable in its weak borrowings from the culture and sounds of club culture on the first single, 'Go Let It Out'. Equally problematic was the drift to weighty balladry in 'Roll It Over'.

In retrospect, the album helped confirm the enormous advances made by the likes of The Beatles, the Rolling Stones and the **Byrds.** In the sixties and seventies, over a series of albums, they continued to point new ways forward for popular music; in the nineties the likes of Oasis and **Pulp** seem unable to make more than snapshot-type classics, albums of real significance, but albums far greater than the body of work of their creators. While Standing on the Shoulder of Giants was only a moderate commercial success, the continual fights during the tour to support it gave added credence to the sense of a band on the edge of (self-) destruction. Later the same year Oasis issued a double live album, Familiar to Millions, recorded at the first of two tempestuous gigs at Wembley stadium in the summer. It was accompanied by a live DVD/video, which also featured documentary footage shot by Grant Gee, director of **Radiohead**'s Meeting People Is Easy.

EBENEZER OBEY
b. 27 August 1942, Abeokuta, Nigeria

Chief Ebenezer Obey is a leading exponent of juju music, a Yoruba style which combines electric guitars with traditional lyrics and percussion instruments.

Obey sang in a mission-school choir and later played 'mambo' street music on agidigbo (thumb piano) but the major influence on his musical development was I. K. Dairo, who popularized juju in the sixties with his band the Blue Spots.

Obey moved to Lagos in the early sixties and played congas with the Fatayi Rolling Dollar band before forming his first group, the International Brothers, in 1964. The group was unique among juju bands in having twin lead guitars and an electric bass. Obey first recorded later in 1964 ('Ewa Woman Ojumi Ri') and had his first hit in 1965, 'Omo Lami'. He had an even bigger hit, 'Olo Mi Gbo Temi', two years later.

During the seventies Obey's style came to be known as 'miliki' (enjoyment), after the title of one of his best-known songs, 'Esa Ma Miliki'. The moralizing lyrics on his recordings for Decca expressed orthodox sentiments on the political and social issues of the day, while the sound was heavier and faster than Dairo's juju music. It also contrasted with the approach of his foremost rival **King Sunny Ade**, who made greater use of Western synthesizer technology. Another difference between the two was religion: Ade's background was that of traditional Yoruba beliefs, Obey's of traditional Christian values. Moreover, whereas Ade became increasingly critical of the Nigerian government, Obey became an unofficial spokesman of sorts, releasing a song explaining why the government switched to driving on the right-hand side, for example, in 1972 and defending the government's austerity programme with *Operation Feed the Nation* (1976).

His first record releases outside Nigeria came in 1980 when Obey licensed six albums to British-based OTI Records. Among them were *Current Affairs* and *What God Has Joined Together*. However, they did not sell beyond the European expatriate Nigerian community. In 1983 Obey's records were issued in Europe through a deal with Virgin which released the funk inflected *Je Ka Jo* and a greatest hits package, *Miliki Plus*. Sterns later released *Solution* (1985). In 1985 and 1986 Obey toured North America and in 1989 recorded *Count Your Blessings*. In the same year, the Dutch label Provogue issued the first CD of Obey's work, *Get Your Jujus Out*.

OCEAN COLOUR SCENE
Steve Cradock; Simon Fowler; Oscar Harrison; Damon Minchella

Following the lead of mod revivalists the **Jam** and the **Faces**, Ocean Colour Scene were one of the most popular bands in Britain in the mid-nineties in the wake of the **Oasis**-led resurgence of traditional guitar-based rock.

Ocean Colour Scene formed from the ashes of the **Velvet Underground**-influenced trio the Fanatics, when Fowler (vocals), Harrison (drums) and Minchella (bass) recruited Cradock (guitar), in Birmingham, England, in 1989. They managed to build up a small fanbase over the next year, signing with local label !Phfft and receiving good reviews for the single 'Sway' (1990) before heading into the studio to record their full-length début. This turned out to be a lengthy process, as !Phfft were acquired by Fontana, who demanded that the band re-record the album three times. After poor sales for *Ocean Colour Scene* (1992) the band left Fontana under acrimonious circumstances.

By 1993 Ocean Colour Scene had almost ceased to exist after Cradock, Fowler and Minchella found themselves playing in **Paul Weller**'s backing band. However, they continued to rehearse, and won the patronage of Oasis's Noel Gallagher, who offered them a support slot on their nationwide tour of 1994. This gave Ocean Colour Scene the required exposure, and won them a deal with MCA. English DJ Chris Evans made their comeback single, 'The Riverboat Song' (1996), the theme to his *TFI Friday* TV show. It reached No. 15 in the UK chart, while *Mosley Shoals* (1996) became one of the year's bestsellers on the back of 'The Day We Caught the Train' and 'You've Got It Bad'. Outside the UK, like the **Kinks** in the sixties and, to a lesser extent, Oasis, the group's Britishness meant that the band remained little more than a cult act.

Ocean Colour Scene returned in 1997 with the rarities collection *B-Sides, Seasides and Free Rides* before the release of *Marchin' Already* later the same year. The first single from the album, 'Hundred Mile High City', became their biggest hit to date, entering the British chart at No. 2. They confirmed their position as one of Britain's most popular bands with their fourth studio album, *One from the Modern* (1999), which included the hit single 'Profit in Peace'.

BILLY OCEAN
b. Leslie Sebastian Charles, 21 January 1950, Trinidad

The most successful British-based soul singer, Billy Ocean had two distinct series of hits, firstly with GTO in the late seventies and then with Jive in the eighties when the film theme 'When the Going Gets Tough (the Tough Get Going)'* (1986) was a worldwide success.

Raised in London's East End, Ocean first sang with local groups Shades of Midnight and Dry Ice before briefly joining bandleader Ken Mackintosh. He recorded as Joshua (for Louvigny-Marquee), as Les Charles for Spark, and as Scorched Earth for Youngblood (1974) before singing to GTO in 1975.

Renamed Billy Ocean, he co-wrote 'Whose Little Girl Are You?' and the Top Ten hit 'Love Really Hurts without You' (1976) with producer Ben Findon. Further hits followed with 'L.O.D. (Love on Delivery)', 'Stop Me (If You've Heard It All Before)' and 'Red Light Spells Danger' (1977). Later releases, such as 'American Hearts' (1979) and 'Are You Ready' (1980) were only minor hits, however, and when GTO collapsed, Ocean signed to Epic.

There he released *Inner Feelings* (1982) before moving to Jive. Produced and co-written by Keith Diamond, Ocean's first single appeared as 'European Queen' in Britain and 'Caribbean Queen'* in America where it reached No. 1. A British re-release of 'Caribbean Queen' brought a Top Ten hit and the title track from *Suddenly* (1984) and 'Lover Boy' were also successful.

Featured on the soundtrack of *The Jewel of the Nile*, the slick 'When the Going Gets Tough' was an international hit. Even more successful was 'There'll Be Sad Songs'*, his second American chart-topper. Later hits included the title track from *Love Zone* (1986) and 'Love Is Forever' (1987). Co-written and produced by Robert John 'Mutt' Lange, the intense 'Get outta My Dreams, Get into My Car'* from *Tear Down These Walls* gave Ocean a third American No. 1. The 1989 *Greatest Hits* collection made the British Top Five, but Ocean did not release another album until *Time to Move on* in 1993. This featured a strong contemporary dance feel, exemplified by the single 'Pressure'. Its sales, however, failed to match those of its predecessors. In 1999 a new collection of Ocean hits, *Love is Forever*, was released, and a new version of 'When the Going Gets Tough' by boy group **Boyzone** topped the UK charts.

PHIL OCHS
b. 19 December 1940, El Paso, Texas, USA, d. 9 April 1976, Far Rockaway, New York

With his dramatic clear voice Ochs was the finest topical folk singer of his generation. Like **Woody Guthrie**, he was as much a celebrator as a harsh critic of America. However, as the liberal climate that spawned him ebbed, Ochs' career floundered. It is only in retrospect that his later work, which confusingly saw him singing rock'n'roll and overwrought would-be epics in the manner of **Bob Dylan**, as well as songs of protest, has been positively revalued.

From a middle-class background, Ochs attended a military academy before going to Ohio State University, where he wrote his first song, 'Ballad of the Cuban Invasion' (which took a pro-Castro stance), and majored in journalism. The journalistic approach was central to his songwriting, a fact signalled by the reference to the motto of the *New York Times* in the title of his début album. He briefly joined the Singing Socialists before travelling to Cleveland and in 1961 to New York, where he soon became one of the group of singers associated with the magazine *Broadside*. Signed to Elektra, his first album was *All the News That's Fit to Sing* (1964), which included the passionate 'The Power and the Glory' and 'Bound for Glory', a tribute to Guthrie, a surprisingly effective adaptation of Edgar Allan Poe's poem 'The Bells', and a number of lesser topical songs ('The Thresher', 'Talking Vietnam Blues').

I Ain't Marchin' Anymore (1965) and *Phil Ochs in Concert* (1966) were far more assured. The first included the best of his early protest songs in the title song, 'Draft Dodger Rag' and 'Here's to the State of Mississippi', while the second included 'There But for Fortune' (a hit for **Joan Baez** in 1965), his first epic 'The Ringing of Revolution', the bitterly comic 'Love Me I'm a Liberal' and 'Changes', his first mature love song.

Pleasures of the Harbor (A&M, 1967) saw Ochs straining to match Dylan on songs like 'The Crucifixion' and the title song. The result was an impressive display of high romanticism (intensified by the backing provided by producer Larry Marks, which included former musical director of the **Four Preps**, pianist Lincoln Mayorga), but more successful were Ochs' deft satires, notably 'Outside of a Small Circle of Friends', one of his best-known songs. *Tape from California* (1968), produced by **Van Dyke Parks**, was less successful. The best of the songs were 'When in Rome', Ochs' answer to Dylan's 'Desolation Row', the

beautifully sung 'Joe Hill' and 'The War Is Over', but more significantly the album introduced the sound of rock'n'roll that remained the one constant in Ochs' subsequent recording career. *Rehearsals for Retirement* (1969), made with the riots at the Democratic Convention of 1968 (which Ochs had attended) in mind, is the singer's bitterest album, an unsuccessful but moving attempt at reassessment. It was followed by *Greatest Hits* (1970, which despite its title and the cover which saw Ochs in a gold lamé suit à la **Elvis Presley** was not a collection of Ochs' 'greatest hits') and his last album, *Gunfight at Carnegie Hall* (1974), in which Ochs sang songs by **Buddy Holly**, Presley and **Merle Haggard** as well as his own compositions in a failed attempt to extend his audience beyond the folk arena.

After his suicide in 1976, A&M released a double compilation album, the aptly titled *Chords of Fame* (1976). Subsequent CD reissues of his early albums by Rykodisc in the nineties and releases of live recordings by Folkways and Rhino further enhanced his reputation. Ochs' story is well told in Marc Eliot's *Death of a Rebel*.

SINEAD O'CONNOR
b. 12 December 1966, Glenageary, Ireland

The controversial Sinead O'Connor made some of the most arresting pop music of the early nineties.

She spent her early years in Dublin where she briefly studied music before joining rock band Ton Ton Macoute in 1985. O'Connor added vocals to soundtrack music composed by U2's The Edge to the film *Captive* before leaving the group to sign a solo recording deal with London-based label Ensign.

O'Connor was a guest vocalist on World Party's *Private Revolution* before releasing 'Troy' (1987) and 'Mandinka' (1988), a UK Top Twenty hit. The début album, *The Lion and the Cobra*, was produced by O'Connor herself and was a minor hit on both sides of the Atlantic. O'Connor's striking appearance with shaved head had attracted considerable publicity and her greatest commercial success came in 1990 when she released a version of the **Prince** composition, 'Nothing Compares 2 U'. With a sparse arrangement by Jazzie B and Nellee Hooper of **Soul II Soul**, O'Connor's impassioned delivery took the track to the top of the charts in the US and the UK. John Murphy's video of the song won numerous awards. Almost immediately, *I Do Not Want What I Haven't Got* topped charts all over the world. Co-produced by O'Connor with Hooper, it included 'I Feel So Different', which incorporated a prayer by the theologian Reinhold Neibuhr, and the traditional-sounding 'I Am Stretched on Your Grave'.

Subsequently, O'Connor's artistic career was side-tracked as she became the target of criticism in the USA for her uncompromising opinions. She refused to perform if the US national anthem was played at one of her concerts and she tore up a picture of the Pope on a prime-time television show.

After the UK hit 'Success Has Made a Failure of Our Home', O'Connor's next album, *Am I Not Your Girl* (1992), contained versions of standard torch-songs such as 'I Want to Be Loved by You', a song associated with Marilyn Monroe. Her only other recordings in the early nineties were contributions to tribute albums to **Cole Porter** (*Red Hot and Blue*, 1991) and **Elton John** and Bernie Taupin (*Two Rooms*, 1992) and an appearance on **Willie Nelson**'s *Across the Borderline* (1993) where she sang **Peter Gabriel**'s 'Don't Give Up' with Nelson. In 1994 she sang 'You Made Me the Thief of Your Heart' on the soundtrack of *In the Name of the Father*.

In 1994 she released *Universal Mother*, which, in view of the growing antagonism to her political state-ments in the nineties, was expected to be roundly denounced. Instead it was celebrated, confirming both her stature as a singer and her ability to remind her audience of uncomfortable issues, notably Ireland and Third World politics. The album's best tracks included her version of **Phil Coulter**'s 'Scorn Not His Simplic-ity', her own 'Fire on Babylon' and the rap 'Famine', as well as a version of **Bob Dylan**'s 'I Believe You'.

The following year O'Connor announced that she would no longer speak to the music press. Her next release was 1997's *The Gospel Oak* EP, followed by a successful retrospective collection, *So Far . . . The Best of Sinead O'Connor*. In 1999 O'Connor was ordained as a catholic priest by the breakaway Order of Mater Dei, at which point she took the name Mother Bernadette Maria. She also signed a new deal with Atlantic in the US the same year. The first album under that contract was *Faith & Courage* (2000). A determined attempt at a mainstream album, it featured the *de rigeur* several producers – including the **Eurythmics**' Dave Stewart – of would-be comeback acts and a slew of far poppier songs than ever before. Predictably, it drew very mixed reviews and moderate sales.

ANITA O'DAY
b. *Anita Colton, 19 December 1919, Chicago, Illinois, USA*

Best-remembered for her appearance in *Jazz on a Summer's Day* – the film of the 1958 Newport Jazz Fes-tival in which she sang **Vincent Youmans**' 'Tea for Two' and 'Sweet Georgia Brown' – O'Day was one of the most inventive jazz singers of the forties, singing in a husky, intimate way on ballads and an exciting, dra-matic way on up-tempo numbers. She was also one of the first female singers to reject a pretty, decorative

appearance. Dressed as often in a suit as in a dress, she projected the image of a professional musician.

In the thirties, often in partnership with **Frankie Laine**, O'Day was a regular participant in the dancing marathons and 'walkathons' then in vogue, in the course of which she first sang professionally. In 1939 she joined vibraphonist Max Miller's trio as vocalist before in 1941 replacing Irene Daye as the singer with **Gene Krupa**'s big band. While trumpeter Roy Eldridge was with the band, she recorded one of the first inter-racial duets with him, the exciting 'Let Me Off Uptown' (Brunswick, 1941) in which her rhythmic phrasing perfectly matched the aggressive style of Eldridge. Her other great hits with Krupa were 'That's What You Think', which featured her almost word-less vocal, and 'Murder He Says'. In 1944 she joined **Stan Kenton**'s band and had an immediate hit with 'And Her Tears Flowed Like Wine', before briefly rejoining Krupa and then going solo.

Relatively inactive for over a decade due to drugs problems, O'Day found new popularity in the late fifties both on record (notably *Anita Sings the Winner*, Verge, 1958) and in performances in Europe. Through-out the sixties and seventies she continued to tour and record, most notably *All the Sad Young Men* (1961), the live album *Anita O'Day at the Berlin Festival* (MPS, 1970) and *Live at the City* (1979), on her own Emily label. Those influenced by O'Day include June Christy, **Julie London** and Chris Connor.

O'Day made occasional appearances in later years, including the fortieth anniversary Stan Kenton con-vention in 1991.

MOLLY O'DAY
b. *LaVerne Lois Williamson, 9 July 1923, McVeigh, Kentucky, USA, d. 5 December 1987, Huntington, West Virginia*

Among the women country singers of the forties Molly O'Day stood out for her unwavering commit-ment to sacred, tragic and 'heart' songs. She had none of **Rose Maddox**'s rowdy humour nor **Kitty Wells**' deserted-wife brooding; rather, like Sara Carter of the **Carter Family**, she had straightforward stories to tell, and she told them straight. In this respect, the artist she most resembled was **Roy Acuff**, a likeness empha-sized by her band's similar blends of fiddle and dobro.

She learned guitar from her brother Cecil (Skeets), who played mandolin and fiddle and was the first family member to work professionally in music, on WCHS in Charleston, West Virginia, in 1939. His sis-ter followed him there as a singer, then began to move round the local radio circuit until she reached WHIS in Bluefield, where she worked with, and soon mar-ried, the singer-guitarist Lynn Davis (b. *Leonard Davis, 15 December 1914, Paintsville, Kentucky*). The couple then worked on the WHAS, Louisville, *Early Morning Frolic*, the *Renfro Valley Barn Dance* and the WNOX, Knoxville, Tennessee, *Mid-day Merry-Go-Round*, where they were heard by **Fred Rose** and signed to Columbia to record one of O'Day's most powerful numbers, 'The Tramp on the Street'. At the same 1946 session O'Day, Davis and their band, the Cumberland Mountain Folks – which included **Mac Wiseman** on bass – recorded the temperance song 'The Drunken Driver' and compositions by Acuff and **Hank Williams**, whom they had met some years before at WAPI, Birmingham, Alabama.

At subsequent sessions in 1947–51 O'Day recorded further Williams numbers, as well as Rose's 'I'll Never See Sunshine Again', and the heart-rending tales of loss, 'At the First Fall of Snow', 'I Heard My Mother Weeping' and 'Teardrops Falling in the Snow'. She and Davis retired from public performing in the fifties to devote themselves to religious work, but made a couple of sacred albums for small labels in the sixties. In 1974 they started a gospel programme on WEMM-FM, a Christian station in Huntington, West Virginia. *And the Cumberland Mountain Folk* (Bear Family, 1992) is the definitive retrospective.

Despite her long absence from the music scene, O'Day's influence on later women singers was considerable, and echoes of her mournful clarity may be heard in the work of Maddox, Rose Lee Maphis (wife of multi-instrumentalist **Joe Maphis**) and, in particular, Wilma Lee Cooper.

Cooper's (*b. Wilma Lee Leary, 7 February 1921, Valley Head, West Virginia*) partnership with her husband, Stoney (*b. 16 October 1918, Harmon, West Virginia, d. 22 March 1977, Nashville, Tennessee*), though musically closer to bluegrass, nonetheless recalled that of O'Day and Davis. The Coopers had a similarly varied radio career but were best known from their spells on the WWVA, Wheeling, West Virgina, *Jamboree* (1954–7) and the *Grand Ole Opry* (from 1957) and hits songs like 'West Virginia Polka', 'Come Walk with Me' (Hickory, 1959) and 'Wreck on the Highway' (Hickory, 1961). In 1974 Wilma Lee was honoured by the Smithsonian Institution as 'First Lady of Bluegrass'. After Stoney's death she continued to work in music, often with their daughter Carol Lee.

ODETTA
b. Odetta Gordon Holmes, 31 December 1930, Birmingham, Alabama, USA

A powerful club performer of spirituals and blues since the early fifties, Odetta became one of the leading figures of the American folk revival a decade later. Both her repertoire and her impassioned style influenced a younger generation of singers, among them **Bob Dylan** and **Joan Baez**.

She moved to Los Angeles in 1936 where she took singing lessons and later studied music at night school. In 1949 she joined a touring company as a member of the chorus of *Finian's Rainbow* and soon afterwards was booked to sing folk and gospel material in San Francisco nightclubs. Her extensive repertoire included many songs that later became staples of the sixties folk-club movement, such as 'House of the Rising Sun', 'Sinner Man' and 'If I Had a Hammer'. She also made the definitive version of 'No More Auction Block for Me', which was later memorably recorded by Dylan.

Odetta appeared in leading New York and Chicago venues and in 1956 made her first recording, *Odetta Sings Ballads and Blues* (Tradition). In the same year Albert Grossman became her manager and in 1957 she recorded a live album at his Chicago folk club, the Gate of Horn. Odetta's first Carnegie Hall appearance was in 1960 when she also sang at the Newport Folk Festival and joined the prestigious Vanguard label. She played Liza on Harry Belafonte's 1961 hit 'Hole in the Bucket'. Her later albums included *Odetta Sings Dylan* (1965), *Ballad for Americans* (1966) and a live Carnegie Hall recording (1967).

In 1968 she took part in the **Woody Guthrie** Memorial Concert in New York and she toured throughout the world in the sixties and seventies, visiting Europe, Africa, Australia and Japan. In 1977 the blues singer and guitarist Louisiana Red (Iverson Minter) became her third husband. She returned to recording after a fifteen-year gap with *Christmas Spirituals* (1989), on which she was reunited with her original bass-player, Bill Lee. Even better was *Blues Everywhere I Go* (MC Records, 2000) on which Odetta (mostly) turned back to the twenties and songs like 'St Louis Blues' and 'Careless Love'. However, the most successful track was her duet with **Dr John** on **Percy Mayfield**'s affecting 'Please Send Me Someone to Love'. *The Essential Odetta* (1989) collects together her most important albums.

Odetta also had a career as a film and stage actress. Among her movies were *The Last Time I Saw Paris* (1954), *Cinerama Holiday* (1955) and *Sanctuary* (1960), Tony Richardson's film of Faulkner's novel. Odetta also appeared in operas by Harry Partch and Gian Carlo Menotti (*The Medium*).

THE OFFSPRING
Bryan 'Dexter' Holland, b. 29 December 1966, Orange County, California, USA; Greg Kreisel, b. 12 January 1965, Glendale, California; Kevin 'Noodles' Wasserman, b. 4 February 1963, Los Angeles, California; Ron Welty, b. 1 February 1971, Long Beach, California

Alongside **Green Day**, the Offspring lead the charge of the many punk-influenced bands to emerge in the mid-nineties.

Formed in 1984 by Holland (vocals), Welty (drums), 'Noodles' (guitar) and Greg K (bass), the Offspring spent several years honing their sound before signing to Nemesis Records for the release of their eponymous début album in 1989. The album sold poorly, but constant touring and an underground hit with *Ignition* (Epitaph, 1993) saw the band's fanbase begin to develop beyond cult status.

With *Smash* (1994) the Offspring added an element of pop appeal to their thrash-punk sound, leading to sales of over four million copies worldwide on the back of the success of the singles 'Self Esteem', 'Gotta Get Away' and the **Nirvana**-like 'Come Out and Play'. The Offspring's subsequent move to Columbia Records led to something of a backlash from the punk scene the band had now turned their backs on, while sales of *Ixnay on the Hombre* (1997) failed to match those of *Smash*. The Offspring returned to international fame with *Americana* (1999), which gave them their first UK No. 1 single, the rap-inspired 'Pretty Fly (For a White Guy)' and the equally emphatic 'Why Don't You Get a Job?'.

THE OHIO PLAYERS

William Beck; Leroy Bonner; Marshall Jones; Ralph Middlebrooks; Walter Morrison; Marvin Pierce; Clarence Satchell; James Williams

The Ohio Players' complex blend of R&B, jazz and **James Brown**-style funk brought them four million-selling singles, including the No. 1 'Fire' (1974) and 'Love Rollercoaster' (1975).

Formed in 1959 in Dayton, Ohio, the group, then known as the Ohio Untouchables, provided the backing for the Falcons' 'I Found a Love' (Lupine, 1962), with searing lead vocals from **Wilson Pickett**. After personnel changes, they became the Ohio Players, joining local label Compass as a house band and recording the minor hit 'Trespassin'' (1968).

After the unsuccessful *Observations in Time* (Capitol, 1969), they were joined by Morrison (keyboards), who proved to be the catalyst for a style which mixed aggressive horn-flavoured jazz-tinged funk with blatantly sexual lyrics. *Pain* (Westbound, 1971) and its title track were R&B hits and the use of sadomasochistic imagery in album artwork made 'Funky Worm'* from *Pleasure* (1973) a Top Twenty pop hit.

Morrison had left to go solo before the Ohio Players signed to Mercury for *Skin Tight** (1974) and the No. 1 pop hits 'Fire' (1975) and 'Love Rollercoaster'. Written by keyboards-player Beck, Pierce (trumpet), bassist Jones and drummer Williams, later successes included 'Fopp' (1976), 'Who'd She Coo' and 'O-H-I-O' (1977). By this time, the group had been supplanted by the newer soul sounds of the **Commodores** and **Earth, Wind and Fire** and in the eighties they label-hopped to

Arista (*Everybody Up*, 1979), Accord (*Young and Ready*, 1980), Boardwalk (*Ouch!* and *Tenderness*, both 1981), and Chip Wilson's Track (*Back*, 1988).

THE O'JAYS

Bobbey Massey, b. Canton, Ohio, USA; Walter Williams, b. 25 August 1942, Canton; Eddie Levert, b. 16 June 1942, Canton; Bill Isles, b. Canton; William Powell, b. 1941, Canton, d. 26 May 1977 (replaced by Sam Strain, replaced by Nathaniel Best, b. 13 December 1960, Miami, Florida, USA)

The O'Jays found international success with some of the best **Gamble and Huff** productions, which mixed sweet sounds with firmly socially conscious lyrics as on their first million-seller 'Back Stabbers' (1972) and the title track of their 1973 album, *Ship Ahoy* (1973), a ten-minute meditation on the arrival of the slave ships in America.

After singing together in a gospel group, Levert and Williams formed the Mascots doo-wop group in 1958 with Powell, Massey and Isles. After their recording début ('Miracles', Wayco, 1961), they renamed themselves the O'Jays in honour of Cleveland disc-jockey Eddie O'Jay and label-hopped their way to Imperial in 1963. Produced by veteran H. B. Barnum, they had R&B success with imitative records like 'Lonely Drifter' (1963, the **Drifters**) and 'Lipstick Traces' (1965, which aped **Allen Toussaint**'s production of Benny Spellman's 1962 hit). 'Stand in for Your Love' (1966) saw the group developing a sweeter sound which was confirmed by the **Thom Bell**-produced 'I'll Be Sweeter Tomorrow' (Bell, 1967), recorded after the departure of Isles.

Signed by Gamble and Huff to their Neptune label as a quartet, the O'Jays had further R&B success with 'One Night After' (1969) and 'Looky Looky (Look at Me)' (1970), records that prefigured the smooth but intense sides of their later work. When Neptune folded, Massey quit to enter production and in 1972 the group, now a trio, signed with Gamble and Huff's newly established Philadelphia International and quickly became one of the mainstays of the label. Their international hits included the American No. 1 'Love Train' (1972), 'Put Your Hands Together', 'For the Love of Money'* (1974), 'I Love Music'* (1975) and 'Use Ta Be My Girl'* (1978), all of which featured the intense, yet restrained, lead vocals of Levert, while their albums, notably *Ship Ahoy* (1973) and *Message in Our Music* (1976), were equally successful.

In 1976 Powell, afflicted by cancer, was replaced by former member of **Little Anthony and the Imperials** Strain. The group continued to record, with Levert and Williams becoming increasingly involved in production, and toured throughout the eighties. Among their biggest hits were 'Forever Mine' (1980), 'Extraordinary Girl' (1984), the R&B No. 1 'Lovin You' (EMI, 1987) and 'Serious Hold on Me' (1989). Later album releases included *Let Me Touch You* (1987), *Serious* (1990) and *Emotionally Yours* (1991), but the group were unable to build on the revival of their fortunes in the late eighties.

In 1986 Levert's son Gerald (*b. 13 July 1966, Cleveland, Ohio, USA*) formed the group Levert with his brother Sean and Marc Gordon. They had a series of hits, including 'Pop Pop Goes My Love' and 'Casanova' (Atlantic), which reached the Top Ten in both America and Britain in 1987. *Just Coolin'* (1988) saw the group experimenting with street styles while *Rope a Dope Style* (1990) saw the trio transformed into fully-fledged rappers. Gerald Levert's solo *Private Line* (East-West, 1992) fused soul ballads and New Jack rhythms in the style of 'Casanova'. In 1993 both Levert and the group charted with *Rope a Dope Style* and *Emotionally Yours*, the title track of which was written by **Bob Dylan**, respectively. The Leverts recorded *Father and Son* in 1995 and in 1997 the O'Jays (produced by Levert) returned to the US charts with *Love You to Tears*. In the same year Levert disbanded his group to establish his own record label, Global Soul, to which he signed the O'Jays, and to concentrate on songwriting and production. He had started producing after his first hits. Major productions include **Barry White**'s comeback single, 'Practice What You Preach' (1997), and **Patti Labelle**'s *Flame* (1997).

DANNY O'KEEFE
b. 1943, Wenatchee, Washington, USA

A blues-inflected singer-songwriter known equally for his intricate word play and doomed romanticism, O'Keefe's only significant hit was the laconic 'Goodtime Charlie's Got the Blues'* (Signpost, 1972), a song later revived by **Willie Nelson** and **Elvis Presley**, among others. He remains of note as a member of the literary, rather than folk-orientated, singer-songwriters that emerged from beneath **Bob Dylan**'s shadow.

O'Keefe travelled from Washington to New York on the folk circuit of the early sixties, turning to songwriting while recuperating from a motorcycle accident. He first recorded for Jerry Dennon's Seattle-based Jerden label ('That Old Sweet Feeling'). Briefly a member of Calliope (with whom he recorded an album on Buddah), he was signed to Cotillion and recorded *Danny O'Keefe* (1971). Produced by **Ahmet Ertegun**, it included an early version of 'Goodtime Charlie' which was reworked a year later under the supervision of **Arif Mardin** on *O'Keefe* (1972). The album also included 'The Road' (later recorded by **Jackson Browne**), a spirited revival of **Hank Williams**' 'Honky Tonkin'' and several wry songs

about the confusion between love and sex (a favourite O'Keefe theme) sung in his expressive, rough tenor voice. Both it and the Arif Mardin-produced *Breezy Stories* (1973), which included the ambitious 'Mad Ruth/The Babe', 'Magdalena' (later recorded by **Leo Sayer**), 'Angel Spread Your Wings' (revived by **Judy Collins**) and an impassioned reading of Spencer Williams' 'Goodbye to Storyville', were critically well received but, like *So Long Harry Truman* (1975), were commercial failures.

After appearing at several benefits in Japan and America to publicize the plight of the whale, O'Keefe returned to recording in 1977 with the superior *American Roulette* (Warners). The most dynamic of his albums, it was both witty ('The Hereafter' with its refrain 'If you ain't hereafter what I'm hereafter, you'll be hereafter I'm gone') and poignant ('In Northern California [Where the Palm Tree Meets the Pine]'). Less successful was *Global Blues* (1979), after which O'Keefe went into semi-retirement, only performing occasionally in the Los Angeles area. In 1985 he issued *The Day to Day* on his own Coldwater Records. The album was subsequently reissued as *Redux* (Beachwood, 1989) and under its original title by Mirimar in 1999. The release of that signalled a return to performing, again mostly in the Los Angeles area, and a further album, *Running from the Devil* (1999). While it missed the production values of his classic earlier albums, *Running* found O'Keefe in fine voice and as precise as ever at documenting the number of angels on a pinhead with a fine degree of acerbity. 'Tonight I'm more than single, tonight I am alone,' he sings on 'Pieces of the Rain'.

MIKE OLDFIELD
b. 15 May 1953, Reading, Berkshire, England

Originally a folk-club singer and rock guitarist, Oldfield with *Tubular Bells* created one of the most popular recordings of the seventies. He later extended this eclectic mood-music approach (in which his only rival prior to the arrival of New Age music was **Jean-Michel Jarre**) to a series of albums, film scores and hit singles.

With his sister Sally, Oldfield had recorded *Sallyangie* (Transatlantic, 1968), a collection of songs with acoustic accompaniment. He next played bass and guitar with the eccentric Kevin Ayers before making the demo tape which became the basis for *Tubular Bells*. After being turned down by several companies, the project was accepted by Richard Branson of Virgin stores. Re-recorded at the newly built Manor Studios, *Tubular Bells* was one of the first releases on the Virgin label in 1973. Of symphonic length, the work was based on a series of simple melodies from folk, rock and classical sources and held together by a central bell-chime motif. The album became a progressive rock sensation in Britain, where it remained on the charts for nearly five years and in America, where its success was aided by the inclusion of extracts on the soundtrack of *The Exorcist* (1973). A single of the film music was a Top Ten hit in 1974. *Tubular Bells* itself went on to sell over 10 million copies worldwide.

The following year Oldfield released *Hergest Ridge*, a somnolent pastoral epic based on the countryside near his home. *Ommadawn* (1975) was more lively and incorporated the **Chieftains**' Paddy Molony on uillean pipes as well as a team of African drummers led by South African exile Julian Bahula. Without emulating the impact of Oldfield's début, both sold well and in 1975 and 1976 he had Christmas hits in Britain with the traditional carol 'In Dulci Jubilo' and the hornpipe 'Portsmouth'.

With arranger David Bedford, previously an Ayers collaborator, Oldfield prepared an orchestral version of *Tubular Bells* which was recorded by the Royal Philharmonic Orchestra in 1975. His next new project was *Incantations* (1978), which included an unsuccessful attempt at a disco single, 'Guilty'. *Exposed* (1979) was recorded at live shows where Oldfield was accompanied by fifty musicians. The studio albums *Platinum* and *QE2* (1980) were less well received but *Five Miles Out* (1982) reached the Top Ten and included the song 'Family Man'. With vocals by Oldfield's regular vocalist Maggie Reilly, the song was also a 1983 hit for **Hall and Oates**.

Reilly's soprano was featured on Oldfield's own bestselling single, 'Moonlight Shadow', from *Crises* (1983). After *Discovery* (1984), Oldfield undertook the film score for Roland Joffe's *The Killing Fields* (1984). Evidence of the pervasive influence of *Tubular Bells* came when in the following year Paul Hardcastle's hit '19' borrowed phrases from it. In 1986 Oldfield moved into the music video field, creating *Pictures in the Dark* with director Peter Claridge.

Islands (1987), with guest vocals from **Bonnie Tyler**, Ayers and Roger Chapman, formerly of **Family**, was followed by *Earth Moving* (1989), featuring Reilly, Anita Hegerland and ex-**Manfred Mann** singer Chris Thompson, and by his least successful album, *Amorok*.

Leaving Virgin after twenty years, Oldfield signed with WEA, for whom he recorded *Tubular Bells II* (1992), which returned to the musical themes of his début even to the extent of once again employing ex-**Bonzo Dog Band** vocalist Vivian Stanshall to recreate the MC role he had played on the original. It was an immediate international success, entering the British chart at No. 1. Oldfield's next project was *Songs of Distant Earth* (1994), based on the novel by Arthur C. Clarke, which included a CD-ROM computer game segment. It was followed by the Celtic-tinged *Voyager*

(1997) before he returned to *Tubular Bells* with *Tubular Bells III* (1998), in which the original material was given the dance/trance treatment. The album was recorded in Ibiza, where Oldfield had settled, and London. In 1999 he toured Europe in support of the album and released the lesser *The Millennium Bell*. First performed in Berlin's Siegessaule Square on Millennium eve, it was brisker and less reflective than early Oldfield to good effect.

WILL OLDHAM
b. Louisville, Kentucky, USA

Using a variety of pseudonyms, including Palace, Palace Music and the Palace Brothers, cult singer-songwriter Will Oldham has produced a series of acclaimed albums steeped in traditional blues, country and folk, in the manner of **Taj Mahal**, remaining a step ahead of the late nineties crop of rustic alternative rock performers. Creating a barely heard whimper of a sound his borrowings from the past were in contrast to the easy-going sound of Keb Mo.

Oldham, who grew up in the bluegrass country of Kentucky, pursued a career as an actor and playwright before turning to music. He appeared in two films, *Matewan* (1987) and *Thousand Pieces of Gold* (1991), and several of his teenage works were published by the Walden Theatre Young Playwrights Project, including *Dustbunnies* and *Plastic Cheese*.

Oldham recorded his first album, the aptly titled *There Is No One What Will Take Care of You* (Drag City, 1993), as Palace Brothers. An impressive début, the album introduced the twin themes of sin and redemption as the mainsprings of his lyrics in '(I Was Drunk at the) Pulpit' and 'Idle Hands Are the Devil's Playthings'. *Days in the Wake* (1993) maintains the bleak tone of its predecessor but has a stronger instrumental backing. *An Arrow through the Bitch* (Domino, 1994) is a UK-only collection of three early singles.

Oldham took the name Palace Songs for the *Hope EP* (1994), recorded with members of Royal Trux and **Stereolab**, before the release of *Viva Last Blues* (1995), credited this time to Palace Music. The album was produced by Steve Albini and veered towards country-rock, relying heavily on the piano and organ of Liam Hayes and brother Ned Oldham's guitar-playing. The superior *Arise Therefore* (1996) saw a return to the primitive acoustic sound of the Palace's early work, accompanied mostly by banjo and occasional percussion, albeit a drum machine. Less folky than its predecessors and more reflective in its use of religious imagery and language, it remains his best album to date.

By this time Oldham had built up a strong live following, working with a band which often included his brothers Ned and Paul on guitar. *Joya* (1997) was the singer's first album to be released under the name Will Oldham, and was similar in tone to *Viva Last Blues*. Oldham received weak reviews for the first time for *Joya* after years of critical adulation, leading to a creative rethink before he returned as Bonnie 'Prince' Billy in 1999. A medley of 'devotional songs' was included on the *Blue Lotus Feet* EP, while *I See a Darkness* was Oldham's most internationally successful release to date.

KING OLIVER
b. Joseph Oliver, 11 May 1885, Louisiana, USA,
d. 10 April 1938, Savannah, Georgia

The leader of the first great New Orleans jazz band, Oliver's cornet style held sway until the arrival of **Louis Armstrong**.

Oliver moved from rural Louisiana to New Orleans as a youth, working as a servant for white families while developing his technique on trombone and later on cornet. By 1910 he was performing with various early jazz bands and marching bands and in 1912 he joined the city's leading group, led by trombonist **Kid Ory**.

Oliver briefly led his own band, taking the young Armstrong under his wing, before rejoining Ory in 1917. During his stay with Ory, Oliver gained the soubriquet 'King' when he succeeded Freddie Keppard as New Orleans' leading cornettist. When Oliver left New Orleans for Chicago in 1919, Armstrong took his place in Ory's line-up. In Chicago, Oliver worked with bass-player Bill Johnson, leader of the Creole Jazz Band – a band that had evolved from a New Orleans ragtime group who emigrated to California in 1909 before moving to the Midwest. Oliver soon took over the leadership of the band which featured Johnny Dodds (clarinet) and Lil Hardin on piano. After spending a year in California, the Creole Jazz Band returned to Chicago in 1922 and Oliver sent for Armstrong to become second cornet.

During 1923 this group made some of the most influential recordings in jazz history. Over forty sides were cut for Gennett, Columbia, Paramount and Okeh, encapsulating the essence of New Orleans jazz. It was essentially ensemble rather than improvising music, one of its main features being the note-perfect cornet duets between Oliver and Armstrong on tracks like 'Snake Rag'. Oliver's muted 'wah-wah' style on 'Dippermouth Blues' inspired the famous 'growling' tone of **Duke Ellington** trumpeter Bubber Miley, while the same tune became **Fletcher Henderson**'s first hit.

This was the high point of Oliver's career. Armstrong left the group in 1924 and Oliver missed a key opportunity in 1927 when he turned down a season at New York's Cotton Club. Ellington took the booking

instead and it proved to be the turning-point of his career. Oliver resumed recording for Vocalion in 1926 with his ten-piece Dixie Syncopaters (which included Ory and clarinettist Barney Bigard) but a serious gum disease increasingly impaired his own playing. On many of his later records, made in 1929–30 for Victor, other players – including his nephew Dave Nelson – took some of the cornet solos.

The effects of the Depression on record sales caused the termination of the Victor contract in 1931 and Oliver formed a touring band which travelled the South. By 1937 this project had come to a halt and Oliver was forced to leave music altogether. He died a year later of bronchial asthma.

GEORGE OLSEN
b. 18 March 1893, Portland, Oregon, USA, d. 18 March 1971, Paramus, New Jersey

Olsen was the leader of one of the most successful dance bands of the twenties, known for its bright, zippy style.

He formed his first band in college and got his big break in 1923 when **Fanny Brice** encouraged Florenz Ziegfeld to put the Olsen band in his production of *Kid Boots*, which starred **Eddie Cantor**. Subsequently the Olsen band was featured in several Broadway productions, including *Good News!* (1927), *Whoopee* (1928) and **Jerome Kern** and Oscar Hammerstein II's *Sunny* (1925), which provided Olsen with his only million-seller, 'Who?' (RCA). From the end of the twenties, the Olsen band, featuring his first wife, Ethel Shutta, and Fran Frey (who with Bob Rice and Jack Fulton, sang on 'Who?') as vocalists, worked regularly on radio. His signature tune was 'Beyond the Blue Horizon', which he often performed with novelty effects. When his sound was deemed too old-fashioned for radio, he turned to playing in hotels.

Following his retirement in 1951, Olsen opened a restaurant in New Jersey.

ALEXANDER O'NEAL
b. 14 December 1954, Natchez, Mississippi, USA

One of the new generation of soul balladeers in the eighties, O'Neal's smooth vocals and stage show made him equally popular in Europe and America.

He grew up in Minneapolis where he sang in clubs before joining Flyte Tyme, the group led by **Jimmy Jam** and **Terry Lewis**, in 1978. When that group evolved into Time, O'Neal began a solo career, issuing the unsuccessful *Playroom* (1980).

After Jam and Lewis had established themselves as songwriters and producers, they supervised *Alexander O'Neal* (Tabu, 1985), which included R&B hits in 'A Broken Heart Can Mend' and 'Innocent', a duet with

Cherelle. He also appeared on 'If You Were Here Tonight', a Cherelle track which became a UK hit in 1986.

After undergoing treatment for drug and alcohol dependency, O'Neal returned with *Hearsay* (1987). Again produced by Jam and Lewis, the album sold strongly in America and Britain, where 'Criticise' reached the Top Five. His UK concerts were sold out and audiences appreciated his suave stagecraft and such touches as inviting an audience member to lie on a brass bed onstage while he serenaded her.

The 1988 Christmas album, *My Gift to You*, was less successful and there was a three-year gap, broken only by the remix album *All Mixed Up*, before the release of *All True Man*. Another Jam and Lewis production, it included the evocative 'Shame on Me' and the rocking 'Used'. In 1993 O'Neal moved to A&M where he was reunited with Cherelle on the former **Marvin Gaye**–Tammi Terrell duet 'Your Precious Love' and also sang a version of **Louis Armstrong**'s 'What a Wonderful World'. Far better was *Love Makes No Sense* (1993) and the retrospective *This Thing Called Love* (1994). In 1996 he settled in London and recorded the UK hit album *Lovers Again*.

YOKO ONO
b. 18 February 1933, Tokyo, Japan

Steeped in avant-garde art and music, Ono was an important influence on **John Lennon**, with whom she created the pared-down music of the Plastic Ono Band after their marriage. She later recorded a number of solo albums.

Ono moved to New York with her family in 1947 and by the late fifties was part of the 'happenings' movement, which aimed to develop alternatives to conventional theatrical and musical performances. Ono gave a concert at Carnegie Hall in 1961 and later toured Japan with the composer John Cage. Her book *Grapefruit*, a collection of instructions for Cageian performances, poems and other writings, was published in 1964.

Ono met Lennon at an exhibition in London in 1966 and in 1968 they collaborated on the tapes that were later released as *Unfinished Music No. 1: Two Virgins* (Apple, 1969). The controversy caused by its sleeve photograph of the couple naked led to the album being distributed in a plain brown wrapper. Musically, *Two Virgins* was a private sound collage as was *Unfinished Music No. 2: Life with the Lions* (Zapple, 1969), which included a recording of the heartbeat of the foetus Ono had miscarried a few months before. *Wedding Album* (Apple, 1969) completed the trilogy before 'Give Peace a Chance' (1969), a mantra-like chant recorded in a Toronto hotel room, was a hit on both sides of the Atlantic. Ono was also

heard wailing above the guitars of Lennon and **Eric Clapton** on the live album *Live Peace in Toronto* (1969). *Yoko Ono/Plastic Ono Band* (1970) featured more improvising vocals, as well as a tape of a rehearsal with **Ornette Coleman**'s quartet.

The next album released under Ono's name was *Fly*, the soundtrack to an avant-garde film which featured several word-game songs like 'Mrs Lennon' and 'Dub Dub'. More significantly, Ono co-wrote the Plastic Ono Band's hit 'Happy Christmas, War Is Over' (1971) and wrote three of the songs on *Some Time in New York City* (1972), including the feminist anthems 'Sisters Oh Sisters' and (with Lennon) 'Woman Is the Nigger of the World'. Similar themes dominated the first album of her own material, *Approximately Infinite Universe* (1973). Soon afterwards she released *Feeling the Space* (1973).

Separation from and reconciliation with Lennon followed by a period of withdrawal from music kept Ono out of the studio until 1980. Then she and Lennon released *Double Fantasy* (Geffen), from which '(Just Like) Starting Over'* reached No. 1 shortly before Lennon was killed.

Ono continued with a solo recording career, releasing *Season of Glass* (Geffen, 1981), whose songs dealt with her bereavement, and *It's Alright* (Polydor, 1982). *Milk and Honey* (1984) repeated the duet approach and contained some of Lennon's unreleased songs. The tribute album *Every Man Has a Woman* (1984) consisted of Ono songs covered by artists ranging from long-time Lennon cohort **Harry Nilsson** to **Elvis Costello**, and included a Lennon vocal on the title track.

In the late eighties Ono concentrated on mounting tribute concerts to Lennon and on guarding his legacy. She oversaw the release of the out-takes album, *Menlove Avenue* (1987), and produced both the movie *Imagine* (1988), which included much previously unseen footage, and a 1988 syndicated radio series on Lennon's life. In 1992 Rykodisc issued *Onobox*, a six-CD retrospective, and in 1993 Ono announced her return to music with *New York Rock*, a musical about a man who is murdered by muggers. It opened off-Broadway in early 1994 and was savaged by critics, being described by one as 'sappy soft-pop'.

ROY ORBISON
b. Roy Kelton Orbison, 23 April 1936, Vernon, Texas, USA, d. 6 December 1988, Hendersonville, Tennessee

With a near-operatic vocal range and a sound once described as 'the slow fall of teardrops', Orbison was one of the most distinctive singers of the sixties. Unusually, he was also able to re-create the full power of his recordings in live performance. Though by the mid-seventies his career seemed to be over, except as an influence ('the radio plays Roy Orbison singing for the lonely' runs a line from **Bruce Springsteen**'s 'Thunder Road', 1975), he had brief renewed success in the eighties as part of the Traveling Wilburys. Of all his interpreters **Chris Isaak** caught his style the best, giving added dimension to the brooding quality of much of Orbison's best work.

The son of an oil driller, Orbison grew up in West Texas and formed the Wink Westerners at the age of thirteen. At college he played with a rockabilly group, the Teen Kings, who included guitarist Johnny 'Peanuts' Wilson and later recorded 'Cast Iron Arm'. The group cut Orbison's 'Ooby Dooby' at **Norman Petty**'s New Mexico studio in 1955 and the single was released on Petty's Jewel label. The following year Orbison re-recorded the song for **Sam Phillips**' Sun label and it became a minor hit. Later Sun rockabilly releases were unsuccessful and Orbison concentrated on songwriting. After the **Everly Brothers** recorded his 'Claudette' (1958), he was signed to Acuff-Rose music publishers and recorded briefly for RCA.

His career only took flight after he joined Fred Foster's newly formed Monument Records. The third release, with Foster producing, was the bestselling lachrymose ballad 'Only the Lonely'* (1960) with its instantly recognizable *a cappella* opening, and its desolate, almost hysterical, climax. Over the next five years, Orbison had eight further Top Twenty hits in America and even more in Britain. They ranged from the agonized 'Cryin''* (1961) and 'It's Over'* (1964) to the yearning 'In Dreams' (which was given an unexpected threatening edge when used by David Lynch in his 1986 film *Blue Velvet*), and the up-tempo 'Mean Woman Blues'* (1964). The most dramatic, however, were the contrasting American No. 1s – 'Oh, Pretty Woman'* (1964) and 'Running Scared'* (1961). The first was an intense romantic song, while the second, like most of Orbison's hits co-written with Joe Melson, built with controlled tension to a cliff-hanging climax in which Orbison's girlfriend chooses him over his rival.

Other memorable recordings of the period were 'Love Hurts' (1962), an early version of the **Felice and Boudleaux Bryant** standard; 'Dream Baby'*, (1962) written by Cindy Walker, author of several songs for **Bob Wills** and **Bing Crosby**; and the exotic 'Leah' (1962). A mark of Orbison's enduring influence was the number and variety of later artists who recorded his songs. They included **Linda Ronstadt** ('Blue Bayou'*, 1977), **Don McLean** ('Crying', 1981) and **Van Halen** ('Oh Pretty Woman', 1982).

Although Orbison was one of the few American solo artists to withstand the British beat-group invasion of 1963–4, his career went into decline in the mid-sixties. In 1965 he left Monument for the larger MGM label where his material (usually written with

Bill Dees, co-author of 'Oh, Pretty Woman') seemed to give less scope for the vocal effects that had been crucial to his earlier success. Only **Don Gibson**'s 'Too Soon to Know' (1966), his last British Top Ten hit, had the melodramatic power of the best Monument sides.

An attempt to launch Orbison on a film career with the singing Western *The Fastest Guitar Alive* (1967) was also unsuccessful and contractual problems with MGM meant that he issued only one new album during the first half of the seventies, although he continued to tour Europe regularly. He recorded *I'm Still in Love with You* for Mercury in 1976 before returning to Monument for *Regeneration* (1977). In 1979 he released *Laminar Flow* (Elektra) and in the following year had his first country hit in a duet with **Emmylou Harris**, 'That Lovin' You Feeling Again', from the film *Roadie*.

During the eighties Orbison's career received a fillip from an unexpected quarter when his voice was featured in 1985 on the soundtrack of Nicholas Roeg's *Insignificance* (singing 'Wild Heart', issued by **Trevor Horn**'s ZTT label), and then *Blue Velvet*. This led to Orbison making an album of re-recordings of his hits with producer T-Bone Burnett (*In Dreams*, Virgin, 1986). Even more successful was the formation of the Traveling Wilburys supergroup with **Bob Dylan**, **George Harrison**, Jeff Lynne (of **ELO**) and **Tom Petty**; their eponymous album, which included a sequel to 'Only the Lonely', 'Lonely No More', was an unexpected hit just prior to Orbison's death in 1988. *Mystery Girl* (1989) and *Roy Orbison and Friends: a Black and White Night*, a live recording made in 1987, were released posthumously. The hit single 'She's a Mystery to Me' was written by members of **U2**.

Orbison's posthumous success continued into the nineties. After its use in the film of the same name, 'Oh, Pretty Woman' was a Top Ten hit in 1990 and the song was the subject of a court case when its publishers sued rap group **2 Live Crew**, who had issued a parody version. In 1992 another posthumously released track, a version of the **Cyndi Lauper** hit 'I Drove All Night', reached the British Top Five and a reissue of Orbison's 1987 duet with **k.d. lang**, 'Crying', made the Top Twenty. A further posthumously-compiled album of new material, *King of Hearts*, was a Top Thirty hit the same year.

ORCHESTRAL MANOEUVRES IN THE DARK
Malcolm Holmes; Dave Hughes (replaced by Martin Cooper); Paul Humphries, b. 27 February 1960, London, England; Andy McCluskey, b. 24 June 1959, Wirral; Graham Weir; Neil Weir

Liverpool's OMD (as Orchestral Manoeuvres in the Dark quickly became known) were one of the first

British synthesizer-based groups to achieve commercial success in the eighties. Their later records retained large audiences through the more traditional virtue of inventive melody lines.

Influenced by **Kraftwerk**, McCluskey (bass, vocals), and Humphries (keyboards, vocals) formed VCL XI in 1976, playing in Hitlers Underpantz and the Id before setting up OMD as a duo in 1978. Early performances also included a drum machine and they were among the first signings to the Manchester label, Factory Records.

The interest aroused by the catchy, quirky 'Electricity' (1979), which showed the influence of the **Tornados**' 1962 hit 'Telstar', led to a contract with Virgin's Dindisc label and a national tour supporting **Gary Numan**. With Holmes (keyboards) and Hughes (drums) replacing the machine, OMD issued an eponymous album in 1980. As Cooper came in for Hughes, the Mike Howlett-produced *Organisation* (1980), which included the Top Ten hit 'Enola Gay' (named after the plane that dropped the atomic bomb on Hiroshima), was released. The following year 'Souvenir', 'Joan of Arc' and 'Maid of Orleans' from *Architecture and Morality* (1981), were also successful.

Later albums like *Dazzle Ships* (1983) and *Junk Culture* (1984) introduced such extraneous effects as electric typewriters and radio signals but OMD's hits continued. 'Genetic Engineering' (1983) was followed by 'Locomotion' and 'Talking Loud and Clear' (1984). With the Neil brothers replacing Holmes and Cooper, the group had its first American success in 1985 with 'So in Love' and 'Secret' from *Crush*. The latter appeared on the soundtrack of *Arthur on the Rocks*.

In 1986 they released *The Pacific Age*, produced by Stephen Hague. Condemned by critics as pretentious, it included tracks dealing with 'the rise of the Pacific Basin countries' and Martin Luther King, as well as the hit single '(Forever) Live and Die'. Shortly after its release, the Weir brothers left the band. A 'best of' compilation, *In the Dark*, followed in 1988, and when Humphreys also left, it seemed this would be the end of OMD's career.

However, McCluskey decided to continue as a soloist, retaining the name OMD and releasing another two Top Ten singles, 'Sailing on the Seven Seas' and 'Pandora's Box'. He formed a touring band with Abe Juckes (drums) and keyboards-players Phil Coxon and Nigel Ipinson. His next album, *Sugar Tax* (1991), was OMD's bestselling album. It featured McCluskey's new writing partners Stuart Kershaw and Lloyd Massett and the trio combined again for *Liberator* (1993). More mainstream in its pop sound than its predecessor, it sold fewer copies, but the band remained a popular live attraction. *Universal* (1998), with its pop-anthem of a single 'Walking on the Milky Way', was more mainstream and more successful. However, their most influential release of the decade was the compilation *The OMD Singles*.

THE ORIGINAL DIXIELAND JAZZ BAND

Eddie Edwards, b. Edwin Branford Edwards, 22 May 1891, New Orleans, Louisiana, USA, d. 9 April 1963, New York; Nick LaRocca, b. Dominick James LaRocca, 11 April 1889, New Orleans, d. 22 February 1961, New Orleans; Alcide Nuñez, b. 17 March 1884, New Orleans, d. 2 September 1934, New Orleans (replaced by Larry Shields, b. 13 September 1893, New Orleans, d. 21 November 1953, Los Angeles, California); Henry Ragas, d. 1918 (replaced by J. Russel Robinson, b. 8 July 1892, Indianapolis, Indiana, d. 30 September 1963, Palmdale, California); Tony Spargo, b. Antonio Sbarbaro, 27 June 1897, New Orleans, d. 30 October 1969, New York

A quintet of white musicians, the ODJB became the first jazz band to make records in 1917. Massive sales led to European tours and an intermittent existence for the group until 1946.

LaRocca (cornet) and Edwards (trombone) had played with Jack Laine, one of the first white jazz bandleaders in New Orleans. In 1916 they joined a group led by drummer Johnny Stein with Nuñez (clarinet) and Ragas (piano), which had a residency in Chicago. Soon afterwards the quartet left Stein, adding drummer Spargo to make up the ODJB. Shields joined later in 1916.

The group's successful New York début led to a recording contract with Victor. Their second release, 'Livery Stable Blues'/'Original Dixieland One-Step', was a bestseller and subsequent record successes, like LaRocca's 'Tiger Rag' and 'At the Jazz Band Ball' (1918), led to a tour of Britain in 1919–20. Both became Dixieland standards and were subsequently recorded by numerous artists. The ODJB became the resident band at the Hammersmith Palais de Danse, emphasizing the importance of the dancing crazes of the era to their success.

Returning to America, the group made further hit records for Victor, including **W. C. Handy**'s 'St Louis Blues' (1921), **Clarence Williams**' 'Royal Garden Blues' (1921) and 'Some of These Days' (1923). While Shields' novelty clarinet-playing influenced **Ted Lewis**, the ODJB's 'corny' style seemed outmoded compared to the new dance orchestras of **Paul Whiteman**, Lewis and others. In 1925 the ODJB disbanded, with LaRocca returning to New Orleans to run his family business and Edwards selling newspapers. The band re-formed in 1936 as Nick LaRocca and his Original Dixieland Band, cutting big-band versions of the twenties repertoire for Victor.

Edwards continued to record, using Shields and Spargo on 1938 tracks for Bluebird and forming an all-star line-up of younger musicians (including

Eddie Condon and Wild Bill Davison) in 1945–6 for sessions released on Commodore as by Eddie Edwards and his Original Dixieland Jazz Band. This material was far superior to the earlier ODJB's music, proving that the band's real significance lay in its being the first jazz band on record, rather than the best.

THE ORIOLES

Sonny Til, b. Earlington Tilghman, 18 August 1925, Baltimore, Maryland, USA, d. 9 December 1981; George Nelson, b. Baltimore, d. 1968; Alexander Sharp, b. Baltimore, d. 1959; Johnny Reed, b. Baltimore; Tommy Gaither, b. Baltimore, d. 1950

With the **Ravens**, the Orioles formed the link between the vocal group sound of the **Ink Spots** and the **Mills Brothers** and the fifties doo-wop groups that followed in their wake. They are best remembered for their classic recording of 'Crying in the Chapel'* (1953) in which Til's cool voice was supported by the spare (mostly wordless) harmonies of the group.

Formed in 1947 in Baltimore as the Vibronaires, they were spotted by songwriter/manager Deborah Chesler, who changed their name, making them (with the Ravens) among the first of many 'bird' groups. She quickly secured them bookings at both the Apollo and on **Arthur Godfrey**'s morning talent show and a contract with Jerry Blaine's Natural (later Jubilee) label. The group had an immediate R&B hit with their first recording, Chesler's 'It's Too Soon to Know' (1948), which introduced a slow, wistful form of harmony singing to vocal-group recordings. The R&B No. 1 'Tell Me So' (1949) was even more innovatory, introducing a wordless falsetto that parallelled Til's lead vocal, which would become a feature of many vocal-group records. 'Crying in the Chapel' (1953), later revived by **Elvis Presley** (1965) and numerous vocal groups, was one of the first R&B hits to cross over to the pop charts.

In 1955 the original group disbanded and Til, who had previously recorded solo for Jubilee, recruited new members. They signed to Vee-Jay and later Charlie Parker Records, mostly re-recording their early hits.

TONY ORLANDO

b. Michael Anthony Orlando Cassavitis, 3 April 1944, New York, USA

In the early sixties Orlando was a teenage heart-throb whose series of hits written by **Don Kirshner**'s Brill Building songsmiths included 'Halfway to Paradise' (**Carole King** and Gerry Goffin) and 'Bless You' (**Barry Mann** and Cynthia Weil). Later he became the lead singer of Dawn, whose 'Tie a Yellow Ribbon

Round the Old Oak Tree'* was the biggest-selling record of 1973.

Of Greek and Puerto Rican origin, Orlando was a member of several New York doo-wop groups (notably the Five Gents) before being signed by Kirshner as a staff writer/demo singer. He sang on the demos for 'Will You Still Love Me Tomorrow' and 'Some Kind of Wonderful', hits for the **Shirelles** and the **Drifters**, respectively, before Kirshner decided to lease his recording of 'Halfway to Paradise' to Epic in 1961. A hit in America – in Britain it was successfully covered by **Billy Fury** – the record was followed by 'Bless You', a dramatic teen ballad, and 'Happy Times Are Here to Stay', his last solo hit: all were well-crafted pop productions, given life by the clarity of Orlando's distinctive voice.

His hitmaking days over, Orlando moved into music publishing, eventually running the April-Blackwood catalogue for Columbia. In 1971, as a favour to producers Hank Medress (a former member of the Tokens, who had a hit with their version of the South African traditional song 'The Lion Sleeps Tonight'* in 1970 on RCA) and David Appell, he re-did the lead vocal on 'Candida' (Bell). Billed as by Dawn, the record and its follow-up, the jaunty American chart-topper 'Knock Three Times' (1971), were both million-sellers. As a result and Orlando and backing singers Thelma Hopkins (*b. 28 October 1948, Louisville, Kentucky*) and Joyce Vincent Wilson (*b. 14 December 1948, Detroit, Michigan*), formerly session singers at Motown, established Dawn as a permanent aggregation.

Their hits, all targeted at the easy-listening market, included a trio of American No. 1s, and fourteen Top Forty hits in the first half of the seventies and made them television and cabaret stars. Their most notable hit was 'Tie a Yellow Ribbon' (1973), written by Irwin Levine and L. Russell Brown, as were most of the group's early hits. The song was reportedly based on a true story – a wife tied a yellow ribbon to a tree signifying that she still loved her husband, who was returning from jail – and Dawn's impact was evident when yellow ribbons were tied to trees coast to coast in America to greet the returning Iran hostages in 1981. Other million-sellers included 'Say Has Anybody Seen My Sweet Gypsy Rose' (1973), 'Steppin' Out' (1974) – by which time the group was billed as Tony Orlando and Dawn – and a remake of **Jerry Butler**'s first solo hit, 'He Will Break Your Heart' (1960), retitled 'He Don't Love You (Like I Love You)' (1975). This was their first release after joining Elektra. Dawn's last hit was another revival, this time of **Sam Cooke**'s 'Cupid' (1976).

In 1977 Orlando briefly left showbusiness after becoming a born-again Christian and when the group broke up Hopkins established herself as an actress.

Subsequently, Orlando returned to performing as both an actor and a solo singer. In 1981 he replaced former British rock'n'roller Jim Dale in the title role of the Broadway musical *Barnum*. With Hopkins and Wilson he re-formed Dawn for cabaret appearances in 1988. Orlando's career was celebrated on the compilation *Tony Orlando and the Best of Dawn* (1995), and Orlando and various Dawns became a staple of the cabaret circuit.

THE ORLONS

Shirley Brickley, b. 9 December 1944; Steve Caldwell, b. 22 November 1942; Marlena Davis, b. 4 October 1944 (replaced by Audrey Brickley); Rosetta Hightower, b. 23 June 1944

A Philadelphia vocal group, the Orlons successfully rode the wave of dance crazes in the early sixties with songs like 'The Wah Watusi' and 'Don't Hang Up'.

The three female members had sung together in junior high school and in 1959 they formed the Orlons with Caldwell singing bass and Brickley as lead vocalist. The name derived from the Cashmeres, a group with whom they frequently appeared and who later became the **Dovells**. In 1960 the Orlons and Dovells became label-mates on Cameo.

Neither Davis's 'I'll Be True' (1960) nor 'Happy Birthday 21' (1961) made an impact but in 1962 the group were given Kal Mann and David Appell's 'Wah Watusi', the song of a dance featured on **Dick Clark**'s *American Bandstand* television show. It was a Top Ten hit, as was the novelty telephone-call follow-up, 'Don't Hang Up'. Members of the group also sang backing vocals on records by other Cameo artists, such as **Bobby Rydell** and Dee Dee Sharp, whose own dance hits included 'Mashed Potato Time' (1962) and 'Do the Bird' (1963).

The Orlons' success continued in 1963 with 'South Street', **Gary US Bonds**' 'Not Me' and 'Cross Fire'. But later records, including an uninspired revival of Bobby Lewis's 'Shimmy Shimmy' and 'Bon Doo Wah' (1964), were only minor hits, though the latter's B-side, 'Don't Throw Your Love Away', became a British No. 1 for the **Searchers**. The Philadelphia sound had been overtaken by Motown and later records like 'Come on Down Baby Baby' and 'No Love but Your Love' were based on the style of groups like **Martha and the Vandellas**. By this time too, Caldwell, his bass lines no longer required, had left, and Brickley's sister Audrey replaced Davis.

Leaving Cameo in 1965, the Orlons recorded briefly for Calla and ABC before splitting up. Hightower moved to England and a career in cabaret, while Shirley Brickley later re-formed the Orlons with Ella Webster and Jimmy Lewis to play oldies concerts.

BETH ORTON

b. December 1970, Norwich, England

Singer-songwriter Orton's début album *Trailer Park* introduced a fresh version of folk music, adding subtle trip-hop rhythms to traditional themes.

Orton made her first foray into the music industry with 'Don't Wanna Know about Evil' (1992), a **John Martyn** cover recorded with William Orbit. She also appeared on Orbit's *Strange Cargo 3* (1993) album, and provided vocals for the first two Red Snapper singles, 'Snapper' and 'In Deep'. Orton began to attract record company interest after singing on 'Alive: Alone', the closing track on the **Chemical Brothers**' début LP, *Exit Planet Dust* (1995).

Signing with Heavenly Recordings for the release of 'She Cries Your Name' (1996), Orton recruited a backing band comprising guitarist Ted Barnes, bassist Ali Friend (also of Red Snapper), Lee Spencer (keyboards) and Wildcat Will (drums) for live performances. Her full-length début, *Trailer Park* (1996), produced by Victor Van Vught (**Nick Cave**) and Andy Weatherall (**Primal Scream**), was instantly proclaimed as one of the year's best albums and went gold in the UK. The singer reached her creative peak with the *Best Bit* EP (1997), which included two tracks recorded with jazz-folk veteran **Terry Callier**. *Central Reservation* (1999) featured further collaborations with Callier and spawned a UK hit single, 'Stolen Car'.

KID ORY

b. Edward Ory, 25 December 1886, La Place, Louisiana, USA, d. 23 January 1973, Hawaii

A founder of the New Orleans trombone style, Ory's was the first black jazz band to make records in 1922. The revival of interest in traditional jazz during the forties brought him out of retirement and gave a new impetus to his career.

He played banjo and trombone in junior bands in La Place before moving to New Orleans – where his brother had a saloon – in 1912. Ory formed a band which was in demand for dances, cabarets and private parties given by wealthy whites. Among its members were clarinettist **Sidney Bechet** and **King Oliver** on cornet. When Oliver moved to Chicago in 1918, Ory replaced him with **Louis Armstrong**.

The following year Ory himself moved to California for medical reasons. With fellow New Orleans musicians Mutt Carey (cornet) and Wade Whaley (clarinet) he formed a band to play at various West Coast venues and in 1922 they made the first recordings of a black jazz band for Sunshine.

In 1925 Ory went to Chicago to play on Armstrong's renowned Hot Five records for Okeh. Over the next few years he also recorded with Oliver's Dixie Syncopaters, with Johnny Dodds (clarinet), **Ma Rainey** and **Jelly Roll Morton**.

During the early thirties Ory played with several West Coast bands before leaving music for chicken farming in 1933. He returned to performing in 1942 with Barney Bigard's group and came to national prominence when he formed a traditional style band to take part in an Orson Welles radio series in 1944. It featured Mutt Carey on trumpet and Jimmy Noone (clarinet). Ory appeared with Armstrong in the film *New Orleans* (1947) and his Creole Jazz Band went on to record for Good Time Jazz and Columbia and performed live until 1955. A new recording of his composition 'Muskrat Ramble' was a minor hit in 1954.

Poor health meant that Ory's later appearances were infrequent, although he performed at his own club in San Francisco until 1961 and appeared at the New Orleans Jazz Festival in 1971. Ory was featured in a number of films, including *Crossfire* (1947) and *The Benny Goodman Story* (1955).

THE OSBORNE BROTHERS
Bobbie, b. 7 December 1931, Hyden, Kentucky, USA; Sonny, b. 29 October 1937, Hyden

The Osborne Brothers were among the most influential artists in bluegrass, introducing not only the distinctive and technically impressive playing of Sonny on banjo and Bobbie on mandolin but innovations in vocal harmony, including switching the lead, tenor and baritone parts between the singers in mid-song. They were also pioneers in the use of amplification and certain instruments, notably the drums.

Bobbie began playing professionally in 1949 and spent about two years with the Lonesome Pine Fiddlers, a respected bluegrass outfit. Sonny spent the summer of 1952, when he was still only fourteen years old, working with **Bill Monroe**, and played on ten of his Decca sides. The brothers made their radio début as a duo in 1953 on WROL, Knoxville, Tennessee, moving in the following year to WJR in Detroit, from which base they established themselves in the Midwest. In 1956 they joined the WWVA, Wheeling, West Virginia, *Jamboree* and signed with MGM. (They had previously been with King and RCA, recording for the latter a superb 1954 session with **Jimmy Martin** that included 'Chalk Up Another One' and '20/20 Vision'.) 'Ruby' (1956), with its eerie, echoing high harmonies, and 'Once More' were their most successful MGM numbers. In 1959 they formed a trio with Benny Birchfield, who sang lead. Bobbie sang tenor and Sonny baritone.

Following the example of **Flatt and Scruggs**, the Osbornes investigated the college and folk-club circuits, appearing at several Newport Folk Festivals.

Signing with Decca in 1963 they recorded *Voices in Bluegrass* (1965), *Up This Hill and Down* (1966), *Modern Sounds* (1967) and numerous other albums. Their best-known single song was **Felice and Boudleaux Bryant**'s 'Rocky Top' (1967), which has since become a bluegrass classic. From the late seventies they recorded for CMH – including a double-album of the Bryants' songs, *From Rocky Top to Muddy Bottom* (1977) – and later for Sugar Hill, in a more traditional style than they have sometimes adopted. Their past contributions to bluegrass were not always welcomed by purists, especially their use of drums, but the Osborne Brothers are the only bluegrass act recognized by the Nashville industry, which has frequently nominated them for Country Music Association Awards.

OSIBISA
Teddy Osei, b. Kumasi, Ghana; Robert Bailey, b. Trinidad, West Indies; Wendell Richardson, b. Antigua, West Indies; Mac Tontoh; Sol Amafio; Loughty Amao, b. Nigeria; Spartacus R, b. Grenada, West Indies (replaced by Jean Mandengue); Kofi Avivor; Princess

For over two decades, Osibisa have been a leading exponent of African-rock fusion music. The group has been equally successful in Europe and West Africa and has been an inspiration to other African musicians.

The band was founded in London in 1969 by Osei, a saxophone and flute player, and drummer Sol Amàrfio. Osei had previously led the Black Star Band, Teddy Osei's Assembly and Cat's Paw. Signing to MCA they recorded a self-titled album, which featured lead vocalist Richardson, and *Woyaya*. Produced by Tony Visconti, both were Top Twenty hits, fusing African and rock music with lengthy guitar solos in the currently fashionable mode established by **Santana**. After releasing *Heads*, the band appeared in the film *Superfly TNT*.

Switching labels to Warner Bros, they issued *Happy Children* (1973) and *Osibirock* (1974). By this time bassist Spartacus R, Richardson and Bailey had left the group. Another move to Bronze in 1976 brought Osibisa's only hit singles, 'Sunshine Day' and 'Dance the Body Music' from the album *Welcome Home*.

In the eighties Osibisa's recordings included *Mystic Energy* (Calibre, 1980), *Live at the Marquee 1983* (Premier, 1984) and *Osibisa Unleashed* (Magnet, 1983). More important was the group's international touring schedule, which took them to Kenya, Senegal, Sierra Leone and India and much of Europe. One of Osibisa's vocalists, Princess, had later chart success with **Stock, Aitken and Waterman**'s 'Say I'm Your No. 1' (1985). A mark of their influence within Ghana was that between 1995 and 1997 Red Steel oversaw the reissue of their entire catalogue.

K. T. OSLIN
b. Kay Toinette Oslin, 15 May 1941, Crossit, Arkansas, USA

As a songwriter Oslin made her mark by articulating the attitudes and concerns of mature women – she called her 1993 greatest hits album *Songs from an Aging Sex Bomb* – in a manner comparable to **Bonnie Raitt**. As a recording artist her approach, in which **Dire Straits** and synthesizers have a role, was moulded by her wide range of musical experiences, which included musical theatre and advertising jingles, before finding success in Nashville in the eighties.

Raised on country music she turned to studying drama and playing folk music in the sixties in the Houston area. She was briefly a member of a trio with cult singer-songwriter Guy Clark, whose début album *Old No. 1* (RCA, 1975), which included 'L.A. Freeway', 'Texas 1947' and the magnificent 'Desperadoes Waiting for the Train', marked one of the beginnings of the eruption of a traditionalist perspective into country music. Oslin sang back-up vocals on Clark's 1978 eponymous outing. That came after a stint in the chorus of *Hello Dolly* on Broadway. During her brief stay with Elecktra she recorded the indicatively titled 'Younger Men (Are Starting to Catch My Eye)' (1981) which, though it sold badly, garnered interest in her as a songwriter. Her breakthrough song was 'Old Pictures', which was a huge hit for the **Judds**. In the wake of that she was signed to RCA and had immediate success with *80s Ladies* (1987), in which she found a way of writing and singing about sexual matters not in the would-be shocking manner of **Millie Jackson** or **Madonna** but as part of a person's life. It included the country chart-toppers 'Do Ya' and 'I'll Always Come Back'. Even better was *This Woman* (1988), which included the moving 'Hey Bobby' and the partly narrated 'Hold Me', a painful song about the break up of a marriage. She followed that with *Love in a Small Town* (1990): a less powerful, but still acutely observed album, it included a wide range of songs, including 'Mary and Willi' and 'Momma Was a Dancer'. Subsequent outings were less successful. In 1993 she made her film début in Peter Bogdanovich's *The Thing Called Love*. The cleverly titled *My Roots Are Showing* (1996), her first studio recording since 1990, saw her covering a collection of other people's songs to little effect. Its risqué cover was much criticized in Nashville.

THE OSMONDS
Alan, b. 22 June 1949, Ogden, Utah, USA; Wayne, b. 28 August 1951, Ogden; Merrill, b. 30 April 1953, Ogden; Jay, b. 2 March 1955, Ogden; Donny, b. Donald Clark Osmond, 9 December 1957, Ogden; Marie, b. 13 October 1959, Ogden; 'Little' Jimmy, b. 16 April 1963, Canoga Park, California

One of the most successful pop-music family acts of all time, the Osmonds between 1971 and 1978 collectively sold some 25 million records and, like fellow teenybopper idols **David Cassidy** and the **Bay City Rollers**, an even greater number of photographs of themselves. In the eighties the Osmonds together and separately turned to country music.

Raised as Mormons, the Osmond children sang regularly at family gatherings. In 1962 the four older brothers appeared in 'Disneyland After Dark'. This led to regular appearances on **Andy Williams'** television shows between 1962 and 1967 and comedian Jerry Lewis's shows (1967–9). During these years, with Donny now a member of the group, they recorded unsuccessfully for Williams' Barnaby label and MCA's Uni subsidiary and toured with **Pat Boone**. Their sound was decidedly middle-of-the-road, but in the wake of the enormous success of the **Jackson Five**, **Mike Curb** signed them to MGM and set about recording the group in a more contemporary manner. The result was the **Rick Hall**-produced American No. 1, 'One Bad Apple'* (1971), the first of a string of international hits (mostly produced by Hall). Among these were **Joe South**'s 'Yo-Yo'* (1971), 'Down by the Lazy River'* and 'Crazy Horses' (1972), which – like the majority of their hits – was written by members of the group. That and their reading of **Johnny Bristol**'s composition 'Love Me for a Reason' (1974) were their best recordings, while *The Plan* (1973) was a concept album inspired by their Mormon beliefs.

In parallel with the group's hits, Donny and Marie recorded together and separately while the youngest brother, Jimmy, also briefly pursued a successful career as a pre-teen idol. He was especially popular in Japan (where he was billed as 'Jimmy Boy') and Britain, where 'Long Haired Lover from Liverpool', a novelty song originally written in response to **The Beatles**' American success a decade earlier, topped the charts in 1972. His other hits were also revivals. They were 'Tweedle Dee' (1973) – a hit for **Lavern Baker** (1955) – and 'I'm Gonna Knock on Your Door', originally a hit for another pre-teen, Eddie Hodges (Cadence, 1961).

Even more committed to revivals of past hits was Donny. After the **Billy Sherrill** composition 'Sweet and Innocent'*, he recorded the Gerry Goffin and **Carole King** songs 'Go Away Little Girl'* (a million-seller for **Steve Lawrence** in 1962) and 'Hey Girl' (a 1963 hit for Freddie Scott on Colpix). But it was mostly to songs associated with fifties teen heartthrobs that Donny turned. Thus, his later hits included 'Puppy Love' and 'Lonely Boy' (1972), originally recorded by **Paul Anka**; **Anthony Newley**'s 'Why' (1972); **Johnny Mathis**'s 'The Twelfth of Never' (1973); **Sonny James**' 'Young Love' (1973); and even **Elvis Presley**'s 'Are You Lonesome Tonight' (1973). Donny's duets with Marie involved a further series of revivals. These included 'I'm Leaving It (All) Up to You' (1974), originally an American No. 1 for Dale and Grace (Montel, 1963); 'Morning Side of the Mountain' (1972), by **Tommy Edwards** (MGM, 1959); 'Deep Purple' (1976), an American No. 1 for another brother and sister act, Nino Tempo and April Stevens (Atco, 1963); 'Ain't Nothing Like the Real Thing' (Polydor, 1976), by **Marvin Gaye** and Tammi Terrell (1968); and '(You're My) Soul and Inspiration' (1978), an American No. 1 for the **Righteous Brothers** (1968).

Marie's solo hits included revivals of 'Paper Roses'* (1973) and 'Who's Sorry Now' (1975), a hit for **Connie Francis** (1958). When her pop hits dried up, she turned, like Francis, to country music, as did the Osmonds after briefly disbanding in 1980. They recorded, with success in the country charts, for Mercury and then Warners, while Marie's Capitol/Curb albums included *There's No Stopping Your Heart* (1986), *I Only Wanted You* (1987) and *All in Love* (1988). Her hits are collected together on *Special Collection* (Curb, 1995).

In 1982 Donny appeared in a revival of **George M. Cohan**'s musical *Little Johnny Jones* and in 1987, after attempting a behind-the-scenes career in music, returned to recording with *Soldier of Love* (Virgin). He followed it with *Eyes Don't Lie* (1989) and its minor hit single, 'My Love Is a Fire'. Donny later appeared in the Toronto production of **Andrew Lloyd Webber** and Tim Rice's *Joseph and the Amazing Technicolour Dreamcoat*.

A new generation of Osmonds emerged in 1992 when four of Alan's sons recorded *Boysterous* (Curb) as the Osmond Boys. Following the group's hit with a reissue of 'Crazy Horses' in the UK, their hits were collected together on *The Very Best of the Osmonds* (1993).

GILBERT O'SULLIVAN

b. Raymond Edward O'Sullivan, 1 December 1946, Waterford, Ireland

A singer-songwriter of the seventies, O'Sullivan's best work owed most to pre-rock musical traditions of music-hall and Denmark Street. His later career lost momentum when he was involved in a six-year law suit.

He moved to England at the age of thirteen and studied art in Swindon where he played in Rick's Blues led by later **Supertramp** keyboards-player

Richard Davies. In 1965 he signed to Columbia for two unsuccessful singles and later (as Gilbert) recorded briefly for Major Minor. In 1970 O'Sullivan was signed by Gordon Mills, manager of **Tom Jones** and **Engelbert Humperdinck**. Mills provided a recording contract – with his own MAM label – and a striking 'Bisto kid' image with short trousers, short hair and cloth cap. O'Sullivan's first single, the clever, riddling 'Nothing Rhymed', reached the British Top Ten and in 1971 he was equally successful with 'We Will' and 'No Matter How I Try'.

His first American success was 'Alone Again (Naturally)'* (1972), which hastened a change of image to a collegiate sweater and long hair. Further million-sellers followed in the cloying 'Clair' (1972), dedicated to Mills' baby daughter, and the up-tempo 'Get Down'. Later records made little impact in America, but O'Sullivan's string of British hits continued with 'Why Oh Why Oh Why' and 'Christmas Song' (1974).

'I Don't Love You but I Think I Like You' (1975) was O'Sullivan's final MAM hit and in 1978 he sued the company for non-payment of royalties and unfair treatment in the terms of his contract. The case did not come to court until 1984, by which time O'Sullivan had moved to Columbia. Despite a Top Twenty single in 'What's in a Kiss' (1980), his two albums for the label – *Off Centre* (1980) and *Life in Rhymes* (1982), produced by **10CC**'s Graham Gouldman – sold poorly.

In 1984 the court found in O'Sullivan's favour and the following year he received £2 million from MAM, plus the full ownership of the copyrights of his songs. He returned to recording with *Frobisher Drive* (1988), which was not released in Britain, and *In the Key of G* (Chrysalis, 1989). Neither album was a commercial success, and an autobiographical touring stage show in 1991 was a major flop. Undaunted, O'Sullivan carried on, releasing *Nothing but the Best* (1991) and *Sounds of the Loop* (1993). More successful in Japan, he released *Live in Japan* (1993), *By Larry* and *The Little Album* (1994) there. In 1997 he issued *Singer Sewing Machine* (Park).

JOHNNY OTIS

b. John Veliotes, 8 December 1921, Vallejo, California, USA

Known as 'The Godfather of Rhythm and Blues', Otis was a seminal figure in the development of R&B on the West Coast of America, a link between the big-band blues of the forties and the harder sounds of the fifties and beyond.

The son of Greek immigrants, Otis was raised in the black quarter of Berkeley and by his teens was proficient on drums, piano and vibes. He first played professionally in the early forties with Count Matthews, who led a strongly blues-influenced dance band. After a further apprenticeship with several touring big bands, he formed his own sixteen-piece orchestra. His first major hit was 'Harlem Nocturne' (Excelsior, 1945) and for the next few years he toured with **Louis Jordan** (who would remain a lasting influence) and others, until in 1947 the big-band era came to a close. Otis then formed a smaller, bluesier aggregation and with Bardu Ali opened the Barrel House Club in Los Angeles. There he discovered **Esther Phillips**, the Robins (later the **Coasters**) and Mel Walker, with whom, as the Johnny Otis Congregation, he recorded for Modern in 1949 and then for Savoy. 1950 was Otis's *annus mirabilis*. That year he topped the R&B charts with 'Double Crossing Blues' and 'Mistrustin' Blues' and had huge hits with 'Deceivin' Blues', 'Far Away Christmas Blues' and 'Rockin' Blues'.

Over the next few years Otis criss-crossed America with the Johnny Otis R&B Caravan, a show that featured such artists as **Big Mama Thornton** (who in 1953, produced by Otis, recorded the original version of 'Hound Dog'), **Jackie Wilson**, **Little Willie John**, **Hank Ballard** and **Johnny Ace**, whose biggest-ever hit, 'Pledging My Love' (1952), Otis produced and arranged. However, Otis's own recordings for **Don Robey**'s Duke label, where his group was virtually the house band, were less successful and his compositions like 'Every Beat of My Heart' only became hits later for **Gladys Knight** (Vee-Jay, 1961) and others. Following the arrival of rock'n'roll, Otis adjusted his style and had a number of hits on Capitol. Among these, most of which featured Marie Adams and the Three Tons of Joy, were 'Willie and the Hand Jive' (1958), covered in Britain by **Cliff Richard** (1960), 'Crazy Country Hop' (1958) and 'Casting My Spell' (1959), while in Britain he had a huge hit with 'Ma He's Making Eyes at Me' (1957), later successfully revived by pre-teen star Lena Zavaroni (Philips, 1974). For all their calculated novelty elements, these and other recordings ('Three Girls Named Molly Doin' the Hully Gully', for example) had at their heart the innocence of Louis Jordan's earlier 'party' records.

After a brief sojourn on King, Otis retired for most of the sixties when he entered Democratic party politics and published an autobiography, *Listen to the Lambs*. He returned to music with *Cold Shot* (Kent, 1969), which spawned the R&B hit 'Country Girl' and featured the guitar-playing of his son Shuggie, whose subsequent solo records included *Here Comes Shuggie* (Epic, 1970).

Otis resurrected the revue format and had success with *Live at Monterey* (Epic, 1970). During the seventies he toured intermittently and formed his own label, Blues Spectrum, on which he issued recordings by R&B pioneers **Charles Brown**, Jordan and **Joe Turner**. However, these recordings, like Otis's own *The New Johnny Otis Show* (Alligator, 1981), are only of historical interest. In the eighties Otis became pastor of the Landmark Community Church in Los Angeles, while in the nineties he performed regularly at a number of local venues.

BUCK OWENS
b. Alvis Edgar Owens, 12 August 1929, Sherman, Texas, USA

In the early sixties, when most Nashville-based country acts were recording with strings, Owens with his band the Buckaroos, in the words of country-music historian Bill C. Malone, 'created a sound that had the hard edge of honky-tonk and the bounce of rockabilly'.

The son of a sharecropper, Owens was raised in Arizona and learned mandolin and guitar while a child; he became a professional musician in his teens. In 1951 he moved to Bakersfield, California, and formed the Schoolhouse Playboys while also working as a session guitarist for Capitol Records on recordings by **Wanda Jackson**, **Sonny James**, **Faron Young** and Tommy Collins (the alias of country songwriter Leonard Snipes), among others. In 1957 after a brief stay with the local Pep label, Owens joined Capitol and in 1959 had his first major success with 'Second Fiddle'. That was a sad song, but his biggest successes were with up-beat numbers which featured guitarist Don Rich and steel-guitarist Tom Brumley (the son of gospel composer Albert E. Brumley, author of the gospel standard 'I'll Fly Away'). They combined to give Owens a hard, rhythmic edge that was later emulated by **Merle Haggard** (who was also based in Bakersfield and later married Owens' former wife Bonnie).

Among Owens' early hits, several co-written with **Harlan Howard**, were 'Excuse Me (I Think I've Got a Heartache)' (1960), 'Fooling Around' and 'Under the Influence of Love' (1961). During this period he also recorded with **Rose Maddox** ('Loose Talk'; 'Mental Cruelty', 1961), but his most influential recordings were the hard-edged 'Act Naturally' (1963), a pop hit better known through its cover by **The Beatles** (1965); 'I've Got a Tiger by the Tail'; 'Waitin' in the Welfare Line' (1965); and 'Tall Dark Stranger' (1969). By now a country superstar, Owens pledged himself to record only country material and sang such ironic patriotic items as 'Made in Japan' (1972). However, after becoming co-host with **Roy Clark** of the long-running *Hee Haw* teleseries in 1969 (the year he had a country hit with **Paul Simon**'s 'Bridge Over Troubled Water'), he set about establishing himself as a publisher and manager of other artists, including Susan Raye (with whom he often duetted in the seventies) and his son Buddy Allan (with whom he recorded the wry 'Too Old to Cut the Mustard', 1971).

Following a change of labels to Warners in 1976, Owens' hits declined. His later records (which included the duet with **Emmylou Harris**, 'Play Together Again, Again', 1979) were less distinctive. More interesting were the recordings he made at the end of the eighties. These included the pointed duet with Dwight Yoakam, one of the new country stars deeply influenced by Owens, 'The Streets of Bakersfield', and the album *Hot Dog!* (Capitol, 1988), which included another Yoakam duet, 'Under Your Spell Again'. Owens toured with Yoakam and released another album which mixed new versions of his old songs with new material, *Act Naturally* (1989).

He remained a popular live act in the United States. In 1990 he re-recorded his hits for Curb, *All Time Greatest Hits, Vol. 1*, but these were only pale shadows of the originals, which were reissued on the Rhino three-CD retrospective, *The Collection* (1992). *Half a Buck* (1996) is a personally chosen collection of Owen's duets with the likes of Rose Maddox, Susan Raye and **Ringo Starr**.

AUGUSTUS PABLO

b. Horace Swaby, 1953, St Andrews, Jamaica

The musician who introduced the piping sound of the melodica to reggae music, Pablo has had many instrumental and dub hits.

A self-taught pianist, he took up the melodica (a hand-held reed instrument with a keyboard) at school, where he also had a sound system. One of his class-mates was Tyrone Downie, later the keyboards player with **Bob Marley**. Swaby's first recordings were 'Iggy Iggy' and 'East of the River Nile' (Aquarius, 1969), produced by Herman Chin-Loy, who gave Swaby the name Augustus Pablo. His first hit was the Clive Chin-produced 'Java' (Randy's, 1969). Soon afterwards, **Lee Perry** brought in Pablo to add melodica solos to such Wailers' tracks as 'Kaya' and 'Sun Is Shining'.

Influenced in part by Milt Jackson's vibraphone-playing for the **Modern Jazz Quartet**, these early records were instrumentals with Eastern-sounding melody lines over a reggae backing. In 1972 Pablo established his own record label, Rockers, and began to experiment with producer **King Tubby** on dub versions of his older material. On *King Tubby Meets Rockers Uptown* (Trojan, 1974) four-track recording technology was used to blank out different instruments to achieve haunting effects. While many dub creators emphasized bass and drum lines, Pablo's work retained the melodica melody line as a central thread.

Pablo's many recordings included reworkings of pop tunes like **Rod McKuen**'s 'Jean', **George Gershwin**'s 'Old Man River' and **Bill Withers**' 'Ain't No Sunshine'. He also produced such artists as the Heptones ('Love Don't Come Easy'), **Big Youth** ('Cassava Rock') and Hugh Mundell ('Afrika Must Be Free by 83'). In 1986 he produced Junior Delgado's *Ragamuffin Year* (Island). He toured the United States in 1985 and in 1990, when he recorded *Blowing with the Wind*, which included traditional Jamaican Nyahbingi drumming. In the same year Profile issued his *We Refuse* in America.

GENE PAGE

b. Los Angeles, USA

One of the leading West Coast studio arrangers, best known for his lush orchestrations, Page worked in the sixties with **Phil Spector** and later with R&B artists like **Solomon Burke**, **Marvin Gaye** and **Barry White**. He made a series of instrumental albums in the seventies and wrote arrangements for such artists as **Elton John** and **Joan Baez**.

Both his father and brother Billy Page were songwriters and he began learning classical piano at the age of five. He won a scholarship to Brooklyn Conservatory in New York before working as a studio arranger. Page's first major success came with the melodramatic string arrangement for the **Righteous Brothers**' 'You've Lost That Lovin' Feelin'' (1964), produced by Spector. In contrast, he created a 'live' club sound on **Dobie Gray**'s 'The "In" Crowd' (1965) before returning to a soulful approach on Solomon Burke's 'Got to Get You off My Mind' (1965).

In the late sixties he became staff arranger for Reprise and then Motown, where he worked with Gaye and **Diana Ross**. The first album to appear under Page's own name was the film score *Blacula* (RCA, 1972), made before he collaborated with Barry White on a series of string-drenched hits. Page also appeared live with White, conducting the Love Unlimited Orchestra. White's success inspired the lush orchestrations of such Page solo albums as *Lovelock* (Atlantic, 1976) and *Close Encounters* (Arista, 1978).

During the seventies and eighties Page provided string arrangements for **Betty Everett**, Ross, Carole Bayer Sager, Deniece Williams, Melissa Manchester, **Manhattan Transfer** and Joan Baez (*Recently*, Goldcastle, 1988), among others.

PATTI PAGE

b. Clara Ann Fowler, 8 November 1927, Claremore, Oklahoma, USA

Best remembered for her evocative double-tracked recording of 'Tennessee Waltz'* (1950), Page, who had fourteen million-sellers in the fifties, was one of the most successful pop singers of her era and one who regularly drew on country music for her repertoire.

She grew up in Tulsa and sang country songs on a local radio station in her teens (she took her stage name from one of the sponsors of her show, the Page Milk Company), before bandleader Jack Rael took her to Chicago and secured her a recording contract with Mercury in 1948. On her first hit, 'Confess' (1948), a double-tracked Page harmonized with herself, a practice which became a feature of many of her fifties recordings. Her first million-seller was the film song 'With My Eyes Wide Open, I'm Dreaming' (1949); this was followed by a revival of **Pee Wee King**'s 'Tennessee Waltz' (originally a country hit for **Cowboy Copas** in 1948), which was one of the most successful records of the year. Like 'Mockingbird Hill'* (1951), 'Tennessee Waltz' was also a hit for guitar virtuoso **Les Paul** and his wife Mary Ford. Page's other million-sellers included 'All My Love' (1950), a French song with English lyrics by Mitchell Parish, who later provided English lyrics to **Domenico Modugno**'s 'Volare' (1958); the country song 'Detour'; 'Mister and Mississippi' (1951), written by Irving Gordon, a writer who specialized in the use of American place names (he also wrote **Perry Como**'s 'Delaware', 1960); and the much-recorded 'Changing Partners' (1953).

Her recording of **Bob Merrill**'s sentimental novelty song 'That Doggie in the Window'* (1953), though it was successfully parodied by country comedians Homer and Jethro (RCA), saw a break with country material. This continued with the lush ballads 'Allegheny Moon'*, 'Old Cape Cod'* (1956) and her last million-seller 'Left Right out of Your Heart' (1958). Page continued to record throughout the sixties, mixing country repertoire ('A City Girl Stole My Country Boy', 1961) with pop songs and had her last major hit with the film theme 'Hush Hush, Sweet Charlotte' (Columbia, 1965). In the seventies she recorded exclusively country material for Mercury, Epic and Harmony, with limited success. She continued touring throughout the eighties.

ROBERT PALMER
b. 19 January 1949, Batley, Yorkshire, England

A talented white soul singer who fronted Vinegar Joe with **Elkie Brooks**, Palmer later transcended his influences to create a glossy and stylish sound in the eighties.

After spending some years in Malta the teenage Palmer led Yorkshire group the Mandrakes before joining the Alan Bown Set in 1968. Led by a jazz trumpeter, the band performed jazz-rock and recorded five albums for Pye, Decca and Island between 1967 and 1971. He next joined Pete Gage's experimental band Dada, where he teamed up with Brooks. The group cut one album for Atlantic before turning into Vinegar Joe, a dynamic soul-rock group that made three Island albums in 1972–3. After Vinegar Joe disbanded, **Chris Blackwell** signed Palmer to a solo contract. The title track of the Steve Smith-produced *Sneakin' Sally through the Alley* (Island, 1974), written by **Allen Toussaint**, was a reworking of **Lee Dorsey**'s original recording and confirmed Palmer's new status as a blue-eyed soul singer. Among the backing musicians on *Pressure Drop* (1975) and *Some People Can Do What They Like* (1976) were members of **Little Feat**.

Palmer, however, did not find a fully individual voice until moving to Nassau in the Bahamas and recording *Double Fun* (1978) and *Secrets* (1979). Self-produced, they gave him American hits with 'Every Kinda People' (1978) and the insistent dance track 'A Bad Case of Lovin' You (Doctor Doctor)' (1979), the latter written by US singer-songwriter Moon Martin, who also wrote Mink Deville's 'Cadillac Walk'. With the unlikely assistance of **Gary Numan**, *Clues* (1980) included the emphatic 'Johnny and Mary' and 'Looking for Clues'.

Palmer took time out to produce albums by **Desmond Dekker** (*Compass Point*, 1981), **Tangerine Dream**'s Peter Baumann and Moon Martin. In 1982 his stage sound was captured on *Maybe It's Live*, which as the title suggests also included some studio tracks, including his biggest British hit, the jaunty, driving 'Some Guys Have All the Luck'.

After releasing *Pride* (1983), Palmer joined pop supergroup Power Station with **Duran Duran** members John Taylor and Andy Taylor. 'Some Like It Hot' and 'Get It on' were 1985 Top Ten hits but Palmer left the group before its first tour. His replacement was British singer Michael Des Barres, formerly of hard rock band Silverhead. Resuming his solo career, Palmer had two No. 1 hits in 1986 with 'Addicted to Love' and 'I Didn't Mean to Turn You on'. Both were slick, sophisticated recordings (promoted by slick, sexy videos featuring mini-skirted models playing in his 'band'), and brought the criticism that he was making 'white soul for snobs'. They were taken from *Riptide* (1985), his final Island recording. A compilation, *Addictions Vol. 1*, was released by Island in 1989.

In 1987 he joined EMI, releasing *Heavy Nova* and the hits 'She Makes My Day' (1988) and 'Simply Irresistible' (1988). He joined forces with **UB40** for a cover of **Bob Dylan**'s 'I'll Be Your Baby Tonight' in 1990. It was a Top Ten hit, as was his medley of **Marvin Gaye**'s 'Mercy Mercy Me'/'I Want You'. Both were taken from the Top Thirty album *Don't Explain* (1990). A second volume of *Addictions* (Island) appeared in 1992, and later that year Palmer released an album of jazz standards, *Ridin' High*. His 1994 album, *Honey*, was recorded at his home studio in Italy. In 1998 he released a compilation of out-takes, *Woke Up Laughing*, and in 1999 his first studio album for some time, *Rhythm & Blues* (Eagle).

NORRIE PARAMOR
b. 1913, England, d. 9 September 1979

The most successful British producer of the fifties and early sixties, Paramor had a decisive influence on the evolution of British pop music in the pre-**Beatles** era.

A pianist and arranger, Paramor graduated from accompanying **Gracie Fields** to playing with various dance bands in the thirties. During the Second World War he was an arranger for Forces' entertainment units. In 1945 he joined Harry Gold and His Pieces of Eight and led session bands for the independent Oriole record company before, in 1952, he was appointed recording director of EMI's Columbia label. He had immediate success with his production of trumpeter Eddie Calvert's evocative reading of 'Oh Mein Papa'* (1953), which topped the British charts and was also an American hit, despite a million-selling vocal version by **Eddie Fisher**. Paramor oversaw the subsequent recordings by the trumpeter (*b. 15 March 1922, Preston, Lancashire, England, d. 7 August 1978, Johannesburg, South Africa*). These included Calvert's version of 'Cherry Pink and Apple Blossom White' (1955), originally recorded by **Perez Prado**, and the exotic 'Zambesi' (1952), a surprise hit when revived by the Piranhas (Dakota, 1982). Calvert later emigrated to South Africa and during the Zimbabwe liberation wars recorded 'Amazing Race', one of the most bizarre right-wing protest songs ever.

In 1954 Paramor began to record orchestral mood music albums (*Emptiona, Zodiac Suite*) in the manner of **Mantovani**. He also formed the Big Ben Banjo Band (and later the Big Ben Hawaiian Band and Big Ben Trad Band) which regularly appeared on television and radio, and, in the manner of **Winifred Atwell**, had hits with the medleys 'Let's Get Together No. 1' (1954) and 'Again' (1955).

In 1956 Paramor made what is claimed to be Britain's first rock'n'roll record with jazz drummer briefly turned rock'n'roller Tony Crombie and his Rockets ('Teach You to Rock'). However, though the record charted, like his fellow established producers in America (notably **Mitch Miller**) Paramor was unsympathetic to rock'n'roll and preferred to work with ballad singers like Michael Holliday and Ruby Murray, whose hits he produced. These included 'The Story of My Life' (1958) and 'Starry Eyed' (1960), both No. 1s for Holliday, and Murray's No. 1, 'Softly Softly' (1955) and 'Goodbye Jimmy Goodbye' (1958). Paramor edged closer to rock'n'roll with his productions of a series of novelty songs for the Mudlarks. The best of these were the inanely pleasing chants 'Lollipop' and 'Book of Love' (1958), covers of American hits by the **Chordettes** and the Monotones (Argo, 1958), respectively. When Paramor decided to record **Cliff Richard** in 1958, he issued Richard's cover-version of Bobby Helm's 'Schoolboy Crush' as the A-side. However, it was the B-side 'Move It', written by Ian Samwell, a member of the Drifters (as the Shadows were then called), that was the hit and launched Richard's career and British rock'n'roll.

Paramor produced more than twenty hits for Richard, including 'Voice in the Wilderness', one of Paramor's many compositions. Others included 'Frightened City' (the Shadows, 1961) and 'Once Upon a Dream' (**Billy Fury**, 1962). He also produced the Avons, who had British success with their cover of Paul Evans' novelty song, 'Seven Little Girls Sitting in the Back Seat' (Guaranteed, 1959), **Frank Ifield**'s hits, many records by the Shadows and Tommy Bruce's surprise hit with his deep-voiced revival of **Fats Waller**'s 'Ain't Misbehaving' (1960). However, Paramor's most celebrated discovery of the period was the big-voiced schoolgirl Helen Shapiro (*b. 28 September 1946, London*). He produced her first hit, 'Don't Treat Me Like a Child', and her pair of British No. 1s, 'You Don't Know'* and 'Walkin' Back to Happiness'* (1961). In retrospect, these records – on which Shapiro's powerful voice is surrounded with over-emphatic choruses and clichéd arrangements – reveal Paramor's unease with pop, in contrast to his contemporary, arranger **John Barry**. Paramor also contributed to numerous British films of the period, including *Expresso Bongo* (1959), *It's Trad Dad* (1960), and *The Young Ones* (1961).

In the wake of The Beatles and demands by groups that they produced themselves or be produced by clearly sympathetic ears, Paramor worked less with rock acts, though he was the producer of the Scaffold's 1968 British chart-topper, 'Lily the Pink'. After leaving EMI, he recorded a number of easy-listening albums for BBC Records with the Midland Radio Orchestra and broadcast regularly with the Orchestra.

MICA PARIS
b. Michelle Warren, 1969, London, England

From a gospel music background, Mica Paris is one of the most stylish soul singers that Britain has produced.

Born in London of Jamaican parents, Paris sang in her grandmother's Pentecostal church as a child. At sixteen, she joined the five-piece gospel group the Spirit of Watts as lead singer. Her move into secular music took place in 1986 when she toured and recorded with Mark Rogers' group Hollywood Beyond.

She signed a recording contract with Island's Fourth & Broadway label, releasing the UK Top Ten hits 'My One Temptation' and 'Like Dreamers Do', which featured a saxophone solo by **Courtney Pine**, in 1988. Her début album, *So Good*, was produced by Peter Vale and Miles Waters, and Will Downing and Roger Christian of the **Christians** were among the guest artists. She also duetted with Downing on the UK hit 'Where Is the Love?' (1989), the **Donny Hathaway–Roberta Flack** classic, before releasing *Contribution*. This time the producers were Andres Levin and Camus Celli and the album included songs composed by **Prince** and **Smokey Robinson**.

Her next album, *Whisper a Prayer*, included productions by **Narada Michael Walden** and former

Heatwave and **Michael Jackson** collaborator Rod Temperton.

CHARLIE PARKER

b. 29 August 1920, Kansas City, Kansas, USA,
d. 12 March 1955, New York

Alto-saxophonist Parker, nicknamed 'Bird' or 'Yardbird', was the most important influence on the development of jazz after 1945. During the early forties he was, with **Dizzy Gillespie**, **Thelonious Monk**, **Kenny Clarke**, and others, one of a small group of New York musicians who turned the dominant swing style inside out to create bebop. As a jazz style, bebop used uncommon harmonies, it emphasized unconventional rhythmic accents and it replaced swing-band riffs with convoluted phrases played in unison. Equally important, bebop represented a revolution in jazz musicians' attitudes. The umbilical link with dance music was cut, leaving the new jazz in a limbo between pop and art. Parker's was the greatest contribution to this musical upheaval because he was one of the most continually creative and imaginative improvisers in the history of jazz. As a soloist he retained a deep feeling for the blues while employing a diamond-hard tone in urgent, headlong rushes of notes to produce improvisations that were models for dozens of younger players. Among those most directly in his debt were Sonny Stitt, **Cannonball Adderley**, Jackie McLean, **Gerry Mulligan** and Eric Dolphy. This compulsive and continuous innovation and the precarious circumstances of the new jazz contributed heavily to Parker's chaotic life and premature death.

After playing baritone sax in a high-school band he took up alto and played in Kansas City with the bands of Lawrence Keyes and Harlan Leonard before joining **Jay McShann**'s orchestra on a permanent basis in 1940. Although McShann's was a conventional blues-based band, Parker's solos on 'Hootie Blues' (1941) and 'Sepia Bounce' (1942) already showed him attempting something different.

Visiting New York with McShann, Parker met bebop pioneers Kenny Clarke and Thelonious Monk, but spent a frustrating period with Noble Sissle's dance band before joining **Earl Hines**' band (1942–3). With Gillespie and other young musicians, the Hines Orchestra was an important precursor of the bebop revolution. In 1944–5 Parker played with such figures as **Billy Eckstine**, Andy Kirk and **Ben Webster** and began to record in his evolving style. He made sides with guitarist Tiny Grimes for Savoy, with Gillespie for Guild ('Salt Peanuts', 'Groovin' High') and with singer Sarah Vaughan ('Mean to Me', Continental, 1945).

The first recordings under Parker's own name included the renowned 'Koko', with its unremitting attack, and the blues 'Billie's Bounce' (Savoy, 1945).

Made with a group that included the young **Miles Davis** on trumpet, these tracks marked the arrival of bebop as a fully fledged alternative to earlier jazz styles. The bulk of the records on which Parker's reputation rests were made in the next three years, for Savoy in New York and Ross Russell's Dial in Los Angeles.

The hundred or so sides (plus even more alternate takes) made for these labels included blues, ballads and bebop originals based on the chords of standard songs. Thus, 'Quasimodo' was derived from **Gershwin**'s 'Embraceable You', 'Stupendous' from ''S Wonderful' and 'Bird Gets the Worm' from **Sigmund Romberg**'s 'Lover Come Back to Me'. The intricate solo from the original blues 'Parker's Mood' (1948) was later given lyrics by jazz singer King Pleasure (Prestige, 1953).

The Dial sessions (released as a six-album set after Parker's death) included such compositions as 'Ornithology', 'Yardbird Suite' and 'A Night in Tunisia'. Among those accompanying Parker were pianists **Erroll Garner** and Dodo Marmorosa. During this period Parker suffered a breakdown which led to a six-month stay in Camarillo mental hospital, later commemorated in the tune 'Relaxing at Camarillo'.

In 1946 he took part in **Norman Granz**'s 'Jazz at the Philharmonic' concerts with **Lester Young** and **Coleman Hawkins** and after 1948 Parker was under contract to Granz's Clef and Verve labels. Although Granz recorded him in 1948–50 with small groups including Davis, and **Bud Powell**, Parker was also recorded with string orchestras, **Machito**'s Latin band and choirs in attempts to find wider audiences for his still eloquent and voluble solos. The critical consensus has been that Parker was uneasy in these settings and reserved his finest work of the fifties for live recordings such as 1953's *Quintet of the Year*, where he played with Gillespie and a superbly supportive rhythm section of Powell, Roach and **Charles Mingus** on bebop standards like 'Salt Peanuts' and 'Night in Tunisia'. In 1953 he also recorded with Davis for Prestige, using the alias Charlie Chan.

From the evidence of numerous off-air tapes and privately made live recordings, it is clear that Parker's finest improvisations were often made in live performance and not in the studio. But by the early fifties his concert and club appearances were notorious for their inconsistency. He died in 1955, worn out by narcotics and alcohol.

The most substantial biography of Parker is *Bird Lives!* (1973) by Ross Russell. In 1988 Clint Eastwood directed the biopic *Bird* in which Parker was played by Forrest Whitaker. The soundtrack, supervised by Lennie Niehaus (released on record by Columbia), used original Parker recordings with new backing tracks.

GRAHAM PARKER

b. 18 November 1950, Camberley, Surrey, England

A highly regarded singer and songwriter who was often compared to **Van Morrison** and **Bruce Springsteen**, Parker did not achieve the commercial success commensurate with his critical reputation.

Guitarist with Way Out while at school, he later busked and played in nightclubs in Gibraltar and Morocco, returning to London in 1971. Like that of **Dire Straits**, Parker's 1975 recording contract (with Vertigo in Britain and Mercury in America) was a result of the playing of a demo tape on Charlie Gillett's *Honky Tonk* show on Radio London.

With backing group the Rumour, including pub-rock veterans from Brinsley Schwarz and Ducks DeLuxe, he cut *Howlin' Wind* (1976). Produced by **Nick Lowe**, another Brinsley Schwarz alumnus, it displayed a tough singing style on a set of songs embodying the values and imagery of rhythm and blues. *Heat Treatment* (1976), produced by Mutt Lange, was in the same vein, but his first chart success came with an EP, *The Pink Parker* (1977), which featured a version of Trammps' 1975 soul hit 'Hold Back the Night'.

Aided by his dynamic live performances, Parker's next four albums reached the British Top Twenty. *Stick to Me* (1977) included **Ann Peebles**' 'I'm Gonna Tear Your Playhouse Down', while *The Parkerilla* (1978) was an undistinguished live set which produced the minor single hit 'Hey Lord Don't Ask Me Questions', a studio remake of a track from his début. The **Jack Nitzsche**-produced *Squeezing out Sparks* (1979) was Parker's bestselling record, and from the same sessions came a new version of the **Jackson Five**'s 1969 million-seller 'I Want You Back'.

Parker next moved to his manager Dave Robinson's Stiff label for *The Up Escalator* (1980). The album included 'Endless Night', a song co-written (and jointly sung) with Springsteen. The Rumour also recorded three albums in 1977–80 and backed American singer-songwriter Garland Jeffreys on his 1980 album *Escape Artist* before disbanding. As a solo artist, Parker moved to RCA for the Jack Douglas-produced *Another Grey Area* (1982) and *The Real Macaw* (1983).

In 1985 he formed a new backing group, the Shot, retaining only Brinsley Schwarz (guitar) from the Rumour. He released *Steady Nerves* on Elektra before returning to RCA in America (Demon in Britain) for *The Mona Lisa's Sister* (1988), co-produced with Schwarz. This was followed by the ambitious *Human Soul* (1989), a semi-concept album with songs split between 'real' and 'surreal' sides. It featured Schwarz and bassist Andrew Bodnar from the Rumour plus Steve Nieve and Pete Thomas from **Elvis Costello**'s band, the Attractions. Later that year, Parker released the superior in concert set, *Live! Alone in America*, which consisted of songs spanning his entire career recorded during a solo American tour. A later companion album was recorded in Japan. 1991's *Struck by Lightning*, which included guest appearances by **The Band**'s Garth Hudson and John Sebastian, was critically acclaimed, but sales were unexceptional. The same fate befell *Burning Questions*, his first under a new deal with Capitol in America. His career to date was summed up on the excellent Rhino Records anthology, *Passion Is No Ordinary Word* (1993). In 1995 he signed with Razor and Tie Records of New York and released *12 Haunted Episodes*. Subsequent albums included the superior *Acid Bubblegum* (1996) and *Loose Monkeys* (1999).

JUNIOR PARKER

b. Herman Parker, 27 March 1932, West Memphis, Arkansas, USA, d. 18 November 1971, Blue Island, Illinois

'Little' Junior Parker suffered from being typed by blues enthusiasts as a down-home artist, located by his harmonica-playing in the same neighbourhood as **Little Walter** or **Sonny Boy Williamson II**. His early recordings in that vein were excellent, but he brought a similar conviction and vocal sensitivity to blues and bluesy pop songs of the kind favoured by **Bobby Bland** and, unlike most artists of his background, took well to the dramatic big-band arrangements of early blues-soul experiments.

He began to work on the Southern blues circuit about 1949, associating with Williamson, **Howlin' Wolf** and others. In Memphis in the early fifties he was part of the circle around **B. B. King** known as the Beale Streeters, but he soon formed his own Blue Flames and recorded for **Sam Phillips**' Sun label the haunting 'Mystery Train' (1953), later taken up by **Elvis Presley**, and the up-tempo 'Feelin' Good', a model for many fifties blues and rockabilly artists. He signed shortly afterwards with Duke and, after a Blue Flames session in the Sun vein, with Pat Hare (guitar), began to work with Bill Harvey's band and similar seven- or eight-piece line-ups. In this he resembled Bland, with whom he toured from 1954 to 1961 and shared a joint début album, *Blues Consolidated* (Duke, 1961).

By the late sixties he was well known in the North and had recorded for Mercury (*Like It Is*, 1968, produced by **Bobby Robinson**), Blue Rock (*Honey-Drippin' Blues*, with two songs by **Doug Sahm**) and Minit (*Blues Man*, 1969). *The Outside Man* (1971), which included **Percy Mayfield**'s 'River's Invitation' and three **Beatles** numbers, was reissued as *Love Ain't Nothin' but a Business Goin' on* on Groove Merchant, which had previously released the fine all-blues set

You Don't Have to Be Black to Love the Blues, its title and cover artwork based on the famous Levy's bread advertisement; Groove Merchant also went on to pair Parker with the organist **Jimmy McGriff** in the disappointing *Good Things Don't Happen Every Day*. Some of these records were released posthumously since in the middle of all this activity Parker died from a brain tumour. *I Tell Stories Sad and True, I Sing the Blues and Play Harmonica Too, It Is Very Funky* (United Artists, 1972), featuring guitarist Wayne Bennett (another Bland connection), and overseen by his long-time producer Sonny Lester, was released after his death.

VAN DYKE PARKS
b. 3 January 1941, Mississippi, USA

Parks' erratic career was structured around uncovering and celebrating the odder corners of American popular music. Most memorably these include the Caribbean influences that lie behind much of it, demonstrated on *The Clang of the Yankee Reaper* (1975) and *Orange Crate Art* (1995), which celebrates the idea of California through a glorification of (aural) surfaces, in the manner of the artform that gives the album its name. As such, his solo albums, which often feature verbal and instrumental montage and dense blocks of sound, were more influential than popular and Parks is best known as a session musician, songwriter, arranger and producer, particularly with the **Beach Boys**.

Born on a military base, Parks moved with his family to Hollywood at the age of thirteen, and became a child actor while studying classical piano. After a brief spell of writing film music in the early sixties, he turned songwriter ('High Coin', recorded by **Bobby Vee**), session musician (he played piano on the **Byrds**' 'Eight Miles High' in 1966 and **Judy Collins**' *Who Knows Where the Time Goes* in 1968) and producer (he produced the Mojo Men's 'Sit Down I Think I Love You' and **Harpers Bizarre**'s version of **Cole Porter**'s 'Anything Goes', both hits in 1967, and the début albums of **Randy Newman** and Collins). His most publicized association of this period was with Brian Wilson of the Beach Boys, with whom he collaborated on songs for the never-released *Smile* album. 'Heroes and Villains' and 'Surf's Up', with typical montage-like lyrics by Parks and music by Wilson, also date from this period.

In 1968 Parks issued *Song Cycle* (Warner Brothers), in which he played off his essentially whimsical sense of pop music against a stately formalism in an effort to document life in the utopia of Southern California. The album, often described as the first example of art-rock, won Parks praise but few sales. His next, the classic *Discover America* (1972), consisting of a mar-

vellous pot-pourri of calypsos about America (be it 'Bing Crosby', 'The Four Mills Brothers' or 'G-Man Hoover'), the Caribbean ('Ode to Tobago') or their interaction ('FDR in Trinidad'), was far more accessible. *The Clang of the Yankee Reaper* (1975), despite its magnificent title track which saw Parks' singing at its best, is a lesser but far more accessible work. At the same time Parks produced albums by the Esso Steel Band and **Mighty Sparrow**.

A decade later came *Jump!* (1984), Parks' charming, but minor, adaptation of the Uncle Remus *Brer Rabbit* folk tales, which also spawned a children's book and a stage show. Ironically, when reissued in Britain in 1986, Parks' early albums outsold *Jump!*. During the eighties Parks continued to arrange and play on sessions, including Peter Case's acclaimed eponymous album (Geffen, 1986). In 1989 he released the less succesful *Tokyo Rose*, a musical meditation on East–West relations and a return to the calypso and Yankee preoccupations of his seventies work. After appearing on the soundtrack of *Crossroads* (1986), Parks played in **Ry Cooder**'s band in 1987–8, appearing on *Get Rhythm* (1987) and touring with him. He also collaborated with producer **Hal Willner** on tribute albums to the music of **Kurt Weill** and the songs from Walt Disney movies (*Lost in the Stars*, 1985, and *Stay Awake*, 1988).

In 1995 he and Brian Wilson reunited for *Orange Crate Art*, which Parks produced and arranged. Credited to both, it is in effect a solo album with Wilson singing Parks' words and melodies. The final track, a rich orchestration of **George Gershwin**'s little-known 'Lullabye', manages to make clear the aural unity of the simple idea of loss and comfort of the Beach Boys at their best with Gershwin's far subtler palette of emotions. Before that track, Wilson's best singing for a decade gives bright voice to a muted celebration of (forties-style) California. In 1998 Parks, whose métier is recorded music, took the unusual step of making a live album, *Moonlighting – Live at the Ash Grove* (Warner). In a similar fashion, in 2000 he acted as concert-master for Brian Wilson's *Pet Sounds* tour.

ALAN PARSONS
b. 1949

A British engineer and producer, Parsons set up the Alan Parsons Project in 1976 with Eric Woolfson to record a series of bestselling concept albums in a progressive rock vein.

From the late sixties Parsons worked at EMI's Abbey Road studios. He was engineer on **The Beatles**' *Abbey Road*, and albums by the **Hollies** and **Paul McCartney**. Nominated for a Grammy award for his work on **Pink Floyd**'s *Dark Side of the Moon* (1973), he graduated to production in 1974, overseeing No. 1

hits by EMI pop bands Cockney Rebel ('Make Me Smile [Come up and See Me]', 1975) and Pilot ('January', 1975).

Leaving EMI, Parsons produced albums by John Miles and **Al Stewart** (*Time Passages*, 1978) and in 1976 issued his first Project album, *Tales of Mystery and Imagination* (Artisa). With arrangements by Andrew Powell (who went on to produce **Kate Bush**), it consisted of a set of mood pieces based on Edgar Allen Poe's stories and performed among others by Pilot, and was a hit in America. *I Robot* (1977) reached the Top Ten, while *Pyramid* was mystically minded and *Eve* (1979) was concerned with male–female relationships.

The big theme of *The Turn of a Friendly Card* (1980) was fate and chance. The album provided Parsons' first hit singles in 'Games People Play' (sung by Lenny Zakatek) and the ballad 'Time', on which Woolfson took the vocals. He also sang 'Eye in the Sky' (1982), the Project's biggest hit and the title track from an album on which ex-**Zombies** vocalist Colin Blunstone was also featured.

Undeterred by critics who regarded his work as pretentious, Parsons issued such further albums as *Ammonia Avenue* (1983), *Vulture Culture* (1985), *Steronomy* (1986) and *Gaudi* (1987). For the compact disc reissue of *Tales* in 1987, Parsons added a narration by Orson Welles.

Parsons later worked with Woolfson on *Freudiana*, a musical show performed in Vienna, before returning to the studio to make *Try Anything Once* (1993). Guest vocalists included Chris Thompson (formerly of **Manfred Mann**'s Earth Band) and **10CC**'s Eric Stewart. Parson's next release was *The Very Best of Life* (Arcade, 1994). He followed that with *On Air* (River North, 1997) before returning briefly in 1998 to oversee EMI's recording studios.

GRAM PARSONS

b. *Cecil Connor, 5 November 1946, Winterhaven, Florida, USA, d. 19 September 1973, Joshua Tree, California*

Parsons was a crucial figure in the development of country-rock. In marked contrast to other rock musicians who adopted country instruments and forms, Parsons, in his work with the **Byrds**, Flying Burritos, and on his solo albums, tried to meld the passion of country music – particularly the harsh, haunting sadness of **George Jones** – with the power of rock. Commercially unsuccessful, he had a profound influence through his recordings and songs on performers like **Elvis Costello** and **Emmylou Harris** (who duetted with him on his solo albums), and on the way country music was seen by the rock audience.

The son of country singer and songwriter Coon Dog Connor, Parsons was raised in Georgia and played guitar from an early age. After his father committed suicide when Parsons was thirteen, he took the name of his mother's second husband and formed a number of bands, the most notable of which were the folkish Shilos, which included Jim Stafford, whose later hits included 'Spiders and Snakes'* (MGM, 1973), and Kent LaVoie, whose later hits as Lobo included 'Me and You and a Dog Named Boo' and 'I'd Love You to Want Me'* (Big Tree, 1971). Material by the Shilos from 1962 was released on Sierra Records in 1979 after Parsons' death. Parsons briefly studied theology at Harvard in 1966 and while there formed the International Submarine Band which recorded the first ever country-rock album, *Safe at Home*, for **Lee Hazelwood**'s LHI label in 1967.

In 1968 Parsons joined the Byrds and was the decisive shaping force in the creation of *Sweetheart of the Rodeo* (1968), the only album he recorded with the group. The Byrds had previously recorded country material – their second album included a version of Porter Wagoner's 'A Satisfied Mind' and *Younger Than Yesterday* (1967) included countryish songs by Chris Hillman – but only from a rock-group standpoint. Parsons introduced the group to the South and the complex and contradictory attitudes to life that country music (and black music, hence the version of **William Bell**'s 'You Don't Miss Your Water') touched on.

The album also included Parsons' first major composition, the intense 'Hickory Wind', about a country boy discovering 'It's a hard way to find out that trouble is real in a far away city with a far away feel', a song that confirmed him as a writer in the mould of **Harlan Howard**.

Even more impressive was *The Gilded Palace of Sin* (A&M, 1969), the début album of the Flying Burrito Brothers, the group Parsons formed with Hillman, steel-guitarist Sneeky Pete Kleinow, Chris Ethridge and Michael Clarke. On the cover Parsons stands wearing a suit by Nudie, tailor to many country stars, but with marijuana leaves and naked ladies in place of the six guns and cowboys beloved of most of Nudie's customers. On the album itself he sang of the evils and anxieties of city life ('Sin City', **Dan Penn**'s 'Dark End of the Street') and the comforts of love ('Hot Burrito W1', 'Hot Burrito W2') in a cracked and breaking voice that, though it lacked the control of, say, Jones or **Merle Haggard**, shared their passion. But if the Parsons stance was essentially traditional, albeit unusual coming from a rock context, his songwriting was innovatory in the way narrative was pared down until the juxtaposition of incidents took upon a mythic, almost surrealistic, edge. The classic example is 'Sin City' in which the city under discussion cannot be protected from 'the Lord's burning rain' even by a 'gold plated door on the 31st floor'.

Burrito Deluxe (1970), which featured future member of the **Eagles** Bernie Leadon, was a lesser album, most notable for the inclusion of **Rolling Stones** Mick Jagger and Keith Richards' 'Wild Horses'. When Parsons left for a solo career, the band continued for several years with a constantly changing line-up, playing a softer, smoother version of country-rock, similar to that of Poco and the Eagles. Among their albums were *Last of the Red Hot Burritos* (1972), *Airborne* (Columbia, 1976) and *Sleepless Nights* (A&M, 1976), a collection of 1970 out-takes by the original group, which featured Parsons singing classic honky-tonk songs and which pointed to Parsons' own solo albums.

The first of these was *GP* (Reprise, 1973), a collection of guilt-ridden ballads interspersed with mysterious evocations of Southern Life ('She', 'The New Soft Shoe') and sweetened by the harmonizing of Emmylou Harris and the guitar of **James Burton**. A critical success, it sold poorly, like the posthumously released *Grievous Angel* (1974), which mined the same territory, most successfully with Parsons and Harris's aching version of **Felice and Boudleaux Bryant**'s 'Love Hurts' and the mordant '$1000 Wedding'.

The strange circumstances of his death, from drug and alcohol abuse, and funeral – his manager kidnapped the corpse and cremated it as the singer would have wished – gave Parsons an immediate cult reputation. A more lasting legacy has come through the exposure given his songs on Harris's string of hit albums and on Costello's records, reissues of his classic recordings and the 1985 biography, *Gram Parsons*, written by Sid Griffin, a founding member of the Long Ryders, one of the second generation of Parsons-influenced country-rockers.

In the eighties and nineties several live performances were released on album. The most noteworthy of these was *Live 1973* (Rhino, 1994). The affecting *Warm Evenings, Pale Mornings, Bottled Blues* (Raven, 1991) collects together important recordings from all the stages of his career. A further mark of his enduring influence were the tribute albums *Commemorativo* (Rhino, 1994), on which mostly alternative acts – but including **Dolly Parton** – performed songs written by and associated with Parsons, and *Return of the Grievous Angel* (Almo, 1999), which was overseen by Harris and served to reintroduce Parsons to a new generation. That was followed in 2000 by *The Gram Parsons Notebooks: The Last Whippoorwill* (Shell Point), a collection of performances of songs and fragments of songs written by Parsons. Included on the album is a pair of tribute songs, recordings of six songs never before recorded by Parsons and a clutch of Parsons' classics, such as 'Hickory Wind'. Among the guest artists were **Ricky Skaggs** and James Burton.

DOLLY PARTON
b. 19 January 1946, Locust Ridge, Tennessee, USA

A household name, Parton has been more celebrated for her extravagant blonde wigs and prominent bosom, which have made her the butt of comedians the world over, than for her songs and recordings. As such, she has been the most successful modern country performer to cross over to the mainstream of American popular culture: recording successful pop songs on her own ('9 to 5'*, 1980), with **Kenny Rogers**, and with **Linda Ronstadt** and **Emmylou Harris** (*Trio*, 1987); building a career for herself as an actress in films like *9 to 5* (1980) and *Rhinestone* (1984); and performing regularly on television and in cabaret at Las Vegas. Her major artistic triumphs are those of the seventies. In a series of mostly self-composed songs that revealed almost as wide a range of concern as **Merle Haggard**, Parton, like **Loretta Lynn**, addressed herself to issues facing women in rural America ('Down from Dover', 'Jolene'), and reminded her audience of the deprivations of the recent past ('In the Good Old Days [When Times Were Bad]', 'Coat of Many Colors'). However, at the end of the nineties, in a burst of creativity she shed the trappings of commercial success and recorded two of her finest albums, *Hungry Again* (1998) and *The Grass Is Blue* (1999), albums on which she returned to her mountain roots.

Born in poverty in rural Tennessee, Parton was the fourth of twelve children. By her teens an accomplished performer and regularly heard on local radio, she first recorded in 1959 ('Puppy Love', Goldband) and in 1964 travelled to Nashville. She signed with Monument records and had her first hit, 'Dumb Blonde', in 1967, just before she joined Porter Wagoner's show as a featured singer. Wagoner (*b. 12 August 1930, West Plains, Missouri*), the host of the long-running *Porter Wagoner* television show, was a hard-edged singer whose major hits included 'Satisfied Mind' (RCA, 1956), the original version of 'The Green Green Grass of Home' (1965), which was later recorded by **Tom Jones** (1967), among others, and 'Carrol County Accident' (1968). He secured Parton a contract with RCA and produced their duets, starting with their version of **Tom Paxton**'s 'The Last Thing on My Mind' (1967), in which her striking soprano meshed perfectly with his tenor.

Her first solo RCA releases, 'Just Because I'm a Woman' and 'In the Good Old Days' (1968), revealed an equally striking writing talent that quickly flowered. Other songs from this period include 'My Blue Ridge Mountain Home' (1969), 'Daddy Come and Get Me', 'Joshua' (1970) – her first country No. 1 – and the classic 'Coat of Many Colors' (1971), a recollection of a patchwork coat made by her mother. In

1974 Parton left Wagoner for a solo career and had a country chart-topper and minor pop hit with 'Jolene'. As her songs were covered by singers like Ronstadt ('I Will Always Love You'), **Maria Muldaur** ('My Tennessee Mountain Home') and Harris ('Coat of Many Colors'), Parton directed her attention increasingly to the pop mainstream. Her success in the country charts continued with No. 1s like 'Here You Come Again' (1977), 'Old Flames Can't Hold a Candle to You' (1980) and 'Think About Love' (1986), but from 1977 onwards she also regularly featured in the pop charts.

Parton's pop hits included 'Here You Come Again'* (1977), written by **Barry Mann** and Cynthia Weil; 'Baby I'm Burnin'' (1979); the theme song to her first feature film, 9 to 5 (1980); and the duet with Kenny Rogers, the **Bee Gees**' 'Islands in the Stream'* (1983). In 1987 Trio (Warners) also produced a hit single for Harris, Ronstadt and Parton with a revival of the **Phil Spector** composition 'To Know Him Is to Love Him'. She reaffirmed her songwriting ability with White Limozeen (Columbia, 1989), produced by Ricky Skaggs. 1990's Eagle When She Flies gave her an American Top Thirty album, and in 1993 she released the successful Slow Dancing with the Moon, with guest appearances from members of the new generation of country stars, including **Vince Gill**, **Mary-Chapin Carpenter** and Billy Ray Cyrus. She ended the year by releasing another collaborative album Honky Tonk Angels, with **Loretta Lynn** and **Tammy Wynette**.

By the late eighties Parton had become an American icon, with a multi-faceted career in film and cabaret as well as on record. She also owned Dollywood, a theme park in Tennessee. In the nineties she continued her acting career with major roles in the TV movie Wild Texas Wind (1991) and Straight Talk (1992) with James Woods, for which she also recorded the soundtrack. Heartsongs (1994) was a live recording. Her greatest success as a songwriter came in 1992, when **Whitney Houston** had a worldwide chart-topper with 'I Will Always Love You'. The Essential Dolly Parton (1995), a retrospective of her RCA days, is the definitive historical collection.

Treasures (Warner, 1996), a collection of versions of other people's songs, including **Kris Kristofferson**, **Neil Young** and **Cat Stevens**, was her last significant album for a major label. On that she was accompanied by a number of non-Nashville guests, which gave her sound a freer feel. She did the same with the rootsy Hungry Again (1998), made for the independent Sugar Hill label after she was dropped by RCA. Even better was The Grass Is Blue (1999), on which with vocal backing from Alison Krauss and Patty Loveless she created compelling versions of songs associated with the **Louvin Brothers**, **Flatt & Scruggs** and **Johnny Cash**, among others.

CHARLEY PATTON
b. 1887, Edwards, Mississippi, USA, d. 28 April 1934, Indianola, Mississippi

Among Mississippi singers of the first blues generation, Charley Patton has been the most celebrated in his own community and the most mythologized among blues devotees. Musically awesome, in person small and sometimes reportedly objectionable, he has the two-edged reputation of a **Woody Guthrie**. He was, nevertheless, the most influential artist of his time and region. Tommy Johnson, the creator of 'Big Road Blues' and 'Canned Heat Blues', left those and a few other songs and guitar riffs to the blues tradition, but Patton bequeathed an entire vocal manner, gruff and barking yet with extraordinary resonance, which has inspired artists from **Howlin' Wolf** to **Captain Beefheart**. Individually his songs are perhaps less widely remembered than Johnson's, but their melodies, verses from them and references to them crop up throughout the history of Deep Southern blues.

He spent much of his life on the Dockery plantation near Ruleville, Mississippi, where he encountered fellow blues singers and guitarists Tommy Johnson and Willie Brown, but he travelled and played throughout northern and central Mississippi and built a name that won him, in 1929, a recording session with Paramount. 'Pony Blues'/'Banty Rooster Blues' and 'Mississippi Boweavil Blues'/'Screamin' and Hollerin' the Blues' introduced his delicate bellow and richly accented, percussive guitar-playing. They sold well – Paramount also issued the latter coupling under the name 'The Masked Marvel', and solicited guesses at the singer's identity – and Patton made, in all, twenty-one singles in 1929–30, as well as accompanying his occasional fiddle-player Henry Sims (with whom, years later, **Muddy Waters** also worked). His last Paramount session was in the company of Willie Brown and **Son House**, whom he had recently come to know as a fellow-worker in Lula, Mississippi.

From 1930 to 1934 Patton led a more settled life in Holly Ridge, Mississippi, playing for local functions. In 1934 he went to New York to record twenty-nine sides for Vocalion, joined on some by his wife, singer Bertha Lee, but only a dozen were ever issued, and he died of a heart condition a few months later.

Patton's imposing style and his songs have been reworked by blues artists of his own day, like House and Brown, and of the next generation, like **Robert Johnson**, Muddy Waters and Howlin' Wolf, whose best-known song, 'Smokestack Lightnin'', is based on Patton's 'Moon Going Down'. Reissues of his work on Origin Jazz Library inspired many of the sixties generation of white blues players in both the United

States and Europe, most notably **Eric Clapton**, who recorded 'Spoonful' with **Cream**. In 1970 guitarist **John Fahey** published the biography *Charley Patton*.

PAUL AND PAULA

Paul, b. Ray Hildebrand, 21 December 1940, Joshua, Texas, USA; Paula, b. Jill Jackson, 20 May 1942, McCaney, Texas

The titles of Paul and Paula's series of hits perfectly evoke the 'high-school' era that bridged the years between the rebellion that was rock'n'roll and the exuberance of **The Beatles**: 'Hey Paula'* (1962), 'Young Lovers', 'First Quarrel', 'Something Old, Something New' and 'First Day Back at School' (1963).

Written by Hildebrand and produced by Major Bill Smith, who also produced Bruce Channel's 'Hey Baby'* (Mercury, 1962), 'Hey Paula''s wonderously innocent romantic simperings took the record to the top of the American charts when Mercury's Philips subsidiary leased it from Smith's LeCam label, who had released the record as by Jill and Ray. Paul and Paula's records lacked the eerie intensity of Dick and Deedee, whose self-produced 'The Mountain's High'* (Liberty, 1961) introduced a similarly short career. However, with their unisex sweaters emblazoned with a 'P' and songs about romance rather than passion, Paul and Paula were far less threatening than Dick and Deedee who, even when singing 'Young and in Love' (1963), had a harder edge.

Of Paul and Paula's subsequent recordings, all devoted to the trials and tribulations of the fictive Paul and Paula, only 'Young Lovers' and 'First Quarrel' were major hits. In 1964 the pair separated when Hildebrand left the music business.

BILLY PAUL

b. Paul Williams, 1 December 1934, Philadelphia, Pennsylvania, USA

A jazz-inflected soul singer of the seventies, Paul found success through his collaboration with producers **Gamble and Huff**.

A childhood friend of comedian Bill Cosby (whose own biggest hit was the novelty 'Little Ole Man', Warners, 1967), Paul first sang on radio in 1945 and studied music at Temple University and other colleges. He sang in Philadelphia jazz clubs, appearing with **Charlie Parker** shortly before the saxophonist's death in 1955. His recording début was 'Why Am I' (Jubilee, 1955) with pianist Tadd Dameron. After army service, he briefly joined Harold Melvin and the Blue Notes in 1961 while continuing to perform on the jazz scene.

In 1967 Gamble signed him to the Neptune label

and produced *Feelin' Good at the Cadillac Club*, a set of showbusiness standards sung in a cocktail-jazz style. *Ebony Woman* (1970) included more contemporary accompaniments on such songs as **Michel Legrand**'s 'Windmills of Your Mind' and **Paul Simon**'s 'Mrs Robinson'. The album entered the R&B chart before the label folded.

When Gamble and Huff regrouped as Philadelphia International, *Goin' East* featured Paul with **Beatles** material and sitars, but it was 'Me and Mrs Jones'* from *360 Degrees* (1973) which found a large pop audience. A tale of infatuation with a married woman, the record reached No. 1 in America and entered the British Top Twenty. 'Thanks for Saving My Life' (1974) was a lesser hit but while Paul's later records sold well to black listeners and entered the British charts, he had no other pop hits in America.

Among his R&B hits were the arrogant 'Am I Black Enough for You' (1973), 'Let's Make a Baby' (1976) and a reworking of **Jerry Butler**'s 1969 million-seller 'Only the Strong Survive' (1977), the title track from an album of socially conscious material. In 1977 he had success in Britain with versions of **Paul McCartney**'s 'Let 'Em in' and **Elton John**'s 'Your Song'.

After a period away from recording, Paul returned with *Lately* (Total Experience, 1985), which included 'Sexual Therapy', a song inspired by **Marvin Gaye**'s 'Sexual Healing'. He moved to Ichiban for *Wide Open* (1988). He later played the cabaret circuit.

LES PAUL

b. Lester Polfuss, 9 June 1915, Waukesha, Wisconsin, USA

Affectionately known as the 'Wizard of Waukesha', Paul's influence on the development of popular music has been immense. He was the inventor of the solid-body electric guitar and a pioneer of multiple recording (over-dubbing), as well as a successful recording artist both on his own ('Lover', 'Brazil', 1948) and with his wife Mary Ford ('How High the Moon', 1951; 'Vaya Con Dios'*, 1953).

Paul's twin concerns as a child were the guitar and electronics. By the age of twelve, he was both a proficient guitarist and had built his first recording machine. As Rhubarb Red he toured with country singer/guitarist Joe Wolverton from 1929 to 1933 and before 1936 performed mostly country material, until the influence of **Django Reinhardt** and **Eddie Lang** led him to play amplified jazz guitar. In 1936 he formed the Les Paul Trio (with Jimmy, the older brother of **Chet Atkins**, and bassist Ernie Newton) and from 1938 to 1940 the group regularly broadcast with **Fred Waring**. Paul continued his electronics experiments and in 1940 built 'The Log' in which guitar strings were fixed to a railroad sleeper without any sound holes and the note was sustained wholly through the electronic amplification of sound. This instrument eventually formed the basis of the Les Paul solid-body Gibson guitar introduced in 1952, after **Leo Fender** had marketed his own solid-body guitar.

During the forties Paul also played with Ben Bernie's Orchestra. He moved to Los Angeles, formed a new trio and played with such artists as **Nat 'King' Cole** and **Bing Crosby**, with whom he recorded the elegant 'It's Been a Long Long Time' (Decca, 1946), his light, lyrical phrasing providing a warm backdrop to Crosby's vocals, even more intimate than Lang's had been in his 1932 recordings with Crosby. Paul also continued experimenting with multiple recordings, in 1948 releasing 'Brazil' and 'Lover' (Capitol), which featured speeded-up sections and over-dubbing to great effect. His first hits were an adaptation of the piano novelty 'Nola' and 'Goofus' in 1950, the year he began recording with Mary Ford.

Vocalist Ford (*b. Colleen Summers, 7 July 1924, Pasadena, California, d. 30 September 1977*) was a former member of **Gene Autry**'s band, who had also played lead guitar with Jimmy Wakely before, in 1947, she teamed up with Paul, marrying him in 1949. Their first joint effort was a version of **Cowboy Copas**'s 1948 country hit 'Tennessee Waltz' (1950), which was an even bigger hit for **Patti Page**, who also specialized in double-tracking. In 1951 the pair had a trio of million-selling records: 'Mockingbird Hill', in which Paul provided a dazzling array of electronic effects behind Ford's double-tracked voice; 'How High the Moon', their most delicate recording; and 'The World Is Waiting for the Sunrise'. However, many of their records, including their biggest-seller 'Vaya Con Dios' (1953), despite their thrilling effects, were bland. Ironically, in view of the importance for it of the electric guitar, rock'n'roll's coming in the mid-fifties ended Paul's recording career. In 1963 Paul and Ford were divorced and Paul spent most of the sixties 'reinventing the electric guitar'.

He returned to recording with *Les Paul Now* (London, 1968), but hearing defects prevented him resuming his career until 1974 when he toured and introduced the Les Paulverisor (a tape-echo device). In 1976 he recorded the imaginative *Chester and Lester* (RCA) with Chet Atkins and in 1978 repeated the process with *Guitar Monsters*. In the eighties and nineties, though retired, he occasionally performed, usually with other guitar virtuosi, including **Jeff Beck** in 1982. In 1992 he performed at a guitar festival in Spain.

In 1991 EMI issued *The Legend and the Legacy*, a four-CD set containing much unreleased material from the early fifties.

PAVEMENT

Mark Ibold, b. 1967, Cincinnati, Ohio, USA; Scott Kannberg, b. 1967, Stockton, California; Stephen Malkimus, b. 1967, Santa Monica, California; Bob Nastanovich, b. 1968, Rochester, New York; Gary Young, b. 1963, Stockton (replaced by Steve West, b. 1967, Richmond, Virginia)

Heavily inspired by the post-punk sound of bands like the **Fall**, Pavement were the perfect embodiment of the nineties lo-fi aesthetic: a blend of skewed, dissonant guitar riffs and knowing lyrical sentiments.

Malkimus (guitar/vocals) and Kannberg (guitar) began recording together in the latter's garage at the tail end of the eighties, releasing a pair of EPs, *Slay Tracks* (1989) and *Demolition Plot J-7* (1990), on the Drag City label. Recruiting bassist Ibold and drummer Young, Pavement recorded a third EP, *Perfect Sound Forever* (1991), before signing with Matador for the release of their début album, *Slanted and Enchanted* (1992), which saw them add percussionist Nastanovich to the line-up. A critical hit, it mixed white noise and pretty melodies to perfection.

After collecting their early work on *Westing (by Musket and Sextant)* (Drag City, 1993) and releasing a pair of sloppy EPs, Pavement replaced Young with West and recorded the acclaimed *Crooked Rain, Crooked Rain* (1994), which included the MTV favourite 'Cut Your Hair' and 'Range Life', a pointed deflation of the egos of alternative rock superstars like **Smashing Pumpkins** and **Stone Temple Pilots**. Calmer than *Slanted*, it eschewed lo-fi aesthetics for a more laid-back and accessible sound.

Wowee Zowee (1995), on which the band attempted a variety of music styles, was poorly received in comparison to its predecessors and saw the band relegated to cult status. Later the same year sacked drummer Young released *Hospital (Big Cat)*, a fitting reflection on his notoriously wild lifestyle. The band's profile rose again in 1997 when they were declared the primary influence on **Blur**'s eponymous fifth album. Sales of *Brighten the Corners* (1997) were boosted accordingly and the band had minor hits with the pop-edged singles 'Shady Lane' and 'Type Slowly'. Pavement had further international success with *Terror Twilight* (1999), recorded by late nineties producer-du-jour Nigel Godrich. The single '. . . and Carrot Rope' made the UK Top Thirty.

TOM PAXTON

b. 11 October 1937, Chicago, Illinois, USA

Paxton was one of the most articulate and prolific topical songwriters of the folk revival of the sixties. He retained a strong following into the eighties and nineties, particularly in Europe.

He studied drama at the University of Oklahoma where he discovered folk music and wrote his first songs. In the early sixties Paxton moved to New York and performed at the Gaslight Club, which issued his first album. Paxton, **Bob Dylan** and **Phil Ochs** were recognized as the leading figures of the new generation of folk songwriters and Paxton compositions appeared in *Broadside* and *Sing Out* magazines.

In 1965 he signed to Jac Holzman's Elektra label and released *Ramblin' Boy*. It included travelling songs in the mode of **Woody Guthrie**, like 'Standing at the Edge of Town', 'Bound for the Mountains and the Sea' and the title track (soon recorded by the **Weavers** and the **Kingston Trio**), as well as the direct political comment of 'Daily News' and 'What Did You Learn in School Today' and Paxton's most admired love songs 'Last Thing on My Mind' (recorded by **Peter Paul and Mary**) and 'My Lady's a Wild Flying Dove'.

On *Ain't That News* (1965) he was accompanied by bassist Felix Pappalardi (later **Cream**'s producer and a member of **Mountain**) on such hard-hitting material as the anti-war 'Lyndon Johnson Told the Nation' and 'Buy a Gun for Your Son'. Paxton's mixture of the amiable, the caustic and the romantic sustained him through such later Elektra albums as *Morning Again* (1968) and *Tom Paxton 6* (1970).

Paxton's continuing popularity in Europe and his success at the 1969 Isle of Wight Festival led him to settle in England and sign to the local branch of Reprise. *Peace Will Come* (1972) was produced by Tony Visconti, and featured backing vocals by **Mary Hopkin** and **Pentangle**'s Danny Thompson on bass. *New Songs for Old Friends* (1973) was a live album with a guest appearance by **Ralph McTell**.

Although he remained a popular live performer, especially in Britain, Paxton's later recordings were intermittent. *Something in My Life* (Private Stock, 1975) was followed by two albums for Vanguard, *New Songs from the Briar Patch* (1977) and *Heroes* (1978), which featured 'The Death of Stephen Biko', the impassioned tribute to the murdered African leader, as well as the gentle satire 'Hand Me Down My Jogging Shoes'. He later recorded for Mountain Railroad (*The Paxton Report*, 1980), Flying Fish (*Even a Grey Day*, 1983), PIP and Cherry Lane. *A Paxton Primer* (Pax, 1986) consists of re-recordings of his best-known songs, while *Tom Paxton Storyteller* (1989) is a compilation from his stay with Warner/Reprise (1965–75).

Paxton's songs were recorded by many other artists, including Peter Paul and Mary ('Going to the Zoo'), **John Denver** (the satire on the American way of death 'Forest Lawn') and **Judy Collins** (the ecological fable 'Whose Garden Was This').

JACK PAYNE
b. John Wesley Vivian Payne, 22 August 1899, Leamington Spa, Warwickshire, England, d. 4 December 1969, Kent

Though neither a remarkable musician nor a notably amiable employer, bandleader Jack Payne wielded great influence on the British dance-band scene in the twenties and thirties, chiefly as director of dance music for the BBC and conductor of its broadcasting Dance Orchestra.

Payne learned to play piano during his childhood in Birmingham. In his late teens he joined the Royal Flying Corps as a pilot; at twenty he left it as an ex-mess bandleader. He then formed a band in the Midlands, but in 1923 moved to London and the following year started a four-year engagement at the Hotel Cecil in the Strand. During this period he made his first records, for Regal. He first broadcast on the BBC in 1925, and in 1928 took over the coveted leadership of the BBCDO, which he held until succeeded by **Henry Hall** in 1932. Among the noteworthy sidemen in Payne's line-up were trumpeter – and later bandleader and disc-jockey – Jack Jackson, and violinist Eric Siday. The singer most associated with the band was Billy Scott-Coomber, who was a member for ten years.

The Payne band made many recordings for British Columbia, Imperial and Rex, usually without any 'hot' content, more often novelties like 'Harmonica Harry' or 'My Brother Makes the Noises for the Talkies'. The latter, with its special effects and comic storyline, led on to more elaborate disc melodramas like 'Little Nell' (Imperial), whose craziness somewhat anticipated that of the **Goons**. The band also made musical short films and appeared in the features *Say It with Music* (1932) and *Sunshine Ahead* (1936).

After the Second World War, Payne became a theatrical agent, but he returned to the music business for a time with his fifties TV show *Off the Record*.

PEARL JAM
Eddie Vedder, b. Edward Mueller, 23 December 1966, Evanston, Illinois, USA; Jeff Ament; Stone Gossard; Mike McCready; Dave Krusen (replaced by Dave Abbruzzese, replaced by Jack Irons)

Pearl Jam, along with **Nirvana**, emerged from the late eighties Seattle scene to become the first superstars of the grunge genre.

This five-piece formed in Seattle in late 1990 from the ashes of two other local bands, Mother Love Bone and Temple of the Dog. Guitarist Gossard and bassist Ament had been in Mother Love Bone, a quintet heavily influenced by Detroit cult bands the Stooges and the **MC5**. They recorded one album, *Apples*, for

Polydor in 1990, but the band split up after the death of vocalist Andrew Wood. The pair then formed Temple of the Dog along with members of fellow Seattle grunge pioneers **Soundgarden**, recording an acclaimed eponymous album for A&M as a tribute to Wood. Ament, Gossard and lead guitarist McCready from Temple of the Dog joined forces with drummer Krusen and vocalist Eddie Vedder to form Pearl Jam, signing to Epic in 1991.

Success was virtually instant, with the début album *Ten* (1991) charting on both sides of the Atlantic, and the band drawing rave reviews for their live shows. In the UK, the album spawned three hit singles, and Pearl Jam toured extensively over the next eighteen months. Vedder and Gossard appeared at the **Bob Dylan** tribute concert at New York's Madison Square Garden in 1992, performing one of the highlights, a version of 'Masters of War', and reflecting their swift elevation to the upper reaches of rock's hierarchy. Gossard led a 'spare time' band called Brad, which recorded *Shame* in 1993. Constant comparisons with Nirvana stoked stories of a feud between the two acts, a subject referred to by the choice of title for the band's second album, *Vs.*, which knocked Nirvana's *In Utero* off the top of the US album chart immediately on release in 1993. The equally successful *Vitalogy* was released a year later. It included 'Spin the Black Circle', a punk-style paean to vinyl.

Later the same year Pearl Jam instigated legal action against Ticketmaster, citing unfair business practice, and refusing to tour because they could not keep ticket prices below $20. The US Justice Department eventually ruled in favour of Ticketmaster. The following year the band began work with **Neil Young** on the *Godfather of Grunge's Mirrorball* (1995). Pearl Jam later released an EP, *Merkinball*, culled from the same sessions, but spent the rest of the year working on side projects. Vedder toured with Hovercraft while McCready issued *Above* as Mad Season alongside **Alice in Chains**' Layne Stanley. Ament recorded an eponymous album in 1996 with Three Fish, a Seattle-based trio.

Pearl Jam reconvened for the experimental *No Code* (1996), the first to feature new drummer Irons. It failed to match the success of its predecessors, lacking a strong single and the support of a tour. In 1997 Gossard recorded a second Brad LP before the release of the acclaimed *Yield* (1998). The album was followed by Pearl Jam's first full-scale tour for several years, documented on the live outing *Live on Two Legs*. The superior *Binaural* (2000) was firmly in the mould of *Vitalogy*, offering high-octane rockers (such as 'Breakerfall' and 'God's Dice') that convince more by sound than words – the group's aggressive attitude seeming oddly out of place in a post-grunge world – interleaved with more thoughtful ballads ('Rival').

ANN PEEBLES
b. 27 April 1947, East St Louis, Missouri, USA

Though her chart hits did not long survive the arrival of disco and jazz-funk, Southern soul singer-composer Peebles brought a raunchiness and intensity to **Willie Mitchell**'s smooth Memphis soul sound. The best examples were the much-covered 'I Can't Stand the Rain' (which, written with her husband Don Bryant and a local deejay, Bernard Miller, was an American Top Forty hit in 1973) and her searing version of the Earl Randle tale of bitter recrimination, 'I'm Gonna Tear Your Playhouse Down' (1973), which provided the model for **Paul Young**'s 1985 million-seller.

Her family was steeped in gospel and by the age of eight she was singing in the church choir under the direction of her father Perry. However, on graduating from High School, under the influence of singers like **Aretha Franklin** and **Otis Redding**, she quit gospel for soul and the church for the nightclubs of St Louis. In 1969 she joined Mitchell's Hi label. Her early recordings were of material associated with established soul performers, but with the release of 'Slipped, Stumbled and Fell in Love' (covered with greater success by **Clarence Carter**) in 1971, on which she soared over the inexorable roll of Southern soul with her own distinctive grainy voice, she found her own style. With 'Playhouse' and later 'Rain', Peebles broached the subject of marital discord that, in the manner of **Millie Jackson**, would provide the subject matter for most of her subsequent songs. However, by the end of the seventies, the formula-bound similarity of most of her recordings, which included 'Old Man with Young Ideas' (1978) and 'If You've Got the Time, I've Got the Love' (1979), the collapse of Hi and the rise of disco left Peebles with a declining audience, ironically despite her growing influence on white singers, including **Alison Moyet**. She returned to recording with *Call Me* (1989) for Mitchell's new Waylo label. Rounder Records later issued *Full Time Love* (Bullseye, 1992), a late exercise in gritty soul on which she was backed by the Memphis Horns.

RALPH PEER
b. 22 May 1892, Kansas City, Missouri, USA, d. 19 January 1960, Hollywood, California

Peer was a pioneering talent scout and record producer working with Southern vernacular music in the twenties and thirties. He holds a greater position in the history of the music industry, as a pioneer of both American and international song-publishing.

The son of a phonograph music and music rolls dealer, he worked for the Kansas City office of Columbia Records between 1911 and 1917, when he was transferred to Chicago. After the First World War he became recording director of the General Phonograph Company's Okeh label in 1920. There he supervised the first blues recording by a black singer, Mamie Smith's 'Crazy Blues' (1920), and conducted the first location recording with portable equipment, in Atlanta in June 1923 – a field trip that yielded the début recordings of **Fiddlin' John Carson**. These included 'Little Old Cabin Down the Lane', reputedly the first commercial recording of country music. In 1926 he went to work for Victor in an arrangement whereby he received little salary but could sign all the repertoire he recorded to a publishing company he jointly owned with Victor. Thereafter his policy with new artists was to insist that they provided new, and if possible their own, material for recording, rather than standard or traditional numbers. This largely financial decision had considerable artistic effect, accelerating the transformation of the hillbilly repertoire from a repository of traditional ballads and lyric folk songs into a medium for the songwriter, both the small-town amateur and the out-of-town professional.

Peer then arranged and conducted field-recording trips in many Southern cities, with most striking success in Bristol, Tennessee, in July–August 1927, when he signed **Jimmie Rodgers** and the **Carter Family**. In 1928 he formed, in association with Victor, Southern Music, which held his fast-growing catalogue of hillbilly and 'race' (blues and jazz) copyrights; he had acquired work by **Jelly Roll Morton**, **Louis Armstrong** and other jazz artists, as well as virtually every original composition recorded for Victor by hillbilly and blues acts.

In 1932 Peer acquired the sole ownership of Southern Music from Victor, and, realizing the limited future of publishing speciality music, began to move into mainstream pop, buttressed by the success of **Hoagy Carmichael**'s 'Rockin' Chair' (1930) and 'Lazy River' (1931). He opened offices in Britain in 1932 and afterwards in Spain, Italy, France (a particularly rich territory) and elsewhere in Europe, as well as in several Latin American countries, whose music Peer studied for its international potential. (A journey to Mexico in 1932 had acquainted him with composer Agustín Lara, who provided Southern with 'Granada'.) This attention was rewarded in the late thirties when Southern acquired what proved to be not only massive international hits but enduring catalogue items: Ary Barroso's 'Baia' (1938) and 'Brazil' (1939), the latter still one of Southern's most valuable holdings; Alberto Dominguez's 'Perfidia' (1939) and 'Frenesi' (1941); and 'Amor' and 'Besame Mucho' (both 1941).

In the ASCAP-BMI conflict of 1940, which Peer later claimed he foresaw, he quickly threw his support behind the new organization by creating Peer International, which became the most extensive single catalogue in BMI. (At the same time he retained the ASCAP association through Southern Music.) He was swift to reconstruct or expand European ties after the Second World War, and was rewarded with the French composition 'Les Trois Cloches' (1945), subsequently a hit for **Edith Piaf** and, as 'The Three Bells', for the **Browns** and several other American acts. The same year saw the British success of Heinz Provost's 'Intermezzo' from the film *Escape to Happiness*, which later became more familiar as the signature tune of the BBC programme *Forces Favourites*.

Peer's companies did not waver at the advent of rock'n'roll – they had publishing interests in, for example, **Little Richard** and **Buddy Holly** – and they maintained a profile in Nashville. Later writers of particular value included **Donovan** and Geoff Stephens, whose 'Winchester Cathedral', a 1966 novelty hit for the New Vaudeville Band (Fontana), is the most recorded work in Southern (London)'s catalogue.

Although Peer remained active in the business during the forties and fifties – he set up a deal, for example, with Walt Disney whereby he obtained copyright in all background music used in Disney cartoons – he spent much of his time pursuing an interest in horticulture, becoming an international authority on camellias, as well as copyright law. His son, Ralph Peer II, succeeded him as President of the Peer-Southern Organisation, now peer music.

Peer's chief assistant at Victor was Eli Oberstein, who joined the A&R department in 1930 to supervise 'race' and popular (and later hillbilly) recording sessions. In 1932–4 he also ran an independent label, Crown, for popular material (including some hillbilly), retaining his Victor connection by having the larger company print his labels. In 1933 he began working on, and from mid-1934 he supervised, Victor's new 35-cent Bluebird label, for which he produced popular 'race', hillbilly and later Mexican material. He left Victor in 1938 – his work being taken over by **Frank Walker**, who passed it on, in 1945, to Steve Sholes – and a year later founded the United States Record Company, which issued a wide range of material, part newly recorded, part leased from earlier catalogues like Gennett and Crown (and, via Crown, Paramount) on Royale and Varsity. In the forties he added to this roster such labels as Hit and in 1946 briefly returned to RCA-Victor as head of A&R. His son Maurice also entered the record industry, overseeing the British arm of CBS before moving to head PolyGram UK in 1986.

TEDDY PENDERGRASS

b. 26 March 1950, Philadelphia, Pennsylvania, USA

During the eighties, Pendergrass was one of the most

successful soul singers in America. A romantic balladeer, he was formerly lead vocalist of Harold Melvin
and the Blue Notes, whose series of soul ballad hits in
the seventies had been produced by **Gamble and Huff**.

A doo-wop group formed in Philadelphia in 1954,
the Blue Notes recorded occasionally for Josie ('If You
Love Me', 1956), Brooke (1959), Val-Ue (the minor hit
'My Hero', 1960) and **Richard Barrett**'s Landa (1964).
For most of the sixties, however, the Blue Notes were
tuxedo-clad supperclub entertainers, singing stan-
dards and show tunes. They recorded a few sides with
Luther Dixon for Chess and with Henry Stone for his
Miami-based TK label.

Turnover of personnel was high and when in 1970
drummer Pendergrass took over on vocals, Melvin (b.
24 May 1941, Philadelphia, Pennsylvania, USA, d. 24
March 1997, Philadelphia) was the only remaining
original member. Thus, when the group signed to
Gamble and Huff's Philadelphia International in 1972,
Melvin had top billing. With Pendergrass's gruff,
impassioned singing, the intense 'I Miss You' was fol-
lowed by two million-sellers, the stately 'If You Don't
Know Me by Now' and 'The Love I Lost' (1973). The
1974 singles 'Satisfaction Guaranteed' and 'Where Are
All My Friends' reached the R&B Top Ten but the fol-
lowing year there were further pop hits with 'Bad
Luck' and 'Wake Up Everybody'. The group also
recorded the original version of 'Don't Leave Me This
Way', which was successfully revived in 1977 by
Thelma Houston and in 1986 by British group the
Communards.

After frequently being mistaken for Harold Melvin,
the lead singer was given the billing 'featuring Teddy
Pendergrass', before beginning a solo career with
Philadelphia International in 1976, recording hits like
'I Don't Love You Anymore' (1976), 'Close the Door'
(an R&B No. 1 in 1978) and 'Turn off the Lights'
(1979). Four albums, including Life Is a Song Worth
Singing (1978) and TP (1980), each sold over a million
copies and he was a popular live performer, touring
with his Teddy Bear Orchestra and playing to packed
houses of female admirers.

With new lead singer David Ebo, the Blue Notes
joined ABC but after the R&B hit 'Reaching for the
World' (1977), their later records for Source and MCA
made little impact. With various Blue Notes, Melvin
returned to the nightclub circuit.

In 1982 Pendergrass was partially paralysed in a
near-fatal car crash. He signed to Asylum in 1983,
releasing Love Language (1984) which included 'Hold
Me', a duet with **Whitney Houston**. He followed it
with the hit albums Workin' It Back (1985) and Joy
(1988), the title track of which was an R&B No. 1. His
later albums included Truly Blessed (1991) and A Little
More Magic (1993), whose producers included **Barry
White** and Leon Huff.

DAN PENN
b. Wallace Daniel Pennington, 16 November 1941,
Vernon, Alabama, USA

Writer of such classics as 'Dark End of the Street', 'Do
Right Woman' and 'Out of Left Field', Penn was one
of the many white Southern writers to be profoundly
influenced by black music.

As a teenager, Penn absorbed the music of **Bobby
Bland** and **Ray Charles** from the radio while singing a
mix of rock'n'roll and country with Benny Cagle and
the Rhythm Swingers, among whose members was
Billy Sherrill. Produced by **Rick Hall**, he recorded his
own 'Crazy Over You' (Spar, 1960) and briefly
fronted his own group, Dan Penn and the Pallbearers,
before turning to songwriting. His first success was 'Is
a Bluebird Blue', a hit for **Conway Twitty** in 1960,
after which he joined forces for a time with Donnie
Fritts. Penn's best-known songs, however, were written with Spooner Oldham. They included 'I'm Your
Puppet' (James and Bobby Purify, Bell, 1966), 'Down
in the Boondocks' (Billy Joe Royal, Columbia 1965)
and the classic cheating song, 'Dark End of the Street',
first recorded by **James Carr** (1967) and since
recorded by artists as diverse as **Richard Thompson**
and **Gram Parsons**. With **Chips Moman**, Penn wrote
'Do Right Woman', originally recorded by **Aretha
Franklin** (1967). He also worked for Oldham's AGP
productions, producing 'The Letter' (1967) by the **Box
Tops**, among other hits, before setting up his own
Beautiful Sounds studio and signing to Bell for the
impressive, albeit erratic, Nobody's Fool (1969).

Relatively inactive in the seventies, Penn became a
born-again Christian in the eighties, recording a gospel
album, produced by Moman. In 1993 he released Do
Right Man (Sire), an album of secular material which
included 'Dark End of the Street' and in 1997 Nobody's
Fool (Repertoire). Then in 1999 he and Oldham
recorded the marvellous live album, Moments from
This Theatre (Bluefive), on which – with just piano
and guitar behind them – the pair transformed a set of
their classic soul compositions into equally compelling
essays in stark singer-songwriting.

HANK PENNY
b. Herbert Clayton Penny, 17 September 1918, Birmingham, Alabama, USA, d. 17 April 1992, Nashville

In the decade after the Second World War, the musically progressive Hank Penny led a series of astutely
picked bands which explored Western swing, discovering strange connections between country music,
humour and big-band jazz.

He gained his first professional experience on
WAPI, Birmingham, Alabama, in 1933, as tenor banjoist in the band of local country personality Hal Burns.

In 1936 he moved to WWL, New Orleans, as a solo singer/guitarist; there he was exposed to the broadcasts from stations in Texas and Oklahoma of the Western swing bands led by **Bob Wills** and **Milton Brown**. Inspired in particular by the records of the latter, he formed his Radio Cowboys, with a similar line-up of fiddle, steel guitar and rhythm. The band worked at stations in Birmingham and Chattanooga, Tennessee, and was signed to Vocalion. Produced by **Art Satherley**, their first session (1938) had a Milton Brown stamp, mixing strains of pop, country and blues.

In 1939 the Radio Cowboys joined the *Crossroads Follies* show on WSB, Atlanta, Georgia. The line-up now included steel-guitarist Noel Boggs, who went on to work with Wills, **Spade Cooley** and his own groups, and songwriter **Boudleaux Bryant**, then a classically trained violinist. After further recordings for Vocalion/Okeh (1939–41), the Radio Cowboys disbanded and Penny left WSB in 1942 for WLW, Cincinnati, Ohio, where he worked on the station's leading country shows, the *Boone County Jamboree* and *Midwestern Hayride*. There he began a long association with the local King label before moving, in 1945, to Hollywood, where he formed a Western dance band on the model of the then immensely popular Cooley. He also did some movie work and hosted his own radio show. His regular sessions for King drew in sidemen like **Merle Travis** and Speedy West, West playing on the 1949 session that produced 'Hillybilly Bebop' and Penny's humorously insulting composition 'Bloodshot Eyes', which was later recorded with great success by **Wynonie Harris**. Penny also worked as a stand-up comic on the nationally networked ABC radio show *Roundup Time* (from 1947) and on Cooley's Saturday-night TV slot.

Ex-Wills steel-guitarist Herb Remington joined the band in 1950, as did singer Mary Morgan, who as Jaye P. Morgan went on to a nightclub career. Penny continued to borrow tunes from the swing bands, such as 'Jersey Bounce' and 'Tuxedo Junction', recorded at his last King date in 1950. Thereafter he recorded with RCA Victor (1950–2) and Decca (1954–7), as well as cutting radio transcriptions of 'cool' Western swing material like 'Progressive Country Music for a Hollywood Flapper', mixed with old black-styled numbers *à la* **Phil Harris**. Morgan's successor was Penny's wife Sue Thompson, who later had a series of pop hits on Hickory with boy's-name titles like 'Norman' (1961) and 'James (Hold the Ladder Steady)' (1962). In the late fifties, however, she and Hank worked in Las Vegas, where he continued to employ superior musicians like **Roy Clark**. He left Las Vegas in 1968 and relocated several times before moving back to the West Coast in 1975, where he began to fill occasional musical engagements, between jobs as an actor (Mel Brooks' *Silent Movie*) or comedian.

PENTANGLE
Terry Cox; Bert Jansch, b. 3 November 1943, Glasgow, Scotland; Jacqui McShee; John Renbourn; Danny Thompson, b. April 1939

Led by two of Britain's leading folk guitarists, Pentangle created an amalgam of jazz, folk and blues music in the early seventies.

By the time Pentangle was formed in 1967, both Jansch and Renbourn had launched solo recording careers with Transatlantic. Jansch played blues and the 'folk-baroque' style developed by **Martin Carthy** and wrote songs (notably the low-key anti-drug piece 'Needle of Death'), while Renbourn specialized in instrumental solos in early and medieval music styles.

The group was completed by South London club singer McShee and the former rhythm section from **Alexis Korner**'s band, Cox (drums) and Thompson (bass). With Shel Talmy producing, the group released an eponymous début album on Transatlantic (Reprise in America) which included the lengthy instrumental 'Pentangling'. By the time *Sweet Child* (1968) was released, Pentangle's manager Jo Lustig had organized extensive international tours for the group.

Basket of Light (1969) was their most successful album and included two minor hits, 'Once I Had a Sweetheart' and 'Light Flight', a television series theme which featured McShee's gentle scat singing. Specialist folk producer Bill Leader took over for *Cruel Sister* (1970), which introduced electric guitars, and *Reflections* (1971).

Pentangle moved to Reprise for *Solomon's Seal* (1972), which featured fuzz guitar from Renbourn on 'Sally Free and Easy' and 'Cherry Tree Carol', one of McShee's most outstanding vocal performances. By this time, the group's music, always refined rather than emotive, had become repetitive and soon afterwards they split. Jansch and Renbourn resumed their solo careers, with the latter recording for **Stefan Grossman**'s Kicking Mule label and later formed the Pentangle-like Ship of Fools with singer Maggie Boyle, releasing an eponymous album (Run River, 1989). In the early nineties Renbourn toured and recorded with Robin Williamson of the **Incredible String Band**.

Jansch joined Charisma to make the country-flavoured *LA Turnaround* (1974), produced by ex-**Monkee** Mike Nesmith, *Santa Barbara Honeymoon* (1975) and the low-key *Avocet* (1979). In 1987 he released *Leather Launderette* (Black Crow) with ex-**Lindisfarne** bassist Rod Clements. Thompson became accompanist to singer/guitarist John Martyn and eventually made his own group albums which featured multi-instrumentalist Tony Roberts. These included *Whatever* (Hannibal, 1987) and *Whatever Next* (Antilles, 1989). The bass player also made fusion recordings with Spanish gypsy band Ketama and Malian kora-player Toumani Diabate (*Songhai*, 1989).

The group briefly re-formed in the early eighties, releasing the disappointing *Open the Door* (Spindrift, 1982). There were occasional tours and recordings after that by various line-ups, including *So Early in the Spring* (1990) on which Jansch and McShee were joined by Clements, Nigel Portman-Smith (bass) and Gerry Conway (drums). *Essential, Vols 1 and 2* (1986) are the best summation of their Transatlantic days, while *Live at the BBC* (Band of Joy, 1995) captures them in live performance from 1969–73.

CARL PERKINS
b. 9 April 1932, Tiptonville, Tennessee, USA, d. 19 January 1998, Jackson, Tennessee

Though 'Blue Suede Shoes'* (1956) was his only major hit, Perkins was one of the key figures of early rock'n'roll. His roots and world view were specifically Southern, but in the songs they inspired, he depicted, like **Chuck Berry** and (to a lesser extent) **Eddie Cochran**, a recognizable teenage world: 'Blue Suede Shoes', 'Put Your Cat Clothes on', 'Dixie Fried'. Similarly, his exciting guitar-playing, which fused the blues of **John Lee Hooker** with the country style of **Bill Monroe** with complete confidence, was an important influence on such diverse artists as **Rick Nelson**, **The Beatles**, who recorded several of Perkins' songs (including 'Matchbox', 'Honey Don't' and 'Everybody's Trying to Be My Baby') and **Creedence Clearwater Revival**.

Born into a poor farming family, Perkins heard the blues and country music equally from an early age and learned guitar from a black sharecropper (a moment affectingly remembered in 'Lake County Cotton Country', Dollie, 1968). In turn, he taught his brothers J.B. and Clayton and by the early fifties the Perkins Brothers Band was playing and broadcasting around the Jackson area. His compositions and singing style were pure country, in the style of his major influence **Hank Williams**, but his guitar style, like that of **Elvis Presley**'s guitarist Scotty Moore, was strongly black influenced. However, when **Sam Phillips** first recorded Perkins it was in a strictly country fashion (the weepie 'Turn Around', Sun, 1955).

However, when Presley left Sun for RCA, Perkins recorded his own composition, the classic 'Blue Suede Shoes', which topped both the country and R&B charts as well as reaching No. 2 in the pop charts. While the lyrics concisely captured the ebullient narcissism of the new teenage culture, the record also included the definitive rockabilly guitar solo. His career was halted by a car accident in 1956 in which his brother J.B. sustained injuries that led to his death in 1958. When Carl returned to performing nine

months later, the momentum was gone. Despite some minor hits (notably 'Boppin' the Blues') and superior recordings ('Dixie Fried', 'Matchbox' – an up-tempo version of a blues first recorded by **Blind Lemon Jefferson** – and 'Right String Baby but the Wrong Yo Yo', 1957), he was overshadowed by **Jerry Lee Lewis** and **Johnny Cash**, Sun's new rock'n'roll stars.

In 1958 Perkins followed Cash to Columbia, where he re-recorded several of his Sun songs to little effect, and in 1963 joined Decca and toured Britain, meeting The Beatles. His career, plagued by alcoholism throughout the early sixties, revived in 1966 when he became a regular member of the Johnny Cash show and wrote Cash's country No. 1 'Daddy Sang Bass' (1968). He also recorded the impressive *Country Boy's Dream* (Dollie, 1968), which revealed him as a sombre and reflective country performer, rejoined Columbia for the surprisingly effective revivalist *Boppin' the Blues* (1969) with the New York-based rock group NRBQ, and scored a country hit with 'Restless' (1969). Better, though not as successful, was 'State of Confusion' (1970). However, his first album for Mercury, *My Kind of Country* (1973), unlike those of Jerry Lee Lewis who was also recording country material, was undistinguished. After the mid-seventies he had modest success as a country performer, interspersed with revivalist albums, the most successful being *Ol' Blue Suede's Back* (Jet, 1978) and the most influential the reissues of his Sun material, which had a deep impact on the late seventies wave of neo-rockabillyists in Britain and America, among whom were the Stray Cats and Robert Gordon.

In the eighties he toured regularly, backed by his sons and, fittingly, he joined with Cash, **Roy Orbison** and Lewis for *Class of '55* (Smash, 1986), a lacklustre celebration of Memphis as the birthplace of rock'n'roll, briefly enlivened by his performance of 'Birth of Rock and Roll', in which he reminded listeners 'I was there when it happened'. Perkins became a member of the Rock'n'Roll Hall of Fame in 1987. Although his later career was hampered by his treatment for throat cancer, he released the creditable *Friends Family & Legends* in 1993, and the tribute album *Go Cat Go* (1996) on which he was aided by the likes of **Eric Clapton** and **Paul Simon**.

LEE PERRY
b. 1936, Kingston, Jamaica

One of the outstanding figures in reggae, the mercurial Perry (also known as 'Scratch', 'The Upsetter' or 'Pipe Cock Jackson') played an important part in the career of **Bob Marley** and in the development of the dub style. In the eighties and nineties, when Perry's glossolalia and graphalalia came to the fore, the result was a unique version of cut-up beat poetry.

In the fifties he worked as an engineer on **Coxsone Dodd**'s sound system. When Dodd moved into recording at Studio One, Perry became a producer. His first recording was **Toots and the Maytals**' 'Six and Seven Books' (1961), a fervent mixture of ska and gospel. He went on to record Shenley Duffus, Delroy Wilson, and his own 'Trials and Crosses'.

One of his first productions after leaving Dodd was 'People Funny Boy' (1968), an attack on his former employer but more importantly a record which introduced the 'rebel beat' of reggae. In 1969 he linked up with Marley and the Wailers to cut a series of fierce tracks, including the Perry compositions 'Small Axe', 'Duppy Conqueror' and '400 Years'. Perry's house band, the Upsetters, went on to form the nucleus of Marley's backing group in the seventies.

From 1968 to 1974 more than one hundred Perry productions were released in Britain on the Upsetter label. They included two albums by the Wailers and the hit instrumental 'Return of Django' by the group he led, the Upsetters (1969), the first in a stream of Italian Western-influenced instrumentals made in Jamaica. He followed that with *Clint Eastwood* and *Eastwood Rides Again* (1970). By now working at his own Black Ark Studio and with the Upsetters as its resident band, Perry also supervised hits by Max Romeo ('War in a Babylon', Unity, 1972) and Junior Murvin (the falsetto-driven 'Police and Thieves', 1976, later covered by the **Clash**).

With **King Tubby**, Perry was an early practitioner of dub and his austere *Blackboard Jungle* (1972) was the genre's first stereo album. He worked closely with the new breed of deejay-toasters like **U-Roy**, **Big Youth** and Dennis Alcapone before visiting Europe for the first time in 1977. He produced Marley's 'Punky Reggae Party' and worked on 'Complete Control' by the Clash in London, although he later professed himself unimpressed by punk's claims to have artistic affinity with reggae.

As Jamaican music shifted from the politico-religious themes and studio experimentation of the seventies, Perry pursued his own path, as well as producing such hits as Susan Cadogan's lovers'-rock version of 'It Hurts So Good' ('Hurt So Good', Magnet, 1975). When Island rejected his *Heart of the Congo* (Runnertelands) album in 1977, Perry responded with the single that included the chorus 'Chris Blackwell is a Vampire', a song in the well-established tradition in Jamaica of the paying of debts in songs, a tradition put to use earlier by **Prince Buster** and Perry himself. The album marked the end of the Black Ark phase of Perry career and, true to type, he burned the studio down later that year.

Subsequently Perry has turned himself into a dadaist typewriter via his magazine *The Upsetter* and ceased producing others in favour of a string of dub

releases, often made with others (the Mad Professor) and often produced by others. In 1981 he toured America with white reggae band the Terrorists. Albums of the eighties, virtually all of which are structured around Perry's stream of consciousness bizarre dystopian ramblings over cut-and-paste dub cuts, include *History Mystery and Prophecy* (Mango, 1984), *Battle of Armageddon* (Trojan, 1986), *Time Boom X De Devil Dead* (U-Sound, 1987), a collaboration with white English producer Adrian Sherwood that is even more manic than usual, and *Mystic Warrior* (RAS, 1989, with the Mad Professor).

In the nineties Perry continued his recording spree with numerous albums, including *From the Secret Laboratory* (Mango, 1990, with Sherwood), *The Quest* (Abraham, 1995), *Dry Acid* (Trojan, 1998) and *Live at Maratime Hall* (Maratime Hall, 1998, with the Mad Professor). At the end of the decade he was reported to be working with the **Beastie Boys**.

PET SHOP BOYS
Christopher Sean Lowe, b. 4 October 1959; Neil Francis Tennant, b. 10 July 1954, North Shields, Northumberland, England

The enigmatic Pet Shop Boys created a series of disco-driven international hits in the late eighties and early nineties. 'West End Girls' (1985) and 'It's a Sin' (1987), featuring a deadpan, mildly camp demeanour, clever lyrics and Stephen Hague's melodramatic, yet minimal, productions, were their most representative outings.

Tennant played cello at school and graduated from the Polytechnic of North London before working in magazine publishing as the London editor for *Marvel* comics and joining the staff of pop paper *Smash Hits*. Lowe was the pianist with Blackpool cabaret group One Under the Eight and was an architecture student when he met Tennant in 1981.

Their enthusiasm for the work of New York hi-energy dance music producer Bobby 'O' Orlando led to the latter supervising 'West End Girls' (Epic, 1984), a minor club hit in America. Next the Pet Shop Boys signed to EMI and released the unsuccessful 'Opportunities (Let's Make Lots of Money)' (1985), before the re-recorded 'West End Girls' became an international hit, reaching No. 1 in America and around Europe. It was produced by Hague, who had previously worked with former **Sex Pistols** mentor **Malcolm McLaren**.

The duo's début album *Please* (1986) provided further hits with 'Love Comes Quickly', a reissued 'Opportunities' and 'Suburbia' while *Disco* comprised remixed versions of the singles. The Pet Shop Boys' success continued in 1987 with 'It's a Sin', a superior gloomy, yet triumphant, celebration of the hedonistic pleasures of life. **Dusty Springfield** was guest vocalist on 'What Have I Done to Deserve This', while 'Rent' (which some commentators saw as a reference to homosexual prostitution) was a double-sided hit with 'Always on My Mind', originally performed by the Pet Shop Boys on a television tribute to **Elvis Presley**, for whom it had been a 1972 hit.

After *Actually* (1987), Tennant and Lowe starred in the poorly received movie *It Couldn't Happen Here* (1988), whose theme song they co-wrote with **Ennio Morricone**. The duo also wrote and produced 'I'm Not Scared' for Patsy Kensit before achieving their fourth British No. 1 with 'Heart'. *Introspective* (1988) included further hits in 'Domino Dancing', 'It's Alright' and 'Left to My Own Devices', produced by **Trevor Horn**. They went on to produce Liza Minnelli's 'Results' (Columbia, 1989) and Springfield's 'In Private' before releasing 'Behaviour' (1990).

The duo contributed to the début album by Electronic (the side project of **New Order** vocalist Bernard Sumner, 1991) and released a 'best of' collection, *Discography*, in 1991. An accompanying tour drew rave reviews for its inventive visuals. They launched their own Spaghetti label in 1992, scoring a hit with the first single by male vocalist Cicero ('Love Is Everywhere'), although later releases were less successful. They produced former **Culture Club** vocalist Boy George's hit version of 'The Crying Game' in 1992 before releasing their own album, *Very*, in 1993. It provided a string of hit singles, including a clever version of the **Village People** camp disco classic 'Go West', all accompanied by effective videos.

Bilingual (1996) saw the group edging towards the knowingness of Gilbert and George (the artists whose subject and material were themselves). It was overshadowed by *Alternative* (1995) a double-album of their earlier B-sides. More interesting was *Twentieth Century Blues – The Songs of Noël Coward* (1998), in which they oversaw the usual suspects (**Elton John**, **Sting**, **Robbie Williams**) offering modern interpretations of the master. **Nightlife** (1999), a meditation on life in the dark, was a further return to form, a melding of dark dreamscapes with direct observation ('New York City Boy', 'You Only Tell Me You Love Me When You're Drunk').

PETER PAUL AND MARY
Peter Yarrow, b. 31 May 1938, New York, USA; Paul Stookey, b. Noel Stookey, 30 December 1937, Baltimore, Maryland; Mary Travers, b. Mary Allin Travers, 9 November 1936, Louisville, Kentucky

One of the first folk revival groups to aim at a mass market, Peter Paul and Mary popularized the songs of **Bob Dylan**, **Gordon Lightfoot**, **Tom Paxton** and others.

The two men and a girl format was the brainchild of **Odetta**'s manager Albert Grossman, who wished to emulate the success of the **Kingston Trio**. He first attempted to form such a group around **Carolyn Hester** in 1960 but settled on Yarrow, Stookey and Travers a year later.

Mary had attended a progressive school where folk song was part of the curriculum and had recorded such Folkways albums as *Bantu Choral Folk Songs* and *Folk Songs of Four Continents* as part of a children's chorus, the Songswappers. Stookey sang in a college rock'n'roll band before drifting into the Greenwich Village folk scene, while Yarrow had taught folk music as an assistant professor at Cornell University.

Grossman signed the close-harmony group to Warners and their eponymous début album provided a hit single in **Pete Seeger** and Lee Hays' 'If I had a Hammer' (1962). But their most successful year was 1963 when for pop radio Peter Paul and Mary were the focal point of the burgeoning folk movement. They had Top Ten hits with 'Puff the Magic Dragon' (a children's song that was accused of harbouring drug references) and 'Blowin' in the Wind' and 'Don't Think Twice It's Alright', songs which brought their author, Dylan, into the public arena. The trio also led the singing at Martin Luther King's civil rights' march on Washington.

The group continued to tour and record throughout the rest of the decade, releasing a total of ten albums. Their most successful singles were Lightfoot's 'For Lovin' Me' (1965), 'I Dig Rock'n'Roll Music' (1967), 'Day Is Done' (1969) and their final song as a group, **John Denver**'s 'Leaving on a Jet Plane'*, a No. 1 in 1969. The trio's respective first solo albums for Warners were called *Peter*, *Paul* and *Mary*. Stookey's album included a hit in the ballad 'Wedding Song (There Is Love)' (1971), which has since become a standard.

He and Yarrow each cut two more albums for Warners, with Yarrow co-writing and producing Mary McGregor's No. 1 hit, 'Torn Between Two Lovers'* (Ariola, 1976). Travers released four Warners albums before joining Chrysalis in 1978 for *It's in Every One of Us*, produced by Vini Poncia. In the same year the trio came together again to record the unsuccessful *Reunion* (Warners).

Peter Paul and Mary performed occasional live concerts and tours in the eighties and nineties, while Travers concentrated on a career as a radio interviewer and Stookey (a born-again Christian) released *Band and Body Works* (Myrrh, 1980) and numerous other gospel albums. *No Easy Walk to Freedom* (Gold Castle, 1986) was a later reunion album whose title track (co-written by Yarrow and Margery Tabankin) was a tribute to Nelson Mandela.

OSCAR PETERSON

b. Oscar Emmanuel Peterson, 15 August 1925, Montreal, Canada

Perhaps the most technically accomplished of post-Second World War jazz pianists, and certainly the most commercially successful, Peterson developed a bop-based style to which he clung, despite the innovations of later generations of musicians.

The child of West Indian immigrants, Peterson abandoned his youthful trumpet studies after contracting tuberculosis. He next took up classical piano, switching to jazz under the influence of **Art Tatum**. Playing in Montreal jazz clubs, Peterson recorded in 1947 for RCA Canada and made a dramatic New York début in a 'Jazz at the Philharmonic' concert organized by **Norman Granz**, who became his manager.

After recording for Verve in 1950 with bassist Major Holley, Peterson formed a piano/bass/guitar trio using the format popularized by **Nat 'King' Cole**, upon whom Peterson modelled himself in his few vocal recordings. Between 1951 and 1958 he performed and recorded copiously with Ray Brown (bass) and guitarist Herb Ellis. The style was chamber jazz but live recordings like those from Stratford, Ontario, in 1957 showed an unusual rapport between the three players. Granz used the trio as a JATP and Verve house rhythm section with such performers as **Lionel Hampton**, **Lester Young** and **Dizzy Gillespie** and also recorded them on selections of tunes from shows such as *My Fair Lady* (1958).

By then Ellis had left to be replaced briefly by drummer Gene Gammage and then by Ed Thigpen, who stayed with Peterson until 1964. The new format allowed Brown to become more exploratory. In 1961 Granz sold Verve to MGM and Creed Taylor became the label's new musical director. Producer Jim Davis gave Peterson a new freedom in his choice of repertoire, resulting in the successful *Night Train* (1963), which included **Duke Ellington** and **Hoagy Carmichael** tunes, and the big-band album arranged by **Count Basie** sideman Ernie Wilkins (*Bursting out with the All-Star Big Band*, 1962).

In 1964 Thigpen and Brown were replaced by former **Cannonball Adderley** rhythm section Sam Jones (bass) and Louis Hayes (drums), with whom Peterson recorded his most ambitious composition, *Canadiana Suite* (1964), for a new label, Mercury. He left Mercury in 1968 and his next releases came from the German MPS label for whom Peterson had made a series of recordings during the mid-sixties. Some of these were solo pieces and their enthusiastic reception contributed to Peterson's decision to dispense with the trio format in 1972.

Peterson's most ambitious recording project was the three-album series *The History of an Artist* (Pablo, 1972–3), which re-created all the stages of his career. In 1974 Granz signed Peterson to his new Pablo label and recorded him extensively as a soloist, and as a small-group leader, most frequently with guitarist Joe Pass and Danish bassist Niels-Henning Orsted Pedersen. In addition Peterson was teamed with singer **Sarah Vaughan** (1978) and trumpeters Gillespie (1974), Clark Terry (1975) and Freddie Hubbard (1982).

In 1990 he composed *The Bach Suite* to commemorate the tercentenary of the classical composer's birth and he undertook reunion tours and recordings with Brown and Ellis. He later recorded for his own Music of the Loons label. Gene Lee's biography *The Will to Swing* (1988) is an exemplary account of Peterson's life and career.

RAY PETERSON

b. 23 April 1939, Denton, Texas, USA

Peterson recorded the original version of the classic death disc 'Tell Laura I Love Her' (RCA, 1960).

Discovered singing in Los Angeles by music-business veteran Stan Shulman, Peterson was signed to RCA in 1958. The possessor of a four-and-a-half-octave voice, he initially recorded such diverse material as the teen ballad 'Let's Try Romance' and a cover of **Little Willie John**'s 'Fever' (1958), before having his first hit with the gentle, countryish 'The Wonder of You' (1959), also recorded by **Rick Nelson** and later a hit for **Elvis Presley** (1970). Peterson then recorded the Jeff Barry and Ben Raleigh composition 'Tell Laura I Love Her'. With its echo-laden tale of a wedding ring and a stock-car-race death, the song, successfully covered by Ricky Valance in Britain on EMI's Columbia label, provoked the answer record 'Tell Tommy I Miss Him' by Marilyn Michaels. After hits with the **Phil Spector**-produced 'Corinna, Corinna' (1960) and 'Missing You' (1961), Peterson returned to the theme of death with 'Give Us Your Blessing' (1963).

From 'Corinna' onwards his records were released on his own Dunes label, on which Curtis Lee had a hit with the Spector productions 'Pretty Little Angel Eyes' and 'Under the Moon of Love' (1961). His hit-making days over, Peterson attempted a career as a country singer on MGM before retiring in the late sixties.

JAMES CAESAR PETRILLO

b. 1892, Chicago, Illinois, USA, d. 23 October 1984, Chicago

Petrillo was President of the American Federation of Musicians (AFM) from 1940 until 1958, and one of America's best-known labour leaders. In 1942 he led a successful boycott of recording that resulted in record companies paying for the Music Performance Trust Fund (which still subsidizes live concerts in North America). A side-effect of the strike was that previously marginal musics, such as country and black music styles, and the companies associated with them, became more solidly established.

Petrillo briefly led a Chicago dance band before turning to union politics, becoming head of Chicago's Local 10 of the AFM in 1922 and President in 1940. In the early thirties he won musicians their first contracts with radio stations and in June 1942, mindful that over 400,000 jukeboxes stocked with records had taken the place of live musicians in clubs and bars, he threatened to lead his 140,000 members on strike against the record companies, unless they helped subsidize live music. The smaller companies with no stockpiles of new recordings capitulated immediately, followed in September 1943 by Decca, then the major pop label in America. Columbia and RCA held out until 1944. Many of the smaller companies specialized in country and R&B and in the temporary absence of new mainstream popular recordings they found a wider audience for their product which they retained after 1944. Other beneficiaries of the ban were band vocalists, like **Frank Sinatra**, who could record without musical accompaniment, and thus began to establish their economic independence of the big bands.

In the sixties Petrillo spearheaded the AFM's drive to integrate the previously racially segregated local branches of the union.

NORMAN PETTY
b. 1927, Clovis, New Mexico, USA, d. 15 August 1984

Composer, pianist and recording studio owner, Petty's role as **Buddy Holly**'s producer was akin to that of **George Martin** with **The Beatles**. Though his musical sensibility was formed in the pre-rock'n'roll aesthetic, Petty's technical and musical skills helped to create the unique sound of Holly's records.

During the fifties the Norman Petty Trio (with Petty on organ and his wife Vi on piano) recorded instrumental pieces. They scored two minor hits in 1957 with 'Almost Paradise' (ABC), a Petty composition that was a Top Thirty hit for **Roger Williams** on Kapp, and 'First Kiss' (Columbia). By that time Petty had set up a studio in Clovis, New Mexico, where early West Texas rock'n'roll singers came to record.

Roy Orbison made his first record, 'Ooby Dooby', at Clovis and he was followed by the Rhythm Orchids from Dumas, Texas, a group featuring Buddy Knox and Jimmy Bowen. Released locally on Triple D, Knox's swinging rockabilly tune 'Party Doll'* and Bowen's teen ballad 'I'm Sticking with You' were national hits on Roulette. Knox's later hits included 'Hula Love' (1957) and 'Lovey Dovey' (1958) and Bowen went on to become a respected country-music producer for **Hank Williams Jnr**, **George Strait**, **Kenny Rogers**, the **Bellamy Brothers** and numerous others.

Knox's initial success led Holly and the **Crickets** to Clovis in 1957. Beginning with 'That'll be the Day', on which he took a co-composer credit, Petty supervised over forty recordings by the group. His approach to studio work was meticulous and atypical of the era and Petty's attitude towards Holly – that he was a 'diamond in the rough' to whom Petty should lend musical polish – brought about a successful creative tension. Petty was also involved in organizing the releases of Holly and the Crickets, with most of the up-tempo numbers appearing under the Crickets' name and the softer songs under Holly's.

Shortly before his death, Holly broke with Petty and began recording in New York. However, Petty continued to record the Crickets and prepared unissued Holly tracks for release. Among the musicians brought in to over-dub backing tracks for the latter were the Fireballs (George Tomsco, Stan Lark and Eric Budd), a Texas group who had a Top Ten hit with 'What a Party' (Atco, 1967) and backed Jimmy Gilmer on his No. 1 record 'Sugar Shack' (Dot, 1963). Both recordings were Petty productions, as was the melodic instrumental 'Wheels'* by the Stringalongs (Warwick, 1961).

During the seventies Petty was less active in the recording field, producing occasional albums, including Baby's *Baby* (Mercury, 1975). He also took part in the annual Buddy Holly weeks organized by **Paul McCartney**, to whom Petty had sold his Nor-Va-Jak publishing company in 1975.

TOM PETTY & THE HEARTBREAKERS
Tom Petty, b. 20 October 1952, Gainesville, Florida, USA; Mike Campbell, b. 1 February 1954, Panama City, Florida; Benmont Tench, b. 7 September 1954, Gainesville; Ron Blair, b. 16 September 1952, Macon, Georgia (replaced by Howie Epstein); Stan Lynch, b. 21 May 1955, Gainesville

Bringing something of the harshness of seventies new-wave music to the sixties guitar-rock tradition, Tom Petty and his group the Heartbreakers melded the ringing guitars of the **Byrds** (and the nasal singing style of its leader Roger McGuinn) with the harder edge of the **Rolling Stones**.

In 1969 Petty joined Florida group Mudcrutch, which included Mike Campbell (guitar) and Benmont Tench (keyboards). The group dissolved in 1974, soon after securing a recording contract with **Leon Russell** and Denny Cordell's Shelter label in Los Angeles. The trio regrouped as Tom Petty and the

Heartbreakers with Stan Lynch (drums) and Ron Blair (bass), releasing an eponymous album in 1976. It contained the distinctly Byrds-like 'American Girl' (later covered by Roger McGuinn) and 'Breakdown', a belated hit in 1978.

You're Gonna Get It! (1978) provided the minor hit 'I Need to Know' but soon after Shelter was bought by MCA, with whom Petty found himself in extended litigation. The dispute was settled when MCA set up the nominally independent label Backstreet for Petty and Nils Lofgren (Petty and the Heartbreakers toured Europe supporting Lofgren in 1977). The new deal bore immediate fruit with *Damn the Torpedoes* (1979), which brought Petty his first American Top Ten single, 'Don't Do Me Like That', and *Hard Promises* (1981). Petty also sang with **Fleetwood Mac**'s Stevie Nicks on the bestselling 'Stop Draggin' My Heart Around' from her *Bella Donna* (1981), duetting again with her in 1985 on a live recording of the **Searchers**' 1964 hit 'Needles and Pins', on the album *Pack Up the Plantation*.

The Top Twenty hit 'You Got Lucky' (1982) came from *Long After Dark*, on which Howie Epstein replaced Blair. Epstein had been bassist for sixties veteran **Del Shannon**, whose 1983 album, *Drop Down and Get Me* Petty produced. The Backstreet label ceased to exist after 1982, and *Southern Accents* appeared on MCA in 1985. It found Petty staunchly expounding Southern mores and included the hit 'Don't Come Around Here No More', produced by the **Eurythmics**' Dave Stewart. In 1987 Petty and the Heartbreakers released *Let Me Up (I've Had Enough)*, which included a song ('Jammin' Me') co-written with **Bob Dylan**, with whom the band had toured in 1986 and 1987. With Dylan, **George Harrison**, **ELO**'s Jeff Lynne and **Roy Orbison**, Petty formed the Traveling Wilburys in 1988, recording an eponymous album for Warners. Harrison also appeared on Petty's solo début, *Full Moon Fever*, co-produced by Lynne. Although billed as a solo recording, most of the Heartbreakers appeared on the album.

By the mid-eighties Petty and the Heartbreakers had established a reputation as accompanists. Following their tours with Dylan, members of the Heartbreakers appeared on *Empire Burlesque* (1985) and *Knocked out Loaded* (1986), which included the Dylan–Petty song 'Got My Mind Made Up'. Tench had also established himself as a sought-after session musician and songwriter, composing material for **Feargal Sharkey**, among other artists. Mike Campbell was also much in demand, most notably playing on the **Eagles**' Don Henley's *Building the Perfect Beast* (1984), co-writing the album's worldwide hit 'The Boys of Summer'. Epstein became co-writer and producer for Carlene Carter and also produced **John Prine**.

A second Traveling Wilburys album, *Volume 3*, was released in 1990, after which Petty was reunited with the Heartbreakers for *Into the Great Wide Open* (1991), again co-produced by Lynne. A 1993 *Greatest Hits*, which featured some new recordings, including a faithful remake of Thunderclap Newman's 1969 hit 'Something in the Air', preceded a move to Warners, with whom Petty signed a three-year deal. Its first fruit was the hugely successful *Wildflowers* (1994), produced by **Rick Rubin**. The stripped-down sound compared favourably to the elaboration of Lynne's productions, and the reflective edge ('King for a Day', 'Time to Move on') made it Petty's best album. *Echo* (1999), billed by Petty and the Heartbreakers, was in the same style but was a lesser outing, only because the songs were less distinctive. Earlier Petty wrote and recorded the soundtrack album *She's the One* (1996).

You Got Lucky (Backyard, 1994) was a tribute album to Petty. Among those performing his compositions were US indie bands Red Red Meat and Throneberry. It was followed by the retrospective set *Playback, 1973–1993* (MCA).

LIZ PHAIR
b. Elizabeth Clark Phair, 17 April 1967, New Haven, Connecticut, USA

Along with **Tori Amos**, Liz Phair was one of the first of a new breed of female performers to emerge in the nineties, paving the way for the likes of **Alanis Morissette** and **Sheryl Crow**.

Raised by wealthy adopted parents, Phair attended art college in Ohio before returning to Chicago and recording 4-track demos under the name Girlysound. One such tape reached the Matador label, which lead to the release of the singer's début album, *Exile in Guyville* (1993). Intended as a feminist riposte to the **Rolling Stones**' *Exile on Mainstreet*, the album was lavished with praise for its frank and confrontational tone, achieving gold status after the success of the single 'Never Said', a rare feat for an independent release. Phair was to suffer a setback soon after, however, as her first full tour was plagued by stagefright.

Whip-Smart (1994) was intended to be the album that broke Phair into the mainstream, having been heavily promoted by Atlantic Records, who had recently acquired Matador. The album entered the US *Billboard* chart at number 27 and spawned a minor hit single in 'Supernova', but poor reviews coupled with a refusal on Phair's part to tour the record meant that it failed to sell beyond her underground fanbase.

Phair's musical output over the next few years was limited to the *Juvenelia* EP (1995) and 'Rocket Boy' (1996). The release of Phair's third album was delayed by the birth of her first child in December 1996, which accounted for the somewhat calmer, more reflective tone of *whitechocolatespaceegg* (1999).

ESTHER PHILLIPS

b. Esther Mae Jones, 23 December 1935, Galveston, Texas, USA, d. 7 August 1984, Los Angeles, California

A versatile singer, much influenced by **Dinah Washington**, Esther Phillips – as Little Esther renamed herself in 1962 – went through phases of singing blues, jazz, standards and even disco, but her intermittent problems with drug addiction often prevented her from making the name she deserved in any of those idioms.

She grew up in Los Angeles, singing in church and at talent shows from an early age. She began recording with **Johnny Otis**, for Savoy and Modern, when she was thirteen and had R&B Top Ten entries with 'Double Crossing Blues' (with the Robins), 'Cupid's Boogie' and 'Mistrusting Blues' (all 1950). She also toured the United States with his Show in 1950–3, and made further records for Federal (a subsidiary of **Syd Nathan**'s King), which produced a minor R&B hit in 'Ring-a-Ding Doo' (1952), and some excellent blues accompanied by Otis's sidemen and, on one occasion, **Ben Webster**. Some of these were composed by the young **Leiber and Stoller**, whose 'Hound Dog' Phillips recorded after the success of **Big Mama Thornton** with the song.

She ceased touring in 1954 and for eight years was virtually absent from the music scene, leaving her home in Houston, Texas, only to record for Savoy in 1956 and 1959. In 1963 she signed with Atlantic, reaching both R&B and pop Top Ten with 'Release Me'* (a British hit for **Engelbert Humperdinck** in 1967) and in 1965 appeared on the British TV show *Ready, Steady, Go* with **The Beatles**, who had commended her 'And I Love Him' as the only tolerable cover-version of any of their songs.

After appearing at the Newport Jazz Festival in 1966, Phillips spent the next three years undergoing drug rehabilitation at clinics like the Synanon Center in Santa Monica, California, where a number of jazz figures had cured their addiction. Returning to music in 1969 she began to lean towards jazz again, recording for Roulette and Epic and appearing at the 1969 and 1970 Monterey Jazz Festivals; she was also reunited with Otis for a TV show. In 1972 she toured Europe with jazz trumpeter Freddie Hubbard. In 1973, now with Kudu, she was nominated for a Grammy award as Best Female R&B Vocalist but was beaten by **Aretha Franklin**, who then gave the award to her as the more deserving candidate. In 1974–5 she won awards from *Rolling Stone* as Best R&B Singer, from *Ebony* as Best Female Blues Singer and from the French Académie du Jazz. Her version of 'What a Difference a Day Makes' (Kudu, 1975) was an international hit, but repeated illness and ill fortune hampered her career in the late seventies and early eighties.

SAM PHILLIPS

b. Samuel C. Phillips, 5 January 1923, Florence, Alabama, USA

One of the most significant individuals in popular-music history, Phillips discovered the young **Elvis Presley** and saw in him the amalgam of black and white musics which became rock'n'roll. Phillips' Sun label also nurtured the careers of **Jerry Lee Lewis**, **Johnny Cash**, **Carl Perkins** and **Charlie Rich**. A mark of the high regard in which Sun was held was the number of tribute records about the label. These included the **Lovin' Spoonful**'s 'Nashville Cats' (1971), **Chip Taylor**'s '(I Want) The Real Thing' (1974) and former leader of **Creedence Clearwater Revival** John Fogerty's 'Big Train from Memphis' (1985).

The son of a tenant farmer, Phillips became an engineer and disc-jockey on stations in Muscle Shoals and Nashville before moving to WREC Memphis in 1946. He also promoted shows and in 1950 he opened his Memphis Recording Service. Although he released one single by blues singer Joe Hill Louis, Phillips and the studio were mainly employed in recording local black artists, including **Howlin' Wolf**, **Bobby Bland** and Jackie Brenston (whose 1951 hit 'Rocket 88' on Chess is often cited as a direct precursor of rock'n'roll) for out-of-town labels like **Leonard Chess**'s Chess and the **Bihari Brothers**' Modern.

Sun was founded in 1952 and its first R&B hit came with **Rufus Thomas**'s 'Bear Cat', an answer to **Big Mama Thornton**'s 'Hound Dog', whose copyright Sun was found to have infringed in a lawsuit. Phillips also released urban blues by **Little Milton** and **Junior Parker**, as well as 'Just Walkin' in the Rain' (1953) by the Prisonaires, a vocal group made up of inmates from the Nashville State Penitentiary. The song became a pop hit for **Johnny Ray** in 1956.

Everything changed for Phillips when Presley walked into his studio in 1954. As more black-orientated labels had emerged, they had sought more control over the recordings they issued. As a result, Phillips turned to white artists. After signing Presley, Philips experimented, recording him on black, country and ballad material until the 'Sun sound' emerged. Backed by Scotty Moore (guitar) and **Bill Black** (bass) from country singer Doug Poindexter's band, Presley's early Sun singles captured an exciting, novel sound in which the urgency of the voice was enhanced by the use of flutter, echo and reverberation.

In 1955 Phillips sold Presley's contract to RCA for $35,000 and groomed Perkins to be the next rock'n'roll star, putting a guitar speaker in the washroom of the 9m x 6m studio to get an over-amplified, heavy tone. Sun had hits in 1956–8 with both Perkins and Cash, though other rockabilly signings like **Charlie Feathers**, **Roy Orbison** and Jack Earls were less successful.

The last of Phillips' great discoveries was pianist/ singer Lewis, who stayed with the label until 1963. After 1958, though, Sun seemed to lose direction and aped teenage trends rather than creating them. Staff producer **Bill Justis** had instrumental hits, while Carl Mann and Rich crooned their way into the charts. Although a new label, Phillips International, was started and new studios were built in Memphis and Nashville, by the mid-sixties Sun had only local distribution.

In 1969 Phillips sold the company to Shelby Singleton and set up a label for Holiday Inn, of which he was a major shareholder. He left music altogether in the seventies to look after a range of business interests, including five radio stations. Among artists recording at Sun studios during the seventies were the **Amazing Rhythm Aces**, whose 'Third Rate Romance' (ABC, 1975) reached the Top Twenty, and **John Prine**, for whom Phillips produced two tracks which appeared on *Pink Cadillac* (1979).

PHISH
Trey Anastasio; Mike Gordon; Page McConnell; Jon Fishman

In the manner of the **Grateful Dead**, Phish made improvisation the centre of their music. However, unlike the Dead, the roots of their improvisatory attitude was jazz rather than folk, thus allowing them a certain irony in their musical references and a far greater degree of humour. Apart from *Billy Breathes* (1996), the group has been largely unable to repeat its live success in the studio. The other lesson Phish learnt from the Dead was, like the **Dave Matthews Band**, to build their reputation through endless touring and by actively encouraging their audience to tape their live performances. While the term Phish-head has not yet followed Deadhead into the rock vocabulary, it seems inevitable that it will eventually.

The group was formed at the University of Vermont, where vocalist Anastasio, bassist Gordon and drummer Fishman were students, in 1983 and solidified in 1985 with the addition of McConnell on keyboards and vocals. They recorded *Junta* (later re-released by Elektra in 1992) themselves in 1988, selling it as a cassette at their shows, and in 1990 released *Lawn Boy*, which stressed both their humour and indicated the epic jams that were henceforth to be a feature of their recordings and performances, on the independent Absolute A Go Go label. Their most structured recording to then, it won them a contract with Elektra, for whom they recorded *A Picture of Nectar* in 1992, which introduced their genre-jumping style in which songs moved from bluegrass to reggae in the twinkling of an eye. By the time of *Hoist* (1993) and the concept album *Rift* (1994), the group had

won themselves a regular place on the American touring circuit and brushed with mainstream success with the radio hits 'Down with Disease' and 'Sample in a Jar'. *A Live One* (1995) captures their live appeal well, while *Billy Breathes* (1996), produced by Steve Lillywhite (who also produced the Dave Matthews Band), is the group's most disciplined outing to date, marrying rock ('Character Zero') with acoustic balladry ('Waste') to good effect. After Anastasio's solo effort *Surrender to the Air*, they released *The Story of the Ghost* (1998), Phish's first US Top 10 album, which included the hit 'Birds of a Feather'. The group followed that in 2000 with *Farmhouse*. Described by several critics as the group's equivalent to the Grateful Dead's *American Beauty*, the album was notable for featuring songs, mostly written by Anastasio, rather than jams, and melodies rather than pyrotechnics. A hit in America where the group toured in support of it, the album was less well received in Europe.

EDITH PIAF
b. Edith Giovanna Gassion, 19 December 1915, Paris, France, d. 10 October 1963, Plascassier

The impassioned Piaf was the most popular French singer of the fifties, powerfully emoting songs of doomed or defiant love. With **Charles Aznavour** and **Maurice Chevalier**, she made the greatest international impact of any French vocalist. Unlike them, however, Piaf achieved recognition through her French-language recordings rather than through English translations.

After travelling with her father, a circus acrobat, she became a Paris street singer in 1931. Two years later she graduated to small clubs where club-owner Louis Leplee gave her the name Piaf. Parisian slang for a sparrow, it alluded to her diminutive stature and waif-like appearance.

In the late thirties Piaf began recording for Polydor, scoring her first hit with the exotic 'Mon Legionnaire' (1937), complete with bugle call. It was written by Raymond Asso and Marguerite Monnot, who provided many of her later songs. Piaf remained in Paris during the German occupation, acting in plays by Jean Cocteau and writing her own songs for the film *Montmartre sur Seine* (1941), in which she appeared.

Two of Piaf's most famous songs, 'La Vie en Rose'* (1946) and 'Les Trois Cloches', were among the first of the 200 she recorded for Pathe-Marconi between 1946 and her death. 'La Vie en Rose' was co-written by Piaf and became her only major American hit. It was later memorably reworked by **Grace Jones** on her *Island Life* (1985), while in translation 'The Three Bells' was a hit in 1959 for Piaf's original accompanists Les Compagnons de la Chanson (EMI Columbia) and for the **Browns** (RCA).

Piaf visited New York in 1947, recording several tracks in English, but for the next decade her success was limited primarily to France where her numerous hits included 'Je t'ai dans la peau' (1952), co-written by **Gilbert Becaud** and her husband Jacques Pills, 'L'Accordioniste' (1955), 'La Goulante de Pauvre Jean' (1954) which, as 'The Poor People of Paris' (1956) was an instrumental hit for **Winifred Atwell** in Britain and for both **Les Baxter** and **Lawrence Welk** in America, and 'La Foule' (1957).

In 1956 Piaf recorded both English translations of French material (**Johnny Mercer**'s lyric to 'Autumn Leaves') and French versions of **Leiber and Stoller**'s 'Black Denim Trousers and Motorcycle Boots' ('L'Homme à la Moto') and Irving Gordon's 'Allen-town Jail' ('Les Prisons de Roy'). But her greatest international success came with the exuberant 'Milord' (1959), by George Moustaki and Monnot, which was a British hit in 1960. This was followed by the proud and magnificent 'Non Je Ne Regrette Rien' (1960), which became as closely associated with Piaf as 'My Way' with **Frank Sinatra**.

By the late fifties drink and drug dependency had taken their toll though one of her last great perform-ances was issued as *Live at the Olympia* (1961) and sold a million copies in France alone. Among the newer composers who supplied songs to Piaf was the accordionist Francis Lai, who later enjoyed success as a bandleader with the *Love Story* theme (Paramount, 1971).

After her death a Paris street was renamed in her honour. Piaf was commemorated in Claude Lelouch's *Edith and Marcel* (1983), which portrayed her romance with a French boxing champion, and in Pam Gems' play *Piaf*, which starred Elaine Paige in Lon-don's West End in 1993. The continuing fascination with her work was underlined by the release of a ten-CD boxed set by EMI France in 1994 and of a tribute album in the same year. Among those performing songs associated with her were **Donna Summer**, **Emmylou Harris** and **Pat Benatar**.

PIANO RED

b. *William Lee Perryman, 19 October 1911, Hampton, Georgia, USA, d. 25 July 1985*

As Piano Red, Perryman was a good-time boogie pianist and singer of fifties R&B. As Dr Feelgood he had a runaway pop hit in 1962 with his effervescent eponymous stomp, which was seized upon by British beat groups and gave one of their seventies successors the name **Dr Feelgood**.

He grew up in Atlanta, where, after winning a radio talent contest in the mid-thirties, he played in clubs. He first recorded in 1936, with **Blind Willie McTell**, at an ARC session in Augusta, Georgia, but the sides

were never issued. Signed in 1950 to Victor, he had immediate success with 'Rockin' with Red'/'Red's Boogie', both of which reached the R&B Top Ten in 1950–1; 'Rockin' with Red', retitled 'She Sure Can Rock Me' (or similar), has been frequently re-recorded by blues, country and rockabilly singers, including **Little Richard**, **Jerry Lee Lewis** and **Charlie Feathers**. 'The Wrong Yo Yo' (Victor, 1951) was a minor R&B hit but became a staple of Piano Red's repertoire and was also covered by non-blues artists like **Carl Perkins**. Red's reciprocal interest in country music yielded versions of **Floyd Tillman**'s 'It Makes No Difference Now' and **Hank Williams**' 'Hey Good Lookin'' (Victor, 1951).

Red continued to make small-group blues and boogie recordings for Victor and its Groove sub-sidiary until 1958. *In Concert* (Groove, 1956), recorded at the Magnolia Ballroom in Atlanta, is the first blues album to have been recorded live on location. He changed his professional name to Dr Feelgood in 1961 and formed a group called the Interns when record-ing his name song for Okeh. The success of 'Dr Feel-good' (1962) brought him several years of nationwide touring. In Britain the song was covered by **Johnny Kidd** and the flip-side 'Mister Moonlight' (sung by Roy Lee Johnson) was included by **The Beatles** on *Beatles for Sale* (1964).

In 1969, as Piano Red again, he began a long-running residency at Muhlenbrink's Saloon in the entertainment complex Underground Atlanta. He recorded albums for local labels and for King (*Hap-piness Is Piano Red*, 1970) and Arhoolie (1972). Also in 1972 he appeared as himself in the television film *The Catcher*. He was invited to the Montreux, Switzer-land, Blues Festival in 1974–5 (documented on Black Lion) and toured Europe in 1977.

His brother Rufus Perryman (b. *23 October 1892, Monroe, Louisiana, d. 2 January 1973, St Louis, Missouri*) was also a singer/pianist. An albino, he was known as Speckled Red. In the twenties he worked in Atlanta and Detroit and then on a Southern medicine-show. In 1929 he recorded a version of the street insult-game 'The Dirty Dozen' for Brunswick, and the following year recorded 'The Right String – but the Wrong Yo Yo', which his brother revived. He contin-ued to travel throughout the South, often with the entertainer Jim Jackson, who had one of the blues' first big sellers with the two-part 'Jim Jackson's Kansas City Blues' (1927). Speckled Red finally settled in St Louis in 1941, becoming a part of the traditional jazz scene there in the fifties. He toured in Europe in 1959–60, recording in England (*Oh! Red*, VJM) and Denmark (*The Dirty Dozen*, Storyville), but on his return to St Louis left music, making only a handful of appearances in the last few years of his life. His intensely stomping piano style, an archaic version of his brother's, showed the influence of ragtime on folk forms like the blues and boogie-woogie.

ASTOR PIAZZOLA
b. 11 March 1921, Mar del Plata, Argentina, d. 4 July 1992

The greatest innovator in the tango genre, Piazzola was a virtuoso player of the Argentinian accordion, the bandoneon.

He was born of Italian parents and lived until 1939 in New York where he studied classical music and jazz. The family returned to Argentina where in the forties Piazzola played with the tango bands of Anibal Troilo and others. In the early fifties he began to compose and perform 'new tango' pieces whose complexity was attacked by traditionalists. Among the most well-known were 'Adios Nonino', 'Balada de un Loco', 'Fuga Y Misterio' (reworked as a 'Tango Rave Mix' by Buenos Aires DJs in the nineties), *Tango Apasionada*, a suite based on short stories by the Argentinian writer Borges, and the opera *Maria de Buenos Aires*.

Piazzola led his own small bands for many years until he was crippled by a stroke in 1990. He was a prolific composer of film scores and he recorded over forty albums. Among these were some late recordings for Kip Hanrahan's American Clave label: *Tango: Zero Hour, La Camorra: The Solitude of Passionate Provocation* and *The Rough Dancer and the Cyclical Night*.

He maintained his early love for jazz by performing with many leading American instrumentalists, notably **Dizzy Gillespie**, **Gerry Mulligan** and **Gary Burton**.

Among the heirs to Piazzola's tango-fusion legacy is Buenos Aires bandleader Jose Colangelo.

WILSON PICKETT
b. 18 March 1941, Prattville, Alabama, USA

With 'In the Midnight Hour' (1965), Pickett introduced a blustering, rhythmic style of soul music which gave him numerous hits during the sixties. With **Otis Redding**, 'The Wicked Pickett' was the best-known soul star of the era.

Pickett's family settled in Detroit when he was a child and he joined gospel group the Violinaires. He moved into secular music with the Falcons in 1959, singing lead (in a style based on that of the Rev. Julius Cheeks of the Sensational Nightingales) on their major R&B hit, the intense, gospel-based ballad 'I Found a Love' (Lupine, 1962). As a result of that success, Pickett went solo, recording for Correctone and for **Lloyd Price**'s Double L ('If You Need Me', covered by **Solomon Burke**, who had the bigger hit), before signing to Atlantic.

After the failure of 'Come Home Baby' (1964), on which producer **Bert Berns** had Pickett crooning, Atlantic's **Jerry Wexler** took Pickett to the Stax studios in Memphis. With songs co-written by guitarist Steve Cropper, the first Memphis session provided the hits 'In the Midnight Hour' (1965) which, with Cropper's stinging riffs, became a leitmotiv for every white soul band of the sixties, '634-5789' (1966) and Eddie Floyd's 'Don't Fight It'. Later hits were recorded at **Rick Hall**'s studio in Muscle Shoals. They included a version of Chris Kenner's 'Land of 1000 Dances' (Pickett's first Top Ten hit), 'Mustang Sally', 'Funky Broadway' (1967) and 'She's Lookin' Good' (1968).

In an attempt to maintain Pickett's crossover status, Atlantic gave him material to cover by **Three Dog Night** (the **Randy Newman** song 'Mama Told Me Not to Come'), **Jimi Hendrix** ('Hey Joe'), **The Beatles** ('Hey Jude', 1969, with Duane Allman of the **Allman Brothers Band** on guitar) and even the cartoon group the Archies, whose 1969 No. 1 'Sugar Sugar' he recorded the following year. However, his next big successes came when he recorded with **Gamble and Huff** in Philadelphia. Backed by Leon Huff's pounding keyboards, 'Don't Let the Green Grass Fool You' (1971) and 'Don't Knock My Love – Pt 1' each sold a million.

In 1973 Pickett moved to RCA where *Mr Magic Man* (1973) and subsequent albums presented him unconvincingly as a mainstream ballad singer. After briefly running his own Wicked label, Pickett made *A Funky Situation* (Big Tree, 1978). Produced by Hall, the album saw a return to his classic style but it was followed by the lesser *I Want You* (EMI America, 1979), *Right Track* (1981) and tracks for Henry Stone's TK label before Pickett joined Motown in 1987. *American Soul Man* (1987) was produced by synthesizer-pioneer Robert Margoulieff (who had worked with **Stevie Wonder**), and contained a new version of 'In the Midnight Hour'. In 1993 he was sentenced to imprisonment on drink-driving charges and was subsequently frequently in trouble over drugs. *It's Harder Now* (Bullseye, 1999) was a recognizable, but lesser, Pickett outing.

A Man and a Half (Rhino, 1992) collects together his essential recordings.

WEBB PIERCE
b. 8 August 1926, nr West Monroe, Louisiana, USA, d. 24 February 1991, Nashville, Tennessee

With a voice of great clarity and penetration and an ineradicable affinity for the blues, Webb Pierce was among the finest honky-tonk singers of the fifties.

He first came to notice on the KWKH, Shreveport, *Louisiana Hayride*, where he was associated with artists like **Faron Young** and **Floyd Cramer**. After a spell in the late forties with Four Star Records (some of whose masters were leased to King), he was signed in 1951 to Decca, where he promptly had hits with 'Wondering' (previously a regional hit, in the thirties, for the cajun Hackberry Ramblers under the name Riverside Ramblers), 'That Heart Belongs to Me' and 'Back Street Affair' (1952), and 'It's Been So Long' and 'There Stands the Glass' (1953).

Pierce joined the *Grand Ole Opry* in 1954, the year of his 'Slowly', a country No. 1 that featured the then novel pedal-steel guitar, played by Budd Isaacs. 'More and More' also topped the country charts in that year, followed in 1955 by 'In the Jailhouse Now' (an adaptation of a song previously recorded by **Jimmie Rodgers**), 'Love, Love, Love' and 'I Don't Care' (co-written with Cindy Walker). In 1956 he teamed with Red Sovine on 'Little Rosa', had a rock'n'roll-inflected hit with 'Teenage Boogie', and was voted Number One Country Male Vocalist in *Cash Box* for the fourth year running. (He won the same award again in 1961–3.)

Pierce's records continued to chart, though at lower positions, throughout the late fifties and early sixties, and he produced many strong-selling albums. By the late sixties he was touring less often, but his 'silver-dollar car' (pictured on the sleeve of his 1962 album *Cross Country*) and guitar-shaped swimming-pool had become Nashville tourist attractions. He left Decca in 1977 and signed to Plantation, recording two volumes of *Greatest Hits*.

COURTNEY PINE
b. 18 March 1964, London, England

The leading figure among a new generation of British jazz musicians, Pine has worked in reggae and pop contexts as well as **John Coltrane**-influenced jazz improvisation.

He learned clarinet before taking up the saxophone which he first played in public at reggae events, accompanying such performers as MCs General Saint and Clint Eastwood. His move into jazz came after he heard **Sonny Rollins**' *Way Out West* album.

Self-taught as a jazz player, Pine worked in the early eighties with the bands of free jazz drummer John Stevens and **Rolling Stones** drummer Charlie Watts. He next worked with other young black players in the Jazz Warriors Big Band as well as his own small groups. He played on the Jazz Warriors' *Out of Many, One People* (1987) which appeared just after his own first album, *Journey to the Urge Within* (Antilles, 1986), established him as the most promising improviser of the era.

In 1988 Delfeayo Marsalis produced *Destiny's Song and the Image of Pursuance* which was followed by

Traditions Beckoning, an EP of songs chosen by Pine and sung by young black vocalists Juliet Roberts and Leroy Osbourne. His ability to work closely with singers was also evidenced by his solo on **Mica Paris**'s 1989 hit 'Like Dreamers Do'.

After releasing *The Vision's Tale*, Pine went to Jamaica to record *Closer to Home* with producer Gussie Clarke and saxophonist Dean Fraser in 1990. It included a version of **Diana Ross**'s 'I'm Still Waiting' sung by English lovers' rock vocalist Carroll Thompson. During the early nineties he has also occasionally led a reggae band combining Jamaican rhythms with jazz-funk horn sounds.

In the Eyes of Creation (1993) found Pine moving closer to his ideal of a British jazz idiom that can encompass Caribbean and Asian music. He played soprano sax on the Eastern-sounding 'Meditation of Contemplation' and included a version of **Bob Marley**'s 'Redemption Song'. He continued touring and recording throughout the nineties, finding a new arena as a guest soloist. Examples of this included his work on the *Evita* film score (1997). More exciting, however, was his solo work, such as *Back in the Day* (Blue Thumb, 2000), which saw him ploughing the rich seam that was soul jazz.

PINK FLOYD
Syd Barrett, b. Roger Keith Barrett, 6 January 1946, Cambridge, England (replaced by David Gilmour, b. 6 March 1944, Cambridge); Nick Mason, b. 27 January 1945, Birmingham; Roger Waters, b. 6 September 1944, Surrey; Rick Wright, b. 28 July 1945, London

In the seventies Pink Floyd developed and refined the strand of progressive rock that dealt in monumental themes and grandiose, stately music. Their 1973 album *Dark Side of the Moon* was one of the most successful recordings of all time, with sales of around 20 million. In the eighties and nineties the group translated that to the live arena with huge commercial success.

Wright (guitar), Waters (bass) and Mason (drums) played together in 1964–5 in student rock groups Sigma 6 and the Abdabs. With art student Barrett on guitar and vocals the group became Pink Floyd (a combination of the names of two early country blues singers) and performed a mixture of R&B and primitive electronic music with light shows.

Pink Floyd were soon among the leading bands on London's nascent underground scene and they signed to EMI. Barrett's quirky 'Arnold Layne' (EMI Columbia, 1966) was a minor hit but in 1967 both the lyrical 'See Emily Play' and *The Piper at the Gates of Dawn* reached the Top Ten. The album's title was taken from a chapter in a favourite Barrett book, *The Wind in the Willows*, and most of its songs featured Barrett's often menacing images of childhood. However, its longest track, the instrumental 'Interstellar Overdrive', indicated the direction the group would follow after Barrett, increasingly erratic in live performances, was replaced by Gilmour in 1968. Barrett became a recluse but in 1970 recorded the idiosyncratic *The Madcap Laughs* and *Barrett*, which were produced by Waters and Gilmour. He did not make any further records although in 1974 he did return briefly to the recording studio in an abortive attempt to record some new songs. In 1988 EMI released *Opel*, a collection of out-takes from his 1970 sessions. A 1993 box set, *Crazy Diamond*, compiled the three albums and added a number of other out-takes.

Without Barrett (although he did appear on two tracks), Pink Floyd released *A Saucerful of Secrets* (1968), which was dominated by longer and more ambitious compositions inspired by outer space exploration, notably 'Set the Controls for the Heart of the Sun'. The increasingly cinematic aspect of Pink Floyd's work was emphasized when they recorded the soundtrack for *More* (1969) and Antonioni used music from the double-album *Ummagumma* (Harvest, 1969) in *Zabriskie Point*, his film about American hippie culture.

Pink Floyd briefly toyed with rock-classical fusions on *Atom Heart Mother* (1970), which included a full-scale orchestra and choir. The inconsistent *Meddle* (1971) and another soundtrack, *Obscured by Clouds* (1972), were the prelude to the group's greatest commercial success, *Dark Side of the Moon* (1973).

With titles like 'Brain Damage', 'Us and Them' and 'Money' (an American Top Twenty hit), the songs were permeated with Waters' gloomy pessimism about contemporary life. Engineered by **Alan Parsons**, the sombre music, making use of tape effects and VCS-3 synthesizers, reinforced the mood of the lyrics. *Dark Side of the Moon* remained in the American album charts for over a decade, and made Pink Floyd international superstars. It reached the charts again in 1993, when a specially remastered edition was issued to mark its twentieth anniversary. *Moon*'s success enabled the group to make fewer but more ambitious recordings and they released only four albums during the next decade. *Wish You Were Here* (1975) was dedicated to Barrett and included a further slice of Waters' bleak philosophy in 'Welcome to the Machine'. With a nod towards George Orwell's *Animal Farm*, *Animals* (1977) contained aggressive guitar lines from Gilmour and abrasive lyrics attacking such targets as clean-up TV campaigner Mary Whitehouse.

Neither album, however, made the impact of *The Wall* (1979), whose central image symbolized the lack of communication Waters found in the modern world. The record spawned both a hit single 'Another

Brick in the Wall' and a film which starred **Bob Geldof**. For the world tour of *The Wall*, Pink Floyd added guitarist Snowy White to the line-up. White had a later hit with 'Bird of Paradise' (Towerbell, 1985). In 2000 EMI released *Is There Anybody Out There, The Wall Live*, a double-album comprising *The Wall* constructed from different performances.

A period of inactivity for the group followed, broken by the release of Waters' 'requiem for the post-war dream', *The Final Cut* (1983). However, both Gilmour and Wright had released solo albums in 1978, while Mason collaborated with **Carla Bley** on *Fictitious Sports* (1981). As a producer, he had worked on records by **Robert Wyatt** in 1974 and 1976, and Gilmour followed his 'discovery' of **Kate Bush** with a co-production credit on the 1986 hit 'Life in a Northern Town' by Dream Academy.

In 1983 Wright left Pink Floyd and rumours of the group's dissolution were rife. Waters' solo career was launched with *Pros and Cons of Hitchhiking* (1984) and in 1987 he released *Radio KAOS*, a concept album which featured 'Four Minutes and Counting', a melodramatic portrayal of a nuclear holocaust. This was preceded by an announcement that he would no longer work with Gilmour and Mason. After he had unsuccessfully attempted to prevent the duo from using the name Pink Floyd, they issued *A Momentary Lapse of Reason* (1987). With Wright returning on keyboards, the album was heavily dominated by Gilmour's writing and singing, and was accompanied by a lavishly staged world tour, captured on the live album *The Delicate Sound of Thunder* (1988).

In 1990 Waters staged an all-star production of *The Wall* on the site of the Berlin Wall, issued on album and video as *The Wall – Live in Berlin* later that year. He followed it with the doomy *Amused to Death* (1992), which featured **Jeff Beck** on lead guitar. Gilmour, Wright and Mason continued as Pink Floyd, releasing the lesser *The Division Bell* (1994), which topped the chart on both sides of the Atlantic. Cluttered with musical references to their own past, it reunited the band with saxophonist Dick Parry, who had played on *Dark Side of the Moon* and *Wish You Were Here*. Parry was one of the eight additional musicians hired by the band for their mammoth world tour in that year. It was followed by the tribute album, *Us and Theme: Symphonic Floyd* (Point, 1995), on which the London Philharmonic Orchestra offered versions of Floyd songs.

GENE PITNEY
b. 17 February 1941, Hartford, Connecticut, USA

A songwriter as well as a recording artist, Pitney had his biggest successes with his dramatic readings of the songs of others, notably **Burt Bacharach**, whose '24

Hours from Tulsa'* (1963) is Pitney's best-known record.

While at school, Pitney became proficient on piano, guitar and drums, formed Jamie and Jane and then performed solo as Billy Brian. His first success was as a writer – he supplied **Rick Nelson** with one of the best teen ballads of the era, 'Hello Mary Lou' (1961) and the **Crystals** with 'He's a Rebel' (1962). He also co-wrote 'Rubber Ball', a hit for **Bobby Vee** (1960), under the pseudonym Orlowski. His first solo hit was 'I'm Gonna Love My Life Away' (Musicor, 1961), on which he over-dubbed all the instruments and multi-tracked all the vocals. But it was the film theme song 'Town without Pity'* (1961) that introduced his strained vocal style which, in the words of one critic, 'managed to combine an over-the-top passion with an extremely precise diction and an overall feel of complete vulnerability'. It was followed by a trio of million-selling songs written by Bacharach and Hal David, 'The Man Who Shot Liberty Valance' (another film theme), 'Only Love Can Break a Heart' (1962) and 'Tulsa', a classic essay in self-pity that revealed Pitney to be the equal of **Gene McDaniels** and **Dionne Warwick** as an interpreter of Bacharach and David's songs.

Through his association with **Phil Spector**, Pitney met and recorded with the **Rolling Stones**, and in turn recorded Jagger and Richards' 'That Girl Belongs to Yesterday' (1964), which was a British hit. It marked a transitional point in Pitney's career. Though he continued to have American hits, including 'Looking Through the Eyes of Love'* (1965) and 'She's a Heartbreaker' (1968), recorded with R&B artists Jerry Williams and **Charlie Foxx**, he became a far bigger star in Europe than America. Thus, while in America Pitney was paired with **George Jones** in an unlikely attempt to revive his career, in Britain his hits stretched to 1974. They included the **Randy Newman** compositions, 'Nobody Needs Your Love' and 'Just One Smile' (1966) and ended with 'Blue Angel' (1974). In Italy, aided by his recording in Italian, his popularity was longer-lasting. Throughout the seventies and eighties Pitney was a regular fixture on the international cabaret scene.

In 1989, in partnership with **Marc Almond**, he returned to the charts with a revival of his 1967 hit, 'Something's Gotten Hold of My Heart' (EMI). The single reached No. 1 in Britain and briefly revived Pitney's career. A 1990 album, *Backstage – The Greatest Hits and More* with new tracks produced by David Courtney (**Leo Sayer**'s former writing partner), was a British Top Twenty hit. He toured larger British venues than before, but was unable to sustain the momentum. Pitney remained, however, a popular and regular visitor to Britain. In 1995 he was the subject of two separate anthology sets, *The Ultimate*

Anthology (One Way) and *The Great Recordings* (Tomato).

THE PIXIES
Black Francis (aka Frank Black), b. Charles Michael Kitteridge Thomson IV, Long Beach, California, USA; Kim Deal, b. Mrs John Murphy, Ohio; Joey Santiago; David Lovering

Mixing punk, garage and elements of early seventies glam-rock, Boston band the Pixies became one of the major indie bands of the late eighties before frontman Black Francis broke the band up to pursue a solo career.

The Pixies were formed in the mid-eighties in Boston by Thomson and college friend Santiago. They recruited bassist Deal and drummer Lovering and began playing around the Boston area, with a sound heavily influenced by **Bob Mould**'s Hüsker Dü. The band recorded several demo tapes, but were unable to solicit much interest from US labels. In 1986 they signed to UK independent label 4AD, releasing their début album, *Come on Pilgrim*, in 1987. The album attracted enthusiastic reviews and topped the UK independent chart, as did the follow-up, *Surfer Rosa* (1988). The band toured Europe in 1988 with labelmates **Throwing Muses**. The tour drew rave reviews and attracted attention from several major labels. An EP, *Gigantic*, followed later in 1988, and the band subsequently signed to the Elektra label in the US, releasing the acclaimed *Doolittle* (1989). A more melodic set than its predecessors, it represented their commercial breakthrough in the UK.

1990 saw *Rolling Stone* writers name the Pixies the best new American band – but frustrated by Thomson's dominance of the band, Deal decided to form her own band, the Breeders, with whom she would record and tour when the Pixies were off the road. Fronted by Deal and Throwing Muses guitarist Tanya Donnelly, the Breeders' line-up was completed by bassist Jo Wiggs (from UK indie band the Perfect Disaster) and drummer Shannon Doughton. With production by Steve Albini, the hardcore veteran who had produced *Surfer Rosa*, the Breeders' début album *Pod* (1990) reached the UK Top Thirty and was warmly received by critics.

The Pixies returned to the fray with *Bossanova* (1990), which found the band adding a stronger sense of melody to the sonic assault of their earlier work. It was another chart album in the US, and when the excellent *Trompe Le Monde* appeared in 1991 it seemed the stage was set for the Pixies to follow **R.E.M.** and cross over from underground status to become a major album-selling act in the US. However, it was the Pixies' last recording, as Thomson broke the band up to pursue a solo career.

Adopting the name Frank Black, he released an eponymous album in 1993. A less frantic work than anything the Pixies had recorded, it sold poorly, despite an enthusiastic reception from the press and hardcore fans. The Breeders released the *Safari* EP, followed by the *Last Splash* album in 1993. More mainstream in its sound than the Pixies' output, it reached the US Top Fifty and would go on to sell nearly a million copies in the US. The single 'Cannonball' was a minor US hit and would later be sampled by the **Prodigy**, forming an integral part of their 1997 UK No. 1 'Firestarter'. In 1995 Deal issued *Pacer* with her new band the Amps. The remaining ex-Pixies, Santiago and Lovering, formed the Martinis, contributing to the soundtrack to *Empire Records* (1997).

Again as Frank Black, Thomson recorded a second solo album, *Teenager of the Year* (1994), although by this stage his fanbase had begun to dwindle to that of a cult act. *The Cult of Ray* (1996), his first album since signing with Sony in Europe and American in the US, was critically acclaimed but again sold poorly. After the collapse of American in 1997 Thomson also left Sony, issuing an eponymous album as Frank Black and the Catholics (Play it Again Sam, 1998). It was followed by *Pistolero* (1999).

PIZZICATO FIVE
Yashuaru Konishi; Keitaro Takanami; Maki Nomiya

A prolific Japanese trio, Pizzicato Five's post-modern mix of sixties pop, soul and disco has earned them a devoted international cult following.

In 1984 Konishi and Takanami, who had met five years previously at Aoyama University in Tokyo, released their first single, 'Audrey Hepburn Complex'. Recruiting female singer Maki Nomiya, the band recorded over fifteen albums of kitsch pop over the next decade for Sony Japan, heavily influenced by Western culture, from *Hawaii Five-O* to **Simon and Garfunkel**. The highlights of this phase of the band's career feature on their début international LP, *Made in USA* (Matador, 1994); a sampler CD, *Five by Five*, was an underground hit in America, by which time Pizzicato Five had become a household name in their homeland, despite the loss of founder member Takanami the previous year.

Continuing to put out albums on a regular basis in Japan, the trio widened their appeal in the US with *The Sound of Music by Pizzicato Five* (Atlantic, 1995), which boasted translated material from some of their more recent albums, *Bossa Nova 2001* and *Overdose*, alongside 'Happy Sad', the band's first single to gain widespread media attention in the UK. To mark the release of *Happy End of the World* (1997), Pizzicato Five performed live outside of Japan for the first time, embarking on an American club tour and playing selected dates in Europe. Pizzicato Five returned in 1999 with *The International Playboy and Playgirl Record*.

PLACEBO
Brian Molko, b. Luxembourg; Stefan Olsdal, b. Sweden; Robert Schultzberg (replaced by Steve Hewitt, b. London, England)

Cosmopolitan three-piece Placebo have achieved international acclaim for their energetic glam-punk sound, exemplified by their biggest hit to date, 'Nancy Boy'.

Androgynous frontman Molko and bassist Olsdal met at school in Luxembourg but didn't begin to work together until after a chance meeting at a London tube station. As Ashtray Heart the duo recruited Schultzberg on drums before replacing him with Hewitt and renaming themselves Placebo. They released a series of singles on independent labels before inking a deal with Hut and recording *Placebo* (1996), which veered from bubblegum-punk to slower, **Velvet Underground**-inspired dissonance, all topped with Molko's penchant for lurid lyrical detail. Having gained their first UK chart entry with 'Teenage Angst', the band hit number four with a re-recorded version of 'Nancy Boy' as sales of their début soared.

Placebo spent much of the next two years on the road, taking in dates on **U2**'s *Popmart* tour and **David Bowie**'s fiftieth birthday party at Madison Square Garden. They also made a cameo appearance in *Velvet Goldmine* (1998), contributing a cover of **T Rex**'s 'Twentieth Century Boy' to the soundtrack. Their second album, *Without You I'm Nothing*, was released later the same year, and included four UK hit singles, 'Pure Morning', 'Every You, Every Me', 'You Don't Care about Us' and a new recording of the title track featuring Bowie. Their third album, the less intense *Black Market Music*, followed in 2000. Featuring the singles 'Taste in Men' and 'Slave to the Wage', it failed to match the critical and commercial success of its predecessors.

THE PLATTERS
Tony Williams, b. 15 April 1928, New Rochelle, New Jersey, USA, d. 14 August 1992; David Lynch, b. 1929, St Louis, Missouri, d. 2 January 1981; Herbert Reed; Zola Taylor; Paul Robi

The most successful black doo-wop group of the fifties, the Platters sold over 50 million records with their fusion of R&B harmonizing and symphonic arrangements, first introduced in their 1955 million-seller 'Only You'. Unlike those of many of their contemporaries, their recordings were only rarely covered by white acts, partly because so many were of past pop hits.

Just as the **Coasters** were largely the creation of writer-producers **Leiber and Stoller**, so the Platters were created by Buck Ram. Ram (*b. 1907, Chicago, Illinois, d. 1 January 1991*) was a lawyer turned songwriter and arranger who worked with the bands of **Duke Ellington** and **Count Basie** in the late thirties and early forties. Among the hits he wrote were 'Afterglow' (Leo Reisman, Victor, 1936), 'At Your Beck and Call' (**Jimmy Dorsey**, 1938) and the ballad 'Twilight Time', which was used by the Three Suns (Hit, 1944) as their theme and was a hit for **Les Brown** in 1945. Following a nervous breakdown Ram retired from the music business, only returning in 1953 as booking agent. According to Ram, blues singer Linda Hayes ('Yes I Know', Hollywood Records) introduced him to her brother Tony Williams and, enchanted by his pure tenor, Ram formed the Platters round him. However, **Ralph Bass** claimed that he discovered Williams and the group, which certainly recorded unsuccessfully for Federal, and that **Syd Nathan** released the group to Ram in 1954.

Whether or not Ram tailormade the group, he was responsible for their distinctive romantic sound and clear phrasing which won the Platters immediate acceptance among whites. Also, he sought aggressively to place them on a major label. Following the Penguins' success with **Jesse Belvin**'s ethereal 'Earth Angel' (Dootone, 1955), Ram, their manager, secured contracts for both the Penguins and Platters with Mercury. The Penguins soon faded, but the Platters' reworking of Ram's 'Only You' (with Ram himself on piano), which the group had previously recorded for Federal, led to a string of international million-sellers. These included 'The Great Pretender' (1955), 'My Prayer' (1956), a 1939 translation of Georges Boulanger's 'Avant de Mourir' by **Jimmy Kennedy** (whose 'Harbour Lights' and 'Red Sails in the Sunset' the group also recorded in 1960), a reworking of Ram's own 'Twilight Time' and a majestic revival of **Otto Harbach** and **Jerome Kern**'s 'Smoke Gets in Your Eyes' (1958).

Though the Platters appeared in the rock'n'roll movies *The Girl Can't Help it* and *Rock Around the Clock* (1956), their sound owed little to either rock'n'roll or the harder black vocal-group sounds of such contemporaries as the **Clovers** or **Hank Ballard** and the Midnighters; rather it harked back to that of the **Ink Spots.** When their hits declined in 1960, Williams went solo and was replaced by Sonny Turner and for the next five years the group underwent several changes of line-up so that by the end of the decade there were some twenty groups all over the world calling themselves 'The Platters', each featuring

at least one 'original member'. In 1966 the official group, now dubbed Buck Ram's Platters, returned to charts with 'I Love You 1000 Times' and had a further hit in 1967 with 'With This Ring', their first release on Musicor, but by then the various Platters had become members of the international nightclub circuit.

THE POGUES

Shane McGowan, b. 25 December 1957, Kent, England; Philip Chevron, b. Philip Ryan, 17 June 1957, Dublin, Ireland; James Fearnley, b. 10 October 1954, Manchester, England; Andrew Rankien, b. 13 November 1953, London; Jem Finer, b. Jeremy Finer, 29 July 1955, Dublin, Ireland; Spider Stacy, b. Peter Stacy, 14 December 1958, Eastbourne, England; Cait O'Riordan (replaced by Daryl Hunt, b. 4 May 1950, Bournemouth); Terry Woods

One of the lesser noted effects of the punk explosion of the seventies was its impact on folk music, which had become, in its way, as insular and inward-looking as rock music at the time. Bands like Edward II and the Red Hot Pokers and the Oyster Band made use of the urgency of punk to revitalize folk music and make of it a music of contemporary comment. Of such groups the Pogues were the most commercially successful, the meeting point of the **Clancy Brothers** and the **Sex Pistols**.

McGowan formed the Nipple Erectors in the aftermath of punk which, after a name change to Pogue Mahone (which means 'kiss my arse' in Gaelic) and a partial switch in styles as more former Irish folkies joined, was invited to tour with the **Clash**. Despite their anarchic stage antics the band was signed to Stiff in 1984 and recorded *Red Roses for Me*. While 'Streams of Whiskey' was both noteworthy and self-indulgent, 'Dark Streets of London' was a fine song. It was followed by the **Elvis Costello**-produced *Rum Sodomy and the Lash* (1985). Probably their most satisfying album it included a resonant reworking of **Ewan MacColl**'s 'Dirty Old Town', an evocative version of Eric Bogle's anti-war song 'And the Band Played Waltzing Matilda' and the fetching 'A Pair of Brown Eyes', which was a minor UK hit. After that they briefly joined forces with the Dubliners for 'The Irish Rover' (1987).

Adding ex-**Steeleye Span** and Sweeney's Men instrumentalist Terry Woods, the Pogues moved to Island for *If I Should Fall from Grace with God* (1988), which was produced by Steve Lillywhite and included the hit single 'Fairytale of New York', a duet between McGowan and Kirsty MacColl, daughter of Ewan and wife of Lilllywhite. Then, just before a planned American tour in support of **Bob Dylan**, McGowan collapsed from alcohol abuse and the band played without him. The subdued *Peace and Love* (1989), as if in response to McGowan's incapacity, was a more democratic album with songs from every group member. *Hell's Ditch* (1990) was centred on McGowan's songwriting but sold poorly, especially in comparison with the single recorded with the Dubliners in celebration of the success of the Irish football team in the World Cup, 'Jack's Heroes', and in 1991 McGowan left the group to be replaced by former singer with the **Clash**, Joe Strummer. In June 1992 Strummer left and Stacy became lead singer.

The Pogues' next album was *Waiting for Herb* (1993), while McGowan returned with a new band, the Popes. His live performances were as unsteady as before but the group's first album, *The Snake* (ZTT, 1994), was well received. More commercially successful was the follow-up, *The Crock of Gold* (1997).

THE POINTER SISTERS

Anita, b. 23 January 1948, Oakland, California; Bonnie, b. 11 July 1950, Oakland; June, b. 1954, Oakland; Ruth, b. 1946, Oakland

A versatile black vocal group, the Pointer Sisters enjoyed considerable success in the seventies and eighties in collaboration with producer Richard Perry.

Children of a minister of religion, they first sang in church before working as session singers for San Francisco producer David Rubinson. They recorded the unsuccessful 'Don't Try to Take the Fifth' (Atlantic, 1972) before Rubinson signed them to Blue Thumb. The **Allen Toussaint** R&B song 'Yes We Can Can' was a Top Twenty hit but it was the Pointer Sisters' mixture of forties standards with jazz, soul and pop which made them in demand for live and TV performances.

The group's versatility was underlined when 'Fairytale' (1974) was both a country and pop hit and 'How Long (Betcha Got a Chick on the Side)' (1975) reached No. 1 in the R&B charts. The Pointer Sisters appeared in the film *Car Wash* (1976) but a dispute with Blue Thumb over unpaid royalties led to a hiatus in their recording career. Bonnie left the group to join Motown, where she had solo hits with 'Heaven Must Have Sent You' (1979) and a revival of the **Four Tops'** 1965 success 'I Can't Help Myself' (1980). During the eighties she recorded for Epic.

The remaining sisters signed to Richard Perry's Planet label, where they enjoyed three million-selling singles in 1978–81. Adding a contemporary rock feel to their sound, Perry produced **Bruce Springsteen**'s 'Fire' from *Energy* (1978), the **Doobie Brothers**-influenced 'He's so Shy' from *Special Things* (1980) and 'Slow Hand' from *Black and White* (1981). *So Excited* (1982) provided further success with 'American Music' and 'I'm So Excited', which was a Top Ten hit when reissued two years later.

The more dance-orientated *Break Out* (1984) gave the Pointers a trio of hits in 'Automatic', 'Jump (for My Love)' (1984) and 'I Need You' (1985). *Contact* (1985) included the hit 'Dare Me' and in 1986 they released *Hot Together* (RCA), once again produced by Perry. Anita recorded a Preston Glass-produced solo album *Love for What It Is* before in 1988 the sisters had further R&B hits with 'He Turned Me Out' and 'I'm in Love' from the album *Serious Slammin'*. A brief stay with Motown produced the unexceptional *Right Rhythm* (1990), and the sisters moved to SBK Records in 1992, releasing *Only Sisters Can Do That* (1993). They continued to tour but recorded less in the nineties.

POISON

Bret Michaels, b. 15 March 1963, Pittsburgh, Pennsylvania, USA; Rikki Rockett, b. 8 August 1959, Mechanicsburgh, Pennsylvania; Matt Smith; Cecil 'CC' DeVille, b. 14 May 1962, Brooklyn, New York (replaced by Richie Kotzen, b. 1970, Birdsboro); Bobby Dall, b. 2 November 1962, Florida

Poison were part of the second wave of glam-metal bands which emerged in the US in the wake of such groups as **Motley Crüe**, W.A.S.P. and Ratt. Like those artists, Poison toured frequently and enjoyed huge success in the late eighties.

Vocalist Michaels and drummer Rockett first teamed up in Pittsburgh band the Spectres before forming Paris (not to be confused with the band of the same name formed in the seventies by ex-**Fleetwood Mac** guitarist Bob Welch) with bassist Dall and guitarist Matt Smith in 1983. Renamed Poison, the band moved to Los Angeles in 1984, where the experienced DeVille (something of an LA band veteran) replaced Smith the following year. A heavy gigging schedule eventually brought the band to the attention of Enigma Records, linked to major label Capitol, who signed the band in 1986. Their début album, *Look What the Cat Dragged in* (1986), drew comparisons with **Kiss**, combining catchy choruses with heavy riffing and DeVille's incendiary fretwork.

The band embarked on a non-stop touring schedule to promote the album, which included the hit singles 'Talk Dirty to Me' and 'I Won't Forget You' and went on to sell over three million copies. The follow-up, *Open Up and Say . . . Aah!* (1988), was an even bigger success, and the ballad 'Every Rose Has its Thorn' topped the US chart as well as giving Poison its first UK hit single. Another lengthy bout of touring followed the album's release, after which the band took time off the road to record the third album, *Flesh and Blood* (1990).

Amid rumours of a split and dogged by health and drug problems, the band undertook a marathon twelve-month tour after the release of *Flesh and Blood* (1990). The tour provided material for the live album *Swallow This Live* (1991), whose sales were disappointing compared to those of its predecessors. Shortly after its release DeVille left Poison to form his own band. His replacement was guitar *wunderkind* Kotzen, who had already released three instrumental solo albums at the age of twenty-one.

The first album by the new line-up, *Native Tongue*, appeared in 1993 and showed a new blues-rock approach with instrumental support supplied by **Lynyrd Skynyrd** keyboard-player Billy Powell and the Tower of Power brass section. The definitive anthology is *Greatest Hits, 1986–1996* (1997).

THE POLICE

Stewart Copeland, b. 19 July 1952, Virginia, USA; Sting, b. Gordon Matthew Sumner, 27 October 1951, Wallsend, Tyne and Wear, England; Andy Summers, b. 31 December 1942, Blackpool, Lancashire

Sting's cleverly constructed lyrics and the group's reggae-styled rhythms made the Police one of the most successful rock bands of the late seventies and early eighties.

Drummer Copeland had recorded with progressive rock band Curved Air and guitarist Summers with R&B group Zoot Money's Big Roll Band ('Big Time Operator', EMI Columbia, 1966) and **Mike Oldfield** before forming the Police in 1977. Bassist Sting had played in jazz-rock group Last Exit in Newcastle and met Copeland and Summers when all three played in Strontium 90, an occasional jazz-rock band led by ex-Gong member Mike Howlett. Managed by Copeland's brother Miles, the Police adopted a punk-rock approach for 'Fall Out' (Illegal, 1977), produced by former **Velvet Underground** member **John Cale**. The band was given a bleached-blonde look to appear in a chewing-gum commercial and in 1978 the Police released 'Can't Stand Losing You' while Copeland made 'Don't Care' (A&M) as Klark Kent.

A brief American tour was followed by the release of *Outlandos d'Amour* (A&M, 1978). Produced by Nigel Gray, it included 'Roxanne', a Sting song about a prostitute, which was a minor American hit and which reached the British Top Twenty. The reissued 'Can't Stand Losing You' was even more successful. *Reggatta de Blanc* (1979) was a No. 1 album which included two No. 1 singles, the anthemic 'Message in a Bottle' and 'Walking on the Moon' (1979). Both featured Sting's jazzy, hoarse vocals and Summers's edgy, dynamic guitar attack which was created with fuzz, delay and tape loops in conjunction with fragmentary chords and frequent changes of rhythm. **Sly and Robbie** later produced Sheila Hylton's reggae version of Sting's 'The Bed's Too Big Without You' (Island,

1981). After the lesser hits 'So Lonely' (1980) and 'Six Pack', the group broke through in America with 'Don't Stand So Close to Me' (1980) – a cry of a teacher to a student with a nod to Nabokov's *Lolita* – and 'De Do Do Do, De Da Da Da' from *Zenyatta Mondatta* (1981). The title was Sanskrit for 'top of the world' and Copeland and Summers contributed compositions to the album.

The title of *Ghost in the Machine* contained a further literary reference (to Arthur Koestler's book about the mind–body relationship) of the kind that caused some reviewers to call Sting pretentious. Producer Hugh Padgham helped to give the album a louder, more polished sound and both the joyous, calypso-flavoured 'Every Little Thing She Does Is Magic' and the philosophical 'Spirits in the Material World' were transatlantic hits, while 'Invisible Sun', with its Irish theme, reached No. 2 in Britain despite the banning of its accompanying video by the BBC. **Grace Jones** recorded a version of the album's 'Demolition Man' on her *Nightclubbin'* (1981).

Sting's powerful evocation of jealousy, 'Every Breath You Take' (1983), topped the charts on both sides of the Atlantic. It came from what was to be the final Police album, *Synchronicity*, whose other single hits were 'Wrapped Around Your Finger', 'Synchronicity II' and 'King of Pain' (1984).

By now each member of the band was absorbed in solo projects and during 1985 the Police performed together only once. In 1986 recording sessions for a new album were begun and abandoned before the band formally split up.

Since then, Copeland, Sting and Summers have all performed and recorded separately. Sting's solo career is detailed in a separate entry. Even while the Police were fully active, Summers had recorded *I Advance Masked* (1982) and *Bewitched* with fellow guitarist **Robert Fripp**. He subsequently made a number of solo albums, including *XYZ* (1987), *Golden Wire* (1989), *Charming Snakes* (1990), on which he was joined by Sting, **Herbie Hancock** and others, and *World Gone Strange* (1991). Later records included *Synaesthesia* (CMP, 1995) and *The Last Days of Mr X* (RCA, 1997).

Copeland's later work was divided between his interest in African rhythms, film scores and the group Animal Logic. He first travelled in West Africa in 1985 to record local drumming styles for *The Rhythmatist*. His first film work was for Francis Ford Coppola's *Rumblefish* (1984). Copeland later wrote the scores for *Wall Street* (1987), *Talk Radio* (1988) and *The Quickening* (1989), among others, with more recent scores including *The Pallbearer* (1996) and *Four Days in September* (1997). He also composed the opera *Holy Blood and Crescent Moon* (1989) and the television operetta *Horse Opera*. In 1989 he formed Animal Logic with drummer **Stanley Clarke** and Los Angeles singer-songwriter Deborah Holland, releasing a self-titled album in 1989.

Message in a Box: The Complete Recordings (1992) over-documents the Police's career.

POMUS AND SHUMAN

Jerome E. Felder Pomus, b. 27 June 1925, New York, USA, d. 14 March 1991, New York; Mort Shuman, b. 12 November 1936, New York, d. 4 November 1991, London

Pomus and Shuman were one of the most prolific and successful songwriting teams of the rock'n'roll era, equally adept at pinning down the innocent anguish of teenage love ('Teenager in Love'), as writing for black vocal groups (the **Drifters**, 'Save the Last Dance for Me') or Elvis Presley ('Little Sister', 'A Mess of Blues'). While earlier mainstream writers, such as **Harold Arlen**, were blues influenced, Pomus and Shuman's best songs were blues based. Further, they were, like their contemporaries **Leiber and Stoller** – who produced many Drifters' recordings of Pomus and Shuman songs – one of the few writing teams of the fifties to continue successfully into the sixties and beyond.

From an early age Pomus immersed himself in the New York R&B scene as a singer and writer. Among his earliest compositions were the blues ballad 'Still in Love' (1951), 'Boogie Woogie, Country Girl' (co-written by Reginald Asby, 1955), both hits for **Joe Turner**; the plaintive 'Lonely Avenue' (**Ray Charles**, 1956); 'Young Blood' (co-written with Leiber and Stoller for the **Coasters**, 1957); and 'Heartlessly' (Dawn, 1956), the most successful of his own **Mose Allison**-like records. In 1958 Pomus released 'I'll Kiss and Make Up' by the Crowns, who later became the Drifters, on his own R&B label.

Pomus and Shuman began writing together in early 1958, and after joining publishers Hill and Range soon found success with a series of gimmicky pop songs in 1959, including 'I'm a Man' (**Fabian**), 'Plain Jane' (**Bobby Darin**), and their first major hit 'Teenager in Love', which was sympathetically interpreted by the sad-voiced **Dion** with backing from the Belmonts.

Even more influential was their string of hits for the Drifters: 'Save the Last Dance for Me', 'I Count the Tears', 'This Magic Moment' (1960), 'Sweets for My Sweet' (1961, later memorably covered by the **Searchers**, 1963) and the double-sided hit for **Ben E. King**, 'Here Comes the Night', co-written with **Phil Spector**, and 'Young Boy Blues', a Shuman–Spector composition. Both, but particularly Pomus, regularly wrote with Spector. The other main recipient of Pomus and Shuman's songs was Presley. He recorded the soulful 'A Mess of Blues' (1960), the playful 'His Latest Flame', 'Little Sister', 'Surrender' (1961), 'She's Not You' (1962) and the lightweight film theme 'Viva Las Vegas' (1964), among others, and continued to

record their work into the seventies. Other hits included 'Seven Day Weekend' (**Gary US Bonds**) and 'Spanish Lace' (**Gene McDaniels**) in 1962, 'Can't Get Used to Losing You' (**Andy Williams**, 1963) and 'Suspicion' (Terry Stafford, Crusader, 1964).

In 1964 the pair went to England, where **Jack Good** had earlier devoted a whole edition of his *Oh Boy!* television show to their work. The following year Pomus suffered a fall that left him wheelchair bound. This, and the lack of demand for their rock material now that, in the wake of **The Beatles**, groups were writing their own songs, led to the dissolution of their partnership. Shuman provided hits for several British artists, including the **Small Faces** ('Sha La La La Lee', which he co-wrote with English writer and one-time pop star Kenny Lynch, whose biggest hit was a cover of the Drifters' 'Up on the Roof', HMV, 1962); the **Hollies** ('Here I Go Again'); and Billy J. Kramer ('Little Children', EMI Columbia, 1964). In 1966 Shuman teamed up with producer **Jerry Ragavoy** to write songs for deep-soul singer **Howard Tate** ('Get It While You Can', 'Look at Granny Run, Run'). Shuman then settled in Paris, where he provided several songs for **Johnny Hallyday** and wrote, produced and starred in the stage show based on translations of **Jacques Brel** songs, *Jacques Brel Is Alive and Well and Living in Paris*, which was later mounted in London and New York. Shuman subsequently recorded a series of solo albums for the French Philips label, including *Amerika* and *Imagine . . .*, which included a version of 'Save the Last Dance for Me'. In 1988 he wrote with lyricist Don Black the musical *Budgie*, starring **Adam Faith**.

After a lengthy period of inactivity Pomus began writing with **Dr John**, first on John's own albums, *City Lights* (1978) and *Tango Palace* (1979), and then for **B. B. King**, most of whose 1981 Grammy-winning album *There Must Be a Better World Somewhere* they wrote, including the title song. Pomus also wrote several songs with one-time American punk rocker Mink De Ville on his 1980 album, *Le Chat Bleu* (Capitol). **Lou Reed**'s 1992 album *Magic and Loss* was a collection of songs about Pomus' fight against cancer, to which he had succumbed in 1991. In that year he became the first white musician to be awarded the Pioneer Award of the Rhythm & Blues Foundation. The tribute album *Till the Night Is Gone* (Rhino, 1995) saw the likes of **Bob Dylan**, **Los Lobos**, Dr John, Lou Reed and **The Band** performing songs written by Pomus.

BRIAN POOLE AND THE TREMELOES

Brian Poole, b. 3 November 1941, Dagenham, Essex, England; Rick Westwood, b. 7 May 1943, Dagenham; Alan Howard, b. 1942, Bromley, Kent (replaced in 1966 by Len 'Chip' Hawkes, b. 11 November 1946, London,

replaced in 1974 by Aaron Woolley); Alan Blakely,
b. 1 April 1942 (replaced in 1975 by Bob Benham); Dave
Munden, b. 2 December 1943, Dagenham

Though, like the **Dave Clark Five** with whom they
shared a policy of covering American hits, Brian
Poole and the Tremeloes rose to success at the time of
the British beat boom, they were only tangentially
connected to the movement.

Formed in 1959 in Dagenham, the group's repertoire initially consisted almost entirely of songs associated with **Buddy Holly** and the **Crickets**, with Poole
even wearing Holly-type spectacles. After several
appearances on the radio show *Saturday Club*, they
signed with Decca, releasing *Big Hits of '62* on the
company's budget Ace of Clubs label. Their first hits
came in 1963 on Decca with covers of **The Beatles'**
album track 'Twist and Shout' (itself a cover of the
Isley Brothers 1962 recording) and of **Berry Gordy's**
'Do You Love Me', an American hit for the **Contours**
(1962) and later revived by the Dave Clark Five (1964).
Their eclecticism was confirmed in 1964 with revivals
of **Roy Orbison's** 'Candy Man' (1961), the Crickets'
'Someone, Someone' (1959), and in 1965 with the
Browns' 'Three Bells' (1959) and 'I Want Candy', a hit
for the Strangeloves (Bang, 1965). Despite success in
Europe where they toured, the group never made an
impact in America and in 1966, as the beat-group
boom lost its momentum, Poole left the group for an
unsuccessful solo career before returning to his original occupation as a butcher. He briefly returned to
recording for Tramline in 1981 and as a member of
the Corporation (alongside Reg Presley of the **Troggs**
and Mike Pender of the **Searchers**) in 1989.

With new member Hawkes, the Tremeloes returned to the charts with the **Cat Stevens** composition
'Here Comes My Baby' (Columbia, 1967), the first of
their trio of million-sellers. The others were an
impressive revival of the **Four Seasons'** album track
'Silence Is Golden' and the **Mitch Murray** and Peter
Callander composition 'Even the Bad Times Are
Good' in 1967. Callander was also partly responsible
for 'Suddenly You Love Me' (1968), after which they
turned to gentler harmonies. Their mawkish version
of **Bob Dylan's** 'I Shall Be Released' (1968) was only a
minor hit but group members Blakely and Hawkes
provided them with their last hits, including '(Call
Me) Number One' (1969) and 'Me and My Life'
(1970). Their hitmaking days over, the group retired
to the European cabaret and revivalist circuit while
Poole occasionally hung up his apron to join them.

Hawkes' son Chesney began his recording career in
1991 with a British No. 1, 'The One and Only', while
his daughters Shellie and Karen recorded with some
success as Alisha's Attic (*Alisha Rules the World*,
1996).

COLE PORTER
b. 9 June 1891, Peru, Indiana, USA, d. 15 October 1964,
Santa Monica, California

In the biopic *Night and Day* (1946) Porter was played
by Cary Grant. While Grant was physically completely dissimilar to Porter (a dandy in his youth, he
was severely crippled after a riding accident in 1937),
the casting was aesthetically correct with Grant's easy,
sophisticated elegance evoking Porter's minor-key
melodies with their witty, ingenious, urbane lyrics.
Porter wrote over twenty Broadway musicals but,
with the notable exception of *Kiss Me Kate* (1948),
most were little but song collections held together by
the flimsiest of narratives. His *métier* was the individual song, often risqué, as in 'Let's Do It' (with its erudite listing of the amatory habits of much of the
animal kingdom). Though he lived for lengthy periods in Europe and brought a cultured sophistication
to his lyric writing, far removed from the direct simplicities of **Irving Berlin**, Porter's wordplay was profoundly American in its use of slang and everyday
language.

Porter was the grandson of a multi-millionaire. His
possessive mother paid to have his composition 'The
Bobolink Waltz' published when Porter was eleven.
While at Yale he developed the playboy, dilettante
lifestyle that he was to hide behind throughout his life
and turned decisively to music, writing a football
song for the University and songs for several revues in
1915. In 1916 he wrote his first show, *See America First*,
which despite a minor hit ('I've a Shooting Box in
Scotland') failed. Porter retreated to Paris where he
married rich socialite Linda Thomas and completed
his society education. He continued writing throughout the twenties but only had limited success until
1928's 'Let's Do It' (the title replaced 'Let's Misbehave'
which was judged too suggestive even for a show
called *Paris*), a hit for **Paul Whiteman**, among others.

That song (memorably revived by **Noël Coward** on
Live at Las Vegas) marked the watershed in Porter's
career. In the next decade he had success after success
with songs which Broadway historian Stanley Green
has described as 'perpetuating all that was glamorous
in the twenties . . . with bright and brittle rhythms'.
Among these were 'Night and Day' (1932), introduced
by **Fred Astaire** in *The Gay Divorce* (filmed 1934 as *The
Gay Divorcee*), and recorded by **Eddy Duchin** (1934),
Charlie Barnet (1940), **Frank Sinatra** (1942) and **Bing
Crosby** (1944), among others; 'I Get a Kick out of You'
(1934), a hit for both **Ethel Merman** and Paul Whiteman in 1935 and revived by Gary Shearston (Charisma,
1974); and 'You're the Top' (1934), a hit for Porter
himself (Victor, 1935). 'Miss Otis Regrets' (1934, a hit
for **Ethel Waters**) was written for Monty Wooley to
sing at a party and later reprised by him in *Night and*

Day, while among those who recorded the lush 'Begin the Beguine' (1934) were **Xavier Cugat** (1935), **Artie Shaw** (1938) and Sinatra (1946). 'My Heart Belongs to Daddy' (1938) was memorably sung by Marilyn Monroe in the 1960 film *Let's Make Love*, and 'Anything Goes' (1934) was revived by **Harpers Bizarre** (1967).

In the mid-thirties Porter began writing for the movies with equal ease. Among his film songs were 'I've Got You under My Skin' (1936, a hit for **Ray Noble** and later parodied by **Stan Freberg**, 1951); 'In the Still of the Night' (1937, a hit for **Tommy Dorsey**); 'You'd Be So Nice to Come Home to' (1943, a hit for **Dinah Shore**); the cowboy-song parody 'Don't Fence Me in' (1944, which was a hit for Bing Crosby with the **Andrew Sisters**, and **Sammy Kaye**, 1945, among others); and the brash 'Be a Clown' (1948, sung by **Judy Garland** and **Gene Kelly** in the **Arthur Freed**-produced *The Pirate*).

That brashness was first heard in his score for the successful Broadway show *DuBarry Was a Lady* (1939, filmed 1943), written by Porter after a riding accident lost him the use of both legs. While 'Ev'ry Time We Say Goodbye' (1944, a hit for **Benny Goodman**, 1945 and closely associated with **Ella Fitzgerald**) caught the mood of wartime America, too many of Porter's songs of this period either repeated the brittle emotions of his earlier work or saw him toying uneasily with sentimentality (as in 'Ev'rything I Love' from *Let's Face It*, 1941). Then came *Kiss Me Kate* (1948, filmed 1953). Based on Shakespeare's *The Taming of the Shrew*, it included the showbusiness standard 'Another Op'nin', Another Show', 'Too Darn Hot', 'Wunderbar' (another of Porter's parodies, this time of Viennese operetta), and the classic, 'Always True to You in My Fashion'. He wrote other stage shows, including *Can Can* (1953, filmed 1960, which included 'I Love Paris') and *Silk Stockings* (1954, filmed 1957) but his major success of the fifties was the jaunty score to the film *High Society* (1956). Starring Sinatra, Bing Crosby and **Louis Armstrong**, it featured 'Now You Has Jazz', a reworking of 'Well, Did You Evah?' from *DuBarry Was a Lady*, 'I Love You Samantha' and 'True Love', Porter's last big hit in a duet by Crosby and Grace Kelly.

Following the amputation of his right leg in 1958, Porter retired. The resilience of Porter's *œuvre* was demonstrated in 1990 when a variety of contemporary pop artists created new versions of his songs on *Red Hot and Blue*, an Aids charity album. In 1994 Koch International released Porter performing twenty-two of his own compositions. These comprised demos made for *Jubilee* and *Can-Can*. Among the latter were five songs that were not in the Broadway show, including 'Who Said Gay Paree?' and 'I Do', which subsequently supplied the melody for *High Society*'s 'Who Wants to Be a Millionaire?'.

PORTISHEAD

Geoff Barrow, b. 9 December 1971, Walton-in-Gordano, Avon, England; Beth Gibbons, b. 4 January 1965, Devon; Adrian Utley, b. 1957, England

Portishead emerged in the early 1990s from Bristol, a city that also produced **Massive Attack**, Tricky and **Soul II Soul** member Nellie Hooper. Their cinematic sound, which owed at least as much to sixties spy thrillers and singers like **Julie London** as it did to contemporary hip-hop, was characterized by the combination of Gibbons' fragile, tortured vocals with the dense, dark and complex backings created by Barrow and Utley.

Gibbons was already a stalwart of the local pub-rock and jazz scene when she met Barrow, who had worked as a studio engineer on the recording of Massive Attack's *Blue Lines* album. Utley, recruited shortly afterwards by Barrow, was also a respected jazz guitarist playing the local circuit. Given the cinematic qualities of their music, it is hardly surprising in retrospect that the group's first real project was a short film, *To Kill a Dead Man*, and its accompanying soundtrack. This brought the band to the attention of Go Discs' Go! Beat arm, with whom the band released two singles, 'Numb' and 'Sour Times', before issuing their début album, *Dummy*, in 1994.

The album gained an audience through word-of-mouth, enough so to make its third single, 'Glory Box', a Top Twenty hit early in 1995. This followed on from excellent press reaction to the album, which was dubbed the first masterpiece of a new genre, 'trip-hop'. *Dummy* went on to win the UK's Mercury Music Prize later in 1995. Portishead's eponymous second album was released in 1997, preceded by the single 'All Mine'. Although *Dummy* had spawned a host of imitators, *Portishead* showed little evolution from the début album. It was well received critically and commercially, however, and was followed in November 1998 by a live album and video, *PNYC*, recorded at New York's Roseland Ballroom with full orchestral accompaniment to reproduce live the band's rich recorded sound.

SANDY POSEY

b. Martha Sharp, 18 June 1945, Jasper, Alabama, USA

Like the more successful **Tammy Wynette**, Posey's anthemic songs about the place of woman, notably the self-penned 'Born a Woman' and 'Single Girl' (1966), have been contrastingly interpreted as both submissive and assertive. In fact the lyric and Posey's performance of 'Woman' identified the pleasures and sadnesses of marriage, just as in 'Single Girl' she captured the two faces of independence.

Raised in the deep South, Posey worked as a

receptionist at **Chip Moman**'s AGP studios before graduating to session singer. She sang back-up on recordings by **Joe Tex**, **Bobby Goldsboro**, **Bobby Bare** and **Percy Sledge** (including 'When a Man Loves a Woman', 1966). A demo of 'Born a Woman', featuring her clean, light voice, led to a contract with MGM and, produced by Moman, the song was her first hit in 1966. She followed it with 'Single Girl', **John D. Loudermilk**'s 'What a Woman in Love Won't Do' and former member of the **Four Preps** Ed Cobb's 'I Take It Back', both in 1967. The latter was formula-ridden but album tracks like her stately version of **Otis Redding**'s 'I've Been Loving You Too Long' (1966), were more effective.

Posey did not record again until 1970 when she signed with Columbia where, supervised by Wynette's producer **Billy Sherrill**, she had a country hit with 'Bring Him Home Safely to Me' (1971). Reunited with Moman, she had further country hits with revivals of the **Chordettes**' 'Born to Be with You' (1977) and 'Chapel of Love' (1978), a No. 1 hit for the Dixie Cups in 1964 (Red Bird). Since the eighties she has recorded only infrequently.

BUD POWELL

b. Earl Powell, 27 September 1924, New York, USA, d. 31 July 1966, New York

With **Thelonious Monk**, Powell was the most creative modern jazz pianist. His powers of invention were often compared to those of **Charlie Parker**, while the later stages of his erratic career inspired the film *Round Midnight* (1986).

The son of stride pianist William Powell, Bud began playing the piano aged six. He first studied classical music, switching to jazz at fifteen when he played with Valaida Snow and the Sunset Royals. With Monk he played at Minton's, the birthplace of bebop.

Powell's first records were made with the swing band of Cootie Williams, recording with him for Capitol, Majestic and Hit (*Echoes of Harlem*, 1944). Having developed a dynamic, vigorous bebop piano style, he recorded frequently in the late forties. In 1946 he appeared on records by trombonist J. J. Johnson, ('Coppin' the Bop', Savoy), trumpeter Fats Navarro and drummer **Kenny Clarke** (Victor).

The following year he made his first recording with Parker ('Cheryl', Savoy), while his own 'Bud's Bubble', recorded with drummer **Max Roach** for Roost, displayed his rhythmic virtuosity. 1949 brought a collaboration with saxophonist Sonny Stitt for Prestige while **Sonny Rollins** joined Powell's recording group on 'Bouncing with Bud' (Blue Note). The pianist was reunited with Parker in 1950 on 'Street Beat' (Dial) while their partnership continued at the saxophonist's last great performance, the Toronto concert of 1953,

recorded as *The Quintet of the Year* (Verve). On the same occasion, Powell made a trio recording with Roach and bassist **Charles Mingus**.

By the mid-fifties a series of mental breakdowns had taken their toll and Powell's music became sombre and inconsistent. He continued to record for Verve, Blue Note, and Victor with *The Lonely One* (Verve, 1955) and *The Scene Changes* (Blue Note, 1959) coming closest to recapturing the brilliance of his earlier work. Shortly afterwards, Powell moved permanently to Paris, returning to America only shortly before his death. There he recorded with such visiting Americans as saxophonists Johnny Griffin (*Bud in Paris*, Xanadu, 1960) and **Coleman Hawkins** (*Hawk in Germany*, Black Lion 1960). Powell also worked with Dexter Gordon (*Our Man in Paris*, Blue Note, 1963), who acted the central role in *Round Midnight*, a portrait of an expatriate jazz musician in Paris in the early sixties. *Bouncing with Bud* (Delmark, 1962) marked the début of bassist Neils-Henning Orsted Pedersen, who later accompanied **Oscar Peterson**.

DICK POWELL

b. Richard Ewing Powell, 14 November 1904, Mountain View, Arkansas, USA, d. 3 January 1963, Hollywood, California

Better remembered for his wavy-haired, apple-cheeked good looks than his pleasant, robust tenor, Powell was the juvenile lead who adorned most of Warners' backstage musicals of the thirties, most frequently in partnership with **Ruby Keeler**.

Educated at Little Rock College, where he learned to play a variety of musical instruments, Powell pursued a part-time career on graduation as a singer, joining the Royal Peacock Orchestra in Louisville, Kentucky, in 1925. In 1928 he made his recording début on Vocalion with Charlie Davis's Orchestra and, in 1930, when Hollywood turned to the mass production of musicals with sound, he was signed by Warners. In 1932 he made his screen début as a crooner in *Blessed Event* and in 1933 he played opposite Keeler in the epochal *42nd Street*, which introduced the format of the backstage musical and the spectacular choreography of Busby Berkeley. It was followed by *Gold Diggers of 1933* and *Footlight Parade* (1933), all featuring songs by **Harry Warren** and Al Dubin, and Keeler.

In these films Powell introduced, respectively, the bright 'Young and Healthy', the risqué 'Petting in the Park', 'I've Got to Sing a Torch Song' and 'Honeymoon Hotel'. In *Dames* (1934), Powell introduced the Warren–Dubin standard 'I Only Have Eyes for You', which later became a staple of doo-wop groups and was memorably recorded by the **Flamingos** (1959) and revived by Art Garfunkel (Columbia, 1975). Powell had hits with recordings of several of his film songs on Vocalion until 1935 and then Decca. *Thanks a Million* (1935), in which he played a crooner running for governor, gave him a hit with his Decca recording of the **Gus Kahn** title song. Though he was still in demand for musicals and his records sold well, Powell later sought, at first unsuccessfully, work outside musicals. Other songs he introduced included **Irving Berlin**'s 'I've Got My Love to Keep Me Warm' (*On the Avenue*, 1937); Warren and **Johnny Mercer**'s 'You Must Have Been a Beautiful Baby' (*Hard to Get*, 1938); and **Harold Arlen** and Mercer's 'Hit the Road to Dreamland' (*Star Spangled Rhythm*, 1943).

Finally, with *Murder My Sweet* (1945), in which he played Raymond Chandler's Philip Marlowe, Powell established a new image for himself outside the musical and went on to become a dramatic actor of note and a film director. In the fifties, with *Four Star Playhouse* (1952), he was one of the pioneers of television drama.

PEREZ PRADO
b. Panteleon Perez Prado, 11 December 1916, Mantanzas, Cuba, d. 14 September 1989, Mexico City

Known as 'El Rey del Mambo', Prado was responsible for the popularity of the mambo in America in the fifties and had two of the most successful records of the decade, 'Cherry Pink and Apple Blossom White'* (1955) and 'Patricia'* (1958).

A pianist with the famous Orquesta Casino de la Playa in Cuba in the forties, Prado moved to Mexico in 1948, formed his own band there and began recording for RCA. He specialized in recording mambos, mostly instrumentals, replete with grunts, cowbells and the like, along with the contrasting brass and sax riffs characteristic of the music. His recordings included 'Mambo No 5', 'Caballo Negro' (1948) and 'Que Rico el Mambo' (1949), which were also released in America by RCA for the Latin market. However, the mambo craze began after arranger and bandleader (and later producer of **Frank Sinatra**'s ambitious *Trilogy*, 1980) Sonny Burke while on holiday in Mexico heard Prado's 'Que Rico el Mambo' and successfully covered it in America as 'Mambo Jambo' (1950). A mark of the music's success was that when Prado first toured the West Coast of America, with **Stan Kenton** trumpeter Pete Candoli, he drew sell-out crowds. He was less successful in New York where, in contrast to **Machito** and **Tito Puente**, his music was considered over-simplified and commercialized by Latins.

In the early fifties Prado had several minor hits, including a piano version of **Moises Simons**' 'The Peanut Vendor' (1953), but the mambo's breakthrough into the mainstream came as a result of a series of novelty songs by established artists in 1954.

These included **Rosemary Clooney** ('Mambo Italiano'* written by **Bob Merrill**), **Perry Como** ('Papa Loves to Mambo'*), **Ruth Brown** (whose 'Mambo Baby' topped the R&B charts) and even **Bill Haley** ('Mambo Rock'). Less successful pieces of opportunism included 'Jingle Bell Mambo', 'I Saw Mommy Doing the Mambo' (an adaptation of **Tommie Connor**'s 'I Saw Mommy Kissing Santa Claus') and 'We Wanna See Santa Do the Mambo'. Prado's own greatest success came in 1955 with 'Cherry Blossom'. After being featured in the film *Underwater*, his recording of the song, featuring trumpeter Billy Regis, topped the American and British charts, despite being covered in Britain by Eddie Calvert (EMI Columbia). The song had unlikely origins for a mambo. It was written by Jacques Larue and Louis Gay as 'Cerise Rose et Pommer Blanc' in Paris in 1950 and after Prado's first recording of it (in 1951) was given an English lyric by Mack David, the brother of **Burt Bacharach**'s collaborator, Hal David.

Though Prado continued to sell large numbers of records in Latin America, his subsequent American hits were only minor until 'Patricia' (1958), which, unusually for the time, topped both the pop and R&B charts. His last American hit was the lacklustre 'Patricia Twist' (1962).

A far more enduring star in South America, Prado continued to tour there until he retired in the early seventies when he settled in Italy. His elder brother Damos was also a bandleader and composer who specialized in the mambo. In 1994 he had a surprise British hit when 'Guaglione' was used in a television commercial for Guinness.

PREFAB SPROUT
Paddy McAloon, b. 7 June 1957, Durham, England; Martin McAloon, b. 4 January 1962, Durham; Wendy Smith, b. 31 May 1963, Durham; Mick Salmon; Neil Conti, b. 12 February 1959, London

Prefab Sprout attracted a devoted cult following and critical acclaim in the eighties with a series of sophisticated, wordy albums featuring the songs of vocalist Paddy McAloon which drew comparisons with **Steely Dan**. Like that band, Prefab Sprout was largely studio-bound but failed to achieve the same level of success as the more jazz-influenced US act.

Paddy McAloon formed the band in Consett in north-east England in 1982 while studying English at nearby Newcastle University. With a line-up which included McAloon's bassist brother Martin, co-vocalist Smith and drummer Salmon, the band played in the Durham and Newcastle area before recording their début single, 'Lions in My Own Garden' (1982), on their own label, Candle. The single brought the band to the notice of local independent label Kitchenware, which released the follow-up, 'The Devil Has All the Best Tunes', in 1983.

The next single, 'Don't Sing', was an attempt by McAloon to condense Graham Greene's novel *The Power and the Glory* into a four-minute pop song. It was taken from the début album, *Swoon* (1984). With Neil Conti on drums, the band's second album, *Steve McQueen*, appeared in 1985 to an ecstatic reception from critics. Like much of Prefab Sprout's subsequent material, it was produced by **Thomas Dolby**, whose studio mastery was reflected in the vast improvement of the album's sound compared with its trebly predecessor. The album included the haunting 'When Love Breaks Down', which was a British hit.

The next self-produced Prefab Sprout album was to be titled *Protest Songs*. However, although recorded, the album did not appear, and the band did not re-emerge until 1988, when they released McAloon's 'Cars and Girls', a wry appraisal of **Bruce Springsteen**'s lyrical concerns. It preceded the album *From Langley Park to Memphis*, which showcased McAloon's versatility as a writer, from the straight rock of 'The Golden Calf' through the cod **Frank Sinatra**-isms of 'Hey Manhattan!' to the cinematic sweep of 'Venus of the Soup Kitchen'. The album sold well in Europe, boosted by the atypical synth-pop hit single, 'The King of Rock'n'Roll'.

With no tour to keep the band in the public eye, the tapes of *Protest Songs* were dusted down and released in 1989, while McAloon worked on material for the band's next album. The three-year-old recordings proved to be well worthy of release and contained two of McAloon's best songs in 'Dublin' and 'Pearly Gates'. The 'official' follow-up to *From Langley Park to Memphis* appeared in 1990. An ambitious suite of songs on the theme of fame and its effects, *Jordan: The Comeback* received mixed reviews, but again made the UK Top Ten and even prompted the band to embark on a short series of live dates. This was the prelude to a period of comparative inactivity with the band reuniting only to record two new tracks for the Prefab Sprout 'best of' album *A Life of Surprises* (1992). The enigmatic McAloon did not re-emerge until 1994 when he composed songs for the BBC TV 'music biz' drama serial *Crocodile Shoes*, starring actor/singer Jimmy Nail. He also issued an album of gospel-styled inspirational songs, *The Atomic Hymn Book* (1996). In 1997 Prefab Sprout returned to the studio for *Andromeda Heights*, another essay in quirky sophistication.

ELVIS PRESLEY
b. Elvis Aaron Presley, 8 January 1935, Tupelo, Mississippi, USA, d. 16 August 1977, Memphis, Tennessee

With eighteen American No. 1s and hundreds of gold records from around the world, Elvis Presley was the first rock'n'roll star. In his prime, during the fifties, he combined in his performances the image of rebellious youth also associated with James Dean with an intense fusion of black and white Southern musics – gospel, R&B and country. Above all, he shared with **Bing Crosby**, **Frank Sinatra**, **Billie Holiday** and few other popular singers the intuitive ability to grasp the essence of a song and the vocal technique to express it – and transcend it when, as happened all too often, his material was inferior. Such were his power and attraction that even in the seventies, when his performances were ridiculed by many critics, Presley still drew thousands to Las Vegas.

Legend has it that Presley was the white boy singing black music that **Sam Phillips** was seeking in order to make a fortune. What is clear is that Presley's musical background contained an unprecedented confluence of black and white popular musics and that his first recordings displayed a unique amalgamation of those influences. In addition, tracks like 'That's All Right Mama' and 'My Baby Left Me' personified a joy in singing and music-making that was unequalled in rock until the emergence of **The Beatles**.

His fifties recordings inspired two generations of rockabilly and rock musicians, but during the sixties Presley and his manager Colonel Tom Parker concentrated on a long series of indifferent films, effectively insulating the singer from the profound changes taking place in rock. For a brief period during the late sixties he hooked into the work of contemporary white Southern songwriters before in the final years of his life he concentrated on presenting a live show designed for Las Vegas and the cabaret audience.

Presley was born into a poor white sharecropping family in the rural South. His early musical education came from the church (where he absorbed white gospel), school (his principal entered him for a talent show at the age of ten which he won singing the sentimental 'Old Shep') and his black neighbours (which meant an exposure to R&B).

In 1948 the Presleys moved to Memphis and Elvis worked as a truck-driver after leaving high school. In 1954 he made a private recording at Sam Phillips' studio of the **Ink Spots** ballad 'My Happiness', the first of several such records which led Phillips to record him with bassist Bill Black and guitarist Scotty Moore. His first Sun single coupled a frantic version of **Arthur Crudup**'s blues 'That's All Right Mama' with **Bill Monroe**'s bluegrass song 'Blue Moon of Kentucky'. A local hit, the record had radio listeners assuming the singer was black and it brought Presley and his group (with drummer D. J. Fontana) live dates billed as 'The King of Western Bop'.

More R&B standards were chosen for his next singles. 'Good Rockin' Tonight' (1955) had been written by **Roy Brown** and was a 1948 hit for **Wynonie Harris**. It was followed by the more archaic 'Milkcow Blues' and Arthur Gunter's recent hit 'Baby Let's Play House'. By now Presley was becoming well known in the South through live appearances and a regular spot on the *Louisiana Hayride* radio show. He released one more Sun single, a pulsating version of **Junior Parker**'s 'Mystery Train', before RCA bought his contract for an unprecedented $35,000 in late 1956. Informal recordings made at Sun with **Johnny Cash**, **Carl Perkins** and **Jerry Lee Lewis** were first officially released by RCA in 1990 as the Million Dollar Quartet.

The move to RCA led to **Hank Snow**'s former manager, Col. Tom Parker, taking control of Presley's career. Parker's subsequent role has been much criticized by later commentators, but the signing of the singer to a major label like RCA (in the face of stiff competition from Columbia's **Mitch Miller**) was a decisive step in the development of rock music. Soon other labels sought their own 'Presleys', thus initiating the careers of such artists as **Gene Vincent** and **Eddie Cochran**.

RCA could give Presley national promotion, notably through networked TV shows on some of which his performance was censored to protect viewers from his gyrating pelvis. While later commentators saw this move as the start of an inexorable artistic decline in Presley's work, his first RCA albums included covers of **Carl Perkins**' 'Blue Suede Shoes', **Ray Charles**' 'I Got a Woman', **Little Richard**'s 'Tutti Frutti' and the **Drifters**' 'Money Honey'. But a shift in his approach was evident with his first No. 1, 'Heartbreak Hotel' (1956), written by Mae Boren Axton, mother of **Hoyt Axton**. Its hyperbolic expression of adolescent heartache showed that, as well as being the consummate rockabilly vocalist, Presley now spoke for and to a (mostly white) teenage audience, although his version of teen *angst* was more powerful than those of his followers.

From 1956 to 1968 the majority of Presley's hits came from skilled professional songwriters who submitted their work via Freddie Bienstock, hired by Parker to run Presley's music-publishing company. Prominent among the writers of over twenty hits (of which twelve reached No. 1) in 1956–60 were **Otis Blackwell**, whose jaunty 'Don't Be Cruel' (1956) introduced the vocal harmonies of the Jordanaires, a Nashville-based quartet, and **Leiber and Stoller** with the raucous R&B-flavoured 'Hound Dog'* (1956), 'Jailhouse Rock'* (1957) and 'King Creole'* (1958). The last two were title songs from movie vehicles for Presley, the first of which had been *Love Me Tender*, whose insipid theme song enabled the singer to display his considerable aptitude for crooning.

During his army service (1958–60) the market was supplied with reissued material plus a number of early tracks made during the Sun period. The first post-Army recordings introduced new writers in Aaron Schroeder and **Pomus and Shuman**, plus a decisive shift towards big and beat ballads. Schroeder co-wrote 'It's Now or Never'* (1960), whose melodic debt to the Italian standard 'O Sole Mio' was underlined by tinkling mandolins. This was followed by a revival of 'Are You Lonesome Tonight?'* (a 1927 hit for **Al Jolson** and **Henry Burr**) and **Hugo and Luigi**'s lush 'Can't Help Falling in Love with You'*, which gave full scope for Presley's husky vibrato. Pomus and Shuman, attuned to the newer teenage market catered for by such singers as **Bobby Rydell** and the Drifters, supplied the up-tempo 'Mess of Blues' (1961), 'Little Sister' and 'His Latest Flame'.

Significantly, Presley's only million-seller between 1962 and 1969 – 'Return to Sender' – came from Blackwell. During those years songs took second place to films, of which he turned out three a year. The movies had an average of seven songs and usually portrayed a clean-limbed Elvis defeating hoodlums and getting a girl. They varied from lightweight musicals in exotic locations (*Blue Hawaii*, 1961) through beach-party movies (*Girls, Girls, Girls*, 1962) to the occasional dramatic feature (*Charro*, 1969). None of the movies or their music measured up to Michael Curtiz's *King Creole*, a dynamic showbiz musical which remains Presley's best film.

Throughout the sixties film songs such as 'Do the Clam' and 'Puppet on a String' (1965) dominated Presley's steady output of albums and singles. From 1966, however, a change was evident. Presley's singles included a revival of Ketty Lester's 1962 arrangement of the forties ballad 'Love Letters', R&B singer **Jimmy Reed**'s 'Big Boss Man' (1967) and **Jerry Reed**'s 'US Male' (1968).

A 'new' Presley was hailed when he recorded a television special in 1968 whose centrepiece was a recreated jam session with early colleagues Moore and Fontana. In that year he returned to Memphis for an epochal recording session produced by **Chips Moman**. Among the thirty-plus tracks were three million-sellers with some of his most powerful performances for years. **Mac Davis**'s moving 'In the Ghetto' was followed by the intense Mark James ballad 'Suspicious Minds' and 'Don't Cry Daddy' by Davis. The bulk of the Memphis tracks appeared on two albums, *From Elvis in Memphis* and *Memphis/Vegas*, a two-record set whose other part was taken from a live show in Las Vegas, which was to become the symbol of Presley's work in the seventies, just as Memphis had been in the fifties and Hollywood in the sixties.

While the show included a reprise of his early hits, the essence of the Vegas Presley was evident in the 1970 singles 'The Wonder of You'*, the country ballad

'There Goes My Everything', and the melodramatic reading of **Mickey Newbury**'s 'American Trilogy' from 1971. Presley played Las Vegas more than a dozen times during the seventies and he toured the United States annually with the Vegas show. His well-documented physical decline in these years was reflected in a series of lacklustre new recordings, *Promised Land* (1974), *From Elvis Presley Boulevard* (1976) and *Moody Blue* (1977), whose shortcomings were cruelly exposed by RCA's scholarly compilations from the fifties, *A Legendary Performer* (1974) and *The Sun Sessions* (1976).

Presley died of heart failure only weeks after the first of what would become a series of exposés of his private life had been published. The most detailed of these was the debunking biography by Albert Goldman (1981), while the most balanced account of the period to 1971 remains Jerry Hopkins' *Elvis* (1971).

The most exhaustive account of Presley's early years is Peter Guralnick's *Last Train to Memphis*. The most unusual tribute to Presley was Ral Donner's *1935–1977: I've Been Away for a While Now* (Piccadilly, 1980), on which a skilled Presley impersonator (who had a 1961 hit on Gone with 'You Don't Know What You've Got') narrated and sang the Elvis saga. Donner (*b. 10 February 1943, Chicago, Illinois, d. 6 April 1984*) also appeared on the soundtrack of the biographical documentary *This Is Elvis* (1981). Through groups like the Stray Cats, rockabilly came briefly to the forefront of pop in the early eighties, while **Shakin' Stevens**' series of hits throughout the decade showed a clear indebtedness to Presley.

Regular reissues of Presley material took place in the years following his death, with RCA enjoying particularly heavy sales in 1985, a half-century after his birth, and on the tenth anniversary of his death in 1987.

Interest in Presley and his work remained at a high level in the nineties. In 1990 *The Last Temptation of Elvis* contained versions of his songs by such artists as **Bruce Springsteen**, **Hall and Oates** and the **Jesus and Mary Chain**. In 1993 the American post office issued an Elvis stamp and in the same year RCA began a scholarly programme of reissues with a five-CD set *The King of Rock'n'Roll, the Complete 50s Masters*. This was followed by *From Nashville to Memphis, the Essential 60s Masters Vol. 1* (1994) and by the end of the decade his career had been covered in great detail. The life behind the records was also exhaustively covered, most notably in Peter Guralnick's two-volume biography *Last Train to Memphis* (1994), which covered his rise, and *Careless Love* (1999), which covered his downfall. The second volume showed how Presley's film career took precedence over his recording career and how his protective circle of friends and minders cut him off (willingly) from reality. As such the account went a long way in explaining how the joyous pleas-ures of music-making – a mark of his fifties recordings – were denied Presley in subsequent decades.

In 1999 Presley, who had become the butt of tabloid journalists who regularly noted his presence in unlikely places, took part in the beyond the grave tour, *Elvis the Concert*. In this regular sidemen, such as James Burton and Ronnie Tutt, appeared as a backing band to a video projection of Presley. The tour was a commercial success.

BILLY PRESTON
b. 9 September 1946, Houston, Texas, USA

A soul and gospel organist, Preston recorded with both **The Beatles** and the **Rolling Stones**. During the seventies he enjoyed a series of solo hits, both vocal and instrumental.

In 1956 Preston played **W. C. Handy** as a child in the biopic *St Louis Blues*, and later performed with A. A. Allen's gospel troupe and with **Andrae Crouch** in Los Angeles' Cogic Singers. After touring Europe with **Sam Cooke** and **Little Richard** in 1962, Preston played on Cooke's 'Little Red Rooster' and recorded a 1964 album for Cooke's label, SAR. After Cooke's death, Preston cut *The Wildest Organ in Town* (1966) for Capitol.

By the time of *The Most Exciting Organ Ever* (Vee-Jay, 1967), Preston had joined **Ray Charles**' orchestra, after playing in the house band of **Jack Good**'s television show *Shindig*. While touring Britain, Preston was signed to Apple by **George Harrison** and he played on The Beatles' hits 'Get Back' and 'Let It Be'. For Apple he recorded *That's the Way God Planned It* (1969), whose title song was a British hit. *Encouraging Words* was issued in the same year and in 1971 Preston played with Harrison on *All Things Must Pass* and at the 'Concert for Bangladesh' in New York.

With the demise of Apple, Preston moved to A&M and enjoyed his first American successes with a series of pop and R&B hits based on funky riffs and hoarse vocals. They included 'Outa Space' (1972), the No. 1 'Will It Go Round in Circles', 'Space Race' (1973) and 'Nothing from Nothing' (1974), which also topped the charts. In 1974, having contributed to each of the group's albums since *Sticky Fingers* (1971), he toured with the Rolling Stones. The following year **Joe Cocker** had a hit with Preston's 'You Are so Beautiful'.

After recording *A Whole New Thing* (1977), Preston appeared in the title role of the ill-considered film of *Sgt Pepper's Lonely Hearts Club Band*, and signed to Motown where a duet with Syreeta Wright, 'With You I'm Born Again' (1979), featured in the film *Fast Break*, was a Top Ten hit. Later Motown albums included *The Way I Am* (1981) and *Pressing on* (1982). In 1980 the gospel label Myrrh released Preston's *Universal Love*. In 1989 Preston toured with **Ringo Starr** and in 1990 recorded for Ian Levine's Motor City Records, including further duets with Syreeta. He recorded little in the rest of the decade.

JOHNNY PRESTON

b. John Preston Courville, 18 August 1939, Port Arthur, Texas, USA

Preston is best remembered as the chronicler of the tragic love of Running Bear for Little White Dove in 'Running Bear'* (1959).

He formed the Shades while at high school and was signed to Mercury by Shelby Singleton on the advice of J. P. Richardson (*b. Jape Richardson, 24 October 1930, Sabine Pass, Texas, d. 3 February 1959, Clear Lake, Iowa*). A singer, songwriter and disc-jockey, Richardson had international success as the Big Bopper with his half-spoken, half-squealed rendition of his own composition 'Chantilly Lace'* (Mercury, 1958) before his death in the plane crash that also killed **Buddy Holly** and **Ritchie Valens** in 1959. Prior to that, reportedly inspired by a commercial for Dove soap, he wrote and produced 'Running Bear' for his protégé Preston, with **George Jones** providing the insistent 'oom-pah-pah' Indian chant in the background. Release of the record was postponed for some six months after Richardson's death, but despite its huge success Preston had few further hits. These included the countryish **Jack Clement**-produced 'Cradle of Love'; a remake of **Shirley and Lee**'s 1955 hit 'I Feel so Good', retitled 'Feel so Fine' (1960); and a reworking of **Little Willie John**'s 1959 R&B hit 'Leave My Kitten Alone' (1961). In 1962 Preston retired from the music business.

THE PRETENDERS

Martin Chambers, b. 4 September 1951, Hereford, England (replaced by Blair Cunningham); Pete Farndon, b. 12 June 1952, Hereford, d. 14 April 1983, London (replaced by T. M. Stevens); James Honeyman-Scott, b. 4 November 1956, Hereford, d. 16 June 1982 (replaced by Robbie McIntosh); Chrissie Hynde, b. 7 September 1951, Akron, Ohio, USA

Led by singer, guitarist and writer Chrissie Hynde, the Pretenders' early inspiration was the British punk era, but they found success in the eighties as a classic rock band, featuring Hynde's sensual, hard-edged vocals.

After studying at Kent State University, Hynde moved to London in 1973 and worked as a rock journalist. After an unsuccessful attempt to form a band in Paris, she returned to Akron and joined R&B group Jack Rabbit. Back in England in 1975 she linked up with **Malcolm McLaren** and many of the musicians who went on to form the early punk bands. She recorded pseudonymously as part of the Moors Mur-

derers, a gimmicky attempt to shock, before Dave Hill signed her to Real Records. With bassist Farndon, formerly of Australian band the Bushwackers, Hynde formed the Pretenders. The group also included former members of Cheeks (a band led by ex-**Mott the Hoople** player Verden Allen), Honeyman-Scott (guitar) and Chambers (drums), who joined after their first single, 'Stop Your Sobbing' (Real, 1978). Written by the **Kinks**' Ray Davies and produced by **Nick Lowe**, the song was a minor hit in Britain.

The band's eponymous first album was produced by Chris Thomas and included 'Brass in Pocket' (1979), which featured Hynde's tough but lyrical singing and was a British No. 1, reaching the Top Twenty in America on Sire. Further hits followed with 'Talk of the Town' (1980) and 'Message of Love' (1981). *Pretenders II* (1981) included a further British hit with another Davies composition, 'I Go to Sleep'. By now, Davies and Hynde were one of rock's higher profile couples, and they had a daughter, Natalie, in 1983.

During 1982 and 1983 the Pretenders underwent upheaval when Farndon left and Honeyman-Smith died of a drugs overdose. After recording 'Back on the Chain Gang' (1982), later featured in the film *King of Comedy*, the group released nothing for over a year before '2000 Miles' was a Christmas hit in 1983. *Learning to Crawl* (1984) included the American hit 'Middle of the Road'. Hynde married Jim Kerr of **Simple Minds** in the same year.

In 1985 Hynde duetted with Ali Campbell on **UB40**'s remake of Sonny and **Cher**'s 'I Got You Babe' before the Pretenders had their first British hit for two years when 'Don't Get Me Wrong' from *Get Close* reached the Top Ten in 1986. Featuring a number of session musicians, the Jimmy Iovine-produced album included a further hit with 'Hymn to Her'. In 1988 Hynde and UB40 had another hit with their version of Lorna Bennett's reggae song 'Breakfast in Bed'.

Chambers, having left the band, played with various other acts, including (ex-**Eurythmics**) Dave Stewart. His replacement, Cunningham, who had been in British pop band Haircut 100, played on the patchy *Packed!* (1990), released the year she and Kerr divorced, and on a variety of one-off tracks the Pretenders recorded for charity albums and film soundtracks at this time, including *Tame Yourself* (1991) and a remake of **10CC**'s 'I'm Not in Love' (1993). The line-up of the band was ever-changing, and among the guitarists who recorded or toured as Pretenders were Johnny Marr (ex-**Smiths**) and Billy Bremner (ex-Rockpile with **Dave Edmunds** and **Nick Lowe**). In 1994 Hynde was reunited with Chambers and added Adam Seymour (guitar) and Andy Hobson (bass) for *Last of the Independents*, which was both a marginal critical and commercial success, in contrast to the acoustic reworkings of the group's best-known songs,

The Isle of View (1995). The group continued to contribute recordings to films, including *G.I. Jane* (1997), before releasing the lacklustre studio album *Viva el Amor* (1999).

THE PRETTY THINGS
Phil May, b. 9 November 1944, Kent, England; Dick Taylor, b. 28 January 1943; Brian Pendleton; John Stax, b. 6 April 1944; Viv Prince, b. 9 August 1944 (replaced 1965 by Skip Alan, b. Alan Skipper, 11 June 1948, London); John Povey, b. 20 August 1942, London; Peter Tolson, b. 10 September 1951, Bishops Stortford, Hertfordshire; Gordon Edwards, b. 26 December 1946, Southport, Lancashire; Jack Green, b. 12 March 1951, Glasgow, Scotland

Despite their name, the Pretty Things were the hardest- and harshest-sounding British R&B band of the sixties. However, unlike their contemporaries the **Rolling Stones** they were unable to translate this image into commercial success beyond their R&B beginnings, and disbanded, only to re-form three times in the seventies and eighties.

Formed at Sidcup Art College in 1962 by May and Taylor (the original bassist with the Rolling Stones), the group took their name from the title of a song by their dominant influence **Bo Diddley**. With Pendleton (guitar) and Stax (bass) they quickly established themselves on the art-school circuit and were signed by Fontana in 1963 on the crest of the R&B boom. Alarmed by their raw sound, Fontana insisted that Prince, one-time drummer with the Dauphin Street Trad Band, joined the inexperienced band, but the group's first single, 'Rosalyn', coupled with a version of **Jimmy Reed**'s 'Big Boss Man' (1964), saw no diminution of their uninhibited approach. Only a minor hit, it was followed by two British Top Twenty hits, 'Don't Bring Me Down' (1964), which was banned in America, adding further to their outrageous image, and 'Honey I Need' (1965). 'Honey' was written by the group but most of their eponymous début album (1965) consisted of energetic versions of **Chuck Berry**, Reed and Bo Diddley material.

Following the Stones, the Pretty Things graduated to soul, recording a version of **Solomon Burke**'s 'Cry to Me' (1965), among other soul material, but the group lacked the necessary cohesion to develop their own musical identity and were ill-equipped to respond to the record company's continued demand for new product as their chart career ebbed. As a result, after a series of disappointing singles and albums (including *Emotions*, 1967) and several personnel changes, the group left Fontana.

With a reorganized line-up, the group signed to EMI's progressive Harvest label and released *S. F. Sorrow* (1968), featuring drummer Twink (John Adler), who afterwards joined the Pink Fairies. Written by May and Taylor and based on a short story by May, the album was one of the first 'rock operas' and remarkably similar to **The Who**'s *Tommy*, released later that year, in structure if not execution. Produced by Norman Smith (who later had several hits of his own as balladeer Hurricane Smith, including 'Don't Let It Die', 1971, and 'Oh Babe What Would You Say', 1972, on EMI's Columbia label), *S. F. Sorrow* was a critical success; like the apocalyptic *Parachute* (1969), however, it failed commercially and the group broke up. Taylor worked as a producer for **Hawkwind** in 1971 and then left the music business for several years. Retaining the group name, May recruited new members Edwards, Green and Alan and recorded *Freeway Madness* (Warners, 1973) before signing to **Led Zeppelin**'s Swan Song label for *Silk Torpedo* (1974) and *Savage Eye* (1975) only to break up the group again in 1976. With Alan, he went on to the short-lived Fallen Angels, while the rest of the band briefly carried on as Metropolis. In 1980 a re-formed Pretty Things consisting of Taylor, Povey and Tolson released *Cross Talk* (Warners, 1980). After that version of the Pretty Things folded in 1982, May and Taylor put together yet another line-up to play the British pub circuit and tour Europe where the group retained a following in 1985. *Live at Heartbreak Hotel* (1985) is from this period. Later that year Taylor left to join one-time punk group the Mekons, which on albums like *Fear and Whiskey* (Sin, 1985) and *Honky Tonkin'* (1987) attempted a fascinating synthesis of traditional folk music with country music and rock'n'roll. With producer Mark St John on drums, May and Taylor later led the Pretty Things on *Out of the Island*, which included a revival of **Barry McGuire**'s 'Eve of Destruction' (Trax, 1989). There were occasional later live performances.

In 1993 group members sued their former record companies over alleged non-payment of royalties and in the same year Fontana issued *Get a Buzz*, a compilation of their recordings for the label.

ANDRÉ PREVIN
b. Andreas Ludwig Prewin, 6 April 1929, Berlin, Germany

In his long career Previn first worked successfully behind the scenes as a film composer and arranger and then became the musical director of the London and Pittsburgh Symphony Orchestras. In Britain, he won further fame as the liberal representative of the cause of good music.

The cousin of Charles Previn, head of Universal's music department in the thirties, he was raised in Hollywood and while studying composition with Mario Castenuovo-Tedesco, became an arranger with MGM in 1948. An accomplished jazz and classical pianist, his scores were noticeably more tuneful than symphonic. Most representative were the Oscar-nominated *Gigi* and *Porgy and Bess* (both 1958), while more interesting were his work on *The Subterraneans* (1960), in which he also appeared as a pianist, improvising in the style of **Art Tatum**, and the harsh score for *Elmer Gantry* (1960).

In the sixties, in addition to his film scores, he also started writing songs with his second wife Dory Langdon (*b. 22 October 1935, Woodbridge, New Jersey, USA*) including the Oscar-nominated 'The Faraway Part of Town', which was sung by **Judy Garland** in *Pepe* (1960). On the break up of their marriage in 1965, Dory Previn continued to write (including **Dionne Warwick**'s 1967 million-selling film theme 'Valley of the Dolls'), and in the seventies won acclaim for her declamatory readings of her own angry, confessional songs. Her albums included *Mythical Kings and Iguanas* (United Artists, 1972) and *One A.M. Phone Calls* (1977). She also published her memoirs, *Midnight Baby* (1976), and was involved in the Broadway musical *Mary C. Brown and the Hollywood Sign* (1973).

Previn had recorded in a jazz vein as early as 1945 and during the fifties he recorded several albums with drummer Shelly Manne. However, from the seventies on, Previn concentrated on his career as an orchestral conductor, only recording as a pianist occasionally, notably with **Ella Fitzgerald** on *Nice Work If You Can Get It* (Pablo, 1984), an album of songs by **George Gershwin**. As conductor of the London Symphony Orchestra he recorded numerous classical works, including Grammy-winning recordings of works by Villa-Lobos and Rachmaninoff and *Concerto for Sitar* (EMI, 1971) with **Ravi Shankar**. The energetic Previn became one of the best-known personalities of the classical-music scene, so much so that he was featured in a series of television commercials for hi-fi.

In the eighties he was director of the Royal Philharmonic Orchestra and the Los Angeles Philharmonic and he composed the music for dramatist Tom Stoppard's opera *Every Good Boy Deserves Favour*. In 1991 he made a thirteen-part television series to celebrate the Mozart bicentenary. He returned to the London Symphony Orchestra as conductor laureate in 1992.

ALAN PRICE
b. 19 April 1942, Durham, England

Formerly the organist with R&B group the **Animals**, Price had a varied solo career in the late sixties and seventies. Solo hits with **Screamin' Jay Hawkins** and **Randy Newman** songs were followed by film and television scores and an ambitious autobiographical concept album.

Leaving the Animals in 1966, he formed the jazzy

Alan Price Set, which included future BBC radio producer John Walters on trumpet. A restrained version of Hawkins' 'I Put a Spell on You' and a revival of the 1952 ballad 'Hi Lili Hi Lo' reached the British Top Twenty on Decca in 1966. These were followed by Newman's 'Simon Smith and the Amazing Dancing Bear', Price's own Newmanesque 'House That Jack Built' (1967) and 'Don't Stop the Carnival' (1968), an exuberant **Sonny Rollins** number to which Price added new lyrics, alluding to the situation of Caribbean immigrants to Britain.

Between 1969 and 1971 Price teamed up with **Georgie Fame** for tours, television series and recordings, of which 'Rosetta' (Columbia 1971) was a Top Twenty hit. A collaboration with director Lindsay Anderson led to Price composing scores for stage and screen, notably the 1974 film *Oh Lucky Man!*. Anderson's neo-Brechtian approach influenced Price's ambitious *Between Today and Yesterday* (Warners, 1974), which dealt with the political history of his native North-East of England and Price's own deracinated role as an entertainer. The album included a Top Ten hit in the stirring 'Jarrow Song'.

He went on to record in the same vein for Polydor (*Metropolitan Man*, 1975; *Shouts across the Street*, 1976) and Jet (*Rainbow's End*, 1977; *England My England*, 1978) but none had the impact of *Between Today and Yesterday*. Price also composed further theatre (*Andy Capp*, 1982) and film scores (*Plague Dogs*, 1982) and TV themes, including 'Papers' (Trojan, 1986). In 1989 he released the impressive *Liberty* (Ariola), which featured his regular touring band, including guitarist and co-writer Steve Grant and veteran jazz saxophonist Don Weller. The album included Price's 'Changes' (based on a John Wesley hymn tune), which was used as the music for an award-winning television commercial.

Having briefly rejoined the Animals for *Before We Were So Rudely Interrupted* (1997), in 1998 Price repeated the effort for *Ark*, also touring in support of the album. In 1999 he joined fellow sixties alumni the Blues Bothers and Colin Blunstone on revivalist tours.

LLOYD PRICE
b. 9 March 1933, New Orleans, Louisiana, USA

Though Price was one of the first New Orleans artists to achieve national success with his million-selling 'Lawdy Miss Clawdy', few of his subsequent records had a New Orleans feel to them. Even his version of the traditional folk song 'Stagger Lee'* (1958, and previously an R&B hit for Archibald on Imperial in 1952) was more notable for its intrusive chorus.

From a musical family, Price learned trumpet while at high school and while working at radio station

WBOK auditioned for **Art Rupe**'s Specialty Records, singing 'Lawdy Miss Clawdy' in 1952. Recorded with **Fats Domino** on piano and overseen by **Dave Bartholomew**, it topped the R&B charts and was one of the first black records to sell in significant numbers to whites. His follow-ups, which included a cover of **Smiley Lewis**'s 'Ain't That a Shame' (1953) were less successful and in 1953 Price went into the army. On his return Price based himself in Washington DC and formed KRC Records, on which he recorded the melodramatic ballad 'Just Because' which was a hit when leased to ABC in 1957. He followed that with 'Stagger Lee' (later revived in 1967 by **Wilson Pickett**, who started his solo career on Price's Double L Records, and **Tommy Roe**, 1971) and a string of brash – mostly self-composed – sing-alongs, including 'Personality' and 'I'm Gonna Get Married' (1959), before in the mid-sixties he edged towards cabaret with **Erroll Garner**'s 'Misty' (1963) on Double L.

In the sixties he concentrated on Double L and, from 1969, Turntable Records, named after his nightclub. In 1976, in partnership with boxing impresario Don King, he formed LPG Records, releasing *The Nominee* in 1978. He still tours occasionally and in 1998 performed with **Allen Toussaint** and David Bartholomew at a celebration in honour of **Fats Domino**.

RAY PRICE
b. 12 January 1926, Perryville, Texas, USA

With his deeply expressive voice Price was at his best, in the words of country-music historian Bill C. Malone, singing 'songs of hurt and disappointment'. A protégé of **Hank Williams**, Price broadened his honky-tonk style in the mid-fifties through the addition of a **Bob Wills**-inspired fiddle section on the major hits 'Crazy Arms'* (1956) and 'City Lights'* (1958), before in 1967 he turned in his cowboy suit for a tuxedo, his steel guitar and fiddle for a string section and began recording songs like 'Danny Boy', in search of crossover pop hits.

After studying to be a vet, Price turned to a career in music in 1949. A regular performer on Dallas's *Big D Jamboree*, he signed to Jim Bulleit's Bullet label in 1950 before joining Columbia in 1951. He had his first hit in 1952 with 'Talk to Your Heart'. In the same year he formally took over Williams' backing group, the Drifting Cowboys, only to pass them on to **Ferlin Husky** in 1954 and organize a new band, the Cherokee Cowboys, which over the years included among its members **Roger Miller**, **Willie Nelson**, Johnny Paycheck, Johnny Bush and steel-guitarist Buddy Emmons. It was this band that was featured on the classic Price recordings, 'Release Me' (1954), 'Crazy Arms', **Bill Anderson**'s 'City Lights', **Harlan Howard**'s 'Heartaches by the Number' (1959),

Miller's 'Invitation to the Blues' (1958) and Mel Tillis's 'Burning Memories' (1964). That recording also featured a string section but by 1967 and 'Danny Boy', Price was regularly recording with a forty-seven-piece orchestra.

'Danny Boy' was a pop hit, but Price's biggest pop success came when he returned to a more countrified sound with **Kris Kristofferson**'s 'For the Good Times' (1970). For most of the seventies Price recorded only occasionally (for the gospel label Myrrh, ABC and Monument) before returning to Columbia and the higher reaches of the country charts with *Willie Nelson and Ray Price* (1980), which included a revival of Bob Wills' 'Faded Love'. He later recorded for Dimension (including 'Old Friends', 1982, on which he was partnered by Cherokee Cowboy alumni Nelson and Miller), Warners (including songs from *Honky Tonk Man*, 1982) and Viva (1984) where he was billed as 'Ray Price and the Cherokee Cowboys'. He returned to the country charts in 1988 with 'I'd Do It All Over Again'. Price's most representative album of the nineties, when he recorded little, was *Sometimes a Rose* (1992). Instead he concentrated on the theatre he opened (as did several other country stars) in Branson, Missouri, at which he performed regularly. *Prisoner of Love* (Justice, 2000) was a surprising critical success. An album of standards – it included versions of 'Fly Me to the Moon' and 'What a Wonderful World' as well as remakes of early Price country hits ('Better Class of Losers') – it featured Price's velvet voice, as heard on his classic recording of 'Danny Boy'.

The Essential Ray Price (1991) collects together a representative selection of his Columbia recordings, but far superior is the exhaustive box-set retrospective, *The Honky Tonk Years* (Bear Family, 1996).

CHARLEY PRIDE
b. 18 March 1938, Sledge, Mississippi, USA

Though not the first black to appear at the *Grand Ole Opry* – that honour belongs to **Deford Bailey** – nor the first to have country hits – **Ray Charles** made his groundbreaking country recordings earlier – Pride was the first black country-music superstar. The key to his success was his soft, warm baritone with no trace at all of the blues in it. Other black country singers followed in his wake, notably Stoney Edwards, who had minor hits with **Dallas Frazier**'s 'Hank and Lefty Raised My Country Soul' (Capitol, 1973), **Jesse Winchester**'s 'Mississippi You're on My Mind' (1975) and **Chip Taylor**'s 'Black Bird (Holding Your Head High)' (1976), songs which were given an added dimension by being performed by a black man. But none was as successful as Pride.

One of eleven children born on a sharecropper's

farm, Pride listened to country music on the radio as a child. Between 1954 and 1964 he attempted a career in baseball, briefly playing for the Memphis Red Sox, before a series of injuries halted his career. Encouraged by **Red Foley**, he travelled to Nashville where **Jack Clement** became his manager and producer and **Chet Atkins** signed him to RCA in 1965. His first single, 'Snakes Crawl at Night' (1965), was released without any publicity, but after his first hit, the Clement composition 'Just Between You and Me' (1966), Pride's colour, though it brought him a welter of publicity, was never a matter of controversy. Singing a judicious mix of contemporary (the Frazier composition 'All I Have to Offer You [Is Me]', his first country No. 1 in 1969) and traditional songs (**Hank Williams**' 'Kaw-Liga', 1969), Pride became one of the most successful country singers of the seventies. *The Best of* (1969), unusually for a country album, went gold and he had a string of country chart-toppers, including 'I'm So Afraid of Losing You' (1969), 'Is Anybody Goin' to San Antone', 'Wonder Could I Live There Anymore' and 'I Can't Believe You've Stopped Loving Me' (1970).

Though he had a major pop hit with 'Kiss an Angel Good Morning'* (1971), Pride's subsequent success was restricted to the country charts. This included more than twenty country No. 1s in the seventies and early eighties, among them 'Amazing Love' (1973), 'You Win Again' (1980) and 'Night Games' (1983), until he was surprisingly dropped by RCA in 1986 and joined the independent company 16th Avenue 70550. His luck there was hardly any better; the company rejected his first album, a tribute to **Brook Benton**, in favour of more middle-of-the-road offerings. His hits included 'Shouldn't It Be Easier Than This' and 'Amy's Eyes'. In 1990 he re-recorded his major hits for Curb, before moving on to Honest Entertainment for whom he repeated the trick.

MAXI PRIEST
b. Maxwell Elliott, 1962, Manchester, England

A former sound system DJ, Maxi Priest was the most successful reggae artist to have come from Britain in the late eighties and early nineties.

At the age of fourteen, he had his own sound system, Gladiator Sounds. He next joined the leading south London system Saxon International as a DJ, 'soul rapping' over reggae tracks. Among his associates were later British reggae artists Smiley Culture, Tippa Irie and Philip Levi. His 'Hey Little Girl', written with Paul Robinson (Barry Boom), was released on their own Level Vibes label and became the first · British-made single to reach No. 1 in Jamaica.

In 1985 he signed to the Virgin subsidiary 10 Records, releasing *You're Safe* and *Intentions* (1986),

on which he worked with **Aswad** and sang a version of **Van Morrison**'s 'Crazy Love'. Produced by **Sly and Robbie**, *Maxi* (1988) included the crossover hit 'Wild World', a 'lovers rock' version of the **Cat Stevens** song, a version of **Robert Palmer**'s 'Some Guys Have All the Luck' and a duet with Beres Hammond, 'How Can We Ease the Pain'. In the same year he headlined the Reggae Sunsplash festival at Montego Bay in Jamaica. He followed up with *Bona Fide* (1990), whose collaborators included Jazzie B of **Soul II Soul** and Jamaican producers **Gussie Clarke** and Geoffrey Chung. The album included another pop hit, 'Close to You'.

His later records have included duets with **Shabba Ranks** ('Housecall', 1991) and the UK Asian ragga-rapper Apache Indian ('Just Wanna Know', 1992). More straightforwardly enjoyable was the poppier *Man with the Fun* (Virgin, 1996).

LOUIS PRIMA
b. 7 December 1910, New Orleans, Louisiana, USA,
d. 24 August 1978, New Orleans

An exuberant performer and singer and a fine jazz trumpeter, Prima is best remembered for the series of records he made in partnership with his wife Keely Smith, most notably 'That Old Black Magic'* (1958). His own records were made within the showbusiness aesthetic that made him a star attraction in Las Vegas, but he mixed Neapolitan slang with scat singing, usually to salacious effect – one critic called Prima's voice 'hoarse and horny'. His vocal style recalled **Cab Calloway** and foreshadowed some of the more florid excesses of rock'n'roll performers like **Little Richard**.

The son of Italian immigrants, Prima studied classical violin but by the time he was thirteen he was a member of his older brother Leon's band, playing regularly throughout New Orleans. On graduating from high school, he formed his own band, the Collegiates, and quickly won a reputation for his showmanship. By 1930 Prima was established as a star attraction in New Orleans; in 1932, he played with **Red Nichols**, in 1933 made his first recordings as a member of the Hotch Trio ('Chinatown', Bluebird) and in 1934 he moved to New York where his larger-than-life demeanour won him a Hollywood contract. His film appearances, however, which included *Rhythm on the Range* (1936) and *Rose of Washington Square* (1939), in which he starred with **Al Jolson**, were undistinguished.

During the forties he toured with a big band and recorded for Varsity, Okeh, Majestic (on which he had his first major hit, 'Bell-Bottom Trousers', 1945), RCA ('Civilization', 1947) and Robin Hood ('Oh Babe!', 1949), among others. Records such as 'The Bigger the Figure' (Columbia, 1951), a tribute to larger sized women based on the 'Largo al Factotum' from Rossini's *Barber of Seville*, revealed the growing influence of R&B, while his Las Vegas performances brought a feel of black cabaret to the casinos. However, not all his compositions were in this style. He also co-wrote the romantic 'Sunday Kind of Love', which became a doo-wop classic in its version by the **Harptones**, and his biggest hit was his fast, scat revival with Keely Smith of **Johnny Mercer**'s and **Harold Arlen**'s 'That Old Black Magic' (Capitol, 1958).

Smith (*b. 9 March 1932, Norfolk, Virginia*) was a jazz-influenced singer who joined Prima's band in 1948 and remained with him until 1962. In 1964 she recorded an album of **Beatles** songs. Another central member of Prima's band of the fifties was Sam Butera, whose **Earl Bostic**-like 'dirty' sax solos enlivened 'Jump, Jive and Wail' (1956) and Prima's camp version of 'Buena Sera' (1957), which provided the model both for British trad bandleader **Acker Bilk**'s 1960 version and for Bilk's singing style. Another person decisively influenced by Prima was Ray Ellington, best known as the leader of the quartet that provided the musical interludes for the **Goons**.

After 'I've Got You under My Skin' (1959), Prima's other big hit of the fifties, he moved to Dot where he cut mediocre versions of his earlier recordings interspersed with such material as a cover of **Bert Kaempfert**'s 'Wonderland by Night' (1960), his last major hit. In 1960 he returned to New Orleans and cabaret and in 1969 supplied the voice for King Louis, the orang-utan in *The Jungle Book*. *Zooma, Zooma* (Rhino, 1992) is the definitive retrospective, while *Louis Prima* (1991) collects together his Capitol recordings.

PRIMAL SCREAM

Bobby Gillespie, b. 22 June 1964, Glasgow, Scotland; Jim Navajo; Robert Young; Andrew Innes; Dave Morgan; Henry Olsen; Martin Duffy; Toby Toman; Denise Johnson; Steve Sidelnik; Gary 'Mani' Mounfield; Paul Mulreany; Paul Mooney

Emerging from the shadow of cult indie band the **Jesus and Mary Chain**, Primal Scream broke into the UK charts in 1991 with a startlingly contemporary rock/dance crossover sound which was largely at odds with their previous retro-rock output. In 1992 the band was the first winner of the prestigious Mercury Music Prize.

Vocalist Gillespie had performed with the Wake prior to forming Primal Scream in Glasgow in 1984. In the same year he joined the Jesus and Mary Chain as drummer, playing on their first album, *Psychocandy*, before leaving to concentrate on his own band in late 1985. Primal Scream's first recordings were 'All Fall Down' (1985) and 'Crystal Crescent'/

'Velocity Girl' (1986) for Alan McGee's Creation label. Primal Scream's Innes had originally been the guitarist in McGee's Glasgow-based band the Laughing Apple.

The line-up which recorded the band's début album, *Sonic Flower Groove* (1987), comprised Gillespie, Innes, guitarist/songwriter Navajo, bassist Young and semi-permanent members Morgan (drums) and Duffy (piano). The album was largely nostalgic in sound, drawing on sixties US guitar rockers such as the **Byrds** and **Love**, but suffered from a lack of strong songs. Navajo departed, and Young switched to guitar for *Primal Scream* (1989). This found the band experimenting with a harder-edged, hard rock guitar sound, although Gillespie's fondness for melody was well to the fore on such tracks as 'Ivy, Ivy, Ivy'. The band's live shows at this time found them very much in tune with their punk-rock roots, drawing comparisons with **Iggy Pop**'s Stooges.

Gillespie and Innes were also attracted to the emerging dance scene (and its attendant drug culture). This led to the incorporation of elements of dance into their own material. The largely instrumental single 'Loaded' (1990), assembled by the influential DJ and producer Andy Weatherall from a song by the band, featured a piano part with a strong similarity to that of the **Rolling Stones**' 'Sympathy for the Devil' alongside several samples. By now the band's line-up was Gillespie, Innes, Young, Duffy, bassist Olsen and drummer Toman, who had played with cult Manchester band the Blue Orchids and with ex-**Velvet Underground** chanteuse Nico. The follow-up singles 'Come Together' (1990) and 'Higher than the Sun' (1991), with its drug references, took the band further into dance territory, with the addition of dance vocalist Johnson and, later, percussionist Sidelnik, to the line-up.

The third album, *Screamadelica*, appeared late in 1991, and carried the band's twin obsessions with classic rock (specifically the Rolling Stones circa 1968–1972) and contemporary dance to a new level. As well as the earlier hit singles, it included a spacey version of 'Slip Inside This House', a piece first recorded by sixties Texan acid-rock legends the 13th Floor Elevators, and a pair of bluesy tracks co-produced by veteran Stones producer Jimmy Miller. One of those, 'Movin' on Up', reached the UK Top Ten when it was released as the lead track of the *Dixie-Narco* EP in 1992. *Screamadelica* was voted Britain's 'album of the year' in the Mercury Music Prize awards in 1992.

Having established themselves on the cutting edge of the dance/rock crossover movement, Primal Scream embarked for Nashville to begin recording their fourth album, which emerged in 1994 as *Give Out But Don't Give Up*. It was an unashamedly retrogressive rock set (with an even greater stylistic debt to the Stones), which found the band working with such veterans as Jimmy Miller, **George Clinton**, **Tom Dowd** and the Memphis Horns. Outraging many of their new-found admirers, it was greeted by reviews which ranged from the enthusiastic to the vitriolic. It topped the UK album charts, and was followed by a world tour which drew as many headlines for the band's hedonistic behaviour as for their energetic performances.

After the *Give Out* tour ended in early 1995 the band took a two-year break to recover from their various excesses. Their only recorded output of the period was 'Trainspotting', their contribution to the 1995 film adaptation of Irvine Welsh's cult novel, and the football-themed single 'The Big Man and the Scream Team Meet the Barmy Army Uptown' (1996). The band returned in 1997 with *Vanishing Point* (1997), loosely based around Richard Sarafian's road movie of the same name, and with a membership now including former **Stone Roses** bassist Mani and drummer Mulreany alongside Scream stalwarts Gillespie, Innes, Duffy and Young. Stylistically, *Vanishing Point* was a return to the dance-orientated sound of *Screamadelica*, albeit with darker overtones. In spite of the heavy tone, the album included their biggest hit to date, 'Kowalski', which reached No. 3 in the UK charts. The following year, Primal Scream released the *If They Move, Kill 'Em* EP, which included a reinterpretation of the title track by **My Bloody Valentine**'s Kevin Shields, and *Echo Dek*, an alternative mix of *Vanishing Point* by Andrew Weatherall. In 1999 Gillespie contributed vocals to 'Soul Auctioneer' on Death in Vegas's *The Contino Sessions*, before leading Primal Scream's return after an eighteen-month recording spell on 'Swastika Eyes'. A new album, including much-mooted collaborations with Kevin Shields, the Automator and the **Chemical Brothers**, was promised for early 2000. *Exterminator*, made in collaboration with Shields, and clearly inspired by the sense of tradition that encompasses **Bernard Herrmann**, **Sun Ra**, the Chemical Brothers and **Kraftwerk**, is extraordinary: an album that certainly lives up to the band's name in full. Full of anger and feelings of betrayal, tracks like 'Kill All Hippies' and 'Blood Money' remind one of rock'n'roll's ability to threaten as well as comfort.

PRINCE
b. Prince Rogers Nelson, 7 June 1958, Minneapolis, Minnesota, USA

One of the most controversial and inventive rock musicians of the eighties and nineties, Prince created a synthesis of the major innovations in black popular music since **Jimi Hendrix** and **Sly Stone** had married the spirit of blues and gospel with the techniques of white rock. Ever enigmatic, in the nineties he for a time renounced his name in favour of the title 'The Artist Formerly Known as Prince', before reappearing in a mellower mood as Prince once more in 2000.

Both his parents had been members of the Prince Rogers Band and Prince formed Champagne at high school in 1972 with Andre Cymone and Morris Day. In 1976 he moved to New York, recording instrumental demo tapes later released as *The Minneapolis Genius* (HPL, 1985). Through the personal contacts of his then manager Owen Husney, Prince was signed to Warner in 1978 for a six-figure advance, one of the largest ever for a new artist. Even more remarkably he was allowed to produce and write his début album. The result was *For You*, including 'Soft and Wet/So Blue' which won him attention in the disco market. 'I Wanna Be Your Lover'* from *Prince* (1979) was followed by the appropriately titled *Dirty Mind* (1980), a paean to the joys of sex and his first album to dent the pop charts.

Controversy (1981), with its reliance on synthesizers, saw him edging further towards the mainstream. Combined with his suggestive stage act, songs like 'Do It All Night', 'Head' and 'Jack U Off' confirmed his outrageous image. *Controversy* also introduced songs on social and political topics like 'Ronnie Talks to Russia' and 'Annie Christian', which dealt with gun control. At this period, Prince's backing group was the Time, which included Day and **Jimmy Jam and Terry Lewis**, who went on to become one of the most successful producers of the mid-eighties. Prince himself produced the group's first two albums.

He broadened his thematic range with *1999* (1982), an apocalyptic view of the future of the world which included three hit singles in the title track (his first substantial British hit), 'Little Red Corvette' and 'Delirious'. The album demonstrated Prince's mastery of a range of styles from funk through disco to mainstream rock. *Purple Rain* (1984) was also a film and in turn it spawned hit singles in 'When Doves Cry'*, the sparest of his recordings to date, 'Let's Go Crazy', 'Purple Rain' and 'I Would Die for U'. The album topped the American charts for more than twenty weeks.

With a new backing group, the Revolution, he released *Around the World in a Day* (1985) on his own label. Far more psychedelic in approach and charming rather than compelling, it included the hits 'Raspberry Beret' and 'Pop Life', while 'Paisley Park' (the name of Prince's label) reached the British Top Ten. *Parade* (1986) formed the soundtrack to the lightweight autobiographical *Under the Cherry Moon* film in which Prince again starred. Its most successful song was 'Kiss'. The superior *Sign o' the Times* (1987) found Prince taking a more committed stance, notably on the anti-drugs title song. Critics saw it as a reflection of Sly Stone's *There's a Riot Goin' on*. In the same year he withdrew the so-called *Black* album shortly before its scheduled release although illicit copies were widely circulated.

Lovesexy was released in 1988 and revealed a concern with spiritual themes, as well as the sensuality evident on the hit 'I Wish U Heaven'. Prince's music for the 1989 *Batman* film was equally successful. He later released 'Scandalous' with actress Kim Basinger. Continuing to work at a prodigious rate, he issued *Graffiti Bridge* (1990), the soundtrack to another largely unsuccessful movie, and toured extensively, including one sixteen-night stint at London's Wembley Arena in 1990. The following year he unveiled his new backing band, the New Power Generation, and released *Diamonds and Pearls*. In 1992 he released an album with no title, generally known as the 'symbol' album, after the combined male/female logo which adorned the cover. From it, the controversial 'Sexy MF' was a UK Top Five hit despite being banned by all British radio stations. The following year, Prince announced that he was adopting the symbol as his name (although he had previously announced that he wished to be known as Victor). He also announced that he was retiring from studio work in order to concentrate on film and theatrical projects, closing a chapter in his career by releasing the retrospective *The Hits/The B-Sides*. In 1994 he released the single 'The Most Beautiful Girl in the World'. Issued independently when Warners reportedly told the artist that it was too soon for any new material, it gave him his most successful single yet in Europe where it topped the charts in several countries. It was also a massive hit in America. In its wake Warners officially released the *Black* album (1994) for a limited period. Following that, Prince put further pressure on Warner to release *The Gold Experience*, even appearing in public with what he called the mark of his slavery and calling himself a slave to the label when the company refused. Released in 1995, it sold respectably and was followed by *Chaos & Disorder* (1996). After the independently released live *Emancipation* (1996) – so called because it ended his Warner contract – the four-CD set *Crystal Ball* and *Newpower Soul* (1998), made with the New Power Generation he had sacked earlier in the year, Prince signed with BMG for *Rave Un2 the Joy Fantastic* (Arista, 1999), which returned him to the US Top Twenty.

Among those Prince produced for Paisley Park were such members of his touring band as percussionist/singer Sheila E. (Sheila Escovedo) and Madhouse, a group led by saxophonist Eric Leeds, and **Madonna** (*Like a Prayer*, 1989). Other signings to the label included Mavis Staples of the **Staple Singers** and **George Clinton**. Prince compositions were also recorded successfully by **Chaka Khan** (the No. 1 'I Feel for You'), Melissa Morgan ('Do Me Baby', Capitol, 1986), **Cyndi Lauper** ('When You Were Mine'), **Sheena Easton** ('Sugar Walls' 1985), **Sinead O'Connor** ('Nothing Compares 2 U', 1990) and the **Bangles** ('Manic Monday', 1987).

PRINCE BUSTER
b. Cecil Bustamente Campbell, 28 May 1938, Kingston, Jamaica

Buster was the most influential Jamaican recording star of the pre-reggae early sixties when ska was the dominant form of Jamaican music. His elliptical, allegorical records about the frictions within Jamaican society were also hugely popular with mods in Britain and later influenced the Two-Tone movement of the late seventies, associated with the **Specials** and **Madness** (who took their name from one of Buster's best-known records).

The son of a railroad worker, Buster was named after the Jamaican political leader Alexander Bustamente. He achieved local fame as a boxer before in the late fifties becoming first a security man for **Coxsone Dodd** and then assistant to Duke Reid, who ran one of the most popular sound systems of the day. Reid (who died in 1974) later built the Treasure Island studio and produced several hits for **Derrick Morgan**, the **Skatalites** and **U-Roy**. Buster's first record was 'Little Honey' (1956) and his first hits 'Wash Wash' – a reworking of the spiritual 'Wash My Troubles Away' – and the political tirade 'Sodom and Gomorrah'. Other directly political songs from this period include 'Black Head Chinee Man', a song about the unequal distribution of wealth in Jamaica (and aimed specifically at Morgan's alliance with producer **Leslie Kong**), 'Praise Rather than Raise', 'Time Longer Than Rope' and his moving version of **Sam Cooke**'s 'A Change Is Gonna Come', all of which featured a brass section over a shuffling rhythm.

In 1961 he formed his own short-lived Wild Bells label for which he recorded 'Buster's Shack'. That appeared in Britain on Starlite but Buster's seminal production, the Folkes Brothers' 'Oh Carolina', was released in Britain on Blue Beat. Although Buster had proudly credited Sam Cooke as the composer of 'Change Is Gonna Come', in the spirit of the mores of the day he claimed the copyright of 'Oh Carolina'. After a version by Shaggy sold over a million copies in 1993 on Greensleeves, John Folkes contested this in court and was awarded ownership of the copyright in 1994. Following the British success of 'Oh Carolina' and Eric Morris's 'Humpty Dumpty' Buster's records and productions were regularly released in Britain on Blue Beat. This was unusual for the period and the name Blue Beat quickly became synonymous in Britain with ska. In 1962 Buster adopted the 'Prince' soubriquet and became a prolific recording artist himself. He also started to buy record shops in Jamaica, eventually becoming a leading music retailer there. When Buster toured Britain in 1964, he introduced 'Madness', an oblique comment on Jamaican political unrest and his best-known song, which was recorded by **Georgie Fame**, whose band backed Buster during the tour. Buster followed this with a series of records that invoked such archetypal figures as 'Al Capone' (his only British chart entry in 1967) and the millionaire television detective, 'Burke's Law'. (**Desmond Dekker** had an international hit with the similar '007', 1969.) Mostly instrumentals with shouted interjections – 'Don't call me Scarface/My name is Kerpown!/C-A-P-O-N-E/Kerpown!' – they were followed by numerous songs about 'rude boys' (the street gangs of the Kingston ghettos) by Buster and others including **Bob Marley**. The culmination of these was the trio of records 'Judge Dread', 'Barrister Pardon' and 'Judge Dread Dance', in which a terrifying Ethiopian magistrate hands out sentences of 500 years to the rude boys before pardoning them and joining them in a celebratory dance. Mysterious and oblique records, their appeal can be gauged by the fact that British deejay Alec Hughes appropriated the name Judge Dread for a series of lewd hits in the early seventies, starting with 'Big Six' (Big Shot, 1972), an updating of Buster's own 'Big Five'; the name Judge Dread was later used for the character in a cult comic. More significantly, these records point forward to the rise of the DJ and dub.

Buster himself made several lewd records but his biggest international hit came with his version of the Moonglows' 'The Ten Commandments of Love' (1967), which was also an R&B hit in America. With the rise of reggae, Buster turned to production and running his numerous record shops in Jamaica. In the wake of the Two Tone bands' extensive borrowing from his repertoire – he was even celebrated by **Madness** whose first hit, 'The Prince' (1979), was about Buster – he attempted a comeback with little success, releasing 'Finger' (Arista, 1981).

In the nineties his seminal recordings were reissued in various forms in Japan, the US (on Rhino), and in the UK as *Fabulous* (Sequel, 1993).

JOHN PRINE
b. 10 October 1946, Maywood, Illinois, USA

Originally compared to **Bob Dylan** for his laconic, drawling delivery of his angry songs, John Prine created songs which, though more country orientated, in many ways prefigured the blue-collar concerns that were to run through much of the work of **Bruce Springsteen**.

The son of a steelworker and union official, Prine took up the guitar and started writing songs in the early sixties after serving in the army for two years. Discovered by **Paul Anka** singing **Hank Williams** songs in 1970, he was signed to Atlantic in 1970 and released an eponymous **Arif Mardin**-produced album. It included his best-known early songs: the bitter depiction of a drug-dependent Vietnam veteran 'Sam Stone', 'Hello in There', about the neglect of the elderly, and the eloquent depiction of working-class concerns, 'Six o'Clock News'. *Diamonds in the Rough* (1972) contained similarly styled vignettes, resembling the work of **Danny O'Keefe** but more corrosive, notably 'The Late John Garfield Blues' and 'Yes, I Guess They Oughta Name a Drink After You'. More countryfied was *Sweet Revenge* (1973), which included the autobiographical 'Grandpa Was a Carpenter', before Prine opted for a harder rock'n'roll sound for the commercial failure *Common Sense* (1975), which closed with a version of **Chuck Berry**'s 'You Never Can Tell'.

The fine, sombre *Bruised Orange* (Asylum, 1978) produced by long-time associate **Steve Goodman**, returned Prine to an acoustic mode and included the bleak, yet hilarious, 'Sabu Visits the Twin Cities Alone' and the love song 'If You Don't Want My Love', co-written with **Phil Spector**. Another commercial failure, it was followed by the harder sounding *Pink Cadillac* (1979), recorded in **Sam Phillips'** Sun studios, and including a version of **Elvis Presley**'s 'Let's Play House', and the lesser *Storm Windows* (1980). In 1981 Prine left Asylum and in 1986 he released the engaging *Aimless Love* on his own Ol' Boy label. This was followed by the low-key *German Afternoons* (1987), which included the melancholy 'Speed of the Sound of Loneliness', and a live double-album featuring such backing musicians as Goodman, **Bonnie Raitt** and **David Bromberg**.

In 1991 Prine released the acclaimed *The Missing Years*, one of his finest collections of songs. Produced by **Tom Petty & the Heartbreakers'** bassist Howie Epstein, it featured guest appearances by Petty and members of his band plus Bruce Springsteen, Bonnie Raitt, **Albert Lee** and Phil Everly. Prine later wrote a song for **John Mellencamp**'s film, *Falling from Grace*, in which he had a cameo role. In 1993 he released *A John Prine Christmas*. In the same year Rhino released the fine anthology *Great Days*. *Lost Dogs and Mixed Blessings* appeared in 1995. After a two-year battle with cancer Prine returned to recording in 1999 with *In Spite of Ourselves* (Oh Boy), on which he duetted with, among others, **Lucinda Williams**, Idris DeMent and **Emmylou Harris**. On it the sentimental touch evident on *Great Days* was given even greater expression. In the same year he also appeared alongside Billy Bob Thornton in the comedy *Daddy and Them*, directed by Thornton.

P. J. PROBY
b. James Marcus Smith, 6 November 1938, Houston, Texas, USA

One of the more colourful figures in sixties pop, Proby's powerful tenor was put to best use in a handful of hit singles and in stage musical appearances organized by **Jack Good**.

Proby had unsuccessfully recorded in Hollywood as Jet Powers before Good brought him to England in 1964. An up-tempo histrionic reading of the 1933 ballad 'Hold Me' (Decca) was a Top Ten hit and the formula was repeated with the 1928 **DeSylva, Brown and Henderson** composition 'Together'. Moving to Liberty, Proby had four further hits in 1964–5. 'Somewhere' and 'Maria' were overheated versions of songs from **Leonard Bernstein**'s *West Side Story*, while 'Let the Water Run Down' was a cover of **Ben E. King**'s recording of the **Bert Berns** composition. Proby's crowning glory, however, was 'I Apologise'. With the aid of an exaggerated Texas drawl, he tore the heart out of **Billy Eckstine**'s lachrymose 1951 ballad.

Proby's career took a sudden downturn when he became the target of a press campaign following incidents in which his trousers split on-stage during a package tour headlined by **Cilla Black**. Although he had a Top Thirty hit in America with the cajun song 'Niki Hoeky' (1967), his later Liberty albums, including *Enigma* (1967) and *What's Wrong with My World* (1968), attracted little attention, despite the fact that members of **Led Zeppelin** were among the backing musicians on *Three Week Hero* (1969).

He returned to prominence in 1970 when Good cast him as Cassio in the London production of *Catch My Soul*, a rock version of *Othello*. For a while in the seventies Proby played the variety club circuit in Britain and in 1978 he took part in Good's show *Elvis*. During the eighties Proby was based in the north of England but remained musically virtually inactive. In 1985 he released a version of Ed Cobb's 'Tainted Love' on the Manchester-based Savoy label, which in 1994 issued an album of Proby's occasional recordings of the eighties which included a version of the **Sex Pistols**' 'Anarchy in the UK' and a recitation of T. S. Eliot's poem *The Waste Land*. In 1996 he briefly returned to the stage in a revival of Jack Good's musical *Elvis*.

PROCUL HARUM
Gary Brooker, b. 29 May 1945, London, England; Matthew Fisher, b. Matthew Charles Fisher, 7 March 1946, London; Bobby Harrison, b. 28 June 1943 (replaced by B. J. Wilson, b. 18 March 1947, London, d. 1989, Oregon, USA); David Knights, b. 28 June 1945 (replaced by Chris Copping, b. 29 August 1945, replaced by Alan Cartwright, b. 10 October 1945); Keith Reid,

b. 10 October 1946; Ray Royer, b. 8 October 1945 (replaced by Robin Trower, b. 9 March 1945, London, replaced by Dave Ball, b. 30 March 1950, replaced by Mick Grabham); Pete Solley

With its ethereal organ passages borrowed from Bach, quasi-surreal lyrics and portentous vocals, Procul Harum's 'A Whiter Shade of Pale'* (1967) epitomized one side of the progressive rock of the sixties. Though the group went on to pioneer classical–rock fusions by recording with a symphony orchestra, they never recaptured their initial impact. Guitarist Robin Trower had some later success as a solo artist.

Singer Brooker first recorded as a member of the Paramounts, an R&B group which also included Trower, Wilson (drums) and bassist Copping. The group had a minor hit with a version of the **Coasters**' 'Poison Ivy' (Parlophone, 1964) but split up in 1966. Brooker next formed a writing partnership with lyricist Reid and Procul Harum was organized to perform the duo's songs. The line-up for the début single, 'A Whiter Shade of Pale' (Deram, 1967), included guitarist Royer, drummer Harrison, Fisher (keyboards) and Knights on bass. Produced by Denny Cordell, the record eventually sold over 10 million copies worldwide and its British success was repeated by 'Homburg' (Regal Zonophone), for which Trower and Wilson rejoined Brooker.

Procul Harum, however, were essentially an album and live concert band. An eponymous début album (released by A&M in America) was followed by *Shine on Brightly* (1968), whose 'In Held Was I' suite included special effects like circus sounds and sirens, and the superior *A Salty Dog* (1969). Among the latter's tracks was the harsh 'The Devil Came from Kansas' and the wistful title song. The album was produced by Fisher, who subsequently left the group for a solo recording career with RCA and Vertigo.

With the addition of Copping on bass and organ, the Paramounts were reunited in Procul Harum and it was their guitarist, Trower, who dominated *Broken Barricades* (1971). His 'Song for a Dreamer' was dedicated to **Jimi Hendrix** and heralded a lengthy solo career for Trower as a guitar hero. After *Twice Removed from Yesterday* (Chrysalis, 1973), he recorded more than a dozen further albums, many with former Stone the Crows singer Jimmy Dewar, while *BLT* (1981) and *Truce* (1982) were collaborations with **Jack Bruce**. In the nineties he worked with **Bryan Ferry**, producing *Taxi* (1993).

With new members Ball (guitar) and Cartwright (bass), Procul Harum had a surprise hit in 1972 with a reworking of 'Conquistador' (first recorded on their début album), part of *Live in Edmonton*, recorded in Canada with the Edmonton Symphony Orchestra. With the group now signed to Chrysalis in Britain,

Grabham replaced Ball for *Grand Hotel* (1973), *Exotic Birds and Fruit* and *Ninth* (1975). None matched the ingenuity or success of the group's early work, however, and Procul Harum split up in 1977 after releasing the weak *Something Magic*.

Brooker released the solo albums *No More Fear of Flying* (Chrysalis, 1979), *Lead Me to the Water* (1982) and *Echoes in the Night* (Mercury, 1986), before joining **Eric Clapton**'s touring band in the late eighties. He also wrote the music for several ballets.

Brooker, Reid, Fisher and Trower reunited as Procul Harum in 1991, releasing *The Prodigal Stranger* with **Big Country** drummer Mark Brzezicki. Wilson had died two years previously. As Trower was unwilling to play live, ex-Quiver guitarist Tim Renwick joined for a successful American tour. A second bout of American dates in 1992 featured only Brooker from the original band, and soon afterwards he announced that Procul Harum no longer existed. Brooker also performed live in the early nineties as a member of **Rolling Stones** bassist Bill Wyman's occasional R&B band, Willy & the Poorboys. *30th Anniversary Anthology* (Westside, 1997) is the definitive retrospective.

PRODIGY
Liam Howlett, b. 21 August 1971, Braintree, Essex, England; Keith Flint, b. 17 September 1969, Braintree; Maxim Reality, b. Keeti Palmer, 21 March 1967; Leeroy Thornhill

Prodigy were the most successful of the UK dance/ rock acts to appear in the nineties, their riotous, post-punk dance sound arguably making them the heirs to the **Sex Pistols**.

Howlett, the creative force behind the band, was originally a hip-hop fan, but his experience of the UK rave and acid house scene of the late eighties turned him on to the harder, underground dance music of Joey Beltram and Meat Beat Manifesto. A demo tape mixing this harder dance sound with speeded-up hip-hop beats won him a deal with XL in 1990, and the Prodigy released its first single, 'What Evil Lurks', early in 1991. 'Charly', a rave anthem built around a seventies UK public information film for children, gave the group a UK No. 3 later that year. Despite the record's novelty element, more hits followed. 'Everybody in the Place', 'Out of Space' and 'Wind It Up' were all UK Top 5 hits over the next two years, while their first album, *Experience* (1992), was a Top Twenty hit. The band's popularity was sustained by their genuine status within the UK rave scene. They were a powerful live as well as recording band, Flint's striking post-punk image and Thornhill's dancing providing the on-stage drama for Howlett's music.

The Prodigy's next hit, 'One Love', marked a transition for the band, as Howlett began to explore a more poppy sound, using more commercial vocals and rock guitars over the same crashing dance beats. Their second album, *Music for the Jilted Generation* (1994), took this new sound further, and was nominated for the UK's Mercury Music Prize. The album contained further hits in 'No Good (Start the Dance)', 'Voodoo People' and 'Poison'. Following the album, the band played at the UK's Glastonbury festival and toured Europe, Australia, Japan and America. Prodigy (the 'The' vanished around 1996) took their combination of frenetic post-punk vocal chants, white noise and dance beats to its most extreme form with the track 'Firestarter', a UK No. 1 hit in March 1996. The single earned the band the scorn of a moralizing UK tabloid press, but this only seemed to fuel their success, their next single 'Breathe' becoming their second UK No. 1 later that year.

The Fat of the Land (1997) was released to staggering commercial success and notable critical acclaim, entering the US album chart at No. 1, and also hitting the top spot in the UK and twenty-four other countries. The album has since sold more than 10 million copies worldwide. The band was much criticized for the third single from the album, 'Smack My Bitch Up', which while not actually advocating violence against women added little of intelligence to the public debate about the issue. The title came from a track by US rap group Ultramagnetic MCs, one of whom, Kool Keith, guested on one of the tracks on the album, 'Diesel Power'. Howlett released a DJ mix album in 1999, *Prodigy Presents the Dirtchamber Sessions Volume 1*.

In 2000, as the group began recording its fourth album, provisionally titled *Always Outnumbered, Never Outgunned*, dancer Thornhill announced he was leaving the group to concentrate on his own music under the name Flightcrank.

PROFESSOR LONGHAIR
b. Henry Roeland (Roy) Byrd, 19 December 1918, Bogalusa, Louisiana, USA, d. 30 January 1980, New Orleans, Louisiana

Perhaps the most influential pianist to emerge from the New Orleans scene since **Jelly Roll Morton**, Longhair's role in the city's musical history was only widely acknowledged in his later life and, more, since his death. He was the mentor of **Fats Domino**, **Dr John**, who recorded several homages, most notably 'Memories of Professor Longhair', **Huey 'Piano' Smith** and **Allen Toussaint**, to name only the most visible of his pupils.

In the thirties he made his living as a street entertainer or gambler, not playing piano regularly until the late forties, when he worked in New Orleans clubs with his Four Hairs, later renamed the Shuffling

Hungarians to record for Talent (1949). He went on to Mercury (1949), Atlantic (1949, 1953), Federal (1951) and many small labels, often recycling favourite themes like 'Tipitina', 'Bald Head', 'Big Chief' (recorded by Dr John on *Gumbo*, 1972) and 'Go to the Mardi Gras' in his hoarse, half-yodelling vocal style, over subtle but vigorous rumba-based piano rhythms. Locally prominent musicians like saxophonists Lee Allen and Red Tyler sometimes worked on these sessions.

He found new opportunities for work in the sixties, and his career only began to recover in 1971, when he appeared at the New Orleans Jazz and Heritage Fair (at which he would henceforth be a constant headliner). By 1973 he was being invited to the Newport and Montreux Jazz Festivals and his recording career was revived. *Rock'n'Roll Gumbo* (Blue Star, 1974) was followed by *Live on the Queen Mary* (Harvest, 1978), recorded at a 1975 party given by Linda and **Paul McCartney**. Longhair visited Britain for the only time in 1978, a single concert preserved on JSP (*The London Concert*, 1981). The double-album *The Last Mardi Gras*, recorded in 1978 at the New Orleans Tipitina club (named after his most famous number), was not released until after his death (Atlantic, 1982). What was probably his last session, *Crawfish Fiesta* (Alligator, 1980), with Dr John on guitar, also came out posthumously. In 1987 Rounder issued *Houseparty New Orleans Style*, previously unreleased recordings from 1971–2, and in 1994 Sequel reissued *New Orleans Piano*, which was also from the early seventies, with the addition of a couple of unreleased tracks.

Longhair is remembered not only for his records but for his crazy costumes and stage act and his irrepressible Mardi Gras party spirit, which none of his followers managed to duplicate.

ARTHUR PRYSOCK
b. 2 January 1929, Spartanburg, North Carolina, USA, d. 21 June 1997, Hamilton, Bermuda

Heavily influenced by **Billy Eckstine**, Prysock's rich baritone enabled him to sustain his career over five decades. Despite his relative lack of record success, he was a mainstay of the cabaret and concert-hall circuits.

He moved to Hartford, Connecticut, to work in the aircraft industry in the early forties and while singing with a local band was spotted in 1944 by bandleader **Buddy Johnson**, who signed him as male vocalist. Prysock sang on several of Johnson's hits first on Decca ('Jet My Love', 1947, and 'I Wonder Where Our Love Has Gone', 1948) and Mercury ('Because', 1950). In 1952 Prysock went solo and signed with Decca. He had an immediate R&B hit, 'I Didn't Sleep a Wink Last Night' (1952), but, his popularity as a live performer with black audiences notwithstanding, he was

essentially a band and ballad – not an R&B – singer. Nonetheless, he recorded R&B classics like **Roy Brown**'s 'Good Rocking Tonight'.

In the sixties Prysock joined Old Time, where he had an R&B hit with a fine version of **Ray Noble**'s thirties ballad, 'The Very Thought of You' (1960), and a pop hit with 'It's Too Late Baby, It's Too Late' (1965) and Verve ('A Working Man's Prayer', 1968). In the seventies, in the wake of successful reissues of his recordings, he had a surprise disco hit with 'When Love Is New' (Old Time, 1977), and in 1985 recorded his first new album, *Arthur Prysock* (Milestone), in almost a decade to critical and commercial approval.

PUBLIC ENEMY
Chuck D, b. Carlton Ridenhour, 1 August 1960, Long Island, New York, USA; Flavor Flav, b. William Drayton, 16 March 1959, Long Island, USA; Terminator X, b. Norman Rogers; Professor Griff, b. Richard Griffin

The longest established of politically-committed rap groups, Public Enemy express a black nationalist philosophy through their bestselling recordings. The period 1988–90 represented Public Enemy at the height of their powers. The two albums from that period are among the finest rap albums ever made.

The group originated at Adelphi University in Long Island, where Chuck D and Hank Shocklee mixed a college radio show at the invitation of station director Bill Stephney in 1982. Shocklee and Chuck D later made their own tapes, including a track called 'Public Enemy Number 1'.

By 1986 the duo had assembled a rap and hip-hop ensemble under the name Public Enemy. Among its fluctuating membership were MC Flavor Flav and DJ Terminator X. In 1987 they signed a recording deal with **Rick Rubin** of Def Jam. The group was promoted by Def Jam in alliance with the **Beastie Boys**, touring with the white rap outfit and provoking the same fervour from young Americans and fear from middle Americans.

Shocklee and Stephney had now become the group's managers and producers. The début album *Yo! Bum Rush the Show* (1987) introduced a new political awareness into New York rap. It featured Chuck D's compelling, stentorian delivery, which contrasted strongly with the caustic asides of Flav, rap's original court jester. In the same year they had US hits with the singles 'Don't Believe the Hype' and 'Bring the Noise', which was featured in the film *Less Than Zero*.

Hip-hop was an emerging and worrying cultural force for much of white America. Public Enemy were among the main sources of concern, and an album containing tracks such as 'You're Gonna Get Yours' and 'Mi Uzi Weighs a Ton' hardly set conservative minds at rest. The group's shock value was visual as well as sonic, their live shows featuring their male on-stage dancers, the S1Ws, in cages carrying fake Uzi machine-guns. But unlike the Beastie Boys, Public Enemy were using shock tactics to articulate a more overtly political agenda, as was evident even early on in tracks like 'Rightstarter (Message to a Black Man)'.

The follow-up album, *It Takes a Nation of Millions to Hold Us Back* (1988), replaced the electro beats of its predecessor with a funkier, tougher sound, making liberal use of **James Brown** samples. Lyrically, the album also marked an advance, the band portraying themselves as political fugitives at odds with the white American establishment on 'Black Steel in the Hour of Chaos', and attacking drug-dealing on 'Night of the Living Bassheads'. Tours of the US with the Beastie Boys and of Europe with LL Cool J helped *It Takes a Nation of Millions . . .*, which also included 'Rebel Without a Pause', to reach the UK Top Ten and the US pop Top Fifty. 1989 saw just one Public Enemy release, 'Fight the Power', the title song from Spike Lee's film *Do the Right Thing* and a huge com-mercial and critical success. It was again lyrically con-troversial, taking a swipe at white American icons such as **Elvis Presley** and John Wayne. Fresh contro-versy followed when the group's 'minister of informa-tion' (a term borrowed from the Black Panther party) Professor Griff was accused of anti-semitism. He left Public Enemy and later recorded for Luke Records, home of **2 Live Crew**.

'Fight the Power' was also included on *Fear of a Black Planet* (1990), which maintained the style of *It Takes a Nation of Millions . . .*, but gave the band's songs a more theatrical setting. This was perhaps a lesson learnt from the way skits and interludes had added freshness and continuity to **De La Soul**'s land-mark *Three Feet High and Rising* a year earlier. The result was their most commercially successful album until then. Hit singles included 'Welcome to the Ter-rordome', '911 Is a Joke', featuring Flav as lead rapper, and the coruscating 'Brothers Gonna Work It Out'. The album was more thematically specific than its predecessor, tackling issues including interracial mar-riages ('Fear of a Black Planet') and the white domi-nation of the film industry on the set's stand-out track, 'Burn Hollywood Burn'.

The group were now adept at manipulating media outrage at their lyrics and stage shows to enhance their reputation as anti-establishment spokesmen for a disenfranchised Black American community. The classic example of this on *Fear* was 'Incident at 66.6 FM', which used excerpts from US radio show phone-ins to satirize the often mindless criticism of the group.

Apocalypse '91 the Enemy Strikes Black (1991) included the hits 'Can't Truss It', 'Nighttrain' and 'Shut 'Em Down', the latter two remixed to com-pelling effect by Pete Rock and featuring his partner, rapper C. L. Smooth. The album also featured a fine Flavor Flav cameo on 'More News at Eleven'. *Greatest Misses* (1992) mixed new tracks and remixes, and was well-received without creating many waves, itself unusual for a Public Enemy release.

By now, rap was moving on towards gangsta rap, a genre in which simple controversy took the place of social issues. Public Enemy were also the first rap group to have their material covered by other artists, an idea that would have seemed absurd at the genre's inception. Those paying tribute to Chuck D and his band included **Duran Duran** on an ill-advised inter-pretation of '911 Is a Joke'. More successful covers came from Tricky with 'Black Steel' and Delaneys Rhythm Section with 'Rebel'.

Muse Sick-N-Hour Mess Age (1994) showed a mel-lowing of the familiar PE sound, although the lyrical content remained as hardcore as ever, notably on 'But Can You Kill the Nigger in You?', which featured a guest appearance from **Isaac Hayes**. In the same year Chuck D undertook a college lecture tour which led to the solo album *The Autobiography of MistaChuck* (1996) in conjunction with a book of the same title. In 1998 Public Enemy regrouped to record the lesser *He Got Game* for the Spike Lee film of the same name. The album was poorly received critically, the princi-pal criticism being that the group was trying too hard to reproduce the west coast G-Funk sound which had been so pervasive in hip-hop in the late nineties. The appearance of former **Crosby, Stills & Nash** singer David Crosby as a guest vocalist also raised a few eye-brows.

In 1999 Public Enemy found themselves at odds with their record label over PE's decision to release some new tracks over the internet. This dispute esca-lated, with PE releasing a new album, *There's a Poison Going on*, via the Internet nearly two months before it would be available in record shops. They subse-quently left Def Jam for Internet record company Atomic Pop. 2000 finally saw the release of Flavor Flav's much-delayed solo album, aptly titled *It's About Time*.

GARY PUCKETT AND THE UNION GAP

Gary Puckett, b. 17 October 1942, Hibbing, Minnesota, USA; Dwight Bement, b. 28 December 1945, San Diego, California; Kerry Chater, b. 7 August 1945, Vancouver, Canada; Mutha Withem, b. 22 August 1946, San Diego; Paul Wheatbread, b. 8 February 1946, San Diego

The Union Gap had four million-sellers with their catchy version of blue-eyed soul.

Formed in 1967 in San Diego as the Outlaws, they won local fame for their ability to duplicate current hits. Signed to Columbia in 1968, the group took their name from the historic town of Union Gap where Puckett had grown up and they adopted Civil War uniforms as their gimmick. At Columbia they were produced by Jerry Fuller, who had had a series of minor hits on Challenge (including 'Tennessee Waltz', 1959, and 'Shy Away', 1961) and written several of **Rick Nelson**'s hits, notably 'Travelin' Man', 'Young World' and 'It's Up to You'. His first success as a producer was the Knickerbockers' **Beatles** pastiche 'Lies' (Challenge, 1966).

The Union Gap's first hit, 'Woman Woman'* (1967), defined their style, with Puckett's sturdy vocals supported by a full sound. In 1968 they followed it with the anthemic 'Young Girl'*, which topped the British charts and was a hit again when reissued in 1974, 'Lady Willpower'* and 'Over You'*, all remarkably similar sounding and all written by Fuller. Their last hit came in 1969 with 'This Girl Is a Woman Now' after which they disbanded with Puckett and Chater pursuing unsuccessful solo careers.

TITO PUENTE
b. 20 April 1923, Harlem, New York City, USA, d. 31 May 2000

One of the most prolific mambo bandleaders in Latin music, Puente, who was featured in the film *The Mambo Kings* (1992), recorded more than a hundred albums in Afro-Cuban and salsa styles. His mix of high-energy drumming and delicate vibraphone playing, supported by a flamboyant band, often with **Celia Cruz** as vocalist, won him the title of 'El Rey del Timbal', or simply 'El Rey'.

Born in America of Puerto Rican parents, Puente initially wanted to be a dancer. Following a serious leg injury, he switched to music, becoming a multi-instrumentalist (piano, saxophone, percussion) and composer. He first played with José Curbelo, then joined **Machito**. After serving in the US Marines, he studied composition at the Juillard School of Music and worked as an arranger. In 1947 he formed the Piccadilly Boys and after several recordings from the independent SMC in 1948 was among the first signings to Tico, a label established by **George Goldner** to cater for the growing New York audience for Latin music. Puente's 'Abaniquito' (1949) was one of the first mambo recordings to sell in large numbers to non-Latins.

His mambo style was always closer to its Afro-Cuban roots than that of **Perez Prado**. During the fifties Puente's band became one of New York's leading Latin orchestras, regularly performing at the Palladium dance hall, backing the genre's most successful singers and performing with such leading jazz musicians as **Stan Kenton** and **Dizzy Gillespie**.

Among the performers who passed through the band were **Mongo Santamaria** and conga-player Ray Barretto, who later had a Top Twenty hit wih 'El Watusi' (Tico, 1963). Puente's outstanding recording from this era was *Dance Mania* (RCA, 1958), which included 'Hong Kong Mambo' and 'El Cayuco' and featured vocalist Santos Colon.

In the sixties Puente recorded for GNP in Los Angeles and made the first of his collaborations with **Celia Cruz**, *Cuba Y Puerto Rico* (1965). In the seventies Puente's band was one of the focuses of the new salsa style, deriving from Cuban rhythms. In 1971 **Carlos Santana** had a Top Twenty hit with Puente's arrangement of 'Oye Como Va' and in 1977 Puente reunited with Colon for *The Legend*, the title track of which was written by **Ruben Blades**. Among his recordings of the eighties were several for Concord Picante, the salsa label of the Concord Jazz company. In 1991 he recorded his 100th album, *The Mambi King*. This was followed by *Royal T* (1993) and *Golden Latin All Stars in Session* (1994) with Santamaria, Hilton Ruiz and others.

The 1997 box set, *Commemorating Tito Puente: 50 Years of Swing*, contains recordings from all stages of his career, while Steve Loza's biography *Tito Puente and the Making of Latin Music* offers a comprehensive account of the importance of Latin music to the development of American popular music in general. The tribute song 'El Cien', which included Celia Cruz among others, was released in 1999 to mark the issuing of his 100th album.

PUFF DADDY
b. Sean Combs, 4 November 1970, Harlem, New York, USA

As well as being one of the most important label heads of the decade, Combs carved out a niche as a successful solo artist in the mid-nineties, blending the 'gangster rap' ethos with classic pop and soul samples to create a commercialized variation of the genre.

Combs made his first foray into the music industry while studying at Howard University in Washington DC, convincing his childhood friend Heavy D to take him on as an intern at Uptown Records. He quickly worked his way up to the position of A&R executive and won the role of executive producer on Father MC's *Father's Day* (1990). After producing **Mary J. Blige**'s highly successful début, *What's the 411?* (1992), Combs laid the foundations for his own Bad Boy Entertainment label, and within two years had signed hip-hop stars the Notorious BIG (*b. Christopher Wallace, 21 May 1972, Brooklyn, New York, d. 6 March 1997*) and Craig Mack. Wallace's début, *Ready to Die* (1995), was eventually certified double platinum, and spawned a US Top Ten hit single, 'Big Poppa'.

Combs spent the next two years signing an array of top R&B/rap talent, notably Faith Evans and 112, as well as producing for **TLC**, **Mariah Carey** and **Aretha Franklin**. However, Combs and Wallace were by this stage embroiled in a high-profile feud with Death Row Records boss Marion 'Suge' Knight and label star **2Pac Shakur**, which culminated in the shooting of both Shakur and Wallace by unknown gunmen, as BIG's 'Hypnotize' stood at the top of the US charts. The rapper would soon have a posthumous hit with the somewhat prophetic *Life after Death* (1997), while Combs had an international number one hit as Puff Daddy with the tribute single 'I'll Be Missing You', built around a sample from the **Police**'s 'Every Breath You Take'. Puff Daddy's début album, *No Way Out* (1997), was also a worldwide success, winning the Grammy Award for Best Rap Album.

In the late nineties Combs branched out his Bad Boy empire to include restaurants, films, clothing manufacture and the publication of a magazine. As Puff Daddy he had another massive hit single with 'Come with Me', as included on the soundtrack to *Godzilla* (1998), which was based loosely around **Led Zeppelin**'s 'Kashmir' and featured original guitarist Jimmy Page. In 1999 Combs unleashed the second Puff Daddy album, *Forever*. In 2000 he returned to the public eye when he was arrested, in the company of his girlfriend, Latino superstar Jennifer Lopez, for possession of an illegal weapon.

PULP

Nick Banks, b. 28 July 1965, Rotherham, England; Jarvis Cocker, b. 19 September 1963, Sheffield; Candida Doyle, b. 25 August 1963, Belfast, Ireland; Steve Mackey, b. 10 November 1966, Sheffield; Russell Senior; Mark Webber, b. 14 September 1970, Chesterfield

Having spent over a decade on the cusp of stardom, Pulp finally cracked the mainstream market in the mid-nineties with 'Common People', a perfect encapsulation of the Britpop aesthetic.

Jarvis Cocker formed the first incarnation of Pulp in 1978 with an ever-changing selection of local musicians. The band soon began to play on the Sheffield club circuit and found themselves championed by DJ John Peel, for whom they recorded a live session in 1981. Pulp gradually built up a cult following with the release of *It* (Red Rhino, 1982) and *Freaks* (Fire, 1986), which were by turns reminiscent of the **Smiths** and a keyboard-driven **Nick Cave and the Bad Seeds**.

By 1989 Cocker had solidified the band's line-up, recruiting Senior (violin), Webber (guitar), Mackey (bass), Doyle (keyboards) and Banks (drums) to record *Separations*. While the album failed to gain release until 1992, Pulp hit their stride with a series of singles in the early nineties in which Cocker detailed

the seedy underbelly of suburban life with his idiosyncratic dry humour. 'Razzmatazz', 'Babies' and 'My Legendary Girlfriend' were highly acclaimed, while *His and Hers* (1994), Pulp's first album for Island Records, débuted in the UK Top Ten and spawned the hit single 'Do You Remember the First Time?'.

After the release of *Masters of the Universe* (Fire, 1995), a collection of early singles, Pulp recorded the album that would see them finally break through into the mainstream. *Different Class* (1995), one of the strongest albums of the Britpop era, achieved multiple-platinum status on the strength of the singles 'Common People', 'Disco 2000' and 'Sorted for E's and Wizz'. Pulp's profile rose considerably in 1996 as they won the Mercury Music Prize, while Cocker gained notoriety for storming the stage at the Brit Awards in protest against **Michael Jackson**'s performance. The band were reduced to a five-piece later in the year with the departure of Senior, the longest-serving member of Pulp after Cocker, before issuing *Countdown: 1992–1983*, a compilation of pre-*His and Hers* material.

Pulp made a conscious decision to spend the following year out of the public eye before returning with *This Is Hardcore* (1998), a bleak treatise on the power of pornography, that had its origins in the sexual innuendo of *Different Class*'s 'I Spy'. The album was a much less commercial affair than its predecessor and left the band's popularity waning, despite respectful reviews. In 1999 Cooking Vinyl repackaged the band's first four albums in the *Pulped (83–92)* boxed set.

PURE PRAIRIE LEAGUE

Craig Lee Fuller, b. 18 July 1949, Portsmouth, Ohio, USA; George Powell, b. North Carolina; John Call; Jim Lantham; Jim Caughlin

Pure Prairie League is probably as well known for its record sleeves as its recordings. Most featured illustrator Norman Rockwell's depiction of Luke as a disreputable-looking, ageing cowboy. He is holding a record, 'Dreams of Long Ago', on their eponymous début album (1972), being kicked out of a saloon for *Bustin' Out* (1972), stranded in the desert for *Two Lane Highway* (1975) and struggling with a recalcitrant pair of boots on *If the Shoe Fits* (1976). These gentle, nostalgic images capture the feel and tone of the group very well. Certainly the images mark the group's very different take on country rock to the more abrasive one of **Gram Parsons**. His far more radical take on country music can be seen on the sleeve of one of the genre's seminal albums, *The Gilded Palace of Sin* (1969), the début album of the Flying Burrito Brothers, the group Parsons formed after leaving the **Byrds**. On it Parsons stands wearing a suit by Nudie, tailor to many country stars, but with marijuana leaves and naked ladies in place of the six guns and cowboy motifs beloved of most of Nudie's customers.

Formed in Columbus, Ohio, and taking their name from the women's temperance union in the Western *Dodge City* (1939), the group were signed by RCA in 1971 and released their eponymous album the next year. The album consisted largely of songs written by lead vocalist Fuller (including the sprightly 'Tears' and 'You're Between Me', which is one of the few pop songs to make reference to another contemporary pop group, McKendree Spring, which is best remembered for making the first recording of the McGarrigles' 'Heart Like a Wheel') and Powell ('It's All One Me'). The sound was less dynamic than that of the **Eagles**, but it had an appealing warmth in the manner of a later country-rock band, the **Amazing Rhythm Aces**. While the melding of country and rock influences is seen as commonplace now, the best moments of Pure Prairie League show how fragile this union was in the early seventies.

During the making of *Bustin' Out* the band's non-writing members drifted away. One effect was to give greater freedom to Mick Ronson, a former sidekick of **David Bowie**, whose elegant string arrangements gave even greater prominence to Fuller's voice, particularly on 'Amie' and 'Falling in and out of Love'. However, with poor sales and a lead singer in jail for draft avoidance, RCA dropped the group, only to quickly re-sign a re-formed version created around Powell and new writer and guitarist Larry Goshorn, when 'Amie' became a surprise hit in 1975. However, the group's subsequent RCA recordings, which included *Two Lane Highway*, *If the Shoe Fits* and *Just Fly* (1978), largely consisted of session musicians, albeit some of the stature of **Chet Atkins**, in support of Powell and Goshorn. When Powell quit in 1977, a mark of how far the band had become a franchise rather than a group was that, after moving to Casablanca in 1980, their only (and biggest) hit, 'Let Me Love You Tonight', featured **Vince Gill**, who was passing through the band as part of his career.

Fuller, who after leaving the band in 1975 had formed American Flyer, briefly returned to the group in 1985 before quitting once again to join the latest version of **Little Feat** in 1988.

In the nineties both Mercury (into which Casablanca was subsumed) and RCA issued several collections. The best of these is *Greatest Hits* (RCA, 1999).

SUZI QUATRO

b. 3 June 1950, Detroit, Michigan, USA

Leather-suited bass-player and singer Quatro offered a hard-rock image (in contrast to the rock'n'roll revivalist image of Mud or the softer rock of Smokie) on a series of seventies hits produced and written by **Chinn and Chapman**. Like Mud and Smokie she never managed to outgrow the image.

Quatro's father led a jazz band while her elder brother Michael was a leading promoter in the Midwest. In 1966 Suzi (as Suzi Soul) and her sister Patti formed the Pleasure Seekers, an all-female rock group. The band recorded 'Good Kind of Hurt' (Mercury, 1967), changed its name to Cradle in 1970 but split up soon afterwards. Patti Quatro later played guitar with another female band, Fanny, which recorded for Reprise (*Charity Ball*, 1971; *Fanny Hill*, 1972) and Casablanca.

After seeing Suzi Quatro playing in New York, **Mickie Most** signed her to his RAK label. Moving to England, she recorded the unsuccessful 'Rolling Stone', after which Most brought in Chinn and Chapman as producers. During 1973–4 the duo provided Quatro with six British hits. Capitalizing on her big voice and leather-clad stage presence, the songs were cartoon evocations of the rock lifestyle: 'Can the Can', '48 Crash', 'Daytona Demon', 'Devil Gate Drive', 'Too Big' and 'The Wild One'. With guitarist Len Tuckey (whom she later married), Quatro formed a touring band.

On 'Your Mama Won't Like Me' (1975), Chinn and Chapman switched to a disco-tinged approach but the record failed. Quatro's next hit came in 1978 with 'If You Can't Give Me Love' but she had only one further British Top Twenty Single, 'She's in Love with You' (1979). Her only American hit came in the same year with 'Stumblin' in'*, a duet with Chris Norman, lead singer of Smokie, another Chinn–Chapman band.

Quatro next signed to Dreamland, the label started by her producers, releasing *Rock Hard* (1980). She later recorded *Main Attraction* (Polydor, 1982), but concentrated in the eighties on TV and stage work, appearing in the American sitcom *Happy Days* and starring in a British production of **Irving Berlin**'s *Annie Get Your Gun* (1986). She had a brief career as a television hostess, during which she continued to record, releasing *Saturday Night Special* (Biff Records) in 1987 and *Rock 'Till You Drop* in 1989. She co-wrote

an unsuccessful musical with playwright Willy Russell, *Tallulah Who?*, which ran briefly in 1991. The definitive retrospective is *The Wild One* (1994). She still occasionally plays live in Britain.

QUEEN

John Deacon, b. 19 August 1951, Leicester, England; Brian May, b. 19 July 1947, Middlesex; Roger Meadows-Taylor, b. 26 July 1949, Norfolk; Freddie Mercury, b. Frederick Bulsara, 5 September 1946, Zanzibar, d. 24 February 1991, London

One of Britain's most successful rock groups of the seventies and eighties, Queen was launched as a glam-and-glitter band but developed a winning and durable blend of showmanship that highlighted Freddie Mercury's distinctive vocals.

The band's origins lay in Smile, formed in 1967 by guitarist May and drummer Taylor with singer Tim Staffell. One single was produced by Lou Reizner for Mercury before Staffell joined Humpy Bong, a group led by former **Bee Gee** Colin Stafford. Mercury, who had been singing with heavy blues band Wreckage, joined in 1970 and soon after the group became Queen. With electronics student Deacon on bass, they signed to Trident Productions in 1972.

In what was then a novel move, Trident, primarily a studio operation, financed the début eponymous album, produced by John Anthony and Roy Thomas Baker, before leasing it to EMI. Its 1973 release was preceded by a revival of the **Beach Boys**' 1969 hit, 'I Can Hear Music' by Mercury masquerading as 'Larry Lurex'. The mildly mystical 'Seven Seas of Rhye' (1974) from *Queen II* was the group's first hit, followed by the close-harmonized, dynamic 'Killer Queen' from *Sheer Heart Attack* (1974).

'Now I'm Here' was followed by the path-breaking 'Bohemian Rhapsody'*, a six-minute single in three movements which was equally notable as the first single whose success was closely tied to its music video, directed by Bruce Gowers. A British No. 1 for two months, and later a re-released hit in both the US (1992) and the UK, 'Bohemian Rhapsody' and the next hit 'Somebody to Love' (1976) were included on *A Night at the Opera*. While *A Day at the Races* borrowed another Marx Brothers title, its sales paled before those of *News of the World* (1977), which included such bombastic anthems as 'We Will Rock You' and 'We Are the Champions'*.

From the late seventies the group became the

monarchs of stadium rock, making international tours with a lavish stage show, which transferred well on to video. Record sales burgeoned in the wake of Queen's live popularity. Although musically undistinguished, 'Fat Bottomed Girls' and 'Don't Stop Me Now' from *Jazz* (1978) were European hits. The in-concert *Live Killers* gave the band another hit album, and 1980's *The Game* brought Queen their greatest American success when both 'Crazy Little Thing Called Love'* and 'Another One Bites the Dust'* reached No. 1. The album provided further British hits in 'Save Me' and 'Play the Game' while 'Flash', the playful theme song from the film *Flash Gordon*, also reached the Top Ten.

The outstanding songs from *Hot Space* (1982) were 'Body Language' and 'Las Palabras de Amor', which looked forward to 'Barcelona' (Polydor, 1987), Mercury's successful collaboration with Spanish opera singer Montserrat Caballe. 'Under Pressure', a duet between **David Bowie** and Mercury was a British No. 1 in 1981, while the 1984 Queen album *The Works* provided a transatlantic hit single with the mildly mocking 'Radio Gaga' and three further British Top Twenty entries led by the histrionic 'I Want to Break Free'.

In 1985 Queen made an acclaimed appearance at Live Aid and later released the utopian song 'One Vision'. *A Kind of Magic* (1986) included the hit 'Who Wants to Live Together', and was followed by another in-concert set, *Live Magic*. In the eighties three of the foursome embarked on solo projects, with varying degrees of success. Solo records included Taylor's *Fun in Space* (1981), *Strange Frontier* (1984) and *Shove It* (with his own band, the Cross, 1988), May's *Star Fleet Project* (1983) and Mercury's *Mr Bad Guy* (1985), with its hits 'Love Kills' and 'I Was Born to Love You'. Mercury had even greater solo success with a melodramatic revival of the **Platters**' 'The Great Pretender' (1987).

After a period of concentrating on their solo projects, the band were reunited for 1989's *The Miracle*, which included more international hit singles, most notably 'I Want It All'. In a high-profile move, the band signed in America to the Walt Disney organization's Hollywood Records in 1990, releasing *Innuendo* (1991) with its six-minute title track that recalled the 'Bohemian Rhapsody' era when released as a single. The lengthy recording sessions for the album had been delayed by Mercury's ill health.

Mercury died from an Aids-related illness in November 1991. His death sparked a revival of interest in Queen's back catalogue, and a reissued 'Bohemian Rhapsody' (which had been featured in the film *Wayne's World*) was a big international hit. A 1986 concert was released as *Live at Wembley*, a collection of Mercury's solo recordings was repackaged as *The Freddie Mercury Album* and a reissued 'Barcelona' made the British Top Five in 1992. The same year, the

three remaining members of Queen organized an all-star charity concert at Wembley stadium as a tribute to Mercury. A recording from the event featuring **George Michael** on vocals topped the British singles chart in 1993.

Brian May returned to solo work after Mercury's death. In 1992 he released *Back to the Light* and the hit single 'Driven by You', originally written for a television commercial. He formed a touring band, which could be heard on *Live at the Brixton Academy* (1994). In the same year Taylor released his own solo album, *Happiness*, while a year later *Made in Heaven*, which was credited to Queen featuring Freddie Mercury and included revised recordings of material recorded before his death, was an international hit and gave rise to another wave of reissues. The most notable of these was *Queen Rocks* (1997). May continued his solo career with *Another World* (1998) and Taylor's *Electric Fire* (1998).

QUEEN LATIFAH
b. Dana Owens, 18 March 1970, Newark, New Jersey, USA

The leading female rapper, Queen Latifah has built a business empire as well as recording several best-selling albums focusing on feminist themes and issues.

At high school Owens formed a female vocal trio, Ladies Fresh. After meeting DJ Mark the 45 King, she became involved with rap music. Taking the name Queen Latifah (Arabic for 'delicate and sensitive'), she recorded 'Wrath of My Madness' and 'Dance with Me' in 1988.

Her début album, *All Hail the Queen* (Tommy Boy, 1989), included a guest appearance by Monie Love on 'Ladies First' and 'Evil that Men Do', a lyric about urban decay. The album sold over a million copies. Her second album, *Nature of a Sista* (1991), featured the reggae-inflected 'Sexy Fancy', and offered a taster of the musical diversity that was to follow. Her next album, *Black Reign* (1993), saw her moving to the Motown label for a record that welded jazz, R&B, hip-hop and reggae elements. Male rappers appearing with her included **Kurtis Blow** and Heavy D on 'If It Ain't Ruff'. The album also included the deep soul of 'Winki's Theme', dedicated to her late brother, and 'U.N.I.T.Y.', a powerful attack on rap's misogynistic tendencies.

At this point in her career, Latifah was strongly associated with New York's Native Tongues rap collective. This loose grouping also included **De La Soul**, with whom she collaborated successfully on the hit 'Mama Gave Birth to the Soul Children'.

In 1993 she established Flavor Unit, her own label and management company, which also diversified into film and real estate. Acts managed by the company included rappers Naughty By Nature, Onyx and singer Faith Evans. Its first hit was Zhan's 'Hey Mr D.J.'. During the mid- and late nineties Latifah gravitated more and more towards an acting career, appearing in the films *Jungle Fever*, *My Life*, *Juice*, *Sphere* and the US TV sitcom *Living Single*. She returned to her musical roots for 1998's *Order in the Court*, recorded on her own label.

QUEENSRYCHE
Chris De Garmo, b. 14 June 1963, Wenatchee, Washington, USA; Eddie Jackson; Scott Rockenfield, b. 15 June 1963, Seattle, Washington; Geoff Tate, b. 14 January 1959, Stuttgart, Germany; Michael Wilton, b. 23 February 1962, San Francisco, California

Seattle-based five-piece Queensryche enjoyed considerable success in the late eighties and early nineties with their twin guitar-led blend of 'socially aware' rhetoric and progressive rock. Musically retrogressive, they nevertheless attracted a sizeable American audience.

In 1981 the band was formed as the Mob in Bellvue, Washington, by five high-school friends: guitarists De Garmo and Wilton, vocalist Tate, bassist Jackson and drummer Rockenfield. Signing to Seattle independent label 206 Records, the renamed band released a four-track EP, *Queen of the Ryche*, in 1983. Although the EP showed the strong influence of the contemporary metal scene, its progressive rock leanings and Tate's distinctive voice marked the band out as sufficiently different to attract the attention of major labels and Queensryche signed to EMI in 1984.

The Warning, produced in London by James Guthrie, disappointed both fans and critics but the band re-established itself by extensive touring, crossing the US as support act to a number of major metal bands. Queensryche's second album, *Rage for Order*, did not appear until 1986, but its heavily studio-orientated sound was a marked improvement.

Even better was the ambitious concept album *Operation Mindcrime* (1988), loosely based on George Orwell's novel *1984*. It sold over one million copies worldwide, picking up ecstatic reviews in the heavy-metal press. Following the pattern of one album every two years, the band released *Empire* in 1990 and enjoyed immediate major success. A multi-million-seller, the album included the hit singles 'Silent Lucidity', a dreamy, almost psychedelic ballad, 'Best I Can' and 'Jet City Woman'. More touring followed, but the lasting success of *Empire* meant that the band was able to take a lengthy break before beginning work on their fifth album. *Promised Land* appeared in 1994 and immediately entered the US Top Ten, confirming the band's hard-won status in the rock hierar-

chy. In 1995 EMI released a multimedia version of *Promised Land*, including a CD-ROM, and 1997's *Hear on the Now Frontier*. That and 1999's *Q2K*, on which their former producer replaced de Garmo as guitarist to good effect, saw the band's style largely unchanged.

? AND THE MYSTERIANS
?, b. Rudy Martinez, 1945, Mexico; Robert Balderrama, b. 1950, Mexico; Frank Rodriguez, b. 9 March 1951, Crystal City, Texas, USA; Frank Lugo, b. 15 March 1947, Welasco, Texas; Edward Serrato, b. 1947, Mexico

Though they actually had two hits, ? and the Mysterians were in many ways the epitome of the one-hit-wonder syndrome. With its insistent, piping organ and Martinez's teenage poetry, and helped by his wonderfully naïve alias – for some years Martinez was only photographed in sunglasses – '96 Tears'* (1966) is both silly and timeless. An American No. 1, it inspired imitations by countless garage bands and its raucous simplicity has been acknowledged as an important influence on seventies punk rock, notably the **Stranglers**, who had a 1990 British hit with the song.

All the group members were raised in Michigan and first played together in 1962 as XYZ in the Detroit area. Taking the name ? and the Mysterians, they recorded '96 Tears', reputedly in the living room of their manager's house, for her independent Pa-Go-Go label. After it became a local hit Cameo released the record nationally. The equally simple 'I Need Somebody' (1966) gave the group their only other Top Forty hit. After three more singles and an eponymous album the group disbanded. In 1981, in the wake of Garland Jeffreys' minor hit with '96 Tears', Martinez formed a new, shortlived ? and the Mysterians for revival concerts. The group re-formed in 1985 for the beguiling *The Dallas Reunion Tapes* (ROIR), a record which uncannily re-created the sound of the sixties.

QUICKSILVER MESSENGER SERVICE
Gary Duncan, b. 4 September 1946, San Diego, California, USA; John Cipollina, b. 24 August 1943, Berkeley, California, d. 29 May 1989, San Francisco; David Freiberg, b. 24 August 1938, Boston, Massachusetts; Greg Elmore, b. 4 September 1946, San Diego; Jim Murray; Dino Valenti, b. 7 October 1943, New York, d. 16 November 1994; Nicky Hopkins, b. 24 February 1944, London, England

Never as successful as either the **Grateful Dead** or **Jefferson Airplane**, Quicksilver Messenger Service were perhaps the most representative San Francisco band. The sleeve of *Happy Trails* (1969) is a perfect example of the work of George Hunter, one of the most important San Francisco poster artists, while the guitar interplay on their side-long reworking of **Bo Diddley**'s 'Who Do You Love?' exemplified the extended improvisation that was central to so much of the city's psychedelic music.

Formed in 1965 by Duncan (guitars), Freiberg (bass), Elmore (drums), Murray (vocals) and guitarist Cipollina (whose godfather was **Jose Iturbi**), the group featured in the film *Revolution* (1968) alongside other San Francisco musicians **Steve Miller** and Country Joe and the Fish (whose leader was **Country Joe McDonald**). However, by the time of the film's release, Murray had left the group and as a foursome they signed to Capitol. The eponymous début album (1968) featured extended numbers like 'The Fool', but showed them uneasy in the studio. Accordingly they recorded most of *Happy Trails*, their most successful album, live.

The band was then ruptured when Valenti, who was originally to have been the group's lead guitarist before a jail sentence, formed the shortlived Outlaws with Duncan. The latter was replaced by pianist Hopkins, best known for his work with the **Rolling Stones**, for the minor *Shady Grove* (1969). Valenti (who as Chester A. Powers had written 'Hey Joe', which was memorably recorded by the **Byrds**, **Love** and **Jimi Hendrix**, among others, and was a chart hit for the Leaves on Mira in 1966, and 'Get Together', a hit for the **Youngbloods**, RCA, 1969) rejoined Quicksilver with Duncan for *Just for Love* (1970), their most commercially successful album. By the time of *What About Me*, made without either Cipollina or Hopkins, Valenti was the undisputed leader of the group that had the minor US hit 'Fresh Air' (1970).

Cipollina formed the shortlived Copperhead, who recorded an eponymous album on Columbia (1973), and in 1971 Freiberg left to join Jefferson Starship. Quicksilver recorded two further undistinguished albums (*Quicksilver*, 1972, and *Comin' Thru*, 1973) with pick-up musicians, before in 1975 Cipollina and Freiberg re-formed the group for *Solid Silver*. The guitarist subsequently recorded with such artists as Man, Nick Gravenites and former **Country Joe McDonald** guitarist Barry Melton. His death was associated with emphysema. In the eighties Quicksilver Messenger Service lived on as a Gary Duncan-led group which recorded in 1987, but this incarnation had little to do with the original group, which found a new generation of fans with the reissue of the early albums and compilations, such as *Sons of Mercury* (1994) and *The Ultimate Journey* (1995).

FREDDY QUINN
b. Manfred Petz, 1932, Vienna, Austria

Known simply as Freddy, singer and actor Quinn was the most successful German singer of the fifties and sixties, selling more than 20 million records, even though, like Adriano Celentano, **Johnny Hallyday**, Heintje and Raphael, he remained largely unknown outside continental Europe.

His childhood was dominated by the disruption of war. In 1945 he escaped to Belgium and supported himself by working for Amercian GIs before travelling Europe as a member of a circus. In 1951 he worked as a merchant seaman and in 1953 settled in Germany and began singing as Freddy Quinn. His first big hit was a German-language version of **Dean Martin**'s 1955 million-selling hit 'Memories Are Made of This', 'Heimweh'* (Polydor) in 1956. Other hits include 'Heimatalos'* (1958), co-written by Lotar Olias (who wrote or co-wrote virtually all his songs), the film theme 'Die Gitarre und das Meer'* (1959), 'Unter Freemden Sternen'* (1960), and a revival of one of the best-known tango tunes ever, Sebastian Yradier's 1877 composition 'La Palomo'* (1961). In 1962 he had a hit with 'Junge Komm Bald Weider'* (1962) from the musical *Homesick for St Pauli*, in which he also appeared. An English-language version of the song was released in the United States in 1963 as 'Son Come Home Soon'. Another hit was the dramatic ballad 'Vergangen, Vergessen, Vorueber'* (1964).

Quinn also appeared in more than ten films.

RADIOHEAD

Colin Greenwood, b. 26 June 1969, Oxford, England;
Jonny Greenwood, b. 5 November 1971, Oxford; Ed
O'Brien, b. 15 April 1968, Oxford; Phil Selway, b. 23 May
1967, Hemingford Grey, Cambridgeshire; Thom Yorke,
b. 7 October 1968, Wellingborough, Northamptonshire

After relatively inauspicious beginnings as a **U2**-
inspired quintet stigmatized by the self-loathing of
their 'Creep' single, Radiohead found themselves
credited with reinventing the modern rock genre on
OK Computer (1997).

Singer-songwriter Yorke, guitarist O'Brien, bassist
Colin Greenwood and drummer Selway began playing together as On a Friday in 1987 after meeting at
sixth-form college in Oxford, England, but didn't
decide to pursue music as a career until the early
nineties, at which point they recruited younger
Greenwood sibling Jonny (guitar/keyboards). Renaming themselves Radiohead, the band earned a deal
with Parlophone in 1993 for the release of their début,
Pablo Honey. The album was ignored until the
grungey 'Creep' became a hit in the US, pushing
worldwide sales close to one million. This proved to
be a double-edged sword, however, as the band were
soon written off as one-hit wonders.

The lead track on the *My Iron Lung* EP (1994), with
its intricate guitar layering and schizophrenic dynamics, was the first indication that Radiohead were a band
of note. By this time they had also become a powerful
live act. *The Bends* (1995) was hailed as a flawed masterpiece on its release and drew comparisons with
R.E.M., whom Radiohead were to support when they
toured Europe later that year. The album sold well
internationally on the strength of the singles 'High and
Dry', 'Fake Plastic Trees', 'Just' and 'Street Spirit (Fade
Out)' as the band embarked on an eighteen-month
world tour.

After contributing 'Lucky' to *Help* (1995), released
in support of the War Child charity, Radiohead
released their third album, *OK Computer* (1997).
Instantly declared a classic of modern times, the
album was an inventive blend of **The Beatles** and DJ
Shadow, swathed in washes of effects-laden guitar and
keyboards. 'Paranoid Android', likened to **Queen**'s
'Bohemian Rhapsody' for its elaborate structure and
choral arrangement, narrowly missed topping the UK
chart, while the album sold five million copies worldwide and saw the band nominated for two Grammys
and four Brit Awards. Radiohead were lavished with

further praise for *Meeting People Is Easy* (1998), an
on-the-road documentary directed by Grant Gee.
They followed that with *Kid A* (2000), a determinedly
experimental outing that reprised the themes of *OK
Computer* – alienation and isolation – but without
either the guitar pyrotechnics or vocal grandeur of
that album. Deemed disappointing by many, the
album was a step away from the progressive-rock
stylings of its predecessor, with songs ranging from
the sparse, Rhodes-driven opener 'Everything in its
Right Place' to the horn-led cacophony of 'The
National Anthem' and the breakbeat-driven
'Idioteque'. The album was also notable for the
unusual methods of promotion employed by the
band: no singles were issued and neither were there
any promotional video clips or photo shoots. Instead
the band issued a series of digitally altered portraits
and a collection of 'blips' – short animated advertisements set to excerpts from the album and shown on
music television programming and over the internet.

GERRY RAFFERTY
b. 16 April 1947, Paisley, Scotland

Rafferty is a singer and songwriter capable of combining memorable melodies with well-crafted lyrics, in
the manner of **Paul McCartney**. His blend of folk and
rock influences was most successful in the seventies
with the group Stealer's Wheel and with his international solo hit 'Baker Street'* (1978).

During the early sixties Rafferty was lead singer
with semi-professional Paisley beat groups the Censors and the Mavericks. As he began to write songs, he
moved into the Scottish folk-club circuit, joining Billy
Connolly in the Humblebums. They recorded *Humblebums* (Transatlantic, 1969) and *Open up the Door*
(1970) before splitting up. Connolly went on to a
career as a stand-up comic, cutting albums for
Transatlantic, Polydor and Virgin and reaching No. 1
in Britain with a parody of **Tammy Wynette**'s
'D.I.V.O.R.C.E.' (Polydor, 1975).

Rafferty next cut a solo album, *Can I Have My
Money Back?* (Transatlantic, 1971). Produced by Hugh
Murphy, it had a soft-rock sound and several of the
backing musicians went on to form the nucleus of
Stealer's Wheel. Chief among them was Joe Egan, a
former Maverick, who co-wrote with Rafferty 'Stuck
in the Middle with You' (A&M, 1973). With vocal harmonies mixing the **Everly Brothers** and **Bob Dylan**'s
nasal intonation, the single was a Top Ten hit on both

sides of the Atlantic. The song was taken from *Stealer's Wheel*, which like *Ferguslie Park* (1974) was produced by **Leiber and Stoller**. 'Star' from the latter was a Top Twenty American hit but *Right or Wrong* (1975) made little impact. The distinctive sleeve designs of the Stealer's Wheel albums were drawn by another Paisley alumnus, John Patrick Byrne, who later wrote the acclaimed teleseries *Tutti Frutti* (1987).

Contractual and management problems led to the duo splitting up and a hiatus in Rafferty's recording career. He returned in 1978 with the Murphy-produced *City to City* (United Artists), which included 'Baker Street' with its stirring sax solo by Raphael Ravenscroft and lyrics of big-city alienation. The album provided further American hits in 'Right Down the Line' and 'Home and Dry'. Egan released the unsuccessful *Out of Nowhere* (Ariola, 1979), produced by **Leo Sayer**'s songwriting partner, David Courtney.

Rafferty's chart success continued with *Night Owl* (1979), whose title track was a British hit, while 'Days Gone Down' and 'Get It Right Next Time' reached the American Top Twenty. *Snakes and Ladders* (1980) included the powerful social comment of 'The Garden of England' and was a Top Twenty hit in Britain, but *Sleepwalking* (Liberty, 1982) sold poorly.

Rafferty spent the mid-eighties away from the limelight but returned to produce (with Murphy) 'Letter from America' (Chrysalis, 1987) by the Scottish duo the Proclaimers. The following year he released *North and South* (London), an album whose songs, including the autobiographical 'Shipyard Town', showed a renewed emphasis on Rafferty's Celtic roots. Later albums included *A Wing and a Prayer* (1993), another stylish collection, and *Over My Head* (1995). *One More Dream* (1995) is the definitive compilation.

JERRY RAGAVOY
b. 1935, Philadelphia, Pennsylvania, USA

A master of deep soul music, Ragavoy wrote and produced classics of the genre by Garnet Mimms, Lorraine Ellison, **Howard Tate** and others in the sixties.

Of Italian extraction, Ragavoy wrote his first song at the age of eight. He absorbed black music working in a ghetto record store, where he discovered vocal group the Castelles. With shopowner Herb Slotkin, he formed Grand Records to release tracks by the group. After 'My Girl Awaits Me' (1954) was a minor hit, Ragavoy wrote 'This Silver Ring' for the group.

Leaving Grand, Ragavoy took time off to study piano and absorbed classical music influences which would colour his later string-filled orchestrations. In the early sixties he worked as an arranger ('Disappointed', Claudine Clark, Chancellor, 1962) before he co-wrote (with Ed Marshall, author of **Frankie Avalon**'s 'Venus') and produced his first hit, the falsetto-led 'Wonderful

Dream' by the Majors (Imperial, 1962).

At the same time Ragavoy met **Bert Berns**, with whom he wrote 'Cry Baby'. Mimms' impassioned recording included backing vocals by **Dionne Warwick** and Cissy and Thelma Houston, mother and aunt of **Whitney Houston**. A Top Ten hit on United Artists in 1963, the song was memorably revived in 1969 by **Janis Joplin**.

Now established in New York, Ragavoy created such later hits as 'Baby Don't You Weep' for Mimms while working with **Aretha Franklin**'s sister Erma ('Piece of My Heart', Shout, 1967 – another song covered by Joplin), Irma Thomas ('Time Is on My Side', 1964, first recorded by trombonist Kai Winding and a big hit for the **Rolling Stones**) and **Gene Pitney** ('Mecca', 1963). In 1966 he became East Coast A&R chief for Warners, recording the Enchanters, Roy Redmond and Lorraine Ellison for Loma.

A former pop-gospel singer with the Golden Chords, Ellison's finest moment was the transcendent 'Stay with Me Baby' on which Ragavoy pitted her soaring, pleading soprano against a forty-six-piece orchestra that had initially been booked for a **Frank Sinatra** session. Although only a minor hit, this soul aria was the most complete realization of Ragavoy's orchestral approach and was the third of his productions to be taken up by Janis Joplin. Ragavoy also produced Ellison's *Heart and Soul* and *Stay with Me* (1969).

For Howard Tate, Ragavoy wrote the mournful, atmospheric 'Ain't Nobody Home' (Verve, 1966) and 'Look at Granny Run Run', later recorded by **Ry Cooder**. He also produced **Miriam Makeba**'s 'Pata Pata' (Reprise, 1967). In 1969 Ragavoy opened his Hit Factory recording studio and in 1973 set up the short-lived Rags label.

He continued to write and produce throughout the seventies. Among those with whom he worked were **Paul Butterfield** (*Keep on Moving*, 1969), Tate (*Burglar*, Atlantic, 1972), **Bonnie Raitt** (*Streetlights*, 1974), Warwick (*Then Came You*, 1975), Major Harris (*How Do You Take Your Love*, RCA, 1978) and Peggy Blue (*I Got Love*, MCA, 1980).

RAGE AGAINST THE MACHINE
Tim Commerford, b. Irvine, California, USA; Tom Morello, b. 30 May 1964, New York; Zach de la Rocha, b. 1967, Irvine, California; Brad Wilk, b. 5 September 1968, Portland, Oregon

Highly politicized, LA-based quartet Rage Against the Machine were one of the first bands to successfully blend rock and hip-hop, becoming one of the most popular guitar bands of the nineties in the US in the process.

They came together in 1991 when de la Rocha

(vocals), Commerford (bass), Morello (guitar) and Wilk (drums), all veterans of the LA music scene, began to earn a loyal fanbase on the south coast with their highly political blend of rap, metal and punk. Signing to Epic the following year, they released their eponymous début, a selection of radical assaults on the state of the nation, the cover of which was a provocative image of a Buddhist monk's self-immolation. By 1994 the album had achieved platinum status on the strength of the singles 'Freedom' and 'Killing in the Name', inspiring a whole genre of new bands.

Rage Against the Machine's long-awaited second album, *Evil Empire* (1996), entered the *Billboard* chart at number one after the band caused controversy by hanging upside-down US flags on their amplifiers for a performance of the hit single 'Bulls on Parade' on *Saturday Night Live*. Having concluded a lengthy world tour in 1997, Rage Against the Machine concentrated their energies on political activity, campaigning and performing at benefits in favour of the exploitation of workers and a variety of oppressed minorities.

MA RAINEY

b. Gertrude Melissa Nix Pridgett, 26 April 1886, Columbus, Georgia, USA, d. 22 December 1939, Georgia

The first of the great women blues singers, Rainey was a direct influence on **Bessie Smith** and others. Her recordings of the twenties, on which her accompanists included **Louis Armstrong** and **Thomas A. Dorsey**, were among the biggest-sellers of the era.

A child of entertainers, she worked in the touring tent shows of the South, marrying Will Rainey in 1904. The couple toured as 'The Assassinators of the Blues' and, after they separated, Ma Rainey worked with such troupes as the Rabbit Foot and Al Gaines' Minstrels before forming her own touring show. The climax of the show occurred when Rainey stepped from a giant phonograph to join her Georgia Jazz Band, a group led by pianist Georgia Tom, later the gospel-music pioneer Thomas A. Dorsey.

Beginning as a singer of minstrel and vaudeville material, Rainey claimed to have first heard the blues in Missouri in 1902. By the time she cut her first records for Paramount, her repertoire was dominated by the genre. Between 1923 and 1929 Rainey cut nearly a hundred titles, including her best-known songs 'See See Rider Blues' (with Armstrong and **Fletcher Henderson** on piano), 'Oh My Babe Blues' (with **Coleman Hawkins**), 'Shave 'Em Dry' and 'Deep Moanin' Blues' (with Dorsey and guitarist Tampa Red).

The Depression ended both her recording career and her travelling show. After touring for three years with Boise de Legge's Bandana Babes, Rainey retired from showbusiness in 1933. Most of her recordings were later reissued in album form, but they suffer from the notoriously poor quality of Paramount's studio recordings and 78 r.p.m. pressings. In 1984 she was the subject of the Broadway play *Ma Rainey's Black Bottom*.

MARVIN RAINWATER

b. Marvin Percy, 2 July 1925, Wichita, Kansas, USA

A big-voiced singer in the manner of **Frankie Laine**, Rainwater had five million-selling records in the late fifties in addition to his best-remembered hit, the rock'n'roll-inflected 'Whole Lotta Woman' (1958).

A full-blooded Cherokee Indian (who regularly performed in Indian head-dress), Rainwater took his mother's maiden name when he began singing professionally on his discharge from the navy in 1945. In 1946 he joined **Red Foley** on his *Ozark Jubilee Radio Show* as a regular guest, and after a run of appearances on the **Arthur Godfrey** *Talent Scouts* TV show was signed to MGM in 1955. His second MGM release was the self-penned 'Gonna Find Me a Bluebird'* (1956). In 1957 he duetted with **Connie Francis** on 'Majesty of Love'* and in 1958 topped the British charts with the emphatic 'Whole Lotta Woman'. His banner year was 1959, when he had hits with 'My Love Is Real'*, his own 'My Brand of Blues' and one of **John D. Loudermilk**'s early compositions, 'Half-Breed'.

In 1960 Rainwater left MGM to record for Warners, United Artists and his own Brave Records with little success and in the mid-sixties suffered a throat infection that caused him to stop singing for several years. *Classic Recordings* (Bear Family, 1992) is the definitive anthology.

BONNIE RAITT

b. 8 November 1949, Los Angeles, California, USA

One of the best female singers of the seventies and eighties, Raitt's work benefited from her use of blues and folk mannerisms not as decoration but as a means of interpreting and giving emotional depth to the songs she recorded. The classic example of this process is her moving, definitive version of Eric Kaz's oft-recorded 'Love Has No Pride' on *Give It Up*. Although her approach had not markedly changed, Raitt found a new mass audience for her work in the nineties.

The daughter of John Raitt, who appeared in the original production of several Broadway musicals, including **Rodgers and Hammerstein**'s *Carousel* (1945) and *The Pajama Game* (1954), Raitt was raised in Los Angeles. She went to Radcliffe College in Boston in 1967 and became part of the local folk and blues scene, performing alongside **Howlin' Wolf**, **Fred McDowell** and **Sippie Wallace** (who was a major influence), among others. Signed to Warners, she released an eponymous début album in 1971; the album featured her own bottleneck guitar and support from bluesman **Junior Wells**, **Jimmy Reed**'s brother A.C. and Freebo (who played fretless bass on all her early albums), and songs by **Robert Johnson** ('Walking Blues') and Wallace (a memorable version of 'Woman Be Wise'), performed in a sensitive, emotional blues style. It was followed by the classic *Give It Up* (1972) which saw her extending her range as a writer ('Nothing Seems to Matter') and singer ('Love Has No Pride', 'Stayed Too Long at the Fair'). However, the album's intimate feel did not prevent her from dedicating it 'to the people of North Vietnam'.

Taking My Time (1973) saw a further shift from acoustic to electric instrumentation with support from **Taj Mahal**, **Van Dyke Parks**, and Bill Payne and Lowell George from **Little Feat**. It contained songs from **Jackson Browne** ('I Thought I Was a Child') and **Randy Newman** ('Guilty'), alongside material by McDowell, **Mose Allison** and others. Although *Taking My Time* was a moderate commercial success, Warners set about attempting to broaden Raitt's audience with a series of artistically miscalculated albums. The first of these was *Streetlights* (1974), which was overproduced by **Jerry Ragavoy**, his slick arrangements leaving little space for Raitt's expressive voice. *Home Plate* (1975) was partially redeemed by versions of **Allen Toussaint**'s 'What Do You Want the Girl to Do' and former **Eagle** J. D. Souther's 'Run Like a Thief'. *Sweet Forgiveness* (1977) included her revival of **Del Shannon**'s 'Runaway', her only hit single, and was her biggest-selling album, while *The Glow* (1979) saw producer Peter Asher try to prettify her voice in the manner of his work with **Linda Ronstadt**.

A founder member of Musicians United for Safe Energy, Raitt appeared at the 1979 Madison Square Garden concert organized by Jackson Browne. Her 1982 album *Green Light* saw a return to a live sound with support from ex-**Small Faces** Ian McLagen. After that, despite successful tours, Raitt was dropped by Warners, returning only for the restrained *Nine Lives* (1986), part of which had been recorded in 1983. It included another Eric Kaz song, 'Angel'. Far better was the Grammy-winning *Nick of Time* (Capitol, 1989) made in the year she duetted with **John Lee Hooker** on his 1949 classic 'I'm in the Mood for Love' on *The Healer*. *Nick of Time* was a slow but steady seller, topping the American albums chart exactly a year after its release. It finally established Raitt as a major act. Among the best things on the album were **John Hiatt**'s 'Thing Called Love' and Michael Ruff's 'Cry on My Shoulder'. Following its success, Warner issued the compilation album *The Bonnie Raitt Collection* (1993).

While in the past her mature love songs had seemed out of fashion and various producers had tried to smooth out her sound, on *Nick of Time* Raitt's image of a strong, independent, sensual woman and the sound (courtesy of producer **Don Was**) fitted perfectly. 1990's *Luck of the Draw* repeated the formula of *Nick of Time*, adding yearning ('I Can't Make You Love Me' by Nashville writers Mike Reid and Allen Shamblin) to the mix of emotions she confidently explored. *Longing in Their Hearts* (1994), rather more raucous than her previous hits, rose equally effortlessly to the top of the American charts. It included a fine rendition of **Richard Thompson**'s 'Dimming of the Day'. *Road Tested* (1995) was a lesser live outing; far better was *Fundamental* (1998).

Throughout the nineties Raitt made guest appearances on several albums, including **Willie Nelson**'s *Across the Borderline* (joining him on a fine version of 'Getting Over You'), *A Tribute to Stevie Ray Vaughan* (1996) and *The Songs of Pete Seeger* (1998). Raitt was also a board member of the Rhythm and Blues Foundation, set up to benefit needy musicians.

THE RAMONES

Dee Dee Ramone, b. Douglas Colvin, 18 September 1952, Fort Lee, Virginia, USA (replaced by CJ Ramone, b. 1965); Joey Ramone, b. Jeffrey Hyman, 19 May 1952, Forest Hills, New York, USA; Johnny Ramone, b. John Cummings, 8 October 1951, New York City, USA; Tommy Ramone, b. Thomas Erdelyi, 29 January 1952, Budapest, Hungary (replaced by Marky Ramone, b. Marc Bell); Ritchie Ramone, b. Richard Beau

The stripped-down buzz-saw guitar sound and breathless tempo of the Ramones' music was one of the most important foundation stones of seventies punk rock. The band's off-beat humour carried them through to the mid-nineties.

Formed in 1974 with Dee Dee and Johnny on bass and guitar, respectively, plus Joey on drums, the band's early line-up was completed when Tommy took over on drums, allowing Joey to concentrate on singing. One of the founders of punk, the group became one of the cult bands appearing at CBGBs in New York, finishing their act with the catchphrase cry, 'gabba gabba hey'. They were signed by Seymour Stein to his Sire label and released *Ramones* in 1976. The tracks, including 'Now I Wanna Sniff Some Glue' and 'Blitzkrieg Bop', were strip-cartoon versions of sub-cultural life and had an average length of under two minutes.

Ramones Leave Home (1976) included parodic lyrics ('You're Gonna Kill That Girl') and nostalgic ones ('Oh Oh I Love Her So'), and in 1977 the group released the anthemic 'Sheena Is a Punk Rocker' from *Rocket to Russia*, a Top Thirty hit in Britain, where the group had toured the previous year. The band's first four studio albums and the definitive in-concert set

It's *Alive* (1979) were co-produced by Tommy Erdelyi/ Ramone, who left the band after the 1978 British tour captured on the live album, to be replaced by Bell, formerly in ex-**Television** bassist Richard Hell's band, the Voidoids.

With the decline of punk, the Ramones' records became more orthodox. *Road to Ruin* (1978) had songs lasting more than three minutes and a cover of the **Searchers**' 1964 hit 'Needles and Pins', while **Phil Spector** was brought in to produce *End of the Century* (1980) with its British hit, 'Baby I Love You', a revival of the **Ronettes** hit (also produced by Spector). Spector had previously worked on the band's contributions to the soundtrack of the film *Rock'n'Roll High School* (1979), in which they also appeared. Former **10CC** member Graham Gouldman supervised *Pleasant Dreams* (1981) and the producer of *Subterranean Jungle* (1983) was Ritchie Cordell, who had been responsible for the hits of **Tommy James and the Shondells**. The latter album included the quirky 'Everytime I Eat Vegetables I Think of You' and featured a guest appearance from guitarist Walter Lure, formerly with (ex-**New York Dolls** guitarist) Johnny Thunders' Heartbreakers. After its release, Marky left the band, replaced by Ritchie, formerly of New York band the Velveteens.

The Ramones found a new popularity in the mid-eighties through *Too Tough to Die* (Beggars Banquet, 1985), which was produced by Erdelyi and Ed Stasium and won prizes at the New York Music Awards as did their witty parody of USA for Africa's 'We Are the World' video which accompanied 'Something to Believe in', a single taken from *Animal Boy* (1986). *Halfway to Sanity* featured a guest appearance by Debbie Harry (of **Blondie**), and was Richie's last album with the band. Marky rejoined for *Brain Drain* (1989), the first release under a new deal with Chrysalis, produced by **Bill Laswell**. It included the theme song for the Stephen King horror film *Pet Sematary*.

The Ramones entered the nineties with a solid following among heavy metal and punk fans. Dee Dee left the band for an unlikely career as a rap artist. He later formed his own rock band, the Chinese Dragons. He subsequently returned to the verities of straight-ahead rock'n'roll with a series of solo albums. The best of these was the Chris Spedding-produced *Hop Around* (Corazong, 2000) in which he express-trained through fifteen songs in 32 minutes. With CJ on bass, the Ramones toured extensively, releasing the live album *Loco Live* (1991). They released the fine *Mondo Bizarro* (1992), which contained a version of the **Doors**' 'Take It as It Comes', pointing the way towards *Acid Eaters* (1993), a complete album of their favourite songs from the sixties, including **The Who**'s 'Substitute'. Both were commercial failures, as was *Adios Amigos* (1995), and after a lengthy farewell tour the group disbanded. Joey also collaborated with General Johnson (of **Chairman of the Board**) on 'Rockaway Beach (On the Beach)', a 'beach music' track.

SHABBA RANKS
b. Rexton Fernando Gordon, 17 January 1966, Sturgetown, Jamaica, West Indies

As Jamaican dancehall and ragga styles began to find favour with the dance music and rap aficionados of London and New York, big record companies began to consider their potential as crossover styles. The charismatic and tough-talking Shabba Ranks was one of the first exponents of the new Jamaican music to be promoted to international pop audiences.

As DJ Don he had worked in the clubs of Kingston before making his first commercial recordings with Jammys and Bobby Digital. He took the name Shabba Ranks from a notorious Kingston underworld figure. Incorporating rap elements, his first local hits on the Digital B label included 'Best Baby Girl', 'Get Up Stand Up' and 'Wicked in Bed'. Like most of his contemporaries he eschewed the 'culture' (religious, social and political) themes associated with the **Bob Marley** reggae generation in favour of 'slackness' (sexual explicitness and obscenity).

His early hits were issued by UK label Greensleeves in 1990 on *Golden Touch*, while *Rapping with the Ladies* included duets with such singers as Deborah Glasgowe, Krystal and J. C. Lodge. By 1991 Shabba Ranks was recognized as the leading exponent of dancehall and he was in demand as a partner for UK-based artists such as **Scritti Politti** (their version of **The Beatles** 'She's a Woman') and **Maxi Priest** ('Housecall').

The latter track appeared on *As Raw as Ever* (Epic, 1991), his début album for a major label. It went on to sell over a million copies in the US. For the follow-up, *Xtra Naked* (1992), Shabba Ranks was joined by a plethora of soul and rap talent. The hit single 'Slow and Sexy' featured Johnny Gill and was produced by **Jimmy Jam and Terry Lewis** while **Queen Latifah** appeared on 'What'cha Gonna Do?' His tracks were used in the films *Deep Cover* ('Mr Loverman') and *Addams Family Values* (1993, 'Family Affair', a version of the **Sly Stone** hit).

Shabba Ranks' career development was impeded by his own 'family values', however. Homophobic remarks on a UK television show in 1992 caused him to be banned from several US appearances the following year.

TOM RAPP

On his own and with the group Pearls Before Swine, Rapp produced some of the most engaging and idiosyncratic music of the late sixties and early seventies. An evocative, painterly writer – the covers of Rapp's albums, which include paintings by Bosch, Bruegel the elder and Millais, are as revealing of his sensibilities as the sword-and-sorcery imagery of many heavy-metal bands – Rapp edged his way from the New York avant-garde towards the mainstream. However, unlike his British counterparts the **Incredible String Band**, Rapp never achieved more than a cult following.

Formed in 1967 in New York, Pearls Before Swine originally comprised Rapp, Wayne Harley, Lane Lederer and Roger Crissinger. This line-up recorded *One Nation Underground* (ESP, 1967) on which Rapp, with autoharp and clavinet prominent behind him, softly sang imagist songs about love in the abstract, in the detached fashion of **Lou Reed**. *Balaklava* (1968), described by one critic as 'acid folk', continued in the same vein with added emphasis on sound effects. For *These Things Too* (Reprise, 1969) Rapp's wife Elisabeth joined the fluctuating group and the album saw a broadening of approach, to include **Bob Dylan**'s 'I Shall Be Released'. It was followed by the classic *The Use of Ashes* (1970). Recorded in Nashville with Norbert Putnam, Charlie McCoy and Buddy Spicher among the session men, it was the most accessible of Rapp's albums. It included some of his best songs: 'The Jeweler', in which he particularized his sense of doom in the bizarre image of a jeweller trying to make pristine again the old coins brought to him; 'Rocket Man' with its quiet despair; the philosophical 'Song about a Rose'; and the evocative 'When the War Began'.

After . . . *Beautiful Lies You Could Live in* (1971), which saw the group billed as Tom Rapp/Pearls Before Swine, Rapp re-recorded much of his early material for *Familiar Songs* (1972). *Stardancer* (Blue Thumb, 1972) was the best of his later albums and included the anti-Vietnam-war song 'Fourth Day of July'. After *Sunforest* (1973) Rapp did not record for over 25 years. Then, in 1999, he released *A Journal of the Plague Year* (Woronzow) on which, as ever, he attempted a sombre literariness set against a layered landscape of despair.

Constructive Melancholy (Birdman, 1998) is the definitive retrospective.

THE RASCALS
Eddie Brigati, b. 22 October 1946; Felix Cavaliere, b. 29 November 1943; Gene Cornish, b. 14 May 1945; Dino Danelli, b. 23 July 1945

Based in New York, the Rascals were among the earliest and best of white-soul harmony groups. 'Groovin''* (1967), their most famous international hit, foreshadowed a style of ethereal R&B that would be perfected by black groups like the **Isley Brothers** and **Earth, Wind and Fire**.

Brigati (vocals), guitarist Cornish and Cavaliere (organ, vocals) had been members of Joey Dee and the Starliters, a group which came to fame through a series of dance records, including 'Peppermint Twist'* (Roulette, 1961) and a version of the Isleys' 'Shout' (1962). In 1964, with drummer Danelli (who had played with both **Lionel Hampton** and **Little Willie John**), they formed the Young Rascals.

The group were signed to Atlantic by **Ahmet Ertegun** and the dynamic, rhythmic 'Good Lovin'', produced by **Tom Dowd**, reached No. 1 in 1966. The following year **Arif Mardin** supervised 'Groovin'', which featured Brigati's soaring vocals on a song which, in its evocation of a euphoric mood, was New York's response to the new California vocal sounds of such groups as **The Mamas and the Papas** and **Harpers Bizarre**. This was followed by 'A Girl Like You' and 'How Can I Be Sure?' (1967), a 1972 British No. 1 for **David Cassidy**. Like 'Groovin'', it was a Brigati–Cavaliere composition.

Dropping the adjective 'Young', the group moved towards progressive rock and psychedelic philosophy with the 1968 albums *Once Upon a Dream, Time Peace* and *Freedom Suite* and the million-selling singles 'A Beautiful Morning' and 'People Got to Be Free', Cavaliere's response to the assassinations of Robert Kennedy and Martin Luther King and the group's third No. 1. After the 1969 hits 'See' and 'Carry Me Back', their records were less successful and with *Search and Nearness* (1970) the group explored jazz–rock fusions. The Rascals moved to Columbia and deeper into mysticism for *Peaceful World* (1971) and *Island of Real* (1972), but split up soon afterwards.

Cavaliere went on to a solo recording career with Bearsville (*Destiny*, 1975), Epic (*Treasure*, 1976, and *Castles in the Air*, 1980, which included the hit 'Only a Lonely Heart Sees') and Karambalage, the label owned by producer **Don Was**. He also produced albums by Jimmy Spheeris and **Laura Nyro**. Cornish and Danelli formed Bulldog, recording albums for MCA and Buddah; Danelli later worked with Steve Van Zandt. Danelli, Cornish and Cavaliere regrouped in 1988 for an extensive American tour. *Anthology* (Rhino, 1992) collected together their best recordings. It was followed by Cavaliere's first solo album in more than a decade, *Dreams in Motion* (1994).

THE RASPBERRIES
Eric Carmen, b. 11 August 1949, Cleveland, Ohio, USA; Wally Bryson, b. 18 July 1949, Gastonia, North Carolina; Jim Bonfanti, b. 17 December 1948, Windber, Pennsylvania; Dave Smalley, b. 10 July 1949, Oil City, Pennsylvania

Like the Knickerbockers, whose only major hit was 'Lies' (Challenge, 1966), the Raspberries were initially highly imitative of **The Beatles**. But where the Knickerbockers could only repeat the past, the Raspberries, like **Elton John**, were able to build on it, creating a dynamic pop sound that was a precursor of power pop and gave the group (and, later, lead singer Eric Carmen) a series of hits throughout the seventies and early eighties.

Formed in 1970, the group were veterans of the Cleveland rock scene which, unusually, was strongly influenced by a wide range of British groups, including the **Small Faces**, **The Who** (whose mod dress the Raspberries imitated) and the **Kinks**, as well as The Beatles. Bonfanti drummed on the Outsiders' hit 'Time Won't Let Me' (Columbia, 1966) before joining the Mods with Smalley and Bryson. With a name change to the Choir, they had a minor hit with 'It's Cold Outside' (Roulette, 1967). Carmen had recorded solo and with the Quick for Epic.

In 1971 tyro producer Jimmy Ienner signed them to Capitol and the suggestive 'Go All the Way'* (1972) from their impressive eponymous début album became their first hit. *Fresh Raspberries* (1973) included the hits 'I Wanna Be with You' and 'Let's Pretend', both written by Carmen, but after *Side Three* (1973) Bonfanti and Smalley left the band in protest at the increasingly lush sound Carmen was seeking for his romantic songs of adolescent love, and formed the shortlived Dynamite. With new members Michael McBride (previously a member of Cyrus Erie with Carmen) and Scott McCarl, the Raspberries made *Starting Over* (1974). A concept album about the joys and tribulations of stardom, it was introduced by the anthemic 'Overnight Sensation (Hit Record)' which, in contrast to the world-weariness of the **Byrds** earlier 'So You Wanna Be a Rock'n'Roll Star', succinctly summed up the aspirations of the new generation of would-be popsters in Carmen's pleading refrain 'I just wanna hit record'. However, it got no higher than the Top Twenty and the group disbanded with Carmen going solo.

With Ienner once more producing, Carmen had immediate success with the lush *angst* of 'All by Myself'* (Arista, 1976), his only British hit either with the Raspberries or solo, which typified his eponymous album. Later hits, including 'She Did It' (1978) and 'Change of Heart', saw him moving further into **Barry Manilow** territory. After a series of disappointing albums for Arista, Carmen signed with Geffen and returned to the charts in 1985 with 'I Wanna Hear It from Your Lips'. He had a further hit in 1987 with 'Hungry Eyes' (RCA), a song featured in the film *Dirty Dancing* (1986), and followed it with 'Make Me Lose Control'. He contributed 'Reason to Try' to the 1988 Olympics album *One Moment in Time* but subsequently was unable to capitalize on the revival in his fortunes.

Capitol Collectors (1991) collects together the best of their Capitol recordings to good effect.

THE RAVENS
Jimmy Ricks; Maithe Marshal; Warren Suttles; Leonard Puzey

Dubbed 'the granddaddy of the R&B groups', the Ravens, with the **Orioles**, bridged the gap between the white-orientated harmonies of the **Inkspots** and the **Mills Brothers** and the blacker sounds of the doo-wop groups that followed them. They were also responsible for popularizing the practice of vocal groups taking the names of birds. Among the many groups who followed suit were the Orioles (originally called the Vibranaires), the Robins (later the **Coasters**), the **Flamingos**, the Penguins, the Cardinals and the Larks.

Formed in 1946 in New York and as influenced by the more jazzy sounds of the Delta Rhythm Boys as by the Mills Brothers, the group recorded with only moderate success for Hub and King ('Bye Bye Baby Blues', 1947) with Marshal as lead singer, until bassist Ricks began singing lead. Their first major hit was **Jerome Kern** and Oscar Hammerstein II's 'Ole Man River' (National, 1947) – previously a hit for **Paul Robeson** – from *Show Boat*, which had just been revived on Broadway. Co-produced by Herb Abramson (later one of the founders of Atlantic), the song featured Ricks' vibrant voice over a strong rhythm. They followed it with two more show tunes, a reworking of **Kurt Weill**'s 'September Song' and **Irving Berlin**'s 'White Christmas' (1948). However, though most of their repertoire was standards ('Deep Purple', 'Summertime') and covers of current pop hits ('Count Every Star' a hit for Ray Anthony, Capitol, 1950), they occasionally covered material by other vocal groups (including the Orioles' 'It's Too Soon to Know', 1948).

Though the Ravens had little chart success in the fifties – the exceptions being the harder-edged 'I Don't Have to Ride No More' (1950) and 'Rock Me All Night Long' (Mercury, 1952) – they exerted considerable influence on the gospel-inspired groups that followed. Thus it was their version, the first by a black group, that formed the model for the **Drifters**' classic recording of 'White Christmas' in 1954, and **Clyde McPhatter**'s group the Dominoes chose to record 'Sixty Minute Man' (1951) with bass Billy Brown taking the lead, in imitation of the Ravens. In 1950 a much-changed line-up left National for Columbia, then Okeh (1951), Mercury (1952), Jubilee (1955), Argo (1956) and Savoy in 1957, where they ended their career with a coupling of 'Silent Night' and 'White Christmas'.

LOU RAWLS
b. 1 December 1937, Chicago, Illinois, USA

Like **Nat 'King' Cole**, Lou Rawls developed a successful cabaret and supperclub vocal style from a solid
base in blues, soul and jazz. With a three-octave
range, he also developed a form of rhythmic monologue in the sixties. He has released over sixty albums.

With school friend **Sam Cooke**, Rawls sang in
gospel groups the Highway QCs and the Soul Stirrers
(1955–8). After military service Rawls followed Cooke
to Los Angeles and joined the Pilgrim Travelers
before his career as a gospel singer was curtailed by a
serious car accident in 1958.

When he was able to recommence his career,
Cooke had moved on to the world of pop music and
Rawls followed suit. Aspiring producers **Herb Alpert**
and **Lou Adler** produced 'Love Love Love' (Shardee,
1959) and further singles on Candix before Rawls
signed to the West Coast's biggest label, Capitol.
There he was teamed with pianist Les McCann on
Stormy Monday (1961). In 1962 he backed Cooke on
the hit 'Bring It on Home to Me'.

His mixture of supperclub ballads, polite blues and
jazz performed with a small combo propelled Rawls
into the top rank of cabaret artists. Although his
smooth voice was well-suited to Cole-style crooning,
his gospel roots were never far from the surface and
his sixth album, *Live* (Capitol, 1966), which featured a
dynamic reading of **John D. Loudermilk**'s 'Tobacco
Road', was a Top Ten hit while 'Love Is a Hurtin'
Thing' (1966), the half-spoken 'Dead End Street'
(1967) and the **Isaac Hayes**–David Porter song 'Your
Good Thing (Is About to End)' were also highly successful. In 1967 Rawls appeared at the Monterey Pop
Festival.

At the end of the decade Rawls joined MGM for *A
Natural Man* (1971), whose title track was his only pop
hit until **Gamble and Huff** revived his recording
career by producing 'You'll Never Find Another Love
Like Mine'* (Philadelphia International, 1975), his
only British hit. Other R&B bestsellers from this
period included 'See You When I Git There' (1977)
and 'Let Me Be Good to You' (1979). Rawls also sang
on Budweiser beer commercials, even titling *When
You've Heard Lou, You've Heard It All* (1977) after the
Budweiser slogan.

In 1982 he moved to Epic, releasing *Now Is the Time*
(1982), *When the Night Comes* (1983), which was produced by **Dr Hook** producer Ron Haffkine and
included songs by Shel Silverstein, and *Close Company* (1984). In 1988 he signed to the revived Blue
Note jazz label to record such albums as *At Last*
(1990) and *Portrait of the Blues* (1993), on which he
was joined by **Buddy Guy**, **Lionel Hampton** and
Phoebe Snow. Rawls also entered television produc-

tion, working on music shows and telethons in partnership with **Dick Clark** and others. Since the eighties
he has had a promotional contract with Budweiser
beer in the United States.

JOHNNY RAY
*b. John Alvin Ray, 10 January 1927, Dallas, Oregon,
USA, d. 24 February 1990, Los Angeles*

Known as 'The Nabob of Sob' and 'Prince of Wails'
for his histrionic stage performances in which he
would often break down and cry, Ray was one of the
most controversial recording artists of the immediate
pre-rock'n'roll era. Though this approach, which
brought him three gold records, pointed back to the
exuberance of **Al Jolson** and forwards to the greater
excesses of rock'n'roll, many critics found his style
(on record as well as in live performance) distasteful
in contrast to the staid warblings of, say, **Perry Como**.
However, Ray was a more complex figure than this
suggests. He acknowledged the influence of gospel
and recorded several songs associated with black acts,
notably the 1956 million-seller 'Just Walking in the
Rain', originally recorded by the Prisonaires (Sun,
1953). Nonetheless, his records seem mannered rather
than intense. Thus his version of the **Drifters**' R&B
hit 'Such a Night' (1954), which despite being banned
for its suggestiveness in America topped the British
charts, was recorded as a straightforward dramatic
piece and lacks the wit and understanding of the lyric
of the original. After 'Cry'* (1951), issued on Columbia's Okeh subsidiary normally used by the company
for black artists, Ray was transferred to the Columbia
label and he had no more R&B hits.

Of American Indian ancestry, Ray partially lost his
hearing as a child and had to use a hearing aid. In the
forties he sang in clubs across America before, with
the help of **Lavern Baker**'s manager Al Green, he got
regular work at the Flame Club in Detroit. Signed to
Okeh, he released the self-penned 'Whiskey and Gin'
(1951), which encouraged **Mitch Miller** to give 'Cry'
to Ray to record. Supporting Ray with little more
than a strummed guitar and the cooing voices of the
Four Lads, Miller perfectly set the stage for Ray's
highly mannered expressions of anguish in which he
stretched notes and emphasized words in the manner
of **Al Hibbler**. The result was a multi-million-seller,
aided by the popularity of the B-side, Ray's own
composition, the sentimental 'The Little White
Cloud That Cried'. He followed it with a revival of
the 1927 **DeSylva, Brown and Henderson** composition 'Here I Am Broken-Hearted'* (1951) and Harry
Richman's 1930 song, 'Walking My Baby Back
Home'* (1952).

Subsequently, until 'Just Walking in the Rain'*
(1956), Ray had greater success outside America, par-

ticularly in Britain where his melodramatic style won him a large following. His British hits included 'Somebody Stole My Girl' (Philips, 1953), a pair of duets with **Doris Day** ('Ma Says, Pa Says' and 'Let's Walk Thata-Way', 1953), a revival of **Fats Waller**'s 'Ain't Misbehavin'' (1956), 'Just Walking in the Rain' and 'Yes Tonight, Josephine', a chart-topper and his last major British hit. These records saw Ray edging closer to a mainstream approach, which was confirmed by his appearance in the film *There's No Business Like Show Business* (1955) in which he played the singer who decides to become a priest and sang **Irving Berlin**'s 'Alexander's Ragtime Band' and 'If You Believe'. His chart career at an end, Ray turned to cabaret where his sobbing performances made him a regular attraction at the Las Vegas casinos throughout the sixties and seventies.

CHRIS REA
b. 4 March 1951, Middlesbrough, Cleveland, England

A rock balladeer whose best songs dwell on his North-East England roots, Rea made his greatest impact in Germany and Britain in the mid-eighties.

From an Italian–Irish background, slide guitarist Rea did not take up the instrument until the age of twenty-two. His earliest influences were Joe Walsh and **Ry Cooder** and in 1975 he joined local rock band Magdalene, which at one point included vocalist David Coverdale, later leader of **Whitesnake**. As Beautiful Losers, the band won a *Melody Maker* contest with Rea's songs.

By this time Rea had signed a solo recording contract with Michael Levy's Magnet, the label which launched Alvin Stardust's career. Produced by Gus Dudgeon, *Whatever Happened to Benny Santini?* (1978) included the big ballad 'Fool If You Think It's Over', an American Top Twenty hit on United Artists. The song was successfully revived by British singer **Elkie Brooks** in 1982.

Deltics (1979) included keyboards-players Rod Argent (formerly of the **Zombies**) and Pete Wingfield among the backing musicians but despite the minor hit 'Diamonds' (1979), neither it nor *Tennis* (1980) sold well. The next album, the Jon Kelly-produced *Chris Rea* (1982), introduced former **Jeff Beck** sideman Max Middleton (keyboards), who became a mainstay of Rea's touring band. In 1981 Rea played on **Rolling Stone** Bill Wyman's solo album and later took part in Wyman's *Willie and the Poor Boys* project.

His career regained momentum when Irish and German audiences responded to the reflective *Water Sign* (1983) and Rea undertook long club tours in Europe. *Shamrock Diaries* (1985) included the nostalgic 'Stainsby Girls' and 'Steel River', a moving account of the effects of industrial decline on his home town. It was the first of his albums to sell over a million copies throughout Europe.

On the Beach (1986) included a German song 'Auf Immer und Ewig' and a new version of the title track was a British hit in 1988. *Dancing with Strangers* (1987) included 'Loving You Again' and 'Let's Dance', which reached the British Top Twenty while *New Light Through Old Windows* (Warners, 1988) contained re-recorded versions of Rea's best-known songs. He turned to film-making with the motor-racing movie *La Passione* (1996), the soundtrack of which included a duet with **Shirley Bassey**. The title track from *The Road to Hell* (inspired by London's orbital motorway) was a Top Ten hit in 1989, and the parent album topped the British chart. *Auberge* (1991) was another commercial success. Rea's later albums included *God's Great Banana Skin* (1992) and *Espresso Logic* (1993), which was almost too tasteful with its mix of pessimism and related accompaniment. *The Best of Chris Rea* (1994) is the best of the several compilations of his work. After the lesser *The Blue Café* (1998), Rea made the mistake of appearing in the Michael Winner film *Parting Shots* (1999). He returned to form with the relaxed *King of the Beach* (2000).

RED HOT CHILI PEPPERS
Anthony Kiedis, b. 1 November 1962, Grand Rapids, Michigan, USA; Michael 'Flea' Balzary, b. 16 October 1962, Melbourne, Australia; Jack Irons, b. California, USA; Hillel Slovak, b. Israel, d. June 1988; Jack Sherman; Cliff Martinez; Chad Smith; John Frusciante; Dave Navarro

The Red Hot Chili Peppers were one of the first US acts in the mid-eighties to enjoy success with a style of music that fused elements of funk, hard rock and punk, a mixture which also brought rewards for bands like Fishbone and **Faith No More**.

Drummer Irons and guitarist Slovak had first formed a band while at school together, before teaming up with bassist Flea (the son of jazz trumpeter Walter Urban Jr) in hard rock/garage band Anthym in the early eighties. Kiedis, the son of actor Blackie Dammett, was a friend of the band, regularly acting as compère at their gigs before joining as lead vocalist. The band changed its name to the Red Hot Chili Peppers and signed to EMI in 1983, but owing to contractual difficulties neither Irons nor Slovak could appear on the eponymous début album released in 1984, their respective places being taken by Martinez and Sherman. The album was generally disappointing, but the inventiveness of the band's songwriting drew some praise and their high-octane live shows were well received. Slovak replaced Sherman (who would later unsuccessfully sue the band over his sacking) and funk veteran **George Clinton** was drafted in to produce the second album, *Freaky Styley* (1985), which concentrated on the funk/soul side of the band's material and featured ex-**James Brown** hornmen Maceo Parker and Fred Wesley. On the return of Irons the band recorded *The Uplift Mofo Party Plan* and the *Abbey Road* EP (both 1988), which attracted almost as much attention for its **Beatles** pastiche cover shot – in which the band appeared naked apart from socks over their genitals – as for its musical content. The recordings captured the band's mixture of **Jimi Hendrix**-style rock and Clinton-esque funk in its full glory.

In 1988 Slovak died from a heroin overdose, and when a distraught Irons quit the band, the Chilis' future was in some doubt. Kiedis and Balzary recruited guitarist Frusciante and drummer Smith to record *Mother's Milk* (1989), their most successful album yet. This provided them with a hit single in a version of **Stevie Wonder**'s 'Higher Ground' and established them as a major rock act. The band moved to Warner Bros for *Blood Sugar Sex Magick* (1991). Produced by hard-rock maestro **Rick Rubin**, it was a major chart success in the US and provided the group with hits in 'Under the Bridge' and 'Breaking the Girl'. The band toured extensively to promote the album, but after the Japanese leg of a world tour in 1992 Frusciante quit, replaced by Arik Marshall, who in turn was replaced by Dave Navarro, from highly rated US rock act Jane's Addiction. In late 1992 EMI released a career retrospective, the ironically titled *What Hits?*, and in early 1994 the band enjoyed a Top Ten hit in the UK with a track from *Blood Sugar . . .*, 'Give It Away'.

After appearing at Woodstock '94, the Red Hot Chili Peppers began work on their next studio album, released the following year as *One Hot Minute*. The album débuted at No. 1 on the US *Billboard* charts but failed to match the standard set by *Blood Sugar Sex Magick*. After a year-long world tour the band took a lengthy break, with Flea joining Navarro in a re-formed Jane's Addiction for a US tour and album in 1997. Navarro then announced his intention to leave the Chili Peppers to concentrate on his new solo project, Spread, prompting the return of Frusciante for *Californication* (1999). Their best-received album for some time, it displayed an engaging meld of jagged introspection and high-energy rock and included the hit singles 'Scar Tissue' and 'Around the World'.

LEON REDBONE
b. 1941 Toronto, Canada

A charming eccentric, the gruff-voiced Redbone carved out a small career for himself with spirited (but decidedly laid-back) versions of the classic songs of the twenties and thirties performed in a manner that neatly mixed pastiche with homage. But, like

Dan Hicks, another performer devoted to the past, Redbone could never enter the mainstream except as a novelty artist.

After performing in clubs in Toronto in the early seventies where he won plaudits from a number of rock stars from **Bob Dylan** to **Bonnie Raitt**, Redbone was signed by Warner. His début album, *On the Track* (1976), is his definitive statement. It includes affectionate readings of 'Sweet Mama Hurry Home', **Fats Waller**'s 'Ain't Misbehavin'' (with Joe Venuti on violin), **Hoagy Carmichael**'s 'Lazybones' and a gently funny reading of 'Polly Wolly Doodle'. The album, which featured **Don McLean** on banjo, won Redbone immediate cult status and sold moderately well. *Double Time* (1977) and *Champagne Charlie* (1978) were more of the same and again sold better than expected thanks to Redbone's frequent appearances on the US network television show *Saturday Night Live*.

1981 saw Redbone on Emerald City for *From Branch to Branch*, on which he performed **Hank Williams**' 'Your Cheating Heart' and 'When You Wish upon a Star'. In 1986 he moved to August for *Red to Blue* on which **Hank Williams Jnr** and Mac Rebennack (**Dr John**) guested. Though these sold poorly Redbone was in high demand in America as a voice-over artist for television commercials and in the UK won himself a new clutch of followers when his version of 'Lazybones' was used on a television commercial for British Rail. *Christmas Island* (1989), a collection of Christmas songs, was Redbone's most camp album but *Up a Lazy River* (1992), which saw the singer surrounded by a much more layered sound, was a return to form. A further point of departure was that it included several Redbone originals.

OTIS REDDING
b. 9 September 1941, Dawson, Georgia, USA,
d. 10 December 1967, Wisconsin

One of the most original vocal stylists of the sixties, Otis Redding's emotive soul singing brought him pop as well as R&B hits. His career was cut short by his death in a plane crash.

The son of a minister, he joined Johnny Jenkins and the Pinetoppers in the late fifties and recorded the **Little Richard**-influenced 'Shout Bamalama' (Bethlehem, 1960). Other singles on Finer Arts and Alshire flopped before Redding sang his own 'These Arms of Mine' (Volt, 1963) during a Jenkins recording session at Stax in Memphis. The single was an R&B Top Twenty hit, and Redding followed up with his classic slow ballad 'Pain in My Heart', a showcase for his histrionic, baroque approach. Based on Irma Thomas's 'Ruler of My Heart' (Minit, 1962), it was only a minor pop hit but it helped to establish Redding as one of the most popular artists on the black touring circuit of the South. From the beginning, his career was guided by Phil Walden, a white Southerner who went on to manage other soul stars and set up Capricorn Records, for which the **Allman Brothers Band** recorded.

During 1964–5 Redding consolidated his reputation with 'Come to Me', 'Chained and Bound' and two of his most-covered songs, 'Mr Pitiful' and 'I've Been Loving You Too Long' (co-written with **Jerry Butler**). Both displayed the tight call-and-response interplay of voice and horns that was the hallmark of Redding's best records, while 'Loving' remains one of soul's most moving and complex love songs. It was also Redding's first Top Thirty pop hit.

'Respect' (1965) also sold well but the song's reputation rests on **Aretha Franklin**'s impassioned and dignified reading which sold a million two years later. Redding next recorded 'I Can't Turn You Loose', a raucous up-tempo song which exemplified his use of a stuttering technique to signify the overwhelming pressure of emotion on the singer. The choice of the **Rolling Stones**' 'Satisfaction' (1966) as a single was recognition of Redding's stature among white European audiences. His version of **Smokey Robinson**'s 'My Girl' had been a British hit in 1965, and his songs were quickly absorbed into the repertoire of white soul bands. A European tour in 1966 was a resounding success.

Redding did not make a similar impact on the white American market until his appearance, backed by **Booker T. and the MGs**, at the Monterey Pop Festival in 1967. Before that he released as singles three of his best slow-ballad performances. 'My Lover's Prayer' featured a sombre duet between horns and voice; 'Fa Fa Fa Fa Fa (Sad Song)' was based on a horn pattern which Redding himself sang on the advice of producer **Jerry Wexler**; his rendition of 'Try a Little Tenderness' was a startling transformation of a somewhat trite sentimental ballad written in 1932 by Harry Woods, author of 'When the Red Red Robin Comes Bob Bob Bobbin' Along'.

His biggest hit of 1967 was a cover of **Sam Cooke**'s 'Shake', taken from the album *Otis Blue*. Redding's version of **Charles Brown**'s 1947 seasonal hit 'Merry Christmas Baby' was released shortly before he and four members of his band, the Bar-Kays, died in a plane crash. Ironically, if inevitably, the first posthumous release, the elegiac '(Sittin' on) The Dock of the Bay'*, reached No. 1 in the pop charts. It had been written by Redding and Steve Cropper after the Monterey concert. A prolific recording artist, Redding left behind numerous tracks which were later issued by Atlantic. They included the joyous 'Hard to Handle', 'Love Man' and 'Tell the Truth'.

Shortly before his death Redding had formed his own label, Jotis, to issue records by new artists. He also produced his protégé Arthur Conley, whose recording of Redding's 'Sweet Soul Music' (Atlantic, 1967) was a million-seller. In 1982 the Reddings, his two sons and a nephew, released *Steamin' Hot* (Epic), which included a version of '(Sittin' on) The Dock of the Bay'.

Otis Redding's own alternate takes of that song were included on *It's Not Just Sentimental* (Stax/Ace), a collection of previously unreleased material issued in 1991. The definitive anthology is *Dock of the Bay* (1998).

HELEN REDDY
b. 25 October 1941, Melbourne, Australia

Reddy is best remembered for the self-penned 'I Am Woman'* (1972), the first of her trio of American No. 1s which became an anthem of the American women's liberation movement in the seventies.

The daughter of an actress and a comedian, Reddy first appeared on stage at the age of four and throughout her childhood toured with her parents. In 1966 she won a trip to New York in a talent contest and settled there. She had no success until she secured a contract with Capitol in 1971 and later that year she had her first chart entry with Tim Rice and **Andrew Lloyd Webber**'s 'I Don't Know How to Love Him'. In Britain the song was a minor hit for **Petula Clark** and Yvonne Elliman (MCA, 1972), who had created the role of Mary Magdalene in the original British production of *Jesus Christ Superstar*.

Reddy's breakthrough came when her rearranged version of 'I Am Woman' was used in the 'women's lib' comedy *Stand Up and Be Counted*. In retrospect an overly idealized vision of womanhood (especially when compared to more realistic descriptions of a woman's situation by country and soul singers like **Tammy Wynette** and **Millie Jackson**), the song and Reddy's bright performance captured the mood of the times. Reddy followed it with 'Peaceful' and a second No. 1, 'Delta Dawn'*, which had been a country hit for **Tanya Tucker** in 1972 and was also recorded by **Bette Midler**. Other hits of this period included 'Leave Me Alone (Ruby Red Dress)'* (1973) and 'Keep on Singing' (1974). On these she sang in a clear, straightforward manner but far more impressive was her chilling interpretation of the mysterious 'Angie Baby'* (1974). Written by Alan O'Day (who in 1977 had his own No. 1 with 'Undercover Angel' on Pacific), the song gave Reddy another American No. 1 and was her only substantial British hit.

Though she had other hits, including her version of **Leon Russell**'s 'Bluebird', 'Ain't No Way to Treat a Lady' (1975) and 'You're My World' (1977), Reddy devoted most of the late seventies to other projects. In 1975 she became the host of the television rock show *Midnight Special* and appeared in the movies *Airport '75*, *Pete's Dragon* (1975) and *Sgt Pepper's Lonely Hearts*

Club Band (1978). In 1979 she left Capitol for MCA, recording a trio of lacklustre albums, *Play Me Out* (1981), *Imagination* (1983) and *Take It Home*. She later appeared in Broadway musicals and in a one-woman show. Later recordings included *When I Dream* (1996).

DON REDMAN
b. Donald Matthew Redman, 29 July 1900, Piedmont, West Virginia, USA, d. 30 November 1964, New York City

A multi-instrumentalist and bandleader, Redman's most important contribution to jazz was as an arranger. In the mid-twenties his charts for **Fletcher Henderson** broke new ground with their sophisticated use of harmonies, counterpoint and contrasting rhythms. In the following decade he worked for nearly every major orchestra.

The son of a music teacher, he learned several wind instruments as a child although his principal instrument was the alto-sax. He studied music in Chicago and New York before joining Billy Paige's Broadway Syncopators in 1923. The following year Redman recorded with Henderson and became his staff arranger. The Henderson band's recordings of the mid-twenties opened new horizons for jazz ensemble-playing. Among Redman's contributions were 'TNT', on which **Louis Armstrong** took a memorable solo, 'Words', with its saxophone harmonies, and 'Whiteman Stomp'. Originally written for **Paul Whiteman**'s band, this featured an innovative mix of short solos and ensemble breaks.

From 1927 to 1931 Redman wrote arrangements for McKinney's Cotton Pickers, with whom he recorded (as a vocalist) 'Gee Baby Ain't I Good to You' (Victor), which became a jazz standard. The band's other major hits were 'Milenberg Joys' (1928) and 'If I Could Be with You One Hour Tonight' (1930). Redman's next move was to form his own orchestra which he led throughout the thirties, playing at Connie's Inn in New York and broadcasting regularly on the radio. The band featured singer Harlan Lattimore, who billed himself as 'the black Bing Crosby', but it also recorded such Redman classics as 'Chant of the Weed' (Brunswick, 1931), a paean to marijuana, and an arrangement of 'Sweet Sue', which used a 'swing choir' (a variation on the call-and-response style). Redman's skills on clarinet and soprano sax were displayed on tracks like 'Sophisticated Lady' (1933) and 'Tea for Two'. His composition 'How'm I Doin'?' was successfully recorded by the **Mills Brothers**. The Redman band also recorded for Bluebird ('Margie', 1939) and **Irving Mills**' Variety ('Exactly Like You', 1937).

During the thirties Redman also contributed arrangements to other orchestras, notably those of Whiteman, **Isham Jones** and **Nat Shilkret**. After dissolving his own band in 1940, he concentrated on composing and arranging, only occasionally forming bands for tours or broadcasts. Among those for whom he wrote were **Tommy Dorsey** ('Deep Purple'), **Count Basie** ('Five o'Clock Whistle'), **Harry James**, **Jimmie Lunceford** and **Ella Fitzgerald**; he was also musical director for Pearl Bailey during the fifties.

JERRY REED
b. Jerry Hubbard, 20 March 1937, Atlanta, Georgia, USA

A fast-picking country guitarist and teller of tall tales ('Amos Moses'*, 'Tupelo Mississippi Flash'), Reed wrote two of **Elvis Presley**'s best songs of the late sixties ('US Male' and 'Guitar Man'), before establishing himself as an actor with his larger-than-life persona in a number of 'good ole boy' movies.

The son of an amateur musician, Reed learned the guitar as a child and played at local dances in his teens. In 1955 he was signed to Capitol as a writer (providing **Gene Vincent** with 'Crazy Legs') and recorded in a rockabilly style for the label. After army service, he joined Columbia and in 1962 had minor country hits with the instrumentals 'Goodnight Irene' (a reworking of the **Weavers**' hit) and 'Hully Gully Guitars', before becoming a session guitarist in Nashville. Signed to RCA, he had a country hit with his own composition 'Guitar Man' (1967), which Presley recorded a year later. This led to Presley also recording Reed's 'US Male' (1968).

Reed's own records veered from fast-picking, fast-talking stories to bland ballads. The best of them was 'Amos Moses' (1972), a tale of the Alabama swamps, which was coupled with his reworking of Arthur Longbrake's novelty song 'The Preacher and the Bear', earlier a million-seller for **Arthur Collins** (1905), and a hit for **Phil Harris** (1947). 'Amos' and 'When You're Hot, You're Hot'* (1972) were Reed's only pop hits.

He cut two superior albums of guitar duets with **Chet Atkins**, *Me and Jerry* (1970) and *Jerry and Me* (1971), and had a further country No. 1 with the comic 'Lord Mr Ford' (1973), but though he continued to record intermittently – he had another country chart-topper in 1982 with 'She's Got the Goldmine (I Got the Shaft)' – Reed concentrated on films in the seventies. Among those in which he appeared are *WW and the Dixie Dance Kings* (1974), *Gator* (1976) and *Smokey the Bandit* (1977) and its sequels. His later albums include *Half & Half* (1979), on which half the songs were instrumentals, *The Interesting Jerry Reed Sings Jim Croce* (1980) and the minor *Lookin' at You* (Capitol, 1986). Far better was the album he made with Chet Atkins, *Sneakin' Around* (1992). In 1998 he formed the Old Dogs with **Bobby Bare**, **Mel Tillis** and **Waylon Jennings**, and recorded an eponymous album (Atlantic).

JIMMY REED
b. Mathis James Reed Leland, 6 September 1925, Dunleith, Mississippi, USA, d. 29 August 1976, Oakland, California

Reed's lazy, slack-jawed singing and hypnotic guitar patterns were one of the blues' most readily identifiable sounds in the fifties and sixties, and Reed one of its most popular artists.

He began to work in music in 1948, in the clubs of Chicago and nearby Gary, Indiana, with blues singer John Brim. Soon afterwards he began a long musical association with guitarist Eddie Taylor (*b. 29 January 1923, Benoit, Mississippi, d. 25 December 1985, Chicago, Illinois*), with whom he had grown up. Taylor played bass guitar, with Reed on lead guitar and harmonica, on Reed's first record, 'High and Lonesome'/'Roll and Rhumba' (Chance, 1954). This was also issued as the first single on the new Vee-Jay label, for which Reed recorded for the next eleven years. His third release, 'You Don't Have to Go', was one of the R&B hits of 1954, followed by 'Ain't That Lovin' You Baby' (1956), 'Honest I Do' (1957), 'Take out Some Insurance' (1959), 'Baby What You Want Me to Do' (1959), 'Big Boss Man' (1960), 'Bright Lights, Big City' (1961) and 'Shame Shame Shame' (1963).

From 1955 until well into the sixties Reed was a major attraction on the black circuit across America. He visited England in 1963–4 – several of his hits had been recycled by Liverpool contemporaries of **The Beatles**, as well as by other groups such as the **Rolling Stones** ('Honest I Do') – and Europe with the American Folk Blues Festival in 1968. After recording nearly forty singles and a dozen albums for Vee-Jay, he signed with ABC-Bluesway in 1965 to produce *The New Jimmy Reed Album* (1967) and four further sets. Further albums came on Roker (1970) and Blues on Blues (1971), but in the seventies his career was frequently interrupted by ill-health, and on recordings from those last years his diction is almost impenetrable and his once captivating rhythm sluggish.

His style had left a permanent impression on the blues before his death, his foremost admirers including the South Louisiana artists Slim Harpo, Silas Hogan and Lazy Lester. Harpo had Reed-like hits with 'I'm a King Bee' (Excello, 1957), later recorded by the Rolling Stones, and 'Rainin' in My Heart' (Excello, 1961).

LES REED
b. 24 July 1935, Woking, Surrey, England

The composer of 'It's Not Unusual'*, the song that established **Tom Jones**, Reed was one of the most successful British songwriters of the sixties.

The son of an amateur impresario, Reed played in local groups before doing his military service with the military band of the Royal East Kent Regiment. On his discharge he played piano with various bands before joining the **John Barry** Seven in 1958. While with Barry, Reed started writing songs. With Geoff Stephens he wrote 'Tell Me When' (a hit for the Applejacks, Decca, 1964), 'Leave a Little Love' (**Lulu**, 1965) and with Jones' manager Gordon Mills, 'It's Not Unusual'. He then teamed up with lyricist Barry Mason (*b. 12 July 1935, Wigan, Lancashire*).

Together the pair produced a lengthy series of lightweight, catchy songs, carefully written with specific artists in mind. Among these were 'Here It Comes Again' (the Fortunes, Decca, 1965), 'I'm Coming Home' and 'Delilah'* (Jones), 'The Last Waltz'*, 'Les Bicyclettes de Belsize', 'Winter World of Love' (**Engelbert Humperdinck**) and 'Everybody Knows' (the **Dave Clark Five**). Reed also maintained his partnership with Stephens, composing 'Daughter of Darkness' (Jones) and 'There's a Kind of Hush' (**Herman's Hermits**, later even more successfully revived by the **Carpenters**). With **Tony Macaulay**, he wrote 'Love Grows Where My Rosemary Goes' (Edison Lighthouse, Bell, 1970).

Mason went on to work as a solo songwriter, composing 'You Just Might See Me Cry' and singing lead on Our Kid's hit version (Polydor, 1976). He provided Jones with 'Say You'll Stay Until Tomorrow' and Demis Roussos with 'When Forever Has Gone'. He later wrote the musicals *Miranda* (1980) and *American Heroes*, which was first issued as an album (Warners, 1980, featuring former member of the **Move** Carl Wayne). In the seventies Reed moved from writing chart-orientated material to writing songs for well-established artists. Among those who have recorded his material were **Connie Francis** ('You Bring Out the Best of the Woman in Me'), **Bing Crosby** ('That's What Life Is All About', his last recording), **Teresa Brewer**, **Steve Lawrence** and **Shirley Bassey**. He also composed several scores for films, including *Girl on a Motorcycle* (1968) and *One More Time* (1969), supplied songs for *Alfie* (1966) and the remake of *The Lady Vanishes* (1979), and theme tunes for the British television series *George and Mildred* and *To the Manor Born*.

LOU REED
b. Louis Firbanks, 2 March 1943, Brooklyn, New York, USA

Reed's distinctive approach as singer and songwriter has influenced a wide range of rock artists in the seventies, eighties and nineties. His work with the **Velvet**

Underground was a vital reference point for the glam-rock of **David Bowie** (with whom Reed later collaborated) as well as colouring the stance of punk rock in the late seventies. Reed's music and demeanour also had a major effect on the art-rock scene, affecting such musicians as **Roxy Music** and **Talking Heads**. His solo catalogue of some twenty albums displays an unevenness of quality and an unnerving penchant for sudden shifts of style and approach.

After leaving the Velvet Underground in 1970, Reed signed to RCA and recorded his eponymous début album in England in 1972. It made little impact but it was followed by the successful *Transformer* (1972). Produced by Bowie and his guitarist-arranger Mick Ronson, the album included the hit single 'Walk on the Wild Side', a vignette of New York's demi-monde. The Bob Ezrin-produced *Berlin* (1973) was a powerful and disturbing song cycle about a perverse and doomed relationship.

Rock'n'Roll Animal (1974) was a concert recording which found Reed in a basic rock'n'roll mood with guitarists Dick Wagner and Steve Hunter who later joined **Alice Cooper**. (Another album from the same concerts appeared in 1975 as *Lou Reed Live*.) *Rock'n'Roll Animal* was followed by *Sally Can't Dance* (1974), which mixed soul-music influences with Reedesque lyrics on songs like 'Ennui' and 'Kill Your Sons'. Produced by former **Blood, Sweat and Tears** member Steve Katz, *Sally* was Reed's most commercially successful album, but *Metal Machine Music*, an album entirely consisting of electronic noise and feedback (1975), was his poorest seller. Reed's motive for releasing it has been cited as a move to obtain release from his contract with RCA. The reflective *Coney Island Baby* featured Reed the songwriter and soon afterwards he moved to Arista.

Rock'n'Roll Heart was a slapdash affair, but the return to the sidewalk as the setting for the bleak narratives of *Street Hassle* (1976) brought critical acclaim. After the poorly received *The Bells* (1979), Reed released *Growing up in Public* (1980), a set of stronger songs written with keyboards-player Michael Fonfara.

The eighties brought a new contract with RCA and *The Blue Mask* (1982), a collaboration with new-wave players Doane Perry and Robert Quine (guitar) and jazz-rock bassist Fernando Saunders. Perry was replaced by ex-Material drummer Fred Maher on *Legendary Hearts* (1983) and *Live in Italy* (1984). Quine was absent from the excellent *New Sensations* (1984), which preceded *Mistrial* (1986), co-produced with Saunders and which included a rap number, 'The Original Wrapper'.

In the same year Reed had a surprise hit with his film theme version of **Sam and Dave**'s 'Soul Man', sung with Sam Moore of the original duo. He ended the decade triumphantly with the widely praised *New*

York (Sire, 1989) and *Songs for Drella* (1990), a tribute to Andy Warhol, recorded with **John Cale**. A sombre work, it set the tone for 1992's *Magic and Loss*, an album of songs on the themes of death and illness inspired by the loss of two of Reed's close friends, one of whom was the songwriter **Doc Pomus**. Although sales were poor, it was critically acclaimed, as was the RCA boxed set *Between Thought and Expression*, collecting the best moments of Reed's RCA and Arista career and released simultaneously with his book of lyrics and poetry of the same name. Reed's reunion with Cale and Velvet drummer Maureen Tucker's appearance on *New York* (Reed repaid the compliment by playing on two of Tucker's own albums) paved the way for the reunion of the original Velvet Underground in 1993.

After the release of the live set *MCMXCIII* Reed returned to his solo career, issuing the eclectic *Set the Twilight Reeling* (1996). It featured the anti-republican live track 'Sex with Your Parents Part II (Motherfucker)', proving Reed still had it in him to stir up controversy. By contrast, the following year saw his 1972 composition, the sombre 'Perfect Day' (from *Transformer*), chosen by the BBC to be re-recorded for the Comic Relief charity by an all-star cast (ranging from Bowie and **U2**'s Bono to **Dr John** and opera singer Leslie Garrett). Surprisingly, the juxtaposition of moods worked and a further compilation volume, *Perfect Day: The Best of Lou Reed*, and the live recording *Perfect Night* followed in 1998. Far less successful was *Ecstasy* (2000), a hugely self-indulgent recording presenting Reed as a grumpy (rather than bemused) observer of (mostly New York) low life.

REEF

Jack Bessant, b. 19 March 1971, Wella, Somerset, England; Dominic Greensmith, b. 2 June 1970, Denby, Derbyshire; Kenwyn House, b. 1 August 1970, Tiverton, Devon; Gary Stringer, b. 18 June 1973, Litchfield, Staffordshire

Inspired by the sixties British R&B of the **Rolling Stones** and **Led Zeppelin**, Reef rose to fame in the mid-nineties with their traditional, upbeat rock, viewed by many as a positive antidote to the many bleak, downcast bands around at the time.

Stringer (vocals), House (guitar), Bessant (bass) and Greensmith (drums) met while music students in London. They formed Reef in 1993 and based themselves in the English village of Street, Somerset, a stone's throw from the site of the Glastonbury festival. After signing with Sony Reef found a degree of popularity as the main support act on **Paul Weller**'s 1994 UK tour. *Replenish* (1995) sold well after the success of 'Naked', which was the song used in a witty advert for Sony's Mini Disc system and suggested the band was American.

Reef crossed over into the mainstream with 'Place Your Hands' (1996), written about the death of Stringer's grandfather. *Glow* (1997), which had a more polished production than its predecessor, subsequently topped the British album chart before the band embarked on a successful tour of Europe and Asia. Reef then returned in 1999 with *Rides*, featuring the hit single 'I've Got Something to Say'. Less adventurous, but almost as successful, was *Getaway* (2000), the group's poppiest outing to date, particularly on songs like 'Hold on' and 'Set the Record Straight'.

DELLA REESE

b. Dellareese Taliaferro, 6 July 1932, Detroit, Michigan, USA

A ballad singer who was highly influenced by **Dinah Washington**, Reese retained more of the harder sounds of her gospel roots than most female singers of her generation.

From the age of six Reese sang in her church choir and by the age of thirteen was a member of **Mahalia Jackson**'s gospel troupe. She sang gospel for over a decade, with Jackson, **Clara Ward** and Beatrice Brown and the Inspirational Singers, among others, before in 1956 turning to secular music and securing a regular engagement in Detroit's Flame Club (where **Lavern Baker** and **Johnny Ray** had been discovered). At first she sang only standards, but under the guidance of Lee Magrid, who signed her to Jubilee in 1957 and got her a job singing with Erskine Hawkins' band, she broadened her repertoire, though, unlike many other ex-gospel singers, she rarely sang secularized versions of gospel songs. Her first Jubilee recording was 'In the Still of the Night' (1957) and her first hit later that year was 'And That Reminds Me', which led to her being signed by **Hugo and Luigi** to RCA, where she had her biggest hits. These included the R&B chart-topper 'Don't You Know'* (1959), an adaptation by Bobby Worth of 'Musetta's Waltz' from Puccini's *La Bohème*, 'Not One Minute More' (1959) and 'Someday' (1960).

Reese's new pop orientation saw her out of step with most black music, which was rediscovering its gospel roots in soul, but led to a successful career in cabaret. In the sixties she recorded with limited success for ABC and in the seventies for Avco-Embassy, where she was reunited with Hugo and Luigi. In 1980 she returned to RCA for *The Classical Della*, a collection of songs that, like 'Don't You Know', were adapted from pieces of classical music.

JIM REEVES

b. 20 August 1923, Galloway, Texas, USA, d. 31 July 1964, Nashville, Tennessee

A soft-voiced country singer best remembered for his recording of 'He'll Have to Go'*, 'Gentleman Jim' Reeves' career is a testament to the power of death as a promotional device: after his death in a plane crash, sales of his records increased considerably.

Raised on a farm, Reeves made his first radio broadcast at the age of nine, but initially attempted a career in sport. When an injury ended his baseball days in 1947, he became a deejay and started performing throughout East Texas, briefly becoming a sideman with **Moon Mullican**. In 1949 he recorded for the Macy label.and in 1952 joined Abbott, for whom he had his first major country hits 'Mexican Joe'* and 'Bimbo'* (1953). They were straightforward country songs but his recordings for RCA (which he joined in 1955) saw him following **Eddy Arnold** in edging towards the pop mainstream with **Chet Atkins**' 'Nashville sound'. This was particularly noticeable on his first major RCA hit, 'Four Walls'* (1957), on which strings and choruses replaced fiddle and steel guitar and Reeves' voice was warmer and lower. Much better, and more interesting, was his recording of 'He'll Have to Go' (1959). The song, written by Joe and Audrey Allison, was firmly set in the honky-tonk milieu but the performance (in contrast to his earlier country hit of that year, **Roger Miller**'s 'Billy Bayou'), was pure pop with Reeves intoning his love with velvet softness. It presaged a series of similarly styled offerings, the most notable being a revival of 'I Love You Because'* (which though by a country songwriter, Leon Payne, had earlier been a pop hit for **Al Martino** in 1963), 'Welcome to My World' (both 1964) and 'Distant Drums', released in 1966 after his death. Reeves was also one of the first country stars to record an album composed entirely of pop songs, *A Touch of Velvet* (1961).

Reeves was popular throughout Africa, particularly in Nigeria (where, along with such singers as **Kitty Wells**, he was known as a 'sentimental artist') and in South Africa, where he toured with Atkins and **Floyd Cramer** in 1962. He returned there in 1963 to film *Kimberley Jim*. Reeves' posthumous success in the country charts continued throughout the sixties and seventies and he even charted in the eighties with electronically created duets with Deborah Allen ('Take Me in Your Arms and Hold Me', 1980) and **Patsy Cline** ('Have You Ever Been Lonely', 1981).

DJANGO REINHARDT

b. Jean Baptiste Reinhardt, 23 January 1910, Liverchies, Belgium, d. 16 May 1953, Samois, France

One of the early masters of the jazz guitar, Reinhardt was both a superb technician and an original improviser. The first great European jazz musician, he influenced almost all later practitioners of the instrument, through his recordings with violinist **Stephane Grappelli**.

From a gypsy family, he travelled throughout Europe and North Africa as a child before settling near Paris. He learned violin, banjo and guitar, and played in clubs and cafés from 1923. Reinhardt's first recording was as banjo accompanist to accordionist Jean Vaissade in 1928. He was invited to join **Jack Hylton**'s orchestra but in November 1928 lost two fingers of his left hand in a fire in his caravan. He modified his technique and developed a remarkable jazz style, primarily from listening to the records of **Joe Venuti**, **Louis Armstrong** and **Duke Ellington**. He continued to record as accompanist to singer Jean Sablon ('Rendezvous sous la Pluie', Pathe-Marconi, 1935) and bandleader Louis Vola but the turning point of his career was his meeting with Grappelli in 1934.

They formed the Quintet of the Hot Club of France with Reinhardt's brother Joseph, one of the two rhythm guitarists. With the encouragement of critic Hugues Panassie, the Quintet recorded more than fifty tracks for Decca, Gramophone and Panassie's own Swing label. Characterized by Reinhardt's dazzling single-string runs, they included both standard ballads ('Shine', 1936, **Fats Waller**'s 'Ain't Misbehavin'', 1937, and **Gus Kahn**'s 'I'll See You in My Dreams', 1939 – probably the best example of Reinhardt's improvising skill) and original compositions like 'Nuages' (1940) and 'Djangology'. He also recorded with such visiting Americans as **Coleman Hawkins** (**Hoagy Carmichael**'s 'Star Dust', 1935), violinist Eddie South ('Daphne', 1937), and trumpeter Rex Stewart ('Montmarte', 1939).

At the outbreak of war in 1939 the Quintet were in England, where Grappelli stayed until 1945. Reinhardt, however, returned to Paris, forming a new quintet that included clarinettist Hubert Rostaing and experimenting with amplified guitar. 'Moppin' the Bride' (1947) showed the influence of bebop on Reinhardt although the electric guitar work on *Django in Rome* (EMI, 1950) and other records lacked the innovatory character of his pre-war recordings. He resumed his partnership with Grappelli in 1946.

Reinhardt left his mark on numerous later acoustic jazz guitarists, among them British player Diz Disley who accompanied Grappelli in the sixties, and Birelli Lagrene, another gypsy virtuoso who recorded *Inferno* (Blue Note, 1988).

R.E.M.

Michael Stipe, b. 4 January 1960, Decatur, Georgia, USA; Peter Buck, b. 6 December 1956, Athens, Georgia; Bill Berry, b. 31 July 1958, Hibbing, Maine; Mike Mills, b. 17 December 1958, Georgia

One of the most popular rock groups of the late eighties and early nineties, R.E.M., with their thick, layered guitar sound that echoed (but only echoed) bands as various as the **Byrds** and the **Troggs** (whom R.E.M. would later work with) were also a critics' favourite from their very first recordings.

Formed in Athens in 1980 the band took the name from the acronym for Rapid Eye Movement. 'Radio Free Europe' (1981) released on the local Hib-tone label was voted best independent single of the year and led to the group being signed to IRS. The five-track *Chronic Town* (1982) saw guitarist Buck still playing too many arpeggios but provided a showcase for Stipe's weird, sometimes mumbled, lyrics. With its anthemic melodies and yearning lyrics *Murmur* (1983) was the band's breakthrough album. In its wake a re-recorded version of 'Radio Free Europe' was an American hit. *Reckoning* (1984) was another step into the mainstream: the group's sound was pared down without any loss of intensity and Stipe's songs were more conventional in form, but still mysterious. Even more commercially successful was *Fables of the Reconstruction* (1985). **Joe Boyd**'s production seemed too folksy for a group that was transforming itself into a guitar band par excellence but Stipe's meditations upon history ('Can't Get There from Here' and 'Feeling Gravity's Pull') took his songwriting to a new peak. On *Life's Rich Pageant* (1986) the shift from the Byrds to the Troggs as an influence was completed. Produced by **John Mellencamp**'s regular collaborator Don Gehman, the album caught the band looking back to a past where political activism made sense and forward to an uncertain future. However, where others preached Stipe was able to conjure ideas rather than state them.

Dead Letter Office (1987) was a collection of B-sides and cover-versions. In the same year R.E.M. released *Document*, their last album of new material for IRS. It included the catchy babble 'It's the End of the World as We Know It (I Feel Fine)' and the simple ballad 'The One I Love', a mark of how confident they had become. In 1988 IRS released a Greatest Hits (*Eponymous*) and the group released their first album for Warner, *Green*, which included the singles 'Stand' and 'Orange Crush' and their most explicitly political song to date, 'World Leader Pretend'. On 'Pop Song 89' they poked fun at themselves and their success. In between that and *Out of Time* (1991), members of the group initiated several solo projects. The most notable of these were Stipe's series of public service commercials on Aids, abortion and racism, and the rest of the group's touring and recording with **Warren Zevon** as the Hindu Love Gods. *Out of Time* confirmed the band's continued experimentation: the big guitar sound was replaced by more edgy rhythms, and harmonies (with **B-52** Kate Pierson) were foregrounded. 'Radio Song' and 'Losing My Religion' were as elliptical and ironic as ever but the denser, brooding songs like 'Me in the Honey' and 'Texarcana' were more moving.

After taking a break, in the course of which the group worked on *From Andover to Athens* (1992) for the Troggs and individual members guested on albums by the likes of **The Band**'s Robbie Robertson and **Billy Bragg**, the group returned to the fray with *Automatic for the People* (1992). Its ruminative tone was complemented by its (mostly) acoustic feel and R.E.M.'s songs remained as mysterious as ever. Most of the songs, excepting the simple satires ('Ignoreland') on Reagan's America, retained the questioning stance of earlier albums but with a gloomier touch; with 'Everybody Hurts' the band scored one of the most simply affecting hits of the decade. 1994's *Monster* was a back to basics rock album. While this stripped-down sound was less affecting than *Automatic*'s engaging acoustics, the songs, notably 'What's the Frequency' and 'I Don't Sleep, I Dream', were as powerful as ever.

R.E.M. chose to record their next album live on stage and in soundchecks as they toured *Monster*; the result, *New Adventures in Hi-Fi* (1996), was in a similar vein to its predecessor but refreshingly free of that record's sometimes overbearing guitar experimentation. It featured the **Patti Smith** collaboration 'E-Bow the Letter' amongst a trio of hit singles also including 'Electrolite' and 'Bittersweet Me'. By the time the *Monster* tour was completed, however, three of the band's quartet had been hospitalized at various points, most seriously when Berry collapsed from a cerebral aneurysm on stage in Switzerland. The band was forced to record their eleventh album as a trio after the departure of the drummer in 1997, claiming that he no longer wished to live the rock'n'roll lifestyle. *Up* (1998) was less successful commercially than the rest of the band's nineties output, taking a more sombre, keyboard-based approach reminiscent in places of Suicide and **Can**. In spite of poor sales, however, the album included several moments of beauty, notably the singles 'Suspicion' and 'Daysleeper'.

REO SPEEDWAGON

Neal Doughty, b. 29 July 1946, Evanston, Illinois, USA; Alan Gratzer, b. 9 November 1948, Syracuse, New York (replaced by Bryan Hitt, b. 5 January 1954); Terry Luttrell (replaced by Kevin Cronin, b. 6 October 1951, Evanston); Greg Philbin (replaced by Bruce Hall, b. 3 May 1953, Champaign, Illinois); Gary Richrath, b. 18 October 1949, Peoria, Illinois (replaced by Dave Amato, b. 3 March 1953); Jesse Harms, b. 6 July 1952

One of the pioneers of stadium rock, REO Speed-

wagon mixed hard-rock riffs with pop hooks and had a series of hits in the eighties, over a decade after the band's formation.

In 1968 drummer Gratzer and keyboards-player Doughty named the group after the 1911 fire-engine designed by Ransom Eli Olds and with Irving Azoff (later to become the **Eagles** manager and head of MCA Records) as manager, they grew in popularity in the Midwest. Signed to Epic, they released an eponymous début album of bar-band rock in 1971 with Luttrell on lead vocals, Richrath on guitar and bassist Philbin.

After the Paul Leka-produced *REO Two* (1972), Cronin took over as singer for the **Doobie Brothers**-influenced *Ridin' the Storm out* (1973) before being briefly replaced by Michael Murphy on *Lost in a Dream* (1974), produced by Bill Halverson. Throughout the rest of the decade, REO Speedwagon toured frequently and consolidated their position through annual album releases, which included *You Get What You Play for* (1977) and *You Can Tune a Piano But You Can't Tuna Fish* (1978).

The band's breakthrough came with the release of their tenth album, *Hi Infidelity* (1980). Starting with the No. 1 'Keep on Lovin' You'*, it produced four hit singles. 'Take It on the Run' (1981) reached the Top Ten, while both 'Don't Let Him Go' and 'In Your Letter' entered the Top Thirty. REO Speedwagon's momentum was maintained by the success of 'Keep the Fire Burnin'' and 'Sweet Time' from *Good Trouble* (1982) and the No. 1 'Can't Fight This Feeling' from *Wheels Are Turnin'* (1984).

Life as We Know It (1986) was the group's fourteenth album for Epic. It provided Top Twenty singles with 'That Ain't Love' and 'In My Dreams'. With the line-up of Doughty, Cronin and Hall augmented by ex-**Ted Nugent** band guitarist Amato, drummer Hitt and keyboards-player Harms, the band recorded the minor *The Earth, a Small Man, His Dog and a Chicken* (1990), while Richrath released his first album with his own band, *Only the Strong Survive*, in 1992. *Building the Bridge* (1996), the group's first new album in over five years, saw them moving further into power-balladry, a move that 1999's *The Ballads* confirmed.

HARRY RESER

b. 17 January 1896, Piqua, Ohio, USA, d. 27 September 1965, New York

During the twenties and thirties Reser was generally acknowledged to be the world's most accomplished banjoist. Even today his influence is felt, through his tuition books as much as his records, by players of all stringed instruments.

His first instrument was guitar, but in his teens he

switched to banjo, inspired by the instrument's pioneers Vess L. Ossman and Fred Van Eps. After gaining experience with dance bands in the Midwest, he moved to New York in 1921 and made his way into the dance-band scene there. He recorded both in bands and, from 1922, solo, playing ragtime on the tenor banjo, on tunes as difficult as Zez Confrey's piano exhibition-piece 'Kitten on the Keys'. In 1925 he began a decade-long weekly NBC radio programme. He also began a series of 'hot' recordings for Brunswick with the Six Jumping Jacks.

From the mid-thirties to mid-fifties he toured continuously and worked on a series of tutor books on banjo, guitar and ukelele techniques. His last engagement was as guitarist in the pit orchestra for the Broadway production of *Fiddler on the Roof*; he was found dead in his place one evening before the show began.

HARRY REVEL
b. 21 December 1905, London, England, d. 3 November 1958, New York, USA

Revel and lyricist Mack Gordon were one of the most prolific and successful song writing teams for films in the thirties.

Revel studied piano as a child and in his teens left home to tour Europe with a 'Hawaiian' band. He settled in Berlin in the twenties where he composed light music (the score to the operetta *Was Frauen Traumen*) before returning to London to write the music for *Andre Charlot's Revue of 1927*. At the same time he started writing American-styled pop songs (including 'I'm Going Back to Old Nebraska', co-written with American bandleader Noble Sissle, and 'Just Give the Southland to Me'). On the strength of these, he emigrated to America in 1929 and joined forces with Mack Gordon to write the all-black show *Fast and Furious* (1930) and songs for *Ziegfeld Follies of 1931*.

Gordon (*b. Morris Gittler, 21 June 1904, Warsaw, Poland, d. 1 March 1959, New York*) emigrated to America as a child and became first a boy soprano in a minstrel show and then a vaudevillian before meeting Revel, who persuaded him that songwriting was a more lucrative career. From the start, the pair were better at writing individual songs than show material. Thus, although they wrote a couple more shows before travelling to Hollywood in 1932, their first success was the pop song 'Under the Harlem Moon', a hit for **Fletcher Henderson** (Columbia), **Don Redman** (Brunswick) and violinist-bandleader Joe Rines (Victor), among others.

In Hollywood, where they worked first for Paramount (1933–6) and Fox (1936–8), the pair had immediate success with 'Did You Ever See a Dream

Walking'. Introduced by Ginger Rogers in *Sitting Pretty* (1933) and a big hit for **Eddy Duchin** and **Bing Crosby**, the song was the first of many about dreams. Others include 'With My Eyes Wide Open, I'm Dreaming' (1934), 'Afraid to Dream' (1937) and 'I've Got a Date with a Dream' (1938). The pair's best-remembered songs include 'Stay as Sweet as You Are' (1934), 'Paris in the Spring' – one of British bandleader **Ray Noble**'s first hits after moving to America (1935) – and 'Goodnight My Love' (1936). In 1942 they started organizing troop shows, after which Revel teamed up with first Morter Green and then Paul Francis Webster to write material for several films before turning to composing instrumental suites (*Music for Peace of Mind*, 1947) for his own publishing company Realm.

Gordon also formed successful partnerships with other composers. With **Harry Warren** he wrote 'Down Argentine Way' (1940) and 'I Yi Yi Yi Yi' (1941) for **Carmen Miranda**, and 'Chattanooga Choo-Choo' (1941) and 'I've Got a Girl in Kalamazoo' (1942), both of which were memorably recorded by **Glenn Miller**. The pair also wrote the oft-revived 'The More I See You' (originally recorded by **Dick Haymes** and **Harry James** in 1945) and 'There Will Never Be Another You', a hit for **Woody Herman** in 1942 and **Sammy Kaye** in 1943. Both songs provided **Chris Montez** with hits in 1966. With Joseph Myrow, Gordon wrote 'You Make Me Feel So Young', a hit for Dick Haymes in 1946 and later memorably recorded by **Frank Sinatra** (1956).

PAUL REVERE AND THE RAIDERS
Paul Revere, b. Paul Revere Dick, 7 January 1942, Boise, Ohio, USA; Mark Lindsay, b. 9 March 1942, Cambridge, Ohio; Phil Violk; Michael Smith; Drake Levin; Joe Correro, b. 19 November 1946, Greenwood, Massachusetts; Freddy Weller, b. 9 September 1947, Atlanta, Georgia; Charlie Coe, b. 19 November 1944

Like their contemporaries the **Monkees**, the Raiders were swept to success through television exposure. Thus, while their appeal was therefore primarily to teenybopper audiences (and they were much maligned by critics as a result), their records, like those of the Monkees, were among the best pop productions of their time.

Formed in Caldwell, Ohio, and known originally as the Downbeats, the group's mainstays were pianist Revere and singer/instrumentalist Lindsay, whose honking sax was the feature of their first release, 'Like Long Hair' (Gardena, 1961). In 1962, by now outfitted in the pseudo-Revolutionary War costumes that became their trademark, they moved to Portland, Oregon, and were the first rock group to be signed to Columbia. In 1963 they recorded an early rock version of **Richard Berry**'s 'Louie Louie' only to be beaten to the national charts by the Kingsmen on Wand. Though their later records were smoother sounding, none lost the defiant stance that rock'n'roll had represented in the fifties and the wave of British groups had recaptured in the sixties. In this, they were aided by producer Terry Melcher and **Barry Mann** and Cynthia Weil, who provided them with their first Top Ten successes, 'Kicks' and 'Hungry' (1966), which followed the Lindsay–Revere compositions, 'Steppin' Out' and 'Just Like Me' (1965), their first hits. The group's immediate success, however, was undisputedly the result of being chosen by **Dick Clark** to be featured regularly on his daily television show *Where the Action Is*.

Though never successful abroad, Paul Revere and the Raiders' American hits continued until 1969 when Lindsay left for a solo career, and included 'Him or Me – What's It Gonna Be?' (1967) and 'Let Me' (1969). Among the many people who were briefly Raiders was Joe Frank, who later as part of the trio Hamilton, Frank and Reynolds had a pair of million-selling singles, 'Don't Pull Your Love' (ABC, 1971) and 'Falling in Love' (Playboy, 1975).

On his own, Revere had a series of moderate hits, the best of which was 'Arizona' (1969), but the Raiders had their biggest hit (now recording without the Paul Revere prefix) when 'Indian Reservation'* (1971) was an American No. 1. Written by **John D. Loudermilk**, the protest song had earlier provided Don Fardon with Top Twenty hits in America (GNP, Crescendo, 1968) and Britain (Young Blood, 1970). Produced by Lindsay and featuring Weller on lead vocals, it marked the end of the group's hitmaking days.

Lindsay and Revere later frequently put the band back together for the rock'n'roll revival circuit. Weller, who in the sixties had written several songs with **Tommy Roe** (including 'Dizzy'*, 1968, and 'Jam Up, Jelly Tight'*, 1969), joined **Joe South**'s touring band and eventually established himself as a country singer with a string of minor hits in the seventies. These included South's 'Games People Play' and 'Another Night of Love' before he was dropped by Columbia in 1980. In 1983 Lindsay and Revere appeared with another set of Raiders for *Paul Revere Rides Again*, the same year the anthology *Kicks* was released in the UK.

DEBBIE REYNOLDS

b. *Mary Frances Reynolds, 1 April 1932, El Paso, Texas, USA*

Best remembered as the pert, fresh-faced *ingénue* of *Singing in the Rain* (1952), Reynolds made the million-selling records, 'Aba Daba Honeymoon' (1950) and 'Tammy' (1957), which revealed Hollywood's change in attitudes towards music in the course of the decade. The first was a novelty number from a family musical, the second, a sentimental theme song aimed at the new teenage audience.

Reynolds grew up in Hollywood and was signed to Warner Brothers after winning a talent contest in 1948. In 1950 she joined MGM for whom she appeared as a bright and bouncy youngster in a number of films, including *Rain* and *Two Weeks to Love*, in which she duetted on 'Aba Daba' with Carleton Carpenter. In 1956 she married crooner **Eddie Fisher**, with whom she appeared in *Bundle of Joy* (1956), but it was *Tammy and the Bachelor*, in which she played a backwoods tomboy who nurses an injured pilot back to health and falls in love with him, that brought her renewed international chart success. The film theme was also a hit for the **Ames Brothers**. In 1966 she appeared in *The Singing Nun*, a biopic about Sister Luc-Gabrielle who in 1963 had a surprise international hit and American No. 1 with 'Dominique'* (Philips), a eulogy to St Dominic, the founder of the Dominican order. Soon after the film's release the Singing Nun, as the sister had been tagged, left her Belgian convent and under her real name (Jeanine Deckers) less successfully recorded 'Glory Be to God for the Golden Pill', a song in praise of the birth-control pill.

In 1973, as her film career wound down, Reynolds appeared in the successful Broadway revival of *Irene*, the show that had introduced 'Alice Blue Gown' in 1919, and later mounted the extravagant revue *The Debbie Reynolds Show*.

BUDDY RICH

b. *Bernard Rich, 30 September 1917, New York, USA, d. 2 April 1987*

One of the most controversial jazz drummers, Rich's dazzling technique was widely recognized, although many critics regarded his work as unnecessarily brash.

The child of a vaudeville couple called Wilson and Rich, he was featured in the act as 'Baby Traps, the Drum Wonder' by the age of four. He led his own band at eleven and played his first jazz gigs with Art Shapiro and Hot Lips Page. After joining clarinettist Joe Marsala's band in 1938, where he was billed as 'the fastest drummer in the world', Rich moved into the big league of swing bands, playing with **Harry James**, **Artie Shaw** and **Tommy Dorsey**, with whose orchestra he stayed from 1941 to 1944. Rich was one of the Dorsey band's featured soloists, notably on 'Quiet Please'.

Rich became close friends with Dorsey's vocalist **Frank Sinatra** and after the drummer left the marines in 1946, Sinatra helped him to finance a Buddy Rich Big Band. The move was a financial failure and from 1947 Rich joined many of **Norman Granz**'s 'Jazz at the Philharmonic' tours, playing on numerous Verve recordings, including *Drum Battle*, a collaboration with **Gene Krupa**. In the late forties he also recorded with **Bud Powell** and **Charlie Parker**.

During the fifties Rich formed bands for tours and television shows, but his best work was done with James (1953–4 and 1956–7) and Dorsey (1954–5). He resumed his collaboration with James in 1961 and in 1966 left to form a new Buddy Rich Big Band. He maintained the big format until shortly before his death, touring throughout the United States and abroad. The band showed a strong rock influence in the rhythm section, recording for Liberty, RCA and smaller labels. Among Rich's albums were *Mercy Mercy* (Liberty, 1968), *The Roar of '74* (RCA, 1974) and *The Man from Planet Jazz* (Ronnie Scotts, 1980).

CHARLIE RICH

b. 14 December 1932, Colt, Arkansas, USA

In the course of his long career Rich, perhaps more than any other country-based artist, has suffered from being mis-labelled. In the fifties at Sun he was recorded for the most part as a would-be **Elvis Presley** ('Lonely Weekends'*, 1960), and in the sixties as either a country balladeer or novelty rock'n'roller, until finally he achieved international success in the seventies as a country crossover artist with 'Behind Closed Doors'* and 'The Most Beautiful Girl in the World'* (1973). Yet, like many country artists, Rich's roots were equally in the blues – he wrote and originally recorded 'Who Will the Next Fool Be', a Top Ten R&B hit for **Bobby Bland** in 1962 – while his playing reveals the complex interplay of jazz and cocktail-lounge piano. Furthermore, his (and his wife's) compositions, notably 'Sittin' and Thinkin'' and 'Life Has Its Little Ups and Downs', delineated the sorrows of everyday life with a rare precision.

Rich briefly studied music at the University of Arkansas and while in the air force formed the Velvetones, a jazz combo in the style of **Stan Kenton**, which featured his wife-to-be Margaret as vocalist. His reputation as a jazz pianist led to session work with Sun in 1958, but **Sam Phillips** refused to record him in his own right until Rich could play in the style of **Jerry Lee Lewis**. Early recordings ('Whirlwind', 1958) show Rich attempting this, but success came with the self-penned ballad 'Lonely Weekends', sung in the manner of Presley and all but ruined by the intrusive chorus. More sympathetic was producer **Billy Sherrill**, whose work with Rich (which included 'Fool' and 'Sittin'') highlighted the introspection of the songs and the haunted quality of his singing and piano-playing.

When Phillips closed down Sun in 1962, Rich briefly recorded for RCA's Groove subsidiary ('Big Boss Man', 1963) before moving to Smash. He had an immediate hit with **Dallas Frazier**'s novelty song 'Mohair Sam' (1965) but his other recordings saw producer Jerry Kennedy straining to recapture the sound of 'Lonely Weekends'. Rich's best recording from this period was the album *Sings Country and Western* (Hi, 1967), a selection of **Hank Williams** songs. In 1968 Rich joined Epic where he was reunited with Sherrill and had his first major country hit for some time with the smooth 'I Take It on Home' (1972). Then came the lush 'Behind Closed Doors', a perfect example of the countrypolitan trend within country music. Produced by Sherrill, it set the sound of Rich's recordings for the next few years, a sound which, though it brought Rich further success (including 'The Most Beautiful Girl in the World', 1973 – Rich's second American No. 1; 'A Very Special Love Song', 1974; and 'Every Time You Touch Me', 1975), quickly became formula ridden. In 1979, after his hits dried up, Rich joined Elektra and had success with 'I'll Wake You Up When I Get Home'. Later records were only moderately successful in the country charts but he returned to his best form with *Pictures and Paintings* (Sire, 1992), which included an atmospheric version of one of his finest songs, 'Feel Like Going Home'. The three major stages of his career are documented in three anthologies: *Lonely Weekends: the Sun Years* (Avi, 1996), *The Complete Smash Sessions* (Mercury, 1992) and *Feel Like Going Home* (Columbia, 1997).

CLIFF RICHARD

b. Harry Roger Webb, 14 October 1940, Lucknow, India

With a hit-parade career stretching over five decades, Cliff Richard has been the only British rock'n'roll star to ride the changing musical trends from the sixties through to the nineties. He has succeeded through a judicious choice of songs and an ability to frame his clear, warm and precise singing voice with arrangements which incorporated elements of most new trends in rock. His middle-of-the-road image and lifestyle have also made him one of British television's favourite rock stars.

Moving to England in 1948, Richard's musical ambitions were fired by hearing **Elvis Presley** and after a brief period with a skiffle group he formed the Drifters with drummer Terry Smart in 1957. With the addition of Ian Samwell on lead guitar, the group won a talent contest and were signed to EMI's Columbia label by **Norrie Paramor** in 1958. The first Cliff Richard and the Drifters single was a cover of Bobby Helm's American hit 'Schoolboy Crush', backed by Samwell's 'Move It'.

Aided by exposure on Radio Luxembourg and an appearance on **Jack Good**'s *Oh Boy!* television show, 'Move It' eventually reached No. 2. In demand for package tours, Richard reorganized his backing group to include guitarists Bruce Welch and Hank Marvin, later adding Jet Harris (bass). Samwell left to concentrate on songwriting, providing Richard's next hits, 'High Class Baby' (1958) and 'Mean Streak' (1959).

Richard's first film role, in *Serious Charge*, aided the success of **Lionel Bart**'s 'Living Doll' (1959), a softer beat ballad which heralded a move away from up-tempo rock'n'roll. A brief American tour helped the song into the American Top Thirty and caused a name change for Richard's backing group. Faced with legal action on behalf of the black vocal group the **Drifters**, the British band became the **Shadows**.

Over the next four years, Richard had seventeen Top Ten hits in Britain. Three of his five No. 1s ('Please Don't Tease', 1960; 'I Love You', 1960; 'Summer Holiday', 1963) were written by the Shadows, who also provided the precise guitar-based accompaniments with Marvin's clipped single-string solos. Richard's other songs came from many sources. Paramor wrote 'Voice in the Wilderness' (1960); Samwell contributed 'Fall in Love with You' (1960); 'I'm Looking out the Window' and 'Do You Wanna Dance' were revivals of hits by **Peggy Lee** and Bobby Freeman; and the composers of 'Nine Times out of Ten' (1960, **Otis Blackwell**) and 'The Young Ones' (1962, Sid Tepper and Roy Bennett) were also songwriters for Presley. Like Presley, Richard also starred in a series of youth-orientated movies, beginning with *Expresso Bongo* (1960), Sidney J. Furie's *The Young Ones* (1962) and *Summer Holiday* (1963).

The pace of Richard's career slackened only slightly during the mid-sixties with twelve Top Ten hits in the five years that climaxed with 'Congratulations' (1968), written by Bill Martin and **Phil Coulter** for the Eurovision Song Contest. The pick of the rest were the country-flavoured 'The Minute You're Gone', recorded in Nashville in 1965, 'Blue Turns to Grey' (1966), an uncharacteristic ballad from Jagger and Richard of the **Rolling Stones**, and the atmospheric 'The Day I Met Marie', composed by Marvin.

1969 saw further success with Raymond Froggatt's 'Big Ship' and 'Throw Down a Line', a duet with Marvin, but Richard's fortunes, artistically as well as commercially, took a downturn in the first half of the seventies. Most of his songs came from the chirpy end of British songwriting, notably **Mitch Murray** and Peter Callander's coy 'Goodbye Sam, Hallo Samantha', Roger Cook and **Roger Greenaway**'s 'Sunny Honey Girl' (1971), and two songs by Guy Fletcher and Doug Flett which offered nebulous politico-religious sentiments, 'Sing a Song of Freedom' (1971) and another Eurovision contender, 'Power to All Our Friends' (1973).

With Welch as producer, the dramatic 'Devil Woman'* (1976) and Terry Britten's 'Miss You Nights' (1976) marked a change in direction for Richard. Like others among his best records of the next decade, it harnessed his unimpaired vocal skills to a lyric and backing track that were contemporary without being simply modish. The 1979 No. 1 'We Don't Talk Anymore' was the beginning of a fruitful partnership with writer/producer Alan Tarney, who had first written for Richard in 1972 ('Living in Harmony').

'Devil Woman' and 'We Don't Talk Anymore' were Richard's first Top Ten hits in America and the sequence of transatlantic success continued with B. A. Robertson's 'Carrie' (1980), 'Dreamin'', 'A Little in Love' (1981) and 'Daddy's Home' (1982), a reworking of **Shep and the Limelites**' 1961 doo-wop classic. During the eighties Richard also recorded duets with **Olivia Newton-John** ('Suddenly', 1980) and Phil Everly of the **Everly Brothers** ('She Means Nothing to Me', 1983).

In 1986 his career came full circle when he participated in a parodic recording of 'Living Doll' with comedy group the Young Ones. He also took a leading role in *Time*, a musical conceived by former sixties pop idol **Dave Clark**. The 1987 album *Satisfaction Guaranteed* was again produced by Tarney. The following year 'Mistletoe and Wine' was Britain's Christmas No. 1, while Richard kept abreast of pop trends by using **Stock, Aitken and Waterman** to write and produce 'Just Don't Have the Heart'. His later hits were compiled on the million-selling *Private Collection* (1988). 1989 saw Richard notch up his 100th British hit, followed by an unlikely duet with **Van Morrison** on 'Whenever God Shines His Light' and the hit album *Stronger*.

Richard started the nineties with four hits, including the gospel song 'Saviour's Day' (the British Christmas No. 1 of 1990), and a live album recorded during a Wembley stadium concert the previous year, *From a Distance . . . The Event*. Others appearing at The Event had included the **Kalin Twins**, with whom Richard had toured in 1958. 1991's *Together with Cliff Richard* reached the British Top Ten and preceded a major British tour, which included sixteen London dates at Wembley Arena. In 1993 proof of Richard's continued appeal was provided when *The Album* topped the British chart in its first week of release. It included new songs by such writers as **Nik Kershaw** and Pete Sinfield, once of **King Crimson**.

He continued the experiment started with *Time* with *Heathcliff* (1994), a musical based on Emily Brontë's *Wuthering Heights*, which he toured Britain with to terrible notices and full houses. In 1995 he released *Songs from Heathcliff* and won equal amounts of fame and infamy for his impromptu serenading of the Centre Court audience at Wimbledon during a downpour that stopped play. For this he was supported by a bevy of tennis stars. He continued having hits in the nineties (including 'Had to Be', 1995, a duet with Olivia Newton-John from *Heathcliff*, and 'Real as I Wanna Be', 1995). However, the emphasis was on the past, as in the collections *At the Movies, 1959–1974* (1996) and the deservedly well-received *The Rock'n'roll Years* (1997). When his contract with EMI was not revived Richard turned adversity to his advantage. He turned his Chrysalis recording of 'The Millennium Prayer' – a setting of 'The Lord's Prayer' to the tune of 'Auld Lang Syne' – into a UK chart-topper despite getting no airplay, using his Christian fanbase as a marketing tool.

LIONEL RICHIE
b. Lionel Brockman Richie Jnr, 20 June 1949, Tuskegee, Alabama, USA

Former lead singer of the **Commodores**, Richie became the most popular crossover black ballad singer of the eighties, occupying a similar position to that of **Nat 'King' Cole** in the sixties and **Smokey Robinson** in the seventies.

Richie studied economics at Tuskegee Institute before becoming a full-time saxophonist, singer and writer with the Commodores in 1968. While the group's early albums for **Berry Gordy**'s Motown label were dominated by hard funk numbers, in the mid-seventies Richie's soft ballads gradually came to the fore. He wrote the American pop hits 'Sweet Love' (1976) and 'Just to Be Close to You', as well as the lush 'Easy' (1977) and 'Three Times a Lady' (1978), all of which were international million-sellers.

In 1980 Richie wrote **Kenny Rogers**' No. 1 hit 'Lady'* and the following year he duetted with **Diana Ross** on the chart-topping film theme 'Endless Love'*, described by one critic as a 'sugar-coated aria'. Soon afterwards he left the Commodores to pursue further projects as a writer, producer and singer. *Lionel Richie* (1982) included three Top Ten hits in 'Truly'*, 'You Are' and 'My Love', but *Can't Slow Down* (1983) sold 15 million worldwide and contained six American Top Ten singles among its eight tracks.

Among them were the two million-selling No. 1s, the up-tempo 'All Night Long (All Night)' and the plangent 'Hello' (1984). By now Richie was recognized as one of the most potent pop songwriters and in 1985 he provided the Oscar-winning No. 1 hit 'Say You, Say Me' for the film *White Nights*, wrote and sang music for Pepsi commercials and co-wrote with **Michael Jackson** the charity song 'We Are the World'* for USA for Africa.

Dancing on the Ceiling (1986) continued Richie's triumphant progress. It included songs in country, funk, pop and MOR ballad style and both the title track and 'Love Will Conquer All' were major worldwide hits. Richie maintained a low profile following the success of *Ceiling*, beset by marital problems and

a number of operations on his vocal chords. In 1992 he released the 'best of' set, *Back to Front*, which contained three new tracks – his first recordings to be released in six years. The same year, he left Motown to sign with Mercury Records. His first studio album, co-produced with **Jimmy Jam & Terry Lewis**, was the hugely successful *Louder than Words* (1996). Less successful, his smooth balladry seeming increasingly out of style, was *Time* (1998), despite the compilation *The Love Songs* hitting the Top Five earlier in the year.

JONATHAN RICHMAN
b. 16 May 1951, Boston, Massachusetts, USA

With his bizarre, childlike but poetic lyrics and idiosyncratic singing, Richman found a considerable European audience in the late seventies, scoring hit singles in England.

With the **Velvet Underground** as a major influence, Richman formed the Modern Lovers in 1970 with drummer David Robinson, bassist Rolfe Anderson and guitarist John Felice, who would later record with his own band, the Real Kids. After line-up changes which saw Jerry Harrison (keyboards) and Ernie Brooks (bass) join Richman and Robinson, the band came to the attention of Warner Bros, who allocated then-staff producer (ex-**Velvet Underground**) John Cale to supervise their first recordings. However, during the sessions, band and label parted company. **Kim Fowley** supervised some further demo tapes (released by Bomp! as *The Original Modern Lovers* in 1981) but in 1973 the group split up. Harrison later joined **Talking Heads**.

In 1975 Richman signed to the small West Coast label Beserkley, appearing solo on the tongue-in-cheek *Beserkley Chartbusters* (1975) album and releasing *Jonathan Richman & the Modern Lovers* (1976) with a new band which included only Robinson from the previous line-up. Also in 1976, Beserkley issued the Cale tracks as *Modern Lovers*. Songs with titles like 'Hospital' and 'Pablo Picasso' expressed Richman's oblique vision, while a 1975 re-recording of 'Roadrunner', with insistent riffs and monotone vocals, reached the British Top Ten in 1977. Richman repeated the success with the deadpan instrumental 'Egyptian Reggae' from *Rock'n'Roll with the Modern Lovers* (1977), on which Robinson was replaced by drummer D. Sharpe, completing a line-up which included bassist Curly Keranen (later replaced by Asa Brebner) and guitarist Leroy Radcliffe.

The next album was a concert recording and *Back in Your Life* (1979) included 'Abdul and Cleopatra' and 'I'm Nature's Mosquito'. Richman broke the band up and during the early eighties played club dates, releasing only one album, *Jonathan Sings!*

(1982). In 1985 he signed to the British label Rough Trade. Among the tracks on *Rockin' and Romance* (1985) were 'Chewing Gum Wrapper' and 'Vincent Van Gogh'. This was followed by *It's Time for Jonathan Richman and the Modern Lovers* (1986), which found the singer in an even more minimalist frame of mind. In 1988 Richman switched labels to Rounder, who issued *Modern Lovers 88*. His backing group now consisted of Brenan Totten (guitar) and Johnny Avila (drums).

Rounder released an eponymous 1990 album, which featured more of Richman's increasingly self-parodic, idiosyncratic songs, including 'I Eat with Gusto, Damn! You Bet' and 'Fender Stratocaster', a paean to his guitar. The same year saw the entertaining and self-explanatory *Jonathan Sings Country*, on which Richman tackled songs made famous by **Tammy Wynette**, **Marty Robbins** and **Skeeter Davis**. His later recordings were of variable quality, the best of them being *I, Jonathan* (1992), which included the typically quirky 'I Was Dancing in the Lesbian Bar' and his tribute to his original inspiration 'Velvet Underground'. In 1994 he released *Jonathan, Te Vas a Emocionar!* (Hey Jonathan, You're Getting All Emotional), Spanish-language versions of his best-known songs. In the same year he issued a new album, *You Must Ask the Heart* (Rounder), which he quickly followed with *Surrender to Jonathan* (Warner, 1996). *Collection* (Rhino, 1995) is the best anthology of his career.

NELSON RIDDLE
b. 1 June 1921, Oradell, New Jersey, USA, d. 6 October 1985, Los Angeles, California

Though Riddle had chart success as an orchestra leader ('Lisbon Antigua'*, 1956), and wrote the scores for several films (including *Lolita*, 1962, and *The Great Gatsby*, 1974, for which he won an Oscar), he is best known for his work as an arranger in the fifties for **Frank Sinatra** and **Nat 'King' Cole** and in the eighties for **Linda Ronstadt**.

The son of a commercial artist and amateur musician, Riddle learned piano as a child, later graduating to trombone (his father's instrument). After leaving high school, he joined the bands of Charlie Spivak and Jerry Wald as trombonist and arranger. While with **Tommy Dorsey**, he was drafted into the army in 1944 and on his discharge in 1945 joined **Bob Crosby** and travelled with him to the West Coast, settling there in 1947 as a staff arranger for NBC Radio. In 1950 he was asked by **Les Baxter** to supply arrangements for Nat 'King' Cole and following Cole's success with 'Mona Lisa'* (1950) and 'Too Young'* (1951) became one of Cole's regular collaborators. Riddle also arranged **Ella Mae Morse**'s 1952 hit 'Blacksmith Blues'* and began to record for Capitol as a band-

leader. His hits of this period include 'Brother John' (1954) – an adaptation of the traditional French song 'Frère Jacques' – 'Lisbon' and the exotic 'Port au Prince' (1956). But his most influential work was with Sinatra, with whom Riddle worked throughout Sinatra's seven-year stay with the company.

As an arranger Riddle was equally adept at creating intimate moods (*In the Wee Small Hours*, 1955, thought by many to be Sinatra's most compelling album), elegant soundscapes for the singer's exercises in mournful balladry (*Only the Lonely*, 1958), and the cool delights of *Songs for Swingin' Lovers* (1956), Sinatra's most commercially successful Capitol album. Among the million-selling records Riddle arranged for Sinatra were 'Young at Heart' (1953), 'Love and Marriage' (1955) and 'All the Way' (1957). Riddle's association with Sinatra led to his first film commission in 1956 when he worked on Sinatra's *Johnny Concho*. In the same year Riddle had a hit with the theme to *The Proud Ones*. Like his contemporary **Henry Mancini**, Riddle also wrote for television, where his greatest successes were the theme music for *The Untouchables* (1959) and *Route 66* (1962).

For most of the sixties and early seventies Riddle worked as a staff arranger for Sinatra's Reprise records (though he only rarely worked with Sinatra himself) and wrote film scores. In 1982 Riddle was asked by Linda Ronstadt's producer Peter Asher to arrange and conduct the orchestra for her collection of fifties standards. He re-created his rich orchestration and full instrumentation for the impressive *What's New* (1983), which included three songs from Sinatra's *Only the Lonely* ('What's New', 'Guess I'll Hang My Tears out to Dry' and 'Good-Bye'). Less successful was their second album, *Lush Life* (1984), which included a reverential remake of the Cole hit, 'When I Fall in Love' (equally faithful to Riddle's sound was the Rick Astley revival of the song in 1987, produced by **Stock, Aitken and Waterman**). In the same year Riddle also arranged a rather cloying album of standards by opera star **Kiri Te Kanawa**, *Blue Skies*. After Riddle's death, Ronstadt released the last of their collaborations, *For Sentimental Reasons* (1986).

RIDE
Andy Bell; Loz Colbert; Mark Gardner; Stephan Queralt

Ride, along with **My Bloody Valentine**, were at the forefront of the style dubbed 'Shoegazing' by critics to describe the heads down, motionless approach of a number of British independent bands of the nineties. Ride had a more direct, melodic approach than many of their peers, but fell apart just as they reached the cusp of stardom. Guitarist Andy Bell was to earn further success in the late nineties as the chief creative force behind Hurricane #1.

Ride came together in 1988 in Oxfordshire, England, and comprised Bell, Gardner (vocals/guitar), Colbert (drums) and Queralt (bass). The band soon gained a reputation for the intensity of their live performances and signed to Creation for the release of their eponymous début EP. The droning psychedelia of the *Play* EP (1990) earned Ride their first UK chart entry, while the acclaimed *Nowhere*, issued later the same year, confirmed their mastery of the style with songs like 'Vapour Trail' that managed to be both plodding and spacey, and the effective title song with its **Pink Floyd**-like echoes. Although *Going Blank Again* (1992) spawned a Top Ten single, 'Leave Them All Behind', it was not the breakthrough success Ride had anticipated. Frustrated, the band took a year off to rethink their options.

Carnival of Light (1994) heralded a more conventional rock sound, but served only to alienate Ride's existing following while also failing to find them a new audience. Tensions between Bell and Gardner grew as the quartet recorded *Tarantula* in 1995, and by the time the album was released the following year Ride had split up.

In 1996 Bell formed a new band, Hurricane #1, with singer Alex Lowe, bassist Will Pepper and drummer Gareth Farmer. The band's sound was closer to labelmates **Oasis** than Ride, and proved a greater commercial success. *Hurricane #1* (1997) spawned three hit singles, 'Chain Reaction', 'Just Another Illusion' and 'Step into My World'. The UK top five hit 'Only the Strongest Will Survive' preceded the release of the album of the same name. In 1999 Bell left to join Oasis.

JOSHUA RIFKIN
b. 22 April 1944, New York, USA

Pianist, musicologist and arranger, Rifkin was among those responsible for the revival of popular interest in **Scott Joplin** in the seventies.

Rifkin studied composition at the Juilliard School of Music and musicology at Princeton before travelling to Germany in 1961 to study under Stockhausen. Throughout this period, he also played jazz and ragtime piano and in 1964 made his first recordings for Elektra as a member of the Even Dozen Jug Band, with John Sebastian (later a member of the **Lovin' Spoonful**), **Stefan Grossman** and the Steve Katz Jug Band. While with Elektra, he also recorded *The Baroque Beatles Book* (1966) and arranged *Wildflowers* (1967) and other pieces for **Judy Collins**.

Appointed Professor of Music at Brandeis and musical director of the Elektra subsidiary, Nonesuch Records, he continued recording in an eclectic fashion. Among his albums of the late sixties were *Baroque Fanfares and Sonatas for Brass* and Eric Salz-

man's *The Nude Paper Sermon* with actor Stacy Keach as narrator. But it was his collection of pieces by Joplin, *Piano Rags* (1970), that won Rifkin (and ragtime) a popular audience when it topped the classical charts in 1971, the year concert-pianist Vera Brodsky published her *Collected Works of Scott Joplin* and the Lincoln Centre mounted the highly successful *An Evening with Scott Joplin* at which Rifkin was one of the featured artists. The climax of this revival of ragtime came when 'The Entertainer' and other Joplin tunes, adapted by **Marvin Hamlisch**, were featured extensively in *The Sting* (1974). The title of his 1980 recording *Digital Ragtime* indicated his concern to save vintage recordings through digital technology.

THE RIGHTEOUS BROTHERS
Bobby Hatfield, b. 10 April 1940, Beaver Dam, Wisconsin, USA; Bill Medley, b. 19 September 1940, Santa Ana, California

The vocalists on one of **Phil Spector**'s greatest productions, 'You've Lost That Lovin' Feelin''* (1964), the Righteous Brothers were among the finest exponents of blue-eyed soul.

Ex-member of local group the Paramours, baritone Medley teamed up with the high tenor singer Hatfield in 1962. During a residency at a Santa Ana club they were signed by Ray Maxwell to his Moonglow label. As the Righteous Brothers they had minor hits with a revival of **Don and Dewey**'s 'Koko Joe', Medley's 'Little Latin Lupe Lu' (1963) and 'My Babe' before **Jack Good** featured the duo on his *Shindig* television show (Maxwell later issued further 1963 tracks and a version of **Ray Charles**' 'Georgia on My Mind' was a minor hit in 1965).

As a result of that TV appearance, Spector signed them to his Philles label, producing a melodramatic version of **Barry Mann**'s and Cynthia Weil's 'You've Lost That Lovin' Feelin'' on which Medley's deeper voice chased Hatfield's pleading falsetto to a thrilling denouement. The record was a No. 1 hit in America and Britain. The formula was repeated on 'Just Once in My Life' (1965) and revivals of **Roy Hamilton**'s fifties hits 'Ebb Tide' and 'Unchained Melody'. The latter was a re-released hit in 1990.

In 1966 the duo moved to Verve where another Mann–Weil soul-flavoured ballad, '(You're My) Soul and Inspiration'*, topped the charts. 'He' and 'Go Ahead and Cry' were lesser hits but later Verve singles foundered. In Britain the Righteous Brothers had hits with a reissue of the Spector version of the **Vera Lynn** wartime ballad 'White Cliffs of Dover' and a revival of the **Harry Belafonte** hit 'Island in the Sun' (Verve) from *Standards* (1968).

Later that year Medley went solo, recording the minor hits 'Brown Eyed Woman' and 'Peace Brother

Peace' for MGM. Hatfield recruited Jimmy Walker (formerly of the **Beatles**-inspired Knickerbockers, whose 'Lies' had been a 1966 hit on Challenge) and retained the Righteous Brothers name for live shows and unsuccessful records. A reunion of Medley and Hatfield resulted in the Top Ten death disc 'Rock'n'Roll Heaven' (Haven, 1974), a tasteless ode to dead rock stars composed by Alan O'Day, who also wrote 'Angie Baby' for **Helen Reddy** and later recorded the No. 1 'Undercover Angel' (Pacific, 1977).

There were further hits with 'Give It to the People' (1974) and 'Dream on' before the duo returned to obscurity, re-emerging for the occasional show. Medley released *Right Here and Now* (Planet, 1982), with a title track by Mann and Weil and production by Richard Perry, and later enjoyed considerable success with '(I've Had) The Time of My Life' (RCA, 1987), a duet with **Jennifer Warnes** from the film *Dirty Dancing*, and a revival of the **Hollies**' 'He Ain't Heavy, He's My Brother' (Scotti Bros, 1988). When 'Unchained Melody' was included in the hit movie *Ghost*, the song became a hit once again, in both the original and a re-recorded version. Released as a follow-up, 'You've Lost That Lovin' Feelin'' made the British Top Five at the end of 1990. The success of the reissues led the duo to team up once again, and they toured extensively in the early nineties.

Anthology (Rhino, 1990) is the definitive career retrospective.

TEDDY RILEY
b. 1966, Harlem, New York City, USA

Riley has been the one of the most influential figures in recent black dance music by combining contemporary hip-hop with more traditional vocal styles in his 'New Jack Swing' work with vocal group Guy and his 'swingbeat' productions for **Michael Jackson**, **Bobby Brown**, **Mary J. Blige** and other artists.

His first public appearance as a vocalist was in partnership with his future brother-in-law Omar Chandler. The duo won a talent contest at Harlem's Apollo Theatre when Riley was sixteen. He next formed and produced tracks by the group Kids at Work.

In 1987 Riley created the vocal group Guy with brothers Aaron and Damian Hall. 'Groove Me' (1988) was one of the first examples of New Jack Swing, a softer style of dance music than hip-hop and rap inspired in part by veteran disco group the Gap Band. Riley co-produced the Guy début album with Gene Griffin, the writer of 'Groove Me'. Other Guy hits included 'Piece of My Love' and 'Let's Chill'.

After recording *Future* (1990), Guy split up and Riley concentrated on songwriting and production. Each of the Hall brothers made solo albums.

Riley's first big success as producer had been Keith Sweat's crossover hit 'I Want Her' in 1988. Among his later work as writer or producer has been *Dangerous* by Michael Jackson, for which he produced six tracks, Bobby Brown's 1991 hit 'My Prerogative', Kool Moe Dee's 'How Ya' Like Me Now' and 'New Jack Swing', and 'Rump Shaker' by Wreckx-N-Effect. Riley's younger brother Markell is one half of Wreckx-N-Effect, which was one of the first signings to Teddy Riley's own Future label.

Among Riley's film works are the bestselling title track for *New Jack City* and the R&B chart-topper 'My Fantasy' for Spike Lee's *Do the Right Thing*. In 1994 Riley co-produced hits by Blackgirl and **Hammer**. He and the Hall brothers were also planning to reunite for a final Guy tour and album.

TEX RITTER
b. Woodward Maurice Ritter, 12 January 1905, Pana County, Texas, USA, d. 2 January 1974, Nashville, Tennessee

The first performer to get any recognition for country music in New York and the only entertainer to be elected to both the Cowboy Hall of Fame and Country Music Hall of Fame, Ritter, once dubbed 'The Voice of the Western', was the most important (if not the most successful or influential) singing cowboy to emerge in the wake of **Gene Autry**.

While studying law at the University of Texas, Ritter's already strong interest in cowboy songs was increased through contact with folklorist J. Frank Dobie and collector **John Lomax**. The cowboy and mountain songs which he collected formed the basis of his repertoire when he began singing on KPRC in Houston in 1929. He travelled to New York, where he secured a featured part in Lynn Riggs' folk play, *Green Grow the Lilacs* in 1931 (it later formed the basis of **Rodgers and Hammerstein**'s *Oklahoma!*), and sang cowboy ballads during scene changes. An immediate success, he was greatly in demand for both his songs and for lecture recitals about the cowboy in Eastern colleges; he also performed regularly on a number of New York radio stations before travelling to Hollywood to become a singing cowboy in 1936.

The paucity of their budgets meant that Ritter's Westerns were inferior to those of Autry and **Roy Rogers**, though their musical content was often more interesting. Thus, *Take Me Back to Oklahoma* (1940) featured Ritter and **Bob Wills** duetting on 'Take Me Back to Tulsa' and later films featured **Johnny Bond**, with whom Ritter regularly toured and performed. Ritter's last movie as a singing cowboy was *Flaming Bullets* (1945). In 1942 he was the first country artist to join the newly established Capitol label. A prolific recording artist, Ritter's gentle, rich baritone was heard to good effect on 'There's a New Moon Over

My Shoulder', 'Boll Weevil', 'Have I Stayed Away Too Long', 'Rye Whiskey' and the patriotic Second World War song, 'Gold Star in the Window'.

Ironically, it was an off-camera film performance that once more boosted his career, when he sang the theme song to *High Noon* (1956), written by **Dimitri Tiomkin** and Ned Washington. Westerns had utilized theme songs before – indeed Ritter had sung the themes to *The Marshall's Daughter* (1953) and *Wichita* (1955) – but after 'High Noon' virtually every Western had one. It was, however, **Frankie Laine** who had the bigger hit with 'High Noon'; Ritter's biggest hit was the unabashedly sentimental salute to country music 'I Dreamed of a Hillbilly Heaven', which made the Top Twenty in 1961. By then Ritter had turned his attention back to the cowboy songs he'd begun collecting in his youth and which were once more in vogue, courtesy of both 'High Noon' and the success **Marty Robbins** and others were having with 'fake' gunfighter ballads. The album *Blood on the Saddle* (1960) contains a representative selection of these songs.

Elected to the Country Music Hall of Fame in 1964, Ritter attempted a political career, running, unsuccessfully, for the Senate and for the Governorship of Tennessee, before his death in 1974.

JOHNNY RIVERS
b. John Ramistella, 7 November 1942, New York, USA

A successful publisher and label-owner, Rivers the singer raised the revival of earlier hits to an art-form, selling over 25 million records in the sixties and seventies.

Raised in Louisiana where he played in high-school bands, Rivers' meeting **Alan Freed** in 1957 led to a name change and a recording contract with **George Goldner**'s Gone label, the first of a dozen Rivers recorded for before becoming successful. **Rick Nelson** recorded his 'I'll Make Believe' (1958) and Rivers briefly worked with **Louis Prima** in Las Vegas before in 1961 he settled in Los Angeles, aiming to establish himself as a songwriter. He supported himself by live appearances, specializing in performing rock'n'roll standards.

A meeting with **Lou Adler**, who had just set up Dunhill Productions, led to a contract with Imperial and the 'live' album *Johnny Rivers at the Whiskey a Go Go* (1964), which spawned a trio of Top Twenty hits. All revivals, the songs, **Chuck Berry**'s 'Memphis'* and 'Maybelline', and 'Mountain of Love', originally a hit for Harold Dorman (Rita, 1960), were approached from the same perspective as the British beat groups then hugely popular in America. Later records reflected the twists and turns of fashion. They encompassed blues and R&B ('Midnight Special'; 'Seventh

Son', 1965), folk and folk-rock (**Pete Seeger**'s 'Where Have All the Flowers Gone', 1965), **P. F. Sloan**'s television theme song 'Secret Agent Man'* (1966), proto-punk (a cover of the Standells' local hit '[I Washed My Hands] In Muddy Water', 1966) and Motown covers (the **Four Tops**' 'Baby I Need Your Loving', and **Smokey Robinson**'s 'Tracks of My Tears', 1967). In contrast, Rivers' only American No. 1 was with his own 'Poor Side of Town' (1966).

In 1967 Rivers established his own record label Soul City. He had immediate success with the vocal group the Versatiles, led by Marilyn McCoo and Billy Davis. With a name change to the Fifth Dimension, they had more than ten Top Forty hits between 1967 and 1970, all produced by Rivers and featuring such top-flight studio musicians as Hal Blaine, Larry Knetchtel and Joe Osborn. These included the atmospheric 'Up Up and Away'* (1967) by **Jimmy Webb**, a songwriter signed to Rivers' music-publishing company; **Laura Nyro**'s 'Stoned Soul Picnic'* (1968); the anthemic 'Aquarius'/'Let the Sunshine in'*, from *Hair*; and Nyro's 'Wedding Bell Blues'* – both of which topped the American charts in 1969. In 1970 the group left Soul City for Bell where their hits included **Burt Bacharach** and Hal David's 'One Less Bell to Answer' (1970) and **Tony Macaulay**'s '(Last Night) I Didn't Get to Sleep at All' (1972). McCoo and Davis left the group in 1975 and the following year had an American No. 1 with 'You Don't Have to Be a Star (To Be in My Show)' (ABC). The duo's other hits included 'Your Love' (1977) and 'Look What You've Done to My Heart' (1978).

Rivers himself returned to the charts in 1972 with an energetic revival of **Huey 'Piano' Smith**'s 1957 hit, 'Rocking Pneumonia and the Boogie Woogie Flu'* (United Artists) and continued in the same vein with revivals of **Carl Perkins**' 'Blue Suede Shoes' (1973) and the **Beach Boys**' 'Help Me Rhonda' (Epic, 1975), which featured Brian Wilson on back-up vocals. His last hit was the disco-orientated 'Swayin' to the Music (Slow Dancin')'* (Big Tree, 1977).

Rivers retired from music in 1983 after recording the contemporary gospel set *Not a Through Street*, only emerging to play the occasional charity or tribute concert in the early nineties.

MAX ROACH
b. Maxwell Roach, 10 January 1925, Brooklyn, New York, USA

A protean figure of modern jazz, drummer Roach came to prominence in the forties, accompanying bebop founder **Charlie Parker**. He later led his own groups and composed extended works, including the *Freedom Now Suite* (1958). In the eighties he wrote film and TV scores, worked on video projects and performed with a string quartet led by his daughter Maxine.

As a teenager, Roach was influenced by bebop drummer **Kenny Clarke**, whom he replaced in **Coleman Hawkins**' group. He first recorded in 1943 with Hawkins and joined **Dizzy Gillespie**'s band soon afterwards. During the late forties Roach made many bebop records with Parker (including the first under the alto-sax player's own name in 1945), Tadd Dameron, **Bud Powell**, **Thelonious Monk** and others for Savoy and Dial.

The first group led by Roach included trumpeter **Clifford Brown** and Harold Land or **Sonny Rollins** on tenor sax; he recorded *Three Giants* (Prestige, 1956) with the latter. After Brown's death in 1956, Roach recorded *Jazz in 3/4 Time* with Kenny Dorham (trumpet) and Ray Brown (bass), the title indicating the drummer's interest in unusual time signatures.

We Insist! Freedom Now Suite (Candid, 1958) showed a shift towards lengthy compositions on social or political themes. The suite was written with Oscar Brown Jnr and featured singer Abbey Lincoln (Roach's wife) on such tracks as 'Driva Man', as well as solos from Hawkins and trumpeter Booker Little. Roach's approach to drumming was showcased on *Percussion Bitter Sweet* (Impulse, 1961) while *It's Time* (1961) combined percussion with choral chants.

In 1962 Roach recorded *Speak Brother Speak* with tenor-player Clifford Jordan. *Drums Unlimited* (Atlantic, 1966) was a solo record.

Roach continued his musical experimentation into the eighties and nineties. The Double Quartet combined his own group with a string quartet led by his daughter Maxine Roach, recording *Bright Moments* (Soul Note, 1986). He led the band which accompanied Lincoln on *The World Is Fallen Down*. He also composed music for stage plays by Sam Shepard and collaborated with video artist Kit Fitzgerald, as well as rap musicians.

MARTY ROBBINS

b. Martin D. Robinson, 26 September 1925, Glendale, Arizona, USA, d. 8 December 1982, Nashville, Tennessee

Robbins was one of the most consistent country hit-makers, with records on the country charts every year between 1956 and 1982. His early recordings saw him veer stylistically between tear-stained ballads, rockabilly and pop, but his most memorable were a series of gunfighter ballads, including his best-known recording, 'El Paso'* (1959). In the words of country-music historian Bill C. Malone, 'Robbins was a singing cowboy who had been born just a few years too late.'

Robbins grew up in the Arizona desert with **Gene Autry** and the **Sons of the Pioneers** as his idols. After his discharge from the navy in 1948, he began playing clubs in the Phoenix area, eventually graduating to his own radio and television show, *Western Caravan*, singing cowboy songs and telling tales of the old West. Signed by Columbia in 1952 on the advice of Little Jimmy Dickens (who in 1965 had a novelty hit with 'May the Bird of Paradise Fly up Your Nose', Columbia), Robbins' first hit was the sentimental 'I'll Go on Alone' (1953). It, and subsequent hits (including 'Pretty Words' and 'At the End of a Long Lonely Day'), won Robbins the sobriquet 'Mr Teardrop', until in 1954 he shattered this image by recording the first country version of **Elvis Presley**'s epochal rendering of **Arthur Crudup**'s 'That's All Right' and gained a country Top Ten hit; Presley's own version was unsuccessful outside Memphis.

Columbia next used Robbins to record country versions of pop hits (such as 'Singing the Blues', which was Robbins' first major pop hit, although an even bigger one for **Guy Mitchell**) and then more directly teen-orientated material. Songs in this vein included 'A White Sport Coat (and a Pink Carnation)'*, 'The Story of My Life' (1957) and 'She Was Only Seventeen (He Was One Year More)' (1958), mostly written by Robbins himself. Then, in 1959, he had his first success with a Western-inspired song, the theme song to the film *The Hanging Tree*, followed by his own composition and first international hit 'El Paso'. Originally a five-minute album track on *Gunfighter Ballads and Trail Songs*, the song – with its story of the gunfighter who dies for love – topped the charts and led to a series of similar cowboy ballads, mostly written by Robbins, which though only minor pop hits were enormously influential on country music. Among these were 'Big Iron' (1960), a revival of 'Cool Water' (written by Bob Nolan of the Sons of the Pioneers), 'The Fastest Gun Around' and 'Battle of the Alamo' (1962). In the same period Robbins starred in a number of low-budget Westerns, including *Buffalo Gun* (1958) with fellow country stars **Webb Pierce** and Carl Smith.

Though he later recorded a sequel to 'El Paso', 'El Paso City' (1976), Robbins turned away from cowboy songs in the mid-sixties. Later pop hits included 'Devil Woman' (1962) and 'Ruby Ann' (1963), after which his impact was restricted to the country charts. He had a trio of chart-toppers, 'Ribbon of Darkness' (1965), 'My Woman, My Woman, My Wife' (1970) and a revival of the standard 'Among My Souvenirs' (1976). His musical activity was restricted in later years by heart trouble. A plethora of posthumous releases kept Robbins' name alive amongst the country fraternity, and his recording career was surveyed on a number of compilations in the eighties and nineties, notably on the boxed set from Bear Family, *Marty Robbins Country 1951–58*.

DON ROBERTSON
b. 5 December 1922, Peking, China

Though **Floyd Cramer** is more often identified with the 'slipped-note' style of piano-playing that was a central element of **Chet Atkins**' 'Nashville sound', the style originated with West coast pianist and composer Robertson, who wrote several country hits and had a million-seller himself with his own composition, the instrumental 'The Happy Whistler', in 1956.

The son of a doctor, Robertson studied music at the Chicago Musical College. While there he was deeply influenced by poet and folk historian Carl Sandburg, then working on *The New American Songbag* (1950). In 1947 Robertson went to Los Angeles to become a songwriter and supported himself as a rehearsal pianist at Capitol. His first success, co-written with Hal Blair, was the forlorn ballad 'I Really Don't Want to Know', a hit for **Eddy Arnold** in 1954 and successfully revived by **Tommy Edwards** (1966), Ronnie Dove (Diamond, 1966) and **Elvis Presley** (1971). With Jack Rollins he wrote 'I Don't Hurt Anymore', a million-seller for **Hank Snow** (1955).

Robertson's distinctive piano-playing on the demo version of 'Please Help Me I'm Falling' (a 1960 million-seller for **Hank Locklin**) was copied by Cramer, giving an added sophistication to Atkins' developing 'Nashville sound'. As well as Arnold and Snow, who regularly recorded his compositions, Robertson provided hits for **Les Paul** and Mary Ford ('Hummingbird', 1955), the De John Sisters ('No More', Epic, 1955), the **Chordettes** ('Born to Be with You', 1956), **Al Martino** ('I Love You More and More Each Day', 1964) and *Bonanza* teleseries actor Lorne Greene, who, in the guise of his Ben Cartwright persona, narrated the story of 'Ringo'* (RCA, 1964).

Robertson's most surprising success, however, was with the instrumental 'The Happy Whistler' (1956), which in Britain was covered by dance-band leader Cyril Stapleton on Decca. In 1964 he recorded an album of his hits, *Heart on My Sleeve* (RCA), and in 1972 was made a member of the Nashville Songwriters' Association's Hall of Fame.

PAUL ROBESON
b. Leroy Bustill, 9 April 1898, Princeton, New Jersey, USA, d. 23 January 1976, Philadelphia, Pennsylvania

Best remembered for his resonant, rumbling version of 'Ol' Man River' (1928) by **Jerome Kern** and Oscar Hammerstein (later of **Rodgers and Hammerstein**), Robeson was one of the most important black performers and spokesmen of his time. His recitals were largely responsible for the growth of interest in spirituals in mainstream America, while as an actor he starred in a number of films and plays, notably *Oth-*

ello (1943), one of the longest-running Shakespearian productions on Broadway. An activist in the struggle for black rights, he won enormous respect in Europe and the USSR for his frequently expressed avowals of internationalism and socialism. In America, however, this stand made him a target for McCarthyism and blacklisting and Robeson, still a symbol of black pride, retreated into seclusion in the late sixties.

The son of a minister and teacher, Robeson won a scholarship to Rutgers, where he was part of the All-American football team in 1917 and 1918. On his graduation a year later he studied at the Columbia Law School, but though he was admitted to the New York bar in 1923, his experiences of racial discrimination led him to take up the theatre rather than law. He had appeared in amateur productions while at Columbia and in 1922 Eugene O'Neill offered him a part in *Emperor Jones*. He refused but two years later had resounding success in that and O'Neill's *All God's Chillun Got Wings*. In 1925 Robeson's first concert of spirituals with Lawrence Brown inspired Kern to write the spiritual-like 'Ol' Man River' (which Robeson sang in the London production of *Showboat* in 1928 and the 1935 film). Several of his recordings of spirituals were hits, including 'Steal Away' (Victor, 1925) and 'Deep River' (1927).

In the thirties Robeson travelled to Europe to give concerts and appeared in the British film *Sanders of the River* (1934), which like his performance in *King Solomon's Mines* (1937) was later criticized for its 'Uncle Tom' attitudes. More significantly, in 1934 he made the first of many trips to the Soviet Union and in 1937 sang in Spain to the International Brigade. In 1939 he performed the world première of **Earl Robinson**'s 'Ballad for Americans' and during the war gave many concerts. In 1947 he turned increasingly to politics and his outspoken praise of the USSR led to attacks at benefit concerts and in 1950 to the State Department revoking his passport. When it was returned after worldwide pressure, he settled in Britain. After retiring from singing and acting in 1961 due to illness, he returned to America in 1963, living in seclusion until his death in 1976. A definitive biography of Robeson by Martin Bauml Duberman was published in 1989.

DON ROBEY
b. 1 November, 1903, Houston, Texas, USA, d. 16 June 1975, Houston

Better known to blues and soul scholars as Deadric Malone, the pseudonym he used to copyright the songs he bought outright from other writers, Robey made his Duke label a pioneering black-owned record company. Though few of his artists had long-term mainstream success, the gospel-based blues style of the likes of **Bobby Bland** and **Junior Parker** were subsequently hugely influential.

The owner of a record store and the Bronze Peacock club in Houston, Robey established Peacock in 1949 to record **Clarence 'Gatemouth' Brown** while he was appearing at his club. He had his first success with the gospel groups the **Five Blind Boys of Mississippi** ('Our Father', 1951), the **Dixie Hummingbirds** and the Nightingales. He recorded **Little Richard** early in his career and in 1954 had national success with **Johnny Ace** on the Duke label, which he had bought from disc-jockey James Mattis in 1952. Unlike other independent labels, such as the **Bihari Brothers'** Modern Records, which acted as clearing houses for masters recorded by others, from the start Duke (which Robey made his leading label), like **Syd Nathan**'s King Records, centralized its operations with Robey and in-house producer Joe Scott (the leader of Bobby Bland's band) overseeing production and Evelyn Johnson running the Buffalo Booking agency which ensured that Duke acts were always able to tour in support of their latest releases. The company even established its own record manufacturing plant.

Though Robey, whose penchant for showy diamonds and bodyguards won him the sobriquet 'Black Caesar', soon retired from day-to-day running of the company, the integrated structure he established made Duke the most successful black-owned company prior to **Berry Gordy**'s Motown. After Johnny Ace's pop hits, in the late fifties and early sixties Duke had numerous R&B hits with Bland and Parker, whose Texas style of blues influenced the emergence of Southern soul. Among other artists who recorded for Duke were Marie Adams, Jimmy McCracklin, **Big Mama Thornton** and **O. V. Wright**.

In 1973 Robey sold his labels to ABC. Galen Gart's *Duke/Peacock Record: An Illustrated History* (1990) tells the Don Robey story in great detail.

LEO ROBIN
b. 6 April 1900, Pittsburgh, Pennsylvania, USA

One of the most successful and versatile Hollywood songwriters, Robin's film songs included 'Louise' (1929), **Maurice Chevalier**'s first American hit; the oft-recorded 'Beyond the Blue Horizon' (1930), a hit for **Jeanette MacDonald** and revived by **Hugo Winterhalter** (1951); 'Blue Hawaii' (1937), a hit for **Bing Crosby** and revived by **Elvis Presley** in his 1961 film of the same title; and the Oscar-winning 'Thanks for the Memory' (1938), introduced by Bob Hope in *The Big Broadcast of 1938*.

A former reporter, Robin went to New York to become a playwright, only concentrating on songwriting after the success of *Hit the Deck* (1927). Writ-

ten in collaboration with **Vincent Youmans**, it included 'Hallelujah', a hit for **Nat Shilkret**. In the wake of this he was paired by his publisher with **Richard Whiting** to write songs for Paramount. Among their successes were 'Louise', 'Beyond the Blue Horizon' and 'My Ideal', for *Playboy of Paris* (1930), which provided hits for Chevalier (1931) and **Jimmy Dorsey** (1944). In 1932 Robin teamed up with Ralph Rainger (*b. 7 October 1901, New York, USA, d. 23 October 1942, Beverly Hills, California*), his regular collaborator for some six years. Together they wrote songs for over forty films. Their first was *A Bedtime Story*, in which Chevalier was partnered by the six-month-old Babe LeRoy, and their first hit 'Please', introduced by Crosby. Among their greatest successes were 'Love in Bloom' (later used by comedian Jack Benny as his theme song), 'June in January' (1934), the exotic 'Blue Hawaii' and 'Whispers in the Dark' (1937), all sung first by Crosby. With Lewis Genser, Robin wrote 'Love Is Just Around the Corner' (1935).

After Rainger's death in 1942, Robin wrote with a variety of composers, including **Jerome Kern** ('In Love in Vain', 1946), a hit for **Dick Haymes** and the first major hit for Richard Whiting's daughter, Margaret, on Capitol; Arthur Schwarz ('A Girl in Calico', 1947); and **Harold Arlen** ('Hooray for Love' and 'For Every Man There's a Woman', 1948). His last major success came in 1949 when with **Jule Styne** he wrote the score for the Broadway musical *Gentlemen Prefer Blondes* (filmed 1953), which included the oft-recorded 'Diamonds Are a Girl's Best Friend'. Less successful was his last Broadway show, *The Girl in Pink Tights* (1954), for which Robin fashioned lyrics to music by **Sigmund Romberg** after the latter's death.

BOBBY ROBINSON

One of the great black pioneers of R&B, Robinson used the retail store he owned on Harlem's 125th Street in New York for more than forty years as a base for various highly successful record labels.

The popularity of his shop attracted many local musicians as well as the owners of several of the newly formed independent labels, and he soon began to produce music in addition to selling it over the counter. He formed his first label, Robin Records, in 1951, changing its name to Red Robin in 1953. Initially recording local sax-player Morris Lane, he soon attracted the attention of the slowly emerging doo-wop market and recorded the Vocaleers, the Mello Moods and the Du-Droppers, among other vocal groups. The label also featured New York-based bluesmen like **Champion Jack Dupree**, and **Brownie McGhee and Sonny Terry**. Robinson subsequently established Whirlin' Disc Records exclusively to record doo-wop. Among his signings to the label were the **Chantels**, and Lewis (brother of **Frankie**) **Lymon** and the Teenchords.

His other label included Enjoy, Everlast, Fire and Fury. On these, all of which lasted well into the sixties, he enjoyed several big hits, including 'Kansas City' (**Wilbert Harrison**, 1959), 'Fannie Mae' (Buster Brown, 1959), Bobby Marchan's version of saxophonist Big Jay McNeely's composition 'There Is Something on Your Mind' (1960), 'Ya Ya' (**Lee Dorsey**, 1961), 'Soul Twist' (**King Curtis**, 1962), and 'Letter Full of Tears' (**Gladys Knight and the Pips**, 1962). In 1960 promotion man Marshall Sehorn, who had brought Dorsey to Robinson, was influential in breaking Chicago blues singer **Elmore James** into the R&B chart with 'The Sky Is Crying' – an influential record on the emerging R&B scene in Britain – on Robinson's Fire label, a major coup for his labels, and a personal high point in Robinson's career.

By the mid-sixties, after fifteen years of nurturing much of New York's emerging black talent, Robinson – unable to afford the advance royalty payments artists were now expecting – returned to retailing full-time. Always a believer in the principle of giving teenage groups the chance to make a record, rather than signing them for a long-term career, Robinson did not get back into recording until the mid-seventies arrival of rap, a genre he compared to the emergence of doo-wop. Once more, he was able to find artists eager to make a record without considering the consequences of a hit record. He revived Enjoy and produced **Grandmaster Flash**'s first records. Flash eventually moved to Sugarhill and major stardom and Robinson again returned to retailing. His shop remained a major attraction for discerning record collectors the world over.

EARL ROBINSON
b. Earl Hawley Robinson, 2 July 1910, Seattle, Washington, USA, d. 20 July 1991

An important figure in the development of the American folk revival, Robinson was a song-collector, songwriter and composer of orchestral works and TV and film music. Among his collaborators were **Woody Guthrie**, **Yip Harburg** and **Paul Robeson**, while both **Three Dog Night** and Greyhound had seventies hits with his multi-racial anthem 'Black and White'.

From a musical family, he graduated in music from the University of Washington in 1933. Robinson next travelled to China and across America, linking up with such singers as **Leadbelly**, Guthrie and **Pete Seeger**. He sang the songs he had collected for **Alan Lomax**'s Library of Congress recordings. Among the best known of his compositions was 'Joe Hill', a tribute to the murdered union leader, which was recorded most memorably by **Joan Baez**.

Robinson's interest in large-scale works began in the mid-thirties when he joined a Workers' Theater Project in New York. From 1937 to 1943 he conducted the American People's Chorus, with whom Robeson recorded Robinson's 'Ballad for Americans' (RCA Victor, 1939). He took part in a number of folk-music radio series and in 1943 moved to Hollywood, providing songs for such films as *A Walk in the Sun*, *California* and *Romance of Rosie Ridge*. With Millard Lampell, formerly of the Almanac Singers, Robinson composed the cantata 'The Lonesome Train' whose first performance in 1948 starred **Harry Belafonte**.

In 1952 Robinson was blacklisted for his left-wing sympathies and returned to New York, becoming a school guitar teacher. In later years he began to compose again, specializing in song cycles or cantatas, and often writing to civic commissions. In 1968 he composed *Illinois People* for the state of Illinois, while *To the Northwest Indian* was an orchestral piece performed in Spokane in 1974.

SMOKEY ROBINSON
b. William Robinson, 19 February 1940, Detroit, Michigan, USA

With his group the Miracles, Smokey Robinson was an essential element in the success of Motown Records. During the sixties he was **Berry Gordy**'s right-hand man, discovering new talent, songwriting and producing. While such compositions as 'My Guy', 'The Tracks of My Tears', 'Get Ready', 'The Tears of a Clown' and 'I Second That Emotion' made him one of the leading popular songwriters of the last forty years, Robinson's ethereal tenor was equally renowned as one of the music's most expressive voices.

Robinson formed the Miracles at high school in 1955 with vocalists Pete Moore (*b. 19 November 1939, Detroit*), Bobby Rogers (*b. 19 February 1940, Detroit*), Ron White (*b. 5 April 1939, Detroit, d. 26 August 1995*) and Claudette Rogers (*b. 1942 Detroit*), whom he later married. Robinson based his own style on Nolan Rogers of the Diablos doo-wop group, who recorded for the local Fortune label. In 1958 Gordy produced recordings by the Miracles including 'Got a Job', an answer disc to the Silhouettes' 'Get a Job', which he leased to Chess.

When Gordy started his own company in 1959 it was the Miracles who provided its first big pop hit with Robinson's 'Shop Around' (Tamla, 1960). While singing on numerous Miracles' hits over the next decade, Robinson began to write and produce for many artists on Tamla-Motown's growing roster. His first successes came with **Mary Wells**, whose 1962 Top Ten successes 'The One Who Really Loves You', 'You

Beat Me to the Punch' and 'Two Lovers' he wrote and produced. But Robinson's songwriting credentials were firmly established when the Miracles' American Top Ten hit 'You've Really Got a Hold on Me' (1963) was covered by **The Beatles**, and Wells' version of his 'My Guy' (1964) reached No. 1.

From the mid-sixties he provided the **Temptations** with such songs as 'The Way You Do the Things You Do' (1964), 'My Girl' (a No. 1 in 1965) and 'Get Ready' (1966), while continuing to take lead vocals on Miracles hits like the magisterial 'Tracks of My Tears' (1965), 'I Second That Emotion' (1967) and 'The Tears of a Clown' (1970), co-written with **Stevie Wonder**. He also wrote hits for **Marvin Gaye** (the R&B No. 1, 'Ain't That Peculiar', 1965), the **Marvelettes** ('The Hunter Gets Captured by the Game', 1965), the **Four Tops** ('Still Water Love', 1970) and the **Supremes** ('I'll Try Something New', 1969).

In 1971 Robinson left the Miracles in order to supervise Motown's move to Los Angeles. With new member Billy Griffin, the Miracles' only later pop hits were the Latin-tinged 'Do It Baby' (1974) and the disco-styled No. 1 'Love Machine (Part 1)' (1975). In 1976 the group moved to Columbia with little success and later disbanded. In 1986 a re-formed Miracles led by Bobby Rogers recorded for Hitsburgh, a label owned by Al Cleveland, co-writer of 'I Second That Emotion'.

Smokey (1973) was Robinson's first solo album while *Pure Smokey* (1974) and *A Quiet Storm* (1975) contained the respective hits 'Baby Come Close' and 'Baby That's Backatcha'. More successful were 'Cruisin'' (1979) from *Where There's Smoke* and the million-selling title track from *Being with You* (1981), produced by George Tobin.

During the eighties Robinson released an album a year. Some seemed little more than perfunctory although *Essar* (1984) and *One Heartbeat* (1987), with a guest appearance by the Temptations, had moments to compare with his sixties heyday. He was less active in the nineties and *Love, Smokey* (1990) was an unexceptional effort. His achievements as a songwriter and performer were marked by the four-volume boxed set *The 35th Anniversary Collection* (Motown, 1994).

TOM ROBINSON
b. 1 July 1950, Cambridge, England

Songwriter, singer and guitarist, Robinson rose to prominence during Britain's punk era, though his most successful songs were in the mainstream rock idiom and many of his lyrics took the form of protest songs.

With Hereward Kaye and Raphael Doyle he formed the acoustic trio Café Society in 1973 and signed to the **Kinks**' Konk label. The group released a Ray Davies-produced album in 1975. In the following year, Robinson set up the Tom Robinson Band (TRB) with Danny Kustow (guitar), Mark Ambler (keyboards) and Dolphin Taylor on drums. Signed to EMI, the TRB had a Top Ten hit with the raucous '2–4–6–8 Motorway' (1977), and followed this with an EP of political songs, *Rising Free. Power in the Darkness* (1978), which contained Robinson's sardonic 'Glad to Be Gay', was also a British hit.

Now a rising star, Robinson co-wrote songs with **Peter Gabriel** and **Elton John** before recording the **Todd Rundgren**-produced *TRB 2* (1979). The album's lack of impact caused the dissolution of the band and Robinson re-emerged with the more experimental Sector 21, which included one-time **Troggs** bassist Jo Burt and Stevie B. (drums). The band recorded one album for **Police** manager Miles Copeland's IRS label in 1980. Of the TRB members, Kustow joined ex-**Sex Pistols** bassist Glen Matlock in the Spectres and Taylor joined Belfast punk survivors Stiff Little Fingers.

Robinson, now based in Germany, included some of the Gabriel songs on *North by Northwest* (1982), released on his own Panic label. Returning to Britain, he toured with a new group including drummer Steve Laurie and had a major hit with the harsh 'War Baby' (Panic, 1983). The follow-up, 'Listen to the Radio: Atmospherics', was less successful.

Forming a new label, Castaway, Robinson released *Hope and Glory* (1984) and *Still Loving You* (1987), which was a surprise hit in Italy. *Midnight at the Fringe* (Dojo, 1987) was recorded live at the Edinburgh Festival and in the same year the original Tom Robinson Band played a reunion concert. Its success led the group to tour during 1989. The subsequent live in Berlin set *Tango* (1990) was unremarkable and Robinson developed a parallel career as a radio presenter in the early nineties, while continuing to perform, particularly at political benefit concerts. In 1994 he briefly returned to recording with *Love over Rage*, featuring the minor hit 'Roaring Days'.

CARSON ROBISON
b. 4 August 1890, Chetopa, Kansas, USA, d. 24 March 1957, Poughkeepsie, New York

'He was a modern Nashville figure in embryo,' wrote Robert Coltman in a celebrated essay, 'in his mastery of the music business as singer, songwriter, sideman, arranger, music entrepreneur, creator of image, blender of country-and-western music.' In particular, Robison was the most versatile country songwriter of the twenties and thirties – less prolific than **Bob Miller**, but with a finer sense of melody and poetry.

Robison began his musical career as a guitarist with dance bands in Kansas City in 1920. From 1922 he built a reputation as a radio entertainer over the local station KDAF, where he met **Wendell Hall**. Together they went to New York to record for Victor, Robison taking the opportunity to exhibit his talent for whistling. He was hired as a staff guitarist and occasional whistler, and in the latter capacity had a later hit with Felix Arnolt's piano novelty 'Nola' (Victor, 1926). As a guitarist he accompanied **Vernon Dalhart** on his historic tracks 'Wreck of the Old '97'/'The Prisoner's Song' (Victor, 1924). They continued to record together, Robison very much the junior partner at first, though once he started to sing tenor harmony on the records he was given joint credit with Dalhart. 'My Blue Ridge Mountain Home' (Victor, 1927) was an especially successful Robison composition for the duo, but in addition to songs of wife, home and mother Robison was a facile writer of topical numbers about train and ship wrecks, storms, fires and crimes. He also wrote an anti-evolutionist piece, (under the pseudonym Carlos B. McAfee) 'The John T. Scopes Trial', about the schoolteacher arraigned for teaching Darwinism to young Tennesseans.

As well as working with Dalhart, Robison put in thousands of studio hours accompanying other hillbilly artists and popular singers like **Gene Austin** and **Frank Crumit**. He also headed a jazz line-up, Carson Robison's Kansas City Jack-Rabbits, on a coupling of 'Stuff' and 'Nonsense', issued in Victor's 'race' series (1929). By that time he had broken with Dalhart and teamed with **Frank Luther** on lush Western duets like 'The Utah Trail', 'When It's Springtime in the Rockies' and 'Sleepy Rio Grande'. For his own jaunty 'Left My Gal in the Mountains' he enlisted guitarist **Roy Smeck**. The duo worked together until 1932, recording prolifically for other companies as well as Victor, sometimes as the Carson Robison Trio, whose third member was Luther's wife Zora Layman.

Robison's next band, initially called his Pioneers, later Buckaroos, employed the banjo- and guitar-playing Mitchell Brothers (John and Bill), multi-instrumentalist Frank Novak (an in-demand New York session musician who had worked with Bob Miller and others) and singer Pearl Pickens. In 1932 they made a nationwide tour, performing at the White House, and then visited Britain and Australasia. They toured Britain again in 1936 and 1939, by which time they were well known from their programmes on Radio Luxembourg. Recordings were made for many of the British labels and Robison was the bestselling country recording artist of his day in Britain, with the possible exception of **Jimmie Rodgers**.

From this peak of international celebrity Robison slipped slowly, in the forties, back to the rank of old radio pro. He had some success with '1942 Turkey in the Straw' (Bluebird), one of a batch of wartime topical songs that included 'We're Gonna Have to Slap That Dirty Little Jap (And Uncle Sam's the Man That Can Do It)', and later with some square-dance records and a quaint venture into the newest sound of the fifties, 'Rockin' and Rollin' with Granmaw' (MGM, 1956). His most potent piece of work, however, was the rustic narration 'Life Gets Tee-jus, Don't It?' (1946), recorded both by himself and by the actor Peter Lind Hayes. Apparently off the same shelf as **Woody Guthrie**'s talking blues, **Hoagy Carmichael** and **Johnny Mercer**'s 'Lazybones' and **Hank Williams**' 'Luke the Drifter' monologues, it was distinguished from them by the air – one that Robison's work always had – of being journalism rather than autobiography, observed and noted down from a reporter's box above the playing-field of Southern Life.

ROCKET FROM THE CRYPT
Apollo 9; Atom; JC 2000; ND; John Reis, aka Speedo; Petey X

One of the few rock'n'roll bands to achieve widespread fame in the nineties, punk-inspired sextet Rocket from the Crypt have built up a devoted following for their energetic, horn-driven sound.

Inspired by the similarly named Rocket from the Tomb, a raw, pre-punk rock band from the mid-seventies, John Reis formed the band in San Diego in 1990. All six members of the band took on pseudonyms, with Reis becoming Speedo alongside JC 2000 (trumpet), Atom (drums), ND (guitar), Apollo 9 (sax) and Petey X (bass). After the release of *Paint as a Fragrance* (Headhunter, 1991), the band toured the US, earning themselves a strong underground following just as **Nirvana** were bringing alternative rock into the mainstream. *Circa: Now!* saw RFTC earn a deal with Interscope Records, while their profile rose further after the release of *All Systems Go* (1993), a collection of early singles.

Apparently on the brink of stardom, Speedo took the unusual step of concentrating on his lo-fi, alternative rock side project, Drive Like Jehu, for the next year, recording *Yank Crime* (1994), the follow-up to an eponymous 1992 début. Rocket from the Crypt returned with a vengeance in 1995, releasing an EP, *The State of Art Is on Fire*, and two new albums, *Hot Charity* and *Scream, Dracula, Scream*, the latter spawning a UK Top Twenty hit single, 'On a Rope', which was heavily reminiscent of the **MC5**.

Having spent the previous two years on tour, developing an impressive international following, the band returned with *RFTC* (1998), which saw them move towards a more traditional fifties rock'n'roll sound and away from the garage sound of their earlier work.

RODGERS AND HAMMERSTEIN

Richard Rodgers, b. 28 June 1902, New York, USA, d. 30 December 1979, New York; Oscar Hammerstein II, b. Oscar Greely Glendenning Hammerstein, 12 July 1895, New York, d. 23 August 1960, Philadelphia, Pennsylvania

During the forties and fifties Rodgers and Hammerstein brought about profound changes in the Broadway musical. In contrast to the sophisticated and acidic **Lorenz Hart** (Rodgers' previous lyricist), Oscar Hammerstein, a screenwriter as well as a lyricist, had a broad conception of the function of the musical. Originally a writer of operettas (*Rose Marie*, 1924, with **Rudolf Friml**; *The Desert Song*, 1926, with **Sigmund Romberg**), Hammerstein's major seminal works with **Jerome Kern** (*Show Boat*, 1927) and later Rodgers (*Oklahoma!*, 1943) were more free-flowing musicals in which song, dance and story were carefully interwoven in order to celebrate what Rodgers called Hammerstein's 'three inter-related themes – nature, music and love'. The effect was equally liberating for Rodgers, whose collaboration with Hammerstein was warmer and more melodic than his earlier works with Hart. This decisive shift is confirmed by the fact that whereas with Rodgers and Hart, the words were written to the music, in the case of Rodgers and Hammerstein, the music followed the words.

The grandson of an opera impresario and the son of a theatre manager, Hammerstein briefly studied law at Columbia University before adopting the name Oscar Hammerstein II and securing a job as stage manager from his uncle Arthur in 1917. After the failure of his first professionally staged work, the non-musical *The Light* (1919), Arthur suggested he work with Herbert Stothart (*b. 11 September 1885, Milwaukee, Wisconsin, USA, d. 1 February 1949, Los Angeles, California*), a veteran Broadway composer and co-author with **Kalamar and Ruby** of 'I Wanna Be Loved by You' (1928), and **Otto Harbach**, librettist and lyricist to Friml's early operettas. The trio's first success was *Tickle Me* (1920), which was followed by *Wildflower* (1923), with additional music by **Vincent Youmans**, *Rose Marie* (1924) and *The Desert Song* (1926) with Romberg replacing Stothart. With Harbach and **George Gershwin**, Hammerstein also wrote *Song of the Flame* (1925), but his breakthrough came when Jerome Kern invited him to write the libretto and lyrics to *Show Boat* (1927), the success of which signalled the end of the dominance of the operetta tradition and the rise of the musical play.

Even more important than the number of hit songs *Show Boat* produced ('Ol' Man River', 'Can't Help Lovin' Dat Man' and 'Bill', whose lyric was co-authored by **P. G. Wodehouse**) was the concern of Kern and Hammerstein to treat their subject, Edna Ferber's sprawling novel about life on the Mississippi, seriously, and to integrate the songs fully into the plot. The classic case is 'Ol' Man River', which Hammerstein, who (uncredited) co-directed the show on its first appearance on Broadway, specifically wrote as the opening number to set the tone of the piece. The opening words – 'Tote that barge, lift that bale, git a little drunk an' you end in jail' – caught the feel of the Mississippi and indicated the sympathy the writers had for their characters. Later, intending precisely the same effect, Hammerstein wrote 'Oh What a Beautiful Morning' to establish the outdoor, optimistic feel of *Oklahoma!*.

Hammerstein and Kern had two further Broadway successes, *Sweet Adeline* (1929, filmed 1935) and *Music in the Air* (1932, filmed 1934), which introduced 'I've Told Ev'ry Little Star', but the thirties was a lean period for the lyricist. He spent most of the decade in Hollywood, where he worked on several musicals, including *Viennese Night* (1930), *The Night Is Young* (1935), for which he and Romberg wrote 'When I Grow Too Old to Dream', a hit for **Nelson Eddy**, *Show Boat* (1936) and his one great artistic (but not commercial) cinematic success, *High, Wide and Handsome* (1937), which he also scripted, with uncredited assistance from director Rouben Mamoulian. Described by one critic as 'an extraordinary fusion of Brecht and Broadway', the film, like *Show Boat* a panoramic musical, was about the discovery of oil in Pennsylvania in 1859 and its heroic farmer-prospectors anticipated those of *Oklahoma!*. It introduced the delicate 'The Folks That Live on the Hill', a hit for **Guy Lombardo** (1937). Hammerstein's last major collaboration with Kern was the moving 'The Last Time I Saw Paris'. Inspired by news of the German occupation of Paris and featured in *Lady Be Good* (1941), it won an Oscar and was a hit for **Kate Smith**.

Returning to Broadway, Hammerstein was working on *Carmen Jones* (1943, filmed 1954 with **Harry Belafonte**), an updating of George Bizet's *Carmen*, when Rodgers invited him to collaborate on a musical based on Lynn Riggs' play *Green Grow the Lilacs*. Rodgers (like Lorenz Hart and Hammerstein a product of Columbia University) had previously only written with Hart. But, despite their great past successes, the partnership with Hart had collapsed soon after their greatest triumph, *Pal Joey* (1940), under the weight of Hart's growing alcoholism. When Hart rejected *Green Grow the Lilacs* as unsuitable subject matter, Rodgers turned to Hammerstein. The result was *Oklahoma!* (1943, filmed 1955 with **Gordon MacRae**) and an eighteen-year partnership.

Although on the surface a simple love story, *Oklahoma!*'s deeper theme was the celebration of rural values. It was this, at a time of war, that struck such a resonant chord with American audiences. Important elements in the show's success were Mamoulian's direction and Agnes De Mille's inventive and restrained choreography, but it was Rodgers and Hammerstein's vision that made it such a landmark musical. Its effects were visible in the most unlikely places: after seeing it, Republic's chief Herbert J. Yates ordered that **Roy Rogers**' musical Westerns should be styled after the show, and the original cast recording (Decca) was a huge hit, the first such, and helped establish the pattern of hit Broadway albums in the fifties. Alfred Drake, who acted in the show, had a hit with 'Surrey with the Fringe on Top', and both **Frank Sinatra** and **Bing Crosby** had big hits with the show's other memorable songs, 'Oh What a Beautiful Morning' and 'People Will Say We're in Love'. Later revivals, such as the UK National Theatre's hugely successful one in 1999, gave equal emphasis to the black ('My Room') as to the celebratory.

Carousel (1945, filmed 1956), a reworking of Ferenc Molnar's *Liliom* (1921), was equally ambitious, moving the musical play even closer to opera. Among the songs it included were 'Soliloquy', 'June Is Bustin' out All Over', the idyllic 'When the Children Are Asleep' and the triumphant 'You'll Never Walk Alone'. Recorded by Sinatra and **Judy Garland** at the time, it was later revived by **Roy Hamilton** (1954) and **Gerry and the Pacemakers** (1963), and has since become a perennial favourite with crowds at British football matches. The musical was revived with great success in London (and subsequently Broadway) in 1992. Less successful was *Allegro* (1947), one of the few of Rodgers and Hammerstein's musicals not to be an adaptation. Then came *South Pacific* (1949, filmed 1958), considered by many to be the duo's greatest work. Suggested by the show's director Joshua Logan, it was based on two stories by James Michener and carefully blended escapism (the idyllic island the story is set in) with realism (the time is war) and has an underlying theme of anti-racism firmly articulated in 'You've Got to Be Carefully Taught' (later memorably recorded by **Ian Matthews**). Among the numbers it introduced were 'Some Enchanted Evening', 'Bali Hi' (both hits for Sinatra, Crosby and **Perry Como**), 'Younger Than Springtime', 'There Is Nothing Like a Dame' and 'Happy Talk', which in 1982 was a surprise British No. 1 for former member of the **Damned**, Captain Sensible (A&M). The original production was also unusual in featuring an opera bass, Enzio Pinza; later, during the vogue for 'operatic' versions of musicals in the eighties, a recording featuring Kiri Te Kanawa, José Carreras, Mandy Patimkin and **Sarah Vaughan** was released (Columbia, 1986).

Rodgers and Hammerstein followed *South Pacific* with the exotic *The King and I* (1951, filmed 1956,

1999), a show closely associated with Yul Brynner who starred in it on Broadway, on film and in numerous revivals. That show included 'Hello Young Lovers' (a hit for Perry Como and **Paul Anka**, 1960) and 'Getting to Know You'. After several minor works, the best of which was *Flower Drum Song* (1958, filmed 1961), Rodgers and Hammerstein produced their last and most successful musical, *The Sound of Music* (1959, filmed with **Julie Andrews** in 1965). The soundtrack album remained in the charts for over seven years, *South Pacific*'s for over five. Disliked by many for its excessive sentimentality – the show told the story of the Trapp Family and included the much-parodied 'My Favourite Things' – *The Sound of Music* saw an onset of aesthetic conservatism in Rodgers and Hammerstein and was the crudest example of Hammerstein's celebration of 'nature, music and love'. Also in the show were 'Climb Ev'ry Mountain', 'Do-Re-Me' and 'Edelweiss', a British hit for balladeer Vince Hill (EMI Columbia, 1967).

After Hammerstein's death, Rodgers wrote his own lyrics to *No Strings* (1962) and collaborated with **Stephen Sondheim** on *Do I Hear a Waltz* (1965). His last show was *Two by Two* (1970).

JIMMIE RODGERS

b. 8 September 1897, Pine Springs, Mississippi, USA, d. 26 May 1933, New York

Rodgers was the first artist to extend a reputation made in Southern hillbilly music into the world of American popular song. Though not the first white Southern singer to draw on the blues, nor the first to employ the yodel, 'America's Blue Yodeler' did, in effect, create the blue yodel form by which so many of his successors were inspired, from **Gene Autry** and **Jimmie Davis** to **Hank Williams**, **Lefty Frizzell** and **Merle Haggard**. His influence, however – so pervasive that he has been called the 'Father of Country Music' – stems from his entire output, which, besides blues-derived material, included parlour ballads, fragments of traditional song, railroad and hobo narratives and out-and-out novelties; and from his ingratiating style, which sounded remarkably vivid on records.

He grew up in Meridian, Mississippi, learning to play banjo and guitar as a child. Forced out of his first career on the railroads through tuberculosis, he was working as a private detective and playing banjo in a local string band in Asheville, North Carolina, when he heard that Victor's **Ralph Peer** planned to make records in Bristol, Tennessee. On 4 August 1927, three days after the recording début of the **Carter Family**, he cut his first record singing to his own guitar accompaniment 'The Soldier's Sweetheart' and an old yodel song, 'Sleep, Baby, Sleep'. Four months later

Peer summoned him to Victor's studios in Camden, New Jersey, where he cut the first 'Blue Yodel' (beginning 'T for Texas . . .'), a worldwide million-seller.

In all there were thirteen sides in the (mostly) numbered blue yodel series, and several more in a similar vein, but at the same time Rodgers was singing, and sometimes writing or reshaping, numerous state praise songs ('Mississippi River Blues', 'Jimmie's Texas Blues', 'Peach Picking Time in Georgia'), sentimental numbers about family and home ('Mother, the Queen of My Heart', 'Home Call') and railroad songs, like 'Waitin' for a Train' or the ostensibly autobiographical 'Jimmie the Kid', which accorded with another of his sobriquets, 'The Singing Brakeman' (also the title of the 1929 short feature in which he made his only film appearance). In less than six years he recorded over 100 songs, variously accompanied by his own guitar, Hawaiian trios, string bands both white (such as one led by fiddler Clayton McMichen of **Gid Tanner**'s Skillet-Lickers) and black (the Louisville Jug Band), studio orchestras, Texas fiddle bands prefiguring Western swing, and on one occasion **Louis Armstrong** and his pianist wife Lil Hardin Armstrong ('Blue Yodel No. 9', 1930). Originally issued on Victor, these recordings were licensed to companies in Britain, Australia and India and at home to the mail-order-store label Montgomery Ward, and were re-released on the home market in the thirties on Bluebird. An often-quoted story has it that customers in rural general stores would order a gallon of milk, a dozen eggs and the latest Jimmie Rodgers record.

Between sessions Rodgers toured for the Loew's and Keith vaudeville circuits (1928–9), built himself a home ('Yodeler's Paradise') in Kerrville, Texas, moved to San Antonio in 1930, did a charity tour with monologist Will Rogers (1931), and had a radio show on KMAC, San Antonio (1932). Progressively weakened by TB (about which he wrote two blues), he fulfilled with difficulty his last recording engagement and died in his hotel a few days later.

Soon afterwards his wife Carrie wrote a selective biography, *My Husband Jimmie Rodgers* (1935). She also initiated a 'Rodgers industry', maintained by their daughter Anita Rodgers Court, which helped to bring about the annual celebrations in Meridian (since 1953), an early appearance on reissue albums – RCA eventually reinstated almost his entire output on seven albums – and membership of the Country Music Hall of Fame (1961). A commemorative postage stamp was issued in 1978. Of the considerable literature that has sprung up round him, Nolan Porterfield's *Jimmie Rodgers: The Life and Times of America's Blue Yodeler* (1979) is the most valuable.

No other figure in country music has been so imitated. Many minor performers based their entire act on blue yodels and other Rodgers-like material, and even artists who would later show some individuality, like Gene Autry and Cliff Carlisle, played Rodgers tunes for a few years. Entire albums of Rodgers' songs have been recorded as tributes by **Hank Snow**, Lefty Frizzell and Merle Haggard (*Same Train, Different Time*, 1969), while the stamp of his style is plain in much of the work of **Bill Monroe**, Hank Williams and, especially, **Ernest Tubb** – whose first recordings, in 1937 were not only in Rodgers' manner but accompanied by one of Rodgers' guitars. Generations later Rodgers' music was still a potent element in the vernacular amalgam, whether half-parodied, as by British group the Fendermen in 'Mule Skinner Blues' (Top Rank, 1960), or lovingly remembered by Southern rock musicians like the **Allman Brothers Band**. **Van Morrison** and Haggard (*Same Train, Different Time*, 1969) are among those who have participated in tribute albums to Rodgers. The most recent of these is *The Songs of Jimmie Rodgers* (1997).

NILE RODGERS
b. 19 September 1952, New York, USA

One of the most sought-after record producers of the eighties, Rodgers established himself as a member of top dance-music group Chic.

A New York guitarist, Rodgers worked at Harlem's Apollo Theater before forming the Big Apple Band in 1976 with bassist Bernard Edwards (*b. 31 October 1952, Greenville, N. Carolina*) and drummer Tony Thompson. After a brief foray as new-wave group Allah and the Knife-Wielding Punks, they added singers Alfa Anderson and Norma Jean Wright to become Chic. The new group had immediate success with the disco track 'Dance Dance Dance (Yowsah Yowsah Yowsah)'* (Atlantic, 1977). The follow-up, 'Everybody Dance', on which Luci Martin replaced Wright, reached the British Top Ten. The second album, *C'est Chic* (1978), included the multi-million-seller and American No. 1 'Le Freak' (1979), which featured Edwards' incisive bass lines. The group had further hits with the hypnotic 'I Want Your Love'* and their second American No. 1 'Good Times'*.

Later albums like *Real People* (1980) and *Take It Off* (1981) sold less well but by now Rodgers and Edwards had turned their attention to producing other artists. In 1979 they supervised 'Spacer' (Carrere) by Eurodisco singer Sheila B. Devotion, followed by **Sister Sledge**'s first hits 'We Are Family'* and 'He's the Greatest Dancer' as well as producing successful tracks by **Carly Simon** and **Blondie** singer Debbie Harry (*Koo Koo*).

The distinctive Chic production formula mixed up-beat stylized string charts with Edwards' original bass technique and Rodgers' equally inventive lead guitar. Among the triumphs, however, were failures; sessions with **Aretha Franklin** and **Johnny Mathis** were scrapped when the artists complained of the duo's intransigence in the studio, while **Diana Ross** extensively remixed her Rodgers–Edwards-produced *Diana* album, which included the No. 1 single 'Upside Down'.

After *Tongue in Chic* (1982), Chic split up and Rodgers began a solo career as artist and producer. He recorded *Adventures in the Land of the Good Groove* (1983) and *B-Movie Matinee* (Warners, 1985) and worked with many other artists. Among his productions were **David Bowie**'s *Let's Dance* (1983), **Duran Duran**'s *Notorious* (1986), **Jeff Beck**'s *Flash* (1985), Mick Jagger's 'Let's Work' (1987), **Grace Jones**' *Inside Story* (1986), **Al Jarreau**'s *L Is for Lover* (1986) and **Madonna**'s *Like a Virgin* (1985). Rodgers also recorded and performed with the Honeydrippers, the group formed by ex-**Led Zeppelin** vocalist Robert Plant, and in 1987 with Outloud (Warners). He continued to concentrate on production in the early nineties before teaming up once again with Edwards in 1992 for a short-lived Chic reunion. This produced one unexceptional album, *Chic-Ism* (1992), but after its release Rodgers returned to production, notably with Bowie on 1993's *Black Tie White Noise*, which topped the UK album chart.

Later productions included former lead singer of **Van Halen** Dave Lee Roth's *Your Filthy Little Mouth* (1994) and Samantha Cole's eponymous album (1997).

TOMMY ROE

b. *Thomas David Roe, 9 May 1942, Atlanta, Georgia, USA*

Despite the simplicity of his records (which for the most part were either derivative of **Buddy Holly** or pure bubblegum), Roe was a surprisingly resilient pop star, topping the American charts in both 1962 ('Sheila'*) and 1969 ('Dizzy'*).

While at Brown High School, Roe formed his first band, the Satins, and aged sixteen signed with Judd Records, releasing his own Holly-styled composition, the ebullient 'Sheila' in 1960. However, it was not until he was signed by Felton Jarvis to ABC and re-recorded the song (originally as the B-side of 'Save Your Kisses') with **Jerry Reed** on guitar, that he had his first hit. He followed this with the exuberant 'Everybody' (1963) before his career was interrupted by military service.

In 1966 Roe returned to the charts with the nonsense chants 'Sweet Pea'* and 'Hooray for Hazel'. Then, in 1969, with Steve Barri producing, Roe returned to the sound of 'Sheila' with 'Dizzy' (a song he co-wrote with Freddy Weller, a one-time member of **Paul Revere and the Raiders**) and had a further

American No. 1. Roe, however, never developed as a writer beyond chronicling the coy problems of teenage passion and even Barri's bright production could not disguise the vacuity of Roe's last major hit, the bubblegum 'Jam up Jelly Tight'* (1969). He followed this with a more interesting revival of **Lloyd Price**'s 'Stagger Lee' (1971). Later in the seventies he recorded for MGM South (1972–3) and Movement (1976–8). During the eighties Roe enjoyed limited success on the American country charts, and in 1991 British band the Wonder Stuff and comedian Vic Reeves had a British No. 1 hit with a camp revival of 'Dizzy'.

KENNY ROGERS

b. *Kenneth Donald Rogers, 21 August 1937, Houston, Texas, USA*

The possessor of a warm baritone, Rogers was the most successful country artist of the late seventies and early eighties and the only one to reach the pop charts consistently. He achieved this with a series of duets with such singers as **Kim Carnes**, **Sheena Easton** and **Dolly Parton** and by actively seeking songs from writers outside the country field, including **Lionel Richie** and the **Bee Gees**. In 2000, without the support of a major label, he returned to the top of the country charts with the single 'Buy Me a Rose', on his own Dreamcatcher label.

The son of a dock worker and the younger brother of independent producer and label-owner Lelan Rogers, he formed the Scholars while at high school and had a regional hit with 'That Crazy Feeling' (Carlton, 1958). At the University of Houston he played jazz with the Bobby Doyle Trio and later was a member of the barber-shop quartet, the Lively Ones, before he joined the New Christy Minstrels in 1966. Formed in 1961 by Randy Sparks at the height of the folk boom, the group took its name from E. P. Christy, whose minstrel troupe had been the most successful of the nineteenth century. Like Christy's original troupe, the New Minstrels sang the songs of **Stephen Foster** but as folk songs with modern arrangements, and at the same time they recorded numerous contemporary songs, including their three hits, 'Green, Green', 'Saturday Night' (Columbia, 1963) and 'Today' (1964).

When Rogers joined, the group's hitmaking days were over and within a year he and Mike Settle left to form the First Edition (later Kenny Rogers and the First Edition). Signed to Reprise, they had immediate success with **Mickey Newbury**'s 'Just Dropped in (To See What Condition My Condition Was in)' (1968), a typical 'clever' country song which was mistakenly regarded as being psychedelic by pop commentators and gave the group a mildly hippie image. Even more successful was his recording of Mel Tillis's 'Ruby,

Don't Take Your Love to Town'* (1969). Actually written in response to the Korean War, the song (about a disabled soldier and his wife) was given a new resonance by growing disquiet about the Vietnam War within America. Other hits by the group included **Woody Guthrie**'s 'Reuben James' (1969) and **Mac Davis**'s 'Something's Burning' (1970).

In 1972 Rogers left the group for a solo career but it wasn't until he joined United Artists in 1976 and began recording in a country vein that he returned to the pop (and country) charts with 'Love Lifted Up'. Even more successful was 'Lucille'* (1977) – another tale of an unfaithful wife – Don Schlitz's 'The Gambler'* (1977), 'She Believes in Me'* and 'Coward of the County'* (1979). Most of these were story-songs and both 'The Gambler' and 'Coward' formed the basis of telefilms, *The Gambler* (1980), *The Gambler II* (1983) and *Coward of the County* (1981), starring Rogers. He confirmed his country orientation with duets with Dottie West ('Every Time Two Fools Collide' and 'Anyone Who Isn't Me Tonight', 1978) and 'Love the World Away' from the film *Urban Cowboy* (1979) before 'Lady' (1980), which was written and produced by Richie, gave Rogers his first No. 1 on both the country and pop charts.

Throughout the eighties, as well as his own solo hits, which included 'I Don't Need You' (1981), 'All My Life' (1983), 'This Woman' (RCA, 1984) and 'Morning Desire' (1986), Rogers, like **Willie Nelson**, embarked on a screen career and recorded a series of duets. Among these were 'Don't Fall in Love with a Dreamer' (1980) with Kim Carnes, 'What About Me', with Carnes and James Ingram, a country version of **Bob Seger**'s 1979 hit 'We've Got Tonight' (1983) with Sheena Easton and, most dramatic, the Bee Gees' composition and American No. 1 'Islands in the Stream' (RCA, 1983) with Dolly Parton, with whom he also recorded a Christmas album. His later records included *They Don't Make 'Em like They Used to* (1986) and *Something Inside so Strong* (Warners, 1989). In the early nineties Rogers concentrated on live and TV work. He signed to Giant Records in 1993, releasing the formulaic *If Only My Heart Had a Voice*. *Timepiece* (Atlantic, 1994) was a collection of standards such as 'My Funny Valentine' and 'You Are So Beautiful', produced by **David Foster**.

When, in 1998, Rogers found himself deemed old rather than new country – and without a record deal as a result – he established his own label, Dreamcatcher. Initially it marketed the albums he had retained the rights to, but in 1999 he made his first new recording for the label, 'The Greatest', a paean to baseball, and *She Rides Wild Horses*. He promoted both not through country radio but through public appearances at baseball games and sports television programmes. Both were a success and he followed it

in 2000 with the country chart-topping 'Buy Me a Rose', which he promoted through the television series *Touched by an Angel*, an episode of which was written around the song.

Rogers' son, Kenny Rogers Jnr, recorded the pop song 'Take Another Step Closer' (Cypress, 1989). *Greatest Hits* (HIPP, 1996) is the most representative of several hits collections, while the four-CD set *A Retrospect* (EMI, 1999) is the definitive anthology.

SHORTY ROGERS
b. Milton M. Rajonsky, 14 April 1924, Great Barrington, Massachusetts, USA

A leading modern jazz trumpeter and arranger, Rogers was a key figure in the West Coast school of the fifties.

After classical training at New York's High School of Music and Art, Rogers played briefly with vibraphonist Red Norvo in 1942, before spending three years in the army. Returning to civilian life, he joined **Woody Herman** and recorded with the first and second Herds in 1945–7. He next worked with **Stan Kenton** during the latter's 'progressive jazz' phase of the late forties.

Moving to Los Angeles, Rogers formed his own group and in 1951, with **Gerry Mulligan**, recorded his own compositions 'Didi' and 'Sam and the Lady' (Capitol) in the light, cool style which became known as West Coast jazz. The group also included Jimmy Giuffre (clarinet) and drummer Shelly Manne, who both appeared on *Cool and Crazy* (RCA) as part of a seventeen-piece big band led by Rogers. A small-group version of the sound appeared on *West Coast Blues* (Atlantic) and Rogers also contributed his composition 'Shapes Motions Colors' to *Shelly Manne and His Men Vol. 2* (Contemporary, 1954).

In 1952 Rogers, Giuffre and Mulligan recorded some R&B tracks as Boots Brown and his Blockbusters.

During the sixties and seventies Rogers was in semi-retirement, but he later formed a partnership with his former Kenton colleague Bud Shank (alto sax), recording for Concord and Concept. He also performed with Britain's National Youth Jazz Orchestra.

ROY ROGERS
b. Leonard Slye, 5 November 1911, Duck Run, Ohio, USA, d. 6 July 1998

Though Rogers' screen career outlasted that of fellow singing cowboys **Gene Autry** and **Tex Ritter**, he never sold records in the same quantities as they did. However, the group he originally founded, the **Sons of the Pioneers**, who brought smooth, melodious harmonies to their romantic Western ballads, were probably the most influential of all the 'Western' groups.

Born on a farm in Southern Ohio, he moved with his family to California in 1930, where he worked as a fruit picker. There, after guesting as a vocalist with various groups in the migratory workers' camps, he formed the Sons of the Pioneers in 1934. A typical, if sweeter sounding, country band of the period, the group's entry into movies, with *The Old Homestead*, and their supporting Autry in his first starring picture, *Tumbling Tumbleweeds* (both 1935), brought about the decisive shift in their style and career. Slye quit the group for a solo career as a singing cowboy, first as Dick Weston and then as Rogers in his first starring series Western for Republic, *Under Western Skies* (1938). The group supported Rogers in his films until 1948 and *Grand Canyon Trail* when they were replaced by a virtual carbon copy, the Riders of the Purple Sage (whose name was to inspire the country-rock band of the seventies, New Riders of the Purple Sage).

Many of Rogers' songs were written by members of the Pioneers, including such Western classics as 'Tumbling Tumbleweeds' and 'Cool Water'. In the late forties a few were contributed by **Jule Styne**, then a contract songwriter with Republic, who also provided Autry with the occasional song. In contrast to Rogers, who had little direct influence outside the series Western, the Pioneers found a wider audience.

When Rogers' succeeded Autry at the box-office as 'King of the Cowboys' in 1942, Republic increased the budgets of his films. More interestingly, on the direct orders of studio boss Herbert J. Yates, who had been very impressed with **Rodgers and Hammerstein**'s 1943 Broadway smash *Oklahoma!*, Republic also increased and further stylized the musical content of the films. In 1947 Rogers married his frequent co-star Dale Evans (*b. Frances Smith, 31 October 1912, Uvalde, Texas*), whose strict religious views strongly influenced him. He made his last film for Republic, *Pals of the Golden West*, in 1951, and, after briefly hosting his own TV show, turned to business before the growing nostalgia market brought him out of retirement in the early seventies. He recorded the **Tommy 'Snuff' Garrett** composition 'Hoppy, Gene and Me', which was a minor hit, and returned to the screen as a hard-working cowboy, simple denims replacing the gaudy costumes of old, in *Mackintosh and T.J.* (1975). Subsequently he made regular appearances on TV shows such as *The Muppets*, usually with Evans.

He came out of retirement in 1991 to record *Tribute of Roy Rogers* (RCA), a collection of duets with such contemporary country singers as **Clint Black**, **K. T. Osklin** and **Kathy Mattea**.

The 'Roy Rogers and Dale Evans Museum' in Victorville, California, which documents his career and which Rogers himself maintained, includes the stuffed and mounted body of his famous palomino horse, Trigger (*b. 1932, d. 3 July 1965*).

THE ROLLING STONES

Mick Jagger, b. Michael Philip Jagger, 26 July 1943, Dartford, Kent, England; Brian Jones, b. Lewis Brian Hopkins-Jones, 28 February 1942, Cheltenham, Gloucestershire, d. 3 July 1969, Sussex (replaced by Mick Taylor, b. 17 January 1948, Hertfordshire, replaced by Ron Wood, b. 1 June 1947, London); Keith Richard(s), b. Keith Richards, 18 December 1943; Ian Stewart, b. 1938, d. 12 December 1985; Charlie Watts, b. 2 June 1941, London; Bill Wyman, b. William Perks, 24 October 1936, London

For the decade following their first recordings in 1963 the Rolling Stones were among the major artists who shaped the development of rock music. At the heart of the band was Jagger's mannered but powerful black-influenced singing and Richard's incisive rhythm guitar. While their rebellious image ensured high record sales, it was in live performance that the Stones lived up to their reputation as 'the greatest rock'n'roll band in the world'. From the mid-seventies, the quality of Jagger–Richard's songs declined and later records only intermittently recaptured the power of the group's early work. Thus, although they continued to record, in the eighties and nineties it was their tours that made the headlines.

The British R&B movement of the early sixties was initiated by a number of older musicians who had been in trad bands or skiffle groups. Such performers – among them slide guitarist Brian Knight, Geoff Bradford, Cyril Davies and **Alexis Korner** – drew to them a younger cadre of singers and guitarists whose primary inspiration lay in the more contemporary Chicago rhythm and blues of **Muddy Waters** and the rock'n'roll of **Chuck Berry**. The roots of the Rolling Stones lay in this milieu. Jagger had sung with Korner's band, for whom Watts was a regular drummer, while Jones had played with Knight. By late 1962 the Stones' line-up was virtually complete and early in 1963 they began an eight-month residency at the Crawdaddy Club, Richmond, as a six-piece with Stewart (later their road manager) on piano.

Through their manager Andrew Loog Oldham, the group recorded an up-tempo version of Berry's 'Come on' (Decca, 1963) and **John Lennon** and **Paul McCartney**'s 'I Wanna Be Your Man', which was their first Top Twenty hit. While their stage act still included references to the original blues recordings they were reworking, the shift away from the purism in the Stones' approach was underlined by the choice of **Buddy Holly**'s 'Not Fade Away' and **Bobby Womack**'s soul song 'It's All Over Now' (1964) as single releases.

The band's early albums, *The Rolling Stones* (1964),

Rolling Stones No. 2 (1965) and *Out of Our Heads* (1965), were equally eclectic in their sources, mingling material from Waters and Berry with songs first recorded by Irma Thomas ('Time Is on My Side'), the **Drifters** ('Under the Boardwalk'), **Marvin Gaye** ('Can I Get a Witness'), **Don Covay** ('Mercy Mercy') and rock'n'roll singer Dale Hawkins ('Suzie Q'). The common denominator was Jagger's impassioned singing and the group's rebellious long-haired image which brought growing popularity among teenage audiences and a string of British No. 1s in 1964–5. These included 'It's All Over Now', **Willie Dixon**'s slow blues 'Little Red Rooster' and three of the first songs to be written by Richard and Jagger: 'The Last Time' was a conventional soul-based piece but '(I Can't Get No) Satisfaction' and 'Get off My Cloud' introduced themes of frustration, elation and aggression which mirrored the anger and energy of the Stones' sound. '19th Nervous Breakdown' and 'Paint It Black' (1966) were in a similar vein. The American Top Ten hit 'Mother's Little Helper' came from *Aftermath* (1966), the first of a trio of albums which foregrounded the Rolling Stones as a progressive rock group whose songs commented on the social scene and expressed current preoccupations. While such songs as 'Out of Time' (a British No. 1 for Chris Farlowe, Immediate, 1966) from *Aftermath* used soulmusic structures, *Between the Buttons* (1967) had a lighter, English rock touch (reminiscent of the **Kinks** or **The Who**), and *Their Satanic Majesties' Request* was a psychedelic album complete with sitar-playing from Jones.

1967 was a watershed year for the Rolling Stones. A series of police raids culminated in jail sentences for Jagger, Jones and Richard on drugs charges (which were quashed on appeal), while the group perfected the rock/blues/country music mélange which would form the basis of the Stones' sound for the next two decades. It was first heard on the 1968 single 'Jumping Jack Flash' and on *Beggars Banquet*, the group's most assured album, which included the menacing 'Sympathy for the Devil', the poetic countrified 'No Expectations' and the sardonic anthem 'Salt of the Earth'.

Increasingly marginalized by the success of Jagger and Richard as songwriters, Jones left the group in 1969. Only days after he was replaced by former **John Mayall** guitarist Taylor, he drowned in a swimming pool at his home. 'Honky Tonk Women' reached No. 1 in Britain and America but the year ended in further tragedy when a fan was killed at a free concert in Altamont, California, an event which formed a focal point for the documentary film *Gimme Shelter* (1970).

Let It Bleed (1970) contained some of the group's strongest songs in 'Gimme Shelter' and 'You Can't Always Get What You Want'. In the same year, *One Plus One* – Jean-Luc Godard's film of the Stones in

the studio – was released, and Jagger had starring roles in *Ned Kelly* and *Performance*. After the live recording *Get Yer Ya-Yas Out* (1970), the group made *Sticky Fingers*, the first release on their own label which was distributed by Atlantic. With a sleeve design and logo by Andy Warhol, both the album and 'Brown Sugar' were massive hits.

The double-album *Exile on Main Street* (1972) with its hit single 'Tumbling Dice' marked the end of a highly creative phase for the group. Although they had an American No. 1 ('Angie' 1973) from the inconsistent *Goat's Head Soup* (recorded in Jamaica), the Rolling Stones lost momentum in the mid-seventies. The success of *It's Only Rock'n'Roll* (1974) couldn't disguise the banality of some of the music and soon afterwards Taylor left for a solo career that included work with **Carla Bley** and **Jack Bruce**, **Bob Dylan** and intermittent solo recordings, including a 1979 solo album on Columbia. In the early nineties he released *Stranger in This Town* (1990) and played with American singer-guitarist Carla Olson (*Carla Olson & Mick Taylor Live*, 1990).

Guest guitarists Wayne Perkins and Harvey Mandel appeared on *Black and Blue* (1976) along with Wood, who toured America and Europe with the band. The European dates were captured on *Love You Live* (1977). Distribution of the band's label switched to EMI after the live album, and by the recording of *Some Girls* (1978), the first release under the new deal, Wood had become a permanent member of the group. 'Miss You' from *Some Girls* became the group's first American No. 1 for five years.

During the early eighties the group remained among the most popular live performers in the world but neither *Emotional Rescue* (1980) nor *Tattoo You* (1981) matched their earlier work. Another world tour produced the patchy live album *Still Life* (1982), but the banning of the video for the title track of *Undercover* (1983) drew more attention. In 1985 the Rolling Stones signed their label to Columbia, releasing *Dirty Work* (1986). Produced by Steve Lillywhite, it included the hit singles 'Harlem Shuffle' (a revival of the Bob and Earl 1963 song) and 'One Hit'. By this time, however, individual group members were spending more time on solo projects.

Wyman had a 1983 British Top Twenty hit with 'Si Si Je Suis un Rock Star' (A&M), and released solo albums in 1974, 1976, 1982 and 1993. He also formed an all-star band for charity gigs, Willie & the Poor Boys, releasing an eponymous album in 1985. Jagger released the **Bill Laswell**-produced *She's the Boss* (1985) and the Dave Stewart-produced *Primitive Cool* (1987), on both of which **Jeff Beck** played guitar. In 1993 he released his most consistent solo album, *Wandering Spirit*. With **David Bowie**, he also had a hit with **Martha and the Vandellas**' 'Dancing in the

Streets' (EMI-America, 1985), a performance taken from the Live Aid benefit concert. He also continued with his sporadic acting career, appearing in the sci-fi thriller *Freejack* (1992).

Both Wood (whose solo career dated back to his days in the **Faces**) and Watts made their own albums. Watts had played live with his jazz-blues big band made up of leading British musicians but he used a quintet for the impressive 1991 set of standard ballads *Warm & Tender*. Richards (the 's' had been added in the early seventies) directed the music for *Hail Hail Rock'n'Roll* (1987), Taylor Hackford's concert film about Chuck Berry, and cut the well-received solo album *Talk Is Cheap* (Virgin, 1988). He followed that with the 1991 live album *At the Hollywood Palladium* featuring his own band the X-Pensive Winos and in 1992 released the superior *Main Offender*. In the late eighties and early nineties he also recorded with a number of other artists, notably **Tom Waits** and Berry's pianist Johnnie Johnson.

In 1989 the group laid further claim to their 'greatest rock'n'roll band' title with a major tour and the release of *Steel Wheels*, their best album in a decade. The tour produced an unexceptional live album, *Flashpoint* (1991), which included two new studio tracks. In 1991 the band signed to Virgin Records in a multi-million pound three-album deal. Wyman, who had several outside interests, had been increasingly unhappy in the band in the late eighties and announced his final departure in 1993. He formed his own group, Bill Wyman's Rhythm Kings, which recorded and performed occasionally. The group's best album was *Groovin'* (Papillon, 2000). On it an expanded group, which included **Georgie Fame**, former **Procol Harum** member Gary Booker and former Rolling Stone Mick Taylor recorded a mix of Wyman originals ('Tomorrow Night') and versions of classics, including the title track (originally recorded by the **Rascals**), the **Lovin Spoonful**'s 'Daydream' and **Screamin' Jay Hawkins**' 'I Put a Spell on You'.

For *Voodoo Lounge* (1994), Wyman was replaced by American bassist Darryl Jones, who also took part in their subsequent world tour. The tour was hugely successful and the album won the group their best reviews (and sales) for some time.

In 1995 their recording of 'Start Me Up' was used as the launch theme for the Windows '95 operating system and the group issued their first CD-ROM, an interactive version of *Voodoo Lounge*. That was followed by *Stripped* (1996), which included a superior version of Bob Dylan's 'Like a Rolling Stone' and was their most impressive album for some time. In 1997 they embarked upon yet another lengthy world tour, *Bridges to Babylon*, and in 1998 were the subject of the tribute album *Cover You*, on which the likes of **Johnny Winter**, **Steve Earle** and **Tina Turner** did just

that to Stones' songs. In 1999, the year Jagger and Jerry Hall divorced, the band released the live offering *No Security*.

HENRY ROLLINS
b. 13 February 1961, Washington DC, USA

Crop-haired, musclebound and tattooed, Henry Rollins made an unlikely nineties' Renaissance man. In addition to performing music, which merged rap, metal and funk, his myriad activities have included film acting, the authorship of several books, and performances which mixed stand-up comedy with social comment. Rollins also runs his own music- and book-publishing companies.

Brought up by his mother, who introduced him to jazz and soul music as a (hyperactive) child, the teenage Rollins developed a taste for heavy metal at high school before being converted to punk/hardcore at a gig by pioneering black punk outfit Bad Brains in 1979. He joined local band S.O.A. in 1980, releasing the *No Policy* EP before joining LA-based hardcore band Black Flag in 1981, taking over from vocalist Dez Cadenza, who switched to rhythm guitar. The line-up for *Damaged* (1981) also included guitarist Greg Ginn, bassist Chuck Dukowski and drummer Robo.

Black Flag toured constantly for the next five years and released six further albums, on their own SST label, including *My War* (1982), *Loose Nut* (1985) and *Family Man* (1984), a spoken-word and instrumental album which reflected Rollins' growing interest in the area. He began doing spoken-word performances in 1983 and later alternated spoken-word tours with his live work with his own band.

Black Flag broke up in 1986 after recording *Who's Got the 10½*. Rollins next recorded the solo album *Hot Animal Machine* (1987) and the EP *Drive by Shooting* (1987) as Henrietta Rollins & the Wife-Beating Child Haters. Rollins and guitarist Haskett recruited bassist Andrew Weiss and drummer Sim Cain from Gone (a former Black Flag support group) to form the Rollins Band in 1987, recording the album *Life Time*. The follow-up mini-album, *Do It* (1988), included versions of songs by the **Velvet Underground**, **Chuck Berry** and legendary UK psychedelic shockers the Pink Fairies.

Alongside the Rollins Band's intense live schedule, the singer continued his spoken-word performances, releasing four CDs of this material – *Big Ugly Mouth*, *Sweatbox*, *Live at McCabes* and *Human Butt* – from 1987 onwards. The Rollins Band's *Hard Volume* (1989) and *Turned on (Live in Vienna)* (1990) confirmed the band's reputation for no-frills, aggressive punk-metal, with occasional jazz inflections thrown in. Rollins worked with Weiss on the *Wartime* EP (1990), which included a version of the **Grateful Dead**'s 'Franklin's

Tower', but the following year was marred by the murder of Rollins' friend Joe Cole (a former Black Flag roadie). Rollins and Cole had been returning from a gig when Cole was murdered as they reached the apartment they shared in Los Angeles. The Rollins Band's bluesy *The End of Silence* (1992) was overshadowed by Cole's death, which also formed the central point of Rollins' spoken-word performances that year, captured on *The Boxed Life* and the video *Talking from the Box* (1993).

Rollins had launched his own book-publishing company 2.13.61 in 1984, publishing titles by Exene Cervenka (from LA band X), Vietnam veteran Bill Shields and **Iggy Pop**. Rollins' own written output was prodigious, including collections of short stories, poetry and autobiography, most notably 1993's epic *Black Coffee Blues* and *Now Watch Him Die* (inspired by Cole's death).

In 1993 Rollins also made his Hollywood début in *The Chase*, starring Charlie Sheen, and guested on Iggy Pop's well-received album *American Caesar*. In 1994 the Rollins Band resumed its activities with *Weight*, its first album with ex-Defunkt bassist Melvin Gibbs, who added a funkier element than on previous albums. The band's most successful album, it reached the US Top Fifty. One track, 'Volume 4', dealt with the death of Cole, while another, 'Civilized', was an attack on the misogynistic, violence-glamourizing side of the gangsta-rap movement.

Rollins ended 1994 by publishing a book of reminiscences of his Black Flag days, *Get in the Van*, which also spawned another spoken-word album. The Rollins Band's next album, *Come in and Burn*, didn't appear until 1997. Rollins spent much of the intervening period writing *Do I Come Here Often* (1997), the second volume of the *Black Coffee Blues* series, and publishing the work of a variety of authors, including Hubert Selby Jr, through 2.13.61, which by now also included a record label. His next spoken-word release was the relaxed, comic *Think Tank* (1998). The third *Black Coffee Blues* book, *Smile, You're Travelling*, was published in 1999.

SONNY ROLLINS
b. *Theodore Walter Rollins, 7 September 1929, New York, USA*

Rollins has been one of the major tenor-saxophone players of modern jazz. He began with a bebop approach and in the sixties developed his own response to the avant-garde revolution led by **Ornette Coleman** and **John Coltrane**. In a parallel manner to **Miles Davis**, Rollins devised a style that retained bebop roots while moving towards a method in which lengthy free-association solos were often based on tunes from many sources.

His brother played violin and his sister was a church pianist, but Rollins' early jazz influences were **Coleman Hawkins** and **Charlie Parker**, with both of whom he later recorded. During the early fifties he also played with pianists **Bud Powell** and **Thelonious Monk**. Rollins' first important solo record was *Moving Out* (Prestige, 1954), but the springboard for the development of an individual approach to improvisation was his work in 1956–7 with drummer **Max Roach** and trumpeter **Clifford Brown**.

After cutting *Three Giants* (Prestige, 1956), Rollins made *Saxophone Colossus*, which included the calypso 'St Thomas'. On *Tenor Madness* (1956) he recorded with Coltrane, while *Way Out West* (Contemporary, 1958) included such songs as **Johnny Mercer**'s 'I'm an Old Cowhand', and *Newk's Time* (Blue Note) used **Richard Rodgers**' 'Surrey with a Fringe on Top'. With drummer Philly Jo Jones, Rollins made two live albums at New York's Village Vanguard and a 1958 reunion with Roach resulted in *Freedom Suite* (Candid), an extended composition inspired by the black civil rights struggle.

Rollins was in temporary retirement in 1959–61. He returned to record for RCA a series of albums which displayed a new synthesis. *The Bridge* and *What's New* (with the calypso 'Don't Stop the Carnival', later a pop hit for **Alan Price**) were followed by *Our Man in Jazz* (1962), a collaboration with new-wave trumpeter **Don Cherry**. The film soundtrack *Alfie* (Impulse 1965) was Rollins' most commercially successful record.

Ill health caused a lengthy lay-off in the late sixties but after 1972 he performed and recorded steadily, primarily for Milestone. Following the release of *The Cutting Edge* (an acclaimed performance at the Montreux Jazz Festival in 1974, which included Rufus Harley on bagpipes), Rollins experimented with electric music. *Nucleus* was an orthodox funk album, while *The Way I Feel* was a jazz-rock fusion effort.

Later records included *Don't Stop the Carnival* (1978) and *Sunny Days Stormy Nights* (1985). Rollins' most ambitious work in the eighties was his *Concerto for Tenor Saxophone and Orchestra*, first performed in 1985 with the Yomiuri Nippon Symphony Orchestra in Japan.

Among his subsequent recordings for Milestone are *Falling in Love with Jazz* (1990) with Branford Marsalis and Jack de Johnette, *Here's to the People* (1991) and *Old Flames* (1993).

SIGMUND ROMBERG
b. *29 July 1887, Nagy Kaniza, Hungary, d. 9 November 1961, New York, USA*

Like **Franz Lehár** and **Rudolf Friml**, Romberg found success with his Viennese operettas, notably *The*

Student Prince. He was, however, a far more versatile composer than his forerunners.

Sent to Vienna to study engineering, Romberg immersed himself in the world of Viennese music and in 1909 emigrated to America. He settled in New York and supported himself as a pianist in cafés, forming his own orchestra in 1912. Though only moderately successful, his early compositions ('Some Smoke', 'Leg o' Mutton Rag') attracted the attention of Broadway producers J. J. and Lee Shubert, who employed him as their house composer. His first work for them was *The Whirl of the World* (1914), but his first great success was the sentimental *Maytime* (1917), an adaptation of the Viennese operetta *Wie einst im Mai*, with book and lyrics by Rida Johnson Young. (When it was filmed with **Jeannette MacDonald** and **Nelson Eddy** in 1937, only the waltz 'Will You Remember?' was retained from the original score and a new story was used.) Another adaptation of a Viennese operetta (*Das Dreimaderlhaus*) was *Blossom Time* (1921), a fictionalized version of Franz Schubert's youth for which Romberg rearranged several pieces of Schubert's music. He followed this with one of the greatest successes of the decade, *The Student Prince* (1924), which included the traditional 'Gaudeamus Igitur', 'The Drinking Song' and 'Serenade' and was memorably filmed in 1954 with **Mario Lanza** singing (but not performing) the title role.

The Student Prince was firmly in the operetta tradition but *The Desert Song*, for which Romberg teamed up with Oscar Hammerstein II and **Otto Harbach**, was more modern and was filmed in 1929, 1943 and 1953. The trio next created the extravagant *New Moon* (1928), which also featured a disguised hero and introduced the standard 'Lover Come Back to Me' with which **Paul Whiteman** and **Rudy Vallee**, among others, had big hits in 1929. As well as writing shows throughout the thirties, Romberg wrote the scores for several films, including *Viennese Nights* (1930), *The Night Is Young* (1953) – which featured his and Hammerstein's 'When I Grow Too Old to Dream' (a hit for Nelson Eddy in 1936) – and *Broadway Serenade* (1938). In the forties he toured America with his own orchestra which recorded 'Zing Zing – Zoom Zoom' with **Perry Como** (RCA) and regularly appeared on radio. His final Broadway show was *Up in Central Park* (1945), written with Herbert and **Dorothy Fields**, a musical set at the turn of the century and filmed in 1948 with **Deanna Durbin** and **Dick Haymes**.

In 1954 Romberg himself was the subject of the film *Deep in My Heart*, in which he was played by Jose Ferrer.

ANN RONELL
b. 28 December 1908, Omaha, Nebraska, USA

The first woman to compose and conduct film music in Hollywood, Ronell was also a prolific songwriter.

On graduating from Radcliffe University, Ronell taught music and worked as a rehearsal pianist for Broadway musicals in the late twenties. Throughout the thirties and forties she worked in the theatre, adapting classics, including *The Magic Flute* (1937), and writing the libretto (with Vicki Baum) for the opera *Martha* (1939) and the lyrics for the folk-opera *Oh Susanna* (1947). At the same time she worked as a songwriter for films. Her first notable success was 'Who's Afraid of the Big Bad Wolf?' (1933), which she co-wrote with Walt Disney's musical director Frank E. Churchill for the highly popular cartoon, *Three Little Pigs*. It was during this period that she wrote the classic 'Willow Weep for Me', which has been recorded by numerous performers, most notably by **Billie Holiday** and **Frank Sinatra**.

While working for Disney she met and married producer Lester Cowans. It was his production of *The Story of G.I. Joe* (1945) that saw Ronell move into scoring film music. Her work on that film won an Oscar nomination for the best score. Other scores include *One Touch of Venus* (1948), the Marx Brothers film *Love Happy* (1949) and *The Main Street to Broadway* (1953).

After her retirement in the early sixties, Ronell served on the boards of a variety of music foundations and institutions.

THE RONETTES
Veronica 'Ronnie' Bennett, b. 10 August 1943, New York, USA; Estelle Bennett, b. 22 July 1944, New York; Nedra Talley, b. 27 January 1946, New York

Though their songs were among the most romantic he produced, the Ronettes were the most threatening girl group of the sixties, due to the obsessive sound **Phil Spector** gave their records, coupled with their decidedly working-class notions of glamour – heavy eyeshadow and piled-up hair.

Comprising two sisters and their cousin, the Ronettes began life as a teenage dance-act, the Dolly Sisters. In 1961, at the height of the twist craze, they were employed by the Peppermint Lounge as dancers and were featured in the film *Twist Around the Clock*. Signed to Colpix, they released several records as Ronnie and the Relatives in 1961, and then as the Ronettes ('You Bet I Would', 1962), and worked as back-up singers before meeting Spector, who signed them to his Philles label in 1963.

The intensity of the Ronettes' first Philles release, 'Be My Baby'* (1963), the company's biggest-ever hit, stemmed from the melding of their sultry voices and **Ellie Greenwich** and Jeff Barry's plea for eternal love, with the most symphonic version ever of Spector's 'wall of sound'. It was followed in 1964 by the equally intense 'Baby I Love You' and a trio of lesser hits, '(The Best Part of) Breakin' Up', 'Do I Love You' and the distinctive 'Walking in the Rain', which won Spector his only Grammy award, for 'special effects'. After two minor hits in 1965, 'Born to Be Together' and 'Is That What I Get for Loving You', which featured tremulous lead vocals from Ronnie, Spector, who was running down Philles, allowed Jeffy Barry to produce them. The result gave them their last chart entry, 'I Can Hear Music' (1965), which was a bigger hit for the **Beach Boys** when they revived the song in 1969.

Following the demise of Philles in 1966, Ronnie married Spector. The group briefly signed with A&M (1969) and Buddah (1973, the year she and Spector separated). Following the break up of the Ronettes, Ronnie Spector pursued a solo career rather than join the rock'n'roll revival circuit. She appeared on the début album of Southside Johnny and the Ashbury Dukes, *I Don't Want to Go Home* (Epic, 1976), as a guest vocalist and recorded a solo album, *Siren* (Red Shadow, 1980), and several singles, including 'Say Goodbye to Hollywood', which **Billy Joel** wrote specially for her.

After a long gap, Ronnie returned to recording with *Unfinished Business* (Columbia, 1987). In 1990 she published her autobiography, *Be My Baby. The Best of The Ronettes* (ABKO, 1992) is the definitive collection.

LINDA RONSTADT
b. 15 July 1946, Tucson, Arizona, USA

Ronstadt has been one of the most adventurous female singers of the rock era. She has recorded in a wide variety of styles, including the light operetta of **Gilbert and Sullivan**, R&B and country music, and with artists as diverse as **Nelson Riddle** and **Ruben Blades**. In the course of her career, like **Dolly Parton** and **Emmylou Harris** (with whom she recorded *Trio*, 1987) and **Blondie**'s Debbie Harry, Ronstadt has also managed to live with the burden of a sex-symbol image, while introducing the songs of such writers as **Kate and Anna McGarrigle** and **Elvis Costello** to her huge mainstream following.

Of Mexican and German extraction, Ronstadt grew up listening to **Elvis Presley**, **Hank Williams** and the Mexican folk songs her father played (to which she returned with the evocative *Canciónes de Mi Padre*, 1987). She formed a trio with her brother and sister while at high school, and in 1964 joined the Stone Poneys with Kenny Edwards and Bob Kimmel. Signed to Capitol, the country-rock group's second album produced a surprise Top Twenty hit, 'Different Drum' (1967), written by **Monkee** Mike Nesmith, but by this time the group had broken up and Ronstadt

had gone solo. *Silk Purse* (1970), her second solo album, included the hit 'Long Long Time', but her early work (gathered together on *Retrospective*, 1977) was generally hesitant, with her singing more often ragged than controlled. The most notable feature of *Linda Ronstadt* (1972) was that during its production her backing group evolved into the **Eagles**. The decisive change in her career came when former teen-idol Peter Asher became her producer with *Don't Cry Now* (Asylum, 1973).

Asher (*b. 22 June 1944, London, England*), the brother of actress Jane Asher, formed the soft-voiced harmony duo Peter and Gordon with Gordon Waller; they had some ten hits in the mid-sixties, starting with 'World without Love'* and 'Nobody I Know'* (EMI Columbia/Capitol in America, 1964), both written by **John Lennon** and Jane's boyfriend **Paul McCartney**. Particularly successful in America where their 'Englishness' was much appreciated, the duo's further hits included a pair of revivals in 1964, 'True Love Ways'* (**Buddy Holly**) and 'To Know You Is to Love You' (the Teddy Bears, the group formed by **Phil Spector**), and 'Lady Godiva'* (1966) and 'Knight in Rusty Armour' (1967), songs similar in style to several of **Herman's Hermits**' American hits. When the duo separated, Waller briefly attempted a solo career and Asher turned to production with **James Taylor**, whom he signed to **The Beatles**' Apple label.

In 1973 Asher took control of Ronstadt's career as producer and manager. Their first album together was erratic, but *Heart Like a Wheel* (1974), her last album for Capitol, was West Coast rock at its best. Asher's production is clean-cut and Ronstadt's tremulous, throbbing voice and phrasing reveals a clear understanding of the songs. Equally important was Asher's song selection which mixed classics of the rock era (the **Betty Everett** hit 'You're No Good', Ronstadt's first American No. 1, the **Everly Brothers** 'When Will I Be Loved', the album's other hit single, and Buddy Holly's 'It Doesn't Matter Anymore') with material by contemporary songwriters (Anna McGarrigle's 'Heart Like a Wheel', Lowell George of **Little Feat**'s 'Willin'').

Another key figure in the album's success was musician and arranger Andrew Gold (*b. 2 August 1951, Burbank, California*). The son of film composer Ernest Gold, he was a former member of Bryndle with Karla Bonoff and Wendy Waldman (both frequent collaborators of Ronstadt's) and ex-Stone Poney Edwards. When the group broke up, Gold and Edwards joined Ronstadt and, while the leader of her backing group, Gold had hits of his own – the disturbing 'Lonely Boy' (Asylum, 1977) and 'Thank You for Being a Friend' (1978). Though subsequent releases were less successful, in 1987 he returned to the charts with 'Bridge to Your Heart' (RCA) with one-time member of 10CC, Graham Gouldman, as Wax.

Gold also appeared on Ronstadt's follow-up albums to *Wheel*, *Prisoner in Disguise* (1975), *Hasten Down the Wind**(1976) and *Simple Dreams** (1977), which saw her repeating the formula of *Wheel* with great commercial success. The albums spawned numerous hits, including revivals of **Martha and the Vandellas**' 'Heatwave', **Smokey Robinson**'s 'Tracks of My Tears', Holly's 'That'll Be the Day' and 'It's So Easy', **Roy Orbison**'s 'Blue Bayou'* and even the **Rolling Stones**' 'Tumbling Dice'. Increasingly, however, Ronstadt's singing became mannered, emotional but never passionate, particularly on **Chuck Berry**'s 'Back in the USA' from *Living in the USA* (1978). That album also included her version of Elvis Costello's 'Alison', which prefigured her enthusiastic embrace of the ideals of American new-wave music on *Mad Love* (1980). As well as three further songs by Costello, Ronstadt included three by Mark Goldberg, a member of the Cretones, who played on the album.

Though the album (which included the hit,'How Do I Make You') did not sell as well as previous releases, the experience was clearly a liberating one for Ronstadt, who continued to broaden the range of her activities. She appeared in Joseph Papp's innovative production of Gilbert and Sullivan's *Pirates of Penzance* (1981) and the 1983 film, and sang in a revival of *La Bohème* at the New York Public Theater (1981). Similarly, after the weak *Get Closer* (1982), Ronstadt, who had earlier recorded such standards as Oscar Hammerstein and **Sigmund Romberg**'s 'When I Grow Too Old to Dream', made a trio of albums of standards – *What's New* (1983), *Lush Life* (1984) and *For Sentimental Reasons* (1986) – with arranger Nelson Riddle, who in the fifties had won great acclaim for his work with **Frank Sinatra**. In a similar vein, in 1987 she finally completed the long-planned project of an album with Dolly Parton and Emmylou Harris, *Trio* '(1987), and (with **Joe Jackson**) guested on Ruben Blades' *Escenas* (1985) and **Paul Simon**'s *Graceland* (1986). That was a prelude to *Canciónes de Mi Padre* (Songs for My Father, 1987) in which Ronstadt sang in Spanish a selection of *rancheras* (Mexican cowboy) standards, including 'Los Laureles' and 'Por un Amor'.

A hit duet with **Neville Brother** Aaron on **Barry Mann** and Cynthia Weil's 'Don't Know Much' heralded the 1989 album *Cry Like a Rainstorm, Howl Like the Wind*. She co-produced (with George Massenburg) and sang on Neville's 1991 solo album *Warm Your Heart* and also appeared on the follow-up, *The Grand Tour* (1993). Her solo career continued with two more Spanish language albums in 1992, *Mas Canciónes* and *Frenesi*, before she returned to English-language releases with *Winter Light* in 1993. In the same year she co-produced **Jimmy Webb**'s first album in several years, *Suspended Belief*. However, for most of the nineties she appeared as a guest on other people's records, including the Muppets (*Kermit Unplugged*, 1994), **Frank Sinatra** (*Duets II*, 1995), **Randy Newman** (*Faust*, 1995) and Aaron Neville (*To Make Me Who I Am*, 1997). Other records from this period included the set of lullabies (*Dedicated to the One I Love*, 1996), the pop outing *We Ran* (1998), *Trio II* (1999), a run-of-the-mill outing on which she was reunited with Harris and Parton, and the superior *Western Wall: The Tucson Sessions* (1999), on which, partnered by Harris, she delved into country and blues with a purpose.

EDMUNDO ROS
b. 7 December 1910, Trinidad

The leader of the most popular Latin American dance band in the UK since **Geraldo**, Ros's biggest success was 'Wedding Samba'* (1949).

Ros travelled to London in 1937 and by 1939 was drumming at various London clubs. In 1941 he formed his own band, Rumba with Ros, and signed with Decca. He appeared regularly on the radio throughout the forties on such shows as *The Golden Slipper Club* and *Mr Ros and Mr Ray* (the Ray being Ray Ellington, best remembered for the musical interludes he provided for the **Goons**) and in 1949 had an international hit with 'Wedding Samba', which despite its name was written as a Yiddish tune, 'Der Nayer Sher', in 1940. The song was also an American hit for **Guy Lombardo** and the **Andrews Sisters** with **Carmen Miranda**. Among Ros's many albums was *Rhythms of the South* (Decca, 1957).

DAVID ROSE
b. 15 June 1910, London, England, d. 28 August 1990, Burbank, California

Though he had a long and varied career, Rose is best remembered for the raucous, evocative instrumental 'The Stripper'* (1962).

Raised in Chicago, Rose studied piano as a child and went to the Chicago College of Music. After working as a pianist-arranger for NBC in Chicago, Rose formed an orchestra for the Mutual Broadcasting system in Hollywood in 1938 and, reportedly, after cuts in costs left him with only a string section, began composing and arranging purely for strings. The result was 'Holiday for Strings'* (Victor, 1944), a tune he revived less successfully as 'Holiday for Trombones' (MGM, 1957). Throughout the fifties Rose worked in television, including *Bonanza*, and recorded with his orchestra for MGM. He had a surprise hit with 'Calypso Melody'* (1957), one of the many tunes written to cash in on the calypso craze, and it was his orchestra that supplied the backing to one of **Connie Francis**'s million-sellers, 'My Happiness' (1959).

In 1958 Rose wrote and recorded 'The Stripper' for the television show *Burlesque*. When finally released in 1962 (originally as the B-side to a version of 'Ebb Tide'), the record topped the American charts and sold several million copies worldwide. After that, Rose returned to television work as the musical director of the teleseries *Little House on the Prairie*, in 1981 appearing in one episode as a train engineer (outside music his greatest passion was trains).

FRED ROSE
b. 1897, Evansville, Indiana, USA, d. 1954, Nashville, Tennessee

The most prolific composer of country songs in the forties and early fifties, Rose was a one-time pop singer and pianist whose background and previous work was entirely different from those of **Hank Williams** and **Roy Acuff**. Yet Rose collaborated with Williams in some of his most successful songs, and with Acuff formed a music-publishing company that controlled a number of the most important copyrights in country music, including many by Rose himself.

He grew up in St Louis and in his teens sang and played piano in Chicago honky-tonks. His early compositions were in the popular idiom of their time: they included 'Doo Dah Blues' (1922), 'Honestly and Truly' (1924), 'Deep Henderson' and ''Deed I Do' (both 1926). He also recorded his own and others' songs as a singer/pianist on Brunswick.

He went to Nashville in 1933 to work on radio. Accustoming himself to the subjects and styles of country songwriting, in 1941 he composed 'Be Honest with Me', 'I'm Trusting in You' and 'Tears on My Pillow'. Rose devoted himself thereafter to talent-scouting, publishing and songwriting in Nashville. Among his most famous compositions are 'Kaw-Liga' and 'A Mansion on the Hill' for Williams, the latter written with Williams; 'Roly Poly' and 'Home in San Antonio' for **Bob Wills**; 'Blue Eyes Crying in the Rain', notably revived in 1975 by **Willie Nelson**; 'Take These Chains from My Heart', best known in **Ray Charles**' 1963 version; 'Crazy Heart', 'No One Will Ever Know' and 'We Live in Two Different Worlds'.

After Rose's death, his partnership with Acuff in the Acuff–Rose publishing company was maintained by his son Wesley Rose (1912–1990).

DIANA ROSS
b. 26 March 1944, Detroit, Michigan, USA

Originally lead singer with the **Supremes**, Ross became the leading female black pop singer of the seventies, starring in films and cabaret as well as appearing regularly in the charts.

With the highly successful trio billed as Diana Ross

and the Supremes by 1967, Motown Records founder **Berry Gordy** had already put the spotlight on the lead singer before the group disbanded at the end of 1969. Ross's first eponymous solo album (1970) was produced by **Ashford and Simpson** and included a Top Twenty hit in the lilting 'Reach out and Touch (Somebody's Hand)'. The singer's penchant for melodrama was given full rein on 'Ain't No Mountain High Enough', an American No. 1 previously recorded by **Marvin Gaye** and Tammi Terrell. Ashford and Simpson provided a further Top Twenty hit in 'Remember Me' (1971) while 'I'm Still Waiting' was a British No. 1.

Although Gordy's career strategy for Ross hinged as much on screen, supperclub and album success as the singles charts, Ross had three more No. 1s in the seventies. The Miller–Masser ballad 'Touch Me in the Morning' (1973) was followed by the wistful 'Do You Know Where You're Going to?' (1975) – the theme from *Mahogany*, in which Ross had a starring role, while 'Love Hangover' (1976) had a disco flavour and also topped the R&B charts.

Her film career had begun with the leading role in the **Billie Holiday** biopic *Lady Sings the Blues* (1973), in which Ross gave a creditable version of Holiday's singing. However, both *Mahogany* (which Gordy directed) and *The Wiz*, a black version of *The Wizard of Oz* in which Ross took the **Judy Garland** part, were critical and commercial failures.

Although she had sharp disagreements with them, the arrival of **Nile Rodgers** and Bernard Edwards as producers of *Diana* (1980) saw an upturn in Ross's fortunes. 'Upside Down'* harnessed her evocative soprano to a contemporary disco sound and it reached No. 1. The same album included the Top Ten hit 'I'm Coming Out' and the following year Ross and **Lionel Richie** topped the charts with 'Endless Love'*, the most successful of a series of duets with such singers as Marvin Gaye ('You Are Everything', 1974) and **Julio Iglesias** ('All of You', 1984).

In 1981 Ross severed a twenty-year connection with Motown and signed to RCA. She produced *Why Do Fools Fall in Love* and had hits with the title track (a revival of the **Frankie Lymon** classic) and 'Mirror Mirror'. *Silk Electric* (1983) included the Top Ten hit 'Muscles'. After *Swept Away* (1984), Barry Gibb of the **Bee Gees** produced *Eaten Alive*, with **Michael Jackson** duetting on the title track. The album also included the Supremes-like 'Chain Reaction' a British No. 1.

Red Hot Rhythm and Blues (1987) was produced by **Tom Dowd** and was Ross's homage to the R&B tradition, containing versions of the **Drifters**' 'There Goes My Baby' and the Bobbettes' 'Mr Lee', as well as a song by **Simply Red**'s Mick Hucknall. *Greatest Hits Live* (1989) was recorded during her 1989 world tour. She returned to Motown for the Nile Rodgers-produced

Workin' Overtime (1989). *The Force behind the Power* (1991) reached the British Top Twenty and included the Top Five single, 'When You Tell Me that You Love Me'. Sell-out UK tours in 1991 and 1992 preceded a return to *Lady Sings the Blues* territory on *Live . . . Stolen Moments* (1993), an in-British concert set on which Ross tackled jazz and blues standards. This sold disappointingly, but the compilation *One Woman . . . The Ultimate Collection* confirmed her long-standing appeal when it climbed to the upper reaches of the European album chart later that year. That set the pattern for the nineties when Ross's original albums, which included *Take Me Higher* (1995) and *The Voice of Love* (1996), were overshadowed by reissues such as *40 Golden Motown Greats* (1998). She started the twenty-first century unsteadily when her US tour with a makeshift Supremes in support was a commercial failure.

NINO ROTA
b. 31 December 1911, Milan, Italy, d. 10 April 1979

Just as the music of **Bernard Herrmann** conjures up the images of Alfred Hitchcock, so Rota's music is associated with the films of Federico Fellini, with whom he collaborated over a period of some twenty-five years. During this time he also wrote for other Italian directors and won international recognition for his operas and symphonies. In America, he was best known for the melodic scores for *The Godfather* (1972) and *The Godfather Part II* (1974), for which he won an Oscar.

A child prodigy – he wrote an oratorio at the age of eleven – Rota wrote his first film score in 1933 for *Treno Popolare* and began his association with Fellini with *The White Sheik* (1952). Though his concert music and operas were known for their complexity, Rota's film scores, in the words of one critic, 'were noted for their appealing simplicity and were usually melodic and memorable'. As well as his work for Fellini, Rota collaborated frequently with Luchino Visconti (including *Rocco and His Brothers*, 1960, and *The Leopard*, 1963). His score for *The Godfather* included a love theme which provided both **Al Martino** (who also appeared in the film) and **Andy Williams** with hits in 1972. The score of *Godfather III* (1990) made extensive use of his music for the earlier films in the series.

ROXETTE
Per Gessle, b. 12 February 1959, Halmstad, Sweden; Marie Fredriksson, b. 29 May 1958, Halmstad

Swedish duo Roxette became Sweden's most successful musical export since **Abba**. They sold some 30 million albums with their catchy, sixties-influenced pop-rock in the late eighties and early nineties and, unlike Abba, found real success in the US where their clean good looks and bright pop sound found favour with the MTV generation.

Vocalist Fredriksson and guitarist/singer Gessle (a former member of new-wave band Gyllene Tider) had each made two solo albums when the formation of a duo was suggested by former Abba manager Thomas Johannson in 1985. Under the name Roxette, and using the material and musicians assembled by Gessle for a planned solo album, the pair recorded an English-language single, 'Never-Ending Love', which was an immediate hit in Scandinavia. In 1986 they released *Pearls of Passion*.

Import copies of the second Roxette album, *Look Sharp* (1988), and one track in particular, 'The Look', filtered through to the US, where the song entered the US Top 100 purely on radio plays. 'The Look' topped the US singles chart in the spring of 1989 and the album was a US Top Thirty hit. There were two more US chart-toppers in 'Listen to Your Heart' and 'It Must Have Been Love'. The latter was featured on the soundtrack of the film *Pretty Woman*.

After releasing the third Roxette album, *Joyride* (1991), with its attendant hits in the title track and 'Fading Like a Flower', the duo undertook their first-ever world tour. During this period Roxette recorded their fourth album, a mixture of live recordings, new studio works and two songs taped in a Buenos Aires hotel room. *Tourism* (1992) sold poorly in the US, but was successful in the UK and Europe, yielding further hit singles.

After remaining inactive for most of 1993 because of the birth of Fredriksson's daughter, the pair released *Crash! Boom! Bang!* (1994). They also toured with a live band that included bassist Anders Herrlin and guitarist Michael Andersson. The album featured the European Top Twenty hits 'Sleeping in My Car' and 'Fireworks' but was less successful in the US. Even more successful in Europe was the greatest hits collection, *Don't Bore Us Get to the Chorus* (1995). In 1999 they toured extensively in support of *Have a Nice Day*. After a label change to edel America they had a further US hit with the anthemic ballad 'I Wish I Could Fly' (2000).

ROXY MUSIC
Brian Eno, b. 15 May 1948, Woodbridge, Suffolk, England; Bryan Ferry, b. 26 September 1945, Washington, Tyne and Wear; Andy Mackay, b. 23 July 1946; David O'List (replaced by Phil Manzanera, b. 31 January 1951, London); Graham Simpson (replaced by Rik Kenton, replaced by John Porter); Paul Thompson, b. 13 May 1951, Jarrow, Tyne and Wear

A highly influential art-rock group in the seventies,

Roxy Music was built around **Bryan Ferry**'s matinée-idol stage presence, his quirky, unsettling songs and the (for the time) advanced electronic sounds conjured up by **Brian Eno**. In the eighties the group's work shifted towards a lush romanticism while Ferry, Manzanera and, to a lesser extent, Mackay pursued parallel solo careers.

A former student of pop painter Richard Hamilton and a school teacher, Ferry had fronted Gasboard, a Newcastle-based soul and R&B band. He travelled to London in 1970 to form an 'avant rock' group with ex-Gasboard bassist Simpson, saxophonist and synthesizer-player Mackay and electronics expert Eno. Thompson joined on drums and former Nice guitarist O'List was soon replaced by Manzanera from progressive band Quiet Sun. O'List later formed Jet with Andy Ellison, ex-**Marc Bolan**'s band John's Children.

Simpson was ousted before the group was signed to Island where former **King Crimson** member Pete Sinfield produced *Roxy Music* (1972), very much a pop-art artefact, from the period pin-up on the sleeve to the collage effect of 'Re-make/Re-model' which put **Duane Eddy**-style guitar next to bluebeat sax and jazz piano-playing in the style of Cecil Taylor. The bouncy 'Virginia Plain' was a Top Ten hit as was 'Pyjamarama', neither of them included on the band's début. Porter took over on bass for the second album (he would be replaced by a string of temporary bassists for the rest of the band's career, including ex-the Big Three member John Gustafson and future **Adam and the Ants** member Gary Tibbs). *For Your Pleasure* (1973) included the parodic 'Do the Strand' and the eerie 'In Every Dream Home a Heartache', a love song to an inflatable sex doll.

For *Stranded* (1973), Eno was replaced by former Curved Air violinist Eddie Jobson. 'Street Life' was another Top Ten hit while 'A Song for Europe' accurately parodied the musical style of the Eurovision Song Contest. With *Country Life* (1974) and its banal hit 'All I Want Is You', the momentum of innovation slowed down and it virtually stopped with *Siren* (1975), where only 'Love Is the Drug', Roxy Music's first American hit (and a hit again in Britain when reissued in 1996), stood out.

The group was then put on hold for three years (a stop-gap live album *Viva!* was released in 1976) while Ferry made solo albums, Manzanera followed his impressive 1974 début *Diamond Head* with an album recorded with his old band Quiet Sun – *Mainstream* (1975), *K Scope* (1978) and, with Eno and the band 801, *801 Live* (1976) and *Listen Now* (1977). McKay had already made a start at a solo career with the stylish-but-camp *In Search of Eddie Riff* (1974) and *Resolving Contradictions*.

A rejuvenated Roxy Music returned with *Manifesto*

(1979) which reached the American Top Thirty and provided British hits with the lilting 'Dance Away' and 'Angel Eyes'. *Flesh and Blood* (1980) brought further success with the more mainstream 'Over You' (1981) and 'Oh Yeah (On the Radio)'. The same year, Roxy Music released a faithful reading of **John Lennon**'s 'Jealous Guy' as a tribute to the dead ex-**Beatle**.

The climax of this phase of the group's evolution was *Avalon* (1982) whose drifting, idyllic 'Avalon' and 'More than This' both reached the British Top Ten. By now the core of the band was the trio of Mackay, Manzanera and Ferry, who promptly jettisoned Roxy Music to return to solo activity. The live mini-album *Musique/The High Road* (1983) was the band's last release, although a 1982 concert was later released as *Heart Still Beating* (1990) and several compilations also appeared. Manzanera followed Ferry's example after releasing an eponymous album with Mackay as the Explorers (1985). He released *Guitarissimo* (EG) in 1986 and *Southern Cross* the following year before launching his own Expression label with another album with his sax-playing former colleague, *Manzanera & Mackay* (1990). After some ten years travelling in Latin America, Manzanera returned to the studio with *Vozero* (Expression, 1999), on which, again in partnership with Mackay (and with occasional vocal support from **Robert Wyatt**), he explored Latin music in a series of extended pieces. *The Manzanera Collection* (Virgin, 1995) is an anthology of Manzanera's solo work and *The Thrill of It All* (1996) is the definitive Roxy Music retrospective.

HARRY ROY

b. 12 January 1900, London, England, d. 1 February 1971, London

A popular British bandleader of the thirties, Roy was known as 'King of the Hot-Cha', a reference to his penchant for novelty items such as 'Leicester Square Rag' and 'Sarawakee', written in honour of his wife, the daughter of the Rajah of Sarawak.

A clarinettist, Roy first worked professionally in his brother Sidney's band, the Darnswells, in 1914. Later the brothers formed the Original Lyric Five and replaced the **Original Dixieland Jazz Band** when that group left its residency at London's Hammersmith Palais in 1920. This group evolved into the Original Chricton Lyricals and by the late twenties were playing regularly at various West End restaurants in London. After a tour of Europe in 1930, Roy took over leadership of the band and in 1933 started to broadcast and appear in various revues. The band recorded prolifically for Decca and Parlophone (often as Harry Roy's Tigermuffins, which featured the twin pianos of Ivor Moreton and Dave Kaye), mostly in a novelty vein with Roy's strident singing prominent.

His recording career came to an end after the Second World War and unlike other bandleaders, such as **Billy Cotton** or **Geraldo**, unable to diversify into variety or band management, Roy left showbusiness.

MIKLOS ROZSA
b. 18 April 1907, Budapest, Hungary, d. 1995, Hungary

A film and television composer, best remembered as the author of the theme for *Dragnet* and for his use of the theramin, an electronic instrument, to suggest psychological disorder in his Oscar-winning score for Alfred Hitchcock's *Spellbound* (1945), Rozsa was equally at home in the world of the historical epic and won an Oscar for *Ben Hur* (1959), regarded by many as one of the finest scores ever written for a Hollywood movie. He was also one of the few Hollywood composers to continue to write concert music and be accepted by the concert world as a serious composer. In recognition of this dual career he called his autobiography *Double Life*.

Rozsa took up the violin at the age of five and in his twenties, while still in Hungary, wrote several ballets. One of these attracted the attention of director Jacques Feyder, who commissioned him to write his first score, *Knight without Armour* (1936), which included several songs for **Marlene Dietrich**. This led to Rozsa's scoring several, mostly exotic, films for fellow Hungarian Alexander Korda in Britain, including *The Four Feathers* (1939) and *The Thief of Bagdad* (1940). After this he travelled to Hollywood, where he worked mainly on psychological dramas. These included *Double Indemnity* (1944), *The Lost Weekend* (1945), *The Killers* (1946), the central motif of which he later used as the theme for the *Dragnet* teleseries, which provided bandleader Ray Anthony with a hit in 1953 (Capitol), *Brute Force* and the Oscar-winning *A Double Life* (1947), *Criss Cross* (1949) and *The Asphalt Jungle* (1950).

In all these films Rozsa's scores intensified rather than romanticized the violence and brutality of the worlds depicted. Later he adapted several of the scores as 'The Background to Violence' suite. With the success of *Quo Vadis* (1951), Rozsa became identified with a series of historical films in which he adopted an equally realistic approach, basing his scores on music of the time (often using instruments of the period). Among the best scores in this vein were those for *El Cid* and *King of Kings* (both 1961).

Following the revival of interest in film music in the seventies, which led to scores by **Max Steiner** and **Eric Wolfgang Korngold** being made available on albums, Rozsa conducted the Royal Philharmonic Orchestra in 1984 in excerpts from several of his scores on *Immortal Music of Miklos Rozsa* (Memoir).

RICK RUBIN
b. 1963, Long Island, New York, USA

As a producer and record company chief, Rubin has made a major contribution to the rap and heavy metal movements of the past decade.

Rubin became involved with rap music while a student at New York University. His first production was 'It's Yours' by T La Rock and Jazzy J in 1983. He launched the Def Jam label with his partner Russell Simmons the following year by issuing 'I Need a Beat' by LL Cool J. After the success of early singles, Def Jam concluded a distribution agreement with CBS. This led to the Rubin-produced **Beastie Boys'** *Licensed to Ill* and **Run DMC**'s *Raising Hell*. Both included rap–heavy rock fusions, an indication of the route Rubin's later work would take. The label's most successful rap artists were **Public Enemy**.

In 1988 Rubin and Simmons ended their partnership. Simmons remained in New York to concentrate on R&B recordings with Def Jam while Rubin moved to Los Angeles to set up the Def American label. His first signing was thrash-metal group Slayer, whose *Reign in Blood* (1989) he produced. Among the other early signings to the label were Danzig, Masters of Reality and British groups the Cult and Wolfsbane. Def American also released albums by the controversial right-wing stand-up comedian Andrew Dice Clay.

Rubin later expanded the label's range to include rap (the Geto Boys), mainstream rock (**Black Crowes**) and British indie music (the **Jesus and Mary Chain**). During this period he also produced albums by acts not signed to the label. His major productions included the Cult's *Electric* (Sire, 1987), the **Red Hot Chili Peppers'** commercial breakthrough, *Blood Sugar Sex Magick* (Warner, 1991), and **Tom Petty**'s *Wildflowers* (1994).

In 1993 he ceremonially buried the word 'Def', claiming its radical edge had been destroyed. The first major project for his new American Recordings label was **Johnny Cash**'s *American Recordings* (1994), an album of songs by contemporary writers. Subsequent productions for American included **Donovan**'s *Sutras* (1996) and a further album by Cash (*Unchained*, 1997).

RUN DMC
Joseph 'Run' Simmons, b. 24 November 1966, New York City, USA; Darryl 'DMC' McDaniels, b. 31 May 1964, New York City; DJ Jam Master Jay, b. Jason Mizzell, 1965, New York

As the founders of 'hardcore rap', Run DMC took hip-hop back to the street, from where it has seldom strayed since. Their insistence on 'keeping it real' paved the way for the later politicized rap of **Public Enemy** and **Boogie Down Productions**, and set the tone for the next decade of rap. Run DMC were also the first globally famous rap crew, appearing on both MTV and the cover of *Rolling Stone* magazine.

The trio went to school together in the Hollis suburb of New York's Queens district. Simmons' elder brother was Russell Simmons, who set up the hip-hop management company Rush Productions in the early 1980s, and later formed the record label Def Jam with **Rick Rubin**. Russell Simmons encouraged his brother and McDaniels to form a rap group, which they did, taking the names Run and DMC and enlisting their friend Mizell as their DJ.

The group signed to Profile Records in 1983, releasing their début single 'It's Like That'/'Sucker MCs' the same year. The tracks sounded like no others in rap at the time, utilizing contemporary teenage street jargon over sparse drum-machine beats and Jam Master Jay's skilful scratching. As well as a new sound, Run DMC also gave hip-hop a new image, rejecting the sub-**George Clinton** jumpsuit finery of **Grandmaster Flash** and his ilk in favour of streetwear, particularly sports clothing by Adidas and Puma. 'It's Like That' was a Top Twenty R&B hit, as was its follow-up, 'Hard Times'. Their eponymous début album appeared on Profile in 1984 and was a huge success, becoming the first rap album to achieve gold status.

The release of their second album, *King of Rock* (1985), saw Run DMC as the most popular and influential rappers in the US, underscored by their appearance in the rap movie *Krush Groove*, which was loosely based on Russell Simmons' life. Under the influence of Def Jam bosses Simmons and Rubin, they were also using more rock and heavy metal riffs, often played by session guitarist Eddie Martinez, as the backing for their raps. Hits from the LP included the title track and 'My Adidas', a hymn to the fashionable running shoes whose manufacturers had signed a sponsorship deal with the group. Their rap/rock hybrid broke into the mainstream in 1986 with their third album, *Raising Hell*. The album, a US Top Ten hit, also included the groundbreaking Top Ten single 'Walk This Way', a rap cover-version of a song by US rock band **Aerosmith** with guest appearances from two members of the band, singer Steve Tyler and guitarist Joe Perry. The album ultimately went platinum in the US, and also spawned the hits 'You Be Illin'' and 'It's Tricky'.

Run DMC released *Tougher than Leather* in 1988, but by now the rap world was beginning to change, with the emergence of hardcore political rappers like Public Enemy and Boogie Down Productions. The album still sold well, but the band's audience was starting to move on to newer acts, and it spawned no significant hit singles. The group also contributed to the soundtrack of *Ghostbusters II* in 1989 and to the television show tie-in *The Beavis and Butt-head Experience* in 1993.

1990's *Back from Hell* sold poorly, marking the start of a difficult period for the band. McDaniels lapsed into alcoholism, and Simmons faced a rape charge. After McDaniels dried out and the charges against Simmons were dismissed, both rappers became born-again Christians, touting their religious conversion on the 1993 album *Down with the King*, whose title track was a Top Ten R&B hit. However, a mark of just how unthreatening they, and a large slice of rap, had become was their contribution to the rap seasonal album, *A Very Special Christmas* (1997). The group continued to tour, and in 1998 enjoyed unexpected pop success with a tough house remix of 'It's Like That' by New York dance producer Jason Nevins. The definitive retrospective is *Together Forever – Greatest Hits 83–98* (1998).

TODD RUNDGREN
b. 22 June 1948, Upper Darby, Pennsylvania, USA

One of the most admired record producers in seventies rock, Rundgren, who also had a prolific recording career as a writer, singer and founder member of the progressive rock group Utopia, was one of the first rock musicians to embrace the Internet.

At high school in 1965 he formed Money and at college was a member of blues band Woody's Truck Stop. Under the influence of British rock as purveyed by **The Who**, **Cream** and the **Yardbirds** (after one of whose songs it was named), the group became the Nazz. Two albums were released in 1968–9 by Screen Gems-Columbia but it was not until after the band had split up that 'Hello It's Me' (1970) was a minor hit. Their third album, *Nazz III*, appeared in 1971.

Former Woody's manager Paul Fishkin signed Rundgren to Albert Grossman's Bearsville company. As a resident engineer/producer at the company's studio, Rundgren worked on albums by American Dream, Halfnelson (later to become **Sparks**), **Jesse Winchester**, Chicago blues harmonica-player James Cotton, **Paul Butterfield** and **The Band**.

Meanwhile, *Runt* (Ampex, 1970) gave him a hit single with the sparkling 'We Gotta Get You a Woman'. The following year Rundgren released the less successful *Ballad of Todd Rundgren* but also produced Badfinger's *Straight Up* with its million-selling single 'Day by Day'. On the ambitious double-album *Something/Anything* (Bearsville, 1972), Rundgren played nearly every instrument and won critical comparisons with **The Beatles**, **Carole King**, **Jimi Hendrix** and Motown. The album provided hit singles with 'I Saw the Light' and a reworked 'Hello It's Me'.

From 1973 Rundgren pursued three parallel careers as solo artist, producer and member of Utopia, a band with featured synthesizer-player Jean Yves Labat and whose initial stage act was focused on a geodesic dome. The group's 1974 début album was preceded by the grandiose *A Wizard, A True Star*, whose nineteen tracks included a song cycle dealing with the theme of rock superstardom.

During the mid-seventies both Rundgren and Utopia released annual albums. The solo work veered from the Eastern mysticism of *Initiation* (1975), with its thirty-six-minute instrumental 'A Treatise on Cosmic Fire', to the rock styling of *Faithful* (1976), whose revivals of sixties material included a hit in the **Beach Boys**' 'Good Vibrations'. Among Utopia's ambitious projects was the concept album *Ra* (1976).

Productions during this period included *Stagefright* (**The Band**, 1970), *Great Speckled Bird* (**Ian and Sylvia**, 1970), *War Babies* (**Hall and Oates**, 1974), *The New York Dolls* (1973), *We're an American Band* (**Grand Funk Railroad**, 1973), *L* (Steve Hillage, 1973) and *Bat Out of Hell* (**Meat Loaf**, 1977). These demonstrated Rundgren's wide range as a producer. Later productions, for **Patti Smith** (*Wave*, 1979), **Tom Robinson** (*TRB 2*, 1979) and the Psychedelic Furs (*Forever Now*, 1982), showed that he could also work with new-wave artists. In 1979 he built his own video studio. Later albums supervised by Rundgren included work by Shaun Cassidy (*Wasp*, 1980), Jim Steinman (*Bad and Good*, 1981), Lords of the New Church (*Live for Today*, 1986), and Canadian band the Pursuit of Happiness (*Love Junk*, 1988).

His own records for Bearsville continued with *Healing* (1981) and *The Ever Popular Tortured Artist Effect* (1982) but with the demise of the label he moved to Warners for *A Cappella* (1985), which multi-tracked and sampled Rundgren's voice. Among Utopia's later albums were *Swing to the Right* (Network, 1982) and *Oblivion* (Passport, 1983). The group split in 1986, leaving behind the compilation *Trivia* (1987), although they briefly re-formed in 1992, an event captured on *Redux '92 – Live in Japan*.

Ever ambitious, Rundgren's next move was to turn late British playwright Joe Orton's rejected Beatles film script, *Up Against It*, into a musical. It ran briefly in New York, and one song from the project appeared on *Nearly Human* (1989). Rundgren mixed live work (which produced 1991's in-concert set *2nd Wind*) with production over the next three years, during which he became increasingly involved with the emerging interactive technology. In 1993 he issued *No World Order*, billed as the world's first album to be made available as an interactive CD. His commitment to new media resulted in him becoming a consultant to online service provider CompuServe in the mid-nineties, releasing a further interactive CD (*The Individualist*, 1995) and being the first major rock star to establish his own website. By now completely in control of his own career, he created a subscription service for his fanbase through which they could regularly

download new works (music, writings). At the same time he recorded new versions of past material for Angel (for example, *With a Twist*, 1997, on which he added a bossa nova rhythm to past songs) and toured in the guise of a lounge act.

ART RUPE
b. 1919, Pittsburgh, Pennsylvania, USA

Rupe was the founder of Specialty Records, the most important West Coast independent R&B label of the fifties. Among the artists who recorded for it were **Little Richard**, **Lloyd Price**, **Guitar Slim** and **Roy Milton**.

The son of European immigrants, Rupe was raised in Pittsburgh where he grew up listening to black music. After graduating from high school, he travelled to Los Angeles to study at UCLA and while there joined Atlas Records in the early forties. Despite issuing records by **Frankie Laine** and **Nat 'King' Cole**, then recording as the King Cole Trio ('My Lips Remember Your Kiss', 1943), the company failed and in 1944 Rupe formed Jukebox Records with the aim of recording black acts. His first signings were the Sepia Tones and Roy Milton. He produced Milton's hits 'Boogie No. 1' (1944) and 'R. M. Blues'* (1945), both influential jump-blues songs that anticipated the more raucous sounds of fifties rhythm and blues. In 1946 Rupe formed Specialty and had success with Milton's pianist Camille Howard ('X-temporaneous Boogie', 1948). He started recording gospel in 1947, including the **Swan Silvertones** ('Trouble in My Way') and later the Soul Stirrers, whose lead singer was **Sam Cooke** ('Touch the Hem of His Garment'). Greater success came with the impassioned balladry of **Jimmy and Joe Liggins** ('Pink Champagne', 1950), and the soft balladry of **Percy Mayfield** ('Please Send Me Someone to Love'*, 1950) and **Jesse Belvin** ('Dream Girl', 1953, recorded as Jesse and Marvin).

In 1952, after hearing **Fats Domino**, Rupe travelled to New Orleans in search of new acts. Through **Dave Bartholomew** he found and recorded Price, whose 'Lawdy Miss Clawdy'* was the biggest-selling R&B record of 1952. Also in New Orleans, Rupe found Guitar Slim, whose emotional 'The Things I Used to Do' (1954) was to become a modern blues classic. An even more important discovery was Little Richard, who opened the white rock'n'roll market to Specialty with a series of hits beginning with the frenetic 'Tutti Frutti' (1955), subject of a bland cover by **Pat Boone**.

The success of Little Richard led Rupe to record several more artists in a similar fashion. The first was pianist **Larry Williams**, whose major hits were 'Short Fat Fannie'*, 'Bony Moronie'* (1957) and 'Dizzy Miss Lizzy' (1958). Like Little Richard, Williams was unable to escape from the shadow of his fifties hits and after

leaving Specialty he only recorded intermittently.
There was also **Don and Dewey**. But most exciting of
Specialty's Little Richard sound-alike recordings was
Jerry Byrne's 'Lights Out' (1958), the singer's only hit.
A rock'n'roll classic, the song, co-written by **Dr John**,
produced by Harold Battiste and featuring the
pounding piano of Art Neville of the **Neville
Brothers**, was performed by the seventeen-year-old
white Southerner in an electrifying, impassioned
manner.

In 1959, with the first wave of rock'n'roll coming to
an end and having difficulties with his producers and
an increasingly erratic Little Richard, Rupe abruptly
closed down Specialty. He turned to investments in
oil and real estate, only reviving Specialty in the late
sixties with a series of carefully documented reissues
initially under the direction of Barret Hansen.

RUSH

*Geddy Lee, b. 29 July 1953, Toronto, Canada; Alex Life-
son, b. 27 August 1953, Surnie, British Columbia; John
Rutsey (replaced by Neil Peart, b. 12 September 1952,
Hamilton, Ontario)*

The leading Canadian heavy-metal band, Rush's
three-piece line-up was based on such sixties models
as **Cream** and the **Jimi Hendrix** Experience.

Singer and bassist Lee formed the group at high
school in 1969 with Rutsey (drums) and Lifeson (guitar). The group built up a local following for their
melodic hard rock and in 1973 released an album on
their own Moon label. The record was leased by Mercury for US distribution. Peart joined for *Fly by Night*
(Mercury, 1975) and added his penchant for rambling,
science-fiction and fantasy lyrics to Lee's tunes and
high-pitched singing. *2112* (1976) was a concept album
based on the work of novelist-philosopher Ayn Rand
and brought accusations of neo-fascism which Rush
denied.

A Farewell to Kings (1977), which featured 'Cygnus
X-1', the tale of a descent into a black hole in space,
was recorded at Rockfield, a studio in Wales. It was
followed by the bestselling *Hemisphere* (1978) and *Permanent Waves* (1980), which included a British hit
single in 'Spirit of the Radio'. With *Moving Pictures*
(1981) and *Signals* (1982), Rush shifted towards
briefer, more precise songs and 'New World Man'
(1982) was a Top Twenty hit. Lee also sang on the
novelty hit 'Take Off' by Canadian television characters Bob and Doug McKenzie (satirists Dave Thomas
and Rick Moranis).

For *Grace under Pressure* (1984), Rush replaced
their long-serving co-producer Terry Brown with
Peter Henderson. *Power Windows* (1985), produced by
Peter Collins, included string sections and a choir. In
1987 the group released the well-received *Hold Your

Fire, their twelfth studio album, and in 1989 the live
set, *Show of Hands*. It was followed the same year by
the unremarkable *Presto*, their first for their new label,
Atlantic. The band, as always, toured heavily to promote the album, which made the US Top Twenty.
The follow-up, *Roll the Bones* (1991), was more successful, giving the band a US Top Five album, and
1993's *Counterparts* repeated the trick, reaffirming
Rush's major league status after almost a quarter century of existence. In 1996 Lifeson issued his first solo
album, *Victor*, and the band returned to the US Top
Five with *Test for Echo*, in support of which the band
toured for two years, eventually releasing the live set
Different Stages in 1998.

OTIS RUSH
b. 29 April 1934, Philadelphia, Mississippi, USA

A contemporary of **Buddy Guy** and **Magic Sam**, and
often grouped with them as an instigator of the West
Side Chicago blues style of the late fifties, Rush was
one of the most intense performers of his generation.
Crying and groaning the blues to a flurry of guitar
notes, he made so awesome an impact with his first
recordings that he afterwards found it hard to measure up to his own past.

He moved to Chicago in his teens and by 1955 was
leading a club band. Between 1956 and 1958 he made a
series of singles for Cobra with seasoned accompanists like Walter 'Shakey' Horton (harmonica),
Harold Ashby (tenor) and Lafayette Leake or Little
Brother Montgomery (piano). These ranged from
jump blues ('Jump Sister Bessie') and pop songs
('Violent Love') to the magnificent turbulence of 'I
Can't Quit You Baby' (his first release), 'Groaning the
Blues', 'Checking on My Baby', 'All Your Love' and
'Double Trouble'. He also played on other people's
sessions: he was, for example, the guitarist on Guy's
début single (Artistic, 1958).

Subsequent signings to Chess (1960) and Duke
(1962) were briefer and less productive, though each
elicited a first-rate performance: 'So Many Roads, So
Many Trains' on Chess, 'Homework' on Duke. Contractually bound to the latter, Rush did not record
again until 1965, when he participated in Sam Charters' *Chicago/The Blues/Today!* series on Vanguard. In
the following year he toured Europe with the American Folk Blues Festival. He made his first full album
appearance in 1969 on the Atlantic subsidiary Cotillion: *Mourning in the Morning*, produced, to little
critical approval, by **Mike Bloomfield** and Nick
Gravenites, who wrote much of the material. Duane
Allman of the **Allman Brothers Band** played guitar
on the date. A 1971 Capitol session, produced by Rush
and Gravenites, did him greater justice but was not
released; it was finally licensed to Bullfrog and issued

in 1976 as *Right Place, Wrong Time*. Over the next few years Rush's career was interrupted by personal problems. He toured Europe again in 1974, with fellow Chicago blues-singer/guitarist Jimmy 'Fast Fingers' Dawkins, and 1977, and Japan in 1974–5, returning to Chicago to cut *Cold Day in Hell* (Delmark). His subsequent albums were drawn from his earlier visits to Japan (*So Many Roads*, Delmark, 1978), Sweden (*Troubles, Troubles*, Sonet, 1978) and France (*Screamin' and Cryin'*, Black and Blue, 1979) and, while his old Cobra sides were reissued several times over on different labels, he did not cut a new album until *Tops*, recorded at the San Francisco blues festival of 1985. In 1994 he delivered a studio set which lived up to his reputation, *Ain't Enough Comin' in* (This Way Up). It contained reworkings of his own 'Homework' and 'She's a Good 'Un' alongside songs by **Sam Cooke** and **Albert King**. A critical success, it was followed by *This Way* (Mercury, 1994). His first recording for a major label in over a decade, *This Way* saw Rush in an up-tempo rather than intense mood on songs associated with the likes of **Ray Charles**, **B. B. King** and **Percy Mayfield**. It was followed by the live *So Many Roads* (Delmark, 1996).

Rush made a strong impact on the British R&B movement of the sixties. **John Mayall** was a notable disciple, re-creating 'All Your Love' with **Eric Clapton** on guitar, 'Double Trouble' with Peter Green and 'I Can't Quit You Baby' with Mick Taylor. His influence continued to be felt in the eighties through performers such as **Stevie Ray Vaughan**, who named his band Double Trouble after Rush's theme song. *Cobra Recordings, 1956–1958* (Flyright, 1989) is the definitive compilation of Rush's most creative period.

TOM RUSH

b. 8 February 1941, Portsmouth, New Hampshire, USA

One of the leading singers of the folk revival of the sixties, Rush played a major role in bringing to a wide audience the early songs of such writers as **Joni Mitchell**, **Jackson Browne** and **James Taylor**, while in *The Circle Game* (1968) he produced one of the classics of the genre. In the eighties he formed his own company, Maple Hill Productions.

As a Harvard student Rush was originally a rock guitarist but he later became drawn into the Boston folk scene. After recording for a small local company, Rush was signed by Paul Rothchild to Prestige, releasing *Got a Mind to Ramble* and the Sam Charters-produced *Blues, Songs and Ballads* (1963) which showed the strong blues emphasis among Boston singers. After graduating in 1964, Rush joined Elektra and released an eponymous album. He appeared at leading festivals and released *Take a Little Walk with Me* (1966).

Mitchell's 'The Circle Game' provided the title for Rush's 1968 album which was organized as a song cycle and established his reputation for championing songs by new writers. Among them were Browne's 'Shadow Dream Song', Taylor's 'Something in the Way She Moves' and 'No Regrets', Rush's most famous composition which was a 1976 British hit for the **Walker Brothers**. In 1970 he moved to Columbia, releasing three albums in a year. *Tom Rush* was followed by the David Briggs-produced *Wrong End of the Rainbow* (which included Taylor's 'Sweet Baby James') and *Merrimack County*.

During the seventies Rush's performances were intermittent and he recorded only the country-influenced *Ladies Love Outlaws* (1974). He returned to full-time musical activity in 1982, releasing *New Year* (1983) and *Late Night Radio* (1984) on his own Nightlight label.

In 1989 Fantasy reissued an expanded version of Rush's first two albums as *Blues and Ballads*, which in its mix of traditional folk and blues songs stands as a perfect snapshot of the coffee-house folk scene of the early sixties.

JIMMY RUSHING

b. James Andrew Rushing, 26 August 1902, Oklahoma, USA, d. 8 June 1972, New York

Nicknamed 'Mr Five by Five', Rushing was **Count Basie**'s vocalist from 1935 to 1948 and became the leading exponent of big-band blues singing.

As a child he learned violin and piano and sang in California in 1924 with **Jelly Roll Morton**. Returning to the Midwest, Rushing joined the Billy King Revue and when bassist Walter Page left to form his Blue Devils, Rushing followed, singing on the 1929 recording of 'Blue Devil Blues'. He made further records like 'Liza Lee' with Benny Moten's band, which included Basie on piano.

After Moten's death in 1935, Rushing joined Basie and made many successful recordings with him. Rushing's style developed as he shouted the three-line blues stanzas against the hard-blowing horns of the orchestra. Among the songs most associated with him were 'Good Morning Blues' (Decca, 1937), 'Sent for You Yesterday (And Here You Come Today)' (1938), 'Evil Blues' (1939), 'Goin' to Chicago' (Columbia, 1941), 'Rusty Dusty Blues' (1941) and 'Jimmy's Blues' (1944). **Jimmy Witherspoon**, Joe Williams (a later Basie singer) and Walter Brown were among those who were influenced by Rushing's Kansas City blues shouting style.

Leaving Basie, Rushing appeared with his own group, which often included a rhythm section drawn from the Basie orchestra. His recordings for Columbia included *Little Jimmy Rushing and the Big Brass*

(1954) and *The Odyssey of James Rushing Esq* (1956). He later toured with Basie's orchestra, **Benny Goodman**'s band and Buck Clayton's All Stars. In 1969 Rushing appeared in the film *The Learning Tree*.

The You and Me That Used to Be (RCA, 1971) was recorded shortly before Rushing's death from leukaemia.

GEORGE RUSSELL
b. 23 June 1923, Cincinnati, Ohio, USA

Composer and pianist Russell was one of the most erudite of modern jazz musicians, publishing volumes of music theory as well as writing a number of extended works.

The son of a music teacher, Russell played drums briefly with Benny Carter before turning to arranging and composing. In the mid-forties he wrote arrangements for various bands including those of **Earl Hines**, **Artie Shaw** and **Count Basie**. Ill-health prevented him working with **Charlie Parker** but in 1947 **Dizzy Gillespie**'s orchestra, with conga drummer Chano Pozo, recorded his 'Cubana Be' and 'Cubana Bop' while 'Ezz-Thetic' was recorded by Lee Konitz in 1951.

In 1953 Russell published *The Lydian Chromatic Concept of Tonal Organization* which advocated the use of scales or 'modes' instead of chords as the basis of jazz improvisation. On *Cross-Section Saxes* (Decca, 1958) he provided themes and arrangements for alto-sax-player Hal McCusick, who had played on Russell's *The Jazz Workshop* (RCA, 1956). With the arrival of the album, Russell was able to compose large-scale works such as *New York NY* (1958, an evocation of city street sounds) and *Jazz in the Space Age* (1960), which featured piano duets by Paul Bley and **Bill Evans**.

Russell formed a small group with **Eric Dolphy** (soprano sax) and trumpeter Don Ellis to record *Ezz-Thetics* (Riverside, 1961). Russell settled in Scandinavia in the mid-sixties, developing a system of 'vertical forms' which involved the simultaneous appearance of different sounds and rhythms. Electronic sounds were over-dubbed on organ improvisations on *Electronic Sonata for Souls Loved by Nature* (Strata East, 1969), while the big-band work *Living Time* (Columbia) brought together bebop, Latin, rock, blues and free-form sounds.

After 1969 he was teaching at the New England Conservatory and Russell spent much of the seventies writing a second instalment of his theoretical work. He returned to the studio with a large orchestra for *New York Big Band* (Soul Note, 1978) and *Live in an American Time Spiral*. *The African Game* (Blue Note, 1983) took as its theme the evolution of humanity and in the mid-eighties Russell's Living Time orchestra toured America and Europe where such British musicians as **Courtney Pine** (tenor sax) and pianist

Django Bates of the Loose Tubes experimental big band joined him.

LEON RUSSELL
b. Hank Wilson, 2 April 1941, Lawton, Oklahoma, USA

A multi-instrumentalist, writer and producer, Russell, like **Doug Sahm**, represents a rich fusion of lived (if not entirely digested) musical influences. In the late sixties he emerged from the anonymity of session work to take centre stage briefly with a series of brooding, intense, yet decidedly down-home albums. These were accompanied by the contrasting image of Russell as master of ceremonies to an ever-changing cast of Woodstock era superstars.

Russell studied piano and trumpet as a child before turning to rock'n'roll with fellow Tulsa-based musicians David Gates (later of **Bread**), Carl Radle and **J. J. Cale**. In 1956–7 he toured (as a guitarist) with **Ronnie Hawkins** and **Jerry Lee Lewis**, whose influence can be seen on Russell's first recordings, 'Swanee River' and 'All Right', frantic piano pieces recorded in Oklahoma and leased to Chess in 1959. In 1958 he moved to Los Angeles where with **James Burton** and Delaney Bramlett he joined the regular backing group of **Jack Good**'s *Shindig* televison show and became a session pianist. As such he played on numerous hits produced by **Phil Spector** and a wide range of recordings, including movie star Walter Brennan's mournful monologue 'Old Rivers' and its charming flipside, 'The Epic Ride of John H. Glenn' (Liberty, 1962), the **Byrds**' 'Mr Tambourine Man' (1965), **Herb Alpert**'s 'A Taste of Honey' (1965) and Bob Lind's 'Elusive Butterfly' (World Pacific, 1966). In 1965–6 Russell arranged Gary Lewis (son of comedian Jerry) and the Playboys' series of hits, including the American No. 1 'This Diamond Ring'*, 'Count Me in', 'Save Your Love for Me' and 'She's Just My Style' (Liberty, 1965). On the recommendation of Lewis's producer, **Tommy 'Snuff' Garrett**, Russell arranged the 1967 hits of **Harpers Bizarre** ('Feelin' Groovy' and 'Come to the Sunshine').

Russell's own recordings were very different. 'Misty' (A&M, 1966) was a country-styled version of the **Errol Garner** song while *Asylum Choir* (Smash, 1968), made with Texan songwriter Marc Benno, featured Russell's gospel piano and hard-edged vocals and had an emotional power that was unusual for the period. However, the album failed commercially, as did the belated and lesser sequel, *Asylum Choir II* (Shelter, 1971). Benno went on to make three more solo albums for A&M but had more success as a songwriter, his compositions being recorded by **Rita Coolidge** and **Georgie Fame**, among others. More significant for Russell's future was his involvement in Delaney and Bonnie's début album, *Accept No Substi-*

tute (Elektra, 1969), which he arranged. In the course of making that album, he met **Rita Coolidge** and the musicians who would eventually become Mad Dogs and Englishmen.

In 1970 he made his solo album début. Released on Shelter, the label he and producer Denny Cordell set up in association with Blue Thumb, *Leon Russell* saw the one-time super session musician backed by a galaxy of stars, including **Steve Winwood**, **Eric Clapton**, **Joe Cocker**, **George Harrison**, **Ringo Starr** and **Rolling Stones** Charlie Watts and Bill Wyman. Surprisingly the mix worked with Russell's fierce piano-playing and raspy singing finding sympathetic support from his backing group. Included on the album were two classic love songs to Coolidge, 'A Song for You' (later memorably recorded by **Willie Nelson**) and 'Delta Lady', a hit for Joe Cocker (1969) for whom Russell organized the Mad Dogs and Englishmen tour that made Russell a star when it was filmed and recorded in 1970. Now in great demand, Russell in 1971 recorded the superior *Leon Russell and the Shelter People*, wrote the reflective 'Superstar', a huge hit for the **Carpenters**, wrote and recorded with Clapton, **Bob Dylan** ('Watching the River Flow') and Harrison ('Bangla Desh') and appeared at the 'Concert for Bangladesh', before suffering a breakdown.

Carney (1972), which like **The Band**'s *Stage Fright* (1970) explored the personal costs of live performance, saw a different, mellower Russell and included the hit single 'Tight Rope'. Even more reflective was *Hank Wilson's Back* (1973) on which Russell essayed faithful interpretations of such country classics as **Moon Mullican**'s 'I'll Sail My Ship Alone' and **George Jones**' 'She Thinks I Still Care' with a backing group that included veteran country session men Billy Byrd and Harold (brother of **Owen**) **Bradley**, as well as **Pete Drake** and long-time Russell associates Carl Radle and J. J. Cale. Henceforth, Russell's albums would be far less frenetic than his early work. These included *Stop All That Jazz* (1974), with its fine version of **Mose Allison**'s 'Smashed', and *Wedding Album*, made with his wife, one-time back-up singer Mary McCreary, in the same year (1976) that **George Benson** had a huge hit with Russell's 'This Masquerade'. Russell ended the decade with *Willie and Leon* and *One for the Road* (Columbia, 1979), both made with Willie Nelson. The latter album featured a broad spectrum of material from pop standards to country classics, but more surprising was *Leon Russell and the New Grass Revival* (Warners, 1981) which saw Russell leading a progressive bluegrass band.

For several years after *Hank Wilson Volume II* (1984) Russell devoted most of his time to his video facility Paradise Video, while without him the New Grass band had several country hits including 'Unconditional Love' (Capitol, 1987). In 1991 he returned to live performance, and in 1992 released the laid-back *Anything Can Happen* (Virgin), co-produced by **Bruce Hornsby**. After a break he followed this with the countryfied *Legend in My Time, Hank Wilson Vol. III* (Ark, 1998) and the rockier *Face in the Crowd* (Sagestone, 1999). In the interim EMI issued the two-CD anthology *Gimme Shelter* (1996).

BOBBY RYDELL
b. Robert Louis Ridarelli, 26 April 1940, Philadelphia, Pennsylvania, USA

Like **Fabian**, Rydell was one of the clutch of teen-idols who rose to fame in the years between the advent of rock'n'roll and the emergence of **The Beatles**, with clean-cut images and the assistance of regular appearances on **Dick Clark**'s *American Bandstand*.

By the age of ten a veteran of the Philadelphia club circuit and a regular guest on **Paul Whiteman**'s *Teen Club* TV talent show, Rydell joined the local rock'n'roll group Rocco and the Saints, which featured **Frankie Avalon** on trumpet, in 1957. After Rydell was turned down by Capitol, Decca and RCA, his manager Frankie Day established his own label, Venise, and recorded Rydell singing 'Fatty, Fatty' (1958) with no success.

That came only after Kal Mann and Bernie Lowe of Cameo signed Rydell and provided him with a series of teen ballads, complete with cloying choruses to croon, and secured regular guest appearances on *American Bandstand*. The result was a trio of million-sellers penned by the label-owners: 'We Got Love', 'Wild One' (1959) and 'Swinging School' (1960). Cameo next tried to take Rydell up-market with finger-snapping revivals of **Domenico Modugno**'s 'Volare'* (1960) and **Johnny Mercer** and **Harold Arlen**'s 'That Old Black Magic' (1962). More interesting was the decision to record Rydell in England, where his records had only sold moderately. The result was 'Forget Him'* (1963), written by **Tony Hatch**, the producer and composer of several of **Petula Clark**'s hits. That was Rydell's last major hit. Like so many solo artists of his time, his image and music were made old-fashioned by The Beatles.

In 1965 Rydell moved to Capitol and then to RCA and Reprise (1968) with little success, before in the revivalist seventies he returned to the charts with a re-recording of 'Sway' (Pip, 1976), one of his best-known Cameo hits. He later had the high school in the rock revival film *Grease* (1978) named after him and became a regular on the oldies circuit.

MITCH RYDER AND THE DETROIT WHEELS
Mitch Ryder, b. William Levise, 26 February 1945, Detroit, Michigan, USA; James McCarty, b. 1947,

Detroit; Joseph Kubert, b. 1947, Detroit, d. 16 June 1991, Detroit; John Badanjek, b. 1948, Detroit

Unlike other blue-eyed soul singers of his generation, Ryder was committed to the harsher, shouting styles of the fifties rather than the smoother sounds of the sixties, the decade in which he had his greatest success.

During his teens Ryder briefly sang with a black vocal quartet, the Preps, before forming Bill Lee and the Rivierias in 1965. Their imitation of **James Brown**'s sock-it-to-me revue format won a large local following in the Detroit area but records on Garrie and Hyland failed. Signed by producer **Bob Crewe**, the group had a huge international hit with their amalgam of **Chuck Willis**'s 'C. C. Rider' and **Little Richard**'s 'Jenny, Jenny' as 'Jenny Take a Ride'*, under the name Mitch Ryder and the Detroit Wheels on Crewe's New Voice label. They followed it with similarly frenetic offerings, remarkable for their assimilation of black musical styles. Among these were 'Little Latin Lupe Lu' (1966), previously recorded by the **Righteous Brothers** (1963) and the Kingsmen (Wand, 1964), the medley 'Devil with the Blue Dress'/'Good Golly Miss Molly', and 'Sock It to Me Baby!' (1967). Crewe then convinced Ryder to leave the group for a shortlived solo career during which his only hit was 'What Now My Love' (Dyna Voice, 1967), a revival of **Shirley Bassey**'s 1962 hit.

After *The Detroit Memphis Experience* (Dot, 1969), produced by guitarist Steve Cropper, Ryder reformed the Detroit Wheels under the abbreviated name of Detroit for the impressive *Detroit* (Paramount, 1971). When it failed to sell, Ryder left the music business. He returned in 1978 with *How I Spent My Vacation* (Seeds and Stems), followed by *Naked But Not Dead* (1980), *Live Talkies* (1981) and *Got Change for a Million* (1981). By now Ryder was based in Germany, and several of his later albums only appeared there. In 1982 he released *Smart Ass* (Safari) before recording the **John Mellencamp**-produced *Never Kick a Sleeping Dog* (Riva, 1983), produced by John Mellencamp. Both were lesser works, showing Ryder to be uneasy once outside the broad area of soul and R&B. Still an impressive live performer, Ryder was a strong influence on **Bruce Springsteen**, who throughout the eighties regularly featured Ryder's hit singles, as 'Detroit Medley', in his stage act. In 1987 Ryder returned to recording with the topical novelty 'Good Golly, Ask Ollie' (SOS). Still a major draw in Germany, he recorded the live set *Red Blood and White Mink* (1989) in Berlin. On it he tackled songs by the **Velvet Underground**, the **Rolling Stones** and James Brown, as well as revisiting his own back catalogue. Later recordings included *The Beautiful Toulang Sunset* (1990), *La Gash* (1992) and *Rite of Passage* (1994). The most representative anthology is *The Best of Mitch Ryder and the Detroit Wheels* (1994).

SADE

b. Folasade Adu, 16 January 1959, Ibadan, Nigeria

A British-based soul-jazz singer with hints of Astrud Gilberto and **Steely Dan**, Sade was the most successful of a new generation of black British artists to emerge in the mid-eighties. With an artful mixture of strong melodies and Latin rhythms her first two albums sold a total of over 10 million copies worldwide.

Daughter of a Nigerian professor of Economics and white British mother, she moved to England with her mother in 1964. She studied fashion design at St Martin's College of Art in London and joined Latin group Ariva in 1981. This became a soul-funk band, Pride, whose members included saxophone-player and former clarinet teacher Stuart Matthewman, Hull-born Paul Denman (bass), Andrew Hale (keyboards), and guitarist Ray St John with whom she wrote 'Smooth Operator', Pride's most popular song.

When Sade signed to Epic in 1983, Matthewman, Hale and Denman formed the nucleus of her recording band. Produced by Robin Millar, *Diamond Life* (1984) provided a British hit with the lilting 'Your Love Is King' while the cool and sophisticated 'Smooth Operator' reached the American Top Ten.

In 1985 Sade released *Promise*, which emulated the success of its predecessor and included further hits in 'The Sweetest Taboo' and 'Never So Good as the First Time' (1986).

After a period of semi-retirement, during which she made a cameo appearance in *Absolute Beginners*, Sade returned in 1988 with *Stronger than Pride*. Retaining a low-key atmosphere, 'Love Is Stronger than Pride' was an American hit and the band was joined by ex-Wham! backing singer Leroy Osbourne for a world tour. Another lengthy gap preceded the arrival of *Love Deluxe* (1992). Adhering to the blueprint of its predecessors, it was another worldwide hit, reaching the American Top Five. In 1994 Epic released *The Best of Sade*. Matthewman, Denman and Hale, Sade's long-term backing band, released their own album, *Sweetback*, in 1996.

DOUG SAHM

b. Doug Saldana, 6 November 1941, San Antonio, Texas, USA, d. 18 November 1999, Taos, New Mexico

Sahm is one of the most original exponents of Tex-Mex music, an amalgam of country music, R&B and the Mexican *conjunto*. He enjoyed brief chart success with 'She's About a Mover' (1965) and 'Mendocino'* (1969) but his greater importance lay in the awareness he created among rock audiences and musicians of the Tex-Mex synthesis. Among those with whom he collaborated were **Bob Dylan** and members of **Creedence Clearwater Revival**.

By the age of six he was singing and playing steel guitar on station KMAC in San Antonio. He recorded as Little Doug ('Rollin' Rollin', Sarg, 1955) before forming the Knights blues band in 1958. Drawing on the repertoire of **T-Bone Walker**, **Bobby Bland** and **Junior Parker**, Sahm developed his own approach in club performances and through records for such labels as Warrior, Harlem, Personality and Renner. A selection of these recordings was reissued as *Doug Sahm: San Antonio Rock* (Norton, 2000).

In 1964 he formed the Sir Douglas Quintet for a residency at the Blue Note lounge in San Antonio. With **Huey P. Meaux** producing, the group cut the riff-laden 'She's About a Mover' (Tribe, 1965) which featured Augie Meyer on Vox organ. With their Anglicized name, the Quintet were presented as a British-style beat group, and the record was a Top Twenty hit, but its sequel, 'When the Rains Came', was less successful.

Sahm moved to San Francisco where he made the experimental, psychedelically tinged *Sir Douglas Quintet + 2 (Honkey Blues)* (Smash, 1968) with a new line-up. *Mendocino* (1969), whose ebullient title track was a Top Thirty hit, and the Meaux-produced *Together After Five* (1970), however, saw a return to the Tex-Mex sound with Meyer again to the fore. The album found Sahm reflecting on the San Francisco experience on songs like 'At the Crossroads' (later revived by **Mott the Hoople**), 'Texas Me' and 'Lawd I'm Just a Country Boy in This Great Big Freaky City'. The less satisfactory *1+1+1=4* (1970), containing the impassioned 'Be Real', was partly produced in Nashville by Jerry Kennedy.

The Return of Doug Saldana (Philips, 1971) was Sahm's first album under his own name and his last for Philips. The enthusiasm of **Jerry Wexler** for Sahm's by now mature blend of Texas music resulted in a contract with Atlantic and *Doug Sahm and Band* (1973) featured an all-star line-up including Dylan, **Dr John**, **David Bromberg** and saxophonist David 'Fathead' Newman. The album displayed the range of Sahm's influences – from **Bob Wills** through T-Bone Walker to the **Delmore Brothers** – but despite critical acclaim neither it nor *Texas Tornado* (1974) sold well and Sahm spent the rest of the decade label-hopping.

Among his records were the mellow *Groover's Paradise* (Warners, 1974), produced by ex-Creedence member Doug Clifford, who would later become a regular member of the Quintet; *Texas Rock for Country Rollers* (Dot, 1976), a Meaux production that included the whimsical 'You Can't Hide a Redneck Under Hippy Hair'; the bar-band concert album *Live Love* (Texas Re-Cord Company, 1977); and *Hell of a Spell* (Takoma, 1980). A subsequent reunion of the Quintet resulted in *Border Wave* (1981). *Rio Medina* (Sonet, 1984), which included 'Anymore – A Tribute to Johnny Ace', marked a return to Sahm's and Texas music's past. His later eighties albums include the two live albums with the Quintet, *Wanted Very Much Alive* (1987) and *Back to the 'Dillo* (1988), and the superior *Juke Box Music* (1988), which included versions of (mostly Texan) obscure R&B and rock'n'roll recordings.

The one fixed point in Sahm's various bands, Meyer also made a series of solo albums. Among them were *Western Head Music Co* (Polydor, 1977), *Finally in Light* (Texas Re-Cord Company, 1979) and *San Antonio Saturday Night* (Sonet, 1986), on which Meyer produced and accompanied several chicano musicians including **Flaco Jimenez**. In partnership with Amos Garret he also made *The Return of the Formerly Brothers* (Rykodisc, 1989), another essay in roots music.

Meyer and Jiminez joined Sahm and country singer **Freddy Fender** in the Texas Tornados, recording an eponymous album in 1990, followed by *Zone of Our Own* (1991) and *Hangin' on by a Thread* (1992). In 1994 Sahm, Meyers and Clifford teamed up with Sahm's sons Shawn and Shandon plus guitarists Louis Ortega and John Jorgensen to form another (seven-piece) version of the Sir Douglas Quintet, recording the excellent *Daydreaming at Midnight* for Elektra. While many of Sahm's nineties recordings had a slap-dash feel to them, all were enthralling examples of roots music. The best of these was *The Last Real Texas Blues Band* (1997), which saw him performing old blues songs and Tex-Mex songs with affection and expertise. His last album was the countrified *The Return of Wayne Douglas* (2000) which, while it aped the title of his 1971 album, actually saw him more assured reworking Dylan's 'Love Minus Zero/No Limit' than as a would-be country singer.

SAINT ETIENNE

Sarah Cracknell, b. 12 April 1967; Bob Stanley, b. 25 December 1964, Croydon, Surrey, England; Pete Wiggs, b. 15 May 1966, Croydon

Before Britpop, Saint Etienne were among the leading exponents of sixties-influenced pop in the UK, combining breezy melodicism with subtle club beats.

Saint Etienne were formed in 1988 by Stanley and Wiggs, who had spent the early eighties compiling party tapes in Croydon. After relocating to Camden, the duo started work on the dance-pop project, dreamt-up by Stanley while working as a music journalist, recruiting a variety of session singers for early singles before settling on Cracknell for their full-length début, *Foxbase Alpha* (Heavenly, 1991). The album became an indie hit on the strength of 'Nothing Can Stop Us' and a cover of **Neil Young**'s 'Only Love Can Break Your Heart', while the success of 'You're in a Bad Way' propelled the band's second album, *So Tough* (1993), into the mainstream.

After the release of *You Need a Mess of Help to Stand Alone* (1993), a perfunctory compilation of B-sides and rarities, and the *X-Mas '93* EP, Saint Etienne recorded *Tiger Bay* (1994), which had a more cinematic feel than its predecessors but failed to achieve the same volume of sales. A singles collection, *Too Young to Die* (1995), saw the band's profile rise again after 'He's on the Phone' became their biggest hit to date.

Saint Etienne took an extended break following the release of *Casino Classics* (1996), a collection of remixes. Cracknell issued a solo album, while Stanley and Wiggs worked as scouts at EMI, having previously founded Caff Records in the late eighties, releasing singles by **Pulp** and the **Manic Street Preachers**. The band reconvened in 1998 to record *Good Humour* (1998), which included the European hit single 'Sylvie'. *Sound of Water* (Sub Pop, 2000) saw the group's sound less clubby and more *après* club, with more relaxed rhythms and a more stripped-down sound with less space for their poppier inflections. It included the club hit 'Heart Failed (In the Back of a Taxi)'.

BUFFY SAINTE-MARIE
b. 20 February 1941, Saskatchewan, Canada

Buffy Sainte-Marie was one of the outstanding writers and singers of the sixties folk revival.

Of North American Indian descent, she studied at the University of Massachusetts and travelled to New York after graduation. Her intense, pure soprano (to which a celebrated vibrato was later added) soon won her a following in the Greenwich Village folk clubs. She signed to Vanguard in 1964 and recorded *It's My Way* (1964), *Many a Mile* (1965), *Little Wheel Spin* (1966) and *Fire, Fleet and Candle Light* (1967).

During these years several of Sainte-Marie's songs became widely known in versions by other artists. The effective anti-war ballad 'Universal Soldier' was a hit in America for **Glen Campbell** (Capitol, 1965) and in Britain was one of **Donovan**'s earliest recordings

(Pye, 1965), while the dramatic love song 'Until It's Time for You to Go' was first recorded by **Bobby Darin** in 1966 and then by dozens of singers from Sonny and **Cher** to **Elvis Presley**, for whom it was a 1972 hit. **Bobby Bare** had a country hit with her 'Piney Wood Hills' (1967).

While her anti-drug song 'Cod'ine' was a club favourite, Sainte-Marie was best known for a number of powerful pieces depicting the plight of the American Indians, notably 'Now That the Buffalo's Gone' and 'My Country 'Tis of Thy People You're Dying'. Sainte-Marie also organized educational projects to assist the Indian community.

I'm Gonna Be a Country Girl Again (1968) and subsequent albums were recorded in Nashville. In 1970 Sainte-Marie wrote and sang the theme song for the film *Soldier Blue*. *Moonshot* (1972), produced by Norbert Putnam, contained 'Native North American Child', another statement about the Indian peoples, and the minor hit 'Hey Mister, Can't You See'.

After ten years with Vanguard, Sainte-Marie moved to MCA for the full-scale rock albums *Buffy* (1974), *Changing Woman* (1975) and *Sweet America* (1976). She also worked for several years on the children's television series *Sesame Street* and in 1983 won an Oscar for 'Up Where We Belong', the theme from *An Officer and a Gentleman*, co-written with her husband **Jack Nitzsche** and recorded by **Joe Cocker** and **Jennifer Warnes**. She recorded with the **Neville Brothers** on 1990's *Brother's Keeper* before resuming her own recording career in 1992 with the well-received *Coincidence and Likely Stories* (Chrysalis).

RYUICHI SAKAMOTO
b. 17 January 1952, Tokyo, Japan

Ryuichi Sakamoto first came to international notice as a member of pioneering Japanese electronic trio Yellow Magic Orchestra in the late seventies. In the eighties he became known for his collaborative work with a string of artists from **Iggy Pop** to Brian Wilson of the **Beach Boys** and for his film soundtracks, one of which, *The Last Emperor*, won an Academy Award in 1987.

Sakamoto's father was a literary editor and his mother a hat designer, and he was encouraged to pursue a creative career from an early age – he wrote his first piano piece at the age of four, and began studying composition at the University of Tokyo at the age of ten. During his teens, he began listening to the avant-garde compositions of John Cage and Steve Reich as well as the more conventional rock'n'roll output of **The Beatles** and the **Rolling Stones**. In 1978 he formed the self-mockingly titled Yellow Magic Orchestra with fellow keyboard-players Haruomi Hosono and Yukihero Takahashi. The trio, with an

image which parodied the stereotypical Japanese tourist, targeted Europe and America rather than Japan, and were hailed as the East's answer to **Kraftwerk**, with admirers such as **David Bowie** and **XTC**'s Andy Partridge. YMO were unable to make a major impression on the albums market outside Japan, however, with their one UK success coming in the shape of the 1980 Top Twenty single, 'Computer Game (Theme from the Invaders)', which cashed in on the then-current Space Invaders computer game craze. The trio's influence on a number of European acts and later on the 1990s dance scene, with numerous records sampling from their seven albums, was widespread (a dance remix album of their best-known material, *Hi-Tech/No Crime*, would appear in 1992), but in 1983, after completing two world tours, they split up.

Sakamoto had recorded a solo album in 1978, although it was not widely available, and his first bona fide recording came in 1980 with B-2 Unit, which featured Andy Partridge. The follow-up, *Hidariuendo* (Left-Handed Dream) (1981), continued the collaborative theme, featuring vocals by Robin Scott, a UK vocalist and keyboard player who, like Sakamoto, had enjoyed an early electro-pop hit in the UK (as M, with 'Pop Musik', 1979). He then teamed up with former **Japan** vocalist **David Sylvian** on the 1982 single 'Bamboo Music', the first in a series of collaborations in a partnership which would continue for a decade. Sakamoto's next project was the film soundtrack for *Merry Christmas Mr Lawrence*, the Japanese POW drama starring David Bowie and Tom Conti, in which Sakamoto himself had a major role. The score drew extensive critical acclaim for its mixture of western and Japanese themes, and included a hit single in the shape of Sylvian and Sakamoto's theme song 'Forbidden Colours'. Over the next decade, Sakamoto would mix his film score work with other recordings, notably *Illustrated Musical Encyclopaedia* (1986), which featured keyboard-player/producer **Thomas Dolby**, and *Neo Geo* (1987), which featured guest appearances from a number of other artists, including Iggy Pop on the single 'Risky'. His most successful film score during this period was for Bertolucci's *The Last Emperor* (1987) which featured **Talking Heads'** **David Byrne**, and he went on to score the same director's *Sheltering Sky* (1991).

In 1990 Sakamoto made his home in New York and continued to turn out work at a remarkable rate. *Beauty* (Virgin, 1990), a world-music soundscape mixing elements of Eastern, Western and African musics, featured contributions from **The Band**'s Robbie Robertson, Sly Dunbar and former Beach Boy Brian Wilson. He toured Japan with a jazz-orientated band in late 1991 and released *Heartbeat* in 1992, with contributions from dance and rap artists alongside those of

African musician **Youssou N'Dour**, ex-**J. Geils Band** harmonica-player Magic Dick and avant-garde jazz sax-player John Lurie. The album also continued his partnership with Sylvian on the minor hit 'Heartbeat Returning to the Womb'. Sakamoto composed the opening music for the 1992 Olympic Games before beginning work on the **Aztec Camera** album *Dreamland* (1993), which he co-produced. In 1993 it was reported that Sakamoto had re-formed Yellow Magic Orchestra, recording an album's worth of material with the proposed title *Technodon*, but the album remains unreleased. Subsequently, Sakamoto concentrated on his soundtrack work and, in 1993, released the album of his music for Oscar-winning director Oliver Stone's US TV series, *Wild Palms*. In 1994 he continued his relationship with Bertolucci by composing the soundtrack of *Little Buddha*. Later film soundtracks included *Love Is the Devil* (1998) and *Snake Eyes* (1999).

SALT'N'PEPA
Salt, b. Cheryl James, 28 March 1969, New York City, USA; Pepa, b. Sandra Denton, 9 November 1969, Kingston, Jamaica; DJ Spinderella, b. Dee Dee Roper

Sometimes scorned by the hardcore rap community, Salt'N'Pepa achieved international pop success without sacrificing their street-smart wit and commitment to presenting a female perspective on social and sexual topics.

While working in telephone sales in New York, James and Denton composed an answer rap to Doug E. Fresh's 'The Show'. This was recorded by Hurby Azor as part of a college course on audio and subsequently issued in 1985 as 'Show Stoppa' by Super Nature on the local Pop Art label. It was a minor R&B hit and the duo chose Salt'N'Pepa (from a line in the song) as their future stage name. With Azor (now Hurby Love Bug) again producing and DJ Spinderella providing beats and samples, they issued the playful 'My Mike Sounds Nice', a version of the **Otis Redding**/Carla Thomas soul hit 'Tramp', and 'Chick on the Side' on Next Plateau in 1987.

Salt'N'Pepa's crossover to wider pop audiences came with the album *Hot, Cool & Vicious*, which included the Top Twenty hit 'Push It'. It was followed in 1988 by *A Salt with a Deadly Pepa*, which included a rap treatment of the **Isley Brothers**' 1961 classic 'Twist and Shout' as well as 'Shake Your Thang' and 'Get Up Everybody (Get Up)'. In the same year the group had its first overseas success when both 'Push It' and 'Twist and Shout' became British hits.

Blacks' Magic (1990) contained further hit singles with 'Do You Want Me?' and 'Let's Talk about Sex', which included a forthright message about the danger of AIDS. The group's pace of activity slowed when both Denton and James had babies, but they were back in the studio to record *Very Necessary* in 1993. Earlier in the year they had performed at the inauguration of US President Clinton and in 1994 they appeared at Woodstock '94.

They enjoyed another hit single in 1994 with 'Whatta Man', a collaboration with funky soul divas **En Vogue**, but their star was beginning to wane, outshone by the emerging generation of female gangsta rappers, such as Lil Kim. In 1996 they contributed to an all-star version of *The Songs of West Side Story* (singing 'Gee Officer Krupke') and sang **Diana Ross**'s 'Upside Down' on the soundtrack of *Space Jam*. They followed that with their first new album in several years, *Brand New* (Red Ant, 1997), which featured contributions from **Sheryl Crow** and **Queen Latifah**, among others. In 1999 they began a lengthy tour in support of *That Was Then, This Is Now* (2000).

SAM AND DAVE
Sam Moore, b. 12 October 1935, Miami, Florida, USA; David Prater, b. 9 May 1937, Ocilla, Georgia, d. 9 April 1988, Syracuse, Georgia

Best remembered for 'Soul Man'* (1967), Sam and Dave were among the most gospel-influenced soul stars of the sixties, their voices answering and echoing both each other and the solid riffs of the Stax house band. Their records also served as the launch pad for **Isaac Hayes** and David Porter, Stax's most prolific in-house writing and production team.

Moore and Prater met while singing gospel in 1958 and teamed up to sing secular music in clubs in the Miami area. Signed by Roulette in 1960, they remained with the label until 1964 but their records, produced by **Henry Glover**, failed. Moving to Atlantic in 1965, they were leased to Stax and sent to Memphis to record with Hayes and Porter. After a pair of failures came 'You Don't Know Like I Know' (1966) with Prater's rougher, thicker voice supporting Moore's higher-pitched emphatic lead vocals while behind them the Stax house band offered an equally punchy support. It was followed by a string of hits, virtually all written and produced by Hayes and Porter, including 'Hold on, I'm Coming'*, 'You Got Me Hummin'' (1966), 'Soul Man' (1967) and 'I Thank You'* (1968), which though less successful outside America were highly influential.

When Stax ceased independent operation in 1968, the duo returned to Atlantic where they scored a big hit with the insistent 'Soul Sister, Brown Sugar' (1969) before, in 1970, they split, Moore remaining with Atlantic and Prater joining Alston. Despite bad feeling between them, Moore and Prater teamed up throughout the seventies for occasional recordings on United Artists and Atlantic and for live performances.

The success in 1979 of *The Blues Brothers* film, in which John Belushi and Dan Aykroyd sang 'Soul Man' in a manner clearly derived from that of Sam and Dave, prompted Moore and Prater briefly to renew their partnership. In the eighties each regularly toured with a variety of partners, both billed as Sam and Dave until the latter's death in a car crash. In 1987 Moore recorded yet another version of 'Soul Man' with **Lou Reed** for the film of the same name. Moore continued to record to little effect in the early nineties, including a duet with **Conway Twitty** on 'Rainy Night in Georgia', which appeared on the 1994 compilation *Rhythm, Country and Blues*. Sam and Dave's legacy of rumbustious soul stompers was collected on the aptly titled *Sweat'N'Soul – The Anthology* (Rhino, 1993).

DAVID SANBORN
b. 30 July 1945, Tampa, Florida, USA

The most popular of American jazz-based saxophonists of the eighties, Sanborn's approach had much in common with that of **King Curtis**. His influence on a generation of studio players is evident from the strident sax sound which characterized a large number of eighties American television series themes.

Growing up in St Louis, Sanborn took up alto sax as physical therapy after contracting polio. He played in his high-school band and his early influences included **Ray Charles** sideman Hank Crawford. He studied at Northwestern University before moving to California, joining **Paul Butterfield**'s band in 1967 and recording with Butterfield until 1975. Sanborn also toured and recorded with such artists as **Stevie Wonder**, **James Taylor**, **B. B. King**, **James Brown** and **David Bowie**. In the early seventies he began a lengthy association with **Gil Evans**, appearing on such Evans albums as *Svengali* (Atlantic) and *Priestess* (Antilles). By the early eighties he had become the most sought-after alto-player for recording sessions.

The **Brecker Brothers** were among the players on *Taking Off* (Warners, 1975), his first solo album, while *Sanborn* (1976) included guest vocalists **Paul Simon**, Phoebe Snow and Patti Austin. Sanborn's hard-blowing alto-playing on later records like *Heart to Heart* (1978) and *Voyeur* (1981) brought him an increased following and his ninth album, *Straight to the Heart* (1985) was the biggest-selling jazz album of the year. *Close-Up* (Reprise, 1988) was almost as successful.

Another Hand (1991) marked a change of label (to Elektra) and of direction as Sanborn worked with avant-garde guitarist Bill Frisell as well as the rhythm section of **Charlie Haden** and Jack de Johnette. In 1992 he released the expressive *Upfront*. Even better was *Pearls* (1995) on which with the support of an orchestra he offered impassioned readings of classics such as 'Try a Little Tenderness' and 'Smoke Gets in Your Eyes'.

MONGO SANTAMARIA
b. Ramos Santamaria, 7 April 1922, Havana, Cuba

One of the most accomplished Latin percussionists of the sixties and beyond, Santamaria performed with many leading jazz musicians and also explored the Afro-Cuban roots of his music.

Originally studying violin, he switched to congas before leaving Cuba for Mexico in 1948 with his cousin and fellow percussionist Armando Peraza. They recorded traditional Afro-Cuban music and moved to New York to join **Tito Puente**. They played with **Perez Prado** before in the mid-fifties joining the West Coast Latin jazz bandleader and vibraphone-player Cal Tjader, with whom they had formerly worked in **George Shearing**'s 1953 augmented group. Santamaria's congas and Willie Bobo's timbales were prominent on Tjader's *Concert by the Sea* (Vocalion, 1959). Peraza later joined **Carlos Santana**'s group.

Forming his own polyrhythmic group with Bobo, Santamaria recorded *Afro-Roots* (Prestige, 1961), which included the Latin-jazz standard 'Afro Blue', and *Skins* (Milestone, 1962) before he had a hit single with the sinuous 'Watermelon Man' (Battle, 1963). 'Yeh Yeh' (1963) was less successful (though **Georgie Fame** had a British No. 1 with a vocal version, with lyrics by Jon Hendricks [of **Lambert, Hendricks and Ross**]) and Santamaria signed to Columbia in 1965, scoring a minor hit 'Cloud Nine' in 1969. During the sixties the members of his band included **Chick Corea**, **Herbie Hancock** (who wrote 'Watermelon Man') and Hubert Laws.

Santamaria toured extensively in Europe, Africa and Japan, and continued to record regularly. In 1975 he released *Afro India* (Voyo) with Colombian flautist Justo Almario and two years later won a Grammy. In 1981 he made *Summertime* (Pablo) with **Dizzy Gillespie** while *Soy Yo* (1987) featured Charlie Palmieri (piano) and Piro Rodriguez in arrangements by Marty Sheller. *Olé Ola* was released in 1989. He continued recording in the nineties, mostly in a Latin vein. Albums from this period include *Mambo Mongo* (1992) and *Mongo Returns* (1995).

CARLOS SANTANA
b. 20 July 1947, Autlan, Mexico

Santana, the major figure in sixties attempts to fuse Latin music and rock using Afro-Cuban rhythms and white blues guitar styles, became the comeback king in the nineties when, after a lengthy period without any hits, he returned to the top of the US charts in

1999 with one of the bestselling albums of the year, *Supernatural* (Arista).

The son of a Mexican mariachi violinist, Carlos Santana formed the Santana Blues Band in 1967 with Greg Rolie (keyboards) and David Brown (bass). After playing at San Francisco's Fillmore West, the group's 1969 performance at Woodstock led to a contract with Columbia. *Santana* reached the top of the album charts and included the hit single 'Evil Ways'. For two years, the band was one of America's most successful acts. *Abraxas* (1970) included a hit version of **Fleetwood Mac**'s 'Black Magic Woman' and a Top Twenty single in **Tito Puente**'s 'Oye Como Va'. *Santana III* added Afro-Cuban percussionist Coke Escovedo to the band and provided the hit 'Everybody's Anything' (1971).

In 1972 Santana brought in keyboards-player Tom Coster and percussionist and former colleague of **Mongo Santamaria** Armando Peraza for *Caravanserai*, and collaborated unsuccessfully with drummer **Buddy Miles** on a live album. The following year he announced his conversion to the Hinduism of Sri Chimnoy, adding Devadip to his name. *Love Devotion Surrender* (1973) was recorded with fellow adept **John McLaughlin** and for the next decade Santana recorded group and solo albums in parallel.

Borboleta (1974) was an acclaimed jazz–rock fusion album with guest artists Airto and Flora Purim but frequent personnel changes in the group meant that only Coster remained after the Top Ten album *Amigos* (1976). *Moonflower* (1977) included a minor hit with a revival of the **Zombies**' 'She's Not There' (1977). Carlos Santana solo albums like *Oneness* and *The Swing of Delight* (1980) assembled such leading jazz soloists as **Herbie Hancock** and **Weather Report**'s Wayne Shorter.

Santana's Latin-rock formula continued to work into the eighties. The group enjoyed Top Twenty hits with ex-Zombie Russ Ballard's 'Winning' from *Zebop!* (1981) and 'Hold on' from *Shango* (1982). **Willie Nelson** guested on the solo album *Havana Moon* (1983) before Santana was reunited with Miles for a 1984 live recording. The group toured with **Bob Dylan** in 1985 and in 1987 released *Freedom* which featured Peraza, Coster and Miles on lead vocals. Santana's Grammy award-winning solo instrumental album *Blues for Salvador* followed later that year. In 1988 the live compilation *Viva Santana* was a minor hit and the following year Santana guested on **John Lee Hooker**'s comeback album *The Healer*. Another group album, *Spirits Dancing in the Flesh* followed in 1990. Although their record sales were disappointing, the band were still a potent live force and toured regularly in the early nineties. *Milagro* appeared on Santana's own label, Guts and Grace (through Polydor), in 1992 and was followed by the spirited live album *Sacred Fire* in 1993.

The following year Carlos issued *Brothers*, a collaboration with his brother Jorge (of the group Malo) and his nephew Carlo Hernandez. In 1986 Carlos Santana produced the music for *La Bamba*, the film based on the life of **Ritchie Valens**, which brought Latin–pop fusions to a new generation of listeners.

He continued touring and recording throughout the late eighties and nineties, but few of his albums (which included *Spirits Dancing in the Flesh*, 1990, *Milagro*, 1992, and *The Santana Brothers*, 1994) troubled chart statisticians. It seemed, as often was the case with veteran artists, that the sales of reissues would overshadow those of new albums. Reissues of this period included *Dance of the Rainbow Serpent* (1995), *The Best of Santana* and *The Ultimate Santana* (both 1998). Then, in 1999, Santana moved to Arista and recorded *Supernatural* (which featured guest appearances by the likes of **Eric Clapton**) to enormous critical and commercial – it sold some five million copies in the US alone – acclaim.

ART SATHERLEY
b. 19 October 1889, Bristol, Avon, England, d. 10 June 1986, Fountain Valley, California, USA

A pioneer of the American record industry, 'Uncle Art' Satherley, as he was known to many of his artists, was responsible for discovering and developing much of the blues and hillbilly talent of the twenties and thirties.

Fascinated by what he had read of America, Satherley left England in 1913, and on his arrival there found work grading lumber for the Wisconsin Chair Company. In 1918 the company went into the phonograph business and Satherley became, successively, technical supervisor, salesman and producer for their Paramount label, whose virtually unrivalled blues catalogue included **Ma Rainey**, **Blind Lemon Jefferson** and **Blind Blake**. He also developed the strategy of advertising Paramount releases in black newspapers like the *Chicago Defender*, thereby circumventing retailers who were committed to the established Victor or Columbia labels. The first hit record he oversaw was 'My Lord's Gonna Move this Wicked Race' (1923) by the Norfolk Jubilee Quartet.

In 1929 he left to work in New York for QRS, and soon afterwards Plaza, which was finding success selling records through chain stores like Sears, Roebuck. In August 1929 Plaza merged with other New York labels into the American Record Company. Now travelling round the South to look for talent, Satherley became acquainted with hillbilly music as well as the more familiar blues and jazz. While the majority of ARC recordings were done in New York or Chicago, and, later, Los Angeles, Satherley also set up sessions, using portable equipment, in Southern cities like

Birmingham, Alabama (where he first recorded **Roy Acuff**), Hot Springs, Arkansas, Jackson, Mississippi and Dallas, Texas. Among his signings were **Big Bill Broonzy**, the **Carlisle Brothers**, **Blind Boy Fuller**, **Memphis Minnie**, **Bob Wills** and **Gene Autry**, whose huge hit 'That Silver-Haired Daddy of Mine'* (1931), which Satherley produced, virtually reopened the country record market in the Depression.

Satherley worked with Columbia (which bought ARC in 1938) until 1952, continuing to specialize in what was now called country talent. **Spade Cooley, Al Dexter, Rose Maddox, Bill Monroe, Ray Price** and **Floyd Tillman** were among the scores of country acts he signed and produced. His assistant for many years was Don Law, who went on to become a leading record producer himself. 'Uncle Art' was voted a member of the Country Music Hall of Fame in 1971.

JOE SATRIANI
b. 15 July 1957, Long Island, USA

Satriani is one of the few guitar teachers who went on to become guitar heroes in their own right. Although worlds apart in terms of style, the only other significant guitarist also to do this was the British guitarist **Bert Weedon**, who swapped his *Play in a Day* instructional manual for a brief chart career in the fifties and a longer one in the revivalist seventies. Most other guitar teachers, such as the famed Ivor Moirants, preferred the anonymity of the classroom and the instructional book to the dangers and delights of the stage.

A respected guitarist in hard-rock circles, Satriani was initially a teacher – he taught Kirk Hammett of **Metallica** and Steve Vai – before emerging as an artist in his own right in the late eighties with a series of largely instrumental albums featuring his technically accomplished style. In the nineties Satriani's fast and flash yet melodic guitar playing led to work with rock's hierarchy. Mick Jagger asked him to replace **Jeff Beck** in his band on a tour of the Far East and he temporarily joined **Deep Purple** after Richie Blackmore left during the band's 1993–4 world tour.

As a child in Long Island, Satriani was brought up on a diet of jazz and soul, later moving on to listen to the British 'blues boom' guitarists of the late sixties – he cites the ex-**Yardbirds Eric Clapton**, Jeff Beck and Jimmy Page as major influences. He won a reputation for his impressive playing technique and took to guitar teaching.

Along with his tutoring, Satriani also played with bands and travelled overseas in the early eighties, forming the Squares on his return to the US in 1982. In 1984 he recorded a self-financed eponymous instrumental EP in 1984 before joining California-based singer-songwriter Greg Kihn's band, with

whom he recorded *Love and Rock'n'Roll* (1986). Leaving Kihn in 1986, Satriani recorded the instrumental album *Not of this Earth*, which (although criticized as sounding 'like heavy metal without the vocals') won him admirers in the hard-rock press and sold respectably in the US. Released on the Epic label, 1987's follow-up, *Surfing with the Alien*, like its predecessor played almost exclusively by Satriani, sold over one million copies in the US.

Satriani formed a band in 1988, recruiting bassist Stu Hamm and drummer Jonathan Mover before recording the hit EP *Dreaming 11*. His next album, *Flying in a Blue Dream*, included several self-penned songs, with Satriani himself providing the vocals.

After a major tour, Satriani began work on an album with Hamm and Mover, but dissolved the band after a lengthy period and re-recorded the album with bassist Matt Bissonette and his drummer brother. The wholly instrumental *The Extremist* (1992) was Satriani's most commercially successful album. In 1993 he released the career retrospective *Time Machine*, which included out-takes from previous albums, live material from the *Extremist* world tour and new recordings with both line-ups of his band. Among his later recordings are *Joe Satriani* (Epic, 1995), on which he was partnered by Eric Johnson and Vai, *In Concert* (1997) and the lesser *Crystal Planet* (1998).

LEO SAYER
b. Gerard Hugh Sayer, 21 May 1948, Brighton, Sussex, England

Sayer was one of the more exuberant British singer-songwriters of the seventies.

At art college, Sayer formed Terraplane Blues. Moving to London, he joined Patches, for whom he wrote songs with David Courtney, a former drummer with **Adam Faith**'s backing group. Faith financed a single by the group and the recording of a Sayer solo album. Before the release of *Silverbird* (Chrysalis, 1973), **The Who**'s Roger Daltrey had a No. 1 hit with the dramatic Courtney–Sayer song 'Giving It All Away'. Sayer's own album also provided a No. 1 in 'The Show Must Go on', with which Sayer introduced his clown persona for television appearances. In America, it was successfully covered by **Three Dog Night**.

Just a Boy (1974) included 'One Man Band' and his first American hit, 'Long Tall Glasses'. This was followed by the British success 'Moonlighting' (1975) and a change of producer to Richard Perry. From *Endless Flight* (1976) Sayer had contrasting American No. 1 singles in the disco-influenced 'You Make Me Feel Like Dancing' (co-written with Vini Poncia) and the Carole Bayer Sager–Albert Hammond ballad

'When I Need You'. The album also provided a lesser hit in 'How Much Love' but *Thunder in My Heart* (1977) and *Leo Sayer* (1978) were less successful.

Cliff Richard associate Alan Tarney was Sayer's next producer. He supervised *Living in a Fantasy* (1980), which included the transatlantic hit, **Bobby Vee**'s 'More Than I Can Say'. *World Radio* (1982) and *Have You Ever Been in Love* (1983) were produced by **Arif Mardin** and the title track of the latter was a British hit, as was 'Orchard Road' (1983). After a long gap, he returned to live performance with a British tour in 1988. Disputes with former manager Faith and former label Chrysalis took up much of Sayer's time in the late eighties and early nineties, when he released only one album, the unsuccessful *Cool Touch* (1990). After finally winning back the rights to his back catalogue in 1992, Sayer's 'You Make Me Feel Like Dancing' recharted in the UK in 1998, the year he issued the best of his later albums, *I'm Going Home*. The definitive anthology is *All the Best* (1993).

BOZ SCAGGS
b. William Royce Scaggs, 8 June 1944, Ohio, USA

Originally the vocalist with **Steve Miller**'s band, Scaggs became a leading white soul singer of the seventies.

Scaggs played in high-school band the Marksmen with Miller before forming the Ardells with pianist and later music writer Ben Sidran and Miller at the University of Wisconsin. During the mid-sixties he played in Europe, recording *Boz* (Polydor, 1966) in Sweden. He rejoined Miller for the albums *Children of the Future* (1968) and *Sailor* (1969) before cutting *Boz Scaggs* (Atlantic, 1969). Featuring Duane Allman of the **Allman Brothers Band** and co-produced by *Rolling Stone* publisher Jann Wenner, the album's strong blues feeling, notably on 'Loan Me a Dime' impressed critics but failed to find an audience.

Scaggs now formed a group with drummer George Rains and signed to Columbia for the Glyn Johns-produced *Moments* (1971) and *Boz Scaggs and Band* (1972). After *My Time* (1972), the veteran soul arranger **Johnny Bristol** supervised *Slow Dancer* (1974). The soul influence was more pronounced on *Silk Degrees* (1976). Produced by Joe Wissert with future **Toto** members David Hungate (bass) and David Paich (keyboards) among the musicians, it gave Scaggs a Top Ten hit with 'Lowdown'. The album also included his biggest British success in 'What Can I Say' and a transatlantic hit in 'Lido Shuffle' (1977).

Two Down Then Left (1977) was also successful but the peak of Scaggs' popularity came with *Middle Man* (1980). With **Carlos Santana** on guitar, the album provided four Top Twenty hits in 'Breakdown Dead Ahead', 'Jojo', 'Look What You've Done to Me' and 'Miss Sun'. Scaggs did not record again until 1988

when the Steve Levine-produced 'Heart of Mine' from *Other Roads* was a hit. Another lengthy absence from the recording studio followed until he signed to Virgin Records, releasing the critically acclaimed *Some Change* in 1994. The album was co-produced by former Flame and **Beach Boys** member Ricky Fataar. The definitive career retrospective is *My Time* (1998).

VICTOR SCHERTZINGER
b. 8 April 1880, Mahony City, Pennsylvania, USA, d. 26 October 1941, Hollywood, California

Film director, composer and lyricist, Schertzinger was one of the most versatile artists working in the field of popular music in the twentieth century.

After studying music in Europe, Schertzinger toured there as a concert violinist before returning to America. He led pit orchestras in New York before travelling to Hollywood in 1916 to compose the accompanying music to Thomas Ince's silent film, *Civilization*. He swiftly graduated to directing films, and with the coming of sound, Schertzinger turned to making musicals after providing the score for the **Maurice Chevalier** and **Jeanette MacDonald** vehicle *The Love Parade* (1929). He was one of the eleven directors who worked on the all-star revue *Paramount on Parade* (1930) and thereafter specialized in musicals, usually featuring his own songs. Among the films he directed were *Heads Up* (1930), *One Night of Love* (1934), the title song of which, written with **Gus Kahn**, gave **Grace Moore** her biggest hit, and a pair of 'Road' outings with **Bing Crosby** and Bob Hope, *Singapore* (1940) and *Zanzibar* (1941).

Schertzinger's most ambitious film was *Something to Sing About* (1937), which he co-scripted and directed as well as scored, but his most successful film as director and composer was *The Fleet's in* (1942), released after his death. It featured **Betty Hutton** and a trio of songs written by Schertzinger with **Johnny Mercer**: 'Tangerine', 'Arthur Murray Taught Me Dancing in a Hurry' and 'I Remember You', a hit for **Jimmy Dorsey** and later **Frank Ifield**.

LALO SCHIFRIN
b. 21 June 1932, Buenos Aires, Argentina

A prolific and eclectic composer of nearly eighty film scores, Schifrin's work was influenced by jazz, particularly the work of **Dizzy Gillespie**, with whom he toured in the early sixties, Latin American styles and classical music.

From a musical family – his father was the conductor of the Teatro Colón in Buenos Aires for over thirty years – Schifrin studied composition in Paris and played jazz piano in the evenings in the early fifties. After meeting Gillespie in 1956, he moved to

874

New York and began writing for television as well as arranging music for bands, including **Xavier Cugat**'s. For Gillespie he wrote 'Gillespiana' (1961) and most of *Dizzy on the French Riviera* (1962). During this period he recorded the hit album *Bossa Nova – New Brazilian Jazz* (Audio Fidelity, 1962).

After working with **Quincy Jones** and **Cannonball Adderley** (*Dialogues for Jazz Quintet and Orchestra* 1969), Schifrin concentrated on film composition. His scores included *The Cincinnati Kid* (1965), *Bullitt* (1968), *Dirty Harry* (1971) and *The Eagle Has Landed* (1976), while for television he wrote the themes to *Mission Impossible* (1966) and *Starsky and Hutch* (1975). More unusual was his 'score' for the documentary *The World of Insects* for which Schifrin gave an ensemble of jazz and chamber musicians notes for the individual sequences from which they improvised.

In the nineties he conducted a recording of his song-cycle *Canto Aztecas* with **Placido Domingo**.

ARTHUR SCHWARTZ
*b. 25 November 1900, Brooklyn, New York, USA,
d. 4 September 1984*

With Howard Dietz, Schwartz wrote both the unofficial anthem of showbusiness, 'That's Entertainment', and the brooding, intimate 'Dancing in the Dark'.

The son of a lawyer, Schwartz opted for songwriting rather than law as a career, after graduating from the Columbia Law School, where he had written songs for college shows. His first published song was 'Baltimore MD, You're the Only Doctor for Me', which was featured in *The Grand Street Follies* (1925), and he had several songs in similar small revues before meeting Dietz in 1927. Their first success came in 1929 when Dietz rewrote a lyric **Lorenz Hart** had supplied for one of Schwartz's college show tunes to produce 'I Guess I'll Have to Change My Plan' (later a hit for **Rudy Vallee**). Their greatest early success was *The Band Wagon* (1931), which starred Adele and **Fred Astaire**, for which they wrote all the songs, including 'Dancing in the Dark', an immediate hit for artists as varied as **Bing Crosby**, **Ben Selvin** and **Fred Waring**.

Dietz (*b. 8 September 1896, New York, d. 30 July 1983, New York*), once described by director Ernst Lubitsch as 'the man who writes hit shows on MGM stationery', was director of publicity for the studio for over thirty years. While there, he coined the mottos 'Ars Gratia Artis' and 'More stars than there are in Heaven', created the studio's trademark Leo the Lion, and passed to posterity some of Sam Goldwyn's entertaining malapropisms (even reputedly 'writing' some of them). Before teaming up with Schwartz, Dietz wrote with **Jerome Kern** ('If Only We Could Lead a Merry Mormon Life') and **George Gershwin** ('Heaven and Earth'). Schooled in writing songs for

revues, where the emphasis was on wit rather than feeling, Dietz brought an element of playfulness to his writing with Schwartz. Thus as well as 'Dancing', *The Band Wagon* included the witty reflection on the Depression, 'I Might as Well Be Miserable with You'.

Throughout the thirties Schwartz and Dietz contributed to numerous Broadway and West End shows, including *Revenge with Music* (1934), which featured 'You and the Night and the Music', *At Home Abroad* (1935), which featured 'Love Is a Dancing Thing', a British hit for **Jessie Matthews**, and *Between the Devil* (1937). That show failed and as a result the pair dissolved their partnership. After one show with **Dorothy Fields** (*Stars in Your Eyes*, 1939), Schwartz belatedly followed his fellow Broadway songwriters to Hollywood. There, in addition to songwriting ('They're Either Too Young or Too Old', 1943, a hit for **Jimmy Dorsey**, and 'A Girl in Calico', 1946), he turned to production. Among his notable films as producer were the Rita Hayworth musical *Cover Girl* (1944), which featured songs by Jerome Kern and **Ira Gershwin**, and *Night and Day* (1946), which romantically told the story of **Cole Porter**.

After the Second World War Schwartz once more collaborated on several shows with Dietz, but their only substantial success was 'That's Entertainment', written specifically for the 1953 film version of *The Band Wagon*. The song later provided the name for collections of MGM film clips in 1974 and 1976. Schwartz's biggest success after the war was the show *A Tree Grows in Brooklyn* (1951) with lyrics by Fields. In the same year Dietz wrote the first of his English adaptations of operas for the Metropolitan Opera House, *La Bohème*.

In the late sixties Schwartz retired to England and in 1975 recorded an album of his songs produced by nostalgia enthusiast Alan Dell, *From the Pen of Arthur Schwartz* (RCA).

THE SCORPIONS
Klaus Meine, b. 25 May 1948, Hannover, Germany; Rudolf Schenker, b. 31 August 1948, Hildersheim; Michael Schenker, b. 10 January 1955, Sarstedt; Lothar Heinberg; Wolfgang Dziony; Francis Buchholz, b. 19 February 1950, Hannover (replaced by Ralph Bieckermann, b. 8 August 1962, Lubeck); Jurgen Rosenthal; Ulrich Roth; Rudy Lenners; Herman Rarebell, b. 18 November 1953, Lebach; Mathias Jabs, b. 25 October 1955, Hannover

The most successful hard-rock band to emerge from Germany, the Scorpions survived several line-up changes to score their greatest success almost twenty years into their career when they began the nineties with their biggest-ever hit, taken from their fourteenth album.

The Schenker brothers, both guitarists, formed the band in Dusseldorf in 1971 with vocalist Meine, bassist Heinberg and drummer Dziony, signing to RCA Records for their first album, *Lonesome Crow*, in 1972. The album, produced by Dieter Dierks (who would fulfil the same role for the band's next twelve albums), was particularly noted for the exciting guitar playing of Michael Schenker, but he left the band in 1973 to join British hard-rockers **UFO**, with whom he would record six albums. Heinberg and Dziony also left the band, replaced by Buchholz and Rosenthal, respectively, before the Scorpions recorded the second album, *Fly to the Rainbow* (1974), as a four-piece. Later that year, Roth joined the band as lead guitarist, with Lenners replacing Rosenthal in 1975. With a settled line-up, the band began drawing plaudits for their combination of hard-edged metallic rock and melody, and sales of the next two albums, *In Trance* (1975) and *Virgin Killer* (1976), in Europe and Japan showed encouraging growth – although in the UK they were best known for the controversial cover and title of the latter set. Extensive touring and the replacement of Lenners by Rarebell preceded *Taken by Force* (1978) and the live album *Tokyo Tapes* (1979), which saw the band beginning to make more headway in the US and UK, particularly for their trademark 'power-ballads'.

In 1978 Michael Schenker left UFO, rejoining the Scorpions briefly and playing on some tracks on their first UK chart album, *Lovedrive* (1979, their début for the Harvest label), which included a UK hit single, 'Is There Anybody There?'. However, he collapsed onstage during a European tour and was permanently replaced by Jabs. Schenker went on to enjoy a successful solo career. The band began touring more regularly in the US, and subsequent albums *Animal Magnetism* (1980) and *Blackout* (1982) saw them achieve the long-awaited breakthrough in the US and UK. The *Love at First Sting* album gave them their first US hit single, 'Rock You Like a Hurricane' in 1984, and another live album, *World Wide Live* (1985) consolidated their success. In 1986 they played their first gig in what was then the Eastern Bloc, in Budapest, and in 1988 became the first western hard-rock act to play in the USSR.

1988's *Savage Amusement*, their last with producer Dierks, was an even greater success. After it they changed labels to Phonogram worldwide. The first album for the label, *Crazy World* (1989), contained the international No. 1 'Winds of Change', an anthemic track inspired by political changes in Eastern Europe which was recorded in three languages and topped the chart in twelve countries. The album, produced by Keith Olsen and with songs co-written by **Bryan Adams**' writing partner Jim Vallance, sold over seven million copies. Yet another line-up change followed, with Bieckermann replacing the long-serving Buchholz. In 1992 the band played Germany's biggest-ever peacetime rally, 'Artists for Freedom', before 180,000 people, and in 1993 released the long-awaited new album, *Face the Heat*, recorded with producer Bruce Fairbairn (best known for his work with **Aerosmith**, **Bon Jovi** and **AC/DC**). *Pure Instinct* (1995), which the band supported with a North American tour, was almost as successful. They repeated the process for the lesser *Eye to Eye* (1999), which featured new drummer Kottak.

JACK SCOTT
b. Jack Scafone, 28 January 1938, Windsor, Ontario, Canada

Best remembered for the brooding ballads, 'My True Love'* (Carlton, 1958), 'What in the World's Come Over You'* and 'Burning Bridges'* (both Top Rank, 1960), Scott developed his unusual clipped vocal manner singing Southern-styled rockabilly.

The son of Italian immigrants, Scott was signed to ABC-Paramount by Jack Carlton in 1957, and then to Carlton's own label in 1958. His rockers (which include the fine 'Two-Timing Woman' and 'Baby She's Gone') failed, but 'My True Love' (originally the B-side of the up-tempo 'Leroy') was a hit and henceforth Scott was seen as a mournful balladeer. After another hit, 'Goodbye Baby' (1958), Scott, who wrote most of his material, left Carlton for Top Rank, where he expressed his growing devotion to country music with *I Remember Hank Williams* (1960) and *Old Time Religion* (1962).

A move to Capitol in 1961 produced several minor hits but the records were more noticeable for the insistent strings. Subsequently, he recorded unsuccessfully for Groove, RCA and GRT. In 1973 he briefly joined Dot and recorded a series of introspective singles (including 'Insane' and 'As You Take a Walk Through My Mind'). In 1977 he made the first of a series of low-key tours of Europe, where his early records were revered by rockabilly cultists and revived by such artists as **Shakin' Stevens**. *Classic Scott* (Bear Family, 1990) is the definitive anthology.

RAYMOND SCOTT
b. Harry Warnow, 10 September 1908, Brooklyn, New York, USA, d. 8 February 1994, Van Nuys, California

A composer, pianist, bandleader and inventor of a wide range of electronic musical instruments, in his career Scott neatly united the concerns of a **Thomas Edison** with the wit and energy of **Philip Glass**, **Spike Jones**, **Stan Freberg** and **Henry Rollins**. His music, described by one critic as 'a beguiling mix of programme music, jazz and Tin Pan Alley', won him •

critical applause in the late thirties. In the forties many of his compositions were regularly used by Warner Bros as the soundtracks to the studio's *Merrie Melodies* and *Loony Tunes* cartoon series. The titles of his compositions, 'Dinner Music for a Pack of Hungry Cannibals', 'War Dance for Wooden Indians' and 'Reckless Night on Board an Ocean Liner', were often as expressive as those of the cartoons they accompanied.

The son of a music-shop owner, Scott (who changed his name in 1936) played piano from an early age. He wanted to study science but was persuaded by his family to study music at what was to become the Juilliard School of Music. On graduating in 1931 Scott joined the CBS Radio Orchestra (of which the conductor was his brother Mark) as a pianist and later in 1936 formed his own group, the Quintette (which actually had six members). It was this group that introduced many of the short compositions (many derived from the advertising jingles Scott wrote) that would later be featured in the Warner Bros cartoons. The groups recorded briefly for **Irving Mills**' Master label ('Twilight in Turkey', 'The Toy Trumpet' and 'Dinner Music for a Pack of Hungry Cannibals', 1937) and later for Columbia ('Huckleberry Duck', 1940) and Decca ('Secret Agent'). Many of these compositions were cut and pasted passages from songs the band recorded at rehearsals. This gave them an arbitrary, almost choppy feeling which would be further intensified when they were married to the schizophrenic visuals of the Warner Bros cartoons.

In 1937 Scott began writing film music for 20th Century Fox, which was usually performed by the Quintette. Among the films featuring Scott's compositions were *Ali Baba Goes to Town* (1937) and *Happy Landing* (1938), both of which featured the Quintette on screen, and *Rebecca of Sunny Brook Farm* in which **Shirley Temple** sings and dances with Bill 'Bojangles' Robinson to 'The Toy Trumpet'.

In 1939 Scott left CBS to form his own big band but his greatest success came in 1943 when Warner Bros' music director Carl Stallings started using Scott compositions as incidental music. These helped fix Scott's tunes in America's national memory, so much so that fifty years later in 1992 the tunes were again featured in the hit *Ren and Stimpy* show. Earlier, to help create the cartoon effect needed for the film *Honey I Shrunk the Kids*, the title music borrowed extensively from 'Powerhouse', the tune used over forty times in the Warner Bros cartoons.

In 1949 Scott replaced his brother Mark as the bandleader on the hit radio (and then television) show *Your Hit Parade*. He composed the TV show's theme, 'Be Happy Go Lucky', which was sung by his second wife Dorothy Collins.

He recorded albums for his own label, AudioVox, and others and at one time auditioned **Bo Diddley**,

but his main preoccupation from the mid-fifties onwards was tinkering with electronics. Many of his radio commercials had featured sound effects, often generated electronically by a machine he devised and called Karloff in 1948. Other electronic machines he invented were the Clavivox, a keyboard instrument which produced sinuous whining sounds, and a scanning radio which tuned into radio stations automatically. Mostly working from his own laboratory, Manhattan Research, in the early sixties Scott developed prototype synthesizers and sequencers. His most complex machine was the Electronium, which attempted to marry artificial intelligence to electronics in the form of a machine that could actually compose music. Stories about this came to the attention of Motown Founder **Berry Gordy**, who in 1972 hired Scott to head up Motown's electronic music research department in Los Angeles. In 1977 he retired from Motown and continued composing ('Beautiful Little Butterfly', 1986) until 1987 when a series of strokes made it virtually impossible for him to work.

In the nineties, in the wake of renewed interest in Scott, selections of his works were reissued on CD. *Reckless Night and Turkish Twilights* (Columbia, 1992), produced by Irwin Chusid, the curator of the Raymond Scott Archive, features thirties recordings, including the original version of 'Powerhouse'. *The Raymond Scott Project: Powerhouse, Vol. 1* is a complementary set of Quintette radio recordings from 1935 to 1940 which highlights the Quintette's experimental approach, while *The Carl Stalling Project* (Warner, 1990) consists of the actual soundtracks of numerous classic cartoons (without dialogue). Produced by **Hal Willner**, the album confirms how zany Scott's music was and how inventively it was programmed and edited – with the melodies often being either compressed or stretched – by Stalling.

The albums *Soothing Sounds for Babies* (Basta, 1997) and *Manhattan Research Inc* (2000) included mostly unissued electronic material created by Scott. The first was a three-CD expansion of an album of electronic soundscapes intended to stimulate the intelligence of babies, while the second includes the abstract music from adverts for fifties and sixties products, such as spark plugs and theme parks, which were seen as being futuristic at the time. Lavishly illustrated and documented, the CD sets confirm Scott's musicianship as much as his technological interests.

RONNIE SCOTT
b. Ronald Schatt, 28 January 1927, London, England, d. 23 December 1996

An outstanding jazz tenor-saxophonist, Ronnie Scott became the most important figure in the British jazz scene through his London club, which attracted the leading figures of the genre for over three decades.

The son of a musician, Scott acquired his first saxophone at the age of fourteen and joined Johnny Claes' swing band in 1943 which appeared in the **George Formby** film *George in Civvy Street*. A British disciple of bebop (and a member of 'Geraldo's Navy', so named because **Geraldo** booked the band on the *Queen Mary*, Scott regularly travelled back and forth to New York) he played in the late forties in the big bands of **Ambrose**, Jack Parnell and **Ted Heath**. With **Johnny Dankworth** and others he started Club Eleven in 1948 as a centre for British modern jazz playing but the club closed in 1950 after a police drugs raid.

Scott formed his first band in 1952 with Vic Feldman (vibes) and Benny Green (baritone sax), recording *Great Scott* (Esquire). He was a session man on **Tommy Steele**'s 'Rock with the Caveman' (1957) the year that Scott and Tubby Hayes (*1935–73*), widely regarded as the most gifted of British jazz players, formed the Jazz Couriers. With Hayes on tenor sax and vibes, the group recorded *The Message from Britain* and *The Jazz Couriers in Concert* before splitting up in 1959.

Scott opened his club in 1959 but continued to perform with the big band led by **Kenny Clarke** and Francy Boland and with a group of younger British players, including baritone-sax-player John Surman and Tony Oxley (drums). During the seventies the Ronnie Scott group was based at the club and included Irish guitarist Louis Stewart and trumpeter Dick Pearce. His story is entertainingly told in John Fordham's biography *Let's All Join Hands and Contact the Living* (1986).

GIL SCOTT-HERON
b. 1 April 1949, Chicago, Illinois, USA

Poet turned songwriter and singer, Scott-Heron used a jazz-rock backdrop for his highly political songs. His style formed a bridge between laid-back soul singers like **Bill Withers** and the later rap artists.

While at Pennsylvania's Lincoln University, Scott-Heron and keyboards-player Brian Jackson recorded a musical setting of his book of verse *Small Talk at 125th and Lenox* (Flying Dutchman, 1972). He next released *Free Will* and *Pieces of a Man* (1973), which included some of his most famous pieces, notably 'The Revolution Will Not Be Televised', 'Whitey on the Moon' and 'Lady Day and John Coltrane'.

Scott-Heron was signed to the newly formed Arista label in 1974, and *The First Minute of a New Day* (1975) featured his new group the Midnight Band. His political commentary 'Johannesburg' (1976) appeared on his best-known album, *From South Africa to South*

California. During the late seventies he composed several songs on the topic of nuclear power, notably 'We Almost Lost Detroit' and 'Shut 'Em Down' from *1980*.

At the end of the seventies Scott-Heron split up with Jackson and formed a new touring group, the Amnesia Express. His later recordings included *Reflections* (1981) and *Moving Target* (1982) which featured the moving blues 'Blue Collar' and the ambitious 'Black History/The World'. As a new generation of rap and jazz-funk fans discovered his work, Scott-Heron remained a popular live attraction and occasionally toured in Europe. After he left Arista in 1985 a drug problem limited his work. He returned to recording with the superior *Spirits* (TVT, 1994) and in the second half of the decade started to tour regularly.

SCREAMING TREES
Gary Lee Conner; Van Conner; Mark Lanegan; Mark Pickerel (replaced by Barrett Martin)

Screaming Trees were one of the few US alternative rock bands to outlive the grunge boom of the early nineties, going on to produce their most acclaimed work, *Dust*, in 1996. Lead singer Lanegan also recorded a series of successful solo albums.

Screaming Trees were formed in 1984 when brothers Gary (guitar) and Van (bass) Conner met singer Lanegan in their home town of Ellensburg, Washington. With the addition of drummer Pickerel they recorded the *Other Worlds* EP before the release of their début, *Clairvoyance* (Velvetone, 1985). The band was picked up by SST Records the following year, gradually building up a strong fanbase with three albums – *Even and Especially When* (1987), *Invisible Lantern* (1988) and *Buzz Factory* (1989) – inspired by the **Stooges** and late sixties garage rock and psychedelia.

After recording a pair of EPs – *Change Has Come* (1989) and *Something about Today* (1990) – for Sub Pop, Screaming Trees signed to Epic, releasing *Uncle Anaesthesia* (1991), which featured new drummer Barrett Martin. Produced by **Soundgarden**'s Chris Cornell, the album was a polished distillation of the band's earlier work, but at the same time saw the group significantly begin to replace the simple rage and aggression central to grunge with a tighter and more constructed rock sound. The quartet broke on to the world stage with their contribution to the *Singles* (1992) soundtrack, 'Nearly Lost You', before issuing the gold album *Sweet Oblivion* (1992), which heralded a new artistic maturity. The album was followed by a year-long world tour alongside **Soul Asylum** and **Alice in Chains**.

Before making their sixth album, Screaming Trees took an extended break, during which time Lanegan, who had already made the solo outing *Winding Sheet* in 1990, recorded *Whiskey for the Holy Ghost* (1994), a more acoustic-based, melancholy affair than the band's work. The Conners and Martin spent the hiatus working with an array of Seattle-based musicians on underground releases, most notably *Above* (1995) by Mad Season, a grunge 'supergroup' which also featured members of **Pearl Jam** and Alice in Chains.

Screaming Trees returned in 1996 with their most successful album to date, *Dust*; produced by George Drakoulias, the album expanded the band's sound to take in strings and keyboards and spawned a hit single, 'All I Know'. In the manner of the **Grateful Dead** three decades before them, the album saw the band add a rustic (folk and country) feel to their assured psychedelia.

SCRITTI POLITTI
Green, b. Green $trohmeyer-Gartside, 22 June 1956, Cardiff, Wales; Matthew K; Tom Morley (replaced by Fred Maher); Mike McEvoy; David Gamson

Starting out as an avant-garde punk group, Scritti Politti evolved into one of the more original dance-disco groups of the mid-eighties.

Inspired by the live shows of the **Clash** and the **Sex Pistols**, singer/guitarist Green formed the band in Leeds in 1978 with fellow art students, taking the name from an Italian phrase describing political texts. Moving to London and adding drummer Morley, Scritti Politti issued the angular 'Skank Bloc Bologna' (St Pancras, 1978), a cut-up of various musical styles and political slogans. The sleeve of the single carried detailed information on costings in an attempt to encourage others to make their own records.

After further singles, Scritti Politti cut *Songs to Remember* (Rough Trade, 1982). With McEvoy on synthesizers and produced by Adam Kidron, the album allied more accessible pop, reggae and jazz sounds to songs like 'Asylums in Jerusalem' and 'Jacques Derrida', named after the contemporary French philosopher. Soon afterwards, all members (except Green) left the band, with Morley signing to Zarjazz, the label owned by **Madness**. Green recruited New York avant-garde players Gamson and drummer Maher, who had worked with guitarist Fred Frith and **Bill Laswell**, and signed to Virgin for *Cupid and Psyche* (1985). The album had taken three years to complete.

With **Arif Mardin** producing, the album's opulent sound combined with Green's ethereal voice and gnomic lyrics provided a series of hit singles. They included the British Top Ten entries 'Wood Beez (Pray Like Aretha Franklin)', 'Absolute' and 'The Word Girl', and the American success 'Perfect Way', which reached No. 1 in 1984.

Green's songs were recorded by other artists, including **Madonna**, **Miles Davis** and **Chaka Khan** with Davis on trumpet, before Scritti Politti returned to recording with 'Oh Patti (Don't You Worry About Loverboy)' and *Provision* (1988). The nineties began promisingly for Green with a pair of hits in 1991, a cover of **The Beatles**' 'She's a Woman' featuring rising reggae star **Shabba Ranks** and a version of **Gladys Knight and the Pips**' 'Take Me in Your Arms and Rock Me' with another reggae guest star, Sweetie Irie. His only other appearance on record in the early part of the decade came on the album *Music of Quality and Distinction Vol. 2* (1991) by **Heaven 17** spin-off BEF.

Green remained out of the public eye until 1999, when he issued the fourth Scritti Politti album, *Anhomie and Bonhomie*. Drawing on grunge and hip-hop (the album featured Rawkus rapper Mos Def heavily), *Anhomie* was a multi-layered gem, but failed to match the success of Green's earlier works. 'Tinseltown to the Boogiedown' was a minor hit single in the UK.

THE SEARCHERS
Mike Pender, b. Mike Prendergast, 3 March 1942, Liverpool, England; John McNally, b. 30 August 1941, Liverpool; Tony Jackson, b. 16 July 1940, Liverpool; Chris Curtis, b. Christopher Crummey, 16 August 1941, Liverpool

At one point second only to **The Beatles** in popularity in Liverpool, the Searchers, like the Fab Four, broadened their repertoire from its original R&B and rock'n'roll base, but unlike The Beatles and other beat groups, such as the **Hollies**, they never became writers and were unable to develop further. Thus, after their initial success, which included a trio of British No. 1s, 'Sweets for My Sweet' (1963), 'Needles and Pins'* and 'Don't Throw Your Love Away' (1964), they were condemned to retread their early hits on the revival circuit in the seventies, eighties and nineties.

Formed in 1961 as the backing group to Johnny Sandon (later a member of the Merseybeat group the San Remo Four), the group took their name from the John Ford film (a catchphrase from which had already supplied **Buddy Holly** with the title of 'That'll Be the Day' in 1957). Like other Merseybeat groups, they built up an extensive repertoire of obscure American R&B and rock'n'roll songs, many learned from records brought home by the 'Cunard Yanks', sailors who worked on the transatlantic liners that then docked in Liverpool. Similarly, like The Beatles, the Searchers perfected their stagecraft in the Hamburg clubs and, after The Beatles' early hits, were signed to Pye by **Tony Hatch** in 1963. They had a hit with their first single, a crisply produced version of **Pomus and Shuman**'s 'Sweets for My Sweet', originally recorded by the **Drifters**. Their début album, *Meet the Searchers* (1963), included energetic versions of R&B standards (the revival of the **Coasters**' 'Love

Potion No. 9' was their biggest American hit in 1964 on Kapp). But the gentler high-pitched harmonies of 'Sweets' and the jangly guitars of **Pete Seeger**'s 'Where Have All the Flowers Gone', also on the album, pointed forward to the folk-rock sounds with which the Searchers next experimented, foreshadowing the **Byrds**' move in this direction.

The nursery-rhyme-like 'Sugar and Spice' (1963), penned by Hatch, saw the group marking time but with the release of 'Needles and Pins', written by **Cher**'s then partner Sonny Bono and **Jack Nitzsche** and earlier an American hit for **Jackie DeShannon**, the group achieved their moment of stylistic perfection. If the lyric was lightweight, the group's recording featured a fuller production, an affecting 'Pins-a' refrain and tight harmonies. It was followed by a soft-voiced revival of the **Orlons**' 'Don't Throw Your Love Away' (1964), after which Jackson, disgruntled by the new gentle sound, left the group for a solo career. He was replaced by Frank Allen, from Cliff Bennett and the Rebel Rousers, and the Searchers continued in a folk-rock vein. Their hits included DeShannon's 'When You Walk in the Room', 'What Have They Done to the Rain' (1964), written by Malvina Reynolds, author of the protest song 'Little Boxes', and **P. F. Sloan**'s 'Take Me for What I'm Worth' (1965), the group's last British Top Twenty entry.

In 1966 Curtis left to form Roundabout and was replaced by Johnny Blunt (and then Billy Adamson in 1969), and the group left Pye and, in the absence of chart hits, turned to cabaret. They briefly joined RCA ('Desdemona', 1971) and later were signed by Sire, who released the impressive *The Searchers* (1979) and *Love's Melodies* (1981). Following its commercial failure, the group (minus Pinder after 1985) returned to the lucrative cabaret and rock revival circuits. The band took legal action against Pinder in 1988 to stop him billing his own band as 'Mike Pinder's Searchers' and, after a further album, *Hungry Heart* (Arista, 1993), continued to perform into the nineties. *The Complete Collection* (Rhino, 1996) is just that.

JON SECADA
b. 1959, Havana, Cuba

Jon Secada had substantial success in the early nineties with his slickly packaged but lightweight Latin dance-pop which appealed to a huge cross-over audience in the US. He was the precursor of a flood of Latin stars in the nineties, including Enrique Iglesias, Marc Anthony, Christina Aguilera and Ricky Martin.

The son of Cuban immigrants, Secada was brought up in Miami, Florida. After completing his conservatory training, he went on to study at the University of Miami, where he gained a Bachelor's degree in Music and a Master's degree in Jazz Vocal Performance. In

1987 Secada's song-writing talents brought him to the attention of Cuban émigrée vocalist **Gloria Estefan** and her manager husband Emilio. Managed by Emilio Estefan, Secada joined Estefan's backing band as a vocalist, touring with her until late 1991.

Estefan recorded one of Secada's songs on her 1989 US Top Ten album *Cuts Both Ways* and gave him a featured slot on her 1991 world tour. He also co-wrote six tracks and sang on her 1991 album *Into the Night*, including the American chart-toppers 'Coming Out of the Dark' and 'Can't Forget You'.

Groomed for stardom by the Estefan organization, Secada embarked on his solo career in 1992 with an eponymous début album, which featured songs and backing vocals by Gloria Estefan and was co-produced by Emilio. The first single from the album, 'Just Another Day', was an international hit, and a Spanish-language version topped the US Latin charts for three months. Other hit singles in 'Do You Believe in Us' and 'Angel' followed, and the album went on to sell over four million copies worldwide. His Spanish-language album *Otra Dias Mas Sin Verte* (1992) was the bestselling Latin album of the year in the US.

Secada released *Heart, Soul & a Voice* in 1994. It included the hit singles 'If You Go' (co-written with Emilio Estefan), which stayed in the US charts for almost the whole year, 'Mental Picture' and 'Where Do I Go from You', composed by **Diane Warren**. Later the same year he recorded *Si Te Vas*, a second album of Spanish-language material. Subsequent outings *Amor* (1995) and *Secada* (1997), which was produced in part by **Jimmy Jam and Terry Lewis** and included the minor hit 'Too Late Too Soon', were better received critically than commercially. In their wake, he spent the rest of the nineties writing and producing for the likes of Martin and Jennifer Lopez. He returned to recording in his own right with the (mostly) English-language album *Better Part of Me* (Epic, 2000), which was firmly aimed at the mainstream with its mix of power-ballads ('There's No Sunshine Anymore') and lightweight dance tracks ('Stop').

NEIL SEDAKA
b. 13 March 1939, Brooklyn, New York, USA

A songwriter and singer, Sedaka was a graduate of the Brill Building school of skilful teenage ballads, along with **Carole King** and **Ellie Greenwich**. Like King, he survived a barren period in the sixties, successfuly re-emerging as both a writer and performer in the following decade.

From a Turkish family background, Sedaka trained as a classical pianist before turning to pop songwriting with lyricist Howard Greenfield. Working at publisher **Don Kirshner**'s Aldon Music, they had their first hit with the ebullient 'Stupid Cupid' (1958) by **Connie Francis**, while other Sedaka–Greenfield songs were recorded by **Clyde McPhatter**, **Lavern Baker** and **Dinah Washington**.

The following year Sedaka recorded the Top Twenty hit 'The Diary' (RCA), but his first major success came with 'Oh Carol' (dedicated to King) and the frantic 'I Go Ape'. Sedaka's bright, unaccented voice and chubby good looks made him the **Paul Anka** of the early sixties and he had eight further hits in four years. They included 'Stairway to Heaven' (1960); the chirpy 'Calendar Girl' (1961), with its litany of the months of the year; 'Little Devil' into which Sedaka tried to inject a note of excitement with a few squeals; and the mournful 'Breaking Up Is Hard to Do' (1962) his only No. 1.

By 1963 Sedaka was twenty-four and his days as a teen-idol over. He and Greenfield continued to compose, however, and provided hits for Jimmy Clanton ('Venus in Blue Jeans', 1962), the Fifth Dimension ('Working on a Groovy Thing', 1969), **Tom Jones** ('Puppet Man', 1971) and **Captain and Tennille**, who reached No. 1 with 'Love Will Keep Us Together'* (1975) and also recorded Sedaka's 'You Never Done It Like That' (1978).

By this point Sedaka had begun a new recording career. After the unsuccessful *Emergence* (RCA, 1972), he made *The Tra La Days Are Over* (MGM, 1973) with the musicians who later formed **10CC**. Its best tracks showed a new maturity in the psychological insight of 'Standing on the Inside' and the self-analysis and intensity of 'Our Last Song Together', a song inspired by the break up of his partnership with Greenfield. Both were hits in Britain where Sedaka was able both to retain his nostalgic audience and sell them his new material.

The title track of *Laughter in the Rain* (1974) re-established Sedaka in America where it reached No. 1 on **Elton John**'s Rocket label. 'The Immigrant', a lucid song inspired by **John Lennon**'s treatment by the US government, was also a success. Elton John himself provided backing vocals on a further No. 1, 'Bad Blood'* (1975), which was followed by a new, slower version of 'Breaking Up Is Hard to Do' and 'Love in the Shadows' (1976).

In 1977 Sedaka signed to Elektra, recording *A Song and Now* (1981) which included the hit duet with his daughter Dara, 'I Should've Never Let You Go'. He later joined **Mike Curb**'s company, releasing *In the Pocket* (MCA, 1984) before publishing an autobiography, *Laughter in the Rain* (1987). Later records were few and far between, although Sedaka toured Britain regularly and had a Top Ten hit there with the compilation *Timeless* in 1991.

THE SEEDS

Sky Saxon, b. Richard Marsh; Daryl Hooper; Jon Savage; Rick Andridge

Best remembered for 'Pushin' Too Hard' (1967), the Seeds were one of several garage bands who produced naïve, but arresting versions of psychedelia.

Formed in Los Angeles in the mid-sixties and strongly influenced by the **Rolling Stones**, the group tried a variety of names (including the Amoeba) before as the Seeds they were signed to Gene Norman's GNP Crescendo label. Early B-sides revealed their debts to the Stones ('The Other Place') and **Little Richard** ('Daisy Mae'), but 'Can't Seem to Make You Mine' (1965) saw the group achieving a distillation of influences, with Saxon's angry vocals and a simplistic organ riff prominent. Their eponymous début album (1965) developed this sound further and produced their biggest success, 'Pushin''.

However, by the time the song had become a national hit, the group had developed further, retaining their sound but adding a 'sociocultural' element to their songwriting. The result was *Future* (1967), a classic of the psychedelic era. As well as the hit 'Thousand Shadows' the album included such songs as 'March of the Flower Children', 'Travel with Your Mind' and 'Where Is the Entranceway to Play' and won Saxon and producer Marcus Tybalt a cult reputation. After the insipid pseudo-blues album, *A Full Spoon of Seedy Blues* (1969), which came complete with a cloying liner note by **Muddy Waters**, the group briefly joined MGM in 1971 before splitting up. Saxon spent most of the seventies and eighties outside the music business, resurfacing only occasionally. In 1987 he released *Destiny's Children* (Jem), a record which did no more than confirm his cult appeal. *Evil Hoodoo* (Edsel, 1988) is the best retrospective so far available.

PETE SEEGER

b. 3 May 1919, New York, USA

In a career spanning half a century and as many albums, Seeger was the embodiment of the continuity of the folk revival. As a writer, singer, teacher, organizer and editor, he was closely associated with such figures as **Woody Guthrie**, the **Weavers** and **Don McLean**.

All three of the children of Harvard musicologist Charles Seeger became musicians. Peggy settled in England, forming a partnership with **Ewan MacColl**, Mike formed the **New Lost City Ramblers** to play traditional 'old-time' country music, while Pete left Harvard in 1938 to assist **Alan Lomax** in his song-collecting trips through the American South.

He began to perform on banjo, guitar and vocals

and in 1940 formed the Almanac Singers with Lee Hays and Millard Lampell. The group recorded union songs and peace anthems for Eric Bernay's Keynote company before Guthrie joined in 1941. The Almanacs made a national tour and an album of pro-war songs (*Dear Mr President*) before disbanding when the various members joined the war effort.

After army service, Seeger became director of People's Songs, a loose organization devoted to arranging performances and publishing protest material. This activity was succeeded by the periodicals *Sing Out!* (1950) and *Broadside* (1961), both of which Seeger helped to found. His first commercial success as a singer came in 1948 when he and Hays formed the Weavers and signed a recording deal with Decca. With **Gordon Jenkins** providing orchestral arrangements, the group had a number of pop hits including Seeger's version of the East African song 'Wimoweh'. The Weavers' progress was blighted by blacklisting and Seeger did not clear his name of charges of 'un-American activities' until 1962; he was barred from appearing on television until the late sixties.

He left the group in 1958, recording solo albums for Folkways, Tradition and Columbia, to whom he was signed by **John Hammond** in 1960. Among his numerous albums for the label were *Story Songs* (1961), *We Shall Overcome* (1963), *Big Muddy* (1967) and *Rainbow Race* (1972). Most contained a mixture of traditional American material, contemporary compositions and songs from around the world. Never a prolific writer, Seeger translated or extended existing material to create several of the most popular songs of the revival, notably 'If I Had a Hammer' (a hit for both **Peter Paul and Mary**, 1962, and **Trini Lopez**, 1963); 'Guantanamera' (successfully covered in 1966 by the Sandpipers); 'Where Have All the Flowers Gone?' (of which there were hit versions by the **Kingston Trio**, 1962, **Marlene Dietrich**, 1965, and **Johnny Rivers**, 1965); 'Turn Turn Turn'; and 'The Bells of Rhymney'. The last two, settings of words from the Old Testament and Welsh poet Idris Davies, respectively, were folk-rock hits for the **Byrds** in 1965. *The World of Pete Seeger* (1973) collects together the best of his Columbia recordings.

Seeger's attitude towards the new singers of the sixties was benevolent, although he found electric music distasteful and continued to record with acoustic-guitar backings. The most important of his later protégés was McLean, who had worked with Seeger on the Clearwater Project, an ecological movement calling for the cleaning-up of the Hudson River.

He continued to tour and record into the seventies and eighties, when he formed a partnership with Arlo Guthrie for numerous concerts and several albums, including *Together in Concert* (Warners, 1975) and *Precious Friend* (1982). The two-CD set *Singalong*

Demonstration Concert (Folkways, 1980) is an affectionate snapshot of a Seeger concert.

In 1993 Seeger published *Where Have All the Flowers Gone?*, a collection of his compositions. In the same year Vanguard released previously unissued performances by Seeger at the Newport festival in 1963–5. In 1998 Appleseed issued the tribute album *Where Have All the Flowers Gone: The Songs of Pete Seeger*, which featured the likes of **Bonnie Raitt** and **Jackson Browne** singing songs associated with Seeger.

THE SEEKERS
Judith Durham, b. 3 July 1943; Athol Guy, b. 5 January 1940, Victoria, Australia; Keith Potger, b. 2 March 1941, Colombo, Sri Lanka; Bruce Woodley, b. 25 July 1942, Melbourne, Australia

A successful commercial folk group of the early sixties, the Seekers' format was revived several years later as the New Seekers, who converted the Coca-Cola jingle 'I'd Like to Teach the World to Sing'* (1971) into a chart-topping single.

After a series of Australian hits, the Seekers came to England where 'I'll Never Find Another You' (EMI Columbia, 1965) reached No. 1. An American Top Ten hit on Capitol and written and produced by **Dusty Springfield**'s brother Tom, the record's tight vocal harmonies behind Durham's pure lead singing recalled the formula of his own group, the Springfields. Woodley co-wrote with **Paul Simon** the Cyrkle's American No. 1 'Red Rubber Ball' (Columbia, 1966).

Over the next two year the Seekers had seven more British hits, all Springfield compositions except for Simon's 'Someday One Day', Malvina Reynolds' 'Morningtown Ride' and Kenny Young's 'When Will the Good Apple Fall'. The most impressive of these songs was the stately ballad 'The Carnival Is Over' (1965) and the most successful the film theme 'Georgy Girl', which sold a million in America.

The group split up in 1967 when Durham left to pursue a solo career which faltered after the minor hit 'Olive Tree' (1967). Two years later, Potger put together the New Seekers. Its members included Lyn Paul (*b. 16 February 1949, Melbourne*), Eve Graham (*b. 13 April 1943, Perth, Scotland*), Peter Doyle (*b. 28 July 1949, Melbourne*), Marty Kristian (*b. 27 May 1947, Leipzig, Germany*) and Paul Layton (*b. 4 August 1947, Beaconsfield, England*).

After reaching the American Top Twenty on Elektra with a pop-folk treatment of **Melanie**'s 'What Have They Done to My Song, Ma' (Philips, 1970), the group switched to a mainstream pop approach. Delaney Bramlett's 'Never Ending Song of Love' (1970) was the first of a series of Top Ten hits, which included **Roger Greenaway** and Roger Cook's 'I'd

Like to Teach the World to Sing' (Polydor, 1971), 'Beg, Steal or Borrow' (1972) and **Harry Chapin**'s 'Circles'. After lesser success with a revival of the **Fleetwoods**' 1959 hit 'Come Softly to Me' (1972) and 'Pinball Wizard'/'See Me Feel Me', an incongruous medley of songs from **The Who**'s *Tommy* (1973), the New Seekers had their second British No. 1 with the **Tony Macaulay**–Geoff Stephens ballad 'You Won't Find Another Fool like Me'.

'I Get a Little Sentimental over You' (1974) reached the Top Ten before the group was dissolved. Paul attempted a solo career with 'It Oughta Sell a Million' (Polydor, 1975) and during the eighties she moved into the country-music field.

The other New Seekers re-formed in 1976 and signed to Columbia where they found only intermittent success with the Top Thirty songs 'I Wanna Go Back' (1977) and 'Anthem (One Day in Every Week)' (1978).

In 1994, almost thirty years after their first British success, the original Seekers re-formed and toured Britain to packed houses. The lasting appeal of their individual brand of pop-folk was proven when a compilation, *Carnival of Hits* (EMI), reached the Top Ten that year.

BOB SEGER

b. 6 May 1945, Ann Arbor, Michigan, USA

Comparable in many ways to **Bruce Springsteen**, Seger was a local hero in the Midwest in the sixties and early seventies. He later found national success with songs which reflected blue-collar concerns and feelings, coupled with an untiring approach to touring and live performance.

A leading figure on the Detroit rock scene, Seger recorded a series of local hits in the mid-sixties. Among them were 'East Side Story' (Hideout, 1964), the **P. F. Sloan**-styled 'Persecution Smith' and 'Heavy Music' (Cameo, 1966). The latter was an anthem to the rock tradition of which Seger was a part, while 'Ballad of the Yellow Beret' (Are You Kidding Records, 1966) was an answer song to Staff Sgt Barry Sadler's right-wing protest hit 'Ballad of the Green Berets'* (RCA, 1966).

Signing to Capitol after Cameo closed down, Seger released another anti-war song, '2+2=?', before 'Ramblin' Gamblin' Man' reached the Top Twenty in 1969. Although well received by critics, such albums as *Noah* (1969), *Mongrel* (1970) and the acoustic *Brand New Morning* (1971) were commercial failures. In 1971 Seger worked with the duo Teegarden and Van Winkle whose 'God Love and Rock'n'Roll' (Westbound) had been a 1970 hit. They accompanied him on *Smokin' O.P.'s* (1972), on which Seger performed songs by **Chuck Berry** ('Let It Rock'), Stephen Stills

('Love the One You're With'), **Bo Diddley** ('Bo Diddley') and **Tim Hardin** ('If I Were a Carpenter').

Seger also recorded for Reprise *Back in 72* (1973) and *Seven* (1974), on which he was backed for the first time by the Silver Bullet Band, which featured guitarist Drew Abbott and Robyn Robbins on keyboards. Re-signing with Capitol, Seger featured ballads on *Beautiful Loser* (1975) but it was the live double-album *Live Bullet* (1976) which brought his first national success. The title track of *Night Moves* (1977) gave him his first Top Ten single.

Seger was now established as a guardian of the rock'n'roll flame and he enjoyed numerous hits over the next decade. Only the gruff ballad 'We've Got Tonite' from *Stranger in Town* (1979) made any British impact but the American successes included 'Fire Lake' and the title track from *Against the Wind* (1980), 'Tryin' to Live My Life without You' from *Nine Tonight* (1981), Rodney Crowell's 'Shame on the Moon' from *The Distance* (1983) and 'Shakedown' (MCA, 1987) from the movie *Beverly Hills Cop II*, which gave Seger an American No. 1 single. 1986's *Like a Rock* was Seger's last album of the decade, and over the next five years Seger limited himself to making guest appearances on other people's albums, including **Little Feat**'s *Let It Roll* (1988) and **Aaron Neville**'s *Warm Your Heart* (1991). He returned to the American album charts with the **Don Was**-produced *The Fire Inside*, a well-crafted collection which included a version of **Tom Waits**' 'Blind Love'.

In 1994 Capitol released a *Greatest Hits* album by Seger and the Silver Bullet Band, while in 1995 Seger had renewed success with *It's a Mystery*, his first wholly self-produced album.

BEN SELVIN

b. 1898, d. 15 July 1980, Manhasset, New York, USA

Selvin was probably the most prolific English-language recording artist of all time. He reputedly recorded over 9,000 titles under thirty-nine aliases for numerous different labels. Selvin was also responsible for the first dance record to sell a million copies, 'Dardanella' (Victor, 1920).

Selvin formed his first recording band, Selvin's Novelty Orchestra, in 1917. His first hit was 'I'm Forever Blowing Bubbles' (Victor, 1919) which was soon followed by 'Dardanella' (which he also recorded for Paramount). Written by Felix Barnard, Johnny S. Black and Fred Fisher (and originally titled 'Turkish Tom Toms') in 1919, Selvin's recording of the tune sold a million copies within a year and more than six million copies in all. When Selvin retired in 1963, RCA-Victor presented him with a gold disc for its huge sales.

Throughout the twenties Selvin recorded his syn-

copated dance music on a variety of labels, including
Okeh ('Afghanistan', 1920), Lyric ('The Japanese
Sandman', 1921, earlier a hit for **Paul Whiteman**),
Emerson, Arto, Banner, Brunswick and Vocalion,
before in the thirties he signed with Columbia. On
most of his recordings Selvin himself sang, but on
several he supported others, including **Irving Kaufman** ('Yes We Have No Bananas', Vocalion, 1923),
Ethel Waters ('I Got Rhythm', Columbia, 1931), **Ruth
Etting** ('Dancing with Tears in My Eyes', Columbia,
1930) and **Kate Smith** ('My Mom', Columbia, 1932).

Essentially a recording artist rather than a performer, Selvin employed top sidemen for many of his
records. These included Bunny Berigan ('Just One
More Chance', 1931), **Benny Goodman** ('Dancing in
the Dark', 1931), **Tommy Dorsey** (1929–31) and **Glenn
Miller**. Selvin's last major success was the original hit
version of **Harry Warren**'s widely-recorded 'I Only
Have Eyes for You' (1934), also a hit for **Eddy Duchin**
in the same year. In later years Selvin worked for the
Muzak Corporation making background music, established Majestic Records with one-time Mayor of New
York Jimmy Walker, and acted as a consultant to RCA
Victor, Columbia and other music organizations.

SEPULTURA

*Igor Cavalera, b. Belo Horizonte, Brazil; Max Cavalera,
b. Belo Horizonte; Paulo Pinto Jr., b. Belo Horizonte;
Jairo T (replaced by Andreas Kisser), b. Belo Horizonte*

A Brazilian heavy-metal quartet, Sepultura gradually
became one of the most popular acts of the genre in
the mid-nineties.

Sepultura was formed in 1984 by brothers Max
(vocals) and Igor (drums) Cavalera with then schoolfriends Jairo T (guitar) and Pinto Jr. (bass), releasing
a pair of generic metal albums, *Bestial Devastation*
and *Morbid Visions*, in their homeland to mild success. After replacing Pinto Jr. with Kisser the band
recorded *Schizophrenia* (1987), earning them a
devoted international underground following.
Beneath the Remains (1989) and *Arise* (1991) saw the
band mature artistically, speaking out against the cor-
rupt Brazilian political system in their lyrics to a fierce
backing which drew comparisons with **Metallica**.

Sepultura signed to Epic in 1993, releasing *Chaos
AD*, their first album to chart in the US. After touring
with the likes of Ministry and **Black Sabbath**'s Ozzy
Osbourne the band issued *Roots* (1996), which saw
them combine the usual metal riffing with rhythms
drawn from traditional Amazonian drumming.
'Roots Bloody Roots', in which Cavalera spoke of the
plight of the Xavantes Indians, was a minor hit single
in the UK.

After an extensive world tour Max Cavalera quit
the band over creative differences, forming Soulfly in

1997 and releasing an eponymous album the following
year on Roadrunner Records. Sepultura planned to
continue with a new vocalist.

DAVID SEVILLE
*b. Ross Bagdasarian, 27 January 1919, Fresno, Califor-
nia, USA, d. 16 January 1972*

Actor and songwriter Seville is best remembered as the
creator of the Chipmunks, who had a trio of million-
selling novelty records in 1958–9.

Of Armenian extraction, Seville travelled to New
York to become an actor at the age of nineteen. On
his demob from the army in 1945, he first attempted
to become a grape grower but returned to the music
business when his folky 'Come on-a My House', co-
written with his cousin, playwright William Saroyan
and first recorded by Seville's wife Kay Armen, was
picked up by **Mitch Miller** and transformed into a
million-seller for **Rosemary Clooney** (1951). Other
songwriting successes included 'Hey Brother Pour the
Wine' (**Dean Martin**, 1954) and during this period he
resumed his acting career with bit parts in films like
Alfred Hitchcock's *Rear Window* (1954).

'Witch Doctor'* (Liberty, 1958) was the first record
he released under the Seville pseudonym. A novelty
song that featured an insistent nonsense chorus, 'Oo-
ee, oo-ah-ah/Ting-tang, walla-walla bing bang', it was
only possible because the new technology of making
records with tape recorders allowed music and voices
to be speeded up and slowed down. It inspired a slew
of imitations in 1958, notably actor Sheb Wooley's
'Purple People Eater'* (MGM) and Seville's own 'The
Bird on My Head'. Even more successful was 'The
Chipmunk Song'* (1958), which introduced the Chipmunks (Alvin, Si and Theodore). On this Seville
played with the format of the recording process in the
manner of **Stan Freberg** as well as, once more, using
speeded-up voices.

Further hits by the Chipmunks included 'Alvin's
Harmonica'* and 'Ragtime Cowboy Joe'* (1959), a
revival of **Johnny Marks**' perennial Christmas
favourite 'Rudolph the Red-Nosed Reindeer' (1960)
and Seville's commentary on the twist craze, 'Alvin
Twist' (1962). The Chipmunks were given their own
television series in 1961 and in 1964 Seville turned his
creations loose on **The Beatles** with *The Chipmunks
Sing The Beatles*. Though Seville retired the characters
in 1967, after his death Ross Jnr and his wife Janice
Armen revived them in 1980 for *Chipmunk Punk* and
the sequel *Urban Punk*. As a result, in 1983 the Chipmunks were once more given their own television
series.

In 1992 the Chipmunks returned to the recording
studio to make a hit album of well-known country
songs.

THE SEX PISTOLS

Paul Cook, b. 20 July 1956, London, England; Steve Jones; Glen Matlock (replaced by Sid Vicious, b. John Beverley, 10 May 1957, London, d. 2 February 1979, New York, USA); Johnny Rotten, b. John Lydon, 30 January 1956

Although their recording career lasted less than three years, the Sex Pistols have had a greater impact on rock music than any British group since **The Beatles**. Among the founders of punk rock, the group rapidly became regarded as its quintessential exponents and inspired the formation of dozens of other bands, some of which became leading British artists of the eighties. With other pioneer punk groups the Pistols were also acknowledged as an influence by the grunge rock groups of the USA. Although the surviving members continued to perform and record in the eighties and nineties, none of their work approached the power or impact of 'Anarchy in the UK' (1976) or 'God Save the Queen' (1977).

As the Swankers, Jones (guitar), Cook (drums) and Matlock (bass) had begun to rehearse under the aegis of **Malcolm McLaren** before Lydon (now renamed Rotten) joined in 1975. As the Sex Pistols, the group began to perform live at the end of the year, combining original songs with sixties material by the **Monkees**, **The Who** and others. During 1976 they appeared regularly on the London pub and club circuit, drawing media comment for the violent behaviour of their followers and headlining a 'Punk Festival' in September. In October they signed to EMI and released the Chris Thomas-produced 'Anarchy in the UK'. The crashing guitar chords and Rotten's minatory delivery of the strong protest lyric made it a minor hit before a notorious interview on a London television show turned the group into national celebrities.

As a result, the Sex Pistols were banned from many halls and EMI cancelled their contract. With Beverley (Sid Vicious) replacing Matlock (who formed the Rich Kids with Midge Ure, later to join **Ultravox**, then formed the Spectres with ex-**Tom Robinson** guitarist Danny Kustow), the group were signed to A&M and 'God Save the Queen' was announced as their next record before the label lost its nerve following another disturbance at the reception held after the public signing of the A&M contract outside the gates of Buckingham Palace. The single, another snarling attack on the political status quo, was eventually released by Virgin (and by Warners in the US) to coincide with the official celebrations of the twenty-fifth anniversary of Elizabeth II's accession. Despite a blanket broadcasting ban, 'God Save the Queen' reached No. 2 in Britain.

Like the earlier records, 'Pretty Vacant' had an incantatory force plus a catchy chorus and both it and 'Holidays in the Sun' were Top Ten hits. The album *Never Mind the Bollocks, Here's The Sex Pistols* was released late in 1977. In addition to the singles, it included 'EMI', a coruscating attack on the group's former record company.

A poorly organized American tour and increasing dissatisfaction with McLaren's attempt to produce a film featuring the group prompted Rotten to leave early in 1978. He formed Public Image Limited (PIL) with Keith Levene (guitar, ex-the **Clash**) and bassist Jah Wobble (John Wardle), recording an eponymous album which used dub techniques and other avant-garde elements. The remaining trio released 'No One Is Innocent', recorded with exiled train-robber Ronald Biggs, plus their last classic track, Vicious's graffiti-covered version of **Paul Anka**'s 'My Way', after which **Frank Sinatra**'s rendition could never seem the same.

McLaren's movie project was directed by Julien Temple and released in 1978 as *The Great Rock'n'Roll Swindle*, but the group itself disintegrated after Vicious died of a heroin overdose – a saga portrayed in Alex Cox's *Sid and Nancy* (1986), whose musical director was the Clash's Joe Strummer. Virgin and McLaren continued to release Sex Pistols records throughout 1979, achieving Top Ten hits with sloppy revivals of **Eddie Cochran**'s 'Something Else' and 'C'mon Everybody' and the original 'Silly Thing'. Three more albums of out-takes and reissues were released during 1979, including the appropriately titled *Flogging a Dead Horse*. The band had their revenge in 1986 when they sued McLaren for money owed, picking up £1 million in an out-of-court settlement.

In their post-Pistols work, the remaining members continued to emphasize the contrasting sides of the group's music. Lydon (the name Rotten had now been dropped) remained an *agent provocateur*, challenging audiences with the avant-garde approach of later PIL albums like *Metal Box* (1980), *Flowers of Romance* (1981) and *This Is What You Want, This Is What You Get* with its eerie, repetitive hit 'This Is Not a Love Song' (1984). **Bill Laswell** produced Lydon's *Album* (1986), on which Ginger Baker played drums. 'Disappointed' from *PIL 9* was a minor British hit in 1989. The ironically titled compilation *Greatest Hits . . . So Far* followed in 1990, and the following year Lydon was reunited with Levene to release their last album as PIL (Lydon had been the only constant in the band's fifteen-year history), *That What Is Not*. Dropped by Virgin, Lydon signed a solo deal with Atlantic. He had occasionally collaborated with other artists including NY art-rock outfit the Golden Palominos (*Visions of Excess*, 1985) and hip-hop artist **Afrika Bambaataa** (as Timezone), and in 1993 had a hit with British dance act **Leftfield**, 'Open Up'. He also briefly essayed an acting career, appearing with Harvey Keitel in *Cop Killer* (1983).

In 1980 Cook and Jones formed the Professionals, a hard-rock band, who released the unimpressive *I Didn't See It Coming* (1981). Cook returned in 1985 with the Chiefs of Relief while Jones worked with **Iggy Pop** and released the solo albums *Mercy* (MCA, 1987) and *Fire & Gasoline* (1989). Matlock had continued to work on his own and with a number of other artists, including Iggy Pop and ex-**New York Dolls** guitarist Johnny Thunders, before publishing his autobiography, *I Was a Teenage Sex Pistol*. In 1993 he returned with a new band, the Mavericks.

In 1992, the year in which a reissued 'Anarchy in the UK' charted again in Britain, Virgin released the comprehensive Sex Pistols compilation *Kiss This*, which made the British Top Ten. In the manner of a group like **Herman's Hermits**, in 1996 the Sex Pistols re-formed (with Matlock on bass) for a lucrative *Pretty Vacant* tour and live album (*Filthy Lucre*).

Lydon published an autobiography, *Rotten: No Irish, No Blacks, No Dogs*, in 1994 but the definitive biography of the band remains *England's Dreaming* by Jon Savage.

THE SHADOWS

Jet Harris, b. Terence Hawkins, 6 July 1939 (replaced by Brian Licorice Locking, replaced by John Rostill, b. 16 June 1942); Hank B. Marvin, b. Brian Robson Rankin, 28 October 1941, Newcastle, Tyne and Wear, England; Tony Meehan, b. 2 March 1942, London (replaced by Brian Bennett, b. 9 February 1940, London); Bruce Welch, b. 2 November 1941, Bognor Regis, Sussex

Originally the backing group for **Cliff Richard**, the Shadows recorded with him, wrote songs for him and appeared in his films. In their own right, the group dominated instrumental pop music in Britain in the years between the demise of skiffle and the rise of R&B and Merseybeat. Their embellishment of simple, strong melody lines with tremolo and echo inspired numerous young musicians to take up electric guitar. Indeed the image of a teenager, tennis racquet raised like a guitar, while anxiously eyeing his feet to make sure he's got the dance step right, was an enduring one from the early sixties.

Guitarists Marvin and Welch had been in Newcastle skiffle groups and, moving to London, joined the Vipers where they met Harris. The duo were recruited to accompany Richard on 'Move It' (1958) and formed the nucleus of his touring band, the Drifters, which Harris (bass) and Meehan (drums) joined in 1959. The group first recorded for EMI's Columbia label in that year but it was not until their name was changed (to avoid confusion with the black American vocal group) that they reached No. 1 with 'Apache' (1960).

Written by Jerry Lordan and produced by **Norrie Paramor**, the tune featured Marvin's twangy guitar and Meehan's Hollywood-style war-drums. An American hit for Danish guitarist Jorgen Ingmann (Atco) and revived in 1981 by the Sugarhill Gang (Sugar Hill), 'Apache' initiated a sequence of singles that brought the Shadows nearly twenty Top Twenty hits in five years. For the most part these were conceived on the same lines as film themes, with the sound attempting to illustrate the images evoked by the tune's title. In 1960-1, these were tough, rhythmic pieces about urban life (**Michael Carr**'s 'Man of Mystery', 'FBI' and 'Frightened City') or exotic locations ('Kon-Tiki', 'The Savage').

Lordan's 'Wonderful Land' (a 1962 No. 1) included a string section and ushered in a series of softer tunes. Among them were 'Dance on' (a 1963 vocal hit for Kathy Kirby) and three pieces composed by group members: 'Foot Tapper' (1963), 'Theme for Young Lovers' and 'The Rise and Fall of Flingel Bunt' (1964). This switch in style was partly responsible for the departure of Harris in 1962. Signing to Decca, he reached the Top Twenty with a **Duane Eddy**-inspired version of 'Main Theme from "The Man with the Golden Arm"' before teaming up with Meehan, who had been replaced in the Shadows by Bennett. The duo emulated their former colleagues in 1963 by having three major hits. 'Diamonds' and 'Scarlett O'Hara' were composed by Lordan and 'Applejack' by Les Vandyke, author of **Adam Faith**'s hits. Their career was ended when Harris and singer Billie Davis were involved in a serious car accident and Meehan had only a small solo hit with 'Song for Mexico' (Decca, 1964) before fading from view.

1965 brought the Shadows' first vocal hits with 'Mary Anne' and the **Barry Mann**–Cynthia Weil ballad 'Don't Make My Baby Blue'. It also brought the end of their run of hits. After 'War Lord', the group's records sold poorly and in 1969 the Shadows disbanded.

Marvin and Welch continued their singing career in a **Crosby Stills and Nash**-influenced group with Australian guitarist John Farrar, recording *Marvin Welch and Farrar* and *Second Opinion* (both 1971). Farrar and Welch together produced the early records of **Olivia Newton-John** while Welch later went on to supervise several of Richard's albums in the mid-seventies.

The trio joined up with Bennett to record *Rocking with Curly Leads* (1973), which marked the group's re-formation. After playing a 1974 charity concert with Richard, the Shadows represented Britain in the 1975 Eurovision Song Contest, singing 'Let Me Be the One'. While Marvin cut the acclaimed *Guitar Syndicate* (EMI, 1977) with leading session players, the TV-advertised *20 Golden Greats* (1977) topped the charts and went on to sell a million copies in Britain.

Now consisting of Bennett, Marvin and Welch, the

Shadows toured in the late seventies and had hits with precisely played versions of **Andrew Lloyd Webber**'s 'Don't Cry for Me Argentina' (1978) and 'Theme from "The Deer Hunter" (Cavatina)' (1979). Their final hit for EMI was 'Riders in the Sky' (1980), the 1949 **Vaughn Monroe** million-seller which had been adapted for beat groups in 1961 by American group the Ramrods.

In 1981 the Shadows signed to Polydor, recording *Change of Address* (1981), *Life in the Jungle* (1982), *Guardian Angel* (1984), *XXV* (1985), *Moonlight Shadows* (1986) and *Simply Shadows* (1987). *Steppin' to The Shadows* (1989) was a British Top Twenty hit and followed the group's trusted formula of covering recent pop hits. The same approach was taken on *Reflections* (1990), *Themes and Dreams* (1991) and *Shadows in the Night* (1993). Marvin released the solo albums *Into the Light* and *Heartbeat* in 1992 and 1993, respectively, both reaching the British Top Twenty. The latter contained a duet on 'Wonderful Land' between Marvin and one of his biggest fans, Mark Knopfler of **Dire Straits**. However, the culmination of the affection in which the group was held was *Twang! – A Tribute to Hank Marvin & The Shadows* (Ark, 1996) on which a variety of guitarists paid homage to the group.

Marvin continued his solo career with *Hank Plays Holly* (1996) and *Hank Plays Live* (1997).

SHAKESPEARS SISTER
Siobhan Marie Deidre Fahey, b. 10 September 1958, Dublin, Ireland; Marcella Detroit, b. Marcy Levy, 21 June 1959, Detroit, Michigan, USA

In their short career, Shakespears Sister produced a brief catalogue of polished and dramatic pop songs which outstripped the individual members' previous efforts in different guises.

Vocalist Fahey had been a founder member of successful UK pop trio **Bananarama**, but left the group shortly after marrying Dave Stewart of **Eurythmics** in 1987. The following year, she teamed up with singer/guitarist Levy in Los Angeles. Levy had first come to attention as a backing vocalist with **Eric Clapton** in 1974, singing on four of his albums and co-writing his 1978 US Top Five hit 'Lay Down Sally'. Naming themselves after an essay by Virginia Woolf which in turn had given a title to a song by the **Smiths** (adding their own ungrammatical mis-spelling), Fahey and Levy, now renamed Detroit, signed to London Records and released their début single, 'Break My Heart', in 1989. It was not a hit, but the superior 'You're History' made the Top Ten later the same year. The début album was a hit and drew praise for the duo's contrasting vocal techniques – particularly Detroit's mock-operatic mannerisms – and for its quality pop song-writing.

The more assured follow up, *Hormonally Yours* (1992), was recorded after a long gap while the duo concentrated on their families – the title refers to the fact that both were pregnant during the sessions. It was a major success and provided their biggest hit, the dramatic 'Stay', which topped the UK singles chart for almost two months and reached the US Top Five. The follow-up, 'Hello (Turn Your Radio on)', was a smaller hit later in 1992, but by then rumours of friction between the duo were beginning to circulate. Shakespears Sister split the following year, with Detroit the first to emerge as a solo singer, releasing the minor hit 'I Believe' in early 1994, followed by the album *Jewel* which lacked the tension which had enlivened the best of Shakespears Sister's work.

SHALAMAR
Jeffrey Daniels, b. 24 August 1957, Los Angeles, California, USA (replaced by Micki Free); Gerald Brown (replaced by Howard Hewitt, b. 1 October 1957, Akron, Ohio, replaced by Sidney Justin); Jody Watley, b. 30 January 1961, Chicago, Illinois (replaced by Delisa Davis)

An American disco group with British Northern soul fans, Shalamar had a number of pop hits in the early eighties. Each member subsequently had a solo career.

Los Angeles promoter Dick Griffey used session musicians to record 'Uptown Festival' (1977), a medley of hits from **Berry Gordy**'s Motown label for Soul Train, a label associated with Northern soul promoter Simon Soussan. When the record was a pop hit in both America and Britain, Griffey signed Watley and Daniels, dancers on the American TV show *Soul Train* and vocalist Brown to perform as Shalamar.

Disco Gardens was issued on Griffey's Solar label and included the British hit 'Take That to the Bank' (1979) while the distinctive voice of Hewitt replaced Brown on Shalamar's biggest American success, 'Second Time Around'* (1979) from *Big Fun*. With producer Leon Sylvers, the trio had a succession of American R&B and British pop hits. Among them were 'I Owe You One' (1980), 'Make That Move' (1981), 'A Night to Remember' (1982) and 'Dead Giveaway' (1983).

At this point Daniels and Watley left the group to follow solo careers, with the latter joining MCA to record the R&B No. 1 'Looking for a New Love' (1987). Free and Davis joined Hewitt to make *Heartbreak* (1984), which included the Grammy-winning 'Don't Get Stopped in Beverly Hills' from the film *Beverly Hills Cop*. But later singles like 'Disappearing Act' and 'Amnesia' were stylistically unfocused and sold poorly.

Hewitt now left, recording a solo album for Elektra

in 1990 (*Howard Hewitt*). His replacement was Justin, a former backing vocalist for Shalamar, but, after *Wake Up* (1990), the group dissolved. Watley had minor success with the (mostly) self-penned *Affairs of the Heart* (1992), which saw her recording more ballads than hitherto, and *Intimacy* (1993), as did Hewitt with *How Fast Forever Goes* (1993) and *It's Time* (1995). More successful was Watley's *Flower* (1998). However, all were overshadowed by the success of the anthology *The Collection* (1994).

SHAM 69

Mark Doidie Cain; Albie Maskall (replaced by Dave 'Kermit' Treganna); Dave Parsons; Jimmy Pursey, b. 9 February 1955, Surrey, England

Although leader Pursey's aggressively proletarian anthems attracted supporters of the neo-fascist National Front, the resulting controversy did not prevent punk band Sham 69 enjoying considerable commercial success in 1978–9.

The group was formed in 1975 by Pursey and bassist Maskall as a hard-rock band playing such songs as 'Let's Rob a Bank', 'Hey Little Rich Boy' and 'Borstal Breakout'. Ex-Excalibur guitarist Parsons and drummer Cain joined before the examples of the **Sex Pistols** and the **Ramones** transformed Sham 69's style.

With Treganna on bass, the group cut an EP, produced by ex-**Velvet Underground** member **John Cale**, for Miles Copeland's Step Forward label in 1977. Soon afterwards they were signed to Polydor and in 1978 had a series of hit singles with 'Borstal Breakout', 'Angels with Dirty Faces', 'If the Kids Are United' and 'Hurry up Harry'. Resembling soccer chants in their simple sing-along choruses, all were delivered by Pursey in an uncompromising and unadorned vocal style. The albums *Tell Us the Truth* and *That's Life* sold equally well. Pursey also turned to production on *Teenage Warning* (Warners) by the Angelic Upstarts, a band from the North-East of England whose concerns were similar to those of Sham 69.

The following year 'Questions and Answers' and 'The Hersham Boys' were Top Twenty hits and *The Adventures of the Hersham Boys* reached the Top Ten of the album charts. However, Pursey now decided to disband the group in order to make the more introspective solo albums *Imagination Camouflage* (Epic, 1980) and *Alien Orphan* (1981). Neither pleased critics or record-buyers and after producing an album by the Cockney Rejects and translating the lyrics for an album by French heavy-metal band Trust (Columbia, 1981), he faded from view.

After playing with the Wanderers and Framed, Parsons rejoined Pursey in 1987 to relaunch Sham 69. Signing to Legacy, they released 'Rip and Tear' (1988).

They continued to record without any commercial success into the nineties, also touring regularly, particularly in Europe. In 1993 they released the album *Information Libre* and played a number of punk revival concerts with an augmented line-up, including saxophone and keyboards, and the following year undertook a full-scale British tour.

THE SHAMEN

Colin Angus, b. 24 August 1961, Aberdeen, Scotland; Will Sin, b. Will Sinnott, 23 December 1960, d. 23 May 1991; Richard 'Mr C.' West; Derek McKenzie, b. 27 February 1964, Aberdeen; Keith McKenzie, b. 30 August 1961, Aberdeen; Peter Stephenson, b. 1 March 1962, Ayr

UK band the Shamen went through several incarnations, moving from indie guitar rockers to psychedelic revivalists in the eighties, before eventually finding UK success as a dance act in the nineties.

The Shamen began life as the Colin Angus-led Alone Again Or in their native Aberdeen in the early eighties. With a suitably sixties-sounding name (taken from a song by **Love**) and with the then *de rigueur* fringes and jangly guitars which characterized the Scottish scene as typified by **Aztec Camera**, Orange Juice and Josef K, the band briefly recorded for Polydor Records in 1984.

The Shamen came into existence in 1985 with a line-up of bassist Angus, the McKenzie brothers and Stephenson. The band released a pair of unexceptional independent singles which continued Angus' fascination with sixties psychedelia, at the same time gradually incorporating elements of the then current dance scene into their live work. The début album, *Drop* (1987), summed up their psychedelic rock period, and keyboards-player Sinnott had replaced McKenzie before the Shamen released 'Christopher Mayhew Says' in 1987. The first of their recordings to show the fruits of their interest in dance, it was a minor indie chart success and set the scene for a series of increasingly dancefloor-orientated recordings during the following year.

The second Shamen album, *In Gorbachev We Trust*, appeared in 1988, the year that Angus and Sinott reduced the band to a duo and moved to London. The pair's heavy involvement in the capital's dance scene and their fondness for the attendant drug culture set the tone for the band's new direction as unveiled on the *Phorward* mini-album in 1989. A fully-fledged dance album, it formed the soundtrack to their high-energy stage show, which married a rock presentation, complete with a 'real' band, with dance music, club-style lighting and DJs. The duo added London rapper Mr C for the next album, *En-Tact*, which reached the UK Top Forty in 1990. There were minor hits with 'Pro-Gen' and 'Make It Mine', and in

1991 they reached the UK Top Thirty with the single 'Hyperreal', which featured guest vocalist Plavka.

After Sinnott drowned while swimming off Tenerife, Angus released a new version of 'Pro-Gen' as 'Move Any Mountain'. The Shamen, now consisting of Angus, Mr C and a cast of supporting musicians and vocalists, enjoyed their biggest hit yet when the single made the UK Top Five, also reaching the US Top Forty.

The parent album, *Progeny*, was a UK Top Thirty hit in late 1991 and the following year the band consolidated its position with 'L.S.I. (Love Sex Intelligence)', which made the Top Ten. The follow-up single, the novelty drugs song 'Ebeneezer Goode' (a hymn to the designer drug Ecstasy, with a chorus which chanted 'E,s are good . . .'), gave the band a No. 1 hit, and was the first in a string of successful singles to be taken from the *Boss Drum* (1992) album. A world tour followed, and an album of remixes, *Different Drum*, appeared in 1993. Less successful was *On Air* (1994) and *Axis Mutatis* (1995). After the greatest hits set, *The Shamen Collection* (1998), the group established their own website and promised that all later recordings would be only available via the Internet. The first was *Uv* (1999).

THE SHANGRI-LAS
Mary Ann Ganser, d. 1971; Marge Ganser, d. 1976; Betty Weiss; Mary Weiss

Guided by producer **Shadow Morton**, the Shangri-Las recorded a series of dramatic teen ballads which featured the keening voices of Mary and Betty Weiss.

The Weiss sisters and the Ganser twins were schoolfriends in Queens, New York, when they were discovered in 1964 by Morton, a staff producer for **Leiber and Stoller**'s Red Bird label. With arranger Artie Butler (who had previously played piano on the Jaynetts' mysterious 'Sally Go Round the Roses', Tuff, 1963), Morton produced the quartet on his **Phil Spector**-influenced 'Remember (Walking in the Sand)'* (1964).

With its seagull sound effects and abrupt changes of pace, the record was a Top Ten hit. The sound of a motorcycle engine revving up opened 'Leader of the Pack' (1964), written by Morton with Jeff Barry and **Ellie Greenwich**. It reached No. 1 and inspired the parody 'Leader of the Laundromat' (Roulette, 1964) by the Detergents, a group led by Ron Dante, who later created the Archies with Barry and **Don Kirshner**. In 1985 'Leader of the Pack' was used as the title of the Broadway show devised around the songs of Barry and Greenwich, starring Greenwich herself. The Shangri-Las' follow-up was the less successful, more conventional 'Give Him a Great Big Kiss'.

While 'Out in the Streets' (1965) – in which the protagonist has to surrender her biker boyfriend to

his buddies – was only a minor hit, the Barry–Greenwich death song 'Give Us Your Blessings' reached the Top Thirty. It was the prelude to the Shangri-Las' final Top Ten entry, 'I Can Never Go Home Any More', on which Mary Weiss's voice quivered with wailing anguish.

By 1966, the era in which such groups as the **Ronettes**, Dixie Cups and the Shangri-Las had flourished was drawing to a close. 'Long Live Our Love', with its solemn references to 'fighting overseas' and interpolation of 'When Johnny Comes Marching Home', reached the Top Forty but 'He Cried' and 'Past Present and Future' were commercial failures. The latter, however, was Morton's most grandiose conception, with Weiss reciting the teen-*angst* lyric over the melody from Beethoven's *Moonlight Sonata*.

The group released later Red Bird singles, including a version of **Jay and the Americans**' 'He Cried' and an early **Nilsson** song, 'Paradise', before Morton took them to Mercury in 1967. After two unsuccessful singles, the Shangri-Las split up in 1969. Mary Ann Ganser died in 1971 but the other three members briefly re-formed in 1977 after which they faded from view. However, the longevity of the Shangri-Las' music was underlined in 1988 when the remaining original group members took legal action against a new group of 'Shangri-Las' playing dates in the United States. Mary and Betty Weiss performed the following year at a sixties reunion event in New Jersey.

RAVI SHANKAR
b. 1919 Benares, India

Shankar was the most respected exponent in India of the classical repertoire for the sitar. The 'echoing' sound produced by the elaborate stringed instrument was much in demand by rock musicians of the sixties and Shankar found himself at the heart of the flower-power and underground music scene, a role he bore with equanimity and good humour.

The younger brother of a folk ensemble leader, Shankar began to learn the sitar with Ustad Allauddin Khan in 1938. He first performed in America in 1956 and did much to popularize Indian classical music there and in Europe. In 1966 **George Harrison** studied sitar with Shankar, having used the instrument on **The Beatles**' 'Norwegian Wood'. Shankar subsequently appeared at the Monterey Pop Festival (1967), Woodstock (1969) and the Harrison-organized Concert for Bangladesh (1971). His recordings during this period included *East Meets West* (with classical violinist Yehudi Menuhin).

While the rock fashion for sitar passed, during the seventies and eighties Shankar maintained a busy schedule of teaching, performing and recording. He taught at the University of California and gave concerts in all the major cities of the world. Shankar also wrote music for ballets and films, notably Richard Attenborough's *Gandhi* (1982).

His later albums included *Concert for Sitar* (EMI, 1971) with **André Previn**, and a collaboration with Japanese classical musicians (*East Greets East*). In 1987 he signed to Private Music, the label owned by former **Tangerine Dream** member Peter Beumann. He recorded *Tana Mana*, with Harrison among the guest musicians working with synthesizers for the first time, followed by *Inside the Kremlin* (Private Music, 1989), recorded in the USSR. *Passages* (1990) was a collaboration with **Philip Glass**.

Among his tabla (percussion) players were Chatur Lal, Alla Rakha and Kumar Bose. During the eighties his son, Shubho Shankar, frequently performed on sitar with him.

In 1989 Shankar devised and composed *Ghanashayam – a Broken Branch*, a stage work which mixed music, drama and dance from the Eastern and Western traditions. It was performed in Britain by the City of Birmingham Touring Opera. *The Highlights* (1996), a one-volume edition of the earlier four-CD set *In Celebration* (1993), is the best introduction to his music. He taught his daughter Anoushka, who, after accompanying him on second sitar in her teens, released her first record, *Anoushka* (Angel), in 1998. Consisting mostly of her father's compositions, it was followed by *Anourag* (2000), on which she was accompanied by Shankar. In the same year she toured in the US both in support of her album and with her father as part of a tour celebrating his 70th year in the music business and 80th birthday.

DEL SHANNON
b. *Charles Westover, 30 December 1939, Coopersville, Michigan, USA, d. 9 February 1990, Santa Clara, California*

Best remembered for the anguished 'Runaway'* (1961) with its galloping beat, echo-laden musitron (an electronic organ and forerunner of the synthesizer) and its harsh vocals, Shannon was one of the few artists of the immediate pre-**Beatles** era to write his own material.

Spotted by disc-jockey Ollie McLaughlin while singing at a club in Battle Creek, Michigan, in 1960, Shannon was signed by pop veterans Harry Balk and Irving Micahnik (managers of **Little Willie John** and later **Johnny and the Hurricanes**). With co-writer Max Crook on organ, 'Runaway' (Big Top) was one of the biggest-selling records of 1961. It was followed by the similarly desperate-sounding 'Hats off to Larry'* (1961) and a trio of Top Forty hits, culminating with 'Little Town Flirt' (1963). He was especially popular in Britain – his recording of 'Swiss Maid'

(London, 1962) was a Top Five record in Britain but only a minor hit in America. While touring Britain, Shannon heard The Beatles perform 'From Me to You' and his 1963 recording of it gave Lennon and McCartney their first American hit, and a higher chart placing than The Beatles' own version of the song. Following disagreements with his managers and publishers Shannon left Big Top for Amy, where he was successful with a remake of **Jimmy Jones**' 'Handy Man' (1964) and his own 'Keep Searchin'* (1965). But though the recordings revealed a new sophistication, Shannon's songs remained throwbacks to an earlier era.

In 1966 he joined Liberty where he worked unsuccessfully with **Leon Russell** before in 1969 setting up as a producer. His hits included his own discovery Smith ('Baby It's You', Dunhill, 1969) and **Brian Hyland** ('Gypsy Woman', 1970). He continued performing – like **Roy Orbison**, Shannon could re-create his recorded sound on stage – and attempted comebacks with records produced by **ELO**'s Jeff Lynne (including 'Cry Baby Baby Cry', United Artists, 1973) and **Dave Edmunds** ('And the Music Plays on', 1974). In 1982 he returned to the charts with the **Tom Petty**-produced 'Sea of Love' (originally a 1959 hit for Phil Phillips) from *Drop Down and Get Me* (Network), after which he signed with Warners. The liaison was unproductive, however, and Shannon reluctantly returned to playing the nostalgia circuit. While on prescribed antidepressant drugs, he committed suicide in 1990. *Rock on!*, his second album with Jeff Lynne, appeared the following year. Again featuring Petty, it was enthusiastically received. *Looking Back: The Biggest Hits* (1991) is the definitive collection.

FEARGAL SHARKEY
b. *13 August 1958, Londonderry, Northern Ireland*

Former lead singer with punkish pop group the Undertones, Sharkey, with his distinctive quavering vocal style, was briefly a successful solo artist in the late eighties.

In 1976 a group of schoolfriends formed the Undertones, intending the name as a parody of Irish showbands. The early influences on joint leaders Sharkey and songwriter John O'Neill (guitar, b. *26 August 1957, Londonderry*), (John's brother) Damian O'Neill (guitar), Mickey Bradley (bass), and drummer Billy Doherty were the **Rolling Stones** and **Dr Feelgood**. The arrival of records by the **Ramones** and the **New York Dolls** gave their style a punk inflection.

After recording the *Teenage Kicks* EP for Belfast label Good Vibrations, the Undertones were signed to Sire. Between 1979 and 1983 they recorded four albums and scored three Top Twenty hits: 'Jimmy Jimmy' (1979) from the eponymous début album, and the quirky 'My Perfect Cousin' and 'Wednesday Week' from the most successful album, *Hypnotised* (1980).

The more sophisticated *Positive Touch* was less successful and *The Sin of Pride* (1983) was the group's final release. Sharkey went on to join Vince Clarke (**Alison Moyet**'s Yazoo partner) in the Assembly, singing the hit 'Never Never' (Mute, 1983). He recorded 'Listen to Your Father' (1984) for **Madness**'s Zarjazz label before reaching No. 1 with the doleful 'A Good Heart' (Virgin, 1985). An eponymous début album was produced by Dave Stewart of **Eurythmics** and 'You Little Thief' (1986) reached the British Top Ten. In 1988 he issued *Wish*, produced by Danny Kortchmar. Sales were disappointing and after one other album, 1991's *Songs from the Mardi Gras*, Sharkey next put his singing career on hold to join Polydor Records' A&R department. In 1994 he started performing occasionally while working for interactive label ESP.

The O'Neill brothers formed That Petrol Emotion, which took a harder-edged direction than the Undertones' punk-pop approach, adding a funk element and more direct, political lyrics. The group recorded *Manic Pop Thrill* (Demon, 1985) before moving to Polydor for *Babble* (Polydor, 1987). Both received positive reviews, but sales were poor. The band switched to Virgin for *End of the Millennium Psychosis Blues* (1988). The band released 1993's *Fireproof* on their own label. It again collected enthusiastic reviews but, disillusioned by their lack of commercial success, the band announced their break-up in early 1994, recording their final concerts for a live album.

The Undertones' brief career is the subject of the retrospective *Teenage Kicks* (1994).

CECIL SHARP

b. 22 November 1859, London, England, d. 23 June 1924, London

A leading folk-song collector in Britain and America, Sharp's methods and publications were the greatest single influence on the character and direction of the folk-song revival in England.

A professional music teacher and principal of the Hampstead Conservatoire of Music, Sharp's interest in folk song was aroused in 1903 by the singing of a Somerset gardener, John England. Sharp wrote down the words and music, the first of over 5,000 songs and ballads he would collect and publish. .

In 1907 Sharp published *English Folk Song: Some Conclusions* in which he expressed his view that true folk songs were those not composed by individuals but 'evolved by the many'. He also took a leading role in the Folk Song Society (later the English Folk Dance and Song Society), arguing for the teaching of folk song in schools and encouraging the revival of tradi-

tional dances like maypole and morris. Among the most famous dance tunes collected by Sharp was 'Country Gardens', which was later arranged by **Percy Grainger** and, with added lyrics, was a 1962 pop hit for **Jimmie Rodgers** (Roulette).

With his assistant Maud Karpeles, Sharp went to the Appalachian mountains of West Virginia in 1916, noting hundreds of songs with roots in the English folk tradition.

The material collected by Sharp and his EFDSS colleagues inspired developments both in classical music as composers like Benjamin Britten and Ralph Vaughan Williams discovered folk tunes as the basis of their national music, and in the popular field. Sharp's concept of the true folk song was broadly shared by the revivalists of the fifties, notably **Ewan MacColl** and **A. L. Lloyd**, even if some criticized him for modifying lyrics he felt to be improper. In addition, the corpus of songs he collected provided the repertoire for later electric folk groups.

In 1930 Cecil Sharp House in London was erected 'in memory of Cecil Sharp who restored to the English people the songs and dances of their country'. It became the headquarters of the EFDSS.

ARTIE SHAW

b. Arthur Jacob Arshawsky, 23 May 1910, New York, USA

One of the leading swing bandleaders and clarinettists of the thirties and forties, Shaw was noted for his outspoken attacks on the commercialization of the music.

Growing up in Connecticut, Shaw learned ukulele and tenor saxophone before taking up clarinet. His first permanent engagement was with violinist Austin Wylie's band in 1929–31. He later joined Irving Aaronson's Commanders and undertook radio and recording work. Shaw's first significant recordings were made with Bunny Berigan in 1936, the year he organized his own band with a swing section. This group recorded for Brunswick, as did Shaw's orthodox big band which he formed in 1937.

After moving to RCA, Shaw had massive hits in 1938 with **Cole Porter**'s 'Begin the Beguine'* and his own compositions 'Nightmare'* and 'Back Bay Shuffle'. **Billie Holiday** (on whose earlier recording sessions Shaw had worked) sang briefly with the orchestra but Shaw's regular vocalist was Helen Forrest, who was featured on recordings of 'Deep Purple' and 'All the Things You Are'. Among Shaw's other hits were 'Goodnight Angel' (1938), 'Thanks for Ev'rything' (1939), 'Fresni' and 'Adios Marquita Linda' – two Mexican songs featuring Anita Boyer on vocals – and 'Dancing in the Dark' (1941). His arrangers of the forties included the young **Ray Conniff**.

In 1949 Shaw experimented unsuccessfully with a fusion of classical music and jazz, and the addition of works by bebop arrangers Tadd Dameron and Eddie Sauter was not appreciated by his audiences. He reverted to his swing style until 1954 when he retired from live performance. After living in Spain, he returned to America in 1960 to concentrate on writing for the theatre. He published an autobiography, *The Trouble with Cinderella*, in 1952.

A new Artie Shaw Orchestra led by Dick Johnson was formed in 1983, and two years later Shaw was the subject of the jazz documentary, *Time Is All You've Got*.

SANDIE SHAW

b. *Sandra Goodrich, 26 February 1947, Dagenham, Essex, England*

Always a harder-edged version of **Cilla Black**, British vocalist Sandie Shaw nonetheless also capitalized on American soft-soul styles in the sixties. However, where Black entered the entertainment mainstream in the seventies and eighties, Shaw subsequently retreated to the fringes.

A former Ford car worker, Shaw was discovered by **Adam Faith**'s manager Eve Taylor and signed to Pye in 1964. Her gamine profile and miniskirt plus bare feet helped to make a cover of **Burt Bacharach** and Hal David's 'There's Always Something There to Remind Me' (1964) a No. 1 hit. Many of Shaw's later records were composed by Chris Andrews, who had written Faith's 1963 hit 'The First Time'. His use of jerky rhythms on such songs as the calypso-flavoured 'Girl Don't Come' (1964) and the No. 1 'Long Live Love' (1965) complemented Shaw's somewhat breathless soprano.

Andrews also provided her with the Top Ten hits 'Message Understood' and 'Tomorrow' (1966) but her greatest commercial success came with **Phil Coulter** and Bill Martin's 'Puppet on a String', which won the Eurovision Song Contest in 1967. By now Shaw's style had diverged from the rock mainstream and only the 1969 novelty 'Monsieur Dupont' (translated from the French by Peter Callander) gave her comparable success.

Shaw married fashion designer Jeff Banks in 1968 and was semi-retired during the seventies, returning to recording in 1982 when she sang 'Anyone Who Had a Heart' on *Quality Songs . . .*, an album by BEF, an offshoot from **Heaven 17**. Ironically this Bacharach–David song had been associated in the sixties with Shaw's rival, Black. Shaw went on to collaborate with the **Smiths** on a minor hit, 'Hand in Glove' (Rough Trade, 1984).

Briefly signed to Polydor in 1986, she released a faithful cover of Lloyd Cole's 'Are You Ready to Be

Heartbroken' but neither it nor the follow-up, **Patti Smith**'s 'Frederick', made any noticeable impression on the charts. She recorded *Hello Angel* (1988) for Rough Trade. It featured songs by ex-Smiths vocalist **Morrissey** and indie favourites the **Jesus and Mary Chain**, but failed to sell. Now married to film producer Nik Powell, Shaw published her autobiography *The World at My Feet* in 1991, and in 1993 made a rare appearance on record, singing on a version of the **Rolling Stones**' 'Gimme Shelter' with indie band Cud, released to raise money for a housing charity. She followed that with *Nothing Less than Brilliant* (1998), another foray into alternative balladry.

GEORGE SHEARING

b. *George Albert Shearing, 13 August 1919, London, England*

Composer of one of the best-known jazz standards, 'Lullaby of Birdland' (1952), George Shearing developed with his quintet in the late forties a sound in which piano, vibes and guitar blended together to produce an intimate sound which gave the group two decades of success.

Born blind, he studied piano as a child, and after touring Britain with an all-blind band under the leadership of Claude Bampton, joined **Ambrose** in the thirties and later the **Ted Heath** orchestra. He first recorded in 1938 for Decca, but though a regular winner of the *Melody Maker* poll as Best British Pianist, he only found international success when jazz critic **Leonard Feather** invited him to America in 1947. Feather was also instrumental in putting together the George Shearing Quintet, which originally included Margie Hyams (vibes), Chuck Wayne (guitar), Denzil Best (drums) and John Levy, later Shearing's manager (bass). One of their first recordings, an instrumental version of **Harry Warren**'s film song 'September in the Rain'* (MGM, 1949), was an immediate success and established the popularity of the quintet. In 1954 Shearing added a conga player and in 1956 joined Capitol, for whom he recorded prolifically on his own, gaining a minor British hit with his version of the classical adaptation 'Baubles Bangles and Beads' (1962) and with others, including **Peggy Lee** (*Beauty and the Beat*, 1960), **Nat 'King' Cole** (*Nat 'King' Cole Sings and George Shearing Plays*, 1962, which included the hit 'Let There Be Love'), and **Mel Tormé**.

In the sixties he briefly formed a big band before in 1967 dissolving the quintet; subsequently he has toured and recorded intermittently. Albums from this period include the superior *Blues Alley and Jazz* (Concorde, 1979), *Top Drawer*, with Mel Tormé (1983), the trio set *I Hear Rhapsody* (1992) and his first quintet-styled recording for over ten years, the critically well-received *The Shearing Sound* (Telarc, 1994).

ANNE SHELTON
b. 10 November 1927, Dulwich, London, England, d. 31 July 1994

Like **Vera Lynn**, Anne Shelton is closely associated with memories of the Second World War. She was the first to sing and record **Tommie Connor**'s English lyric to 'Lili Marlene' (first popularized by **Lale Anderson** and subsequently a hit for **Marlene Dietrich**), and in 1979 reprised **Sammy Fain**'s evocative 'I'll Be Seeing You' in *Yanks*, John Schlesinger's film about the American forces stationed in wartime Britain.

Shelton made her first radio broadcast at the age of twelve and while still a teenager joined **Ambrose**, with whom she sang throughout the forties. During the war she regularly entertained the troops, performing with **Glenn Miller** when he was in Britain in 1944. Unusually for a British artist, she had American hits in the forties, including 'Be Mine' (Decca, 1949) and 'Galway Bay' (1949), which was a bigger hit for **Bing Crosby**, and in 1950 successfully toured there. In the fifties, however, she found it increasingly difficult to find suitable material and most of her British hits failed in America. The one exception was her British No. 1, 'Lay Down Your Arms' (Philips, 1959), a song whose military imagery was complemented by both her strong clear voice and wartime associations; even that, however, was a bigger hit for the **Chordettes**. Her biggest British hits of the decade included **Harry Von Tilzer**'s 'I'm Praying to St Christopher' (HMV, 1953), 'Arrivederci Darling' (1955), 'Seven Days' (Philips, 1956), originally recorded by **Clyde McPhatter** (1955) and a cover-version hit for the **Crew Cuts** (1956), and 'The Village of St Bernadette' (1959), a bigger American hit for **Andy Williams**. Her last hit was a cover of **Petula Clark**'s 'Sailor'.

Shelton continued touring and appearing on television in Britain throughout the sixties and seventies and in the eighties devoted much of her time to charity work for the armed forces.

SHEP AND THE LIMELITES
James 'Shep' Sheppard, b. New York, USA, d. 24 January 1970; Clarence Bassett, b. New York; Charles Baskerville, b. New York

Shep and the Limelites produced some of the most delicate and romantic recordings of the doo-wop era, including 'Daddy's Home' (1961), which was later successfully revived by former **Jackson Five** member Jermaine Jackson (Motown, 1973) and **Cliff Richard** (1982).

In 1956 Sheppard, then leader of the Heartbeats, wrote and recorded the hesitant, wistful 'A Thousand Miles Away' (Rama). It and subsequent offerings, including 'Everybody's Somebody's Fool' (1957), were only minor hits but 'Thousand Miles' quickly became one of the best-loved doo-wop recordings. After the group had disbanded, it was successfully reissued. Sheppard next formed Shep and the Limelites and recorded the similarly styled answer song to 'Thousand Miles', 'Daddy's Home' (Hull, 1961). With its cool backing, featuring vibes and a soft sax, and Sheppard's expressive lead vocals, the record was even more successful, reaching No. 2 on the American charts. It was followed by a series of equally romantic, feathery singles all written by Sheppard, which, in the manner of **Paul and Paula**, charted the course of the lovers introduced in 'A Thousand Miles Away'. These included 'Three Steps from the Altar' (1961), 'Our Anniversary', 'What Did Daddy Do' (1962) and 'Remember Baby' (1963), their last chart hit. They continued to record for Hull until 1967 and 'I'm a Hurting Inside', after which the label folded and the group disbanded.

After Sheppard's death and the renewed interest in 'Daddy's Home' and 'A Thousand Miles Away', which in 1982 was featured in the film *Diner*, a Shep and the Limelites line-up re-formed to play revival concerts.

ARCHIE SHEPP
b. 24 May 1937, Fort Lauderdale, Florida, USA

With a distinctive, hoarse tone on tenor saxophone, composer and teacher Shepp was one of the leading figures in the jazz new wave of the seventies.

Raised in Philadelphia, where he played with local jazz and R&B groups, Shepp studied drama and moved to New York in 1959, aiming to work in the theatre. Instead he joined Cecil Taylor's group, recording three albums with the pianist in 1960–1, including *The World of Cecil Taylor* (Barnaby, 1960). He went on to form the New York Contemporary Five with **Don Cherry** and John Tchicai, making an eponymous album in Copenhagen for Polydor. It included 'The Funeral', a Shepp composition dedicated to the black civil rights leader Medgar Evers whose murder had also inspired **Bob Dylan**'s 'Only a Pawn in Their Game'.

In 1965, the year his play *The Communist* was first performed, he recorded with **John Coltrane** (*Ascension*) and on Coltrane's recommendation was given a solo contract by Bob Thiele of Impulse. Shepp's albums for the label included *Four for Trane* (a collection of Coltrane compositions), *Fire Music, On This Night* and *Mama Too Tight* (1967), whose 'Portrait of Robert Johnson' drew on **James Brown**'s brand of soul music. They established Shepp's status as an original composer and improviser who united the older traditions of black music with a free-form approach to structure. He went on to record a series of albums for BYG in Paris, notably *Poem for Malcolm* (1969), inspired by black-power leader Malcolm X.

During the seventies and eighties Shepp spent a large proportion of his time writing plays and teaching, becoming a professor at the University of Massachusetts in 1978. As well as duets with **Max Roach**, his recordings explored black music traditions in albums of blues and gospel recordings with singer Joe Lee Wilson and pianist Horace Parlan (*Goin' Home*, 1977). *Bird Fire* (1978) was one of three Shepp records devoted to the music of **Charlie Parker**.

Shepp's later recordings included *Mama Too Tight* (1982), *Downhome New York* (1986) and *In Memory of . . .* (1988), which was made with Chet Baker shortly before the trumpeter's death.

As well as his own stage plays and poetry, he composed music for a stage biography of **Billie Holiday** by Aishah Rahman.

BILLY SHERRILL
b. Phil Campbell, 5 November 1938, Winston, Alabama, USA

The most successful country producer of the modern era, Sherrill was responsible for two of the genre's most important recordings, **Tammy Wynette**'s 'Stand by Your Man'* (1968) and **Charlie Rich**'s 'Behind Closed Doors'* (1973), as well as many others, most of which he also co-wrote. Where country producers in search of pop success before him, such as **Chet Atkins**, had toned down the country instrumentation of their productions in favour of strings and choruses, Sherrill blended orthodox country instruments (notably the steel guitar) with orchestras to provide a sweeping, yet spare, backdrop for his artists. On 'Stand by Your Man', for instance, Wynette's anguished singing is saved from being merely melodramatic by the formal and intensifying arrangement Sherrill provides. Though many of his later productions were accused of cocooning artists in sweetness, Sherrill had a far wider range of interests and his production of **Elvis Costello**'s *Almost Blue* (1981) demonstrated a willingness to experiment.

The son of a travelling evangelist, Sherrill played piano at his father's revivalist meetings as a youth, before in 1955 switching to saxophone as a member of rockabilly group Benny Cagle and the Rhythm Swingsters. In 1956 he left that group to join the more R&B-orientated Fairlanes, another member of which was **Rick Hall**, with whom Sherrill began writing songs. During this period he also recorded in a rockabilly vein ('Like Making Love', Mercury, 1958, which was covered in Britain by **Marty Wilde**). After selling a number of songs to Nashville publishers, including 'Achin' Breakin' Heart' (later a hit for **George Jones**)

in 1962), Sherrill and Hall established Fame Music which, in the sixties – after Sherrill had gone to work for **Sam Phillips** in his newly established Nashville studio in 1960 – became the basis of Hall's Fame studio. In Nashville, Sherrill produced Rich, recording him in a more bluesy, introspective manner (notably on 'Who Will the Next Fool Be', 1961), and **Jerry Lee Lewis**. When Phillips, who Sherrill always says taught him all he knows about production, closed down the studio in 1964, Sherrill joined Columbia. There he worked mostly for the label's R&B subsidiary Okeh, for whom he produced Ted Taylor's 1965 R&B hit 'Stay Away from My Baby' and several releases by the **Staple Singers**.

Sherrill's decisive break with rhythm and blues came in 1966 when his production of the tear-jerking ballad 'Almost Persuaded', which he co-wrote with regular collaborator Glenn Sutton (the then husband of **Lynn Anderson**), gave David Houston a country No. 1 on Epic. Sherrill's further similarly styled hits for Houston included 'You Mean the World to Me' (1967), 'Already It's Heaven' (1968) and 'My Elusive Dreams' (1967), all country chart-toppers. That last song was a duet with Wynette, the artist with whom Sherrill achieved his greatest successes. Wynette's impassioned, yet controlled, vocals blended perfectly with Sherrill's increasingly formal production style and gave added bite to the songs about how 'sometimes it's hard to be a woman' (the opening lines of 'Stand by Your Man'), which Sherrill, Sutton and Wynette took as their subject matter. Their first collaboration was 'Apartment #9' (1966), co-written by Johnny Paycheck (another artist produced by Sherrill). It was quickly followed by Wynette's first country No. 1, 'I Don't Wanna Play House' (1967), the epochal 'D-I-V-O-R-C-E' (1968), and the biggest-selling single ever by a female country artist, 'Stand by Your Man' (1968). These recordings have often been too easily dismissed by critics as socially regressive (particularly in contrast to songs like **Helen Reddy**'s 'I Am Woman', 1972). More interesting was the parody by Scottish comedian Billy Connolly who, in 1975, the year a re-release of 'Stand by Your Man' topped the British charts, had a British No. 1 with his version of 'D-I-V-O-R-C-E' on Polydor.

Sherrill, by now Columbia's Nashville recording chief, continued producing hits for Wynette into the seventies (occasionally with her husband George Jones, including 'Golden Ring', 1976) and eighties. He was also successful with **Tanya Tucker**, whose 'Delta Dawn' (1972) and other outings he masterminded, and Rich, whose career he revived with 'Behind Closed Doors' and 'The Most Beautiful Girl in the World'* (1973). Other artists with whom he worked include **Marty Robbins** (*All Around Cowboy*, 1979), J. Lacy Dalton (*Hard Times*, 1980), Jones (virtually everything between 1972 and 1990) and **Ray Charles** (*Friendships*, 1984). Perhaps his most interesting collaboration of the eighties, however, was with Costello. The Sherrill-produced *Almost Blue* included the British Top Ten hit 'A Good Year for the Roses' (1981) and Sherrill's own 'Too Far Gone'. In the early nineties he retired.

NAT SHILKRET
b. 25 December 1895, New York, USA

Nat Shilkret was a leading bandmaster of the twenties and early thirties who also became an all-purpose accompanist and musical director at many recording sessions.

Trained as a classical clarinettist, he played with the New York Philharmonic, the New York Symphony and the orchestra of the Metropolitan Opera House. He also worked in the concert bands of **John Philip Sousa** and Arthur Pryor. He began to work for Victor Records at the start of the twenties, one job of many being to supervise the first recordings of Southern traditional fiddling, by Eck Robertson in 1922. (He also accompanied Robertson on piano on some tunes.) From the mid-twenties he conducted the company's 'house' orchestra, sometimes as an anonymous accompanying unit for singers, sometimes in special guises like the Victor Salon Orchestra or International Novelty Orchestra, but most often as the Victor Orchestra, functioning as a production-line for versions of current popular songs and tunes. Some of those hits were his own work, such as 'Jeannine, I Dream of Lilac Time' (1928), 'Down the River of Golden Dreams' (1930) and 'The First Time I Saw You' (1937).

In 1935 Shilkret went to Hollywood to work in films as an arranger, conductor and musical director. In the following year he worked on the radio programme *Camel Caravan*, and later on *Relaxation Time* (1938–9). Still associated with Victor, he conducted the orchestra on such successes as Allen Jones' 'Donkey Serenade' (1939).

His brother Jack Shilkret was a pianist, songwriter and bandleader who also had a recording band on Victor and worked in radio in the mid-thirties.

THE SHIRELLES
Shirley Owens, b. 10 June 1941, Passiac, New Jersey, USA; Addie 'Micki' Harris, b. 22 January 1940, Passiac, d. 10 June 1982, Los Angeles, California; Doris Coley Kenner, b. 2 August 1941, Passiac; Beverly Lee, b. 3 August 1941, Passiac

Best remembered for their breathy version of **Carole King**'s 'Will You Love Me Tomorrow?'* (1960), the Shirelles were one of the most enduring groups of the

girl-group era and formed the link between the harder-edged vocal style of the **Chantels** and the fluffier, 'little girl' sound of the groups that followed in their wake.

Formed in high school in 1958 as the Poquelles, the Shirelles were signed to Florence Greenberg's small Tiara label and had an immediate hit with their own composition, the bouncy 'I Met Him on a Sunday', when it was leased to Decca. However, subsequent Decca recordings failed and it was only when Greenberg set up Scepter Records and brought in producer and songwriter Luther Dixon that the group returned to the charts. A former member of the Four Buddies ('I Will Wait', Savoy, 1951), Dixon was co-author of several hits, notably 'Sixteen Candles' (the **Crests**, 1958), 'Big Boss Man' (**Elvis Presley**, 1960) and 'Hundred Pounds of Clay' (**Gene McDaniels**, 1961). The group's first recording with Dixon was a remake of the **Five Royales**' 'Dedicated to the One I Love'. Clearly patterned after the Chantels' recordings, it was only a minor hit in 1959, but a million-seller when reissued in 1961 in the wake of the group's later success. More unusual (and suggestive) was the West Indian-flavoured 'Tonight's the Night'* (1969), co-written by Owens and Dixon, which was covered by the **Chiffons**. Even more successful was the follow-up 'Will You Love Me Tomorrow?', which took the central situation of the earlier song a stage further with its blend of what critic Charlie Gillett has called 'vulnerable and suppliant availability'. An American No. 1 and one of the most played of 'golden oldies', the song has since been recorded by numerous artists, including the **Four Seasons** (1968), **Roberta Flack** (1972) and King herself (on *Tapestry*, 1971). In 1983 the Shirelles themselves re-recorded the song with **Dionne Warwick**.

There followed a series of big hits for the group, including Dixon's plaintive 'Mama Said' and **Burt Bacharach**'s 'Baby It's You' (1961), on which Bacharach himself sang backing to Owens' lead vocal and which with 'Boys' was recorded by **The Beatles** on their début album. The series climaxed with the Shirelles' second American No. 1, Dixon's plangent 'Soldier Boy'* (1962). However, after a few more records Dixon left Scepter to form his own Ludix records and after one more Top Ten hit, 'Foolish Little Girl' (1963), the group's career went into decline. In 1964, the year **Manfred Mann** had a British hit with their version of the Shirelles' 'Sha-La-La', they sued Scepter over unpaid royalties, only returning to recording in 1967 with 'Last Minute Miracle', their last chart entry. After further recordings for Bell and RCA, the group broke up in 1976. Owens had left in 1975 and cut a solo album for Prodigal followed in 1977 by *Lady Rose* (RCA), recorded under her married name of Alston. The remaining Shirelles have since occasionally re-formed for revival concerts. In 1983 they provided backing vocals on **Dionne Warwick**'s version of 'Will You Love Me Tomorrow'. A further mark of how far the recording had sunk into the public's subconscious was the clever use made of it by Tom Stoppard in his play *The Real Thing* (1982), which contrasted the idealized descriptions of love in pop songs like it with the difficulties of actually being in (and out) of love.

SHIRLEY AND LEE

Shirley Pixley, b. 19 June 1936, New Orleans, Louisiana, USA; Leonard Lee, b. 29 June 1935, New Orleans, d. 26 October 1976

A teenage vocal duo, Shirley and Lee's hits of the early fifties included the R&B standard 'Let the Good Times Roll'.

A demo tape made by the couple at Cosimo Matassa's studio in New Orleans persuaded Eddie Mesner to sign them to Aladdin in 1952. 'I'm Gone' reached the R&B Top Ten and launched a series of boy-meets-girl hits which were accompanied by frequent magazine articles on the 'Sweethearts of the Blues'. Shirley's high-pitched girlish voice was echoed by Jamaican Millie Small on her 1964 hit 'My Boy Lollipop'.

With production by **Dave Bartholomew** and accompaniment from leading New Orleans session players, 'Rock All Night', 'Rockin' with the Clock' and 'Lee's Goofed' (1954) were minor hits before the Lee-composed 'Feel So Good' reached the R&B Top Ten in 1955. This was followed by the rollicking 'Let the Good Times Roll' (1956), whose energetic sax solo by Lee Allen (whose own biggest hit was the **Allen Toussaint**-produced 'Walking with Mr Lee', 1957) helped to make it a pop hit.

The song was later revived by producer Bunny Sigler (Parkway, 1967) and gave its name to a 1973 film of a rock revival show in which Shirley and Lee appeared. After the minor hit 'I Feel Good' (1956) and the demise of Aladdin, the duo moved to Imperial and Warwick where they had some success with a remake of 'Let the Good Times Roll' (1960) and 'Well-a Well-a' (1961).

They returned briefly to Imperial in 1961 before separating in 1963. Lee recorded in New Orleans for Imperial and Bartholomew's Broadmoor label while Shirley moved to Los Angeles. There she worked with Jesse Hill (a New Orleans singer whose biggest hit had been 'Ooh Poo Pah Doo', Minit, 1967) as Shirley and Jesse and sang on numerous recording sessions, including those for the **Rolling Stones**' *Exile on Main Street* (1972) and **Dr John**'s *Gumbo*. In 1975 she re-emerged as Shirley and Company on 'Shame Shame Shame' (Vibration), produced by Sylvia Robinson,

formerly partner of **Mickey Baker** in the male-female duo Mickey and Sylvia. In 1988 Shirley won half the royalties from 'Let the Good Times Roll' in a court case brought against Lee's family.

DINAH SHORE

b. Frances Rose Shore, 1 March 1917, Winchester, Tennessee, USA, d. 24 February 1994, Beverly Hills, California

Best remembered for her sensuous recordings of 'Blues in the Night'* (1941) and the possessor of what one critic has called 'a silky, light-as-air voice', Shore was one of the most popular recording stars of the forties.

While at Vanderbilt University, Shore sang on Nashville radio and took the name Dinah after using 'Dinah' as her signature tune. In 1937 she travelled to New York and sang on radio before joining **Xavier Cugat** as guest vocalist. She made her recording début with Cugat ('The Breeze and I', 1940) but her big break came later that year when she became a regular on **Eddie Cantor**'s radio show. Her first hit was 'Yes My Darling Daughter' (Bluebird, 1940), which was an adaptation of a traditional Russian melody. An even bigger hit for **Glenn Miller**, the song was successfully revived by Eydie Gorme in 1962. However, the song that established Shore was **Harold Arlen** and **Johnny Mercer**'s film theme, 'Blues in the Night'. That led to her appearing in several movies, including *Up in Arms* (1944), in which she sang Arlen's 'Now I Know' and 'I'll Walk Alone' (Victor), and the **Jerome Kern** biopic *Till the Clouds Roll By* (1946), in which she sang the oft-recorded 'Smoke Gets in Your Eyes'. When her film career ended Shore returned to radio and joined Columbia. Her hits of the forties included 'The Gypsy' (1946), **Al Jolson**'s 'Anniversary Song' (1947), the Oscar-winning 'Buttons and Bows'* (1948) from the Bob Hope film, *Paleface*, and **Sammy Fain**'s 'Dear Hearts and Gentle People' (1949).

In the fifties, as her hits declined with the advent of rock'n'roll, Shore established herself as a television star with a long-running show, in the mould of **Perry Como**'s. In the sixties she recorded only intermittently and in the seventies became a television chat-show hostess.

SHOWADDYWADDY

Dave Bartram, b. 1953; Malcolm Allured; Romeo Challenger; Russ Fields; Billy Gask; Al James; Trevor Oakes; Rod Teas

A tongue-in-cheek British rock'n'roll revival band, Showaddywaddy had numerous British hits in the seventies.

Taking their name from the chanted phrase in the

backing vocals of the **Maurice Williams** composition 'Little Darlin'' (1957), a million-seller for the Diamonds, Showaddywaddy were formed in the Leicester area in 1973. Initially playing the cabaret circuit the group appeared on the TV talent show *New Faces* and were signed to Bell. During 1974 they had hits in Britain and Europe with 'Hey Rock'n'Roll', 'Rock'n'Roll Lady' and 'Hey Mr Christmas'. Written by the group's eight members, they were produced by Mike Hurst.

During 1975 the self-penned 'Sweet Music' and 'Heavenly' were less successful than covers of **Eddie Cochran**'s 'Three Steps to Heaven' and **Buddy Holly**'s 'Heartbeat'. Later revivals, however, were drawn from the more diluted regions of late fifties and early sixties rock. Versions of Curtis Lee's 'Under the Moon of Love' (1976, Showaddywaddy's only No. 1), the **Kalin Twins**' 'When' (Arista, 1977) and **Marv Johnson**'s 'You Got What It Takes' were Hurst's final productions and from 'Dancin' Party' the group's records were self-produced.

Showaddywaddy's commercial success reached a peak in 1976–8 when the band had seven successive Top Ten hits, concluding with cover-versions of two 1961 songs, the Jarmels' 'A Little Bit of Soap' and Curtis Lee's 'Pretty Little Angel Eyes'. Later records like **Chuck Berry**'s 'Sweet Little Rock'n'Roller' (1979) and **Bobby Darin**'s 'Multiplication' (1981) were only minor hits and in 1982 the group moved to RCA. After unsuccessfully reviving **Barry Mann**'s 'Who Put the Bomp', Showaddywaddy faded from view.

In the first half of the nineties they returned to live performance, making regular appearances on the British cabaret circuit.

SHEL SILVERSTEIN
b. 1932, Chicago, Illinois, USA

Composer of such songs as 'Sylvia's Mother' and 'Queen of the Silver Dollar', author, cartoonist and performer Silverstein, who is probably best described in fifties jazz parlance as a 'hipster', was one of the most unlikely of country songwriters of recent times. His narrative songs, particularly those he wrote for **Dr Hook**, were similar in style to those **Leiber and Stoller** provided for the **Coasters**, with the difference that behind them was a gentle parody of country songwriting in general as humorous episodes and puns were pushed to extreme lengths.

Raised in Chicago, where he listened to jazz and blues, Silverstein was a staff artist for *Stars and Stripes* magazine during his army service in the fifties. After leaving the army he worked successfully as a cartoonist, particularly in *Playboy* magazine, for some fifteen years. With the advent of the folk boom of the early sixties, Silverstein turned his satiric interest to folk

music and released *Inside Folk* (1961), which included 'The Unicorn Song' which has since been recorded often by folk singers. Throughout the sixties and seventies he published collections of his cartoons (*Grab My Box*) and illustrated children's books (*Uncle Shelley's ABC*, *The Giving Tree*, 1972) but turned increasingly to songwriting. In 1967 he released an eponymous album (Cadet) and in 1969 had his first popular success when **Johnny Cash** sold a million copies of Silverstein's 'A Boy Named Sue'. In 1971 **Loretta Lynn** took his 'One's on the Way' to the top of the country charts.

In the early seventies Silverstein used Dr Hook as the main outlet for his songwriting. He provided them with their first hits, 'Sylvia's Mother' (1972) and 'The Cover of Rolling Stone'* (1973) – which inspired **Buck Owens**' take-off, 'The Cover of Music City News' – and wrote all the material on their first albums, including the bitter-sweet 'Queen of the Silver Dollar', which has since been memorably recorded by **Marianne Faithfull** and **Emmylou Harris**. Silverstein's own recordings, such as *Freaking at the Freakers Ball* (Columbia, 1979), which included 'Don't Give a Dose to the One You Love the Most' (a song used in several anti-VD campaigns), and *The Great Conch Train Robbery* (Flying Fish, 1984) were less successful.

In 1973 Silverstein teamed up with **Bobby Bare**, who recorded an album of his songs, *Lullabys, Legends and Lies*, which spawned a pair of Top Ten country hits, 'Daddy What If' and 'Marie Laveau' (1974). This partnership continued over several concept albums into the eighties, including most notably *Drinkin' from the Bottle, Singing from the Heart* (1983). During this period Silverstein turned to writing children's books (such as *A Light in the Attic*, 1980) and recorded the hilarious solo album *The Great Conch Train Robbery* (Flying Fish, 1980). The partnership with Bare later formed the basis of the *Old Dogs* album (1998) on which Bare, partnered by **Mel Tillis**, **Waylon Jennings** and **Jerry Reed**, recorded a number of Silverstein compositions.

VICTOR SILVESTER
b. 25 February 1901, Wembley, Middlesex, England, d. 14 August 1978, France

An orchestra leader for more than thirty years, Victor Silvester had an influential voice in determining what popular music Britons listened to and how they used it, through his promotion of 'strict tempo' dance music.

The son of a north London vicar, he ran away from boarding-school to be a dance host in a West End restaurant. Returning home, he studied at the Trinity and London Colleges of Music, dancing in the evenings. In 1922 he won the 'World's Dancing

Championship' at London's Queen's Hall. Then, in collaboration with beauty queen Dorothy Newton, whom he later married, he opened an academy to teach a more formal style of dancing than **Vernon and Irene Castle**. In 1935 he formed his first Ballroom Orchestra, and two years later began broadcasting. He directed the *BBC Dancing Club*, which had an audience of millions, and later *Television Dancing Club*. He also wrote the million-selling *Modern Ballroom Dancing* and numerous other instructional books. His records for Columbia (which included 'Blue Danube', 'Tales from the Vienna Woods', 'Valse des Fleurs' and 'La Cumparsita') sold chiefly to dance enthusiasts, but a series of sides made in 1943–4 by a small group called Victor Silvester's Jive Band, featuring jazz-conscious musicians like George Chisholm (trombone) and Tommy McQuater (trumpet), appealed to 'hot' music fans, though they too were labelled 'for jive dancing', in response to the arrival in Britain (through the US servicemen stationed in the country) of modern American styles.

Victor Silvester Jnr led his father's band in the eighties.

SIMON AND GARFUNKEL

Art Garfunkel, b. 5 November 1942, New York, USA;
Paul Simon, b. Paul Frederic Simon, 13 October 1942,
Newark, New Jersey

Garfunkel's soaring 'choir-boy' tenor and **Simon**'s well-crafted songs made Simon and Garfunkel among the most successful and influential acts in sixties rock. Taking their cue equally from the folk-rock of **Bob Dylan** and the harmonies of the **Everly Brothers**, the duo opened the way for a flood of soft-voiced singer-songwriters. After they parted company in 1970, Garfunkel concentrated on film acting, making occasional solo recordings, while Simon went on to a distinguished career as a solo writer and performer.

The two met at high school in New York and in 1957 wrote and recorded 'Hey Schoolgirl' (Big) as Tom and Jerry. Very much in the Everlys' vein, it was a minor hit, unlike later singles on Big, Hunt and Ember. While continuing to study, Simon wrote (sometimes with **Carole King**) and recorded as Tico and the Triumphs ('Motorcycle', Amy, 1962) and Jerry Landis ('The Lone Teen Ranger', 1963) while Garfunkel released unsuccessful singles for Octavia and Warwick as Artie Garr.

By 1963, when Simon (as Paul Kane) recorded the protest song 'He Was My Brother' (Tribute), both he and Garfunkel were strongly influenced by the folk revival. The following year Simon visited England, learning songs like 'Scarborough Fair' from such figures as **Martin Carthy**. On his return to New York, Columbia signed Simon and Garfunkel, releasing the Tom Wilson-produced *Wednesday Morning 3 A.M.* It included a mixture of restrained versions of folk-club standards like Dylan's 'The Times They Are a-Changin'' and Simon originals such as 'The Sounds of Silence' and 'Bleecker Street'.

The album sold poorly and Simon returned to England, re-recording 'Brother' for Oriole and a solo acoustic album, *The Paul Simon Songbook* (1965), for the newly established British branch of Columbia. Among its tracks were 'I Am a Rock', 'Kathy's Song', **Davy Graham**'s 'Anji', and the first version of the satirical 'A Simple Desultory Philippic'. He also produced an eponymous album by Jackson C. Frank (EMI Columbia, 1965), had compositions covered by Harvey Andrews and Val Doonican and co-wrote with Bruce Woodley 'Red Rubber Ball' (a 1966 US hit for the Cyrkle) and 'Someday, One Day', a British Top Twenty hit for Woodley's group the **Seekers**.

In the meantime, the success of folk-rock records by Dylan, the **Byrds** and others led Wilson to add bass, drums and electric guitar to Simon and Garfunkel's 'The Sounds of Silence'. The resulting single reached No. 1 in America at the end of 1965 (in Britain it was covered by ballad harmony group the Bachelors). Reunited, the duo recorded *Sounds of Silence* (Columbia, 1966), which was essentially an electric version of Simon's British solo album. During 1966 'Homeward Bound' and 'I Am a Rock' were transatlantic hits and Simon and Garfunkel also released *Parsley, Sage, Rosemary and Thyme*. The album found Simon trying out various styles, from the sombre introspection of 'Patterns' and the romanticism of 'For Emily, Wherever I May Find Her' to the ebullient pop of 'The 59th Street Bridge Song (Feelin' Groovy)', a hit for **Harpers Bizarre** in 1967. The up-beat 'A Hazy Shade of Winter' was a Top Twenty hit in America and in 1988 was successfully revived by the **Bangles**.

By now Simon and Garfunkel were consciously orientating themselves to college audiences (in the same way as **Dave Brubeck** had a decade earlier). In 1967 they appeared at the Monterey Festival, released the adroit 'At the Zoo' and the semi-psychedelic 'Fakin' It' and were signed to provide the soundtrack for Mike Nichols' film about contemporary youth, *The Graduate*. Released in 1968, the soundtrack album contained instrumental pieces by Dave Grusin, several old Simon compositions and only one new song, 'Mrs Robinson'*, which reached No. 1. The success of the film also helped to give Simon and Garfunkel the top three slots in the American album chart in June 1968.

In contrast, the first side of *Bookends* (1968) was a concept song cycle leading from youth ('Save the Life of My Child') through the evocative 'America', both a love song and a meditation on the state of the nation, to old age ('Old Friends'). During 1969 the enigmatic

'The Boxer' (later recorded by Dylan on *Self Portrait*, 1970) was a hit, Garfunkel filmed *Catch 22* with Nichols, and the duo made their first tour with a backing group.

The following year marked the artistic and commercial peak of the duo's career, as well as its demise. *Bridge Over Troubled Water* included some of Simon's most accomplished writing, on such songs as 'The Only Living Boy in New York' and 'Cecilia'*, while the polished arrangement and Garfunkel's solo voice on the title track made it a multi-million-seller. Inspired by a **Swan Silvertones** song and **Phil Spector**'s 'wall of sound', 'Bridge Over Troubled Water' was later covered by more than two hundred artists from **Elvis Presley** to **Aretha Franklin**. 'Cecilia' and 'El Condor Pasa' were later hits from the album.

Soon after its release, Simon's musical ambitions and Garfunkel's acting commitments forced the dissolution of the partnership. There were two later reunions. In 1975 the duo recorded the dynamic 'My Little Town', which appeared on solo albums by each and was a Top Ten hit single. Six years afterwards, Simon and Garfunkel gave a free concert in New York, releasing *The Concert in Central Park* (Geffen, 1982)

During the seventies and eighties Garfunkel acted in such films as *Carnal Knowledge* (1971) and *Bad Timing* (1980) and cut a series of solo albums, beginning with the Halee-produced *Angel Clare* (1973), which included the Top Ten single 'All I Know'. *Breakaway* (1975), produced by Richard Perry, provided hits with 'My Little Town', **Gallagher and Lyle**'s title track and a revival of the **Flamingos**' 1959 arrangement of **Harry Warren** and Al Dubin's 'I Only Have Eyes for You'. **Jimmy Webb**'s songs provided the basis for Garfunkel's most critically acclaimed album, *Watermark* (1978), while a revival of **Sam Cooke**'s 'Wonderful World' (1978) was an American hit with guest singers **James Taylor** and Simon, and 'Bright Eyes' (1979), the theme from the film *Watership Down*, reached No. 1 in Britain. Later recordings included *Scissors Cut* (1981) and *Lefty* (1988). Garfunkel's only subsequent new recordings were issued on *Up 'Til Now* (1993), which included older unreleased tracks, such as the original acoustic version of 'The Sounds of Silence'.

Following their 1982 reunion, Simon and Garfunkel toured America, and they would occasionally team up again over the next decade, often at charity fund-raising events. In 1993 they played a two-week season at a New York theatre.

CARLY SIMON
b. 25 June 1945, New York, USA

Simon began as a singer-songwriter whose subject matter was the foibles and *angst* of the well-to-do, rather than the bleak view from a bedsit that was the perspective of many of her seventies contemporaries. Her most memorable recording was 'You're So Vain'* (1972) on which, with cutting sarcasm, she sang of the playboy-lover, 'You're so vain, I bet you think this song is about you'.

The youngest daughter of Richard Simon, co-founder of the Simon and Schuster publishing house, Simon formed the Simon Sisters with her elder sister Lucy after leaving Sarah Lawrence College, and had a minor hit with the folky 'Winkin', Blinkin' and Nod' (Kapp, 1964). In 1966 she started recording an album with members of **The Band** only for the project to fall apart and she left the music business until 1970 when she was signed to Elektra. Her first eponymous album included the Top Ten hit, the acutely observed 'That's the Way I Always Heard It Should Be' (1971). Co-written with lyricist and screenwriter Jacob Brackman, the song introduced the theme of the lonely rich that would dominate most of her seventies work. The title track of her second album *Anticipation* (1971) gave her another hit, but more significant was *No Secrets* (1972). It was produced by Richard Perry, who gave her a slicker and more sophisticated sound, and included 'You're So Vain', on which Simon's confident voice was prominently supported by Mick Jagger's back-up vocals. *Hotcakes* (1974) included the sombre 'Haven't Got Time for the Pain' and a duet with her husband **James Taylor**, an exuberant revival of **Charlie and Inez Fox**'s 1963 hit 'Mockingbird'*. Subsequent albums were only moderately successful and Simon's only big hits of the period were the theme song to the James Bond movie *The Spy Who Loved Me*, 'Nobody Does It Better'* (1977), her revival in partnership with Taylor of the **Everly Brothers** 1958 hit 'Devoted to You' (1978) and 'You Belong to Me' (1978), which she co-wrote with Michael McDonald, a one-time member of the **Doobie Brothers**, and which saw her edging away from her autobiographical stance.

In the eighties Simon had a hit 'Jesse'* (Warners, 1980) and divorced Taylor in 1982. In 1981, anticipating **Linda Ronstadt**, she released *Torch*, an album of standards by such songwriters as **Hoagy Carmichael** ('I Get Along without You Very Well'), after which she went into semi-retirement, only resurfacing in 1987 with *Coming Round Again* (Arista), the mellow title track of which was featured in the film *Heartburn* and gave her a big hit. Another film theme, 'Let the River Run' (from *Working Girl*, 1988), was equally successful the following year.

The 1988 album *Greatest Hits Live* featured Simon playing her back catalogue to an invited audience. It was followed by the album of standards, *My Romance* (1990), and her first collection of new material in three years, *Have You Seen Me Lately* (1990). In 1992 she released the soundtrack to the movie *This Is My Life*. Simon published her first children's book, *Amy and the Dancing Bear*, in 1989, and followed it with *The Boy of the Bells* in 1990. Her interest in writing for children led to the composition of the opera *Romulus Hunt*, which opened in New York in 1993. In 1994 she released her first album of original songs for some time, *Letters Never Sent*, which featured **Roseanne Cash** and **Eurythmic** Dave Stewart, among others. In 1997 she recorded another album of standards, *Film Noir*, which was co-produced by **Jimmy Webb**. *The Bedroom Tapes* (2000), her first collection of original songs for over five years, saw her both introspective ('Scars') and witty ('Your Dearest Friends'), confirming that the songwriting tradition she grew out of was Broadway rather than the Brill Building.

The three-CD retrospective *Clouds in My Coffee, 1965–1995* (Arista, 1995) covered all the stages of her career.

JOE SIMON
b. 2 September 1943, Simmesport, Louisiana, USA

Simon was one of several black singers with Southern roots who had success interpreting country material for black and pop audiences. Unlike **Charley Pride**, however, Simon did not embrace country music completely.

After moving to California in his teens, Simon sang gospel but retained his strong affinity with country music on releases on Irral and Hush (where he sang with the Goldentones), which showed the strong influence of **Ray Charles**. In 1965 he was signed by Vee-Jay and had an R&B hit with 'Let's Do It Over'. On that label's collapse he went to Nashville, where he was signed by legendary disc-jockey turned producer John 'R'. Richbourg to Sound Stage Seven, a subsidiary of Fred Foster's Monument label. Utilizing the cream of Nashville session men, Richbourg and Simon produced a steady stream of country-inflected R&B hits between 1966 and 1970, including 'Teenager's Prayer' and 'That's the Way I Want Our Love'. The artistic peak of this stage of his career was his intense version of **Waylon Jennings**' 'The Chokin' Kind' (1969), an R&B chart-topper and Top Twenty pop hit.

He joined Spring Records in 1970, and after the pop hit 'Your Time to Cry', was assigned to Philadelphia-based producers **Gamble and Huff** in 1971. They immediately came up with two million-sellers, 'Drowning in a Sea of Love' (1971) and 'The Power of Love' (1972), which set Simon's strangled, intense vocals against a highly arranged backdrop. He continued recording country material, including **Kris Kristofferson**'s 'Help Me Make It Through the Night' which he made before **Gladys Knight**'s hit version.

Then, like so many soul singers, he took refuge in disco with 'Step by Step' (1973), his only UK hit, and 'Get Down, Get Down (Get on the Floor)'* (1975), his biggest international hit. Prior to this he had a hit with his own composition, 'Theme from Cleopatra Jones' (1973), from one of the many blaxploitation films of the seventies.

After several years in relative obscurity, he appeared on Mello-O-Soun in 1984 (where he was produced by his old partner Richbourg) and in 1985 joined Compleat Records, releasing *Mr Right*. He has performed only intermittently in the nineties.

PAUL SIMON
b. Paul Frederic Simon, 13 October 1942, Newark, New Jersey, USA

Following the break-up of **Simon and Garfunkel**, Paul Simon had a fluctuating solo career. Artistic and commercial success in the early seventies was followed by an abortive attempt to enter film-making. His return to recording – *Graceland* (1986), a collaboration with South African musicians – was both an international bestseller and one of the most influential records of the eighties.

The stark arrangements of many of the songs on the intense *Paul Simon* (Columbia, 1972) inspired critical comparisons with **John Lennon**'s *Plastic Ono Band* (1970), but its two hit singles were jaunty fusions of rock with other musics. 'Mother and Child Reunion' was reggae-based and recorded in Jamaica, while 'Me and Julio Down by the Schoolyard' evoked New York's Latin traditions. This multi-cultural emphasis was underlined when Simon toured in 1973 with Peruvian ensemble Urubamba and the Jessy Dixon Singers gospel group. 'Loves Me Like a Rock'*, from *There Goes Rhymin' Simon* (1973), was gospel-based, while the album also included the anthemic 'American Tune', the summation of Simon's attempts to create metaphors for his feelings about the moral and political direction of his country.

The concert recording *Live Rhymin'* (1974) was followed by *Still Crazy After All These Years* (1975), whose title track introduced a major preoccupation of Simon's later work – the attempt to explore the issues arising from getting older in a musical form rooted in adolescent moods and images. The album included the catchy, wry 'Fifty Ways to Leave Your Lover'* (1976).

Simon's only release during the rest of the decade was the downbeat 'Slip Sliding Away' (1977), a Top Ten hit taken from the compilation *Greatest Hits, Etc.* He turned away from recording towards the cinema, appearing in Woody Allen's *Annie Hall* (1977) and writing, producing and starring in the unsuccessful *One Trick Pony*. The accompanying soundtrack album (Warners, 1980) included the powerful ballad 'How the Heart Approaches What It Yearns' while the title song was a minor hit.

A reunion with Garfunkel for a New York open-air concert led to plans for a new album by the duo which were later abandoned. Simon's next release was the low-key and introverted *Hearts and Bones* (1983), whose highlight was 'The Late Great Johnny Ace', a tribute both to Lennon and to the fifties music which had inspired the teenage Simon. The *Graceland* project began in 1985 with recording sessions in Johannesburg which were the subject of fierce controversy because of the international cultural boycott of South Africa. Released in 1986, the resulting album included contributions from Mbaqanga players Ray Phiri (guitar), the Ladysmith Black Mambazo choir (which recorded a 1987 album for Warners), Latino-rock group **Los Lobos** (who later had international success with their revival of **Ritchie Valens**' 'La Bamba'), **Linda Ronstadt** and cajun band Rockie Dopsie and the Twisters.

In marked contrast to **Malcolm McLaren**'s *Duck Rock* (1983), which had appropriated African sounds as novelties, the sound and feel of *Graceland* confirmed a growing interest in African music, particularly in Europe, where the album sold more copies than in America, though it reached No. 1 on both continents. However, despite its strong African dimension (and Simon's commitment to the Sowetan musicians who later toured with him), *Graceland*'s central concerns remained decidedly American. The record's first hit single 'You Can Call Me Al' reprised some of Simon's fundamental themes, while the title track's search for salvation took for its central image **Elvis Presley**'s former home. Another compilation, *Negotiations and Love Songs*, followed in 1988.

Two years in the making and inspired by Brazilian music and the poetry of Caribbean writer Derek Walcott, *Rhythm of the Saints* appeared in 1990. He spent most of the next year touring in support of the album, and one of the dates from the tour provided the live album *Paul Simon's Concert in the Park* (1991). He married American singer-songwriter Edie Brickell in 1992, co-producing her 1994 single 'Tomorrow Comes' and album *Picture Perfect Morning*. In 1993 Simon guested on **Willie Nelson**'s acclaimed album *Across the Borderline*.

The three-CD set *1964–1993* (1994) was the definitive retrospective of Simon's career up to that point. In 1995 he began working on *Capeman*, a musical based on the imprisonment of a Puerto Rican gang member in the fifties for the killing of a white gang member. In part clearly a reworking of *West Side Story*, Simon's musical, which was eventually staged in 1998, sought to highlight the racism that was obscured in that musical. The musical eventually

turned out to be one of the greatest disasters ever staged on Broadway, its explicit account of racism and violence being out of kilter with the revivalist spirit then dominant on the great white way. Similarly, the album of songs from the show that Simon issued, *Songs from the Capeman* (1998), was the least successful of his nineties outings. Clearly a homage to the music he had heard in his teens, it was one of the few examples (excepting **Dion** and the **Rascals**) of an outsider capturing the sinuous pleasures behind the seeming formality of fifties doo-wop. That album's commercial failure led to Simon retreating in great part to the whimsy and pleasantry that had always been part of his work on *You're the One* (2000). Rhythmically as inventive as ever – the album featured drum legend Steve Gadd and regular accompanists bassist Bakithi Kumalo and guitarist Vincent Nguini – the songs' observations – of the gap between hopes and reality on the title track, for example – seem less penetrating than the mysteries Simon conjured up on *Graceland* or the sombre truths he examined in *The Capeman*. The result was a charming album that was light in weight as well as in spirit.

NINA SIMONE
b. Eunice Waymon, 21 February 1933, Tryon, North Carolina, USA

One of the most gifted soul-jazz pianist/singers of any era, Simone's career has spanned four decades. The political intensity and generic range of her work made her more popular in Europe than America.

Simone grew up in the gospel tradition and went on to study music at the Juilliard School in New York. She also taught piano before making her first recordings for Bethlehem. Among them was a swooping, intense version of 'I Love You Porgy'* (1959) from **George Gershwin**'s *Porgy and Bess* which reached the Top Twenty and the jaunty, jazzy 'My Baby Just Cares for Me', which was a belated hit when re-released in Britain on Charly in 1987.

She next recorded for Colpix, mixing ballads (Jesse Mae Robinson's 'The Other Woman'), blues ('Trouble in Mind', 1961), rhythm and blues (**Screamin' Jay Hawkins**' 'I Put a Spell on You') and her own compositions (the soulful 'Please Don't Let Me Be Misunderstood'). The last two songs were successfully covered in Britain by **Alan Price** (1966) and the **Animals** (1965).

During the late sixties Simone became a poet laureate of the civil rights movement, writing a series of hard-hitting eloquent songs which she recorded for RCA. They included a setting of Langston Hughes' poem 'Backlash Blues', 'Mississippi Goddam' (like **Bob Dylan**'s 'Only a Pawn in Their Game', inspired by the murder of Medgar Evers), 'Old Jim Crow' and

'Why? The King of Love Is Dead' (dedicated to Dr Martin Luther King). Her 'Young Gifted and Black' (1969) was a big British hit for the Jamaican singers **Bob and Marcia** in 1970. Simone also recorded highly personal versions of current and recent pop and show tunes and in Britain had Top Ten hits with 'Ain't Got No – I Got Life' (1968, from *Hair*) and the **Bee Gees**' 'To Love Somebody' (1969).

It Is Finished (1972) was the appropriate title of her final RCA album and Simone's militant approach led to her being ostracized by the American showbusiness establishment. She next recorded *Baltimore* (1978), whose title track was composed by **Randy Newman**, for Creed Taylor's CTI label.

Simone's later career was marred by a reputation for unpredictability, but the success of 'My Baby Just Cares for Me' prompted reissues of much of her best work of the sixties and some new recordings. These included *Live at Ronnie Scott's* (1989) and *A Single Woman* (1994). She regularly toured the UK in the nineties.

She published an autobiography, *I Put a Spell on You*, in 1992.

MOISES SIMONS
b. 1888, Cuba, d. 1945, Havana

Simons was a prolific Cuban composer who wrote 'El Manisero'. Introduced to America and Britain by Don Azpiazu and his Havana Casino Orchestra as the 'The Peanut Vendor' in 1931, the song was a huge success and confirmed the growing interest in Latin-American music in the US.

The song was discovered by Herbert Marks, son of music publisher E. B. Marks, while honeymooning in Cuba in 1930. He commissioned Louis Rittenberg to write an English lyric but it was not until Azpiazu's brother-in-law Marion Sunshine and Wolfe Gilbert produced a more suitable version that the song was a hit. Cuban bandleader Azpiazu's Victor recording created a sensation and sold a million within a year, an unusual achievement at the height of the Depression. The song was also featured in the 1931 film *The Cuban Love Song*, performed by Lawrence Tibbett.

Gilbert later wrote an English lyric for Simons' 'Marta', which was adopted by **Arthur Tracy** as his radio signature tune, and for 'Mama Inez', another early influential Cuban composition by Eliseo Grenet.

SIMPLE MINDS
Charlie Burchill, b. 27 November 1959, Glasgow, Scotland; Derek Forbes (replaced by John Giblin); Jim Kerr, b. 9 July 1959, Glasgow; Brian McGee (replaced by Kenny Hyslop, replaced by Mel Gaynor, b. 29 May 1960); Michael McNeill, b. 20 July 1958

In the eighties Simple Minds, like **U2**, graduated from small clubs to stadium venues with a brand of socially aware and moralizing song.

Born in Glasgow, Kerr (vocals) and Burchill (guitar) were members of punk group Johnny and the Self-Abusers, which recorded 'Saints and Sinners' in 1977 for Chiswick. The following year they formed Simple Minds with Forbes (bass), McGee (drums) and McNeill (synthesizers). Their first album, *Life in a Day* (Zoom, 1979), showed the influence of such artists as **Roxy Music** and **David Bowie**, but *Real to Real Cacophony* found the group mixing rock and experimental sounds, reflecting their burgeoning interest in electronic music. Both albums were produced by John Leckie.

A 'futurist' approach was apparent on *Empires and Dance* (Arista, 1980), whose songs had an aura of menace and panic. The group shifted its stance yet again when Steve Hillage, a former member of progressive rock band Gong, was brought in to produce the twin albums *Sons and Fascination* and *Sister Feelings Call* (Virgin, 1981). The enthusiastic following built up by frequent tours took the albums into the British Top Twenty but Simple Minds' breakthrough to commercial success came with *New Gold Dream* (1982) and its hit singles 'Promised You a Miracle' and 'Glittering Prize'.

McGee had been replaced by Hyslop (formerly with Midge Ure of **Ultravox** in Slik) during the protracted recording of *New Gold Dream*, which also featured his permanent replacement Gaynor. The Steve Lillywhite-produced *Sparkle in the Rain* (1984) had a full-blown stadium rock sound and provided further Top Twenty records with 'Waterfront' and 'Speed Your Love to Me'. Although Simple Minds had toured America with the **Pretenders** (whose Chrissie Hynde Kerr later married), they had no chart success there until they recorded Keith Forsey's 'Don't You (Forget About Me)'* (A&M, 1985), the theme song from the film *The Breakfast Club*. An American No. 1, it also gave the band its biggest British hit.

In the same year the group's new status was underlined when they were chosen to appear at Live Aid. *Once Upon a Time* (1985) was given a grander stadium-rock sound by producers Bob Clearmountain and Jimmy Iovine and sold over four million copies worldwide. *In the City of Light* (1987), a live double-album, topped the British chart but was less successful in America. In 1988 the band played 'Mandela Day', their tribute to the imprisoned South African political leader, at a Wembley Stadium concert marking his seventieth birthday. It was featured on *Street Fighting Years* (1989), which reached No. 1 in nine countries and included the band's British No. 1 single 'Belfast Child', based on the traditional Irish lament 'She Moved through the Fair'.

The band, which was now basically the Kerr–Burchill duo, with additional members drafted in for studio or live work, released *Real Life* in 1991. Featuring the hit single 'Let There Be Love', it preceded another lengthy world tour. The band was largely inactive for the next two years, during which Virgin released the career retrospective *Glittering Prizes 81/92* (1992). Divorced from Hynde, in 1992 Kerr married actress Patsy Kensit (who would subsequently marry **Oasis**'s Liam Gallagher in 1997). In 1995 the band issued *Good News from the Next World*, the first album of new material for several years. Only moderately successful, the band label-hopped to Chrysalis for *Neapolis* (1998), which saw a return to the group's earlier sound to good commercial effect.

SIMPLY RED
Tony Bowers; Mick Hucknall, b. 8 June 1960; Chris Joyce; Tim Kellett; Fritz McIntyre; Sylvan Richardson (replaced by Aziz Ibrahim); Ian Kirkham; Janette Sewell

A British soul-based group, Simply Red, in Hucknall, had the most acclaimed new blue-eyed soul singer of the eighties and became a massively successful act in the nineties, selling over eight million copies of their 1991 album *Stars*.

As Manchester art students, Hucknall and bassist Brian Turner formed punk group the Frantic Elevators in the late seventies. Starting out under the influence of the **Sex Pistols** and **Captain Beefheart**, the group gradually moved towards soul and R&B, recording several independent singles, including 'Holding Back the Years' (1982), for a local label shortly before disbanding.

Hucknall put together a new band to perform soul standards and his own compositions. After early personnel changes, Simply Red signed to Elektra and cut *Picture Book* (1985) with ex-Durutti Column members Joyce (drums) and Bowers (bass), plus Richardson (guitar), McIntyre (keyboards) and sax-player Kellett. Produced by Stewart Levine, the album included the British hit 'Money's Too Tight to Mention', a cover of the Valentine Brothers' disco hit.

International success came with a new arrangement of the pensive ballad 'Holding Back the Years' (1986) and Hucknall was invited to contribute a song for **Diana Ross** as well as collaborating with Lamont Dozier (of **Holland, Dozier and Holland**) on material for *Men and Women* (1987). The Alex Sadkin-produced album provided further hits with 'The Right Thing', 'Infidelity' and **Cole Porter**'s 'Ev'ry Time We Say Goodbye'. In 1987 Ibrahim joined Simply Red on guitar, replacing Richardson.

Levine returned to supervise *A New Flame* (1989) with its hit version of Harold Melvin and the Blue Notes' 1972 hit 'If You Don't Know Me by Now', which topped the American chart. The album also contained songs co-written with Dozier and Joe Sample of the **Crusaders** and was a worldwide success, selling over six million copies. Hucknall was now a considerable media star (he even appeared as a cartoon character in *Viz* comic) and took up residence in Italy as a tax exile.

Levine again produced 1991's *Stars*. Entirely written by Hucknall the album was a massive success, selling over three million copies in Britain alone, and spun off a string of hit singles, including 'Something Got Me Started', 'For Your Babies' and the title track. A lengthy world tour produced the live EP *Montreux*, which reached the British Top Twenty.

Simply Red's fourth album appeared in 1995, by which time guitarist Ibrahim had left to replace John Squire in the **Stone Roses**. Once again split between soulful ballads and light R&B, *Life* topped the charts across Europe, as did the lead-off single 'Fairground'. However, the album was less successful in the US than its predecessor. *Blue* (1997) was in much the same vein, and was followed a year later by *Live at the Lyceum*. *Love and the Russian Winter* saw Hucknall move towards house music with mixed results.

THE SIMPSONS
Homer Simpson (voiced by Dan Castellaneta); Marge Simpson (Julie Kavner); Bart Simpson (Nancy Cartwright); Lisa Simpson (Yeardley Smith); Maggie Simpson (Matt Groening)

In the nineties the garishly coloured, simply-drawn Simpson family were the most successful cartoon act since **Don Kirshner**'s Archies in the sixties. They were also clearly the product of a far less innocent age.

The Simpsons first came to life in 1987 in a string of thirty-second animated pieces on the US TV show starring British comedienne and singer Tracey Ullman. Ullman had had UK Top Ten hits in 1983 with 'Breakaway', 'They Don't Know' and 'Move Over Darling'. The dysfunctional Simpson family was created by Matt Groening, a former Los Angeles music critic who had created a successful syndicated cartoon strip, 'Life Is Hell', which at its mid-eighties peak ran in over 200 US newspapers.

The Simpsons were an immediate hit with the US public and were given their own TV series in 1990. The 'star' of the show for younger audiences was the street-smart, anarchic son of the family, Bart, whose string of catchphrases such as 'Eat my shorts' or 'Don't have a cow, man' adorned T-shirts throughout the US. The other members of the family included the grumpy, permanently bemused father and avid bowler, Homer (a safety inspector at a nuclear power plant), the cloying mother and refugee from a fifties sit-com, Marge, daughter Lisa – a saxophone-playing blues fan – and the baby, Maggie.

The massive merchandising success of *The Simpsons* was repeated in Europe, despite the fact that the series was only accessible to the small percentage of viewers with satellite or cable TV. In 1990 the series' popularity led to an album featuring the family, *The Simpsons Sing the Blues*, which included hit singles in 'Do the Bartman' and 'Deep Deep Trouble', the former a UK No. 1. Both were rap tracks featuring Bart and typified the approach of producer John Boylan, who had insisted on sacrificing parody in favour of musical credibility. To that end, the album featured appearances from **B. B. King**, **Dr John**, the **Byrds'** Roger McGuinn and Buster Poindexter (aka ex-**New York Doll** David Johansen), while the non-original material included **Albert King**'s blues standard 'Born Under a Bad Sign', **Billie Holiday**'s 'God Bless the Child' and **Chuck Berry**'s 'School Days'.

Groening's brightly coloured but crudely drawn characters set a trend in animation which saw the arrival in the early nineties of the Simpson's spiritual successors, *Ren and Stimpy*, created by John Kricfalusi for the Nickleodeon children's TV channel, MTV's parody of its own viewers, *Beavis and Butt-Head*, and *South Park*, which spawned a film, *South Park, Bigger, Longer & Uncut* (1999), which in turn included the recording 'Blame Canada', a song that owed its existence to *The Simpsons*.

FRANK SINATRA
b. Francis Albert Sinatra, 12 December 1915, Hoboken, New Jersey, USA, d. 15 May 1998, Los Angeles, California

If **Bing Crosby** was the most important of the crooners, Sinatra – affectionately known as 'ole blue eyes' – was the greatest of the singers whose style grew out of the music of the swing bands of the thirties. As one of the many obituaries succinctly put it, he was 'the voice of the century'. Generally regarded as the finest interpreter of Broadway show tunes, Sinatra influenced a generation of singers. Shaping his style during a big-band apprenticeship with **Tommy Dorsey**, Sinatra acknowledged **Billie Holiday**'s ability to imbue lyrics with deep emotion as a primary model. Even more than Holiday, however, he was a songwriter's favourite, interpreting and drawing out the essence of a lyric, whether forlorn or joyous. His early successes as a solo artist both hastened the emancipation of the vocalist from the role of a big-band member and provoked the first outbreak of teenage hysteria and fan-worship. After a period when he lost popularity, Sinatra's fortunes were restored by the **Nelson Riddle**-arranged 'Young at Heart' (1954) and a series of atmospheric albums like the melancholic *In the Wee Small Hours of the Morning* (1955). In 1961 he

became one of the first popular musicians to set up his own record label, Reprise. Among numerous vocalists who adopted elements of the Sinatra style were **Matt Monro**, **Vic Damone** and Jack Jones.

Sinatra first sang with the Hoboken Four vocal group, winning an amateur talent contest in 1935. His growing local reputation as a solo singer led to a contract with the newly-formed **Harry James** and his orchestra in 1939. He sang (uncredited) on the band's 'From the Bottom of My Heart' before joining Tommy Dorsey's band where in less than three years he sang on some ninety recordings for Victor.

In that time Sinatra developed a vocal style highly attuned to dance rhythms and to swing. Among his Dorsey recordings were numerous songs by **James Van Heusen** and Burke, **Irving Berlin** and **Frank Loesser**. Such was Sinatra's own popularity by 1942 that against Dorsey's wishes he persuaded Victor to record him as a solo artist on 'Night and Day' (Bluebird, 1942).

The following year Sinatra left the band to work as a soloist, joining the network radio show *Your Hit Parade* and inciting fanatical audience responses from teenage 'bobby-soxers'. The strike called by American Federation of Musicians president **James Caesar Petrillo** prevented recording sessions until in 1943 Decca's **Jack Kapp** recorded **Dick Haymes** *a cappella*. Columbia, enjoying success with a reissue of 'From the Bottom of My Heart' under Sinatra's name, followed suit by signing him and, with backing by the Bobby Tucker Singers, had hits with **Harry Warren** and Mack Gordon's 'You'll Never Know' and 'People Will Say We're in Love' from **Rodgers and Hammerstein**'s *Oklahoma!*.

In a decade with Columbia Sinatra recorded more than 250 songs, mostly with arranger Axel Stordahl, who created a soft, opulent sound with swirling strings, understated rhythms and woodwinds. The most popular vocalist of the mid-forties, Sinatra's hits included **Johnny Mercer**'s 'Dream' (1945), 'Nancy (With the Laughing Face)', 'Day by Day', 'The Coffee Song' (1946), 'The Things We Said Last Summer' and 'Full Moon and Empty Arms', based on a theme by Rachmaninov.

In 1950 **Mitch Miller** arrived at Columbia as head of A&R but his enthusiasm for cover-versions of country and R&B hits was not shared by Sinatra, whose sales and popularity slumped in the late forties. He worked unsuccessfully with the orchestras of **Hugo Winterhalter**, **Percy Faith** and Morris Stoloff. At Miller's behest, he even cut the novelty song 'Mama Will Bark' (1950).

Sinatra moved to Capitol in 1953 where Riddle's strings-based arrangement on the No. 1 'Young at Heart'* (1954) revitalized his singing career at the same time as he won an Oscar for his dramatic role in

From Here to Eternity. Legend has it that Sinatra secured the role through Mafia connections, a story retold in Francis Ford Coppola's *The Godfather* (1971) in which **Al Martino** played a character loosely based on Sinatra.

With Riddle and producer Voyle Gilmore, Sinatra also crafted a bestselling series of eight-song ten-inch albums that began with *Songs for Young Lovers* (1954) and *Swing Easy*. By 1955 R&B and rock'n'roll were beginning to have an impact and Sinatra even cut the rocking 'Two Hearts Two Kisses' with Dave Cavanaugh, producer of **Peggy Lee**'s 'Fever'. Sinatra, however, topped the charts with the swinging 'Learnin' the Blues'* and had further hits with the **Sammy Cahn**/ Van Heusen songs 'Love and Marriage'* (the first song to become a hit after being featured in a TV show) and the film theme '(Love Is) The Tender Trap'.

During the late fifties Sinatra recorded profusely. Among his 1956 successes were 'Hey Jealous Lover' and *Songs for Swinging Lovers*, which included **Cole Porter**'s 'I've Got You Under My Skin' and Myrow and Gordon's 'You Make Me Feel So Young'. In 1957 he sang Cahn and Van Heusen's ballad 'All the Way'*, which won an Oscar, while **Gordon Jenkins** arranged *A Jolly Christmas from Frank Sinatra*, which included 'Have Yourself a Merry Little Christmas'.

From this position of strength, Sinatra became one of rock'n'roll's most outspoken critics, although 'Witchcraft' (1958) was to be his last major single hit for eight years. With Cavanaugh now producing, however, the downbeat *Only the Lonely* (1958), which included Mercer's 'Blues in the Night' and 'One for My Baby', *Come Fly with Me*, with its 'touristic' songs 'April in Paris', 'London by Night' and 'Blue Hawaii', and *Nice'n'Easy* (1960) were all hit albums. On these albums he perfected his *bel canto*-based style with legato phrasing, seemingly effortless breath control and an ability to read the emotions behind the songs he sang.

In 1961 Sinatra set up his own Reprise label, issuing *Sinatra Swings*, whose title had to be changed from *Swing Along with Me* when Capitol claimed it was too similar to their own Sinatra album, *Come Swing with Me*. Headed by Mo Ostin, Reprise also released albums by **Sammy Davis Jnr**, **Dean Martin**, Bing Crosby and **Trini Lopez** before a majority shareholding was sold to Warners in 1963, but the label's mainstay was Sinatra himself.

With arrangers like ex-**Count Basie** man Johnny Mandel (*Ring a Ding Ding*, 1961), **Billy May** (*Sinatra Swings*) and former Dorsey associate Sy Oliver (*I Remember Tommy*), the Reprise Sinatra took on more of a jazz tinge. He made two albums with Basie (*Sinatra–Basie*, 1963, and *It Might as Well Be Swing*, 1964, arranged by **Quincy Jones**) and later worked with **Duke Ellington** and **Ella Fitzgerald**. The contrasting

Sinatra and Strings found Sinatra returning to classic ballads like **Hoagy Carmichael**'s 'Star Dust' and Porter's 'Night and Day' on arrangements by Don Costa, while he also collaborated on a bossa nova album with **Antonio Carlos Jobim** (1967).

In the mid-sixties Sinatra had occasional pop hits like 'Softly as I Leave You' (a British hit for Monro in 1964) and 'It Was a Very Good Year' and, in 1966, 'Strangers in the Night'*, the **Bert Kaempfert** melody with lyrics by Charles Singleton and Eddie Snyder, reached No. 1 in thirteen countries. Further success followed with the up-tempo 'That's Life' (1966) and a lightweight duet with his daughter Nancy, 'Somethin' Stupid'* (1967), a No. 1 hit. Nancy (to whom 'Nancy [With the Laughing Face]' had been dedicated) had previously reached No. 1 with the novelty 'These Boots Were Made for Walking' (1966) and subsequently partnered writer/producer **Lee Hazelwood** on such duets as 'Jackson' and 'Some Velvet Morning'.

While he made numerous Reprise albums in the mid-sixties, many involved re-recordings with Riddle of earlier Sinatra songs. More original were the mellow *September of My Years* (1965), which included **Kurt Weill**'s 'September Song' and 'It Gets Lonely Early', and *A Man Alone* (1969), a collection of songs by **Rod McKuen**, one of a number of contemporary singer-songwriters whose work Sinatra now began to record. Among the others were **John Lennon** and **Paul McCartney** ('Yesterday'), **Joni Mitchell** ('Both Sides Now'), **John Hartford** ('Gentle on My Mind') and **Paul Simon** ('Mrs Robinson'). Sinatra's best-known record of the period, however, was the old-fashioned big ballad 'My Way'* (1969). Originally a French tune 'Comme d'Habitude' with English lyrics written by **Paul Anka**, the song became Sinatra's signature tune during the seventies when his recording career took third place to acting and live appearances in Las Vegas. His only new releases of the decade were *Ol' Blue Eyes Is Back* (1973), whose title referred to a 1970 'retirement' decision and which included **Stephen Sondheim**'s 'Send in the Clowns', while *The Main Event* (1974) was a live recording.

The ambitious *Trilogy* (1980) was a three-album set divided into past, present and future. It included the lively 'Theme from New York, New York', a minor hit. Sinatra later released *She Shot Me Down* (1981) with its version of the former Sonny and **Cher** hit 'Bang Bang (My Baby Shot Me Down)', and *LA Is My Lady* (1984) on Quincy Jones' Qwest label. Later recordings were sporadic and there were several health scares, but Sinatra soldiered on, playing a surprisingly large number of concerts, including the occasional European visit.

In 1993 he made an unlikely return to the upper regions of the American album chart with *Duets* (Capitol), on which he revisited thirteen Sinatra classics with a variety of guest artists. These included French crooner **Charles Aznavour**, **Tony Bennett**, **Barbra Streisand** and, less predictably, U2 vocalist Bono and soul singer **Luther Vandross**. Though a sequel, *Duets II*, quickly followed in 1994, *Duets* was more notable for its technical achievements – many of the tracks were recorded with Sinatra and his partner thousands of miles apart – than anything else.

Sinatra also appeared in more than fifty films, beginning with a 1935 short featuring the Hoboken Four. In 1945 he won a special Oscar for the anti-prejudice short *The House I Live in*, whose title song was written by Lewis Allen (who wrote Holiday's 'Strange Fruit') and **Earl Robinson**, author of 'Ballad for Americans', but Sinatra's first major role was in *Higher and Higher* (1944). He had starring roles in such musical films as *Anchors Aweigh* (1945) and *On the Town* (1950) with **Gene Kelly**, *Young at Heart* (1955) with **Doris Day**, *Guys and Dolls* with Marlon Brando, *High Society* (1956) with Crosby and **Louis Armstrong** and Rodgers and **Hart**'s *Pal Joey* (1957). Although he sang 'My Kind of Town' in *Robin and the Seven Hoods* (1964), following his Oscar-winning performance in *From Here to Eternity* (1953), the majority of Sinatra's roles were non-singing. They included starring parts in *The Manchurian Candidate* (1962), *Tony Rome* (1967), *The Detective* (1968) and *The First Deadly Sin* (1980).

SIOUXSIE AND THE BANSHEES

Siouxsie, b. Susan Dallion, 27 May 1957; Sid Vicious, b. John Ritchie, 10 May 1957, London, England, d. 2 February 1979, New York, USA (replaced by Kenny Morris, replaced by Budgie, b. Peter Clark, 21 August 1957); Marco Pironni, b. 27 April 1959 (replaced by John McKay, replaced by John McGeogh, replaced by Robert Smith, b. 21 April 1959, replaced by John Carruthers, replaced by Jon Klein); Steve Severin, b. 25 September 1955; Martin McCarrick

One of the more adventurous of the early British punk groups, Siouxsie and the Banshees are more significant for the inspiration they gave to later artists than for their considerable European commercial success.

Siouxsie was one of the 'Bromley contingent' who followed the **Sex Pistols** in their earliest days and in September 1976 she performed a twenty-minute medley of the **Isley Brothers**' 'Twist and Shout', 'The Lord's Prayer' and **Bob Dylan**'s 'Knocking on Heaven's Door' at the London punk-rock festival. One of her accompanists was Vicious but when the Banshees re-emerged a few months later they included bassist Severin (formerly Steve Havoc), Morris (drums) and McKay (guitar).

Among the most uncompromising of punk groups, the group did not release a record for two years, when

'Hong Kong Garden' (Polydor, 1978) reached the Top Ten. By then, the early primal punk aesthetic had given way to a stylized approach in which the influence of singers like the **Velvet Underground**'s Nico was apparent. The accompanying album, *The Scream*, was produced by Steven Lillywhite and included 'Metal Postcard', inspired by the photomontages of John Heartfield, and a stark version of **The Beatles**' 'Helter Skelter'.

After *Join Hands* (1979) ex-Slits drummer Budgie and ex-Magazine guitarist McGeogh joined for *Kaleidoscope* (1980). With ex-Sex Pistol Steve Jones contributing a cameo on guitar, the album included the hit 'Happy House'. *Ju Ju* (1981) was followed by *A Kiss in the Dreamhouse* (1982), McGeogh's last recording with the group. Robert Smith of the **Cure** joined on guitar and he and Severin recorded *Blue Sunshine* as Glove (1983) on Wonderland, the Banshees' own label. Siouxsie and Budgie had enjoyed a minor hit in 1981 as the Creatures with 'Mad-Eyed Screamers' and reached the Top Ten with a version of **Mel Tormé**'s jazzy 'Right Now' in 1983. The Banshees themselves returned to the charts with another Beatles cover, 'Dear Prudence', which reflected their growing interest in late sixties rock. They were by now a considerable live attraction in Britain, although sales of the live album *Nocturne* (1983) were disappointing.

Hyena (1984) was produced by Mike Hedges and for *Tinderbox* (1986) the band was joined by former Clock DVA guitarist Carruthers. Siouxsie and the Banshees were able to indulge their penchant for the past when they released *Through the Looking Glass* (1987), a collection of cover-versions from which Dylan's 'This Wheel's on Fire' became a British hit. By this time McCarrick (from **Marc Almond**'s band) had joined the band on keyboards and Klein on guitar. *Peepshow* appeared in 1988 and included the British hit 'Peek-a-Boo'. The album was a minor hit in America, where the band were signed to Geffen Records.

Although seemingly poised for an American breakthrough, the Banshees were largely inactive in 1989–90, with Siouxsie and Budgie (now a married couple) recording and touring as the Creatures. They returned in 1991 with the consistent *Superstition*. However, after an American tour, the band again opted for a lengthy lay-off, broken only by the single 'Face to Face' (1992), written for the movie *Batman Returns* and included on the second hits collection, *Twice upon a Time* (1992).

The group's last album was the **John Cale**-produced *The Rapture* (1995), which they toured in support of. After they finally broke up in 1996, Cleopatra Records issued the tribute album *Reflections in the Looking Glass*, in which various US indie bands offered their own interpretations of songs associated with the group.

SISTER SLEDGE

Debbie Sledge, b. 1955, Philadelphia, Pennsylvania, USA; Joni Sledge, b. 1957, Philadelphia; Kathy Sledge, b. 1959, Philadelphia; Kim Sledge, b. 1958, Philadelphia

A disco-soul vocal group, Sister Sledge's greatest impact came with 'We Are Family'* (1979), produced by **Nile Rodgers** and Bernard Edwards, which became the anthem of both gay rights' activists and the Pittsburgh Pirates baseball team.

From a musical family (their grandmother had been an opera singer), the girls performed in church from an early age. They were still only aged between twelve and sixteen when (as Sisters Sledge) they recorded the Marty Bryant-produced 'Time Will Tell' (1971) for the Philadelphia Money Back label. The quartet also sang backing vocals on recording sessions for **Gamble and Huff** before signing to Atlantic in 1973.

Their first singles for the company, 'The Weatherman' and the British hit 'Mama Never Told Me' (1975), were produced in Philly-soul style by Tony Bell but later records were made in New York with Tony Sylvester. *Circle of Love* (Atco, 1975) and *Together* (Cotillion, 1977) sold poorly and it was not until 'He's the Greatest Dancer' (1979) and 'We Are Family' that they enjoyed pop success. The first of Rodgers and Edwards' hits as producers, the records influenced the sound of much disco music over the following few years.

The Chic duo produced *Love Somebody Today* but were replaced by **Narada Michael Walden** for *All American Girls* (1981). In the following year Sister Sledge had a Top Thirty hit with a revival of Mary Wells' 1964 hit 'My Guy'. *When the Boys Meet the Girls* (1985) gave the group a British No. 1 with the jaunty 'Frankie', but the group were unable to maintain their momentum and subsequent releases sold poorly. 'Here to Stay' (Parlophone, 1988) was taken from the film *Playing for Keeps*. The sisters' twentieth anniversary as a vocal group was marked by the release of the compilation *The Very Best of Sister Sledge* (Rhino, 1993), which included inferior remixes of some of their finest moments. It was a Top Thirty hit. Earlier Kathy Sledge released her own solo album, *Heart* (Epic, 1992).

RONI SIZE

b. 1968, England

Bristol jungle producer Size's Reprazent collective created the genre's first genuine crossover success in the album market with *New Forms* (1997), which gained jungle an audience outside its underground clubs and specialist record shops.

The son of Jamaican immigrants, Size grew up in Bristol. His first musical influences were his brothers' collections of Studio One reggae, soul and rare groove, but it was the eighties hip-hop film *Wild Style* which inspired him to become a DJ. Expelled from school at the age of sixteen, he attended parties organized by the local Wild Bunch sound system, which was later to evolve into **Massive Attack**, and decided to set up a DJ sound system of his own.

Through this he met another local soul and hip-hop fan, DJ Krust. Krust had previously been part of the Fresh 4, which had enjoyed a club and UK Top Ten hit in 1989 with a cover of **Rose Royce**'s 'Wishing on a Star'. Size and Krust began writing together in 1992. The pair's early work was picked up by Bryan G and Jumpin' Jack Frost's V Recordings label, but in 1993 Size and Krust formed their own label, Full Cycle, with two other like-minded DJs, DJ Die and DJ Suv. Suv, like Krust, had earlier been part of the Fresh 4.

The group shared similar musical tastes, but were also being inspired by the breakbeat house and jungle scene emerging in the UK in the early 1990s, and by London DJs like Fabio and Grooverider. But while those DJs were creating a new sound by speeding up drum loops from house or hip-hop records, the Full Cycle crew approached from a lighter, jazzier angle. Early recordings were sparse, featuring light, deliberately non-aggressive percussion, and, taking a cue from reggae, made use of a warm bass sound.

The future direction of the group was most clearly marked out on Size's 'It's a Jazz Thing' and DJ Krust's 'Jazz Note' (both V Recordings). A compilation of Full Cycle recordings, *Music Box*, appeared in 1996, the same year Size and his collective signed to Gilles Peterson's Talkin Loud label as Reprazent. Reprazent's *Reasons for Sharing* EP was released in November 1996 and featured singer Onallee on the lead track, 'Share the Fall'. The use of a vocalist was a departure for the group, and a sign of what was to follow on their 1997 album, *New Forms*. On the album, the sparse textures of the earlier Full Cycle material were embellished with samples and acoustic bass, most strikingly on the superior 'Brown Paper Bag'. Onallee appeared on four tracks, including the singles 'Heroes' and 'Watching Windows', while the title track featured US female rapper Bahamadia.

The long album – it was over two hours long – met with universal critical acclaim, praised for extending the boundaries of jungle, or drum'n'bass as it was becoming known. *New Forms* was a surprise winner of the UK's prestigious Mercury Music Prize in 1997. Its victory heralded the arrival of jungle as a musical form taken seriously by the mainstream and gained Size and Reprazent a following outside jungle's UK homeland, notably among New York's house aristocracy. **Masters at Work**'s Nu Yorican Soul project was also signed to Talkin Loud, and Size remixed one of the singles from the *Nu Yorican Soul* album, 'It's Alright, I Feel It'.

Size re-emerged in 1999 with a new drum'n'bass project, Breakbeat Era, working with Reprazent's DJ Die and female vocalist Leonie Laws. The three had already collaborated as Scorpio on a track called 'Breakbeat Era', which appeared on the 1996 *Music Box* compilation. The group, which aimed for a tougher sound than Reprazent, released *Ultra Obscene* (XL Recordings, 1999).

Size and Reprazent's follow-up album, *In the Mode* (2000), had a mixed reception. The menacing 'Out of the Game' and the wry 'Play the Game' were powerful offerings, but too much of the album was lightweight sloganizing.

RICKY SKAGGS
b. 18 July 1954, Cordell, Kentucky, USA

More than any other artist of the eighties, Skaggs restored to country music a part of the strength it derives from its own sense and use of tradition – a tradition that had often, in the sixties and seventies, been ignored or scorned by both artists and producers intent on creating a country music more closely aligned with mainstream American pop. Skaggs was well placed to figure in a 'roots' movement, having started his career playing rigorously authentic bluegrass. Unlike some contemporaries with similar credentials, however, he preserved the values of that music, as well as much of its repertoire and style, in his own, and gained remarkable international success at the cost of few artistic compromises.

The son of amateur musicians in eastern Kentucky, Skaggs began playing at the age of five, first mandolin, then guitar and fiddle. At seven he performed on **Flatt and Scruggs**' TV show, and at fifteen he joined Ralph Stanley (of the **Stanley Brothers**) as mandolin player and vocalist. With his fellow teenage member of the Clinch Mountain Boys, singer/guitarist Keith Whitley, he cut his first album in 1971, *Tribute to the Stanley Brothers* (Jalyn), followed by another Whitley–Skaggs collaboration, *Second Generation Bluegrass* (Rebel, 1972), and, in his own name, *That's It* (Rebel, 1975). By that time he had worked with the Washington DC bluegrass band the Country Gentlemen (1972–4) and with banjo-player J. D. Crowe's New South (1974–5), recording with both, for Vanguard and Rounder, respectively.

In 1975 he formed the progressive bluegrass group Boone Creek, which expressed some of his interest in styles outside bluegrass, such as Western swing and honky-tonk. The band recorded for Rounder (*Boone Creek*, 1977) and Sugar Hill (*One Way Track*, 1978) and then broke up. Skaggs next joined **Emmylou Harris**'s Hot Band, arranging her bluegrass album *Roses in the Snow* (Warner, 1980). Harris appeared on his critically regarded *Sweet Temptation* (Sugar Hill,

1979), as did singer/guitarist Tony Rice, a colleague from New South days who joined him in the duo album *Skaggs and Rice* (Sugar Hill, 1980) to re-create the style of the country brother acts of the past. Skaggs was also playing with the Whites, a family singing group (father Buck and daughters Sharon and Cheryl) whose Warner records he produced.

In 1981 he married Sharon White, signed with Epic and recorded *Waitin' for the Sun to Shine*, which topped the country charts. Subsequent sets *Highways and Heartaches* (1983), *Don't Cheat in Our Hometown* (1984) and *Country Boy* (1984) all reproduced that success and received gold awards for US sales. Skaggs also had major chart hits with several singles from these albums, notably **Bill Monroe**'s song 'Uncle Pen' (from *Don't Cheat in Our Hometown*), the first bluegrass number by a solo artist ever to reach No. 1 in *Billboard*'s country charts. In 1985 Skaggs toured Europe, recording his most exciting album, *Live in London* (Epic, 1985), with a guest appearance by **Elvis Costello**.

Love's Gonna Get Ya! (Epic, 1986) featured, amidst more conventional country and bluegrass repertoire, a duet with **James Taylor**. 'Love Can't Ever Get Better Than This', a duet with White, earned them a Country Music Association award in 1987 as Vocal Duo of the Year. Skaggs himself seldom failed to carry away several titles at each of the annual CMA awards ceremonies for several years after 1982, the year in which he was also inducted as the youngest member of the *Grand Ole Opry*. He later released *Comin' Home to Stay* (1988) and *Kentucky Thunder* (1989). The same year, he produced **Dolly Parton**'s *White Limozeen*.

The sales of 1991's excellent *My Father's Son* failed to match his critical reputation. In 1993 he was named chairman of the campaign to build an international bluegrass music museum in Kentucky. *Solid Ground* (1995), his first album for Atlantic, which included a version of Harry Chapin's 'Cat's in the Cradle', was a return to commercial and critical form. He followed that with the ultra-traditional *Bluegrass Rules!* (1997) on his own Skaggs label and in 1998 appeared with a host of country stars on Columbia's *Tribute to Tradition* album.

THE SKATALITES
Roland Alphonso; Lloyd Brevette; Don Drummond, d. 21 April 1971; Jah Gerry; Lloyd Knibbs; Tommy McCook; Jackie Mittoo, b. 1948; Johnny Moore; Lester Stirling

Instrumental group the Skatalites were the foremost exponents of ska music in Jamaica. As well as making their own recordings, the band accompanied such performers as the Wailers, **Toots and the Maytals** and **Derrick Morgan**.

The group was led by tenor-sax-player McCook, who, like Drummond, learned music at Alpha Boys School in Kingston and also played with Count Ossie's Rastafarian drummers. From 1954 to 1962 he played in a dance band in Nassau, Bahamas.

Ska itself developed when Jamaican sound-system operators like **Coxsone Dodd** moved into record production, employing local musicians to emulate the New Orleans R&B of **Fats Domino** and **Dave Bartholomew**. The style added to rhythm and blues the guitar and syncopated bass of the earlier mento (a kind of Jamaican calypso), giving an emphasis to the after-beat of each bar. McCook's group with Drummond (trombone), Mittoo (piano), Moore (trumpet), Alphonso and Stirling (saxes) added jazz elements, while Brevette (bass) and Knibbs (drums) prefigured later reggae rhythm sections in their playing. The first band to play ska live as well as on record, the Skatalites' earliest hits for Dodd included 'Road Block' and the film theme 'Exodus'. They also recorded 'Dick Tracy', 'Independent Anniversary Ska' and 'Sandy Gully'.

The group went on to make records for Duke Reid's Treasure Isle label ('Twelve Minutes to Go') and Phillip Yapp's Top Deck (*Ska Boo Da Ba*). Their only British hit was 'Guns of Navarone'. Recorded in 1965 and released in 1967 by Island with vocals by **Lee Perry** it was their most representative recording. The Skatalites' outstanding soloist was Drummond, whose playing on such tracks as 'Man in the Street', 'Confucius' and 'Treasure Isle' justified his reputation as a world-class jazz trombonist. His career was ended by mental illness and he committed suicide in 1971.

The Skatalites dissolved in late 1965, with Mittoo becoming Dodd's house producer and Alphonso forming the Soul Brothers, and enjoying a solo hit with 'Phoenix City' (Doctor Bird, 1966). McCook recorded the rock-steady hit 'Last Train to Expo 67' with the Melodians. In 1975 the group briefly reformed and recorded *African Roots* (United Artists, 1977). In 1984 a version of the band re-formed for the Sunsplash concerts in Jamaica and Britain and recorded *Scattered Lights*. The later *Stretching out* (1986) consisted for the most part of versions of songs associated with them. In 1989 the group toured Japan with **Prince Buster** as guest vocalist.

Buster, Toots Hibbert (of **Toots and the Maytals**) and Lester Bowie were among the guest performers on *Hi-Bop Ska* (Shanakhie, 1994), which found McCook and Alphonso on top form.

PETER SKELLERN
b. 1947, Bury, Lancashire, England

Songwriter, singer and pianist, Skellern had a series of hits in the seventies with quirky pop songs delivered with an unusual mix of balladeer (**Hoagy Carmichael**) and English regional inflection (**George Formby**). Later in his career, he concentrated on stage and television appearances.

He graduated from London's Guildhall College of Music in 1968 and after a brief career as a concert pianist joined rock band Harlan County and recorded for the British label Nashville in 1971. He subsequently signed to Decca, releasing the Top Ten hit 'You're a Lady' (1972), which featured a brass band and a lush string arrangement behind his plaintive voice. The song was later covered by **Johnny Mathis**, Telly Savalas and Jack Jones.

The Derek Taylor-produced *Not without a Friend* (1973) mixed ragtime tunes and intimate ballads while *Holding My Own* (1974) paid homage to music-hall comedy. The rock backing of 'Hold on to Love' (1975) gave him a Top Twenty hit and in the same year Skellern moved to Island for *Hard Times* (1975), produced by Meyer Shagaloff. In 1977 he moved to Mercury for the Geoffrey Haslam-produced *Kissing in the Cactus*, which included a revival of 'Love Is the Sweetest Thing', with accompaniment from the Grimethorpe Colliery Band.

Among later albums were *Astaire* (1979), an album of songs associated with **Fred Astaire**, and *A String of Pearls* (1982). In 1984 he formed the short-lived group Oasis with Mary Hopkin and cellist Julian Lloyd-Webber, brother of Andrew. Skellern also composed theme songs for British television series, including *Me and My Girl* (1987). After *Lovelight* in 1987, Skellern largely abandoned his recording career.

SKID ROW
Dave 'The Snake' Sabo; Sebastian Bach, b. Sebastian Bierk, 3 April 1968, Bahamas; Scotti Hill; Rob Affuso; Rachel Bolan, b. 9 February 1964

This US five-piece found almost immediate success with their formulaic hard rock in the late eighties and early nineties following their virtual adoption by Jon Bon Jovi.

New Jersey-born guitarist Sabo and bassist Bolan formed Skid Row in 1986 when they split the band they were in and recruited local drummer Affuso and second guitarist Hill. Demos were recorded, then vocalist Bach was poached from Toronto-based glammetal band Madam X, completing Skid Row's lineup. Sabo approached his childhood friend Jon Bon Jovi, then enjoying massive success worldwide with his band's distinctive brand of pop-metal, and asked him to help with the project. Skid Row were swiftly signed to **Bon Jovi**'s management company, and shortly after that signed to Atlantic Records. The band were introduced to US audiences on Bon Jovi's

1989 tour, the year they released their first album, *Skid Row*. The album was a skilful blend of hard-rock influences such as **Kiss** and **Motley Crüe** plus the more commercial elements of punk rock – particularly Bolan's guitar style, which was reminiscent of the **Sex Pistols**' Steve Jones.

The combination of commercial hard rock and a classic 'wasted' rock'n'roll image, with frontman Bach's teen idol looks and manic on-stage demeanour, proved irresistible to US audiences, who swiftly put the album into the Top Ten. The band also enjoyed two US Top Ten singles in 1989 and made the album chart in the UK following a UK visit supporting Bon Jovi. However, the relationship with Bon Jovi soured following a dispute over publishing royalties. Various legal problems delayed the recording of the band's second album, which did not appear until 1991. *Slave to the Grind*, a major step forward for the band in its embracing of metal and rejection of the poppier, Bon Jovi-esque elements of their début album, delighted critics and widened Skid Row's audience, with the album achieving multi-platinum status in the US.

In 1992 Atlantic issued an EP collecting their non-album B-sides, *B-Sides Ourselves*. *Subhuman Race* followed in 1995. A return to their earlier style, it was the least successful of their later albums.

SKUNK ANANSIE
Ace; Cass; Mark; Skin

Drawing on the heavily politicized sounds of **Public Enemy** and **Rage Against the Machine**, Skunk Anansie became one of the most popular British guitar bands of the mid-nineties with their blend of fierce rock and anthemic balladry.

Comprising vocalist Skin, guitarist Ace, bassist Cass and drummer Mark, Skunk Anansie signed to One Little Indian within five months of their formation in London, England, in 1994, releasing 'Selling Jesus' and 'I Can Dream' to mild acclaim. *Paranoid and Sunburnt* (1995) soon achieved gold status on the strength of breakthrough single 'Weak', which entered the UK Top Twenty.

The band toured constantly for the next year, earning support slots with the likes of the **Sex Pistols** and **Lenny Kravitz**, which helped them to build up an impressive international following. *Stoosh* (1996) was a more controlled affair than their début, veering from the aggressive metal of 'Yes, It's Fucking Political' to the graceful, string-laden single 'Hedonism (Just Because It Feels Good)', which became their biggest hit to date. Skunk Anansie returned in 1999 with their third album, *Post Orgasmic Chill*, spawning 'Charlie Big Potato', which made the UK Top Ten in the same week that the band headlined the final night at the last Glastonbury festival of the millennium.

SKY
Herbie Flowers; Tristan Fry; Francis Monkman (replaced by Steve Gray); Kevin Peek, b. Australia; John Williams, b. Melbourne, Australia

A group composed of virtuosi from both the classical and rock spheres, Sky recorded a series of successful instrumental albums in the early eighties.

Already established as a leading acoustic guitar soloist for his performances and recordings of Bach, **Malcolm Arnold**, Rodrigo and others, Williams recorded *Changes* (Fly, 1977), an album of popular pieces arranged by Stanley Myers and *Travelling* (1978), produced by session bassist Flowers.

The success of that album led the pair to found Sky to perform soft-rock arrangements of classical themes. They added former Curved Air keyboards-player Monkman, session guitarist Peek and top percussionist Fry, who had played with the London Philharmonic Orchestra as well as with **Peter Skellern** and **Frank Sinatra**. With a mixture of their own compositions ('Westway') and such classical pieces as 'Gymnopedies' by Eric Satie (whose work had also been recorded by **Frank Zappa** and **Blood, Sweat and Tears**), *Sky* (Ariola, 1979) reached the British Top Ten.

Sky 2 (1980) was a double-album which went to No. 1 in Britain and featured Monkman's 'Fifo' and the British Top Ten hit 'Toccata'. International tours were followed by further hit albums, *Sky 3* (1981) and *Forthcoming* (1982). Later records like *Cadmium* (1983) and *The Great Balloon Race* (Epic, 1985) were less successful. By this time Williams had left and session musician Gray had replaced Monkman. The group subsequently broke up and the individual members returned to their solo careers.

SLADE
Noddy Holder, b. Neville Holder, 15 June 1946, Walsall, England; Dave Hill, b. 4 April 1950, Fleet Castle; Jimmy Lea, b. 14 June 1950, Wolverhampton; Don Powell, b. 10 September 1950, Bilston

Thunderous British rockers of the early seventies, Slade are best remembered for Holder's screaming vocals and the felicitous liberties they took with the English language in their song titles ('Mama Weer All Crazee Now', 'Gudbuy T'Jane', 1972, and the classic 'Cum on Feel the Noize', 1973). The group survived the end of Slade mania, like **Gary Glitter**, by mocking their earlier threatening image and transforming themselves into cheerful celebrators of the rock'n'roll tradition, along the way returning their 1973 Christmas chart-topper 'Merry Xmas Everybody'* to the British charts no less than eight times in subsequent years.

Formed in Wolverhampton at the height of the British beat boom in 1965 as the 'N Betweens, Hill, Lea, Holder and Powell were all veterans of various semi-professional bands. They first recorded under the auspices of **Kim Fowley** for British Columbia in 1966 (a cover of the [**Young**] **Rascals**' 'You Better Run') and in 1969 signed with Fontana as Ambrose Slade. Their début album, *Beginnings*, saw them performing material associated with **Frank Zappa** and the **Moody Blues**, but their live performances were firmly in the rock'n'roll tradition of **The Beatles**. Signed by Chas Chandler, a one-time member of the **Animals** who had gone into management (most successfully with **Jimi Hendrix**), the group's name was shortened to Slade and they were given a new, aggressive 'bovver boy' skinhead image. It brought them notoriety but little success until in 1971 they scored their first hit with 'Get Down and Get with It' (Polydor), a revival of a song by Bobby Marchan (one-time singer with **Huey 'Piano' Smith**). That was a prelude to a series of stomping chants as often heard echoing around Britain's football grounds as on the radio. All penned by Holder and Lea, Slade's hits included six British No. 1s, 'Coz I Luv You' (1971) – successfully revived by American heavy-metal group Quiet Riot (Pasha, 1983) – 'Take Me Bak 'Ome', 'Mama Weer All Crazee Now', 'Gudbuy T'Jane' (1972), 'Cum on Feel the Noize', 'Skweeze Me, Pleeze Me' and 'Merry Xmas Everybody' (1973), and gave the group the reputation of a people's band, especially in live performance.

The film *Slade in Flame* (1974) saw them attempting to broaden their audience but a failed attempt to conquer America in 1975–6 lost them their British audience to the new punk groups. Regular appearances in the charts with 'Merry Xmas Everybody' and constant touring kept the group together until the EP *Slade Alive at Reading '80* (Cheap, 1980) saw their successful reincarnation as a jolly, rather than posturing, heavy-metal band. They continued throughout the eighties with sporadic chart success, including their first successes in America, with 'Run Runaway' and 'My Oh My' (Columbia), both Top Forty hits in 1984. Slade's subsequent British RCA releases ('7 Year Bitch', 'Do You Believe in Miracles', 1985) were only minor hits and the group, like their sixties beat-boom contemporaries, took to the club circuit where their once-threatening songs were greeted with affectionate nostalgia.

Slade made another attempt at recapturing past glories with *You Boyz Make Big Noize* (RCA, 1987), but when it flopped, they decided to split up. Holder became a local success in Birmingham as a radio deejay, but willingly re-formed the band in 1991. The British Top Thirty single 'Radio Wall of Sound' (1991) heralded a return to Polydor and was included on the compilation *Wall of Hits*, the first of many that would follow, later that year. Holder subsequently left the group again but the others persevered as Slade II. That group had muted success with *Emergency* (1993) and *Keep on Rockin'* (1996). However, sales of those paled beside those of *Feel the Noize – Greatest Hits* (1996). Holder successfully brought his cheerful tough-guy image first to radio as a disc jockey and then to television, first as a regular on game shows and quizzes and then as an actor in the British television comedy series *The Grimleys*.

PERCY SLEDGE
b. 25 November 1941, Leighton, Alabama, USA

With his clear, majestic phrasing, Sledge's début recording 'When a Man Loves a Woman'* (1966) was one of the great soul anthems of the mid-sixties. It confirmed his mastery of the country-influenced Southern soul style.

He sang in school and in church before joining the Esquires Combo while working as a nurse. In 1966 local disc-jockey Quin Ivy recorded Sledge on the slow, melodic ballad 'When a Man Loves a Woman' with Spooner Oldham on Farfisa organ. Released through Atlantic, the record topped both R&B and pop charts and inspired the progressive rock hit 'A Whiter Shade of Pale' (1967) by **Procul Harum**. **Bobby Robinson**'s 'Warm and Tender Love' used the same formula and included **Sandy Posey** among the backing vocalists.

Oldham and **Dan Penn** composed two of Sledge's best records, 'It Tears Me Up' (1966) and 'Out of Left Field' (1967) and he followed these with a string of singles which were R&B successes but only minor pop hits. They included 'Love Me Tender' (1967), the magisterial 'Take Time to Know Her' (1968), which reached the pop Top Twenty, and 'Any Day Now' (1969), a revival of Chuck Jackson's 1962 hit.

Sledge's potent mix of country and soul was out of fashion in the seventies, but he continued to record for Atlantic (the wonderful 'Stop the World Tonight', 1970, and **Kris Kristofferson**'s 'Help Me Make It Through the Night') while *I'll Be Your Everything* (Capricorn, 1974) showed an especially strong country input. George Soule's title song was an R&B Top Twenty hit and other tracks included versions of **Charlie Rich**'s 'Behind Closed Doors' and **Dallas Frazier**'s 'If This Is the Last Time'.

In the late seventies and eighties Sledge continued to perform in the South, re-recording his hits for Stan Shulman's Kilo label in 1980 and making a country-orientated album for Monument, *Wanted Again* (1987). In 1987 'When a Man Loves a Woman' was again a British hit after being used in a TV commercial for jeans. Sledge's first album of new songs for many years was *Blue Night* (1994), on which he was accompanied by **Bobby Womack**, Steve Cropper (of **Booker T. and the MGs**) and former **Rolling Stones** guitarist Mick Taylor.

It Tears Me Up (Rhino, 1992) is the definitive career retrospective.

P. F. SLOAN
b. Philip Greg Schlein, 1944, New York, New York, USA

Sloan had only one minor hit, 'Sins of a Family' (1965), but he has an assured place in the history of popular music as the composer of **Barry McGuire**'s 'Eve of Destruction'* (1965), the song that – with the **Byrds**' 'Mr Tambourine Man' (1965) – signalled the decisive impact of **Bob Dylan** on rock. He was also the subject of **Jimmy Webb**'s evocative 'P. F. Sloan'.

When in 1964 **Lou Adler** set up his Dunhill productions, his first signings were songwriters and tyro producers Sloan and Steve Barri. They had an immediate local hit in California with 'Tell 'Em I'm Surfin'' (Imperial, 1965) as the Fantastic Baggys and recorded and produced the cult classic *Surfin' Craze*. Later that year, influenced by the protest songs of Dylan, Sloan wrote 'Eve' which, when gruffly declaimed by former member of the New Christy Minstrels McGuire, gave Adler's newly established label its first American No. 1. The first protest song to attract a mass pop audience beyond the folk-music fraternity, it was attacked by many and received the accolade of a right-wing answer record, 'Dawn of Correction' (Decca, 1965), by former members of **Danny and the Juniors**, Johnny Madara and Dave White, as the Spokesmen. Sloan and Barri provided McGuire with an eponymous album and several follow-ups to little avail. Equally unsuccessful, but more interesting as a period piece, was Sloan's own *Songs of Our Times* (Dunhill, 1965) which revealed an even deeper debt to Dylan.

Still in partnership with Barri, Sloan turned to production for the Grass Roots and wrote songs for the **Turtles** ('You Baby', 1966), the **Searchers**, **Herman's Hermits** and others before in 1972 Sloan and Barri split up. Barri continued as a producer of a wide range of acts (from **Bobby Bland** to **Cher**), while Sloan returned to performing. His **Tom Dowd**-produced *Measure of Pleasure* (Atco, 1968) was more elliptical, revealing the influence of **Fred Neil**, but still firmly in the protest vein of his earlier work. *Raised on Records* (Epic, 1972) was a lesser work which saw Sloan attempting to become a more intimate singer-songwriter. After that, Sloan's disappearance from the music business inspired 'P. F. Sloan', in which Webb contrasted Sloan's 'Eve of Destruction' and its strong, if simple, protest about social ills, with the depoliticized songwriting of the early seventies when 'Nixon's come and bound to stay'.

Later sightings of Sloan included an appearance at a New York songwriters concert in 1993 with **Taj Mahal**. *Anthology* (1993) collects together his most representative recordings.

SLY AND ROBBIE
Sly Dunbar, b. Lowell Fillmore Dunbar, 10 May 1952, Kingston, Jamaica; Robbie Shakespeare, b. 27 September 1953, Kingston

Jamaica's most prolific session musicians, Sly and Robbie graduated from reggae's best-known rhythm section to become leading producers of dub music in the eighties. Subsequently they played on albums by many top rock artists.

Shakespeare heard American music on the radio as a child but his first major influence was **Bob Marley**'s bass-player Aston Barrett, whom Shakespeare succeeded in the Hippie Boys in 1970. Dunbar had been a follower of **Skatalites**' drummer Lloyd Knibbs before working during the mid-seventies with Shakespeare in the Revolutionaries, the house band of Channel One studio. In this capacity they defined the militant sound that swept Jamaica in the mid-seventies. Also in the band was keyboards-player Ansil Collins, who recorded the British No. 1 'Double Barrel' (Technique, 1971) with his brother Dave. On records by the Mighty Diamonds, the Wailing Souls, I Roy and others, the Revolutionaries developed a style known as 'Rockers'. At its heart was the close-knit bass and drum rhythm, with the drum sound characterized by extensive use of rim-shots.

The duo formed the Taxi label in the mid-seventies and their first single, 'Soon Forward', with **Gregory Isaacs** on vocals, was a Jamaican No. 1. As Word Sound and Power, Sly and Robbie backed **Peter Tosh** on *Legalise It* (1976) and toured with the ex-Wailer. They also accompanied **Jimmy Cliff**, **Burning Spear**, **Big Youth** and Bunny Wailer. By 1979 Dunbar was experimenting with an electronic drum kit and the resulting sound, scattered with random squeaks and clangs, once more revolutionized reggae rhythms. As producers, Sly and Robbie worked with leading Jamaican harmony group Black Uhuru (Puma Jones, Michael Rose and Duckie Simpson) on *Sinsemilla* (1980), *Red* (1981) and *Chill Out* (1982). In 1980 Taxi signed an international distribution deal with **Chris Blackwell**'s Island company.

By the eighties Sly and Robbie were in demand for sessions with such rock singers as **Grace Jones** (*Warm Leatherette*, 1980), **Ian Dury** (*Lord Upminster*, 1981) and **Bob Dylan** (*Empire Burlesque*, 1985). They also played on tracks by **Fela Kuti**, remixed by **Bill Laswell** who in turn collaborated on the Sly and Robbie album, *Language Barrier* (Celluloid, 1985).

In 1987 they released the Laswell-produced *Rhythm*

Killers, whose guest performers included former **George Clinton** associate Bootsy Collins and New York rap vocalist Shinehead. The album provided a British hit in 'Boops (Here to Go)'. *The Summit* was released in 1988 and *Silent Assassin I* (1990) was produced by American rapper KRS-1.

DJ Riot (1990) included vocals by Jamaican raggamuffin artists. The duo also produced 'Twist and Shout' and other tracks by Chaka Demus and Pliers, one of several reggae artists whose work crossed over into the British pop charts in the early nineties. Later productions included *Man with the Fun* (Maxi Priest, 1996), *Passion* (Lady Saw) and *It's on Tonight* (Sam Salter, both 1997).

THE SMALL FACES
Ronnie Lane, b. 1 April 1946, London, England; Steve Marriott, b. 30 January 1947, London, d. 20 April 1991, Arkeston, Essex; Kenny Jones, b. 16 September 1948, London; Jimmy Winston (replaced 1965 by Ian McLagan, b. 12 May 1945, London, d. 4 June 1997, England

Named for their slight height and desire to be, in mod parlance, a 'face' – as in **The Who**'s early recording, 'I'm the Face' (1964) – the Small Faces were the British mod group *par excellence*. From the beginning Marriott and Lane wrote most of the group's material, including 'All or Nothing' (1966) – a classic example of 'blue-eyed soul' – and, like the **Kinks**' Ray Davies, developed a particularly English style of songwriting, notably on 'Itchycoo Park'* (1967) and 'Lazy Sunday' (1968). However, the group were unable to make the transition from chart band to album group and broke up in the mid-sixties. Marriott joined **Peter Frampton** to form Humble Pie and the rest of the group, as the Faces, became **Rod Stewart**'s backing band.

A child actor who, like **Phil Collins**, appeared in **Lionel Bart**'s *Oliver* in the role of the Artful Dodger, Marriott met bassist Lane in 1965, discovering a shared interest in R&B and soul. With the addition of organist Winston and drummer Jones the quartet became the Small Faces. Like countless other British beat groups they began playing R&B and soul – even to the extent of 'borrowing' the riff from **Solomon Burke**'s 'Every Body Needs Somebody to Love' for their first recording, 'Whacha Gonna Do About It' (Decca, 1965). Produced and co-written by Ian Samwell, one-time guitarist with **Cliff Richard** and composer of Richard's first hit 'Move It' (1958), the record was a hit, as was the Mort Shuman (of **Pomus and Shuman**) and Kenny Lynch composition 'Sha La La La Lee' (1966), which featured McLagan (from Boz and the Boz People) on Hammond organ. If McLagan's arrival deepened the group's sound, the decisive shift came when Marriott and Lane took over responsibility for their material. After 'Hey Girl', the impassioned 'All or Nothing' and the imaginative 'My Mind's Eye' (1966), for their first release on Immediate they produced 'Here Comes the Nice' (1967), one of the few drugs songs (about amphetamine, *the* mod drug) not to be banned.

The superior *Ogden's Nut Gone Flake* (1968) was notable for its intricate sleeve (one of the first of the complex sleeves that soon became the norm for rock albums), its early use of phasing and Stanley Unwin's linking narrative (in his usual twisted English) on side two. But, though it topped the British album charts, it was overshadowed by the success of 'Itchycoo Park', the group's only significant American hit. Originally intended as a parody of Scott McKenzie's 'San Francisco (Be Sure to Wear Flowers in Your Hair)'* (Ode, 1967) – 'I feel inclined to blow my mind, get hung up, feed the ducks with a bun' – the song has since become the archetypal example of English psychedelia. Sung in broad cockney, 'Lazy Sunday' (1968) looked back to the music-hall tradition of London's East End. But, after the relative failure of 'The Universal' (1968), Marriott left to form Humble Pie with Frampton in 1969. After one more album, *Autumn Stone* (1969), an engaging collection of their Immediate singles and live recordings, the rest of the group joined Stewart as the Faces.

Humble Pie (Marriott, Frampton, Greg Ridley from Spooky Tooth and Jerry Shirley) had an immediate hit with 'Natural Born Bugie' (Immediate, 1969), but from the start the band's sound was an uneasy compromise between the straight-ahead rock of Marriott and the gentler, acoustic inclinations of Frampton. Their best albums were *Humble Pie* (A&M, 1970), which included Marriott's witty account of the demise of Immediate, 'Theme from Skint (See You Later Liquidator)', and the raucous *Live at the Fillmore* (1971), after which Frampton left for a solo career. The group continued (*Thunderbox*, 1974, *Street Rats*, 1975) until Marriott too left for a solo career (*Marriott*, 1976). Marriott and Shirley resurrected the Humble Pie name in 1980, releasing two albums (*On to Victory*, 1980, and *Go for the Throat*, 1981) before disbanding.

Having elected to form the Faces with one-time members of the **Jeff Beck** group Stewart and Ron Wood, in preference to working as a backing group, the remaining Small Faces saw themselves becoming just that as Stewart's solo career took off. They recorded with Stewart as the Faces (*First Step*, 1970, *Long Player*, 1971, and *A Nod's as Good as a Wink to a Blind Horse*, 1971, which included the hit 'Stay with Me') but more often were reduced to being his support on lengthy American tours. This led to Lane leaving after *Ooh La La* in 1973 to form the folky-sounding Slim Chance with whom he recorded three albums and had two surprise hit singles in Britain, 'How Long' and 'The Poacher' (1974). He recorded the album *Rough Mix* (1977) with **The Who**'s Pete Townshend (like Lane, a follower of guru Meher Baba) and his own solo album, *See Me* (Gem, 1979), before his career was affected by multiple sclerosis. He moved to America in the mid-eighties, where he continued to play occasional live dates when his illness permitted.

Lane was replaced by Japanese bassist Tetsu Yamauchi (formerly with **Free**), who played on the live album *Overture and Beginners* (1974) and two singles, before the Faces split in the wake of Rod Stewart's departure in 1975. With both Marriott's career and the Faces' in decline (and Wood joining the **Rolling Stones**), the original members of the Small Faces briefly re-formed, without Lane, after the success of the reissue of 'Itchycoo Park' (1975) and 'Lazy Sunday' (1976) for a series of lacklustre albums: *Playmates* (Atlantic, 1977, which featured **Joe Brown** on guitar), *78 in the Shade* (1978) and *For Your Delight* (Virgin, 1980). McLagan released two solo albums (*Troublemaker*, 1979, and *Bump in the Night*, 1980) and in the eighties regularly gigged with the Rolling Stones, while concentrating on session work. Jones replaced Keith Moon as The Who's drummer, and later formed the Law with ex-**Bad Company** vocalist Paul Rodgers. Marriott continued to play London's pub and club circuit and in 1989 released the uneven *30 Seconds to Midnight* (Trax), his first studio recording for several years.

Marriott teamed up with Frampton again in 1990, recording demos for a proposed Humble Pie reunion. The project was scrapped after Marriott's death in a house fire in 1991, but some recordings surfaced on later Frampton albums.

The definitive retrospectives are *The Decca Anthology* (1996) and *The Immediate Years* (1995), which were followed by the tribute album *Long Agos and Worlds Apart* (1997) on which a number of indie acts, including **Ocean Colour Scene** and **Paul Weller**, contributed tracks.

SMASHING PUMPKINS
Billy Corgan, b. 17 March 1967, Chicago, Illinois, USA; Jimmy Chamberlin, b. 10 June 1964, Joilet, Illinois; James Iha, b. 26 March 1968, Elk Grove, Illinois; D'Arcy Wretzky, b. 1 May 1968, South Haven, Mississippi

One of the most successful American bands of the nineties, Smashing Pumpkins' dreamlike psychedelia paved the way for the futuristic progressive rock that **Radiohead** would later make their own.

Smashing Pumpkins formed in the late eighties when Corgan (guitar/vocals) met Iha (guitar) while working in a Chicago record store. With the addition of bassist Wretzky and drummer Chamberlin the band earned a strong live following in the Midwestern area before recording their début. *Gish* (Caroline, 1990), named after American silent actress Lillian Gish, was an imaginative blend of heavy alternative rock and forceful melodicism, underpinned by Chamberlin's jazzy time-keeping, which went on to sell over a million copies. Significantly, where other indie bands of the time mostly sought to disrupt the aural experience, *Gish* was far more roots-based, evoking the multi-layered approach of **Queen** and similar bands of that generation.

Having toured solidly for over two years Smashing Pumpkins recorded *Siamese Dream* (1993) with Butch Vig, taking inspiration from the innovation of the likes of **Jimi Hendrix** and **John Coltrane**. The album was instantly acclaimed as one of the classics of the alternative rock genre for its inventive layering of guitars and subtle use of strings. It spawned a trio of international hit singles – 'Disarm', 'Today' and 'Cherub Rock' – and achieved triple-platinum status in the US and earned the quartet a worldwide following. Its successor, the aptly titled *Mellon Collie and the Infinite Sadness* (1995), was an even more ambitious project, a two-disc set composed equally on piano and guitar and spanning over two hours of multi-textured experimentation. The release of the album led to a lengthy worldwide tour marred by the sacking of Jimmy Chamberlin in July 1996 for his continual substance abuse, which had become public after the death of touring keyboardist Jonathan Melvoin from a heroin overdose.

Corgan claimed to have exhausted the guitar-rock genre on *Mellon Collie*, opting to embrace electronica on the refined *Adore* (1998), which saw the band employ programmed percussion alongside the services of **Soundgarden**'s Matt Cameron rather than find a full-time replacement for Chamberlin. Compared to its predecessors, with sales of only three million *Adore* was seen as a commercial failure. In response to this, in mid-1999 the freshly detoxed Chamberlin returned to the fold. The group toured immediately and quickly recorded *MACHINA/The Machines of God* (2000). Another exercise in *angst*, it melded the stance of *Mellon Collie* with the elegance of *Adore* to great effect on songs like 'Stand Inside Your Love' and 'With Every Light'.

After the album's completion Wretzky was replaced by former **Hole** bassist Melissa Auf der Maur and manager Sharon Osbourne quit. *MACHINA* failed to match the critical and commercial success of its predecessors, and the band announced their decision to split up after completing an almost year-long tour. Later the same year the band issued a final album, *MACHINA II: Friends and Enemies of Modern Music*, exclusively over the internet. *MACHINA II* was made up of tracks recorded during the sessions for its predecessor.

ROY SMECK

b. 6 February 1900, Reading, Pennsylvania, USA,
d. 1994

During the first half of the twentieth century no
stringed-instrument player in popular music was
more influential than Roy Smeck. Though an enormously prolific recording artist, he affected other
musicians most through his series of bestselling
instrumental tuition books.

Raised in New York, Smeck showed an early aptitude for guitar, autoharp, banjo and ukulele. **Sol
Hoopii** inspired his Hawaiian guitar-playing, **Eddie
Lang** his flat-picking and **Harry Reser** his approach
to the banjo. Working on the RKO vaudeville circuit,
he developed an act whose showmanship compen-
sated for his not also being a vocalist: he would 'tap-
dance' with his fingers while playing the ukulele, or
play uke and harmonica at the same time – without
using a neck-rack. Early Warners' movie shorts documented his act.

With the decline of vaudeville, Smeck spent a great
deal of time in the New York studios as a session
stringed-instrument player on pop, hillbilly and
sometimes jazz and blues recordings. Among the
major artists he accompanied, most often on Hawaiian or standard guitar but also sometimes on banjo,
ukulele or harmonica, were **Vernon Dalhart**, **Carson
Robison**, **King Oliver** and **Clarence Williams**. He
also led, well into the thirties, a series of small groups,
including his Vita Trio, playing Hawaiian treatments
of current popular material. Throughout, he was
publishing his many instructional books.

Smeck continued to be active into the sixties,
recording albums for ABC-Paramount, Kapp (*Roy
Smeck and His Magic Uke*, 1965) and other labels.

BESSIE SMITH

b. 15 April 1894, Chattanooga, Tennessee, USA,
d. 26 September 1937, Clarksdale, Mississippi

The greatest of all the women who have sung the
blues, Bessie Smith brought to the idiom, on material
of very variable quality and style, an unmatched
intensity of expression, subtlety of inflection and
beauty of tone. By her example she imparted lessons
in phrasing to jazz instrumentalists, as well as designing a model of blues singing for her contemporaries
and successors, from **Billie Holiday** and **Dinah
Washington** to **Janis Joplin**.

Smith developed her skills during the second
decade of the century in travelling shows, working for
a time with **Ma Rainey**. In the early twenties she
worked with bands and in vaudeville in Atlantic City
and Philadelphia, before embarking on a recording
career with Columbia in 1923. She was promptly suc-

cessful with 'Down Hearted Blues'/'Gulf Coast Blues'*
(the B-side of which had been a hit the previous year
for Alberta Hunter on Paramount) and its follow-ups,
generally accompanied on piano by **Clarence
Williams** or **Fletcher Henderson**. In 1924 she initiated Columbia's new 'race' catalogue (the 14000-D
series) with 'Chicago Bound Blues', and later that year
she collaborated with **Louis Armstrong** in her
immortal version of 'The St Louis Blues'. Other
favourite accompanists were Joe Smith and Tommy
Ladnier (cornet), Charlie Green (trombone), **Don
Redman** (clarinet/alto), Buster Bailey (clarinet) and
James P. Johnson (piano).

She also recorded a few duets with her fellow
Columbia artist Clara Smith (b. c. 1894, Spartanburg,
South Carolina, d. 2 February 1935, Detroit, Michigan):
a fine singer, known as 'The Queen of the Moaners',
whose recording career spanned much the same
period (1923–32), she had no outstanding successes,
bar 'Chicago Blues' (1924).

Besides blues, Smith also recorded popular songs
like 'I Ain't Got Nobody' (1925) and **Irving Berlin**'s
'Alexander's Ragtime Band' (1927); suggestive pieces –
'I Want Ev'ry Bit of It' (1926), 'Need a Little Sugar in
My Bowl' (1931); and the mock-gospel 'On Revival
Day' (1930), but few of them approached the quality
of statuesque blues performances like 'Young
Woman's Blues' (1926) or 'Back-Water Blues' (1927,
about that year's disastrous Southern floods).

Throughout the twenties she was a headline attraction at black theatres across the country, often touring her own shows *Harlem Frolics*, *Yellow Girl Revue*,
Steamboat Days and *Happy Times*. In 1929 she made a
short film, a dramatization of her now-celebrated *St
Louis Blues*. She recorded her last Columbia sides in
1931, but two years later **John Hammond** recalled her
to cut a session for the company's subsidiary Okeh.
She was backed by **Jack Teagarden**, trumpeter
Frankie Newton, tenor saxophonist Chu Berry and,
on the roistering 'Gimme a Pigfoot', **Benny Goodman**. The four-song date found her not only in good
voice but evidently adaptable to the peppier rhythms
of what would be called the swing era. But there were
no subsequent sessions, and she returned to touring,
in more humble revues. On one such trip she was
injured in a road accident in northern Mississippi and
died, possibly from shock and delayed treatment; the
early accounts alleging racist carelessness seem to
have been mistaken.

In addition to several biographies, the best of
which is Chris Albertson's *Bessie* (1972), her life and
music inspired other writings – including Edward
Albee's 1959 play *Death of Bessie Smith* – and writers,
James Baldwin and Amiri Baraka (Leroi Jones)
among them. Her musical influence has been more
diffuse than almost any other figure in the blues: she

has been acknowledged as a model by **Mahalia Jackson**, **Odetta**, **Jimmy Rushing**, Teagarden and innumerable blueswomen. Her complete works were reissued by Columbia on five double-albums (1971–3).

ELLIOTT SMITH
b. 1969, Dallas, Texas, USA

Acclaimed singer-songwriter Smith found himself propelled into the spotlight when one of his songs was chosen as the main theme to the Matt Damon/ Robin Williams movie *Good Will Hunting*.

He achieved mild success in Northwest America as a member of Heatmiser, recording a pair of albums for Frontier Records in the early nineties (*Dead Air*, 1993, and *Cop and Speeder*, 1994). Perhaps sensing the impending demise of the band, Smith released *Roman Candle* (Cavity Search) in 1994. Moving away from the aggressive rock of Heatmiser, the album drew comparisons with **Nick Drake** and **Paul Simon** for its soft vocal style and finger-picked folk sound. The following albums, *Elliott Smith* (Kill Rock Stars, 1995) and *Either/Or* (1997), won Smith a cult following in the US.

Smith's break came when 'Miss Misery' was chosen as the theme to the hit movie *Good Will Hunting* (1997), earning him an Oscar nomination and a chance to perform the song at the 1998 Academy Awards ceremony. 'Miss Misery' found its way into the US Top Forty and sent sales of *Either/Or* towards the platinum mark.

Capitalizing on his recent mainstream exposure, Smith released *XO* (1998), which spawned a minor UK hit single, 'Waltz #2'. Moody and lo-fi, the album was as austere as ever, signalling no change of direction as Smith moved from the independent sector to the mainstream. Equally sombre was *Figure 8* (2000), which, despite a rounder sound, was essentially a collection of sixties-styled, bedsitter-type, mournful ballads.

HUEY 'PIANO' SMITH
b. 26 January 1934, New Orleans, Louisiana, USA

As a New Orleans pianist, Smith formed the stylistic link between **Professor Longhair** and **Allen Toussaint**. He is best remembered as the author and original performer of the oft-recorded 'Rockin' Pneumonia and the Boogie Woogie Flu' (1957) and 'High Blood Pressure' (1958), both good-time New Orleans party records with a strong *mardi gras* feel.

Aged fifteen, Smith joined the trio led by **Guitar Slim** and made his début solo recording in 1953 ('You Made Me Cry', Savoy). Always a hesitant vocalist, he had greater success as a session pianist, appearing on **Little Richard**'s first Specialty recordings (including 'Tutti Frutti', 1955) and records by **Lloyd Price**, **Smi-**

ley Lewis (for whom he provided the catchy introduction to 'I Hear You Knockin'', 1955) and others. When Johnny Vincent left Specialty to form his own Ace label in 1955, Smith was one of his first signings. However, it was only when Smith teamed up with the Clowns vocal group (which included Gerri Hall, Eugene Francis, Billy Roosevelt and lead singer Bobby Marchan, who in 1955 had a local hit on Ace with Smith's 'Little Chicken Wah Wah') that he had any national success, first with 'Rockin' Pneumonia' and then 'Don't You Just Know It' (1958), his biggest hit. Already dependent on Marchan's histrionics, Smith's solo career was virtually ended in 1959 when first Marchan left the Clowns and then Vincent replaced Smith and Hall's vocals on the Smith-penned 'Sea Cruise' with those of white teenager **Frankie Ford**. Further, the success of the humorous **Coasters**-like 'Rockin' Pneumonia' gave Smith a reputation as a provider of novelty material that he could not shake off and many of his subsequent recordings, such as 'Tu-ber-cu-lucas and the Sinus Blues' (1959), were derivative of his earlier hits. The power of 'Rockin' Pneumonia' was further confirmed in 1972 when **Johnny Rivers** had a million-seller with his revival of it.

In 1960 Smith joined Imperial, only to have Vincent dig out an old Smith recording, add a new vocal and give Smith his last national chart hit, 'Popeye' (1962). Though Smith continued to record throughout the sixties for local labels (including Pitter-Pat and Spinit) under various names (the Pitter Pats, the Hueys), his material remained rooted in fifties New Orleans rhythm and blues. In the seventies Smith quit music and became a gardener, only performing intermittently.

After a brief solo career (which included an impassioned reading of 'There Is Something on Your Mind', Fury, 1960), Marchan too returned to New Orleans, where he performed regularly.

JIMMY SMITH
b. James Oscar Smith, 8 December 1925, Norristown, Pennsylvania, USA

A prolific recording artist, Smith was the most prominent jazz-blues Hammond organ player of the late fifties and early sixties. His sound and his repertoire were major influences on the British R&B movement of the sixties.

His first instrument was bass but he also played piano before the example of Wild Bill Davis led to a switch to Hammond in 1953. In 1956 Smith signed to Blue Note and made a series of albums in the hard bop style with such musicians as drummer **Art Blakey**, trumpeter Lee Morgan, guitarist **Kenny Burrell** and saxophonists Hank Mobley and Stanley

Turrentine. Smith replaced the heavily chorded big-band-inspired sound of organ-led groups, like that of **Bill Doggett**, with a swirling, punchy approach which adapted for organ elements of the piano styles of Horace Silver and **Bud Powell** and which proved highly popular.

With Turrentine and Burrell he made the Top Thirty hits *Midnight Special* (1962) and *Back at the Chicken Shack* (1963) and had even greater success when he moved to Verve. There, Creed Taylor produced *Bashin'* (1962), which included a hit single version of **Elmer Bernstein**'s film theme 'Walk on the Wild Side' where Smith was accompanied by a big band directed by Oliver Nelson.

Among his other Verve albums were *Hobo Flats* (1963), *The Cat* (1964), *Organ Grinder Swing* (1965) and *Got My Mojo Workin'* (1966), whose title track, a version of a **Muddy Waters** song, was a minor pop hit in both America and Britain. During the mid-sixties Smith's sound was emulated by such British musicians as **Graham Bond**, **Georgie Fame**, Zoot Money and **Brian Auger**. His American followers included **Jimmy McGriff** and Jack McDuff.

With the arrival of electric pianos and synthesizers, Smith's organ riffs and occasional gruff vocals came to seem outmoded and his records for Mercury in the early seventies were less successful. Later in the decade he concentrated on religious activities but re-emerged with *Off the Top* (Elektra-Musician, 1982). In 1986 he signed to the revived Blue Note label where his recordings included *Prayer Meeting* (1988) and *The Master* (1994), which once again teamed him with Burrell. *Walk on the Wild Side* (1995) collected together the best of his Verve recordings.

KATE SMITH

b. Kathryn Elizabeth Smith, 1 May 1907, Greenville, Virginia, USA, d. 17 June 1986, Raleigh, North Carolina

Smith is best remembered for her powerful version of **Irving Berlin**'s 'God Bless America' (Victor), which she first performed on Armistice Day (11 November) 1938 and which many saw as America's second national anthem. Significantly, her recording of the song was coupled with 'The Star Spangled Banner'.

An untrained soprano, Smith left nursing for vaudeville and was featured in the musical *Honeymoon Lane* in 1926, as a buffoon named Tiny Little who was ridiculed because of her large size. A career as the butt of fat jokes beckoned, from which she was rescued by manager Ted Collins who redirected her career away from Broadway towards radio. In 1931 she secured her first radio show and introduced her theme song 'When the Moon Comes over the Mountain' (which she co-wrote with Harry Woods and Howard Johnson). Within two years, dubbed 'The

First Lady of Radio', she was the highest-paid woman on radio and used her shows – at one point she had three running at the same time – to launch a slew of successful recordings (she made over 2,000) on Decca, Victor and (after 1940) Columbia. Among these were 'The Music Goes Round and Round', 'I'll Walk Alone', 'The Last Time I Saw Paris', 'Rose O'Day'* and 'Did You Ever See a Dream Walking?', all performed in a clear, forceful manner. In 1933 she starred as herself in the film *Hello Everybody*, the title of which was based on the opening line to her radio shows. Already an American institution, Smith's singing of 'God Bless America', a tune Berlin wrote for his 1918 musical *Yip Yip Yaphank* and then omitted, thinking it too sentimental, established her image as a patriotic reflection of the nation's hopes and aspirations. During the Second World War she inspired the sale of millions of dollars-worth of war bonds.

After the war, however, Smith's career faltered. By now a dispenser of advice and chat as well as a singer, and despite a series of television shows – including *The Kate Smith Show* (1950–4), the first major daytime television programme – she seemed increasingly out of time. She recorded only sporadically throughout the sixties, though she sang 'God Bless America' at special occasions with increasing frequency, before illness ended her career in the seventies.

PATTI SMITH

b. 30 December 1946, Chicago, Illinois, USA

Writer and poet, Patti Smith became one of the most striking and adventurous members of the New York punk new wave in the seventies, through her unorthodox singing and songwriting.

A member of New York's artistic avant-garde, Smith's poetry collections of the early seventies included *Devotions for Arthur Rimbaud* and *Cowboy Mouth*, co-written with playwright Sam Shepard. **Todd Rundgren** used a Smith poem as a sleeve note on *A Wizard, A True Star* (1973), and she also provided lyrics for **Blue Oyster Cult**. She teamed up with rock critic and guitarist Lenny Kaye in 1972, recording an arresting variant of **Jimi Hendrix**'s version of 'Hey Joe' (1974) for Mer, a label financed by photographer Robert Mapplethorpe. The single featured **Television** guitarist Tom Verlaine, Smith's beau at the time.

A central figure in the growing punk scene at clubs like CBGB's, Smith formed her own band, the Patti Smith Group, and signed to Arista, releasing *Horses* in 1975. With Ivan Kral (bass), Jay Dee Daugherty (drums) and Richard Sohl (piano), the **John Cale**-produced album contained Smith/Kaye originals and versions of rock standards like **Van Morrison**'s 'Gloria' and Chris Kenner's 'Land of 1000 Dances', while Smith's dramatic live performances offered reinterpretations of such songs as **The Who**'s 'My Generation'. After *Radio Ethiopia* (1976), Smith had a hit single with a relatively conventional version of **Bruce Springsteen**'s 'Because the Night' from *Easter* (1978). The album also included a revival of 'Privilege (Set Me Free)', the theme song from the 1967 film.

Waves (1979), produced by **Todd Rundgren**, contained more emphatic religious themes and provided a minor British hit with 'Frederick'. Smith then retired from music to start a family, returning in 1988 with 'People Got the Power' and a new album *Dream of Life*, produced by Jimmy Iovine and her husband, ex-**MC5** guitarist Fred 'Sonic' Smith. However, it was a one-off, and Smith's only releases in the early nineties were contributions to the film soundtrack *Until the End of the World* (1992) and to a 1993 charity compilation. She was recording a new solo album with her husband at the time of his death in 1994. After recording 'Walkin' Blind' specifically for the film *Dead Man Walking* (1996), Smith, with Kaye again co-producing, made *Gone Again* (1996) and *Peace and Noise* (1997). She continued this high work-rate after her long hiatus with *Gung Ho* (2000), in which she returned to the religious themes of *Waves*. It included 'One Voice' (which was dedicated to Mother Theresa) and the hectoring 'Strange Messengers', in which Smith lectured black Americans about their past.

Lenny Kaye enjoyed a successful career as a producer in the eighties and nineties, notably with singer-songwriter **Suzanne Vega**.

WILL SMITH
b. 25 September 1968, Philadelphia, Pennsylvania, USA

Smith stood at the forefront of the commercialization of the rap genre in the late eighties. He quickly translated his pop version of rap into television success as *The Fresh Prince of Bel-Air* and then made the even more difficult transition from rap and television to film and solo artist in the nineties.

Smith and Jeff Townes first began collaborating as Jazzy Jeff and the Fresh Prince in the mid-eighties. After becoming local live favourites the duo had a US hit with 'Girls Ain't Nothing But Trouble' from their début, *Rock the House* (1987). On the strength of the international hit single 'Parents Just Don't Understand', their second album, *He's the DJ, I'm the Rapper* (1988), became one of the first hip-hop releases to achieve double-platinum status. Smith and Townes' pop sheen offered a non-violent alternative to their harder-edged contemporaries, helping to sell rap music to a white audience for the first time.

Following the release of *And in this Corner . . .* (1989) Smith was offered the lead role in the sitcom *The Fresh Prince of Bel-Air*, which ran until 1996 and

brought Smith an international audience. During this time Smith continued to work intermittently with Townes. At the same time his acting career blossomed. The duo scored their biggest hit in 1991 with 'Summertime', drawn from *Homebase*. The rapper made his first feature film appearances in 1993, taking supporting roles in *Where the Day Takes You* and the acclaimed *Six Degrees of Separation*; the same year Jazzy Jeff and the Fresh Prince issued their final album, *Code Red*.

Having starred in *Bad Boys* (1995), Smith took the leading roles in a pair of science-fiction blockbusters, *Independence Day* (1996) and *Men in Black* (1997), making him one of the hottest properties in Hollywood. Smith topped the UK chart with the *Men in Black* theme before releasing his solo début, *Big Willie Style* (1997), which included the international hit singles 'Gettin' Jiggy wit It' and 'Just the Two of Us'. Smith had another worldwide hit with the theme to *Wild, Wild West*, in which he also starred, before returning to the pop charts with 'Will2K' from his *Willennium* (1999) album.

THE SMITHS
Mike Joyce, b. 1 June 1963; Johnny Marr, b. John Maher, 31 October 1963; Steven Patrick Morrissey, b. 22 May 1959, Manchester, England; Andy Rourke; Craig Gannon

One of the most fêted British rock bands in the eighties, the Smiths' appeal was based on Marr's inventive guitar parts and **Morrissey**'s eloquently gloomy lyrics which expressed what one critic called 'bedsit existentialism' through portrayals of schoolboy brutalities, unsuccessful love affairs and adolescent *angst*.

As a teenager, Morrissey unsuccessfully submitted scripts for the television soap opera *Coronation Street* and ran a fan club for the **New York Dolls**. Impressed by punk rock and local Manchester groups the **Buzzcocks** and the **Fall**, he edited fanzines, published booklets on the Dolls and James Dean and wrote for the music press. He formed the Smiths with Marr and bassist Rourke in 1982. They were later joined by ex-Victim drummer Joyce.

Signing to Rough Trade (Sire in America), the group released 'Hand in Glove' (1983) before their John Porter-produced eponymous début album was a Top Ten hit. 'This Charming Man' (1983) and 'What Difference Does It Make?' were Top Thirty hits before the Smiths collaborated with **Sandie Shaw** on a new version of 'Hand in Glove' (Rough Trade, 1984).

Later that year they released *Hatful of Hollow*, a collection which included live sessions from the John Peel radio show, while the singles 'Heaven Knows I'm Miserable Now' (described by one admiring critic as 'a hymn of drunken melancholy') and 'William, It Was Really Nothing' were also successful.

In 1985 the Smiths reached No. 1 with *Meat Is Murder* (1985). Among its tracks were 'Barbarism Begins at Home' and 'The Headmaster Ritual', while the title song promoted the virtues of vegetarianism. 'The Boy with the Thorn in His Side' was a Top Twenty hit later in the year. The threat of nuclear radiation in the wake of the Chernobyl disaster inspired the Top Ten hit 'Panic' (1986) with its unusual refrain 'hang the deejay'. The group's later singles included 'Ask' and 'Shoplifters of the World Unite'.

The 1986 album *The Queen Is Dead* was in part a lament for the British lifestyle of the forties and fifties. In 1987 Rough Trade released *The World Won't Listen*, a collection of singles and remixed tracks, and in 1988, *Rank*, a live show recorded in 1986, which featured newly recruited second guitarist Gannon, formerly with **Aztec Camera**. In a controversial move for a group regarded as the leading 'independent' band, the Smiths signed to EMI in 1987. Before releasing any records, however, they announced their dissolution. Their back catalogue was signed to Warners, who released two 'best of' compilations in 1992. The Smiths' influence continued to be felt well after their demise through the work of other British bands such as **James** and **Suede**. *The Singles Collection* was issued in 1995.

Marr began a low-key solo career which saw him work with **Bryan Ferry**, **Billy Bragg**, **Talking Heads** and the **Pretenders**. He joined art-rock band **The The** in 1989, playing on *Mind Bomb* (1989) and co-writing *Dusk* (1993). In 1990 he formed Electronic with **New Order** vocalist Bernard Sumner. Rourke and Joyce played with Irish vocalist **Sinead O'Connor** and the Fall spin-off the Adult Net, before briefly joining a re-formed Buzzcocks in 1991.

1991 was also the year the pair began legal action against Morrissey and Marr, believing it to be unfair that they only received a 10% share of the group's earnings. While Rourke settled out of court, Joyce eventually won his case in 1996, with Mr Justice Weeks labelling Morrissey 'devious, truculent and unreliable'. In 1999 Rourke and Joyce had formed a new band with former **Stone Roses** guitarist Aziz Ibrahim. In between recording as Electronic, Marr lent his guitar-playing ability to the **Pet Shop Boys**' *Bilingual* and **M People**'s *Fresco* (both 1997).

HANK SNOW
b. *Clarence Eugene Snow, 9 May 1914, Liverpool, Nova Scotia, Canada, d. 20 December 1999*

Gifted with one of the richest and most distinctive voices in country music, Hank Snow developed the style of his idol **Jimmie Rodgers** into a mainstream country manner, at the same time turning his childhood obsession with American cultural images –

especially the railroad and the West – into the resources of an evocative songwriter. As a Canadian weaver of tales about America, he stood unequalled until the arrival of Robbie Robertson of **The Band**.

Inspired by Western movies and Rodgers' records, Snow embarked on a career in country music in 1933 with a radio show on station CHNS, Halifax, Nova Scotia, singing and playing guitar as 'Hank, the Singing Ranger'. In 1936 he signed with the Canadian branch of RCA Victor and recorded busily for their, and later the American, Bluebird label. Supported by fellow Rodgers devotee **Ernest Tubb**, he made his first appearance in the USA in 1944. Tubb was also behind Snow's recruitment to the cast of the *Grand Ole Opry* in January 1950 – shortly before he established himself beyond dispute by writing and recording 'Golden Rocket' and the million-selling 'I'm Movin' on', both No. 1 country hits in 1950. (In a 1963 *Billboard* poll 'I'm Movin' on' was voted deejays' all-time favourite country record.) He then became an American citizen and moved to Nashville.

Through the fifties and sixties (still with RCA) Snow had many country chart entries, notably the Don Robertson composition 'I Don't Hurt Anymore'* (1954) and the tongue-twisting gazetteer 'I've Been Everywhere' (1962), an anglicized version of which was recorded by Rolf Harris. He also recorded guitar duets with **Chet Atkins**. Among his more than a hundred albums were tributes to his first inspiration, *Songs of Jimmie Rodgers* (1960) and *In Memory of Jimmie Rodgers* (1970). He had earlier acknowledged his debt by taking a leading role in the first Jimmie Rodgers Memorial Day at Meridian, Mississippi, in 1953 (and earlier still by naming his son Jimmie Rodgers Snow). Snow Jnr had a brief career in country music (having a pop hit as Jimmie Rodgers with 'English Country Garden', 1962) before becoming a Nashville minister and TV evangelist.

Snow remained a pillar of the *Grand Ole Opry* into the eighties. In 1994 he published his autobiography *The Hank Snow Story*.

SOFT MACHINE
Daevid Allen, b. Australia; Kevin Ayers, b. 16 August 1945, Kent, England (replaced by Hugh Hopper, b. 1945); Mike Ratledge, b. 1943; Robert Wyatt (replaced by Phil Howard, replaced by John Marshall); Elton Dean (replaced by Karl Jenkins); John Etheridge

Among the earliest of British underground rock bands, Soft Machine evolved in the seventies into highly skilled exponents of jazz-rock, with an ever-shifting line-up.

The group's origins lay in the Wilde Flowers, a jazz/soul band formed in Canterbury in 1963 by Wyatt (drums), Hopper (bass), his brother Brian (sax and guitar), Ayers (vocals) and Richard Sinclair, a guitarist who later led Caravan, a durable progressive-rock band that made ten albums during the seventies. By 1966 they had become Soft Machine (named after the William Burroughs novel), and included Wyatt, Ayers (bass), Allen (guitar) and Ratledge (keyboards). Its principal features were the surreal and witty songs of Wyatt and Ayers. After performing in a French production of the Picasso play, *Désir Attrapé par la Queue*, the group became an integral part of London's nascent underground scene, releasing 'Love Makes Sweet Music' (Polydor, 1967).

Soon afterwards Allen left to form Gong, a French-based progressive rock band whose albums for BYG and Virgin chronicled the annals of the planet Gong and various pixies and teapots. The remaining trio toured America with **Jimi Hendrix** and cut an eponymous album for Probe in New York in 1968 with producer Tom Wilson. Ayers then left the group and embarked on an erratic solo career. After recording *Joy of a Toy* (Harvest, 1969), he toured with his group the Whole World, which included classical arranger and composer David Bedford and guitarist **Mike Oldfield**. During the mid-seventies he recorded *Whatevershebringswesing* (1972), *Bananamour* (1973), *The Confessions of Dr Dream* (1974), which featured ex-**Velvet Underground** vocalist Nico, and *Sweet Deceiver*, with piano from **Elton John** (1975). Among his various sidemen during this period was future **Police** guitarist Andy Summers. Ayers recorded two further inconsistent albums in the late seventies. His eighties albums included 1983's *Diamond Jack and the Queen of Pain*, *As Close as You Think* (1986) and *Falling Up* (Virgin, 1988). Resident in Spain, he continued to record sporadically, most notably on 1992's *Still Life with Guitar*.

Adding Hopper on bass, Wyatt and Ratledge cut *Soft Machine Vol. 2* (Probe, 1969), which contained seventeen tracks. Saxophonist Elton Dean joined for *Third* (Columbia, 1970) and *Fourth* (1971), a double-album with one composition on each side. Wyatt was the next to leave, forming Matching Mole and going on to a lengthy solo career. Howard joined on drums for a year, but was replaced by Marshall from Ian Carr's **Nucleus**, who played on *Fifth* (1972).

The following year Hopper left the group, releasing the concept album *1984* (Columbia, 1973) and later forming Isotope and Soft Heap, whose members included Dean. Marshall and the former Nucleus composer, pianist and sax-player Jenkins (who joined Soft Machine in 1973) were the mainstay of the group throughout the seventies. From *Bundles* (Harvest, 1975), which featured guitarist Allan Holdsworth, Soft Machine's music showed more mainstream jazz-rock leanings, especially after the departure of the remaining founder-member Ratledge in 1976. With Jenkins

he later became a leading composer of music for TV commercials. *Softs* (1976) featured sax-player Alan Wakeman while violinist Ric Sanders, from Ashley Hutchings' **Albion Band**, played on *Alive and Well in Paris* (1978). The final Soft Machine album, *In the Land of Cockayne* (1981), included bassist **Jack Bruce** among its personnel.

STEPHEN SONDHEIM
b. 22 March 1930, New York, USA

The author of the oft-recorded 'Send in the Clowns', composer and lyricist Sondheim was the most influential composer of musicals of the last quarter of the century. Where earlier Broadway writers (notably **Rodgers and Hammerstein**, with whom Sondheim studied) had produced musicals in which song and libretto were dramatically interwoven, Sondheim (usually in partnership with director Harold Prince) created what several critics have termed 'concept musicals'. The most commercially successful of these was *Sweeney Todd* (1979). That said, however strong the concept, in marked contrast to the event musicals of **Andrew Lloyd Webber**, Sondheim's works dealt in understatement rather than grandiloquence.

The son of a New York dress manufacturer, Sondheim went to school with Oscar Hammerstein II's son and, under Hammerstein's guidance, wrote four musicals while at college. He studied with avant-garde composer Milton Babbitt and in the early fifties contributed music to a variety of Broadway shows. His breakthrough came when **Leonard Bernstein** invited him to contribute lyrics to the epochal *West Side Story* (1957, filmed 1961). The show introduced 'Something's Coming', 'Maria' (a hit for **P. J. Proby**, Liberty, 1965, and **Johnny Mathis**, 1960), 'America', 'Tonight' (an instrumental hit for pianists Ferrante and Teicher, United Artists, 1961) and 'Somewhere', a hit for Proby in 1964. Sondheim followed this with *Gypsy* (1958) on which he collaborated with **Jule Styne** and which included 'Small World', a hit for Johnny Mathis in 1959, and 'Everything's Coming up Roses'. His first show as composer and lyricist was *A Funny Thing Happened on the Way to the Forum* (1962, filmed 1967). The innovatory *Company* (1970), Sondheim's first collaboration with Prince, was a critical success. It introduced 'The Ladies Who Lunch' and 'Side by Side'. However, neither it nor *Follies* (1971), which included 'Broadway Baby', produced any hit songs.

The turning point in Sondheim's career was *A Little Night Music* (1973, filmed 1978) which was based on Ingmar Bergman's 1953 film *Smiles of a Summer Night*. A meditation on the meaning of love, it introduced the sombre 'Liaisons' and, most notably, 'Send in the Clowns', a million-seller for **Judy Collins** (1975) and recorded by artists as varied as **Frank Sinatra** and Elizabeth Taylor. The ambitious *Pacific Overtures* (1976), which told the story of Japan's emergence from isolation in the nineteenth century to a dominant position in world trade, was only a critical success until its revival in 1988. It was followed by *Sweeney Todd* (1979), the most spectacular of Sondheim's shows.

Earlier in Britain the revue *Side by Side by Sondheim* (1976, transferred to Broadway 1977) had confirmed the writer's cult reputation. *Sunday in the Park with George* (1984), a meditation on the nature of creativity based on the painting 'A Sunday Afternoon on the Island of La Grande Jatte' by Georges Seurat, was a surprise hit on Broadway, though the second act added after its off-Broadway début was largely ineffectual and seemed there only to lengthen the piece.

The range of Sondheim's interests was confirmed by his next two works, *Into the Woods* (1991) and *Assassins* (1992). The first was a marvellously intricate blending and interweaving of a number of fairy tales which tersely questioned the simple idea of happy endings by continuing the fairy tales. Full of intricate rhyming and surprising shafts of melody, it is the most playful of Sondheim's musicals. *Assassins*, which celebrated America's gun culture as a way of life and death, along the way making heroes of a selection of presidential assassins, is a far darker work. The two shows also indicated the latitude Sondheim allowed his directors. The first was elaborately fashioned, the second sparse. 1993 saw a British revival of *Sweeney Todd* which transformed it from his most spectacular show to his most intimate to great effect, along the way highlighting the theme of unrequited love in the playing of Julia McKenzie.

Sondheim's next Broadway musical was *Passion* (1994). His third collaboration with James Lapine (who had been the librettist of both *Woods* and *Sunday in the Park*), *Passion* is based on the film *Passione d'Amore* (1981). Another of his essays in obsession, *Passion* is doubly unusual for its explicit treatment of sexuality and for being an almost seamless mix of speech, singing and music. In this it is, with *Sweeney Todd*, the most 'through sung' of Sondheim's musicals.

Further evidence of Sondheim's belated acceptance in America was the revival of past commercial failures in the eighties and nineties and the number of opera companies who included his 'musicals' in their repertoire. The latest of these was the revival in 2000 of *Saturday Night*, a revival of a musical written in 1954. Similarly, **Barbra Streisand**'s chart-topping *The Broadway Album* (1985) featured eight Sondheim songs spanning the whole of his writing career. Another mark of Sondheim's stature was Sony Classical's tribute album, *Color and Light: Jazz Sketches on Sondheim*, which featured **Herbie Hancock** and

Grover Washington, among others. *A Collectors Sondheim* (RCA, 1985) is a three-CD compilation of songs from most of his shows.

SONIC YOUTH

Thurston Moore, b. 25 July 1958, Coral Gables, Florida, USA; Kim Gordon, b. 28 April 1953, Rochester, New York; Lee Ranaldo, b. 3 February 1956, Glen Cove, New York; Steve Shelley, b. 23 June 1953, Midland, Missouri

The missing link between the sixties New York art-noise of the **Velvet Underground** and the early nineties grunge movement, Sonic Youth achieved lasting cult status with a series of uncompromising albums in the eighties and nineties and gained a reputation as one of the most innovative and important US bands of the era.

Guitarists Moore and Ranaldo first teamed up in the late seventies 'guitar choir' organized by avant-garde New York composer Glenn Branca to perform his work. Recruiting bassist Gordon (another Branca alumnus) and drummer Richard Edson in 1981, the band released its eponymous live début album the following year. Raw and experimental, the album merged their avant-garde background and fascination with the possibilities of noise with the intensity of the emerging hardcore scene, but created little interest outside New York. Edson was replaced by Jim Sclavunos, who in turn gave way to Bob Bert by the time of the recording of the second album, *Confusion is Sex* (1983). The mini-album *Kill Yr Idols* and the full-length follow-up *Sonic Death* (1984) saw the band refining their technique, reaching a peak in 1985 with *Bad Moon Rising*. The album, which included the Charles Manson-inspired 'Death Valley '69', co-written with NY poetess/performance artist Lydia Lunch, received enthusiastic reviews, particularly in the UK where the band had a devoted cult audience.

Drummer Shelley (ex-the Crucifucks) replaced Bert for 1986's *E.V.O.L.*, which included two **Madonna** 'tributes'. The band's fascination with the pop idol continued with their release of a version of one of her biggest hits as 'Into the Groove(y)' in 1987, and a year later they released a spin-off LP, *The Whitey Album*, as Ciccone Youth. 1987's *Sister* was another critical success, but it was the impressive sales enjoyed by *Daydream Nation* which convinced a major label to sign up what by then had become arguably America's most important 'underground' band.

Geffen Records released *Goo*, the first album under the band's new deal, in 1990. By now the band was also drawing praise from counter-culture figures of earlier generations such as **Iggy Pop**, who joined the band on stage, and **Neil Young**, with whom they toured the US in 1991. The riff-orientated *Dirty* (1992) was met with mixed reviews, some critics feeling it was too similar to *Goo*, but the band's concurrent incendiary live shows belied any accusations that they had lost their edge.

Recorded while Gordon and Moore were expecting their first child, 1994's *Experimental Jet Set, Trash and No Star* was more restrained than its predecessor, but paradoxically less commercial, typified by the acoustic 'Winner's Blues' and the dry humour of 'Doctor's Orders'. *Goo* had included 'Tunic (Song for Karen)', dedicated to Karen Carpenter, another of the band's unlikely heroines, and in 1994 they contributed a cover of the **Carpenters**' 'Superstar' (written by **Leon Russell**) to a tribute album, *If I Were a Carpenter*.

In 1988 Sonic Youth recorded the soundtrack for the experimental movie *Made in the USA*, an album of which was released in 1995, and Moore played in the band which performed as the early **Beatles** for the soundtrack of the film *Backbeat* (1993). Moore and Shelley recorded an album and EP with original punk idol (ex-**Television** bassist) Richard Hell as Dim Stars in 1992, and played several low-key dates as a duo in 1994. Moore also contributed to **R.E.M.**'s 1994 album *Monster* and in the same year Shelley played with re-formed UK female punk band the Raincoats. Kim Gordon formed her own band, Free Kitten, releasing a pair of hip-hop flavoured albums, *Call Now* (1993) and *Nice Ass* (1995). In April 1994 she unveiled her own line of fashions, X Girl Clothing, in New York.

After issuing *Screaming Fields of Sonic Love* (1995), a compilation volume of pre-*Goo* tracks, Sonic Youth headlined the Lollapalooza touring festival, largely to raise the funds necessary to build their own studio. *Washing Machine* (1996) earned the band their strongest reviews since *Daydream Nation* but the band's output for the next two years was confined to a series of patchy, untitled EPs on their own SYR imprint. Their next major label release was *A Thousand Leaves* (1998), which featured the modestly successful single 'Sunday' and a track written in tribute to recently deceased beat poet Allen Ginsberg, 'Hits of Sunshine'.

The group returned to their art roots for *SYR 4: Goodbye 20th Century* (Smells Like Records, 1999), which featured their versions of a wide range of avant-garde works, from **Yoko Ono**'s 'Voice Piece for Soprano' to George Macuunias's 'Piano Piece #13'. The result, as one critic put it, was 'quite jolly and bracing for about two listens'. Less compelling was *NYC Ghosts* (2000), which saw the group returning again to their roots, this time to little effect.

THE SONS OF THE PIONEERS
Len Slye, b. Leonard Franklin Slye, 5 November 1911, Cincinnati, Ohio, USA; Bob Nolan, b. Robert Clarence

Nobles, 1 April 1908, New Brunswick, Canada; Tim Spencer, b. Vernon Spencer, 13 July 1908, Webb City, Missouri, d. 26 April 1974, Apple Valley, California; Hugh Farr, b. Thomas Hubert Farr, 6 December 1903, Llano, Texas (1943–58, replaced 1960 by Wade Ray, b. 6 April 1913, Evansville, Indiana); Karl Farr, b. Karl Marx Farr, 25 April 1909, Rochelle, Texas, d. 20 September 1961, West Springfield, Massachusetts; Lloyd Perryman, b. 29 January 1917, Ruth, Arkansas, d. 31 May 1977, California; Pat Brady, b. Robert Ellsworth O'Brady, 31 December 1914, Toledo, Ohio, d. 27 February 1972, Colorado Springs, Colorado; Ken Carson, b. Hubert Ken Carson, Colgate, Oklahoma, d. 7 April 1994, Jacksonville, Florida; Shug Fisher, b. George Clinton Fisher, 26 September 1907, Chickasha, Oklahoma; Ken Curtis, b. Curtis Wayne Gates, 2 July 1916, Lamar, Colorado; Lloyd Tommy 'Spike' Doss, b. 26 September 1920, Weiser, Idaho; Dale Warren, b. 1 June 1925, Summerville, Kentucky; Deuce Spriggens; Roy Lanham, b. 16 January 1923, Corbin, Kentucky

The outstanding Western singing group in country music, the Sons of the Pioneers devoted more than half a century to instilling in the American consciousness a love and respect for the history and environment of the Old West. A score or more members maintained the group's name in an unbroken career that embraced movies, radio, TV, recordings and personal appearances.

The group was founded in Los Angeles in late 1933 by singer/guitarist Slye, who later as **Roy Rogers** had a hugely successful career as a singing cowboy. The other charter members were Nolan, a former chautauqua (travelling tent show) singer and occasional poet, and Spencer, an amateur singer/banjoist with some nightclub experience. All three had previously sung with the Rocky Mountaineers, one of several country acts around Los Angeles. Another was the Beverly Hill Billies, which included **Elton Britt** and Stuart Hamblen, later the writer of 'This Old House' and for many years leader of a popular Western gospel group. Country music had been heard in California since the mid-twenties, from such artists as the cowboy singer Harry 'Mac' McClintock, who helped popularize the Wobblies' quasi-anthem 'Hallelujah, I'm a Bum', Len Nash and His Country Boys and a duo who called themselves the Rolling Stones.

Broadcasting on the Hollywood station KFWB as the Pioneer Trio, Slye, Nolan and Spencer developed a practised style of three-part singing with harmonized yodelling, initially accompanied by Slye's guitar. In 1934 they added fiddler Hugh Farr, changed their name to the Sons of the Pioneers and began recording, for Decca, such Nolan compositions as 'Way Out There' and 'Tumbling Tumbleweeds' (Decca), which became test-pieces for the many Western trios that followed in their wake. In the following year they added Farr's brother Karl on guitar and made the first of many movie appearances in *The Old Homestead*. They partnered **Bing Crosby** in *Rhythm on the Range* (1936) and later, under contract to Columbia (1937–41), appeared in twenty-eight Charles Starrett Westerns. They also appeared in a couple of **Gene Autry** features for Republic, *The Big Show* and *The Old Corral* (both 1936).

Following the departure of Slye in 1937, the group, which had already added singer Perryman, brought in bass-player/comedian Brady. Their first extended stay away from California was in Chicago in 1940, but they were already widely known to radio listeners from their hundreds of electrical transcriptions for Standard and Thesaurus; from 1940 they also recorded them for Orthacoustic. Of their regular recordings, one of the most popular was Nolan's composition 'Cool Water' (Decca, 1941). During the Second World War both Perryman and Brady left for army service and were replaced by Carson, formerly with a similar trio called the Ranch Boys, and bass-player/comedian Fisher. The group was reunited in 1946, now signed to RCA Victor, for whom they remade 'Cool Water' and 'Tumbling Tumbleweeds'.

In 1949, the year of their last major hit, Spencer's 'Room Full of Roses', the other founder-members quit, Spencer being replaced by a former pop singer, Curtis, and Nolan by Doss; Perryman took over the leadership. Curtis's presence and the more elaborate accompaniments provided by RCA drew the group's work closer to mainstream pop music, and they occasionally recorded with pop artists like **Vaughn Monroe** ('Cool Water', 1948) and **Perry Como**. In 1950 they made their most significant contribution to Western film when they supplied the vocal score for John Ford's *Wagon Master*, from which the long-running TV series *Wagon Train* was derived. They also appeared with John Wayne in *Rio Grande* (Republic, 1950) and *The Searchers* (Warner Bros, 1956).

On Curtis's departure in 1953 (he later became well-known to TV viewers as 'Festus' in *Gunsmoke*), the group signed singer Warren and veteran singer/bass-player/bandleader Spriggens, who had worked with Californian Western swing bands in the style of Tex Williams'. After a brief spell with Coral (1954), they returned to RCA Victor, staying on the label for the next twenty-one years and recording such durable albums as *How Great Thou Art* (1957) and *Cool Water* (1959). Personal tensions led to the departure in 1958 of Hugh Farr, who was replaced in 1960 by fiddler Ray, while Karl Farr's death in 1961 led to the signing of guitarist Lanham. There were other personnel changes in the years following, ex-members often returning for second and third spells alongside younger hands. By the early seventies the group had

earned various civic awards and tributes from Western organizations, and its reputation remained unchallenged afterwards.

From the start the Sons of the Pioneers' carefully worked-out harmonies inspired other country singers, among them **Johnny Bond** and Jimmy Wakely, while Nolan's vivid sense of landscape more or less set the tone for later Western songwriting. The group's legacy of repertoire and vocal technique was inherited in the seventies by the Nashville-based trio Riders in the Sky.

SOUL ASYLUM

Pat Morley (replaced by Grant Young, b. 5 January 1964, Iowa City, Iowa, USA, replaced by Sterling Campbell); Karl Mueller b. 27 July 1962, Minneapolis, Minnesota; Dan Murphy, b. 12 July 1962, Duluth, Michigan; Dave Pirner, b. 16 April 1964, Green Bay, Wisconsin

If **Bob Seeger** and **Grand Funk Railroad** could claim to be the contrasting rock voices of the American Midwest in the seventies, Soul Asylum could claim to be the representative voice of the late eighties.

Singer/guitarist Pirner, guitarist Murphy and bassist Mueller formed Loud Fast Rules in 1981, recruiting drummer Morley the following year and renaming themselves Soul Asylum. The début album *Say What You Will* (Twin Tone, 1984) was a heady mix of garage punk and youthful inexperience. Produced by Hüsker Dü's **Bob Mould**, it sold only to a cult, localized fanbase. In 1986 the band issued two new studio albums – *Made to Be Broken* and *While You Were Out* – and a collection of out-takes and live recordings, *Time Incinerator*, by which time they had replaced Morley with Young and evolved into a tighter unit, albeit still without commercial success.

Soul Asylum signed to A&M for the release of *Hang Time* (1987): Dismissed by some, in view of the group's previous efforts, as an over-produced blend of punk-pop and heavy rock, it marked a significant evolution. It was followed by *And the Horse They Rode in on* (1990), arguably the band's finest artistic statement to date, which saw them part company with A&M after it failed to meet sales expectations. Soul Asylum re-emerged two years later on Columbia and finally broke into the mainstream. The hit single 'Runaway Train' was unrepresentative of the overall sound of *Grave Dancers Union*, but managed to send sales of the album, which also spawned 'Black Gold' and 'Somebody to Shove', over the four million mark.

Let Your Dim Light Shine (1995), which marked the recording début of former **Duran Duran** drummer Campbell, failed to repeat the success of its predecessor in spite of the more commercial sheen added by producer Butch Vig (best known for his work with **Garbage**). Soul Asylum returned in 1998 with *Candy* *from a Stranger*, after which the band were left looking for a fourth drummer following the amicable departure of Campbell.

SOUL II SOUL

Jazzie B, b. Beresford Romeo, 26 January 1963, London, England; Nellee Hooper; Philip Harvey; Caron Wheeler, b. 19 January 1963

Britain's Soul II Soul produced an elegant hybrid of soul, reggae and hip-hop in the late 1980s and early 1990s, winning them critical and mainstream success at home and abroad.

Soul II Soul's founder was Jazzie B, born in England of Antiguan parents. His first ambition was to be a professional soccer player, but he opted instead to train as a studio engineer. At the same time he and Harvey established Soul II Soul as a reggae sound system in 1982. Soul II Soul grew over the next few years to become one of London's leading promoters of warehouse parties. Their success enabled them to open music and clothing stores, while Jazzie B became a well-known figure on London's black music pirate radio scene.

In 1985 the Soul II Soul collective was joined by Nellee Hooper, a former member of Bristol's Wild Bunch sound system and erstwhile cohort of **Massive Attack**. With Hooper's musicianship and Jazzie B's ear for new sounds, Soul II Soul became a recording group in 1987 with the release of 'Fairplay', which featured Rose Windross on vocals. After releasing 'Feel Free' with lead singer Do-Reen, Soul II Soul had their first hit in 1989 with 'Keep on Movin''.

The track's plangent vocals were sung by Caron Wheeler, a former member of such UK soul bands as Afrodiziak and Brown Sugar. With its syncopated hip-hop beats, sparse but elegant arrangement and lush vocals, 'Keep on Movin'' was a huge hit in the UK and the US. Its follow-up, 'Back to Life (However Do You Want Me?)', drew on the same basic elements, again featured Wheeler on vocals, and was a UK No. 1 pop hit. Both featured on *Club Classics Volume One* (1989), which was also a huge success on both sides of the Atlantic, selling two million copies in the US.

Drawing on the cream of British black musicians and singers, Hooper and Jazzie B had created a sound which distilled the best of the soul, reggae and hip-hop that had featured in their DJ careers. Hooper and Jazzie B were now in demand as producers. Hooper would subsequently work with **Sinead O'Connor**, **Madonna** and, most memorably, **Björk** on the Icelandic singer's eclectic and ambitious solo album, *Debut* (1993). His place in the international musical firmament was confirmed when he produced the title song, written by Bono and The Edge from **U2** and

sung by **Tina Turner**, from the James Bond film *Goldeneye*. Jazzie B meanwhile co-produced **James Brown**'s 1993 comeback album *Universal James* and worked with the **Fine Young Cannibals**, **Neneh Cherry** and **Maxi Priest**.

The group, increasingly built around Jazzie B, returned with *Volume II – 1990 A New Decade* (1990). Wheeler had by this stage left the group to record her first solo album, the soulful and intelligent *UK Blak* (1990) for RCA. Jazzie B himself rapped on the hit single 'Get a Life', and brought in vocalists Kym Mazelle and Victoria Wilson-James, who appeared on another single, 'A Dream's a Dream'. The album also featured a cameo from UK jazz saxophonist **Courtney Pine**.

Jazzie B's attempts to record other artists for his Funki Dred label were frustrated by an abortive deal with Motown, but he released *Volume III – Just Right* in 1992, which spawned the hits 'Joy' and 'Wish', and also marked Wheeler's return to the fold.

The group's classic soul sound was rather overtaken by newer sounds as the 1990s progressed. After a 1993 greatest hits package and a fourth studio album, *Volume V – Believe* (1995), the group were dropped by Virgin in 1996, but bounced back to release *Time for Change* on Island in 1997. A tenth anniversary re-release of their début album in 1999 served to remind the world of their talents.

DAVID SOUL

b. David Solberg, 28 August 1943, Chicago, Illinois, USA

Transformed into a heart-throb by his portrayal of Hutch in the 'buddy, buddy' detective teleseries *Starsky and Hutch* (1975–9), Soul briefly essayed a complementary career as a soft-voiced balladeer.

The son of a Lutheran minister and classical concert singer, Soul grew up in Germany and in the sixties attempted a career as a folk singer. He had a period of brief celebrity as 'the covered man' – he sang in a ski mask – on American television before turning to acting. In the wake of his success in *Starsky and Hutch*, Soul resurrected his music career and industry veteran Larry Uttal signed him to the recently established Private Stock Records. After an eponymous début album (1976), he teamed up with songwriter **Tony Macaulay** for a series of hits. These included 'Don't Give Up on Us'* (1976), a British and American No. 1, 'Goin' in with My Eyes Open' and 'Silver Lady' (1977). Always a bigger attraction in Britain than America, Soul's subsequent hits ('Let's Have a Quiet Night in', 1977, and 'It Sure Brings Out the Love in Your Eyes', 1978) failed in America. In the eighties he recorded only intermittently (*The Best Days of My Life*, Energy, 1982) before giving up music to concentrate on his acting career.

SOUNDGARDEN

Matt Cameron, b. 28 November 1962, Olympia, Washington, USA; Chris Cornell, b. 20 July 1964, Seattle, Washington; Kim Thayil, b. 4 September 1960, Seattle; Hiro Yamamoto, b. 13 April 1961, Park Forest (replaced by Ben Shepard)

Emerging from the embryonic Seattle grunge scene in the late eighties, Soundgarden, with their post-modernist version of post-punk heavy metal, became one of the major alternative rock acts of the nineties.

Having previously played in a variety of local bands, vocalist/guitarist Cornell formed Soundgarden with Olympia students Thayil (guitar) and Yamamoto (bass) in 1984, gaining a strong reputation for their live performances in the Northwest area after the addition of drummer Cameron to the line-up. Two Sub Pop EPs, *Screaming Life* (1986) and *Fopp* (1987), rooted heavily in the arena rock of **Black Sabbath** and **Led Zeppelin**, preceded *Ultramega OK* (SST, 1988). Including a highly dramatic reading of **Howling Wolf**'s 'Smokestack Lightning', it showed the band to be less reliant on Cornell's vocal mimicry of Robert Plant than before. By this stage the band had developed enough of an underground fanbase to attract the attention of A&M, with whom the band signed in 1989.

Louder than Love was released to positive reviews in 1989, eventually earning the band a Grammy nomination, but the band were left without a bassist after the departure of Yamamoto. Former **Nirvana** guitarist Jason Everman filled in for a lengthy American tour, after which Shepard joined, boosting the band's sound considerably on *Badmotorfinger* (1991), which achieved platinum status in the US and lead to a high-profile spot on the 1992 Lollapalooza. On the brink of mainstream success, Cornell and Cameron took a break from Soundgarden to join members of **Pearl Jam** in a grunge-rock supergroup, Mother Love Bone. The quartet returned in 1994 with *Superunknown**, taking a more psychedelic approach and achieving massive international success on the strength of 'Spoonman' and 'Black Hole Sun', which won two Grammys. Two solid years of touring preceded the release of *Down on the Upside* (1996), which featured the hit singles 'Pretty Noose' and 'Blow Up the Outside World' but failed to match the sales of *Superunknown*. After another worldwide tour Soundgarden split in 1997, allowing Cameron to take up the vacant position of Pearl Jam drummer, while Cornell launched his solo career in 1999 with 'Can't Change Me' from *Euphoria Morning*. A mark of how far Cameron had come from his beginnings was his 1997 US Top Thirty recording, with Eleven, of 'Ave Maria'.

JOHN PHILIP SOUSA

b. 6 November 1854, Washington, DC, USA, d. 6 March 1932, Reading, Pennsylvania

Sousa was 'The March King' of America and the composer of 'Stars and Stripes Forever' (1897). Despite his disdain for what in a 1906 article he called 'the menace of mechanical music', he was the first bandleader to record with commercial success, with the US Marine Band (1890) and then with his own band (1895).

After studying the violin and trombone, Sousa joined the US Marine Band in 1867. In 1872 he left to play in various theatre orchestras before returning to the Marine Band as director in 1880, remaining there until 1892. The Band's recording of Sousa's 'Semper Fidelis' (Columbia, 1890) was the first record to top the American charts and was followed later in the year by the equally successful 'Washington Post' and 'The Thunderer'. These recordings helped to establish the Band as the most popular marching band in America, eclipsing that led by Patrick Gilmore (co-author of the Civil War classic 'When Johnny Comes Marching Home', 1863). In 1892 Sousa formed his own band and toured America and Europe with great success. For two decades from 1895 onwards, Sousa recorded prolifically, including some tunes for dancing ('Happy Days in Dixie', 'La Czarine', 1897) as well as the stirring marches – 'a march should make a man with a wooden leg step out', he once succinctly explained – with which he made his reputation. Sousa's major recording successes included 'El Capitan March' (Columbia, 1895), which he later used as the theme of *El Capitan* (1896), one of the several comic operettas he wrote; 'Stars and Stripes Forever' (1897); 'In the Good Old Summertime' (Victor, 1903), with a vocal refrain by Harry MacDonough (with **Henry Burr** the most successful tenor of the early recording era); and 'Liberty Loan March' (1918), one of the few recordings issued under his name which he actually conducted.

From the beginning of his recording career, Sousa, who is generally regarded as the first to use the derisive phrase 'canned music', took no interest in the recording process, preferring to leave his concert master Arthur Pryor to supervise the band's recordings (the fees being paid to Sousa for the use of his name). Thus, in 1902 Sousa signed an exclusive contract with Victor, but it was Pryor who actually took charge of the recording sessions. This led in 1904 to Pryor forming his own band, which rapidly became second only to Sousa's. Among Pryor's recordings, which showed a broader-based repertoire than Sousa's own, were 'A Coon Band Contest', 'In the Shade of the Old Apple Tree' (Victor, 1905), **George M. Cohan**'s 'You're a Grand Old Flag' (1907) and **Nora Bayes**' 'Shine on Harvest Moon' (1910).

During the First World War, Sousa became director of all America's navy bands and afterwards returned to touring. His views on 'canned music' notwithstanding, Sousa was a prime mover with **Victor Herbert** in seeking greater copyright protection for the composers of music. As well as various instructional treatises on musical instruments, Sousa published three novels and an autobiography, *Marching Along* (1928).

JOE SOUTH
b. 28 February 1940, Atlanta, Georgia, USA

More successful as a songwriter than a recording artist, South, like **Dallas Frazier**, brought a sombre and reflective eye to his stories about Southern life and mores.

South took up guitar in his teens and in 1957 briefly played in a band led by steel-guitarist **Pete Drake** before being signed by music publisher Bill Lowry. He had a minor hit with 'The Purple People Eater Meets the Witch Doctor' (1958) – an answer record to **David Seville**'s 'Witch Doctor' – on Lowry's NRC label, before moving to **Rick Hall**'s Muscle Shoals studio as a session guitarist and writer. Among his writing successes were 'Untie Me' by black vocal group the Tams (Arlen, 1962), whose later hits included the British chart-topper 'Hey Girl Don't Bother Me' (Probe, 1971), and a series of hits for fellow Atlanta singer Billy Joe Royal. These included the 'wrong side of town' ballad 'Down in the Boondocks' (Columbia, 1965), 'I've Got to Be Somebody' (1966) and 'Hush' (1967), which gave **Deep Purple** their first American Top Ten hit in 1968. At the same time, he played on numerous sessions, including *Nashville Skyline* (**Bob Dylan**, 1969), 'The Sounds of Silence' (**Simon and Garfunkel**, 1965) and several recordings by **Aretha Franklin** and **Wilson Pickett**.

In 1968 he signed with Capitol and released *Introspect*, one of the first albums to make extensive use of multi-track facilities, which allowed South to sing and play nearly all the vocal and instrumental parts himself. It included the oft-recorded 'Games People Play' (South's first hit and subsequently revived by the **Spinners** as 'They Just Can't Stop It', 1975, and **Alan Parsons**, 1981); 'Rose Garden', subsequently a million-seller for **Lynn Anderson** (1970); and 'These Are Not My People', a 1969 country hit for Freddy Weller, a member of **Paul Revere and the Raiders**, who had their last Top Forty hit with another song from *Introspect*, 'Birds of a Feather' (1971).

Most of these versions lacked the bite of South's own performances. An exception was **Brook Benton**'s R&B hit with the title track of South's second album, *Don't It Make You Want to Go Home* (1969). That included 'Walk a Mile in My Shoes', South's last Top Twenty hit. After the similar *So the Seeds Are Growing*

(1971), South retired to Hawaii following the death of his brother Tommy. There he recorded *A Look Inside Midnight Rainbows* (1974). He later released the lesser *Midnight Rainbows* (Island, 1975) and *To Have, to Hold and to Let Go* (1976), on which he was backed by members of the **Atlanta Rhythm Section**. He subsequently worked in music publishing.

The Best of Joe South (1992) is the definitive anthology.

SPACEMEN 3
Pete Bain; Natty Brooker; Jason Pierce, b. 1967, Rugby, England; Kate Radley; Sonic Boom, b. Pete Kember, Rugby

Spacemen 3 were an avant-garde rock band who developed a cult following in the late eighties for their expansive, feedback-laden psychedelia, which was heavily influenced by the **Velvet Underground** and Suicide. Subsequently co-founder Jason Pierce left in 1990 to form Spiritualized.

Kember and Pierce formed Spacemen 3 in 1982 alongside bassist Bain and drummer Brooker, building a loyal local fanbase for their droning rock soundscapes, eventually releasing *Sound of Confusion* (Fire) in 1986 to mild acclaim. *The Perfect Prescription* (1987) and *Playing with Fire* (1989), which included the minor hit 'Revolution', earned the quartet a strong underground following in the US, but by the time *Recurring* (1991) was released Pierce and Kember were no longer on speaking terms. The album is essentially Spacemen 3's *White Album*, with the two songwriters recording separately. In spite of this, *Recurring* is a worthy coda to the band's eight-year career. The band also released a series of live albums, most notably *Performance* (1989), and various retrospective compilations, including *The Singles* (1995). Spacemen 3's status as one of the most influential guitar bands of the eighties was confirmed with the release of a tribute album on Fire Records in 1998, which features contributions from an array of bands who owe a debt to their sound, including **Mogwai**.

While Kember would go on to produce ever-more experimental offerings as Spectrum and Experimental Audio Research, Pierce opted for a refinement of the Spacemen 3 sound, adding brass and strings to his trademark droning feedback. Recruiting girlfriend Kate Radley on keyboards alongside bassist Sean Cook and drummer Damon Reece, Pierce rode the crest of the minimalist independent wave on *Laser-Guided Melodies* (1992) before going in search of the 'pure sound' on *Pure Phase* (1995). The band reached its peak on the critically lauded *Ladies and Gentlemen We Are Floating in Space* (1997), an aural document of the break-up of Pierce's relationship with Radley, developing a wider international fanbase on the strength of the UK hit singles 'I Think I'm in Love' and 'Come Together' and a US tour in support of **Neil Young**. *Live at the Royal Albert Hall* (1998) was recorded on the band's 1997 tour, backed by the London Community Gospel Choir and a string quartet alongside Pierce's now customary horn-led live band.

SPANDAU BALLET

Tony Hadley, b. 2 June 1960, London, England; John Keeble, b. 6 July 1959; Gary Kemp, b. 15 October 1959, London; Martin Kemp, b. 10 October 1962, London; Steve Norman, b. 25 March 1960

With such groups as **Ultravox** and **ABC**, Spandau Ballet led the new-romantic trend in eighties rock music in Britain. Their glossy, well-crafted songs, initially developed from England's thriving disco scene, were a reaction against the rough edges of punk.

The band grew out of a schoolboy group, the Gentry. Its members were *habitués* of the London club scene and formed their own label, Reformation, before signing to Chrysalis in 1980. With Hadley on vocals, Gary Kemp (guitar), Norman (saxophone), Martin Kemp (bass) and drummer Keeble, *Journeys to Glory* (1981) included the hits 'To Cut a Long Story Short', 'The Freeze' and 'Musclebound'. Produced by Richard James Burgess, whose electro-jazz group Landscape had a Top Ten single with 'Einstein a Go-Go' (RCA, 1981), the album featured a blend of synthesizers and guitars.

Horns were added for the funky 'Chant No. 1 (Don't Need This Pressure on)' from *Diamond* (1982). Later international disco hits included 'Instinction', 'Lifeline' and 'Communication', while both 'True' and 'Gold' (the 1984 Olympic Games anthem) were successful in America as well as Europe. *Parade* (1984) repeated the white-dance-music formula and gave Spandau Ballet four more British hits, including 'Only When You Leave' (1983) and 'Round and Round' (1985). The group appeared at Live Aid in the same year.

After a lengthy legal dispute with Chrysalis, Spandau Ballet signed to Columbia, releasing *Through the Barricades* (1986), an album of 'committed' material, which included the hit 'Fight for Ourselves', whose left-wing sympathies confounded the group's critics. The unremarkable *Heart Like a Sky* was issued in 1989, the year that the Kemps began filming *The Krays*, a biography of the notorious criminal twins of the 'Swinging Sixties'.

The band and their label fell out over the latter's refusal to release *Heart Like a Sky* in America, and Spandau Ballet subsequently split up in 1990. Hadley recorded the solo album *The State of Play* (EMI, 1992), which included a trio of minor chart hits ('Lost in Your Love', 'For Your Blue Eyes Only' and 'The Game of Love'), and the Kemps continued their acting careers. Gary played **Whitney Houston**'s manager

in *The Bodyguard*. *The Best of Spandau Ballet* appeared in 1991, the same year that rap group PM Dawn had a worldwide hit with 'Set Adrift on Memory Bliss', based on samples from Spandau's 'True'.

In 1999, the year Martin Kemp joined the cast of UK soap opera *Eastenders*, Gary Kemp won a High Court action brought against him by the former members of Spandau Ballet (bar his brother) for a share in his publishing royalties. A year later Hadley released another solo album, the minor *Obsession* (Alma, 2000), which featured former Spandau drummer John Keeble among the backing band.

THE SPANIELS

James 'Pookie' Hudson, b. 11 June 1934, Gary, Indiana, USA; Ernest Warren, b. Gary (replaced 1955 by James Cochran); Willis C. Jackson, b. Gary (replaced 1955 by Donald Porter); Opal; Courtney Jnr, b. Gary (replaced by Carl Rainge); Gerald Gregory, b. Gary

The Spaniels featured one of the most varied repertoires of the doo-wop groups of the fifties. They sang jump blues ('House Cleaning'), novelty songs ('Automobiles') and ballads ('False Love') with equal ease, but their forte lay in arrangements which contrasted the bass and tenor vocal parts, as on their best-remembered recording, 'Goodnight Sweetheart, Goodnight' (Vee-Jay, 1954).

Consisting of former students of Roosevelt High School in Gary, Indiana, and originally called Pookie Hudson and the Hudsonaires, the group was the first act signed by Vivian and Calvin Carter to their newly established Vee-Jay label in 1953. Their first recording, the plaintive 'Baby It's You' (1943), was leased to Chance Records and it was not until 1954 and the cool-sounding 'Goodnight' – one of the first teen ballads of the rock'n'roll era – that they appeared on Vee-Jay. That song, written by Hudson and Calvin Carter, was covered by the **McGuire Sisters**, who had the bigger pop hit, and Johnnie and Jack (RCA), who had a country hit with it. Following their reorganization in 1955 as a result of several members being called up for army service, the Spaniels had further R&B hits, including 'You Painted Pictures' (1955) and their final Vee-Jay recording, 'I Know' (1960), before disbanding. Hudson recorded solo for several small labels before, in 1970, a re-formed Spaniels once more charted with 'Fairy Tales' on Calla and later re-recorded 'Goodnight' for Buddah.

In later years the group was largely inactive, only re-forming for occasional revival concerts.

OTIS SPANN

b. 21 March 1930, Jackson, Mississippi, USA, d. 24 April 1970, Chicago, Illinois

Otis Spann's reputation initially rested on his firm, detailed piano-playing in the **Muddy Waters** band, but grew as he exposed his considerable skills as a soloist. He sang, in a thick Mississippi accent, blues about Southern rural life, interspersed with blues hits of the thirties and forties and an occasional boogie, all over rolling, crowded piano lines.

A piano player since early childhood, Spann began his career in music while living in Chicago in the early fifties. He first recorded with Waters in 1952 ('Standing Around Crying', Chess) and joined the band full-time in 1953, replacing the brilliant Big Maceo (*b. Major Merriweather, 31 March 1905, Atlanta, Georgia, d. 26 February 1953, Chicago*), a singer/pianist whose forties partnership with Tampa Red had produced the classic version of 'Worried Life Blues' (Bluebird, 1941) and 'Chicago Breakdown' (Bluebird, 1945). Maceo's rich piano textures and hoarse, smoky singing greatly influenced the younger man, who often remade 'Worried Life' and others of Maceo's compositions.

During the fifties and part of the sixties Spann was a house pianist for Chess, recording with **Howlin' Wolf**, **Bo Diddley** and many other artists. He also made a small number of sides in his own name, including 'It Must Have Been the Devil' (Checker, 1955), one of his personal favourites. He toured Britain with Waters in 1958 and played the Newport Jazz Festival in 1960, commemorating the closing of the event by singing a 'Goodbye Newport Blues' hastily written for the occasion by the poet Langston Hughes. Soon afterwards he made his album début with *Otis Spann Is the Blues* (Candid, 1960), which he shared with singer/guitarist Robert 'Junior' Lockwood. Still with Waters, he toured Europe in 1963 with the American Folk Blues Festival, recording in Denmark for Storyville, and Britain in 1964 with the American Blues Caravan, recording *The Blues of Otis Spann* (Decca). Now recognized as an artist in his own right, rather than simply a band pianist – though he continued to work with Waters until his death – he recorded for Prestige (1965), Testament (1966), Bluesway (1966–8), Blue Horizon (1969, with **Fleetwood Mac**) and Vanguard (1969). He also accompanied, on record, fellow Chicago blues artists Johnny Young, Johnny Shines and **Buddy Guy**, as well as his then wife Lucille on *Cry Before I Go* (Bluesway, 1969).

SPARKS

Ron Mael, b. August 1948, Culver City, California, USA; Russell Mael, b. October 1953, Santa Monica, California

Sparks were an American duo who found their greatest success in Europe. During the mid-seventies they had a series of hits featuring Russell Mael's arresting falsetto and Ron Mael's curious lyrics. Later work

with **Giorgio Moroder** in Germany pre-dated the early eighties vogue for electro-pop.

As teenagers they modelled for mail-order catalogues before forming Urban Renewal Project in 1967 and then Halfnelson with guitarist and studio engineer Earl Mankey. The group was signed to Bearsville and **Todd Rundgren** produced an eponymous début album in 1971 which included the minor hit 'Wonder Girl'. Shortly after its release, the band changed its name to Sparks.

The Maels made a promotional trip to Europe before the release of *A Woofer in Tweeter's Clothing* (1973) but its poor American sales, coupled with the duo's positive reception in Britain, led them to record *Kimono My House* (1974) for Island in London. Work permit problems had prevented the rest of the band joining them in Britain, and the album featured a new all-British line-up.

Produced by Muff Winwood, the album included the Top Ten singles 'This Town Ain't Big Enough for the Both of Us', with its staccato chorus, and 'Amateur Hour' which dealt with adolescent anxieties. Further hits followed with the subdued 'Never Turn Your Back on Mother Earth' and 'Something for the Girl with Everything' (1975) but *Propaganda* (1974) and *Indiscreet* were poorly received.

Returning to America, the Maels signed to Columbia for *Big Beat* (1976). When this failed to stimulate interest, Sparks moved to Germany to record the disco-styled 'The Number One Song in Heaven' (Virgin, 1979), 'Beat the Clock' and 'When I'm with You'. Produced by Moroder, these were European hits, as were *Number One in Heaven* and *Terminal Jive* (1980).

While those albums inspired the work of such British bands as **Depeche Mode**, **Duran Duran** and the **Human League**, Sparks returned to America, signing to Atlantic for *Angst in My Pants* (1982) and *In Outer Space* (1983). They later recorded *Music That You Can Dance to* (Consolidated Allied, 1987) and the self-produced *Interior Design* (1988) on their own Fine Art label.

Over the next few years the duo recorded rarely. The fine career retrospective, *Profile: The Ultimate Collection* (Rhino), appeared in 1994, the year they returned to Britain for live shows to coincide with the release of *Gratuitous Sex and Senseless Violins. Balls* (Recognition, 2000) was a minor offering.

BRITNEY SPEARS

b. 2 December 1981, Kentwood, Louisiana, Texas, USA

Prodigious pop singer Spears rose to global superstardom while still in her mid-teens, prefiguring a new wave of female teen-orientated popsters, such as Christine Aguilera, whose single 'Genie in a Bottle' (BMG) was also a No. 1 US hit in 1999.

· Having spent her summers studying at the Off-Broadway Dance Centre in New York from an early age, Spears began appearing in TV commercials in the late eighties before landing a leading role in the *Mickey Mouse Club Show* on the Disney Channel in 1992. After two years of working in television Spears opted for a music career, signing to Jive Records in 1997. She began work the following year on her début album alongside production duo Eric Foster and Max Martin, who had written for **Whitney Houston** and the **Backstreet Boys**.

. . . Baby One More Time became a huge international success on its release, with the title track and lead-off single topping the charts in over thirty countries including Britain and the US, a feat which Spears was to repeat with 'Sometimes'. The singer planned to embark on a full world tour the following year after the completion of her high-school studies. She followed that with the equally successful *Oops . . . I Did It Again*, the title track of which was another international No. 1. The ever-so slightly suggestive title was partnered by carefully leaked information that 'Britney intended to remain a virgin until Mr Right came along' in a marketing move that cleverly melded *Mary Poppins* and *Lolita*.

THE SPECIALS

John Bradbury; Jerry Dammers, b. Gerald Dankin, 22 May 1954, India; Lynval Golding, b. 24 July 1951, Coventry, England; Terry Hall, b. 19 March 1959, Coventry; Horace Panter; Roddy Radiation, b. Rod Byers; Neville Staples, b. 11 April 1956, Christiana, Jamaica

One of the few bands to invent a music movement (albeit shortlived), the Specials pioneered Two-Tone, a revival of ska with contemporary lyrics. Of the group members' later projects, only the Fun Boy Three had commercial success, but Dammers remained an influential spokesman for such causes as Artists Against Apartheid in the late eighties.

The group's origins lay in several Coventry groups. Singer Hall had been with punk band Squad, Roddy Radiation in the Wild Boys and Dammers (keyboards), Panter (bass) and guitarist Golding in the Coventry Automatics, an unsuccessful attempt to fuse punk and roots reggae. In 1977 Special AKA (taking their name from the 'special' one-off records made for the early Jamaican sound systems) toured with the **Clash** and in 1979 formed the Two-Tone label (reflecting the band's and the music's racial integration) to release the Top Ten hit 'Gangsters', a tribute to **Prince Buster**'s 'Al Capone'. **Elvis Costello** produced the group's eponymous début album, which included the Specials' second hit, a revival of **Laurel Aitken**'s 'A Message to You Rudy'. A home for other

ska-revivalists, Two-Tone had more success in 1979 with **Madness** ('The Prince', dedicated to Prince Buster), the Beat (**Smokey Robinson**'s 'Tears of a Clown') and the Selecter ('On My Radio').

1980 brought more hits with a live EP 'Too Much Too Young', 'Rat Race' and 'Stereotype', while the Selecter – featuring singer Pauline Black – reached the Top Thirty with 'Three Minute Hero' and 'Missing Words'. Both the Beat and Madness had left Two-Tone to set up their own labels. *More Specials* (1980) moved away from the strict ska form but sold strongly and was followed by the prophetic protest song 'Ghost Town' (1981), which topped the British charts as the country was torn by inner-city riots. The Specials' own performances were also troubled by racial violence and Hall and Dammers were arrested at one concert after trying to prevent fights in the audience.

Soon afterwards, Hall, Staples and Golding left to form the Fun Boy Three, which eschewed the increasingly direct political stance of the Specials for quirky pop lyrics. Their eponymous début made the British Top Ten and the trio had a string of hits in 1981–3, including 'Tunnel of Love' (1982), 'Our Lips Are Sealed' (also a hit for US band the Go-Gos) and 'It Ain't What You Do It's the Way That You Do It' (1983). The latter was recorded with the female vocal group **Bananarama**, on whose first hit 'Really Saying Something' (Deram, 1983) the male trio had sung.

David Byrne of **Talking Heads** produced Fun Boy Three's second album, *Waiting*, but in 1984 the group split with Hall re-emerging with a new band, Colourfield. They released two albums, *Virgins and Philistines* (1985) and *Deception*, before splitting in 1986. In 1990 Hall released *Ultra Modern Nursery Rhymes* (Chrysalis) as part of the trio Terry, Blair and Anouchka. The highlights of his career were collected on *Terry Hall, the Collection* in 1993, the year his new band with **Eurythmics**' Dave Stewart, Vegas, released its eponymous début album. Among Staple's later productions was 'We've Got Feelings Too' (1994) by Bindu, a group which featured his vocalist daughter Sheena.

With Radiation and Panter also leaving the Specials, Dammers and Bradbury regrouped as Special AKA, recording 'The Boiler' (1983), a harrowing tale of rape sung by former Bodysnatchers member Rhoda Dakar, before Dammers' incantatory 'Nelson Mandela' reached the British Top Ten in 1984. It was featured on the album *In the Studio*. The following year the group split but Dammers continued his musical-political activities by collaborating on 'Starvation', a ska-reggae charity record, and organizing the Nelson Mandela 70th Birthday Party at Wembley Stadium in 1988. Among those appearing were **Simple Minds**, **Stevie Wonder**, **Whitney Houston** and **Tracy Chapman**.

Dammers appeared at the 1990 Wembley concert

to celebrate Mandela's release, but maintained a low profile for the next few years, re-emerging in 1993 with a one-night-a-week club in London's Covent Garden. A retrospective, *The Specials Singles*, appeared in 1991, when it made the British Top Ten. It was followed by two live albums, *Too Much Too Young* (Receiver) and *Live at the Moonlight Club* (both 1991), after which the group members pursued various solo projects. Hall released *Home* (1995) and *Laugh* (1997), by which time the band re-formed for *Today's Specials* (1996). They toured extensively in support of it and the later *Guilty Til Proved Innocent* (1998).

PHIL SPECTOR
b. Philip Harvey Spector, 26 December 1940, Bronx, New York, USA

During the sixties Spector did more than anyone to establish the role of the record producer as creative artist. He created numerous hits with the **Ronettes**, **Shangri-Las**, **Crystals** and others using his 'wall of sound'. This combined an R&B rhythm section with a liberal use of echo and multiple tracking and large studio bands including string sections. Spector himself called the resulting records 'little symphonies for the kids'. Almost as significant in creating the image of Spector as a lonely, tormented genius was his reclusive, erratic personality. Although he went on to work with **The Beatles**, **Leonard Cohen** and the **Ramones**, his later success was intermittent.

He moved to Los Angeles as a child, playing piano and guitar in high-school bands with drummer **Sandy Nelson** and **Kim Fowley**. At the age of seventeen, he formed the Teddy Bears with schoolmates Annette Kleinbard and Marshall Leib, writing and producing the lachrymose teen ballad 'To Know Him Is to Love Him' (Dore, 1958). The title of the record, which was an international hit, was based on an inscription on Spector's father's grave.

Later records for Imperial ('Oh Why', 1959) were less successful and Spector next worked with **Lee Hazelwood**, who masterminded **Duane Eddy**'s hits, while Kleinbard, as Carol Connors, went on to write 'Hey Little Cobra' (Columbia, 1964) for the Ripchords and 'Gonna Fly Now (Theme from *Rocky*)' (United Artists), an American No. 1 for Bill Conti in 1977. Spector made 'I Really Do' (Trey, 1959) with the Spector Three before working as an assistant in New York to **Leiber and Stoller**. These early apprenticeships helped him to shape his own sound. From Hazelwood he learned the use of echo while Leiber and Stoller showed him how to marry heavy string arrangements with complex Latin-American rhythms.

In New York, Spector co-wrote **Ben E. King**'s 'Spanish Harlem' and **Gene Pitney**'s 'Dream for Sale' before producing his first big hits on the Dune label.

These included **Ray Peterson**'s 'Corrine Corrina' (1960) and 'Pretty Little Angel Eyes' by Curtis Lee (1961). Spector went on to supervise the Paris Sisters' 'I Love How You Love Me' (Gregmark, 1961) and 'Second Hand Love' by **Connie Francis** (1962).

As productions, however, these were varied and anonymous. The first flowering of Spector's distinctive approach did not occur until he and Lester Sill formed their own Philles label in 1961. Beginning with the Top Twenty hit 'There's No Other (Like My Baby)' by the Crystals he began to perfect the Spector sound at Goldstar studios in Los Angeles where he brought together such session players as Earl Palmer and Hal Blaine (drums), **Leon Russell** and Nino Tempo (piano), **Glen Campbell** and Barney Kessell (guitars) and Larry Knechtel (keyboards). With **Jack Nitzsche** as arranger, Spector's studio group often had three drummers, bassists and keyboards players plus numerous guitars and horns. An autocrat, he bought out Sill in 1962 and had little regard for his singers, treating them as no more than an element in the production mix. Thus, he brought in top session singer **Darlene Love** to sing lead on such tracks as the Crystals' 'He's a Rebel' (written by Pitney) and Bob B. Soxx and the Blue Jeans' update of 'Zip-a-De-Doo-Dah'.

In 1963 Love made '(Today) I Met the Boy I'm Going to Marry' under her own name. With the Crystals' 'Da Doo Ron Ron' and 'Then He Kissed Me' plus the Ronettes' plaintive 'Be My Baby' and 'Baby I Love You' (1964), it marked the final stage in the evolution of the 'wall of sound'. Perhaps the apotheosis of this phase of Spector's career was *A Christmas Gift for You* (1963), a concept album featuring interpretations of seasonal songs by all the Philles artists.

The following year Spector sat in on sessions for the first **Rolling Stones** album (co-writing 'Little by Little') and had further success with the Ronettes (the anthemic '[The Best Part of] Breakin' Up') before discovering a white duo, the **Righteous Brothers**. Their powerful harmonies on Cynthia Weil and **Barry Mann**'s 'You've Lost That Lovin' Feelin'' created blue-eyed soul and led to further hits, including remakes of **Roy Hamilton**'s 'Unchained Melody' and 'Ebb Tide'. Spector's masterpiece, however, was the monumental, operatic 'River Deep Mountain High', co-written with **Ellie Greenwich** and Jeff Barry and recorded by **Ike** and **Tina Turner**. Although this and 'A Love Like Yours' were British hits, their failure in America signalled the end of the era of Spector's commercial dominance.

Comedian Lenny Bruce made an album for Philles before the label closed down in 1967 and Spector took parts in television series and the film *Easy Rider* but made no further records until he produced Sonny Charles and the Checkmates' only hit, 'Black Pearl' (A&M, 1969). Through The Beatles' business manager

Allen Klein, Spector was next brought in to produce **John Lennon**'s 'Instant Karma' and salvage the album *Let It Be*, whose unmixed tapes were victim of the growing estrangement between **Paul McCartney** and Lennon.

Spector continued to supervise much of the Apple label output up to 1972, including **George Harrison**'s *All Things Must Pass* (1970), the live *Concert for Bangladesh* (1972) and Lennon's *John Lennon/Plastic Ono Band* (1971) and *Some Time in New York City* (1972). While working on tracks for what would become Lennon's *Rock'n'Roll*, Spector had a serious car accident which put him out of action for nearly a year.

He returned in 1975 (the year of his divorce from Veronica Wright, former lead singer of the Ronettes) as a label owner, concluding deals with Warners and Polydor to reissue much of the Philles catalogue. His new recordings from this period included **Dion**'s 'Born to Be with You' (1975) and singles by **Cher** and Jerri Bo Keno, none of which enhanced his reputation. The label deal came to an end in 1977 and Spector returned to freelance production, working with Leonard Cohen (*Death of a Ladies Man*, 1977), the Ramones (*End of the Century*, 1980) and **Yoko Ono** (*Seasons of Glass*, 1981). During the eighties Spector was largely inactive. In 1988 he hired Allen Klein to resolve a royalty dispute with Leiber and Stoller's publishing company and to re-market his classic recordings. Subsequently a series of 'best of' compilations featuring the highlights of his sixties output was released. The four-CD set *Back to Mono* (ABKCO, 1991) is the definitive career retrospective, while *Early Productions, 1958–1961* (Rhino, 1983) explores the beginnings of his career.

A 1989 biography, *He's a Rebel* by Marc Ribowsky, was withdrawn after Spector sued the author and publisher for libel.

LEN SPENCER
b. Leonard Garfield Spencer, 12 February 1867, Washington DC, USA, d. 15 December 1914

Known nationally in the 1890s, Spencer was America's first recording star. Moreover, his 'Arkansas Traveler', released on several labels between 1900 and 1902, is generally regarded as the first song to sell a million copies on record.

Spencer was the son of a renowned educational reformer, who had developed the Spencerian method of penmanship taught in American schools at the turn of the century, and a suffragist and political activist. His repertoire initially included both the songs of the first generation of professional songwriters such as **Stephen Foster** ('The Old Folks at Home', New Jersey, 1902) and James Bland ('Carry Me Back

to Old Virginny', 1903, later a million-seller for **Alma Gluck**) and the latest pop songs of the day, 'Ta-Ra-Ra-Boom Der-E' (written and recorded in 1890), 'Mamie Come and Kiss Your Honey Boy' (1893) and 'Little Alabama Coon' (1895). This ear for a song led him to record one of **George M. Cohan**'s earliest hit songs, 'I Guess I'll Have to Telegraph My Baby' (Columbia, 1899) – also a hit for **Arthur Collins** – and 'Everything Is Ragtime Now' (1899) – one of the earliest celebrations of the new music – as well as several 'coon' songs of the day, including Ernest Hogan's (now notorious) 'All Coons Look Alike to Me'.

However, following the success of the comic 'Arkansas Traveler' (first recorded for Columbia in 1900 and subsequently on Edison and Victor, with Charles D'Almaine on violin, in 1902), Spencer turned almost entirely to comedy, either on his own or in partnership with **Ada Jones**. His hits included several devoted to the exploits of Reuben Haskins ('Ride on a Cyclone Auto', 1903; 'Ride 'Round the World in His Airship', 1904), and parodies ('The Transformation Scene from *Dr Jekyll and Mr Hyde*', 1905). His last hit was a duet with the noted tenor **Billy Murray**, 'Two Gentlemen from Ireland' (Edison, 1910).

SPICE GIRLS
Victoria Beckham, aka 'Posh Spice', b. Victoria Adams, 17 April 1975, Goff's Oak, Hertfordshire, England; Emma Lee Bunton, aka 'Baby Spice', b. 21 January 1976, London; Melanie Jayne Chisholm, aka 'Sporty Spice', b. 12 January 1974, Liverpool; Melanie Gulzar, aka 'Scary Spice', b. Melanie Janine Brown, 29 May 1975, Leeds; Geraldine Estelle Halliwell, aka 'Ginger Spice', b. 6 August 1972, Watford

After topping the charts in twenty-two countries with 'Wannabe' in 1996, the Spice Girls established themselves as one of the most successful pop bands of the decade. In their wake came a number of female vocal groups aimed predominantly at the teenage market the success of the Spice Girls had identified. However, more than any of the other groups that followed them the Spice Girls were of sociological and cultural interest as well as being a mere pop phenomenon. Going hand in hand with their 'girl next door' image was their 'girl power' philosophy, a post-modern take on traditional feminist values advocating strength of character, confidence and individuality. The quintet took a break after the departure of apparent leader Halliwell in 1998, laying the foundations for future solo careers.

Geri, Mel B, Mel C, Emma and Victoria came together in 1995 after responding to an advertisement placed in *Stage* magazine by father and son management duo Chris and Bob Herbert, before deciding to forge their own route to stardom. Under the guidance of Simon Fuller the quintet spent the next year working on their début album with songwriters Richard Stanard and Matt Rowe and production duo Absolute, whose previous credits include **Al Green** and **Mica Paris**. The aspirational bubblegum pop of 'Wannabe' soon rose to the top of the British chart upon its release in July 1996, while 'Say You'll Be There' set a trend of UK number one singles that would continue with '2 Becomes 1' and the double A-side 'Mama'/ 'Who Do You Think You Are?'. After *Spice* had become one of the year's biggest sellers in the UK the group set their sights on the rest of the world, equalling their British success across Europe, Asia and the US as they began a mammoth world tour.

Within a year the Spice Girls had recorded a second album, *Spiceworld* (1997), which included four more hit singles – 'Spice Up Your Life', 'Too Much', 'Stop' and 'Viva Forever' – of which only 'Stop' failed to top the UK charts. In addition, the quintet starred in *Spiceworld the Movie*, a lacklustre, but highly successful, send-up of their rise to fame, with Richard E. Grant taking the role of their svengali-like manager, based on the recently sacked Fuller.

The Spice Girls were reduced to a quartet in 1998 when Halliwell suddenly left, claiming that she wished to devote more of her time to promoting health issues, which she could not fit into the group's schedule. She subsequently was appointed a UN Ambassador with the brief of raising the profile of women's health issues. After her departure the remaining Spice Girls took an extended break following an exhaustive world tour, reconvening only for 'Goodbye', a tribute to their former colleague which saw them become the only band other than **The Beatles** to achieve the coveted Christmas number one in Britain for three consecutive years.

Brown was the first Spice Girl to launch a solo career, topping the UK chart with 'I Want You Back' (1998), written and produced by **Missy 'Misdemeanor' Elliot**. Her second single, a cover of **Cameo**'s 'Word Up' (1999), was a comparative flop, only reaching the top Twenty. Chisholm's first step towards solo work was as guest vocalist on **Bryan Adams**' 'When You're Gone' (1998), after which she released 'Going Down' from the rock-edged *Northern Star* (1999). In between work as a UN Ambassador Halliwell found time to release *Schizophonic* (1999), spawning a pair of hit singles, 'Look at Me' and 'Mi Chico Latino'. The success of Halliwell's autobiography, *If Only*, confirmed her successful transformation from pop personality to fully fledged media icon.

Both Brown and Adams married their partners in 1999, dancer Jimmy Gulzar and footballer David Beckham, respectively, while also giving birth to their first children. Brown and Gulzar subsequently separated in 2000, while Adams set her feet on a tentative media career in the manner of Halliwell.

All four remaining Spice Girls continued to give precedence to their solo careers for much of 2000. Adams had a UK hit single with 'Buggin'', a collaboration with UK Garage producers True Steppers and former Another Level vocalist Dane Bowers, while Bunton released a successful cover of 'What I Am' alongside dance act Tin Tin Out. Chisholm reissued her *Northern Star* album with an added dance flavour after her attempt to cross over into the indie market failed and hit the top of the UK charts with 'I Will Turn to You'. Brown recorded a lacklustre R&B-flavoured solo album, *Hot*, which featured production contributions from the likes of Rodney Jenkins, Blackstreet's **Teddy Riley** and **Jimmy Jam and Terry Lewis**.

The Spice Girls reconvened later in the year for the release of their third album, *Forever*. It featured little variation from the formula of its predecessors but was still a huge international success and included the single 'Holler'.

THE SPINNERS
Bobby Smith, b. 10 April 1937, Detroit, Michigan, USA; Henry Fambrough, b. 10 May 1935, Detroit; Billy Henderson, b. 9 August 1939, Detroit; George W. Dixon; G. C. Cameron, b. Detroit (replaced by Philippe Wynne, b. 3 April 1941, Detroit, d. 14 July 1984, replaced by John Edwards)

Known in Britain as the Detroit Spinners, to distinguish them from the Spinners folk group, the Spinners, like the **Drifters**, kept abreast of the changing fashions in black vocal music through regular changes of their lead singer.

Organized by **Harvey Fuqua** in 1957 as the Moonglows, the group became the Spinners and had their first R&B hit, featuring Fuqua singing lead, with 'That's What Girls Are Made for' (Tri-Phi, 1961). After records on Harvey and Time, the Spinners moved to Motown when Fuqua sold his labels to **Berry Gordy** in 1965. With Cameron as lead vocalist they had several R&B hits (including 'Truly Yours', 1966) and two pop hits ('I'll Always Love You', 1965, and the **Stevie Wonder**-written and produced 'It's a Shame', 1970) before moving to Atlantic in 1971. With Wynne replacing Cameron, they had success with a series of lush, **Thom Bell**-produced close-harmony ballads, including 'I'll Be Around'* (1972), 'Could It Be I'm Falling in Love'*, 'One of a Kind (Love Affair)'* (1973), the chart-topping 'Then Came You'* with **Dionne Warwick(e)** (1974), 'They Just Can't Stop It (Games People Play)'* (1975) and 'The Rubberband Man'* (1976). Following the departure of Wynne for an unsuccessful solo career on the Atlantic subsidiary Cotillion, the group returned to the charts with a new lead singer, the sweet-voiced Edwards, and producer, Michael Zager. They reworked past hits and incorporated some new lyrics on 'Working My Way Back to You (Forgive Me Girl)'* (1980), a version of the **Four Seasons**' 1966 hit, and 'Cupid (I've Loved You for a Long Time)' (1980), a version of **Sam Cooke**'s 1961 hit. They subsequently recorded for Mirage and Volt with little success. For Atlantic, they recorded *Crossfire* (1984) and *Lovin' Feelings* (1985), moving to Volt for *Down to Business* (1989). The group continued to play revival shows well into the nineties.

A One of a Kind Love Affair (Rhino, 1991) is the definitive career anthology.

SPIRIT

Mark Andes, b. 19 February 1948, Philadelphia, Pennsylvania, USA (replaced by Al Staehely, b. Texas); Randy California, b. Randolph Craig Woolfe, 20 February 1951, Los Angeles, California, d. 2 January 1997 (replaced by John Christian Staehely, b. Texas); Ed Cassidy, b. 4 May 1931, Chicago, Illinois; Jay Ferguson, b. 10 May 1947, Burbank, California; John Locke, b. 25 September 1934, Los Angeles

One of the most admired West Coast rock bands of the late sixties, Spirit's music mingled jazz and rock elements.

Cassidy was a veteran jazz drummer who had played with **Thelonious Monk** and **Gerry Mulligan** before joining **Ry Cooder** and **Taj Mahal** in early folk-rock band the Rising Sons in 1965. He next played with the Red Roosters, which included California (guitar), Ferguson (vocals) and bassist Andes. That group split up soon afterwards, with California and Cassidy moving to New York where the former sat in with **Jimi Hendrix**, but in 1967 the quartet formed Spirits Rebellious with pianist Locke. The name was taken from a book by Kahlil Gibran.

As Spirit, the group recorded an eponymous album for **Lou Adler**'s Ode label, followed by *The Family That Plays Together* (1968), which had arrangements by Marty Paich and included a hit single, 'I Got a Line on You' (1969). After *Clear Spirit* (1969), which included music from the soundtrack of Jacques Demy's *The Model Shop*, the group moved to Epic for their most successful album, *The Twelve Dreams of Dr Sardonicus*. Produced by David Briggs, it featured such songs as 'Nature's Way', 'Animal Zoo' and 'Mr Skin'.

At this point, Ferguson and Andes left to form Jo Jo Gunne with Matt Andes (guitar) and Curly Smith (drums) and record a Top Thirty hit, 'Run Run Run' (Asylum, 1972). After that group split in 1974, Ferguson went on to a solo career that included the Top

Ten hit 'Thunder Island' (Asylum, 1978). Spirit made *Feedback* (1972) with the Staehely brothers, but after Epic rejected the concept album *Potatoland* (it was eventually issued independently in 1981), Spirit split. California worked on English singer Peter Hammill's *The Silent Corner* (Charisma, 1973) and cut the eccentric solo album *Captain Kopter and the Twirlybirds* (Epic, 1972) with Hendrix bassist Noel Redding, Cassidy and Locke.

With the latter two plus bassist Barry Keene, he reformed Spirit for *Spirit of 76* (Mercury, 1975) and the group was joined by the Andes brothers for *Son of Spirit* (1976). With Cassidy and California as the nucleus, further Spirit albums included *Future Games (A Magical Kahvana Dream)* (1977) and *The Thirteenth Dream* (1984).

Spirit signed to IRS Records in 1989, releasing *Rapture in the Chamber* (1989) and *Tent of Miracles* (1990). The band continued to tour occasionally into the early nineties, releasing *California Blues* (Were) in 1997.

Time Circle, 1968–1973 (Sony, 1993) and *The Collection* (Castle, 1992) are the most representative collections.

VICTORIA SPIVEY

b. 15 October 1906, Houston, Texas, USA, d. 3 October 1976, New York

Her rasping voice and narrow range lacked the grandeur of **Bessie Smith** or the grace of **Ethel Waters**, but Victoria Spivey made a number of idiosyncratic and affecting records in the twenties and thirties, seldom leaving the direct path of the blues, and often accompanied by the finest of contemporary jazzmen.

She learned to play piano as a child and in her teens worked in local clubs and theatres. Moving to St Louis in 1926 she recorded, with her own piano accompaniment, 'Black Snake Blues' (Okeh). Its success earned her further recording dates with Okeh (1926–9), Victor (1929–30) and other labels. She composed most of her material, favouring as subjects reptiles, crime and tuberculosis, on which she wrote a famous 'T. B. Blues' (Okeh, 1927). Often accompanied on guitar by **Lonnie Johnson**, she recorded with him the suggestive duet 'Toothache Blues' (Okeh, 1928). She also recorded in 1929 with **Louis Armstrong** on Okeh and trumpeter Henry 'Red' Allen's New York Orchestra (more or less the Luis Russell Band) on Victor, cutting 'Funny Feathers' with both, and with Allen the superb 'Moaning the Blues' session.

Meanwhile Spivey had been appearing in revue and in King Vidor's all-black movie *Hallelujah!* (1929). She continued to work both in vaudeville and as a blues recording artist throughout the thirties, ending the decade in the New York and travelling productions of the musical revue *Hellzapoppin'*. From the late forties she was based in New York, playing jazz venues and hotel lounges.

Reunited in 1961 with Johnson, Spivey played club dates and recorded two albums for Prestige-Bluesville; for the same label she also brought out of retirement her contemporaries Alberta Hunter and Lucille Hegamin for the album *Songs We Taught Your Mother*. The following year she started the Spivey label to issue her own new recordings, made with jazz friends like tenor saxophonist Buddy Tate, as well as a reissue collection, and new product by old friends like Johnson and singer/pianist Roosevelt Sykes (including *The Queen and Her Knights*, 1963). She also encouraged young musicians, both black and white, among them **Bob Dylan**, who played harmonica on a session by **Big Joe Williams**. In 1963 she toured Europe with the American Folk Blues Festival and for the next dozen years appeared at similar events all over the US, an enthusiastic, if sometimes eccentric, promoter of the blues.

Two sisters, Addie 'Sweet Pease' Spivey and Elton Spivey, 'The Za Zu Girl', had less distinguished touring and recording careers.

DUSTY SPRINGFIELD
b. Mary O'Brien, 16 April 1939, London, England, d. 2 March 1999, Los Angeles, California, USA

Of all the white female singers to emerge from Britain in the sixties, Springfield, with her husky, breathy voice, made the greatest use of R&B and soul models on recordings like 'I Only Want to Be with You'* (1963) and 'You Don't Have to Say You Love Me'. However, unlike such male compatriots as **Rod Stewart** and **Joe Cocker**, she never fitted into the role of 'blue-eyed soul singer' and, excluded from the mainstream of rock in the seventies, drifted inconclusively between cabaret and soul approaches, before finding fame again through her association with the **Pet Shop Boys** in the late eighties.

After singing with the Lana Sisters, Dusty Springfield formed the Springfields with her brother Tom and Tim Field in 1960. They had a series of British successes, including the folky 'Island of Dreams' and 'Say I Won't Be There' (Philips, 1963) and a surprise American million-seller with their version of the country song 'Silver Threads and Golden Needles' (1962). When the trio split up, Springfield's strong vocals on 'I Only Want to Be with You', despite being cocooned in composer Ivor Raymonde's jaunty production, revealed a strong R&B influence. It was the first of a lengthy series of hits in both Britain and America that included her melodramatic reading of **Burt Bacharach**'s 'I Just Don't Know What to Do with Myself', a cool version of the same writer's 'Wishin' and Hopin'' (1964), and her impassioned interpretation of the big ballad 'You Don't Have to Say You Love Me' (1966). The best of her British recordings, the Italian song was written by V. Pallavincini and P. Donnaggio as 'Io Che Non Vivo (Senzate)' and translated into English by Simon Napier-Bell and Vicki Wickham (it was later revived successfully by **Elvis Presley**, 1971). Other hits of the period included a subtle reading of **Carole King**'s 'Goin' Back', 'All I See Is You' (1966) and 'The Look of Love' (1967) from the James Bond film *Casino Royale*.

After a brief period in which she turned to cabaret, Springfield left Philips, signed to Atlantic and settled in America where she recorded what is generally regarded as her best album, *Dusty in Memphis* (1969). Produced by **Jerry Wexler**, it included the transatlantic hit, the hard-edged 'Son of a Preacher Man', which was later revived by **Aretha Franklin**. Her last British hit, it was followed in America by **Michel Legrand**'s film song 'Windmills of Your Mind' (1969), a British hit for Noel Harrison (Reprise, 1969), and **Jerry Butler**'s 'A Brand New Me' (1969). After leaving Atlantic, Springfield was produced less sympathetically and her seventies albums were lesser works. They included *Cameo* (ABC, 1973), *It Begins Again* (Mercury, 1978) and *Living without Your Love* (1979). A lone single for 20th Century was followed by the disco-styled *White Heat* (Casablanca, 1983).

In 1987 she returned to the British charts in collaboration with the Pet Shop Boys with 'What Have I Done to Deserve This?' and recorded a duet with Richard Carpenter of the **Carpenters**, 'Something in Your Eyes'. Springfield resumed her solo career in 1989 with the Pet Shop Boys-produced hits 'Nothing Has Been Proved' and 'In Private'. The collaboration provided four tracks for *Reputation* (1990). In 1994 the career retrospective *Goin' Back* returned Springfield to the British Top Five. It was released simultaneously with the boxed set *Dusty – The Legend of Dusty Springfield*. However, subsequent recordings failed to revive her solo career and she retired from view for most of the nineties.

RICK SPRINGFIELD
b. Richard Springthorpe, 23 August 1949, Sydney, Australia

After surviving a brief spell as a teen-idol, Springfield enjoyed success as a rock singer in the eighties with the aid of a starring role in a television soap-opera.

The son of a British army officer, Springfield's first groups were the Jordy Boys, Rock House and Zoot, who reached No. 1 in Australia with 'Speak to the Sky'. Recorded in London, *Beginnings* (Capitol, 1972) included a new version of the song which became a

Top Twenty hit in America. After the unsuccessful *Comic Book Heroes* (Columbia, 1974), he joined **Wes Farrell**'s Chelsea label but the company folded soon after the release of *Wait for the Night* (1976), whose backing musicians included **Elton John**'s rhythm section Dee Murray (bass) and Nigel Olsson (drums). Springfield then turned to television, in 1981 landing the role of Dr Noah Drake in *General Hospital*. The same year he signed to RCA, and 'Jessie's Girl'* from *Working Class Dog* reached No. 1. The Keith Olsen-produced album also included the lesser hit, 'I've Done Everything for You'.

During the following three years, nine of Springfield's singles reached the Top Thirty. The most successful were 'Don't Talk to Strangers' from *Success Hasn't Spoiled Me Yet* (1982), 'Affair of the Heart' from *Living in Oz* (1983) and 'Love Somebody' from the film *Hard to Hold* (1984), in which Springfield appeared as a rock star. His later albums included *Tao* (1985) and *Rock of Life* (1988). *Greatest Hits* (1989) is just that.

BRUCE SPRINGSTEEN

b. *Bruce Frederick Joseph Springsteen, 23 September 1949, Freehold, New Jersey, USA*

In 1974 critic (and future Springsteen manager) Jon Landau wrote 'I saw rock'n'roll's future and its name is Bruce Springsteen'. Perhaps surprisingly, Springsteen's subsequent career all but justified that claim as his popularity grew and his style was closely and consciously developed as an extension of the rock tradition leading from **Elvis Presley** and **Chuck Berry** through **The Beatles** and **The Who**. By the eighties, as his writing matured, he could reasonably be called the poet of blue-collar America and his spare, muscular, observational songs be compared equally to those of **Woody Guthrie**, Berry and **Steve Earle**, the other great poet of the dispossessed. More problematic was his live show, which was the most widely admired in rock despite being criticized for its (flag-waving) conservative musical stance.

Of Irish-Italian parentage, the young Springsteen led a double musical life. As a member of such bands as Steel Mill and Dr Zoom and the Sonic Boom, he played the bars of New Jersey, but he also performed in Greenwich village as a solo singer-songwriter. It was as the latter that **John Hammond** signed him to Columbia in 1972. Produced by Springsteen's manager, Mike Appel, *Greetings from Asbury Park, NJ* (1973) mixed acoustic tracks with accompaniments by Springsteen's band. It included 'Blinded by the Light' and 'Spirit in the Night', which were hits for **Manfred Mann** in 1976–7.

Led by Clarence Clemons (saxes) and Gary Tallent (bass), Springsteen's E Street Band was more heavily featured on *The Wild, the Innocent and the E. Street Shuffle* (1973). Reviewers compared his voice to those of **Van Morrison** and **Wilson Pickett**, but the album's weakest aspect was its lengthy **Dylan**-esque lyrics. These were replaced on *Born to Run* (1975) by a more evocative and economical rock approach and the album's title track became his first hit and one of Springsteen's best-known songs. The touring band had now been joined by guitarist Miami Steve Van Zandt, who had played in Dr Zoom and the earlier line-up of the E Street Band, and worked with vocal group the **Dovells** and Southside Johnny and the Asbury Jukes, whose 1976 début album he produced.

The momentum of Springsteen's career was interrupted by a legal dispute with Appel which prevented him from releasing *Darkness on the Edge of Town* until 1978. With Landau now installed as manager and producer, this was the first of a trio of albums whose dominant tone was one of brooding thoughtfulness. In the same year Springsteen's songs enjoyed further chart success when the **Pointer Sisters** ('Fire'*) and **Patti Smith** ('Because the Night') took his compositions into the Top Twenty.

'Hungry Heart' and 'Fade Away' were among the hits from the 1980 double-album *The River*, whose title song was a sombre tale of small-town life. The peak of this realist phase was reached with *Nebraska* (1982), which was recorded at 'demo' quality on four-track recording equipment to avoid the high gloss of studio technology.

It took a move to mainstream rock on *Born in the USA* (1984), however, for Springsteen to achieve superstar status. With sales of over 12 million, the album also spawned five hit singles. Besides the title track, these were 'Dancing in the Dark', 'Cover Me', 'I'm on Fire' and 'Glory Days'. 'Born in the USA' itself combined patriotism with an underdog stance but caused controversy among those who felt Springsteen had capitulated to American chauvinism.

In 1985 he undertook a mammoth tour with Nils Lofgren replacing Van Zandt, who as well as recording the first in a number of solo albums as Little Steven & the Disciples of Soul ('Men Without Women', 1982) had organized the 'Sun City' project, a multi-artist charity recording which highlighted the apartheid policies of South Africa and in which Springsteen participated. Van Zandt and the Disciples of Soul would continue to record throughout the eighties, although without much commercial success. Springsteen's *Live 1975–85* (1986) was a five-album collection of club and concert recordings which included both originals and his covers of such songs as Edwin Starr's 'War', **Sam and Dave**'s 'Raise Your Hand', **Woody Guthrie**'s 'This Land Is Your Land' and **Tom Waits**' 'Jersey Girl'. Hit singles from the live collection included 'War' and 'Fire'.

The low-key *Tunnel of Love* (1987) found Springsteen at the height of his songwriting powers. Both 'Brilliant Disguise' and the album's title track reached No. 1 in America. Springsteen later took part in the *Human Rights Now!* world tour with **Peter Gabriel**, Sting, Tracy Chapman and Senegalese musician **Youssou N'Dour**. He also recorded two Woodie Guthrie songs for *A Vision Shared* (Columbia, 1988), a tribute to Guthrie and **Leadbelly**.

After a world tour in 1988, Springsteen took a break from recording and touring, announcing the break-up of the E Street Band in late 1989. In 1991 he began working on a new album with new musicians, retaining only Bittan from the E Street days. In 1992 he simultaneously released two albums, *Human Touch* and *Lucky Town*. Reviews and sales were poorer than expected, but Springsteen's subsequent world tour was a sell-out. A TV appearance in 1992 provided the live album *In Concert – MTV Plugged* (1993), on which he performed mainly stripped-down versions of the strongest material from the two 1992 albums. In 1994 Springsteen had one of his biggest hits worldwide with the sombre 'Streets of Philadelphia', the title song of the movie *Philadelphia*. In 1995 Sony issued the compilation album, *Greatest Hits*.

The brooding, mostly acoustic *The Ghost of Tom Joad* (1995) was a moving celebration of a wide range of American losers. Springsteen toured extensively in support of it, sometimes with a re-formed E Street Band and, most notably in Europe, with a stripped-down band. *18 Tracks* (1999) was a lesser album.

Born to Run (1981) and *Glory Days* (1987) by Dave Marsh were detailed official biographies, while Bobbie Ann Mason's novel, *In Country* (1985), took Springsteen's vision of America as a central motif and explored its impact on his listeners. *Tracks* (1998), a lavish four-CD collection of out-takes, unreleased material and alternative takes, gives a good sense of how exploratory Springsteen was in the studio, while *One Step Up/Two Steps* (1997), a tribute album from the likes of **David Bowie**, **Joe Cocker** and others, only confirmed how good an interpreter of his own songs Springsteen was.

SPYRO GYRA
Manolo Barendra; Jay Beckenstein; Eli Konikoff (replaced by Richie Morales, replaced by Joel Rosenblatt); David Samuels; Rick Strauss (replaced by Julio Fernandez); Jeremy Wall (replaced by Tom Schuman)

Spyro Gyra were the most commercially successful of the second wave of jazz-rock fusion groups who followed such innovators as **Weather Report** and **Herbie Hancock**. Eight of the group's first ten albums reached No. 1 in the jazz charts.

The band was founded in Buffalo, New York, by Beckenstein (saxes, lyricon) and keyboards-player Wall in 1977. Produced by Richard Calandra, their eponymous début album was self-distributed and included 'Shaker Song', which became a minor hit after the group signed to MCA's Infinity label. The catchy title track of *Morning Dance* (1978) was a pop hit in both America and Britain. After *Catching the Sun* (MCA, 1980), the **Brecker Brothers** were guest musicians on *Carnival* (1980). Spyro Gyra's Latin-jazz influences were emphasized after 1983 when guitarist Fernandez, Morales (drums) and Barendra (percussion) joined the band.

Later albums included the live *Access All Areas* (1985) and *City Kids* (1985). Soon after working on *Breakout* (1986), Spyro Gyra's long-time producer Calandra died. In 1987 the group released *Stories without Words* and, in 1989, *Point of View*. Percussionist Sammy Figueroa joined for *Three Wishes* (GRP, 1992), which varied the Spyro Gyra formula by omitting synthesizers from the line-up. After twelve years with the band, vibes- and marimba-player Samuels left in 1994 to form the Caribbean Jazz Project with steel-pan-player Andy Narello. The band continued with *Love and Other Obsessions* (1995).

SQUEEZE
Chris Difford, b. 11 April 1954, London, England; Jools Holland, b. Julian Holland (replaced by Paul Carrack, b. April 1951, Sheffield, replaced by Don Snow, b. 13 January 1957, Kenya); Harry Kakoulli (replaced by John Bentley, b. 16 April 1951, London, replaced by Keith Wilkinson); Gilson Lavis, b. 27 June 1951, Bedford (replaced by Pete Thomas); Matt Irving; Andy Metcalfe; Glenn Tilbrook, b. 31 August 1957, London

Difford and Tilbrook's articulate songwriting made Squeeze one of the most impressive British rock groups in the early eighties.

The group was formed in 1973 when lyricist Difford joined forces with Holland (keyboards) and guitarist/singer Tilbrook who had been playing in pub bands. The line-up was completed by bassist Kakoulli and experienced session drummer Lavis. Despite the fact that their songs owed more to **The Who** or the **Kinks**, Squeeze were promoted as a punk band and the EP *Packet of Three* (Deptford Fun City, 1978) was produced by former **Velvet Underground** member **John Cale**.

The group was signed to A&M and Cale supervised most of the début eponymous album, from which 'Take Me I'm Yours' was a hit. Both the title track and 'Up the Junction' from *Cool for Cats* (1979) were equally successful. The songs were tuneful, wry, literate descriptions of slices of South London life. *Argy Bargy* (1980) included the playful 'Pulling Mussels

(From the Shell)' as well as the hit 'Another Nail in My Heart'.

After Holland left for a solo career, initially backed by the Millionaires, and to compère the TV music programme *The Tube*, Squeeze was joined by Carrack, who had had an American No. 1 as a member of Ace with 'How Long' (Anchor, 1974). He sang lead vocals on the minor American hit 'Tempted' from *East Side Story* (1981). Produced by **Elvis Costello**, the album also included the country-styled 'Labelled with Love'.

With Carrack leaving for work with **Nick Lowe**, then Mike and the Mechanics, and a solo recording career, Snow joined Squeeze for *Sweets from a Stranger* (1982), the final record before the group split. The two songwriters formed Difford and Tilbrook, releasing a poorly received eponymous album in 1984, while Lavis and bassist Bentley played sessions.

The following year, Squeeze re-formed with Difford, Tilbrook, Lavis, Holland and new bassist Wilkinson. The hurriedly recorded *Cosi Fan Tutti Frutti* (1985) was disappointing but *Babylon and on* (1987), which introduced second keyboard-player Metcalfe (ex-**Robyn Hitchcock**'s Soft Boys), included some of Difford and Tilbrook's most assured writing on such tracks as 'Tough Love', 'In Today's Room' and the hit 'Hourglass'. The lesser *Frank* followed in 1989, and after an American tour to promote it, Holland again left the band to be briefly replaced by Irving. Holland released the solo album, *A World of His Own* (IRS, 1990) (followed by *The Full Compliment*, 1991, and *The A–Z of the Piano*, 1993) and resumed his career as a TV presenter. He subsequently formed the Jools Holland Big Band.

Dropped by A&M, Squeeze marked time by releasing the live album *A Round and A Bout* (1990) on IRS, before signing to Reprise for *Play* (1991). Sales, however, were disappointing, and the band's association with the label was short. A&M issued the *Greatest Hits* set in 1992, following which they re-signed the band. Elvis Costello's drummer Thomas and keyboard-player Steve Nieve had played live with the band in 1992, and the former joined the band (and Carrack rejoined) for *Some Fantastic Place* (1993), a return to form fifteen years after their début. *Ridiculous* (1995), which included the minor hit 'Heaven Knows', was equally good, but despite winning critical approval, Difford and Tilbrook's tricksy and witty songs were clearly out of kilter with the times and both albums sold poorly. The group continued to tour. In 2000 Difford and Carrack collaborated on a further Carrack solo album, *Satisfy My Soul* (Carrackuk), a pleasant rather than compelling exercise in blue-eyed soul on which Carrack himself was presented as Mr Everything: producer, accompanist, singer and label owner.

JO STAFFORD
b. 12 November 1920, Coalinga, California, USA

A clear-voiced singer with no touch of vibrato, Stafford was one of the most versatile vocalists of the forties. Her cool voice was a key feature in the recordings of the Pied Pipers ('Dream'*, 1945), while as Cinderella G. Stump she recorded the million-selling parody of country music (and country accents), 'Temptation' (1947) – or 'Tim-tayshun' as the song was billed on the label. In the fifties her biggest hits included the jaunty 'Shrimp Boats'* (1951) and a version of **Hank Williams**' 'Jambalaya'* (1952).

Stafford started singing as part of a family act, the Stafford Sisters, who made their radio début, singing country-styled material, in 1935. In 1941 she became a member of the Pied Pipers, the vocal group featured by **Tommy Dorsey**. Formed in 1937 as an octet, they had joined Dorsey in 1939 as a quartet and in 1942 backed **Frank Sinatra**, then Dorsey's featured male singer, on 'There Are Such Things'* (Victor). In 1945 the Pied Pipers (which then comprised Stafford, John Huddlestone, Chuck Lowry and Clark Yokum) had their own million-seller with 'Dream' (Capitol), written by **Johnny Mercer** with whom they recorded 'Candy' that same year. After Stafford left in 1945, the group (with new member June Hutton) had further hits, the most notable of which was their dreamy version of 'My Happiness'* (1948), which was also a million-seller for John and Sandra Steele (Damon).

Stafford began her solo career on Capitol with versions of songs popularized in films, including 'That's for Me' (1945) from *State Fair*, and 'White Christmas' (1946) from *Holiday Inn*, but her first big success came in partnership with Red Ingle and his Natural Seven with the parody of **Arthur Freed** and **Nacio Herb Brown**'s 'Temptation' as done by a 'hillbilly' band. Ingle, a former saxophonist with **Ted Weems** and occasional partner in mayhem with **Spike Jones** ('Chloe', 1945), repeated the joke with equal success on his own with 'Cigarettes, Whusky and Wild, Wild Women'* (1948), originally written by Tim Spencer of the **Sons of the Pioneers**. Later in the mid-fifties, with her husband and fellow Dorsey alumnus Paul Weston, whose band backed her on almost all her recording sessions, she returned to this comic vein, when as Jonathan and Darlene Edwards they recorded a series of take-offs of popular singers of the day.

In 1948 Stafford and **Gordon MacRae** had a million-seller with their version of 'Say Something Sweet to Your Sweetheart' (originally recorded by **Anne Shelton** and Sam Browne in Britain) and in 1949 repeated their success with 'My Happiness'*, one of the several songs written (in 1868) by music publisher Septimus Winner under his Alice Hawthorne pseudonym. In 1950, following **Mitch Miller**'s appointment as head of popular music at Columbia, Stafford joined the label. Miller immediately gave her country hits to cover, including several by Williams that climaxed with her version of 'Jambalaya' (1952). Equally successful was the folky-sounding 'Shrimp Boats'* (1951), written by Weston, and **Pee Wee King**'s 'You Belong to Me'* (1952). More unusual was 'Make Love to Me!'* (1954), a version of the 1923 jazz instrumental 'Tin Roof Blues' with a new lyric by Bill Norvas and Allan Copeland. Her last major hit was 'Almost Tomorrow' (1955), a cover of the Dream Weavers' million-selling record (Decca).

Afterwards Stafford regularly toured and appeared on television, but recorded only intermittently.

THE STANLEY BROTHERS
Carter Glen Stanley, b. 27 August 1925, McClure, Virginia, USA, d. 1 December 1966; Ralph Edmond Stanley, b. 25 February 1927, McClure

With **Bill Monroe** and **Flatt and Scruggs**, the Stanley Brothers were the great style-makers of early bluegrass. While Monroe and Scruggs contributed an original instrumental approach, the Stanley Brothers' effect and influence stemmed from their raw, emotional duet and trio vocal harmonies, the sound of which has passed into bluegrass syntax.

From a background of banjo-playing relatives, hillbilly radio and the 'lined-out' hymns of the local Baptist church, the Stanley Brothers made their professional début in 1946 with Roy Sykes and the Blue Ridge Mountain Boys. They soon left, taking the band's mandolin-player Darrell 'Pee Wee' Lambert, hiring a fiddler, and becoming the Stanley Brothers and the Clinch Mountain Boys. They joined the WCYB, Bristol, Tennessee, Farm and Fun Time show and made their first recordings for the small Rich-R-Tone label in Johnson City, Tennessee. These included old mountain songs 'Little Glass of Wine' and 'Man of Constant Sorrow', alongside Monroe repertoire like 'Molly and Tenbrooks'. Carter sang lead, Lambert or Ralph tenor. They then moved to WPTF, Raleigh, North Carolina, and were signed by **Art Satherley** to Columbia, a move which precipitated Monroe's switch to Decca. The Columbia recordings (1949–52), more rough-edged than Monroe's early sides (their only forerunners in recorded bluegrass), possessed a primitive power – in particular on 'A Vision of Mother', 'Lonesome River' and 'The White Dove' – that has never been matched.

For a short spell in 1951 Carter worked with Monroe, developing his lead-singing skills in recordings like 'Uncle Pen' and 'Sugar Coated Love'. Reunited with Ralph, he returned to WCYB, and in 1954 the brothers signed with Mercury, where Flatt and Scruggs had preceded them. Here the 'high lonesome'

character of their work was exchanged for a hot, fast-moving ensemble that bore out **Alan Lomax**'s celebrated definition of bluegrass as 'folk music with overdrive'. Despite its quality, however, their Mercury work could not compete in the market with rock'n'roll, and the Stanleys left the label in 1958 to work, from a base in Florida, on tours and radio shows. They recorded for Starday and, for much of the sixties, King. Their first album for the latter included such future standards as 'How Mountain Girls Can Love' and 'Clinch Mountain Backstep'. Company pressure to reduce the role of the fiddle and mandolin and emphasize the guitar, which is played as a lead rather than rhythm instrument by pickers like George Shuffler and Bill Napier, is evident in their many King recordings.

The Stanleys took part in a European folk caravan in 1965, but their working schedule at home was less prestigious, and Carter's death in 1966 was probably hastened by life on the road. Ralph formed a new group in early 1967 with lead-singer and guitarist Larry Sparks, who went on to lead a succession of good bands himself in the seventies and eighties. Sparks was succeeded by Roy Lee Centers, whose voice was remarkably similar to Carter Stanley's. By the early seventies, the Clinch Mountain Boys, back among the leading bluegrass bands and recording for Rebel, included the teenaged Keith Whitley (guitar) and **Ricky Skaggs** (mandolin). Centers' murder in 1974 and the departure of Whitley and Skaggs to play in younger-styled bands were setbacks that Ralph in time overcame, and he continued to head sturdily traditional line-ups and maintain his distinguished standing in bluegrass. He appeared in Japan, and recorded regularly for Rebel in the eighties.

A mark of the Stanley Brothers' continuing influence was that traditionally inclined contemporary artists turned to their repertoire in the eighties. They included former **Byrds** member Chris Hillman and **Emmylou Harris**, who recorded a version of Ralph's 'The Darkest Hour Is Just Before Dawn' in 1980. Harris was one of a number of Stanley's admirers who appeared with him on *Saturday Night and Sunday Morning* (1993). A double-album mixing sacred and secular material, it included duets by Stanley with Ricky Skaggs, **Tom T. Hall**, **George Jones** and others.

LISA STANSFIELD
b. 11 April 1966, Rochdale, Lancashire, England

Blessed with a convincing mellow soul voice and distinctive looks, Stansfield emerged from the crowded UK dance scene of the late eighties to enjoy considerable success in Europe and the US.

Born in Rochdale (previously best known as birthplace of Depression-era star **Gracie Fields**), Stansfield appeared in local talent contests before, in her teens, being hired as a children's TV presenter. She formed the soul/funk act Blue Zoo with former schoolfriends Andy Morris and Ian Devaney in 1984 and signed to Arista records in 1986. They released one album, *Big Thing*, later that year.

Although the compositions of the trio showed promise, the album failed to sell, and Stansfield moved on, singing on the 1989 dance hit 'People Hold on' by Coldcut. Her guest vocal on the track convinced Big Life Records to sign her as a solo act, with Morris and Devaney in tow as co-writers/producers/musicians. Coldcut produced her début solo single, the energetic 'This Is the Right Time' (1989), which reached the UK Top Twenty, but it was the follow-up which made the major break-through. The irresistible mid-tempo 'All Around the World' effortlessly crossed over from the dance market and topped the charts around the world.

The début album, *Affection* (1989), was equally successful, with worldwide sales well over the four million mark. It reached the Top Five in the UK and in America, where 'All Around the World' was a major hit in 1990, making the Top Ten. Further hit singles 'Live Together' (1990) and 'What Did I Do to You?' (1990) followed, before Stansfield, Devaney and Morris began work on the second album. Preceded by the UK hit 'All Woman', *Real Love* (1992) again reached the European charts but it was a lesser album than its predecessor.

1993 started promisingly with the Top Ten success of 'Someday (I'm Coming Back)', taken from the multi-million-selling soundtrack to the **Whitney Houston** movie *The Bodyguard*, and continued with another hit, 'In All the Right Places'. *So Natural* (1993), her next album, was a commercial rather than critical success. She followed that with the much better *Lisa Stansfield* (1997), which included a fine version of **Diane Warren**'s 'I Cried My Last Tear Last Night'. In 1998 Arista released the hit collection *The Number 1 Remixes*.

THE STAPLE SINGERS

Roebuck 'Pops' Staples, b. 28 December 1915, Winona, Mississippi, USA; Cleotha Staples, b. 1934, Drew, Mississippi; Mavis Staples, b. 1940, Chicago, Illinois; Pervis Staples, b. 1935, Drew; Yvonne Staples, b. 1939, Chicago

One of America's leading gospel groups in the fifties, the Staple Singers were distinguished by Pop Staples' bluesy guitar and Mavis's earthy lead singing. From the early sixties the group moved into secular music, finding their greatest success with message songs reflecting the mood of the black community in the era of civil rights.

Growing up on the same plantation as **Charley Patton**, Pop Staples learned the blues guitar style which underpinned the group's later sound. He turned to spiritual singing with the Gold Trumpets before moving to Chicago in 1936. There, he joined the Trumpet Jubilees and heard the gospel music pioneers **Thomas A. Dorsey** and Sallie Martin. In 1951 he formed a family group with his four children, recording 'Sit Down Servant' (United, 1953), before signing to Vee-Jay. Yvonne left the group in 1955, only rejoining when Pervis was called up for military service four years later. At Vee-Jay 'Uncloudy Day' (1955) became the Staples' first hit. Like such later successes as 'This May Be the Last Time' (1958), 'Amazing Grace' and 'Stand by Me' – all of which were adapted for pop success by the **Rolling Stones**, **Judy Collins** and **Ben E. King**, respectively – the song featured the husky, searing contralto of Mavis with Pop Staples' understated but effective guitar accompaniment.

Leaving Vee-Jay in 1962, the group recorded *Great Day*, *Hammer and Nails* (1963) and other folk-gospel albums for Riverside before moving to Columbia where **Larry Williams** produced the secular 'Why Am I Treated So Bad' and a cover of **Buffalo Springfield**'s 'For What It's Worth' (1967), which was a minor pop hit. The following year the Staple Singers signed to Stax, where Al Bell added a contemporary soul accompaniment to further message lyrics aimed at the black community.

After 'The Ghetto' (1968) and 'Long Walk to DC' (1969), the group performed **Al Kooper**'s 'Brand New Day' in *The Landlord* (1970). Their first major hits came with 'Respect Yourself' (1971), a revived hit for Bruce Willis (RCA, 1987), and the reggae-flavoured No. 1 'I'll Take You There'* (1972). The million-selling 'If You're Ready (Come Go with Me)' (1973) appeared on *Be What You Are* which, with *City in the Sky* (1974), was the Staples' most acclaimed album. A **Curtis Mayfield** film theme, 'Let's Do It Again'* (Curtom), reached No. 1 in 1975.

In 1976 the group moved to Warners for *Pass It on* and *Unlock Your Mind* (1978), later recording for 20th-Century Fox. Signed to Epic, they recorded the strong contemporary set *Turning Point* (1984), which yielded an airplay hit with their cover of **Talking Heads**' 'Slippery People' (the Staples also covered the same band's 'Life During Wartime'). From 1968 Mavis Staples pursued a solo career beginning with an eponymous album which included songs associated with **Otis Redding**, **Sam Cooke** ('You Send Me'), **Dusty Springfield** and others. Her 1971 R&B hit 'I Have Learned to Do Without You' appeared on the Don Davis-produced *Only for the Lonely* and in the same year Mavis appeared in *Soul to Soul*, the film of a Ghanaian concert.

In general, though, her solo recordings failed to match the Staple Singers tracks as she followed a

Mayfield soundtrack album (*A Piece of the Action*, 1977) with disco singles and the disappointing *Love Gone Bad* (Phono, 1983), a collaboration with **Holland, Dozier and Holland**. In 1987 she signed to **Prince**'s Paisley Park label, recording *Time Waits for No One* (1989), co-produced by Bell and Prince, and *The Voice* (1995).

More satisfying were Pops Staples' solo recordings which mixed blues and gospel standards with his own material. *Peace to the Neighborhood* (1992) was produced by **Bonnie Raitt** and **Ry Cooder**, who also produced two of the tracks on the slightly less impressive *Father Father* (1994), on which Staples covered Curtis Mayfield's 'People Get Ready'. Also in 1994 the Staple Singers appeared on the various artists hit album *Rhythm, Country and Blues*, performing **The Band**'s 'The Weight' with country star Marty Stuart (they had previously performed the song with The Band in the 1977 concert movie *The Last Waltz*). The group continued to tour throughout the nineties.

KAY STARR

b. Katherine La Verne Starks, 21 July 1922, Dougherty, Oklahoma, USA

An uninhibited bluesy singer in the forties, Starr had her greatest commercial success with a series of brash numbers in the fifties, climaxing in the anodyne novelty outing 'Rock and Roll Waltz'* (1956), the first single by a female singer to top the American charts in the rock era, and the first to include 'rock and roll' in its title.

When her family moved to Memphis in 1937, Starr sang with **Joe Venuti**'s orchestra and later with **Glenn Miller**, **Bob Crosby** and **Charlie Barnet** before in 1945 she joined Capitol as a solo artist. After her first hit, 'You Were Only Foolin' (While I Was Falling in Love)' (1948), she turned to country material (**Pee Wee King**'s 'Bonaparte's Retreat', 1950) and recorded several duets with **Tennessee Ernie Ford**, including 'I'll Never Be Free' (1950) and 'Oceans of Tears' (1951), before the jaunty 'Wheel of Fortune'* (1952) became her biggest hit. A cover of the Cardinals' R&B hit (Atlantic, 1952) and later revived by **Lavern Baker** (1960), the song's success made a pop singer of Starr and her subsequent hits (which included 'Side by Side' and 'Changing Partners', 1953) were far slicker than the unrequited-love songs with which she'd made her name.

The culmination of this trend was her RCA recording of Dick Ware and Shorty Allen's 'Rock and Roll Waltz', an example of the uneasy compromises between rock'n'roll and established popular music of the mid-fifties. After the success of 'My Heart Reminds Me' (1957), Starr returned to Capitol where she had a series of minor hits with country songs, including a revival of 'I'll Never Be Free' (1961) and **Jim Reeves**' 1959 hit 'Four Walls' (1962). More interestingly, she returned to her roots on a series of albums including *Jazz Singer* (1960) and the collection of standards *Movin' on Broadway* (1963). *Kay Starr and Count Basie* (1968) was also in this vein.

RINGO STARR
b. Richard Starkey, 7 July 1940, Liverpool, England

In contrast to the more exploratory and innovatory solo careers of his fellow **Beatles**, Starr successfully sustained his cheerful, easy-going Beatles persona in a series of pop hits throughout the seventies. In the process he became one of the grand old men of rock.

The first of The Beatles to record solo, Starr's *Sentimental Journey* (Apple, 1970) was a lacklustre collection of standards remembered from his childhood. That was followed by the **Pete Drake**-produced collection of country songs *Beaucoups of Blues* (1970) – Starr had generally sung country songs on the few occasions he sang lead with The Beatles, such as **Carl Perkins**' 'Matchbox' and **Buck Owens**' 'Act Naturally'. His first chart success came with the defiant declaration of his independence from The Beatles, 'It Don't Come Easy'* (1971), and 'Back off Boogaloo' (1972), both self-penned and produced by **George Harrison**.

Even more successful was *Ringo** (1973), produced by Richard Perry whom Starr had met while working with **Nilsson**. On the album (at different times) Starr was given support by Harrison, **John Lennon** and **Paul McCartney**. The album included a pair of American No. 1s, 'Photograph'* and 'You're Sixteen'* (a revival of **Johnny Burnette**'s 1960 hit), a third Top Ten hit, 'Oh My My', and Lennon's 'I'm the Greatest', which told the story of Starr's Beatles days. *Goodnight Vienna* (1974) featured two further hits, a revival of the **Platters**' 1954 recording 'Only You' and 'No No Song'. Following a move to Polydor (Atlantic in the US) for three albums, including the 1978 covers set *Bad Boy* and the solitary American hit single 'A Dose of Rock'n'Roll' (1976), Starr moved to Boardwalk for *Stop and Smell the Roses* (Boardwalk, 1981), which included his last American hit, 'Wrack My Brain', written and produced by Harrison. After the failure of *Old Wave* (RCA, 1983), Starr recorded only intermittently. In 1985, the year his son Zak made his first album, Starr made a guest appearance on the protest record 'Sun City' (Manhattan) by Artists United Against Apartheid.

Starr's musical career during the rest of the eighties was largely confined to making guest appearances on other people's albums until he returned to live performing with the All-Starr Band in 1989. The line-up included former members of **The Band**, **Bruce**

Springsteen's sax-player Clarence Clemmons, Nils Lofgren, ex-**Eagles** guitarist Joe Walsh and **Dr John**. In 1991 he signed to the Private Music label, releasing *Time Takes Time* and touring with the All Starr Band to promote it. The *Live at Montreux* album, recorded during the tour, was released in 1993. Although pleasantly easy-going affairs, neither album enjoyed any commercial success. In 1994, along with McCartney and Harrison, he added music to tracks recorded by Lennon for The Beatles' *Anthology* series. He also contributed to the tribute album to **Nilsson**, *For the Love of Harry* (1995), singing 'Lay Down Your Arms'. He returned to performing with Ringo and His All-Starr band, which toured intermittently throughout the nineties as a revivalist band of sorts, with its floating cast (which included at various times **Peter Frampton**, Dave Mason, **Todd Rundgren**, **Procol Harum**'s Gary Booker and **Jack Bruce**) each parading their moment in the sun.

Starr also essayed a film career with parts in such films as *Candy* (1967) and *That'll Be the Day* (1973), the year he made his directorial début with *Born to Boogie*, a documentary about **Marc Bolan**'s T. Rex. In 1981 he starred in *Caveman* and married his co-star Barbara Bach. In 1984 Starr commenced a new career as a narrator of the television series derived from the Rev. Awdry's *Railway Stories* series of children's books devoted to Thomas the Tank Engine and his friends. The series was a major success in Britain, America and Japan, where Starr was in great demand as a voice-over artist for commercials.

CANDI STATON
b. 1943, Hanceville, Alabama, USA

With **Ann Peebles**, Staton was one of the most emotive female Southern soul singers of the late sixties.

Staton began her career in gospel music at the age of ten, and became a member of the Jewel Gospel Trio, which toured the South in the sixties. In 1968 she made an impromptu appearance in a Birmingham, Alabama, nightclub singing the only secular song she knew, **Chips Moman** and **Dan Penn**'s 'Do Right Woman'. On the strength of her reading of that song, she was booked on a Southern tour with blind singer-songwriter **Clarence Carter**, whom she eventually married.

Carter took her to his producers at Fame Studios and **Rick Hall** signed her to his Fame label. Staton's first hit was a powerful reading of Carter's 'I'd Rather Be an Old Man's Sweetheart (Than a Young Man's Fool)', which she followed with the superior album *I'm Just a Prisoner* (1969). Later hits included a soul working of **Tammy Wynette**'s 'Stand By Your Man' (1970) and a version of **Mac Davis**'s much-recorded 'In the Ghetto' (1972).

After divorcing Carter, Staton signed with Warners in 1974. There, under the guidance of producer Dave Crawford, she edged towards the emerging dance music area. In 1976 the transformation was complete with the exhilarating international hit 'Young Hearts Run Free', one of the best dance records of its time. She charted again in 1977 with 'Nights on Broadway' and in 1978 with 'Victim'. By the end of the decade, however, with disco on the wane and Southern soul virtually an anachronistic form, her career crumbled. She recorded for Crawford's LA label in 1980 before signing to Sugarhill where she enjoyed a brief revival in 1982 with 'Suspicious Minds', a song, like 'In the Ghetto', associated with **Elvis Presley**, after which she returned to gospel music and albums such as *Love Lifted Me* (Betecah, 1988) and *Stand Up and Be a Witness* (1990). She returned, briefly, to secular music and the charts with 'You Got the Love' in 1991, a collaboration with the Source which became a hit again when remixed and re-released in 1996. *The Best of Candi Staton* (1995) is just that.

STATUS QUO
Francis Rossi, b. 29 April 1949, London, England; Alan Lancaster, b. 7 February 1949, London (replaced by John Edwards); Richard Parfitt, b. 12 October 1948, London; John Coghlan, b. 19 September 1946, London (replaced by Peter Kircher, b. 21 January 1948, London, replaced by Jeff Rich)

After nearly a decade of struggling and changing styles to suit the times, Status Quo rediscovered the verities of the twelve-bar riff in the seventies and found huge success with a music that was initially dubbed 'the non-thinking man's Canned Heat' by critics. By the end of the eighties, however, they had had a dozen Top Five albums in Britain and won affectionate admiration from both critics and audiences. They even managed to make John Fogerty's (of **Creedence Clearwater Revival**) 'Rocking All Over the World' *their* song when they used it to open the Wembley Stadium section of Live Aid.

Schoolfriends guitarist Rossi and bassist Lancaster formed the Spectres instrumental group in 1962, playing material by the **Shadows** and **Johnny and the Hurricanes**. With the addition of drummer Coghlan in 1963 they became a British beat boom group and in 1966 were signed to Pye, releasing a cover of **Ben E. King** and **Shirley Bassey**'s 1963 hit 'I Who Have Nothing'. When that failed they changed their name to Traffic Jam and turned to psychedelia with 'Almost But Not Quite There' (1967) before adopting the name Status Quo and releasing 'Pictures of Matchstick Men' (1968). With Rossi's quasi-surrealistic lyrics and an exotic guitar line made even stranger by the then fashion for phasing, the song was a European million-seller. In the same year guitarist Parfitt, a veteran of the Butlins holiday-camp circuit, joined but despite a further British hit, the **Marty Wilde** composition 'Ice in the Sun', the group's lightweight version of psychedelia (*Picturesque Matchstickable Messages*, 1968) failed. An attempt by Pye to remodel them as a **Bee Gees**-type harmony group in 1969 was equally unsuccessful and in 1970 the group redefined themselves as a good-time R&B group with the twin guitars and almost sing-along harmonies of 'Down the Dustpipe'.

A hit, 'Dustpipe', was followed by the similarly styled 'In My Chair' and the albums *Ma Kelly's Greasy Spoon* (1970) and *Dog of Two Heads* (1971), after which a dispute with Pye left them without a release until 'Paper Plane' (Vertigo, 1973). During this hiatus they toured continually and won themselves a committed 'wanna-be' head-waving, guitar-miming denim-clad following. *Piledriver* (Vertigo, 1973) gave the band the breakthrough they had worked for for so long when it reached the British Top Five. *Hello* (1973) entered the British album charts at No. 1 and was followed by a stream of hit albums plus singles including 'Down Down' (1975); 'Rain' (1976), a version of **Hank Thompson**'s 1952 Country hit 'Wild Side of Life'; 'Rockin' All Over the World' (1977), by which time Andy Bown, one-time member – with **Peter Frampton** – of the Herd, had become a semi-permanent member of the group; 'Whatever You Want' (1979), their most representative record; 'What You're Proposing' (1980); and a revival of **Hank Williams**' 1951 hit 'Dear John' (1982).

Unaffected by the punk movement, Status Quo found themselves celebrated as a 'people's band' and in the eighties, despite the replacement of Coghlan by Peter Kirchner in 1982, their hits continued unabated. Among them were 'Marguerita Time' (1983), a remake of **Dion**'s 1962 hit 'The Wanderer' (1984), the **Dave Edmunds**-produced 'Rollin' Home' (1986) and 'Burning Bridges' (1989). From 1983 onwards Lancaster had been an increasingly peripheral member of the band and he finally left in 1984, although he rejoined the band for their Live Aid appearance. Kircher also left in 1985. With a new line-up which saw Rossi, Parfitt and Bown joined by drummer Rich and bassist Edwards, the band soldiered on, releasing the Edmunds-produced *In the Army Now*, the title track of which gave them one of their biggest hit singles in 1986.

Subsequently the band's album sales began to drop, although they were still a considerable live attraction, with a set which included a staggering number of hits (almost fifty British Top Fifty entries) and a catholic selection of cover-versions invariably including the **Doors**' 'Roadhouse Blues' and **Chuck Berry**'s 'Bye Bye Johnny'. Quo had by the early nineties become a showbiz institution, and attracted possibly the broadest age range of any successful British act of the rock

era, with the exception of **Cliff Richard**. In 1994 they topped the British singles chart backing the Manchester United football team on 'Come on You Reds'.

Rossi and Parfitt co-wrote *Status Quo*, a band autobiography, in 1993, the year they started on their *Just for the Record* world tour. Albums from this period include *Thirsty Work* (1994) and *Don't Stop* (1996), from which the single 'Fun, Fun Fun', a reworking of the **Beach Boys** song on which several of the Beach Boys sang back-up vocals, was a minor hit despite getting no airplay on BBC's Radio 1 in the UK – on the basis that the group were too old. A few years later another British veteran, **Cliff Richard**, was to translate a similar controversy into a chart-topping single with 'Millennium Prayer' (1999). Rossi's solo album, *King of the Doghouse* (1996), was overshadowed by *Whatever You Want – The Best of Status Quo* (1997), which was a large European hit. The title track was subsequently used in a television commercial. *Famous in the Last Century* (Universal, 2000) was a dire collection of covers ('Roll Over Beethoven', 'Sweet Home Chicago', etc).

TOMMY STEELE
b. Thomas Hicks, 17 December 1936, Bermondsey, London, England

Britain's first rock'n'roll star, Steele was also the first to desert rock'n'roll for the greener pasture of 'all-round entertainment'. However, in contrast to many similar refugees from the world of pop music, Steele managed to match the innocence of his early recordings with the charm – and ambition – of much of his later work.

A one-time merchant seaman, Hicks formed a skiffle trio with Mike Pratt and **Lionel Bart** in London. He was spotted by John Kennedy, who signed him up, renamed him Steele and got him a recording contract with Decca Records. The result, in great part due to Kennedy's astute marketing of Steele, was that Steele became a teenage idol literally overnight and 'Rock with the Cavemen' a Top Twenty hit in 1956. This meteoric rise is documented in *The Tommy Steele Story* (1957), Steele's first film, and with even more glee in *Tommy Steele* (1958), Kennedy's biography of his protégé's rock'n'roll years.

Steele co-wrote a number of his early hits with Bart and Pratt ('Rock with the Cavemen', 1956; 'Water, Water'; 'Handful of Songs', 1957) but initially his biggest hits were covers of American records – **Guy Mitchell**'s 'Singing the Blues' (his only British chart-topper in 1956) – and recordings of American compositions – such as 'Nairobi' (1958) by Guy Merrill, the writer of most of Mitchell's hits. His later rock'n'roll hits, such as the overwrought 'Tallahassee Lassie' (1959), another cover-version, saw Steele decidedly uncomfortable. Far more indicative of how Steele's career would develop were his last significant pop hits, 'Little White Bull' (1959) and 'What a Mouth' (1960). 'Bull', written by Steele, Pratt and Bart, came from his fourth film, *Tommy the Toreador*, and was straightforwardly sentimental, while 'Mouth', Steele's version of **R. P. Weston**'s fifty-year-old music-hall classic, was performed with far more gusto and cockney zest. These were the qualities that Steele projected, with varying degrees of success, for the rest of his career on stage and screen.

Steele marked his defection from the world of rock with an appearance in *She Stoops to Conquer* at the Old Vic in 1960. His first great popular success, however, was in the musical written specifically for him by David Heneker, *Half a Sixpence* (1963). Based on H. G. Wells' comic novel *Kipps*, the show transferred to Broadway (with Steele) in 1965 and was filmed (again with Steele) in 1967. From then on he committed himself to films – starring in *Finian's Rainbow* (1968) and *Where's Jack?* (1969) – and the stage – *Hans Andersen* (1974), which he also directed, and *Singing in the Rain* (1983), which, though his singing and dancing were coarser than **Gene Kelly**'s, Steele made into an extraordinary popular success in London.

In 1974 Steele composed and recorded his musical autobiography, *My Life, My Song. Tommy Steele's 20 Greatest Hits* (Decca, 1990) is the definitive career retrospective.

STEELEYE SPAN
Tim Hart; Ashley Hutchings (replaced by Rick Kemp); Gay Woods; Terry Woods (replaced by Martin Carthy, replaced by Bob Johnson); Maddy Prior; Nigel Pegrum; John Kirkpatrick; Peter Knight

With **Fairport Convention**, Steeleye Span were the most successful English electric-folk band of the seventies. Beginning as a grouping of former acoustic musicians, the band evolved a winning formula of traditional songs plus heavy-rock backings.

The band was formed in 1969 by folk-revival singers Hart and Prior (who had already recorded for Pegasus), Ashley Hutchings (bass), who had recently left Fairport, and Irish musicians Gay Woods (concertina) and Terry Woods (guitar), who had played in folk-rock group Sweeney's Men. They recorded the formal, restrained *Hark! The Village Wait* (RCA, 1970).

The Woods left soon afterwards to form the Woods Band which recorded five albums for Greenwich, Rockburgh, Mooncrest and Polydor, and Terry Woods later joined the **Pogues**. Steeleye Span recruited leading folk guitarist **Martin Carthy** and fiddler Knight for *Please to See the King* (Charisma, 1971), which included the mesmeric ballad 'Lovely on the Water' with Prior's voice accompanied by

Knight's mandolin. After recording *Ten Man Mop* (1971), Carthy returned to solo work and Hutchings left to form the **Albion Band**, whose decidedly English music was purged of the Celtic elements he detected in Steeleye.

The addition of the more rock-orientated bassist Kemp and electric guitarist Johnson (a former partner of Knight) completed the formula which brought Steeleye Span's greatest commercial success. On songs like 'King Henry' (from *Below the Salt*, Chrysalis, 1973), Johnson worked out rock-styled melodies to folk lyrics, while five-part *a cappella* harmonies were featured on 'Gaudete', the Latin carol which gave the group a British hit at Christmas 1973. After *Parcel of Rogues* (1973), on which the band's sound was becoming heavier, Steeleye Span added a drummer, Pegrum from Gnidrolog.

Over the next few years, the band toured extensively in America, Australia and Europe, adding an electronic mummers' play to their act. *Now We Are Six* featured **David Bowie** on saxophone on a revival of **Phil Spector**'s 'To Know Him Is to Love Him', but the album's most significant tracks were 'Thomas the Rhymer' and 'Seven Hundred Elves', which Johnson's arrangements turned into heavy-metal folk. It was Steeleye Span's first Top Twenty album and *Commoner's Crown* (1975), which featured the **Goons**' Peter Sellers on one track, sold almost as strongly.

Mike Batt was the surprise choice as producer for *All Around My Hat* (1975), whose title track was a British hit, and the less successful *Rocket Cottage* (1976), which included 'Fighting for Strangers', a montage of three songs segued together. Johnson and Knight then left the group to record their concept album *The King of Elfland's Daughter*, based on the fantasy novel by Lord Dunsany, with guest appearances by **Alexis Korner** and **Mary Hopkin**. Their replacements were Carthy and concertina virtuoso Kirkpatrick, who played on *Storm Force 10* (1977), with its two Bertolt Brecht–**Kurt Weill** songs, 'The Black Freighter' and 'The Wife of the Soldier'. The band broke up shortly afterwards with a concert recording, *Live at Last*, released in 1978.

While Carthy and Kirkpatrick later formed Brass Monkey, Hart and Prior embarked on solo recording careers which made little impact; the latter also recorded as a duo with June Tabor. In 1980 the 1972–6 line-up (including Johnson and Knight) reassembled to tour and record *Sails of Silver*. Produced by Gus Dudgeon, it included piano and woodwind, as well as songs composed by the band. The band played occasional festivals and tours in later years, releasing such albums as *Back in Line* (Flutterby, 1986) and *Tempted and Tried* (Chrysalis, 1989).

Spanning the Years (1995), with liner notes by Prior, is the definitive career retrospective.

STEELY DAN

Jeff Skunk Baxter, b. 13 December 1948, Washington DC, USA; Walter Becker, b. 1950, Queens, New York; Denny Dias; Donald Fagen, b. 1948, Passaic, New Jersey; Jim Hodder, b. 1948, d. 5 June 1990, Point Arena, California; David Palmer

The brainchild of Becker and Fagen, Steely Dan were one of the most highly regarded rock bands of the seventies. Their songs were an ambitious attempt to translate the languages of modern fiction and of jazz into the rock idiom. The result was a highly controlled music of immaculate surfaces which contrasted with the luxuriant emotionalism of the rock mainstream.

After leaving Bard College, New York State, bassist Becker and Fagen (keyboards) composed the soundtrack for the Richard Pryor film *You Gotta Walk It Like You Talk It* and briefly played in Demian with guitarist Dias before joining oldies group **Jay and the Americans**.

In 1971 Gary Katz signed the duo as songwriters to ABC-Dunhill and the following year produced *Can't Buy a Thrill* by Steely Dan. The group, whose name was taken from the writing of William Burroughs, included Hodder (drums), singer Palmer (ex-Myddle Class) and guitarist Baxter. The album provided Top Twenty hits in the lilting 'Do It Again' and the exhilarating 'Reelin' in the Years' (1973). Palmer left before the recording of *Countdown to Ecstasy* (1973). When, after an unsuccessful tour, Becker and Fagen, now on lead vocals, decided to concentrate on studio work, Baxter left to join the **Doobie Brothers**.

Pretzel Logic (1974) included the plaintive hit 'Rikki Don't Lose That Number' but more importantly it introduced a strong jazz emphasis with a version of **Duke Ellington**'s 'East St Louis Toodle-oo' on which Becker used wah-wah guitar to simulate Bubber Miley's 'growling' trumpet sound. By now, the two songwriters were using large numbers of session players like **Crusaders**' guitarist Larry Carlton, who appeared on *Katy Lied* (1975).

The Royal Scam (1976) was followed by the best-selling *Aja* (1977) and its hit singles 'Peg' and 'Deacon Blue' (1978). Steely Dan had further success with 'FM (No Static at All)' (MCA, 1978), the title song from the John A. Alonzo film. Although the poor critical reception of *Gaucho* (MCA, 1980) precipitated Steely Dan's dissolution, both 'Hey Nineteen' and 'Time Out of Mind' sold well.

In the eighties Fagen contributed to the score of Martin Scorsese's *King of Comedy*, released the acclaimed *The Nightfly* (Warners, 1982) and contributed to the score of *Arthur* (1988). Becker produced *Flaunt the Imperfection* (Virgin, 1985) by British group China Crisis before linking up with Fagen as a session player on *Zazu* (A&M, 1987), the Katz-produced début

album by Rosie Vela. Becker went on to produce US singer-songwriter **Rickie Lee Jones** (*Flying Cowboys*, 1989). In 1988 Fagen (who had been working for American film magazine *Première*) contributed 'Century's End' to the film soundtrack *Bright Lights Big City*.

In 1990 Becker and Fagen began work on the latter's second solo album, although work on it was interrupted by Fagen's involvement in the Rock and Soul Revue, a live event featuring **Michael McDonald** and **Boz Scaggs**, which produced the album *The New York Rock and Soul Revue – Live at the Beacon* (1992). The Fagen album, *Kamakiriad*, appeared in 1993 to ecstatic reviews, and Becker and Fagen toured America as Steely Dan in 1993 and 1994. Becker's *11 Tracks of Whack* (Giant, 1994) was produced by Fagen. A career retrospective boxed set, *Citizen Steely Dan: 1972–1980*, was issued in 1993.

The long-awaited *Two Against Nature* (RCA, 2000) was one of the few reunion albums that didn't seem driven by financial concerns. Where *Alive in America* (1995) was a pleasant live set of their greatest hits, *Two Against Nature* took off from *Aja*, as if nothing had happened in the twenty years since *Gaucho*. Detached in its mix of cynical descriptions of unwise affairs ('Negative Girl', 'Cousin Dupree'), restrained playing, bizarre lyrics ('Gas Lighting Abbie') and complex melodies, all bound together in the cleanest of productions, the offering slotted almost too neatly into Becker and Fagen's discography, as ever dividing the critics who saw it alternately as an example of consummate craftsmanship or bland 'sessionmanship'.

MAX STEINER

b. Maximilian Raoul Steiner, b. 10 May 1888, Vienna, Austria, d. 28 December 1971, Hollywood, California, USA

Steiner was one of the most prolific Hollywood composers – he scored over 300 films – and one of the first to co-ordinate precisely music and image. He won three Oscars for his scores, which were emotional and lyrical and often built around motifs associated with characters.

A musical prodigy, he graduated from the Imperial Academy of Vienna at the age of thirteen. The following year he wrote the operetta *The Beautiful Greek Girl* and was a professional conductor by the time he was sixteen, before studying with Robert Fuchs and Gustav Mahler. In 1914, at the invitation of Florenz Ziegfeld, he travelled to America to help orchestrate his shows. For over ten years he orchestrated and conducted Broadway shows for George White, Ziegfeld and **Victor Herbert** before going to Hollywood in 1929 after the advent of sound. His first score was *Rio Rita* (1929) after which, in 1930, he was made head of music at RKO; his first significant one, however, was *King Kong*

(1933), which melded music and sound effects with great success. *The Informer* (1935) was Steiner's first Oscar-winning score – the others were *Now Voyager* (1942) and *Since You Went Away* (1944) – and his first to relate sound and image precisely. He popularized the use of the click-track among Hollywood composers as a means of securing absolute co-ordination between music and action.

Moving to Warners, Steiner scored, among others, *The Charge of the Light Brigade* (1936), *Jezebel* (1938) and *Dark Victory* (1939), before he was loaned to David O. Selznick for *Gone with the Wind* (1939), his longest, most complex (Steiner quoted many traditional Southern tunes and even some songs by **Stephen Foster**) and best-remembered score.

In the forties Steiner alternated romantic (*Casablanca*, 1942) and dramatic (*The Big Sleep*, 1946) with more ambitious works, notably his score for *The Treasure of the Sierra Madre* (1946). He continued his high work rate throughout the fifties (including *The Caine Mutiny*, 1953, and *The Searchers*, 1956), only slowing down in the sixties. His last score was *Two on a Guillotine* (1965).

STEPPENWOLF

John Kay, b. Joachim F. Krauledat, 12 April 1944, Tilsit, Germany; Michael Monarch, b. 5 July 1950, Los Angeles, California, USA; Goldy McJohn, b. 2 May 1945; Jerry Edmonton, b. 24 October 1946, Canada; Nick St Nicholas, b. 28 September 1943, Hamburg, Germany; George Bondio, b. 3 September 1945, New York

A hard-rock band of the late sixties, Steppenwolf's mix of social disaffection and biker image brought them great success with 'Born to Be Wild'* and 'Magic Carpet Ride'* (1968), before in the seventies they lost their way amidst the many heavy-metal groups that came in their wake.

Kay, a refugee from East Germany, settled in Toronto in 1958 where he later formed the blues-orientated Sparrow with Edmonton and McJohn. Signed to Dunhill, with a name change to Steppenwolf (after the Herman Hesse novel) and new members Monarch and John Russell Morgan, the band had immediate success with the biker anthem 'Born to Be Wild' which, with **Hoyt Axton**'s 'The Pusher', was featured in *Easy Rider* (1968). The similarly styled 'Magic Carpet Ride' was equally successful but by the time of 'Rock Me'* (1969), from *Candy* – despite Kay's stated radical politics – the band had become merely another hard-rock ensemble.

After a few more hits, including 'Move Over' and 'Monster' (1970), the band broke up in 1972. Kay briefly pursued a solo career ('I'm Moving on', 1972) before forming a new version of Steppenwolf in 1974 for one more hit, 'Straight Shootin' Woman'

(Mums). When that group split in 1976, Kay once more returned to his solo career (*All in Good Time*, Mercury, 1978) before in 1980 touring as John Kay and Steppenwolf. In 1987 Kay put together a further version of Steppenwolf (including keyboardist Michael Wilk, guitarist Rocket Ritchotte and drummer Ron Hurst) for *Rock and Roll Rebels* (Qwil). The new band (again billed as John Kay and Steppenwolf) released a second album, *Rise and Shine* (IRS, 1990), and toured regularly in the early nineties.

Born to Be Wild (1991) is the definitive anthology, while *Magic Carpet Ride* by Kay offers an insider's story of the group.

STEREOLAB

Joe Dilworth (replaced by Andrew Ramsay); Tim Gane; Martin Kean (replaced by Duncan Brown, replaced by Richard Harrison); Morgane Lhote; Gina Morris (replaced by Mary Hansen); Sean O'Hagan; Laetitia Sadier

A prolific retro-futurist collective, Stereolab have earned a devoted international following for their blend of subtle, Krautrock-inspired electronica and the ethereal vocals of Sadier, which were reminiscent of Francoise Hardy.

Guitarist Gane fronted Marxist pop quartet McCarthy during the late eighties before he formed Stereolab with Parisian chanteuse Sadier at the turn of the decade. After creating their own Duophonic label the pair set about releasing a series of singles, later collected on *Switched on* (1992). With bassist Kean and drummer Dilworth Stereolab issued *Peng!* (1991), which also featured backing vocalist Morris, who would be replaced by Hansen soon after. The album's mechanical rhythms and intertwining harmonies earned the band a loyal underground following, which would be enhanced by a pair of albums released the following year. *The Groop Played Space Age Bachelor Pad Music* and *Transient Random Noise Bursts with Announcements* again drew heavily on Neu! and **Kraftwerk**, and saw Dilworth and Kean replaced by Ramsay and Brown.

Stereolab's profile rose in 1994 when 'Ping Pong' became a minor UK hit. Its attendant album, *Mars Audiac Quintet*, heralded a more sophisticated sound for the band, who by this stage had begun to move away from the mere assimilation of their influences. The seven tracks featured on *Music for the Amorphous Body Study Centre* (1995) were originally composed to accompany an exhibition by sculptor Charles Long, and featured string arrangements by the High Llamas' Sean O'Hagan, who had also contributed to some of the band's earlier material. *Refereed Ectoplasm (Switched on Volume Two)* is a collection of more obscure singles recorded since 1993 for various independent labels. Produced by **Tortoise**'s John McEntire, the acclaimed *Emperor Tomato Ketchup* (1996) is Stereolab at their artistic peak, and includes collaborations with a host of international avant-garde musicians, notably Sonic Boom (formerly of **Spacemen 3**) and jazz flautist Herbie Mann.

Having signed a US distribution deal with Elektra, Stereolab returned with a new line-up for their most successful album to date, *Dots and Loops* (1997). The album marked the recording début of keyboardist Lhote and bass-player Harrison as well as featuring erstwhile collaborators McEntire and O'Hagan, and had a brass-led, jazzy feel. The band spent much of the next eighteen months working on side projects, releasing only the third volume of the *Switched on* series in 1998, before returning with the double-album *Cobra and Phases Group Play Voltage in the Milky Night* (1999).

STEREOPHONICS
Stuart Cable, b. Cwmaman, Wales; Kelly Jones, b. Cwmaman; Richard Jones, b. Cwmaman

One of a flood of Welsh bands to emerge in the wake of the **Manic Street Preachers**' rise to fame, Stereophonics quickly became one of the biggest guitar bands in Britain in the late nineties.

Inspired by classic heavy-rock bands such as **Led Zeppelin** and **AC/DC**, childhood friends Kelly Jones (vocals/guitar), Cable (drums) and Richard Jones (bass) began playing together in 1992, combining crunching guitar chords with pop melodies to striking effect. After forging a strong local fanbase, Stereophonics became the first band to be signed to V2 Records in 1996 after the underground success of 'More Life in a Tramp's Vest'. Their début, *Word Gets Around* (1996), won praise for its direct rock sound and Jones' honest portrayal of small-town life in his lyrics. The album achieved gold status in the UK, spawning the hit singles 'Local Boy in the Photograph', 'A Thousand Trees' and 'Traffic'.

The Stereophonics continued to grow in popularity over the next year, touring solidly and making a series of well-received festival appearances. Their second album, *Performance and Cocktails* (1999), topped the British charts and saw the band find increasing success in Europe.

STETSASONIC
Prince Paul, b. Paul Hutson; Daddy O, b. 1961, Brooklyn, New York, USA; Delite; Fruitkwan; DBC

More influential than commercially successful, New York rap group Stetsasonic is best remembered for producing one of the genre's timeless classics, 'Talkin' All That Jazz'.

Stetsasonic began life as the Stetson Brothers in Brooklyn around 1981. By 1984 they were good enough to win a local radio rap competition, leading to a deal with New York's Tommy Boy label and a first single, 'Just Say Stet', in 1985. Their first, critically acclaimed album, *On Fire* (1987), was followed later that year by *A.F.R.I.C.A.*, an attack on South Africa's apartheid regime. That album won the praise of prominent US black leader Jesse Jackson and was a forerunner of the politically Afrocentric outlook of later New York rap groups, including **Public Enemy** and the **Jungle Brothers**.

1988 saw the release of 'Talkin' All That Jazz' and the group's best album, *In Full Gear*. Making extensive use of a bassline sampled from Lonnie Liston Smith's 'Expansions', 'Talkin' All That Jazz' was an eloquent defence of hip-hop's production process and its use of samples and breaks from old soul, R&B and jazz records: 'Rap brings back old R&B, and if we would not, people could have forgot.' Like *A.F.R.I.C.A.*, the track was a glimpse into rap's immediate future, looking ahead to the jazz-rap experiments of **Gang Starr**. A third album, *Blood Sweat and No Tears* (1991), was well received critically, but by this time the group had been overtaken, at least commercially, by other US rap acts.

Ironically, the highest-profile Stetsasonic members since that third album have been those producing the rap acts that helped eclipse the group. Prince Paul produced **De La Soul**'s *Three Feet High and Rising* album and also worked with white Jewish rap act Third Bass. Daddy-O has also since worked with **Queen Latifah**, Big Daddy Kane and **Mary J. Blige**. 1998 saw a revival of 'Talkin' All That Jazz', remixed for the house clubs by France's super-hip **Dimitri from Paris**.

CAT STEVENS
b. Steven Georgiou, 21 July 1947, London, England

A soft-voiced songwriter and singer with a gift for strong melody lines (and a weakness for simplistic philosophizing), Stevens recorded prolifically during the seventies.

Of Greek-Swedish parentage, Stevens was an acoustic guitarist and singer as a student. He was discovered by ex-Springfields member Mike Hurst, who produced the quirky 'I Love My Dog' (1966), the first release on Deram, Decca's progressive rock label. It was a minor hit but the portrait of an old-fashioned shopkeeper, 'Matthew and Son', and 'I'm Gonna Get Me a Gun' reached the Top Ten. Other Stevens compositions were hits for P. P. Arnold ('The First Cut Is the Deepest', Immediate, 1967; revived in 1973 by **Rod Stewart**) and the **Tremeloes** (the bouncy 'Here Comes My Baby').

Ill health caused Stevens to withdraw from recording for two years and on his return he presented himself not as a pop composer but as a singer-songwriter in the **James Taylor**, **Carole King** mould. Using medieval instruments, the Paul Samwell-Smith-produced *Mona Bone Jakon* (1970) included a British hit in the madrigal-styled 'Lady D'Arbanville' but it was *Tea for the Tillerman* (1971) which brought Stevens a following in America, where he reached the Top Twenty with 'Wild World' (a British hit for **Jimmy Cliff** in the previous year and a future hit for Maxi Priest in 1988).

Teaser and the Firecat (1971) included further hits with 'Peace Train' and the nineteenth-century hymn 'Morning Has Broken', while the title of *Catch Bull at Four* (1972), taken from Zen Buddhism, indicated a concern with Eastern religion. The album's sparky, urgent 'Can't Keep It in' sold well in Britain. Recorded in Jamaica with **Phil Upchurch** among the accompanists, *Foreigner* (1972) contained a lengthy and sententious song cycle and was less popular. *Buddha and the Chocolate Box* (1973) resumed the series of hits with 'Oh Very Young'. A pleasing revival of **Sam Cooke**'s 'Another Saturday Night' was Stevens' last big success and the later albums *Numbers* (1975), *Isitzo* (1976), for which David Kershenbaum replaced Samwell-Smith, and *Back to Earth* (1978) sold poorly.

In 1997 Stevens announced his conversion to Islam, took the name Yusuf Islam and left the music business. Among his later compositions were 'A Is for Allah', which was written and recorded in celebration of the birth of his daughter Hasanah and was much bootlegged, and 'Afghanistan: Land of Islam'. He subsequently issued the predominantly spoken-word album *The Life of the Last Prophet* (Mountain of Light, 1995). He followed this with *A Is for Allah* (2000), a two-CD set and 68-page hardback book that aimed to teach the Arabic alphabet to children.

Career anthologies include the eighteen-track *The Very Best of Cat Stevens* (1990, reissued 2000).

RAY STEVENS
b. Ray Ragsdale, 24 January 1939, Clarkdale, Georgia, USA

Like **Stan Freberg** and **Spike Jones**, Stevens was a master parodist who used special effects and unusual sounds to make his comic points on such novelty recordings as 'Ahab the Arab'* and 'The Streak'* (1974). He also had major hits with more mainstream material, including 'Everything Is Beautiful'* (1970) and a country-styled version of the standard 'Misty' (1975).

Raised in Atlanta, Stevens was signed to Bill Lowry's music-publishing company in 1958 and made his recording début with a parody of the comic-strip character 'Sergeant Preston of the Yukon' (Prep, 1958). When that failed, Stevens moved to Mercury for 'Jeremiah Peabody's Poly Unsaturated Quick Dissolving Fast Acting Pleasant Tasting Green and Purple Pills' (1961), the first of a series of novelty hits which included 'Ahab the Arab' (1962) and 'Harry, the Hairy Ape' (1963). 'Mr Businessman' (Monument, 1968) was more seriously intentioned but 'Gitarzan'* and his revival of **Leiber and Stoller**'s 'Along Came Jones' (1969) saw Stevens returning to parody. Then, after being signed to Barnaby by **Andy Williams**, on whose television show Stevens was a frequent guest, he had his first American No. 1 with 'Everything Is Beautiful' (1970).

Stevens next recorded in a country vein ('Turn Your Radio on', 1971) before returning to comedy with his comment on the craze for streaking – running naked at public events – 'The Streak' (1974). With few exceptions, notably his country version of the **Erroll Garner** classic 'Misty' (1975), Stevens' later work was confined to the comedy field. His hits include parodies of the **Glenn Miller** standard 'In the Mood' (on which, billed as the Henhouse Five Plus Too, Warners, 1977, Stevens constructed the tune entirely from the squawks of chickens), 'Mississippi Squirrel Convention' (MCA, 1984), 'It's Me Again Margaret' (1985) and *I Have Returned* (MCA, 1986). The later *Beside Myself* (1989) included another novelty hit 'I Saw Elvis in a UFO'. Later albums included *He Thinks He's Ray Stevens* (1994), but his biggest success of the nineties was the video *Ray Stevens: Comedy Video Classics* (1993), which was the bestselling music video of the year. *Collection* (1993) brings together all his hits.

SHAKIN' STEVENS
b. Michael Barrett, 4 March 1948, Ely, Wales

Beginning his career as an **Elvis Presley**-influenced rock'n'roll revivalist, Stevens became one of Britain's most successful singers and teen idols of the eighties.

Originally formed as the Backbeats in Penarth, South Wales, Shakin' Stevens and the Sunsets recorded *A Legend* (Parlophone, 1970). Produced by **Dave Edmunds**, it contained versions of fifties songs by **Jack Scott** ('Leroy'), **Tiny Bradshaw** ('The Train Kept a Rollin'') and Jerry Byrne ('Lights Out'), as well as the original 'Spirit of Woodstock'.

The group recorded with little success for Columbia (1971), Contour (1972) and Philips (1974) before Stevens was chosen by **Jack Good** to take the title role in his stage musical tribute to Presley, *Elvis*, and in his revived *Oh Boy!* television show. An eponymous solo album for Track appeared in 1978 and the following year Stevens moved to Epic where he had hits with 'Hot Dog' (1980) and a cover of 'Marie Marie' by

American roots-rockers the Blasters from the Mike Hurst-produced *Take One*, before a rockabilly-styled revival of **Rosemary Clooney**'s 1954 hit 'This Ole House' (1981) reached No. 1.

Usually with former disc-jockey Stuart Colman as producer, the clean-cut singer had found a following which spanned the age-groups. Over twenty more British hits followed during the decade, none of which was successful in America. The songs were a mixture of fifties revivals and new songs which had a rock'n'roll flavour. Among the cover-versions were Jim Lowe's 'Green Door' (a No. 1 for Stevens), 'I'll Be Satisfied' (1982), written by **Berry Gordy** for **Jackie Wilson** in 1959, **Ricky Nelson**'s 'It's Late' (1983) and **Holland, Dozier and Holland**'s 1964 song for the **Supremes** 'Come See About Me'. Stevens himself wrote the No. 1 'Oh Julie' (1982) and 'Teardrops' while other new compositions were Billy Livsey's 'Give Me Your Heart Tonight' (1982), Bob Heatlie's 'Cry Just a Little Bit' (1983), 'Merry Christmas Everybody' (a seasonal No. 1 in 1985) and the Mike Leander–**Gary Glitter** number 'A Little Boogie Woogie (In the Back of My Mind)'. 'A Rockin' Good Way' (1984) was a duet with **Bonnie Tyler**.

His last British Top Ten single was a faithful copy of the **Emile Ford** 1959 hit 'What Do You Want to Make Those Eyes at Me for?' in 1987. Stevens continued to tour successfully in Britain into the nineties, at the same time securing a series of minor hits, including 'How Many Tears Can You Hide?' (1988), 'Jezebel' (1989), 'I Might' and a reworking of 'Pink Champagne' (both 1990). *The Epic Years* (1995) is the definitive anthology.

AL STEWART
b. 5 September 1945, Glasgow, Scotland

A product of the British folk scene of the sixties, Stewart's later popularity with American college audiences was built on a series of lengthy songs dealing with historical events.

He grew up in Bournemouth, playing lead guitar in future disc-jockey Tony Blackburn's group, the Sabres. Inspired by **Bob Dylan**, Stewart became an acoustic singer-songwriter, playing on the London club circuit and rooming in 1965 with **Paul Simon**. **Led Zeppelin**'s Jimmy Page played on the unsuccessful 'The Elf' (Decca, 1966) but the following year Stewart released *Bedsitter Images* (Columbia). Its title summed up the introspective stance of many contemporary British singer-songwriters and though it was over-burdened with extraneous string arrangements by producer Roy Guest, the album included strong material from his club set, such as 'Swiss Cottage Manoeuvres' and 'Clifton in the Rain'.

Love Chronicles (1969) was notable for its eighteen-minute title track on which Stewart sang the word 'fucking', while *Zero She Flies* (1970) included 'Small Fruit Song' – a folk-baroque guitar solo in the manner of **Pentangle**'s John Renbourn – and 'Manuscript', the first of the historical narratives, set in 1914. The unimpressive *Orange* (1972), which included **Rick Wakeman** among the backing musicians, was followed by *Past, Present and Future* (1973, released by Janus in America), an album entirely devoted to historical themes. Among the tracks were 'Post World War Two Blues' and 'Nostradamus'.

After *Modern Times*, with its look back at the folk era, 'Soho, Needless to Say', Stewart had his first hit single with the melodic title track to *Year of the Cat* (1977), released in Britain on RCA. For *Time Passages* (1978), a further selection of songs on historical themes, Stewart's American distribution moved to Arista and again the title track reached the Top Ten. 'Song on the Radio' (1979) and 'Midnight Rocks' (1980) were lesser hits.

Among the albums released by Stewart in the eighties were the studio/live mix *Indian Summer* (1981), *Russians and Americans* (1984) and *The Last Days of the Century* (Enigma, 1988). He continued to record and tour throughout the nineties and played live regularly, particularly in California, where he settled to oversee his vineyard interests. Albums from this period include the live outing *Rhymes in Rooms* (1993), *Seemed Like a Good Idea at the Time* (1996) and *Midnight Rocks* (1998). *Chronicles* (1991) remains the best anthology to date.

JIM STEWART
b. 1930, Middleton, Tennessee, USA

Stewart was the founder of Stax, a pivotal label in the history of black music. **Berry Gordy**'s Motown group of labels, equally influential in the development of black music in the sixties and early seventies, depended for their success on a streamlined version of R&B. In marked contrast, Stax created a relaxed style of music that drew upon and melded together the various musics and cultures of the South to create what historian Peter Guralnick called 'Sweet Soul Music', the title of his 1987 book about the phenomenon. The subtitle of the book – 'Rhythm and Blues and the Southern Dream of Freedom' – is equally instructive, pointing to the fact that throughout the period of its influence, much of Stax's output reflected the concerns of the black consciousness movement in America, most notably in the Wattstax concert the label organized in 1972.

Stewart graduated from Memphis State University in 1956 in preparation for a career in banking but spare-time fiddle-playing in Western swing bands led to him recording Fred Bylar's 'Blue Rose', a straight country offering, in 1957. A year later he formed Satellite Records with his sister Estelle Axton. Her son, Packy, played in high-school group the Royal Spades that included guitarist Steve Cropper and bassist Dick Dunn, and they became the backbone of the operation. In spite of the lack of success of the first singles on the label, in 1960 they leased a disused theatre on Memphis's McLemore Avenue in order to expand the operation. Their first notable visitor was **Rufus Thomas** (among other activities, a deejay on the local black station). Always a supporter of local labels, Thomas suggested they record him and his seventeen-year-old daughter duetting on a song called "Cause I Love You". It was released in August 1960 and became a hit in the South when leased to Atlantic Records. Stewart followed this with 'Gee Whiz', a solo recording by Carla Thomas, which gave the company its first national pop hit in 1961. By the middle of 1961 the Royal Spades – now augmented by horns and the keyboards of **Booker T.** – had become the Mar-Keys and recorded the instrumental 'Last Night' on the label. Through the intervention of Atlantic's **Jerry Wexler**, it became an immediate hit on Atlantic, eventually climbing to No. 3 on the pop charts. In response to the publicity surrounding the record's success, another label threatened to sue Stewart, claiming the name Satellite. He renamed the company Stax, from the first two letters of his own and his sister's names.

The label soon attracted local and statewide talent, and within three years had signed **William Bell**, **Otis Redding**, **Isaac Hayes**, David Porter, Eddie Floyd, **Sam and Dave** and **Johnnie Taylor**. By 1966 the label's studios were also being used by other Atlantic artists, including **Wilson Pickett**, and the label itself was scoring as many pop hits as its major black rival Motown in Detroit. In 1967 Al Bell joined the label as its first black executive, and Redding – Stax's major artist – died. This led to the end of Stax's partnership with Atlantic, although Atlantic retained ownership of all past recordings, and in 1968 Stewart sold the company to Gulf and Western. Hits came quickly, largely due to Hayes, whose experiments with symphonic arrangements were very successful in the album market. Other Stax artists to have hits in the late sixties include Taylor, the **Staple Singers** and Booker T.

In 1970 Stewart and Bell bought the company back with loans from Polydor, its then European licensee. By this time Stax had changed from a family concern into a multi-million-dollar corporation and many of the artists, with the label since its inception, became increasingly critical of its direction. In 1972 Bell, now running the company, organized the giant Wattstax concert in Los Angeles and, at Stewart's request, signed a lucrative distribution deal with CBS to buy Stewart out of the company. However, the deal collapsed and by 1975 Stax was rocked by charges of financial illegalities, including bank fraud and tax evasion. On 26 January 1976 the label closed its doors. The most important Southern-based soul label was eventually auctioned by a Memphis bank and its assets purchased by California-based Fantasy Records, who continued to keep the label's rich heritage of Southern soul available in their catalogue.

Stewart was ruined by the collapse. He made a brief return to the record business with the Houston Connection label in 1983. Al Bell later worked for Berry Gordy at Motown and founded his own company Bellmark in 1989. In the nineties it became one of America's most successful gospel and rap labels and distributors.

An attempt by Fantasy to reactivate the label in Memphis in 1979 under the control of writer-producer David Porter failed.

JOHN STEWART
b. 5 September 1939, San Diego, California, USA

Beginning as a folk singer and writer, Stewart's atmospheric, querulous-voiced, country-influenced ballads (similar in approach to those of **Gordon Lightfoot**) won a considerable following in the seventies. In the eighties he enjoyed some success with a more rock-orientated approach.

As a rock'n'roll guitarist he formed John Stewart and the Furies, recording 'Rocking Anna' (Vita) before joining the folk revival in 1958. His compositions 'Molly Dee' and 'Green Grasses' were recorded by the **Kingston Trio**. With John Montgomery and Mike Settle, Stewart formed the Cumberland Three in 1960 to record three albums for Roulette. A year later he replaced Dave Guard in the Kingston Trio and remained with the group until 1967. He next planned to work first with John Phillips (of **The Mamas and the Papas**) and then **John Denver**. But though the ethos of Stewart's later work was close to that of Denver, his commercial impact proved to be far less.

Stewart's most successful song turned out to be the ballad 'Daydream Believer' which, in the hands of the **Monkees**, reached No. 1 in 1967. In that year Stewart formed a duo with Buffy Ford, recording *Signals Through the Glass* (Capitol, 1968). He went on to make a series of critically praised solo albums produced by Nik Venet, each of which contained highly crafted love songs and commentaries on the American scene. *California Bloodlines* (Capitol, 1969) included 'Mother Country', a tribute to Robert Kennedy for whom Stewart had campaigned – he later recorded the equally affecting 'The Last Campaign' – and 'July You're a Woman'. *The Lonesome Picker Rides Again* (Warners, 1971) had an acoustic version of 'Daydream Believer' and the elegiac 'All the

Brave Horses'. *The Phoenix Concerts Live* (RCA) is a testament to his charisma in person.

Bombs Away Dream Babies (RSO, 1979) marked a change of direction. Produced by **Fleetwood Mac**'s Lindsey Buckingham it provided a Top Ten single with 'Gold' on which Stewart sang with Stevie Nicks. Another duet with Nicks, 'Midnight Wind' (1979), and 'Lost Her in the Sun' (1980) were lesser hits.

Stewart's later albums included *The Trio Years* (1986), which featured new versions of songs written during his Kingston Trio days and was made with fellow Kingston alumnus Nick Reynolds, *Punch the Big Guy* (1987), on which he duetted with **Nanci Griffith**, and the superior live outing *Neon Beach*. The reissue album *California Bloodlines Plus* (1991) added five tracks from *Willard* (1970) to the original album, while *Turning Love into Gold* (1995) sampled all the stages of his career.

ROD STEWART

b. Roderick David Stewart, 10 January 1945, London, England

With **Elton John**, Rod Stewart was the most successful British singer of the seventies. In one week in 1971 'Maggie May' and the album from which it came, *Every Picture Tells a Story**, simultaneously topped the singles and album charts in Britain and America. A noted member of the London R&B community in the mid-sixties, Stewart won critical acclaim for his solo work as a compassionate songwriter and emotive interpreter of other people's material (*Gasoline Alley*, 1970), but his greatest success came with a series of rowdy, Jack the Laddish exuberant songs, most notably 'Do Ya Think I'm Sexy?'* (1978). With this transition came a glitzy Hollywood lifestyle which made Stewart the epitome of all that the punk rockers of the late seventies stood against, before in the eighties and nineties, his music unchanged, he found new audiences almost as easily as he lost wives.

London-born but of Scottish origins, Stewart first sought a career in football (as a passionate supporter he recorded 'Ole Ola' with Scotland's national soccer team in 1978) before in the early sixties travelling Europe as an itinerant folk singer. In 1963 he returned to London and played harmonica with Jimmy Powell and the Five Dimensions before joining Long John Baldry's Hoochie Coochie Men in 1964 as second singer. Baldry later had an unlikely brief period of success as a big-voiced ballad singer with **Tony Macaulay**'s 'Let the Heartaches Begin' (Pye, 1967), a British No. 1, and 'Mexico' (1968). In 1965 Stewart formed Steampacket, which included **Brian Auger** among its members, but the band folded a year later as the London R&B scene faded. During this period, dubbed 'Rod the Mod', Stewart made his first record-

ings, 'Good Morning Little Schoolgirl' (Decca, 1964) and **Sam Cooke**'s 'Shake' (EMI Columbia, 1966), on which he was backed by Brian Auger's band. Stewart also worked as a session musician, playing harmonica on Millie's **Chris Blackwell**-produced 'My Boy Lollipop' (Fontana, 1964), the first Jamaican record to achieve real commercial success in Britain.

In 1966, with future members of **Fleetwood Mac** Mick Fleetwood and Peter Green, Stewart performed in the short-lived Shotgun Express before in 1967, with **Jeff Beck** and Ron Wood, forming the Jeff Beck Group. After successful American tours and two albums (*Truth*, 1968; *Beck-Ola*, 1969) on which Stewart's searing vocals complemented Beck's guitar pyrotechnics (**Led Zeppelin** would later use a similar formula), Stewart left both to pursue a solo career and lead the Faces, the group formed by Wood and former members of the **Small Faces**. This split (with Stewart signed to Vertigo/Mercury and the Faces, who backed Stewart on his first solo albums, to Warners) initially had a positive effect. With the Faces, Stewart perfected a good-time rock'n'roll sound, while on his own he revealed a more expressive and introspective vocal style that perfectly suited the autobiographical songs he wrote for *An Old Raincoat Won't Let You Down* (1969) and *Gasoline Alley* (1970). Moreover, Stewart's period as a folk singer had given him both a broader-based repertoire and a wider range of experiences than his fellow alumni of British rhythm and blues. Included on the first two albums were the traditional 'Man of Sorrow', **Ewan MacColl**'s 'Dirty Old Town' and **Bob Dylan**'s 'Only a Hobo', as well Stewart's own compassionate musings, 'Lady Day' and 'Joe Lament'. A prominent feature of the albums was Martin Quittenton's acoustic guitar. Also in 1970 Stewart added lead vocals to 'In a Broken Dream' which, when finally issued in 1972 (Youngblood) as by Python Lee Jackson, was an international hit.

Every Picture Tells a Story (1971) was the most commercially successful of his early albums. As well as the autobiographical title track and 'Maggie May'*, co-written by Quittenton, it included a sensitive reading of **Tim Hardin**'s 'Reason to Believe' and an impassioned reworking of the **Temptations** 1966 hit 'I Know (I'm Losing You)', which had been revived less pleasingly a year earlier by Rare Earth (Rare Earth). The similarly styled *Never a Dull Moment* (1972), which featured a pair of hits, 'Angel' and 'You Wear It Well', **Sam Cooke**'s 'Twistin' the Night Away' and the blues classic 'I'd Rather Go Blind', was almost as successful. However, the next few years were not productive. Tension grew between Stewart and the Faces and Warners and Mercury fought over Stewart's contract. As a result, after a desultory live album and *Smiler* (1974), Stewart and the Faces parted and the singer joined Warners.

Atlantic Crossing (1975), produced by **Tom Dowd**, saw Stewart backed by sessionmen (including most of **Booker T. and the MGs**). Clinical in feel, it included two British hits, a reworking of the **Isley Brothers'** 'This Old Heart of Mine' and the soaring 'Sailing', written by Gavin Sutherland who with his brother Ian led one of the better British pub-rock bands and had their own British hit, 'Arms of Mary' (CBS, 1976). Much better was *A Night on the Town* (1976). As well as 'Tonight's the Night'* an American No. 1, it included the sombre 'The Killing of Georgie', an account of the murder of a young homosexual, and **Cat Stevens'** 'The First Cut Is the Deepest'.

Stewart fronted his own band, which included Phil Chen on bass, Carmine Appice from **Vanilla Fudge** on drums (both had played with Jeff Beck) and Jim Cregan (ex-**Family**) on guitar, on a series of successful American tours and at the same time became a regular target of the gossip columns for his hedonistic lifestyle and tempestuous relationship with actress Britt Ekland. With no hint of self-parody this filtered through to his work on hits such as 'Hot Legs' and 'Do Ya Think I'm Sexy?' (1978). Though Stewart's critical reputation declined, his albums and singles continued to sell in large numbers. His international hits of the eighties included 'Passion' (1980), 'Young Turks' (1981), 'Baby Jane' (1983) and a British No. 1 with **Robert Palmer**'s 'Some Guys Have All the Luck' (1984), which earlier had been a hit for the Persuaders (Atco, 1973). *Camouflage* (1984) reunited him with Beck, who also played a handful of American dates with Stewart. In 1986 Stewart returned to the American Top Twenty with 'Love Touch' from the film *Legal Eagles*, 'Lost in You' (1988) and 'Forever Young', from *Out of Order* (1988).

In 1989 the boxed set *Storyteller/The Complete Anthology 1964–1990* was released. It included a newly recorded version of **Tom Waits'** 'Downtown Train', a Top Ten hit on both sides of the Atlantic. 1991's *Vagabond Heart* included another fine cover-version, 'Broken Arrow' by **The Band**'s Robbie Robertson. The following year was largely devoted to touring, with only one new recording emerging, a hit version of another Waits song, the haunting 'Tom Traubert's Blues'. His next album, *Lead Vocalist* (1993), was a mix of new songs and tracks from his Beck, Faces and earlier solo days. An MTV show provided his second album of the year, the acoustic *Unplugged . . . and Seated*, which reunited him with Wood. From it, Stewart's interpretation of **Van Morrison**'s 'Have I Told You Lately That I Love You' gave him yet another Top Five single. He ended the year with the international hit 'All for Love', taken from the movie *The Three Musketeers*, on which he sang with **Sting** and **Bryan Adams**. This temporarily had the effect of transforming Stewart into a ballad singer (*If We Fall*

in Love Tonight, 1996), but more substantial was *When We Were the Boys* (1998) on which Stewart offered his own versions of songs associated with **Oasis** ('Cigarettes and Alcohol') and the like. He toured exhaustively throughout the nineties.

STING
b. Gordon Matthew Sumner, 27 October 1951, Wallsend, Tyne and Wear, England

Following the dissolution of the **Police** in 1984, songwriter, bass-player and vocalist Sting developed a second career as a film actor. At the same time his records, which mostly saw him as a purveyor of sophisticated, jazz-tinged meaningful ballads, won him a new generation of fans. Critical accusations that his attempts to deal with broad political and philosophical issues were pretentious left Sting's millions of followers unmoved. He gave a number of concerts to publicize the work of Amnesty International and to save the Amazonian rain forests, and started his own record label.

His first solo hit had been a version of Vivian Ellis's thirties' musical song 'Spread a Little Happiness' (1982) from the film *Brimstone and Treacle*, in which he also starred. In 1985, however, he embarked on the ambitious *The Dream of the Blue Turtles* (1985), co-produced in Barbados with Pete Smith. The album spawned the American hits 'If You Love Somebody Set Them Free' and 'Fortress Round Your Heart' as well as 'The Russians', which reached the British Top Twenty. Among the musicians involved was Branford Marsalis, saxophonist brother of **Wynton Marsalis**, who also played with drummer Omar Hakim in 1985–6 when the group played Amnesty charity concerts.

The live *Bring on the Night* (1986) preceded *Nothing Like the Sun* (1987), whose title was taken from Shakespeare's sonnets. The album included the poignant ballad 'Be Still My Beating Heart' and the powerful 'They Dance Alone (Gueca Solo)', dealing with the plight of political prisoners in Chile. Among those playing on the album were Mark Knopfler of **Dire Straits**, **Gil Evans** and **Eric Clapton**. In 1988 Sting played further dates for Amnesty as well as launching the Pangaea label to provide a platform for world music and experimental artists such as tango star **Astor Piazzolla** and composer Kip Hanrahan.

The next studio album, *The Soul Cages* (1991), was more musically and lyrically complex. With guitarist Dominic Miller and keyboards-player David Sancious and co-produced by Hugh Padgham, it included the hit 'All This Time'. *Ten Summoner's Tales* (1993) was again produced with Padgham and like its predecessors was released to coincide with a world tour. In 1994 Sting sang with **Bryan Adams** and **Rod Stewart** on the hit film theme 'All for Love' and duetted with

Tammy Wynette on her album of duets, *Without Walls*, on a reworking of 'Every Breath You Take'. In the same year A&M issued *Fields of Gold*, a selection of his work from the previous decade, which included two new songs, 'When We Dance' and 'The Cowboy Song'. *Mercury Falling* (1996) was followed, after the lengthy obligatory tour, by *Brand New Day* (1999). As arty as ever – the opening track, 'Fill Her Up', was inspired by Edward Hopper's 1940 painting *Gas* – the album, a Top Twenty hit in both the UK and US, was made more accessible by taking love for its subject. The result, especially when compared to the nostalgia that attracted so many of his peers, was an innovative and exciting outing that mixed bossa nova riffs and *chansonnier*-styled songs to good and surprising effect.

Sting's acting career has included roles in Ken Russell's *Quadrophenia* (1979), based on **The Who**'s 1973 concept album, Chris Petit's *Radio on* (1980), *Dune* (1984), *Plenty* (1985), *Storm Warrior* (1988) and *Stormy Monday* (1988). He appeared on stage in a production of **Kurt Weill** and Bertolt Brecht's *The Threepenny Opera* in 1989 in Washington DC. His song 'Englishman in New York' was used as the theme of *Stars and Bars* (1988).

STOCK, AITKEN AND WATERMAN

Matt Aitken, b. 25 August 1956, England; Mike Stock, b. 3 December 1951; Peter Waterman, b. 15 January 1947

With their slogan 'the sound of a bright young Britain', writer-producers Stock, Aitken and Waterman established their own 'hit factory' on the model of **Berry Gordy**'s Motown in the mid- and late-eighties. During the latter half of the eighties they had more than fifty hit singles with such artists as Rick Astley, **Kylie Minogue**, **Jason Donovan**, Mel and Kim, and Sinitta.

In 1974 Pete Waterman, who owned a specialist soul record shop, was working as a disc-jockey at a Coventry ballroom. His contribution to the success of Alvin Stardust's 'My Coo Ca Choo' (1975) led Magnet label-owners Michael Levy and Pete Shelley to sign Waterman as a promotion man and then A&R scout. He discovered Adrian Baker, whose 'Sherry' reached the Top Ten in 1975, and remixed the **Lee Perry**-produced 'Hurt So Good' (1975) by Susan Cadogan. The record was a Top Ten hit and the Waterman-produced 'Love Me Baby' reached the Top Thirty. The following year he co-wrote and co-produced 'Alright Baby' by Stevenson's Rocket.

Waterman subsequently worked for MCA Music, went into independent production with Peter Collins (producer of Musical Youth and **Nik Kershaw**) and in 1984 teamed up with guitarists and keyboards-players Aitken and Stock. As Agents Aren't Aeroplanes the duo released the unsuccessful 'The Upstroke' (RCA, 1984) and produced the disco-styled British No. 1 'You

Spin Me Around (Like a Record)' by Dead or Alive (Epic, 1984). As a trio SAW had their first successes with Divine's 'You Think You're a Man' (Proto, 1984), Hazell Dean's hi-energy disco favourite 'Searchin'' (Proto) and the pared-down sounds of Sinitta's 'So Macho' (Fanfare, 1986), the prototype of their subsequent hits.

In 1987 the trio produced numerous British hits, including **Bananarama**'s 'I Heard a Rumour' (London); Mel and Kim's 'F.L.M. (Fun Love Money)' (Supreme); ex-model Samantha Fox's 'Nothing Gonna Stop Me Now' (Jive); Sinitta's 'Toy Boy'; and their own 'Roadblock', a skilful pastiche of **James Brown**-style soul. 'Roadblock' was later at the centre of a controversy over sampling when SAW won a lawsuit against 4AD Records for copyright infringement by the Marrs hit 'Pump Up the Volume' (1987). Their later successes included 'You'll Never Stop Me Loving You' by Sonia (Chrysalis, 1989) and tracks for established artists **Donna Summer** ('This Time I Know It's for Real') and **Cliff Richard** ('I Just Don't Have the Heart').

In general, the SAW sound was more important than the artist, but in the late eighties the trio successfully developed the careers of two contrasting teen-idols on their own PWL label – *Neighbours* soap-opera star Kylie Minogue and Rick Astley. For Minogue they developed a jaunty, carefree sound on such British hits as 'I Should Be So Lucky', a remake of the **Carole King** composition 'The Loco-Motion' (1988), 'Je Ne Sais Pas Pourquoi', and the duet with her soap-opera 'husband', Jason Donovan, 'Especially for You' (1988). For Donovan, SAW created British No. 1s with 'Too Many Broken Hearts' and a revival of Brian Hyland's 1961 hit 'Sealed with a Kiss'.

They were even more successful with Rick Astley (*b. 6 February 1966, Warrington, England*), whose 'Never Gonna Give You Up'* was Europe's bestselling single of 1987 and an American chart-topper in 1988 (on RCA). In 1987 he had further success with a brooding remake of **Nat 'King' Cole**'s 'When I Fall in Love' and in 1988 he returned to the top of the British and American charts with 'Together Forever' on which the staccato dance rhythms were more muted than in past productions. Astley's later hits included 'She Wants to Dance with Me' (1988), 'Take Me to Your Heart' and 'Hold Me in Your Arms'.

The trio produced Band Aid II's 1989 re-make of 'Do They Know It's Christmas?' and there were later hits, notably from Sybil ('Walk on By', 1990). However, the team broke up in the nineties as first Stock (in 1991) and Aitken (1993) left to pursue independent production careers. Waterman had now achieved the unlikely status of a grand old man of pop and in 1992 became a director of the Performing Rights Society. He returned to the teen idol fray in the late nineties with Steps (*Steptacular*, 1999, which included several hit singles), whose career he oversaw and records he produced, in tandem with various sets of younger ears.

THE STONE ROSES

Ian George Brown, b. 20 February 1963, Ancoats, Lancashire, England; Mani, b. Gary Michael Mounfield, 16 November 1962, Crampsall, Greater Manchester; Reni, b. Alan John Wren, 10 April 1964, Manchester (replaced by Robbie Maddix); John Thomas Squire, b. 24 November 1962, Broadheath, Lancashire (replaced by Aziz Ibrahim); Nigel Ippinson

Blending melodic, sixties guitar-pop with eighties dance beats, the Stone Roses were the most important British group of the late eighties/early nineties. They stood at the forefront of the 'Madchester' scene, which also included the **Charlatans** and the **Happy Mondays**, while vocalist Brown was the primary influence on **Oasis** frontman Liam Gallagher. However, the band failed to capitalize on the success of their eponymous 1989 début, and slowly dismantled after eventually releasing a follow-up five years later.

Originally known as English Rose, the Stone Roses were formed in 1985 by Brown, guitarist Squire and drummer Reni. After recruiting bassist Mani they developed a dedicated following in and around Manchester, releasing their début single, 'So Young', in 1987. 'Sally Cinnamon' attracted the attention of Silvertone Records, who signed the band the following year. The third single, 'Elephant Stone', introduced their psychedelic edge as well as Brown's formless vocalizing, paving the way for the band's full-length début.

The Stone Roses (1989) was a startlingly original set, blending Acid House rhythms with hook-laden sixties guitar-pop. It included the classic singles 'I Am the Resurrection' and 'She Bangs the Drums', largely responsible for bringing the 'Madchester' scene into the mainstream, alongside the Happy Mondays' 'Step on'. The album was swiftly followed by 'Fools Gold', which became the Stone Roses' first UK Top Ten hit, and the optimistic 'One Love'. In 1990 the band organized their own festival on Spike Island in Widnes, where 30,000 fans witnessed a legendary set which proved to be the Stone Roses' final live performance for five years.

After their Spike Island performance the Stone Roses began a lengthy legal battle with Silvertone over their desire to leave the label. The band eventually won the case and signed to Geffen in 1991, but it would be a further three years before they issued any new material. *Second Coming* (1994), heavily influenced by **Led Zeppelin**, met with a mixed reaction on its release, while comeback single 'Love Spreads'

stalled at No. 2 in the UK charts. Before the band could begin a full international tour Reni left the band, apparently discontent with his share of the band's songwriting, which on *Second Coming* was dominated by Squire. On the eve of a headlining appearance at Glastonbury, Squire broke his collarbone in a freak cycling accident.

While support for the Stone Roses dwindled, their contemporaries began to shine once again, as the Charlatans and Happy Mondays frontman Shaun Ryder staged successful comebacks. The band eventually embarked on a series of UK dates in late 1995 with new drummer Maddix (formerly of Rebel MC) and additional keyboardist Ippinson, a year after the release of *Second Coming*. This proved to be the band's final tour, however, as Squire announced his plan to form a new band in May 1996. The Stone Roses made one final appearance, at the 1996 Reading Festival, with guitarist Ibrahim, before founding members Brown and Mani disbanded the group. A commemorative edition of their début was issued on its tenth anniversary in 1999, complete with additional tracks and an interactive element. Two compilation volumes have also been issued: *Made of Stone* is a collection of non-album tracks, while *The Complete Stone Roses* features the best of their early material.

In 1997 Squire made his recording début with new band the Seahorses, formed with singer Chris Helme, whose vocal style was somewhat reminiscent of Brown. The Seahorses issued one album, *Do It Yourself* (Geffen), before splitting up. Squire has since been working with former **Verve** bassist Simon Jones on an as-yet unnamed project. Ian Brown recorded a low-key solo album, *Unfinished Monkey Business*, in 1998 with guitarist Ibrahim, before being jailed for six months for threatening behaviour on an aeroplane. The following year Ibrahim began working with the former **Smiths** rhythm section of Andy Rourke and Mike Joyce, while Brown issued *Golden Greats*, described by many as the best work of any of the former Stone Roses since their 1989 début. Reni has not spoken to the music press since leaving the Stone Roses in 1995, but is believed to be planning a solo career. Bassist Mani joined **Primal Scream** in 1996, shortly after the Stone Roses split.

STONE TEMPLE PILOTS

Dean DeLeo, b. 23 August 1961, New Jersey, USA; Robert DeLeo, b. 2 February 1966, New Jersey; Eric Kretz, b. 7 June 1966, Santa Crize, California; Scott Weiland, b. 27 October 1967, San Diego, Texas

A US rock quartet inspired by the seventies arena rock of **Aerosmith** and **Kiss**, Stone Temple Pilots rose to international fame in the midst of the grunge boom of the early nineties but were held back from superstardom by the heroin addiction of lead singer Weiland.

Formed at the start of the nineties in San Diego as Shirley Temple's Pussy, the group soon drew comparisons with **Pearl Jam**, mainly for the vocal similarities between Weiland and Eddie Vedder. Signed to Atlantic on the basis of their touring reputation, the group, which featured the DeLeo brothers on guitars – Robert (bass) and Dean (lead), with drummer Kretz and Weiland – achieved triple-platinum status with *Core* (1992). That album included the arena anthem 'Plush', which was a hit single, and the controversial 'Sex Type Thing', a song about date rape. Within two years the band had topped the US chart with *Purple* (1994), which included a series of sexually explicit songs, and were beginning to gain recognition in Britain and across Europe.

The band was forced to take an extended break after touring in support of *Purple* in order that Weiland could curb his drug addiction. After watching their lead singer go in and out of rehabilitation and, briefly, prison, Stone Temple Pilots recorded *Tiny Music . . . Songs from the Vatican Gift Shop* (1996), but were unable to tour because of Weiland's difficulties. The album, which entered the *Billboard* charts at No. 4 only to slip down, saw the group successfully extending their range. The quartet returned to touring in support of *Interstate Love Songs* (1998) and in the same year Weiland released a solo album, *12 Bar Blues*.

JESSE STONE

b. 12 November 1901, Atchison, Kansas, USA, d. 1 April 1999, Florida

Best remembered as the author of the seminal 'Shake Rattle and Roll', arranger and composer Stone was one of the first songwriters to incorporate the solid backbeat of rock'n'roll into fifties R&B.

From a showbusiness family, Stone made his first stage appearance at the age of four with a performing dog act. By his teens a veteran of vaudeville, he formed his first band, Jesse Stone and His Blues Serenaders, in 1926; they recorded his 'Starvation Blues' (Okeh, 1927). Later he worked as an arranger in Kansas City for Meritt and Brunswick before in the early thirties moving to New York under the patronage of **Duke Ellington**. In New York he worked first as an arranger at the Apollo Theater and then for **Chick Webb** and **Jimmie Lunceford** (1939), as well as fronting his own band and recording ('Snakey Feelings', Variety, 1937). After the success of 'Idaho' (a hit for **Benny Goodman** and Alvino Rey, 1942), he turned increasingly to songwriting in the forties and only recorded intermittently ('Get It While You Can', RCA, 1949).

On the formation of Atlantic in 1947, Stone became the company's staff arranger and was responsible for re-orientating **Ahmet Ertegun** from the fluid rhythms of jazz to a more danceable form of rhythm and blues with a strong bass line. The classic example was 'Cole Slaw' (Frank Culley, 1948 – an even bigger hit for **Louis Jordan**, 1949), an adaptation of Stone's earlier composition, 'Sorghum Switch', which had been a hit for **Jimmy Dorsey** (1942). Stone also recorded the song for RCA (1949). Throughout the early fifties Stone worked as an arranger and rehearser of Atlantic's vocal group signings, as well as a writer. His songs included a trio of witty accounts of the power of money, 'Money Honey' (the **Drifters**, 1953), 'It Should Have Been Me' (**Ray Charles**) and 'Your Cash Ain't Nothin' but Trash' (the **Clovers**, 1954).

Stone had his greatest success with 'Shake Rattle and Roll' which he wrote under his Charles Calhoun pseudonym. An R&B hit for **Joe Turner** (1954), it was even more successful, becoming an anthem of rock'n'roll, when bowdlerized – in the original at the song's beginning the protagonists are in bed – by **Bill Haley**. More successful was the similarly styled follow-up Stone provided for Turner, 'Flip Flop and Fly'* (1955). Stone also wrote for **Ruth Brown** another song based on the same strong backbeat, 'As Long as I'm Moving'. During this period he recorded occasionally for Atlantic, MGM and Groove. Then in 1955, following a dispute over royalties, he left Atlantic to work as an arranger at Aladdin. When that company collapsed in 1956, Stone turned publisher and established Roosevelt Music, among whose first signings was **Otis Blackwell**. In the sixties and early seventies he worked briefly for Capitol, Epic and Reprise before finally retiring to Florida in 1983. In 1991 Atlantic issued *It's My Time*.

LEW STONE

b. 28 May 1898, London, England, d. 13 February 1969

Stone was the leader of one of the most successful British dance bands of the thirties. He was also responsible for **Al Bowlly**'s best recordings.

While a pianist with Bert Ralton's band, Stone established himself as a freelance arranger, working for **Ambrose** and other bands in the late twenties. In 1931 he joined **Roy Fox**'s band as pianist and in 1932, when Fox fell ill, briefly took over the band – which included trumpeter **Nat Gonella** and vocalist Bowlly – and Fox's residency at London's Monseigneur Restaurant. His Tuesday night radio broadcasts won him a reputation as an inventive arranger and his hundred or so recordings with Bowlly between 1932 and 1938, commencing with 'Nightfall' (Decca), were noticeably more restrained than Bowlly's other recordings, because, in the words of Albert McCarthy, the 'basic astringency in his arranging style prevented sentiment descending to bathos'. Stone's only American hit, **Jimmy Kennedy**'s 'Isle of Capri' (1935), featured Gonella on vocals.

Between 1931 and 1935, in addition to leading the band and his recording and broadcasting activities, Stone was musical director for British and Dominion Films. As such, with his band, he appeared in several films, including *A Night Like This* (1932) and *Bitter Sweet* (1933), as well as writing and arranging music for some forty more. In 1935, the year he left Decca for Regal Zonophone, he published *Harmony and Orchestration for the Modern Dance Band*. Throughout the later thirties he led (mostly pick-up) bands at various London residencies while at the same time working as musical director of several musicals. Such was his fame that, in 1938, with **Mantovani**, he was invited to play at the opening of Billy Butlin's holiday camp at Clacton.

During the war, as Lew Stone and his Stone-Crackers, Stone recorded his most jazzy sides for Decca (1942) with George Chisholm on trombone, and toured military camps and ballrooms with a larger band. After the war, he led smaller groups at London cafés and hotels and continued to broadcast until the sixties, at the same time working as an agent.

SLY STONE
b. Sylvester Stewart, 15 March 1944, Dallas, Texas, USA

One of the great innovators in contemporary black music, Sly Stone's late-sixties records laid the foundations for the funk and disco sounds of the following decade. After 1974 his own career faltered and he never recaptured the impact of his early work despite the fact that a new generation of rappers in the nineties regarded him as their precursor.

Raised in San Francisco, he studied music and composition before, as Sylvester Stewart, he recorded 'Long Time Away' in 1960. He became a disc-jockey and worked for fellow deejay Tom Donahue's local Autumn label, producing future **Jefferson Airplane** singer Grace Slick's group the Great Society, the Beau Brummels ('Just a Little', 1965) and Bobby Freeman ('C'mon and Swim', 1964).

Sly and the Family Stone was formed in 1966 with Cynthia Robinson (trumpet), Fred Stewart (guitar) and bassist Larry Graham – who later formed Graham Central Station, which had a big hit with 'Your Love' (Reprise, 1975). After releasing a single on the local Loadstone label, the group signed to Epic for *A Whole New Thing*. Their first hit came with the polyrhythmic title track to *Dance to the Music* (1968), while 'Everyday People' (1969) topped both pop and R&B charts.

A triumphant appearance at the Woodstock Festival clinched the band's popularity with white audiences. 'Hot Fun in the Summertime' (1969) reached No. 2, while both 'Thank You (Falettin Me Be Mice Elf Again)'* (1970) and 'Family Affair'* (1971) topped the charts. Other Sly and the Family Stone favourites with live audiences included 'I Want to Take You Higher' and 'Stand!', the title track to the group's third album.

'Family Affair' came from *There's a Riot Goin' on* (1971), which replaced the carefree psychedelic sentiments of earlier songs with a more determined political stance on songs like 'Don't Call Me Nigger, Whitey' and 'Runnin' Away'. The album was soon followed by similar forthright statements from **Curtis Mayfield**, the **Temptations** and others, but Sly Stone's increasingly erratic stage performances – in 1971 twelve of his forty scheduled appearances had to be cancelled – and growing drug dependency marred his artistic progress.

Fresh (1973) brought another big hit in 'If You Want Me to Stay', but also included a banal version of the former **Doris Day** hit, 'Que Sera Sera'. It was followed by *Small Talk* (1974), which divided critics' opinion among those who found it musically experimental and those who heard a self-indulgent celebration of Stone's recent marriage and parenthood. After the release of *High on You* (1975), Stone was reported to be bankrupt and the disappointing *Heard Ya Missed Me* did not appear until 1978. The following year he moved to Warners for *Back on the Right Track*, but by now he was being outstripped by those whom he had taught, like **George Clinton** and the **Ohio Players**.

During the eighties Stone's output was meagre. He worked with Clinton on Funkadelic's *Electric Spanking of War Babies* (1981) and recorded his own *Ain't but One Way* (A&M, 1983). His next recording was a duet with Martha Davis (of the Motels) on **Joan Armatrading**'s 'Love and Affection' for the soundtrack of *Soul Man* (1986).

In the nineties Stone's career was again blighted by drug problems.

ERNEST V. STONEMAN
b. 25 May 1893, Carroll County, Virginia, USA, d. 14 June 1968, Nashville, Tennessee

Unique among country musicians, Ernest 'Pop' Stoneman not only lived through, but participated in, the technological development of the record industry from phonograph cylinder to stereo album. He also presided over what may be, after the **Carter Family**, the 'second clan' of country music.

A carpenter and amateur musician on guitar and autoharp, Stoneman was inspired to make records by his low opinion of the early country hit 'Wreck of the Old '97' (Okeh, 1923), by the Virginia singer, guitarist and harmonica-player Henry Whitter. After a cautious start, in the late twenties he became one of the busiest hillbilly recording artists, working for Okeh, Victor and Gennett to produce string-band instrumentals, 'heart' songs, hymns, ballads and 'rural sketches' like 'Possum Trot School Exhibition' (Victor, 1928). Stoneman recruited for these sessions several distinguished musicians from his Galax, Virginia, neighbourhood, an area then (and still) rich in traditional country music. He also documented, by recording them, more old songs than anyone of his time except A. P. Carter.

In the early thirties the Stoneman family, which eventually included thirteen children, moved to Washington DC, where, after some lean times, Ernest secured regular work outside music. His recording activity was limited to an obscure session with his eldest son Eddie (Vocalion, 1934). In the late forties, however, with many of the children in their teens, he organized a family band to perform locally on Connie B. Gay's *Gaytime Show*. In 1956 there followed a family bluegrass band, the Bluegrass Champs. Various combinations appeared on the *Grand Ole Opry* and at folk-song clubs during the fifties and sixties, and there were Stoneman Family albums for Folkways, Starday, MGM and other labels.

Meanwhile some of the second-generation Stonemans began to make their own name, most notably Scott, whose fiery and unrestrained bluegrass fiddling with groups like the Kentucky Colonels left its mark on another generation of players. The family name in country music is maintained by Donna, who plays mandolin, Ronnie (banjo) and others of 'Pop's' children and grandchildren.

GEORGE STRAIT

b. 18 May 1952, Poteet, Texas, USA

With **Ricky Skaggs** the most successful of the traditionally inclined country singers who emerged in the mid-eighties, Strait found favour with a strong, warm voice that was reminiscent of, if not as flexible as, **Merle Haggard**'s. Backing it were the twin fiddles and the honky tonk sounds of Texas rather than the sweet countrypolitan sound in vogue when he started recording.

The son of a teacher and a cattle rancher, Strait began singing while in the army, taking for his models **George Jones**, Haggard and **Lefty Frizzell**. After his discharge in 1975 he briefly recorded for D Records (1976) while completing a degree in agriculture. Signed to MCA in 1980 he had immediate success with 'Unwound' (1981). During the remainder of the decade, he had ten No. 1s, including 'Fool Hearted

Memory' (1982), 'Amarillo by Morning' (1983), 'Does Fort Worth Ever Cross Your Mind', his most renowned recording, 'You Look So Good in Love' (1984), 'The Chair' (1986) and 'If You Ain't Lovin' (You Ain't Livin)' (1988), which he co-wrote with his regular producer Jimmy Bowen. While these were mostly straightforward love songs, albums such as *Something Else* (1986) included more reflective offerings, notably 'Lefty's Gone', a haunting tribute to Frizzell written by Sanger D. Shafer, author of many of Strait's hits, and such easygoing evocations of the honky tonk era as 'Dance Time in Texas'. *Ocean Front Property* (1987) provided him with the country classic 'All My Ex's Live in Texas'.

Albums from this period were *Beyond the Blue Neon* (1989), which included 'Hollywood Squares', *Livin' It Up* (1990), which included 'Lonesome Radio Cowboy' and 'Amen', and the lesser *Chill of an Early Fall* (1991). In 1992 he made a creditable acting début in *Pure Country*, for which he provided the unremarkable soundtrack. It was followed in 1994 by the lesser *Easy Come, Easy Go* (MCA), which lacked the energy of earlier releases. Far better was the chart-topping *Lead on* (1994), which included the country hit 'The Big One'. His other major hit from this period was 'Check Yes or No' (1995). *Strait out of the Box* (1995) is a four-CD retrospective that fully documents his career – it includes all thirty-two country chart-toppers – up to that point.

Blue Clear Sky (1996) included the moving 'I Can Still Make Cheyenne', a rodeo rider's desperate telephone call to his loved one about his financial prospects. It invited comparison with the equally affecting **Lyle Lovett** song 'Farther Down the Line', which was memorably recorded by **Willie Nelson** on *Across the Borderline* (1993). Later Strait albums included *Carrying Your Love With Me* (1997), *One Step at a Time* (1998), which was one of his biggest pop hits, and *Always Never the Same* (1999). In 2000 his duet with Alan Jackson, 'Murder on Music Row', became a *cause célèbre* for its claim that traditional country music had been killed by 'the almighty dollar and the lust for worldwide fame'. The record was only a minor hit.

THE STRANGLERS

Jet Black, b. Brian Duffy, 26 August 1938; Jean Jacques Burnel, b. 21 February 1952, London, England; Hugh Cornwell, b. 28 August 1949, London; Dave Greenfield

Emerging during the punk era with a reputation for distasteful and controversial lyrics, the Stranglers found longer-term success as a mainstream rock band.

Cornwell had played guitar with **Richard Thompson** in the London-based Emil and the Detectives and the Swedish group Johnny Sox before meeting bassist Burnel in 1974 and forming the Guildford Stranglers with drummer Black and keyboards-player Greenfield. They dropped the prefix in 1975. They supported **Patti Smith** on her 1976 début British tour and later that year they signed to United Artists, releasing their début single 'Grip' in 1977, which appeared on *Rattus Norvegicus IV* (1977), along with the Top Ten hit 'Peaches' (whose voyeuristic lyrics were changed to permit radio play). The politically orientated single 'Something Better Change' followed, like its predecessors featuring Cornwell's gruff vocals and Greenfield's distinctive organ sound which showed a strong influence from the **Doors**.

With its litany of 'great names', the title track of *No More Heroes* was equally successful. The group's string of hits extended into 1979 with 'Five Minutes', 'Nice 'n' Sleazy' and 'Duchess', though a cover of **Burt Bacharach**'s 'Walk on By' was less successful. The albums *Black and White* (1978) and *Live (X-Cert)* (1979) were both sizeable hits, and Burnel's solo effort *Euroman Cometh* (1979) – a pretentious manifesto for a Euro-culture – made the British Top Forty. The same year Cornwell's low-key collaboration with Robert Williams (ex-**Captain Beefheart**'s band), *Nosferatu*, failed to chart. The Top Five album *The Raven* (1979) preceded *Themeninblack* (1980) – a concept album about the mystery of UFOs – which found the group grappling with grand themes: it even had a parody of the Lord's Prayer, 'Hallo to Our Men'. The superior *La Folie* (1981) was on a smaller scale and produced the group's biggest hits in the uncharacteristic waltz-time ode to heroin 'Golden Brown' and sentimentality of 'Strange Little Girl' (1982).

A move to Epic led to further hits including 'European Girl' (from *Feline*, 1983), 'Skin Deep' (from *Aural Sculpture*), and 'Nice in Nice' and 'Big in America' from *Dreamtime* (1986), an album whose title track dealt with the religious beliefs of Australian aboriginals.

In a reversion to the style of their earlier work, the Stranglers' biggest hit in the eighties was a primitive reworking of the **Kinks**'s 'All Day and All of the Night' (1988), taken from the film soundtrack *Permanent Record*. In the same year Cornwell released the solo album *Wolf* (Virgin). In 1989 the Stranglers performed the theme music for the BBC2 *Floyd's American Pie* cookery teleseries – an indication of their newfound respectability.

After *10*, which included a hit version of **? & the Mysterians**' '96 Tears', Cornwell left the band. His last live appearance with the Stranglers was released in 1993 as *Saturday Night Sunday Morning* (Castle). He released a well-received solo album, *Wired*, in 1993 and *Guilty* in 1997. The remaining Stranglers recruited ex-Vibrators guitarist John Ellis and vocalist Paul

Roberts to replace Cornwell and released the lacklustre *Stranglers in the Night* on British independent label China Records in 1992. They followed this with *About Time* (1995), *Written in Red* (1997) and *Coup de Grace* (1998). None of these maintained the bite of earlier albums. The group continued to tour throughout the nineties.

BARBRA STREISAND
b. Barbara Joan Streisand, 24 April 1942, Brooklyn, New York, USA

A powerful and dramatic singer and actress, Streisand's career demonstrated how separate the popular- and rock-music traditions were in the fifties and sixties and how in the seventies and eighties they came together. Though a child of the rock era, she first won success on Broadway and in Hollywood with the stage and film version of *Funny Girl* (1964, 1968) before re-orientating her career towards the rock marketplace with *Stoney End* (1970) and the 'rock' remake of *A Star Is Born* (1976). There followed a series of solo hits ('The Main Event'*, 1979; 'Woman in Love'*, 1980) and duets with **Neil Diamond** ('You Don't Bring Me Flowers'*, 1978), **Donna Summer** ('No More Tears [Enough Is Enough]'*, 1979), Barry Gibb of the **Bee Gees** ('Guilty', 1980) and Don Johnson ('Till I Loved You', 1988). At the same time, in the manner of her rock contemporaries (rather than the popular-music stars of the past she initially modelled herself on), she took complete control of her career, directing, writing and performing in her most personal project, *Yentl* (1983), and later *Prince of Tides* (1991).

Streisand's first Broadway success was in *I Can Get It for You Wholesale* (1962), which led to the lead in *Funny Girl* (1964), the musical based on incidents in the life of **Fanny Brice**. Her versions of **Bob Merrill** and **Jule Styne**'s intimate 'People' – her first major hit (Columbia, 1964) – and the brash 'Don't Rain on My Parade' featured her powerful, yet controlled voice. An overnight star, Streisand won an Oscar for her performance in the 1968 film *Funny Girl* (which added 'My Man', the song most closely associated with Brice) and later appeared in the 1975 sequel *Funny Lady*. In 1969 she starred in the film version of the similar *Hello Dolly*, the title song of which gave **Louis Armstrong** an American No. 1 in 1964, the year the Broadway show opened, and in *On a Clear Day You Can See Forever*.

Though her albums, mostly of standards such as *The Barbra Streisand Album* (1963), sold reasonably well, her only other hit recording of the period was 'Second Hand Rose' (1966). Another song associated with Brice, who had a hit with it in 1922, 'Rose' successfully traded on Streisand's gawky, hand-me-down image. Then, in 1970, Columbia Records' Clive Davis, who had successfully extended the chart careers of other mainstream artists (including **Andy Williams**) by getting them to record contemporary material, persuaded Streisand to work with producer Richard Perry. The result was *Stoney End*, whose **Laura Nyro**-penned title track was a Top Ten hit. The Oscar-winning film theme 'The Way We Were'*, co-written by **Marvin Hamlisch**, gave Streisand her first American No. 1 in 1973, but the fusion of the contemporary image she had established in films like *What's Up Doc?* (1972) and *For Pete's Sake* (1974) with her new approach to music came in *A Star Is Born* (1976). An updated reworking of the 1954 film, with Streisand and **Kris Kristofferson** in the parts originally played by **Judy Garland** and James Mason, it included an American No. 1, 'Evergreen', which she co-wrote with **Paul Williams**. She followed it with another collection of contemporary songs, *Streisand Superman* (1977), which included her version of **Billy Joel**'s 'New York State of Mind'. In its wake came the hit duets (with Diamond, Summer and Gibb, who also produced and co-wrote most of the songs on *Guilty**, 1980, Streisand's biggest-selling album). In the eighties on both record and film she turned her attention to the past with *Memories** (1981), *Broadway* (1986) and *Yentl* (1983), which also provided the hit 'The Way He Makes Me Feel'. In 1987 she revived her wacky comedienne persona in the film *Nuts*. *Prince of Tides* (1991) was another personal work.

Streisand returned to her roots to record the album of 'songs from the shows', *Back to Broadway* (1993), which also included songs from the then unseen **Andrew Lloyd Webber** musical, *Sunset Boulevard*. It included the hit 'Ordinary Miracles' by Marvin Hamlisch with Marilyn and Alan Bergman. Hamlisch led the orchestra when, in 1994, she played her first concerts in Britain since she had appeared in *Funny Girl* in the sixties. *Barbra – The Concerts: Live at Madison Square Garden* was issued in the same year.

In 2000 she commenced on a short farewell tour, *Timeless*, producing a show that told her life-story through song and audio-visual aids that suggested – as was not the case with most farewell tours – she really was saying goodbye to the stage.

LESLIE STUART

b. Thomas Augustine Barrett, 15 March 1864, Southport, Lancashire, England, d. 27 March 1928, Richmond, Surrey

As 'Lily of Laguna' approaches its centenary, still known or half-known by perhaps a majority of British people, its composer Leslie Stuart has achieved music-hall immortality. If his other achievements, both in that idiom and in musical comedy, are included, he

rates among the greatest composers of light music in the last hundred years – a judgement endorsed by, among others, **Eubie Blake** and **Jerome Kern**.

By the age of fifteen he had become the organist of St John's Cathedral, Salford. He went on to hold a similar position in Manchester, in which city he also organized many classical concerts. In his thirties, under his assumed name, he started working in musical comedy and enjoyed enormous success with *Florodora*, which introduced his first hit song, 'Tell Me Pretty Maiden'. *Florodora* was first produced in London in 1899 and in New York in 1900, and revived several times in both cities until as late as 1931. Other works in this vein included *The Silver Slipper* (1901), *The Belle of Mayfair* (1906), *Havana* (1908), *The Slim Princess* (1911) and *Peggy* (1911).

He also wrote for music-hall artists during the eighties and nineties, one of his early successes being the patriotic *Soldiers of the Queen* (1881). His best-known songs were written for the American 'coon' singer Eugene Stratton, among them 'I May Be Crazy', 'Little Dolly Daydream' (1897) and 'Lily of Laguna' (1898). Their association ended after a quarrel at a race meeting and Stuart spent many years in relative obscurity, but shortly before his death he appeared as a solo act at the London Palladium where, the story goes, he quietly played his most celebrated tunes to an audience that slowly realized it was in the presence of their forgotten creator.

In later years the joint legacy of Stratton and Stuart was loyally shouldered by G(eorge) H. Elliott, 'the chocolate coloured coon', who maintained the blackface song tradition on the British variety stage into the fifties and formed a link between the old days and the popular stage and TV production *The Black and White Minstrel Show*.

THE STYLISTICS

James Dunn, b. 4 February 1950, Philadelphia, Pennsylvania, USA; Airron Love, b. 8 August 1949, Philadelphia; Herbie Murrell, b. 27 April 1949, Lane, South Carolina; James Smith, b. 16 June 1950, New York; Russel Thompkins Jnr, b. 21 March 1951, Philadelphia

With Thompkins' pure, high tenor and **Thom Bell**'s finely judged arrangements, the Stylistics made some of the most distinctive soft-soul records of the seventies.

During the mid-sixties Thompkins, Love and Smith had been members of Philadelphia vocal group the Monarchs while Murrell and Dunn had been part of the Percussions. Both groups disbanded in 1968 and the quintet combined to form the Stylistics. The following year the new group recorded 'You're a Big Girl Now' by their guitarist Robert Douglas and road manager Marty Bryant for local label Sebring. When the doo-wop-flavoured song had become a Philly hit, it was picked up for national distribution by **Hugo and Luigi**'s Avco Embassy.

Avco signed the group and Thom Bell was brought in to produce a stream of ethereal, bestselling singles. He set the sweetness of Thompkins' high tenor against an electronically phased introduction on 'You Are Everything'* (1971), written by Bell and Linda Creed, and followed up with 'Betcha by Golly, Wow'* (1972) from the eponymous début album. *Stylistics 2* (1972) included the gently rocking 'I'm Stone in Love with You'*, the group's first British Top Ten hit, which was faithfully covered the following year by **Johnny Mathis**.

The hits continued with 'Break Up to Make Up'* (1973); a revival of **Burt Bacharach** and Hal David's 1964 hit for **Dionne Warwick**, 'You'll Never Get to Heaven (If You Break My Heart)'; 'Rockin' Roll Baby'; and the Stylistics' biggest success 'You Make Me Feel Brand New'* (1974). 'Let's Put It All Together' was Bell's last production for the group. With **Van McCoy**'s arrangements and songs by George David Weiss, Hugo and Luigi took over production. But while the more saccharine 'Star on a TV Show' (1975) and 'Sing Baby Sing' were only minor hits in America, British audiences remained loyal and 'Can't Give You Anything (But My Love)' reached No. 1.

The Stylistics' series of British hits continued with 'Na Na Is the Saddest Word' (1976), 'Can't Help Falling in Love' and '16 Bars'. In 1977 the group switched to their producers' new H&L label but '7000 Dollars and You' was their final European success.

The group continued to record prolifically, making *Sun and Soul* (1977) and *Wonder Woman* (1978) for H&L before moving to Mercury for *Love Spell* (1979). Dunn left the group before the remaining members returned to the Philly fold by signing to **Gamble and Huff**'s Philadelphia International label in 1980. *Hurry Up This Way Again* (1980) was followed by *1982*, which included a version of Bacharach–David's 'There's Always Something There to Remind Me'.

The group later released *Some Things Never Change* (Virgin, 1985). In 1992 they released the seasonal album *The Stylistics Christmas* and the following year the undistinguished *Love Talk*. They continued touring throughout the nineties.

Greatest Hits (1996) is the definitive retrospective.

JULE STYNE

b. *Jules Kerwin Stein, 31 December 1905, London, England, d. 20 September 1994, New York City, USA*

A prolific film and stage musical composer, Styne's sequence of hit songs stretched from 'Since You' (1941) to 'People' (1971). His lyricists included **Frank Loesser**, **Sammy Cahn**, **Leo Robin** and **Stephen Sondheim**.

A child prodigy – at three he duetted with **Harry Lauder** – Styne emigrated to America with his family in 1913, where at the age of nine he was a piano soloist with Chicago Symphony Orchestra. Turning to popular music, he had his first success with 'Sunday' (1927), a hit for **Gene Austin**. Styne led his own band before moving to New York, where he began twin careers as a singing coach for actors and a songwriter.

Styne moved to Hollywood as a vocal coach for 20th-Century Fox and in 1935 joined Republic as a staff songwriter. There he was teamed with Loesser, composing 'Since You' for Dorothy Lamour to sing in *Sailors on Leave* and 'I Don't Want to Walk Without You' from *Sweater Girl* (1942), a hit for Helen Forrest with **Harry James**' band and for **Bing Crosby** and **Dinah Shore**.

When Loesser went into the army, Styne worked with Cahn on 'There Goes That Song Again' (1944), sung by Harry Babbitt with **Kay Kyser**'s orchestra in *Carolina Blues* and successfully revived in Britain in 1961 by Gary Miller (Pye). Among the film songs composed by Cahn and Styne were such hits as 'I Still Get Jealous'* by **Gordon MacRae** (Decca, 1947) from *High Button Shoes* and 'It's Magic'*, first sung by **Doris Day** in *Romance on the High Seas* (1948) and covered in the same year by **Dick Haymes**, MacRae, **Tony Martin** and **Sarah Vaughan**.

The first Broadway hit for Cahn and Styne was *High Button Shoes*, which introduced MacRae's 'I Still Get Jealous' and Day's 'Papa Won't You Dance with Me'. In 1949 Styne wrote the Broadway show *Gentlemen Prefer Blondes* with Leo Robin. Featuring 'Diamonds Are a Girl's Best Friend', it was filmed in 1953 with Marilyn Monroe and revived as *Lorelei* in 1973.

In 1951 Styne began a regular collaboration with Betty Comden (b. *3 May 1917, Brooklyn, New York*) and Adolph Green (b. *2 December 1915, Brooklyn*), who had previously partnered Judy Holiday in the musical comedy group the Revuers. The duo's lyrics and librettos revealed a fascination with the many aspects of New York and their first success came in partnership with **Leonard Bernstein** with *On the Town* (1944, filmed 1949).

With Styne they wrote *Two for the Aisle* (1951) and *The Bells Are Ringing* (1956, filmed 1960), in which Holiday introduced the wistful 'The Party's Over', a hit for Doris Day and in Britain for **Lonnie Donegan**. The trio's later plays like *Do Re Mi* (1960) and *Hallelujah Baby!* (1967) were less successful than Comden and Green's film writing for producer **Arthur Freed**, *Singin' in the Rain* (1952), *The Band Wagon* (1953) and *It's Always Fair Weather* (1955), for which **André Previn** wrote the music.

Styne's own biggest hit of the fifties was the Oscar-winning theme song 'Three Coins in the Fountain' (1954), a million-seller for the **Four Aces** and a hit for

Frank Sinatra, while his penchant for expansive, brash melodies was well suited to the showbusiness theme of *Gypsy* (1959, filmed 1962), a musical based on the life of striptease artist Gypsy Rose Lee. With lyrics by Sondheim, the show starred **Ethel Merman** and introduced 'Some People' and the frequently recorded 'Everything's Coming Up Roses'.

Though he wrote more Broadway shows, Styne's only other major success was *Funny Girl* (1964, filmed 1968), written with **Bob Merrill**. Also based on a showbusiness star, this time **Fanny Brice**, it featured **Barbra Streisand** and introduced 'Don't Rain on My Parade' and 'People', later a hit for the Tymes (Columbia, 1968).

STYX

John Curulewski (replaced by Tommy Shaw, b. 1954); Dennis DeYoung, b. 18 February 1947, Chicago, Illinois, USA; Chuck Panozzo, b. 20 September 1947, Chicago; John Panozzo, b. 20 September 1947, Chicago, d. 16 July 1996, Chicago; James Young, b. 14 November 1948, Chicago

With **Foreigner**, Styx were the leading American exponents of eclectic art-rock or 'pomp rock' during the seventies. They mixed theatrical elements with massive light shows and churning rhythms.

Formed in Chicago by twins Chuck Panozzo (bass), John Panozzo (drums) and singer/keyboards-player DeYoung, the group became the Tradewinds with the addition of guitarists Young and Curulewski in 1968. As Styx (the underground river of Hades in Greek mythology) they recorded *Styx I* (1972) for Chicago label Wooden Nickel. Tracks like 'Movement for the Common Man' and 'Mother Nature's Matinee' typified the ambitious lyrics of the group's principal songwriter DeYoung.

Numerous live shows and two more albums during the next three years built up a following which made 'Lady' (1975), from *Equinox*, their début album for A&M, a Top Ten hit. *Equinox* also included Styx's first mini-epic, 'Suite Madame Blue'. At this point guitarist-singer Shaw joined and the group's strengthened harmonies helped to make them one of the leading bands on the stadium rock circuit of the late seventies. 'Lorelei' (1977) was a minor hit but *The Grand Illusion* (1978) provided a Top Ten single with 'Come Sail Away'.

Though every A&M release was a bestseller, 1979–81 were Styx's most successful years. *Cornerstone* provided the million-selling No. 1 'Babe' (1979) while Top Ten hits 'Too Much Time on My Hands' and 'The Best of Times' appeared on *Paradise Theater* (1981), a chart-topping album which dealt with the state of the nation. Though critics were lukewarm about the robot theme of the concept album *Kilroy*

Was Here (1983), 'Mr Roboto' sold a million and 'Don't Let It End' reached the Top Ten.

In 1984 the group released the live *Caught in the Act* and then disbanded for what was intended to be a temporary period. Shaw embarked on a solo career with *Girls with Guns* (Atlantic, 1984) and *Ambition* (1987) while DeYoung released *Desert Moon* (1978) and *Boomchild* (1988). In 1989 Shaw joined veteran Detroit guitarist **Ted Nugent** in heavy metal 'supergroup' Damn Yankees.

Without Shaw, Styx re-formed in 1990 for *Edge of the Century*, which included the heartfelt 'Not Dead Yet' and the Top Five hit 'Show Me the Way', which caught the patriotic tenor of the times during the Gulf War. When Styx took time off in 1993 DeYoung revived his theatrical ambitions, appearing in *Jesus Christ Superstar* and recording a collection of show tunes, *10 Days on Broadway* (1995). They returned to touring in support of *Return to Paradise* (1997) and *Brave New World* (1998), both of which were made without DeYoung. *Greatest Hits* (1995) is the definitive anthology.

SUEDE

Brett Anderson, b. 27 September 1967, Sussex, England; Bernard Butler, b. 1 May 1970, London (replaced by Richard Oakes); Neil Codling; Justine Frischmann, b. Twickenham; Simon Gilbert; Mike Joyce; Mat Osman, b. 9 October 1967, Sussex

Before being overtaken by Britpop and its principle players **Blur** and **Oasis**, Suede were responsible for bringing glamour back to pop music, becoming one of the most popular British guitar bands of the nineties.

Schoolfriends Osman (bass) and Anderson (vocals) moved to London in the late eighties and recruited guitarist Butler from an advert in the *NME*. Adding guitarist Frischmann and a drum machine for their early live performances, the band subsequently began to work with Joyce, formerly of the **Smiths**. In 1992, by which time Joyce had been replaced by Gilbert and Frischmann had left to form **Elastica**, Suede had generated enough interest to appear on the cover of the *Melody Maker* before releasing their first single. 'The Drowners' soon became a chart hit in the UK, winning unanimous praise for its simple, chiming guitar lines and Anderson's sexually ambiguous lyrics.

After securing their reputation with 'Animal Nitrate' Suede unleashed their eponymous début (Nude, 1993), which was one of the fastest-selling début albums in British history, spawning further hit singles in 'So Young' and 'Metal Mickey', before gaining their highest chart entry to date for the epic 'Stay Together'. The band gained further exposure when the album won them both the 1993 Mercury Music

Prize and the Brit Award for Best New Band. However, Butler was to quit over 'creative differences' during the making of the prog-influenced *Dog Man Star* (1994), leaving the band without a guitarist and a new album to promote.

Anderson quickly drafted in an unknown seventeen-year-old, Richard Oakes, but the band faced a backlash as they toured in support of the album, while allegations of a heavy drug problem centred around the singer. Suede soon lost their position as the darlings of the British music press to Blur and Oasis, despite the success of the superb 'The Wild Ones' as a single. The band also had to alter their name in the US, becoming the London Suede in the wake of threatened legal action from a Baltimore folk singer.

Suede took a break to reassess their position after promoting *Dog Man Star*, eventually returning with *Coming Up* (1996), a collection of radio-friendly glam-pop songs. The album was a huge international success on the strength of the singles 'Trash', 'Lazy', 'The Beautiful Ones' and 'Saturday Night' as Suede embarked on a lengthy world tour. As they released their fourth album, *Head Music* (1999), which had been given a polished, hi-tech veneer by producer Steve Osbourne (**Happy Mondays**), Suede were hailed by many as the best British band of the decade, achieving a total of sixteen consecutive hit singles with 'Electricity', 'She's in Fashion' and 'Everything Will Flow'.

After leaving Suede, Bernard Butler worked with a number of different artists before embarking on a solo career. Having lent his guitar skills to artists including **Neneh Cherry**, Butler began a short-lived collaboration with singer David McAlmont. A pair of **Phil Spector**-inspired soul-pop singles, 'Yes' and 'You Do', were lavished with praise by the critics before another creative dispute caused them to split. Their entire recorded output is included on *The Sound of McAlmont* (1995). In 1998 Butler released his solo début, taking vocal duties for the first time on *People Move On* (Creation), heavily inspired by Nick Drake and the west-coast soft rock of **Fleetwood Mac**. 'Stay' and 'Not Alone' both made the British Top Ten. Butler returned the following year with the heavier *Friends and Lovers*.

DONNA SUMMER

b. LaDonna Gaines, 31 December 1948, Boston, Massachusetts, USA

Achieving fame with the controversial 'Love to Love You Baby'* (1976), Summer was the most successful disco singer of the late seventies, having ten million-selling singles. She later moved into mainstream soul and rock-ballad singing.

Influenced by **Mahalia Jackson**, she sang in gospel choirs as a child. After singing briefly in 1967 with Boston rock group Crow, Donna Gaines joined the German cast of *Hair!*, settling in Munich in 1970 and taking her first husband's name, Sommer. After she sang backing vocals on a **Three Dog Night** recording session, producers Pete Bellotte and **Giorgio Moroder** signed Sommer to sing their European disco hits 'Hostage' (Oasis, 1974) and 'Lady of the Night'.

The success of the reissued 'Je T'Aime . . . Moi Non Plus' by **Serge Gainsbourg** with its erotic moans from Jane Birkin (Antic, 1974) inspired Moroder and Bellotte to make 'Love to Love You Baby' in 1975; on the record Sommer panted equally suggestively over synthesized disco rhythms. It sold poorly in Europe but a seventeen-minute version was released by Neil Bogart on his Casablanca label and, despite being denounced by the Rev. Jesse Jackson, was first a club hit and then sold a million in 1976 in a shortened version. Banning by the BBC did not prevent the song reaching the Top Ten in Britain.

Summer (Bogart had changed the spelling) followed with the Moroder-produced *Love Trilogy* (1976) and the disco concept album *Four Seasons of Love* (1977) before the hypnotic, repetitive 'I Feel Love'* became a British No. 1. The track came from *I Remember Yesterday*, which also demonstrated Summer's versatility with the girl-group-sounding 'Love's Unkind' and the salsa-flavoured 'Black Lady'. After releasing *Once Upon a Time*, a 'disco opera' based on the Cinderella story, Summer appeared in the film *Thank God It's Friday* (1978), singing Paul Jabara's Grammy-winning 'Last Dance'*.

Jimmy Webb's 'MacArthur Park'* (first a hit for actor Richard Harris in 1968) was given the Moroder disco treatment on the double-album *Live and More* (1978), which reached No. 1, as did 'Hot Stuff'* and Summer's own title track from *Bad Girls* (1979). A double-album, *Bad Girls* mixed Eurodisco with American rock and softer ballads, composed by Summer. This move towards the mainstream was confirmed by 'No More Tears (Enough Is Enough)'*, (1979) a duet with **Barbra Streisand** which reached No. 1.

When Bogart sold Casablanca to PolyGram in 1980, Summer left for the newly formed Geffen label where the title track from *The Wanderer* was another million-seller. The album also included 'I Believe in Jesus', through which Summer announced that she was born again. Label chief David Geffen rejected the next Moroder-produced album and brought in **Quincy Jones** for *Donna Summer* (1982), which included **Bruce Springsteen**'s 'Protection' as well as the hit single 'Love Is in Control (Finger on the Trigger)'.

Summer's later successes included 'She Works Hard for the Money' (Mercury, 1983) and a revival of the **Drifters**' 1959 hit 'There Goes My Baby' from *Cats* *without Claws* (1984). Both were produced by Michael Omartian but Richard Perry took over for *All Systems Go* (Warners, 1987), which brought more chart success with the Brenda Russell composition 'Dinner with Gershwin'.

In an unexpected switch of producer, British hit-makers **Stock, Aitken and Waterman** came in for *Another Place and Time* (1989). 'This Time I Know It's for Real' and 'I Don't Wanna Get Hurt' were hit singles from the album. Subsequent singles were less successful, although Summer remained a popular live act, particularly in Europe. She later concentrated on painting. In 1994 she recorded 'Melody of Love (Wanna Be Love)' with producers Clivilles and Cole of **C&C Music Factory** and *Christmas Spirit*, her first seasonal offering. In 1996 the *I'm a Rainbow* double-album made in 1981 but not released was finally issued. In 1998 she was reunited with Moroder for the minor hit 'Carry on'.

The Donna Summer Anthology (1993) is the best career retrospective available.

SUN RA

b. Herman Sonny Blount, 22 May 1914, Birmingham, Alabama, USA, d. 30 May 1993

A pianist and keyboards player, Sun Ra led his rehearsal band-cum-commune, the Solar Arkestra, for over thirty years. Looking both forwards (through his 'intergalactic music') and back to the African polyrhythmic roots of jazz, he made an important contribution to avant-garde jazz during the seventies and eighties.

He settled in Chicago in the thirties and played with **Fletcher Henderson** in 1946–7, making his first recording the following year with former **Dave Brubeck** bassist Eugene Wright. Already active in black community organizations, Sun Ra began gathering the nucleus of the Arkestra during the early fifties. Among them were bassist Ronnie Boykins and saxophonists John Gilmore (a later influence on **John Coltrane**), Pat Patrick and Marshall Allen.

The band was run in a highly disciplined autocratic way by Sun Ra and its self-contained nature was underlined by the founding of its own Saturn label, whose often hand-labelled records documented the Arkestra's progress. There were parallel recordings for other labels, beginning with the Chicago-based Transition and Delmark (*Sound of Joy*, 1957). Live performances often took on a ritualistic character with band members in robes and some wearing headgear with flashing lights. The shows frequently consisted of continuous playing with abrupt shifts from one style and one soloist to another.

Sun Ra's own playing was characterized by a range of styles (from cocktail jazz to **McCoy Tyner**-like

modernism) and a passion for new keyboards technology. As early as 1956 he was using electric piano, graduating to celeste, electric organ and Moog synthesizer, whose sonic range was perfectly suited to Sun Ra's eclecticism and the futuristic mythologies of more programmatic works like *Pictures of Infinity* (1969) and *The Solar Myth Approach*. One of his finest synthesizer efforts was 'Cosmic Explorer' on *Nuits de la Fondation Maeght* (Shandar, 1970).

In 1960 the Arkestra spent some months in Montreal before relocating in New York, where it recorded for ESP (*Heliocentric Worlds of Sun Ra*, 1965). The group visited Europe in 1970 and Egypt the following year. Among over 100 musicians who passed through the Solar Arkestra were many who became leading jazz figures. They included tenor-saxophonist Pharoah Sanders, who played with Coltrane and **Archie Shepp**, bassist Wilbur Ware, and Julian Priester, who worked with **Ray Charles** and **Herbie Hancock**. Later albums included *Solo Piano Vol. 1* (1977), *Sunrise in Different Dimensions* (1989) and *Purple Night* (1990) with **Don Cherry**.

A stroke in 1990 left Sun Ra with limited mobility but the Arkestra continued to tour and record until his death.

SUPERGRASS

Gaz Coombes, b. 8 March 1976, Brighton, Sussex, England; Danny Goffey, b. 7 February 1974, London; Mickey Quinn, b. 17 December 1970, Oxford

Starting life as an energetic punk-pop trio at the height of Britpop, Supergrass soon turned to melancholy psychedelia, becoming one of Britain's premier guitar bands of the nineties.

After releasing 'Just Got Back Today' (Nude, 1992) as the Jennifers, Coombes (vocals/guitar) and Goffey (drums) renamed themselves Supergrass. They recorded 'Caught by the Fuzz' (1994) with bassist Quinn and, after sending a demo to a number of labels, were signed by Parlophone later in the year. After confirming their reputation with 'Mansize Rooster' and 'Lenny', Supergrass hit the UK Top Ten with *I Should Coco* (1995) before 'Alright' propelled them into the mainstream. The breezy, piano-led single made the British Top Three as well as earning the band an underground following in the US.

Supergrass returned to recording two years later after a hectic touring schedule with the critically acclaimed *In It for the Money* (1997). While 'Richard III', 'Late in the Day' and 'Going Out' all made the UK Top Forty, the mature, multi-textured psychedelia of their second album failed to repeat the success of the band's début, struggling to achieve gold status. The band took a break after promoting the album before releasing their eponymous third album *Supergrass*

(1999), which had echoes of the playful nature of **The Beatles**' later recordings and included the hit singles 'Pumping on Your Stereo' and 'Moving'.

SUPERTRAMP
Richard Davies, b. 22 July 1944, England; Roger Hodgson, b. 21 March 1950, Portsmouth, Hampshire; Richard Palmer (replaced by Frank Farrell, b. Birmingham, replaced by Dougie Thompson, b. 1951, Scotland); Bob Miller (replaced by Kevin Currie, replaced by Bob Siebenberg); David Winthrop, b. 27 November 1948, New Jersey, USA (replaced by John Anthony Helliwell, b. 1945, England)

A British progressive rock group of the late sixties, Supertramp established a following in Europe and America that ensured the group's survival into the eighties.

Keyboards-player Davies had been a member of R&B groups in the Reading area with the future **Gilbert O'Sullivan** before joining the Joint. When that group failed, he found a Dutch backer to finance Supertramp, whose name was taken from W. H. Davies's *Autobiography of a Supertramp*. The band had a songwriting nucleus of Davies and singer/guitarist Hodgson.

Adding guitarist Palmer and drummer Miller, the group made an eponymous album for A&M in 1971. *Indelibly Stamped* (1972), made with a different rhythm section, was equally unsuccessful. The breakthrough came with *Crime of the Century* (1974), for which Supertramp recruited what would be a permanent rhythm section of bassist Thompson from the Alan Bown Set (**Robert Palmer**'s former group) and drummer Siebenberg, who had played with London pub-rock pioneers Bees Make Honey. Ex-Bown saxophonist Helliwell also joined at this point.

Crime of the Century reached the British Top Ten and the catchy 'Dreamer' (1975) was a Top Twenty hit. Both *Crisis? What Crisis?* (1975) and *Even in the Quietest Moments* (1977) sold well in Britain, but Supertramp made little impact in America until they turned to transatlantic themes on *Breakfast in America* (1979). 'The Logical Song' and 'Take the Long Way Home' were Top Ten hits there while the title track reached the Top Ten in Britain.

After the live album *Paris* (1980), Supertramp released . . . *famous last words* . . . (1982) from which Hodgson's 'It's Raining Again' was a British hit. Soon afterwards he left the group to make the solo albums *Eye of a Storm* (1985) and *Hai Hai* (1987). The remaining quartet recorded the lacklustre *Brother Where You Bound* (1985) and the jaunty *Free as a Bird* (1987). A world tour in 1988 was followed by the release of *Live in 88*, after which the band disintegrated, only to re-form for *Some Things Never Change* (1997), which, with significant tour support, was surprisingly successful.

The Very Best of Supertramp (1997) is the only anthology to date.

THE SUPREMES
Diana Ross, b. Diane Ross, 26 March 1944, Detroit, Michigan, USA (replaced 1969 by Jean Terrell, b. 6 November 1955, Texas); Florence Ballard, b. 30 June 1943, Detroit, d. 22 February 1976, Detroit (replaced 1967 by Cindy Birdsong, b. 15 December 1939, Camden, New Jersey); Mary Wilson, b. 6 March 1944, Detroit

With twelve American No. 1s and some twenty million-selling records to their credit, the Supremes were the most successful and longest-lasting female vocal group of the sixties. As such, they formed the launching pad for **Berry Gordy**'s and Motown's musical assault on the white American market, and later for the solo career of **Diana Ross**.

Formed in 1959 by Ross, Ballard, Wilson and Betty Anderson as the Primettes, the group regularly performed with the Primes, the forerunner of the **Temptations**. With Barbara Martin replacing Anderson they recorded unsuccessfully for Lupine in 1960, before being signed by Gordy to Motown. After 'I Want a Guy' (Tamla, 1961), Martin left the group whose first singles, produced by **Smokey Robinson** and mostly featuring Ballard's tougher lead vocals, were only minor hits. Their first Top Forty hit, 'When the Lovelight Starts Shining through His Eyes' (Motown, 1963), came after Gordy handed them over to the writing and production team of **Holland, Dozier and Holland**. That was followed by a trio of No.1s, the groundbreaking 'Where Did Our Love Go?'* (later successfully revived by Donnie Elbert, All Platinum, 1971), 'Baby Love'* and 'Come See About Me', on which Ross's bright, cooing vocals perfectly complemented the metallic sheen of the productions.

In the wake of their international success, the Supremes were the first of Motown's acts to be processed through its charm school where they were groomed to perform, in the words of the school's director Maxine Powell, 'in only two places: Buckingham Palace and the White House'. In 1965, a year after they had toured Britain – where they had been fêted by **The Beatles** and others as a soul group – they recorded *Live at the Copa* to signal their newfound sophistication and Gordy's mainstream aspirations. Their act now as precisely choreographed as the production of their records, the Supremes and Holland, Dozier and Holland's hits continued unabated. Their American No.1s included 'Stop in the Name of Love'* 'Back in My Arms Again'*, 'I Hear a Symphony'* (1965), 'You Can't Hurry Love'* (later revived by **Phil Collins**, 1982), 'You Keep Me Hangin' on'* (1968), (which was extensively reworked by **Vanilla Fudge**, also in 1968), 'Love Is Here and Now You're Gone', the film theme 'The Happening' (on which Birdsong, a former member of **Patti Labelle and the Blue Belles**, replaced Ballard, who had been sacked by Gordy), and 'Reflections'* (1967), the first of their records to be billed as by Diana Ross and the Supremes. 'Love Child'* (1968) was their first major hit after they stopped working with Holland, Dozier and Holland, but a more significant split followed 'Someday We'll Be Together'* (1969), when Ross left the group to be replaced by Terrell.

Like most Motown artists, the Supremes frequently recorded with their label-mates. With the Temptations they made 'I'm Gonna Make You Love Me' (1968) and with the **Four Tops** a remake of **Ike** and **Tina Turner**'s collaboration with **Phil Spector**, 'River Deep Mountain High' (1970). With the departure of Ross, the Supremes' chart career rapidly declined. After 'Stoned Love' (1970) 'Nathan Jones' (1971) and 'Floy Joy' (1972), Wilson and Birdsong left the group and in 1976 the new group had one more hit, 'I'm Gonna Let My Heart Do the Walking' (1976), before it too disbanded. In 1980 Wilson toured Britain, where the Supremes' later records had been more successful than in America and where in 1974 a reissued 'Baby Love' had returned to the Top Twenty, with a pair of backing singers as Mary Wilson and the Supremes – Motown owned the name, thus she couldn't bill herself as the Supremes. A year later the Broadway show *Dreamgirls* told the story of the Supremes from the perspective of Ballard, who had died in poverty, depicting Gordy as a manipulative tycoon and Ross as his puppet. Wilson published her own version, *Dreamgirl: My Life as a Supreme*, in 1984.

Diana Ross & The Supremes: 40 Golden Motown Greats (1998) is the definitive anthology. The miscalculated Diana Ross/Supremes tour of 2000 only served to revive the animosity between those that saw the Supremes as a vocal *group* and those who worshipped at the shrine of diva Ross.

THE SWAN SILVERTONES

Claude Jeter, b. 1915, Montgomery, Alabama, USA; Rev. Robert Crenshaw; Solomon J. Womack; Paul Ownes

Led by Claude Jeter, generally acclaimed as 'The Master of Falsetto', the Swan Silvertones were one of the sweetest-sounding jubilee gospel groups of the postwar era. Jeter's gentle, whispered falsetto formed the basis of **Curtis Mayfield**'s work with the **Impressions** and was later echoed by the **Temptations**. The Swan Silvertones' recording of 'Mary Don't You Weep', which included the line 'I'll be a bridge over deep water if you trust in my name', was the inspiration for **Paul Simon**'s oft-recorded 'Bridge over Troubled Water'* (1970).

The son of a lawyer, Jeter sang in church and, after working as a miner in Kentucky, formed the Four Harmony Kings in 1938 with two other miners and his brother. In the early forties, after John Myles (later their manager) joined, they began broadcasting on WBIR in Knoxville, Tennessee, changing their name to the Silvertones (to avoid confusion with the Kings of Harmony). Swan was added after they were sponsored by the Swan Brothers' bakery. Though they specialized in the quiet harmony singing – on radio they all sang into one microphone – of folk songs like **Stephen Foster**'s 'Old Black Joe', as well as traditional gospel material, Jeter added a hard-voiced vocalist, Solomon Womack, when they signed to King in 1945. With a changed line-up of Jeter, Womack, Myles and Robert Crenshaw (and later Paul Owens) they joined **Art Rupe**'s Specialty label in 1951 and recorded their most pop-orientated material. In 1955 they switched to Vee-Jay, adding guitarist Linwood Hargrove and a new hard singer, Louis Johnson. There, they recorded their best-remembered songs, 'Mary Don't You Weep', 'Saviour Pass Me Not' and 'How I Got Over' (1959), which they had earlier recorded for Speciality.

In the mid-sixties Jeter retired to become a minister in Detroit, but the group, led by Myles and Johnson, continued to perform.

BILLY SWAN

b. 12 May 1942, Cape Giradeau, Missouri, USA

Best remembered for 'I Can Help' (1974), with its simple rolling organ set against the singer's sprightly pleading, Swan was a writer, session musician and recording artist whose work drew on the wide spectrum of Southern musical styles.

Swan's first success came when 'Lover Please', which he wrote for his group Mirt Mirley and the Rhythm Steppers in 1958, was recorded first by **Bill Black** (1960) and then **Clyde McPhatter**, who had an international hit with it in 1962. In the mid-sixties Swan moved to Nashville as a songwriter and replaced **Kris Kristofferson** as the janitor at Columbia's studio to support himself. He produced Tony Joe White – including his biggest hit 'Polk Salad Annie' (1969) – and toured as a member of Kristofferson's backing band. During this period he also toured and recorded with Kinky Friedman, who briefly won critical approbation for his outlandish country recordings (notably *Sold American*, Vanguard, 1973, which included 'Ride 'Em Jewboy' and the controversial 'Ballad of Charles Whitman', and *Lasso from El Paso*, Epic, 1976, on which he was backed by **Eric Clapton** and **Bob Dylan**, among others).

Signed to Monument, reportedly on the unlikely basis that he sounded like **Ringo Starr**, Swan produced in the title track of his début album *I Can Help* one of the bestselling records of 1974. A mixture of Southern rock'n'roll and blues-inflected country, it was one of the best examples of the reflective mood of many recordings of the period. The follow-up, a sensuous slow version of the **Elvis Presley** 1956 hit 'Don't Be Cruel', was a minor hit in the UK in 1975, but though the album and its sequels *Rock'n'Roll Moon* (1975), which included the relaxed 'Everything's the Same (Ain't Nothing Changed)', and *Billy Swan* (1976) were critical successes they failed commercially. After the lesser *You're OK, I'm OK* (A&M, 1978) and a lengthy period working as a session man in Nashville, Swan in 1986 briefly linked up with former member of the **Eagles** Randy Meisner, in the group Black Tie, before rejoining Kristofferson, recording *Repossessed* (1986) and *Third World Warrior* (1990) and touring with him. He was also a regular collaborator with singer/songwriter/producer T-Bone Burnett, appearing on several of his albums in the eighties and nineties.

Billy Swan's Best (Red Barron, 1993) only begins to suggest how eclectic a mixture of country, soul and pop the music of Swan was.

THE SWEET

Brian Connolly, b. Brian McManus, 5 October 1948, Middlesex, England, d. 10 February 1997; Steve Priest, b. 23 February 1950, Middlesex; Frank Torpy (replaced by Mick Stewart, replaced by Andy Scott, b. 30 July 1949, Wrexham, Wales); Mick Tucker, b. 17 July 1948, Middlesex

A British bubblegum group renowned for their outrageous costumes, Sweet had a dozen hits written by **Chinn and Chapman** in the seventies.

Singer Connolly replaced Ian Gillan (later of **Deep Purple**) in Harrow soul band Wainwright's Gentlemen in 1965 with drummer Tucker joining soon afterwards. With Torpy (guitar) and Priest (bass) they recorded as Sweet in 1968–70 for Fontana ('Slow Motion') and Parlophone ('Lollipop'). With Phil Wainman as producer, their first Chinnichap song, the catchy 'Funny Funny' (RCA, 1971) with its echoes of the Archies 'Sugar Sugar'* (Calendar, 1969), was a British Top Twenty hit. 'Co Co' sold even better but the more complex 'Alexander Graham Bell' did less well. However, 'Poppa Joe' and the American million-seller (on Bell) 'Little Willy' successfully repeated the 'Funny Funny' formula, while the harder-sounding 'Wig Wam Bam' showed a slight change of style.

Each single was accompanied by a change of stage outfit for television appearances and with the British No. 1 'Blockbuster', which began with police sirens wailing (1973), Sweet took on what one reviewer called a 'cheerily androgynous' image inspired by **David Bowie**. As the songs got heavier – 'Hell

Raiser', 'The Ballroom Blitz', 'Teenage Rampage' (1974) – Connolly's suggestive stage antics caused the group to be banned from appearing on the Mecca dance-hall circuit.

The Bowie influence was also apparent in 'The Six Teens', Chinn and Chapman's more serious lyric about teenage life. In 1975 the group issued a declaration of independence from their writers and producers. The self-produced 'Fox on the Run' (another million-seller in America) and 'Action' reached the Top Twenty, after which the hits dried up.

The difficulty of going beyond the bubblegum audience was shown by the lack of success of the progressive-rock-orientated *Give Us a Wink* (1976) and *Off the Record* (1977). A switch of label to Polydor provided a final international hit with 'Love Is Like Oxygen' (1978). Connolly left soon afterwards and after making *A Cut Above the Rest* (1979), *Water's Edge* (1980) and *Identity Crisis* (1981), Sweet disbanded.

The band briefly re-formed without Connolly in 1985 and again in 1988 with Scott and Tucker joined by vocalist Mal McNulty, bassist Jeff Brown and keyboard-player Steve Mann. They released the album *Live at the Marquee* (1990) and toured clubs regularly on the crest of a wave of seventies nostalgia. Connolly retired from the music business when he contracted a disabling muscular condition.

The Best of Sweet (EMI, 1993) is the best compilation of their trashy delights.

THE SWINGING BLUE JEANS

Ray Ennis, b. 26 May 1942, Liverpool, England; Ralph Ellis, b. 8 March 1942, Liverpool (replaced 1965 by Terry Sylvester, b. 8 January 1945, Liverpool); Les Braid, b. 15 September 1941, Liverpool; Norman Kuhlke, b. 12 June 1942, Liverpool

The Swinging Blue Jeans are best remembered for their frantic 'Hippy Hippy Shake' (1963), a classic example of the coarse, energetic versions of black American hits that were the staple diet of the British beat groups of the mid-sixties. However, like so many groups of the beat-boom era, they were unable either to reproduce consistently the intensity of their stage act on record or, through songwriting, develop their own musical identity.

Originally a traditional jazz band, the Bluegenes were formed in 1958 by Ennis (vocals, guitar), Braid (bass), Kuhlke (drums) and Ellis (guitar). After residencies in Hamburg and at Liverpool's Cavern club, the group signed to HMV as the Swinging Blue Jeans (the name change following their sponsorship by a jeans' manufacturer) in 1963 in the wake of **Beatles** hysteria. 'Too Late Now' was only a minor hit but their revival of Chan Romero's 1958 Del Fi recording

'Hippy Hippy Shake' reached No. 2 in Britain (and was a hit a year later in America on Imperial). It set the pattern for their subsequent releases, all revivals of black hits. These included **Little Richard**'s 'Good Golly Miss Molly', **Betty Everett**'s 'You're No Good' (1964) and **Dionne Warwick**'s 'Don't Make Me Over' (1966). That record saw them attempting a more sophisticated sound with which they continued when Sylvester (a former member of the Escorts) replaced Ellis in 1965. However, the lack of original material and their old-fashioned image ('smart' blue jeans and matching leather waistcoats) told against the group and in 1968, after the departure of Sylvester to join the **Hollies**, they retreated to the cabaret circuit.

In 1974 the group recorded the unimpressive *Brand New and Faded* (Dart), before once more returning to cabaret and European tours. By this time only Braid and Ennis remained from the original line-up. They continued to play as a cabaret act into the early nineties. *Hippy Hippy Shake* (EMI, 1993) is the definitive career retrospective.

DAVID SYLVIAN
b. David Batt, 23 February 1958, Lewisham, London, England

Former **Japan** frontman Sylvian, once described as 'the most beautiful man in the world', carved out a distinctive solo career on the borderline between avant-garde and ambient music in the eighties and nineties. He performed and recorded with a variety of collaborators.

Shortly before Japan split in 1982, Sylvian had released the hit single 'Bamboo Music', a collaboration with ex-Yellow Magic Orchestra musician **Ryuichi Sakamoto**. This inaugurated an occasional musical partnership which would continue for a decade. With Japan defunct, Sylvian contributed the theme 'Forbid-den Colours' to Sakamoto's soundtrack of the film *Merry Christmas Mr Lawrence*. His first solo album, *Brilliant Trees* (1984), was a logical progression from his last recordings with Japan, and reached the Top Five in the UK, providing him with a hit single, 'Red Guitar'. In the same year Sylvian had the first exhibition of his photographic work in London.

Despite the critical and commercial success of *Brilliant Trees* it would be nearly two years before the release of its follow-up, *Gone to Earth* (1986), although a cassette-only album of experimental pieces, *Alchemy – An Index of Possibilities*, appeared in 1985 (it later appeared on CD in Japan). A sprawling, looser work than its predecessor, *Gone to Earth* was markedly less successful, and the next album, *Secrets of the Beehive* (1988), continued the trend.

At this point, Sylvian began to work with ex-**Can** member Holger Czukay, releasing two ambient albums, *Plight and Premonition* (1988) and *Flux and Mutability* (1989). With his solo career apparently faltering, Sylvian re-formed Japan, releasing the patchy *Rain Tree Crow* (1991), which was neither an artistic nor a commercial success.

Sylvian now re-established his partnership with Sakamoto, recording 'Heartbeat Returning to the Womb' (1992) with Sylvian's girlfriend Ingrid Chavez on vocals. Sylvian's next partner was another devotee of experimentation in music, veteran guitarist **Robert Fripp** (ex-**King Crimson**). The pair recorded *The First Day* (1993), a largely successful collaboration which featured Chavez. Fripp and Sylvian also toured together, issuing the live *Damage* in 1994. In the same year the duo issued a seventeen-minute dance single, 'Darshan (the Road to Graceland)', which was remixed by Future Sounds of London, leading members of a new generation of British experimentalists. His much delayed solo album *Dead Bees on a Cake* (Virgin) finally appeared in 1999 to little effect.

TAJ MAHAL

b. Henry St Clair Fredericks, 17 May 1942, New York City, USA

Like **Ry Cooder**, Taj Mahal found his inspiration in the roots of American popular musics. During the seventies and eighties he created a rich brew of blues, ragtime, jazz, R&B, reggae, calypso, African and Bahamian styles.

Of Caribbean descent, Taj Mahal's earliest influences came from the whole range of Afro-American music. After graduating from the University of Massachusetts, he moved to Los Angeles where in 1965 he formed the Rising Sons folk-rock band with Cooder, Jesse Ed Davis, Gary Marker and Ed Cassidy (later of **Spirit**). The material recorded by the group was eventually released in 1992 as *The Rising Sons*. The nucleus of that group played on *Taj Mahal* (Columbia, 1967), which was produced by David Rubinson. The album contained the haunting 'Celebrated Walking Blues' and exuberant reworkings of **Blind Willie McTell**'s 'Statesboro Blues' and **Sleepy John Estes**' 'Leavin' Trunk'. *Natch'l Blues* (1968), on which Mahal mostly played banjo, harmonica and guitar on re-creations of country blues styles and sounds, also included an impassioned Southern soul rendering of **William Bell**'s 'You Don't Miss Your Water (Till Your Well Runs Dry)'. The double-album *Giant Steps/De Ole Folks at Home* (1969) consisted of an electric set of blues and an acoustic set and included the ironic 'Ain't Gwine Whistle Dixie (Any Mo')' and a reworking of **Lloyd Price**'s 1959 chart-topper 'Stagger Lee', which he returned to its folk roots. It was followed by a live album, *The Real Thing* (1971), on which he was accompanied by a tuba section and a string quartet.

The title of *Recycling the Blues* (1971) summed up Mahal's early seventies work, which included the soundtrack to the film *The Sounder* (1972), in which he also appeared. Beginning with *Mo' Roots* (1974) – on which **Bob Marley** produced Mahal's version of his own 'Slave Driver' and 'Johnny Too Bad', sung by **Jimmy Cliff** in *The Harder They Come* – Mahal looked outwards to the West Indies, addressing reggae and calypso themes. His final albums for Columbia were *Music Keeps Me Together* (1975) and *Satisfied'n'Tickled Too* (1976). In 1977 Mahal's score for the biopic *Brothers*, which dealt with the lives of black activists George Jackson and Angela Davis, was released by Warners. His studio albums for the label included *Music Fuh Ya* (1977) and *Evolution* (1978).

A 1979 live album for Crystal Clear was followed by a second in concert set *Live* (1981) and *Take a Giant Step* (1983). After a period of semi-retirement, Mahal returned in 1987 to renew his partnership with Jesse Ed Davis on the mellow *Taj* (Gramavision). It was followed by another live album, *Live and Direct*, and the studio set *Mule Bone* (1991) and presaged a period of intense activity from Taj Mahal. He returned to the studio to record *Like Never Before* (Private Music, 1992) and *Dancing the Blues* (1994). One of his best albums, it included songs by **Fats Domino**, **T-Bone Walker** and **Percy Mayfield** alongside his own material. Later albums included *An Evening of Acoustic Music*, *Phantom Blues* (both 1996) and *Sacred Islands* (1998). Earlier anthologies (*Anthology*, 1976, *The Best of Taj Mahal*, 1981, and *The Collection*, 1987) tended to concentrate on earlier, more accessible recordings. The most comprehensive to date, which also includes a number of unreleased tracks, is *In Progress & in Motion, 1965–1998* (Columbia, 1998). It captures well the diversity, power and idiosyncrasies that are Taj Mahal.

TALKING HEADS

David Byrne, b. 14 May 1952, Dumbarton, Scotland; Chris Frantz, b. 8 May 1951, Fort Campbell, Kentucky, USA; Jerry Harrison, b. 21 February 1949, Milwaukee, Wisconsin; Tina Weymouth, b. 22 November 1950, Coronado, California

One of the most widely admired groups of the eighties, Talking Heads mixed mainstream rock instrumentation in their music with leader **David Byrne**'s New York avant-garde sensibilities and interest in African and Arabian rhythms. Later works, notably *True Stories* (1986), were conceived by Byrne in visual as well as musical terms.

In 1970 Frantz and Byrne formed rock band the Artistics (aka Autistics) at the Rhode Island School of Design in New York. Frantz had previously played drums with the Beans while Byrne had formed a duo called Bizadi to busk in California and Baltimore. In 1974 Weymouth (bass) joined and the group was renamed Talking Heads.

Critical attention was focused on the band after they supported the **Ramones** at CBGBs, the club which became the centre of the New York 'punk' scene in the mid-seventies. In 1976 Seymour Stein signed Talking Heads to his Sire label and after releasing their début single, 'Love Goes to Building on Fire'

(1976), the band added ex-**Jonathan Richman** keyboard-player Harrison. He joined in time to record the Tony Bongiovi-produced *Talking Heads 77*, (1977) which featured the dramatic 'Psychokiller'.

Brian Eno produced *More Songs About Buildings and Food* (1978), which included an American Top Thirty hit in a cover of **Al Green**'s 'Take Me to the River'. The partnership with Eno continued on *Fear of Music* (1979) and *Remain in Light* (1980) and the Englishman's experience in avant-garde musical explorations enabled Byrne to expand Talking Heads' musical vocabulary to include non-Western and non-rock elements. The summation of this process was the evocative 'Once in a Lifetime' from *Remain in Light* whose sound combined African polyrhythms with the more deliberated repetitions of **Philip Glass**. The eloquence of the music was matched by the video, on which Byrne worked with choreographer/singer Tony Basil, who later had a No. 1 hit with 'Mickey' (Chrysalis, 1982). It was among the first music videos to be given a place in the Museum of Modern Art's permanent collection.

In the early eighties Talking Heads briefly suspended operations while its members worked on separate projects. Byrne collaborated with Eno on the experimental album *My Life in the Bush of Ghosts* (EG, 1981), and also released albums of his music from Twyla Tharp's ballet *The Catherine Wheel* (1981) and, later, Robert Wilson's opera *The Knee Plays* (1985). He also produced the **Specials** spin-off group the Fun Boy Three and the **B-52s**. Frantz and Weymouth, meanwhile, formed Tom Tom Club with Weymouth's sisters Loric, Laura and Lani plus Jamaican keyboards-player Tyrone Downie. 'Genius of Love' from their eponymous album was a disco hit while 'Wordy Rappinghood' reached the British Top Ten. Harrison recorded *The Red and the Black*.

The Name of This Band Is Talking Heads (1982) was a collection of live recordings and the group's next studio album was *Speaking in Tongues* (1983), with its Top Ten hit 'Burning Down the House'. Talking Heads' subsequent tour, with extra guitarist Alex Weir (who had played with the **Brothers Johnson**), was filmed by Jonathan Demme and formed the basis of the acclaimed film *Stop Making Sense* (1984) and its accompanying album, the first under a new deal with EMI.

Little Creatures (1985) included the British hits 'The Road to Nowhere' and 'And She Was'. It was followed by *True Stories*, a linking series of anecdotes about eccentric dwellers in small-town America. The concept was realized by Byrne both as a sequence of songs and as a film which he both directed and appeared in, as the narrator. Henceforth images would be as important as music to Byrne.

In 1988 Talking Heads released their last album before the group dissolved, *Naked*, a collection of songs recorded partly in Paris with producer Steve Lillywhite and musicians who included **Level 42** producer Wally Badarou (keyboards) and guitarist Yves N'Djock. By building tracks from riffs and vocal sounds, Byrne managed to deal successfully with such grand themes as the character of human nature. It was followed by the career retrospective *Once in a Lifetime/Sand in the Vaseline* (1992).

The group members pursued their own projects. Frantz and Weymouth released further Tom Tom Club records (*Close to the Bone*, 1983, *Boom Chi Boom Boom*, 1988) and *Dark Sneak Love Action* (1992). They supervised an album by **Bob Marley**'s children, Ziggy Marley and the Melody Makers, and produced Manchester band **Happy Mondays** (. . . *Yes Please*, 1992). Harrison recorded two albums, toured with his own group, Casual Gods (which recorded *Casual Gods*, 1988, and *Walk on Water*, 1990, on Sire), and also worked as a producer. His productions included *God Shuffled His Feet* (Crash Test Dummies, 1993), *Throwing Copper* (Live, 1994) and an eponymous album by Neurotic Outsider (1996). Late in 1996 the members of Talking Heads, bar Byrne, re-formed to tour and record as Heads. Their first album was *No Talking Just Heads*.

Byrne explored world music through a number of releases and compilations on his own Luka Bop label, including *Rei Mo Mo* (1989), *Brazilian Classics* and *The Forrest* (both 1991). That was followed by his first official solo album, *Uh-Oh* (1992), which was received respectfully rather than joyfully, particularly in contrast to the *Once in a Lifetime* anthology. Far better, albeit less quirky, was *David Byrne* (1994). In 1995 Byrne issued a book of photos, *Strange Rituals*, music for the film *Blue in the Face*, on which he was a producer, and in 1997 a further solo album, *Feelings*.

TANGERINE DREAM

Edgar Froese, b. 6 June 1944; Connie Schnitzler (replaced by Christophe Franke, b. 4 April 1942, replaced by Ralf Wadephal); Klause Schultze (replaced by Peter Baumann, b. 1953, Berlin, Germany); Johannes Schmelling (replaced by Paul Haslinger); Klaus Kruger

Pioneers in the use of synthesizers, Tangerine Dream produced an abstract but melodic music that was widely used on film soundtracks and was a precursor of the new-age music of the eighties and of the work of such performers as **Jean Michel Jarre**. The group also worked on the design and development of new equipment for leading synthesizer manufacturers.

Guitarist Froese started his first rock band in 1964, with the approach becoming increasingly experimental. In 1968 he formed Tangerine Dream with Schnitzler (guitars and cello) and Schultze (percussion), recording *Electronic Meditation* (1970) for Rolf Kaiser's Berlin-based Ohr-Music. The group's name came from a line in **The Beatles**' song 'Lucy in the Sky with Diamonds'. Both Schnitzler and Schultze left soon afterwards, the latter to form Ash Ra Temple before moving on to a solo recording career that included *Blackdance* (Brain, 1974), *Timewind* (1975) and *Dig It* (1980).

With the addition of Franke (flute, synthesizers) and briefly Schroyer (organ), Tangerine Dream recorded the space-inspired *Alpha Centauri* (1971). With Baumann (synthesizers), they developed an abstract keyboard-based approach on the double-album *Zeit* (1972) and *Atem* (1973), which were released in Britain by Polydor. Moving to Virgin after a legal dispute with Kaiser, the trio of Froese, Franke and Baumann released *Phaedra* (based on the Greek tragedy) and *Rubycon* (1975). In 1974–5 they gave a series of performances in cathedrals in France and England.

After releasing *Ricochet* (1976) and *Stratosphere*, the group composed their first film soundtrack for *The Sorcerer*. The group's film music is markedly different from other film composers. Where most film composers centre their work on the dramatic action of a story and the characters, Tangerine Dream's film music is more akin to mood music. It is preparatory and scene setting, rather than dramatic and intensifying. Baumann left the group in 1977 and later founded the Private Music label, releasing albums by such artists as **Ravi Shankar**, Andy Summers (of the **Police**), Leo Kottke and Nona Hendryx (of **Patti Labelle and the Blue Belles**). Drummer Klaus Kruger was added for *Cyclone* and *Force Majeure* (1978), after which he left, joining **Iggy Pop**'s band in 1979. A new keyboards player, Schmelling, joined for *Tangram* (1980) and *Exit* (1981). The band later signed to Jive, releasing such albums as *Poland*, *Parc* and *Livemiles* (1988).

Tangerine Dream's later film scores included those for *Thief* (1981), *Firestarter*, *Wavelength*, *Heartbreakers* and *Legend* (1987), for whose American release the group's work replaced a score by **Jerry Goldsmith** that was rejected. The band's later albums included *Optical Race* (1988), *Lily on the Beach* (1989) and *Melrose*. With only Froese remaining from the original line-up, Tangerine Dream signed to Baumann's Private Music label in 1992, releasing *Rockoon*. By 1994 the group, which also included saxophonist Linda Spa, guitarist Zlatki Perica and Froese's son Jerome, had started recording shorter, song-based pieces.

Tangents, 1973–1983 (Capitol, 1992) is a partial career retrospective.

GID TANNER
b. *James Gideon Tanner, 6 June 1884, Thomas Bridge, Georgia, USA, d. 13 May 1960, Dacula, Georgia*

A figure of character and charm, Gid Tanner was the nominal leader of early country music's best-known and most influential string band, the Skillet-Lickers.

He was one of the first Southern fiddlers to make records, starting soon after his fellow Georgian **Fiddlin' John Carson** in the spring of 1924, when he cut old-time songs and fiddle tunes with singer/guitarist Rily Puckett. Songs predominated in these and subsequent sessions, since Tanner was a rough fiddler and better known for his comedy routines and falsetto part-singing. In 1926, probably at the instigation of Frank Walker, who had signed him to Columbia, a larger group was formed, with Tanner, Clayton McMichen and Bert Layne on fiddles, Puckett (guitar) and Fate Norris (banjo). Adapting the name of an earlier Atlanta group, the Lick the Skillet Band, they called themselves the Skillet-Lickers. Tanner probably took primary credit because he was already known from records, though several members of the group, notably McMichen, had been familiar for some time to North Georgia radio listeners through their appearances on Atlanta's WSB.

The band's first recordings were immediately successful, selling hundreds of thousands of copies throughout the South. Musicians were impressed by Puckett's idiosyncratic guitar runs and the distinctive multiple-fiddle sound, with its characteristic choppy *spiccato* bowing. The 'fiddle section' was soon augmented by the outstanding Lowe Stokes. The Skillet-Licker circle, which also included singer/banjoist Arthur Tanner (Gid's brother) and singer/guitarists Hugh Cross and Claude W. Davis, provided many recording combinations for Columbia and Brunswick engineers on their field-trips to Atlanta in 1927–31; among these were McMichen's Melody Men and Stokes's North Georgians, who often performed jazz and popular tunes. They also had an enormous following for their recordings of comic sketches with musical interludes, notably the fourteen-part (seven-record) sequence *A Corn Licker Still in Georgia* (1927–30).

Tension between McMichen's progressive approach and Tanner's archaic minstrelsy eventually split the Skillet-Lickers. Gid and his son Gordon made their last recordings, with Puckett and mandolinist Ted Hawkins, for Bluebird in 1934. The million-selling 'Down Yonder' from this session remained in catalogue until well into the fifties. Puckett contined to work on radio, and record for Bluebird and Decca, until 1940. Layne led a band in the Cincinnati area until the end of the thirties. Stokes lost his right hand in a shooting incident on Christmas Day 1930, learned to play again with an artificial hand and worked in the Southwest in the forties and fifties.

Clayton McMichen formed his Georgia Wildcats, with singer/guitarist Hoyt 'Slim' Bryant and others, and broadcast on various stations in the Upper South throughout the thirties, recording for Columbia (1931), Crown (1932) and Decca (1937–9). He also accompanied **Jimmie Rodgers** on a 1932 Victor date. 'I'm Gonna Learn to Swing' (Decca, 1938) described his musical policy: 'Get me a job in a big jazz band,/I'm gonna learn to swing/Don't give a heck about corny fiddling,/It's driving me insane.' Blues, swing tunes and waltzes like 'Sweet Bunch of Daisies' formed the bulk of the Wildcats' repertoire, but McMichen continued to perform traditional fiddle tunes, though in a modern style, and held the rank of National Fiddling Champion, apparently undefeated, from 1934 to 1949. **Merle Travis** was among the musicians who passed through the Wildcats' ranks. McMichen's last working base was in Louisville, Kentucky, where he appeared on radio and TV until his retirement in 1954.

Gordon Tanner was best known in later years as a fiddle-maker, but he preserved the legacy by leading, in the seventies, his Junior Skillet-Lickers. His fiddling was documented shortly before his death in 1982 on an album for Folkways.

HOWARD TATE
b. 1943, Macon, Geogia, USA

A passionate vocalist and emotive guitarist, Tate's *Get It While You Can* (Verve, 1966) is a classic example of blues-drenched, dramatic soul. It was produced by **Jerry Ragavoy** in New York with wistful horns, a piping gospel organ and a heavy backbeat.

Born in Macon, Tate grew up in Philadelphia singing in various gospel groups, with **Bill Doggett**'s band and vocal group the Gainors before coming to the attention of Ragavoy in the mid-sixties. Though Tate's was a blues voice, Ragavoy chose to envelop his fine interpretive vocals in the surging rhythms of contemporary soul. Thus, even the R&B standards ('How Blue Can You Get' and 'Everyday I Have the Blues') were completely recast by him. The sessions produced considerable soul hits, in the haunting 'Ain't Nobody Home', the dramatic reading of 'Part Time Love' and the dance record 'Look at Granny Run Run' (all 1966), which were also minor American pop hits. Subsequently Tate had lesser hits on **Lloyd Price**'s Turntable label in 1969–70 (including the powerful 'These Are the Things That Make Me Know You're Gone', 1969) before being reunited with Ragavoy for *Burgler* (Atlantic, 1972), which had much of the feel of their earlier collaborations, but was not as successful. Subsequently he recorded for Epic and various minor labels.

ART TATUM
b. Arthur Tatam, 13 October 1909, Toledo, Ohio, USA, d. 5 November 1956, Los Angeles, California

Tatum was the most technically advanced jazz pianist of the twenties and thirties. Equivalent in stature to **Earl Hines**, he was a major influence on the young **Erroll Garner**.

Partially blind from birth, he learned piano, guitar, violin and accordion as a child. From 1926 to 1932 he was active in Ohio, leading bands, playing in clubs and on radio WSPD in Toledo. After pianist Joe Turner heard him play, Tatum took a job in New York in 1932 as **Adelaide Hall**'s accompanist. The following year he began a solo career as a live performer and recording artist. With a repertoire of standard ballad and jazz tunes, he cut 'Tiger Rag' and 'Indiana' for Decca in 1933 and later led a six-piece band on 'I've Got My Love to Keep Me Warm' and 'Body and Soul' (1937).

During the thirties Tatum played in Chicago and Hollywood, and toured Europe. Although working principally as a solo pianist, he led a trio of Tiny Grimes (guitar) and Slam Stewart (bass) in 1943–5. For the last decade of his life he made annual concert tours, including the 1952 'Piano Parade' with Garner and boogie-woogie pianist **Pete Johnson**.

The latter stages of his recording career took place under the guidance of **Norman Granz**, who organized a marathon series of 120 tracks in 1953–4. Granz later grouped Tatum with a variety of artists including **Lionel Hampton**, **Ben Webster**, Barny Kessel, Benny Carter and **Buddy Rich**.

His final recording was *Art Tatum in Person* (20th Century Fox, 1956), made shortly before his death.

RICHARD TAUBER
b. Ernest Seifert, 16 May 1892, Linz, Austria, d. 8 January 1948, London, England

A lyric tenor, Tauber is best remembered for his recording of **Franz Lehár**'s 'You Are My Heart's Delight' from *The Land of Smiles* (1931), re-recorded in 1946 as 'Yours in My Heart Alone'.

A recording star in Germany in the twenties on Odeon, Tauber moved between opera and operetta before in 1930 turning to films. He starred in several German films of the early thirties (including *Das Lockende Ziel*, 1930, which he also produced, and *Die Grosse Attraktion*, 1931) before fleeing to London where he appeared in *The Land of Smiles*, an English-language reworking of Lehar's *Die Gelbe Jacke*. In Britain, he joined HMV and resumed his film career with a series of slight operettas, including *Blossom Time* (1934), loosely based on the life of Franz Schubert; *Heart's Desire* (1935), for which he also wrote the songs; and *Waltz Time* (1945), which also featured Anne Ziegler and Webster Booth. Zeigler and Booth began singing together in 1940 and continued for some twenty years. Their tours and frequent radio appearances kept alive the spirit of operetta long after the genre's demise. During the same period Tauber appeared in several London shows, including *Old Chelsea* (1943), which he wrote. Most, however, derived from his films. In 1946 he appeared on Broadway in *Yours in My Heart*, another revision of *The Land of Smiles*.

CHIP TAYLOR
b. James Wesley Voight, 1940, New York, USA

Singer, producer and songwriter, Taylor is best known as the author of the oft-recorded 'Wild Thing'. A million-selling record for the **Troggs** (1966), the song was later memorably recorded by **Jimi Hendrix**, humorously by comedian Bill Minkin under the pseudonym of Senator Bobby on a record produced by Taylor himself (Parkway, 1967), and provided British group Fancy with a further American Top Twenty hit in 1974 (Big Tree). However, 'Wild Thing' was unrepresentative of Taylor's later work and in the seventies he won widespread critical praise for his own recordings of his quirky, observant songs.

The younger brother of actor Jon Voight, Taylor played in country groups around New York in his teens and in the late fifties recorded in a rockabilly vein for King. In the sixties he turned to songwriting with great success. Among his songs were 'I Can't Let Go' (the **Hollies**, 1966); 'Any Way That You Want Me' and 'Step out of Your Mind' (the American Breed, Acta, 1967, 1968, respectively); 'Story Book Children' (1967) and 'Country Girl, City Man' (1968) by Billy Vera and Judy Clay (better remembered for her duets with **William Bell**); 'I Can Make It with You' (**Jackie DeShannon**, 1967); 'Angel of the Morning' (Merilee Rush, Bell, 1968, and an even bigger hit for Juice Newton, Capitol, 1981); and 'Take Me for a Little While' (**Vanilla Fudge**, 1968). Taylor also wrote in a more mainstream country fashion for such artists as **Waylon Jennings**, **Bobby Bare**, **Eddy Arnold** and **Chet Atkins**.

In 1967 Taylor and Al Gorgoni produced **James Taylor** and his first group, the Flying Machine. With Trade Martin they formed the trio Gorgoni, Martin and Taylor and recorded a pair of countryish albums for Buddah (*Gorgoni, Martin and Taylor*, 1971, and *Gotta Get Back to Cisco*, 1972). More interesting was Taylor's solo album, *Gasoline* (1972), which included his own version of 'Angel of the Morning' and introduced guitarist John Platania, later a mainstay of **Van Morrison**'s backing group, and the wry humour ('Swear to God Your Honor') that was to be a regular feature of his subsequent work. His best album, *Chip Taylor's Last Chance* (1974), followed a move to Warners.

In contrast to his earlier work which had in the

main consisted of love songs, *Last Chance* revealed a broader range of interests and saw Taylor alternately humorous ('I Read It in Rolling Stone' and '101 in Cashbox', which laconically told the story of his own commercially unsuccessful recording of 'Angel of the Morning') and reflective. These latter songs included Taylor singing jauntily about his odd position as a city-born country singer ('I Wasn't Born in Tennessee', which interpolated choruses from **Merle Haggard**'s 'Okie from Muskogee' to good effect), with gruff intimacy about social change (the sombre 'The Coalfields of Shickshinny') and about the music of the fifties that he grew up with ('[I Want] The Real Thing', in which he celebrated the days 'when Sun meant more than the daylight shining down on Memphis, Tennessee'). Like *Some of Us* (1974) and *This Side of the Big River* (1975), *Last Chance* was a critical success but sold poorly. Subsequently Taylor recorded lesser albums for Columbia (*Somebody Shot Out of the Jukebox*, 1976) and Capitol (*Saint Sebastian*, 1979). When that album failed commercially Taylor gave up music to become a full-time gambler – a topic often treated in his songs – for some fifteen years, before recording a collection of hits he had written for others, *Hit Man* (1996), on his own Train Wreck label. That presaged a return to the recording of low-key albums, probably the best of which was the personal *The Living Room Tapes* (1997).

JAMES TAYLOR
b. 12 March 1948, Boston, Massachusetts, USA

With **Carole King** the most representative singer-songwriter of the early seventies, Taylor's skilful lyrics evoking the pains of drug-addiction and mental illness won him a fervent cult following. The most successful of his eighties records were often low-key revivals of pop hits of the fifties and sixties, while by the nineties, as a grand old man of folk, he was offering equally low-key versions of his own sixties classics.

From a musical family, he played in his elder brother Alex's R&B group the Flying Corsayers before forming the King Bees in 1966 with bassist Danny Kortchmar. As Flying Machine they recorded tracks with Al Gorgoni and **Chip Taylor**. 'Night Owl' was released in 1967. In 1968 Peter Asher introduced Taylor's songs to **Paul McCartney**, who signed him to Apple. An eponymous solo album was released in 1969 and Taylor's songs were covered by **Tom Rush** ('Something in the Way She Moves') and **Bobbie Gentry**.

With Kortchmar (now known as Danny Kootch) and Carole King, Taylor next recorded *Sweet Baby James* (Warners, 1970). Produced by Asher, the record came to embody the new soft rock of the early seventies. The songs ranged from the humour of 'Steamroller' to the poetic melodrama of 'Fire and Rain' and the gentle lullaby of the title track.

None of Taylor's later albums matched *Sweet Baby James*, though *Mud Slide Slim and the Blue Horizon* (1971) included another tuneful lullaby, 'You Can Close Your Eyes', and an international hit in King's 'You've Got a Friend'. The album's country flavour was enhanced by **John Hartford** (banjo) and Richard Greene (fiddle). **Linda Ronstadt** made a guest appearance on *One Man Dog* (1972) while Taylor had a further Top Ten hit with a revival of **Charlie and Inez Foxx**'s 'Mockingbird', on which he duetted with his then wife, **Carly Simon**. In the wake of Taylor's success both his sister Kate and younger brother Livingston recorded for Columbia and Epic, respectively.

Taylor had sporadic hits in the mid-seventies, mostly with somewhat anaemic interpretations of soul and rock standards like **Holland, Dozier and Holland**'s 'How Sweet It Is' (1975), originally a 1965 hit for **Marvin Gaye**, **Jimmy Jones**' 1960 million-seller 'Handy Man' (Columbia, 1977) and **Sam Cooke**'s '(What a) Wonderful World' (1978), made with **Simon and Garfunkel**. During the eighties his output slowed with only 'Her Town Too' (1981), a duet with J. D. Souther, reaching the charts. During the decade Taylor appeared at a number of anti-nuclear concerts with such artists as **Jackson Browne** and **Linda Ronstadt**. In 1986 he released *That's Why I'm Here*, which included a duet with **Ricky Skaggs**. *Never Die Young* (1988) was his most commercially successful album for seven years.

He toured heavily in 1990 before recording *New Moon Shine* (1991), another American Top Forty album. Taylor duetted with Garfunkel on the **Everly Brothers** classic 'Crying in the Rain' for Garfunkel's *Up 'Til Now* album. His own return to touring was marked by the in-concert set *James Taylor Live* (1993), an American Top Twenty success that reflected his enduring appeal. Unusually, the interactive hits package *Greatest Hits Live* (1995) was overshadowed by the sales of Taylor's new album, *Hourglass* (1997). A collection of gentle songs, it featured **Stevie Wonder** and reached the US Top Ten and went on to be a platinum album. In 1998 Taylor toured Europe extensively.

JOHNNIE TAYLOR
b. 5 May 1938, Crawfordsville, Arkansas, USA

An influential vocalist, Taylor was one of the most consistent blues-based adult-orientated soul singers, with a rich vibrant delivery. He remained a favourite with black Southern audiences for two decades after his first major hits in 1968.

His earliest gospel records were made for Chance and with the Five Echoes in 1955 for Vee-Jay. Two years later he replaced **Sam Cooke** in the Soul Stirrers

and in 1963 he moved into secular music with Cooke's Sar label. He had little commercial success, however, until he joined Stax in 1965. With production by **Isaac Hayes** and David Porter, his early releases like 'I Got to Love Somebody's Baby' (1966) were firmly blues based but in 1968 he scored a pop Top Ten hit with 'Who's Makin' Love'*. The song was covered by Little Johnny Taylor (*b. John Young, 1940, Memphis, Tennessee*), a rival blues and soul vocalist whose own big hit, 'Part Time Love' (Galaxy, 1963), had itself been covered by Johnnie Taylor. **Howard Tate** successfully revived 'Part Time Love' in 1966 while Little Johnny had later R&B hits on Stan Lewis's Ronn label in 1971–2 and in the late eighties was recording for Ichiban.

'Who's Makin' Love' was a classic example of Southern soul, whose wry lyrics and irresistible beat led to a series of big R&B hits for Taylor. These included 'Take Care of Your Homework' (1969), which reached the pop Top Twenty, 'Testify (I Wanna)', 'Steal Away' (1970) and the R&B No. 1s 'Jody's Got Your Girl and Gone' (1971) and 'I Believe in You'* (1973).

With the demise of Stax, Taylor moved to Columbia and immediately found a crossover audience with 'Disco Lady' (1975) from *Eargasm*, produced in Detroit by Don Davis. The single sold over two million copies in America but later releases, including *Rated Extraordinaire* (1977) and *Disco 9000* (1977), made little impact.

Taylor next recorded *Just Ain't Good Enough* (1983), with arrangements by **Gene Page**, for the Los Angeles label Beverly Glen before signing to Malaco and returning to a more classic R&B approach. *This Is Your Night* (1984), *Wall to Wall* (1985), *Lover Boy* (1986) and *Crazy 'Bout You* (1989) all sold well.

Chronicle (1977), which includes all the major hits, documents his stay with Stax, while *Rated X-Traordinaire* (Columbia, 1996) collects together his lesser Columbia recordings of the late seventies.

JACK TEAGARDEN
b. Weldon John Teagarden, 29 August 1905, Vernon, Texas, USA, d. 15 January 1964, New Orleans, Louisiana

The leading exponent of the trombone in traditional and early big-band jazz, Teagarden was also one of the greatest stylists in blues-jazz singing. As well as leading his own groups, he played with both **Paul Whiteman** and **Louis Armstrong** for a number of years.

Teagarden's father was an amateur trumpeter and his brother Charlie (trumpet) and sister Norma (piano) went on to become professional musicians. During the twenties Teagarden played with such bands as those of Peck Kelly, Doc Ross and Johnny Johnson, with whom he made his recording début in 1927. In 1928 Teagarden moved to New York and joined Ben Pollack's band. He stayed with Pollack for four years but also recorded frequently with Armstrong, **Benny Goodman**, **Eddie Condon**, **Red Nichols**, **Eddie Lang**, **Hoagy Carmichael** and others. Among Teagarden's own records were 'Someone Stole Gabriel's Horn' (Columbia, 1933) and 'I've Got It' (1934).

In 1933 Teagarden joined Whiteman as a featured soloist in live performance and on recordings of a wide variety of material, including the novelty item 'Three Little Fishes' (1939), the ballad 'Christmas in Harlem' (1934) and the classical adaptation 'Moon Love' (1939), based on a theme from Tchaikovsky.

From 1939 to 1947 he ran his own big band, recording for Varsity, Viking and Brunswick ('The Sheik of Araby', 1939) before joining Decca in 1941. There, Teagarden recorded a swing version of Rachmaninov's 'Prelude in C Sharp Minor' (1941) and 'A Hundred Years from Today'. Wartime conscription caused frequent line-up changes and the big band was never an unqualified artistic success.

The orchestra was disbanded in 1947 and Teagarden joined Armstrong's All Stars to play Dixieland jazz on tours to Europe. With the group he recorded 'Jack Armstrong Blues' (RCA, 1947). Live performances featured such songs as 'Rockin' Chair' and 'St James' Infirmary'.

Teagarden left Armstrong in 1951 to form his own All Stars, who enjoyed considerable success throughout the fifties with a relaxed brand of Dixieland jazz. Among his recordings of this period were *Jazz Ultimate* (Capitol) with Bobby Hackett and *T for Trombone* (Jazztone), on which he re-recorded earlier hits like 'Stars Fell on Alabama' and 'St James' Infirmary'.

TEARS FOR FEARS
Roland Orzabel, b. 22 August 1961; Curt Smith, b. 24 June 1961

Among the most popular of British pop writers and singers in the eighties, Tears for Fears' 'Everybody Wants to Rule the World' (retitled 'Everybody Wants to Run the World') was adopted as the theme tune for the Sport Aid famine relief event in 1986.

Orzabel (guitar and keyboards) and Smith (bass and synthesizers) went to school together in the West Country city of Bath, playing together in Graduate, a ska-influenced group. Taking the name Tears for Fears from a book by Arthur ('primal scream') Janov, the duo signed to Phonogram in 1981.

After two unsuccessful singles, 'Mad World' reached the Top Ten in 1982. It was the first of a long series of hits distinguished by bright harmonies and thoughtful lyrics and melodies. 'Change' and 'Pale Shelter' came from *The Hurting* (1983), produced by Chris Hughes, who had previously worked with **Adam Ant**. The duo had by this time been augmented by Ian Stanley (keyboards) and Manny Elias (drums).

Songs from the Big Chair (1985) provided the group with four British hits and brought American success when 'Shout' and 'Everybody Wants to Rule the World' both reached No. 1. Later hits included 'Mother's Talk' and 'Head over Heels'. For *The Seeds of Love* (1989) the duo replaced programming with a 'live' approach to recording. Among the accompanists were **Phil Collins** and Kansas City soul singer Oleta Adams, whose 1990 début *Circle of One* the duo contributed to. The cod-psychedelic 'Sowing the Seeds of Love' and the album were Top Ten hits in America.

Despite the huge success of *Seeds*, the duo split in 1991. Smith signed to Mercury as a solo artist, and Orzabel kept the Tears for Fears name, recording a new track, 'Laid So Low' (1992), for inclusion on the hits compilation *Tears Roll Down* (1992). Like the first non-Smith album, *Elemental* (1993), it was a Top Five hit in Britain, but sales in America were relatively disappointing. Smith released his solo début, *Soul on Board*, in 1993. In 1995 the band moved to Epic for *Raoul and the King of Spain*, while in 1998 Smith formed Mayfield and established his own label Zerodisc for *Mayfield*.

TEENAGE FANCLUB
Norman Blake; Gerard Love; Francis MacDonald (replaced by Brendan O'Hare, replaced by Paul Quinn); Raymond McGinley

Drawing on **Neil Young** and the **Byrds**, Teenage Fanclub were the most commercially successful of a number of whimsical Scottish guitar-pop bands to emerge in the nineties, forging a style that was a million miles away from the laddish arrogance of the same decade's Britpop scene.

After playing together as members of the BMX Bandits in the late eighties, guitarist/vocalist Blake and drummer MacDonald called on bassist Love and guitarist McGinley to record their 1990 début, *Catholic Education*. The band's rich blend of layered guitars and harmonic vocals won them a strong localized fanbase and attracted the attention of Creation Records' Alan McGee, who signed them for the release of *The King* (1991). MacDonald soon returned to the BMX Bandits and was replaced by Brendan O'Hare for the recording of the acclaimed *Bandwagonesque* (1991), the pinnacle of the band's creativity, which drew comparisons with Big Star and **The Beatles**, spawning a minor hit single, 'The Concept', a humorous tale of **Status Quo** fandom.

Teenage Fanclub's fourth album displayed a marked country influence while taking a more angry tone than its predecessors. *Thirteen* (1993) also saw the band move to DGC and included 'Gene Clark', a tribute to the Byrds' late guitarist. *Grand Prix* (1995) marked the recording début of drummer Paul Quinn after O'Hare left to join **Mogwai**. The album was a commercial success after being lavished with praise by the music press, spawning minor hit single 'Mellow Doubt', and featured another tribute to one of the band's heroes, 'Neil Jung'. *Songs from Northern Britain* (1997) consolidated Teenage Fanclub's new-found success, reaching the UK Top Ten.

TELEVISION

Billy Ficca; Richard Hell, b. Richard Myers, 2 October 1949, Lexington, Kentucky, USA (replaced by Fred Smith); Richard Lloyd; Tom Verlaine, b. Thomas Miller, 13 September 1949, New Jersey

With **Patti Smith**, **Blondie**, **Talking Heads** and others, Television were part of the influential New York semi-punk, art-rock scene of the late seventies. Hell had a considerable solo career, as did Verlaine, when the band dissolved in 1978. A nineties reunion was critically successful, but commercially disappointing.

Myers (bass) and Miller (guitar) met at school and took their stage names after moving to New York in 1968. With drummer Ficca, they formed the short-lived Neon Boys before Verlaine began working as a solo guitarist/singer. A meeting with Lloyd (lead guitar) led to the formation of Television in 1974. With Hell's spiky hair and safety-pinned ripped clothing (an idea later used by **Malcolm McLaren** for the **Sex Pistols**) and such songs as 'Blank Generation' and 'Love Comes in Spurts', the pioneering American punk group were soon a popular attraction at such clubs as CBGBs.

In 1975 Hell left and former Blondie member Smith joined the band on bass. The same year **Brian Eno** produced demo recordings of the group that were rejected by Island Records. Their first release was 'Little Johnny Jewel' on the small Ork label (1975). Verlaine was closely associated with Patti Smith, playing guitar on her early single 'Hey Joe' (1974), publishing a joint volume of poetry (*The Night*, 1975) and playing on her first album, *Horses* (1975).

Television signed to Elektra and recorded *Marquee Moon* (1977), produced by Andy Johns. Both the title track and 'Prove It' were minor hits in Britain. But, after making *Adventure* (1978), the group suddenly split up (a 'posthumous' album, recorded live in 1978, *The Blow Up* subsequently appeared on a New York independent label).

Verlaine's eponymous 1979 album was very much in Television's style. His later records included *Dreamtime* (1981), *Words from the Front* (1982), *Cover* (1984) and *Flash Light* (Fontana, 1987). Although they all adhered to Television's skeletal twin guitar, bass and drum blueprint, they were largely bereft of the tension which had made the band's work so compelling. In 1990 he released *The Wonder*, after which he parted company with Fontana, releasing the instrumental album *Warm and Cool* on Rough Trade in 1992. Fred Smith played on all Verlaine's solo albums, usually alongside Patti Smith's old drummer Jay Dee Daugherty.

Hell, by contrast, moved towards British-style punk by joining (ex-**New York Dolls**) Johnny Thunders' Heartbreakers and forming the Voidoids in 1976. He recorded *Blank Generation* (Stiff, 1977) and the **Nick Lowe**-produced 'The Kid with the Replaceable Head' (1979). In 1979 he made his acting début (effectively playing himself) in the punk exploitation movie *Blank Generation* and in 1982 starred in the film *Smithereens*. The same year, his second album *Destiny Street* was released, some three years after it was recorded. Hell subsequently announced his intention to quit music, releasing a collection of rarities and live material as his own epitaph *R.I.P.* (1985). Voidoids guitarist Robert Quine went on to join **Lou Reed**'s band with latterday drummer Fred Maher, whose predecessor Marc Bell had joined the **Ramones**. The power of Hell's late seventies live shows was captured on the archive live album *Funhunt*, which appeared in 1990. Hell subsequently concentrated on journalism and poetry, resuming his musical career in 1991 on an EP recorded with members of **Sonic Youth** as the Dim Stars. An album followed before Hell issued his own solo EP, *Three New Songs*, in 1992.

Lloyd's first solo album was the sixties rock-styled *Alchemy* (Elektra, 1980), which he followed with the more guitar-driven *Field of Fire* (1985) and the live album *Real Time* (1986). In 1990 he was heavily featured on *Meet John Doe*, the solo album by the leader of Los Angeles band X, and in 1991 played on *Girlfriend*, the critically acclaimed album by American singer-songwriter Matthew Sweet, with whom he would later tour. Various members of the Voidoids also played with Sweet. Ficca joined the Waitresses, whose 'I Know What Boys Like' was a minor hit in 1981, before moving into session work.

Influential on a number of British bands, notably **U2** and **Echo and the Bunnymen**, Television were persuaded to re-form in 1991, releasing an eponymous album for Capitol the following year and touring America and Europe. When the album failed the group disbanded again. In 1996 Virgin released the Tom Verlaine career retrospective, *The Millers Tale*.

SHIRLEY TEMPLE
b. 23 April 1928, Santa Monica, California, USA

The most successful of child film stars, Shirley Temple's career barely outlived the thirties, the decade in which she was among the biggest box-office attractions, child or adult, in the movies. Despite her undoubted talents, the passing of the years has revealed most of her films to be brittle confections. However, while her recordings, which include 'On the Good Ship Lollipop' (1934) and 'Animal Crackers in my Soup' (1935), never matched the volume of toys, soaps and dolls that were sold under her name at the time, they remain her most affecting and enduring contributions to popular culture.

The daughter of a bank cashier, she took dancing lessons at the age of three and made her first films at the age of four. These were part of the *Baby Burlesks* series which consisted of take-offs of popular movies of the day and called upon Temple to impersonate such stars as **Marlene Dietrich** (*The Incomparable More Legs Sweetrick*). She signed to Fox at the age of six, where her singing of 'Baby Take a Bow' at the climax of *Stand Up and Cheer* (1934) launched her career as the innocent child who could right all wrongs, unite estranged couples and almost rewrite history – 'You're almost nice enough to be a Confederate' she tells President Lincoln in *The Littlest Rebel* (1935). In *Bright Eyes* (1934), the first film to be built around her, she sang 'Lollipop' (Brunswick), written by **Richard Whiting** and Sidney Clare, the song most closely identified with her (though **Rudy Vallee** had the bigger hit in 1935). A perennial children's favourite, the song's innocent visions of plenty struck a deep chord at the time. A year later in *Curly Top* (named after her famous hair-style, just as *Dimples*, 1936, was titled for another of her characteristic features) she introduced 'Animal Crackers'.

An accomplished dancer, Temple partnered Bill 'Bojangles' Robinson in four films and given strong direction – as in *Wee Willie Winkie* (1937, by John Ford) and *Heidi* and *Rebecca of Sunnybrook Farm* (1938, by Allan Dwan) – showed herself to be a capable actress. However, unlike **Deanna Durbin** and **Judy Garland**, she was unable to manage the transition from child to gangly teenager and her film career as a star came to an abrupt end in the forties.

She returned to showbusiness in 1957 with the tele-series *Shirley Temple's Storybook*. In the sixties she devoted herself to Republican politics as Shirley Temple Black (after her marriage in 1950 to businessman Charles Black) and later filled various ambassadorial positions.

THE TEMPTATIONS
Melvin Franklin, b. David English, 12 October 1942, Montgomery, Alabama, USA, d. 23 February 1995; Eddie Kendricks, b. 17 December 1939, Birmingham, Alabama, d. 5 October 1992, Birmingham, Alabama (replaced by Damon Harris, b. 3 July 1950, Baltimore, Maryland, replaced by Glenn Leonard, b. 1948, Washington DC, replaced by Ron Tyson, b. 1948, North Carolina); Eldridge Bryant (replaced by David Ruffin, b. 18 January 1941, Whyknot, Mississippi, d. 1 June 1991, Philadelphia, replaced by Dennis Edwards, b. 3 February 1943, Birmingham, replaced by Louis Price, b. 1953, Chicago, Illinois, replaced by Ali-Ollie Woodson, b. 1951, Detroit, Michigan); Otis Williams, b. Otis Miles, 30 October 1941, Texakarna, Texas; Paul Williams, b. 2 July 1939, Birmingham, d. 17 August 1973, Birmingham (replaced by Richard Street, b. 5 October 1942, Detroit)

With a history stretching over three decades, the Temptations were one of the most popular black vocal groups of all time. Like the **Inkspots** and the **Mills Brothers** in an earlier era and their near-contemporaries the **Drifters**, the group were able to appeal beyond their core black audience. They did so by modifying their style to take in soul ballads, black rock and disco. The group also had remarkable lead singers in Eddie Kendricks and David Ruffin, plus the songwriting and production genius of **Smokey Robinson** (1963–6) and **Norman Whitfield** (1966–73).

The original quintet of Bryant (lead), Otis Williams (baritone), Franklin (bass), Paul Williams (lead) and Kendricks (tenor, falsetto) were founded as the Elgins and became the Primes before **Berry Gordy** signed them to Motown in 1960. By the time Ruffin replaced Bryant in 1961 they were the Temptations and early singles on Miracle were doo-wop ballads, with 'Dream Come True' (Gordy, 1962) becoming their first R&B hit.

When Gordy assigned Robinson to produce the group, Kendricks sang lead on Robinson's 'The Way You Do the Things You Do', which reached the pop Top Twenty and began a long series of hit singles. The greatest of the Robinson productions was the ethereal 'My Girl'* (1965) an American No. 1 and later an international hit for **Otis Redding**. After 'It's Growin'', another romantic song given an extra edge by Ruffin's plaintive, almost hoarse voice, 'Since I Lost My Baby' (1965) and 'My Baby', Whitfield took over from Robinson. With 'Ain't Too Proud to Beg' (1966), he injected a slightly tougher edge by bringing Ruffin's gospel-tinged baritone even further forward.

With songwriting partners including Barrett Strong and Brian Holland of **Holland, Dozier and Holland**, Whitfield supervised seventeen American Top Twenty hits in seven years. Ruffin emoted intense love songs like '(I Know) I'm Losing You' (1966) and 'I Wish It Would Rain' (1968) before leaving for an uneven solo career in 1968. His most successful records were 'My Whole World Ended (The Moment You Left Me)' (Motown, 1969) and the **Van McCoy**-produced 'Walk Away from Love' (1975).

With ex-**Contours** vocalist Edwards, the Temptations entered a psychedelic period with 'Cloud Nine' (1969), 'Run Away Child, Running Wild' (1969), the No. 1 'I Can't Get Next to You', 'Psychedelic Shack' (1970) and Whitfield's most grandiose production and most ambitious lyrics, 'Ball of Confusion (That's What the World Is Today)'.

After 'Just My Imagination (Running Away with Me)' had reached No. 1, Kendricks and Paul Williams left the group. The latter had serious drink and drugs problems and died two years later. Kendricks had immediate solo R&B hits with 'Can I' (Motown, 1971) and 'Eddie's Love' (1972) but his greatest triumph was the six-minute pop No. 1 'Truckin''*. Followed by 'Boogie Down', produced and written by Leonard Caston and Frank Wilson, it was a prototype disco single but his later efforts for Arista and Atlantic made little impact.

Harris replaced Kendricks in the group and sang lead on their fourth No. 1, 'Papa Was a Rolling Stone' (1972). 'Masterpiece' (1973) was Whitfield's final production for the Temptations and subsequent releases like 'Let Your Hair Down' (1974) and 'Shakey Ground' (1975) were lesser hits. In 1976 the group left Motown to record unsuccessfully for Atlantic in the disco idiom, returning to the fold in 1980 when Gordy himself produced *Power*.

With **Rick James** producing, Kendricks and Ruffin returned for the *Reunion* hit album and tour in 1982. Two years later the Temptations proved their resilience with the techno-pop influenced 'Treat Her Like a Lady', a British Top Twenty hit, while *To Be Continued* (1986) and 'I Wonder Who She's Seeing Now' (1987) were R&B hits. The following year the group backed actor Bruce Willis on his successful reworking of the Drifters' 'Under the Boardwalk' (RCA). In 1989 the Temptations released *Special*.

While Otis Williams and Franklin remained in the group from the 1960 line-up, Kendricks and Ruffin worked as a duo in the eighties, appearing at Live Aid, recording *Live at the Apollo* (RCA, 1986) with **Hall and Oates** and making their own *Ruffin and Kendricks* (RCA, 1988). Ruffin died of a suspected drug overdose in 1991, the same year Kendricks had major surgery for cancer (he died the following year). Also in 1991 the Temptations released their fiftieth album, *Milestone*. They subsequently toured Britain in 1992 and 1994 as part of a package with fellow Motown survivors, titled *Giants of Motown*. In the same year Motown released a five-CD career retrospective, *Emperors of Soul*, while in 1998 the group returned to the US charts with *Phoenix Rising*.

1OCC

Eric Stewart, b. 20 January 1945, Manchester, England; Kevin Godley, b. 7 October 1945, Manchester; Graham Gouldman, b. 10 May 1946, Manchester; Lol Creme, b. 19 September 1947, Manchester

Perpetrators of a series of witty pop hits, 1OCC brought an affectionate, historical perspective into seventies rock, a perspective that was the result of the individual group members' wide experience of sixties music. In the eighties they were among the first rock musicians to embrace video and technology in a big way.

Stewart was lead guitarist with Wayne Fontana and the Mindbenders, a Manchester beat group that had several hits, including the American No. 1 'Game of Love' (Fontana, 1965). After Fontana left, the Mindbenders had another No. 1 with 'A Groovy Kind of Love' (1966). Stewart was soon the only remaining original member of the group and, after subsequent records failed to sell, he disbanded the Mindbenders at the end of 1968. At that time, Gouldman was playing bass with the Mindbenders, though he had enjoyed great success as a songwriter. Originally with Godley in Manchester band the Mockingbirds, he went on to write for the **Yardbirds** ('For Your Love', 'Heart Full of Soul'), the **Hollies** ('Bus Stop') and **Herman's Hermits** ('No Milk Today'). In 1969 he and Stewart joined forces with Godley and Creme to cut an album of the latter's songs intended for Giorgio Gomelsky's Marmalade label.

Only one single was released from that project, but the quartet moved on to cut some tracks at Stewart and Gouldman's Strawberry Studios near Manchester for the Kasenatz–Katz operation in New York. Kasenatz and Katz were the major producers of bubblegum music and in 1970 one of these tracks (written by Gouldman) appeared as 'There Ain't No Umbopo' by Crazy Elephant. A tongue-in-cheek approach to bubblegum was evident in the records the four musicians next made, under the name Hotlegs. Their first single, 'Neanderthal Man' (Fontana, 1970), was a major hit in Europe and North America. It and the subsequent Hotlegs album, *Songs* (called *Thinks School Stinks* in the US), foreshadowed the approach of 1OCC.

Hearing 'Umbopo' led **Neil Sedaka** to record two albums at Strawberry with the Hotlegs team in 1971–2. At the same time, the tracks which formed the first 1OCC album were being laid down. Signing to **Jonathan King**'s UK label, the quartet released the fifties pastiche 'Donna' (1972), which was followed by their best single, 'Rubber Bullets'.

A No. 1 hit in 1973, this was a cartoon version of 'Jailhouse Rock' with **Beach Boys** harmonies and a topical reference in the title to the Irish situation. Other British hits followed (including 'The Dean and

I', 1973, and 'Wall Street Shuffle', 1974) before 10CC had their first American hit with the contrasting 'I'm Not in Love' (1975), a lush ballad that exemplified Godley and Creme's increasing concern with the potential of studio sound.

Two albums – *10CC* (1973) and *Sheet Music* (1974) – were cut for UK before the band was signed in 1975 by Phonogram for a reported $1 million advance. Subsequent British Top Ten records included 'Life Is a Minestrone' and 'Art for Art's Sake' (1975), whose refrain 'Money for God's Sake' summed up 10CC's ambivalence towards the commercial pop scene their songs were both part of and distanced from.

In late 1976 Godley and Creme left the group to concentrate on new projects, including the development of the 'Gizmo', a guitar synthesizer. Continuing to tour with a band that now included guitarist Stewart Tosh from Pilot and keyboards-player Tony O'Malley (ex-Kokomo), Stewart and Gouldman had further hits with 'The Things We Do for Love'* and the reggae spoof 'Dreadlock Holiday' (Mercury, 1978).

Later records were less successful, however, and Andrew Gold joined them for *Ten out of Ten* (1982). Gold and Gouldman later formed Wax, releasing *American English* (RCA, 1987). Both also worked as producers, Gouldman for **Gilbert O'Sullivan** and the **Ramones**, Stewart for fellow Manchester group Sad Café. The guitarist went on to play with **Paul McCartney** on *Tug of War* (1982).

As recording artists, Godley and Creme tended to move into the avant-garde area, which had always been one component of 10CC's success. Albums like *Consequences* (1977) and *L* (1978) were criticized for being confused and pretentious, but in the eighties their career took an upturn as they returned to a more accessible style for the British hits 'Under Your Thumb', 'Wedding Bells' (both 1981) and 'Cry' (1985). The latter's success was helped by an imaginative accompanying video, one of many Godley and Creme had directed. *Goodbye Blu Sky* (Polydor, 1988) was a collection of quirky songs by the duo with backings dominated by harmonica solos.

In returning to and exploiting an earlier interest in film, Godley and Creme became one of the top production teams in music video. They created award-winning videos for **Herbie Hancock** ('Rockit'), **Frankie Goes to Hollywood** ('Two Tribes'), **Duran Duran** and the **Police**, as well as directing the film of the 'Sun City' anti-apartheid recording in 1986. The verve and wit of the early 10CC records found a new home in these music videos and Godley and Creme formed the Video Label in 1985 and released *The History Mix Volume I*, a collection of their audiovisual work together. Creme directed the video for **Tom Jones**' 'If I Only Knew' in 1994.

In 1991 Gouldman and Stewart briefly resurrected the 10CC name, recording the undistinguished *Meanwhile*, on which both Godley and Creme made appearances. *Mirror, Mirror* (Avex, 1995) included an acoustic version of 'I'm Not in Love'. More substantial was the double-CD anthology of the original group's recordings, *The Things We Do for Love* (1996).

TEN CITY
Byron Stingily; Herb Lawson; Byron Burke

A vocal house/garage group from Chicago, Ten City's sound was built around the soaring falsetto of Byron Stingily, who enjoyed club and chart success as a solo artist after the band's demise.

The group met in Chicago in 1985, and first recorded under the name Ragtyme, releasing two singles, 'I Can't Stay Away' and 'Fix It Man'. In 1986 the trio signed to Atlantic and changed their name to Ten City. Working with US house legend Marshall Jefferson as their producer, the group recorded a début single, 'Devotion', which was a huge and immediate hit. With Jefferson at the helm, the band scored further hits with 'Right Back to You' and 'That's the Way Love Is', both taken from their début album, *Foundation* (1988).

Ten City's star burned brightly in dance and club circles on two further albums for Atlantic, *State of Mind* (1990) and *No House Big Enough* (1992), but their lack of mainstream commercial success led the label to drop them in 1993. Ten City co-wrote another club hit, *Fantasy*, with New York's **Masters at Work**, and recorded a fourth album, *That Was Then, This Is Now*, on Columbia in 1994, but after that the band broke up.

Stingily rejected a solo deal, choosing instead to concentrate on songwriting and production, working with Kim English on her garage hit 'Nitelife' and also Michael Watford. In 1996 he returned to recording on New York's Nervous label with 'Love You the Right Way' and 'Don't Fall in Love'. He followed up with 'Sing a Song' and 'Get Up', both massive club hits in 1997, the latter remixed by Germany's Mousse T. His début solo album, *The Purist* (1998), however, met with a distinctly lukewarm critical and commercial reception.

TEN YEARS AFTER
Alvin Lee, b. Graham Barnes, 19 December 1944, Nottingham, England; Chick Churchill, b. 2 January 1946, Flint; Leo Lyons, b. 30 November 1943, Bedford; Ric Lee, b. 20 October 1945, Staffordshire

One of the earliest rock 'guitar heroes', Alvin Lee's frantic playing was immortalized in *Woodstock* (1970), the film of the 1969 festival.

With Dave Quickmire (drums), Lee and bassist

Lyons formed the Jaybirds in Nottingham in 1961. Like **The Beatles**, the group developed an extrovert style through frequent residencies in Hamburg. In 1965 Quickmire was replaced by Ric Lee from local band the Mansfields and the band moved to London, providing music for the stage adaptation of Alan Sillitoe's *Saturday Night and Sunday Morning* (which was set in Nottingham). They also worked for publishers Southern Music, playing on demo discs and backing vocal group the Ivy League, who had two Top Ten hits in 1965.

Increasingly committed to rhythm and blues, the band took on as manager Chris Wright, who later formed Chrysalis Records, and changed their name to Ten Years After, a reference to the foundation of rock'n'roll in 1956. Keyboards-player Churchill was added shortly before they cut their first, eponymous, album for Deram, a Decca subsidiary, in 1967. Its heavy blues sound caught the mood of the second British blues boom, predating **Led Zeppelin**'s recording début by a year. The next album, *Undead*, was a Top Thirty hit in Britain and was followed by four Top Ten albums between 1969 and 1971, including *Stonedhenge* (1969) and *Cricklewood Green* (1970). Ten Years After's only hit singles were 'Love Like a Man' in Britain in 1970 and 'I'd Love to Change the World' (Columbia, 1971) in America.

The pyrotechnics of the ten-minute Woodstock version of 'I'm Going Home' made the band firm favourites in America, but by 1974 the punishing touring schedule led to the break-up of the group, which briefly reunited for a 'farewell' tour the following year. Lee continued to record and perform, first with Tom Compton (drums) and Mick Hawksworth (bass) as Ten Years Later, then as the Alvin Lee Band with various musicians, including ex-**Rolling Stone** Mick Taylor and Fuzzy Samuels (bass). After 1975 Churchill became a music publisher while Lyons produced albums by Chrysalis acts **UFO** and Bridget St John.

In 1988 the original quartet re-formed and recorded *About Time* (1989), supervised by **ZZ Top** producer Terry Manning. They toured extensively over the next two years. In 1994 Lee released the pleasant but minor solo album *Nineteen Ninety Four*, on which **George Harrison** made a cameo appearance.

The Essential Ten Years After (1991) collects together their most notable recordings. Lee's solo albums of the nineties include *Zoom* (1992) and *I Hear You Knockin'* (1994). The group, which toured throughout the decade, recorded *Solid Rock* in 1997.

TODD TERRY
b. 18 April 1967, Brooklyn, New York, USA

Along with **Masters at Work**, Terry has been the defining influence in New York house of the late eighties and nineties, famed as much for DJ sets featuring only his own work as for his dense, sample-heavy production style.

Terry began DJing as a teenager in the early eighties, playing hip-hop as part of the Scooby Doo Crew. As house music began to evolve in Chicago and New York later in the decade, Terry became more interested in the new genre, releasing his first house production, 'Alright Alright', in 1987. A year later, he collaborated with New York rappers the **Jungle Brothers** on 'I'll House You', a seminal early house/hip-hop hybrid which featured on the rappers' début album.

The track helped establish Terry, and he enjoyed further club hits that year, as the Todd Terry Project, with 'Weekend' and 'Bango (To the Batmobile)'. Under this and a variety of other aliases, Terry enjoyed a string of hits during house's formative years, most notably Black Riot's 'A Day in the Life', Sound Design's 'Can You Feel It?' and Royal House's 'Can You Party?'. As well as writing his own material, Terry was also in huge demand as a remixer, his clients including **Sting**, **Björk**, **Tina Turner** and Annie Lennox of the **Eurythmics**.

Terry set up Freeze Records in 1992 with William Socolov, whose Fresh and Sleeping Bag labels had provided the outlet for much of his early work. The new label became the vehicle for Terry's *Unreleased Project* series of EPs over the next few years.

Terry's star rose even higher in 1995 with perhaps his most celebrated remix, Everything But the Girl's 'Missing'. The track became a huge club and pop hit, selling over three million copies globally. That year also saw the release of *A Night in the Life of Todd Terry*, a 'live' album of one of his DJ sets recorded at the UK's Hard Times house club.

On the back of these successes, Terry released a more song-orientated garage album in 1997, *Ready for a New Day*, which featured Jocelyn Brown and former Weather Girls singer Martha Wash performing together on the hit single 'Something Going on in My Soul'. The album met with a moderate response, some critics suggesting he was far better as a remixer and producer than as a songwriter.

Having explored hip-hop and mastered house, 1999 saw Terry experimenting, successfully, it should be said, with a new style – jungle – on the track 'Blackout'.

JOE TEX
b. Joseph Arrington Jnr, 8 August 1933, Baytown, Texas, USA, d. 13 August 1982, Navasota, Texas

With four million-selling records and numerous hits to his credit, Tex was one of the most successful soul artists of the sixties and one of the very few to survive into the seventies. His broader significance lay in his adaptation of the format of white country music to black gospel singing and preaching styles.

While at high school he sang gospel and in 1954 won a local talent contest that took him to New York. He recorded for King (1955–7), Ace (1958–60) and Anna (1960) in a wide variety of styles, ranging from **Little Richard** imitations to pop novelties. He had more success as a writer, supplying hits to **Jerry Butler** and **James Brown**, among others. Then in 1961 he was signed by Nashville publisher Buddy Killen to his Big Tree Music. So impressed was Killen with Tex that he started up Dial Records specifically to market Tex and his growing folio of songs. Killen's productions on Tex's early Dial releases were cluttered and fussy until, in 1964, he took Tex to **Rick Hall**'s studio to cut 'Hold What You've Got'*. The song introduced Tex the preacher – a persona he frequently returned to – here offering advice to young lovers. Behind him Killen created a cleaner, more insistent sound, a subdued version of the 'Stax sound' **Booker T. and the MGs** were producing in Memphis. The result was the first Southern soul song to make the American Top Ten. Other hits in the same vein followed: 'A Woman Can Change a Man', 'I Want to (Do Everything for You)', 'A Sweet Woman Like You' and the majestic 'The Love You Save' (all 1965). If on occasion Tex's sermons sounded too calculated and lacked the raw commitment of a **Solomon Burke**, his dance records ('The Letter Song', 1966, and 'Skinny Legs and All'*, 1967) were as witty as they were catchy.

In 1970 he briefly became a minister before returning to the charts with 'I Gotcha'* in 1972. Then followed a lean period in which Tex alternated dance records with country material before his final big hit, the novelty dance piece 'Ain't Gonna Bump No More (With No Big Fat Woman)'* (Epic, 1977). His death was the result of a heart attack.

The Hits & More (Ichiban, 1992) is the definitive anthology.

TEXAS
Eddie Campbell; Ally McErlaine; Johnny McElhone, b. 31 October 1968, Glasgow, Scotland; Stuart Kerr, b. 16 March 1963, Glasgow (replaced by Richard Hynd); Sharleen Spiteri, b. 7 November 1967, Glasgow

Scottish rock band Texas became one of the most popular bands in the UK in the late nineties, blending the classic soul of **Marvin Gaye** with contemporary guitar-led pop.

Texas was formed in 1986 when former Altered Images bassist McElhone began collaborating with singer/guitarist Spiteri. Taking their name from the Wim Wenders film *Paris, Texas* (1985), after recruit-

ing guitarist McErlaine and drummer Kerr from other local bands they began touring the UK, earning a deal with Phonogram in 1988. Début album *Southside* (1988) soon achieved platinum status on the strength of the single 'I Don't Want a Lover', before the band's traditional, bluesy sound was overshadowed by the burgeoning 'Madchester' scene.

Mother's Heaven (1991) saw Hynd replace Kerr and sold well across Europe but failed to match the success of *Southside* in the UK. After releasing *Rick's Road* (1993) and touring America the quartet took an extended break in 1994, before resurfacing with a new soulful direction three years later to greater success.

Driven by subtle trip-hop rhythms and a strong vocal performance by Spiteri, *White on Blonde* (1997) became one of the bestselling albums of the year in Britain on the back of the hit singles 'Say What You Want', 'Halo' and 'Black Eyed Boy', and featured keyboardist Campbell for the first time. Texas toured solidly and had another British hit with a new version of 'Say What You Want' recorded with Wu Tang Clan rapper Method Man before consolidating their position as one of Britain's most popular bands with *The Hush* (1999), which, despite sounding like out-takes from the earlier album, managed to duplicate its success, particularly in Europe.

SISTER ROSETTA THARPE
b. Rosetta Nubin, 20 March 1915, Cotton Plant, Arkansas, USA, d. 9 October 1973, Philadelphia, Pennsylvania

A charismatic figure in the black gospel music of the forties and fifties, Rosetta Tharpe was second only to **Mahalia Jackson** in nurturing white interest in that music. But whereas Jackson employed relatively sober instrumental accompaniment, usually on keyboards, and often had choral support, Tharpe played her own bluesy guitar and worked with small groups of blues-based musicians. Both textually and contextually, Tharpe's gospel was fundamentalist and 'sanctified', and thus rawer and more secularly swinging than Jackson's testimony.

She sang in church as a girl, but in New York worked with the **Cab Calloway** band (1938–9) while beginning a recording career with the gospel solos 'Rock Me'/'The Lonesome Road' (Decca, 1938). Influential later recordings included 'I Looked down the Line (and I Wondered)' (1939) and 'God Don't Like it' (1943). She also sang with **Lucky Millinder** (1941–3), recording 'Trouble in Mind', 'Rock Me' and 'Shout, Sister, Shout' (1941) and appearing in several soundies (short films for visual jukeboxes). From 1943 she concentrated on gospel and made a series of exuberant and very popular sides for Decca, both solos and duets with her mother Katie Bell Nubin or Marie Knight, including 'Up Above My Head'. Her biting electric guitar brought an urban blues flavour which was intensified by such accompanists as pianist Sammy Price.

She continued to perform in jazz contexts (though singing only gospel material) and appeared at many European festivals in the fifties and sixties, recording albums from time to time, often for French labels.

MIKIS THEODORAKIS
b. Michalis Theodorakis, 29 July 1925, Chios, Greece

The most outstanding Greek composer of the post-Second World War era, Theodorakis sought to fuse orchestral writing with popular songs and traditional bouzouki music. A leading political activist, he was twice imprisoned for his beliefs. Outside Greece, he is best known for his film music.

His participation on the Communist side in the Greek Civil War of the late forties resulted in a jail sentence which lasted until 1952. He spent the rest of the decade in exile in Paris, composing classical pieces. On returning to Greece in 1960, Theodorakis joined the popular-music movement which sought to create an amalgam of rural folk song, Byzantine church music and the urban bouzouki style. He formed an ensemble to perform his own songs which included a strong protest element. Its most renowned members were singers Maria Farantouri and George Kapernaros. Released on EMI Columbia, Theodorakis's material outsold all others in Greece during the mid-sixties.

During the sixties Theodorakis composed the scores for some twenty-five films. Among them were Cacoyannis's Electra (1962) and Zorba the Greek (1964), whose theme was an American hit for Herb Alpert (1966). Later film scores included Z (1968), Serpico and State of Siege (both 1973).

From 1967 to 1970, he was kept either in prison or under house arrest by the Greek military dictatorship and was freed after an international campaign led by other musicians and composers. Much of Theodorakis's later work took the form of song cycles.

In 1976, the year Theodorakis became a member of the Greek Parliament, Sven-Bertil Taube recorded an album of English translations of Theodorakis's songs for EMI. He left politics in 1986 and returned to film composition, most notably with the music for the Turkish film Sis (1989).

THIN LIZZY
Eric Bell (replaced by Gary Moore, b. 1953, Ireland, replaced by Brian Robertson); Brian Downey; Phil Lynott, b. 20 August 1951, Dublin, d. 4 January 1986; Scott Gorham, b. 17 March 1951, Santa Monica, California, USA

An erratic hard-rock band led by bass guitarist/writer Lynott, Thin Lizzy recorded over a dozen albums in its twelve-year history.

Lynott's career began with Dublin soul band Black Eagles, and he went on to form Skid Row with lead guitarist Gary Moore in 1969. He left the group to start Orphanage with Downey (drums) and Bell, a former guitarist with Them. As Thin Lizzy, they were signed to Decca by Frank Rodgers (brother of singer Clodagh Rodgers, whose hits included 'Come Back and Shake Me', RCA, 1969, and 'Jack in the Box', 1971). Their eponymous début album was produced in 1971 by Scott English, who had a Top Twenty hit with 'Brandy' (Horse) in the same year.

The record's unusual combination of Jimi Hendrix-style guitar pyrotechnics and Irish folk elements failed to achieve commercial success; neither did the follow-up Shades of a Blue Orphanage (1972). In 1973, however, their novelty version of the traditional 'Whiskey in the Jar' was a Top Ten hit. Bell left after the release of Vagabonds of the Western World (1973) and after Moore rejoined Lynott briefly, Thin Lizzy added two new guitarists, Scotsman Robertson and American Gorham.

The group moved to Mercury for Nightlife (1974), Fighting and Jailbreak (1976), which included the rousing international hit, 'The Boys Are Back in Town'. Moore, who had been playing with jazz-rock band Colosseum, replaced the injured Robertson on Bad Reputation (1977), with its British hit 'Dancin' in the Moonlight (It's Caught Me in the Spotlight)' and Live and Dangerous (1978).

The late seventies were Thin Lizzy's most successful years as 'Rosalie – Cowgirl's Song' (1978), 'Waiting for an Alibi' (1979) and 'Do Anything You Want to' reached the British Top Twenty. In 1980 Snowy White replaced Moore, whose solo hit 'Parisienne Walkways' (1979) had featured Lynott's singing, and the group's 'Killer on the Loose' entered the Top Ten. For Renegade (1982), keyboards-player Darren Wharton was added but after Thunder and Lightning the following year, the group split, leaving behind a final live album Life – Live (1984), which featured appearances by all the band's former guitarists. Lynott looked set to extend a solo career that had already produced two albums (Solo in Soho, 1980, and The Philip Lynott Album, 1982) and a hit with 'Yellow Pearl' (1981), the theme for television's Top of the Pops, co-written by Midge Ure of Ultravox, who had played with Thin Lizzy in 1979. He collaborated with Moore on the raucous Top Ten record, 'Out in the Fields' (1985) before drugs and other health problems led to his premature death.

Soldier of Fortune (1986) chronicles the band's career in some detail. It was followed a decade later by the even more lavish The Very Best of Thin Lizzy

(1996), which led to a reissued 'The Boys Are Back in Town' becoming a minor hit in the UK. In the same year Lynott's mother published the biography *The Phil Lynott Story*.

B. J. THOMAS
b. Billy Joe Thomas, 27 August 1942, Houston, Texas, USA

A resilient and versatile singer, Thomas recorded mainly in a country vein. However, he is best remembered as the singer of the effervescent Oscar-winning film song 'Raindrops Keep Fallin' on My Head'* (1969), his only international hit, from *Butch Cassidy and the Sundance Kid*.

In 1957 Thomas joined the Triumphs, a seven-piece band which played around the Houston area until the mid-sixties when their version of **Hank Williams**' 'I'm So Lonesome I Could Cry', recorded on the local Pacemaker label (1965), was picked up by Scepter for national release in 1966. A million-seller, it led to Thomas leaving the group for a solo career and a shift in style to a smoother sound that produced further hits, including 'Mama' (1966), 'The Eyes of a New York Woman' and Mark James' 'Hooked on a Feeling'* (1968). That record was later covered in Britain by **Jonathan King** in 1971 and King's novelty arrangement of the song, recorded by the Swedish sextet Blue Swede, was a million-seller in 1974 (EMI) and the first American chart-topper by a Swedish group, three years before **Abba** repeated the process with 'Dancing Queen'*.

In 1969 Thomas had his greatest success with **Burt Bacharach**'s 'Raindrops'. Further hits included 'I Just Can't Help Believing' (1970), 'No Love at All' (1971) and 'Rock and Roll Lullaby' (1972), which featured **Duane Eddy** on guitar and back-up vocals by **Darlene Love**. The track came from *Billy Joe Thomas*, a collection of songs by contemporary writers – including **Stevie Wonder**, **Carole King**, **Barry Mann** and Cynthia Weil, **Jimmy Webb**, Mark James and one-time member of the **Lovin' Spoonful** John Sebastian – on which the writers helped provide the backing to Thomas's interpretations of their songs. After that album, Thomas switched unsuccessfully to Paramount, only returning to the charts with the decidedly countryish '(Hey Won't You Play) Another Somebody Done Somebody Wrong Song'* (ABC, 1975), co-authored and produced by **Chips Moman**. The following year Thomas became a born-again Christian.

His 1977 Myrrh gospel album *Home Where I Belong*, also the title of his autobiography in which he told of his drug addiction in the early seventies, won a Grammy. Subsequently Thomas mixed gospel and secular recordings. These latter, all firmly in a country style, included 'Some Love Songs Never Die' (MCA,

1981), 'She Meant Forever When She Said Goodbye' (Cleveland International, 1983) and a duet with **Ray Charles**, 'Rock and Roll Shoes' (1984). He later sang the theme to the television series *Growing Pains*. Later albums include *Throwing Rocks at the Moon* (1985). Then, in 1989, he briefly moved away from country for the duet with **Dusty Springfield**, 'As Long as We've Got One Another'.

Greatest Hits (Rhino, 1990) and *More Greatest Hits* (Varese, 1995) are the definitive collections.

RUFUS THOMAS
b. 28 March 1917, Collierville, Texas, USA

Thomas has run the gamut of black entertainment. He began his career in 1935 as a comedian with the Rabbit Foot Minstrels and by the early forties in Memphis was a deejay on the black-owned WDIA station (a show he ran until the mid-seventies). He started to host talent shows on Beale Street, which were instrumental throughout the decade in the development of the careers of **B. B. King**, **Bobby Bland**, **Junior Parker**, **Ike Turner** and Roscoe Gordon, among others. In the sixties he had considerable success as a recording artist.

He recorded briefly in 1941, and again in 1949, but made his first real impact on **Sam Phillips**' Sun label with 'Bearcat' in 1953. The record was equally famous as Sun's first national hit, and for its plagiarism of **Leiber and Stoller**'s 'Hound Dog'. His radio show and talent-spotting activities became more important during the fifties but in 1961 he recorded a duet with his daughter Carla for the Satellite label owned by **Jim Stewart** and Estelle Axton. 'Cause I Love You', a minor hit, led to Carla's solo recording of the ethereal 'Gee Whiz (Look at His Eyes)' (1961). Produced by **Chips Moman**, the record became a major hit after being picked up for national distribution by Atlantic Records. Satellite quickly changed its name to Stax, and Thomas was able in later years to lay claim to having helped start two of America's most influential labels. Carla Thomas had further solo hits on both Atlantic and Stax, including 'I'll Bring It Home to You' (Atlantic, 1962) and 'B-A-B-Y' (Stax, 1966), as well as recording successful duets with **Otis Redding** ('Tramp', 'Knock on Wood', 1967).

Rufus Thomas himself had a huge hit with one of the novelty records, 'Walking the Dog' (Stax, 1963) – covered the following year by the **Rolling Stones** – and continued with such dance-craze records as 'Can Your Monkey Do the Dog' (1964), 'Do the Funky Chicken' (1970), 'Do the Push and Pull' (1971), 'Breakdown' (1971) and 'Do the Funky Penguin' (1972), as well as several fine blues ('Night Time Is the Right Time', 'Did You Ever Love a Woman?' and 'Fine and Mellow').

After the collapse of Stax, Thomas recorded one

album for AVI (*Blues in the Basement*, 1975), then remained inactive until the 1986 release *Rappin' Rufus* (Ichiban), which saw the self-styled 'oldest living teenager' as at home with rap as he had been with R&B. He later recorded 'Do the Funky Somethin'' (1992) with Fred Schneider of the **B-52s**. The song later provided him with the title of the career retrospective (Rhino, 1996).

THE THOMPSON TWINS
Tom Bailey, b. 18 June 1957, Halifax, England; Chris Bell; Alannah Currie, b. 20 September 1959, Auckland, New Zealand; Peter Dodd, b. 27 October 1953, Chesterfield, England; Joe Leeway, b. 1957, London; John Roog; Jane Shorter

A British group devoted to making 'cross-cultural' dance music, the Thompson Twins found international success after reducing their numbers from seven to three and adopting electronic instruments.

The group was formed in Chesterfield in 1977 by singer Bailey, Dodd (guitar), Bell (drums) and Roog (guitar). Taking their name from characters in Hergé's *Tintin* comic books, the group played funk/dance music. They added Shorter (saxophone) and Leeway (percussion) and released 'Squares and Triangles' and 'She's in Love with Mystery' on the independent Dirty Discs label before signing in 1981 to T, a subsidiary of the German-owned Hansa company, which was later absorbed by Arista.

The Thompson Twins demonstrated their political commitment by playing a 'No Nukes' tour of British colleges before recording *A Product of* (Arista, 1981) and *Set* (1982). With the departure of most of the members, the group became a trio with New Zealander Currie (keyboards, saxophone, vocals) joining Bailey and Leeway who began recording with synthesizers and drum machines replacing their previous guitars and percussion sound. Ironically, shortly after the group slimmed down, 'In the Name of Love', taken from *Set*, was a dance hit in America.

Their first British pop hits were 'Love on Your Side' (1983) and the quirky 'We Are Detective' from the Alex Sadkin-produced *Quick Step and Sidekick*. American success followed with 'Hold Me Now' (1983) and the catchy 'Doctor Doctor' (1984) from *Into the Gap*, co-produced by Sadkin and Bailey. The album provided further British hits in 1984 with 'You Take Me Up' and 'Sisters of Mercy'.

Nile Rodgers was brought in to co-produce *Here's to Future Days* (1985), which included the anti-heroin song 'Don't Mess with Dr Dream' and 'Lay Your Hands on Me', which reached the American Top Ten. In the same year the group appeared at Live Aid. After Leeway left the group in 1986, Currie and Bailey released *Close to the Bone*. The duo later wrote 'I

Want That Man' for Deborah Harry of **Blondie** and signed to Warners, releasing *Big Trash* (1989) with little commercial success. *Queer* failed to chart, and in 1993 the duo re-emerged as Babble, recording *The Stone* (Warner). In 1994 they relocated to New Zealand, continuing to work under the Babble name. *Love, Lies & Other Strange Things* (1996) is the definitive career retrospective.

HANK THOMPSON
b. Henry William Thompson, 3 September 1925, Waco, Texas, USA

Hank Thompson and his Brazos Valley Boys were the most commercially successful Western swing band of the fifties and sixties. Much of their material, however, had a more mainstream country approach and could well be called honky-tonk.

In his late teens, Thompson broadcast as a singer-guitarist over the local station WACO in a show called *Hank the Hired Hand*. After wartime service in the navy, he returned to Waco to work on KWTX and formed the first Brazos Valley Boys to play dances around central Texas. He recorded for Globe (1946) and Bluebonnet (1947) before signing with Capitol in 1948. On that label, he had Top Ten country hits with 'Humpty Dumpty Heart'* (1948), 'Whoa Sailor' and 'Green Light' (both 1949) and 'Waiting in the Lobby of Your Heart' (1952). 'Wild Side of Life'* (1952), which shared the melody of **Roy Acuff**'s 'Great Speckled Bird' and sparked **Kitty Wells**' answer song 'It Wasn't God Who Made Honky Tonk Angels', was his first No. 1.

The next two years produced numerous hits, some written by Thompson with his band vocalist Billy Gray; these included 'You Can't Have My Love' (1954), which featured a vocal duet by Gray and **Wanda Jackson**. Thompson became a major draw, both for concert appearances and on the county-fair and rodeo circuits. He stayed with Capitol until 1966, logging scores of country chart singles and producing several high-selling albums. The Brazos Valley Boys were rated top country band by both *Billboard* and *Cashbox* from 1953 to 1966. Thompson later signed with Warners (1966–7) and ABC/Dot, for whom he recorded *Back in the Swing of Things* (1976), which included an affectionate look back at his early career, 'Big Band Days'.

The Bear Family twelve-CD box set *Hank Thompson and his Brazos Valley Boys* (1996) is the definitive collection.

RICHARD THOMPSON
b. 3 April 1949, London, England

A founder member of folk-rock band **Fairport Con-**

vention, Thompson became an influential songwriter and guitarist in the seventies and eighties.

After recording six albums with the band between 1967 and 1970, Thompson left to pursue a solo career, playing sessions on albums by Sandy Denny, John Cale, Ashley Hutchings' Albion Country Band and **Nick Drake** before recording *Henry the Human Fly* (Island, 1972). Dominated by Thompson's melancholic temperament, songs like 'Roll Over Vaughan Williams', 'Nobody's Wedding' and 'The Old Changing Way' found him mixing the rock and folk traditions effectively.

The mood deepened on *I Want to See the Bright Lights Tonight*, on which Thompson shared the credits with his vocalist wife, Linda, who sang lead on 'Down Where the Drunkards Roll' and the title track. In 'When I Get to the Border' Thompson contemplated death; in 'Calvary Cross', which featured one of his most impressive guitar solos, he dealt with the bleakness of most relationships; and he dispensed cautionary advice about life 'outside the nursery door' in 'The End of the Rainbow'. With Fairport guitarist Simon Nicol the couple toured in 1974 as Sour Grapes, making *Hokey Pokey* (1974). Produced by Nicol, the album included one of Thompson's finest slow ballads, 'A Heart Needs a Home'. With its sparse arrangements, *Pour Down Like Silver* (1976) was made after the Thompsons' conversion to Sufism. It maintained the low-key atmosphere of the earlier work with such songs as 'Beating the Retreat' and 'Night Comes in'.

Religious commitments contributed to a three-year absence from the studio for Thompson, with only the retrospective double-album *Guitar/Vocal* (1976) appearing until he signed to Chrysalis in 1978. With Linda, he cut *First Light* (1978) and *Sunnyvista* (1979) for the label before forming Elixir to release the instrumental album *Strict Tempo* (1981).

Shoot Out the Lights (1982) brought critical acclaim in America where a new generation of guitar groups were beginning to acknowledge the influence of Thompson's blend of folk and rock guitar styles. Soon afterwards the couple separated, with Linda signing to Warners for the Hugh Murphy-produced *One Clear Moment* (1985), which included 'Telling Me Lies'. Co-written with Betsy Cook, the song appeared on *Trio* (1987) by **Dolly Parton**, **Linda Ronstadt** and **Emmylou Harris**. *Dreams Fly Away* (Hannibal, 1996) is a twenty-track anthology of her solo career.

Richard went on to join **Joe Boyd**'s Hannibal label, which reissued his early albums as well as releasing the mournful *Hand of Kindness* (1983) and *Small Town Romance* (1984), a live recording of a solo acoustic concert. He later recorded for Polydor (*Across a Crowded Room*, 1985; *Daring Adventures*, 1986), and Capitol (the Mitchell Froom-produced

Amnesia, 1988). Despite critical acclaim, these albums sold poorly. *Rumour and Sigh*, which included the bitter 'Read about Love' and gloriously indulgent 'God Loves a Drunk', made the British Top Forty, but 1992's *Sweet Talker* failed to maintain the momentum. In 1994 he toured with bassist Danny Thompson and former Fairport drummer Dave Mattacks. In 1993 Rykodisc released the superb boxed set *Watching the Dark*, a career retrospective containing much unreleased material.

Thompson also wrote television music (*The Marksman*, 1988) produced albums by **Loudon Wainwright**, made countless session appearances and guest appearances with others, notably with guitarists Fred Frith and Henry Kaiser on *Live, Love, Larf and Loaf* (1988), which included an impressive Thompson original, 'Drowned Dog Black Night', and an irreverent version of the **Beach Boys**' 'Surfin' USA'.

Watching the Dark was followed by two tribute albums, Dave Burland's *His Master's Choice* (1992) and *Beat the Retreat* (Capitol, 1994), on which **Los Lobos** ('Down Where the Drunkards Roll'), **Bonnie Raitt** ('When the Spell Is Broken') and **R.E.M** ('Wall of Death'), among others, offered interpretations of Thompson songs. These, and particularly the latter which was very well received, raised Thompson's profile. They were followed by a series of superior albums, including *Mirror Blue* (1994) and the double-album *You? Me? Us?* (1996), which included 'Razor Dance' and two wonderful songs of observation and imagination, 'Cold Kisses' and 'The Woods of Darney'. The double-album was Thompson's high point of the nineties. One CD was acoustic, the other electric. Henceforth his songs would be a staple element of the repertoire of folk-oriented performers.

Industry (1997), made in partnership with Danny Thompson, had a wide scope but was not as successful. *Mock Tudor* (1999), a concept album of sorts about the changing patterns of love and desolation in London's suburbs, had stronger songs ('Walking the Long Miles Home'). As usual, despite their critical plaudits, none of the albums sold particularly well.

CLAUDE THORNHILL
b. 10 August 1909, Terre Haute, Indiana, USA, d. 1 July 1965, Caldwedd, New Jersey

Thornhill was the leader of one of the most sophisticated big bands of the forties, known for its progressive arrangements, many of which were supplied by **Gil Evans**.

After studying at the Cincinnati Conservatory and Philadelphia's Curtis Institute, and playing in various bands in the Midwest, pianist Thornhill travelled to New York in the early thirties. There he played with **Paul Whiteman** and **Benny Goodman** (1934) and performed – alongside **Glenn Miller** – and worked as an arranger in **Ray Noble**'s American Band (1935–6). He also worked frequently as a session musician, notably with **Billie Holiday** (including 'Getting Some Fun out of Life', 1937, and 'I'm Gonna Lock My Heart', 1938), and recorded ('Gone with the Wind', 'Loch Lomond', Vocalion, 1937) and toured with vocalist Maxine Sullivan, before first working with Evans in 1938.

In 1941 Thornhill, encouraged by Miller, formed his own band and signed with Columbia, recording several tone poems (including his theme song 'Snowfall', 1941) and classical adaptations ('Concerto for Two', 1941). After wartime service, Thornhill re-formed his big band and once more hired Evans as arranger. It was Evans' progressive arrangements for Thornhill, many of which are included in the reissue album *The Real Birth of the Cool*, that inspired **Miles Davis** to hire Evans, but more successful commercially were Thornhill's recordings with Fran Warren. These included a lush version of **Louis Prima**'s 'Sunday Kind of Love' (1947). The adverse economic climate of the late forties led Thornhill, like many others, to break up his band in 1948. In the fifties he led big bands and small groups but did not record.

BIG MAMA THORNTON
b. Willie Mae Thornton, 11 December 1926, Montgomery, Alabama, USA, d. 25 July 1984, Los Angeles, California

One of the foremost tough female singers in fifties rhythm and blues, Thornton made her name with the original version of **Leiber and Stoller**'s 'Hound Dog', an R&B No. 1 in 1953, which **Elvis Presley** later made one of his archetypal early RCA recordings. She was versatile enough to work in contexts as disparate as big-band soul-blues in the style of **Bobby Bland**, with a Chicago bar band, and with acoustic country-blues guitarist **Fred McDowell**.

A minister's daughter, she grew up listening to the records of **Bessie Smith** and **Memphis Minnie** and taught herself to play harmonica and drums. In the forties she toured the South in Sammy Green's Hot Harlem Revue, as a singer, dancer and comedienne. She settled in Houston, Texas, in 1948, working local clubs, and signed with Peacock in 1951, recording on some occasions with the **Johnny Otis** band. She also toured with Otis's Rhythm and Blues Caravan (1952), **Junior Parker** and **Johnny Ace** (1953–4) and **Clarence 'Gatemouth' Brown** (1956). In 1957 she settled on the West Coast. She toured Europe with the American Folk Blues Festival in 1965, recording her first album, *In Europe* (Arhoolie), in London with fellow troupers McDowell, Walter 'Shakey' Horton (harmonica) and **Buddy Guy**. *Big Mama Thornton Vol. 2* (Arhoolie,

1966) put her with the **Muddy Waters** band. She was now working at jazz festivals and universities as well as black clubs. *Stronger Than Dirt* (Mercury, 1969) included pop standards, versions of 'Born Under a Bad Sign' and **Bob Dylan**'s 'I Shall Be Released', and her own 'Ball and Chain', which in an earlier, live, version for Arhoolie greatly impressed, and was memorably copied by, **Janis Joplin**.

The early seventies were less eventful, though she toured Europe again with the AFBF in 1972, but in 1975 she signed with Vanguard and quickly cut *Sassy Mama*, a studio set with Cornell Dupree (guitar), and *Jail*, recorded in concert in two Northwestern prisons. Her final album was *Live Together*, with **Clifton Chenier**, for Crazy Cajun. In the eighties she appeared less frequently, because of ill-health, though she performed memorably in the *L.A. Blues* episode of the documentary series *Repercussions*, made for British Channel 4 TV in 1984.

THREE DOG NIGHT
Danny Hutton, b. 10 September 1946, Buncrana, Ireland; Chuck Negron, b. 8 June 1942, Bronx, New York, USA; Cory Wells, b. 5 February 1942, Buffalo, New York

Three Dog Night's pop sensibilities and sprightly harmonies, featuring three lead singers, resulted in ten million-selling records in the early seventies. The group members wrote few songs, preferring instead to record other people's compositions. While their versions were generally blander than the originals, the group provided valuable exposure for contemporary songwriters. **Laura Nyro** ('Eli's Coming', 1969), **Nilsson** ('One', 1969, the group's first million-seller) and **Randy Newman** ('Mama Told Me [Not to Come]'*, 1970, the group's first American No. 1) all had their first major success when Three Dog Night recorded their songs.

Raised in America, Hutton had a minor hit with the self-produced and composed 'Roses and Rainbows' (Hanna-Barbara Records, 1965). In the same year he joined MGM as a producer. There he worked with Wells' group the Enemies. Then, in 1968, Wells and Hutton – who, like Stephen Stills, failed his audition to become a member of the **Monkees** – formed Three Dog Night. They added Negron, whose clear tenor complemented Wells' soul-styled singing voice and Hutton's gruffer vocals, and instrumentalists Mike Allsup (guitar), Jim Greenspoon (keyboards), Joe Schermie (bass) and Floyd Sneed (drums). Signed to Dunhill, they had an immediate hit with their prettified version of 'Try a Little Tenderness' (1969), a prettified reworking of **Otis Redding**'s 1966 hit. With the vital difference that their sources were for the most part white contemporary singer-songwriters, 'Tenderness' set the pattern for their later hits.

These included 'Easy to Be Hard'* (1969), from the musical *Hair*; 'Joy to the World' (1971), by **Hoyt Axton**; 'Liar'* (1971), by Russ Ballard of Argent, the group formed by former member of the **Zombies** Rod Argent; **Paul Williams**' 'Just an Old Fashioned Love Song' (1971); and Axton's 'Never Been to Spain' (1972). More interesting was 'Black and White'* (1972). The song was written in 1954 by David, father of actor Alan, Arkin and **Earl Robinson** (author of the classic union ballad 'Joe Hill' and 'Ballad for Americans', memorably recorded by **Paul Robeson** in 1940) in response to the historic Supreme Court decision 'Brown versus Board of Education' which banned segregation in America's public schools. In 1971 the reggae group Greyhound's lilting version (Trojan), the first commercial release of the song, was a European hit and this inspired Three Dog Night to record it.

Later hits included 'Shambala'* (1973), **Leo Sayer**'s 'The Show Must Go on'* and **Allen Toussaint**'s 'Play Something Sweet (Brickyard Blues)' (1974). Following Hutton's departure in 1976, Wells and Negron continued to perform with Jay Gruska as Three Dog Night until in 1981 Hutton returned. A career retrospective, *The Three Dog Night Story*, appeared in 1993. A further one, *Celebrate*, appeared in 1998.

THROWING MUSES
Tanya Donelly, b. Rhode Island, USA; Kristin Hersch, b. 1966, Rhode Island; Leslie Langston (replaced by Bernard Georges); David Narcizo

One of the most important underground bands of the eighties, Throwing Muses' blend of obtuse rock and shimmering pop earned them many admirers before tension between half-sisters Hersch and Donelly caused them to split in the mid-nineties. Both have since gone on to solo careers.

Hersch and Donelly formed Throwing Muses at high school in 1983, employing various local musicians until the recruitment of drummer Narcizo and bassist Langston. Signing to British independent label 4AD the quartet recorded their eponymous début album in 1986, introducing an anguished sound that drew heavily on Hersch's mental instability, the result of a bipolarity that often caused her to hallucinate. The same themes dominated *House Tornado* (1988) and *Hunkpa* (1989), which saw Throwing Muses develop a larger fanbase having signed to Sire Records. With the release of *The Real Ramona* (1991) the band edged towards a more commercial, classic pop sound, but by this stage tension between the band's creative siblings had brought about the departure of Donelly.

Hersch recorded the fourth Throwing Muses album, *Red Heaven* (1992), with Narcizo and bassist

Georges before focusing her attention on a solo career. *Hips and Makers* (1994) continued in the same vein as *Red Heaven*, once again delving into the singer's health problems, with an ethereal musical backdrop provided by Lenny Kaye, formerly of **Patti Smith**'s band, and featuring a guest appearance from **R.E.M.**'s Michael Stipe. *Strings* (1994) put the same songs in an orchestral setting before Hersch reformed Throwing Muses for two final LPs, *University* (1995) and *Limbo* (1996). After a final tour as a three-piece the band officially broke up in 1997. Since the split Hersch has issued two new albums of her own material, *Strange Angels* (1998) and *Sky Motel* (1999), and a collection traditional folk songs, *Down in the Willow Garden* (1998).

Donelly enjoyed a brief stint in the Breeders, fronted by former **Pixies** bassist Kim Deal, playing on *Pod* (1992) before forming her own band, Belly, with brothers Tom (guitar) and Chris (drums) Gorman. The trio released two albums of hook-laden guitar-pop, *Star* (1993) and *King* (1995), before Donelly decided on a solo career, recording the acclaimed *Love Songs for Underdogs* (1997).

FLOYD TILLMAN
b. 8 December 1914, Ryan, Oklahoma, USA

Floyd Tillman was a pivotal figure in honky-tonk music, as both singer and songwriter. Vocally, his relaxed timing and strong jazz and blues leanings anticipated the stylistic direction that was later pursued by **Willie Nelson**, while as a lyricist he was one of the original architects of the 'cheating song' genre, typified by his 1949 hit 'Slipping Around'. What **Jimmie Rodgers** did for railroads in country music, Tillman did for adultery.

As a young man he admired Rodgers and **Vernon Dalhart**, but gained his first professional experience in the early thirties with the San Antonio-based singer-guitarist-bandleader Adolph Hofner. Later, as singer and rhythm guitarist, he joined the bands of Leon Selph (the Blue Ridge Playboys) and Cliff Bruner. In 1938 he wrote what would become his most famous song, 'It Makes No Difference Now'; it was recorded by Hofner (Bluebird, with Tom Dickey and the Show Boys), Bruner (Decca) and **Jimmie Davis** (Decca), to whom Tillman sold a half share in the number. All these versions were substantial Southwestern hits, enabling Tillman to record in his own name (for Decca). He was successful again with 'They Took the Stars out of Heaven' (1942) and 'Each Night at Nine', a major country song of 1943.

Signing with Columbia in 1946, he had further hits with 'Drivin' Nails in My Coffin' (1946) and 'I Love You So Much It Hurts' (1947) before the nationwide success of 'Slipping Around'. After leaving the label in

1954 he performed and recorded only occasionally for Sims, Cimarron, Musicor, Crazy Cajun and Gilley's. *Floyd Tillman and Friends* (Gilley's) included duets with Nelson and **Merle Haggard**. A member of BMI's 'Millionaire Club', which recognizes songs that have received over a million airplays, he was voted into the Country Music Hall of Fame in 1984.

JOHNNY TILLOTSON
b. 20 April 1939, Jacksonville, Florida, USA

Best remembered for the quintessential teen ballad 'Poetry in Motion'* (1960), the clear-voiced Tillotson was one of the first country performers to turn successfully to pop.

Tillotson began performing in his teens and in 1958 was signed to Cadence. His early records were mostly slow ballads ('Dreamy Eyes', 1958, and a hit when reissued in 1962, and a cover of **Johnny Ace**'s 1955 hit 'Pledging My Love', 1959). It was only with the addition of the chirpy, bouncy rhythmic accompaniment of 'Poetry', however, that Tillotson found real success. More accomplished was the self-composed 'It Keeps Right on a-Hurtin'' (1962), later recorded by **Elvis Presley**, but his version of **Hank Locklin**'s 'Send Me the Pillow You Dream on' (1962) saw Tillotson edging toward the smooth countrypolitan sound being pioneered by **Chet Atkins**. 'Talk Back Trembling Lips' (MGM, 1963) and his version of **Don Gibson**'s 'Heartaches by the Number' (1965), Tillotson's last major pop hit, were similarly styled.

After his hits declined, Tillotson recorded 'Tears on My Pillow' (1969) for Jimmy Bowen's Amos label, and attempted careers in cabaret and then acting before in the seventies returning to country music with an eponymous album (United Artists, 1977).

TINDERSTICKS
David Boulter; Mark Cornwill; Neil Fraser; Dickon Hinchcliffe; Al McCauley; Stuart Staples

One of the most distinctive British bands of the nineties, Tindersticks drew on the dark pop of **Leonard Cohen** and **Scott Walker** for a series of critically acclaimed albums that blended mellow orchestrations with mumbled vocals.

Vocalist Staples, violinist Hinchcliffe and keyboard-player Boulter performed together in Asphalt Ribbons before forming Tindersticks in Nottingham in 1992 with guitarist Fraser, bassist Cornwill and drummer McCauley. After releasing a series of singles, most notably 'Marbles' (1993), independently, the band were signed by This Way Up for the release of their eponymous début double-album. Its melancholy arrangement, taking in muted trumpet, bassoon and layered strings, and mournful vocals drew unanimous praise and earned the band a devoted following. It was followed by a version of **John Barry**'s 'We Have All the Time in the World' (1994) and an exceptional live recording, *Amsterdam 8th September 1994*. Tindersticks returned in 1995 with their second untitled album, largely in the same vein as its predecessor, and their second live recording, *The Bloomsbury Theatre 12.3.95*, on which the band was accompanied by a 26-piece orchestra, lifting their earlier material to an even higher level.

Tindersticks disappeared for much of 1996, surfacing only on the soundtrack to the Claire Denis movie *Nénette et Boni* and on a version of 'A Marriage Made in Heaven' recorded with actress Isabella Rossellini. Their third album, *Curtains* (1997), marked the end of the first phase of the Tindersticks' career, the best of which is collected on *Straw Donkeys* (1998). In 1999 they released their strongest album to date, *Simple Pleasures*, which saw the band take a new classic soul direction and included a version of 'If You're Looking for a Way Out', originally popularized by Odyssey, alongside the minor hit single 'Can We Start Again?'.

DIMITRI TIOMKIN
b. 10 May 1899, St Petersburg, Russia, d. 11 November 1979, London, England

A versatile film composer, Tiomkin was among the first to have his film music released on record (*Duel in the Sun*, 1946) and to have commercial success when other artists recorded his title songs. The Oscar-winning 'High Noon' was a hit for both **Tex Ritter** and **Frankie Laine** (1952) and 'Friendly Persuasion' was a hit for **Pat Boone** in 1956. Both were written with lyricist Ned Washington.

A graduate of the St Petersburg Conservatory of Music, Tiomkin was originally a concert pianist. He turned to composing and conducting in 1919, in which capacity he introduced **George Gershwin**'s music to Europe. In 1925 he went to America and, after writing ballet music for films, settled in Hollywood. His first full score was *Alice in Wonderland* (1933). Among the 150 or so films he scored were *Lost Horizon* (1937), *Only Angels Have Wings* (1938), *Red River* (1948), *Strangers on a Train* (1950), *Giant* (1956) and *Rio Bravo* (1959). Known for his lush romanticism, Tiomkin frequently made use of indigenous folk music (particularly in his Western scores) and often borrowed from classical composers. His famous acceptance speech for the Oscar he received for *The High and the Mighty* (1954) pointed out the great debt owed by Hollywood to classical composers in general. Tiomkin's recording of his theme to 'The High and the Mighty' (Coral) was his only hit.

In the sixties Tiomkin wrote mostly epics (*55 Days at Peking*, 1963, and *The Fall of the Roman Empire*,

1964) and Westerns (*The War Wagon*, 1967) before moving into production with *Mackenna's Gold* (1969) and *Tchaikovsky* (1970), a biography of the composer which Tiomkin also directed.

TLC
Lisa 'Left Eye' Lopez, b. 27 May 1971, Philadelphia, Pennsylvania, USA; Rozonda 'Chilli' Thomas, b. 27 February 1971, Atlanta; Tione 'T-Boz' Watkins, b. 26 April 1970, Des Moines, Iowa

One of the most successful exponents of the early nineties blend of hip-hop and R&B, female trio TLC rose to international prominence with 'Waterfalls', their biggest hit to date.

TLC were assembled in 1991 by Pebbles, who had found success as a solo artist in the late eighties. The début album *Ooooooooh . . . On the TLC Tip** (1992) earned the trio immediate success in the US, establishing their distinctive vocal style, the sugary blend of T-Boz's lead vocals, Chilli's harmonizing and Left Eye's rapping. The album, which also introduced TLC's feminist mentality and unashamed sexuality, predating the **Spice Girls**' 'girl power' ideology by half a decade, featured three *Billboard* Top Ten singles: 'Ain't 2 Proud 2 Beg', 'What about Your Friends' and 'Baby-Baby-Baby'.

TLC achieved international stardom with their sophomore effort *Crazy Sexy Cool* (1994), which sold over four million copies on the strength of 'Waterfalls', 'Creep' and 'Red Light Special'. The album earned the trio two Grammy Awards, but its success was marred somewhat by the arrest of Lopez for burning down the house she shared with US footballplayer André Rison. After promoting the album determinedly the group took a two-year hiatus in 1996 as Watkins battled sickle-cell anaemia and Thomas gave birth to a son. They returned in 1999 with *Fanmail*. The tenth most successful album of the year in the US, it included the international hit singles 'No Scrubs', the second bestselling single of the year in the US, and 'Unpretty', the twentieth bestselling single of the year in the US.

TOMPALL AND THE GLASER BROTHERS
Tompall Glaser, b. 3 September 1933, Spalding, Nebraska, USA; Charles 'Chuck' Glaser, b. 27 February 1936, Spalding; James 'Jim' Glazer, b. 16 December 1937, Spalding

With **Waylon Jennings** and **Willie Nelson**, the Glasers were leaders of the 'outlaw' movement that did much to preserve country as a distinct musical tradition and to make it accessible to the younger, rock audience.

Professional musicians since their teens, the Glasers

travelled to Nashville in 1958 and signed first to **Marty Robbins**' Robbins label and then Decca in 1959, as Tompall and the Glaser Brothers. It was, however, as session and back-up musicians that they first made their mark. They provided the smooth harmonies behind several of Robbins' hits (notably 'El Paso', which they later recorded themselves) and supported Robbins and **Johnny Cash** on tour. During this period they mostly recorded in a folk manner and their only success was in the pop charts with the novelty, 'On Top of Spaghetti' (Kapp, 1963).

In 1966 they joined MGM and, with **Jack Clement** handling production, began a string of hits with **John Hartford**'s 'Gentle on My Mind'. During the late sixties, the brothers also became very active behind the scenes. Tompall wrote such songs as 'Stand Beside Me' and the classic 'Streets of Baltimore' (with **Harlan Howard**), while Chuck turned producer, working with Jimmy Payne, Hartford and Kinky Friedman (whose outrageous 'Ride 'Em Jewboy' and *Sold American*, Vanguard, 1973, were critical, if not popular, successes), and Jimmy signed a solo contract with Monument. At the same time they offered support, and studio time in their Glaser Studios, to new progressive country writers, including **Mickey Newbury**, Steve Young and Friedman, as well as aligning themselves with the 'outlaw' movement.

In 1973 the group split up to concentrate on their various solo careers. Tompall, who appeared on the classic *Wanted: The Outlaws* (RCA, 1976) with Nelson, Jennings and Jesse Colter, was the most successful; Chuck suffered a massive stroke in 1975. They re-formed in 1978, and in 1981 they joined Elektra but by 1983 they were recording separately again. This time Jim (who with Jimmy Payne had written the million-selling 'Woman, Woman' for **Gary Puckett**) was the more successful with a string of romantically inclined soft-voiced country hits on Noble Vision, including 'When You're Not a Lady' (1982) and 'You're Getting to Me Again' (1984). Tompall's later albums included *Nights on the Borderline* (1986), the self-explanatory *Collection of Ballads from World War II* (1987) and *The Rogue* (1992).

TOOTS AND THE MAYTALS
Raleigh Gordon, b. Ralphus Gordon, 1945, Jamaica; Toots Hibbert, b. Frederick Hibbert, 1946, Maypen, Jamaica; Jerry Matthias, b. Nathaniel Matthias, 1945, Jamaica

The Maytals' 'Do the Reggay' (1968) was the first song to refer to Jamaica's most famous musical genre, and the group was reggae's most accomplished vocal trio, bringing together gospel and Rastafarian traditions with the secular fervour of such singers as **Solomon Burke**.

Hibbert was the son of a leader of the Pukkamina cult (whose ritual influenced reggae) and he moved from the countryside to Kingston at the age of fifteen. As the Vikings, he and backing singers Matthias and Gordon first recorded in 1962 when the ragged, lively 'Hallelujah', produced by **Coxsone Dodd**, was a hit. Other singles in a similar ska vein included 'Come into My Parlour', 'I Am in Love' and 'Six and Seven Books of Moses'. Renamed the Maytals, the trio recorded 'Little Slea', 'Domino' and 'Ska War' for **Prince Buster** in 1964. In the same year the Maytals topped the Jamaican charts with the **Byron Lee**-produced 'It's You'/'Daddy' and in 1966 they had the first of three Jamaican Song Festival victories with 'Bam Bam'.

'Do the Reggay', 'Pressure Drop' and '54–46' were among the classic Maytals tracks produced by **Leslie Kong** and in 1970 'Monkey Man' was a minor British hit on Trojan. After Kong's death the trio returned to Lee for the more cosmopolitan 'Funky Kingston' and 'In the Dark'. However, it was the inclusion of 'Pressure Drop' and 'Sweet and Dandy' on the soundtrack of *The Harder They Come* (1972) that introduced the group to a wider international audience. In 1975 they signed to **Chris Blackwell**'s Island label for the rock–reggae fusion of *Funky Kingston* and *Reggae Got Soul* (1977), which included **Steve Winwood** on organ.

Later albums included *Pass the Pipe* (1979), *Live!* (1981, recorded in London), *Knockout* (1982) and *Toots in Memphis* (1988), a collection of soul and R&B standards, for Island's Mango subsidiary. In 1994 Toots sang on a new album by the **Skatalites**.

Time Tough (1996) is the definitive career retrospective.

MEL TORMÉ

b. Melvin Howard Tormé, 13 September 1925, Chicago, Illinois, USA

Actor, composer and multi-instrumentalist, Tormé was the most jazz influenced of the crooners who established themselves in the late forties at the close of the big-band era. Originally known as 'The Velvet Fog' for his smooth, mellow voice, he gained a new reputation in the late fifties and sixties with a far more fluid, rhythmic cool style, even scoring a pop hit with 'Comin' Home Baby'.

After acting in radio soap operas in his teens, Tormé joined the band led by Chico Marx (of the Marx Brothers) as vocalist and in 1943 made his film début in *Higher and Higher*. He then formed the vocal group the Mel-Tones, which recorded with **Artie Shaw** ('I Got the Sun in the Morning', 1946) and **Bing Crosby** ('Day by Day', 1946), as well as under its own name ('It's Dreamtime', Musicraft, 1947). During this period Tormé also had success as a songwriter, most

notably with 'The Christmas Song', first recorded by **Nat 'King' Cole** in 1946.

In 1947 he joined Capitol as a solo artist, scoring his first No. 1 with 'Careless Love' (1949) and regularly partnering **Peggy Lee** on record ('The Old Master Painter', 1950). In 1954 he recorded a live album, *Mel Tormé at the Crescendo* (GNP), which gave him a surprise British hit with his slick, speeded-up jazz version of **Richard Rodgers** and **Lorenz Hart**'s 'Mountain Greenery' (Vogue, 1956).

Generally more successful in live performance than on record, where his cool style sometimes seemed mannered, Tormé had a surprise pop hit in 1962 with his Atlantic recording of 'Comin' Home Baby'. He later recorded for several labels, mixing contemporary songs (*Right Now*, Columbia, 1966; *Raindrops Keep Falling on My Head*, Capitol, 1970) and collaborations with **George Shearing** (*An Evening at Charlie's*, Concord, 1982, *Vintage Year*, 1988), **Cleo Laine** and **Buddy Rich**.

THE TORNADOS

George Bellamy, b. 8 October 1941, Sunderland, Tyne and Wear, England; Heinz Burt, b. 24 July 1942, Hargen, Germany; Alan Caddy, b. 2 February 1940, London, England, d. 16 August 2000, London; Clem Cattini, b. 28 August 1939, London; Roger Laverne, b. Roger La Vern Jackson, 11 November 1938, Kidderminster, Worcestershire

The first British group to top the American charts, the Tornados are best remembered for their ethereal organ-dominated instrumental 'Telstar'* (1962).

The group (of whom guitarist Caddy and drummer Cattini had previously backed **Johnny Kidd** as the Pirates, later backing **Tommy Steele**'s brother Colin Hicks, who was briefly a big star in Italy, as the Cabin Boys) was put together by producer **Joe Meek**. It was created to accompany Meek's acts (which included John Leyton, Michael Cox, Mike Berry and Ken Charles) in live performance and to act as session musicians. In 1962, while acting as **Billy Fury**'s backing group, they made their first recording, 'Love and Fury' (Decca). That and the Caddy- and Cattini-written 'Popeye Twist' failed, but the Meek-penned follow-up 'Telstar' – inspired by watching the first live television pictures transmitted via the Telstar satellite – was an international hit. Laverne's swirling organ sound, however, quickly became formulaic and after further hits in 1963 – 'Globetrotter', 'Robot' and 'Dragonfly' – and a lacklustre album (*Away from It All*, 1964) the group members left for various solo projects. The most successful was bassist Heinz whose series of minor hits included 'Just Like Eddie' (Decca, 1963), a homage to **Eddie Cochran**, and 'Country Boy' (1963), both written by Meek's house writer Geoff Goddard.

Caddy briefly worked as a session musician before becoming a producer, specializing in covers of current hits, first in the UK (Avenue Records) and then in Canada.

Following Meek's suicide in 1967, the group officially broke up, briefly re-forming (without Caddy), in 1975 to record an updated version of 'Telstar' (SRT) and in 1991 to play at a Joe Meek tribute concert. Heinz became a stalwart of the revival circuit, while Cattini established himself as a session drummer.

Telstar, The Original Sixties Hits of The Tornados (MCI, 1994) is the definitive anthology.

TORTOISE

Dan Bitney; Bundy K Brown (replaced by David Pajo, replaced by Jeff Parker); John Herndon; Doug McCombs; John McEntire

As the leading exponents of the 'post-rock' genre, the instrumental collective Tortoise have enjoyed widespread underground support in the nineties, attempting to emphasize the importance of percussion and bass over guitar and vocals with an expansive sound inspired by Krautrock and free jazz.

Bassist McCombs and drummer Herndon began experimenting together in 1990, at first intending to record and produce in the vein of **Sly and Robbie**. With the addition of producer/percussionist McEntire, guitarist Brown and drummer Bitney, all veterans of the Chicago indie-rock scene, the quintet recorded their acclaimed eponymous début in 1993 for Thrill Jockey, which drew on the experimental sounds of **Can** and Faust. The album proved highly influential and established a devoted following for the band, allowing its members to begin work on a variety of side projects, notably Gastr del Soul (McEntire and Brown) and Eleventh Dream Day (McCombs). *Tortoise* also inspired an album of remixes by the likes of Jim O'Rourke, Steve Albini and Brad Wood, *Rhythms, Resolutions and Clusters* (1995). The *Gamera* 12" followed on **Stereolab**'s Duophonic label.

Before starting work on the second Tortoise album Brown left to devote his time to record production, and was replaced by David Pajo, who had previously won acclaim for his work with Slint on the albums *Tweez* (1989) and *Spiderland* (1991), and on **Palace Music**'s *Viva Last Blues*. *Millions Now Living Will Never Die* (1996) took its name from an old Jehovah's Witness tract, and was lavished with praise on both sides of the Atlantic, namely for the 21-minute opener 'Djed', which was intended to represent the work of a club disc jockey. The album's success brought about a series of remix EPs, which saw Spring Heel Jack, UNKLE and Jim O'Rourke attempt to rework its six expansive tracks. Pajo left the band soon after to concentrate on his Aerial M project, while McEntire pro-

duced a number of Stereolab recordings. Tortoise recruited Parker (guitar/keyboards) for *TNT* (1998), which saw the band move away from their recent forays into electronica, returning instead to the sound of their début. *TNT* featured contributions from Autechre and another influential Chicago-based figure, Derrick Carter.

PETER TOSH
b. Winston Hubert McIntosh, 9 October 1944, West-moreland, Jamaica, d. 12 September 1987, Kingston

With **Bob Marley**, Tosh was a founder member of the Wailers, the most combative and influential reggae group of the mid-sixties. After leaving Marley in 1974, Tosh recorded a series of uncompromising solo albums before he was murdered in 1987. They were characterized by caustic social comment and the innovative reggae arrangements of **Sly and Robbie**.

The Wailers were formed in 1963 and in later years Tosh recorded as Peter Touch on such occasional solo singles as 'Selassie Serenade' (Bullet, 1969) and 'The Return of Al Capone' (Unity, 1969). After leaving the group, Tosh recorded for his own Intel-Diplo H.I.M. label, whose title proclaimed Tosh's Rastafarian faith. His first solo album was *Legalize It* (released in Britain by Virgin and in America by Columbia in 1976), whose title track was an attack on the laws concerning marijuana. After recording *Equal Rights* (1977), with its version of the Wailers 'Get up Stand up', Tosh and his Word Sound and Power band (including Sly Dunbar and Robbie Shakespeare) took part in the **Rolling Stones**' world tour and subsequently signed to the group's label.

Bush Doctor (Rolling Stones, 1978), which included contributions from Mick Jagger and Keith Richards, was followed by *Mystic Man* (1979) and *Wanted Dead and Alive* (1981). When the Rolling Stones label wound down, Tosh signed to EMI for *Mama Africa* (1983), with a title track featuring soul singer **Betty Wright**. The album was produced by Chris Kimsey, who had previously worked with the Stones, and included the political commentary 'Peace Treaty' and a reggae version of **Chuck Berry**'s 'Johnny B. Goode', a minor hit in Britain.

Later records included *Captured Live* (1984) and *No Nuclear War* (1987). Tosh was murdered by gangsters attempting to extort money from him.

TOTO
David Hungate, b. Los Angeles, California, USA; Bobby Kimball, b. Robert Toteaux, 29 March 1967, Vinton LA (replaced by Fergie Fredrikson, b. 15 May 1951, Louisiana, replaced by Joseph Williams, replaced by Jean-Michel Byron); Steve Lukather, b. 4 October 1957,

Los Angeles; David Paich, b. 25 June 1954, Los Angeles; Jeff Porcaro, b. 1 April 1954, Los Angeles, d. 5 August 1992, Los Angeles; Mike Porcaro, b. 29 May 1955, Los Angeles; Steve Porcaro, b. 2 September 1957, Los Angeles

A group of former top session players, Toto found success in the eighties with a series of polished, tuneful pop albums.

The Porcaro brothers, Lukather and Paich (son of film composer Marty Paich) played in high-school band Still Life in California's San Fernando Valley. All went on to become successful session or backing musicians, with drummer Jeff Porcaro touring with Sonny and **Cher** before joining **Boz Scaggs'** band in 1976 with Paich (keyboards) and Hungate (bass). Paich co-wrote songs which appeared on Scaggs' *Silk Degrees* (1976) and composed the Cheryl Lynn hit 'Got to Be Real'* (Columbia, 1979). The future members of Toto played sessions for numerous artists, including **Leo Sayer**, **Alice Cooper**, **Steely Dan**, Valerie Carter and **Hall and Oates**.

In 1978 the trio formed Toto (the name of the dog in *The Wizard of Oz*) with Lukather (guitar) and singer Kimball. Their eponymous album for Columbia (with string arrangements by Marty Paich) produced the Top Ten hit 'Hold the Line'*. '99', from *Hydra* (1979), was a lesser hit but after *Turn Back* (1981), the group released their most successful album, *Toto IV* (1982). It included three Top Ten hits in 'Rosanna' (dedicated to actress Rosanna Arquette), the catchy 'Africa', an American No. 1 and the band's biggest British hit, and 'I Won't Hold You Back'. In 1982 members of the group also composed the Tubes' hit 'Talk to You Later'.

By now Mike Porcaro had joined on bass and Kimball left the group, in 1987 joining MGM, the heavy-rock band formed by former **Whitesnake** members Bernie Marsden, Mel Galley and Neil Murray. Former Trillion singer Fredrikson briefly joined the band and took lead vocals on *Isolation* (1984). In turn he was replaced by writer and singer Williams, who appeared on *Fahrenheit* (1986). **Miles Davis** appeared on one track, and 'I'll Be over You' was a hit.

For *The Seventh One* (1988), Toto brought in outside producers George Massenburg (who had worked with **Earth, Wind and Fire**), and **Phil Collins** and former **Little Feat** pianist Bill Payne. The album included the **Jimmy Webb** song 'Home of the Brave'. In 1991 the band toured with a new line-up which saw vocalist Byron join Jeff and Michael Porcaro, Paich and Lukather. A hits collection, *Past to Present*, followed in 1990. All the band members continued to find lucrative work as session men, and the long-term future of Toto was thrown into doubt when Jeff Porcaro died of an apparently drugs-related heart attack in 1992, shortly before the release of *Kingdom of*

Desire. British drummer Simon Phillips (another veteran sessioneer) stepped in for a British tour later that year and also played in America with the band in 1993. In 1999 they mounted a world tour in support of *Minefields*.

In 1984 Toto provided the soundtrack for the science-fiction film *Dune*.

TOURE KUNDA

Michel Abissila, b. Algeria; Belinga Bens, b. Cameroon; Michel Billiez, b. France; Jean-Claude Bonaventure, b. France; Samspon Goustillias, b. France; Dioup Nebou, b. Ivory Coast; Amadou Toure, b. Casamance, Senegal, d. 25 January 1983; Ismail Toure, b. Casamance; Sixu Toure, b. Casamance; Ousmane Toure, b. Casamance

One of African music's leading groups, Toure Kunda (the Toure or elephant family) combined traditional lyrics and melodies with modern Western instrumental and production techniques. While they were extremely successful in France, where they were based, the heterogeneous character of Toure Kunda's music made them less appealing to the new audience for 'world music' which developed in the late eighties.

Having travelled to Paris in the mid-seventies, Ismail Toure and his half-brother Sixu recorded the reggae-influenced *Ismail and Sixu* (1977). The group Toure Kunda was formed in Paris in the late seventies when Amadou joined his brothers in France. Featuring close vocal harmonies, the band's repertoire was centred on the language and songs of the Sengalese initiation rite Djamba Dong but with Western instrumentation and rhythmic borrowings from soukous, highlife, funk and reggae. Signing to Celluloid, Toure Kunda released their first Afro-rock album, *Em'Ma/Africa* in 1980.

This was followed by *Turu* before the group's growing popularity was sapped by the sudden death of Amadou. The group recorded *Amadou Tilo* in his memory and a fourth half-brother, Ousmane, joined as harmony vocalist. *Casamance au Clair de Lune* (1983) was recorded using only traditional acoustic instruments, the tambour, balafon and guitar but Toure Kunda took a full multinational backing group to perform in four African countries in 1984. These concerts were recorded to form the double-album *Live Paris – Ziquinchor* (1985), with saxophonists Billiez and Bens, Dioup (backing vocals) guitarist Bonaventure and Goustillias on piano. In 1984 Toure Kunda appeared on the famine relief record 'Tam Tam pour l'Ethiopie' (Phonogram).

In 1985 Celluloid brought in **Bill Laswell** to produce the high-tech *Natalia*. Guest musicians included synthesizer-player Bernie Worrell but the album sold poorly.

In 1988 they returned to Senegal, adding another

brother, Hamidou, to the line-up. Back in Paris, the group moved to Trama Records for whom they recorded the impressive *Salam* (1990), their most accessible album for some time. *1983–1984* (Celluloid, 1986) is a useful compilation of their earlier recordings.

ALLEN TOUSSAINT
b. 14 January 1938, New Orleans, Louisiana, USA

Songwriter, session musician, arranger, producer and recording artist, Toussaint was the driving force behind the New Orleans music of the sixties, just as **Dave Bartholomew** had been in the fifties. His productions marked a shift from rolling, piano-led rhythms, reprised in his production of **Ernie K-Doe**'s classic 'Mother-in-Law' (1961), to the more urgent sounds of his hits with **Lee Dorsey** whose spare intensity presaged the sound of funk. His own recordings, particularly the triumphant *Southern Nights* (1975), were more relaxed and evocative.

From a musical family, Toussaint formed his first band with **Snooks Eaglin** in 1951 and in 1957 briefly replaced **Huey 'Piano' Smith** in **Shirley and Lee**'s touring band. In the same year he was hired by Bartholomew as a session pianist. In this capacity he played on various recordings by **Fats Domino** and **Lloyd Price**, while acting as arranger on several recordings for Johnny Vincent's Ace label, including Lee Allen's hit instrumental 'Walkin' with Mr Lee' (1958). In the same year he recorded his début album, as Al Tousan, *The Wild Sounds of New Orleans* (RCA). An instrumental album, it showed his stylistic debt to **Professor Longhair** and his deftness at mimicry, and introduced 'Java', later a million-seller for trumpeter Al Hirt (1963), whose other major hit was Buddy Killen's (manager and producer of **Joe Tex**) and **Billy Sherrill**'s 'Sugar Lips'* (1964).

In 1959 Toussaint was hired by Joe Banashak of Minit Records as the company's principal producer. He also recorded for the label as Allen Orange ('Heavenly Baby', 1959), and later with the Stokes (including the instrumental 'Whipped Cream', 1964, later the title track of **Herb Alpert**'s 1965 chart-topping album and subsequently used as the theme for the television show *The Dating Game*). Among his successful productions, many of which he also wrote under his Naomi Neville pseudonym, were Jesse Hill's 'Ooh Poo Pah Do', 'Mother-in-Law' (1960), Chris Kenner's 'I Like It Like That', the Showmen's hymn to rock'n'roll 'It Will Stand' (1961), and Irma Thomas's passionate ballad 'Ruler of My Heart' (1962). Between 1963 and 1965 Toussaint was in the army and on his release left Minit to form Sansu, an independent production company, with Marshall Sehorn, one-time assistant of **Bobby Robinson**. Their first success came with Lee Dorsey, whose 'Ya Ya' (1961) Toussaint had supervised. The dance tune 'Ride Your Pony' (1965) led to a series of Toussaint-written and -produced hits, including 'Working in a Coalmine', the oft-recorded 'Get out My Life Woman' and 'Holy Cow' (1966).

After Dorsey's last hit, 'Everything I Do Gonna Be Funky' (1969), Toussaint had further success with the Meters, the group led by the **Neville Brothers** and comprising leading New Orleans session musicians. The Meters' hits included 'Sophisticated Cissy' and 'Cissy Strut' (Josie, 1969), records which prefigured Toussaint's exercises in funk with Dorsey on the magnificent *Yes We Can* (Polydor, 1970). All the songs on *Yes We Can*, including 'Sneaking Sally Thru the Alley' (later the title track of **Robert Palmer**'s 1974 album) and 'Yes We Can' (a hit for the **Pointer Sisters**, 1973), bar one, were written by Toussaint. The exception was **Joe South**'s 'Games People Play', which with its wry comments on the ability of most people to lead lives of self-deception, suggested the concerns that Toussaint went on to develop as a songwriter.

The solo album *Toussaint* (Tiffany, 1970) included reworkings of several Lee Dorsey hits and also saw Toussaint in a mellower vocal mood on 'From a Whisper to a Scream', a revival of **Joe Simon**'s 1969 **Harlan Howard**-written hit 'The Chokin' Kind' and the reflective 'What Is Success'. Although not commercially successful, it led to Toussaint working on **The Band**'s *Cahoots* (1971) and *Rock of Ages* (1972), after which Toussaint began to produce mainstream rock artists. Among these were Frankie Miller, whose best album *High Life* (Chrysalis, 1974) included several Toussaint songs ('Brickyard Blues', a hit for **Three Dog Night**; 'Shoorah Shoorah', first recorded by **Betty Wright**); **Dr John** (*In the Right Place*, 1973; *Desitively Bonnaroo*, 1974); Labelle ('Lady Marmalade'*, 1975); and **Paul Simon** (whose 'Tenderness' on *There Goes Rhymin' Simon*, 1973, he arranged).

For these artists Toussaint provided a tougher sound, akin to his later work with Dorsey, but on his own recordings, notably *Life, Love and Faith* (Warners, 1972) and the magisterial *Southern Nights* (1975), whose title track gave **Glen Campbell** a million-seller and American No. 1 in 1977, Toussaint developed a warmer, intimate sound that perfectly captured the questioning tone of songs like 'What Do You Want the Girl to Do' and 'When the Party's Over'. However, though critically acclaimed, neither these nor the lesser *Motion* (1978), produced by **Jerry Wexler**, were commercially successful and Toussaint retreated into inactivity for most of the eighties. In 1978 he supervised the music for Louis Malle's New Orleans-based film *Pretty Baby* and in 1987 in a surprise move, since Toussaint had always been a diffident performer, he was musical director for **Ruth Brown** in the Broadway musical *Staggerlee*. In 1994 he duetted with guitarist **Chet Atkins** on his own 'Southern Nights' on the concept album *Rhythm, Country and Blues* (MCA). Later albums include the sombre *Connected* (NYNO, 1996) and the lesser *A New Orleans Christmas* (1998).

The Allen Toussaint Collection (Warner, 1991) is a lacklustre bits and pieces anthology of his Warner recordings.

TOYAH

b. Toyah Ann Willcox, 18 May 1958, Birmingham, England

An actress and singer, Toyah's flamboyant concert performances brought her a series of neo-punk hits in the early eighties.

While studying at drama school in 1977, Toyah appeared in a television play. That led to a leading role in Derek Jarman's controversial punk-inspired film *Jubilee* (1977), in which she wrote and sang 'Nine to Five', and a part in *Quadrophenia* (1979), the film version of **The Who**'s concept album. In the same year she formed a band with Joel Borgen (guitar) and Peter Bush (keyboards).

Signing to Safari, Toyah recorded a 'mini-album', *Sheep Farming in Barnet* (1979), and released the single 'Victims of the Riddle', which she co-wrote with Borgen. During 1980 she maintained her twin careers, expressing her interest in the occult on *The Blue Meaning* and releasing the live album *Toyah! Toyah! Toyah!*. Commercial success eluded the group until 'It's a Mystery' (1981) reached the Top Ten, followed by Toyah's best-known song, 'I Want to Be Free', and *Anthem*.

Scorned by the critics for her jejune philosophizing, Toyah nevertheless retained a youthful following in Britain and both *The Changeling* and *Warrior Rock – Toyah on Tour* (1982) were hits. *Love is the Law* and 'The Vow' (1983) were less successful, however, and she concentrated on acting roles in 1983–4.

After *Minx* (Epic, 1985), Toyah teamed up with **Robert Fripp**, whom she later married. Fripp worked on her 1987 album *Desire*, which contained a successful revival of Martha and the Muffins' hit 'Echo Beach' (Dindisc, 1980). With Fripp, she also released *The Lady or the Tiger* (1987) and the same year she played Sally Bowles in *Cabaret* in London's West End. In 1988 she released the intense *Prostitute* (EG). Again with her husband, she formed Fripp, Fripp, which was renamed Sunday All Over the World, and released one album, *Kneeling at the Shrine* (1991). In 1994 Wilcox released another solo album, the dance-orientated *Dreamchild*.

ARTHUR TRACY

b. Abraham Alter-Traterofski, 25 June 1900, Kamieni-etz, Podolosk, Ukraine, d. 6 October 1997

Arthur Tracy, 'The Street Singer', became one of the leading variety artists of the thirties on both sides of the Atlantic by deftly synthesizing the popular images of the gypsy troubadour, the drifting cowboy and the insouciant hero of Viennese operetta.

Little is known of Tracy's early life beyond the fact that his family emigrated to the US in 1906 when he was six and he was given the name Tracy. One account of his early life has him embarking on street-singing as a boy, another confines him to the profession of accountancy. What is certain is that he entered the American musical theatre in a Shubert Brothers' production of *Blossom Time*, a show with music by Franz Schubert, arranged by **Sigmund Romberg** and first staged on Broadway in 1921. Singing with dance bands, he made a name on American radio, enhanced by the success of his record 'Marta (Rambling Rose of the Wildwood)' (Brunswick, 1931), which he sang to his own piano-accordion accompaniment. The tune of 'Marta' was the work of the Cuban **Moises Simons**, who also wrote 'The Peanut Vendor' (1930); the English lyrics were by L. Wolfe Gilbert. Tracy appeared in the film *The Big Broadcast of 1932* and in the same year worked on the Chesterfield radio show with **Ruth Etting** and the **Boswell Sisters**. His transatlantic popularity was such that many of his American-made recordings were issued only in Britain, and in 1935 he moved there to work in clubs and make movies like *Limelight* (1936), *The Street Singer* (1937) and *Follow Your Star* (1938).

On records he displayed his florid approach, pitched somewhere between **Nelson Eddy** and **Slim Whitman**, on dramatic ballads of the roving life – keywords like 'gypsy', 'wander' and 'serenade' appear in many of his song titles – interspersed with cowboy numbers, some genuine like 'The Last Round Up' (Decca, 1933) and some pastiche, like 'Ole Faithful' (Decca, 1934), written by **Michael Carr**. He then sought this rural flavour in songs with different exotic resonances: Irish, Scottish, Pacific ('On the Beach at Bali-Bali', Decca, 1936), and even Yiddish. (Tracy's gentleman-of-the-road attire, however, with slouch hat and rakish neckerchief, never lost the reassuring Englishness of a rattling yarn by Jeffrey Farnol.)

In 1939 he returned to the US, where he recorded, for English wartime consumption, a version of the **Bob Wills**' hit 'San Antonio Rose' and 'Arthur Tracy's Message for England' (Decca, 1940). His career waned over the next decade, though he found a loyal British audience on his return in 1948. He was still making occasional guest appearances on American TV in the sixties.

TRAVIS

Andy Dunlop, b. Glasgow, Scotland; Fran Healy,

b. Glasgow; Dougie Payne, b. Glasgow; Neil Primrose, b. Glasgow

Scottish independent rock group Travis won their initial reputation with their impassioned live shows. They developed a more considered attitude in which, almost by default, they came to represent the angst that **Oasis**'s celebratory anthems obscured. The key moment in this transition was *The Man Who* (1999) album, which asked the perennial question 'Why Does It Always Rain on Me?'.

Healy (vocals/guitar), Dunlop (guitar) and Payne (bass) met as students at the Glasgow School of Art in 1990 before dropping out of college and forming Travis with drummer Primrose. After six years of determined live performance at local venues the band attracted the attention of Independiente, which was set up by Andy McDonald after the collapse of his Go Discs company, with the self-released single 'All I Wanna Do Is Rock'. The fledgling label's first signing in 1996, Travis built up a nationwide following touring in support of Oasis and **Catatonia**. Their début album *Good Feeling* (1997), which included the singles 'U16 Girls', 'Happy', 'Tied to the 90s' and 'More Than Us', all of which neatly captured the current trend for anthemic rock, reached the UK Top Ten.

Far more compelling was *The Man Who* (1999), a collection of acoustic-led ballads with a more mature, melancholic feel than its predecessor. Neatly described by one critic as 'presenting angst in a more accessible fashion than **Radiohead**', the album rose to the top of the British chart on the strength of a series of triumphant festival appearances and a trio of hit singles: 'Writing to Reach You', 'Driftwood' and 'Why Does It Always Rain on Me?'. The success of its questioning stance marked one of the first cracks in the celebration of (teenage) excess that Oasis represented at their most basic. The subsequent success of Coldplay's *Parachute* (Parlophone, 2000) suggested that student angst would be a significant theme in British rock in the first decade of the twenty-first century.

MERLE TRAVIS

b. 29 November 1917, Ebenezer, Kentucky, USA, d. 20 October 1983, Tahlequah, Oklahoma

One of the most accomplished and versatile figures in the history of country music, Travis was particularly noted for his brilliant songwriting and the creation of a distinctive and influential style of guitar-playing.

As a boy, he learned banjo from his father but moved on to guitar and began to develop a mode of picking with thumb and index finger, based on a banjo technique. Other local musicians – among them Mose Rager and Ike Everly, father of the **Everly Brothers** – were already playing in this fashion and applying it to jazz tunes which were more chordally sophisticated than the average country song. Travis began travelling the country and playing wherever he could, eventually working with Clayton McMichen (a one-time associate of **Gid Tanner**) and his Georgia Wildcats (1937). From the late thirties to the mid-forties he was based at WLW, Cincinnati, Ohio, playing regularly on the *Boone County Jamboree* (later the *Midwestern Hayride*). He was associated with Grandpa Jones and the **Delmore Brothers**, singing with them in the influential gospel group, the Brown's Ferry Four. In 1943 he also participated in the first recordings on the local King label, cutting a solo under the pseudonym Bob McCarthy and a duet with Jones as the Shepherd Brothers.

After war service, Travis moved to California and worked with the Western swing bands of Cliffie Stone, Ray Whitley and others; he also did session work for King with **Hank Penny**. He joined Capitol and had some success with his own compositions 'Divorce Me C.O.D.', 'So Round, So Firm, So Fully Packed' (based on a Lucky Strike cigarette ad), 'Sweet Temptation' (later recorded by **Ricky Skaggs**) and 'Dark as a Dungeon', recorded by himself, **Rose Maddox**, and later by innumerable artists. He also devised 'Smoke, Smoke, Smoke That Cigarette' for Tex Williams, modelling it on the **Bert Williams**' song 'The Darktown Poker Club'. His most enduring composition, however, was 'Sixteen Tons', which came to be seen as the archetypal coalfield protest piece, though he himself preferred to call it merely 'a fun song'. He recorded it on the album *Folk Songs of the Hills* (1947), but it did not reach a wide audience until revived by **Tennessee Ernie Ford** in 1955 (and later by many others).

Meanwhile 'Travis-style' picking, with its 'choked' sound from the heel of the picking hand damping the strings, was exercising an enormous influence on guitar players everywhere, from **Doc Watson** (who named his son Merle) to **Chet Atkins** (who did the same with his daughter). The album *Walkin' the Strings* (1959) provided a remarkable display of blues guitar solos. This was an acoustic set, but Travis had earlier come up with what was, in effect, a rough blueprint of the first solid-body electric guitar, built for him by Paul Bigsby and subsequently developed by **Leo Fender**.

In the late fifties and sixties Travis appeared on many TV shows and at folk festivals, made a memorable cameo appearance singing 'Re-entlistment Blues' in *From Here to Eternity* (1954), worked as a scriptwriter for the **Johnny Cash** TV show, and was for a time a cast member of the *Grand Ole Opry*. He took part in the **Nitty Gritty Dirt Band**'s *Will the Cir-*

cle Be Unbroken? project (1972) and recorded with Atkins (RCA, 1971, produced by **Jerry Reed**) and **Joe Maphis**, with whom he cut *Country Guitar Giants* (1979), one of several albums he made for CMH; another, *The Merle Travis Story* (1980), reinstated him in a Western swing setting, with former **Bob Wills** sideman Alex Brashear (trumpet), Herb Remington (steel guitar) and Johnny Gimble (fiddle). He was elected to the Country Music Hall of Fame in 1977.

RANDY TRAVIS
b. Randy Bruce Traywick, 4 May 1959, Marshville, North Carolina, USA

Travis was one of the first of the new traditionalists of country music to establish himself. His début Warner album, *Storms of Life* (1986), was a million-seller.

His father, an occasional performer, encouraged Travis to perform from an early age. In his teens Travis formed a band with brother Ricky (guitar) and David (bass). The band played locally but its activities were curtailed by Travis's juvenile delinquency. While on probation in 1977 he was discovered by Lib Hatcher, a club owner who gave him regular work. She financed his first recording, 'She's My Woman' (Paula, 1979), and *Randy Ray Live at the Nashville Palace* (1982) – Travis was using the name Ray then. That brought him to the attention of Warners, who after another name change issued the immaculate *Storms of Life* (1986). 'On the Other Hand' and 'Diggin' Up Bones', the former an internal debate about an extra-marital affair conducted with the typical brevity of a country songwriter ('on the other hand, there's a golden band'), and the latter an account of a solitary man going through the jewellery of a departed wife, neatly capture the traditional feel of the album. Both songs which featured decidedly unemphatic backings were country chart-toppers. They were followed by six further chart-toppers from *Always and Forever* (1987) and *Old 8x10* (1988). These included 'Forever and Forever, Amen' and 'Deeper Than the Holler'.

No Holding Back (1989) included a reworking of **Brook Benton**'s 'It's Just a Matter of Time' that presaged a widening of interests. That was confirmed later that year with the collection of Christmas songs *An Old Time Christmas* and *Heroes and Friends* (1990), on which he duetted with a series of guests including **Merle Haggard**, **Dolly Parton**, **Willie Nelson**, **George Jones** and, most surprisingly, **Roy Rogers** (with whom he sang 'Happy Trails'), **B. B. King** and film star Clint Eastwood. *High Lonesome* (1991) included a further pair of No. 1s, 'Hard Rock Bottom of Your Heart' and 'Forever Together', while in 1994 he released *This Is Me*, produced by Kyle Lehning.

Generally less successful in the nineties, in part because of greater competition from other would-be traditionalists, *Wind in the Wire* (1993) saw him exploring Western music, while 1996's *Full Circle* saw him broadening his range, looking backwards to honky tonk and forward to rock (Mark Knopfler's 'Are We in Trouble Now'). However, neither move was particularly successful commercially. He also appeared on *Come Together* (1995), a celebration of **The Beatles** by country artists, singing 'Nowhere Man'.

In 1997 Travis moved to Deamworks and contributed to the multi-artist album *Tribute to Tradition* (Columbia), singing 'Same Old Train' with **Merle Haggard**, **Ricky Skaggs** and **Emmylou Harris**, among others. *A Man Made out of Stone* (Dreamworks, 1999) saw Travis attempting a stripped-down version of his traditional stance with some success.

Greatest Hits Vols 1 and *2* (1992, 1994) collect together the important stages of his career to date.

CHARLES TRENET
b. 18 May 1913, Narbonne, France

One of the most imaginative French *chansonniers*, Trenet brought to his songs of precise recollection and observation – like **Van Morrison**'s his songs are scattered with the place names of his past – a painter's eye for detail and to his singing a cool microphone style that perfectly matched them.

In his teens he studied painting before opting for a career as a singer. Describing in his songs either an idealized past or a sunny present Trenet won immediate success in the provinces and after 1936, where his vitality and optimism caught the spirit of the times, in Paris. He quickly became hugely popular, especially after his first film, *La Route Enchantée* (1938), and sales of his records and sheet music were vast. Recordings from this period include the emphatic 'Je Chante' and 'Fleur Bleu' (Pathe-Marconi, 1937), 'Y'a d'La Jolie', 'Boum' and the surreal 'La Polka du Roi' (1938).

His biggest hit came after the war with the haunting 'La Mer' (1948). A description of local sea-side scenes from La Nouvelle and Argeles (both resorts near Narbonne) the song saw the sea as infinite and unchanging yet caring, a sight full of memories to offer succour. The song's majesty is further amplified by Trenet's relaxed, confident performance. It is, with 'La Jardin Extraordinaire' (1957), a description of a surreal garden where the ducks speak English and the statuary dances at night, the most representative of Trenet's songs. Later 'La Mer' would be frequently recorded by numerous artists. Among them were pianist Roger Williams, who had an instrumental hit with the song in 1956 and, as 'Beyond the Sea', **Bobby Darin** in 1960. Songs from the fifties include 'La Folle

Complainte' (1951), one of his few sad songs, 'Coin de Rue' (1954) and the autobiographical 'La Porte Du Garage' (1957). In the fifties Trenet frequently performed in one-man shows at the Olympia Music Hall in Paris. In the sixties he left Pathe for Barclay and then CBS. During this period he wrote several novels.

After the obligatory series of farewell tours at the end of the seventies Trenet was coaxed out of retirement in 1983 for a farewell tour of Canada, after which he returned to occasional performing, appearing in Paris in 1986. In 1992 he recorded an album for Atlantic. His story is told in *La Ballade de Charles Trenet* (1984) and *Charles Trenet* (1989).

A TRIBE CALLED QUEST
Q-Tip, b. Jonathan Davis, 20 November 1970, New York, USA; Ali Shaheed Muhammed, b. 11 August 1970, Brooklyn, New York; Phife, b. Malik Taylor, 10 April 1970, Brooklyn, New York

Consistently intelligent and tasteful New York rappers, the Tribe made some of the best, most accessible hip-hop of the 1990s, mixing light and heavy rhymes over their trademark laid-back jazz-laced beats.

The group formed while its members were still at school in New York, and released their début single, the Roy Ayers-sampled 'Description of a Fool', on Jive in 1989. The band were from the beginning part of New York's Native Tongues collective, Q-Tip appearing on 'Buddy' on **De La Soul**'s 1989 début LP. Tribe's own début album, *People's Instinctive Travels and the Paths of Rhythm*, arrived in 1990 in a rap world still getting its head around De La Soul's fresh, Afrocentric perspectives.

Travels was very much in the De La Soul vein, with greater emphasis on funky beats and jazz samples. The album produced three big hit singles, 'I Left My Wallet in El Segundo', 'Bonita Applebum' and 'Can I Kick It?', which was built around a sample from Lou Reed's 'Walk on the Wild Side'. The band's sense of humour was also evident in titles such as 'Pubic Enemy', an early B-side dealing with the perils of venereal disease. In addition, Q-Tip also enjoyed chart success with a guest appearance on **Deee-Lite**'s huge pop hit 'Groove Is in the Heart'.

Like De La Soul, Tribe's sophomore album, *The Low End Theory* (1991), was a harder, sparser affair, with a slightly more world-weary attitude discernible on cuts like 'Check the Rhime' and 'Showbusiness'. As the album's title suggested, a harder, bass-heavy sound was also in evidence, partly attributable to the contributions of veteran jazz bassist Ron Carter.

Midnight Marauders (1993) was preceded by the hit single 'Award Tour', and maintained the harder, still heavily jazz-driven sound of its predecessor. The band toured heavily in 1994, and spent a quiet 1995 before

issuing *Beats, Rhymes and Life* (1996), which débuted at No. 1 on the US album charts. Perhaps the Tribe's most expansive and complete recording, the album mixed rapping and soul vocals from Faith Evans on the hit 'Stressed Out', and saw a return to the richer use of samples that had characterized their début.

Q-Tip made another guest appearance on **Masters at Work**'s Nu Yorican Soul project in 1997, before the release of the Tribe's fifth album, *The Love Movement*, in 1998. This met with a more subdued critical and commercial response, and while touring in support of the album the band decided to split up.

The former members were not slow to embark on new projects. In 1999 Q-Tip released his solo album, *Amplified* (Arista), which included the hits 'Breathe and Stop' and 'Vivrant Thing'. Ali Shaheed, meanwhile, teamed up with former En Vogue singer Dawn Robinson and ex-Tony Toni Tone vocalist Raphael Saadiq to form a new R&B band, Lucy Pearl, whose eponymous début album was released on Virgin in 2000, preceded by the single 'Dance Tonight'.

TRAVIS TRITT
b. 9 February 1963, Marietta, Georgia, USA

One of the most potent songwriters in the new generation of country musicians, Tritt's songs confirm his oft-stated belief that 'country music is the soundtrack to the lives of working people'.

He was a soloist in the children's choir of his local church and learned the guitar at the age of eight. His first efforts at songwriting were influenced by such composers as **John Denver** and **James Taylor**. After school, Tritt worked in the trucking business but devoted himself full-time to music from the mid-eighties, singing his own songs as a solo guitarist. Signed by Warner, his first album, *Country Club* (1990), included the No. 1 hit 'Help Me Hold on', 'I'm Gonna Be Somebody' and 'Drift Off to Dream'.

Mixing country, rock and bluegrass elements, *It's All about to Change* appeared the following year. **Little Feat** played on 'Bible Belt', a song about television evangelists, while the agonies of divorce were the subject of 'Here's a Quarter, Call Someone Who Cares', and Tritt sang bluegrass harmonies with Marty Stuart on Stuart's 'The Whiskey Ain't Working'. The next album was *T-R-O-U-B-L-E* (1992), the title song being a cover of an **Elvis Presley** song. The album also included a version of **Buddy Guy**'s 'Leave My Girl Alone'.

Gregg Brown produced *Ten Feet Tall and Bulletproof* (1994), a Top Twenty pop hit which produced the hit country singles 'Foolish Pride' and 'Can I Fool You with My Heart?'. Tritt also published an autobiography with the same name as the album. *Restless Kind*, co-produced with **Don Was**, was perhaps his

grittiest album ever, alternatively poking fun and celebrating the outlaw image he had embraced.

Greatest Hits (1995) is just that. In 1997 he con-
tributed to the multi-artist album Tribute to Tradition
(Columbia), singing 'Same Old Train' with **Merle
Haggard**, **Ricky Skaggs**, **Randy Travis** and **Emmylou
Harris**, among others.

THE TROGGS

Ronnie Bond, b. Ronald Bullis, 4 May 1943, Andover,
Hampshire, England, d. 13 November 1992, Winchester
(replaced by Tony Murray, replaced by Dave Maggs);
Chris Britton, b. 21 January 1945, Watford (replaced by
Richard Moore); Peter Staples, b. 3 May 1944, Andover
(replaced by Peter Lucas); Reg Presley, b. Reginald Ball,
12 June 1943, Andover

The Troggs found great success in the mid-sixties
through the unlikely combination of Presley's moody,
almost spoken, vocals and a simple but emphatic beat
backing that was occasionally lightened by an ocarina.
Though their most influential recording was **Chip
Taylor**'s 'Wild Thing'* (1966), Presley wrote most of
their hits, including 'With a Girl Like You'* (1966)
and the softer 'Love Is All Around'* (1967). Nonetheless, the group were unable to develop beyond either
the beat-boom sound or the rustic image with which
they started. Within a couple of years of their international hits, they had retreated to the cabaret circuit.

Formed in Andover in 1965 as the Troglodytes, the
group were signed to CBS by manager Larry Page for
'Lost Girl' (1966). 'Wild Thing' (Fontana) brought
them international success and won them the odd
claim to fame as the only group to top the American
charts with a disc that was simultaneously released on
two labels, Atlantic and Fontana. Later **Jimi Hendrix**
regularly featured 'Wild Thing' in his stage act. Less
sophisticated in their suggestive sexuality than **Dave
Dee, Dozy, Beaky, Mick and Tich**, the Troggs' appeal
rested on the harmony between the naïvety of Presley's singing (and lyrics) and the group's sound.
Among their hits were 'I Can't Control Myself'
(1966), the first release on Page One Records, the label
formed by their manager and **Dick James**, which was
banned in several countries, 'Anyway That You Want
Me' (1966) and 'Give It to Me' (1967). There was a
hint of the drug culture in the equally successful
'Night of the Long Grass' (1967).

In 1968 the group left Page and toured Europe,
recording for Hansa (Hip Hip Hooray), and in 1969
bass-player Tony Murray replaced Staples. Regulars
on the cabaret circuit, they returned to recording after
a bootleg tape of the group in the studio that revealed
Presley's limited foul-mouthed vocabulary and the
group's musical incompetence won them renewed
cult fame. For Page's Penny Farthing label they

attempted a version of the **Beach Boys**' 'Good Vibrations' but their best work from this period was the
live recording The Troggs: Live at Max's Kansas City
(Basement, 1980), which mixed new and old material,
and Black Bottom (New Rose, 1981), which was
recorded in Europe. The group continued to tour
throughout the eighties, regularly appearing at sixties
revival concerts.

The band's material had been popular with punk
and new wave bands on both sides of the Atlantic in
the late seventies (the **Buzzcocks** had covered 'I Can't
Control Myself', ex-**Television** bassist Richard Hell 'I
Can Only Give You Everything' and LA band X 'Wild
Thing'). In the eighties **R.E.M.** were among the bands
who frequently played Troggs songs in their live set.
In 1991 the Troggs, now consisting of Presley, Britton,
Lucas and Maggs, recorded tracks with members of
R.E.M. in Athens, Georgia. The result was the minor
Athens Andover (1992). In 1994 Scottish band **Wet
Wet Wet** had an international hit with a version of
'Love Is All Around' from the soundtrack of the film
Four Weddings and a Funeral.

DORIS TROY
b. Doris Payne, 1937, New York, USA

A songwriter and session singer, Troy is best remembered for her composition 'Just One Look', an American hit for her in 1963, a British hit for the **Hollies** in
1965 and for Faith, Hope and Charity (RCA) in 1976.

The daughter of a baptist preacher, Troy sang
gospel in her teens before joining the Halos jazz trio.
In 1960 she wrote Dee Clark's hit 'How About That'
(Abner) and in 1962 joined Atlantic. Her staccato
handling of 'Just One Look' gave her her only American pop hit and 'Whatcha Gonna Do About It' (1964)
her only British success. After brief stays with Capitol
and Calla in 1969, she settled in Britain where she
worked as a session singer, most notably on **Pink
Floyd**'s Dark Side of the Moon. Troy later recorded for
Apple, People and Polydor (Stretching Out, 1976).
During the eighties she appeared in the off-Broadway
musical Mamma I Want to Sing, which was presented
in London in 1995 with **Chaka Khan** as co-star.

ERNEST TUBB
b. 9 February 1914, Crisp, Texas, USA, d. 6 September
1984, Nashville, Tennessee

Though inspired by **Jimmie Rodgers**, Ernest Tubb
spent fifty years in country music supported by a different musical inheritance – that of the Texas honky-
tonk sound exemplified in his 'Walkin' the Floor over
You'* (1941). A performer of character and grit, he
was held in high regard for his sincerity, generosity
and commitment to country-music's values.

He began his career on KONO, San Antonio, Texas (1934–5), later working on stations in San Angelo and Fort Worth, where he was the 'Gold Chain Troubadour' for a local flour company, before joining the *Grand Ole Opry* in 1943. (He remained a cast member until his death.) Early Rodgers-styled recordings for Bluebird were unsuccessful, but on switching in 1940 to Decca, he crystallized his drawling, slightly off-key singing style and had success with 'Blue-Eyed Elaine' and other sides that featured the electric guitar of Fay 'Fatty' Smith, Eddie Tudor, Jimmie Short and, later, Billy Byrd.

In the late forties and early fifties he was among the most successful and influential artists in country music, enjoying many chart hits and touring continuously with his Texas Troubadours. Key recordings from this period include 'Blue Christmas', 'Letters Have No Arms' and 'I Ain't Going Honky Tonkin'' Anymore'. He also recorded with the **Andrews Sisters** and made several movie appearances, among them *Ridin' West* (1942), *Jamboree* (1944) and *Hollywood Barn Dance* (1947), all B-pictures. In 1947 he opened what would become one of Nashville's most famous landmarks, the Ernest Tubb Record Shop on Broadway, close to the then home of the *Opry* in the Ryman Auditorium. It was from the shop that he broadcast his WSM *Midnight Jamboree* show every Saturday night after the *Opry*. In later years the show went out from the Number 2 store near Opryland.

Tubb maintained his gruelling performance schedule for much of the sixties and seventies, though latterly troubled by illness. He also helped the careers of many other artists, including **Hank Snow**, **Hank Williams**, **Patsy Cline**, **Loretta Lynn** and **Willie Nelson**. Some of his most notable recordings in these years were 'Thanks a Lot' (1963), 'Mr and Mrs Used to Be' with Lynn (1964), and the enduring 'Waltz Across Texas', a hit in 1965, the year he was voted into the Country Music Hall of Fame. A tribute album to celebrate his sixty-fifth birthday, *The Legend and the Legacy* (Cachet, 1979), included contributions by Nelson, Lynn, **Merle Haggard**, **George Jones**, and many others.

Tubb's eldest son Justin (*b. 20 August 1935, San Antonio, Texas*) had a moderately successful career as a country singer and composer from the early fifties, joining the *Opry* in 1955 and recording for Decca (1953–9), Starday (1960–2), RCA (1962–7) and Paramount. His most successful song was 'Lonesome 7–7203' (1963) for **Hawkshaw Hawkins**. Where Ernest had earlier campaigned to rid country music of its demeaning 'hillbilly' tag, Justin was as fierce an opponent of progressive country music, which he believed was driving more traditional styles off the air, and took up with obvious enthusiasm the late-seventies flag-waver 'What's Wrong with the Way We're Doing It Now?'.

Walking the Floor over You (Bear Family, 1996) is the definitive career retrospective.

ORRIN TUCKER
b. 17 February 1911, St Louis, Missouri, USA

Bandleader Tucker is best remembered for 'Oh Johnny, Oh'* (1939), the revival of a First World War song much enlivened by vocalist Bonnie Baker's risqué squeals and sighs.

A staid dance-band leader, Tucker had little record success until Baker joined him as vocalist. They followed 'Johnny' (Columbia), which had been composed in 1917 by Ed Rose and Abe Olman, with the similarly styled 'Stop! It's Wonderful' (1939) and 'Pinch Me' (1940). After Baker left, Tucker, who composed much of the band's material and occasionally sang himself ('Apple Blossoms and Chapel Bells', 1940; 'Dear Mom', 1942), replaced her with first Scotte Marsh and later Helen Lee. His later bands were musically far better but commercially less successful. After the demise of the big-band era at the end of the forties, Tucker fronted several smaller groups for nightclub residencies and appeared occasionally on television.

SOPHIE TUCKER
b. Sonia Kalish, 13 January 1884, Russia, d. 9 February 1966, New York, USA

Known as 'The Last of the Red Hot Mamas', as much for her brassy, flamboyant image as for her robust, raucous singing style, Tucker was the first white woman to record **W. C. Handy**'s 'St Louis Blues' and one of the biggest recording stars of the vaudeville era.

Born while her family was *en route* from Russia to America, Tucker grew up in Boston under the name of Abuza and first sang in public in 1905 in her father's restaurant. Under her married name of Tucker she went to New York in 1906 where she began her career singing in blackface at the Old Music Hall. Originally billed as a 'coon shouter', she had dispensed with burned cork and was calling herself a ragtime singer by the time of her first appearance in the *Ziegfeld Follies* (in 1909) and her first (cylinder) recordings for Edison in 1910 ('That Loving Rag'). In 1911 she recorded her first version of Shelton Brooks' 'Some of These Days', which with the same writer's 'Darktown Strutters Ball' was one of the numbers most closely associated with her. Tucker's 1927 Columbia recording of 'Days', backed by the **Ted Lewis** band, eventually sold over a million copies.

Tucker's association with ragtime continued throughout the twenties and included such recordings as **Irving Berlin**'s 'International Rag', and 'Bugle

Call Rag' (1927). Following the demise of vaudeville in the thirties she turned to cabaret and a series of undistinguished films, including *Honky Tonk* (1929) and *Broadway Melody of 1938* (1937).

While she had a further million-seller with 'My Yiddishe Momme' (Columbia, 1928), on which she was supported by Ted Shapiro, her regular accompanist for some forty-six years, Tucker was at her best in live performance. For over thirty years, she criss-crossed America and regularly visited Europe, singing the songs associated with her and, increasingly in the later years, offering semi-spoken humorous homilies about life in general ('Life Begins at Forty', 'You Can't Sew a Button on a Heart', 'Make It Legal, Mr Segal').

TANYA TUCKER
b. Tanya Denise Tucker, 10 October 1958, Seminole, Texas, USA

A fiery-voiced country singer, Tanya Tucker recorded her first hits as a fourteen-year old. She later briefly deserted country music for the rock market with little success.

Tucker grew up in Phoenix, Arizona, and by the age of nine was singing at local fairs. In 1971 she had a small part in the film *Jeremiah Johnson* and a year later **Billy Sherrill** signed her to Columbia. Her version of Alex Harvey's 'Delta Dawn' was the first in a series of country hits produced by Sherrill. They included 'What's Your Mama's Name?', 'Blood Red and Going Down' (1973) and the controversial 'Would You Lay with Me in a Field of Stone' (1974), which topped the country charts and confirmed Tucker's image as a country Lolita.

The following year, Tucker moved to MCA, scoring her only pop hit with 'Lizzie and the Rainman'. With **Tommy 'Snuff' Garrett** as producer, her country successes included 'You've Got to Hold on to Me' (1976), 'It's a Cowboy Lovin' Night' and 'Texas (When I Die)' (1978). With *TNT* (1978) and *Tear Me Apart* (produced by Mike Chapman of **Chinn and Chapman**), Tucker presented herself as a raunchy rock artist, recording things like **Buddy Holly**'s 'Not Fade Away', but the albums sold poorly.

She retained her country following, however, recording duets with her then beau **Glen Campbell** and reaching the country Top Ten with 'Pecos Promenade' (which was featured in the film *Smokey and the Bandit*, 1980) and 'I Feel Right' (Arista, 1982). Jerry Crutchfield took over as producer for *Girls Like Me* (Capitol, 1986), which contained four country Top Ten hits, including 'I'll Come Back as Another Woman' and 'It's Only Over for You'. Tucker maintained her hold over country-music audiences with *Love Me Like You Used to* (1987) and *Strong Enough to Bend* (1988). In 1988 she entered a clinic to be treated

for alcohol and drug addiction, and she did not record again until 1990, when she returned with *Tennessee Woman*. This was followed by *What Do I Do About Me* (1991), *Lizzie & the Rainman* and *Can't Hide from Yourself* (1992). In 1993 she was among the artists paying tribute to the **Eagles** on the album *Common Thread* (Giant) and the following year duetted with **Little Richard** on the various artists set *Rhythm, Country & Blues* (MCA).

Tucker's later albums included the minor but best-selling *Soon* (1993) and *Complicated* (1997). Her hits are collected together on *Boxed Set* (1994).

IKE TURNER
b. Ikear Luster Turner, 5 November 1931, Clarksdale, Mississippi, USA

Though later overshadowed by the success of his wife **Tina Turner**, Ike was an important R&B talent scout in the fifties and his recording of 'Rocket "88"' (1951) is generally considered to be one of the first rock'n'roll recordings.

Turner learned piano from blues musician Pinetop Perkins and by 1945 was working as a disc-jockey on WROX. With schoolfriends he formed the Kings of Rhythm, who recorded 'Rocket "88"' for **Sam Phillips**' Memphis studio. Released on Chess under singer Jackie Brenston's name, it was an R&B hit in 1951 and was covered by **Bill Haley** later that year.

Turner himself became a talent scout for both Phillips and the **Bihari Brothers**, who owned Modern Records. Among those whose early records he produced were **Howlin' Wolf**, **B. B. King** and **Elmore James**. Turner's own records were often released under such pseudonyms as Lover Boy and he recorded with his first wife Bonnie as Ike and Bonnie ('Way Down in the Congo', Sun, 1953).

In 1955 Turner moved north to St Louis, signing his new Kings of Rhythm to **Syd Nathan**'s Federal label. He continued to record and produce prolifically for such labels as Joyce, Stevens, Artistic, Cobra and Planet and in 1957 met Annie Bullock (the future Tina Turner), who made her first records as Little Ann.

After her marriage to Ike, Tina recorded the duet 'A Fool in Love' (Sue, 1960), a pop hit, and the slow blues ballad with Ike's mesmeric guitar riff, 'It's Gonna Work out Fine' (1961) – on which she duetted with **Mickey Baker** – reached the Top Twenty. After further success with 'I Idolize You' and 'Poor Fool' (1962), the couple moved to Los Angeles, where Ike set up a series of labels including Prann, Sony, Innis and Teena. Throughout the early sixties the Ike and Tina Turner Revue toured constantly, with backing singers the Ikettes who included P. P. Arnold, Bonnie Bramlett and Claudia Lennear.

Ike and Tina continued to record for Loma (the

gospel-styled 'I Can't Believe What You Say', 1964) and the Biharis' Kent label but had no further chart success until **Phil Spector** produced 'River Deep Mountain High' (1966) on which Tina's powerful voice soared against the orchestral backing. The record was a big British hit where a cover of the **Holland, Dozier and Holland** song 'A Love Like Yours' also reached the Top Twenty. The couple toured with the **Rolling Stones** in 1969.

After making *The Hunter* (Blue Thumb, 1969) and *Her Man, His Woman* (Capitol, 1970), the couple signed to United Artists in 1971, reworking pop material like **The Beatles**' 'Come Together' (1969) and 'Get Back' (1970) and **Creedence Clearwater Revival**'s 'Proud Mary'* (1971). Tina's 'Nutbush City Limits' (1973) was their last hit together before Ike's drugs problems contributed to a decline in the couple's output.

In 1975 they separated, with Ike Turner recording the solo album *I'm Tore Up* (1978) in his Bolic studio, which was destroyed by fire in 1982. Another solo album, *My Confessions*, appeared in 1988, but in 1990 Ike's continuing drugs problems led to him being imprisoned for eighteen months. On his release in 1991 he returned to performing with a re-formed the Ikettes comprising Janette Bazell, Marcia Thomas and Tina lookalike Barbara Cole.

Proud Mary: The Best of Ike & Turner (EMI, 1991) is the definitive career retrospective.

JOE TURNER

b. 18 May 1911, Kansas City, Missouri, USA, d. 23 November 1985, Inglewood, California

The original and greatest 'blues-shouter', Turner did much to create the jazz-blues singing style in which the voice is used less to narrate than to contribute a quasi-instrumental melody strand to the orchestral texture. Many of the songs for which he was known were celebratory routines, little more interesting as texts than a football-crowd chant, but he conveyed in them the air of a joyously partying musician jamming endlessly on blues changes, his intonation and sense of time almost always flawless. This spirit, attached to more pointed lyrics, made him one of the few R&B figures of the fifties to succeed with the white audience for early rock'n'roll.

A Kansas City bartender in his youth, he sang with local bands led by Bennie Moten, Andy Kirk and **Count Basie**, but it was his partnership with the pianist **Pete Johnson** that made him nationally famous in the late thirties and throughout the forties, especially after their appearances at the 1938–9 'Spirituals to Swing' concerts at New York's Carnegie Hall. Turner recorded for Vocalion with Johnson, for Decca with Johnson, **Art Tatum** or pianist Sammy

Price, then for National (1945–7), Aladdin (1949), Imperial (1950) and other labels before signing in 1951 with Atlantic, for whom he had an immediate hit with 'Chains of Love'. 'Honey Hush' (1952, cut in New Orleans with **Fats Domino** on piano) also charted, but Turner's biggest rock'n'roll record was 'Shake Rattle and Roll' (1954), later covered in a muted version by **Bill Haley**. This chart status landed him a place on national touring packages organized by **Alan Freed**. He had lesser hits with 'Flip, Flop and Fly' (1955) and a version of the traditional blues 'Corrine, Corrina' (1956). He also confirmed his status as a blues-singer with *Boss of the Blues* (Atlantic, 1956), an album with jazz sidemen like Johnson and Pete Brown (alto) that has come to be regarded as a classic of its genre. He appeared at the Newport Jazz Festival in 1958, then visited Europe with Johnson in a 'Jazz at the Philharmonic' tour.

In the sixties Turner was based in New Orleans. He revisited Europe in 1965 to tour with **Humphrey Lyttelton**, in 1966 with the American Folk Blues Festival and several times in the seventies. By then his work at home was chiefly at jazz and blues festivals and in the studio for **Norman Granz**'s Pablo label, on which he cut albums with Basie groups, blues-bands or collections of star instrumentalists; also, on one occasion, with **Jimmy Witherspoon**. Though troubled by illness he spent his last years in only fitful retirement, and months before his death was working in public with Witherspoon.

TINA TURNER

b. Annie Mae Bullock, 26 November 1938, Brownsville, Tennessee, USA

Following a successful partnership with her ex-husband **Ike Turner**, Tina Turner became one of the most dynamic and spectacular performers of the eighties and nineties.

After separating from Ike Turner in 1975, she appeared as the Acid Queen in Ken Russell's film of **The Who**'s *Tommy*. She recorded the unsuccessful *Acid Queen* (United Artists, 1975) and *Rough* (1979). Apparently condemned to the oldies circuit, she found her career revived when she did guest vocals on **Norman Whitfield**'s 'Ball of Confusion' for **Heaven 17** in 1982.

The group's Martin Ware and Greg Walsh produced Turner's version of **Al Green**'s 'Let's Stay Together'* (Capitol, 1983), which became a big international hit. Turner then recorded *Private Dancer** (1984). The album included revivals of **Ann Peebles**' 'I Can't Stand the Rain' and **The Beatles**' 'Help', and new songs by **Dire Straits**' Mark Knopfler and **David Bowie**, and provided her with three hits: 'What's Love Got to Do with It' (by Terry Britton and Graham

Lyle, formerly of **Gallagher and Lyle**), 'Better Be Good to Me', and Knopfler's title track. The album eventually sold over ten million copies.

Her success continued with 'We Don't Need Another Hero' (1985), which was featured on the soundtrack of *Mad Max Beyond Thunderdome*, a film in which she also appeared. In the same year she undertook a world tour, supported by **Bryan Adams**, who duetted on the hit 'It's Only Love'.

After the American success of 'One of the Living' (1985), Turner released the multi-million-selling *Break Every Rule* (1986), produced by Britten and Rupert Hine. To promote the album she undertook a fourteen-month world tour involving 230 concerts with a backing group which included James Ralston (guitar), Jack Bruno (drums), Bob Feit (bass) and pianist/singer John Miles, whose British hits had included 'Music' (Decca, 1976).

The album had guest appearances from **Phil Collins** and **Steve Winwood** and it included the pop hits 'Typical Male', 'Two People' (1987) and 'What You Get Is What You See'. In 1988 she released *Live in Europe* and had a further international hit with **Robert Palmer**'s 'Addicted to Love'. The next year Turner recorded *Foreign Affair* with its Top Ten singles 'The Best' and 'I Don't Wanna Lose You'.

Turner spent much of 1990 on the road, playing to over three million people and cementing her superstar status. The singles collection *Simply the Best* followed in 1991. She announced her retirement from touring in 1992, and the following year released *What's Love Got to Do with It?*, the soundtrack to the successful biopic of the same name. The film was based on Tina's 1986 book, *I Tina*, while the album contained reworkings of material originally recorded with Ike and three new songs. A new live version of 'Sweet Mary' was released as a single in 1994. It was followed by the studio album *Wildest Dreams* (1996), the first in seven years, and *Twenty Four Seven* (1999), a collection of superior pop songs, which she again toured in support of.

The three-CD set *The Collected Recordings* (1995) documents her solo career.

THE TURTLES

Howard Kaylan, b. Howard Lawrence Kaplan, 22 June 1945, New York, USA; Mark Volman, b. 19 April 1944, Los Angeles, California; Al Nichol, b. 31 March 1945, Los Angeles; Chuck Portz, b. 28 March 1945, Los Angeles; Donald Ray Murray, b. 8 November 1945, Los Angeles

Initially a surf group, the Turtles managed to adjust to the fashions of the sixties, moving from the folk-rock of **Bob Dylan**'s 'It Ain't Me Babe' (1965) to the wistful romanticism of 'Happy Together'* (1967). What distinguished them from other groups of the period was their detached, irreverent view of the world of pop. Thus 'Elenore', from *The Turtles Present the Battle of the Bands* (1968), found the group impersonating a variety of bands to hilarious effect. A deft putdown of 'moon and june' love songs, 'Elenore' includes the line 'You're my pride and joy, etcetera'. Volman's and Kaylan's wit and humour was even more in evidence during their later career as the Phlorescent Leech and Eddie (later abbreviated to Flo and Eddie).

As the Crossfires, they were one of the numerous surf groups in the Los Angeles area in the early sixties. Following the failure of early records 'Fiberglass Jungle' (Capco, 1963), 'Santa and the Sidewalk Surfer' and 'One Potato, Two Potato' (Lucky Token, 1964), they changed their name to the Crosswind Singers and their repertoire to folk. Signed to White Whale in 1965 and renamed the Turtles, they had an immediate hit with their calculated version of 'It Ain't Me Babe'. Far better was the follow-up, **P. F. Sloan**'s tale of adolescent *angst* 'Let Me Be' (1966), before the group deserted protest for the good-time sounds of 'You Baby' (1966), another Sloan composition. 1967 brought their biggest hits, both written by Gary Bonner and Alan Gordon: the wistful 'Happy Together' and the jaunty 'She'd Rather Be with Me'*. In 1968 the group started to produce their own records with the satiric *Battle of the Bands*, in which they impersonated such archetypal groups as the Fabulous Dawgs, the Atomic Enchilada and Nature's Children. Equally interesting but less commercially successful, mostly because it lacked the gloss of their earlier work, was *Turtle Soup* (1969), produced by Ray Davies of the **Kinks**, an important influence on the group. The Turtles' last major hit was 'You Showed Me' (1969), written by Roger McGuinn and Gene Clark of the **Byrds**, another major influence.

In 1970 the group broke up and Volman and Kaylan joined **Frank Zappa** as the Phlorescent Leech and Eddie and had prominent roles in *Live at the Fillmore* (1971) and the film and album *200 Motels* (1972), which also featured **Ringo Starr** and **Theodore Bikel**. After leaving Zappa, the pair released a series of albums on which they combined mainstream songs with send-ups of rock's excesses. These included *Flo and Eddie* (Columbia, 1973), *Moving Targets* (1976) and the reggae-styled *Rock Steady with Flo & Eddie* (1981). They also sang back-up vocals for acts as varied as **Marc Bolan**, **Bruce Springsteen** ('Hungry Heart', 1980), **Blondie** and the reunited **Jefferson Airplane** (1989). Having acquired the rights to the name, the duo toured as the Turtles in the late eighties and early nineties on the American oldies circuit.

As well as their records, Volman and Kaylan wrote record columns in various music publications, hosted a talk show and served as genial commentators on the excesses of contemporary rock.

While *Happy Together* (1975) remains the definitive retrospective, in the eighties Rhino issued many rarities, including *Wooden Head* (1982) and *Shell Shock* (1987), all with extensive notes by Volman and Kaylan.

SHANIA TWAIN
b. 28 August 1965, Timmins, Ontario, Canada

Emerging in the mid-nineties with *The Woman in Me*, Twain become the most popular country-music performer since **Garth Brooks**, using seductive music video images to achieve international stardom.

Twain began performing in local clubs and bars in Ontario, Canada, as a child before the death of her parents in a car crash in 1986 forced her to take responsibility for her four younger brothers. Regaining her independence in the early nineties, Twain signed to Mercury and recorded her eponymous début album in 1993. It achieved modest success in the US and across Europe upon its release in 1993, spawning a pair of minor hit singles, 'What Made You Say That' and 'Dance with the One that Brought You'. Subsequently, Twain married producer Robert 'Mutt' Lange, best known for his work with **Def Leppard** and **AC/DC**, and began work on her second album.

The Woman in Me (1995) was a marked change in direction, clearly influenced by the heavy-rock production methods of Twain's new husband. The album spawned three US No. 1 singles, 'Any Man of Mine', 'No One Needs to Know' and '(If You're Not in it for Love) I'm Outta Here!', and achieved worldwide sales of over nine million copies. Twain repeated the feat with *Come on Over*. Released to positive reviews at the end of 1997, it included her biggest hit outside the US to date, 'That Don't Impress Me Much' (1999), and saw her dominate the European charts with its mix of raunch and sentimentality, with a veneer of hard rock.

CONWAY TWITTY
b. Harold Lloyd Jenkins, 1 September 1933, Friars Point, Mississippi, USA, d. 5 June 1993

Unlike **Carl Perkins**, who was at his best singing rockabilly, rock'n'roll was only a phase in Twitty's career. Thus, though he turned from country music to rock'n'roll under the influence of **Elvis Presley**, his hits, which included the melodramatic 'It's Only Make Believe'* (1958), were beat ballads and were sung in a similar style to the hits that made him one of the biggest country stars of the seventies and eighties.

The son of a riverboat pilot, Jenkins formed a country band, the Phillips County Ramblers, in his teens. On his discharge from the army in 1955, under the influence of Presley, he broadened the band's repertoire, retitled it the Rockhousers, took the name Conway Twitty and, like so many Southern hopefuls, auditioned unsuccessfully for **Sam Phillips**. Signed to Mercury, Twitty recorded in the style of Presley ('I Need Your Lovin'', 1957) but only achieved success after switching to MGM in 1958.

'It's Only Make Believe', co-written with drummer Jack Nance, set the singer's intense, mournful style and initiated a series of hits, including 'The Story of My Love', 'Mona Lisa' (1959), a revival of the **Nat 'King' Cole** 1950 hit which was also successful in 1959 for Carl Mann (Philips), and a new version of the 1913 composition 'Danny Boy' (1959). That was followed by 'Lonely Boy Blue'* (1960), a song written for the Presley film *King Creole* (1958) as 'Danny', and one of **Dan Penn**'s earliest compositions, 'Is a Bluebird Blue?' (1960), before Twitty, by now a veteran of quickie rock'n'roll movies (*Platinum High School*, *Sex Kittens Go to College*, 1960) headed for the cabaret market. Initially successful with 'C'Est Si Bon' (1961), his career soon floundered and he moved to ABC and then Decca in 1965 where, with **Owen Bradley** producing, he returned to country-styled material.

In 1966 Twitty had his first country hit, 'Guess My Eyes Were Bigger Than My Heart', and in 1968 his first No. 1, 'Next in Line'. This was followed by some forty country No. 1s, including 'To See My Angel Cry' (1969), 'Fifteen Years Ago' (1970), 'She Needs Someone to Hold Her' (1972), 'You've Never Been This Far Before' (1973, also a pop hit), 'There's a Honky Tonk Angel' (1974), 'Happy Birthday Darlin'' (1979) and 'Rest Your Love on Me' (1980). Twitty also regularly recorded duets with **Loretta Lynn**, including a trio of No. 1s, 'After the Feeling Is Gone' (1971), 'Louisiana Woman, Mississippi Man' (1973) and 'As Soon as I Hang up the Phone' (1974). On all these songs Twitty's voice fell midway between the expressiveness of a **Merle Haggard** and the warmth of a **Kenny Rogers**, but unlike so many of his contemporaries he never sought crossover success. Instead he preferred to market himself exclusively to the country audience, as in the Twitty City theme park he established on the outskirts of Nashville in 1982, the year he left Decca/MCA for Elektra.

Two years later Twitty moved to Warners where among his hits were a duet with his daughter Joni Lee, 'I Don't Know About Love (The Moon Song)' (1984), and 'Falling for You for Years' (1987). By 1989 Twitty was back with MCA. *Home on Old Lonesome Road* (1989) and *Crazy in Love* (1990) saw him teamed with the new breed of Nashville sessionmen to good effect. His final recording was a duet with Sam Moore (of **Sam and Dave**) on the album *Rhythm, Country and Blues*.

2 LIVE CREW
David Mr Mix Hobbs; Chris Fresh Kid-Ice Won Wong; Brother Marquis Ross; Luther Campbell

2 Live Crew was an unremarkable Miami-based rap team who gained international notoriety when their 1990 album *As Nasty as They Wanna Be* was declared obscene by a Florida judge. The group subsequently traded successfully for a while on their reputation for sexually explicit lyrics.

Formed in 1985 as a relatively unadventurous proponent of the Miami dance sound pioneered by the likes of **KC and the Sunshine Band**, the group released *2 Live Crew Is What We Are* (1986) and *Move Somethin'* (1988), which included copious rapping and sampling, before the arrival of writer and producer Campbell. In the manner of **Prince Buster**, and while borrowing the name Luke Skyywalker from *Star Wars* (1977), Campbell provided such tracks as 'Me So Horny', a Top Forty hit in the US, 'We Want Some Pussy' and 'Dick Almighty' for *As Nasty as They Wanna Be*, which ultimately met with an obscenity ruling in a Florida court. The band's case was supported by a number of free-speech advocates, and Campbell recorded a solo album, *Banned in the USA*, The title track, based on **Bruce Springsteen**'s *Born in the USA*, was a Top Twenty hit. The band then followed up with *As Clean as They Wanna Be*, which drew fresh legal controversy in the shape of a lawsuit from the publishers of **Roy Orbison**'s 'Pretty Woman', to which Campbell had added predictably obscene lyrics. The case eventually reached the US Supreme Court, which ruled in 2 Live Crew's favour.

The arrival of US west coast gangsta rap in the 1990s quickly left the band looking more obsolete than obscene. This view was reinforced by the two 1991 concert recordings, *Sports Weekend (As Nasty as They Wanna Be Part II)* and *Sports Weekend (As Clean as They Wanna Be Part II)*. On these albums the audience joined in good-naturedly, completing the group's rhymes. Campbell later released *Luke in the Nude* (1993).

2 UNLIMITED
Anita Doth, b. 28 December 1971, Amsterdam, The Netherlands (replaced by Marjon van Iwaarden, b. 18 June 1974, Kruiningen); Ray Slijngaard, b. 28 June 1971, Amsterdam (replaced by Romy van Ooijen, b. 18 November 1971, Amsterdam)

A Dutch techno-pop outfit, 2 Unlimited, who achieved over 18 million sales in the nineties, are best remembered for the hit single 'No Limits' (1993).

Eurodance producers Phil Wilde and Jean-Paul DeCoster began the 2 Unlimited project in 1990, soon recruiting Slijngaard and Doth to add their voices to the single 'Get Ready for This' (1991), which immediately became a European hit. *Get Ready* (1992) achieved global sales of three million, while a version of the title track became the group's only Top Forty hit in the US after being used at sporting events. *No Limits* (1993) topped album charts across Europe, while the single 'No Limits' was an international number one. 'Faces', 'Let the Beat Control Your Body' and 'Maximum Overdrive' were all highly successful in the UK. *Real Things* (1994) was equally successful, earning gold status on the day of its release in Britain and spawning further hit singles in 'No One', 'Here I Go' and 'Nothing Like the Rain'.

After issuing the compilation volume *Hits Unlimited* (1995), Slijngaard quit the group to maintain his X-Ray label, while Doth pursued a career in TV and radio. Wilde and DeCoster announced plans to revive 2 Unlimited in 1998 with two new singers. Van Ooijen and van Iwaarden fronted the singles 'Wanna Get Up', 'Edge of Heaven' and 'Never Surrender', and released an album, *II* (1998), but failed to match the success of the earlier incarnation of the group.

2PAC SHAKUR
b. Tupac Amaru Shakur, 16 June 1971, New York City, USA, d. 13 September 1996, New York City

Briefly one of the nineties most popular and controversial rap stars, Tupac (or 2Pac) Shakur mixed successful gangsta rap recordings with film work.

Raised in the Bronx and Harlem districts of New York, then Baltimore, before moving to Marin City, California, Shakur's mother encouraged his interest in theatre, briefly enrolling him in the Baltimore School of the Performing Arts. Shakur left home in 1988 when the family moved to California, and formed a group, Strictly Dope, with a friend, Ray Luv. His real introduction to rap came through Digital Underground, with whom he toured and recorded for a short time in 1990.

In November 1991 he released his début, *2Pacalypse Now* (Interscope), which promptly achieved gold status in the US. Shakur also made his film début a few months later with a role in Ernest Dickerson's *Juice*. Then his music was cited as a factor in the shooting of a Texas state trooper. The suspect had a tape of *2Pacalypse Now* in his car at the time of the shooting. Henceforth, controversy became a central element of his career. Later the same year a six-year-old child died following a fight involving Shakur, although charges against the rapper over the incident were later dismissed.

Strictly for My N.I.G.G.A.Z. was released in February 1993, and contained the crossover hit 'I Get Around'. The album went platinum in the US, and later that year Shakur resumed his film career opposite Janet Jackson in *Poetic Justice*.

In November 1993 Shakur was charged over the alleged sexual assault of a nineteen-year-old fan, but before his trial began he completed another film role in *Above the Rim*. At trial in November 1994 Shakur was convicted of sexual assault and given a sentence of between eighteen months and four-and-a-half years. But a day after his conviction he was shot in New York, an attack Shakur later linked to east coast rap stars **Notorious B.I.G.** and **Sean 'Puffy' Combs**.

Shakur finally began serving his sentence at New York's Rickers Island penitentiary on 14 February 1995. While in prison, Shakur's third album, *Me Against the World*, was released, taking just seven months to go double platinum. Shakur was released from prison in October 1995 after a $1.4 million parole deal was arranged by Marion 'Suge' Knight, head of Los Angeles-based hip-hop label Death Row Records, to which Shakur subsequently signed.

His first album for the label, 1996's *All Eyez on Me*, went quintuple platinum, and Shakur appeared later that year with another of rap's bad boys, Snoop Doggie Dogg, in the video of *Americaz Most Wanted*. Shakur also completed two more film appearances that year, *Bullet* and *Gridlocked*. Returning to New York in September 1996 for the MTV Music Video Awards Show, Shakur was involved in a fight and was shot four times, dying six days later in hospital in Las Vegas. There was speculation that Shakur's killing marked another chapter in the US east/west coast rap feud, which was fuelled further by Notorious B.I.G.'s own murder in Los Angeles in March 1997.

A posthumous 2Pac Shakur *Greatest Hits* package was released in 1998, featuring four previously unreleased tracks.

BONNIE TYLER
b. Gaynor Hopkins, 8 June 1951, Skewen, Wales

One of the most dramatic rock-ballad singers of the late seventies and eighties, Tyler's torch-singer approach was best heard on the grandiose 'Total Eclipse of the Heart'* (Columbia, 1983).

A Welsh club singer, she was discovered by writer/ producers Steve Wolfe and Ronnie Scott, whose 'Lost in France' (RCA, 1976) Tyler took into the British Top Ten. 'More Than a Lover' from the Dave Mackay-produced *The World Starts Tonight* was less successful but the raucous **Rod Stewart**-like 'It's a Heartache' (1977) sold a million in America.

Diamond Cut (1979, produced by Robin Geoffrey Cable) and the Hugh Murphy-produced *Goodbye to the Island* (1981) made little impact, although 'Married Men' (1979, the theme from the film of Jackie Collins' *The World is Full of Married Men*) was a

minor hit. In 1983 Tyler signed to Columbia, where **Meatloaf**'s mentor Jim Steinman matched the melodrama of her powerful voice with his compositions on *Faster than the Speed of Night*. Russell Mulcahy's video for 'Total Eclipse of the Heart' perfectly matched the bombast of Tyler's performance and the single topped both the British and American charts.

The following year, Tyler reached the British Top Ten with 'A Rockin' Good Way', a duet with **Shakin' Stevens**, while 'Holding out for a Hero' was used on the soundtrack of *Footloose* and was a transatlantic hit. The song appeared on her next collaboration with Steinman, *Secret Dreams and Forbidden Fire*, which also included a majestic duet with **Todd Rundgren**, 'Loving You's a Dirty Job But Somebody's Gotta Do It'.

Tyler returned in 1988 with a new songwriter-producer, Desmond Child, on 'Hide Your Heart', and took part in **George Martin**'s recording of Dylan Thomas's *Under Milk Wood*. In the early nineties she moved to Germany where her brash, highly melodramatic style was much favoured. *Bitterblu* (1992) was a big hit across Northern Europe.

McCOY TYNER
b. 11 December 1938, Philadelphia, Pennsylvania, USA

After accompanying **John Coltrane** on some of his most memorable recordings, pianist Tyner had a distinguished career as a soloist and group leader in the seventies and eighties. He was one of the most prolific recording artists in modern jazz.

At the age of fifteen he was leading an R&B band but studies at Granoff Music School introduced him to the music of **Bud Powell** and **Thelonious Monk**. He played with **Max Roach**, **Sonny Rollins** and Lee Morgan before coming to wider notice as a member of the Art Farmer–Benny Golson Jazztet.

From 1960 to 1965 he was a member of Coltrane's group, playing on such albums as *My Favorite Things* (1960), *A Love Supreme* (1964) and *Ascension* (1965). Tyner became known for the ferocity of his attack and for what *Downbeat* called his 'Chopinesque virtuosity' and began his recording career as a leader with *Inception* (Impulse, 1962), accompanied by the rhythm section of the Coltrane group.

After leaving Coltrane, Tyner worked without a regular group and recorded several uneven albums for Blue Note with guest artists, the best of which was *The Real McCoy* (1967) with drummer **Elvin Jones**. In 1972 he formed a new group to play at the Newport Jazz Festival with ex-**Weather Report** drummer Alphonse Mouzon and Calvin Hall (bass). The trio's *Sahara* (Milestone, 1972) began a series of bestselling albums that included the tribute to Coltrane, *Echoes of a Friend* (1973) and *Sama Layuca*, recorded with a larger group of four percussionists and Aza Lawrence, former saxophonist with **Ike** and **Tina Turner**.

Tyner consolidated his reputation in the eighties through frequent tours with a series of groups whose members included violinist John Blake, trumpeter Freddie Hubbard, Avery Sharp (bass) and Louis Hayes (drums).

Signing to Blue Note in 1989 he issued a trilogy of solo albums. *Revelations* was followed by *Things Ain't What They Used to Be* (1991), on which he duetted with guitarist John Scofield and tenor sax-player George Adams, and *Soliloquy*, which contained pieces associated with Coltrane. *Manhattan Moods* (1994) teamed Tyner with vibes-player Bobby Hutcherson.

U2

*Bono, b. Paul Hewson, 10 May 1960, Dublin, Ireland;
Adam Clayton, b. 13 March 1960, Chinnor, Oxfordshire,
England; The Edge, b. David Evans, 8 August 1961,
Barking, Essex; Larry Mullen, b. Laurence Mullen, 1
October 1961, Dublin*

By the late eighties, Irish group U2 had become the
most popular rock band in the world. Led by singer/
lyricist Bono, U2 stood directly in a tradition of
relentless stadium sound combined with intense,
strong-minded songs whose pedigree stretched back
to **Bob Dylan** and **John Lennon**.

The quartet met at school in 1977 in Dublin and
began as Feedback by playing cover-versions of songs
by the **Beach Boys** and the **Rolling Stones** and parodies of the **Bay City Rollers** at a school talent contest,
with Evans on guitar, Clayton (bass) and Mullen
(drums). A further inspiration was the **Clash**, who
played in Dublin in that year. Bono and Edge
acquired their stage names and the group became first
the Hype and then U2 before winning a talent contest
in Limerick in 1978.

With ex-Spud manager Paul McGuinness handling their career, U2 released the Chas de Whalley-
produced 'Out of Control' (Columbia, 1979), which
became an Irish hit. Now one of the country's leading rock bands, U2 signed to **Chris Blackwell**'s
Island label, releasing the Martin Hannett-produced
'11 o'Clock Tick Tock' in Britain. Steve Lillywhite
supervised *Boy* (1980), a critically acclaimed, sombre
evocation of adolescence.

After their first major American tour, 'Fire' from
October (1981) was a minor hit in Britain. The album
reached the Top Twenty, many of its songs dramatiz-
ing the conflict between Bono's evangelical Christian
commitment and the world of rock'n'roll. The songwriting of the Bono–Edge team reached a new peak on
War (1983). The powerful and poetic 'Sunday Bloody
Sunday' fused Bono's feelings about religious schism
with a direct reference to the political history of
Northern Ireland, while international terrorism was
the theme of 'Seconds'. Both 'New Year's Day' (a song
inspired by the Polish Solidarity movement) and 'Two
Hearts Beat as One' reached the British Top Twenty.

During their next American tour, U2 played a free
concert at the Red Rocks natural ampitheatre in Colorado. The performance was filmed and released as
an album and bestselling video under the name *Under
a Blood Red Sky*.

Brian Eno and **Daniel Lanois** were brought in to
produce *The Unforgettable Fire* (1984), transforming
and enhancing the group's studio sound. The album
was a major international success and included Top
Ten British hits with the title track and 'Pride', dedicated to Martin Luther King and the group's first
American hit.

In 1985 U2 took part in Live Aid and the following
year performed on the 'Conspiracy of Hope' tour for
Amnesty International. The hugely successful *The
Joshua Tree* (1987), which topped the British and
American charts, received critical acclaim and
included the hit singles 'I Still Haven't Found What
I'm Looking for' and 'With or Without You'. The
group also set up the Mother label, based in Dublin,
with the aim of providing opportunities for young
Irish musicians.

The band's next major project was *Rattle and Hum*
(1988), a film and soundtrack double-album made on
the 'Joshua Tree' tour of America. It provided hit singles with 'Desire', 'Angel of Harlem' and 'When Love
Comes to Town', on which the group was joined by
B. B. King. The album again topped the charts on
both sides of the Atlantic.

Taking advantage of their superstar status, the
group took a break before returning to the studio to
record *Achtung Baby*, which reunited them with Eno
and Lanois. A more experimental album than its two
predecessors, it nonetheless made No. 1 in America
and provided five hit singles, including 'The Fly' (a
British chart-topper). The hugely successful tour promoting the album, 'The Zoo TV Tour', was a complex
multi-media event, involving nightly satellite links to
other parts of the world. After the tour, the band
changed their work pattern by immediately releasing
another album, *Zooropa* (1993), which took the experimental edge of *Achtung Baby* a stage further. Produced by Eno, it included a collaboration with
Johnny Cash on 'The Wanderer'. On its release, the
band immediately embarked on a further set of 'Zoo
TV' dates, after which they decided to take an
extended break.

U2's next release was 'Hold Me, Thrill Me, Kiss Me,
Kill Me' (1995), the glam-rock theme to *Batman For-
ever*. Produced by Nellee Hooper (**Björk, Soul II
Soul**), the single was a major hit across Europe and
the US. It was quickly followed by the collaborative
Original Soundtracks Volume One, credited to the Pas-
sengers (essentially U2, Eno and guest vocalist
Pavarotti). The album spawned the haunting single

'Miss Sarajevo' but was generally met with indifference critically and commercially. The following year, as U2 prepared their next album, Clayton and Mullen provided the theme to the Tom Cruise vehicle *Mission: Impossible*.

After a lengthy delay as the band struggled to complete its recording, *Pop* was issued in early 1997. Drawing on modern electronic dance techniques and the production skills of Howie B, *Pop* included a handful of hit singles, notably the UK No. 1 'Discotheque'. On the extravagant 'PopMart' world tour U2 emerged from a giant plastic lemon on to a huge stage surrounded by vast video screens in a similar vein to 'Zoo TV'. In 1998 they issued the first in a series of planned retrospectives, *The Best of 1980–89*, and had a hit with a reworking of an early B-side, 'The Sweetest Thing'. In 2000 the band released the much-delayed *All That You Can't Leave Behind*. Produced by Eno and Lanois, the album's sound saw a return to that of 1984's *The Unforgettable Fire* (also produced by Eno and Lanois). Eschewing the eclecticism of *Pop*, the band returned to their earlier anthemic style with songs like 'Beautiful Day' and 'Walk on' which featured a big guitar sound with Bono's richly romantic voice well to the fore. The result was a solid rather than adventurous outing.

UB40

James Brown, b. 21 November 1957; Alastair Campbell, b. 2 February 1959, Birmingham, England; Robin Campbell, b. 25 December 1954; Earl Falconer, b. 23 January, 1959, Birmingham; Norman Hassan, b. 26 January 1958; Brian Travers, b. 7 February 1959; Michael Virtue, b. 19 January, 1957, Birmingham; Astro, b. Terence Wilson, 24 June 1957, Birmingham

A successful multi-racial British reggae group of the eighties, UB40 were noted for the political and social comment of their early songs and for their independence from the mainstream music industry, epitomized by their setting up of their own record label.

The Campbell brothers were the children of Birmingham-based folk singers Lorna and Ian Campbell. Inspired by the **Weavers**, the Ian Campbell Group was formed in 1959. Among its members were Dave Swarbrick and Dave Pegg, who went on to join **Fairport Convention**. Ian Campbell was the author of the anti-nuclear anthem 'The Sun Is Burning', which appeared on **Paul Simon**'s first solo album in 1965.

Taking the name UB40 from the Unemployment Benefit card, the group was formed in 1977 by the Campbells (guitar, vocals), Brown (drums), Falconer (bass) and Travers (saxophone). They evolved a softer reggae style, akin to lovers' rock, which was allied to lyrics about colonialism and unemployment on *Sign-*

ing Off (1979), produced by Steve Gibbons Band drummer Bob Lamb for the local Graduate label. With the addition of reggae toaster (talkover vocalist) Astro (*b. Terence Wilson*) and percussionist Norman Lamount, Ali Campbell's plaintive lead singing took the double-sided 'King'/'Food for Thought', **Randy Newman**'s 'I Think It's Going to Rain Today' and 'The Earth Dies Screaming' into the British Top Ten in 1980.

The following year UB40 formed their own label, Dep International, to release *Present Arms*, which included their best-known song, 'One in Ten', whose title referred to the proportion of jobless in the British population. The political emphasis faded on *Labour of Love* (1983), on which UB40 covered such reggae standards as the **Neil Diamond** composition 'Red Red Wine' (a 1983 No. 1 and minor American hit), **Jimmy Cliff**'s 'Many Rivers to Cross' (1983) and 'Cherry Oh Baby' (1984). Other hits written by the group included 'Please Don't Make Me Cry' (1983), 'If It Happens Again' (1984) and 'Don't Break My Heart' (1985).

Geffrey Morgan (1984) and *Beggariddim* (1985) were less successful, but the group scored a second British No. 1 with a revival of Sonny and **Cher**'s 'I Got You Babe' (1985), on which the **Pretenders**' Chrissie Hynde duetted with Ali Campbell (a pairing repeated in 1988 on 'Breakfast in Bed'). In 1986 UB40 played in Russia, later releasing a video of the tour (*CCCP: The Video Mix*). The title track of *Rat in the Kitchen* (1986) was a hit in 1987, the year that UB40 recorded a cover of the **Jackson Five**'s 'Almost Tomorrow'.

The band had been making steady progress in the United States since *Labour of Love* reached the Top Forty in 1984, and a reissue of 'Red Red Wine' from that album gave them an American No. 1 in 1988. Later album releases included *UB40* (1988) and *Labour of Love II* (1990), another set of cover-versions which included the American Top Ten hit 'The Way You Do the Things You Do', originally a hit for the **Temptations** in 1964. Also in 1990 UB40 had a Top Ten hit in Britain with **Robert Palmer** on a version of **Bob Dylan**'s 'I'll Be Your Baby Tonight'. The band had another massively successful album in *Promises and Lies* (1993), which included a further international No. 1 with a remake of **Elvis Presley**'s 'Can't Help Falling in Love'. A former studio engineer with the group, Bitty McLean, had a big British hit in the same year with 'It Keeps Raining', a revival of a **Fats Domino** song.

Later albums included *Guns in the Ghetto* (1997) and the various-artist outing *UB40 Presents the Dancehall Album* (1998), for which the group acted as the backing band for a number of Jamaican toasters.

The hits are collected on *The Best of . . . Volume 1* (1987) and *Volume 2* (1996).

UFO

Mick Bolton (replaced by Larry Wallis, replaced by Bernie Marsden, replaced by Michael Schenker, b. Germany, replaced by Paul Chapman); Phil Mogg, b. 1951, London, England; Danny Peyronel; Paul Raymond (replaced by Neil Carter); Pete Way (replaced by Paul Gray); Jim Simpson; Atomic Tommy M; Lawrence Archer; Clive Edwards

One of the more durable of British heavy-metal groups, UFO found greater success in Europe and America than at home.

During the late sixties Way (bass), Mogg (vocals) and Bolton (guitar) were members of London rock band Hocus Pocus. Adding Andy Parker (drums) and changing their name to UFO, the group recorded *UFO 1* (1970) for independent label Beacon. The album was a hit in Japan where *Flying* (1971) and a version of **Eddie Cochran**'s 'C'mon Everybody' were also successful. A tour of the country produced *UFO Live in Japan* (1972). After Bolton's departure, Wallis and Marsden briefly held the lead guitar job, before leaving for the Pink Fairies and Wild Turkey, respectively.

In 1973 the group signed to Chrysalis for *Phenomenon* (1974), which included the minor hit 'Doctor Doctor' and 'Rock Bottom' and introduced lead guitarist Schenker from German rock band the **Scorpions**, who later became the first internationally famous heavy-metal band from a non-English-speaking country. UFO toured America before recording *Force It* (1975), produced by former **Ten Years After** bass-player Leo Lyons and briefly brought in Peyronel on keyboards for *No Heavy Petting* (1976). The group became a five-piece with the addition of guitarist Raymond and reached the Top Thirty on both sides of the Atlantic with *Lights Out* (1977). The live double-album *Strangers in the Night* was a Top Ten hit in Britain.

Schenker left to briefly rejoin the Scorpions and then formed the Michael Schenker Group. That group's début album, *MSG*, entered the British Top Ten in 1981. **George Martin** produced UFO's next Top Twenty album, *No Place to Run*, after which Raymond joined Schenker's group. *Obsessions* (1978), which featured Chapman and Neil Carter on guitars, was followed by two more British hit albums before Way left to form his own band, leaving Mogg the only original member on UFO's thirteenth album, *Mechanix*.

After recording *Making Contact* (1983), the group was temporarily disbanded but Mogg, Raymond and Gray (bass) re-formed UFO with Japanese–American guitarist Atomik Tommy M to release *Misdemeanour* (1985). The band were unable to recapture past glories and split up once again, only to re-emerge in 1991 with a line-up of Mogg, Way, guitarist Archer and drummer Edwards. They recorded the album *High Stakes and Desperate Men* (1991) and toured heavily, reuniting with Schenker for Japanese and American dates in 1994. Schenker, Mogg and Gray formed the basis of the band that recorded the lacklustre *Covenant* (SPV, 2000), which was made even more unappealing by including a far superior seven-track live album from 1995.

ULTRAVOX

Warren Cann, b. 20 May 1952, Victoria, Canada; Chris Cross, b. Christopher St John, 14 July 1952, London, England; Billie Currie, b. 20 May 1952, Victoria; John Foxx, b. Dennis Leigh, Chorley, England; Midge Ure, b. James Ure, 10 October 1954, Cambuslang, Scotland

The career of Ultravox had two distinct phases. Under the leadership of Foxx, they developed an influential electro-pop sound during the late seventies. When Foxx was replaced by Ure, the group found success with ambitious rock ballads, notably 'Vienna' (1980), which typified the new-romantic reaction against punk.

Singer Foxx and bassist Cross played together in Stones Rose and Tiger Lily, developing a glam-rock sound which emerged on a version of **Fats Waller**'s 'Ain't Misbehavin'' (Gull, 1975). With Currie (synthesizer, keyboards, violin), Steve Shears (guitar) and Cann (drums), they became Ultravox in 1976, recording an eponymous album for Island, produced by **Brian Eno** and Steve Lillywhite. This was followed by *Ha Ha Ha* and *Systems of Romance* (co-produced by Conny Plank in 1978), which displayed a lush synthesizer-based sound, influencing the style of such bands as **Depeche Mode** and the **Human League**. By this point Robin Simon had replaced Shears.

The albums sold poorly, however, and in 1979 Island dropped the group, with Foxx leaving for a solo career, recording *Metamatic* (Virgin, 1980), *The Garden* (1981), *The Golden Section* (1983) and *In Mysterious Ways* (1985). Ure was recruited by the remaining members as the new lead singer. His previous experience had included a spell with teenybop group Slik, whose 1976 No. 1 'Forever and Ever' (Bell) was written by **Phil Coulter** and Bill Martin, and the Rich Kids, led by former **Sex Pistols** bassist Glen Matlock.

The mixture of Currie's wash of synthesizers and Ure's vibrant tenor made the Plank-produced 'Vienna' and 'All Stood Still' Top Ten hits on Chrysalis in 1981. *Rage in Eden* (1981) brought further success with 'The Thin Wall' and 'Voice'. The following year Ure had a solo hit with a soulful revival of **Tom Rush**'s 'No Regrets' while Ultravox's 'Reap the Wild Wind' and 'Hymn' reached the Top Twenty. Currie and Ure were also members of the new-

romantic studio band Visage. Led by Steve Strange
(*b. Steve Harrington, 28 May 1959, Wales*), Visage's
hits included 'Fade to Grey' (Polydor, 1981), 'Mind of
a Toy' and 'Night Train' (1982).

By now a mainstream rock band, Ultravox maintained their popularity in 1984 with the Top Twenty
hits 'Dancing with Tears in My Eyes' and 'Love's
Great Adventure'. They later released *U-Vox* (1986),
which included a collaboration with the **Chieftains**,
but the group's activity was interrupted by Ure's
involvement with Band Aid (he co-wrote 'Do They
Know It's Christmas?' with **Bob Geldof**) and his solo
recording: his rock crooning on 'If I Was' from *The
Gift* brought a No. 1 hit in 1985 and in 1988 he released
Answers (Answers to Nothing). Meanwhile, Currie
recorded the solo instrumental album *Transportation*
(IRS, 1987) before forming the band Humania. The
band flopped, and Currie released the solo album
Stand Up and Walk before he unsuccessfully
attempted to revive the Ultravox name, touring and
recording an album in Germany with a new line-up.

Ure continued with his own solo career, releasing
the moderately successful album *Pure* (1991) with its
British hit single 'Cold Cold Heart'. Even more successful was *Breathe* (1996), released in the same year
Currie assembled another version of Ultravox to tour
and record (*Ingenuity*, Resurgence). The best of Ure's
solo material and work with Ultravox was compiled
on the album *If I Was* (1993).

UNCLE TUPELO
*Jay Farrar, b. 26 December 1966, Belleville, Illinois,
USA; Michael Heidorn (replaced by Ken Coomer); Max
Johnson; John Stirratt; Jeff Tweedy, b. 25 August 1967,
Belleville*

Drawing equally on **Gram Parsons** and **Black Flag**,
Uncle Tupelo were the catalysts for a new wave of
bands blending traditional country elements with
contemporary, guitar-led rock in the nineties.

Guitarist/singer Farrar and bassist/vocalist Tweedy
began playing together in punk cover band the Primitives in the mid-eighties before combining their noisy
guitar style with a love of traditional country music
and forming Uncle Tupelo. Recruiting drummer Heidorn, the band built up their reputation as a live band
on the club circuit before signing to Rockville for the
release of the ironically titled *No Depression* (1990),
which was named after a **Carter Family** song and in
turn was taken as the title in 1995 of the UK fanzine
that championed alternative country music. With the
support of college radio Uncle Tupelo developed a
nationwide following, bolstered by critical praise for
their sophomore effort, *Still Feel Gone* (1991). The
band's third release was a 'live in the studio' set,
March 16–20 (1992), produced by Peter Buck. Their

association with the **R.E.M.** guitarist attracted the
attention of Sire Records, who signed the band later
the same year.

For their major label début, *Anodyne* (Sire, 1993),
Uncle Tupelo expanded their line-up to include
multi-instrumentalist Johnson and bassist Stirratt,
allowing Tweedy to switch to guitar. Farrar's duet
with **Doug Sahm** signalled one modern root of the
alternative country movement. *Anodyne*, which also
marked the recording début of Coomer after the
ousting of drummer Heidorn, was bolstered respectively, and won the band new fans across the US. By
1994, however, tension between the band's two
founding members had led to the departure of Farrar,
leading Tweedy to assume full control of the group,
which he renamed Wilco. The new band's first
release, *AM* (1995), garnered further acclaim, which
surprised many who had assumed Farrar was the real
talent behind Uncle Tupelo. Wilco built up an international following with their second album, *Being
There* (1996), which drew as much on psychedelia and
soul as country rock. The success of the album led to
Wilco being chosen to work with **Billy Bragg** on an
album of previously unrecorded songs by **Woody
Guthrie**, *Mermaid Avenue* (Elektra, 1998). The band
followed this collaborative effort with the superior
Summer Teeth (Reprise, 1999). In the same year it
recorded 'One Hundred Years from Now' for the
Gram Parsons tribute album *Return of the Grievous
Angel* (Almo). Wilco returned to Guthrie, again in
collaboration with Bragg, for *Mermaid Avenue Vol. 2*
(2000), on which they rather than Bragg took centre
stage, reminding listeners that Guthrie was a celebrator as much as a critic of America.

Having left Uncle Tupelo, Jay Farrar went on to
found Son Volt with original drummer Heidorn
alongside siblings Dave (guitar and fiddle) and Jim
(bass) Boquist. While falling short of Wilco's success,
Son Volt have built up a devoted fanbase with three
albums of stark country-tinged rock, *Trace* (1995),
Straightaways (1997) and *Wide Swing Tremolo* (1998),
all of which highlighted what one critic has called Farrar's 'gentle despondency'.

UNDERWORLD
*Darren Emerson, b. 1973, Essex, England; Rick Smith,
b. 1962, Wales; Karl Hyde*

Underworld were leading figures in the new generation of nineties dance acts, using twisted versions of
Detroit techno and British drum'n'bass as the backings for Karl Hyde's dark, disjointed vocals.

Hyde and Smith met in Cardiff in 1981, when Hyde
was playing with new wave band the Screen Gems
and Smith was studying electronics. The pair formed
a band, Freur, which enjoyed brief and modest pop

success, recording two albums for CBS in 1984 and 1985.

Freur disbanded, but Hyde and Smith in 1987 formed the first version of Underworld. Like Freur, the group enjoyed modest success, releasing two albums of unremarkable **Prince**- and **Eurythmics**-influenced funk in 1987 and 1988, and touring the US with the Eurythmics in 1989. This changed following the arrival of Emerson in 1990. A part-time techno DJ, Emerson met Smith through a mutual friend in London. Now a trio, Underworld self-financed the release of a new single, 'The Hump'/'Mother Earth' (1991), which was enthusiastically received in London's specialist dance record shops.

After an appearance at the Glastonbury festival in 1992, the band's career moved up a gear in 1993, with two singles released on the UK's Junior Boy's Own label under the Lemon Interrupt alias. Also on JBO the same year they released what they regarded as the first real Underworld singles, 'Mmm . . . Skyscraper I Love You' and 'Cowgirl'/'Rez', characterized by a hard, rock-edged techno sound and Hyde's menacing spoken vocals.

The new Underworld's first album, *Dubnobass-withmyheadman* (1994), was released to huge critical acclaim. Live appearances followed over the next eighteen months, with the band, with Hyde on guitar, becoming part of the first generation of dance acts that could draw crowds at festivals more usually associated with rock. Their follow-up album, *Second Toughest in the Infants* (1996), saw the band making use of a broader palette of sounds, using both slower and faster jungle-influenced beats than the band's familiar heavy techno stomp. In the same year Underworld scored their first hit single with 'Born Slippy (Nuxx)'. Originally a 1995 B-side, it was given a new lease of life through its prominent use in the hit UK film *Trainspotting*.

The band kept a low public profile over the next two years. A new track, 'Moaner', appeared on the soundtrack to *Batman and Robin* (1997) and there were some remixes, including **Depeche Mode**'s 'Barrel of a Gun'. After live performances at UK festivals late in 1998 a new album, *Beaucoup Fish*, finally appeared early in 1999, containing the hit single 'King of Snake'. The album retained its predecessor's diverse range of beats, while also evincing a slightly more US disco-flavoured approach to the group's house anthems. Emerson quit the group in 2000.

PHIL UPCHURCH
b. *Chicago, Illinois, USA*

A blues/jazz guitarist, Upchurch had one major pop hit with the dance classic 'You Can't Sit Down'* (1961) and was a leading Chicago and New York session player.

A studio bassist, Upchurch worked regularly for Chess Records in Chicago, backing R&B performers like **Howlin' Wolf** and **Muddy Waters** as well as soul stars the **Dells** and **Jerry Butler**. 'You Can't Sit Down' was made as a two-part instrumental single for the Texas label Boyd and Part 2 reached the Top Thirty. Subsequent attempts to capitalize on this success, such as *Twist the Big Hit Dances* (United Artists, 1962), failed, but the tune itself, with added lyrics by Dee Clark and Kal Mann, was an even bigger hit for the **Dovells** on Cameo-Parkway in 1963. The Upchurch version entered the British Top Forty on Sue in 1966.

Upchurch later recorded jazz guitar pieces for Milestone (*Feeling Blue*, 1968) and Cadet (*The Way I Feel*, 1969). *Phil Upchurch* (Marlin) was co-produced by **George Benson**, on whose later Warners albums Upchurch played bass. During the early seventies Upchurch recorded *Darkness Darkness* (1972) and *Lovin' Feelin'* (1973), which included **Curtis Mayfield** and **Carole King** compositions and was produced by Tommy LiPuma for the West Coast label Blue Thumb. He also played sessions for label-mates Ben Sidran and Arthur Adams. His own later albums included *Upchurch Tennyson*, made with singer-pianist Tennyson Stephens for Creed Taylor's Kudu (1975), *Name of the Game* (Jam, 1984), produced by Esmond Edwards, *All I Want* (1992) and *Whatever Happened to the Blues* (1992) with the **Staple Singers**.

His session playing in the seventies and eighties showed a mastery of many styles, from blues (**Jimmy Reed**, **Bo Diddley**) through funk (**Grover Washington**, **Crusaders**), soul (Jerry Butler, **Bobby Bland**) to white rock (**Cat Stevens**, Barry Melton of **Country Joe McDonald**'s Fish).

URIAH HEEP
Mick Box, b. 8 June 1947, London, England; David Byron, b. 29 January 1947, Essex, d. 28 February 1985 (replaced by John Lawton, replaced by Peter Goalby); Ken Hensley, b. 24 August 1945 (replaced by John Sinclair); Alex Napier (replaced by Keith Baker, replaced by Lee Kerslake); Paul Newton (replaced by Gary Thain, d. 1975, replaced by John Wetton, replaced by Trevor Bolder, replaced by Bob Daisley, replaced by Trevor Bolder)

Uriah Heep were among the most durable of the British heavy-rock bands that emerged in the early seventies. With only limited record success, the group remained popular on the heavy-metal touring circuit and by the end of the eighties had performed in forty countries.

Singer Byron and Box (guitar) formed the Stalkers in 1965, and with the addition of Newton (bass) and Napier (drums), the band became Spice a year later.

Byron also recorded vocals for cover-version albums on the budget Avenue label. In 1969 Spice was signed by producer Gerry Bron. Becoming Uriah Heep, the group added Baker (drums) and Hensley, a keyboards player who had worked with future **John Mayall** and **Rolling Stones** guitarist Mick Taylor in the Gods and with Cliff Bennett in Toe Fat. Uriah Heep recorded *Very 'Eavy, Very 'Umble* (Vertigo, 1970), a collection of tracks which ranged from the folk-rock of Tim Rose's 'Come Away Melinda' to the hard rock of 'Gypsy'.

Salisbury (1971) veered towards the symphonic rock of **Deep Purple** with a sixteen-minute title track and the addition of a twenty-six-piece orchestra. *Look at Yourself* (1971) was issued on Bron's newly formed Bronze label. It was followed by *Demons and Wizards* (1972), which included Hensley's sword-and-sorcery song 'The Wizard' and a new rhythm section, former Toe Fat drummer Kerslake and Thain on bass. The album marked the band's first commercial success, reaching the Top Thirty in both Britain and America.

After *The Magician's Birthday* (1972), the group released *Uriah Heep Live* (1973). *Sweet Freedom* (1973) was another hit but after *Wonderworld*, with arrangements by jazz composer Michael Gibbs, former **Family** member Wetton replaced Thain, who died of a drug overdose a few months later. *Return to Fantasy* (1975) was Uriah Heep's biggest British hit but soon afterwards both Wetton and Byron left the group. The singer formed Rough Diamond with former **Colosseum** guitarist Clem Clempson, and went on to make two solo albums, *Baby Faced Killer* (Arista, 1978) and *This Day and Age* (1980), and *On the Rocks* (Creole, 1981) with a new group.

Uriah Heep recruited Lawton from Lucifer's Friend as lead vocalist on *Firefly* (1977), *Innocent Victim* and *Fallen Angel* (1978). The new bass guitarist was former **David Bowie** sideman Bolder. When Lawton left the group, Lone Star's John Sloman sang on *Conquest* (1980), after which Hensley quit the band to develop a solo career. Ex-Trapeze vocalist Goalby appeared on *Abnominog* (1982), along with keyboards-player Sinclair and bassist Daisley, who was replaced by the returning Bolder in 1983.

Determined touring had maintained a strong international following for the group but following the collapse of Bronze, the next album to be released was *Equator* (Portrait, 1985). In 1987, when Uriah Heep became the first heavy-metal group to perform in

Moscow, Bernie Shaw (vocals) and Phil Lanzon (keyboards) from Grand Prix had joined the band. Later albums included *Live in Moscow* (1988), *Raging Silence* (1989), *Still 'Eavy, Still Proud* (1990) and *Different World* (1991).

The four-CD set *A Time of Revelation* (Essential, 1996) documents every stage of their career.

U-ROY
b. Ewart Beckford, 1942, Kingston, Jamaica

Although he did not invent the form, U-Roy was the first great exponent of disc-jockey talkover music. Developing the technique while playing reggae singles in dance halls, he went on to record his own shouted comments, call-and-response style, into existing rock-steady records.

Originally inspired by sound-system man Count Machuki, who worked for both **Coxsone Dodd** and **Prince Buster**, U-Roy worked during the sixties with Dickie's Dynamic and Sir George Atomic before joining **King Tubby** in 1968. While other deejays like King Stitt had evolved a toasting, talkover style using nonsense rhymes, U-Roy introduced a fast-flowing jive-talk manner expressing Rastafarian sentiments and using shouts, shrieks and screams.

In 1970 he recorded with producer King Reid and had three big hits on Treasure Isle, 'Wake the Town' (based on Alton Ellis' 1966 rock-steady hit, 'Girl, I've Got a Date'), 'Rule the Nation' and 'Wear You to the Ball'.

For two years Jamaica's bestselling artist, his popularity dropped as his material became weaker and as new deejays like **Big Youth** and I-Roy emerged with heavier rhythms.

His career revived in 1975 when he recorded with Bunny Lee and Prince Tony, and in 1976 he signed to Virgin. The British label released *Dread in a Babylon*, his best album, *Natty Rebel* (1976) and *Rasta Ambassador* (1977), on which U-Roy was joined by **Sly and Robbie**. U-Roy also recorded in the late seventies for Live and Love.

He later set up his own Stur Gav (Stereograph) label to record newer deejays like Charlie Chaplin and in 1985 U-Roy released *Line up and Come*, which included 'Dance Hall Memory', a song recalling his early years on the sound systems. In 1991 he starred in a deejay revivalist concert in London and in 1992 released the traditionally styled *Rock with I* (RAS).

RITCHIE VALENS

b. Richard Valenzuela, 13 May 1941, Los Angeles, California, USA, d. 3 February 1959, Clear Lake, Iowa

A singer who combined rock'n'roll with Mexican-American music, Valens' pioneering role as a chicano musician was commemorated in the 1986 biopic, *La Bamba*.

From a Mexican-American family, Valens formed the Silhouettes at high school, developing a style which mingled rock'n'roll with Latin music. In 1958 he was signed to Bob Keene's Del-Fi label. With producer Rene Hall – an associate of **Bumps Blackwell** who later wrote arrangements for **Sam Cooke** – Valens released his own composition, the catchy 'Come on Let's Go' (1958). A minor hit in America, the song reached the British Top Ten in a cover-version by **Tommy Steele**.

His next single combined a mournful teen ballad, 'Donna', with 'La Bamba', a rock arrangement of a traditional Mexican dance tune. The record was a double-sided million-seller in 1959, with **Marty Wilde** successfully covering 'Donna' in Britain. The song itself went on to become a standard of American popular music, recorded by artists as diverse as the **Crickets**, the **Ventures** and the Mormon Tabernacle Choir. The Latin chord sequence of 'La Bamba' quickly became part of the vocabulary of rock, reappearing in such songs as the **Isley Brothers**' 'Twist and Shout' (1960) and **Bert Berns**' production of 'Hang on Sloopy' for the **McCoys** (1965).

Valens had taken part in the filming of *Go Johnny Go* shortly before he died in the plane crash which also killed **Buddy Holly** and the Big Bopper. Del-Fi issued a number of posthumous tracks, including the minor hit 'That's My Little Susie', 'Ooh My Head', 'Stay Beside Me' and 'Cry Cry Cry'.

After Valens' death, Keen signed another chicano singer, Chan Romero (b. 27 July 1941, Billings, Montana). His 'Hippy Hippy Shake' was a 1963 British hit for the **Swinging Blue Jeans**. Later chicano rock musicians included **Chris Montez**, **Carlos Santana**, **Freddy Fender** and **Los Lobos**, whose lead singer, David Hidalgo, re-created Valens' singing in *La Bamba* (1986). The film's musical director was Santana.

CATERINA VALENTE

b. 14 January 1931, Paris, France

With **Edith Piaf** one of the few Europeans to find international success in the fifties, Valente is best remembered for her recording of 'The Breeze and I'* (1956).

Born into an Italian showbusiness family – her mother was a circus clown and her father an accordionist – Valente made her professional stage début at the age of five and spent most of her teens travelling Europe with her family, appearing in circuses and cabaret. In 1945 she took up the guitar and in the fifties started her solo career as a nightclub artist, singing in English, French, German, Spanish, Italian and Swedish. In 1953 she signed with Polydor and had immediate success with her version of Cuban composer Ernesto Lecuona's 'Malagueña', later recorded by numerous artists including **Connie Francis** (1960), and **Edmundo Ros**. Valente had even greater success with her thrilling version of Lecuona's 'Andalucia' (with English lyrics by Al Stillman) and 'The Breeze and I' (Decca), which reached both the British and American charts and established her on the international cabaret circuit with a repertoire centred on exotic material such as **Moises Simons**' 'The Peanut Vendor', and 'Besame Mucho', sung in a variety of languages.

In 1963 she appeared with such stars as **Anne Shelton**, **Maurice Chevalier**, **Doris Day** and **Nana Mouskouri**, singing 'La Golondrina' on the million-selling *All Star Festival* (United Nations). Organized by the United Nations Commission for Refugees, the album was one of the last charity records to feature 'popular' artists. Later successful charity records, such as the **George Harrison**-organized *Concert for Bangladesh* and Band Aid's 'Do They Know It's Christmas?' (1984), would (almost exclusively) feature rock artists.

By the seventies and *This Is Me* (Pye, 1975) Valente had added more contemporary material, including the **Carpenters**' 1970 hit 'We've Only Just Begun', to her repertoire. She did not record in the eighties or nineties.

RUDY VALLEE

b. Hubert Prior Vallee, 28 July 1901, Island Pond, Vermont, USA, d. 3 July 1986, California

The first singer to be called a 'crooner' and the first to induce mass hysteria among his fans, the soft-voiced, wavy-haired Vallee had a second career as a Hollywood actor.

The son of a pharmacist, Vallee took up the saxophone in his teens, and formed his own band in 1921 while at the University of Maine (whose college song, 'The Stein Song', released in 1930 on Victor, was one of his first hits). He later switched to Yale (its 'glee club' theme, 'The Whiffenpoof Song', he recorded with little success in 1937, but which, re-recorded was his last major hit on Enterprise in 1946) and played his way through college as a member of several bands, including the Savoy Havana band which – while in Britain in 1924 – was the first dance band to broadcast regularly. On graduating, after briefly playing with **Vincent Lopez** in 1927, he formed the Connecticut Yankees in 1928. When his shows at New York's Heigh Ho Club were broadcast, he won instant success for what one critic called the 'gracious sex appeal' of his plaintive voice. In contrast to big-voiced shouters such as **Al Jolson**, Vallee's intimate, smooth-voiced crooning, like that of **Bing Crosby**, was perfectly suited to both the radio microphone and the new process of electrical recording.

After recording for Harmony ('Marie', 1929) Vallee joined Victor, for whom he made the two songs most closely associated with him, the film theme 'The Vagabond Lover', which gave him his early nickname, and 'My Time Is Your Time' (1929), the theme to his long-running radio show. Among his many hits of the thirties, mostly derived from film and Broadway shows, were 'As Time Goes By' (1931), which was even more successful when reissued in 1943 in the wake of **Dooley Wilson**'s performance in *Casablanca*; 'Let's Put out the Lights'; **Harold Arlen** and **Yip Harburg**'s 'Brother Can You Spare a Dime?' (Columbia, 1932); another college drinking song, 'There Is a Tavern in the Town' (Victor, 1934); a cover-version of **Shirley Temple**'s 'On the Good Ship Lollipop' (1935); and 'Vieni, Vieni' (1937). At the same time, Vallee worked in films, first as a romantic lead in lesser musicals, including *George White's Scandals* (1934), in which he reprised his Broadway role, and *Gold Diggers of Paris* (1938), before in *Palm Beach Story* (1942) he switched to comedy with great success, especially when parodying stiff-shirted, pince-nez-wearing versions of his earlier Hollywood self.

During the war he was director of the US Coast Guards Band, before once more returning to Hollywood. His stiff-shirt firmly in place, Vallee had great success in the Broadway (1961) and screen (1966) versions of **Frank Loesser**'s *How to Succeed in Business Without Really Trying*. In the early seventies he tried unsuccessfully to have the name of the Los Angeles street on which he lived changed to Rue de Vallee.

VAN HALEN
Eddie Van Halen, b. 26 January 1957, Nijmegen, Holland; David Lee Roth, b. 10 October 1955, Bloomington,

USA; Alex Van Halen, b. 8 May 1955, Nijmegen; Michael Anthony, b. 20 June 1955, Chicago, Illinois, USA; Sammy Hagar, b. 13 October, 1947, Monterey (replaced Gary Cherone, b. 24 July 1961, Malden, Minnesota)

Built around the stunning guitar-playing of Eddie Van Halen, this four-piece survived the potentially catastrophic departure of their frontman David Lee Roth at what seemed to be the pinnacle of their career to re-establish themselves as one of the leading heavy-metal acts of the eighties.

The Van Halen brothers, whose family had moved to Pasadena in California in the mid-sixties, joined forces with vocalist Roth in 1973 to form a heavy rock band, Mammoth. All three had played in local bands before meeting. Recruiting bassist Anthony from another local band, Snake, they played regularly in clubs and as support around the Los Angeles area before changing the name to Van Halen in 1975. A 1976 demo produced by **Kiss** bass-player Gene Simmons failed to attract any major label interest, but Warner Bros signed the band in 1977 after a recommendation from producer Ted Templeman. The Templeman-produced 1978 début, *Van Halen*, attracted attention for Eddie Van Halen's guitar pyrotechnics and Roth's tongue-in-cheek lyrics. Their outrageous cover of the **Kinks**' 'You Really Got Me' gave the band their first US Top Forty hit. The album was a US hit, selling over 2 million copies, and charted in the UK following the band's début British shows later that year. The follow-up, *Van Halen II*, was even more successful, and precipitated a massive world tour which would last almost a year. Throughout the tour, frontman Roth attracted headlines for his combination of posing and outrageous athleticism, creating a large-than-life character which would find full expression in the band's promotional videos.

Women and Children First (1980), *Fair Warning* (1981) and *Diver Down* (1982) saw the band increasing their popularity and sales globally, swiftly becoming one of the rock world's biggest names. By now, Eddie Van Halen was regularly topping polls as leading guitarist, a fact acknowledged by **Michael Jackson** and his producer **Quincy Jones**, who asked him to play on the 1983 'Beat It' single. The band's sixth album, *1984*, marked a new departure for the band with its heavy use of synthesizers and was their most successful in the UK, giving them a hit single with the poppy 'Jump', which hit No. 1 in the US. In 1985 Roth issued *Crazy from the Heat*, a solo EP of cover-versions including songs by the **Beach Boys** and the **Lovin' Spoonful**, and later that year announced his departure from Van Halen.

In Roth's place, the remaining members recruited

veteran vocalist Hagar (ex-Montrose), who had released eleven solo albums and would continue his own career alongside his work with Van Halen. The band's first album with Hagar, *5150* (1986, named after Eddie Van Halen's own studio where it was recorded), was an even bigger chart success than its predecessor, reaching No. 1 in the US, and was swiftly followed up the charts by Roth's début long-player, *Eat 'Em and Smile*. Roth hired another talented guitar player, Steve Vai (ex-**Frank Zappa**), for the album and lengthy tour which followed, with a set which mixed his own material, some Van Halen songs and covers. His second album, *Skyscraper* (1988), was another Transatlantic success, as was *A Little Ain't Enough* (1991), although both showed Roth moving away from the eclectic approach of his early solo recordings in favour of a straightforward hard-rock approach.

With Hagar settled in the band, Van Halen returned to live work in 1988, followed by the release of *OU812*, which again hit the top slot in the US. More touring followed, after which the band took time off before reconvening for the 1991 album *For Unlawful Carnal Knowledge* (1991), another international bestseller. Shows from the tour promoting the album were recorded for 1993's *Right Here Right Now*, which also included material from their 1986–7 and 1988–9 tours. In 1995 they released the bestselling *Balance*. The next year Hagar acrimoniously left the band and released a solo album, *Marching to Mars* (1997). *Van Halen III* (1998), the first album with Cherone as lead vocalist, was a US hit and the band supported it with a worldwide tour.

Best of Volume I (1996) is just that. A year later Roth released a similar offering, *The Best*.

JAMES VAN HEUSEN
b. *Edward Chester Babcock, 26 January 1913, Syracuse, New York, USA, d. 7 February 1990, Rancho Mirage, California*

A prolific songwriter, Van Heusen, in partnership with lyricists Johnny Burke and later **Sammy Cahn**, supplied Oscar-winning songs to **Bing Crosby** ('Swinging on a Star', 1944) and **Frank Sinatra** ('All the Way', 1957; 'High Hopes', 1959; and 'Call Me Irresponsible', 1963).

After a spell as a radio announcer, during which he adopted the name Van Heusen (after the shirt company), his first hit was written with, and recorded by, **Jimmy Dorsey** ('It's the Dreamer in Me', 1938). In the same year he formed a partnership with bandleader Eddie De Lange which produced 'Deep in a Dream' (**Artie Shaw**), 'Heaven Can Wait' (the Casa Loma Orchestra, featuring **Pee Wee Hunt**, 1939) and 'All This and Heaven Too', a hit for both Jimmy and

Tommy Dorsey. The pair also wrote the music for the Broadway swing version of *Midsummer Night's Dream, Swingin' the Dream* (1939), which included 'Darn that Dream', a No. 1 hit for **Benny Goodman** with **Mildred Bailey** on vocals (1940). Even more important was Tommy Dorsey's success with 'Polka Dots and Moonbeams'. The song announced a new writing partnership, Van Heusen and Burke (b. 3 October 1908, Antioch, California, d. 25 February 1964, New York) and it was sung by Sinatra, who regularly solicited material from its writers after going solo in 1942.

Following the success of their first film songs, Crosby commissioned the pair to write extensively for him. In total, Van Heusen, with Burke and later Cahn, wrote songs for some twenty Crosby films, including six of the seven *Road* movies. Among their hits for Crosby were 'Moonlight Becomes You' (1942), 'Personality' (1945), 'Swingin on a Star' (1944, later reworked by Big Dee Irwin, Dimension, 1963) and 'Aren't You Glad You're You' (1945). During the Second World War, Van Heusen, an enthusiastic flier, worked under his real name (which Crosby confusingly used as his character name in the *Road* movies) as a test pilot for the Lockheed Corporation. In 1954, when Burke fell ill, Van Heusen teamed up with Cahn, who had just dissolved his partnership with **Jule Styne**.

Writing mostly for Sinatra, the pair's songs were even more wise-cracking and blustery than Van Heusen's collaborations with Burke. They also wrote some of Sinatra's most effective melancholic ballads. Among the songs they provided for Sinatra were 'The Tender Trap', 'Love and Marriage' (1955), 'Come Fly with Me' (1958), 'Pocketful of Miracles' (1961) and the frequently recorded hymn to Chicago, 'My Kind of Town' (1964). Attempts at Broadway shows (which included *Skyscraper*, 1965, and *Walking Happy*, 1966) were less successful and their last major composition was 'Star' (1968), the title song of the musical about Gertrude Lawrence starring **Julie Andrews**.

DAVE VAN RONK
b. *30 June 1936, Brooklyn, New York, USA*

A central figure in the American folk revival of the sixties, white blues singer Van Ronk was an important influence on the young **Bob Dylan**.

In the early fifties he played banjo with the Brute Force Jazz Band and in 1957 he began to perform with the Folksingers Guild, building up a knowledge of folk blues unusual among his Greenwich Village contemporaries. His repertoire of the early sixties contained such songs as 'House of the Rising Sun', **Blind Lemon Jefferson**'s 'See That My Grave Is Kept Clean' (both of which later appeared on Dylan's début album), 'Candy Man', 'Poor Lazarus' and 'Dink's Song'.

Van Ronk first recorded for Lyrichord in 1958 with a jug band whose members included future blues collector and **Country Joe McDonald** producer Sam Charters. He signed to **Moe Asch**'s Folkways for *Sings Earthy Ballads and Blues* (1959) and *Black Mountain Blues* (1960). Blues continued to predominate on *Folksinger* (1963), which included 'Cocaine Blues' and a cover of Dylan's 'He Was a Friend of Mine'. On *Inside* (1964), his most enduring work, Van Ronk performed such traditional songs as 'Fair and Tender Ladies' and 'House Carpenter', before playing at the Newport Folk Festival with a jazz-inflected jug band in the **Gus Cannon** mould, also recording with them for Mercury. He briefly recorded in a folk-rock vein with *Dave van Ronk and the Hudson Dusters* (1967), but quickly retreated to solo acoustic recordings.

Maintaining his distance both from the protest-song movement and from folk-rock, Van Ronk recorded only occasional albums for Verve in the late sixties. In 1974 he appeared with Dylan at a New York concert for Chilean political prisoners and recorded *Songs for Aging Children* (Cadet), produced by Michael Brovsky. He later released *Sunday Street* (Philo, 1976), which included versions of **Scott Joplin** ragtime tunes and **Joni Mitchell**'s 'That Song About the Midway', and the Mitch Greenhill-produced *Somebody Else, Not Me* (1980). In 1985 he released an intriguing album of his own compositions, *Going Back to Brooklyn* (Gazell).

Perhaps his most surprising later recording was 1989's *Inside Dave van Ronk*, on which he attempted versions of songs by **Randy Newman** and others with an over-lush string backing. Far better were the re-issues of his earlier recordings, such as *The Folkway Years* (1991) and *Inside* (1969), which paired *Inside* and *Folksinger*. These consolidated his reputation as the most intense white singer of traditional blues in the sixties folk revival.

LUTHER VANDROSS
b. 20 April 1951, New York, USA

After a lengthy career as a session singer and a 'back-room' influence on soul music, Vandross emerged as a major artist with *Never Too Much* (1981). The possessor of a contemporary, somewhat mannered, vocal style, Vandross acknowledged his debt to his soul roots by including at least one sixties hit on each of his albums.

Vandross came from a musical background – an elder sister had sung with the **Crests** – and one of his compositions ('Everybody Rejoice') was used in 1972 in the Broadway show *The Wiz*, which was based on

The Wizard of Oz and filmed in 1978 with **Diana Ross** and **Michael Jackson** in the starring roles. After establishing himself as a session vocalist, he worked as singer and arranger on **David Bowie**'s *Young Americans* (1975), which included the Vandross song 'Fascination'. This led to further session work with producer **Arif Mardin** and artists as diverse as **Bette Midler**, **Carly Simon** and **Quincy Jones**. Vandross was also established as a vocalist for commercial jingles, singing ads for 7-Up and Kentucky Fried Chicken, among others.

In 1976–7 he recorded with his own group Luther for Cotillion, having minor R&B hits with 'It's Good for the Soul' and 'This Close to You'. He went on to provide lead vocals for Italian studio band Change on the disco hits 'Lover's Holiday'/'Glow of Love' and 'Searching', which reached the British Top Twenty in 1980. As a result, he began a solo career with Epic and produced *Never Too Much*, whose title track was a Top Forty hit.

Forever, for Always, for Love (1982) was also successful and soon afterwards Vandross was brought in to produce **Aretha Franklin**'s *Jump to It* (1982) and *Get It Right* (1983). He also made hit duet with **Dionne Warwick**, 'How Many Times Can We Say Goodbye' (1983), and arranged and sang on several tracks of Diana Ross's *Silk*.

Vandross's own later work included *Busybody* (1983) and *The Night I Fell in Love* (1985), with the successful single 'Till My Baby Comes Home'. *Give Me the Reason* (1987) included the hits 'Stop to Love', 'I Really Didn't Mean It' and 'There's Nothing Better Than Love', a duet with Gregory Hines and an R&B No. 1. In 1988 he released *Any Love*, a Top Ten album in Britain and America. In 1989 the compilation *The Best of Love* was another trans-Atlantic hit.

Power of Love in 1991 gave Vandross his seventh consecutive million-selling album in America and provided hit singles in 'Power of Love/Love Power' (a reissued hit in the UK in 1995) and 'Don't Want to Be a Fool'. In 1992 his duet with **Janet Jackson** on 'The Best Things in Life Are Free' from the movie soundtrack *Mo' Money* was his biggest British hit (and a reissued hit again in 1995). In 1993 he notched up yet another hit album with *Never Let Me Go*, on which he covered the **Bee Gees**' 'How Deep Is Your Love?'. In 1994 he had a European hit with his version of Stephen Stills' (of **Crosby, Stills and Nash**) 'Love the One You're With'. Like his duet with **Mariah Carey** on 'Endless Love' (the **Lionel Richie** and **Diana Ross** hit), it came from *Songs*, Vandross's album of cover-versions.

Later albums included the seasonal outing *This Is Christmas* (1995) and *Your Secret Love* (1996). His hits are collected on *The Best of Love, Vol. 1* (1992) and *Vol. 2* (1997).

VANGELIS
b. *Evanghelos Odyssey Papathanoussiou, b. 24 May 1943, Athens, Greece*

A keyboards and synthesizer player, Vangelis enjoyed success in partnership with Jon Anderson, lead singer of **Yes**, and as a composer of scores for such films as *Chariots of Fire* and *Blade Runner*.

In the mid-sixties he formed Aphrodite's Child with singer Demis Roussos, recording the European hit 'Rain and Tears' (Mercury, 1968). The group recorded several albums, including *It's Five o'Clock* (1969) and *666 – The Apocalypse of St John* (1972), before splitting up. Roussos had a successful solo career as a bravura ballad singer, with such hits as 'Happy to Be on an Island in the Sun' (Philips, 1975), 'Can't Say How Much I Love You' (1976) and 'When Forever Has Gone' (1977).

Vangelis released the soundtrack album *L'Apocalypse des Animaux* (Polydor, 1973) before basing himself in London to record the British hits *Heaven and Hell* (RCA, 1976), with vocals by the English Chamber Choir and Anderson, and *Albedo 39*, a concept album which included the voices of astronauts landing on the moon. *Beaubourg* (1978) mixed jazz, electronics and rock but Vangelis had greater success in collaboration with Anderson. 'I Hear You Now' from *Short Stories* (Polydor, 1980), an experiment with ambient music, and the haunting 'I'll Find My Way Home' from *The Friends of Mr Cairo* (1981) both reached the British Top Ten.

His most popular piece was the theme for *Chariots of Fire* (1981), an American No. 1 as well as a European hit. Vangelis went on to compose film music for *Blade Runner* (1982), *The Bounty* (1984), *Mask* (1985), *City* (1990) and *1492 – Conquest of Paradise* (1992). Highlights of his soundtrack work were collected on the album *Themes* (Polydor, 1989). In 1988 Vangelis signed to the Arista label, releasing *Direct* (1988) and *Page of Life*, which saw him reunited with Anderson. In 1994 Warner released his soundtrack to *Blade Runner* to critical acclaim. Later albums included *Voices* (1996) and *El Greco* (1998).

Portrait (1996) is a partial 'best of'.

VANILLA FUDGE
Mark Stein, b. 11 March 1947, Bayonne, New Jersey, USA; Vince Martell, b. 11 November, 1945, Bronx, New York; Tim Bogert, b. 27 August 1944, New York; Carmine Appice, b. 15 December 1946, Staten Island, New York

The meeting point of psychedelia and heavy rock, Vanilla Fudge are best remembered for their stretched-out, gothic versions of other people's hits, notably the **Supremes**' 'You Keep Me Hangin' on' (1968).

The group evolved from two New York bar bands, the Pigeons (Bogert, bass, and Stein, organ) and the Vagrants (Appice, drums, and Martell, guitar), which like the **Rascals** specialized in blue-eyed soul. In 1967 they took the name Vanilla Fudge, signed with Atlantic and had immediate success with their **Shadow Morton**-produced eponymous début album. As well as the single 'You Keep Me Hangin' on', the album included readings of **The Beatles**' 'Eleanor Rigby', **Curtis Mayfield**'s 'People Get Ready' and **Cher**'s 'Bang Bang'. Dominated by Stein's organ, these symphonic exercises, which mixed crude gospel harmonies with wide-screen arrangements, reached their climax on *The Beat Goes on* (1968), which included a pompous twelve-minute history of the music of the past twenty-five years and their last major hit, a version of **Patti Labelle and the Blue Belles**' 1966 Atlantic outing 'Take Me for a Little While'. Their extended version of **Donovan**'s 'Season of the Witch' from *Renaissance* (1968) revealed the limits of the group's symphonic-variations idea of rock and after two lesser albums the group broke up in 1970.

Appice and Bogert formed Cactus before joining up with **Jeff Beck** in the shortlived Beck, Bogert and Appice, and Stein formed the equally shortlived Boomerang. By the late seventies Appice was a respected session drummer and regular member of **Rod Stewart**'s backing group. In 1982 the group re-formed and released *Mystery* (Atco, 1983). They split in 1984, re-forming again in 1988 to play Madison Square Garden with other Atlantic acts in celebration of the label's fortieth anniversary.

FRANKIE VAUGHAN
b. *Francis Abelson, 3 February 1928, Liverpool, England*

Despite a lengthy list of British chart successes, Vaughan is best remembered in live performance where, with top hat and cane, he enlivened his theme song 'Give Me the Moonlight' with high kicks. An emphatic, expressive, big-voiced singer of the old style, Vaughan had the misfortune to emerge at the same time as rock'n'roll and subsequently his hits were mostly cover-versions of material ill-suited to him.

Vaughan first sang professionally with the Yorkshire Dance Band Revue while at Leeds College of Art and, after briefly attempting a career as a commercial artist, made his recording début in 1950 on Decca. After signing with HMV he had his first major hit in 1954 with **Jimmy Kennedy**'s 'Istanbul'. However, within a year, like his American contemporaries, he was recording lacklustre cover-versions of R&B and rock'n'roll songs. In 1955 he moved to Philips and covered Georgia Gibbs' million-selling 1955 cover of

Lavern Baker's 'Tweedle Dee' on Mercury and the Fontane Sisters' 1955 cover-version of Boyd Bennet's 'Seventeen' on Dot. Subsequent covers included American hits of all kinds: 'Green Door' (a million-seller for Jim Lowe, Dot, 1956), 'Garden of Eden' (Joe Valino, Vik, 1956, and Vaughan's first British No. 1 in 1957), 'Kisses Sweeter Than Wine' (Jimmie Rodgers, Roulette, 1957), Perry Como's 'Kewpie Doll' (1958), Edith Piaf's 'Milord' (1960), Gene McDaniels' 'Tower of Strength' (1961, Vaughan's second British No. 1), and a pair of European-orientated dance records, 'Don't Stop Twist' (1962) and 'Loop-De-Loop' (1963). Vaughan's one American success was the ballad 'Judy' (Epic, 1958).

From the late fifties on Vaughan appeared frequently on TV and in cabaret and in 1960, after several British films, went to Hollywood to co-star with Marilyn Monroe in Let's Make Love. He had few hits in the sixties, the major exceptions being 'There Must Be a Way' (1967) and 'Nevertheless' (1968). In the seventies and eighties he recorded less frequently, devoting himself to charity work for the Boys' Club movement and occasional performances.

SARAH VAUGHAN

b. 27 March 1924, Newark, New Jersey, USA, d. 3 April 1990, Los Angeles, California

One of the greatest interpreters of a lyric to emerge since the Second World War, Vaughan was second only to Ella Fitzgerald as a jazz singer. Her best-known recordings were the thrilling duet with Billy Eckstine, 'Passing Strangers' (1957), and her only million-seller 'Broken Hearted Melody' (1959).

The daughter of a laundress, Vaughan sang in the church and studied piano as a child. After she won an amateur contest at Harlem's Apollo Theater in 1943, Earl Hines signed her as a singer and second pianist on the advice of Eckstine. A year later, when Eckstine formed his own big band, Vaughan went with him. Her first recordings in 1945 were firmly in a small-group jazz mould, notably her fine, cool reading of 'Lover Man' (Musicraft, 1945) on which she was partnered by Dizzy Gillespie and Charlie Parker. But, like Eckstine, she had greater success with romantic ballads into which she breathed life with her wide vocal range and precise timing. Among her hits were 'Nature Boy' (Musicraft, 1948), later successfully revived by Bobby Darin (1961), 'I'm Crazy to Love You' (Columbia, 1950) and 'My Tormented Heart' (1952). In 1953 she joined Mercury and recorded a memorable version of Kurt Weill's 'September Song' (1954) with trumpeter Clifford Brown. Her other Mercury records were more pop orientated. They included the show song 'Whatever Lola Wants' (1955), 'C'Est la Vie' (1955) and even a cover of 'Banana Boat

Song' (1957), the calypso popularized by Harry Belafonte and parodied by Stan Freberg.

Her greatest success came with 'Broken Hearted Melody' (1959). Co-written by Burt Bacharach's regular writing partner Hal David, it presaged a more contemporary approach to singles (she also recorded 'A Lover's Concerto', 1966, a cover of the Toys' 1965 Dyno Voice recording). By the end of the decade, though 'Passing Strangers' was a British hit again when reissued in 1969, Vaughan was concentrating on touring, sometimes appearing with symphony orchestras, occasionally with just bass and drums. She continued to tour and record throughout the eighties. Her last performance before her death from lung cancer was in Back on the Block, the tribute film to Quincy Jones.

STEVIE RAY VAUGHAN

b. 3 October 1954, Dallas, USA, d. 27 August 1990, East Troy

A gifted blues-rock guitarist, Stevie Ray Vaughan was partly responsible for the blues revival of the late eighties and nineties.

Born in Dallas, Vaughan was heavily influenced in his musical tastes by his elder brother, Jimmie, a guitarist who would eventually form leading Texan R&B practitioners the Fabulous Thunderbirds in the late seventies. Along with electric blues, Stevie Ray developed an interest in the more rock-orientated output of Cream and Jimi Hendrix, who would remain a lasting influence. Having been taught to play by his brother, Vaughan joined several bands while at high school, eventually dropping out to join his brother in Austin at the age of eighteen. There he joined Paul Ray & the Cobras, recording a single, 'Texas Clover', in 1974, before leaving to form Triple Threat with local vocalist Lou Ann Barton, bassist Jackie Newhouse and drummer Chris Layton in 1977. The band changed their name to Double Trouble (taking their name from an Otis Rush classic) in 1979 and, when Barton left shortly after, Vaughan became lead singer.

The band toured constantly, generally billed as Stevie Vaughan and Double Trouble, enhancing the guitarist's reputation and attracting the attention of veteran producer Jerry Wexler, who organized a performance at the 1982 Montreux Jazz Festival. With new bassist Tommy Shannon, the band played to a Festival audience which included David Bowie and Jackson Browne, both of whom were greatly impressed. Browne offered the band studio time in Los Angeles, and Bowie hired Vaughan to work on his forthcoming album. When the R&B-slanted Let's Dance appeared in 1982, the reviews universally applauded Vaughan's Albert King-styled guitar playing, but an argument over billing led to his pulling out of Bowie's subsequent world tour.

Stevie Ray Vaughan and Double Trouble signed to Epic Records in 1983, releasing the exceptional *Texas Flood*. Boosted by good reviews and the band's incessant touring, the album reached the US Top Forty. *Couldn't Stand the Weather* appeared the following year. Displaying more of a rock sound, it eventually sold over one million copies in the US and included a version of Hendrix's 'Voodoo Chile (Slight Return)', a Vaughan stage favourite. Keyboard-player Reese Wynans was added to Double Trouble's line-up in 1985, playing on *Soul to Soul*, which found Vaughan adding jazz inflections to his trademark blues-rock. The same year also saw Vaughan produce an album, *Strike Like Lightning*, for one of his heroes, **Lonnie Mack**.

While Vaughan underwent a drink and drug rehabilitation programme, Epic released a stop-gap live album, the disappointing *Live Alive*, in 1987. Recovered, Vaughan returned to touring and to the studio to record *In Step*. The album appeared in 1989 and was acclaimed as his best work yet, reaching the US Top Forty and charting in the UK.

In 1990 Stevie Ray finally recorded with his brother Jimmie, but soon after was killed in a helicopter crash flying home from a concert in Wisconsin. When the Vaughan Brothers' *Family Style* was released a few months later, it became Stevie Ray Vaughan's biggest chart success, reaching the US Top Ten.

The posthumous compilation of unreleased studio recordings *The Sky Is Crying* (1991) was equally successful. A 1980 live recording, *In the Beginning*, appeared in 1993. In November 1993 the citizens of Austin erected a statue to Vaughan on the shores of Town Lake. Jimmy Vaughan's 1994 album *Strange Pleasure* included the song 'Six Strings Down', a fitting tribute to the guitarist whose death, according to **B. B. King**, was 'a loss not just to music, but to people as a whole'. It was followed by *A Tribute to Stevie Ray Vaughan* (1996), on which the likes of **Eric Clapton**, **Buddy Guy**, **Robert Cray** and **Dr John** recorded songs in his honour.

BILLY VAUGHN
b. 12 April 1931, Glasgow, Kentucky, USA, d. 26 September 1991, Escondido, California

A highly successful orchestra leader who had four million-selling records in the fifties, Vaughn was even more influential as the musical director of Randy Wood's Dot Records, which specialized in producing cover-versions of R&B and rock'n'roll hits.

While attending Western Center College in Bowling Green in 1952, Vaughn formed the vocal quartet the Hilltoppers with fellow students Jimmy Sacca,

Don McGuire and Seymour Spiegleman. Their hits included 'Trying' (Dot, 1952 – written by Vaughn), a version of **Johnny Mercer** and **Gordon Jenkins**' 'P.S. I Love You'* (1953), a cover of the **Platters**' 'Only You' (1955) and Terry Gilkyson's 'Marianne' (Columbia, 1957). By this time, Vaughn, originally the group's musical director, had established his own studio orchestra and became Dot's musical director. With label-owner Wood (who ran the biggest mail-order record shop in the South) choosing the records to cover, Vaughn provided the sweetened soundalike orchestrations for the Fontane Sisters' million-selling version of the Charms' 'Hearts of Stone' (De Lux, 1954), Gale Storm's million-selling cover of **Smiley Lewis**'s 'I Hear You Knocking' (1955) and many others, including **Pat Boone**'s hits.

Vaughn's own hits were, for the most part, similarly sweetened versions of other artists' hits. 'Melody of Love'* (1954), an adaptation of 'Melodie d'Amour', was also a hit for the **Four Aces** and **Frank Sinatra**, among others; 'The Shifting Whispering Sands' (1955) was a cover of Rusty Draper's million-selling Mercury recording; and 'Raunchy' was a cover of **Bill Justis**'s 1957 million-seller. His brisk revival of 'Sail Along Silv'ry Moon'* (1957) won him a large German following and most of his subsequent recordings were targeted at Europe as much as America. These included 'Tumbling Tumbleweeds' (1958), 'La Paloma'* (1958) and 'Wheels'* (1961), co-written by **Buddy Holly**'s original producer **Norman Petty**. A million-seller for the String-a-Longs (Warwick), the tune was also recorded by the **Ventures** (1961). Vaughn's last hit was a cover of **The Beatles**' 'Michelle' (1966).

BOBBY VEE
b. Robert Thomas Velline, 30 April 1943, Fargo, North Dakota, USA

In marked contrast to such contemporaries as **Fabian** and **Bobby Rydell**, who offered jaunty, tame, puppy-fat versions of the threatening sexuality of **Elvis Presley**, the coy-voiced Vee took as his model the more ambiguous **Buddy Holly**. But whereas Holly took control of his own career, Vee's was masterminded by **Tommy 'Snuff' Garrett** and his fussy, precisely syncopated productions, and was dependent on songs from the new breed of songwriters working out of the Brill Building, notably **Carole King** and Gerry Goffin. Together singer, producer and songwriters gave perfect expression to the melodramas of high-school life in songs such as 'Take Good Care of My Baby'* and 'Run to Him'* (1961), Vee's most typical recordings.

The son of Norwegian immigrants, Vee formed the Shadows band with his elder brother Bill while in high school. The group's big break came when in 1959 they substituted for Holly after his death when the rock'n'roll tour he had been on arrived in Fargo. That led to the recording of the Bobby Vee-composed 'Suzie Baby' for the local Soma label, which was picked up for national distribution by Liberty (1959). Though the group remained with Vee until 1963, with the youthful **Bob Dylan** reportedly playing piano at one gig, Liberty from the start concentrated on Vee as a solo act. After a failed cover-version of **Adam Faith**'s 'What Do You Want', Garrett recorded Vee in Clovis at the studio Holly had regularly used. His first major hit was the string-laden revival of the **Clovers'** 1956 hit 'Devil or Angel'* (1960) which he followed with the **Gene Pitney** co-written 'Rubber Ball'* (1960). The restrained Vee sound now successfully established, Goffin and King and other Brill Building writers provided him with a series of hits moulded around the repressed, caring persona he projected. Among these were 'Take Good Care of My Baby', 'Run to Him'* (1961), with its wave-like rhythms which never reach a resolution, the petulant 'How Many Tears' (1961), the plaintive 'Please Don't Ask About Barbara', the wistful 'Sharing You' (1962), and the almost triumphant 'The Night Has a Thousand Eyes'* (1962).

In contrast to his singles and film appearances (*Play It Cool*, 1962; *Just for Fun*, 1963), Vee's albums, which included *Meets the Crickets* (1963) and *I Remember Buddy Holly* (1964) which he recorded with the **Crickets**, were more reflective. Despite his widespread international popularity, Vee's career did not long outlast **The Beatles** and he turned to cabaret in the mid-sixties. Then in 1967 he had a surprise hit with 'Come Back When You Grow Up'* which he followed with the medley 'My Girl/My Guy' (1968). In 1972 he recorded *Nothing Like a Sunny Day* under his real name for United Artists, which included a reworking of 'Take Good Care of My Baby', before reverting to Bobby Vee to play the revival circuit. Vee was a regular visitor to Britain, where a 1980 compilation, *The Bobby Vee Singles Album*, made the British Top Five. In 1992 he released a self-financed album, *The Last of the Great Rhythm Guitar Players*.

SUZANNE VEGA
b. *12 August 1959, Santa Monica, California, USA*

A literate songwriter whose songs are based on compassion and observation rather than confession, Vega captured the sensibilities of the late eighties in a series of striking albums.

A dance student at New York's High School for the Performing Arts, Vega did the round of the folk clubs in Greenwich Village in the late seventies. By 1982 she had been featured in several issues of CooP, a local songwriters magazine, and in 1984 was signed to

A&M. Her eponymous début album (1985) was co-produced by former rock critic turned guitarist (with **Patti Smith**) Lenny Kaye. It is a classic example of bedsitter folk music, the observation of city life from a narrow, slightly introverted, perspective. The carefully constructed and almost coldly performed 'Marlene on the Wall' and 'Small Blue Thing' were surprise European hits, boosting the album's sales. 'Luka', a memorable depiction of domestic violence, from her second, stronger, album, *Solitude Standing* (1987), gave her her first American hit. An even more surprising hit was the remixed version of her *a cappella* rendition 'Tom's Diner' by two British deejays, DNA, in 1990. In the same year she released the lesser *Days of Open Hand*.

99.9F (1992) added dance-music elements to Vega's characteristic approach on such tracks as 'Blood Makes Noise' and 'When Heroes Go Down'. Vega took a lengthy break before issuing *Nine Objects of Desire* (1996), a return to the tone of her earlier material. A 'best of' collection was issued in 1998.

THE VELVET UNDERGROUND
John Cale, b. 5 December, 1940, Garnant, Wales (replaced by Doug Yule); Sterling Morrison, b. Holmes Sterling Morrison Jr, 29 August, 1942, Long Island, USA (replaced by Willie Alexander), d. 30 August 1995; Nico, b. Christa Paffgen, 16 October 1938, Cologne, Germany, d. 18 July 1988, Ibiza, Spain; Lou Reed, b. Lewis Allen Reed, 2 March 1942, Long Island, New York (replaced by Walter Powers); Angus MacLise, d. Katmandu, Nepal, 1979 (replaced by Maureen Tucker, b. 1945, New Jersey, replaced by Billy Yule)

Although the classic line-up only played together for three years, the Velvet Underground were among the most influential of sixties rock bands. The mix of **John Cale**'s avant-garde temperament and **Lou Reed**'s harsh street poetry dealing with taboo topics like sex and drugs was a corrosive alternative to the flower-power optimism of many of their contemporaries. Among those whose debt to the Velvet Underground can be clearly traced are **David Bowie, Patti Smith, Roxy Music, Blondie** and the **Sex Pistols**.

A classical viola player and pianist, Cale went to America in 1963 on a scholarship. Having studied the work of John Cage, he performed with another noted avant-gardist, LaMonte Young, before meeting Reed, at the time working as a staff songwriter for Pickwick Records. To promote one of his songs, a dance-craze parody titled 'The Ostrich' (Pickwick, 1965) recorded by Reed and various in-house session men as the Primitives, the label put together a band to back Reed with Cale on bass, fellow Young sideman Tony Conrad on guitar and drummer Walter DeMaria. The record flopped, but Reed and Cale resolved to continue working together. Recruiting Reed's ex-college friend Morrison on guitar and another ex-Young percussionist Angus MacLise, they performed on the avant-garde circuit in New York under various names before becoming the Velvet Underground in 1965, at which time Tucker replaced Maclise.

They accompanied Andy Warhol's travelling multimedia show 'The Exploding Plastic Inevitable' and met *chanteuse* Nico, who sang lead on three of the songs on the band's début album, *The Velvet Underground and Nico* (MGM, 1967). With a sleeve design featuring a peelable banana by Warhol, who also received a producer credit, the album featured Reed's alternately fearful and joyous celebration of drug-taking 'Heroin', the urgent 'Waiting for the Man', plus Nico's cool, precise singing on the icy 'Femme Fatale' and Cale's innovative viola playing on 'Venus in Furs'. *White Light/White Heat* (1968), recorded without Nico, was louder and harsher. It included the seventeen-minute 'Sister Ray' and 'The Gift', a horror story written by Reed with a deadpan narration by Cale.

Cale left soon afterwards and without him Reed's songwriting skills took centre stage on *The Velvet Underground* (1970). With Doug Yule from Boston group Glass Menagerie on bass, the album included the lyrical ballads 'Candy Says', 'Pale Blue Eyes' and 'Afterhours', which was sung by Tucker. The song-based approach was maintained on *Loaded* (Atlantic, 1970), a mix of fervent ballads like 'Oh Sweet Nuthin'' and 'New Age' and such pulsating rock songs as 'Sweet Jane' and 'Rock and Roll'. Tucker did not play on the album as she was pregnant at the time, and was temporarily replaced by Yule's brother Billy, who also played live with the band in 1970.

Before the release of *Loaded*, however, Reed had also left the group, retiring from music for almost two years before re-emerging as a solo artist. The returning Tucker and Morrison elected to continue with Yule as the band's figure-head and recruited Boston musicians Alexander (guitar, keyboards) and Powers (vocals, guitar). Morrison was next to leave, and after a short European tour (the band's first), the Velvets split up. Doug Yule kept the band name going for *Squeeze* (Polydor, 1972), essentially a solo album. After the final demise of the band, two live recordings from 1969–1970 were issued, with *Live at Max's Kansas City* (Atlantic, 1972) Reed's final performance with the group. The excellent *1969 Live* (Mercury, 1974) was superior in both sound and performance.

Some measure of the Velvets' continued importance was provided in 1985 when *VU* (Polydor), a collection of previously unreleased tracks from 1967–8, sold more copies than had the group's four albums on their first release. A more uneven second volume, *Another View*, followed in 1986.

Morrison left music for an academic career, while Tucker raised a family before launching a low-key solo career in 1982 with *Playin' Possum*. A 1987 EP featured two old Velvets' songs, and Reed and members of **Sonic Youth** appeared on *Life in Exile After Abdication* (1989). Reed, Cale and Morrison all contributed to *I Spent a Week There the Other Night* (1991), one track of which featured the four members together on record for the first time since 1968. Yule had a low-key post-Velvets career, recording two late seventies albums with country-rock band American Flyer (whose vocalist Craig Fuller would later join **Little Feat** before quitting music).

Cale and Reed both had distinguished careers in the next three decades and Cale was also involved in Nico's solo recording career. Along with Reed and Morrison, he played on her début, *Chelsea Girl* (Verve, 1968), and subsequently arranged *Marble Index* (Elektra, 1969). He produced *Desert Shore* (Reprise, 1971) and *The End* (Island, 1974), which included a controversial rendering of the German anthem 'Das Lied der Deutschen' ('Deutschland über Alles'). After taking part in a live recording *June 1 1974* (Island) with Cale, **Brian Eno** and Kevin Ayers (ex-**Soft Machine**), Nico went into semi-retirement, acting in a few low-budget European films before re-emerging in 1978 as a live performer, adopted as an icon by punk bands such as **Siouxsie and the Banshees**. 1981's *Drama of Exile* (Aura) included a new version of the Velvet Underground's 'Waiting for My Man'. *Do or Die* (1983) was a live recording. Dogged by her heroin addiction, she later settled in Manchester, England (recording the Cale-produced *Camera Obscura*, 1985), and, having kicked her drug habit, died after a cycling accident in 1988. Several live recordings appeared posthumously.

In 1989 Tucker made a cameo appearance on Reed's album *New York*, drumming on 'Dime Store Mystery', a tribute to the band's late former mentor, Warhol. Reed and Cale were next to be reunited, releasing the album based on Warhol's life, *Songs for Drella* (1990). In June 1990 an impromptu reunion of the Velvet Underground took place at a Warhol convention in Jouy-en-Josas, France. Subsequently, Morrison toured in Tucker's band, appearing on the live album *Oh No, They're Recording This Show*. These events laid the groundwork for a full-scale reunion of the Velvets in 1993, when Reed, Cale, Morrison and Tucker toured Europe to ecstatic audiences. The in-concert album *Live MCMXCIII* followed later that year, but planned American dates were scrapped after reports of constant in-fighting among the group members and shortly afterwards Cale, Reed and Tucker resumed their solo careers. Tucker released another idiosyncratic collection, *Dogs Under Stress* (New Rose 1993).

The seventy-five-track *Peel Slowly and See* (1995) is the definitive career retrospective, while *Loaded (Fully*

Loaded) (1997) was a thirty-three-track 'complete version' of the band's 1970 album.

THE VENTURES

Bob Bogle, b. 6 January 1937, Portland, Oregon, USA; Don Wilson, b. 10 February 1937, Tacoma, Washington; Nokie Edwards, b. 9 May 1939, Lahoma, Oklahoma; Howie Johnston, b. 1938, Washington, d. 1988

With sales of over 50 million records, the Ventures were both the most prolific and most successful instrumental group of their era. In contrast to the raucous style of **Johnny and the Hurricanes** and the ponderous, melodramatic approach of **Duane Eddy**, the Ventures' sound, like that of the **Shadows**, was clean, spare and melodic with lots of tremolo. But, whereas the British group were known for their atmospheric records, the Ventures' best recordings ('Walk Don't Run'*, 1960, and 'Perfidia'*, 1961) were more exciting and electric, driven by Edwards' pulsating bass and Johnston's economical drumming.

Founder members Bogle and Wilson met in Seattle, Washington. Both accomplished guitarists, they were inspired not by rock'n'roll but by **Chet Atkins**, whose 1957 recording of jazz guitarist Johnny Smith's 'Walk Don't Run' provided the model for their own version. With the addition of the **James Burton**-influenced Edwards and Johnston the group became the Ventures and released 'Walk Don't Run' on Blue Horizon, a label specially formed by Wilson's mother to further the group's career. Picked up by Dolton, the record initiated a series of instrumental hits. The best of these were a dynamic version of Alberto Dominguez's much-recorded 1913 composition, 'Perfidia', 'Ram-Bunk-Shush' (1961) and 'Lullaby of the Leaves'.

However, what had once been innovatory soon became clichéd and by the time of 'Walk Don't Run '64'* the Ventures sounded archaic. Nonetheless, they had further hits, including a surprise million-seller with the television theme 'Hawaii Five-O' (1969), and their albums – mostly of cover-versions – which saw them religiously following each new musical fashion, sold in large quantities in America. These included *The Ventures Play Telstar and the Lonely Bull* (1963), *Surfing with The Ventures* (1964), *Guitar Freakout* (1967) and *Super Psychedelics* (1968). During this period the line-up of the group fluctuated. In 1962 bassist Edwards and lead guitarist Bogle switched roles and Mel Taylor (*b. 24 September 1934, New York, USA, d. 11 August 1996*) replaced Johnston, while session guitarist Jerry McGhee joined in 1967.

Relegated to the margins of the popular mainstream in America and Europe, the Ventures' precise playing won them a huge and long-lasting following in Japan. Following their first tour of the country in 1962, in the sixties and seventies the Ventures sold some 30 million records there and recorded over ten albums, mostly live, specifically for the Japanese market. Included on these were a number of 'instrumental impressions of Japan'. Several of these were recorded, with additional Japanese lyrics, by local singers, including 'Kyoto No Koi' (Toshiba, 1970) and 'Kyoto Bojyo' (1971), million-sellers for Yuko Nagisa, who regularly toured with the group. Another mark of the Ventures' influence in Japan was the number of Japanese groups who recorded tribute albums to them. Typical of these was *The Blue Jeans Go to The Ventures Melodies* (1965), which consisted largely of Japanese versions of the Ventures' versions of other people's hits. In 1972 the group was elected to the Music Conservatory of Japan, the first foreigners to be so honoured. *The Jim Croce Songbook* (1974), which was followed by *The Ventures Play The Carpenters* (1975), started a new series of albums.

They played regularly on the American nostalgia circuit into the nineties. *Walk Don't Run* (1990) is the definitive hits collection.

JOE VENUTI

b. Giuseppe Venuti, 16 September 1903, South Philadelphia, Pennsylvania, USA, d. 14 August 1978, Seattle, Washington

With **Stephane Grappelli**, Venuti was the most technically gifted of the first generation of jazz violinists. Known as 'the mad fiddler from Philly', Venuti's most important recordings were made with guitarist **Eddie Lang**.

He met Lang at school and by 1921 they were performing professionally in Atlantic City. Venuti went on to jobs in the bands of **Red Nichols** and Jean Goldkette before moving to New York. From 1924 he was involved in dozens of recording sessions. With Lang he recorded some seventy tracks for Victor and Columbia before the guitarist's death in 1933. They included 'Wild Cat', 'Stringing the Blues' (1926), 'Four String Joe', 'Really Blue' and 'Little Girl' (1931), with songwriter **Harold Arlen** on vocals. Venuti also made records with **Bix Beiderbecke**, **Tommy** and **Jimmy Dorsey** ('Jig Saw Puzzle Blues', 1933), Frankie Trumbauer, and many others.

From 1929 to 1930 Venuti played in **Paul Whiteman**'s band, appearing in *King of Jazz* (1930), on the set of which prankster Venuti reportedly poured flour into a tuba. After joining Roger Wolfe Kahn's band in 1932, he visited Europe and founded his own band in 1935. This was wound up in 1944 when he moved to California to work at MGM studios. Venuti also continued to perform live and during the fifties had a radio show in Los Angeles.

After recording with saxophonist Zoot Sims (*Joe and Zoot*, Chiascuro, 1966), Venuti made a highly acclaimed appearance at the 1968 Newport Festival. He continued to tour America and Europe in the seventies, recording with numerous musicians, including singer Marian McPartland, and the Dutch Swing College Band for Parlophone.

MIKE VERNON
b. 19 November 1944, Harrow, Middlesex, England

Record-producer Vernon was a leading figure in the British blues scene of the sixties, working with **Johnny Mayall**, **Eric Clapton** and **Fleetwood Mac**. Among his later successes were records by Dutch group Focus, funk band Bloodstone and the Olympic Runners, a soul group in which he also played. In the eighties Vernon produced the early albums of **Level 42** before returning to producing mostly blues in the nineties.

A choirboy, Vernon met blues enthusiast and future Savoy Brown producer Neil Slaven at school. At Croydon Art College he played in the Mojo Men before joining Decca in 1964. His earliest productions were by American artists Curtis Jones, **Larry Williams** and **Otis Spann**. While producing Mayall's *Bluesbreakers* (1966), which featured Clapton, and *A Hard Road* (1967), as well as **David Bowie**'s *Images* (1967) for Decca, Vernon started his own Purdah, Outasite and Blue Horizon labels to issue material by both American and British artists.

Signing a distribution deal for Blue Horizon with Columbia in 1968, Vernon released albums by Chicken Shack, Duster Bennett, Jellybread and Fleetwood Mac, whose hits 'Need Your Love So Bad' (1968) and the No. 1 'Albatross' Vernon produced. After winding up Blue Horizon, his next discovery was Focus, led by singer Thijs Van Leer and Jan Akkerman (guitar). 'Hocus Pocus' (Polydor/Sire, 1973) was an American Top Ten hit while 'Sylvia' (1973) reached the British Top Ten. Akkerman later became a leading exponent of New Age music.

With Bloodstone, an eight-piece soul band from Kansas City, Vernon cut the million-selling 'Natural High' (London, 1973) and eight albums throughout the seventies. The Olympic Runners' recording career kept pace, with nine releases between 1974 and 1979. The group was made up of session players, plus Vernon and ex-Jellybread keyboards-player Pete Wingfield. Their disco-orientated records sold well in R&B markets and 'Get It While You Can' (Polydor, 1978) and 'Sir Dancealot' (1979) were minor British hits. Wingfield had a transatlantic hit with 'Eighteen with a Bullet' (Island, 1975) and in the eighties produced **Dexy's Midnight Runners**, the Pasadenas and the Proclaimers.

Vernon's own later production work involved British doo-wop revivalists Rocky Sharpe and the Replays (*Rock It to Mars*, 1980) and Level 42 (*Level 42,*

1981, *The Pursuit of Accidents*, 1982), a funk group in similar mould to the Olympic Runners. He worked on an album by New Orleans singer **Frankie Ford** and in 1985 launched the Brand New label, signing London pub band Johnny and the Roccos. In 1988 he revived Blue Horizon to release R&B albums by the British-based De Luxe Blues Band, Dana Gillespie, Lazy Lester and other contemporary blues acts. He subsequently set up another blues label, Indigo, for which he produced albums by **Robert Johnson** contemporary Honeyboy Edwards (*Delta Bluesman*, 1992), Lightnin' Slim (*London Gumbo*) and new acts Jay Owens (*The Blues Soul of Jay Owens*, 1994) and Sherman Robertson. In 1994 he signed a deal with East West Records which saw new albums, including by Owens and Robertson (*Here and Now*, 1996), appear on the Code Blue label.

THE VERVE
Richard Ashcroft, b. 11 September 1971, Billinge, Lancashire, England; Simon Jones, b. 29 July 1972, Wigan; Nick McCabe, b. 14 July 1971, Wigan; Peter Salisbury, b. 24 September 1971, Wigan; Simon Tong, b. 1972

Originally a British psychedelic rock quartet, the Verve found international fame in the late nineties with the zeitgeist-capturing anthems on the aptly titled *Urban Hymns*.

Singer-songwriter Ashcroft, bassist Jones and drummer Salisbury began playing together at sixth-form college in Wigan in 1989. With the addition of local guitarist McCabe they took the name Verve and soon earned a deal with Virgin subsidiary Hut Records on the strength of their expansive, tripped-out live performances and the shamanistic presence of Ashcroft. After honing their sound and releasing a handful of singles, notably 'All in the Mind' and 'She's a Superstar', Verve issued *A Storm in Heaven* (1993). The album was lavished with praise by critics on both sides of the Atlantic, but its expansive psychedelia failed to generate commercial interest, while the same fate befell an album of B-sides and rarities, *No Come Down* (1994), intended primarily for the American market. The same year the band was forced to add the definite article to its name after the threat of legal action from jazz label Verve Records. *A Northern Soul* (1995) took a more song-based approach than its predecessor, and as a result achieved stronger sales. However, just as 'History' put them within reach of stardom, the Verve announced that they were to split after a tempestuous performance at the T in the Park festival.

Undeterred by the split, caused essentially by the musical differences between McCabe and himself, Ashcroft returned to the studio and soon enlisted the help of Jones and Salisbury, as well as keyboardist/

guitarist Tong. After rehearsing with former **Suede** guitarist Bernard Butler, it became clear to Ashcroft that the band needed the mercurial guitar skills of Nick McCabe, and eventually asked him to return to the fold in 1997. The Verve had a huge hit with their comeback single, the string-laden epic 'Bittersweet Symphony', before topping the UK charts with the mournful ballad 'The Drugs Don't Work'. *Urban Hymns* (1997) then cemented the Verve's position as one of the most popular bands in Britain, becoming one of the year's bestsellers. Success proved not to last, however, as McCabe quit for the second time shortly after a massive gig at the Haigh Hall in Wigan. After fulfilling their touring commitments with the assistance of slide guitarist BJ Cole, the band ended months of speculation by announcing that they would not be playing together again.

Ashcroft spent the bulk of 1999 working on his début solo album *Alone with Everybody* (2000), which featured drummer Salisbury and wife Kate Radley, formerly keyboardist with Spiritualized, in support. A commercial success, the album missed the sense of the times that made *Urban Hymns* so compelling. Instead it merely veered between stirring and bland balladry, best instanced by the lead single 'A Song for the Lovers'.

VILLAGE PEOPLE

Alex Briley, b. 12 April 1951; David Hodo, b. July 1947, New York, USA; Glenn Hughes, b. 18 July 1950; Randy Jones; Felipe Rose; Victor Willis (replaced by Ray Simpson, replaced by Miles Jaye)

A disco-styled vocal group, the Village People purveyed a camp version of the gay-club style to the mass pop audience in the early eighties.

The brainchild of producer Jacques Morali (*b. 1941, d. 15 November 1991, Paris, France*), who had created the Ritchie Family hits 'Brazil' (20th Century, 1975) and 'The Best Disco in Town' (Marlin, 1976), the group was formed around lead vocalist Willis. Dressed as macho stereotypes (biker, cop, cowboy, building worker, and so on) the group built up a club following with gay-related songs like 'San Francisco' and 'Fire Island'.

In 1977 they signed to Casablanca, released an eponymous album and went on to have three million-selling hits. 'Macho Man' (1978) was followed by the controversial 'Y.M.C.A.'* (1978). Despite the surface innocence of the lyric, the group were accused of hinting that the august institution harboured gay activity. The jaunty 'In the Navy'* (1979) was the most camp of the Village People's offerings.

Willis was replaced by Simpson, brother of Valerie Simpson of **Ashford and Simpson**. With him, the band cut the unsuccessful *Cruisin'* (1979) and *Go West* (1979) and appeared with the Ritchie Family in the poorly received disco movie *Can't Stop the Music* (1980), directed by Nancy Walker. In Britain both 'Go West' and 'Can't Stop the Music' were pop hits.

In a vain attempt to retrieve the Village People's flagging fortunes, Morali turned to a new-romantic approach on *Renaissance* (1981). In contrast, 'Sex over the Phone' from *New York City* (Record Shack, 1985) saw a return to the group's heavy innuendo. The Village People's next lead singer was Miles Jaye, who was later signed by **Teddy Pendergrass** to his Top Priority label before enjoying black chart success with *Miles* (Island, 1987) and *Irresistible* (1989). In the nineties a new version of Village People appeared on the cabaret circuit in Britain and Europe. A remixed version of 'Y.M.C.A.' was a minor British hit and the re-formed act had chart success in Germany in 1994 when they made a single with the German World Cup soccer squad.

GENE VINCENT

b. Eugene Vincent Craddock, 11 February 1935, Norfolk, Virginia, USA, d. 12 October 1971, Los Angeles, California

Unlike **Elvis Presley** who swiftly managed the change from threatening, swaggering sex symbol to patriotic soldier and movie star, Gene Vincent remained an unrepentant and increasingly anachronistic rock'n'roll singer. Within two years of 'Be-Bop-a-Lula'* (1956), along with Presley's Sun recordings perhaps the purest example of Southern-styled rock'n'roll, his career was over in America. His last years were mostly spent in Europe where, clad in black leathers, he further intensified his original greasy, working-class image and confirmed his role as the keeper of the rock'n'roll flame.

The son of a shipyard worker, Vincent began singing while in the navy. In 1955 he shattered his left leg in an auto accident and began performing at country-music shows in the Norfolk area. A demo of his own composition 'Be-Bop-a-Lula', made with the Blue Caps (Cliff Gallup, Jack Neal, Willie Williams and Dickie Harrell), led to a contract with Capitol, who saw Vincent as a Presley soundalike. On the studio recording that followed, Vincent's gentle voice was strengthened and given a cutting edge by use of echo while Gallup's swirling guitar lines gave an extra dimension to the simple rhythms of the song. Vincent's spirited performance of 'Be-Bop-a-Lula' was also a high point of Frank Tashlin's classic rock'n'roll film, *The Girl Can't Help It* (1956). The follow-up 'Race with the Devil' (1956) was a British hit but failed in America and it was only with the double-sided hit 'Lotta Lovin''/'Wear My Ring'* (1957) that Vincent returned to the American charts. The former was a routine rocker and the latter a ballad (penned by **Don Kirshner** and **Bobby Darin**), complete with cooing harmony voices; both featured a changed Blue Caps line-up, with Johnny Meeks replacing Gallup and **Buck Owens** on rhythm guitar.

After the lesser 'Dance to the Bop' (1958) Vincent, plagued by bad advice and bad luck, was unable to sustain his American career. He moved to Britain where, dressed in black leather by **Jack Good**, he had further hits, including a reworking of **Al Dexter**'s 'Pistol Packing Mama' (1960) and 'She She Little Sheila' (1961). He also toured with **Eddie Cochran** (and was further injured in the car crash that killed Cochran), appeared in films, notably Dick Lester's *It's Trad Dad* (1962), and regularly toured Europe before his archaic style lost favour with audiences in the beat-group era dominated by **The Beatles**. He signed with EMI's Columbia label and recorded, backed with a Liverpudlian group, the Shouts, before returning to America in 1965. There he re-recorded his old hits for Challenge before returning to Britain in 1969. By now in poor health and reduced to appearing with pick-up bands, he recorded *I'm Back and I'm Proud* (1969) for Dandelion, the label set up by progressive disc-jockey John Peel, and in 1970 made two albums for Kama Sutra (including *The Day the World Turned Blue* – also the title of Britt Hagerty's biography of Vincent) before his death.

Though few of the later recordings are of real interest, Vincent's legacy remains potent. He was celebrated in **Ian Dury**'s affecting 'Sweet Gene Vincent' (1976). In 1993 **Jeff Beck** released *Crazy Legs*, an album of Vincent songs, as a tribute to Blue Caps guitarist Cliff Gallup. *The Best of Gene Vincent* (Capitol, 1988) is the definitive anthology of his creative period.

EDDIE 'CLEANHEAD' VINSON
b. 18 December 1917, Houston, Texas, USA, d. 2 July 1988

A raunchy big-band blues-shouter, whose hoarse delivery characteristically twirled into a squeaky, whooping falsetto at the ends of lines, Vinson was also an accomplished bebop alto-saxophonist in the style of **Charlie Parker** and the writer of several blues popular with other musicians, like 'Kidney Stew', 'Old Maid Boogie' and 'Person to Person'. He gained his sobriquet from his bald head.

He studied saxophone in high school (1934–6), toured with Milt Larkins' band alongside **Illinois Jacquet** (1936–40) and moved to New York in 1942, joining the big band led by ex-**Duke Ellington** trumpeter Cootie Williams to appear in movie shorts and record for Okeh, Hit and Capitol. He formed his own band in 1945, recording for Mercury, working in New York and St Louis and touring with an **Ink Spots** show (1947–9). His records included the humorous **Louis Jordan**-styled blues 'Kidney Stew' (1947) and the **Pete Johnson–Joe Turner** composition 'Cherry Red'. Based in Chicago, he next recorded for King

(1949–52), remaking some of his Mercury hits but suffering from King's more assiduous promotion of the not dissimilar **Wynonie Harris**. He rejoined Williams briefly in 1954 and then left music for more than a decade, returning only to make *Cleanhead's Back in Town* (Bethlehem, 1957) with members of the **Count Basie** orchestra and a Riverside session with Nat and **Cannonball Adderley** (1961).

Cherry Red (Bluesway, 1967) was followed by several European tours with **Jay McShann**. *Wee Baby Blues* (Black and Blue, 1969) was made in France with McShann, tenor saxophonist Hal Singer and **T-Bone Walker**. In the seventies he worked with **Johnny Otis** and returned often to Europe for tours, festivals and recording dates. He also teamed up with the Boston R&B band Roomful of Blues for tours and a 1982 album on Muse.

BOBBY VINTON
b. Stanley Robert Vinton, 16 April 1935, Canonsburg, Pennsylvania, USA

A bland balladeer, Vinton is best remembered for his lugubrious version of 'Blue Velvet'* (1963), which was chillingly recontextualized in David Lynch's 1986 thriller. Vinton survived the musical revolution associated with **The Beatles** better than his fellow teen-idols by turning to a repertoire of mainstream material and revivals.

A multi-instrumentalist, Vinton was a member of a big band while at high school and played trumpet in a military band while in the army. On his discharge in 1960, he formed his own big band. Signed to Epic, he released big-band versions of contemporary hits, *Dancing at the Hop* and *Bobby Vinton Plays for His L'il Darlin's* (1961). However, success only came when he turned to singing and recorded the American No. 1 'Roses Are Red (My Love)'* (1962), co-written by Paul Evans, who in 1959 had a million-seller with the novelty song 'Seven Little Girls' (Guaranteed). 'Roses' was followed by a string of hits, all firmly in the teen-ballad mould, including 'I Love You the Way You Are' (Diamond, 1962), a recording he made before joining Epic; 'Over the Mountain (Across the Sea)', a revival of Johnnie and Joe's 1957 Chess hit; and the **Burt Bacharach** composition 'Blue on Blue' (1963). That led to an album of 'blue' songs, among which was Vinton's revival of **Tony Bennett**'s 1951 hit 'Blue Velvet'. Arranged by Bacharach and recorded in Nashville with **Floyd Cramer**, Grady Martin and Charlie McCoy in support, the song gave Vinton his second American No. 1. It was followed by a series of revivals, including a version of **Vaughn Monroe**'s 1945 million-seller 'There I've Said It Again'* (1963), June Christy's (**Stan Kenton**'s band singer) 1942 Capitol hit 'My Heart Belongs to Only You' and 'Tell Me Why' (1964), a 1952 success for both **Eddie Fisher** and the **Four Aces**. Later that year Vinton returned to the No. 1 spot with his own composition, 'Mr Lonely' (1964).

By now well ensconced on the cabaret circuit, Vinton caught the revivalist mood of the late sixties with a series of highly successful supperclub versions of early sixties pop ballads. Among them were 'Please Love Me Forever' (1967), originally a hit for Cathy Jean and the Roommates (Valmor, 1961); 'Just as Much as Ever', Bob Beckman (Decca, 1959); 'Take Good Care of My Baby', **Bobby Vee** (1961); 'Halfway to Paradise', **Tony Orlando** (1961); 'I Love How You Love Me'* (1968), the Paris Sisters (Gregmark, 1961); a reworking of **Phil Spector**'s Teddy Bears' hit 'To Know Him Is to Love Him' (1958) as 'To Know You Is to Love You' (1969); 'Every Day of My Life', the **McGuire Sisters** (Coral, 1956); and 'Sealed with a Kiss' (1972), **Brian Hyland** (1962).

In 1974, after leaving Epic for ABC, Vinton had a huge hit with his own 'My Melody of Love'*, which he sang partially in Polish. His last major hit came a year later with an updated version of the **Andrews Sisters**' 1939 hit 'Beer Barrel Polka'. Afterwards Vinton concentrated on television (where he had his own show, 1975–8) and the cabaret circuit. In 1980 he moved to Tapestry and had a minor hit with 'Make Believe It's Your First Time'. Vinton later signed to **Mike Curb**'s MCA/Curb label, releasing *Timeless* (1989). In 1990 a reissued 'Blue Velvet' made the British Top Ten, following its use in the David Lynch movie of the same name and in a skin-care television advertisement. Later recordings included *Kissing Christmas* (1994) and *16 Most Requested Songs* (1996).

HARRY VON TILZER

b. 8 July 1872, Detroit, Michigan, USA, d. 10 January 1946, New York

A founding father of Tin Pan Alley – he even claimed the phrase was coined in his office – Von Tilzer was the most successful songwriter of the first decade of the twentieth century, and one of the first to establish his own music-publishing firm. In this capacity he published some of the first songs of **Irving Berlin** and **George Gershwin**.

From a musical family (his brothers Albert and Will also became songwriters), Von Tilzer became a tumbler in a circus at the age of fourteen, before switching to burlesque and then vaudeville where he formed a double act with George Sidney (the Humorous Germans). At the same time he wrote songs for his fellow performers in a variety of styles, from sentimental ballads to German dialect songs. His first hit was 'I Love You Both' (1892). Introduced by Lottie Gilson in Chicago, its success led Von Tilzer to settle in New York. There in 1898 he had his first major hits, the ballad 'My Old New Hampshire Home' (lyrics by Andrew Sterling), which was recorded by George J. Gaskin and Frank Stanley (both Columbia, 1898), among others, and the coon song 'I'd Leave My Happy Home for You' (lyrics by Will A. Heelan), which was one of the first hits of **Arthur Collins** (1899).

Though Von Tilzer sold the copyright of these songs (which eventually sold a million copies of sheet music), he was made a partner by the publishers, Shapiro and Bernstein, for whom he wrote his next great success, 'A Bird in a Gilded Cage' (1900). A sentimental ballad about a girl who married for money rather than love, it articulated a perennial theme in popular song which has continued to the present (as in the **Eagles**' 'Lyin' Eyes', 1975) and was a hit for Jere Mahony (Edison), Steve Porter (Columbia) and Harry Macdonough (Edison), among others. With his royalties Von Tilzer followed the lead of **Charles K. Harris** and set up his own publishing firm in 1902.

Among his most successful songs were 'On a Sunday Afternoon', a hit for J. Aldrich Libby (Edison, 1902) who a decade earlier had introduced Harris's 'After the Ball'; 'Down Where the Wurzburger Flows', introduced by **Nora Bayes** and a hit for Arthur Collins (1903); 'Please Go 'Way and Let Me Sleep' (1903); 'Wait Till the Sun Shines Nellie' (1905), a hit for Harry Tally (Victor, 1906) and subsequently revived by numerous artists, including **Bing Crosby** (1941); one of the earliest dance tunes, 'Cubanola Glide', a hit for **Billy Murray** (1910); and the vaudeville classic 'I Want a Girl Just Like the Girl That Married Dear Old Dad' (1911). These songs showed Von Tilzer's versatility, but by the twenties, despite one last major hit ('Just Around the Corner', 1925), he was clearly out of sympathy with the more hectic mood of the times and devoted the rest of his career to supervising his publishing interests.

Of Von Tilzer's brothers, Albert (*b. 29 March 1878, Indianapolis, Indiana, d. 1 October 1956, Los Angeles, California*) was the most successful. Briefly a plugger for his brother, Albert set up as an independent publisher in 1903. His first hit, 'Teasing' (1903), written with Cecil Mack, established a partnership with Billy Murray, who regularly recorded Albert's songs. Other hits included 'Honey Boy' (1907); 'Smarty' (1908); 'Take Me out to the Ball Game' (1908); 'Give Me the Moonlight, Give Me the Girl (And Leave the Rest to Me)' (1917), one of the many songs he wrote with Lew Brown of **Desylva, Brown and Henderson**, which was later revived by **Frankie Vaughan** who took it as his theme song; 'I'll Be with You in Apple Blossom Time', a hit for **Henry Burr** in 1920 and later revived by the **Andrews Sisters** (1941); 'Dapper Dan', a hit for **Frank Crumit** (1922); and 'Roll Along Prairie Moon', a hit for Smith Ballew (Melotone, 1935), one of the many singing cowboys to emerge in the wake of **Gene Autry**.

LOUDON WAINWRIGHT

b. Loudon Wainwright III, 5 September 1946, Chapel Hill, North Carolina, USA

A quirky singer-songwriter, more akin to **Randy Newman** than **James Taylor**, Wainwright made his name in America in the seventies but found greater popularity in Europe in the eighties and nineties than in America.

The son of a journalist, Wainwright's early listening was jazz, show tunes and folk revival artists like **Joan Baez** and **Jack Elliott**. At high school he formed the Highlanders folk group and a jug band called Tri-acre Company. Wainwright studied acting at Carnegie Tech. in Pittsburgh, where he met singer George Gerdes, who encouraged his songwriting.

By 1968 Wainwright was playing folk clubs in New York and Boston and the following year he signed to Atlantic. An eponymous début album (1970) featured the anecdotal 'Central Square Song' and the wryly confessional 'I Don't Care'. It established the mood of sombre humour that would run through all his work. *Album II* (1971) was more accessible, ranging from the wry innocence of 'Be Careful There's a Baby in the House' to the humorous account of life on the road, 'Motel Blues', and the serenity of the traditional song 'Old Paint'.

Wainwright moved to Columbia for *Album III* (1972), which included the poignant 'Red Guitar', and a revival of **Leiber and Stoller**'s 'Smokey Joe's Cafe' and the surprise novelty hit, 'Dead Skunk'.

Attempted Moustache (1974) was produced in Nashville by Bob Johnston and included the raucous 'Down Drinking at the Bar', the politically incorrect song about his baby, 'Rufus Is a Tit Man', and the deceptively gentle 'Swimming Song', which was also recorded by Wainwright's then wife **Kate McGarrigle**. After *Unrequited* (1975), Wainwright signed to Arista. *T-shirt* (1976), which included pointed political comment in 'Bicentennial' and 'Just Like President Thieu', was followed by *Final Exam* (1978). He next joined British label Radar for *A Live One* (1980). Released in America by Rounder, it included new versions of 'Red Guitar' and 'Down Drinking at the Bar'.

As an actor Wainwright appeared in the stage musical *Pump Boys and Dinettes*, in the television series *M.A.S.H.* and the film *Jacknife* (1988). His later records included *Fame and Wealth* (1983), *I'm Alright* (Demon, 1985), and the ironically titled *More Love Songs* (1986), co-produced by **Richard Thompson**, an artist whose wit could be even more mordant. He moved to Silvertone for *Therapy* (1989), and in 1992 released the superior *History* (Virgin). Equally fine was the critically acclaimed, if ironically titled, live album *Career Moves* (1993). Less successful was *Grown Man* (1995). *Social Studies* (Rykodisc, 1999) was both a return to form and to the satirical songs that Wainwright had started out performing. It contained a collection of topical songs about matters American.

TOM WAITS

b. 7 December 1949, Pomona, California, USA

Waits was an idiosyncratic writer and singer, drawing on Edward Hopper's paintings, beat generation authors, Broadway composers and jazz singers for a style which brought him a cult following in the seventies. In the eighties and nineties he found wider success as both a singer and an actor.

His early club act with songs and monologues attracted manager Herb Cohen, who had previously worked with **Tim Buckley** and **Frank Zappa**. He recorded in 1971 for Cohen's Straight Records, but nothing was released. Material from this period would later appear on a pair of albums, *The Early Years Vol. 1 & 2* (Edsel/Straight, 1990 and 1992). Waits subsequently signed to Asylum for the Jerry Yester-produced *Closing Time* (1973), which included 'Ol' 55', later covered by the **Eagles**, and 'Martha', recorded by Buckley. Bones Howe supervised *Heart of Saturday Night* (1974) and the live set *Nighthawks at the Diner* (1975), on which Waits moved away from singer-songwriter territory towards jazz.

Noted jazz players Shelly Manne (drums) and Lew Tabackin (saxophone) appeared on *Small Change* (1976) and *Foreign Affairs* (1977), maintaining the jazz flavour, but *Blue Valentine* (1978), with a rasping version of **Stephen Sondheim** and **Leonard Bernstein**'s 'Somewhere', moved towards a rock and R&B sound. *Heartattack and Vine* (1980) contained 'Jersey Girl', which became part of **Bruce Springsteen**'s stage repertoire. Waits was also a strong influence on the singer **Rickie Lee Jones**, whose 'Chuck E's in Love' (Warners) was a big transatlantic hit in 1979.

Waits left Asylum in 1981, and the label released the compilation *Bounced Checks* after his departure. Waits composed the score for Francis Ford Coppola's *One from the Heart* (1982), duetting with **Crystal**

Gayle on some of the songs. He later had small roles in Coppola's *Rumblefish* (1983) and *The Cotton Club* (1985). Waits moved to Island for *Swordfishtrombones* (1983), which used brass bands and showed the influence of composer Harry Partch. The album included 'Soldier's Things', later recorded by **Paul Young**.

Rain Dogs (1985), with guitar work by the **Rolling Stones**' Keith Richards, was followed by the ambitious *Frank's Wild Years* (1987). A song cycle based on a play by Waits and his wife Kathleen Brennan, the album was an expansion of the storyline of a song from *Swordfishtrombones*. The music was again eclectic, based on silent film piano music, **Kurt Weill** and even **Ennio Morricone**. In 1986 Waits starred in Jim Jarmusch's film *Down by Law* and in 1988 he appeared in *Ironweed* as well as releasing the live album and film *Big Time*. In the following year, **Rod Stewart** had a big hit with Waits's 'Downtown Train'. The same year, he carried on with his cinematic career in *Candy Mountain* and *Cold Feet*. In 1990 Waits won $2.5m damages as a result of a lawsuit against an American snack company that had used an impersonation of his voice in a television commercial without his permission.

Waits later released his soundtrack album from the Jarmusch movie *Night on Earth*, followed by the critically acclaimed *Bone Machine* (1992), which again featured Richards who co-wrote, sang and played on 'That Feel'. His acting career progressed with a supporting role in *Bram Stoker's Dracula* (1992). He also appeared in the Jarmusch short *Coffee and Cigarettes* alongside **Iggy Pop** and in Robert Altman's *Short Cuts* (1993). *The Black Rider* (1990), featured songs from a musical co-written with avant-garde author William Burroughs. In 1995 Holly Cole released *Temptation*, a collection of reworkings of Waits's songs, and in 1996 Waits contributed recordings to the soundtrack of *Dead Man Walking*. In 1998 the career retrospective *Beautiful Maladies* was warmly received, preparing the way for *Mule Variations* (1999). His greatest critical and commercial success of the decade, the album saw him melding anger and sentimentality to perfection, its rough-hewn sound giving it added grandeur. The album, co-produced and written with his wife Kathleen Brennan, was similar in tone to *Swordfishtrombones* in its mix of gritty love songs and raw blues tales. It also featured the powerful single 'Big in Japan'.

RICK WAKEMAN
b. 18 May 1949, London, England

A keyboards player and composer, Wakeman was a member of the Strawbs and **Yes** before embarking on an erratic solo career in the seventies.

After learning classical piano as a child, he joined a local blues band at the age of fourteen and later briefly attended the Royal College of Music. In the late sixties he began work as a session musician, contributing to hits by Clive Dunn ('Grandad', EMI Columbia, 1970), Edison Lighthouse (the British No. 1 'Love Grows Where My Rosemary Goes', Bell, 1969) and Brotherhood of Man ('United We Stand', Deram, 1970) and to **David Bowie**'s 'Space Oddity' (1969).

Wakeman next joined the Strawbs, a folk-rock band led by Dave Cousins and with whom Sandy Denny had sung before the formation of **Fairport Convention**. He played on four of the group's A&M albums, including the minor hits *Just a Collection of Antiques* (1970) and *From the Witchwood* (1971). He also continued his session work, notably on Bowie's *Hunky Dory* and **Lou Reed**'s 1972 solo début. In 1971–4 Wakeman was a member of Yes, rejoining the group in 1976 for a further two-year stint.

His solo career began in 1973 with the baroque *The Six Wives of Henry VIII*, the first of a trio of orchestral suites based on literary and historical themes. They were as overblown as **Paul Whiteman**'s earlier exercises in 'symphonic jazz'. A rendering of Jules Verne's *Journey to the Centre of the Earth* (1974) was followed by *The Myths and Legends of King Arthur and the Round Table* (1975), staged as an ice spectacular with forty-five-piece orchestra and forty-eight-strong choir. In the same year Wakeman composed the score for Ken Russell's *Lisztomania*. Science fiction was the inspiration for the verbose *No Earthly Connection* (1976) while *White Rock* (1977) was written for a film about the Winter Olympics.

With tracks like 'Judas Iscariot' and 'The Breathalyser', *Criminal Record* was a further attempt at a concept album. After *Rhapsodies* (1979), he left A&M and with Tim Rice as lyricist and guest singer **Chaka Khan** recorded the successful *1984* (Charisma, 1981), a musical version of George Orwell's novel.

Wakeman's film work continued with music for *The Burning* (1982), *G'Ole* (1983), Russell's *Crimes of Passion* and *Phantom of the Opera* (1990). He recorded *Silent Night* (TBG, 1985) and in 1987 released a religious opus, *The Gospels* (Stylus). By now he was also developing a career as an exponent of new-age music with *Country Airs* (Coda, 1986). In 1989 he toured and recorded with the ex-Yes line-up, Anderson, Wakeman, Bruford and Howe, and toured as part of an expanded Yes line-up in 1991.

His later solo albums included *Suite of Gods* (1988), *Time Machine* (1988), *Zodiaque* (1988) and *Sea Airs* (1990). He also recorded with his son and his wife, former model Nina Carter. In the mid-nineties Wakeman enjoyed a further career as a minor television personality, appearing regularly on British game shows.

NARADA MICHAEL WALDEN
b. 23 April 1952, Kalamazoo, Michigan

Originally a jazz-fusion drummer, Walden went on to a career as a solo artist and in the mid-eighties became one of the most successful producers of black pop music.

In 1974 he joined **John McLaughlin**'s Mahavishnu Orchestra. Like the band's leader a disciple of Sri Chimnoy, Walden played on *Apocalypse* (1974), *Visions of the Emerald Beyond* (1975) and *Inner Worlds* (1976).

During the late seventies he was a prolific session drummer, contributing to albums by **Jeff Beck**, **Weather Report**, Jaco Pastorius, Roy Buchanan, **Chick Corea**, **Santana** and **Robert Fripp**. Walden's own recording career began with the **Tom Dowd**-produced *Garden of Love Light* (Atlantic, 1977), on which his accompanists included Beck, Santana and singer Cissy Houston. *I Cry I Smile* (1978) was followed by *Awakening* (1979), with the **Brecker Brothers** among the backing musicians.

Bob Clearmountain was brought in to produce *Dance of Life* (1979), which provided a British Top Ten hit in 'I Shoulda Lovedyah', and *Victory* (1980). In the mid-eighties he moved to Warners and *Divine Emotions* (1988) was a British hit.

Walden's production career began with Stacy Lattisaw's disco hit 'Jump to the Beat' (Cotillion, 1980) and **Sister Sledge**'s *All American Girls* (1981). He later worked with **George Benson** and **Don Cherry** but Walden's greatest success as a producer came in 1986–7 when he was named top singles producer by *Billboard*. Among the hits he was responsible for were **Aretha Franklin**'s 'Freeway of Love' (1985), 'Who's Zoomin' Who' and her duet with **George Michael**, 'I Knew You Were Waiting' (1985); Jermaine Stewart's 'We Don't Have to Take Our Clothes Off' (1986); Starship's 'Nothing's Gonna Stop Us Now' (1987); and a trio of US chart-toppers for **Whitney Houston**, 'How Will I Know', 'The Greatest Love of All' and 'Saving All My Love for You'. Walden subsequently produced Houston's second album, *Whitney* (1987), which produced four more Top Ten hits, including 'I Wanna Dance with Somebody (Who Loves Me)'.

In the nineties Walden remained in demand as writer and producer. Artists whom he produced hits for include **Mariah Carey** ('I Don't Wanna Cry', 1991), Tevin Campbell (*T.E.V.I.N.*, 1991), Angela Bofill ('Too Tough', 1992), the **O'Jays** (*Emotionally Yours*, 1992), **Diana Ross** (*Take Me Higher*, 1995) and **Steve Winwood** (*Junction Seven*, 1997).

THE WALKER BROTHERS
Gary Leeds, b. 3 September 1944, Glendale, California, USA; John Walker, b. John Maus, 12 November 1943, New York; Scott Walker, b. Noel Scott Engel, 9 January 1944, Hamilton, Ohio

A highly successful white vocal group of the mid-sixties, the Walker Brothers combined melodramatic string-laden productions (of the kind associated with **Dusty Springfield**) with the minor key symphonic elements pioneered by **Phil Spector**. Scott Walker went on to make some critically acclaimed solo records.

Scott Engel, a protégé of **Eddie Fisher**, was a session bass player in Hollywood, working with **Jack Nitzsche**. He teamed up with guitarist Maus to record for Tower as the Dalton Brothers in 1964 before adding drummer Leeds. As the Walker Brothers the trio cut the Nitzsche-produced 'Love Her' (Mercury, 1965), which showed the influence of Spector's work with the **Righteous Brothers**.

The group moved to Britain where Johnny Franz produced the even more grandiose 'Make It Easy on Yourself'* (Philips, 1965). A **Burt Bacharach** and Hal David song and a 1962 hit for **Jerry Butler**, it featured Scott Walker's rich baritone and reached No. 1. The similarly styled 'My Ship Is Coming in' and 'The Sun Ain't Gonna Shine Anymore' (1966), written by **Bob Crewe** and Bob Gaudio, were also big hits.

By now the trio had become teen-idols throughout Europe and their chart success continued with '(Baby) You Don't Have to Tell Me' and 'Another Tear Falls', another Bacharach–David composition recorded earlier by **Gene McDaniels** (Liberty, 1962). They recorded the film theme 'Deadlier Than the Male' (1967) and a version of **Bert Berns**' 'Stay with Me Baby' before splitting up.

Each group member began a solo singing career, with Gary and John enjoying minor hits with 'You Don't Love Me' (Columbia, 1967) and 'Annabella' (Philips, 1967), respectively. Scott Walker had a more substantial impact, with a series of albums which increasingly focused on **Jacques Brel**'s bitter-sweet songs in English translation by Mort Shuman (formerly of **Pomus and Shuman**). *Scott 2* (1968) included a hit with the harsh 'Jackie' as well as songs by **Tim Hardin** and Walker himself. The softer ballad 'Joanna' (1968), composed by **Tony Hatch** and Jackie Trent, was followed by a Top Twenty hit with **Tony Macaulay** and Geoff Stephens' 'The Lights of Cincinatti' (1969).

After *'Till the Band Comes in* (1972), Scott moved to Columbia for the Del Newman-produced *Stretch* (1973), which included a version of **Dan Penn** and Spooner Oldham's 'A Woman Left Lonely'. The country influence was maintained on *We Had It All* (1974) before he was reunited with Leeds and Maus to record *Lines* (GTO, 1976), which included a hit version of **Tom Rush**'s 'No Regrets'. After *Nite Flights* (1978), the group again disbanded.

Scott Walker's earlier work gained him cult status among the new wave of the early eighties, with his material being revived by **Marc Almond** and the Teardrop Explodes. His bleak, elliptical compositions on *Climate of Hunter* (Virgin, 1984) gained widespread critical acclaim but sold poorly. In 1991, in the wake of the renewed attention he got after the release of the compilation album *Boy Child* with notes by Almond, Walker signed to Fontana Records for *Tilt* (1992). However, it was overshadowed by the compilation set *No Regrets: The Best of The Walker Brothers*. In 2000 Walker followed in the footsteps of **Elvis Costello** and **Nick Cave** and organized the *Meltdown* festival at London's Royal Festival Hall.

FRANK WALKER
b. c. 1890, Fly Summit, New York, USA, d. 1965

Producer/talent scout Frank Walker, along with **Ralph Peer** and **Art Satherley**, founded the great twenties catalogues of country, blues and gospel recordings.

He started his career in banking, and in 1921, having served in the First World War and spent a short spell in the concert booking business, joined the Artists and Repertoire department of the Columbia Phonograph Company. He soon began to record country music, and in 1925 initiated a special catalogue for it under the title 'Old Familiar Tunes'. By 1931 it totalled more than 750 releases, and was particularly strong in string-band music, much of it from members of the Atlanta, Georgia, circle of musicians that included **Gid Tanner** and his Skillet Lickers, fiddler Clayton McMichen and the blind singer-guitarist Riley Puckett. From this group also came most of the topical humorous sketches like 'Corn Licker Still in Georgia' and 'Prohibition – Yes or No?', which Columbia recorded in greater depth and with more success than any of its rivals. Other artists to record prolifically for the catalogue included singer-banjoist Charlie Poole and his North Carolina Ramblers and the 'citybilly' singers **Vernon Dalhart** and **Bob Miller**.

Walker visited Southern centres like Atlanta and Dallas once or twice a year to engage in several days of recording activity, assisted by local talent scouts, including Atlanta's Dan Hornsby and Bill Brown. He also gathered material for the parallel 'race' series of jazz and blues records and was responsible, in 1923, for signing **Bessie Smith**. In New Orleans in 1928 he made the first recordings of Louisiana cajun music, by singer-accordionist Joseph Falcon.

Walker left Columbia to become a vice-president of RCA Victor (1938–45), then joined MGM, where his most famous signing was **Hank Williams**. After serving for many years as president of MGM he retired to become a consultant to Loew's Inc., MGM's parent company.

JERRY JEFF WALKER
b. Ronald Clyde Crosby, 16 March 1942, Oneonta, New York State, USA

A leading light of the new wave of country performers who made Austin, Texas, their base in the seventies, Walker's best-known song is the oft-recorded 'Mr Bojangles', a hit for the **Nitty Gritty Dirt Band** in 1971.

From a musical family, Walker became a folk singer on graduating from high school in 1959. He sang his way around America in the early sixties before forming the folk-rock band Circus Maximus with Bob Bruno in 1967. After recording an album for Vanguard, that group broke up and Walker cut *Driftin' Way of Life* (Vanguard, 1969) before signing with Atlantic. He first recorded 'Mr Bojangles', an evocative description of an old street dancer, as the title track of his début album for the company in 1969. In the early seventies he joined MCA and settled in Austin. **Willie Nelson**, Guy Clark (one of whose best songs, 'L.A. Freeway', gave Walker a country hit in 1973) and Townes Van Zandt soon followed. Less assured a singer than Nelson, less autobiographical than Clark (whose other songs include 'Texas – 1947' and 'Desperadoes Waiting for a Train', both, like 'L.A. Freeway', from *Old No. 1*, RCA, 1975, for which Walker wrote the sleeve note), and more relaxed and less cryptic than Van Zandt (whose Tomato albums include *Our Mother the Mountain*, 1978), Walker at his best (*Viva Terlingua*, 1973; *A Man Must Carry on*, 1977) essayed a good-time version of country music with a folk and rock'n'roll inflection. By the end of the seventies, after Walker stopped touring and recording with the Lost Gonzo Band in favour of solo appearances, his music became more reflective.

In 1978 Walker joined Elektra for two lesser albums before returning to MCA for *Reunion* (1981). It was followed in 1982 by *Cowjazz*, and in 1986 Walker toured Britain with Clark. His later albums included *Gypsy Songman* (1988), *Live at Guene Hall* (1989), *Navajo Rug* (1991) and *Hill Country Rain* (1992). In 1994 Walker released *Viva Luckenbach*, recorded in Texas with his new band, the Gonzo Compadres.

Gypsy Songman (Rykodisc, 1987) and *Must Carry on Vols 1 & 2* (MCA, 1997) are representative collections.

JUNIOR WALKER
b. Autry deWalt Walker, 1942, Blythesville, Arkansas, USA, d. 23 November 1995, Battle Creek, Michigan

Perhaps the most anachronistic star on Motown, sax-player Walker was more in tune with the honkers of the fifties, like **Earl Bostic**, than the slick soul of **Berry Gordy**'s company.

Discovered by **Harvey Fuqua** and signed to his

Tri-Phi label, Walker scored some local hits in Detroit on Harvey in 1962 (including 'Brainwasher' and 'Twistlackawanna'), before Fuqua sold out to Gordy. Walker's first Motown hit came in 1965 with the raucous dance epic 'Shotgun' (Soul), which reached No. 4 on the American chart. The flip-side of 'Shotgun', 'Hot Cha', was a big hit in Jamaica where its slow, sensual rhythms were akin to the ska music of the time. Other hits of the period included 'Shake and Fingerpop', the compelling '(I'm a) Roadrunner' (1965), and instrumental versions of other Motown hits, including **Marvin Gaye**'s 'How Sweet It Is (To Be Loved by You)' (1966) and the **Supremes**' 'Come See About Me' (1967). All were functional dance records, featuring Walker's rasping sax interjections over simple organ (played by Vic Thomas), bass, guitar and drum backings and, as such, were totally at odds with the more sophisticated outpourings of mainstream Motown.

By 1969 Walker had moved on to more elaborate arrangements and enjoyed his biggest hit in that year with 'What Does It Take (To Win Your Love)'. His last American hit was in 1972 with 'Walk in the Night', but he continued to make the British charts until 1973 with 'Way Back Home' and 'Take Me Girl I'm Ready'. He left Motown in 1978, but returned briefly in 1983 for one album, *Blow the House Down*. In the intervening years he signed with **Norman Whitfield**'s Whitfield label and enjoyed great success providing a sax solo for rock group **Foreigner** on their 1981 hit 'Urgent'.

Throughout the eighties Walker was a regular on the revival circuit.

T-BONE WALKER

b. Aaron Thibeaux Walker, 28 May 1910, Linden, Texas, USA, d. 16 March 1975, Los Angeles, California

No blues guitarist had a longer or more far-reaching influence on the history of his instrument than Walker, who stands at the head of a line which includes **Lowell Fulson**, **B. B. King**, **Freddie King** and **Albert Collins**, as well as innumerable second-rank figures. His knowledge of the guitar's vocabulary was more extensive than any of his blues contemporaries, and it was largely through him that the more sophisticated chords, already familiar to jazz players, were incorporated into blues practice. Playing with immense rhythmic subtlety and variety, he would slip with almost playful ease in and out of double-tempo passages. His conversational singing and sharp city-dweller's lyrics, broadly similar in tone to **Louis Jordan**'s (and somewhat modelled on **Leroy Carr**'s), were widely adopted as progressive models by young artists of the forties and fifties, anxious to shed the rustic trappings of down-home juke-joint blues.

He grew up in Dallas, where he taught himself guitar and began performing in his teens, working with a travelling medicine show. He recorded a single for Columbia in 1929, as Oak Cliff T-Bone. In the thirties he worked with jazz bands, moving, in 1934, to the West Coast, where he was among the earliest musicians to use electrically amplified guitar. Joining Les Hite's Cotton Club Orchestra in 1939, he recorded with them in the following year. In 1942 he made his first recording in the style that was to become his own, 'I Got a Break, Baby'/'Mean Old World' (Capitol), accompanied by a trio led by boogie-woogie pianist Freddie Slack. His reputation was made by a series of recordings for Black and White (1946–7), later leased to Capitol, which included the definitive version of 'Call It Stormy Monday', later recorded by **Bobby Bland** and many other artists, and 'T-Bone Shuffle'. In contrast to the harmonica-and-guitar ensembles of contemporary Chicago, Walker worked with bands fronted by two or three horns, a format that was maintained in his Imperial sessions of 1950–4, which often featured tenor saxophonist and arranger **Maxwell Davis**.

Throughout the late forties and early fifties Walker was a major touring attraction on the black circuit. In 1955, after an ulcer operation, he began to work less; he had just signed with Atlantic, but took over four years to record enough material for one album, the outstanding *T-Bone Blues* (1960), which put him among accompanists like **Plas Johnson** (tenor), Lloyd Glenn (piano) and jazz guitarist Barney Kessel. In the sixties he maintained his reduced touring schedule, but visited Europe with the first American Folk Blues Festival (1962) and returned in 1965, 1966 (with a 'Jazz at the Philharmonic' package) and 1968–9, when he made *Feeling the Blues* for the French label Black and Blue. He had previously signed with Bluesway and cut *Stormy Monday Blues* (1967) and *Funky Town* (1968).

Walker next made the French-recorded *Good Feelin'* (Polydor, 1970), which featured **Manu Dibango** on keyboards and saxophones and won a Grammy award. He visited Europe again in 1972, playing the Montreux Jazz Festival, then cut *Very Rare* (Reprise, 1973), an elaborate double-album produced by **Leiber and Stoller**, with guest appearances by **Dizzy Gillespie**, flautist Herbie Mann and saxophonists **Gerry Mulligan**, Al Cohn and Zoot Sims. By that time the testimonials of musicians like B. B. King were helping to bring him the prestige he deserved, but illness forced him to stop working in 1974.

SIPPIE WALLACE

b. Beulah Thomas, 11 November 1898, Houston, Texas, USA, d. 1 November 1986, Houston

A majestic singer in the 'classic' blues idiom of the

mid-twenties, Sippie Wallace outlived nearly all her contemporaries to bring her stately style to audiences two generations later.

She came from a highly musical family: one of her brothers, George W. Thomas Jnr, was a musician, songwriter and publisher; another, Hersal, was a celebrated pianist, for whom she wrote his best-known number, 'Suitcase Blues'; and her niece Hociel Thomas was a singer and pianist popular in Chicago in the late twenties. Wallace herself moved to Chicago in 1923, already experienced as a travelling-show singer and pianist. Almost at once she was recording for Okeh ('Up the Country Blues'/'Shorty George Blues'), and in her three and a half years' association with the label worked with **Clarence Williams**, **Louis Armstrong**, **Sidney Bechet**, **King Oliver** and **Perry Bradford**. Sides with Armstrong like 'Special Delivery Blues'/'Jack of Diamonds Blues' (1926), or the later Victor recording of 'I'm a Mighty Tight Woman' (1929) with Johnny Dodds, are masterpieces of jazz accompaniment.

She retired from performing in 1929 to work for the Leland Baptist Church in Detroit, but made brief returns to the business, including one in 1945 to record with **Albert Ammons** (Mercury), and another in 1966 for the American Folk Blues Festival tour, during which she recorded a fine album, *Sippie Wallace Sings the Blues* (Storyville), accompanied on piano by herself, and by Little Brother Montgomery and Roosevelt Sykes. After that she appeared often at blues and folk festivals until serious illness confined her to a wheelchair in 1970. She returned to performance with the support of **Bonnie Raitt**, who had been singing her songs like 'Women Be Wise', and the two toured together at intervals during the seventies, an association commemorated by a 1982 Atlantic set with guest appearances by Raitt and accompaniment by Jim Dapogny's Chicago Jazz Band.

FATS WALLER

b. Thomas Wright Waller, 21 May 1904, New York, USA, d. 15 December 1943, Kansas City, Missouri

An exuberant performer and pianist, Waller is best remembered for such compositions as 'Ain't Misbehavin'' and 'Honey Suckle Rose' (both 1929) and the novelty recording 'Your Feet's Too Big' (1939).

The son of a Harlem Baptist minister, Waller took up the piano at the age of six and in 1918 won a talent contest playing **James P. Johnson**'s 'Carolina Shout'. After studying with the stride pianist, Waller was one of the first artists to be signed by **Ralph Peer** after he inaugurated the Okeh 'race' series in 1920 with Mamie Smith's 'You Can't Keep a Good Man Down'. Walter's first recording was 'Muscle Shoals Blues' in 1922. During the early twenties he made numerous piano

rolls and worked as a silent-movie pianist and at various theatres. He recorded with McKinney's Cotton Pickers, **Fletcher Henderson** (1926) and Johnson (1929), as well as releasing organ solos in 1926–7 on Victor. Waller also played piano accompaniment for such artists as **Adelaide Hall**, **Bessie Smith** and **Gene Austin**.

His first published composition was 'Squeeze Me' (1925), with lyrics by publisher Clarence Williams, before he established a writing partnership with Andy Razoff. In 1928 he collaborated with Johnson on the score for the all-black revue *Keep Shufflin'* and in 1929, again with Razoff, for another all-black revue *Hot Chocolates*, wrote 'Ain't Misbehavin'' (a hit for Waller himself, **Louis Armstrong**, **Ruth Etting** and revived by **Teddy Wilson** in 1937), 'I've Got a Feeling I'm Falling', with lyrics by Billy Rose (a hit for Gene Austin), and the oft-recorded 'Honeysuckle Rose' (a hit for Fletcher Henderson in 1933, and Waller himself and Tommy and **Jimmy Dorsey** in 1935). Other Razoff–Waller collaborations included 'My Very Good Friend the Milkman' and 'Blue Turnin' Gray over You' (1929). During the thirties Waller composed 'I'm Crazy 'Bout My Baby' (1932), 'Keepin' out of Mischief Now', the stride-piano standard 'Handful of Keys' (1933), and the dynamic 'The Joint Is Jumpin'' (1938). Waller's solo recording of 'Handful', played against a darkened set with a floodlight illuminating piano and empty stool, was one of the highlights of the Broadway musical about him, *Ain't Misbehavin'* (1978).

In the thirties Waller also had several long-running radio shows and played clubs with a variety of bands. In 1934 he began a series of recordings for Victor as Fats Waller and his Rhythm, a five-piece backing group. As well as his own songs, his most successful records included the novelty pieces 'Your Feet's Too Big' and 'I'm Gonna Sit Right Down and Write Myself a Letter' (1935), by Fred Ahlert and Joe Young.

In the late thirties Waller unsuccessfully ran a big band. He died of pneumonia *en route* from Los Angeles to New York.

Waller's screen appearances included 'soundies' (for visual jukeboxes) of his most famous songs. He also appeared in *Hooray for Love, King of Burlesque* (1936) and the **Irving Mills**-produced *Stormy Weather* (1943) with **Lena Horne**, **Cab Calloway** and **Dooley Wilson**.

WAR

Papa Dee Allen, b. 19 July 1931, Wilmington, Delaware, USA, d. 30 August 1988; Harold Brown, b. 17 March 1946, Long Beach, California; B. B. Dickerson, b. 3 August 1949, Torrance, California; Lonnie Jordan, b. 21 November 1948, San Diego, California; Charles Miller, b. 2 June 1939, Olathe, Kansas; Lee Oskar, b. Oskar Levetin Hansen, 24 March 1948, Copenhagen, Denmark; Howard Scott, b. 15 March 1946, San Pedro, California

War found success in the seventies with a sound that combined the Latin rock of **Santana** with the funk-rock of **Sly Stone**.

During the late sixties the band were known variously as Señor Soul, the Romeos, the Creators or the Night Shift as they played the bars of Southern California. They were signed by producer-manager Jerry Goldstein (a former member of the Strangeloves and ex-producer of the **McCoys**) as a backing band for Eric Burdon, one-time singer with the **Animals**.

With addition of white harmonica-player Oskar, the group recorded two albums with Burdon as well as the hit 'Spill the Wine'* (1970). In 1970–1 they undertook a world tour which culminated in a jam session with **Jimi Hendrix** shortly before the guitarist's death. Neither this nor the many live recordings made by Goldstein were released.

When Burdon left, the group made an eponymous first album for United Artists which featured guitarist Scott, saxophonist Miller, Jordan on keyboards and harmonica-player Oskar. 'Slippin' into Darkness'* from *All Day Music* (1971) reached the Top Ten and *The World Is a Ghetto* (1972) topped the album charts while its title track and 'The Cisco Kid' (1973), a tribute to the group's chicano followers, sold a million. *Deliver the Word* (1973) provided further Top Twenty hits in 'Gypsy Man' and 'Me and Baby Brother'.

A management dispute preceded the release of *Why Can't We Be Friends* (1975), which included Top Ten singles in the million-selling title track and 'Low Rider', War's first British success on Island. In 1977 Goldstein took the group to MCA but only the disco-flavoured 'Galaxy' (1978) made any impact.

War re-emerged in 1982 with *Outlaw* (RCA) and *Life Is So Strange* (1983) but line-up changes and weak solo ventures by Oskar (*Before the Rain*, MCA, 1978) and Jordan (*Different Moods of Me*, MCA, 1978) had taken their toll. Despite Goldstein's ownership of the name, members of the group recorded independently as War, scoring a minor British hit with an insipid version of the **Rascals**' 'Groovin'' (1984). They later returned to Goldstein, who in 1987 also resumed the management of Burdon. Later that year War had an R&B hit with a new version of 'Low Rider' (Lax). Goldstein's Avenue label released a new studio album, *Peace Sign*, in 1994, and *War Anthology, 1970–1994*, a re-recording of their best-known material, in 1995.

CLARA WARD

b. 21 August 1924, Philadelphia, Pennsylvania, USA, d. 16 January 1973, Los Angeles, California

A mainstay of the Ward Singers (one of the first gospel groups to feature multiple soloists), Clara Ward was one of the greatest stylists in gospel music. Her nasal vibrant alto won her the sobriquet 'queen of the moaners' and was a formative influence on **Aretha Franklin**.

Her mother, Gertrude, was born in South Carolina, and moved to Philadelphia where in 1931 she formed the Ward Singers as a family group with daughters Clara and Willa. Soon Clara became the star of the show and by 1943, performing the modern gospel songs of **Thomas A. Dorsey** and Sally Martin, the Ward Singers were the leading sacred vocal group.

Clara sang lead on 'How I Got Over', recorded on the local Gotham label, but the group's greatest commercial success came when they recorded for Savoy such Rev. W. H. Brewster compositions as 'Surely God Is Able' (which introduced the waltz rhythm to gospel) and 'Packin' Up', with Marion Williams on lead. Clara's 'This Little Light of Mine' was later secularized by **Ray Charles** as 'This Little Girl of Mine'.

From the early fifties the Ward Singers (now including **Della Reese**) toured with the Rev. C. L. Franklin, whose daughter Aretha based her early vocal style on that of Clara, now the undisputed leader of the group. The singers became increasingly flamboyant in their costume and showmanship and after the group appeared at the Newport Jazz Festival in 1957, Williams and group members left to form the Stars of Faith. The regrouped Ward Singers moved towards white audiences, from 1961 performing at Las Vegas and on television as well as touring Europe, Vietnam and Australia. Their albums for Verve mixed soul, pop and gospel. In 1972 the Singers signed to United Artists and provided backing vocals for **Canned Heat**'s *New Age* (1973).

Marion Williams went on to star with Alex Bradford in the musical *Black Nativity*. Written by Langston Hughes, it toured Europe in 1962–3. In 1965 she began a solo recording career for Atlantic, singing jazz and pop material as well as gospel songs. She died in 1994, aged sixty-six.

FRED WARING

b. Frederick M. Waring, 9 June 1900, Tyrone, Pennsylvania, USA, d. 29 August 1984, State College, Pennsylvania

A popular dance-band leader of the twenties, Waring had even greater success in the forties with his Pennsylvanians, singing 'glee club' versions of collegiate songs ('The Whiffenpoof Song'*, which he recorded with **Bing Crosby**, 1947) and adaptations of traditional material ('Twas the Night Before Christmas'*, 1942).

In 1916 with his brother Tom (a mainstay of Waring's subsequent aggregations) on piano, banjoist

Waring formed Waring's Banjazzatra. When he left Pennsylvania State College, this became the nucleus of his first orchestra, Waring's Collegians. As Fred Waring's Pennsylvanians this group recorded mostly instrumental sides for Columbia and then Victor. His first hit was 'Sleep' (Victor, 1923), after which he soon specialized in collegiate-type songs rather than dance music, forming a glee club in which he and his brother took most of the lead vocals. Material from this period included 'Freshie' (1926), 'Sweetheart of Sigma Chi' (1927), 'Laugh, Clown, Laugh', which was based on a theme from *I Pagliacci*, **Victor Herbert**'s 'Ah Sweet Mystery of Life' (1928), and **Harry Warren**'s 'I Found a Million Dollar Baby (In a Five-and-Ten Cent Store)' (1931).

In 1933 Waring secured a long-running radio show, graduating to television in 1949, and in 1942, after joining Decca, had his first million-seller with an adaptation of Clement Clarke Moore's poem ''Twas the Night Before Christmas', with music by Ken Darby, a staff composer for the Walt Disney studio. When released as a long-playing album in 1954, the Pennsylvanians' collection of similarly themed forties recordings, *Christmas Songs*, reputedly sold a million copies. During this time he also appeared in films, including *Varsity Show* (1937), and recorded with other Decca artists, notably Crosby (including the free adaptation of Rudyard Kipling's poem 'Gentlemen Rankers', 'The Whiffenpoof Song', originally a minor hit for **Rudy Vallee** in 1937, and 'Way Back Home', 1949).

In the fifties and sixties, in addition to his recording and television work, Waring wrote numerous college songs to order, published band and choral arrangements of hundreds of traditional songs and ran his own nightclub, the Shawnee Inn, in Pennsylvania.

JENNIFER WARNES
b. 3 March 1947, Seattle, Washington, USA

Warnes' biggest hits were her American chart-topping duets with **Joe Cocker**, 'Up Where We Belong' (Island) from the film *An Officer and a Gentleman* (1983), and Bill Medley (of the **Righteous Brothers**), 'I've Had the Time of My Life' (RCA) from the film *Dirty Dancing* (1987), but her high critical reputation rests on her much-acclaimed collection of songs by **Leonard Cohen**, *Famous Blue Raincoat* (1986).

A child prodigy, she appeared (as Jennifer Warren) on the Smothers Brothers' long-running television show in the late sixties. There she met Mason Williams (who in 1968 had an American million-seller with *Classical Gas*, Warner) with whom she briefly recorded before taking the lead in the West Coast production of *Hair*. She recorded unsuccessfully for Parrot and Reprise (where she was produced by **John**

Cale in 1972) before signing with Arista in 1975. Her biggest hits for the label were 'Right Time of the Night' (1977) and 'I Know a Heartache When I See One' (1979) while her most interesting recordings were 'I'm Restless' and 'Shot Through the Heart'. In 1980 she won an Oscar for the first of her film theme songs, 'It Goes like It Goes' from *Norma Rae*, and in 1982 sang **Randy Newman**'s 'One More Hour' on the film *Ragtime*.

Warnes first worked with Cohen in 1973 and in 1979 created the vocal arrangements for his *Recent Songs*. In the wake of her enormous success with her film themes she persuaded RCA in 1986 to allow her to do an album of Cohen songs, ranging from his first album (*Bird on a Wire*) to his most recent (*First We Take Manhattan*). Her brooding production, which made great play with insistent rhythms behind many of the songs, helped set the tone for Cohen's subsequent recordings and brought Cohen, who guested on that album's 'Joan of Arc', to a new audience. In 1988 she guested on Cohen's *I'm Your Man* and in 1992 recorded the self-produced *The Hunter* (Private Music). On it she was assisted by **Richard Thompson**, **Van Dyke Parks** and **Steely Dan** member Donald Fagen.

DIANE WARREN
b. 1956, Van Nuys, California, USA

With over sixty US Top Ten singles and four Oscar nominations since 1983, Warren is the most successful composer of hit songs of recent times. She is also among the most conservative, with the classic Tin Pan Alley ability to create a 'hook' for a three-minute song and the versatility to write for the R&B, pop and hard rock idioms and for artists as diverse as **Aerosmith** and **Barbra Streisand**.

Warren's parents bought her a guitar when she was eight and she began songwriting at fourteen. Her first success came in 1983 when her songs were recorded by dance music diva **Laura Branigan** ('Solitaire') and soul vocal group DeBarge (the No. 1 'Rhythm of the Night').

Warren's subsequent songs have been divided between her own compositions and those co-written with other specialists in three-minute tunes aimed at the charts. With Albert Hammond, Warren co-wrote 'Nothing's Gonna Stop Us Now' for **Jefferson Starship** in 1985, the **Chicago** hit 'Look Away' and 'Don't Turn Around' for **Aswad** in 1988. The song was successfully revived by Swedish vocal group Ace of Base in 1994. One of her most successful partnerships has been with **Michael Bolton**. Together they composed 'How Can We Be Lovers', 'When I'm Back on My Feet Again', 'Walk Away', 'Time, Love and Tenderness' and 'Completely'.

Warren is also skilled at providing a hit single for 'album artists' who usually compose their own music. She was brought in to co-write tracks with **Bon Jovi** ('Wild Is the Wind') and Cheap Trick ('Wherever I Would Be', 1991) as well as delivering the Starship and Aswad hits in collaboration with Hammond. She was also responsible for the **Belinda Carlisle** single 'I Get Weak'.

For **Cher**, Warren supplied 'If I Could Turn Back Time', 'Love and Understanding' and 'Save Up All Your Tears'. In the soul field her successes include **Patti Labelle**'s 'If You Asked Me to', 'It Isn't, It Wasn't . . . It Ain't' by **Whitney Houston** and **Aretha Franklin**, 'Set the Night to Music' for **Roberta Flack** and **Maxi Priest**, and Expos's 'Your Baby Never Looked Good in Blue'. Warren's dance hits included Taylor Dayne's 'Love Will Lead You Back', a 1989 No. 1, and Milli Vanilli's 'Blame It on the Rain'.

Among other artists who have recorded Diane Warren compositions are **Ringo Starr**, **Toni Braxton** ('Un-break My Heart'), **Gloria Estefan** ('Reach', 'The One I Gave My Heart to'), **Jon Secada**, **Diana Ross**, Cheap Trick, Bad English, **Céline Dion** ('Because You Love Me'), **Mariah Carey**, **Boyz II Men** ('I Will Get There') and **Joan Jett**. Warren has benefited from the increasingly close relationship between the music and film industries in recent years, providing songs for such films as *Ghostbusters*, *Mannequin* ('Nothing's Gonna Stop Us Now'), *Vice Versa* and the James Bond movie *Licence to Kill*. Her Oscar nominations for best song include Céline Dion's 'Because You Loved Me' from *Up Close and Personal* (1997), Aerosmith's 'I Don't Want to Miss a Thing' from *Armageddon* (1998) and 'Music of My Heart' from the film of the same name (2000). The first of her compositions to become an advertising jingle was Cher's 'If I Could Turn Back Time'.

HARRY WARREN

b. Salvatore Guaranya, 24 December 1893, Brooklyn, New York, USA, d. 22 September 1981, Los Angeles, California

In the words of one critic, 'the most prolific and durable of all Hollywood composers', Warren produced a stream of hit film songs – mostly in partnership with Al Dubin – over two decades.

The child of Italian immigrants, Warren taught himself accordion and piano in his teens while working as a circus and stage hand and later as a songplugger. His first successes as a composer included 'Rose of the Rio Grande' (1922), 'Back Home in Pasadena' (1924, with lyrics by Edgar Leslie), which was revived during the British trad boom by the Temperance Seven (Parlophone, 1961), and 'Nagasaki' (1928, with Mort Dixon). During this period he also

contributed songs to revues, including 'I Found a Million Dollar Baby (In a Five-and-Ten Cent Store)' (1931), an early hit for **Bing Crosby**, after which he was taken to Hollywood to work with Dubin.

Dubin (*b. 10 July 1891, Zurich, Switzerland, d. 1943, New York*), a lawyer turned lyricist, was already established in Hollywood ('Tiptoe Through the Tulips with Me', 1929) when Warner Brothers producer Darryl Zanuck paired him with Warren for the epochal musical *42nd Street* (1932). Remembered for Busby Berkeley's grandiose staging of the musical numbers, which for the first time took full account of the new mobility of the camera, the film (which featured Warren and Dubin in bit parts as songwriters) revived the backstage musical, paired **Dick Powell** and Ruby Keeler for the first time, and introduced 'You're Getting to Be a Habit with Me', 'Shuffle off to Buffalo' and the anthemic title song. Though the best of their songs were specifically created for the highly artificial world of the Hollywood musical, few other composers could either write so directly for the screen or capture the mix of exaggerated ups and downs that was Hollywood's reaction to the Depression, best typified by the opening and closing numbers of *Gold Diggers of 1933*, the celebratory, major-key 'We're in the Money' and the affecting, minor-key 'Remember the Forgotten Man'.

Before their partnership ended in 1938, the pair wrote songs for some twenty musicals. These included *Roman Scandals* (1933, which introduced 'Keep Young and Beautiful'), *Moulin Rouge* (1934, 'The Boulevard of Broken Dreams'), *Twenty Million Sweethearts* ('I'll String Along with You'), *Dames* ('I Only Have Eyes for You'), *Gold Diggers of 1935* (the Oscar-winning 'Lullaby of Broadway'), *Broadway Gondolier* (1935, 'Lulu's Back in Town') and *Melody for Two* (1937, 'September in the Rain'). Among those who introduced their songs were Powell, **Eddie Cantor**, **Al Jolson** and **Rudy Vallee**, while 'I Only Have Eyes for You' provided hits for **Ben Selvin** and **Eddy Duchin** (1934) and was memorably revived by the black vocal group the **Flamingos** (1959).

Before his death, Dubin wrote several hits with other composers, notably 'South American Way' with **Jimmy McHugh**, which was sung by **Carmen Miranda** in the 1949 film *Down Argentina Way* (the title song of which was written by Warren and Mack Gordon), and 'Anniversary Waltz', with Dave Franklin, a hit for Bing Crosby in 1941. Warren was even more successful. With **Johnny Mercer** he wrote 'Jeepers Creepers', 'You Must Have Been a Beautiful Baby' (1938) and the Oscar-winning 'On the Atcheson, Topeka and the Santa Fe' (1946), sung by **Judy Garland** in *The Harvey Girls*. He also wrote with Mack Gordon (better known for his collaborations with **Harry Revel**) the Oscar-winning 'You'll Never

Know' (1943), a hit for **Dick Haymes**, **Frank Sinatra** and revived by **Rosemary Clooney** (1953), among others; 'Chattanooga Choo-Choo' (1941) and 'I've Got a Girl in Kalamazoo' (1942), both hits for **Glenn Miller**; and 'The More I See You', a hit for **Harry James** and Haymes in 1945, and revived by **Chris Montez** in 1966.

Warren continued writing at a lesser pace into the fifties, providing **Dean Martin** with his 1953 hit 'That's Amore' and **Vic Damone** with 'An Affair to Remember' (1957) before retiring in the early sixties.

DIONNE WARWICK

b. 12 December 1941, East Orange, New Jersey, USA

A distinctive, high-register, pop-soul ballad singer, Warwick had numerous hits with **Burt Bacharach** songs and productions during the sixties. After a fallow period in the seventies, she enjoyed renewed success in a middle-of-the-road soul style after joining Clive Davis's Arista label in 1979.

With her sister Dee Dee, Warwick was a member of gospel group the Drinkard Singers, who recorded for Savoy in the fifties. With Dee Dee, Doris Troy and Cissy, mother of **Whitney Houston** she sang backing vocals on the **Drifters**' 'Mexican Divorce' and other sessions before signing to Scepter in 1962. With its skipping title phrase and prominent string arrangement, the Bacharach–Hal David song 'Don't Make Me Over' became the first of a dozen Top Thirty hits written by the duo for Warwick in the sixties. Among the others were 'Anyone Who Had a Heart' (1963), covered in Britain by **Cilla Black**; the desolate 'Walk on By' (1964), with its french horn obbligato; 'Message to Michael' (1966), a new version of the 1964 **Adam Faith** hit 'Message to Martha'; the film themes 'Alfie' (1967), also covered by Cilla Black, 'I Say a Little Prayer'* and 'Valley of the Dolls' (1968); and 'Do You Know the Way to San José?'. 'This Girl's in Love with You' (1969) was another gender-switched song, following **Herb Alpert**'s 'This Guy's . . .', while the plaintive 'I'll Never Fall in Love Again' (1970) from the Broadway musical *Promises Promises* was a British hit for **Bobbie Gentry**.

Warwick spent the seventies recording for Warners with a variety of contemporary producers. Brian Holland and Lamont Dozier of **Holland, Dozier and Holland** supervised *Just Being Myself* (1973), while **Jerry Ragavoy** was responsible for *Then Came You* (1975), made at a time when Warwick had added an 'e' to her surname after consulting a numerologist. The title track, a duet with the **Spinners**, was the singer's first American No. 1 in 1974. Its producer, **Thom Bell**, also oversaw *Track of the Cat* (1975), while *A Man and a Woman* (1977) was a set of duets with **Isaac Hayes**, recorded live.

At Arista, Davis brought in **Barry Manilow** to produce 'I'll Never Love This Way Again' (1979) and *Dionne*, both of which sold a million. Later hits included 'Déjà Vu' (1979), **Bee Gee** Barry Gibb's 'Heartbreaker' (1982), the British success 'All the Love in the World' (1983) and the No. 1 Aids charity record 'That's What Friends Are for' (1985), which was written by Bacharach and Carole Bayer Sager.

In 1987 Warwick made *Reservations for Two*, an album of duets which provided hits with the title track (sung with Kashif) and 'Love Power' (sung with Jeffrey Osborne). The 1990 compilation *Love Songs* reached the British Top Ten, but the tribute album *Dionne Warwick Sings the Songs of Cole Porter* (1990) was less successful. She spent much of the next three years in charity work, appearing at countless fundraising benefits, before releasing *Friends Can Be Lovers* (1993), on which she sang the first new material penned by Bacharach and David in almost two decades. She followed that with a collection of Brazilian songs, *Aquerela Do Brasil* (1994). She continued to tour throughout the decade.

Dee Dee Warwick's solo career included records on **Leiber and Stoller**'s Tiger label, Jubilee ('You're No Good', 1964) and Mercury, where she made the original version of 'I'm Gonna Make You Love Me' (a 1969 hit for the **Supremes** and **Temptations**) and the R&B hit 'Foolish Fool' (1969). During the seventies and eighties she had further releases on Atlantic, Mercury, Private Stock, RCA and Buddah.

DON WAS

b. Donald Fagenson, 13 September 1952, Detroit, Michigan, USA

A highly enigmatic figure, Don Was made his reputation as one half of the quirky Was Not Was. He subsequently became a renowned producer of such mature talents as **Bob Dylan**, **Bonnie Raitt** and the **Rolling Stones**.

As a Detroit teenager he was first inspired by seeing **Iggy Pop** at a high school sock-hop. He and his schoolfriend David Weiss began experimenting with tape-recorded sound before Weiss moved to Los Angeles to work as a journalist. Fagenson spent much of the seventies playing bass in jazz groups in the Detroit area.

In 1980 Weiss returned to Detroit and the pair decided to create 'mutant dance' music using rhythms recorded by Fagenson in the city's clubs and Weiss's off-the-wall lyrics. Calling themselves Don Was and David Was, jointly Was Not Was, they recorded the eccentric club favourites 'Wheel Me Out' and 'Out Come the Freaks' plus a self-titled album for the Ze label.

Over the next decade there were three more albums

on which Was Not Was used veteran soul singers Sweet Pea Atkinson and Sir Harry Bowens and numerous guests to deliver their witty and sophisticated pastiches of dance, jazz and soul styles. *Born to Laugh at Tornadoes* (1983) was followed by *What's up Dog?* with its surprise hit 'Walk the Dinosaur'. *Are You Okay?* (1990) included contributions from Iggy Pop, **Leonard Cohen** and the Roches.

The remix album *Hello Dad, I'm in Jail* (1992) was the finale for Was Not Was. By then Don Was was working full-time as a producer. His first success in this role came with Bonnie Raitt's *Nick of Time* in 1990. He followed up with the Dylan album *Under a Red Sky* and tracks by **Paula Abdul**, Cohen, Iggy Pop and **Bob Seger**.

Was later expanded his range to include the rai-rock fusion of **Khaled**, the country/R&B duets of *Rhythm, Country and Blues* and the 1994 Rolling Stones album, *Voodoo Lounge*. His first film work was as music supervisor for *Backbeat* (1993), the biography of former **Beatles** member Stuart Sutcliffe.

In 1993 he started his own label, Karambolage, and in 1994 made the critically acclaimed documentary about **Beach Boy** Brian Wilson, *I Just Wasn't Made for These Times*. Recent productions include albums by Johnny Clegg (*In My African Dreams*, 1994), Felix Cavaliere, formerly of the **Rascals** (*Dreams in Motion*, MCA, 1994), **Kris Kristofferson** (*A Moment of Forever*, Justice, 1995) and **Travis Tritt** (*The Restless Kind*, 1996). He also oversaw the tribute albums *It's Now or Never: A Tribute to Elvis Presley* (1994), *Rhythm, Country and Blues* (1994) and *The Songs of Jimmie Rodgers* (1997).

DINAH WASHINGTON
b. *Ruth Lee Jones, 29 August 1924, Tuscaloosa, Alabama, USA, d. 14 December 1963, Detroit, Michigan*

Known as 'The Queen of the Blues', Washington was one of the most influential female vocalists of the post-war years, in particular for the strong jazz and gospel inflection, similar to that of **Ray Charles**, she brought to her fifties recordings.

Raised in Chicago, Washington sang in church choirs as a teenager and joined the Sallie Martin Singers (the group led by the former associate of **Thomas A. Dorsey**) after a brief period as a nightclub singer. Hearing **Billie Holiday** in 1941, she returned to secular music with regular appearances at Chicago's Garrick Club under the name Washington. There she was heard by **Lionel Hampton**, whose band she joined in 1943. Only interested in band recordings, Decca refused to record her with Hampton and Washington's first recordings were made by **Leonard Feather** for the independent Keynote label with members of the Hampton band in support. These

included 'Evil Gal Blues' and 'Salty Papa Blues' (1943) and were mostly in a blues vein.

After leaving Hampton in 1946 and signing to Mercury as a solo singer in 1948, Washington was used by the company virtually as a living jukebox, recording what might be called reverse cover-versions: singing pop, jazz, country and R&B hits for the mainstream black audience. In 1948 she recorded the **Orioles**' 'It's Too Soon to Know'; in 1950 (along with **Lucky Millinder**) covered Paul Gayten and Annie Laurie's Regal recording, 'I'll Never Be Free'; and in 1951 followed **Tony Bennett** in recording **Hank Williams'** 'Cold, Cold Heart'. The following year both Washington and **Kay Starr** had huge hits with a version of the Cardinals' Atlantic recording 'Wheel of Fortune'. Ironically, her biggest R&B hit of this period, Feather's 'Baby Get Lost' (1949), was itself covered by Billie Holiday, Washington's great stylistic influence, at the behest of Decca's **Milt Gabler**.

From the mid-fifties onwards Washington turned increasingly to jazz and it was such a recording, a lilting version of 'What a Difference a Day Makes' (1959), that became her first major pop hit. In the same year her appearance in *Jazz on a Summer's Day* was one of the film's highlights. Her subsequent hits were mostly revivals of popular songs of the thirties and forties. Among them were 'Love Walked in' (1960), **Harry Warren**'s 'September in the Rain' (1961) and 'Where Are You?' (1962), her first recording for Roulette where she worked with arranger Don Costa and producer Henry Glover. Interspersed with these were several duets with **Brook Benton**, more sensuous and less stately than **Billy Eckstine** and **Sarah Vaughan**'s 'Passing Strangers' (1957) collaboration but clearly inspired by that recording. They included 'Baby (You Got What It Takes)', Washington's only million-seller, and 'A Rockin' Good Way (To Mess Around and Fall in Love)' (1960).

GROVER WASHINGTON JUNIOR
b. *12 December 1943, Buffalo, New York, USA*

One of the most successful saxophonists of the seventies and eighties, Washington graduated from mellow jazz-funk to popular middle-of-the-road collaborations with such singers as **Bill Withers** and **Patti Labelle**.

The son of a professional saxophone player, Washington moved to Philadelphia in the early sixties, playing with various small combos. He made his recording début with organist Charles Earland (*Living Black!*) and did studio work before his playing in organist Johnny Hammond Smith's *Breakout* (1970) led to a contract with veteran jazz producer Creed Taylor's Kudu label.

Taylor had previously replaced **Norman Granz** at

Verve, but Kudu was intended to bring jazzy instrumental music to a broad audience. Supervised by Taylor and his arranger Bob James, the Kudu roster of artists operated in a workshop atmosphere which gave Kudu recordings a similar sound. Washington's earliest releases were arrangements of hits like **Marvin Gaye**'s 'Inner City Blues' (1972) but *Mr Magic* (1975) contained original compositions and was a pop hit. Washington also appeared on Kudu albums by Dave Grusin, Eric Gale and Randy Weston.

By 1978 Kudu was in financial difficulties and Washington's contract was transferred to the company's distributor Motown. After the commercial failure of *Reed Seed* (1978), Washington negotiated a deal with Elektra under which he recorded alternate albums for each label. *Paradise* (Elektra, 1979) was a flop, while *Skylarkin'* (Motown, 1980) did better. However, *Winelight* (Elektra, 1980) included the American No. 2 'Just the Two of Us', with Withers as guest vocalist, and a version of **Bob Marley**'s 'Jamming'. This was followed by *Come Morning* (1982) and *The Best Is Yet to Come* (1983) featuring Patti Labelle. In 1985 he made *Togethering* with guitarist Kenny Burrell for the revived Blue Note label. Washington later provided music for the Bill Cosby television show and in 1987 he released *Strawberry Moon* (Columbia), with guest vocalists Jean Carne and **B. B. King**, which included the R&B instrumental hit 'Summer Nights'. *Time Out of Mind* appeared in 1989.

In 1991 he released the superior MOR-styled *Next Exit* (Columbia), which featured jazz vocalist Nancy Wilson and included a synth-driven remake of the **Dave Brubeck** hit, 'Take Five'. *All My Tomorrows* (1994) found him back in a jazz groove with arrangements by Slide Hampton.

THE WATERBOYS
Mike Scott, b. 14 December 1958, Edinburgh, Scotland; Anthony Thistlethwaite, b. 31 August 1955, Leicester, England; Karl Wallinger, b. 19 October 1957, Prestatyn, Wales; Kevin Wilkinson

In his guise as the Waterboys, Scottish singer and songwriter Mike Scott produced a string of albums since 1982 covering a variety of styles, from straight rock to traditional Irish music.

A contributor to one of Scotland's first fanzines during the early days of punk, Scott formed his first band of note, Another Pretty Face (Scott, vocals/guitar; John Caldwell, lead guitar; Crigg, drums; and Jim Geddes, bass) in Edinburgh in 1978. 'All the Boys Love Carrie' (New Pleasures, 1979), with its '**Bruce Springsteen** meets the **Clash**' sound, brought the band to the attention of Virgin Records, but after a string of unsuccessful singles, line-up changes and a change of name to the Red and the Black, the band were

dropped. Scott and Caldwell re-emerged on the Ensign label as Funhouse with another unsuccessful single, the dramatic 'Out of Control' (1982), which set the tone for much of Scott's later work.

An unproductive link-up with Lenny Kaye (ex-**Patti Smith** Group) in New York prefaced Scott's return to the UK, where he recruited the first Waterboys line-up (taking the name from a line in **Lou Reed**'s 'The Kids'), with Thistlethwaite (saxophone), Kevin Wilkinson (drums) and bassist Nick Linden, releasing a single, 'A Girl Called Johnny' (1983), on his own Chicken Jazz label. A tribute to his heroine Patti Smith, the single was not a hit, but picked up enough airplay to convince Ensign to sign the group.

The Waterboys' eponymous début album for the label saw the arrival of multi-instrumentalist Karl Wallinger, and although it failed to chart, it won good reviews and attracted a devoted fanbase, encouraged by some high-octane live shows. The follow-up, *A Pagan Place* (1984), was a powerful collection which drew comparisons with **U2**, but the breakthrough did not arrive until 1985's *This Is the Sea*, which saw the band reduced to the core of Scott, Thistlethwaite and Wallinger. A Top Forty album in the UK, it gave Scott his first UK Top Thirty single with 'The Whole of the Moon' (which would be a bigger hit when reissued in 1990) and saw the first appearance on a Waterboys record of Irish violinist Steve Wickham, who had played with **Sinead O'Connor** and In Tua Nua. The album's mystic themes led to comparisons with **Van Morrison** and Irish poet W. B. Yeats, and Scott duly relocated Waterboys operations to Ireland, his new 'spiritual home'.

Wallinger left the Waterboys to form his own band, World Party, which would enjoy success with a number of sixties-influenced albums, and Scott, Thistlethwaite and Wickham based themselves in Galway and began to assemble a floating line-up of Irish musicians for the lengthy recording sessions which would eventually produce the album *Fisherman's Blues* (1988). A mixture of folk-rock and traditional Irish music, it proved to be the Waterboys' biggest album to date, reaching the UK Top Twenty, and included a version of Van Morrison's 'Sweet Thing'. Live shows at this time were dominated by Scott's new-found love of Irish folk music, despite the presence in the band of former Patti Smith Group drummer Jay Dee Daugherty, and there was little surprise when 1990's *Room to Roam* turned out to be a whimsical collection of folk-influenced ditties. Shortly after its release, Wickham and Scott parted company.

The Waterboys then toured the UK with a pared-down line-up of Thistlethwaite, drummer Ken Blevins and bassist Trevor Hutchinson, playing little of the material from the new album and displaying Scott's rediscovered love of rock music. A 'best of' set appeared in 1991, and in 1992 the reinvigorated Scott signed to Geffen Records. He recorded *Dream Harder* (1993), a return to form and his first rock album since 1985, mainly in New York and without any previous band members. He followed that with *Bring 'Em All in* (1995) and the superior *Still Burning* (1997). Even more interesting is *A Rock in the Weary Land* (RCA, 2000) on which Scott sampled the delights of sampling and gospel choirs to good effect. The result was a ragged but exciting album.

The definitive collection is *The Whole of the Moon* (EMI, 1998).

ETHEL WATERS

b. 31 October 1896, Chester, Pennsylvania, USA,
d. 1 September 1977, Chatsworth, California

Ethel Waters started her career as a blues singer nicknamed 'Sweet Mama Stringbean'; she ended it regarded as one of her era's most accomplished and sensitive interpreters of popular songs, equally at home with blues, jazz, vaudeville and show tunes. As such she was a model for **Mildred Bailey**, **Lena Horne** and many other black cabaret artists. She was also a pioneer as a black personality in American showbusiness, earning a number of theatrical awards seldom, if ever, before given to a black artist.

She worked in vaudeville from 1917, and from 1921 with **Fletcher Henderson**. Her first recording, for Cardinal in 1921, was followed by many for the black-owned Black Swan label (1921–3), including the hits 'Oh Daddy'/'Down Home Blues' (1921), 'Tiger Rag' (1922) and 'Georgia Blues' (1923), then for Vocalion (1923–4), Paramount (1924) and Columbia (1925–31). The cornettist Joe Smith, who also recorded with **Bessie Smith**, was a frequent accompanist on her records, and she also did sessions with pianists **James P. Johnson** and **Clarence Williams**.

Replacing Florence Mills in *Plantation Revue* (1925), she became familiar in revue in New York, Chicago, Philadelphia and elsewhere; she also led her own touring troupe. After a movie début in *On with the Show* (1929, described as 'the first dialog motion picture in natural colors'), she travelled to England for a long residency at the Café de Paris in London. Back in New York, she appeared in the revues *Blackbirds of 1930*, Dixie to Broadway and *From Broadway Back to Harlem* (both 1932) and in 1933's *Stormy Weather*. Her version of **Harold Arlen**'s title song to the revue (Brunswick) remains Waters' best remembered recording. For Brunswick she also recorded with **Duke Ellington** (1932), and in addition worked with him in *Cotton Club Parade*.

By this time she was known as a vocalist versatile beyond the blues. She had recorded with **Tommy** and **Jimmy Dorsey** ('Birmingham Bertha'/'Am I Blue?',

Columbia, 1929) and **Benny Goodman** (1933), and starred on network radio, the first black woman to do so. Throughout the thirties and early forties she continued to work in revue, appear in movie shorts and record for Decca, Liberty and Bluebird. From 1942, and particularly after her success in *Cabin in the Sky* (1943), Waters began to be offered more substantial film acting roles, as in *Pinky* (1949), for which she received a Negro Actors' Guild award and an Academy Award nomination for Best Supporting Actress. She also held office in black actors' unions. Playing on Broadway in *The Member of the Wedding* (1950–1), she received the New York Drama Critics' Award as Best Actress; the 1953 film of the play garnered her another Academy Award nomination. From the late fifties Waters worked with the evangelist Billy Graham, but continued to appear in films (including *The Sound and the Fury*, 1959), on television, and in stock company productions of *The Member of the Wedding* (1964, 1970). After 1972 she made few public appearances because of ill-health. She told her story in the books *His Eye Is on the Sparrow* (1951) and *To Me It's Wonderful* (1972).

MUDDY WATERS

b. McKinley Morganfield, 4 April 1915, Rolling Fork,
Mississippi, USA, d. 30 April 1983, Chicago, Illinois

Like **Bill Monroe** and **Bob Wills**, Waters was an architect of a new music. Chicago blues, like Monroe's bluegrass or Wills' Western swing, though rooted in earlier forms, is firmly stamped with the personality and musical thinking of one man. An extraordinarily potent singer and guitarist, he conceived a new kind of band music, gathered the ideal musicians to execute it, and led them with an authority and magnetism unmatched by any of his contemporaries. His was the greatest single influence on the British blues boom of the sixties when his 'Got My Mojo Working' and 'Hoochie Coochie Man' were among the most played songs by white R&B groups.

He grew up near Clarksdale, Mississippi, learning harmonica and guitar and playing for local functions. He was recorded by **Alan Lomax** for the Library of Congress Archive of Folk Song in 1941 and 1942, playing both solo and in a string band led by Henry 'Son' Simms, formerly the fiddle-playing partner of **Charley Patton**. Moving to Chicago in 1943 he began to play in the clubs, aided by **Big Bill Broonzy** and **Sonny Boy Williamson I**. A 1946 Columbia session lay in the vaults until many years later; his first issued recordings in his own name were for **Leonard Chess**'s Aristocrat label in 1947. Subsequent sides for Aristocrat and Chess dramatically highlighted his bottleneck guitar-playing and trenchant vocals, as on 'I Can't Be

Satisfied' (1948), a two-part 'Rollin' and Tumblin" ·
(1950) and 'Rollin' Stone' (1950), which later provided
a name for the English group. Also in 1950 he first
recorded with harmonica-player **Little Walter**, in the
following year adding guitarist Jimmy Rogers (*b.
James A. Lane, 3 June 1924, Ruleville, Mississippi*) and
drummer Elgar Edmonds. With these he created the
nucleus of a hugely influential band and began a
series of superb Chess recordings that formed much
of the standard repertoire of Chicago-style blues, such
as 'Hoochie Coochie Man' and 'Just Make Love to
Me' (1953). By the mid-fifties **Otis Spann** had also
joined the band on piano, while Little Walter was
sometimes replaced by Walter Horton, as on 'Just to
Be with You' (1956), or James Cotton, as on 'Got My
Mojo Working' (1957).

The success of such recordings – many of them collected on the classic album *The Best of Muddy Waters*
(Chess, 1959) – led to nationwide tours, from which
Waters returned to semi-residencies at the Chicago
clubs Smitty's Corner and Pepper's Lounge. In the
late fifties he embarked on project albums with a collection of Broonzy songs (1959), followed by a live
recording from the Newport Jazz Festival (1960), an
acoustic *Muddy Waters – Folk Singer* (1964) and
Muddy, Brass and the Blues (1966).

A first overseas tour, to Britain, was organized by
Chris Barber in 1958. He returned to Europe with the
1963 American Folk Blues Festival, the 1964 Blues Car-
avan, and frequently thereafter, and appeared at the
Newport and other jazz and folk festivals in the
United States. He responded, or was persuaded to
respond, to the psychedelic rock phenomenon with
Electric Mud (Cadet Concept, 1968), and was joined
by **Rory Gallagher**, **Steve Winwood** and **Georgie
Fame** (as Georgie Fortune) on *The London Muddy
Waters Sessions* (Chess, 1972).

In the mid- and late seventies he chiefly worked the
US college and festival circuits, until his band, which
included Pinetop Perkins (piano) and Luther Johnson
Jnr (guitar), left him in 1980 after a management dispute. (Its members subsequently worked as the Legendary Blues Band.) A tour with **Johnny Winter** led
to the latter producing, and playing on, four
admirable albums for Blue Sky: *Hard Again* (1977),
I'm Ready (1978), *Muddy 'Mississippi' Waters Live*
(1979) and *King Bee* (1981).

Ten years after his death, British blues-rock vocalist
Paul Rodgers (**Free/Bad Company**) released the
album *Tribute to Muddy Waters* (1993) on which he
tackled Waters' material, largely in a hard-rock style,
backed by a number of noted guitarists including **Jeff
Beck**, Brian May (**Queen**), Carlos **Santana** and Slash
(**Guns N' Roses**). *The Chess Box* (1990) is the best
anthology, while *The Complete Muddy Waters*
(Charly, 1992) is just that with 205 tracks.

DOC WATSON
*b. Arthel Watson, 2 March 1923, Deep Gap, North Car-
olina, USA*

Doc Watson arrived on the American folk-music
scene through his role in a documentary recording of
an elderly old-time singer, at a time when he himself
was chiefly playing popular music. He immediately
won a large following for his warm, unpretentious
manner, his love of a wide range of music and, above
all, his remarkable facility on guitar. An outstanding
flat-picker, he revealed new possibilities in the playing
of old-time fiddle tunes and blues and belongs, with
Maybelle Carter of the **Carter Family**, **Merle Travis**
and **Chet Atkins**, among the creators of modern
American acoustic guitar-playing.

Born blind into a large musical family, he took up
harmonica and banjo as a child, and later guitar. In
the fifties he joined an all-purpose band, playing electric guitar on pop, rock'n'roll and country material in
local clubs, but he continued to play and sing old-
time music at home. Through his association with the
veteran musician Clarence 'Tom' Ashley, he came to
the attention of folk-music enthusiast Ralph Rinzler.
His first recorded work, on *Old Time Music at
Clarence Ashley's* (Folkways, 1960), led to concert and
club work in New York, an appearance at the 1963
Newport Folk Festival, and a series of albums (supervised by Rinzler) for Vanguard, beginning with *Doc
Watson* (1964).

In the following year he began to work with his
son, guitarist Merle (*b. 8 February 1949, Deep Gap,
d. 23 October 1985, Lenoir, North Carolina*), whom he
had named after Merle Travis. *Doc Watson and Son*
(1965) was followed by *Southbound* (1966), *Home
Again* (1967) and other albums, which mixed traditional Appalachian ballads and lyric folk songs with
compositions by **Jimmie Rodgers**, the **Delmore
Brothers**, **Mississippi John Hurt** and other figures of
the twenties and thirties. All these records were keenly
studied by up-and-coming guitarists.

Eclipsed by the explosive fusion of folk and rock
forms, Doc Watson regained his standing in the seventies with a contribution to the **Nitty Gritty Dirt
Band**'s *Will the Circle Be Unbroken?* set (United
Artists, 1971) and his Poppy albums with Merle, *Then
and Now* (1973) and *Two Days in November* (1974),
both Grammy award-winners. Their music had not
remained static. Inspired by Duane Allman of the **Allman Brothers Band**, Merle was playing more slide
guitar and inspired by Merle, Doc's repertoire had
become more diverse, including songs associated with
Bob Dylan and **Elvis Presley**. They also used
Nashville session musicians. In 1973 they made the
first full-time addition to their act, the electric bassist
T. Michael Coleman. Over the next twelve years they

continued to work in the United States (less often overseas), recording for United Artists, Flying Fish and Sugar Hill. Doc also joined Chet Atkins on *Reflections* (RCA, 1980). This productive and generally creative period was ended by Merle's 1985 death in a farming accident, which hastened Doc's already planned semi-retirement. *On Praying Ground* (1990) and *Remembering Merle* (1992) are among the few new albums he made in the nineties.

The Vanguard Years (1995) is the best anthology.

JOHNNY GUITAR WATSON

b. 3 February 1935, Houston, Texas, USA, d. 19 May 1996

One of the most original blues guitarists of the fifties, Watson had a more varied career than most of his contemporaries. Never afraid to embrace new developments in black music, he continued to have hit records in later decades while retaining his blues roots.

In 1950 he moved to Los Angeles, already influenced by the Texas blues styles of **T-Bone Walker** and **Clarence 'Gatemouth' Brown**. He joined the Chuck Higgins Band on piano in 1952, making his recording début singing 'Motor Head Blues' (Combo). This led to a contract with the King subsidiary Federal where, as Young John Watson, he recorded 'Highway 60' and the futuristic instrumental 'Space Guitar' (1952), which used reverb and feedback.

Watson moved to the **Bihari Brothers**' Modern in 1955 where Joe Bihari added the 'Guitar' to his name after the current hit movie *Johnny Guitar*. His most successful release for the label was a version of Earl King's 'Those Lonely Lonely Nights' (1955). During the late fifties he developed a spectacular stage act which included playing the guitar with his teeth.

He recorded for minor West Coast labels before **Johnny Otis** signed him to King again, producing the R&B hit 'Cuttin' in' (1961) and 'Gangster of Love', later revived by white bluesman **Steve Miller**. Watson then teamed up with **Larry Williams**, recording as a duo the superior *Two for the Price of One* (Okeh, 1965) and touring Britain, where they made a live album produced by Guy Stevens.

Watson added lyrics to 'Mercy Mercy Mercy', the Joe Zawinul (later of **Weather Report**) tune recorded by **Cannonball Adderley** (which he produced). The vocal version was an R&B hit for Marlena Shaw on Cadet and reached the pop Top Ten as sung by the Buckinghams (Columbia, 1967). Through Adderley, Watson signed to Fantasy in 1972, playing a mixture of progressive rock and R&B on *Listen* (1973) and the superb *I Don't Want to Be Alone, Stranger* (1976), from which 'I Don't Want to Be a Lone Ranger' was a minor hit in 1975. He also worked on albums by **Percy Mayfield** and **Betty Everett**.

'Signing to **Dick James**' British-based DJM label, Watson moved into disco territory for *Ain't That a Bitch* (1976), which featured the international hit 'I Need It'. The title track of *A Real Mother for Ya* (1977) was a minor hit in Britain and America. Watson made six more albums for DJM, including *Love Jones* (1980) and *Johnny and the Family Clone* (1981), before moving to A&M for the innovative *That's What Time It Is* (1982). He later released occasional singles on local Los Angeles labels, including 'Strike on Computers' (Valley Vue, 1984), but was largely inactive thereafter, recording *Strike on Computers* (1987), *Bow Wow* (1994) and contributing the occasional guest solo to **Frank Zappa** albums in the late eighties.

LU WATTERS

b. Lucious Watters, 19 December 1911, Santa Cruz, California, USA, d. 5 November 1989, Santa Rosa, California

Like **Ken Colyer** in England, Watters was a trumpeter who led a revival of 'traditional' jazz in the forties and fifties. With his Yerba Buena Band he sought to recreate what he imagined the jazz style of New Orleans in the early part of the century to have been.

From the late twenties he worked as a ship's musician and later joined Carol Lofner's dance band. Watters had formed his first jazz band in 1925 and throughout the thirties he led small groups in the San Francisco area before forming the Yerba Buena group in 1939. The band also featured Turk Murphy (trombone) and second trumpeter Bob Scobey and had soon gained a student following.

Drawing on the music of **King Oliver** and **Jelly Roll Morton**, the band built up a repertoire of blues, ragtime tunes and stomps, recording such titles as 'Muskrat Ramble', 'Memphis Blues' and 'Tiger Rag' for Good Time Jazz in 1941–2. By the mid-forties Watters' Yerba Buena Jazz Band had inspired such bands as Graeme Bell's in Australia and George Webb's Dixielanders in England. In turn these units spearheaded a trad movement that later included British bandleaders **Humphrey Lyttelton** and **Chris Barber**.

Watters served in the Second World War before reforming the Yerba Buena Band in 1946. Scobey and Murphy had left the band by 1949 when 'Frankie and Johnny', 'High Society' and 'My Little Bimbo' were recorded. In 1950 Watters moved to Clef to cut further tracks, including 'When the Saints Go Marching in' and 'Skid-dat-de-dat'. In the early fifties he left music to study geology, returning briefly to performance before retiring in 1959.

WEATHER REPORT

Airto Moreira, b. 5 August 1941, Brazil (replaced by Dom Um Romão); Alphonse Mouzon, b. 21 November

1948, Charleston, South Carolina, USA (replaced by Eric Gravatt, replaced by Ngudu, replaced by Peter Erskine, b. 5 May 1954, Somers Point, New Jersey, replaced by Omar Hakim); Wayne Shorter, b. 25 August 1933, New Jersey; Miroslav Vitous, b. Czechoslovakia (replaced by Alphonse Johnson, replaced by Jaco Pastorius, b. 1 December 1951, Norristown, Pennsylvania, d. 1987, Florida); Joe Zawinul, b. Josef Zawinul, 7 July 1932, Vienna, Austria

The group that did most to define the nature of jazz-rock in the seventies, Weather Report made more than twenty albums and inspired the formation of numerous other bands.

In his youth Zawinul studied piano at the Vienna Conservatoire, turning to jazz after 1945. In 1959 he moved to America where he briefly worked with Maynard Ferguson (whose band included Wayne Shorter) and **Dinah Washington** before joining **Cannonball Adderley** in 1961. The composer of the jazz-funk hit 'Mercy Mercy Mercy' (1967), Zawinul was a key member of the band until in 1969 he joined **Miles Davis**'s group, where he was reunited with tenor-saxophonist Shorter who had previously played with **Art Blakey**'s Jazz Messengers (1959–64). Zawinul wrote the title tune of In a Silent Way (1969) and played on Bitches Brew (1969), records which marked the trumpeter's first major move into electric music.

Weather Report was founded in 1971 by Shorter and Zawinul to develop a kind of fusion music based on Zawinul's mastery of atmosphere and Shorter's love of the exotic and gifts as a melodic improviser. The group which made the eponymous début album for Columbia included Brazilian percussionist Moreira and Czech bassist Vitous. By the time of I Sing the Body Electric (1972), Weather Report's frequent personnel changes had begun with the arrival of Gravatt (drums) and Um Romão, another Latin percussionist. The album included excerpts from a live performance in Tokyo, as well as Zawinul's ambitious 'Unknown Soldier', an attempt to portray war and its aftermath.

The music moved closer to rock on Sweetnighter (1973), named after an anti-bedwetting preparation, and later records like Mysterious Traveler (1974) and Tailspinnin' (1975) showed greater concern with studio techniques and new synthesizer technology. Zawinul used an ARP 2600 on the latter album, moving to an Oberheim polyphonic for Black Market (1976). For one track of that album Weather Report added bassist Jaco Pastorius, whose brilliant fretless playing soon made him a featured member of the group.

Heavy Weather (1977) was the group's most commercially successful album, with Zawinul's 'Birdland' (later memorably recorded by **Manhattan Transfer**) establishing itself as a jazz-rock standard. With the addition of Erskine (drums), Weather Report remained a quartet from 1978 until 1982, cutting Mr Gone (1978), 8.30 (1979) and Night Passages (1980). Both Erskine and Pastorius then left for solo careers, the latter forming Word of Mouth and recording with **Joni Mitchell**. In the mid-eighties his musical career was disrupted by drugs problems and his premature death occurred after a fight outside a nightclub.

Procession (1983) included former **David Sanborn** and **George Benson** drummer Omar Hakim and the first vocals on a Weather Report album, from Manhattan Transfer's Janis Siegel. Domino Theory (1984) and Sportin' Life (1985) followed and both Zawinul and Shorter made solo recordings before reuniting to make This Is This (1986), Weather Report's final album. Zawinul went on to form Weather Update with Erskine and guitarist Steve Khan, while Shorter established his own quartet.

THE WEAVERS
Ronnie Gilbert; Lee Hays, b. 14 March 1914, Little Rock, Arkansas, USA, d. 26 August 1981, New York City; Fred Hellerman, b. 13 May 1927, New York; Pete Seeger, b. 13 May 1919, New York City (replaced by Erik Darling, b. 25 September 1933, replaced by Frank Hamilton, replaced by Bernie Krause)

Adapting folk songs to an orchestral format supplied by **Gordon Jenkins**, the Weavers were highly successful during the fifties. Evolving a repertoire that mixed compositions by **Woody Guthrie** and other contemporary writers with traditional material from around the world, they provided a blueprint for the **Kingston Trio** and for many of the other folk groups that emerged in America during that decade.

Agit-prop playwright and singer Hays had gone from Arkansas to New York in 1940, where with **Pete Seeger** and Guthrie he formed the Almanac Singers. Concentrating on topical, political and union songs, the group recorded for Eric Bernay's Almanac Records before blacklisting forced them to disband in 1943.

The Weavers (named after a play by German writer Hauptmann) came together in 1949, adding Gilbert's versatile soprano and Hellerman's baritone to Hays' bass and Seeger's tenor. Their performances at the Village Vanguard attracted the interest both of Columbia's **Mitch Miller** and of Jenkins, who persuaded Decca's **Jack Kapp** to sign the quartet. With string arrangements by Jenkins, the Weavers had a series of hits in 1950–1 beginning with **Leadbelly**'s 'Goodnight Irene'* and a version of the sprightly Israeli song 'Tzena Tzena Tzena'.

This was followed by 'On Top of Old Smokey', which provided a model for Miller's later series of 'singalong' hits. The Weavers' success continued with the East African song 'Wimoweh' – an American No. 1

in 1961 for the Tokens as 'The Lion Sleeps Tonight', a British hit for Karl Denver (Decca, 1964) and a No. 1 for Tight Fit (Jive, 1982) – as well as 'Kisses Sweeter Than Wine', and Guthrie's 'So Long It's Been Good to Know You'.

In 1952 the Weavers' career was abruptly halted by McCarthyite blacklisting and the group disbanded until 1955 when a successful reunion concert at Carnegie Hall led to concert tours of campuses and clubs which did much to stimulate the American folk boom of the late fifties. A live recording was released by Vanguard, for whom the Weavers made further records.

Seeger left in 1958 to be replaced by the Tarriers' **Erik Darling**, who in turn left to form the Rooftop Singers in 1961. The original members plus later replacements appeared on *Reunion* (1963), recorded at the group's penultimate concert. Their final performance came in 1981 at Carnegie Hall and was featured in a film biography of the Weavers, *Wasn't That a Time* (1981).

Ronnie Gilbert later recorded with Holly Near, a feminist folk singer from a younger generation. In 1994 Omega issued *Kisses Sweeter than Wine*, a concert recording from the fifties. Doris Willens' biography of Hays, *Lonesome Traveler* (1988), provides an insider's view of the group's history.

CHICK WEBB
b. William Henry Webb, 10 February 1909, Baltimore, Maryland, USA, d. 16 June 1939, Baltimore

Described by **Gene Krupa** as 'the little giant of the drums', Webb was one of the great drummer–bandleaders of the swing era. He is best remembered for 'A-Tisket, A-Tasket'* (1938) on which the featured vocalist was **Ella Fitzgerald**.

A hunchback, Webb formed his first band in the late twenties. Among its original members were guitarist John Trueheart and **Louis Jordan**. In 1931 he secured a residency at New York's Savoy ballroom, celebrated in his most famous original recording, saxophonist and band arranger Edgar Sampson's 'Stompin' at the Savoy' (Columbia, 1934), which subsequently became a jazz classic and provided **Benny Goodman** with one of his biggest hits in 1937. Sampson's dramatic arrangements, trumpeter Taft Jordan's **Louis Armstrong** impressions and Webb's showmanship made the band one of the hottest of the thirties. When in 1935, after winning a talent contest, Fitzgerald joined, Webb restructured the band around her, even becoming her legal guardian after her mother's death. The result was a more sinuous, less dramatic sound, heard at its best on such recordings as 'Sing Me a Sweet Song (And Let Me Dance)', 'I'll Chase the Blues Away' (Decca, 1936) and 'I Got a Guy' (1938).

Their greatest collaboration was the nursery rhyme adapted by Fitzgerald 'A-Tisket, A-Tasket', which featured Louis Jordan on saxophone. The biggest-selling record of the thirties, the song was also a hit for **Tommy Dorsey**. Webb's other hit recordings included 'Undecided' and 'Tain't What You Do (It's the Way That You Do It)' (1939).

After Webb's death, Fitzgerald led the band until 1942 before embarking on a hugely successful solo career.

JIMMY WEBB
b. 15 August 1946, Elk City, Oklahoma, USA

Although Webb's own expressive but austere performances of his songs were far too quirky to achieve success, in the smoother versions by **Glen Campbell** ('By the Time I Get to Phoenix', 1967; 'Wichita Lineman', 1968), Richard Harris and **Donna Summer** ('MacArthur Park'*, 1968 and 1978, respectively) and the Fifth Dimension ('Up Up and Away'*, 1967), Webb's songs were huge hits, making him one of the most successful songwriters of the sixties.

The son of a minister, Webb grew up in rural Oklahoma and spent his teenage years in California. This mix of innocent Americana (seen in the fully realized characters of songs like 'Phoenix' and 'Wichita Lineman') and sophistication lies behind the best of Webb's work. In 1965 he moved to Los Angeles and worked for Motown's publishing company Jobete, who published his 'Honey Come Back', later a minor hit for Chuck Jackson (Motown, 1969) and a major one for Campbell (1970). Success came when Webb met **Johnny Rivers**, who recorded 'Phoenix' on *Changes* (1967) and matched him with the Fifth Dimension, whom Rivers had just signed to his Soul City label. The result was 'Up, Up and Away' (1967). In the same year Campbell recorded 'Phoenix' and in 1968–9 Webb had successes with the epic 'MacArthur Park' (from actor Richard Harris's *A Tramp Shining*, Dunhill, all the songs on which were written by Webb), 'The Worst That Could Happen' (Brooklyn Bridge, Buddah, the group led by former member of the **Crests**, Johnny Maestro) and 'Wichita Lineman' and 'Galveston' (Campbell).

With his songs now being regularly featured by such artists as **Frank Sinatra** and **Andy Williams**, Webb, who had first recorded as a member of Strawberry Children in 1967 and had seen Epic release an album of his demos, *Jim Webb Sings Jim Webb* (1968), turned singer-songwriter with *Words and Music* (Reprise, 1970). That album included his own version of 'P. F. Sloan', which took for its subject the often misunderstood composer of **Barry McGuire**'s 'Eve of Destruction' (1965). However, it and most of his subsequent albums (which included *Letters*, 1972; the

George Martin-produced *El Mirage*, Atlantic, 1977; and *Angel Heart*, 1982), in contrast to the more directly confessional work of **Carole King** and **James Taylor**, were poorly received. Though several of these later songs were memorably recorded by the likes of **Judy Collins** ('The Moon Is a Harsh Mistress', 1975) and **Ian Matthews** ('Met Her on a Plane', 1974), few were hits. The major exceptions were 'All I Know', which gave Art Garfunkel (of **Simon and Garfunkel**) his first major solo hit (Columbia, 1973) and 'Highwayman', the title track of the joint album by **Johnny Cash**, **Willie Nelson** and **Kris Kristofferson**, and a huge hit in 1985. In 1993 the compilation *Archive* was followed by the new solo album *Suspending Disbelief*, produced by **Linda Ronstadt** and George Massenburg. It included his own versions of some of his best songs of the past decade and featured David Crosby, ex-**Eagles** member Don Henley and Ronstadt as backing vocalists.

Webb also worked as a producer with the **Supremes** (1972), **Cher** (the lacklustre *Stars*, 1975) and his sister Susan, who often sang back-up on his own albums.

BEN WEBSTER

b. Benjamin Francis Webster, 27 March 1909, Kansas City, Missouri, USA, d. 20 September 1973, Amsterdam, Netherlands

One of the most successful mainstream jazz saxophonists of the forties and fifties, Webster's versatility encompassed raucous, swinging up-tempo tunes and melodic, breathy ballads. A leading soloist in the **Duke Ellington** band of the early forties, he went on to a solo career, basing himself in Europe where he was especially popular.

Webster's first instruments were the violin and piano, which he played in a silent cinema in Texas before joining Dutch Campbell's band. He learned tenor sax from **Buddy Johnson**, later a member of the bands of **Louis Armstrong** and **Earl Hines**. During the early thirties Webster performed with several Midwest and Southwest bands, recording with Bennie Moten ('Moten Stomp', Victor, 1932), whose Eddie Durham's arrangements are regarded as classics of big-band swing, Ellington ('Stormy Weather', 1933) and Benny Carter ('Dream Lullaby', EMI Columbia, 1934).

During the remainder of the decade Webster played with numerous orchestras, including those of **Fletcher Henderson** and **Cab Calloway**, and recorded with **Billie Holiday** ('What a Little Moonlight Can Do', 1935), Willie Bryant ('The Voice of Old Man River', RCA, 1935), **Teddy Wilson** ('Sweet Lorraine', 1939) and **Jack Teagarden** (1940).

Previously overshadowed by **Coleman Hawkins**, Webster made his reputation as a leading soloist during 1940–3 when he toured and recorded with Ellington. His playing was featured on such tracks as 'All Too Soon', 'Cottontail', 'Sidewalks of New York' (1940) and 'Just a-Settin' and a-Rockin'' (1941). His greatest contribution to Ellington's work came in the suite *Black, Brown and Beige*, which was premièred in New York in 1943.

He later played with **Woody Herman** ('Basie's Basement', Columbia, 1944) before becoming a central figure in **Norman Granz**'s 1949 'Jazz at the Philharmonic' tour. He appeared on several JATP recordings and Granz supervised further sessions with such partners as **Art Tatum** (Pablo, 1955), his mentor Coleman Hawkins (*Tenor Giants*, Verve, 1959) and trumpeter Harry 'Sweets' Edison (*Blues for Basie*, Verve, 1958).

From 1964 Webster based himself in Europe, recording prolifically for Alan Bates' Black Lion label. *Atmosphere for Lovers and Thieves* and *Saturday Night at the Montmartre* were among his best efforts for the company. *My Man* (Inner City, 1973) was recorded live in Copenhagen a few months before Webster's death.

BERT WEEDON

b. 10 May 1920, East Ham, London, England

With Jim Sullivan, Bert Weedon was a leading British session guitarist of the fifties. He had a lasting influence on a whole generation of British guitarists, as much for his *Play in a Day* instructional manual – which sold over two million copies – and frequent radio appearances, as for his series of solo hits.

Weedon took up the guitar at the age of twelve and after turning professional became a pioneer of the electric guitar in Britain. In the forties he played with various dance and big bands, including those of **Ted Heath**, **Mantovani** and Ronnie Aldrich. He also accompanied **George Shearing** and **Stephane Grappelli** before becoming a featured soloist on BBC dance-band broadcasts and recording with **Max Jaffa** ('April in Paris', EMI Columbia, 1954). Too old to become a rock'n'roller himself, he took enthusiastically to the new music, though always refining and giving delicacy to the urgent American models he imitated. He became a leading session player, taking solos on early recordings by **Adam Faith**, **Marty Wilde**, **Tommy Steele** and **Frankie Vaughan**.

After briefly recording for Parlophone, his own first hit was Arthur Smith's 1945 tune 'Guitar Boogie Shuffle' (Top Rank, 1959), a cover of the Virtues' American hit (Hunt, 1959). Others included 'Nashville Boogie' (1959), 'Big Beat Boogie' and, perhaps his purest piece, a reworking of the 1916 piano piece 'Twelfth Street Rag' (1960). By this time his playing was being eclipsed by the **Shadows**, whose 'Apache' (1960) he unsuccessfully covered. Weedon's hits continued into 1961 ('Sorry Robbie', 'Ginchy', 'Mr Guitar') and he regularly appeared on radio, but with the advent of guitarists like **Duane Eddy** and later beat groups his anachronistic image told against him.

Weedon continued to make albums and in the revivalist atmosphere of the seventies had two surprising hits, *Rocking at the Roundhouse* (Warwick, 1970) and 22 *Golden Guitar Greats*, which topped the British charts in 1977. He was less active in the eighties and nineties.

Other guitarists active in Britain in the fifties and early sixties included Rhet Stoller, who had a minor hit with the **Ventures**-inspired 'Chariot' (Decca, 1961), and Wout Steenhous, like Weedon a fixture on radio.

TED WEEMS
b. Wilfred Theodore Weymes, 26 September 1901, Pitcairn, Pennsylvania, USA, d. 6 May 1963, Tulsa, Oklahoma

The dance band headed by Ted Weems was not only among the most popular American combinations of the twenties and thirties but also a proving-ground for several notable singers, in particular **Perry Como**.

Weems formed his first band in 1922 with his brother Art (trumpet) and others; within a year they had a hit record with 'Somebody Stole My Gal' (Victor, 1923). Written by vaudevillian Leo Wood in 1918, the song was later used by British bandleader **Billy Cotton** as a signature tune. In 1929 the band based itself in Chicago, secured a radio show and had success with the novelty record 'Piccolo Pete'*, composed by Phil Baxter, an early member of **Paul Whiteman**'s band. The sequel was 'Harmonica Harry'.

In the early thirties the band's singers included Parker Gibbs, Red Ingle (later a key member of **Spike Jones**' band), Country Washburne – who took the vocal on the hit version of 'Oh Mo' nah' (Victor, 1931) – and Elmo Tanner, a proficient whistler who was featured on Weems' 1933 million-seller 'Heartaches'. Joe Haymes was responsible for many of these arrangements. Como started singing with the band in 1936.

In 1942 the band broke up because of the demands of military service. Weems re-formed a group in 1945, and a couple of years later enjoyed success with the film song 'Micken' and with a reissue of 'Heartaches'. By the mid-fifties, however, he was working as a deejay on a Memphis radio station.

KURT WEILL
b. 2 March 1900, Dessau, Germany, d. 3 April 1950, New York, USA

Mixing elements of classical opera with the jazz, dance and popular music of America, Weill was one of the most original composers of the twentieth century. Like his fellow émigré the film director Fritz Lang, his career was divided between Germany and America. But where Lang's American films were accepted as the equal of his work in Germany (after for a long time being dismissed as 'mere' Hollywood), Weill's American work has still to emerge from the shadow of his famous collaborations with Bertolt Brecht, particularly after the hugely successful revival of *The Threepenny Opera* on Broadway in 1954. A successful and inventive practitioner in the world of the Broadway musical there was a continuity in Weill's work and concerns, from the assimilation of American influences in Germany to his later operation within the confines of the commercial American theatre. Brecht and Weill's *The Threepenny Opera* is in the repertoire of countless opera companies while its most famous song, 'Mack the Knife', in the words of Peter Keepnews 'has found its way into the act of practically every lounge singer in America (no small feat for a song celebrating the exploits of a cold-blooded killer)'. The widespread recordings of the Maxwell Anderson–Weill 'September Song', which range from **Bing Crosby** through **Willie Nelson** and **Jimmy Durante** to Lou Reed, testify equally to the vibrancy of the later work.

The son of a cantor, Weill studied with Englebert Humperdinck and Ferruccio Busoni, during which time he devoted himself to modernistic symphonic compositions, and briefly served as the director of the Luchenscheid opera company. In 1925 he wrote the one-act opera *Der Protagonist* with playwright Georg Kaiser and in 1927 set a series of Brecht's poems to music as a one-act opera, *Mahagonny Songspiel*. Staged in a boxing ring at Baden-Baden, the opera's combination of Brecht's sardonic social commentary and Weill's jangly, almost dissonant, dance music, American-influenced but still retaining the flavour of a German beer hall, resulted in a *succès de scandale*.

In 1928 the pair adapted John Gay's *The Beggar's Opera* as *Die Dreigroschenoper* (*The Threepenny Opera*) in which Weill's wife **Lotte Lenya** took the role of Jenny. A mark of its success was that within five years it had been translated into some twenty languages and performed over 10,000 times in Europe, even briefly reaching Broadway in 1933; it was filmed in 1930. Among the songs it introduced were 'The Ballad of Mack the Knife', an instrumental hit for **Lawrence Welk**, Dick Hyman* (MGM) and **Billy Vaughn** (1956) and a vocal hit for **Louis Armstrong**, **Bobby Darin** (1959) and **Ella Fitzgerald** (1960), among others; the biting satire 'What Keeps Mankind Alive' (later recalled in **Randy Newman**'s equally mordant 'God's Song'); and 'Pirate Jenny', memorably recorded by **Judy Collins**. The insistent social commentary of Brecht's libretto and lyrics neatly caught what Lotte Lenya described as 'those nervous days when the Strauss waltz was still playing to people who were listening for something else', while in the music Weill sought to create a genuine union of music and popular theatre. In 1929 the pair's *Happy End* (which included 'Surabaya Johnny') was briefly staged before being banned and in 1930 *Mahagonny* (which included 'Alabama Song', later recorded by the **Doors**), with its surrealistic vision of America, was revived in a three-act version. After Weill and Georg Kaiser's state-of-the-nation opera *Der Silbersee* was banned in 1933 Weill fled from Germany.

He briefly worked in France (writing his last major collaboration with Brecht, *The Seven Deadly Sins*, 1933) and England (the comic operetta *A Kingdom for a Cow*, 1935) before settling in New York in 1935. There he collaborated with playwright Paul Green on the anti-war *Johnny Johnson* which, though a critical success when mounted by the Group Theater on Broadway in 1936, was a commercial failure. That was followed by the commercial success *Knickerbocker Holiday* (1938, filmed 1944) which, though set in colonial times, had a contemporary theme. In it Walter Huston introduced Weill's most recorded American song, 'September Song', a hit for Crosby, **Frank Sinatra** (1946), **Stan Kenton** (1951) and **Liberace** (1952). Equally successful was the musical satire of psychoanalysis *Lady in the Dark* (1938) with lyrics by **Ira Gershwin**, his first since his brother's death. It included 'Tchaikovsky', which became forever associated with **Danny Kaye**. The light-hearted fantasy *One Touch of Venus* (1943, filmed 1948), with lyrics by celebrated wits Ogden Nash and S. J. Perelman, included the hit 'Speak Low' (**Guy Lombardo**, 1944). During this period Weill wrote his only film score, the bizarre fantasy *Where Do We Go from Here* (1945), also with Ira Gershwin.

For these Weill provided discrete songs, but other works proclaimed his continuing commitment to a form of musical theatre that commented on its times, in the manner of his German works. Among these were his setting of Brecht's 'Ballad of the Soldier's Wife' to music as part of the war effort, *Street Scene* (1947), with a libretto by Elmer Rice and lyrics by black poet Langston Hughes (which included the **Benny Goodman** pop hit 'Moon-Faced, Starry-Eyed'). His final Broadway musical was *Lost in the Stars* (1949), an adaptation of Alan Paton's *Cry the Beloved Country*, with Maxwell Anderson as librettist and lyricist. That title was used for Hal Willner's 1985 A&M collection of disparate readings of Weill's music, including Lou Reed's incisive interpretation of 'September Song', **Tom Waits**' 'What Keeps Man Alive' and **Carla Bley**'s haunting version of the title track.

Weill died in 1950, before he could complete his musical interpretation of Mark Twain's *Huckleberry Finn* and before the enormous popular success of Marc Blitzstein's translation of *The Threepenny Opera* (1954) and subsequently of 'Mack the Knife', with Lotte Lenya reprising her original role, virtually obliterated his American work for several decades. It was in the wake of that that 'Mack the Knife' entered the American popular consciousness. In the eighties Lenya's renderings of Weill's and Brecht's songs gave way to less mannered and stagebound interpretations typified by Bettina Jonic (*The Bitter Mirror*, Transatlantic, 1975), Ute Lemper (Decca, 1988) and Dagmar Krause (*Supply and Demand*, Hannibal, 1986), while Weill's biographer Ronald Sanders (*The Days Grow Short*, 1980) focused attention on Weill's work in America as well as Germany.

ELISABETH WELCH
b. 27 February 1908, New York, New York, USA

Famed for introducing the Charleston to Broadway in *Runnin' Wild* in 1923 and **Cole Porter**'s 'Love for Sale' in *The New Yorkers* (1931), Welch won renewed fame after the Second World War in Europe as a preserver of the flame of the classic Broadway songs.

Of mixed American Indian, African and Scottish descent, Welch appeared in numerous obscure New York night-spots before getting her break with *Runnin' Wild*. After that she regularly appeared in all-black revues on and off Broadway, including *Chocolate Dandies* (1924) and *Blackbirds* (1928), with which she went to Paris. After returning to New York for *Runnin' Wild*, Welch settled in London in 1933 where she regularly appeared in revues and shows and at various night-clubs. Among the shows she appeared in were *Nymph Errant* (1930), *Glamorous Night* (1935), *Arc de Triomphe* (1943), *Happy and Glorious* (1945), *Penny Plain* (1951) and *Pay the Piper* (1954). Though her stage appearances became rarer in the sixties she continued to appear on the radio and in revue and to record. Albums from this period include *Elisabeth Welch Sings the Irving Berlin Songbook* (1958). In 1973 she returned to the stage in *Pippin* and later in 1976 she starred in a show devised for her by Caryl Brahms and Ned Sherrin, *I Gotta Show*.

By now a legendary figure, Welch continued to make appearances, particularly at charity events, and to record. Thus in 1980 she appeared singing 'Stormy Weather' in Derek Jarman's film of *The Tempest*. Later recordings include *In Concert* (1986), *Where Have You Been?* (1987) and *This Thing Called Love* (1989). In 1989 she appeared in a one-night revival of *Nymph Errant* and in 1993 at an Aids benefit concert in London.

LAWRENCE WELK

b. 11 March 1903, Strasburg, North Dakota, USA,
d. 17 May 1992, Santa Monica, California

Though Welk's self-styled 'champagne music' was widely disregarded by musicians, he was one of America's longest-serving bandleaders and continued his career in music publishing and the record industry long after the heyday of the big bands.

Born on a farm in a German immigrant community, Welk learned the accordion in his youth and took up a career in music when he was twenty-one. Just as in the twenties Adolf Hofner led a Texas-based country dance band whose repertoire was mostly Czechoslovakian in origin, so Welk's initial repertoire was mostly German-styled polkas and waltzes. But, whereas Hofner turned to honky-tonk music in his performances in the dance halls of the Southwest, Welk, in the thirties, sought to refine his music. Although his sound retained a country inflection for several decades (and in 1945 he recorded 'Shame on You' with **Red Foley** on Decca), as his band increased in size throughout the thirties Welk 'sweetened' its sound. In 1939 he took 'Bubbles in the Wine' (Vocalion) as his theme tune and called his sound 'champagne music'. In contrast to most big bands who played for urban audiences, Welk aimed his music at middle America. He initially enjoyed only modest recording success (on Vocalion, Okeh and Decca) but, after the demise of the big bands at the end of the forties, Welk secured a residency in Pacific Ocean Park, California, in 1951. With that as his base, and with a nationally broadcast television show (1955–7) to showcase his music, he had a series of hits throughout the fifties, mostly cover-versions of other people's recordings. The climax of his recording career was the American chart-topper 'Calcutta'* (Dot, 1961).

Among his hits were **Kurt Weill**'s 'The Theme from the Threepenny Opera' (Coral, 1956), also a hit for **Louis Armstrong** and **Billy Vaughn**; 'The Poor People of Paris' (1956), also a hit for **Les Baxter** and **Chet Atkins** and in Britain for **Winifred Atwell**; and a cover of **Floyd Cramer**'s 'Last Date' (Dot, 1960). 'Calcutta', a German tune initially called 'Tivoli Melody', which was covered by the **Four Preps**, reached No. 1 a few weeks after fellow German **Bert Kaempfert** had a No. 1 hit with another instrumental 'Wonderland by Night'.

In the sixties and seventies Welk devoted most of his time to his growing publishing and real-estate interests which, in the eighties, extended to recording when he purchased the catalogue of Vanguard Records, the leading folk-revival label of the sixties. His lively autobiography *Wunnerful, Wunnerful,* was a bestseller.

PAUL WELLER

b. Paul John William Weller, 25 May 1958, Woking,
Surrey, England

The leader of the **Jam** from 1975 to 1982, Weller had a prolific later career in white soul band Style Council and as a solo artist.

Style Council was formed in 1982 with keyboards-player Mick Talbot, previously with mod group the Merton Parkas and **Dexy's Midnight Runners**. Other members included female singer D. C. Lee, whom Weller would later marry. The Style Council continued Weller's run of British hits, beginning with 'Speak Like a Child' and 'Long Hot Summer' in 1983. The cool jazz approach of 'My Ever Changing Moods' (1984) from *Café Bleu* gave the group their only American hit on Geffen. Compared to the social realism of the Jam's material, many of Weller's new songs were explicit in their political commitment, and the Style Council frequently played benefits for left-wing political causes. With **Billy Bragg**, Weller led the 'Red Wedge' tour in support of the Labour Party.

My Favourite Shop (1985) was a well-crafted series of funk-grounded songs on such topics as industrial decline, political violence and social change. It included the hit 'Walls Come Tumbling Down', which was also featured on the live album *Home and Abroad* (1986).

The 1987 album, *The Cost of Loving*, was in the same vein and featured rap group the Dynamic Three and Lee singing 'A Woman's Story'. In 1988 the band released its final album, *Confessions of a Pop Group*. A compilation of out-takes and rarities, *Here's Some That Got Away*, appeared in 1993.

Weller signed as a solo artist to UK independent label Go! Discs in 1992, releasing an eponymous début album later that year. It made the UK Top Ten and provided him with a British hit single, the sixties-styled 'Uh Huh Oh Yeh'. His second solo album, *Wild Wood* (1993), heavily influenced by **Steve Winwood**'s late sixties band Traffic, gave him his biggest hit since 1987. It included the hit singles 'Sunflower', 'Hung Up' and the title track, and was followed by the concert recording *Live Wood*. By the time Weller issued his third solo album, *Stanley Road* (1995), he had been adopted as a father-figure by the new breed of sixties-influenced rock groups, notably **Oasis** and **Ocean Colour Scene**. Later the same year Weller recorded a cover of **The Beatles**' 'Come Together' for the *Help* benefit album with **Paul McCartney** and Oasis's Noel Gallagher. It was at this session that the derogatory 'dadrock' label originated.

In 1997 *Heavy Soul* cemented Weller's position as one of the UK's most popular rock performers. The following year he issued a greatest hits compilation,

Modern Classics, which included the new single 'Brand New Start'. Weller enlisted the help of string arranger Robert Kirby, famed for his work with **Nick Drake**, to work on his fifth solo album, *Heliocentric*, which showed Weller to be still angry, still coming to terms with his past, but doing so in a softer and more contemplative manner. This was reflected in the album's sound, which was acoustic and less horn-driven than in the past. The surprising result saw Weller edging closer in perspective to the likes of **Richard Thompson** and **Van Morrison**.

JUNIOR WELLS
b. Amos Wells, 9 December 1934, Memphis, Tennessee, USA, d. 15 January 1998

One of the bright hopes of the post-war generation of Chicago bluesmen, singer and harmonica-player Junior Wells became, with his partner **Buddy Guy**, a travelling ambassador for the blues. A just inheritor of the stylistic legacies of both **Sonny Boy Williamson**s, he was a dramatic player and singer with a powerful stage presence.

He went to live in Chicago in 1946, was working in bands by 1948, and by 1952–3 was experienced enough to replace **Little Walter** in the **Muddy Waters** band. He recorded, under the influence of Sonny Boy Williamson I, for States (1953–4), making the first of many versions of 'Hoodoo Man'. Subsequent work on Mel London's Chief and Profile labels (1957–62) practically phased out his harmonica-playing to emphasize his sexily confident singing on titles like 'Little by Little', 'Come on in This House' and 'Messin' with the Kid'. He worked regularly at the Chicago blues venues Pepper's Lounge and Theresa's, from 1958 often with Guy, who accompanied him on his début album *Hoodoo Man Blues* (Delmark, 1966) and the subsequent Vanguard sets *It's My Life, Baby!* (1966, partly recorded at Pepper's) and *Coming at You* (1968), a studio set with brass arrangements that drew in ex-**Duke Ellington** trumpeter Clark Terry. Wells and Guy went to Europe with the 1966 American Folk Blues Festival, and on many subsequent occasions, working with, among others, the **Rolling Stones**. Tours also took them to Africa (1967–8), Australia (1972) and Japan (1975). Their club act was caught in the documentaries *Chicago Blues* (1970) and *Blues Entre les Dents* (1972).

South Side Blues Jam (Delmark, 1971), with Guy and **Otis Spann**, and *On Tap* (Delmark, 1975) showed that Wells had not been artistically sapped by his frequent separations from his Chicago audience, but European recordings with Guy in the seventies and eighties did not consistently demonstrate the exciting empathy that the artists could display in favourable conditions. They continued to play live together, but Guy's increasing success as a soloist from the late eighties led to the duo parting company.

In 1991 Wells released *Harp Attack* with fellow blues harmonica stylists James Cotton, Carey Bell and Billy Branch. *1957–1966* (Paula, 1991) collects together his important early recordings.

KITTY WELLS
b. Muriel Deason, 30 August 1918, Nashville, Tennessee, USA

More than anyone else, Kitty Wells made a role for the female country singer of the post-second World War period, clearing the ground for **Loretta Lynn**, **Tammy Wynette** and other women who challenged the male hegemony in country music. Her piercing, aching tones became the quintessential country voice of desolation and atonement.

In 1938, two years after her radio début, she joined the duo Johnnie and Jack – Johnnie Wright, whom she had just married, and Jack Anglin – and sang with them on a number of Southeastern radio stations. In 1947 they became cast-members of the *Louisiana Hayride*, which made their national reputation. After recording with Johnnie and Jack, and briefly in her own name, for RCA Victor, she signed with Decca and had the historic country No. 1 'It Wasn't God Who Made Honky Tonk Angels'* (1952), written by **Jay Miller** as a woman's answer to **Hank Thompson**'s 'Wild Side of Life'. No record has a better claim to have turned public opinion, formerly unenthusiastic, in favour of women country singers.

The trio joined Nashville's *Grand Ole Opry* in 1952. Wells extended her list of hits with such records as 'I'm Paying for That Back Street Affair' (1953), 'One by One' and 'As Long as I Live' (both 1954 duets with **Red Foley**), 'Making Believe' (1955), 'I Can't Stop Loving You' (1958) and 'Mommy for a Day' (1959). In 1959 she signed a lifetime contract with Decca. Among her successes in the sixties were 'Heartbreak U.S.A.', a country No. 1 in 1961, and 'Will Your Lawyer Talk to God?' (1962). She had frequent minor hits until the mid-seventies, by which time she had recorded several hundred singles and more than forty albums. In 1969 she and Wright began a syndicated TV programme, *The Kitty Wells/ Johnny Wright Family Show*. She published a book, *Favorite Songs and Recipes*, in 1973, and in 1976 was elected to the Country Music Hall of Fame. She continued to record in the eighties for independent country labels, notably in 1987 with fellow country veteran Roy Drusky. In 1988 she contributed to **k. d. lang**'s *Shadowlands*. *Country Music Hall of Fame* (MCA, 1991) is a representative anthology, while *Queen of Country* (Bear Family, 1996) is the definitive four-CD retrospective.

MARY WELLS
b. 13 May 1943, Detroit, Michigan, USA, d. 26 July 1992

Best remembered for 'My Guy' (1964), Wells was the first female star of **Berry Gordy**'s Motown company.

In 1959 she brought her 'Bye Bye Baby' to Gordy, who released the song which became a Top Ten R&B hit. Subsequently, **Smokey Robinson** was assigned to Wells as producer and songwriter. In 1962–4 Wells had a sequence of seven hits. It began with 'The One Who Really Loves You' (1962), 'You Beat Me to the Punch' and 'Two Lovers', Robinson's clever lyric in which Wells' two men turn out to be two sides of a 'split personality'. With their light, bouncy rhythms and Wells' high, sweet voice, those songs and the later 'What's Easy for Two Is So Hard for One' and 'Laughing Boy' fulfilled Motown's intention to provide black music aimed squarely at teenage listeners.

'My Guy' (1964) was Motown's first No. 1 pop hit and also its first international success, notably in Britain where it reached the Top Ten and was highly praised by **The Beatles**. The song was a reissued hit there in 1972. Following 'My Guy', Wells recorded 'What's the Matter with You Baby' and 'Once upon a Time' as duets with **Marvin Gaye**.

Disagreements with Gordy over the terms of her contract led Wells to join 20th-Century Fox but 'Ain't It the Truth' (1964) and 'Use Your Head' (1965) were only minor hits. For the rest of the decade she label-hopped to Atlantic ('Dear Lover', 1966), Jubilee ('Dig the Way I Feel', 1969) and Epic.

During the seventies Wells was married to **Bobby Womack**'s brother Cecil and her sporadic recordings included tracks for Reprise. She later re-recorded her Motown hits for such nostalgia packages as *The Old the New and the Best of Mary Wells* (Allegiance, 1984), produced by **Crusaders** trombonist Wayne Henderson, and *Keeping My Mind on Love* (1990) for British producer Ian Levine.

Her death was caused by throat cancer.

R. P. WESTON
b. 1878, Islington, London, England, d. 6 November 1936, London

Weston was a prolific writer of comic songs whose career extended beyond the heyday of music hall into writing for shows and films in the twenties and thirties. His best songs were topical and speciality items written for specific performers. These included **Harry Champion** ('I'm 'Enery the Eighth I Am'; 'What a Mouth'), Billy Williams ('When Father Papered the Parlour'), (Eric) Courtland and (Walter) Jeffries ('Goodbye-ee') and Stanley Holloway ('With Her Head Tucked Underneath Her Arm' and 'My Word You Do Look Queer').

In 1905 Weston formed the double act Conway and Weston, writing most of the duo's material with Fred Murray. The pair were more successful with the material they produced for Harry Champion, including 'The End of Me Old Cigar' (1910); 'What a Mouth' (1911), later successfully revived by **Tommy Steele** (1960); ''Enery the Eighth' (1911), which was later a million-seller for **Herman's Hermits** (1965); and 'Any Old Iron', later a hit for former member of the **Goons** Peter Sellers (1957). Written in broad cockney, these songs captured the delights, rather than the privations, of working-class life at the turn of the century. Similarly joyful were the songs Weston wrote with F. J. Barnes for Billy Williams, 'When Father Papered the Parlour' and 'The Hobnailed Boots That Farver Used to Wear'. However, Weston's greatest commercial successes came with the songs he wrote with Bert Lee (*b. 11 June 1880, Ravensthorpe, Yorkshire, d. 27 January 1947, London*).

A former piano-tuner, Lee had his first success in partnership with George Arthur when Clarice Mayne introduced their 'Josh-ua' (HMV, 1910), and later co-wrote with singer Harry Fragson the jaunty 'Hello! Hello! Who's Your Lady Friend' (1913). In 1915, at the suggestion of their music publisher, Weston and Lee joined forces. An early hit was one of the best-remembered songs from the First World War, 'Goodbye-ee', which in 1965 was affectionately revived by satirists Peter Cook and Dudley Moore (Decca).

The twenties saw the pair writing songs to order for revues and musicals (*A–Z*, 1921, which starred **Jack Buchanan**) as well as novelty songs ('Paddy McGinty's Goat', 'What I Want Is a Proper Cup of Coffee') and speciality material for **Gracie Fields** ('We're Living at the Cloisters', 1928), **Peter Dawson** ('The Legion of the Lost') and Stanley Holloway, for whom they wrote many laconic comic monologues. Weston and Lee also operated as 'show doctors', adapting American musicals for the English stage.

In the thirties they harked back to the broad humour of their music-hall songs with numbers such as 'Olga Pullofski the Beautiful Spy' and 'And the Great Big Saw Came Nearer and Nearer' (1936). After Weston's death, Lee continued writing with his son, Harris Weston; their biggest success was the oft-recorded 'Knees up Mother Brown'.

WET WET WET
Marti Pellow, b. Mark McLoughlin, 3 March 1966, Clydebank, Scotland; Graeme Clark, b. 15 April 1966, Glasgow, Scotland; Tom Cunningham, b. 22 June 1965, Glasgow; Neil Mitchell, b. 8 June 1967, Helensburgh, Scotland

Like Mick Hucknall and **Simply Red**, Wet Wet Wet are a former punk and post-punk group who found success after turning to white soul music. Marti Pellow's blue-eyed soul stylings places him in a long tradition of British vocalists that includes **Joe Cocker**, **Robert Palmer** and Hucknall.

Originally known as the Vortex Motion and fronted by lead singer Pellow, keyboards-player Mitchell, Clark (bass) and Cunningham (drums) cut their musical teeth in 1982 on cover-versions of songs by the **Clash**. They found the name Wet Wet Wet in a **Scritti Politti** song and after becoming well respected on the live circuit in Scotland were signed to Phonogram in 1985.

Disputes over producers delayed the release of Wet Wet Wet's first single until early 1987. Tracks recorded in Memphis, Tennessee, with **Willie Mitchell** were initially rejected by Phonogram but the company relented to allow a remixed Mitchell track, 'Wishing I Was Lucky', to be issued. It was a UK Top Ten hit and later in 1987 *Popped in Souled out* topped the British charts.

There were further hits with 'Angel Eyes (Home and Away)' and 'Temptation' before the group had their first UK No. 1 single with a version of **The Beatles**' 'With a Little Help from My Friends', a track from a multi-artist charity record.

The Memphis Sessions, an eight-track album of the Mitchell recordings, was issued in advance of a new studio album, *Holding Back the River* (1989). Like earlier Wet Wet Wet recordings this made no impact in the USA.

At home, however, Wet Wet Wet's popularity was increasing. *High on the Happy Side* was another No. 1 hit in 1992 while *Live at the Royal Albert Hall* reached the Top Ten in 1993. In 1994 they had a European hit with a revival of the **Troggs**' 'Love Is All Around', which was featured in the hit film *Four Weddings and a Funeral* (1994). They followed that with *Picture This* (1995) and *10* (1997), the first of which was a European success but failed in the US, despite a lengthy promotional tour there. The group disbanded in 1998.

JERRY WEXLER

b. 10 January 1917, New York, USA

With **Ahmet and Nesuhi Ertegun**, Wexler was an architect of the Atlantic record company. His principal achievement was to relaunch the career of **Aretha Franklin**, while he was highly influential in ensuring the success of the new Southern soul music of the sixties.

After army service Wexler wrote songwriters' biographies for the copyright organization BMI before working at *Billboard* magazine where he claimed to have renamed the Race chart Rhythm and Blues. In 1953 he joined Atlantic as office manager but was soon involved in the creative output of the label. Later, he

and the Erteguns bought out Atlantic's co-founder Herb Abramson.

With Ahmet Ertegun he chose songs, supervised recordings and promoted releases by the **Drifters**, **Lavern Baker**, the **Clovers**, **Ivory Joe Hunter**, **Joe Turner** and **Ray Charles**. Wexler, Ertegun and composer/arranger **Jesse Stone** even provided background shouts on Turner's classic 'Shake, Rattle and Roll' (1954). Wexler also encouraged **Phil Spector** as a young producer and in 1960 signed **Solomon Burke**, supervising his version of the **Patsy Cline** and **Faron Young** country hit 'Just out of Reach' before placing Burke with **Bert Berns**.

Having signed a distribution deal with **Jim Stewart**'s Stax label in 1960, Wexler took **Wilson Pickett** to record at the label's Memphis studios in 1965 and later at **Rick Hall**'s studio in Muscle Shoals, Alabama, where Wexler also supervised Franklin to make 'I Never Loved a Man (The Way I Loved You)' (1967). It was the first of a dozen hits produced by Wexler, arranged by **Arif Mardin** and engineered by **Tom Dowd**. The trio also worked on **Dusty Springfield**'s *Dusty in Memphis* (1968), widely regarded as the English singer's best album.

A tireless propagandist for the new Southern music, both black and white, Wexler's use of Duane Allman of the **Allman Brothers Band** on Franklin sessions brought the guitarist his first recognition. In 1970 he set up Criteria Studios in Miami, where **Eric Clapton**'s group Derek and the Dominoes later recorded. Wexler also set up a shortlived Nashville office for Atlantic, which resulted in the signing of Troy Seals, **Willie Nelson** (*Phases and Stages*, 1974) and **John Prine**.

During the seventies Wexler spent less time in the studio though he produced such artists as British singer Maggie Bell (*Queen of the Night*, 1974), **Dr John** (*Gumbo*, 1972) and **Doug Sahm** (*Doug Sahm and Band*, 1973). In 1975 he began to undertake freelance production for outside labels (often in partnership with Barry Beckett), working with the **Staple Singers**, **Tony Orlando** (*Tony Orlando*, Elektra, 1978), **Dire Straits** (*Communique*, 1979), **Bob Dylan** (*Saved*, 1980), **Santana** (*Havana Moon*, Columbia, 1983) and **Donovan** (*Lady of the Stars*, Allegiance, 1983).

He was later in semi-retirement in Florida, producing occasional albums such as **Etta James**' *The Right Time* (1993). In 1993 he published an autobiography, *Rhythm and the Blues: A Life in American Music*, with David Ritz.

WHITE ZOMBIE

Ivan dePrume (replaced by Phil Buerstatte, replaced by John Tempersta); Tom Five (replaced by John Ricci); Sean Yseult, b. Sean Reynolds; Rob Zombie, b. Robert

Cummings, 12 January 1966, Haverhill, Massachusetts, USA

One of the most popular heavy-metal acts of the nineties, White Zombie stood ahead of many of their peers with their sample-laden, hi-tech production methods. Singer/guitarist Zombie has since embarked on a successful solo career after splitting the band in 1998.

Cummings formed the band in 1985 while working as a production assistant on the cult children's TV series *Pee-Wee's Playhouse*, recruiting bassist Yseult, drummer dePrume and guitarist Five and taking the stage name Rob Zombie. He continued to work in the television industry and as a magazine art editor as the band achieved moderate success within the heavy-metal scene in the late eighties, and released four albums of heavy rock reminiscent of **Nick Cave**'s first band, the Birthday Party, and the **MC5**. *Psycho-Head Blowout* (1986) and *Soul Crusher* (1987) were based around typical juvenile metal stylings, while new guitarist Ricci gave *Make Them Die Slowly* (1989) and *God of Thunder* (1990) a tighter sound, steeped in classic rock riffing.

White Zombie earned their mainstream breakthrough with *La Sexorcisto: Devil Music Volume One* (1992), before cementing their popularity with *Astro Creep: 2000, Songs of Love, Destruction and Other Synthetic Delusions of the Electric Head* (1995). The album's enhanced production and a pyrotechnic-laden live show helped the band become one of the most popular heavy-rock bands in the US, and allowed Cummings to make a foray into animation (a hallucinatory sequence in *Beavis and Butthead Do America*, 1996) and film direction, although his plan to work on the third part of *The Crow* series was halted by Miramax Films.

In the midst of a lengthy world tour White Zombie issued *Supersexy Swingin' Sounds* (1996), a collection of remixes of tracks from the *Astro Creep . . .* album. Cummings then set to work on his solo début, *Hellbilly Deluxe* (1998), which followed in the same vein as recent White Zombie material. When the album became more successful than his work with the band, Cummings decided to disband White Zombie and embark on a full-time solo career.

BARRY WHITE
b. 12 September 1944, Galveston, Texas, USA

The king of what one critic called 'smooch disco', White created a type of intimate soul ballad that featured a string-smothered but intensely rhythmic backing. Hugely successful in the mid-seventies he paved the way for such eighties soul crooners as **Luther Vandross** and **Alexander O'Neal**.

White grew up in Los Angeles, where he became a church organist and joined R&B group the Upfronts in 1960. The following year he joined Rampart Records as an arranger, recording as Lee Barry, and played keyboards on Bob and Earl's 1963 hit 'Harlem Shuffle'. He next worked at the local Bronco Records as A&R chief where he discovered the **Diana Ross**-styled Felice Taylor ('I Feel Love Coming on', 1967), Viola Wills (who had a later British hit with a revival of 'Gonna Get Along without You Now', Ariola, 1979) and the vocal group Love Unlimited.

White took the trio (Diana Taylor and sisters Linda and Glodean James) to Uni where his wispy ballad, arranged by **Gene Page**, 'Walking in the Rain with the One I Love'* (1972) was a Top Twenty hit. The group later concentrated on providing backings for White's own efforts but they had a further hit in 1975 with 'I Belong to You' (20th Century).

White's solo recording career began when he signed to Russ Regan's new 20th Century label and topped the R&B charts with the half-spoken part-grunted 'I'm Gonna Love You Just a Little More Baby' (1973). This began a five-year cycle of hits which included further million-sellers in 'Never, Never Gonna Give Ya Up', 'Can't Get Enough of Your Love' (1974), 'You're the First, the Last, My Everything' and 'It's Ecstasy When You Lay Down Next to Me' (1977). With Page's participation, White also produced instrumental hits by the Love Unlimited Orchestra, 'Love's Theme'* (1973) and 'Satin Soul' (1975). The standard ballad nature of many of White's songs was underlined by the fact that they were covered by such artists as **Andy Williams**, **Glen Campbell** and pianists **Roger Williams** and Ferrante and Teicher.

After a half-speed version of **Billy Joel**'s 'Just the Way You Are' and a half-hearted attempt at 'Sha La La Means I Love You' (1979), White's record sales went into decline. He wrote film scores for *Together Brothers* and *Our Man Friday* but disappeared from view in the early eighties. He returned in 1987 with *The Right Night and Barry White* (A&M), his first album since 1982's *Change*. 'Sho You Right' was a British hit. *The Man Is Back* was released in 1989. *Put Me in Your Mix* followed in 1991, but neither it nor 1993's *Love Is the Icon* made any significant sales impact. In 1993 PolyGram released the career retrospective boxed set *Just for You* and in 1994 White returned to the US Top Twenty with *The Icon Is Love*, which included the hit 'Practice What You Preach'. In the late nineties his intimate voice won him a number of voice-overs on television commercials. He returned to recording in 1999 with *Staying Power* (BMG), on which he included two versions of 'The Longer We Make Love', one with **Chaka Khan**, the other with **Lisa Stansfield**.

JOSH WHITE

b. 11 February 1915, Greenville, South Carolina, USA,
d. 5 September 1969, Manhasset, New York

Coming from an apparently conventional blues
singer's background, Josh White exchanged his black
audience for the sophisticated folk-song *aficionados* of
Manhattan, whom he offered, in the words of Arnold
Shaw, 'matinée sexuality, bell-like diction and pop
appeal . . . his slick showmanship made him a pre-
Belafonte black sex idol'.

As a child he worked as a guide for the local street-
singer Blind John Henry Arnold, and went on to perform that role for the more celebrated **Blind Willie
Johnson**, **Blind Blake** and Blind Joe Taggart, recording with the last-named, singing and playing guitar,
for Paramount (1928). In 1932 he moved to New York,
where he broadcast and recorded (1932–6) for ARC,
singing sacred songs in his own name and blues
under the pseudonym 'Pinewood Tom'. In 1939 he
formed the Josh White Singers to work at Café Society, and appeared with **Paul Robeson** in the show
John Henry. He also worked with **Leadbelly**, **Woody
Guthrie** and **Brownie McGhee and Sonny Terry**.
During the Second World War he sang for the US
Office of War Information (radio programmes that
were also heard in Britain through the BBC), toured
for the State Department with the **Golden Gate Quartet**, and continued recording on folk-music labels like
Keynote, Asch and Disc. An accomplished and individual guitarist – he had recorded creditable accompaniments to **Leroy Carr** in 1934 – and an unusual
blues singer, he now concentrated on gospel and
work songs with groups like his Carolinians (Columbia, 1940) or 'message' compositions like 'Southern
Exposure' (Keynote, 1941), 'Ball and Chain Blues' and
'Silicosis Is Killin' Me'.

After the war, and for the next twenty years, he held
his position as a popular folk-song interpreter, using
material as diverse as the traditional ballad 'Lord Randall, My Son', 'Waltzing Matilda', the eighteenth-
century drawing-room piece 'The Lass with the Delicate Air' and numbers associated with **Billie Holiday**
('Strange Fruit') and **Bessie Smith**. He worked in concert halls and coffee-houses and appeared in numerous films and plays. In 1950–1 he toured Europe,
recording in France (Vogue) and Britain (EMI
Columbia). His US recordings were chiefly for Elektra
(1954–62) and Mercury (1962–4). He returned to
Britain in 1956 (recording with local jazzmen for
Nixa), 1961, 1965 and 1967, by which time, however, he
had lost his ability to appeal to the new devotees of
authentic black music, whether blues or Motown.

His son Josh White Jnr and daughters Beverly, Fern
and Judy have all followed careers in music. Josh Jnr
worked with his father from his teens but spent more
time as an actor. After his father's death he commemorated him in his own concerts, but also drew on the
work of contemporary songwriters like **Gordon
Lightfoot**. In 1978 he signed with Vanguard and
recorded *Josh White Jr*.

PAUL WHITEMAN

*b. 28 March 1890, Denver, Colorado, USA, d. 29
December 1967, Doylestown, Pennsylvania*

A flamboyant personality and the most popular bandleader of the twenties, the decade in which he had
thirty American No. 1s, Whiteman was a controversial
figure in jazz circles. His self-promoted role as 'The
King of Jazz', the title of a 1930 film in which he
starred, was hotly disputed by jazz players and critics.
Notwithstanding his employment of **Bix
Beiderbecke**, **Tommy** and **Jimmy Dorsey**, **Joe
Venuti**, **Eddie Lang**, **Jack Teagarden**, and other
respected jazzmen in his various bands, his music
bore little relationship to either the hot jazz of the
twenties or the swing music that followed. Similarly,
his, and arranger Ferde Grofé's, experiments with
'symphonic jazz' were considered by many to be
pompous and pretentious. His important role in the
history of popular music was summed up by Herman
D. Kenin, who called Whiteman not 'The King of
Jazz' but 'The King of the Jazz Age'.

The son of a music teacher, Whiteman studied violin in his youth and joined the Denver Symphony
Orchestra as a viola player, graduating to the San
Francisco Symphony Orchestra in 1916. After brief
service as a navy bandmaster, he formed his first
band, which featured **Henry Busse** on trumpet, in
San Francisco in 1919. After moving to New York in
1920 he was signed to Victor. Whiteman's first success
was the oft-recorded 'Whispering' (1920), which sold
over two million copies and was later successfully
revived by **Les Paul** (1951), **Gordon Jenkins** (1951) and
Whiteman himself (1954), among others. Whiteman's
fuller, smoother sound was a huge hit with New
York's high society – 'we could look out and see the
Vanderbilts, Drexel Biddles, Goulds and the rest
dancing to our music' he wrote in his autobiography
Jazz (1926). 'Whispering' initiated a string of further
instrumental hits. These were mostly conventional
dance-band material and show tunes: 'My Mammy'
(1921), revived by **Al Jolson** in 1928; 'Stumbling', 'Do
It Again', 'Hot Lips' (featuring Busse), 'Three o'Clock
in the Morning' (all 1922) and 'Linger Awhile'* and
'Parade of the Wooden Soldiers' (both 1923). But
what distinguished the Whiteman orchestra, beyond
its sheer size, was its leader's showmanship and insistence on being more than a 'mere' bandleader. More
indicative of Whiteman's aspirations was his 1921
recording of 'Song of India', an adaptation of a theme

from Rimsky-Korsakov's opera *Sadko*. In 1922 White-man made his Broadway début in *George White's Scandals of 1922* and in 1923 the band travelled to the UK, where its sophisticated sound influenced **Jack Hylton** and other British bandleaders.

The climax of Whiteman's concern with presenta-tion and notions of 'symphonic jazz' was the concert at New York's Aeolian Hall (12 February 1924) where he led a twenty-three-piece orchestra in what he styled *An Experiment in Modern Music*. Among the material presented was **George Gershwin**'s 'Rhapsody in Blue' (which Whiteman, who had personally commissioned it, recorded with Gershwin on piano later that year) and symphonic arrangements of songs by **Irving Berlin**, a suite of serenades by **Victor Herbert** and complex arrangements of Zez Confrey's piano novelty 'Kitten on the Keys'. While 'Rhapsody in Blue' justi-fied the notion of 'symphonic jazz', the other pieces have not lasted in the manner presented by White-man. Though the concerts (repeated several times in 1924) were a cultural success and confirmed White-man's elevated position within popular music, within a few years Whiteman himself turned his back on such experimentation and started to employ jazz musicians of real stature. He also turned increasingly to record-ing songs with vocalists, rather than instrumentals.

In 1927 Beiderbecke was the first serious jazzman to be lured by the high wages Whiteman offered and the increasing freedom he provided his band mem-bers, as his arrangements, though still complex, grew more sensitive. In the same year Whiteman hired **Bing Crosby** and Al Rinker as the basis of his Rhythm Boys vocalists. The recordings from this period show Whiteman at his best. His material and musicians were better than before. 'Changes' (1928), for example, featured both the Rhythm Boys and one of Beiderbecke's best cornet solos, and such was Whiteman's stature that **Hoagy Carmichael** ('Wash-board Blues') and **Paul Robeson** ('Ol' Man River', 1928) occasionally guested on his recordings. Hits of this period included **DeSylva, Brown and Hender-son**'s 'Birth of the Blues' (1926), 'In a Little Spanish Town', **Walter Donaldson**'s 'My Blue Heaven', which featured **Red Nichols** on trumpet (1927), Crosby singing 'Ol' Man River' (1928), **Vincent Youmans**' 'Great Day' (1929), 'Body and Soul' (1930) and 'All of Me' with **Mildred Bailey**.

In 1930 Whiteman's fame was further established by *King of Jazz*, a filmed music revue built almost entirely around him. It was the first of several films, in all of which he played himself. These included the George Gershwin biopic *Rhapsody in Blue* (1945), and *The Fabulous Dorseys* (1947), his last screen appear-ance. However, despite his twice re-forming his band (in 1938 and 1940), his later thirties recordings were less successful than the more modern sounds of the

Dorsey brothers and **Benny Goodman** and he briefly stopped recording.

In 1942 Whiteman joined Capitol, recording with **Billie Holiday** ('Travelin' Light', on which Holiday was billed as 'Lady Day') and **Johnny Mercer** ('The Old Music Master', 1943) before disbanding his orchestra in 1944 to become musical director of the ABC radio network. His last major hit was a rework-ing of 'Whispering' (Coral, 1954) and he made his last public appearance in 1962.

WHITESNAKE

David Coverdale, b. 21 September 1951, Saltburn, Tyne and Wear, England; Vivian Campbell; David Dowle (replaced by Ian Paice, b. 29 June 1948, Nottingham, replaced by Cozy Powell, replaced by Tommy Aldridge, b. 15 August 1950); Brian Johnson (replaced by Pete Sol-ley, replaced by Jon Lord, b. 9 June 1941, Leicester); Bernie Marsden (replaced by Mel Galley); Mick Moody (replaced by John Sykes, replaced by Adrian Vanden-berg, b. 31 January 1954, Netherlands); Neil Murray (replaced by Colin Hodgkinson, replaced by Murray, replaced by Rudi Sarzo, b. 18 November 1950)

Led by former **Deep Purple** singer Coverdale, the blues-inflected Whitesnake became one of the most explicitly macho heavy-metal bands of the seventies and eighties.

After the demise of Deep Purple in 1976, Coverdale recorded the solo albums *White Snake* (Purple, 1977) and *North Winds* (1978). Whitesnake was formed from the session and touring musicians who accom-panied him. Guitarist Moody was a former fellow-student at Middlesbrough Art College and had played lead on Juicy Lucy's Top Twenty version of **Bo Didd-ley**'s 'Who Do You Love' (Vertigo, 1970), which had earlier been memorably revived in 1963 by **Ronnie Hawkins** and a group that included future members of **The Band**. Marsden had been the guitarist with such heavy rock groups as **UFO**, Wild Turkey (1971–2, a band led by former **Jethro Tull** bassist Glenn Cor-nick) and Babe Ruth (1975–6). Whitesnake also included ex-**Colosseum** bassist Murray, Dowle (drums) and Johnson (keyboards).

After touring with the **Police**, the group signed to United Artists. Before the release of *Trouble* (1978), however, Solley had come and gone, while *Lovehunter* (1979) featured ex-Purple members Paice and Lord. Coverdale's emphatically macho lyrics earned Whitesnake's music the epithet 'cock rock', though the blues influence was maintained in a cover of **Bobby Bland**'s 'Ain't No Love in the Heart of the City', featured on the EP *Long Way from Home* (1979). 'Ready an' Willing (Sweet Satisfaction)' (1980) was a Top Ten hit and was followed by the double concert album *Live . . . in the Heart of the City. Come an' Get*

It (1981) included the Top Twenty hit 'Don't Break My Heart Again' while *Saints an' Sinners* (1982) reached the Top Ten. Extensive personnel changes now brought in former Trapeze guitarist Galley, ex-Back Door and **Alexis Korner** bassist Hodgkinson, and Powell. Before the release of *Slide It in* (1984), ex-**Thin Lizzy** guitarist Sykes replaced Moody, and Lord left to take part in the Deep Purple reunion of 1984.

Now a four-piece band, Whitesnake toured extensively in America but the band disintegrated in 1986 during recording sessions which saw the arrival of Dutch guitarist Vandenberg. He was kept on when Coverdale put together a new version of Whitesnake to promote the album which eventually emerged, *Whitesnake 1987*. The new line-up was completed by former **Black Oak Arkansas** and Ozzy Osbourne drummer Aldridge, Osbourne's bassist Sarzo and guitarist Vivian Campbell. *1987* turned out to be the most successful album of the group's career, selling over ten million copies and providing American and British hits with 'Still of the Night' and 'Is This Love'. Campbell had departed by the time *Slip of the Tongue* appeared in 1989. He later joined **Def Leppard**. The band toured heavily in support of the album in 1990, but Coverdale disbanded Whitesnake later that year to concentrate on solo work. However, his next move was to form a duo with ex-**Led Zeppelin** guitarist Jimmy Page for the album *Coverdale Page*, which reached the Top Five on both sides of the Atlantic in 1993. *Restless Heart* (1997) was credited to David Coverdale and Whitesnake, while the solo album *Into the Light* (EMI, 2000) saw Coverdale trading on his blues roots to little effect. *Greatest Hits* (1994) is just that.

DAVID WHITFIELD
b. 2 February 1926, Hull, Yorkshire, England, d. 16 January 1980, Sydney, Australia

A light-voiced operatic tenor, Whitfield was one of the few British singers to achieve success in America in the pre-rock'n'roll fifties.

After his discharge from the Royal Navy in 1950, Whitfield worked as a labourer while singing in clubs in the Hull area. He made his radio début later that year in Hughie Green's Radio Luxemburg talent show *Opportunity Knocks*. In the early fifties he graduated to club and concert work before in 1953 he was signed by Bunny Lewis to Decca. His first hit was 'Bridge of Sighs', written by the prolific British songwriter Billy Reid, who was also responsible for a trio of million-sellers: 'The Gypsy' (the **Ink Spots**, 1946), 'A Tree in the Meadow' (Margaret Whiting, Capitol, 1948) and 'I'm Walking Beside You' (**Eddie Fisher**, 1953). In 1954 Whitfield had two British No. 1s: 'Answer Me', a cover of **Frankie Laine**'s 1953 hit which was successfully revived by Barbara Dickson (RSO, 1976), and

'Cara Mia'*, his biggest American hit (on London). The latter (and 'Beyond the Stars', 1955) was pseudonymously written by Lewis and **Mantovani**, who accompanied Whitfield on the recording, while **Tolchard Evans** provided the singer with 'Ev'rywhere' (1955) and 'My September Love'. The music for Whitfield's other American hit, 'Smile' (1954), was written by Charles Chaplin for his film *Modern Times* (1936). Other songs by Chaplin, who wrote the scores to most of his films, including the Oscar-nominated oft-recorded theme to *Limelight* (1952) and 'This Is My Song', a million-seller for **Petula Clark** in 1967.

Unlike such contemporaries as **Frankie Vaughan**, Whitfield never recorded rock'n'roll material and, after his last Top Twenty hit, a version of **Lerner and Loewe**'s 'On the Street Where You Live' (1958), he moved to HMV in 1961, releasing 'This Heart of Mine'. He attempted a career in light opera in 1963.

NORMAN WHITFIELD
b. 1943, New York, USA

A songwriter and record producer, Whitfield came to prominence through his work with such Motown artists as **Marvin Gaye** and the **Temptations**. After leaving the company, Whitfield's greatest success was with Rose Royce.

Whitfield worked as producer and writer with Thelma Records (whose artists included future Temptations member Richard Street) before joining **Berry Gordy**'s Motown company in 1962, where he enjoyed his first Top Ten hit with Marvin Gaye's 'Pride and Joy'. For the next few years Whitfield worked with the company's lesser acts, including the Marvelettes and the Velvelettes. In 1967 he formed a songwriting team with Barrett Strong (*b. 5 February 1941, Mississippi*), whose 1960 hit 'Money' had been covered by **The Beatles**. One of their earliest collaborations was 'I Heard It Through the Grapevine', a No. 1 hit for **Gladys Knight and the Pips** in 1968.

As a result of these successes, Whitfield and Strong supplanted **Holland, Dozier and Holland** as Motown's top production team. After reworking 'Grapevine' with Gaye, they made a series of records with the Temptations which incorporated elements of the 'black power' feeling within the black community as well as the stylistic advances of **Sly Stone** and **Jimi Hendrix**. Among them were the pioneering 'Cloud Nine' (1968) and 'Message from a Black Man' (1969), with its refrain 'say it loud – I'm black and I'm proud'. Later Whitfield–Strong hits for the Temptations included 'Psychedelic Shack' (1970), 'Ball of Confusion' and 'Papa Was a Rolling Stone' (1973), while the duo also wrote and produced 'War' (1970) by Edwin Starr and Rare Earth's 'I Just Want to Celebrate' (1971).

After the Temptations left Motown, Whitfield was less successful in applying the 'acid-soul' formula to the Undisputed Truth. In 1976 he took the group with him when he set up Whitfield Records, with distribution through Warners. But Whitfield's greatest post-Motown triumph came with Rose Royce, formed from the backing group for the Temptations and Undisputed Truth. With singer Gwen Dickey, they reached No. 1 on MCA with the film theme 'Car Wash'* (1976). Later hits included 'I Wanna Get Next to You' (1977) and In Full Bloom (Whitfield, 1978) which included the haunting ballad 'Love Don't Live Here Anymore', later recorded by **Madonna** on Like a Virgin (1984). The opening riff from Rose Royce's 'Is It Love You're After?' was used in 1988 by British dance act S'Express for its hit 'Theme from S'Express'.

In 1981 Whitfield closed his label and went into semi-retirement.

RICHARD A. WHITING

b. 12 November 1891, Peoria, Illinois, USA, d. 10 February 1938, Beverly Hills, California

The father of singer Margaret Whiting and author of 'Till We Meet Again' (1918), with **George M. Cohan**'s 'Over There' (1918) one of the most widely recorded American songs of the First World War, Whiting was also one of the most successful songwriters of the thirties.

Raised in Detroit and educated at the Harvard Military Academy in Los Angeles, Whiting returned to Detroit in 1915 to work as a copy boy and then songplugger at the Jerome H. Remick music publishing company. Later that year he had his first success with 'It's Tulip Time in Holland', with words by Dave Radford, which was recorded by **Henry Burr**, among others. Ray Egan supplied the words for 'Till We Meet Again', which topped the charts for Burr and **Vernon Dalhart** in 1919. Whiting continued his collaboration with Egan into the twenties when their hits included 'The Japanese Sandman' (1920), a hit for **Paul Whiteman** and **Nora Bayes**, among others, and successfully revived by **Benny Goodman** (1935); the oft-recorded 'Ain't We Got Fun' (1921), with additional lyrics by **Gus Kahn**; and 'Sleepy Time Gal' (1926), a hit for **Ben Selvin** and **Gene Austin** and revived by **Harry James** (1944).

In 1929 Whiting was teamed by publisher Max Dreyfus with **Leo Robin** and together the pair wrote numerous film songs, beginning with 'Louise', **Maurice Chevalier**'s first American hit. With Buddy DeSylva (of **DeSylva, Brown and Henderson**) and **Nacio Herb Brown**, he contributed 'You're an Old Smoothie' and 'Eadie Was a Lady', recorded by **Ethel Merman**, **Cab Calloway** and **Al Bowlly** in Britain, to the stage musical Take a Chance (1932, filmed 1933).

But his greatest successes were film songs: 'On the Good Ship Lollipop' (1934, recorded by **Shirley Temple**), the anthemic 'Hooray for Hollywood' and 'Too Marvellous for Words' (1937). This last song was written with **Johnny Mercer**, Whiting's last regular collaborator, who, after Whiting's death in 1938, encouraged Margaret Whiting in her singing career, signing her to Capitol in 1942.

Margaret (b. 22 July 1924, Detroit, Michigan) remains closely associated with the haunting 'Moonlight in Vermont'* (1944), one of her first recordings. Other million-sellers include 'A Tree in the Meadow' (1948), by British songwriter Billy Reid (who also wrote million-sellers for the **Ink Spots**, 'The Gypsy', 1946, and **Eddie Fisher**, 'I'm Walking Behind You', 1953) and 'Slipping Around' (1949), a duet with country singer Jimmy Wakely. She recorded **Max Steiner**'s 'My Own True Love', a vocal version of the main theme from Gone With the Wind, with words by Hal David, and made several albums of her father's songs in the fifties. For **Norman Granz**'s Verve label she recorded The Jerome Kern Songbook, an album similar in style to the songbook albums of **Ella Fitzgerald**.

SLIM WHITMAN

b. Otis Dewey Whitman Jnr, 20 January 1924, Tampa, Florida, USA

A sweet-voiced vocalist able effortlessly to slip into falsetto or yodel, Whitman had his greatest success with simple, yearning romantic ballads in the fifties ('Indian Love Call'*, 1952; 'Rose Marie'* and 'Secret Love'*, 1954). These won him a lasting reputation, particularly in Europe, where he regularly toured to sell-out audiences. In the seventies and eighties these resulted in a series of bestselling albums (The Very Best of, 1976, Red River Valley, 1977, and All My Best, 1980, most of which were marketed through television) that confirmed his role as a heartthrob for the middle-aged.

While pursuing a career in baseball, Whitman began singing to supplement his income in 1948. This led to a contract with RCA in 1949, where he had only moderate success as a country singer (most notably with the Western song 'Casting My Lasso to the Sky', 1950). In 1952 he joined Imperial and had an immediate hit with his yodelling version of **Rudolf Friml**'s 'Indian Love Call' from the operetta Rose Marie, previously a hit for **Paul Whiteman** (1925) and best remembered in the 1937 version by **Nelson Eddy** and **Jeanette MacDonald**. That record set the pattern of Whitman's subsequent hits, which included the two million-sellers 'Secret Love' (a hit for **Doris Day** in 1953) and 'Rose Marie' itself. The success of these recordings overseas – 'Rose Marie' topped the British charts for eleven weeks in 1955 – led to Whitman

touring Europe and the Far East as a romantic balladeer from the sixties onwards, while in America he
had continued, but lesser, success in the country
charts.

In the wake of the success of Whitman's television-
advertised albums in Europe in the seventies, United
Artists and then Cleveland International promoted
All My Best and *Songs I Love to Sing* (1981), respectively, in a similar manner in America. Whitman continued to record and tour throughout the eighties and
nineties, latterly with his son Byron, who sang with
him on *Magic Moments* (1990).

ROGER WHITTAKER
b. 22 March 1936, Nairobi, Kenya

A singer-guitarist, Whittaker built a large following in
Europe and America in the eighties for his gentle
middle-of-the-road ballads.

The child of emigrants from England, Whittaker
learned Swahili as a child, singing African songs. After
army service he briefly studied in South Africa before
performing in Nairobi nightclubs. In 1959 he began a
university course in Wales and after making charity
recordings was signed by Jack Baverstock to Fontana
in 1961. A cover of **Jimmy Dean**'s 'Steel Men' was a
minor hit and a networked television series for Ulster
television established Whittaker on the British club
and cabaret circuit.

In 1967 Whittaker was a prize-winner at the
Knokke Song Festival in Belgium and as a result his
own 'Mexican Whistler' and a version of 'If I was a
Rich Man' from the Bock–Harnick musical *Fiddler on
the Roof* were hits in continental Europe. His first
British success came with the lilting 'Durham Town
(The Leavin')' (EMI Columbia, 1969) and 'I Don't
Believe in If Anymore'. In the same year Whittaker
won the Rio Festival competition with his 'New
World in the Morning'.

There were lesser British hits with 'Why' (1971) and
'Mammy Blue', a cover of a Spanish song, before
Whittaker broke through in America with the Top
Twenty song 'The Last Farewell' (RCA, 1975), whose
lyrics were written by a listener to Whittaker's BBC
radio series. During the rest of the decade and
throughout the eighties Whittaker toured frequently,
having further hits in Germany where 'Albany' (1982)
reached No. 1.

He next formed his own Tembo label (the name
means elephant in Swahili). Whittaker had a surprise
British hit in 1986 with the traditional 'Skye Boat
Song', a duet with singer/comedian Des O'Connor,
who in 1968 had a No. 1 with **Les Reed** and Barry
Mason's 'I Pretend' (EMI Columbia). *The Genius of
Love* (1986) was produced by **Shadows**' guitarist
Bruce Welch. In the eighties and early nineties he

continued to record, often releasing several albums
each year. Among his later albums were *Live from the
Tivoli* (1989), *The Country Collection* (1991) and *You
Deserve the Best* (1991). His thirtieth anniversary
album, *Celebration*, was issued by Ariola in 1993.

THE WHO
*Roger Harry Daltrey, b. 1 March 1945, London, Eng-
land; John Alec Entwistle, b. 9 October 1946, London;
Keith Moon, b. 23 August 1947, London, d. 7 September
1978 (replaced by Kenny Jones, b. 16 September 1948,
London); Peter Dennis Blandford Townshend, b. 19
May 1945, London*

During the seventies The Who and the **Rolling Stones**
were both billed 'the greatest rock'n'roll band in the
world', notably for the power and aura of their live
shows. But while the Stones' music was rooted in the
past, in a mélange of black American genres, The
Who's work was increasingly subject to guitarist
Townshend's more ambitious forward-looking grand
designs. Following an early series of outstanding
songs of teenage realism ('My Generation', 1965) and
playful insight ('Pictures of Lily', 1967), the group's
first, and in many ways most successful, major project
was the rock-opera *Tommy* (1969), which was successfully restaged in a grand theatrical manner on
Broadway in the early nineties. This tale of hero-wor-
ship had its introspective dimension (when the
Tommy character is seen as an analogue of a rock
star), but it was with *Quadrophenia* (1973) that Townshend's self-consciousness tended to destabilize the
work as a whole. If in later years both Townshend's
commitment to rock and the cohesion of The Who as
a group fell away, in their prime The Who were
amongst the few to establish the claims of progressive
rock to contain the elements of a major art form.

The son of a dance-band saxophonist, Townshend
had played banjo with Entwistle (trumpet) in trad-
jazz groups while still at school. Entwistle later joined
Daltrey and drummer Doug Sanden in rock band the
Detours and in 1963 Townshend was added on guitar.
The group's repertoire of **Duane Eddy** and **Beatles**
numbers had been discarded in favour of soul and
R&B by the time ex-Beachcombers drummer Moon
joined in 1964. As the High Numbers, they recorded
the unsuccessful 'I'm the Face'/'Zoot Suit' (Fontana),
songs written by manager Peter Meaden to capitalize
on the band's mod associations.

Soon afterwards the quartet had new managers (Kit
Lambert and Chris Stamp) and a new name, The
Who. Lambert and Stamp encouraged Townshend to
incorporate guitar-smashing into the group's stage
act, intensified the mod image and took the group to
Kinks' producer Shel Talmy. During 1965 Townshend's power chords and defiant lyrics, Daltrey's

snarling voice and Moon's demonic drumming brought The Who three British Top Ten hits which neatly encapsulated the bafflement, irritations and exubérance of their audience and youth in general: 'I Can't Explain' (Brunswick), 'Anyway Anyhow Anywhere' and the anthemic 'My Generation', with its 'hope I die before I get old' refrain.

A 1966 move to the independent Reaction label brought a lawsuit from Decca subsidiary Brunswick and from Talmy, who had been replaced by Lambert after the success of 'Substitute' (1966), whose oddball lyrics gave the first glimpse of the surreal side of Townshend's imagination. For a few months both labels released Who singles, with the joyous 'I'm a Boy' and the portrait of a seaside eccentric, 'Happy Jack', on Reaction selling better than Brunswick's 'It's a Legal Matter'. Reaction also released A Quick One (1966), which included the song cycle 'A Quick One While He's Away'.

The following year brought a further label change – to Lambert and Stamp's Track. 'Pictures of Lily' and the powerful 'I Can See for Miles' were Top Ten hits and The Who also recorded a version of 'The Last Time' to show their solidarity with Jagger and Richards after the latter's arrest on drugs charges. 1967 also saw the release of The Who Sell Out, an album of songs linked by spoof radio ads and containing another 'mini-opera', 'Rael'. This was the prelude to the release of Tommy (1969), Townshend's remarkable rock opera dealing with the life of a 'deaf dumb and blind boy' whose prowess on the pinball table makes him a guru for millions.

Performed by The Who on a world tour of opera houses, the songs ranged from the joyous 'Pinball Wizard' through 'I'm Free' to the sombre 'Smash the Mirror'. Tommy was first produced on stage by Lou Reizner in 1973 and then filmed by Ken Russell in 1975 (with **Tina Turner** and **Elton John**). After performing at the Woodstock Festival, the group released Live at Leeds (1970), which contained heavy-rock versions of **Eddie Cochran**'s 'Summertime Blues' and **Johnny Kidd**'s 'Shakin' All Over'.

That album closed the most prolific phase of the group's recording career. During the seventies they released only four albums of new material and in the eighties just three. Who's Next (1971) contained the tough song of disillusionment 'Won't Get Fooled Again' as well as songs originally written by Townshend for a new rock opera, Lifehouse. Songs originally written for Lifehouse, 'Let's See Action', 'Join Together' (1972) and 'Relay' (1973), also sold well before the release in 1973 of Quadrophenia.

A more complex project than Tommy, it was more flawed. The song cycle combined a nostalgic look back at the early sixties and the mod experience with a psychological exploration of the four sides of the central character's personality. Although each side was 'played' by one member of the group, this was more than ever Townshend's vision, at a time when other Who members were embarking on solo work.

Entwistle's grim humour, first evidenced on 'Boris the Spider' (1966), was further expressed on Smash Your Head against the Wall (Track, 1971), Whistle Rhymes (1972), Rigor Mortis Sets in (1973) and Mad Dog (1975), while Daltrey reached the Top Ten with **Leo Sayer**'s wistful 'Giving It All Away' (1973) from the Sayer-penned solo album Daltrey. He followed it with the lesser Ride a Rock Horse (1975) and One of the Boys (1977). Moon also made a solo album, Two Sides of the Moon (Polydor, 1975), but won more acclaim for his role in **David Essex**'s films That'll Be the Day (1973) and Stardust (1974). Townshend himself had earlier recorded Who Came First (1972), with its version of **Jim Reeves**' 'There's a Heartache Following Me', dedicated to the guru Meher Baba. Townshend had previously contributed to two privately pressed albums of music by Baba devotees.

The Who by Numbers (1975) and Who Are You (1978) included the respective hits 'Squeeze Box' and 'Who Are You' but were lesser works. Each member continued with solo projects – Rough Mix (1977), Townshend's collaboration with ex-**Small Faces** member Ronnie Lane, was exceptional – and the sudden death of Moon in 1978 (from an overdose of a sedative drug) put the future of The Who into question. The group, however, added Jones (formerly of their great mod rivals the Small Faces) and continued to tour and to undertake projects, including the soundtrack for Franc Roddam's film version of Quadrophenia (1979), whose cast included **Sting** of the **Police**. The Kids Are Alright (1979) was a film history of the band, put together as a memorial to Moon, which spawned a memorable live soundtrack album.

A reissue of the banal 'Long Live Rock', featuring the original line-up and taken from the 1974 album of out-takes Odds & Sods, made the charts in 1979, while the new version of The Who made the unimpressive Face Dances (1981), produced by Bill Szymczyk. 'You Better You Bet' reached the American Top Twenty but after releasing It's Hard (1982) and undertaking a lengthy American tour, the group announced that their touring days were over. A live album, Who's Last, was released in 1984, but the band were reunited to perform at Live Aid in 1985.

In the eighties Townshend released Empty Glass (1980), All the Best Cowboys Have Chinese Eyes (1982), the video/concept album White City (1985) and two volumes of demos, Scoop (1983) and Another Scoop (1987). He also published a volume of poetry and prose, Horse's Neck, and toured with a new band, the Deep End (Deep End Live, 1986). Iron Man (Virgin,

1989), a Townshend song sequence based on Ted Hughes' children's book, included performances from **John Lee Hooker**, Entwistle and Daltrey.

Daltrey pursued an acting career (which included appearances in *Lisztomania*, 1975, and *McVicar*, 1979) while still regularly making records. These included *Parting Should Be Painless* (1984), *Under a Raging Moon* (Ten, 1986) and *Can't Wait to See the Movie*. After intense speculation about the band's future, The Who regrouped (with Simon Phillips on drums) for a 1989 North American and European tour, which included some all-star performances of *Tommy*. Performances from the tour were captured on a triple live album. After the tour, The Who disbanded again. Daltrey resurrected his acting career and regularly toured, often singing music associated with The Who, as in 1994 when he appeared in 'Daltry Sings Townshend' at New York's Carnegie Hall with arrangements by Michael Kamen.

Townshend released yet another concept album, the intermittently rewarding *Psychoderelict* (1993), a 'radio play' with a semi-autobiographical lead character, an ageing rock star with a drink problem. More successful was a Broadway stage version of *Tommy* on which Townshend collaborated with Des MacAnuff. It included a new Townshend song, 'I Believe My Own Eyes', and won five Tony awards in 1993. The cast album was produced by **George Martin**. In 1999 Townshend finally released *Lifehouse*. Originally intended as the sequel to *Tommy*, it was launched as a BBC concert. In its wake Townshend began to release a series of archive recordings on his Eel Pie label.

In 1994 MCA/PolyGram released a Who career retrospective boxed set, *30 Years of Maximum R&B*, with much unreleased material including the band's landmark performance at the 1969 Woodstock Festival. Reissues have since followed at regular intervals. One of the most interesting was *BBC Sessions* (2000), the early tracks of which saw the group in the midst of the transition from R&B to art rock.

KIM WILDE
b. Kim Smith, 18 November 1960, London, England

The daughter of fifties pop star Marty Wilde, Kim Wilde enjoyed a fluctuating career in the eighties and nineties which nevertheless, in terms of longevity and chart success, far outstripped her father's.

Wilde had been singing backing vocals on her father's live appearances on the UK cabaret circuit when a demo she had recorded with her brother Ricky (who had an unsuccessful pop career as a would-be teen idol behind him) brought her to the attention of producer **Mickie Most**, who signed her to his RAK label in 1980. Managed by her mother (Joyce Baker, a former member of British vocal group the Vernon Girls) and with her father and brother acting as producers and songwriters, Wilde released her first single, 'Kids in America', in 1981. A classic example of guitar-driven pop wish-fulfilment, it was an immediate success. Another hit followed with 'Chequered Love', like the début accompanied by a video which emphasized her photogenic qualities.

Her UK Top Five début album, *Kim Wilde*, largely written by brother Ricky, followed later that year, with another successful single, 'Water on Glass', taken from it. The next single, the less obviously commercial 'Cambodia' (1981), was a UK hit and established Wilde as a major act in Europe, particularly France where it sold over one million copies. A second album, *Select*, followed in 1982, and reached the UK Top Twenty, as did the single 'View from a Bridge' but subsequent singles sold disappointingly. Brief US chart success came in 1982, when 'Kids in America' charted, but Wilde was unable to build momentum in the US market. Later that year she undertook her first live dates. In the UK, her third RAK album, *Catch as Catch Can* (1983), flopped.

A move to MCA in 1984 initially failed to revive Wilde's career, although the album *Teases and Dares* did chart briefly late that year in the UK and enjoyed minor success in the US. Dave Edmunds remixed the rockabilly-styled 'Rage to Love' single (1985) which saw Wilde back in the Top Twenty, but it was the release of 'You Keep Me Hanging on', her version of the **Supremes**' 1966 hit, taken from her second MCA album, *Another Step* (1986), which provided her with her biggest hit in the UK and throughout Europe.

Wilde's high profile remained intact as she charted on a various artists charity single of **The Beatles**' 'Let It Be' in 1987, and with a duet featuring UK soul singer Junior Giscombe. Later that year she hit the No. 1 spot in the US with 'You Keep Me Hanging on'. The single revived *Another Step*, which charted in the US and again in the UK, but again Wilde was unable to sustain her success. Another charity record, a duet with comedian Mel Smith, gave her another UK hit in 1987, but her 1988 album *Close* again sold poorly on release.

Following a European tour supporting **Michael Jackson**, a change in direction towards dance material saw Wilde enjoy three consecutive UK Top Ten singles in 1988, and *Close* subsequently sold in large quantities. However, the next two albums, *Love Moves* (1990) and *Love Is* (1992), plus their attendant singles, sold comparatively modestly. In 1993 a successful revival of the 1978 Yvonne Elliman hit 'If I Can't Have You' preceded MCA's release of a compilation, *The Singles Collection 1981–1993*. After *Now & Forever* (1996) she retired.

MARTY WILDE
b. Reginald Leonard Smith, 15 April 1936, Blackheath, London, England

With **Cliff Richard** and **Tommy Steele** one of the stalwarts of British rock'n'roll, Wilde found renewed success in the eighties as the manager of his daughter **Kim Wilde**, who had a series of bright pop hits, most of which were produced by his son Ricky.

A former member of the Hound Dogs skiffle group, Wilde was performing as Reg Patterson in London in 1957 when he was discovered by Steele's manager Larry Parnes. Parnes promptly changed his name, added him to his 'stable of stars' and signed him to Philips. Wilde's first record, a cover of **Jimmie Rodgers**' million-seller 'Honeycomb' (Roulette, 1957) failed, but a year later his atmospheric version of the death song 'Endless Sleep', originally recorded by Jody Reynolds (Demon, 1957), was a British Top Five hit. Subsequently **Jack Good** made Wilde a resident artist on his TV rock show *Oh Boy!* and the host of its sequel *Boy Meets Girl*. On these, his sultry looks and **Elvis Presley**-ish voice made him a *bona fide* teen-idol – he even had a girls' magazine named after him, *Marty*. However, though he was also a writer – he composed his best record and his last major hit 'Bad Boy' (1959), which was his only American success – Wilde was rarely allowed to record his own material. Among his cover-versions were **Ritchie Valens**' 'Donna', **Dion and the Belmonts**' 'A Teenager in Love' and Phil Philips' 'Sea of Love' (Mercury), all hits in 1959. This material suited his light, brooding voice, but, unlike **Billy Fury** who was also forced into covering American hits in the sixties, Wilde was less successful and his only subsequent Top Ten record saw him imitating the coyness of **Bobby Vee** ('Rubber Ball', 1961). He later recorded unsuccessfully for EMI Columbia (1964), Decca (as the Wilde Three with his wife and future **Moody Blues** singer Justin Hayward, 1965), Philips ('Abergavenny', 1969), Magnet (1973) and Kaleidoscope (1982).

Another reason for Wilde's demise as a teen idol was his marriage in 1959 to Joyce Baker, a member of the Vernon Girls dance troupe who, named after the football pools company for whom many of them originally worked, regularly appeared on Good's television shows. Later members formed a backing group, also called the Vernon Girls, and had several British chart successes, notably with their 1962 covers of **Clyde McPhatter**'s 'Lover Please' (Decca) and Little Eva's American chart-topper on Dimension, 'The Loco-Motion'.

In the seventies Wilde became the manager and producer of his son, Ricky, whom he promoted unsuccessfully as a British rival to Little Jimmy of the

Osmonds. Both father and son had greater success with daughter Kim.

ANDY WILLIAMS
b. Howard Andrew Williams, 3 December 1928, Wall Lake, Iowa, USA

A minor cabaret artist of the forties, Williams was one of several popular performers who achieved recording success on the back of rock'n'roll in the fifties. However, it was not until the sixties, when television enabled him to display his relaxed singing style and easy-going fireside personality, that he became a superstar.

Williams and his three elder brothers were encouraged to sing by their father. By the late thirties they were singing professionally as staff artists on radio stations in Des Moines, Chicago and Cincinnati before moving to California in 1943. There the brothers soon found film and radio session work. They made their recording début as backing singers for **Bing Crosby** on the Academy Award-winning song 'Swinging on a Star'* from *Going My Way* (1944). That same year Andy dubbed Lauren Bacall's singing voice in *To Have and Have Not*. Next, the brothers teamed up with comedienne Kay Thompson in 1947 and worked the cabaret circuit with varying degrees of success until 1952, when Andy finally went solo.

He recorded unsuccessfully for Columbia and then, in the 'folk' manner popularized by **Mitch Miller**, for the RCA subsidiary, Label X, before signing to Archie Bleyer's Cadence label in 1955. By then a resident singer, alongside **Steve Lawrence** and Eydie Gormé, on Steve Allen's influential *Tonight* television show, Williams did not find record success until 1956 when his version of 'Canadian Sunset' (a million-seller for **Hugo Winterhalter**) hit the Top Ten. However, the song that established him was 'Butterfly'. Written by Kal Mann and Bernie Lowe, the joint founders of the Philadelphia-based Cameo Records, and closely modelled on **Elvis Presley**'s recording of 'Don't Be Cruel', 'Butterfly' was a million-seller for Charlie Gracie in 1957. Gracie's record laid the foundations for Cameo's subsequent success with **Fabian**, **Bobby Rydell** and **Chubby Checker**. But Williams' gentler version was the bigger hit, topping the American and British charts.

Subsequent Top Ten hits saw him edging back to the mainstream, performing popular (rather than pop) songs which highlighted his smooth delivery and clear enunciation: 'I Like Your Kind of Love', a duet with Peggy Powers (1957); 'Are You Sincere' (1958); 'The Hawaiian Wedding Song'*, 'Lonely Street' and 'The Village of Bernadette' (all 1959). Then, in 1961, Williams changed record labels, joining Columbia – he later bought Cadence so as to control his earlier recordings – and found a new agent who secured him a weekly television show on CBS, where his relaxed manner brought immediate success.

His first big hit on Columbia, and his best-remembered pop performance, was the **Pomus and Shuman** composition 'Can't Get Used to Losing You'* (1963), which twenty years later was successfully revived by the British group the Beat (Go Feet). But more significant was the 1962 album *Moon River and Other Great Movie Themes**, produced by Robert Mersey. Throughout the sixties and seventies, as the market for popular music declined compared to that for rock, Williams regularly recorded well-known film and show tunes which he could showcase on his television shows, as a way of increasing his chances of chart success and album sales. Hits of this type included 'Days of Wine and Roses' (1963), 'On the Street Where You Live' (1964), '(Where Do I Begin) Love Story' (1971) and 'Love Theme from "The Godfather"' (1972). Williams was also one of the first popular performers regularly to include songs from contemporary writers on his albums. Thus, one of his biggest hits of the seventies was **Neil Sedaka**'s 'Solitaire' (1974) from the album of the same title for which producer Richard Perry provided a contemporary but 'adult' sound around Williams' soothing tenor.

By then, however, the charts were virtually irrelevant to Williams. A rich man, forever in the public eye through his television specials and golf tournaments, Williams was a fixture in the world of popular entertainment.

In 1994 Laserlight released his *Greatest Hits Live*, recorded at the Moon River theatre in Branson, Missouri.

BERT WILLIAMS
b. Egbert Austin Williams, 12 November 1874, New Providence, Nassau, Bahamas, d. 4 March 1922, New York

Bert Williams was one of the first and greatest names in black American showbusiness, and a pioneering black presence on the Broadway musical stage. In addition to being a consummate comedian, he was also a considerable songwriter, in both capacities wielding great influence upon other black artists of the 1910s and 20s, such as Shelton Brooks.

Williams initially worked with George W. Walker, and they made their Broadway début in *The Gold Bug* (1896); this was followed by appearances in the all-black shows *The Policy Shop* (1900), *In Dahomey* (1903) and others. In 1906 they formed the Negro Actors' Society to safeguard the rights of black performers.

Williams and Walker ended their association in 1909, and in 1910 Florenz Ziegfeld gave Williams a leading part in his *Follies*, the first time a black actor had been so featured in a white revue. Williams worked in Ziegfeld shows almost every year up to 1919, a familiar figure in top hat, shabby dress suit and oversized shoes. Among the songs he popularized, on Columbia records as well as in person, were his own compositions 'Nobody' (1905) and 'Let It Alone' (1906), both with lyrics by Alex Rogers, and 'That's a-Plenty' (1909). He was also associated with **Irving Berlin**'s 'Woodman, Woodman, Spare That Tree' (1911) and the comic song 'The Darktown Poker Club' (1917), both of which were recorded in Williams' spirit a generation later by **Phil Harris**. Later admirers have included **Ry Cooder**, who recorded 'Nobody' on *Jazz* (Warners, 1978), and **Randy Newman**. Williams was the subject of a biography by Ann Charters, *Nobody: The Story of Bert Williams* (1970).

BIG JOE WILLIAMS
b. 16 October 1903, Crawford, Mississippi, USA, d. 17 December 1982, Macon, Mississippi

Big Joe Williams lived, and retained his abilities, longer than almost all of his contemporaries, the first generation of Mississippi blues singers. He changed his working pattern to fall in with the blues revival of the sixties but little changed in his music, which continued to express with remarkable communicative power both the rural culture of his youth and the faster urban tempo of his later life.

He left home as a boy to travel and occasionally work as singer-guitarist at local functions. In the late 1910s and early twenties he toured with medicine and minstrel shows. Although it was long believed among collectors that he had recorded earlier, he did not appear on record until 1935, when he cut the first version of his 'Highway 49' for Bluebird. At subsequent Bluebird sessions he introduced 'Baby Please Don't Go' (1935), whose 1941 remake, probably more than any other version of this traditional blues theme, exposed it to white blues musicians in the sixties; 'Crawlin' King Snake' (1941), later recorded by **John Lee Hooker**; and 'Someday Baby' (1941). On some of those dates, and throughout a 1947 Columbia session, he was brilliantly accompanied by **Sonny Boy Williamson I** (harmonica). The interplay of their instruments, over the rhythm laid by bass and drums, resembled the new down-home blues-band styles that were beginning to emerge in Chicago from younger men like **Little Walter** and **Muddy Waters**.

Throughout the thirties, forties and fifties Williams was an incessant rambler, working in Chicago, St Louis, and in the South. He recorded his first album, *Piney Woods Blues* (Delmark, 1961) in St Louis. It was followed by *Tough Times* (Arhoolie, 1961), *Blues on Highway 49* (Delmark, 1962) and sets for Folkways

(1962) and Bluesville (1962–3). He visited Europe with the 1963 American Folk Blues Festival, recording in Denmark for Storyville. *Classic Delta Blues* (Milestone, 1965) was a collection of songs associated with **Charley Patton** and **Robert Johnson**, for which he used a six-string guitar; normally he played a nine-string instrument which he had adapted himself. By contrast, *Hand Me down My Old Walking Stick* (Liberty, 1969), recorded in London with producer **Mike Batt**, featured amplified guitar and a less contemplative, more public repertoire. He worked in Europe several times in 1971–3, and Japan in 1974, but in the later seventies was hampered by ill-health, and some of the work from that period that has since been issued (on Ornament and L+R) was informally recorded by enthusiasts at his home in Crawford, Mississippi, where he was also filmed for blues documentaries.

Williams had many acquaintances who were amateur musicians, and several collections of rural blues performances on Testament and Storyville were drawn from that circle. Of particular interest for his primitive vocal and guitar style was John Wesley Macon, 'Mr Shortstuff', who recorded with Williams' help in 1964 for Spivey and Folkways.

CLARENCE WILLIAMS
b. 8 October 1898, Plaquemine Delta, Louisiana, USA, d. 6 November 1965, Queens, New York

Pianist, bandleader, composer, arranger, music publisher and talent scout, Williams was one of the first black figures to wield power in the American music industry, particularly in the recording field.

He grew up in New Orleans, playing piano semi-professionally from his teens. He also worked in vaudeville as a dancer with Armand J. Piron, later a bandleader and Williams' partner in a music publishing firm. He opened a music store in Chicago, then in 1918 a publishing house in New York. From 1922 to 1930 he was A&R manager for the black catalogue of Okeh Records, signing innumerable jazz and blues artists and setting up, and often playing on, their sessions; among them were **Louis Armstrong**, **Sidney Bechet** and **Bessie Smith**. He also recorded prolifically as singer, pianist, jug-blower or merely leader with various groups of his own, such as his Blue Five, Blue Seven and Washboard Band, whose widely varying instrumental line-ups allowed Williams to show his considerable versatility as an arranger. Some of these recordings – including 'Cushion Foot Stomp' (1927) or his own 'Organ Grinder Blues' (1928, 1933), also recorded by **Victoria Spivey** and **Ethel Waters** – have passed into the standard repertoire of the traditional jazz band. The vocalist on some of them was his wife Eva Taylor, while his sidemen included noteworthy jazzmen like Ed Allen (cornet), reeds-players

Bechet, Cecil Scott and Buster Bailey and pianist **James P. Johnson**, as well as, more briefly, **King Oliver** and **Coleman Hawkins**. During this period he composed, or co-composed with collaborators like Spencer Williams, such future standards as 'Sugar Blues' (1923), 'Baby Won't You Please Come Home', 'Royal Garden Blues', and 'West End Blues', memorably recorded by Armstrong.

Williams' recordings for Vocalion in the early thirties drew in white musicians like steel-guitarist **Roy Smeck** and singers Dick Robertson and Chick Bullock, and took on a light-hearted 'novelty' approach analogous to some contemporary hillbilly bands, as in **Bob Miller**'s 'Swaller-Tail Coat' (1933) or 'Milk Cow Blues' (1935). He continued to lead recording bands until the mid-thirties, then devoted more of his time to songwriting. In 1943 he sold his publishing interests to Decca and became a Harlem storekeeper.

Eva Taylor, who had been particularly active on radio during the thirties, retired in the early forties, but after her husband's death visited Europe several times, performing and recording with admirers of his music in England, Denmark and Sweden.

DON WILLIAMS
b. 27 May 1939, Floydada, Texas, USA

A deep-voiced, intimate country singer, Williams relied heavily on acoustic instruments, particularly guitar and dobro, in his music. The resulting, 'folksy', laid-back sound was equally well received in Europe and America.

The son of a mechanic, Williams was raised in Corpus Christi and on his discharge from the army in 1963 formed Strangers Two with Lofton Kline. With the addition of Susan Taylor in 1964 the group became the Pozo-Seco Singers, adopted a more folk-rock sound and signed with Columbia. 'Time' (1966) led to a series of hits, including 'I Can Make It with You', 'Look What You've Done' (1966) and **Doug Kershaw**'s oft-recorded 'Louisiana Man' (1967). Their hitmaking days over, the group disbanded in 1971 and Williams briefly left the music business.

He returned as a songwriter on a solo album by Taylor, settled in Nashville and in 1973, after working for **Jack Clement**'s music publishing companies, released *Don Williams Vol. 1* on Clement's own JMI label. Primarily intended as a showcase for Williams' writing and that of Bob McDill and Wayland Hoyfield, it resulted in a country hit, 'In the Shelter of Your Eyes'. This initiated a lengthy series of (mostly self-produced) hits that included 'We Should Be Together' (ABC, 1974), 'You're My Best Friend' (1975), ''Til the Rivers All Run Dry' (1976), 'Tulsa Time' (1978) and 'I Believe in You' (1980), his only major American pop hit. During the late seventies

Williams was particularly successful in Europe, scoring a British Top Twenty hit with 'I Recall a Gypsy Woman' (1976) and *Visions* (1976) and the television-promoted *Images* (K-Tel, 1978). He also appeared in the 'good ole boy' movie *W.W. and the Dixie Dance Kings* (1974), in which he first wore the battered stetson that, along with his gentle, romantic songs, has since become his trademark. Williams' songs have been recorded by **Eric Clapton** ('We're All the Way'), **Kenny Rogers** and **Johnny Cash**, among others.

In the eighties his hits included 'Love on a Roll' (MCA, 1983), 'Stay Young' (1984), 'Walking a Broken Heart' (1985), 'Heartbeat in the Darkness' (Capitol, 1986) and 'Another Place Another Time' (1988). In 1987 he decided to take a year off from music, re-emerging in 1989 on RCA, enjoying further success with 'I've Been Loved by the Best' and 'One Good Well'. His later albums included *As Long as I Have You* (1989), *True Love* (1990) and *Currents* (1992), all displaying Williams' distinctive laid-back folksy charm. A 1993 British concert recording was released as *An Evening with Don Williams* in 1994. In 1998 he released *I Turn the Page* on his own Giant label.

HANK WILLIAMS

b. Hiram Hank Williams, 17 September 1923, Mt Olive, Alabama, USA, d. 1 January 1953, West Virginia

The deepest-dyed of all country singers, Hank Williams made a mark upon the canvas of country music that has proved ineradicable, his songs and style having been ceaselessly remixed to yield a range of secondary colours, from the lonesome honky-tonk blues of **Webb Pierce** and **Ray Price** to the sturdy independence of **Merle Haggard**. He also imparted a tint of his plain man's pithiness to the popular music of his day, grounding its fantasies for a while in the reality of a dirt-poor farm boy.

After an early childhood spent in rural southern Alabama, Williams lived in Greenville, where he encountered a black street-singer, Rufe Payne, who gave him, as he was to say later, 'all the musical training I ever had'. His family then moved to Montgomery, where he made his first public appearance, in about 1937, singing a topical blues about the Works Progress Administration (a New Deal agency) at an Empire Theater amateur night. This was followed by a regular spot on the local station WSFA and shows at various venues in southern Alabama. He formed his first band and gave it a name, the Drifting Cowboys, that he would carry with him throughout his career. At that time he was greatly influenced, as both singer and songwriter, by **Roy Acuff**, a background clearly visible in such early compositions as 'Six More Miles (to the Graveyard)'.

Williams dropped out of school at nineteen and after an unsuccessful attempt to join the US Army went to work in a Mobile shipyard. In the summer of 1944 he returned to music, forming a new band and adding a second singer, Audrey Sheppard Guy, whom he married. In 1946 he signed to publisher **Fred Rose**, who put him under contract and placed 'Six More Miles' and other numbers with **Molly O'Day**, who recorded them shortly afterwards for Columbia. Williams and Rose built the most profitable collaboration, artistic and financial, in the history of country music. How much Rose contributed to the songs themselves remains uncertain, though the most probable conclusion is, as one of the singer's biographers has put it, that 'Williams produced the gems and Rose polished them'. Certainly Rose was responsible for much of the management of Williams' career, from setting up his sessions to organizing his bookings.

Williams' first recordings were for the small New York label Sterling in December 1946. In the following spring he signed with MGM, charting with his first release, the blues 'Move It on Over', and following up with such low-life anthems as 'Honky Tonkin'', though the sacred number 'I Saw the Light', which became one of his best-known compositions, was also a hit. In August 1948 he joined the cast of the *Louisiana Hayride* on KWKH, Shreveport, a move that made him known throughout the Southwest. He established his recording career firmly with the 1949 country No. 1 'Lovesick Blues', and in the summer of that year finally attained what he had long worked towards, and because of his reputation as a heavy drinker been denied: a place on the *Grand Ole Opry*. Thereafter his position among the leading artists of country music was unassailable.

While Williams' records unfailingly reached the country market – 1950, for example, made substantial hits out of 'Long Gone Lonesome Blues' and 'Why Don't You Love Me' – Rose felt that the songs could also make an impact in mainstream pop, and eventually succeeded in placing 'Cold, Cold Heart' with Columbia's **Mitch Miller**. Thus, in 1951, Williams had the country hit with the song while the young **Tony Bennett** turned it into a pop million-seller. Subsequently Williams' numbers were taken up by **Frankie Laine** (the embryonic rock'n'roll of 'Hey Good Lookin''*, 1951), **Jo Stafford** (the cajun-flavoured 'Jambalaya [on the Bayou]'* 1952, with guitar-playing by the young **Chet Atkins**) and innumerable other pop artists. When making his records Williams drew on a pool of Nashville studio musicians, including Zeke Turner (guitar), Jerry Byrd (steel) and Tommy Jackson (fiddle), but on tour his Drifting Cowboys were seldom without fiddler Jerry Rivers and steel-player Don Helms, whose distinctive bluesy approaches contributed significantly to Williams' modified honky-tonk ensemble sound.

Acceptance by the Nashville establishment did not curb Williams' drinking; he was also, since a back injury, dependent on painkilling drugs, and in consequence his performances were frequently late or unsatisfactory. He was divorced from Audrey in May 1952, and in August suspended by the *Opry*. He went back to Shreveport and in October married Billie Jean Jones Eshlimar in New Orleans at a showy double ceremony: an afternoon rehearsal and evening wedding that were both open to anyone who had bought a ticket – 28,000 people are said to have attended.

In the early hours of New Year's Day 1953, Williams died in the back of his car on the way to an engagement in Canton, Ohio. His funeral in Montgomery was witnessed by many country music figures and 25,000 members of the public. 'Your Cheatin' Heart' and 'Kaw-Liga', recorded at his last session, in Nashville in September, were coupled on a posthumous release which topped both *Billboard* and *Cashbox* country charts for months. Williams' back catalogue, too, was boosted by the publicity surrounding his death and his elevation to country music's Valhalla (he was elected to the Hall of Fame in 1961), and in 1953–64 his name sold twenty million records. 'Your Cheatin' Heart', which became perhaps his best-known song, recorded by over 300 other artists, also provided a title for a low-budget 1964 biopic. A far better film, Peter Bogdanovich's *The Last Picture Show* (1971), though not concerned with Williams himself, made brilliant use of his songs to convey the atmosphere of growing up in the early post-war Southwest.

Williams' chief gift as a songwriter was to marry words and music in simple but direct and memorable combinations. 'Nobody I know', **Mitch Miller** has said, 'could use basic English so effectively,' while the critic Henry Pleasants has remarked that 'Hank's melodies were the music of language'. This natural conversational quality has impressed and guided country songwriters ever since. As a singer he belongs in the blues tradition of **Jimmie Rodgers**, but he removed the ironic distance between the Rodgersian 'I' and his listeners, communicating with extraordinary sympathy the texture of everyday emotional life. The country singers who have re-used his songs, very often in album-length commemorations, are too numerous to list, and it is no exaggeration to say that nearly all the important figures of the fifties and sixties have drawn to some degree on his stylistic legacy. Thus as late as 1967 **Tim Hardin** wrote and recorded 'Tribute to Hank Williams' while Williams' son **Hank Williams Jnr** summed up the feelings of dissatisfaction with the countrypolitan movement in country music with the emphatic 'Are You Sure Hank Done It This Way?' (1981), and **Leonard Cohen** included a verse about him in 1988's 'Tower of Song'.

With the development of a 'New Country' idiom, singers like **Dwight Yoakam** and **Randy Travis** and country-rock acts such as Jason and the Scorchers reaffirmed the strength of Hank Williams' music in the eighties and nineties. In 1991 Polydor issued the comprehensive boxed set *The Original Singles Collection . . . Plus*, and in 1993 a collection of songs from Williams' late forties radio shows, *Health and Happiness Shows*. The same year, a compilation was released which combined some of Williams' best-known material with his son's biggest hits as *The Best of Hank and Hank*. In 1995 The The released the tribute album *Hanky Panky*.

HANK WILLIAMS JNR
b. Randall Hank Williams Jnr, 26 May 1949, Shreveport, Louisiana, USA

Few other artists in the history of popular music have borne such a heavy family burden as **Hank Williams Jnr**. The son of **Hank Williams**, he was embroiled in Hank Snr's life from his early years, patching together songs from fragments left by him and from the age of fourteen, when he officially took the name Hank Williams Jnr, performing with his mother, Audrey Williams, numerous versions of his father's songs. The culmination of this was his singing them in the 1964 biopic about his father *Your Cheatin' Heart*. Since becoming an established artist in his own right, the weight of being the son of Hank Williams has hardly been alleviated. Hank Jnr's life has, for the most part, been a more public version of his father's hedonistic race to death, and in his recordings he sought alternately to obliterate and proudly celebrate his father. These include 'Standing in the Shadow (Of a Very Famous Man)' (1966) and 'Family Tradition' (1979), in which Hank Jnr specifically explained his drinking and womanizing in terms of a family tradition. Similarly, his versions of **Waylon Jennings**' 'Are You Sure Hank Done It This Way?' and **Kris Kristofferson**'s 'If You Don't Like Hank Williams' (1981) were both given greater resonance by being performed by Hank Jnr. In marked contrast to his earlier recordings of his father's songs, later recordings ('Kaw-Liga', 'Honky Tonkin'', 1980, and 'Move It on Over', 1982), performed over heavy-rock backing but with a strong traditional feel, saw Hank Jnr battling again with his father's all-pervasive spirit. Far more commercially inclined in the manner of **Frank Sinatra**'s *Duets* albums was *Three Generations of Hank* (Curb, 1996), on which electronic wizardry allowed Hank Snr and Jnr and his son Hank Williams III to sing together.

His parentage notwithstanding, Williams was also a child of rock'n'roll – the band he formed in high school was Randall and the Rockets. After his initial success on MGM, for whom he recorded prolifically in the sixties, as 'the son of Hank Williams', Williams reorientated himself towards the new mix of rock, blues and country music emerging in the South in the mid-seventies. The first indication of this was *Hank Williams Jnr and Friends* (1975), recorded with members of the **Allman Brothers Band**, the **Charlie Daniels Band** and the Marshall Tucker Band, the last two the most countryfied of the southern boogie bands. This move was confirmed by the Waylon Jennings-produced *New South* (Warners, 1977), which saw Williams as a fully fledged member of the 'outlaw' movement within country music. That album came after a climbing accident which nearly cost Williams his life and required the surgical reconstruction of his face.

His huge success – in 1982 he had eight albums on the country charts at the same time – was heavily dependent on the traditional themes of the outlaw movement, macho songs ('I Fought the Law', 1978; 'Whiskey Bent and Hell Bound', 1979) and defiant celebrations of the new/old South ('Dixie on my Mind', 1981, 'A Country Boy Can Survive', 1982, and the controversial 'If the South Woulda Won', 1988). Occasionally interspersed with these were more reflective songs, including 'Old Habits' (1980). Later albums included *Man of Steel* (1982), *Hank Live* (1987) and *Born to Boogie* (1988). *Lone Wolf* (1990) included a duet with **Jimmy C. Newman**. Although his record sales slipped from the late eighties onwards, he continued to release albums, including *America – The Way I See It* (1990), *Pure Hank* (1992) and *Maverick* (1992). Later (and lesser) albums included *Out of Left Field* (1993) and *The Raw Deal* (1994), while *Three Generations of Hank* (1997) was one of the most bizarre tribute albums ever. Courtesy of the magic of overdubbing it featured Hank Snr, Jnr and his son Hank Williams III on a collection of Hank Williams' songs. In the manner of Frank Sinatra's *Duets*, the result was of greater technological than artistic interest. Since then Williams has recorded only sporadically.

JOHN WILLIAMS

b. *John Towner Williams, 8 February 1932, New York, USA*

Best known for his Oscar-winning, stirring scores to *Jaws* (1975) and *Star Wars* (1977), Williams was a prolific film composer. He also regularly worked as a conductor, notably with the Boston Symphony Orchestra.

The son of drummer Johnny Williams, he was raised in New York and educated at UCLA and the Juilliard School of Music. In the early fifties he began working as a session pianist and recorded extensively,

mostly in a jazz vein, for Kapp, Beth, RCA and Dot, before later in the decade turning to writing for television (*M-Squad*, *Wagon Train*) and then films. His early films included *Bachelor Flat* (1962) and *None But the Brave* (1965) and he won his first Oscar for the orchestration of *Fiddler on the Roof* (1971), in the wake of which he worked almost exclusively with big-budget movies. His score provided much of the excitement of *Towering Inferno* (1974) and he was responsible for the threatening opening theme to *Jaws* (1975), a hit for him (MCA) and one of the best-known pieces of film music of modern times. His music for *Star Wars* was more symphonic and even more commercially successful. The theme music gave Williams another hit (20th-Century Fox) and the group Meco an American No. 1 and million-seller on Millennium with their disco treatment of several of the film's musical themes. Subsequently Meco 'disco-ized' further themes from Williams' scores, including those to *Close Encounters of the Third Kind* (1978) and the *Star Wars* sequels, *The Empire Strikes Back* (1980) and 'Ewok Celebration' from *Return of the Jedi* (1983).

Williams himself had chart success with 'The Theme from Close Encounters of the Third Kind' (Arista, 1978) and has continued to write scores. Among these were *Superman* (1978), for which he provided a very successful folksy feel to the evocative sequence of Superman/Clark Kent's childhood on earth, the two Indiana Jones films, *Raiders of the Lost Ark* (1981) and *Indiana Jones and the Temple of Doom* (1984), *The Witches of Eastwick* (1987) and *Empire of the Sun* (1988).

He remained among the most sought-after film composers in the nineties, scoring such blockbusters as *Jurassic Park* (1993), *Schindler's List* (1993), *Nixon* (1995), *The Lost World* and *Seven Years in Tibet* (both 1997) and *Angela's Ashes* (1999), for which he was nominated for an Oscar.

LARRY WILLIAMS

b. *Lawrence E. Williams, 10 May 1935, New Orleans, Louisiana, USA, d. 2 January 1980, Los Angeles, California*

Briefly a rival in popularity to his label-mate **Little Richard**, Williams is best remembered for a trio of self-composed, frantic, alliterative celebrations of his girlfriends, 'Short Fat Fannie'*, 'Bony Moronie'* (1957) and 'Dizzy Miss Lizzie' (1958).

In 1953 Williams moved to San Francisco, where he formed his own band, the Lemon Drops, and played piano for **Roy Brown** and **Percy Mayfield**. In 1955 he joined **Lloyd Price**'s band and returned to New Orleans, where he was signed by **Art Rupe** to his Specialty label. A cover of Price's 'Just Because' (1957) failed, but the Little Richard soundalike 'Short Fat

Fannie' was an international hit. That and his other hits and compositions of 1957–8 were particularly influential among the British beat groups of the early sixties, notably **The Beatles**. Williams' 'Slow Down', 'Bad Boy' and 'Dizzy Miss Lizzie' (1958) were regularly performed by The Beatles in 1962–3. Interestingly, **John Lennon**, who subsequently recorded 'Bony Moronie' on *Rock'n'Roll* (1975), generally sang lead, as he did on The Beatles' recording of 'Dizzy Miss Lizzie', while **Paul McCartney** sang lead on the group's versions of the songs of Little Richard.

In the sixties Williams formed a partnership with **Johnny 'Guitar' Watson** which produced several R&B hits, including a version of the **Cannonball Adderley** hit 'Mercy, Mercy, Mercy' (Okeh, 1967) and 'Nobody' (1968), and such albums as *The Larry Williams Show* (Decca, 1964), recorded in London by blues enthusiast **Mike Vernon**, and *Two for the Price of One* (Okeh, 1967). After a lengthy period of retirement, he returned to recording with the lacklustre *That Larry Williams* (Fantasy, 1978) before committing suicide in 1980.

LUCINDA WILLIAMS
b. 26 January 1953, Lake Charles, USA

While hardly prolific, having released only four albums of original material in over twenty years, singer-songwriter Williams has melded country music, blues and folk in a unique manner that is probably only possible in the American South West. There traditions remain vibrant, allowing performers to naturally turn from traditional songs such as 'Great Speckled Bird' and 'Motherless Children' to writing their own material. Even more independently minded than, say, **Mary Chapin Carpenter** or **Lyle Lovett,** Williams' influence has been more stealthy, but equally important, than most coming from the folk-blues spectrum. Among those who have, consciously or not, echoed Williams' meld of introspection and exuberance is **Texas**.

The daughter of an American college professor (and a friend of **Tom T. Hall**), after spending her childhood moving around from Southern USA to Mexico and Chile, Williams settled in Austin, Texas, in her early twenties. She began playing in local folk clubs, mixing her own compositions with traditional songs, with little success. In 1979 she made her début album, *Ramblin' on My Mind* (Folkways), a collection of country-blues standards recorded in an afternoon at the studios of the Malco blues label. She followed it with her first set of original material, *Happy Woman Blues* (1980). Both failed to generate commercial interest and Williams took a seven-year break from her recording career.

She eventually signed to Rough Trade after relocating to Los Angeles in the late eighties, releasing her acclaimed eponymous third album, a mature blend of country, folk and blues given a firm rock context. It included her best-known song, 'Passionate Kisses', later recorded by Carpenter on her best album *Come on, Come on*, and 'Crescent City', recorded by **Emmylou Harris** on *Cowgirl's Prayer*. However, more indicative of the charm and urgency of the album, which was co-produced by her long-time guitarist Gurf Morlix, was the opening cut, 'I Just Wanted to See You So Bad'. The album's critical success led to a deal with RCA in 1989. However, Williams moved to the independent Chameleon Records before issuing any new material, preferring the creative freedom afforded to her by the smaller label. *Sweet Old World* (1992) was her first album to have any commercial impact in the US. It included the **Bonnie Raitt**-sounding 'Hot Blood' and the emphatic 'Something about What Happens When We Talk', and was subsequently named as one of the albums of the year by a slew of American critics.

Another long hiatus preceded Williams' fifth release, *Car Wheels on a Gravel Road* (Mercury, 1998), which was the singer's most successful international release. Where before her songs had merely documented the travails (and pleasures) of working-class life, *Car Wheels* brought an assured familiarity to its subjects. Williams' performance was similarly assured, but even more impressive was the emphatic soundscape behind the songs and Williams' convincing voice, which gave the songs even greater authenticity. This was largely the result of **Steve Earle**, who co-produced the album.

MARY LOU WILLIAMS
b. Mary Elfrieda Scruggs, 8 May 1910, Atlanta, Georgia, USA, d. 28 May 1981, Durham, North Carolina

Pianist, composer and arranger, Williams' career spanned the Kansas City style of the thirties and the modern jazz of the post-Second World War period.

She grew up in Pittsburgh and was inspired to become a professional pianist by theatre musician and arranger Lovie Austin. As Mary Lou Burleigh she recorded with alto-saxophonist John Williams' band in 1927 for Paramount and Gennett. Williams, whom she later married, joined Andy Kirk's Clouds of Joy. When Kirk was signed to a recording contract by **Jack Kapp** of Brunswick, Mary Lou Williams joined the band as writer and soloist on such tracks as the **Earl Hines**-influenced 'Messa Stomp' and 'Corky Stomp' (1929). Williams stayed with Kirk until 1942, growing in stature as an arranger, and providing scores for such bandleaders as **Louis Armstrong**, **Benny Goodman** and **Tommy Dorsey**.

In 1936 Kapp signed the Kirk group to his Decca

label and Williams was involved in such recordings as 'Walkin' and Swingin'' (1936) and 'Overhand'. From 1942 to 1944 she worked as an arranger for **Duke Ellington**, composing 'Trumpet No End' for him. During the late forties Williams worked with bebop pioneers **Dizzy Gillespie** and **Bud Powell**, recording for **Moe Asch**'s Disc and Asch labels as well as providing Goodman with a bebop arrangement of 'Stealing Apples'. She also recorded with an all-woman group featuring guitarist Mary Osborne for *Girls in Jazz* (RCA, 1946), produced by **Leonard Feather**, played solo dates in New York City and created her *Zodiac Suite*, which was performed by the New York Philharmonic at its première and recorded by Williams for Asch's Folkways label.

For the next three decades Williams continued to combine composing, performing and recording. She wrote the mass *Black Christ of the Andes* (MPS) and played at numerous festivals in both America and Europe, where she lived in 1952–4. With Gillespie, she recorded the *Zodiac Suite* at Newport (Verve, 1957) and was recorded by **Norman Granz** at Montreux (Pablo, 1978). Among Williams' other records were *Don Carlos Meets Mary Lou* (with Don Byas, Vogue, 1954) and *My Mama Pinned a Rose on Me* (Pablo, 1979).

From 1977 to her death, Williams taught at Duke University in South Carolina and in 1980 she set up a Foundation to help children study with leading jazz players.

MAURICE WILLIAMS AND THE ZODIACS

Maurice Williams, b. 26 April 1938, Lancaster, North Carolina, USA; Willie Bennet; Henry Gaston; Charles Thomas

'Stay', written by Williams and featuring his wailing, exciting falsetto, was an American No. 1 in 1960. The group's only major hit, it was successfully revived by the **Hollies**, whose raucous version was a British Top Ten hit in 1963; the **Four Seasons**, whose shrill rendition reached the American Top Twenty in 1964; and, most surprisingly, by **Jackson Browne**, who scored another American Top Twenty hit in 1978 with his low-key reworking of the song.

Formed in Lancaster as the Charms in 1955, the group signed with Excello as the Gladiolas and scored a minor hit in 1957 with Williams' composition, the Latin-inflected 'Little Darlin'. The **Diamonds**' cover-version of the song became a transatlantic million-seller. They continued recording with little success, as the Royal Charms and Excellos, before moving to New York and joining Herald in 1959 as the Zodiacs. Subsequent similar-sounding discs to 'Stay' failed and in 1963 the group folded, leaving Williams to pursue an unsuccessful solo career before re-forming the Zodiacs to join the rock'n'roll revival circuit of the late sixties.

MAYO WILLIAMS

One of the leading black talent agents and recording managers, Williams worked for the Paramount and Decca companies in the twenties and thirties. Among those whose careers he guided were **Blind Lemon Jefferson**, while a new version of Williams' production, 'Drinkin' Wine Spo De a Dee' by Stick McGhee gave **Ahmet Ertegun**'s Atlantic its first hit in 1949.

A former college football star, Williams worked as a booking agent and supplied blues artists to Paramount when the label started a 'race' records series in 1922. He was soon appointed as recording director for the company, with **Art Satherley** among his team of assistants. Papa Charlie Jackson's 'Lawdy Lawdy Blues' (1924) was one of Paramount's first successes while Williams also signed Jefferson and **Blind Blake** to Paramount. The inventive Williams named the Paramount 12000 series 'The Popular Race Record' and regularly organized writing contests among artists.

He also recorded the early songs of **Big Bill Broonzy** plus classic blues singers **Ma Rainey** and Ida Cox before leaving Paramount in 1927 to start the shortlived Black Patti label, only the second black-owned record company to be formed. The first had been Black Swan (1921–4), set up by **W. C. Handy**'s business partner Harry Pace. Black Patti (the name came from the nickname of opera singer Sissieretta Jones) released tracks by Mississippi blues singer Sam Collins and cornettist Willie Hightower ('Boar Hog Blues'). After the company failed, Williams joined the Vocalion label, recording Henry Thomas (Ragtime Texas) and Memphis singer Jim Jackson on 'Goin' to Kansas City' (1927). The record was a bestseller and the song became a blues standard.

Williams' next success was the risqué 'It's Tight Like That' (1928) by Tampa Red and Georgia Tom, the future gospel composer **Thomas A. Dorsey**. The label covered the song with a jazz version by Jimmy Noone and a guitar instrumental by Tampa Red. Of greater artistic worth was **Leroy Carr**'s 'How Long Blues' (1928), the first of a hundred tracks Carr made for Vocalion, which in 1931 was acquired by the American Recording Corporation (ARC).

Soon afterwards Williams moved on to supervise urban blues recording for **Jack Kapp**'s Decca, producing Bumble Bee Slim and Kokomo Arnold, whose 'Milk Cow Blues' was widely covered by Western swing bands and by **Elvis Presley** (1957). In the jazz sphere, Williams produced Herb Morand's Harlem Hamfats in 1936–8. The group's 'Oh Red' and 'Lake Providence Blues' mixed New Orleans jazz and country blues in a way which foreshadowed the jump band R&B of artists like **Louis Jordan**.

In the forties Williams established his own Harlem label, on which the original version of 'Drinkin' Wine' appeared. He also supervised Louis Jordan sessions and in the fifties had his own Ebony label for which Little Brother Montgomery recorded.

PAUL WILLIAMS
b. 19 September 1940, Omaha, Nebraska, USA

A songwriter, singer and actor, Williams is best remembered for the hits he wrote for the **Carpenters** ('We've Only Just Begun'*, 1970; 'Rainy Days and Mondays'*, 1972), **Three Dog Night** ('An Old-Fashioned Love Song'*, 1971), **Helen Reddy** ('You and Me Against the World', 1974) and **Dionne Warwick** ('That's What Friends Are for', 1985). As well as recording in his own right, he acted in films and wrote the music for several movies, notably *A Star Is Born*, whose theme 'Evergreen'*, co-written with **Barbra Streisand**, won an Oscar as best film song of 1976.

A former apprentice jockey, the diminutive Williams entered films as a stunt man and actor (*The Loved One*, 1964). While continuing his acting career, he turned to songwriting in the mid-sixties with Biff Rose and in 1967 with composer Roger Nichols. The songs they (and after 1975 Williams and Ken Ascher) wrote for the Carpenters and others were notable for their easy romanticism and lush melodies which recalled the Broadway ballads of the thirties. In marked contrast were the songs of his brother Mentor, the best of which (such as the **Dobie Gray** hit 'Drift Away', 1973) were firmly in the rock'n'roll tradition. But though Williams' songs were hugely successful for others, his own recordings, which included *Someday Man* (Reprise, 1970) and *Life Goes on* (A&M, 1973), were more good-timey than singer-songwriter, and made little impact. More successful were his regular appearances in cabaret in Las Vegas which began in the early seventies.

In 1974 he brought both aspects of his career together when he starred in and wrote the music and songs for Brian De Palma's rock remake of *Phantom of the Opera*, *Phantom of the Paradise*. This led to further film-music projects, including *A Star Is Born* and the intriguing Alan Parker film *Bugsy Malone* (1976). A gentle parody of the thirties gangster film entirely acted by children, it was enlivened by Williams' own performance of a series of pastiche songs, among which were 'My Name Is Tallulah', 'So You Want to Be a Boxer' and the witty title song. Afterwards Williams continued to record sporadically, and to act in and write music for films, including *The End* (1977) and *The Muppet Movie* (1979).

ROBBIE WILLIAMS
b. 13 February 1974, Stoke on Trent, England

Robbie Williams first came to fame as a member of Take That, the most successful British teenage vocal group since the sixties. After the break-up of the group in 1996 Williams found international success as a solo performer. This was in marked contrast to the group's main songwriters, Barlow (*b. 20 January 1971, Frodsham, England*) and Owen (*b. 27 January 1974, England*), who struggled to match their earlier success. Williams' mix of naughty boy campery and laddish behaviour caught the tenor of the times in a way that Barlow's balladry didn't. The remaining members, Jason Orange (*b. 10 July 1970, Manchester*) and Howard Donald (*b. 28 April 1968, Manchester*), decided against pursuing solo careers.

Barlow, Owen and Williams first performed together as Cutest Rush before producer Nigel Martin Smith took over their management and allied them with former breakdancers Orange and Donald, forming Take That. Aimed both at the gay club scene and teen-pop audiences, Take That first came to prominence over the suggestive nature of the promotional video accompanying their début single, 'Do What U Like' (Dance UK, 1991). Subsequent releases 'Promises' and 'Once You've Tasted Love' (1992) were minor UK hits before a cover of Tavares' 'It Only Takes a Minute' reached No. 7 in the charts. *Take That and Party* (1992) spawned three more Top Ten singles: 'A Million Love Songs', 'Could It Be Magic' (a cover of a **Barry Manilow** song) and 'Why Can't I Wake Up with You?'.

Although Take That spent much of 1993 attempting unsuccessfully to crack the American market, they managed to achieve a pair of number one singles in the UK: 'Pray' and the **Lulu** collaboration 'Relight My Fire'. *Everything Changes* (1993) achieved vast sales across Europe and Canada as well as in Britain. By the time Take That began to record their third album, they were beginning to lose their status as the most popular band in Britain to the guitar-pop of **Blur** and **Oasis**. Barlow responded to this change in the music mood of the time with the acclaimed 'Back for Good', which moved away from Take That's dance-pop past towards a classic pop sound. The single topped the British chart and become the band's only US hit. However, Williams had already begun to move away from the band, and his departure on the eve of the release of *Nobody Else* (1995) both signalled the end of Take That's reign and began a lengthy legal dispute with his former manager. The remaining members officially announced their decision to split in February 1996, signing off with a highly successful greatest hits collection and their final number one single, a cover of the **Bee Gees**' 'How Deep Is Your Love?'.

Songwriter Barlow was the first member of Take That to launch a solo career, topping the British charts with 'Open Road' from his début album of the same name in 1996. However, his popularity soon began to dwindle, as his songs edged towards MOR, alienating his teenage fanbase while failing to impress a more mature market. Williams kick-started his career as a solo performer with a cover of **George Michael**'s 'Freedom '90', before releasing a series of singles, notably 'Old Before I Die', heavily influenced by his new friends in Oasis, which were increasingly unpopular. This decline was ended with the jocular Williams managing to represent himself as a post-modernist music-hall turn. Seen from this perspective, 'Angels' and 'Let Me Entertain You' were huge hits, sending his début album, *Life Thru a Lens* (1997), towards multiple platinum status. The follow up, *I've Been Expecting You* (1998), confirmed his position as Britain's most popular solo performer and included the number one single 'Millennium', based around a string sample from **John Barry**'s score to *You Only Live Twice*. In 1999 Williams set his sights on the American market with *The Ego Has Landed*, a compilation of the best tracks from his first two releases. However, just as Oasis and others before him had failed to achieve success in the US because of their innate Britishness, so Williams also failed to find mainstream success there.

Owen's solo career began promisingly with the indie-rock single 'I Am What I Am', but his album *Green Man* (1997), a blend of **Radiohead** and **Paul Weller**, was a flop. Orange and Donald have remained out of the limelight since Take That's split. The former turned his hand to acting, starring in British TV mini-series *Killer Net* (1998), while the latter has written UK hit singles for pop-dance singer Kavana, among others.

Williams returned to centre stage with *Sing When You're Winning* (2000). Co-written with Guy Chambers, as were his earlier albums, this had much more of the feel of 1993's *The Open Book*, the only album ever made by Chambers' group the Lemon Trees, possibly because Chambers also acted as the album's co-producer with Steve Power, the engineer on *Open Book*. Less clownish than *I've Been Expecting You*, while still awash with Williams' typically *faux naif* lyrics, the songs showed a more caring and less swaggering side to Williams. It was a critical and commercial success.

ROGER WILLIAMS
b. Louis Wertz, 1925, Omaha, Nebraska, USA

Williams sold more records than any other popular pianist in the fifties. His rivals included **Winifred Atwell** and Russ Conway in Britain and Ferrante and

Teicher and **Liberace** in America, but only the flamboyant Liberace ever rivalled him in popularity, and that by virtue of the high camp of his live performances.

The son of a music teacher, multi-instrumentalist Williams enrolled in New York's Juilliard School of Music in 1951 and subsequently won a regular spot on *Arthur Godfrey's Talent Scouts*. Spotted by **Jack Kapp**, he was signed to Kapp Records and had an American No. 1 with his romantic version of the film theme 'Autumn Leaves' (1955), despite covers by Steve Allen, **Mitch Miller**, **Victor Young**, Jackie Gleason and the Ray Charles Singers, all of whose versions also charted. Among his many hits were versions of 'La Mer (Beyond the Sea)' (1956), later revived by **Bobby Darin**; 'Near You' (1958), a revival of **Francis Craig**'s 1947 hit; 'Autumn Leaves' (1965); and the film theme 'Born Free', his last big hit in 1966. In the sixties the duo (Arthur) Ferrante and (Louis) Teicher supplanted Williams in the higher reaches of the charts with a series of more melodramatic film themes. These included 'Theme from the Apartment', 'Exodus' (1960), 'Tonight' (1961), from *West Side Story*, 'Midnight Cowboy' (1968) and a most unlikely version of **Bob Dylan**'s 'Lay Lady Lay' (1969), all on United Artists.

In the seventies Williams continued to record for MCA (the company which had taken over Kapp) and Bainbridge, and to play the cabaret circuit. He retired in the eighties.

TONY WILLIAMS
b. 12 December 1945, Chicago, Illinois, USA, d. 23 February 1997

A teenage prodigy as a jazz drummer, Williams was the mainstay of **Miles Davis**'s group from 1963 to 1969. He later divided his time between jazz-rock experiments with such musicians as **John McLaughlin** and **Jack Bruce** and more conventional jazz activity.

The son of saxophonist Tillmon Williams, he grew up in Boston and took up the drums at the age of ten. In 1962 he moved to New York to play on Jackie McLean's *One Step Beyond* (1963). Soon afterwards he joined Davis where his unorthodox approach was a catalyst for the trumpeter's series of stylistic shifts during the sixties. Often providing compositions for the group, Williams played on such albums as *Seven Steps to Heaven* (1963), *Nefertiti* (1967) and *In a Silent Way* (1969). He also recorded with **Eric Dolphy** (*Out to Lunch*, 1964) and **Charles Lloyd** as well as leading his own group on *Life Time* (Blue Note, 1965) and *Spring* (1966).

It was Williams who brought McLaughlin from England to New York and in 1969 the pair formed Lifetime with another former Davis musician, organist

Larry Young. *Emergency* (Polydor, 1969) was followed by *Turn It Over* (1970), on which one-time **Cream** bassist Bruce joined the group.

With the departure of McLaughlin and Bruce, later Lifetime albums were made with a shifting personnel. After *Ego* (1971) and *The Old Bum's Rush* (1972) the group was disbanded with Williams returning to the jazz scene. In 1975 he set up a new fusion band with former **Soft Machine** guitarist Allan Holdsworth to record *Believe It* and *Million Dollar Legs* (Columbia, 1976). In the same year Williams played with VSOP, a group led by **Herbie Hancock** which re-created the style of the Miles Davis bands of the sixties. He also joined VSOP II in 1984.

The Joy of Flying (Columbia, 1979) was a solo album while in 1986 Williams signed to the revived Blue Note label, releasing *Foreign Intrigue* and *Civilisation* (1987). His later recordings included *Native Heart* (1990) and *The Story of Neptune* (1992).

SONNY BOY WILLIAMSON

Sonny Boy Williamson I, b. John Lee Williamson, 30 March 1914, Jackson, Tennessee, USA, d. 1 June 1948, Chicago, Illinois; Sonny Boy Williamson II, b. Aleck Ford (later Aleck/Alex 'Rice' Miller), 5 December 1899, Glendora, Mississippi, d. 25 May 1965, Helena, Arkansas

Two blues artists have been known by this name, the younger, confusingly, having apparently used it first.

Sonny Boy Williamson I, as John Lee Williamson has come to be known, was the most influential harmonica player of the thirties and forties, his instrumental phrases rhythmically interwoven with his singing to create a unified style new in blues. He was associated in the twenties and early thirties with fellow-Tennesseans **Sleepy John Estes** and mandolinist Yank Rachell. Moving to Chicago in 1934, he began recording for RCA Victor's Bluebird label in 1937, his second release, 'Good Morning, (Little) School Girl', becoming one of his best-known numbers and eventually a standard. It became part of the repertoire of white blues groups in the sixties, being recorded by the **Yardbirds**, among others. He collaborated, on his own recordings and often on theirs, with Rachell, **Big Joe Williams**, pianist Walter Davis and singer/guitarist Robert Lee McCoy (later known as Robert Nighthawk). By 1947 he had made more than one hundred sides for Bluebird (1937–45) and RCA Victor (1945–7), and a further score with Williams for Bluebird and Columbia. He would undoubtedly have played a significant role in fifties Chicago blues – whose style he had already helped to mould – had he not been murdered by a mugger while on his way home from a job.

Junior Wells demonstrated his debt to Williamson by recording new versions of his 'Early in the Morn-

ing', 'Hoodoo Hoodoo' and 'Better Cut That Out' within the space of a few months. Other harmonica players touched by his example include Billy Boy Arnold, whose 'I Wish You Would' and 'I Ain't Got You' (Vee-Jay, 1955) were popular with British R&B bands in the sixties, Snooky Pryor and **Little Walter**, whose début single 'I Just Keep Loving Her' (Ora Nelle, 1947) was another Williamson remake.

Sonny Boy Williamson II, remembered by many of his contemporaries as 'Rice' Miller, was equally influential, despite his singular style: a bleating sound, great rhythmic subtlety, sly half-spoken vocals and a predilection, especially in later years, for rambling autobiographical narratives.

By his own account he was already working as an itinerant musician before John Lee Williamson was born, but under what name is not known for certain. In the thirties he travelled widely as a one-man-band, later working fitfully with **Elmore James**, **Robert Johnson** and **Howlin' Wolf**. By the early forties, teamed with guitarist Robert Junior Lockwood and based in Helena, Arkansas, he was broadcasting on KFFA's *King Biscuit Time* and travelling around the Delta region with the sponsor's King Biscuit Entertainers, who included pianist Willie Love and drummer James 'Peck' Curtis. He worked with James again in the early fifties, also making his first recordings, for Trumpet (1951–4), among them the first of several versions of 'Eyesight to the Blind', 'Nine Below Zero' and the bizarre 'Mighty Long Time', accompanied only by harmonica and vocal bass. He also made periodic trips to Detroit, where he recorded as accompanist to singer-guitarist Baby Boy Warren, and Chicago, where he began an eight-year stay with Chess subsidiary Checker in 1955 ('Don't Start Me to Talkin''). Sides like those collected on *Down and Out Blues* (Chess, 1959) were part of the primer of British R&B, along with 'Help Me' (1963), which used an organ riff based on **Booker T. and the MGs**' 'Green Onions', and, from the same session, 'Bring It on Home' (1963).

He first visited Europe with the 1963 American Folk Blues Festival. In Denmark he recorded extraordinary free-form blues on two Storyville albums with guitarist Matt Murphy and **Memphis Slim**, while in England he made a Mercury set with the Yardbirds line-up that included **Eric Clapton**. He returned to Europe in the two following years, recording his final album, *Don't Send Me No Flowers* (Marmalade, 1965), with the British group **Brian Auger** and the Trinity. In 1991 the best of his fifties and early sixties output was collected on *The Chess Years*.

CHUCK WILLIS

b. 31 January 1928, Atlanta, Georgia, USA, d. 10 April 1958, Atlanta

Willis is best remembered for the sinuous 'C. C. Rider' (1957), raucously revived by **Mitch Ryder** as 'Jenny Take a Ride' (1967), and the simple but effective 'What Am I Living for'* (1956), which was later revived by **Wilbert Harrison** and **Solomon Burke**, among others. Willis's short career encapsulated the dramatic changes in black music during the fifties, and the decisive influence of Atlantic Records on those changes. He began as a blues balladeer and jump-blues singer and ended as a singer of rock'n'roll-inflected R&B material, pointing the way forward to soul.

After performing in talent shows in his teens, Willis graduated to singing with the bands of Ron Mays and Red McAllister in Atlanta in 1946, and in 1951 was signed to Columbia's subsidiary Okeh. A year later came his first hit record, the soft blues ballad 'My Story', coupled with a lively remake of **Louis Jordan**'s 'Caldonia' (1945) which showed the contrasting sides of Willis's vocal style. His cover of **Fats Domino**'s melancholic 'Going to the River' (1953) was another R&B hit, but more representative of the dark side of his balladry were his own 'Change My Mind' and 'I Don't Mind If I Do' (1954). Even better were his last hits for Okeh, the bluesy 'You're Still My Baby' and 'I Feel So Bad' (1954), later a hit for **Elvis Presley** (1961).

The forties, after-hours feel of Willis's work disappeared after he joined Atlantic in 1956. Apart from the intrusive vocal choirs on some songs (a failing of many Atlantic recordings of the period), the **Jesse Stone** arrangements were far more modern and less cluttered, even though in the main they were made with the same musicians, notably Sam 'the Man' Taylor on sax and **Mickey Baker** on guitar.

The intense, self-penned 'It's Too Late' (1956), affectingly recorded by **Buddy Holly** in 1957 and **Otis Redding** in 1966, gave Willis an R&B hit but his first pop hit came with an adaptation of **Ma Rainey**'s 1925 classic blues 'C. C. Rider' (1957). The song also gave Willis, previously known as 'The Sheik of the Blues', the tag 'King of the Stroll' when **Dick Clark** described the record as perfect for the new dance. Willis's follow-up, 'Betty and Dupree', was similarly fashioned from traditional materials (a folk song and the tune of **Robert Johnson**'s 'Four Till Late') but his last hit, 'Hang up My Rock and Roll Shoes' (1958), felicitously melded rhythm and blues and rock'n'roll. He died in hospital during treatment for a stomach complaint.

HAL WILLNER

b. 1957, Philadelphia, Pennsylvania, USA

Once described as a musical *provocateur*, Willner masterminded evocative and unusual tribute albums to figures as diverse as Walt Disney and **Charlie Mingus**. As such he is the father of the stream of tribute albums that have become a major feature of nineties rock.

A fan of modern jazz and **Frank Zappa**, Willner worked in the late seventies as musical supervisor of the American cult show *Saturday Night Live*. Using the contacts he had developed in New York's music world, he organized his first homage, *Amacord/Nino Rota* (1981), a selection of themes by the composer of the scores to Frederico Fellini's films. Among those who took part were **Wynton Marsalis**, Steve Lacy, **Carla Bley** and Deborah Harry of **Blondie**. *That's the Way I Feel Now* (1984) featured the work of jazz pianist **Thelonious Monk** as seen through the eyes of **Dr John**, **Gil Evans**, Bley and **Joe Jackson**, amongst others. Released on Jackson's label A&M it led to a close association between Willner and A&M. The company also underwrote *Lost in the Stars* (1985), which was devoted to the songs of **Kurt Weill**. The most highly acclaimed of Willner's productions, it included a magisterial version of 'September Song' from **Lou Reed**, **Sting** singing 'Mack the Knife' and sterling contributions from Bley, **Van Dyke Parks**, **Tom Waits**, **Marianne Faithfull** and others. In the late eighties Willner masterminded the innovative American television show *Night Music*, which followed his own albums in mixing classical, jazz, pop and almost anything else. One show featured **Conway Twitty** jamming with avant-garde group the Residents.

The most controversial of Willner's tribute albums was that devoted to Disney, *Stay Awake* (1988). A collection of versions of music from Disney's animated films, the project so alarmed the Disney studio that they refused permission for either Mickey Mouse or Donald Duck to be portrayed on the album's sleeve. Willner's cast for this included **Sun Ra**, **Suzanne Vega**, cult fifties torch singer Yma Sumac, Waits, **Harry Nilsson** and a coy **Ringo Starr** intoning 'When You Wish Upon a Star'. *Weird Nightmare* (1992) is the most ambitious Willner album to date. A tribute to Mingus, it interpolated between the music tracks extracts from Mingus' books read by a variety of figures, including Chuck D from rap group **Public Enemy**, novelist Hubert Selby and **Leonard Cohen**. The project also marked a change of direction for Willner. For the first time he used a house band, led by avant-garde guitarist Bill Frisell, for the entire project. Other members included **Elvis Costello** and **Rolling Stones** Keith Richards and Charlie Watts.

BOB WILLS

b. 6 March 1905, Limestone County, Texas, USA, d. 13 May 1975, Fort Worth, Texas

To some extent the inventor, and undoubtedly the chief propagator of Western swing, Bob Wills had, like **Bill Monroe** or **Muddy Waters**, a pivotal influence upon the course of American popular music. From a background of old-time fiddling and the ragtime-flavoured string-band music of the Southwest, he blended these strains with the jazz and blues that had fascinated him since his childhood – he would later claim that he was influenced by the songs of black workers alongside him in the cottonfields – and devised a hybrid country band music more instrumentally diverse, more omnivorous of repertoire, than anything that had gone before. Western swing became, like bluegrass, a musical dialect, a method of transforming material as wildly discrete as **Jimmie Rodgers** blues, Mexican polkas, New Orleans jazz tunes and honky-tonk weepers.

His father was an old-time fiddler, and Wills grew up in that tradition, though he was never more than a passable player. In the early thirties he worked with the Light Crust Doughboys, a string band sponsored by the Burrus Mill flour company; **Milton Brown** was the group's singer. They recorded together for Victor in 1932 as the Fort Worth Doughboys, where they were based, and broadcast on KFJZ. This first recording showed both men's interest in contemporary black music, 'Nancy Jane' being taken from the 1930 recording by the Famous Hokum Boys, a **Big Bill Broonzy** group.

Released by his sponsors in 1933, Wills worked briefly in Waco, Texas, then took a group, which he was to name the Texas Playboys, to Tulsa, Oklahoma, where they became the resident band at Cain's Dancing Academy and broadcast daily over KVOO. Soon they were on the road continuously throughout the Southwest. Signing in 1935 with Vocalion (which later became Okeh, then Columbia), they recorded over the next few years such enduring numbers as 'Maiden's Prayer', 'Steel Guitar Rag'/'Swing Blues No. 1', 'Silver Bells', 'That's What I Like 'Bout the South', 'Time Changes Everything' and the enormous 1940 hit 'New San Antonio Rose', which became their theme-song and was a huge pop hit for **Bing Crosby** (1941). Outstanding members of the early Playboys included steel-guitarist Leon McAuliffe (1917–88) (often called on by Wills in the famous words 'Take it away, Leon!'), pianist Al Stricklin, guitarist Eldon Shamblin and the expressive singer Tommy Duncan, who combined the bluesiness of Jimmie Rodgers with the warmth and romance of Bing Crosby.

During the Second World War Wills took the band to California, where they worked on a circuit of giant ballrooms round Los Angeles, playing for the munitions-factory and shipyard workers as they came off their round-the-clock shifts. Many of these were old Wills fans from the Southwest who had left in the Okie migration, and they quickly gave Wills massive personal and radio status on the West Coast. Now leading a band of fourteen or sixteen pieces, Wills was the premier Western swing leader, rivalled only – but closely – by **Spade Cooley**. As well as recording for Columbia, the Texas Playboys made a series of transcriptions for Tiffany (1945–7), designed for circulation to radio stations. Made in relaxed circumstances, these sides show the band at their best, bristling with adventurous musicians like fiddlers Louis Tierney and Joe Hoiley, steel players Herb Remington and Noel Boggs, guitarist Lester 'Junior' Barnard and electric mandolinist Tiny Moore.

After the war, in common with the big swing band-leaders, Wills had to economize, and his groups diminished as his drinking increased. His reputation ensured him more or less constant work in the Southwest, but he held on to few of his best musicians, some of whom broke away to build their own Western swing bands. He left Columbia in 1947 and recorded for MGM (1947–54), Decca (1955–7), Liberty (1960–3), Longhorn (1964–5) and Kapp (1965–9). In the early seventies he enjoyed the recognition accorded him by **Merle Haggard**, who made *A Tribute to the Best Damn Fiddle Player in the World (or, My Salute to Bob Wills)* (Capitol, 1970), **Waylon Jennings**, in his song 'Bob Wills Is Still the King', and, from a different direction, by the Western swing-loving rock'n'roll band **Commander Cody**'s Lost Planet Airmen. Another Western swing revivalist group, **Asleep at the Wheel**, organized a 1994 tribute album to Wills on Liberty. In 1973 Haggard organized a reunion recording session with many of the original Playboys, during which Wills suffered a stroke; he remained in a coma for eighteen months before his death. The record, *For the Last Time* (United Artists, 1974), was followed by a series of reissues of his earlier (chiefly Columbia) work that continued into the eighties. In the nineties an eight-volume series of radio recordings was issued under the generic title of *The Tiffany Transcriptions*.

Several of Wills' brothers worked with him and then led their own bands. Bass-players Luke and Billy Jack had fairly short careers as leaders, but banjoist Johnny Lee (*b. 1912, Limestone County, Texas, d. 25 October 1984, Tulsa, Oklahoma*) ran a series of good bands for many years. He recorded a highly influential version of 'Milk Cow Blues' (Decca, 1941), and had a hit with 'Rag Mop' (Bullet, 1949), covered for the pop market by the **Ames Brothers**. He was active into the early eighties, leading one of the two ex-Playboys line-ups that were carrying on in the Wills tradition and recording for Flying Fish (*Reunion*, 1978) and Delta (*Dance All Night*, 1980). The other veterans' band, which retained the Playboys' name and was headed by Leon McAuliffe, continued to work on the Western swing circuit in the late eighties.

DOOLEY WILSON

*b. Arthur Wilson, 3 April 1894, Tyler, Texas, USA,
d. 30 May 1953, Los Angeles, California*

Wilson is best remembered for his appearance as Sam in Michael Curtiz's *Casablanca* (1942), in which he sang (among other numbers) the Herman Hupfeld composition 'As Time Goes by'.

A teenage minstrel performer, Wilson graduated to vaudeville and the stage. While a member of the Illinois Pekin Stock Company he changed his first name to Dooley in honour of 'Mr Dooley', an Irish song he performed to much acclaim with an Irish brogue and in whiteface. He then took up jazz drumming, formed the Red Devils and toured Europe in the twenties, before returning to America in 1930, where he appeared in Orson Welles' and John Houseman's Federal Theater production of the all-black musical *Cabin in the Sky* as Little Joe. On the strength of this he travelled to Hollywood and a succession of 'pullman porter' parts before securing the role of Sam. His performance as the bar pianist perfectly mixed pixie-like vivacity and weariness, while his rendition of 'As Time Goes by' (for which the piano was dubbed by Elliot Carpenter) was a perfect blend of sentimentality and pragmatism in the manner of **Hoagy Carmichael**. The potency of Wilson's performance (and its, often misquoted, introduction, 'Play it Sam . . . play "As Time Goes by"') was demonstrated in 1977 when a soundtrack recording of it reached the British Top Twenty. However, *Casablanca* did little for Wilson's career as either a singer or actor and, after supporting roles in various minor films, he faded into obscurity.

JACKIE WILSON

b. 9 March 1934, Detroit, Michigan, USA, d. 21 January 1984, New Jersey

A pioneer R&B showman, Wilson possessed one of the genre's most stratospheric and influential voices. His style drew on both the blues of **Roy Brown** and **Clyde McPhatter**'s R&B but it transcended them. Whether he sang hard-core blues, semi-operatic ballads or Tin Pan Alley schmaltz, Wilson held his audiences until the seventies. His career was cut short by serious illness in 1975.

As a teenager Wilson was a boxing champion but he also grew up among such aspirant singers as **Little Willie John** and Levi Stubbs (later of the **Four Tops**). His first models were **Al Jolson** and Roy Brown and in 1951 he was discovered at a talent show by **Johnny Otis**. Two years later Wilson replaced McPhatter as lead singer of the Dominoes.

During his four years with the group Wilson sang lead on such R&B hits as 'Have Mercy Baby' (Federal, 1952) and the soaring 'Rags to Riches' (1955). In 1957

Al Green, former manager of **Johnny Ray** and **Lavern Baker**, secured Wilson a solo contract with Brunswick, where **Berry Gordy** composed the exhilarating 'Reet Petite' (1957), a Top Ten hit in Britain. Gordy and Wilson followed this with the lavishly arranged ballads 'To Be Loved' (1958) and Wilson's first American Top Ten hit 'Lonely Teardrops', originally written for Roy Brown.

When Green died in 1958 his assistant Nat Tarnopol directed Wilson towards the lucrative cabaret market with such semi-operatic songs as 'Night' (1960), based on Saint-Saëns' 'Samson and Delilah', the Top Ten hit 'Alone at Last', taken from a theme by Tchaikovsky, and 'My Empty Arms' (1961), a version of Leoncavallo's 'On with the Motley' from *I Pagliacci*. However, he also reached the Top Twenty in 1960 with the blues ballads 'Doggin' Around' and 'A Woman, a Lover, a Friend'. This was Wilson's most successful period when he broke box-office records all over America, was criticized by the middle-class black press for his suggestive stage act, and in 1961 was shot by a besotted fan in a New York hotel lobby.

After 'Baby Workout' (1962), a curious big-band hybrid, Wilson's sales declined with the rise of new soul stars and the separation of the black from the white pop market. Such records as 'Squeeze Her – Tease Her' (1964) and 'Danny Boy' (1965) were unsuccessful and it was not until Tarnopol (later president of Brunswick) brought in Chicago producer Carl Davis that Wilson regained his popularity. 'Whispers' (1966) and the exuberant '(Your Love Keeps Lifting Me) Higher and Higher' (1967) were major pop hits. The latter charted belatedly in Britain in 1969 and again in 1975.

Other successes of the Chicago period included 'Since You Showed Me How to Be Happy' (1967) and **Van McCoy**'s 'I Get the Sweetest Feeling' (1968). Later releases failed to find a significant audience, however, and Wilson's career went into rapid decline. By the mid-seventies he was reduced to appearances on **Dick Clark**'s oldies package shows and in 1975 he collapsed on stage in Camden, New Jersey, of a stroke which caused massive brain damage and left him virtually comatose until his death.

Britain had a brief Wilson revival in 1986–7 when 'Reet Petite' reached No. 1 and 'I Get the Sweetest Feeling' was a Top Ten hit.

TEDDY WILSON

b. Theodore Wilson, 24 November 1912, Austin, Texas, USA, d. 31 July 1986, New Britain, Connecticut

A key figure in the formation of the sophisticated, economical mainstream-jazz piano style, Wilson was a masterly accompanist of several major singers. He played a key role in breaking down segregation in jazz when he joined **Benny Goodman**'s previously all-white organization in 1936.

The child of middle-class parents, he majored in music at Talladega College, Alabama, and played with various bands in Detroit and Chicago before making his first records accompanying **Louis Armstrong** in 1933. That year **John Hammond** recorded him with Benny Carter and went on to place him with Goodman and **Billie Holiday** for many fine recordings during the thirties, beginning with 'What a Little Moonlight Can Do' (Brunswick, 1935). He also worked with **Mildred Bailey** and **Ella Fitzgerald** ('Melancholy Baby', 1936) at this time, as well as cutting solo sides for Brunswick.

From 1936 to 1939 Wilson was a member of Goodman's quartet, but left to form an orchestra and then a sextet of his own before rejoining Goodman from 1944 to 1946. After that, he combined work for the CBS radio network with frequent recording dates and solo tours of Europe. In 1962 he performed in Moscow with Goodman. He appeared (as himself) in the 1955 biopic *The Benny Goodman Story*.

Although he recorded in 1945 with **Dizzy Gillespie** and **Charlie Parker**, Wilson was unmoved by bebop. His style was based on the less energetic playing of **Earl Hines** and **Art Tatum**, to which he added an elegance which, though neat, never strayed into the realms of cocktail-lounge piano. Among his last recordings were two impressive tribute albums: *Striding after Fats* (for **Fats Waller**) and *With Billie in Mind*.

ANGELA WINBUSH
b. St Louis, Missouri, USA

Although black music has numerous female singing stars, there are few women writing and producing in the idiom. Winbush is among the most well established of these, equally accomplished as a singer, writer, instrumentalist, arranger and producer.

After studying music at Howard University in Washington DC, Winbush quickly established herself as a vocalist and songwriter. With a four-octave range she was part of **Stevie Wonder**'s backing group Wonderlove by the end of the seventies and she sang on recording sessions for **Dolly Parton** and others. Parton, Lenny Williams and Alton McClain were among the first to record her songs.

From 1980 until 1986 she worked with Rene Moore as Rene and Angela. Together they wrote and recorded three albums for Capitol and one for PolyGram. The latter, *Street Called Desire*, included the R&B hits 'Save Your Love (For No. 1)', 'Your Smile' and 'No How, No Way'. Moore and Winbush also produced tracks for **Janet Jackson**'s début album, Odyssey and Evelyn 'Champagne' King.

Amid recriminations and a lawsuit, Rene and Angela split up in 1987. As a solo singer, Winbush recorded *Sharp* (1987) and *Real Thing* (1989), which included 'Lay Your Troubles Down', a duet with Ronald Isley (of the **Isley Brothers**), whom she later married. Winbush moved to Elektra in 1993 to record *Angela Winbush*. Contributors to the album included George Duke (piano), Ernie Isley (guitar) and arranger **Thom Bell**.

Among artists to have recorded Winbush songs are Lalah Hathaway, Stephanie Mills, **Sheena Easton** and the Isley Brothers.

JESSE WINCHESTER
b. James R. Winchester, 17 May 1944, Shreveport, Louisiana, USA

Winchester's best work was recorded in Canada, where he settled to avoid the draft, and detailed his longing for the South in a series of sharply etched, elegiac songs, many of which were later recorded by such folk-orientated performers as **Ian Matthews**, **Joan Baez** and **Tim Hardin**. Among them were 'Biloxi', 'Brand New Tennessee Waltz', 'Yankee Lady', 'Midnight Bus', 'Mississippi, You're on My Mind' (which was given a further ironic twist when it was a hit for black country singer Stoney Edwards, Capitol, 1975) and 'Defying Gravity'.

The son of a pacifist air-force captain, Winchester was raised in Memphis and played in rock'n'roll bands in his youth. While studying in Germany, he received his draft notice and in 1967 settled in Canada, playing in local groups until meeting Robbie Robertson of **The Band**, who secured him a recording contract with Ampex. His eponymous Robertson-produced début album (1971) won huge critical acclaim for the passion, notwithstanding the singer's low-key performance, which Winchester articulated. However, it and the **Todd Rundgren** co-produced *3rd Down, 110 to Go* (Bearsville, 1972) sold poorly.

More successful was *Learn to Love It* (1974) which saw Winchester singing in French ('L'Air de la Louisiane') and dealing with his opposition to the Vietnam war ('Pharoah's Army'). On the album Winchester was supported by noted session guitarist Amos Garrett and members of the Russell Smith- and Barry Burton-led group, the **Amazing Rhythm Aces**. He recorded a pair of Smith's songs, the wry tale of willing seduction 'Third Rate Romance' and the enigmatic 'The End Is Not in Sight'. The group's own recording of 'Romance' gave them their only major hit (ABC, 1975) and led to a series of similarly low-key albums, including *Stacked Deck* (1975) and *Too Stuffed to Jump* (1976), which melded country, blues and rock to superior effect.

Winchester became a Canadian citizen in 1973, but

toured America in support of *Let the Rough Side Drag*
(1976) after President Carter's 1977 amnesty for draft
evaders. *Nothin' but a Breeze* (1977) and *A Touch on
the Rainy Side* (1978) saw Winchester performing
mostly story- and love songs that lacked the wit and
passion of his earlier work, while *Talk Memphis*
(1981), produced by **Willie Mitchell**, featured a harder
sound than before and provided his only hit single,
'Say What'. *Humour Me* (1988) was a lesser album. It
was overshadowed by the anthology *The Best of Jesse
Winchester* (Rhino, 1989), which collected together
the best of his Bearsville recordings.

JOHNNY WINTER

*b. John Dawson Winter III, 23 February 1944, Leland,
Mississippi, USA*

An outstanding white blues guitarist, Winter and his
brother Edgar (*b. 28 December 1946, Beaumont, Texas,
USA*) enjoyed fame as progressive rock stars in the
early seventies. He later returned to his blues roots,
recording and touring with **Muddy Waters** and other
R&B musicians.

From a musical family, the brothers were raised in
Beaumont, Texas, and played soul, rock and blues in
such Texas bands as Johnny and the Jammers
(recording 'Schoolday Blues', Dart, 1959), Gene Terry
and the Downbeats, It and Them, and Black Plague.
After travelling to Chicago in 1962, where he played
with **Mike Bloomfield**, Johnny returned to Texas
where he recorded for local labels. In 1968 he formed
a blues trio with Tommy Shannon (bass) and drummer Red Turner.

A *Rolling Stone* article on the band, which stressed
the albino Winter's outlandish appearance, led New
York club-owner Steve Paul to become Winter's manager. Clive Davis signed the guitarist to Columbia for
a $300,000 advance and his début album for the label
contained such blues standards as **Sonny Boy
Williamson**'s 'Good Morning Little Schoolgirl' and
Elmore James' 'Mean Mistreater'. Its success led Liberty to release *The Progressive Blues Experiment*, an
early Winter demo tape. Other early recordings made
for Texas labels were reissued by Janus as *About Blues*
(1971) and *Before the Storm*.

The three-sided double-album *Second Winter* was
more rock-orientated and included a version of **Bob
Dylan**'s 'Highway 61 Revisited'. In 1971 Winter re-
formed his group with Rick Derringer (guitar) and
former **McCoys**, Randy Hobbs (bass) and Randy
Zehringer (drums). After releasing *And* and *And Live*
(1971), Winter's drug problems forced him into retirement until 1973 when he returned with *Still Alive and
Well*. This was followed by *Saints and Sinners* (1974)
and *John Dawson Winter III*, issued through Paul's
Blue Sky label.

Leading his own band, White Trash, on saxophone
and keyboards, Edgar Winter (*b. 28 December 1946,
Beaumont, Texas*) had hits with the No. 1 'Frankenstein'* (Epic, 1973), from *They Only Come out at
Night*, and 'Free Ride'. His group included bassist and
singer Dan Hartman, who later had solo hits with
'Instant Replay'* (Blue Sky, 1978) and the film theme
'I Can Dream about You' (MCA, 1984). Hartman
went on to enjoy a successful career as a soul/dance
writer and producer, working with **James Brown** and
the **Average White Band**, but died in 1994 from an
Aids-related illness. In 1976 Edgar rejoined his brother
to re-create their Texas R&B sound on *Together*. He
later released *Recycled* (1977), *The Edgar Winter
Album* and *Standing on Rock* (1981) before concentrating on session work for the rest of the eighties. In the
early nineties he enjoyed success providing songs for
films, and in 1994 released *I'm Not a Kid Anymore*
(L+R), which included a remake of 'Frankenstein'.

Waters joined Johnny Winter for *Nothin' but the
Blues* (1977) and the veteran Chicago bluesman subsequently signed to Blue Sky, with Winter producing
and playing lead guitar on several of his albums. Winter later moved to Bruce Iglauer's Chicago-based Alligator label, releasing *Guitar Slinger* (1984). *Serious
Business* (1985) was followed by *Third Degree* (1986),
on which he was accompanied by **Dr John** as well as
his original rhythm section, Shannon and Turner.
Winter of '88 (1988) was recorded for MCA's Voyager
label. He followed it with *Let Me in* (1991) and *Hey,
Where's Your Brother?* (1992). The answer to that
question was provided that same year, when the Winters appeared together at a Connecticut club. They
subsequently toured in 1993. Both also recorded separately, Edgar releasing *Winter Blues* (Eagle, 1999) and
Johnny a pair of live albums, *Live at the Dallas International Motor Speedway* (Magnum, 1994) and *Live in
NYC '97* (Pointblank).

HUGO WINTERHALTER

*b. 15 August 1909, Wilkes-Barre, Pennsylvania, USA,
d. 17 September 1973, New York*

As musical director of RCA as well as an orchestra
leader, Winterhalter was an important force in fifties
pop, arranging and conducting his string-laden
orchestra behind **Eddy Arnold**, **Kay Starr**, **Perry
Como**, the **Ames Brothers** and, most successfully of
all, **Eddie Fisher**.

Winterhalter studied violin as a child, switching to
saxophone while at college, where he led the campus
orchestra. On graduation he worked as a music
teacher, before moving to New York where he played
with various bands, including those of Larry Clinton
and Will Bradley. In 1944 he became an arranger for
Tommy Dorsey and throughout the forties worked in

that capacity for **Vaughn Monroe**, **Billy Eckstine**, **Jimmy Dorsey** and, briefly, **Count Basie**. In the same period he also arranged for MGM and Columbia Records, the label on which he made his recording début ('Jealous Heart', 1949).

Within a year, Winterhalter moved to RCA as musical director, supervising the career of the label's mainstream popular singers. Though not as strong-minded a producer as **Mitch Miller**, for example, Winterhalter also sought mostly hard-edged singers, rather than the softer balladeers who had dominated in the forties. Among the numerous hits he arranged and for which he provided orchestral backing were 'Tell Me Why'*, 'I'm Walking Behind You'* (Fisher, 1952, 1953), 'Naughty Lady of Shady Lane'* (the Ames Brothers, 1954), 'Wanted'* (Como, 1954), 'Cattle Call'* (Arnold, 1955) and 'Rock and Roll Waltz'* (Starr, 1956).

Winterhalter also had a series of hits in his own right. These ranged from film themes (a cover of **Anton Karas**' 'Theme from the Third Man', 1950, 'Across the Wide Missouri', 1951), to pop songs ('I Need You So', 1950, which featured **Don Cornell** on vocals) and instrumentals. It was one of these, a boogie-inflected version of 'Canadian Sunset' (1956) with Eddie Heywood (who had previously played with **Billie Holiday**) on piano, that gave Winterhalter his only million-seller, despite a cover-version by **Andy Williams**.

Winterhalter continued to record throughout the fifties and in the sixties turned to arranging music for Broadway and television.

STEVE WINWOOD
b. Stephen Philip Winwood, 12 May 1948, Birmingham, England

Possessor of one of the most expressive white soul voices, Winwood was successively the vocalist with the Spencer Davis Group, Traffic and Blind Faith. In the eighties he enjoyed renewed success as a solo performer.

In 1962 he was pianist with the Muff Woody Jazz Band, led by his brother Muff (*b. Mervyn Winwood, 15 June 1945, Birmingham*). With drummer Pete York (*b. 15 August 1942, Birmingham*) and guitarist and singer with another trad band Spencer Davis (*b. 11 July 1942, Swansea, Wales*), the Winwoods next formed the Rhythm and Blues Quartet, performing material by such artists as **John Lee Hooker** and **Ray Charles**.

Re-named the Spencer Davis Group, they were signed by **Chris Blackwell**, who placed them with Fontana and produced cover-versions of Hooker's 'Dimples', the Soul Sisters' 'I Can't Stand It' and the minor hit 'Every Little Bit Hurts', a cover of Brenda

Holloway's American hit written by Ed Cobb, formerly of the **Four Preps**.

The group's first big success came in 1966 with a reworking of reggae singer **Jackie Edwards**' 'Keep on Running' and 'Somebody Help Me'. Featuring Winwood's powerful, plaintive lead vocals and a tightly controlled, urgent sound, both reached No. 1. Winwood himself composed the American hits 'Gimme Some Loving' (1967) and 'I'm a Man'. Co-written with producer Jimmy Miller, the latter was successfully covered by **Chicago** in 1971.

Winwood recorded three albums with the Spencer Davis Group, including *Autumn 66* on which his interpretations of **Percy Sledge**'s 'When a Man Loves a Woman' and the standard 'Nobody Knows You When You're Down and Out' confirmed his place as the creative centre of the band. Soon afterwards he left the group to form progressive rock band Traffic. Muff Winwood also moved on, to Island Records' A&R department, eventually heading the A&R team of British Columbia in 1980, and later setting up the Sony subsidiary label, Soho Square. Davis continued with the group before going solo with *It's Been So Long* (United Artists, 1971).

Traffic included drummer Jim Capaldi (*b. 24 August 1944, Evesham, Worcestershire*), guitarist Dave Mason (*b. 10 May 1947, Worcester*) from Deep Feeling and ex-Locomotive flautist Chris Wood (*b. 24 June 1944, Birmingham, d. 12 July 1983, London*). They created a highly eclectic mix of folk, rock, blues and jazz on *Mr Fantasy* (Island, 1967) and the hits 'Paper Sun' and 'Hole in My Shoe', which, with the **Small Faces**' 'Itchycoo Park', were the epitome of British psychedelia. Equally significant was the band's decision to retreat to a cottage in the country in order to prepare the album, a practice which soon became commonplace. Traffic's title theme for the film *Here We Go Round the Mulberry Bush* (1968) also reached the British Top Ten.

Mason left for a solo career after the recording of *Traffic* (1968), which including his classic composition 'Feelin' Alright', later a hit for **Joe Cocker**. *Last Exit* (1969) was released after Winwood had broken up the group to join the shortlived 'supergroup' Blind Faith with **Eric Clapton** and Ginger Baker. By 1970, however, Wood, Capaldi and Winwood had regrouped and kept Traffic going until 1975 with a succession of backing musicians. The six albums from this second phase of the band's existence included *John Barleycorn Must Die* (1970), with its haunting version of the traditional folk title song, *Welcome to the Canteen* (1972), for which Mason rejoined Traffic, and *When the Eagle Flies* (1974), which featured Winwood's keyboard-playing.

After the dissolution of Traffic, each member followed a solo career. Capaldi made a series of albums for Island which included *Short Cut Draw Blood* (1975), which provided a hit in a version of **Boudleaux Bryant**'s 'Love Hurts'. The most successful of the members of the band, though, was Winwood.

During the mid-seventies he recorded with Japanese composer and multi-instrumentalist Stomu Yamashta (*Go*, 1976) and the New York salsa band Fania All Stars (*Delicate and Jumpy*, 1976). He recorded an eponymous solo album in 1977 with Capaldi contributing lyrics but had no commercial success until the synthesizer-dominated *Arc of a Diver* (1981) reached the American Top Ten. The **Bonzo Dog Band**'s Viv Stanshall wrote the lyrics for the title track while Will Jennings (co-author of 'Somewhere in the Night', a hit in 1976 for **Helen Reddy** and in 1979 for **Barry Manilow**, and of the **Crusaders**' 'Street Life', 1979, and 'One Day I'll Fly Away', 1981) collaborated on the Top Ten hit 'While You See a Chance'.

Jennings also co-wrote *Talking Back to the Night* (1982) with Winwood, while *Back in the Highlife* (1986) was the most successful of his solo albums, with **Chaka Khan** duetting on the transatlantic hit 'Higher Love'. In 1987 Winwood moved to Virgin, releasing 'Roll with It' (1988), the hit title track from his fifth solo album. Maintaining his laid-back schedule, Winwood released the follow-up, *Refugees of the Heart*, over two years later. Another American Top Thirty album, it included a track co-written with Capaldi, and the duo went on to resurrect the Traffic name and form a new band for 1994's *Far from Home* (Virgin). This Traffic line-up performed at Woodstock '94.

The Finer Things (1995) was a four-CD career retrospective of Winwood's days at Island. It was followed by the **Narada Michael Walden**-produced *Junction Seven* (1997), which Winwood toured in support of.

MAC WISEMAN

b. 23 May 1925, Crimora, Virginia, USA

With his warm, soft-edged voice Mac Wiseman could have concentrated on a career as a mainstream country singer. However, his own tastes repeatedly drew him back to the styles of his youth, old-time singing and bluegrass.

In the mid-forties he worked as a deejay on WSVA, Harrisburg, Virginia, and sang and played guitar with local groups. In 1946–7 he worked with **Molly O'Day**, singing and playing bass. He went on to host the WCYB *Farm and Fun Time* in Bristol, Virginia, where he met **Flatt and Scruggs**, who had recently left **Bill Monroe**. He was a charter member in 1948 of their Foggy Mountain Boys, but left at the beginning of 1949 to work on the WSB, Atlanta, Georgia *Barn Dance*. A few months later he joined Monroe, and sang lead on his recording of 'Can't You Hear Me Callin'' (Columbia).

In 1951, now working on the *Louisiana Hayride*, Wiseman started a recording career in his own name on Dot, and over the next few years had hits with 'Shackles and Chains', ''Tis Sweet to Be Remembered', 'Ballad of Davy Crockett',·'Love Letters in the Sand' (a pop hit for **Pat Boone**), and his greatest success, 'Jimmy Brown the Newsboy'. In 1953 he joined the WRVA, Richmond, Virginia, *Old Dominion Barn Dance*. He was Dot's country A&R manager from 1957 to 1961, but returned to recording for Capitol (1961–6), then Dot for a short time before joining RCA in 1969. He had become a regular attraction at bluegrass festivals but his appeal was broad enough to earn him a place at mainstream events like the annual British country music festival at Wembley, where he first appeared in 1973. In the early seventies he cut several albums for RCA, three of them with Lester Flatt.

During the seventies he played frequently on the US college circuit, finding there a new audience for the old folk songs he had always preferred. Signing in the late seventies to the specialist bluegrass label CMH he cut new versions of his now celebrated Dot recordings on *The Mac Wiseman Story* (1976). He also made an album of forties and fifties country hits with Western swing accompaniments, *Songs that Made the Jukebox Play* (1974), and *Mac Wiseman Sings Gordon Lightfoot* (1974), among others. In 1986 he returned to Dot (now owned by MCA) for *Once More with Feeling*. In 1992 he narrated the documentary about bluegrass *High Lonesome* and in 1988 recorded *Mac, and Del* (Groove Grass) in tandem with **Doc Watson** and Del McCoury.

WISHBONE ASH

Andy Powell, b. 8 February 1950; Martin Turner, b. 1 October 1947, Torquay, Devon, England (replaced by Trevor Bolder); Ted Turner, b. David Alan Turner, 2 August 1950 (replaced by Laurie Wisefield); Steve Upton, b. 24 May 1946, Wrexham, Wales

Featuring the twin lead guitars of Powell and Ted Turner, Wishbone Ash were one of the most musically ambitious British rock bands of the mid-seventies.

Drummer Upton had played with the Scimitars and other local groups before joining Martin Turner (bass) and Glen Turner (guitar) in the Empty Vessels in 1966 in the Devon resort town of Torquay. As Tanglewood, the trio moved to London, but Glen Turner left soon afterwards. Now handled by Miles Copeland, future manager of the **Police** and Curved Air, they recruited Ted Turner from Birmingham blues band King Biscuit, and Powell from soul group the Sugarband. Wishbone Ash was designed on the model of the **Allman Brothers Band** or the Jimmy Page/**Jeff Beck** version of the **Yardbirds**, with duetting lead guitarists.

The group built up a following on the college circuit, recording an eponymous début album for MCA in 1970. Ted Turner played on **John Lennon**'s *Imagine* before Wishbone Ash released *Pilgrimage* (1972), which included Jack McDuff's 'Vas Dis'. *Argus* (1973), which, like the earlier records, was produced by Derek Lawrence, was their biggest-selling and most representative album. It mixed historical themes ('Warrior', 'The King Will Come') with bravura instrumental passages.

Ted Turner left the group after *Wishbone 4* (1973), to be replaced by Wisefield from Home, a rock band which recorded three albums for Columbia in 1970–3. Later albums were recorded in America where the group played the burgeoning stadium circuit, and included *There's the Rub* (1974), produced in Miami by Bill Szymczyk, and *Locked in* (1976), with **Tom Dowd** supervising.

Wishbone Ash continued to record annual albums into the eighties, despite the departure of Martin Turner in 1980 and the addition of vocalist Claire Hammill, who later became a leading figure in British New Age music. After *Two Barrels Burning* (AVM, 1982), the group disbanded.

The original quartet re-formed in 1987 to cut the instrumental *Nouveau Calls* for Copeland's No Speak label, and they continued to perform into the nineties, largely playing their early seventies back catalogue. *Illuminations* (1996) was their first album of new material for several years. It was followed by *Trance Visionary* (1997), which saw the group foregoing the verities of twin-guitar-styled rock and embracing dance music, and in 2000 by *Psychic Terrorism* (Ration), which continued in the same vein, even to the extent of including a bonus album of remixes.

The four-CD set *Distillation* (1997) is the definitive anthology.

BILL WITHERS

b. 4 July 1938, Slab Fork, West Virginia, USA

A black singer-songwriter (rather than soul singer), Withers is best remembered for 'Lean on Me'* and 'Use Me'.

He was discovered by Clarance Avant fitting toilets into 747 planes in Los Angeles and signed to his Sussex label in 1971. His début album, *Just as I Am*, was produced by **Booker T.** and included MGs Duck Dunn and Al Jackson in the rhythm section. The album featured 'Ain't No Sunshine' (a British hit for **Michael Jackson** in 1972) and 'Grandma's Hands' (one of the finest evocations of the matriarchal aspects of black American society) and proved Withers to be a songwriter of immense talent. His second album, *Still Bill* (1972), included the oft-recorded

'Lean on Me' and 'Use Me'. After further albums for Sussex, he signed to Columbia in 1975, recording some six albums, without particular success. His biggest hit for the label was 'Lovely Day' (1978). His only later successes were as guest vocalist on others' records: the **Crusaders**' 'Soul Shadows' (1980) and **Grover Washington Jnr**'s 'Just the Two of Us' (1981). In 1985 he released *Watching You Watching Me*, and a version of 'Lean on Me' by dance act Club Nouveau reached the British Top Five in 1987. In 1988 a remix of 'Lovely Day' by Dutch deejay Ben Liebrand reached the British Top Ten, and, in 1992, Withers re-signed with Atlantic Records.

Lean on Me (1995) is a patchy greatest hits album.

JIMMY WITHERSPOON

b. 8 August 1923, Gurdon, Arkansas, USA, d. 18 September 1997, Los Angeles, California

Like **Joe Turner**, Witherspoon sang blues not only in jazz settings but with jazz conceptions of time, dynamics and phrasing. Unlike Turner he was not unremittingly loyal to the blues, and in the seventies experimented with new repertoires, though his finest work drew either its form or its feeling from the blues. Initially influenced by Turner, **Jimmy Rushing** and **Big Bill Broonzy**, he sweetened their flavour with a smooth and wheedling delivery.

While on wartime service he sang with the band led by emigré jazz pianist Teddy Weatherford in Calcutta. In 1944 he replaced singer Walter Brown in the **Jay McShann** band, recording with them, over the next four years, for Philo/Aladdin, Mercury, Supreme and Down Beat/Swing Time; he also recorded with other accompanists on Modern (1947–51). 'Tain't Nobody's Business' (Supreme) was a substantial 1949 hit, remaining on the *Billboard* R&B chart for more than thirty weeks.

After leaving McShann he worked across the United States in his own name. He appeared at some of Gene Norman's 'Just Jazz' concerts in Pasadena, California, recording 'No Rollin' Blues', another hit. In 1952 he signed with the King subsidiary Federal. By 1956 he was working with the New Orleans jazz band led by Wilbur and Sidney de Paris, and in the following year he was reunited on RCA Victor with McShann and also recorded for that label with the **Jesse Stone** band. His sluggish career progress was revitalized by a magnificent performance at the 1959 Monterey Jazz Festival, among jazz company like **Earl Hines**, **Coleman Hawkins** and **Ben Webster**, and Webster was also on hand, with **Gerry Mulligan**, for an appearance later that year at the Renaissance Club in Hollywood; both occasions were memorably caught on albums for HiFi Jazz.

During the sixties 'Spoon' (as he had come to be

known) continued to work under jazz leaders like Webster, trumpeter Buck Clayton and **Count Basie**, often touring outside the US and recording prolifically for Prestige. *Handbags and Gladrags* (ABC, 1971), with Joe Walsh, showed him updating his repertoire, and in the same year he collaborated with Eric Burdon of the **Animals** at festivals and on *Guilty!* (United Artists). He was also teamed with jazz organists Brother Jack McDuff (*The Blues Is Now*, Verve, 1968) and Richard 'Groove' Holmes (*Groovin' and Spoonin'*, Olympic, 1974). Over the next fifteen years he maintained his rank as a leading jazz-blues singer by festival and nightclub appearances, overseas tours and numerous albums, often recorded in Europe, like the 1984 set with drummer Panama Francis and the re-created Savoy Sultans (Black and Blue). He was troubled by ill-health in the mid-eighties but showed an undiminished appetite for singing on *Midnight Lady Called the Blues* (Muse, 1986), a set written and produced by **Dr John** and Doc Pomus of the **Pomus and Shuman** writing team. A burst of activity in the early nineties saw him release *Call Me Baby* (1991), *Live at the Norodden Blues Festival* with guitarist Robben Ford and the excellent *The Blues, the Whole Blues and Nothin' but the Blues* (1992), the first release on Indigo, the new label formed by long-term admirer **Mike Vernon**. Even better was *Blowin' in from Kansas City* (Capitol, 1993).

Spoon So Easy (MCA, 1990) documents his Chess years, *Jay's Blues* (Charly, 1996) his stay with Federal.

P. G. WODEHOUSE
b. Pelham Grenville Wodehouse, b. 15 October 1881, Guildford, Surrey, England, d. 14 February 1975, Long Island, New York, USA

With Evelyn Waugh, Wodehouse was the leading British comic novelist of the 20th century. As such he is best remembered these days for his chronicles of the Blandings estate and its pig-loving Lord Emsworth and the precisely, comically plotted escapades of Bertram Wooster, the perpetual innocent and archetypal 'silly ass', who is steered clear of scheming aunts and swooning young women by his unflappable manservant Jeeves. These novels (and stories) are set in a seemingly timeless Edwardian world, in which baby talk and classical allusions supplant all notions of reality.

Wodehouse's contribution to the American musical is markedly different. As critic Mark Steyn put it, 'Had Wodehouse died in 1918, he would have been remembered not as a British novelist but as the first great lyricist of the American musical.' Moreover, his stage work was revolutionary. In place of the artifice of the operetta as constructed by the likes of **Rudolf Friml**, **Franz Lehar** and **Sigmund Romberg**, Wodehouse as a lyricist brought a naturalism to a field where it was hitherto unknown. As such he was the forerunner of **Lorenz Hart**, **Ira Gershwin** and all those who sought to ground the American musical in reality.

Educated at Dulwich College, Wodehouse worked briefly in a London bank before becoming a freelance writer. At first closely associated with the London *Globe*, he achieved immediate success with a variety of characters, including Psmith and Jeeves (who first appeared in 1919). From 1904 he travelled regularly to the US, where he settled in 1914 – he was declared unfit for service during WWI. He continued writing novels and also worked as a drama critic for *Vanity Fair*. After meeting **Jerome Kern** in 1915, with fellow émigré Guy Bolton, Wodehouse provided libretto and lyrics (mostly) for Kern for over ten years. His most enduring lyric is that for 'Bill', which was written for *Oh Lady! Lady!!* (1918) but dropped before the show opened and later revived with slightly rewritten lyrics for the groundbreaking *Show Boat* (1927). It has a conversational quality – 'I love him/Because he's – I don't know/Because he's just/My Bill' – that is aeons away from the world of operetta. Indeed, all his best songs, to quote Steyn again, 'gave ordinary folks a plausible singing voice on the American stage'. Many of the shows, which include *Oh Boy!*, *Leave It to Jane* (both 1917), *The Cabaret Girl* (1922), *Sitting Pretty* (1924) and *Oh Kay!* (1926), are also notable for integrating song into the fabric of the musical. Among Wodehouse's best songs are 'Till the Clouds Roll By', 'The Sirens Song' and 'March of the Musketeers'.

When Wodehouse moved to France in 1934 he severed his ties with Broadway. When interned after the German invasion of France, Wodehouse unwisely made a series of broadcasts for the Germans, which led to him being called a traitor. Accordingly, after the war he settled again in the US. He was knighted just weeks before his death.

Bolton and Wodehouse's *Bring on the Girls!: The Improbable Story of Our Life in Musical Comedy with Pictures to Prove It* (1953) is an affectionate look back at that period.

BOBBY WOMACK
b. 4 March 1944, Cleveland, Ohio, USA

Although recognition came late, as both a writer and singer Womack was an important and catalytic influence on the development of black music in the seventies and eighties. He absorbed gospel music from his father and soul from **Sam Cooke** before becoming one of the first contemporary black artists to make an impact on British rock when the **Rolling Stones** recorded his 'It's All Over Now' in 1964.

Womack's father, Friendly Womack, organized his

sons into the Womack Brothers Gospel Quartet until Cooke's move into secular music prompted them to follow suit and become the Valentinos. For Cooke's Sar label they cut the Bobby Womack compositions 'Looking for a Love' (1962) and 'It's All Over Now' (1964), later covered by the **J. Geils Band** (1972) and the Stones, respectively.

After Cooke's death in 1965, Womack incurred widespread disapproval by marrying the singer's widow. He embarked on a songwriting career, providing material for **Wilson Pickett** ('People Make the World' and 'I'm a Midnight Mover'). After making the unsuccessful 'Trust Me' for Atlantic, Womack moved to Keyman and Minit where he had minor pop hits with versions of 'Fly Me to the Moon' and **The Mamas and the Papas**' 'California Dreamin'' (1968). He also worked on sessions for **Janis Joplin** and on **Sly Stone**'s *There's a Riot Goin' on* (1971).

When Minit was purchased by United Artists, Womack, now based with **Rick Hall** at Muscle Shoals, was given artistic freedom to develop his own version of black rock on *Communication* (1971) and *Understanding* (1972). 'That's the Way I Feel About 'Cha'' (1971) was a pop hit, and his R&B Top Ten entries included the No. 1 'Woman's Got to Have It' and Jim Ford's 'Harry Hippie'.

After a dispute over the title of his collection of country songs *BW Goes CW* (1976) – Womack's own title had been *Move over Charley Pride and Give Another Nigger a Chance* – he moved to Columbia and Arista with lacklustre results, due in part to a serious drug problem.

He re-emerged in 1980 as the vocalist on the **Crusaders**' 'Inherit the Wind' and returned to form with *The Poet* (Beverly Glen, 1981), an album which unfashionably returned to soul roots in an age of disco. Both the album and 'If You Think You're Lonely Now' were R&B hits. After *Poet 2* was equally successful, Womack recorded one album for Motown before moving to MCA in 1985. *So Many Rivers*, the **Chips Moman**-produced *Womagic* (1986) and *The Last Soul Man* (1987), with a guest appearance by Sly Stone, consolidated his role as the guardian of a soul tradition that laid stress on impassioned singing and well-constructed songs. In 1986 Womack re-established his relationship with the Stones, playing on *Dirty Work* and producing a solo album for Ron Wood. He later signed to Solar, recording *Save the Children* (1989). He toured regularly over the next five years, regularly visiting Britain. In 1994 he released *Resurrection* (Slide), an album of new songs, while the superior collection *Midnight Mover* brought together his best work from 1967 to 1976.

In the mid-eighties Womack's brother Cecil and sister-in-law Linda (the daughter of Sam Cooke), began a recording career as Womack and Womack.

Already a successful songwriting team they had written 'A Woman's Gotta Have It' for Bobby Womack, and numerous songs for **Teddy Pendergrass** including 'Love TKO', 'I Just Called to Say' and 'I Can't Live without Your Love'. *Womack and Womack* (Elektra, 1983) was followed by *Love Wars* (1984), produced by Stewart Levine. After recording *Radio M.U.S.I.C. Man* (1985), the duo set up the Sar II label, named after Sam Cooke's original. In 1986 they released *Star Bright* (EMI-Manhatten), moving to Island's 4th and Broadway label for *Conscience* (1988), which included the British hit 'Teardrops'. *Family Spirit* (RCA, 1991) was less successful.

Midnight Mover (1993) is the definitive anthology.

STEVIE WONDER
b. Steveland Morris, 13 May 1950, Saginaw, Michigan, USA

For over four decades, Stevie Wonder has been a major figure in both black and rock music. He came to prominence as a child prodigy and during the sixties made a string of hit singles with the aid of the Motown team of writers and producers. Taking full control of his career in 1971, Wonder used the newest electronic technology to create a black variety of progressive rock. The best of his later work found him adapting newer trends in black music to his gift for creating simple yet effective lyrics. He also became a respected elder statesman in the black music community, notably through his involvement in the successful campaign to achieve a national holiday in honour of civil rights leader Martin Luther King, for whom Wonder wrote 'Happy Birthday'.

Blind from birth, he grew up in Detroit where he listened to **Ray Charles**, **B. B. King**, **Johnny Ace** and **Jimmy Reed**. By the age of eight he was proficient on bongos, harmonica, piano and drums. In 1960 Ronnie White of the Miracles brought Stevie to the attention of **Berry Gordy**, who signed him to Hitsville USA. He released the unsuccessful singles 'Mother Thank You' and 'I Call It Pretty Music' before the gospel-influenced harmonica vehicle 'Fingertips Part II'* (Tamla, 1963) was successful. Recorded live and released as by Little Stevie Wonder, it reached No. 1 in America. *The Twelve-Year-Old Genius* (1963) was also a major hit.

The following year Wonder appeared in the films *Muscle Beach Party* and *Bikini Beach*, but 'Hey Harmonica Man', a cover of Tommy Tucker's 'Hi Heel Sneakers', *A Tribute to Uncle Ray* and *The Jazz Soul of Little Stevie* (1963) sold poorly. 'Uptight (Everything's Alright)' (1966) marked a switch of style to Motown soul and was a hit on both sides of the Atlantic. Further hits from the *Uptight* album during 1966 included 'Nothing's Too Good for My Baby', **Bob Dylan**'s 'Blowin' in the Wind' and 'A Place in the Sun'.

Over the next five years, Wonder consolidated his position as a leading pop artist with eight more Top Twenty hits. Co-written with Motown staff writers, notably Sylvia Moy and Henry Cosby, they included 'I Was Made to Love Her'* (1967), 'For Once in My Life'* (1968), 'My Cherie Amour'* (1969), 'Yester-Me, Yester-You, Yesterday'* and 'Signed, Sealed, Delivered I'm Yours'* (1970), co-written with Syreeta Wright, whom he married.

In 1971 he changed direction both financially and artistically. Wonder set up Taurus Productions to make his records which were leased to Motown. He spent the year working on synthesizer music with Bob Margoulieff and Malcolm Cecil who had created Tonto's Expanding Head Band to record the instrumental *Zero Time* (Embryo, 1971). Wonder's synthesizer experiments produced *Music of My Mind* (1972) and the dramatic, polyrhythmic 'Superstition'*, his second American No. 1.

Wonder's move towards a rock audience was underlined by his 1972 tour with the **Rolling Stones** and the melodic ballad 'You Are the Sunshine of My Life'* (1973) from *Talking Book*, which was made up of further tracks from the synthesizer sessions. Wonder's increasing socio-political awareness was expressed in 'Living for the City' (1973), an anthem for ghetto-dwellers from *Innervisions*, which also included 'All in Love Is Fair', later recorded by both **Frank Sinatra** and **Barbra Streisand**.

A serious road accident in August 1973 interrupted his career and *Fulfillingness' First Finale* (1974) contained some older material as well as the critique of liberalism 'You Haven't Done Nothing'* (another American No. 1, with background vocals from the **Jackson Five**) and 'Boogie on Reggae Woman'*.

In 1975 he renegotiated his Motown contract at a reputed 20 per cent royalty rate and $13 million advance. The double-album *Songs in the Key of Life* (1976) was Wonder's most ambitious to date and one of the most important records of the decade. It provided two No. 1s in 'I Wish' and 'Sir Duke', dedicated to **Duke Ellington**, as well as the memorable 'Isn't She Lovely', a British hit for David Parton (Pye, 1977). After a long period of preparation, the primarily instrumental *Journey Through the Secret Life of Plants* (1979) was condemned as esoteric by the critics. *Hotter Than July* (1980) was more favourably received as Wonder drew on reggae and rap in songs like 'Master Blaster (Jammin')' and 'Happy Birthday'. 'That Girl' and 'Do I Do' were included in the compilation album *Original Musiquarium* (1982) and in the same year Wonder recorded 'Ebony and Ivory' with **Paul McCartney**.

He won an Oscar for 'I Just Called to Say I Love You' from the film *The Woman in Red* (1984). *In Square Circle* (1985) included the No. 1 'Part Time

Love' and 'It's Wrong (Apartheid)'. Wonder's next album was the highly praised *Characters* (1987) and he had later hits in 1988 with duets with **Michael Jackson** ('Get It') and **Julio Iglesias** ('My Love'). Working at a slower rate than in the past, Wonder wrote the music for the Spike Lee film *Jungle Fever* (1991), and enjoyed an American Top Thirty success with the soundtrack album. He toured Europe in 1992, but spent much of the period 1991–94 working on a proposed new album. In 1995 he released an album of new songs, *Conversation Peace*, and in 1996 issued the greatest hits collection *Song Review*. The four-CD retrospective *At the Close of the Century* (2000), issued in the run-up to Wonder's 50th birthday, confirmed the huge significance of his career and the dramatic changes he had brought about for black music as a whole.

LINK WRAY
b. Lincoln Wray, 2 May 1930, Fort Bragg, North Carolina, USA

Wray was the creator of the influential 'Rumble'* (1958), which introduced to the world the fuzz-tone guitar sound and the idea of distortion as part of the guitarist's armoury of sounds.

Part North American Indian, Wray played in various country and then rock'n'roll groups with his brothers Doug and Vernon before recording 'Rumble' (allegedly in 1954, though it did not chart until 1958 on Cadence). An aural simulation of a bar brawl, in which reverberation and distortion are laid over a harsh, menacing riff (that predated the attempts of heavy-metal guitarists by over a decade), 'Rumble' and 'Rawhide'* (Epic, 1959), strongly influenced **The Who**'s Pete Townshend and **Jeff Beck**.

Though he continued to record, Wray had only one more minor hit ('Jack the Ripper', Swan, 1963) before in 1965 he retired to farm in Accokeek, Maryland. There he built a primitive recording studio (Wray's Three Track Shack) and in 1971 recordings made there were released on *Link Wray* (Polydor) to critical acclaim. Less confident than **Lonnie Mack**'s similarly themed seventies work, the album featured Wray's hoarse vocals and a mellower guitar sound. It was followed by a series of lesser albums, including *Be What You Want* (Virgin, 1973), whose backing musicians included the **Grateful Dead**'s Jerry Garcia and **Commander Cody**, and *Stuck in Gear* (1976), before he teamed up with neo-rockabilly singer Robert Gordon for *Robert Gordon with Link Wray* (Private Stock, 1977). Later solo albums included *Live at El Paradiso* (Instant, 1980), *Wild Side of the City Lights* (1988) and *Indian Child*, issued by British label Creation in 1993.

Guitar Preacher (1995) documents his stay with Polydor, while the three-volume series *Missing Links* (1996) collects together his rare recordings.

BETTY WRIGHT
b. 21 December 1953, Miami, Florida, USA

Part of the Miami soul scene which also included **KC and the Sunshine Band**, Wright was one of the most exuberant black singers of the seventies. She retained her popularity with soul music audiences into the nineties.

She sang with her brothers and sisters in the gospel group Echoes of Joy before making her first single at the age of thirteen. After recording for Solid Soul and Deep City she signed to Henry Stone's Alston label. Wright's 1968 ballad 'Girls Can't Do What the Guys Do' was a pop and R&B hit. The tougher 'He's Bad Bad Bad' (1968) preceded the Top Ten single 'Clean Up Woman' (1971) with its guitar work by Willie Hale. Written by Steve Alaimo (whose own biggest hit had been 'Every Day I Have to Cry', Checker, 1963), 'Clean Up Woman' was a warning song about 'the other woman' and was followed by the similar 'The Baby Sitter' and 'Secretary'.

In 1974 she released 'Shoorah Shoorah', a cover of a New Orleans number recorded by **Allen Toussaint** with British singer Frankie Miller. 'Where Is the Love' (1975) was a Grammy award-winning song written by KC's Harry Casey and Richard Finch. After cutting seven albums with Alston, Wright moved to Epic in 1981 where André Fisher produced an eponymous album of funk/disco material which contained a track recorded with **Stevie Wonder**, 'What Are You Going to Do with It'.

She returned to the higher reaches of the R&B charts in 1988 with *Mother Wit* (on her own Ms B label) and its hit R&B singles 'No Pain, No Gain' and 'After the Pain'. *4U2NJOY* (1989) contained the further hit 'From Pain to Joy'. Her next release was *Passion and Compassion* (1990).

Best of Betty Wright (Rhino, 1992) is just that.

LAWRENCE WRIGHT
b. 15 February 1888, Leicester, England, d. 19 May 1964, London

Dubbed the 'Edgar Wallace of songwriters', so prolific and successful was he, Wright was also an important music publisher, and one of the first to set up shop in London's Denmark Street, Britain's 'Tin Pan Alley'.

The son of a violin teacher and music-shop proprietor, Wright studied piano and violin as a child and worked on his father's market stall selling sheet music in his teens. After performing as a member of a concert party, he wrote his first song ('Down By the Stream') in 1905, and set up his own market stall to sell sheet music in Leicester. His first hit was the topical 'Coronation Waltz' (1910) and his first great success as a publisher 'Don't Go Down the Mine Daddy',

which he bought for £5 and sold over a million copies of in the wake of the 1910 Whitehaven pit disaster in which 136 men died. On the basis of these successes, Wright opened a shop in Denmark Street in 1911 and quickly established himself as a leading publisher.

Though he had an enduring fondness for topical songs (which ranged from 'Amy, Wonderful Amy', 1930 – dedicated to aviatrix Amy Johnson – to 'The Festival of Britain', 1950), Wright's best compositions were old-fashioned sentimental ballads such as 'Blue Eyes' (1915), his first big success under his Horatio Nicholls' pseudonym; other names Wright used were Gene Williams, Everett Lynton and Betsy O'Hagan. Further major hits for Wright (mostly under the Nicholls pseudonym) were 'That Old Fashioned Mother of Mine' (1919); the oft-recorded 'Among My Souvenirs' (1927), co-written with regular collaborator Edgar Leslie and a hit for **Paul Whiteman** (1928) and **Connie Francis** (1959) and memorably sung by **Hoagy Carmichael** in *The Best Years of Our Lives* (1946); and 'Shepherd of the Hills' (1927).

If many of his songs were old-fashioned, Wright was nonetheless one of the first British songwriters to spot the growing interest in American themes in Britain and to take advantage of it, notably with the waltz 'Wyoming' (which was an American hit when it was recorded by Charles Hart, Victor, 1921). Similarly, Wright bought the rights to more American hits than other British publishers. At the same time, as both an outlet for the songs he published and to test their appeal, he produced the annual summer show *On with the Show* for thirty-two years (1924–56). Famous for American-style publicity stunts, Wright flew **Jack Hylton** and his orchestra around the Blackpool tower in 1927 with the band playing 'Me and Jane in a Plane' while dropping copies of the song on to the crowds below, and he offered a £1,000 prize to anyone who could produce a straight banana to publicize 'I've Never Seen a Straight Banana' (1926). Wright was also involved in founding *The Melody Maker* in 1926, intending the magazine to become a promotional vehicle for his growing catalogue, in the manner of **Irving Mills** in America.

In 1943 Wright suffered a stroke that confined him to a wheelchair from which he continued to supervise his empire, publishing rock'n'roll material as well as more traditionally inclined popular songs. He retired in the late fifties.

O. V. WRIGHT
b. Overton Vertis Wright, 9 October 1939, Memphis, Tennessee, USA, d. 16 November 1980

Wright was a soul singer whose gospel background gave an impassioned, sanctified anguish to his recordings. Though he did not achieve significant success outside the R&B charts in his own lifetime, since his death Wright has been widely acclaimed as one of the last great Southern soul singers.

In his teens he recorded with the Sunset Travelers gospel group on **Don Robey**'s Peacock label and then joined the Spirit of Memphis Quartet and the influential the Highway QCs (which numbered **Sam Cooke** and **Johnnie Taylor** among its alumni). He made his first secular recording for Goldwax in 1964 (featuring 'That's How Strong My Love Is' – later a big hit for **Otis Redding** – on the flip-side) before being signed by Robey to his Backbeat label. His second single, the plaintive ballad 'You're Gonna Make Me Cry', was a big R&B hit and established the basic style of all of Wright's subsequent recordings, the singer's voice regularly cracking and squeaking with emotion as the backing churned relentlessly on. Other hits in this vein include such soul classics as 'Eight Men, Four Women' (1967), 'Ace of Spade' (with its splendidly gruff, yet plaintive B-side 'Afflicted', 1970) and 'A Nickel and a Nail' (1971).

These last singles, like most of his work after 1967, were overseen by **Willie Mitchell** at the Hi studio in Memphis and were much more complex productions, in which horns and strings alternated with a gospel guitar. Thus his superior 1973 album, *Memphis Unlimited*, saw him mixing straight gospel material ('I'm Going Home to Live with God') with social comment ('Ghetto Child' and 'He's My Son Just the Same') and soul balladry ('I've Been Searching' and the magnificent 'I'd Rather Be Blind, Crippled and Crazy').

After Robey sold his companies to ABC in 1973, Wright, after a few singles for ABC (including 'Nobody but You', 1975) signed with Mitchell's Hi Records. He recorded a trio of albums, the best of which were *Into Something I Can't Shake Loose* (1977) and *The Bottom Line* (1978), on which his voice, now heavier but more authoritative, showed grave passion.

His death in 1980 came after a lengthy illness. *The Soul of O. V. Wright* (MCA, 1992) is the definitive anthology.

ROBERT WYATT
b. Robert Ellidge, 28 January 1945, Bristol, England

A founder member of and drummer with **Soft Machine**, Wyatt became an idiosyncratic but influential solo performer, collaborating with such artists as **Elvis Costello** in the eighties.

Wyatt made his first solo album, *End of an Ear* (Columbia, 1969), two years before he left Soft Machine to form Matching Mole with Phil Miller (guitar), keyboardists Dave Macrae and David Sinclair, and Bill McCormick (bass). An eponymous début album for Columbia (1972) was followed by *Lit-*

tle Red Record (1973), which included **Brian Eno** on synthesizers. After the band split up, Miller joined Hatfield and the North and Wyatt sang on the band's first album. The group also included Dave Stewart and Barbara Gaskin, who later had a British No. 1 hit with a revival of **Lesley Gore**'s 'It's My Party' (Stiff, 1981).

Shortly afterwards, an accident left Wyatt paralyzed from the waist down. His drumming career was at an end but he continued to record, having a surprise British hit in 1974 with an eccentric version of the **Monkees**' 'I'm a Believer' (Virgin). Wyatt next applied his thin but evocative voice to Chris Andrews' hit 'Yesterday Man' (Decca, 1964), but it sold less well. He returned to the Matching Mole mode of surreal lyrics in jazz settings on *Rock Bottom* (1974) and *Ruth Is Stranger than Richard* (1975), though the inclusion of 'Song for Che' on the latter indicated the political edge that came to dominate his subsequent work.

Wyatt's occasional releases between 1978 and 1982 were collected on *Nothing Can Stop Us* (Rough Trade, 1983). They included versions of the Cuban song 'Guantanamera', an earlier hit for the Sandpipers (A&M, 1966), **Billie Holiday**'s 'Strange Fruit', 'Stalin Wasn't Stallin'', a Second World War gospel-style song first recorded by the **Golden Gate Quartet**, and the minor British hit 'Shipbuilding' (Rough Trade, 1963), an Elvis Costello composition inspired by the Falklands conflict.

'The United States of Amnesia' and 'The British Road' were among Wyatt's own songs which appeared on *Old Rottenhat* (1986), another politically charged outing. After a lengthy break, it was followed by the superior *Dondestan* (1991). In 1992 he released the five-song mini-album *A Short Break* (Voiceprint), which included four wordless 'songs' where Wyatt's inimitable voice was treated as an instrument. His recordings of the previous decade were reissued on *Mid Eighties* (Rough Trade, 1993). Wyatt later collaborated with the electronic group Ultramarine.

TAMMY WYNETTE
b. Virginia Wynette Pugh, b. 5 May 1942, nr Tupelo, Mississippi, USA, d. 6 April 1998

Wynette was one of the most successful female country singers of all time, not least because the melodrama of her own life – which included five marriages (including one to **George Jones**) and a kidnapping in 1979 – led both commentators and audiences to blur the distinction between her personal life and professional career (a French critic called her the **Edith Piaf** of America). In the words of country-music historian Bill C. Malone, 'her clear expressive, pleading voice tore at the emotions and pulled . . . listeners into her orbit of personal experience, making them feel that her songs of hurt and loneliness, which were somehow tempered by hope, mirrored their own and the singer's lives'. Additionally, songs like 'Stand by Your Man'*, one of the several about the tribulations of womanhood written by Wynette, have often been attacked by feminists as ideologically regressive. However, while these elements have contributed significantly to her popularity within country circles and to her status as an icon outside them, Wynette's recordings were both more complex and far better crafted than their reputation suggests.

Raised on a farm by her grandparents after the death of her father, Wynette sang in church as a child and worked as a beautician before travelling to Nashville where, in 1966, she was signed to Epic by **Billy Sherrill** (who subsequently produced and co-wrote most of her classic recordings). Though her first hits, such as 'Your Good Girl's Gonna Go Bad', 'I Don't Wanna Play House' (1967) and 'D-I-V-O-R-C-E' (1968), were written for her (mostly by Sherrill and Glen Sutton), they introduced the theme bluntly detailed in the opening line of her own 'Stand by Your Man' (1968): 'Sometimes it's hard to be a woman'.

On that recording, her only major crossover pop hit, the dominant feature of Sherrill's pared-down **Phil Spector**-style production was the counterbalancing of steel guitar and strings to provide a dramatic background for Wynette's searing voice. The result was less a paean to masculine dominance than a confessional account of the gap between ideals and reality. Very quickly both Sherrill's productions and Wynette's singing became formula-ridden, with the results depending entirely on the suitability of the song to the formula. While 'Almost Persuaded' (1968) was a classic track, her version of **John Hartford**'s 'Gentle on My Mind' (1968) was almost a mockery of the song, with Wynette's crying voice overpowering the lyric. More successful examples of her style were the hits 'Good Lovin'' (1971), 'Woman to Woman'

(1974) and 'Womanhood' (1978), but more interesting were the recordings she made with George Jones during the period of their marriage (1969–75) and later. On these, which include 'We're Gonna Hold on' (1972), 'Golden Ring' (1976) and 'Two Storey House' (1980), her breathy voice perfectly complemented Jones' more pliable blues-inflected sound. Many of the songs they recorded together and individually ("Til I Can Make It on My Own', 1974) were specifically written for them and thus the various stages of their relationship were documented on record.

In the eighties Wynette turned to television, securing a role in the daytime soap *Washington*, but, unlike **Dolly Parton**, she did not break into the mainstream of American entertainment, mainly because though her material was often pop-orientated ('I Just Heard a Heartbreak', 1983; 'Sometimes When We Touch', 1985), Wynette's singing on albums like *Higher Ground* (1987), on which she duetted with **Ricky Skaggs**, among others, and *Next to You* (1989) remained more faithful to country styles than Parton's. Wynette's autobiography, *Stand by Your Man*, was filmed in 1982.

Wynette's first nineties album, *Heart Over Mind* (1990), was another country hit, but the following year she scored one of her unlikeliest successes as guest vocalist on the British Top Five single 'Justified and Ancient' by dance/rock mavericks **KLF**. In 1993 she returned to her roots with *Honky Tonk Angels*, recorded with Parton and **Loretta Lynn**. This was followed by one of her best albums, *Without Walls* (1994). Later recordings included *One* (1995), a duet with Jones. Her last recording was a duet with former **Beach Boy** Brian Wilson, 'In My Room' (1998).

Anniversary (1987) and *Collectors Edition* (1998) are the definitive hits collections, while *Remembered* (1998) is a tribute album on which artists as diverse as **Elton John** and **Roseanne Cash** sing songs associated with her.

XTC

Andy Partridge, b. 11 December 1953, Malta; Colin Moulding, b. 17 August 1955, Swindon, England; Barry Andrews, b. London; Terry Chambers, b. 18 July, 1955, Swindon; Dave Gregory, b. Swindon

An intrinsically English group, XTC grew out of the UK punk movement of 1976–7 to develop into a moderately successful pop act in the late seventies before their mixture of art-school rock, Olde English themes and late sixties psychedelia gained them a devoted US cult following in the eighties.

Guitarist/vocalist Partridge, bassist/vocalist Moulding and drummer Chambers had first teamed up in Swindon rock band Star Park, changing the name and musical direction to Helium Kidz when punk appeared in 1976. The arrival of keyboards-player Andrews in 1977 completed the line-up, and they signed to Virgin Records later that year. The EP *3-D* (1977) and particularly its lead track 'Science Friction' set the tone for the early part of XTC's career, with Partridge's fondness for puns (exemplified by the band's name) and both his and Moulding's pop sensibilities to the fore, backed by Andrews' quirky keyboard style. The band's perceived middle-class background, their musical proficiency and their off-beat lyrics marked them apart from most of their spikier contemporaries, particularly in the eyes of the UK music press, and the début album *White Music* (1978), with its version of **Jimi Hendrix**'s 'All Along the Watchtower', confirmed their unwillingness to be part of the punk scene. The follow-up, *Go2* (1978), featured more of Andrews' influence, with less of the pop tones of the début, and came with an additional EP, *Go+*, which found the band experimenting with extended dub versions of songs from the album. The conflict between Partridge and Moulding's vision of the band and the less traditional approach espoused by Andrews apparent on *Go2* saw the latter depart XTC in early 1979. He teamed up with guitarist **Robert Fripp** in the League of Gentlemen, recorded as a solo artist and played with **Iggy Pop** (*Soldier*, 1980) before forming his own band, Shriekback, which released several albums.

Rather than replace Andrews with another keyboards player, the band recruited long-time friend and guitarist Gregory, whose first appearance with the band was on the more lightweight 'Life Begins at the Hop', which reached the UK Top Sixty in 1979. The subsequent album, *Drums and Wires* (the title a reference to Andrews' departure), appeared later that year.

With a markedly different, less deliberately 'difficult' sound to its predecessors, it provided the band with a UK Top Twenty hit in Moulding's ironic 'Making Plans for Nigel'. Partridge, the band's most prolific songwriter, released a solo single in 1980 and the band scored another pair of UK hits before releasing *Black Sea*, which reached the US Top Fifty. Despite Partridge's preference for the studio environment, the band toured heavily throughout 1981, taking time off to record the double-album *English Settlement* (1982), which gave them their biggest UK hit single, 'Senses Working Overtime'. However, when Partridge collapsed twice in a matter of weeks in 1982 (exhaustion and a stomach ulcer were diagnosed), the band abandoned stage work.

After Terry Chambers left, subsequently moving to Australia and joining new wave rock band Dragon, the remaining trio released *Mummer* (1983), which saw Partridge's fascination with disappearing English culture draw comparisons with the **Kinks**. After *The Big Express* (1984) the band recorded *Skylarking* (1986) in the US with producer **Todd Rundgren**. Ironically, a one-off mini-album, *25 o'Clock*, which the group had recorded as spoof psychedelic band the Dukes of Stratosfear the year previously, had sold twice as many copies in the UK as *The Big Express*, and the band were therefore encouraged by Virgin to record a follow-up, *Psionic Psunspots*, which appeared in 1987. It was enthusiastically received, and the band incorporated many of its sixties stylings into the next XTC album, *Oranges and Lemons* (1989), possibly their best album. It returned the band to the UK Top Thirty and was their most successful in the US, but they were unable to capitalize on that success. In 1992 XTC released the minor *Nonsuch*, which featured **Fairport Convention** drummer Dave Mattacks and was produced by Gus Dudgeon, who had previously worked with **Elton John** and **David Bowie**.

Partridge's individual projects of the nineties included writing lyrics for a Captain Sensible album (*The Greatest Living Englishman*, 1993) and *Through the Hill* (1994), an ambient album with Harold Budd. *Fossil Fuel* (1996) was a compilation album of XTC singles and *Apple Venus Volume 1* (1999) the group's first album of new material for over five years. The group followed this rather quickly with *Wasp Star* (*Apple Venus Volume 2*) (2000). As quirky as ever, the album – nine songs by Partridge and three by Moulding – saw the duo offering pop songs with an independent bent to good effect.

JIMMY YANCEY
b. 20 February 1898, Chicago, Illinois, USA, d. 17 September 1951, Chicago

The apparent simplicity and artlessness of Jimmy Yancey's playing masked an extraordinary sense of rhythm and dynamics, so delicate that many have judged him among the most moving of all blues pianists. Though generally regarded as a boogie-woogie player, he had little of the technical command of his friend **Meade Lux Lewis** (who composed a 'Yancey Special' in tribute to him), but he did devise, or at least popularize, a left-hand figure (the 'Yancey bass') than runs through innumerable blues, from the **Delmore Brothers**' 'Blues Stay Away from Me' (King, 1946) to Pee Wee Crayton's 'Blues After Hours' (Modern, 1949) and **Guitar Slim**'s 'The Things That I Used to Do' (Specialty, 1954).

His family background was musical and as a child he worked in vaudeville, as both singer and dancer. He learned piano from his brother Alonzo and from 1915 onwards began to play at various functions around Chicago, though after 1925 he never did so for a living; he had a day-job as groundkeeper for the Chicago White Sox baseball team. He first recorded in 1939 for Solo Art. Sessions in 1939–40 for Victor introduced some of the tunes that would be most closely associated with him: 'State Street Special', 'Tell 'Em About Me', '35th and Dearborn'. He sometimes sang, hesitantly and movingly, as on 'Death Letter Blues' (Session, 1943).

His wife 'Mama' Yancey (b. Estella Harris, 1 January 1896, Cairo, Illinois) was also an affecting singer, though never a professional one. She joined him on several recording dates, her specialities including 'How Long Blues', 'I Received a Letter' and 'Make Me a Pallet on the Floor' (all Session, 1943). Their last collaboration was in 1951 for Atlantic. After Jimmy's death from diabetes she recorded with pianists Don Ewell (Windin' Ball, 1952), Little Brother Montgomery (Riverside, 1961) and Chicagoan blues specialist Art Hodes (Verve-Folkways, 1965).

YANNI
b. Kalamata, Greece

A veteran of 'New Age' music in the eighties, keyboard-player Yanni found a large American audience in the early nineties for his complexly arranged instrumental electronic compositions.

Born and brought up in Greece, at the age of fourteen Yanni was a member of his country's national swimming team. In America he initially trained as a psychologist at the University of Minnesota. A largely self-taught musician, he began working as a studio musician and jingles' composer before moving full-time into writing and production.

After releasing his first album independently, Yanni signed as an artist with the Private Music label set up by ex-**Tangerine Dream** member Peter Baumann and released six albums during the eighties, culminating in *Niki Nana* (1989). This was followed by the compilation album *Reflections of Passion* (1990), a collection of romantic themes which sold over one million copies in the US. A less successful second compilation, *In Celebration of Life*, was issued in 1991. *Dare to Dream* (1992) was followed by the in-concert set *Live at the Acropolis* (1994), a two-million-seller in the US.

Yanni's music, which has drawn comparisons with **Vangelis** and Tangerine Dream, also proved popular with film TV producers and commercial makers, resulting in the claim that in 1992 he was the US's most often heard composer. His collaboration with **Malcolm McLaren** in 1991 on music for a British Airways commercial based on a piece by Delibes won several awards. Yanni's relationship with US soap star Linda Evans won him a newfound mainstream audience.

THE YARDBIRDS
Keith Relf, b. 22 March 1943, Richmond, Surrey, England, d. 14 May 1976, London; Jim McCarty, b. 25 July 1943, Liverpool; Paul Samwell-Smith, b. 8 May 1943, Twickenham (replaced 1966 by Jimmy Page, b. 9 April 1944, London); Anthony Topham, b. 1947 (replaced 1963 by Eric Clapton, b. 30 March 1945, Ripley, Surrey, replaced 1965 by Jeff Beck, b. 24 June 1944, Surrey); Chris Dreja, b. 11 November 1946, Surbiton, Surrey

The three successive lead guitarists of the highly influential Yardbirds personified the changes in (London-based) British rock of the sixties: from blues (**Eric Clapton**) through the beginnings of psychedelia (**Jeff Beck**) to heavy rock (Jimmy Page, who formed **Led Zeppelin** as a direct descendant of the Yardbirds.)

As was the case with many British groups of the early sixties, Samwell-Smith (bass), Relf (vocals), Dreja (guitar) and McCarty (drums) met while performing in school and folk-club bands. They formed the Metropolitan Blues Quartet in 1963, which became the Yardbirds with the addition of lead guitarist Topham. With the arrival of Clapton to replace Topham, who chose to remain at art school but later recorded *Ascension Heights* (Blue Horizon, 1970), the line-up of the Yardbirds Mark 1 was confirmed. Like the **Rolling Stones**, whose residency at Richmond's Crawdaddy Club they took over, the group's music was rooted in Chicago blues and an early recording, the live *The Yardbirds* (recorded 1964, issued in 1975, Charly), saw them performing 'purist' versions of songs by **Chuck Berry**, **Bo Diddley** and **Howlin' Wolf**. During this period they also recorded *Sonny Boy Williamson and The Yardbirds* (issued by Philips, 1965). Signed by manager Giorgio Gomelsky to EMI's Columbia label, their first single (a version of Billy Boy Arnold's 1956 Vee-Jay recording, 'I Wish You Would', 1964) was similarly purist in intent, but by the time of the live album *Five Live Yardbirds* (1964) Clapton's guitar work was innovative rather than merely derivative. At the same time, with Samwell-Smith now producing, the group began to distance themselves from R&B and after their first hit, 'For Your Love' (1965), written by Graham Gouldman, later of **10CC**, and featuring **Brian Auger** on harpsichord rather than a guitar solo, Clapton quit to join **John Mayall** and was replaced by Beck.

Denounced by Clapton as 'commercial pop', the string of international hits – issued on Epic in America – that followed, including 'Heart Full of Soul', 'Still I'm Sad' (1965), 'Shapes of Things' and 'Over Under Sideways Down' (1966), saw the group creating a genuinely progressive sound. In this they were similar in attitude to **Procul Harum** and **Pink Floyd**, groups which also had strong blues roots, rather than the Stones and the **Animals**. Central to this phase of the Yardbirds' sound was Beck's exploratory approach to the guitar as an electronic instrument and Samwell-Smith's production, which incorporated elements of Gregorian chant ('Still I'm Sad'), electronic effects and feedback and Indian sounds (the sitar-style guitar of 'Over Under Sideways Down') into their records. When Samwell-Smith left to concentrate on production (most successfully with **Cat Stevens**) Page, who had originally been invited to replace Clapton, joined.

This line-up recorded the innovatory 'Happenings Ten Years Time Ago' (1966) and was featured in Antonioni's portrait of 'Swinging London', *Blow Up* (1966), smashing their guitars in the manner of **The Who** during a performance of 'Stroll on', a reworking of **Tiny Bradshaw**'s 'The Train Kept a-Rollin''. After a brief period in which Beck and Page shared lead-guitar duties, Beck departed and the group, now a foursome, turned unsuccessfully to producer **Mickie Most** in search of further pop hits (particularly in the US where 'Little Games', 1967, was a success). In 1968 the group disbanded to pursue solo careers.

Page formed the New Yardbirds to fulfil the group's outstanding engagements and this group evolved into Led Zeppelin. Dreja became a photographer and McCarty and Relf turned to folk music, forming Renaissance which recorded an eponymous Samwell-Smith-produced album (Island, 1978). Samwell-Smith later concentrated on production, notably with British 'Goth' band All About Eve, who enjoyed considerable British success in the late eighties. In the eighties Dreja, Samwell-Smith and McCarty occasionally played together as the Yardbirds and as Box of Frogs on the London pub circuit. As Box of Frogs, they had released two albums on Epic in the early eighties. Topham and McCarty played together on the pub circuit in the late eighties and early nineties, and in 1989 McCarty formed the British Invasion All-Stars with other sixties veterans, releasing an album of oldies as *Regression*. He also played with ex-members of the **Pretty Things** as the Pretty Things Yardbirds Blues Band.

YELLO
Dieter Meier; Boris Blank

Quirky Swiss duo Yello set a style for sophisticated synth-pop in the eighties which was later successfully adopted by acts such as the **Pet Shop Boys** and **Erasure**. Their sound also set the blueprint for much of the heavily sampled electronic dance music which was in vogue in the early nineties.

Born into a wealthy banker's family, Meier's colourful background included a period as a professional poker player and a spell in the Swiss national golf team. He released two singles through the Zurich-based independent Periphery Perfume label with his band Fresh Colour before turning to filmmaking. He hired Blank to provide soundtrack music. A former truck driver and television repairman, Blank had been working on a series of electronic compositions for Periphery Perfume.

The pair collaborated on a performance piece dreamed up by Meier entitled 'Dead Cat', which was premièred in Zurich in 1979. This led to the release of Yello's first single 'I T Splash'. A tape of their material reached avant-garde US band the Residents who, impressed by Meier's concepts and deadpan vocals and by Blank's inventive soundscapes, released Yello's début album on their Ralph label.

Solid Pleasure appeared in 1980. A bewildering mix of cinematic themes – spy movies, science fiction and just plain weirdness – and disco rhythms, it was a commercial flop, although UK label Do It released the 'Bostisch' single, which became a club favourite. In the US the track was also popular in clubs where it was used by the emerging rappers as a basis for their then-new 'scratch' mixes. A second album, *Claro Que*

Si, appeared in 1981. Again a club and critical hit, it included 'Pinball Cha Cha', which won acclaim for its inventive promotional video, directed by Meier (as would be all their subsequent promos). The following year Meier directed his first full-length movie, *Jetzt und Alles*, after which he was reunited with Blank to work on the third Yello album.

In 1983 UK independent Stiff Records released *You Gotta Say Yes to Another Excess*, which provided Yello with a UK hit single, 'I Love You', and a sizeable European success, 'Lost Again'. A move to Elektra Records produced the stylish *Stella* (1985) and a US hit in 'Oh Yeah', but it was a switch to the Mercury label in 1986 which produced their greatest commercial successes. A compilation remix album *1980–85: The New Mix in One Go* was a favourite with clubbers, and the new album, *One Second* (1987), made the UK Top Fifty. It found the duo adding guest vocalists to their already heady cocktail, most notably **Shirley Bassey** (on 'The Rhythm Divine') and Scottish vocalist Billy MacKenzie from UK band the Associates. A subsequent reworking of an earlier track as the acid house-styled 'The Race' gave the duo their biggest international hit in 1988, when it reached the UK Top Ten.

The single's success helped the next album, *Flag* (1988), to over one million sales worldwide, although the follow-up, *Baby* (1989), was less successful. As Meier became more involved in his film projects, Mercury released the *Essential Yello* compilation in 1992 and Blank turned to outside production with the solo album from Billy MacKenzie, *Outernational* (1992). Yello returned in 1994 with *Zebra*, a typically eccentric collection on which the Glenn Miller swing of 'S.A.X.' sat comfortably alongside the trademark twisted dance/funk items such as 'Tremendous Pain' or 'How How', which ironically borrowed from the contemporary dance scene which Yello themselves had inspired.

Essential (1992) is a representative compilation.

YES

Jon Anderson, b. 25 October 1944, Accrington, Lancashire, England (replaced by Trevor Horn); Pete Banks (replaced by Steve Howe, b. 8 April 1947, London); Bill Brufords, b. 17 May 1949, London (replaced by Alan White, b. 14 June 1949, Durham); Tony Kaye (replaced by Rick Wakeman, b. 18 May 1949, London, replaced by Patrick Moraz, b. 24 June 1948, Morges, Switzerland, replaced by Wakeman, replaced by Geoff Downes); Chris Squire, b. 4 March 1948, London

Yes were one of the most ambitious and proficient progressive rock bands of the seventies. With a sound based on Anderson's distinctive high-pitched tenor voice and **Rick Wakeman**'s imaginative use of syn-

thesizer technology, the group had ten hit albums before disbanding in 1980. They reunited several times thereafter, with mixed success.

In 1962 Anderson joined his brother Tony's rock/soul cover-version group the Warriors. After unsuccessful singles for Decca, Anderson moved from group to group until in 1968 he formed Mabel Greer's Toyshop with Squire (bass) and Banks (guitar) from underground band Syn. With the addition of keyboards-player Kaye (from Bitter Sweet) and Brufords (drums), they became Yes. One of the first British signings to Atlantic, the group's eponymous début album showed strong **Crosby Stills and Nash** vocal influences and resembled **Emerson Lake and Palmer** in its use of classical motifs. *Time and a Word* (1970) included versions of Stephen Stills' 'Everydays' and **Richie Havens**' 'No Opportunity Necessary' and was a minor hit. It was co-produced by Eddie Offord who supervised the group's next five albums.

Shortly afterwards Banks was replaced by Howe, who had played guitar on Tomorrow's 'My White Bicycle' (Parlophone, 1967), one of the best examples of British psychedelia. Tomorrow broke up after producer Mark Wirtz made the successful 'Excerpt from a Teenage Opera' with Tomorrow vocalist Keith West. Howe's fluency in a range of guitar styles gave Yes a fuller sound. Almost as important in establishing the group's identity were Roger Dean's accomplished and surreal sleeve illustrations for their albums.

The Yes Album (1971) included 'I've Seen All Good People' and 'Yours Is No Disgrace', Anderson compositions which became staples of the band's live set. When Kaye left to form Flash with Banks – the group made three albums for Sovereign in 1972–3 – his replacement Wakeman brought a richer keyboards sound to the band.

'Roundabout' from *Fragile* (1971) was Yes's first American hit and *Close to the Edge* (1972) found the group venturing into extended compositions with the four-part title track. After Brufords went to **King Crimson** (replaced by White, ex-**John Lennon**'s Plastic Ono Band), the triple live *Yessongs* (1973) and the symphonic concept album *Tales from Topographic Oceans* (1973, inspired by Paramhansa Yogananda's *Autobiography of a Yogi*) continued the trend, but the following year Wakeman left the band.

The new keyboards player, Moraz, had played with Refuge (a trio including ex-Nice bassist Lee Jackson and drummer Brian Davison). In two years with the group he played only on *Relayer* (1974) and on live recordings issued in 1980 as *Yesshows*. Moraz went on to make numerous solo albums, write film scores and work with the **Moody Blues**. On his departure, Wakeman returned for *Going for the One* (1977), which included the band's biggest British hit, 'Wonderful

Stories', and *Tormato* (1978), whose 'Don't Kill the Whale' reached the Top Forty. Although these albums showed a move back to shorter songs, the group was now losing momentum and when both Anderson and Wakeman left for solo careers in 1979, the remaining members recruited **Trevor Horn** and Geoff Downes who, as Buggles, had recorded the hit 'Video Killed the Radio Star' (Island, 1979). After *Drama* (1980), Yes ceased to exist for three years.

When they returned with the dance/R&B-influenced *90125* (1983), the line-up was Anderson, Squire, Kaye, White and guitarist Trevor Rabin, who had played with Streetband and **Manfred Mann**, as well as making solo albums for Chrysalis. The band released a mini-album from the subsequent world tour, *9012 Live: The Solos* (1985).

While Horn went on to become a top producer, both Howe and Anderson recorded prolifically outside the Yes format. After making *Beginnings* (1975) and *The Steve Howe Album* (1979), solo works which displayed his virtuosity, the guitarist set up Asia with Downes, drummer Carl Palmer and former **Family** and **Roxy Music** bassist John Wetton, scoring American hits with the stadium-rock songs 'Heat of the Moment' (Geffen, 1982) and 'Don't Cry' (1983). He later founded GTR with Steve Hackett, releasing *GTR* and the American hit single, 'When the Heart Rules the Mind' (Arista, 1986). He released *Turbulence*, his first solo album in over a decade, in 1991. Beginning with *Olias of Sunhillow* (1976) Anderson made five solo albums for Atlantic on which he developed his interest in mythological themes. *In the City of Angels* (Columbia, 1988) included songs co-written with Lamont Dozier (formerly of **Holland, Dozier and Holland**). In 1980 he began a fruitful collaboration with **Vangelis**. Among their recordings were *Short Stories* (Mercury, 1980), which included the hit 'I'll Find My Way Home' (1981), and *Friends of Mr Cairo* (1982).

By 1988 the various members of the group were split into two warring camps. The name Yes was owned by a band led by Squire with Kaye, Rabin and White which recorded *Big Generator* (Atco, 1987). Meanwhile other Yes alumni toured as Anderson, Brufords, Wakeman and Howe, releasing 'Brother of Mine' (Arista, 1989) and an eponymous album (1989). In 1991, the disputes seemingly settled, a re-formed Yes including the erstwhile ABW&H members plus Kaye, Squire, White and Rabin, toured the United States, and the album *Union* was a hit both there and in Britain. However, the reunion was relatively brief, and in 1992 Anderson, Kaye, Squire, White and Rabin released *Talk*. Howe, Brufords and Anderson, meanwhile, appeared on an album with the London Philharmonic Orchestra, *The Symphonic Music of Yes* (1993).

In 1994 Yes continued with the interactive CD-ROM *Yes Active*, while Anderson released two solo outings, *Change We Must* and *Deseo*. They were followed by the live albums *Keys to Ascension* (1996) and *Keys to Ascension Volume 2* (1997), with Howe back in the group, and the studio set *Open Your Eyes* (1997). *Beyond and Before/Something's Coming* (1998) was a double-CD set of recordings made by the band for the BBC. Igor Khoroshev (*b. 14 July 1965, Moscow, Russia*) joined for their 1998 US tour in support of *Friends and Relatives*. *The Ladder* (Eagle Rock, 1999) included a tribute to **Bob Marley**, while Anderson continued recording in a New Age vein with *The More You Know* (Eagle, 1998).

DWIGHT YOAKAM
b. 23 October 1956, Pikesville, Kentucky, USA

Yoakam has proved far more dedicated to a roots notion of country music than other 'men in hats' among the generation which came to fame in the late eighties. His work relied heavily on the spare sounds developed by **Lefty Frizzell** in the forties and fifties and **Buck Owens** in the sixties.

After failing to find work in Nashville, Yoakam moved to Los Angeles in 1978, where he played country music in clubs and supported **Los Lobos**. In 1984 he recorded an EP on the independent Oak label which included his version of **Johnny Horton**'s classic 'Honky Tonk Man'. That led to him being signed by Warners who in 1986 released the Pete Anderson-produced *Guitars, Cadillacs, etc.*, which included a reworked version of 'Honky Tonk Man'. It was an American country hit and a radio hit in Europe. Yoakam subsequently had hits with material as diverse as a reworking of **Elvis Presley**'s 'Little Sister' (1987) and Frizzell's 'Always Late' (1988), both of which were featured on *Hillbilly Deluxe*, along with a bleak version of **Harlan Howard**'s classic 'Heartaches by the Number'.

Both these albums were highly autobiographical, drawing on Yoakam's Kentucky childhood, but his next, *Buenos Noches from a Lonely Room* (1988), was full of anger and self-recrimination. One of its highpoints was a rock remake of Owens' 'Streets of Bakersfield', on which he was joined by its writer. Later in the year Yoakam returned the favour by duetting with Owens on 'Under Your Spell Again' on Owens' comeback album *Hot Dog* (Capitol). Other remakes included versions of **Hank Locklin**'s 'Send Me the Pillow' and **Johnny Cash**'s 'Ring of Fire'. Even better was the more optimistic *If There Was a Way* (1990) which included the hit 'You're the One' and an enjoyable reworking of **Wilbert Harrison**'s anthemic 'Let's Work Together'. The superior *This Time* (1993) was more mellow. It included the hits 'Ain't That Lonely

Yet' and **Gene Pitney**'s 'A Thousand Miles from Nowhere' and remained in the country charts for nearly two years. It was followed by the mostly self-penned *Gone* (1995). He also appeared on *Tribute to Tradition* (1997) with the likes of **Merle Haggard** and **Travis Tritt**. In the same year he appeared in the film *Slingblade* and released *Under the Covers*, a collection of his versions of other people's songs. Some were conventional, countryish, re-readings (such as **Danny O'Keefe**'s 'Good Time Charlie's Got the Blues'), but others were quite radical, notably the big-band version of the **Kinks**' 'Tired of Waiting for You'. He followed that with the hits collection *Last Chance for a Thousand Years* (1999). In 2000 he released his début film as director (and co-writer), *South of Heaven, West of Hell*, and the acoustic set, *dwightyoakamacoustic.net*, on which he trawled through his back catalogue with only his own strumming to accompany him. The result was intriguing rather than compelling.

VINCENT YOUMANS
b. 27 September 1898, New York, USA, d. 5 April 1946, Denver, Colorado

Youmans is best remembered as the composer of *No, No Nanette* (1925), the musical that probably best caught the buoyant mood of the twenties.

The son of a hatter, Youmans, after briefly working in a Wall Street brokerage firm during the First World War, joined the navy and helped organize shows for fellow servicemen. During this time he also wrote his first songs, including 'Hallelujah', which later was one of the successes of *Hit the Deck* (1927). On his discharge he became a song-plugger and rehearsal pianist before being invited to co-compose (with Paul Lannin) the Broadway musical *Two Little Girls in Blue* (1921) with lyricist **Ira Gershwin**. That produced 'Oh Me, Oh My' (a hit for **Frank Crumit**), but Youmans' first great success was *Wildflower* (1923), with book and lyrics by **Otto Harbach** and Oscar Hammerstein (later of **Rodgers and Hammerstein**). Firmly in the operetta tradition – the plot concerns a strong-willed heroine who must keep her temper for six months to secure a vast inheritance – it introduced the oft-recorded 'Bambolina', a big hit for **Paul Whiteman** (1923). *No, No Nanette* was equally fantastical in plot but the music had a more contemporary ring, and 'Tea for Two' and the chirpy 'I Want to Be Happy' (written with lyricist Irving Caesar) have subsequently become among the most representative songs of the decade and recorded by many artists. **Teddy Wilson** (1937), **Art Tatum** (1939) and **Vincent Lopez** (1925) are among those who recorded 'Tea' while there were memorable versions of 'Happy' by **Red Nichols** (1930) and **Benny Goodman**. After major restructuring before reaching Broadway, the show became one of the most successful musicals of the twenties and was filmed three times (in 1930, 1940 and 1950 as *Tea for Two*). Youmans became his own producer for his subsequent Broadway musicals, but apart from *Hit the Deck*, which included 'Sometimes I'm Happy' (revived by Benny Goodman, 1935, and **Sammy Kaye**, 1937, and filmed in 1930 and 1955), none was successful and in 1933 Youmans followed the trail of songwriters who left Broadway for Hollywood.

There, he had immediate success with 'The Carioca' (later revived by **Les Paul**, 1952) and 'Flying Down to Rio' (1933), the title song of **Fred Astaire**'s début movie with Ginger Rogers, which gave Astaire one of his earliest hit recordings. Dogged by ill-health, Youmans contracted tuberculosis in 1934 and spent most of his remaining life in sanatoria, only returning to Broadway to mount the ill-fated extravaganza *The Vincent Youmans Ballet Revue* (1943), an ambitious mix of Latin-American and classical music, including Ravel's *Daphnis and Chloe*. Choreographed by Leonide Massine, it lost some $4 million.

FARON YOUNG
b. 25 February 1932, Shreveport, Louisiana, USA, d. 10 December 1996

Originally highly imitative of **Hank Williams**, Young found mainstream success in the sixties and seventies ('Hello Walls'*, 1961; 'Four in the Morning'*, 1972) without deserting traditional country styles.

Raised on a farm, Young became a featured vocalist with **Webb Pierce** in 1950 and in 1951 signed with the independent Gotham label ('Tattle Tale Tears') before joining Capitol Records. Though his first major hit, his own 'Goin' Steady' (1953), dealt with teenage themes, it was firmly in the honky-tonky mould of Hank Williams and throughout the fifties Young sang with a pronounced whine. During this period he also appeared in several low-budget movies, mostly Westerns, including *Hidden Guns* (1956). Far smoother were his first country chart-toppers, 'Country Girl' (1959) and 'Hello Walls', one of the first of **Willie Nelson**'s songs to be recorded by an established artist. In 1963 Young switched labels to Mercury and throughout the sixties regularly toured Europe where 'Four in the Morning' became a huge pop hit. At the same time, he established various property and publishing interests in Nashville, including *Music City News*, the trade journal of country music. In the seventies Young recorded for MCA with less success.

Live Fast, Love Hard (Country Music Foundation, 1995) documents his honky-tonk period with Capitol Records, while *The Classic Years* (Bear Family, 1996) is a five-CD account of his days at the label.

LESTER YOUNG

b. Lester Willis Young, 27 August 1909, Woodville, Mississippi, USA, d. 15 March 1959, New York

Nicknamed 'Prez' (for President), Young was a key figure in the development of modern jazz tenor-saxophone-playing. Alone, he replaced the dominance of **Coleman Hawkins**' rounded, beefy style with a slimmer, darting soulful lyricism. On record his most famous partnership was with singer **Billie Holiday** and while he survived the bebop revolution, his most lasting influence was on a generation of mainstream jazz players including **Stan Getz**, Al Cohn and Zoot Sims.

As a child he played drums and then sax in the Young family band which toured the Midwest carnival circuit. Young joined Art Bronson's band in 1928, played briefly with **King Oliver** and then moved to Minneapolis, where he played with the Original Blue Devils in 1932. His distinctive style, influenced by **Bix Beiderbecke** associate Frankie Trumbauer, led him to Kansas City and **Count Basie**'s group in 1933. After an unsuccessful interlude with **Fletcher Henderson**, where his originality went unappreciated, Young made his recording début in 1936 with members of Basie's orchestra. **John Hammond** produced 'Lady Be Good' and 'Shoe Shine Swing' for Columbia.

With Basie, Young featured in saxophone duels with the more musically conservative Herschel Evans and recorded and broadcast extensively between 1937 and 1940. However, his best work was done with such small groups as the Kansas City Six ('Countless Blues' for **Milt Gabler**'s Commodore label in 1938) and the Kansas City Seven ('Lester Leaps in', Columbia, 1939). Young also played with **Benny Goodman** and **Charlie Christian** but among his most highly praised records of the thirties were the Holiday titles. Versions of current pop hits made for the jukebox market, they included 'A Sailboat in the Moonlight' (Brunswick, 1937) and 'Mean to Me' (1937). *A Musical Romance* (Columbia, 1977), the second volume of *The Lester Young Story*, contains a selection of these tracks.

Leaving Basie, Young unsuccessfully led his own group before moving to Los Angeles in 1941 to play with a band led by his drummer brother Lee. There he recorded with **Nat 'King' Cole** on piano, in a heavier and more reflective style. Returning to New York, he rejoined Basie and made some of his finest small group recordings for Keynote and Signature in 1943–4. He was also featured in the famous short film *Jammin' the Blues* (1944), directed by Gjon Mili.

While in the army he was court-martialled and imprisoned for using marijuana. Following his release in 1945, Young's work seldom recaptured the incandescence of his thirties records, partly because his progress was dogged by the myriad young saxophon-ists eagerly emulating his earlier style. After cutting 'DB Blues' (a reference to the detention barracks) for the West Coast Aladdin label in 1945, Young settled into a career pattern that involved annual tours with **Norman Granz**'s 'Jazz at the Philharmonic', though his introspective approach never quite fitted the barnstorming mood of JATP. During the fifties Young regularly played club dates with his own groups of young musicians (such as Connie Kay, later of the **Modern Jazz Quartet**) and made records for Granz's Clef and Verve labels. The highlights of Young's later recording career included the 1952 version of 'There'll Never Be Another You' with **Oscar Peterson** and the 1956 album *Jazz Giants* with pianist **Teddy Wilson**. He died after collapsing with stomach problems during an engagement in Paris.

NEIL YOUNG

b. 12 November 1945, Toronto, Canada

One of the most enigmatic songwriters, singers and guitarists to emerge in the sixties, Young had recorded more than twenty solo albums by the end of the century. Although his songs consistently expressed a melancholic and pessimistic view of personal and political relationships, Young's music veered into heavy rock, fifties rock'n'roll and electronic synthesizer sounds, while retaining a country undertow. Ironically, in the nineties, when he produced the acoustic *Harvest Moon* and *Unplugged* probably his most optimistic albums, his earlier electric material became a major influence on the so-called 'grunge' movement.

He spent his early years in Winnipeg, playing in high-school bands the Classics and the Squires in 1963. Returning to Toronto, Young joined the growing folk scene, eventually forming the Mynah Birds with **Rick James** and Bruce Palmer. He next moved to Los Angeles with Palmer, where he played with **Buffalo Springfield** between 1966 and 1968.

Young's reputation as an aggressive lead guitarist and emotive songwriter won him a solo contract with Reprise, the label originally formed by **Frank Sinatra**. He released 'The Loner' (1968) from an eponymous solo album which had string arrangements by **Jack Nitzsche**. For *Everybody Knows This is Nowhere* (1969) Young was joined by Crazy Horse, formerly a bar band consisting of Danny Whitten (guitar), Billy Talbot (bass) and Ralph Molina (drums). The first of many albums co-produced with David Briggs, it included 'Down by the River', 'Cinnamon Girl' and 'Cowgirl in the Sand'.

In 1969–70 Young toured with **Crosby, Stills and Nash** as CSN and Y, contributing 'Helpless' to *Déjà Vu* and composing the quartet's hit 'Ohio', which dealt with the shooting of anti-war student protestors by National Guardsmen. His next solo album, *After the Gold Rush* (1970), included a hit single in the lilting ballad 'Only Love Can Break Your Heart', as well as a notably mournful version of **Don Gibson**'s 'Oh Lonesome Me' and the title track's evocation of the lost dreams of the sixties. The six-minute 'Southern Man' was a powerful attack on racism which provoked **Lynyrd Skynyrd** to respond with 'Sweet Home Alabama' (1974). The album also introduced guitarist Nils Lofgren (b. 1952 *Chicago, Illinois*), whose group Grin had recorded for Briggs' label, Spin. Lofgren toured with Young in 1973 and 1982, and later worked with **Bruce Springsteen**, also attracting a cult following with his own frequent solo albums.

Harvest (1972), which apart from 'The Needle and the Damage Done' was a lighter album, was Young's greatest commercial success, with 'Heart of Gold'* reaching No. 1 in America and 'Old Man' entering the Top Forty. Nitzsche returned to provide string arrangements for the overblown 'A Man Needs a Maid'. The eccentric retrospective *Journey Through the Past* (a soundtrack to an obscure experimental movie) and the live *Time Fades Away* preceded Young's next album of new songs, *On the Beach* (1974), whose 'Revolution Blues' and 'Ambulance Blues' expressed a gloomy view of life under President Nixon. Centring on the drugs-induced deaths of Whitten and a former CSN and Y roadie, *Tonight's the Night* (1975) was both darker in mood and more powerful.

Zuma (1976) found Young venturing into historical narrative with 'Cortez the Killer' and soon afterwards he recorded the bestselling *Long May You Run* with Stills. **Linda Ronstadt** sang backing vocals on *American Stars'n'Bars* (1977) while the acoustic-flavoured *Comes a Time* (1978) provided a minor British hit with a version of **Ian and Sylvia**'s 'Four Strong Winds' (1979). *Rust Never Sleeps* (1979) was also the title of Young's last tour for eight years with Crazy Horse, which now included guitarist Frank Sampedro. On the album were 'Out of the Blue', Young's statement on the arrival of punk rock and the **Sex Pistols**, and 'Powderfinger', one of the most powerful of his later songs.

During the eighties Young adopted a meandering course. *Hawks and Doves* (1980) contained more of his occasional political ruminations, while *Re*ac*tor* (1981) and *Trans* (1983) found him experimenting with vocoders and synthesizers. In contrast, *Everybody's Rockin'* (Geffen, 1983) turned the clock back to the fifties with versions of songs first recorded by **Elvis Presley**, **Jimmy Reed**, **Johnny Cash** and **Buddy Holly**. The nostalgic mood deepened on the country-styled *Old Ways* (1985) and its hit 'Get Back to the Country', while *Landing on Water* (1986), with songs like 'Hippie Dream' and 'Bad News Beat',

brought critical accusations that Young was now a Reaganite.

Although the criticism of American foreign policy on 'Long Walk Home' and 'Midstream Vacation' from *Life* (1987) provided evidence to the contrary, the album (which reunited Young with Crazy Horse and Briggs) was poorly received. The iconoclastic performer returned to the limelight when the title track of *This Note's for You* (Reprise, 1988), an attack on the commercial sponsorship of rock music, was initially banned by MTV. After the release of *American Dream* (1988), the first CSNY album since 1971, he recorded the superior *Freedom* (1989).

Young began the nineties in fine style with the powerful *Ragged Glory*, again featuring Crazy Horse, with whom he toured in 1991. His influence on a new generation of bands was acknowledged when **Sonic Youth** accepted the invitation to open for him on his American dates that year. Young's feedback-driven performances from the tour were captured on the exemplary live album *Weld* (1991). After the gutsy rock approach of the two previous albums, Young switched direction for the mellow *Harvest Moon* (1992), a twenty-year-on nod back to *Harvest*, which was his most commercially successful album since 1979. In 1993 an American television performance produced the *Unplugged* album, on which Young (accompanied by a band which included Lofgren) revisited his back catalogue with drastically revamped acoustic versions of 'Like a Hurricane' and 'Transformer Man', among others.

For subsequent live dates, Young worked with veteran R&B band **Booker T. and the MGs**, but in 1994 Young and Crazy Horse teamed up once again to record the sombre *Sleeps with Angels*. This included the damning 'Piece of Crap' – 'Saw it on the tube, bought it on the phone . . . it's a piece of crap' – which reiterated the sentiments of 'This Note's for You'.

Young then began working with grunge band **Pearl Jam**, who backed him on a US tour and on the provocative *Mirrorball* (1995). However, for legal reasons Pearl Jam's name could not feature on the cover and the album was not as successful as expected. Reunited once again with Crazy Horse, Young issued *Broken Arrow* (1996), a less song-based collection than his recent output, built around the expansive title track. The following year provided a meandering, electric guitar soundtrack to Jim Jarmusch's *The Year of the Horse*, which was accompanied by a two-disc live set. In 1998 Young embarked on his first full tour with Crazy Horse in almost eight years and, as if to show just how contrary he could be, in 1999 rejoined Crosby, Stills and Nash for *Looking Forward*. More revealing was *Silver and Gold* (2000). In part a throwback to the sound of *Harvest Moon*, the album saw Young in nostalgic mood – as on 'Buffalo Springfield Again', in which his rejoining Crosby, Stills and Nash was explained – and for the first time imagining himself as old ('Daddy Went Walkin'').

PAUL YOUNG

b. Paul Anthony Young, 17 January 1956, Luton, Bedfordshire, England

Young was one of the most successful of the expressive white soul singers of the eighties.

A former car worker, he played bass with semi-pro band Kat Kool and the Kool Kats before joining North London soul group Streetband in 1978. Produced by **Ian Dury** associate Chas Jankel, Streetband had a hit with the novelty record 'Toast'/'Hold on' (Logo, 1978). Young also sang on the group's albums, London (1979) and Dilemma.

With Streetband members Ian Kewley (keyboards) and Mick Pearl (bass), Young next formed Q-Tips, a popular club and college band specializing in soul standards. The group made an eponymous Bob Sargeant-produced album for Chrysalis in 1980 which included Eddie Floyd's 'Raise Your Hand', with Floyd himself on guest vocals.

Q-Tips split in 1982 and Young signed to Columbia as a solo artist. He recorded the unsuccessful 'Iron out the Rough Spots' and 'Love of the Common People' (a version of Nicky Thomas's 1970 hit on Trojan) before a revival of **Marvin Gaye**'s 'Wherever I Lay My Hat' reached the Top Ten in 1983. No Parlez (1983) included further hits in 'Come Back and Stay' (a minor American success) and the reissued 'Common People' as well as a reworking of Joy Division's 'Love Will Tear Us Apart'.

The Secret of Association (1984) included an American No. 1 in 'Every Time You Go Away' (composed by Daryl Hall of **Hall and Oates**) and three further British hits. 'I'm Gonna Tear Your Playhouse Down' was first recorded by **Ann Peebles** in 1973, while the sombre 'Everything Must Change' and 'Tomb of Memories' were Young originals. Young chose to feature his own songs (co-written with Kewley) on the lesser Between Two Fires (1987). He was largely inactive during 1988–9, but re-emerged in 1990 with Other Voices, which found him once again tackling other writers' material, including the American Top Ten hit 'Oh Girl', originally a 1972 success for US soul act the Chi-lites. The hits compilation From Time to Time (1991) topped the British chart and provided him with another British hit, a cover of **Crowded House**'s 'Don't Dream It's Over'. Another period of inactivity preceded the 1993 release of the stylish but minor The Crossing. In 1997 he signed with East West for the poorly received Paul Young.

VICTOR YOUNG

b. 8 August 1900, Chicago, Illinois, USA, d. 11 November 1956, Palm Springs, California

A prolific film composer, Young was noted for his romantic scores. Regarded by many critics as archetypal 'Hollywood music' for their opulence, they were hugely popular with film producers and audiences.

Raised in Poland, Young studied at the Warsaw Conservatory, returning to America in the twenties. He worked as a violinist and arranger for several dance bands and in the thirties became musical director for two radio networks where he worked with **Al Jolson**, among others. He formed his own orchestra which recorded for Brunswick (1931–4) and Decca (1934–54). Among his hits were numerous film themes, including 'Who's Afraid of the Big Bad Wolf?' (1933), 'She's a Latin from Manhattan' (1935), **Anton Karas**' 'Theme from the Third Man' (1950) and **Dimitri Tiomkin**'s 'The High and the Mighty' (1954).

In 1935 Young settled in Hollywood to write film scores and songs. The songs included 'Sweet Sue' (1928), later a hit for the **Mills Brothers** (1932) and **Tommy Dorsey** (1939); 'I Don't Stand a Ghost of a Chance', a hit for **Bing Crosby** and Ted Fio Rito (Brunswick, 1932), for whom Young had worked as an arranger; and 'Can't We Talk It Over' (Crosby, and the Mills Brothers, 1932, and the **Andrews Sisters**, 1950). Perhaps his most evocative songs were 'Stella by Starlight' (memorably recorded by both **Harry James** and **Frank Sinatra**, 1947) and 'My Foolish Heart', which he wrote with his regular collaborator, lyricist Ned Washington, and was one of the biggest hits of 1950 when it was recorded by **Gordon Jenkins**, **Hugo Winterhalter** and **Billy Eckstine**, among others.

Even more influential were his numerous film scores, which included For Whom the Bell Tolls (1944, and thought by many to be his finest film work), Scaramouche (1950), Shane (1952), Three Coins in a Fountain (1953) and Around the World in Eighty Days (1956), for which he won an Oscar.

THE YOUNGBLOODS

Jesse Colin Young, b. Perry Miller, 11 November 1944, New York, USA; Jerry Corbitt, b. Tifton, Georgia; Joe Bauer, b. 26 September 1941, Memphis, Tennessee; Banana, b. Lowell Levinger, 1946, Cambridge, Massachusetts

A harder-edged folk-rock group than the **Lovin' Spoonful**, the Youngbloods' only major hit, the anthemic 'Get Together'* (1969), with **Joni Mitchell**'s 'Woodstock', typified the optimism of much late-sixties American youth culture.

Young went to school with **Simon and Garfunkel** and dropped out of college to join the Greenwich Village folk circuit, recording the solo albums *Soul of a City Boy* (Capitol, 1963) and *Youngblood* (Mercury, 1964), the latter with John Sebastian in support. He formed a duo in 1965 with Corbitt (guitar), later adding Bauer (drums) and Banana to become the Youngbloods. The group fulfilled Young's contractual obligations with Mercury with *Two Trips* (1966, released 1967) and in 1967 signed to RCA. Their eponymous début album included the good-timey 'Grizzly Bear' and 'Get Together' (written by **Quicksilver Messenger Service**'s Dino Valenti). Following their move to California, the group adopted a looser style, seen at its best on the **Charlie Daniels**-produced *Elephant Mountain*, made without Corbitt in the year a re-released 'Come Together' gave them a Top Ten

hit. That album included the haunting 'Darkness, Darkness', later recorded by **Ian Matthews**, **Mott the Hoople** and **Jesse Winchester**. As a trio, the group signed to Warner Brothers who gave them their own label, Raccoon, on which they released a series of pleasant but inconsequential albums, including the live *Rock Festival* (1970) and *Good and Dusty* (1971) with Michael Kane on bass.

In 1972 the group disbanded and all the members embarked on solo careers. The most successful was Young who, in the manner of Sebastian, recorded a series of gentle, folky albums featuring his light, supple voice. Among these were *Songbird* (Warners, 1975) and *American Dreams* (Elektra, 1978). In the eighties Young briefly re-formed the Youngbloods and released the solo album *The Highway Is for Heroes* (Cypress, 1987).

FRANK ZAPPA

b. 21 December 1940, Baltimore, Maryland, USA,
d. 4 December 1993

Bandleader, composer, guitarist, humorist and rock politician, Zappa pursued an idiosyncratic but respected course over more than a quarter of a century. He was also among the most prolific of rock artists, releasing over fifty albums. More than 200 musicians appeared on stage or on record with him, including long-term collaborator **Captain Beefheart**, **Little Feat**'s Lowell George and jazz violinist Jean-Luc Ponty.

Zappa grew up in Southern California, inspired equally by doo-wop (he wrote the elegiac 'Memories of El Monte' for the Penguins, Original Sound, 1963) and the classical avant-garde music of Stravinsky and Edgard Varese. He played in bar bands, wrote for low-budget movies (*Run Home Slow*, 1965) and recorded singles in his own studio as Ned and Nelda, Baby Ray and the Ferns and Brian Lord and the Midnighters before joining the Soul Giants in 1964. The band soon switched from white soul to Zappa's quirky, sarcastic songs and became the Muthers. With singer Ray Collins, Jimmy Carl Black (drums), Roy Estrada (bass) and Elliott Ingber (guitar), the group was signed by manager Herb Cohen to Verve, who insisted on a name change to the Mothers of Invention.

Freak Out! (1966) was one of the first rock double-albums and introduced Zappa's characteristic technique of shifting abruptly between contrasting styles, moods, sentiments and techniques. The record included sentimental pop ('Wowie Zowie'), social protest ('Who Are the Brain Police?') and audience provocation ('You're Probably Wondering Why I'm Here'). Between tracks Zappa and producer Tom Wilson added snatches of conversation and other sound effects.

For *Absolutely Free* (1967), keyboards-player Don Preston and saxophonists Bunk Gardner and Jim Motorhead Sherwood were added. The record introduced a jazz flavour to the acerbic lyrics of 'Brown Shoes Don't Make It' and 'Plastic People'. The sleeve of *We're Only in It for the Money* (1967) was a parody of **The Beatles**' *Sgt Pepper's Lonely Hearts Club Band* and the album lampooned the hippy movement in songs like the savage 'Flower Punk', sung to the tune of 'Hey Joe'.

The first album credited to Zappa alone was the sound collage *Lumpy Gravy*, which was followed by *Cruisin' with Ruben and the Jets* (1968) on which the Mothers lovingly and precisely re-created the sound of a fifties vocal group.

With a growing international reputation as an underground hero, Zappa launched the first of his multi-media projects, *Uncle Meat*. The 1969 double-album, the first on Cohen's Bizarre label was intended as a movie soundtrack, though an audiovisual *Uncle Meat*, a collection of film clips from Zappa's career, did not appear until 1988.

Burnt Weeny Sandwich (1970) and the live collection *Weasels Ripped My Flesh* marked the end of the first phase of the Mothers of Invention. The group split, with Estrada and George forming Little Feat and Black and Gardner recording for Uni as Geronimo Black. Zappa himself moved into production for Bizarre, where he was responsible for Beefheart's classic *Trout Mask Replica* (1969), *Permanent Damage* by female ensemble the GTO's and *An Evening with Wild Man Fischer* (1969), an unaccompanied set by an eccentric Los Angeles street singer.

In another unexpected move, Zappa next featured his own impressive jazz-rock guitar work on *Hot Rats* (1970). The wholly instrumental album also included electric violin-playing from Sugarcane Harris (formerly of **Don and Dewey**) and the French virtuoso Jean-Luc Ponty (*b. 29 September 1942, Avranches*). Ponty had previously recorded for Pacific Jazz with **George Duke** and made his own album of Zappa tunes, *King Kong* (Pacific Jazz, 1970).

Zappa's first collaboration with classical musicians was a 1970 concert performance of *200 Motels* with Zubin Mehta and the Los Angeles Philharmonic. *200 Motels* was filmed the following year as 'a surrealistic documentary of life on the road', featuring **Ringo Starr**. By now a new touring group had been assembled with former **Turtles** members Howard Kaylan and Mark Volman on vocals. *Just Another Band from LA* (1972) contained live recordings by this group and was compiled by Zappa when confined to a wheelchair after being dragged from a London stage by an irate audience member. In the same year he released the instrumental *Waka/Jawaka* and *The Grand Wazoo*, a jazz-based concept album.

The aggressive, misogynist *Overnite Sensation* (1973) was followed by a Top Ten hit in *Apostrophe*, whose title track was co-written by Zappa and **Jack Bruce**. Despite this commercial success, Zappa's career lost artistic momentum in the mid-seventies when he was reunited with a harmonica-playing Beefheart on *Bongo Fury* (1975) and cut *Zoot Allures* (1976) with a new touring band featuring Ruth Underwood. *Sheik Yerbouti* (released in 1979 on a new label, Zappa), a Top Thirty hit, caused controversy over its portrayal of Arab and Jewish stereotypes and featured guitarist Adrian Belew, later to play with **David Bowie**, **King Crimson** and Bears.

During the eighties Zappa maintained his prodigious recorded output, releasing three volumes of a rock-opera, *Joe's Garage*, in 1980 and three more of *Shut Up and Play Your Guitar* (1981), issued on another of his labels, Barking Pumpkin. His greatest commercial triumph was 'Valley Girl' (1982), a satire on Southern California youth culture featuring his fourteen-year-old daughter Moon Unit. Zappa returned to a classical/rock format on *With the LSO* (1983) and asked the rhetorical question *Does Humor Belong in Music?* in 1985.

Though primarily a marginal figure with a significant cult following, Zappa returned to centre stage in 1985 when he figured prominently in the campaign against the so-called Parents Music Resource Centre (PMRC) which sought to censor rock lyrics. He testified before a Congressional Committee and issued *Frank Zappa Meets the Mothers of Prevention* in 1986, when he also recorded *Jazz from Hell* on synclavier. *The Hard Way* followed in 1988, after which Zappa began his own programme of reissuing live performances previously only available on bootlegs. He released an eight-CD set of bootlegs, *Beat the Boots!*, in 1991, plus two new albums, *The Best Band You Never Heard* and *Make a Jazz Noise Here*. Later that year he announced he was suffering from cancer. He carried on working, however, and conducted a series of interviews in 1992 during which he discussed his battle with the disease. He released his final albums, *Yellow Shark* and *Civilization Phaze III*, in 1993 and 1995, respectively. The following year the English 'Zappologist' Ben Watson published a lengthy critical biography, *Frank Zappa, The Negative Dialectics of Poodle Play*.

Strictly Commercial (1995) was a single-album anthology, while in the same year Relativity Records released the first batch of all Zappa's fifty-three albums, each one newly remastered. In 1996 Warner added the four-CD set *Luther* to the pile, and in 1998 Ryko a single CD, *Mystery Disc*, of recently discovered out-takes and demos.

Dweezil Zappa first played guitar with his father in 1982 at the age of twelve, co-writing 'My Mother Is a Space Cadet' (1983) with Frank Zappa's guitarist Steve Vai. His later solo albums for Chrysalis included the Beau Hill-produced *My Guitar Wants to Kill Your Mama* (1988). He also enjoyed a successful career as a presenter on satellite/cable channel MTV.

WARREN ZEVON
b. 24 January 1947, Chicago, Illinois, USA

Guitarist and pianist Warren Zevon emerged in the seventies as one of America's most gifted singer-songwriters. Like many such before him, however, he was unable to convert huge critical acclaim into record sales.

Born of Russian and Scottish descent, Zevon had early hopes of becoming a classical composer before discovering folk and blues in his teens. A period as an unsuccessful session musician led to work writing television jingles in the late sixties and his first appearances as a songwriter on singles by Nino Tempo & April Stevens and the **Turtles**. He released a few singles under various pseudonyms for the Turtles' own label before signing to Imperial Records for his début album, *Wanted Dead or Alive* (1970). Disappointed at its lack of success, he joined the **Everly Brothers** band as musical director, touring and recording with the duo in the early seventies. He released his eponymous second solo album, produced by Jackson Browne and featuring **Fleetwood Mac** members Stevie Nicks and Lindsey Buckingham, in 1976 to enthusiastic reviews. The ironic and melancholic stance of many of the songs on *Warren Zevon* drew comparisons with **Randy Newman**, and two, 'Poor Poor Pitiful Me' and 'Hasten Down the Wind', were subsequently covered by a number of artists, most notably **Linda Ronstadt**.

The follow-up, *Excitable Boy* (1978), gave Zevon his first international hit single with the tongue-in-cheek rocker 'Werewolves of London', later featured in the successful John Landis film, *American Werewolf in London*. His best album, it included many of his most admired songs, such as 'Roland the Headless Thompson Gunner' and 'Accidentally Like a Martyr'. His fourth album, *Bad Luck Streak in Dancing School*, again drew ecstatic reviews and the single 'Jeannie Needs a Shooter', co-written with **Bruce Springsteen**, drew the attention of a wider audience. After a live album (*Stand in the Fire*, 1981) and the disappointing concept album *The Envoy* (1982), alcohol problems saw him retire from recording activity for almost five years, although he continued to tour.

Zevon re-emerged on Virgin in 1987 with the excellent *Sentimental Hygiene*, on which he dealt with his 'missing years' in the lyrics of several songs, employing the services of **R.E.M.** as backing band, with other guest appearances from **Bob Dylan**, **Neil Young** and Don Henley. The basic unit of Zevon and Pete Buck, Michael Mills and Bill Berry (all from R.E.M.) also recorded an album of cover-versions under the name Hindu Love Gods, which would eventually be released in 1990. A 'best of' from Asylum, *A Quiet Normal Life* (1988), preceded *Transverse City* (1989), which was less successful and displayed Zevon's newly acquired love of computers and synthesizers. It was followed by 1992's appropriately titled *Mr Bad Example* (Giant).

In 1993 Zevon released a solo acoustic live album, *Learning to Flinch*, culled from a lengthy world tour and including three new songs. *Life'll Kill You* (Artemis, 1999) included a version of **Steve Winwood**'s 'Back in the High Life Again', but was more noteworthy for the clutch of Zevon originals all bristling with malice and naked emotions, such as 'I Was in the House when the House Burned Down'.

THE ZOMBIES

Rod Argent, b. 14 June 1945, St Albans, Hertfordshire, England; Paul Atkinson, b. 19 March 1946, Cuffley; Colin Blunstone, b. 24 June 1945, Hatfield; Hugh Grundy, b. 6 March 1945, Winchester, Hampshire; Chris White, b. 7 March 1943, Barnet

One of the most technically accomplished British beat groups of the sixties, the Zombies retained a strong cult following for years after their dissolution in 1968. Both Argent and Blunstone had later success as solo artists.

The group was formed at school as the Sundowners by Argent (piano), Atkinson (guitar), Grundy (drums) and singer Blunstone. Playing covers of current hits, they became the Mustangs and then the Zombies in 1962, adding bassist White. With music taking second place to studies, the band had decided to split when they won a Decca recording contract in a talent contest.

Their first release, Argent's ethereal beat ballad 'She's Not There' (1964), featured Blunstone's singular breathy vocals. It was a British Top Twenty hit and reached No. 2 in America on Parrot. The Zombies' début album *Begins Here* also featured 'Tell Her No', a Top Ten hit in America in 1965. The group toured extensively in America but later singles like 'She's Coming Home' were unsuccessful.

In 1967 the Zombies were signed by Derek Everett to the newly formed British arm of Columbia, recording the imaginative *Odyssey and Oracle*. The group had split up before the release of 'Time of the Season', a million-seller in America on Date. They briefly reformed to make the unsuccessful 'Imagine the Swan' and 'It Don't Work Out' but Argent and White had already planned their own group, Argent.

White remained backstage as producer and songwriter while Argent included drummer Robert Henrit (*b. 2 May 1944, Broxbourne, Herts*), bass-player Jim Rodford (*b. 7 July 1945, St Albans*) and Russ Ballard (*b. 14 June 1945, St Albans*), who had previously played guitar with **Adam Faith**'s backing group the Roulettes, and with Unit 4+2, whose 'Concrete and Clay' (Decca, 1965) had been a British No. 1.

The prolific Argent made several self-produced albums in five years for Columbia, achieving two major hits with 'Hold Your Head Up' (1972) and 'God Gave Rock and Roll to You' (1973). After writing such hits as 'Liar' (**Three Dog Night**, 1971) and 'I Don't Believe in Miracles' (Blunstone, 1972), Ballard left to concentrate on songwriting, creating 'New York Groove' for Hello (Bell, 1975). Argent cut one album for RCA before the keyboardist dissolved the band in 1976. Rod Argent's later work included such solo albums as *Moving Home* (MCA, 1978) and the mainly instrumental *Red House* (MMC, 1988). He also accompanied saxophonist Barbara Thompson, **Johnny Dankworth** and **The Who**'s Roger Daltrey, as well as composing television themes and jingles and operating as a freelance producer for the likes of Tanita Tikaram (*Ancient Hearts*, 1988) and Labbi Siffre (*Man of Reason*, 1991).

Of the other Zombies, Atkinson and Grundy worked for Columbia's A&R department (with the former moving on to RCA and MCA) while Blunstone pursued a fitful solo career in the seventies and eighties. As Neil McArthur he re-recorded 'She's Not There' (Deram, 1969) before signing to Columbia for the wistful, well-crafted *One Year* (1971), which featured a Top Twenty hit in the delicate reading of Denny Laine's 'Say You Don't Mind'. After *Ennismore* (1972), he cut three lesser albums before moving to **Elton John**'s Rocket label for *Late Nights in Soho* (1979). With keyboards-player Dave Stewart, Blunstone successfully revived Jimmy Ruffin's 1966 hit 'What Becomes of the Broken Hearted?' (Stiff, 1981) but had a lower profile in later years, singing on albums by **Alan Parsons**, forming Keats with several Parsons alumni and recording as a soloist for IRS in 1988.

Despite the brevity of the group's career, Zombies records were frequently reissued and more than one group of imposters took to the American rock revival circuit. The genuine Zombies, however, steadfastly refused to re-form until 1991, when Blunstone, Grundy and White teamed up to record the unsuccessful *New World* after 'Time of the Season' had been used in the film *Awakenings*. Blunstone made a pair of new albums, *Echo Bridge* (1991) and *The Light Inside* (1998), but these were overshadowed by the anthology *In the Time of Colin Blunstone* (1991) and the four-CD career retrospective *Zombie Heaven* (1997).

ZUCCHERO
b. Aldelmo Fornaciari, 1956, Italy

A major star in his native Italy in the eighties and nineties, Zucchero was unable to achieve any sustained success outside his homeland with his **Joe Cocker**-styled blues-rock.

Zucchero formed his first band in Bologna in the late seventies, having studied veterinary medicine in the city. Finding little success as a performer, he turned to songwriting with more luck in the early eighties. He launched his own career in 1986 with *Respetto*, but it was the follow-up *Blues* (1987) which made the breakthrough, selling over one million copies in Italy. From it, the ballad 'Senz' Una Donna' ('Without a Woman') was a hit throughout mainland Europe. The album *Ora Incenso Birra* (1989) was another major seller.

In 1991 a re-recorded English/Italian language version featuring **Paul Young** reached the Top Five in the UK. It was taken from the previous year's album, *Zucchero Fornaciari*, which featured English language songs and guest appearances from **Eric Clapton** and veteran R&B organist **Jimmy Smith**. The album subsequently charted in the UK, but Zucchero was unable to sustain the momentum, and later releases sold poorly. His two other UK hits in the early nineties were both duets, 'Diamante' (1992) with soul vocalist Randy Crawford and the more unexpected 'Miserere' with opera star Luciano Pavarotti. The latter song, which reached the UK Top Twenty in 1992, was written by **U2**'s Bono.

Zucchero later appeared at Woodstock '94.

ZZ TOP

Frank Beard, b. 11 July 1949, Frankston, Texas, USA;
Billy Gibbons, b. 16 December 1949, Houston, Texas;
Dusty Hill, b. 19 May 1949, Dallas, Texas

With an incongruous mixture of Rip Van Winkle beards, heavy blues guitar music and videos that were both lascivious and self-mocking, ZZ Top were one of the most popular rock bands of the mid-eighties.

The trio was formed in 1970 by three experienced Texas musicians. Gibbons was the son of the conductor of the Houston Philharmonic Orchestra and had played in the Saints, Coachmen and Ten Blue Flames before forming the psychedelic band the Moving Sidewalks, whose '99th Floor' (Tantara, 1967) was a local hit. Hill's mother had been a big-band singer and her guitarist son had accompanied **Freddie King**,

recorded with his brother Rocky for Paradise and Ara as the Warlocks and formed the American Blues with drummer Beard, recording albums for Karma (1967) and Uni (1969).

With manager/producer Bill Ham, ZZ Top signed to London and released *The First Album* (1971). As a result of constant touring in the South, 'Francine' from *Rio Grande Mud* (1972) was a regional hit, while *Tres Hombres* (1973) brought a minor national success with 'La Grange' and was the first of ZZ Top's string of million-selling albums. 'Tush' from *Fandango* (1975) was the group's first Top Twenty single.

In 1976 ZZ Top undertook their ambitious Worldwide Texas Tour, whose stage set featured a Southwestern panorama complete with cacti and longhorn cattle, and released *Tejas*, whose tracks included 'Arrested for Driving While Blind'. The group was inactive in 1977–9 and on returning to recording signed with Warners for *Deguello* (1979), from which came the hit 'I Thank You', and *El Loco* (1981).

Eliminator (1983) saw the introduction of synthesizer and drum machine and was ZZ Top's most successful album, giving the trio a Top Ten hit with 'Legs'. This period also saw the group become video stars as Tim Newman directed a series of quirky accompaniments to such tracks as 'Gimme All Your Lovin'' (1984), the band's biggest British hit, and 'Sharp Dressed Man'.

ZZ Top's popularity increased with *Afterburner*, one of the biggest-selling records of 1985. It included the Top Ten hits 'Sleeping Bag', 'Stages' and 'Rough Boy'. *Recycler* was released in 1990, and was another major success. The band toured extensively in 1991 and marked the end of their deal with Warners by releasing the compilation *Greatest Hits* (1992), including the newly recorded **Elvis Presley** cover, 'Viva Las Vegas'. They signed to RCA in a high-profile multi-million dollar deal, releasing *Antenna* (1994), which saw them return to a rootsier R&B sound. In the same year they released *One Foot in the Blues*, a collection of unreleased blues recordings. They continued in that vein with *Rhytmeen* (1996), which they supported with a North American tour.

The Best of ZZ Top (1994) is just that.

Index of Song and Album Titles

Song titles are set in roman type and album titles in italics. Where a title refers to both a song and an album the page reference to the album has been set in italics

A, 499
A Cappella, 860
A Is for Allah, 946, *946*
A l'Olympia, 266
A Los Seis a Nueva York Los Salvajes del Ritmo, 92
A Mi Manera, 384
A Mis 33 Años, 469
A–Z of the Piano, The, 936
Aaron Neville's Soulful Christmas, 714
Aba Daba Honeymoon, 829
Abacab, 378
Abandoned Luncheonette, 413
Abandoned Shopping Trolley Hotline, 390
Abaniquito, 804
Abba Gold, 1
Abba: The Album, 1
Abba-esque, 2, 312
Abbamania, 2
Abbasalutely, 2
Abbey Road, 67, 647, 755, 820
ABC, 478
ABCs of Love, The, 606
Abdul Abulbul Amir, 233
Abdul and Cleopatra, 832
Abele Dance, 263
Abergavenny, 1056
Abigail Beecher, 154
Abilene, 417, 599
Abnominog, 1009
Abominable Showman, The, 603
About Blues, 1071
About This Thing Called Love, 322
About Time, 956, 977
Above, 762, 878
Above and Beyond, 458
Abracadabra, 2, 673
Abraham, Martin and John, 266, 480
Abraxas, 871
Abriendo Puertas, 315
Absolute, 878
Absolute Beginners, 484
Absolute Benson, 77
Absolute Game, The, 83
Absolute Torch and Twang, 563
Absolutely, 630
Absolutely ABC, 2
Absolutely Free, 1091
Academy in Peril, The, 150
Acadie, 714

Ac-cent-tchu-ate the Positive, 662, 663
Accept No Substitute, 863
Access All Areas, 935
Accidentally Born in New Orleans, 553
Accidentally Like a Martyr, 1092
Accidentally on Purpose, 254
Accidents of Birth, 474
Accordioniste, L', 774
Ace 90 Skank, 459
Ace of Spades, 699, *1079*
Acertate Mas, 16
Achin' Breakin' Heart, 893
Achtung Baby, 563, 1004
Acid Bubblegum, 754
Acid Eaters, 815
Acid Queen, 998
Acknowledge Your Own History, 520
Acme, 511
Acoustic, 321, 724
Across a Crowded Room, 982
Across a Wire: Live in New York City, 221
Across from Midnight, 198
Across the Borderline, 294, 444, 713, 734, 814, 900, 955
Across the Universe, 354
Across the Wide Missouri, 1072
Act Like Nothing's Wrong, 552
Act Naturally, 748, 749, 939
Act of War, 482, 503
Action, 154, 964
Actually, 768
Addicted to Love, 532, 751, 999
Addictions Vol. 1, 751
Addictions Vol. 2, 751
Addio, Addio, 681
A.D.I.D.A.S., 552
Adios Amigos, 815
Adios Marquita Linda, 890
Adios Nonino, 775
Adolescent Sex, 490
Adono, 274
Adore, 913
Adrenalize, 254
Advance, 106
Adventure, 973
Adventures in Modern Recording, 455
Adventures in the Land of the Good Groove, 846

Adventures of Grandmaster Flash on the Wheels of Steel, The, 397
Adventures of the Hersham Boys, The, 887
Adventures of Wheels of Steel, 397
Aerial Ballet, 722
Aero Zeppelin, 10
Affair of the Heart, 887, *934*
Affair to Remember, An, 1033
Affection, 938
Affectionate Melanie, 659
Afflicted, 1079
Afghanistan, 883
Afghanistan: Land of Islam, 946
Afraid to Dream, 828
A.F.R.I.C.A., 945
Africa, 640, 989
Africa Centre of the World, 40
Africa/Brass, 206, 274, 511
Africadelic, 263
African Piano, 466
African Portraits, 466
African Roots, 908
African Sketchbook, 466
African Waltz, 8, 242
Afrijazzy, 263
Afrika Must Be Free by 83, 750
Afrika Shox, 51, 573
Afro Blue, 369, 870
Afro India, 870
Afro-Cuban Jazz Moods, 384
Afro-Roots, 870
After All, 177, 181
After Bathing at Baxters, 494
After Hours, 690
After Midnight, 150, 186
After the Ball, 425, 1023
After the Ball: Forty Years of Melody, 425
After the Feeling Is Gone, 1000
After the Fire Is Gone, 607
After the Gold Rush, 1088
After the Hurricane, 647
After the Lights Go Low, 444
After the Love Has Gone, 298, 346
After the Lovin', 462
After the Pain, 1078
After the Rain, 573, 624, 712
After the Satellite Sings, 711
After the Storm, 229
After the War, 690

After the Watershed, 163
After You've Gone, 567
Afterburner, 1094
Afterglow, 272, 780
Aftermath, 724, 849
Afternoon Delight, 258
Aftershock, 40
Aftertones, 466
Again, 241, 479, 752
Against All Odds, 205
Against the Wind, 882
Age Ain't Nothin' but a Number, 528
Age of Consent, 208
Age of Plastic, The, 455
Age to Age, 397
Agent Provocateur, 345
Agents of Fortune, 98
Ages of Mann, 635
Agitation Sell-Out Waltz, 329
Agua de Luna, 92
Ah Sunflower, 361
Ah Sweet Mystery of Life, 441, 1031
Ahab the Arab, 946
Ahmad's Blues, 485
Ahnongay, 472
Ai A Mwana, 51
Ai No Corrida, 514
Aicha, 532
Aida, 623
Aimless Love, 799
Ain't but One Way, 954
Ain't Enough Comin' in, 862
Ain't Even Done with the Night, 660
Ain't Ever Satisfied, 297
Ain't Going Down (Til the Sun Comes Up), 123
Ain't Gonna Bump No More (With No Big Fat Woman), 978
Ain't Gonna Rain No Mo', 587
Ain't Gonna Worry, 375
Ain't Got No – I Got Life, 901
Ain't Gwine Whistle Dixie (Any Mo'), 966
Ain't Had Enough Fun, 588
Ain't It the Truth, 1046
Ain't Love a Good Thing, 356
Ain't Misbehavin', 28, 752, 819, 820, 826, 1006, 1029
Ain't No Love in the Heart of the City, 94, 1050
Ain't No Money, 166
Ain't No Mountain High Enough, 32, 121, 363, 374, 579, 855
Ain't No Pleasing You, 175
Ain't No Stoppin' Us Now, 84
Ain't No Sunshine, 481, 750, 1074
Ain't No Way to Treat a Lady, 821

Ain't No Woman (Like the One I've Got), 350
Ain't Nobody, 532
Ain't Nobody Better, 472
Ain't Nobody Here But Us Chickens, 518
Ain't Nobody Home, 812, 969
Ain't Nothin' but a Houseparty, 74
Ain't Nothin' Like the Real Thing, 549
Ain't Nothing Going on but the Rent, 579
Ain't Nothing Like the Real Thing, 32, 374, 747
Ain't She Sweet, 10, 65, 66, 522
Ain't That a Bitch, 1038
Ain't That a Shame, 58, 107, 275, 794
Ain't That Good News, 213
Ain't That Just Like Me, 449
Ain't That Lonely Yet, 1085
Ain't That Lovin' You Baby, 823
Ain't That Lovin' You (for More Reasons Than One), 471
Ain't That News, 761
Ain't That Peculiar, 279, 374, 841
Ain't Too Proud to Beg, 974
Ain't 2 Proud 2 Beg, 986
Ain't Understanding Mellow, 144
Ain't We Got Fun, 1052
Air de la Louisiane, L', 1070
Air That I Breathe, The, 450
Airborne, 757
Airhead, 273
Aja, 943
Akoustic Band, 216
Al Capone, 799, 928
Al Fin del Camino, 114
Al's Big Deal, 552
Alabam, 215
Alabama Blues, 577
Alabama Live, 12
Alabama Song, 279, 577, 1043
Alabamy Bound, 155, 260, 302
Aladdin Sane, 110, 638
Alagbon Close, 556
Alarm Clock, 431
Albany, 1053
Albatross, 341, 1020
Albedo 39, 1014
Albert, 537
Albert Flasher, 406
Album, 225, 884
Album, The, 831
Album II, 1024
Album III, 1024
Alchemy, 973
Alchemy – An Index of Possibilities, 965
Alchemy Live, 267
Alexander Graham Bell, 79

Alexander O'Neal, 739
Alexander's Ragtime Band, 78, 203, 222, 231, 819, 914
Alexis Korner's Blues Incorporated, 553
Alf, 703
Alfie, 45, *851*, 1033
Alice Blue Gown, 711, 829
Alice's Restaurant, 408
Alien, 37
Alien Orphan, 887
Aliens Ate My Buick, 273
Aliens, The, 226
Alimony, 212, 344
Alisha Rules the World, 784
Alison, 219, 854
Alive!, 546
Alive: Alone, 744
Alive and Kicking, 255
Alive and Well in Paris, 919
Alive in America, 943
Alive in Concert, 585
Alive, She Cried, 280
Alive Tonight, 145
Alive II, 546
Alive III, 546
All About Good Little Girls and Bad Little Boys, 48
All about Me, 559
All About My Girl, 620
All Alone Am I, 571
All Alone This Christmas, 601
All Along the Watchtower, 292, 440, 1081
All American Alien Boy, 700
All American Boy, 615
All American Girls, 906, 1026
All Around Cowboy, 893
All Around My Hat, 942
All Around the World, 278, 484, 504, 588, 731, 938
All Because of You, 4
All Boy, 216
All by Myself, 124, 267, 275, 817
All Change, 564
All for Love, 7, 950
All for Me Grog, 591
All God's Chillun Got Rhythm, 522
All Grown Up, 235
All Hail the Queen, 808
All I Could Do Was Cry, 486
All I Do Is Dream of You, 359
All I Ever Need Is You, 177, 373
All I Have to Do Is Dream, 134, 153, 320, 378

All I Have to Offer You (Is Me), 795
All I Know, 878, 898, 1041
All I Need Is a Miracle, 378
All I Really Want, 693
All I Really Want to Do, 147, 177
All I See Is You, 933
All I Wanna Do, 232
All I Wanna Do Is Rock, 992
All I Wannna Do Is Make Love to You, 436
All I Want, 54, 513, *1008*
All I Want for Christmas Is a Beatle, 515
All I Want for Christmas Is My Two Front Teeth, 515
All I Want for Christmas Is You, 157
All I Want Is You, 857
All I Want to Do, 292
All I Want to Do in Life, 192
All in a Night's Work, 526
All in Good Time, 944
All in Love, 747
All in Love Is Fair, 1077
All in My Mind, 257
All in the Family, 169
All in the Mind, 1020
All Is Full of Love, 86
All Killer, No Filler, 582
All la Glory, 53
All Mine, 785
All Mixed Up, 740
All Mod Cons, 484
All My Best, 1052, 1053
All My Best Years, 1
All My Ex's Live in Texas, 955
All My Life, *126*, 255, 847
All My Love, *134*, 325, 751
All My Relations, 592
All My Tomorrows, 1035
All My Trails, 718
All Night Long, 295, 488, 832
All of a Sudden, 444
All of Me, 48, 113, *156*, 1050
All of Me Loves All of You, 62, 220
All of My Friends Were There, 543
All of My Heart, 2
All of the Good Ones Are Taken, 700
All of You, 469, 855
All or Nothing, 487, 558, 912
All Out of Love, 12
All Over the Place, 54
All Over the World, 257
All Right, 231, 863
All Right Now, 357, 358
All Set, 145
All She Wants to Do Is Dance, 296
All Shook Up, 91, 555

All Star Festival, 1010
All Stood Still, 1006
All Systems Go, 842, 961
All That I Need, 114
All That You Can't Leave Behind, 1005
All that You Have Is Your Soul, 172
All the Best, 873
All the Best Cowboys Have Chinese Eyes, 1054
All the Boys Love Carrie, 1035
All the Brave Horses, 948
All the Faces of Buddy Miles, 669
All the Good Times, 724
All the Good Uns, 465
All the King's Horses, 373, 569
All the Love in the World, 1033
All the Magic, 59
All the Man That I Need, 458
All the News That's Fit to Sing, 733
All the Sad Young Men, 734
All the Things We Are, 133
All the Things You Are, 530, 890
All the Time, 472
All the Way, 150, 833, 904, 1012
All the Way . . . A Decade of Song, 267
All the Way from Memphis, 700
All the Young Dudes, 111, 700, 700
All These Things, 714
All Things Must Pass, 284, 427, 790, 930
All This and Heaven Too, 1012
All This for a Song, 406
All This Time, 950
All Those Years Ago, 427
All Through the Night, 566
All Time Greatest Hits, Vol. 1, 749
All Time High, 214
All Too Soon, 1041
All True Man, 740
All Woman, 938
All You Can Eat, 563
All You Had to Do Was Tell Me, 688
All You Need Is Love, 516
All Your Goodies Are Gone, 194
All Your Love, 632, 861, 862
All-American Boy, The, 55
Allegheny Moon, 751
Allegria, 384
Allen Toussaint Collection, The, 991
Allentown, 502
Allentown Jail, 774
Alley Oop, 17, 351, 356
Allies, 229
Alligator Man, 671
Alligator Wine, 433
Alligator Woman, 152

Allman Brothers Band, The, 15
Allnighter, The, 296
Allons à Lafayette, 3
Almaz, 234
Almighty Fire, 355
Almo Caribena, 92, 315
Almost a Gentleman, 691
Almost Blue, 219, 893, 894
Almost But Not Quite There, 940
Almost Cut My Hair, 229
Almost Like Being in Love, 577
Almost Paradise, 436, 770
Almost Persuaded, 487, 893, 1080
Almost Saturday Night, 226, 302
Almost Tomorrow, 937, 1005
Alone, 436
Alone Again (Naturally), 747
Alone Again Or, 240, 600
Alone and Acoustic, 409
Alone at Last, 1069
Alone in the Night, 385
Alone on a Rainy Night, 74
Alone with Everybody, 1021
Along Came Jones, 196, 946
Along Comes a Woman, 181
Along Comes Mary, 34
Along the Red Ledge, 413
Alpert and Masekela, 649
Alpha Centauri, 968
Alphabet City, 2
Already It's Heaven, 893
Alright, 479, 490, 961
Alright Again!, 126
Alright Alright, 651, 977
Alright Baby, 951
Alright Jack, 13
Alright, Okay You Win, 572
Alright Tonight, 3
Also sprach Zarathustra (2001), 550
Alter Nations, 558
Alternate Title, 684
Alternative, 768
Aluna Loluwa, 8
Alvin Twist, 883
Alvin's Harmonica, 883
Always, 201
Always and Forever, 437, 993
Always in My Heart, 211
Always in the Way, 425
Always Late, 360, 1085
Always Never the Same, 955
Always on My Mind, 768
Always . . . Patsy Cline, 193
Always Say Goodbye, 410
Always True to You in My Fashion, 785
AM, 1007
Am I Black Enough for You, 759
Am I Blue?, 1036
Am I Losing You, 675
Am I Not Your Girl, 734

Am I That Easy to Forget, 462
Amacord/Nino Rota, 1067
Amadou Tilo, 989
Amanda, 109, *119*
Amandla, 248
Amapola, 280
Amarillo, 425
Amarillo by Morning, 955
Amateur Hour, 927
Amazing Grace, 47, *192*, 204, 385, 714, 938
Amazing Grace (Used to Be Her Favourite Song), 18
Amazing Love, 795
Amazing Race, 752
Ambassador, 263
Amber Waves of Grain, 411
Ambition, 959
Ambulance Blues, 1088
Ambush, 659
Amen, 470, 955
America, 81, 309, 598, 897, 919
America Eats Its Young, 194
America, I Believe in You, 242
America in Concert, 19
America the Beautiful, 174
America – The Way I See It, 1061
American Beauty, 400, 773
American Beauty Rose, 44
American Caesar, 469, 851
American City Suite, 228
American Country Gothic, 417
American Dream, 229, 478, 724, *1088*
American Dreamer, *148*, 729
American Dreams, 1090
American English, 976
American Fool, 660
American Garage, 666
American Girl, 771
American Gothic, 5, 503
American Hearts, 732
American in Paris, An, 380
American Moonshine and Prohibition Songs, 716
American Music, 781
American Patrol, 653, 671
American Pie, 451, 625, 632
American Prayer, An, 280
American Pride, 12
American Recordings, 166, 858
American Roulette, 737
American Soul Man, 775
American Stars'n'Bars, 1088
American Stonehenge, 471
American Trilogy, 718, 790
American Tune, 899
American Woman, 406
Americana, 736
Americanization of Oooga Booga, The, 649
Americano, El, 332

Americanos, 354
Amerika, 783
AmeriKKKa's Most Wanted, 466
Amie, 806
Amigos, 24, 586, 871
Ammonia Avenue, 756
Amnesia, 886, 982
Among My Souvenirs, 353, *353*, 1078
Among the Living, 25
Among the Stars, 689
Amor, 469, 763, 879
Amor Gitana, 332
Amorica, 87
Amorok, 738
Amos Moses, 822
Amoureuse, 503
Amplified, 994
Amplified Heart, 321
Amsterdam, 47, 119, 120
Amsterdam 8th September 1994, 985
Amused to Death, 777
Amy Grant, 397
Amy, Wonderful Amy, 1078
Amy's Eyes, 795
Anaheim, Azusa and Cucamunga Sewing Circle, Book Review and Timing Association, The, 490
Anam, 312
Anarchy in the UK, 659, 699, 800, 884, 885
Anastasia, 108
Anatomy of a South African Village, 466
Ancient and Modern, 286
Ancient Hearts, 1093
And, 1071
And a Time to Dance, 594
And Along Came Jones, 512
. . . and Carrot Rope, 760
And Her Mother Came Too, 135, 726
And Her Tears Flowed Like Wine, 734
And His Mother Called Him Bill, 307
And I Love Him, 772
And I Love You So, 625
And in this Corner . . ., 917
And It Stoned Me, 694
. . . And Justice for All, 665
And Live, 1071
And Now the Runaways!, 499
And Russia Is Her Name, 422
And She Was, 967
And That Reminds Me, 825
And the Band Played Waltzing Matilda, 780
And the Bull Walked Around, Olay, 529

And the Cumberland Mountain Folk, 735
And the Great Big Saw Came Nearer and Nearer, 1046
And the Hits Just Keep on Comin', 685
And the Horse They Rode in on, 922
And the Music Plays on, 889
And the Tears Flowed Like Wine, 529
And Then He Took up Golf, 233
And Then Some, 711
And When I Die, 97, 728
And You Smiled, 685
And Your Dream Comes True, 63
Andalucia, 1010
Andmoreagain, 600
Andromeda Heights, 788
Angel, 49, 388, 631, 650, 814, 879, 949
Angel Clare, 898
Angel Cried, An, 475
Angel Eyes, 857, 1047
Angel Face, 386
Angel Fingers, 703
Angel Heart, 1041
Angel of Harlem, 1004
Angel of the Morning, 683, 970
Angel Spread Your Wings, 737
Angel Station, 635
Angel with a Lariat, 302, 562
Angela Jones, 599, 658
Angela Winbush, 1070
Angels, 1065
Angels & Cigarettes, 164
Angels Listened in, The, 227
Angels with Dirty Faces, 887
Angie, 395, 849
Angie Baby, 821, 835
Angst in My Pants, 927
Anhomie and Bonhomie, 878
Animal, 254
Animal Boy, 815
Animal Crackers, 260
Animal Crackers in my Soup, 974
Animal Magnetism, 875
Animal Nitrate, 959
Animal Zoo, 932
Animalize, 546
Animals, 777
Anita O'Day at the Berlin Festival, 734
Anita Sings the Winner, 734
Anji, 897
Anna, 13
Anna Lee, 486
Annabella, 1026
Annie Christian, 797
Annie Had a Baby, 51
Annie I'm Not Your Daddy, 533

Annie Mae's Café, 588
Annie's Aunt Fanny, 51
Annie's Song, 258, 274, 369
Anniversary, 381, 1080
Anniversary Albums, 341
Anniversary Song, 510, 895
Anniversary Waltz, 1032
Annual Waltz, 429
Anodyne, 1007
Another Brick in the Wall, 777
Another Cycle, 193
Another Day, 611
Another Day in Paradise, 205
Another Green World, 311
Another Grey Area, 754
Another Hand, 870
Another Hand Shakin' Goodbye, 356
Another Music in a Different Kitchen, 145
Another Nail in My Heart, 936
Another Night, 355, *450*
Another Night of Love, 829
Another One Bites the Dust, 808
Another Op'nin', Another Show, 785
Another Part of Me, 481
Another Perfect Day, 699
Another Place and Time, 961
Another Place, Another Time, 581, 1059
Another Rock'n'Roll Christmas, 386
Another Sad Love Song, 44, 118
Another Saturday Night, 213, 946
Another Scoop, 1054
Another Side of Bob Dylan, 292
Another Side of Rick, 711
Another Somebody Done Somebody Wrong Song, 683
Another Step, 1055
Another Suitcase in Another Hall, 593
Another Tear Falls, 616, 1026
Another Ticket, 187
Another Time, Another Place, 333
Another View, 1018
Another World, 808
Anourag, 889
Anoushka, 889
Answer Me, 1051
Answer My Love, 202
Answers (Answers to Nothing), 1007
Antenna, 1094
Anthem, 991
Anthem of the Sun, 400
Anthem (One Day in Every Week), 882
Anthology, 67, 68, 119, 174, 612, 647, 816, 835, 911, 940, 966
Anthology, 1961–1977, 470

Anthology 1, 302, 305, 350, 376, 403, 427, 434, 489, 539
Anthology 2, 68, 305, 427
Anthology 3, 68
Anthony Braxton, 118
Antichrist Superstar, 638, 639
Anticipation, 898
Anticloning, 541
Antmusic, 25
Ants Marching, 246
Anutha Zone, 272
Any Day Now, 44, 47, 257, 675, 910
Any Dream Will Do, 278, 593
Any Kind of Man, 359
Any Love, 650, *1013*
Any Man of Mine, 1000
Any Old Iron, 170, 393, 1046
Any Old Place with You, 428
Any Place I Hang My Hat Is Home, 663
Any Road, 406
Any Time Any Place/And on and on, 479
Any Way That You Want Me, 970
Any Way You Want It, 187
Anymore, 284
Anymore – A Tribute to Johnny Ace, 867
Anyone at All, 540
Anyone for Tennis, 133
Anyone Who Had a Heart, 45, 89, 438, 891, 1033
Anyone Who Isn't Me Tonight, 847
Anything Can Happen, 864
Anything for You, 314
Anything Goes, 149, 424. 755, 785
Anything Is Possible, 381
Anything You Can Do, 79
Anything You Can Do I Can Do Better, 463
Anything You Want, 427
Anytime, 336
Anytime . . . Anywhere, 214
Anyway, 328
Anyway Anyhow Anywhere, 1054
Anyway That You Want Me, 995
Anyway the Wind Blows, 150
Anywhere I Wander, 564
Aoxomoxoa, 400
Apache, 885, 1041
Apartment #9, 893
Apasionado, 17
Apocalypse, 624, 1026
Apocalypse des Animaux, L', 1014
Apocalypse '91 the Enemy Strikes Black, 803
Apollo Nine, 25
Apostrophe, 1091
Appetite for Destruction, 407, 728

Apple Bed, The, 443
Apple Blossom Time, 413
Apple Blossoms and Chapel Bells, 996
Apple for the Teacher, An, 231
Apple Honey, 441
Apple of My Eye, 349
Apple Stretching, The, 512
Apple Venus Volume 1, 1081
Applejack, 885
Apples, 761
Apples & Lemons, 130
Approaching Day, 228
Approximately Infinite Universe, 740
'Appy 'Ampstead, 531
April in Paris, 287, 372, 422, 904, 1041
April in Portugal, 61
April Love, 108, 323
April Showers, 259, 510
Aqualung, 498
Aquarium, 26
Aquarius, 26, 836
Aquerela Do Brasil, 1033
Arabesque, 660
Aravah Aravah, 585
Arbour Zena, 492
Arc of a Diver, 105, 1073
Arcadie, 563
Architecture and Morality, 742
Archive, 1041
Archive: 1967–1975, 378
Are 'Friends' Electric?, 727
Are We Having Fun Yet?, 86
Are We in Trouble Now, 993
Are You Experienced?, 440
Are You from Dixie?, 99
Are You Gonna Go My Way, 554
Are You Lonesome Tonight?, 747, 789
Are You Man Enough?, 350
Are You Okay?, 1034
Are You Ready, *136*, 732
Are You Ready to Be Heartbroken, 891
Are You Sincere, 1056
Are You Sure Hank Done It This Way?, 90, 683, 1060
A-Reet-a-Voutie, 366
Aren't You Glad You're You, 230, 1012
Arena, 289
Areo-Plain, 429
Aretha, 355
'Arf a Pint of Ale, 305
Argus, 1074
Argy Bargy, 935
Aria, 86
Arise, 883
Arise Therefore, 738
Arista Years, The, 401

Ariverderci Roma, 564
Arizona, 829
Ark, 24, 793
Ark 2, 377
Arkansas Traveler, 162, 511, 930
Armchair Theatre, 305
Armed & Dangerous, 25
Armed Forces, 219
Arms of Love, 447
Arms of Mary, 950
Arms of Orion, The, 298
Army Arrangement, 565
Army Arrangements, 557
Army Blues, 94
Army of Me, 86
Arnold Layne, 113, 776
Around Midnight, 206
Around the World, 239, 622, 820
Around the World in a Day, 797
Around the World in Eighty
   Days, 639
Arranger's Touch, The, 318
Arrested for Driving While
   Blind, 1094
Arrival, 1
Arrivederci Darling, 892
Arrow through the Bitch, An, 738
Ars Longa Vita Brevis, 309
Art Deco, 178
Art for Art's Sake, 976
Art of Defense, 559
Art of Excellence, The, 77
Art of Falling Apart, The, 16
Art of Parties, 491
Art Official Intelligence, 251
Art Tatum in Person, 969
Artful Dodger, The, 701
Arthur, 543
Arthur Alexander, 13
Arthur Lee & Love, 600
Arthur McBride, 116
Arthur Murray Taught Me Danc-
   ing in a Hurry, 463, 663, 873
Arthur Prysock, 802
Arthur Tracy's Message for Eng-
   land, 991
Arthur's Theme, 45, 231
Artificial Intelligence, 151
Artistic Hair, 392
Artistry in Bolero, 529
Artistry in Percussion, 529
Artistry in Rhythm, 529
As Above, So Below, 7
As Clean as They Wanna Be, 1001
As Close as You Think, 919
As Falls Wichita, So Falls Wichita
   Falls, 666
As I Live and Bop, 381
As I Love You, 60
As Long as He Needs Me, 57, 60
As Long as I Have You, 1059
As Long as I Live, 1045

As Long as I'm Moving, 953
As Long as I'm Singing, 244
As Long as She Needs Me, 249
As Long as We've Got One
   Another, 980
As Long as You Love Me, 46
As Nasty as They Wanna Be, 1001
As Raw as Ever, 815
As Soon as I Hang up the Phone,
   607, 1000
As Tears Go By, 326
As Time Goes By, 334, 334, 424,
   435, 588, 722, 1011, 1069
As You Take a Walk Through
   My Mind, 875
Ascension, 206, 892, 1002
Ascension Heights, 1083
Ashes in Your Mouth, 659
Ashes to Ashes, 111
Asian Rut, 696
Ask, 918
Ask Me, 352
Ask Me What You Want, 482
Ask Rufus, 532
Asking for It, 448
Asleep at the Wheel, 33
Ass Pocket o' Whiskey, An, 511
Assassing, 642
Assault and Battery, 513
Association, The, 34
Astaire, 908
Astoria: Portrait of the Artist, 77
Astounding 12-String Guitar of
   Glen Campbell, The, 153
Astral Weeks, 694
Astro Creep: 2000, Songs of Love,
   Destruction and Other Syn-
   thetic Delusions of the Electric
   Head, 1048
Astronauts and Heretics, 273
Asylum, 546
Asylum Choir, 863
Asylum Choir II, 863
Asylums in Jerusalem, 878
At Abbey Road, 1963–1966, 450
At Abbey Road, 1966–1970, 450
At Carnegie Hall, 623
At Folsom Prison, 166
At Home, 636
At Last, 486, 818
At My Front Door, 3, 107
At Seventeen, 466
At Sundown, 276, 282
At the Close of the Century, 1077
At the Club, 285
At the Crossroads, 866
At the Drop of a Hat, 574
At the Drop of Another Hat, 574
At the Edge, 401
At the End of a Long Lonely Day,
   837
At the Fairfield Hall, Croydon, 136

At the First Fall of Snow, 735
At the Gate of Horn, 662
At the Hollywood Bowl, 647
At the Hollywood Palladium, 850
At the Hop, 243
At the Jazz Band Ball, 73, 742
At the Movies, 1959–1974, 832
At the Pershing, 485
At the Ryman, 426
At the Speed of Sound, 611
At the Swing Cats Ball, 518
At the Village Vanguard, 511
At the Woodchopper's Ball, 441
At the Zoo, 897
At This Moment, 516
At Worst . . . , 236
At Your Beck and Call, 780
Atem, 968
Athens Andover, 995
A-Tisket, A-Tasket, 1040
Atkins-Travis Traveling Show,
   The, 36
Atlanta Rhythm Section, 37
Atlantic Crossing, 950
Atlantic Realm, 312
Atlantis, 267, 277
Atmosphere for Lovers and
   Thieves, 1041
Atom Heart Mother, 777
Atom Shop, 711
Atomic, 96, 96
Atomic Dog, 194
Atomic Hymn Book, The, 788
Atomic Mr Basie, The, 59, 246
Attack Me with Your Love, 152
Attack of the Giant Ants, The, 96
Attack of the Grey Lantern, 639
Attack of the Killer B's, 25
Attempted Moustache, 1024
Attica State, 576
Attitude, 178
Auberge, 819
Audrey Hepburn Complex, 779
Auf Immer und Ewig, 819
Auf Wiedersehen Sweetheart,
   608
August, 187
August and Everything After, 221
Auld Lang Syne, 597, 660
Auntie Maggie's Remedy, 346
Aura, 8, 248
Aural Sculpture, 956
Austin Sessions, The, 555
Australia, 637
Authority Song, 660
Authority Stealing, 557
Autoamerican, 96, 183
Autobahn, 554
Autobiography of MistaChuck,
   The, 803
Autogeddon, 215
Automatic, 498, 781, 827

Automatic for the People, 569, 827
Automobiles, 926
Autumn, 5
Autumn Almanac, 543
Autumn in New York, 288
Autumn Leaves, 274, 372, 485, 524, 774, 1065
Autumn 66, 1072
Autumn Song, 695
Autumn Stone, 912
Aux Armes Etc., 367
Avalanche, 168, 702
Avalon, 334, 510, 857, *857*
Avalon Sunset, 327, 695
Avant de Mourir, 528, 780
Ave Maria, 924
Avenger, The, 300
Average Guy, 272
Avocet, 765
Awakening, 485, 1026
Award Tour, 994
Away from It All, 987
Awesome Power of a Fully Operational Mothership, The, 195
Awful, 448
Axe, 406
Axe Victim, 710
Axel F, 693
Axis: Bold as Love, 440
Axis Mutatis, 888
Ay Ai Ai/Where Did You Go Last Night, 176
Ay Te Deju en San Antonio, 500
Ay-Tête-Fee, 176
Azucar Negra, 235

B-A-B-Y, 434, 980
B-52s, The, 43
B Movie Boxcar Blues, 613
*B*Witched*, 83
Babbacombe Lee, 324
Babble, 890
Babe, 959
Babies, 805
Babooshka, 143
Baby, 320, 706, 770, *1084*
Baby (You've Got What It Takes), 78, 1034
Baby Baby, 398
Baby Come Back, 398
Baby Come Close, 841
Baby Come to Me, 514
Baby Did a Bad Bad Thing, 475
Baby Do Ya Wanna Bump, 328
Baby Do You Wanna Bump?, 104
Baby Don't Change Your Mind, 549, 615
Baby Don't Do It, 127, 337
Baby Don't Forget My Number, 328
Baby Don't Get Hooked on Me, 247

Baby Don't Go, 177
Baby Don't Go Too Far, 471
Baby Don't You Weep, 812
Baby Faced Killer, 1009
Baby Get Lost, 331, 1034
Baby Go Go, 559
Baby I Don't Care, 575, 679
Baby I Love You, 302, 355, 404, 539, 815, 853, 929
Baby, I Love Your Way, 352
Baby I Need Your Loving, 350, 836
Baby I'm a Want You, 119
Baby I'm Back, 550
Baby I'm Burnin', 758
Baby I'm Lonely, 472
Baby I'm Yours, 615
Baby It's Cold Outside, 48, 336, 518, 595, 596, 663
Baby It's You, 889, 894, 926
Baby James Harvest, 55
Baby Jane, 950
Baby Let Me Follow You Down, 291, 698
Baby Let Me Hold Your Hand, 173
Baby Let Me Take You Home, 23, 698
Baby Let's Play House, 302, 789
Baby Love, 449, 649, 962, 963
Baby Lover, 188
Baby Make It Soon, 644
Baby Makes Her Blue Jeans Talk, 271
Baby Now That I've Found You, 610
. . . *Baby One More Time*, 928
Baby Plays Around, 219
Baby Please Don't Go, 694, 727, 1057
Baby Scratch My Back, 671
Baby She's Gone, 875
Baby Sitter, The, 1078
Baby Take a Bow, 974
Baby Talk, 9, 490
Baby That's Backatcha, 841
Babe the Rain Must Fall, 585, 623
Baby What You Want Me to Do, 823
Baby Won't You Please Come Home, 1058
Baby Workout, 1069
Baby, You Can Get Your Gun!, 296
(Baby) You Don't Have to Tell Me, 1026
Baby-Baby-Baby, 986
Babyface, 44
Babylon, 255, 271, 717
Babylon and on, 936
Babylon by Bus, 643
Bach – Goldberg Variations, 492

Bach Goes to Town, 391
Bachelorette, 86
Back, 736
Back and Forth, 152
Back and Fourth, 586
Back at the Chicken Shack, 37, 141, 916
Back Bay Shuffle, 890
Back by Popular Demand, 98
Back Country Suite, 15
Back Door Wolf, 459
Back for Good, 1064
Back for More, 635
Back from Hell, 859
Back from Rio, 148
Back Here on Earth, 584
Back Home, 82, 220
Back Home in Pasadena, 1032
Back Home in Tennessee, 276
Back in Black, 4
Back in Business, 547
Back in Line, 942
Back in My Arms Again, 962
Back in 72, 882
Back in the Day, 776
Back in the High Life Again, 1093
Back in the Highlife, 1073
Back in the Night, 270
Back in the Saddle Again, 39
Back in the Swing of Things, 981
Back in the USA, 656, 854
Back in the USSR, 502
Back in Your Life, 832
Back of Love, The, 299
Back of My Mind, 231
Back off Boogaloo, 939
Back on the Block, 124, 514, 551, 1015
Back on the Chain Gang, 791
Back on the Right Track, 954
Back on Top, 695
Back Stabbers, 736
Back Street Affair, 776
Back Street Crawler, 358
Back to Avalon, 596
Back to Back, 119
Back to Basics, 117, 656, 721
Back to Broadway, 957
Back to Earth, 946
Back to Front, 832
Back to Life (However Do You Want Me?), 923
Back to Mono, 930
Back to New Orleans, 12
Back to the 'Dillo, 867
Back to the Blues, 616
Back to the Centre, 116
Back to the Delta, 207
Back to the Egg, 611
Back to the Future Live, 33
Back to the Grindstone, 675
Back to the Groove, 234

Back to the Hop, 243
Back to the Light, 808
Back to the Night, 27
Back to the Roots, 654
Back to the Sh.t, 482
Back to the Streets, 221
Back Together Again, 338, 430
Back Up Train, 402
Backfield in Motion, 171
Backhand, 492
Backlash Blues, 900
Backstabbers, 74, 370
Backstage – The Greatest Hits and More, 778
Backstreet Boys, 46
Backstreet's Back, 46
Backwater Blues, 506, 914
Bad, 481, 514, 615
Bad and Good, 860
Bad Animals, 436
Bad Attitude, 657
Bad Bad Boy, 709
Bad Bad Leroy Brown, 228
Bad Bad Whiskey, 248, 669
Bad Blood, 880
Bad Boy, 314, 939, 1056, 1062
Bad Boys, 666, 917
Bad Case of Lovin' You (Doctor Doctor), A, 751
Bad Days, 339
Bad Eye, 679
Bad for Good, 657
Bad Girls, 693, 960
Bad Goodbye, A, 90
Bad Influence, 224, 224
Bad Love, 720
Bad Luck, 764
Bad Luck Streak in Dancing School, 1092
Bad Medicine, 102
Bad Moon Rising, 226, 920
Bad News Beat, 1088
Bad Penny Blues, 609, 658
Bad Reputation, 499, 979
Bad Seed/Mutiny, The, 168
Bad Time, 396, 493
Badge, 225
Badmotorfinger, 924
Bag Full of Soul, 620
Baggy Trousers, 630
Baghdad, 706
Bags' Groove, 248
Bahania, 384
Baia, 763
Bailamos, 469
Baja Sessions, 475
Baker Street, 811, 812
Bakersfield Bound, 148
Balabu, 236
Balada de un Loco, 775
Balaklava, 816
Balance of Power, 304

Bald Head, 802
Balham, Gateway to the South, 393
Bali Ha'i, 572
Bali Hi, 844
Ball, 473
Ball and Chain, 517, 983
Ball and Chain Blues, 1049
Ball of Confusion, 438, 975, 998, 1051
Ball Park Incident, 703
Ballad for Americans, 288, *735*, 838, 840, 905, 984
Ballad of a Teenage Queen, 165, 192
Ballad of Billy the Kid, 407
Ballad of Bonnie and Clyde, The, 327, 707
Ballad of Cat Ballou, The, 202
Ballad of Charles Whitman, 963
Ballad of Davy Crockett, The, 146, 1073
Ballad of East Rider, The, 147
Ballad of Forty Dollars, 415
Ballad of Go Go Brown, The, 438
Ballad of Ira Hayes, The, 165
Ballad of Jed Clampett, The, 340
Ballad of Lucy Jordan, 326
Ballad of Mack the Knife, The, 1042
Ballad of Paladin, The, 300
Ballad of Penny Evans, The, 392
Ballad of Sally Rose, The, 425
Ballad of the Cuban Invasion, 733
Ballad of the Fallen, The, 410
Ballad of the Green Berets, 882
Ballad of the Soldier's Wife, 1043
Ballad of the Yellow Beret, 882
Ballad of Todd Rundgren, 859
Ballad of You and Me and Pooneil, The, 494, 710
Ballade pour Adeline, 191
Ballads, The, 827
Ballads & Blues, 690
Ballbreaker, 5
Ballerina, 687
Ballroom Blitz, The, 964
Balls, 927
Balls to Picasso, 474
Baltimore, 134, 720, 901
Baltimore MD, You're the Only Doctor for Me, 874
Bam Bam, 987
Bama Lama Bama Lou, 589
Bamba, La, 228, 594, 598, 688, 900, 1010
Bamboleo, 384
Bambolina, 1086
Bamboo Music, 868, 965
Banana Boat (Day-O), 356
Banana Boat Song, 60, 73, 194, 244, 567, 1015

Banana Republic, 376
Banana Republics, 392
Banana Wind, 137
Bananamour, 919
Banba, 312
Band, The, 52, 53
Band and Body Works, 768
Band Kept Playin', The, 97
Band of Gold, 10, 210, 449
Band on the Run, 611
Band Played Waltzing Matilda, The, 185
Bandstand, 328
Bandstand Hop, 115
Bandwagonesque, 972
Bandy the Rodeo Clown, 54
Bang!, 354
Bang Bang, 724, 1014
Bang Bang Bang, 172
Bang Bang (My Baby Shot Me Down), 177, 904
Bangers and Mash, 393
Bangla Desh, 427, 864
Bango (To the Batmobile), 977
Bang-Shang a-Lang, 546
Bankrupt, 271
Banks of Pontchartrain, The, 116
Banks of the Ohio, The, 721
Banned in the USA, 1001
Banquet in Blues, 654
Bantu Choral Folk Songs, 768
Banty Rooster Blues, 758
Baptize Me in Wine, 433
Barabajagal, 277
Barbara Allen, 535
Barbarism Begins at Home, 918
Barbed Wire Blues, 270
Barbed Wire Kisses, 498
Barbie Girl, 26
Barbra Streisand Album, The, 956
Barbra – The Concerts: Live at Madison Square Garden, 957
Barcelona, 318, 808
Bare Trees, 341
Bare Wires, 654
Barefoot Boy, 218
Bark, 494
Barking at the Moon, 88
Barnacle Bill the Sailor, 518, 606
Barnestorming, 56
Barnstorm, 295
Baron von Tollbooth and the Chrome Nun, 495
Baroque Beatles Book, The, 834
Baroque Fanfares and Sonatas for Brass, 834
Barracuda, 436
Barrel House Bessie, 691
Barrel of a Gun, 259, 1008
Barrelhouse, Boogie & the Blues, 696
Barrelhouse Piano, 582

Barrett, 777
Barrister Pardon, 799
Barry Manilow, 637
Bartender Blues, 512
Basement Tapes, The, 52, 292
Bashin', 916
Basie's Basement, 1041
Basin Street Blues, 210, 211, 231
Basket Case, 402
Basket of Light, 765
Basketball, America, 98
Bass Culture, 507
Bass Goin' Crazy, 20
Bass Strings, 616
Basslines, 565
Bastards, 699
Bat Out of Hell, 657, *657, 860*
Bat Out of Hell II: Back into Hell, 657
Battle, The, 511
Battle of Armageddon, 767
Battle of Evermore, 569
Battle Hymn of the Republic, 718
Battle of New Orleans, The, 277, 285, 424, 456, 687
Battle of Who Could Care Less, The, 76
Battle of the Alamo, 837
Battle of the Field, The, 13
Battle Rages on, The, 254
Baubles Bangles and Beads, 891
Baxters, 494
Bayou Country, 226
BBC Sessions, 199, 570, 1055
B'Boom, 536
BDP Live Hardcore, 106
Be a Clown, 372, 527, 528, 785
Be a Man, 448
Be Bop a Lula, 65
Be Bop Baby, 641, 711
Be Careful There's a Baby, 1024
Be for Real, 201
Be Glad for the Song Has No Ending, 471
Be Good to Yourself, 519
Be Happy, 95
Be Happy Go Lucky, 876
Be Here Now, 731
Be Honest with Me, 855
Be Mine, 892
Be My Baby, 176, 554, 724, 852, 929
Be My Girl, 715
Be My Guest, 275
Be My Little Baby Bumble Bee, 706
Be My Little Bumble Bee, 511
Be My Love, 150, 274, 275, 563
Be Near Me, 2
Be Prepared, 574
Be Real, 866
Be Still My Beating Heart, 950

Be the One, 478
Be True to Your School, 712
Be What You Are, 938
Be What You Want, 1077
Be Yourself, 558
Be Yourself Tonight, 317
Beach Boys in Concert, The, 63
Beach Boys Today, The, 63
Beach Party, 536
Beachcomber, 244
Beacon Street Collection, 725
Beale Street Blues, 420
Beans and Cornbread, 518
Bear Cat, 772, 980
Bear Cat Crawl, 582
Beard of Stars, A, 101
Beast in Me, The, 603
Beaster, 701
Beasts of No Nation, 557
Beat, 536
Beat Dis, 51
Beat Goes on, The, 177, *1014*
Beat It, 481, 615, 1011
Beat Me Daddy Eight to the Bar, 207
Beat Surrender, 484
*Beat That *?!! Drum*, 712
Beat the Boots!, 1092
Beat the Clock, 927
Beat the Retreat, 982
Beatin' the Odds, 682
Beating the Retreat, 982
Beatitude, 161
Beatle Girls, The, 647
Beatles Concerto, 393
Beatles for Sale, 66, 774
Beatnik, 170
Beats, Rhymes and Life, 994
Beaubourg, 1014
Beaucoup Fish, 1008
Beaucoups of Blues, 284, 939
Beautiful Buffalo River, 286
Beautiful Day, 1005
Beautiful Dreamer, 347
Beautiful Dreams, 251
Beautiful Freak, 303
Beautiful Friends, 75
. . . *Beautiful Lies You Could Live in*, 816
Beautiful Little Butterfly, 876
Beautiful Loser, 882
Beautiful Love, 215
Beautiful Maladies, 1025
Beautiful Morning, A, 816
Beautiful Noise, 262
Beautiful Ones, The, 960
Beautiful Stranger, 631
Beautiful Toulang Sunset, The, 865
Beautiful Vision, 695
Beauty, 868
Beauty and the Beast, 134, 266

Beauty and the Beat, 157, 572, 891
Beauty Lies, 343
Beauty on a Back Street, 413
Beauty School Dropout, 39
Beauty Stab, 2
Beaver, 170
Be-Baba-Leba, 461
Bébé le Strange, 436
Be-Bop Grandma, 138
Be-Bop Medley, 532
Be-Bop-a-Lula, 1021
Because, 187, 209, 802
Because I Love You, 327
Because of the Wind, 309
Because of You, 61, 76, 261, 325
Because the Night, 917, 934
Because They're Young, 300
Because You Love Me, 1032
Because You Loved Me, 266, 1032
Because You're You, 441
Beck Ola, 70, 949
Beckology, 70
Becoming More Like Alfie, 268
Bed of Roses, 102, *667*
Bed's Too Big Without You, The, 782
Bedlam Bridge, 668
Bedroom, The, 132
Bedroom Tapes, The, 899
Beds Are Burning, 668
Bedside of a Neighbor, 337, 388
Bedsitter, 16
Bedsitter Images, 947
Bedtime for Democracy, 252
Bedtime Stories, 44, 631
Bee a Brother, 517
Beechwood 4-5789, 649
Been There Done That, 269
Beer Barrel Polka, 23, 1023
Beer Cans on the Moon, 361
Beer Drinking Woman, 661
Beethoven (I Love to Listen to), 317
Beethoven Was Deaf, 696
Beetlebum, 100
Before and After, 233, 615
Before and After Science, 311
Before I Let Go, 656
Before I Let You Go, 656
Before the Deluge, 132
Before the Flood, 53, 293
Before the Next Teardrop Falls, 332, 658
Before the Rain, 1030
Before the Storm, 1071
Before These Crowded Streets, 246
Before This Day Ends, 284
Before We Were So Rudely Interrupted, 24, 793
Beg, Steal or Borrow, 882
Beg Your Pardon, 223
Beggar on a Beach of Gold, 378

Beggariddim, 1005
Beggars Banquet, 849
Beggin' My Baby, 588
Begin the Beguine, 34, 236, 469, 785, 890
Beginnings, 910, 933, 1085
Begins Here, 1093
Behaviour, 768
Behind a Painted Smile, 476
Behind Blue Eyes, 182
Behind Closed Doors, 588, 830, 893, 910
Behind the Mask, 342
Behind the Sun, 187
Bei Mir Bist Du Schön, 23, 149
Being a Girl, 639
Being Boiled, 461
Being Green, 695
Being There, 1007
Being with You, 841
Belafonte '89, 73
Belafonte at Carnegie Hall, 73
Beleza Tropical, 148
Belfast Child, 901
Believe, 177
Believe It, 1066
Believe Me If All Those Endearing Young Charms, 614
Believe What You Say, 139, 142, 711
Believers, 625
Belinda, 157, 771
Bell Bottom Blues, 44, 199
Belladonna, 342
Bell-Bottom Trousers, 795
Belle of Avenue A, The, 361
Belleau Woods, 123
Bells, The, 127, 625, 824
Bells Are Ringing, The, 583
Bells of Dublin, The, 182
Bells of Normandy, The, 319
Bells of Rhymney, The, 147, 881
Belly Up, 271
Bellyful of Blue Thunder, 691
Belo Horizonte, 624
Belonging, 492
Below the Salt, 942
Bemba Colora, 235
Ben, 481
Ben Crawley Steel Co, 703
Ben Folds Five, 76
Bend Me Shape Me, 70, 532
Bend Sinister, 326
Bends, The, 811
Beneath Still Waters, 356
Beneath the Mask, 216
Beneath the Remains, 883
Benefit, 498
Benny and Us, 39, 539
Bent Out of Shape, 254
Berimbau, 235
Berlin, 824

Berlin Theatre Songs by Kurt Weill, 577
Bermuda, 227, 349
Bernadette, 350, 449
Bernard Herrman, 443
Besame Mucho, 280, 763, 1010
Beserkley Chartbusters, 832
Beserkley Years, The, 151
Beside Myself, 946
Besides, 701
Bess, You Is My Woman Now, 380
Best, The, 999
Best Always, 375
Best Baby Girl, 815
Best Band You Never Heard, The, 1092
Best Bit, 744
Best Days of My Life, The, 923
Best Disco in Town, The, 1021
Best Film Music of Georges Delarue, 255
Best Friends, 559
Best I Can, 809
Best I Could Do, 1997–1988, The, 661
Best Is Yet to Come, The, 1035
Best Love, The, 144
Best of, 606, 633, 795
Best of Arrested Development, The, 31
Best of Betty Wright, 1078
Best of Both Worlds, The, 642
Best of Candi Staton, The, 940
Best of Carnival, The, 571
Best of Chris Rea, The, 819
Best of Don McLean, The, 625
Best of Doug Kershaw, The, 531
Best of Gene Vincent, The, 1022
Best of Hank and Hank, The, 1060
Best of Howard Jones, The, 513
Best of James, The, 485
Best of Jesse Winchester, The, 1071
Best of Joe South, The, 925
Best of Little Walter, The, 590
Best of Love, Vol. 1, The, 1013
Best of Love, Vol. 2, The, 1013
Best of Matumbi, 109
Best of Me, The, 7
Best of Mitch Ryder and the Detroit Wheels, The, 865
Best of Muddy Waters, The, 1037
Best of My Love, 295, 310
Best of Nick Cave, The, 169
Best of 1980–89, The, 1005
Best of Sade, The, 866
Best of Santana, The, 871
Best of Sellers, 393, 647
Best of Spandau Ballet, The, 926
Best of Steve Miller 1968–1973, The, 674
Best of Sweet, The, 964

Best of Taj Mahal, The, 966
Best of the Christians, The, 184
Best of the EMI Years Vol. 1, The, 442
Best of the Marcels, The, 641
Best of the Ronettes, The, 853
Best of the 20th Century Boy, 101
Best of Thomas Mapfumo, The, 640
Best of Times, The, 959
Best of Van Morrison, The, 694
Best of . . . Volume 1, The, 1005
Best of . . . Volume 2, The, 1005
Best of ZZ Top, The, 1094
(Best Part of) Breakin' Up, (The), 853, 929
Best Thing That Ever Happened to Me, 548
Best Things in Life Are Free, The, 259, 1013
Best Way to Travel, The, 689
Best Years of Our Lives, The, 262
Bestial Devastation, 883
Bestiality of the Bonzo Dog Band, 105
Bet Yer Life I Do, 457
Betcha by Golly Wow, 74, 958
Bête Noire, 333
Beth, 546
Betta Listen, 251
Bette Davis Eyes, 159, 259
Better Be Good to Me, 999
Better Class of Loser, 479
Better Class of Losers, 794
Better Cut That Out, 1066
Better Generation, 495
Better Git It in Your Soul, 395
Better Living through Chemistry, 330
Better Man, A, 90
Better Part of Me, 879
Better Together, 652
Betty and Dupree, 1067
Between 10th and 11th, 172
Between a Rock and a Hard Place, 164
Between Friends, 139
Between Nothingness and Eternity, 624
Between the Buttons, 849
Between the Devil and the Deep Blue Sea, 26
Between the Lines, 278, 466
Between the Sheets, 476
Between the Wars, 116
Between Thought and Expression, 824
Between Today and Yesterday, 793
Between Two Fires, 1089
Beware (The Funk Is Everywhere), 51
Bewitched, 360, 558, 782

Bewitched, Bothered and Bewildered, 428
Beyond and Before/Something's Coming, 1085
Beyond the Blue Horizon, 739, 839
Beyond the Blue Neon, 955
Beyond the Eyes, 398
Beyond the Missouri Sky, 666
Beyond the Sea, 244, 391, 993
Beyond the Season, 123
Beyond the Stars, 1051
Beyond the Sunset, 121, 344
Bible Belt, 994
Bicentennial, 1024
Bicentennial Gathering, 669
Bicyclettes de Belsize, Les, 823
Big All Round, 127
Big Apple Bash, The, 627
Big Bad John, 252
Big Balls, 4
Big Band Bossa Nova, 514
Big Band Days, 981
Big Band Percussion, 437
Big Band Sound of Gene Krupa, The, 556
Big Beat, 927
Big Beat Boogie, 1041
Big Blon' Baby, 581
Big Blow, 263
Big Blue Frog, 98
Big Boss Band, 77
Big Boss Man, 521, 789, 792, 823, 830, 894
Big Boy Blue, 336
Big Boy Pete, 276
Big Break, The, 82
Big Brother, 111
Big Cheese, 723
Big Chief, 802
Big City, 591
Big Daddy, 661
Big 'Ead, 146
Big Express, The, 1081
Big Five, 799
Big 4, 384
Big Four Poster Bed, 571
Big Fun, 472, *886*
Big Generator, 1085
Big Girls Don't Cry, 3, 349
Big Guitar, 115, *115*
Big Gun, 5
Big Hits of '62, 784
Big in America, 956
Big in Japan, 1025
Big Iron, 837
Big Log, 569
Big Love, 342
Big Mama Thornton Vol. 2, 983
Big Man, *8*, 348
Big Man and the Scream Team Meet the Barmy Army Uptown, The, 797

Big Muddy, 881
Big Noise from Winnetka, 231
Big One, The, 86, 955
Big Ones, 10
Big Picture, The, 504
Big Poppa, 804
Big Question, The, 655
Big Reunion, The, 439
Big Road Blues, 758
Big Rock Candy Mountain, 477
Big Scary Animal, 158
Big Science, 21
Big Ship, 831
Big Six, 799
Big Spender, 334
Big Star, 493
Big Stuff, 318
Big Table Murphy, 356
Big Thing, 289, 938
Big Three-O, The, 332
Big Time, 185, *1025*
Big Time Operator, 782
Big Time Sensuality, 86
Big Top Halloween, 10
Big Town, 116
Big Train, 645
Big Train (From Memphis), 226, 772
Big Ugly Mouth, 850
Big Up, 35
Big Wide World, 587
Big Willie Style, 917
Big World, 480
Big Yellow Taxi, 398, 679
Bigger Than America, 438
Bigger the Figure, The, 795
Bigger They Come, The, 352
Biggest Aspidistra in the World, The, 334
Biggest Man, 575
Biko, 366
Bilbo Is Dead/Union Man Blues, 178
Bilingual, 768, 918
Bill, 530, 692, 843, *1075*
Bill Bailey, Won't You Please Come Home, 203
Bill Drummond, 547
Bill Evans Album, The, 318
Bill Monroe and Stars of the Bluegrass Hall of Fame, 687
Bill Monroe for Breakfast, 416
Bill Monroe's Uncle Pen, 687
Billericay Dickie, 290
Billie Jean, 481
Billie Joe, 378
Billie's Bounce, 41, 753
Billy Austin, 296, 297
Billy Bayou, 825
Billy Breathes, 773
Billy Burnette, 139
Billy Don't Be a Hero, 707

Billy Is a Runaway, 468
Billy Joe Thomas, 980
Billy Swan, 964
Billy Swan's Best, 964
Biloxi, 652, 1070
Bim Bam Boom, 413
Bimbo, 542, 825
Binaural, 762
Bing and Louis, 663
Bing Crosby, 755
Bingo Master's Breakout, 326
Biograph, 291, 293
Biography, A, 660
Bip Bop Bip, 221
Bird Dog, 134, 320
Bird Fire, 893
Bird Gets the Worm, 753
Bird in a Gilded Cage, A, 203, 1023
Bird Noises, 668
Bird of Paradise, 777
Bird on a Wire, 201, *423*, *1031*
Bird on My Head, The, 883
Birdboy, 178
Birdland, 561, 636, 1039
Birds of a Feather, 773, 925
Birds of Fire, 624
Birds, the Bees and the Monkees, The, 684
Birdy, 563
Birima, 710
Birmingham Bertha, 1036
Birth, 492
Birth and Rebirth, 118
Birth of Rock and Roll, 766
Birth of the Blues, The, 259, 260, 1050
Birth of the Cool, 248, 318, 705
Birthday Concert, The, 60
Birthday Thank You Tommy from Vietnam, 672
Bitch Is Back, The, 503
Bitches Brew, 216, 248, 624, 1039
Bite the Hand, 2
Bits and Pieces, 187
Bitter Mirror, The, 1043
Bitter Tears, 165
Bitterblu, 1002
Bitterness of Life, 549
Bittersweet, 449
Bittersweet Me, 827
Bittersweet Symphony, 1021
Bixieland, 210
Bizarre Fruit, 610
Black, 86, 798
Black Album, The, 240
Black and Blue, 849
Black and Blue Rhythm, 464
Black and Dekker, 255
Black and White, 445, 481, *781*, 840, 956, 984
Black and White Rag, 37

Black Betty, 568
Black Bird (Holding Your Head High), 794
Black Bottom, 259, 260, 995
Black Brown and Beige, 307, 480, 1041
Black, Brown and White, 124
Black Cat, 479
Black Christ of the Andes, 1063
Black Codes (From the Underground), 645
Black Coffee, 14
Black Denim Trousers, 575, 687
Black Denim Trousers and Motorcycle Boots, 774
Black Eyed Boy, 978
Black Eyed Boys, The, 707
Black Eyed Man, 223
Black Freighter, The, 942
Black Gold, 922
Black Head Chinee Ma, 692, 798
Black History/The World, 877
Black Hole Sun, 924
Black Lady, 960
Black Love, 10
Black Magic, 632
Black Magic Woman, 341, 519, 871
Black Man, 520
Black Man's Burdon, 24
Black Market, 1039
Black Market Music, 779
Black Moon, 310
Black Moses, 434
Black Music for White People, 433
Black Night, 125, 253
Black Nights, 362
Black Pearl, 620, 929
Black People, 640
Black Peter, 400
Black President, 557
Black Rat Swing, 661
Black Reign, 808
Black Requiem, 514
Black Rider, The, 1025
Black Rose, 151
Black Saint and Sinner Lady, 676
Black Sea, 1081
Black Sheets of Rain, 701
Black Skin Boy, 110
Black Skinned Blue Eyed Boy, 398
Black Snake Blues, 932
Black Snake Diamond Role, 447
Black Steel in the Hour of Chaos, 803
Black Tie, White Noise, 111, 700, 846
Black to the Future, 650
Black Velvet Band, 220
Black Water, 279
Blackberry Boogie, 344
Blackberry Way, 703

Blackboard Jungle, 767
Blackdance, 968
Blackheart Man, 644
Blackjack, 126
Blackout, 875, 977
Blacks' Magic, 869
Blacksmith Blues, 696, 833
Blackstrap Molasses, 289
Blacula, 750
Blah Blah Blah, 469
Blame Canada, 903
Blame It on Me, 565
Blame It on the Bossa Nova, 501, 567
Blame It on the Rain, 1032
Blame it on the Weatherman, 83
Blame It on Your Heart, 459
Blank Generation, 973, 973
Blast!, 354
Blaze Away, 594
Blaze of Glory, 102, 480
Blazing Away, 326
Blazing Fire, 692
Bleach, 723
Bleecker and MacDougal, 710
Bleecker Street, 897
Bless its Little Pointed Head, 494
Bless Our Love, 170
Bless this House, 250
Bless You, 638, 743
Bless Your Beautiful Hide, 663
Blessed Are . . ., 47
Blessed Easter, 153
Blessing of Tears, A, 360
Blimp, The, 72
Blind, 328
Blind before I Stop, 657
Blind Boy Fuller No. 2, 362
Blind Joe Death, 322
Blind Love, 882
Blind Man, 588
Blind Willie McTell, 627
Blinded by the Light, 635, 934
Blindfold Test, 331
Bliss, 20
Blitzkrieg Bop, 814
Blob, The, 44
Block Rockin' Beats, 175
Blockbuster, 964
Blonde on Blonde, 292, 551, 700
Blondie and Beyond, 96
Blood and Chocolate, 219, 603
Blood and Roses, 183
Blood Brother, 656
Blood Brothers, 108
Blood Makes Noise, 1017
Blood Money, 797
Blood on Blood, 102
Blood on the Dancefloor, 482
Blood on the Saddle, 836
Blood on the Tracks, 293
Blood Red and Going Down, 997

Blood Red Roses, 614
Blood Sugar Sex Magick, 820, 858
Blood Sweat and No Tears, 945
Blood, Sweat and Tears, 97, 165
Blood Vibes, 651
Bloodflowers, 238
Bloodline, 258
Bloodnock's Rock'n'Roll, 356, 393
Bloodshot Eyes, 426, 765
Bloody Buccaneers, 387
Bloomsbury Theatre 12.3.95, The, 985
Bloop Bleep, 525
Blossom Fell, A, 202
Blow Away, 427
Blow by Blow, 70, 647
Blow Joe Blow, 85
Blow the House Down, 1028
Blow the Wind Southerly, 333
Blow Up, The, 973
Blow Up the Outside World, 924
Blow Up Your Video, 5
Blow Your Face Out!, 376
Blow Your Whistle, 526
Blowin' Away, 47
Blowin' in from Kansas City, 1075
Blowin' in the Wind, 49, 211, 216, 291, 292, 326, 432, 542, 768, 1076
Blowing Kisses in the Wind, 3
Blowing with the Wind, 750
Blowing Your Mind, 694
BLT, 800
Blue, 67, 335, 679, 902
Blue Afternoon, 135
Blue and the Gray, The, 284
Blue Angel, 778
Blue Bayou, 741, 854
Blue Bell Knoll, 199
Blue Belles of Harlem, 307
Blue Blood Blues, 697
Blue Blue Day, 382
Blue Café, The, 819
Blue Champagne, 280
Blue Christmas, 996
Blue Clear Sky, 955
Blue Collar, 877
Blue Danube, 282, 897
Blue Danube Waltz, 115
Blue Days – Black Nights, 450
Blue Devil Blues, 862
Blue Earth, 493
Blue Eyes, 1078
Blue Eyes Crying in the Rain, 115, 629, 712, 855
Blue Frontier, 119
Blue Guitar, 689
Blue Guitars, 562
Blue Hat for a Blue Day, 443
Blue Hawaii, 839, 904
Blue Hotel, 475
Blue Is the Colour, 68
Blue Jays, 689

Blue Jean Bop, 612
Blue Jeans Go to The Ventures Melodies, The, 1019
Blue Jungle, 411
Blue Light, Red Light, 210
Blue Lines, 650, 785
Blue Lotus Feet, 739
Blue Mask, The, 824
Blue Meaning, The, 991
Blue Monday, 58, 275, 421, 427, 583, 716
Blue Moon, 293, 300, 428, 462, 641
Blue Moon of Kentucky, 686, 788
Blue Moon Swamp, 226
Blue Moves, 503
Blue Night, 911
Blue Notes for Johnny, 620
Blue Nun, 163
Blue Obsession, 279
Blue on Blue, 1022
Blue Prelude, 496
Blue Ridge Rangers, 226
Blue Rondo à la Turk, 133, 492
Blue Room, The, 428
Blue Rose, 947
Blue Savannah, 312
Blue Shadows, 362
Blue Skies, 79, 245, 330, 713, *833*
Blue Skies Black Heroes, 627
Blue Skies of Montana, 675
Blue Skinned Beast, 630
Blue Sky, 717
Blue Sky Mining, 668
Blue Star, 392
Blue Suede Shoes, 576, 766, 789, 836
Blue Sunshine, 905
Blue Tango, 61
Blue Trane, 206
Blue Tune, 447
Blue Turnin' Gray Over You, 1029
Blue Turns to Grey, 831
Blue Valentine, 1024
Blue Velvet, 195, 1022, 1023
Blue Yodel No. 9, 845
Blueberry Hill, 15, 29, 31, 63, 275, 671
Bluebird, 136, 426, 821
Blue-Eyed Darlin', 648
Blue-Eyed Elaine, 996
Bluegrass Instrumentals, 686
Bluegrass Rules!, 907
Blueprint, 37
Blues, 440, 1094
Blues, The, 720
Blues 'n' Jazz, 538
Blues After Hours, 1082
Blues Alive, 690
Blues Alley and Jazz, 891
Blues Alone, The, 654

Blues and Ballads, 862
Blues and Jazz Guitar, 50
Blues and Me, The, 50, 327
Blues and Roots, 676
Blues and Then Some, 655
Blues at Carnegie Hall, 681
Blues Balladeer, 76
Blues Band, 154
Blues Before Sunrise, 160
Blues Boy, 704
Blues Breakers, 186
Blues Breakers – John Mayall with Eric Clapton, 654
Blues Consolidated, 754
Blues Everywhere I Go, 735
Blues Eyes Crying in the Rain, 713
Blues for Allah, 400
Blues for Basie, 1041
Blues for Greeney, 690
Blues for Salvador, 871
Blues for the Lost Days, 655
Blues for Waterloo, 609
Blues from Laurel Canyon, 654
Blues from the Gutter, 288
Blues Garni, 372
Blues Groove, 620
Blues in Green, 318
Blues in Greens: Bach Ground, 16
Blues in Orbit, 318
Blues in the Basement, 981
Blues in the East, 565
Blues in the Night, 26, 109, 441, 605, 609, 662, 663, 895, 904
Blues in the Night (the Early Show), 487
Blues in the Night (the Late Show), 487
Blues in Thirds, 69
Blues Incorporated, 553
Blues Is King, 538
Blues Is Now, The, 1075
Blues Man, 754
Blues of Otis Spann, The, 927
Blues on Bach, 681
Blues on Broadway, 131
Blues on Highway 49, 1057
Blues on the Ceiling, 710
Blues on the Downbeat, 508
Blues, Rags and Hollers, 291
Blues, Songs and Ballads, 862
Blues Soul of Jay Owens, The, 1020
Blues Stay Away from Me, 115, 139, 257, 1082
Blues Summit, 538
Blues, the Whole Blues and Nothin' but the Blues, The, 1075
Blues with a Feeling, 590
Blues You Can Use, 94
Bluesbreakers, 1020
Bluesiana Triangle, 272
Bluesology, 681

Bluestime, 376
Blue-Tailed Fly, 477
Blunted on Reality, 361
Blur, 100
B-Movie Matinee, 846
Bo Diddley, 263, 352, 432, 451, 882
Bo Diddley Goes Surfing, 264
Bo Diddley Is Jesus, 498
Boar Hog Blues, 1063
Boat That I Row, The, 604, 698
Boatman's Call, The, 169
Boats, Beaches, Bars & Ballads, 137
Bob Dylan, 291
Bob Dylan Live, 291
Bob Dylan's Dream, 164
Bob Wills and Tommy Duncan, 724
Bob Wills Is Still the King, 1068
Bobby, 125
Bobby Bare and Friends, 55
Bobby Bare Sings Lullabies, Legends and Lies, 55
Bobby Charles, 173
Bobby Vee Singles Album, The, 1017
Bobby Vinton Plays for His L'il Darlin's, 1022
Bobolink Waltz, The, 784
Boces, 663
Bodacious DF, 494
Bodies and Souls, 636
Body and Soul, 315, *381*, 431, *480*, 969, 1050
Body Count, 467
Body Heat, 514
Body Language, 194, 808
Bodyguard, The, 44
Bodyswerve, 56
Boggy Depot, 14
Bohemian Rhapsody, 807, 808, 811
Boiled Beef and Carrots, 170
Boiler, The, 928
Boingo, 306
Bold Fenian Men, 185
Bolero, 190, 218
Bolero at the Savoy, 556
Boll Weevil, 568, 836
Boll Weevil Song, The, 78
Bomb (These Sounds Fall into My Mind), The, 651
Bomber, 699
Bombs Away Dream Babies, 949
Bon Doo Wah, 744
Bon Jovi, 102
Bona Drag, 696
Bona Fide, 795
Bonaparte's Retreat, 542, 939
Bone Machine, 1025
Boney M Megamix, 104
Bonfire, 5

Bong, Bongo, Bongo, 724
Bongo Fury, 1092
Bonita Applebum, 994
Bonnie and Clyde, 10
Bonnie Raitt Collection, The, 814
Bonny Bunch of Roses, 324
Bony Moronie, 432, 860, 1061, 1062
Boobs a Lot, 361
Boogaloo Party, The, 340
Boogie at Midnight, 131
Boogie Chillen, 452
Boogie Chillun, 85
Boogie Down, 975
Boogie My Blues Away, 691
Boogie Nights, 437
Boogie No. 1, 860
Boogie on Reggae Woman, 1077
Boogie Rock, 12
Boogie with Canned Heat, 154
Boogie Wonderland, 298, 310
Boogie Woogie, 33, 282
Boogie Woogie Bugle Boy, 23, 667
Boogie Woogie, Country Girl, 783
Boogie Woogie Fiddle Blues, 242
Boogie Woogie on St Louis Blues, 125, 446
Boogie Woogie Stomp, 20
Booglie Wooglie Piggie, The, 23
Book of Days, 312
Book of Dreams, 673
Book of Love, 539, 752
Bookbinder's Kid, 123
Bookends, 897
Boom Boom, 216, 452, 453
Boom Chi Boom Boom, 967
Boom-Bang-a-Bang, 604
Boomchild, 959
Boomer's Story, 212, 315
Boone Creek, 907
Boops (Here to Go), 912
Booted, 94
Booth and the Bad Angel, 485
Bootie Call, 14
Bootleg, 294
Bootleg Him, 553
Bootleg Series, Vols 1–3, The, 294
Bootlegs and B Sides, 466
Booty Butt, 174
Bop Doo Wop, 636
Bop till You Drop, 212, 532
Boppin' the Blues, 766, 766
Borboleta, 871
Border Song, 503
Border Town at Midnight, 245
Border Wave, 867
Borderline, 212, 444, 602, 631
Boredom, 602
Boris the Spider, 1054
Born a Woman, 683, 785, 786

Born Again, 88, 184, 720
Born Dead, 467
Born for Trouble, 713
Born Free, 1065
Born in a Trunk, 371
Born in Captivity, 424
Born in Chicago, 144
Born in Mississippi Raised Up in Tennessee, 452
Born in the USA, 934, *934*, *1001*
Born into the '90s, 528
Born Slippy (Nuxx), 1008
Born to Be, 659
Born 2 B Blue, 674
Born to Be My Baby, 102
Born to Be Together, 853
Born to Be Wild, *351*, 944, *944*
Born to Be with You, 183, 266, 302, 786, 838, 930
Born to Boogie, 101, 1061
Born to Laugh at Tornadoes, 1034
Born to Lose, 239, 515
Born to Love, 339
Born to Run, 354, *934*
Born Tuff, 398
Born Under a Bad Sign, 74, 107, 537, 903, 983
Born Walden Robert Cassotto, 244
Born Yesterday, 302, 320
Borscht Riders in the Sky, 516
Borstal Breakout, 887
Boss Drum, 888
Boss of the Blues, 998
Bossa Nova Baby, 501
Bossa Nova Bird, The, 256
Bossa Nova – New Brazilian Jazz, 874
Bossa Nova 2001, 779
Bossanova, 778
Bostisch, 1083
Boston, 109
Botch-a-Me, 195
Both Sides, 205
Both Sides Now, 204, 312, 395, 678, 679, *679*, 904
Bottle Let Me Down, The, 142, 410
Bottleneck and Slide Guitar, 405
Bottom Line, The, 1079
Boulder to Birmingham, 425
Boulders, 703
Boulevard, 132
Boulevard of Broken Dreams, The, 1032
Boum, 993
Bounced Checks, 1024
Bouncing Off the Satellites, 43
Bouncing with Bud, 786, *786*
Bound for Glory, *376*, 733
Bound for the Mountains and the Sea, 761
Bouquet of Roses, 29

Bourgeois, Les, 120
Bourgie Bourgie, 549
Bow Wow, 1038
Bowling Green, 320
Box of Rain, 400
Boxed Life, The, 851
Boxed Set, 536, 609, 997
Boxer, The, 293, 898
Boy, 604, *1004*
Boy from New York City, The, 245, 575, 636, 697
Boy from Nowhere, A, 516
Boy in the Gallery, The, 592
Boy Named Sue, A, 166, 896
Boy with the Arab Strap, The, 75
Boy with the Note, The, 627
Boy with the Thorn in His Side, The, 918
Boys, 329
Boys and Girls, 333, 461
Boys Are Back in Town, The, 422, 979, 980
Boys Don't Cry, 237
Boys for Pele, 20
Boys in the Back Room, The, 264
Boys of Summer, The, 296, 771
Boys Won't Leave the Girls Alone, The, 185
Boysterous, 747
Boyz N the Hood, 728
Boz, 873
Boz Scaggs, 873
Boz Scaggs and Band, 873
Brace Yourself, 555
Brain, 521
Brain Capers, 700
Brain Damage, 109, 777
Brain Drain, 815
Brain Salad Surgery, 309
Brainwasher, 1028
Brand New, 869
Brand New and Faded, 965
Brand New Cadillac, 533
Brand New Day, *97*, 551, 938, *951*
Brand New Key, 659
Brand New Me, 74, 933
Brand New Morning, 882
Brand New Start, 1045
Brand New Tennessee Waltz, 1070
Brand New Z. Z. Hill, The, 445
Branded Man, 411
Brandy, 637, 979
Branigan, 117
Branigan 2, 117
Brasil, 636
Brass Construction 1,2 and 3, 117
Brass in Pocket, 791
Brassed Up, 635
Brave, 642
Brave New World, 474, 673, 959
Brazil, 236, 759, 760, 763, 1021

Brazilian Classics, 967
Brazilian Love Affair, A, 287
Brazilian Soul, 16
Bread and Roses, 204, 641
Break Every Rule, 999
Break It to Me Gently, 571
Break It Up, 98
Break My Mind, 599, 886
Break Out, 781
Break the News to Mother, 425
Break Up to Make Up, 958
Breakaway, 259, 368, 555, 898, 902
Breakbeat Era, 907
Breakdown, 771, 980
Breakdown Dead Ahead, 873
Breakerfall, 762
Breakfast in America, 962
Breakfast in Bed, 791, 1005
Breakin' Away, 492
Breakin' Through the B.S., 264
Breakin' Up Is Hard to Do, 167, 658, 880
Breaking Away, 438
Breaking Hearts, 503
Breaking Silence, 466
Breaking the Ethers, 594
Breaking the Girl, 820
Breaking the Law, 519
Breaking Us in Two, 480
Breakout, 193, 935, 1034
Breaks, The, 98
Breath of Heaven – A Christmas Collection, 383
Breathalyser, The, 1025
Breathe, 801, *1007*
Breathe Again, 118
Breathe and Stop, 994
Breathless, *365*, 581
Breeze and I, The, 236, 280, 895, 1010
Breezin', 77
Breezy Stories, 737
Brel, 120
Brenda Lee, 571
Brenda Lee Christmas, 571
Brewing Up with Billy Bragg, 116
Brian Wilson, 64
Brick, 76
Brick by Brick, 469
Brickhouse, 208
Bricks and Mortar, 484
Brickyard Blues, 990
Bride Stripped Bare, The, 333
Bridge, The, 502, 851
Bridge Between, The, 536
Bridge Is Over, The, 106
Bridge of Sighs, *627*, 1051
Bridge Over Troubled Water, 119, 153, 355, 702, 748, 898, *898*, 963
Bridge to Your Heart, 853
Brigade, 437
Brigg Fair, 395

Bright Eyes, 60, 898
Bright Lights and Country Music, 711
Bright Lights, Big City, 170, 823
Bright Moments, 837
Bright Size Life, 665
Bright Sun, 22
Brighten the Corners, 760
Brighter Than a Thousand Suns, 534
Brightest Smile in Town, The, 272
Brilleaux, 270
Brilliant Corners, 683
Brilliant Disguise, 935
Brilliant Trees, 965
Brimful of Asha, 330
Brindisi, 386
Bring Back the Thrill, 336
Bring 'Em All in, 1036
Bring Him Back Home, 649
Bring Him Home Safely to Me, 786
Bring It on, 390, *390*
Bring It on Down to My House, Honey, 605
Bring It on Home, 1066
Bring It on Home to Me, 23, 108, 213, 818
Bring It to Jerome, 263
Bring Me the Head of Yuri Gagarin, 434
Bring on the Dancing Horses, 299
Bring on the Night, 950
Bring on the Boys Home, 169, 449
Bring the Family, 444, 603
Bring the Noise, 25, 802
Bring Your Daughter to the Slaughter, 474
Bringing It All Back Home, 216, 292
Bristol Stomp, 282
Bristol Twistin' Annie, 282
Bristol's Creme, 121
Britannia Rag, 37
British Concert, 702
British Road, The, 1079
British Steel, 519
Broadsword and the Beast, 499
Broadway, 957
Broadway Album, The, 275, 920
Broadway Baby, 919
Broadway in Rhythm, 210
Broken, 723
Broken Arrow, 137, 950, *1088*
Broken Barricades, 800
Broken Down Angel, 709
Broken English, 326
Broken Frame, 258
Broken Ground, 164
Broken Heart Can Mend, A, 739
Broken Hearted Me, 705

Broken Hearted Melody, 1015
Broken Toy Shop, 303
Brontosaurus, 703
Brontosaurus Stomp, 348
Bronx Blues, 266
Brood, The, 122
Brother Can You Spare a Dime?, 112, 230, 422, 667, *1011*
Brother John, 833
Brother Louie, 457, 553
Brother of Mine, 1085
Brother, the Great Spirit Made Us All, 133
Brother to Brother, 476
Brother Where You Bound, 962
Brother's Keeper, 868
Brotherhood, 279, 716
Brotherhood of Man, 596
Brothers, 871
Brothers and Sisters, 15
Brothers Gonna Work It Out, 175
Brothers Gonna Work It Out, 803
Brothers in Arms, 47, 267
Brothers' Keeper, 714
Brown Eyed Girl, 226, 652, 694
Brown Eyed Handsome Man, 81, 451, 612
Brown Eyed Woman, 834
Brown Girl in the Ring, 104
Brown Paper Bag, 906
Brown Shoes Don't Make It, 1091
Brown Sugar, 589, 849
Brown's Ferry Blues, 257
Brownsville Blues, 315
Brownsville Girl, 293
Bruised Orange, 799
Brutal, 717
Brutal Planet, 215
Brutal Youth, 219, 603
Bryter Layter, 283
B-Sides Ourselves, 909
Bubble Rock Is Here to Stay, 541
Bubblegum, Bop Ballads and Boogie, 228
Bubbles in the Wine, 1044
Buck Naked, 148
Bud in Paris, 786
Bud's Bubble, 786
Budapest, 635
Buddha and the Chocolate Box, 946
Buddy, 994
Buddy Bolden Stomp, 101
Buddy Bolden's Blues, 101
Buddy Holly, 451
Buddy Holly Story, The, 451
Buena Sera, 796
Buena Vida, 472
Buenos Noches from a Lonely Room, 1085
Buffalo Gals, 624

Buffalo Skinner, 308
Buffalo Skinners, The, 83
Buffalo Soldier, 340
Buffalo Springfield Again, 136, 1089
Buffalo Stance, 178
Buffy, 868
Bug, 265
Buggin', 931
Bugle Call Rag, 155, 670, 996
Buhaina's Delight, 93
Buhloone Mindstate, 251
Build a Bridge, 520
Build Me Up Buttercup, 610, 635
Building a Mystery, 623
Building the Bridge, 827
Building the Perfect Beast, 296, 771
Built to Last, 401
Bulletproof Heart, 149, 513
Bullfrog Blues, 122
Bullinamingvase, 424
Bulls on Parade, 813
Bumble Bee, 661
Bumble Boogie, 351
Bummed, 421
Bummin' Around, 252
Bump, The, 220
Bump in the Night, 913
Bump n' Grind, 528
Bumpin', 688
Bundles, 919
Bungle in the Jungle, 499
Bunny Hop Mambo, 307
Bunny Sings the Wailers, 644
Buona Sera, 86
Burglar, 541, 812, 969
Burke's Law, 799
Burlesque, 328
Burn, 253
Burn down the Cornfield, 487
Burn Hollywood Burn, 84, 803
Burrr on, 720
Burn the Honky Tonk Down, 512
Burned, 299
Burnin', 239, 558, 643
Burnin' for You, 98
Burnin' Old Memories, 652
Burning Bridges, 237, 875, 941
Burning Down the House, 517, 967
Burning London, 191
Burning Memories, 794
Burning of the Midnight Lamp, The, 440
Burning Questions, 754
Burning the Ballroom Down, 18
Burning Up, 631
Burnt Weeny Sandwich, 1091
Burrito Deluxe, 757
Bursting Out with the All-Star Big Band, 769
Burundanga, 234

Bury Me Under the Weeping Willow, 162
Bus Driver's Prayer & Other Stories, The, 290
Bus Stop, 348, 449, 975
Bus Stop Song, The, 348
Buscando America, 92
Bush Doctor, 988
Business as Usual, 662
Busted, 165, 458
Buster Brown, 679
Buster Goes Berserk, 718
Buster's Happy Hour, 718
Buster's Shack, 798
Bustin' Out, 488, 805, 806
Bustin' Out of L-Seven, 488
Busybody, 1013
But Can You Kill the Nigger in You?, 803
But I Do, 173
But Not for Me, 348, 485
. . . *But Seriously*, 205
But Seriously Folks . . . , 295
But Two Came By, 164
But You're Mine, 177
Buttercorn Lady, 93
Butterfly, 157, 450, 1056
Button Up Your Overcoat, 259, 315
Buttons and Bows, 895
Buy a Gun for Your Son, 761
Buy Me a Rose, 846, 847
Buy Me for the Rain, 724
Buzz Factory, 877
BW Goes CW, 1076
By a Sleepy Lagoon, 197, 487
By a Waterfall, 323
By All Means Necessary, 106
By Larry, 747
By Request, 114
By the Beautiful Sea, 706
By the Blue Hawaiian Waters, 531
By the Fireside, 725
By the Light of the Moon, 594
By the Light of the Silvery Moon, 706, 726
By the Time I Get to Phoenix, 153, 434, 1040
By the Time this Night Is Over, 134, 365
By Your Side, 87
Bye Bye Baby, 62, 1046
Bye Bye Baby Blues, 817
Bye Bye Blackbird, 568
Bye Bye Blues, 152
Bye Bye Johnny, 82, 941
Bye Bye Love, 134, 319, 320
Byker Hill, 164
Byrdhouse, 233
Byrdmaniax, 148
Byrds, 147, 148
Byzantium, 290

Ça Plane Pour Moi, 122
Cab Calloway, 152
Cab Calloway – Best of the Big Bands, 152
Cab Calloway Stands in for the Moon, 152
Caballo Negro, 787
Cabbage Alley, 714
Cabin in the Sky, 287
Cabinessence, 63
Cadillac Rag, 429
Cadillac Walk, 751
Cadmium, 909
Café Bleu, 1044
Cahoots, 53, 695, 990
Cajun in the Blues Country, 530
Cajun Pogo, 671
Cajun Queen, The, 252
Cajun Swamp Music Live, 176
Cajun Way, The, 530
Cal, 220
Calcutta, 1044
Caldonia, 365, 441, 518, 539, 1067
Calendar Girl, 880
California, 19
California Album, 94
California Bloodlines Plus, 949
California Bloodlines, 948
California Blues, 932
California Cottonfields, 356
California Dreamin', 633, 1076
California Girls, 63
California Here I Come, 259, 510
California Love, 269
California Nights, 394
California Rehearsals, The, 253
California Uber Alles, 252
Californication, 820
Call, The, 592
Call Her Your Sweetheart, 468
Call It Stormy Monday, 1028
Call Me, 37, 96, 117, 430, 688, 693, 762
Call Me (Come Back Home), 402
Call Me Baby, 1075
Call Me Irresponsible, 1012
Call Me Mr In-Between, 477
(Call Me) Number One, 784
Call Me Up Some Rainy Afternoon, 511
Call Now, 921
Call on Me, 72, 94, *94*, 224
Calling All Stations, 378
Calling All Workers, 197
Calling America, 304
Calling Card, 368
Calling Dr Jazz, 246
Calling Occupants of Interplanetary Craft, 160
Calvary Cross, 982
Calypso, 73, 258
Calypso King of Trinidad, The, 669

Calypso Melody, 854
Cambodia, 1055
Camden Town, 630
Cameo, 933
Cameosis, 152
Camera Obscura, 1018
Caminando, 92
Camorra: The Solitude of Passion-
 ate Provocation, La, 775
Camouflage, 950
Camptown Races, 347
Can Blue Men Sing the Whites?,
 105
Can Box, 153
Can Can You Party?, 501
Can I, 975
Can I Fool You with My Heart?,
 994
Can I Get a Witness, 129, 374,
 449, 849
Can I Have My Money Back?, 811
Can I Kick It?, 994
Can I Play with Madness, 474
Can I Take You Home Little Girl,
 285
Can of Bees, 446
Can the Can, 183, 698, 807
Can We, 308
Can We Start Again?, 985
Can You Dig It, 684
Can You Do It, 4
Can You Feel It?, 977
Can You Feel the Love Tonight,
 504
Can You Jerk Like Me, 211
Can You Party?, 977
Can Your Monkey Do the Dog,
 980
Can't Buy a Thrill, 943
Can't Buy Me Love, 66, 337
Can't Change Me, 924
Can't Fight This Feeling, 827
Can't Forget You, 879
Can't Get Enough, 46, 398
Can't Get Enough of Your Love,
 1048
Can't Get It out of My Head, 304
Can't Get Over (the Bossa Nova),
 567
Can't Get There from Here, 826
Can't Get Used to Losing You,
 335, 783, 1057
Can't Give You Anything (But
 My Love), 958
Can't Help Falling in Love, 460,
 958, 1005
Can't Help Falling in Love with
 You, 789
Can't Help Lovin' Dat Man, 843
Can't Help Loving That Man,
 372, 530
Can't Hide from Yourself, 997

Can't Keep It in, 946
Can't Let Go, 157
Can't Let Her Go, 114
Can't Quit You, 569
Can't Say How Much I Love
 You, 1014
Can't Seem to Make You Mine,
 880
Can't Shake Loose, 1
Can't Slow Down, 832
Can't Smile Without You, 637
Can't Stand Losing You, 782
Can't Stand Still, 5
Can't Stay Away from You, 314
Can't Stop Dreaming, 413
Can't Stop the Love, 656
Can't Stop the Music, 1021
Can't Stop This Thing I've
 Started, 7
Can't Truss It, 803
Can't Wait to See the Movie, 1055
Can't We Talk It Over, 1089
Can't You Heah Me Callin',
 Caroline?, 240
Can't You Hear Me Callin', 1073
Can't You Hear My Heartbeat?,
 442
Can't You See That She's Mine,
 187
Can'tcha Say You Believe in Me,
 109
Canadian Impressions, Songs of
 Britain, 329
Canadian Pacific, 417
Canadian Railroad Trilogy, 584
Canadian Sunset, 1056, 1072
Canadiana Suite, 769
Canciónes de Mi Padre, 853, 854
Candida, 743
Candle in the Wind, 502, 503, 504
Candleland, 299
Candlelight, 318
Candles, 438
Candles in the Rain, 659
Candy, 84, 152, 405, 469, 663, 936,
 944
Candy Apple Grey, 701
Candy from a Stranger, 922
Candy Girl, 125
Candy Kisses, 29
Candy Man, 249, 710, 719, 784,
 1013
Candy Man Blues, 463
Candy Says, 1018
Candyman, 246
Canned Ham, 404
Canned Heat, 36, 154, 490
Canned Heat Blues, 758
Canned Music, 445
Canned Wheat Packed by Guess
 Who, 406
Cannonball, 779

Canto Aztecas, 874
Cantos de Amor, 384
Cao, Cao, Mani Picao Seeco, 234
Capitan March, El, 924
Capitol Collectors, 817
Capitol Years, The, 153
Captain and Me, The, 279
Captain Fantastic and the Brown
 Dirt Cowboy, 503
Captain Kopter and the Twirly-
 birds, 932
Captain Marvel, 381
Captain Saint Lucifer, 728
Captured, 519
Captured Angel, 342
Captured Live, 988
Car Button Cloth, 575
Car Car, 408
Car Wash, 1052
Car Wheels on a Gravel Road,
 1062
Cara Mia, 493, 639, 1051
Caramelos, 234
Caravan, 300, 307
Caravan of Love, 68, 476
Caravanserai, 871
Cardiff Rose, 147
Career Moves, 1024
Career of Evil, 98
Carefree Highway, 585
Careless Love, 735, 987
Careless Whisper, 666
Cargo, 662
Caribbean Blue, 312
Caribbean Queen, 732
Caribbean Sunset, 150
Caribou, 503
Carino, 610
Carioca, The, 1086
Carl Stalling Project, The, 876
Carla Olson & Mick Taylor Live,
 849
Carmel, 234
Carney, 864
Carnival, 361, 935
Carnival in Venice, 487
Carnival Is Over, The, 881
Carnival of Hits, 882
Carnival of Light, 834
Carol, 81
Carol of the Bells, 346
Carole Bayer Sager, 45
Carole King: Writer, 540
Carolina (I Remember You), 242
Carolina in the Morning, 276
Carolina Moon, 38
Carolina Shout, 506, 1029
Carolyn Hester, 443
Carreterra, 469
Carrie, 316, 831
Carrie Anne, 449
Carrie Brown, 297

Carrol County Accident, 757
Carry Me Back, 816
Carry Me Back to Old Virginny, 347, 386, 387, 930
Carry on, 229, 961
Carry on Up the Charts, 68
Carrying a Torch, 516
Carrying Your Love With Me, 955
Cars, 727, 728
Cars and Girls, 788
Cartoon Heroes, 26
Cartridge, 591
Carved in Stone, 699
Casa Loma Stomp, 462
Casamance au Clair de Lune, 989
Casanova, 268, 737
Cascade, The, 517
Case of You, A, 679
Casey Jones, 400, 445, 706
Casey Jones – the Union Scab, 445
Casino Classics, 867
Cassava Rock, 750
Cast Iron Arm, 741
Casting My Lasso to the Sky, 1052
Casting My Spell, 748
Castle House Rag, 316
Castle Walk, The, 168, 316
Castles in the Air, 625, *816*
Castles in the Sand, 199
Casual Gods, 967
Cat, The, 916
Cat Food, 536
Cat Scratch Fever, 727
Cat Squirrel, 498
Cat's in the Cradle, 172, 907
Cat's Squirrel, 225
Catch, The, 709
Catch a Falling Star, 209
Catch a Fire, 643
Catch as Catch Can, 1055
Catch Bull at Four, 946
Catch One, 457
Catch the Fall, 491
Catch the Wind, 277
Catch Us If You Can, 188
Catching the Sun, 935
Caterina, 460
Caterpillar, The, 238
Catfish Rising, 499
Catherine Wheel, The, 967
Catholic Education, 972
Cathy's Clown, 320, 416, 618
Cats vs Chicks, 331
Cats without Claws, 960
Cattle Call, 30, 1072
Caught by the Fuzz, 961
Caught in a Trap I Can't Walk Out 'Cause I Love You Too Much Baby, 19
Caught in the Act, 959
Caught in the Net, 55

Caught Up, 482
Caught Up in the Rapture, 49, 95
Caught Up in You, 609
Cause Cheap Is How I Feel, 223
Cause I Love You, 948, 980
Causing a Commotion, 631
Caution Horses, The, 223
Cayuco, El, 804
C. C. Rider, 82, 865, 1067
Cecil Sharp, 13
Cecilia, 898
Celebrate, 550, 984
Celebrate Life, 708
Celebrate Me Home, 596
Celebrated Walking Blues, 966
Celebration, 550, *1053*
Celebration for a Gray Day, 329
Celebrity Skin, 448
Celia and Johnny, 235
Cellophane Symphony, 489
Celluloid Heroes, 544
Cement Mixer, 366
Centerfield, 226
Centerfold, 376
Central Heating, 437
Central Reservation, 744
Central Square Song, 1024
Centre Stage, 314
Century's End, 943
Ceremony, 716
Cerise Rose et Pommer Blanc, 787
Certain Smile, A, 323, 651
C'est Bon la Vie, 702
C'est Chic, 845
C'est La Vie, 83, 1015
C'est Si Bon, 29, 525, 547, 1000
Cha Cha, 122
Cha Dooky Doo, 714
Chain Gang, 213
Chain Lightning, 625
Chain of Fools, 217, 221, 355
Chain Reaction, 234, 834, 855
Chained and Bound, 821
Chains, 540, 545
Chains and Things, 538
Chains of Love, 107, 312, 998
Chair, The, 955
Chaka, 532, 641
Chaka Khan, 532
Chalk Farm to Camberwell, 683
Chalk Mark in a Rain Storm, 679
Chalk Up Another One, 745
Challenge Cup, 8
Chamber Music, 694
Chameleon, *350*, *420*, *558*
Champ, The, 206
Champagne Charlie, 820
Champagne Jam, 37
Championship Wrestling, 552
Chamunora, 640
Chance, 83

Chances Are, 651
Change, 972, *1048*
Change Has Come, 175, 877
Change Is Gonna Come, A, 53, *139*, 213, 243, 640, 798
Change Is Now, 147
Change My Mind, 1067
Change of Address, 886
Change of Heart, 566, 817
Change of Season, 413
Change of the Century, 202, 410
Change Partners, 34, 79, 280
Change the World, 44
Change up the Groove, 40
Change We Must, 1085
Change (Will Do You Good), A, 232
Change with the Times, 615
Changeling, The, 991
Changes, 73, 230, 487, 492, 579, 684, 733, 793, 909, *1040*, *1050*
Changes in Attitude, 137
Changes One, 677
Changes Two, 677
Changin', 117
Changing for You, 180
Changing Horses, 471
Changing Partners, 751, 939
Changing Woman, 868
Chanson d'Amour, 636
Chanson de Prevert, La, 367
Chant Down Babylon, 644
Chant No. 1 (Don't Need This Pressure on), 926
Chant of the Weed, 822
Chantilly Lace, 582, 791
Chanting Dread inna Fine Style, 85
Chaos AD, 883
Chaos & Disorder, 798
Chapel of Love, 404, 697, 786
Chappo, 328
Chaquita, 187
Character Zero, 773
Characters, 1077
Charade, 525
Chariot, 188, 189, *1042*
Charity Ball, 807
Charles, 83
Charleston, 506
Charleston Rag, 92
Charley My Boy, 706
Charlie Big Potato, 909
Charlie Brown, 196, 712
Charlie Connais Pas, 416
Charlie Daniels, 242
Charlotte Anne, 215
Charly, 801
Charmaine, 348, 639
Charmed Life, 468
Charming Snakes, 782
Charmless Man, 100

Chase, The, 123
Chasin' that Neon Rainbow, 479
Chasing for the Breeze, 35
Chattahoochee, 479
Chattanooga Choo-Choo, 412, 424, 670, 671, 1033
Chattanooga Shoeshine Boy, 343
Che, 204
Cheap Thrills, 517
Cheatin' Woman, 344
Check the Rhime, 994
Check Yes or No, 955
Check Your Head, 65
Checkin' Out the Ghosts, 159
Checking on My Baby, 861
Checkmate, 184
Chee Chee-Oo-Chee (Sang the Little Bird), 209
Cheek to Cheek, 34, 79, 286
Cheerful Insanity of Giles, Giles and Fripp, The, 535
Cheers Then, 52
Cheeseburger in Paradise, 137
Chelsea Bridge, 307
Chelsea Girl, 1018
Chemical Wedding, The, 474
Chemical World, 100
Chequered Love, 1055
Cherchez la Femme, 533
Cherish, 34, 167, 550, 631
Cherkazoo and Other Stories, 254
Cherokee, 56, 653, 725
Cherokee Boogie, 704
Cherokee Canyon, 381
Cherry Blossom, 787
Cherry Bomb, 661
Cherry Cherry, 262
Cherry Oh Baby, 1005
Cherry Pie, 147, 351
Cherry Pink and Apple Blossom White, 752, 787
Cherry Red, 1022, *1022*
Cherry Tree Carol, 765
Cherub Rock, 913
Cheryl, 786
Chess Box, The, 1037
Chess Masters, 270
Chess Years, The, 1066
Chest Fever, 53
Chester, 561
Chester and Lester, 36, 760
Chestnut Mare, 147
Chestnut Street Incident, 660
Chevalier de Paris, Le, 264
Chevy Chase, The, 92
Chewing Gum Wrapper, 833
Chi Mai, 694
Chicago 16, 181
Chicago 18, 181
Chicago 19, 181
Chicago II, 181
Chicago VII, 181

Chicago XI, 181
Chicago Blues, 266, 914
Chicago Breakdown, 927
Chicago Line, 654
Chicago Piano Vol. 1, 314
Chicago Revisited, 485
Chicago/The Blues/Today!, 861
Chic-Ism, 846
Chick a Boom, 541
Chick on the Side, 869
Chickasaw County Child, 378
Chicken and the Hawk, The, 574
Chicken Cordon Bleus, The, 392
Chicken Shack Boogie, 669
Chicken Skin Music, 212, 500
Chicken Strut, 714
Chief, 276
Chieftains II, 181
Chieftains IV, 181
Chieftains V, 182
Chieftains Celebration, A, 182
Child in Time, 253, *254*
Child Is Father to the Man, 96
Child of God, A, 482
Child's Adventures, A, 326
Child's Claim to Fame, 137
Child's Play, 617
Childhood and Memory, 5
Children of Darkness, 329
Children of the Future, 673, 873
Children of the World, 71
Children's Marching Song, 30
Children's Songs, 216
Chill Factor, 411
Chill of an Early Fall, 955
Chill Out, 453, 547, 911
Chim Chim Cher-ee, 22
Chime Bells, 121
Chimes Blues, 27
Chimurenga for Justice, 640
Chimurenga Singles, The, 640
China Girl, 469
Chinatown, 703, 795
Chinatown, My Chinatown, 36
Chinese Checkers, 106
Chinese Mule Train, 516
Chinese Way, The, 579
Chip Chip, 616
Chip Taylor's Last Chance, 970
Chipmunk Punk, 883
Chipmunk Song, The, 883
Chipmunks Sing The Beatles, The, 883
Chiquitita, 1
Chirping Crickets, 451
Chloe, 515, 936
Choba B CCCP (Back in the USSR), 612
Choice of Colors, 470
Choke, 68
Chokin' Kind, The, 899, 990
Chonk Charlie Chonk, 184

Choo Choo Ch'Boogie, 365, 518
Choo Choo Train, 113
Choonie on Chon, 127
Chopin '66, 724
Chords of Fame, 733
Chorus, 312, *312*
Chosen Few, The, 265
Chosen People, 544
Chris Isaak, 475
Chris Rea, 819
Christian Automobile, 268
Christian Life, The, 147
Christians, The, 184
Christmas, 601
Christmas Album, The, 262, 346
Christmas Album Vol. II, 262
Christmas Alphabet, 437
Christmas and the Bead of Sweat, 728
Christmas (Baby Please Come Home), 601
Christmas Day in the Cook-house, 691
Christmas Gift for You, A, 929
Christmas in Harlem, 662, 972
Christmas in My Heart, 353
Christmas in Washington, 297
Christmas Interpretations, 114
Christmas Is a Special Day, 275
Christmas Island, 23, 329, 820
Christmas Like a Lullaby, 258
Christmas Rapping, 98
Christmas Sing Along with Mitch, 672
Christmas Song, The, 201, 747, 987
Christmas Songs, 1031
Christmas Spirit, 961
Christmas Spirituals, 735
Christmas Through Your Eyes, 315
Christmas Time in Washington, 408
Christmas with BabyFace, 44
Christmas with Placido Domingo, 274
Christopher Columbus, 439, 471
Christopher Mayhew Says, 887
Christopher Robin, 659
Christy Moore Folk Collection, The, 690
Chronic, The, 269
Chronic Town, 826
Chronicle, 971
Chronicle of the Black Sword, 434
Chronicles, 947
Chronologie, 491
Chuck E's in Love, 515, 588, 1024
Chug-a-Lug, 673
Church, 602
Church Bells Will Ring, 262
Church of Anthrax, 150

Church of the Poison Mind, 236
Church Street Sobbin' Blues, 562
Ciao Ciao Bambino, 681
Cicero Park, 457
Cid, El, 573
Cielito Lindo, 332
Cien, El, 804
Cigarettes and Alcohol, 950
Cigarettes, Whusky and Wild, Wild Women, 516, 936
Cimarron, 103
Cinderella, 383
Cinderella Theory, 194
Cindy Oh Cindy, 244, 336
Cindy So Loud, 239
Cinemagic, 405
Cinnamon Girl, 1087
Circa: Now!, 842
Circle Game, The, 679, 862, 862
Circle in the Sand, 157
Circle Is Small (I Can See It in Your Eyes), The, 585
Circle of Love, 673, 906
Circle of One, 972
Circle Sky, 684
Circles, 882
Circus, 312, 554
Circus Animals, 56
Ciribiribin, 487
Cisco Kid, The, 1030
Cissy Strut, 714, 990
Cities of the Heart, 133, 690
Cities on Flame with Rock'n'Roll, 98
Citizen Steely Dan: 1972–1980, 943
Citizen Wayne, 656
City, 147
City Girl Stole My Country Boy, A, 751
City in the Sky, 938
City Kids, 935
City Lights, 21, 463, 783, 794
City of Angels, 693
City of Glass, 529
City of New Orleans, 392, 408
City Streets, 540
City to City, 812
Civilisation, 1066
Civilised Man, Unchain My Heart, 198
Civilization, 795
Civilization Phaze III, 1092
Civilized, 851
C. J. Fish, 616
CK, 532
Clair, 19, 210, 747
Clair de lune, 476
Claire de Lune, 647
Clairvoyance, 877
Clairvoyant, The, 474
Clang of the Yankee Reaper, The, 755

Clap for the Wolfman, 406
Clapping Song, The, 309, 352
Clapton Chronicles, The, 187
Clarabella, 66
Clarinet à la King, 391
Clarke Duke Project, The, 190
Claro Que Si, 1083
Clash, The, 191
Class, The, 175
Class and Subject, 459
Class of '55, 226, 766
Classic Blue, 60, 689
Classic Case – the Music of Jethro Tull, A, 499
Classic Delta Blues, 1058
Classic Hits Live, The, 345
Classic Recordings, 813
Classic Scott, 875
Classic Tranquillity, 220
Classic Years, The, 1086
Classical Della, The, 825
Classical Gas, 119, 1031
Classical Nana, 702
Classics, 45
Classics by Moonlight, 565
Classics up to Date, 565
Claudette, 741
Claudia, 627
Clayton Delaney, 415
Clean Shirt, 497
Clean Up Woman, 704, 1078
Cleanhead's Back in Town, 1022
Cleaning Windows, 695
Clear Sailin', 147
Clear Spirit, 932
Clear Water, 173
Clearings, The, 368
Clementine, 244
Cleo at Carnegie: The 10th Anniversary Concert, 559
Clever Trevor, 290
Cliches, 113
Click Song, 633
Cliff Hangar, 193
Clifton in the Rain, 947
Climb Ev'ry Mountain, 22, 60, 844
Clinch Mountain Backstep, 937
Clint Eastwood, 767
Clones of Dr Funkenstein, 194
Close, 1055
Close Company, 818
Close Encounters, 750
Close the Door, 485, 764
Close to Me, 238
Close to My Heart, 527
Close to the Bone, 967
Close to the Edge, 1084
Close (to the Edit), 286
Close to the Wind, 324
Close to You, 45, 160, 795
Close Up the Honk Tonks, 148

Close Your Eyes, 615
Close-Up, 870
Closed for Business, 639
Closeness, 410
Closer, 716
Closer I Get to You, The, 338, 430
Closer Look, A, 44
Closer to Home, 396, 776
Closer to Jesus, 483
Closer to the Flame, 302
Closer to You, 150
Closer You Get, The, 12
Closing Time, 601, 1024
Cloud Nine, 427, 521, 870, 975, 1051
Cloudburst, 561
Cloudbusting, 143
Cloudcuckoo Land, 585
Clouds, 678
Clouds in My Coffee, 1965–1995, 899
Clouds Taste Metallic, 339
Clowns to the Left, Jokers to the Right, 575
Club Classics Volume One, 923
Club Fantasia Megamix, 666
Club Tropicana, 666
Clue, The, 727
Clues, 751
Clutching at Straws, 642
Clyde Ankle, 356
CM: Cornelius Remixes, 216
C'mon and Love Me, 546
C'mon and Swim, 954
C'Mon Billy, 429
C'mon C'mon, 208
C'mon Everybody, 197, 586, 884, 1006
C'Mon Kids, 105
Co Co, 964
Coal Miner's Daughter, 607
Coalfields of Shickshinny, The, 970
Coat of Many Colors, 757, 758
Cobra and Phases Group Play Voltage in the Milky Night, 945
Cobra Recordings, 1956–1958, 862
Cocaine, 150
Cocaine Blues, 1013
Cocktails, 516
Cocktails for Two, 515
Coconut, 722
Coconut Pudding Vendor, The, 235
Coconut Telegraph, 137
Cocoye, El, 234
Cocteau Signature Tunes, 711
Cod'ine, 868
Coda, 569
Code Red, 917
Code Selfish, 327
Coffee An', 445

Coffee Blues, 602
Coffee Song, The, 903
Coffin for Head of State, 557
Cohen and Casey in the Army, 435
Cohen at the Prizefight, 435
Cohen Buys a Wireless Set, 435
Cohen Calls His Tailor on the Phone, 434
Cohen Live, 201
Cohen on the Telephone, 434, 497
Cohen's Recruiting Speech, 434
Coin de Rue, 994
Coincidence and Likely Stories, 868
Cokey, 391
Cold as Ice, 345
Cold Blow and the Rainy Night, 689
Cold, Cold Heart, 76, 77, 325, 672, 1007, 1034, 1059
Cold Day in Hell, 862
Cold Grey Light of Dawn, 604
Cold Hearted, 2
Cold Kisses, 982
Cold Shot, 748
Cold Snap, 203, 614
Cold Spring Harbor, 502
Cold Sweat, 128
Cold Turkey, 576
Coldblooded, 488
Coldest Days of My Life, (The), 180
Coldest Rap, The, 484
Cole Slaw, 953
Colette, 364
Collaboration, 681
Collected Recordings, The, 999
Collected Works of Scott Joplin, 834
Collection, The, 431, 701, 749, 833, 887, 932, 946, 966
Collection 1979–86, The, 397
Collection of Ballads from World War II, 986
Collection of Songs Representing an Enthusiasm for Recording 1984–1990, A, 339
Collectors Edition, 1080
Collectors Sondheim, A, 920
College Man, 521
Collins Mix, 203
Colombe, La, 120, 204
Colonel Bogey, 30
Color and Light: Jazz Sketches on Sondheim, 920
Color My Life, 610
Color of Love, The, 283
Color of My Love, The, 266
Color of the Blues, 512
Color of Your Dreams, 540

Colossal Head, 594
Colour, 184
Colour and the Shape, The, 723
Colour by Numbers, 236
Colours, 277
Coltrane Dreams, 532
Columbia, 113
Comb Your Hair and Curl It, 181
Combat Rock, 191
Combined Harvester, 659
Come a Little Bit Closer, 493
Come a Little Closer, 329
Come and Get It, 67
Come and Get These Memories, 449, 645
Come and Stay with Me, 259, 326
Come as You Are, 32, 376, 723
Come Away Melinda, 204, 1009
Come Back and Finish What You Started, 549
Come Back and Shake Me, 979
Come Back and Stay, 1089
Come Back Baby, 443, 502, 710
Come Back Lover, 149
Come Back My Love, 245
Come Back Silly Girl, 578
Come Back to Me, 479
Come Back to Sorrento, 594
Come Back When You Grow Up, 1017
Come by Me, 210
Come Dancing, 544
Come Down, Ma Ev'ning Star, 140
Come Fill Your Glass with Us, 185
Come Find Yourself, 363
Come Fly with Me, 94, 150, 653, 904, 1012
Come from the Heart, 652
Come from the Shadows, 47
Come Get It!, 488
Come Go with Me, 64, 257
Come Hell and High Water, 254
Come Home, 485
Come Home Baby, 775
Come in and Burn, 851
Come into My Parlour, 987
Come into Our World, 310
• Come Live with Me, 134, 438
Come Monday, 137
Come Morning, 1035
Come My Way, 326
Come on, 82, 848
Come on, Come on, 159, 1062
Come on Die Young, 682
Come on Down Baby Baby, 744
Come on Down to My Boat, 329
Come on Eileen, 261
Come on Feel the Lemonheads, 575
Come on in My Kitchen, 509
Come on in This House, 1045
Come on Let's Go, 594, 615, 1010

Come on, Let's Play with Pearlie Mae, 48
Come on Little Angel, 265
Come on Over, 71, 1000
Come on Over Here, 118
Come on Over to My Place, 285
Come on Pilgrim, 778
Come on You Reds, 941
Come on-a My House, 672, 883
Come Out and Play, 736
Come Out Fighting Genghis Smith, 423
Come Rain or Come Shine, 26, 272, 663
Come Sail Away, 959
Come See About Me, 947, 962, 1028
Come Softly to Me, 342, 882
Come Sunday, 447
Come Swing with Me, 904
Come Take a Trip in My Air-Ship, 706
Come Talk to Me, 366
Come Taste the Band, 253
Come to Me, 121, 508, 651, 821
Come 2 My House, 533
Come to the Sunshine, 424, 863
Come Together, 9, 555, 613, 796, 926, 993, 998, 1044, 1090
Come Together, America Salutes The Beatles, 581
Come Undone, 289
Come up the Years, 494
Come Walk with Me, 735
Come Where My Love Lies Dreaming, 614
Come with Me, 805
Comedy, 86
Come-on-a My House, 195
Comes a Time, 1088
Comic Book Heroes, 934
Comin' Back to Me, 515
Comin' Home Baby, 987
Comin' Home to Stay, 907
Comin' Thru, 810
Coming at You, 1045
Coming in on a Wing and a Prayer, 622
Coming on Strong, 571, 571
Coming Out, 636
Coming Out of the Dark, 879
Coming Right at Ya, 33
Coming Round Again, 898
Coming Thro' the Rye, 387, 660
Coming Up, 960
Comme d'Habitude, 904
Comme Dans un Film, 657
Commemorating Tito Puente: 50 Years of Swing, 804
Commemorativo, 757
Comment te dire Adieu, 208
Commodores 13, 208

Common One, 695
Common People, 805
Common Sense, 799
Common Thread, 997
Common Thread: Songs of the Eagles, 296
Commoner's Crown, 942
Communication, 926, 1076
Communiqué, 267, 1047
Community Music, 33
Company Policy, 164
Compartments, 332
Compas, 384
Compass, The, 229
Compass and Chart, 653
Compass Point, 255, 751
Complete Buddy Holly, The, 451
Complete Collection, The, 879
Complete Communion, 177
Complete Control, 767
Complete '50s Chess Recordings, The, 453
Complete Guitarist, The, 395
Complete Imperial Recordings, The, 203
Complete Johnny Kidd & The Pirates, The, 534
Complete Muddy Waters, The, 1037
Complete Recordings, The, 509
Complete Smash Sessions, The, 830
Complete Stone Roses, The, 952
Complete Studio Recordings, The, 570
Completely, 1031
Completely Hooked, 271
Completely Well, 538
Complicated, 997
Compositions, 49
Computer Game (Theme from the Invaders), 868
Computer Games, 194
Computer World, 554
Concept, The, 972
Concert, 238
Concert at Newport, 452
Concert by the Sea, 372, 870
Concert Classics, 18
Concert Creations for Guitar, 16
Concert for Bangladesh, 293, 930, 1010
Concert for Sitar, 889
Concert for the People, A, 55
Concert in Central Park, The, 898
Concerto for Group and Orchestra, 253, 254
Concerto for Guitar and Orchestra, 624
Concerto for Sitar, 793
Concerto for Tenor Saxophone and Orchestra, 851

Concerto for Trumpet, 487
Concerto for Two, 647, 983
Concerto in B Goode, 82
Concerto in F, 380
Concerts Bremen and Lausanne, 492
Concerts in China, The, 491
Concrete and Clay, 1093
Concubine de l'Hemoglobine, La, 657
Condor Pasa, El, 898
Coney Island Baby, 824
Conferring with the Moon, 5
Confess, 250, 750
Confessin' the Blues, 626
Confessions of a Pop Group, 1044
Confessions of Dr Dream, The, 919
Confide in Me, 677
Confluence, 466
Confrontation, 644
Confucius, 908
Confusion, 640, 716
Confusion Is Sex, 920
Conga, 314
Congratulations, 8, 220, 831
Congregation, 10
Connected, 991
Connection, 304, 304
Connections, 431
Connie Francis and Hank Williams Jnr Sing Great Country Hits, 353
Connie Francis Sings Great Jewish Favourites, 353
Conqueror, The, 692
Conquest, 1009
Conquistador, 800
Conscience, 1076
Conscious, 33, 591
Conscious Party, 644
Consequences, 976
Consider Yourself, 57
Conspiracy of Hope, 660
Constipation Blues, 433
Constrictor, 215
Construction Time Again, 258
Constructive Melancholy, 816
ConstruKction of Light, 536
Contact, 781
Contact from the Underworld of Redboy, 53
Continental, The, 34
Contino Sessions, The, 797
Contrasts for Clarinet, Violin and Piano, 391
Contribution, 752
Control, 479, 484
Controversy, 797
Conversation Peace, 1077
Conversations with Myself, 318
Convoy, 287, 555
Cookbook, The, 246

Cooking Breakfast for the One I Love, 120
Cool and Crazy, 847
Cool Cat Blues, 327
Cool for Cats, 935
Cool in a Kaftan, 712
Cool It Now, 125
Cool Operator, 712
Cool River, 619
Cool Ruler, 475
Cool Shake, 257
Cool Sound of Albert Collins, The, 203
Cool Touch, 873
Cool Water, 687, 837, 848, 922, 922
Cooleyhigh Harmony, 114
Coon Band Contest, A, 924
Cop and Speeder, 915
Cop Killer, 467
Copa Rota, La, 332
Copacabana, 637
Copeland Special, 216
Copenhagen, 73
Copper Blue, 701
Copperhead Road, 297
Coppin' the Bop, 786
Coquette, 597
Corazón, El, 296, 297, 408
Core, 953
Corinna, Corinna, 769
Corky Stomp, 1062
Corn Licker Still in Georgia, 968, 1027
Corn Pickin' and Slick Slidin', 142
Cornerstone, 959
Cornflake Girl, 20
Coronation Rag, 37
Coronation Waltz, 1078
Correct Use of Soap, 145
Corridors of Power, 690
Corrine, Corrina, 929, 998
Corruption, 640, 640
Cortez the Killer, 1088
Coryell, 217
Coryell/Lanphere, 218
Cosas del Amor, 469
Cosi Fan Tutti Frutti, 936
Cosmic Explorer, 961
Cosmic Girl, 490
Cosmic Thing, 43
Cosmic Wheels, 278
Cosmo's Factory, 226
Cost of Loving, The, 1044
Costafine Town, 427
Cottage for Sale, 299
Cotton Fields, 568
Cotton Jenny, 585
Cottonfields, 542
Cottontail, 1041
Could It Be Forever?, 167, 329
Could It Be I'm Falling in Love?, 74, 931

Could It Be Magic, 1064
Could You Be Loved, 644
Couldn't Stand the Weather, 1016
Count Every Star, 817
Count Me in, 863
Count on Me, 495
Count Talent and the Originals, 97
Count Your Blessings, 732
Countdown: 1992–1983, 805
Countdown to Ecstasy, 943
Countdown to Extinction, 659
Counterfeit EP, 258
Counterparts, 861
Counting Teardrops, 344
Countless Blues, 1087
Country, 516
Country Airs, 1025
Country Blues Guitar, 405
Country Boy, 53, 58, 134, 541, *907*, 987
Country Boy Can Survive, A, 1061
Country Boy's Dream, 766
Country Classics, 417
Country Club, 994
Country Collection, The, 1053
Country Cooking, 620
Country Fever, 711
Country Fool, 169
Country Gardens, 395, 890
Country Gentleman, 36
Country Girl, 748, 1086
Country Girl, City Man, 970
Country Gospel, 483
Country Guitar Giants, 993
Country House, 100, 731
Country Is Going to War, The, 523
Country Life, 857
Country Line Special, 552
Country Love Songs, 599
Country Morning, 368
Country Music Hall of Fame, 247, 1045
Country Music Is Here to Stay, 463
Country Pedigree, 33
Country Preacher, 8
Country Songs for City Folks, 581
Country Songs for Kids, 416
Country Steel Guitar, 284
Country Steel Guitar of Pete Drake, The, 284
Coup de Grace, 956
Couple in Spirit, 37
Couple of Swells, A, 79
Court and Spark, 679
Court Room, The, 163
Courtship of Barney and Eileen, The, 511
Cousin Caruso, 706
Cousin Dupree, 943
Cousin Norman, 644

Covenant, 1006
Cover, 973
Cover Me, 934
Cover of Music City News, The, 896
Cover of Rolling Stone, The, 271, 896
Cover Shot, 314
Cover You,, 850
Coverdale Page, 1051
Covers, 321
Cow Cow Blues, 696
Cow Cow Boogie, 696
Cow Finger and Mosquito Pie, 433
Cowabonga, 660
Coward of the County, 847
Cowboy, 161
Cowboy Jimmy Joe, 200
Cowboy on the Moon, 560
Cowboy Song, The, 951
Cowboy's Work Is Never Done, A, 177, 373
Cowboyography, 465
Cowboys, 312
Cowboys to Girls, 369, 472
Cowgirl, 1008
Cowgirl and the Dandy, The, 571
Cowgirl in the Sand, 1087
Cowgirl's Prayer, 426, 1062
Cowjazz, 1027
Cowpuncher's Cantata, 146
Coz I Luv You, 910
Cracked Rear View, 453
Crackers International, 312
Cracking Up, 498
Cracklin' Rosie, 262
Cradle of Love, 468, 791
Crash, 246, 461
Crash! Boom! Bang!, 856
Crash Landing, 440
Crashin' in, 173
Crawfish Fiesta, 802
Crawlin' King Snake, 280, 1057
Crawling from the Wreckage, 302
Crawling King Snake, 452
Crawling Up a Hill, 654
Crazy, 193, 377, 712
Crazy Arms, 581, 794
Crazy Blues, 114, 115, 763
Crazy 'Bout You, 971
Crazy 'Bout You Baby, 227
Crazy Country Hop, 748
Crazy, Crazy, Baby, 332
Crazy, Crazy, Crazy, 338
Crazy Diamond, 777
Crazy for You, 380, 631
Crazy from the Heart, 75
Crazy Heart, 855
Crazy Horses, 746, 747
Crazy in Love, 1000
Crazy Legs, *70*, 822, *1022*
Crazy Little Guitar Man, 344

Crazy Little Thing Called Love, 808
Crazy Love, 16, *795*
Crazy Mama, 150
Crazy Man Crazy, 412
Crazy Nights, 546
Crazy on You, 436
Crazy Over You, 764
Crazy Sexy Cool, 986
Crazy Steal, A, 450
Crazy Words, Crazy Tune, 233
Crazy World, 875
Crazy World of Arthur Brown, The, 124
Creation, 692
Creation of Love, 56
Creator, 575
Creatures of the Night, 546
Creep, 811, 986
Creeque Alley, *633*, *725*
Creeque Alley: The History of The Mamas and the Papas, 634
Creole Love Call, 307, 414
Crepuscule with Nellie, 684
Crescendo in Drums, 152
Crescent City, 1062
Crescents, 511
Crest of a Knave, 499
Crew Cuts Go Folk, The, 227
Crew Necks and Khakis, 227
Cricklewood Green, 977
Cried Like a Baby, 130
Crime of the Century, 962
Crimes of Passion, 76
Criminal Minded, 106
Criminal Record, 1025
Criminal Tango, 635
Crimson and Clover, 450, 489, 499
Crises, 738
Crisis? What Crisis?, 962
Criticise, 740
Crock of Gold, The, 781
Crocodile Rock, 503
Crocodiles, 299
Croix, Les, 68
Crooked Rain, Crooked Rain, 760
Croonin', 705
Crosby Stills and Nash, 229
Cross Country, 776
Cross Fire, 744
Cross Purposes, 89
Cross Road Blues, 509
Cross Talk, 792
Cross that Line, 513
Cross Your Heart, 141
Crossfire, 504, *932*
Crossing, The, 83, 1089
Crossing Muddy Waters, 444
Crossroads, *102*, *172*, 186, *187*, *755*
Cross-Section Saxes, 863
Crown of Creation, 494
Crucifixion, The, 733

Crucify Me, 20
Cruel Sister, 765
Cruel Summer, 52
Cruel to Be Kind, 603
Cruisin', 841, 1021
Cruisin' with Ruben and the Jets, 1091
Crumbling Down, 660
Crusade, 654
Crush, 103, 742
Crushed by the Wheels of Industry, 438
Cry, 348, 356, 375, 818, 976
Cry Baby, 80, 655, 812
Cry Baby Baby Cry, 889
Cry Before I Go, 927
Cry Cry Cry, 165, 1010
Cry Just a Little Bit, 947
Cry Like a Baby, 112, 113, 355, 683
Cry like a Rainstorm, Howl like the Wind, 714, 854
Cry Me a River, 198, 598
Cry Myself to Sleep, 520
Cry of Love, 440
Cry of the Wild Geese, The, 560, 646, 664, 672
• Cry of the Wild Goose, 146, 344
Cry on My Shoulder, 814
Cry to Me, 80, 138, 139, 792
Cryin', 562, 741
Crying, 625, 675, 741
Crying Game, The, 236, 611, 768
Crying in the Chapel, 337, 389, 743
Crying in the Rain, 11, 320, 540, 971
Crying My Heart Out Over You, 340
Crying Over You, 108
Crying Waiting Hoping, 451
Crypt Style, 510
Cryptic Writings, 659
Crystal Ball, 798
Crystal Blue Persuasion, 489
Crystal Crescent, 796
Crystal Planet, 872
Crystal Silence, 141
CSN, 229
C. T. A. 102, 147
C30, C60, C90 Go, 623
Cuanto Le Gusto, 678
Cuba Y Puerto Rico, 804
Cuban Fire, 529
Cuban Love Song, 334, 621
Cubana Be, 863
Cubana Bop, 863
Cubanola Glide, 1023
Cube, 194
Cucula, 235
Cuddle up a Little Closer, Lovey Mine, 422, 706
Cuddly Toy, 722
Cult Classics, 98
Cult of Ray, The, 779

Cum on Feel the Noize, 909, 910
Cumberland Gap, 277
Cumparsita, La, 897
Cup Full of Dreams, 276
Cup of Coffee, a Sandwich and You, A, 135
Cupid, 213, 708, 743
Cupid and Psyche, 642, 878
Cupid (I've Loved You for a Long Time), 932
Cupid's Boogie, 772
Cupid's in Fashion, 40
Curiosities on the Farm, 691
Curious Feeling, A, 378
Curly, 186, 703
Current, 438
Current Affairs, 732
Currents, 1059
Curtains, 985
Curtis, 655
Cushion Foot Stomp, 1058
Cut Above the Rest, A, 964
Cut Across Shorty, 197
Cut the Cake, 39
Cut the Crap, 191
Cut Your Hair, 760
Cuts Both Ways, 314, 879
Cuts Like a Knife, 7
Cuts to the Chase, 431
Cutter, The, 299
Cuttin' in, 1038
Cuttin' the Boogie, 20
Cuttin' Up, 276
Cutting Edge, The, 256, 851
Cyberpunk, 468
Cycles, 218, 279
Cyclone, 968
Cygnus X-1, 861
Cypress Avenue, 694
Czarine, La, 924

Da Capo, 600
Da Doo Ron Ron, 167, 235, 237, 404, 652, 724, 728, 929
Da Funk, 239
Da Real World, 308
Dachau Blues, 72
Daddy, 618, 987
Daddy Come and Get Me, 757
Daddy Cool, 245
Daddy Could Swear, I Declare, 121
Daddy Don't You Walk So Fast, 329, 707
Daddy Frank (the Guitar Man), 411
Daddy Rolling Stone, 91
Daddy Sang Bass, 766
Daddy Went Walkin', 1089
Daddy What If, 896
Daddy's Home, 84, 257, 478, 831, 892
Daddy's Honky Tonk, 54

Dagenham Dave, 696
Daily News, 761
Daily Operation, 370
Daisies of the Galaxy, 303
Daisy Got Me Crazy, 549
Daisy Mae, 880
Dallas, 479
Dallas Blues, 85
Dallas Reunion Tapes, The, 809
Daltrey, 1054
Damage, 965
Damaged, 850
Dame Nellie Melba, 660
Damn Right I Got the Blues, 409
Damn the Torpedoes, 771
Damned Damned Damned, 240, 603
D'Amour ou d'Amitié, 266
Dan Is the Man in the Van, 668
Dana My Love, 328
Dance a Little Light, 137
Dance All Night, 1068
Dance Away, 857
Dance Band on the Titanic, 172
Dance Dance, Dance, 63, 845
Dance (Disco Heat), 363
Dance for Two People, 395, 405
Dance Hall at Louse Point, 429
Dance Hall Don, 475
Dance Hall Memory, 1009
Dance Hits, 438
Dance into the Light, 205
Dance Little Lady, 222
Dance Mania, 804
Dance Naked, 661
Dance of Life, 1026
Dance of the Rainbow Serpent, 871
Dance on, 885
Dance Soca Party, 31
Dance Stance, 261
Dance the Body Music, 745
Dance Time in Texas, 955
Dance to the Bop, 1022
Dance to the Music, 502, 954
Dance Tonight, 994
Dance with Arthur Brown, 125
Dance with Me, 285, 808
Dance with Me Henry, 51, 85, 460, 486
Dance with the Devil, 712
(Dance with the) Guitar Man, 300
Dance with the One that Brought You, 1000
Dance . . . Ya Know It!, 125
Dance Your Life Away, 586
Dancepieces, 385
Dancer, 619
Dancer with Bruised Knees, 619
Dancin', 575
Dancin' in the Moonlight (It's Caught Me in the Spotlight), 979 •

Dancin' on the Edge, 500
Dancin' with Them Brung Me Propper, 297
Dancing at the Hop, 1022
Dancing Cowboys, 75
Dancing Floor, 474
Dancing Girls, 531
Dancing in the Dark, 49, 874, 883, 890, 934
Dancing in the Street, 111, 377, 589, 645, 728, 849
Dancing in Your Head, 202
Dancing Machine, 478
Dancing on the Ceiling, 428, 832
Dancing on the Edge, 613
Dancing Queen, 1, 169, 980
Dancing Shoes, 669
Dancing the Blues, 966
Dancing with Strangers, 819
Dancing with Tears in My Eyes, 883, 1007
Dandy, 442, 699
Dandy in the Underworld, 101
Dang Me, 673
Danger Zone, 596, 655, 693
Dangerous, 289, 481, 835
Dangerous Acquaintances, 326
Dangerous Age, 46
Dangerous Curves, 500
Danglin' on a String, 169
Daniel and the Sacred Harp, 53
Danny, 1000
Danny Boy, 444, 594, 794, 1000, 1069
Danny O'Keefe, 737
Danny's Song, 596, 705, 705
Danse Macabre, 590
Daphne, 826
Dapper Dan, 259, 1023
Darcy's Song, 653
Dardanella, 882
Dare, 461
Dare Me, 781
Dare to Dream, 721, 1082
Daring Adventures, 982
Dark as a Dungeon, 992
Dark at the End of the Tunnel, 305
Dark End of the Street, 160, 212, 415, 682, 690, 756, 764
Dark Horse, 427
Dark Intervals, 492
Dark Is the Night, 11
Dark Lady, 177
Dark Ride, The, 653
Dark Side of the Moon, 755, 776, 777, 995
Dark Side of the Room, 653
Dark Side of Town, The, 401
Dark Sneak Love Action, 967
Dark Star, 400, 401, 401
Dark Streets of London, 780
Dark Town Strutters' Ball, 203

Dark Was the Night, 505
Dark Was the Night – Cold Was the Ground, 505
Darkest Hour Is Just Before Dawn, The, 937
Darkest Street in Town, 186
Darklands, 498
Darkness Darkness, 1008, 1090
Darkness on the Edge of Town, 934
Darkness on the Face of the Earth, 712
Darktown Poker Club, The, 426, 992, 1057
Darktown Strutters Ball, The, 116, 129, 996
Darlin', 63, 167, 516
Darling Be Home Soon, 602
Darling, Dear I Know, 256
Darn That Dream, 391, 1012
Darshan (the Road to Graceland), 965
Das Kabinett, 711
Das Lied der Deutschen, 1018
Dat Dere, 93
Daughter of Darkness, 516, 823
Daughter of Time, 205
Dave Stewart & The Spiritual Cowboys, 317
Davenport Blues, 73
David Ackles, 5
David Bowie, 110
David Byrne, 148, 967
David Cassidy, 167
David Foster, 346
David Live, 111
David Watts, 484, 543
David White Tricker, 243
David's Album, 47
Davy the Fat Boy, 719
Davy's on the Road Again, 635
Daw Da Hiya, 436
Dawn (Go Away), 349
Dawn of Correction, 621, 911
Day, The, 44
Day at the Races, A, 807
Day by Day, 231, 348, 859, 903, 987
Day Dreaming, 355
Day Dreams about Night Things, 675
Day I Met Marie, The, 831
Day in Day out, 231
Day in the Life, A, 688, 977
Day Is Done, 768
Day of the Jackal, 586
Day the Rains Came Down, The, 68
Day the World Turned Blue, The, 1022
Day to Day, The, 737
Day Trip to Bangor, 13

Day We Caught the Train, The, 732
Daydream, 157, 850
Daydream Believer, 684, 705, 948
Daydream Nation, 920, 921
Daydreamer, 167
Daydreaming at Midnight, 867
Daydreams, 602
Daylight Again, 229
Days, 614
Days Gone Down, 812
Days in Paradise, 690
Days in the Wake, 738
Days Like This, 695
Days of Future Passed, 689
Days of Open Hand, 1017
Days of Wine and Roses, 634, 1057
Daysleeper, 827
Daytona Demon, 807
Dazzle Ships, 742
DB Blues, 1087
D.E. 7th, 302
De Do Do Do, De Da Da Da, 782
De La Soul Is Dead, 251
De Panama a Nueva York, 92
Deacon Blue, 943
Dead Air, 915
Dead Bees on a Cake, 491, 965
Dead Cat, 1083
Dead End Street, 543, 818
Dead Flowers, 39
Dead from the Waist Down, 168
Dead Giveaway, 886
Dead Heart, The, 668
Dead Letter Office, 826
Dead Man's Curve, 490
Dead Man's Party, 305
Dead Ringer, 657
Dead Ringer for Love, 177, 657
Dead Set, 401
Dead Skunk, 1024
Deadicated, 401
Deadlier Than the Male, 1026
Deadline, 263
Deadweight, 69
Deal It Out, 226
Dealer, The, 217
Dean and I, The, 975
Dear Beverly, 549
Dear Elaine, 703
Dear Hearts and Gentle People, 323, 895
Dear Ivan, 252
Dear John, 941
Dear John Letter, 463
Dear Lady Twist, 104
Dear Landlord, 292
Dear Lover, 1046
Dear Mom, 996
Dear Mr Gable, 371
Dear Mr President, 881

Dear Old Southland, 69, 567
Dear Prudence, 905
Dearest Beverley, 193
Dearly Beloved, 530, 663
Death and the Flower, 492
Death Certificate, 466
Death Letter Blues, 1082
Death May Be Your Santa Claus, 700
Death of a Clown, 543
Death of a Ladies Man, 201, 930
Death of a Salesman, 392
Death of an Unpopular Poet, 137
Death of Floyd Collins, The, 240
Death of Luther King, 288
Death of Rock and Roll, The, 629
Death of Stephen Biko, The, 761
Death or Glory, 424
Death Ray Boogie, 508
Death Trip, 468
Death Valley '69, 920
Death Wish, 420
Debonair, 10
Deborah, 101
Debravation, 96
Début, 86, 923
Decade, 289
Decade of Darkness (1991–2000), The, 51
Decade of Decadence, 699
Decade of Hits, A, 242
Decca Anthology, The, 913
Decca Skiffle Sessions 1956-7, The, 207
Deceivin' Blues, 748
December 1963 (Oh What a Night), 350
Deception, 928
Deck of Cards, 146
Deconstructed, 142
Dede Dinah, 39
Dedicated, 668
Dedicated Follower of Fashion, 543
Dedicated Hound, 586
Dedicated to the One I Love, 60, 338, 633, 854, 894
Dedication, 104
Deed I Do, 391, 455, 670, 855
Deed Is Done, The, 682
Deep Deep Trouble, 903
Deep End Live, 1054
Deep Harlem, 73
Deep Henderson, 855
Deep in a Dream, 1012
Deep in the Heart of Nowhere, 377
Deep in the Night, 487
Deep in Your Heart, 116
Deep Inside My Heart, 295
Deep Moanin' Blues, 813
Deep Purple, 253, 339, 747, 817, 822, 890

Deep Purple in Rock, 253
Deep River, 838
Deep South Suite, 307
Deep Space/Virgin Sky, 495
Deeper, 256
Deeper Love, A, 149, 355
Deeper Than the Holler, 993
Deeper Underground, 490
Def Dumb and Blonde, 96
Defender, 368
Defenders of the Faith, 519
Definitely Maybe, 730
Definitely What, 37
Definition of Soul, 139
Defying Gravity, 1070
Deguello, 1094
Dehumanizer, 89
Dein Ist Mein Ganzes Herz, 574
Déjà Vu, 229, 1033, *1087*
Delaware, 209, 751
D'Electrified, 90
Delicado, 325
Delicate, 243
Delicate and Jumpy, 1073
Delicate Sound of Thunder, The, 777
Delightful, 421
Delilah, 516, 823
Delilah Jones, 621
Delirious, 797
Deliver the Word, 1030
Deliverance Will Come, 12
Della and the Dealer, 40
Delta Blues, 617
Delta Bluesman, 1020
Delta Dawn, 496, 821, 893, 997
Delta Lady, 198, 214, 864
Deltics, 819
Delusion, 7
Democracy, 535
Demolition Man, 782
Demolition Plot J-7, 760
Demon in Disguise, 122
Demon's Theme, 138
Demons and Wizards, 1009
Denis, 96
Dennis Coulson, 368
Departure, 519
Der Fuehrer's Face, 515
Der Nayer Sher, 854
Derringer, 615
Desafinado, 381, 501, 561
Descendants of Smith, 424
Description of a Fool, 994
Desdemona, 101, 879
Dese Dem Dose, 670
Deseo, 1085
Desert Moon, 959
Desert Shore, 151, 1018
Desert Song, 422
Desert Wind, 435
Deserter's Songs, 664

Design for Life, A, 637
Desire, 71, 293, 360, 427, 991, 1004
Desire Walks on, 437
Desitively Bonnaroo, 272, 990
Desolation Angels, 46
Desolation Row, 292, 733
Desperado, 295
Desperadoes Waiting for the Train, 746, 1027
Destination Anywhere, 102
Destiny, 315, 478, 532, 816
Destiny Calling, 485
Destiny Street, 973
Destiny's Children, 880
Destiny's Song and the Image of Pursuance, 776
Destroyer, 546
Detour, 751
Detroit, 865
Detroit City, 55, 239, 516, 646
Detroit Medley, 865
Detroit Memphis Experience, The, 865
Deuce, 98, 368
Deuces Wild, 539
Deutschland uber Alles, 151, 1018
D'Eux, 266
Devil Came from Kansas, The, 800
Devil Comes Back to Georgia, The, 242
Devil Gate Drive, 183, 698, 807
Devil Girl, 113
Devil Got My Woman, 488, *488*
Devil Has All the Best Tunes, The, 788
Devil Inside, 473
Devil or Angel, 195, 364, 1017
Devil Went Down to Georgia, The, 242
Devil with a Blues Dress, 227, 865
Devil with an Angel's Smile, 472
Devil Woman, 831, 837
Devil's Elbow, 530
Devil's Haircut, 69
Devo Presents the Adventures of the Smart Patrol, 260
Devoted to You, 898
Devotion, 976
Dew Drops in the Garden, 253
Dexter Blues, 627
Dialogue for Jazz Combo and Symphony, 133
Dialogues for Jazz Quintet and Orchestra, 874
Diamante, 1094
Diamantina Cocktail, 590
Diamond, 926
Diamond Cut, 1002
Diamond Dogs, 111
Diamond Girl, 170
Diamond Head, 857

Diamond Jack and the Queen of Pain, 919
Diamond Life, 866
Diamond of Dream, 471
Diamonds, 17, 267, 819, 885
Diamonds and Pearls, 351, *798*
Diamonds and Rust, 47, *718*
Diamonds and Rust in the Bull-ring, 47
Diamonds Are a Girl's Best Friend, 839, 958
Diamonds Are Forever: The Remix Album, 60
Diamonds in the Rough, 799
Diana, 24, 218, 846, 855
Diana Ross & The Supremes: 40 Golden Motown Greats, 963
Diana with Marvin, 374
Diary, The, 880
Diary of a Band, 654
Dick Almighty, 1001
Dick Farina and Eric von Schmidt, 329
Dick Tracy, 908
Dick's Picks No. 1, 401
Dick's Picks Vol 4, 401
Did She Mention My Name?, 584
Did Ya, 544
Did You Ever Love a Woman?, 980
Did You Ever See a Dream Walking?, 286, 828, 916
Did You See Jackie Robinson Hit That Ball?, 505
Diddy Wah Diddy, 72
Didi, 532, 847
Didn't I (Blow Your Mind This Time), 255, 715
Die Gittare und das Meer, 522, 810
Diesel and Dust, 668
Diesel Power, 801
Different Beat, A, 114
Different Class, 805
Different Corner, A, 666
Different Drum, 685, 853, *888*
Different Drummer, 476
Different Kind of Tension, A, 145
Different Moods of Me, 1030
Different Stages, 861
Different Strokes, 221
Different Therefore Equal, 614
Different World, 1009
Difficult to Cure, 254
Dig a Little Deeper, 480
Dig All Night, 309
Dig It, 968
Dig My Mood, 603
Dig the New Breed, 484
Dig the Way I Feel, 1046
Dig Your Own Hole, 175
Diga Diga Doo, 674

Diggin' Up Bones, 993
Diggy Liggy Lo, 207, 530
Digital Ragtime, 834
Digital, 389
Dilemma, 1089
Dim, Dim the Lights, 412
Dim Lights, Thick Smoke (and Loud, Loud Music), 641
Dimanche à Orly, 68
Dime Store Mystery, 1018
Dimming of the Day, 814
Dimples, 452, 1072
Dinah, 231, 399, 555
Dingly Dell, 586
Dink's Song, 1013
Dinner Music for a Pack of Hungry Cannibals, 876
Dinner Music for People Who Aren't Very Hungry, 516
Dinner with Gershwin, 961
Dio Come Ti Amo, 681
Dion, 266
Dion Chante Plamondon, 266
Dionne, 1033
Dionne Warwick Sings the Songs of Cole Porter, 1033
Dippermouth Blues, 739
Direct, 1014
Dirk Wears White Sox, 24
Dirt, 14
Dirty, 371, 920
Dirty Dawg, 715
Dirty Deeds Done Dirt Cheap, 4
Dirty Diana, 481
Dirty Dozen, The, 774
Dirty Laundry, 296, 655, *701*
Dirty Mind, 797
Dirty Old Town, 614, 780, 949
Dirty Water, 349
Dirty Work, 221, 849, 1076
Disappear, 473
Disappearing Act, 886
Disappointed, 812, 884
Disarm, 913
Disc Jockey Jump, 556, 705
Discipline, 536
Disco, 767
Disco Baby, 615
Disco Gardens, 886
Disco: La Passione, 60
Disco Lady, 971
Disco 9000, 971
Disco Reggae, 571
Disco 2000, 805
Discography, 768
Discotheque, 1005
Discover America, 755
Discovery, 304, 738
Discreet Repeat, 652
Disintegration, 238
Disney Girls, 64
Disorder at the Border, 383

Disposable Teens, 638
Disraeli Gears, 225, 283, 701
Disregard of Timekeeping, The, 570
Distance, The, 882
Distant Drums, 825
Distant Shore, A, 320
Distant Thunder, 35
Distillation, 1074
Ditty Wa Ditty, 212
Diva, 317, 355, 615
Divine Emotions, 1026
Divine Madness, 630, 667
Divine Miss M, The, 667
Division Bell, The, 777
D.I.V.O.R.C.E., 220, 811, 893, 1080
Divorce Me C.O.D., 992
Dixie, 306, 412, 718
Dixie Chicken, 123, *587*
Dixie Flyer, 720
Dixie Fried, 766
Dixie Lee, 462
Dixie on my Mind, 1061
Dixie-Narco, 796
Diz and Getz, 381
Dizzy, 384, 829, 846
Dizzy Heights, 585
Dizzy Miss Lizzie, 576, 860, 1061, 1062
D.J. for a Day, 415
DJ Riot, 912
Django, 681
Django in Rome, 826
Djangology, 826
Djed, 988
Djobi Djoba, 384
Djupa Andertag, 1
D'Natural Blues, 674
Do Anything You Want to, 979
Do Baby Do, 526
Do Fries Go with That Shake?, 194
Do I Do, 1077
Do I Love You, 853
Do I Make Myself Clear, 486
Do I Worry?, 472
Do It, 850
Do It Again, 63, 156, 943, 1049
Do It All Night, 797
Do It Baby, 841
Do It Good, 526
Do It Properly, 149
Do It with Feeling, 134
Do It Yourself, 290, 952
Do Me Again, 479
Do Me Baby, 798
Do Not Pass Me By, 418
Do Nothing Till You Hear From Me, 15
Do or Die, 1018
Do Re Mi, 408, 661

Do Right Man, 764
Do Right Woman, 355, 415, 764, 940
Do Right Woman – Do Right Man, 682
Do That to Me One More Time, 156
Do the Bartman, 903
Do the Bird, 744
Do the Bop, 243
Do the Clam, 789
Do the Freddie, 357
Do the Funky Chicken, 980
Do the Funky Penguin, 980
Do the Funky Somethin', 981
Do the New Continental, 282
Do the Push and Pull, 980
Do the Reggay, 549, 986, 987
Do the Strand, 857
Do They Know It's Christmas?, 377, 666, 951, 1007, 1010
Do Wah Diddy Diddy, 635
Do What U Like, 1064
Do What You Do, 478
Do Ya, 304, 472, 703, 746
Do Ya Think I'm Sexy?, 949, 950
Do You Believe in Love, 303, 581
Do You Believe in Magic?, 167, 602, 602
Do You Believe in Miracles, 910
Do You Believe in Us, 879
Do You Get Enough Love, 370
Do You Know the Way to San José?, 45, 1033
Do You Know Where You're Going to?, 855
Do You Love Me?, 187, 211, 784
Do You Love What You Feel?, 472
Do You Mind, 718
Do You Really Want to Hurt Me?, 236
Do You Remember, 205
Do You Remember the First Time?, 805
Do You See My Love (for You Growing), 121
Do You Wanna Dance?, 633, 831
Do You Wanna Get Funky?, 149
Do You Wanna Touch Me (Oh Yeah!), 386
Do You Want Me?, 869
Do You Want to Dance, 667
Do You Want to Know a Secret?, 3
Do You Want to Touch Me (Oh Yeah), 499
Doc Watson, 1037
Doc Watson and Son, 1037
Dock of the Bay, 102, 821
Doctor, The, 279
Doctor Doctor, 981, 1006

Doctor Jazz, 697
Doctor My Eyes, 132, 478
Doctor's Orders, 921
Doctorin' the Tardis, 386, 547
Document, 826
Does Anybody Really Know What Time It Is?, 181
Does Fort Worth Ever Cross Your Mind, 955
Does He Love You, 618
Does Humor Belong in Music?, 1092
Does Your Chewing Gum Lose Its Flavour, 277
Doesn't Somebody Want to Be Wanted, 167
Dog and Butterfly, 436
Dog Days, 37
Dog Eat Dog, 25, 273, 679
Dog Man Star, 960
Dog of Two Heads, 941
Dogg Food, 269
Doggfather, 269
Doggie House Boogie, 691
Doggin' Around, 1069
Doggy Dogg World, 269
Doggystyle, 269
Dogs Under Stress, 1018
Doin' Our Own Dang, 251, 520
Doin' What Comes Naturally, 664
Doing All Right with the Boys, 386
Doing Our Thing, 163
Doing Things, 562
Doing What Comes Naturally, 463
Doll Dance, 130
Doll Parts, 448
Dollar Done Fell, The, 409
Dollar Down, A, 585
Dolores, 282
Dolphin, The, 381
Dolphins, The, 136, 710
Doma Sportova . . . Live in Zagreb, 20/5/94, 163
Domani, 564
Dominion, 625
Dominique, 829
Domino, 694, 987
Domino Dancing, 768
Domino Theory, 1039
Don Carlos Meets Mary Lou, 1063
Don McLean Christmas, 625
Don Quixote, 531
Don Williams Vol. 1, 1058
Don't Answer Me, 707
Don't Ask Me Why, 317
Don't Be Afraid of the Dark, 224
Don't Be Angry, 130, 227
Don't Be Cruel, 89, 91, 125, 332, 789, 964, 1056

Don't Be That Way, 48
Don't Believe the Hype, 802
Don't Blame Me, 334, 621
Don't Blow Your Mind, 214
Don't Bogart That Joint, 351, 587
Don't Bore Us Get to the Chorus, 856
Don't Break My Heart, 1005
Don't Break My Heart Again, 1051
Don't Break the Heart That Loves You, 353
Don't Bring Lulu, 260
Don't Bring Me Down, 23, 304, 540, 792
Don't Bring Me Your Heartaches, 707
Don't Call Me from a Honky Tonk, 458
Don't Call Me Mama Anymore, 633
Don't Call Me Nigger, Whitey, 954
Don't Call My Name, 244
Don't Care, 782
Don't Change on Me, 174
Don't Cheat in Our Hometown, 907
Don't Come Around Here No More, 771
Don't Come Home a-Drinkin' (With Lovin on Your Mind), 607
Don't Cry, 407, 1085
Don't Cry Beautiful Edith, 545
Don't Cry Daddy, 247, 789
Don't Cry for Me, Argentina, 593, 631, 886
Don't Cry My Love, 608
Don't Cry Now, 853
Don't Cry Out Loud, 123
Don't Do Me Like That, 771
Don't Do That, 699
Don't Doubt Yourself, 147
Don't Doubt Yourself Babe, 259
Don't Dream It's Over, 232, 1089
Don't Ever Change, 228
Don't Explain, 448, 751
Don't Fall in Love, 976
Don't Fall in Love with a Dreamer, 159, 847
(Don't Fear) The Reaper, 98
Don't Fence Me in, 23, 230, 785
Don't Fight It, 519, 775
Don't Get Around Much Anymore, 306, 447
Don't Get Hooked on Me, 415
Don't Get Me Wrong, 791
Don't Get Stopped in Beverly Hills, 886
Don't Give a Dose to the One You Love the Most, 896

Don't Give Up, 143, 232, 734
Don't Give Up on Us, 611, 923
Don't Go, 703
Don't Go Breaking My Heart, 503
Don't Go Down the Mine Daddy, 1078
Don't Hang Up, 744
Don't It Make My Brown Eyes Blue, 375
Don't It Make You Want to Go Home, 925
Don't Kill the Whale, 1085
Don't Knock My Love – Pt 1, 775
Don't Know Much, 714, 854
Don't Leave Me This Way, 208, 458, 764
Don't Leave Your Records in the Sun, 429
Don't Let Go, 417, 434, 636
Don't Let Him Go, 827
Don't Let It Die, 55, 792
Don't Let It End, 959
Don't Let It Get You Down, 234
Don't Let Love Slip Away, 479
Don't Let Me Suffer, 474
Don't Let Our Love Start Slippin' Away, 383
Don't Let the California Earthquake Scare You Away, 404
Don't Let the Green Grass Fool You, 775
Don't Let the Sun Catch You Crying, 379
Don't Let the Sun Go Down on Me, 503
Don't Let's Be Beastly to the Germans, 222
Don't Look Back, 109, 335, 403, 453, 710
Don't Look Back in Anger, 731
Don't Lose Your Grip on Love, 603
Don't Make Me Over, 45, 965, 1033
Don't Make My Baby Blue, 885
Don't Marry Her, 68
Don't Mess Around with Bill, 649
Don't Mess Me Up, 703
Don't Mess up a Good Thing, 59
Don't Mess with Dr Dream, 981
Don't Mind if I Do, 236
Don't Need a Gun, 468
Don't Pass Me By, 84
Don't Pay the Ferryman, 251
Don't Play That Song, 355, 539
Don't Pull Your Love, 829
Don't Push Your Luck, 49
Don't Rain on My Parade, 664, 956, 959
Don't Rob Another Man's Castle, 23, 29

Don't Rock the Jukebox, 478, 479
Don't Say Nothin' Bad About My Baby, 540
Don't Send Me No Flowers, 1066
Don't Shoot Me, I'm Only the Piano Player, 503
Don't Sing, 788
Don't Sit Under the Apple Tree, 671
Don't Sleep in the Subway, 189, 430
Don't Speak, 725
Don't Stand Another Chance, 479
Don't Stand Me Down, 261
Don't Stand So Close to Me, 782
Don't Start Crying Now, 694
Don't Start Me to Talkin', 1066
Don't Stop, 342, 467, 941
Don't Stop Believin', 519
Don't Stop Me Now, 808
Don't Stop . . . Planet Rock, 51
Don't Stop the Carnival, 137, 793, 851, 851
Don't Stop the Dance, 333
Don't Stop (Till You Get Enough), 481
Don't Stop Twist, 1015
Don't Stop Your Love, 107
Don't Sweat the Technique, 43
Don't Take It Personal, 478
Don't Take Love for Granted, 604
Don't Take Your Guns to Town, 165
Don't Talk to Strangers, 934
Don't Think Twice, 349
Don't Think Twice It's All Right, 292, 308, 768
Don't Throw Your Love Away, 744, 878, 879
Don't Toss Us Away, 622
Don't Tread, 727
Don't Treat Me Like a Child, 609, 752
Don't Try This at Home, 117
Don't Try to Take the Fifth, 781
Don't Turn Around, 35, 1031
Don't Walk Away, 350, 710
Don't Wanna Know about Evil, 744
Don't Wanna Lose You, 314
Don't Want to Be a Fool, 1013
Don't Worry, 364
Don't Worry Baby, 63
Don't Worry Be Happy, 561
Don't Worry Mum, 702
Don't You Feel My Leg, 704
Don't You (Forget About Me), 901
Don't You Just Know It, 915
Don't You Know, 825

Don't You Know I Love You, 195
Don't You Rock Me, Daddy-O, 629
Don't You Think It's Time, 174, 659
Don't You Think This Outlaw Bit's Done Got out of Hand, 497
Don't You Want Me, 461
Donald the Dub, 233
Donald Where's Your Troosers, 566
Dondestan, 1079
Done by the Forces of Nature, 520
Done with Mirrors, 9
Dong-Dong-Di-Ki-Di-Ki-Dong, 387
Donkey Cart, 169
Donkey Serenade, The, 359, 894
Donna, 975, 1010, 1056
Donna e Mobile, La, 367
Donna Riccia, La, 681
Donna Summer, 960
Donna Summer Anthology, The, 961
Donna, the Prima Donna, 266
Donny Hathaway Live, 430
Donovan, 278, 421
Doo Bop, 249
Doo Dah Blues, 855
Doo Wah Diddy Diddy, 404
Doo Wop (That Thing), 361
Doodlin', 93
Doolin-Dalton, 132
Doolittle, 778
Door Peeper, 140
Door to Door, 161
Doors, The, 279
Doors Box Set, The, 280
Doot Doot Dow, 505
Dope Sucks, 122
Doppelganger, 533
Dorando, 78
Doraville, 37
Do-Re-Mi, 22, 281, 844
Dose, 16
Dose of Rock'n'Roll, A, 939
Dots and Loops, 945
Dottie, 243
Double Barrel, 549, 911
Double Cross, 579
Double Crossing Blues, 59, 196, 748, 772
Double Dutch, 624
Double Fantasy, 576, 740
Double Fun, 751
Double – Live, 123
Double Time, 820
Double Trouble, 31, 654, 861, 862
Double Vision, 345
Doug Sahm and Band, 866, 1047
Doug Sahm: San Antonio Rock, 866

Doughnut in Granny's Green-house, The, 105
Douglas James Kershaw, 531
Down and Out Blues, 1066
Down Argentina Way, 231, 828
(Down at) Papa Joe's, 521
Down at Rachel's Place, 635
Down at the Beach Club, 169
Down at the Old Bull and Bush, 345
Down at the Station, 366
Down by the Jetty, 270
Down by the Lazy River, 746
Down by the River, 227, 279, 1087
Down by the Riverside, 231
Down by the Stream, 1078
Down by the Water, 429
Down Down, 941
Down, Down, Down, 629
Down Drinking at the Bar, 1024
Down from Dover, 757
Down Hearted Blues, 914
Down Home, 446
Down Home Blues, 445, 1036
Down Home Girl, 196
Down Home Rag, 316
Down in Mexico, 196
Down in the Boondocks, 764, 925
Down in the Groove, 191, 293
Down in the Tube Station at Midnight, 484
Down in the Valley, 138
Down in the Willow Garden, 984
Down on Bending Knee, 216
Down on the Banks of the Ohio, 99
Down on the Corner, 226
Down on the Farm, 483, 588
Down on the Upside, 924
Down South Summit Meetin', 454
Down That Road, 650
Down the Aisle, 185, 558
Down the Dustpipe, 941
Down the River of Golden Dreams, 894
Down the Road, 305, 691
Down the Road Apiece, 81, 691
Down to Business, 932
Down to Earth, 137, 254
Down to Zero, 27
Down Under, 441, 662
Down Where the Drunkards Roll, 982
Down Where the Wurzburger Flows, 62, 203, 1023
Down with Disease, 773
Down with the King, 859
Down Yonder, 296, 968
Downhill Drag, 36
Downhome New York, 893
Downtown, 11, 189, 430
Downtown Train, 159, 950, 1025

Downward Spiral, The, 723
Dozin' at the Knick, 401
Dr Beat, 314
Dr Buzzard's Original Savannah Band Meets King Pennett, 533
Dr C.C., 164
Dr Dre Presents . . . The After-math, 269
Dr Dre – 2001, 270
Dr Feelgood, 699, 774
Dr Feelgood and the Interns, 270
Dr Heckle and Mr Jive, 662
Dr Hook and the Medicine Show, 271
Dr John Plays Mac Rebennack, 272
Draft Dodger Rag, 348, 733
Draft Morning, 147
Drag, 563
Drag City, 490
Draggin' the Line, 489
Dragnet, 437
Dragonfly, 495, 987
Drake 400 Suite, The, 392
Drama, 455, 1085
Drama of Exile, 1018
Draw the Line, 9
Dre Day, 269
Dread Beat 'n' Blood, 507
Dread in a Babylon, 1009
Dread Locks Dread, 84
Dreadlock Holiday, 976
Dream, 466, 903, 936
Dream a Little Dream of Me, 633
Dream Baby, 741
Dream Come True, 974
Dream for Sale, 929
Dream Girl, 75, 860
Dream Harder, 1036
Dream into Action, 513
Dream Letter, 136
Dream Lover, 244
Dream Lullaby, 1041
Dream Merchant, 363
Dream of Gerontius, 61
Dream of Life, 626, 917
Dream of the Blue Turtles, The, 645, 950
Dream on, 9, 835
Dream Street, 479
Dream Weaver, 492, 591
Dream's a Dream, A, 923
Dreamboat, 199
Dreamboat Annie, 436
Dreamchild, 991
Dreamer, 94, 34, 962
Dreamin', 139, 373, 831
Dreamin' My Dreams, 326
Dreaming, 96, 143, 340, 610
Dreaming 11, 872
Dreaming of Me, 258
Dreaming of the Master Suite, 31

Dreamland, 42, 87, 869
Dreamlover, 157
Dreams, 16, 217, 342
Dreams Fly Away, 982
Dreams in Motion, 816, 1034
Dreams of a Lifetime, 375
Dreams of Long Ago, 805
Dreams of Reason Produce Mon-sters, 491
Dreams of You, 627
Dreamtime, 413, 956, 973
Dreamy Devon, 319
Dreamy Eyes, 348, 985
Dreamy Melody, 561, 562
Dreidel, 625
Dress, 429
Dress You Up, 631
Dressed to Kill, 546
Drift Away, 102, 401, 1064
Drift Away, Loving Arms, 401
Drift Off to Dream, 994
Driftin' Way of Life, 1027
Drifting Blues, 125, 296
Driftwood, 992
Drinkin' from the Bottle, Singing from the Heart, 896
Drinkin' My Baby Goodbye, 242
Drinkin' Wine, 1064
Drinkin' Wine Spo-Dee-O-Dee, 283, 313, 619, 1063
Drinking Again, 218
Drinking in My Sunday Dress, 622
Drinking Song, The, 852
Drip Drop, 266
Drip Fed Fred, 630
Driva Man, 837
Drive, 161
Drive by Shooting, 850
Drive on, 700
Drive Thru Booty, 330
Driven by You, 808
Drivin', 543
Drivin' Nails in My Coffin, 984
Drivin' Wheel, 343
Driving, 321
Driving Sideways, 541
Driving to Damascus, 84
Driving Wheel, 402
Drop, 887
Drop Down and Get Me, 771, 889
Drop Down Mama, 315
Drop the Pilot, 27
Drown in My Own Tears, 386
Drowned Dog Black Night, 982
Drowners, The, 959
Drowning in a Sea of Love, 899
Drugs Don't Work, The, 1021
Drum Battle, 830
Drum Is a Woman, A, 307
Drum Party, 712
Drum Thing, The, 511

Drummin' Man, 556
Drummin' up a Storm, 712
Drums and Wires, 1081
Drums Are My Beat, 712
Drums Unlimited, 837
Drunken Driver, The, 735
Drunken Hearted Man, 509
Dry, 429
Dry Acid, 767
Dry Votin' – Wet Drinkin' – Better Than Thous, Hypocritical Blues, 669
D.T.K., 717
Duane A Go Go, 300
Duane Allman: An Anthology, 15
Duane Eddy, 300
Duane Goes Dylan, 300
Duane's Tune, 16
Dub Be Good to Me, 330
Dub Dub, 740
Dub from the Roots, 537
Dublin, 788
Dubnobasswithmyheadman, 1008
Duchess, 956
Duck Down, 106
Duck Rock, 455, 624, 900
Dude, The, 514
Dude (Looks Like a Lady), 9
Dueces Wild, 187
Duel in the Sun, 985
Duelling Banjos, 244
Duets, 95, 118, 426, 469, 549, 563, 904, 905, 1061
Duets II, 558, 854, 905
Duke, 378
Duke Elegant, 272
Duke Ellington Classics, 609
Duke Ellington meets Coleman Hawkins, 431
Duke Ellington Presents the Dollar Brand Trio, 466
Duke of Earl, 170, 171, 245
Duke's Choice, 676
Dukes of Hazzard, The, 497
Dum Dum, 259, 571
Dumb, 371
Dumb Blonde, 757
Dummy, 785
Dungaree Doll, 336
Duo, 118
Duotones, 365
Duppy Conqueror, 643, 767
Duran Duran (The Wedding Album), 289
Durham Town (The Leavin'), 1053
Dusk, 918
Dust, 877, 878
Dust Bowl Ballads, 407
Dust Bowl Refugees, 407
Dust in the Wind, 546
Dust My Blues, 486

Dust My Broom, 154, 486
Dusty in Memphis, 933, 1047
Dusty Old Dust, 407, 408
Dusty – The Legend of Dusty Springfield, 933
Duty Now for the Future, 260
dwightyoakamacoustic.net, 1086
D. W. Washburn, 196
D'yer Maker, 569
Dylan, 293
Dylan & the Dead, 293, 401
Dynaflow Blues, 509
Dynamic Fashioned Way, 459
Dynamite, 478, 571
Dynasty, 546
D'You Know What I Mean, 731

$E = MC^2$, 693
'E Dunno Where 'E Are, 305
E Pluribus Funk, 396
Each and Every One, 320
Each Night at Nine, 984
Eadie Was a Lady, 664, 1052
Eagle, The, 497
Eagle When She Flies, 758
Eagles, The, 295
Eagles Live, 295
Eargasm, 971
Earl Hines at Home, 446
Early Autumn, 381
Early Bird Catches the Worm, The, 691
Early Days, 570
Early in the Morning, 244, 385, 451, 1066
Early Morning Rain, 417, 465, 584
Early Productions, 1958–1961, 930
Early Tapes, The, 579
Early Tracks, 297
Early Years, The, 713
Early Years Vol. 1, The, 1024
Early Years Vol. 2, The, 1024
Earth, 138, 495
Earth, a Small Man, His Dog and a Chicken, The, 827
Earth & Sun & Moon, 668
Earth and Sky, 229
Earth Angel, 75, 76, 227, 780
Earth Dies Screaming, The, 1005
Earth Jones, 511
Earth Moving, 642, 738
Earth Song, 482
Earth Song, Ocean Song, 454
Earth Songs, 258
Earth Wants You, The, 15
Earthbound, 536
Earthling, 112
Earthquake Weather, 191
Earthspan, 471
Earthwords and Music, 429
East, 56
East Coasting, 318, 676

East Greets East, 889
East Meets West, 888
East of Midnight, 585
East of the River Nile, 750
East of the Sun, 383
East of the Sun, West of the Moon, 11
East River Drive, 190
East Side Story, 219, 882
East St Louis Toodle-oo, 943
Easter, 494, 917
Easter Island, 555
Easter Parade, 597
Eastern Sounds, 566
East-West, 144
Eastwood Rides Again, 767
Easy, 208, 832
Easy Baby, 632
Easy Come, Easy Go, 955
Easy Going Me, 325
Easy Lover, 205, 298
Easy Money, 515, 588
Easy to Be Hard, 984
Eat a Peach, 283
Eat It, 481, 615
Eat Starch, Mom?, 494
Eat the Rich, 699
Eat to the Beat, 96, 183, 404
Eat Your Heart Out Sandy Nelson, 712
Eaten Alive, 855
Eazy Duz It, 728
Ebb Tide, 169, 417, 834, 855, 929
Ebeneezer Goode, 888
Ebony and Ivory, 611, 1077
Ebony Eyes, 320, 599
Ebony Rhapsody, 307
Ebony Woman, 759
E-Bow the Letter, 827
E.C. Was Here, 187
Echo, 771
Echo Beach, 563, 991
Echo Bridge, 1093
Echo Dek, 797
Echoes in the Night, 801
Echoes of a Friend, 1002
Echoes of an Era, 29, 532
Echoes of Harlem, 786
Echoes of the Duke, 609
Eclectic, 84
Ecstasy, 707, 824
Eddie Cochran: The Boxed Set, 198
Eddie Condon's World of Jazz, 210
Eddie Fisher at the Winter Garden, 336
Eddie My Love, 85, 107, 183
Eddie's Love, 975
Eddie's Twister, 562
Eddy Grant, 398
Edelweiss, 22, 844
Eden, 320
Edgar Winter Album, The, 1071

Edge of Forever, 609
Edge of Heaven, 1001
Edge of Seventeen, 342
Edge of the Century, 959
Education, 140
Edutainment, 106
Efil4Zaggin, 728
Ege Bamyasi, 153
Eggplant That Ate Chicago, The, 155, 403
Ego, 1066
Ego Has Landed, The, 1065
Ego Trip, 98
Egyptian Reggae, 832
Eh Cumpari, 564
8 Frames a Second, 627
801 Live, 857
845 Stomp, 108
Eight Men, Four Women, 1079
Eight Miles High, 34, 147, *387*, 755
8.05, 680
8.30, 1039
Eighteen, 214
Eighteen Inches of Rain, 465
18 'Til I Die, 7
18 Tracks, 935
Eighteen Wheels and a Dozen Roses, 652
Eighteen with a Bullet, 1020
1812 Overture, 702
18 Yellow Roses, 244
18th Letter, The, 43
Eighth Day, 288
Eighth of January, 285
80s Ladies, 746
80/81, 666
81, The, 369
86 Years of Eubie Blake, The, 93
Einstein a Go-Go, 926
Einstein on Fire, 434
Eisenhower Blues, 576
Either/Or, 915
Ekaya, 466
Ekstasis, 565
Elastic Rock, 726
Elastica, 304
Elder, The, 546
Eldorado, 304
Eleanor Rigby, 67, 503, 1014
Elected, 214
Electra Blues, 616
Electric, 858
Electric Africa, 263
Electric Avenue, 398
Electric Café, 554
Electric Church, 669
Electric Connection, 287
Electric Fire, 808
Electric Honey, 605
Electric Ladyland, 440, 551
Electric Landlady, 614

Electric Light Orchestra, 304
Electric Mud, 1037
Electric Music for the Mind and Body, 616
Electric Spanking of War Babies, 954
Electric Warrior, 101
Electric Youth, 381
Electricity, 72, 742, 960
Electrolite, 827
Electronic Meditation, 968
Electronic Sonata for Souls Loved by Nature, 863
Electronic Sounds, 427
Electro-Shock Blues, 303
Elegant Slumming, 610
Elegantly Wasted, 473
Elégie, 386
Elemental, 972
Elements, The, 574
Elenore, 999
Elephant Mountain, 1090
Elephant Stone, 952
Elephant's Memory, 242
Eleven Cent Cotton Forty Cent Meat, 240, 670
1100 Bel Air Place, 469
11 o'Clock Tick Tock, 1004
11 Tracks of Whack, 943
11th Hour Melody, 444
Elf, The, 947
Eli and the 13th Confession, 728
Eli's Coming, 728, 983
Eliminator, 1094
Elis and Tom, 501
Elisabeth Welch Sings the Irving Berlin Songbook, 1043
Elite Hotel, 425
Elizabeth on the Bathroom Floor, 303
Elizabethan Serenade, 392
Ella B, The, 18
Ella Speed, 587
Ellington Is Forever, 141
Elliott Smith, 915
Elmer Bernstein by Elmer Bernstein, 80
ELO II, 304
Eloise, 240
Elton John, 503
Elusive Butterfly, 863
Elvis Lives on the Moon, 586
Em'Ma/Africa, 989
Emancipation, 798
Emancipation of Hugh Masekela, The, 649
Embarrassment, 630
Embraceable You, 34, 753
Emergence, 880
Emergency, 910, 1066
Emergency on Planet Earth, 489
Emerson Lake and Powell, 310

EMI, 884
Emily, 503
Eminence Front, 579
Emmerdale, 156
Emociones, 469
Emotional Rescue, 849
Emotional Violence, 152
Emotionally Yours, 737, 1026
Emotions, *157*, 571, 792
Emperor Tomato Ketchup, 945
Emperors of Soul, 975
Empire, 809
Empire Burlesque, 293, 771, 911
Empires and Dance, 901
Emptiona, Zodiac Suite, 752
Empty Arms, 463
Empty Glass, 1054
Empty Rooms, 654
Empty Sky, 503
Enchanted, 17
Enchanted Forest, The, 369
Enchanted Island, 348
Enchanted Sea, 521
Encomium, 570
Encore, *19*, *38*, 690
Encouraging Words, 790
End, The, *151*, 279, *1018*
End Is Not in Sight, The, 18, 1070
End of an Ear, 1079
End of My Old Cigar, The, 170, 1046
End of Our Road, The, 548
End of Silence, The, 851
End of the Century, 815, 930
End of the Innocence, 296
End of the Millennium Psychosis Blues, 890
End of the Rainbow, The, 982
End of the Road, 44, 114
End of the World, The, 36, 249
Endless, 438
Endless Boogie, 452
Endless Flight, 872
Endless Love, 208, 832, 855, 1013
Endless Night, 754
Endless Sleep, 1056
Endless Summer, 62, 63
Energy, 781
Energy of Love, 472
Engine, 19
England My England, 793
England Swings, 673
England's Glory, 290
English Country Garden, 395, 918
English Settlement, 1081
Englishman in New York, 951
Enigma, 800
Enjoy the Silence, 258
Enjoy Yourself, 478, 677
Enlightenment, 695
Ennismore, 1093
Ennui, 824

Enola Gay, 742
Enrique, 469
En-Tact, 887
Enter Sandman, 665
Entering the Dragon, 459
Entertainer, The, 418, 506, 517, 834
Entre la Jeunesse et la Sagesse, 619
Entreat, 238
Envoy, The, 1092
Epic, 324
Epic Ride of John H. Glenn, The, 863
Epic Years, The, 947
Epiphany, 533
Epistrophy, 190, 683
Eponymous, 826
Equal Rights, 988
Equally Cursed and Blessed, 168
Equator, 1009
Equinox, 959
Equinoxe, 491
Erase/Rewind, 156
Erasure, 312
Eric B. Is President, 43
Eric Clapton, 186
Ernie (The Fastest Milkman in the West), 430
Erotica, 631
Esa Ma Miliki, 731
Escalator, 699
Escalator Over the Hill, 95, 133
Escapade, 479
Escape, 519
Escape Artist, 754
Escape from Broadway, 272
Escenas, 92, 854
Escenas de Amor, 332
Escucha Me, 384
E.S.P., 71, 420
Especially for You, 278, 677, 951
Espresso Logic, 819
Essar, 841
Essence to Essence, 278
Essential, 1084
Essential Dolly Parton, The, 758
Essential Etta James, The, 487
Essential George Jones, The, 512
Essential Jack Elliott, The, 308
Essential King Crimson, Frame by Frame, The, 536
Essential Odetta, The, 735
Essential Ray Price, The, 794
Essential Recordings, 166
Essential Ronnie Milsap, 675
Essential Ten Years After, The, 977
Essential Tom T. Hall, The, 416
Essential, Vols 1 and 2, 766
Essential Willie Nelson, The, 713
Essential Yello, 1084
Essex, 704
Este Mundo, 384

Et Maintenant, 68
Eternal Flame, 54, 500
Eton Rifles, 484
Eugene Record, The, 180
Euphoria, 437
Euphoria Morning, 924
Euroman Cometh, 956
Europe '72, 400
European Concert, 681
European Girl, 956
European Queen, 732
Eurythmics Live 1983–1989, 317
Evangeline, 199
Eve, 756
Eve of Destruction, 490, 621, 792, 911, 1040
Eve's Volcano (Covered in Sin), 215
Even a Grey Day, 761
Even and Especially When, 877
Even Better Than the Real Thing, 730
Even Cowgirls Get the Blues, 22, 563
Even in the Quietest Moments, 962
Even the Bad Times Are Good, 707, 784
Evening at Charlie's, An, 987
Evening of Acoustic Music, An, 966
Evening Star, 360
Evening with Don Williams, An, 1059
Evening with Harry Belafonte and Miriam Makeba, An, 633
Evening with the Allman Brothers, An, 16
Evening with Wild Man Fischer, An, 1091
Ever Fallen in Love, 145, 335
Ever Popular Tortured Artist Effect, The, 860
Ever Since the World Ended, 15
Ever the Winds, 185
Everclear, 19
Evergreen, 299, 957, 1064
Everlasting First, The, 600
Everlovin', 711
Everly Brothers, The, 302, 320
Every Beat of My Heart, 51, 548, 748
Every Body Needs Somebody to Love, 912
Every Breath You Take, 782, 805, 951
Every Day I Have the Blues, 362
Every Day I Have to Cry, 1078
Every Day I Have to Cry Some, 13
Every Day of My Life, *101, 1023*
Every Good Boy Deserves Favour, 689
Every Grain of Sand, 293

Every Heaven, 105
Every Hour, 588
Every Kinda People, 751
Every Little Bit Hurts, 348, 1072
Every Little Movement, 592
Every Little Movement Has a Meaning of Its Own, 422
Every Little Step, 125
Every Little Thing She Does Is Magic, 782
Every Man Has a Woman, 740
Every Night, 171
Every Night About This Time, 275
Every One's a Winner, 457
Every Picture Tells a Story, 949
Every Rose Has its Thorn, 781
Every Time Two Fools Collide, 847
Every Time You Go Away, 413, 1089
Every Time You Touch Me, 830
Every Turn of the World, 231
Every You, Every Me, 779
Everybody, 631, 846
Everybody Dance, 845
Everybody Do the Click, 332
Everybody Everybody, 87
Everybody Has the Blues, 77
Everybody Here Wants You, 135
Everybody Hurts, 827
Everybody in the Place, 801
Everybody Knows This Is Nowhere, 1087
Everybody Knows, 188, 823
Everybody Likes to Cha Cha, 213
Everybody Loves a Nut, 192
Everybody Loves a Rain Song, 683
Everybody Loves a Winner, 74, 106
Everybody Loves Me but You, 571
Everybody Loves My Baby, 28
Everybody Loves Somebody, 646
Everybody Must Get Stoned, 277
Everybody Needs Love, 548
Everybody Needs Somebody to Love, 80, 138, 139
Everybody Rag with Me, 522
Everybody (Rap), 49
Everybody Rejoice, 1013
Everybody Stand Up and Clap Your Hands, 338
Everybody Up, 736
Everybody Wants to Rule the World, 972
Everybody Wants to Run the World, 972
Everybody's Anything, 871
Everybody's Been Burned, 147
Everybody's Cryin' Mercy, 15
Everybody's Doin' It, 79

Everybody's in Showbiz, Everybody's a Star, 543
Everybody's Rockin', 1088
Everybody's Somebody's Fool, 892
Everybody's Sweetheart, 383
Everybody's Talkin', 710, *710*, 722
Everybody's Trying to Be My Baby, 766
Everyday, 205, 450
Everyday I Have the Blues, 969
Everyday I Write the Book, 219
Everyday Is a Winding Road, 232
Everyday People, 30, 355, 500, 954
Everyday with You Girl, 37
Everydays, 1084
Everyone Can Rock and Roll, 413
Everyone Is Everybody Else, 55
Everyone's Gone to the Moon, 541
Everything, 54
Everything Changes, 1064
Everything Counts, 258
Everything Falls Apart, 701
Everything from Jesus to Jack Daniels, 416
Everything I Do Gonna Be Funky, 281, 990
(Everything I Do) I Do It for You, 6, 7, 192
Everything I Have Is Yours, 300
Everything I Love, 479
Everything I Own, 108, 119, 236
Everything in its Right Place, 811
Everything Is Beautiful, 946
Everything Is Everything, 361, *430*
Everything Is Peaches Down in Georgia, 10
Everything Is Playing, 602
Everything Is Ragtime Now, 930
Everything Louder Than Everything Else, 699
Everything Must Change, 1089
Everything Must Go, 636
Everything that Touches You, 34
Everything Will Flow, 960
Everything Your Heart Desires, 413
Everything Zen, 142
Everything's Alright Forever, 105
Everything's Coming up Roses, 919, 959
Everything's Coming Up Rosie, 195
Everything's the Same (Ain't Nothing Changed), 964
Everything's Tuesday, 169
Everytime I Eat Vegetables I Think of You, 815
Everywhere, 342
Evil Blues, 862
Evil Empire, 813
Evil Gal Blues, 331, 1034
Evil Hoodoo, 880

Evil Is Going on, 459
Evil that Men Do, 474, 808
Evil Ways, 519, 651
Evil Woman, 304
E.V.O.L., 920
Evolution, 114, 450, 484, 519, 966
Ev'ry Time We Say Goodbye, 337, 785, 902
Ev'rything I Love, 785
Ev'rywhere, 319, 1051
Ewa Woman Ojumi Ri, 731
Ewok Celebration, 1061
Exactly Like You, 334, 621, 822
Excalibur, 226
Except the New Girl, 475
Excerpt from a Teenage Opera, 1084
Excerpts from Swine Lake, 653
Excitable Boy, 1092
Exclusivamente Latino, 211
Excursion on the Version, 330
Excuse Me (I Think I've Got a Heartache), 458, 748
Exercises, 709
Ex-Girlfriend, 725
Exhale (Shoop Shoop), 458
Exile, 728
Exile in Guyville, 771
Exile on Main Street, 771, 849, 895
Exiles, 343
Exit, 968
Exit O, 297
Exit Planet Dust, 175, 744
Exitos de, Los, 332
Exodus, 639, 643, 908, 1065
Exodus and Other Great Themes, 639
Exorcizing the Evil Spirits from the Pentagon, 361
Exotic Birds and Fruit, 801
Expansions, 492, 945
Expecting to Fly, 725
Experience, 375, 801
Experience the Divine: Greatest Hits, 667
Experimental Jet Set, Trash and No Star, 921
Experimental Remixes EP, 510
Experiments with Mice, 242
Expletive Deleted, 324
Explosive Little Richard, The, 589
Exposed, 32, 699, 738
Exposures, 360
Express Yourself, 631
Expression, 206
Expressway to Your Heart, 369
Expressway to Your Skull, 669
Exquisite Nana M, The, 702
Extended Play, 333
Extensions, 636
Extensions of a Man, 430
Exterminator, 797

External Idol, The, 88
Extra Classic, 474
Extra Texture (Read All About It), 427
Extra Width, 510
Extraordinary Girl, 736
Extrapolation, 624
Extras, 484
Extreme II Pornograffitti, 321
Extremist, The, 872
Extremities, Dirt and Repressed Emotions, 534
Extricate, 327
Eye, 447
Eye in the Sky, 756
Eye Know, 251
Eye of a Storm, 962
Eye of the Zombie, 226
Eye to Eye, 532, 875
Eyes Don't Lie, 747
Eyes of a New York Woman, The, 980
Eyes of a Stranger, 44
Eyes without a Face, 468
Eyesight to the Blind, 1066
Ezz-Thetic, 863
Ezz-Thetics, 274, 863

Fa Fa Fa Fa Fa (Sad Song), 821
Fables of the Reconstruction, 113, 826
Fabulous, 799
Face Dances, 1054
Face in the Crowd, 864
Face It, 387
Face of the Nation, The, 660
Face the Heat, 875
Face the Music, 304, 715
Face to Face, 615, 905
Face Value, 204
Facelift, 14
Faces, 1001
Faces I've Been, The, 229
Faces of Fame, The, 327
Facing You, 492
Facts and Fictions, 33
Fade Away, 934
Fade to Black, 267
Fade to Grey, 1007
Faded Love, 259, 794
Fading Like a Flower, 856
Fahrenheit, 989
Fair and Tender Ladies, 1013
Fair Oak Fusions, 242
Fair Thee Well to Harlem, 662
Fairground, 902
Fairplay, 923
Fairport Live, 324
Fairweather Johnson, 453
Fairy Tale, 277
Fairy Tales, 926
Fairytale, 781

Fairytale of New York, 614, 690, 780
Faith, *238*, 666, *666*
Faith & Courage, 734
Faithful, 860
Faithful Hussar, 437
Faithfull, 326
Faithfull Forever, 326
Faithfully, 519
Faithless, 326
Faithless Love, 153
Faithless Lover, 604
Fake Friends, 500
Fake Plastic Trees, 811
Fakin' It, 897
Falcon and the Snowman, The, 666
Falklands Suite, 151
Fall at Your feet, 233
Fall Down, 432
Fall in Love with You, 831
Fall on You, 680
Fall out, 782
Fallen Angel, 1009
Fallen Star, The, 179
Fallin' out of Love, 618
Falling Apart at the Seams, 644
Falling for You for Years, 1000
Falling in and out of Love, 806
Falling in Love, 829
Falling in Love Again, 264
Falling in Love with Jazz, 851
Falling in Love with Love, 428
Falling Into You, 266
Falling Rain Blues, 507
Falling Up, 919
False Accusations, 224
False Knight on the Road, The, 183
False Love, 926
False Start, 600
Fame, 111, *512*, 576
Fame and Fortune, 46
Fame and Wealth, 1024
Fame at Last, 327
Familiar Songs, 816
Familiar to Millions, 731
Family Affair, *418*, 815, 954
Family Album, 199
Family Bible, 207, 712
Family Entertainment, 328
Family Groove, 714
Family Man, 738, *850*
Family Reunion, 370
Family Spirit, 1076
Family Style, 1016
Family That Plays Together, The, 932
Family Tradition, 1060
Family Values, 552, *552*
Famine, 734
Famous Blue Raincoat, 1031

Famous in the Last Century, 941
. . . *famous last words . . .* , 962
Fancy, 378
Fancy Our Meeting, 135
Fandango, 1094
Fanfare for Louis, 30
Fanfare for the Common Man, 310
Fanfare for the Warriors, 31
Fanmail, 986
Fannie Mae, 840
Fanny Hill, 807
Fans, 624
Fantasma, 216
Fantastic Chi-Lites, The, 180
Fantastic Day, 443
Fantastic Expedition of Dillard and Clark, Through the Morn-ing Through the Night, The, 147
Fantastic Star, 17
Fantasy, 87, 157, *540*, 976
Far Away Christmas Blues, 748
Far Beyond the Castle Walls, 251
Far East Suite, 307
Far from Home, 1073
Faraway Part of Town, The, 793
Fare You Well Old Joe Clark, 162
Farewell Cream, 225
Farewell Farewell, 324
Farewell My Own, 382
Farewell to Kings, A, 861
Farewell to Storyville, 211
Farm Relief Song, 240
Farmer John, 276
Farmhouse, 773
Farover, 140
Farther Along, 148
Farther Down the Line, 955
Fascinating Rhythm, 379
Fascination, 461, 1013
Fast Car, 172
Fast Women and Slow Horses, 270
Faster Than the Speed of Night, 1002
Fastest Gun Around, The, 837
Fastlove, 667
Fat, 615
Fat Angel, 494
Fat Bottomed Girls, 808
Fat Man, The, 58, 275, 692
Fat of the Land, The, 801
Fate of Nations, 570
Fate Stay with Me, 692
Father and Son, 114, *737*
Father Father, 939
Father Figure, 666
Father of Night, 293
Father's Day, 804
Father's Eyes, 397
Fathers and Sons, 144, 645
Fats and Me, 507
Fatty, Fatty, 864

Fault, The, 652
Faust, 720, 854
Favourite Shirts (Boy Meets Girl), 443
FBI, 885
F. D. R. Blues, 288
FDR in Trinidad, 755
Fear, 150
Fear and Whiskey, 792
Fear of a Black Planet, *84*, 803, 803
Fear of Music, 360, 967
Fear of the Dark, 474
Fearless, 328
Feather Merchant's Ball, 210
Feats Don't Fail Me Now, 588
Feb 27, '71, 415
Feedback, 932
Feel Free, 923
Feel Like Change, 86
Feel Like Going Home, 830, *830*
Feel Like I'm Fixin' to Die Rag, 616, 617
Feel Like Making Love, 46, *338*, 616
Feel My Power, 418
Feel So Fine, 791
Feel So Good, 895
Feel So Right, 12
Feel the Fire, 134
Feel the Noize – Greatest Hits, 910
Feel the Warm, 559
Feel What You Feel, 138
Feelin' Alright, 1072
Feelin' Bitchy, 482
Feelin' Good, 754
Feelin' Good at the Cadillac Club, 759
Feelin' Groovy, 863
Feeling Blue, 1008
Feeling Good, 719
Feeling Gravity's Pull, 826
Feeling Is Gone, The, 94
Feeling the Blues, 1028
Feeling the Space, 740
Feelings, 148, 967
Feels Good to Feel Good, 310
Feels Like the First Time, 345
Feenin, 138
Feet Up (Pat Him on the Po-Po), 678
Fegmania, 447
Feliciano!, 332
Feline, 956
Felix Kept on Walking, 545
Felix Pappalardi and Creation, 702
Feliz Encuentra, 235
Female Trouble, 559
Femme de Mon Pote, Le, 150
Femme Fatale, 1018
Fender Stratocaster, 833

Ferguslie Park, 812
Fernando, 1, 211
Ferry Cross the Mersey, 184, 354
Festival of Britain, The, 1078
Fever, 91, 504, 536, 572, 615, 769, 904
Fever in Fever Out, 605
Fiberglass Jungle, 999
Fictitious Sports, 777
Fiddle Fire: 25 Years of the Charlie Daniels Band, 242
Fiddler on the Rock, 276
Fidgety Feet, 73
Fields of Fire, 83, 973
Fields of Gold, 951
Fifo, 909
15 Big Ones, 63
Fifteen Years Ago, 1000
Fifth, 919
5th Album, 204
Fifth Dimension, 147
50 Original Tracks, 375
Fifty Ways to Leave Your Lover, 899
54–46, 35, 987
59th Street Bridge Song, 357, 424, 897
Fight for Ourselves, 926
Fight for Your Mind, 423
Fight (No Matter How Long), 71
Fight the Power, 476, 803
Fighting, 979
Fighting for Strangers, 942
Fighting Side of Me, The, 411
Figure 8, 915
File Under Easy Listening, 701
File under Rock, 398
Filet of Soul, 490
Filipino Baby, 215
Fill Her Up, 951
Filles de Kilimanjaro, 420
Film Encores, 639, 640
Film Festival, 169
Film Music 1966–87, 694
Film Noir, 899
Filthy Lucre, 885
Fin de Siècle, 268
Final Battle, The, 254
Final Countdown, The, 316, 316
Final Cut, The, 777
Final Damnation, 240
Final Exam, 1024
Finally Got Myself Together (I'm a Changed Man), 470
Finally in Light, 867
Finbegin, 498
Find a Way, 397
Find Out, 190
Fine and Mellow, 448, 980
Fine Art of Surfacing, 376
Fine Brown Frame, 505, 605
Fine Cuts, 591

Fine Romance, A, 34, 530
Fine Wine, 21
Finer Things, The, 1073
Finest, The, 335
Finger, 799
Finger of Suspicion, 437
Finger Pickin', 688
Finger Poppin' Time, 51
Fingernails, 309
Fingertips Part II, 1076
Fings Ain't What They Used to Be, 146
Finkel's Cafe, 552
Finn Brothers, The, 233
Fins, 137
Fire, 124, 472, 736, 781, 934, 1004
Fire and Desire, 488
Fire & Gasoline, 885
Fire and Ice, 76
Fire and Rain, 492, 971
Fire and Romance, 393
Fire and Water, 357
Fire Brigade, 703
Fire Dances, 534
Fire, Fleet and Candle Light, 867
Fire Inside, The, 882
Fire Island, 1021
Fire It Up, 488
Fire Lake, 882
Fire Music, 892
Fire of Unknown Origin, 98
Fire on Babylon, 734
Fire on the Bayou, 714
Fire on the Mountain, 641
Fire on the Strings, 641, 641
Fireball, 253
Fireball Mail, 6
Fireball Zone, 161
Firebird and Petrouchka, The, 218
Firecracker, 595
Firefly, 77, 1009
Fireman, The, 612
Fireproof, 890
Fires of Eden, 204
Firestarter, 779, 801
Firesticks, 35
Fireworks, 28, 856
Firin' Up, 383
First Album, 361, 1094
First and Last, 609
First Band on the Moon, 156
First Born, 619
First Circle, 666
First City, 607
First Class Mary Brown, 596
First Cut Is the Deepest, The, 309, 945, 950
First Date, First Kiss, First Love, 489
First Day, The, 360, 491, 965
First Day Back at School, 759
First Girl I Ever Loved, 470

First I Look at the Purse, 211
First Impressions, 470
First Kiss, 770
First Light, 982
First Minute of a New Day, The, 877
First Person, 591
First Quarrel, 759
First Question Award, 216
First Step, 912
First Take, 338
First Take Chapter Two, 338
First Time, The, 325, 891
First Time Ever I Saw Your Face, The, 338, 613, 614, 702
First Time I Met the Blues, 408
First Time I Saw You, The, 894
First Water, 358
First We Take Manhattan, 1031
Firstborn Is Dead, The, 168
Fish Ain't Bitin', 449
Fish and Chips, 552
Fish Cheer, 616
Fisherman's Blues, 1035
Fistful of Alice, A, 215
Fistful of Metal, 25
Fit as a Fiddle, 359
Fit to Be Tied, 500
5, 554
Five and Dime, 5
Five Bridges Suite, 309
Five by Five, 779
5 D, 147
$5.98 EP – Garage Days Revisited, The, 665
Five Fathoms, 321
Five Feet High and Rising, 165
Five Foot Two, Eyes of Blue, 260
5 4 3 2 1, 634
Five Guys Named Moe, 518
500 Miles Away from Home, 55
Five Leaves Left, 283
Five Live Yardbirds, 186, 1083
Five Miles Out, 738
Five Minutes, 956
Five Minutes More, 150
Five o'Clock Whistle, 822
Five o'Clock World, 215
5.01 Blues, 411
Five Seasons, The, 324
5150, 345, 1012
5000 Spirits or the Layers of the Onion, The, 470
Five to One, 279
5-10-15 Hours, 131
Fix It Man, 976
Fixed, 723
Fiyo on the Bayou, 714
Fizz Water, 92
Flaco's First, 500
Flag, 1084
Flag Party, 398

Flame, 265, 558, 737
Flaming Pie, 305, 612, 647
Flamingo, 108
Flash, 70, 808, 846
Flash Harry, 722
Flash Light, 973
Flash to the Beat, 397
Flashback, 211
Flashdance . . . What a Feeling, 693
Flashpoint, 850
Flat Baroque and Berserk, 424
Flat Earth, The, 273
Flat Foot Floogie, 366
Flat Out, 98
Flaunt It, 467, 693
Flaunt the Imperfection, 943
Flavours, 406
Flea Circus, 521
Fleetwood Mac, 342
Flesh and Blood, 781, 782, 857
Flesh of My Skin, 459
Fleur Bleu, 993
Fleures Musicales du Camerooun, 263
Flick of the Switch, 4
Flight NAACP 105, 672
Flight of Icarus, 474
Flight of the Bumble Bee, 487
Flint Hill Special, 340
Flip Flop, 606
Flip, Flop and Fly, 953, 998
Flip Your Wig, 701
Flirtation Waltz, 37
Flirtin' with Disaster, 682
F.L.M. (Fun Love Money), 951
Flo and Eddie, 999
Flogging a Dead Horse, 884
Floral Dance, The, 250
Flower, 887
Flower Children, 361
Flower Punk, 1091
Flower that Shattered the Stone, The, 258
Flowers, 310
Flowers in the Dirt, 219, 612
Flowers in the Rain, 703
Flowers of Evil, 701
Flowers of Romance, 884
Floy Joy, 963
Floyd Tillman and Friends, 985
Flux and Mutability, 965
Fly, 740
Fly, The, 175, 1004
Fly Away, 554
Fly by Night, 861
Fly Dude, 620
Fly Like an Eagle, 673, 673
Fly Me to the Moon, 50, 794, 1076
Fly on the Wall, 4
Fly Robin Fly, 104
Fly to the Rainbow, 875

Flyer, 405
Flying, 251, 1006
Flying Colours, 251
Flying Cowboys, 515, 943
Flying Down to Rio, 1086
Flying Home, 184, 336, 419, 483
Flying in a Blue Dream, 872
Flying Saucers Rock'n'Roll, 192
FM: Fantasma Remixes, 216
FM (No Static at All), 943
Focus, 381
Fog on the Tyne, 586, 586
Foggy Day, A, 34
Foggy, Foggy Dew, 477
Foggy Mountain Breakdown, 340
Foggy River, 343
Foghat, 343
Fold Your Hands Child, You Walk Like a Peasant, 75
Folie, La, 956
Folk Ballads, 432
Folk Blues and All Points in Between, 395
Folk Blues and Beyond, 395
Folk Blues of John Lee Hooker, The, 452
Folk City, 490
Folk Country, 496
Folk Lore of John Lee Hooker, The, 452
Folk Matinée, 585
Folk 'n' Roll, 490
Folk Roots, New Routes, 395
Folk Songs, 410
Folk Songs from Just About Everywhere, 85
Folk Songs of Four Continents, 768
Folk Songs of the Hills, 992
Folkjokeopus, 423
Folks Who Live on the Hill, The, 530, 572, 843
Folkways: A Vision Shared, 408, 589
Folle Complainte, La, 993
Follow My Mind, 193
Follow the Boys, 353
Follow the Flag, 720
Follow the Leader, 43, 552
Follow the Yellow Brick Road, 422
Follow You Follow Me, 378
Followers of Saint Julian, 215
Fontessa, 681
Food for Thought, 1005
Food, Glorious Food, 57
Fool, 436, 565, 810
Fool Am I, A, 707
Fool at the Wheel, 588
Fool Britannia, 393
Fool Circle, 709
Fool, Fool, Fool, 195
Fool Hearted Memory, 955

Fool if You Think It's Over, 123, 819
Fool in Love, A, 997
Fool No. 1, 571
Fooled Around and Fell in Love, 144, 495
Fooling Around, 458, 748
Foolish Beat, 381
Foolish Fool, 1033
Foolish Little Girl, 894
Foolish Pride, 994
Foolishments, 691
Foolkiller, 37
Fools Gold, 952
Fools Rush in, 78, 435, 663, 671, 711
Foot Tapper, 885
Football Rock'n'Roll, 413
Footloose, 596
Footsteps, 567, 638
Footstompin' Music, 396
Footstomping – Part 1, 82
Fopp, 736, 924
For a Friend, 208
For All Seasons, 399
For All the Cows, 723
For All the Seasons of Your Mind, 465
4 All the Sistas Around Da World, 308
For All We Know, 119, 160
For Alto, 118
For America, 132
For Dancers Only, 605
For Ellington, 681
For Emily, Wherever I May Find Her, 897
For Ever, 353
For Every Man There's a Woman, 839
For Free, 679
(For) God, Country and My Baby, 139
(For God's Sake) Give More Power to the People, 180
For Lovin' Me, 465, 584, 768
For Mama, 41
For Men Only, 482
For My Broken Heart, 618
For My Lover, 172
For No One, 67
For No Reason at All in C, 562
For Once in My Life, 1077
For Our Children, 3
For Pence and Spicey Ale, 164
For Pete's Sake, 284
For Rent, 489
For Segregationists Only, 672
For Sentimental Reasons, 833, 854
For Teenagers Only, 217
For the Beauty of Wynona, 563
For the Boys, 667

For the Cool in You, 44
For the Feet, 667
For the Good Times, 794
For the Heart, 667
For the Last Time, 411, 1068
For the Love of Harry, 722, 940
For the Love of Money, 736
For the Memories Vols 1&2, 625
For the Noo, 250
For the Record, 199
For the Record: 41 Number One
   Hits, 12
For the Roses, 679
For Those Who Are About to
   Rock, 4
For Tinkerbell, 168
For Tomorrow, 100
For Trio, 118
For Two Pianos, 118
4U2NJOY, 1078
For What It's Worth, 136, 537, 938
For Whom the Bell Tolls, 71
For You, 711, 797
For You, for Me, for Evermore,
   435
For Your Babies, 902
For Your Blue Eyes Only, 926
For Your Delight, 913
For Your Love, 37, 975, 1083
For Your Pleasure, 310, 857
For Your Precious Love, 143, 470
Forbidden, 89
Forbidden Colours, 868, 965
Forbidden House, 491
Forbidden Melody, 422
Force, The, 550
Force behind the Power, The, 856
Force It, 1006
Force Majeure, 968
Forces of Victory, 507
Fore, 581
Foreign Affair, 999
Foreign Affairs, 1024
Foreign Intrigue, 1066
Foreigner, 946
Foreman and Frazier, 84
Forest Flower, 492, 592
Forest Lawn, 761
Forever, 63, 125, 173, 204, 284, 481,
   550, 703, 805, 931
Forever and Ever, 220, 1006
Forever and Forever, Amen, 993
Forever Autumn, 689
Forever Blue, 475
Forever Changes, 600
Forever, for Always, for Love, 1013
Forever Gold, 476
Forever I'll Stay, 451
(Forever) Live and Die, 742
Forever Mine, 736
Forever Now, 579, 860
Forever Together, 993

Forever Young, 73, 293, 950
Forever Your Girl, 2
Forget About the World, 239
Forget Him, 864
Forget Me Not, 523, 608, 645
Forgetting, 352
Forgive Me John, 463
Forgiven Not Forgotten, 217
Forgotten Town, 184
Forgotten Years, 668
Forrest, The, 967
Forthcoming, 909
40th Anniversary Celebration, A,
   642
Fortress Round Your Heart, 950
Fortunate Son, 225
Forty Days, 52, 432
40 Golden Motown Greats, 856
Forty Miles of Bad Road, 300
Forty Years – The Artistry of Tony
   Bennett, 77
48 Crash, 807
Forty-Niner, 580
Forward March, 692
Fossil Fuel, 1081
Foul Play, 127
Foule, La, 774
Foundation, 976
Fountain of Sorrow, 47, 132
4, 345, 369
Four, 99
Four Calendar Café, 199
Four Chords and Several Years
   Ago, 581
Four Eyes, 720
458489 – A Sides, 327
458489 – B Sides, 327
Four for Trane, 892
400 Years, 643, 767
461 Ocean Boulevard, 187
Four in the Morning, 1086
Four Mills Brothers, The, 755
Four Minutes and Counting, 777
4% Pantomime, 695
Four Sail, 600
4 Seasons of Loneliness, 114
Four Seasons of Love, 693, 960
Four String Joe, 1019
Four Strong Winds, 55, 465, 496,
   1088
Four Symbols, 569
4,000 Weeks Holiday, 290
Four Till Late, 225, 1067
Four Walls, 825, 939
Four Way Street, 229
Four Winds and Seven Seas, 44
4-Track Demos, 429
Fourteen 14K Folksongs, 585
Fourth, 919
Fourth Day of July, 816
4th of July (Asbury Park), 450
Fox on the Run, 415, 635, 964

Foxbase Alpha, 867
Foxtrot, 377
Foxy Lady, 237
Fragile, 723, 1084
Fragments of a Rainy Season, 151
Frakctured, 536
Framed, 33, 196
Frames, 37
Frampton Comes Alive!, 352
Frampton Comes Alive II, 352
Francine, 1094
Frank, 936
Frank Chacksfield Plays . . . , 169
Frank Zappa Meets the Mothers of
   Prevention, 1092
Frank's Wild Years, 1025
Frankenchrist, 252
Frankenstein, 615, 1071
Frankie, 906
Frankie and Johnnie, 78, 294,
   1038
Franklin's Tower, 850
Fraulein, 567
Freak, Le, 845
Freak Out!, 351, 509, 1091
Freaking at the Freakers Ball, 896
Freaks, 805
Freaky Dancin', 152
Freaky Deaky, 40
Freaky Styley, 820
Freberg Underground Show No. 1,
   356
Fred Neil, 710
Freddie Freeloader, 561
Freddie King Is a Blues Master,
   541
Freddie Mercury Album, The, 808
Freddie's Dead, 655
Frederick, 891, 917
Free, 357, 651
Free and Easy, 522
Free and Equal, 288
Free and Equal Blues, The, 422
Free and in Love, 482
Free as a Bird, 67, 305, 962
Free at Last, 357
Free Bird, 608
Free for All, 657, 727
Free Girl, 74
Free Jazz, 177, 202, 206, 274, 410
Free Man in Paris, 679
Free Ride, 1071
Free Satpal Ram, 33
Free the People, 220
Free to Be Me, 121
Free Wheelin', 158
Free Will, 877
Free Your Mind and Your Ass
   Will Follow, 194
Freeborn Man, 648
Freedom, 272, 288, 397, 666, 813,
   871, 1088

Freedom at Point Zero, 495
Freedom Come Freedom Go, 403
Freedom for the Stallion, 460
Freedom for the World, 24
Freedom Knows My Name, 660
Freedom '90, 1065
Freedom Now, 172
Freedom Now Suite, 836
Freedom of Choice, 260
Freedom Sound, 234
Freedom Street, 108, 549
Freedom Suite, 816, 851
Freefall, 369
Freeway Madness, 792
Freeway of Love, 355, 1026
Freewheelin' Bob Dylan, The, 291
Freeze, 122
Freeze, The, 203, 926
Freeze-Frame, 376
Freight Train Boogie, 257
Freight Train Heart, 56
French, 145
French Concertos, 645
French Cooking, 190
French Kissin' in the USA, 96
French Record, 619
Frenesi, 763, 854
Frenz Experiment, The, 327
Fresco, 610, 918
Fresh, 954
Fresh Air, 810
Fresh Cream, 225
Fresh Evidence, 368
Fresh Fruit for Rotting Vegetables,
  252
Fresh Fruit in Foreign Places, 533
Fresh Horses, 123
Fresh Poison, 122
Fresh Raspberries, 817
Freshie, 1031
Freshman Favorites, 348
Fresni, 890
Friday I'm in Love, 238
Friday in San Francisco, 624
Friday on My Mind, 298
Fried, 215
Friend in California, A, 411
Friend of Mine, 588
Friend of the Devil, 148
Friend or Foe, 25
Friendly Fire, 650
Friendly Persuasion, 108, 347, 985
Friends, 43, 503, 538, 667
Friends and Countrymen, 650
Friends and Lovers, 960
Friends and Neighbours, 220
Friends and Relatives, 1085
Friends Can Be Lovers, 1033
Friends Family & Legends, 766
Friends in High Places, 512
Friends in Love, 652
Friends in Low Places, 123

Friends of Mr Cairo, 1014, 1085
Friendships, 894
Frightened City, 752, 885
Frisco Mabel Joy, 718
Frobisher Drive, 747
Frog Princess, The, 268
Froggie Went A-Courtin', 294
From a Distance, 404, 642, 652,
  667
From a Distance . . . The Event,
  831
From a Japanese Screen, 531
From a Spark to a Flame, 251
From a Whisper to a Scream, 990
From Andover to Athens, 827
From Branch to Branch, 820
From Clare to Here, 627, 627
From Despair to Where, 636
From Elvis in Memphis, 683, 789
From Elvis Presley Boulevard, 790
From Every Stage, 47
From Four Until Late, 509
From Genesis to Revelation, 377
*From Graceland to the Promised
  Land*, 411
From Her to Eternity, 168
From Here to Eternity, 191
From Humble Origins, 225
From Langley Park to Memphis,
  788
From Luxury to Heartache, 236,
  642
From Mantovani with Love, 640
From Me to You, 66, 889
From Monday to Sunday, 443
From My Heart, 652
*From Nashville to Memphis, the
  Essential 60s Masters Vol. 1*, 790
From Pain to Joy, 1078
*From Rocky Top to Muddy Bot-
  tom*, 745
From Russia with Love, 685
From Small Things Big Things
  Come, 302
*From South Africa to South Cali-
  fornia*, 877
From the Beginning, 309
From the Bottom of My Heart,
  689, 903
From the Choirgirl Hotel, 20
From the Cradle, 187
From the Highlands, 329
From the Land of Sky-Blue
  Water, 387
*From the Muddy Banks of the
  Wishkah*, 723
From the Pen of Arthur Schwartz,
  874
From the Secret Laboratory, 767
From the Underworld, 245, 352
From the Witchwood, 1025
From this Moment on, 209

From Time to Time, 1089
*From Where I Stand: The Black
  Experience in Country Music*,
  48
Frontiers, 519
Frostbite, 203
Frosty, 203
Frosty the Snow Man, 38
Frozen, 631
Fruit Tree, 284
Fruitcakes, 137
***k the Millennium, 548
Fuck the Police, 728
Fuga Y Misterio, 775
Fugazi, 642
Fugee La, 361
Fugitive, The, 378
Fugs (Kill for Peace), The, 361
Fujiyama Mama, 482
Fulfillingness' First Finale, 1077
Full Circle, 280, 497, 993
Full Clip: A Decade of Gang Starr,
  370
Full Compliment, The, 936
Full House, 324, 376
Full Moon, 116
Full Moon and Empty Arms, 903
Full Moon, Dirty Hearts, 473
Full Moon Fever, 771
Full of Fire, 402
Full Sail, 596
Full Spoon of Seedy Blues, A, 880
Full Time Love, 762
Fun, Fun, Fun, 62, 63, 941
Fun in Space, 808
Fun Lovin' Criminal, 363
Function at the Junction, 589
Fundamental, 814
Funeral, The, 892
Funeral Pyre, 484
Fung, The, 728
Funhunt, 973
Funke Funke Wisdom, 551
*Funkentelechy vs the Placebo Syn-
  drome*, 194
Funky Broadway, 775
Funky Headhunter, The, 418
Funky Kingston, 987, 987
Funky Serenity, 582
Funky Situation, A, 775
Funky Stuff, 550
Funky Town, 1028
Funky Worm, 736
Funny, 76
Funny Familiar Forgotten Feel-
  ings, 516, 718
Funny Feathers, 932
Funny Funny, 964
Funny How Time Slips Away,
  712, 713
Funny Way of Laughing, 115, 477
Further Along, 147

Further Down the Spiral, 723
Further up the Road, 52, 94
Futurama, 710
Future, 201, 496, 835, 880
Future Days, 153
Future Games (A Magical Kahvana Dream), 932
Future Listening!, 253
Future Mrs 'Awkins, The, 179
Future Reconstructions: Ritual of the Solstice, 434
Future Shock, 254, 420

G Force, 365
G N' R Lies, 407
G Plays G: the Piano Rolls, 380
Gaia: One Woman's Journey, 721
Gal That Got Away, The, 380
Galaxy, 1030
Galbi, 435
Gallis Pole, The, 568
Galloping on the Guitar, 36
Galveston, 153, 1040
Galway Bay, 230, 892
Gambler, The, 847
Gamblin' Bar Blues, 661
Game, The, 299, *808*
Game of Love, The, 926, 975
Gamera, 988
Games Lovers Play, 565
Games People Play, 4, 756, 829, 925, 990
Games That Lovers Play, 336
Games without Frontiers, 366
Gangsta Gangsta, 728
Gangsta Tripping, 330
Gangster Moderne, 657
Gangster of Love, 1038
Gangsters, 928
Gangsters of the Groove, 438
Garage Inc, 665
Garbage, 371
Garden, The, 685, 1006
Garden of Eden, The, 486, 1015
Garden of England, The, 812
Garden of Joy, 704
Garden of Love, 488
Garden of Love Light, 1026
Garden Party, 642, 711
Gardens of Harlem, The, 94
Garlands, 198
Garvey's Ghost, 140
Gary's Bar, 19
Gas Food Lodging, 7
Gas Lighting Abbie, 943
Gash, La, 865
Gasoline, 970
Gasoline Alley, 123, *949*
Gates of Eden, 292
Gates of Paradise, The, 360
Gathering Flowers for the Master's Bouquet, 629

Gaucho, 943
Gaudeamus Igitur, 852
Gaudete, 942
Gaudi, 756
Gave You My Love, 549
Gay Caballero, A, 233
Gay Nineties, Songs of the South, 606
Gee, 389, 490
Gee Baby (I'm Sorry), 56
Gee Baby Ain't I Good to You, 822
Gee, Jimmy, that's Swell, 527
Gee Officer Krupke, 869
Gee Whizz, 682, 948, 980
Geechy Joe, 152
Geffrey Morgan, 1005
Geisha Girl, 595
Gemini Suite, 30
Gems, 558
Gems for Ever, 639
Gene Clark, 973
General Johnson, 169
Generation Swine, 699
Generation Terrorists, 636
Generations, 141
Generations of Hank, The, 1060
Genesis, 378
Genesis Live, 377
Genetic Engineering, 742
Genevieve, 614
Genie in a Bottle, 927
Genius & Soul, 174
Genius Hits the Road, 174
Genius of Love, 967, *1053*
Genius of Ray Charles, The, 174
Genius Plus Soul Equals Jazz, 174, 514
Geno, 261
Gentle Giant, 566
Gentle on My Mind, 153, 429, 496, 646, 904, 986, 1080
Gentleman, 10, 556
Gentlemen Rankers, 1031
Gentlemen Take Polaroids, 491
Genuine Imitation Life Gazette, 349
Genuine Tong Funeral, A, 141
Geoff and Amos, 704
Geometrid, The, 75
George Harrison, 427
Georgia Blues, 1036
Georgia on My Mind, 73, 158, 174, 390, 501, 713, 834
Georgia Tom, 281
Georgy Girl, 881
German Afternoons, 799
Germ-Free Adolescence, 703
Gershwin Songbook, 336
Gertcha, 175
Get a Buzz, 792
Get a Grip, 10

Get a Hold on Me, 342
Get a Job, 840
Get a Life, 923
Get Away, 125, 327
Get Back, 67, 790, 998
Get Back to the Country, 1088
Get Close, 791
Get Closer, 170, *854*
Get Dancin', 228, 329
Get Down, 170, 171, 747
Get Down and Get with It, 910
Get Down, Get Down (Get on the Floor), 899
Get Down Tonight, 526, *526*
Get Happy, 26, 219
Get It, 51, 302, 1077
Get It on, 101, 289, 751
Get It Outcha System, 482
Get It Right, 355, 1013
Get It Right Next Time, 812
Get It While You Can, 783, 953, 969, 1020
Get Lucky, 590
Get Me on Your Mind, 626
Get Me to the Church on Time, 564, 578
Get Me to the World on Time, 305
Get Myself Arrested, 390
Get off My Cloud, 849
Get on the Good Foot, 128
Get on Top, 136
Get Out, 56
Get Out My Life Woman, 144, 990
Get Out of My Cube, 273
Get Out of My Life Woman, 281
Get Outta My Dreams, Get into My Car, 732
Get Ready, 840, 841, *1001*
Get Ready for This, 1001
Get Real, 354
Get Rhythm, 212, 755
Get Right, Church, 246
Get That Feeling, 439
Get Together, 810, 1089, 1090
Get Up, 976
Get Up Everybody (Get Up), 869
Get Up I Feel Like Being a Sex Machine, 128
Get Up Stand Up, 643, 815, 988
Get Up with It, 248
Get with It, 331
Get Yer Ya-Yas Out, 849
Get Your Jujus Out, 732
Get Your Wings, 9
Getaway, 297, 825
Getcha Back, 64
Getcha Rocks Off, 254
Gettin' Jiggy wit It, 917
Getting Better, 390
Getting Mighty Crowded, 319

Getting Out of Hand, 54
Getting Over You, 814
Getting Ready, 541
Getting Some Fun out of Life, 983
Getting the Holy Ghost Across, 711
Getting to Know You, 844
Getz–Byrd, 381
Getz–Gilberto, 381, 501
Ghanashayam – a Broken Branch, 889
Ghetto, The, 77, 430, 651, 938
Ghetto Blaster, 234
Ghetto Child, 1079
Ghetto Life, 488
Ghetto Music – The Blueprint of Hip Hop, 106
Ghetto Supastar, 361
Ghost in the Machine, 782
Ghost of Tom Joad, The, 935
(Ghost) Riders in the Sky, 687
Ghost Town, 928
Ghosts, 491
Ghostyhead, 515
G.I. Jive, 518
Giannina Mia, 359
Giant of Rock'n'Roll, 432
Giant Steps, 105, 206, 666
Giant Steps/De Ole Folks at Home, 966
Giants of Motown, 975
Giants of the Organ in Concert, 620
Gift, The, *484, 1007*, 1018
Gift from a Flower to a Garden, 277
Gigantic, 778
Gil Evans, 318
Gil Evans Plays Hendrix, 318
Gilded Palace of Sin, The, 756, 805
Gillespiana, 874
Gilly Gilly Ossenfeffer Katzenellen Bogen By the Sea, 146
Gimme a Pigfoot, 92, 914
Gimme a Pigfoot and a Bottle of Beer, 418
Gimme Back My Bullets, 608
Gimme Hope Jo'Anna, 398
Gimme Shelter, 849, *864*, 891
Gimme Some Loving, 1072
Gimme Some Time, 339
Gin and Juice, 269
Gin Soaked Boy, 268
Gina, 651
Ginchy, 1042
Ginger, You're Barmy, 170
Ginny Come Lately, 464
Girl at Her Volcano, 515
Girl Called Johnny, A, 1035
Girl Can't Help It, The, 245

Girl Crazy, 457
Girl Don't Come, 891
Girl from Ipanema, The, 381, 501
Girl from the North Country, 164, 166, 292
Girl I Love You, 413
Girl I Used to Know, A, 512
Girl in Calico, A, 839, 874
Girl in My Dreams, 76
Girl Is Mine, The, 481, 611
Girl, I've Got a Date, 1009
Girl Like You, A, 816
Girl of My Best Friend, 389
Girl That I Marry, The, 79
Girl with the Golden Braids, The, 209
Girl You Know It's True, 328
Girl, You'll Be a Woman Soon, 262
Girlfriend, 973
Girls Ain't Nothing but Trouble, 730, 917
Girls and Boys, 100
Girls Can't Do What the Guys Do, 1078
Girls Girls Girls, 698
Girls in Jazz, 331, 1063
Girls Just Wanna Have Fun, 49, 566, 567
Girls L.G.B.N.A.F., 467
Girls Like Me, 997
Girls on Film, 288
Girls Talk, 302
Girls with Guitars, 520
Girls with Guns, 959
Gish, 371, 913
Gitarzan, 946
Give 'Em Enough Rope, 191
Give a Little Love, 35, 62
Give and Take, 193
Give Him a Great Big Kiss, 888
Give Ireland Back to the Irish, 611
Give It Away, 180, 820
Give It to Me, 376, 995
Give It to the People, 835
Give It to The Soft Boys, 446
Give It Up, 526, *813*, 814
Give It Up or Turnit a Loose, 128
Give Me a Saddle, I'll Trade You a Car, 13
Give Me Back My Heart, 602
Give Me Convenience or Give Me Death, 252
Give Me Just a Little More Time, 169, 449, 677
Give Me Love (Give Me Peace on Earth), 427
Give Me One Reason, 172
Give Me the Moonlight, 1014
Give Me the Moonlight, Give Me the Girl, 259, 1023
Give Me the Night, *77*, 437, *514*

Give Me the Reason, 1013
Give Me the Simple Life, 523
Give Me the Time, 707
Give Me Your Heart Tonight, 947
Give Me Your Love, 560
Give My Regards to Broadway, 200, 706
Give Out But Don't Give Up, 194, 283, 796
Give Peace a Chance, 29, 456, 554, 576, 740
Give U My Heart, 118
Give Us a Wink, 964
Give Us Your Blessing, 769, 888
Give Your Baby a Standing Ovation, 256
Givin' Up Givin' in, 56
Giving It All Away, 872, 1054
Giving It Back, 476
Giving It Up, 615
Giving It Up for Your Love, 613
Giving Up, 430, 548
Giving You the Best That I Got, 49
Glad All Over, 187, 364
Glad It's All Over, 240
Glad to Be Gay, 841
Gladys' Leap, 324
Glamour, 544
Glamour Boy, 406
Glasgow Belongs to Me, 566
Glass, 267
Glass Onion, 642
Glassworks, 385
Glenn Yarbrough and the Limeliters, 585
Glider, 707
Gliding Bird, 425
Glint at the Kindling, A, 471
Glittering Prize, 901
Glittering Prizes 81/92, 902
Global Blues, 737
Globe, The, 191
Globe of Frogs, 447
Globe Sessions, The, 232
Globetrotter, 987
Gloomy Sunday, 448
Gloria, 117, 315, 453, 541, 694, 695, 916
Glorified Magnified, 635
Glory Be to God for the Golden Pill, 829
Glory Box, 785
Glory Days, 934
Glory of Gershwin, The, 380
Glory of Love, The, 181, 346, 602
Gloryhalastoopid, 194
Gloryland, 413
Glorylands, 484
Glow, 488, 492, 814, 825
Glow of Love, 1013

Glow Worm, The, 515, 674
Glycerine, 142
G-Man Hoover, 755
Go, 688, 1073
Go Ahead and Cry, 834
Go All the Way, 817
Go Away Little Girl, 540, 567, 746
Go Cat Go, 766
Go Deep, 479
Go Down Gamblin', 97
Go for Broke, 652
Go for the Throat, 912
Go for Your Life, 702
(Go) Get It, 666
Go Help the Outcasts, 667
Go Home Girl, 13
Go Jimmy Go, 186
Go Let It Out, 731
Go Now, 689, 698
Go on and on, 549
Go See the Doctor, 551
Go to Heaven, 401
Go to the Mardi Gras, 802
Go West, 768, 1021, 1021
Go Wild in the Country, 623
Go Your Own Way, 342
Go+, 1081
Go2, 1081
Goat's Head Soup, 849
Gob Is a Slob, A, 250
God, 20, 178
God Be with Our Boys Tonight, 614
God Bless America, 78, 79, 408, 916
God Bless the Child, 448, 492, 903
God Don't Like it, 978
God Gave Rock'n'Roll to You, 546, 1093
God Love and Rock'n'Roll, 882
God Loves a Drunk, 164, 982
God of Thunder, 1048
God Only Knows, 63
God Save the Queen, 25, 354, 700, 884
God Save the Queen/Under Heavy Manners, 360
God Shuffled His Feet, 967
God, Time and Causality, 322
God's Beautiful City, 589
God's Cop, 421
God's Dice, 762
God's Gonna Separate the Wheat from the Tares, 480
God's Great Banana Skin, 819
God's Song, 720, 1042
Godfather of Grunge's Mirrorball, 762
Godfathers of Threatt, 551
Goin' Away Blues, 508
Goin' Back, 147, 540, 933, 933
Goin' Back to New Orleans, 272

Goin' Down Slow, 154, 459
Goin' East, 759
Goin' Gone, 652
Goin' Home, 275, 893
Goin' in with My Eyes Open, 611, 923
Goin' Out of My Head, 578, 587, 688
Goin' Places, 17
Goin' Steady, 1086
Goin' to Brownsville, 212
Goin' to Chicago, 862
Goin' to Kansas City, 1063
Goin' to the River, 275
Goin' Up the Country, 154
Going Away, 403, 680
Going Back to My Roots, 449
Going Blank Again, 834
Going Down, 931
Going Down to Liverpool, 447
Going for Broke, 398
Going for the One, 1084
Going Home, 304
Going Loco in Acapulco, 350
Going Out, 961
Going Places, 478
Going Public, 64
Going to Get My Baby out of Jail, 171
Going to the Bank, 208
Going to the River, 1067
Going to the Zoo, 408, 761
Going to Your Funeral, 303
Going Underground, 484, 635
Gold, 926, 949
Gold Against the Soul, 636
Gold Chain Troubadour, 996
Gold Experience, The, 798
Gold Hits, 581
Gold Mother, 485
Gold Star in the Window, 836
Golden Age of Noël Coward, The, 222
Golden Age of Rock'n'Roll, 700
Golden Age of Wireless, The, 273
Golden Apples of the Sun, 204
Golden Brown, 956
Golden Calf, The, 788
Golden D, The, 100
Golden Dustman, The, 305
Golden Filth, 361
Golden Flute, The, 566
Golden Greats, 952
Golden Heart, 267
Golden Hits, St Louis to Frisco, 82
Golden Latin All Stars in Session, 804
Golden Ring, 512, 893, 1080
Golden Rocket, 918
Golden Scarab, The, 280
Golden Section, The, 1006
Golden Teardrops, 339

Golden Time of Day, 656, 656
Golden Touch, 815
Golden Wire, 782
Golden Years, 111, 234, 699
Golondrina, La, 1010
Gone, 463, 1086
Gone Again, 917
Gone Clear, 263
Gone Fishing, 231
Gone from Danger, 47
Gone Gone Gone, 331
Gone to Earth, 965
Gone to the Country, 716
Gone Troppo, 427
Gone with the Wind, 983
Gonna Build a Mountain, 719
Gonna Capture Your Heart, 644
Gonna Catch You, 87
Gonna Find Me a Bluebird, 813
Gonna Fly Now (Theme from Rocky), 929
Gonna Get Along without You Now, 1048
Gonna Get Through, 559
Gonna Lay Down My Old Guitar, 257
Gonna Make You a Star, 314
Gonna Make You Sweat (Everybody Dance Now), 149
Gonna Take a Miracle, 558, 728
Goo, 920, 921
Good and Bad Times, The, 234
Good and Dusty, 1090
Good As I Been to You, 294
Good Citizen, 669
Good Dirty Fun, 615
Good Enough, 125
Good Feeling, 992, 1028
Good for Your Soul, 305
Good Fortune, 429
Good Golly, Ask Ollie, 865
Good Golly Miss Dolly, 589
Good Golly Miss Molly, 90, 581, 589, 865, 965
Good Good Whiskey, 248
Good Guys, 26
Good Heart, A, 622, 890
Good Hearted Woman, 713
Good Humour, 867
Good Idea Son, A, 146, 719
Good Kind of Hurt, 807
Good King Bad, 77
Good Life, 472
Good Lovin', 195, 641, 816, 1080
Good Lovin' Ain't Easy to Come by, 374
Good Man, Good Woman, 613
Good Man Is Hard to Find, A, 365
Good Mornin' Blues, 568, 862
Good Morning, 359
Good Morning Britain, 42
Good Morning Dear, 468

Good Morning Heartache, 131
Good Morning Judge, 426
Good Morning Little Schoolgirl, 400, 949, 1066, 1071
Good Morning Starshine, 227
Good News Comin', 520
Good News from the Next World, 902
Good Night Sweetheart, 725
Good Old Boys, 720
Good Old Rock'n'Roll, 188
Good Rockin' Tonight, 131, 426, 788, 802
Good Rocking Daddy, 85, 486
Good Singin' Good Playin', 396
Good Son, The, 169
Good Stuff, 43
Good Thing, 335
Good Thing Going, 220
Good Things Don't Happen Every Day, 620, 755
Good Time Charlie's Got the Blues, 1086
Good Times, 56, 845
Good Timin', 64, 513, 514
Good Trouble, 827
Good Vibes, 141
Good Vibrations, 62, 63, 715, 860, 995
Good Woman, 549
Good Year for the Roses, A, 219, 512, 894
Good, the Bad and the Ugly, The, 92
Good-Bye, Good Luck, God Bless You, 140
Goodbye, 453, 496, 833, 931
Goodbye Baby, 875
Goodbye Baby (Baby Goodbye), 329
Goodbye Blu Sky, 976
Goodbye Blues, 617, 674
Goodbye Broadway, Hello France, 706
Goodbye Cruel World, 219
Goodbye Girl, 119
Goodbye Jimmy Goodbye, 752
Goodbye My Love, 386
Goodbye Newport Blues, 927
Goodbye Pork Pie Hat, 676, 679
Goodbye Sam, Hello Samantha, 707, 831
Goodbye to Love, 160
Goodbye to Storyville, 737
Goodbye to the Island, 1002
Goodbye Yellow Brick Road, 503
Goodbye-ee, 1046
Goodness Gracious Me, 393
Goodnight Angel, 890
Goodnight Irene, 496, 568, 672, 704, 822, 1039
Goodnight Kathleen, 56

Goodnight Mrs Flintstone, 348
Goodnight My Love, 76, 85, 113, 828
Goodnight Sweetheart, 112
Goodnight, Sweetheart, Good-night, 621, 926
Goodnight Vienna, 939
Goodtime Charlie, 737
Goodtime Charlie's Got the Blues, 737
Goody Goody, 606
Goody Two Shoes, 25
Goofus, 760
Google Eye, 698
Goonies Are Good Enough, 566
Gorgoni, Martin and Taylor, 970
Gorilla, 105
Gospel Duets, 98
Gospel Nights, 704
Gospel Oak, The, 734
Gospel Plow, The, 291
Gospel Road, 166
Gospels, The, 1025
Got a Girl, 348
Got a Job, 840
Got a Mind to Ramble, 862
Got Change for a Million, 865
Got My Mind Made Up, 771
Got My Mind Set on You, 427
Got My Mojo Workin', 144, 916, 1036, 1037
Got Myself Together, 651
Got the Blues, 495
Got the Bull by the Horns, 456
Got the Time, 25, 480
Got to Be Real, 989
Got to Be There, 481
Got to Get You into My Life, 174, 298
Got to Get You off My Mind, 139, 750
Got to Give It Up, 374
Gotta Band, 342
Gotta Get Away, 736
Gotta Get Back to Cisco, 970
Gotta Let this Hen Out, 447
Gotta Lotta Love, 467
Gotta Serve Somebody, 293
Gotta Travel on, 293
Gottle O'Geer, 324
Goulante du Pauvre Jean, La, 61, 774
GP, 142, 425, 757
Grabbin' Blues, 84
Grace, 135
Grace under Pressure, 861
Graceland, 176, 212, 594, 633, 649, 710, 854, 899, 900
Graduation Day, 348, 475
Graffitti Bridge, 798
Gram Parsons Notebooks: The Last Whippoorwill, The, 757

Gran Turismo, 156
Granada, 763
Grand Coulee Dam, 407
Grand Funk Lives, 396
Grand Hotel, 801
Grand Illusion, The, 959
Grand Prix, 973
Grand Tour, The, 511, 714, 854
Grand Wazoo, The, 287, 1091
Grandad, 1025
Grandma Harp, 411
Grandma's Hands, 1074
Grandpa (Tell Me About the Good Old Days), 520
Grandpa Was a Carpenter, 799
Grange, La, 1094
Granite Creek, 680
Grape 69, 680
Grape Live, 680
Grass Is Blue, The, 757, 758
Grasshopper, 150
Grateful Dead, 400
Grateful When You're Dead, 556
Gratuitous Sex and Senseless Violins, 927
Grave Dancers Union, 922
Gravity, 128, 365
Gravity's Rainbow, 76
Grazing in the Grass, 649
Great American Dream, 284
Great Australian Legend, The, 591
Great Balloon Race, The, 909
Great Balls of Fire, 91, 581
Great Concert of Charles Mingus, The, 676
Great Concert of Eric Dolphy, The, 274
Great Conch Train Robbery, The, 896
Great Dance Hits, 170
Great Day, 938, 1050
Great Days, 799
Great Electric Show and Dance, The, 454
Great Escape, The, 100
Great Fatsby, The, 702
Great Filling Station Holdup, The, 137
Great Gosh A'Mighty, 589
Great Gospel Songs, 344
Great Hits of 1964, The, 109
Great Imposter, The, 259, 342
Great Mahalia Jackson, The, 480
Great Move, 703
Great Pretender, The, 356, 780, 808
Great Recordings, The, 778
Great Scott, 877
Great Speckled Bird, 6, 162, 465, 860, 981, 1062
Great Wall of China, 502
Greatest, The, 847

Greatest Beats, 265
Greatest Funkin' Hits, 195
Greatest Hits, 22, 97, 108, 109, 169, 185, 317, 328, 355, 365, 458, 520, 551, 588, 589, 596, 618, 674, 682, 732, 733, 771, 776, 806, 847, 882, 934, 935, 936, 958, 959, 980, 995, 1051, 1094
Greatest Hits, Etc., 899
Greatest Hits from the Fourth Decade, 128
Greatest Hits Live, 625, 855, 898, 971, 1057
Greatest Hits – Live, 12, 519
Greatest Hits 1965–1992, 177
Greatest Hits 1966–1992, 262
Greatest Hits, 1985–1995, 102
Greatest Hits, 1986–1996, 782
Greatest Hits . . . So Far, 884
Greatest Hits Vol. 1, 993
Greatest Hits Vol. 2, 993
Greatest Live Show on Earth, The, 581
Greatest Living Englishman, The, 1081
Greatest Love of All, The, 458, 1026
Greatest Misses, 803
Greco, El, 1014
Greedy Gal, 692
Green, 265, 826
Green & Guitar: The Best of Peter Green, 1977–81, 341
Green Door, The, 616, 947, 1015
Green Eye of the Little Yellow God, The, 691
Green Eyes, 280
Green Fields of Foreverland, The, 75
Green Grasses, 948
Green Green, 621, 846
Green Green Grass of Home, The, 1, 516, 757
Green Light, *814*, 981
Green Man, 1065
Green Manalishi, 341
Green Onions, 37, 106, 107, 1066
Green River, 225, 496
Green Tie on the Little Yellow Dog, The, 691
Greenback Dollar, 40, 542
Greenfields, 542
Greensleeves, 141, 639
Greeting from the Gutter, 317
Greetings from Asbury Park, NJ, 934
Greetings from LA, 136
Greetings from the West, 343
Gresford Mining Disaster, The, 13
Grey Day, 630
Grievous Angel, 142, 425, 757

Grinder Man Blues, 661
Gringing Stone, 690
Grip, 956
Gris Gris, 271
Grits Ain't Groceries, 504, 588
Grizzly Bear, 1090
Groaning the Blues, 861
Groeten uit Grollo, 122
Groop Played Space Age Bachelor Pad Music, The, 944
Groove Approved, 378
Groove Is in the Heart, 252, 994
Groove Line, The, 438
Groove Me, 835
Groovemaster, 31
Groover's Paradise, 226, 867
Groovin', 106, 816, 850, 1030
Groovin' and Spoonin', 1075
Groovin' High, 383, 753
Groovin' with Jacquet, 483
Groovy Decay, 447
Groovy Kind of Love, A, 45, 205, 558, 975
Groovy Situation, 171
Grope Need, 361
Grow Old with Me, 159
Growing Pains, 344
Growing up in Hollywood Town, 349
Growing up in Public, 824
Grown Man, 1024
Grown Up Baby, 306
GTR, 1085
Guaglione, 787
Guantanamera, 17, 454, 702, 881, 1079
Guaranteed, 579
Guardian Angel, 886
Guardian Angels, 520
Guava Jelly, 643, 708
Gudbuy T'Jane, 909, 910
Guess I'll Hang My Tears out to Dry, 833
Guess My Eyes Were Bigger Than My Heart, 1000
Guess Things Happen That Way, 165, 192
Guess Who, 76, *538*
Guess Who's Back?, 43
Guide, The, 710
Guilty, 24, 71, 206, 738, 814, 956, 956, 957, 1075
Guilty Til Proved Innocent, 929
Guitar Blues, 35
Guitar Boogie, 333
Guitar Boogie Shuffle, 1041
Guitar Concerto and Serenade, 30
Guitar Forms, 141
Guitar Freakout, 1019
Guitar from Ipanema, 16
Guitar Man, 119, *150*, 822
Guitar Monsters, 760

Guitar Player, 395
Guitar Preacher, 1077
Guitar Shop, 70
Guitar Slinger, 1071
Guitar Sounds of James Burton, The, 142
Guitar Speaks, 702
Guitar Syndicate, 885
Guitar Town, 297
Guitar/Vocal, 982
Guitarissimo, 857
Guitars and Women, 615
Guitars, Cadillacs, etc., 1085
Gula Matari, 514
Gulf Coast Blues, 914
Gum Tree Canoe, 429
Gumbo, 271, 802, 895, 1047
Gunfight at Carnegie Hall, 349, 733
Gunfighter Ballads and Trail Songs, 837
Gung Ho, 917
Guns in the Ghetto, 1005
Guns of Brixton, 330
Guns of Navarone, 272, 908
Gunslinger, 560
Guy Is a Guy, A, 673
Gymnopedies, 909
Gypsy, 342, 472, 895, 1009, 1051, 1052
Gypsy Cadillac, 465
Gypsy Cried, The, 185
Gypsy Honeymoon, 159
Gypsy Love Song, 441
Gypsy Man, 1030
Gypsy Songman, 1027
Gypsy Woman, 464, 470, 889
Gypsys, Tramps and Thieves, 177, 373

Ha!, 534
Ha Cha Cha, 117
Ha Cha Cha (Acieed Mix), 117
Ha Ha Ha, 1006
Ha Ha Said the Clown, 635
Had to Be, 831
Hada Raykoum, 532
Hai Hai, 962
Hail H.I.M., 140
Haile Selassie, 12
Hair, 223
Hair of Spun Gold, 465
Hair of the Dog, 709
Hal-an-Tow, 13
Haley's Juke Box, 413
Half & Half, 822
Half a Buck, 749
Half As Much, 195, 672
Half Awake, 655
Half the Way, 375
Half-Breed, 177, 373, 813
Halfway to Heaven, 316

Halfway to Paradise, 364, 540, 743, 1023
Halfway to Sanity, 815
Hall of Fame, 689, 724
Hall of the Mountain Grill, 433
Hallelujah, 472, 839, 987, 1086
Hallalujah Freedom, 644
Hallelujah I Love Her So, 174
Hallelujah I Love Him So, 572
Hallelujah I Love You So, 571
Hallelujah, I'm a Bum, 921
Hallo to Our Men, 956
Hallucination Engine, 565
Halo, 978
Halo 'Round the Moon, 297
Hamlet, 416
Hammer and Nails, 938
Hampstead Incident, 277, 326
Hand Cut, 136
Hand Held in Black and White, 455
Hand in, 891
Hand in Glove, 917
Hand in Hand, 693
Hand in My Pocket, 693
Hand It Over, 265
Hand Me Down My Jogging Shoes, 761
Hand Me Down My Old Walking Stick, 1058
Hand Me Down My Walking Cane, 387
Hand of Kindness, 113, 982
Hand on Your Heart, 677
Hand to Mouth, 47
Handbags and Gladrags, 635, 1075
Handful of Beauty, A, 624
Handful of Keys, 1029
Handful of Songs, A, 57, *561*, 941
Handle with Care, 427
Hands of Time, 573
Hands Off She's Mine, 335
Handsome, 290
Handy Man, 91, 513, 514, 889, 971
Hang 'Em High, 106
Hang in Long Enough, 205
Hang on in There Baby, 121
Hang on Sloopy, 80, 329, 582, 615, 1010
Hang on to a Dream, 423
Hang on to Your Love, 278
Hang Time, 922
Hang up My Rock'n'Roll Shoes, 53, 1067
Hangin' on a Thread, 332
Hangin' on by a Thread, 500, 867
Hangin' Tough, 497, 715
Hanging Around the Observatory, 444
Hanging Fire, 193
Hanging on the Telephone, 96

Hangman's Beautiful Daughter, The, 471
Hank, 560
Hank and Lefty Raised My Country Soul, 794
Hank Live, 1061
Hank Plays Holly, 886
Hank Plays Live, 886
Hank Thompson and his Brazos Valley Boys, 981
Hank Williams Hits, 516
Hank Williams Jnr and Friends, 1061
Hank Wilson Volume II, 864
Hank Wilson's Back, 864
Hanky Panky, 404, 489, *1060*
Happening, The, 449, 963
Happenings Ten Years Time Ago, 1083
Happiness, 330, *808*
Happiness Heartaches, 38
Happiness Is a Thing Called Joe, 26, 422
Happiness Is Just Around the Bend, 37
Happiness Is Piano Red, 774
Happy, 244, 573, 992
Happy Anniversary, 590
Happy Being Lonely, 180
Happy Birthday, 1076, 1077
Happy Birthday Darlin', 1000
Happy Birthday Rock'n'Roll, 534
Happy Children, 745
Happy Christmas, War Is Over, 740
Happy Club, The, 377
Happy Days Are Here Again, 10
Happy Days in Dixie, 924
Happy Daze, 586
Happy End of the World, 779
Happy Endings, 58, *319*
Happy Feet, 10
Happy Go Lucky Girl, 451
Happy Heart, 565
Happy Hour, 68
Happy House, 905
Happy in Hell, 184
Happy Jack, 1054
Happy Sad, *135*, 779
Happy Talk, 240, 844
Happy Times Are Here to Stay, 743
Happy to Be on an Island in the Sun, 1014
Happy to Make Your Acquaintance, 596
Happy Together, 251, 999, *1000*
Happy Trails, *809*, *810*, 993
Happy Whistler, The, 838
Happy Woman Blues, 1062
Happy Xmas (War Is Over), 576
Harbour Lights, *456*, 525, 528, 780

Hard Act to Follow, 180
Hard Again, 1037
Hard Ain't It Hard, 542
Hard at Play, 581
Hard Bop, 93
Hard Day, 666
Hard Day's Night, A, 66, 393, 582
Hard Habit to Break, 181
Hard Lovin' Loser, 329
Hard Luck Blues, 131
Hard Nose the Highway, 695
Hard Promises, 771
Hard Rain, 293
Hard Rain's Gonna Fall, A, 291, 333
Hard Road, A, 654, 1020
Hard Rock Bottom of Your Heart, 993
Hard Rope and Silken Twine, 471
Hard Station, 116
Hard Stuff, The, 656
Hard Time Killin' Floor Blues, 488
Hard Times, *131*, 294, 482, 574, 859, *893*, 908
Hard Times Come Easy, 103
Hard to Earn, 370
Hard to Handle, 87, 821
Hard to Say, 343
Hard to Say I'm Sorry, 181, 346
Hard Travellin', 308
Hard Volume, 850
Hard Way, The, 90, 297, 1092
Hardcore Jollies, 194
Hardcore Vol. 1, Vol. 2, 260
Harder Than the Rest, 140
Harder They Come, The, 630, 966
Hard-Hearted Hannah, 10
Hardline According to Terence Trent d'Arby, The, 438
Hardly Getting Over It, 701
Hark! The Village Wait, 942
Harlem Chocolate Babies on Parade, 506
Harlem Jazz Scene 1941, 184, 190
Harlem Nocturne, 536, 748
Harlem Shuffle, 849, 1048
Harlem Street Singer, 246
Harlequin, 405
Harlequin Melodies, 718
Harmonica According to, 405
Harmonica Harry, 761, 1042
Harmony, 201, 705
Harmony Row, 133
Harp Attack, 1045
Harper Valley P.T.A., 415, 537
Harpers Bizarre 4, 424
Harrigan, 706
Harry, 722
Harry Hippie, 1076
Harry Lime Theme, 524

Harry, the Hairy Ape, 946
Harvest, 725, 1088
Harvest for the World, 184, 476
Harvest Moon, 1087, 1088
Has Anybody Here Seen Kelly?, 62, 345
Has He Got a Friend for Me?, 622
Hasten Down the Wind, 854, 1092
Hat Full of Stars, 567
Hate Your Friends, 575
Hatful of Hollow, 917
Hats off to Harper, 424
Hats off to Larry, 889
Haunted House, 89
Haunting Melody, The, 510
Havana Moon, 871, 1047
Have a Cigar, 424
Have a Drink on Me, 277
Have a Good Time, 131, 134
Have a Little Faith, 198
Have a Nice Day, 856
Have a Whiff on Me, 277
Have I Got a Deal for You?, 618
Have I Stayed Away Too Long, 836
Have I the Right?, 245, 659
Have I Told You Lately that I Love You?, 39, 622, 950
Have Mercy Baby, 59, 625, 1069
Have Mercy Judge, 82
Have Mercy Miss Percy, 589
Have You Ever Been in Love, 873
Have You Ever Been Lonely, 193, 825
Have You Ever Loved a Woman?, 7, 541
Have You Heard?, 186, 654
Have You Never Been Mellow, 721
Have You Seen Her?, 180, 418
Have You Seen Me Lately, 898
Have Yourself a Merry Little Christmas, 371, 372, 904
Haven't Got Time for the Pain, 898
Having Church, 192
Hawaii Five-O, 1019
Hawaiian Wedding Song, The, 1056
Hawk, The, 432
Hawk in Germany, 786
Hawk, 1953–1961, 432
Hawks and Doves, 1088
Hay Foot, Straw Foot, 422
Hazy Shade of Winter, A, 54, 897
He, 444, 834
He Ain't Heavy, He's My Brother, 450, 835
He Beeped When He Should Have Bopped, 383
He Can't Fill My Shoes, 582

He Cried, 888
He Don't Love You (Like I Love You), 743
He Don't Really Love You, 255
He Got Game, 803
He Hit Me, 540
He Hit Me (and It Felt Like a Kiss), 235
He Knows You Know, 642
He Stopped Loving Her Today, 512
He Thinks He'll Keep Her, 159
He Thinks He's Ray Stevens, 946
He Turned Me Out, 781
He Was a Friend of Mine, 148, 1013
He Was My Brother, 897
He Was Really Sayin' Somethin', 52
He Wasn't Man Enough, 118
He Who Rides the Tiger, 503
He Will Break Your Heart, 143, 743
He'll Have to Get Under – Get Out and Get Under (to Fix up His Automobile), 706
He'll Have to Go, 138, 825
He's a Real Gone Guy, 605
He's a Rebel, 235, 601, 724, 778, 929
He's a Tramp, 572
He's Back, 215
He's Bad Bad Bad, 1078
He's Coming, 40
He's Gone, 171
He's Gonna Step on You Again, 386
He's Got the Power, 404
He's Got the Whole World in His Hands, 266
He's My Rock, 571
He's My Son Just the Same, 1079
He's on the Phone, 867
He's So Fine, 182, 427
He's So Shy, 781
He's Sure the Boy I Love, 235, 601, 638
He's Sure the Man I Love, 601
He's the DJ, I'm the Rapper, 917
He's the Greatest Dancer, 845, 906
He's the Man, 374
Head, 684, 797
Head Games, 345
Head Injuries, 668
Head Music, 960
Head on the Door, The, 238
Head Over Heels, 3, 198, 972
Head to the Sky, 297
Headed for the Future, 262
Headhunters, 420
Headin' Down into the Mystery Below, 429

Headin' Down the Highway, 239
Headless Cross, 88
Headlines & Deadlines, 11
Headmaster Ritual, The, 918
Headquarters, 684
Heads, 745
Heads and Tails, 171
Heal the World, 481
Healer, The, 452, 814, 871
Healing, 860
Healing Game, The, 695
Healing Hand, 503
Healing Hands of Time, 712, 713
Healing the Wounds, 234
Health and Happiness Shows, 1060
Hear My Song Violetta, 594
Hear No Evil, 565
Hear on the Now Frontier, 809
Heard Ya Missed Me, 954
Hearsay, 740
Heart, 436, 768, 906
Heart and Soul, 389, 490, 581, *812*
Heart Failed (In the Back of a Taxi), 867
Heart Full of Soul, 70, 975, 1083
Heart in Motion, 398
Heart Is a House for Love, A, 256
Heart Land, 520
Heart Like a Sky, 926
Heart Like a Wheel, 461, 618, 619, 806, 853, *853*
Heart Needs a Home, A, 982
Heart of a Coon, 306
Heart of a Nigger, 306
Heart of Chicago, 1967–1997, The, 181
Heart of Glass, 96
Heart of Gold, 1088
Heart of Mine, 873
Heart of My Heart, 217
Heart of Rock'n'Roll, The, 581, *581*
Heart of Saturday Night, 1024
Heart of Stone, 102, 107, *177*
Heart of the City, 603
Heart of the Congo, 767
Heart on My Sleeve, 333, 368, *368*, *838*
Heart on the Wall, 96
Heart Over Mind, 705, 1080
Heart Shaped Box, 723
Heart Shaped World, 475
Heart, Soul & a Voice, 879
Heart Still Beating, 857
Heart Strings, 249
Heart to Heart, 538, 870
Heart Won't Lie, The, 618
Heart's Filthy Lesson, The, 112
Heart's Horizon, 492
Heartache All Over the World, 503

Heartaches, 641, 1042
Heartaches by the Number, 458, 496, 678, 794, 985, 1085
Heartattack and Vine, 433, *1024*
Heartbeat, 106, 579, 868, 886, 896
Heartbeat City, 161
Heartbeat in the Darkness, 1059
Heartbeat Returning to the Womb, 869, 965
Heartbeats Accelerating, 619
Heartbreak, 886
Heartbreak Hotel, 40, 150, 164, 356, 789
Heartbreak U.S.A., 1045
Heartbreaker, 71, 76, *357*, 1033
Heartless, 436
Heartlessly, 783
Heartlight, 262
Hearts and Bones, 900
Hearts and Flowers, 27
Hearts in Motion, 12
Hearts of Stone, 226, 344, 1016
Hearts on Fire, 7, 295
Heartsongs, 758
Heat, The, 118, 559
Heat Is on, The, 296
Heat, Light & Sound, 164
Heat of Heat, 484
Heat of the Beat, 40
Heat of the Moment, 1085
Heat of the Night, 7
Heat Treatment, 754
Heat Wave, 79, 330
Heatseeker, 5
Heatwave, 449, 645, 854
Heaven, 7
Heaven and Earth, 874
Heaven and Hell, *88*, *480*, 536, *1014*
Heaven and Paradise, 257
Heaven and Sea, 145
Heaven Can Wait, 1012
Heaven Help the Child, 718
Heaven in my Hands, 579
Heaven Is a Place on Earth, 157
Heaven Just Knows, 303
Heaven Knows, 936
Heaven Knows I'm Miserable Now, 917
Heaven Must Have Sent You, 781
Heaven or Las Vegas, 199
Heaven Up Here, 299
Heavenly, 651, 896
Heavenly Baby, 990
Heavy, 473
Heavy Duty Festival, 303
Heavy Fuel, 267
Heavy Heavy Hits, The, 630
Heavy Horses, 499
Heavy Music, 882
Heavy Nova, 751
Heavy Soul, 1044

Heavy Weather, 1039
Hedgehog's Song, The, 470
Hedonism (Just Because It Feels Good), 909
Hee Haw, 168
Heebie Jeebies, 28
Heimatalos, 810
Heimweh, 810
Hejira, 679
Helen of Troy, 150
Heliocentric, 1045
Heliocentric Worlds of Sun Ra, 961
Hell Bent for Leather, 519
Hell Low, 270, 467
Hell of a Spell, 867
Hell Raiser, 964
Hell's Ditch, 781
Hellbilly Deluxe, 1048
Hello, 832, 941
Hello Again . . . Mary Lou, 433
Hello America, 254
Hello and Goodbye, 135
Hello Angel, 891
Hello Central Give Me Heaven, 425
Hello Dad, I'm in Jail, 1034
Hello Dolly, 29, 109
Hello! Hello! Who's Your Lady Friend, 1046
Hello How Are You, 298
Hello I Love You, 279
Hello I Must Be Going!, 205
Hello in There, 799
Hello It's Me, 859
Hello Little Girl, 65
Hello Mary Lou, 142, 711, 778
Hello Momma, 497
Hello Mudduh, Hello Fadduh!, 435
Hello Nasty, 65
Hello Spaceboy, 112
Hello (Turn Your Radio on), 886
Hello Vietnam, 415
Hello Walls, 712, 1086
Hello Woman, 531
Hello Young Lovers, 844
Help, 52, 66, 240, *548*, 612, 811, 998, *1044*
Help Is on Its Way, 590
Help Me, 520, 679, 1066
Help Me Girl, 70
Help Me Hold on, 994
Help Me Make It Through the Night, 452, 548, 555, 899, 910
Help Me Rhonda, 63, 836
Help Me Somebody, 337
Help Wanted, 180
Help Yourself, 576
Helpless, 1087
Helter Skelter, 905
Hemisphere, 861

Henderson Stomp, 439
Henry the Human Fly, 982
Henry's Dream, 169
Her Man, His Woman, 998
Her Town Too, 971
Here and Now, 178, 1020
Here Come the Warm Jets, 310
Here Comes My Baby, 784, 945
Here Comes Santa Claus, 38
Here Comes Shuggie, 748
Here Comes the Nice, 912
Here Comes the Night, 604, 694, 717, 783
Here Comes the Rain Again, 317
Here Comes the Sun, 67, 431
Here Comes Trouble, 46
Here I Am Broken-Hearted, 818
Here I Am (Come and Take Me), 402
Here I Go, 1001
Here I Go Again, 449, 783
Here I Sit, 722
Here in My Heart, 648
Here in the Real World, 479
Here Is Barbara Lynn, 607
Here It Comes Again, 823
Here It Is, 479
Here My Dear, 374
Here She Comes, 693
Here to Stay, 906
Here We Are Again, 616
Here We Go, 149
Here You Come Again, 638, 758
Here's a Quarter, Call Someone Who Cares, 994
Here's Some That Got Away, 1044
Here's the Man, 94
Here's to My Lady, 195
Here's to the Ladies, 77
Here's to the People, 851
Here's to the State of Mississippi, 733
Hereafter, The, 737
Hergest Ridge, 738
Heritage, 298, 310, 454
Herman and Minnie, 511
Herman Brood and his Wild Romance, 122
Hero, 157, 229
Hero in Your Own Hometown, 159
Heroes, *31*, *311*, *360*, *761*, 906
'Heroes', 111
Heroes and Friends, 512, 993
Heroes and Villains, 62, 755
Heroin, 468, 1018
Hersham Boys, The, 887
Hesitation Blues, 130
Hex Enduction Hour, 326
Hey, 469
Hey! Ba-Ba-Re-Bop, 419

Hey Baby, 613, 759
Hey! Bo Diddley, 263
Hey Bobby, 746
Hey Boy Hey Girl, 175
Hey Brother Pour the Wine, 883
Hey Deanie, 167
Hey Dixie, 401
Hey Elvira, 356
Hey Girl, 746, 912
Hey Girl Don't Bother Me, 925
Hey God, 102
Hey Good Looking, 194, 774, 1059
Hey Harmonica Man, 1076
Hey Jealous Lover, 904
Hey Joe, 134, 440, 600, 775, 810,
 916, 973, 1091
Hey Joe, Hey Moe, 54
Hey Jude, 15, 415, 731, 775
Hey Little Cobra, 929
Hey Little Girl, 795
Hey Little Rich Boy, 887
Hey Lord Don't Ask Me Ques-
 tions, 754
Hey Luciani, 327
Hey Mama, 129
Hey Man Smell My Finger, 194
Hey Manhattan!, 788
Hey Mister, Can't You See, 868
Hey Mr Christmas, 896
Hey Mr DJ, 615, 809
Hey Nineteen, 943
Hey Now Hey, 514
Hey Paula, 759
Hey Presto, 86
Hey Rock'n'Roll, 896
Hey Schoolgirl, 897
Hey Sheriff, 530
Hey Stoopid, 215
Hey That's No Way to Say Good-
 bye, 338
Hey There, 195, 249
Hey Western Union Man, 144
Hey, Where's Your Brother?, 1071
(Hey Won't You Play) Another
 Somebody Done Somebody
 Wrong Song, 980
Hey World, 644
Hi!, 435
Hi De Ho, 97
Hi Diddle Diddle, 352
Hi Heel Sneakers, 212, 332, 1076
Hi Hi Hazel, 261
Hi Hi Hi, 611
Hi Ho Silver Lining, 70
Hi Infidelity, 827
Hi Lili Hi Lo, 793
Hi-Bop Ska, 908
Hickory Wind, 147, 239, 756, 757
Hidariuendo, 868
Hidden Charms, 269
Hidden Treasures, 637, 659
Hide and Seek, 513

Hide Nor Hair, 655
Hide Your Heart, 1002
Hideaway, *190*, 541
Hidin', 570
Hi-Fi, 489
High and Dry, 811
High and Lonesome, 823
High and Mighty Hawk, The, 431
High and the Mighty, The, 985,
 1089
High Blood Pressure, 915
High Civilization, 71
High Class Baby, 831
High Coin, 259, 755
High Cost of Living, *635*, 668
High Country Snows, 343
High Crime, 492
High Hat, 236
High Hopes, 150, 1012
High Horse, 724
High Land, Hard Rain, 41
High Life, 990
High Lonesome, 993, 1073
High Lonesome Sound, 383, 715
High Mileage, 479
High 'n' Dry, 254
High Noon, 560, 836, 985
High on Emotion, 251
High on the Happy Side, 1047
High on the Hog, 53, 88
High on You, 954
High Priest, 113
High Priest of Harmful Matter,
 252
High School Confidential, 325
High School Dance, 176
High School USA, 103
High Society, 296, 697, 1038
High Stakes and Desperate Men,
 1006
High Tech Redneck, 512
High Time, *635*, 656
High Voltage, 4
High Wire, 476
Higher and Higher, 214, 438, 987
Higher Ground, *258*, 820, *1080*
Higher Love, 532, 1073
Higher Power, 49, 191
Higher the Mountain, The, 189
Highlights, The, 889
Highlights from the Main Event,
 721
Highway 49, 1057
Highway Is for Heroes, The, 1090
Highway Patrolman, 166
Highway 60, 1038
Highway 61 Revisited, 97, 292, 551,
 1071
Highway Song, 608
Highway to Hell, 4
Highwayman, *166*, 497, 555, *683*,
 713, 1041

Highwayman 2, 497
Highwayman II, 555, 683, 713
Highways and Heartaches, 907
Hi-Ho Silver Lining, 698
Hill Billie Blues, 629
Hill Country Rain, 1027
Hillbilly Boogie, 257
Hillbilly Deluxe, 1085
Hillbilly Jazz, Vols 1 and 2, 122
Hillybilly Bebop, 765
Hilversum Session, The, 41
Him or Me – What's It Gonna
 Be?, 829
Hines Plays Duke Ellington, 446
Hip Hip Hooray, 995
Hip Hug Her, 106
Hip to Be Square, 580
Hippie Dream, *1088*
Hippy Gumbo, 101
Hippy Hippy Shake, 364, 964,
 965, *965*, 1010
Hips and Makers, 984
Hi-Res, 309
His and Hers, 805
His Band and Street Choir, 694
His Excellency Is Dead, 523
His Latest Flame, 783, 789
His Master's Choice, 982
Hissing of Summer Lawns, The,
 679
Historic Reunion, 162
History, 1020, 1024
History Mix Volume I, The, 976
History Mystery and Prophecy,
 767
History of an Artist, The, 769
History of the Grateful Dead, 400
HIStory: Past, Present and Future,
 482
History Repeating, 60
Hit and Miss, 57
Hit List, 500
Hit Man, 970
Hit Me with Your Best Shot, 76
Hit Me with Your Rhythm Stick,
 290
Hit that Perfect Beat, 208
Hit the Road Jack, 85, 171, 174,
 298, 655
Hit the Road to Dreamland, 663,
 787
Hit to Death in the Future Head,
 339
Hitch Hike, 374, 645
Hitchin' a Ride, 402
Hi-Tech/No Crime, 868
Hitomi, 322
Hits, 123, 205, 679
Hits & More, The, 978
Hits of Sunshine, 921
Hits of The Beatles, 724
Hits of the Sixties, 608

Hits/The B-Sides, The, 798
Hits Unlimited, 1001
Hittin' the Bottle, 184
HMS Donovan, 278
HO, 413
Hobnailed Boots That Farver Used to Wear, The, 1046
Hobo Blues, 452
Hobo Flats, 916
Hobo Joe, 354
Hobo's Lullaby, 408
Hocus Pocus, 1020
Hog Calling Blues, 544
Hoist, 773
Hokey Cokey, The, 528
Hokey Pokey, 982
Hokoyo, 640
Hold Back the Night, 754
Hold It, 273
Hold It Now Hit It, 65
Hold Me, *117*, *342*, *522*, *746*, *764*, 800
Hold Me Baby, 669
Hold Me Close, 314
Hold Me in Your Arms, 951
Hold Me Now, 981
Hold Me, Thrill Me, Kiss Me, 315, 1004
Hold Me Tight, 708
Hold Me till the Mornin' Comes, 24
Hold My Hand, 217, 453
Hold on, 64, 362, 603, 623, 825, 871, 1089
Hold on I'm Comin', 217, 333, 434, 869
Hold on to Love, 908
Hold Out, 132
Hold the Line, 989
Hold What You've Got, 415, 978
Hold Your Fire, 861
Hold Your Hand Out, Naughty Boy, 345
Hold Your Head Up, 1093
Holding Back the River, 1047
Holding Back the Years, 902
Holding My Own, 908
Holding on with Both Hands, 649
Holding out for a Hero, 1002
Hole, The, 387
Hole Hearted, 321
Hole in My Shoe, 1072
Hole in the Bucket, 735
Hole in the Ground, 647
Holiday, 631
Holiday for Strings, 515, 854
Holiday for Trombones, 854
Holiday in Cambodia, 252
Holidays in Eden, 642
Holidays in the Sun, 884
Holland, 63
Holler, 931

Holliedaze, 450
Hollies Sing Buddy Holly, The, 450
Hollies Sing Dylan, 450
Hollis Brown, 292
Holly Days, 612
Holly in the Hills, 450
Holly Jolly Christmas, A, 642
Hollywood and Broadway, 192
Hollywood Be Thy Name, 272
Hollywood Musicals, The, 634, 652
Hollywood Squares, 955
Hollywood Swinging, 550
Hollywood Town Hall, 493
Holy Bible, The, 636
Holy Cow, 281, 990
Holy Night, 172
Holy One, 332
Holy Smoke, 474
Holy Water, 46
Holy Wood (In the Shadow of the Valley of Death), 638
Homage, 635
Homage to Duke, 405
Homage to the Queen, 30
Homburg, 800
Home, 929
Home Again, 204, 1037
Home and Abroad, 1044
Home and Dry, 812
Home Before Dawn, 204
Home Call, 845
Home for Christmas, 398
Home Free, 342
Home in San Antonio, 855
Home Invasion, 467
Home Is Where the Heart Is, 167
Home Is Where the Music Is, 649
Home Lovin' Man, 403, 610
Home Movies, 321
Home of the Brave, 22
Home of the Brave, 638, 989
Home on Old Lonesome Road, 1000
Home on the Range, 606
Home Plate, 814
Home Town, 528
Home Town Girl, 159
Home Where I Belong, 980
Homebase, 917
Homebrew, 178
Homegrown, 416
Homeland, 633
Homeless Brother, 625
Homely Girl, 180
Homenaje a Benny More, 235
Hometown Honeymoon, 12
Homeward Bound, 897
Homework, *239*, *376*, *861*, *862*
Homme à la Moto, L', 774
Hommy, 235
Homogenic, 86

Homosapien, 145
Honaloochie Boogie, 700
Honest I Do, 823
Honestly and Truly, 855
Honey, 157, 389, *751*
Honey Baby, 526
Honey Bee, 375
Honey Bop, 482
Honey Boy, 1023
Honey Chile, 645
Honey Come Back, 1040
Honey Don't, 766
Honey Hush, 201, 998
Honey I Need, 792
Honey Love, 285, 625
Honey Suckle Rose, 1029
Honey Wheat and Laughter, 705
Honey-Drippin' Blues, 754
Honey's Dead, 498
Honeycomb, 460, 664, 1056
Honeydripper, The, 584
Honeymoon Hotel, 786
Honeysuckle Rose, 439, 1029
Hong Kong Blues, 158, 561
Hong Kong Garden, 905
Hong Kong Mambo, 804
Honky Chateau, 503
Honky Tonk, *10*, *126*, *273*, *521*, *536*, 708
Honky Tonk Amnesia, *54*, *54*
Honky Tonk Angels, 607, 758, 1080
Honky Tonk Blues, 261
Honky Tonk Christmas, 479
Honky Tonk Demos, The, 267
Honky Tonk Girl: The Collection, 607
Honky Tonk Hardwood Floor, 456
Honky Tonk Heroes, 496
Honky Tonk Man, 456, 1085
Honky Tonk Masquerade, 309
Honky Tonk Queen, 54
Honky Tonk '65, 628
Honky Tonk Train Blues, 231, 309, 582, 599
Honky Tonk Woman, 416, 502
Honky Tonk Women, 849
Honky Tonk Years, The, 794
Honky Tonkin', 737, 792, 1059, 1060
Honky's Ladder, 10
Honolulu Lulu, 490
Honour Thy Father and Mother, 255
Honour Your Father, 549
Hoochie Coochie Man, 82, 266, 1036, 1037
Hoodoo, 703
Hoodoo Hoodoo, 1066
Hoodoo Man, 1045
Hoodoo Man Blues, 1045

Hooked, 168
Hooked on a Feeling, 980
Hooker 'n' Heat, 452
Hoople, The, 700
Hooray for Captain Spaulding, 523
Hooray for Hazel, 846
Hooray for Hollywood, 663, 1052
Hooray for Love, 839
Hooray Hooray, 104
Hootenanny in London, 164
Hootie Blues, 627, 753
Hoots Mon, 348
Hooverville, 184
Hop Around, 815
Hope, 650, 738
Hope and Glory, 350, 841
Hopelessly Devoted to You, 721
Hoppy, Gene and Me, 848
Horace Silver and the Jazz Messengers, 93
Horizons, 138
Hormonally Yours, 886
Horse Latitudes, 279
Horse with No Name, A, 18
Horses, 151, 916, 973
Horses and Trees, 133, 225, 565
Hospital, 832
Hospital (Big Cat), 760
Hostage, 960
Hot, 931
Hot and Sweet, 669
Hot Animal Machine, 850
Hot August Night, 262
Hot August Night II, 262
Hot Blast, 614
Hot Blood, 221, 1062
Hot Blooded, 345
Hot Burrito W1, 756
Hot Burrito W2, 756
Hot Buttered Soul, 434
Hot Cha, 1028
Hot Charity, 842
Hot Child in the City, 183
Hot Chili Mama, 176
Hot, Cool & Vicious, 869
Hot Diggidy Doug, 531
Hot Diggity (Dog Ziggity Boom), 209
Hot Dog, 749, 946, 1085
Hot Dog Buddy Buddy, 412
Hot Feet, 447
Hot Fun in the Summertime, 954
Hot Hot Hot, 31, 718
Hot House, 456
Hot House Flowers, 645
Hot in the City, 467
Hot in the Shade, 546
Hot Legs, 950
Hot Lips, 143, 1049
Hot Love, 101, 314
Hot Nights, 350

Hot Pants (She Got to Use What She Got, to Get What She Wants), 128
Hot Potatoes, 92
Hot Property, 438
Hot Rats, 276, 1091
Hot Rod Lincoln, 103, 207
Hot Space, 808
Hot Spot, 392
Hot Stuff, 960
Hot Together, 781
Hot Water, 137, 579
Hotcakes, 898
Hotel California, 295, 295
Hotter Than July, 1077
Hottest New Group in Jazz, The, 561
Hound Dog, 574, 748, 772, 789, 980, 983
Hound Dog Man, 322
Hounds of Love, 143
Hourglass, 19, 936, 971
hours . . ., 110, 112
House at Pooh Corner, 596
House Carpenter, 1013
House Cleaning, 926
House of Blue Lights, 81, 221, 254, 691, 696
House of Cards, 159
House of Love, 398
House of the Rising Sun, 23, 46, 291, 308, 416, 698, 735, 1012
House Party, 107
House That Jack Built, 793
House Tornado, 984
House with Love in It, A, 608
Housecall, 795, 815
Houseparty New Orleans Style, 802
Houses of the Holy, 569
Housewives' Choice, 549, 692
Houston, 646
How About That, 325, 995
How Am I Supposed to Live Without You?, 102, 117
How Are Things in Glocca Morra?, 423, 595
How Blue, 618
How Blue Can You Get, 969
How Can a Poor Man Stand Such Times and Live, 212
How Can I Be Sure?, 167, 816
How Can I Love You More?, 610
How Can I Miss You When You Won't Go Away, 445
How Can I Unlove You?, 22
How Can We Be Lovers, 102, 1031
How Can We Ease the Pain, 795
How Can You Mend a Broken Heart?, 71
How Come You Do Me Like You Do?, 38

How Could You Believe Me When I Said I Loved You, When You Know I've Been a Liar All My Life, 35
How Deep Is the Ocean, 572
How Deep Is Your Love?, 71, 1013, 1064
How Do I Make You, 854
How Do You Do It?, 379, 379, 647, 706
How Do You Sleep, 576
How Do You Stop, 679
How Do You Take Your Love, 812
(How Does It Feel to Be) On Top of the World, 299
How Fast Forever Goes, 887
How Great Thou Art, 713, 922
How Hard It Is, 517
How High?, 173
How High the Moon, 336, 375, 381, 435, 556, 705, 759, 760
How High's the Watergate Martha?, 199
How How, 1084
How I Got Over, 480, 963, 1030
How I Quit Smoking, 560
How I Spent My Vacation, 865
How I Wrote Elastic Man, 326
How Insensitive, 501
How Late'll Ya Play 'Til?, 122
How Little We Know, 158, 663
How Live Is, 438
How Long, 35, 267, 603, 913, 936
How Long (Betcha Got a Chick on the Side), 781
How Long Blues, 1063, 1082
How Long, How Long Blues, 160
How Many Tears, 1017
How Many Tears Can You Hide?, 947
How Many Times Can We Say Goodbye, 1013
How Men Are, 42, 438
How Mountain Girls Can Love, 937
How Much Is That Doggie in the Window?, 437, 664
How Much Love, 873
How Sweet It Is, 121, 971
How Sweet It Is to Be Loved by You, 449, 1028
How the Heart Approaches What It Yearns, 900
How the Hell Do You Spell Rhythm?, 18
How to Be a Zillionaire, 2
How to Win an Election, 393
How Was it for You?, 485
How Will I Know, 458, 1026
How Will the Wolf Survive?, 594
How Ya Gonna Keep 'Em Down on the Farm, 276

How Ya' Like Me Now, 551, 835
How'd You Like to Spoon with Me, 529
How'm I Doin'?, 822
How's Tricks, 133
Howard and David, 75
Howard Hewitt, 887
Howlin' Wind, 754
Howlin' Wolf, 459
Howlin' Wolf Album, The, 459
Howling Wind, 603
Hoy Hoy, 588
HQ, 424
Hubba-Hubba-Hubba, A, 209
Hubble Bubble Toil and Trouble, 635
Huckleberry Duck, 876
Huckleback, The, 48, 536
Hula Love, 450, 770
Hulet, 35
Hully Gully Baby, 282
Hully Gully Guitars, 822
Human, 461, 484
Human Ball, 615
Human Behaviour, 86
Human Being, 717, 718
Human Butt, 850
Human Nature, 19
Human Racing, 531
Human Soul, 754
Human Touch, 935
Human's Wheels, 661
Human's Lib, 513
Humble Pie, 912
Humblebums, 811
Humeresque, 597
Hummingbird, 538, 838
Humour Me, 1071
Hump, The, 1008
Humpin' Around, 125
Humpty Dumpty, 327, 798
Humpty Dumpty Heart, 981
Hums, 602
Hundred Mile High City, 732
Hundred Pounds of Clay, A, 616, 894
Hundred Years from Today, A, 972
Hundreds and Thousands, 208
Hung Up, 1044
Hunger, 102, 466
Hungry, 638, 829
Hungry Again, 757, 758
Hungry Eyes, 410, 411, 817
Hungry for Love, 534
Hungry Heart, 879, 934, 999
Hungry Like the Wolf, 289
Hunkpa, 984
Hunky Dory, 110, 1025
Hunter, 86, *96*, *998*, *1031*
Hunter Gets Captured by the Game, The, 649, 841

Hunting High and Low, 11
Hunting of the Snark, The, 60
Hurdy Gurdy Man, 277
Hurricane, 293
Hurricane Hattie, 193, 549
Hurricane #1, 834
Hurry on Down, 605
Hurry up Harry, 887
Hurry Up This Way Again, 958
Hurt, 417
Hurt by Love, 352
Hurt So Bad, 578, 587
Hurt So Good, 767, 951
Hurting, The, 972
Hurts So Good, 482, 660
Husbands and Wives, 673
Hush, 253, 556, 925, *978*
Hush 'n' Thunder, 566
Hush Hush, Sweet Charlotte, 751
Hush-a-Bye, 529
Hustle, The, 615
Hyden, 415
Hydra, 989
Hyena, 905
Hymn, 1006
Hymn to Her, 791
Hymns to the Silence, 695
Hyperactive, 273
Hyperreal, 888
Hypnotised, 890
Hypnotize, 805
Hypocrite, 643
Hysteria, 254, 461

I, 217
I Advance Masked, 360, 782
I Ain't Going Honky Tonkin' Anymore, 996
(I Ain't Gonna Play) Sun City, 49
I Ain't Got No Home, 407
I Ain't Got Nobody, 914
I Ain't Got You, 1066
I Ain't Marchin' Anymore, 733
I Almost Lost My Mind, 107, 462
I Am a Rock, 897
I Am a Town, 159
I Am Cold, 178
I Am . . . I Said, 262
I Am in Love, 987
I Am Love, 478
I Am Not Afraid, 649
I Am Only Human After All, 287
I Am Stretched on Your Grave, 733
I Am the Black Gold of the Sun, 651
I Am the Blues, 269
I Am the Law, 25
I Am the Living, 193
I Am the Mob, 168
I Am the Resurrection, 952
I Am the Walrus, 306

I Am What I Am, 376, *582*, 1065
I Am Woman, 394, 821, 893
I Apologize, 300, 800
I Believe, 6, 560, 886
I Believe I Can Fly, 528
I Believe in Father Christmas, 309
I Believe in Jesus, 960
I Believe in Music, 247
I Believe in You, 403, 971, 1058
I Believe My Own Eyes, 1055
I Believe My Time Ain't Long, 486
I Believe the South Is Gonna Rise Again, 389
I Believe You, 734
I Belong to You, 1048
I Bet He Don't Love You, 472
I Blame the Government, 163
I Blow Minds for a Living, 252
I Call It Pretty Music, 1076
I Call Your Name, 633
I Can Dream, 909
I Can Dream about You, 1071
I Can Dream, Can't I?, 23, 323, 496
I Can Hear Music, 63, 807, 853
I Can Hear the Grass Grow, 702
I Can Help, 963, *963*
I Can Make It with You, 970, 1058
I Can Never Go Home Any More, 697, 888
I Can Only Disappoint U, 639
I Can Only Give You Everything, 995
I Can Put My Trust in Jesus, 480
I Can See Clearly Now, 174, 193, 643, 708, *708*
I Can See for Miles, 1054
I Can See Your House from Here, 666
I Can Sing a Rainbow, 256
I Can Still Make Cheyenne, 955
I Can Take or Leave Your Loving, 610
I Can Tell, 534
I Can Understand It, 363
I Can Wait, 297
I Can't Be Satisfied, 1036
I Can't Believe What You Say, 998
I Can't Believe You've Stopped Loving Me, 795
I Can't Control Myself, 995
I Can't Even Get the Blues, 618
I Can't Explain, 1054
I Can't Get Next to You, 402, 975
(I Can't Get No) Satisfaction, 849
I Can't Get No Sleep, 651
I Can't Get Started without You, 287, 288
I Can't Give You Anything but Love, 28, 334, 621

I Can't Go for That (No Can Do), 413
I Can't Go on Living without You, 502
I Can't Hear a Word You Say, 131
I Can't Hear You, 319
I Can't Help It, 52, 721
I Can't Help Myself, 350, 449, 781
(I Can't Help You) I'm Fallin' Too, 249, 595
I Can't Keep from Crying, 551
I Can't Let Go, 449, 970
I Can't Live without Your Love, 1076
I Can't Make You Love Me, 814
I Can't Quit Her, 96
I Can't Quit You Baby, 269, 861, 862
I Can't Stand It, 187, 1072
I Can't Stand It No More, 352
I Can't Stand Still, 296
I Can't Stand the Rain, 680, 762, 998
I Can't Stand up for Falling Down, 219
I Can't Stay Away, 976
I Can't Stay Mad at You, 249
I Can't Stop Loving You, 174, 381, 382, 1045
I Can't Stop Talking About It, 567
I Can't Tell a Waltz from a Tango, 199
I Can't Tell the Bottom from the Top, 450
I Can't Turn You Loose, 821
I Caught Your Act, 460
I Confess, 24
I Could Be Persuaded, 75
I Could Have Danced All Night, 539, 578
I Could Never Miss You (More Than I Do), 604
(I Could Only) Whisper Your Name, 210
I Could Write a Book, 527
I Couldn't Get High, 361
I Couldn't Live Without Your Love, 189, 430
I Couldn't Sleep a Wink Last Night, 622
I Count the Tears, 783
I Cover the Waterfront, 448
I Cried a Tear, 50
I Cried for You, 359, 448
I Cried My Last Tear, 526
I Cried My Last Tear Last Night, 938
I Crossed My Fingers, 325
I Cry I Smile, 1026
I Did What I Did for Maria, 707
I Didn't Mean to Turn You on, 751

I Didn't See It Coming, 885
I Didn't Sleep a Wink Last Night, 802
I Didn't Want to Need You, 436
I Die You Die, 727
I Dig Rock'n'Roll Music, 768
I Do, 376, 479, 595, 785
I Do Love You, 303
I Do Not Play No Rock'n'Roll, 618
I Do Not Want What I Haven't Got, 733
I Don't Believe in If Anymore, 1053
I Don't Believe in Miracles, 1093
I Don't Believe You've Met My Baby, 599
I Don't Care, 776, 1024
I Don't Have to Ride No More, 817
I Don't Hurt Anymore, 838, 918
I Don't Know, 179, 619
I Don't Know About Love (The Moon Song), 1000
I Don't Know Anybody Else, 87
I Don't Know How to Love Him, 593, 821
I Don't Know What You've Got (But It's Got Me), 221
I Don't Know Where I Stand, 678
I Don't Know Why, 206
I Don't Know Why You Don't Want Me, 166
I Don't Like Mondays, 298, 376
I Don't Like the Drugs (But the Drugs Like Me), 638
I Don't Love You Anymore, 600, 764
I Don't Love You but I Think I Like You, 747
I Don't Mind, 127
I Don't Mind If I Do, 1067
I Don't Need It to Rain, 136
I Don't Need You, 847
I Don't Sleep, I Dream, 827
I Don't Stand a Ghost of a Chance, 1089
I Don't Wanna Cry, 157, 1026
I Don't Wanna Dance, 398
I Don't Wanna Fight, 604, 698
I Don't Wanna Get Hurt, 961
I Don't Wanna Live without Your Love, 181
I Don't Wanna Lose You, 999
I Don't Wanna Miss a Thing, 10
I Don't Wanna Play House, 893, 1080
I Don't Want a Lover, 978
I Don't Want Nobody, 505
I Don't Want Our Loving to Die, 245
I Don't Want to Be a Lone Ranger, 1038

I Don't Want to Be a One Night Stand, 618
I Don't Want to Be Alone, Stranger, 1038
I Don't Want to Cry, 257
I Don't Want to Go Home, 853
I Don't Want to Go on Without You, 503, 689
I Don't Want to Go to Chelsea, 219
I Don't Want to Have to Marry You, 132
I Don't Want to Live Without You, 345
I Don't Want to Miss a Thing, 1032
I Don't Want to Spoil the Party, 167
I Don't Want to Talk About It, 320
I Don't Want to Wake up Feeling Guilty, 74
I Don't Want to Walk Without You, 958
I Don't Want to Walk without You Baby, 595
I Don't Want Your Love, 289
I Dream of You, 282
I Dreamed of a Hillbilly Heaven, 836
I Drove All Night, 567, 741
I Eat with Gusto, Damn! You Bet, 833
I Fall in Love too Easily, 150
I Fall to Pieces, 193, 458
I Feel a Cry Coming on, 595
I Feel a Song Coming on, 334, 621
I Feel Alright, 297
I Feel Fine, 66
I Feel for You, 532, 641, 798
I Feel Free, 111, 225
I Feel Good, 895
I Feel Like Buddy Holly, 60
I Feel Love, 17, 208, 693, 960
I Feel Love Coming on, 1048
I Feel Lucky, 159
I Feel Pretty, 81, 589
I Feel Right, 997
I Feel So Bad, 1067
I Feel So Different, 733
I Feel So Good, 791
I Fell in Love, 163
I Forgot More Than You'll Ever Know, 249
I Forgot to Be Your Lover, 74, 468
I Forgot to Remember to Forget, 331
I Fought the Law, 1061
I Found a Cure, 32
I Found a Love, 736, 775
I Found a Million Dollar Baby (In a Five-and-Ten Cent Store), 1031, 1032

I Found Love, 622
I Found Somebody, 296
I Found Someone, 177
I Get a Kick out of You, 784
I Get a Little Sentimental Over You, 610, 882
I Get Along without You Very Well, 898
I Get Around, 63, 1001
I Get Ideas, 648
I Get Joy, 403
I Get Lonely, 479
I Get the Sweetest Feeling, 615, 1069
I Get Weak, 157, 1032
I Give You My Word, 286
I Go Ape, 880
I Go Shout Plenty, 557
I Go to Extremes, 502
I Go to Sleep, 791
I Got a Break, Baby, 1028
I Got a Guy, 1040
I Got a Line on You, 932
I Got a Name, 228
I Got a Right to Sing the Blues, 26
I Got a Woman, 174, 620, 789
I Got Dem Old Kozmic Blues Again, Mama!, 517
I Got Love, 812
I Got My Mind Made Up, 579
I Got Next, 106
I Got Plenty o' Nuttin', 380
I Got Rhythm, 664, 883
I Got the Music in Me, 503
I Got the Sun in the Morning, 79, 987
I Got to Love Somebody's Baby, 971
I Got to Tell Somebody, 319
I Got You Babe, 176, 326, 791, 1005
I Got You (I Feel Good), 128
I Gotcha, 978
I Gotta Go Get My Baby, 120
I Guess I'll Have to Change My Plan, 874
I Guess I'll Have to Telegraph My Baby, 200, 203, 930
I Guess That's Why They Call It the Blues, 503
I Guess the Lord Must Be in New York City, 722
I Had a Dream, 434
I Had a Dream I Was Falling through a Hole in the Ozone Layer, 253
I Had the Craziest Dream, 487
I Had Too Much to Dream Last Night, 305
I Hadn't Anyone Till You, 15
I Hang My Head and Cry, 39

I Hate the White Man, 424
I Hate to Sing, 95
I Hate You, 675
I Have a Boyfriend, 182
I Have a Dream, 1
I Have But One Heart, 241
I Have Dreamed, 685
I Have Learned to Do Without You, 938
I Have Returned, 946
I Haven't Got a Pot to Cook in, 688
I Hear a Rhapsody, 391
I Hear a Symphony, 962
I Hear Rhapsody, 891
I Hear Talk, 136, *136*
I Hear You Knockin', 977
I Hear You Knocking, 58, 107, 301, 583, 614, 915, 1016
I Hear You Now, 1014
I Hear You Rockin', 302
I Hear Your People Singing, 286
I Heard a Rumour, 52, 951
I Heard It Through the Grapevine, 226, 374, 548, 1051
I Heard My Mother Weeping, 735
I Heard That, 514
I Heard the Bells on Christmas Day, 642
I Honestly Love You, 721
I Hope You're Sitting Down/Jack's Tulips, 560
I Idolize You, 997
I, Jonathan, 833
I Just Called to Say, 1076
I Just Called to Say I Love You, 1077
I Just Can't Help Believing, 638, 980
I Just Can't Make My Eyes Behave, 511
I Just Can't Stop Loving You, 481
I Just Don't Have the Heart, 951
I Just Don't Know What to Do with Myself, 45, 933
I Just Fall in Love Again, 705
I Just Heard a Heartbreak, 1080
I Just Keep Loving Her, 1066
I Just Started Hatin' Cheatin' Songs Today, 54
I Just Wanna Be Your Girl, 49
I Just Want to Be, 152
I Just Want to Be Wanted, 571
I Just Want to Be Your Everything, 71
I Just Want to Celebrate, 1051
I Just Want to Make Love to You, 343
I Just Wanted to See You So Bad, 1062
I Just Wasn't Made for These Times, 63, *1034*

I Keep Forgettin', 257
I Keep Forgettin' (Every Time You're Near), 279
I Keep Wanting You, 259
I Knew It All the Time, 187
I Knew the Bride, 302
I Knew You Were Waiting, 355, 666, 1026
I Know, 705, 926
I Know a Heartache When I See One, 1031
I Know a Place, 189, 430
I Know an Old Lady (Who Swallowed a Fly), 477
I Know Darn Well I Can Do without Broadway (But Can Broadway Do without Me?), 289
I Know Him So Well, 89, 593
I Know (I'm Losing You), 949, 974
I Know It's Going to Happen Someday, 111
I Know One, 123
I Know What Boys Like, 973
I Know What I Like, 377
I Know What I'm Here for, 485
I Know Where I'm Going, 204, 417
I Know Where It's At, 14
I Know You Got Soul, 330
I Know You Love Me Not, 37
I Know You're out There Somewhere, 689
I Left My Heart in San Francisco, 77, 105, 490
I Left My Sugar Standing in the Rain, 323
I Left My Wallet in El Segundo, 994
I Lie, 607
I Like It, 379, 706
I Like It Like That, 188, 990
I Like My Baby's Pudding, 426
I Like the Likes of You, 422
I Like Your Kind of Love, 1056
I Like Your Style, 457
I Look to Heaven, 647
I Looked down the Line (and I Wondered), 978
I Love a Lassie, 566
I Love a Piano, 706
I Love Dixie Blues, 411
I Love Everybody, 602
I Love Her, 707
I Love How You Love Me, 638, 929, 1023
I Love L.A., 720
I Love Men, 547
I Love Music, *100*, 736
I Love My Dog, 945
I Love My Fruit, 688

I Love Paris, 573, 785
I Love Rock'n'Roll, *499*, 693
I Love the Life I Live, 15, *15*
I Love the Night Life, 651
I Love the Sound of Breaking Glass, 603
I Love the Way You Love, 394, 508
I Love to Boogie, 101
I Love to Love, 651
I Love You, 831, 1084
I Love You a Thousand Ways, 360
I Love You Avenue, 443
I Love You Baby, 357
I Love You Because, 648, 825
I Love You Both, 1023
I Love You (for Sentimental Reasons), 201, 389
I Love You More and More Each Day, 838
I Love You More and More Every Day, 648
I Love You 1000 Times, 780
I Love You Porgy, 900
I Love You Ringo, 176
I Love You Samantha, 785
I Love You So, 171, 573
I Love You So Much, 523
I Love You So Much It Hurts, 984
I Love You the Way You Are, 1022
I Loved You Yesterday, 602
I Loves You Porgy, 380
I May Be Crazy, 957
I May Be Poor But I'm Honest, 211
I Met Her in Church, 113
I Met Him on a Sunday, 728, 894
I Might, 947
I Might as Well Be Miserable with You, 874
I Miss You, 764
I Miss You Baby, 508
I Miss You So, 587
I Missed Again, 205
I Need a Beat, 858
I Need a Lover, 76, 660
I Need a Man, 317, 512
I Need It, 1038
I Need Somebody, 809
I Need Someone, 445
I Need to Know, 771
I Need You, 257, 603, 781
I Need You Baby, 82
I Need You Now, 336
I Need You So, 462, 1072
I Need Your Lovin', 417, 1000
I Never Cry, 215
I Never Loved a Man the Way That I Love You, 355, 1047

I Never Saw a Better Night, 662
I Only Get the Feeling, 257
I Only Have Eyes for You, 339, 527, 578, 786, 883, 898, 1032
I Only Want to Be with You, 62, 317, 933
I Only Wanted You, 747
I Outgrew the Wagon Train, 465
I Owe You One, 886
I Pity the Fool, 94, *94*
I Pity the Poor Immigrant, 292
I Pray for You, 692
I Pretend, 1053
I Promise to Remember, 606
I Pronounce You, 630
I Put a Spell on You, 124, 226, 433, 793, 850, 900
I Read It in Rolling Stone, 970
I Really Didn't Mean It, 1013
I Really Do, 929
I Really Don't Want to Know, 138, 303, 838
I Recall a Gypsy Woman, 1059
I Received a Letter, 1082
I Remember, 631
I Remember Blind Joe Death, 322
I Remember Buddy Holly, 451, 1017
I Remember Duke, Hoagy & Strayhorn, 485
I Remember Hank Williams, 875
I Remember It Well, 578
I Remember Tommy, 282, 904
I Remember Yesterday, 960
I Remember You, 280, 468, 663, 873
I Robot, 756
I Saw Elvis in a UFO, 946
I Saw Her Again, 633
I Saw Her Standing There, 66
I Saw It on TV, 226
I Saw Mommy Doing the Mambo, 787
I Saw Mommy Kissing Santa Claus, 211, 220, 515, 560, 787
I Saw the Light, 520, *686*, 859, 1059
I Saw Three Ships a Sailing, 182
I Say a Little Prayer, 45, 355, 1033
I Say, I Say, I Say, 312
I Scare Myself, 273, 445
I Second That Emotion, 491, 840, 841
I See a Darkness, 739
I Shall Be Released, 53, 292, 784, 816, 983
I Shot the Sheriff, 187, 643
I Should Be So Lucky, 677, 951
I Should Coco, 961
I Should Have Known Better, 368
I Should've Never Let You Go, 880
I Shoulda Lovedyah, 1026

I Sing the Body Electric, 1039
I Sold My Heart to the Junkman, 558
I Spent a Week There the Other Night, 1018
I Spy, 805
I Spy for the FBI, 471
I Stand Alone, 551
I Started a Joke, 369, 431
I Still Believe in You, 383
I Still Carry You Around, 297
I Still Get a Thrill, 711
I Still Get Jealous, 626, 958
I Still Have Dreams, 137
I Still Haven't Found What I'm Looking for, 1004
I Sucked My Boss's Dick, 560
I Surrender Dear, 683
I Survived, 325
I T Splash, 1083
I Take It Back, 786
I Take It on Home, 830
I Talk to the Trees, 578
I Tell Stories Sad and True, I Sing the Blues and Play Harmonica Too, It Is Very Funky, 755
I Thank You, 869, 1094
I Think, 60
I Think I Love You, 167
I Think I'm in Love, 925
I Think I'm Paranoid, 371
I Think It's Going to Rain Today, 204, 719, 1005
I Think It's Love, 478
I Think the Answer's Yes, 68
I Think We're Alone Now, 489, 499
I Thought I Was a Child, 814
I Thought It Was You, 420
I Threw Away the Rose, 410
I Told You So, 514
I, Too, Have Seen the Woods, 533
I Took My Harp to a Party, 334, 373
I Turn the Page, 1059
I Understand, 357
I Ups to Him and He Ups to Me, 289
I Wah Dub, 109
I Waited Too Long, 50
I Wake Up Crying, 257
I Walk the Line, 165
I Wanna Be a Cowboy's Sweetheart, 687
I Wanna Be Around, 77
I Wanna Be Kate, 143
I Wanna be Loved By You, 523, 843
I Wanna Be Selfish, 32
I Wanna Be with You, 817
I Wanna Be Your Dog, 468
I Wanna Be Your Lover, 797

I Wanna Be Your Man, 848
I Wanna Dance With Somebody, 458, 1026
I Wanna Do It to You, 144
I Wanna Get Funky, 537
I Wanna Get Next to You, 1052
I Wanna Give You Some Love, 257
I Wanna Go Back, 882
I Wanna Hear It from Your Lips, 817
I Wanna Hold Your Hand, 66
I Wanna Love Him So Bad, 697
I Wanna Play for You, 190
I Wanna Play House with You, 30
I Wanna Roo You, 695
I Wanna Stay with You, 368
(I Wanna) Testify, 194
I Wanna Walk You Home, 275
I Want a Girl Just Like the Girl That Married Dear Old Dad, 1023
I Want a Guy, 962
I Want a New Drug, 581
I Want Candy, 615, 623, 784
I Want Ev'ry Bit of It, 914
I Want Her, 835
I Want It All, 808
I Want It Now, 152
I Want It That Way, 46
I Want More, 153
I Want My Roots, 603
I Want That Man, 96, 981
(I Want) The Real Thing, 772, 970
I Want to (Do Everything for You), 978
I Want to Be a Hippy, 288
I Want to Be Free, 991
I Want to Be Happy, 1086
I Want to Be Loved by You, 734
I Want to Be with You, 12
I Want to Be with You Always, 360
I Want to Break Free, 808
I Want to Go with You, 30
I Want to Hold Your Hand, 402
I Want to Know What Love Is, 345
I Want to See the Bright Lights Tonight, 982
I Want to Spend Christmas with Elvis, 545
I Want to Stay Here, 567
I Want to Take You Higher, 954
I Want You, 141, 292, *374*, 751, 775
I Want You Back, 52, 308, 478, 754, 931
I Want You to Be My Baby, 561
I Want You to Be My Girl, 606
I Want Your Love, 845

I Want Your Sex, 666
I Was Born to Love You, 808
I Was Checkin' Out, She Was Checkin' in, 221
I Was Dancing in the Lesbian Bar, 833
(I Was Drunk at the) Pulpit, 738
I Was in the House when the House Burned Down, 1093
I Was Kaiser Bill's Batman, 403
I Was Made for Lovin' You, 546
I Was Made to Love Her, 1077
I Was Such a Fool, 389
I Was Warned, 224
(I Washed My Hands) In Muddy Water, 836
I Wasn't Born in Tennessee, 970
I Went to a Marvellous Party, 222
I Went to Your Wedding, 515
I (Who Have Nothing), 363, 396, 516, 539, 940
I Will Always Love You, 383, 458, 758
I Will Come to You, 421
I Will Follow Him, 189, 460
I Will Get There, 114, 1032
I Will Survive, 375, 376
I Will Turn to You, 931
I Will Wait, 894
I Will Wait for You (If It Takes Forever), 573
I Wish, 1077
I Wish I Could Fly, 856
(I Wish I Had) Johnny's Cash and Charley's Pride, 192
I Wish It Could Be Christmas Everyday, 703
I Wish It Would Rain, 974
I Wish U Heaven, 798
I Wish You Would, 1066, 1083
I Wished on the Moon, 230
I Woke Up in Love This Morning, 167
I Won't Dance, 286, 334
I Won't Forget You, 781
I Won't Hold You Back, 989
I Won't Let the Sun Go Down on Me, 531
I Wonder, 166, 235, 370, 371
I Wonder How She Knows, 126
I Wonder Where My Baby Is Tonight?, 141, 706
I Wonder Where Our Love Has Gone, 802
I Wonder Where She Is Tonight, 284
I Wonder Where You Are Tonight, 103
I Wonder Who She's Seeing Now, 975
I Wonder Who's Kissing Her Now, 140

I Wonder Why, 265
I Would Die for U, 797
I Would Do Anything for Love (But I Won't Do That), 658
I Write the Songs, 64, 167, 637
I Yi Yi Yi Yi, 828
(I'd Be) A Legend in My Time, 382, 675
I'd Do It All Over Again, 375, 794
I'd Leave My Happy Home for You, 1023
I'd Like to Teach the World to Sing, *210*, 403, 881
I'd Love to Change the World, 977
I'd Love You All Over Again, 479
I'd Love You to Want Me, 756
I'd Never Find Another You, 364
I'd Rather Be an Old Man's Sweetheart (Than a Young Man's Fool), 940
I'd Rather Be Blind, Crippled and Crazy, 1079
I'd Rather Go Blind, 486, 949
I'd Rather Leave While I'm in Love, 214
I'd Really Love to See You Tonight, 455
I'll Always Come Back, 746
I'll Always Love My Mama, 472
I'll Always Love You, 646, 931
I'll Be Around, 931
I'll Be Doggone, 374
I'll Be Good to You, 124, 532
I'll Be Home, 107, 339, 719
I'll Be Missing You, 805
I'll Be Over You, 989
I'll Be Satisfied, 393, 947
I'll Be Seeing You, 323, 338, 892
I'll Be Sweeter Tomorrow, 736
I'll Be There, 157, 458, 478, 603
I'll Be Thinking of You, 232
I'll Be True, 744
I'll Be with You in Apple Blossom Time, 23, 1023
I'll Be Your Baby Tonight, 751, 1005
I'll Be Your Everything, 910
I'll Be Your Shelter (in Time of Storm), 471
I'll Bet You, 194
I'll Bring It Home to You, 980
I'll Build a Stairway to Paradise, 379
I'll Chase the Blues Away, 1040
I'll Come Back as Another Woman, 997
I'll Come Running Back to You, 213
I'll Cry for You, 316
I'll Cry Instead, 198
I'll Find It Where I Can, 582

I'll Find My Way Home, 1014, 1085
I'll Find You, 319
I'll Fly Away, 748
I'll Get By, 206, 435
I'll Get Over You, 375
I'll Go Crazy, 127
I'll Go on Alone, 837
I'll Go on Loving You, 479
I'll Have to Say I Love You in a Song, 228
I'll Hold You in My Heart, 29
I'll House You, 520, 977
I'll Keep Holding on, 649
I'll Kiss and Make Up, 783
I'll Make Believe, 836
I'll Make Love to You, 114
I'll Make the Living, If You Make the Loving Worthwhile, 171
I'll Meet You Halfway, 167
I'll Never Be Free, 344, 674, 939, 1034
I'll Never Fall in Love Again, 45, 378, 516, 1033
I'll Never Find Another You, 881
I'll Never Get Over You, 516, 534
I'll Never Love This Way Again, 1033
I'll Never See Sunshine Again, 735
I'll Never Smile Again, 282
I'll Pick a Rose for My Rose, 508
I'll Play the Blues for You, 537
I'll Sail My Ship Alone, 704, 864
I'll Say She Does, 259, 522
I'll See You in My Dreams, 302, 513, 522, 826
I'll Step Aside, 103
I'll Stick Around, 723
I'll String Along with You, 1032
I'll Take Care of You, 94
I'll Take You Home Again Kathleen, 594
I'll Take You There, 938
I'll Try Something New, 841
I'll Wake You Up When I Get Home, 830
I'll Walk Alone, 895, 916
I'm a Bear in a Ladies' Boudoir, 303
I'm a Believer, 262, 684, 1079
I'm a Better Man, 462
I'm a Big Girl Now, 525
I'm a Blues Man, 446
I'm a Boy, 1054
I'm a Country Boy, 608
I'm a Fool, 436, 646
I'm a Fool for You, 160
I'm a Fool to Care, 239, 658
I'm a Gambler, 588
I'm a Hog for You Baby, 196
I'm a Honky Tonk Girl, 607

I'm a Hurting Inside, 892
I'm a King Bee, 671, 823
I'm a Lonesome Fugitive, 22, 411
I'm a Lover Not a Fighter, 671
I'm a Man, 181, 263, 322, 783, 1072
I'm a Midnight Mover, 1076
I'm a Mighty Tight Woman, 1029
I'm a Rainbow, 961
I'm a Rattlesnakin' Daddy, 362
(I'm a) Roadrunner, 1028
I'm a Soldier, 337
(I'm a) Stand by My Woman Man, 675
I'm a Telling You, 144
I'm a Tiger, 604
I'm a Woman, 575, 704
I'm a Wonderful Thing, Baby, 533
I'm Alive, *132*, 449
I'm Alright, 596, *1024*
(I'm Always Hearing) Wedding Bells, 336
I'm an Old Cowhand, 445, 662, 663, 851
I'm Back and I'm Proud, 351, 1022
I'm Bad, 351
I'm Breathless, 631
I'm Coming Home, 74, 516, 823
I'm Coming Home Cindy, 598
I'm Coming Home Virginia, 230
I'm Coming Out, 855
I'm Confessin', 28
I'm Crazy 'Bout My Baby, 1029
I'm Crazy to Love You, 1015
I'm Crying, 23, 412
I'm Dead, 720
I'm Doin' Fine Now, 74, 329
I'm Down, 9
I'm Every Woman, 532
I'm Falling in Love with Someone, 441, 614
I'm Forever Blowing Bubbles, 882
I'm Free, 596, 1054
I'm Getting Sentimental Over You, 282
I'm Girl Scoutin', 472
I'm Going Back to Old Nebraska, 828
I'm Going Home, *873*, 977
I'm Going Home to Live with God, 1079
I'm Gone, 895
I'm Gonna Be a Country Girl Again, 868
I'm Gonna Be a Wheel Some Day, 275
I'm Gonna Be an Engineer, 614
I'm Gonna Be Somebody, 994
I'm Gonna Be Strong, 638
I'm Gonna Forget About You, 224
I'm Gonna Get Married, 794

I'm Gonna Get Me a Gun, 945
I'm Gonna Hire a Wino to Decorate our Home, 360
I'm Gonna Knock on Your Door, 746
I'm Gonna Learn to Swing, 969
I'm Gonna Leave, 271
I'm Gonna Let My Heart Do the Walking, 963
I'm Gonna Lock My Heart, 983
I'm Gonna Love My Life Away, 778
I'm Gonna Love That Guy, 437
I'm Gonna Love You Just a Little More Baby, 1048
I'm Gonna Make You Love Me, 963, 1033
I'm Gonna Make You Mine, 185
I'm Gonna See My Baby, 605
I'm Gonna Sit Right Down and Write Myself a Letter, 1029
I'm Gonna Step on You Again, 421
I'm Gonna Tear Your Playhouse Down, 754, 762, 1089
I'm Henry the Eighth, I, Am, 170, 442, 698, 1046
I'm Here, 176
I'm in a Dancing Mood, 18, 135
I'm in a Phone Booth, Baby, 537
I'm in Korea, 576
I'm in Love, 322, 781
I'm in Love Again, 58, 275, 558
I'm in the Mood, 452
I'm in the Mood for Love, 334, 608, 621, 814
I'm in You, 352
I'm into Something Good, 442, 540
I'm Jimmy the Well-Dressed Man, 289
I'm Just a Prisoner, 940
I'm just a Singer in a Rock and Roll Band, 689
I'm Just Wild about Harry, 92
I'm Leaving It All Up to You, 276, 332, 747
I'm Looking for the Man that Wrote the Merry Widow Waltz, 706
I'm Looking out the Window, 831
I'm Mad, 179
I'm Movin' on, 174, 918, 944
I'm Nature's Mosquito, 832
I'm Needing You, Wanting You, 257
I'm Never Gonna Change, 332
I'm No Angel, 16
I'm Not a Juvenile Delinquent, 606
I'm Not a Kid Anymore, 1071
I'm Not Ashamed, 94

I'm Not in Love, 791, 976
I'm Not Scared, 768
(I'm Not the) Revolution Kind, 177
I'm Old Fashioned, 530, 663
I'm on a Roll, 272
I'm on a See-Saw, 18
I'm on Fire, 934
I'm on My Way to Canaan, 480
I'm on the Outside (Looking in), 587
I'm Only Human After All, 422
I'm Out of Your Life, 32
I'm Paying for That Back Street Affair, 1045
I'm Praying to St Christopher, 892
I'm Putting All My Eggs in One Basket, 34
I'm Ready, 44, 269, 1037
I'm Ready for Love, 121
I'm Real, 128
I'm Restless, 1031
I'm Sending a Letter to Santa, 211
I'm Sitting on Top of the World, 233, 260
I'm So Afraid of Losing You, 795
I'm So Ashamed, 356, 393
I'm So Bored with the USA, 191
I'm So Excited, 781
I'm So Glad, 488
I'm So Lonely I Could Cry, 222
I'm So Lonesome I Could Cry, 658, 980
I'm So Proud, 470
I'm So Tired, 67
I'm Sorry, 258, 571
I'm Sticking with You, 770
I'm Still Here, 547
I'm Still in Love, 272
I'm Still in Love with You, 297, 402, 741
I'm Still Standing, 503
I'm Still Waiting, 776, 855
I'm Stone in Love with You, 958
I'm Telling the Birds, I'm Telling the Bees (How I Love You), 416
I'm Telling You Now, 357, 707
I'm the Face, 912, 1053
I'm the Greatest, 939
I'm the Leader of the Gang (I Am!), 386
I'm the Man, 25, 480
I'm the One (For Your Love Tonight), 40
I'm the Urban Spaceman, 105
I'm Thinking Tonight of My Blue Eyes, 162
I'm Tired Crying Over You, 505
I'm Tired of Getting Pushed Around, 335

I'm Tired of Singing My Songs in Las Vegas, 320
I'm Tore Up, 998
I'm Trusting in You, 855
I'm Waiting Just for You, 107, 674
I'm Walkin', 58, 275, 416, 711
I'm Walking Backwards for Christmas, 393
I'm Walking Behind You, 472, 1052, 1072
I'm Walking Beside You, 336, 1051
I'm Walking to New Orleans, 173
I'm with You, 613
I'm Your Baby Tonight, 44, 458
I'm Your Boogie Man, 526
I'm Your Fan, 201
(I'm Your) Hoochie Coochie Man, 269
I'm Your Man, 201, 666, 1031
I'm Your Puppet, 764
I'm Your Pusher, 467
I'm Yours, 217
I'se 'Gwine Back to Dixie, 387
I've a Shooting Box in Scotland, 784
I've Always Been Country, 463
I've Always Been Crazy, 497
I've Always Wanted to Do This, 133
I've Been a Bad Bad Boy, 385, 635
I've Been Everywhere, 918
I've Been Expecting You, 1065
I've Been in Love Before, 264
I've Been Lonely for So Long, 560
I've Been Loved by the Best, 1059
I've Been Loving You Too Long, 487, 786, 821
I've Been Searching, 1079
I've Been Thinking, 134
I've Been to a Marvellous Party, 268
I've Done Everything for You, 934
I've Got a Date with a Dream, 828
I've Got a Feeling I'm Falling, 1029
I've Got a Girl in Kalamazoo, 828, 1033
I've Got a Lovely Bunch of Coconuts, 220, 525, 647
I've Got a Pocketful of Dreams, 230
I've Got a Reason, 137
I've Got a Tiger by the Tail, 748
I've Got Five Dollars and It's Saturday Night, 239, 512
I've Got It, 972
I've Got Love on My Mind, 202
I've Got My Love to Keep Me Warm, 79, 129, 787, 969

I've Got Something to Say, 825
I've Got the Girl, 230
I've Got the Rock'n'Rolls Again, 9
I've Got the World on a String, 26
I've Got those Fleetwood Mac, Chicken Shack, John Mayall, Can't Fail Blues, 105
I've Got to Be Somebody, 925
I've Got to Go Back Home, 100
I've Got to Sing a Torch Song, 786
I've Got to Use My Imagination, 540, 548
I've Got You, 375
I've Got You Under My Skin, 178, 349, 785, 796, 904
I've Gotta Be Me, 249
I've Gotta Get a Message to You, 71
I've Grown Accustomed to Her Face, 578
I've Had Enough, 618
I've Had the Time of My Life, 835, 1031
I've Heard That Song Before, 487
I've Lost You, 652
I've Never Seen a Straight Banana, 1078
I've Seen All Good People, 1084
I've Told Ev'ry Little Star, 530, 843
I've Waited So Long, 718
Ian Matthews Live, 653
Ice in the Sun, 941
Ice Man Cometh, The, 144
Ice on Fire, 503
Ice on Ice, 144
Ice on the Motorway, 270
Ice Pickin', 203
Ice'n'Hot, 144
Iceberg/Freedom of Speech . . . Just Watch What You Say, The, 467
Iceman, 203
Ich Bin von Kopf bis Fuss auf Liebe Eingestellt, 264
Ichabod and I, 105
Icon Is Love, The, 484, 1048
Ida Sweet as Apple Cider, 130, 155, 233, 721
Idaho, 953
Ideal for Living, An, 716
Ideal World, 184
Ideas Are Like Stars, 159
Identity Crisis, 964
Idiot, The, 468
Idiot Wind, 293
Idioteque, 811
Idle Hands Are the Devil's Playthings, 738
Idlewild, 320
Idlewild South, 15

If, 119, 209, 319, 373, 479, 646
If a Woman Answers, 638
If Could Turn Back Time, 177
If Dogs Run Free, 293
If Drinking Don't Kill Me (Her Memory Will), 512
If Ever I See You Again, 338
If Ever I Would Leave You, 578
If He Really Knew Me, 418
If I Can't Have You, 1055
If I Could, 314
If I Could Be with You One Hour Tonight, 506, 822
If I Could Make a Living, 479
If I Could Only Fly, 411
If I Could Only Remember My Name, 229
If I Could Only Win Your Love, 425
If I Could Turn Back Time, 1032
If I Didn't Care, 167, 471
If I Follow My Heart, 127
If I Get Lucky, 233
If I Had a Boat, 601
If I Had a Hammer, 218, 598, 735, 768, 881
If I Had a Talking Picture of You, 259
If I Had My Way I'd Tear the Building Down, 505
If I Knew You Were Coming I'd've Baked a Cake, 664
If I Loved You, 417
If I Needed You, 425
If I Only Had Time, 385
If I Only Knew, 310, 976
If I Ruled the World, 77, 98, 393, 719
If I Said You Had a Beautiful Body Would You Hold It Against Me, 75
If I Should Fall Behind, 266
If I Should Fall from Grace with God, 780
If I Was, 1007, *1007*
If I Was a Rich Man, 1053
If I Wasn't So Romantic, I'd Shoot You, 615
If I Were a Bell, 206
If I Were a Carpenter, *160*, 166, 244, 350, 423, 452, 496, 882, 921
If I Were the Chief of Police, 425
If I Were the Woman You Wanted, 601
If I Were Your Woman, 548
If I'd Been the One, 609
If It Ain't Ruff, 808
If It Happens Again, 1005
If It Makes You Happy, 232
If It Was So Simple, 317
If It Wasn't for the 'Ouses in Between, 305

If It Weren't for Him, 383
If It's So Baby, 196
If It's Wednesday It Must Be Wembley, 438
If Loving You Is Wrong, 471, 482
(If Loving You Is Wrong) I Don't Want to Be Right, 641
If Not for You, 293, 721
If Only, 421
If Only My Heart Had a Voice, 847
If Only We Could Lead a Merry Mormon Life, 874
If That Ain't Country, 199
If That's What It Takes, 279
If the Kids Are United, 887
If the Shoe Fits, 805, 806
If the South Woulda Won, 1061
If There Was a Way, 1085
If They Move, Kill 'Em, 797
If This Is Our Last Time, 571
If This Is the Last Time, 910
If This Isn't Love, 423
If Tomorrow Never Comes, 123
If We Fall in Love Tonight, 283, 484, 950
If We Make It Through December, 410, 411
If We Only Have Love, 120
If You Ain't Lovin' (You Ain't Livin), 955
If You Asked Me to, 558, 1032
If You Believe, 819
If You Can Believe Your Eyes and Ears, 633
If You Can't Give Me Love, 807
If You Can't Lick 'Em . . ., 727
If You Change Your Mind, 166
If You Could Read My Mind, 585
If You Don't Know Me By Now, 370, 764, 902
If You Don't Like Hank Williams, 1060
If You Don't Want My Love, 799
If You Go, 879
If You Go Away, 119
If You Got the Money, Honey, I've Got the Time, 360
If You Gotta Go, Go Now, 323, 635
If You Gotta Make a Fool of Somebody, 357
If You Leave Me Now, 181
If You Let Me Stay, 243
If You Love Me, 432, 454, 764
If You Love Somebody Set Them Free, 950
If You Love These Blues, Play 'Em as You Please, 97
If You Need Me, 139, 775
If You Really Want Me to, I'll Go, 613

If You Remember Me, 418
If You Saw Thro' My Eyes, 652
If You See Her, 618
If You See Him, 618
If You See Him/If You See Her, 618
If You See My Savior, 281
If You Should Go, 52
If You Think You Know How to Love Me, 183
If You Think You're Lonely Now, 1076
If You Tolerate This Your Children Will Be Next, 637
If You Wanna Be Happy, 104
If You Want Blood – You've Got It, 4
If You Want Me to Stay, 954
If You Were Here Tonight, 740
If You Were the Woman and I Was the Man, 223
If You Were with Me Now, 677
If You're Ever in My Arms Again, 134
If You're Feeling Sinister, 75
If You're Looking for a Way Out, 985
(If You're Not in it for Love) I'm Outta Here!, 1000
If You're Ready (Come Go with Me), 938
If You've Got the Time, I've Got the Love, 762
If Your Girl Only Knew, 308
ifyoubelivein, 601
Iggy Iggy, 750
Ignition, 736
Ignoreland, 827
Ike's Rap, 434
Iko Iko, 271, 566
Il Faut Savoir, 41
Il Flor Che Aveci a Me, 614
Ill Communication, 65
Ill Wind, 27, 286
Illuminations, 1074
Illustrated Musical Encyclopaedia, 868
Im Nin Alu, 435
Image of a Girl, 351
Images, 193, 1020, 1059
Imaginary Lover, 37
Imaginary Roads, 5
Imagination, 64, 137, 548, 822
Imagination Camouflage, 887
Imagine, 99, *537*, 575, 576, *576*, 783, 1074
Imagine Heaven, 432
Imagine the Swan, 1093
Imaginos, 98
Imitation of Love, An, 482
Immaculate Collection, The, 631
Immediate Years, The, 913

Immigrant, The, 880
Immigrant Song, 569
Immigrés, 710
Immortal Classics, 639
Immortal Music of Miklos Rozsa, 858
Imperial Ballroom, 219
Importance of the Rose, The, 68
Impossible Bird, The, 603
Impressions, 206, 274
Impressions of the Middle East, 40
In a Big Country, 83
In a Broken Dream, 949
In a Chinese Temple Garden, 531
In a Free Land, 701
In a Golden Coach, 220
In a Heavy Bag, 362
In a Jam, 447
In a Little Spanish Town, 1050
In a Mellotone, 447
In a Metal Mood: No More Mister Nice Guy, 108
In a Mist, 73
In a Monastery Garden, 531
In a New Age, 718
In a Persian Market, 531
In a Priest Driven Ambulance, 339, 663
In a Sentimental Mood, 272, 652
In a Silent Way, 216, 248, 624, 1039, 1065
In All Language, 202
In All the Right Places, 938
In America, 241
In Between Days, 238
In C, 554
In Celebration, 889
In Celebration of Life, 1082
In Christ There Is No East or West, 322
In Concert, 141, 204, 397, 408, 711, 774, 872, 1043
In Concert, MIDEM 81, 485
In Concert – MTV Plugged, 935
In Concert with The Dub Band, 507
In Concert, Zurich, Oct 28 1979, 216
In Crowd, The, 333, 401, 582, 750
In Deep, 744
In Disneyland, 357
In Dreams, 741, *741*
In Dulci Jubilo, 738
In Europe, 983
In Every Dream Home a Heartache, 857
In Flagrante Delicto, 727
In Flight, 77
In Full Bloom, 1052
In Full Gear, 945
In Gorbachev We Trust, 887
In Hades, 691

In Held Was I, 800
In Hoagland, 159, 561
In Hoagland 81, 327
In It for the Money, 961
In Jail, 691
In London, 120, 368, 492, 618
In Love in Vain, 839
In Love with the Memory of You, 595
In Memory of . . . , 893
In Memory of Elizabeth Reed, 15
In Memory of Jimmie Rodgers, 918
In My African Dreams, 1034
In My Back Yard, 15
In My Book, 298
In My Chair, 941
In My Dreams, 827
In My House, 488
In My Life, 67, 68, 204, *204*, 229, 647
In My Lifetime, 683
In My Little Bottom Drawer, 334
In My Merry Oldsmobile, 706
In My Own Time, 328
In My Room, 63, 397, 1080
In My Time of Dyin', 505
In Mysterious Ways, 1006
In 'n' Out, 488
In Northern California (Where the Palm Tree Meets the Pine), 737
In Old Lisbon, 169
In on, 302
In Outer Space, 927
In Person, 474
In Pictures, 12
In Pieces, 123
In Praise of Older Women . . . and Other Crimes, 533
In Private, 768, 933
In Progress & in Motion, 1965–1998, 966
In Search of a Song, 415
In Search of Amelia Earhart, 652
In Search of Eddie Riff, 857
In Search of Manny, 605
In Search of Space, 433
In Search of the Lost Chord, 689
In Search of the Thirteenth Note, 368
In Search of the Turtle's Navel, 5
In Spite of Ourselves, 799
In Square Circle, 1077
In Step, 1016
In Strict Tempo, 16
In Style, 717, 718
In the Air Tonight, 205
In the Army Now, 302, 941
In the Bad, Bad Old Days, 610
In the Basement, 486
In the Beginning, 1016
In the City, 484

In the City of Angels, 1085
In the City of Light, 901
In the Cool Cool Cool of the Evening, 158, 663
In the Court of the Crimson King, 535
In the Dark, 40, *401*, 742, 987
In the Dark Green Woods, 185
In the Days before Rock'n'Roll, 695
In the Evening by the Moonlight, 387
In the Eyes of Creation, 776
In the Garden, 317
In the Ghetto, 43, 94, 247, 789, 940
In the Good Old Days, 757
In the Good Old Summer Time, 706, 924
In the Hall of the Mountain King, 301
In the Heat of the Night, 76
In the Hot Seat, 310
In the Jailhouse Now, 776
In the Key of G, 747
In the Land of Cockayne, 919
In the Land of Harmony, 523
In the Late of the Night, 118
In . . . the Life of Chris Gaines, 123
In the Light, 492
In the Long Grass, 376
In the Middle of a Heartache, 483
In the Middle of the House, 200, 687
In the Midnight Hour, 107, 400, 775
In the Mode, 907
In the Mood, 508, 599, 670, 946
In the Morning, 268
In the Mystic Land of Egypt, 531
In the Name of Love, 981
In the Name of the Father, 422
In the Navy, 1021
In the Night, 586
In the Pink, 369
In the Pocket, 880
In the Right Place, 272, 990
In the Running, 513
In the Shade of the Old Apple Tree, 522, 924
In the Shelter of Your Eyes, 1058
In the Skies, 341
In the Still of the Night, 63, 114, 265, 301, 785, 825
In the Still of the Nite, 338
In the Studio, 928
In the Summertime, 155
In the Time of Colin Blunstone, 1093
In the Upper Room with Jesus, 480
In the Wake of Poseidon, 536

In the Wee Small Hours, 833
In the Wee Small Hours of the Morning, 903
In the Woodshed She Said She Would, 334
In These Arms, 102
In This House on This Morning, 645
In Thoughts of You, 364
In Through the Out Door, 569
In Times Like These, 616
In Today's Room, 936
In Too Deep, 378
In Touch, 489
In Trance, 875
In Utero, 142, 723, 762
In Walked Bud, 683
In Your Eyes, 77
In Your Letter, 827
In Your Mind, 333
In Your Room, 54
In-a-Gadda-Da-Vida, 473
Inarticulate Speech of the Heart, 694, 695
Incandescence, 153
Incantations, 738
Inception, 1002
Incesticide, 10, 723
Inchworm, 525
Incident at 66.6 FM, 803
Incomplete, 1980–1985, 535
Incredible Jazz Guitar, 688
Incredible! Live!, 616
INCredible Sound of Drum'n'Bass, 389
Indelibly Stamped, 962
Independence, 604, *604*
Independence Cha Cha, 263
Independent Anniversary Ska, 908
Indestructible, 350
Indian Child, 1077
Indian Lake, 223
Indian Love Call, 301, 359, 617, 1052
Indian Reservation, 599, 829
Indian Rope, 172
Indian Summer, 947
Indiana, 555, 969
Indianola Mississippi Seeds, 538
Indians, 25
Indiscreet, 927
Individualism of Gil Evans, The, 318
Individualist, The, 860
Indomitable, 100
Industry, 982
Inertia Creeps, 650
Inez in Memphis, 352
Inferno, 826
Infidelity, 902
Infidels, 267, 293
Infinite McCoys, 615

Infinity, 519
Infinity Within, 253
Inflated Tear, The, 545
Information, 302
Information Libre, 887
Infotainment Scam, The, 327
Ingenue, 563
Ingenuity, 1007
Inglan Is a Bitch, 507
Ingrid Bergman, 117, 408
Inherit the Wind, 1076
Initial Success, 712
Initiation, 860
Inka Dinka Do, 289
Innamarata, 76
Inner City Blues, 375
Inner City Blues – The Music of Marvin Gaye, 30
Inner City Life, 374, 388, 1035
Inner Feelings, 732
Inner Mounting Flame, The, 624
Inner Worlds, 624, 1026
Innervisions, 1077
Innocent, 739
Innocent Age, The, 343
Innocent Eyes, 229
Innocent Lies, 489
Innocent People Cry, 474
Innocent Victim, 1009
Innocents, The, 312
Innuendo, 808
Insane, 875
Inside Folk, 896
Inside from Way Out, The, 65
Inside Information, 345
Inside Job, 266, 296
Inside Out, 418
Inside Story, 513, 846
Inside the Fire, 214
Inside the Kremlin, 889
Inspiration, 123, 656
Instant Groove, 676
Instant Hero, 531
Instant Karma, 930
Instant Knockout, 31
Instant Replay, 684, 1071
Instinct, 469
Instinction, 926
Instrumental Versions of Simon and Garfunkel, 218
Intakes, 711
Intentions, 795
Interesting Jerry Reed Sings Jim Croce, The, 822
Intergalactic, 65
Interior Design, 927
Interiors, 167
Interlude, 551
Intermezzo, 241, 763
Internal Combustion, 154
Internal Exile, 642
International, 367

International Playboy and Playgirl Record, The, 779
International Rag, 79, 996
International Thief Thief, 557
International Velvet, 168
Internationale, The, 117
Interplay, 318
Interstate Love Songs, 953
Interstellar Overdrive, 777
Intimacy, 887
Intimate Ella, The, 337
Intimate Evening with Anne Murray . . . Live, An, 705
Into Battle, 455
Into Each Life a Little Rain Must Fall, 472
Into Each Life Some Rain Must Fall, 336
Into Something I Can't Shake Loose, 1079
Into the Fire, 7, *7*
Into the Great Wide Open, 771
Into the Groove, 631
Into the Groove(y), 920
Into the Light, 251, 314, 886, 1051
Into the Music, 695
Into the Mystic, 694
Into the Night, 879
Into the Purple Valley, 212
Into the Valley, 83
Introducing the Hardline According to Terence Trent D'Arby, 243
Introspect, 925
Introspective, 768
Intuition, Montreux III, 318
Invasion, 546
Invincible, 76
Invincible Summer, 563
Invisible Hits, 446
Invisible Lantern, 877
Invisible Sun, 782
Invisible Touch, 378
Invitation to the Blues, 673, 794
Invitation to the Caribbean, 31
I.O.U., 252, 475
Ira Louvin, 600
Irish Evening: Live at the Grand Opera House, Belfast, An, 182
Irish Heartbeat, 182, 695
Irish Immigrant, The, 614
Irish Rover, The, 614, 780
Irish Tour 74, 368
Irish Uprising, The, 185
Iron Behind the Velvet, The, 690
Iron Fist, 699
Iron Man, 15, 274, 1054
Iron Muse, The, 591
Iron out the Rough Spots, 1089
Ironic, 693
Irresistible, 1021
Is a Bluebird Blue?, 764, 1000

Is Anybody Goin' to San Antone, 795
Is Everybody in Your Family as Dumb as You Is?, 691
Is It Love You're After?, 1052
Is It True, 698
Is It Wrong, 384
Is Nothing Sacred, 658
Is She Really Going out with Him?, 480
Is That All There Is?, 572, 575
Is That What I Get for Loving You, 853
Is There Anybody Out There, The Wall Live, 777
Is There Anybody There?, 875
Is This Desire?, 429
Is This Love, 643, 703, 1051
Is This What You Want, 427
Is You Is (Or Is You Ain't My Baby), 518
Is Your Love in Vain, 293
Isaac Hayes Movement, The, 434
Isis, 293
Isitzo, 946
Isla Bonita, La, 631
Island, 116, 328
Island Girl, 503
Island in the Sun, 73, 469, 571, 834
Island Life, 773
Island of Dreams, 933
Island of Lost Souls, 96
Island of Real, 816
Islands, 536, 738
Islands in the Stream, 758, 847
Isle of Capri, 220, 335, 528, 954
Isle of Sirens, 470
Isle of View, The, 792
Isley Brothers, The, 476
Ismail and Sixu, 989
Isn't Anything, 707
Isn't It a Wonder, 114
Isn't It Romantic, 180, 428
Isn't It Strange, 586
Isn't Life Strange, 689
Isn't She Lovely, 430, 1077
Isn't This a Lovely Day, 79
Isobel, 86
Isolation, 989
Israelites, The, 255, 549
Issues, 552
Istanbul, 348, 1014
It, 805
It Ain't Exactly Entertainment, 540
It Ain't Gonna Rain No More, 416, 568
It Ain't Me Babe, 292, 490, 999
It Ain't Necessarily So, 208, 380
It Ain't Over Til It's Over, 554
It Ain't What You Do It's the Way That You Do It, 52, 928
It Begins Again, 933

It Could Happen to You, 131
It Couldn't Happen Here, 694
It Crawled into My Hand, Honest, 361
It Doesn't Have to Be, 312
It Doesn't Matter Anymore, 24, 451, 853
It Don't Come Easy, 939
It Don't Hurt No More, 130
It Don't Mean a Thing, 511
It Don't Mean a Thing if It Ain't Got That Swing, 120, 675
It Don't Work Out, 1093
It Gets Lonely Early, 904
It Goes like It Goes, 1031
It Had to Be You, 302, 513, 522
It Happened One Bite, 445
It Hurts Me, 242
It Hurts Me Too, 486, 654
It Hurts So Good, 767
It Hurts to Be Alone, 272
It Is Finished, 901
It Is the Business of the Future to Be Dangerous, 434
It Isn't Fair, 217, 525
It Isn't, It Wasn't . . . It Ain't, 1032
It Keeps Raining, 1005
It Keeps Right on a-Hurtin', 985
It Makes No Difference Now, 247, 774, 984
It Mek, 255, 549
It Might as Well Be Swing, 904
It Might as Well Rain until September, 464, 540, 545
It Must Have Been Love, 856
It Must Have Been the Devil, 927
It Only Takes a Minute, 541, 1064
It Only Took a Minute, 129
It Oughta Sell a Million, 882
It Should Have Been Me, 173, 953
It Started with a Kiss, 457
It Sure Brings Out the Love in Your Eyes, 923
It Takes a Nation of Millions to Hold Us Back, 803
It Takes All Night Long, 386
It Takes Believers, 384
It Takes Two, 374
It Takes Two to Tango, 48
It Tears Me Up, 910, 911
It Took a Lot of Drinkin' to Get That Woman Over Me, 54
It Was a Good Day, 466
It Was a Very Good Year, 431, 904
It Was Almost Like a Song, 675
It Was Always Easy to Find an Unhappy Woman, 54
It Was I, 147, 351
It Was So Beautiful, 711
It Was the Whiskey Talking (Not Me), 582

It Wasn't God Who Made Honky Tonk Angels, 162, 671, 981, 1045
It Wasn't Me, 82
It Will Stand, 169, 990
It Won't Be Wrong, 146
It'll Be Me, 192
It's a Big Daddy Thing, 84
It's a Blue World, 348
It's a Cowboy Lovin' Night, 997
(It's a Fresh Wind That) Blows Against the Empire, 494
It's a Great Big Shame, 305
It's a Heartache, 1002
It's a Jazz Thing, 906
It's a Legal Matter, 1054
It's a Lonely Town, 616
It's a Long Way There, 590
It's a Long Way to Tipperary, 345, 614, 706
It's a Mad Mad Mad World, 505
It's a Man's Man's Man's World, 128, 534, 695
It's a Man's World, 466
It's a Mistake, 662
It's a Mystery, 882, 991
It's a Shame, 931
It's a Shame about Ray, 575
It's a Sin, 767
It's About Time, 366, 803
It's Alive, 815
It's All about to Change, 994
It's All in the Game, 303
It's All One Me, 806
It's All Over, 539
It's All Over Now, 848, 849, 1075, 1076
It's All Right, 325, 470, 655, 768
It's Alright, 740
It's Alright, I Feel It, 906
It's Always You, 230
It's Been a Long, Long Time, 231, 760
It's Been So Long, 622, 776, 1072
It's Better to Have, 221
It's Better to Have It, 607
It's Called a Heart, 258
It's Cold Outside, 817
It's De-Lovely, 286
It's Different for Girls, 480
It's Dreamtime, 987
It's Ecstasy When You Lay Down Next to Me, 1048
It's Five o'Clock, 1014
It's Getting Better, 633, 638
It's Gonna Work out Fine, 997
It's Good for the Soul, 1013
It's Good News Week, 541
It's Got to Be Someone I Love, 511
It's Great When You're Straight, Yeah!, 421
It's Growin', 974

It's Hard, 1054
It's Hard to Be Humble, 247
It's Harder Now, 775
It's in Every One of Us, 768
It's It, 86
It's Just a Matter of Time, 78, 489, 993
It's Late, 139, 711, 947
(It's Like a) Sad Old Kinda Movie, 610
It's Like That, 859
It's Like This, 515
It's Like We Never Said Good-bye, 403
It's Magic, 150, 250, 958
It's Me Again Margaret, 946
It's My Delight, 549
It's My Life, Baby!, 1045
It's My Mother's Birthday Today, 211
It's My Party, 394, 514, 1079
It's My Time, 953
It's My Way, 867
It's Nice to Go Traveling, 653
It's No Crime, 44
It's No Good, 259
It's No Secret, 494
It's Nobody's Fault But Mine, 505
It's Not Enough, 495
It's Not for Me to Say, 651
It's Not Just Sentimental, 821
It's Not Unusual, 516, 534, 823
It's Now or Never, 789
It's Now or Never: A Tribute to Elvis Presley, 1034
It's Oh So Quiet, 86
It's on (Dr Dre 187um) Killa, 728
It's on Tonight, 912
It's Only a Movie, 328
It's Only a Paper Moon, 26, 336
It's Only Love, 7, 333, 999
It's Only Make Believe, 364, 1000
It's Only Over for You, 997
It's Only Rock'n'Roll, 497, 849
It's Only the Beginning, 523
It's Over, 741
It's Raining, 245
It's Raining Again, 962
It's Really You, 130
It's Right Here for You, 115
It's Serious, 152
It's So Easy, 451, 854
It's So Hard Being a Loser, 211
It's So Hard to Say Goodbye to Yesterday, 114
It's Such a Small World, 167
It's the Dreamer in Me, 1012
It's the End of the World as We Know It (I Feel Fine), 826
It's the Same Old Song, 350, 449
It's the Way of the World, 520
It's Tight Like That, 281, 1063

It's Time, 642, 668, 837, 887
It's Time for Jonathan Richman and the Modern Lovers, 833
It's Time for Love, 180
It's Too Late, 389, 540, 651, 1067
It's Too Late Baby, It's Too Late, 802
It's Too Late to Stop Now, 695
It's Too Soon to Know, 743, 817, 1034
It's Tough to Be a God, 504
It's Tricky, 859
It's True Love, 607
It's Tulip Time in Holland, 1052
It's Up to You, 711, 804
It's Wrong (Apartheid), 1077
It's You, 987
It's Your Call, 618
It's Your Thing, 476
It's Yours, 858
Italian Street Song, The, 441
Italian Twilight, 531
Italian X-Rays, 674
Itchycoo Park, 610, 912, 913, 1072
Itsy Bitsy Teenie Weenie Yellow Polka Dot Bikini, 464
Ivan M Tribe, 595
Ivory Tower, 107
Ivy, Ivy, Ivy, 796
Ixnay on the Hombre, 736
Izzy Stradlin and the Ju-Ju Hounds, 407

Jack and Diane, 660
Jack Armstrong Blues, 972
Jack in the Box, 979
Jack Kerouac's Last Dream, 308
Jack O'Roses, 400
Jack of Diamonds Blues, 1029
Jack the Ripper, 1077
Jack U Off, 797
Jack's Heroes, 781
Jackie, 120, 259, 283, 1026
Jackie Wilson Said, 261, 695
Jackpot, 586
Jackson, 166, 436, 904
Jacksons, The, 478
Jacob's Ladder, 581
Jacques, 17
Jacques Derrida, 878
Ja-da, 505
Jagged Little Pill, 692, 693
Jah Kingdom, 140
Jah Live, 643
J'ai bu, 41
J'ai Deux Amours, 50
Jail, 983
Jailbreak, 979
Jailhouse Rock, 574, 789, 975
Jalousie, 560
Jam Up, Jelly Tight, 829, 846
Jamaica's Golden Hits, 571

Jamais le Dimanche, 21
Jambalaya, 226, 379, 672, 936, 937, 1059
James Bond Theme, 505
James Dean, 132
James Gang Rides Again, The, 295
James (Hold the Ladder Steady), 382, 765
James Last in Scotland, 565
James Last Plays the Music of Andrew Lloyd Webber, 565
James Monroe High School Presents DBOSB Goes to Washington, 533
James Taylor Live, 971
James II, 485
Jamie, 449
Jammin' Me, 771
Jamming, 643, 1035
Janet, 479
Janet Jackson, 479
Janet Jackson's Rhythm Nation 1814, 479
Janey's Blues, 465
Janie Jones, 191
Janie's Got a Gun, 10
Janis, 517
Janis Ian, 466
Janis Joplin in Concert, 517
January, 61, 756
Japanese Restaurant Song, 729
Japanese Sandman, The, 62, 883, 1052
Japanese Whispers, 238
Jar of Flies, 14
Jardin Extraordinaire, La, 993
Jarre Live, 491
Jarrow Song, 793
Jason Donovan's Poof?, 541
Java, 645, 750, 990
Java Jive, 472, 636
Javanaise, La, 367
Jawbone, 53
Jay's Blues, 1075
Jazz, 212, 559, 808, 1057
Jazz Around Midnight, 337
Jazz Composers Orchestra, 217
Jazz Couriers in Concert, The, 877
Jazz Experiment, 676
Jazz from Hell, 1092
Jazz Giants, 1087
Jazz Goes to College, 133
Jazz Goes to Junior College, 133
Jazz Impressions of New York, 133
Jazz in 3/4 Time, 837
Jazz in the Space Age, 318, 863
Jazz Music, 370
Jazz Note, 906
Jazz Rock Guitar, 405
Jazz Samba, 381, 501
Jazz Samba Encore, 381
Jazz Singer, 350, 939

Jazz Soul of Little Stevie, The, 1076
Jazz the African Sound, 620
Jazz Thing, 370
Jazz Ultimate, 972
Jazz Workshop, 318, 863
Jazz-Blues Fusion, 654
Jazz-Rock Guitar, 50
Jazzabelle, 704
Jazzbuhne Berlin, 202
Jazzman, 540
Jazzmatazz, 370
Jazznocracy, 604
J. B. Lenoir, 577
JBeez Wit the Remedy, 521
Je Chante, 993
Je Ka Jo, 732
Je Ne Sais Pas Pourquoi, 677, 951
Je t'ai dans la Peau, 68, 774
Je t'aime . . . Moi Non Plus, 367, 960
Je t'Attends, 41
Je Veux Me Promener, 416
Je Voyais Déjà, 41
Jealous Guy, 430, 576, 857
Jealous Heart, 462, 1072
Jealous Kind, The, 613
Jealous of You, 353
Jealousy, 364, 560
Jean, 227, 623, 750
Jeannie Needs a Shooter, 1092
Jeannie with the Light Brown Hair, 346
Jeannine, I Dream of Lilac Time, 894
Jeans on, 403
Jeep Is Jumping, The, 447
Jeepers Creepers, 256, 663, 1032
Jeff Beck Group, 70
Jeff Beck Live with the Jan Hammer Group, 70
Jefferson Airplane Takes Off, 494
Jehovah Kill, 215
Jelly Jelly, 299, 446
Jelly Roll Blues, 697
Jennie Lee, 490
Jennifer, 151
Jennifer Eccles, 449
Jennifer Juniper, 278
Jenny Jenny, 589, 865
Jenny Take a Ride, 865, 1067
Jeremiah Peabody's Poly Unsaturated Quick Dissolving Fast Acting Pleasant Tasting Green and Purple Pills, 946
Jeremiah Was a Bullfrog, 40
Jeremy Spencer and the Children, 341
Jericho, 53
Jerome Kern Songbook, The, 1052
Jerry and Me, 822
Jerry Garcia Band, The, 401
Jersey Bounce, 765

Jersey Girl, 934, 1024
Jersey Thursday, 277
Jerusalem, 100
Jesse, 466, 898
Jessica, 15, 499
Jessie's Girl, 934
Jessie's Jig and Other Favorites. Words We Can Dance To, 392
Jesu Joy of Man's Desiring, 627
Jesus and Mary Chain Hate Rock'n'Roll, The, 498
Jesus Children of America, 268
Jesus Is Just Alright, 278
Jesus Is the Answer, 232
Jesus Make Up My Dying Bed, 505
Jesus of Cool, 603
Jesus to a Child, 667
Jesus Walked the Water, 268
Jesus Was a Capricorn, 555
Jesus Will Answer Prayer, 268
Jet, 611
Jet Airliner, 673
Jet City Woman, 809
Jet My Love, 802
Jeun Ko'ku, 556
Jewel, 886
Jewel in the Crown, 324
Jeweler, The, 816
Jezebel, 560, 947
Jig Saw Puzzle Blues, 1019
Jim Croce Songbook, The, 1019
Jim Dandy, 50, 87, 88, 308
Jim Jackson's Kansas City Blues, 580, 774
Jim Webb Sings Jim Webb, 1040
Jimbrowski, 520
Jimmie Cracked Corn, 504
Jimmie the Kid, 845
Jimmie's Texas Blues, 845
Jimmy and Wes, 688
Jimmy Brown the Newsboy, 1073
Jimmy Jimmy, 889
Jimmy Mack, 449, 645
Jimmy Page and the Black Crowes Live at the Greek, 87, 570
Jimmy's Blues, 862
Jimone, 485
Jingle Bell Mambo, 787
Jingle Bell Rock, 571
Jingle Bells, 23, 230
Jingle Jangle, 546
Jingle, Jangle, Jingle, 557, 595
Jinx, 368
Jitter Bug, 152
Jive Bunny – The Album, 501
Jive Samba, The, 8
Jive Talkin', 71, 641
Jivin' Around, 273
J.K. All the Way, 541
J. Mood, 645
Joan Armatrading, 27

Joan of Arc, 742, 1031
Joanna, 430, 550, 1026
Joanne, 685
Job Description, 479
Jocko Homo, 260
Jody's Got Your Girl and Gone, 971
Joe and Rose Lee Maphis, King of the Strings, 641
Joe and Zoot, 1019
Joe Cocker Live, 198
Joe Ely, 309
Joe Frazier (He Prayed), 140
Joe Hill, 47, 445, 733, 840, 984
Joe Lament, 949
Joe Satriani, 872
Joe's Garage, 1092
Joey, Joey, Joey, 572
Johannesburg, 877
John Barleycorn Must Die, 1072
John Cougar, 660
John Dawson Winter III, 1071
John Deere Tractor, 520
John Fogerty, 226
John Hartford, 429
John Hartford Collection, A, 429
John Henry, 277, 580, 585
John Lennon/Plastic Ono Band, 576, 930
John Mayall Plays John Mayall, 654
John Mellencamp, 661
John Prine Christmas, A, 799
John T. Scopes Trial, The, 842
John Wesley Harding, 284, 292
Johnny and Mary, 751
Johnny and the Family Clone, 1038
Johnny Angel, 9
Johnny B. Goode, 81, 266, 416, 698, 988
Johnny Be Bad, 82
Johnny Chrome and Silver, 278
Johnny Come Home, 335
Johnny Come Lately, 297
Johnny Hallyday Sings America's Rockin' Hits, 416
Johnny Johnson, 577
Johnny Loves Me, 638
Johnny Mathis' Greatest Hits, 651
Johnny Reb, 456
Johnny Reggae, 541
Johnny Remember Me, 658
Johnny Rivers at the Whiskey a Go Go, 836
Johnny Too Bad, 966
Johnny's Theme, 24
Join Hands, 905
Join Together, 1054
Joining You, 693
Joint Is Jumpin', The, 1029

Jojo, 873
Joker, The, 673, 674, 719
Joker Went Wild, The, 373, 464
Joko, 710
Jole Blon, 451, 496, 530, 536, 704
Jolene, 757, 758
Jollification, 585, 704
Jolly Christmas from Frank Sinatra, A, 904
Jon Spencer Blues Explosion, The, 510
Jonah, 388
Jonathan Richman & the Modern Lovers, 832
Jonathan Sings!, 832
Jonathan Sings Country, 833
Jonathan, Te Vas a Emocionar!, 833
Jordan: The Comeback, 788
Joseph Locke, 594
Josh White Jr, 1049
Joshua, 757, 1046
Joshua Journeyed to Jericho, 268
Joshua Judges Ruth, 515, 602
Joshua Tree, The, 311, 563, 1004
Jour où il Pluie Viendra, Le, 68
Journal of the Plague Year, A, 816
Journey, 519, 642, 700
Journey of the Sorcerer, 295
Journey Through the Past, 1088
Journey Through the Secret Life of Plants, 1077
Journey to Love, 190
Journey to the Center of the Mind, 727
Journey to the Urge Within, 776
Journey's End, 337
Journey's Inward, 138
Journeyman, 187, 224, 427
Journeys to Glory, 926
Joy, 764, 923
Joy and Blues, 644
Joy and Pain, 656, 656
Joy of a Toy, 919
Joy of Flying, The, 1066
Joy That Floods My Soul, The, 432
Joy to the World, 40, 984
Joya, 738, 739
Joybringer, 635
Joyful Noise unto the Creator, A, 368
Joyride, 638, 856
Joyspring, 126
Ju Ju, 905
Jubilation, 53
Jubilee Concert, 277
Jubiliation T. Cornpone, 663
Judas Iscariot, 1025
Judds Collection, The, 520
Judge Dread, 799
Judge Dread Dance, 799
Judge Not, 127, 549, 643
Judith, 204

Judy, 336, 1015
Judy at Carnegie Hall, 372
Judy Collins No. 3, 204
Judy Sings Dylan . . . Just Like a Woman, 204
Judy's Turn to Cry, 394
Jug of Punch, The, 185
Jugulator, 519
Juju Music, 8
Juke, 179, 590
Juke Box Music, 867
Jukebox Cannonball, 412
Jukin', 636
Julian Cope Presents 20 Mothers, 215
Julie Ann, 220
Juliet Letters, The, 219
Julio, 469, 469
July You're a Woman, 948
Jump, 755, 1011
Jump (for My Love), 781
Jump into the Fire, 722
Jump, Jive and Wail, 796
Jump on the Wagon, 211
Jump Over, 154
Jump Sister Bessie, 861
Jump They Say, 111
Jump to It, 355, 1013
Jump to the Beat, 1026
Jump Up, 571
Jumpin' Blues', The, 627
Jumpin' Jive, 480
Jumping Bean, 329
Jumping Jack Flash, 355, 849
Jumping Jive, 152
Junction Seven, 1026, 1073
June 1 1974, 151, 311, 1018
June in January, 230, 839
June Is Bustin' out All Over, 844
Junge Komm Bald Weider, 810
Jungle Boogie, 550
Jungle Brother, 521
Jungle Hop, 276
Jungle Swing, 216
Junk Culture, 742
Junker's Blues, 288
Junkyard, 168
Junta, 773
Jus Reach, 368
Just, 811
Just a Baby's Prayer at Twilight, 140
Just a Boy, 872
Just a Closer Walk with Thee, 580
Just a Collection of Antiques, 1025
Just a Dream, 124, 186
Just a Girl, 725
Just a Little, 954
Just a Little Bit Better, 442
Just a Little Bit of You, 481
Just a Little Lovin' Will Go a Long Long Way, 29

Just a Lucky So and So, 126
Just a Season, 147
Just a Song Before I Go, 229
Just a Touch of Love Everyday, 149
Just a Woman, 607
Just Ain't Good Enough, 971
Just an Illusion, 703
Just an Old Fashioned Girl, 547
Just an Old Fashioned Love Song, 984
Just Another Band from East LA, 594
Just Another Band from LA, 1091
Just Another Day, 879
Just Another Illusion, 834
Just Another Injustice, 396
Just Around the Corner, 1023
Just as I Am, 12, 1074
Just as Much as Ever, 1023
Just a-Settin' and a-Rockin', 1041
Just Be Good to Me, 330, 484
Just Be True, 170
Just Because, 621, 794, 1061
Just Because I'm a Woman, 757
Just Before the Bullets Fly, 16
Just Being Myself, 1033
Just Between Us, 174
Just Between You and Me, 795
Just Can't Get Enough, 258
Just Come Home, 460
Just Coolin', 737
Just Don't Have the Heart, 831
Just Dropped in (To See What Condition My Condition Was in), 718), 846
Just Family, 190
Just Fly, 806
Just for Love, 810
Just for You, 44, 549, 1048
Just Give the Southland to Me, 828
Just Good Friends, 368
Just Good Old Rock'n'Roll, 305
Just Good Ole Boys, 54
Just Got Back Today, 961
Just Keep Walking, 473
Just Let Me Look at You, 334
Just Like a Woman, 292, 635
Just Like Eddie, 197, 659, 987
Just Like Gold, 41
Just Like Me, 829
Just Like President Thieu, 1024
(Just Like) Starting Over, 740
Just Like the First Time, 479
Just Lookin', 173
Just Make Love to Me, 269, 1037
Just My Imagination (Running Away with Me), 975
Just Once, 514
Just Once in My Life, 834
Just One Look, 334, 449, 995

Just One More Chance, 883
Just One Smile, 778
Just One Time, 382
Just out of Reach, 138, 1047
Just Push Play, 171
Just Say I Love Her, 241
Just Say Ozzy, 88
Just Say Stet, 945
Just Say You Love Me, 180
Just Tell Them That You Saw Me, 284
Just the Two of Us, 917, 1035, 1074
Just the Way You Are, 502, 1048
Just to Be Close to You, 832
Just to Be with You, 1037
Just Try to Picture Me Down Home in Tennessee, 276
Just Walking in the Rain, 672, 772, 818, 819
Just Wanna Know, 795
Just When You're Thinkin' Things Over, 173
Just You 'n' Me, 181
Justified and Ancient, 548, 1080
Justify My Love, 554, 631
Justus, 685
Juvenelia, 771

K, 556
K Scope, 857
K Sera Sera, 548
Ka-Ding-Dong, 262
Kajun Klu Klux Klan, 672
Kalamazoo, 670
Kaleidoscope, 905
Kamakiriad, 943
Kandy Korn, 72
Kansas City, 427, 574, 598, 840
Karma Chameleon, 236
Kashmir, 569, 805
Kassie Jones, 580
Kate and Anna McGarrigle, 113
Kathy Mattea, 652
Kathy's Song, 897
Katrina, 577
Katy Lied, 943
Kaw-Liga, 795, 855, 1060
Kay Starr and Count Basie, 939
Kaya, 643, 750
Kaycee on My Mind, 508
Kayleigh, 642
K.C. Lovin', 574
KC Ten, 526
Keep a Knockin', 115, 589
Keep Each Other Warm, 136
Keep It Comin', 32, 149
Keep It Comin' Love, 526
Keep Moving, 630
Keep on, 613
Keep on Dancing, 61, 208, 541, 682
Keep on Lovin' You, 445, 827

Keep on Loving Me, 319
Keep on Movin', 923
Keep on Moving, 144, 812
Keep on Pumpin' It, 677
Keep on Pushin, 470
Keep on Rockin', 910
Keep on Running, 303, 1072
Keep on Sailing, 652
Keep on Singing, 232, 821
Keep on the Sunny Side, 162
Keep Right on to the End of the Road, 566
Keep Searchin, 889
Keep that Same Old Feeling, 234
Keep the Faith, 102
Keep the Fire, 596
Keep the Fire Burnin', 827
Keep the Home Fires Burning, 222, 250, 614, 726
Keep the Music Playing, 60
Keep Young and Beautiful, 1032
Keep Your Eye on Me, 17
Keep Your Lamp Trimmed and Burning, 505
Keeper of the Castle, 350
Keeper of the Flame, 613
Keepin' out of Mischief Now, 1029
Keeping My Mind on Love, 1046
Keith Jarrett at the Blue Note, 493
Kelly Watch the Stars, 11
Ken Colyer in New Orleans, 207
Kenny G, 365
Kenny G Live, 365
Kentucky, 99
Kentucky Hills of Tennessee, The, 207
Kentucky Thunder, 907
Kentucky Waltz, 30, 686
Kentucky Woman, 253, 262
Kermit Unplugged, 854
Kevin Carter, 637
Kewpie Doll, 1015
Key, The, 27
Key to My Life, 114
Keynsham, 105
Keys of the Kingdom, 689
Keys to Ascension, 1085
Keys to Ascension Volume 2, 1085
Keys to the City, 583
Keys to Your Heart, 191
Keystone 3, 93
Kick, 473
Kick Inside, The, 142
Kick it to the Curb, 124
Kick Out the Jams, 51, 98, 656
Kicking a Dead Pig, 682
Kicking Against the Pricks, 168
Kicking the Gong Around, 152
Kicks, 638, 829, 829
Kid, The, 90
Kid A, 811

Kid Blue, 540
Kid Inside, The, 660
Kid with the Replaceable Head, The, 973
Kiddio, 78
Kidney Stew, 1022
Kids, The, 1035
Kids in America, 698, 1055
Kids of the Baby Boom, 75
Kiko, 37, 594
Kill 'Em All, 665
Kill All Hippies, 797
Kill at Will, 466
Kill City, 468
Kill Me in the Morning, 178
Kill the Poor, 252
Kill Uncle, 696
Kill Your Sons, 824
Kill Yr Idols, 920
Killer on the Loose, 979
Killer on the Rampage, 398
Killers, 474
Killin' Time, 90
Killing an Arab, 237
Killing Floor, 97, 459
Killing in the Name, 813
Killing Is My Business . . . and Business Is Good, 659
Killing Machine, 519
Killing Me Softly, 361
Killing Me Softly with His Song, 338
Killing Moon, The, 299
Killing of Georgie, The, 950
Kiln House, 341
Kilroy Was Here, 959
Kim Carnes, 159
Kim Wilde, 1055
Kimono My House, 927
Kind of Blue, 7, 8, 206, 248, 317, 318
Kind of Boy You Can't Forget, The, 404
Kind of Magic, A, 808
King, 984, 972, 1005
King Bee, 1037
King Creole, 574, 789
King Curtis Plays the Great Memphis Hits, 537
King, Does the King's Things, 537
King for a Day, 771
King Freddie and His Dreaming Knights, 357
King Harvest (Has Surely Come), 53
King Henry, 942
King Heroin, 127
King Holiday, 98
King Jazz, 69
King Kong, 287, 1091
King Midas in Reverse, 449
King of America, 219
King of Bongo Bong, The, 405

King of Elfland's Daughter, The, 942
King of Fools, 256
King of Hearts, 741
King of New York, 363
King of Pain, 782
King of Rock, 859
King of Rock'n'Roll, The, 589, 788
King of Rock'n'Roll, the Complete 50s Masters, The, 790
King of Snake, 1008
King of Stage, 125
King of the Beach, 819
King of the Blues, 538
King of the Doghouse, 941
King of the Gospel Singers, The, 589
King of the Road, 673
King of the World, 669
King Porter Stomp, 391, 439, 609, 691, 696, 697
King Puck, 690
King Rocker, 467
King Soul, 536
King Tubby Meets Rockers Uptown, 750
King Tubby Meets Roots Radics Dangerous Dub, 537
King Tubby's Specials, 537
King Tut, 724
King Will Come, The, 1074
King without a Crown, 2
King's New Clothes, The, 525
King's Record Shop, 166
Kingdom Blow, 98
Kingdom of Desire, 989
Kingdom of the Street, 266
Kings of the Wild Frontier, 25
Kingsize, 105
Kinks, The, 543
Kinky Afro, 421
Kirya, 435
Kiss, 286, 516, 797
Kiss an Angel Good Morning, 795
Kiss, Hotter Than Hell, 546
Kiss in the Dark, A, 260
Kiss in the Dreamhouse, A, 905
Kiss Me Again, 441
Kiss Me Baby, 173
Kiss Me Deadly, 467
Kiss Me Honey, Honey, Kiss Me, 60
Kiss Me, Kiss Me, Kiss Me, 238
Kiss My Ass, 25, 123, 546
Kiss of Fire, 648
Kiss of the Spider Woman, 579
Kiss on My List, 413
Kiss the Lips of Life, 534
Kiss This, 885
Kiss You All Over, 183
Kisses on the Wind, 178

Kisses Sweeter Than Wine, 460, 1015, 1040, *1040*
Kissin', 322
Kissing Christmas, 1023
Kissing in the Back Row of the Movies, 285, 403, 611
Kissing in the Cactus, 908
Kissing to Be Clever, 236
Kitten on the Keys, 598, 828, 1050
Kizz My Black Azz, 728
K-Jee, 363
Knee Deep in Bluegrass, 686
Knee Deep in the Blues, 672, 678
Knee Deep in the Hoopla, 495
Knee Plays, The, 967
Kneeling at the Shrine, 360, 991
Knees up Mother Brown, 1046
Knife, 42
Knight in Rusty Armour, 853
Knights of the Sound Table, 152
Knightsbridge, 197
Knnillssonn, 722
Knock Dem Dead, 31
Knock Knock Who's There?, 454
Knock on Wood, 107, 980
Knock Three Times, 743
Knocked 'Em in the Old Kent Road, 179
Knocked Out Loaded, 293, 771
Knocking on Heaven's Door, 293, 905
Knockout, 987
Knowing Me, Knowing You, 1
Knowledge Is King, 551
Ko Ko Mo, 209, 227, 339
Kohouept, 502
Koko, 753
Koko Joe, 834
Kokomo, 64, 634
Koln Concert, The, 492
Kon-Tiki, 161, 885
Koo, Koo, 96, 845
Kool Aid, 191
Kool and the Gang, 550
Kootchi, 178
Korea Blues, 576
Korn, 552
Kosmic Blues, 517
Kowalski, 797
KRS-One, 106
Kutche, 532
Kylie, 677
Kyoto Bojyo, 1019
Kyoto No Koi, 1019

L, 860, 976
L Is for Lover, 492, 846
L.A. County, 601
L.A. Freeway, 746, 1027
LA Is My Lady, 904
La La I Love You, 74
La La Means I Love You, 255

L.A. Midnight, 538
La Sexorcisto: Devil Music Volume One, 1048
LA Turnaround, 765
La Vern Baker Sings Bessie Smith, 50
LA Woman, 280, 468
La's, The, 564
Labelled with Love, 261, 936
Labour of Love, 1005
Labour of Love II, 1005
Labour of Lust, 603
Lacklustre Me, 11
Ladder, The, 1085
Ladder of Love, The, 339
Ladies and Gentlemen: The Best of George Michael, 667
Ladies and Gentlemen We Are Floating in Space, 925
Ladies First, 808
Ladies Love Outlaws, 496, 862
Ladies of the Canyon, 678
Ladies Who Lunch, The, 919
Ladies' Night, 550
Lady, 832, 847, 959
Lady Be Good, 1087
Lady Bird, 436
Lady Came from Baltimore, The, 244
Lady Coryell, 217
Lady D'Arbanville, 946
Lady Day, 949
Lady Day and John Coltrane, 877
Lady Eleanor, 586
Lady Godiva, 385, 853
Lady in Red, The, 251
Lady Is a Tramp, The, 401, 402, 428
Lady Luck, 271
Lady Madonna, 275, 612
Lady Marmalade, 14, 228, 558, 990
Lady of Spain, 319, 336
Lady of the Night, 960
Lady of the Stars, 278, 1047
Lady or the Tiger, The, 991
Lady Rose, 894
Lady Samantha, 503
Lady Sings the Blues, 509
Lady Soul, 355
Lady Willpower, 804
Lady Writer, 267
Laid, 485
Laid Back Girl, 656
Laid So Low, 972
Lake County Cotton Country, 766
Lake Providence Blues, 1063
Lamb Lies Down on Broadway, The, 377
Lambeth Walk, The, 373
L.A.M.F., 717

Laminar Flow, 741
Land of 1000 Dances, 415, 589, 775, 916
Land of Dreams, 720
Land of Make Believe, The, 136
Land of Many Churches, 411
Land Speed Record, 701
Landing on Water, 1088
Landlord, 549, *938*
Landlords and Tenants, 12
Language Barrier, 911
Language of Life, The, 320
Language of Love, The, 343, 599
Lara's Theme, 192, 210, 492
Larf and Sing, 328
Large as Life but Twice as Natural, 395
Large Black Dick, 22
Larger Than Life, 541
Lark Rise to Candleford, 13
Larks Tongue in Aspic Part IV, 536
Larks' Tongues in Aspic, 536
Larry Carlton, 234
Larry Williams Show, The, 1062
Las Palabras de Amor, 808
Laser-Guided Melodies, 925
Lass of Killiecrankie, The, 566
Lass with the Delicate Air, The, 1049
Lasso from El Paso, 658, 963
Last Campaign, The, 948
Last Century Modern, 253
Last Chance, 970
Last Chance for a Thousand Years, 1086
Last Child, 9
Last Christmas, 666
Last Concert, 681
Last Dance, 960
Last Date, 224, *274*, 1044
Last Day on Earth, 151
Last Days and Time, 297
Last Days of Mr X, The, 782
Last Days of the Century, The, 947
Last Dog and Pony Show, The, 701
Last Exit, 565, 1072
Last Farewell, The, 1053
Last Goodbye, 135
Last Kiss, The, 167
Last Laugh, The, 267
Last Love of My Life, 22
Last Mango in Paris, 137
Last Mardi Gras, The, 802
Last Minute, The, 620
Last Minute Miracle, 894
Last Morning, 271
Last Night, 106, 590, 682, 948
(Last Night) I Didn't Get to Sleep at All, 836
Last Night When We Were Young, 26

Last Nite, 234
Last of Old England, in South America, 565
Last of the British Blues, 654
Last of the Great Rhythm Guitar Players, The, 1017
Last of the Independents, 791
Last of the Red Hot Burritos, 757
Last of the True Believers, 404
Last Protest Singer, The, 172
Last Real Texas Blues Band, The, 867
Last Rebel, The, 609
Last Record Album, The, 588
Last Round-Up, The, 230, 991
Last Session, 124, 568, 627
Last Song, The, 503
Last Soul Man, The, 1076
Last Splash, 779
Last Stop: This Town, 303
Last Temptation, The, 215
Last Temptation of Elvis, The, 266, 790
Last Thing on My Mind, The, 52, 204, 761, 757
Last Time, The, 849, 1054
Last Time Around, 137
Last Time I Saw Paris, The, 530, 843, 916
Last Time I Saw Richard, The, 679
Last Train to Clarksville, 684
Last Train to Expo 67, 908
Last Train to Hicksville, 445
Last Train to Transcentral, 548
Last Waltz, The, *53, 272, 432, 462*, 823
Late for the Sky, 132
Late Great Johnny Ace, The, 5, 900
Late in the Day, 961
Late John Garfield Blues, The, 799
Late Night, 405
Late Night Brubeck, 133
Late Night Grande Hotel, 404
Late Night Radio, 862
Late Nights in Soho, 1093
Lately, 77, *759*
Later Alligator, 173
Later for You Baby, 173
Later That Year, 652
Latest and Greatest, 22
Latin American Suite, 307
Latter Days, 570
Laugh, 929
Laugh at Me, 177
Laugh, Clown, Laugh, 1031
Laugh? I Nearly Bought One, 535
Laughing, 406
Laughing All the Way to the Cleaners, 575

Laughing Boy, 1046
Laughing Gnome, The, 110, 718
Laughing Policeman, The, 506
Laughing Song, The, 367, 506
Laughter, 270, 290
Laughter and Lust, 480
Laughter in the Rain, 880
Laundromat Blues, 537
Laura, 372, 529
Laura, What's He Got That I Ain't Got?, 78
Laureles, Los, 854
Lavender, 642
Lavender Blue, 477, 536
Lawd I'm Just a Country Boy in This Great Big Freaky City, 866
Lawdy Lawdy Blues, 1063
Lawdy Miss Clawdy, 58, 793, 794, 860
Lawn Boy, 773
Lawrence Welk Hee-Haw-Counter-Revolution Polka, The, 189
Laws Must Change, The, 654
Lawyer Clark Blues, 315
Lawyers in Love, 132
Lay Down (Candles in the Rain), 432, 659
Lay Down, Sally, 33, 187, 886
Lay Down Your Arms, 183, 892, 940
Lay Down Your Weary Tune, 146
Lay It All Out, 638
Lay It Down, 223
Lay Lady Lay, 292, 476, 1065
Lay Your Hands on Me, 981
Lay Your Love on Me, 698
Lay Your Troubles Down, 1070
Layla, *15*, 186, *283*
Layla and Other Assorted Love Songs, 186
Laziest Gal in Town, The, 264
Lazy, 960
Lazy Line Painter Jane, 75
Lazy Old Sun, 543
Lazy River, 158, 210, 244, 674, 763
Lazy Sunday, 912, 913
Lazybones, 158, 541, 602, 662, 820, 842
Lazzarella, 681
Le Chat Bleu, 783
Lead and How to Swing It, The, 516
Lead Me on, 94, 397
Lead Me to the Water, 801
Lead on, 955
Lead Vocalist, 950
Leadbelly, 568
Leader, 386
Leader of the Laundromat, 697, 888

Leader of the Pack, 404, 697, 888
League of Gentlemen, The, 360
Leah, 741
Lean on Me, 1074, *1074*
Leaning on a Lamp-post, 346, 373, 442
Leap of Faith, 596
Leap Up and Down and Wave Your Knickers in the Air, 541
Learn to Love It, 1070
Learnin' the Blues, 904
Learning the Game, 451
Learning to Crawl, 791
Learning to Flinch, 1093
Learning to Live Again, 123
Leather and Lace, 296, 342
Leather Jackets, 503
Leather Launderette, 765
Leave a Light on, 157
Leave a Little Love, 604, 823
Leave in Silence, 258
Leave Me Alone (Ruby Red Dress), 821
Leave My Girl Alone, 994
Leave My Kitten Alone, 504, 791
Leave the Guns at Home, 49, 403
Leave Them All Behind, 834
Leave Your Hat on, 487
Leavin' Trunk, 966
Leaving of Liverpool, The, 185
Leaving on a Jet Plane, 258, 768
Lebanon, The, 461
Led Zeppelin, 570
Led Zeppelin II, 569
Led Zeppelin III, 424, 569
Led Zeppelin IV, Untitled, 569
Lee's Goofed, 895
Left My Gal in the Mountains, 842
Left Right out of Your Heart, 751
Left to My Own Devices, 768
Leftism, 572
Lefty, 898
Lefty's Gone, 360, 955
Leg o' Mutton Rag, 852
Legacy, 500, 583, 596, 639
Legacy: A Tribute to Fleetwood Mac's Rumours, 217, 342
Legacy and the Legend, The, 284
Legacy of the Blues Vol. 12, The, 454
Legal Man, 75
Legalise It, 911, 988
Legend, 198, 311, 609, 644, 804, 946
Legend and the Legacy, The, 760, 996
Legend in His Spare Time, A, 432
Legend in My Time, Hank Wilson Vol. III, 864
Legend of Andrew McGraw, 625
Legend of John Henry's Hammer, The, 165

Legend of Sleepy John Estes, The, 315
Legend of Xanadu, 245
Legendary Deford Bailey: Country Music's First Black Star, The, 48
Legendary Hearts, 824
Legendary Lefty Frizzell, The, 360
Legendary, Lovely Marlene, The, 264
Legendary Paul Butterfield Rides Again, The, 145
Legendary Performer, A, 790
Legendary Son House/Father of Folk Blues, The, 457
Legion of the Lost, The, 1046
Legrand Jazz, 573
Legs, 1094
Leicester Square Rag, 857
Leilani, 230
Leisure, 99
Leisure Suite, 617
Lelolia, 332
Lemon Incest, 367
Lemon Tree, 598
Lemonade Song, The, 4
Lenny, 961
Leo Sayer, 873
Leon Russell, 864
Leon Russell and the New Grass Revival, 864
Leon Russell and the Shelter People, 864
Leroy, 875, 946
Les Bicyclettes de Belsize, 462
Les Paul Now, 760
Les Stances à Sophie, 31
Leslie West Band, The, 702
Leslie West – Mountain, 701
Less Than Zero, 219
Lessons in Living, 15
Lessons in Love, 579
Lester Leaps in, 1087
Lester 'n' Mac, 341
Lester Young Story, The, 1087
Let 'Em in, 611, 759
Let a Smile Be Your Umbrella, 323
Let Her Cry, 453
Let Her Down Easy, 243
Let Him Have It, 261
Let It All Hang Out, 541
Let It Alone, 1057
Let It Be, 52, 65, 67, 67, 790, 930, 1055
Let It Be Me, 144, 153, 319, 320, 378, 458
Let It Bleed, 551, 849
Let It Loose, 314
Let It Rock, 882
Let It Roll, 588, 882
Let It Snow, 114
Let Love in, 169

Let Love Rule, 554
Let Me, 829
Let Me Be, 999
Let Me Be Good to You, 818
Let Me Be the Man My Daddy Was, 180
Let Me Be the One, 595, 885
Let Me Be There, 721
Let Me Be Your Lover, 271
Let Me Be Your Wings, 637
Let Me Belong to You, 464
Let Me Call You Sweetheart, 140
Let Me Entertain You, 1065
Let Me Go Home Whiskey, 669
Let Me Go Lover, 120
Let Me Go Rock'n'Roll, 546
Let Me in, 1071
Let Me in Your Life, 355
Let Me Know (I Have a Right), 376
Let Me Love You Tonight, 806
Let Me Off Uptown, 108, 556, 734
Let Me Tickle Your Fancy, 478
Let Me Touch You, 737
Let Me Up (I've Had Enough), 771
Let Off Sup'm, 475
Let the Beat Control Your Body, 1001
Let the Four Winds Blow, 58, 275
Let the Good Times Roll, 58, 518, 539, 895
Let the Heartaches Begin, 502, 610, 949
Let the Music Do the Talking, 9
Let the Music Take Your Mind, 550
Let the People Sing, 373
Let the Rhythm Hit 'Em, 43
Let the River Run, 898
Let the Rough Side Drag, 1071
Let the Slave (Price of Experience), 695
Let the Sunshine in, 836
Let the Water Run Down, 800
Let Them Eat Bingo, 330
Let Them Talk, 504
Let There Be Drums, 712
Let There Be Love, 202, 891, 902
Let There Be Peace on Earth, 383
Let There Be Rock, 4
Let Your Dim Light Shine, 922
Let Your Hair Down, 975
Let Your Love Flow, 75
Let Your Yeah Be Yeah, 193
Let's All Sing Like the Birdies Sing, 319
Let's Burn, 163
Let's Call the Whole Thing Off, 34, 380
Let's Chill, 835
Let's Dance, *111*, 438, 688, 819, 846, 1015

Let's Do It, 222, 784
Let's Do It Again, 655, 938
Let's Do It (Let's Fall in Love), 547
Let's Do It Over, 899
Let's Do the Freddie, 357
Let's Face the Music and Dance, 34, 79
Let's Fall in Love, 286
Let's Get Back to Me and You, 479
Let's Get Buck Naked and Fuck, 467
Let's Get It on, 121, 374
Let's Get It Started, 418
Let's Get It Up, 4
Let's Get Serious, 478
Let's Get Together No. 1, 752
Let's Go Crazy, 797
Let's Go Get Stoned, 32, 292, 362
Let's Go Out to the Programs, 268
Let's Go Round Again, 40
Let's Go Streaking, 51
Let's Go to Bed, 238
Let's Go to San Francisco, 253
Let's Go Trippin', 63, 490
Let's Groove, 298
Let's Hang on, 245, 349, 637
Let's Have a Party, 37, 482, 483, 641
Let's Have a Quiet Night in, 611, 923
Let's Have Another Party, 37
Let's Hear It for the Boy, 287, 651
Let's Jump the Broomstick, 571
Let's Make a Baby, 759
Let's Make Sure We Kiss Goodbye, 383, 398
Let's Make Up and Be Friendly, 105
Let's Misbehave, 784
Let's Party, 501
Let's Play House, 799
Let's Pretend, 604, 817
Let's Put It All Together, 460, 615, 958
Let's Put It Back Together Again, 582
Let's Put out the Lights, 1011
Let's Put the Fun Back in Rock'n'Roll, 154
Let's Rob a Bank, 887
Let's Rock 'n' Roll, 37
Let's See Action, 1054
Let's Slip Away, 559
Let's Stay Together, 402, 438, 680, 998
Let's Stick Together, 333, *333*, 427
Let's Take a Walk Around the Block, 422
Let's Take an Old Fashioned Walk, 511, 706

Let's Take the Long Way Home, 663
Let's Talk About Love, 266, 540
Let's Talk about Sex, 869
Let's Talk About Us, 534
Let's Think About Living, 134
Let's Try Romance, 769
Let's Twist Again, 175, 416
Let's Wait Awhile, 479
Let's Walk Thata-Way, 819
Let's Work, 846
Let's Work Together, 154, 427, 1085
Lethal Injection, 466
Lets Get It on, 10
Lets Get Started, 14
Lets Talk About Love, 267
Letter, The, 112, 198, 683, 764
Letter from America, 812
Letter from Home, 666
Letter Full of Tears, 221, 364, 548, 840
Letter Song, The, 978
Letter That Johnny Walker Read, The, 33
Letter That Never Came, The, 284
Letter to an Angel, A, 186
Letter to Myself, A, 180
Letter to The Beatles, A, 348
Letters, 1040
Letters Have No Arms, 996
Letters Never Sent, 899
Level Best, 579
Level 42, 1020
Level with Me, 617
Levi Stubbs' Tears, 116
Levitation, 225, 591
Lexicon of Love, The, 2, 455
Liaisons, 919
Liar, 984, 1093
Liberace Piano Favourites, 584
Liberation, 181, 268
Liberation Music Orchestra, 410
Liberator, 742
Liberian Suite, 307
Liberty, 793
Liberty Loan March, 924
Libra, 469
Library of Congress Recordings, The, 568
Licensed to Ill, 64, 858
Lick, 575
Lick It Up, 546
Lido Shuffle, 873
Lie to You for Your Love, 75
Liege and Lief, 323
Lies, 804, 816, 835
Life, 156, 902, 1088
Life after Death, 805
Life and Limb, 164
Life and Love, 298

Life and Times, 228
Life as We Know It, 827
Life Begins at Forty, 997
Life Begins at the Hop, 1081
Life During Wartime, 938
Life Gets Tee-jus, Don't It?, 842
Life Goes on, 1064
Life Has Its Little Ups and Downs, 830
Life in a Day, 901
Life in a Northern Town, 777
Life in Exile After Abdication, 1018
Life in One Day, 513
Life in Prison, 147
Life in Rhymes, 747
Life in the Fast Lane, 295
Life in the Jungle, 886
Life in the Modern World, 234
Life in Tokyo, 491
Life Is a Dance, 149, 532
Life Is a Minestrone, 976
Life Is a Rollercoaster, 114
Life Is a Song Worth Singing, 764
Life Is Beautiful, 560
Life Is But a Dream, 424
Life Is Just a Bowl of Cherries, 260, 664
Life Is Peachy, 552
Life Is So Peculiar, 518
Life Is So Strange, 1030
Life Is Suicide, 655
Life Is Sweet, 239, 622
Life Is What You Make It, 417
Life – Live, 979
Life, Love and Faith, 990
Life of Riley, 585
Life of Surprises, A, 788
Life of the Last Prophet, The, 946
Life on Your Own, 461
Life Thru a Lens, 1065
Life Time, 850, 1065
Life'll Kill You, 1093
Life's a Riot with Spy vs Spy, 116
Life's Been Good to Me, 295
Life's Railway to Heaven, 18
Life's Rich Pageant, 826
Life's Too Good, 86
Lifehouse, 1055
Lifeline, 926
Lifetime Friends, 589
Light, The, 51, 194
Light & Heavy, 473
Light Flight, 765
Light Inside, The, 1093
Light My Fire, 279, 332, 442, 650
Light Years, 216, 677
Lightfoot, 584
Lightnin' in New York, 454
Lightnin' Strikes, 185
Lightning Strikes Twice, 682
Lights, 519
Lights of Cincinatti, The, 1026

Lights Out, 271, *376*, 714, *861*, 946, 1006
Lights Out, Sweet Dreams, 522
Like a Baby, 282
Like a Hurricane, *148*, 1088
Like a King, 423
Like a Prayer, 631, *798*
Like a Rock, 882
Like a Rolling Stone, 52, 97, 292, 551, 643, 850
Like a Virgin, 631, 846, 1052
Like an Old Fashioned Waltz, 324
Like an Old Time Movie, 633
Like Brother Like Sister, 403
Like Clockwork, 376
Like Dreamers Do, 752, 776
Like Flies on Sherbert, 113
Like It Is, 754
Like Long Hair, 351, 828
Like Making Love, 893
Like Never Before, 966
Like to Get to Know You Well, 513
Like You Do, 585
Lilac Wine, 123
Lili Marlene, 20, 21, 211, 264, *264*, 892
Lillie Lou, 322
Lily Maybelle, 56
Lily of Laguna, 957
Lily on the Beach, 968
Lily Rosemary and the Jack of Hearts, 293
Lily the Pink, 105, 752
Limbo, 984
Limbo Rock, 170, 175
Limehouse Blues, 222
Limelight, 169, 392
Linda Ronstadt, 853
Line Up, 304
Line Up and Come, 1009
Linger Awhile, 1049
Link Wray, 1077
Linton Kwesi Johnson in Dub, 507
Lion, The, 710
Lion and the Cobra, The, 733
Lion Sleeps Tonight, The, 182, 460, 743, 1040
Lionel Richie, 832
Lionheart, 143
Lions in My Own Garden, 787
Lipstick Killers, 717
Lipstick on Your Collar, 353
Lipstick Traces, 526, 736
Liquid Acrobat as Regards the Air, 471
Liquid Skin, 390
Liquor Store Came First, The, 493
Lisa Stansfield, 938
Lisbon Antigua, 833
Lisdoonvarna, 690

Listen, 1038
Listen Like Thieves, 473
Listen Now, 857
Listen People, 442
Listen to Me, 450, 451
Listen to the Band, 685
Listen to the Lion, 695
Listen to the Music, 278
Listen to the Radio: Atmospherics, 841
Listen to What the Man Said, 611
Listen to Your Father, 630, 890
Listen to Your Heart, 856
Listen Up, 49
Listen without Prejudice Vol. I, 666
Lita, 500
Lithium, 723
Little Alabama Coon, 930
Little Album, The, 747
Little Big Horn, 705
Little Bit Me, A Little Bit You, A, 684
Little Bit More, A, 34, 271
Little Bit of Love, 357
Little Bit of Rain, 710
Little Bit of Soap, A, 896
Little Bitty Pretty One, 478, 606
Little Bitty Tear, A, 115, 477
Little Black Book, 157, 252
Little Boogie Woogie (In the Back of My Mind), A, 947
Little Boxes, 879
Little Boy, 235
Little Boy Sad, 139
Little Boy That Santa Claus Forgot, The, 211, 608
Little Brown Jug, 670
Little by Little, 130, 929, 1045
Little Chicken Wah Wah, 915
Little Children, 783
Little Creatures, 967
Little Criminals, 720
Little Damozel, The, 726
Little Darlin', 262, 896, 1063
Little Deuce Coupe, 63
Little Devil, 880
Little Diane, 266
Little Dolly Daydream, 957
Little Drummer Boy, 111
Little Earthquakes, 20
Little Egypt, 196, 644
Little Eva, 369
Little Feat, 587
Little Games, 1083
Little Ghetto Boy, 368
Little Girl, The, 27, 201, 470, 1019
Little Girl and the Dreadful Snake, The, 648
Little Glass of Wine, 937
Little Good News, A, 705
Little Grass Shack, 453

Little Gray Home in the West, 387
Little Green Apples, 673
Little Head, 444
Little Honda, 237
Little Honey, 798
Little in Love, A, 831
Little Jeannie, 503
Little Jimmy Rushing and the Big Brass, 862
Little John Special, 674
Little Johnny Jewel, 973
Little Kix, 639
Little Latin Lupe Lu, 834, 865
Little Lies, 342
Little Light Music, A, 499
Little Love Affairs, 404
Little Love and Understanding, A, 68
Little Love Letters, 163
Little Mama, 195
Little Miss Dangerous, 727
Little More Love, A, *169*, 721
Little More Magic, A, 764
Little Nell, 761
Little of What You Fancy (Does You Good), A, 592
Little Old Cabin Down the Lane, 763
Little Old Lady from Pasadena, 490
Little Old Log Cabin in the Lane, The, 161
Little Ole Man, 759
Little Ole Wine Drinker Me, 646
Little Queen, 436
Little Red Caboose Behind the Train, 670
Little Red Corvette, 797
Little Red Monkey, 169
Little Red Record, 1079
Little Red Riding Hood, 356
Little Red Rooster, 213, 269, 790, 849
Little Respect, A, 312, 703
Little Richard Is Back, 589
Little Richard Live, 589
Little Rosa, 776
Little Sandy Sleighfoot, 252
Little Sheila, 12, 91
Little Shoemaker, The, 188, 460
Little Sister, 783, 789, 1085
Little Skipper, 711
Little Slea, 987
Little South of Sanity, A, 10
Little Star, 266
Little Suite (Sound), 31
Little Sweetheart of the Prairie, 670
Little Talk with Jesus, A, 281
Little Things, *142*, 389
Little Time, A, 68

Little Too Late, 76
Little Touch of Schmilsson in the Night, A, 496, 722
Little Town Flirt, 889
Little Wheel Spin, 867
Little White Bull, 57, 942
Little White Cloud That Cried, The, 818
Little White Lies, 276, 435, 496, 597
Little Willy, 964
Little Wing, 217, 318
Little Woman You're So Sweet, 362
Live, 5, 122, 163, 216, 225, 294, 343, 476, 480, 519, 558, 618, 643, 719, 818, 966, 987
Live Acoustic America, 513
Live After Death, 474
Live Alive, 1016
Live! Alone in America, 754
Live and Dangerous, 979
Live and Direct, 35, 966
Live and Improvised, 97
Live and Kickin', 33, 195
Live and Learn, 575
Live and Let Die, 407
Live and Let Live!, 212
Live and Loud, 88
Live and More, 338, 960
Live and Uncensored, 482
Live and Unreleased, 440
Live at Blues Alley, 645
Live at Budokan, 293
Live at Burnley, 288
Live at Caesar's Palace, 516
Live at Café au Go-Go, 452
Live at Donington, 474
Live at Dusseldorf, 122
Live at El Paradiso, 1077
Live at Guene Hall, 1027
Live at Heartbreak Hotel, 792
Live at Las Vegas, 784
Live at Last, 942
Live at Leeds, 534, 1054
Live at Liberty Lunch, 309
Live at Luther College, 246
Live at Maratime Hall, 767
Live at Max's Kansas City, 1018
Live at McCabes, 850
Live at McCabe's Guitar Shop, 437
Live at Monterey, 748
Live at Montreux, 940
Live at Pep's, 566
Live at Red Rocks, 689
Live at Red Rocks 8:15:95, 246
Live at Ronnie Scott's, 901
Live at Sin-E, 135
Live at the Acropolis, 1082
Live at the Apollo, 128, 413, 434, 538, 708, 975

Live at the BBC, 66, 766
Live at the Bottom Line, 729
Live at the Brixton Academy, 808
Live at the City, 734
Live at the Copa, 962
Live at the Dallas International Motor Speedway, 1071
Live at the Dancing Slipper, 207
Live at the Deer Head Inn, 492
Live at the Fillmore, 82, 492, 673, 912, 999
Live at the Fillmore East, 15
Live at the Fillmore, February 1969, 148
Live at the Fillmore West, 537
Live at the Harlem Square Club, 213
Live at the Hollywood Bowl, 280
Live at the Hollywood Palace, 8
Live at the Hollywood Palladium, 129, 558
Live at the LA Troubadour, 324
Live at the Lyceum, 902
Live at the Marquee, 964
Live at the Marquee 1983, 745
Live at the Moonlight Club, 929
Live at the Norodden Blues Festival, 1075
Live at the Olympia, 774
Live at the Opry, 687
Live at the Point, 690
Live at the Regal, 538
Live at the Ritz, 264
Live at the Roxy Theatre, 64
Live at the Royal Albert Hall, 310, 926, 1047
Live at the Star Club Hamburg, 505
Live at the Village Vanguard, 206
Live at the Witch Trials, 326
Live at Tipitina's Vol. II, 714
Live at Watkins Glen, 53
Live at Wembley, 657, 808
Live at Winterland '68, 517
Live Baby Live, 473
Live Bootleg, 9
Live Bullet, 882
Live Cream, 225
Live Dead, 400
Live Era '87–'93, 407
Live Fast, Love Hard, 1086
Live Feeding Frenzy, 137
Live for Today,, 860
Live Forever, 730
Live from Albertane, 421
Live from Austin, 613
Live from Central Park, 232
Live from Mars, 148
Live from Neon Park, 588
Live from Paris and Conarky, 633
Live from the Bataclan, 135
Live from the Fall, 99

Live from the Tivoli, 1053
Live in an American Time Spiral. The African Game, 863
Live in China, 182
Live in Concert, 13, 622
Live in Dublin, 690
Live in Edmonton, 800
Live in 88, 962
Live in Europe, 283, 287, 368, 999
Live in Italy, 824
Live in Japan, 70, 427, 607, 747
Live in Las Vegas, 275
Live in London, 704, 907
Live in Moscow, 1009
Live in New Orleans, 656
Live in New York City, 576
Live in NYC '97, 1071
Live in Tasmania, 322
Live in Texas, 602
Live! In the Air Age, 710
Live . . . in the Heart of the City. Come an' Get It, 1050
Live in the UK, 271
Live It Up, 229, 718
Live Jam, 484
Live Jazz, 265
Live Ju Ju, 8
Live Killers, 808
Live?!; Like a Suicide,* 407
Live Love, 867
Live, Love, Larf and Loaf, 982
Live Magic, 808
Live MCMXCIII, 1018
Live 1973, 757
Live 1975–85, 934
Live '91, 263
Live on Beale Stereet, 94
Live on Planet Earth, 714
Live on the Queen Mary, 802
Live on Two Legs, 762
Live One, A, 773, 1024
Live! One Night Only, 558
Live Paris – Ziquinchor, 989
Live Peace in Toronto, 576, 740
Live Rhymin', 232, 899
Live Seeds, 169
Live Shit! Binge & Purge, 665
Live Songs, 201
Live . . . Stolen Moments, 856
Live Talkies, 865
Live: The Mongoloid Years, 260
Live: The Way We Walk, 378
Live Through This, 448, 723
Live to Tell, 631
Live Together, 938, 983
Live Wire, 645
Live Wire/Blues Power, 537
Live with Archie Shepp, 620
Live with the Oakland Symphony Orchestra, 432
Live Wood, 1044
Live (X-Cert), 956

Live Your Life Be Free, 157
Live-Evil, 492
Livemiles, 968
Liverpool, 354
Liverpool Oratorio, 612
Livery Stable Blues, 742
Lives in the Balance, 132
Livid, 96
Livin' Doll, 57, 831
Livin' in the USA, 673
Livin' It Up, 955
Livin' on a Prayer, 102
Livin' the Blues, 154
Livin' Thing, 304
Living a Little, Laughing a Little, 725
Living After Midnight, 519
Living All Alone, 370
Living and Dying in 3/4 Time, 137
Living Black!, 1034
Living End, The, 701
Living Eyes, 71
Living for the City, 1077
Living for the Spangled Moment, 711
Living in a Fantasy, 873
Living in America, 127, 128
Living in Fear, 289
Living in Harmony, 831
Living in Oz, 934
Living in Reverse, 653
Living in the 20th Century, 674
Living in the Material World, 427
Living in the Past, 498, 499
Living in the USA, 854
Living Legend of Carmen Miranda, The, 678
Living My Life, 512
Living Next Door to Alice, 698
Living on the Front Line, 398
Living Room Tapes, The, 970
Living Time, 318, 863
Living Together, 45
Living without Your Love, 933
Living Years, The, 378
Liza, 510, 522, 527, 605
Liza Jane, 383
Liza Lee, 862
Liza with a Z, 372
Lizard, 536
Lizzie and the Rainman, 997, *997*
Load, 665
Loaded, 153, 796, *1018*
Loaded (Fully Loaded), 1018
Loading Zone, 190
Loads, 422
Loan Me a Dime, 873
Local Boy in the Photograph, 945
Local Color, 15
Loch Lomond, 983
Locked in, 1074
Loco, El, 1094

Loco Live, 815
Loco-Motion, The, 396, 540, 545, 677, 742, 951, 1056
L.O.D. (Love on Delivery), 732
Lodger, 111, 311
Lodi, 226
Lofty Fake Anagram, 141, 217
Lofty's Roach Shuffle, 210
Logical Progression, 138, *138*
Logical Song, The, 962
Lola, 543
Lola Versus Powerman and the Moneygoround, Part One, 543
Lollipop, 184, 752, 964
Londinium, 168
London, 1089
London Blues, 609
London by Night, 904
London Calling, 191
London Concert, The, 802
London Gumbo, 1020
London Howlin' Wolf Sessions, The, 459
London Kid, 491
London Muddy Waters Sessions, The, 1037
London o Hull 4, 68
London Pride, 222
London Recordings, The, 660
London Session, 582
London Sessions, 82
London Town, 611
London Waltz, 329
London's Burning, 191
Lone Ranger, The, 630
Lone Star State of Mind, 404
Lone Teen Ranger, The, 897
Lone Wolf, 1061
Lonelier Than This, 297
Loneliest Man in the World, The, 317
Lonely at the Top, 719
Lonely Avenue, 173, 594, 783
Lonely Ballerina, 639
Lonely Boy, 24, 218, 747, 853
Lonely Boy Blue, 1000
Lonely Bull, 17, *17*
Lonely City, 659
Lonely Days, 71
Lonely Drifter, 736
Lonely Island, 213
Lonely Just Like Me, 13
Lonely Lover, 475
Lonely Man, 588
Lonely Night (Angel Face), 156
Lonely No More, 741
Lonely Ol' Night, 660
Lonely One, The, 786
Lonely People, 19
Lonely Soldier, 474
Lonely Street, 1056
Lonely Surfer, The, 724

Lonely Teardrops, 226, 464, 475, 1069
Lonely Teenager, 265
Lonely Things, The, 623
Lonely This Christmas, 183, 698
Lonely Town, 417
Lonely Weekends, 521, 702, 830
Lonely Weekends: the Sun Years, 830
Lonely Wine, 384
Lonely Years, 654
Loner, The, 1087
Lonesome, 325
Lonesome Christmas Blues, 92
Lonesome Crow, 875
Lonesome Death of Hattie Carroll, The, 164, 292
Lonesome Jubilee, The, 661
Lonesome Loser, 590
Lonesome No More, 368
Lonesome Picker Rides Again, The, 948
Lonesome Radio Cowboy, 955
Lonesome River, 937
Lonesome Road, The, 38, 978
Lonesome 7–7203, 432, 996
Lonesome Standard Time, 652
Lonesome Tears in My Eyes, 66
Lonesome Town, 612
Lonesome Train, The, 840
Long After Dark, 771
Long Ago and Far Away, 380, 527, 530
Long Agos and Worlds Apart, 913
Long As I Can See the Light, 226
Long Black Veil, *182*, 360
Long Cool Woman in a Black Dress, 403, 450
Long Distance Voyager, 689
Long Gone Lonesome Blues, 1059
Long Haired Lover from Liverpool, 746
Long Hard Look, 345
Long Harvest, The, 183, 613
Long Hot Summer, 1044
Long John Silver, 494
Long Journey Home, The, 182
Long Line Rider, 244
Long Live Love, 721, 891
Long Live Our Love, 888
Long Live Rock, 1054
Long Live the Chief, 59
Long Live the Kane, 84
Long Lonesome Blues, 495
Long Long Time, 853
Long Long Way from Home, 345
Long May You Run, 1088
Long Player, 912
Long Run, The, 295
Long Shot Kick the Bucket, 549
Long Tall Glasses, 872
Long Tall Sally, 107, 416, 543, 589

Long Tall Shorty, 221
Long Time Away, 954
Long Time Comin', 97
Long Time Gone, 229
Long Train Running, 52, 279
Long Walk Home, 1088
Long Walk to DC, 938
Long Way from Home, 1050
Long Way from Lubbock, 228, 570
Long Way Home, A, 126
Longer, 343
Longer We Make Love, The, 1048
Longfellow Serenade, 262
Longhaired Redneck, 199
Longing in Their Hearts, 814
Longneck Bottle, 123
Longview, 402
Look, The, 856
Look at Granny Run, Run, 783, 812, 969
Look at Me, 401, 451, 931
Look at That Face, 719
Look at the Fool, 136
Look at Yourself, 1009
Look Away, 181, 1031
Look Before You Leap, 692
Look for a Star, 430
Look for the Silver Lining, 260
Look in My Eyes, 171
Look Inside Midnight Rainbows, A, 925
Look into the Future, 519
Look Mama, 513
Look of Love, The, 2, 45, 394, 455, 631, 650, 933
Look on Yonder Wall, 486
Look on Yonder's Wall, 233
Look Sharp, 480, 856
Look Through Any Window, 449
Look Through My Window, 633
Look to the Rainbow, 492
Look What the Cat Dragged in, 781
Look What They Done to My Song, Ma, 174
Look What You Done for Me, 402
Look What You've Done, 1058
Look What You've Done to Me, 873
Look What You've Done to My Heart, 836
Look-Ka Py Py, 714
Lookin' at You, 822
Lookin' for Love, 384
Lookin' Out My Back Door, 226
Looking after No. 1, 376
Looking Back, 78
Looking Back: The Biggest Hits, 889
Looking Back to See, 132
Looking East, 132

Looking for a Love, 376, 1076
Looking for a New Love, 886
Looking for Christmas, 90
Looking for Clues, 751
Looking for Jack, 662
Looking for that Perfect Beat, 51
Looking Forward, 229, 1088
Looking the World Over, 661
Looking Through the Eyes of Love, 778
Looking Up at Down, 124
Looks Like a Job for . . . , 84
Looks Like Rain, 718
Looks Like We Made It, 637
Looky Looky (Look at Me), 736
Loony on the Bus, 424
Loop Di Love, 541
Loop-De-Loop, 1015
Loopzilla, 194
Loose Ends, 440
Loose Fit, 421
Loose Monkeys, 754
Loose Nut, 372, *850*
Loose Salute, 685
Loose Shoes & Tight Pussy, 113
Loose Talk, 629, 748
Loosey's Rap, 488
Lop-sided, Overloaded and It Wiggled When I Rode It, 464
Lorca, 135
Lord Franklin, 164
Lord Lankin, 164
Lord Mr Ford, 822
Lord of the Dance, 164
Lord of the Highway, 309
Lord Randal, 292
Lord Randall, My Son, 1049
Lord Upminster, 290, 911
Lord's Prayer, The, 480, 905
Lorelei, 959
Los Angeles Sessions, 557
Loser, 69
Loser's Weepers, 487
Losing Battle, 271
Losing My Religion, 827
Losing You, 571
Lost Again, 1084
Lost Chord, The, 250, 382
Lost Dogs and Mixed Blessings, 799
Lost Girl, 995
Lost Her in the Sun, 949
Lost Highway, 7
Lost in a Dream, 827
Lost in France, 1002
Lost in Music, 327
Lost in the Fifties Tonight, 675
Lost in the Stars, 755, 1067
Lost in You, 950
Lost in Your Eyes, 381
Lost in Your Love, 926
Lost John, 277
Lost Live Album, The, 549

Lost Love, 655
Lost Without Your Love, 119
Lot About Livin', A, 479
Lots of Love and I, 100
Lotta Lovin', 1021
Lottie Mo, 280
Lotus Blossom, 307
Lou Reed Live, 824
Loud and Proud, 709
Louder Than Love, 924
Louder Than Words, 832
Louie Louie, 82, 83, *83*, 427, 468, 469, 699, 829
Louis and His Friends, 29
Louis, Country & Western, 192
Louis Prima, 796
Louise, 180, 461, 839, 1052
Louise Goffin, 540
Louise Louise, 231
Louisiana, 73
Louisiana Cajun Country, 531
Louisiana Love, 704
Louisiana Man, 512, 530, 1058
Louisiana Woman, Mississippi Man, 607, 1000
Lovable, 213
Love, 42, 561, 600
Love Action, 461
Love Ain't Nothin' but a Business Goin' on, 754
Love Alive, 432
Love All the Hurt Away, 355
Love Among the Cannibals, 495
Love and Affection, 27, *27*, 954
Love and Dancing, 461
Love & Danger, 309
Love & Fear, 56
Love and Fury, 987
Love and Happiness, 18, 651
Love & Hate, 56
Love and Kisses, 336
Love & Liberty, 384
Love and Marriage, 150, 833, 904, 1012
Love and Other Bruises, 12
Love and Other Obsessions, 935
Love and Rock'n'Roll, 872
Love and the Russian Winter, 902
Love and Understanding, 1032
Love at First Sting, 875
Love at Last, 451
Love at the Five and Dime, 404, 652
Love at the Greek, 262
Love Attack, 434
Love Ballad, 77
Love Beach, 310
Love Bites, 145
Love Buzz, 723
Love Came to Me, 266
Love Can Be Found Anywhere (Even in a Guitar), 203

Love Can Build a Bridge, 520
Love Can't Ever Get Better Than This, 907
Love Cats, 238
Love Changes Everything, 593
Love Child, 963
Love Chronicles, 947
Love Comes in Spurts, 973
Love Comes Quickly, 767
Love Corporation, 460
Love Deluxe, 866
Love Devotion Surrender, 624, 871
Love Don't Come Easy, 750
Love Don't Live Here Anymore, 1052
Love for Sale, 337, 485, 1043
Love for What It Is, 781
Love, God, Murder, 166
Love Goes to Building on Fire, 966
Love Gone Bad, 939
Love Grows Where My Rosemary Goes, 610, 823, 1025
Love Gun, 546
Love Hangover, 855
Love Has Found a Way, 127
Love Has No Pride, 102, 813, 814
Love Her, 1026
Love Her Madly, 280
Love Hurts, 134, 177, 709, 741, 757, 1073
Love I Can Feel, A, 452
Love I Lost, The, 764
Love in a Small Town, 746
Love in an Elevator, 9
Love in Bloom, 230, 839
Love in Exile, 398
Love in Store, 342
Love in the First Degree, 12, 52
Love in the Shadows, 880
Love in Vain, 509
Love Is, 1055
Love Is a Battlefield, 76
Love Is a Fire, 617
Love Is a Hurtin' Thing, 818
Love Is a Many Splendored Thing, 126, 323, 347
Love Is a Stranger, 317
Love Is a Wonderful Thing, 102, 476
Love Is All Around, 995, 1047
Love Is All We Need, 303
Love Is Always Seventeen, 119
Love Is Blue, 70, 192, 256, 698
Love Is Everywhere, 768
Love Is Forever, 733
Love Is Here and Now You're Gone, 963
Love Is in Control (Finger on the Trigger), 960
Love Is in the Air, 169
Love Is Just Around the Corner, 839

Love Is Life, 457
(Love Is Like a) Baseball Game, 472
Love Is Like a Violin, 528
Love Is Like Oxygen, 964
Love Is Love, 553
Love Is on a Roll, 403
Love Is Overdue, 474
Love Is Strange, 50, 629
Love Is Stronger Than Pride, 866
Love Is the Drug, 857
Love Is the Healing, 616
Love Is the Icon, 1048
Love Is the Law, 991
Love Is the Only Feeling, 278
Love Is the Sweetest Thing, 112, 725, 908
(Love Is) The Tender Trap, 904
Love Is the Thing, 496
Love Is Thicker Than Water, 71
Love It to Death, 215
Love Jones, 1038
Love Junk, 860
Love Kills, 693, 808
Love Language, 764
Love Lessons, 214
Love Letters, 348, 625, 703, 789
Love Letters in the Sand, 108, 1073
Love Lifted Me, 940
Love Lifted Up, 847
Love Like a Man, 977
Love Like Blood, 534, 723
Love Like Yours, A, 929, 998
Love Lion, 280
Love Locked Out, 18
Love, Love, Love, 171, 195, 262, 430, 438, 776, 818
Love Machine (Part 1), 841
Love Makes a Woman, 180
Love Makes No Sense, 740
Love Makes Sweet Music, 919
Love Makes the World Go Round, 664
Love Man, 821
Love Me Baby, 951
Love Me by Name, 394
Love Me Do, 66, 486, 613, 647
Love Me for a Reason, 121, 746
Love Me for the Reason, 114
Love Me Forever, 567
Love Me I'm a Liberal, 733
Love Me Like I Love You, 62
Love Me Like You Used To, 997
Love Me or Leave Me, 249, 276, 315, 334, 455, 523
Love Me or Love Me Not, 149
Love Me Still, 533
Love Me Tender, 538, 910
Love Me with a Feeling, 561, 632
Love Meeting Love, 579
Love Minus Zero/No Limit, 292, 867

Love Missile F1-11, 467
Love Movement, The, 994
Love Moves, 1055
Love Natty, 692
Love Needs, 424
Love Needs a Heart, 425
Love Not Money, 320
Love of My Life, 164
Love of the Common People, 496, 1089
Love of the Loved, 89
Love on a Roll, 1059
Love on the Airwaves, 368
Love on the Beat, 367
Love on the Rocks, 262
Love on Your Side, 981
Love or Physical, 32
Love Over and Over, 619
Love Over Gold, 267
Love Over Rage, 841
Love Over-Due, 128
Love Plus One, 443
Love Potion No. 9, 196, 878
Love Power, 1033
Love Really Hurts without You, 732
Love Remembers, 77
Love Resurrection, 703
Love Rhymes, 319
Love Rollercoaster, 736
Love Rustler, 613
Love Sensation, 87
Love Shack, 43
Love Shoulda Brought You Home, 44, 118
Love, Smokey, 841
Love So Fine, A, 182
Love So Right, 71
Love Somebody, 934
Love Somebody Today, 906
Love Song, 238, 240, 705, 705
Love Song to a Stranger, 47
Love Songs, 271, 832, 1033
Love Songs for Underdogs, 984
Love Songs of the World, 192
Love Spell, 958
Love Spreads, 952
Love Stinks, 376
Love Stories, 251
Love Story, 601
Love Supreme, A, 49, 206, 511, 1002
Love Takes Time, 157
Love Talk, 958
Love the Life You Live, 550
Love the One You're With, 229, 476, 882, 1013
Love the World Away, 847
Love Theme from 'The Godfather', 1057
Love TKO, 1076
Love to Hate You, 312

Love to Love You, 693
Love to Love You Baby, 960
Love Touch, 950
Love Tracks, 625
Love Train, 354, 736
Love Trap, 139
Love Travels, 652
Love Trilogy, 960
Love Unlimited, 363
Love Walked in, 339, 1034
Love Wars, 1076
Love Will Conquer All, 832
Love Will Find a Way, 92
Love Will Keep Us Together, 156, 880
Love Will Lead You Back, 1032
Love Will Never Do (Without You), 479
Love Will Tear Us Apart, 716, 1089
Love Won't Let Me Wait, 255
Love You All My Lifetime, 533
Love You Live, 849
Love You Save, The, 478, 978
Love You the Right Way, 976
Love You to Tears, 737
Love Zone, 732
Love-in, 592
Love's Been Good to Me, 623
Love's Been Rough on Me, 487
Love's Easy Tears, 199
Love's Gonna Get Ya!, 907
Love's Gonna Getcha, 106
Love's Got a Hold on Me, 127
Love's Got a Hold on You, 479
Love's Great Adventure, 1007
Love's Made a Fool of You, 228
Love's Melodies, 879
Love's Street and a Full Road, 139
Love's Theme, 1048
Love's Unkind, 960
Loveboat, *312*, 677
Loved One, 473
Lovedrive, 875
Lovefool, 156
Lovehunter, 1050
Loveless, 371, 707
Loveliest Night of the Year, The, 563
Lovelight, 908
Lovelines, 160
Lovelock, 750
Lovely Day, 1074
Lovely on the Water, 942
Lovely One, 478
Lovely Sweet Banks of the Moy, The, 182
Lovely to Look At, 334
Lover, 428, 572, 759, 760
Lover and His Lass, A, 242
Lover Boy, 732, *971*
Lover Come Back to Me, 753, 852

Lover in Me, The, 44, *298*
Lover Man, 448, 1015
Lover Overboard, 549
Lover Please, 626, 963, 1056
Lover's Concerto, A, 1015
Lover's Holiday, 1013
Lover's Question, A, 78, 625
Loverboy, 169
Lovers, 44
Lovers Again, 740
Lovers Always Forgive, 548
Lovers Never Say Goodbye, 339
Lovers of the World Unite, 403
Lovers Who Wander, 266
Loves Me Like a Rock, 268, 899
Lovescapes, 262
Lovesexy, 798
Lovesick Blues, 468, 625, 1059
L-O-V-E-U, 117
Lovey, 575
Lovey Dovey, 770
Lovin' Feelin', 1008
Lovin' Feelings, 932
Lovin' Machine, 426
Lovin' Things, 644
Lovin', Touchin', Squeezin', 519
Lovin' You the Way I Do, 93
Loving Blind, 90
Loving Her Was Easier (Than Anything I'll Ever Do Again), 555
Loving You, 588, 737
Loving You Again, 819
Loving You Is a Natural Thing, 675
Loving You Is Where I Belong, 73
Loving You's a Dirty Job (But Someone's Gotta Do It), 657, 1002
Lovingly Yours, 482
Low, 111, 112, 311
Low Budget, 544
Low End Theory, 521, 994
Low Life, 716
Low Rider, 1030
Low Symphony, 385
Lowdown, 873
Lowlife, 565
L.S.I. (Love Sex Intelligence), 888
Lucille, 497, 589, 847
Luck Be a Lady, 596
Luck of the Draw, 116, *613*, *814*
Luckenback Texas, 683
Lucky, 811
Lucky Day in Hell, 303
Lucky Lips, 131, 574
Lucky Man, 309
Lucky Number, 122, 273
Lucky One, The, 117
Lucky Star, 631
Lucky Steels the Wheel, 33
Lucky Town, 935

Lucretia McEvil, 97
Lucy in the Sky with Diamonds, 503, 968
Lucy Jordan, 271
Luka, 575, 1017
Luke in the Nude, 1001
Lukoli, 353
Lullabies with a Difference, 27
Lullaby of Birdland, 891
Lullaby of Broadway, 1032
Lullaby of the Leaves, 1019
Lullaby to Tim, 450
Lullabye, 755
Lullabys, Legends and Lies, 896
Lulu's Back in Town, 1032
Lumpy Gravy, 1091
Lumumba Héros National, 353
Lush Life, 833, 854
Lust for Life, *468*, *469*, 517
Luther, 1092
Luther Ingram, 471
Luxury Gap, The, 438
Luxury Liner, 425
Lydia, 422
Lydia the Tattooed Lady, 422
Lyin' Eyes, 295, 1023
Lyin' to Myself, 167
Lyle Lovett and his Large Band, 602
Lyndon Johnson Told the Nation, 761
Lyonia, 437
Lyric Suite for Sextet, 216
Lyrics of Fury, 43

Ma Baker, 104
Ma He's Making Eyes at Me, 748
Ma Kelly's Greasy Spoon, 941
Ma Says, Pa Says, 819
Mabasa, 640
Mac, Doc and Del, 1073
Mac Wiseman Sings Gordon Lightfoot, 1073
Mac Wiseman Story, The, 1073
Macalla, 311
MacArthur Park, 9, 350, 496, 960, 1040
MACHINA/The Machines of God, 913
MACHINA II: Friends and Enemies of Modern Music, 913
Machine and Soul, 728
Machine Gun, 208
Machismo, 152, 390
Machito, 628
Macho Man, 1021
Mack the Knife, 29, 169, 244, 313, 337, 1042, 1043, 1067
Mad About the Boy, 222
Mad About You, 157
Mad Dog, 304, *1054*
Mad Dogs and Englishmen, 222

Mad Love, 854
Mad Man Blues, 270
Mad Not Mad, 630
Mad Ruth/The Babe, 737
Mad Shadows, 700
Mad World, 972
Madam Butterfly, 624
Madame George, 694
Madame Sherry, 422
Madcap Laughs, The, 777
Made Again, 642
Made in America, 160
Made in England, 504
Made in Heaven, 808
Made in Japan, 748
Made in USA, 779
Made of Stone, 952
Made to Be Broken, 922
Mad-Eyed Screamers, 905
Madman Across the Water, 503
Madness, 327, 799
Madness, The, 630
Madrugada, 660
Madstock, 630
Maestoso, 55
Magazine, 436, 515
Magdalena, 737
Magenta Haze, 447
Maggie May, 949
Maggot Brain, 194
Magic, 350, 721
Magic and Loss, 783, 824
Magic Balladeer, The, 477
Magic Carpet Ride, 397, 944
Magic Hour, 564
Magic in the Air, 586
Magic Man, 436
Magic Moments, 44, 209, 1053
Magic Music, 522
Magic of Christmas, The, 123
Magical Mirror, 387
Magical Ring, 311
Magician's Birthday, The, 1009
Mágico, 410
Magnetic Fields, 491
Magnetic South, 685
Magnificent Music Machine, The, 415
Maid in Heaven, 710
Maid of Constant Sorrow, A, 204
Maid of Orleans, 742
Maiden's Prayer, 1068
Main Attraction, 807
Main Course, 71, 641
Main Event, The, 218, 904, 956
Main Offender, 558, 850
Main Street Breakdown, 36
Main Theme from 'The Man with the Golden Arm', 885
Maire, 312
Majesty of Love, 352, 813
Majesty of the Blues, The, 645

Majorca, 188
Make 'Em Laugh, 130, 528
Make a Jazz Noise Here, 1092
Make a Little Magic, 724
Make Believe, 62
Make Believe It's Your First Time, 1023
Make Believe World, 604
Make It Big, 666
Make It Easy on Yourself, 45, 144, 1026
Make It Happen, 157
Make It Legal, Mr Segal, 997
Make It Mine, 887
Make It with You, 119
Make Love to Me!, 937
Make Me a Pallet on the Floor, 101, 1082
Make Me Laugh, 25
Make Me Lose Control, 817
Make Me Smile, 181
Make Me Smile (Come up and See Me), 756
Make My Home Wherever I Hang My Hat, 216
Make No Mistake (He's Mine), 159
Make No Mistake (She's Mine), 159, 675
Make Sure You Know Your Classroom, 381
Make That Move, 886
Make the World Go Away, 30
Make Them Die Slowly, 1048
Make Your Own Kind of Music, 638
Makin' Friends, 209
Makin' It on the Street, 702
Makin' Moves, 117
Makin' Music, 126
Makin' Whoopee, 523, 722
Making Believe, 1045
Making Contact, 1006
Making History, 507
Making It Again, 433
Making Love, 338
Making Love Out of Nothing at All, 11
Making Movies, 267
Making Plans for Nigel, 1081
Making Whoopee, 155
Making Your Mind Up, 136
Makossa Rock, 565
Maladjusted, 696
Malagueña, 1010
Malice in Wonderland, 253
Malpractice, 270
Malt and Barley Blues, 368, 635
Malted Milk, 509
Mam Kin, 9
Mama, 353, 378, 931, 980
Mama, La, 41

Mama Africa, 988
Mama Can't Buy You Love, 503
Mama Gave Birth to the Soul Children, 251, 808
Mama Guitar, 217, 564
(Mama) He Treats Your Daughter Mean, 131
Mama He's Crazy, 520
Mama Inez, 901
Mama Let Me Lay It on You, 362
Mama Loocie, 374
Mama Never Told Me, 906
Mama Said, 554, 894
Mama Sang a Sad Song, 21
Mama Talk to Your Daughter, 576
Mama, Tell Them What We're Fighting for, 287, 415
Mama Told Me (Not to Come), 719, 775, 983
Mama Too Tight, 892, 893
Mama Tried, 400, 411
Mama Weer All Crazee Now, 909, 910
Mama Will Bark, 903
Mama's Got a Girlfriend Now, 423
Mama's Pearl, 478
Mambi King, The, 804
Mambo Baby, 131, 787
Mambo Italiano, 195, 664, 787
Mambo Jambo, 787
Mambo King, 235
Mambo Mongo, 870
Mambo No 5, 787
Mambo Rock, 412, 787
Mamie Come and Kiss Your Honey Boy, 930
Mamma Mia, 1
Mammy Blue, 1053
Mamouna, 334
Man, 178, 547
Man Alone, A, 623, 904
Man and a Half, A, 775
Man and a Woman, A, 1033
Man Called Destruction, A, 113
Man Called E, A, 303
Man from Laramie, The, 648
Man from Planet Jazz, The, 830
Man I Love, The, 372, 379, 391, 572, 684
Man in Black, The, 166
Man in the Bowler Hat, The, 647
Man in the Box, 14
Man in the Hills, 140
Man in the Mirror, The, 481
Man in the Sky, 121
Man in the Street, 480, 908
Man Is a Man, A, 250
Man Is Back, The, 1048
Man Machine, 554
Man Made Out of Stone, A, 993

Man Must Carry on, A, 1027
Man Needs a Maid, A, 725, 1088
Man Needs a Woman, A, 160
Man of Constant Sorrow, 291, 937
Man of Mystery, 161, 885
Man of Reason, 1093
Man of Sorrow, 949
Man of Steel, 1061
Man of the World, 341
Man of Words/Man of Music, 110
Man Sized Job, 679
Man That Got Away, The, 26, 135, 371, 380
Man Who, The, 992
Man Who Found the Lost Chord, The, 289
Man Who Put the Germ in Germany, The, 62
Man Who Shot Liberty Valance, The, 45, 778
Man Who Sold the World, The, 110, 604
Man Whose Head Expanded, 326
Man with the Child in His Eyes, The, 143
Man with the Fun, 795, 912
Man with the Horn, The, 248
Man without Love, A, 462
Mañana, 572
Manchild, 178
Mandela, 656
Mandela Day, 901
Mandinka, 733
Mandy, 637
Mangoes, 195
Manhattan, 337, 428
Manhattan Moods, 1003
Manhattan Research Inc, 876
Manhattan Skyline, 11
Manhole, 495
Manhood, 261
Manic Depression, 70
Manic Monday, 54, 500, 798
Manic Nirvana, 570
Manic Pop Thrill, 890
Manifestations, 85
Manifesto, 857
Manilow Sings Sinatra, 637
Manisero, El, 901
Mannenberg, 466
Manners and Physique, 25
Mansion of Aching Hearts, The, 203
Mansion on the Hill, A, 855
Mansize Rooster, 961
Manu Dibango, 263
Manuscript, 947
Many a Mile, 867
Many Rivers to Cross, 154, 193, 1005
Manzanera & Mackay, 857

Manzanera Collection, The, 857
Map of Dreams, 711
Map of the World, A, 666
Maple Leaf Rag, 92, 517
Maple on the Hill, 632
Marathon, 190
Marble Index, 151, 1018
Marbles, 985
Marc, 101
March from Bridge on the River Kwai, 672
March of the Flower Children, 880
March of the Mods, 599
March of the Musketeers, 360, 1075
March or Die, 699
March 16–20, 1007
Marcus Garvey, 140, 140
Marcus Garvey Dread, 85
Mardi Gras, 226
Mardi Gras Mambo, 714
Margaritaville, 137
Margaritaville Cafe Light Night Menu, 137
Margie, 605, 822
Marguerita Time, 941
Maria, 81, 96, 616, 800, 919
Maria Elena, 280
Mariah Carey, 157
Marianne, 646, 1016
Marianne Faithfull, 326
Marie, 282, 1011
Marie from Sunny Italy, 78
Marie Laveau, 55, 896
Marie Marie, 946
Marieke, 119, 120
Marigold Sky, 413
Marijuana, 361
Mark Farner, 396
Mark Twang, 429
Market Square Heroes, 642
Marketplace, 644
Marlene Dietrich at the Café Paris, 264
Marlene on the Wall, 1017
Marquee Moon, 973
Marrakesh Express, 229
Marriage Made in Heaven, A, 985
Marriage on the Rocks, 727
Married Men, 1002
Married Woman Blues, 315
Marriott, 912
Marry an Ugly Woman, 104
Mars Audiac Quintet, 944
Mars, the Bringer of War, 310
Marsalis Standard Time, 645
Marseillaise, La, 367
Marshall Mathers LP, The, 270
Marta, 901, 991
Martha, 1024
Martha Reeves, 645

Marty Robbins Country 1951–58, 837
Marvin Welch and Farrar, 885
Mary, 95, 768
Mary and Willi, 746
Mary Anne, 885
Mary Don't You Weep, 963
Mary Had a Little Lamb, 301, 611
Mary Hamilton, 46
Mary Is Coming, 11
Mary Jane, 488
Mary Lee, 221
Mary Lou, 52, 85, 432
Mary's Boy Child, 73, 104
Mas Canciónes, 854
Mas Exitos des Jose Feliciano, 332
Mashed Potato Time, 744
Mashed Potatoes, 128
Masochism Tango, The, 574
Masque, 635
Masquerade, 83
Masquerade Is Over, The, 424
Mass in F Minor, 305
Massa's in de Cold, Cold Ground, 347
Massachusetts, 71
Masses Against the Classes, 637
Master, The, 141, 375, 916
Master and Servant, 258
Master Blaster (Jammin'), 1077
Master Guitarist, Vols 1 & 2, 8
Master of Bluegrass, 687
Master of Puppets, 665
Master of the Game, 550
Master of the Hawaiian Guitar, 453
Master Song, 201
Master's Voice, The, 222
Masterjam, 514
Masterpiece, 476, 975
Masterplan, The, 731
Masters of Puppets, 665
Masters of the Universe, 805
Masters of War, 204, 292, 762
Matador, 516
Matapedia, 113, 619
Match Box Blues, 495, 581
Matchbox, 766, 939
Material Girl, 631
Matters of the Heart, 172
Matthew and Son, 945
Matthews' Southern Comfort, 652
Mattress of Wire, 41
Mau Mau Stomp, 170
Maverick, 1061
Max Q, 473
Maxi, 795
Maximum Joy, 354
Maximum Overdrive, 1001
May I Have the Next Romance with You, 653
May the Bird of Paradise Fly up Your Nose, 837

May the Sun Shine, 709
Maybe, 56, 171
Maybe Baby, 451
Maybe I Do, 287
Maybe I Know, 394
Maybe I'm Amazed, 611
Maybe It's Live, 751
Maybe the People Would Be the Times, or Between Clark and Hilldale, 600
Maybe This Time, 372
Maybe Tomorrow, 364
Maybe You'll Be There, 496
Maybellene, 81, 179, 358, 379, 836
Mayfield, 972
McCartney, 611
McCartney II, 611
McDonald's Cave, 348
McGarrigle Hour, The, 619
McGuinn, Hillman and Clark, 147
MCMXCIII, 824
McNamara's Band, 230
MCs Act Like They Don't Know, 106
Me and a Gun, 20
Me and Baby Brother, 1030
Me and Bobby McGee, 400, 413, 517, 555, 555, 585
Me and Jane in a Plane, 464, 1078
Me and Jerry, 36, 822
Me and Julio Down by the Schoolyard, 899
Me and Mrs Jones, 370, 759
Me and My Arrow, 722
Me and My Chauffeur, 661
Me and My Chauffeur Blues, 661
Me and My Girl, 908
Me and My Girl (Night-Club-bing), 314
Me and My Life, 784
Me and My Shadow, 583
Me and My Woman, 424
Me and the Boys, 242
Me and You, 180
Me and You and a Dog Named Boo, 756
Me Cyan Believe It, 507
Me in the Honey, 827
Me Myself I, 27
Me No Pop I, 533
Me So Horny, 1001
Me the Peaceful Heart, 604
Meadowlark, 276
Mean, Mean Man, 482
Mean Mistreater, 1071
Mean Mistreater Mama, 160
Mean Old 'Frisco Blues, 233
Mean Old World, 590, 1028
Mean Streak, 831
Mean to Me, 448, 753, 1087
Mean Woman Blues, 266, 741
Meaning of Love, The, 258

Meanwhile, 976
Measure of Pleasure, 283, 911
Meat Is Murder, 918
Mecca, 812
Mecca for Moderns, 561
Mechanical Animals, 638
Mechanix, 1006
Medal Song, 236
Meddle, 777
Medicine Man, 228
Meditation, 501
Meditation of Contemplation, 776
Medusa, 317
Meet el Presidente, 289
Meet John Doe, 973
Meet Me in St Louis, Louis, 706
Meet Me on the Corner, 146, 586
Meet on the Ledge, 323
Meet the Searchers, 878
Meeting by the River, A, 212
Meeting Over Yonder, 470
Meets the Crickets, 1017
Mei Kuei, 560
Mein Kampf, 354
Mek We Dweet, 140
Mel Tormé at the Crescendo, 987
Melancholy Baby, 1070
Melancholy Blues, 28
Melinda the Mouse, 336
Mellon Collie and the Infinite Sadness, 913
Mellow Doubt, 973
Mellow Gold, 69
Mellow Madness, 124, 514
Mellow Yellow, 277, 698
Melodie d'Amour, 19, 1016
Melody Fair, 604
Melody in A Major, 303
Melody in F, 282
Melody in 4–F, 525
Melody Nelson, 367
Melody of Love, 961, 1016
Melrose, 968
Melt, 572
Melting Pot, 173, 403
Members Only, 94
Memorial Beach, 11
Memories, 329, 522, 957
Memories Are Made of This, 285, 646, 810
Memories of Days Gone By, 338
Memories of El Monte, 1091
Memories of Professor Longhair, 272
Memories of You, 93, 195
Memory, 637
Memory Serves, 565
Memphis, 82, 628, 836
Memphis Blues, 316, 420, 1038
Memphis in June, 158
Memphis Sessions, The, 1047
Memphis, Tennessee, 82, 263, 432

Memphis Two-Step, 40
Memphis Underground, 217
Memphis Unlimited, 1079
Memphis/Vegas, 789
Men and Women, 902
Men Without Women, 934
Menace, 304
Mendocino, 619, 658, 866, 866
Menlove Avenue, 576, 740
Mental Cruelty, 629, 748
Mental Picture, 879
Mer, La, 244, 391, 993
Mer (Beyond the Sea), La, 1065
Mercedes Benz, 517
Merciful God, 8
Mercury, 19
Mercury Falling, 951
Mercy, 232, 885
Mercy Mercy, 221, 830, 849
Mercy Mercy Me, 751
Mercy Mercy Me (the Ecology), 374
Mercy, Mercy, Mercy, 7, 8, 234, 1038, 1062
Merge, 49
Merkinball, 762
Merle Travis Story, The, 993
Mermaid Avenue, 117, 1007
Mermaid Avenue Vol. 1, 408
Mermaid Avenue Vol. 2, 117, 408, 1007
Merrimack County, 862
Merry Christmas Baby, 125, 821
Merry Christmas Everybody, 909, 910, 947
Merry Christmas . . . Have a Nice Life, 567
Merry, Merry Christmas, 715
Merry Widow Waltz, The, 573
Merry-Go-Round, 550
Merrymakers, The, 197
Mes Mains, 68
Mesopotamia, 43
Mess Around, 174
Mess of Blues, A, 783, 789
Messa Stomp, 1062
Message, The, 397
Message from a Black Man, 1051
Message from Beat Street, 397
Message from Britain, The, 877
Message from Missouri, A, 319
Message from the Country, 703
Message from the People, A, 174
Message in a Bottle, 782
Message in a Box: The Complete Recordings, 783
Message in Our Music, 736
Message Is Love, The, 49
Message Man, 398
Message of Love, 791
Message to Martha, 325, 1033
Message to Michael, 1033

Message to the Young, 459
Message to You Rudy, A, 12, 591, 928
Message 2 (Survival), 397
Message Understood, 891
Messin' with the Kid, 1045
Messina, 596
Messing About on the River, 430
Messing with the Blues, 127
Met Her on a Plane, 1041
Metal Box, 884
Metal Circus, 701
Metal Guru, 101
Metal Machine Music, 824
Metal Mickey, 959
Metal Postcard, 905
Metal Rhythm, 728
Metal Works 73–93, 519
Metallic KO, 468, 469
Metallica, 665
Metamatic, 1006
Metamorphoses, 491
Metamorphosis, 473
Metro Music, 563
Metropolitan Man, 793
Mexicali Rose, 39
Mexican Divorce, 44, 1033
Mexican Joe, 825
Mexican Whistler, 1053
Mexico, 610, 949
Mezzamorphosis, 256
Mezzanine, 199, 650
Mi Bella Donna, 274
Mi Chico Latino, 931
Mi Tierra, 315
Mi Uzi Weighs a Ton, 802
Miaow, 68
Michael, 542
Michael Bolotin, 101
Michael Caine, 630
Michael Hutchence, 473
Michael McDonald, 279
Michael Row the Boat, 277
Michelle, 403, 1016
Micken, 1042
Mickey, 967
Mickey Dolenz Puts You to Sleep, 684
Mickey One, 381
Mid Eighties, 1079
'Mid the Green Fields of Virginia, 425
Middle Aged Crazy, 582
Middle Class Revolt, 327
Middle Man, 873
Middle of Nowhere, 421
Middle of the Road, 791
Middle Passage, 133, 225
Middle-Class White Boy, 14
Midnight at the Fringe, 841
Midnight at the Lost and Found, 657

Midnight at the Oasis, 704
Midnight Believer, 234
Midnight Blue, 45, *141*
Midnight Bus, 1070
Midnight Call Blues, 562
Midnight Cowboy, 1065
Midnight Gambler, 560
Midnight Hour Blues, 160
Midnight in Chelsea, 102
Midnight in Montgomery, 478
Midnight Lady Called the Blues, 272, *1075*
Midnight Lady, 697
Midnight Lightning, 440
Midnight Love, 367, 375
Midnight Marauders, 994
Midnight Mover, 683, 1076
Midnight on the Water, 122
Midnight Postcards, 325
Midnight Rainbows, 925
Midnight Rider, 15, *489*
Midnight Rocks, 947, *947*
Midnight Special, 207, 552, 568, *568*, 836, *916*
Midnight Stroll, 224
Midnight Sun, 17
Midnight Train to Georgia, 458, 548
Midnight Wind, 949
Midnite Vultures, 70
Midstream Vacation, 1088
Mighty Cloud of Joy, 668
Mighty High, 668
Mighty Like a Rose, 119, 219
Mighty Long Time, 1066
Mighty, Mighty Spade and Whitey, 470
Mighty Quinn, 292, 635
Migration, 727
Mike Brecker, 119
Mike Heron, 471
Mike Heron's Reputation, 471
Milagro, 871
Milenburg Joys, 696, 697, 822
Miles, 1021
Miles Ahead, 318
Miles from Home, 223
Miles of Aisles, 679
Miles Smiles, 248, 420
Milestone, 975
Milestones, 8, 206
Miliki Plus, 732
Milk and Alcohol, 270
Milk and Honey, 576, 740
Milk and Kisses, 199
Milk Cow Blues, 231, 629, 1058, 1063, 1068
Milkcow Blues, 789
Millennium, 46, 298, 1065
Millennium Bell, The, 738
Millennium Prayer, The, 832, 941
Miller's Cave, 55

Millers Tale, The, 973
Million Dollar Baby, 243
Million Dollar Bash, 541
Million Dollar Legs, 1066
Million Dollar Secret, 461
Million Love Songs, A, 1064
Million Mile Reflections, 242
Millionaires, 485
Millions Now Living Will Never Die, 988
Milord, 774, 1015
Minatures, 700
Mind Blowing Decisions, 437, 438
Mind Bomb, 918
Mind Games, 576
Mind of a Toy, 1007
Mine All Mine, 152
Minefields, 989
Miner's Dream of Home, The, 545
Minesota Fats, 505
Minglewood Blues, 154
Mingus, 677, 679
Mingus Ah Um, 676
Mingus Oh Yeah, 544, 676
Minneapolis Genius, The, 797
Minnie the Moocher, 151, 152, 675
Minnie the Moocher's Wedding Day, 26, 152
Minor Earth, Major Sky, 11
Minority, 402
Minotaur Song, 471
Minstrel and the Queen, 470
Minstrel Boy, The, 204, 614
Minstrel in the Gallery, 499
Minuetto Allegretto, 60
Minute by Minute, 279
Minute You're Gone, The, 489, 831
Minx, 991
Miracle, The, 808
Miracle Row, 466
Miracles, 495, 736
Miracles – The Holiday Album, 365
Mirage, 342, 431, 489
Mirage, El, 647, 1041
Mirror Blue, 982
Mirror in the Bathroom, 335
Mirror Man, 461
Mirror Mirror, 855, 976
Mirrorball, 1088
Mirrors, 572
Misdemeanour, 1006
Miseducation of Lauryn Hill, The, 361
Miserere, 1094
Misfits, 544
Misplaced Childhood, 642
Miss Chatelaine, 563
Miss Jamaica, 193, 549
Miss Misery, 915

Miss Otis Regrets, 264, 784
Miss Sarajevo, 1005
Miss Sun, 873
Miss the Mississippi and You, 375
Miss Williams' Guitar, 493
Miss World, 448
Miss You, 849
Miss You Like Crazy, 202
Miss You Much, 479
Miss You Nights, 831
Misses, 679
Missing, 321, 977
Missing Links, 1077
Missing . . . Presumed Having a
    Good Time, 267
Missing Words, 928
Missing Years, The, 799
Missing You, 251, 471, 769
Mission to Moscow, 391
Mission to Please, 476
Missionary Man, 317
Mississippi Boweavil Blues, 758
Mississippi Goddam, 900
Mississippi Mud, 73
Mississippi Queen, 701
Mississippi River Blues, 845
Mississippi Squirrel Convention,
    946
Mississippi, You're on My Mind,
    794, 1070
Mister and Mississippi, 344, 751
Mister Charlie, 454
Mister Heartbreak, 21
Mister Meadowlark, 231, 663
Mister Moonlight, 774
Misterioso, 684
Mistletoe and Wine, 831
Mistress Music, 140
Mistrial, 824
Mistrustin' Blues, 748, 772
Misty, 372, 434, 651, 794, 946
Misty Blue, 450
Misty Islands of the Highlands,
    528
Misty Roses, 423
Misunderstanding, 378
Misunderstood, 24
Mix, The, 554
Mixed Bag, 430
Mixed Bag II, 431
Mixed Elixir, 447
Mixed Up, 87, 238
Mixed Up Shook Up Girl, 369
MLK, 47
Mmm . . . Skyscraper I Love You,
    1008
MmmBop, 421
Mo' Money, 484
Mo' Roots, 966
Moaner, 1008
Moanin', 93, 676
Moaning the Blues, 932

Moby Grape, 680
Mock Tudor, 982
Mocking Bird, The, 348
Mockingbird, 351, 352, 898, 971
Mockingbird Hill, 751, 760
Model, The, 554
Model Girl, 227
Modern Adventures of Plato,
    Diogenes and Freud, 96
Modern Classics, 1045
Modern Day Romance, 724
Modern Don Juan, 450
Modern Girl, 298, 657
Modern Life Is Rubbish, 100
Modern Lovers, 832
Modern Lovers 88, 833
Modern Music, 710
Modern Sounds, 745
Modern Sounds in Country and
    Western Music, 174
Modern Times, 495, 947
Modular Mix, 11
Mogwai Fear Satan, 682
Mohair Sam, 356, 830
Mojo Man, 432
Molly, 389
Molly and Tenbrooks, 686, 937
Molly Dee, 948
Molly Maguires, The, 220
Molly on the Shore, 704
Mom and Dad's Waltz, 360
Moment of Forever, A, 555, 1034
Moment of Truth, 370
Momentary Lapse of Reason, A,
    777
Moments, 873
Moments from This Theatre, 764
Moments to Remember, 348
Momma Hated Diesels, 207
Momma Was a Dancer, 746
Mommy for a Day, 458, 1045
Mommy What Happened to the
    Christmas Tree, 504
Mon Legionnaire, 773
Mona Bone Jakon, 946
Mona, 263
Mona Lisa, 61, 201, 202, 704, 833,
    1000
Mona Lisa's Lost Her Smile, 199
Mona Lisa's Sister, The, 754
Monday Monday, 633
Mondo Bizarro, 815
Money, 66, 394, 777, 1051
Money and Cigarettes, 187
Money Changes Everything, 334
Money for Nothing, 267
Money Honey, 62, 285, 625, 789,
    953
Money in my Pocket, 127
Money's Too Tight to Mention,
    902
Mongo Returns, 870

Mongoloid, 260
Mongrel, 882
Monique, 31
Monk's Music, 684
Monkees Present, The, 684
Monkey, The, 58, 666
Monkey Man, 987
Monkey Time, The, 470
Monsieur, 188
Monsieur Dupont, 707, 891
Monsoon, 590
Monster, 827, 921, 944
Monterey, 24
Montmarte, 826
Montreux, 384, 902
Mony Mony, 468, 489, 499
Mooch, The, 307
Mood Indigo, 29, 306, 307, 675
Moods, 325
Moody Blue, 790
Moody River, 108
Moody Woman, 144
Moody's Mood for Love, 561
Moon & Cypress, 15
Moon and the Melodies, The, 199
Moon Going Down, 758
Moon Got in My Eyes, The, 230
Moon Hop, 692
Moon Is a Harsh Mistress, The,
    1041 •
Moon Love, 671, 972
Moon Over Naples, 522, 648
Moon River, 144, 274, 634, 662,
    663
Moon River and Other Great
    Movie Themes, 1057
Moon Safari, 11
Moonchild, 72
Moondance, 327, 694
Moondog Matinée, 53, 524
Moondreams, 435, 451
Moon-Faced, Starry-Eyed, 392,
    663, 1043
Moonflower, 871
Moonglow, 156
Moonlight Bay, 706
Moonlight Becomes You, 230,
    713, 1012
Moonlight Blues, 419
Moonlight in Vermont, 653, 1052
Moonlight Serenade, 670
Moonlight Shadow, 738
Moonlight Shadows, 886
Moonlighting, 872
Moonlighting – Live at the Ash
    Grove, 755
Moonshine Kate, 162
Moonshot, 868
Moonstruck, 683
Moontan, 387
Mope-Itty Mope, 282
Moppin' the Bride, 826

Morbid Visions, 883
More and More, 290, 776
More Good Old Rock'n'Roll, 188
More Greatest Hits, 293, 980
More Gregory, 475
More I See You, The, 435, 688, 828, 1033
More Life in a Tramp's Vest, 945
More Love, 159
More Love Songs, 1024
More Miles per Gallon, 669
More Money for You and Me, 348
More News at Eleven, 803
More Oar, 680
More of Everything for Everybody, 330
More of the Greatest Live Show on Earth, 581
More of the Monkees, 684
More of Tom Lehrer, 574
More Sing Along with Mitch, 672
More Songs About Buildings and Food, 311, 967
More Specials, 928
More Than a Feeling, 109
More Than a Lover, 1002
More Than a New Discovery, 728
More Than Ever, 97
More Than I Can Say, 228, 873
More Than I Know, 572
More Than Physical, 52
More Than the Sun, 86
More Than This, 857
More Than Us, 992
More Than Words, 321
More Whiskey, 12
More You Know, The, 1085
Morento, 640
Morgan Magan, 181
Morgan the Pirate, 329
Morgen, 522
Moribond, Le, 120, 623
Mornin', 492
Morning After, The, 274, *376*
Morning Again, 761
Morning Dance, 935
Morning Desire, 847
Morning Dew, 204, 260, 301
Morning Glory, 135, 653
Morning Gold, 167
Morning Has Broken, 946
Morning Side of the Mountain, 747
Morning Train, 298
Morningtown Ride, 881
Morris on, 13
Morrison Hotel, 280
Mortelle Randonnée, 95
Mos' Scocious: Anthology, 272
Mosaic Thump, 251
Mosaique, 384

Moscow Night, 133
Mose Alive!, 15
Mose Allison Sings & Plays, 15
Mose in Your Ear, 15
Moses, 299
Moses Smote the Water, 285
Moss Side Story, 7
Most Beautiful Girl in the World, The, 428, 798, 830, 893
Most Exciting Organ Ever, The, 790
Most Happy Fella, The, 348
Most of All, 363
Motel Blues, 1024
Moten Stomp, 1041
Mother, 389, 576
M-O-T-H-E-R (A Word That Means the World to Me), 140
Mother and Child Reunion, 549, 899
Mother Country, 948
Mother Earth, 662, 1008
Mother Fist and Her Five Daughters, 17
Mother Goose Rhymes, 606
Mother Lode, 596
Mother Nature Calls, 564
Mother Nature's Matinee, 959
Mother Popcorn (You Got to Have a Mother for Me), 128
Mother Russia, 586
Mother Thank You, 1076
Mother, the Queen of My Heart, 845
Mother Time, 616
Mother Wit, 1078
Mother-in-Law, 526, 990
Mother's Children Have a Hard Time, 505
Mother's Heaven, 978
Mother's Little Helper, 849
Mother's Milk, 820
Mother's Only Sleeping, 686
Mother's Spiritual, 729
Mother's Talk, 972
Motherless Child, 258
Motherless Children, 1062
Mothership Connection, 194
Mothership Reconnection, 239
Motion, 990
Motivation, 228
Motley Crüe, 699
Motor Booty Affair, 194
Motor Head Blues, 1038
Motorcycle, 897
Motorcycle Emptiness, 636
Motown Junk, 636
Motown Remembers Marvin, 375
Motownphilly, 114
Mott, 700
Mott the Hoople – Live, 700
Moulin Rouge, 639

Mountain, The, 297
Mountain Climbing, 701
Mountain Greenery, 428, 987
Mountain Moods, 119
Mountain Music, 12
Mountain of Love, 836
Mountain's High, The, 759
Mountains of Mourne, 625
Mournful Serenade, 697
Mourning in the Morning, 861
Mouse, The, 537
Mouvement Ewondo, 263
Move, The, 703
Move Any Mountain, 730, 888
Move Closer, 516
Move It, 752, 830, 885, 912
Move It on Over, 1059, 1060
Move on Up, 655
Move on Up a Little Higher, 268, 480
Move Over, 944
Move Over Charley Pride and Give Another Nigger a Chance, 1076
Move Over Darling, 250, 902
Move Somethin', 1001
Move Them Niggers North, 672
Move with Me, 136
Movement, 716
Movement for the Common Man, 959
Movements: The 30th Anniversary Anthology, 703
Movie Album: As Time Goes By, The, 262
Movie Star, 84, 474
Movies, 153
Movies and Me, 242
Movin', 117, 962
Movin' and Groovin', 300, 436
Movin' on Broadway, 939
Movin' on Up, 610, 796
Moving Hearts, 690
Moving Home, 1093
Moving on, 52, 654
Moving Out, 851
Moving Pictures, 153, 861
Moving Target, 877
Moving Targets, 999
Mr and Mrs Murphy, 511
Mr and Mrs Used to Be, 996
Mr Bad Example, 1093
Mr Bad Guy, 808
Mr Bass Man, 641
Mr Blue, 123, 342, 348
Mr Bojangles, 122, *283*, 724, 1027
Mr Businessman, 946
Mr Censor Man, 654
Mr Crow and Sir Norman, 304
Mr Crumb, 420
Mr Fantasy, 1072
Mr Five by Five, 696

Mr Gone, 1039
Mr Guitar, 1042
Mr Happy Go Lucky, 661
Mr Jelly Lord, 697
Mr Jones, 221
Mr Jordan, 576
Mr Know It All, 475
Mr Lee, 855
Mr Lonely, 402, 1023
Mr Love Pants, 291
Mr Loverman, 815
Mr Lucky, 452, 453
Mr Magic, 1035
Mr Magic Man, 775
Mr Moonlight, 345
Mr Music, 640
Mr Natural, 71
Mr Pitiful, 821
Mr Policeman, 488
Mr Porter, 698
Mr Right, 899
Mr Roboto, 959
Mr Sandman, 183, 374, 425
Mr Showmanship, 349
Mr Skin, 932
Mr Soul, 137
Mr Spaceman, 147
Mr Tambourine Man, 119, 146,
    146, 259, 292, 659, 863, 911
Mr Tanner, 171
Mr Teardrop, 837
Mr Telephone Man, 125
Mr Volunteer, 284
Mr Wendell, 30
Mr Wonderful, 341, 460, 572
Mrs Brown, 442
Mrs Brown, You've Got a Lovely
    Daughter, 442, 698
Mrs Lennon, 740
Mrs Mills' Medley, 37
Mrs Robinson, 218, 575, 759, 897,
    904
Mrs Worthington, 222
MSG, 1006
MTA, 542
MTV Unplugged, 7
MTV Unplugged EP, 157
MTV Unplugged NYC, 44
Much Better Tomorrow, A, 100
Mud Slide Slim and the Blue
    Horizon, 971
Muddy, Brass and the Blues, 1037
Muddy 'Mississippi' Waters Live,
    1037
Muddy River, 164
Muddy Waters Blues, 46
Muddy Waters – Folk Singer, 1037
Mulder and Scully, 168
Mule Bone, 966
Mule Skinner Blues, 695, 845
Mule Train, 146, 344, 468, 560,
    672, 687

Mule Variations, 1025
Muleskinner Blues, 277
Mull of Kintyre, 66, 611
Multikulti, 178
Multiplication, 244, 896
Mummer, 1081
Mummy, The, 622
Mundial, El, 274
Munki, 498
Murder Ballads, 169, 429, 677
Murder He Says, 734
Murder on Music Row, 955
Murder Was the Case, 269
Murky World of Barry Adamson,
    The, 7
Murmur, 826
Muscle Shoals Blues, 1029
Musclebound, 926
Muscles, 481, 855
Muse, 512
Muse Sick-N-Hour Mess Age, 803
Musetta's Waltz, 825
Music, 138, 540, 632, 999
Music and Arts Seminar Chicago
    Mass Choir, 432
Music and Me, 481
Music Bank, 14
Music Box, 157, 906, 907
Music by Ry Cooder, 212
Music for a New Society, 151
Music for Airports, 310, 311
Music for Films, 311
Music for Moderns, 636
Music for My Mother, 194
Music for Non Musicians, 310
Music for Peace of Mind, 828
Music for Pleasure, 240, 717
Music for Supermarkets, 491
Music for the Amorphous Body
    Study Centre, 944
Music for the Jilted Generation,
    801
Music for the Knee Plays, 148
Music for the Masses, 258
Music for the Millions (A
    l'Olympia), 119
Music for the Motorway, 640
Music for the Native Americans,
    53
Music from Big Pink, 52, 53, 390
Music from the Films of François
    Truffaut, 255
Music Fuh Ya, 966
Music Goes Round and Round,
    The, 282, 414, 916
Music Hath Charms, 10
Music in 12 Parts – Parts I & II,
    385
Music in a Doll's House, 328
Music Keeps Me Together, 966
Music Matador, 274
Music, Music, Music, 120

Music of Bill Monroe, The, 687
Music of Brazilian Masters, 16
Music of John Barry, The, 57
Music of My Heart, 1032
Music of My Mind, 1077
Music of Quality and Distinction,
    438
Music of Quality and Distinction
    Vol. 2, 878
Music Sounds Better with You,
    239
Music Spoken Here, 624
Music That You Can Dance to,
    927
Music to Be Born, 401
Music to Watch Girls By, 227
Music Works Showcase '88, 89, 90,
    189
Musical Chairs, 453
Musical Doctor, 591
Musical Romance, A, 1087
Musical Shapes, 163
Musings of a Creekdipper, 493
Musique/The High Road, 857
Muskrat Ramble, 231, 745, 1038
Must Be Madison, 599
Must Carry on Vol. 1, 1027
Must Carry on Vol. 2, 1027
Must of Got Lost, 376
Musta Notta Gotta Lotta, 309
Mustang Sally, 775
Mustang Wine, 296
Muswell Hillbillies, 543
Mutations, 70
Muthaphuckkin G's, 269
Mutiny, 314
Mutiny in the Brass Section, 280
Mwandishi, 420
My Abstract Heart, 17
My Adidas, 859
My Aim Is True, 219, 580, 603
My Babe, 142, 269, 590, 834
My Baby, 974
My Baby Just Cares for Me, 113,
    155, 276, 523, 900, 901
My Baby Left Me, 226, 233, 788
My Baby Must Be a Magician,
    649
My Baby Said Yes, 231, 518
My Baby Thinks He's a Train,
    166
My Baby's Gone, 600
My Baby's in Love with Another
    Guy, 504
My Back Pages, 292
My Beauty, 261
My Best Friend's Girl, 161
My Bird of Paradise, 140
My Blue Heaven, 38, 275, 276,
    605, 1050
My Blue Ridge Mountain Home,
    757, 842

My Bonnie, 65, 66
My Bonnie Lies Over the Ocean, 522
My Bonny Lad, 333
My Boy Lollipop, 91, 895, 949
My Brand of Blues, 813
My Brother Jake, 357
My Brother Makes the Noises for the Talkies, 761
My Buddy, 276, 442
My Buddy Seat, 237
My Camera Never Lies, 136
My Cello, 445
My Cherie Amour, 1077
My Confessions, 998
My Coo Ca Choo, 951
My Country, 720
My Country Man, 84
My Country 'Tis of Thy People You're Dying, 868
My Cup Runneth Over, 19
My Dad, 638
My Days Are Numbered, 96
My Defences Are Down, 79
My Ding-a-Ling, 58, 82
My Dixie Darling, 163, 277
My Earlier Years, 174
My Early Burglary Years, 696
My Edge of the Razor, 444
My Elusive Dreams, 893
My Empty Arms, 1069
My Ever Changing Moods, 1044
My Eyes Adored You, 227, 350
My Fantasy, 835
My Father, 204
My Father, My Son, 77
My Father's Son, 907
My Favorite Fantasy, 615
My Favorites of Hank Williams, 512
My Favourite Game, 156
My Favourite Mistake, 232
My Favourite Shop, 1044
My Favourite Things, 22, 206, 844, *1002*
My Feeling for the Blues, 541
My Fingers Do the Talking, 582
My First Love, 243
My Flying Saucer, 117, 408
My Foolish Heart, 496, 1089
My Friends Are Gonna Be Strangers, 22, 411
My Funny Valentine, 428, 847
My Gal Sal, 203, 284
My Generation, 467, 917, 1053, 1054
My Gift to You, 740
My Girl, 630, 821, 841, 974
My Girl Awaits Me, 812
My Girl/My Guy, 1017
My Girl Sloopy, 329
My Goal's Beyond, 624

My Grandfather's Clock, 233
My Guitar Wants to Kill Your Mama, 1092
My Guy, 840, 841, 906, 1046
My Handy Man, 158
My Happiness, 352, 788, 854, 936
My Head, My Bed, My Red Guitar, 489
My Heart, 28
My Heart Belongs to Daddy, 547, 785
My Heart Belongs to Only You, 1022
My Heart Cries for You, 678
My Heart Goes Crazy, 437
My Heart Has a Mind of Its Own, 353
My Heart Is an Open Book, 44
My Heart Is Yours, 427
My Heart Reminds Me, 939
My Heart Stood Still, 428
My Heart Will Go on, 267
My Hero, 764
My Home Town, 24, 211
My Home's in Alabama, 12
My Honey and Me, 471
My Human Gets Me Blues, 72
My Ideal, 839
My Innocence, 729
My Iron Lung, 811
My Jamaican Guy, 512
My Jug and I, 655
My Kind of Blues, 538
My Kind of Country, 618, 766
My Kind of Girl, 685, 719
My Kind of Town, 150, 905, 1012
My Kinda Girl, 44
My Lady's a Wild Flying Dove, 761
My Last Date (With You), 249
My Legendary Girlfriend, 805
My Life, *95*, 502
My Life for a Song, 274
My Life in the Bush of Ghosts, 148, 311, 967
My Lips Remember Your Kiss, 860
My Little Bimbo, 1038
My Little Girl, 228
My Little One, 644
My Little Red Book, 600
My Little Town, 898
My Lonely Sad Eyes, 622
My Lord's Gonna Move this Wicked Race, 871
My Love, 189, 469, 611, 832, 1077
My Love Is a Fire, 747
My Love Is Real, 813
My Love Is Your Love, 458
My Lover's Prayer, 821
My Mama Pinned a Rose on Me, 1063

My Mammy, 276, 509, 510, 1049
My Man, 120, 956, *1041*
My Man a Sweet Man, 482
My Man o' War, 158
My Marge, 703
My Melancholy Baby, 175, 303, 641
My Melody, 74
My Melody of Love, 1023
My Memories of You, 424
My Merry Go Round, 708
My Mike Sounds Nice, 869
My Mind's Eye, 912
My Mom, 883
(My) Money Never Runs Out, 155
My Mother Is a Space Cadet, 1092
My Music, 596
My My My, 44
My Name Is Albert Ayler, 41
My Name Is Death, 470
My Name Is Tallulah, 1064
My Nation Underground, 215
My Oh My, 26, 910
My Old Dutch, 179
My Old Flame, 515
My Old Kentucky Home, 347
My Old Man, 290
My Old Man Said 'Follow the Van', 592
My Old Man's a Dustman, 277
My Old Man's a Fireman on the Elder-Dempster Line, 277
My Old New Hampshire Home, 1023
My One Desire, 139
My One Temptation, 752
My Only Lover, 474
My Other Love, 399
My Own True Love, 1052
My People, 307
My People Were Fair and Had Sky in Their Hair but Now They're Content to Wear Stars in Their Brows, 101
My Perfect Cousin, 461, 890
My Philosophy, 106
My Prayer, 268, 471, 528, 780
My Prerogative, 44, 125, 835
My Pussycat, 82
My Real Name Is 'Arold, 450
My Resistance Is Low, 561, 622
My Rockin' Days, 228
My Romance, 898
My Room, 844
My Roots Are Showing, 746
My September Love, 319, 1051
My Sex, 304
My Sharona, 183
My Ship Is Coming in, 1026
My Side of the Bed, 54

My Simple Heart, 56
My Son, My Son, 608
My Song, 5, 492, 664
My Story, 1067
My Strongest Weakness, 520
My Sweet Lord, 182, 427
My Tambourine, 82
My Tennessee Mountain Home, 704, 758
My Testament, 483
My Thang, 128
My Thanks to You, 353
My Time, 873
My Time Is Your Time, 1011
My Toot Toot, 501
My Tormented Heart, 1015
My Town, 619
My True Love, 875
My Truly, Truly Fair, 664, 678
My Very Good Friend the Milkman, 1029
My Very Special Guests, 512
My War, 850
My Way, 24, 192, 218, 384, 502, 774, 884, 904
My Way: a Musical Tribute to Rev. Dr Martin Luther King, 547
My White Bicycle, 709, 1084
My Whole World Ended, 121, 975
My Wife's Gone to the Country (Hurrah! Hurrah!), 78
My Woman, My Woman, My Wife, 837
My Woman's Man, 245
My Word You Do Look Queer, 1046
My World, 174
My Wubba Dolly, 336
My Yiddishe Momme, 997
Mysteries, The, 13
Mysterioso, 299
Mysterious Film World of, The, 443
Mysterious Rhinestone Cowboy, The, 199
Mysterious Traveler, 1039
Mystery, 1014
Mystery Dance, 219
Mystery Disc, 1092
Mystery Girl, 741
Mystery Lady, 487
Mystery of Life, 192, 441
Mystery to Me, 341
Mystery Train, 426, 754, 789
Mystery White Boy, 135
Mystic Energy, 745
Mystic Eyes, 694
Mystic Man, 988
Mystic Realms, 138
Mystic Warrior, 767
Mythical Kings and Iguanas, 793
Mythos, 264

Myths and Legends of King Arthur and the Round Table, The, 1025

Na Na Hey Hey Kiss Him Goodbye, 52
Na Na Is the Saddest Word, 958
Nach'l Blues, 551
Nachts Schient die Sonne, 693
Nadine, 82
Nagasaki, 1032
Nairobi, 941
Naked, 824, 967
Naked Baby Photos, 76
Naked But Not Dead, 865
Naked Eye, 605
Naked in the Rain, 534
Naked Lunch, 202
Naked Songs, 515
Naked Thunder, 254
Name Game, The, 309, 644
Name of the Game, The, 1, 1008
Name of This Band Is Talking Heads, The, 559, 967
Naming of Names, 614
Nancy Boy, 779
Nancy Jane, 1068
Nancy (With the Laughing Face), 903, 904
Nantucket Sleighride, 701
Naomi, 627
Nashville, 465
Nashville Boogie, 1041
Nashville Cats, 602, 772
Nashville Collection, The, 211
Nashville Sessions, The, 646, 683
Nashville Skyline, 166, 242, 284, 292, 711, 925
Nasty, 2
Nat 'King' Cole Sings and George Shearing Plays, 891
Nat Gonella Story, The, 390
Natalia, 565, 989
Natch'l Blues, 966
Nathalie, 68
Nathan Jones, 52, 963
National Anthem, The, 811
National Front Disco, The, 696
Native Heart, 1066
Native North American Child, 868
Native Son, 7, 596
Native Tongue, 782
Natty Dread, 643
Natty Rebel, 1009
Natural Act, 555
Natural Born Bugie, 912
Natural Born Killaz, 270
Natural Born Lover, 275
Natural Elements, 624
Natural High, 1020
Natural Ingredients, 605
Natural Man, 299, 438, 818
Natural One, 265

Natural Woman, 540
Naturally, 150
Nature Boy, 77, 201, 244, 1015
Nature of a Sista, 808
Nature's Baby, 616
Nature's Disappearing, 654
Nature's Way, 932
Naughty, 532
Naughty Lady of Shady Lane, The, 19, 1072
Naughty Little Dogs, 469
Naughty Operetta, 653
Navajo, 250
Navajo Rag, 465
Navajo Rug, 1027
Navidad, 384
Naxalite, 33
Nazareth, 709
Nazi Punks Fuck Off, 252
Nazz III, 859
Ndodemnyama – Free South Africa, 51
Ne Me Quitte Pas, 120, 622
Ne Partez Pas Sans Moi, 266
Neanderthal Man, 975
Neapolis, 902
Near the Soft Boys, 446
Near You, 223, 512, 1065
Nearly Good, 704
Nearly Human, 860
Nearly Lost You, 877
Nearness of You, The, 158
Nebraska, 934
Neck and Neck, 36, 267
Need a Little Sugar in My Bowl, 914
Need to Belong, 144
Need You, 489
Need You Tonight, 473
Need Your Love So Bad, 341, 504, 1020
Needle and the Damage Done, The, 1088
Needle of Death, 765
Needles and Pins, 176, 259, 430, 698, 724, 771, 815, 878, 879
Nefertiti, 1065
Negative, 639
Negative Girl, 943
Negative Theater, 161
Negotiations and Love Songs, 900
Negro Inside Me, The, 7
Neighborhood, The, 594
Neil Jung, 973
Neither Fish nor Flesh, 243
Neither One of Us (Wants to Be the First to Say Goodbye), 548
Nel Blu Dipinto di Blu, 681
Nelson Mandela, 710, 928
Neo Geo, 565, 868
Neon Beach, 949
Neroli, 311

Nerve Net, 311
Nervous, 651
Nervous on the Road, 603
Nervous Track, The, 651
Nessun dorma, 275
Nested, 729
Net, The, 590
Netherlands, 343
Neutronica, 278
Nevada Fighter, 685
Never, 436
Never a Dull Moment, 949
Never Alone, 397
Never Be Anyone Else But You,
  142, 711
Never Be Clever, 122
Never Be You, 166
Never Been in Love, 295
Never Been Rocked Enough, 613
Never Been to Spain, 40, 496, 984
Never Break a Promise, 112
Never Can Say Goodbye, 208,
  375, *375*, 434, 478
Never Die Young, 971
Never Do a Tango with an
  Eskimo, 211
Never Ending Song of Love, 881
Never Ever, 14
Never for Ever, 143
*Never Get Out of These Blues
  Alive*, 452
Never Goin' Back, 602
Never Gonna Give You Up, 144,
  951
Never Had It So Good, 675
Never Introduce Your Donah to
  a Pal, 305
Never Kick a Sleeping Dog, 865
Never Let Her Go, 119
Never Let Me Down, 111
Never Let Me Down Again, 258
Never Let Me Go, *156*, 655, *1013*
Never Like This Before, 74
*Never Mind the Bollocks, Here's
  The Sex Pistols*, 884
Never My Love, 34
Never Never, 312, 703, 890
Never, Never Gonna Give Ya Up,
  1048
Never on Sunday, 21, 184, 218,
  582, 702
Never Said, 771
Never So Good as the First Time,
  866
Never Surrender, 1001
Never Tear Us Apart, 473
Never Told a Soul, 267
Never Too Much, 1013
Never Turn Back, 444
Never Turn Your Back on
  Mother Earth, 258, 927
Never Will I Hurt My Baby', 459

Never-Ending Love, 856
Nevermind, 14, 371, 723
Nevertheless, 1015
Neville-ization, 714
New, 725
New Adventures in Hi-Fi, 827
New Affair, 310
New Age, 1018, *1030*
New Arrangement, 259
New Art Riot, 636
New Attitude, 558
New Beginning, 172
New Beginning (Mamba Seyra),
  136
New Boots and Panties!!, 290
New Chapter, 35
New Chatauqua, 665
New Christ Cardiac Hero, 465
New Craas Massahkah, 507
New Day Dawning, 520
New Day Rising, 701
New Directions, 714
New England, A, 116, 614
New Flame, A, 902
New Forms, 388, 906
New Girl in School, 113, 490
New Gold Dream, 901
New Grass, 41
New It Ain't Gonna Ran No Mo'
  – Part 3, 416
New Jack Swing, 835
New Jazz Conceptions, 318
New Jersey, 102
New Jimmy Reed Album, The, 823
New Johnny Otis Show, The, 748
New Jole Blon, 704
New Kid in Town, 137, 295
New Life, 258
New Light Through Old Windows,
  819
New Moon Shine, 971
New Morning, 122, 293, 551
New Mule Skinner Blues, 686
New, New Minglewood Blues,
  400
New Orleans, 104, 266
New Orleans Bound, 671
New Orleans Christmas, A, 991
New Orleans Heat, 537
New Orleans Joy, 276
New Orleans Joys, 54
New Orleans Piano, 802
New Orleans Street Singer, 296
New Orleans Suite, 307
New Orleans to London, 207
New Rap Language, The, 551
New Ray of Sunshine, 401
New Record by MBV, The, 707
New Rhumba, 485
New Rose, 240
New Routes, 604
New San Antonio Rose, 230, 1068

New Sensations, 824
New Skin for the Old Ceremony,
  201
New Soft Shoe, The, 757
New Song, 513
New Songs for Old Friends, 761
New Songs from the Briar Patch,
  761
New South, 1061
New Speedway Boogie, 400
New Standard, 420
New Tattoo, 699
New Toy, 273
New Traditionalists, 260
New Values, 468
New Violin Summit, 276
New Wave, The, 239
New World, 1093
New World Man, 861
New World Order, 655
New World Record, A, 304
New Year, 862
*New Year, New Band, New Com-
  pany*, 654
New Year's Day, 1004
New York, 824, 1018
New York Big Band, 863
New York City, 1021
New York City Boy, 768
New York Dolls, The, 860
New York Eye and Ear Control, 41
New York Groove, 546, 1093
New York Mining Disaster, 164
New York Mining Disaster 1941,
  71
New York, New York, 527
New York NY, 863
*New York Rock and Soul Revue –
  Live at the Beacon, The*, 943
New York State of Mind, 502,
  626, 957
New York Tendaberry, 728
New York's a Lonely Town, 697
New Zealand Suite, The, 392
Newer Stuff, The, 685
Newk's Time, 851
*Newly Discovered Early American
  Folk Songs*, 285
Newpower Soul, 798
News, The, 586
News of the World, 807
Next, 119, *519*
Next . . ., 709
Next Exit, 1035
Next in Line, 1000
Next Time I Fall, The, 181, 397
Next to You, 1080
*Nexus – Through the Eyes of John
  Lee*, 55
Niagara Theme, 486
Nice Ass, 921
Nice in Nice, 956

Nice 'n' Easy, 904
Nice 'n' Sleazy, 956
Nice Work If You Can Get It, 34, 337, 380, 793
Nicely Out of Tune, 586
Nick Lowe and His Cowboy Outfit, 219, 603
Nick Mason's Fictitious Sports, 95
Nick of Time, 159, 814, 1034
Nick the Knife, 603
Nickel and a Nail, A, 1079
Nico, 95
Niecy, 74
Nigga Ya Love to Hate, The, 466
Night, 350, 1069
Night After Night, 107
Night and Day, 34, 181, 286, 320, 480, 713, 784, 903, 904
Night at Birdland, A, 126
Night at the Opera, A, 807
Night at the Playboy Mansion, A, 265
Night Beat, 213
Night Boat to Cairo, 630
Night Calls, 198
Night Chicago Died, The, 707
Night Comes in, 982
Night Fever, 71
Night Flight, 689
Night Games, 795
Night Has a Thousand Eyes, The, 1017
Night Hunting Time, 116
Night I Fell in Love, The, 1013
Night in San Francisco, A, 695
Night in the Life of Todd Terry, A, 977
Night in the Ruts, 9
Night in Tunisia, A, 383, 446, 532, 753
Night Life, 712, 713
Night Moves, 882
Night Music, 480
Night Nurse, 475
Night of Fear, 702
Night of the Living Bassheads, 803
Night of the Long Grass, 995
Night on the Town, 456, 950
Night Owl, 812, 970
Night Owls, The, 590
Night Passages, 1039
Night People, 281
Night Rains, 466
Night Ride Home, 679
Night Song, 485
Night the Light Went on in Long Beach, The, 304
Night They Drove Old Dixie Down, The, 47, 53
Night Time, 534
Night Time Is the Right Time, 980

Night to Remember, A, 566, 886
Night Train, 127, 769, 1007
Night Was Made for Love, The, 422
Night with Daddy G, A, 104
Night You Murdered Love, The, 2
Nightbird, 342
Nightbirds, 558
Nightclubbing, 512, 782
Nightfall, 953
Nightfly, The, 943
Nighthawkin', 136
Nighthawks at the Diner, 1024
Nightingale, 132, 540
Nightlife, 539, 979
Nightmare, 890
Nightrider, 242
Nights in Manhattan – Live, 653
Nights in White Satin, 123, 277, 689
Nights on Broadway, 641, 940
Nights on the Borderline, 986
Nightshift, 208, 208
Nighttrain, 803
Nightwatch, 596
Nightwatchman, 19
Niki Hoeky, 800
Niki Nana, 1082
Nikita, 503, 531
Nilsson Schmilsson, 722
Nilsson sings Newman, 719, 722
Nina Hagen, 122
Nine, 423
Nine Below Zero, 1066
Nine Lives, 10, 814
Nine Objects of Desire, 1017
9012 Live: The Solos, 1085
90125, 455, 1085
911 Is a Joke, 803
Nine Times out of Ten, 831
9 to 5, 298, 408, 757, 991
Nine Tonight, 882
19, 738
1980, 877
1980–85: The New Mix in One Go, 1084
1984, 111, 532, 919, 1011, 1025
1987 (The JAMs 45 Edits), 547
1987 (What the Fuck Is Going on?), 547
1983–1984, 990
1982, 958
1957–1966, 1045
1942 Turkey in the Straw, 842
Nineteen Ninety Four, 977
1999, 797
1992 – The Love Album, 163
1916, 699
1964–1993, 900
1969 Live, 1018
1913 Massacre, 408

1935–1977: I've Been Away for a While Now, 790
19 Years, 113
19th Nervous Breakdown, 849
99, 989
Ninety-Nine and One-Half (Won't Do), 107
99.9F, 1017
99 Years, 21
99th Floor, 1094
96 Tears, 84, 396, 809, 956
Ninth, 801
Ninth Wave, 600
Nipple to the Bottle, 512
Nitegroove, 264
Nitelife, 976
Nitty Gritty, The, 308
Nixon, 561
No Clause 28, 236
No Code, 762
No Come Down, 1020
No Competition, 43
No Depression, 1007
No Doubt about It, 457
No Earthly Connection, 1025
No Easy Walk to Freedom, 768
No Education = No Future (Fuck the Curfew), 682
No Exit, 96
No Expectations, 47, 849
No Fear No Die, 466
No Fences, 123
No Frills, 396, 579
No Fun, 468
No Good (Start the Dance), 801
No Guru No Method No Teacher, 695
No Guts . . . No Glory, 682
No Heavy Petting, 1006
No Help Wanted, 157
No Holding Back, 993
No House Big Enough, 976
No How, No Way, 1070
No If, 238
No Jacket Required, 205
No Jive, 709
No Letter Today/Born to Lose, 239
No Limits, 1001, 1001
No Lookin' Back, 279
No Love at All, 980
No Love but Your Love, 744
No Man Is an Island, 127
No Man Walks Alone, 138
No Man's Land, 502
No Matter How I Try, 747
No Matter What, 67, 114
No Matter Who You Vote for, the Government Always Gets in, 105
No Me Dejes De Querer, 315
No Mean City, 709

No Milk Today, 975
No Money Down, 81
No More, 838
No More Auction Block for Me, 735
No More Cocoons, 252
No More Fear of Flying, 801
No More Games/Remix Album, 715
No More Heroes, 956
No More Lonely Nights, 612
No More Mr Nice Guy, 214, *370*
No More Rhyme, 381
No More Slavery, 361
No More Tears, 88
No More Tears (Enough Is Enough), 312, 956, 960
No More the Fool, 123
No No Song, 40, 939
No, Not Much, 348
No Nuclear War, 988
No Omega, 43
No One, 1001
No One Cares, 496
No One Else on Earth, 520
No One Is Innocent, 884
No One Knows, 265
No One Needs to Know, 1000
No One Will Ever Know, 855
No Opportunity Necessary, 1084
No Other, *147*, 235
No Other Arms, No Other Lips, 347
No Pain, No Gain, 1078
No Parlez, 716, 1089
No Particular Place to Go, 82
No Place to Run, 1006
No Policy, 850
No Prayer for the Dying, 474
No Prima Donna, 695
No Protection, 495, 650
No Pussyfooting, 310, 360
No Quarter, 569, *570*
No Rain, 95
No Regrets, 862, 1006, 1026
No Resemblance Whatsoever, 343
No Rest for the Wicked, 88
No Rollin' Blues, 1074
No Roses, 13
No Ruinous Feud, 471
No Scrubs, 44, 986
No Secrets, 898
No Security, 850
No Sleep at All, 699
No Sleep Til Hammersmith, 699
No Sleep Till Brooklyn, 64
No Strings, 298
No Sweat, 97
No Talking Just Heads, 967
No Time for Talk, 231
No Time to Kill, 90, *90*
No Time to Live, 38

No Time to Lose, 232
No Tricks, 208
No Way Back, 256
No Way Out, 805
No Woman No Cry, 104, 361, 643
No World Order, 860
No. 2 – Life with the Lions, 576
No. 10, 406
No. 10 Upping Street, 191
Noah, 882
Nobody, 1057, 1062
Nobody but Me, 476
Nobody but You, 260, 1079
Nobody Does It Better, 45, 418, 898
Nobody Else, 1064
Nobody I Know, 853
Nobody Knows the Way I Feel, 69
Nobody Knows What a Redhead Mama Can Do, 323
Nobody Knows You When You're Down and Out, 576, 1072
Nobody Likes Sad Songs, 675
Nobody Lives without Love, 455
Nobody Loves Me Like You, 339
Nobody Loves Me Like You Do, 705
Nobody Needs Your Love, 778
Nobody Wins, 571
Nobody's Business, 344
Nobody's Darling but Mine, 247, 468
Nobody's Diary, 703
Nobody's Fool, 443, 596, *764*
Nobody's Fool but Your Own, 725
Nobody's Home, 90
Nobody's Perfect, 254
Nobody's Sweetheart, 306, 674
Nobody's Wedding, 982
Noche de Cuatro Lunas, 469
Nocturne, 905
Nod's as Good as a Wink to a Blind Horse, A, 912
Noël Coward in Las Vegas, 222
Nola, 598, 691, 760, 842
Nominee, The, 794
Non Je Ne Regrette Rien, 774
Non Stop, 469
Non-Stop Dancing 65, 565
Non-Stop Erotic Cabaret, 16
Nona, 558
Nonsense, 842
Nonstop, 128
Nonsuch, 1081
Norma Waterson, 164
Norman, 382, 599, 765
North and South, 812
North by Northwest, 841
North Country Blues, 291
North Country Boy, 173

North Dakota, 602
North Marine Drive, 320
North of a Miracle, 443
North on South Street, 17
North Star, 385, *385*
North to Alaska, 456
North Winds, 1050
Northern Journey, 465
Northern Lights, 584
Northern Soul, 610, 1020
Northern Star, 931
North-South, 145
Norwegian Wood, 67, 496, 888
Nosferatu, 956
Nostradamus, 947
Not a Through Street, 836
Not Alone, 960
Not Dark Yet, 294
Not Dead Yet, 959
Not Fade Away, 400, 451, 724, 848, 997
Not Forgotten, 572
Not Just Knee Deep, 195
Not Me, 744
Not of this Earth, 241, 872
Not One Minute More, 825
Not Satisfied, 35
Not So Sweet Martha Lorraine, 616
Not the Lovin' Kind, 646
Not the Only One, 116
Not Till Tomorrow, 627
Not without a Friend, 908
Nothin' but a Breeze, 1071
Nothin' but the Blues, 1071
Nothin' Heavy, 75
Nothin' Matters and What if It Did, 660
Nothin''s Gonna Stop Us Now, 495
Nothing but the Best, 747
Nothing but the Tail Lights, 90
Nothing but the Truth, 92
Nothing Can Divide Us, 278
Nothing Can Stop Me, 170
Nothing Can Stop Us, 867, 1079
Nothing Compares 2 U, 733, 798
Nothing Else Matters, 665
Nothing from Nothing, 790
Nothing Gonna Stop Me Now, 951
Nothing Has Been Proved, 933
Nothing in Rambling, 661
Nothing Lasts Forever, 299
Nothing Less Than Brilliant, 891
Nothing Like a Sunny Day, 1017
Nothing Like the Rain, 1001
Nothing Like the Sun, 950
Nothing Matters Without Love, 149
Nothing Rhymed, 747
Nothing Says I Love You Like I Love You, 144

Nothing Seems to Matter, 814
Nothing Takes the Place of You, 33
Nothing to Fear, 305
Nothing Was Delivered, 147
Nothing Without You, 559
Nothing's Gonna Stop Us Now, 1026, 1031, 1032
Nothing's Too Good for My Baby, 1076
Notice to Appear, 654
Notorious, 289, 500, 846
Notorious Byrd Brothers, 146, 147
Nottamun Town, 323
Nous Vivons Ensemble, 585
Nouveau Calls, 1074
Nouveau Western, 657
Novacaine for the Soul, 303
November Rain, 407
Now, 46, 241, 431, 648, 649, 880
Now & Forever, 1055
Now Ain't the Time for Your Tears, 219
Now and for Always, 417
Now and Zen, 570
Now I Got Worry, 511
Now I Know, 525, 895
Now I Wanna Sniff Some Glue, 814
Now I'm Here, 807
Now Is the Hour, 230
Now Is the Time, 692, 818
Now It Can Be Told, 330
Now She Cares No More for Me/ My Kind of Carrying on, 89
Now That the Buffalo's Gone, 868
Now! That's What I Call Quite Good, 68
Now Those Days Are Gone, 136
Now Voyager, 71
Now We Are Six, 499, 942
Now We're Thru, 644
Now You Has Jazz, 29, 231, 785
Now You Know, 348
Now You See It . . . Now You Don't, 119
Nowadays Clancy Can't Even Sing, 136
Nowhere, 834
Nowhere Man, 993
Nowhere to Run, 449, 645
N'ssi, 532
Nu Yorican Soul, 651, 906
Nuages, 218, 713, 826
Nuclear Blues, 97
Nuclear Furniture, 495
Nucleus, 851
Nude Paper Sermon, The, 834
Nuff Respect, 84
Nugent, 727
Nuggets, 305

Nuits de la Fondation Maeght, 41, 961
Numb, 785
Number 5, 673
Number Nine Dream, 576
Number of the Beast, 474
Number 1 Remixes, The, 938
Number One Crush, 371
Number One in Heaven, 927
Number One Man, 613
Number One Song in Heaven, The, 927
#1's, 157
Number 10, 150
Number 12, 55
Numbers, 554, 946
Numero Uno, 87
Nursery Cryme, 377
Nut Rocker, 301, 351
Nutbush City Limits, 998
Nuthin' but a 'G' Thang, 269
Nuthin' Fancy, 608
NYC Ghosts, 921
Nylon Curtain, The, 502

O Boso, 263
O D O O, 557
O La Soca, 31
007, 255, 549, 799
O Soave Fanciulla, 660
O Sole Mio, 789
O Superman, 21
O Terra Addio, 614
Oar, 680
Oasis, 339, 596
Ob-La-Di Ob-La-Da, 644
Oblivion, 860
Oblivious, 41, 42
Obscure Alternatives, 490
Observations in Time, 736
Obsession, 926
Obsessions, 1006
Obsolete, 657
Ocean Front Property, 955
Ocean Rain, 299
Oceans of Tears, 939
Octave, 689
Octavius, 242
October, 1004
Octopus, 461
Odds & Sods, 1054
Ode to Billie Joe, 78, 378, 408, 415
Ode to Duke Ellington, 466
Ode to Tobago, 755
Ode Years, The, 540
Odelay, 69, 70
Odessa, 71
Odetta Sings Ballads and Blues, 735
Odetta Sings Dylan, 735
Odyssey and Oracle, 1093
Odyssey of James Rushing Esq, The, 863

Odyssey through O2, 491
Oedipus Shmoedipus, 7
Of Rivers and Religion, 322
Off Centre, 747
Off the Beatle Track, 647
Off the Coast of Me, 533
Off the Ground, 612
Off the Record, 964
Off the Top, 916
Off the Wall, 481, 514
Off to See the Lizard, 137
Offbeat of Avenues, The, 636
Offering, 218
Offramp, 666
O. G. Original Gangster, 467
Ogden's Nut Gone Flake, 912
Ogni Volta, 694
Oh, 462
Oh Babe!, 795
Oh Babe What Would You Say?, 55, 792
Oh Baby, 607
Oh Baby (We've Got a Good Thing Going), 658
Oh Boy, 451, 698
Oh, by Jingo, 259
Oh Carol, 540, 880
Oh Carolina, 798
Oh Daddy, 1036
Oh Darling, 581
Oh Dem Golden Slippers, 347, 387
Oh Diane, 342
Oh Girl, 180, 1089
Oh Happy Day, 431, 702
Oh How I Hate to Get up in the Morning, 79
Oh How She Could Yacki Hacki Wicki Wacki Woo (That's Love in Honolulu), 203
Oh! How That German Could Love, 78
Oh Johnny, Oh, 996
Oh Julie, 947
Oh Lonesome Me, 382, 1088
Oh Lord, Search My Heart, 246
Oh Me, Oh My, 380, 1086
Oh Me, Oh My, I'm a Fool for You Baby, 604
Oh Mein Papa, 336, 752
Oh Mercy, 293, 563
Oh Monah, 390, 1042
Oh! Mr Porter, 592
Oh My Babe Blues, 813
Oh My God, 407
Oh My My, 939
Oh! Neil, 540
Oh No, 208
Oh No! It's Devo, 260
Oh No, Not My Baby, 257, 540, 635
Oh No, They're Recording This Show, 1018

Oh! Oh! Antonio, 345
Oh Oh I Love Her So, 814
Oh Patti (Don't You Worry About Loverboy), 878
Oh People, 558
Oh Pretty Woman, 741
Oh Red, *774*, 1063
Oh Sherrie, 519
Oh! Susannah, 147, 346
Oh Sweet Nuthin', 1018
Oh Very Young, 946
Oh Way, 337
Oh Well, 341
Oh What a Beautiful Morning, 843, 844
Oh What a Circus, 314
Oh What a Dream, 131
Oh What a Night, 256
Oh What a Pal Was Mary, 523
Oh Why, 929
Oh Yeah, *526*, 857, 1084
Oh Yeah Maybe Baby, 235
Oh Yes I Can, 229
Oh You Beautiful Girl, 706
Oh You Pretty Thing, 442
Oh You Pretty Things, 110
O-H-I-O, 736
Ohio, 1087
Oignons, Les, 69
Oil on Canvas, 491
OK Computer, 256, 811
O'Keefe, 737
Okie Dokie Stomp, 126
Okie from Muskogee, 410, 411, 970
Oklahoma Borderline, 383
Oklahoma Hills, 407
Oklolona River Bottom Band, 378
Ol' Blue Eyes Is Back, 218, 496, 904
Ol' Blue Suede's Back, 766
Ol' Blues Singer, The, 362
Ol' Eon, 465
Ol' 55, 623, 652, 1024
Ol' Man River, 530, 838, 843, 1050
Ol' Waylon, 497
Old 8x10, 993
Old Before I Die, 1065
Old Bitch Warrior, 660
Old Black Joe, 386, 581, 963
Old Bum's Rush, The, 1066
Old Cape Cod, 751
Old Changing Way, The, 982
Old Dan Tucker, 162
Old Dan's Records, 585
Old Devil Moon, 423
Old Dog Tray, 347
Old Dogs, 896
Old Dogs, Children and Watermelon Wine, 415
Old Dope Peddler, The, 574

Old Fashioned Love, 322
Old Fashioned Way, 459, 506
Old Fat Robin, The, 560
Old Flames, 851
Old Flames Can't Hold a Candle to You, 758
Old Folks, 120, 688
Old Folks at Home, The, 346, 347, 386, 660, 930
Old Friends, 673, 794, 897
Old Habits, 1061
Old Hen Cackled and the Rooster's Going to Crow, The, 161
Old Jim Crow, 900
Old Kentucky Home, 719
Old Lamplighter, The, 525
Old Maid Boogie, 1022
Old Man, The, 220, 600, 1088
Old Man Down the Road, The, 226
Old Man Moses, 28
Old Man River, 750
Old Man with Young Ideas, 762
Old Master Painter, The, 987
Old Music Master, The, 1050
Old No. 1, 746, 1027
Old Paint, 1024
Old Payola Roll Blues, The, 322, 356
Old Pictures, 746
Old Raincoat Won't Let You Down, An, 949
Old Rivers, 863
Old Rottenhat, 1079
Old Shep, 343, 788
Old Smokey, 505
Old Soldiers Never Die, 570
Old Straight Track, The, 586
Old the New and the Best of Mary Wells, The, 1046
Old Time Christmas, An, 993
Old Time Music at Clarence Ashley's, 1037
Old Time Religion, 875
Old Times, New Times, 662
Old Trick, New Dog, 167
Old Uncle Ned, 347
Old Wave, 939
Old Ways, 399, 1088
Old-Fashioned Love Song, An, 1064
Old-Fashioned Way, The, 41
Old-Fashioned Wedding, An, 79
Older, 667
Older Stuff, The, 685
Ole, 274
Ole Buttermilk Sky, 158
Ole ELO, 304
Ole Faithful, 161, 991
Ole Man River, 817
Ole Ola, *870*, 949

Ole Slewfoot, 456
Olga Pullofski the Beautiful Spy, 1046
Olias of Sunhillow, 1085
Olive Tree, 881
Oliver Twist, 622
Oliver's Army, 219
Olo Mi Gbo Temi, 731
Omaha, 319, 680
OMD Singles, The, 742
Ommadawn, 738
Omo Lami, 731
On a Carousel, 449
On a Day Like Today, 7
On a Roll, 74
On a Rope, 842
On a Slow Boat to China, 344, 557, 595
On a Sunday Afternoon, 1023
On a Wonderful Day Like Today, 719
On Air, 471, 756, 888
On and on, 548
On Bended Knee, 173
On Broadway, 77, *191*, 285, 545, 637, 638
On Doing an Evil Deed Blues, 322
On Entre OK, On Sorte KO, 353
On Every Street, 267, 383
On Fire, 945
On Land, 311, 563
On Movement, 645
On My Own, 45, 279, 558, 617
On My Radio, 928
On Our Own, 125
On Praying Ground, 1038
On Revival Day, 914
On Tap, 1045
On Target, 31
On the Alamo, 513
On the Atcheson, Topeka and the Sante Fe, 663, 1032
On the Banks of the Ohio, 686
On the Banks of the Wabash, 284
On the Beach, 169, *169*, 452, *819*, *1088*
On the Beach at Bali-Bali, 991
On the Boards, 368
On the Border, 295
On the Double, 387
On the Good Ship Lollipop, 974, 1011, 1052
On the Line, 104
On the Move, 325
On the Night, 267
On the Old Front Porch, 511
On the Other Hand, 993
On the Other Side, 586
On the Rebound, 224
On the Road Again, *120*, 154, 713
On the Road to Kingdom Come, 172

On the Rocks, 1009
On the South Bound, 341
On the Street Where You Live,
    241, 336, 578, 1051, 1057
On the Strength, 397
On the Sunny Side, 704
On the Sunny Side of the Street,
    334, 621
On the Threshold of a Dream, 689
On the Track, 820
On the Way Home, 137
On the Wings of a Dove, 463
On the Wings of a Nightingale,
    320
On This Night, 892
On Through the Night, 254
On Time, 396
On to Victory, 912
On Top of Old Smokey, 496, 687,
    1039
On Top of Spaghetti, 986
On Tour!, 186
On Treasure Island, 282
On with the Motley, 393, 1069
On Your Feet or on Your Knees, 98
On Your Way Down, 587
Once, 143, 424
Once a Day, 21
Once I Had a Sweetheart, 765
Once I Was, 135, *136*
Once in a Lifetime, 719, 967, *967*
*Once in a Lifetime/Sand in the
    Vaseline*, 967
Once in a Very Blue Moon, 404,
    601
Once in a While, 652
Once More, 745
Once More with Feeling, 1073
Once Upon a Dream, 752
Once Upon a Dream, Time Peace,
    816
Once Upon a Summertime, 573
Once Upon a Time, 374, *901*, *960*,
    1046
Once You Get Started, 532
Once You've Tasted Love, 1064
One, *485*, *503*, *512*, *722*, *983*, *1080*
One After 909, 65
One A.M. Phone Calls, 793
One and Only, The, *364*, 531, 784
One Bad Apple, 415, 746
One Belief Away, 116
One Better Day, 630
One by One, 343, 1045
One Clear Moment, 982
One Day at a Time, *47*, 382
One Day I'll Fly Away, 234, 1073
One Day in New York, 113
One Day in Your Life, 481
One Dime Blues, 495
One Emotion, 90
One Fair Summer Evening, 404

One Fine Day, 182, 540
One Fing 'n' Annuver, 175
One Foot in the Blues, 1094
One Foot in the Grave, 69
One for My Baby, 26, 455, 662,
    663, 904
One for the Road, 544, 713, 864
One from the Vault, 401
One Good Well, 1059
One Great Thing, 83
One Heartbeat, 841
One Hell of a Woman, 247
One Hit, 849
One Hot Minute, 820
101 Damnations, 163
101 in Cashbox, 970
100% Columbian, 363
One Hundred Ways, 514
One Hundred Years from Now,
    1007
One I Gave My Heart to, The, 1032
One I Love, The, 826
One I Loved Back Then, The, 512
One in a Million, 308
One in Ten, 1005
One Inch Rock, 101
One Jump Ahead of the Devil, 465
One Less Bell to Answer, 45, 836
*One Lord, One Faith, One Bap-
    tism*, 355
One Love, 801, 952
One Man, 579
One Man Band, 872
One Man Clapping, 485
One Man Dog, 971
One Million Billionth of a Mil-
    lisecond on a Sunday Morn-
    ing, 339
One Mint Julep, 174, 195
One Moment in Time, *71*, 458,
    817
One Monkey Don't Stop No
    Show, 169
One More Cup of Coffee, 293
One More Dream, 812
One More for the Road, 126, 608
One More Fucking Time, 700
One More Hour, 1031
One More Matinee, 267
One More Mile, 287
One More Night, 89, 205
One More Payment, 90
One More Song, 296
One More Story, 181
One More Sunrise, 522
One More Time, 482
One More Try, 666
One Nation Under a Groove, 194,
    195, 466
One Nation Underground, 816
One Night, 198, 583
One Night After, 736

One Night in Heaven, 610
One Night Love Affair, 7
One Night of Love, 522
One Night of Sin, 198
One Note Samba, 501
10538 Overture, 304
One o'Clock Jump, 33, 58, 391,
    487
One of a Kind (Love Affair), 931
One of a Kind Love Affair, A, 932
One of the Boys, 1054
One of the Fortunate Few, 613
One of the Glory Boys, 442
One of the Living, 999
One of the Ruins That Cromwell
    Knocked About a Bit, 592
One of These Nights, 295
One of Those Days in England,
    424
One of Those Nights, 136
One on the Right Is on the Left,
    The, 192
1. Outside, 112
One Piece at a Time, 166
One Piece Topless Bathing Suit,
    490
One Plus One, 385
1+1+1=4, 866
One Potato, Two Potato, 999
1 Record, 113
One Road More, 309
One Rose: The Capitol Years, The,
    629
One Second, 1084
One Step at a Time, 955
One Step Beyond, 630, *1065*
One Step Closer, 256, 279
One Step Up/Two Steps, 935
One Summer Night, 262, *490*
One Sweet Day, 114, 157
One That You Love, The, 12
One Thing, The, *102*, 473
One to Another, 173
One to One, 513, 540
One Toke Over the Line, 343
One True Passion, 716
One, Two, I Love You, 308
(1–2–3–4–5–6–7) Count the Days,
    352
One Vision, 808
One Voice, 917
One Way Track, 907
One Who Really Loves You, The,
    840, 1046
One Woman, 402
One Woman Man, 512
*One Woman . . . The Ultimate
    Collection*, 856
One Year, 1093
One You Love, The, 296
1-2-3, 243, 282
One's on the Way, 607, 896

Oneness, 871
Only a Fool Breaks His Own
  Heart, 669
Only a Hobo, 949
Only a Lad, 305
Only a Lonely Heart Sees, 816
Only a Paper Moon, 422
Only a Pawn in Their Game, 892,
  900
Only a Rose, 359
Only Daddy That'll Walk the
  Line, 497
Only for the Lonely, 938
Only Happy When It Rains, 371
Only in America, 493, 575
Only in My Dreams, 381
Only in My Mind, 618
Only Light on My Horizon Now,
  644
Only Living Boy in New York,
  The, 898
Only Love, 702
Only Love Can Break a Heart,
  778
Only Love Can Break Your
  Heart, 651, 1088
Only One I Know, The, 172
Only One Love, 417
Only One Woman, 71
Only Sisters Can Do That, 781
Only Sixteen, 213, 271
Only the Lonely, 475, 489, 741,
  833, 904
Only the Strong Survive, 74, 144,
  759, 827
Only the Strongest Will Survive,
  834
Only the Young, 519
Only Thing That Looks Good on
  Me Is You, 7
Only Wanna Be With You, 453
Only Way Is Up, The, 35
Only When You Leave, 926
Only Women Bleed, 215
Only You, 703, 779, 780, 939, 1016
Onobox, 740
Onward Christian Soldiers, 480
Ooby Dooby, 741, 770
Ooh La La, 558, 912
Ooh La La La (Let's Go Down),
  550
Ooh Las Vegas, 425
Ooh Look-a There, Ain't She
  Pretty, 401
Ooh My Head, 1010
Ooh Poo Pah Doo, 271, 895, 990
Ooh to Be Ah, 289
Ooh Wee Baby, 714
Ooh Yeah!, 413
Oo-La-La-Limbo, 243
Oooby Dooby, 226
Oooooooh . . . On the TLC Tip, 986

Oop-Shoop, 227
Oops . . . I Did It Again, 928
Opel, 777
Open, 37
Open Arms, 519
Open Book, The, 1065
Open Letter to My Teenage Son,
  An, 279
Open Our Eyes, 297
Open Road, 278, 1065
Open Sesame, 550
Open the Door, 766
Open the Door Richard, 59
Open Thy Lattice Love, 347
Open Up, 572, 884
Open Up and Say . . . Aah!, 781
Open Up the Door, 811
Open Your Eyes, 704, 1085
Open Your Heart, 631
Opening of Doors, The, 5
Operation Feed the Nation, 732
Operation Heartache, 355
Operation Mindcrime, 809
Operator, 228, 589, 636
Opportunities (Let's Make Lots
  of Money), 767
Opposites Attract, 2
Optical Race, 968
Opus de Bop, 381
Opus No. 1, 282
Ora Incenso Birra, 1094
Orange, 510, 947
Orange, L', 68
Orange Blossom Special, 166
Orange Coloured Sky, 529
Orange Crate Art, 64, 755
Orange Crush, 826
Oranges and Lemons, 1081
Orchard Road, 873
Orchestra Siciliana Plays Carla
  Bley, 95
Order in the Court, 809
Ordinary Man, 690
Ordinary Miracles, 418, 957
Ordinary World, 289
Organ Grinder Blues, 1058
Organ Grinder Grinds All Day,
  The, 319
Organ Grinder Swing, 916
Organic, 198
Organisation, 742
Orgasm Addict, 145
Orgasmostron, 699
Orgy in Rhythm, 93
Original, 572
Original Cohen, The, 511
Original Dixieland One-Step, 742
Original Faubus Fables, 274
Original Modern Lovers, The, 832
Original Musiquarium, 1077
Original Recordings, 445
Original Sin, 473, 657

Original Singles Collection . . .
  Plus, The, 1060
Original Soundtracks Volume
  One, 1004
Original Wrapper, The, 824
Orinoco Flow, 312
Ornette!, 202
Ornithology, 753
Orphans and Outcasts Vol. 1, 653
Orphans and Outcasts Vol. 2, 653
Osage Stomp, 155
Osibirock, 745
Osibisa Unleashed, 745
Osmium, 194
Ossie's Dream, 175
Ostrich, The, 1017
Other Aspects, 274
Other Box Set, The, 499
Other Man's Grass, The, 430
Other Place, The, 880
Other Roads, 873
Other Side of Life, The, 689
Other Side of Love, The, 703
Other Side of the Mirror, The, 342
Other Side of this Life, 494, 710,
  710
Other Two and You, The, 716
Other Voice Too (A Trip Back to
  Bountiful), 405
Other Voices, 280, 532, 1089
Other Voices, Other Rooms, 404,
  443
Other Woman, The, 900
Other Worlds, 877
Otherness, 199
Otis Blue, 283, 821
Otis Spann Is the Blues, 927
Otra Dias Mas Sin Verte, 879
Ouch!, 736
Ouija Board, Ouija Board, 696
Our Anniversary, 892
Our Baby, 608
Our Child, 691
Our Father, 337, 839
Our House, 630
Our House Is Rockin', 644
Our Last Song Together, 880
Our Lips Are Sealed, 928
Our Little Nipper, 179
Our Love, 202
Our Man in Jazz, 851
Our Man in Paris, 786
Our Mother the Mountain, 1027
Out Come the Freaks, 1033
Out Deh, 475
Out Here, 600
Out Here on My Own, 218, 394
Out in the Fields, 979
Out in the Streets, 888
Out of a Clear Blue Sky, 288
Out of Breath and Scared to
  Death of You, 662

Out of Control, 727, 1004, 1035
Out of Left Field, 764, 910, 1061
Out of Many, One People, 776
Out of Nowhere, 230, 296, 812
Out of Order, 950
Out of Our Heads, 221, 724, 849
Out of Our Loop, 119
Out of Sight, 128
Out of Space, 801
Out of the Blue, 18, 304, 381, 1088
Out of the Cool, 318
Out of the Cradle, 342
Out of the Dark, 271
Out of the Game, 907
Out of the Island, 792
Out of the Long Dark, 727
Out of the Rain, 487
Out of the Storm, 133
Out of the Wood, 141
Out of the Woodwork, 148
Out of the World, 238
Out of Their Skulls, 534
Out of This World, 316, 430
Out of Time, 106, 205, 709, 826,
  849
Out of Town, 146, 719
Out of Work, 104
Out to Lunch, 274, 1065
Outa Space, 790
Outernational, 1084
Outland, 728
Outlandos d'Amour, 782
Outlaw, 616, 1030
Outlaw Is Just a State of Mind, 22
Outlaws, 497
Outrider, 570
Outside, 667
Outside: from the Redwoods, 596
Outside Lookin' in, 620
Outside Man, The, 754
Outside of a Small Circle of
  Friends, 733
Outside the Gate, 534
Outside the Gates of Heaven, 185
Outward Bound, 274
Over and Over, 188, 702
Over My Head, 341, 812
Over My Heart, 117
Over My Shoulder, 653
Over the Mountain (Across the
  Sea), 1022
Over the Rainbow, 26, 164, 280,
  371, 422, 582, 671
Over the Sea to Skye, 182
Over There, 62, 140, 165, 200, 201,
  203, 1052
Over Under Sideways Down, 70,
  1083
Over You, 357, 714, 804, 857
Overcoats, 444
Overdose, 779
Overhand, 1063

Overkill, 662, 699
Overnight Angels, 700
Overnight Sensation, 699, 1091
Overnight Sensation (Hit
  Record), 817
Overture and Beginners, 913
Ovo, 366
OX15, 499
Oxford Town, 292
Oxygène, 491
Oxygène 7–13, 491
Oy Veh Baby, 111
Oye Como Va, 804, 871
Ozark Mountain Blues, 151
Ozzman Cometh, The, 88
Ozzmosis, 88

Pablo Honey, 811
Pablo Picasso, 832
Pacer, 779
Pachelbel Canon, The, 369
Pacific Age, The, 742
Pacific Coast Rambler, 493
Pacific Standard Time, 318
Pack Up the Plantation, 771
Pack up Your Sorrows, 329
Pack Up Your Troubles, 345
Packed!, 791
Packet of Three, 935
Packin' Up, 1030
Paddy McGinty's Goat, 1046
Paddy on the Road, 689
Padstow Lifeboat, 30
Pagan Love Song, 130, 359
Pagan Place, A, 1035
Page of Life, 1014
Paid in Full, 43, 43, 435
Pain, 736
Pain in My Heart, 820
Painkiller, 519
Paint Another Picture, 601
Paint as a Fragrance, 842
Paint It Black, 849
Painted from Memory, 45, 219
Painted Head, 423
Painter Man, 104
Painter Passing Through, A, 585
Paintings of the Soul, 398
Pair of Brown Eyes, A, 780
Paisley Park, 797
Palace Springs, 434
Pale Blue Eyes, 1018
Pale Shelter, 972
Pale Sun, Crescent Moon, 223
Palisades Park, 154
Palomo, La, 810, 1016
Pan American Blues, 47, 48, 157
Pandemonium, 535
Pandemonium Shadow Show, 722
Pandora's Box, 541, 742
Pandora's Golden Heebie Jeebies,
  34

Panic, 918
Pan-O-Rama, 299
Papa Don't Preach, 631
Papa Don't Take No Mess – Part
  1, 128
Papa Loves Mambo, 209
Papa Loves to Mambo, 787
Papa Was a Rolling Stone, 975,
  1051
Papa Won't You Dance with Me,
  958
Papa-Oom-Mow-Mow, 351
Papa's Dream, 594
Paper Doll, 674
Paper in Fire, 661
Paper Plane, 941
Paper Roses, 489, 747
Paper Sun, 1072
Paperback Writer, 66, 555
Papers, 793
Para Vigo Me Voy, 236
Parachute, 792, 992
Parade, 797, 926
Parade of the Wooden Soldiers,
  1049
Paradise, 472, 722, 888, 1035
Paradise and Lunch, 212
Paradise by the Dashboard Light,
  657
Paradise City, 407
Paradise in Gazankulu, 73
Paradise Is Here, 116
Paradise Lost, 245, 352
Paradise Theater, 959
Paradise with an Ocean View, 617
Paradisiaque, 657
Parallel Lines, 96, 183, 360
Paranoid, 88
Paranoid and Sunburnt, 909
Paranoid Android, 811
Parapluies de Cherbourg, Les, 702
Parc, 968
Parcel of Rogues, 942
Parchman Farm, 15
Pardon My Southern Accent,
  462, 662
Parents Just Don't Understand,
  917
Paris, 624, 962
Paris All Star Blues, 627
Paris Concert, 118, 318
Paris Encounter, 141
Paris in the Spring, 828
Paris Is a Lonely Town, 423
Paris 1919, 150
Paris Sessions, 616
Parisian Pierrot, 221
Parisienne Walkways, 690, 979
Parker's Mood, 561, 753
Parkerilla, The, 754
Parklife, 100
Parrot and the Monkey, The, 668

Parsley Sage Rosemary and Thyme, 164, *897*
Part of the Plan, 342
Part of the Search, 566
Part Time Love, 969, 971, 1077
Part Two, 305
Parting Should Be Painless, 1055
Partisan, The, 201
Partners, 500
Party, 469, 615
Party Doll, 450, 567, 646, 770
Party Doll and Other Favourites, 159
Party Mix, 43
Party Mix/Mesopotamia, 43
Party of One, 302, 603
Party Pops, 37
Party Time, 98
Party's Over, The, 712, 958
Paso, El, 837, 986
Paso City, El, 837
Pass It Around, 183
Pass It on, 938
Pass It on Down, 12
Pass Me By, 332, 415
Pass the Pipe, 987
Passages, 385, 889
Passing Strangers, 300, 1015, 1034
Passion, *74, 912, 950*
Passion and Compassion, 1078
Passion Dance, 17
Passion Grace and Fire, 624
Passion Is No Ordinary Word, 754
Passion Works, 436
Passionate Kisses, 159, 1062
Passport, 702
Past Light, 5
Past Present and Future, 286, 888, 947
Past to Present, 989
Pastiche, 636
Pastures of Plenty, 407
Pat Metheny Group, The, 665
Pat-a-Cake, 412
Pata Pata, 263, 633, 633, 812
Pata Pata 2000, 633
Patches, 163, 169, 415
Patricia, 787
Patricia Twist, 787
Pattern Disruptive, 16
Patterns, 897
Paul, 768
Paul Butterfield Blues Band, 144
Paul Is Live, 612
Paul Revere Rides Again, 829
Paul Simon, 899
Paul Simon Songbook, The, 897
Paul Simon's Concert in the Park, 900
Paul Young, 1089
Paul's Boutique, 64
Pavane for a Dead Princess, 218

Pavarotti and Friends, 102
Paxton Primer, A, 761
Paxton Report, The, 761
Pay to the Piper, 169
Paying the Cost to Be the Boss, 76
Peace, 317
Peace and Love, 780
Peace and Noise, 917
Peace Be Still, 192
Peace Brother Peace, 834
Peace in our Time, 83
Peace in the Valley, 281, 343
Peace on Earth, 111, *617*
Peace Sells . . . But Who's Buying?, 659
Peace Sign, 1030
Peace to the Neighborhood, 939
Peace Train, 946
Peace Treaty, 988
Peace Will Come, 659, *761*
Peaceful World, 816
Peach Picking Time in Georgia, 845
Peaches, 956
Peanut Vendor, The, 235, 529, 628, 787, 991, 1010
Pearl, 426, *517, 563*
Pearl in the Shell, 513
Pearl's a Singer, 122, 575
Pearls, 123, 540, 870
Pearls of Passion, 856
Pearly Gates, 788
Pearly-Dewdrops' Drops, 198
Peasants, Pigs and Astronauts, 556
Pecos Promenade, 997
Peddlin', 449
Pedro Navaja, 92
Peek-a-Boo, 905
Peel Slowly and See, 1018
Peepshow, 905
Peg, 943
Peggy Lee Songbook: There'll Be Another Spring, The, 572
Peggy Sue, 228, 451
Peggy Sue Got Married, 451
Peggy Suicide, 215
Pelican West, 443
Pendulum, 226
Penetration, 468
Penetrator, 727
Peng!, 944
Penitentiary Blues, 199
Pennies from Heaven, 472
Pennsylvania 6-5000, 670
Penny Lane, 67, 630, 703
Pentangling, 765
Penthouse and Pavements, 438
Pent-up House, 126
People, *513*, 664, 956, 958, 959
People Are People, 258
People Are Strange, 279, 299

People Decessiòn, 692
People Everyday, 30
People Funny, Boy, 272, 767
People Get Ready, 470, *655*, 939, 1014
People Got the Power, 917
People Got to Be Free, 816
People Hold on, 938
People Like Us, 633
People Like You and People Like Me, 386
People Make the World, 1076
People Move on, 960
People of the World, 140
People Time, 381
People United Will Never Be Defeated, A, 410
People Who Grinned Themselves to Death, The, 68
People Will Say We're in Love, 844, 903
People's Instinctive Travels and the Paths of Rhythm, 994
People's Parties, 679
Peppermint Twist, 175, 386, 708, 816
Percussion Bitter Suite, 274
Percussion Bitter Sweet, 837
Percussion Discussion, 676
Perdido, 447
Perfect, 317
Perfect Day, 114, 824
Perfect Day: The Best of Lou Reed, 824
Perfect Funk, 420
Perfect Isn't Easy, 637
Perfect Love, 656
Perfect Night, 824
Perfect Prescription, The, 925
Perfect Sound Forever, 760
Perfect Stranger, A, 326
Perfect Strangers, 254
Perfect 10, 68
Perfect Way, 878
Perfect World, 581
Perfectly Good Guitar, 444
Perfidia, 391, 763, 1019
Performance, 925
Performance and Cocktails, 945
Perhaps Love, 258, 274
Period of Transition, A, 695
Permanent Damage, 1091
Permanent Record, 191
Permanent Vacation, 9
Permanent Waves, 861
Persecution Smith, 882
Persistence of Time, 25
Person to Person, 1022
Personal Best, 722
Personal Jesus, 258
Personal Touch, 457
Personality, 218, 230, 663, 794, 1012

Personality Crisis, 717
Perspective, 19, 711
Perspex Island, 447
Perverted by Language, 326
Pet Sounds, 62, 63, 64, 68
Pet Sounds Sessions, The, 64, 68
Petaluma, 404
Pete Green's Fleetwood Mac: Live at the BBC, 341
Peter, 768
Peter and Sophia, 393
Peter Cottontail, 39
Peter Frampton, 352
Peter Gabriel, 366
Peter Gabriel Plays Live, 366
Peter Gunn, 286, 300, 516, 634, 634
Petite Fleur, 54, 69
Petting in the Park, 786
P. F. Sloan, 218, 911, 1040
Phaedra, 968
Phantom Blues, 966
Phantom Melody, 531
Phantom of the Opry, 284
Phantoms, 586
Pharoah's Army, 1070
Phases and Stages, 713, 1047
Phases of Reality, 74
Phat Planet, 573
Phenix, 8
Phenomenon, 1006
Phil Ochs in Concert, 733
Phil Upchurch, 1008
Philadelphia Freedom, 413, 503
Philadelphia Lawyer, 629
Philip Bailey, 298
Philip Lynott Album, The, 979
Philosopher's Stone, The, 695
Phobia, 544
Phoenix, 530, 558
Phoenix City, 272, 908
Phoenix Concerts Live, The, 949
Phoenix Rising, 975
Phone Booth, 224
Phonogenic, 660
Phorward, 887
Photograph, 254, 660, 939
Photographer, The, 385
Photographs and Memories, 229
Physical, 721
Physical Graffiti, 569
Physical Presence, A, 579
Pianist, Arranger, Composer, Conductor, 160
Piano Concerto in G, 346
Piano Improvisations, 216
Piano Man, 502
Piano Parade, 969
Piano Piece #13, 921
Piano Rags, 834
Piccolo Pete, 1042
Pick a Bale of Cotton, 277

Pick a Dub, 459, 537
Pick Me up on Your Way Down, 458
Pick up a Gun, 627
Pick up the Pieces, 39
Pick up Your Tears, 348
Pick Yourself Up, 530
Pickin' up the Pieces, 137
Picture Book, 902
Picture of Nectar, A, 773
Picture of You, A, 114, 129
Picture Perfect Morning, 900
Picture This, 96, 581, 1047
Pictures, 309
Pictures and Paintings, 830
Pictures at an Exhibition, 309
Pictures at Eleven, 569
Pictures of Infinity, 961
Pictures of Lily, 134, 1053, 1054
Pictures of Matchstick Men, 940
Pictures on My Wall, The, 299
Picturesque Matchstickable Messages, 941
Pie Jesu, 593
Piece of Crap, 1088
Piece of Mind, 474
Piece of My Heart, 80, 355, 517, 812
Piece of My Love, 835
Piece of the Action, 136, 939
Pieces of a Man, 877
Pieces of the Rain, 737
Pieces of the Sky, 425
Pieces of You, 500
Pied Piper, 100
Pienso en Ti, 651
PIL 9, 884
Piledriver, 941
Pilgrim, 187
Pilgrimage, 1074
Pill, The, 607
Pills, 717
Pills and Soap, 219
Pills 'n' Thrills and Bellyaches, 421, 730
Piltdown Rides Again, 348
Pimpin' Ain't Easy, 84
Pin Ups, 110, 298, 334
Pinball Cha Cha, 1084
Pinball Wizard, 503, 882, 1054
Pinch Me, 996
Pine Grove Blues, 4
Piney Wood Hills, 868
Piney Woods Blues, 1057
Ping Pong, 944
Pink & Black, 296, 297
Pink Bedroom, 444
Pink Cadillac, 202, 773, 799
Pink Champagne, 584, 860, 947
Pink Houses, 660
Pink Moon, 283
Pink Panther, The, 109, 634

Pink Parker, The, 754
Pinker and Prouder Than Previous, 603
Pins and Needles, 6
Pioneers Who Got Scalped, 261
Piove, 681
Pipe Liner's Blues, 704
Pipedream, 586
Piper at the Gates of Dawn, The, 776
Pipes of Peace, 612, 647
Pirate Jenny, 204, 577, 1042
Pirate Ship, The, 678
Pirates, 515
Pisces, Aquarius, Capricorn and Jones Ltd, 684
Piscipada, La, 681
Pistol Packin' Mama, 23, 230, 261, 1022
Pistola y el Corazon, La, 594
Pistolero, 779
Pithecanthropus Erectus, 676
Pitter Patter, 130
Pittsburgh, Pennsylvania, 678
Pity for the Lonely, 471
Pizzamania, 330
Place in the Sun, A, 1076
Place in the World, A, 159
Place without a Postcard, 668
Place Your Hands, 825
Placebo, 779
Plain and Fancy, 75
Plain Dirt Fashion, 724
Plain Jane, 244, 783
Plains Music, 635
Plaisir d'Amour, 460
Plan, The, 746
Plan Your Revolution, 654
Plane Wreck at Los Gatos, 408
Planet Drum, 401
Planet Earth, 288
Planet Rock, 51, 554
Planet Waves, 53, 293
Plantation Days, 151
Plastic Ono Band, 899
Plastic People, 1091
Plastic Surgery Disasters, 252
Plateaux of Mirror, The, 311
Platinum, 385, 738
Platinum Breakz, 388
Play, 834, 936
Play a Simple Melody, 79
Play Dead, 29
Play Me Backwards, 47
Play Me Like You Play Your Guitar, 300, 611
Play Me Out, 822
Play One More, 465
Play Something Sweet (Brickyard Blues), 984
Play that Barber-Shop Chord, 706
Play the Blues, 376

Play the Game, 709, 808, 907
Play the Game Right, 644
Play to Me Gypsy, 528
Play to Win, 438
Play Together Again, Again, 749
Playback, The, 128
Playback, 1973–1993, 771
Playboy, 148, 649
Playin' Favorites, 625
Playin' Possum, 1018
Playing, 410
Playing My Thing, 107
Playing to Win, 711, 725
Playing with Fire, 925
Playmates, 913
Playroom, 739
Pleasant Dreams, 815
Pleasant Valley Sunday, 540, 684
Please, 767, 839
Please Accept My Love, 538
Please Be Kind, 48
Please Come Home for Christmas, 125
Please Don't Ask About Barbara, 1017
Please Don't Go, 526
Please Don't Let Me Be Misunderstood, 23, 900
Please Don't Make Me Cry, 1005
Please Don't Talk About Me When I'm Gone, 713
Please Don't Tease, 831
Please Don't Tell Me How the Story Ends, 675
Please Don't Touch, 534, 699
Please Forgive Me, 7
Please Go, 387
Please Go 'Way and Let Me Sleep, 1023
Please Hammer Don't Hurt 'Em, 418
Please Help Me, 595
Please Help Me I'm Falling, 224, 595, 838
Please Let Me Love You, 146
Please Let Me Wonder, 63
Please Love Me, 538
Please Love Me Forever, 1023
Please Mr Gravedigger, 110
Please Mr Johnson, 505
Please Mr Please, 721
Please Mr Postman, 160, 449, 649, 702
Please No More Sad Songs, 304
Please Please Me, 3, 66, 66, 545
Please Please Please, 60, 127, 708
Please Send Me Someone to Love, 363, 655, 735, 860
Please Stay, 44, 285
Please Talk to My Heart, 332
Please to See the King, 942
Please (You Got That . . .), 174

Please Yourself, 52
Pleasure, 736
Pleasure and Pain, 271
Pleasure One, 438
Pleasure Principle, The, 479, 727
Pleasures of the Harbor, 733
Pledging My Love, 5, 120, 185, 303, 417, 748, 985
Plight and Premonition, 965
Plot Thickens, The, 369
Plug Tunin', 251
Plume de Ma Tante, La, 460
Plush, 953
PNYC, 785
Po' Folks, 21
Poacher, The, 913
Pocket Full of Gold, 383
Pocketful of Miracles, 150, 1012
Pod, 778, 984
Poem for Malcolm, 893
Poems, Prayers and Promises, 258
Poet, The, 1076
Poet, Fool or Bum, 436
Poet in My Window, 404
Poet 2, 1076
Poetic Champions Compose, 695
Poetry in Motion, 985
Poincianna, 567
Point of Entry, 519
Point of No Return, 616
Point of View, 109, 935
Points in Time, Vols 1–6, 138
Poison, 215, 801
Poison Arrow, 2, 455
Poison Ivy, 196, 800
Poison Years, 701
Poisoning Pigeons in the Park, 574
Poland, 968
Police and Thieves, 191, 767
Police in Helicopter, 452
Police on My Back, 398
Policy of the Truth, 258
Political Science, 720
Political World, 293
Politician, 225
Polk Salad Annie, 963
Polka Dot Rag, 69
Polka Dots and Moonbeams, 1012
Polka du Roi, La, 993
Pollution, 401
Polly Wolly Doodle, 104, 820
PollyWog Stew, 64
Polonaise in A, 286
Polonaise in B Flat, 476
Poncho and Lefty, 411, 713
Ponder Blues, 620
Pontiac, 601
Pontius Pilate's Decision, 645
Pony Blues, 758
Pony Ride, 251

Pony Time, 175, 221
Pool It!, 685
Pool Shark, The, 287
Poor Boy, 505
Poor Fool, 997
Poor Jenny, 134
Poor Lazarus, 1013
Poor Little Fool, 711
Poor Little Rich Girl, 222
Poor Me, 325
Poor Natty, 475
Poor Old Prurient Interest Blues, The, 429
Poor People of Paris, The, 37, 61, 774, 1044
Poor Poor Pitiful Me, 1092
Poor Side of Town, 836
Pop, 1005
Pop Goes the Weasel, 718
Pop Life, 52, 797
Pop Musik, 868
Pop Pop, 515
Pop Pop Goes My Love, 737
Pop Scene, 99
Pop Singer, 661
Pop Singer's Fear of the Pollen Count, The, 268
Pop Song 89, 826
Pop Symphonies, 565
Pop! – The First 20 Hits, 312
Pop Trash, 289
Popeye, 915
Popeye Joe, 526
Popeye Twist, 987
Popeye Waddle, 221
Poppa Joe, 964
Poppa's Got a Brand New Bag, 128
Popped in, Souled out, 680, 1047
Popsicle, 490
Popsicles and Icicles, 351
Por un Amor, 854
Porch, The, 601
Porch Light, 224
Porcupine, 299
Porgy, 448
Porgy and Bess, 8, 174, 379, 380, 559
Pornography, 238
Porpoise Song, 684
Port au Prince, 833
Porte Du Garage, La, 994
Portfolio, 431, 512
Portishead, 785
Portland Town, 308
Portrait, 343, 1014
Portrait in Jazz, 318
Portrait of an American Family, 638
Portrait of My Love, 567, 685
Portrait of Robert Johnson, 892
Portrait of the Blues, 94, 818

Portraits, 426
Portsmouth, 738
Positive, 134
Positive Touch, 890
Positively 4th Street, 292
Possible Dream, The, 245
Possibly Maybe, 86
Possum Trot School Exhibition, 955
Post, 86
Post Historic Monsters, 163
Post Orgasmic Chill, 909
Post World War Two Blues, 947
Postcard, 454
Postcards from Home, 443
Potato Head Blues, 28, 158
Potatoland, 932
Pottery Pie, 704
Pour Down Like Silver, 982
Pour Some Sugar on Me, 254
Pouring Water on a Drowning Man, 160
Powderfinger, 223, 1088
Power, 467, 975
Power and the Glory, The, 653, 733
Power Corruption and Lies, 716
Power in the Darkness, 841
Power in the Music, 406
Power of Gold, The, 343
Power of Love, 117, 253, 266, 275, 354, 581, 899, 1013
Power of Love/Love Power, 1013
Power of Ten, 251
Power to All Our Friends, 831
Power to the People, 576
Power Windows, 861
Powerage, 4
Powerhouse, 876
Powerslave, 474
Practice What You Preach, 737, 1048
Prairie Home Invasion, 252
Praise, 472
Praise Rather Than Raise, 798
Praise the Lord, 595
Praise the Lord and Pass the Ammunition, 557, 595
Praise without Raise, 692
Praise You, 330
Pray, 1064
Pray Along with Little Richard, 589
Prayer and a Jukebox, A, 587
Prayer Changes Things, 480
Prayer Meeting, 916
Prayers on Fire, 168
Preacher, The, 93
Preacher and the Bear, The, 203, 426, 822
Preacher and the Slave, The, 445
Preachin' Blues, 509

Preachin' the Blues, 457
Precious Cargo, 660
Precious Friend, 408, 881
Precious Jewel, 6
Precious Lord, Take My Hand, 281, 481
Precious Time, 76
Predator, The, 466
Predictable, 544
Pre-Flyte, 237
Prelude, 562
Prelude in C Sharp Minor, 972
Prelude No. 2, 141
Prelude to a Kiss, 447
Premier Hits, 728
Premières Symptomes, 11
Premonition, 226, 352
Presence, 569
Present Arms, 1005
Present Company, 466
Presenting I-Roy, 189
Presenting Isaac Hayes, 434
Preservation, 544
President Kennedy, 315
Press to Play, 612
Pressed Rat and Warthog, 225
Pressing on, 790
Pressure, 732
Pressure Drop, 751, 987
Presto, 861
Pretender, The, 132
Pretenders II, 791
Pretty Baby, 522
Pretty Blue Eyes, 567
Pretty Boy Floyd, 147
Pretty Flamingo, 225
Pretty Fly (For a White Guy), 736
Pretty Girl Is Like a Melody, A, 79, 330
Pretty Hate Machine, 722
Pretty Little Angel Eyes, 769, 896, 929
Pretty Much Your Standard Ranch Stash, 685
Pretty Noose, 924
Pretty on the Inside, 447
Pretty Paper, 712
Pretty Vacant, 500, 884
Pretty Woman, 1001
Pretty Words, 837
Pretzel Logic, 943
Price, The, 138
Price of Love, The, 320
Pride, 751
Pride and Joy, 1051
Pride (In the Name of Love), 149, 1004
Priest, They Called Him, The, 723
Priestess, 318, 870
Primal George Duke, The, 287
Primal Scream, 796
Prime Time, 625

Primitive, 262
Primitive Cool, 849
Primitive Dance, 116
Primitive Love, 314
Primrose Hill, 630
Prince, 797
Prince, The, 630, 799, 928
Prince Charming, 25
Prince of Darkness, 84
Prince of Peace, 369
Principle of Moments, The, 569
Prison, The, 685
Prison Bound Blues, 160
Prisoner in Disguise, 854
Prisoner of Love, 127, 206, 209, 299, 794
Prisoner's Song, The, 240, 671, 842
Prisoners of Paradise, 316
Prisons de Roy, Les, 774
Private Audition, 436
Private Beach Party, 475
Private Collection, 831
Private Dancer, 998
Private Eyes, 413
Private Investigations, 267
Private Jives, 365
Private Life, 512
Private Line, 737
Private Number, 74, 107
Private Practice, 270
Private Revolution, 733
Private Waters in the Great Divide, 533
Privilege (Set Me Free), 917
Problem Child, 4
Problems, 134, 320
Procession, 1039
Procol's Ninth, 575
Prodigal Stranger, The, 801
Prodigy Presents the Dirtchamber Sessions Volume, 801
Product, 145
Professional Widow, 20
Profile: The Ultimate Collection, 927
Profit in Peace, 732
Profoundly in Love with Pandora, 290
Pro-Gen, 730, 887, 888
Progeny, 888
Progression Sessions, The, 138
Progressive Blues Experiment, 351, 1071
Progressive Country Music for a Hollywood Flapper, 765
Prohibition – Yes or No?, 1027
Projections, 551
Promenade, 268
Promise, 866
Promise Me You'll Remember, 210

Promised Land, 127, 671, 790, 809
Promised You a Miracle, 901
Promises, 1064
Promises and Lies, 1005
Pronounced Lehnerd Skinnerd, 608
Pronto Monto, 619
Propaganda, 927
Pros and Cons of Hitchhiking, 777
Prose Combat, 657
Prospect Before Us, The, 13
Prosperous, 689
Prostitute, 360, 991
Protect the Innocent, 699
Protection, 321, 650, 960
Protest Songs, 788
Proud Mary, 139, 225, 226, 998
Proud Mary: The Best of Ike &
    Turner, 998
Prove It, 973
Provision, 878
ProzaKc Blues, 536
Prune Song, The, 233
P.S. I Love You, 416, 1016
Psalm of Dub, 537
Psionic Psunspots, 1081
Psychedelic Shack, 975, 1051
Psychedelic Worm, 505
Psychic Terrorism, 1074
Psycho, 443
Psycho Circus, 547
Psycho-Head Blowout, 1048
Psychocandy, 498, 796
Psychoderelict, 1055
Psychokiller, 967
P. T. 109, 252
P'tit Clown de ton Coeur, Le, 416
Pubic Enemy, 994
Public Enemy Number 1, 802
Pucker Up, 349
Pucker Up Buttercup, 121
Puff the Magic Dragon, 768
Pull Up to the Bumper, 512
Pulling Mussels (From the Shell),
    935
Pulped (83–92), 805
Pump, 9, 10
Pump Up the Volume, 435, 951
Pumping on Your Stereo, 962
Punch and Judy, 642
Punch the Big Guy, 949
Punch the Clock, 219
Punky Reggae Party, 643, 767
Puppet Man, 880
Puppet on a String, 108, 220, 273,
    789, 891
Puppy Love, 24, 747, 757
Puppy Song, 167, 722
Pure, 585, 728
Pure and Crooked, 653
Pure and Simple, 500
Pure Hank, 1061
Pure Instinct, 875

Pure Morning, 779
Pure Phase, 925
Pure Pop for Now People, 603
Pure Religion, 246
Pure Shores, 14
Pure Smokey, 841
Purist, The, 976
Purple, 953
Purple Acoustic Tape, The, 595
Purple Haze, 266, 440
Purple Heather, 695
Purple Night, 961
Purple People Eater, 883
Purple People Eater Meets the
    Witch Doctor, The, 925
Purple Rain, 797, 797
Pursuit of Accidents, The, 579, 1020
Push It, 371, 869
Pusher, The, 40, 944
Pushin' Too Hard, 880
Pushover, 486
Puss in Boots, 25, 717
Pussy Cats, 722
Pussy Price, 12
Put a Light in the Window, 348
Put a Little Love in Your Heart,
    259, 317, 403, 480
Put It in Your Ear, 145
Put It Where You Want It, 234
Put Me in Your Mix, 1048
Put on Your Old Gray Bonnet,
    706
Put Your Cat Clothes on, 766
Put Your Hands Together, 736
Put Your Head on My Shoulder,
    24
Put Your Love in Me, 457
Put Yourself in My Place, 476,
    677
Put Yourself in My Shoes, 90
Puttin' It Together, 511
Puttin' on the Smile, 393
Puttin' on the Style, 277, 325
Putting the Heart back into the
    City, 368
Puzzle Song, The, 309
Pyjamarama, 857
Pyramid, 644, 756
Pyromania, 254

Q: Are We Not Men? A: We Are
    Devo, 260
QE2, 738
Q2K, 809
Quadrophenia, 10, 1054
Quaker Girl, A, 683
Quality of Mercer, The, 609
Quality Songs . . . , 891
Quarter to Three, 103, 104, 266
Quartet, 118
Quartet West, 410
Quasimodo, 753

Que Alegria, 624
Que Rico el Mambo, 787
Que Sera, Sera, 250, 261, 954
Queen and Her Knights, The, 933
Queen Elvis, 447
Queen for a Day, 94
Queen Is Dead, The, 918
Queen of Clubs, 526
Queen of Country, 1045
Queen of the Hop, 244
Queen of the House, 673
Queen of the Night, 1047
Queen of the Ryche, 809
Queen of the Silver Dollar, 896
Queen Rocks, 808
Queen II, 807
Queen's Suite, 307
Queens of Noise, 499
Queer, 371
Quelquechose de Tennessee, 416
Quench, 68
Quest, The, 767
Question, 689
Question of Balance, A, 689
Question of Time, A, 133, 258
Questions and Answers, 666, 887
Qui Seme le Vent Recolte le
    Tempo, 657
Quick One, A, 1054
Quick One While He's Away, A,
    1054
Quicksand, 449, 645
Quicksilver, 810
Quiereme Mucho, 469
Quiet Life, 490, 544
Quiet Night of Quiet Stars, 501
Quiet Normal Life, A, 1092
Quiet Please, 829
Quiet Storm, 134, 841
Quiet Sun – Mainstream, 857
Quiet Whiskey, 426
Quinella, 37
Quintet of the Year, 753, 786
Quit Dreaming and Get on the
    Beam, 710
Quit Playin' Games (with My
    Heart), 46

R, 528
R&B at the Flamingo, 327
R&B from the Marquee, 391, 552
R&R Junkie, 122
Ra, 860
Rabbit, 175
Race, The, 1084
Race Is on, The, 302, 512
Race Track, 668
Race with the Devil, 88, 1021
Racing with the Moon, 687
Radancer, 644
Radar Love, 387
Radiation, 642

Radio City, 113
Radio Ethiopia, 917
Radio Free Europe, 826
Radio Gaga, 808
Radio KAOS, 777
Radio M.U.S.I.C. Man, 1076
Radio Musicola, 531
Radio One, 440
Radio Song, 827
Radio Wall of Sound, 910
Radioactivity, 554
Rael, 1054
Rafi's Revenge, 33
Rag Doll, 261, 349
Rag Mop, 19, 223, 419, 1068
Ragamuffin Man, 635
Ragamuffin Year, 750
Rage for Order, 809
Rage Hard, 354
Rage in Eden, 1006
Rage to Love, 1055
Ragged Glory, 1088
Ragging the Baby to Sleep, 510
Ragin' Cajun, The, 531
Raging Silence, 1009
Rags to Riches, 77, 325, 1069
Rags to Rufus, 532
Ragtime Cowboy Jew, 405
Ragtime Cowboy Joe, 463, 883
Railroads 1, 322
Railway Hotel, 60
Rain, 308, 332, 941
Rain and Tears, 1014
Rain Dance, 406
Rain Dogs, 1025
Rain in Spain, The, 578
Rain or Shine, 435
Rain, the Park and Other Things,
The, 223
Rain Today, 719
Rain Tree Crow, 965
Rainbow, *157, 170, 644*
Rainbow in Curved Air, A, 150,
385, 554
Rainbow Race, 881
Rainbow Riot, 273
Rainbow Rising, 254
Rainbow Road, 13
Rainbow Seeker, 234
Rainbow's End, 793
Raindancing, 703
Raindrops, 980
Raindrops Keep Falling on My
Head, 45, 980, 987
*Rainforests, Oceans and Other
Themes*, 322
Raining in My Heart, 671, 823, 134
Rainy Day People, 585
Rainy Day Women Nos 12 and
35, 292
Rainy Days and Mondays, 160,
472, 1064

Rainy Night in Georgia, 78, 870
Raise, 298
Raise the Pressure, 717
Raise Your Fist and Yell, 215
Raise Your Hand, 934, 1089
Raised on Radio, 519
Raised on Records, 911
Raising Hell, 858, 859
Ralph Albert and Sydney, 627
Ram, 611
Ram It Down, 519
Ram-Bunk-Shush, 273, 1019
Ramblin', 308, 509
Ramblin' Boy, 761
Ramblin' Gamblin' Man, 882
Ramblin' Man, 15
Ramblin' on my Mind, 187, 509,
1062
Ramblin Rose, 202
Ramona, 29, 38
Ramones, 814
Ramones Leave Home, 814
Rancho DeLuxe, 137
Rancho Rock, El, 170
Randy Lynn Rag, 340
*Randy Ray Live at the Nashville
Palace*, 993
Randy Scouse Git, 684
Range Life, 760
Rank, 918
Rant'n'Rave with the Stray Cats,
302
Raoul and the King of Spain, 972
Rap Payback, 128
Rape Me, 723
Rappers' Delight, 397
Rappin' Rufus, 981
Rapping with the Ladies, 815
Rapture, 49, 96, *905*
Rapture in the Chamber, 932
Rare, Live and Classic, 47
Rare Precious and Beautiful, 71
Raspberry Beret, 797
Rasputin, 104, 712
Rasta Ambassador, 1009
Rasta Communication, 459
Rasta Don't Fear, 692
Rastaman Vibration, 643
Rat Bastard, 447
Rat in the Kitchen, 1005
Rat Race, 285, 928
Rat Trap, 376
Rated Extraordinaire, 971
Rattle and Hum, 192, 1004
Rattus Norvegicus IV, 956
Raunch and Roll, 88
Raunchy, 273, 300, 521, 1016
Rave on, 451, 698
Rave on John Donne, 695
Rave Un2 the Joy Fantastic, 798
Raven, The, 956
Raw, 84

Raw and the Cooked, The, 335
Raw and the Remixed, The, 335
Raw Deal, The, 1061
Raw Deluxe, 521
Raw Like Sushi, 178
Raw Power, 110, 468
Raw Sienna, 343
Rawhide, 560, 686, 1077
Rawlinson End, 105
Ray Charles Live at Newport, 283
Ray Conniff in Moscow, 211
Ray of Light, 631
*Ray Stevens: Comedy Video Clas-
sics*, 946
*Raymond Scott Project: Power-
house, Vol. 1, The*, 876
Razor Dance, 982
Razor's Edge, The, 5
Razorblade Suitcase, 142
Razzle-Dazzle, 412
Razzmatazz, 805
*Re*ac*tor*, 1088
Reach, 1032
Reach for the Sky, 16
Reach Out, 350
Reach Out and Touch (Some-
body's Hand), 32, 855
Reach Out I'll Be There, 350, 375,
449
Reaching for the Sky, *134, 339*
Reaching for the World, 764
Reaching to the Converted, 117
Read 'Em and Weep, 637
Read about Love, 982
Read My Lips, 208
Read My Mind, 618
Ready an' Willing (Sweet Satis-
faction), 1050
Ready as Hell, 88
Ready for a New Day, 977
Ready or Not, 345, 361
Ready or Not Here I Come, 255
Ready Steady Go, 467
Ready Teddy, 90
Ready to Die, 804
Real, 158
Real American, 615
Real American Folk Song, The,
379, 380
Real as I Wanna Be, 832
Real Birth of the Cool, The, 983
Real Boogie Woogie, The, 662
Real Buddy Holly Story, The, 451
Real Dead One, A, 474
Real Great Escape, 218
Real Life, 145, 902
Real Live One, A, 474
Real Love, 68, 95, 279, 305, *938*
Real Macaw, The, 754
Real McCoy, The, 1002
Real Men Wear Black, 152
Real Mother for Ya, A, 1038

Real People, 845
Real Ramona, The, 984
Real Slim Shady, The, 270
Real Thing, 966, 1070
Real Things, 1001
Real Time, 973
Real to Real Cacophony, 901
Real to Reel, 642
Real Ugly Woman, 574
Real Wild Child, 228, 469, 720
Reality, 588
Reality Check, 75
Really, 150
Really Blue, 1019
Really Rosie, 540
Really Saying Something, 928
Reap the Wild Wind, 1006
Reason, The, 540
Reason to Believe, 423, 949
Reason to Try, 817
Reasons for Sharing, 906
Reasons to Be Cheerful (Part 3), 290
Reba, 618
Rebel Girl, 445
Rebel Heart, 217
Rebel Music, 644
Rebel Rouser, 300
Rebel Souls, 35
Rebel Warrior, 33
Rebel Without a Pause, 803
Rebels without a Clue, 75
Re-Birth of the Cool, 705
Recapitulation, 141
Recent Songs, 201, 1031
Recently, 47, 750
Reckless, 7, 51
Reckless Blues, 28
Reckless Love and Bold Adventure, 629
Reckless Night and Turkish Twi-lights, 876
Reckless Night on Board an Ocean Liner, 876
Reckoning, 401, 826
Recollections, 220
Reconsider Baby, 179, 362
Reconstruction, 649
Recovering the Satellites, 221
Recovery, 59
Recurring, 925
Recurring Dream, 701
Recurring Dream: The Very Best of Crowded House, 233
Recycled, 1071
Recycler, 1094
Recycling the Blues, 966
Red, 67, 164, 208, 911
Red and Gold, 324
Red and the Black, The, 98, 559, 967
Red Balloon, 188

Red Black and Green, 40
Red Blood and White Mink, 865
Red Card, 328
Red Dirt Girl, 426
Red Guitar, 965, 1024
Red Haired Stranger, 713
Red Heaven, 984
Red Hot and Blue, 178, 209, 469, 734, 785
Red Hot & Country, 652
Red Hot & Dance, 667
Red Hot (Reputation), 386
Red Hot Rhythm and Blues, 855
Red House, 537, 1093
Red Light, 691
Red Light Special, 986
Red Light Spells Danger, 732
Red Neck Hippie Romance, 55
Red Nightgown Blues, 247
Red Octopus, 495
Red Red Wine, 1005
Red River Rock, 504
Red River Rock 67, 505
Red River Valley, 504, *1052*
Red Rooster, The, 459
Red Rose Speedway, 611
Red Roses for a Blue Lady, 218, 522
Red Roses for Gregory, 475
Red Roses for Me, 219, 780
Red Rubber Ball, 881, 897
Red Sails in the Sunset, 275, 528, 668, 780
Red Shoes, *143*, 219
Red Sky, 302
Red to Blue, 820
Red We Want Is the Red We've Got in the Old Red, White and Blue, The, 528
Red's Boogie, 774
Redemption Song, 776
Redemption Songs, 644
Red-Headed Music Maker, The, 416
Redneck Wonderland, 668
Redux, 737
Redux '92 – Live in Japan, 860
Reed Seed, 1035
Reel Music, 182
Reel to Real, 600
Reelin' in the Years, 943
Re-entlistment Blues, 992
Reet Petite, 393, 1069
Refereed Ectoplasm (Switched on Volume Two), 944
Reflections, 36, *44*, *765*, *877*, *886*, *963*, *1038*
Reflections in a Crystal Wind, 329
Reflections in the Looking Glass, 905
Reflections of My Life, 644
Reflections of Passion, 1082
Reflex, The, 289

Refugees of the Heart, 1073
Refuse to Be Burnt Out, 361
Reg Dwight's Piano Goes Pop, 503
Regeneration, 741
Reggae Got Soul, 987
Reggae Greats, 475
Reggae on Broadway, 643
Reggatta de Blanc, 782
Regression, 1083
Rehearsals for Retirement, 733
Reheated, 154
Rei Mo Mo, 148, 967
Reign in Blood, 858
Reincarnations of a Lovebird, 676
Rejoice, 310
Rejoicing, 410, 666
Rejuvenation, 714
Rekooperation, 552
Relativity Suite, 95, 177
Relax, 354
Relaxing at Camarillo, 753
Relay, 1054
Relayer, 1084
Release Me, 64, 462, *772*, *794*
Release of an Oath: the Kol Nidre, 305
Release the Pressure, 572
Relight My Fire, 604, 1064
Reload, 517, 665
Remain in Light, 559, 967
Re-make/Re-model, 857
Remasters, 570
Remasters II, 570
Remedies, 271
Remember, 61, 220, 326
Remember Baby, 892
Remember Clifford, 126
Remember I Love You, 462
Remember Me, 584, 855
Remember Me This Way, 386
Remember Pearl Harbor, 525
Remember the Forgotten Man, 527, *1032*
Remember the Time, 481
Remember Two Things, 246
Remember (Walking in the Sand), 697, 888
Remember You're a Womble, 60
Remembered, 1080
Remembering Merle, 1038
Remembrance Day, 7
Reminisce, 95
Reminiscing, 451, 536, 590, *590*
Reminiscing in Tempo, 307
Remix Collection, The, 114
Remixes, 469
Remixes in the Key of B, 125
Remnants, 570
Renaissance, 1014, 1021
Renaissance Fair, 147
Renancer, 314
Rendezvous, 231, 324, 491

Rendezvous sous la Pluie, 826
Renegade, 979
Renegades of Funk, 51
Reno Nevada, 329
Rent, 768
REO Two, 827
Repeat When Necessary, 302
Replenish, 824
Replicas, 727
Repossessed, 555, 964
Representing the Mambo, 588
Reproduction, 461
Republic, 716
Reputation, 933
Requiem, 275, 593
Requiem for a Harlequin, 199
Rescue Me, 31, 59
Reservations for Two, 1033
Resolving Contradictions, 857
Respect, 283, 355, 447, 618, 701,
    821
Respect Yourself, 938
Respectable, 475
Respetto, 1094
Rest in Peace, 321
Rest of the Dream, 724
Rest Your Love on Me, 1000
Restful Mind, 218
Restless, 375, 534, 766, 768
Restless Eyes, 466
Restless Heart, 1051
Restless Kind, 994, 1034
Restless Stranger, The, 19
Results, 372
Resurrection, 1076
Retard Girl, 447
Retox/Detox, 438
Retroactive, 254
Retrosectable, 273
Retrospect, A, 847
Retrospective, 5, 167, 853
Return of Al Capone, The, 988
Return of Da Boom Bap, 106
Return of Django, 767
Return of Doug Saldana, The, 866
Return of Manticore, The, 310
Return of Rock, 581
Return of Saturn, 725
Return of the Arkansas Traveler,
    The, 511
Return of the Brecker Brothers, 119
*Return of the Formerly Brothers,
    The*, 867
Return of the Grievous Angel, 426,
    757, 1007
Return of the Juju King, The, 8
Return of the Los Palmas Seven,
    630
Return of the Real, 467
*Return of the Repressed: Anthol-
    ogy*, 322
Return of the Space Cowboy, 489

Return of Wayne Douglas, The,
    867
Return to Fantasy, 1009
Return to Forever, 190, 216
Return to Me, 646
Return to Paradise, 959
Return to Pooh Corner, 596
Return to Sender, 91, 789
Return to Zero, 109
Reuben James, 847
Reunion, 88, 89, 141, 185, 266, 320,
    617, 768, 975, 1027, 1040, 1068
Reunion in Central Park, 552
Reunion Live, 520
Reveille Rock, 504
Revelation, 600
Revelation: Revolution '69, 602
Revelations, 491, 534, 1003
Revenge, 317, 546
Reverberation, 299
Reverence, 498
Reverend Black Grape, 422
Reverend Mr Black, 542
Reverie, 502
Reverse Willie Horton, A, 510
Revolution, 140, 925
Revolution Blues, 1088
Revolution by Night, 98
Revolution 909, 239
Revolution Will Not Be Tele-
    vised, The, 877
Revolutions of Time, 713
Revolver, 66, 67
Revues, The, 222
Reward, 215
Rez, 1008
RFTC, 842
Rhapsodies, 1025
Rhapsody and Blues, 234
Rhapsody in Blue, 379, 1050
Rhapsody in the Rain, 185
Rhiannon, 342, 497
Rhinestone Cowboy, 153
Rhumboogie, 23
Rhyme Pays, 467
Rhymes and Reasons, 258, 540
Rhymes in Rooms, 947
Rhythm & Blues, 751
Rhythm and Blues Alibi, 390
Rhythm and Romance, 166
Rhythm and Stealth, 51, 573
Rhythm and the Blues, The, 446
Rhythm, Country and Blues, 36,
    549, 558, 589, 997, 870, 939, 991,
    1000, 1034
Rhythm Divine, The, 60, 1084
Rhythm Is Going to Get You, 314
Rhythm Is My Business, 337
Rhythm Is Our Business, 149
Rhythm Killers, 565, 911
Rhythm Nation, 479
Rhythm of Love, 49, 677

Rhythm of the Night, 1031
Rhythm of the Rain, 278, 343
Rhythm of the Saints, 119, 900
Rhythmatist, The, 782
Rhythms of the South, 854
*Rhythms, Resolutions and
    Clusters*, 988
Rhytmeen, 1094
Ribbon of Darkness, 584, 837
Rice, 164
Rice, Red Beans and Turnip
    Greens, 588
Rich Girl, 413
Rich Man's Woman, 122
Richard Clayderman Plays Abba,
    192
Richard P. Havens, 1983, 431
Richard Rodgers' Broadway, 23
Richard III, 961
Richest Man, The, 134
*Richie Havens Sings The Beatles
    and Dylan*, 431
Richland Woman Blues, 463
Rick Sings Nelson, 711
Rick's Road, 978
Ricochet, 120, 968
Rid of Me, 429
Riddle, The, 531
Ride, The, 199
Ride a Rock Horse, 1054
Ride a White Swan, 101
Ride Again, 18
Ride Captain Ride, 473
Ride 'Em Jewboy, 963, 986
Ride Like the Wind, 231
Ride My See-Saw, 689
Ride on, 690
Ride on a Cyclone Auto, 930
Ride on Time, 86, 87
Ride, Ride, Ride, 22
Ride 'Round the World in His
    Airship, 930
Ride the Lightning, 665
Ride This Train, 165
Ride with Bob, 33, 411
Ride Your Pony, 281, 990
Rider Please Pass By, 47
Riders in the Sky, 477, 886
Riders on the Storm, 280
Rides, 825
Ridiculous, 936
Ridin' the Storm Out, 827
Riding High, 230, 751
Riding with the King, 187, 444, 539
Riff Raff, 302
Rift, 773
Right Back to You, 976
Right by You, 229
Right by Your Side, 317
Right Church but the Wrong
    Pew, The, 203
Right Down the Line, 812

Right for the Time, 497
Right Here and Now, 835
Right Here Right Now, 330
Right Night and Barry White, The, 1048
Right Now, 905, *987*
Right of Passage, 164
Right or Wrong, *166*, *483*, *812*
Right Place, Wrong Time, 862
Right Rhythm, 781
Right, Said Fred, 647
Right Side Up, 627
Right String – but the Wrong Yo Yo, The, *766*, *774*
Right Stuff, The, *333*
Right There, 449
Right Thing, The, *902*
Right Time, The, *130*, *487*, *1047*
Right Time of the Night, 1031
Right Time Right Place, 142
Right to Love, The, *482*
Right Track, 775
Right Turn on Blues, 620
Rightstarter (Message to a Black Man), 803
Rigor Mortis, 152
Rigor Mortis Sets in, 1054
Rikki Don't Lose That Number, 328, *943*
Rill Thing, The, 589
Ring a Ding Ding, 904
Ring of Fire, 165, *166*, *192*, *1085*
Ring out Solstice Bells, 499
Ring Ring, 1
Ring Ring Ring (Ha Ha Hey), 251
Ring them Bells, 585
Ring-a-Ding-Doo, *59*, *772*
Ringing of Revolution, The, *733*
Ringo, *838*, *939*
Ringside at Condon's, 210
Rio, 289
Rio Grande Mud, 1094
Rio Medina, 867
Riot in Cell Block No. 9, *82*, *196*, *483*, *574*
Riot on Sunset Strip, 349
R.I.P., 973
Rip and Tear, 887
Rip Her to Shreds, 96
Rip It to Shreds, 24
Rip It Up, 90, *207*, *589*
Rip Rig and Panic, 545
Ripple, 400
Riptide, 751
Rise, 17
Rise and Fall, 630
Rise and Fall of Flingel Bunt, The, 885
Rise and Fall of Ziggy Stardust and the Spiders from Mars, The, 110
Rise and Shine, 35, *944*

Rise Up Like the Sun, 13, *619*
Rising, 278
Rising for the Moon, 324
Rising Free, 841
Rising of the Moon, The, 185
Rising Sons, The, 966
Risingson, 650
Risk, 659
Risky, 868
Rite of Passage, 865
Rite of Strings, 190
Rite Time, 153
Ritmo en el Corazon, 235
Rival, 762
River, The, *314*, *357*, *934*
River Deep, Mountain High, *404*, *724*, *929*, *963*, *998*
River of Dreams, 502
River of Souls, 343
River of Time, 520
River Road and Other Stories, 465
River Stay Away from My Door, 568
River's Invitation, *655*, *754*
Riverboat Shuffle, 158
Riverboat Song, The, 732
Rivers of Babylon, *104*, *549*
Riverside Blues, 27
R. M. Blues, *676*, *860*
R.O.C.K. in the USA, 660
Ro Ro Rosey, 694
Road, The, *544*, *737*
Road Block, 908
Road Goes on Forever, The, *166*, *702*
Road Hog, 599
Road I'm on, The, 266
Road Rage, 168
Road Songs, 40
Road Tested, 814
Road to Cairo, 37
Road to Ensenada, 602
Road to Hell, The, 819
Road to Loch Lomond, The, 319
Road to Nowhere, The, 967
Road to Ruin, 815
Roadblock, 951
Roadhouse Blues, 941
Roadrunner, *147*, *832*
Roamin' in the Gloamin', 566
Roanoke, 686
Roar of '74, The, 830
Roaring Days, 841
Roaring Silence, 635
Robbie Robertson, 53
Robert de Niro's Waiting, 52
Robert Fripp and the League of Crafty Guitarists, 360
Robert Gordon with Link Wray, 1077
Robert Johnson Songbook, The, 341

Roberta, 422
Roberta Flack Featuring Donny Hathaway, 430
Robin Hood, 485
Robot, 987
Robot Man, 353
Robots, The, 554
Rochdale Cowboy, 346
Rock a Little, 342
Rock All Night, 895
Rock and Roll, 109, *1018*
Rock and Roll Hoochie Coo, 615
Rock and Roll Is Here to Stay, 243
Rock and Roll Love Letter, 62
Rock and Roll Lullaby, 980
Rock and Roll Music, 63, 81
Rock and Roll Rebels, 944
Rock and Roll Rhapsody, 347
Rock and Roll Shoes, 980
Rock and Roll Waltz, *939*, *1072*
Rock Around the Clock, 365, *411*, *412*, *722*
Rock Around the Country, 413
Rock Bottom, 1006, *1079*
Rock Festival, 1090
Rock Hard, 64, *807*
Rock in a Hard Place, 9
Rock in the Weary Land, A, 1036
Rock Is Dead, 638
Rock Island, 499
Rock Island Line, 54, *217*, *243*, *276*, *277*, *356*, *552*, *568*, *589*
Rock It to Mars, 1020
Rock Little Baby, 371
Rock Lobster, 43
Rock Lomond, 413
Rock Love, 673
Rock Me, *944*, *978*
Rock Me All Night Long, 817
Rock Me Baby, *167*, *187*, *539*
Rock Me Mama, *233*, *671*
Rock Me Tonight, 479
Rock My Soul, 388
Rock'n'Me, 673
Rock'n'Roll, *576*, *699*, *718*, *930*, *1062*
Rock'n'Roll Ain't Noise Pollution, 4
Rock'n'Roll All Nite, 546
Rock'n'Roll Animal, 824
Rock'n'Roll Baby, 154
Rock'n'Roll Fantasy, *46*, *544*
Rock'n'Roll from Planet Earth, 617
Rock'n'Roll Gumbo, 802
Rock'n'Roll Heart, 824
Rock'n'Roll Heaven, 835
Rock'n'Roll (I Gave You the Best Years of My Life), 247
Rock'n'Roll Is Dead, 554
Rock'n'Roll Lady, 896
Rock'n'Roll Lullabye, 638

Rock'n'Roll Moon, 964
Rock'n'Roll Music, 82
Rock'n'Roll Parts 1 and 2, 386
Rock'n'Roll Resurrection, 432
Rock'n'Roll with the Modern
    Lovers, 832
Rock'n'Roll Woman, 136
Rock'n'Roll Years, The, 832
Rock'n'Soul, 482
Rock of Ages, 53, 254, 990
Rock of Life, 934
Rock of the Westies, 503
Rock on, 314, 889
Rock Solid, 208
Rock Steady, 44
Rock Steady with Flo & Eddie, 999
Rock the Boat, 459, 460
Rock the Casbah, 191
Rock the House, 917
Rock the House Live, 437
Rock the Joint, 412
Rock 'Till You Drop,.807
Rock with I, 1009
Rock with the Cavemen, 57, 877,
    941
Rock with You, 481
Rock You Like a Hurricane, 875
Rock Your Baby, 526
Rocka Rolla, 519
Rockabilly Blues, 166
Rockabilly Kings, 331
Rockabilly's Main Man, 331
Rock-a-Bye Your Baby With a
    Dixie Melody, 355, 510
Rockafella Skank, 330
Rockaway Beach (On the Beach),
    815
Rockbird, 96
Rocket Boy, 771
Rocket Cottage, 942
Rocket '88', 179, 412, 772, 997
Rocket Man, 143, 503, 816
Rocket to Russia, 814
Rockin' & Driftin', 285
Rockin' 50s Rock'n'Roll, 228
Rockin' All Over the World, 226,
    940, 941
Rockin' Alone (In an Old
    Rockin' Chair), 669, 670
Rockin' and Rollin' with Gran-
    maw, 842
Rockin' and Romance, 833
Rockin' Around the Christmas
    Tree, 571, 642
Rockin' at Midnight, 569
Rockin' at the Fillmore, 352
Rockin' at the Star Club, 66
Rockin' Blues, 748
Rockin' Chair, 48, 158, 512, 763,
    972
Rockin' Good Way, A, 78, 947,
    1002, 1034

Rockin' Goose, 505
Rockin' in Rhythm, 307
Rockin' Mary, 170
Rockin' My Life Away, 582
Rockin' Pneumonia and the
    Boogie Woogie Flu, 915
Rockin' Robin, 481
Rockin' Roll Baby, 958
Rockin' Soul, 460
Rockin' the Country, 512
Rockin' the Forest, 265
Rockin' the Oldies, 412
Rockin' Through the Rye, 412
Rockin' with Red, 774
Rockin' with the Clock, 895
Rockin' with the Rhythm, 520
Rocking Anna, 948
Rocking at the Roundhouse, 1042
Rocking Chair, 73, 158
Rocking Down the Highway, 279
Rocking in Rhythm, 306
Rocking Pneumonia and the
    Boogie Woogie Flu, 836
Rocking with Curly Leads, 885
Rockit, 82, 420, 565, 976
Rockney, 175
Rockoon, 968
Rockpile, 302
Rock-Rockola, 691
Rocks, 9
Rocky, 328
Rocky Mountain Way, 295
Rocky Road to Dublin, The, 181
Rocky Top, 133, 745
Rodgers and Hart Songbook, 428
Roger McGuinn, 147
Roger Young, 596
Rogue, The, 986
Rolaids, Doan's Pills and Prepa-
    ration H, 287
Roland the Headless Thompson
    Gunner, 1092
Roll 'Em, 487
Roll 'Em Pete, 508
Roll Along Prairie Moon, 1023
Roll and Rhumba, 823
Roll Away the Stone, 700
Roll It Over, 731
Roll on down the Highway, 406
Roll on Ruby, 586
Roll Over Beethoven, 81, 304, 416,
    941
Roll Over Vaughan Williams, 982
Roll the Bones, 861
Roll with It, 731, 1073
Roll with Me Henry, 51, 82, 460,
    486
Roll with the Punches, 720
Rollercoaster, 83
Rollin' and Tumblin', 154, 1037
Rollin' Home, 302, 941
Rollin' Rollin', 866

Rollin' Stone, 179, 807, 1037
Rollin' Thunder, 75
Rolling Stones, The, 848
Rolling Stones No. 2, 849
Rolling Thunder, 616
Roly Poly, 855
Roman Candle, 915
Romance, 18, 1070
Romance in the Night, 332
Romances for Saxophone, 645
Romantic?, 461
Romantic Warrior, 190
Romantically Yours, 375
Rome Remains Rome, 153
Romeo, 188, 528
Romeo and Juliet, 267
Rompin' Stompin' Blues, 520
Ron Goodwin Conducts the New
    Zealand Symphony Orchestra,
    392
Ronan, 114
Ronnie Hawkins, 432
Ronnie Milsap, 675
Ronnie Talks to Russia, 797
Room at the Top, 25
Room Full of Roses, 29, 384, 525,
    922
Room to Roam, 1035
Room With a View, 222, 653
Roomin' House Boogie, 669
Rooster, 14
Roots, 319, 320, 883
Roots Bloody Roots, 883
Roots of Lightnin' Hopkins, The,
    454
Roots of the Grateful Dead, 401
Roots of Vouty, 366
Roots to Branches, 499
Rope a Dope Style, 737
Ropin' the Wind, 123
Rosalie, 525
Rosalie – Cowgirl's Song, 979
Rosalyn, 792
Rosanna, 989
Rose and a Babe Ruth, A, 417, 599
Rose Garden, 22, 562, 925
Rose Is Still a Rose, A, 355
Rose Maddox Sings Bluegrass, 629
Rose Marie, 359, 422, 1052
Rose O'Day, 916
Rose of Arizona, 428
Rose of England, 603, 726
Rose of No Man's Land, The, 545
Rose of the Rio Grande, 1032
Rose, Rose I Love You, 457, 560
Roses and Rainbows, 983
Roses Are Red, 25, 523, 1022
Roses in September, 711
Roses in the Snow, 425, 907
Roses of Picardy, 250
Rosetta, 327, 446, 793
Rosie, 324

Rotterdam, 68
Rough, 998
Rough and Ready, 70
Rough Boy, 1094
Rough Dancer and the Cyclical Night, The, 775
Rough Mix, 913, 1054
Rough-House 88, 691
Roulette, 37
Round About Midnight, 93, 274, 683
Round and A Bout, A, 936
Round and Round, 926
Round Midnight, 123, 318
Round the Outside! Round the Outside!, 624
Roundabout, 288, 1084
Route 101, 17
Route 66, 437, 598
Roving Kind, The, 496, 672, 678
Row! Row! Row!, 511
Roxanne, 667, 782
Roxy Music, 857
Roy Orbison and Friends: a Black and White Night, 741
Roy Smeck and His Magic Uke, 914
Royal Ancestry, 307
Royal Garden Blues, 73, 742, 1058
Royal Jam, 234
Royal Rappin's, 434, 482
Royal Scam, The, 943
Royal T, 804
Royal Vol. 1, 118
Rrrracket Time, 432
Rubber Ball, 778, 1017, 1056
Rubber Bullets, 975
Rubber Lover, 253
Rubber Soul, 66, 67
Rubberband Man, The, 931
Ruby, 745
Ruby Ann, 837
Ruby Baby, 266
Ruby, Don't Take Your Love to Town, 846
Ruby Tuesday, 163, 659, 709
Rubycon, 968
Rudies Don't Fear, 692
Rudolph the Red-Nosed Reindeer, 38, 211, 230, 515, 642, 883
Rudy Got Married, 12
Rudy the Fifth, 711
Ruffin and Kendricks, 975
Rufus Featuring Chaka Khan, 532
Rufus Is a Tit Man, 1024
Rufusized, 532
Rule the Nation, 1009
Ruler of My Heart, 820, 990
Rum and Coca-Cola, 23
Rum and Limonada, 23
Rum Sodomy and the Lash, 185, 780

Rumble, 1077
Rumble in the Jungle, 221
Rumour, The, 53, 721
Rumour and Sigh, 982
Rumour Has It, 618
Rumours, 342
Rump Shaker, 835
Rum-Tiddle-Tiddle, 510
Run Aground, 485
Run Around, 99
Run Away Child, Running Wild, 975
Run Devil Run, 611, 612
Run for Home, 586
Run for Your Life, 136
Run Like a Thief, 814
Run, Rabbit, Run, 340, 373
Run Run Look and See, 464
Run Run Run, 459, 932
Run Runaway, 910
Run Through the Jungle, 226
Run to Him, 1016, 1017
Run to You, 7
Run with the Pack, 46
Runaround Sue, 265
Runaway, 102, 217, 495, 651, 814, 889
Runaway, The, 368
Runaway Bunion, 220
Runaway Horses, 157
Runaway Run, 421
Runaway Train, 167, 240, 503, 922
Runaways, The, 351
Running Away, 40, 656, 954
Running Bear, 489, 512, 791
Running Free, 474
Running from the Devil, 737
Running in the Family, 579
Running on Empty, 132
Running Out of Fools, 355
Running Scared, 741
Running up That Hill (A Deal with God), 143
Runt, 859
Rush Rush, 3
Russian Roulette, 450
Russians, The, 950
Russians and Americans, 947
Rust in Piece, 659
Rust Never Sleeps, 1088
Rusty Dusty Blues, 862
Rusty Old Halo, 40
Ruth Is Stranger Than Richard, 1079
Ry Cooder, 212
Rye Whiskey, 836

S&M, 665
'S Wonderful, 210, 379, 753
S-90 Skank, 84
Sabbath Bloody Sabbath, 88
Sabotage, 150

Sabre Dance, 301
Sabu Visits the Twin Cities Alone, 799
Sack o'Woe, 8
Sacre Francais, 265
Sacrebleu, 265
Sacred Fire, 871
Sacred Islands, 966
Sacred Songs, 360, 413
Sacrifice, 503, 728
Sad and Lonely and Blue, 298
Sad Movies (Make Me Cry), 382, 599
Sad Songs (Say So Much), 503
Sad Street, 94
Sad Sweet Dreamer, 430
Sad Waters Far from Me, 169
Sad Wings of Destiny, 519
Sad-Eyed Lady of the Lowlands, 292
Sadie Salome, Go Home, 78
Safari, 779
Safe as Milk, 212
Safe at Home, 436, 756
Safe from Harm, 650
Sag Mir Wo die Blumen Sind, 264
Saga of The Beatles, The, 505
Saginaw, Michigan, 360
Sahara, 532, 1002
Said and Done, 114
Said I Loved You . . . But I Lied, 102
Sail Along Silv'ry Moon, 1016
Sail Away, 719
Sail Away Ladies, 629
Sail on, 208
Sail on Sailor, 63
Sailboat in the Midnight, A, 447
Sailboat in the Moonlight, A, 1087
Sailin', 159
Sailin' Shoes, 587
Sailing, 231, 950
Sailing on the Seven Seas, 742
Sailing to Philadelphia, 267
Sailor, 673, 718, 873, 892
Sailor's Life, A, 323
Sails, 36
Sails of Silver, 942
Saint Huck, 168
Saint Sebastian, 970
St Dominic's Preview, 695
St George and the Dragonet, 356
St Giles Cripplegate, 725
St James Hospital, 619
St James' Infirmary, 972
St Julian, 215
St Louis, 298
St Louis Blues, 28, 130, 151, 220, 280, 316, 322, 420, 735, 742, 914, 996

St Stephen, 400
St Swithin's Day, 164
St Thomas, 851
St Valentine's Day Massacre, 699
Saints and Sinners, *14*, 901, *1051*, *1071*
Saints Rock'n'Roll, 412
Sal's Got a Sugar Lip, 277
Salam, 990
Salisbury, 1009
Sally, 334
Sally Can't Dance, 824
Sally Cinnamon, 952
Sally Free and Easy, 765
Sally Go Round the Roses, 888
Sally Was a Good Old Girl, 598
Sallyangie, 737
Salt of the Earth, 849
Salt Peanuts, 383, 753
Salt with a Deadly Pepa, A, 869
Salty Dog, 463, *800*
Salty Papa Blues, 1034
Salute, 585
Sam, 721
Sam and the Lady, 847
Sam Stone, 799
Sam's Song, 231
Sama Layuca, 1002
Sambo (Toda Menina Baiana), 327
Same Old Lang Syne, 343
Same Old Song, The, 541
Same Old Train, 993, 995
Same Sweet Girl, The, 595
Same Train, Different Time, 411, 845
Sampadelic Relics and Dancefloor Oddities, 253
Sample in a Jar, 773
Sample Some of Dis, Sample Some of Dat, 195
Samson and Delilah, 1069
San Antonio Rose, 224, 231, *713*, 991
San Antonio Saturday Night, 867
San Antonio Sound, 500
San Fernando Valley, 496
San Francisco, *19*, 1021
San Francisco (Be Sure to Wear Flowers in Your Hair), 9, 633, 912
San Francisco Bay, 308
San Francisco Bay Blues, 362
San Francisco Days, 475
San Francisco '83, 537
San Francisco Nights, 24
Sanborn, 870
Sanctuary, 266, *376*, 474
Sanders' Truckstop, 361
Sandinista!, 191, 398
Sandstorm, 564
Sandy Gully, 908

Sang Pour Sang, 417
Sangoma, 633
Santa Ana Winds, 392
Santa and the Sidewalk Surfer, 999
Santa Baby, 547
Santa Barbara Honeymoon, 765
Santa Fe, 75
Santana, 871
Santana Brothers, The, 871
Santana III, 871
Santiago, 182
Sap, 14
Sara, 342
Sara Smile, 413
Sarawakee, 857
Sassy Mama, 983
Satan Rejected My Soul, 696
Satchmo: A Musical Autobiography, 29
Satellite, 246
Satin Sheets, 75
Satin Soul, 1048
Satisfaction, 260, 283, 821
Satisfaction Feeling, 127
Satisfaction Guaranteed, 764, *831*
Satisfied Mind, 147, 438, 756, 757
Satisfied'n'Tickled Too, 966
Satisfy My Soul, 936
Saturday Afternoon, 494
Saturday Gigs, 700
Saturday in the Park, 181
Saturday Night, 62, 122, 621, 846, 960
Saturday Night and Sunday Morning, 937
Saturday Night at the Bull and Mouth, 614
Saturday Night at the Montmartre, 1041
Saturday Night at the Movies, 285
Saturday Night Fever, 71, 550
Saturday Night Fish Fry, 48, 518, 539
Saturday Night Is the Loneliest Night of the Week, 150, 370
Saturday Night Special, 4, 608, *807*
Saturday Night, Sunday Morning, 458, *956*
Saturday Nite, 298
Saturday Sunshine, 45
Saturdays, 251
Saturnz Return, 106, 389
Saucerful of Secrets, A, 777
Savage, 317
Savage, The, 885
Savage Amusement, 875
Savage Eye, 792
Save a Prayer, 289
Save for a Rainy Day, 490

Save His Soul, 99
Save It! Save It!, 648
Save Me, 245, 342, 421, 563, 808
Save Our Planet Earth, 193
Save the Children, 472, 1076
Save the Land, 396
Save the Last Dance for Me, 285, 493, 539, *539*, 783
Save the Life of My Child, 897
Save the Overtime (for Me), 549
Save Up All Your Tears, 1032
Save Your Heart for Me, 373
Save Your Kisses, 846
Save Your Love for Me, 863
Save Your Love (for No. 1), 1070
Save Your Nights for Me, 274
Saved, 50, 293, 574, *1047*
Saved by the Bell, 71
Saving All My Love for You, 458, 1026
Saviour Pass Me Not, 963
Saviour's Day, 831
Savoy Blues, 507
S.A.X., 1084
Saxophone Colossus, 851
Saxophone Improvisations Series F, 118
Say Goodbye to Hollywood, 502, 853
Say Has Anybody Seen My Sweet Gypsy Rose, 743
Say I Won't Be There, 933
Say I'm Your No. 1, 745
Say It, 87
Say It in Private, 392
Say It Isn't So, 470
Say It Loud (I'm Black and I'm Proud), 51, 127, 128
Say It With Music, 330
Say Man, 263
Say No Go, 251
Say Say Say, 481, 611
Say Something, 647
Say Something Sweet to Your Sweetheart, 626, 936
Say What, 1071
Say What You Want, 978
Say What You Will, 922
Say When, 122
Say You Don't Mind, 1093
Say You Love Me, 342
Say You, Say Me, 832
Say You'll Be There, 931
Say You'll Stay Until Tomorrow, 516, 823
Says My Heart, 48
Scandalous, 798
Scar Tissue, 820
Scarborough Fair, 164, 292, 897
Scarecrow, 660
Scarlet Ribbons, 132
Scarlett O'Hara, 885

Scars, 899
Scary Monsters, 111, 360
Scat Song, The, 152
Scattered Lights, 908
Scene Changes, The, 786
Scenes from the South Side, 456
Scheherazade, 218
Schizophonic, 931
Schizophrenia, 60, 883
Schizophrenic, 321
School Day, 81, 196
School Days, 190, 903
School for Sweet Talk, 403
School Is Out, 104
School's Out, 64, 214
Schoolboy Crush, 752, 830
Schoolboys in Disgrace, 544
Schoolday Blues, 1071
Schpritz, 122
Science Fiction, 202
Science Friction, 1081
Science of Things, The, 142
Scissors Cut, 898
Scoobie Snacks, 363
Scoop, 1054
Scorching Beauty, 473
Score, The, 361
Scorn Not His Simplicity, 734
Scottish Soldier, A, 566
Scoundrel Days, 11
Scream, 482
Scream, The, 905
Scream, Dracula, Scream, 842
Scream in Blue: Live, 668
Screamadelica, 796, 797
Screamin' and Cryin', 862
Screamin' and Hollerin' the
    Blues, 758
Screamin' the Blues, 433
Screaming Fields of Sonic Love,
    921
Screaming for Vengeance, 519
Screaming Life, 924
Screaming Target, 189
Screen Gems, 123
Script for a Jester's Tears, 642
Sea Airs, 1025
Sea Cruise, 226, 344, 625, 915
Sea of Heartbreak, 382
Sea of Love, 569, 889, 1056
Sea of Tranquillity, 220
Sea Shells, 572
Seal, 455
Sealed with a Kiss, 278, 464, 951,
    1023
Search and Destroy, 468
Search and Nearness, 816
Search for the Hero, 610
Searchers, The, 879
Searchin', 196, 449, 508, 574, 951,
    1013
Searching for Simplicity, 16

Searching for the Young Soul
    Rebels, 261
Season of Glass, 740
Season of Light, 729
Season of the Witch, 278, 1014
Season's End, 642
Seasons in the Sun, 120, 623
Seasons of Glass, 930
Sebadoh, The, 265
Secada, 879
Second Coming, 589, 952
Second Fiddle, 748
Second Generation Bluegrass, 907
Second Hand Love, 929
Second Hand Rose, 956
Second Helping, 608
Second Opinion, 885
2nd Set, 16
Second Spring, 652
Second Thoughts, 232
Second Time, The, 256
Second Time Around, 150, 515,
    886
Second Toughest in the Infants,
    1008
Second Wind, 17, 37, 613, 860
Second Winter, 1071
Second-Hand Rose, 120
Secondhand Daylight, 145
Seconds, 1004
Seconds of Pleasure, 302
Seconds Out, 377
Secret, 742
Secret Agent, 876
Secret Agent Man, 260, 836
Secret Dreams and Forbidden
    Fire, 1002
Secret Gardens, 204
Secret History, A, 268
Secret Language of Birds, The, 499
Secret Life of Harpers Bizarre, 424
Secret Life of J. Eddy Fink, The, 465
Secret Life of the Love Song, The,
    169
Secret Love, 221, 250, 323, 332,
    667, 1052
Secret Messages, 304
Secret of Association, The, 1089
Secret Omen, 152
Secret Passion – The Arias, 102
Secret Rendezvous, 457
Secret Secrets, 27
Secret Storm, 653
Secret Story, 666
Secret Treaties, 98
Secret World Live, 366
Secretary, 1078
Secretly, 460
Secrets, 118, 234, 751
Secrets of the Beehive, 965
Secrets of the Sea, 117, 408
Section 43, 616

Security, 366, 487
Seduction, The, 565
See, 816
See Emily Play, 776
See How It Runs, 164
See Me, 913
See Me Feel Me, 882
See My Baby Jive, 703
See My Friends, 543
See Reverse Side for Title, 704
See Saw, 107, 355, 363
See See Rider, 50, 580
See See Rider Blues, 813
See That My Grave Is Kept
    Clean, 291, 495, 1012
See the Big Man Cry, Mama, 600
See the Funny Little Clown, 389
See What the Boys in the Back-
    room Will Have, 595
See You, 258
See You at the 'Go Go', 401
See You Later Alligator, 173, 365,
    412
See You on the Other Side, 663
See You When I Git There, 818
See-Saw, 217, 221
Seeds, 368
Seeds and Stems, 207
Seeds of Love, The, 972
Seek and You Shall Find, 375
Seemed Like a Good Idea at the
    Time, 947
Seer, The, 83
Sefronia, 136
Selassie Serenade, 988
Select, 1055
Selected Classical Works for Gui-
    tar and Flute, 16
Self Control, 117, 117
Self Esteem, 736
Self Portrait, 122, 293, 530, 898
Self-Made Man, A, 148
Selling England by the Pound, 377
Selling Jesus, 909
Selling That Stuff, 281
Selmasongs, 86
Semi Detached Suburban Mr
    James, 635
Semper Fidelis, 924
Send a Message, 476
Send in the Clowns, 204, 626,
    904, 919
Send It, 32
Send It to Me, 549
Send Me the Pillow, 1085
Send Me the Pillow You Dream
    on, 595, 646, 985
Señor (Tales of Yankee Power),
    293
Sense, 585
Sense of Danger, 650
Sense of Place, A, 654

Sense of Wonder, A, 695
Senses Working Overtime, 1081
Sensual World, The, 143
Sent for You Yesterday (And Here You Come Today), 862
Sentimental Hygiene, 1092
Sentimental Journey, 129, 250, 647, 713, 939
Senz' Una Donna, 1094
Separate Lives, 205, 642
Separate Ways (Worlds Apart), 519
Separations, 805
Sepia Bounce, 753
September, 298
September in the Rain, 597, 713, 891, 1032, 1034
September of My Years, The, 150, 496, 904
September Song, 289, 584, 817, 904, 1015, 1042, 1043, 1067
September Song; The Music of Kurt Weill, 169
Sequel, 172
Serenade, 262, 852
Serenade in Blue, 392
Serenade to a Cuckoo, 498
Serenity, 381
Sergeant Preston of the Yukon, 946
Serious, 737
Serious Business, 1071
Serious Hits – Live, 205
Serious Hold on Me, 737
Serious Slammin', 781
Served Live, 33
Serves You Right to Suffer, 376
Serving 190 Proof, 411
Sessions, 163, 710
Set, 710
Set Adrift on Memory Bliss, 926
Set Me Free, 438
Set the Controls for the Heart of the Sun, 777
Set the Night to Music, 339, 1032
Set the Record Straight, 825
Set the Twilight Reeling, 824
Set You Free This Time, 146
Setting Son, 731
Setting Sons, 484
Setting Sun, 175
Seven, 485, 882
7 and 7 Is, 600
Seven and the Ragged Tiger, 289
Seven Bridges Road, 47, 652
Seven Come Eleven, 184
Seven Day Weekend, 717, 783
Seven Days, 227, 892
Seven Deadly Sins, The, 577
Seven Degrees North, 8
Seven Drunken Nights, 220
Seven Gypsies, 395

Seven Hundred Elves, 942
Seven Letters, 539
Seven Little Girls, 1022
Seven Little Girls Sitting in the Back Seat, 464, 523, 752
Seven Seals, 109
Seven Seas, 299
Seven Seas of Rhye, 807
Seven Seconds, 178
Seven Seconds Away, 710
7 Songs for Quartet and Chamber Orchestra, 141
Seven Souls, 565
Seven Spanish Angels and Other Hits, 174
Seven Standards, 118
Seven Steps to Heaven, 1065
7000 Dollars and You, 958
7800 Degrees Fahrenheit, 102
Seven Turns, 16
Seven Year Ache, 166
7 Year Bitch, 910
Seven Year Itch, 487
Seven Years with the Wrong Woman, 670
7-Tease, 278
Sevens, 123
Seventeen, 107, 344, 1015
17–11–70, 503
Seventeen Seconds, 238
Seventh Heaven, Peanut Butter and Padlock, 579
Seventh One, The, 989
Seventh Sojourn, 689
Seventh Son, 15, 836
Seventh Son of a Seventh Son, 474
Seventh Star, 88
Seventh Wave, 660
78 in the Shade, 913
77, 454
Sex and Drugs and Rock and Roll, 290
Sex and Violence, 106
Sex as a Weapon, 76
Sex, Cars & God, 351
Sex Drive, 513
Sex Me, 528
Sex of It, The, 533
Sex on the Streets, 330
Sex Over the Phone, 1021
Sex Type Thing, 953
Sex with Your Parents Part II (Motherfucker), 824
Sexcrime (Nineteen Eightyfour), 317
Sextant, 420
Sextet, 95
Sexual Healing, 375, 759
Sexual Therapy, 759
Sexuality, 117
Sexy Boy, 11
Sexy Eyes, 271

Sexy Fancy, 808
Sexy MF, 798
S. F. Sorrow, 792
Sgt Pepper's Lonely Hearts Club Band, 67, 298, 600, 1091
Sha La La, 635
Sha La La La Lee, 783, 912
Sha La La Means I Love You, 1048
Shabooh Shoobah, 473
Shackles and Chains, 1073
Shaday, 435
Shades, 150
Shades of a Blue Orphanage, 979
Shades of Bix, 73
Shades of Deep Purple, Book of Talieysyn, 253
Shades of Two Worlds, 16
Shadow Dancing, 71
Shadow Dream Song, 862
Shadow Knows, The, 328
Shadow Waltz, 230
Shadowlands, 562, 571, 1045
Shadows, 338, 585, 676
Shadows and Light, 634, 679
Shadows in the Night, 886
Shadows of the Night, 76
Shadrack, 388
Shady Grove, 810
Shady Lane, 760
Shady Lies, 652
Shake, 821, 949
Shake a Hand, 50, 344
Shake a Leg, 549, 692
Shake a Tail Feather, 227
Shake and Fingerpop, 1028
Shake Hands and Walk Away Crying, 185
Shake It, 652
Shake Me Up, 588
Shake Rattle and Roll, 412, 953, 998, 1047
(Shake, Shake, Shake) Shake Your Booty, 526
Shake Sherry, 211
Shake the Disease, 258
Shake Your Body, 478
Shake Your Head from Side to Side, 149
Shake Your Love, 381
Shake Your Money Maker, 87
Shake Your Thang, 869
Shakedown, 882
Shakedown Street, 401
Shaken and Stirred, 569
Shaken, Not Stirred, 2, 29, 469
Shaker Song, 935
Shakermaker, 730
Shakespeare and All That Jazz, 242, 559
Shakey Ground, 975
Shakin' All Over, 406, 534, 1054

Shakin' the Blues Away, 315
Shaking the Tree, *366*, 710
Sha-La-La, 894
Shambala, 984
Shame, 762
Shame and Sin, 224
Shame on Me, 55, 740
Shame on the Moon, 882
Shame on You, 214, 1044
Shame Shame Shame, 333, 583, 823, 895
Shameless, 123
Shamen Collection, The, 888
Shamrock Diaries, 819
Shang-a-Lang, 62
Shango, 871
Shangri-La, 543
Shape of Jazz to Come, The, 202
Shapes Motions Colors, 847
Shapes of Things, 1083
Share My Life, 472
Share My World, 95, 484
Share the Fall, 906
Share the Land, 406
Share What You've Got, 74
Share Your Love with Me, 53, 94
Sharing the Night Together, 271
Sharing You, 1017
Shark in Jet's Clothing, A, 96
Sharp, 1070
Sharp Dressed Man, 1094
Shaun Cassidy, 167
Shave 'Em Dry, 813
Shaved Fish, 576
Shazam, 703
Sh-Boom, 227, 356, 363
She, 25, 41, *210*, 218, 219, 426, 489, 757
She Ain't Worth It, 125
She and I, 12
She Bangs the Drums, 952
She Believes in Me, 847
She Belongs to Me, 711
She Blinded Me with Science, 273
She Bop, 566
She Came from Fort Worth, 652
She Cried, 493
She Cries Your Name, 744
She Did It, 817
She Didn't Say 'Yes', 422, 530
She Don't Know Me, 102
She Don't Understand Him, 259
She Don't Use Jelly, 339
She Drives Me Crazy, 335
She Even Woke Me Up to Say Goodbye, 582, 718
She Is His Only Need, 520
She Is Still a Mystery, 602
She Kissed Me, 243
She Loves You, 66, 647
She Makes My Day, 751

She Means Nothing to Me, 320, 831
She Meant Forever When She Said Goodbye, 980
She Moved Through the Fair, 323, 395, 901
She Needs Someone to Hold Her, 1000
She Never Spoke Spanish to Me, 309
(She Put the) Wamee (on Me), 433
She Rides Wild Horses, 847
She Sang Hymns out of Tune, 722
She Say Oom Dooby Doom, 638
She She Little Sheila, 1022
She Shot Me Down, 218, 904
She Sold Magic, 185
She Sure Can Rock Me, 774
She Talks to Angels, 87
She Thinks I Still Care, 226, 511, 512, 864
She Took You for a Ride, 714
She Wants to Dance with Me, 951
She Wants to Rock, 82
She Was Bred in Old Kentucky, 706
She Was Only Seventeen (He Was One Year More), 837
She Went to the City, 284
She Works Hard for the Money, 960
She Would Have Been Faithful, 181
She'd Rather Be with Me, 999
She's a Fool, 394
She's a Good 'Un, 862
She's a Heartbreaker, 352, 778
She's a Hum Dum Dinger, 247
She's a Lady, 24, 516, 602
She's a Lassie from Lancashire, 345
She's a Latin from Manhattan, 1089
She's a Mystery to Me, 741
She's a Star, 485
She's a Superstar, 1020
She's a Woman, 815, 878
She's About a Mover, 658, 866
She's Already Made Up Her Mind, 602
She's as Beautiful as a Foot, 98
She's Coming Home, 1093
She's Gone, 413, 691
She's Got Claws, 727
She's Got that Vibe, 528
She's Got the Goldmine (I Got the Shaft), 822
She's Got the Rhythm, 479
She's Got You, 193
She's in Fashion, 960

She's in Love with Mystery, 981
She's in Love with You, 807
She's Just My Style, 373, 863
She's Leaving Home, 117
She's Lookin' Good, 775
She's Making Whoopee in Hell Tonight, 507
She's My Baby, 720
She's My Woman, 993
She's Not There, 871, 1093
She's Not You, 783
She's on It, 64
She's Out of My Life, 481
She's So Fine, 298
She's So High, 99
She's So Unusual, 566
She's Strange, 152
She's the Boss, 565, 849
She's the One, 771
Shearing Sound, The, 891
Sheela-Na-Gig, 429
Sheena Is a Punk Rocker, 814
Sheep, 68
Sheep Farming in Barnet, 991
Sheer Heart Attack, 807
Sheer Magic, 86
Sheet Music, 976
Sheik of Araby, The, 20, 116, 555, 972
Sheik Yerbouti, 1092
Sheila, 451, 846
Shell Shock, 1000
Shelly Manne and His Men Vol. 2, 847
Shelter, 622
Shelter of Your Arms, The, 249
Sheltered Life, 163
Shepherd Moons, 312
Shepherd of the Hills, 464, 1078
Sheriff Fatman, 163
Sherry, 3, 227, 349, 951
Shifting Whispering Sands, The, 1016
Shimmy Shimmy, 744
Shimmy, Shimmy, Ko-Ko-Bop, 358, 587
Shine, 35, *39*, *40*, 129, 155, 212, 231, 316, 559, 826
Shine on, 352
Shine on Brightly, 800
Shine on Harvest Moon, 62, 141, 315, 587, 924
Shinin' on, 396
Shining Star, 297
Ship Ahoy, 736
Shipbuilding, 219, 1079
Ships in the Night, 710
Shipyard Town, 812
Shirley Lee, 142
Sh-La-La (Make Me Happy), 402
Sho You Right, 1048
Shoals of Herring, 591, 614

Shock of the Hour, 728
Shock the Monkey, 366
Shoe Shine Drag, 697
Shoe Shine Swing, 1087
Shoiki Remixed, 557
Shoo-doo-Bedoo, 363
Shoo-Fly Pie and Apple Pan
    Dowdy, 529
Shoop Shoop Song, The, 177, 319
Shoorah Shoorah, 990, 1078
Shoot Out the Lights, 113, 982
Shoot You Full of Love, 427
Shooting Star, 114
Shooting Straight in the Dark, 159
Shop Around, 156, 394, 840
Shoplifters of the World Unite,
    918
Shoppin' for Clothes, 196
Short Album about Love, A, 268
Short Back and Sides, 700
Short Break, A, 1079
Short Cut Draw Blood, 1073
Short Eyes, 655
Short Fat Fannie, 176, 589, 860,
    1061
Short Haired Woman, 454
Short Life of Trouble, 99
Short People, 720
Short Shorts, 349, 551
Short Stories, 171, 703, 1014, 1085
Shorty George Blues, 1029
Shot of Love, 293
Shot of Rhythm and Blues, 13,
    379, 534
Shot of Rhythm and Soul, A, 13
Shot Through the Heart, 1031
Shotgun, 1028
Shotgun Boogie, 344
Shotgun Willie, 713
Should I Stay, Or Should I Go,
    191
Shoulder Pads, 327
Shouldn't I Know, 313
Shouldn't It Be Easier Than This,
    795
Shout, 80, 260, 460, 476, 604, 816,
    972
Shout and Shimmy, 127
Shout at the Devil, 698
Shout Bamalama, 820
Shout for Joy, 20
Shout Parts 1 and 2, 475
Shout, Shout! (Knock Yourself
    Out), 265
Shout, Sister, Shout, 978
Shouting and Pointing, 700
Shouting Stage, The, 27
Shouts across the Street, 793
Shove It, 808
Show, The, 869
Show a Little Love, 304
Show Her, 675

Show Me, 261
Show Me Heaven, 600
Show Me the Way, 352, 959
Show Must Go on, The, 872, 984
Show of Hands, 360, 861
Show Some Emotion, 27
Show Stoppa, 869
Show Time, 500
Show You the Way to Go, 478
Show Your Hand, 39
Showbiz Blues, 122
Showbusiness, 994
Showdown, 203, 216, 304, 368
Showroom Dummies, 554
Shows, The, 222
Showstoppers, 637
Showtime, 212, 224
Shrimp Boats, 936, 937
Shrine of St Cecilia, The, 424
Shropshire Lad, A, 287
Shuffle Off, 13
Shuffle Off to Buffalo, 527, 1032
Shumba, 640
Shut 'Em Down, 803, 877
*Shut Up and Dance (The Dance
    Mixes)*, 2
Shut Up and Die Like an Aviator,
    297
Shut Up and Kiss Me, 159
Shut Up and Play Your Guitar,
    1092
Shutov Assembly, The, 311
Shy Away, 804
Shy Boy, 52
Si Si Je Suis un Rock Star, 849
Si Te Vas, 879
Si Tu Dois Partir, 323
Siamese Cat Song, The, 572
Siamese Dream, 371, 913
Siamese Friends, 652
Sick and Tired, 156
Side by Side, 230, 919, 939
Side Saddle, 37
Side Three, 817
Sideman Serenade, 122
Sidewalks, Fences and Walls, 139
Sidewalks of New York, 1041
Sidi Boumedienne, 532
Siembra, 92
Sign o' the Times, 797
Sign Your Name, 243
Si Tu Dois Partir, 323
Signals, 861
Signals Through the Glass, 948
Signed D.C., 600
Signed, Sealed and Delivered, 215
Signed, Sealed, Delivered I'm
    Yours, 1077
Signing Off, 1005
Signs of Life, 164
S'il Suffisait d'aimer, 267
Silence Is Golden, 784
Silent Assassin I, 912

Silent Corner, The, 932
Silent Lucidity, 809
Silent Night, 153, 230, 817, 1025
Silent Running, 378
Silent Spring, 423
Silhouette, 365
Silhouetted in Light, 148
Silhouettes, 227, 262, 442
Silicosis Is Killin' Me, 1049
Silk, 1013
Silk Degrees, 873, 989
Silk Electric, 855
Silk Purse, 853
Silk Torpedo, 792
Silkie, The, 204
Silky Soul, 656
Silly Games, 110
Silly Love Songs, 169, 611
Silly Putty, 190
Silly Thing, 884
Silver, 723
Silver and Gold, 474, 1088
Silver Bells, 1068
Silver Lady, 923
Silver Machine, 433
Silver Shield, The, 288
Silver Threads and Golden Nee-
    dles, 933
Silver Tongued Devil and I, The,
    555
Silverbird, 325, 872
Silvertone, 475
Simmer Down, 272, 643
Simon Smith and His Amazing
    Dancing Bear, 424, 719, 793
Simple Desultory Philippic, A,
    897
Simple Dreams, 854
Simple Pleasures, 985
Simple Simon, 473
Simple Song, 601
Simple Things, 540
Simple Twist of Fate, 47, 293
Simply Irresistible, 751
Simply Shadows, 886
Simply the Best, 999
Simply the Truth, 452
Simpsons Sing the Blues, The, 903
Sin, 347
Sin After Sin, 519
Sin City, 18, 425, 426, 756
Sin of Pride, The, 890
Sinatra and Strings, 218, 904
Sinatra Swings, 904
Sinatra–Basie, 904
Since I Don't Have You, 625
Since I Fell for You, 505
Since I Lost My Baby, 974
Since I Met You Baby, 463, 489
Since You, 958
Since You Showed Me How to Be
    Happy, 1069

Sincerely, 358, 363, 621
Sing a Little Song, 255
Sing a Little Song of Heartache, 629
Sing a Simple Song of Freedom, 423
Sing a Song, 297, 976
Sing a Song of Freedom, 831
Sing About Love, 22
Sing Along with Mitch, 672
Sing Along World, 598
Sing as We Go, 334, 335
Sing Baby Sing, 958
Sing It with Joe, 37
Sing Me a Sad Song, 410
Sing Me a Song, 633
Sing Me a Sweet Song (And Let Me Dance), 1040
Sing Me Back Home, 410, 411
Sing Out, 585
Sing, Sing, Sing, 391, 487, 555
Sing When You're Winning, 1065
Singalong Collection, The, 146
Singalong Demonstration Concert, 881
Singalongamax, 145, 146
Singalongawaryears, 146
Singapore Sorrows, 306, 437
Singer Sewing Machine, 747
Singer/Songwriter Project, 329
Singin' in the Rain, 130, 289, 302, 359
Singin' to My Baby, 197
Singin' with the Big Bands, 637
Singing the Blues, 73, 302, 562, 672, 678, 837, 941
Single Girl, 683, 785, 786
Single Life, 152
Single Man, 503, 623
Single Woman, A, 901
Singles, 14, 704, 723, 925
Singles Collection 1981–1993, The, 1055
Singles Collection, The, 199, 250, 918
Singles '81–'85, The, 259
Singles '86–'98, The, 259
Singles: 1969–1973, The, 159
Sings Country and Western, 830
Sings His Best for Capitol, 675
Sings Woody Guthrie, 308
Sink the Bismarck, 456
Sinner Man, 558, 735
Sins of a Family, 911
Sinsemilla, 911
Sioux City Sue, 412
Sippie Wallace Sings the Blues, 1029
Sippin' with Cisco, 274
Sipping Cider, 670
Sir Dancealot, 1020
Sir Douglas Quintet + 2 (Honkey Blues), 866

Sir Duke, 1077
Sir Patrick Spens, 164
Siren, 853, 857
Sirens Song, The, 1075
Sirius, 311
Sister, 653, 920
Sister Feelings Call, 901
Sister Golden Hair, 19
Sister Ray, 1018
Sisters, 443
Sisters Are Doing It for Themselves, 317, 355
Sisters of Avalon, 567
Sisters of Mercy, 201, 981
Sisters Oh Sisters, 740
Sit Down, 485
Sit Down I Think I Love You, 755
Sit Down Old Friend, 266
Sit Down Servant, 938
Sit Down You're Rocking the Boat, 596
Sittin' and Thinkin', 830
Sittin' in, 596
Sittin' in the Balcony, 197, 599, 599
Sittin' in the Park, 327
(Sittin' on) The Dock of the Bay, 107, 821
Sitting in Limbo, 193
Sitting in the Park, 374
Six, 639, 639
Six and Seven Books, 767
Six and Seven Books of Moses, 987
Six Cold Feet in the Ground, 161
Six Days on the Road, 286
Six More Miles (to the Graveyard), 1059
Six o'Clock News, 799
Six Pack, 142, 782
Six Pack on the Dashboard, 493
666 – The Apocalypse of St John, 1014
Six Strings Down, 1016
Six Teens, The, 964
634-5789, 107, 415, 775
Six Wheel Chaser, 582
Six Wives of Henry VIII, The, 1025
16 Bars, 958
Sixteen Candles, 226, 894
16 Most Requested Songs, 1023
Sixteen Stone, 142
Sixteen Tons, 344, 992
Sixty Minute Man, 59, 625, 817
60 Years of Music America Hates Best, 516
69/96, 216
69, The Los Angeles Sessions, 556
Size Isn't Everything, 71
Ska Boo Da Ba, 908
Ska War, 987
Skaggs and Rice, 907
Skank Bloc Bologna, 878

Skeleton Keys, 653
Skeleton on the Roundabout, 304
Skeletons in the Closet, 305
Sketches for My Sweetheart the Drunk, 135
Sketches of Life, 234
Sketches of Spain, 248, 249, 318, 681
Skid Row, 909
Skid-dat-de-dat, 1038
Skies of America, 202
Skiffle Sessions – Live in Belfast, The, 55, 272, 277, 695
Skiffling Strings, 392
Skin Deep, 437, 956
Skin Diva, 559
Skin I'm in, 169
Skin Mechanic, 728
Skin Tight, 736
Skin Up Pin Up, 639
Skinhead Train, 12
Skinny Jim, 197
Skinny Legs and All, 978
Skinny Minnie, 413
Skins, 870
Skip James: the Greatest of the Delta Blues Singers, 488
Skip James Today!, 488
Skokiaan, 348
Skull Wars, 534
Skunk Funk, 369
Skweeze Me, Pleeze Me, 910
Sky, 909
Sky 2, 909
Sky 3, 909
Sky Is Crying, The, 486, 840, 1016
Sky Is Falling and I Want My Mommy, The, 252
Sky Is Too High, The, 100
Sky Island, 583
Sky Motel, 984
Sky Pilot, 24
Skye Boat Song, 1053
Skylark, 158, 663
Skylarking, 1035, 1081
Skyliner, 56
Skynyrd Friends, 609
Skyscraping, 2
Slade Alive at Reading '80, 910
Slang, 255
Slanted and Enchanted, 760
Slash's Snake Pit, 407
Slave Driver, 643, 966
Slave to Love, 333
Slave to the Grind, 909
Slave to the Rhythm, 512
Slave to the Wage, 779
Slavery Days, 140
Slaves and Masters, 254
Slay Tracks, 760
Sledgehammer, 366
Sleep, 108, 504, 1031

Sleep, Baby, Sleep, 844
Sleeping Bag, 1094
Sleeping in My Car, 856
Sleeping on the Job, 275
Sleeping With the Past, 503
Sleepless Nights, 586, 757
Sleeps with Angels, 1088
Sleepwalker, 544
Sleepwalking, 812
Sleepy Head, 276
Sleepy Man Blues, 704
Sleepy Rio Grande, 606, 842
Sleepy Time Gal, 141, 1052
Sleepy Time Time, 225
Slide Area, The, 212
Slide Away the Screen, 627
Sliding Doors, 26
Slightly Fabulous Limeliters, The,
    585
Slightly out of Tune, 561
Slim Shady LP, The, 270
Slim's Jam, 366
Slip and Slide, 328
Slip Away, 163, 415
Slip Inside This House, 796
Slip of the Tongue, 1051
Slip Sliding Away, 899
Slip-in Mules, 486
Slipped, Stumbled and Fell in
    Love, 762
Slippery People, 938
Slippery When Wet, 102, 208
Slippin' and Slidin', 483, 589
Slippin' Away, 147
Slippin' in, 409
Slippin' into Darkness, 1030
Slipping Around, 984, 1052
Sloppy Seconds, 271
Sloth, 324
Slouching Towards Bethlehem,
    679
Slow and Sexy, 815
Slow Boat to China, 392
Slow Dancer, 873
Slow Dancing with the Moon, 758
Slow Dazzle, 150
Slow Down, 1062
Slow Down World, 278
Slow Drag, 472
Slow Hand, 781
Slow Motion, 370, 964
Slow Poke, 432, 542
Slow Ride, 343
Slow Train Coming, 267, 293
Slow Train to Dawn, 178
Slow Turning, 444
Slow Twistin', 175
Slow Walk, 273
Slowhand, 187
Slowly, 252, 776
Slug Line, 444

Slyfi, 317
Smack My Bitch Up, 801
Smackwater Jack, 514
Small Axe, 643, 767
Small Blue Thing, 1017
Small Change, 1024
Small Fruit Song, 947
Small Talk, 954
Small Town, 660
Small Town Boy, 208
Small Town Romance, 982
Small Town Talk, 173, 272
Small World, 581, 919
Smart Ass, 865
Smarty, 1023
Smash, 736
Smash the Mirror, 1054
Smash Your Head against the
    Wall, 1054
Smashed, 864
Smells Like Children, 638
Smells Like Teen Spirit, 20, 723
Smiddy Burn, 324
Smile, 63, 64, 319, 494, 729, 755,
    1051
Smiler, 949
Smiley Smile, 63
Smilin' Through, 559
Smiling Men with Bad Reputa-
    tions, 471
Smoke and Strong Whiskey, 690
Smoke Gets in Your Eyes, 333,
    348, 422, 530, 780, 870, 895
Smoke on the Water, 253
Smoke, Smoke, Smoke That Cig-
    arette, 207, 992
Smoker You Drink the Player You
    Get, The, 295
Smokestack Lightning, 459, 758,
    924
Smokey, 841
Smokey Joe's Café, 196, 574, 1024
Smokie – Part 2, 89
Smokin' in the Boys Room, 698
Smokin' O.P.'s, 882
Smoking Gun, 224
Smooth Noodle Maps, 260
Smooth Operator, 84, 866
Smooth Sailin', 476
Smuggler's Blues, 296
Snake, The, 781
Snake Bite Love, 699
Snake Document Masquerade, 351
Snake in the Grass, 245
Snake Rag, 739
Snakes and Ladders, 812
Snakes Crawl at Night, 795
Snakey Feelings, 953
Snapper, 744
Snatching It Back, 163, 164
Snaz, 709
Sneak Attack, 669

Sneakin' Around, 36, 822
Sneakin' Suspicion, 270
Sneakin' up Behind You, 119
Sneaking Sally Through the
    Alley, 281, 751, 990
Sniper and Other Love Songs, 171
Sno-Cone, 203
Snooker Loopy, 175
Snow Blind Friend, 40
Snow White and the Seven
    Dwarfs, 606
Snowbird, 705
Snowbound, 218
Snowfall, 983
Snuff Garrett's Texas Opera Co,
    373
So, 366, 563, 710
So Alone, 717
So Cold the Night, 208
So Early in the Spring, 766
So Excited, 781
So Far, 388
So Far Away, 540
So Far So Good, 7
So Far, So Good . . . So What?, 659
So Far . . . The Best of Sinead
    O'Connor, 734
So Fine, 76, 596
So Glad You're Mine, 233
So Good, 114, 752
So Good to Be Back Home
    Again, 317
So Good Together, 618
So I Can Love You, 310
So in Love, 742
So in to You, 37
So It Goes, 603
So Lonely, 782
So Long, 313, 408
So Long Bannatyne, 406
So Long Harry Truman, 737
So Long It's Been Good to Know
    You, 1040
So Long Marianne, 201
So Macho, 951
So Many Rivers, 1076
So Many Roads, 52, 862
So Many Roads, So Many Trains,
    861
So Many Ways, 78
So Natural, 938
So Rare, 280
So Real, 135
So Rebellious a Lover, 148
So Red the Rose, 289
So Round, So Firm, So Fully
    Packed, 992
So Sad, 320
So the Seeds Are Growing, 925
So Tough, 867
So What, 295, 561
So You Think You're in Love, 447

So You Want to Be a Boxer, 1064
So You Want to Be a Rock and
  Roll Star, 147, 493, 817
So You Win Again, 457
So Young, 952, 959
Soaky in the Pooper, 560
Soap Opera, 544
Sobbin' Women, 663
Soca Baptism, 398, 669
Soca Diva, 398
Social Studies, 1024
Society's Child, 171, 465, 697
Sock It 2 Me, 308
Sock It to Me Baby, 227, 865
Soda Fountain Rag, 306
Sodom and Gomorrah, 798
Soft, 116, 273
Soft and Sweet, 263
Soft and Wet/So Blue, 797
Soft Boys 1976–81, The, 446
Soft Bulletin, The, 339
Soft Lights and Sweet Music, 79
Soft Machine Vol. 2, 919
Soft Parade, The, 279
Soft Swing, 15, 381
Softly as I Leave You, 685, 904
Softly Softly, 752
Softly Whispering I Love You,
  403
Softs, 919
Soho, Needless to Say, 947
Solar Fire, 635
Solar Myth Approach, The, 961
Solar Plexus, 727
Solar Wind, 583
Sold, 236
Sold American, 963, 986
Soldier, 469, 1081
Soldier Boy, 894
Soldier of Fortune, 979
Soldier of Plenty, 132
Soldier's Joy, 285
Soldier's Sweetheart, The, 844
Soldier's Things, 1025
Soldiers of Metal, 25
Soldiers Who Want to Be
  Heroes, 622
Solid, 32
Solid and Country, 89
Solid Ground, 907
Solid Pleasure, 1083
Solid Rock, 977
Solid Silver, 810
Soliloquy, 844, 1003
Solitaire, 117, 1031, 1057
Solitude/Solitaire, 181
Solitude Standing, 1017
Solo, 324, 387, 625
Solo Flight, 184
Solo Piano Vol. 1, 961
Solomon's Seal, 765
Solsbury Hill, 366, 513

Solution, 732
Soma Coba, 263
Some Candy Talking, 498
Some Change, 873
Some Day, 359
Some Enchanted Evening, 98,
  493, 844
Some Fantastic Place, 936
Some Friendly, 172
Some Girls, 849
Some Great Reward, 258
Some Guys Have All the Luck,
  751, 795, 950
Some Hearts, 320
Some Kind of Bliss, 677
Some Kind of Wonderful, 243,
  285, 396, 396, 409, 743
Some Kinda Fun, 688
Some Like It Hot, 289, 751
Some Love Songs Never Die, 980
Some Might Say, 731
Some of These Days, 28, 742, 996
Some of Those Days, 583
Some of Us, 970
Some Old Bullshit, 64
Some Other Guy, 56
Some People, 959
Some People Can Do What They
  Like, 751
Some People's Lives, 667
Some Rainy Morning, 224
Some Smoke, 852
Some Things Never Change, 958,
  962
Some Time in New York City, 576,
  740, 930
Some Velvet Morning, 436, 904
Somebody Bad Stole the Wed-
  ding Bell, 547
Somebody Else's Troubles, 392
Somebody Help Me, 303, 1072
Somebody Like That, 153
Somebody Loves You, 379
Somebody Shot Out of the
  Jukebox, 970
Somebody Stole My Gal, 1042
Somebody to Love, 494, 807
Somebody to Shove, 922
Somebody's Been Sleeping, 449
Someday, 74, 157, 825
Someday Baby, 1057
Someday I'll Find You, 222
Someday (I'm Coming Back),
  938
Someday Man, 1064
Someday One Day, 881, 897
Someday Someway, 649
Someday They're Coming Home
  Again, 62
Someday We'll Be Together, 121,
  963
Someday We'll Look Back, 411

Somedays, 178
Somedays You Eat the Bear, 652
Someone Else's Baby, 325
Someone Should Leave, 618
Someone, Someone, 784
Someone Stole Gabriel's Horn,
  972
Someone to Care for Me, 522
Someone to Watch Over Me, 379,
  515
Someone's Looking at You, 376
Someone's Taken Maria Away,
  325
Somethin Els, 133
Somethin' Else, 197, 589
Somethin' Stupid, 904
Something, 67
Something about Today, 877
Something About What Happens
  When We Talk, 1062
Something About You, 579
Something/Anything, 859
Something Better Change, 956
Something Else, 8, 543, 884, 955
Something Else Again, 431
Something for the Girl with
  Everything, 927
Something for the Pain, 102
Something for the Weekend, 268
Something Going on in My Soul,
  977
Something Got Me Started, 902
Something Happens, 444
Something Here in My Heart, 610
Something in Blue, 684
Something in My Life, 761
Something in the Air, 771
Something in the Night, 383
Something in the Way She
  Moves, 862, 970
Something in Your Eyes, 933
Something Inside So Strong, 847
Something Magic, 801
Something More, 300
Something Old, Something New,
  759
Something Sweet, Something
  Tender, 274
Something to Believe in, 655, 815
Something to Remember, 631
Something to Remember You
  By, 406
Something to Talk About, 705
Something You Got, 257
Something's Burning, 247, 847
Something's Coming, 919
Something's Gonna Jump Out of
  the Bushes, 130
Something's Got a Hold on Me,
  486
Something's Gotta Give, 249, 621,
  663

Something's Gotten Hold of My Heart, 17, 403, 778
Sometimes, 312, 703, 928
Sometimes a Rose, 794
Sometimes Always, 498
Sometimes Good Guys Don't Wear White, 349
Sometimes I'm Happy, 391, 439, 1086
Sometimes When We Touch, 369, 559, 638, 1080
Somewhere, 800, 919, 1024
Somewhere Beyond the Blue Horizon, 617
Somewhere in Afrika, 635
Somewhere in England, 427
Somewhere in My Heart, 42
Somewhere in the Night, 1073
Somewhere in the Stars, 166
Somewhere in Time, 474
Somewhere My Love, 210
Somewhere Other Than the Night, 123
Somewhere Over the Rainbow, 713
Somewhere Tonight, 459
Son Come Home Soon, 810
Son of a Preacher Man, 933
Son of Hickory Holler's Tramp, The, 356
Son of My Father, 693
Son of Schmilsson, 722
Son of Spirit, 932
Son of the South, 199
Son This Is She, 659
Song, A, 647, 880
Song about a Rose, 816
Song Book, 100
Song Cycle, 755
Song for a Dreamer, 800
Song for Che, 1079
Song for Europe, A, 857
Song for Love, 321
Song for Me, A, 328
Song for Mexico, 885
Song for the Lovers, A, 1021
Song for Whoever, 68
Song for You, A, 864
Song from Moulin Rouge, The, 325
Song Is Born, A, 16
Song of India, 282, 1049
Song of Life, 572
Song of the Flame, 422
Song of the Vagabonds, 359
Song of the Volga Boatmen, 671
Song on the Radio, 947
Song Review, 1077
Song Slowly Song, 135
Song Sung Blue, 262
Song to Che, 410
Song to Remember, A, 286
Song to the Siren, 175, 198

Song to Woody, 291, 408
Song 2, 100
Song X, 202, 666
Songbird, 365, 1090
Songhai, 766
Songs, 259, 574, 975, 1013
Songs & Crazy Dreams, 116
Songs for a Tailor, 133, 726
Songs for Distingué Lovers, 448
Songs for Drella, 151, 824, 1018
Songs for Sale, 199
Songs for Swinging Lovers, 833, 904
Songs for Swinging Sellers, 393, 574, 647, 685
Songs for the Jet Set, 218
Songs for Torching, 448
Songs for Young Lovers, 904
Songs from a Room, 201
Songs from Alphabet Zoo, 627
Songs from an Aging Sex Bomb, 746
Songs from Heathcliff, 831
Songs from Liquid Days, 385
Songs from Northern Britain, 973
Songs from the Big Chair, 972
Songs from the Capeman, 900
Songs from the Last Century, 667
Songs from the Mardi Gras, 890
Songs from the Mirror, 642
Songs from the Victorious City, 286
Songs from the Wood, 499
Songs from Theatreland, 639
Songs I Love to Sing, 1053
Songs in the Key of Life, 1077
Songs in the Key of X, 215, 311
Songs of Bessie Smith, The, 120
Songs of Distant Earth, 738
Songs of Faith and Devotion, 258
Songs of Faith and Devotion – Live, 258
Songs of Freedom, 644
Songs of Jimmie Rodgers, The, 695, 845, 918, 1034
Songs of Leonard Cohen, 201
Songs of Love, 19
Songs of Love and Hate, 201
Songs of Our Times, 911
Songs of Pete Seeger, The, 814
Songs of the Depression, 715
Songs of the Famous Carter Family, 163
Songs of the Heart, 705
Songs of the North, 606
Songs of the Seashore, 369
Songs of West Side Story, The, 558, 589, 869
Songs Our Daddy Taught Us, 319
Songs that Made the Jukebox Play, 1073
Songs to a Seagull, 678

Songs to Grow on, 308
Songs to Learn and Sing, 299
Songs to Remember, 878
Songs We Taught Your Mother, 933
Songstress, The, 49
Songwriter, 555
Songwriters for the Stars, 346
Sonic Boom Boy, 467
Sonic Death, 920
Sonic Flower Groove, 796
Sonny Boy, 259, 510
Sonny Boy Williamson and The Yardbirds, 1083
Sons and Fascination, 901
Sons of Mercury, 810
Soon, 230, 997
Soon Forward, 475, 911
Soothing Sounds for Babies, 876
Sopa de Pichon, 628
Sophisticated Beggar, The, 423
Sophisticated Cissy, 714, 990
Sophisticated Lady, 307, 675, 822
Sorghum Switch, 953
Sorrow Will Come in the End, 696
Sorry Robbie, 1042
Sorry Seems to be the Hardest Word, 198
Sorry Suzanne, 450, 610, 611
Sorted for E's and Wizz, 805
SOS, 1
Soul & Inspiration, 638
Soul Alive, 139
Soul Alone, 413
Soul Auctioneer, 797
Soul Bossa Nova, 265
Soul Brothers, 174
Soul Cages, The, 950
Soul Crusher, 1048
Soul Deep, 113, 683
Soul Food Man, 427
Soul Gestures in Southern Blue, 645
Soul Inside, 16
Soul Kiss, 721
Soul Limbo, 106
Soul Makossa, 263
Soul Man, 107, 434, 824, 869, 870
Soul Meeting, 536
Soul Motion, 276
Soul Murder, 7
Soul My Way, 581
Soul of a City Boy, 1090
Soul of O. V. Wright, The, 1079
Soul of the Blues, 139
Soul on Board, 972
Soul Provider, 102
Soul Searchin', 296
Soul Serenade, 536, 679
Soul Shadows, 1074
Soul Sister, Brown Sugar, 869

Soul Survives, The, 131
Soul Syndrome, 128
Soul Time, 309
Soul to Soul, 1016
Soul, Tramp, Now!, 362
Soul Trane, 511
Soul Twist, 536, 840
Soulful Dress, 486
Soulful Mood of Marvin Gaye, The, 374
Soulful Strut, 582
Soulfully, 232
Soultrane, 206
Sound Affects, 484
Sound Elixir, 709
Sound Museum, 253
Sound of Confusion, 925
Sound of Fury, The, 129, 364, 391
Sound of Joy, 961
Sound of Lies, The, 493
Sound of McAlmont, The, 960
Sound of Music, The, 22, 105, 844
Sound of Music by Pizzicato Five, The, 779
Sound of Philadelphia, The, 370
Sound of 65, The, 103, 133
Sound of Speed, The, 498
Sound of Spring, 582
Sound of the Crowd, 461
Sound of Water, 867
Sound of White Noise, 25
Sound on Sound, 710
Sound System, 565
Sound Venture, 327
Sound Your Funky Horn, 526
Soundhouse Tapes, The, 474
Sounds – and Stuff Like That, 514
Sounds from the Street, 484
Sounds of Science, The, 65
Sounds of Silence, The, 897, 897, 898, 925
Sounds of the Loop, 747
Sounds the Ritual Echo, 711
Soundscapes, Live in Argentina, 536
Soup, 95
Sour Times, 785
Source, The, 397
Sourcelab, 11
South African Experience, 591
South America, Take It Away, 23
South American Way, 678, 1032
South Bronx, 106
South of the Border, 17, 18, 39, 161, 528
South Rampart Street Parade, 231
South Side Blues Jam, 1045
South Street, 744
South's Gonna Do It, The, 241, 242
Southbound, 1037
Southern Accents, 771

Southern Cross, 857
Southern Exposure, 128, 1049
Southern Folk Heritage, 597
Southern Harmony and Musical Companion, The, 87
Southern Journey, 597
Southern Man, 608, 1088
Southern Nights, 36, 153, 990, 990
Southpaw Grammar, 696
Southside, 978
Southtown USA, 521
Souvenir, 742
Souvenirs, 342
Soweto, 31
Sowing the Seeds of Love, 972
Soy Yo, 870
Space Guitar, 1038
Space Oddity, 110, 110, 111, 1025
Space Race, 790
Space Ritual, 433
Space Ritual 2, 434
Spaceman, 722
Spaceman Came Travelling, A, 251
Spacer, 845
Spaces, 217
Spaghetti Incident?, The, 407, 709, 718
Spain, 513
Spaniard that Blighted My Life, The, 510
Spanish Eddie, 117
Spanish Eyes, 130, 522, 648, 713
Spanish Guitar, 118
Spanish Harlem, 271, 355, 537, 539, 574, 633, 929
Spanish Is the Loving Tongue, 585
Spanish Lace, 616, 783
Spanish Omega, 459
Spanish Train and Other Stories, 251
Spanning the Years, 942
Sparkle, 152, 355
Sparkle in the Rain, 901
Sparky's Magic Piano, 554
Sparrow Come Back, 669
Sparrow in the Tree Top, 678
Spasticus Autisticus, 290
Speak and Spell, 258
Speak Brother Speak, 837
Speak Like a Child, 1044
Speak Low, 1043
Speak of the Devil, 475
Speak to the Sky, 933
Speaking in Tongues, 559, 967
Speaking of Dreams, 47
Special, 193, 371, 975
Special Christmas, A, 172
Special Collection, 747
Special Delivery Blues, 1029
Special Things, 781

Specials Singles, The, 929
Specters, 98
Speech, 30
Speechless, 570
Speed King, 253
Speed of the Sound of Loneliness, 159, 799
Speed Your Love to Me, 901
Speeding Time, 9, 540
Speedoo, 196
Speedy Gonzales, 108
Spellbound, 3, 3
Spend the Night, 476
Spice, 931
Spice of Life, 636
Spice Up Your Life, 931
Spiceworld, 931
Spicks and Specks, 71
Spiderland, 988
Spiders and Snakes, 75, 756
Spiderwebs, 725
Spike, 219
Spike Driver Blues, 463
Spike Jones in Stereo, 516
Spill the Wine, 24, 1030
Spin Away, 349
Spin of the Wheel, 40
Spin the Black Circle, 762
Spinner, 311
Spinning Around, 677
Spinning Coin, 655
Spinning Wheel, 97
Spiral Scratch, 145
Spiral Staircase, 627
Spirit, 454, 500, 713
Spirit in the Night, 934
Spirit in the Sky, 403, 404
Spirit of New Orleans, 58
Spirit of 76, 932
Spirit of the Age, 434
Spirit of the Place, 727
Spirit of the Radio, 861
Spirit of the World, 727
Spirit of Woodstock, 946
Spirits, 493, 877
Spirits Colliding, 116
Spirits Dancing in the Flesh, 871
Spirits in the Material World, 782
Spirits Rejoice, 41
Spiritual Unity, 41
Spitfire, 495
Splendid, 218
Splinter Group, 341
Splish Splash, 244
Spooky, 37
Spoon, 246
Spoon So Easy, 1075
Spoonful, 225, 266, 269, 759
Spoonman, 924
Sporting Life, 569, 1039
Sporting Life Blues, 619
Sports, 581

Sports Weekend (As Clean as They Wanna Be Part II), 1001
Sports Weekend (As Nasty as They Wanna Be Part II), 1001
Spread a Little Happiness, 950
Spring, 1065
Spring Fever, 615
Spring of the Year, 726
Spring Will Be a Little Late This Year, 290, 596
Springer, The, 256
Square the Circle, 27
Squares and Triangles, 981
Squeeze, 1018
Squeeze Box, 1054
Squeeze Her – Tease Her, 1069
Squeeze Me, 1029
Squeezing Out Sparks, 725, 754
Squire, 586
Squirrel and G-Man Twenty Four Hour Party People Plastic Face Carnt Smile (White Out), 421
Stack O'Lee, 302
Stacked Deck, 18, 1070
Stage, 111
Stagefright, 53, 860, 864
Stages, 1094
Stagger Lee, 218, 793, 794, 846, 966
Stained Class, 519
Stainsby Girls, 819
Stairway to Heaven, 143, 569, 880
Stakes Is High, 251
Stalin Wasn't Stallin', 1079
Stan Freberg Presents the United States of America, 356
Stan Getz: Gold, 381
Stand, 826, 954
Stand and Deliver, 25
Stand Back, 342
Stand Beside Me, 986
Stand by Me, 384, 493, 539, 574, 938
Stand by Your Man, 602, 893, 940, 1080
Stand in for Your Love, 736
Stand in the Fire, 1092
Stand Inside Your Love, 913
Stand Tall, 406
Stand Up, 498
Stand Up and Be a Witness, 940
Stand Up and Walk, 1007
Stand Up for Jesus, 303
Standard Time, 645
Standards, 492, 834
Standing Around Crying, 927
Standing at the Burying Ground, 618
Standing at the Crossroads, 486
Standing at the Edge of Town, 761
Standing in the Grits Line, 221
Standing in the Light, 579

Standing in the Line of Fire, 104
Standing in the Shadow (Of a Very Famous Man), 1060
Standing in the Shadows of Love, 350
Standing My Ground, 126
Standing on a Beach – The Singles, 238
Standing on Rock, 1071
Standing on the Corner, 348, 596
Standing on the Inside, 880
Standing on the Shoulder of Giants, 731
Standing on the Top, 488
Standing on the Verge of Getting It, 194
Standing out on the Highway, 268
Standing Stone, 611, 612
Standing Tall, 198, 234
Standing Together, 77
Standing Too Close to the Flames, 199
Stanley Clarke, 190
Stanley Road, 1044
Star, 312, 812, 984, 1012
Star Bright, 1076
Star Dust, 158, 184, 826, 904
Star Fleet Project, 808
Star on a TV Show, 958
Star People, 248
Star Spangled Rhythm, 26
Star Spangled Springer, 300
Star Turtle, 210
Star-Spangled Banner, The, 332, 440, 458, 614, 618, 916
Stardancer, 816
Stardust, *107*, 202, 314, 513, 645, 713
Staring at the Sun, 579
Starless and Bible Black, 536
Starlight, Star Bright, 441
Starry Eyed, 752
Starry Eyed and Bollock Naked, 163
Starry Night, 469
Stars, 177, 466, 902, 1041
Stars and Stripes Forever, 924
Stars Fell on Alabama, 972
Stars of Track and Field, 75
Stars We Are, The, 17
Starsailor, 136
Start, 484
Start Me Up, 850
Starting Five, The, 620
Starting Over, 576, *618*, 817
Starting Up, 703
Starvation, 928
Starvation Blues, 953
State Occasion, 329
State of Affairs, 550
State of Art Is on Fire, The, 842

State of Confusion, 544, 766
State of Euphoria, 25
State of Mind, 976
State of Play, The, 926
State of Shock, 478
State of the Art, 620
State of the Heart, 159
State Street Special, 1082
State Trooper, 222
Stately Homes of England, The, 222
Statesboro Blues, 966
Station to Station, 111
Statues, 701
Status Quo, 941
Stay, 132, 449, 595, 886, 960, 1063
Stay as Sweet as You Are, 828
Stay Awake, 755, 1067
Stay Away from My Baby, 893
Stay Beside Me, 1010
Stay Free, 32
Stay Here, 567
Stay in My Corner, 256
Stay on These Roads, 11
Stay Together, 959
Stay with Me, 812, 912
Stay with Me Baby, 812, 1026
Stay Young, 473, 1059
Stayed Too Long at the Fair, 814
Stayin' Alive, 71
Staying Power, 1048
Steady Nerves, 754
Steal Away, 415, 838, 971
Stealer's Wheel, 812
Stealin' Back, 627
Stealin' Home, 652
Stealing Apples, 1063
Steamboat, 285
Steamer, The, 381
Steamin' Hot, 821
Steaming Jungle, 459
Steamroller, 970
Steel Bars, 102
Steel Claw, 116
Steel Guitar Rag, 1068
Steel Men, 1053
Steel Rail Blues, 417
Steel River, 819
Steel Town, 83
Steel Wheels, 558, 850
Stein Song, The, 1011
Stella, 1084
Stella by Starlight, 492, 1089
Stella Maris, 13
Step by Step, 227, 715, 899
Step Further, A, 343
Step in the Arena, 370
Step Inside Love, 89
Step Inside This House, 602
Step into a World, 106
Step into My World, 834
Step It up and Go, 362

Step Off, 397
Step on, 421, 952
Step Out of Your Mind, 970
Stephane Grappelli Plays Jerome Kern, 399
Steppin' Out, 27, 77, 180, 186, 332, 480, 480, 743, 829
Steppin' Out of Babylon, 100
Steppin' to the Shadows, 886
Steptacular, 952
Stereopathic Soul Manure, 69
Stereotype, 928
Stereotypes, 100
Steronomy, 756
Steve Howe Album, The, 1085
Steve McQueen, 273, 788
Steve Miller Band Box Set, 674
Stick to Me, 754
Stick to Your Guns, 698
Stick-Up, 169, 232, 449, 601
Stickin' to My Guns, 487
Sticky Fingers, 618, 724, 790, 849
Stiff Upper Lip, 5
Still, 21, 208, 378, 716
Still Alive and Well, 1071
Still Believes, 122
Still Bill, 1074
Still Burning, 1036
Still Caught Up, 482
Still Crazy After All These Years, 160, 899
Still 'Eavy, Still Proud, 1009
Still Feel Gone, 1007
Still Got the Blues, 690
Still I'm Sad, 1083
Still in Love, 783
Still in Saigon, 241, 242
Still Life, 849
Still Life (Talking), 666
Still Life with Guitar, 919
Still Losing You, 675
Still Loving You, 841
Still of the Night, 1051
Still Water Love, 841
Still Waters, 71
Still Within the Sound of My Voice, 153
Stir It Up, 643, 708
Stockholm Sweetnin', 126
Stolen Car, 744
Stolen Moments, 444
Stomp, 124
Stomp 442, 25
Stomp Your Feet, 306
Stompin' at the Savoy, 391, 471, 1040
Stone Blue, 343
Stone Free, 70
Stone in Love with You, 74
Stone Love, 550
Stone Roses, The, 952
Stoned and Dethroned, 498

Stoned Love, 963
Stoned out of My Mind, 180
Stoned Soul Picnic, 728, 836
Stonedhenge, 977
Stonehenge, 431
Stones, 262
Stones in the Road, 47, 159
Stoney End, 728
Stood There Amazed, 465
Stood Up, 224, 641, 711
Stooges, The, 468
Stool Pigeon, 533
Stoosh, 909
Stop, 129, 312, 879, 931
Stop All That Jazz, 864
Stop and Smell the Roses, 247, 939
Stop Draggin' My Heart Around, 342, 771
Stop in the Name of Love, 449, 450, 962
Stop! It's Wonderful, 996
Stop, Look and Listen, 670
Stop Me (If You've Heard It All Before), 732
Stop Pretending, 505
Stop Stop Stop, 449
Stop the War, 178, 396
Stop the World, 321
Stop the World Tonight, 910
Stop to Love, 1013
Stop Your Sobbing, 544, 791
Stop Your Tickling Jock, 566
Stories from the City, Stories from the Sea, 429
Stories from the Nerve Bible, 22
Stories of Johnny, 17
Stories Told and Untold, 46
Stories We Can Tell, 603
Stories without Words, 935
Storm, The, 690
Storm Force 10, 942
Storm Front, 345, 502
Storm in Heaven, A, 1020
Storm Windows, 799
Stormbringer, 253
Stormcock, 424
Storms of Life, 993
Storms, 404
Stormwatch, 499
Stormy, 37
Stormy Monday, 446, *818*
Stormy Monday Blues, 299, 570, *1028*
Stormy Weather, 26, 27, 455, 679, *1041, 1043*
Story Book Children, 970
Story of a Starry Night, The, 671
Story of Bo Diddley, The, 263
Story of My Life, The, 44, 752, 837
Story of My Love, The, 1000
Story of Neptune, The, 1066

Story of the Clash Vol. 1, The, 191
Story of the Ghost, The, 773
Story of the Knoxville Girl, 99
Story Songs, 881
Story Untold, A, 227
Storyteller, The, 415, 544
Storyteller/The Complete Anthology 1964–1990, 950
Storyville, 53
Straight Ahead, 397
Straight Between the Eyes, 254
Straight, Clean and Simple, 705
Straight from the Heart, 7, 16, *134*
Straight No Chaser, 8
Straight on, 436
Straight on 'Til Morning, 99
Straight out the Jungle, *251*, 520, 520
Straight Outta Compton, 728
Straight Shooter, 46
Straight Shootin', 445
Straight Shootin' Woman, 944
Straight to the Heart, 375, *870*
Straight Up, 2, 427, 859
Straightaways, 1007
Straighten Up and Fly Right, 201
Strait Out of the Box, 955
Stranded, 436, *857*
Stranded in the Jungle, 85, 196, 351
Strange Angels, 22, 984
Strange Are the Ways of Love, 399
Strange Brew, 186, 225
Strange Cargo 3, 744
Strange Days, 279
Strange Frontier, 808
Strange Fruit, 365, 448, 905, 1049, 1079
Strange Glue, 168
Strange I Know, 649
Strange Little Girl, 956
Strange Magic, 304
Strange Messengers, 917
Strange Pleasure, 1016
Strange Things Happening, 655
Strange Town, 484
Strange Weather, 326
Strangelands, 125
Strangelove, 258
Stranger, The, 502
Stranger in Paradise, 77, 347
Stranger in the House, 219
Stranger in this Town, 102, 849
Stranger in Town, 882
Stranger on the Shore, 85, 86, 313
Stranger Things Have Happened, 685
Strangers in the Night, 130, 522, 904, *1006*
Stranglers in the Night, 956
Stratosphere, 968

Straw Donkeys, 985
Straw Donkeys . . . The Singles, 163
Strawberries Oceans Ships Forest, 612
Strawberry Fair, 718
Strawberry Fields Forever, 67, 647, 703
Strawberry Letter 23, 124
Strawberry Moon, 1035
Stray, 42
Stray Cats, 302
Streak, The, 946
Streams of Whiskey, 780
Street Angel, 342
Street Beat, 786
Street Called Desire, 1070
Street Dreams, 36
Street Fighting Years, 901
Street Hassle, 824
Street Legal, 293
Street Life, 234, 857, 1073
Street Life '92, 332
Street Opera, 32
Street Player, 532
Street Rats, 912
Street Songs, 488
Street Spirit (Fade Out), 811
Street Survivors, 608, 609
Street Talk, 519
Street Tough, 539
Streetfighter, 350
Streetlife Serenade, 502
Streetlights, 812, 814
Streetnoise, 37
Streets, 122
Streets of Bakersfield, 749, 1085
Streets of Baltimore, 55, 239, 458, 986
Streets of Laredo, 619
Streets of London, 73, 627
Streets of Philadelphia, 935
Streisand Superman, 957
Stressed Out, 994
Stretching Out, 582, 908, 995
Strict Tempo, 982
Strictly Commercial, 1092
Strictly Dubwise, 109
Striding after Fats, 1070
Strike Like Lightning, 1016
Strike on Computers, 1038, *1038*
Strike Up the Band, 380
Striking It Rich, 445
String of Pearls, A, 908
Stringing the Blues, 562, 1019
Strings, 984
Strip Mine, 485
Strip Polka, 557
Stripped, 850
Stripper, The, 854, 855
Stripper Vicar, 639
Stroll, The, 262
Stroll on, 1083

Strolling with Bones, 81
Strong Enough, 579
Strong Enough to Bend, 997
Strong Persuader, 203, 224
Stronger, 831
Stronger Than Dirt, 983
Stronger Than Pride, 866
Struck by Lightning, 754
Strugglin' Lady, 588
Strut, 298
Strut Your Material, 670
Strutter, 546
Struttin', 124
Stubborn Kind of Fellow, A, 374, 645
Stuck in Gear, 1077
Stuck in the Middle with You, 575, 811
Stuck With You, 581
Student Demonstration Time, 197
Student Prince, The, 563
Studio, 223
Study in Frustration, A, 439
Stuff, 842
Stumble, The, 541, 654
Stumble and Fall, 601
Stumblin' in, 183, 807
Stumbling, 1049
Stupendous, 753
Stupid Cupid, 353, 545, 880
Stupid Girl, 371
Stupid, Stupid, Stupid, 421
Stupidity, 270
Stutter, 304, 485
Stuttering Cindy, 331
Stylistics Christmas, The, 958
Stylistics 2, 958
Styx I, 959
Subhuman Race, 909
Substance, 716
Substitute, 376, 815, 1054
Subterranean Homesick Blues, 82, 292, 722
Subterranean Jungle, 815
Subtle as a Flying Mallet, 302
Suburban Attitudes, 599
Suburban Voodoo, 603
Suburbia, 767
Subway to the Country, 5
Success, 607
Success Has Made a Failure of Our Home, 734
Success Hasn't Spoiled Me Yet, 934
Success Is the Word, 106
Such a Day, 608
Such a Night, 285, 308, 625, 818
Such Sweet Thunder, 307
Sucker MCs, 859
Suckin' a Big Bottle of Gin, 309
Sucu Sucu, 437
Suddenly, 721, 732, 831
Suddenly There's a Valley, 398, 564

Suddenly You Love Me, 707, 784
Suedehead, 696
Suedehead: The Best of Morrissey, 696
Sugar, 506
Sugar and Spice, 879
Sugar Babe, 131
Sugar Bee, 671
Sugar Blues, 1058
Sugar Coated Iceberg, 585
Sugar Coated Love, 671, 937
Sugar Daddy, 75
Sugar Foot Stomp, 391, 487
Sugar Foot Strut, 231
Sugar Lips, 645, 990
Sugar Magnolia, 400
Sugar Plum, 186
Sugar Rum Cherry, 307
Sugar Shack, 770
Sugar Sugar, 183, 541, 546, 775, 964
Sugar Tax, 742
Sugar Town, 436
Sugar Walls, 298, 798
Sugarbush, 250, 560
Sugarcane's Got the Blues, 276
Sugarfoot Rag, 343
Sugarfoot Stomp, 439
Sugartime, 200, 621
Suicide Blonde, 473
Suicide Is Painless (The Theme from Mash), 636
Suitcase Blues, 1029
Suite for Susan Moore and Damian, 423
Suite for the Single Girl, 144
Suite: Judy Blue Eyes, 229
Suite Madame Blue, 959
Suite of English Dances, 30
Suite of Gods, 1025
Suite Thursday, 307
Sultans of Swing, 267
Summer, 682
Summer Breeze, 170, 476
Summer Days (and Summer Nights), 63
Summer Holiday, 831
Summer in Paradise, 64
Summer in the City, 602
Summer Knows, 573
Summer Means Fun, 63, 490
Summer Nights, 326, 721, 1035
Summer of Last Year, 652
Summer of '78, 637
Summer of '69', 7
Summer Set, 86
Summer Side of Life, 585
Summer Teeth, 1007
Summer (The First Time), 389
Summer's Love, 171
Summerlove Sensation, 62
Summertime, 66, 69, 213, 221, 380, 492, 517, 641, 817, *870*, 917

Summertime Blues, 196, 197, 298, 479, 1054
Summertime City, 60
Summertime in England, 695
Summit, The, 912
Sun Ain't Gonna Shine Anymore, The, 177, 1026
Sun Always Shines on TV, The, 11
Sun and Soul, 958
Sun and Steel, 473
Sun Arise, 565
Sun City, 92, 939, 976
Sun Comes Up, It's Tuesday Morning, 223
Sun Explosion, 263
Sun Goddess, 583
Sun Goes Down, The, 579
Sun Has Got Its Hat on, The, 373
Sun Is Burning, The, 1005
Sun Is Shining, 486, 750
Sun Moon and Herbs, The, 271
Sun Sessions, The, 790
Sunburst Finish, 710
Sunday, 921, 958
Sunday and Me, 262, 493
Sunday Bloody Sunday, 220, 576, 1004
Sunday Concert, 585
Sunday Girl, 96
Sunday Kind of Love, 257, 424, 490, 618, 796, 983
Sunday Morning Christian, 458
Sunday Morning Coming Down, 166, 496, 555
Sunday Will Never Be the Same, 634, 636
Sundown, 277, 585
Sunfighter, 494
Sunflower, 1044
Sunforest, 816
Sunlight, 420, 642
Sunny, 327, 422, 438
Sunny Afternoon, 602
Sunny Days Stormy Nights, 851
Sunny Goodge Street, 277
Sunny Honey Girl, 831
Sunny '76, 439
Sunny Side of Life, 99
Sunny Side of the Mountain, 432, 648
Sunny Side of the Street, The, 282
Sunnyvista, 982
Sunrise in Different Dimensions, 961
Sunset and Other Beginnings, 660
Sunset down in Somerset, 319
Sunset Trail, The, 161
Sunshine After the Rain, 122
Sunshine Cake, 230
Sunshine Day, 498, 745
Sunshine, Lollipops and Roses, 394, 417

Sunshine of Your Love, 133, 186, 225
Sunshine of Your Smile, The, 614
Sunshine Superman, 277, 278, 698, 712
Sunshower, 458
Supa Dupa Fly, 308
Super Dude One, 221
Super Freak, 418, 488
Super Kiumba, 263
Super Psychedelics, 1019
Super Session, 97
Super Trouper, 1
Supercalifragilisticexpialidocious, 22
Superfly, 655, *655*
Supergrass, 961
Supernatural, 871
Supernatural Thing (Part 1), 539
Supernova, 771
Superrappin', 396
Supersession, 551
Supersexy Swingin' Sounds, 1048
Supersonic, 730
Superstar, 160, 214, 864, 921
Superstition, 905, 1077
Superstitious, 316
Superstitious Giants, 617
Superunknown, 924
Supper Time, 79
Supper's Ready, 377
Suppertime, 247
Supply and Demand, 113, 1043
Supposed Former Infatuation Junkie, 693
Supremes Sing Rodgers and Hart, The, 428
Sur La Mer, 689
Sur Ma Vie, 41
Surabaya Johnny, 1043
Sure as I'm Sitting Here, 444
Surely God Is Able, 1030
Surf City, 63, 490, *490*
Surf City and Other Swinging Cities, 490
Surf's Up, 63, 755
Surfer Girl, 63
Surfer Rosa, 778
Surfin', 63
Surfin' Craze, 911
Surfin' on a New Wave, 134
Surfin' Safari, 63
Surfin' U.S.A., 63, 82, 982
Surfing with the Alien, 872
Surfing with The Ventures, 1019
Surprisingly Cilla, 89
Surrealistic Pillow, 494
Surrender, 32, *175,* 783
Surrender to Jonathan, 833
Surrender to the Air, 773
Surrey with the Fringe on Top, 264, 485, 844, 851

Survival, 644
Survival of the Fittest, 727
Survivor, 24, 638
Survivors, The, 166
Susan's House, 303
Susana Hoffs, 54
Susannah, 347
Susannah's Still Alive, 543
Sushi, 642
Suspended Belief, 854
Suspending Disbelief, 1041
Suspicion, 783, 827
Suspicious Minds, 335, 438, 497, 789, 940
Sussudio, 205
Sutras, 278, 858
Suzanne, 201
Suzanne Beware of the Devil, 591
Suzie Baby, 1017
Suzie Q, 142, 226, 849
Svengali, 870
Swaller-Tail Coat, 1058
Swallow This Live, 782
Swallowed, 142
Swamp Grass, 530
Swamp Thing, 624
Swanee, 379, 510
Swanee River, 863
Swanee River Boogie, 20
Swastika Eyes, 797
Sway, 732, 864
Swayin' to the Music (Slow Dancin'), 836
Swear to God Your Honor, 970
Sweat, 550
Sweat'N'Soul – The Anthology, 870
Sweatbox, 850
Swedish Rhapsody, 639
Sweet Adeline, 140, 706
Sweet America, 868
Sweet and Dandy, 987
Sweet and Innocent, 746
Sweet and Low, 704
Sweet and Sour Tears, 174
Sweet Angeline, 700
Sweet Baby, 190, 287
Sweet Baby James, 970, 971
Sweet Bitter Love, 100
Sweet Blindness, 728
Sweet Bunch of Daisies, 969
Sweet Caroline, 262
Sweet Child, 765
Sweet Child o' Mine, 407
Sweet Cocaine, 710
Sweet Deceiver, 919
Sweet Dream, 498
Sweet Dreams, 317, *317,* 382, 425, 618, 638
Sweet Emotion, 9
Sweet Evil, 615
Sweet Forgiveness, 814
Sweet Freedom, 279, *1009*

Sweet Gene Vincent, 290, 1022
Sweet Georgia Brown, 713, 734
Sweet Harmony, 509, 704
Sweet Hitch-Hiker, 226
Sweet Home Alabama, 608, 1088
Sweet Home Chicago, 509, 941
Sweet Illusion, 644
Sweet Inspiration, 355, 458
Sweet Jane, 222, 622, 1018
Sweet Jenny Lee, 130
Sweet Kitty Wells, 535
Sweet Little Angel, 538
Sweet Little Rock and Roller, 675, 896
Sweet Little Sixteen, 63, 81, 82, 581
Sweet Lorraine, 1041
Sweet Love, 49, 208, 832
Sweet Mama Hurry Home, 820
Sweet Mary, 999
Sweet Memories, 718, *718*
Sweet Music, 896
Sweet Nothin's, 571
Sweet Oblivion, 877
Sweet Old World, 1062
Sweet Passion, 355
Sweet Pea, 846
Sweet Potato Pie, 224
Sweet Potatoes, 704
Sweet Rain, 216, 381
Sweet Revenge, 718, 799
Sweet Seasons, 540
Sweet Sixteen, 468, 538
Sweet Soul Music, *332*, 821, 947
Sweet Sue, 822, 1089
Sweet Sugar Lips, 523
Sweet Surrender, 623
Sweet Talker, 982
Sweet Talkin' Guy, 182
Sweet Tears, 651
Sweet Temptation, *907*, 992
Sweet Thing, 95, 532, 1035
Sweet Things, 533
Sweet Time, 827
Sweet Violets, 688
Sweet Water Jones, 637
Sweet Woman Like You, A, 978
Sweetback, 866
Sweeter Than the Flowers, 704
Sweetest Gift, The, 520
Sweetest Girl, 630
Sweetest One, 226
Sweetest Smile, 86
Sweetest Taboo, The, 866
Sweetest Thing, The, 1005
Sweetheart of Sigma Chi, 1031
Sweetheart of the Rodeo, 74, 146, 147, 724, 756
Sweetheart Time, 276
Sweethearts of the Blues, 895
Sweethearts on Parade, 28, 597
Sweetnighter, 1039

Sweets for My Sweet, 285, 430, 783, 878
Sweets from a Stranger, 936
Swept Away, 413, 855
Swimming Song, 1024
Swing, 473, 636
Swing Along with Me, 904
Swing and Turn Jubilee, 443
Swing Blues No. 1, 1068
Swing Easy, 904
Swing Is Here, 555
Swing Mr Charlie, 371
Swing of Delight, The, 871
Swing Street, 533, 637
Swing the Mood, 501
Swing Time Cowgirl, 687
Swing to Bop, 184
Swing to the Right, 860
Swingin on a Star, 1012
Swingin' Low, 659
Swingin' Sweethearts, 392
Swinging Best of, The, 33
Swinging Doors, 142
Swinging Down the Lane, 513
Swinging on a Star, 230, 1012, 1056
Swinging School, 864
Swinging Shepherd Blues, 337, 437
Swiss Cottage Manoeuvres, 947
Swiss Maid, 889
Switched on, 944, 945
Swoon, 788
Swordfishtrombones, 1025
Swords, 572
Sylvia, 627, 1020
Sylvia's Mother, 270, 271, 896
Sylvie, 867
Sympathy, 511
Sympathy for the Devil, 407, 796, 849
Symphonic Fusions, 242
Symphonic Music of Yes, The, 1085
Symphony, 241
Symphony in One Movement, 480
Symphony Sessions, 346
Synaesthesia, 782
Synchro System, 8
Synchronicity, 782
Synchronicity II, 782
Syncopated Musical Show Made in America, A, 79
Synkronized, 490
SYR 4: Goodbye 20th Century, 921
Systems of Romance, 1006

T for Trombone, 972
T-Bird Rhythm, 603
T-Bone Blues, 1028
T-Bone Shuffle, 1028

T-Shirt, 228, 1024
Ta-Ra-Ra-Boom Der-E, 930
Tadpoles, 105
Tahiti, 314
Tail Gunner, 620
Tails, 595
Tailspinnin', 1039
Tain't Nobody's Business, 1074
Tain't What You Do (It's the Way That You Do It), 1040
Tainted Love, 16, 349, 800
Taj, 966
Taj Mahal, 966
Take a Bow, 44
Take a Giant Step, 966
Take a Little Walk with Me, 509, 862
Take a Look, 202, 579
Take a Message to Mary, 134
Take a Pair of Sparkling Eyes, 382
Take Another Step Closer, 847
Take Care of Your Homework, 971
Take Five, 133, 1035
Take Good Care of My Baby, 540, 545, 1016, 1017, 1023
Take Good Care of Yourself, 56
Take Heart, 329
Take It as It Comes, 815
Take It Easy, 132, 295
Take It Easy Chicken, 639
Take It Easy on Me, 590
Take It from Me, 141
Take It Home, 234, 538, 822
Take It Like a Man, 406
Take It Off, 251, *845*
Take It on the Run, 827
Take It to the Limit, 295, 487
Take Love Easy, 337
Take Me Back, 587
Take Me Back to Tulsa, 261, 835
Take Me Bak 'Ome, 910
Take Me for a Little While, 558, 970, 1014
Take Me for What I'm Worth, 879
Take Me Girl, I'm Ready, 121, 1028
Take Me Higher, 856, 1026
Take Me Home, *75*, 177
Take Me Home Country Roads, 258, 721
Take Me I'm Yours, 935
Take Me in the Lifeboat, 632
Take Me in Your Arms and Hold Me, 825
Take Me in Your Arms and Love Me, 548
Take Me in Your Arms and Rock Me, 878
Take Me in Your Arms (Rock Me), 279

Take Me Now, 119
Take Me Out to the Ball Game, 706, 1023
Take Me to the Limit, 160
Take Me to the River, 402, 680, 967
Take Me to Your Heart, 951
Take Me to Your Heart Again, 604
Take My Breath Away, 693
Take My Love, 504
Take No Prisoners, 682
Take Off, 861
Take Off Your Uniform, 444
Take on Me, 11
Take on the World, 519
Take One, 684, 947
Take out Some Insurance, 823
Take That and Party, 1064
Take That Situation, 443
Take That to the Bank, 886
Take the A Train, 152, 307
Take the Long Way Home, 962
Take the Message Everywhere, 232
Take These Chains from My Heart, 855
Take This Job and Shove It, 199
Take Time to Know Her, 910
Take Your Memory with You, 383
Taken by Force, 875
Taker, The, 496
Takin' Off, 420
Taking a Chance on Love, 288, 391
Taking Care of Business, 98, 406
Taking My Time, 618, 814
Taking Off, 870
Taking Tiger Mountain (by Strategy), 311
Taking Your Shoes Off, 224
Tales for Beginners, 229
Tales from the Vienna Woods, 897
Tales from Topographic Oceans, 1084
Tales of Brave Ulysses, 225
Tales of Kidd Funkadelic, 194
Tales of Mystery and Imagination, 756
Tales of the Great Rum Runners, 400
Talk, 1085
Talk Back Trembling Lips, 985
Talk Dirty to Me, 781
Talk Is Cheap, 558, 850
Talk Memphis, 1071
Talk of the Town, 791
Talk on Corners, 217
Talk to Me, 342, 384, 504
Talk to the Animals, 719
Talk to You Later, 989

Talk to Your Heart, 794
Talkin' 'Bout a Revolution, 172
Talkin' About You, 173
Talkin' All That Jazz, 265, 945
Talkin' Blues, 644
Talking Back to the Night, 1073
Talking Book, 1077
Talking from the Box, 851
Talking Heads 77, 967
Talking in Your Sleep, 136, 375, 403
Talking Loud and Clear, 742
Talking Loud and Saying Nothing, 128
Talking New York, 291
Talking Timbuktu, 212
Talking to the Man in the Moon, 178
Talking Vietnam Blues, 733
Talking with the Taxman About Poetry, 116
Tall Dark Stranger, 748
Tallahassie Lassie, 154, 941
Tallest Trees, 206
Tallyman, 70
Tam Lin, 591
Tam Tam pour l'Afrique, 263
Tam Tam pour l'Ethiopie, 377, 989
Tame Yourself, 791
Taming the Tiger, 679
Tammy, 19, 829
Tampico, 529
Tana Mana, 889
Tangents, 1973–1983, 968
Tangerine, 280, 569, 663, 873
Tangled, 443
Tangled Mind, 239
Tangled Up in Blue, 293
Tango, 469, 628, *841*
Tango della Gelosia, 353
Tango in the Night, 342
Tango Palace, 783
Tango Rave Mix, 775
Tango: Zero Hour, 775
Tangram, 968
Tantamount to Treason Vol. 1, 685
Tao, 934
Tap Turns on the Water, 553, 698
Tape from California, 349, 733
Tapestry, 9, 342, 539, 540, 625, 894
Tapestry Revisited, 540
Tapo Mago, 153
Tar Beach, 603
Tarantula, 834
Tarka, 377
Tarkus, 309
Tarot Suite, 60
Tart's Song, 435
Taste in Men, 779
Taste of Bitter Love, 549

Taste of Chocolate, 84
Taste of Honey, A, 17, 863
Taste of Yesterday's Wine, A, 411
Taster, 498
Tattle Tale Tears, 1086
Tattoo, 199
Tattoo You, 849
Tattooed Millionaire, 474
Tattva, 556
Taxes on the Farmer Feeds Us All, 212
Taxi, 171, 172, *334*, *800*
Taxi Driver, 443
Taxloss, 639
T. B. Blues, 932
Tchaikovsky, 380, 525, 1043
Tea for the Tillerman, 946
Tea for Two, 399, 734, 822, 1086
Tea for Two Cha Cha, 282
Teach Me Tonight, 372
Teach You to Rock, 752
Teacher Don't Teach Me Nonsense, 557
Tear Down These Walls, 732
Tear Fell, A, 120
Tear It Up, 139
Tear Me Apart, 997
Tear Off, 113
Tear the Roof off the Sucker (Give up the Funk), 194
Teardrop, 332, 650
Teardrops, 563, 947, 1076
Teardrops Falling in the Snow, 735
Teardrops from My Eyes, 283
Teardrops on Your Letter, 51
Teardrops Will Fall, 212
Tearing My Soul Apart, 354
Tears, 357, 806
Tears Are Not Enough, 2, 7, 377, 433
Tears at the Grand Ole Opry, 482
Tears from My Eyes, 131
Tears in Heaven, 186, 187
Tears of a Clown, 335, 840, 841, 928
Tears of Rage, 53
Tears of Stone, 182
Tears on My Pillow, 587, 621, 677, 708, 855, 985
Tears Roll Down, 972
Teaser and the Firecat, 946
Teases and Dares, 1055
Teasing, 1023
Technique, 716
Technobush, 649
Technodon, 869
Teddy Bear Duke and Psycho, 438
Teddy Bears' Picnic, 414, 528
Teen Commandments, The, 708
Teenage Angst, 779
Teenage Boogie, 776

Teenage Dream, 101
Teenage Kicks, 889, 890
Teenage Meeting, 217
Teenage Rampage, 964
Teenage Warning, 887
Teenager in Love, 265, 348, 783, 1056
Teenager of the Year, 779
Teenager Sings the Blues, A, 708
Teenager's Mother, 412
Teenager's Prayer, 711, 899
Tejas, 1094
Telecasting, 324
Telefone (Long Distance Love Affair), 298
Telegram, 86
Telegram Sam, 101
Telephone Line, 304
Television, 272
Television Eye, 654
Tell 'Em About Me, 1082
Tell 'Em I'm Surfin', 911
Tell Her No, 1093
Tell Him I'm Not Home, 257
Tell It Like It Is, 436, 714
Tell Laura I Love Her, 404, 460, 769
Tell Mama, 487
Tell Me a Story, 468, 560
Tell Me Darling, 303
Tell Me on a Sunday, 593
Tell Me Pretty Maiden, 203, 957
Tell Me So, 743
Tell Me Something, 327, 695
Tell Me Something Good, 532
Tell Me the Truth, 561
Tell Me When, 461, 611, 823
Tell Me Why, 265, 336, 347, 520, 520, 1022, 1072
Tell the Truth, 338, 821
Tell Tommy I Miss Him, 769
Tell Us the Truth, 887
Tellin' Stories, 172, 173
Telling Lies, 112
Telling Me Lies, 982
Telstar, 534, 658, 659, 742, 987, 988
Telstar, The Original Sixties Hits of The Tornados, 988
Temma Harbour, 454
Temper Temper, 389
Temperamental, 321
Temple of Love, 436
Temple of Low Men, 233
Temporary Music, 565
Temps, Les, 657
Temps Mort, 657
Temptation, 108, 130, 209, 230, 320, 359, 438, 716, 936, 1025, 1047
Tempted, 936
Tempted and Tried, 942
10, 956, 1047

Ten, 762
Ten Cents a Dance, 158, 315, 428
Ten Commandments of Love, 363, 587, 643, 799
Ten Days in Prison, 196
10 Days on Broadway, 959
Ten Feet Tall and Bulletproof, 994
Ten Good Reasons, 278
Ten Little Bottles, 103
Ten Man Mop, 942
10,9,8,7,6,5,4,3,2,1, 668
Ten Out of Ten, 976
Ten Rapid, 682
10 Song Demo, 167
Ten Summoner's Tales, 950
Ten to One It's Murder, 669
Ten Years Are Gone, 654
10CC, 976
Tend the Fire, 616
Tender, 100
Tender Is the Night, 304
Tender Lover, 44
Tender Prey, 168
Tender Trap, The, 1012
Tenderly, 77, 522
Tenderness, 492, 736, 990
Tenderness Junction, 361
Tenement Symphonies, 17
Tenement Symphony, The, 648
Tennessee, 30
Tennessee Blues, 173
Tennessee Border, 412
Tennessee Firebird, 141
Tennessee Flat Top Box, 166
Tennessee River, 12
Tennessee Saturday Night, 343
Tennessee Stud, 285
Tennessee Waltz, 215, 542, 750, 751, 760, 804
Tennessee Woman, 997
Tennessee's Not the State I'm in, 309
Tennis, 819
Tenor Giants, 1041
Tenor Madness, 851
Tenor Saxophone, 339
Tent of Miracles, 932
Tequila, 170
Tequila Sunrise, 295
Terence Trent D'Arby's Symphony or Damn Exploring: The Tension Inside the Sweetness, 243
Terminal Jive, 927
Terminator, 388
Terrapin Station, 401
Terrible Operation Blues, 281
Terror Twilight, 760
Terry Hall, the Collection, 928
Terry Waite Says, 327
Tessa's Torch Song, 48
Tessie (You Are the Only, Only), 706

Test for Echo, 861
Testify (I Wanna), 971
Tetris, 593
T.E.V.I.N., 1026
Texarcana, 827
Texas 1947, 746
Texas Cannonball, 541
Texas Clover, 1015
Texas Fever, 110
Texas Flood, 1016
Texas Folk Songs, 597
Texas Gold, 33
Texas Me, 866
Texas – 1947, 1027
Texas Rock for Country Rollers, 658, 867
Texas Sharecropper and Songster, 587
Texas Songster Volume 2, 587
Texas Swing, 126
Texas Tornado, 867
Texas Tornados, 332, 500
Texas Trilogy, 602
Texas Twister, 216
Texas (When I Die), 997
Tex-Mex Breakdown, 500
Thank God I'm a Country Boy, 258
Thank Heaven for Little Girls, 180, 578
Thank U, 693
Thank You, 20, 289
Thank You (Falettin Me Be Mice Elf Again), 954
Thank You for Being a Friend, 853
Thank You Pretty Baby, 78
Thanks a Lot, 996
Thanks a Million, 522
Thanks for Ev'rything, 890
Thanks for Nothing, 130
Thanks for Saving My Life, 759
Thanks for the Memory, 839
Thanks I'll Eat It Here, 588
That Ain't Love, 827
That Black Snake Moan, 495
That Chick's Too Young to Fry, 303
That Crazy Feeling, 846
That Did It, 94
That Doggie in the Window, 751
That Don't Impress Me Much, 1000
That Feel, 1025
That Girl, 1077
That Girl Belongs to Yesterday, 778
That Girl Could Sing, 132
That Heart Belongs to Me, 776
That Lady, 476
That Lady (Part 1), 476
That Larry Williams, 1062

That Lovin' You Feelin' Again, 425, 741
That Loving Rag, 996
That Lucky Old Sun, 560
That Mesmerizing Mendelssohn Tune, 78
That Old Black Magic, 26, 241, 249, 663, 795, 796, 864
That Old Fashioned Mother of Mine, 1078
That Old Feeling, 323
That Old Gang of Mine, 260
That Old Sweet Feeling, 737
That Ole Devil Called Love, 703
That Same Old Feeling, 610
That Silver Haired Daddy of Mine, 38, 872
That Someone Must Be You, 605
That Song About the Midway, 678, 1013
That Sounds Good to Me, 501
That Summer, 123
That Thing Called Love, 115
That Was Then but This Is Now, 2
That Was Then, This Is Now, 685, 869, 976
That Was Your Mother, 176
That What Is Not, 884
That'll Be the Day, 65, 67, 450, 451, 770, 854, 878
That'll Work, 82
That's All, 378
That's All Right, 179, 233, 837
That's All Right Mama, 788
That's Amore, 646, 1033
That's a-Plenty, 1057
That's Entertainment, 359, 874
That's for Me, 936
That's How Love Is, 457
That's How Strong My Love Is, 1079
That's It, 907
That's Just the Way It Is, 205
That's Life, *887*, 904
That's Mister Landlord, 30
That's My Desire, 85, 559
That's My Home, 86
That's My Little Susie, 1010
That's My Story, 452
That's Right, 77
That's Rock'n'Roll, 167
That's the Bag I'm in, 710
That's the Stuff You Gotta Watch, 505
That's the Way, 569
That's the Way God Planned It, 790
That's the Way I Always Heard It Should Be, 898
That's the Way I Feel About 'Cha', 1076

That's the Way I Feel Now, 684, 1067
That's the Way I Like It, 526
That's the Way I Wanna Rock'n'Roll, 5
That's the Way I Want Our Love, 899
That's the Way It Should Be, 107
That's the Way Love Goes, 479
That's the Way Love Is, 976
That's the Way of the World, 297
That's What Friends Are for, 45, 1033, 1064
That's What Girls Are Made for, 931
That's What I Like, 175, 501
That's What I Like About the South, 426, 1068
That's What It's Like to Be Lonesome, 21
That's What Life Is All About, 823
That's What Love Is All About, 102
That's What Love Will Do, 129
That's What Mama Say, 470
That's What the Good Book Says, 196
That's What Time It Is, 1038
That's What You Think, 734
That's When I Cried, 514
That's Why I'm Here, 971
Theatre of Pain, 698
Their Greatest Hits, 457
Their Satanic Majesties' Request, 849
Them Changes, 669
Them Update Blues, 362
Theme for Young Lovers, 885
Theme from 'A Summer Place', 325, 578
Theme from Cleopatra Jones, 899
Theme from Close Encounters of the Third Kind, The, 1061
Theme from Harry's Game, 311
Theme from Here to Eternity, 693
Theme from New York, New York, 904
Theme from Picnic, The, 621
Theme from S'Express, 1052
Theme from Shaft, 434
Theme from Skint (See You Later Liquidator), 912
Theme from the Apartment, 1065
Theme from 'The Deer Hunter' (Cavatina), 886
Theme from the High and the Mighty, The, 61
Theme from the Third Man, 1072, 1089

Theme from the Threepenny Opera, The, 1044
Theme from the Umbrellas of Cherbourg, 326
Theme to Love Story, The, 640
Theme to Staccato, 80
Themeninblack, 956
Themes, 1014
Themes and Dreams, 886
Then and Now, 685, 1037
Then Came the Last Days of May, 98
Then Came You, 74, *812*, 931, *1033*
Then He Kissed Me, 235, 404, 724, 929
Then Play on, 341
Then There Were Three, 378
Then Who Am I, 356
Therapy, 1024
There Ain't No Good Chain Gang, 497
There Ain't No Umbopo, 975
There and Back, 70
There Are Bad Times Just Around the Corner, 222
There Are Such Things, 282, 936
There But for Fortune, 47, 733
There But for the Grace of God, 533
There Comes a Time, 318
There Goes My Baby, 285, 539, 574, 855, 960
There Goes My Everything, 356, 462, 790
There Goes My First Love, 285
There Goes Rhymin' Simon, 899, 990
There Goes That Song Again, 958
There Goes the Neighborhood, 295
There I've Said It Again, 687, 1022
There Is, 256, 256
There Is a Ghost in the House, 326
There Is a Love, 704
There Is a Mountain, 277
There Is a Tavern in the Town, 1011
There Is Always One More Time, 538
There Is No Greater Love, 513
There Is No One What Will Take Care of You, 738
There Is Nothing Left to Lose, 723
There Is Nothing Like a Dame, 844
There Is Power in the Union, 445
There Is Something on Your Mind, 840, 915
There Must Be a Better World Somewhere, 783
There Must Be a Way, 1015
There Must Be an Angel, 317

There She Goes, 564
There Stands the Glass, 776
(There Was a) Tall Oak Tree, 139
There Will Never Be Another
You, 688, 828
There'll Be a Hot Time in the
Old Town Tonight, 162
There'll Be Sad Songs, 732
There'll Be Some Changes Made,
210
There'll Come a Time, 319
There'll Never Be Another You,
1087
There's a Bond Between Us, 103,
133
There's a Boy Down the Chip
Shop Swears He's Elvis, 614
There's a Heartache Following
Me, 1054
There's a Honky Tonk Angel,
1000
There's a Kind of Hush, 442, 611,
823
There's a Light Beyond These
Woods, 404
There's a Little Lane Without a
Turning (On the Way to
Home Sweet Home), 140
There's a New Moon Over My
Shoulder, 835
There's a New Star up in Heaven
(Baby Lindy Is up There), 670
There's a New World, 528
There's a Pawnshop on a Corner
in Pittsburgh, Pennsylvania,
664
There's a Poison Going on, 803
There's a Riot Goin' on, 196, 798,
954, 1076
There's a Small Hotel, 428
There's a Star-Spangled Banner
Waving Somewhere, 121, 670
There's Always Something There
to Remind Me, 891, 958
There's Always Tomorrow, 135
There's More to Love, 208
There's No Business Like Show
Business, 78, 79, 463, 664
There's No Easy Way, 514
There's No Other (Like My
Baby), 235, 929
There's No Other Way, 99
There's No Place Like America
Today, 655
There's No Stopping Your Heart,
747
There's No Sunshine Anymore,
879
There's No Way, 12
There's Nothing Better Than
Love, 1013
There's Only One of You, 348

There's Something About a Sol-
dier, 373
There's Something Wrong with
You, 433
There's the Rub, 1074
These Are My Songs, 91
These Are Not My People, 925
These Are Special Times, 267
These Are the Things That Make
Me Know You're Gone, 969
These Arms of Mine, 820
These Blues, 126
These Boots Are Made for
Walkin', 436, 904
These Days, 102, 652
These Dreams, 436, 437
These Eyes, 406
These Foolish Things, 333
These Things Too, 816
They All Laughed, 34, 379
They Call Me the Fat Man, 275
They Call the Wind Maria, 542,
578
They Call the Wind Mariah, 156
They Can't Take That Away from
Me, 34, 379, 380
They Dance Alone (Gueca Solo),
950
They Didn't Believe Me, 529
They Don't Dance Like Carmen
No More, 137, 677
They Don't Know, 902
They Don't Make 'Em like They
Used to, 847
They Just Can't Stop It, 925, 931
They Martyr Mantras, 236
They Never Came Home, 690
They Only Come Out at Night,
1071
They Play She Sings, 249
They Said It Couldn't Be Done,
397
They Say It's Wonderful, 664
They Took the Stars out of
Heaven, 984
They're Either Too Young or
Too Old, 874
They're Gonna Tear Down the
Grand Ole Opry, 429
Thick as a Brick, 498
Thicker Plot, A, 369
Thief in the Night, 287
Thieves Like Us, 716
Thieving Magpie (La Gazza
Ladra), The, 642
Thigh High, 314
Thin Wall, The, 1006
Thing, The, 426
Thing Called Love, 814
Things, 244
Things Ain't What They Used to
Be, 1003

Things Can Only Get Better, 513
Things I Used to Do, The, 173,
860
Things That I Used to Do, The,
406, 1082
Things That Make You Go
Hmmm, 149
Things We Do for Love, The,
976, 976
Things We Said Last Summer,
The, 903
Think, 127, 338, 355
Think About Love, 758
Think About That, 591
Think About Your Children, 454,
456
Think It Over, 451
Think of Laura, 231
Think of One, 645
Think of What You've Done, 343
Think Tank, 851
Think Twice, 266
Think Visual, 544
Thinking About Little Willie John
and a Few Nice Things, 504
Thinking of Woody Guthrie, 616
Thinking of You, 336, 596
Third, 919
Third Album, The, 113
Third Decade, The, 31
Third Degree, 101, 1071
3rd Down, 110 to Go, 1070
Third Face of Fame, 327
Third Man, The, 53
Third Rate Romance, 18, 773,
1070
Third Reich 'n' Roll, 261
Third Stage, 109
Third Time Lucky (First Time I
Was a Fool), 343
Third World Warrior, 555, 964
Thirsty Work, 941
13, 100, 304, 426
Thirteen, 973
Thirteen and Good, 106
Thirteenth Dream, The, 932
30th Anniversary Anthology, 801
Thirty Days, 81
30 Pieces of Silver, 692
30 Seconds Over Winterland, 494
30 Seconds to Midnight, 913
30 Something, 163
30 Years of Maximum R&B, 1055
35th and Dearborn, 1082
35th Anniversary Collection, The,
841
33 1/3, 427
32–20 Blues, 488
This Ain't a Love Song, 102
This Beach Is Mine, 398
This Charming Man, 917
This Christmas, 558

This Close to You, 1013
This Could Be Magic, 389
This Day and Age, 1009
This Diamond Ring, 373, 863
This Flight Tonight, 709
This Girl Is a Woman Now, 804
This Girl's in Love with You, 1033
This Golden Ring, 403, 551
This Guy's in Love with You, 17, 45
This Heart of Mine, 359, 1051
This Here, 8
This Is a Call, 723
This Is a Lovely Way to Spend an Evening, 622
This Is Always, 372
This Is Another Day, 232
This Is Big Audio Dynamite, 191
This Is Christmas, 1013
This Is Hardcore, 805
This Is It, 404, 450, 581, 596
This Is Just a Modern Rock Song, 75
This Is Me, 993, 1010
This Is My Night, 532
This Is My Song, 189, 393, 1051
This Is My Truth: Tell Me Yours, 637
This Is My Year for Mexico, 375
This Is Not a Love Song, 884
This Is Not America, 666
This Is Our Music, 202
This Is the Army, Mr Jones, 79
This Is the Modern World, 484
This Is the Place, 540
This Is the Right Time, 938
This Is the Sea, 1035
This Is the Thanks I Get, 607
This Is the Time – The Christmas Album, 102
This Is the World Calling, 377
This Is This, 1039
This Is Tim Hardin, 423
This Is Tomorrow, 333
This Is What You Want, This Is What You Get, 884
This Is Why I Love You So, 393
This Is Your Bloody Valentine, 707
This Is Your Night, 971
This Land Is Your Land, 79, 407, 408, 934
This Last Night in Sodom, 16
This Little Bird, 326
This Little Girl, 104
This Little Girl of Mine, 1030
This Little Girl's Gone Rockin', 131
This Little Light of Mine, 1030
This Magic Moment, 285, 493, 783
This Masquerade, 77, 864
This May Be the Last Time, 938

This Mess We're in, 429
This Nation's Saving Grace, 326
This Note's for You, 1088
This Note's for You, 1088
This Old Heart of Mine, 449, 476, 950
This Old House, 921
This Ole House, 195, 947
This One's for the Children, 715
This Should Go on Forever, 658, 671
This Side of Paradise, 161
This Side of the Big River, 970
This Silver Ring, 812
This Strange Engine, 642
This Thing Called Love, 740, 1043
This Time, 7, 118, 236, 492, 660, 1085
This Time Around, 421
This Time I Know It's for Real, 951, 961
This Town Ain't Big Enough for the Both of Us, 927
This Was, 498
This Way, 862
This Way My Way, 705
This Wheel's on Fire, 37, 53, 292, 905
This Whole World, 63
This Will Be, 202
This Woman, 746, 847
This Woman's Work, 143
This Year's Model, 219
Thomas the Rhymer, 942
Thoroughbred, 540
Those Lazy-Hazy-Crazy Days of Summer, 202
Those Lonely Lonely Nights, 1038
Those Pleasant Days, 405
Those Were the Days, 225, 453, 454
Those Who Are About to Die Salute You, 205
Thou Shalt Not Steal, 319, 357, 599
Thou Swell, 428
Thought I'd Died and Gone to Heaven, 7
Thoughts and Words, 147
$1000 Wedding, 757
Thousand Leaves, A, 921
Thousand Miles Away, A, 892
Thousand Miles from Nowhere, A, 1086
Thousand Roads, 229
Thousand Shadows, 880
Thousand Stars, A, 364, 688
Thousand Trees, A, 945
Thrak, 536
THRaKaTTaK, 536
Thread the Needle, 163
3AM Eternal, 548
Three Bells, 36, 132, 763, 773, 784

Three Car Garage: The Independent Recordings '95–'96, 421
Three Coins in the Fountain, 347, 958
3 Compositions of New Jazz, 118
Three Dog Night Story, The, 984
Three Feet High and Rising, 251, 803, 945
Three Generations of Hank, 1061
Three Giants, 126, 837, 851
Three Girl Rhumba, 304
Three Girls Named Molly Doin' the Hully Gully, 748
Three Hearts in the Happy Ending Machine, 413
360 Degrees, 759
360 (Oh Yeah), 251
Three Imaginary Boys, 237
Three Line Whip, 327
Three Lions, 585
Three Little Fishes, 557, 583, 972
Three Little Maids, 382
Three Little Words, 523
Three Minute Hero, 928
Three New Songs, 973
Three o'Clock Blues, 85, 362, 363, 538
Three o'Clock in the Morning, 522, 1049
Three of a Perfect Pair, 536
Three Piece, 228
III Sides to Every Story, 321
Three Snakes & One Charm, 87
Three Stars, 197, 451, 599
Three Steps from the Altar, 892
Three Steps to a Phone, 458
Three Steps to Heaven, 197, 896
Three Times a Lady, 208, 832
Three Times in Love, 489
3 x 7=21, 58
Three Week Hero, 800
Three Wishes, 935
3 Years, 5 Months and 2 Days in the Life of . . . , 30
3-D, 1081
3/5 of a Mile in Ten Seconds, 494
Threepenny Opera, The, 6
Thresher, The, 733
Thrill Is Gone, The, 85, 260, 538, 539, 713
Thrill of It All, The, 857
Thriller, 46, 437, 481, 514, 560
Throb, 141
Through the Barricades, 926
Through the Hill, 1081
Through the Looking Glass, 905
Through the Storm, 350, 355, 503
Through the Years, 386
Throw Down a Line, 831
Throwin' Down, 488
Throwing Copper, 967
Throwing It All Away, 378

Throwing Rocks at the Moon, 980
Thrust, 420
Thumbelina, 525
Thunder, 289
Thunder and Lightning, 979
Thunder in My Heart, 873
Thunder Island, 932
Thunder on the Run, 405
Thunder Road, 741
Thunder Rolls, The, 123
Thunderball, 2
Thunderbox, 912
Thunderbyrd, 147
Thunderer, The, 924
Thunderstruck, 5
Thursday Afternoon, 311
Tickeration, 152
Ticket to Ride, 160
Tickle Me, 422
Tide Is High, The, 96, 451, 452
Tie a Yellow Ribbon Round the
   Old Oak Tree, 743
Tied to the 90s, 992
Tiempos, 92
Tierra Gitana, 384
Tiffany Transcriptions, The, 1068
Tiger, 322
Tiger Bay, 867
Tiger Feet, 183, 698
Tiger Rag, 306, 399, 562, 674, 742,
   969, 1036, 1038
Tiger Rose, 400
Tigermilk, 75
Tigers Will Survive, 652, 653
Tight Rope, 864
Tighter, Tighter, 489
Tijuana Jail, The, 542
Tijuana Moods, 676
Tikniver I Hjertet, 11
'Til I Can Make It on My Own,
   1080
('Til) I Kissed You, 320
'Til the Rivers All Run Dry, 1058
'Til Things Are Brighter, 166
*Til We Outnumber Them . . . The
   Songs of Woody Guthrie*, 408
Till Hell Freezes Over, 296
Till I Gain Control Again, 425
Till I Hear from You, 531
Till I Loved You, 275, 956
Till I Waltz Again with You, 120
Till My Baby Comes Home, 1013
Till the Boys Come Home, 250,
   726
Till the Clouds Roll By, 1075
Till the End of Time, 209
Till the Night Is Gone, 594, 783
*Till the Night Is Gone: A Tribute
   to Doc Pomus*, 272
Till We Meet Again, 1052
Till You Love Me, 618
Till You Say You'll Be Mine, 721

Tim Hardin, 423
Tim Hardin II, 423
Tim Moore's Farm, 454
Time, *160, 304, 668, 756, 832,
   1058*
Time After Time, 248, 344, 566,
   688
Time and a Word, 1084
Time Between, 147, 148
Time Boom X De Devil Dead, 767
Time Changes Everything, 1068
Time Circle, 1968–1973, 932
Time Don't Run out on Me, 540
Time Exposure, 190
Time Fades Away, 1088
Time for Change, 923
Time Has Come Today, 500
Time Has Come, The, 690
Time Honoured Ghosts, 55
Time in a Bottle, 228
Time Incinerator, 922
Time Is on My Side, 812, 849
Time Is the Master, 452
Time Is Tight, 106
Time Is Time, 71
Time Longer Than Rope, 798
Time, Love and Tenderness, *102,
   1031*
Time Loves a Hero, 588
Time Machine, 872, 1025
Time of No Reply, 284
Time of Revelation, A, 1009
Time of the Season, 1093
Time on My Hands, 112
Time Out, 133
Time out for the Burglar, 478
Time out of Mind, *291, 294, 563,
   943, 1035*
Time Passages, 756, 947
Time Passes By, 652
Time Pie, 554
Time Takes Time, 940
Time – The Album, 188
Time to Kill, 53
Time to Move on, *732, 771*
Time Tough, 987
Time Traveller, 689
Time Waits for No One, 939
Time Will Tell, 87, 906
Time Won't Let Me, 817
Timeless, 388, 880, 1023
Timeless (The Classics), 102
Timepiece, 847
Times Like These, 142
Times of Our Lives, 204
Times They Are a-Changin', The,
   291, 292, 292, 294, 431, 897
TimeSpace, 342
Timewind, 968
Timtayshun, 515
Tin Drum, 491
Tin Machine II, 111

Tin Man, 19
Tin Roof Blues, 937
Tinderbox, 905
Ting-a-Ling, 195
Tings and Times, 507
Tiniest Wham, The, 653
Tinseltown to the Boogiedown,
   878
*Tiny Music . . . Songs from the
   Vatican Gift Shop*, 953
Tipitina, 802
Tipperary, 528
Tippler's Tales, 324
Tips, 21
Tips of My Fingers, 21, 189
Tiptoe Through the Tulips with
   Me, 1032
Tired, 48
Tired of Being Alone, 402, 679
Tired of Toein' the Line, 139
Tired of Waiting for You, 543,
   1086
'Tis a Story That Shall Live For-
   ever, 545
'Tis Sweet to Be Remembered,
   1073
Tishomingo Blues, 447
Tisket a Tasket, A, 336
Tit-Willow, 230, 382
Tivoli Melody, 1044
TNT, *4, 822, 988, 997*
To a Sleeping Beauty, 252
To All the Girls I've Loved
   Before, 469, 712
To Be Continued, 434, 975
To Be in Love, 651
To Be Loved, 1069
To Bring You My Love, 429
To Cut a Long Story Short, 926
To Each His Own, 472, 648
To Have, to Hold and to Let Go,
   925
To Kingdom Come, 53
To Know Him Is to Love Him,
   712, 758, 929, 942, 1023
To Know You Is to Love You,
   538, 853, 1023
To Lefty from Willie, 713
To Live in the Past, 655
To Love Somebody, 71, 102, 160,
   209, 901
To Make Me Who I Am, 854
To My First Love, 250
*To Our Children's Children's
   Children*, 689
To Ramona, 292
To See My Angel Cry, 1000
To Sir with Love, 604
To the Aisle, 338
To the Bone, 544, 555
To the Door of the Sun (Alla
   Porte del Sol), 649

To the End, 100
To the Limit, 27
To the Other Man, 471
To the Power of Three, 310
To the Top, 35
To Venus and Back, 20
To You I Belong, 83
Toad, 225
Toast, 1089
Tobacco Road, 23, 599, 698, 818
Tobermory, 566
Toccata, 909
Today, 621, 846, 913
Today and Now, 431
Today I Met the Boy I'm Going
  to Marry, 404, 601, 929
Today I Sing the Blues, 355
Today I Started Loving You
  Again, 226, 410, 411, 426
Today's Specials, 929
Today's Themes for Young Lovers,
  325
Toes Across the Floor, 95
Together, 218, 299, 353, 472, 616,
  800, 906, 1071
Together After Five, 658, 866
Together Again, 129, 479, 538
Together Again . . . Live, 94
Together Alone, 233
Together At Last, 192, 565
Together for the First Time . . .
  Live, 94, 538
Together Forever, 951
Together Forever – Greatest Hits
  83–98, 859
Together in Concert, 881
Together in Electric Dreams, 461,
  693
Together with Cliff Richard, 831
Togethering, 1035
Togetherings, 141
Tokoloshe Man, 386
Tokyo Joe, 333
Tokyo Live, 624
Tokyo Rose, 755
Tokyo Tapes, 875
Tom Cat, 244
Tom Cat and Pussy Blues, 247
Tom Cat Blues, 697
Tom Cat Goodbye, 728
Tom Dooley, 277, 542
Tom Lehrer in Concert, 574
Tom Paxton 6, 761
Tom Paxton Storyteller, 761
Tom Rush, 862
Tom Tom Turnaround, 183, 698
Tom Traubert's Blues, 950
Tom's Diner, 1017
Tomb of Memories, 1089
Tommy, 235, 416, 503, 544, 647,
  882, 1054
Tommy Gun, 191

Tommy Makem and Liam Clancy,
  185
Tommy Steele's 20 Greatest Hits,
  942
Tomorrow, 124, 208, 485, 649, 891
Tomorrow Belongs to Me, 709
Tomorrow Comes, 900
Tomorrow Is a Long Time, 465
Tomorrow Never Comes, 103
Tomorrow Night, 507, 850
Tomorrow the Green Grass, 493
Tomorrow Today, 492
Tomorrow's Just Another Day,
  630
Tongue in Chic, 846
Tongue Tied Jill, 331
Tonic for the Troops, A, 376
Tonight, *111*, 81, 336, *350*, 452, 919,
  1065
Tonight at Noon, 676
Tonight I Celebrate My Love, 339
Tonight I Celebrate My Love for
  You, 134
Tonight, I'll Say a Prayer, 567
Tonight I'm Singing Just for You,
  616
Tonight She Comes, 161
Tonight, Tonight, Tonight, 378
Tonight We Love, 646, 647, 648
Tonight's the Night, 139, 182, 894,
  950, *1088*
Tonin', 636
Tons of Sobs, 357
Tony Orlando, 1047
Tony Orlando and the Best of
  Dawn, 744
Too Big, 807
Too Close for Comfort, 567
Too Darn Hot, 785
Too Drunk to Fuck, 252
Too Dumb for New York City –
  Too Ugly for LA, 497
Too Expensive, 459
Too Far Gone, 894
Too Fast for Love, 698
Too Fat Polka, 387
Too Good to Be Forgotten, 180
Too Hot, 285
Too Hot to Handle, 437, *437*
Too Late for Goodbyes, 576
Too Late Now, 964
Too Late to Worry, 261
Too Late Too Soon, 879
Too Legit to Quit, 418
Too Long in Exile, 327, 453, 695
Too Low for Zero, 503
Too Many Broken Hearts, 278,
  951
Too Many Miles from Broadway,
  200
Too Many Parties, Too Many
  Pals, 412

Too Marvellous for Words, 527,
  662, 663, 1052
Too Much, 931
Too Much Lovin', 338
Too Much Monkey Business, 82
Too Much Mustard, 316
Too Much Time on My Hands,
  959
Too Much, Too Little, Too Late,
  651
Too Much Too Soon, 697, 717
Too Much Too Young, 928, 929
Too Nice to Talk to, 335
Too Old to Cut the Mustard, 157
Too Old to Rock'n'Roll, Too
  Young to Die, 499
Too Rye Ay, 261
Too Shy, 289
Too Soon to Know, 741
Too Stuffed to Jump, 18, 1070
Too Tough, 1026
Too Tough to Die, 815
Too Weak to Fight, 163
Too Wicked, 35
Too Wild Too Long, 512
Too Young, 61, 202, 481, 548, 833
Too Young to Die, 867
Took the Last Train, 119
Toot Toot, 531
Toot, Toot, Tootsie! Goodbye,
  510
Toothache Blues, 932
Toots in Memphis, 987
Top, The, 238
Top Drawer, 891
Top Gun, 693
Top of the Pops, 461
Top of the World, 160
Topanga, 662
Tops, 862
Torch, 16, *898*
Tore Up, 130
Torero, 564
Tormato, 1085
Torment and Torreros, 16
Torn Between Two Lovers, 768
Tortoise, 988
Torture, 478
Tossin' and Turnin', 392
Total Devo, 260
Total Eclipse of the Heart, 657,
  1002
Totales Turns, 326
Totally Wired, 326
Toto IV, 989
Tottenham Tottenham, 175
Toucan Do It Too, 18
Touch, 156, *317*
Touch Me, 279, 499
Touch Me in the Morning, 855
Touch More Schmilsson, A, 722
Touch of Gray, 401

Touch of Velvet, A, 825
Touch of Your Hand, The, 422
Touch of Your Lips, The, 725
Touch on the Rainy Side, A, 1071
Touch Sensitive, 484
Touch the Feeling, 144
Touch the Hem of His Garment, 213, 860
Touch the Sky, 540
Touch the World, 298
Touching the Ghost, 314
Tough Love, 936
Tough Times, 1057
Tougher Than Leather, 859
Tougher Than the Rest, 321
Toughest Tenors, 246
Toulouse Street, 278
Tour, The, 95
Tour de France, 554
Tour de La Question, La, 657
Tourism, 856
Toussaint, 990
Tower of Song, 1060
Tower of Strength, 45, 385, 616, 1015
Town Called Malice, 484
Town Hall Concert, 676
Town I Loved So Well, The, 220
Town Where I Was Born, The, 284
Town without Pity, 778
Toxiques, 710
Toy Boy, 951
Toy Theatre Suite, The, 592
Toy Trumpet, The, 876
Toyah! Toyah! Toyah!, 991
Toys in the Attic, 9, 9
TP, 764
Tra La La Days Are Over, The, 880
Trace, 1007
Traces, 37
Track of the Cat, 1033
Tracks, 570, 935
Tracks of Life, 476
Tracks of My Tears, The, 836, 840, 841, 854
Tracy Chapman, 172
Trade Test Transmissions, 145
Tradition, 454
Traditional Tunes of the Child Ballads, The, 183
Traditions Beckoning, 776
Traffic, 945, 1072
Traffic from Paris, 515
Tragedy, 342, 426
Tragic Kingdom, 725
Tragic Romance, 215
Tragic Songs of Life, 600
Trailer Park, 744
Train a Comin', 297
Train and the River, 218
Train in Vain, 191

Train Kept a-Rollin', 116, 139, 946, 1083
Train of Memories, 652
Train of Thought, 11
Train Time, 225
Train to Rhodesia, 85
Train, Train, 608
Trains and Boats and Planes, 45
Trainspotting, 797
Tramaine, 432
Tramp, 248, 362, 869, 980
Tramp on the Street, 629, 735
Tramp Shining, A, 1040
Tramp the Dirt Down, 219
Trampoline, 215
Trance, 153
Trance Visionary, 1074
Traneing in, 206
Trans, 1088
Trans Europe Express, 554, 554
Transblucency, 704
Transcendental Blues, 297
Transcendental Waterfall, 322
Transformation Scene from Dr Jekyll and Mr Hyde, The, 930
Transformed by Time, 598
Transformer, 110, 824
Transformer Man, 1088
Transient Random Noise Bursts with Announcements, 944
Transmissions from the Satellite Heart, 339
Transportation, 1007
Transverse City, 1092
Trapped By a Thing Called Love, 679
Trash, 215, 717, 718, 960
Travel Log, 150
Travel with Your Mind, 880
Travelers & Thieves, 99
Travelin', 489
Travelin' Band, 226
Travelin' in Heavy Traffic, 221
Travelin' Light, 1050
Travelin' Shoes, 388
Traveling Wilburys, The, 305, 427
Travellin' Man, 417, 711, 804
Travelling, 909
Travelling People, The, 614
Travelling Without Moving, 490
Travelogue, 461
Travels, 666, 666
TRB 2, 841, 860
Treacherous, 714
Treason (It's Just a Story), 215
Treasure, 198, 816
Treasure Isle, 908
Treasure of Love, 625
Treasured Hits and Hidden Treasures, 450
Treasures, 758
Treasures Vol. 1, 189

Treat Her Like a Lady, 975
Treat Her Right, 658
Treatise on Cosmic Fire, A, 860
Tree in the Meadow, A, 472, 1051, 1052
Trees, 567
Tremendous Pain, 1084
Tremolo, 707
Trench Town Rock, 643
Tres Hombres, 1094
Trespass, 377
Trespassin', 736
Trial by Fire, 519
Trials and Crosses, 767
Tribe, The, 503
Tribute, 88, 128, 172
Tribute of Roy Rogers, 848
Tribute to a King, 74, 107
Tribute to Blackwell, A, 178
Tribute to Buddy Holly, 174, 451, 659
Tribute to Curtis Mayfield, A, 655
Tribute to Hank Williams, 1060
Tribute to Miles Davis, A, 420
Tribute to Muddy Waters, 1037
Tribute to Stevie Ray Vaughan, A, 814, 1016
Tribute to the Best Damn Fiddle Player in the World (or My Salute to Bob Wills), A, 411, 1068
Tribute to the Music of Bob Wills, 33
Tribute to the Stanley Brothers, 907
Tribute to Tradition, 907, 993, 995, 1086
Tribute to Uncle Ray, A, 1076
Tribute to Willie Dixon, A, 269
Trick Bag, 714
Trick of the Night, A, 52
Trick of the Tail, A, 204, 377
Trick or Treat, 116
Trilogy, 218, 309, 496, 787, 904
Trini Lopez in London, 598
Trini Lopez Live at PJ's, 598
Trini Tracks, 598
Trinity Sessions, The, 222, 223
Trio, 426, 757, 758, 853, 854, 982
Trio 99–00, 666
Trio II, 426, 854
Trio Years, The, 949
Trip Down Sunset Strip, A, 150
Trip to Hyden, 415
Triple Exposure, 609
Tripping the Live Fantastic, 612
Tristan und Isolde, 81
Tristano, 395
Tristesse Durera, La, 636
Triumph, 478
Triumvirate, 97, 272, 419
Trivia, 860

Troggs: Live at Max's Kansas City, The, 995
Trois Cloches, Les, 132, 763, 773
Trojan Souls, 667
Trolley Song, The, 372
Trombonology, 282
Trompe Le Monde, 778
Trooper, The, 474
Tropic Appetites, 95
Tropical Gangsters, 533
Troubadour, 150
Troubilizing, 161
T-R-O-U-B-L-E, 994
Trouble, 1050
Trouble Bound, 192
Trouble in Mind, *587,* 674, 900, 978
Trouble in My Way, 860
Trouble in Paradise, *147, 227, 492, 720*
Trouble Is a Lonesome Town, 436
Trouble Man, 178, 515
Troublemaker, 913
Troubles, Troubles, 862
Trout Mask Replica, 1091
Troy, 733
Truce, 800
Truck Driver Blues, 239, 287
Truck Stop Girl, 587
Trucker's Prayer, 287
Truckin', 400, 975
Truckin' My Blues Away, 362
Trucking Little Woman, 124
Truckload of Lovin', 537
True, 926
True Blue, 631
True Colors, 566
True Colours, 232
True Faith, 716
True for You, 116
True Hearted Girl, A, 164
True Love, *76,* 231, 296, 785, *1059*
True Love Travels on a Gravel Road, 10, 603
True Love Ways, 451, 853
True Religion, 244
True Stories, 966, 967
True Stories and Other Dreams, 204
True to Life, 174
Truganini, 668
Truly, 832
Truly Blessed, 764
Truly Fine Citizen, 680
Truly, Truly Fair, 241
Truly Western Experience, A, 562
Truly Yours, 931
Trumpet Africa, 649
Trumpet Concertos, 645
Trumpet No End, 1063
Trust, 219
Trust in Me, 48, 198

Trust Me, 1076
Trust Your Heart, 204
Truth, 70, 698, 949
Truth and Time, 402
Try, 356
Try a Little Tenderness, 492, 821, 870, 983
Try Anything Once, 756
Try for the Sun, 277
Try It Before You Buy It, 98
Try Me, 60, 127
Try Me I'm Real, 94
Try Some of This, 493
Try Whistling This, 233
Tryin' to Get Heaven, 294
Tryin' to Live My Life without You, 882
Tryin' to Love Two, 74
Trying, 1016
Trying to Get You, 180
Trying to Hold on to My Woman, 449
Trying to Live My Life without You, 679
Trying to Make a Fool of Me, 255
Tu Immenso Amor, 332
Tu-ber-cu-lucas and the Sinus Blues, 915
Tubeway Army, 727
Tubular Bells, *105, 385, 467, 737, 738*
Tubular Bells II, 455, 738
Tubular Bells III, 738
Tucker – the Man and his Dream, 480
Tuesday Night Music Club, 232
Tuff Enough, 526
Tuff Enuff, 302
Tug of War, 611, 647, 976
Tula Ndivile, 633
Tulane, 82
Tulips from Amsterdam, 146
Tulsa Time, 1058
Tumbleweed Connection, 5, 503
Tumbling Dice, 849, 854
Tumbling Tumbleweeds, 39, 230, 848, 921, 1016
Tune in Tomorrow, 645
Tunic (Song for Karen), 921
Tunnel of Love, 928, *935*
Tupelo, 168
Tupelo Honey, 695
Tupelo Mississippi Flash, 822
Turbo, 519
Turbulence, 1085
Turbulent Indigo, 679
Turkish Tom Toms, 882
Turn Around, 766
Turn Around and Love You, 214
Turn Around Look at Me, 153
Turn Back, 989
Turn Back the Hands of Time, 336

Turn Back Time, 26
Turn It on Again, 378
Turn It Out, 559
Turn It Over, 1066
Turn Me Loose, 322, *501*
Turn of a Friendly Card, The, 756
Turn off the Lights, 764
Turn on Tune in Cop out, 330
Turn on Your Lovelight, 94, 400, 401
Turn the Page, 497
Turn to Red, 534
Turn! Turn! Turn!, 146, *146,* 454, 881
Turn Your Radio on, 99, 946
Turned on (Live in Vienna), 850
Turning Love into Gold, 949
Turning Point, 654, 938
Turnstiles, 502
Turtle Soup, 999
Turtles Present the Battle of the Bands, The, 999
Turu, 989
Tush, 500, 1094
Tusk, 342
Tutti Frutti, 107, 416, 588, 789, 860, 915
Tutu, 248, 287
Tuxedo Junction, 636, 670, 671, 765
TV Eye, 468
Twang!, 267
Twang! – A Tribute to Hank Marvin & The Shadows, 886
Twangin', 302
'Twas the Night Before Christmas, 1030
Tweakin', 194
Tweedle Dee, 50, 460, 746, 1015
Tweez, 988
Twelfth of Never, 651, 673, 747
Twelfth Street Rag, 462, 1041
12 Bar Blues, 953
Twelve Deadly Cins . . . and Then Some, 567
12 Dimensions, 1965–1972, 148
Twelve Dreams of Dr Sardonicus, The, 932
Twelve Gates to the City, 246
12 Haunted Episodes, 754
Twelve Minutes to Go, 908
12 Play, 528
12 Songs, 719
Twelve Years of Tears, 17
Twelve-Year-Old Genius, The, 1076
20th Anniversary of Rock'n'Roll, 264
Twentieth Century Blues, 222, 326
Twentieth Century Blues – The Songs of Noël Coward, 768
Twentieth Century Boy, 101, 779

20, 210
Twenty Flight Rock, 197, 207
Twenty Four Seven, 999
20 Golden Greats, 885
Twenty 1, 181
20,000 Watts R.S.I., 668
Twenty Tiny Fingers, 200, 485
Twenty Years of Dirt, 724
20 Years of Manfred Mann's Earth Band 1971–1991, 635
Twenty Years of Romance, 156
25th Anniversary, 499, 669
25th Anniversary Album, 598
25th Anniversary Reunion, 133
21st Century Schizoid Man, 535
25, 210
25 Miles, 121
25 o'Clock, 1081
25 or 6 to 4, 181
25 Thumping Great Hits, 188
Twenty-Four Hours from Tulsa, 45, 777
24 Nights, 187
Twenty-Four Robbers, 605
21 at 33, 503
Twenty-One Years, 669, 670
26 Miles, 348, 641
23 Solo Piano Pieces for La Naissance de L'Amour, 151
22 Golden Guitar Greats, 1042
20–20 Blues, 488
20/20, 77
20/20 Vision, 648, 745
Twice Nightly, 442
Twice Removed from Yesterday, 800
Twice upon a Time, 905
Twilight in Turkey, 876
Twilight Time, 780
Twilight Zone, 387
Twilight Zone/Twilight Tone, 636
Twin House, 218
Twin Sons of Different Mothers, 343·
Twingy Baby, 694
Twinkle, Twinkle, Little Star, 80
Twinlights, 199
Twist, The, 51, 175, 243
Twist and Shout, 66, 80, 228, 475, 784, 869, 905, 912, 1010
Twist of Fate, 721
Twist the Big Hit Dances, 1008
Twist Twist Señora, 104
Twist-Her, 89
Twisted, 561, 679
Twisted Tenderness, 717
Twistin', 322
Twistin' in the Wind, 309
Twistin' Knights at the Round Table, 413
Twistin' the Night Away, 213, 949

Twistin' U.S.A., 243
Twistlackawanna, 1028
II, 44, 114, 1001
Two Against Nature, 943
2.00 am Paradise Cafe, 637
Two Angels, 493
Two Barrels Burning, 1074
2 Becomes 1, 931
Two Bit Monsters, 444
Two Days Away, 122
Two Days in November, 1037
Two Down Then Left, 873
Two Faces Have I, 185
Two Fires, 56
Two for the Price of One, 1038, 1062
2–4–6–8 Motorway, 841
Two Gentlemen from Ireland, 930
Two Heads Are Better Than One, 103
Two Hearts, 662
Two Hearts Beat as One, 1004
Two Hearts, Two Kisses, 107, 904
200 More Miles, 223
200 Motels, 287, 999
Two Lane Highway, 805, 806
Two Little Boys, 143
2 Live Crew Is What We Are, 1001
Two Lovers, 841, 1046
Two Minute Warning, 258
Two More Bottles of Wine, 613
Two Occasions, 44
Two of a Kind, 244, 663
Two of Us, The, 583
Two Out of Three Ain't Bad, 657
Two People, 999
Two Pina Coladas, 123
2+2=?, 882
Two Ring Circus, 312
Two Rooms, 143, 198, 413, 503, 734
Two Sides of the Moon, 1054
Two Six Packs Away, 287
Two Sleepy People, 158, 595
Two Steps Behind, 254
Two Steps from the Blues, 94
Two Storey House, 1080
2000 BBF, 417
2000 Miles, 791
2000 Years: The Millennium Concert, 502
2112, 861
2300 Jackson Street, 478
2400 Fulton Street, 495
Two Tribes, 354, 976
Two Triple Cheese (Side Order of Fries), 207
Two Trips, 1090
Two Years of Torture, 655
Two-Timing Woman, 875
2XS, 709

Twyford Down, 369
Tycoon, 593
Type Slowly, 760
Typical Male, 999
Tyr, 89
Tyranny and Mutation, 98
Tzena, Tzena, Tzena, 241, 496, 672, 1039

U, 3, 471
U Can't Touch This, 418, 488
U Got the Look, 298
U16 Girls, 992
UB40, 1005
UB40 Presents the Dancehall Album, 1005
UFO Live in Japan, 1006
UFO 1, 1006
Ugly Duckling, The, 525
Uh Huh Oh Yeh, 1044
Uh-huh, 660
Uh-Oh, 148, 967
UK Blak, 923
UK Jive, 544
Ukulele Lady, 233
Ultimate, The, 511
Ultimate Anthology, The, 778
Ultimate Collection, The, 488, 517
Ultimate Dr John, The, 272
Ultimate Journey, The, 810
Ultimate Santana, The, 871
Ultimate Sin, The, 88
Ultra, 259
Ultra Modern Nursery Rhymes, 928
Ultra Obscene, 907
Ultramega OK, 924
Um Homem de Aquarius, 501
Um, Um, Um, Um, Um, Um, 470
Umbrella Man, 340
Umbriago, 289
Ummagumma, 777
Una Paloma Blanca, 541
Unanswered Prayers, 123
Unauthorised Biography of Reinhold Messner, The, 76
Unavailable, 580
Unbreak My Heart, 118, 1032
Unchain My Heart, 138
Unchained, 166, 858
Unchained Melody, 61, 417, 444, 834, 835, 929
Unchallenged, 127
Uncle Albert, 611
Uncle Anaesthesia, 877
Uncle Arthur, 110
Uncle Charlie and His Dog Teddy, 724
Uncle Jam Wants You, 194
Uncle John's Band, 400
Uncle Meat, 1091

Uncle Pen, 907, 937
Uncle Sam, 630
Uncloudy Day, 938
Unconditional Love, 153, 864
Uncovered, 590
Undead, 977
Undecided, 19, 1040
Under a Blood Red Sky, 1004
Under a Raging Moon, 1055
Under a Red Sky, 1034
Under Milk Wood, 454, 516, 647
Under Pressure, 808
Under the Boardwalk, 22, 80, 285, 574, 849, 975
Under the Bridge, 14, 820
Under the Bridges of Paris, 547
Under the Cover of Night, 287
Under the Covers, 1086
Under the Green Oak Tree, 4
Under the Harlem Moon, 828
Under the Influence, 479
Under the Influence of Love, 748
Under the Moon of Love, 769, 896
Under the Pink, 20
Under the Red Sky, 294
Under the Rose, 13
Under the Table and Dreaming, 246
Under Wraps, 499
Under Your Spell Again, 749, 1085
Under Your Thumb, 976
Undercover, 849
Undercover Angel, 821, 835
Underground, 111, 532
Underground Music, 339
Underground System, 557
Underneath the Arches, 340, 414
Underneath the Colours, 473
Understanding, 1076
Underwater Moonlight, 446
Undiscovered Soul, 103
Undun, 406
Une Very Stylish Fille, 265
Uneasy Rider, 242
Unexpectedly, 115
Unfaithful Servant, 53
Unfinished Business, 853
Unfinished Monkey Business, 952
Unfinished Music No. 1 – Two Virgins, 576, 740
Unfinished Music No. 2: Life with the Lions, 740
Unfinished Revolution, 690
Unfinished Sympathy, 650, 730
Unforeseen Blessings, 31
Unforgettable, 202, 346
Unforgettable Fire, The, 311, 563, 1004, 1005
Unforgettable – With Love, 202
Unguarded, 397

Unhalfbricking, 323
Unicorn, 101
Unicorn Song, The, 896
Uninvited, 693
Union, 1085
Union City Blue, 96
Union Man, 107
Union of the Snake, 289
Unison, 266
Unite, 550
United, 208, 519
United Kingdom, 19
United States, 21
United States of Amnesia, The, 1079
United We Stand, 1025
U.N.I.T.Y., 808
Unity, 51, 128
Universal, 742
Universal, The, 100, 912
Universal James, 128, 149, 923
Universal Love, 790
Universal Mother, 734
Universal Soldier, 867
University, 984
Unknown Pleasures, 716
Unknown Soldier, 279, 424, 1039
Unleaded, 570
Unleashed in the East, 519
Unlimited, 618
Unlock Your Mind, 938
Unmasked, 546
Uno Mundo, 137
Unorthodox Behaviour, 204
Unplugged, 30, 186, 187, 612, 693, 1087, 1088
Unplugged . . . and Seated, 950
Unplugged in New York, 723
Unpretty, 44, 986
Unreleased Project, 977
Unrequited, 1024
Unsquare Dance, 133
Unsuccessful Blues, 454
Untasted Honey, 652
Unter Freemden Sternen, 810
Untie Me, 925
Until It's Time for You to Go, 868
Until the Night, 502
(Until Then) I'll Suffer, 607
Until You Come Back to Me (That's What I'm Gonna Do), 355
Untitled, 147, 148
Unusual Heat, 345
Unwound, 955
Up, 2, 39, 827
Up a Lazy River, 820
Up a Tree, 75
Up Above My Head, 978
Up Around the Bend, 226
Up Escalator, The, 754

Up for the Down Stroke, 194
Up from the Skies, 515
Up in the Streets of Harlem, 80, 285
Up Jumps Da Boogie, 308
Up on Cripple Creek, 53
Up on It, 10
Up on the Roof, 285, 540, 545, 783
Up on the Roof – Songs of the Brill Building, 262
Up the Country Blues, 1029
Up the Junction, 935
Up This Hill and Down, 745
Up 'Til Now, 898, 971
Up to No Good, 376
Up to Our Hips, 172
Up Township, 649
Up Up and Away, 836, 1040
Up Where We Belong, 198, 725, 868, 1031
Upchurch Tennyson, 1008
Upfront, 870
Uplift Mofo Party Plan, The, 820
Uprising, 644
Upside Down, 498, 846, 855, 869
Upstairs at Eric's, 703
Upstroke, The, 951
Uptight, 1076
Uptight (Everything's Alright), 1076
Uptown, 235, 638, 714
Uptown Avondale, 10
Uptown Festival, 886
Uptown Girl, 502
Uptown Top Ranking, 272
Urban Blues, 452
Urban Bushmen, 31
Urban Guerrilla, 433
Urban Gypsy, 119
Urban Hymns, 1020, 1021
Urban Punk, 883
Urgent, 1028
Uriah Heep Live, 1009
Us, 366, 563
Us and Them, 777
Us and Theme: Symphonic Floyd, 777
Us and Us Only, 173
US Male, 789, 822
USA Union, 276, 654
Use Me, 1074
Use of Ashes, The, 816
Use Ta Be My Girl, 736
Use Your Head, 1046
Use Your Illusion I, 407
Use Your Illusion II, 407
Used, 740
Utah Trail, The, 842
Utopia, 230
Uv, 888
U-Vox, 1007

V, 130
V Deep, 376
Vagabond Heart, 950
Vagabond Lover, The, 1011
Vagabond Shoes, 241
Vagabonds of the Western World, 979
Valentine Melody, 135
Valentyne Suite, 205
Valleri, 684
Valley Girl, 1092
Valley Hi, 652
Valley of Tears, 275
Valley of the Dolls, 467, 793, 1033
Valley Road, The, 456
Valotte, 576
Valse des Fleurs, 897
Vamp, The, 706
Van Lose Stairway, 695
Vanessa, 437
Vanguard Years, The, 1038
Vanishing Point, 797
Vanishing Race, 12
Vapour Trail, 834
Variations, 593
Various Positions, 201
Varsity Drag, 259, 315
Vas Dis, 1074
Vauxhall and I, 696
Vaya Con Dios, 759, 760
Veedon Fleece, 695
Vegas, 317
Vegetable Man, 446, 447
Vegetarians of Love, The, 377
Velocity Girl, 796
Velvet Mood, 448
Velvet Rope, The, 479
Velvet Underground, 833, 1018
Velvet Underground and Nico, The, 1018
Vendome, 681
Ventura Highway, 19
Ventures Play Telstar and the Lonely Bull, The, 1019
Ventures Play The Carpenters, The, 1019
Venupelli Blues, 399
Venus, 39, 52, 812
Venus and Mars, 611
Venus as a Boy, 86
Venus in Blue Jeans, 186, 880
Venus in Furs, 1018
Venus of the Soup Kitchen, 788
Vergangen, Vergessen, Vorueber, 810
Verities and Balderdash, 171
Vermin in Ermine, 17
Version 2.0, 371
Very, 768
Very Best . . . Beyond, The, 345
Very Best of, The, 219, 1052
Very Best of Cat Stevens, The, 946

Very Best of Joan Armatrading, The, 27
Very Best of Level 42, The, 579
Very Best of Life, The, 756
Very Best of Ron Goodwin, The, 392
Very Best of Sister Sledge, The, 906
Very Best of Supertramp, The, 962
Very Best of the Osmonds, The, 747
Very Best of Thin Lizzy, The, 979
Very 'Eavy, Very 'Umble, 1009
Very Necessary, 869
Very Rare, 1028
Very Special Christmas, A, 211, 859
Very Special Love, A, 708
Very Special Love Song, A, 830
Very Thought of You, The, 112, 164, 496, 594, 725, 802
Vesti La Giubba, 102, 165
Veteranz Day, 84
Vibrator, 243
Victim, 940
Victim of Love, 7, 703
Victim of the Peace, 590
Victims of Life's Circumstances, 613
Victims of Romance, 633
Victims of the Future, 690
Victims of the Riddle, 991
Victor, 861
Victoria, 326, 543
Victorialand, 199
Victory, 550, 1026
Video Killed the Radio Star, 288, 454, 1085
Vie des Hommes, La, 353
Vie en Rose, La, 29, 115, 264, 648, 667, 773
Vieillir, 120
Vieni, Vieni, 1011
Vienna, 288, 1006
Viens Danser le Twist, 416
Vietnam, 193
Vietnam Blues, 287, 288
View from a Bridge, 698, 1055
View from the Ground, 19
View from the Hill, The, 689
View from the House, 159
View to a Kill, A, 289
Vigil in the Wilderness of Mirrors, 642
Village Green Preservation Society, The, 543
Village Life, 420
Village of Bernardette, The, 1056
Village of St Bernadette, The, 892
Vincent, 625
Vincent Van Gogh, 833
Vindaloo, 100
Vindicator, 600

Vintage Collection, 512
Vintage Violence, 150
Vintage Year, 987
Viola Lee Blues, 154
Violator, 258
Violent Love, 861
Violet, 448
Violin Summit, 399
Violins No End, 399
V.I.P., 521
Virgin Beauty, 202
Virgin Fugs (for Adult Minds Only), 361
Virgin Islands Suite, 307
Virgin Killer, 875
Virgin Suicides, The, 11
Virginia Plain, 857
Virgins and Philistines, 928
Virgo Vibes, 40
Virtual Insanity, 490
Virtual XI, 474
Vision of Love, 157
Vision of Mother, A, 937
Vision Shared, A, 661, 935
Vision's Tale, The, 776
Visions, 1059
Visions of Dennis Brown, 127
Visions of Excess, 133, 884
Visions of Johanna, 292
Visions of the Emerald Beyond, 624, 1026
Visitor, The, 342
Vital Idol, 468
Vitalogy, 762
Viva!, 857
Viva Bobby Joe, 398
Viva Bossa Nova, 16
Viva el Amor, 792
Viva Espana, 565
Viva Forever, 931
Viva Hate, 696
Viva Las Vegas, 783, 1094
Viva Last Blues, 738, 739, 988
Viva Luckenbach, 1027
Viva Santana, 871
Viva Terlingua, 1027
Vive le Rock, 25
Vivir, 469
Vivrant Thing, 994
Vocalese, 561, 636
Vogts Villa, 11
Vogue, 631
Voice, 939, 1006
Voice and Guitar of Jose Feliciano, The, 332
Voice from on High, A, 648
Voice in the Wilderness, 752, 831
Voice of Africa, 633
Voice of Love, The, 856
Voice of Old Man River, The, 1041
Voice of the Heart, 160
Voice Piece for Soprano, 921

Voices, 413, 1014
Voices in Bluegrass, 745
Voices in Love, 348
Voices in the Sky, 689
Vol. 1, 669
Volare, 113, 192, 621, 646, 649, 681, 751, 864
Volcano, 137
Volga Vouty, 307
Volume 1, 569
Volume 3, 427, 771
Volume 4, 851
Volume 8 – The Threat Is Real, 25
Volume II – 1990 A New Decade, 923
Volume II – The New Reality, 370
Volume III – Just Right, 923
Volume V – Believe, 923
Volunteered Slavery, 545
Volunteers, 494
Voodoo Chile, 440, 1016
Voodoo Lounge, 850, 1034
Voodoo People, 801
Voodoo Woman, 389
Vote for Love, 163
Vow, 371, 991
Voyage, 690
Voyage of the Acolyte, 377
Voyager, 738
Voyeur, 519, 870
Voz, una Guitarra, Una, 332
Voz y la guitarra de Jose Feliciano, 332
Vozero, 857
Vroom, 536
Vs., 762
VU, 1018
Vulture Culture, 756

Wabash Blues, 513
Wabash Cannonball, 6, 412
Wack Wack, 582
Waddlin' at the Waldorf, 280
Wade in the Water, 582
Wah Wah, 311, 485
Wah Watusi, The, 744
Waif Me, 723
Wait a Minute, 122
Wait for the Night, 934
Wait Till My Bobby Gets Home, 404, 601
Wait Till the Sun Shines Nellie, 1023
Wait Till the Work Comes Round, 305
Waitin' for a Train, 845
Waitin' for the Night, 351, 499
Waitin' for the Robert E. Lee, 706
Waitin' for the Sun to Shine, 907
Waitin' in the Welfare Line, 748
Waiting, 928
Waiting for a Girl Like You, 345

Waiting for an Alibi, 979
Waiting for Columbus, 588
Waiting for Cousteau, 491
Waiting for Herb, 781
Waiting for My Man, 1018
(Waiting for) The Ghost Train, 630
Waiting for the Man, 1018
Waiting for the Punchline, 321
Waiting for the Rain, 649
Waiting for the Sun, 279, 493
Waiting for You, 585
Waiting in School, 139, 641
Waiting in the Lobby of Your Heart, 981
Waiting to Exhale, 44
Waitress in a Donut Shop, 619, 704
Waka/Jawaka, 1091
Wakafrika, 263
Wake Me Up Before You Go Go, 666
Wake of the Flood, 400
Wake the Town, 1009
Wake Up, 40, 105, 396, 887
Wake Up and Make Love with Me, 290
Wake Up Baby, 613
Wake Up Boo, 105
Wake Up Call, 655
Wake Up Everybody, 764
Wake Up Little Susie, 134, 320
Wakin Up, 191
Waking Hour, The, 491
Waking Up the Neighbours, 7
Waking Up with the House on Fire, 236
Walk, The, 238
Walk a Mile in My Shoes, 925
Walk Away, 685, 1031
Walk Away from Love, 615, 975
Walk Away Renee, 350
Walk Don't Run, 1019, *1019*
Walk Hand in Hand, 648
Walk in the Black Forest, A, 522
Walk in the Night, 1028
Walk in the Sun, 456
Walk into Light, 499
Walk Like a Man, 3, 349
Walk Like an Egyptian, 54, 500
Walk of Life, 267
Walk on, *109*, 444, 618, 619, 1005
Walk on By, 45, 434, 951, 956, 1033
Walk on Gilded Splinters, 271
Walk on the Wild Side, 354, 824, *916, 916*, 994
Walk on Water, 967
Walk Out to Winter, 41
Walk Right Back, 320
Walk Right in, 155, 244
Walk Right Up to the Sun, 255
Walk the Dinosaur, 1034

Walk the Dog & Lite the Lite, 729
Walk the Way the Wind Blows, 652
Walk This Way, 9, 859
Walk Through This World with Me, 512
Walk Under Ladders, 27
Walkaway, 564
Walkin', 553, 698
Walkin' and Swingin', 1063
Walkin' Away, 90
Walkin' Back to Happiness, 752
Walkin' Blind, 917
Walkin' in the Rain, 493
Walkin' in the Sun, 153
Walkin' in the Sunshine, 673
Walkin' the Floor Over You, 995
Walkin' the Strings, 992
Walkin' with Mr Lee, 990
Walking a Broken Heart, 1059
Walking a Changing Line, 653
Walking After Midnight, 193, 222
Walking Away a Winner, 652
Walking Back to Happiness, 609
Walking Blues, 814
Walking by Myself, 591
Walking in a Dream, 138
Walking in Space, 514
Walking in the Rain, 724, 853
Walking in the Rain with the One I Love, 1048
Walking into Clarksdale, 570
Walking My Baby Back Home, 818
Walking My Cat Named Dog, 227
Walking on Sunshine, *398*, 446
Walking on the Milky Way, 742
Walking on the Moon, 782
Walking Stick Boogie, 197
Walking Tall, 707
Walking the Dog, 980
Walking the Floor Over You, 996
Walking the Long Miles Home, 982
Walking to New Orleans, 58, 275
Walking with Mr Lee, 895
Walking Wounded, 321
Wall, The, 326, 377, 777
Wall – Live in Berlin, The, 777
Wall of Death, 982
Wall of Hits, 910
Wall Street Shuffle, 976
Wall to Wall, 971
Wallflower, 85
Walls and Bridges, 576
Walls Can Fall, 512
Walls Come Tumbling Down, 1044
Walter, 543
Waltz Across Texas, 996
Waltz Darling, 624

Waltz #2, 915

Waltz Was Born in Vienna, A, 577

Waltzing Matilda, 250, 369, 1049

Wand'rin' Star, 578

Wanderer, The, 261, 265, 941, 960, 1004

Wandering Cowboy, 121

Wandering Spirit, 849

Wang Dang Doodle, 269, 459

Wang Wang Blues, 143

Wanna Get Up, 1001

Wannabe, 930, 931

Want Ads, 169, 232, 449, 601

Wanted, 648, 1072

Wanted Again, 910

Wanted Dead and Alive, 988

Wanted Dead or Alive, 122, 351, 1092

Wanted: The Outlaws, 713, 986

Wanted Very Much Alive, 867

War, 643, 934, 1004, 1051

War and Peace Vol. I: The War Disc, 467

War and Peace Vol. II: The Peace Disc, 270, 467

War Anthology, 1970–1994, 1030

War Babies, 413, 860

War Baby, 841

War Child, 499

War Dance for Wooden Indians, 876

War Heroes, 440

War in a Babylon, 767

War Is Over, The, 733

War Lord, 885

War of Nerves, 14

War of the Worlds, The, 689

War Paint, 638

War Song, 236

Warakurna, 668

Ward One: Along the Way, 88

Wardance, 534

Warehouse and Other Stories, 701

Warm and Cool, 973

Warm and Tender, 189, 721, 850

Warm and Tender Love, 910

Warm Evenings, Pale Mornings, Bottled Blues, 757

Warm Leatherette, 512, 911

Warm Your Heart, 714, 854, 882

Warmed Over Kisses, 464

Warming Up to the Ice Age, 444

Warning, 402, 809

Warning Sign, 443

Warpaint, 430

Warren Zevon, 1092

Warrior, 1074

Warrior on the Edge of Time, 433

Warrior Rock – Toyah on Tour, 991

Warriors, 727

Warriors of the Wasteland, 354

Warsaw Concerto, The, 125

Wartime, 850

Warts'n'Audience, 290

Was This the Time?, 369

Wash My Troubles Away, 798

Wash Wash, 798

Washable Ink, 444

Washboard Blues, 158, 1050

Washing Machine, 921

Washington Post, 924

Washington Square, 516

Wasn't Born to Follow, 147, 540

Wasp, 860

Wasp Star (Apple Venus Volume 2), 1081

Waste, 773

Wasted, 254

Wasted Days and Wasted Nights, 332, 658

Wasted Life Blues, 506

Wasted on the Way, 229

Watch Out!, 270

Watching Scotty Grow, 389

Watching the Dark, 113, 982

Watching the Detectives, 219

Watching the River Flow, 864

Watching Windows, 906

Watching You Watching Me, 1074

Water from the Well, 182

Water from the Wells of Home, 166

Water of Dreams, 627

Water of Love, 520

Water on Glass, 1055

Water Sign, 819

Water Song, 471

Water, Water, 57, 941

Water's Edge, 964

Waterbed in Trinidad, 34

Watercolors, 665

Waterfall, 193

Waterfalls, 986

Waterfront, 901

Waterhouse Posse, 537

Waterloo, 1, 599

Waterloo Sunset, 543

Watermark, 312, 898

Watermelon Man, 420, 870

Watermelon Weather, 231

Waterson: Carthy, 164

Watusi, El, 804

Wave, 501, 860

Wavelength, 695

Waves, 60, 917

Way Back Home, 84, 234, 1028, 1031

Way Back in the 1960s, 470

Way Beyond Blue, 168

Way Down in the Congo, 997

Way Down Yonder in New Orleans, 154, 490, 567

Way Down Yonder, 242

Way He Makes Me Feel, The, 957

Way I Am, The, 790

Way I Feel, The, 584, 851, 1008

Way I Want to Touch You, The, 156

Way It Is, The, 456

Way It Used to Be, The, 403

Way of a Clown, The, 587

Way Out, 564

Way Out There, 921

Way Out West, 776, 851

Way We Make a Broken Heart, The, 166

Way We Were, The, 548, 957

Way You Do the Things You Do, The, 214, 841, 974, 1005

Way You Look Tonight, The, 34, 334, 530, 578

Way You Make Me Feel, The, 481

Wayfaring Sons, 662

Waylon and Company, 497

Waylon and Willie, 497, 713

Waylon Jennings Sings Ol' Harlan, 496

Wayne Kramer's Deathtongue, 656

Ways of a Woman in Love, The, 165

Wayward Wind, The, 369, 398, 468

We All Have a Star, 234

We All Live Happily Together, 298

We All Sleep Alone, 177

We All Stand Together, 612

We Almost Lost Detroit, 877

We Are All Living in One Place, 385

We Are Detective, 981

We Are Family, 845, 906

We Are in Love, 210, 325

We Are Motorhead, 699

We Are One, 656

We Are Rude, 591

We Are Slaves in Our Country, 640

We Are the Champions, 807

We Are the Vegetables, 473

We Are the World, 73, 377, 481, 514, 815, 832

We Belong, 76

We Built This City on Rock'n'Roll, 495

We Can Be Together, 494

We Can Fly, 223

We Can Make It Together, 567

We Can Talk, 53

We Can Work It Out, 66, 532

We Can't Dance, 378

We Didn't Start the Fire, 502

We Die Young, 14

We Don't Have to Take Our Clothes Off, 1026

We Don't Need Another Hero, 368, 999

(We Don't Need This) Fascist Groove Thang, 438
We Don't Talk Anymore, 831
We Don't Work for Free, 397
We Free Kings, 544
We Got By, 492
We Got Love, 864
We Got the Love, 532
We Got to Get Our Thing Together, 256
We Gotta Get Out of this Place, 23, 292, 638
We Gotta Get You a Woman, 859
We Have All the Time in the World, 985
We in There, 106
We Insist! Freedom Now Suite, 837
We Just Couldn't Say Goodbye, 48
We Kill the World (Don't Kill the World), 104
We Live Here, 666
We Live in Two Different Worlds, 855
We Love You Bay City Rollers, 603
We Love You Like a Rock, 268
We Meet Again, 646
We Must Be Ready, 201
We Must Believe in Magic, 375
We Ran, 854
We Refuse, 750
We Shall Be Free, 123
We Shall Overcome, 46, *881*
We Should Be Together, 1058
We Take Mystery (To Bed), 727
We Three Kings of Orient Aren't, 163
We Too Are One, 317
We Two, 590
We Wanna See Santa Do the Mambo, 787
We Want Some Pussy, 1001
We Will, 747
We Will Fall, 469
We Will Rock You, 807
We Wish You a Merry Christmas, 210
We'll All Go Riding on a Rainbow, 568
(We'll Be) United, 369, 472
We'll Gather Lilacs, 726
We'll Meet Again, 147, 608
We'll Talk About It Later, 726
We're a Couple of Swells, 372
We're a Winner, 470
We're All Alone, 214
We're All the Way, 1059
We're an American Band, 396, 860
We're Going to Hang out Our Washing on the Siegfried Line, 161, 340, 528

We're Going to Love, 303
We're Going Wrong, 225
We're Gonna Go Fishing, 595
We're Gonna Have to Stop the Dirty Little Jap, 674, 842
We're Gonna Hold on, 512, 1080
We're Gonna Make It, 588
We're Gonna Rock, 371
We're in the Money, 527, 1032
We're in This Love Together, 492
We're Living at the Cloisters, 1046
We're Not Making Love Anymore, 102
We're off to See the Wizard, 422
We're Only in It for the Money, 1091
We're the Best of Friends, 134
We're the Talk of the Town, 629
We've Got Feelings Too, 928
We've Got It Goin' on, 46
We've Got Tonight, 298, 847, 882
We've Only Just Begun, 160, *210*, 1010, 1064
Weak, 909
Weak in the Presence of Beauty, 703
Weakness Is a Thing Called Man, 655
Wear My Ring, 1021
Wear You to the Ball, 1009
Weary Blues, 621
Weasels Ripped My Flesh, 276, 1091
Weather Bird, 446
Weather with You, 233
Weatherman, The, 906
Weaver's Answer, The, 328
Wedding Album, 740, 864
Wedding Bell Blues, 728, 836
Wedding Bells, 976
Wedding of the Painted Doll, The, 130
Wedding Samba, 678, 854
Wedding Song (There Is Love), 768
Wednesday Morning 3 A.M, 897
Wednesday Night Prayer Meeting, 676
Wednesday Night Waltz, 606
Wednesday Week, 890
Wee Baby Blues, 1022
Wee Doech an' Doris, A, 566
Wee Tam and the Big Huge, 471
Weekend, 197, 977
Weekend in LA, 77
Weight, 851
Weight, The, 53, 259, 709, 939
Weird Nightmare, 219, 1067
Weird Nightmare: Meditation on Mingus, 677
Weird Science, 305
Weirdo, 172

Weisse Rosen Aus Athen, 702
Welcome Back, 603
Welcome Back My Friends, to the Show that Never Ends, 309
Welcome Here, Kind Stranger, 116
Welcome Home, 540, 745
Welcome My Love, 227
Welcome to My World, 825
Welcome to Paradise, 402
Welcome to the Beautiful South, 68
Welcome to the Canteen, 1072
Welcome to the Club, 124, *700*
Welcome to the Cruel World, 423
Welcome to the Jungle, 407
Welcome to the Machine, 777
Welcome to the Neighbourhood, 658
Welcome to the Pleasuredome, 354, 379
Welcome to the Show, 55
Welcome to the Story, 368
Welcome to the Terrordome, 803
Welcome to the Working Week, 219
Welcome to Wherever You Are, 473
Weld, 1088
Well All Right, 451
Well Below the Valley, The, 689
Well Did You Evah?, 231, 469, 785
Well, I Told You, 171
Well-a Well-a, 895
Welsh World of Mary Hopkin, The, 454
Werewolves of London, 1092
Wes and Friends, 688
West, 19
West Coast Blues, 92, 847
West End Blues, 28, 1058
West End Girls, 767
West of Oz, 349
West Side Soul, 632
West Side Story, 529
West Virginia Mine, 259
West Virginia Polka, 735
Western Head Music Co, 867
Western Stars, 563
Western Union Man, 74
Western Wall: The Tucson Sessions, 854
Westing (by Musket and Sextant), 760
Westminster Waltz, 329
Westway, 909
Wet Dream, 692
Whacha Gonna Do About It, 912
Wham, 628
Wham! Rap (Enjoy What You Do?), 666
Whammy, 43
Wharf Rat, 668
What a Crazy World We're Living in, 129

What a Difference a Day Makes, 772, 1034
What a Fool Believes, 279, 596
What a Fool I Was, 655
What a Guy, 404
What a Little Moonlight Can Do, 448, 1041, 1070
What a Long Strange Trip It's Been, 400
What a Mouth, 170, 942, 1046
What a Party, 275, 770
What a Surprise, 227
What a Waste, 290
What a Woman in Love Won't Do, 786
What a Wonderful World, 29, 708, 713, 740, 794, 971
What About Love, 436
What About Me, 159, 810, 847
What About Your Friends, 986
What Am I Gonna Do, 344
What Am I Living for, 1067
What Another Man Spills, 560
What Are You Doing the Rest of Your Life, 573
What Are You Going to Do with It, 1078
What Are You Going to Do with Your Life?, 299
What Becomes of the Broken Hearted?, 1093
What Can I Do, 217
What Can I Say, 873
What 'Cha Gonna Do for Me, 532
What Comes Naturally, 298
What Cowgirls Do, 383
What Did Daddy Do, 892
What Did I Do to You?, 938
What Did You Learn in School Today, 761
What Difference Does It Make?, 917
What Do I Do About Me, 997
What Do You Do in the Infantry, 595
What Do You Want, 325, 451, 1017
What Do You Want from Me?, 717
What Do You Want the Girl to Do, 814, 990
What Do You Want to Make Those Eyes at Me for?, 344, 706, 947
What Does It Take, 121, 365, 1028
What Evil Lurks, 801
What Fi Goh Rave, 507
What God Has Joined Together, 732
What Goes Around, 450
What Goes on, 333
What Have I Done to Deserve This?, 768, 933

What Have They Done to My Song, Ma, 659, 881
What Have They Done to the Rain, 879
What Hits?, 820
What I Am, 931
What I Did for Love, 418
What I Want Is a Proper Cup of Coffee, 1046
What If We Went to Italy, 159
What in the World's Come Over You, 875
What Is a Man, 121
What Is and What Never Should Be, 87, 570
What Is Life?, 427, 721
What Is Love, 513
What Is Success, 990
What Is This Thing Called Love?, 158
What Is Truth, 166
What Keeps Man Alive, 1043
What Keeps Mankind Alive, 1042
What Kind of Fool, 719
What Kind of Fool Am I?, 60, 249, 718
What Kind of Love Is This, 708
What Kind of Man Would I Be, 181
What Kinda Boy You Lookin' for (Girl), 457
What Kinda Deal Is This?, 157
What Lack of Love Has Done, 604
What Led Me to This Town, 494
What Made Milwaukee Famous (Has Made a Loser Out of Me), 581
What Made You Say That, 1000
What Now My Love?, 60, 68, 865
What She Does Best, 22
What the Dickens, 242, 559
What the World Needs Now, 480
What the World Needs Now Is Love, 45, 259
What Time Is Love?, 548
What to Do, 451
What Was It You Wanted, 294
What We Did on Our Holidays, 323
What Were Once Vices Are Now Habits, 279
What Will I Tell My Heart, 424
What Will Mary Say, 651
What Would You Say, 246
What Wouldn't I Do for That Man, 692
What You Get Is What You See, 999
What You Hear Is What You Get, 46
What You Need, 473
What You See Is What You Sweat, 355

What You're Proposing, 941
What'cha Gonna Do?, 625, 815
What'd I Say, 174, 244, 581, 658
What'll I Do, 140
What's Bin Did and What's Bin Hid, 277
What's Cooking, 357
What's Easy for Two, 472
What's Easy for Two Is So Hard for One, 1046
What's Funk?, 396
What's Going on, 85, 271, 374, 374, 430, 431, 566
What's in a Kiss, 747
What's in the Box?, 105
What's Inside, 27
What's Love Got to Do with It, 368, 998, 999
What's New, 833, 833, 851, 854
What's New Pussycat, 516
What's Shakin'?, 97, 144
(What's So Funny 'Bout) Peace Love and Understanding, 603
What's the 411?, 95, 804
What's the Frequency, 827
What's the Matter with You Baby, 374, 1046
(What's the Story) Morning Glory?, 100, 731
What's This, 556
What's THIS For . . .!, 534
What's up Dog?, 1034
What's Wrong with My World, 800
What's Wrong with the Way We're Doing It Now?, 996
What's Your Mama's Name?, 997
What's Your Name, 609
Whatcha Gonna Do About It, 995
Whatever, 730, 765
Whatever & Ever Amen, 76
Whatever Gets You through the Night, 576
Whatever Happened to Baby Jane, 505
Whatever Happened to Benny Santini?, 819
Whatever Happened to Jugula, 424
Whatever Happened to the Blues, 1008
Whatever Lola Wants, 264, 460, 1015
Whatever Next, 765
Whatever Turns You on, 702
Whatever You Want, 941
Whatever You Want – The Best of Status Quo, 941
Whatever's for Us, 27
Whatevershebringswesing, 919
Whatta Man, 869
Wheel, 854

Wheel, The, 167
Wheel in the Sky, 519
Wheel Me Out, 1033
Wheel of Fortune, 939, 1034
Wheel of the Wagon Is Broken, The, 161
Wheels, 425, 770, 1016
Wheels Are Turnin', 827
Wheels Cha Cha, 599
Wheels of Fire, 225, 283
When, 464, 523, 896
When a Man Loves a Woman, 415, 667, 786, 910, 1072
When a Woman Loves a Man, 496
When All the Pieces Fit, 352
When an Old Cricketer Leaves the Crease, 424
When Day Is Done, 143
When Do I Get to Be Called a Man, 124
When Doves Cry, 797
When Father Papered the Parlour, 1046
When Forever Has Gone, 823, 1014
When Frances Dances with Me, 511
When Heroes Go Down, 1017
When I Been Drinking, 124
When I Call Your Name, 383
When I Close My Eyes, 44
When I Come Around, 402
When I Come Home, 303
When I Dream, 822
When I Fall, 297
When I Fall in Love, 201, 202, 266, 496, 578, 833, 951
When I Get to Heaven, 466
When I Get to the Border, 982
When I Grow Too Old to Dream, 462, 843, 852, 854
When I Grow Up (To Be a Man), 62
When I Look into Your Heart, 383
When I Lost You, 79
When I Need You, 873
When I Stop Dreaming, 600
When I Take My Morning Promenade, 592
When I Take My Sugar to Tea, 109
When I Think of You, 479
When I Was Young, 24
When I'm Away from You, 75
When I'm Back on My Feet Again, 1031
When I'm Cleaning Windows, 346
When I'm Dead and Gone, 367, 635

When I'm Gone, 348
When I'm with You, 927
When in Rome, 733
When It's Sleepy Time Down South, 28
When It's Springtime in Alaska, 456
When It's Springtime in the Rockies, 606, 842
When Jesus Lived in Galilee, 443
When Johnny Comes Marching Home, 441, 687, 888, 924
When Love Breaks Down, 788
When Love Comes to Town, 538, 1004
When Love Finds You, 383
When Love Is New, 802
When My Baby Smiles at Me, 583
When My Little Girl Is Smiling, 285, 344
When My Man Comes Home, 505
When My Ship Comes in, 90
When My Sugar Walks down the Street, 38, 621
When Revolution Comes, 85
When Rock'n'Roll Came to Trinidad, 202
When Shadows Gather, 614
When She Was My Girl, 350
When Smokey Sings, 2
When Something Is Wrong with My Baby, 558
When That Midnight Choo-Choo Leaves for Alabam', 79, 203
When the Boys Meet the Girls, 906
When the Children Are Asleep, 844
When the Eagle Flies, 1072
When the Fingers Point, 184
When the Going Gets Tough, 114, 732, 733
When the Guardsman Started Crooning on Parade, 211
When the Heart Rules the Mind, 1085
When the Lovelight Starts Shining through His Eyes, 962
When the Moon Comes Over the Mountain, 916
When the Music's Over, 279
When the Night Comes, 818
When the Party's Over, 990
When the Rain Comes Down, 289
When the Rains Came, 866
When the Red Red Robin Comes Bob Bob Bobbin' Along, 821
When the Saints Go Marching in, 522, 1038
When the Snow Is on the Roses, 489
When the Spell Is Broken, 982

When the Sun Begins to Shine, 276
When the Sun Goes Down, 160, 509
When the War Began, 816
When the Year Ends in 1, 175
When Two Worlds Collide, 582, 673
When We Dance, 951
When We Get Married, 472
When We Was Fab, 427
When We Where the Boys, 950
When Will I Be Loved?, 320, 853
When Will I See You Again?, 56
When Will the Good Apple Fall, 881
When You Believe, 157, 458
When You Fall in Love, 296
When You Feel the Feeling You Was Feeling, 357
When You Get Right Down to It, 74
When You Gonna Learn?, 489
When You Know You're Not Forgotten by the Girl You Can't Forget, 120
When You Love a Woman, 519
When You Say Nothing at All, 114
(When You Say You Love Somebody) From the Heart, 550
When You Tell Me that You Love Me, 856
When You Walk in the Room, 259, 879
When You Want 'Em, You Can't Have 'Em, When You Have 'Em, You Don't Want 'Em, 379
When You Were Mine, 798
When You Were Sweet Sixteen, 209
When You Wish Upon a Star, 265, 302, 645, 671, 820, 1067
When You Wore a Tulip (And I Wore a Big Red Rose), 527
When You're a Boy, 54
When You're Gone, 7, 931
When You're Hot, You're Hot, 822
When You're in Love with a Beautiful Woman, 271
When You're Not a Lady, 986
When You're Smiling, 448
When You're Young and in Love, 615, 649
When You've Got a Little Springtime in Your Heart, 653
When You've Heard Lou, You've Heard It All, 818
Whenever God Shines His Light, 831
Whenever I Call You Friend, 596
Whenever We See the Dark, 499

Whenever We Wanted, 661
Where Are All My Friends, 764
Where Are You?, 1034
Where Are You Now?, 90, 430
Where Are You Now My Son?, 47, 329
Where Can I Go Without You, 572
Where Did Our Love Go?, 449, 962
Where Do Broken Hearts Go, 458
(Where Do I Begin) Love Story, 1057
Where Do I Go from You, 879
Where Have All the Flowers Gone?, 264, 431, 542, 640, 836, 879, 881, 881
Where Have I Known You Before, 190
Where Have You Been?, 13, *1043*
Where I Should Be, 352
Where Is My Man, 547
Where Is the Entranceway to Play, 880
Where Is the Love? , 338, 430, 752, 1078
Where Is Your Heart, 325
Where It's At, 69
Where or When, 265, 428, 578, 667
Where Teardrops Fall, 293
Where the Blue of the Night Meets the Gold of the Day, 230
Where the Boys Are, 353
Where the Day Takes You, 917
Where the Wild Roses Grow, 677
Where There's a Will There's a Way, 337, 628
Where There's Smoke, 841
Where There's Woman, 72
Where We Belong, 114
Where's the Dress?, 54
Where's the Love, 421
Where's the Money, 445
Wherever I Lay My Hat, 1089
Wherever I May Roam, 665
Wherever I Would Be, 1032
Which Side Are You on, 171
Which Way You Goin' Billy?, 623
Whiffenpoof Song, The, 227, 1011, 1030, 1031
While You See a Chance, 1073
While You Were Out, 922
Whip in My Valise, 24
Whip It, 260
Whiplash, 468, 485
Whiplash Smile, 468
Whipped Cream, 990
Whipped Cream and Other Delights, 17
Whippin' Piccadilly, 390
Whip-Smart, 771

Whirlwind, 830
Whiskey Ain't Working, The, 994
Whiskey and Gin, 818
Whiskey Bent and Hell Bound, 1061
Whiskey for the Holy Ghost, 877
Whiskey in the Jar, 979
Whisper a Prayer, 752
Whisper Your Name, 210
Whispering, 351, 383, 1049, 1050
Whispering Bells, 257
Whispering Grass, 472
Whispering Hope, 626
Whispering Jack, 590
Whispering Pines of Nevada, The, 319
Whispering Your Name, 703
Whispers, 1069
Whispers in the Dark, 231, 839
Whistle Down the Wind, 443
Whistle Rhymes, 1054
Whistler, The, 499
Whistling Coon, The, 506
Whistling the Blues Away, 416
White Album, The, 67
White Christmas, 38, 78, 79, 230, 285, 447, 625, 647, 817, 936
White City, 1054
White Cliffs of Dover, 608, 834
White Dove, The, 937
White Heat, 604, *933*
White Jazz, 462
White Light, 147
White Light/White Heat, 1018
White Lightning, 512
White Limozeen, 758, 907
White Lines (Don't Do It), 397
White Music, 1081
White Noise, 728
White on Blonde, 978
White Rabbit, *77*, 494
White Riot, 191
White Rock, 1025
White Room, 133, 225, 232, 547
White Rose of Athens, The, 702
White Silver Sands, 115
White Snake, 1050
White Sport Coat and a Pink Carnation, A, 137, 837
White Sport Coat and a Pink Crustacean, A, 137
White Wedding, 467, 485
whitechocolatespaceegg, 771
Whiter Shade of Pale, A, 317, 800, 910
Whites Off Earth Now, 222
Whitesnake 1987, 1051
Whitey Album, The, 920
Whitey on the Moon, 877
Whitney, 458, 1026
Who?, 739
Who Am I?, 479, 615

Who Are the Brain Police?, 1091
Who Are You, 1054, *1054*
Who by Numbers, The, 1054
Who Came First, 1054
Who Can I Turn to?, 77, 719
Who Can It Be Now, 662
Who Do You Love?, 52, 263, 432, 472, 810, 1050
Who Do You Think You Are?, 931
Who Don Mon Man, 195
Who Gets Your Love, 108
Who Knows Where the Time Goes?, 204, 323, *755*
Who Loves You, 350
Who Made Who, 4
Who Needs Love Like That, 312
Who Needs You, 348
Who Put the Bomp, 638, 896
Who Really Cares, 466
Who Said Gay Paree?, 785
Who Sell Out, The, 1054
Who Snuck the Wine in the Gravy?, 108
Who Threw the Whiskey in the Well, 426
Who Wants to Be a Millionaire?, 785
Who Wants to Live Together, 808
Who Will Answer?, 19
Who Will Save Your Soul?, 500
Who Will the Next Fool Be?, 18, 830, 893
Who Wouldn't Love Me, 557
Who'd She Coo, 736
Who'll Buy My Memories?, 713
Who'll Stop the Train, 225, 413
Who's Afraid of the Big Bad Wolf?, 852, 1089
Who's Afraid of Y2K?, 75
Who's Been Foolin' You, 233
Who's Been Talkin', 224
Who's Cheatin' Who?, 588
Who's Crying Now, 519
Who's Gonna Fill Her Shoes, 512
Who's Gonna Love Me, 587
Who's Got the 101/2, 850
Who's Last, 1054
Who's Makin' Love, 971
Who's Next, 1054
Who's Sorry Now, 352, 523, 747
Who's That Girl, 317
Who's That Lady, 476
Who's the Badman?, 572
Who's Your Baby, 546
Who's Zoomin' Who, 355, 1026
Whoa Sailor, 981
Whoever's in New England, 618
Whole Lotta Love, 269, 553, 569
Whole Lotta Loving, 275
Whole Lotta Shakin' Goin' on, 192, 483, 581
Whole Lotta Woman, 211, 813

Whole New Thing, A, 790, 954
Whole New World, 134, 593
Whole Oates, 413
Whole of the Moon, The, 1035, 1036
Whole Thing Started with R'n'R, The, 280
Whoopin', 620
Whose Garden Was This, 761
Whose Little Girl Are You?, 732
Why?, 39, 208, 628, 718, 747, 1053
Why Am I, 759
Why Am I Treated So Bad, 8, 938
Why Blackmen Dey Suffer, 557
Why Can't I Wake Up with You?, 1064
Why Can't We Be Friends, 1030
Why Can't We Be Lovers, 449
Why Can't We Live Together?, 418
Why Can't You, 173
Why Did She Fall for the Leader of the Band, 528
Why Did You Put Your Shoes Under My Bed, 221
Why Do Fools Fall in Love?, 107, 262, 606, 855
Why Do Lovers Break Each Other's Heart?, 601
Why Does It Always Rain on Me?, 992
Why Don't They Understand, 417
Why Don't We Do It in the Road?, 362
Why Don't You Do Right?, 392, 572
Why Don't You Get a Job?, 736
Why Don't You Love Me, 1059
Why Dontcha, 702
Why Haven't I Heard from You?, 618
Why Lady Why, 12
Why Me, 555
Why Must We Die?, 619
Why Not Me, 520
Why Oh Why Oh Why, 747
Why Pick on Me, 349
Why Robinson Crusoe Got the Blues, 545
Why Should I Cry?, 559
Why? The King of Love Is Dead, 901
Why the Long Face, 84
Why the Stars Come out Tonight, 726
Why Was I Born?, 241
Why Women Go Wrong, 507
Wichita Lineman, 153, 1040
Wichita Train Whistle Sings, 685
Wicked Game, 475, 475
Wicked in Bed, 815

Wicked Man, 24
Wide Awake in Dreamland, 76
Wide Boy, 531
Wide Open, 759
Wide Open Space, 639
Wide Prairie, 612
Wide River, 674
Wide Swing Tremolo, 1007
Wide Wings, 284
Widow Maker, 648
Wife of the Soldier, The, 942
Wig Wam Bam, 964
Wiggle Wiggle, 294
Wild!, 312
Wild America, 469
Wild and Frantic Little Richard, The, 589
Wild and Peaceful, 488, 550
Wild Boys, 289
Wild Cat, 1019
Wild Frontier, 690
Wild Heart, 342, 741
Wild Honey, 63
Wild Horses, 757
Wild Is the Wind, 1032
Wild Life, 611
Wild Mood Swings, 238
Wild Mountain Thyme, 204, 695
Wild Night, 661, 695
Wild One, 720, 807, 807, 864
Wild Ones, The, 960
Wild Places, The, 343
Wild Planet, 43
Wild Root, 441
Wild Seed, 11
Wild Side of Life, 162, 671, 941, 981, 1045
Wild Side of the City Lights, 1077
Wild Sounds of New Orleans, The, 990
Wild Tchoupitoulas, The, 714
Wild, the Innocent and the E. Street Shuffle, The, 934
Wild Thing, 440, 486, 970, 995
Wild Things Run Fast, 679
Wild West, 480
Wild Wind, 659
Wild Woman Do, 202
Wild Wood, 1044
Wild World, 193, 729, 795, 946
Wild Youth, 467
Wilder, 215
Wilderness Road and Jimmy Driftwood, The, 285
Wildest Dreams, 999
Wildest Organ in Town, The, 790
Wildflower, 346, 422
Wildflowers, 204, 771, 834, 858
Wildlife, 700
Wildwood Flower, 46, 162
Will It Go Round in Circles, 790
Will Power, 133, 480

Will the Circle Be Unbroken, 6, 162, 163, 724, 992, 1037
Will the Circle Be Unbroken, Volume 2, 724
Will the Wolf Survive?, 497
Will to Live, The, 423
Will You, 288
Will You Love Me Tomorrow?, 334, 540, 545, 894
Will You Marry Me?, 3
Will You Remember?, 852
Will You Still Love Me?, 181
Will You Still Love Me Tomorrow, 743
Will Your Lawyer Talk to God?, 1045
Will2K, 917
Willard, 949
Willennium, 917
Willette, 257
William Bloke, 117
William, It Was Really Nothing, 917
William Tell Overture, 515
Willie and Leon, 864
Willie and the Hand Jive, 159, 748
Willie and the Poor Boys, 226, 819
Willie Nelson and Ray Price, 794
Willie the Wandering Gypsy and Me, 496
Willie, Waylon and Me, 199
Willin', 587, 853
Willing to Forgive, 44
Willow in the Wind, 652
Willow Weep for Me, 852
Wimoweh, 460, 496, 881, 1039
(Win Place or Show) She's a Winner, 472
Winchester Cathedral, 611, 763
Wind and Wuthering, 377
Wind Beneath My Wings, 369, 642, 667
Wind Cries Mary, The, 440
Wind in the Wire, 993
Wind It Up, 801
Windfall, 711
Winding Sheet, 877
Windmills of Your Mind, 573, 759, 933
Window up Above, The, 512
Windows and Walls, 343
Windpower, 273
Winds of Change, 352, 495, 559, 875
Windsor Waltz, The, 608
Windy, 34, 688
Wine, 97
Wine Yuh Body, 31
Winelight, 1035
Wing and a Prayer, A, 812
Winging and Singing, 207
Wings of Tomorrow, 316

Wings Over Manhattan, 653
Winki's Theme, 808
Winkin', Blinkin' and Nod, 898
Winner in You, 558
Winner Takes It All, The, 1
Winner's Blues, 921
Winning, 871
Winter Blues, 1071
Winter Light, 854
Winter of '88, 1071
Winter Wonderland, 597
Winter World of Love, 462, 823
Winter's Tale, A, 60, 314
Wire Brush Stomp, 556
Wired, 70, 647, 956
Wish, 238, 890, 923
Wish Me Luck as You Wave Me
 Goodbye, 335
Wish You Were Here, 424, 777
Wish You Were Here Tonight, 174
Wishbone 4, 1074
Wishin' and Hopin', 933
Wishing, 260
Wishing I Was Lucky, 1047
Wishing on a Star, 906
Wishing Well, 243, 357
Witch Doctor, 26, 390, 883, 925
Witch's Promise, The, 498
Witchcraft, 904
Witches and Devils, 41
Witchy Woman, 295
With a Girl Like You, 995
With a Little Help from my
 Friends, 107, 117, 129, 198, 1047
With a Little Luck, 611
With a Song in My Heart, 428
With a Twist, 860
With All My Heart, 188
With Billie in Mind, 1070
With Every Light, 913
With Everything I Feel in Me, 355
With God on Our Side, 292, 563
With Her Head Tucked Under-
 neath Her Arm, 1046
With My Eyes Wide Open, I'm
 Dreaming, 750, 828
With My Little Stick of Blackpool
 Rock, 346
With or Without You, 1004
With Pen in Hand, 389
With the Beatles, 66, 649
With the LSO, 1092
With These Hands, 516
With This Ring, 780
With You I'm Born Again, 790
Without a Net, 401
Without a Sound, 265
Without Love, 166, 516
Without the Aid of a Safety Net, 84
Without Walls, 951, 1080
Without You, 722
Without You I'm Nothing, 779

Wizard, The, 101, 1009
Wizard, A True Star, A, 860, 916
Wizard of Ragtime Piano, The, 93
Woke Up Laughing, 751
Woke Up This Morning, 538
W.O.L.D., 172
Wolf, 956
Wolf and Leopard, 127
Wolfking of LA, The, 633
Wolverine Blues, 697
Wolves and Leopards, 127
Womack and Womack, 1076
Womagic, 1076
Woman, 45, 178, 576
Woman, a Lover, a Friend, A,
 1069
Woman Across the Water, 541
Woman and a Man, A, 158
Woman Be Wise, 814
Woman Can Change a Man, A,
 978
Woman I Am, The, 533
Woman in Love, 56, 675, 956
Woman in Me, The, 1000
Woman Is the Nigger of the
 World, 576, 740
Woman Left Lonely, A, 517, 1026
Woman to Woman, 559, 1080
Woman Woman, 804, 986
Woman, Your Love, 54
Woman's Got to Have It, 1076
Woman's Story, A, 1044
Woman's Story: Compilation, A, 17
Woman's World, 465
Womanhood, 1080
Wombling Song, The, 60
Wombling White Tie and Tails,
 60
Women Be Wise, 1029
Women in Uniform, 474
Women of Ireland, 182
Women's Love Rights, 449
Women's Work, 172
Wommat, 710
Won't Get Fooled Again, 1054
Won't You Come Home Bill Bai-
 ley?, 244
Won't You Try, 494
Wonder, The, 973
Wonder Could I Live There Any-
 more, 795
Wonder Girl, 927
Wonder of You, The, 769, 789
Wonder Woman, 958
Wonderful, 25, 488, 630
Wonderful Christmastime, 611
Wonderful Dream, 812
Wonderful Girl, 265
Wonderful Land, 885, 886
Wonderful Life, 86
Wonderful Stories, 1084
Wonderful! Wonderful!, 651

Wonderful, Wonderful Copen-
 hagen, 525
Wonderful World, 9, 213, 442, 898
Wonderful World, Beautiful
 People, 193
Wondering, 3, 776
Wonderland, 312
Wonderland by Night, 796, 1044
Wonderwall, 427, 731
Wonderworld, 1009
Wood, 289
Wood & The Wire, The, 324
Wood Beez (Pray Like Aretha
 Franklin), 878
Woodchopper's Ball, 210, 599
Wooden Head, 1000
Wooden Heart (Muss I' Denn),
 522
Woodface, The, 233
Woodman, Woodman, Spare
 That Tree, 426, 1057
Woods of Darney, The, 982
Woodstock, 229, 652, 679, 1089
Woody Woodpecker's Song, 525,
 557
Woofer in Tweeter's Clothing, A,
 927
Woortcha!, 175
Word Gets Around, 945
Word Girl, The, 878
Word of Mouth, 378, 544
Word Up, 152, 931
Words, 114, 184, 822
Words and Music, 1040
Words for the Dying, 151
Words from the Front, 973
Words of Love, 451, 633
Wordy Rappinghood, 967
Work of Heart, 424
Work Rest and Play, 630
Work Song, 144, 619, 704
Work Songs, 688
Work That Body, 579
Work with Me Annie, 51, 59, 82,
 450, 486
Workbook, 701
Workers' Playtime, 117
Workin' at the Car Wash Blues,
 228
Workin' Band, 724
Workin' It Back, 764
Workin' Overtime, 856
Working Class Dog, 934
Working Class Hero, 99, 159, 326,
 576
Working Class Man, 56
Working Classical, 612
Working in a Coalmine, 990
Working in the Coal Mine, 260,
 281, 520
Working Man's Blues, 27
Working Man's Prayer, A, 802

Working My Way Back to You, 349, 932
Working on a Building of Love, 169
Working on a Groovy Thing, 880
Workingman's Dead, 400, 401
Works, The, 216, 531, 808
Works Vol 1, 310
Workshop of the Telescopes, 98, 98
World Championship Ballroom Dances, 599
World Class, 442
World Clique, 252
World Destruction, 51
World Falling Down, 181
World Gone Strange, 782
World Gone Wrong, 294
World I Used to Know, 623
World in Motion, *132*, 716
World in My Eyes, 258
World Is a Ghetto, The, 1030
World Is Fallen Down, The, 837
World Is Full of Married Men, The, 1002
World Is Made of Stone, The, 567
World Is Stone, The, 593
World Is Waiting for the Sunrise, The, 760
World Leader Pretend, 826
World Machine, 579
World of Cecil Taylor, The, 892
World of His Own, A, 936
World of Morrissey, The, 696
World of Pain, 225
World of Pete Seeger, The, 881
World Outside, The, 347
World Radio, 873
World Should Know, The, 140
World Shut Your Mouth, *215*, 215
World Starts Tonight, The, 1002
World Wide Live, 875
World Within, The, 234
World Without Dave, A, 163
World Without Love, 853
World Won't Listen, The, 918
World's Fair, 108
Worldwide, 321
Worldwide Love, 590
Worried Life, 927
Worried Life Blues, 927
Worried Man, A, 542
Worried Mind, 239
Worry Bomb, 163
Worst That Could Happen, The, 227, 329, 1040
Wot, 240
Would?, 14
Would I Lie to You, 317
Would Ya Like More Scratchin', 624
Would You Believe, 174

Would You Lay with Me in a Field of Stone, 199, 997
Wouldn't It Be Good, 531
Wouldn't It Be Luverly, 578
Wouldn't It Be Nice, 63
W.O.W., 546
Wow, *143*, *680*
Wowee Zowee, 760
Wowie Zowie, 1091
Woyaya, 745
Wrack My Brain, 939
Wrap Around Joy, 540
Wrap Her Up, 503, 666
Wrapped Around Your Finger, 782
Wrapping Paper, 225
Wrath of My Madness, 808
Wreck of the Edmund Fitzgerald, 585
Wreck of the Old '97, 240, 706, 842, 955
Wreck on the Highway, 6, 735
Wrecking Ball, 426, 563
Write Me a Few Lines, 618
Writing on the Wall, 136
Writing to Reach You, 992
Written in Red, 956
Wrong End of the Rainbow, 862
Wrong Idea, The, 525
Wrong Road Again, 375
Wrong Way Up, 151, 311
Wrong Yo Yo, The, 774
Wrote for Luck, 730
W. S. Walcott Medicine Show, The, 53
Wun'erful, Wun'erful!, 356
Wunderbar, 785
Wunderland bei Nacht, 522
Wuthering Heights, *142*, 143
Wyatt Earp, 374
Wynonna, 520
Wyoming, 639, 1078
Wyoming Lullaby, 319

X, 473
X Factor, The, 474
X Offender, 96
X-Mas '93, 867
X-Static, 413
X-temporaneous Boogie, 860
Xanadu, 721
Xerox, 24
XL1, 145
XO, 915
Xplora, 366
Xtra Naked, 815
XTRMNTR, 707
XXV, 886
XYZ, 782

Y Kant Tori Read?, 20
Y'a d'La Jolie, 993

Ya Ya, 281, 674, 840, 990
Ya Ya Twist, 281
Yada Yada, 122
Yah Moh B There, 514
Yakety Axe, 36
Yakety Yak, 196, 298, 536
Yama, Yama Man, The, 511
Yancey Special, 582
Yank Crime, 842
Yankee Doodle, The, 200
Yankee Lady, 1070
Yankee Rose, 354
Yankie Doodle Dandy, 706
Yardbird Suite, 15, 753
Yardbirds, The, 1083
Yarira, 640
Ya-Ta-Ta, Yah-Ta-Ta (Talk, Talk, Talk), 231
Yazoo Basin Boogie, 405
Year of Decision, 56
Year of the Cat, 947
Year That Clayton Delaney Died, The, 415
Years of Tears, 94
Yeh Yeh, 327, 870
Yellow Bird, 547, 571
Yellow Brick Road, 72
Yellow Dog Blues, 391, 420
Yellow Man, 719
Yellow Moon, 563, 714
Yellow Pearl, 979
Yellow Rose of Texas, The, 356, 672
Yellow Shark, 1092
Yellow Submarine, 68
Yemenite Songs, 435
'Yep!', 300
Yer Album, 295
Yerself Is Steam, 663
Yes, 960
Yes Active, 1085
Yes Album, The, 1084
Yes I Do, 705
Yes, I Guess They Oughta Name a Drink After You, 799
Yes I Know, 780
Yes I'm Ready, 369, 526
Yes, It's Fucking Political, 909
Yes My Darling Daughter, 895
Yes Open, 710
Yes Please, 421, 620, 967
Yes Sir, That's My Baby, 6, 276, 523
Yes Tonight, Josephine, 819
Yes We Can, *281*, 990, *990*
Yes We Can Can, 781
Yes We Have No Bananas, 706, 883
Yesshows, 1084
Yessongs, 1084
Yesterday, 67, 274, 647, 685, 904
Yesterday Has Gone, 17

Yesterday Man, 1079

Yesterday Once More, 160

Yesterday, When I Was Young, 189

Yesterday's Wine, 512

Yester-Me, Yester-You, 121

Yester-Me, Yester-You, Yester-day, 1077

Yi Yi Yi Yi, 678

Yield, 762

Ying Tong Song, 393

Y.M.C.A., 1021

Yo! Bum Rush the Show, 802

Yo Frankie, 266

Yodel Songs, 121

Yodelling Yippie, 361

Yoko Ono/Plastic Ono Band, 740

You, 355, 424, 427

You Ain't Heard Nothing Yet, 336, 509

You Ain't Seen Nothin' Yet, 406

You Ain't Woman Enough, 607

You Always Hurt the One You Love, 515, 674

You and I, 375, 488

You and Me Against the World, 1064

You and Me Both, 703

You and Me That Used to Be, The, 863

You and the Night and the Music, 874

You and Your Baby Blues, 139

You Are, 832

You Are Everything, 855, 958

You Are My Destiny, 24, 218

You Are My Heart's Delight, 969

You Are My Jersey Lilly, 510

You Are My Lucky Star, 286, 359

You Are My Sunshine, 20, 247

You Are Not Alone, 482, 528

You Are So Beautiful, 198, 790, 847

You Are the Sunshine of My Life, 1077

You Baby, 911, 999

You Baby You, 389

You Be Illin', 859

You Beat Me to the Punch, 840, 1046

You Belong to Me, 898, 937

You Belong to the City, 296

You Bet I Would, 852

You Bet Your Love, 420

You Better Leave That Woman Alone, 173

You Better Move on, 13

You Better Run, 910

You Better Sit Down Kids, 177

You Better You Bet, 1054

You Bought It, You Name It, 295

You Boyz Make Big Noize, 910

You Bring Out the Best of the Woman in Me, 823

You Brought a New Kind of Love to Me, 180, 323

You Came a Long Way from St Louis, 490

You Can Call Me Al, 900

You Can Close Your Eyes, 971

You Can Depend on Me, 571

You Can Do It, 401

You Can Do It Baby, 651

You Can Do Magic, 19

You Can Get It If You Really Want, 193, 255, 549

You Can Have Her, 417

You Can Leave Your Hat on, 517

You Can Make It if You Try, 139

You Can Run, 221

You Can Run but You Can't Hide, 138

You Can Suit Yourself, 173

You Can Tune a Piano But You Can't Tuna Fish, 827

You Can't Always Get What You Want, 216, 849

You Can't Catch Me, 81

You Can't Get a Man with a Gun, 463, 664

You Can't Get What You Want (Till You Know What You Want), 480

You Can't Have My Love, 981

You Can't Hide a Redneck Under Hippy Hair, 867

You Can't Hurry Love, 205, 449, 962

You Can't Judge a Book by the Cover, 263

You Can't Keep a Good Man Down, 1029

You Can't Put Your Arms around a Memory, 718

You Can't Roller Skate in a Buffalo Herd, 673

You Can't Sew a Button on a Heart, 997

You Can't Sit Down, 282, 1008

You Can't Win, 481

You Deserve the Best, 1053

You Didn't Have to Be So Nice, 602

You Didn't Want Me, 538

You Do, 960

You Don't Bring Me Flowers, 132, 262, 956

You Don't Care, 537

You Don't Care about Us, 779

You Don't Have to Be a Star (To Be in My Show), 836

You Don't Have to Be Black to Love the Blues, 755

You Don't Have to Go, 180, 607, 823

You Don't Have to Say You Love Me, 933

You Don't Know, 609, 752

You Don't Know Like I Know, 434, 869

You Don't Know Me, 174

You Don't Know My Mind, 648

You Don't Know What You've Got, 389, 790

You Don't Love Me, 1026

You Don't Mess Around with Jim, 228, 228

You Don't Miss a Thing, 30

You Don't Miss Your Water, 74, 147, 756, 966

You Don't Own Me, 394

You Gave Me a Mountain, 560

You Get What You Play for, 827

You Give Good Love, 458

You Give Love a Bad Name, 102

You Got It (The Right Stuff), 715

You Got Lucky, 771, 771

You Got Me Hummin', 869

You Got Soul, 708

You Got the Love, 532, 940

You Got What It Takes, 394, 508, 896

(You Gotta) Fight for Your Right (To Party), 64

You Gotta Move, 618

You Gotta Say Yes to Another Excess, 1084

You Gotta Sin to Get Saved, 622

You Have to Cry Sometime, 559

You Haven't Done Nothing, 1077

You Haven't Heard the Last of Me, 54

You Hurt Me, 504

You Just Might See Me Cry, 823

You Keep Me Hangin' on, 438, 449, 697, 962, 1014, 1055

You Know I Love You, 538

You Know I Love You . . . Don't You, 513

You Left the Water Running, 607

You Lie, 618

You Lift Me up to Heaven, 618

You Light up My Life, 108, 237

You Little Thief, 890

You Look So Good in Love, 955

You Love Us, 636

You Made Me Believe in Magic, 62

You Made Me Cry, 915

You Made Me Love You, 371, 487, 510

You Made Me So Very Happy, 97

You Made Me the Thief of Your Heart, 734

You Make Loving Fun, 342, 500

You Make Me Feel Brand New, 44, 74, 958

(You Make Me Feel Like) A Natural Woman, 355

You Make Me Feel Like Dancing, 872, 873

You Make Me Feel (Mighty Real), 363

You Make Me Feel So Young, 828, 904

You May Swing, 653

You? Me? Us?, 982

You Mean the World to Me, 118, 893

You Might Be Surprised, 40

You Might Need Somebody, 234

You Must Ask the Heart, 833

You Must Believe in Spring, 573

You Must Have Been a Beautiful Baby, 230, 244, 663, 787, 1032

You Must Love Me, 593, 631

You Need a Mess of Help to Stand Alone, 867

You Need Hands, 146, 567

You Need Love, 269, 569

You Needed Me, 705

You Never Can Tell, 799

(You Never Can Tell) C'est la Vie, 425

You Never Done It Like That, 880

You Never Even Called Me by My Name, 199

You Never Know Who Your Friends Are, 551

You Only Tell Me You Love Me When You're Drunk, 768

You Ought to Be with Me, 402

You Oughta Know, 693

You Painted Pictures, 926

You Rascal You, 28

You Really Got a Hold on Me, 729

You Really Got Me, 543, 544, 1011

You Said, 478

You Saved My Soul, 406

You Say the Sweetest Things, Baby, 330

You Say You Don't Love Me, 145

You Scare Me to Death, 101

You Send Me, 90, 120, 213, 938

You Sexy Thing, 456, 457

You Shook Me, 569

You Should be Dancing, 71

You Should Have Told Me You Were . . ., 533

You Should See the Rest of the Band, 122

You Showed Me, 585, 999

You Spin Me Around (Like a Record), 951

You Stepped out of a Dream, 130, 522, 648

You Still Want Me, 543

You Take Me Up, 981

You Take My Breath Away, 149

You Talk Too Much, 344

You Think You're a Man, 951

You Took Advantage of Me, 73, 428

You Took the Words Right Out of My Mouth, 657

You Turn Me on, I'm a Radio, 679

You Upset Me, Baby, 538

You Waited Too Long, 470

You Want It Back, 521

You Want It, You Got It, 7

You Wear It Well, 949

You Well-Meaning Brought Me Here, 627

You Were Made for Me, 357, 707

You Were Meant for Me, 93, 130, 359, 500

You Were Never Lovelier, 663

You Were on My Mind, 465, 465

You Were Only Fooling, 241, 939

You Will Never Miss Your Mother Until She Is Gone, 162

You Win Again, 71, 275, 696, 795

You Won't Be Satisfied Until You Break My Heart, 336

You Won't Find Another Fool Like Me, 610, 882

You Won't See Me, 705

You Won't See Me Cry, 64

You, You, You, 19

You'd Be So Nice to Come Home to, 785

You'd Better Move on, 415

You'll Answer to Me, 559

You'll Be in My Heart, 205

You'll Lose a Good Thing, 332, 607, 658

You'll Never Be the Same, 648

You'll Never Find Another Love Like Mine, 818

You'll Never Get to Heaven (If You Break My Heart), 958

You'll Never Know, 331, 435, 903, 1032

You'll Never Know What You're Missing, 344

You'll Never Stop Me Loving You, 951

You'll Never Walk Alone, 138, 153, 379, 417, 844

You're a Big Girl Now, 957

You're a Grand Old Flag, 201, 706, 924

You're a Lady, 908

You're a Million Miles from Nowhere When You're One Little Mile from Home, 276

You're a Part of Me, 159

You're a Pink Toothbrush, 146

You're a Pink Toothbrush, I'm a Blue Toothbrush, 485

You're a Wonderful One, 449

You're All I Need, 558, 699

You're All I Need to Get By, 32

You're an Old Smoothie, 1052

You're Between Me, 806

You're Breaking My Heart, 241

You're Driving Me Crazy, 28, 105, 276, 597

You're Getting Even While I'm Gettin' Odd, 376

You're Getting to Be a Habit with Me, 230, 1032

You're Getting to Me Again, 986

You're Gonna Get It!, 771

You're Gonna Get Yours, 802

You're Gonna Kill That Girl, 814

You're Gonna Make Me Cry, 1079

You're Gonna Need Magic, 417

You're Gonna Need Me, 224, 607

You're Good to Me, 247

You're Growing Cold, Cold, Cold, 200

You're Having My Baby, 24, 415

You're History, 886

You're in a Bad Way, 867

You're in Love, 399

You're Just a Dream Come True, 513

You're Living All Over Me, 265

You're Lucky to Me, 93

You're Making Me High, 118

You're More Than a Number in My Little Red Book, 285, 403, 611

You're Moving Out Today, 45

You're My Best Friend, 1058

You're My One and Only Love, 711

(You're My) Soul and Inspiration, 747, 834

You're My Thrill, 679

You're My World, 89, 443, 821

You're Never Alone with a Schizo, 700

You're No Good, 108, 291, 319, 449, 853, 965, 1033

You're OK, I'm OK, 964

You're Probably Wondering Why I'm Here, 1091

You're Running Wild, 599

You're Safe, 795

You're Sixteen, 139, 939

You're So Good to Me, 63

You're So Vain, 898

You're Still My Baby, 1067

You're Still New to Me, 298

You're Still Standing There, 297

You're the Cream in My Coffee, 259

You're the First Time I've Thought about Leaving, 618
You're the First, the Last, My Everything, 1048
You're the Inspiration, 181
You're the One, 900, 1085
You're the One That I Want, 381, 721
You're the Only Dancer, 259
You're the Only World That I Know, 489
You're the Reason God Made Oklahoma, 360
You're the Reason I'm Living, 244
You're the Top, 34, 784
You're the Voice, 590
You'se a Viper, 636
You've Been Untrue, 255
You've Come a Long Way, Baby, 330
You've Got a Friend, 338, 540, 678, 971
You've Got a Lot to Answer for, 168
You've Got It Bad, 732
You've Got My Mind Messed Up, 160
You've Got to Be Carefully Taught, 844
You've Got to Hold on to Me, 997
(You've Got to) Move Two Mountains, 508
You've Got to Pick a Pocket or Two, 57
You've Got Your Troubles, 403
You've Lost That Lovin' Feeling, 47, 413, 545, 637, 638, 750, 834, 835, 929
You've Made Me So Very Happy, 348
You've Never Been This Far Before, 1000
You've Really Got a Hold on Me, 841
Young Abe Lincoln, 217, 460
Young Americans, 111, 111, 1013
Young and Healthy, 786
Young and in Love, 759
Young and Ready, 736
Young at Heart, 833, 903
Young Blood, 46, 66, 196, 582, 783
Young Boy Blues, 783
Young Brigham, 308
Young, Gifted and Black, 100, 641, 901
Young Girl, 804

Young Girl Blues, 277
Young Guns (Go for It), 666
Young Hearts Run Free, 940
Young Love, 227, 479, 488, 489, 747
Young Lovers, 759
Young Man, Older Woman, 482
Young Man's Blues, 15
Young Ones, The, 831
Young Parisians, 24
Young Team, 682
Young Turks, 950
Young Woman's Blues, 914
Young World, 711, 804
Youngblood, 1090
Younger Generation, 602
Younger Girl, 237
Younger Men (Are Starting to Catch My Eye), 746
Younger Than Springtime, 844
Younger Than Yesterday, 146, 147, 756
Your Arsenal, 696, 700
Your Baby Is a Lady, 259
Your Baby Never Looked Good in Blue, 1032
Your Body's Callin', 528
Your Cash Ain't Nothing but Trash, 195, 953
Your Cheating Heart, 174, 820, 1060
Your Cool Mystery, 184
Your Dearest Friends, 899
Your Disco Needs You, 677
Your Eyes are Dreaming, 303
Your Face, My Ass, 560
Your Feet's Too Big, 1029
Your Filthy Little Mouth, 846
Your Funeral, My Trial, 168
Your Generation, 467
Your Good Girl's Gonna Go Bad, 1080
Your Good Thing (Is About to End), 504, 818
Your Love, 472, 836, 954
Your Love Is King, 866
(Your Love Keeps Lifting Me) Higher and Higher, 1069
Your Love Looks Good on Me, 171
Your Mama Don't Dance, 596
Your Mama Won't Like Me, 807
Your Mother's Son in Law, 448
Your Old Love Letters, 103
Your Place or Mine, 460
Your Precious Love, 32, 363, 374, 740

Your Saving Grace, 673
Your Secret Love, 1013
Your Smile, 1070
Your Song, 492, 503, 759
Your Time to Cry, 899
Your Wildest Dreams, 689
Yours in My Heart Alone, 969
Yours Is My Heart Alone, 574
Yours Is No Disgrace, 1084
Yours, 608
Youthanasia, 659
Yo-Yo, 746
YUI Orta, 700
Yvonne's Special Revolution, 127

Z Cars, 437
Z Zelebration, 446
Zabadak!, 245
Zaireeka, 339
Zambesi, 752
Zazu, 943
Zebop!, 871
Zebra, 1084
Zeit, 968
Zen Arcade, 701
Zenyatta Mondatta, 782
Zero She Flies, 947
Zero Time, 1077
Zero Tolerance for Silence, 666
Zimbabwe, 644
Zimmerman Blues, 627
Zing Zing – Zoom Zoom, 852
Zingalamundi, 30
Zip, 428
Zip Gun City, 101
Zip-a-Dee-Doo-Dah, 185, 601, 929
Zodiac Suite, 1063
Zodiac Variations, 242
Zodiaque, 1025
Zombie Birdhouse, 469
Zombie Heaven, 1093
Zombie Soca, 31
Zone of Our Own, 867
Zone of Your Own, 332
Zoolook, 491
Zoom, 977
Zooma, Zooma, 796
Zooropa, 1004
Zoot Allures, 1092
Zoot Suit, 1053
Zu Zu Man, 271
Zucchero Fornaciari, 1094
Zulu Nation Throwdown Part One, 51
Zuma, 1088